WEBSTER'S New Spanish-English Dictionary

WEBSTER'S
New Spanish-English Dictionary

Created in Cooperation with
the Editors of
Merriam-Webster

This 2002 edition published by arrangement with Federal Street Press, a division of Merriam-Webster, Incorporated

The Popular Group, LLC
1700 Broadway
New York, New York 10019

ISBN 1-59027-064-9

Printed in the United States of America

06 07 08 14 13 12 11

Contents — Índice

Preface

WEBSTER'S NEW SPANISH-ENGLISH DICTIONARY is a completely new dictionary designed to meet the needs of English and Spanish speakers in a time of ever-expanding communication among the countries of the Western Hemisphere. It is intended for language learners, teachers, office workers, tourists, business travelers—anyone who needs to communicate effectively in the Spanish and English languages as they are spoken and written in the Americas. This new dictionary provides accurate and up-to-date coverage of current vocabulary in both languages, as well as abundant examples of words used in context to illustrate idiomatic usage. The selection of Spanish words and idioms was based on evidence drawn from a wide variety of modern Latin-American sources and interpreted by trained Merriam-Webster bilingual lexicographers. The English entries were chosen by Merriam-Webster editors from the most recent Merriam-Webster dictionaries, and they represent the current basic vocabulary of American English.

All of this material is presented in a format that emphasizes convenience and ease of use, clarity and conciseness of the information presented, precise discrimination of senses, and frequent inclusion of example phrases showing words in actual use. Also included are pronunciations (in the International Phonetic Alphabet) for all English words, full coverage of irregular verbs in both languages, a section on basic Spanish grammar, a table of the most common Spanish abbreviations, and a detailed Explanatory Notes section that answers any questions the reader might have concerning the use of this book.

Eileen M. Haraty
Editor

Explanatory Notes

Entries

1. Main Entries

A boldface letter, word, or phrase appearing flush with the left-hand margin of each column of type is a main entry or entry word. The main entry may consist of letters set solid, of letters joined by a hyphen, or of letters separated by a space:

cafetalero[1], **-ra** *adj*. . .
eye–opener. . . *n*. . .
walk out *vi* . . .

The main entry, together with the material that follows it on the same line and succeeding indented lines, constitutes a dictionary entry.

2. Order of Main Entries

Alphabetical order throughout the book follows the order of the English alphabet, with one exception: words beginning with the Spanish letter *ñ* follow all entries for the letter *n*. The main entries follow one another alphabetically letter by letter without regard to intervening spaces or hyphens; for example, *shake-up* follows *shaker*.

Homographs (words with the same spelling) having different parts of speech are usually given separate dictionary entries. These entries are distinguished by superscript numerals following the entry word:

hail[1]. . . *vt*. . .

hail[2] *n*. . .

hail[3] *interj*. . .

madrileño[1], **-ña** *adj*. . .

madrileño[2], **-ña** *n*. . .

Numbered homograph entries are listed in the following order: verb, adverb, adjective, noun, conjunction, preposition, pronoun, interjection, article.

Homographs having the same part of speech are normally included at the same dictionary entry, without regard to their different semantic origins. On the English-to-Spanish side, however, separate entries are made if the homographs have distinct inflected forms or if they have distinct pronunciations.

3. Guide Words

A pair of guide words is printed at the top of each page, indicating the first and last main entries that appear on that page:

fregar • fuego

4. Variants

When a main entry is followed by the word *or* and another spelling, the two spellings are variants. Both are standard, and either one may be used according to personal inclination:

jailer *or* **jailor**. . . *n*. . .
quizá *or* **quizás** *adv*. . .

Occasionally, a variant spelling is used only for a particular sense of a word. In these cases, the variant spelling is listed after the sense number of the sense to which it pertains:

electric. . . *adj* **1** *or* **electrical**. . .

Sometimes the entry word is used interchangeably with a longer phrase containing the entry word. For the purposes of this dictionary, such phrases are considered variants of the headword:

bunk[2] *n* **1** *or* **bunk bed**. . .

angina *nf* **1** *or* **angina de pecho** **:** angina . . .

Variant wordings of boldface phrases may also be shown:

> **madera** *nf*. . . **3 madera dura** *or* **madera noble**. . .
>
> **atención**[1] *nf*. . . **2 poner atención** *or* **prestar atención**. . .

5. Run-On Entries

A main entry may be followed by one or more derivatives or by a homograph with a different functional label. These are run-on entries. Each is introduced by a boldface dash and each has a functional label. They are not defined, however, since their equivalents can be readily derived by adding the corresponding foreign-language suffix to the terms used to define the entry word or, in the case of homographs, simply substituting the appropriate part of speech:

> **illegal**. . . *adj* **:** ilegal **— illegally** *adv*
> (the Spanish adverb is *ilegalmente*)
>
> **transferir**. . . *vt* TRASLADAR **:** to transfer **— transferible** *adj*
> (the English adjective is **transferable**)
>
> **Bosnian** *n* **:** bosnio *m,* -nia *f* **— Bosnian** *adj*
> (the Spanish adjective is *bosnio, -nia*)

On the Spanish side of the book, reflexive verbs are sometimes run on undefined:

> **enrollar** *vt* **:** to roll up, to coil **— enrollarse** *vr*

The absence of a definition means that *enrollarse* has the simple reflexive meaning "to become rolled up or coiled," "to roll itself up."

6. Bold Notes

A main entry may be followed by one or more phrases containing the entry word or an inflected form of the entry word. These are bold notes. Each bold note is defined at its own numbered sense:

> **álamo** *nm* **1 :** poplar **2 álamo temblón :** aspen
>
> **hold**[1]. . . *vi*. . . **4 to hold to :**. . . **5 to hold with :**. . .

If the bold note consists only of the entry word and a single preposition, the entry word is represented by a boldface swung dash **~**.

> **pegar** . . . *vi* . . . **3 ~ con :** to match, to go with . . .

The same bold note phrase may appear at two or more senses if it has more than one distinct meaning:

> **wear**[1]. . . *vt*. . . **3 to wear out :** gastar <he wore out his shoes. . . > **4 to wear out** EXHAUST **:** agotar, fatigar <to wear oneself out . . .> . . .
>
> **estar** . . . *vi* . . . **15 ~ por :** to be in favor of **16 ~ por :** to be about to <está por cerrar . . .> . . .

If the use of the entry word is commonly restricted to one particular phrase, then a bold note may be given as the entry word's only sense:

> **ward**[1]. . . *vt* **to ward off :**. . .

Pronunciation

1. Pronunciation of English Entry Words

The matter between a pair of brackets [ ] following the entry word of an English-to-Spanish entry indicates the pronunciation. The symbols used are explained in the International Phonetic Alphabet chart on page 25a.

The presence of variant pronunciations indicates that not all educated speakers pronounce words the same way. A second-place variant is not to be regarded as less acceptable than the pronunciation that is given first. It may, in fact, be used by as many educated speakers as the first variant, but the requirements of the printed page are such that one must precede the other:

tomato [tə'meɪt̬o, -'mɑ-]. . .

When a compound word has less than a full pronunciation, the missing part is to be supplied from the pronunciation at the entry for the unpronounced element of the compound:

gamma ray ['gæmə]. . .

ray ['reɪ]. . .

smoke[1] ['smo:k]. . .

smoke detector [dɪ'tɛktər]. . .

In general, no pronunciation is given for open compounds consisting of two or more English words that are main entries at their own alphabetical place:

water lily *n* **:** nenúfar *m*

Only the first entry in a series of numbered homographs is given a pronunciation if their pronunciations are the same:

dab[1] ['dæb] *vt*. . .

dab[2] *n*. . .

No pronunciation is shown for principal parts of verbs that are formed by regular suffixation, nor for other derivative words formed by common suffixes.

2. Pronunciation of Spanish Entry Words

Spanish pronunciation is highly regular, so no pronunciations are given for most Spanish-to-English entries. Exceptions have been made for certain words (such as foreign borrowings) whose Spanish pronunciations are not evident from their spellings:

pizza ['pitsa, 'pisa] . . .

footing ['fuˌtɪŋ]. . .

Functional Labels

An italic label indicating a part of speech or some other functional classification follows the pronunciation or, if no pronunciation is given, the main entry. The eight traditional parts of speech, adjective, adverb, conjunction, interjection, noun, preposition, pronoun, and verb, are indicated as follows:

daily[2] *adj*. . .

vagamente *adv*. . .

and. . . *conj*. . .

huy *interj*. . .

jackal. . . *n*. . .

para *prep*. . .

neither[3] *pron*. . .

leer. . . *v*. . .

Verbs that are intransitive are labeled *vi,* and verbs that are transitive are labeled *vt.* Entries for verbs that are both transitive and intransitive are labeled *v;* if such an entry includes irregular verb inflections, it is labeled *v* immediately after the main entry, with the labels *vi* and *vt* serving to introduce transitive and intransitive subdivisions when both are present:

deliberar *vi* **:** to deliberate

necessitate. . . *vt* **-tated; -tating :** necesitar, requerir

satisfy. . . *v* **-fied; -fying** *vt*. . . — *vi*. . .

Two other labels are used to indicate functional classifications of verbs: *v aux* (auxiliary verb) and *v impers* (impersonal verb).

may. . . *v aux, past* **might**. . .

haber[1]. . . *v aux* **1 :** have. . . — *v impers* **1 hay :** there is, there are. . .

Gender Labels

In Spanish-to-English noun entries, the gender of the entry word is indicated by an italic *m* (masculine), *f* (feminine), or *mf* (masculine or feminine), immediately following the functional label:

magnesio *nm*. . .

galaxia *nf*. . .

turista *nmf*. . .

If both the masculine and feminine forms are shown for a noun referring to a person, the label is simply *n:*

director, -tora *n*. . .

Spanish noun equivalents of English entry words are also labeled for gender:

amnesia. . . *n* **:** amnesia *f*

earache. . . *n* **:** dolor *m* de oído

gamekeeper. . . *n* **:** guardabosque *mf*

Inflected Forms

1. Nouns

The plurals of nouns are shown in this dictionary when they are irregular, when plural suffixation brings about a change in accentuation or in the spelling of the root word, when an English noun ends in a consonant plus *-o* or in *-ey,* when an English noun ends in *-oo,* when an English noun is a compound that pluralizes any element but the last, when a noun has variant plurals, or whenever the dictionary user might have reasonable doubts regarding the spelling of a plural:

> **tooth**. . . *n, pl* **teeth**. . .
>
> **garrafón** *nm, pl* **-fones**. . .
>
> **potato**. . . *n, pl* **-toes**. . .
>
> **abbey**. . . *n, pl* **-beys**. . .
>
> **cuckoo**[2] *n, pl* **-oos**. . .
>
> **brother–in–law**. . . *n, pl* **brothers–in–law** . . .
>
> **quail**[2] *n, pl* **quail** *or* **quails**. . .
>
> **hábitat** *nm, pl* **-tats**. . .
>
> **tahúr** *nm, pl* **tahúres**. . .

Cutback inflected forms are used for most nouns on the English-to-Spanish side, regardless of the number of syllables. On the Spanish-to-English side, cutback inflections are given for nouns that have three or more syllables; plurals for shorter words are written out in full:

> **shampoo**[2] *n, pl* **-poos**. . .
>
> **calamity** . . . *n, pl* **-ties**. . .
>
> **mouse** . . . *n, pl* **mice**. . .
>
> **sartén** *nmf, pl* **sartenes**. . .
>
> **hámster** *nm, pl* **hámsters**. . .
>
> **federación** *nf, pl* **-ciones**. . .

If only one gender form has a plural which is irregular, that plural form will be given with the appropriate label:

> **campeón, -ona** *n, mpl* **-ones** **:** champion

The plurals of nouns are usually not shown when the base word is unchanged by the addition of the regular plural suffix or when the noun is unlikely to occur in the plural:

apple. . . *n* : manzana *f*

inglés[3] *nm* : English (language)

Nouns that are plural in form and that regularly occur in plural constructions are labeled as *npl* (for English nouns), *nmpl* (for Spanish masculine nouns), or *nfpl* (for Spanish feminine nouns):

knickers. . . *npl*. . .

enseres *nmpl*. . .

mancuernas *nfpl*. . .

Entry words that are unchanged in the plural are labeled *ns & pl* (for English nouns), *nms & pl* (for Spanish masculine nouns), *nfs & pl* (for Spanish feminine nouns), and *nmfs & pl* (for Spanish gender-variable nouns):

deer. . . *ns & pl* . . .

lavaplatos *nms & pl*. . .

tesis *nfs & pl* . . .

rompehuelgas *nmfs & pl* . . .

2. Verbs

ENGLISH VERBS

The principal parts of verbs are shown in English-to-Spanish entries when they are irregular, when suffixation brings about a change in spelling of the root word, when the verb ends in *-ey,* when there are variant inflected forms, or whenever it is believed that the dictionary user might have reasonable doubts about the spelling of an inflected form:

break[1]. . . *v* **broke**. . . ; **broken**. . . ; **breaking**. . .

drag[1]. . . *v* **dragged; dragging**. . .

monkey[1]. . . *vi* **-keyed; -keying**. . .

label[1]. . . *vt* **-beled** *or* **-belled; -beling** *or* **-belling**. . .

imagine. . . *vt* **-ined; -ining**. . .

Cutback inflected forms are usually used when the verb has two or more syllables:

multiply. . . *v* **-plied; -plying**. . .

bevel[1]. . . *v* **-eled** *or* **-elled; -eling** *or* **-elling**. . .

forgo *or* **forego**. . . *vt* **-went; -gone; -going**. . .

commit . . . *vt* **-mitted; -mitting** . . .

The principal parts of an English verb are not shown when the base word is unchanged by suffixation:

delay[1]. . . *vt*

pitch[1]. . . *vt*

SPANISH VERBS

Entries for irregular Spanish verbs are cross-referenced by number to the model conjugations appearing in the Conjugation of Spanish Verbs section:

abnegarse {49} *vr*. . .

volver {89} *vi*. . .

Entries for Spanish verbs with regular conjugations are not cross-referenced; however, model conjugations for regular Spanish verbs are included in the Conjugation of Spanish Verbs section beginning on page 44a.

Adverbs and Adjectives

The comparative and superlative forms of English adjective and adverb main entries are shown when suffixation brings about a change in spelling of the root word, when the inflection is irregular, and when there are variant inflected forms:

wet[2] *adj* **wetter; wettest**. . .

good[2] *adj* **better**. . . ; **best**. . .

evil[1]. . . *adj* **eviler** *or* **eviller; evilest** *or* **evillest**. . .

The superlative forms of adjectives and adverbs of two or more syllables are usually cut back; the superlative is shown in full, however, when it is desirable to indicate the pronunciation of the inflected form:

early[1]. . . *adv* **earlier; -est**. . .

gaudy. . . *adj* **gaudier; -est**. . .

secure[2] *adj* **-curer; -est**. . .

but

young[1]. . . *adj* **younger** [ˈjʌŋgər]; **youngest** [-gəst]. . .

At a few entries only the superlative form is shown:

mere *adj, superlative* **merest**. . .

The absence of the comparative form indicates that there is no evidence of its use.

The comparative and superlative forms of adjectives and adverbs are usually not shown when the base word is unchanged by suffixation:

quiet[3] *adj* **1**. . .

Usage

1. Usage Labels

Two types of usage labels are used in this dictionary—regional and stylistic. Spanish words that are limited in use to a specific area or areas of Latin America, or to Spain, are given labels indicating the countries in which they are most commonly used:

guarachear *vi Cuba, PRi fam*. . .

bucket. . . *n* :. . . cubeta *f Mex*

The following regional labels are used in this book: *Arg* (Argentina), *Bol* (Bolivia), *CA* (Central America), *Car* (Caribbean), *Chile* (Chile), *Col* (Colombia), *CoRi* (Costa Rica), *Cuba* (Cuba), *DomRep* (Dominican Republic), *Ecua* (Ecuador), *Sal* (El Salvador), *Guat* (Guatemala), *Hond* (Honduras), *Mex* (Mexico), *Nic* (Nicaragua), *Pan* (Panama), *Par* (Paraguay), *Peru* (Peru), *PRi* (Puerto Rico), *Spain* (Spain), *Uru* (Uruguay), *Ven* (Venezuela).

Since this book focuses on the Spanish spoken in Latin America, only the most common regionalisms from Spain have been included in order to allow for more thorough coverage of Latin-American forms.

A number of Spanish words are given a *fam* (familiar) label as well, indicating that these words are suitable for informal contexts but would not normally be used in formal writing or speaking. The stylistic label *usu considered vulgar* is added for a word which is usually considered vulgar or offensive but whose widespread use justifies its inclusion in this book. The label is intended to warn the reader that the word in question may be inappropriate in polite conversation.

2. Usage Notes

Definitions are sometimes preceded by parenthetical usage notes that give supplementary semantic information:

not. . . *adv* **1** (*used to form a negative*) : no. . .

within² *prep* . . . **2** (*in expressions of distance*) :. . . **3** (*in expressions of time*) : . . .

e[2] *conj* (*used instead of* **y** *before words beginning with i or hi*) **:**. . .

poder[1]. . . *v aux*. . . **2** (*expressing possibility*) **:**. . . **3** (*expressing permission*) **:**. . .

Additional semantic orientation is also sometimes given in the form of parenthetical notes appearing within the definition:

calibrate. . . *vt*. . . **:** calibrar (armas), graduar (termómetros)

palco *nm* **:** box (in a theater or stadium)

Occasionally a usage note is used in place of a definition. This is usually done when the entry word has no single foreign-language equivalent. This type of usage note will be accompanied by examples of common use:

shall. . . *v aux*. . . **1** (*used to express a command*) <you shall do as I say **:** harás lo que te digo> . . .

3. Illustrations of Usage

Definitions are sometimes followed by verbal illustrations that show a typical use of the word in context or a common idiomatic usage. These verbal illustrations include a translation and are enclosed in angle brackets:

lejos *adv* **1 :** far away, distant <a lo lejos **:** in the distance, far off> . . .

make[1]. . . **9** . . .**:** ganar <to make a living **:** ganarse la vida> . . .

Sense Division

A boldface colon is used to introduce a definition:

fable. . . *n* **:** fábula *f*

Boldface Arabic numerals separate the senses of a word that has more than one sense:

laguna *nf* **1 :** lagoon **2 :** lacuna, gap

Whenever some information (such as a synonym, a boldface word or phrase, a usage note, a cross-reference, or a label) follows a sense number, it applies only to that specific numbered sense and not to any other boldface numbered senses:

abanico *nm*. . . **2** GAMA **:**. . .

tonic[2] *n*. . . **2** *or* **tonic water :**. . .

grillo *nm*. . . **2 grillos** *nmpl* **:**. . .

fairy. . . *n, pl* **fairies**. . . **2 fairy tale :**. . .

myself. . . *pron* **1** (*used reflexively*) **:**. . .

pike. . . *n*. . . **3 → turnpike**

atado[2] *nm*. . . **2** *Arg* **:**. . .

Cross-References

Three different kinds of cross-references are used in this dictionary: synonymous, cognate, and inflectional. In each instance the cross-reference is readily recognized by the boldface arrow following the entry word.

Synonymous and cognate cross-references indicate that a definition at the entry cross-referred to can be substituted for the entry word:

scapula. . . **→ shoulder blade**

amuck. . . **→ amok**

An inflectional cross-reference is used to identify the entry word as an inflected form of another word (as a noun or verb):

fue, etc. → ir, ser

mice → mouse

Synonyms

At many entries or senses in this book, a synonym in small capital letters is provided before the boldface colon and the following defining text. These synonyms are all main entries or bold notes elsewhere in the book. They serve as a helpful guide to the meaning of the entry or sense and also give the reader an additional term that might be substituted in a similar context. On the English-to-Spanish side synonyms are particularly abundant, since special care has been taken to guide the English speaker—by means of synonyms, verbal illustrations, or usage notes—to the meaning of the Spanish terms at each sense of a multisense entry.

Abbreviations in this Work

adj	adjective
adv	adverb
Arg	Argentina
Bol	Bolivia
Brit	British
CA	Central America
Car	Caribbean region
Col	Colombia
conj	conjuction
CoRi	Costa Rica
DomRep	Dominican Republic
Ecua	Ecuador
esp	especially
f	feminine
fam	familiar or colloquial
fpl	feminine plural
Guat	Guatemala
Hond	Honduras
interj	interjection
m	masculine
Mex	Mexico
mf	masculine or feminine
mpl	masculine plural
n	noun
nf	feminine noun
nfpl	feminine plural noun
nfs & pl	invariable singular or plural feminine noun
Nic	Nicaragua
nm	masculine noun
nmf	masculine or feminine noun
nmfpl	plural noun invariable for gender
nmfs & pl	noun invariable for both gender and number
nmpl	masculine plural noun
nms & pl	invariable singular or plural masculine noun
npl	plural noun
ns & pl	noun invariable for plural
Pan	Panama
Par	Paraguay
pl	plural
pp	past participle
prep	preposition
PRi	Puerto Rico
pron	pronoun
s	singular
Sal	El Salvador
Uru	Uruguay
usu	usually
v	verb (transitive and intransitive)
v aux	auxiliary verb
Ven	Venezuela
vi	intransitive verb
v impers	impersonal verb
vr	reflexive verb
vt	transitive verb

Pronunciation Symbols

VOWELS

- æ **a**sk, b**a**t, gl**a**d
- ɑ c**o**t, b**o**mb
- a *New England* **au**nt, *British* **a**sk, gl**a**ss, *Spanish* c**a**s**a**
- e *Spanish* p**e**so, j**e**f**e**
- ɛ **e**gg, b**e**t, f**e**d
- ə **a**bout, jav**e**lin, Al**a**b**a**m**a**
- *ə* when italicized as in *ə*l, *ə*m, *ə*n, indicates a syllabic pronunciation of the consonant as in bott**le**, pris**m**, butt**on**
- i ver**y**, an**y**, thirt**y**, *Spanish* p**i**ña
- iː **ea**t, b**ea**d, b**ee**
- ɪ **i**d, b**i**d, p**i**t
- o **O**hio, yell**o**wer, potat**o**, *Spanish* **ó**valo
- oː **oa**ts, **ow**n, z**o**ne, bl**ow**
- ɔ **aw**l, m**au**l, c**au**ght, p**aw**
- ʊ s**u**re, sh**ou**ld, c**ou**ld
- u *Spanish* **u**va, c**u**lpa
- uː b**oo**t, f**ew**, c**oo**
- ʌ **u**nder, p**u**tt, b**u**d
- eɪ **ei**ght, w**a**de, b**ay**
- aɪ **i**ce, b**i**te, t**ie**
- aʊ **ou**t, g**ow**n, pl**ow**
- ɔɪ **oy**ster, c**oi**l, b**oy**
- ɒ *British* b**o**nd, g**o**d
- ø *French* d**eu**x, *German* H**öh**le
- œ *French* b**œu**f, *German* H**ö**lle
- y *French* l**u**ne, *German* f**üh**len
- ʏ *German* f**ü**llt
- ~ (tilde as in ã, ɔ̃, ɛ̃) *French* v**in**, b**on**, bi**en**
- ː indicates that the preceding vowel is long. Long vowels are almost always diphthongs in English, but not in Spanish.

STRESS MARKS

- ˈ high stress **pen**manship
- ˌ low stress penman**ship**

CONSONANTS

- b **b**a**b**y, la**b**or, ca**b**
- β *Spanish* ca**b**o, óva**l**o
- d **d**ay, rea**d**y, ki**d**
- dʒ **j**ust, ba**dg**er, fu**dg**e
- ð **th**en, ei**th**er, ba**th**e
- f **f**oe, tou**gh**, bu**ff**
- g **g**o, bi**gg**er, ba**g**
- ɣ *Spanish* tra**g**ar, da**g**a
- h **h**ot, a**h**a
- j **y**es, vine**y**ard
- ʲ marks palatalization as in *French* digne [dinʲ]
- k **c**at, **k**eep, la**cqu**er, flo**ck**
- l **l**aw, ho**ll**ow, boi**l**
- m **m**at, he**m**p, ha**mm**er, ri**m**
- n **n**ew, te**n**t, te**n**or, ru**n**
- ŋ ru**ng**, ha**ng**, swi**ng**er
- ɲ *Spanish* caba**ñ**a, pi**ñ**a
- p **p**ay, la**p**se, to**p**
- r **r**ope, bu**r**n, ta**r**
- s **s**ad, mi**s**t, ki**ss**
- ʃ **sh**oe, mi**ss**ion, slu**sh**
- t **t**oe, bu**tt**on, ma**t**
- t̬ indicates that some speakers of English pronounce this as a voiced alveolar flap [ɾ], as in la**t**er, ca**tt**y, ba**tt**le
- tʃ **ch**oose, ba**tch**
- θ **th**in, e**th**er, ba**th**
- v **v**at, ne**v**er, ca**v**e
- w **w**et, soft**w**are
- x *German* Ba**ch**, *Scots* lo**ch**, *Spanish* **g**ente, **j**efe
- z **z**oo, ea**s**y, bu**zz**
- ʒ **j**aborandi, a**z**ure, bei**g**e
- ʔ indicates a glottal stop, the sound beginning the syllables in **uh-oh**
- *h, k, p, t* when italicized indicate sounds which are present in the pronunciation of some speakers of English but absent in that of others, so that *whence* [ˈ*h*wɛn*t*s] can be pronounced as [ˈwɛns], [ˈhwɛns], [ˈwɛnts], or [ˈhwɛnts]

Spanish Grammar

Accentuation

Spanish word stress is generally determined according to the following rules:

- Words ending in a vowel, or in *-n* or *-s,* are stressed on the penultimate syllable (*za**pa**to, **lla**man*).
- Words ending in a consonant other than *-n* or *-s* are stressed on the last syllable (*per**diz**, curiosi**dad***).

Exceptions to these rules have a written accent mark over the stressed vowel (***fá**cil, habla**rá**, **úl**timo*). There are also a few words which take accent marks in order to distinguish them from homonyms (*si, sí; que, qué; el, él;* etc.).

Adverbs ending in *-mente* have two stressed syllables since they retain both the stress of the root word and of the *-mente* suffix (***len**ta**men**te, di**fí**cil**men**te*). Many compounds also have two stressed syllables (***lim**piapara**bri**sas*).

Punctuation and Capitalization

Questions and exclamations in Spanish are preceded by an inverted question mark ¿ and an inverted exclamation mark ¡, respectively:

¿Cuándo llamó Ana?
Y tú, ¿qué piensas?

¡No hagas eso!
Pero, ¡qué lástima!

In Spanish, unlike English, the following words are not capitalized:

- Names of days, months, and languages (*jueves, octubre, español*).
- Spanish adjectives or nouns derived from proper nouns (*los nicaragüenses, una teoría marxista*).

Articles

1. Definite Article

Spanish has five forms of the definite article: *el* (masculine singular), *la* (feminine singular), *los* (masculine plural), *las* (feminine plural), and *lo* (neuter). The first four agree in gender and number with the nouns they limit (*el carro,* the car; *las tijeras,* the scissors), although the form *el* is used with feminine singular nouns beginning with a stressed *a-* or *ha-* (*el águila, el hambre*).

The neuter article *lo* is used with the masculine singular form of an adjective to express an abstract concept (*lo mejor de este método,* the best thing about this method; *lo meticuloso de su trabajo,* the meticulousness of her work; *lo mismo para mí,* the same for me).

Whenever the masculine article *el* immediately follows the words *de* or *a,* it combines with them to form the contractions *del* and *al,* respectively (*viene* ***del*** *campo, vi* ***al*** *hermano de Roberto*).

The use of *el, la, los,* and *las* in Spanish corresponds largely to the use of *the* in English; some exceptions are noted below.

The definite article is used:

- When referring to something as a class (*los gatos son ágiles,* cats are agile; *me gusta el café,* I like coffee).
- In references to meals and in most expressions of time (*¿comiste el almuerzo?,* did you eat lunch?; *vino el año pasado,* he came last year; *son las dos,* it's two o'clock; *prefiero el verano,* I prefer summer; *la reunión es el lunes,*

the meeting is on Monday; but: *hoy es lunes,* today is Monday).

- Before titles (except *don, doña, san, santo, santa, fray,* and *sor*) in third-person references to people (*la señora Rivera llamó,* Mrs. Rivera called; but: *hola, señora Rivera,* hello, Mrs. Rivera).
- In references to body parts and personal possessions (*me duele la cabeza,* my head hurts; *dejó el sombrero,* he left his hat).
- To mean "the one" or "the ones" when the subject is already understood (*la de madera,* the wooden one; *los que vi ayer,* the ones I saw yesterday).

The definite article is omitted:

- Before a noun in apposition, if the noun is not modified (*Caracas, capital de Venezuela;* but: *Pico Bolívar, la montaña más alta de Venezuela*).
- Before a number in a royal title (*Carlos Quinto,* Charles the Fifth).

2. Indefinite Article

The forms of the indefinite article in Spanish are *un* (masculine singular), *una* (feminine singular), *unos* (masculine plural), and *unas* (feminine plural). They agree in number and gender with the nouns they limit (*una mesa,* a table; *unos platos,* some plates), although the form *un* is used with feminine singular nouns beginning with a stressed *a-* or *ha-* (*un ala, un hacha*).

The use of *un, una, unos,* and *unas* in Spanish corresponds largely to the use of *a, an,* and *some* in English, with some exceptions:

- Indefinite articles are generally omitted before nouns identifying someone or something as a member of a class or category (*Paco es profesor/católico,* Paco is a professor/Catholic; *se llama páncreas,* it's called a pancreas).

- They are also often omitted in instances where quantity is understood from context (*vine sin chaqueta,* I came without a jacket; *no tengo carro,* I don't have a car).

Nouns

1. Gender

Nouns in Spanish are either masculine or feminine. A noun's gender can often be determined according to the following guidelines:

- Nouns ending in *-aje, -o,* or *-or* are usually masculine (*el traje, el libro, el sabor*), with some exceptions (*la mano, la foto, la labor,* etc.).
- Nouns ending in *-a, -dad, -ión, -tud,* or *-umbre* are usually feminine (*la alfombra, la capacidad, la excepción, la juventud, la certidumbre*). Exceptions include: *el día, el mapa,* and many learned borrowings ending in *-ma* (*el idioma, el tema*).

Most nouns referring to people or animals agree in gender with the subject (*el hombre, la mujer; el hermano, la hermana; el perro, la perra*). However, some nouns referring to people, including those ending in *-ista,* use the same form for both sexes (*el artista, la artista; el modelo, la modelo;* etc.).

A few names of animals exist in only one gender form (*la jirafa, el sapo,* etc.). In these instances, the adjectives *macho* and *hembra* are sometimes used to distinguish males and females (*una jirafa macho,* a male giraffe).

2. Pluralization

Plurals of Spanish nouns are formed as follows:

- Nouns ending in an unstressed vowel or an accented *-é* are pluralized by adding *-s* (*la vaca, las vacas; el café, los cafés*).

- Nouns ending in a consonant other than *-s,* or in a stressed vowel other than *-é,* are generally pluralized by adding *-es* (*el papel, los papeles; el rubí, los rubíes*). Exceptions include *papá* (*papás*) and *mamá* (*mamás*).
- Nouns with an unstressed final syllable ending in *-s* usually have a zero plural (*la crisis, las crisis; el jueves, los jueves*). Other nouns ending in *-s* add *-es* to form the plural (*el mes, los meses; el país, los países*).
- Nouns ending in *-z* are pluralized by changing the *-z* to *-c* and adding *-es* (*el lápiz, los lápices; la vez, las veces*).
- Many compound nouns have a zero plural (*el paraguas, los paraguas; el aguafiestas, los aguafiestas*).
- The plurals of *cualquiera* and *quienquiera* are *cualesquiera* and *quienesquiera,* respectively.

Adjectives

1. Gender and Number

Most adjectives agree in gender and number with the nouns they modify (un chico *alto,* una chica *alta,* unos chicos *altos,* unas chicas *altas*). Some adjectives, including those ending in *-e* and *-ista* (*fuerte, altruista*) and comparative adjectives ending in *-or* (*mayor, mejor*), vary only for number.

Adjectives whose masculine singular forms end in *-o* generally change the *-o* to *-a* to form the feminine (*pequeño* → *pequeña*). Masculine adjectives ending in *-án, -ón,* or *-dor,* and masculine adjectives of nationality which end in a consonant, usually add *-a* to form the feminine (*holgazán* → *holgazana*; *llorón* → *llorona*; *trabajador* → *trabajadora*; *irlandés* → *irlandesa*).

Adjectives are pluralized in much the same manner as nouns:

- The plurals of adjectives ending in an unstressed vowel or an accented *-é* are formed by adding an *-s* (un postre *rico,* unos postres *ricos;* una camisa *café,* unas camisas *cafés*).

- Adjectives ending in a consonant, or in a stressed vowel other than *-é,* are generally pluralized by adding *-es* (un niño *cortés,* unos niños *corteses;* una persona *iraní,* unas personas *iraníes*).
- Adjectives ending in *-z* are pluralized by changing the *-z* to *-c* and adding *-es* (una respuesta *sagaz*, unas respuestas *sagaces*).

2. Shortening

- The following masculine singular adjectives drop their final *-o* when they occur before a masculine singular noun: *bueno* (*buen*), *malo* (*mal*), *uno* (*un*), *alguno* (*algún*), *ninguno* (*ningún*), *primero* (*primer*), *tercero* (*tercer*).
- *Grande* shortens to *gran* before any singular noun.
- *Ciento* shortens to *cien* before any noun.
- The title *Santo* shortens to *San* before all masculine names except those beginning with *To-* or *Do-* (*San Juan, Santo Tomás*).

3. Position

Descriptive adjectives generally follow the nouns they modify (*una cosa útil, un actor famoso*). However, adjectives that express an inherent quality often precede the noun (*la blanca nieve*).

Some adjectives change meaning depending on whether they occur before or after the noun: *un pobre niño,* a poor (pitiable) child; *un niño pobre,* a poor (not rich) child; *un gran hombre,* a great man; *un hombre grande,* a big man; *el único libro,* the only book; *el libro único,* the unique book, etc.

4. Comparative and Superlative Forms

The comparative of Spanish adjectives is generally rendered as *más . . . que* (more . . . than) or *menos . . . que* (less . . . than): *soy más alta que él,* I'm taller than he; *son menos inteligentes que tú,* they're less intelligent than you.

The superlative of Spanish adjectives usually follows the formula *definite article* + (*noun* +) *más/menos* + *adjective: ella es la estudiante más trabajadora,* she is the hardest-working student; *él es el menos conocido,* he's the least known.

A few Spanish adjectives have irregular comparative and superlative forms:

Adjective	Comparative/Superlative
bueno (good)	**mejor** (better, best)
malo (bad)	**peor** (worse, worst)
grande[1] (big, great), **viejo** (old)	**mayor** (greater, older; greatest, oldest)
pequeño[1] (little), **joven** (young)	**menor** (lesser, younger; least, youngest)
mucho (much), **muchos** (many)	**más** (more, most)
poco (little), **pocos** (few)	**menos** (less, least)

[1]These words have regular comparative and superlative forms when used in reference to physical size: *él es más grande que yo; nuestra casa es la más pequeña.*

ABSOLUTE SUPERLATIVE

The absolute superlative is formed by placing *muy* before the adjective, or by adding the suffix *-ísimo* (*ella es muy simpática* or *ella es simpatiquísima,* she is very nice). The absolute superlative using *-ísimo* is formed according to the following rules:

- Adjectives ending in a consonant other than *-z* simply add the *-ísimo* ending (*fácil* → *facilísimo*).
- Adjectives ending in *-z* change this consonant to *-c* and add *-ísimo* (*feliz* → *felicísimo*).
- Adjectives ending in a vowel or diphthong drop the vowel or diphthong and add *-ísimo* (*claro* → *clarísimo; amplio* → *amplísimo*).

- Adjectives ending in *-co* or *-go* change these endings to *qu* and *gu,* respectively, and add *-ísimo* (*rico* → *riquísimo; largo* → *larguísimo*).
- Adjectives ending in *-ble* change this ending to *-bil* and add *-ísimo* (*notable* → *notabilísimo*).
- Adjectives containing the stressed diphthong *ie* or *ue* will sometimes change these to *e* and *o,* respectively (*ferviente* → *fervientísimo* or *ferventísimo; bueno* → *buenísimo* or *bonísimo*).

Adverbs

Adverbs can be formed by adding the adverbial suffix *-mente* to virtually any adjective (*fácil* → *fácilmente*). If the adjective varies for gender, the feminine form is used as the basis for forming the adverb (*rápido* → *rápidamente*).

Pronouns

1. Personal Pronouns

The personal pronouns in Spanish are:

Person	Singular		Plural	
FIRST	**yo**	I	**nosotros, nosotras**	we
SECOND	**tú**	you (familiar)	**vosotros**[2], **vosotras**[2]	you, all of you
	vos[1]	you		
	usted	you (formal)	**ustedes**[3]	you, all of you
THIRD	**él**	he	**ellos, ellas**	they
	ella	she		
	ello	it (neuter)		

[1] Familiar form used in addition to *tú* in South and Central America.
[2] Familiar form used in Spain.
[3] Formal form used in Spain; familiar and formal form used in Latin America.

FAMILIAR VS. FORMAL

The second person personal pronouns exist in both familiar and formal forms. The familiar forms are generally used when addressing relatives, friends, and children, although usage varies considerably from region to region; the formal forms are used in other contexts to show courtesy, respect, or emotional distance.

In Spain and in the Caribbean, *tú* is used exclusively as the familiar singular "you." In South and Central America, however, *vos* either competes with *tú* to varying degrees or replaces it entirely. (For a more detailed explanation of *vos* and its corresponding verb forms, refer to the Conjugation of Spanish Verbs section.)

The plural familiar form *vosotros, -as* is used only in Spain, where *ustedes* is reserved for formal contexts. In Latin America, *vosotros, -as* is not used, and *ustedes* serves as the all-purpose plural "you."

It should be noted that while *usted* and *ustedes* are regarded as second person pronouns, they take the third person form of the verb.

USAGE

In Spanish, personal pronouns are generally omitted (*voy al cine,* I'm going to the movies; *¿llamaron?,* did they call?), although they are sometimes used for purposes of emphasis or clarity (*se lo diré yo,* I will tell them; *vino ella, pero él se quedó,* she came, but he stayed behind). The forms *usted* and *ustedes* are usually included out of courtesy (*¿cómo está usted?,* how are you?).

Personal pronouns are not generally used in reference to inanimate objects or living creatures other than humans; in these instances, the pronoun is most often omitted (*¿es nuevo? no, es viejo,* is it new? no, it's old).

The neuter third person pronoun *ello* is reserved for indefinite subjects (as abstract concepts): *todo ello implica . . . ,* all of this implies . . . ; *por si ello fuera poco . . . ,* as if that weren't enough . . . . It most commonly appears in formal writing and speech. In less formal contexts, *ello* is often either omitted or replaced with *esto, eso,* or *aquello*.

2. Prepositional Pronouns

Prepositional pronouns are used as the objects of prepositions (*¿es para mí?,* is it for me?; *se lo dio a ellos,* he gave it to them).

The prepositional pronouns in Spanish are:

Singular		Plural	
mí	me	**nosotros, nosotras**	us
ti	you	**vosotros**[1]**, vosotras**[1]	you
usted	you (formal)	**ustedes**	you
él	him	**ellos, ellas**	them
ella	her		
ello	it (neuter)		
sí	yourself, himself, herself, itself, oneself	**sí**	yourselves, themselves

[1]Used primarily in Spain.

When the preposition *con* is followed by *mí, ti,* or *sí,* both words are replaced by *conmigo, contigo,* and *consigo,* respectively (*¿vienes conmigo?,* are you coming with me?; *habló contigo,* he spoke with you; *no lo trajo consigo,* she didn't bring it with her).

3. Object Pronouns

DIRECT OBJECT PRONOUNS

Direct object pronouns represent the primary goal or result of the action of a verb. The direct object pronouns in Spanish are:

Singular		Plural	
me	me	**nos**	us
te	you	**os**[1]	you
le[2]	you, him	**les**[2]	you, them
lo	you, him, it	**los**	you, them
la	you, her, it	**las**	you, them

[1]Used only in Spain.
[2]Used mainly in Spain.

Agreement

The third person forms agree in both gender and number with the nouns they replace or the people they refer to (*pintó las paredes,* she painted the walls → *las pintó,* she painted them; *visitaron al señor Juárez,* they visited Mr. Juárez → *lo visitaron,* they visited him). The remaining forms vary only for number.

Position

Direct object pronouns are normally affixed to the end of an affirmative command, a simple infinitive, or a present participle (*¡hazlo!,* do it!; *es difícil hacerlo,* it's difficult to do it; *haciéndolo, aprenderás,* you'll learn by doing it). With constructions involving an auxiliary verb and an infinitive or present participle, the pronoun may occur either immediately before the construction or suffixed to it (*lo voy a hacer* or *voy a hacerlo,* I'm going to do it; *estoy haciéndolo* or *lo estoy haciendo,* I'm doing it). In all other cases, the pronoun immediately precedes the conjugated verb (*no lo haré,* I won't do it).

Regional Variation

In Spain and in a few areas of Latin America, *le* and *les* are used in place of *lo* and *los* when referring to or addressing people (*le vieron,* they saw him; *les vistió,* she dressed them). In most parts of Latin America, however, *los* and *las* are used for the second person plural in both formal and familiar contexts.

The second person plural familiar form *os* is restricted to Spain.

INDIRECT OBJECT PRONOUNS

Indirect object pronouns represent the secondary goal of the action of a verb (*me dio el regalo,* he gave me the gift; *les dije que no,* I told them no). The indirect object pronouns in Spanish are:

Singular		Plural	
me	(to, for, from) me	**nos**	(to, for, from) us
te	(to, for, from) you	**os**[1]	(to, for, from) you
le	(to, for, from) you, him, her, it	**les**	(to, for, from) you, them
se[2]		**se**[2]	

[1]Used only in Spain.
[2]See explanation below.

Position

Indirect object pronouns follow the same rules as direct object pronouns with regard to their position in relation to verbs. When they occur with direct object pronouns, the indirect object pronoun always precedes (*nos lo dio,* she gave it to us; *estoy trayéndotela,* I'm bringing it to you).

Use of *Se*

When the indirect object pronouns *le* or *les* occur before any direct object pronoun beginning with an *l-,* the indirect object pronouns *le* and *les* convert to *se* (*les mandé la carta,* I sent them the letter → *se la mandé,* I sent it to them; *vamos a comprarle los aretes,* let's buy her the earrings → *vamos a comprárselos,* let's buy them for her).

4. Reflexive Pronouns

Reflexive pronouns are used to refer back to the subject of the verb (*me hice daño,* I hurt myself; *se vistieron,* they got dressed, they dressed themselves; *nos lo compramos,* we bought it for ourselves).

The reflexive pronouns in Spanish are:

Singular		Plural	
me	myself	**nos**	ourselves
te	yourself	**os**[1]	yourselves
se	yourself, himself, herself, itself	**se**	yourselves, themselves

[1]Used only in Spain.

Reflexive pronouns are also used:

- When the verb describes an action performed to one's own body, clothing, etc. (*me quité los zapatos,* I took off my shoes; *se arregló el pelo,* he fixed his hair).

- In the plural, to indicate reciprocal action (*se hablan con frecuencia,* they speak with each other frequently).
- In the third person singular and plural, as an indefinite subject reference (*se dice que es verdad,* they say it's true; *nunca se sabe,* one never knows; *se escribieron miles de páginas,* thousands of pages were written).

It should be noted that many verbs which take reflexive pronouns in Spanish have intransitive equivalents in English (*ducharse,* to shower; *quejarse,* to complain; etc.).

5. Relative Pronouns

Relative pronouns introduce subordinate clauses acting as nouns or modifiers (*el libro que escribió . . .*, the book that he wrote . . . ; *las chicas a quienes conociste . . .*, the girls whom you met . . .). In Spanish, the relative pronouns are:

que (that, which, who, whom)

quien, quienes (who, whom, that, whoever, whomever)

el cual, la cual, los cuales, las cuales (which, who)

el que, la que, los que, las que (which, who, whoever)

lo cual (which)

lo que (what, which, whatever)

cuanto, cuanta, cuantos, cuantas (all those that, all that, whatever, whoever, as much as, as many as)

Relative pronouns are not omitted in Spanish as they often are in English: *el carro que vi ayer,* the car (that) I saw yesterday. When relative pronouns are used with prepositions, the preposition precedes the clause (*la película sobre la cual le hablé,* the film I spoke to you about).

The relative pronoun *que* can be used in reference to both people and things. Unlike other relative pronouns, *que* does not take the personal *a* when used as a direct object referring to a person (*el hombre que llamé,* the man that I called; but: *el hombre a quien llamé,* the man whom I called).

Quien is used only in reference to people. It varies in number with the explicit or implied antecedent (*las mujeres con quienes charlamos . . .,* the women we chatted with; *quien lo hizo pagará,* whoever did it will pay).

El cual and *el que* vary for both number and gender, and are therefore often used in situations where *que* or *quien(es)* might create ambiguity: *nos contó algunas cosas sobre los libros, las cuales eran interesantes,* he told us some things about the books which (the things) were interesting.

Lo cual and *lo que* are used to refer back to a whole clause, or to something indefinite (*dijo que iría, lo cual me alegró,* he said he would go, which made me happy; *pide lo que quieras,* ask for whatever you want).

Cuanto varies for both number and gender with the implied antecedent: *conté a cuantas (personas) pude,* I counted as many (people) as I could. If an indefinite mass quantity is referred to, the masculine singular form is used (*anoté cuanto decía,* I jotted down whatever he said).

Possessives

1. Possessive Adjectives

UNSTRESSED FORMS

Singular		Plural	
mi(s)	my	**nuestro(s), nuestra(s)**	our
tu(s)	your	**vuestro(s)**[1], **vuestra(s)**[1]	your
su(s)	your, his, her, its	**su(s)**	your, their

[1]Used only in Spain.

STRESSED FORMS

Singular		Plural	
mío(s), mía(s)	my, mine, of mine	**nuestro(s), nuestra(s)**	our, ours, of ours
tuyo(s), tuya(s)	your, yours, of yours	**vuestro(s)**[1], **vuestra(s)**[1]	your, yours, of yours
suyo(s), suya(s)	your, yours, of yours; his, of his; her, hers, of hers; its, of its	**suyo(s), suya(s)**	your, yours, of yours; their, theirs, of theirs

[1]Used only in Spain.

The unstressed forms of possessive adjectives precede the nouns they modify (*mis zapatos,* my shoes; *nuestra escuela,* our school).

The stressed forms occur after the noun and are often used for purposes of emphasis (*el carro tuyo,* your car; *la pluma es mía,* the pen is mine; *unos amigos nuestros,* some friends of ours).

All possessive adjectives agree with the noun in number. The stressed forms, as well as the unstressed forms *nuestro* and *vuestro,* also vary for gender.

2. Possessive Pronouns

The possessive pronouns have the same forms as the stressed possessive adjectives (see table above). They are always preceded by the definite article, and they agree in number and gender with the nouns they replace (*las llaves mías,* my keys → *las mías,* mine; *los guantes nuestros,* our gloves → *los nuestros,* ours).

Demonstratives

1. Demonstrative Adjectives

The demonstrative adjectives in Spanish are:

Singular		Plural	
este, esta	this	**estos, estas**	these
ese, esa	that	**esos, esas**	those
aquel, aquella	that	**aquellos, aquellas**	those

Demonstrative adjectives agree with the nouns they modify in gender and number (*esta chica, aquellos árboles*). They normally precede the noun, but may occasionally occur after for purposes of emphasis or to express contempt: *en la época aquella de cambio,* in that era of change; *el perro ese ha ladrado toda la noche,* that (awful, annoying, etc.) dog barked all night long.

The forms *aquel, aquella, aquellos,* and *aquellas* are generally used in reference to people and things that are relatively distant from the speaker in space or time: *ese libro,* that book (a few feet away); *aquel libro,* that book (way over there).

2. Demonstrative Pronouns

The demonstrative pronouns in Spanish are orthographically identical to the demonstrative adjectives except that they take an accent mark over the stressed vowel (*éste, ése, aquél,* etc.). In addition, there are three neuter forms—*esto, eso,* and *aquello*—which are used when referring to abstract ideas or unidentified things (*¿te dijo eso?,* he said that to you?; *¿qué es esto?,* what is this?; *tráeme todo aquello,* bring me all that stuff).

Except for the neuter forms, demonstrative pronouns agree in gender and number with the nouns they replace (*esta silla,* this chair → *ésta,* this one; *aquellos vasos,* those glasses → *aquéllos,* those ones).

Spanish Numbers

Cardinal Numbers

1	uno
2	dos
3	tres
4	cuatro
5	cinco
6	seis
7	siete
8	ocho
9	nueve
10	diez
11	once
12	doce
13	trece
14	catorce
15	quince
16	dieciséis
17	diecisiete
18	dieciocho
19	diecinueve
20	veinte
21	veintiuno
22	veintidós
23	veintitrés
24	veinticuatro
25	veinticinco
26	veintiséis
27	veintisiete
28	veintiocho
29	veintinueve
30	treinta
31	treinta y uno
32	treinta y dos
33	treinta y tres
34	treinta y cuatro
35	treinta y cinco
36	treinta y seis
37	treinta y siete
38	treinta y ocho
39	treinta y nueve
40	cuarenta
41	cuarenta y uno
50	cincuenta
60	sesenta
70	setenta
80	ochenta
90	noventa
100	cien
101	ciento uno
102	ciento dos
200	doscientos
300	trescientos
400	cuatrocientos
500	quinientos
600	seiscientos
700	setecientos
800	ochocientos
900	novecientos
1,000	mil
1,001	mil uno
2,000	dos mil
100,000	cien mil
1,000,000	un millón
1,000,000,000	mil millones

Ordinal Numbers

1st	primero, -ra	18th	decimoctavo, -va
2nd	segundo, -da	19th	decimonoveno, -na; *or* decimonono, -na
3rd	tercero, -ra	20th	vigésimo, -ma
4th	cuarto, -ta	21st	vigésimoprimero, vigésimaprimera
5th	quinto, -ta	22nd	vigésimosegundo, vigésimasegunda
6th	sexto, -ta	30th	trigésimo, -ma
7th	séptimo, -ma	40th	cuadragésimo, -ma
8th	octavo, -va	50th	quincuagésimo, -ma
9th	noveno, -na	60th	sexagésimo, -ma
10th	décimo, -ma	70th	septuagésimo, -ma
11th	undécimo, -ma	80th	octogésimo, -ma
12th	duodécimo, -ma	90th	nonagésimo, -ma
13th	decimotercero, -ra	100th	centésimo, -ma
14th	decimocuarto, -ta		
15th	decimoquinto, -ta		
16th	decimosexto, -ta		
17th	decimoséptimo, -ma		

Conjugation of Spanish Verbs

Simple Tenses

TENSE	REGULAR VERBS ENDING IN -AR hablar	
PRESENT INDICATIVE	hablo hablas habla	hablamos habláis hablan
PRESENT SUBJUNCTIVE	hable hables hable	hablemos habléis hablen
PRETERIT INDICATIVE	hablé hablaste habló	hablamos hablasteis hablaron
IMPERFECT INDICATIVE	hablaba hablabas hablaba	hablábamos hablabais hablaban
IMPERFECT SUBJUNCTIVE	hablara hablaras hablara *or* hablase hablases hablase	habláramos hablarais hablaran hablásemos hablaseis hablasen
FUTURE INDICATIVE	hablaré hablarás hablará	hablaremos hablaréis hablarán
FUTURE SUBJUNCTIVE	hablare hablares hablare	habláremos hablareis hablaren
CONDITIONAL	hablaría hablarías hablaría	hablaríamos hablaríais hablarían
IMPERATIVE	 habla hable	hablemos hablad hablen
PRESENT PARTICIPLE (GERUND)	hablando	
PAST PARTICIPLE	hablado	

REGULAR VERBS ENDING IN -ER comer		REGULAR VERBS ENDING IN -IR vivir	
como	comemos	vivo	vivimos
comes	coméis	vives	vivís
come	comen	vive	viven
coma	comamos	viva	vivamos
comas	comáis	vivas	viváis
coma	coman	viva	vivan
comí	comimos	viví	vivimos
comiste	comisteis	viviste	vivisteis
comió	comieron	vivió	vivieron
comía	comíamos	vivía	vivíamos
comías	comíais	vivías	vivíais
comía	comían	vivía	vivían
comiera	comiéramos	viviera	viviéramos
comieras	comierais	vivieras	vivierais
comiera	comieran	viviera	vivieran
or		*or*	
comiese	comiésemos	viviese	viviésemos
comieses	comieseis	vivieses	vivieseis
comiese	comiesen	viviese	viviesen
comeré	comeremos	viviré	viviremos
comerás	comeréis	vivirás	viviréis
comerá	comerán	vivirá	vivirán
comiere	comiéremos	viviere	viviéremos
comieres	comiereis	vivieres	viviereis
comiere	comieren	viviere	vivieren
comería	comeríamos	viviría	viviríamos
comerías	comeríais	vivirías	viviríais
comería	comerían	viviría	vivirían
	comamos		vivamos
come	comed	vive	vivid
coma	coman	viva	vivan
comiendo		viviendo	
comido		vivido	

Compound Tenses

1. Perfect Tenses

The perfect tenses are formed with *haber* and the past participle:

PRESENT PERFECT

he hablado, etc. (*indicative*);
haya hablado, etc. (*subjunctive*)

PAST PERFECT

había hablado, etc. (*indicative*);
hubiera hablado, etc. (*subjuntive*)
or
hubiese hablado, etc. (*subjunctive*)

PRETERIT PERFECT

hube hablado, etc. (*indicative*)

FUTURE PERFECT

habré hablado, etc. (*indicative*)

CONDITIONAL PERFECT

habría hablado, etc. (*indicative*)

2. Progressive Tenses

The progressive tenses are formed with *estar* and the present participle:

PRESENT PROGRESSIVE

estoy llamando, etc. (*indicative*);
esté llamando, etc. (*subjunctive*)

IMPERFECT PROGRESSIVE

estaba llamando, etc. (*indicative*);
estuviera llamando, etc. (*subjunctive*)
or
estuviese llamando, etc. (*subjunctive*)

PRETERIT PROGRESSIVE

estuve llamando, etc. (*indicative*)

FUTURE PROGRESSIVE

estaré llamando, etc. (*indicative*)

CONDITIONAL PROGRESSIVE

estaría llamando, etc. (*indicative*)

PRESENT PERFECT PROGRESSIVE

he estado llamando, etc. (*indicative*);
haya estado llamando, etc. (*subjunctive*)

PAST PERFECT PROGRESSIVE

había estado llamando, etc. (*indicative*);
hubiera estado llamando, etc. (*subjunctive*)
or
hubiese estado llamando, etc. (*subjunctive*)

Use of *Vos*

In parts of South and Central America, *vos* often replaces or competes with *tú* as the second person familiar personal pronoun. It is particularly well established in the Río de la Plata region and much of Central America.

The pronoun *vos* often takes a distinct set of verb forms, usually in the present tense and the imperative. These vary widely from region to region; examples of the most common forms are shown below.

INFINITIVE FORM	hablar	comer	vivir
PRESENT INDICATIVE	vos hablás	vos comés	vos vivís
PRESENT SUBJUNCTIVE	vos hablés	vos comás	vos vivás
IMPERATIVE	hablá	comé	viví

In some areas, *vos* may take the *tú* or *vosotros* forms of the verb, while in others (as Uruguay), *tú* is combined with the *vos* verb forms.

Irregular Verbs

The *imperfect subjunctive,* the *future subjunctive,* the *conditional,* and the remaining forms of the *imperative* are not included in the model conjugations list, but can be derived as follows:

The *imperfect subjunctive* and the *future subjunctive* are formed from the third person plural form of the preterit tense by removing the last syllable (*-ron*) and adding the appropriate suffix:

PRETERIT INDICATIVE, THIRD PERSON PLURAL (querer)	quisieron
IMPERFECT SUBJUNCTIVE (querer)	quisiera, quisieras, etc. *or* quisiese, quisieses, etc.
FUTURE SUBJUNCTIVE (querer)	quisiere, quisieres, etc.

The conditional uses the same stem as the future indicative:

FUTURE INDICATIVE (poner)	pondré, pondrás, etc.
CONDITIONAL (poner)	pondría, pondrías, etc.

The third person singular, first person plural, and third person plural forms of the *imperative* are the same as the corresponding forms of the present subjunctive.

The second person plural *(vosotros)* form of the *imperative* is formed by removing the final *-r* of the infinitive form and adding a *-d* (ex.: *oír → oíd).*

Model Conjugations of Irregular Verbs

The model conjugations below include the following simple tenses: the *present indicative* (*IND*), the *present subjunctive* (*SUBJ*), the *preterit indicative* (*PRET*), the *imperfect indicative* (*IMPF*), the *future indicative* (*FUT*), the second person singular form of the *imperative* (*IMPER*), the *present participle* or *gerund* (*PRP*), and the *past participle* (*PP*). Each set of conjugations is preceded by the corresponding infinitive form of the verb, shown in bold type. Only tenses containing irregularities are listed, and the irregular verb forms within each tense are displayed in bold type.

Conjugation of Spanish Verbs

Each irregular verb entry in the Spanish-English section of this dictionary is cross-referred by number to one of the following model conjugations. These cross-reference numbers are shown in curly braces { } immediately following the entry's functional label.

1 **abolir** *(defective verb)* **:** *IND* abolimos, abolís *(other forms not used); SUBJ (not used); IMPER (only second person plural is used)*

2 **abrir :** *PP* abierto

3 **actuar :** *IND* **actúo**, **actúas**, **actúa**, actuamos, actuáis, **actúan;** *SUBJ* **actúe, actúes, actúe,** actuemos, actuéis, **actúen;** *IMPER* **actúa**

4 **adquirir :** *IND* **adquiero, adquieres, adquiere,** adquirimos, adquirís, **adquieren;** *SUBJ* **adquiera, adquieras, adquiera,** adquiramos, adquiráis, **adquieran;** *IMPER* **adquiere**

5 **airar :** *IND* **aíro, aíras, aíra,** airamos, airáis, **aíran;** *SUBJ* **aíre, aíres, aíre,** airemos, airéis, **aíren;** *IMPER* **aíra**

6 **andar :** *PRET* **anduve, anduviste, anduvo, anduvimos, anduvisteis, anduvieron**

7 **asir :** *IND* **asgo,** ases, ase, asimos, asís, asen; *SUBJ* **asga, asgas, asga, asgamos, asgáis, asgan**

8 **aunar :** *IND* **aúno, aúnas, aúna,** aunamos, aunáis, **aúnan;** *SUBJ* **aúne, aúnes, aúne,** aunemos, aunéis, **aúnen;** *IMPER* **aúna**

9 **avergonzar :** IND **avergüenzo, avergüenzas, avergüenza,** avergonzamos, avergonzáis, **avergüenzan;** *SUBJ* **avergüence, avergüences, avergüence, avergoncemos, avergoncéis, avergüencen;** *PRET* **avergoncé;** *IMPER* **avergüenza**

10 **averiguar :** *SUBJ* **averigüe, averigües, averigüe, averigüemos, averigüéis, averigüen;** *PRET* **averigüé,** averiguaste, averiguó, averiguamos, averiguasteis, averiguaron

11 **bendecir :** *IND* **bendigo, bendices, bendice,** bendecimos, bendecís, **bendicen;** *SUBJ* **bendiga, bendigas, bendiga, bendigamos, bendigáis, bendigan;** *PRET* **bendije, bendijiste, bendijo, bendijimos, bendijisteis, bendijeron;** *IMPER* **bendice**

12 **caber** : *IND* **quepo,** cabes, cabe, cabemos, cabéis, caben; *SUBJ* **quepa, quepas, quepa, quepamos, quepáis, quepan;** *PRET* **cupe, cupiste, cupo, cupimos, cupisteis, cupieron;** *FUT* **cabré, cabrás, cabrá, cabremos, cabréis, cabrán**

13 **caer** : *IND* **caigo,** caes, cae, caemos, caéis, caen; *SUBJ* **caiga, caigas, caiga, caigamos, caigáis, caigan;** *PRET* caí, **caíste, cayó, caímos, caísteis, cayeron;** *PRP* **cayendo;** *PP* **caído**

14 **cocer** : *IND* **cuezo, cueces, cuece,** cocemos, cocéis, **cuecen;** *SUBJ* **cueza, cuezas, cueza, cozamos, cozáis, cuezan;** *IMPER* **cuece**

15 **coger** : *IND* **cojo,** coges, coge, cogemos, cogéis, cogen; *SUBJ* **coja, cojas, coja, cojamos, cojáis, cojan**

16 **colgar** : *IND* **cuelgo, cuelgas, cuelga,** colgamos, colgáis, **cuelgan;** *SUBJ* **cuelgue, cuelgues, cuelgue, colguemos, colguéis, cuelguen;** *PRET* **colgué,** colgaste, colgó, colgamos, colgasteis, colgaron; *IMPER* **cuelga**

17 **concernir** *(defective verb; used only in the third person singular and plural of the present indicative, present subjunctive, and imperfect subjunctive) see* 25 **discernir**

18 **conocer** : *IND* **conozco,** conoces, conoce, conocemos, conocéis, conocen; *SUBJ* **conozca, conozcas, conozca, conozcamos, conozcáis, conozcan**

19 **contar** : *IND* **cuento, cuentas, cuenta,** contamos, contáis, **cuentan;** *SUBJ* **cuente, cuentes, cuente,** contemos, contéis, **cuenten;** *IMPER* **cuenta**

20 **creer** : *PRET* creí, **creíste, creyó, creímos, creísteis, creyeron;** *PRP* **creyendo;** *PP* **creído**

21 **cruzar** : *SUBJ* **cruce, cruces, cruce, crucemos, crucéis, crucen;** *PRET* **crucé,** cruzaste, cruzó, cruzamos, cruzasteis, cruzaron

22 **dar** : *IND* **doy,** das, da, damos, **dais,** dan; *SUBJ* **dé,** des, **dé,** demos, **deis,** den; *PRET* **di, diste, dio, dimos, disteis, dieron**

23 **decir** : *IND* **digo, dices, dice,** decimos, decís, **dicen;** *SUBJ* **diga, digas, diga, digamos, digáis, digan;** *PRET* **dije, dijiste, dijo,**

dijimos, dijisteis, dijeron; *FUT* **diré, dirás, dirá, diremos, diréis, dirán;** *IMPER* **di;** *PRP* **diciendo;** *PP* **dicho**

24 **delinquir :** *IND* **delinco,** delinques, delinque, delinquimos, delinquís, delinquen; *SUBJ* **delinca, delincas, delinca, delincamos, delincáis, delincan**

25 **discernir :** *IND* **discierno, disciernes, discierne,** discernimos, discernís, **disciernen;** *SUBJ* **discierna, disciernas, discierna,** discernamos, discernáis, **disciernan;** *IMPER* **discierne**

26 **distinguir :** *IND* **distingo,** distingues, distingue, distinguimos, distinguís, distinguen; *SUBJ* **distinga, distingas, distinga, distingamos, distingáis, distingan**

27 **dormir :** *IND* **duermo, duermes, duerme,** dormimos, dormís, **duermen;** *SUBJ* **duerma, duermas, duerma, durmamos, durmáis, duerman;** *PRET* dormí, dormiste, **durmió,** dormimos, dormisteis, **durmieron;** *IMPER* **duerme;** *PRP* **durmiendo**

28 **elegir :** *IND* **elijo, eliges, elige,** elegimos, elegís, **eligen;** *SUBJ* **elija, elijas, elija, elijamos, elijáis, elijan;** *PRET* elegí, elegiste, **eligió,** elegimos, elegisteis, **eligieron;** *IMPER* **elige;** *PRP* **eligiendo**

29 **empezar :** *IND* **empiezo, empiezas, empieza,** empezamos, empezáis, **empiezan;** *SUBJ* **empiece, empieces, empiece, empecemos, empecéis, empiecen;** *PRET* **empecé,** empezaste, empezó, empezamos, empezasteis, empezaron; *IMPER* **empieza**

30 **enraizar :** *IND* **enraízo, enraízas, enraíza,** enraizamos, enraizáis, **enraízan;** *SUBJ* **enraíce, enraíces, enraíce, enraicemos, enraicéis, enraícen;** *PRET* **enraicé,** enraizaste, enraizó, enraizamos, enraizasteis, enraizaron; *IMPER* **enraíza**

31 **erguir :** *IND* **irgo** *or* **yergo, irgues** *or* **yergues, irgue** *or* **yergue,** erguimos, erguís, **irguen** *or* **yerguen;** *SUBJ* **irga** *or* **yerga, irgas** *or* **yergas, irga** *or* **yerga, irgamos, irgáis, irgan** *or* **yergan;** *PRET* erguí, erguiste, **irguió,** erguimos, erguisteis, **irguieron;** *IMPER* **irgue** *or* **yergue;** *PRP* **irguiendo**

32 **errar :** *IND* **yerro, yerras, yerra,** erramos, erráis, **yerran;** *SUBJ* **yerre, yerres, yerre,** erremos, erréis, **yerren;** *IMPER* **yerra**

33 **escribir :** *PP* **escrito**

34 **estar :** *IND* **estoy, estás, está,** estamos, estáis, **están;** *SUBJ* **esté, estés, esté,** estemos, estéis, **estén;** *PRET* **estuve, estuviste, estuvo, estuvimos, estuvisteis, estuvieron;** *IMPER* **está**

35 **exigir :** *IND* **exijo,** exiges, exige, exigimos, exigís, exigen; *SUBJ* **exija, exijas, exija, exijamos, exijáis, exijan**

36 **forzar :** *IND* **fuerzo, fuerzas, fuerza,** forzamos, forzáis, **fuerzan;** *SUBJ* **fuerce, fuerces, fuerce, forcemos, forcéis, fuercen;** *PRET* **forcé,** forzaste, forzó, forzamos, forzasteis, forzaron; *IMPER* **fuerza**

37 **freír :** *IND* **frío, fríes, fríe, freímos,** freís, **fríen;** *SUBJ* **fría, frías, fría, friamos, friáis, frían;** *PRET* freí, **freíste, frió, freímos, freísteis, frieron;** *IMPER* **fríe;** *PRP* **friendo;** *PP* **frito**

38 **gruñir :** *PRET* gruñí, gruñiste, **gruñó,** gruñimos, gruñisteis, **gruñeron;** *PRP* **gruñendo**

39 **haber :** *IND* **he, has, ha, hemos,** habéis, **han;** *SUBJ* **haya, hayas, haya, hayamos, hayáis, hayan;** *PRET* **hube, hubiste, hubo, hubimos, hubisteis, hubieron;** *FUT* **habré, habrás, habrá, habremos, habréis, habrán;** *IMPER* **he**

40 **hacer :** *IND* **hago,** haces, hace, hacemos, hacéis, hacen; *SUBJ* **haga, hagas, haga, hagamos, hagáis, hagan;** *PRET* **hice, hiciste, hizo, hicimos, hicisteis, hicieron;** *FUT* **haré, harás, hará, haremos, haréis, harán;** *IMPER* **haz;** *PP* **hecho**

41 **huir :** *IND* **huyo, huyes, huye,** huimos, huís, **huyen;** *SUBJ* **huya, huyas, huya, huyamos, huyáis, huyan;** *PRET* huí, huiste, **huyó,** huimos, huisteis, **huyeron;** *IMPER* **huye;** *PRP* **huyendo**

42 **imprimir :** *PP* **impreso**

43 **ir :** *IND* **voy, vas, va, vamos, vais, van;** *SUBJ* **vaya, vayas, vaya, vayamos, vayáis, vayan;** *PRET* **fui, fuiste, fue, fuimos, fuisteis, fueron;** *IMPF* **iba, ibas, iba, íbamos, ibais, iban;** *IMPER* **ve;** *PRP* **yendo;** *PP* **ido**

44 **jugar :** *IND* **juego, juegas, juega,** jugamos, jugáis, **juegan;** *SUBJ* **juegue, juegues, juegue, juguemos, juguéis, jueguen;** *PRET* **jugué,** jugaste, jugó, jugamos, jugasteis, jugaron; *IMPER* **juega**

45 **lucir :** *IND* **luzco,** luces, luce, lucimos, lucís, lucen; *SUBJ* **luzca, luzcas, luzca, luzcamos, luzcáis, luzcan**

46 **morir :** *IND* **muero, mueres, muere,** morimos, morís, **mueren;** *SUBJ* **muera, mueras, muera, muramos, muráis, mueran;** *PRET* morí, moriste, **murió,** morimos, moristeis, **murieron;** *IMPER* **muere;** *PRP* **muriendo;** *PP* **muerto**

47 **mover :** *IND* **muevo, mueves, mueve,** movemos, movéis, **mueven;** *SUBJ* **mueva, muevas, mueva,** movamos, mováis, **muevan;** *IMPER* **mueve**

48 **nacer :** *IND* **nazco,** naces, nace, nacemos, nacéis, nacen; *SUBJ* **nazca, nazcas, nazca, nazcamos, nazcáis, nazcan**

49 **negar :** *IND* **niego, niegas, niega,** negamos, negáis, **niegan;** *SUBJ* **niegue, niegues, niegue, neguemos, neguéis, nieguen;** *PRET* **negué,** negaste, negó, negamos, negasteis, negaron; *IMPER* **niega**

50 **oír :** *IND* **oigo, oyes, oye, oímos,** oís, **oyen;** *SUBJ* **oiga, oigas, oiga, oigamos, oigáis, oigan;** *PRET* oí, **oíste, oyó, oímos, oísteis, oyeron;** *IMPER* **oye;** *PRP* **oyendo;** *PP* **oído**

51 **oler :** *IND* **huelo, hueles, huele,** olemos, oléis, **huelen;** *SUBJ* **huela, huelas, huela,** olamos, oláis, **huelan;** *IMPER* **huele**

52 **pagar :** *SUBJ* **pague, pagues, pague, paguemos, paguéis, paguen;** *PRET* **pagué,** pagaste, pagó, pagamos, pagasteis, pagaron

53 **parecer :** *IND* **parezco,** pareces, parece, parecemos, parecéis, parecen; *SUBJ* **parezca, parezcas, parezca, parezcamos, parezcáis, parezcan**

54 **pedir :** *IND* **pido, pides, pide,** pedimos, pedís, **piden;** *SUBJ* **pida, pidas, pida, pidamos, pidáis, pidan;** *PRET* pedí, pediste, **pidió,** pedimos, pedisteis, **pidieron;** *IMPER* **pide;** *PRP* **pidiendo**

55 **pensar :** *IND* **pienso, piensas, piensa,** pensamos, pensáis, **piensan;** *SUBJ* **piense, pienses, piense,** pensemos, penséis, **piensen;** *IMPER* **piensa**

56 **perder :** *IND* **pierdo, pierdes, pierde,** perdemos, perdéis, **pierden;** *SUBJ* **pierda, pierdas, pierda,** perdamos, perdáis, **pierdan;** *IMPER* **pierde**

57 **placer** : *IND* **plazco,** places, place, placemos, placéis, placen; *SUBJ* **plazca, plazcas, plazca, plazcamos, plazcáis, plazcan;** *PRET* plací, placiste, plació *or* **plugo,** placimos, placisteis, placieron *or* **pluguieron**

58 **poder** : *IND* **puedo, puedes, puede,** podemos, podéis, **pueden;** *SUBJ* **pueda, puedas, pueda,** podamos, podáis, **puedan;** *PRET* **pude, pudiste, pudo, pudimos, pudisteis, pudieron;** *FUT* **podré, podrás, podrá, podremos, podréis, podrán;** *IMPER* **puede;** *PRP* **pudiendo**

59 **podrir** *or* **pudrir** : *PP* **podrido** *(all other forms based on* pudrir*)*

60 **poner** : *IND* **pongo,** pones, pone, ponemos, ponéis, ponen; *SUBJ* **ponga, pongas, ponga, pongamos, pongáis, pongan;** *PRET* **puse, pusiste, puso, pusimos, pusisteis, pusieron;** *FUT* **pondré, pondrás, pondrá, pondremos, pondréis, pondrán;** *IMPER* **pon;** *PP* **puesto**

61 **producir** : *IND* **produzco,** produces, produce, producimos, producís, producen; *SUBJ* **produzca, produzcas, produzca, produzcamos, produzcáis, produzcan;** *PRET* **produje, produjiste, produjo, produjimos, produjisteis, produjeron**

62 **prohibir** : *IND* **prohíbo, prohíbes, prohíbe,** prohibimos, prohibís, **prohíben;** *SUBJ* **prohíba, prohíbas, prohíba,** prohibamos, prohibáis, **prohíban;** *IMPER* **prohíbe**

63 **proveer** : *PRET* proveí, **proveíste, proveyó, proveímos, proveísteis, proveyeron;** *PRP* **proveyendo;** *PP* **provisto**

64 **querer** : *IND* **quiero, quieres, quiere,** queremos, queréis, **quieren;** *SUBJ* **quiera, quieras, quiera,** queramos, queráis, **quieran;** *PRET* **quise, quisiste, quiso, quisimos, quisisteis, quisieron;** *FUT* **querré, querrás, querrá, querremos, querréis, querrán;** *IMPER* **quiere**

65 **raer** : *IND* rao *or* **raigo** *or* **rayo,** raes, rae, raemos, raéis, raen; *SUBJ* **raiga** *or* **raya, raigas** *or* **rayas, raiga** *or* **raya, raigamos** *or* **rayamos, raigáis** *or* **rayáis, raigan** *or* **rayan;** *PRET* **raí, raíste, rayó, raímos, raísteis, rayeron;** *PRP* **rayendo;** *PP* **raído**

66 **reír** : *IND* **río, ríes, ríe, reímos,** reís, **ríen;** *SUBJ* **ría, rías, ría, riamos, riáis, rían;** *PRET* reí, **reíste, rió, reímos, reísteis, rieron;** *IMPER* **ríe;** *PRP* **riendo;** *PP* **reído**

67 **reñir :** *IND* **riño, riñes, riñe,** reñimos, reñís, **riñen;** *SUBJ* **riña, riñas, riña, riñamos, riñáis, riñan;** *PRET* reñí, reñiste, **riñó,** reñimos, reñisteis, **riñeron;** *PRP* **riñendo**

68 **reunir :** *IND* **reúno, reúnes, reúne,** reunimos, reunís, **reúnen;** *SUBJ* **reúna, reúnas, reúna,** reunamos, reunáis, **reúnan;** *IMPER* **reúne**

69 **roer :** *IND* roo *or* **roigo** *or* **royo,** roes, roe, roemos, roéis, roen; *SUBJ* roa *or* **roiga** *or* **roya,** roas *or* **roigas** *or* **royas,** roa *or* **roiga** *or* **roya,** roamos *or* **roigamos** *or* **royamos,** roáis *or* **roigáis** *or* **royáis,** roan *or* **roigan** *or* **royan;** *PRET* roí, **roíste, royó, roímos, roísteis, royeron;** *PRP* **royendo;** *PP* **roído**

70 **romper :** *PP* **roto**

71 **saber :** *IND* **sé,** sabes, sabe, sabemos, sabéis, saben; *SUBJ* **sepa, sepas, sepa, sepamos, sepáis, sepan;** *PRET* **supe, supiste, supo, supimos, supisteis, supieron;** *FUT* **sabré, sabrás, sabrá, sabremos, sabréis, sabrán**

72 **sacar :** *SUBJ* **saque, saques, saque, saquemos, saquéis, saquen;** *PRET* **saqué,** sacaste, sacó, sacamos, sacasteis, sacaron

73 **salir :** *IND* **salgo,** sales, sale, salimos, salís, salen; *SUBJ* **salga, salgas, salga, salgamos, salgáis, salgan;** *FUT* **saldré, saldrás, saldrá, saldremos, saldréis, saldrán;** *IMPER* **sal**

74 **satisfacer :** *IND* **satisfago,** satisfaces, satisface, satisfacemos, satisfacéis, satisfacen; *SUBJ* **satisfaga, satisfagas, satisfaga, satisfagamos, satisfagáis, satisfagan;** *PRET* **satisfice, satisficiste, satisfizo, satisficimos, satificisteis, satisficieron;** *FUT* **satisfaré, satisfarás, satisfará, satisfaremos, satisfaréis, satisfarán;** *IMPER* **satisfaz** *or* **satisface;** *PP* **satisfecho**

75 **seguir :** *IND* **sigo, sigues, sigue,** seguimos, seguís, **siguen;** *SUBJ* **siga, sigas, siga, sigamos, sigáis, sigan;** *PRET* seguí, seguiste, **siguió,** seguimos, seguisteis, **siguieron;** *IMPER* **sigue;** *PRP* **siguiendo**

76 **sentir :** *IND* **siento, sientes, siente,** sentimos, sentís, **sienten;** *SUBJ* **sienta, sientas, sienta, sintamos, sintáis, sientan;** *PRET* sentí, sentiste, **sintió,** sentimos, sentisteis, **sintieron;** *IMPER* **siente;** *PRP* **sintiendo**

77 **ser :** *IND* **soy, eres, es, somos, sois, son;** *SUBJ* **sea, seas, sea, seamos, seáis, sean;** *PRET* **fui, fuiste, fue, fuimos, fuisteis, fueron;** *IMPF* **era, eras, era, éramos, erais, eran;** *IMPER* **sé;** *PRP* **siendo;** *PP* **sido**

78 **soler** *(defective verb; used only in the present, preterit, and imperfect indicative, and the present and imperfect subjunctive) see* 47 **mover**

79 **tañer :** *PRET* tañí, tañiste, **tañó,** tañimos, tañisteis, **tañeron;** *PRP* **tañendo**

80 **tener :** *IND* **tengo, tienes, tiene,** tenemos, tenéis, **tienen;** *SUBJ* **tenga, tengas, tenga, tengamos, tengáis, tengan;** *PRET* **tuve, tuviste, tuvo, tuvimos, tuvisteis, tuvieron;** *FUT* **tendré, tendrás, tendrá, tendremos, tendréis, tendrán;** *IMPER* **ten**

81 **traer :** *IND* **traigo,** traes, trae, traemos, traéis, traen; *SUBJ* **traiga, traigas, traiga, traigamos, traigáis, traigan;** *PRET* **traje, trajiste, trajo, trajimos, trajisteis, trajeron;** *PRP* **trayendo;** *PP* **traído**

82 **trocar :** *IND* **trueco, truecas, trueca,** trocamos, trocáis, **truecan;** *SUBJ* **trueque, trueques, trueque, troquemos, troquéis, truequen;** *PRET* **troqué,** trocaste, trocó, trocamos, trocasteis, trocaron; *IMPER* **trueca**

83 **uncir :** *IND* **unzo,** unces, unce, uncimos, uncís, uncen; *SUBJ* **unza, unzas, unza, unzamos, unzáis, unzan**

84 **valer :** *IND* **valgo,** vales, vale, valemos, valéis, valen; *SUBJ* **valga, valgas, valga, valgamos, valgáis, valgan;** *FUT* **valdré, valdrás, valdrá, valdremos, valdréis, valdrán**

85 **variar :** *IND* **varío, varías, varía,** variamos, variáis, **varían;** *SUBJ* **varíe, varíes, varíe,** variemos, variéis, **varíen;** *IMPER* **varía**

86 **vencer :** *IND* **venzo,** vences, vence, vencemos, vencéis, vencen; *SUBJ* **venza, venzas, venza, venzamos, venzáis, venzan**

87 **venir :** *IND* **vengo, vienes, viene,** venimos, venís, **vienen;** *SUBJ* **venga, vengas, venga, vengamos, vengáis, vengan;** *PRET* **vine, viniste, vino, vinimos, vinisteis, vinieron;** *FUT* **vendré, vendrás, vendrá, vendremos, vendréis, vendrán;** *IMPER* **ven;** *PRP* **viniendo**

88 **ver** : *IND* veo, **ves, ve, vemos, veis, ven;** *PRET* **vi, viste, vio, vimos, visteis, vieron;** *IMPER* **ve;** *PRP* **viendo;** *PP* **visto**

89 **volver** : *IND* **vuelvo, vuelves, vuelve,** volvemos, volvéis, **vuelven;** *SUBJ* **vuelva, vuelvas, vuelva,** volvamos, volváis, **vuelvan;** *IMPER* **vuelve;** *PP* **vuelto**

90 **yacer** : *IND* **yazco** *or* **yazgo** *or* **yago,** yaces, yace, yacemos, yacéis, yacen; *SUBJ* **yazca** *or* **yazga** *or* **yaga, yazcas** *or* **yazgas** *or* **yagas, yazca** *or* **yazga** *or* **yaga, yazcamos** *or* **yazgamos** *or* **yagamos, yazcáis** *or* **yazgáis** *or* **yagáis, yazcan** *or* **yazgan** *or* **yagan;** *IMPER* yace *or* **yaz**

Spanish–English Dictionary

A

a[1] *nf* **:** first letter of the Spanish alphabet

a[2] *prep* **1 :** to <nos vamos a México : we're going to Mexico> **2** (*used before direct or indirect objects referring to persons*) <¿llamaste a tu papá? : did you call your dad?> <como a usted le guste : as you wish> **3 :** in the manner of <papas a la francesa : french fries> **4 :** on, by means of <a pie : on foot> **5 :** per, each <tres pastillas al día : three pills per day> **6** (*with infinitive*) <enséñales a leer : teach them to read> <problemas a resolver : problems to be solved>

ábaco *nm* **:** abacus

abad *nm* **:** abbot

abadesa *nf* **:** abbess

abadía *nf* **:** abbey

abajo *adv* **1 :** down <póngalo más abajo : put it further down> <arriba y abajo : up and down> **2 :** downstairs **3 :** under, beneath <el abajo firmante : the undersigned> **4 :** down with <¡abajo la inflación! : down with inflation!> **5 ~ de :** under, beneath **6 de ~ :** bottom <el cajón de abajo : the bottom drawer> **7 hacia ~** *or* **para ~ :** downwards **8 cuesta abajo :** downhill **9 río abajo :** downstream

abalanzarse {21} *vr* **:** to hurl oneself, to rush

abanderado, -da *n* **:** standard-bearer

abandonado, -da *adj* **1 :** abandoned, deserted **2 :** neglected **3 :** slovenly, unkempt

abandonar *vt* **1** DEJAR **:** to abandon, to leave **2 :** to give up, to quit <abandonaron la búsqueda : they gave up the search> **— abandonarse** *vr* **1 :** to neglect oneself **2 ~ a :** to succumb to, to give oneself over to

abandono *nm* **1 :** abandonment **2 :** neglect **3 :** withdrawal <ganar por abandono : to win by default>

abanicar {72} *vt* **:** to fan **— abanicarse** *vr*

abanico *nm* **1 :** fan **2** GAMA **:** range, gamut

abaratamiento *nm* **:** price reduction

abaratar *vt* **:** to lower the price of **— abaratarse** *vr* **:** to go down in price

abarcar {72} *vt* **1 :** to cover, to include, to embrace **2 :** to undertake **3 :** to monopolize

abaritonado, -da *adj* **:** baritone

abarrotado, -da *adj* **:** packed, crammed

abarrotar *vt* **:** to fill up, to pack

abarrotería *nf CA, Mex* **:** grocery store

abarrotero, -ra *n Col, Mex* **:** grocer

abarrotes *nmpl* **1 :** groceries, supplies **2 tienda de abarrotes :** general store, grocery store

abastecedor, -dora *n* **:** supplier

abastecer {53} *vt* **:** to supply, to stock **— abastecerse** *vr* **:** to stock up

abastecimiento → abasto

abasto *nm* **:** supply, supplying <no da abasto : there isn't enough for all>

abatido, -da *adj* **:** dejected, depressed

abatimiento *nm* **1 :** drop, reduction **2 :** dejection, depression

abatir *vt* **1** DERRIBAR **:** to demolish, to knock down **2 :** to shoot down **3** DEPRIMIR **:** to depress, to bring low **— abatirse** *vr* **1** DEPRIMIRSE **:** to get depressed **2 ~ sobre :** to swoop down on

abdicación *nf, pl* **-ciones :** abdication

abdicar {72} *vt* **:** to relinquish, to abdicate

abdomen *nm, pl* **-dómenes :** abdomen

abdominal *adj* **:** abdominal

abecé *nm* **:** ABC

abecedario *nm* ALFABETO **:** alphabet

abedul *nm* **:** birch (tree)

abeja *nf* **:** bee

abejorro *nm* **:** bumblebee

aberración *nf, pl* **-ciones :** aberration

aberrante *adj* **:** aberrant, perverse

abertura *nf* **1 :** aperture, opening **2** AGUJERO **:** hole **3 :** slit (in a skirt, etc.) **4** GRIETA **:** crack

abeto *nm* **:** fir (tree)

abierto[1] *pp* **→ abrir**

abierto[2]**, -ta** *adj* **1 :** open **2 :** candid, frank **3 :** generous **— abiertamente** *adv*

abigarrado, -da *adj* **:** multicolored, variegated

abigeato *nm* **:** rustling (of livestock)

abismal *adj* **:** abysmal, vast

abismo *nm* **:** abyss, chasm <al borde del abismo : on the brink of ruin>

abjurar *vi* **~ de :** to abjure **— abjuración** *nf*

ablandamiento *nm* **:** softening, moderation

ablandar *vt* **1** SUAVIZAR **:** to soften **2** CALMAR **:** to soothe, to appease **—** *vi* **:** to moderate, to get milder **— ablandarse** *vr* **1 :** to become soft, to soften **2** CEDER **:** to yield, to relent

ablución *nf, pl* **-ciones :** ablution

abnegación *nf, pl* **-ciones :** abnegation, self-denial

abnegado, -da *adj* **:** self-sacrificing, selfless

abnegarse {49} *vr* **:** to deny oneself

abobado, -da *adj* **1 :** silly, stupid **2 :** bewildered

abocarse {72} *vr* **1** DIRIGIRSE **:** to head, to direct oneself **2** DEDICARSE **:** to dedicate oneself

abochornar *vt* AVERGONZAR **:** to embarrass, to shame **— abochornarse** *vr*

abofetear *vt* **:** to slap

abogacía *nf* **:** law, legal profession

abogado, -da *n* **:** lawyer, attorney

abogar {52} *vi* ~ **por** : to plead for, to defend, to advocate
abolengo *nm* LINAJE : lineage, ancestry
abolición *nf, pl* **-ciones** : abolition
abolir {1} *vt* DEROGAR : to abolish, to repeal
abolladura *nf* : dent
abollar *vt* : to dent
abombar *vt* : to warp, to cause to bulge — **abombarse** *vr* : to decompose, to go bad
abominable *adj* ABORRECIBLE : abominable
abominación *nf, pl* **-ciones** : abomination
abominar *vt* ABORRECER : to abominate, to abhor
abonado, -da *n* : subscriber
abonar *vt* **1** : to pay **2** FERTILIZAR : to fertilize — **abonarse** *vr* : to subscribe
abono *nm* **1** : payment, installment **2** FERTILIZANTE : fertilizer **3** : season ticket
abordaje *nm* : boarding
abordar *vt* **1** : to address, to broach **2** : to accost, to waylay **3** : to come on board
aborigen[1] *adj, pl* **-rígenes** : aboriginal, native
aborigen[2] *nmf, pl* **-rígenes** : aborigine, indigenous inhabitant
aborrecer {53} *vt* ABOMINAR, ODIAR : to abhor, to detest, to hate
aborrecible *adj* ABOMINABLE, ODIOSO : abominable, detestable
aborrecimiento *nm* : abhorrence, loathing
abortar *vi* : to have an abortion — *vt* **1** : to abort **2** : to quash, to suppress
abortista *nmf* : abortionist
abortivo, -va *adj* : abortive
aborto *nm* **1** : abortion **2** : miscarriage
abotonar *vt* : to button — **abotonarse** *vr* : to button up
abovedado, -da *adj* : vaulted
abrasador, -dora *adj* : burning, scorching
abrasar *vt* QUEMAR : to burn, to sear, to scorch
abrasivo[1], **-va** *adj* : abrasive
abrasivo[2] *nm* : abrasive
abrazadera *nf* : clamp, brace
abrazar {21} *vt* : to hug, to embrace — **abrazarse** *vr*
abrazo *nm* : hug, embrace
abrebotellas *nms & pl* : bottle opener
abrelatas *nms & pl* : can opener
abrevadero *nm* BEBEDERO : watering trough
abreviación *nf, pl* **-ciones** : abbreviation
abreviar *vt* **1** : to abbreviate **2** : to shorten, to cut short
abreviatura *nf* → **abreviación**
abridor *nm* : bottle opener, can opener
abrigadero *nm* : shelter, windbreak
abrigado, -da *adj* **1** : sheltered **2** : warm, wrapped up (with clothing)
abrigar {52} *vt* **1** : to shelter, to protect **2** : to keep warm, to dress warmly **3** : to cherish, to harbor <abrigar esperanzas : to cherish hopes> — **abrigarse** *vr* : to dress warmly
abrigo *nm* **1** : coat, overcoat **2** : shelter, refuge
abril *nm* : April
abrillantador *nm* : polish
abrillantar *vt* : to polish, to shine
abrir {2} *vt* **1** : to open **2** : to unlock, to undo **3** : to turn on (a tap or faucet) — *vi* : to open, to open up — **abrirse** *vr* **1** : to open up **2** : to clear (of the skies)
abrochar *vt* : to button, to fasten — **abrocharse** *vr* : to fasten, to hook up
abrogación *nf, pl* **-ciones** : abrogation, annulment, repeal
abrogar {52} *vt* : to abrogate, to annul, to repeal
abrojo *nm* : bur (of a plant)
abrumador, -dora *adj* : crushing, overwhelming
abrumar *vt* **1** AGOBIAR : to overwhelm **2** OPRIMIR : to oppress, to burden
abrupto, -ta *adj* **1** : abrupt **2** ESCARPADO : steep — **abruptamente** *adv*
absceso *nm* : abscess
absolución *nf, pl* **-ciones 1** : absolution **2** : acquittal
absolutismo *nm* : absolutism
absoluto, -ta *adj* **1** : absolute, unconditional **2 en** ~ : not at all <no me gustó en absoluto : I did not like it at all> — **absolutamente** *adv*
absolver {89} *vt* **1** : to absolve **2** : to acquit
absorbente *adj* **1** : absorbent **2** : absorbing, engrossing
absorber *vt* **1** : to absorb, to soak up **2** : to occupy, to take up, to engross
absorción *nf, pl* **-ciones** : absorption
absorto, -ta *adj* : absorbed, engrossed
abstemio[1], **-mia** *adj* : abstemious, teetotal
abstemio[2], **-mia** *n* : teetotaler
abstención *nf, pl* **-ciones** : abstention
abstenerse {80} *vr* : to abstain, to refrain
abstinencia *nf* : abstinence
abstracción *nf, pl* **-ciones** : abstraction
abstracto, -ta *adj* : abstract
abstraer {81} *vt* : to abstract — **abstraerse** *vr* : to lose oneself in thought
abstraído, -da *adj* : preoccupied, withdrawn
abstruso, -sa *adj* : abstruse
abstuvo, etc. → **abstenerse**
absuelto *pp* → **absolver**
absurdo[1], **-da** *adj* DISPARATADO, RIDÍCULO : absurd, ridiculous — **absurdamente** *adv*
absurdo[2] *nm* : absurdity
abuchear *vt* : to boo, to jeer
abucheo *nm* : booing, jeering
abuela *nf* **1** : grandmother **2** : old woman **3 ¡tu abuela!** *fam* : no way!, forget about it!

abuelo *nm* **1 :** grandfather **2 :** old man **3 abuelos** *nmpl* **:** grandparents, ancestors
abulia *nf* **:** apathy, lethargy
abúlico, -ca *adj* **:** lethargic, apathetic
abultado, -da *adj* **:** bulging, bulky
abultar *vi* **:** to bulge — *vt* **:** to enlarge, to expand
abundancia *nf* **:** abundance
abundante *adj* **:** abundant, plentiful — **abundantemente** *adv*
abundar *vi* **1 :** to abound, to be plentiful **2 ~ en :** to be in agreement with
aburrido, -da *adj* **1 :** bored, tired, fed up **2** TEDIOSO **:** boring, tedious
aburrimiento *nm* **:** boredom, weariness
aburrir *vt* **:** to bore, to tire — **aburrirse** *vr* **:** to get bored
abusado, -da *adj Mex fam* **:** sharp, on the ball
abusador, -dora *n* **:** abuser
abusar *vi* **1 :** to go too far, to do something to excess **2 ~ de :** to abuse (as drugs) **3 ~ de :** to take unfair advantage of
abusivo, -va *adj* **1 :** abusive **2 :** outrageous, excessive
abuso *nm* **1 :** abuse **2 :** injustice, outrage
abyecto, -ta *adj* **:** despicable, contemptible
acá *adv* AQUÍ **:** here, over here <¡ven acá! : come here!>
acabado[1], -da *adj* **1 :** finished, done, completed **2 :** old, worn-out
acabado[2] *nm* **:** finish <un acabado brillante : a glossy finish>
acabar *vi* **1** TERMINAR **:** to finish, to end **2 ~ de :** to have just (done something) <acabo de ver a tu hermano : I just saw your brother> **3 ~ con :** to put an end to, to stamp out — *vt* TERMINAR **:** to finish — **acabarse** *vr* TERMINARSE **:** to come to an end, to run out <se me acabó el dinero : I ran out of money>
academia *nf* **:** academy
académico[1], -ca *adj* **:** academic, scholastic — **académicamente** *adv*
académico[2], -ca *n* **:** academic, academician
acaecer {53} *vi* (*3rd person only*) **:** to happen, to take place
acalambrarse *vr* **:** to cramp up, to get a cramp
acallar *vt* **:** to quiet, to silence
acalorado, -da *adj* **:** emotional, heated
acaloramiento *nm* **1 :** heat **2 :** ardor, passion
acalorar *vt* **:** to heat up, to inflame — **acalorarse** *vr* **:** to get upset, to get worked up
acampada *nf* **:** camp, camping <ir de acampada : to go camping>
acampar *vi* **:** to camp
acanalar *vt* **1 :** to groove, to furrow **2 :** to corrugate
acantilado *nm* **:** cliff
acanto *nm* **:** acanthus
acantonar *vt* **:** to station, to quarter
acaparador, -dora *adj* **:** greedy, selfish
acaparar *vt* **1 :** to stockpile, to hoard **2 :** to monopolize
acápite *nm* **:** paragraph
acariciar *vt* **:** to caress, to stroke, to pet
ácaro *nm* **:** mite
acarrear *vt* **1 :** to haul, to carry **2 :** to bring, to give rise to <los problemas que acarrea : the problems that come along with it>
acarreo *nm* **:** transport, haulage
acartonarse *vr* **1 :** to stiffen **2 :** to become wizened
acaso *adv* **1 :** perhaps, by any chance **2 por si acaso :** just in case
acatamiento *nm* **:** compliance, observance
acatar *vt* **:** to comply with, to respect
acaudalado, -da *adj* RICO **:** wealthy, rich
acaudillar *vt* **:** to lead, to command
acceder *vi* **~ a 1 :** to accede to, to agree to **2 :** to assume (a position) **3 :** to gain access to
accesar *vt* **:** to access (on a computer)
accesibilidad *nf* **:** accessibility
accesible *adj* ASEQUIBLE **:** accessible, attainable
acceso *nm* **1 :** access **2 :** admittance, entrance
accesorio[1], -ria *adj* **1 :** accessory **2 :** incidental
accesorio[2] *nm* **1 :** accessory **2 :** prop (in the theater)
accidentado[1], -da *adj* **1 :** eventful, turbulent **2 :** rough, uneven **3 :** injured
accidentado[2], -da *n* **:** accident victim
accidental *adj* **:** accidental, unintentional — **accidentalmente** *adv*
accidentarse *vr* **:** to have an accident
accidente *nm* **1 :** accident **2 :** unevenness **3 accidente geográfico :** geographical feature
acción *nf, pl* **acciones 1 :** action **2** ACTO **:** act, deed **3 :** share, stock
accionamiento *nm* **:** activation
accionar *vt* **:** to put into motion, to activate — *vi* **:** to gesticulate
accionario, -ria *adj* **:** stock <mercado accionario : stock market>
accionista *nmf* **:** stockholder, shareholder
acebo *nm* **:** holly
acechar *vt* **1 :** to watch, to spy on **2 :** to stalk, to lie in wait for
acecho *nm* **al acecho :** lying in wait
acedera *nf* **:** sorrel (herb)
acéfalo, -la *adj* **:** leaderless
aceitar *vt* **:** to oil
aceite *nm* **1 :** oil **2 aceite de ricino :** castor oil **3 aceite de oliva :** olive oil
aceitera *nf* **1 :** cruet (for oil) **2 :** oilcan **3** *Mex* **:** oil refinery
aceitoso, -sa *adj* **:** oily
aceituna *nf* OLIVA **:** olive
aceituno *nm* OLIVO **:** olive tree

aceleración *nf, pl* **-ciones** : acceleration, speeding up
acelerado, -da *adj* : accelerated, speedy
acelerador *nm* : accelerator
aceleramiento *nm* → **aceleración**
acelerar *vt* **1** : to accelerate, to speed up **2** AGILIZAR : to expedite — *vi* : to accelerate (of an automobile) — **acelerarse** *vr* : to hasten, to hurry up
acelga *nf* : chard, Swiss chard
acendrado, -da *adj* : pure, unblemished
acendrar *vt* : to purify, to refine
acento *nm* **1** : accent **2** : stress, emphasis
acentuación *nf, pl* **-ciones** : accentuation
acentuado, -da *adj* : marked, pronounced
acentuar {3} *vt* **1** : to accent **2** : to emphasize, to stress — **acentuarse** *vr* : to become more pronounced
acepción *nf, pl* **-ciones** SIGNIFICADO : sense, meaning
aceptabilidad *nf* : acceptability
aceptable *adj* : acceptable
aceptación *nf, pl* **-ciones** **1** : acceptance **2** APROBACIÓN : approval
aceptar *vt* **1** : to accept **2** : to approve
acequia *nf* **1** : irrigation ditch **2** *Mex* : sewer
acera *nf* : sidewalk
acerado, -da *adj* **1** : made of steel **2** : steely, tough
acerbo, -ba *adj* **1** : harsh, cutting <comentarios acerbos : cutting remarks> **2** : bitter — **acerbamente** *adv*
acerca *prep* **~ de** : about, concerning
acercamiento *nm* : rapprochement, reconciliation
acercar {72} *vt* APROXIMAR, ARRIMAR : to bring near, to bring closer — **acercarse** *vr* APROXIMARSE, ARRIMARSE : to approach, to draw near
acería *nf* : steel mill
acerico *nm* : pincushion
acero *nm* : steel <acero inoxidable : stainless steel>
acérrimo, -ma *adj* **1** : staunch, steadfast **2** : bitter <un acérrimo enemigo : a bitter enemy>
acertado, -da *adj* CORRECTO : accurate, correct, on target — **acertadamente** *adv*
acertante[1] *adj* : winning
acertante[2] *nmf* : winner
acertar {55} *vt* : to guess correctly — *vi* ATINAR : to be accurate, to be on target
acertijo *nm* ADIVINANZA : riddle
acervo *nm* **1** : pile, heap **2** : wealth, heritage <el acervo artístico del instituto : the artistic treasures of the institute>
acetato *nm* : acetate
acético, -ca *adj* : acetic <ácido acético : acetic acid>
acetileno *nm* : acetylene
acetona *nf* **1** : acetone **2** : nail-polish remover
achacar {72} *vt* : to attribute, to impute <te achaca todos sus problemas : he blames all his problems on you>
achacoso, -sa *adj* : frail, sickly
achaparrado, -da *adj* : stunted, scrubby <árboles achaparrados : scrubby trees>
achaque *nm* DOLENCIA : ailment, malady, discomfort
achatar *vt* : to flatten
achicar {72} *vt* **1** REDUCIR : to make smaller, to reduce **2** : to intimidate **3** : to bail out (water) — **achicarse** *vr* : to become intimidated
achicharrar *vt* : to scorch, to burn to a crisp
achicoria *nf* : chicory
achispado, -da *adj fam* : tipsy
achote *or* **achiote** *nm* : annatto seed
achuchón *nm, pl* **-chones** **1** : push, shove **2** *fam* : squeeze, hug **3** *fam* : mild illness
aciago, -ga *adj* : fateful, unlucky
acicalar *vt* **1** PULIR : to polish **2** : to dress up, to adorn — **acicalarse** *vr* : to get dressed up
acicate *nm* **1** : spur **2** INCENTIVO : incentive, stimulus
acidez *nf, pl* **-deces** **1** : acidity **2** : sourness **3** **acidez estomacal** : heartburn
acidificar {72} *vt* : to acidify
ácido[1], **-da** *adj* AGRIO : acid, sour
ácido[2] *nm* : acid
acierto *nm* **1** : correct answer, right choice **2** : accuracy, skill, deftness
acimut *nm* : azimuth
acitronar *vt Mex* : to fry until crisp
aclamación *nf, pl* **-ciones** : acclaim, acclamation
aclamar *vt* : to acclaim, to cheer, to applaud
aclaración *nf, pl* **-ciones** CLARIFICACIÓN : clarification, explanation
aclarar *vt* **1** CLARIFICAR : to clarify, to explain, to resolve **2** : to lighten **3** **aclarar la voz** : to clear one's throat — *vi* **1** : to get light, to dawn **2** : to clear up — **aclararse** *vr* : to become clear
aclaratorio, -ria *adj* : explanatory
aclimatar *vt* : to acclimatize — **aclimatarse** *vr* **~ a** : to get used to — **aclimatación** *nf*
acné *nm* : acne
acobardar *vt* INTIMIDAR : to frighten, to intimidate — **acobardarse** *vr* : to be frightened, to cower
acodarse *vr* **~ en** : to lean (one's elbows) on
acogedor, -dora *adj* : cozy, warm, friendly
acoger {15} *vt* **1** REFUGIAR : to take in, to shelter **2** : to receive, to welcome — **acogerse** *vr* **1** REFUGIARSE : to take refuge **2** **~ a** : to resort to, to avail oneself of

acogida *nf* **1** AMPARO, REFUGIO **:** refuge, protection **2** RECIBIMIENTO **:** reception, welcome

acolchar *vt* **1 :** to pad (a wall, etc.) **2 :** to quilt

acólito *nm* **1** MONAGUILLO **:** altar boy **2 :** follower, helper, acolyte

acomedido, -da *adj* **:** helpful, obliging

acometer *vt* **1** ATACAR **:** to attack, to assail **2** EMPRENDER **:** to undertake, to begin — *vi* **~ contra :** to rush against

acometida *nf* ATAQUE **:** attack, assault

acomodado, -da *adj* **1 :** suitable, appropriate **2 :** well-to-do, prosperous

acomodador, -dora *n* **:** usher, usherette *f*

acomodar *vt* **1 :** to accommodate, to make room for **2 :** to adjust, to adapt — **acomodarse** *vr* **1 :** to settle in **2 ~ a :** to adapt to

acomodaticio, -cia *adj* **:** accommodating, obliging

acomodo *nm* **1 :** job, position **2 :** arrangement, placement **3 :** accommodation, lodging

acompañamiento *nm* **:** accompaniment

acompañante *nmf* **1** COMPAÑERO **:** companion **2 :** accompanist

acompañar *vt* **:** to accompany, to go with

acompasado, -da *adj* **:** rhythmic, regular, measured

acomplejado, -da *adj* **:** full of complexes, neurotic

acondicionado, -da *adj* **1 :** equipped, fitted-out **2 bien acondicionado :** in good shape, in a fit state

acondicionador *nm* **1 :** conditioner **2 acondicionador de aire :** air conditioner

acondicionar *vt* **1 :** to condition **2 :** to fit out, to furnish

acongojado, -da *adj* **:** distressed, upset

acongojarse *vr* **:** to grieve, to become distressed

aconsejable *adj* **:** advisable

aconsejar *vt* **:** to advise, to counsel

acontecer {53} *vi* (*3rd person only*) **:** to occur, to happen

acontecimiento *nm* SUCESO **:** event

acopiar *vt* **:** to gather, to collect, to stockpile

acopio *nm* **:** collection, stock

acoplamiento *nm* **:** connection, coupling

acoplar *vt* **:** to couple, to connect — **acoplarse** *vr* **:** to fit together

acoquinar *vt* **:** to intimidate

acorazado¹, -da *adj* BLINDADO **:** armored

acorazado² *nm* **:** battleship

acordado, -da *adj* **:** agreed upon

acordar {19} *vt* **1 :** to agree on **2** OTORGAR **:** to award, to bestow — **acordarse** *vr* RECORDAR **:** to remember, to recall

acorde¹ *adj* **1 :** in agreement, in accordance **2 ~ con :** in keeping with

acorde² *nm* **:** chord

acordeón *nm, pl* **-deones :** accordion — **acordeonista** *nmf*

acordonar *vt* **1 :** to cordon off **2 :** to lace up **3 :** to mill (coins)

acorralar *vt* ARRINCONAR **:** to corner, to hem in, to corral

acortar *vt* **:** to shorten, to cut short — **acortarse** *vr* **1 :** to become shorter **2 :** to end early

acosar *vt* PERSEGUIR **:** to pursue, to hound, to harass

acoso *nm* ASEDIO **:** harassment <acoso sexual : sexual harassment>

acostar {19} *vt* **1 :** to lay (something) down **2 :** to put to bed — **acostarse** *vr* **1 :** to lie down **2 :** to go to bed

acostumbrado, -da *adj* **1** HABITUADO **:** accustomed **2** HABITUAL **:** usual, customary

acostumbrar *vt* **:** to accustom — *vi* **:** to be accustomed, to be in the habit — **acostumbrarse** *vr*

acotación *nf, pl* **-ciones 1 :** marginal note **2 :** stage direction

acotado, -da *adj* **:** enclosed

acotamiento *nm Mex* **:** shoulder (of a road)

acotar *vt* **1** ANOTAR **:** to note, to annotate **2** DELIMITAR **:** to mark off (land), to demarcate

acre¹ *adj* **1 :** acrid, pungent **2** MORDAZ **:** caustic, biting

acre² *nm* **:** acre

acrecentamiento *nm* **:** growth, increase

acrecentar {55} *vt* AUMENTAR **:** to increase, to augment

acreditación *nf, pl* **-ciones :** accreditation

acreditado, -da *adj* **1 :** accredited, authorized **2 :** reputable

acreditar *vt* **1 :** to accredit, to authorize **2 :** to credit **3 :** to prove, to verify — **acreditarse** *vr* **:** to gain a reputation

acreedor¹, -dora *adj* **:** deserving, worthy

acreedor², -dora *n* **:** creditor

acribillar *vt* **1 :** to riddle, to pepper (with bullets, etc.) **2 :** to hound, to harass

acrílico *nm* **:** acrylic

acrimonia *nf* **1 :** pungency **2 :** acrimony

acrimonioso, -sa *adj* **:** acrimonious

acriollarse *vr* **:** to adopt local customs, to go native

acritud *nf* **1 :** pungency, bitterness **2 :** intensity, sharpness **3 :** harshness, asperity

acrobacia *nf* **:** acrobatics

acróbata *nmf* **:** acrobat

acrónimo *nm* **:** acronym

acta *nf* **1 :** document, certificate <acta de nacimiento : birth certificate> **2 actas** *nfpl* **:** minutes (of a meeting)

actitud *nf* **1 :** attitude **2 :** posture, position

activación *nf, pl* **-ciones 1 :** activation, stimulation **2** ACELERACIÓN **:** acceleration, speeding up

activar *vt* **1 :** to activate **2 :** to stimulate, to energize **3 :** to speed up

actividad *nf* **:** activity

activista *nmf* **:** activist

activo[1], -va *adj* **:** active — **activamente** *adv*

activo[2] *nm* **:** assets *pl* <activo y pasivo : assets and liabilities>

acto *nm* **1** ACCIÓN **:** act, deed **2 :** act (in a play) **3 el acto sexual :** sexual intercourse **4 en el acto :** right away, on the spot **5 acto seguido :** immediately after

actor *nm* ARTISTA **:** actor

actriz *nf, pl* **actrices** ARTISTA **:** actress

actuación *nf, pl* **-ciones 1 :** performance **2 actuaciones** *nfpl* DILIGENCIAS **:** proceedings

actual *adj* PRESENTE **:** present, current

actualidad *nf* **1 :** present time <en la actualidad : at present> **2 actualidades** *nfpl* **:** current affairs

actualización *nf, pl* **-ciones :** updating, modernization

actualizar {21} *vt* **:** to modernize, to bring up to date

actualmente *adv* **:** at present, nowadays

actuar {3} *vi* **:** to act, to perform

actuarial *adj* **:** actuarial

actuario, -ria *n* **:** actuary

acuarela *nf* **:** watercolor

acuario *nm* **:** aquarium

Acuario *nmf* **:** Aquarius, Aquarian

acuartelar *vt* **:** to quarter (troops)

acuático, -ca *adj* **:** aquatic, water

acuchillar *vt* APUÑALAR **:** to knife, to stab

acuciante *adj* **:** pressing, urgent

acucioso, -sa → **acuciante**

acudir *vi* **1 :** to go, to come (someplace for a specific purpose) <acudió a la puerta : he went to the door> <acudimos en su ayuda : we came to her aid> **2 :** to be present, to show up <acudí a la cita : I showed up for the appointment> **3 ~ a :** to turn to, to have recourse to <hay que acudir al médico : you must consult the doctor>

acueducto *nm* **:** aqueduct

acuerdo *nm* **1 :** agreement **2 estar de acuerdo :** to agree **3 de acuerdo con :** in accordance with **4 de ~ :** OK, all right

acuicultura *nf* **:** aquaculture

acullá *adv* **:** yonder, over there

acumulación *nf, pl* **-ciones :** accumulation

acumulador *nm* **:** storage battery

acumular *vt* **:** to accumulate, to amass — **acumularse** *vr* **:** to build up, to pile up

acumulativo, -va *adj* **:** cumulative — **acumulativamente** *adv*

acunar *vt* **:** to rock, to cradle

acuñar *vt* **:** to coin, to mint

acuoso, -sa *adj* **:** aqueous, watery

acupuntura *nf* **:** acupuncture

acurrucarse {72} *vr* **:** to cuddle, to nestle, to curl up

acusación *nf, pl* **-ciones 1 :** accusation, charge **2 la acusación :** the prosecution

acusado[1], -da *adj* **:** prominent, marked

acusado[2], -da *n* **:** defendant

acusador, -dora *n* **1 :** accuser **2** FISCAL **:** prosecutor

acusar *vt* **1 :** to accuse, to charge **2 :** to reveal, to betray <sus ojos acusaban la desconfianza : his eyes revealed distrust> — **acusarse** *vr* **:** to confess

acusatorio, -ria *adj* **:** accusatory

acuse *nm* **acuse de recibo :** acknowledgment of receipt

acústica *nf* **:** acoustics

acústico, -ca *adj* **:** acoustic

adagio *nm* **1** REFRÁN **:** adage, proverb **2 :** adagio

adalid *nm* **:** leader, champion

adaptable *adj* **:** adaptable — **adaptabilidad** *nf*

adaptación *nf, pl* **-ciones :** adaptation, adjustment

adaptado, -da *adj* **:** suited, adapted

adaptador *nm* **:** adapter (in electricity)

adaptar *vt* **1** MODIFICAR **:** to adapt **2 :** to adjust, to fit — **adaptarse** *vr* **:** to adapt oneself, to conform

adecentar *vt* **:** to tidy up

adecuación *nf, pl* **-ciones** ADAPTACIÓN **:** adaptation

adecuadamente *adv* **:** adequately

adecuado, -da *adj* **1** IDÓNEO **:** suitable, appropriate **2 :** adequate

adecuar {8} *vt* **:** to adapt, to make suitable — **adecuarse** *vr* **~ a :** to be appropriate for, to fit in with

adefesio *nm* **:** eyesore, monstrosity

adelantado, -da *adj* **1 :** advanced, ahead **2 :** fast (of a clock or watch) **3 por ~ :** in advance

adelantamiento *nm* **1 :** advancement **2 :** speeding up

adelantar *vt* **1 :** to advance, to move forward **2 :** to overtake, to pass **3 :** to reveal (information) in advance **4 :** to advance, to lend (money) — **adelantarse** *vr* **1 :** to advance, to get in front **2 ~ a :** to forestall, to preempt

adelante *adv* **1 :** ahead, in front, forward **2 más adelante :** further on, later on **3 ¡adelante! :** come in!

adelanto *nm* **1 :** advance, progress **2 :** advance payment **3 :** earliness <llevamos una hora de adelanto : we're running an hour ahead of time>

adelfa *nf* **:** oleander

adelgazar {21} *vt* **:** to thin, to reduce — *vi* **:** to lose weight

ademán *nm, pl* **-manes 1** GESTO **:** gesture **2 ademanes** *nmpl* **:** manners

además *adv* **1 :** besides, furthermore **2 ~ de :** in addition to, as well as

adenoides *nfpl* : adenoids
adentrarse *vr* **~ en** : to go into, to penetrate
adentro *adv* : inside, within
adentros *nmpl* **decirse para sus adentros** : to say to oneself <me dije para mis adentros que nunca regresaría : I told myself that I'd never go back>
adepto¹, -ta *adj* : supportive <ser adepto a : to be a follower of>
adepto², -ta *n* PARTIDARIO : follower, supporter
aderezar {21} *vt* **1** SAZONAR : to season, to dress (salad) **2** : to embellish, to adorn
aderezo *nm* **1** : dressing, seasoning **2** : adornment, embellishment
adeudar *vt* **1** : to debit **2** DEBER : to owe
adeudo *nm* **1** DÉBITO : debit **2** *Mex* : debt, indebtedness
adherencia *nf* **1** : adherence, adhesiveness **2** : appendage, accretion
adherente *adj* : adhesive, sticky
adherirse {76} *vr* : to adhere, to stick
adhesión *nf, pl* **-siones 1** : adhesion **2** : attachment, commitment (to a cause, etc.)
adhesivo¹, -va *adj* : adhesive
adhesivo² *nm* : adhesive
adicción *nf, pl* **-ciones** : addiction
adición *nf, pl* **-ciones** : addition
adicional *adj* : additional — **adicionalmente** *adv*
adicionar *vt* : to add
adicto¹, -ta *adj* **1** : addicted **2** : devoted, dedicated
adicto², -ta *n* **1** : addict **2** PARTIDARIO : supporter, advocate
adiestrador, -dora *n* : trainer
adiestramiento *nm* : training
adiestrar *vt* : to train
adinerado, -da *adj* : moneyed, wealthy
adiós *nm, pl* **adioses 1** DESPEDIDA : farewell, good-bye **2 ¡adiós!** : good-bye!
aditamento *nm* : attachment, accessory
aditivo *nm* : additive
adivinación *nf, pl* **-ciones 1** : guess **2** : divination, prediction
adivinanza *nf* ACERTIJO : riddle
adivinar *vt* **1** : to guess **2** : to foretell, to predict
adivino, -na *n* : fortune-teller
adjetivo¹, -va *adj* : adjectival
adjetivo² *nm* : adjective
adjudicación *nf, pl* **-ciones 1** : adjudication **2** : allocation, awarding, granting
adjudicar {72} *vt* **1** : to adjudge, to adjudicate **2** : to assign, to allocate <adjudicar la culpa : to assign the blame> **3** : to award, to grant
adjuntar *vt* : to enclose, to attach
adjunto¹, -ta *adj* : enclosed, attached
adjunto², -ta *n* : deputy, assistant
adjunto³ *nm* : adjunct
administración *nf, pl* **-ciones 1** : administration, management **2 administración de empresas** : business administration
administrador, -dora *n* : administrator, manager
administrar *vt* : to administer, to manage, to run
administrativo, -va *adj* : administrative
admirable *adj* : admirable, impressive — **admirablemente** *adv*
admiración *nf, pl* **-ciones** : admiration
admirador, -dora *n* : admirer
admirar *vt* **1** : to admire **2** : to amaze, to astonish — **admirarse** *vr* : to be amazed
admirativo, -va *adj* : admiring
admisibilidad *nf* : admissibility
admisible *adj* : admissible, allowable
admisión *nf, pl* **-siones** : admission, admittance
admitir *vt* **1** : to admit, to let in **2** : to acknowledge, to concede **3** : to allow, to make room for <la ley no admite cambios : the law doesn't allow for changes>
admonición *nf, pl* **-ciones** : admonition, warning
admonitorio, -ria *adj* : admonitory
ADN *nm* : DNA
adobar *vt* : to marinate
adobe *nm* : adobe
adobo *nm* **1** : marinade, seasoning **2** *Mex* : spicy marinade used for cooking pork
adoctrinamiento *nm* : indoctrination
adoctrinar *vt* : to indoctrinate
adolecer {53} *vi* PADECER : to suffer <adolece de timidez : he suffers from shyness>
adolescencia *nf* : adolescence
adolescente¹ *adj* : adolescent, teenage
adolescente² *nmf* : adolescent, teenager
adonde *conj* : where <el lugar adonde vamos es bello : the place where we're going is beautiful>
adónde *adv* : where <¿adónde vamos? : where are we going?>
adondequiera *adv* : wherever, anywhere <adondequiera que vayas : anywhere you go>
adopción *nf, pl* **-ciones** : adoption
adoptar *vt* **1** : to adopt (a measure), to take (a decision) **2** : to adopt (children)
adoptivo, -va *adj* **1** : adopted (children, country) **2** : adoptive (parents)
adoquín *nm, pl* **-quines** : paving stone, cobblestone
adorable *adj* : adorable, lovable
adoración *nf, pl* **-ciones** : adoration, worship
adorador¹, -dora *adj* : adoring, worshipping
adorador², -dora *n* : worshipper
adorar *vt* : to adore, to worship
adormecer {53} *vt* **1** : to make sleepy, to lull to sleep **2** : to numb — **ador-**

mecerse *vr* **1 :** to doze off **2 :** to go numb
adormecimiento *nm* **1** SUEÑO **:** drowsiness, sleepiness **2** INSENSIBILIDAD **:** numbness
adormilarse *vr* **:** to doze, to drowse
adornar *vt* DECORAR **:** to decorate, to adorn
adorno *nm* **:** ornament, decoration
adquirido, -da *adj* **1 :** acquired **2 mal adquirido :** ill-gotten
adquirir {4} *vt* **1 :** to acquire, to gain **2** COMPRAR **:** to purchase
adquisición *nf, pl* **-ciones 1 :** acquisition **2** COMPRA **:** purchase
adquisitivo, -va *adj* **poder adquisitivo :** purchasing power
adrede *adv* **:** intentionally, on purpose
adrenalina *nf* **:** adrenaline
adscribir {33} *vt* **:** to assign, to appoint — **adscribirse** *vr* **~ a :** to become a member of
adscripción *nf, pl* **-ciones :** assignment, appointment
adscrito *pp* → **adscribir**
aduana *nf* **:** customs, customs office
aduanero[1], -ra *adj* **:** customs
aduanero[2], -ra *n* **:** customs officer
aducir {61} *vt* **:** to adduce, to offer as proof
adueñarse *vr* **~ de :** to take possession of, to take over
adulación *nf, pl* **-ciones :** adulation, flattery
adulador[1], -dora *adj* **:** flattering
adulador[2], -dora *n* **:** flatterer, toady
adular *vt* LISONJEAR **:** to flatter
adulteración *nf, pl* **-ciones :** adulteration
adulterar *vt* **:** to adulterate
adulterio *nm* **:** adultery
adúltero[1], -ra *adj* **:** adulterous
adúltero[2], -ra *n* **:** adulterer
adultez *nf* **:** adulthood
adulto, -ta *adj & n* **:** adult
adusto, -ta *adj* **:** harsh, severe
advenedizo, -za *n* **1 :** upstart, parvenu **2 :** newcomer
advenimiento *nm* **:** advent
adventicio, -cia *adj* **:** adventitious
adverbio *nm* **:** adverb — **adverbial** *adj*
adversario[1], -ria *adj* **:** opposing, contrary
adversario[2], -ria *n* OPOSITOR **:** adversary, opponent
adversidad *nf* **:** adversity
adverso, -sa *adj* DESFAVORABLE **:** adverse, unfavorable — **adversamente** *adv*
advertencia *nf* AVISO **:** warning
advertir {76} *vt* **1** AVISAR **:** to warn **2 :** to notice, to tell <no advertí que estuviera enojada : I couldn't tell she was angry>
adviento *nm* **:** Advent
adyacente *adj* **:** adjacent
aéreo, -rea *adj* **1 :** aerial, air **2 correo aéreo :** airmail
aeróbic *nm* **:** aerobics
aeróbico, -ca *adj* **:** aerobic
aerobio, -bia *adj* **:** aerobic
aerodinámica *nf* **:** aerodynamics
aerodinámico, -ca *adj* **:** aerodynamic, streamlined
aeródromo *nm* **:** airfield
aeroespacial *adj* **:** aerospace
aerolínea *nf* **:** airline
aeromozo, -za *n* **:** flight attendant, steward *m,* stewardess *f*
aeronáutica *nf* **:** aeronautics
aeronáutico, -ca *adj* **:** aeronautical
aeronave *nf* **:** aircraft
aeropostal *adj* **:** airmail
aeropuerto *nm* **:** airport
aerosol *nm* **:** aerosol, aerosol spray
aeróstata *nmf* **:** baloonist
aerotransportado, -da *adj* **:** airborne
aerotransportar *vt* **:** to airlift
afabilidad *nf* **:** affability
afable *adj* **:** affable — **afablemente** *adv*
afamado, -da *adj* **:** well-known, famous
afán *nm, pl* **afanes 1** ANHELO **:** eagerness, desire **2** EMPEÑO **:** effort, determination
afanador, -dora *n Mex* **:** cleaning person, cleaner
afanarse *vr* **:** to toil, to strive
afanosamente *adv* **:** zealously, industriously, busily
afanoso, -sa *adj* **1 :** eager, industrious **2 :** arduous, hard
afear *vt* **:** to make ugly, to disfigure
afección *nf, pl* **-ciones 1 :** fondness, affection **2 :** illness, complaint
afectación *nf, pl* **-ciones :** affectation
afectado, -da *adj* **1 :** affected, mannered **2 :** influenced **3 :** afflicted **4 :** feigned
afectar *vt* **1 :** to affect **2 :** to upset **3 :** to feign, to pretend
afectísimo, -ma *adj* **suyo afectísimo :** yours truly
afectivo, -va *adj* **:** emotional
afecto[1], -ta *adj* **1 :** affected, afflicted **2 :** fond, affectionate
afecto[2] *nm* CARIÑO **:** affection
afectuoso, -sa *adj* CARIÑOSO **:** affectionate, caring
afeitar *vt* RASURAR **:** to shave — **afeitarse** *vr*
afelpado, -da *adj* **:** plush
afeminado, -da *adj* **:** effeminate
aferrado, -da *adj* **:** obstinate, stubborn
aferrarse {55} *vr* **:** to cling, to hold on
AFI *nm* (*Alfabeto Fonético Internacional*) **:** IPA
affidávit *nm, pl* **-dávits :** affidavit
afgano, -na *adj & n* **:** Afghan
afianzar {21} *vt* **1 :** to secure, to strengthen **2 :** to guarantee, to vouch for — **afianzarse** *vr* ESTABLECERSE **:** to establish oneself
afiche *nm* **:** poster
afición *nf, pl* **-ciones 1 :** enthusiasm, penchant, fondness <afición al de-

porte : love of sports> 2 PASATIEMPO : hobby
aficionado[1], **-da** *adj* ENTUSIASTA : enthusiastic, keen
aficionado[2], **-da** *n* **1** ENTUSIASTA : enthusiast, fan **2** : amateur
áfido *nm* : aphid
afiebrado, -da *adj* : feverish
afilado, -da *adj* **1** : sharp **2** : long, pointed <una nariz afilada : a sharp nose>
afilador *nm* : sharpener
afilalápices *nms & pl* : pencil sharpener
afilar *vt* : to sharpen
afiliación *nf, pl* **-ciones** : affiliation
afiliado[1], **-da** *adj* : affiliated
afiliado[2], **-da** *n* : member
afiliarse *vr* : to become a member, to join, to affiliate
afín *adj, pl* **afines 1** PARECIDO : related, similar <la biología y disciplinas afines : biology and related disciplines> **2** PRÓXIMO : adjacent, nearby
afinación *nf, pl* **-ciones 1** : tune-up **2** : tuning (of an instrument)
afinador, -dora *n* : tuner (of musical instruments)
afinar *vt* **1** : to perfect, to refine **2** : to tune (an instrument) — *vi* : to sing or play in tune
afincarse {72} *vr* : to establish oneself, to settle in
afinidad *nf* : affinity, similarity
afirmación *nf, pl* **-ciones 1** : statement **2** : affirmation
afirmar *vt* **1** : to state, to affirm **2** REFORZAR : to make firm, to strengthen
afirmativo, -va *adj* : affirmative — **afirmativamente** *adj*
aflicción *nf, pl* **-ciones** DESCONSUELO, PESAR : grief, sorrow
afligido, -da *adj* : grief-stricken, sorrowful
afligir {35} *vt* **1** : to distress, to upset **2** : to afflict — **afligirse** *vr* : to grieve
aflojar *vt* **1** : to loosen, to slacken **2** *fam* : to pay up, to fork over — *vi* : to slacken, to ease up — **aflojarse** *vr* : to become loose, to slacken
afloramiento *nm* : outcropping, emergence
aflorar *vi* : to come to the surface, to emerge
afluencia *nf* **1** : flow, influx **2** : abundance, plenty
afluente *nm* : tributary
afluir {41} *vi* **1** : to flock <la gente afluía a la frontera : people were flocking to the border> **2** : to flow
aforismo *nm* : aphorism
aforo *nm* **1** : appraisal, assessment **2** : maximum capacity (of a theater, highway, etc.)
afortunado, -da *adj* : fortunate, lucky — **afortunadamente** *adv*
afrecho *nm* : bran, mash
afrenta *nf* : affront, insult
afrentar *vt* : to affront, to dishonor, to insult
africano, -na *adj & n* : African
afroamericano, -na *adj & n* : Afro-American
afrodisiaco *or* **afrodisíaco** *nm* : aphrodisiac
afrontamiento *nm* : confrontation
afrontar *vt* : to confront, to face up to
afrutado, -da *adj* : fruity
afuera *adv* **1** : out <¡afuera! : get out!> **2** : outside, outdoors
afueras *nfpl* ALEDAÑOS : outskirts
agachadiza *nf* : snipe (bird)
agachar *vt* : to lower (a part of the body) <agachar la cabeza : to bow one's head> — **agacharse** *vr* : to crouch, to stoop, to bend down
agalla *nf* **1** BRANQUIA : gill **2 tener agallas** *fam* : to have guts, to have courage
agarradera *nf* ASA, ASIDERO : handle, grip
agarrado, -da *adj fam* : cheap, stingy
agarrar *vt* **1** : to grab, to grasp **2** : to catch, to take — *vi* **agarrar y** *fam* : to do (something) abruptly <el día siguiente agarró y se fue : the next day he up and left> — **agarrarse** *vr* **1** : to hold on, to cling **2** *fam* : to get into a fight <se agarraron a golpes : they came to blows>
agarre *nm* : grip, grasp
agasajar *vt* : to fête, to wine and dine
agasajo *nm* : lavish attention
ágata *nf* : agate
agave *nm* : agave
agazaparse *vr* **1** AGACHARSE : to crouch **2** : to hide
agencia *nf* : agency, office
agenciar *vt* : to obtain, to procure — **agenciarse** *vr* : to manage, to get by
agenda *nf* **1** : agenda **2** : appointment book
agente *nmf* **1** : agent **2 agente de viajes** : travel agent **3 agente de bolsa** : stockbroker **4 agente de tráfico** : traffic officer
agigantado, -da *adj* GIGANTESCO : gigantic
agigantar *vt* **1** : to increase greatly, to enlarge **2** : to exaggerate
ágil *adj* **1** : agile, nimble **2** : sharp, lively (of a response, etc.) — **ágilmente** *adv*
agilidad *nf* : agility, nimbleness
agilizar {21} *vt* ACELERAR : to expedite, to speed up
agitación *nf, pl* **-ciones 1** : agitation **2** NERVIOSISMO : nervousness
agitado, -da *adj* **1** : agitated, excited **2** : choppy, rough, turbulent
agitador, -dora *n* PROVOCADOR : agitator
agitar *vt* **1** : to agitate, to shake **2** : to wave, to flap **3** : to stir up — **agitarse** *vr* **1** : to toss about, to flap around **2** : to get upset

aglomeración *nf, pl* **-ciones** **1** : conglomeration, mass **2** GENTÍO : crowd
aglomerar *vt* : to cluster, to amass — **aglomerarse** *vr* : to crowd together
aglutinar *vt* : to bring together, to bind
agnóstico, -ca *adj & n* : agnostic
agobiado, -da *adj* : weary, worn-out, weighted-down
agobiante *adj* **1** : exhausting, overwhelming **2** : stifling, oppressive
agobiar *vt* **1** OPRIMIR : to oppress, to burden **2** ABRUMAR : to overwhelm **3** : to wear out, to exhaust
agonía *nf* : agony, death throes
agonizante *adj* : dying
agonizar {21} *vi* **1** : to be dying **2** : to be in agony **3** : to dim, to fade
agorero, -ra *adj* : ominous
agostar *vt* **1** : to parch **2** : to wither — **agostarse** *vr*
agosto *nm* **1** : August **2** **hacer uno su agosto** : to make a fortune, to make a killing
agotado, -da *adj* **1** : exhausted, used up **2** : sold out **3** FATIGADO : worn-out, tired
agotador, -dora *adj* : exhausting
agotamiento *nm* FATIGA : exhaustion
agotar *vt* **1** : to exhaust, to use up **2** : to weary, to wear out — **agotarse** *vr*
agraciado[1], **-da** *adj* **1** : attractive **2** : fortunate
agraciado[2], **-da** *n* : winner
agradable *adj* GRATO, PLACENTERO : pleasant, agreeable — **agradablemente** *adv*
agradar *vi* : to be pleasing <nos agradó mucho el resultado : we were very pleased with the result>
agradecer {53} *vt* **1** : to be grateful for **2** : to thank
agradecido, -da *adj* : grateful, thankful
agradecimiento *nm* : gratitude, thankfulness
agrado *nm* **1** GUSTO : taste, liking <no es de su agrado : it's not to his liking> **2** : graciousness, agreeableness **3** **con ~** : with pleasure, willingly <lo haré con agrado : I will be happy to do it>
agrandar *vt* **1** : to exaggerate **2** : to enlarge — **agrandarse** *vr*
agrario, -ria *adj* : agrarian, agricultural
agravación *nf, pl* **-ciones** : aggravation, worsening
agravante *adj* : aggravating
agravar *vt* **1** : to increase (weight), to make heavier **2** EMPEORAR : to aggravate, to worsen — **agravarse** *vr*
agraviar *vt* INJURIAR, OFENDER : to offend, to insult
agravio *nm* INJURIA : affront, offense, insult
agredir {1} *vt* : to assail, to attack
agregado[1], **-da** *n* **1** : attaché **2** : assistant professor
agregado[2] *nm* **1** : aggregate **2** AÑADIDURA : addition, something added
agregar {52} *vt* **1** AÑADIR : to add, to attach **2** : to appoint — **agregarse** *vr* : to join
agresión *nf, pl* **-siones** **1** : aggression **2** ATAQUE : attack
agresividad *nf* : aggressiveness, aggression
agresivo, -va *adj* : aggressive — **agresivamente** *adv*
agresor[1], **-sora** *adj* : hostile, attacking
agresor[2], **-sora** *n* **1** : aggressor **2** : assailant, attacker
agreste *adj* **1** CAMPESTRE : rural **2** : wild, untamed
agriar *vt* **1** : to sour, to make sour **2** : to embitter — **agriarse** *vr* : to turn sour
agrícola *adj* : agricultural
agricultor, -tora *n* : farmer, grower
agricultura *nf* : agriculture, farming
agridulce *adj* **1** : bittersweet **2** : sweet-and-sour
agrietar *vt* : to crack — **agrietarse** *vr* **1** : to crack **2** : to chap
agrimensor, -sora *n* : surveyor
agrimensura *nf* : surveying
agrio, agria *adj* **1** ÁCIDO : sour **2** : caustic, acrimonious
agriparse *vr* : to catch the flu
agroindustria *nf* : agribusiness
agronomía *nf* : agronomy
agropecuario, -ria *adj* : pertaining to livestock and agriculture
agrupación *nf, pl* **-ciones** GRUPO : group, association
agrupamiento *nm* : grouping, concentration
agrupar *vt* : to group together
agua *nf* **1** : water **2** **agua oxigenada** : hydrogen peroxide **3** **aguas negras** *or* **aguas residuales** : sewage **4** **como agua para chocolate** *Mex fam* : furious **5** **echar aguas** *Mex fam* : to keep an eye out, to be on the lookout
aguacate *nm* : avocado
aguacero *nm* : shower, downpour
aguado, -da *adj* **1** DILUIDO : watered-down, diluted **2** *CA, Col, Mex fam* : soft, flabby **3** *Mex, Peru fam* : dull, boring
aguafiestas *nmfs & pl* : killjoy, stick-in-the-mud, spoilsport
aguafuerte *nm* : etching
aguamanil *nm* : ewer, pitcher
aguanieve *nf* : sleet <caer aguanieve : to be sleeting>
aguantar *vt* **1** SOPORTAR : to bear, to tolerate, to withstand **2** : to hold **3** **aguantar las ganas** : to resist an urge <no pude aguantar las ganas de reír : I couldn't keep myself from laughing> — *vi* : to hold out, to last — **aguantarse** *vr* **1** : to resign oneself **2** : to restrain oneself
aguante *nm* **1** TOLERANCIA : tolerance, patience **2** RESISTENCIA : endurance, strength
aguar {10} *vt* **1** : to water down, to dilute **2** **aguar la fiesta** *fam* : to spoil the party

aguardar *vt* ESPERAR : to wait for, to await — *vi* : to be in store

aguardiente *nm* : clear brandy

aguarrás *nm* : turpentine

agudeza *nf* **1** : keenness, sharpness **2** : shrillness **3** : witticism

agudizar {21} *vt* : to intensify, to heighten

agudo, -da *adj* **1** : acute, sharp **2** : shrill, high-pitched **3** PERSPICAZ : clever, shrewd

agüero *nm* AUGURIO, PRESAGIO : augury, omen

aguijón *nm, pl* **-jones 1** : stinger (of a bee, etc.) **2** : goad

aguijonear *vt* : to goad

águila *nf* **1** : eagle **2 águila o sol** *Mex* : heads or tails

aguileño, -ña *adj* : aquiline

aguilera *nf* : aerie, eagle's nest

aguilón *nm, pl* **-lones** : gable

aguinaldo *nm* **1** : Christmas bonus, year-end bonus **2** *PRi, Ven* : Christmas carol

agüitarse *vr Mex fam* : to have the blues, to feel discouraged

aguja *nf* **1** : needle **2** : steeple, spire

agujerear *vt* : to make a hole in, to pierce

agujero *nm* **1** : hole **2 agujero negro** : black hole (in astronomy)

agujeta *nf* **1** *Mex* : shoelace **2 agujetas** *nfpl* : muscular soreness or stiffness

agusanado, -da *adj* : worm-eaten

aguzar {21} *vt* **1** : to sharpen <aguzar el ingenio : to sharpen one's wits> **2 aguzar el oído** : to prick up one's ears

ahí *adv* **1** : there <ahí está : there it is> **2 por ~** : somewhere, thereabouts **3 de ahí que** : with the result that, so that

ahijado, -da *n* : godchild, godson *m*, goddaughter *f*

ahijar {5} *vt* : to adopt (a child)

ahínco *nm* : eagerness, zeal

ahogar {52} *vt* **1** : to drown **2** : to smother **3** : to choke back, to stifle — **ahogarse** *vr*

ahogo *nm* : breathlessness, suffocation

ahondar *vt* : to deepen — *vi* : to elaborate, to go into detail

ahora *adv* **1** : now **2 ahora mismo** : right now **3 hasta ~** : so far **4 por ~** : for the time being

ahorcar {72} *vt* : to hang, to kill by hanging — **ahorcarse** *vr*

ahorita *adv fam* : right now, right away

ahorquillado, -da *adj* : forked

ahorrador, -dora *adj* : thrifty

ahorrar *vt* **1** : to save (money) **2** : to spare, to conserve — *vi* : to save up — **ahorrarse** *vr* : to spare oneself

ahorrativo, -va *adj* : thrifty, frugal

ahorro *nm* : saving <cuenta de ahorros : savings account>

ahuecar {72} *vt* **1** : to hollow out **2** : to cup (one's hands) **3** : to plump up, to fluff up

ahuizote *nm Mex fam* : annoying person, pain in the neck

ahumar {8} *vt* : to smoke, to cure

ahuyentar *vt* **1** : to scare away, to chase away **2** : to banish, to dispel <ahuyentar las dudas : to dispel doubts>

airado, -da *adj* FURIOSO : angry, irate

airar {5} *vt* : to make angry, to anger

aire *nm* **1** : air **2 aire acondicionado** : air-conditioning **3 darse aires** : to give oneself airs

airear *vt* : to air, to air out — **airearse** *vr* : to get some fresh air

airoso, -sa *adj* **1** : elegant, graceful **2 salir airoso** : to come out winning

aislacionismo *nm* : isolationism

aislacionista *adj & nmf* : isolationist

aislado, -da *adj* : isolated, alone

aislamiento *nm* **1** : isolation **2** : insulation

aislante *nm* : insulator, nonconductor

aislar {5} *vt* **1** : to isolate **2** : to insulate

ajado, -da *adj* **1** : worn, shabby **2** : wrinkled, crumpled

ajar *vt* : to wear out, to spoil

ajardinado, -da *adj* : landscaped

ajedrecista *nmf* : chess player

ajedrez *nm, pl* **-dreces 1** : chess **2** : chess set

ajeno, -na *adj* **1** : alien **2** : of another, of others <propiedad ajena : somebody else's property> **3 ~ a** : foreign to **4 ~ de** : devoid of, free from

ajetreado, -da *adj* : hectic, busy

ajetrearse *vr* : to bustle about, to rush around

ajetreo *nm* : hustle and bustle, fuss

ají *nm, pl* **ajíes** : chili pepper

ajo *nm* : garlic

ajonjolí *nm, pl* **-líes** : sesame

ajuar *nm* : trousseau

ajustable *adj* : adjustable

ajustado, -da *adj* **1** CEÑIDO : tight, tight-fitting **2** : reasonable, fitting

ajustar *vt* **1** : to adjust, to adapt **2** : to take in (clothing) **3** : to settle, to resolve — **ajustarse** *vr* : to fit, to conform

ajuste *nm* **1** : adjustment **2** : tightening

ajusticiar *vt* EJECUTAR : to execute, to put to death

al (*contraction of* **a** *and* **el**) → **a²**

ala *nf* **1** : wing **2** : brim (of a hat)

Alá *nm* : Allah

alabanza *nf* ELOGIO : praise

alabar *vt* : to praise — **alabarse** *vr* : to boast

alabastro *nm* : alabaster

alabear *vt* : to warp — **alabearse** *vr*

alabeo *nm* : warp, warping

alacena *nf* : cupboard, larder

alacrán *nm, pl* **-cranes** ESCORPIÓN : scorpion

alado, -da *adj* : winged

alambique *nm* : still (to distill alcohol)

alambre *nm* **1** : wire **2 alambre de púas** : barbed wire

alameda *nf* **1 :** poplar grove **2 :** tree-lined avenue
álamo *nm* **1 :** poplar **2 álamo temblón :** aspen
alar *nm* **:** eaves *pl*
alarde *nm* **1 :** show, display **2 hacer alarde de :** to make show of, to boast about
alardear *vi* PRESUMIR **:** to boast, to brag
alargado, -da *adj* **:** elongated, slender
alargamiento *nm* **:** lengthening, extension, elongation
alargar {52} *vt* **1 :** to extend, to lengthen **2** PROLONGAR **:** to prolong — **alargarse** *vr*
alarido *nm* **:** howl, shriek
alarma *nf* **:** alarm
alarmante *adj* **:** alarming — **alarmantemente** *adv*
alarmar *vt* **:** to alarm
alazán *nm, pl* **-zanes :** sorrel (color or animal)
alba *nf* AMANECER **:** dawn, daybreak
albacea *nmf* TESTAMENTARIO **:** executor, executrix *f*
albahaca *nf* **:** basil
albanés, -nesa *adj & n, mpl* **-neses :** Albanian
albañil *nmf* **:** bricklayer, mason
albañilería *nf* **:** bricklaying, masonry
albaricoque *nm* **:** apricot
albatros *nm* **:** albatross
albedrío *nm* **:** will <libre albedrío : free will>
alberca *nf* **1 :** reservoir, tank **2** *Mex* **:** swimming pool
albergar {52} *vt* ALOJAR **:** to house, to lodge, to shelter
albergue *nm* **1 :** shelter, refuge **2 :** hostel
albino, -na *adj & n* **:** albino — **albinismo** *nm*
albóndiga *nf* **:** meatball
albor *nm* **1 :** dawning, beginning **2** BLANCURA **:** whiteness
alborada *nf* **:** dawn
alborear *v impers* **:** to dawn
alborotado, -da *adj* **1 :** excited, agitated **2 :** rowdy, unruly
alborotador[1], -dora *adj* **1 :** noisy, boisterous **2 :** rowdy, unruly
alborotador[2], -dora *n* **:** agitator, troublemaker, rioter
alborotar *vt* **1 :** to excite, to agitate **2 :** to incite, to stir up — **alborotarse** *vr* **:** to riot
alboroto *nm* **1 :** disturbance, ruckus **2** MOTÍN **:** riot
alborozado, -da *adj* **:** jubilant
alborozar {21} *vt* **:** to gladden, to cheer
alborozo *nm* **:** joy, elation
álbum *nm* **:** album <álbum de recortes : scrapbook>
albúmina *nf* **:** albumin
albur *nm* **1 :** chance, risk **2** *Mex* **:** pun
alca *nf* **:** auk
alcachofa *nf* **:** artichoke
alcahuete, -ta *n* CHISMOSO **:** gossip
alcaide *nm* **:** warden (in a prison)
alcalde, -desa *n* **:** mayor
alcaldía *nf* **1 :** mayoralty **2** AYUNTAMIENTO **:** city hall
álcali *nm* **:** alkali
alcalino, -na *adj* **:** alkaline — **alcalinidad** *nf*
alcance *nm* **1 :** reach **2 :** range, scope
alcancía *nf* **1 :** piggy bank, money box **2 :** collection box (for alms, etc.)
alcanfor *nm* **:** camphor
alcantarilla *nf* CLOACA **:** sewer, drain
alcanzar {21} *vt* **1 :** to reach **2 :** to catch up with **3** LOGRAR **:** to achieve, to attain — *vi* **1** DAR **:** to suffice, to be enough **2 ~ a :** to manage to
alcaparra *nf* **:** caper
alcapurria *nf PRi* **:** stuffed fritter made with taro and green banana
alcaravea *nf* **:** caraway
alcatraz *nm, pl* **-traces :** gannet
alcázar *nm* **:** fortress, castle
alce[1], etc. → **alzar**
alce[2] *nm* **:** moose, European elk
alcoba *nf* **:** bedroom
alcohol *nm* **:** alcohol
alcohólico, -ca *adj & n* **:** alcoholic
alcoholismo *nm* **:** alcoholism
alcoholizarse {21} *vr* **:** to become an alcoholic
alcornoque *nm* **1 :** cork oak **2** *fam* **:** idiot, fool
alcurnia *nf* **:** ancestry, lineage
aldaba *nf* **:** door knocker
aldea *nf* **:** village
aldeano[1], -na *adj* **:** village, rustic
aldeano[2], -na *n* **:** villager
aleación *nf, pl* **-ciones :** alloy
alear *vt* **:** to alloy
aleatorio, -ria *adj* **:** random, fortuitous — **aleatoriamente** *adv*
alebrestar *vt* **:** to excite, to make nervous — **alebrestarse** *vr*
aledaño, -ña *adj* **:** bordering, neighboring
aledaños *nmpl* AFUERAS **:** outskirts, surrounding area
alegar {52} *vt* **:** to assert, to allege — *vi* DISCUTIR **:** to argue
alegato *nm* **1 :** allegation, claim **2** *Mex* **:** argument, summation (in law) **3 :** argument, dispute
alegoría *nf* **:** allegory
alegórico, -ca *adj* **:** allegorical
alegrar *vt* **:** to make happy, to cheer up — **alegrarse** *vr* **:** to be glad, to rejoice
alegre *adj* **1 :** glad, cheerful **2 :** colorful, bright **3** *fam* **:** tipsy
alegremente *adv* **:** happily, cheerfully
alegría *nf* **:** joy, cheer, happiness
alejado, -da *adj* **:** remote
alejamiento *nm* **1 :** removal, separation **2 :** estrangement
alejar *vt* **1 :** to remove, to move away **2 :** to estrange, to alienate — **alejarse** *vr* **1 :** to move away, to stray **2 :** to drift apart
alelado, -da *adj* **1 :** bewildered, stupefied **2 :** foolish, stupid
aleluya *interj* **:** hallelujah!, alleluia!

alemán[1], **-mana** *adj & n, mpl* **-manes** : German
alemán[2] *nm* : German (language)
alentador, -dora *adj* : encouraging
alentar {55} *vt* : to encourage, to inspire — *vi* : to breathe
alerce *nm* : larch
alérgeno *nm* : allergen
alergia *nf* : allergy
alérgico, -ca *adj* : allergic
alergista *nmf* : allergist
alero *nm* **1** : eaves *pl* **2** : forward (in basketball)
alerón *nm, pl* **-rones** : aileron
alerta[1] *adv* : on the alert
alerta[2] *nf* : alert, alarm
alertar *vt* : to alert
alerto, -ta *adj* : alert, watchful
aleta *nf* **1** : fin **2** : flipper **3** : small wing
aletargado, -da *adj* : lethargic, sluggish, torpid
aletargarse {52} *vr* : to feel drowsy, to become lethargic
aleteo *nm* : flapping, flutter
alevosía *nf* **1** : treachery **2** : premeditation
alevoso, -sa *adj* : treacherous
alfabético, -ca *adj* : alphabetical — **alfabéticamente** *adv*
alfabetismo *nm* : literacy
alfabetizado, -da *adj* : literate
alfabetizar {21} *vt* : to alphabetize
alfabeto *nm* : alphabet
alfalfa *nf* : alfalfa
alfanje *nm* : cutlass, scimitar
alfarería *nf* : pottery
alfarero, -ra *n* : potter
alféizar *nm* : sill, windowsill
alfeñique *nm fam* : wimp, weakling
alférez *nmf, pl* **-reces 1** : second lieutenant **2** : ensign
alfiler *nm* **1** : pin **2** BROCHE : brooch
alfiletero *nm* : pincushion
alfombra *nf* : carpet, rug
alfombrado *nm* : carpeting
alfombrar *vt* : to carpet
alfombrilla *nf* : small rug, mat
alforfón *nm, pl* **-fones** : buckwheat
alforja *nf* : saddlebag
alforza *nf* : pleat, tuck
alga *nf* **1** : aquatic plant, alga **2** : seaweed
algáceo, -cea *adj* : algal
algarabía *nf* **1** : gibberish, babble **2** : hubbub, uproar
álgebra *nf* : algebra
algebraico, -ca *adj* : algebraic
álgido, -da *adj* **1** : critical, decisive **2** : icy cold
algo[1] *adv* : somewhat, rather <es simpático, pero algo tacaño : he's nice but rather stingy>
algo[2] *pron* **1** : something **2 ~ de** : some, a little <tengo algo de dinero : I've got some money>
algodón *nm, pl* **-dones** : cotton
algoritmo *nm* : algorithm
alguacil *nm* : constable
alguien *pron* : somebody, someone
alguno[1], **-na** *adj* (**algún** *before masculine singular nouns*) **1** : some, any <algún día : someday, one day> **2** (*in negative constructions*) : not any, not at all <no tengo noticia alguna : I have no news at all> **3 algunas veces** : sometimes
alguno[2], **-na** *pron* **1** : one, someone, somebody <alguno de ellos : one of them> **2 algunos, -nas** *pron pl* : some, a few <algunos quieren trabajar : some want to work>
alhaja *nf* : jewel, gem
alhajar *vt* : to adorn with jewels
alharaca *nf* : fuss
alhelí *nm* : wallflower
aliado[1], **-da** *adj* : allied
aliado[2], **-da** *n* : ally
alianza *nf* : alliance
aliarse {85} *vr* : to form an alliance, to ally oneself
alias *adv & nm* : alias
alicaído, -da *adj* : depressed, discouraged
alicates *nmpl* PINZAS : pliers
aliciente *nm* **1** INCENTIVO : incentive **2** ATRACCIÓN : attraction
alienación *nf, pl* **-ciones** : alienation, derangement
alienar *vt* ENAJENAR : to alienate
aliento *nm* **1** : breath **2** : courage, strength **3 dar aliento a** : to encourage
aligerar *vt* **1** : to lighten **2** ACELERAR : to hasten, to quicken
alijo *nm* : cache, consignment (of contraband)
alimaña *nf* : pest, vermin
alimentación *nf, pl* **-ciones** NUTRICIÓN : nutrition, nourishment
alimentar *vt* **1** NUTRIR : to feed, to nourish **2** MANTENER : to support (a family) **3** FOMENTAR : to nurture, to foster — **alimentarse** *vr* **~ con** : to live on
alimentario, -ria → **alimenticio**
alimenticio, -cia *adj* **1** : nutritional, food, dietary **2** : nutritious, nourishing
alimento *nm* : food, nourishment
alineación *nf, pl* **-ciones 1** : alignment **2** : lineup (in sports)
alineamiento *nm* : alignment
alinear *vt* **1** : to align **2** : to line up — **alinearse** *vr* **1** : to fall in, to line up **2 ~ con** : to align oneself with
aliño *nm* : seasoning, dressing
alipús *nm, pl* **-puses** *Mex fam* : booze, drink
alisar *vt* : to smooth
aliso *nm* : alder
alistamiento *nm* : enlistment, recruitment
alistar *vt* **1** : to recruit **2** : to make ready — **alistarse** *vr* : to join up, to enlist
aliteración *nf, pl* **-ciones** : alliteration
aliterado, -da *adj* : alliterative

aliviar *vt* MITIGAR : to relieve, to alleviate, to soothe — **aliviarse** *vr* : to recover, to get better
alivio *nm* : relief
aljaba *nf* : quiver (for arrows)
aljibe *nm* : cistern, well
allá *adv* **1** : there, over there **2 más allá** : farther away **3 más allá de** : beyond **4 allá tú** : that's up to you
allanamiento *nm* **1** : (police) raid **2 allanamiento de morada** : breaking and entering
allanar *vt* **1** : to raid, to search **2** : to resolve, to solve **3** : to smooth, to level out
allegado[1], -da *adj* : close, intimate
allegado[2], -da *n* : close friend, relation <parientes y allegados : friends and relations>
allegar {52} *vt* : to gather, to collect
allende[1] *adv* : beyond, on the other side
allende[2] *prep* : beyond <allende las montañas : beyond the mountains>
allí *adv* : there, over there <allí mismo : right there> <hasta allí : up to that point>
alma *nf* **1** : soul **2** : person, human being **3 no tener alma** : to be pitiless **4 tener el alma en un hilo** : to have one's heart in one's mouth
almacén *nm, pl* **-cenes 1** BODEGA : warehouse, storehouse **2** TIENDA : shop, store **3 gran almacén** *Spain* : department store
almacenaje → **almacenamiento**
almacenamiento *nm* : storage <almacenamiento de datos : data storage>
almacenar *vt* : to store, to put in storage
almacenero, -ra *n* : shopkeeper
almacenista *nm* MAYORISTA : wholesaler
almádena *nf* : sledgehammer
almanaque *nm* : almanac
almeja *nf* : clam
almendra *nf* **1** : almond **2** : kernel
almendro *nm* : almond tree
almiar *nm* : haystack
almíbar *nm* : syrup
almidón *nm, pl* **-dones** : starch
almidonar *vt* : to starch
alminar *nm* MINARETE : minaret
almirante *nm* : admiral
almizcle *nm* : musk
almohada *nf* : pillow
almohadilla *nf* **1** : small pillow, cushion **2** : bag, base (in baseball)
almohadón *nm, pl* **-dones** : bolster, cushion
almohazar {21} *vt* : to curry (a horse)
almoneda *nf* SUBASTA : auction
almorranas *nfpl* HEMORROIDES : hemorrhoids, piles
almorzar {36} *vi* : to have lunch — *vt* : to have for lunch
almuerzo *nm* : lunch
alocado, -da *adj* **1** : crazy **2** : wild, reckless **3** : silly, scatterbrained
alocución *nf, pl* **-ciones** : speech, address
áloe *or* **aloe** *nm* : aloe
alojamiento *nm* : lodging, accommodations *pl*
alojar *vt* ALBERGAR : to house, to lodge — **alojarse** *vr* : to lodge, to room
alondra *nf* : lark, skylark
alpaca *nf* : alpaca
alpinismo *nm* : mountain climbing, mountaineering
alpinista *nmf* : mountain climber
alpino, -na *adj* : Alpine, alpine
alpiste *nm* : birdseed
alquilar *vt* ARRENDAR : to rent, to lease
alquiler *nm* ARRENDAMIENTO : rent, rental
alquimia *nf* : alchemy
alquimista *nmf* : alchemist
alquitrán *nm, pl* **-tranes** BREA : tar
alquitranar *vt* : to tar, to cover with tar
alrededor[1] *adv* **1** : around, about <todo temblaba alrededor : all around things were shaking> **2 ~ de** : around, approximately <alrededor de quince personas : around fifteen people>
alrededor[2] *prep* **~ de** : around, about <corrió alrededor de la casa : she ran around the house> <llegaré alrededor de diciembre : I will get there around December>
alrededores *nmpl* ALEDAÑOS : surroundings, outskirts
alta *nf* **1** : admission, entry, enrollment **2 dar de alta** : to release, to discharge (a patient)
altanería *nf* ALTIVEZ, ARROGANCIA : arrogance, haughtiness
altanero, -ra *adj* ALTIVO, ARROGANTE : arrogant, haughty — **altaneramente** *adv*
altar *nm* : altar
altavoz *nm, pl* **-voces** ALTOPARLANTE : loudspeaker
alteración *nf, pl* **-ciones 1** MODIFICACIÓN : alteration, modification **2** PERTURBACIÓN : disturbance, disruption
alterado, -da *adj* : upset
alterar *vt* **1** MODIFICAR : to alter, to modify **2** PERTURBAR : to disturb, to disrupt — **alterarse** *vr* : to get upset, to get worked up
altercado *nm* DISCUSIÓN, DISPUTA : altercation, argument, dispute
alternador *nm* : alternator
alternancia *nf* : alternation, rotation
alternar *vi* **1** : to alternate **2** : to mix, to socialize — *vt* : to alternate — **alternarse** *vr* : to take turns
alternativa *nf* OPCIÓN : alternative, option
alternativo, -va *adj* **1** : alternating **2** : alternative — **alternativamente** *adv*
alterno, -na *adj* : alternate <corriente alterna : alternating current>
alteza *nf* **1** : loftiness, lofty height **2 Alteza** : Highness

altibajos *nmpl* **1 :** unevenness (of terrain) **2 :** ups and downs

altímetro *nm* **:** altimeter

altiplano *nm* **:** high plateau

altisonante *adj* **1 :** pompous, affected (of language) **2** *Mex* **:** rude, obscene (of language)

altitud *nf* **:** altitude

altivez *nf, pl* **-veces** ALTANERÍA, ARROGANCIA **:** arrogance, haughtiness

altivo, -va *adj* ALTANERO, ARROGANTE **:** arrogant, haughty

alto[1] *adv* **1 :** high **2 :** loud, loudly

alto[2], **-ta** *adj* **1 :** tall, high **2 :** loud <en voz alta : aloud, out loud>

alto[3] *nm* **1** ALTURA **:** height, elevation **2 :** stop, halt **3 altos** *nmpl* **:** upper floors

alto[4] *interj* **:** halt!, stop!

altoparlante *nm* ALTAVOZ **:** loudspeaker

altozano *nm* **:** hillock

altruismo *nm* **:** altruism

altruista[1] *adj* **:** altruistic

altruista[2] *nmf* **:** altruist

altura *nf* **1 :** height **2 :** altitude **3 :** loftiness, nobleness **4 a la altura de :** near, up by <en la avenida San Antonio a la altura de la Calle Tres : on San Antonio Avenue up near Third Street> **5 a estas alturas :** at this point, at this stage of the game

alubia *nf* **:** kidney bean

alucinación *nf, pl* **-ciones :** hallucination

alucinante *adj* **:** hallucinatory

alucinar *vi* **:** to hallucinate

alucinógeno[1], **-na** *adj* **:** hallucinogenic

alucinógeno[2] *nm* **:** hallucinogen

alud *nm* AVALANCHA **:** avalanche, landslide

aludido, -da *n* **1 :** person in question <el aludido : the aforesaid> **2 darse por aludido :** to take personally

aludir *vi* **:** to allude, to refer

alumbrado *nm* ILUMINACIÓN **:** lighting

alumbramiento *nm* **1 :** lighting **2 :** childbirth

alumbrar *vt* **1** ILUMINAR **:** to light, to illuminate **2 :** to give birth to

alumbre *nm* **:** alum

aluminio *nm* **:** aluminum

alumnado *nm* **:** student body

alumno, -na *n* **1 :** pupil, student **2 ex–alumno, -na :** alumnus, alumna *f* **3 ex–alumnos, -nas** *npl* **:** alumni, alumnae *f*

alusión *nf, pl* **-siones :** allusion, reference

alusivo, -va *adj* **1 :** allusive **2 ~ a :** in reference to, regarding

aluvión *nm, pl* **-viones :** flood, barrage

alza *nf* SUBIDA **:** rise <precios en alza : rising prices>

alzamiento *nm* LEVANTAMIENTO **:** uprising, insurrection

alzar {21} *vt* **1** ELEVAR, LEVANTAR **:** to lift, to raise **2 :** to erect — **alzarse** *vr* LEVANTARSE **:** to rise up

ama *nf* → **amo**

amabilidad *nf* **:** kindness

amable *adj* **:** kind, nice — **amablemente** *adv*

amado[1], **-da** *adj* **:** beloved, darling

amado[2], **-da** *n* **:** sweetheart, loved one

amaestrar *vt* **:** to train (animals)

amafiarse *vr Mex fam* **:** to conspire, to be in cahoots

amagar {52} *vt* **1 :** to show signs of (an illness, etc.) **2 :** to threaten — *vi* **1 :** to be imminent, to threaten **2 :** to feint, to dissemble

amago *nm* **1** AMENAZA **:** threat **2 :** sign, hint

amainar *vi* **:** to abate, to ease up, to die down

amalgama *nf* **:** amalgam

amalgamar *vt* **:** to amalgamate, to unite

amamantar *v* **:** to breast-feed, to nurse, to suckle

amanecer[1] {53} *v impers* **1 :** to dawn **2 :** to begin to show, to appear **3 :** to wake up (in the morning)

amanecer[2] *nm* ALBA **:** dawn, daybreak

amanerado, -da *adj* **:** affected, mannered

amansar *vt* **1 :** to tame **2 :** to soothe, to calm down — **amansarse** *vr*

amante[1] *adj* **:** loving, fond

amante[2] *nmf* **:** lover

amañar *vt* **:** to rig, to fix, to tamper with — **amañarse** *vr* **amañárselas :** to manage

amaño *nm* **1 :** skill, dexterity **2 :** trick, ruse

amapola *nf* **:** poppy

amar *vt* **:** to love — **amarse** *vr*

amargado, -da *adj* **:** embittered, bitter

amargar {52} *vt* **:** to make bitter, to embitter — *vi* **:** to taste bitter

amargo[1], **-ga** *adj* **:** bitter — **amargamente** *adv*

amargo[2] *nm* **:** bitterness, tartness

amargura *nf* **1 :** bitterness **2 :** grief, sorrow

amarilis *nf* **:** amaryllis

amarillear *vi* **:** to yellow, to turn yellow

amarillento, -ta *adj* **:** yellowish

amarillismo *nm* **:** yellow journalism, sensationalism

amarillo[1], **-lla** *adj* **:** yellow

amarillo[2] *nm* **:** yellow

amarra *nf* **1 :** mooring, mooring line **2 soltar las amarras de :** to loosen one's grip on

amarrar *vt* **1 :** to moor (a boat) **2** ATAR **:** to fasten, to tie up, to tie down

amartillar *vt* **:** to cock (a gun)

amasar *vt* **1 :** to amass **2 :** to knead **3 :** to mix, to prepare

amasijo *nm* **:** jumble, hodgepodge

amasio, -sia *n* **:** lover, paramour

amateur *adj & nmf* **:** amateur — **amateurismo** *nm*

amatista *nf* **:** amethyst

amatorio, -ria *adj* **:** amatory, love

amazona *nf* **1 :** Amazon (in mythology) **2 :** horsewoman
amazónico, -ca *adj* **:** amazonian
ambages *mpl* **sin ~ :** without hesitation, straight to the point
ámbar *nm* **1 :** amber **2 ámbar gris :** ambergris
ambición *nf, pl* **-ciones :** ambition
ambicionar *vt* **:** to aspire to, to seek
ambicioso, -sa *adj* **:** ambitious — **ambiciosamente** *adv*
ambidextro, -tra *adj* **:** ambidextrous
ambientación *nf, pl* **-ciones :** setting, atmosphere
ambiental *adj* **:** environmental — **ambientalmente** *adv*
ambientalista *nmf* **:** environmentalist
ambientar *vt* **:** to give atmosphere to, to set (in literature and drama) — **ambientarse** *vr* **:** to adjust, to get one's bearings
ambiente *nm* **1 :** atmosphere **2 :** environment **3 :** surroundings *pl*
ambigüedad *nf* **:** ambiguity
ambiguo, -gua *adj* **:** ambiguous
ámbito *nm* **:** domain, field, area
ambivalencia *nf* **:** ambivalence
ambivalente *adj* **:** ambivalent
ambos, -bas *adj & pron* **:** both
ambulancia *nf* **:** ambulance
ambulante *adj* **1 :** traveling, itinerant **2 vendedor ambulante :** street vendor
ameba *nf* **:** amoeba
amedrentar *vt* **:** to frighten, to intimidate — **amedrentarse** *vr*
amén *nm* **1 :** amen **2 ~ de :** in addition to, besides **3 en un decir amén :** in an instant
amenaza *nf* **:** threat, menace
amenazador, -dora *adj* **:** threatening, menacing
amenazante → **amenazador**
amenazar {21} *v* **:** to threaten
amenguar {10} *vt* **1 :** to diminish **2 :** to belittle, to dishonor
amenidad *nf* **:** pleasantness, amenity
amenizar {21} *vt* **1 :** to make pleasant **2 :** to brighten up, to add life to
ameno, -na *adj* **:** agreeable, pleasant
amento *nm* **:** catkin
americano, -na *adj & n* **:** American
amerindio, -dia *adj & n* **:** Amerindian
ameritar *vt* MERECER **:** to deserve
ametralladora *nf* **:** machine gun
amianto *nm* **:** asbestos
amiba *nf* → **ameba**
amigable *adj* **:** friendly, amicable — **amigablemente** *adv*
amígdala *nf* **:** tonsil
amigdalitis *nf* **:** tonsilitis
amigo[1], -ga *adj* **:** friendly, close
amigo[2], -ga *n* **:** friend
amigote *nm* **:** crony, pal
amilanar *vt* **1 :** to frighten **2 :** to daunt, to discourage — **amilanarse** *vr* **:** to lose heart
aminoácido *nm* **:** amino acid
aminorar *vt* **:** to reduce, to lessen — *vi* **:** to diminish
amistad *nf* **:** friendship
amistoso, -sa *adj* **:** friendly — **amistosamente** *adv*
amnesia *nf* **:** amnesia
amnésico, -ca *adj & n* **:** amnesiac, amnesic
amnistía *nf* **:** amnesty
amnistiar {85} *vt* **:** to grant amnesty to
amo, ama *n* **1 :** master *m,* mistress *f* **2 :** owner, keeper (of an animal) **3 ama de casa :** housewife **4 ama de llaves :** housekeeper
amodorrado, -da *adj* **:** drowsy
amolar {19} *vt* **1 :** to grind, to sharpen **2 :** to pester, to annoy
amoldable *adj* **:** adaptable
amoldar *vt* **1 :** to mold **2 :** to adapt, to adjust — **amoldarse** *vr*
amonestación *nf, pl* **-ciones 1** APERCIBIMIENTO **:** admonition, warning **2** AMONESTACIONES *nfpl* **:** banns
amonestar *vt* APERCIBIR **:** to admonish, to warn
amoníaco *or* **amoniaco** *nm* **:** ammonia
amontonamiento *nm* **:** accumulation, piling up
amontonar *vt* **1** APILAR **:** to pile up, to heap up **2 :** to collect, to gather **3 :** to hoard — **amontonarse** *vr*
amor *nm* **1 :** love **2 :** loved one, beloved **3 amor propio :** self-esteem **4 hacer el amor :** to make love
amoral *adj* **:** amoral
amoratado, -da *adj* **:** black-and-blue, bruised, livid
amordazar {21} *vt* **1 :** to gag, to muzzle **2 :** to silence
amorfo, -fa *adj* **:** shapeless, amorphous
amorío *nm* **:** love affair, fling
amoroso, -sa *adj* **1 :** loving, affectionate **2 :** amorous <una mirada amorosa : an amorous glance> **3 :** charming, cute — **amorosamente** *adv*
amortiguación *nf* **:** cushioning, absorption
amortiguador *nm* **:** shock absorber
amortiguar {10} *vt* **:** to soften (an impact)
amortizar {21} *vt* **:** to amortize, to pay off — **amortización** *nf*
amotinado[1], -da *adj* **:** rebellious, insurgent, mutinous
amotinado[2], -da *n* **:** rebel, insurgent, mutineer
amotinamiento *nm* **:** uprising, rebellion
amotinar *vt* **:** to incite (to riot), to agitate — **amotinarse** *vr* **1 :** to riot, to rebel **2 :** to mutiny
amparar *vt* **:** to safeguard, to protect — **ampararse** *vr* **1 ~ de :** to take shelter from **2 ~ en :** to have recourse to
amparo *nm* ACOGIDA, REFUGIO **:** protection, refuge
amperímetro *nm* **:** ammeter

amperio *nm* : ampere
ampliable *adj* : expandable, enlargeable, extendible
ampliación *nf, pl* **-ciones** : expansion, extension
ampliar {85} *vt* **1** : to expand, to extend **2** : to widen **3** : to enlarge (photographs) **4** : to elaborate on, to develop (ideas)
amplificador *nm* : amplifier
amplificar {72} *vt* : to amplify — **amplificación** *nf*
amplio, -plia *adj* : broad, wide, ample — **ampliamente** *adj*
amplitud *nf* **1** : breadth, extent **2** : spaciousness
ampolla *nf* **1** : blister **2** : vial, ampoule
ampollar *vt* : to blister — **ampollarse** *vr*
ampolleta *nf* **1** : small vial **2** : hourglass **3** *Chile* : light bulb
ampulosidad *nf* : pompousness, bombast
ampuloso, -sa *adj* GRANDILOCUENTE : pompous, bombastic — **ampulosamente** *adv*
amputar *vt* : to amputate — **amputación** *nf*
amueblar *vt* : to furnish
amuleto *nm* TALISMÁN : amulet, charm
amurallar *vt* : to wall in, to fortify
anacardo *nm* : cashew nut
anaconda *nf* : anaconda
anacrónico, -ca *adj* : anachronistic
anacronismo *nm* : anachronism
ánade *nmf* **1** : duck **2 ánade real** : mallard
anagrama *nm* : anagram
anal *adj* : anal
anales *nmpl* : annals
analfabetismo *nm* : illiteracy
analfabeto, -ta *adj & n* : illiterate
analgésico[1], **-ca** *adj* : analgesic, painkilling
analgésico[2] *nm* : painkiller, analgesic
análisis *nm* : analysis
analista *nmf* **1** : analyst **2** : annalist
analítico, -ca *adj* : analytical, analytic — **analíticamente** *adv*
analizar {21} *vt* : to analyze
analogía *nf* : analogy
analógico, -ca *adj* **1** : analogical **2** : analog <computadora analógica : analog computer>
análogo, -ga *adj* : analogous, similar
ananá *or* **ananás** *nm, pl* **-nás** : pineapple
anaquel *nm* REPISA : shelf
anaranjado[1], **-da** *adj* NARANJA : orange-colored
anaranjado[2] *nm* NARANJA : orange (color)
anarquía *nf* : anarchy
anárquico, -ca *adj* : anarchic
anarquismo *nm* : anarchism
anarquista *adj & nmf* : anarchist
anatema *nm* : anathema
anatomía *nf* : anatomy — **anatomista** *nmf*
anatómico, -ca *adj* : anatomical — **anatómicamente** *adv*
anca *nm* **1** : haunch, hindquarter **2 ancas de rana** : frogs' legs
ancestral *adj* **1** : ancient, traditional **2** : ancestral
ancestro *nm* ASCENDIENTE : ancestor, forefather *m*
ancho[1], **-cha** *adj* **1** : wide, broad **2** : ample, loose-fitting
ancho[2] *nm* : width, breadth
anchoa *nf* : anchovy
anchura *nf* : width, breadth
ancianidad *nf* SENECTUD : old age
anciano[1], **-na** *adj* : aged, old, elderly
anciano[2], **-na** *n* : elderly person
ancla *nf* : anchor
ancladero *nm* → **anclaje**
anclaje *nm* : anchorage
anclar *v* FONDEAR : to anchor
andadas *nfpl* **1** : tracks **2 volver a las andadas** : to go back to one's old ways, to backslide
andador[1] *nm* **1** : walker, baby walker **2** *Mex* : walkway
andador[2], **-dora** *n* : walker, one who walks
andadura *nf* : course, journey <su agotadora andadura al campeonato : his exhausting journey to the championship>
andaluz, -luza *adj & n, mpl* **-luces** : Andalusian
andamiaje *nm* **1** : scaffolding **2** ESTRUCTURA : structure, framework
andamio *nm* : scaffold
andanada *nf* **1** : volley, broadside **2 soltar una andanada a** : to reprimand
andanzas *nfpl* : adventures
andar[1] {6} *vi* **1** CAMINAR : to walk **2** IR : to go, to travel **3** FUNCIONAR : to run, to function <el auto anda bien : the car runs well> **4** : to ride <andar a caballo : to ride on horseback> **5** : to be <anda sin dinero : he's broke> — *vt* : to walk, to travel
andar[2] *nm* : walk, gait
andas *nfpl* : stand (for a coffin), bier
andén *nm, pl* **andenes 1** : (train) platform **2** *CA, Col* : sidewalk
andino, -na *adj* : Andean
andorrano, -na *adj & n* : Andorran
andrajos *nmpl* : rags, tatters
andrajoso, -sa *adj* : ragged, tattered
andrógino, -na *adj* : androgynous
andurriales *nmpl* : remote place
anea *nf* : cattail
anduvo, etc. → **andar**
anécdota *nf* : anecdote
anecdótico, -ca *adj* : anecdotal
anegar {52} *vt* **1** INUNDAR : to flood **2** AHOGAR : to drown **3** : to overwhelm — **anegarse** *vr* : to be flooded
anejo *nm* → **anexo**[2]
anemia *nf* : anemia
anémico, -ca *adj* : anemic
anémona *nf* : anemone
anestesia *nf* : anesthesia

anestesiar *vt* : to anesthetize
anestésico[1], -ca *adj* : anesthetic
anestésico[2] *nm* : anesthetic
anestesista *nmf* : anesthetist
aneurisma *nmf* : aneurism
anexar *vt* : to annex, to attach
anexión *nf, pl* **-xiones** : annexation
anexo[1], -xa *adj* : attached, joined, annexed
anexo[2] *nm* **1** : annex **2** : supplement (to a book), appendix
anfetamina *nf* : amphetamine
anfibio[1], -bia *adj* : amphibious
anfibio[2] *nm* : amphibian
anfiteatro *nm* **1** : amphitheater **2** : lecture hall
anfitrión, -triona *n, mpl* **-triones** : host, hostess *f*
ánfora *nf* **1** : amphora **2** *Mex, Peru* : ballot box
ángel *nm* : angel
angelical *adj* : angelic, angelical
angina *nf* **1** *or* **angina de pecho** : angina **2** *Mex* : tonsil
anglicano, -na *adj & n* : Anglican
angloparlante[1] *adj* : English-speaking
angloparlante[2] *nmf* : English speaker
anglosajón, -jona *adj & n, mpl* **-jones** : Anglo-Saxon
angoleño, -ña *adj & n* : Angolan
angora *nf* : angora
angostar *vt* : to narrow — **angostarse** *vr*
angosto, -ta *adj* : narrow
angostura *nf* : narrowness
anguila *nf* : eel
angular *adj* : angular — **angularidad** *nf*
ángulo *nm* **1** : angle **2** : corner **3 ángulo muerto** : blind spot
anguloso, -sa *adj* : angular, sharp <una cara angulosa : an angular face> — **angulosidad** *nf*
angustia *nf* **1** CONGOJA : anguish, distress **2** : anxiety, worry
angustiar *vt* **1** : to anguish, to distress **2** : to worry — **angustiarse** *vr*
angustioso, -sa *adj* **1** : anguished, distressed **2** : distressing, worrisome
anhelante *adj* : yearning, longing
anhelar *vt* : to yearn for, to crave
anhelo *nm* : longing, yearning
anidar *vi* **1** : to nest **2** : to make one's home, to dwell — *vt* : to shelter
anillo *nm* SORTIJA : ring
ánima *n* ALMA : soul
animación *nf, pl* **-ciones 1** : animation **2** VIVEZA : liveliness
animado, -da *adj* **1** : animated, lively **2** : cheerful — **animadamente** *adv*
animador, -dora *n* **1** : (television) host **2** : cheerleader
animadversión *nf, pl* **-siones** ANIMOSIDAD : animosity, antagonism
animal[1] *adj* **1** : animal **2** ESTÚPIDO : stupid, idiotic **3** : rough, brutish
animal[2] *nm* : animal
animal[3] *nmf* **1** IDIOTA : idiot, fool **2** : brute, beastly person
animar *vt* **1** ALENTAR : to encourage, to inspire **2** : to animate, to enliven **3** : to brighten up, to cheer up — **animarse** *vr*
anímico, -ca *adj* : mental <estado anímico : state of mind>
ánimo *nm* **1** ALMA : spirit, soul **2** : mood, spirits *pl* **3** : encouragement **4** PROPÓSITO : intention, purpose <sociedad sin ánimo de lucro : nonprofit organization> **5** : energy, vitality
animosidad *nf* ANIMADVERSIÓN : animosity, ill will
animoso, -sa *adj* : brave, spirited
aniñado, -da *adj* : childlike
aniquilación *nf* → **aniquilamiento**
aniquilamiento *nm* : annihilation, extermination
aniquilar *vt* **1** : to annihilate, to wipe out **2** : to overwhelm, to bring to one's knees — **aniquilarse** *vr*
anís *nm* **1** : anise **2 semilla de anís** : aniseed
aniversario *nm* : anniversary
ano *nm* : anus
anoche *adv* : last night
anochecer[1] {53} *v impers* : to get dark
anochecer[2] *nm* : dusk, nightfall
anodino, -na *adj* : insipid, dull
ánodo *nm* : anode
anomalía *nf* : anomaly
anómalo, -la *adj* : anomalous
anonadado, -da *adj* : dumbfounded, speechless
anonadar *vt* : to dumbfound, to stun
anonimato *nm* : anonymity
anónimo, -ma *adj* : anonymous — **anónimamente** *adv*
anorexia *nf* : anorexia
anoréxico, -ca *adj* : anorexic
anormal *adj* : abnormal — **anormalmente** *adv*
anormalidad *nf* : abnormality
anotación *nf, pl* **-ciones 1** : annotation, note **2** : scoring (in sports) <lograron una anotación : they managed to score a goal>
anotar *vt* **1** : to annotate **2** APUNTAR, ESCRIBIR : to write down, to jot down **3** : to score (in sports) — *vi* : to score
anquilosado, -da *adj* **1** : stiff-jointed **2** : stagnated, stale
anquilosamiento *nm* **1** : stiffness (of joints) **2** : stagnation, paralysis
anquilosarse *vr* **1** : to stagnate **2** : to become stiff or paralyzed
anquilostoma *nm* : hookworm
ánsar *nm* : goose
ansarino *nm* : gosling
ansia *nf* **1** INQUIETUD : apprehensiveness, uneasiness **2** ANGUSTIA : anguish, distress **3** ANHELO : longing, yearning
ansiar {85} *vt* : to long for, to yearn for
ansiedad *nf* : anxiety
ansioso, -sa *adj* **1** : anxious, worried **2** : eager — **ansiosamente** *adv*
antagónico, -ca *adj* : conflicting, opposing
antagonismo *nm* : antagonism

antagonista[1] *adj* : antagonistic
antagonista[2] *nmf* : antagonist, opponent
antaño *adv* : yesteryear, long ago
antártico, -ca *adj* **1** : antarctic **2 círculo antártico** : antarctic circle
ante[1] *nm* **1** : elk, moose **2** : suede
ante[2] *prep* **1** : before, in front of **2** : considering, in view of **3 ante todo** : first and foremost, above all
anteanoche *adv* : the night before last
anteayer *adv* : the day before yesterday
antebrazo *nm* : forearm
antecedente[1] *adj* : previous, prior
antecedente[2] *nm* **1** : precedent **2 antecedentes** *nmpl* : record, background
anteceder *v* : to precede
antecesor, -sora *n* **1** ANTEPASADO : ancestor **2** PREDECESOR : predecessor
antedicho, -cha *adj* : aforesaid, above
antelación *nf, pl* **-ciones 1** : advance notice **2 con ~** : in advance, beforehand
antemano *adv* **de ~** : in advance <se lo agradezco de antemano : I thank you in advance>
antena *nf* : antenna
antenoche → **anteanoche**
anteojera *nf* **1** : eyeglass case **2 anteojeras** *nfpl* : blinders
anteojos *nmpl* GAFAS : glasses, eyeglasses
antepasado[1]**, -da** *adj* : before last <el domingo antepasado : the Sunday before last>
antepasado[2]**, -da** *n* ANTECESOR : ancestor
antepecho *nm* **1** : guardrail **2** : ledge, sill
antepenúltimo, -ma *adj* : third from last
anteponer {60} *vt* **1** : to place before <anteponer al interés de la nación el interés de la comunidad : to place the interests of the community before national interest> **2** : to prefer
anteproyecto *nm* **1** : draft, proposal **2 anteproyecto de ley** : bill
antera *nf* : anther
anterior *adj* **1** : previous **2** : earlier <tiempos anteriores : earlier times> **3** : anterior, forward, front
anterioridad *nf* **1** : priority **2 con ~** : beforehand, in advance
anteriormente *adv* : previously, beforehand
antes *adv* **1** : before, earlier **2** : formerly, previously **3** : rather, sooner <antes prefiero morir : I'd rather die> **4 ~ de** : before, previous to <antes de hoy : before today> **5 antes que** : before <antes que llegue Luis : before Luis arrives> **6 cuanto antes** : as soon as possible **7 antes bien** : on the contrary
antesala *nf* **1** : anteroom, waiting room, lobby **2** : prelude, prologue
antiaborto, -ta *adj* : antiabortion
antiácido *nm* : antacid
antiadherente *adj* : nonstick
antiaéreo, -rea *adj* : antiaircraft
antiamericano, -na *adj* : anti-American
antibalas *adj* : bulletproof
antibiótico[1]**, -ca** *adj* : antibiotic
antibiótico[2] *nm* : antibiotic
antichoque *adj* : shockproof
anticipación *nf, pl* **-ciones 1** : expectation, anticipation **2 con ~** : in advance
anticipado, -da *adj* **1** : advance, early **2 por ~** : in advance
anticipar *vt* **1** : to anticipate, to forestall, to deal with in advance **2** : to pay in advance — **anticiparse** *vr* **1** : to be early **2** ADELANTARSE : to get ahead
anticipo *nm* **1** : advance (payment) **2** : foretaste, preview
anticlerical *adj* : anticlerical
anticlimático, -ca : anticlimatic
anticlímax *nm* : anticlimax
anticomunismo *nm* : anticommunism
anticomunista *adj & nmf* : anticommunist
anticoncepción *nf, pl* **-ciones** : birth control, contraception
anticonceptivo *nm* : contraceptive
anticongelante *nm* : antifreeze
anticuado, -da *adj* : antiquated, outdated
anticuario[1]**, -ria** *adj* : antique, antiquarian
anticuario[2]**, -ria** *n* : antiquarian, antiquary
anticuario[3] *nm* : antique shop
anticuerpo *nm* : antibody
antidemocrático, -ca *adj* : antidemocratic
antideportivo, -va *adj* : unsportsmanlike
antidepresivo *nm* : antidepressant
antídoto *nm* : antidote
antidrogas *adj* : antidrug
antier → **anteayer**
antiestético, -ca *adj* : unsightly, unattractive
antifascista *adj & nmf* : antifascist
antifaz *nm, pl* **-faces** : mask
antifeminista *adj & nmf* : antifeminist
antífona *nf* : anthem
antígeno *nm* : antigen
antigualla *nf* **1** : antique **2** : relic, old thing
antiguamente *adv* **1** : formerly, once **2** : long ago
antigüedad *nf* **1** : antiquity **2** : seniority **3** : age <con siglos de antigüedad : centuries-old> **4 antigüedades** *nfpl* : antiques
antiguo, -gua *adj* **1** : ancient, old **2** : former **3** : old-fashioned <a la antigua : in the old-fashioned way>
antihigiénico, -ca *adj* INSALUBRE : unhygienic, unsanitary
antihistamínico *nm* : antihistamine
antiimperialismo *nm* : anti-imperialism

antiimperialista *adj & nmf* : anti-imperialist
antiinflacionario, -ria *adj* : anti-inflationary
antiinflamatorio, -ria *adj* : anti-inflammatory
antillano[1], **-na** *adj* CARIBEÑO : Caribbean, West Indian
antillano[2], **-na** *n* : West Indian
antílope *nm* : antelope
antimilitarismo *nm* : antimilitarism
antimilitarista *adj & nmf* : antimilitarist
antimonio *nm* : antimony
antimonopolista *adj* : antimonopoly, antitrust
antinatural *adj* : unnatural, perverse
antipatía *nf* : aversion, dislike
antipático, -ca *adj* : obnoxious, unpleasant
antipatriótico, -ca *adj* : unpatriotic
antirrábico, -ca *adj* : antirabies <vacuna antirrábica : rabies vaccine>
antirreglamentario, -ria *adj* **1** : unlawful, illegal **2** : foul (in sports)
antirrevolucionario, -ria *adj & n* : antirevolutionary
antirrobo, -ba *adj* : antitheft
antisemita *adj* : anti-Semitic
antisemitismo *nm* : anti-Semitism
antiséptico[1], **-ca** *adj* : antiseptic
antiséptico[2] *nm* : antiseptic
antisocial *adj* : antisocial
antitabaco *adj* : antismoking
antiterrorista *adj* : antiterrorist
antítesis *nf* : antithesis
antitoxina *nf* : antitoxin
antitranspirante *nm* : antiperspirant
antojadizo, -za *adj* CAPRICHOSO : capricious
antojarse *vr* **1** APETECER : to be appealing, to be desirable <se me antoja un helado : I feel like having ice cream> **2** : to seem, to appear <los árboles se antojaban fantasmas : the trees seemed like ghosts>
antojitos *nmpl Mex* : traditional Mexican snack foods
antojo *nm* **1** CAPRICHO : whim **2** : craving
antología *nf* **1** : anthology **2 de ~** *fam* : fantastic, incredible
antónimo *nm* : antonym
antonomasia *nf* **por ~** : par excellence
antorcha *nf* : torch
antracita *nf* : anthracite
antro *nm* **1** : cave, den **2** : dive, seedy nightclub
antropofagia *nf* CANIBALISMO : cannibalism
antropófago[1], **-ga** *adj* : cannibalistic
antropófago[2], **-ga** *n* CANÍBAL : cannibal
antropoide *adj & nmf* : anthropoid
antropología *nf* : anthropology
antropológico, -ca *adj* : anthropological
antropólogo, -ga *n* : anthropologist
anual *adj* : annual, yearly — **anualmente** *adv*
anualidad *nf* : annuity
anuario *nm* : yearbook, annual
anudar *vt* : to knot, to tie in a knot — **anudarse** *vr*
anuencia *nf* : consent
anulación *nf, pl* **-ciones** : annulment, nullification
anular *vt* : to annul, to cancel
anunciador, -dora *n* → **anunciante**
anunciante *nmf* : advertiser
anunciar *vt* **1** : to announce **2** : to advertise
anuncio *nm* **1** : announcement **2** : advertisement, commercial
anzuelo *nm* **1** : fishhook **2 morder el anzuelo** : to take the bait
añadido *nm* : addition
añadidura *nf* **1** : additive, addition **2 por ~** : in addition, furthermore
añadir *vt* **1** AGREGAR : to add **2** AUMENTAR : to increase
añejar *vt* : to age, to ripen
añejo, -ja *adj* **1** : aged, vintage **2** : age-old, musty, stale
añicos *nmpl* : smithereens, bits <hacer(se) añicos : to shatter>
añil *nm* **1** : indigo **2** : bluing
año *nm* **1** : year <en el año 1990 : in (the year) 1990> <tiene diez años : she is ten years old> **2** : grade <cuarto año : fourth grade> **3 año bisiesto** : leap year **4 año luz** : light-year **5 Año Nuevo** : New Year
añoranza *nf* : longing, yearning
añorar *vt* **1** DESEAR : to long for **2** : to grieve for, to miss — *vi* : to mourn, to grieve
añoso, -sa *adj* : aged, old
aorta *nf* : aorta
apabullante *adj* : overwhelming, crushing
apabullar *vt* : to overwhelm
apacentar {55} *vt* : to pasture, to put to pasture
apache *adj & nmf* : Apache
apachurrado, -da *adj fam* : depressed, down
apachurrar *vt* : to crush, to squash
apacible *adj* : gentle, mild, calm — **apaciblemente** *adv*
apaciguador, -dora *adj* : calming
apaciguamiento *nm* : appeasement
apaciguar {10} *vt* APLACAR : to appease, to pacify — **apaciguarse** *vr* : to calm down
apadrinar *vt* **1** : to be a godparent to **2** : to sponsor, to support
apagado, -da *adj* **1** : off, out <la luz está apagada : the light is off> **2** : dull, subdued
apagador *nm Mex* : switch
apagar {52} *vt* **1** : to turn off, to shut off **2** : to extinguish, to put out — **apagarse** *vr* **1** : to go out, to fade **2** : to wane, to die down
apagón *nm, pl* **-gones** : blackout (of power)

apalancamiento *nm* **:** leverage
apalancar {72} *vt* **1 :** to jack up **2 :** to pry open
apalear *vt* **:** to beat up, to thrash
apantallar *vt Mex* **:** to dazzle, to impress
apañar *vt* **1 :** to seize, to grasp **2 :** to repair, to mend — **apañarse** *vr* **:** to manage, to get along
apaño *nm fam* **1 :** patch **2** HABILIDAD **:** skill, knack
apapachar *vt Mex fam* **:** to cuddle, to caress — **apapacharse** *vr*
aparador *nm* **1 :** sideboard, cupboard **2** ESCAPARATE, VITRINA **:** shop window
aparato *nm* **1 :** machine, appliance, apparatus <aparato auditivo : hearing aid> <aparato de televisión : television set> **2 :** system <aparato digestivo : digestive system> **3 :** display, ostentation <sin aparato : without ceremony> **4 aparatos** *nmpl* **:** braces (for the teeth)
aparatoso, -sa *adj* **1 :** ostentatious **2 :** spectacular
aparcamiento *nm Spain* **1 :** parking **2 :** parking lot
aparcar {72} *v Spain* **:** to park
aparcero, -ra *n* **:** sharecropper
aparear *vt* **1 :** to mate (animals) **2 :** to match up — **aparearse** *vr* **:** to mate
aparecer {53} *vi* **1 :** to appear **2** PRESENTARSE **:** to show up **3 :** to turn up, to be found — **aparecerse** *vr* **:** to appear
aparejado, -da *adj* **1 ir aparejado con :** to go hand in hand with **2 llevar aparejado :** to entail
aparejar *vt* **1** PREPARAR **:** to prepare, to make ready **2 :** to harness (a horse) **3 :** to fit out (a ship)
aparejo *nm* **1 :** equipment, gear **2 :** harness, saddle **3 :** rig, rigging (of a ship)
aparentar *vt* **1 :** to seem, to appear <no aparentas tu edad : you don't look your age> **2** FINGIR **:** to feign, to pretend
aparente *adj* **1 :** apparent **2 :** showy, striking — **aparentemente** *adv*
aparición *nf, pl* **-ciones 1 :** appearance **2** PUBLICACIÓN **:** publication, release **3** FANTASMA **:** apparition, vision
apariencia *nf* **1** ASPECTO **:** appearance, look **2 en ~ :** seemingly, apparently
apartado *nm* **1 :** section, paragraph **2 apartado postal :** post office box
apartamento *nm* DEPARTAMENTO **:** apartment
apartar *vt* **1** ALEJAR **:** to move away, to put at a distance **2 :** to put aside, to set aside, to separate — **apartarse** *vr* **1 :** to step aside, to move away **2** DESVIARSE **:** to stray
aparte[1] *adv* **1 :** apart, aside <modestia aparte : if I say so myself> **2 :** separately **3 ~ de :** apart from, besides
aparte[2] *adj* **:** separate, special
aparte[3] *nm* **:** aside (in theater)
apartheid *nm* **:** apartheid
apasionado, -da *adj* **:** passionate, enthusiastic — **apasionadamente** *adv*
apasionante *adj* **:** fascinating, exciting
apasionar *vt* **:** to enthuse, to excite — **apasionarse** *vr*
apatía *nf* **:** apathy
apático, -ca *adj* **:** apathetic
apearse *vr* **1** DESMONTAR **:** to dismount **2 :** to get out of or off (a vehicle)
apedrear *vt* **:** to stone, to throw stones at
apegado, -da *adj* **:** attached, close, devoted <es muy apegado a su familia : he is very devoted to his family>
apegarse {52} *vr* **~ a :** to become attached to, to grow fond of
apego *nm* AFICIÓN **:** attachment, fondness, inclination
apelación *nf, pl* **-ciones :** appeal (in court)
apelar *vi* **1 :** to appeal **2 ~ a :** to resort to
apelativo *nm* APELLIDO **:** last name, surname
apellidarse *vr* **:** to have for a last name <¿cómo se apellida? : what is your last name?>
apellido *nm* **:** last name, surname
apelotonar *vt* **:** to roll into a ball, to bundle up
apenar *vt* **:** to aggrieve, to sadden — **apenarse** *vr* **1 :** to be saddened **2 :** to become embarrassed
apenas[1] *adv* **:** hardly, scarcely
apenas[2] *conj* **:** as soon as
apéndice *nm* **1 :** appendix **2 :** appendage
apendicectomía *nf* **:** appendectomy
apendicitis *nf* **:** appendicitis
apercibimiento *nm* **1 :** preparation **2** AMONESTACIÓN **:** warning
apercibir *vt* **1** DISPONER **:** to prepare, to make ready **2** AMONESTAR **:** to warn **3** OBSERVAR **:** to observe, to perceive — **apercibirse** *vr* **1 :** to get ready **2 ~ de :** to notice
aperitivo *nm* **1 :** appetizer **2 :** aperitif
apero *nm* **:** tool, implement
apertura *nf* **1 :** opening, aperture **2 :** commencement, beginning **3 :** openness
apesadumbrar *vt* **:** to distress, to sadden — **apesadumbrarse** *vr* **:** to be weighed down
apestar *vt* **1 :** to infect with the plague **2 :** to corrupt — *vi* **:** to stink
apestoso, -sa *adj* **:** stinking, foul
apetecer {53} *vt* **1 :** to crave, to long for <apeteció la fama : he longed for fame> **2 :** to appeal to <me apetece un bistec : I feel like having a steak> <¿cuándo te apetece ir? : when do you want to go?> — *vi* **:** to be appealing
apetecible *adj* **:** appetizing, appealing
apetito *nm* **:** appetite
apetitoso, -sa *adj* **:** appetizing
apiario *nm* **:** apiary
ápice *nm* **1 :** apex, summit **2** PIZCA **:** bit, smidgen

apicultor, -tora *n* : beekeeper
apicultura *nf* : beekeeping
apilar *vt* AMONTONAR : to heap up, to pile up — **apilarse** *vr*
apiñado, -da *adj* : jammed, crowded
apiñar *vt* : to pack, to cram — **apiñarse** *vr* : to crowd together, to huddle
apio *nm* : celery
apisonadora *nf* : steamroller
apisonar *vt* : to pack down, to tamp
aplacamiento *nm* : appeasement
aplacar {72} *vt* APACIGUAR : to appease, to placate — **aplacarse** *vr* : to calm down
aplanadora *nf* : steamroller
aplanar *vt* : to flatten, to level
aplastante *adj* : crushing, overwhelming
aplastar *vt* : to crush, to squash
aplaudir *v* : to applaud
aplauso *nm* **1** : applause, clapping **2** : praise, acclaim
aplazamiento *nm* : postponement
aplazar {21} *vt* : to postpone, to defer
aplicable *adj* : applicable — **aplicabilidad** *nf*
aplicación *nf, pl* **-ciones 1** : application **2** : diligence, dedication
aplicado, -da *adj* : diligent, industrious
aplicador *nm* : applicator
aplicar {72} *vt* : to apply — **aplicarse** *vr* : to apply oneself
aplique *or* **aplicqué** *nm* : appliqué
aplomar *vt* : to plumb, to make vertical
aplomo *nm* : aplomb, composure
apocado, -da *adj* : timid
apocalipsis *nms & pl* : apocalypse <el Libro del Apocalipsis : the Book of Revelation>
apocalíptico, -ca *adj* : apocalyptic
apocamiento *nm* : timidity
apocarse {72} *vr* **1** : to shy away, to be intimidated **2** : to humble oneself, to sell oneself short
apócrifo, -fa *adj* : apocryphal
apodar *vt* : to nickname, to call — **apodarse** *vr*
apoderado, -da *n* : proxy, agent
apoderar *vt* : to authorize, to empower — **apoderarse** *vr* **~ de** : to seize, to take over
apodo *nm* SOBRENOMBRE : nickname
apogeo *nm* : acme, peak, zenith
apología *nf* : defense, apology
apoplejía *nf* : apoplexy, stroke
apoplético, -ca *adj* : apoplectic
aporrear *vt* : to bang on, to beat, to bludgeon
aportación *nf, pl* **-ciones** : contribution
aportar *vt* CONTRIBUIR : to contribute, to provide
aporte *nm* → **aportación**
apostador, -dora *n* : bettor, better
apostar {19} *v* : to bet, to wager <I bet he's not coming : apuesto que no viene>
apostasía *nf* : apostasy
apóstata *nmf* : apostate
apostilla *nf* : note
apostillar *vt* : to annotate
apóstol *nm* : apostle
apostólico, -ca *adj* : apostolic
apóstrofe *nmf* : apostrophe
apostura *nf* : elegance, gracefulness
apoyacabezas *nms & pl* : headrest
apoyapiés *nms & pl* : footrest
apoyar *vt* **1** : to support, to back **2** : to lean, to rest — **apoyarse** *vr* **1 ~ en** : to lean on **2 ~ en** : to be based on, to rest on
apoyo *nm* : support, backing
apreciable *adj* : appreciable, substantial, considerable
apreciación *nf, pl* **-ciones 1** : appreciation **2** : appraisal, evaluation
apreciar *vt* **1** ESTIMAR : to appreciate, to value **2** EVALUAR : to appraise, to assess — **apreciarse** *vr* : to appreciate, to increase in value
aprecio *nm* **1** ESTIMO : esteem, appreciation **2** EVALUACIÓN : appraisal, assessment
aprehender *vt* **1** : to apprehend, to capture **2** : to conceive of, to grasp
aprehensión *nf, pl* **-siones** : apprehension, capture, arrest
apremiante *adj* : pressing, urgent
apremiar *vt* INSTAR : to pressure, to urge — *vi* URGIR : to be urgent <el tiempo apremia : time is of the essence>
apremio *nm* : pressure, urgency
aprender *v* : to learn — **aprenderse** *vr*
aprendiz, -diza *n, mpl* **-dices** : apprentice, trainee
aprendizaje *nm* : apprenticeship
aprensión *nf, pl* **-siones** : apprehension, dread
aprensivo, -va *adj* : apprehensive, worried
apresamiento *nm* : seizure, capture
apresar *vt* : to capture, to seize
aprestar *vt* : to make ready, to prepare — **aprestarse** *vr* : to get ready
apresuradamente *adv* **1** : hurriedly **2** : hastily, too fast
apresurado, -da *adj* : hurried, in a rush
apresuramiento *nm* : hurry, haste
apresurar *vt* : to quicken, to speed up — **apresurarse** *vr* : to hurry up, to make haste
apretado, -da *adj* **1** : tight **2** *fam* : cheap, tightfisted — **apretadamente** *adv*
apretar {55} *vt* **1** : to press, to push (a button) **2** : to tighten **3** : to squeeze — *vi* **1** : to press, to push **2** : to fit tightly, to be too tight <los zapatos me aprietan : my shoes are tight>
apretón *nm, pl* **-tones 1** : squeeze **2** **apretón de manos** : handshake

apretujar *vt* : to squash, to squeeze — **apretujarse** *vr*
aprieto *nm* APURO : predicament, difficulty <estar en un aprieto : to be in a fix>
aprisa *adv* : quickly, hurriedly
aprisionar *vt* **1** : to imprison **2** : to trap, to box in
aprobación *nf, pl* **-ciones** : approval, endorsement
aprobar {19} *vt* **1** : to approve of **2** : to pass (a law, an exam) — *vi* : to pass (in school)
aprobatorio, -ria *adj* : approving
apropiación *nf, pl* **-ciones** : appropriation
apropiado, -da *adj* : appropriate, proper, suitable — **apropiadamente** *adv*
apropiarse *vr* **~ de** : to take possession of, to appropriate
aprovechable *adj* : usable
aprovechado[1], -da *adj* **1** : diligent, hardworking **2** : pushy, opportunistic
aprovechado[2], -da *n* : pushy person, opportunist
aprovechamiento *nm* : use, exploitation
aprovechar *vt* : to take advantage of, to make good use of — *vi* **1** : to be of use **2** : to progress, to improve — **aprovecharse** *vr* **~ de** : to take advantage of, to exploit
aprovisionamiento *nm* : provisions *pl*, supplies *pl*
aprovisionar *vt* : to provide, to supply (with provisions)
aproximación *nf, pl* **-ciones 1** : approximation, estimate **2** : rapprochement
aproximado, -da *adj* : approximate, estimated — **aproximadamente** *adv*
aproximar *vt* ACERCAR, ARRIMAR : to approximate, to bring closer — **aproximarse** *vr* ACERCARSE, ARRIMARSE : to approach, to move closer
aptitud *nf* : aptitude, capability
apto, -ta *adj* **1** : suitable, suited, fit **2** HÁBIL : capable, competent
apuesta *nf* : bet, wager
apuesto, -ta *adj* : elegant, good-looking
apuntador, -dora *n* : prompter
apuntalar *vt* : to prop up, to shore up
apuntar *vt* **1** : to aim, to point **2** ANOTAR : to write down, to jot down **3** INDICAR, SEÑALAR : to point to, to point out **4** : to prompt (in the theater) — *vi* **1** : to take aim **2** : to become evident — **apuntarse** *vr* **1** : to sign up, to enroll **2** : to score, to chalk up
apunte *nm* : note
apuñalar *vt* : to stab
apuradamente *adv* **1** : with difficulty **2** : hurriedly, hastily
apurado, -da *adj* **1** APRESURADO : rushed, pressured **2** : poor, needy **3** : difficult, awkward **4** : embarrassed
apurar *vt* **1** APRESURAR : to hurry, to rush **2** : to use up, to exhaust **3** : to trouble — **apurarse** *vr* **1** APRESURARSE : to hurry up **2** PREOCUPARSE : to worry
apuro *nm* **1** APRIETO : predicament, jam **2** : rush, hurry **3** : embarrassment
aquejar *vt* : to afflict
aquel, aquella *adj, mpl* **aquellos** : that, those
aquél, aquélla *pron, mpl* **aquéllos 1** : that (one), those (ones) **2** : the former
aquello *pron* (*neuter*) : that, that matter, that business <aquello fue algo serio : that was something serious>
aquí *adv* **1** : here **2** : now <de aquí en adelante : from now on> **3 por ~** : around here, hereabouts
aquiescencia *nf* : acquiescence, approval
aquietar *vt* : to allay, to calm — **aquietarse** *vr* : to calm down
aquilatar *vt* **1** : to assay **2** : to assess, to size up
ara *nf* **1** : altar **2 en aras de** : in the interests of, for the sake of
árabe[1] *adj & nmf* : Arab, Arabian
árabe[2] *nm* : Arabic (language)
arabesco *nm* : arabesque — **arabesco, -ca** *adj*
arábigo, -ga *adj* **1** : Arabic, Arabian **2 número arábigo** : Arabic numeral
arable *adj* : arable
arado *nm* : plow
aragonés, -nesa *adj & n, mpl* **-neses** : Aragonese
arancel *nm* : tariff, duty
arándano *nm* : blueberry
arandela *nf* : washer (for a faucet, etc.)
araña *nf* **1** : spider **2** : chandelier
arañar *v* : to scratch, to claw
arañazo *nm* : scratch
arar *v* : to plow
arbitraje *nm* **1** : arbitration **2** : refereeing (in sports)
arbitrar *v* **1** : to arbitrate **2** : to referee, to umpire
arbitrariedad *nf* **1** : arbitrariness **2** INJUSTICIA : injustice, wrong
arbitrario, -ria *adj* **1** : arbitrary **2** : unfair, unjust — **arbitrariamente** *adv*
arbitrio *nm* **1** ALBEDRÍO : will **2** JUICIO : judgment
árbitro, -tra *n* **1** : arbitrator, arbiter **2** : referee, umpire
árbol *nm* **1** : tree **2 árbol genealógico** : family tree
arbolado[1], -da *adj* : wooded
arbolado[2] *nm* : woodland
arboleda *nf* : grove, wood
arbóreo, -rea *adj* : arboreal
arbusto *nm* : shrub, bush, hedge
arca *nf* **1** : ark **2** : coffer, chest
arcada *nf* **1** : arcade, series of arches **2 arcadas** *nfpl* : retching <hacer arcadas : to retch>
arcaico, -ca *adj* : archaic
arcángel *nm* : archangel
arcano, -na *adj* : arcane

arce *nm* **:** maple tree
arcén *nm, pl* **arcenes :** hard shoulder, berm
archidiócesis *nfs & pl* **:** archdiocese
archipiélago *nm* **:** archipelago
archivador *nm* **:** filing cabinet
archivar *vt* **1 :** to file **2 :** to archive
archivista *nmf* **:** archivist
archivo *nm* **1 :** file **2 :** archive, archives *pl*
arcilla *nf* **:** clay
arco *nm* **1 :** arch, archway **2 :** bow (in archery) **3 :** arc **4 :** wicket (in croquet) **5** PORTERÍA **:** goal, goalposts *pl* **6 arco iris :** rainbow
arder *vi* **1 :** to burn <el bosque está ardiendo : the forest is in flames> <arder de ira : to burn with anger, to be seething> **2 :** to smart, to sting, to burn <le ardía el estómago : he had heartburn>
ardid *nm* **:** scheme, ruse
ardiente *adj* **1 :** burning **2 :** ardent, passionate — **ardientemente** *adv*
ardilla *nf* **1 :** squirrel **2** *or* **ardilla listada :** chipmunk
ardor *nm* **1 :** heat **2 :** passion, ardor
ardoroso, -sa *adj* **:** heated, impassioned
arduo, -dua *adj* **:** arduous, grueling — **arduamente** *adv*
área *nf* **:** area
arena *nf* **1 :** sand <arena movediza : quicksand> **2 :** arena
arenga *nf* **:** harangue, lecture
arengar {52} *vt* **:** to harangue, to lecture
arenilla *nf* **1 :** fine sand **2 arenillas** *nfpl* **:** kidney stones
arenisca *nf* **:** sandstone
arenoso, -sa *adj* **:** sandy, gritty
arenque *nm* **:** herring
arepa *nf* **:** cornmeal bread
arete *nm* **:** earring
argamasa *nf* **:** mortar (cement)
argelino, -na *adj & n* **:** Algerian
argentino, -na *adj & n* **:** Argentinian, Argentine
argolla *nf* **:** hoop, ring
argón *nm* **:** argon
argot *nm* **:** slang
argucia *nf* **:** sophistry, subtlety
argüir {41} *vi* **:** to argue — *vt* **1** ARGUMENTAR **:** to contend, to argue **2** INFERIR **:** to deduce **3** PROBAR **:** to prove
argumentación *nf, pl* **-ciones :** line of reasoning, argument
argumentar *vt* **:** to argue, to contend
argumento *nm* **1 :** argument, reasoning **2 :** plot, story line
aria *nf* **:** aria
aridez *nf, pl* **-deces :** aridity, dryness
árido, -da *adj* **:** arid, dry
Aries *nmf* **:** Aries
ariete *nm* **:** battering ram
arisco, -ca *adj* **:** surly, sullen, unsociable
arista *nf* **1 :** ridge, edge **2 :** beard (of a plant) **3 aristas** *nfpl* **:** rough edges, complications, problems
aristocracia *nf* **:** aristocracy
aristócrata *nmf* **:** aristocrat
aristocrático, -ca *adj* **:** aristocratic
aritmética *nf* **:** arithmetic
aritmético, -ca *adj* **:** arithmetic, arithmetical — **aritméticamente** *adv*
arlequín *nm, pl* **-quines :** harlequin
arma *nf* **1 :** weapon **2 armas** *nfpl* **:** armed forces **3 arma de fuego :** firearm
armada *nf* **:** navy, fleet
armadillo *nm* **:** armadillo
armado, -da *adj* **1 :** armed **2 :** assembled, put together **3** *PRi* **:** obstinate, stubborn
armador, -dora *n* **:** shipowner
armadura *nf* **1 :** armor **2** ARMAZÓN **:** skeleton, framework
armamento *nm* **:** armament, arms *pl*, weaponry
armar *vt* **1 :** to assemble, to put together **2 :** to create, to cause <armar un escándalo : to cause a scene> **3 :** to arm — **armarse** *vr* **armarse de valor :** to steel oneself
armario *nm* **1** CLÓSET, ROPERO **:** closet **2** ALACENA **:** cupboard
armatoste *nm fam* **:** monstrosity, contraption
armazón *nmf, pl* **-zones 1** ESQUELETO **:** framework, skeleton <armazón de acero : steel framework> **2 :** frames *pl* (of eyeglasses)
armenio, -nia *adj & n* **:** Armenian
armería *nf* **1 :** armory **2 :** arms museum **3 :** gunsmith's shop **4 :** gunsmith's craft
armiño *nm* **:** ermine
armisticio *nm* **:** armistice
armonía *nf* **:** harmony
armónica *nf* **:** harmonica
armónico, -ca *adj* **1 :** harmonic **2 :** harmonious — **armónicamente** *adv*
armonioso, -sa *adj* **:** harmonious — **armoniosamente** *adv*
armonizar {21} *vt* **1 :** to harmonize **2 :** to reconcile — *vi* **:** to harmonize, to blend together
arnés *nm, pl* **arneses :** harness
aro *nm* **1 :** hoop **2 :** napkin ring **3** *Arg, Chile, Uru* **:** earring
aroma *nm* **:** aroma, scent
aromático, -ca *adj* **:** aromatic
arpa *nf* **:** harp
arpegio *nm* **:** arpeggio
arpía *nf* **:** shrew, harpy
arpista *nmf* **:** harpist
arpón *nm, pl* **arpones :** harpoon — **arponear** *vt*
arquear *vt* **:** to arch, to bend — **arquearse** *vr* **:** to bend, to bow
arqueología *nf* **:** archaeology
arqueológico, -ca *adj* **:** archaeological
arqueólogo, -ga *n* **:** archaeologist
arquero, -ra *n* **1 :** archer **2** PORTERO **:** goalkeeper, goalie

arquetípico, -ca *adj* : archetypal

arquetipo *nm* : archetype

arquitecto, -ta *n* : architect

arquitectónico, -ca *adj* : architectural — **aquitectónicamente** *adv*

arquitectura *nf* : architecture

arrabal *nm* **1** : slum **2 arrabales** *nmpl* : outskirts, outlying area

arracada *nf* : hoop earring

arracimarse *vr* : to cluster together

arraigado, -da *adj* : deep-seated, ingrained

arraigar {52} *vi* : to take root, to become established — **arraigarse** *vr*

arraigo *nm* : roots *pl* <con mucho arraigo : deep-rooted>

arrancar {72} *vt* **1** : to pull out, to tear out **2** : to pick, to pluck (a flower) **3** : to start (an engine) **4** : to boot (a computer) — *vi* **1** : to start an engine **2** : to get going — **arrancarse** *vr* : to pull out, to pull off

arrancón *nm, pl* **-cones** *Mex* **1** : sudden loud start (of a car) **2 carrera de arrancones** : drag race

arranque *nm* **1** : starter (of a car) **2** ARREBATO : outburst, fit **3 punto de arranque** : beginning, starting point

arrasar *vt* **1** : to level, to smooth **2** : to devastate, to destroy **3** : to fill to the brim

arrastrar *vt* **1** : to drag, to tow **2** : to draw, to attract — *vi* : to hang down, to trail — **arrastrarse** *vr* **1** : to crawl **2** : to grovel

arrastre *nm* **1** : dragging **2** : pull, attraction **3 red de arrastre** : dragnet, trawling net

arrayán *nm, pl* **-yanes 1** MIRTO : myrtle **2 arrayán brabántico** : bayberry, wax myrtle

arrear *vt* : to urge on, to drive — *vi* : to hurry along

arrebatado, -da *adj* **1** PRECIPITADO : impetuous, hotheaded, rash **2** : flushed, blushing

arrebatar *vt* **1** : to snatch, to seize **2** CAUTIVAR : to captivate — **arrebatarse** *vr* : to get carried away (with anger, etc.)

arrebato *nm* ARRANQUE : fit, outburst

arreciar *vi* : to intensify, to worsen

arrecife *nm* : reef

arreglado, -da *adj* **1** : fixed, repaired **2** : settled, sorted out **3** : neat, tidy **4** : smart, dressed-up

arreglar *vt* **1** COMPONER : to repair, to fix **2** : to tidy up <arregla tu cuarto : pick up your room> **3** : to solve, to work out <quiero arreglar este asunto : I want to settle this matter> — **arreglarse** *vr* **1** : to get dressed (up) <arreglarse el pelo : to get one's hair done> **2 arreglárselas** *fam* : to get by, to manage

arreglo *nm* **1** : repair **2** : arrangement **3** : agreement, understanding

arrellanarse *vr* : to settle (in a chair)

arremangarse {52} *vr* : to roll up one's sleeves

arremeter *vi* EMBESTIR : to attack, to charge

arremetida *nf* EMBESTIDA : attack, onslaught

arremolinarse *vr* **1** : to crowd around, to mill about **2** : to swirl (about)

arrendador, -dora *n* **1** : landlord, landlady *f* **2** : tenant, lessee

arrendajo *nm* : jay

arrendamiento *nm* **1** ALQUILER : rental, leasing **2 contrato de arrendamiento** : lease

arrendar {55} *vt* ALQUILAR : to rent, to lease

arrendatario, -ria *n* : tenant, lessee, renter

arreos *nmpl* GUARNICIONES : tack, harness, trappings

arrepentido, -da *adj* : repentant, remorseful

arrepentimiento *nm* : regret, remorse, repentance

arrepentirse {76} *vr* **1** : to regret, to be sorry **2** : to repent

arrestar *vt* DETENER : to arrest, to detain

arresto *nm* **1** DETENCIÓN : arrest **2 arrestos** *nmpl* : boldness, daring

arriate *nm Mex, Spain* : bed (for plants), border

arriba *adv* **1** : up, upwards **2** : above, overhead **3** : upstairs **4 ~ de** : more than **5 de arriba abajo** : from top to bottom, from head to foot

arribar *vi* **1** : to arrive **2** : to dock, to put into port

arribista *nmf* : parvenu, upstart

arribo *nm* : arrival

arriendo *nm* ARRENDAMIENTO : rent, rental

arriero, -ra *n* : mule driver, muleteer

arriesgado, -da *adj* **1** : risky **2** : bold, daring

arriesgar {52} *vt* : to risk, to venture — **arriesgarse** *vr* : to take a chance

arrimado, -da *n Mex fam* : sponger, freeloader

arrimar *vt* ACERCAR, APROXIMAR : to bring closer, to draw near — **arrimarse** *vr* ACERCARSE, APROXIMARSE : to approach, to get close

arrinconar *vt* **1** ACORRALAR : to corner, to box in **2** : to push aside, to abandon

arroba *nf* : arroba (Spanish unit of measurement)

arrobamiento *nm* : rapture, ecstasy

arrobar *vt* : to enrapture, to enchant — **arrobarse** *vr*

arrocero[1], -ra *adj* : rice

arrocero[2], -ra *n* : rice grower

arrodillarse *vr* : to kneel (down)

arrogancia *nf* ALTANERÍA, ALTIVEZ : arrogance, haughtiness

arrogante *adj* ALTANERO, ALTIVO : arrogant, haughty

arrogarse {52} *vr* : to usurp, to arrogate

arrojado, -da *adj* : daring, fearless
arrojar *vt* **1 :** to hurl, to cast, to throw **2 :** to give off, to spew out **3 :** to yield, to produce **4** *fam* **:** to vomit — **arrojarse** *vr* PRECIPITARSE **:** to throw oneself, to leap
arrojo *nm* **:** boldness, fearlessness
arrollador, -dora *adj* **:** sweeping, overwhelming
arrollar *vt* **1 :** to sweep away, to carry away **2 :** to crush, to overwhelm **3 :** to run over (with a vehicle)
arropar *vt* **:** to clothe, to cover (up) — **arroparse** *vr*
arrostrar *vt* **:** to confront, to face (up to)
arroyo *nm* **1** RIACHUELO **:** brook, creek, stream **2 :** gutter
arroz *nm, pl* **arroces :** rice
arrozal *nm* **:** rice field, rice paddy
arruga *nf* **:** wrinkle, fold, crease
arrugado, -da *adj* **:** wrinkled, creased, lined
arrugar {52} *vt* **:** to wrinkle, to crease, to pucker — **arrugarse** *vr*
arruinar *vt* **:** to ruin, to wreck — **arruinarse** *vr* **1 :** to be ruined **2 :** to fall into ruin, to go bankrupt
arrullar *vt* **:** to lull to sleep — *vi* **:** to coo
arrullo *nm* **1 :** lullaby **2 :** coo (of a dove)
arrumaco *nm fam* **:** kissing, cuddling
arrumbar *vt* **1 :** to lay aside, to put away **2 :** to floor, to leave speechless
arsenal *nm* **:** arsenal
arsénico *nm* **:** arsenic
arte *nmf* (*usually m in singular, f in plural*) **1 :** art <artes y oficios : arts and crafts> <bellas artes : fine arts> **2** HABILIDAD **:** skill **3 :** cunning, cleverness
artefacto *nm* **1 :** artifact **2** DISPOSITIVO **:** device
artemisa *nf* **:** sagebrush
arteria *nf* **:** artery — **arterial** *adj*
arteriosclerosis *nf* **:** arteriosclerosis, hardening of the arteries
artero, -ra *adj* **:** wily, crafty
artesanal *adj* **:** pertaining to crafts or craftsmanship, handmade
artesanía *nm* **1 :** craftsmanship **2 :** handicrafts *pl*
artesano, -na *n* **:** artisan, craftsman *m*, craftsperson
artesiano, -na *adj* **:** artesian <pozo artesiano : artesian well>
ártico, -ca *adj* **:** arctic
articulación *nf, pl* **-ciones 1 :** articulation, pronunciation **2** COYUNTURA **:** joint
articular *vt* **1 :** to articulate, to utter **2 :** to connect with a joint **3 :** to coordinate, to orchestrate
articulista *nmf* **:** columnist
artículo *nm* **1 :** article, thing **2 :** item, feature, report **3 artículo de comercio :** commodity **4 artículos de primera necesidad :** essentials **5 artículos de tocador :** toiletries
artífice *nmf* **1** ARTESANO **:** artisan **2 :** mastermind, architect
artificial *adj* **1 :** artificial, man-made **2 :** feigned, false — **artificialmente** *adv*
artificio *nm* **1** HABILIDAD **:** skill **2** APARATO **:** device, appliance **3** ARDID **:** artifice, ruse
artificioso, -sa *adj* **1 :** skillful **2 :** cunning, deceptive
artillería *nf* **:** artillery
artillero, -ra *n* **:** artilleryman *m*, gunner
artilugio *nm* **:** gadget, contraption
artimaña *nf* **:** ruse, trick
artista *nmf* **1 :** artist **2** ACTOR, ACTRIZ **:** actor, actress *f*
artístico, -ca *adj* **:** artistic — **artísticamente** *adv*
artrítico, -ca *adj* **:** arthritic
artritis *nms & pl* **:** arthritis
artrópodo *nm* **:** arthropod
arveja *nf* GUISANTE **:** pea
arzobispado *nm* **:** archbishopric
arzobispo *nm* **:** archbishop
as *nm* **:** ace
asa *nf* AGARRADERA, ASIDERO **:** handle, grip
asado[1], -da *adj* **:** roasted, grilled, broiled
asado[2] *nm* **1 :** roast **2 :** barbecued meat **3 :** barbecue, cookout
asador *nm* **:** spit, rotisserie
asaduras *nfpl* **:** entrails, offal
asalariado[1], -da *adj* **:** wage-earning, salaried
asalariado[2], -da *n* **:** wage earner
asaltante *nmf* **1 :** mugger, robber **2 :** assailant
asaltar *vt* **1 :** to assault **2 :** to mug, to rob **3 asaltar al poder :** to seize power
asalto *nm* **1 :** assault **2 :** mugging, robbery **3 :** round (in boxing) **4 asalto al poder :** coup d'etat
asamblea *nf* **:** assembly, meeting
asambleísta *nmf* **:** assemblyman *m*, assemblywoman *f*
asar *vt* **:** to roast, to grill — **asarse** *vr fam* **:** to roast, to be dying from heat
asbesto *nm* **:** asbestos
ascendencia *nf* **1 :** ancestry, descent **2 ~ sobre :** influence over
ascendente *adj* **:** ascending, upward <un curso ascendente : an upward trend>
ascender {56} *vi* **1 :** to ascend, to rise up **2 :** to be promoted <ascendió a gerente : she was promoted to manager> **3 ~ a :** to amount to, to reach <las deudas ascienden a 20 millones de pesos : the debt amounts to 20 million pesos> — *vt* **:** to promote
ascendiente[1] *nmf* ANCESTRO **:** ancestor
ascendiente[2] *nm* INFLUENCIA **:** influence, ascendancy

ascensión *nf, pl* **-siones 1 :** ascent, rise **2 Fiesta de la Ascensión :** Ascension Day

ascenso *nm* **1 :** ascent, rise **2 :** promotion

ascensor *nm* ELEVADOR **:** elevator

asceta *nmf* **:** ascetic

ascético, -ca *adj* **:** ascetic

ascetismo *nm* **:** asceticism

asco *nm* **1 :** disgust <¡qué asco! : that's disgusting!, how revolting!> **2 darle asco (a alguien) :** to sicken, to revolt **3 estar hecho un asco :** to be filthy **4 hacerle ascos a :** to turn up one's nose at

ascua *nf* **1** BRASA **:** ember **2 estar en ascuas** *fam* **:** to be on edge

asear *vt* **1 :** to wash, to clean **2 :** to tidy up **— asearse** *vr*

asechanza *nf* **:** snare, trap

asechar *vt* **:** to set a trap for

asediar *vt* **1** SITIAR **:** to besiege **2** ACOSAR **:** to harass

asedio *nm* **1 :** siege **2** ACOSO **:** harassment

asegurador[1], -dora *adj* **1 :** insuring, assuring **2 :** pertaining to insurance

asegurador[2], -dora *n* **:** insurer, underwriter

aseguradora *nf* **:** insurance company

asegurar *vt* **1 :** to assure **2 :** to secure **3 :** to insure **— asegurarse** *vr* **1** CERCIORARSE **:** to make sure **2 :** to take out insurance, to insure oneself

asemejar *vt* **1 :** to make similar <ese bigote te asemeja a tu abuelo : that mustache makes you look like your grandfather> **2** *Mex* **:** to be similar to, to resemble **— asemejarse** *vr* **~ a :** to be look like, to resemble

asentaderas *nfpl fam* **:** bottom, buttocks *pl*

asentado, -da *adj* **:** settled, established

asentamiento *nm* **:** settlement

asentar {55} *vt* **1 :** to lay down, to set down, to place **2 :** to settle, to establish **3** *Mex* **:** to state, to affirm **— asentarse** *vr* **1 :** to settle **2** ESTABLECERSE **:** to settle down, to establish oneself

asentimiento *nm* **:** assent, consent

asentir {76} *vi* **:** to consent, to agree

aseo *nm* **:** cleanliness

aséptico, -ca *adj* **:** aseptic, germ-free

asequible *adj* ACCESIBLE **:** accessible, attainable

aserción *nf* **→ aserto**

aserradero *nm* **:** sawmill

aserrar {55} *vt* **:** to saw

aserrín *nm, pl* **-rrines :** sawdust

aserto *nm* **:** assertion, affirmation

asesinar *vt* **1 :** to murder **2 :** to assassinate

asesinato *nm* **1 :** murder **2 :** assassination

asesino[1], -na *adj* **:** murderous, homicidal

asesino[2], -na *n* **1 :** murderer, killer **2 :** assassin

asesor, -sora *n* **:** advisor, consultant

asesoramiento *nm* **:** advice, counsel

asesorar *vt* **:** to advise, to counsel **— asesorarse** *vr* **~ de :** to consult

asesoría *nf* **1 :** consulting, advising **2 :** consultant's office

asestar {55} *vt* **1 :** to aim, to point (a weapon) **2 :** to deliver, to deal (a blow)

aseveración *nf, pl* **-ciones :** assertion, statement

aseverar *vt* **:** to assert, to state

asexual *adj* **:** asexual **— asexualmente** *adv*

asfaltado[1], -da *adj* **:** asphalted, paved

asfaltado[2] *nm* PAVIMENTO **:** pavement, asphalt

asfaltar *vt* **:** to pave, to blacktop

asfalto *nm* **:** asphalt

asfixia *nf* **:** asphyxia, asphyxiation, suffocation

asfixiar *vt* **:** to asphyxiate, to suffocate, to smother **— asfixiarse** *vr*

asga, etc. → asir

así[1] *adv* **1 :** like this, like that **2 :** so, thus <así sea : so be it> **3 ~ de :** so, about so <una caja así de grande : a box about so big> **4 así que :** so, therefore **5 ~ como :** as well as **6 así así :** so-so, fair

así[2] *adj* **:** such, such a <un talento así es inestimable : a talent like that is priceless>

así[3] *conj* AUNQUE **:** even if, even though <no irá, así le paguen : he won't go, even if they pay him>

asiático[1], -ca *adj* **:** Asian, Asiatic

asiático[2], -ca *n* **:** Asian

asidero *nm* **1** AGARRADA, ASA **:** grip, handle **2** AGARRE **:** grip, hold

asiduamente *adv* **:** regularly, frequently

asiduidad *nf* **1 :** assiduousness **2 :** regularity, frequency

asiduo, -dua *adj* **1 :** assiduous **2 :** frequent, regular

asiento *nm* **1 :** seat, chair <asiento trasero : back seat> **2 :** location, site

asignación *nf, pl* **-ciones 1 :** allocation **2 :** appointment, designation **3 :** allowance, pay **4** *PRi* **:** homework, assignment

asignar *vt* **1 :** to assign, to allocate **2 :** to appoint

asignatura *nf* MATERIA **:** subject, course

asilado, -da *n* **:** exile, refugee

asilo *nm* **:** asylum, refuge, shelter

asimetría *nf* **:** asymmetry

asimétrico, -ca *adj* **:** asymmetrical, asymmetric

asimilación *nf, pl* **-ciones :** assimilation

asimilar *vt* **:** to assimilate **— asimilarse** *vr* **~ a :** to be similar to, to resemble

asimismo *adv* **1** IGUALMENTE **:** similarly, likewise **2** TAMBIÉN **:** as well, also

asir {7} *vt* : to seize, to grasp — **asirse** *vr* ~ **a** : to cling to
asistencia *nf* **1** : attendance **2** : assistance **3** : assist (in sports)
asistente[1] *adj* : attending, in attendance
asistente[2] *nmf* **1** : assistant **2 los asistentes** : those present, those in attendance
asistir *vi* : to attend, to be present <asistir a clase : to attend class> — *vt* : to aid, to assist
asma *nf* : asthma
asmático, -ca *adj* : asthmatic
asno *nm* BURRO : ass, donkey
asociación *nf, pl* **-ciones 1** : association, relationship **2** : society, group, association
asociado[1], **-da** *adj* : associate, associated
asociado[2], **-da** *n* : associate, partner
asociar *vt* **1** : to associate, to connect **2** : to pool (resources) **3** : to take into partnership — **asociarse** *vr* **1** : to become partners **2** ~ **a** : to join, to become a member of
asolar {19} *vt* : to devastate, to destroy
asoleado, -da *adj* : sunny
asolear *vt* : to put in the sun — **asolearse** *vr* : to sunbathe
asomar *vt* : to show, to stick out — *vi* : to appear, to become visible — **asomarse** *vr* **1** : to show, to appear **2** : to lean out, to look out <se asomó por la ventana : he leaned out the window>
asombrar *vt* MARAVILLAR : to amaze, to astonish — **asombrarse** *vr* : to marvel, to be amazed
asombro *nm* : amazement, astonishment
asombroso, -sa *adj* : amazing, astonishing — **asombrosamente** *adv*
asomo *nm* **1** : hint, trace **2 ni por asomo** : by no means
aspa *nf* : blade (of a fan or propeller)
aspaviento *nm* : exaggerated movement, fuss, flounce
aspecto *nm* **1** : aspect **2** APARIENCIA : appearance, look
aspereza *nf* RUDEZA : roughness, coarseness
áspero, -ra *adj* : rough, coarse, abrasive — **ásperamente** *adv*
aspersión *nf, pl* **-siones** : sprinkling
aspersor *nm* : sprinkler
aspiración *nf, pl* **-ciones 1** : inhalation, breathing in **2** ANHELO : aspiration, desire
aspiradora *nf* : vacuum cleaner
aspirante *nmf* : applicant, candidate
aspirar *vi* ~ **a** : to aspire to — *vt* : to inhale, to breathe in
aspirina *nf* : aspirin
asquear *vt* : to sicken, to disgust
asquerosidad *nf* : filth, foulness
asqueroso, -sa *adj* : disgusting, sickening, repulsive — **asquerosamente** *adv*
asta *nf* **1** : flagpole <a media asta : at half-mast> **2** : horn, antler **3** : shaft (of a weapon)
ástaco *nm* : crayfish
astado, -da *adj* : horned
áster *nm* : aster
asterisco *nm* : asterisk
asteroide *nm* : asteroid
astigmatismo *nm* : astigmatism
astil *nm* : shaft (of an arrow or feather)
astilla *nf* **1** : splinter, chip **2 de tal palo, tal astilla** : like father, like son
astillar *vt* : to splinter — **astillarse** *vr*
astillero *nm* : dry dock, shipyard
astral *adj* : astral
astringente *adj & nm* : astringent — **astringencia** *nf*
astro *nm* **1** : heavenly body **2** : star
astrología *nf* : astrology
astrológico, -ca *adj* : astrological
astrólogo, -ga *n* : astrologer
astronauta *nmf* : astronaut
astronáutica *nf* : astronautics
astronautico, -ca *adj* : astronautic, astronautical
astronave *nf* : spaceship
astronomía *nf* : astronomy
astronómico, -ca *adj* : astronomical — **astronómicamente** *adv*
astrónomo, -ma *n* : astronomer
astroso, -sa *adj* DESALIÑADO : slovenly, untidy
astucia *nf* **1** : astuteness, shrewdness **2** : cunning, guile
astuto, -ta *adj* **1** : astute, shrewd **2** : crafty, tricky — **astutamente** *adv*
asueto *nm* : time off, break
asumir *vt* **1** : to assume, to take on <asumir el cargo : to take office> **2** SUPONER : to assume, to suppose
asunción *nf, pl* **-ciones** : assumption
asunto *nm* **1** CUESTIÓN, TEMA : affair, matter, subject **2 asuntos** *nmpl* : affairs, business
asustadizo, -za *adj* : nervous, jumpy, skittish
asustado, -da *adj* : frightened, afraid
asustar *vt* ESPANTAR : to scare, to frighten — **asustarse** *vr*
atacante *nmf* : assailant, attacker
atacar {72} *v* : to attack
atado[1], **-da** *adj* : shy, inhibited
atado[2] *nm* **1** : bundle, bunch **2** *Arg* : pack (of cigarettes)
atadura *nf* LIGADURA : tie, bond
atajar *vt* **1** IMPEDIR : to block, to stop **2** INTERRUMPIR : to interrupt, to cut off **3** CONTENER : to hold back, to restrain — *vi* ~ **por** : to take a shortcut through
atajo *nm* : shortcut
atalaya *nf* **1** : watchtower **2** : vantage point
atañer {79} *vi* (*3rd person only*) : to concern, to have to do with <eso no me atañe : that does not concern me>
ataque *nm* **1** : attack, assault **2** : fit <ataque de risa : fit of laughter> **3 ataque de nervios** : nervous break-

down **4 ataque cardíaco** *or* **ataque al corazón :** heart attack

atar *vt* AMARRAR **:** to tie, to tie up, to tie down — **atarse** *vr*

atarantado, -da *adj fam* **1 :** restless **2 :** dazed, stunned

atarantar *vt fam* **:** to daze, to stun

atarazana *nf* **:** shipyard

atardecer[1] {53} *v impers* **:** to get dark

atardecer[2] *v impers* **:** late afternoon, dusk

atareado, -da *adj* **:** busy, overworked

atascar {72} *vt* **1** ATORAR **:** to block, to clog, to stop up **2 :** to hinder — **atascarse** *vr* **1 :** to become obstructed **2 :** to get bogged down **3** PARARSE **:** to stall

atasco *nm* **1 :** blockage **2** EMBOTELLAMIENTO **:** traffic jam

ataúd *nm* **:** coffin, casket

ataviar {85} *vt* **:** to dress, to clothe — **ataviarse** *vr* **:** to dress up

atavío *nm* ATUENDO **:** dress, attire

ateísmo *nm* **:** atheism

atemorizar {21} *vt* **:** to frighten, to intimidate — **atemorizarse** *vr*

atemperar *vt* **:** to temper, to moderate

atención[1] *nf, pl* **-ciones 1 :** attention **2 poner atención** *or* **prestar atención :** to pay attention **3 llamar la atención :** to attract attention **4 en atención a :** in view of

atención[2] *interj* **1 :** attention! **2 :** watch out!

atender {56 } *vt* **1 :** to help, to wait on **2 :** to look after, to take care of **3 :** to heed, to listen to — *vi* **:** to pay attention

atenerse {80} *vr* **:** to abide <tendrás que atenerte a las reglas : you will have to abide by the rules>

atentado *nm* **:** attack, assault

atentamente *adv* **1 :** attentively, carefully **2** (*used in correspondence*) **:** sincerely, sincerely yours

atentar {55} *vi* **~ contra :** to make an attempt on, to threaten <atentaron contra su vida : they made an attempt on his life>

atento, -ta *adj* **1 :** attentive, mindful **2** CORTÉS **:** courteous

atenuación *nf, pl* **-ciones 1 :** lessening **2 :** understatement

atenuante[1] *adj* **:** extenuating, mitigating

atenuante[2] *nmf* **:** extenuating circumstance, excuse

atenuar {3} *vt* **1** MITIGAR **:** to extenuate, to mitigate **2 :** to dim (light), to tone down (colors) **3 :** to minimize, to lessen

ateo[1], **atea** *adj* **:** atheistic

ateo[2], **atea** *n* **:** atheist

aterciopelado, -da *adj* **:** velvety, downy

aterido, -da *adj* **:** freezing, frozen

aterrador, -dora *adj* **:** terrifying

aterrar {55} *vt* **:** to terrify, to frighten

aterrizaje *nm* **:** landing (of a plane)

aterrizar {21} *vi* **:** to land, to touch down

aterrorizar {21} *vt* **1 :** to terrify **2 :** to terrorize — **aterrorizarse** *vr* **:** to be terrified

atesorar *vt* **:** to hoard, to amass

atestado, -da *adj* **:** crowded, packed

atestar {55} *vt* **1** ATIBORRAR **:** to crowd, to pack **2 :** to witness, to testify to — *vi* **:** to testify

atestiguar {10} *vt* **:** to testify to, to bear witness to — *vi* DECLARAR **:** to testify

atiborrar *vt* **:** to pack, to crowd — **atiborrarse** *vr* **:** to stuff oneself

ático *nm* **1 :** penthouse **2** BUHARDILLA, DESVÁN **:** attic

atigrado, -da *adj* **:** tabby (of cats), striped (of fur)

atildado, -da *adj* **:** smart, neat, dapper

atildar *vt* **1 :** to put a tilde over **2 :** to clean up, to smarten up — **atildarse** *vr* **:** to get spruced up

atinar *vi* ACERTAR **:** to be accurate, to be on target

atingencia *nf* **:** bearing, relevance

atípico, -ca *adj* **:** atypical

atiplado, -da *adj* **:** shrill, high-pitched

atirantar *vt* **:** to make taut, to tighten

atisbar *vt* **1 :** to spy on, to watch **2 :** to catch a glimpse of, to make out

atisbo *nm* **:** glimpse, sign, hint

atizador *nm* **:** poker (for a fire)

atizar {21} *vt* **1 :** to poke, to stir, to stoke (a fire) **2 :** to stir up, to rouse **3** *fam* **:** to give, to land (a blow)

atlántico, -ca *adj* **:** Atlantic

atlas *nm* **:** atlas

atleta *nmf* **:** athlete

atlético, -ca *adj* **:** athletic

atletismo *nm* **:** athletics

atmósfera *nf* **:** atmosphere

atmosférico, -ca *adj* **:** atmospheric

atole *nm Mex* **1 :** thick hot beverage prepared with corn flour **2 darle atole con el dedo (a alguien) :** to string (someone) along

atollarse *vr* **:** to get stuck, to get bogged down

atolón *nm, pl* **-lones :** atoll

atolondrado, -da *adj* **1** ATURDIDO **:** bewildered, dazed **2** DESPISTADO **:** scatterbrained, absentminded

atómico, -ca *adj* **:** atomic

atomizador *nm* **:** atomizer

atomizar {21} *vt* FRAGMENTAR **:** to fragment, to break into bits

átomo *nm* **:** atom

atónito, -ta *adj* **:** astonished, amazed

atontar *vt* **1 :** to stupefy **2 :** to bewilder, to confuse

atorar *vt* ATASCAR **:** to block, to clog — **atorarse** *vr* **1** ATASCARSE **:** to get stuck **2** ATRAGANTARSE **:** to choke

atormentador, -dora *n* **:** tormenter

atormentar *vt* **:** to torment, to torture — **atormentarse** *vr* **:** to torment oneself, to agonize

atornillar *vt* **:** to screw (in, on, down)

atorrante *nmf Arg* : bum, loafer
atosigar {52} *vt* : to harass, to annoy
atracadero *nm* : dock, pier
atracador, -dora *n* : robber, mugger
atracar {72} *vi* : to dock, to land — *vt* : to hold up, to rob, to mug — **atracarse** *vr fam* **~ de** : to gorge oneself with
atracción *nf, pl* **-ciones** : attraction
atraco *nm* : holdup, robbery
atractivo[1], **-va** *adj* : attractive
atractivo[2] *nm* : attraction, appeal, charm
atraer {81} *vt* : to attract — **atraerse** *vr* **1** : to attract (each other) **2** GANARSE : to gain, to win
atragantarse *vr* : to choke (on food)
atrancar {72} *vt* : to block, to bar — **atrancarse** *vr*
atrapada *nf* : catch
atrapar *vt* : to trap, to capture
atrás *adv* **1** DETRÁS : back, behind <se quedó atrás : he stayed behind> **2** ANTES : ago <mucho tiempo atrás : long ago> **3 para ~** *or* **hacia ~** : backwards, toward the rear **4 ~ de** : in back of, behind
atrasado, -da *adj* **1** : late, overdue **2** : backwards **3** : old-fashioned **4** : slow (of a clock or watch)
atrasar *vt* : to delay, to put off — *vi* : to lose time — **atrasarse** *vr* : to fall behind
atraso *nm* **1** RETRASO : lateness, delay <llegó con 20 minutos de atraso : he was 20 minutes late> **2** : backwardness **3 atrasos** *nmpl* : arrears
atravesar {55} *vt* **1** CRUZAR : to cross, to go across **2** : to pierce **3** : to lay across **4** : to go through (a situation or crisis) — **atravesarse** *vr* **1** : to be in the way <se me atravesó : it blocked my path> **2** : to interfere, to meddle
atrayente *adj* : attractive
atreverse *vr* **1** : to dare **2** : to be insolent
atrevido, -da *adj* **1** : bold, daring **2** : insolent
atrevimiento *nm* **1** : daring, boldness **2** : insolence
atribución *nf, pl* **-ciones** : attribution
atribuible *adj* IMPUTABLE : attributable, ascribable
atribuir {41} *vt* **1** : to attribute, to ascribe **2** : to grant, to confer — **atribuirse** *vr* : to take credit for
atribular *vt* : to afflict, to trouble — **atribularse** *vr*
atributo *nm* : attribute
atril *nm* : lectern, stand
atrincherar *vt* : to entrench — **atrincherarse** *vr* **1** : to dig in, to entrench oneself **2 ~ en** : to hide behind
atrio *nm* **1** : atrium **2** : portico
atrocidad *nf* : atrocity
atrofia *nf* : atrophy
atrofiar *v* : to atrophy
atronador, -dora *adj* : thunderous, deafening
atropellado, -da *adj* **1** : rash, hasty **2** : brusque, abrupt
atropellamiento *nm* → **atropello**
atropellar *vt* **1** : to knock down, to run over **2** : to violate, to abuse — **atropellarse** *vr* : to rush through (a task), to trip over one's words
atropello *nm* : abuse, violation, outrage
atroz *adj, pl* **atroces** : atrocious, appalling — **atrozamente** *adv*
atuendo *nm* ATAVÍO : attire, costume
atufar *vt* : to vex, to irritate — **atufarse** *vr* **1** : to get angry **2** : to smell bad, to stink
atún *nm, pl* **atunes** : tuna fish, tuna
aturdimiento *nm* : bewilderment, confusion
aturdir *vt* **1** : to stun, to shock **2** : to bewilder, to confuse, to stupefy
atuvo, etc. → **atenerse**
audacia *nf* OSADÍA : boldness, audacity
audaz *adj, pl* **audaces** : bold, audacious, daring — **audazmente** *adv*
audible *adj* : audible
audición *nf, pl* **-ciones 1** : hearing **2** : audition
audiencia *nf* : audience
audífono *nm* **1** : hearing aid **2 audífonos** *nmpl* : headphones, earphones
audio *nm* : audio
audiovisual *adj* : audiovisual
auditar *vt* : to audit
auditivo, -va *adj* : auditory, hearing, aural <aparato auditivo : hearing aid>
auditor, -tora *n* : auditor
auditoría *nf* : audit
auditorio *nm* **1** : auditorium **2** : audience
auge *nm* **1** : peak, height **2** : boom, upturn
augurar *vt* : to predict, to foretell
augurio *nm* AGÜERO, PRESAGIO : augury, omen
augusto, -ta *adj* : august
aula *nf* : classroom
aullar {8} *vi* : to howl, to wail
aullido *nm* : howl, wail
aumentar *vt* ACRECENTAR : to increase, to raise — *vi* : to rise, to increase, to grow
aumento *nm* INCREMENTO : increase, rise
aun *adv* **1** : even <ni aun en coche llegaría a tiempo : I wouldn't arrive on time even if I drove> **2 aun así** : even so **3 aun más** : even more
aún *adv* **1** TODAVÍA : still, yet <¿aún no ha llegado el correo? : the mail still hasn't come?> **2 más aún** : furthermore
aunar {8} *vt* : to join, to combine — **aunarse** *vr* : to unite
aunque *conj* **1** : though, although, even if, even though **2 aunque sea** : at least
aura *nf* **1** : aura **2** : turkey buzzard
áureo, -rea *adj* : golden

aureola *nf* **1** : halo **2** : aura (of power, fame, etc.)
aurícula *nf* : auricle
auricular *nm* : telephone receiver
aurora *nf* **1** : dawn **2 aurora boreal** : aurora borealis
ausencia *nf* : absence
ausentarse *vr* **1** : to leave, to go away **2 ~ de** : to stay away from
ausente[1] *adj* : absent, missing
ausente[2] *nmf* **1** : absentee **2** : missing person
auspiciar *vt* **1** PATROCINAR : to sponsor **2** FOMENTAR : to foster, to promote
auspicios *nmpl* : sponsorship, auspices
austeridad *nf* : austerity
austero, -ra *adj* : austere
austral[1] *adj* : southern
austral[2] *nm* : former monetary unit of Argentina
australiano, -na *adj & n* : Australian
austriaco *or* **austríaco, -ca** *adj & n* : Austrian
autenticar {72} *vt* : to authenticate — **autenticación** *nf*
autenticidad *nf* : authenticity
auténtico, -ca *adj* : authentic — **auténticamente** *adv*
autentificar {72} *vt* : to authenticate — **autentificación** *nf*
autismo *nm* : autism
autista *adj* : autistic
auto *nm* : auto, car
autoayuda *nf* : self-help
autobiografía *nf* : autobiography
autobiográfico, -ca *adj* : autobiographical
autobús *nm, pl* **-buses** : bus
autocompasión *nf* : self-pity
autocontrol *nm* : self-control
autocracia *nf* : autocracy
autócrata *nmf* : autocrat
autocrático, -ca *adj* : autocratic
autóctono, -na *adj* : indigenous, native <arte autóctono : indigenous art>
autodefensa *nf* : self-defense
autodestrucción *nf* : self-destruction — **autodestructivo, -va** *adj*
autodeterminación *nf* : self-determination
autodidacta *adj* : self-taught
autodisciplina *nf* : self-discipline
autoestima *nf* : self-esteem
autogobierno *nm* : self-government
autografiar *vt* : to autograph
autógrafo *nm* : autograph
autoinfligido, -da *adj* : self-inflicted
automación *nf* → **automatización**
autómata *nm* : automaton
automático, -ca *adj* : automatic — **automáticamente** *adv*
automatización *nf* : automation
automatizar {21} *vt* : to automate
automotor, -tora *adj* **1** : self-propelled **2** : automotive, car
automotriz[1] *adj, pl* **-trices** : automotive, car
automotriz[2] *nf, pl* **-trices** : car dealership
automóvil *nm* : automobile
automovilista *nmf* : motorist
automovilístico, -ca *adj* : automobile, car <accidente automovilístico : automobile accident>
autonombrado, -da *adj* : self-appointed
autonomía *nf* : autonomy
autónomo, -ma *adj* : autonomous — **autónomamente** *adv*
autopista *nf* : expressway, highway
autopropulsado, -da *adj* : self-propelled
autopsia *nf* : autopsy
autor, -tora *n* **1** : author **2** : perpetrator
autoría *nf* : authorship
autoridad *nf* : authority
autoritario, -ria *adj* : authoritarian
autorización *nf, pl* **-ciones** : authorization
autorizado, -da *adj* **1** : authorized **2** : authoritative
autorizar {21} *vt* : to authorize, to approve
autorretrato *nm* : self-portrait
autoservicio *nm* **1** : self-service restaurant **2** SUPERMERCADO : supermarket
autostop *nm* **1** : hitchhiking **2 hacer autostop** : to hitchhike
autostopista *nmf* : hitchhiker
autosuficiencia *nf* : self-sufficiency — **autosuficiente** *adj*
auxiliar[1] *vt* : to aid, to assist
auxiliar[2] *adj* : assistant, auxiliary
auxiliar[3] *nmf* **1** : assistant, helper **2 auxiliar de vuelo** : flight attendant
auxilio *nm* **1** : aid, assistance **2 primeros auxilios** : first aid
aval *nm* : guarantee, endorsement
avalancha *nf* ALUD : avalanche
avalar *vt* : to guarantee, to endorse
avaluar {3} *vt* : to evaluate, to appraise
avalúo *nm* : appraisal, evaluation
avance *nm* ADELANTO : advance
avanzado, -da *adj* **1** : advanced **2** : progressive
avanzar {21} *v* : to advance, to move forward
avaricia *nf* CODICIA : greed, avarice
avaricioso, -sa *adj* : avaricious, greedy
avaro[1]**, -ra** *adj* : miserly, greedy
avaro[2]**, -ra** *n* : miser
avasallador, -dora *adj* : overwhelming
avasallamiento *nm* : subjugation, domination
avasallar *vt* : to overpower, to subjugate
ave *nf* **1** : bird **2 aves de corral** : poultry **3 ave rapaz** *or* **ave de presa** : bird of prey
avecinarse *vr* : to approach, to come near
avecindarse *vr* : to settle, to take up residence
avellana *nf* : hazelnut, filbert
avena *nf* **1** : oat, oats *pl* **2** : oatmeal

avenencia *nf* **:** agreement, pact

avenida *nf* **:** avenue

avenir {87} *vt* **:** to reconcile, to harmonize — **avenirse** *vr* **1 :** to agree, to come to terms **2 :** to get along

aventajado, -da *adj* **:** outstanding

aventajar *vt* **1 :** to be ahead of, to lead **2 :** to surpass, to outdo

aventar {55} *vt* **1 :** to fan **2 :** to winnow **3** *Col, Mex* **:** to throw, to toss — **aventarse** *vr* **1** *Col, Mex* **:** to hurl oneself **2** *Mex fam* **:** to dare, to take a chance

aventón *nm, pl* **-tones** *Col, Mex fam* **:** ride, lift

aventura *nf* **1 :** adventure **2** RIESGO **:** venture, risk **3 :** love affair

aventurado, -da *adj* **:** hazardous, risky

aventurar *vt* **:** to venture, to risk — **aventurarse** *vr* **:** to take a risk

aventurero[1], -ra *adj* **:** adventurous

aventurero[2], -ra *n* **:** adventurer

avergonzado, -da *adj* **1 :** ashamed **2 :** embarrassed

avergonzar {9} *vt* APENAR **:** to shame, to embarrass — **avergonzarse** *vr* APENARSE **:** to be ashamed, to be embarrassed

avería *nf* **1 :** damage **2 :** breakdown, malfunction

averiado, -da *adj* **1 :** damaged, faulty **2 :** broken down

averiar {85} *vt* **:** to damage — **averiarse** *vr* **:** to break down

averiguación *nf, pl* **-ciones :** investigation, inquiry

averiguar {10} *vt* **1 :** to find out, to ascertain **2 :** to investigate

aversión *nf, pl* **-siones :** aversion, dislike

avestruz *nm, pl* **-truces :** ostrich

avezado, -da *adj* **:** seasoned, experienced

aviación *nf, pl* **-ciones :** aviation

aviador, -dora *n* **:** aviator, flyer

aviar {85} *vt* **1 :** to prepare, to make ready **2 :** to tidy up **3 :** to equip, to supply

avicultor, -tora *n* **:** poultry farmer

avicultura *nf* **:** poultry farming

avidez *nf, pl* **-deces :** eagerness

ávido, -da *adj* **:** eager, avid — **ávidamente** *adv*

avieso, -sa *adj* **1 :** twisted, distorted **2 :** wicked, depraved

avinagrado, -da *adj* **:** vinegary, sour

avío *nm* **1 :** preparation, provision **2 :** loan (for agriculture or mining) **3 avíos** *nmpl* **:** gear, equipment

avión *nm, pl* **aviones :** airplane

avioneta *nf* **:** light airplane

avisar *vt* **1 :** to notify, to inform **2 :** to advise, to warn

aviso *nm* **1 :** notice **2 :** advertisement, ad **3** ADVERTENCIA **:** warning **4 estar sobre aviso :** to be on the alert

avispa *nf* **:** wasp

avispado, -da *adj fam* **:** clever, sharp

avispero *nm* **:** wasps' nest

avispón *nm, pl* **-pones :** hornet

avistar *vt* **:** to sight, to catch sight of

avituallar *vt* **:** to suppy with food, to provision

avivar *vt* **1 :** to enliven, to brighten **2 :** to strengthen, to intensify

avizorar *vt* **1** ACECHAR **:** to spy on, to watch **2 :** to observe, to perceive <se avizoran dificultades **:** difficulties are expected>

axila *nf* **:** underarm, armpit

axioma *nm* **:** axiom

axiomático, -ca *adj* **:** axiomatic

ay *interj* **1 :** oh! **2 :** ouch!, ow!

ayer[1] *adv* **:** yesterday

ayer[2] *nm* ANTAÑO **:** yesteryear, days gone by

ayote *nm CA, Mex* **:** squash, pumpkin

ayuda *nf* **1 :** help, assistance **2 ayuda de cámara :** valet

ayudante *nmf* **:** helper, assistant

ayudar *vt* **:** to help, to assist — **ayudarse** *vr* **~ de :** to make use of

ayunar *vi* **:** to fast

ayunas *nfpl* **en ~ :** fasting <este medicamento ha de tomarse en ayunas **:** this medication should be taken on an empty stomach>

ayuno *nm* **:** fast

ayuntamiento *nm* **1 :** town hall, city hall **2 :** town or city council

azabache *nm* **:** jet <negro azabache **:** jet black>

azada *nf* **:** hoe

azafata *nf* **1 :** stewardess *f* **2 :** hostess *f* (on a TV show)

azafrán *nm, pl* **-franes 1 :** saffron **2 :** crocus

azahar *nm* **:** orange blossom

azalea *nf* **:** azalea

azar *nm* **1 :** chance <juegos de azar **:** games of chance> **2 :** accident, misfortune **3 al azar :** at random, randomly

azaroso, -sa *adj* **1 :** perilous, hazardous **2 :** turbulent, eventful

azimut *nm* **:** azimuth

azogue *nm* **:** mercury, quicksilver

azorar *vt* **1 :** to alarm, to startle **2 :** to fluster, to embarrass — **azorarse** *vr* **:** to get embarrassed

azotar *vt* **1 :** to whip, to flog **2 :** to lash, to batter **3 :** to devastate, to afflict

azote *nm* **1** LÁTIGO **:** whip, lash **2** *fam* **:** spanking, licking **3 :** calamity, scourge

azotea *nf* **:** flat roof, terraced roof

azteca *adj & nmf* **:** Aztec

azúcar *nmf* **:** sugar — **azucarar** *vt*

azucarado, -da *adj* **:** sweetened, sugary

azucarera *nf* **:** sugar bowl

azucarero, -ra *adj* **:** sugar <industria azucarera **:** sugar industry>

azucena *nf* **:** white lily

azuela *nf* **:** adz

azufre *nm* **:** sulphur — **azufroso, -sa** *adj*

azul *adj & nm* : blue
azulado, -da *adj* : bluish
azulejo *nm* : ceramic tile, floor tile
azulete *nm* : bluing
azuloso, -sa *adj* : bluish
azur[1] *adj* CELESTE : azure
azur[2] *n* CELESTE : azure, sky blue
azuzar {21} *vt* : to incite, to egg on

B

b *nf* : second letter of the Spanish alphabet
baba *nf* **1** : spittle, saliva **2** : dribble, drool (of a baby) **3** : slime, ooze
babear *vi* **1** : to drool, to slobber **2** : to ooze
babel *nf* : babel, chaos, bedlam
babero *nm* : bib
babor *nm* : port, port side
babosa *nf* : slug (mollusk)
babosada *nf CA, Mex* : silly act or remark
baboso, -sa *adj* **1** : drooling, slobbering **2** : slimy **3** *CA, Mex fam* : silly, dumb
babucha *nf* : slipper
babuino *nm* : baboon
bacalao *nm* : cod (fish)
bache *nm* **1** : pothole **2** *PRi* : deep puddle **3** : bad period, rough time <bache económico : economic slump>
bachiller *nmf* : high school graduate
bachillerato *nm* : high school diploma
bacilo *nm* : bacillus
backgammon *nm* : backgammon
bacon *nm Spain* : bacon
bacteria *nf* : bacterium
bacteriano, -na *adj* : bacterial
bacteriología *nf* : bacteriology
bacteriológico, -ca *adj* : bacteriologic, bacteriological
bacteriólogo, -ga *n* : bacteriologist
báculo *nm* **1** : staff, stick **2** : comfort, support
badajo *nm* : clapper (of a bell)
badén *nm, pl* **badenes 1** : (paved) ford, channel **2** : dip, ditch (in a road)
bádminton *nm* : badminton
bafle *or* **baffle** *nm* **1** : baffle **2** : speaker, loudspeaker
bagaje *nm* **1** EQUIPAJE : baggage, luggage **2** : background <bagaje cultural : cultural baggage>
bagatela *nf* : trifle, trinket
bagre *nm* : catfish
bahía *nf* : bay
bailar *vt* : to dance — *vi* **1** : to dance **2** : to spin **3** : to be loose, to be too big
bailarín[1], **-rina** *adj, mpl* **-rines 1** : dancing **2** : fond of dancing
bailarín[2], **-rina** *n, mpl* **-rines 1** : dancer **2** : ballet dancer, ballerina *f*
baile *nm* **1** : dance **2** : dance party, ball **3 llevarse al baile a** *Mex fam* : to take for a ride, to take advantage of
baja *nf* **1** DESCENSO : fall, drop **2** : slump, recession **3** : loss, casualty **4 dar de baja** : to discharge, to dismiss **5 darse de baja** : to withdraw, to drop out
bajada *nf* **1** : descent **2** : dip, slope **3** : decrease, drop
bajar *vt* **1** DESCENDER : to lower, to let down, to take down **2** REDUCIR : to reduce (prices) 3 INCLINAR : to lower, to bow (the head) **4** : to go down, to descend **5 bajar de categoría** : to downgrade — *vi* **1** : to drop, to fall **2** : to come down, to go down **3** : to ebb (of tides) — **bajarse** *vr* **~ de** : to get off, to get out of (a vehicle)
bajeza *nf* **1** : low or despicable act **2** : baseness
bajío *nm* **1** : lowland **2** : shoal, sandbank, shallows
bajista *nmf* : bass player, bassist
bajo[1] *adv* **1** : down, low **2** : softly, quietly <habla más bajo : speak more softly>
bajo[2], **-ja** *adj* **1** : low **2** : short (of stature) **3** : soft, faint, deep (of sounds) **4** : lower <el bajo Amazonas : the lower Amazon> **5** : lowered <con la mirada baja : with lowered eyes> **6** : base, vile **7 los bajos fondos** : the underworld
bajo[3] *nm* **1** : bass (musical instrument) **2** : first floor, ground floor **3** : hemline
bajo[4] *prep* : under, beneath, below
bajón *nm, pl* **bajones** : sharp drop, slump
bajorrelieve *m* : bas-relief
bala *nf* **1** : bullet **2** : bale
balacera *nf* TIROTEO : shoot-out, gunfight
balada *nf* : ballad
balance *nm* **1** : balance **2** : balance sheet
balancear *vt* **1** : to balance **2** : to swing (one's arms, etc.) **3** : to rock (a boat) — **balancearse** *vr* **1** OSCILAR : to swing, to sway, to rock **2** VACILAR : to hesitate, to vacillate
balanceo *nm* **1** : swaying, rocking **2** : vacillation
balancín *nm, pl* **-cines 1** : rocking chair **2** SUBIBAJA : seesaw
balandra *nf* : sloop
balanza *nf* BÁSCULA : scales *pl,* balance
balar *vi* : to bleat
balaustrada *nf* : balustrade
balaustre *nm* : baluster
balazo *nm* **1** TIRO : shot, gunshot **2** : bullet wound
balboa *nf* : balboa (monetary unit of Panama)

balbucear *vi* **1 :** to mutter, to stammer **2 :** to prattle, to babble <los niños están balbuceando : the children are prattling away>

balbuceo *nm* **:** mumbling, stammering

balbucir → **balbucear**

balcánico, -ca *adj* **:** Balkan

balcón *nm, pl* **balcones :** balcony

balde *nm* **1** CUBO **:** bucket, pail **2 en ~ :** in vain, to no avail

baldío[1], **-día** *adj* **1 :** fallow, uncultivated **2 :** useless, vain

baldío[2] *nm* **1 :** wasteland **2** *Mex* **:** vacant lot

baldosa *nf* LOSETA **:** floor tile

balear *vt* **:** to shoot, to shoot at

balero *nm* **1** *Mex* **:** ball bearing **2** *Mex, PRi* **:** cup-and-ball toy

balido *nm* **:** bleat

balín *nm, pl* **balines :** pellet

balística *nf* **:** ballistics

balístico, -ca *adj* **:** ballistic

baliza *nf* **1 :** buoy **2 :** beacon (for aircraft)

ballena *nf* **:** whale

ballenero[1], **-ra** *adj* **:** whaling

ballenero[2], **-ra** *n* **:** whaler

ballenero[3] *nm* **:** whaleboat, whaler

ballesta *nf* **1 :** crossbow **2 :** spring (of an automobile)

ballet *nm* **:** ballet

balneario *nm* **:** spa, bathing resort

balompié *nm* FUTBOL **:** soccer

balón *nm, pl* **balones :** ball

baloncesto *nm* BASQUETBOL **:** basketball

balsa *nf* **1 :** raft **2 :** balsa

balsámico, -ca *adj* **:** soothing

bálsamo *nm* **:** balsam, balm

báltico, -ca *adj* **:** Baltic

baluarte *nm* BASTIÓN **:** bulwark, bastion

bambolear *vi* **1 :** to sway, to swing **2 :** to wobble — **bambolearse** *vr*

bamboleo *nm* **1 :** swaying, swinging **2 :** wobbling

bambú *nm, pl* **bambúes** *or* **bambús :** bamboo

banal *adj* **:** banal, trivial

banalidad *nf* **:** banality

banana *nf* **:** banana

bananero[1], **-ra** *adj* **:** banana

bananero[2] *nm* **:** banana tree

banano *nm* **1 :** banana tree **2** *CA,Col* **:** banana

banca *nf* **1 :** banking **2** BANCO **:** bench

bancada *nf* **1 :** group, faction **2 :** workbench

bancal *nm* **1 :** terrace (in agriculture) **2 :** plot (of land)

bancario, -ria *adj* **:** bank, banking

bancarrota *nf* QUIEBRA **:** bankruptcy

banco *nm* **1 :** bank <banco central : central bank> <banco de datos : data bank> <banco de arena : sandbank> <banco de sangre : blood bank> **2** BANCA **:** stool, bench **3 :** pew **4 :** school (of fish)

banda *nf* **1 :** band, strip **2** *Mex* **:** belt <banda transportadora : conveyor belt> **3 :** band (of musicians) **4 :** gang (of persons), flock (of birds) **5 banda de rodadura :** tread (of a tire, etc.) **6 banda sonora** *or* **banda de sonido :** sound track

bandada *nf* **:** flock (of birds), school (of fish)

bandazo *nm* **:** swerving, lurch

bandearse *vr* **:** to look after oneself, to cope

bandeja *nf* **:** tray, platter

bandera *nf* **:** flag, banner

banderazo *nm* **:** starting signal (in sports)

banderilla *nf* **:** banderilla, dart (in bullfighting)

banderín *nm, pl* **-rines :** pennant, small flag

bandidaje *nm* **:** banditry

bandido, -da *n* BANDOLERO **:** bandit, outlaw

bando *nm* **1** FACCIÓN **:** faction, side **2** EDICTO **:** proclamation

bandolerismo *nm* **:** banditry

bandolero, -ra *n* BANDIDO **:** bandit, outlaw

banjo *nm* **:** banjo

banquero, -ra *n* **:** banker

banqueta *nf* **1 :** footstool, stool, bench **2** *Mex* **:** sidewalk

banquete *nm* **:** banquet

banquetear *v* **:** to feast

banquillo *nm* **1 :** bench (in sports) **2 :** dock, defendant's seat

bañadera *nf* → **bañera**

bañar *vt* **1 :** to bathe, to wash **2 :** to immerse, to dip **3 :** to coat, to cover <bañado en lágrimas : bathed in tears> — **bañarse** *vr* **1 :** to take a bath, to bathe **2 :** to go for a swim

bañera *nf* TINA **:** bathtub

bañista *nmf* **:** bather

baño *nm* **1 :** bath **2 :** swim, dip **3 :** bathroom **4 baño María :** double-boiler

baqueta *nf* **1 :** ramrod **2 baquetas** *nfpl* **:** drumsticks

bar *nm* **:** bar, tavern

baraja *nf* **:** deck of cards

barajar *vt* **1 :** to shuffle (cards) **2 :** to consider, to toy with

baranda *nf* **:** rail, railing

barandal *nm* **1 :** rail, railing **2 :** bannister, handrail

barandilla *nf Spain* **:** bannister, handrail, railing

barata *nf* **1** *Mex* **:** sale, bargain **2** *Chile* **:** cockroach

baratija *nf* **:** bauble, trinket

baratillo *nm* **:** rummage sale, flea market

barato[1] *adv* **:** cheap, cheaply <te lo vendo barato : I'll sell it to you cheap>

barato[2], **-ta** *adj* **:** cheap, inexpensive

baratura *nf* **1 :** cheapness **2 :** cheap thing

barba *nf* **1 :** beard, stubble **2 :** chin

barbacoa *nf* **:** barbecue

bárbaramente *adv* : barbarously
barbaridad *nf* **1** : barbarity, atrocity **2** **¡qué barbaridad!** : that's outrageous!
barbarie *nf* : barbarism, savagery
bárbaro[1] *adv fam* : wildly <anoche lo pasamos bárbaro : we had a wild time last night>
bárbaro[2], **-ra** *adj* **1** : barbarous, wild, uncivilized **2** *fam* : great, fantastic
bárbaro[3], **-ra** *n* : barbarian
barbecho *nm* : fallow land <dejar en barbecho : to leave fallow>
barbero, -ra *n* : barber
barbilla *nf* MENTÓN : chin
barbitúrico *nm* : barbiturate
barbudo[1], **-da** *adj* : bearded
barbudo[2] *nm* : bearded man
barca *nf* **1** : boat **2** **barca de pasaje** : ferryboat
barcaza *nf* : barge
barcia *nf* : chaff
barco *nm* **1** BARCA : boat **2** BUQUE, NAVE : ship
bardo *nm* : bard
bario *nm* : barium
barítono *nm* : baritone
barlovento *nm* : windward
barman *nm* : bartender
barniz *nm, pl* **barnices** **1** LACA : varnish, lacquer **2** : glaze (on ceramics, etc.)
barnizar {21} *vt* **1** : to varnish **2** : to glaze
barométrico, -ca *adj* : barometric
barómetro *nm* : barometer
barón *nm, pl* **barones** : baron
baronesa *nf* : baroness
baronet *nm* : baronet
barquero, -ra : boatman *m*, boatwoman *f*
barquillo *nm* : wafer, thin cookie or cracker
barra *nf* : bar
barraca *nf* **1** CABAÑA, CHOZA : hut, cabin **2** : booth, stall
barracuda *nf* : barracuda
barranca *nf* **1** : hillside, slope **2** → **barranco**
barranco *nm* : ravine, gorge
barredora *nf* : street sweeper (machine)
barrena *nf* **1** TALADRO : drill, auger, gimlet **2** : tailspin
barrenar *vt* **1** : to drill **2** : to undermine
barrendero, -ra *n* : sweeper, street cleaner
barrer *v* : to sweep — **barrerse** *vr* : to slide (in sports)
barrera *nf* OBSTÁCULO : barrier, obstacle <barrera de sonido : sound barrier>
barreta *nf* : crowbar
barriada *nf* **1** : district, quarter **2** : slums *pl*
barrica *nf* BARRIL, TONEL : barrel, cask, keg
barricada *nf* : barricade
barrida *nf* **1** : sweep **2** : slide (in sports)
barrido *nm* : sweeping
barriga *nf* PANZA : belly, paunch
barrigón, -gona *adj, mpl* **-gones** *fam* : potbellied, paunchy
barril *nm* **1** BARRICA : barrel, keg **2** **cerveza de barril** : draft beer
barrio *nm* **1** : neighborhood, district **2** **barrios bajos** : slums *pl*
barro *nm* **1** LODO : mud **2** ARCILLA : clay **3** ESPINILLA, GRANO : pimple, blackhead
barroco, -ca *adj* : baroque
barroso, -sa *adj* ENLODADO : muddy
barrote *nm* : bar (on a window)
barrunto *nm* **1** SOSPECHA : suspicion **2** INDICIO : sign, indication, hint
bártulos *nmpl* : things, belongings <liar los bártulos : to pack one's things>
barullo *nm* BULLA : racket, ruckus
basa *nf* : base, pedestal
basalto *nm* : basalt
basar *vt* FUNDAR : to base — **basarse** *vr* FUNDARSE **~ en** : to be based on
báscula *nf* BALANZA : balance, scales *pl*
base *nf* **1** : base, bottom **2** : base (in baseball) **3** FUNDAMENTO : basis, foundation **4** **base de datos** : database **5 a base de** : based on, by means of **6 en base a** : based on, on the basis of
básico, -ca *adj* FUNDAMENTAL : basic — **básicamente** *adv*
basílica *nf* : basilica
basquetbol *or* **básquetbol** *nm* BALONCESTO : basketball
basset *nm* : basset hound
bastante[1] *adv* **1** : enough, sufficiently <he trabajado bastante : I have worked enough> **2** : fairly, rather, quite <llegaron bastante temprano : they arrived quite early>
bastante[2] *adj* : enough, sufficient
bastante[3] *pron* : enough <hemos visto bastante : we have seen enough>
bastar *vi* : to be enough, to suffice
bastardilla *nf* CURSIVA : italic type, italics *pl*
bastardo, -da *adj & n* : bastard
bastidor *nm* **1** : framework, frame **2** : wing (in theater) <entre bastidores : backstage, behind the scenes>
bastilla *nf* : hem
bastión *nf, pl* **bastiones** BALUARTE : bastion, bulwark
basto, -ta *adj* : coarse, rough
bastón *nm, pl* **bastones** **1** : cane, walking stick **2** : baton **3** **bastón de mando** : staff (of authority)
basura *nf* DESECHOS : garbage, waste, refuse
basurero[1], **-ra** *n* : garbage collector
basurero[2] *nm Mex* : garbage can
bata *nf* **1** : bathrobe, housecoat **2** : smock, coverall, lab coat
batalla *nf* **1** : battle **2** : fight, struggle **3 de ~** : ordinary, everyday <mis

zapatos de batalla : my everyday shoes>

batallar *vi* LIDIAR, LUCHAR : to battle, to fight

batallón *nm, pl* **-llones** : battalion

batata *nf* : yam, sweet potato

batazo *nm* HIT : hit (in baseball)

bate *nm* : baseball bat

batea *nf* **1** : tray, pan **2** : flat-bottomed boat, punt

bateador, -dora *n* : batter, hitter

batear *vi* : to bat — *vt* : to hit

batería *nf* **1** PILA : battery **2** : drum kit, drums *pl* **3** : artillery **4 batería de cocina** : kitchen utensils *pl*

baterista *nmf* : drummer

batido *nm* LICUADO : milk shake

batidor *nm* : eggbeater, whisk, mixer

batidora *nf* : (electric) mixer

batir *vt* **1** GOLPEAR : to beat, to hit **2** VENCER : to defeat **3** REVOLVER : to mix, to beat **4** : to break (a record) — **batirse** *vr* : to fight

batista *nf* : batiste, cambric

batuta *nf* **1** : baton **2 llevar la batuta** : to be the leader, to call the tune

baúl *nm* : trunk, chest

bautismal *adj* : baptismal

bautismo *nm* : baptism, christening

bautista *adj & nmf* : Baptist

bautizar {21} *vt* : to baptize, to christen

bautizo *nm* → **bautismo**

bávaro, -ra *adj & n* : Bavarian

baya *nf* **1** : berry **2 baya de saúco** : elderberry

bayeta *nf* : cleaning cloth

bayoneta *nf* : bayonet

baza *nf* **1** : trick (in card games) **2 meter baza en** : to butt in on

bazar *nm* : bazaar

bazo *nm* : spleen

bazofia *nf* **1** : table scraps *pl* **2** : slop, swill **3** : hogwash, rubbish

bazuca *nf* : bazooka

beagle *nm* : beagle

beatificar {72} *vt* : to beatify — **beatificación** *nf*

beatífico, -ca *adj* : beatific

beatitud *nf* : beatitude

beato, -ta *adj* **1** : blessed **2** : pious, devout **3** : sanctimonious, overly devout

bebé *nm* : baby

bebedero *nm* **1** ABREVADERO : watering trough **2** *Mex* : drinking fountain

bebedor, -dora *n* : drinker

beber *v* TOMAR : to drink

bebida *nf* : drink, beverage

beca *nf* : grant, scholarship

becado, -da *n* : scholar, scholarship holder

becerro, -rra *n* : calf

begonia *nf* : begonia

beige *adj & nm* : beige

beisbol *or* **béisbol** *nm* : baseball

beisbolista *nmf* : baseball player

beldad *nf* BELLEZA, HERMOSURA : beauty

belén *nf, pl* **belenes** NACIMIENTO : Nativity scene

belga *adj & nmf* : Belgian

beliceño, -ña *adj & n* : Belizean

belicista[1] *adj* : militaristic

belicista[2] *nmf* : warmonger

bélico, -ca *adj* GUERRERO : war, fighting <esfuerzos bélicos : war efforts>

belicosidad *nf* : bellicosity

belicoso, -sa *adj* **1** : warlike, martial **2** : aggressive, belligerent

beligerancia *nf* : belligerence

beligerante *adj & nmf* : belligerent

bellaco[1], **-ca** *adj* : sly, cunning

bellaco[2], **-ca** *n* : rogue, scoundrel

belleza *nf* BELDAD, HERMOSURA : beauty

bello, -lla *adj* **1** HERMOSO : beautiful **2 bellas artes** : fine arts

bellota *nf* : acorn

bemol *nm* : flat (in music) — **bemol** *adj*

benceno *nm* : benzene

bendecir {11} *vt* **1** CONSAGRAR : to bless, to consecrate **2** ALABAR : to praise, to extol **3 bendecir la mesa** : to say grace

bendición *nf, pl* **-ciones** : benediction, blessing

bendiga, bendijo, etc. → **bendecir**

bendito, -ta *adj* **1** : blessed, holy **2** : fortunate **3** : silly, simple-minded

benedictino, -na *adj & n* : Benedictine

benefactor[1], **-tora** *adj* : beneficent

benefactor[2], **-tora** *n* : benefactor, benefactress *f*

beneficencia *nf* : beneficence, charity

beneficiar *vt* : to benefit, to be of assistance to — **beneficiarse** *vr* : to benefit, to profit

beneficiario, -ria *n* : beneficiary

beneficio *nm* **1** GANANCIA, PROVECHO : gain, profit **2** : benefit

beneficioso, -sa *adj* PROVECHOSO : beneficial

benéfico, -ca *adj* : charitable, beneficent

benemérito, -ta *adj* : meritorious, worthy

beneplácito *nm* : approval, consent

benevolencia *nf* BONDAD : benevolence, kindness

benévolo, -la *adj* BONDADOSO : benevolent, kind, good

bengala *nf* **luz de bengala 1** : flare (signal) **2** : sparkler

bengalí[1] *adj & nmf* : Bengali

bengalí[2] *nm* : Bengali (language)

benignidad *nf* : mildness, kindness

benigno, -na *adj* : benign, mild

beninés, -nesa *adj & n* : Beninese

benjamín, -mina *n, mpl* **-mines** : youngest child

beodo[1], **-da** *adj* : drunk, inebriated

beodo[2], **-da** *n* : drunkard

berberecho *nm* : cockle

berbiquí *nm* : brace (in carpentry)

berenjena *nf* : eggplant

bergantín *nm, pl* **-tines** : brig (ship)

berilo *nm* : beryl

bermudas *nfpl* : Bermuda shorts
berrear *vi* **1** : to bellow, to low **2** : to bawl, to howl
berrido *nm* **1** : bellowing **2** : howl, scream
berrinche *nm fam* : tantrum, conniption
berro *nm* : watercress
berza *nf* : cabbage
besar *vt* : to kiss
beso *nm* : kiss
bestia[1] *adj* **1** : ignorant, stupid **2** : boorish, rude
bestia[2] *nf* : beast, animal
bestia[3] *nmf* **1** IGNORANTE : ignoramus **2** : brute
bestial *adj* **1** : bestial, beastly **2** *fam* : huge, enormous <hace un frío bestial : it's terribly cold> **3** *fam* : great, fantastic
besuquear *vt fam* : to cover with kisses — **besuquearse** *vr fam* : to neck, to smooch
betabel *nm Mex* : beet
betún *nm, pl* **betunes 1** : shoe polish **2** *Mex* : icing
bianual *adj* : biannual
biatlón *nm, pl* **-lones** : biathlon
biberón *nm, pl* **-rones** : baby's bottle
biblia *nf* **1** : bible **2 la Biblia** : the Bible
bíblico, -ca *adj* : biblical
bibliografía *nf* : bibliography
bibliográfico, -ca *adj* : bibliographic, bibliographical
bibliógrafo, -fa *n* : bibliographer
biblioteca *nf* : library
bibliotecario, -ria *n* : librarian
bicameral *adj* : bicameral
bicarbonato *nm* **1** : bicarbonate **2 bicarbonato de soda** : sodium bicarbonate, baking soda
bicentenario *nm* : bicentennial
bíceps *nms & pl* : biceps
bicho *nm* : small animal, bug, insect
bici *nf fam* : bike
bicicleta *nf* : bicycle
bicolor *adj* : two-tone
bicúspide *adj* : bicuspid
bidón *nm, pl* **bidones** : large can, (oil) drum
bien[1] *adv* **1** : well <¿dormiste bien? : did you sleep well?> **2** CORRECTAMENTE : correctly, properly, right <hay que hacerlo bien : it must be done correctly> **3** : very, quite <el libro era bien divertido : the book was very amusing> **4** : easily <bien puede acabarlo en un día : he can easily finish it in a day> **5** : willingly, readily <bien lo aceptaré : I'll gladly accept it> **6 bien que** : although **7 más bien** : rather
bien[2] *adj* **1** : well, OK, all right <¿te sientes bien? : are you feeling all right?> **2** : pleasant, agreeable <las flores huelen bien : the flowers smell very nice> **3** : satisfactory **4** : correct, right
bien[3] *nm* **1** : good <el bien y el mal : good and evil> **2 bienes** *nmpl* : property, goods, possessions
bienal *adj & nf* : biennial — **bienalmente** *adv*
bienaventurado, -da *adj* **1** : blessed **2** : fortunate, happy
bienaventuranzas *nfpl* : Beatitudes
bienestar *nm* **1** : welfare, well-being **2** CONFORT : comfort
bienhechor[1], **-chora** *adj* : beneficent, benevolent
bienhechor[2], **-chora** *n* : benefactor, benefactress *f*
bienintencionado, -da *adj* : well-meaning
bienvenida *nf* **1** : welcome **2 dar la bienvenida a** : to welcome
bienvenido, -da *adj* : welcome
bies *nm* : bias (in sewing)
bife *nm Arg, Chile, Uru* : steak
bífido, -da *adj* : forked
bifocal *adj* : bifocal
bifocales *nmpl* : bifocals
bifurcación *nf, pl* **-ciones** : fork (in a river or road)
bifurcarse {72} *vr* : to fork
bigamia *nf* : bigamy
bígamo, -ma *n* : bigamist
bigote *nm* **1** : mustache **2** : whisker (of an animal)
bigotudo, -da *adj* : mustached, having a big mustache
bikini *nm* : bikini
bilateral *adj* : bilateral — **bilateralmente** *adv*
bilingüe *adj* : bilingual
bilioso, -sa *adj* **1** : bilious **2** : irritable
bilis *nf* : bile
billar *nm* : pool, billiards
billete *nm* **1** : bill <un billete de cinco dólares : a five-dollar bill> **2** BOLETO : ticket <billete de ida y vuelta : round-trip ticket>
billetera *nf* : billfold, wallet
billón *nm, pl* **billones 1** : billion (Great Britain) **2** : trillion (U.S.A.)
bimestral *adj* : bimonthly — **bimestralmente** *adv*
bimotor *adj* : twin-engined
binacional *adj* : binational
binario, -ria *adj* : binary
binocular *adj* : binocular
binoculares *nmpl* : binoculars
binomio *nm* : binomial
biodegradable *adj* : biodegradable
biodegradarse *vr* : to biodegrade
biodiversidad *nf* : biodiversity
biofísica *nf* : biophysics
biofísico[1], **-ca** *adj* : biophysical
biofísico[2], **-ca** *n* : biophysicist
biografía *nf* : biography
biográfico, -ca *adj* : biographical
biógrafo, -fa *n* : biographer
biología *nf* : biology
biológico, -ca *adj* : biological, biologic — **biológicamente** *adv*
biólogo, -ga *n* : biologist

biombo *nm* MAMPARA : folding screen, room divider
biomecánica *nf* : biomechanics
biopsia *nf* : biopsy
bioquímica *nf* : biochemistry
bioquímico[1], **-ca** *adj* : biochemical
bioquímico[2], **-ca** *n* : biochemist
biosfera *or* **biósfera** *nf* : biosphere
biotecnología *nf* : biotechnology
biótico, -ca *adj* : biotic
bipartidismo *nm* : two-party system
bipartidista *adj* : bipartisan
bípedo *nm* : biped
birlar *vt fam* : to swipe, to pinch
birmano, -na *adj & n* : Burmese
bis[1] *adv* **1** : twice, again (in music) **2** : a, A <artículo 47 bis : Article 47A> <calle Bolívar, número 70 bis : Bolívar Street, number 70A>
bis[2] *nm* : encore
bisabuelo, -la *n* : great-grandfather *m,* great-grandmother *f,* great-grandparent
bisagra *nf* : hinge
bisbisar *vt fam* : to mutter, to mumble
bisecar {72} *vt* : bisect — **bisección** *nf*
bisel *nm* : bevel
biselar *vt* : to bevel
bisexual *adj* : bisexual
bisiesto *adj* **año bisiesto** : leap year
bismuto *nm* : bismuth
bisnieto, -ta *n* : great-grandson *m,* great-granddaughter *f,* great-grandchild
bisonte *nm* : bison, buffalo
bisoñé *nm* : hairpiece, toupee
bisoño[1], **-ña** *adj* : inexperienced, green
bisoño[2], **-ña** *n* : rookie, greenhorn
bistec *nm* : steak, beefsteak
bisturí *nm* ESCALPELO : scalpel
bisutería *nf* : costume jewelry
bit *nm* : bit (unit of information)
bituminoso, -sa *adj* : bituminous
bivalvo *nm* : bivalve
bizarría *nf* **1** : courage, gallantry **2** : generosity
bizarro, -rra *adj* **1** VALIENTE : courageous, valiant **2** GENEROSO : generous
bizco, -ca *adj* : cross-eyed
bizcocho *nm* **1** : sponge cake **2** : biscuit **3** *Mex* : breadstick
bizquera *nf* : crossed eyes, squint
blanco[1], **-ca** *adj* : white
blanco[2], **-ca** *n* : white person
blanco[3] *nm* **1** : white **2** : target, bull's-eye <dar en el blanco : to hit the target, to hit the nail on the head> **3** : blank space, blank <un cheque en blanco : a blank check>
blancura *nf* : whiteness
blancuzco, -ca *adj* **1** : whitish, off-white **2** PÁLIDO : pale
blandir {1} *vt* : to wave, to brandish
blando, -da *adj* **1** SUAVE : soft, tender **2** : weak (in character) **3** : lenient
blandura *nf* **1** : softness, tenderness **2** : leniency
blanqueador *nm* : bleach, whitener
blanquear *vt* **1** : to whiten, to bleach **2** : to shut out (in sports) **3** : to launder (money) — *vi* : to turn white
blanquillo *nm CA, Mex* : egg
blasfemar *vi* : to blaspheme
blasfemia *nf* : blasphemy
blasfemo, -ma *adj* : blasphemous
blazer *nm* : blazer
bledo *nm* **no me importa un bledo** *fam* : I couldn't care less, I don't give a damn
blindado, -da *adj* ACORAZADO : armored
blindaje *nm* **1** : armor, armor plating **2** : shield (for cables, machinery, etc.)
bloc *nm, pl* **blocs** : writing pad, pad of paper
blof *nm Col, Mex* : bluff
blofear *vi Col, Mex* : to bluff
blondo, -da *adj* : blond, flaxen
bloque *nm* **1** : block **2** GRUPO : bloc <el bloque comunista : the Communist bloc>
bloquear *vt* **1** OBSTRUIR : to block, to obstruct **2** : to blockade
bloqueo *nm* **1** OBSTRUCCIÓN : blockage, obstruction **2** : blockade
blusa *nf* : blouse
blusón *nm, pl* **blusones** : loose shirt, smock
boa *nf* : boa
boato *nm* : ostentation, show
bobada *nf* : folly, nonsense
bobalicón, -cona *adj, mpl* **-cones** *fam* : silly, stupid
bobina *nf* CARRETE : bobbin, reel
bobo[1], **-ba** *adj* : silly, stupid
bobo[2], **-ba** *n* : fool, simpleton
boca *nf* **1** : mouth **2 boca arriba** : face up, on one's back **3 boca abajo** : face down, prone **4 boca de riego** : hydrant **5 en boca de** : according to
bocacalle *nf* : entrance to a street <gire a la última bocacalle : take the last turning>
bocadillo *nm Spain* : sandwich
bocado *nm* **1** : bite, mouthful **2** FRENO : bit (of a bridle)
bocajarro *nm* **a ~** : point-blank, directly
bocallave *nf* : keyhole
bocanada *nf* **1** : swig, swallow **2** : puff, mouthful (of smoke) **3** : gust (of air) **4** : stream (of people)
boceto *nm* : sketch, outline
bochinche *nm fam* : ruckus, uproar
bochorno *nm* **1** VERGÜENZA : embarrassment **2** : hot and humid weather **3** : hot flash
bochornoso, -sa *adj* **1** EMBARAZOSO : embarrassing **2** : hot and muggy
bocina *nf* **1** : horn, trumpet **2** : automobile horn **3** : mouthpiece (of a telephone) **4** *Mex* : loudspeaker
bocinazo *nm* : honk (of a horn)
bocio *nm* : goiter
bocón, -cona *n, mpl* **bocones** *fam* : blabbermouth, loudmouth
boda *nf* : wedding

bodega *nf* **1 :** wine cellar **2** *Chile, Col, Mex* **:** storeroom, warehouse **3** (*in various countries*) **:** grocery store

bofetada *nf* CACHETADA **:** slap on the face

bofetear *vt* CACHETEAR **:** to slap

bofetón *nm* → **bofetada**

bofo, -fa *adj* **:** flabby

boga *nf* **:** fashion, vogue <estar en boga : to be in style>

bogotano[1], -na *adj* **:** of or from Bogotá

bogotano[2], -na *n* **:** person from Bogotá

bohemio, -mia *adj & n* **:** bohemian, Bohemian

boicot *nm, pl* **boicots :** boycott

boicotear *vt* **:** to boycott

boina *nf* **:** beret

boiserie *nf* **:** wood paneling, wainscoting

boj *nm, pl* **bojes :** box (plant), boxwood

bola *nf* **1 :** ball <bola de nieve : snowball> **2** *fam* **:** lie, fib **3** *Mex fam* **:** bunch, group <una bola de rateros : a bunch of thieves> **4** *Mex* **:** uproar, tumult

bolear *vt Mex* **:** to polish (shoes)

bolera *nf* **:** bowling alley

bolero *nm* **:** bolero

boleta *nf* **1 :** ballot **2 :** ticket **3 :** receipt

boletería *nf* TAQUILLA **:** box office, ticket office

boletín *nm, pl* **-tines 1 :** bulletin **2 :** journal, review **3 boletín de prensa :** press release

boleto *nm* BILLETE **:** ticket

boliche *nm* **1** BOLOS **:** bowling **2** *Arg* **:** bar, tavern

bolígrafo *nm* **:** ballpoint pen

bolillo *nm* **1 :** bobbin **2** *Mex* **:** roll, bun

bolívar *nm* **:** bolivar (monetary unit of Venezuela)

boliviano[1], -na *adj & n* **:** Bolivian

boliviano[2] *nm* **:** boliviano (monetary unit of Bolivia)

bollo *nm* **:** bun, sweet roll

bolo *nm* **:** bowling pin, tenpin

bolos *nmpl* BOLICHE **:** bowling

bolsa *nf* **1 :** bag, sack **2** *Mex* **:** pocketbook, purse **3** *Mex* **:** pocket **4 la Bolsa :** the stock market, the stock exchange **5 bolsa de trabajo :** employment agency

bolsear *vi Mex* **:** to pick pockets

bolsillo *nm* **1 :** pocket **2 dinero de bolsillo :** pocket change, loose change

bolso *nm* **:** pocketbook, handbag

bomba *nf* **1 :** bomb **2 :** bubble **3 :** pump <bomba de gasolina : gas pump>

bombachos *nmpl* **:** baggy pants, bloomers

bombardear *vt* **1 :** to bomb **2 :** to bombard

bombardeo *nm* **1 :** bombing, shelling **2 :** bombardment

bombardero *nm* **:** bomber (airplane)

bombástico, -ca *adj* **:** bombastic

bombear *vt* **:** to pump

bombero, -ra *n* **:** firefighter, fireman *m*

bombilla *nf* **:** lightbulb

bombillo *nm CA, Col, Ven* **:** lightbulb

bombo *nm* **1 :** bass drum **2** *fam* **:** exaggerated praise, hype <con bombos y platillos : with great fanfare>

bombón *nm, pl* **bombones 1 :** bonbon, chocolate **2** *Mex* **:** marshmallow

bonachón[1], -chona *adj, mpl* **-chones** *fam* **:** good-natured, kindhearted

bonachón[2], -chona *n, mpl* **-chones** *fam* BUENAZO **:** kindhearted person

bonaerense[1] *adj* **:** of or from Buenos Aires

bonaerense[2] *nmf* **:** person from Buenos Aires

bonanza *nf* **1** PROSPERIDAD **:** prosperity <bonanza económica : economic boom> **2 :** calm weather **3 :** rich ore deposit, bonanza

bondad *nf* BENEVOLENCIA **:** goodness, kindness <tener la bondad de hacer algo : to be kind enough to do something>

bondadoso, -sa *adj* BENÉVOLO **:** kind, kindly, good — **bondadosamente** *adv*

bonete *nm* **:** cap, mortarboard

boniato *nm* **:** sweet potato

bonificación *nf, pl* **-ciones 1 :** discount **2 :** bonus, extra

bonito[1] *adv* **:** nicely, well <¡qué bonito canta tu hermana! : your sister sings wonderfully!>

bonito[2], -ta *adj* LINDO **:** pretty, lovely <tiene un apartamento bonito : she has a nice apartment>

bonito[3] *nm* **:** bonito (tuna)

bono *nm* **1 :** bond <bono bancario : bank bond> **2 :** voucher

boqueada *nf* **:** gasp <to give one's last gasp : dar la última boqueada>

boquear *vi* **1 :** to gasp **2 :** to be dying

boquete *nm* **:** gap, opening, breach

boquiabierto, -ta *adj* **:** open-mouthed, speechless, agape

boquilla *nf* **:** mouthpiece (of a musical instrument)

borbollar *vi* **:** to bubble

borbotar *or* **borbotear** *vi* **:** to boil, to bubble, to gurgle

borboteo *nm* **:** bubbling, gurgling

borda *nf* **:** gunwale

bordado *nm* **:** embroidery, needlework

bordar *v* **:** to embroider

borde *nm* **1 :** border, edge **2 al borde de :** on the verge of <estoy al borde de la locura : I'm about to go crazy>

bordear *vt* **1 :** to border, to skirt <el Río Este bordea Manhattan : the East River borders Manhattan> **2 :** to border on <bordea la irrealidad : it borders on unreality> **3 :** to line <una calle bordeada de árboles : a street lined with trees>

bordillo *nm* **:** curb

bordo *nm* **a ~ :** aboard, on board

boreal *adj* **:** northern

borgoña *nf* **:** burgundy

bórico, -ca *adj* : boric <ácido bórico : boric acid>

boricua *adj & nmf fam* : Puerto Rican

borinqueño, -ña → **boricua**

borla *nf* **1** : pom-pom, tassel **2** : powder puff

boro *nm* : boron

borrachera *nf* : drunkenness <agarró una borrachera : he got drunk>

borrachín, -china *n, mpl* **-chines** *fam* : lush, drunk

borracho[1], **-cha** *adj* EBRIO : drunk, intoxicated

borracho[2], **-cha** *n* : drunk, drunkard

borrador *nm* **1** : rough copy, first draft <en borrador : in the rough> **2** : eraser

borrar *vt* : to erase, to blot out — **borrarse** *vr* **1** : to fade, to fade away **2** : to resign, to drop out **3** *Mex fam* : to split, to leave <me borro : I'm out of here>

borrascoso, -sa *adj* : gusty, blustery

borrego, -ga *n* **1** : lamb, sheep **2** : simpleton, fool

borrico *nm* → **burro**

borrón *nm, pl* **borrones** : smudge, blot <borrón y cuenta nueva : let's start on a clean slate, let's start over again>

borronear *vt* : to smudge, to blot

borroso, -sa *adj* **1** : blurry, smudgy **2** CONFUSO : unclear, confused

boscoso, -sa *adj* : wooded

bosnio, -nia *adj & n* : Bosnian

bosque *nm* : woods, forest

bosquecillo *nm* : grove, copse, thicket

bosquejar *vt* ESBOZAR : to outline, to sketch

bosquejo *nm* **1** TRAZADO : outline, sketch **2** : draft

bostezar {21} *vi* : to yawn

bostezo *nm* : yawn

bota *nf* **1** : boot **2** : wineskin

botana *nf Mex* : snack, appetizer

botanear *vi Mex* : to have a snack

botánica *nf* : botany

botánico[1], **-ca** *adj* : botanical

botánico[2], **-ca** *n* : botanist

botar *vt* **1** ARROJAR : to throw, to fling, to hurl **2** TIRAR : to throw out, to throw away **3** : to launch (a ship)

bote *nm* **1** : small boat <bote de remos : rowboat> **2** : can, jar **3** : jump, bounce **4** *Mex fam* : jail

botella *nf* : bottle

botica *nf* FARMACIA : drugstore, pharmacy

boticario, -ria *n* FARMACÉUTICO : pharmacist, druggist

botín *nm, pl* **botines 1** : baby's bootee **2** : ankle boot **3** : booty, plunder

botiquín *nm, pl* **-quines 1** : medicine cabinet **2** : first-aid kit

botón *nm, pl* **botones 1** : button **2** : bud **3** INSIGNIA : badge

botones *nmfs & pl* : bellhop

botulismo *nm* : botulism

boulevard [ˌbule'var] *nm* → **bulevar**

bouquet *nm* **1** : fragrance, bouquet (of wine) **2** RAMILLETE : bouquet (of flowers)

boutique *nf* : boutique

bóveda *nf* **1** : vault, dome **2** CRIPTA : crypt

bovino, -na *adj* : bovine

box *nm, pl* **boxes 1** : pit (in auto racing) **2** *Mex* : boxing

boxeador, -dora *n* : boxer

boxear *vi* : to box

boxeo *nm* : boxing

boya *nf* : buoy

boyante *adj* **1** : buoyant **2** : prosperous, thriving

bozal *nm* **1** : muzzle **2** : halter (for a horse)

bracear *vi* **1** : to wave one's arms **2** : to make strokes (in swimming)

bracero, -ra *n* : migrant worker, day laborer

braguero *nm* : truss (in medicine)

bragueta *nf* : fly, pants zipper

braille *adj & nm* : braille

bramante *nm* : twine, string

bramar *vi* **1** RUGIR : to roar, to bellow **2** : to howl (of the wind)

bramido *nm* : bellowing, roar

brandy *nm* : brandy

branquia *nf* AGALLA : gill

brasa *nf* ASCUA : ember, live coal

brasero *nm* : brazier

brasier *nm Col, Mex* : brassiere, bra

brasileño, -ña *adj & n* : Brazilian

bravata *nf* **1** JACTANCIA : boast, bravado **2** AMENAZA : threat

bravo, -va *adj* **1** FEROZ : ferocious, fierce <un perro bravo : a ferocious dog> **2** EXCELENTE : excellent, great <¡bravo! : bravo!, well done!> **3** : rough, rugged, wild **4** : annoyed, angry

bravucón, -cona *n, mpl* **-cones** : bully

bravuconadas *nfpl* : bravado

bravura *nf* **1** FEROCIDAD : fierceness, ferocity **2** VALENTÍA : bravery

braza *nf* **1** : breaststroke **2** : fathom (unit of length)

brazada *nf* : stroke (in swimming)

brazalete *nm* PULSERA : bracelet, bangle

brazo *nm* **1** : arm **2 brazo derecho** : right-hand man **3 brazos** *nmpl* : hands, laborers

brea *nf* ALQUITRÁN : tar, pitch

brebaje *nm* : potion, brew

brecha *nf* **1** : gap, breach <estar siempre en la brecha : to be always there when needed, to stay in the thick of things> **2** : gash

brécol *nm* : broccoli

brega *nf* **1** LUCHA : struggle, fight **2** : hard work

bregar {52} *vi* **1** LUCHAR : to struggle **2** : to toil, to work hard **3 ~ con** : to deal with

brete *nm* : jam, tight spot

breve *adj* **1** CORTO : brief, short **2 en ~** : shortly, in short — **brevemente** *adv*

brevedad *nf* : brevity, shortness

breviario *nm* : breviary

brezal *nm* : heath, moor
brezo *nm* : heather
bribón, -bona *n, mpl* **bribones** : rascal, scamp
bricolaje *or* **bricolage** *nm* : do-it-yourself
brida *nf* : bridle
brigada *nf* **1** : brigade **2** : gang, team, squad
brigadier *nm* : brigadier
brillante[1] *adj* : brilliant, bright — **brillantemente** *adv*
brillante[2] *nm* DIAMANTE : diamond
brillantez *nf* : brilliance, brightness
brillar *vi* : to shine, to sparkle
brillo *nm* **1** LUSTRE : luster, shine **2** : brilliance
brilloso, -sa *adj* LUSTROSO : lustrous, shiny
brincar {72} *vi* **1** SALTAR : to jump around, to leap about **2** : to frolic, to gambol
brinco *nm* **1** SALTO : jump, leap, skip **2** **pegar un brinco** : to give a start, to jump
brindar *vi* : to drink a toast <brindó por los vencedores : he toasted the victors> — *vt* OFRECER, PROPORCIONAR : to offer, to provide — **brindarse** *vr* : to offer one's assistance, to volunteer
brindis *nm* : toast, drink <hacer un brindis : to drink a toast>
brinque, etc. → **brincar**
brío *nm* **1** : force, determination **2** : spirit, verve
brioso, -sa *adj* : spirited, lively
briqueta *nf* : briquette
brisa *nf* : breeze
británico[1], **-ca** *adj* : British
británico[2], **-ca** *n* **1** : British person **2** **los británicos** : the British
brizna *nf* **1** : strand, thread **2** : blade (of grass)
brocado *nm* : brocade
brocha *nf* : paintbrush
broche *nm* **1** ALFILER : brooch **2** : fastener, clasp **3** **broche de oro** : finishing touch
brocheta *nf* : skewer
brócoli *nm* : broccoli
broma *nf* **1** CHISTE : joke, prank **2** : fun, merriment **3** **en ~** : in jest, jokingly
bromear *vi* : to joke, to fool around <sólo estaba bromeando : I was only kidding>
bromista[1] *adj* : fun-loving, joking
bromista[2] *nmf* : joker, prankster
bromo *nm* : bromine
bronca *nf fam* : fight, quarrel, fuss
bronce *nm* : bronze
bronceado[1], **-da** *adj* **1** : tanned, suntanned **2** : bronze
bronceado[2] *nm* **1** : suntan, tan **2** : bronzing
broncearse *vr* : to get a suntan
bronco, -ca *adj* **1** : harsh, rough **2** : untamed, wild
bronquial *adj* : bronchial
bronquio *nm* : bronchial tube, bronchus
bronquitis *nf* : bronchitis
broqueta *nf* : skewer
brotar *vi* **1** : to bud, to sprout **2** : to spring up, to stream, to gush forth **3** : to break out, to appear
brote *nm* **1** : outbreak **2** : sprout, bud, shoot
broza *nf* **1** : brushwood **2** MALEZA : scrub, undergrowth
brujería *nf* HECHICERÍA : witchcraft, sorcery
brujo[1], **-ja** *adj* : bewitching
brujo[2], **-ja** *n* : warlock *m,* witch *f,* sorcerer
brújula *nf* : compass
bruma *nf* : haze, mist
brumoso, -sa *adj* : hazy, misty
bruñir {38} *vt* : to burnish, to polish (metals)
brusco, -ca *adj* **1** SÚBITO : sudden, abrupt **2** : curt, brusque — **bruscamente** *adv*
brusquedad *nf* **1** : abruptness, suddenness **2** : brusqueness
brutal *adj* **1** : brutal **2** *fam* : incredible, terrific — **brutalmente** *adv*
brutalidad *nf* CRUELDAD : brutality
brutalizar {21} *vt* : to brutalize, to maltreat
bruto[1], **-ta** *adj* **1** : gross <peso bruto : gross weight> <ingresos brutos : gross income> **2** : unrefined <petróleo bruto : crude oil> **3** : brutish, stupid
bruto[2], **-ta** *n* **1** : brute **2** : dunce, blockhead
bucal *adj* : oral
bucanero *nm* : buccaneer, pirate
buccino *nm* : whelk
buceador, -dora *n* : diver, scuba diver
bucear *vi* **1** : to dive, to swim underwater **2** : to explore, to delve
buceo *nm* **1** : diving, scuba diving **2** : exploration, searching
buche *nm* **1** : crop (of a bird) **2** *fam* : belly, gut **3** : mouthful <hacer buches : to rinse one's mouth>
bucle *nm* **1** : curl, ringlet **2** : loop
bucólico, -ca *adj* : bucolic
budín *nm, pl* **budines** : pudding
budismo *nm* : Buddhism
budista *adj & nmf* : Buddhist
buen → **bueno**[1]
buenamente *adv* **1** : easily **2** : willingly
buenaventura *nf* **1** : good luck **2** : fortune, future <le dijo la buenaventura : she told his fortune>
buenazo, -za *n fam* BONACHÓN : kind-hearted person
bueno[1], **-na** *adj* (**buen** *before masculine singular nouns*) **1** : good <una buena idea : a good idea> **2** BONDADOSO : nice, kind **3** APROPIADO : proper, appropriate **4** SANO : well, healthy **5** : considerable, goodly <una buena cantidad : a lot> **6** **buenos días**

: hello, good day **7 buenas tardes** : good afternoon **8 buenas noches** : good evening, good night
bueno[2] *interj* **1** : OK!, all right! **2** *Mex* : hello! (on the telephone)
buey *nm* : ox, steer
búfalo *nm* **1** : buffalo **2 búfalo de agua** : water buffalo
bufanda *nf* : scarf, muffler
bufar *vi* : to snort
bufet *or* **bufé** *nm* : buffet-style meal
bufete *nm* **1** : law firm, law office **2** : writing desk
bufido *nm* : snort
bufo, -fa *adj* : comic
bufón, -fona *n, mpl* **bufones** : clown, buffoon, jester
bufonada *nf* **1** : jest, buffoonery **2** : sarcasm
buhardilla *nf* **1** ÁTICO, DESVÁN : attic **2** : dormer window
búho *nm* **1** : owl **2** *fam* : hermit, recluse
buhonero, -ra *n* MERCACHIFLE : peddler
buitre *nm* : vulture
bujía *nf* : spark plug
bulbo *nm* : bulb
bulboso, -sa *adj* : bulbous
bulevar *nm* : boulevard
búlgaro, -ra *adj & n* : Bulgarian
bulla *nf* BARULLO : racket, rowdiness
bullicio *nm* **1** : ruckus, uproar **2** : hustle and bustle
bullicioso, -sa *adj* : noisy, busy, turbulent
bullir {38} *vi* **1** HERVIR : to boil **2** MOVERSE : to stir, to bustle about
bulto *nm* **1** : package, bundle **2** : piece of luggage, bag **3** : size, bulk, volume **4** : form, shape **5** : lump (on the body), swelling, bulge
bumerán *nm, pl* **-ranes** : boomerang
búnker *nm, pl* **búnkers** : bunker
búnquer *nm* → **búnker**
buñuelo *nm* : fried pastry
buque *nm* BARCO : ship, vessel
burbuja *nf* : bubble, blister (on a surface)
burbujear *vi* **1** : to bubble **2** : to fizz
burbujeo *nm* : bubbling
burdel *nm* : brothel, whorehouse
burdo, -da *adj* **1** : coarse, rough **2** : crude, clumsy <una burda mentira : a clumsy lie> — **burdamente** *adj*
burgués, -guesa *adj & n, mpl* **burgueses** : bourgeois
burguesía *nf* : bourgeoisie, middle class
burla *nf* **1** : mockery, ridicule **2** : joke, trick **3 hacer burla de** : to make fun of, to mock
burlar *vt* ENGAÑAR : to trick, to deceive — **burlarse** *vr* **~ de** : to make fun of, to ridicule
burlesco, -ca *adj* : burlesque, comic
burlón[1], **-lona** *adj, mpl* **burlones** : joking, mocking
burlón[2], **-lona** *n, mpl* **burlones** : joker
burocracia *nf* : bureaucracy
burócrata *nmf* : bureaucrat
burocrático, -ca *adj* : bureaucratic
burrada *nf fam* : stupid act, nonsense
burrito *nm* : burrito
burro[1], **-rra** *adj fam* : dumb, stupid
burro[2], **-rra** *n* **1** ASNO : donkey, ass **2** *fam* : dunce, poor student
burro[3] *nm* **1** : sawhorse **2** *Mex* : ironing board **3** *Mex* : stepladder
bursátil *adj* : stock-market
burundés, -desa *adj & n* : Burundian
bus *nm* : bus
busca *nf* : search
buscador, -dora *n* : hunter (for treasure, etc.), prospector
buscapleitos *nmfs & pl* : troublemaker
buscar {72} *vt* **1** : to look for, to seek **2** : to pick up, to collect **3** : to provoke — *vi* : to look, to search <buscó en los bolsillos : he searched through his pockets>
buscavidas *nmfs & pl* **1** : busybody **2** : go-getter
busque, etc. → **buscar**
búsqueda *nf* : search
busto *nm* : bust
butaca *nf* **1** SILLÓN : armchair **2** : seat (in a theatre) **3** *Mex* : pupil's desk
butano *nm* : butane
buzo[1], **-za** *adj Mex fam* : smart, astute <¡ponte buzo! : get with it!, get on the ball!>
buzo[2] *nm* : diver, scuba diver
buzón *nm, pl* **buzones** : mailbox
byte *nm* : byte

C

c *nf* : third letter of the Spanish alphabet
cabal *adj* **1** : exact, correct **2** : complete **3** : upright, honest
cabales *nmpl* **no estar en sus cabales** : not to be in one's right mind
cabalgar {52} *vi* : to ride (on horseback)
cabalgata *nf* : cavalcade, procession
cabalidad *nf* **a ~** : thoroughly, conscientiously
caballa *nf* : mackerel
caballada *nf* **1** : herd of horses **2** *fam* : nonsense, stupidity, outrageousness
caballar *adj* EQUINO : horse, equine
caballeresco, -ca *adj* : gallant, chivalrous
caballería *nf* **1** : cavalry **2** : horse, mount **3** : knighthood, chivalry
caballeriza *nf* : stable
caballero[1] → **caballeroso**
caballero[2] *nm* **1** : gentleman **2** : knight

caballerosidad *nf* : chivalry, gallantry
caballeroso, -sa *adj* : gentlemanly, chivalrous
caballete *nm* **1** : ridge **2** : easel **3** : trestle (for a table, etc.) **4** : bridge (of the nose) **5** : sawhorse
caballista *nmf* : horseman *m,* horsewoman *f*
caballito *nm* **1** : rocking horse **2 caballito de mar** : seahorse **3 caballitos** *nmpl* : merry-go-round
caballo *nm* **1** : horse **2** : knight (in chess) **3 caballo de fuerza** *or* **caballo de vapor** : horsepower
cabalmente *adv* : fully, exactly
cabaña *nf* CHOZA : cabin, hut
cabaret *nm, pl* **-rets** : nightclub, cabaret
cabecear *vt* : to head (in soccer) — *vi* **1** : to nod one's head **2** : to lurch, to pitch
cabecera *nf* **1** : headboard **2** : head <cabecera de la mesa : head of the table> **3** : heading, headline **4** : headwaters *pl* **5 médico de cabecera** : family doctor **6 cabecera municipal** *CA, Mex* : downtown area
cabecilla *nmf* : ringleader, kingpin
cabellera *nf* : head of hair, mane
cabello *nm* : hair
cabelludo, -da *adj* **1** : hairy **2 cuero cabelludo** : scalp
caber {12} *vi* **1** : to fit, to go <no sé si cabremos todos en el coche : I don't know if we'll all fit in the car> **2** : to be possible <no cabe duda alguna : there's no doubt about it> <cabe que llegue mañana : he may come tomorrow>
cabestro *nm* : halter (for an animal)
cabeza *nf* **1** : head **2 cabeza hueca** : scatterbrain **3 de ~** : head first **4 dolor de cabeza** : headache
cabezada *nf* **1** : butt, blow with the head **2** : nod <echar una cabezada : to take a nap, to doze off>
cabezal *nm* : bolster
cabezazo *nm* : butt, blow with the head
cabezón, -zona *adj, mpl* **-zones** *fam* **1** : having a big head **2** : pigheaded, stubborn
cabida *nf* **1** : room, space, capacity **2 dar cabida a** : to accomodate, to hold
cabildear *vi* : to lobby
cabildeo *nm* : lobbying
cabildero, -ra *n* : lobbyist
cabildo *nm* AYUNTAMIENTO **1** : town or city hall **2** : town or city council
cabina *nf* **1** : cabin **2** : booth **3** : cab (of a truck), cockpit (of an airplane)
cabizbajo, -ja *adj* : dejected, downcast
cable *nm* : cable
cableado *nm* : wiring
cabo *nm* **1** : end <al cabo de dos semanas : at the end of two weeks> **2** : stub, end piece **3** : corporal **4** : cape, headland <el Cabo Cañaveral : Cape Canaveral> **5 al fin y al cabo** : after all, in the end **6 llevar a cabo** : to carry out, to do
caboverdiano, -na *adj & n* : Cape Verdean
cabrá, etc. → **caber**
cabra *nf* : goat
cabrestante *nm* : windlass
cabrío, -ría *adj* : goat, caprine
cabriola *nf* **1** : skip, jump **2 hacer cabriolas** : to prance
cabriolar *vi* : to prance
cabrito *nm* : kid, baby goat
cabús *nm, pl* **cabuses** *Mex* : caboose
cacahuate *or* **cacahuete** *nm* : peanut
cacalote *nm Mex* : crow
cacao *nm* : cacao, cocoa bean
cacarear *vi* : to crow, to cackle, to cluck — *vt fam* : to boast about, to crow about <cacarear un huevo : to brag about an accomplishment>
cacatúa *nf* : cockatoo
cace, etc. → **cazar**
cacería *nf* **1** CAZA : hunt, hunting **2** : hunting party
cacerola *nf* : pan, saucepan
cacha *nf* : butt (of a gun)
cachar *vt fam* : to catch
cacharro *nm* **1** *fam* : thing, piece of junk **2** *fam* : jalopy **3 cacharros** *nmpl* : pots and pans
cache *nm* : cache, cache memory
cachear *vt* : to search, to frisk
cachemir *nm* : cashmere
cachetada *nf* BOFETADA : slap on the face
cachete *nm* : cheek
cachetear *vt* BOFETEAR : to slap
cachiporra *nf* : bludgeon, club, blackjack
cachirul *nm Mex fam* : cheating <hacer cachirul : to cheat>
cachivache *nm fam* : thing <mete tus cachivaches en el maletero : put your stuff in the trunk>
cacho *nm fam* : piece, bit
cachorro, -rra *n* **1** : cub **2** PERRITO : puppy
cachucha *nf Mex* : cap, baseball cap
cacique *nm* **1** : chief (of a tribe) **2** : boss (in politics)
cacofonía *nf* : cacophony
cacofónico, -ca *adj* : cacophonous
cacto *nm* : cactus
cactus *nm* → **cacto**
cada *adj* **1** : each <cuestan diez pesos cada una : they cost ten pesos each> **2** : every <cada vez : every time> **3** : such, some <sales con cada historia : you come up with such crazy stories> **4 cada vez más** : more and more, increasingly **5 cada vez menos** : less and less
cadalso *nm* : scaffold, gallows
cadáver *nm* : corpse, cadaver
cadavérico, -ca *adj* **1** : cadaverous **2** PÁLIDO : deathly pale
caddie *or* **caddy** *nmf, pl* **caddies** : caddy

cadena *nf* **1** : chain **2** : network, channel **3 cadena de montaje** : assembly line **4 cadena perpetua** : life sentence

cadencia *nf* : cadence, rhythm

cadencioso, -sa *adj* : rhythmic, rhythmical

cadera *nf* : hip

cadete *nmf* : cadet

cadmio *nm* : cadmium

caducar {72} *vi* : to expire

caducidad *nf* : expiration

caduco, -ca *adj* **1** : outdated, obsolete **2** : deciduous

caer {13} *vi* **1** : to fall, to drop **2** : to collapse **3** : to hang (down) **4 caer bien** *fam* : to be pleasant, to be likeable <me caes bien : I like you> **5 caer mal** *or* **caer gordo** *fam* : to be unpleasant, to be unlikeable — **caerse** *vr* : to fall down

café[1] *adj* : brown <ojos cafés : brown eyes>

café[2] *nm* **1** : coffee **2** : café

cafeína *nf* : caffeine

cafetal *nm* : coffee plantation

cafetalero[1], **-ra** *adj* : coffee <cosecha cafetalera : coffee harvest>

cafetalero[2], **-ra** *n* : coffee grower

cafetera *nf* : coffeepot, coffeemaker

cafetería *nf* **1** : coffee shop, café **2** : lunchroom, cafeteria

cafetero[1], **-ra** *adj* : coffee-producing

cafetero[2], **-ra** *n* : coffee grower

cafeticultura *nf Mex* : coffee industry

caguama *nf* **1** : large Caribbean turtle **2** *Mex* : large bottle of beer

caída *nf* **1** BAJA, DESCENSO : fall, drop **2** : collapse, downfall

caiga, etc. → **caer**

caimán *nm, pl* **caimanes** : alligator, caiman

caimito *nm* : star apple

caja *nf* **1** : box, case **2** : cash register, checkout counter **3** : bed (of a truck) **4** *fam* : coffin **5 caja fuerte** *or* **caja de caudales** : safe **6 caja de seguridad** : safe-deposit box **7 caja torácica** : rib cage

cajero, -ra *n* **1** : cashier **2** : teller **3 cajero automático** : automated teller machine, ATM

cajeta *nf Mex* : a sweet carmel-flavored spread

cajetilla *nf* : pack (of cigarettes)

cajón *nm, pl* **cajones 1** : drawer, till **2** : crate, case **3 cajón de estacionamiento** *Mex* : parking space

cajuela *nf Mex* : trunk (of a car)

cal *nf* : lime, quicklime

cala *nf* : cove, inlet

calabacín *nm, pl* **-cines** : zucchini

calabacita *nf Mex* : zucchini

calabaza *nf* **1** : pumpkin, squash **2** : gourd **3 dar calabazas a** : to give the brush-off to, to jilt

calabozo *nm* **1** : prison **2** : jail cell

calado[1], **-da** *adj* **1** : drenched **2** : openworked

calado[2] *nm* **1** : draft (of a ship) **2** : openwork

calafatear *vt* : to caulk

calamar *nm* **1** : squid **2 calamares** *nmpl* : calamari

calambre *nm* **1** ESPASMO : cramp **2** : electric shock, jolt

calamidad *nf* DESASTRE : calamity, disaster

calamina *nf* : calamine

calamitoso, -sa *adj* : calamitous, disastrous

calaña *nf* : ilk, kind, sort <una persona de mala calaña : a bad sort>

calar *vt* **1** : to soak through **2** : to pierce, to penetrate — *vi* : to catch on — **calarse** *vr* : to get drenched

calavera[1] *nf* **1** : skull **2** *Mex* : taillight

calavera[2] *nm* : rake, rogue

calcar {72} *vt* **1** : to trace **2** : to copy, to imitate

calce, etc. → **calzar**

calceta *nf* : knee-high stocking

calcetería *nf* : hosiery

calcetín *nm, pl* **-tines** : sock

calcificar {72} *v* : to calcify — **calcificarse** *vr*

calcinar *vt* : to char, to burn

calcio *nm* : calcium

calco *nm* **1** : transfer, tracing **2** : copy, image

calcomanía *nf* : decal, transfer

calculador, -dora *adj* : calculating

calculadora *nf* : calculator

calcular *vt* **1** : to calculate, to estimate **2** : to plan, to scheme

cálculo *nm* **1** : calculation, estimation **2** : calculus **3** : plan, scheme **4 cálculo biliar** : gallstone **5 hoja de cálculo** : spreadsheet

caldas *nfpl* : hot springs

caldear *vt* : to heat, to warm — **caldearse** *vr* **1** : to heat up **2** : to become heated, to get tense

caldera *nf* **1** : cauldron **2** : boiler

caldo *nm* **1** CONSOMÉ : broth, stock **2 caldo de cultivo** : culture medium, breeding ground

caldoso, -sa *adj* : watery

calefacción *nf, pl* **-ciones** : heating, heat

calefactor *nm* : heater

caleidoscopio *nm* → **calidoscopio**

calendario *nm* **1** : calendar **2** : timetable, schedule

caléndula *nf* : marigold

calentador *nm* : heater

calentamiento *nm* **1** : heating, warming **2** : warm-up (in sports)

calentar {55} *vt* **1** : to heat, to warm **2** *fam* : to annoy, to anger **3** *fam* : to excite, to turn on — **calentarse** *vr* **1** : to get warm, to heat up **2** : to warm up (in sports) **3** *fam* : to become sexually aroused **4** *fam* : to get mad

calentura *nf* **1** FIEBRE : temperature, fever **2** : cold sore

calibrador *nm* : gauge, calipers *pl*

calibrar *vt* **:** to calibrate — **calibración** *nf*

calibre *nm* **1 :** caliber, gauge **2 :** importance, excellence **3 :** kind, sort <un problema de grueso calibre : a serious problem>

calidad *nf* **1 :** quality, grade **2 :** position, status **3 en calidad de :** as, in the capacity of

cálido, -da *adj* **1 :** hot <un clima cálido : a hot climate> **2 :** warm <una cálida bienvenida : a warm welcome>

calidoscopio *nm* **:** kaleidoscope

caliente *adj* **1 :** hot, warm <mantenerse caliente : to stay warm> **2 :** heated, fiery <una disputa caliente : a heated argument> **3** *fam* **:** sexually excited, horny

califa *nm* **:** caliph

calificación *nf, pl* **-ciones 1** NOTA **:** grade (for a course) **2 :** rating, score **3** CLASIFICACIÓN **:** qualification, qualifying <ronda de calificación : qualifying round>

calificar {72} *vt* **1 :** to grade **2 :** to describe, to rate <la calificaron de buena alumna : they described her as a good student> **3 :** to qualify, to modify (in grammar)

calificativo[1], -va *adj* **:** qualifying

calificativo[2] *nm* **:** qualifier, epithet

caligrafía *nf* **1** ESCRITURA **:** handwriting **2 :** calligraphy

calistenia *nf* **:** calisthenics

cáliz *nm, pl* **cálices 1 :** chalice, goblet **2 :** calyx

caliza *nf* **:** limestone

callado, -da *adj* **:** quiet, silent — **calladamente** *adv*

callar *vi* **:** to keep quiet, to be silent — *vt* **1 :** to silence, to hush <¡calla a los niños! : keep the children quiet!> **2 :** to keep secret — **callarse** *vr* **:** to remain silent <¡cállate! : be quiet!, shut up!>

calle *nf* **:** street, road

callejear *vi* **:** to wander about the streets, to hang out

callejero, -ra *adj* **:** street <perro callejero : stray dog>

callejón *nm, pl* **-jones 1 :** alley **2 callejón sin salida :** dead-end street

callo *nm* **:** callus, corn

calloso, -sa *adj* **:** callous

calma *nf* **:** calm, quiet

calmante[1] *adj* **:** calming, soothing

calmante[2] *nm* **:** tranquilizer, sedative

calmar *vt* TRANQUILIZAR **:** to calm, to soothe — **calmarse** *vr* **:** to calm down

calmo, -ma *adj* TRANQUILO **:** calm, tranquil

calmoso, -sa *adj* **1** TRANQUILO **:** calm, quiet **2** LENTO **:** slow, sluggish

calor *nm* **1 :** heat <hace calor : it's hot outside> <tener calor : to feel hot> **2 :** warmth, affection **3 :** ardor, passion

caloría *nf* **:** calorie

calórico, -ca *adj* **:** caloric

calque, etc. → **calcar**

calumnia *nf* **:** slander, libel — **calumnioso, -sa** *adj*

calumniar *vt* **:** to slander, to libel

caluroso, -sa *adj* **1 :** hot **2 :** warm, enthusiastic

calva *nf* **:** bald spot, bald head

calvario *nm* **1 :** Calvary **2 :** Stations of the Cross *pl* **3 vivir un calvario :** to suffer great adversity

calvicie *nf* **:** baldness

calvo[1], -va *adj* **:** bald

calvo[2], -va *n* **:** bald person

calza *nf* **:** block, wedge

calzada *nf* **:** roadway, avenue

calzado *nm* **:** footwear

calzador *nm* **:** shoehorn

calzar {21} *vt* **1 :** to wear (shoes) <¿de cuál calza? : what is your shoe size?> <siempre calzaban tenis : they always wore sneakers> **2 :** to provide with shoes

calzo *nm* **:** chock, wedge

calzoncillos *nmpl* **:** underpants, briefs

calzones *nmpl* **:** underpants, panties

cama *nf* **1 :** bed **2 cama elástica :** trampoline

camada *nf* **:** litter, brood

camafeo *nm* **:** cameo

camaleón *nm, pl* **-leones :** chameleon

cámara *nf* **1 :** camera **2 :** chamber, room **3 :** house (in government) **4 :** inner tube

camarada *nmf* **1 :** comrade, companion **2 :** colleague

camaradería *nf* **:** camaraderie

camarero, -ra *n* **1** MESERO **:** waiter, waitress *f* **2 :** bellboy *m,* chambermaid *f* (in a hotel) **3 :** steward *m,* stewardess *f* (on a ship, etc.)

camarilla *nf* **:** political clique

camarógrafo, -fa *n* **:** cameraman *m,* camerawoman *f*

camarón *nm, pl* **-rones 1 :** shrimp **2 :** prawn

camarote *nm* **:** cabin, stateroom

camastro *nm* **:** small hard bed, pallet

cambalache *nm fam* **:** swap

cambiante *adj* **1 :** changing **2** VARIABLE **:** changeable, variable

cambiar *vt* **1** ALTERAR, MODIFICAR **:** to change **2 :** to exchange, to trade — *vi* **1 :** to change **2 cambiar de velocidad :** to shift gears — **cambiarse** *vr* **1 :** to change (clothing) **2** MUDARSE **:** to move (to a new address)

cambio *nm* **1 :** change, alteration **2 :** exchange **3 :** change (money) **4 en cambio :** instead **5 en cambio :** however, on the other hand

cambista *nmf* **:** exchange broker

camboyano, -na *adj & n* **:** Cambodian

cambur *nm Ven* **:** banana

camelia *nf* **:** camellia

camello *nm* **:** camel

camellón *nm, pl* **-llones** *Mex* **:** traffic island

camerino *nm* **:** dressing room

camerunés, -nesa *adj, mpl* **-neses :** Cameroonian

camilla *nf* : stretcher
camillero, -ra *n* : orderly (in a hospital)
caminante *nmf* : wayfarer, walker
caminar *vi* ANDAR : to walk, to move — *vt* : to walk, to cover (a distance)
caminata *nf* : hike, long walk
camino *nm* **1** : path, road **2** : journey <ponerse en camino : to set off> **3** : way <a medio camino : halfway there>
camión *nm, pl* **camiones 1** : truck **2** *Mex* : bus
camionero, -ra *n* **1** : truck driver **2** *Mex* : bus driver
camioneta *nm* : light truck, van
camisa *nf* **1** : shirt **2 camisa de fuerza** : straitjacket
camiseta *nf* **1** : T-shirt **2** : undershirt
camisón *nm, pl* **-sones** : nightshirt, nightgown
camorra *nf fam* : fight, trouble <buscar camorra : to pick a fight>
camote *nm* **1** : root vegetable similar to the sweet potato **2 hacerse camote** *Mex fam* : to get mixed up
campal *adj* : pitched, fierce <batalla campal : pitched battle>
campamento *nm* : camp
campana *nf* : bell
campanada *nf* TAÑIDO : stroke (of a bell), peal
campanario *nm* : bell tower, belfry
campanilla *nf* **1** : small bell, handbell **2** : uvula
campante *adj* : nonchalant, smug <seguir tan campante : to go on as if nothing had happened>
campaña *nf* **1** CAMPO : countryside, country **2** : campaign **3 tienda de campaña** : tent
campañol *nm* : vole
campechana *nf Mex* : puff pastry
campechanía *nf* : geniality
campechano, -na *adj* : open, cordial, friendly
campeón, -peona *n, mpl* **-peones** : champion
campeonato *nm* : championship
cámper *nm* : camper (vehicle)
campero, -ra *adj* : country, rural
campesino, -na *n* : peasant, farm laborer
campestre *adj* : rural, rustic
camping *nm* **1** : camping **2** : campsite
campiña *nf* CAMPO : countryside, country
campista *nmf* : camper
campo *nm* **1** CAMPAÑA : countryside, country **2** : field <campo de aviación : airfield> <su campo de responsabilidad : her field of responsibility>
camposanto *nm* : graveyard, cemetery
campus *nms & pl* : campus
camuflaje *nm* : camouflage
camuflajear *vt* : to camouflage
camuflar → **camuflajear**
can *nm* : hound, dog
cana *nf* **1** : gray hair **2 salirle canas** : to go gray, to get gray hair **3 echar una cana al aire** : to let one's hair down
canadiense *adj & nmf* : Canadian
canal[1] *nm* **1** : canal **2** : channel
canal[2] *nmf* : gutter, groove
canalé *nm* : rib, ribbing (in fabric)
canaleta *nf* : gutter
canalete *nm* : paddle
canalizar {21} *vt* : to channel
canalla[1] *adj fam* : low, rotten
canalla[2] *nmf fam* : bastard, swine
canapé *nm* **1** : hors d'oeuvre, canapé **2** SOFÁ : couch, sofa
canario[1], **-ria** *adj* : of or from the Canary Islands
canario[2], **-ria** *n* : Canarian, Canary Islander
canario[3] *nm* : canary
canasta *nf* **1** : basket **2** : canasta (card game)
cancel *nm* **1** : sliding door **2** : partition
cancelación *nf, pl* **-ciones 1** : cancellation **2** : payment in full
cancelar *vt* **1** : to cancel **2** : to pay off, to settle
cáncer *nm* : cancer
Cáncer *nmf* : Cancer
cancerígeno[1], **-na** *adj* : carcinogenic
cancerígeno[2] *nm* : carcinogen
canceroso, -sa *adj* : cancerous
cancha *nf* : court, field (for sports)
canciller *nm* : chancellor
cancillería *nf* : chancellery, ministry
canción *nf, pl* **canciones 1** : song **2 canción de cuna** : lullaby
cancionero[1] *nm* : songbook
cancionero[2], **-ra** *n Mex* : songster, songstress *f*
candado *nm* : padlock
candela *nf* **1** : flame, fire **2** : candle
candelabro *nm* : candelabra
candelero *nm* **1** : candlestick **2 estar en el candelero** : to be the center of attention
candente *adj* : red-hot
candidato, -ta *n* : candidate, applicant
candidatura *nf* : candidacy
candidez *nf* **1** : simplicity **2** INGENUIDAD : naïveté, ingenuousness
cándido, -da *adj* **1** : simple, unassuming **2** INGENUO : naive, ingenuous
candil *nm* : oil lamp
candilejas *nfpl* : footlights
candor *nm* : naïveté, innocence
candoroso, -sa *adj* : naive, innocent
canela *nf* : cinnamon
canesú *nm* : yoke (of clothing)
cangrejo *nm* JAIBA : crab
canguro *nm* **1** : kangaroo **2 hacer de canguro** *Spain* : to baby-sit
caníbal[1] *adj* : cannibalistic
caníbal[2] *nmf* ANTROPÓFAGO : cannibal
canibalismo *nm* ANTROPOFAGIA : cannibalism
canibalizar {21} *vt* : to cannibalize
canica *nf* **1** : marble **2 canicas** *nfpl* : marbles (toys)
caniche *nm* : poodle

canijo, -ja *adj* **1** *fam* : puny, weak **2** *Mex fam* : tough, hard <un examen muy canijo : a very tough exam>
canilla *nf* **1** : shin, shinbone **2** *Arg, Uru* : faucet
canino[1], **-na** *adj* : canine
canino[2] *nm* **1** COLMILLO : canine (tooth) **2** : dog, canine
canje *nm* INTERCAMBIO : exchange, trade
canjear *vt* INTERCAMBIAR : to exchange, to trade
cannabis *nm* : cannabis
cano, -na *adj* : gray <un hombre de pelo cano : a gray-haired man>
canoa *nf* : canoe
canon *nm, pl* **cánones** : canon
canónico, -ca *adj* **1** : canonical **2 derecho canónico** : canon law
canonizar {21} *vt* : to canonize — **canonización** *nf*
canoso, -sa → **cano**
cansado, -da *adj* **1** : tired <estar cansado : to be tired> **2** : tiresome, wearying <ser cansado : to be tiring>
cansancio *nm* FATIGA : fatigue, weariness
cansar *vt* FATIGAR : to wear out, to tire — *vi* : to be tiresome — **cansarse** *vr* **1** : to wear oneself out **2** : to get bored
cansino, -na *adj* : slow, weary, lethargic
cantaleta *nf fam* : nagging <la misma cantaleta : the same old story>
cantalupo *nm* : cantaloupe
cantante *nmf* : singer
cantar[1] *v* : to sing
cantar[2] *nm* : song, ballad
cántaro *nm* **1** : pitcher, jug **2 llover a cántaros** *fam* : to rain cats and dogs
cantata *nf* : cantata
cantera *nf* : quarry <cantera de piedra : stone quarry>
cántico *nm* : canticle, chant
cantidad[1] *adv fam* : really <ese carro me costó cantidad : that car cost me plenty>
cantidad[2] *nf* **1** : quantity **2** : sum, amount (of money) **3** *fam* : a lot, a great many <había cantidad de niños en el parque : there were tons of kids in the park>
cantimplora *nf* : canteen, water bottle
cantina *nf* **1** : tavern, bar **2** : canteen, mess, dining quarters *pl*
cantinero, -ra *n* : bartender
canto *nm* **1** : singing **2** : chant <canto gregoriano : Gregorian chant> **3** : song (of a bird) **4** : edge, end <de canto : on end, sideways> **5 canto rodado** : boulder
cantón *nm, pl* **cantones 1** : canton **2** *Mex fam* : place, home
cantor[1], **-tora** *adj* **1** : singing **2 pájaro cantor** : songbird
cantor[2], **-tora** *n* **1** : singer **2** : cantor
caña *nf* **1** : cane <caña de azúcar : sugarcane> **2** : reed **3 caña de pescar** : fishing rod **4 caña del timón** : tiller (of a boat)
cañada *nf* : ravine, gully
cáñamo *nm* : hemp
cañaveral *nm* : sugarcane field
cañería *nf* TUBERÍA : pipes *pl*, piping
caño *nm* **1** : pipe **2** : spout **3** : channel (for navigation)
cañón *nm, pl* **cañones 1** : cannon **2** : barrel (of a gun) **3** : canyon
cañonear *vt* : to shell, to bombard
cañoneo *nm* : shelling, bombardment
cañonero *nm* : gunboat
caoba *nf* : mahogany
caos *nm* : chaos
caótico, -ca *adj* : chaotic
capa *nf* **1** : cape, cloak **2** : coating **3** : layer, stratum **4** : (social) class, stratum
capacidad *nf* **1** : capacity **2** : capability, ability
capacitación *nf, pl* **-ciones** : training
capacitar *vt* : to train, to qualify
caparazón *nm, pl* **-zones** : shell, carapace
capataz *nmf, pl* **-taces** : foreman *m*, forewoman *f*
capaz *adj, pl* **capaces 1** APTO : capable, able **2** COMPETENTE : competent **3** : spacious <capaz para : with room for>
capcioso, -sa *adj* : cunning, deceptive <pregunta capciosa : trick question>
capea *nf* : amateur bullfight
capear *vt* **1** : to make a pass with the cape (in bullfighting) **2** : to dodge, to weather <capear el temporal : to ride out the storm>
capellán *nm, pl* **-llanes** : chaplain
capilar *nm* : capillary — **capilar** *adj*
capilla *nf* : chapel
capirotada *nf Mex* : traditional bread pudding
capirotazo *nm* : flip, flick
capital[1] *adj* **1** : capital **2** : chief, principal
capital[2] *nm* : capital <capital de riesgo : venture capital>
capital[3] *nf* : capital, capital city
capitalino[1], **-na** *adj* : of or from a capital city
capitalino[2], **-na** *n* : inhabitant of a capital city
capitalismo *nm* : capitalism
capitalista *adj & nmf* : capitalist
capitalizar {21} *vt* : to capitalize — **capitalización** *nf*
capitán, -tana *n, mpl* **-tanes** : captain
capitanear *vt* : to captain, to command
capitanía *nf* : captaincy
capitel *nm* : capital (of a column)
capitolio *nm* : capitol
capitulación *nf, pl* **-ciones** : capitulation
capitular *vi* : to capitulate, to surrender
capítulo *nm* **1** : chapter, section **2** : matter, subject
capó *nm* : hood (of a car)
capón *nm, pl* **capones** : capon

caporal *nm* **1 :** chief, leader **2 :** foreman (on a ranch)
capota *nf* **:** top (of a convertible)
capote *nm* **1 :** cloak, overcoat **2 :** bullfighter's cape **3** *Mex* COFRE **:** hood (of a car)
capricho *nm* ANTOJO **:** whim, caprice
caprichoso, -sa *adj* ANTOJADIZO **:** capricious, fickle
Capricornio *nmf* **:** Capricorn
cápsula *nf* **:** capsule
captar *vt* **1 :** to catch, to grasp **2 :** to gain, to attract **3 :** to harness, to collect (waters)
captor, -tora *n* **:** captor
captura *nf* **:** capture, seizure
capturar *vt* **:** to capture, to seize
capucha *nf* **:** hood, cowl
capuchina *nf* **:** nasturtium
capuchino *nm* **1 :** Capuchin (monk) **2 :** capuchin (monkey) **3 :** cappuccino
capullo *nm* **1 :** cocoon **2 :** bud (of a flower)
caqui *adj & nm* **:** khaki
cara *nf* **1 :** face **2** ASPECTO **:** look, appearance <¡qué buena cara tiene ese pastel! : that cake looks delicious!> **3** *fam* **:** nerve, gall **4 ~ a** *or* **de cara a :** facing **5 de cara a :** in view of, in the light of
carabina *nf* **:** carbine
caracol *nm* **1 :** snail **2** CONCHA **:** conch, seashell **3 :** cochlea **4 :** ringlet
caracola *nf* **:** conch
carácter *nm, pl* **caracteres 1** ÍNDOLE **:** character, kind, nature **2** TEMPERAMENTO **:** disposition, temperament **3 :** letter, symbol <caracteres chinos : Chinese characters>
característica *nf* RASGO **:** trait, feature, characteristic
característico, -ca *adj* **:** characteristic — **característicamente** *adv*
caracterizar {21} *vt* **:** to characterize — **caracterización** *nf*
caramba *interj* **:** darn!, heck!
carámbano *nm* **:** icicle
carambola *nf* **1 :** carom **2 :** ruse, trick <por carambola : by a lucky chance>
caramelo *nm* **1 :** caramel **2** DULCE **:** candy
caramillo *nm* **1 :** pipe, small flute **2 :** heap, pile
caraqueño[1], -ña *adj* **:** of or from Caracas
caraqueño[2], -ña *n* **:** person from Caracas
carátula *nf* **1 :** title page **2 :** cover, dust jacket **3** CARETA **:** mask **4** *Mex* **:** face, dial (of a clock or watch)
caravana *nf* **1 :** caravan **2 :** convoy, motorcade **3** REMOLQUE **:** trailer
caray → **caramba**
carbohidrato *nm* **:** carbohydrate
carbón *nm, pl* **carbones 1 :** coal **2 :** charcoal
carbonatado, -da *adj* **:** carbonated
carbonato *nm* **:** carbonate
carboncillo *nm* **:** charcoal
carbonera *nf* **:** coal cellar, coal bunker (on a ship)
carbonero, -ra *adj* **:** coal
carbonizar {21} *vt* **:** to carbonize, to char
carbono *nm* **:** carbon
carbunco *or* **carbunclo** *nm* **:** carbuncle
carburador *nm* **:** carburetor
carca *nmf fam* **:** old fogy
carcacha *nf fam* **:** jalopy, wreck
carcaj *nm* **:** quiver (for arrows)
carcajada *nf* **:** loud laugh, guffaw <reírse a carcajadas : to roar with laughter>
carcajearse *vr* **:** to roar with laughter, to be in stitches
cárcel *nf* PRISIÓN **:** jail, prison
carcelero, -ra *n* **:** jailer
carcinogénico, -ca *adj* **:** carcinogenic
carcinógeno *nm* CANCERÍGENO **:** carcinogen
carcinoma *nm* **:** carcinoma
carcomer *vt* **:** to eat away at, to consume
carcomido, -da *adj* **1 :** worm-eaten **2 :** decayed, rotten
cardán *nm, pl* **cardanes :** universal joint
cardar *vt* **:** to card, to comb
cardenal *nm* **1 :** cardinal (in religion) **2 :** bruise
cardíaco *or* **cardiaco, -ca** *adj* **:** cardiac, heart
cárdigan *nm, pl* **-gans :** cardigan
cardinal *adj* **:** cardinal
cardiología *nf* **:** cardiology
cardiólogo, -ga *n* **:** cardiologist
cardiovascular *adj* **:** cardiovascular
cardo *nm* **:** thistle
cardumen *nm* **:** school of fish
carear *vt* **:** to bring face-to-face
carecer {53} *vi* **~ de :** to lack <el cheque carecía de fondos : the check lacked funds>
carencia *nf* **1** FALTA **:** lack **2** ESCASEZ **:** shortage **3** DEFICIENCIA **:** deficiency
carente *adj* **~ de :** lacking (in)
carero, -ra *adj fam* **:** pricey
carestía *nf* **1 :** rise in cost <la carestía de la vida : the high cost of living> **2 :** dearth, scarcity
careta *nf* MÁSCARA **:** mask
carey *nm* **1 :** hawksbill turtle, sea turtle **2 :** tortoiseshell
carga *nf* **1 :** loading **2 :** freight, load, cargo **3 :** burden, responsibility **4 :** charge <carga eléctrica : electrical charge> **5 :** attack, charge
cargado, -da *adj* **1 :** loaded **2 :** bogged down, weighted down **3 :** close, stuffy **4 :** charged <cargado de tensión : charged with tension> **5** FUERTE **:** strong <café cargado : strong coffee> **6 cargado de hombros :** stoop-shouldered
cargador[1], -dora *n* **:** longshoreman *m*, longshorewoman *f*

cargador[2] *nm* **1 :** magazine (for a firearm) **2 :** charger (for batteries)
cargamento *nm* **:** cargo, load
cargar {52} *vt* **1 :** to carry **2 :** to load, to fill **3 :** to charge — *vi* **1 :** to load **2 :** to rest (in architecture) **3 ~ sobre :** to fall upon
cargo *nm* **1 :** burden, load **2 :** charge <a cargo de : in charge of> **3 :** position, office
cargue, etc. → **cargar**
carguero[1], **-ra** *adj* **:** freight, cargo <tren carguero : freight train>
carguero[2] *nm* **:** freighter, cargo ship
cariarse *vr* **:** to decay (of teeth)
caribe *adj* **:** Caribbean <el mar caribe : the Caribbean Sea>
caribeño, -ña *adj* **:** Caribbean
caribú *nm* **:** caribou
caricatura *nf* **1 :** caricature **2 :** cartoon
caricaturista *nmf* **:** caricaturist, cartoonist
caricaturizar {21} *vt* **:** to caricature
caricia *nf* **1 :** caress **2 hacer caricias :** to pet, to stroke
caridad *nf* **1 :** charity **2** LIMOSNA **:** alms *pl*
caries *nfs & pl* **:** cavity (in a tooth)
carillón *nm, pl* **-llones 1 :** carillon **2 :** glockenspiel
cariño *nm* AFECTO **:** affection, love
cariñoso, -sa *adj* AFECTUOSO **:** affectionate, loving — **cariñosamente** *adv*
carioca[1] *adj* **:** of or from Rio de Janeiro
carioca[2] *nmf* **:** person from Rio de Janeiro
carisma *nf* **:** charisma
carismático, -ca *adj* **:** charismatic
carita *adj Mex fam* **:** cute (said of a man) <tu primo se cree muy carita : your cousin thinks he's gorgeous>
caritativo, -va *adj* **:** charitable
cariz *nm, pl* **carices :** appearance, aspect
carmesí *adj & nm* **:** crimson
carmín *nm, pl* **carmines 1 :** carmine **2 carmín de labios :** lipstick
carnada *nf* CEBO **:** bait
carnal *adj* **1 :** carnal **2 primo carnal :** first cousin
carnaval *nm* **:** carnival
carnaza *nf* **:** bait
carne *nf* **1 :** meat <carne molida : ground beef> **2 :** flesh <carne de gallina : goose bumps>
carné *nm* → **carnet**
carnero *nm* **1 :** ram, sheep **2 :** mutton
carnet *nm* **1 :** identification card, ID **2 :** membership card **3 carnet de conducir** *Spain* **:** driver's license
carnicería *nf* **1 :** butcher shop **2** MATANZA **:** slaughter, carnage
carnicero, -ra *n* **:** butcher
carnívoro[1], **-ra** *adj* **:** carnivorous
carnívoro[2] *nm* **:** carnivore
carnoso, -sa *adj* **:** fleshy, meaty
caro[1] *adv* **:** dearly, a lot <pagué caro : I paid a high price>
caro[2], **-ra** *adj* **1 :** expensive, dear **2** QUERIDO **:** dear, beloved
carpa *nf* **1 :** carp **2 :** big top (of a circus) **3 :** tent
carpelo *nm* **:** carpel
carpeta *nf* **:** folder, binder, portfolio (of drawings, etc.)
carpetazo *nm* **dar carpetazo a :** to shelve, to defer
carpintería *nf* **1 :** carpentry **2 :** carpenter's workshop
carpintero, -ra *n* **:** carpenter
carraspear *vi* **:** to clear one's throat
carraspera *nf* **:** hoarseness <tener carraspera : to have a frog in one's throat>
carrera *nf* **1 :** run, running <a la carrera : at full speed> <de carrera : hastily> **2 :** race **3 :** course of study **4 :** career, profession **5 :** run (in baseball)
carreta *nf* **:** cart, wagon
carrete *nm* **1** BOBINA **:** reel, spool **2 :** roll of film
carretel *nm* → **carrete**
carretera *nf* **:** highway, road <carretera de peaje : turnpike>
carretero, -ra *adj* **:** highway <el sistema carretero nacional : the national highway system>
carretilla *nf* **1 :** wheelbarrow **2 carretilla elevadora :** forklift
carril *nm* **1 :** lane <carretera de doble carril : two-lane highway> **2 :** rail (on a railroad track)
carrillo *nm* **:** cheek, jowl
carrito *nm* **:** cart <carrito de compras : shopping cart>
carrizo *nm* JUNCO **:** reed
carro *nm* **1** COCHE **:** car **2 :** cart **3** *Chile, Mex* **:** coach (of a train) **4 carro alegórico :** float (in a parade)
carrocería *nf* **:** bodywork
carroña *nf* **:** carrion
carroñero, -ra *n* **:** scavenger (animal)
carroza *nf* **1 :** carriage **2 :** float (in a parade)
carruaje *nm* **:** carriage
carrusel *nm* **1 :** merry-go-round **2 :** carousel <carrusel de equipaje : luggage carousel>
carta *nf* **1 :** letter **2** NAIPE **:** playing card **3 :** charter, constitution **4** MENÚ **:** menu **5 :** map, chart **6 tomar cartas en :** to intervene in
cártamo *nm* **:** safflower
cartearse *vr* ESCRIBIRSE **:** to write to one another, to correspond
cartel *nm* **:** sign, poster
cártel *or* **cartel** *nm* **:** cartel
cartelera *nf* **1 :** billboard **2 :** marquee
cartera *nf* **1** BILLETERA **:** wallet, billfold **2** BOLSO **:** pocketbook, purse **3 :** portfolio <cartera de acciones : stock portfolio>
carterista *nmf* **:** pickpocket
cartero, -ra *n* **:** letter carrier, mailman *m*

cartilaginoso, -sa *adj* : cartilaginous, gristly
cartílago *nm* : cartilage
cartilla *nf* **1** : primer, reader **2** : booklet <cartilla de ahorros : bankbook>
cartografía *nf* : cartography
cartógrafo, -fa *n* : cartographer
cartón *nm, pl* **cartones 1** : cardboard <cartón madera : fiberboard> **2** : carton
cartucho *nm* : cartridge
cartulina *nf* : poster board, cardboard
carúncula *nf* : wattle (of a bird)
casa *nf* **1** : house, building **2** HOGAR : home **3** : household, family **4** : company, firm **5 echar la casa por la ventana** : to spare no expense
casaca *nf* : jacket
casado¹, -da *adj* : married
casado², -da *n* : married person
casamentero, -ra *n* : matchmaker
casamiento *nm* **1** : marriage **2** BODA : wedding
casar *vt* : to marry — *vi* : to go together, to match up — **casarse** *vr* **1** : to get married **2 ~ con** : to marry
casateniente *nmf Mex* : landlord, landlady *f*
cascabel¹ *nm* : small bell
cascabel² *nf* : rattlesnake
cascada *nf* CATARATA, SALTO : waterfall, cascade
cascajo *nm* **1** : pebble, rock fragment **2** *fam* : piece of junk
cascanueces *nms & pl* : nutcracker
cascar {72} *vt* : to crack (a shell) — **cascarse** *vr* : to crack, to chip
cáscara *nf* **1** : skin, peel, rind, husk **2** : shell (of a nut or egg)
cascarón *nm, pl* **-rones 1** : eggshell **2** *Mex* : shell filled with confetti
cascarrabias *nmfs & pl fam* : grouch, crab
casco *nm* **1** : helmet **2** : hull **3** : hoof **4** : fragment, shard **5** : center (of a town) **6** *Mex* : empty bottle **7 cascos** *nmpl* : headphones
caserío *nm* **1** : country house **2** : hamlet
casero¹, -ra *adj* **1** : domestic, household **2** : homemade
casero², -ra *n* DUEÑO : landlord *m,* landlady *f*
caseta *nf* : booth, stand, stall <caseta telefónica : telephone booth>
casete *nmf* → **cassette**
casi *adv* **1** : almost, nearly, virtually **2** (*in negative phrases*) : hardly <casi nunca : hardly ever>
casilla *nf* **1** : booth **2** : pigeonhole **3** : box (on a form)
casino *nm* **1** : casino **2** : (social) club
caso *nm* **1** : case **2 en caso de** : in case of, in the event of **3 hacer caso de** : to pay attention to, to notice **4 hacer caso omiso de** : to ignore, to take no notice of **5 no venir al caso** : to be beside the point
caspa *nf* : dandruff
casque, etc. → **cascar**
casquete *nm* **1** : skullcap **2 casquete glaciar** : ice cap **3 casquete corto** *Mex* : crew cut
cassette *nmf* : cassette
casta *nf* **1** : caste **2** : lineage, stock <de casta : thoroughbred, purebred> **3 sacar la casta** *Mex* : to come out ahead
castaña *nf* : chestnut
castañetear *vi* : to chatter (of teeth)
castaño¹, -ña *adj* : chestnut, brown
castaño², -ña *nm* **1** : chestnut tree **2** : chestnut, brown
castañuela *nf* : castanet
castellano¹, -na *adj & n* : Castilian
castellano² *nm* ESPAÑOL : Spanish, Castilian (language)
castidad *nf* : chastity
castigar {52} *vt* : to punish
castigo *nm* : punishment
castillo *nm* **1** : castle **2 castillo de proa** : forecastle
casto, -ta *adj* : chaste, pure — **castamente** *adv*
castor *nm* : beaver
castración *nf, pl* **-ciones** : castration
castrar *vt* **1** : to castrate, to spay, to neuter, to geld **2** DEBILITAR : to weaken, to debilitate
castrense *adj* : military
casual *adj* **1** FORTUITO : fortuitous, accidental **2** *Mex* : casual (of clothing)
casualidad *nf* **1** : chance **2 por ~** *or* **de ~** : by chance, by any chance
casualmente *adv* : accidentally, by chance
casucha *or* **casuca** *nf* : shanty, hovel
cataclismo *nm* : cataclysm
catacumbas *nfpl* : catacombs
catador, -dora *n* : wine taster
catalán¹, -lana *adj & n, mpl* **-lanes** : Catalan
catalán² *nm* : Catalan (language)
catálisis *nm* : catalysis
catalítico, -ca *adj* : catalytic
catalizador *nm* **1** : catalyst **2** : catalytic converter
catalogar {52} *vt* : to catalog, to classify
catálogo *nm* : catalog
catamarán *nm, pl* **-ranes** : catamaran
cataplasma *nf* : poultice
catapulta *nf* : catapult
catapultar *vt* : to catapult
catar *vt* **1** : to taste, to sample **2** : to look at, to examine
catarata *nf* **1** CASCADA, SALTO : waterfall **2** : cataract
catarro *nm* RESFRIADO : cold, catarrh
catarsis *nf* : catharsis
catártico, -ca *adj* : cathartic
catástrofe *nf* DESASTRE : catastrophe, disaster
catastrófico, -ca *adj* DESASTROSO : catastrophic, disastrous
catcher *nmf* : catcher (in baseball)
catecismo *nm* : catechism

cátedra *nf* **1** : chair, professorship **2** : subject, class **3 libertad de cátedra** : academic freedom
catedral *nf* : cathedral
catedrático, -ca *n* PROFESOR : professor
categoría *nf* **1** CLASE : category **2** RANGO : rank, standing **3 categoría gramatical** : part of speech **4 de ~** : first-rate, outstanding
categórico, -ca *adj* : categorical, unequivocal — **categóricamente** *adv*
catéter *nm* : catheter
cátodo *nm* : cathode
catolicismo *nm* : Catholicism
católico, -ca *adj & n* : Catholic
catorce *adj & nm* : fourteen
catorceavo *nm* : fourteenth
catre *nm* : cot
catsup *nm* : ketchup
caucásico, -ca *adj & n* : Caucasian
cauce *nm* **1** LECHO : riverbed **2** : means *pl,* channel
caucho *nm* **1** GOMA : rubber **2** : rubber tree **3** *Ven* : tire
caución *nf, pl* **cauciones** FIANZA : bail, security
caudal *nm* **1** : volume of water **2** RIQUEZA : capital, wealth **3** ABUNDANCIA : abundance
caudillaje *nm* : leadership
caudillo *nm* : leader, commander
causa *nf* **1** MOTIVO : cause, reason, motive <a causa de : because of> **2** IDEAL : cause <morir por una causa : to die for a cause> **3** : lawsuit
causal[1] *adj* : causal
causal[2] *nm* : cause, grounds *pl*
causalidad *nf* : causality
causante[1] *adj* **~ de** : causing, responsible for
causante[2] *nmf Mex* : taxpayer
causar *vt* **1** : to cause **2** : to provoke, to arouse <eso me causa gracia : that strikes me as being funny>
cáustico, -ca *adj* : caustic
cautela *nf* : caution, prudence
cautelar *adj* : precautionary, preventive
cauteloso, -sa *adj* : cautious, prudent — **cautelosamente** *adv*
cauterizar {21} *vt* : to cauterize
cautivador, -dora *adj* : captivating
cautivar *vt* HECHIZAR : to captivate, to charm
cautiverio *nm* : captivity
cautivo, -va *adj & n* : captive
cauto, -ta *adj* : cautious, careful
cavar *vt* : to dig — *vi* **~ en** : to delve into, to probe
caverna *nf* : cavern, cave
cavernoso, -sa *adj* **1** : cavernous **2** : deep, resounding
caviar *nm* : caviar
cavidad *nf* : cavity
cavilar *vi* : to ponder, to deliberate
cayado *nm* : crook, staff, crosier
cayena *nf* : cayenne pepper
cayó, etc. → **caer**
caza[1] *nf* **1** CACERÍA : hunt, hunting **2** : game
caza[2] *nm* : fighter plane
cazador, -dora *n* **1** : hunter **2 cazador furtivo** : poacher
cazar {21} *vt* **1** : to hunt **2** : to catch, to bag **3** *fam* : to land (a job, a spouse) — *vi* : to go hunting
cazatalentos *nmfs & pl* : talent scout
cazo *nm* **1** : saucepan, pot **2** CUCHARÓN : ladle
cazuela *nf* **1** : pan, saucepan **2** : casserole
cazurro, -ra *adj* : sullen, surly
CD *nm* : CD, compact disk
cebada *nf* : barley
cebar *vt* **1** : to bait **2** : to feed, to fatten **3** : to prime (a pump, etc.) — **cebarse** *vr* **~ en** : to take it out on
cebo *nm* **1** CARNADA : bait **2** : feed **3** : primer (for firearms)
cebolla *nf* : onion
cebolleta *nf* : scallion, green onion
cebollino *nm* **1** : chive **2** : scallion
cebra *nf* : zebra
cebú *nm, pl* **cebús** *or* **cebúes** : zebu (cattle)
cecear *vi* : to lisp
ceceo *nm* : lisp
cecina *nf* : dried beef, beef jerky
cedazo *nm* : sieve
ceder *vi* **1** : to yield, to give way **2** : to diminish, to abate **3** : to give in, to relent — *vt* : to cede, to hand over
cedro *nm* : cedar
cédula *nf* : document, certificate
céfiro *nm* : zephyr
cegador, -dora *adj* : blinding
cegar {49} *vt* **1** : to blind **2** : to block, to stop up — *vi* : to be blinded, to go blind
cegatón, -tona *adj, mpl* **-tones** *fam* : blind as a bat
ceguera *nf* : blindness
ceiba *nf* : ceiba, silk-cotton tree
ceja *nf* **1** : eyebrow <fruncir las cejas : to knit one's brows> **2** : flange, rim
cejar *vi* : to give in, to back down
celada *nf* : trap, ambush
celador, -dora *n* GUARDIA : guard, warden
celda *nf* : cell (of a jail)
celebración *nf, pl* **-ciones** : celebration
celebrado, -da *adj* CÉLEBRE, FAMOSO : famous, celebrated
celebrante *nmf* OFICIANTE : celebrant
celebrar *vt* **1** FESTEJAR : to celebrate **2** : to hold (a meeting) **3** : to say (Mass) **4** : to welcome, to be happy about — *vi* : to be glad — **celebrarse** *vr* **1** : to be celebrated, to fall **2** : to be held, to take place
célebre *adj* CELEBRADO, FAMOSO : celebrated, famous
celebridad *nf* **1** : celebrity **2** FAMA : fame, renown
celeridad *nf* : celerity, swiftness
celeste[1] *adj* **1** : celestial **2** : sky blue, azure

celeste[2] *nm* : sky blue
celestial *adj* : heavenly, celestial
celibato *nm* : celibacy
célibe *adj & nmf* : celibate
cello *nm* : cello
celo *nm* **1** : zeal, fervor **2** : heat (of females), rut (of males) **3 celos** *nmpl* : jealousy <tenerle celos a alguien : to be jealous of someone>
celofán *nm, pl* **-fanes** : cellophane
celosía *nf* **1** : lattice window **2** : latticework, trellis
celoso, -sa *adj* **1** : jealous **2** : zealous — **celosamente** *adv*
celta[1] *adj* : Celtic
celta[2] *nmf* : Celt
célula *nf* : cell
celular *adj* : cellular
celuloide *nm* **1** : celluloid **2** : film, cinema
celulosa *nf* : cellulose
cementar *vt* : to cement
cementerio *nm* : cemetery
cemento *nm* : cement
cena *nf* : supper, dinner
cenador *nm* : arbor
cenagal *nm* : bog, quagmire
cenagoso, -sa *adj* : swampy
cenar *vi* : to have dinner, to have supper — *vt* : to have for dinner or supper <anoche cenamos tamales : we had tamales for supper last night>
cencerro *nm* : cowbell
cenicero *nm* : ashtray
ceniciento, -ta *adj* : ashen
cenit *nm* : zenith, peak
ceniza *nf* **1** : ash **2 cenizas** *nfpl* : ashes (of a deceased person)
cenizo, -za *n* : jinx
cenote *nm Mex* : natural deposit of spring water
censar *vt* : to take a census of
censo *nm* : census
censor, -sora *n* : censor, critic
censura *nf* **1** : censorship **2** : censure, criticism
censurable *adj* : reprehensible, blameworthy
censurar *vt* **1** : to censor **2** : to censure, to criticize
centauro *nm* : centaur
centavo *nm* **1** : cent (in English-speaking countries) **2** : unit of currency in various Latin-American countries
centella *nf* **1** : lightning flash **2** : spark
centellear *vi* **1** : to twinkle **2** : to gleam, to sparkle
centelleo *nm* : twinkling, sparkle
centenar *nm* **1** : hundred **2 a centenares** : by the hundreds
centenario[1], **-ria** *adj & n* : centenarian
centenario[2] *nm* : centennial
centeno *nm* : rye
centésimo[1], **-ma** *adj* : hundredth
centésimo[2] *nm* : hundredth
centígrado *adj* : centigrade, Celsius
centigramo *nm* : centigram
centímetro *nm* : centimeter
centinela *nmf* : sentinel, sentry
central[1] *adj* **1** : central **2** PRINCIPAL : main, principal
central[2] *nf* **1** : main office, headquarters **2 central camionera** *Mex* : bus terminal
centralita *nf* : switchboard
centralizar {21} *vt* : to centralize — **centralización** *nf*
centrar *vt* **1** : to center **2** : to focus — **centrarse** *vr* **~ en** : to focus on, to concentrate on
céntrico, -ca *adj* : central
centrífugo, -ga *adj* : centrifugal
centrípeto, -ta *adj* : centripetal
centro[1] *nmf* : center (in sports)
centro[2] *nm* **1** MEDIO : center <centro de atención : center of attention> <centro de gravedad : center of gravity> **2** : downtown **3 centro de mesa** : centerpiece
centroamericano, -na *adj & n* : Central American
ceñido, -da *adj* AJUSTADO : tight, tight-fitting
ceñir {67} *vt* **1** : to encircle, to surround **2** : to hug, to cling to <me ciñe demasiado : it's too tight on me> — **ceñirse** *vr* **~ a** : to restrict oneself to, to stick to
ceño *nm* **1** : frown, scowl **2 fruncir el ceño** : to frown, to knit one's brows
cepa *nf* **1** : stump (of a tree) **2** : stock (of a vine) **3** LINAJE : ancestry, stock
cepillar *vt* **1** : to brush **2** : to plane (wood) — **cepillarse** *vr*
cepillo *nm* **1** : brush <cepillo de dientes : toothbrush> **2** : plane (for woodworking)
cepo *nm* : trap (for animals)
cera *nf* **1** : wax <cera de abejas : beeswax> **2** : polish
cerámica *nf* **1** : ceramics *pl* **2** : pottery
cerámico, -ca *adj* : ceramic
ceramista *nmf* ALFARERO : potter
cerca[1] *adv* **1** : close, near, nearby **2 ~ de** : nearly, almost
cerca[2] *nf* **1** : fence **2** : (stone) wall
cercado *nm* : enclosure
cercanía *nf* **1** PROXIMIDAD : proximity, closeness **2 cercanías** *nfpl* : outskirts, suburbs
cercano, -na *adj* : near, close
cercar {72} *vt* **1** : to fence in, to enclose **2** : to surround
cercenar *vt* **1** : to cut off, to amputate **2** : to diminish, to curtail
cerceta *nf* : teal (duck)
cerciorarse *vr* ASEGURARSE **~ de** : to make sure of, to verify
cerco *nm* **1** : siege **2** : cordon, circle **3** : fence
cerda *nf* **1** : bristle **2** : sow
cerdo *nm* **1** : pig, hog **2 carne de cerdo** : pork
cereal *nm* : cereal — **cereal** *adj*
cerebelo *nm* : cerebellum
cerebral *adj* : cerebral
cerebro *nm* : brain

ceremonia *nf* : ceremony — **ceremonial** *adj*
ceremonioso, -sa *adj* : ceremonious
cereza *nf* : cherry
cerezo *nm* : cherry tree
cerilla *nf* **1** : match **2** : earwax
cerillo *nm* (*in various countries*) : match
cerner {56} *vt* : to sift — **cernerse** *vr* **1** : to hover **2 ~ sobre** : to loom over, to threaten
cernidor *nm* : sieve
cernir → **cerner**
cero *nm* : zero
ceroso, -sa *adj* : waxy
cerque, etc. → **cercar**
cerquita *adv fam* : very close, very near
cerrado, -da *adj* **1** : closed, shut **2** : thick, broad <tiene un acento cerrado : she has a thick accent> **3** : cloudy, overcast **4** : quiet, reserved **5** : dense, stupid
cerradura *nf* : lock
cerrajería *nf* : locksmith's shop
cerrajero, -ra *n* : locksmith
cerrar {55} *vt* **1** : to close, to shut **2** : to turn off **3** : to bring to an end — *vi* **1** : to close up, to lock up **2** : to close down — **cerrarse** *vr* **1** : to close **2** : to fasten, to button up **3** : to conclude, to end
cerrazón *nf, pl* **-zones** : obstinacy, stubbornness
cerro *nm* COLINA, LOMA : hill
cerrojo *nm* PESTILLO : bolt, latch
certamen *nm, pl* **-támenes** : competition, contest
certero, -ra *adj* : accurate, precise — **certeramente** *adv*
certeza *nf* : certainty
certidumbre *nf* : certainty
certificable *adj* : certifiable
certificación *nf, pl* **-ciones** : certification
certificado[1], -da *adj* **1** : certified **2** : registered (of mail)
certificado[2] *nm* **1** : certificate **2** : registered letter
certificar {72} *vt* **1** : to certify **2** : to register (mail)
cervato *nm* : fawn
cervecería *nf* **1** : brewery **2** : beer hall, bar
cerveza *nf* : beer <cerveza de barril : draft beer>
cervical *adj* : cervical
cerviz *nf, pl* **cervices** : nape of the neck, cervix
cesación *nf, pl* **-ciones** : cessation, suspension
cesante *adj* : laid off, unemployed
cesantía *nf* : unemployment
cesar *vi* : to cease, to stop — *vt* : to dismiss, to lay off
cesárea *nf* : cesarean, C-section
cese *nm* **1** : cessation, stop <cese del fuego : cease-fire> **2** : dismissal
cesio *nm* : cesium
cesión *nf, pl* **cesiones** : transfer, assignment <cesión de bienes : transfer of property>
césped *nm* : lawn, grass
cesta *nf* **1** : basket **2** : jai alai racket
cesto *nm* **1** : hamper **2** : basket (in basketball) **3 cesto de (la) basura** : wastebasket
cetrería *nf* : falconry
cetrino, -na *adj* : sallow
cetro *nm* : scepter
chabacano[1], -na *adj* : tacky, tasteless
chabacano[2] *nm Mex* : apricot
chacal *nm* : jackal
cháchara *nf fam* **1** : small talk, chatter **2 cháchara**s *nfpl* : trinkets, junk
chacharear *vi fam* : to chatter, to gab
chacra *nf Arg, Chile, Peru* : small farm
chadiano, -na *adj & n* : Chadian
chal *nm* MANTÓN : shawl
chalado[1], -da *adj fam* : crazy, nuts
chalado[2], -da *n* : nut, crazy person
chalán *nm, pl* **chalanes** *Mex* : barge
chalé *nm* → **chalet**
chaleco *nm* : vest
chalet *nm Spain* : house
chalupa *nf* **1** : small boat **2** *Mex* : small stuffed tortilla
chamaco, -ca *n Mex fam* : kid, boy *m*, girl *f*
chamarra *nf* **1** : sheepskin jacket **2** : poncho, blanket
chamba *nf Mex, Peru fam* : job, work
chambear *vi Mex, Peru fam* : to work
chamo -ma *n Ven fam* **1** : kid, boy *m*, girl *f* **2** : buddy, pal
champaña *or* **champán** *nm* : champagne
champiñón *nm, pl* **-ñones** : mushroom
champú *nm, pl* **-pus** *or* **-púes** : shampoo
champurrado *nm Mex* : hot chocolate thickened with cornstarch
chamuco *nm Mex fam* : devil
chamuscar {72} *vt* : to singe, to scorch — **chamuscarse** *vr*
chamusquina *nf* : scorch
chance *nm* OPORTUNIDAD : chance, opportunity
chancho[1], -cha *adj fam* : dirty, filthy, gross
chancho[2], -cha *n* **1** : pig, hog **2** *fam* : slob
chanchullero, -ra *adj fam* : shady, crooked
chanchullo *nm fam* : shady deal, scam
chancla *nf* **1** : thong sandal, slipper **2** : old shoe
chancleta *nf* → **chancla**
chanclo *nm* **1** : clog **2 chanclos** *nmpl* : overshoes, galoshes, rubbers
chancro *nm* : chancre
changarro *nm Mex* : small shop, stall
chango, -ga *n Mex* : monkey
chantaje *nm* : blackmail
chantajear *vt* : to blackmail
chantajista *nmf* : blackmailer
chanza *nf* **1** : joke, jest **2** *Mex fam* : chance, opportunity

chapa *nf* **1** : sheet, panel, veneer **2** : lock **3** : badge
chapado, -da *adj* **1** : plated **2 chapado a la antigua** : old-fashioned
chapar *vt* **1** : to veneer **2** : to plate (metals)
chaparrón *nm, pl* **-rrones 1** : downpour **2** : great quantity, torrent
chapeado, -da *adj Col, Mex* : flushed
chapopote *nm Mex* : tar, blacktop
chapotear *vi* : to splash about
chapucero¹, -ra *adj* **1** : crude, shoddy **2** *Mex fam* : dishonest
chapucero², -ra *n* **1** : sloppy worker, bungler **2** *Mex fam* : cheat, swindler
chapulín *nm, pl* **-lines** *CA, Mex* : grasshopper, locust
chapuza *nf* **1** : botched job **2** *Mex fam* : fraud, trick <hacer chapuzas : to cheat>
chapuzón *nm, pl* **-zones** : dip, swim <darse un chapuzón : to go for a quick dip>
chaqueta *nf* : jacket
charada *nf* : charades (game)
charango *nm* : traditional Andean stringed instrument
charca *nf* : pond, pool
charco *nm* : puddle, pool
charcutería *nf* : delicatessen
charla *nf* : chat, talk
charlar *vi* : to chat, to talk
charlatán¹, -tana *adj* : talkative, chatty
charlatán², -tana *n, mpl* **-tanes 1** : chatterbox **2** FARSANTE : charlatan, phony
charlatanear *vi* : to chatter away
charol *nm* **1** : lacquer, varnish **2** : patent leather **3** : tray
charola *nf Bol, Mex, Peru* : tray
charreada *nf Mex* : charro show, rodeo
charretera *nf* : epaulet
charro¹, -rra *adj* **1** : gaudy, tacky **2** *Mex* : pertaining to charros
charro², -rra *n Mex* : charro (Mexican cowboy or cowgirl)
chascarrillo *nm fam* : joke, funny story
chasco *nm* **1** BROMA : trick, joke **2** DECEPCIÓN, DESILUSIÓN : disillusionment, disappointment
chasis *or* **chasís** *nm* : chassis
chasquear *vt* **1** : to click (the tongue, fingers, etc.) **2** : to snap (a whip)
chasquido *nm* **1** : click (of the tongue or fingers) **2** : snap, crack
chatarra *nf* : scrap metal
chato, -ta *adj* **1** : pug-nosed **2** : flat
chauvinismo *nm* : chauvinism
chauvinista¹ *adj* : chauvinistic
chauvinista² *nmf* : chauvinist
chaval, -vala *n fam* : kid, boy *m,* girl *f*
chavo¹, -va *adj Mex fam* : young
chavo², -va *n Mex fam* : kid, boy *m,* girl *f*
chavo³ *nm fam* : cent, buck <no tengo un chavo : I'm broke>
chayote *nm* : chayote (plant, fruit)
checar {72} *vt Mex* : to check, to verify
checo¹, -ca *adj & n* : Czech
checo² *nm* : Czech (language)
checoslovaco, -ca *adj & n* : Czechoslovakian
chef *nm* : chef
chelín *nm, pl* **chelines** : shilling
cheque¹, etc. → **checar**
cheque² *nm* **1** : check **2 cheque de viajero** : traveler's check
chequear *vt* **1** : to check, to verify **2** : to check in (baggage)
chequeo *nm* **1** INSPECCIÓN : check, inspection **2** : checkup, examination
chequera *nf* : checkbook
chévere *adj fam* : great, fantastic
chic *adj & nm* : chic
chica → **chico**
chicano, -na *adj & n* : Chicano, Chicana *f*
chicha *nf* : fermented alcoholic beverage made from corn
chícharo *nm* : pea
chicharra *nf* **1** CIGARRA : cicada **2** : buzzer
chicharrón *nm, pl* **-rrones 1** : pork rind **2 darle chicharrón a** *Mex fam* : to get rid of
chichón *nm, pl* **chichones** : bump, swelling
chicle *nm* : chewing gum
chicloso *nm Mex* : taffy
chico¹, -ca *adj* **1** : little, small **2** : young
chico², -ca *n* **1** : child, boy *m,* girl *f* **2** : young man *m,* young woman *f*
chicote *nm* LÁTIGO : whip, lash
chiffon *nm* → **chifón**
chiflado¹, -da *adj fam* : nuts, crazy
chiflado², -da *n fam* : crazy person, lunatic
chiflar *vi* : to whistle — *vt* : to whistle at, to boo — **chiflarse** *vr fam* **~ por** : to be crazy about
chiflido *nm* : whistle, whistling
chiflón *nm, pl* **chiflones** : draft (of air)
chifón *nm, pl* **chifones** : chiffon
chilango¹, -ga *adj Mex fam* : of or from Mexico City
chilango², -ga *n Mex fam* : person from Mexico City
chilaquiles *nmpl Mex* : shredded tortillas in sauce
chile *nm* : chili pepper
chileno, -na *adj & n* : Chilean
chillar *vi* **1** : to squeal, to screech **2** : to scream, to yell **3** : to be gaudy, to clash
chillido *nm* **1** : scream, shout **2** : squeal, screech, cry (of an animal)
chillo *nm PRi* : red snapper
chillón, -llona *adj, mpl* **chillones 1** : piercing, shrill **2** : loud, gaudy
chilpayate *nmf Mex fam* : child, little kid
chimenea *nf* **1** : chimney **2** : fireplace
chimichurri *nm Arg* : traditional hot sauce

chimpancé *nm* : chimpanzee
china *nf* **1** : pebble, small stone **2** *PRi* : orange
chinchar *vt fam* : to annoy, to pester — **chincharse** *vr fam* : to put up with something, to grin and bear it
chinchayote *nm Mex* : chayote root
chinche¹ *nf* **1** : bedbug **2** *Ven* : ladybug **3** : thumbtack
chinche² *nmf fam* : nuisance, pain in the neck
chinchilla *nf* : chinchilla
chino¹, -na *adj* **1** : Chinese **2** *Mex* : curly, kinky
chino², -na *n* : Chinese person
chino³ *nm* : Chinese (language)
chip *nm, pl* **chips** : chip <chip de memoria : memory chip>
chipote *nm Mex fam* : bump (on the head)
chipotle *nm Mex* : type of chili pepper
chipriota *adj & nmf* : Cypriot
chiquear *vt Mex* : to spoil, to indulge
chiquero *nm* POCILGA : pigpen, pigsty
chiquillada *nf* : childish prank
chiquillo¹, -lla *adj* : very young, little
chiquillo², -lla *n* : kid, youngster
chiquito¹, -ta *adj* : tiny
chiquito², -ta *n* : little one, baby
chiribita *nf* **1** : spark **2 chiribitas** *nfpl* : spots before the eyes
chiribitil *nm* **1** DESVÁN : attic, garret **2** : cubbyhole
chirigota *nf fam* : joke
chirimía *nf* : traditional reed pipe
chirimoya *nf* : cherimoya, custard apple
chiripa *nf* **1** : fluke **2 de ~** : by sheer luck
chirivía *nf* : parsnip
chirona *nf fam* : slammer, jail
chirriar {85} *vi* **1** : to squeak, to creak **2** : to screech — **chirriante** *adj*
chirrido *nm* **1** : squeak, squeaking **2** : screech, screeching
chirrión *nm, pl* **chirriones** *Mex* : whip, lash
chisme *nm* **1** : gossip, tale **2** *Spain fam* : gadget, thingamajig
chismear *vi* : to gossip
chismoso¹, -sa *adj* : gossipy, gossiping
chismoso², -sa *n* **1** : gossiper, gossip **2** *Mex fam* : tattletale
chispa¹ *adj* **1** *Mex fam* : lively, vivacious <un perrito chispa : a frisky puppy> **2** *Spain fam* : tipsy
chispa² *nf* **1** : spark **2 echar chispas** : to be furious
chispeante *adj* : sparkling, scintillating
chispear *vi* **1** : to give off sparks **2** : to sparkle
chisporrotear *vi* : to crackle, to sizzle
chiste *nm* **1** : joke, funny story **2 tener chiste** : to be funny **3 tener su chiste** *Mex* : to be tricky
chistoso¹, -sa *adj* **1** : funny, humorous **2** : witty
chistoso², -sa *n* : wit, joker
chivas *nfpl Mex fam* : stuff, odds and ends
chivo¹, -va *n* **1** : kid, young goat **2 chivo expiatorio** : scapegoat
chivo² *nm* **1** : billy goat **2** : fit of anger
chocante *adj* **1** : shocking **2** : unpleasant, rude
chocar {72} *vi* **1** : to crash, to collide **2** : to clash, to conflict **3** : to be shocking <le chocó : he was shocked> **4** *Mex, Ven fam* : to be unpleasant or obnoxious <me choca tu jefe : I can't stand your boss> — *vt* **1** : to shake (hands) **2** : to clink glasses
chochear *vi* **1** : to be senile **2 ~ por** : to dote on, to be soft on
chochín *nm, pl* **-chines** : wren
chocho, -cha *adj* **1** : senile **2** : doting
choclo *nm* **1** : ear of corn, corncob **2** : corn **3 meter el choclo** *Mex fam* : to make a mistake
chocolate *nm* **1** : chocolate **2** : hot chocolate, cocoa
chofer *or* **chófer** *nm* **1** : chauffeur **2** : driver
choke *nm* : choke (of an automobile)
chole *interj Mex fam* **¡ya chole!** : enough!, cut it out!
cholo, -la *adj & n* : mestizo
cholla *nf fam* : head
chollo *nm Spain fam* : bargain
chongo *nm Mex* **1** : bun (chignon) **2 chongos** *nmpl Mex* : dessert made with fried bread
choque¹, etc. → **chocar**
choque² *nm* **1** : crash, collision **2** : clash, conflict **3** : shock
chorizo *nm* : chorizo, sausage
chorrear *vi* **1** : to drip **2** : to pour out, to gush out
chorrito *nm* : squirt, splash
chorro *nm* **1** : flow, stream, jet **2** *Mex fam* : heap, ton
choteado, -da *adj Mex fam* : worn-out, stale <esa canción está bien choteada : that song's been played to death>
chotear *vt* : to make fun of
choteo *nm* : joking around, kidding
chovinismo, chovinista → **chauvinismo, chauvinista**
choza *nf* BARRACA, CABAÑA : hut, shack
chubasco *nm* : downpour, storm
chuchería *nf* : knickknack, trinket
chueco, -ca *adj* **1** : crooked, bent **2** *Chile, Mex fam* : dishonest, shady
chulada *nf Mex, Spain fam* : cute or pretty thing <¡qué chulada de vestido! : what a lovely dress!>
chulear *vt Mex fam* : to compliment
chuleta *nf* : cutlet, chop
chulo¹, -la *adj* **1** *fam* : cute, pretty **2** *Spain fam* : cocky, arrogant
chulo² *nm Spain* : pimp
chupada *nf* **1** : suck, sucking **2** : puff, drag (on a cigarette)
chupado, -da *adj fam* **1** : gaunt, skinny **2** : plastered, drunk
chupaflor *nm* COLIBRÍ : hummingbird
chupamirto *nm Mex* : hummingbird

chupar *vt* **1 :** to suck **2 :** to absorb **3 :** to puff on **4** *fam* **:** to drink, to guzzle — *vi* **:** to suckle — **chuparse** *vr* **1 :** to waste away **2** *fam* **:** to put up with **3 ¡chúpate esa!** *fam* **:** take that!

chupete *nm* **1 :** pacifier **2** *Chile, Peru* **:** lollipop

chupetear *vt* **:** to suck (at)

chupón *nm, pl* **chupones 1 :** sucker (of a plant) **2 :** baby bottle, pacifier

churrasco *nm* **1 :** steak **2 :** barbecued meat

churro *nm* **1 :** fried dough **2** *fam* **:** botch, mess **3** *fam* **:** attractive person, looker

chusco, -ca *adj* **:** funny, amusing

chusma *nf* GENTUZA **:** riffraff, rabble

chutar *vi* **:** to shoot (in soccer)

chute *nm* **:** shot (in soccer)

cianuro *nm* **:** cyanide

cibernética *nf* **:** cybernetics

cicatriz *nf, pl* **-trices :** scar

cicatrizarse {21} *vr* **:** to form a scar, to heal

cíclico, -ca *adj* **:** cyclical

ciclismo *nm* **:** bicycling

ciclista *nmf* **:** bicyclist

ciclo *nm* **:** cycle

ciclomotor *nm* **:** moped

ciclón *nm, pl* **ciclones :** cyclone

cicuta *nf* **:** hemlock

cidra *nf* **:** citron (fruit)

ciega, ciegue, etc. → **cegar**

ciego[1], -ga *adj* **1** INVIDENTE **:** blind **2 a ciegas :** blindly **3 quedarse ciego :** to go blind — **ciegamente** *adv*

ciego[2], -ga *n* INVIDENTE **:** blind person

cielo *nm* **1 :** sky **2 :** heaven **3 :** ceiling

ciempiés *nms & pl* **:** centipede

cien[1] *adj* **1 :** a hundred, hundred <las primeras cien páginas : the first hundred pages> **2 cien por cien** *or* **cien por ciento :** a hundred percent, through and through, wholeheartedly

cien[2] *nm* **:** one hundred

ciénaga *nf* **:** swamp, bog

ciencia *nf* **1 :** science **2 :** learning, knowledge **3 a ciencia cierta :** for a fact, for certain

cieno *nm* **:** mire, mud, silt

científico[1], -ca *adj* **:** scientific — **científicamente** *adv*

científico[2], -ca *n* **:** scientist

ciento[1] *adj* (*used in compound numbers*) **:** one hundred <ciento uno : one hundred and one>

ciento[2] *nm* **1 :** hundred, group of a hundred **2 por ~ :** percent

cierne, etc. → **cerner**

cierra, etc. → **cerrar**

cierre *nm* **1 :** closing, closure **2 :** fastener, clasp, zipper

cierto, -ta *adj* **1 :** true, certain, definite <lo cierto es que... : the fact is that...> **2 :** certain, one <cierto día de verano : one summer day> <bajo ciertas circunstancias : under certain circumstances> **3 por ~ :** in fact, as a matter of fact — **ciertamente** *adv*

ciervo, -va *n* **:** deer, stag *m,* hind *f*

cifra *nf* **1 :** figure, number **2 :** quantity, amount **3** CLAVE **:** code, cipher

cifrar *vt* **1 :** to write in code **2 :** to place, to pin <cifró su esperanza en la lotería : he pinned his hopes on the lottery> — **cifrarse** *vr* **:** to amount <la multa se cifra en millares : the fine amounts to thousands>

cigarra *nf* CHICHARRA **:** cicada

cigarrera *nf* **:** cigarette case

cigarrillo *nm* **:** cigarrette

cigarro *nm* **1 :** cigarette **2** PURO **:** cigar

cigoto *nm* **:** zygote

cigüeña *nf* **:** stork

cilantro *nm* **:** cilantro, coriander

cilíndrico, -ca *adj* **:** cylindrical

cilindro *nm* **:** cylinder

cima *nf* CUMBRE **:** peak, summit, top

cimarrón, -rrona *adj, mpl* **-rrones :** untamed, wild

címbalo *nm* **:** cymbal

cimbel *nm* **:** decoy

cimbrar *vt* **:** to shake, to rock — **cimbrarse** *vr* **:** to sway, to swing

cimentar {55} *vt* **1 :** to lay the foundation of, to establish **2 :** to strengthen, to cement

cimientos *nmpl* **:** base, foundation(s)

cinc *nm* **:** zinc

cincel *nm* **:** chisel

cincelar *vt* **1 :** to chisel **2 :** to engrave

cincha *nf* **:** cinch, girth

cinchar *vt* **:** to cinch (a horse)

cinco *adj & nm* **:** five

cincuenta *adj & nm* **:** fifty

cincuentavo[1], -va *adj* **:** fiftieth

cincuentavo[2] *nm* **:** fiftieth (fraction)

cine *nm* **1 :** cinema, movies *pl* **2 :** movie theater

cineasta *nmf* **:** filmmaker

cinematográfico, -ca *adj* **:** movie, film, cinematic <la industria cinematográfica : the film industry>

cingalés[1], -lesa *adj & n* **:** Sinhalese

cingalés[2] *nm* **:** Sinhalese (language)

cínico[1], -ca *adj* **1 :** cynical **2 :** shameless, brazen — **cínicamente** *adv*

cínico[2], -ca *n* **:** cynic

cinismo *nm* **:** cynicism

cinta *nf* **1 :** ribbon **2 :** tape <cinta métrica : tape measure> **3 :** strap, belt <cinta transportadora : conveyor belt>

cinto *nm* **:** strap, belt

cintura *nf* **1 :** waist, waistline **2 meter en cintura** *fam* **:** to bring into line, to discipline

cinturón *nm, pl* **-rones 1 :** belt **2 cinturón de seguridad :** seat belt

ciñe, etc. → **ceñir**

ciprés *nm, pl* **cipreses :** cypress

circo *nm* **:** circus

circón *nm, pl* **circones :** zircon

circonio *nm* **:** zirconium

circuitería *nf* **:** circuitry

circuito *nm* **:** circuit

circulación *nf, pl* **-ciones 1 :** circulation **2 :** movement **3 :** traffic

circular[1] *vi* **1 :** to circulate **2 :** to move along **3 :** to drive

circular[2] *adj* **:** circular

circular[3] *nf* **:** circular, flier

circulatorio, -ria *adj* **:** circulatory

círculo *nm* **1 :** circle **2 :** club, group

circuncidar *vt* **:** to circumcise

circuncisión *nf, pl* **-siones :** circumcision

circundar *vt* **:** to surround — **circundante** *adj*

circunferencia *nf* **:** circumference

circunflejo, -ja *adj* **acento circunflejo :** circumflex

circunlocución *nf, pl* **-ciones :** circumlocution

circunloquio *nm* → **circunlocución**

circunnavegar {52} *vt* **:** to circumnavigate — **circunnavegación** *nf*

circunscribir {33} *vt* **:** to circumscribe, to constrict, to limit — **circunscribirse** *vr*

circunscripción *nf, pl* **-ciones 1 :** limitation, restriction **2 :** constituency

circunscrito *pp* → **circunscribir**

circunspección *nf, pl* **-ciones :** circumspection, prudence

circunspecto, -ta *adj* **:** circumspect, prudent

circunstancia *nf* **:** circumstance

circunstancial *adj* **:** circumstantial, incidental

circunstante *nmf* **1 :** onlooker, bystander **2 los circunstantes :** those present

circunvalación *nf, pl* **-ciones :** surrounding, encircling <carretera de circunvalación : bypass, beltway>

circunvecino, -na *adj* **:** surrounding, neighboring

cirio *nm* **:** large candle

cirro *nm* **:** cirrus (cloud)

cirrosis *nf* **:** cirrhosis

ciruela *nf* **1 :** plum **2 ciruela pasa :** prune

cirugía *nf* **:** surgery

cirujano, -na *n* **:** surgeon

cisma *nm* **:** schism, rift

cisne *nm* **:** swan

cisterna *nf* **:** cistern, tank

cita *nf* **1 :** quote, quotation **2 :** appointment, date

citable *adj* **:** quotable

citación *nf, pl* **-ciones** EMPLAZAMIENTO **:** summons, subpoena

citadino[1], **-na** *adj* **:** of the city, urban

citadino[2], **-na** *n* **:** city dweller

citado, -da *adj* **:** said, aforementioned

citar *vt* **1 :** to quote, to cite **2 :** to make an appointment with **3 :** to summon (to court), to subpoena — **citarse** *vr* **~ con :** to arrange to meet (someone)

cítara *nf* **:** zither

citatorio *nm* **:** subpoena

citoplasma *nm* **:** cytoplasm

cítrico[1], **-ca** *adj* **:** citric

cítrico[2] *nm* **:** citrus fruit

ciudad *nf* **1 :** city, town **2 ciudad universitaria :** college or university campus **3 ciudad perdida** *Mex* **:** shantytown

ciudadanía *nf* **1 :** citizenship **2 :** citizenry, citizens *pl*

ciudadano[1], **-na** *adj* **:** civic, city

ciudadano[2], **-na** *n* **1** NACIONAL **:** citizen **2** HABITANTE **:** resident, city dweller

ciudadela *nf* **:** citadel, fortress

cívico, -ca *adj* **1 :** civic **2 :** public-spirited

civil[1] *adj* **1 :** civil **2 :** civilian

civil[2] *nmf* **:** civilian

civilidad *nf* **:** civility, courtesy

civilización *nf, pl* **-ciones :** civilization

civilizar {21} *vt* **:** to civilize

civismo *nm* **:** community spirit, civic-mindedness, civics

cizaña *nf* **:** discord, rift

clamar *vi* **:** to clamor, to raise a protest — *vt* **:** to cry out for

clamor *nm* **:** clamor, outcry

clamoroso, -sa *adj* **:** clamorous, resounding, thunderous

clan *nm* **:** clan

clandestinidad *nf* **:** secrecy <en la clandestinidad : underground>

clandestino, -na *adj* **:** clandestine, secret

clara *nf* **:** egg white

claraboya *nf* **:** skylight

claramente *adv* **:** clearly

clarear *v impers* **1 :** to clear, to clear up **2 :** to get light, to dawn — *vi* **:** to go gray, to turn white

claridad *nf* **1** NITIDEZ **:** clarity, clearness **2 :** brightness, light

clarificación *nf, pl* **-ciones** ACLARACIÓN **:** clarification, explanation

clarificar {72} *vt* ACLARAR **:** to clarify, to explain

clarín *nm, pl* **clarines :** bugle

clarinete *nm* **:** clarinet

clarividencia *nf* **1 :** clairvoyance **2 :** perspicacity, discernment

clarividente[1] *adj* **1 :** clairvoyant **2 :** perspicacious, discerning

clarividente[2] *nmf* **:** clairvoyant

claro[1] *adv* **1 :** clearly <habla más claro : speak more clearly> **2 :** of course, surely <¡claro!, ¡claro que sí! : absolutely!, of course!> <claro que entendió : of course she understood>

claro[2], **-ra** *adj* **1 :** bright, clear **2 :** pale, fair, light **3 :** clear, evident

claro[3] *nm* **1 :** clearing **2 claro de luna :** moonlight

clase *nf* **1 :** class **2** ÍNDOLE, TIPO **:** sort, kind, type

clasicismo *nm* **:** classicism

clásico[1], **-ca** *adj* **1 :** classic **2 :** classical

clásico[2] *nm* **:** classic

clasificación *nf, pl* **-ciones 1 :** classification, sorting out **2 :** rating **3** CALIFICACIÓN **:** qualification (in competitions)

clasificado, -da *adj* **:** classified <aviso clasificado : classified ad>

clasificar {72} *vt* **1 :** to classify, to sort out **2 :** to rate, to rank — *vi* CALIFICAR

: to qualify (in competitions) — **clasificarse** *vr*

claudicación *nf, pl* **-ciones** : surrender, abandonment of one's principles

claudicar {72} *vi* : to back down, to abandon one's principles

claustro *nm* : cloister

claustrofobia *nf* : claustrophobia

claustrofóbico, -ca *adj* : claustrophobic

cláusula *nf* : clause

clausura *nf* **1** : closure, closing **2** : closing ceremony **3** : cloister

clausurar *vt* **1** : to close, to bring to a close **2** : to close down

clavadista *nmf* : diver

clavado[1], -da *adj* **1** : nailed, fixed, stuck **2** *fam* : punctual, on the dot **3** *fam* : identical <es clavado a su padre : he's the image of his father>

clavado[2] *nm* : dive

clavar *vt* **1** : to nail, to hammer **2** HINCAR : to plunge, to stick **3** : to fix (one's eyes) on — **clavarse** *vr* : to stick oneself (with a sharp object)

clave[1] *adj* : key, essential

clave[2] *nf* **1** CIFRA : code **2** : key <la clave del misterio : the key to the mystery> **3** : clef **4** : keystone

clavel *nm* : carnation

clavelito *nm* : pink (flower)

clavicémbalo *nm* : harpsichord

clavícula *nf* : collarbone

clavija *nf* **1** : plug **2** : peg, pin

clavo *nm* **1** : nail <clavo grande : spike> **2** : clove **3 dar en el clavo** : to hit the nail on the head

claxon *nm, pl* **cláxones** : horn (of an automobile)

clemencia *nf* : clemency, mercy

clemente *adj* : merciful

cleptomanía *nf* : kleptomania

cleptómano, -na *n* : kleptomaniac

clerecía *nf* : ministry, ministers *pl*

clerical *adj* : clerical

clérigo, -ga *n* : cleric, member of the clergy

clero *nm* : clergy

cliché *nm* **1** : cliché **2** : stencil **3** : negative (of a photograph)

cliente, -ta *n* : customer, client

clientela *nf* : clientele, customers *pl*

clima *nm* **1** : climate **2** AMBIENTE : atmosphere, ambience

climático, -ca *adj* : climatic

climatización *nf, pl* **-ciones** : air-conditioning

climatizar {21} *vt* : to air-condition — **climatizado, -da** *adj*

clímax *nm* : climax

clínica *nf* : clinic

clínico, -ca *adj* : clinical — **clínicamente** *adv*

clip *nm* **1** : clip **2** : paper clip

clítoris *nms & pl* : clitoris

cloaca *nf* ALCANTARILLA : sewer

clocar {82} *vi* : to cluck

cloche *nm CA, Car, Col, Ven* : clutch (of an automobile)

clon *nm* : clone

cloqué, etc. → **clocar**

cloquear *vi* : to cluck

clorar *vt* : to chlorinate — **cloración** *nf*

cloro *nm* : chlorine

clorofila *nf* : chlorophyll

cloroformo *nm* : chloroform

cloruro *nm* : chloride

clóset *nm, pl* **clósets 1** : closet **2** : cupboard

club *nm* : club

clueca, clueque, etc. → **clocar**

coa *nf Mex* : hoe

coacción *nf, pl* **-ciones** : coercion, duress

coaccionar *vt* : to coerce

coactivo, -va *adj* : coercive

coagular *v* : to clot, to coagulate — **coagulación** *nf*

coágulo *nm* : clot

coalición *nf, pl* **-ciones** : coalition

coartada *nf* : alibi

coartar *vt* : to restrict, to limit

cobalto *nm* : cobalt

cobarde[1] *adj* : cowardly

cobarde[2] *nmf* : coward

cobardía *nf* : cowardice

cobaya *nf* : guinea pig

cobertizo *nm* : shed, shelter

cobertor *nm* COLCHA : bedspread, quilt

cobertura *nf* **1** : coverage **2** : cover, collateral

cobija *nf* FRAZADA, MANTA : blanket

cobijar *vt* : to shelter — **cobijarse** *vr* : to take shelter

cobra *nf* : cobra

cobrador, -dora *n* **1** : collector **2** : conductor (of a bus or train)

cobrar *vt* **1** : to charge **2** : to collect, to draw, to earn **3** : to acquire, to gain **4** : to recover, to retrieve **5** : to cash (a check) **6** : to claim, to take (a life) **7** : to shoot (game), to bag — *vi* **1** : to be paid **2 llamar por cobrar** *Mex* : to call collect

cobre *nm* : copper

cobro *nm* : collection (of money), cashing (of a check)

coca *nf* **1** : coca **2** *fam* : coke, cocaine

cocaína *nf* : cocaine

cocal *nm* : coca plantation

cocción *nf, pl* **cocciones** : cooking

cocear *vi* : to kick (of an animal)

cocer {14} *vt* **1** COCINAR : to cook **2** HERVIR : to boil

cochambre *nmf fam* : filth, grime

cochambroso, -sa *adj* : filthy, grimy

coche *nm* **1** : car, automobile **2** : coach, carriage **3 coche cama** : sleeping car **4 coche fúnebre** : hearse

cochecito *nm* : baby carriage, stroller

cochera *nf* : garage, carport

cochinada *nf fam* **1** : filthy language **2** : disgusting behavior **3** : dirty trick

cochinillo *nm* : suckling pig, piglet

cochino[1], -na *adj* **1** : dirty, filthy, disgusting **2** *fam* : rotten, lousy

cochino[2], -na *n* : pig, hog

cocido[1], **-da** *adj* **1 :** boiled, cooked **2 bien cocido :** well-done

cocido[2] *nm* ESTOFADO, GUISADO **:** stew

cociente *nm* **:** quotient

cocimiento *nm* **:** cooking, baking

cocina *nf* **1 :** kitchen **2 :** stove **3 :** cuisine, cooking

cocinar *v* **:** to cook

cocinero, -ra *n* **:** cook, chef

cocineta *nf Mex* **:** kitchenette

coco *nm* **1 :** coconut **2** *fam* **:** head **3** *fam* **:** bogeyman

cocoa *nf* **:** cocoa, hot chocolate

cocodrilo *nm* **:** crocodile

cocotero *nm* **:** coconut palm

coctel *or* **cóctel** *nm* **1 :** cocktail **2 :** cocktail party

coctelera *nf* **:** cocktail shaker

codazo *nm* **1 darle un codazo a :** to elbow, to nudge **2 abrirse paso a codazos :** to elbow one's way through

codearse *vr* **:** to rub elbows, to hobnob

códice *nm* **:** codex, manuscript

codicia *nf* AVARICIA **:** avarice, covetousness

codiciar *vt* **:** to covet

codicilo *nm* **:** codicil

codicioso, -sa *adj* **:** avaricious, covetous

codificación *nf, pl* **-ciones 1 :** codification **2 :** coding, encoding

codificar {72} *vt* **1 :** to codify **2 :** to code, to encode

código *nm* **1 :** code **2 código postal :** zip code **3 código morse :** Morse code

codo[1], **-da** *adj Mex* **:** cheap, stingy

codo[2], **-da** *n Mex* **:** tightwad, cheapskate

codo[3] *nm* **:** elbow

codorniz *nf, pl* **-nices :** quail

coeficiente *nm* **1 :** coefficient **2 coeficiente intelectual :** IQ, intelligence quotient

coexistir *vi* **:** to coexist — **coexistencia** *nf*

cofa *nm* **:** crow's nest

cofre *nm* **1** BAÚL **:** trunk, chest **2** *Mex* CAPOTE **:** hood (of a car)

coger {15} *vt* **1 :** to seize, to take hold of **2 :** to catch **3 :** to pick up **4 :** to gather, to pick **5 :** to gore — **cogerse** *vr* AGARRARSE **:** to hold on

cogida *nf* **1 :** gathering, harvest **2 :** goring

cognición *nf, pl* **-ciones :** cognition

cognitivo, -va *adj* **:** cognitive

cogollo *nm* **1 :** heart (of a vegetable) **2 :** bud, bulb **3 :** core, crux <el cogollo de la cuestión : the heart of the matter>

cogote *nm* **:** scruff, nape

cohabitar *vi* **:** to cohabit — **cohabitación** *nf*

cohechar *vt* SOBORNAR **:** to bribe

cohecho *nm* SOBORNO **:** bribe, bribery

coherencia *nf* **:** coherence — **coherente** *adj*

cohesión *nf, pl* **-siones :** cohesion

cohesivo, -va *adj* **:** cohesive

cohete *nm* **:** rocket

cohibición *nf, pl* **-ciones 1 :** (legal) restraint **2** INHIBICIÓN **:** inhibition

cohibido, -da *adj* **:** inhibited, shy

cohibir {62} *vt* **:** to inhibit, to make self-conscious — **cohibirse** *vr* **:** to feel shy or embarrassed

cohorte *nf* **:** cohort

coima *nf Arg, Chile, Peru* **:** bribe

coimear *vt Arg, Chile, Peru* **:** to bribe

coincidencia *nf* **:** coincidence

coincidir *vi* **1 :** to coincide **2 :** to agree

coito *nm* **:** sexual intercourse, coitus

coja, etc. → **coger**

cojear *vi* **1 :** to limp **2 :** to wobble, to rock **3 cojear del mismo pie :** to be two of a kind

cojera *nf* **:** limp

cojín *nm, pl* **cojines :** cushion, throw pillow

cojinete *nm* **1 :** bearing, bushing **2 cojinete de bola :** ball bearing

cojo[1], **-ja** *adj* **1 :** limping, lame **2 :** wobbly **3 :** weak, ineffectual

cojo[2], **-ja** *n* **:** lame person

cojones *nmpl usu considered vulgar* **1 :** testicles *pl* **2 :** guts *pl,* courage

col *nf* **1** REPOLLO **:** cabbage **2 col de Bruselas :** Brussels sprout **3 col rizada :** kale

cola *nf* **1** RABO **:** tail <cola de caballo : ponytail> **2** FILA **:** line (of people) <hacer cola : to wait in line> **3 :** cola, drink **4 :** train (of a dress) **5 :** tails *pl* (of a tuxedo) **6** PEGAMENTO **:** glue **7** *fam* **:** buttocks *pl,* rear end

colaboracionista *nmf* **:** collaborator, traitor

colaborador, -dora *n* **1 :** contributor (to a periodical) **2 :** collaborator

colaborar *vi* **:** to collaborate — **colaboración** *nf*

colación *nf, pl* **-ciones 1 :** light meal **2 :** comparison, collation <sacar a colación : to bring up, to broach> **3 :** conferral (of a degree)

colador *nm* **1 :** colander, strainer **2** *PRi* **:** small coffeepot

colapso *nm* **1 :** collapse **2 :** standstill

colar {19} *vt* **:** to strain, to filter — **colarse** *vr* **1 :** to sneak in, to cut in line, to gate-crash **2 :** to slip up, to make a mistake

colateral[1] *adj* **:** collateral — **colateralmente** *adv*

colateral[2] *nm* **:** collateral

colcha *nf* COBERTOR **:** bedspread, quilt

colchón *nm, pl* **colchones 1 :** mattress **2 :** cushion, padding, buffer

colchoneta *nf* **:** mat (for gymnastic sports)

colear *vi* **1 :** to wag its tail **2 vivito y coleando** *fam* **:** alive and kicking

colección *nf, pl* **-ciones :** collection

coleccionar *vt* **:** to collect, to keep a collection of

coleccionista *nmf* **:** collector

colecta *nf* **:** collection (of donations)

colectar *vt* : to collect

colectividad *nf* : community, group

colectivo[1], -va *adj* : collective — **colectivamente** *adv*

colectivo[2] *nm* **1** : collective **2** *Arg, Bol, Peru* : city bus

colector[1], -tora *n* : collector <colector de impuestos : tax collector>

colector[2] *nm* **1** : sewer **2** : manifold (of an engine)

colega *nmf* **1** : colleague **2** HOMÓLOGO : counterpart **3** *fam* : buddy

colegiado[1], -da *adj* : collegiate

colegiado[2], -da *n* **1** ÁRBITRO : referee **2** : member (of a professional association)

colegial[1], -giala *adj* **1** : school, collegiate **2** *Mex fam* : green, inexperienced

colegial[2], -giala *n* : schoolboy *m*, schoolgirl *f*

colegiatura *nf Mex* : tuition

colegio *nm* **1** : school **2** : college <colegio electoral : electoral college> **3** : professional association

colegir {28} *vt* **1** JUNTAR : to collect, to gather **2** INFERIR : to infer, to deduce

cólera[1] *nm* : cholera

cólera[2] *nf* FURIA, IRA : anger, rage

colérico, -ca *adj* **1** FURIOSO : angry **2** IRRITABLE : irritable

colesterol *nm* : cholesterol

coleta *nf* **1** : ponytail **2** : pigtail

coletazo *nm* : lash, flick (of a tail)

colgado, -da *adj* **1** : hanging, hanged **2** : pending **3 dejar colgado a** : to disappoint, to let down

colgante[1] *adj* : hanging, dangling

colgante[2] *nm* : pendant, charm (on a bracelet)

colgar {16} *vt* **1** : to hang (up), to put up **2** AHORCAR : to hang (someone) **3** : to hang up (a telephone) **4** *fam* : to fail (an exam) — **colgarse** *vr* **1** : to hang, to be suspended **2** AHORCARSE : to hang oneself **3** : to hang up a telephone

colibrí *nm* CHUPAFLOR : hummingbird

cólico *nm* : colic

coliflor *nf* : cauliflower

colilla *nf* : butt (of a cigarette)

colina *nf* CERRO, LOMA : hill

colindante *adj* CONTIGUO : adjacent, neighboring

colindar *vi* : to adjoin, to be adjacent

coliseo *nm* : coliseum

colisión *nf, pl* **-siones** : collision

colisionar *vi* : to collide

collage *nm* : collage

collar *nm* **1** : collar (for an animal) **2** : necklace <collar de perlas : string of pearls>

colmado, -da *adj* : heaping

colmar *vt* **1** : to fill to the brim **2** : to fulfill, to satisfy **3** : to heap, to shower <me colmaron de regalos : they showered me with gifts>

colmena *nf* : beehive

colmenar *nm* APIARIO : apiary

colmillo *nm* **1** CANINO : canine (tooth), fang **2** : tusk

colmilludo, -da *adj Mex, PRi* : astute, shrewd, crafty

colmo *nm* : height, extreme, limit <el colmo de la locura : the height of folly> <¡eso es el colmo! : that's the last straw!>

colocación *nf, pl* **-ciones** **1** : placement, placing **2** : position, job **3** : investment

colocar {72} *vt* **1** PONER : to place, to put **2** : to find a job for **3** : to invest — **colocarse** *vr* **1** SITUARSE : to position oneself **2** : to get a job

colofón *nm, pl* **-fones** **1** : ending, finale **2** : colophon

colofonia *nf* : rosin

colombiano, -na *adj & n* : Colombian

colon *nm* : (intestinal) colon

colón *nm, pl* **colones** : Costa Rican and Salvadoran unit of currency

colonia *nf* **1** : colony **2** : cologne **3** *Mex* : residential area, neighborhood

colonial *adj* : colonial

colonización *nf, pl* **-ciones** : colonization

colonizador[1], -dora *adj* : colonizing

colonizador[2], -dora *n* : colonizer, colonist

colonizar {21} *vt* : to colonize, to settle

colono, -na *n* **1** : settler, colonist **2** : tenant farmer

coloquial *adj* : colloquial

coloquio *nm* **1** : discussion, talk **2** : conference, symposium

color *nm* **1** : color **2** : paint, dye **3 colores** *nmpl* : colored pencils

coloración *nf, pl* **-ciones** : coloring, coloration

colorado[1], -da *adj* **1** ROJO : red **2 ponerse colorado** : to blush **3 chiste colorado** *Mex* : off-color joke

colorado[2] *nm* ROJO : red

colorante *nm* : coloring <colorante de alimentos : food coloring>

colorear *vt* : to color — *vi* **1** : to redden **2** : to ripen

colorete *nm* : rouge, blusher

colorido *nm* : color, coloring

colorín *nm, pl* **-rines** **1** : bright color **2** : goldfinch

colosal *adj* : colossal

coloso *nm* : colossus

coludir *vi* : to be in collusion, to conspire

columna *nf* **1** : column **2 columna vertebral** : spine, backbone

columnata *nf* : colonnade

columnista *nmf* : columnist

columpiar *vt* : to push (on a swing) — **columpiarse** *vr* : to swing

columpio *nm* : swing

colusión *nf, pl* **-siones** : collusion

colza *nf* : rape (plant)

coma[1] *nm* : coma

coma[2] *nf* : comma

comadre *nf* **1** : godmother of one's child **2** : mother of one's godchild **3**

fam : neighbor, female friend **4** *fam* : gossip
comadrear *vi fam* : to gossip
comadreja *nf* : weasel
comadrona *nf* : midwife
comanche *nmf* : Comanche
comandancia *nf* **1** : command headquarters **2** : command
comandante *nmf* **1** : commander, commanding officer **2** : major
comandar *vt* : to command, to lead
comando *nm* **1** : commando **2** : command (for computers)
comarca *nf* REGIÓN : region
comarcal *adj* REGIONAL : regional, local
combar *vt* : to bend, to curve — **combarse** *vr* **1** : to bend, to buckle **2** : to warp, to bulge, to sag
combate *nm* **1** : combat **2** : fight, boxing match
combatiente *nmf* : combatant, fighter
combatir *vt* : to combat, to fight against — *vi* : to fight
combatividad *nf* : fighting spirit
combativo, -va *adj* : combative, spirited
combinación *nf, pl* **-ciones** **1** : combination **2** : connection (in travel)
combinar *vt* **1** UNIR : to combine, to mix together **2** : to match, to put together — **combinarse** *vr* : to get together, to conspire
combo *nm* **1** : (musical) band **2** *Chile, Peru* : sledgehammer **3** *Chile, Peru* : punch
combustible[1] *adj* : combustible
combustible[2] *nm* : fuel
combustión *nf, pl* **-tiones** : combustion
comedero *nm* : trough, feeder
comedia *nf* : comedy
comediante *nmf* : actor, actress *f*
comedido, -da *adj* MESURADO : moderate, restrained
comediógrafo, -fa *n* : playwright
comedor *nm* : dining room
comején *nm, pl* **-jenes** : termite
comelón[1], **-lona** *adj, mpl* **-lones** *fam* : gluttonous
comelón[2] **-lona** *n, pl* **-lones** *fam* : big eater, glutton
comensal *nmf* : dinner guest
comentador, -dora *n* → **comentarista**
comentar *vt* **1** : to comment on, to discuss **2** : to mention, to remark
comentario *nm* **1** : comment, remark <sin comentarios : no comment> **2** : commentary
comentarista *nmf* : commentator
comenzar {29} *v* EMPEZAR : to begin, to start
comer[1] *vt* **1** : to eat **2** : to consume, to eat up, to eat into — *vi* **1** : to eat **2** CENAR : to have a meal **3 dar de comer** : to feed — **comerse** *vr* : to eat up
comer[2] *nm* : eating, dining
comercial *adj & nm* : commercial — **comercialmente** *adv*
comercializar {21} *vt* **1** : to commercialize **2** : to market
comerciante *nmf* : merchant, dealer
comerciar *vi* : to do business, to trade
comercio *nm* **1** : commerce, trade **2** NEGOCIO : business, place of business
comestible *adj* : edible
comestibles *nmpl* VÍVERES : groceries, food
cometa[1] *nm* : comet
cometa[2] *nf* : kite
cometer *vt* **1** : to commit **2 cometer un error** : to make a mistake
cometido *nm* : assignment, task
comezón *nf, pl* **-zones** PICAZÓN : itchiness, itching
comible *adj fam* : eatable, edible
comic *or* **cómic** *nm* : comic strip, comic book
comicastro, -tra *n* : second-rate actor, ham
comicidad *nf* HUMOR : humor, wit
comicios *nmpl* : elections, voting
cómico[1], **-ca** *adj* : comic, comical
cómico[2], **-ca** *n* HUMORISTA : comic, comedian, comedienne *f*
comida *nf* **1** : food **2** : meal **3** : dinner **4 comida basura** : junk food **5 comida rápida** : fast food
comidilla *nf* : talk, gossip
comienzo *nm* **1** : start, beginning **2 al comienzo** : at first **3 dar comienzo** : to begin
comillas *nfpl* : quotation marks <entre comillas : in quotes>
comilón, -lona → **comelón, -lona**
comilona *nf fam* : feast
comino *nm* **1** : cumin **2 me vale un comino** *fam* : not to matter to someone <no me importa un comino : I couldn't care less>
comisaría *nf* : police station
comisario, -ria *n* : commissioner
comisión *nf, pl* **-siones** **1** : commission, committing **2** : committee **3** : percentage, commission <comisión sobre las ventas : sales commission>
comisionado[1], **-da** *adj* : commissioned, entrusted
comisionado[2], **-da** *n* → **comisario**
comisionar *vt* : to commission
comité *nm* : committee
comitiva *nf* : retinue, entourage
como[1] *adv* **1** : around, about <cuesta como 500 pesos : it costs around 500 pesos> **2** : kind of, like <tengo como mareos : I'm kind of dizzy>
como[2] *conj* **1** : how, as <hazlo como dijiste que lo harías : do it the way you said you would> **2** : since, given that <como estaba lloviendo, no salí : since it was raining, I didn't go out> **3** : if <como lo vuelva a hacer lo arrestarán : if he does that again he'll be arrested> **4 como quiera** : in any way

como[3] *prep* **1** : like, as <ligero como una pluma : light as a feather> **2 así como** : as well as

cómo *adv* : how <¿cómo estás? : how are you?> <¿a cómo están las manzanas? : how much are the apples?> <¿cómo? : excuse me?, what was that?> <¿se puede? ¡cómo no! : may I? please do!>

cómoda *nf* : bureau, chest of drawers

comodidad *nf* **1** : comfort **2** : convenience

comodín *nm, pl* **-dines 1** : joker, wild card **2** : all-purpose word or thing **3** : pretext, excuse

cómodo, -da *adj* **1** CONFORTABLE : comfortable **2** : convenient — **cómodamente** *adv*

comodoro *nm* : commodore

comoquiera *adv* **1** : in any way **2 comoquiera que** : in whatever way, however <comoquiera que sea eso : however that may be>

compa *nm fam* : buddy, pal

compactar *vt* : to compact, to compress

compacto, -ta *adj* : compact

compadecer {53} *vt* : to sympathize with, to feel sorry for — **compadecerse** *vr* **1 ~ de** : to take pity on, to commiserate with **2 ~ con** : to fit, to accord (with)

compadre *nm* **1** : godfather of one's child **2** : father of one's godchild **3** *fam* : buddy, pal

compaginar *vt* **1** COORDINAR : to combine, to coordinate **2** : to collate

compañerismo *nm* : comradeship, camaraderie

compañero, -ñera *n* : companion, mate, partner

compañía *nf* **1** : company <llegó en compañía de su madre : he arrived with his mother> **2** EMPRESA, FIRMA : firm, company

comparable *adj* : comparable

comparación *nf, pl* **-ciones** : comparison

comparado, -da *adj* : comparative <literatura comparada : comparative literature>

comparar *vt* : to compare

comparativo[1], **-va** *adj* : comparative, relative — **comparativamente** *adv*

comparativo[2] *nm* : comparative degree or form

comparecencia *nf* **1** : appearance (in court) **2 orden de comparecencia** : subpoena, summons

comparecer {53} *vi* : to appear (in court)

compartimiento *or* **compartimento** *nm* : compartment

compartir *vt* : to share

compás *nm, pl* **-pases 1** : beat, rhythm, time **2** : compass

compasión *nf, pl* **-siones** : compassion, pity

compasivo, -va *adj* : compassionate, sympathetic

compatibilidad *nf* : compatibility

compatible *adj* : compatible

compatriota *nmf* PAISANO : compatriot, fellow countryman

compeler *vt* : to compel

compendiar *vt* : to summarize, to condense

compendio *nm* : summary

compenetración *nf, pl* **-ciones** : rapport, mutual understanding

compenetrarse *vr* **1** : to understand each other **2 ~ con** : to identify oneself with

compensación *nf, pl* **-ciones** : compensation

compensar *vt* : to compensate for, to make up for — *vi* : to be worth one's while

compensatorio, -ria *adj* : compensatory

competencia *nf* **1** : competition, rivalry **2** : competence

competente *adj* : competent, able — **competentemente** *adv*

competición *nf, pl* **-ciones** : competition

competidor[1], **-dora** *adj* RIVAL : competing, rival

competidor[2], **-dora** *n* RIVAL : competitor, rival

competir {54} *vi* : to compete

competitividad *nf* : competitiveness

competitivo, -va *adj* : competitive — **competitivamente** *adv*

compilar *vt* : to compile — **compilación** *nf*

compinche *nmf fam* **1** : buddy, pal **2** : partner in crime, accomplice

complacencia *nf* : pleasure, satisfaction

complacer {57} *vt* : to please — **complacerse** *vr* **~ en** : to take pleasure in

complaciente *adj* : obliging, eager to please

complejidad *nf* : complexity

complejo[1], **-ja** *adj* : complex

complejo[2] *nm* : complex

complementar *vt* : to complement, to supplement — **complementarse** *vr*

complementario, -ria *adj* : complementary

complemento *nm* **1** : complement, supplement **2** : supplementary pay, allowance

completamente *adv* : completely, totally

completar *vt* TERMINAR : to complete, to finish

completo, -ta *adj* **1** : complete **2** : perfect, absolute **3** : full, detailed — **completamente** *adv*

complexión *nf, pl* **-xiones** : (physical) constitution

complicación *nf, pl* **-ciones** : complication

complicado, -da *adj* : complicated

complicar {72} *vt* **1 :** to complicate **2 :** to involve — **complicarse** *vr*

cómplice *nmf* **:** accomplice

complicidad *nf* **:** complicity

complot *nm, pl* **complots** CONFABULACIÓN, CONSPIRACIÓN **:** conspiracy, plot

componenda *nf* **:** shady deal, scam

componente *adj & nm* **:** component, constituent

componer {60} *vt* **1** ARREGLAR **:** to fix, to repair **2** CONSTITUIR **:** to make up, to compose **3 :** to compose, to write **4 :** to set (a bone) — **componerse** *vr* **1 :** to improve, to get better **2 ~ de :** to consist of

comportamiento *nm* CONDUCTA **:** behavior, conduct

comportarse *vr* **:** to behave, to conduct oneself

composición *nf, pl* **-ciones 1** OBRA **:** composition, work **2 :** makeup, arrangement

compositor, -tora *n* **:** composer, songwriter

compostura *nf* **1 :** composure **2 :** mending, repair

compra *nf* **1 :** purchase **2 ir de compras :** to go shopping **3 orden de compra :** purchase order

comprador, -dora *n* **:** buyer, shopper

comprar *vt* **:** to buy, to purchase

compraventa *nf* **:** buying and selling

comprender *vt* **1** ENTENDER **:** to comprehend, to understand **2** ABARCAR **:** to cover, to include — *vi* **:** to understand <¡ya comprendo! : now I understand!>

comprensible *adj* **:** understandable — **comprensiblemente** *adv*

comprensión *nf, pl* **-siones 1 :** comprehension, understanding, grasp **2 :** understanding, sympathy

comprensivo, -va *adj* **:** understanding

compresa *nf* **1 :** compress **2** *or* **compresa higiénica :** sanitary napkin

compresión *nf, pl* **-siones :** compression

compresor *nm* **:** compressor

comprimido *nm* PÍLDORA, TABLETA **:** pill, tablet

comprimir *vt* **:** to compress

comprobable *adj* **:** verifiable, provable

comprobación *nf, pl* **-ciones :** verification, confirmation

comprobante *nm* **1 :** proof <comprobante de identidad : proof of identity> **2 :** voucher, receipt <comprobante de ventas : sales slip>

comprobar {19} *vt* **1 :** to verify, to check **2 :** to prove

comprometedor, -dora *adj* **:** compromising

comprometer *vt* **1 :** to compromise **2 :** to jeopardize **3 :** to commit, to put under obligation — **comprometerse** *vr* **1 :** to commit oneself **2 ~ con :** to get engaged to

comprometido, -da *adj* **1 :** compromising, awkward **2 :** committed, obliged **3 :** engaged (to be married)

compromiso *nm* **1 :** obligation, commitment **2 :** engagement <anillo de compromiso : engagement ring> **3 :** agreement **4 :** awkward situation, fix

compuerta *nf* **:** floodgate

compuesto[1] *pp* → **componer**

compuesto[2], **-ta** *adj* **1 :** fixed, repaired **2 :** compound, composite **3 :** decked out, spruced up **4 ~ de :** made up of, consisting of

compuesto[3] *nm* **:** compound

compulsión *nf, pl* **-siones :** compulsion

compulsivo, -va *adj* **1 :** compelling, urgent **2 :** compulsive — **compulsivamente** *adv*

compungido, -da *adj* **:** contrite, remorseful

compungirse {35} *vr* **:** to feel remorse

compuso, etc. → **componer**

computación *nf, pl* **-ciones :** computing, computers *pl*

computador *nm* → **computadora**

computadora *nf* **1 :** computer **2 computadora portátil :** laptop computer

computar *vt* **:** to compute, to calculate

computarizar {21} *vt* **:** to computerize

cómputo *nm* **:** computation, calculation

comulgar {52} *vi* **:** to receive Communion

común *adj, pl* **comunes 1 :** common **2 común y corriente :** ordinary, regular **3 por lo común :** generally, as a rule

comuna *nf* **:** commune

comunal *adj* **:** communal

comunicación *nf, pl* **-ciones 1 :** communication **2 :** access, link **3 :** message, report

comunicado *nm* **1 :** communiqué **2 comunicado de prensa :** press release

comunicar {72} *vt* **1 :** to communicate, to convey **2 :** to notify — **comunicarse** *vr* **~ con 1 :** to contact, to get in touch with **2 :** to be connected to

comunicativo, -va *adj* **:** communicative, talkative

comunidad *nf* **:** community

comunión *nf, pl* **-niones 1 :** communion, sharing **2 :** Communion

comunismo *nm* **:** communism, Communism

comúnmente *adv* **:** commonly

con *prep* **1 :** with <vengo con mi padre : I'm going with my father> <¿con quién hablas? : who are you speaking to?> **2 :** in spite of <con todo : in spite of it all> **3 :** to, towards <ella es amable con los niños : she is kind to the children> **4 :** by <con llegar temprano : by arriving early> **5 con (tal) que :** as long as, so long as

conato *nm* **:** attempt, effort <conato de robo : attempted robbery>

cóncavo, -va *adj* : concave
concebible *adj* : conceivable
concebir {54} *vt* **1** : to conceive **2** : to conceive of, to imagine — *vi* : to conceive, to become pregnant
conceder *vt* **1** : to grant, to bestow **2** : to concede, to admit
concejal, -jala *n* : councilman *m,* councilwoman *f,* alderman *m,* alderwoman *f*
concejo *nm* : council <concejo municipal : town council>
concentración *nf, pl* **-ciones** : concentration
concentrado *nm* : concentrate
concentrar *vt* : to concentrate — **concentrarse** *vr*
concéntrico, -ca *adj* : concentric
concepción *nf, pl* **-ciones** : conception
concepto *nm* NOCIÓN : concept, idea, opinion
conceptuar {3} *vt* : to regard, to judge
concernir {17} *vi* : to be of concern
concertar {55} *vt* **1** : to arrange, to set up **2** : to agree on, to settle **3** : to harmonize — *vi* : to be in harmony
concesión *nf, pl* **-siones 1** : concession **2** : awarding, granting
concha *nf* : conch, seashell
conciencia *nf* **1** : conscience **2** : consciousness, awareness
concientizar {21} *vt* : to make aware — **concientizarse** *vr* **~ de** : to realize, to become aware of
concienzudo, -da *adj* : conscientious
concierto *nm* **1** : concert **2** : agreement **3** : concerto
conciliador¹, -dora *adj* : conciliatory
conciliador², -dora *n* : arbitrator, peacemaker
conciliar *vt* : to conciliate, to reconcile — **conciliación** *nf*
concilio *nm* : (church) council
conciso, -sa *adj* : concise — **concisión** *nf*
conciudadano, -na *n* : fellow citizen
cónclave *nm* : conclave, private meeting
concluir {41} *vt* **1** TERMINAR : to conclude, to finish **2** DEDUCIR : to deduce, to infer — *vi* : to end, to conclude
conclusión *nf, pl* **-siones** : conclusion
concluyente *adj* : conclusive
concomitante *adj* : concomitant
concordancia *nf* : agreement, accordance
concordar {19} *vi* : to agree, to coincide — *vt* : to reconcile
concordia *nf* : concord, harmony
concretar *vt* **1** : to pinpoint, to specify **2** : to fulfill, to realize — **concretarse** *vr* : to become real, to take shape
concretizar → **concretar**
concreto¹, -ta *adj* **1** : concrete, actual **2** : definite, specific <en concreto : specifically> — **concretamente** *adv*
concreto² *nm* HORMIGÓN : concrete
concubina *nf* : concubine
concurrencia *nf* **1** : audience, turnout **2** : concurrence
concurrente *adj* : concurrent — **concurrentemente** *adv*
concurrido, -da *adj* : busy, crowded
concurrir *vi* **1** : to converge, to come together **2** : to concur, to agree **3** : to take part, to participate **4** : to attend, to be present <concurrir a una reunión : to attend a meeting> **5 ~ a** : to contribute to
concursante *nmf* : contestant, competitor
concursar *vt* : to compete in — *vi* : to compete, to participate
concurso *nm* **1** : contest, competition **2** : concurrance, coincidence **3** : crowd, gathering **4** : cooperation, assistance
condado *nm* **1** : county **2** : earldom
conde, -desa *n* : count *m,* earl *m,* countess *f*
condecoración *nf, pl* **-ciones** : decoration, medal
condecorar *vt* : to decorate, to award (a medal)
condena *nf* **1** REPROBACIÓN : disapproval, condemnation **2** SENTENCIA : sentence, conviction
condenación *nf, pl* **-ciones 1** : condemnation **2** : damnation
condenado¹, -da *adj* **1** : fated, doomed **2** : convicted, sentenced **3** *fam* : darn, damned
condenado², -da *n* : convict
condenar *vt* **1** : to condemn **2** : to sentence **3** : to board up, to wall up — **condenarse** *vr* : to be damned
condensación *nf, pl* **-ciones** : condensation
condensar *vt* : to condense
condesa *nf* → **conde**
condescendencia *nf* : condescension
condescender {56} *vi* **1** : to condescend **2** : to agree, to acquiesce
condición *nf, pl* **-ciones 1** : condition, state **2** : capacity, position **3 condiciones** *nfpl* : conditions, circumstances <condiciones de vida : living conditions>
condicional *adj* : conditional — **condicionalmente** *adv*
condicionamiento *nm* : conditioning
condicionar *vt* **1** : to condition, to determine **2 ~ a** : to be contingent on, to depend on
condimentar *vt* SAZONAR : to season, to spice
condimento *nm* : condiment, seasoning, spice
condolencia *nf* : condolence, sympathy
condolerse {47} *vr* : to sympathize
condominio *nm* : condominium, condo
condón *nm, pl* **condones** : condom
cóndor *nm* : condor
conducción *nf, pl* **-ciones 1** : conduction (of electricity, etc.) **2** DIRECCIÓN : management, direction

conducir {61} *vt* **1** DIRIGIR, GUIAR : to direct, to lead **2** MANEJAR : to drive (a vehicle) — *vi* **1** : to drive a vehicle **2** ~ **a** : to lead to — **conducirse** *vr* PORTARSE : to behave, to conduct oneself

conducta *nf* COMPORTAMIENTO : conduct, behavior

conducto *nm* : conduit, channel, duct

conductor[1], **-tora** *adj* : conducting, leading

conductor[2], **-tora** *n* : driver

conductor[3] *nm* : conductor (of electricity, etc.)

conectar *vt* : to connect — *vi* ~ **con** : to link up with, to communicate with

conector *nm* : connector

conejera *nf* : rabbit hutch

conejillo *nm* **conejillo de Indias** : guinea pig

conejo, -ja *n* : rabbit

conexión *nf, pl* **-xiones** : connection

confabulación *nf, pl* **-ciones** COMPLOT, CONSPIRACIÓN : plot, conspiracy

confabularse *vr* : to plot, to conspire

confección *nf, pl* **-ciones 1** : preparation **2** : tailoring, dressmaking

confeccionar *vt* : to make, to produce, to prepare

confederación *nf, pl* **-ciones** : confederation

confederarse *vr* : to confederate, to form a confederation

conferencia *nf* **1** REUNIÓN : conference, meeting **2** : lecture

conferenciante *nmf* : lecturer

conferencista *nmf* → **conferenciante**

conferir {76} *vt* : to confer, to bestow

confesar {55} *v* : to confess — **confesarse** *vr* : to go to confession

confesión *nf, pl* **-siones 1** : confession **2** : creed, denomination

confesionario *nm* : confessional

confesor *nm* : confessor

confeti *nm* : confetti

confiable *adj* : trustworthy, reliable

confiado, -da *adj* **1** : confident, self-confident **2** : trusting — **confiadamente** *adv*

confianza *nf* **1** : trust <de poca confiaza : untrustworthy> **2** : confidence, self-confidence

confianzudo, -da *adj* : forward, presumptuous

confiar {85} *vi* : to have trust, to be trusting — *vt* **1** : to confide **2** : to entrust — **confiarse** *vr* **1** : to be overconfident **2** ~ **a** : to confide in

confidencia *nf* : confidence, secret

confidencial *adj* : confidential — **confidencialmente** *adv*

confidencialidad *nf* : confidentiality

confidente *nmf* **1** : confidant, confidante *f* **2** : informer

configuración *nf, pl* **-ciones** : configuration, shape

configurar *vt* : to shape, to form

confín *nm, pl* **confines** : boundary, limit

confinamiento *nm* : confinement

confinar *vt* **1** : to confine, to limit **2** : to exile — *vi* ~ **con** : to border on

confirmación *nf, pl* **-ciones** : confirmation

confirmar *vt* : to confirm, to substantiate

confiscar {72} *vt* DECOMISAR : to confiscate, to seize

confitado, -da *adj* : candied

confite *nm* : comfit, candy

confitería *nm* **1** DULCERÍA : candy store, confectionery **2** : tearoom, café

confitero, -ra *n* : confectioner

confitura *nf* : preserves, jam

conflagración *nf, pl* **-ciones 1** : conflagration, fire **2** : war

conflictivo, -va *adj* **1** : troubled **2** : controversial

conflicto *nm* : conflict

confluencia *nf* : junction, confluence

confluir {41} *vi* **1** : to converge, to join **2** : to gather, to assemble

conformar *vt* **1** : to form, to create **2** : to constitute, to make up — **conformarse** *vr* **1** RESIGNARSE : to resign oneself **2** : to comply, to conform **3** ~ **con** : to content oneself with, to be satisfied with

conforme[1] *adj* **1** : content, satisfied **2** ~ **a** : in accordance with

conforme[2] *conj* : as <entreguen sus tareas conforme vayan saliendo : hand in your homework as you leave>

conformidad *nf* **1** : agreement, consent **2** : resignation

confort *nm* : comfort

confortable *adj* CÓMODO : comfortable

confortar *vt* CONSOLAR : to comfort, to console

confraternidad *nf* : brotherhood, fraternity

confrontación *nf, pl* **-ciones** : confrontation

confrontar *vt* **1** ENCARAR : to confront **2** : to compare **3** : to bring face-to-face — *vi* : to border — **confrontarse** *vr* ~ **con** : to face up to

confundir *vt* : to confuse, to mix up — **confundirse** *vr* : to make a mistake, to be confused <confundirse de número : to get the wrong number>

confusión *nf, pl* **-siones** : confusion

confuso, -sa *adj* **1** : confused, mixed-up **2** : obscure, indistinct

congelación *nf, pl* **-ciones 1** : freezing **2** : frostbite

congelado, -da *adj* HELADO : frozen

congelador *nm* HELADORA : freezer

congelamiento *nm* → **congelación**

congelar *vt* : to freeze — **congelarse** *vr*

congeniar *vi* : to get along (with someone)

congénito, -ta *adj* : congenital

congestión *nf, pl* **-tiones** : congestion

congestionado, -da *adj* : congested

congestionamiento *nm* → **congestión**

congestionarse *vr* **1 :** to become flushed **2 :** to become congested

conglomerado[1], -da *adj* **:** conglomerate, mixed

conglomerado[2] *nm* **:** conglomerate, conglomeration

congoja *nf* ANGUSTIA **:** anguish, grief

congoleño, -ña *adj & n* **:** Congolese

congraciarse *vr* **:** to ingratiate oneself

congratular *vt* FELICITAR **:** to congratulate

congregación *nf, pl* **-ciones :** congregation, gathering

congregar {52} *vt* **:** to bring together — **congregarse** *vr* **:** to congregate, to assemble

congresista *nmf* **:** congressman *m,* congresswoman *f*

congreso *nm* **:** congress, conference

congruencia *nf* **1 :** congruence **2** COHERENCIA **:** coherence — **congruente** *adj*

cónico, -ca *adj* **:** conical, conic

conífera *nf* **:** conifer

conífero, -ra *adj* **:** coniferous

conjetura *nf* **:** conjecture, guess

conjeturar *vt* **:** to guess, to conjecture

conjugación *nf, pl* **-ciones :** conjugation

conjugar {52} *vt* **1 :** to conjugate **2 :** to combine

conjunción *nf, pl* **-ciones :** conjunction

conjuntivo, -va *adj* **:** connective <tejido conjuntivo : connective tissue>

conjunto[1], -ta *adj* **:** joint

conjunto[2] *nm* **1 :** collection, group **2 :** ensemble, outfit <conjunto musical : musical ensemble> **3 :** whole, entirety <en conjunto : as a whole, altogether>

conjurar *vt* **1 :** to exorcise **2 :** to avert, to ward off — *vi* CONSPIRAR **:** to conspire, to plot

conjuro *nm* **1 :** exorcism **2 :** spell

conllevar *vt* **1 :** to bear, to suffer **2** IMPLICAR **:** to entail, to involve

conmemorar *vt* **:** to commemorate — **conmemoración** *nf*

conmemorativo, -va *adj* **:** commemorative, memorial

conmigo *pron* **:** with me <habló conmigo : he talked with me>

conminar *vt* AMENAZAR **:** to threaten, to warn

conmiseración *nf, pl* **-ciones :** pity, conmiseration

conmoción *nf, pl* **-ciones 1 :** shock, upheaval **2** *or* **conmoción cerebral :** concussion

conmocionar *vt* **:** to shake, to shock

conmovedor, -dora *adj* EMOCIONANTE **:** moving, touching

conmover {47} *vt* **1** EMOCIONAR **:** to move, to touch **2 :** to shake up — **conmoverse** *vr*

conmutador *nm* **1 :** switch **2 :** switchboard

connivencia *nf* **:** connivance

connotación *nf, pl* **-ciones :** connotation

connotar *vt* **:** to connote, to imply

cono *nm* **:** cone

conocedor[1], -dora *adj* **:** knowledgeable

conocedor[2], -dora *n* **:** connoisseur, expert

conocer {18} *vt* **1 :** to know, to be acquainted with <ya la conocí : I've already met him> **2 :** to meet **3** RECONOCER **:** to recognize — **conocerse** *vr* **1 :** to know each other **2 :** to meet **3 :** to know oneself

conocido[1], -da *adj* **1 :** familiar **2 :** well-known, famous

conocido[2], -da *n* **:** acquaintance

conocimiento *nm* **1 :** knowledge **2** SENTIDO **:** consciousness

conque *conj* **:** so, so then, and so <¡ah, conque esas tenemos! : oh, so that's what's going on!>

conquista *nf* **:** conquest

conquistador[1], -dora *adj* **:** conquering

conquistador[2], -dora *n* **:** conqueror

conquistar *vt* **:** to conquer

consabido, -da *adj* **:** usual, typical

consagración *nf, pl* **-ciones :** consecration

consagrar *vt* **1 :** to consecrate **2** DEDICAR **:** to dedicate, to devote

consciencia *nf* → **conciencia**

consciente *adj* **:** conscious, aware — **conscientemente** *adv*

conscripción *nf, pl* **-ciones :** conscription, draft

conscripto, -ta *n* **:** conscript, inductee

consecución *nf, pl* **-ciones :** attainment

consecuencia *nf* **1 :** consequence, result <a consecuencia de : as a result of> **2 en ~ :** accordingly

consecuente *adj* **:** consistent — **consecuentemente** *adv*

consecutivo, -va *adj* **:** consecutive, successive — **consecutivamente** *adv*

conseguir {75} *vt* **1 :** to get, to obtain **2 :** to achieve, to attain **3 :** to manage to <consiguió acabar el trabajo : she managed to finish the job>

consejero, -ra *n* **:** adviser, counselor

consejo *nm* **1 :** advice, counsel **2 :** council <consejo de guerra : court-martial>

consenso *nm* **:** consensus

consentido, -da *adj* **:** spoiled, pampered

consentimiento *nm* **:** consent, permission

consentir {76} *vt* **1** PERMITIR **:** to consent to, to allow **2** MIMAR **:** to pamper, to spoil — *vi* **~ en :** to agree to, to approve of

conserje *nmf* **:** custodian, janitor, caretaker

conserva *nf* **1 :** preserve(s), jam **2 conservas** *nfpl* **:** canned goods

conservación *nf, pl* **-ciones :** conservation, preservation

conservacionista *nmf* : conservationist
conservador[1], **-dora** *adj & n* : conservative
conservador[2] *nm* : preservative
conservadurismo *nf* : conservatism
conservante *nm* : preservative
conservar *vt* **1** : to preserve **2** GUARDAR : to keep, to conserve
conservatorio *nm* : conservatory
considerable *adj* : considerable — **considerablemente** *adv*
consideración *nf, pl* **-ciones 1** : consideration **2** : respect **3 de ~** : considerable, important
considerado, -da *adj* **1** : considerate, thoughtful **2** : respected
considerar *vt* **1** : to consider, to think over **2** : to judge, to deem **3** : to treat with respect
consigna *nf* **1** ESLOGAN : slogan **2** : assignment, orders *pl* **3** : checkroom
consignar *vt* **1** : to consign **2** : to record, to write down **3** : to assign, to allocate
consigo *pron* : with her, with him, with you, with oneself <se llevó las llaves consigo : she took the keys with her>
consiguiente *adj* **1** : resulting, consequent **2 por ~** : consequently, as a result
consistencia *nf* : consistency
consistente *adj* **1** : firm, strong, sound **2** : consistent — **consistentemente** *adv*
consistir *vi* **1 ~ en** : to consist of **2 ~ en** : to lie in, to consist in
consola *nf* : console
consolación *nf, pl* **-ciones** : consolation <premio de consolación : consolation prize>
consolar {19} *vt* CONFORTAR : to console, to comfort
consolidar *vt* : to consolidate — **consolidación** *nf*
consomé *nm* CALDO : consommé, clear soup
consonancia *nf* **1** : consonance, harmony **2 en consonancia con** : in accordance with
consonante[1] *adj* : consonant, harmonious
consonante[2] *nf* : consonant
consorcio *nm* : consortium
consorte *nmf* : consort, spouse
conspicuo, -cua *adj* : eminent, famous
conspiración *nf, pl* **-ciones** COMPLOT, CONFABULACIÓN : conspiracy, plot
conspirador, -dora *n* : conspirator
conspirar *vi* CONJURAR : to conspire, to plot
constancia *nf* **1** PRUEBA : proof, certainty **2** : record, evidence <que quede constancia : for the record> **3** : perseverance, constancy
constante[1] *adj* : constant — **constantemente** *adv*
constante[2] *nm* : constant
constar *vi* **1** : to be evident, to be on record <que conste : believe me, have no doubt> **2 ~ de** : to consist of
constatación *nf, pl* **-ciones** : confirmation, proof
constatar *vt* **1** : to verify **2** : to state
constelación *nf, pl* **-ciones** : constellation
consternación *nf, pl* **-ciones** : consternation, dismay
consternar *vt* : to dismay, to appall
constipación *nf, pl* **-ciones** : constipation
constipado[1], **-da** *adj* **estar constipado** : to have a cold
constipado[2] *nm* RESFRIADO : cold
constiparse *vr* : to catch a cold
constitución *nf, pl* **-ciones** : constitution — **constitucional** *adj* — **constitucionalmente** *adv*
constitucionalidad *nf* : constitutionality
constituir {41} *vt* **1** FORMAR : to constitute, to make up, to form **2** FUNDAR : to establish, to set up — **constituirse** *vr* **~ en** : to set oneself up as, to become
constitutivo, -va *adj* : constituent, component
constituyente *adj & nmf* : constituent
constreñir {67} *vt* **1** FORZAR, OBLIGAR : to constrain, to oblige **2** LIMITAR : to restrict, to limit
construcción *nf, pl* **-ciones** : construction, building
constructivo, -va *adj* : constructive — **constructivamente** *adv*
constructor, -tora *n* : builder
constructora *nf* : construction company
construir {41} *vt* : to build, to construct
consuelo *nm* : consolation, comfort
consuetudinario, -ria *adj* **1** : customary, habitual **2 derecho consuetudinario** : common law
cónsul *nmf* : consul — **consular** *adj*
consulado *nm* : consulate
consulta *nf* **1** : consultation **2** : inquiry
consultar *vt* : to consult
consultor[1], **-tora** *adj* : consulting <firma consultora : consulting firm>
consultor[2], **-tora** *n* : consultant
consultorio *nm* : office (of a doctor or dentist)
consumación *nf, pl* **-ciones** : consummation
consumado, -da *adj* : consummate, perfect
consumar *vt* **1** : to consummate, to complete **2** : to commit, to carry out
consumible *adj* : consumable
consumición *nf, pl* **-ciones 1** : consumption **2** : drink (in a restaurant)
consumido, -da *adj* : thin, emaciated
consumidor, -dora *n* : consumer
consumir *vt* : to consume — **consumirse** *vr* : to waste away
consumo *nm* : consumption

contabilidad *nf* **1 :** accounting, bookkeeping **2 :** accountancy
contabilizar {21} *vt* **:** to enter, to record (in accounting)
contable[1] *adj* **:** countable
contable[2] *nmf Spain* **:** accountant, bookkeeper
contactar *vt* **:** to contact — *vi* **~ con :** to get in touch with, to contact
contacto *nm* **:** contact
contado[1]**, -da** *adj* **1 :** counted <tenía los días contados : his days were numbered> **2 :** rare, scarce <en contadas ocasiones : on rare occasions>
contado[2] *nm* **al contado :** cash <pagar al contado : to pay in cash>
contador[1]**, -dora** *n* **:** accountant
contador[2] *nm* **:** meter <contador de agua : water meter>
contaduría *nf* **1 :** accounting office **2** CONTABILIDAD **:** accountancy
contagiar *vt* **1 :** to infect **2 :** to transmit (a disease) — **contagiarse** *vr* **1 :** to be contagious **2 :** to become infected
contagio *nm* **:** contagion, infection
contagioso, -sa *adj* **:** contagious, catching
contaminación *nf, pl* **-ciones :** contamination, pollution
contaminante *nm* **:** pollutant, contaminant
contaminar *vt* **:** to contaminate, to pollute
contar {19} *vt* **1 :** to count **2 :** to tell **3 :** to include — *vi* **1 :** to count (up) **2 :** to matter, to be of concern <eso no cuenta : that doesn't matter> **3 ~ con :** to rely on, to count on — **contarse** *vr* **~ entre :** to be numbered among
contemplación *nf, pl* **-ciones :** contemplation — **contemplativo, -va** *adj*
contemplar *vt* **1 :** to contemplate, to ponder **2 :** to gaze at, to look at
contemporáneo, -nea *adj & n* **:** contemporary
contención *nf, pl* **-ciones :** containment, holding
contencioso, -sa *adj* **:** contentious
contender {56} *vi* **1 :** to contend, to compete **2 :** to fight
contendiente *nmf* **:** contender
contenedor *nm* **1 :** container, receptacle **2 :** Dumpster™
contener {80} *vt* **1 :** to contain, to hold **2** ATAJAR **:** to restrain, to hold back — **contenerse** *vr* **:** to restrain oneself
contenido[1]**, -da** *adj* **:** restrained, reserved
contenido[2] *nm* **:** contents *pl,* content
contentar *vt* **:** to please, to make happy — **contentarse** *vr* **:** to be satisfied, to be pleased
contento[1]**, -ta** *adj* **:** contented, glad, happy
contento[2] *nm* **:** joy, happiness
contestación *nf, pl* **-ciones 1 :** answer, reply **2 :** protest
contestar *vt* RESPONDER **:** to answer — *vi* **1** RESPONDER **:** to answer, to reply **2** REPLICAR **:** to answer back
contexto *nm* **:** context
contienda *nf* **1 :** dispute, conflict **2 :** contest, competition
contigo *pron* **:** with you <voy contigo : I'm going with you>
contiguo, -gua *adj* COLINDANTE **:** contiguous, adjacent
continencia *nf* **:** continence
continente *nm* **:** continent — **continental** *adj*
contingencia *nf* **:** contingency, eventuality
contingente *adj & nm* **:** contingent
continuación *nf, pl* **-ciones 1 :** continuation **2 a ~ :** next <lo demás sigue a continuación : the rest follows> **3 a continuación de :** after, following
continuar {3} *v* **:** to continue
continuidad *nf* **:** continuity
continuo, -nua *adj* **:** continuous, steady, constant — **continuamente** *adv*
contonearse *vr* **:** to sway one's hips
contoneo *nm* **:** swaying, wiggling (of the hips)
contorno *nm* **1 :** outline **2 contornos** *nmpl* **:** outskirts
contorsión *nf, pl* **-siones :** contortion
contra[1] *nf* **1** *fam* **:** difficulty, snag **2 llevar la contra a :** to oppose, to contradict
contra[2] *nm* **:** con <los pros y los contras : the pros and cons>
contra[3] *prep* **:** against
contraalmirante *nm* **:** rear admiral
contraatacar {72} *v* **:** to counterattack — **contraataque** *nm*
contrabajo *nm* **:** double bass
contrabalancear *vt* **:** to counterbalance — **contrabalanza** *nf*
contrabandear *v* **:** to smuggle
contrabandista *nmf* **:** smuggler, black marketeer
contrabando *nm* **1 :** smuggling **2 :** contraband
contracción *nf, pl* **-ciones :** contraction
contracepción *nf, pl* **-ciones :** contraception
contrachapado *nm* **:** plywood
contraconceptivo *nm* ANTICONCEPTIVO **:** contraceptive — **contracepción** *nf*
contracorriente *nf* **1 :** crosscurrent **2 ir a contracorriente :** to go against the tide
contractual *adj* **:** contractual
contradecir {11} *vt* DESMENTIR **:** to contradict — **contradecirse** *vr* DESDECIRSE **:** to contradict oneself
contradicción *nf, pl* **-ciones :** contradiction
contradictorio, -ria *adj* **:** contradictory
contraer {81} *vt* **1 :** to contract (a disease) **2 :** to establish by contract

<contraer matrimonio : to get married> **3** : to tighten, to contract — **contraerse** *vr* : to contract, to tighten up
contrafuerte *nm* : buttress
contragolpe *nm* **1** : counterblow **2** : backlash
contrahecho, -cha *adj* : deformed, hunchbacked
contraindicado, -da *adj* : contraindicated — **contraindicación** *nf*
contralor, -lora *n* : comptroller
contralto *nmf* : contralto
contramaestre *nm* **1** : boatswain **2** : foreman
contramandar *vt* : to countermand
contramano *nm* **a ~** : the wrong way (on a street)
contramedida *nf* : countermeasure
contraorden *nf* : countermand
contraparte *nf* **1** : counterpart **2 en ~** : on the other hand
contrapartida *nf* : compensation
contrapelo *nm* **a ~** : in the wrong direction, against the grain
contrapeso *nm* : counterbalance
contraponer {60} *vt* **1** : to counter, to oppose **2** : to contrast, to compare
contraposición *nf, pl* **-ciones** : comparison
contraproducente *adj* : counterproductive
contrapunto *nm* : counterpoint
contrariar {85} *vt* **1** : to contradict, to oppose **2** : to vex, to annoy
contrariedad *nf* **1** : setback, obstacle **2** : vexation, annoyance
contrario, -ria *adj* **1** : contrary, opposite <al contrario : on the contrary> **2** : conflicting, opposed
contrarrestar *vt* : to counteract
contrarrevolución *nf, pl* **-ciones** : counterrevolution — **contrarrevolucionario, -ria** *adj & n*
contrasentido *nm* : contradiction
contraseña *nf* : password
contrastante *adj* : contrasting
contrastar *vt* **1** : to resist **2** : to check, to confirm — *vi* : to contrast
contraste *nm* : contrast
contratar *vt* **1** : to contract for **2** : to hire, to engage
contratiempo *nm* **1** PERCANCE : mishap, accident **2** DIFICULTAD : setback, difficulty
contratista *nmf* : contractor
contrato *nm* : contract
contravenir {87} *vt* : to contravene, to infringe
contraventana *nf* : shutter
contribución *nf, pl* **-ciones** : contribution
contribuidor, -dora *n* : contributor
contribuir {41} *vt* **1** APORTAR : to contribute **2** : to pay (in taxes) — *vi* **1** : contribute, to help out **2** : to pay taxes
contribuyente[1] *adj* : contributing
contribuyente[2] *nmf* : taxpayer
contrición *nf, pl* **-ciones** : contrition
contrincante *nmf* : rival, opponent
contrito, -ta *adj* : contrite, repentant
control *nm* **1** : control **2** : inspection, check **3** : checkpoint, roadblock
controlador, -dora *n* : controller <controlador aéreo : air traffic controller>
controlar *vt* **1** : to control **2** : to monitor, to check
controversia *nf* : controversy
controversial → **controvertido**
controvertido, -da *adj* : controversial
controvertir {76} *vt* : to dispute, to argue about — *vi* : to argue, to debate
contubernio *nm* : conspiracy
contumacia *nf* : obstinacy, stubbornness
contumaz *adj, pl* **-maces** : obstinate, stubbornly disobedient
contundencia *nf* **1** : forcefulness, weight **2** : severity
contundente *adj* **1** : blunt <un objeto contundente : a blunt instrument> **2** : forceful, convincing — **contundentemente** *adv*
contusión *nf, pl* **-siones** : bruise, contusion
contuvo, etc. → **contener**
convalecencia *nf* : convalescence
convalecer {53} *vi* : to convalesce, to recover
convaleciente *adj & nmf* : convalescent
convección *nf, pl* **-ciones** : convection
convencer {86} *vt* : to convince, to persuade — **convencerse** *vr*
convencimiento *nm* : belief, conviction
convención *nf, pl* **-ciones 1** : convention, conference **2** : pact, agreement **3** : convention, custom
convencional *adj* : conventional — **convencionalmente** *adv*
convencionalismo *nm* : conventionality
conveniencia *nf* **1** : convenience **2** : fitness, suitability, advisability
conveniente *adj* **1** : convenient **2** : suitable, advisable
convenio *nm* PACTO : agreement, pact
convenir {87} *vi* **1** : to be suitable, to be advisable **2** : to agree
convento *nm* **1** : convent **2** : monastery
convergencia *nf* : convergence
convergente *adj* : convergent, converging
converger {15} *vi* **1** : to converge **2 ~ en** : to concur on
conversación *nf, pl* **-ciones** : conversation
conversador, -dora *n* : conversationalist, talker
conversar *vi* : to converse, to talk
conversión *nf, pl* **-siones** : conversion
converso, -sa *n* : convert
convertible *adj & nm* : convertible
convertidor *nm* : converter

convertir {76} *vt* **1** : to convert **2** : to transform, to change **3** : to exchange (money) — **convertirse** *vr* ~ **en** : to turn into

convexo, -xa *adj* : convex

convicción *nf, pl* **-ciones** : conviction

convicto[1], -ta *adj* : convicted

convicto[2], -ta *n* : convict, prisoner

convidado, -da *n* : guest

convidar *vt* **1** INVITAR : to invite **2** : to offer

convincente *adj* : convincing — **convincentemente** *adv*

convivencia *nf* **1** : coexistence **2** : cohabitation

convivir *vi* **1** : to coexist **2** : to live together

convocación *nf, pl* **-ciones** : convocation

convocar {72} *vt* : to convoke, to call together

convocatoria *nf* : summons, call

convoy *nm* : convoy

convulsión *nf, pl* **-siones 1** : convulsion **2** : agitation, upheaval

convulsivo, -va *adj* : convulsive

conyugal *adj* : conjugal

cónyuge *nmf* : spouse, partner

coñac *nm* : cognac, brandy

cooperación *nf, pl* **-ciones** : cooperation

cooperador, -dora *adj* : cooperative

cooperar *vi* : to cooperate

cooperativa *nf* : cooperative, co-op

cooperativo, -va *adj* : cooperative

cooptar *vt* : to co-opt

coordenada *nf* : coordinate

coordinación *nf, pl* **-ciones** : coordination

coordinador, -dora *n* : coordinator

coordinar *vt* COMPAGINAR : to coordinate, to combine

copa *nf* **1** : wineglass, goblet **2** : drink <irse de copas : to go out drinking> **3** : cup, trophy

copar *vt* **1** : to take <ya está copado el puesto : the job is already taken> **2** : to fill, to crowd

copartícipe *nmf* : joint partner

copete *nm* **1** : tuft (of hair) **2 estar hasta el copete** : to be completely fed up

copia *nf* **1** : copy **2** : imitation, replica

copiadora *nf* : photocopier

copiar *vt* : to copy

copiloto *nmf* : copilot

copioso, -sa *adj* : copious, abundant

copla *nf* **1** : popular song or ballad **2** : couplet, stanza

copo *nm* **1** : snowflake **2 copos de avena** : rolled oats **3 copos de maíz** : cornflakes

copra *nf* : copra

cópula *nf* : copulation

copular *vi* : to copulate

coque *nm* : coke (fuel)

coqueta *nf* : dressing table

coquetear *vi* : to flirt

coqueteo *nm* : flirting, coquetry

coqueto[1], -ta *adj* : flirtatious, coquettish

coqueto[2], -ta *n* : flirt

coraje *nm* **1** VALOR : valor, courage **2** IRA : anger <darle coraje a alguien : to make someone angry>

coral[1] *nm* **1** : coral **2** : chorale

coral[2] *nf* : choir

Corán *nm* **el Corán** : the Koran

coraza *nf* **1** : armor, armor plating **2** : shell (of an animal)

corazón *nm, pl* **-zones 1** : heart <de todo corazón : wholeheartedly> <de buen corazón : kindhearted> **2** : core **3** : darling, sweetheart

corazonada *nf* : hunch, impulse

corbata *nf* : tie, necktie

corcel *nm* : steed, charger

corchete *nm* **1** : hook and eye, clasp **2** : square bracket

corcho *nm* : cork

corcholata *nf Mex* : cap, bottle top

corcovear *vi* : to buck

cordel *nm* : cord, string

cordero *nm* : lamb

cordial[1] *adj* : cordial, affable — **cordialmente** *adv*

cordial[2] *nm* : cordial (liqueur)

cordialidad *nf* : cordiality, warmth

cordillera *nf* : mountain range

córdoba *nf* : Nicaraguan unit of currency

cordón *nm, pl* **cordones 1** : cord <cordón umbilical : umbilical cord> **2** : cordon

cordura *nf* **1** : sanity **2** : prudence, good judgment

coreano[1], -na *adj & n* : Korean

coreano[2] *nm* : Korean (language)

corear *vt* : to chant, to chorus

coreografía *nf* : choreography

coreografiar {85} *vt* : to choreograph

coreográfico, -ca *adj* : choreographic

coreógrafo, -fa *n* : choreographer

cormorán *nm, pl* **-ranes** : cormorant

cornada *nf* : goring, butt (with the horns)

córnea *nf* : cornea

cornear *vt* : to gore

cornejo *nm* : dogwood (tree)

corneta *nf* : bugle, horn, cornet

cornisa *nf* : cornice

cornudo, -da *adj* : horned

coro *nm* **1** : choir **2** : chorus

corola *nf* : corolla

corolario *nm* : corollary

corona *nf* **1** : crown **2** : wreath, garland **3** : corona (in astronomy)

coronación *nf, pl* **-ciones** : coronation

coronar *vt* **1** : to crown **2** : to reach the top of, to culminate

coronel, -nela *n* : colonel

coronilla *nf* **1** : crown (of the head) **2 estar hasta la coronilla** : to be completely fed up

corpiño *nm* **1** : bodice **2** *Arg* : brassiere, bra

corporación *nf, pl* **-ciones** : corporation

corporal *adj* : corporal, bodily
corporativo, -va *adj* : corporate
corpóreo, -rea *adj* : corporeal, physical
corpulencia *nf* : corpulence, stoutness, sturdiness
corpulento, -ta *adj* ROBUSTO : robust, stout, sturdy
corpúsculo *nm* : corpuscle
corral *nm* **1** : farmyard **2** : corral, pen, stockyard **3** *or* **corralito** : playpen
correa *nf* : strap, belt
correcaminos *nms & pl* : roadrunner
corrección *nf, pl* **-ciones 1** : correction **2** : correctness, propriety **3** : rebuke, reprimand **4 corrección de pruebas** : proofreading
correccional *nm* REFORMATORIO : reformatory
correctivo, -va *adj* : corrective <lentes correctivos : corrective lenses>
correcto, -ta *adj* **1** : correct, right **2** : courteous, polite — **correctamente** *adv*
corrector, -tora *n* : proofreader
corredizo, -za *adj* : sliding <puerta corrediza : sliding door>
corredor[1], -dora *n* **1** : runner, racer **2** : agent, broker <corredor de bolsa : stockbroker>
corredor[2] *nm* PASILLO : corridor, hallway
correduría *nf* → **corretaje**
corregir {28} *vt* **1** ENMENDAR : to correct, to emend **2** : to reprimand **3 corregir pruebas** : to proofread — **corregirse** *vr* : to reform, to mend one's ways
correlación *nf, pl* **-ciones** : correlation
correo *nm* **1** : mail <correo aéreo : airmail> **2** : post office
correoso, -sa *adj* : leathery, rough
correr *vi* **1** : to run, to race **2** : to rush **3** : to flow — *vt* **1** : to travel over, to cover **2** : to move, to slide, to roll, to draw (curtains) **3 correr un riesgo** : to run a risk — **correrse** *vr* **1** : to move along **2** : to run, to spill over
correspondencia *nf* **1** : correspondence, mail **2** : equivalence **3** : connection, interchange
corresponder *vi* **1** : to correspond **2** : to pertain, to belong **3** : to be appropriate, to fit **4** : to reciprocate — **corresponderse** *vr* : to write to each other
correspondiente *adj* : corresponding, respective
corresponsal *nmf* : correspondent
corretaje *nm* : brokerage
corretear *vi* **1** VAGAR : to loiter, to wander about **2** : to run around, to scamper about — *vt* : to pursue, to chase
corrida *nf* **1** : run, dash **2** : bullfight
corrido[1], -da *adj* **1** : straight, continuous **2** : wordly, experienced
corrido[2] *nm* : Mexican narrative folk song
corriente[1] *adj* **1** : common, everyday **2** : current, present **3** *Mex* : cheap, trashy **4 perro corriente** *Mex* : mutt
corriente[2] *nf* **1** : current <corriente alterna : alternating current> <direct current : corriente continua> **2** : draft **3** TENDENCIA : tendency, trend
corrillo *nm* : small group, clique
corro *nm* : ring, circle (of people)
corroborar *vt* : to corroborate
corroer {69} *vt* **1** : to corrode **2** : to erode, to wear away
corromper *vt* **1** : to corrupt **2** : to rot — **corromperse** *vr*
corrompido, -da *adj* CORRUPTO : corrupt, rotten
corrosión *nf, pl* **-siones** : corrosion
corrosivo, -va *adj* : corrosive
corrugar {52} *vt* : to corrugate — **corrugación** *nf*
corrupción *nf, pl* **-ciones 1** : decay **2** : corruption
corruptela *nf* : corruption, abuse of power
corrupto, -ta *adj* CORROMPIDO : corrupt
corsario *nm* : privateer
corsé *nm* : corset
cortada *nf* : cut, gash
cortador, -dora *n* : cutter
cortadora *nf* : cutter, slicer
cortadura *nm* : cut, slash
cortafuego *nm* : firebreak
cortante *adj* : cutting, sharp
cortar *vt* **1** : to cut, to slice, to trim **2** : to cut out, to omit **3** : to cut off, to interrupt **4** : to block, to close off **5** : to curdle (milk) — *vi* **1** : to cut **2** : to break up **3** : to hang up (the telephone) — **cortarse** *vr* **1** : to cut oneself <cortarse el pelo : to cut one's hair> **2** : to be cut off **3** : to sour (of milk)
cortauñas *nms & pl* : nail clippers
corte[1] *nm* **1** : cut, cutting <corte de pelo : haircut> **2** : style, fit
corte[2] *nf* **1** : court <corte suprema : supreme court> **2 hacer la corte a** : to court, to woo
cortejar *vt* GALANTEAR : to court, to woo
cortejo *nm* **1** GALANTEO : courtship **2** : retinue, entourage
cortés *adj* : courteous, polite — **cortésmente** *adv*
cortesano[1], -na *adj* : courtly
cortesano[2], -na *n* : courtier
cortesía *nf* **1** : courtesy, politeness **2 de ~** : complimentary, free
corteza *nf* **1** : bark **2** : crust **3** : peel, rind **4** : cortex <corteza cerebral : cerebral cortex>
cortijo *nm* : farmhouse
cortina *nm* : curtain
cortisona *nf* : cortisone
corto, -ta *adj* **1** : short (in length or duration) **2** : scarce **3** : timid, shy **4 corto de vista** : nearsighted
cortocircuito *nm* : short circuit
corvo, -va *adj* : curved, bent

cosa *nf* **1 :** thing, object **2 :** matter, affair **3 otra cosa :** anything else, something else
cosecha *nf* **:** harvest, crop
cosechador, -dora *n* **:** harvester, reaper
cosechadora *nf* **:** harvester (machine)
cosechar *vt* **1 :** to harvest, to reap **2 :** to win, to earn, to garner — *vi* **:** to harvest
coser *vt* **1 :** to sew **2 :** to stitch up — *vi* **:** to sew
cosmético[1], **-ca** *adj* **:** cosmetic
cosmético[2] *nm* **:** cosmetic
cósmico, -ca *adj* **:** cosmic
cosmonauta *nmf* **:** cosmonaut
cosmopolita *adj & nmf* **:** cosmopolitan
cosmos *nm* **:** cosmos
cosquillas *nfpl* **1 :** tickling **2 hacer cosquillas :** to tickle
cosquilleo *nm* **:** tickling sensation, tingle
cosquilloso, -sa *adj* **:** ticklish
costa *nf* **1 :** coast, shore **2 :** cost <a toda costa : at all costs>
costado *nm* **1 :** side **2 al costado :** alongside
costar {19} *v* **:** to cost <¿cuánto cuesta? : how much does it cost?>
costarricense *adj & nmf* **:** Costa Rican
costarriqueño, -ña → **costarricense**
coste *nm* → **costo**
costear *vt* **:** to pay for, to finance
costero, -ra *adj* **:** coastal, coast
costilla *nf* **1 :** rib **2 :** chop, cutlet **3** *fam* **:** better half, wife
costo *nm* **1 :** cost, price **2 costo de vida :** cost of living
costoso, -sa *adj* **:** costly, expensive
costra *nf* **1 :** crust **2** POSTILLA **:** scab
costumbre *nf* **1 :** custom **2** HÁBITO **:** habit
costura *nf* **1 :** seam **2 :** sewing, dressmaking **3 alta costura :** haute couture
costurera *nf* **:** seamstress *f*
cotejar *vt* **:** to compare, to collate
cotejo *nm* **:** comparison, collation
cotidiano, -na *adj* **:** daily, everyday <la vida cotidiana : daily life>
cotización *nf, pl* **-ciones 1 :** market price **2 :** quote, estimate
cotizado, -da *adj* **:** in demand, sought after
cotizar {21} *vt* **:** to quote, to value — **cotizarse** *vr* **:** to be worth
coto *nm* **1 :** enclosure, reserve **2 poner coto a :** to put a stop to
cotorra *nf* **1 :** small parrot **2** *fam* **:** chatterbox, windbag
cotorrear *vi fam* **:** to chatter, to gab, to blab
cotorreo *nm fam* **:** chatter, prattle
coyote *nm* **1 :** coyote **2** *Mex fam* **:** smuggler (of illegal immigrants)
coyuntura *nf* **1** ARTICULACIÓN **:** joint **2 :** occasion, moment
coz *nm, pl* **coces :** kick (of an animal)
crac *nm, pl* **cracs :** crash (of the stock market)
cozamos, etc. → **cocer**
craneal *adj* **:** cranial
cráneo *nf* **:** cranium, skull — **craneano, -na** *adj*
cráter *nm* **:** crater
creación *nf, pl* **-ciones :** creation
creador[1], **-dora** *adj* **:** creative, creating
creador[2], **-dora** *n* **:** creator
crear *vt* **1 :** to create, to cause **2 :** to originate
creatividad *nf* **:** creativity
creativo, -va *adj* **:** creative
crecer {53} *vi* **1 :** to grow **2 :** to increase
crecida *nf* **:** flooding, floodwater
crecido, -da *adj* **1 :** grown, grown-up **2 :** large (of numbers)
creciente *adj* **1 :** growing, increasing **2 luna creciente :** waxing moon
crecientemente *adv* **:** increasingly
crecimiento *nm* **1 :** growth **2 :** increase
credencial *adj* **cartas credenciales :** credentials
credenciales *nfpl* **:** documents, documentation, credentials
credibilidad *nf* **:** credibility
crédito *nm* **:** credit
credo *nm* **:** creed, credo
credulidad *nf* **:** credulity
crédulo, -la *adj* **:** credulous, gullible
creencia *nf* **:** belief
creer {20} *v* **1 :** to believe **2 :** to suppose, to think <creo que sí : I think so> — **creerse** *vr* **1 :** to believe, to think **2 :** to regard oneself as <se cree guapísimo : he thinks he's so handsome>
creíble *adj* **:** believable, credible
creído, -da *adj* **1** *fam* **:** conceited **2 :** confident, sure
crema *nf* **1 :** cream **2 la crema y nata :** the pick of the crop
cremación *nf, pl* **-ciones :** cremation
cremallera *nf* **:** zipper
cremar *vt* **:** to cremate
cremoso, -sa *adj* **:** creamy
crepa *nf Mex* **:** crepe (pancake)
crepe *or* **crep** *nmf* **:** crepe (pancake)
crepé *nm* **1** → **crespón 2 papel crepé :** crepe paper
crepitar *vi* **:** to crackle
crepúsculo *nm* **:** twilight
crescendo *nm* **:** crescendo
crespo, -pa *adj* **:** curly, frizzy
crespón *nm, pl* **crespones :** crepe (fabric)
cresta *nf* **1 :** crest **2 :** comb (of a rooster)
creta *nf* **:** chalk (mineral)
cretino, -na *n* **:** cretin
creyente *nmf* **:** believer
creyó, etc. → **creer**
crezca, etc. → **crecer**
cría *nf* **1 :** breeding, rearing **2 :** young **3 :** litter
criadero *nm* **:** hatchery
criado[1], **-da** *adj* **1 :** raised, brought up **2 bien criado :** well-bred
criado[2], **-da** *n* **:** servant, maid *f*
criador, -dora *n* **:** breeder

crianza *nf* : upbringing, rearing

criar {85} *vt* **1** : to breed **2** : to bring up, to raise

criatura *nf* **1** : baby, child **2** : creature

criba *nf* : sieve, screen

cribar *vt* : to sift

cric *nm, pl* **crics** : jack

crimen *nm, pl* **crímenes** : crime

criminal *adj & nmf* : criminal

crin *nf* **1** : mane **2** : horsehair

criollo[1], **-lla** *adj* **1** : Creole **2** : native, national <comida criolla : native cuisine>

criollo[2], **-lla** *n* : Creole

criollo[3] *nm* : Creole (language)

cripta *nf* : crypt

críptico, -ca *adj* **1** : cryptic, coded **2** : enigmatic, cryptic

criptón *nm* : krypton

críquet *nm* : cricket (game)

crisálida *nf* : chrysalis, pupa

crisantemo *nm* : chrysanthemum

crisis *nf* **1** : crisis **2 crisis nerviosa** : nervous breakdown

crisma *nf fam* : head <romperle la crisma a alguien : to knock someone's block off>

crisol *nm* **1** : crucible **2** : melting pot

crispar *vt* **1** : to cause to contract **2** : to irritate, to set on edge <eso me crispa : that gets on my nerves> — **crisparse** *vr* : to tense up

cristal *nm* **1** VIDRIO : glass, piece of glass **2** : crystal

cristalería *nf* **1** : glassware shop <como chivo en cristalería : like a bull in a china shop> **2** : glassware, crystal

cristalino[1], **-na** *adj* : crystalline, clear

cristalino[2] *nm* : lens (of the eye)

cristalizar {21} *vi* : to crystallize — **cristalización** *nf*

cristianismo *nm* : Christianity

cristiano, -na *adj & n* : Christian

criterio *nm* **1** : criterion **2** : judgment, sense

crítica *nf* **1** : criticism **2** : review, critique

criticar {72} *vt* : to criticize

crítico[1], **-ca** *adj* : critical — **críticamente** *adv*

crítico[2], **-ca** *n* : critic

criticón[1], **-cona** *adj, mpl* **-cones** *fam* : hypercritical, captious

criticón[2], **-cona** *n, mpl* **-cones** *fam* : faultfinder, critic

croar *vi* : to croak

croata *adj & nmf* : Croatian

crocante *adj* : crunchy

croché *or* **crochet** *nm* : crochet

cromático, -ca *adj* : chromatic

cromo *nm* **1** : chromium, chrome **2** : picture card, sports card

cromosoma *nm* : chromosome

crónica *nf* **1** : news report **2** : chronicle, history

crónico, -ca *adj* : chronic

cronista *nmf* **1** : reporter, newscaster **2** HISTORIADOR : chronicler, historian

cronología *nf* : chronology

cronológico, -ca *adj* : chronological — **cronológicamente** *adv*

cronometrador, -dora *n* : timekeeper

cronometrar *vt* : to time, to clock

cronómetro *nm* : chronometer

croquet *nm* : croquet

croqueta *nf* : croquette

croquis *nm* : rough sketch

cruce[1], **etc.** → **cruzar**

cruce[2] *nm* **1** : crossing, cross **2** : crossroads, intersection <cruce peatonal : crosswalk>

crucero *nm* **1** : cruise **2** : cruiser, warship **3** *Mex* : intersection

crucial *adj* : crucial — **crucialmente** *adv*

crucificar {72} *vt* : to crucify

crucifijo *nm* : crucifix

crucifixión *nf, pl* **-xiones** : crucifixion

crucigrama *nm* : crossword puzzle

crudo[1], **-da** *adj* **1** : raw **2** : crude, harsh

crudo[2] *nm* : crude oil

cruel *adj* : cruel — **cruelmente** *adv*

crueldad *nf* : cruelty

cruento, -ta *adj* : bloody

crujido *nm* **1** : rustling **2** : creaking **3** : crackling (of a fire) **4** : crunching

crujiente *adj* : crunchy, crisp

crujir *vi* **1** : to rustle **2** : to creak, to crack **3** : to crunch

crup *nm* : croup

crustáceo *nm* : crustacean

crutón *nm, pl* **crutones** : crouton

cruz *nf, pl* **cruces** : cross

cruza *nf* : cross (hybrid)

cruzada *nf* : crusade

cruzado[1], **-da** *adj* : crossed <espadas cruzadas : crossed swords>

cruzado[2] *nm* **1** : crusader **2** : Brazilian unit of currency

cruzar {21} *vt* **1** : to cross **2** : to exchange (words, greetings) **3** : to cross, to interbreed — **cruzarse** *vr* **1** : to intersect **2** : to meet, to pass each other

cuaderno *nm* LIBRETA : notebook

cuadra *nf* **1** : city block **2** : stable

cuadrado[1], **-da** *adj* : square

cuadrado[2] *nm* : square <elevar al cuadrado : to square (a number)>

cuadragésimo[1] *adj* : fortieth, forty-

cuadragésimo[2], **-ma** *n* : fortieth, forty- (in a series)

cuadrante *nm* **1** : quadrant **2** : dial

cuadrar *vi* : to conform, to agree — *vt* : to square — **cuadrarse** *vr* : to stand at attention

cuadriculado *nm* : grid (on a map, etc.)

cuadrilátero *nm* **1** : quadrilateral **2** : ring (in sports)

cuadrilla *nf* : gang, team, group

cuadro *nm* **1** : square <una blusa a cuadros : a checkered blouse> **2** : painting, picture **3** : baseball diamond, infield **4** : panel, board, cadre

cuadrúpedo *nm* : quadruped

cuadruple *adj* : quadruple

cuadruplicar {72} *vt* : to quadruple — **cuadruplicarse** *vr*
cuajada *nf* : curd
cuajar *vi* **1** : to curdle **2** COAGULAR : to clot, to coagulate **3** : to set, to jell **4** : to be accepted <su idea no cuajó : his idea didn't catch on> — *vt* **1** : to curdle **2** : to adorn
cual[1] *prep* : like, as
cual[2] *pron* **1 el cual, la cual, los cuales, las cuales** : who, whom, which <la razón por la cual lo dije : the reason I said it> **2 lo cual** : which <se rió, lo cual me dio rabia : he laughed, which made me mad> **3 cada cual** : everyone, everybody
cuál[1] *adj* : which, what <¿cuáles libros? : which books?>
cuál[2] *pron* **1** (*in questions*) : which (one), what (one) <¿cuál es el mejor? : which one is the best?> <¿cuál es tu apellido? : what is your last name?> **2 cuál más, cuál menos** : some more, some less
cualidad *nf* : quality, trait
cualitativo, -va *adj* : qualitative — **cualitativamente** *adv*
cualquier → **cualquiera**[1]
cualquiera[1] (**cualquier** *before nouns*) *adj, pl* **cualesquiera 1** : any, whichever <cualquier persona : any person> **2** : everyday, ordinary <un hombre cualquiera : an ordinary man>
cualquiera[2] *pron, pl* **cualesquiera 1** : anyone, anybody, whoever **2** : whatever, whichever
cuán *adv* : how <¡cuán risible fue todo eso! : how funny it all was!>
cuando[1] *conj* **1** : when <cuando llegó : when he arrived> **2** : since, if <cuando lo dices : if you say so> **3 cuando más** : at the most **4 de vez en cuando** : from time to time
cuando[2] *prep* : during, at the time of <cuando la guerra : during the war>
cuándo *adv & conj* **1** : when <¿cuándo llegará? : when will she arrive?> <no sabemos cuándo será : we don't know when it will be> **2 ¿de cuándo acá?** : since when?, how come?
cuantía *nf* **1** : quantity, extent **2** : significance, import
cuántico, -ca *adj* : quantum <teoría cuántica : quantum theory>
cuantioso, -sa *adj* **1** : abundant, considerable **2** : heavy, grave <cuantiosos daños : heavy damage>
cuantitativo, -va *adj* : quantitative — **cuantitativamente** *adv*
cuanto[1] *adv* **1** : as much as <come cuanto puedas : eat as much as you can> **2 cuanto antes** : as soon as possible **3 en ~** : as soon as **4 en cuanto a** : as for, as regards
cuanto[2]**, -ta** *adj* : as many, whatever <llévate cuantas flores quieras : take as many flowers as you wish>
cuanto[3]**, -ta** *pron* **1** : as much as, all that, everything <tengo cuanto deseo : I have all that I want> **2 unos cuantos, unas cuantas** : a few
cuánto[1] *adv* : how much, how many <¿a cuánto están las manzanas? : how much are the apples?> <no sé cuánto desean : I don't know how much they want>
cuánto[2]**, -ta** *adj* : how much, how many <¿cuántos niños tiene? : how many children do you have?>
cuánto[3] *pron* : how much, how many <¿cuántos quieren participar? : how many want to take part?> <¿cuánto cuesta? : how much does it cost?>
cuarenta *adj & nm* : forty
cuarentavo[1] *adj* : fortieth
cuarentavo[2] *nm* : fortieth (fraction)
cuarentena *nf* **1** : group of forty **2** : quarantine
Cuaresma *nf* : Lent
cuartear *vt* **1** : to quarter **2** : to divide up — **cuartearse** *vr* AGRIETARSE : to crack, to split
cuartel *nm* **1** : barracks, headquarters **2** : mercy <una guerra sin cuartel : a merciless war>
cuartelazo *nm* : coup d'état
cuarteto *nm* : quartet
cuartilla *nf* : sheet (of paper)
cuarto[1]**, -ta** *adj* : fourth
cuarto[2]**, -ta** *n* : fourth (in a series)
cuarto[3] *nm* **1** : quarter, fourth <cuarto de galón : quart> **2** HABITACIÓN : room
cuarzo *nm* : quartz
cuate, -ta *n Mex* **1** : twin **2** *fam* : buddy, pal
cuatrero, -ra *n* : rustler
cuatrillizo, -za *n* : quadruplet
cuatro *adj & nm* : four
cuatrocientos[1]**, -tas** *adj* : four hundred
cuatrocientos[2] *nms & pl* : four hundred
cuba *nf* BARRÍL : cask, barrel
cubano, -na *adj & n* : Cuban
cubertería *nf* : flatware, silverware
cubeta *nf* **1** : keg, cask **2** : bulb (of a thermometer) **3** *Mex* : bucket, pail
cúbico, -ca *adj* : cubic, cubed
cubículo *nm* : cubicle
cubierta *nf* **1** : covering **2** FORRO : cover, jacket (of a book) **3** : deck
cubierto[1] *pp* → **cubrir**
cubierto[2] *nm* **1** : cover, shelter <bajo cubierto : under cover> **2** : table setting **3** : utensil, piece of silverware
cubil *nm* : den, lair
cúbito *nm* : ulna
cubo *nm* **1** : cube **2** BALDE : pail, bucket, can <cubo de basura : garbage can> **3** : hub (of a wheel)
cubrecama *nm* COLCHA : bedspread
cubrir {2} *vt* : to cover — **cubrirse** *vr*
cucaracha *nf* : cockroach, roach
cuchara *nf* : spoon
cucharada *nf* : spoonful
cucharilla *or* **cucharita** *nf* : teaspoon
cucharón *nf, pl* **-rones** : ladle
cuchichear *vi* : to whisper
cuchicheo *nm* : whisper

cuchilla *nf* **1** : kitchen knife, cleaver **2** : blade <cuchilla de afeitar : razor blade> **3** : crest, ridge

cuchillada *nf* : stab, knife wound

cuchillo *nm* : knife

cuclillas *nfpl* **en ~** : squatting, crouching

cuco[1], -ca *adj fam* : pretty, cute

cuco[2] *nm* : cuckoo

cuece, cueza, etc. → **cocer**

cuela, etc. → **colar**

cuelga, cuelgue, etc. → **colgar**

cuello *nm* **1** : neck **2** : collar (of a shirt) **3 cuello del útero** : cervix

cuenca *nf* **1** : river basin **2** : eye socket

cuenco *nm* : bowl, basin

cuenta[1], etc. → **contar**

cuenta[2] *nf* **1** : calculation, count **2** : account **3** : check, bill **4 darse cuenta** : to realize **5 tener en cuenta** : to bear in mind

cuentagotas *nfs & pl* **1** : dropper **2 con ~** : little by little

cuentista *nmf* **1** : short story writer **2** *fam* : liar, fibber

cuento *nm* **1** : story, tale **2 cuento de hadas** : fairy tale **3 sin ~** : countless

cuerda *nf* **1** : cord, rope, string **2 cuerdas vocales** : vocal cords **3 darle cuerda a** : to wind up (a clock, a toy, etc.)

cuerdo, -da *adj* : sane, sensible

cuerno *nm* **1** : horn, antler **2** : cusp (of the moon) **3** : horn (musical instrument)

cuero *nm* **1** : leather, hide **2 cuero cabelludo** : scalp

cuerpo *nm* **1** : body **2** : corps

cuervo *nm* : crow, raven

cuesta[1], etc. → **costar**

cuesta[2] *nf* **1** : slope <cuesta arriba : uphill> **2 a cuestas** : on one's back

cuestión *nf, pl* **-tiones** ASUNTO, TEMA : matter, affair

cuestionable *adj* : questionable, dubious

cuestionar *vt* : to question

cuestionario *nm* **1** : questionnaire **2** : quiz

cueva *nf* : cave

cuidado *nm* **1** : care **2** : worry, concern **3 tener cuidado** : to be careful **4 ¡cuidado!** : watch out!, be careful!

cuidadoso, -sa *adj* : careful, attentive — **cuidadosamente** *adv*

cuidar *vt* **1** : to take care of, to look after **2** : to pay attention to — *vi* **1 ~ de** : to look after **2 cuidar de que** : to make sure that — **cuidarse** *vr* : to take care of oneself

culata *nf* : butt (of a gun)

culatazo *nf* : kick, recoil

culebra *nf* SERPIENTE : snake

culi *nmf* : coolie

culinario, -ria *adj* : culinary

culminante *adj* **punto culminante** : peak, high point, climax

culminar *vi* : to culminate — **culminación** *nf*

culo *nm* **1** *fam* : backside, behind **2** : bottom (of a glass)

culpa *nf* **1** : fault, blame <echarle la culpa a alguien : to blame someone> **2** : sin

culpabilidad *nf* : guilt

culpable[1] *adj* : guilty

culpable[2] *nmf* : culprit, guilty party

culpar *vt* : to blame

cultivado, -da *adj* **1** : cultivated, farmed **2** : cultured

cultivador, -dora *n* : cultivator

cultivar *vt* **1** : to cultivate **2** : to foster

cultivo *nm* **1** : cultivation, farming **2** : crop

culto[1], -ta *adj* : cultured, educated

culto[2] *nm* **1** : worship **2** : cult

cultura *nf* : culture

cultural *adj* : cultural — **culturalmente** *adv*

cumbre *nf* CIMA : top, peak, summit

cumpleaños *nms & pl* : birthday

cumplido[1], -da *adj* **1** : complete, full **2** : courteous, correct

cumplido[2] *nm* : compliment, courtesy <por cumplido : out of courtesy> <andarse con cumplidos : to stand on ceremony, to be formal>

cumplimentar *vt* **1** : to congratulate **2** : to carry out, to perform

cumplimiento *nm* **1** : completion, fulfillment **2** : performance

cumplir *vt* **1** : to accomplish, to carry out **2** : to comply with, to fulfill **3** : to attain, to reach <su hermana cumple los 21 el viernes : her sister will be 21 on Friday> — *vi* **1** : to expire, to fall due **2** : to fulfill one's obligations <cumplir con el deber : to do one's duty> <cumplir con la palabra : to keep one's word> — **cumplirse** *vr* **1** : to come true, to be fulfilled <se cumplieron sus sueños : her dreams came true> **2** : to run out, to expire

cúmulo *nm* **1** MONTÓN : heap, pile **2** : cumulus

cuna *nf* **1** : cradle **2** : birthplace <Puerto Rico es la cuna de la música salsa : Puerto Rico is the birthplace of salsa music>

cundir *vi* **1** : to propagate, to spread <cundió el pánico en el vecindario : panic spread throughout the neighborhood> **2** : to progress, to make headway

cuneta *nf* : ditch (in a road), gutter

cuña *nf* : wedge

cuñado, -da *n* : brother-in-law *m*, sister-in-law *f*

cuño *nm* : die (for stamping)

cuota *nf* **1** : fee, dues **2** : quota, share **3** : installment, payment

cupé *nm* : coupe

cupo[1], etc. → **caber**

cupo[2] *nm* **1** : quota, share **2** : capacity, room

cupón *nm, pl* **cupones 1** : coupon, voucher **2 cupón federal** : food stamp

cúpula *nf* : dome, cupola

cura¹ *nm* : priest
cura² *nf* **1** CURACIÓN, TRATAMIENTO : cure, treatment **2** : dressing, bandage
curación *nf, pl* **-ciones** CURA, TRATAMIENTO : cure, treatment
curandero, -ra *nm* **1** : witch doctor **2** : quack, charlatan
curar *vt* **1** : to cure, to heal **2** : to treat, to dress **3** CURTIR : to tan **4** : to cure (meat) — *vi* : to get well, to recover — **curarse** *vr*
curativo, -va *adj* : curative, healing
curiosear *vi* **1** : to snoop, to pry **2** : to browse — *vt* : to look over, to check
curiosidad *nf* **1** : curiosity **2** : curio
curioso, -sa *adj* **1** : curious, inquisitive **2** : strange, unusual, odd — **curiosamente** *adv*
currículo *nm* → **currículum**
currículum *nm, pl* **-lums 1** : résumé, curriculum vitae **2** : curriculum, course of study
curry ['kurri] *nm, pl* **-rries 1** : curry powder **2** : curry (dish)
cursar *vt* **1** : to attend (school), to take (a course) **2** : to dispatch, to pass on
cursi *adj fam* : affected, pretentious
cursilería *nf* **1** : vulgarity, poor taste **2** : pretentiousness
cursiva *nf* BASTARDILLA : italic type, italics *pl*
curso *nm* **1** : course, direction **2** : school year **3** : course, subject (in school)
cursor *nm* : cursor
curtido, -da *adj* : weather-beaten, leathery (of skin)
curtidor, -dora *n* : tanner
curtiduría *nf* : tannery
curtir *vt* **1** : to tan **2** : to harden, to weather — **curtirse** *vr*
curva *nf* : curve, bend
curvar *vt* : to bend
curvatura *nf* : curvature
curvilíneo, -nea *adj* : curvaceous, shapely
curvo, -va *adj* : curved, bent
cúspide *nf* : zenith, apex, peak
custodia *nf* : custody
custodiar *vt* : to guard, to look after
custodio, -dia *n* : keeper, guardian
cúter *nm* : cutter (boat)
cutícula *nf* : cuticle
cutis *nms & pl* : skin, complexion
cuyo, -ya *adj* **1** : whose, of whom, of which **2 en cuyo caso** : in which case

D

d *nf* : fourth letter of the Spanish alphabet
dable *adj* : feasible, possible
dactilar *adj* **huellas dactilares** : fingerprints
dádiva *nf* : gift, handout
dadivoso, -sa *adj* : generous
dado, -da *adj* **1** : given **2 dado que** : given that, since
dador, -dora *n* : giver, donor
dados *nmpl* : dice
daga *nf* : dagger
dalia *nf* : dahlia
dálmata *nm* : dalmatian
daltónico, -ca *adj* : color-blind
daltonismo *nm* : color blindness
dama *nf* **1** : lady **2 damas** *nfpl* : checkers
damasco *nm* : damask
damisela *nf* : damsel
damnificado, -da *n* : victim (of a disaster)
damnificar {72} *vt* : to damage, to injure
dance, etc. → **danzar**
dandi *nm* : dandy, fop
danés¹, -nesa *adj* : Danish
danés², -nesa *n, mpl* **daneses** : Dane, Danish person
danza *nf* : dance, dancing <danza folklórica : folk dance>
danzante, -ta *n* BAILARÍN : dancer
danzar {21} *v* BAILAR : to dance
dañar *vt* **1** : to damage, to spoil **2** : to harm, to hurt — **dañarse** *vr*
dañino, -na *adj* : harmful
daño *nm* **1** : damage **2** : harm, injury **3 hacer daño a** : to harm, to damage **4 daños y perjuicios** : damages
dar {22} *vt* **1** : to give **2** ENTREGAR : to deliver, to hand over **3** : to hit, to strike **4** : to yield, to produce **5** : to perform **6** : to give off, to emit **7 ~ como** *or* **~ por** : to regard as, to consider — *vi* **1** ALCANZAR : to suffice, to be enough <no me da para dos pasajes : I don't have enough for two fares> **2 ~ a** *or* **~ sobre** : to overlook, to look out on **3 ~ con** : to run into **4 ~ con** : to hit upon (an idea) **5 dar de sí** : to give, to stretch — **darse** *vr* **1** : to give in, to surrender **2** : to occur, to arise **3** : to grow, to come up **4 ~ con** *or* **~ contra** : to hit oneself against **5 dárselas de** : to boast about <se las da de muy listo : he thinks he's very smart>
dardo *nm* : dart
datar *vt* : to date — *vi* **~ de** : to date from, to date back to
dátil *nm* : date (fruit)
dato *nm* **1** : fact, piece of information **2 datos** *nmpl* : data, information
dé → **dar**
de *prep* **1** : of <la casa de Pepe : Pepe's house> <un niño de tres años : a three-year-old boy> **2** : from <es de Managua : she's from Managua> <salió del edificio : he left the building> **3** : in, at <a las tres de la mañana

: at three in the morning> <salen de noche : they go out at night> **4** : than <más de tres : more than three>

deambular *vi* : to wander, to roam

debajo *adv* **1** : underneath, below, on the bottom **2** ~ **de** : under, underneath **3 por** ~ : below, beneath

debate *nm* : debate

debatir *vt* : to debate, to discuss — **debatirse** *vr* : to struggle

debe *nm* : debit column, debit

deber[1] *vt* : to owe — *v aux* **1** : must, have to <debo ir a la oficina : I must go to the office> **2** : should, ought to <deberías buscar trabajo : you ought to look for work> **3** (*expressing probability*) : must <debe ser mexicano : he must be Mexican> — **deberse** *vr* ~ **a** : to be due to

deber[2] *nm* **1** OBLIGACIÓN : duty, obligation **2 deberes** *nmpl Spain* : homework

debidamente *adv* : properly, duly

debido, -da *adj* **1** : right, proper, due **2** ~ **a** : due to, owing to

débil *adj* : weak, feeble — **débilmente** *adv*

debilidad *nf* : weakness, debility, feebleness

debilitamiento *nm* : debilitation, weakening

debilitar *vt* : to debilitate, to weaken — **debilitarse** *vr*

debilucho[1], **-cha** *adj* : weak, frail

debilucho[2], **-cha** *n* : weakling

debitar *vt* : to debit

débito *nm* **1** DEUDA : debt **2** : debit

debut [deˈbut] *nm, pl* **debuts** : debut

debutante[1] *nmf* : beginner, newcomer

debutante[2] *nf* : debutante *f*

debutar *vi* : to debut, to make a debut

década *nf* DECENIO : decade

decadencia *nf* **1** : decadence **2** : decline

decadente *adj* **1** : decadent **2** : declining

decaer {13} *vi* **1** : to decline, to decay, to deteriorate **2** FLAQUEAR : to weaken, to flag

decaiga, etc. → **decaer**

decano, -na *n* **1** : dean **2** : senior member

decantar *vt* : to decant

decapitar *vt* : to decapitate, to behead

decayó, etc. → **decaer**

decena *nf* : group of ten

decencia *nf* : decency

decenio *nm* DÉCADA : decade

decente *adj* : decent — **decentemente** *adv*

decepción *nf, pl* **-ciones** : disappointment, letdown

decepcionante *adj* : disappointing

decepcionar *vt* : to disappoint, to let down — **decepcionarse** *vr*

deceso *nm* DEFUNCIÓN : death, passing

dechado *nm* **1** : sampler (of embroidery) **2** : model, paragon

decibelio *or* **decibel** *nm* : decibel

decidido, -da *adj* : decisive, determined, resolute — **decididamente** *adv*

decidir *vt* **1** : to decide, to determine <no he decidido nada : I haven't made a decision> **2** : to persuade, to decide <su padre lo decidió a estudiar : his father persuaded him to study> — *vi* : to decide — **decidirse** *vr* : to make up one's mind

decimal *adj* : decimal

décimo, -ma *adj* : tenth — **décimo, -ma** *n*

decimoctavo[1], **-va** *adj* : eighteenth

decimoctavo[2], **-va** *nm* : eighteenth (in a series)

decimocuarto[1], **-ta** *adj* : fourteenth

decimocuarto[2], **-ta** *nm* : fourteenth (in a series)

decimonoveno[1], **-na** *or* **decimonono, -na** *adj* : nineteenth

decimonoveno[2], **-na** *or* **decimonono, -na** *nm* : nineteenth (in a series)

decimoquinto[1], **-ta** *adj* : fifteenth

decimoquinto[2], **-ta** *nm* : fifteenth (in a series)

decimoséptimo[1], **-ma** *adj* : seventeenth

decimoséptimo[2], **-ma** *nm* : seventeenth (in a series)

decimosexto[1], **-ta** *adj* : sixteenth

decimosexto[2], **-ta** *nm* : sixteenth (in a series)

decimotercero[1], **-ra** *adj* : thirteenth

decimotercero[2], **-ra** *nm* : thirteenth (in a series)

decir[1] {23} *vt* **1** : to say <dice que no quiere ir : she says she doesn't want to go> **2** : to tell <dime lo que estás pensando : tell me what you're thinking> **3** : to speak, to talk <no digas tonterías : don't talk nonsense> **4** : to call <me dicen Rosy : they call me Rosy> **5 es decir** : that is to say **6 querer decir** : to mean — **decirse** *vr* **1** : to say to oneself **2** : to be said <¿cómo se dice "lápiz" en francés? : how do you say "pencil" in French?>

decir[2] *nm* DICHO : saying, expression

decisión *nf, pl* **-siones** : decision, choice

decisivo, -va *adj* : decisive, conclusive — **decisivamente** *adv*

declamar *vi* : to declaim — *vt* : to recite

declaración *nf, pl* **-ciones 1** : declaration, statement **2** TESTIMONIO : deposition, testimony **3 declaración de derechos** : bill of rights **4 declaración jurada** : affidavit

declarado, -da *adj* : professed, open — **declaradamente** *adv*

declarar *vt* : to declare, to state — *vi* ATESTIGUAR : to testify — **declararse** *vr* **1** : to declare oneself, to make a statement **2** : to confess one's love **3**

: to plead (in court) <declararse inocente : to plead not guilty>
declinación *nf, pl* **-ciones 1** : drop, downward trend **2** : declination **3** : declension (in grammar)
declinar *vt* : to decline, to turn down — *vi* **1** : to draw to a close **2** : to diminish, to decline
declive *nm* **1** DECADENCIA : decline **2** : slope, incline
decodificador *nm* : decoder
decolar *vi Chile, Col, Ecua* : to take off (of an airplane)
decolorar *vt* : to bleach — **decolorarse** *vr* : to fade
decomisar *vt* CONFISCAR : to seize, to confiscate
decomiso *nm* : seizure, confiscation
decoración *nf, pl* **-ciones 1** : decoration **2** : decor **3** : stage set, scenery
decorado *nm* : stage set, scenery
decorador, -dora *n* : decorator
decorar *vt* ADORNAR : to decorate, to adorn
decorativo, -va *adj* : decorative, ornamental
decoro *nm* : decorum, propriety
decoroso, -sa *adj* : decent, proper, respectable
decrecer {53} *vi* : to decrease, to wane, to diminish — **decreciente** *adj*
decrecimiento *nm* : decrease, decline
decrépito, -ta *adj* : decrepit
decretar *vt* : to decree, to order
decreto *nm* : decree
decúbito *nm* : horizontal position <en decúbito prono : prone> <en decúbito supino : supine>
dedal *nm* : thimble
dedalera *nf* DIGITAL : foxglove
dedicación *nf, pl* **-ciones** : dedication, devotion
dedicar {72} *vt* CONSAGRAR : to dedicate, to devote — **dedicarse** *vr* **~ a** : to devote oneself to, to engage in
dedicatoria *nf* : dedication (of a book, song, etc.)
dedo *nm* **1** : finger <dedo meñique : little finger> **2 dedo del pie** : toe
deducción *nf, pl* **-ciones** : deduction
deducible *adj* **1** : deducible, inferable **2** : deductible
deducir {61} *vt* **1** INFERIR : to deduce **2** DESCONTAR : to deduct
defecar {72} *vi* : to defecate — **defecación** *nf*
defecto *nm* **1** : defect, flaw, shortcoming **2 en su defecto** : lacking that, in the absence of that
defectuoso, -sa *adj* : defective, faulty
defender {56} *vt* : to defend, to protect — **defenderse** *vr* **1** : to defend oneself **2** : to get by, to know the basics <su inglés no es perfecto pero se defiende : his English isn't perfect but he gets by>
defendible *adj* : defensible, tenable
defensa[1] *nf* : defense
defensa[2] *nmf* : defender, back (in sports)
defensiva *nf* : defensive, defense
defensivo, -va *adj* : defensive — **defensivamente** *adv*
defensor[1], -sora *adj* : defending, defense
defensor[2], -sora *n* **1** : defender, advocate **2** : defense counsel
defeño, -ña *n* : person from the Federal District (Mexico City)
deficiencia *nf* : deficiency, flaw
deficiente *adj* : deficient
déficit *nm, pl* **-cits 1** : deficit **2** : shortage, lack
definición *nf, pl* **-ciones** : definition
definido, -da *adj* : definite, well-defined
definir *vt* **1** : to define **2** : to determine
definitivamente *adv* **1** : finally **2** : permanently, for good **3** : definitely, absolutely
definitivo, -va *adj* **1** : definitive, conclusive **2 en definitiva** : all in all, on the whole **3 en definitiva** *Mex* : permanently, for good
deflación *nf, pl* **-ciones** : deflation
deforestación *nf, pl* **-ciones** : deforestation
deformación *nf, pl* **-ciones 1** : deformation **2** : distortion
deformar *vt* **1** : to deform, to disfigure **2** : to distort — **deformarse** *vr*
deforme *adj* : deformed, misshapen
deformidad *nf* : deformity
defraudación *nf, pl* **-ciones** : fraud
defraudar *vt* **1** ESTAFAR : to defraud, to cheat **2** : to disappoint
defunción *nf, pl* **-ciones** DECESO : death, passing
degeneración *nf, pl* **-ciones 1** : degeneration **2** : degeneracy, depravity
degenerado, -da *adj* DEPRAVADO : degenerate
degenerar *vi* : to degenerate
degenerativo, -va *adj* : degenerative
degollar {19} *vt* **1** : to slit the throat of, to slaughter **2** DECAPITAR : to behead **3** : to ruin, to destroy
degradación *nf, pl* **-ciones 1** : degradation **2** : demotion
degradar *vt* **1** : to degrade, to debase **2** : to demote
degustación *nf, pl* **-ciones** : tasting, sampling
degustar *vt* : to taste
deidad *nf* : deity
deificar {72} *vt* : to idolize, to deify
dejado, -da *adj* **1** : slovenly **2** : careless, lazy
dejar *vt* **1** : to leave **2** ABANDONAR : to abandon, to forsake **3** : to let be, to let go **4** PERMITIR : to allow, to permit — *vi* **~ de** : to stop, to quit <dejar de fumar : to quit smoking> — **dejarse** *vr* **1** : to let oneself be <se deja insultar : he lets himself be insulted> **2** : to forget, to leave <me dejé las llaves en el carro : I left the keys in

the car> **3 :** to neglect oneself, to let oneself go **4 :** to grow <nos estamos dejando el pelo largo : we're growing our hair long>

dejo *nm* **1 :** aftertaste **2 :** touch, hint **3 :** (regional) accent

delación *nf, pl* **-ciones :** denunciation, betrayal

delantal *nm* **1 :** apron **2 :** pinafore

delante *adv* **1** ENFRENTE **:** ahead, in front **2 ~ de :** before, in front of

delantera *nf* **1 :** front, front part, front row <tomar la delantera : to take the lead> **2 :** forward line (in sports)

delantero[1], -ra *adj* **1 :** front, forward **2 tracción delantera :** front-wheel drive

delantero[2], -ra *n* **:** forward (in sports)

delatar *vt* **1 :** to betray, to reveal **2 :** to denounce, to inform against

delegación *nf, pl* **-ciones :** delegation

delegado, -da *n* **:** delegate, representative

delegar {52} *vt* **:** to delegate

deleitar *vt* **:** to delight, to please — **deleitarse** *vr*

deleite *nm* **:** delight, pleasure

deletrear *vi* **:** to spell <¿como se deletrea? : how do you spell it?>

deleznable *adj* **1 :** brittle, crumbly **2 :** slippery **3 :** weak, fragile <una excusa deleznable : a weak excuse>

delfín *nm, pl* **delfines 1 :** dolphin **2 :** dauphin, heir apparent

delgadez *nf* **:** thinness, skinniness

delgado, -da *adj* **1** FLACO **:** thin, skinny **2** ESBELTO **:** slender, slim **3** DELICADO **:** delicate, fine **4** AGUDO **:** sharp, clever

deliberación *nf, pl* **-ciones :** deliberation

deliberado, -da *adj* **:** deliberate, intentional — **deliberadamente** *adv*

deliberar *vi* **:** to deliberate

deliberativo, -va *adj* **:** deliberative

delicadeza *nf* **1 :** delicacy, fineness **2 :** gentleness, softness **3 :** tact, discretion, consideration

delicado, -da *adj* **1 :** delicate, fine **2 :** sensitive, frail **3 :** difficult, tricky **4 :** fussy, hard to please **5 :** tactful, considerate

delicia *nf* **:** delight

delicioso, -sa *adj* **1** RICO **:** delicious **2 :** delightful

delictivo, -va *adj* **:** criminal

delictuoso, -sa → **delictivo**

delimitación *nf, pl* **-ciones 1 :** demarcation **2 :** defining, specifying

delimitar *vt* **1 :** to demarcate **2 :** to define, to specify

delincuencia *nf* **:** delinquency, crime

delincuente[1] *adj* **:** delinquent

delincuente[2] *nmf* CRIMINAL **:** delinquent, criminal

delinear *vt* **1 :** to delineate, to outline **2 :** to draft, to draw up

delinquir {24} *vi* **:** to break the law

delirante *adj* **:** delirious

delirar *vi* DESVARIAR **1 :** to be delirious **2 :** to rave, to talk nonsense

delirio *nm* **1** DESVARÍO **:** delirium **2** DISPARATE **:** nonsense, ravings *pl* <delirios de grandeza : delusions of grandeur> **3** FRENESÍ **:** mania, frenzy <¡fue el delirio! : it was wild!>

delito *nm* **:** crime, offense

delta *nm* **:** delta

demacrado, -da *adj* **:** emaciated, gaunt

demagogia *nf* **:** demagogy

demagógico, -ca *adj* **:** demagogic, demagogical

demagogo, -ga *n* **:** demagogue

demanda *nf* **1 :** demand <la oferta y la demanda : supply and demand> **2 :** petition, request **3 :** lawsuit

demandado, -da *n* **:** defendant

demandante *nmf* **:** plaintiff

demandar *vt* **1 :** to demand **2** REQUERIR **:** to call for, to require **3 :** to sue, to file a lawsuit against

demarcar {72} *vt* **:** to demarcate — **demarcación** *nf*

demás[1] *adj* **:** remaining <acabó las demás tareas : she finished the rest of the chores>

demás[2] *pron* **1 lo (la, los, las) demás :** the rest, everyone else, everything else <Pepe, Rosa, y los demás : Pepe, Rosa, and everybody else> **2 estar por demás :** to be of no use, to be pointless <no estaría por demás : it couldn't hurt, it's worth a try> **3 por demás :** extremely **4 por lo demás :** otherwise **5 y demás :** and so on, et cetera

demasía *nf* **en ~ :** excessively, in excess

demasiado[1] *adv* **1 :** too <vas demasiado aprisa : you're going too fast> **2 :** too much <estoy comiendo demasiado : I'm eating too much>

demasiado[2], -da *adj* **:** too much, too many, excessive

demencia *nf* **1 :** dementia **2** LOCURA **:** madness, insanity

demente[1] *adj* **:** insane, mad

demente[2] *nmf* **:** insane person

demeritar *vt* **1 :** to detract from **2 :** to discredit

demérito *nm* **1 :** fault **2 :** discredit, disrepute

democracia *nf* **:** democracy

demócrata[1] *adj* **:** democratic

demócrata[2] *nmf* **:** democrat

democrático, -ca *adj* **:** democratic — **democráticamente** *adv*

democratizar {21} *vt* **:** to democratize, to make democratic

demografía *nf* **:** demography

demográfico, -ca *adj* **:** demographic

demoledor, -dora *adj* **:** devastating

demoler {47} *vt* DERRIBAR, DERRUMBAR **:** to demolish, to destroy

demolición *nf, pl* **-ciones :** demolition

demonio *nm* DIABLO **:** devil, demon

demora *nf* **:** delay

demorar *vt* **1** RETRASAR **:** to delay **2** TARDAR **:** to take, to last <la reparación demorará varios días **:** the repair will take several days> — *vi* **:** to delay, to linger — **demorarse** *vr* **1 :** to be slow, to take a long time **2 :** to take too long
demostración *nf, pl* **-ciones :** demonstration
demostrar {19} *vt* **:** to demonstrate, to show
demostrativo, -va *adj* **:** demonstrative
demudar *vt* **:** to change, to alter — **demudarse** *vr* **:** to change one's expression
denegación *nf, pl* **-ciones :** denial, refusal
denegar {49} *vt* **:** to deny, to turn down
denigrante *adj* **:** degrading, humiliating
denigrar *vt* **1** DIFAMAR **:** to denigrate, to disparage **2 :** to degrade, to humiliate
denodado, -da *adj* **:** bold, dauntless
denominación *nf, pl* **-ciones 1 :** name, designation **2 :** denomination (of money)
denominador *nm* **:** denominator
denominar *vt* **:** to designate, to name
denostar {19} *vt* **:** to revile
denotar *vt* **:** to denote, to show
densidad *nf* **:** density, thickness
denso, -sa *adj* **:** dense, thick — **densamente** *adv*
dentado, -da *adj* SERRADO **:** serrated, jagged
dentadura *nf* **1 :** teeth *pl* **2 dentadura postiza :** dentures *pl*
dental *adj* **:** dental
dentellada *nf* **1 :** bite **2 :** tooth mark
dentera *nf* **1 :** envy, jealousy **2 dar dentera :** to set one's teeth on edge
dentición *nf, pl* **-ciones 1 :** teething **2 :** dentition, set of teeth
dentífrico *nm* **:** toothpaste
dentista *nmf* **:** dentist
dentro *adv* **1 :** in, inside **2 :** indoors **3 ~ de :** within, inside, in **4 dentro de poco :** soon, shortly **5 dentro de todo :** all in all, all things considered **6 por ~ :** inwardly, inside
denuedo *nm* **:** valor, courage
denuesto *nm* **:** insult
denuncia *nf* **1 :** denunciation, condemnation **2 :** police report
denunciante *nmf* **:** accuser (of a crime)
denunciar *vt* **1 :** to denounce, to condemn **2 :** to report (to the authorities)
deparar *vt* **:** to have in store for, to provide with <no sabemos lo que nos depara el destino **:** we don't know what fate has in store for us>
departamental *adj* **1 :** departmental **2 tienda departamental** *Mex* **:** department store
departamento *nm* **1 :** department **2** APARTAMENTO **:** apartment
departir *vi* **:** to converse
dependencia *nf* **1 :** dependence, dependency <dependencia emocional **:** emotional dependence> <dependencia del alcohol **:** dependence on alcohol> **2 :** agency, branch office
depender *vi* **1 :** to depend **2 ~ de :** to depend on **3 ~ de :** to be subordinate to
dependiente[1] *adj* **:** dependent
dependiente[2]**, -ta** *n* **:** clerk, salesperson
deplorable *adj* **:** deplorable
deplorar *vt* **1 :** to deplore **2** LAMENTAR **:** to regret
deponer {60} *vt* **1 :** to depose, to overthrow **2 :** to abandon (an attitude or stance) **3 deponer las armas :** to lay down one's arms — *vi* **1** TESTIFICAR **:** to testify, to make a statement **2** EVACUAR **:** to defecate
deportación *nf, pl* **-ciones :** deportation
deportar *vt* **:** to deport
deporte *nm* **:** sport, sports *pl* <hacer deporte **:** to engage in sports>
deportista[1] *adj* **1 :** fond of sports **2 :** sporty
deportista[2] *nmf* **1 :** sports fan **2 :** athlete, sportsman *m,* sportswoman *f*
deportividad *nf Spain* **:** sportsmanship
deportivo, -va *adj* **1 :** sports, sporting <artículos deportivos **:** sporting goods> **2 :** sporty
deposición *nf, pl* **-ciones 1 :** statement, testimony **2 :** removal from office
depositante *nmf* **:** depositor
depositar *vt* **1 :** to deposit, to place **2 :** to store — **depositarse** *vr* **:** to settle
depósito *nm* **1 :** deposit **2 :** warehouse, storehouse
depravado, -da *adj* DEGENERADO **:** depraved, degenerate
depravar *vt* **:** to deprave, to corrupt
depreciación *nf, pl* **-ciones :** depreciation
depreciar *vt* **:** to depreciate, to reduce the value of — **depreciarse** *vr* **:** to lose value
depredación *nf* SAQUEO **:** depredation, plunder
depredador[1]**, -dora** *adj* **:** predatory
depredador[2] *nm* **1 :** predator **2** SAQUEADOR **:** plunderer
depresión *nf, pl* **-siones 1 :** depression **2 :** hollow, recess **3 :** drop, fall **4 :** slump, recession
depresivo[1]**, -va** *adj* **1 :** depressive **2 :** depressant
depresivo[2] *nm* **:** depressant
deprimente *adj* **:** depressing
deprimir *vt* **1 :** to depress **2 :** to lower — **deprimirse** *vr* ABATIRSE **:** to get depressed
depuesto *pp* → **deponer**
depuración *nf, pl* **-ciones 1** PURIFICACIÓN **:** purification **2** PURGA **:** purge **3 :** refinement, polish
depurar *vt* **1** PURIFICAR **:** to purify **2** PURGAR **:** to purge
depuso, etc. → **deponer**
derecha *nf* **1 :** right **2 :** right hand, right side **3 :** right wing, right (in politics)

derechazo *nm* **1 :** pass with the cape on the right hand (in bullfighting) **2 :** right (in boxing) **3 :** forehand (in tennis)
derechista[1] *adj* **:** rightist, right-wing
derechista[2] *nmf* **:** right-winger
derecho[1] *adv* **1 :** straight **2 :** upright **3 :** directly
derecho[2], **-cha** *adj* **1 :** right **2 :** right-hand **3 :** RECTO **:** straight, upright, erect
derecho[3] *nm* **1 :** right <derechos humanos : human rights> **2 :** law <derecho civil : civil law> **3 :** right side (of cloth or clothing)
deriva *nf* **1 :** drift **2 a la deriva :** adrift
derivación *nf, pl* **-ciones :** derivation
derivar *vi* **1 :** to drift **2 ~ de :** to come from, to derive from **3 ~ en :** to result in — *vt* **:** to steer, to direct <derivó la discusión hacia la política : he steered the discussion over to politics> — **derivarse** *vr* **:** to be derived from, to arise from
dermatología *nf* **:** dermatology
dermatológico, -ca *adj* **:** dermatological
dermatólogo, -ga *n* **:** dermatologist
derogación *nf, pl* **-ciones :** abolition, repeal
derogar {52} *vt* ABOLIR **:** to abolish, to repeal
derramamiento *nm* **1 :** spilling, overflowing **2 derramamiento de sangre :** bloodshed
derramar *vt* **1 :** to spill **2 :** to shed (tears, blood) — **derramarse** *vr* **1 :** to spill over **2 :** to scatter
derrame *nm* **1 :** spilling, shedding **2 :** leakage, overflow **3 :** discharge, hemorrhage
derrapar *vi* **:** to skid
derrape *nm* **:** skid
derredor *nm* **al derredor** *or* **en derredor :** around, round about
derrengado, -da *adj* **1 :** bent, twisted **2 :** exhausted
derretir {54} *vt* **:** to melt, to thaw — **derretirse** *vr* **1 :** to melt, to thaw **2 ~ por** *fam* **:** to be crazy about
derribar *vt* **1** DEMOLER, DERRUMBAR **:** to demolish, to knock down **2 :** to shoot down, to bring down (an airplane) **3** DERROCAR **:** to overthrow
derribo *nm* **1 :** demolition, razing **2 :** shooting down **3 :** overthrow
derrocamiento *nm* **:** overthrow
derrocar {72} *vt* DERRIBAR **:** to overthrow, to topple
derrochador[1], **-dora** *adj* **:** extravagant, wasteful
derrochador[2], **-dora** *n* **:** spendthrift
derrochar *vt* **:** to waste, to squander
derroche *nm* **:** extravagance, waste
derrota *nf* **1 :** defeat, rout **2 :** course (at sea)
derrotar *vt* **:** to defeat
derrotero *nm* RUTA **:** course
derrotista *adj & nmf* **:** defeatist
derruir {41} *vt* **:** to demolish, to tear down
derrumbamiento *nm* **:** collapse
derrumbar *vt* **1** DEMOLER, DERRIBAR **:** to demolish, to knock down **2** DESPEÑAR **:** to cast down, to topple — **derrumbarse** *vr* DESPLOMARSE **:** to collapse, to break down
derrumbe *nm* **1** DESPLOME **:** collapse, fall <el derrumbe del comunismo : the fall of Communism> **2 :** landslide
desabastecimiento *nm* **:** shortage, scarcity
desabasto *nm Mex* **:** shortage, scarcity
desabrido, -da *adj* **:** tasteless, bland
desabrigar {52} *vt* **1 :** to undress **2 :** to uncover **3 :** to deprive of shelter
desabrochar *vt* **:** to unbutton, to undo — **desabrocharse** *vr* **:** to come undone
desacato *nm* **1 :** disrespect **2 :** contempt (of court)
desacelerar *vi* **:** to decelerate, to slow down
desacertado, -da *adj* **1 :** mistaken **2 :** unwise
desacertar {55} *vi* ERRAR **:** to err, to be mistaken
desacierto *nm* ERROR **:** error, mistake
desaconsejado, -da *adj* **:** ill-advised, unwise
desacorde *adj* **1 :** conflicting **2 :** discordant
desacostumbrado, -da *adj* **:** unaccustomed, unusual
desacreditar *vt* DESPRESTIGIAR **:** to discredit, to disgrace
desactivar *vt* **:** to deactivate, to defuse
desacuerdo *nm* **:** disagreement
desafiante *adj* **:** defiant
desafiar {85} *vt* RETAR **:** to defy, to challenge
desafilado, -da *adj* **:** blunt
desafinado, -da *adj* **:** out-of-tune, off-key
desafinarse *vr* **:** to go out of tune
desafío *nm* **1** RETO **:** challenge **2** RESISTENCIA **:** defiance
desafortunado, -da *adj* **:** unfortunate, unlucky — **desafortunadamente** *adv*
desafuero *nm* ABUSO **:** injustice, outrage
desagradable *adj* **:** unpleasant, disagreeable — **desagradablemente** *adv*
desagradar *vi* **:** to be unpleasant, to be disagreeable
desagradecido, -da *adj* **:** ungrateful
desagrado *nm* **1 :** displeasure **2 con ~ :** reluctantly
desagravio *nm* **1 :** apology **2 :** amends, reparation
desagregarse {52} *vr* **:** to break up, to disintegrate
desaguar {10} *vi* **:** to drain, to empty
desagüe *nm* **1 :** drain **2 :** drainage
desahogado, -da *adj* **1 :** well-off, comfortable **2 :** spacious, roomy

desahogar {52} *vt* **1** : to relieve, to ease **2** : to give vent to — **desahogarse** *vr* **1** : to recover, to feel better **2** : to unburden oneself, to let off steam
desahogo *nm* **1** : relief, outlet **2 con ~** : comfortably
desahuciar *vt* **1** : to deprive of hope **2** : to evict — **desahuciarse** *vr* : to lose all hope
desahucio *nm* : eviction
desairar {5} *vt* : to snub, to rebuff
desaire *nm* : rebuff, snub, slight
desajustar *vt* **1** : to disarrange, to put out of order **2** : to upset (plans)
desajuste *nm* **1** : maladjustment **2** : imbalance **3** : upset, disruption
desalentar {55} *vt* DESANIMAR : to discourage, to dishearten — **desalentarse** *vr*
desaliento *nm* : discouragement
desaliñado, -da *adj* : slovenly, untidy
desalmado, -da *adj* : heartless, callous
desalojar *vt* **1** : to remove, to clear **2** EVACUAR : to evacuate, to vacate **3** : to evict
desalojo *nm* **1** : removal, expulsion **2** : evacuation **3** : eviction
desamor *nm* **1** FRIALDAD : indifference **2** ENEMISTAD : dislike, enmity
desamparado, -da *adj* DESVALIDO : helpless, destitute
desamparar *vt* : to abandon, to forsake
desamparo *nm* **1** : abandonment, neglect **2** : helplessness
desamueblado, -da *adj* : unfurnished
desandar {6} *vt* : to go back, to return to the starting point
desangelado, -da *adj* : dull, lifeless
desangrar *vt* : to bleed, to bleed dry — **desangrarse** *vr* **1** : to be bleeding **2** : to bleed to death
desanimar *vt* DESALENTAR : to discourage, to dishearten — **desanimarse** *vr*
desánimo *nm* DESALIENTO : discouragement, dejection
desanudar *vt* : to untie, to disentangle
desapacible *adj* : unpleasant, disagreeable
desaparecer {53} *vt* : to cause to disappear — *vi* : to disappear, to vanish
desaparecido[1], **-da** *adj* **1** : late, deceased **2** : missing
desaparecido[2], **-da** *n* : missing person
desaparición *nf, pl* **-ciones** : disappearance
desapasionado, -da *adj* : dispassionate, impartial — **desapasionadamente** *adv*
desapego *nm* : coolness, indifference
desapercibido, -da *adj* **1** : unnoticed **2** DESPREVENIDO : unprepared, off guard
desaprobación *nf, pl* **-ciones** : disapproval
desaprobar {19} *vt* REPROBAR : to disapprove of
desaprovechar *vt* MALGASTAR : to waste, to misuse — *vi* : to lose ground, to slip back
desarmador *nm Mex* : screwdriver
desarmar *vt* **1** : to disarm **2** DESMONTAR : to disassemble, to take apart
desarme *nm* : disarmament
desarraigado, -da *adj* : rootless
desarraigar {52} *vt* : to uproot, to root out
desarreglado, -da *adj* : untidy, disorganized
desarreglar *vt* **1** : to mess up **2** : to upset, to disrupt
desarreglo *nm* **1** : untidiness **2** : disorder, confusion
desarrollar *vt* : to develop — **desarrollarse** *vr* : to take place
desarrollo *nm* : development
desarticulación *nf, pl* **-ciones** **1** : dislocation **2** : breaking up, dismantling
desarticular *vt* **1** DISLOCAR : to dislocate **2** : to break up, to dismantle
desaseado, -da *adj* **1** : dirty **2** : messy, untidy
desastre *nm* CATÁSTROFE : disaster
desastroso, -sa *adj* : disastrous, catastrophic
desatar *vt* **1** : to undo, to untie **2** : to unleash **3** : to trigger, to precipitate — **desatarse** *vr* : to break out, to erupt
desatascar {72} *vt* : to unblock, to clear
desatención *nf, pl* **-ciones** **1** : absentmindedness, distraction **2** : discourtesy
desatender {56} *vt* **1** : to disregard **2** : to neglect
desatento, -ta *adj* **1** DISTRAÍDO : absentminded **2** GROSERO : discourteous, rude
desatinado, -da *adj* : foolish, silly
desatino *nm* : folly, mistake
desautorizar {21} *vt* : to deprive of authority, to discredit
desavenencia *nf* DISCORDANCIA : disagreement, dispute
desayunar *vi* : to have breakfast — *vt* : to have for breakfast
desayuno *nm* : breakfast
desazón *nf, pl* **-zones** INQUIETUD : uneasiness, anxiety
desbalance *nm* : imbalance
desbancar {72} *vt* : to displace, to oust
desbandada *nf* : scattering, dispersal
desbarajuste *nm* DESORDEN : disarray, disorder, mess
desbaratar *vt* **1** ARRUINAR : to destroy, to ruin **2** DESCOMPONER : to break, to break down — **desbaratarse** *vr* : to fall apart
desbloquear *vt* **1** : to open up, to clear, to break through **2** : to free, to release
desbocado, -da *adj* : unbridled, rampant
desbocarse {72} *vr* : to run away, to bolt
desbordamiento *nm* : overflowing
desbordante *adj* : overflowing, bursting <desbordante de energía : bursting with energy>
desbordar *vt* **1** : to overflow, to spill over **2** : to surpass, to exceed **3** : to

burst with, to brim with — **desbordarse** *vr*
descabellado, -da *adj* : outlandish, ridiculous
descafeinado, -da *adj* : decaffeinated
descalabrar *vt* : to hit on the head — **descalabrarse** *vr*
descalabro *nm* : setback, misfortune, loss
descalificar {72} *vt* : to disqualify — **descalificarse** *vr*
descalzarse {21} *vr* : take off one's shoes
descalzo, -za *adj* : barefoot
descansado, -da *adj* **1** : rested, refreshed **2** : restful, peaceful
descansar *vi* : to rest, to relax — *vt* : to rest <descansar la vista : to rest one's eyes>
descansillo *nm* : landing (of a staircase)
descanso *nm* **1** : rest, relaxation **2** : break **3** : landing (of a staircase) **4** : intermission
descapotable *adj & nm* : convertible
descarado, -da *adj* : brazen, impudent — **descaradamente** *adv*
descarga *nf* **1** : discharge **2** : unloading
descargar {52} *vt* **1** : to discharge **2** : to unload **3** : to release, to free **4** : to take out, to vent (anger, etc.) — **descargarse** *vr* **1** : to unburden oneself **2** : to quit **3** : to lose power
descargo *nm* **1** : unloading **2** : defense <testigo de descargo : witness for the defense>
descarnado, -da *adj* : scrawny, gaunt
descaro *nm* : audacity, nerve
descarriado, -da *adj* : lost, gone astray
descarrilar *vi* : to derail — **descarrilarse** *vr*
descartar *vt* : to rule out, to reject — **descartarse** *vr* : to discard
descascarar *vt* : to peel, to shell, to husk — **descascararse** *vr* : to peel off, to chip
descendencia *nf* **1** : descendants *pl* **2** LINAJE : descent, lineage
descendente *adj* : downward, descending
descender {56} *vt* **1** : to descend, to go down **2** BAJAR : to lower, to take down, to let down — *vi* **1** : to descend, to come down **2** : to drop, to fall **3** ~ **de** : to be a descendant of
descendiente *adj & nm* : descendant
descenso *nm* **1** : descent **2** BAJA, CAÍDA : drop, fall
descentralizar {21} *vt* : to decentralize — **descentralizarse** *vr* — **descentralización** *nf*
descifrable *adj* : decipherable
descifrar *vt* : to decipher, to decode
descolgar {16} *vt* **1** : to take down, to let down **2** : to pick up, to answer (the telephone)
descollar {19} *vi* SOBRESALIR : to stand out, to be outstanding, to excel
descolorarse *vr* : to fade
descolorido, -da *adj* : discolored, faded
descomponer {60} *vt* **1** : to rot, to decompose **2** DESBARATAR : to break, to break down — **descomponerse** *vr* **1** : to break down **2** : to decompose
descomposición *nf, pl* **-ciones 1** : breakdown, decomposition **2** : decay
descompresión *nf* : decompression
descompuesto[1] *pp* → **descomponer**
descompuesto[2], **-ta** *adj* **1** : broken down, out of order **2** : rotten, decomposed
descomunal *adj* **1** ENORME : enormous, huge **2** EXTRAORDINARIO : extraordinary
desconcertante *adj* : disconcerting
desconcertar {55} *vt* : to disconcert — **desconcertarse** *vr*
desconchar *vt* : to chip — **desconcharse** *vr* : to chip off, to peel
desconcierto *nm* : uncertainty, confusion
desconectar *vt* **1** : to disconnect, to switch off **2** : to unplug
desconfiado, -da *adj* : distrustful, suspicious
desconfianza *nf* RECELO : distrust, suspicion
desconfiar {85} *vi* ~ **de** : to distrust, to be suspicious of
descongelar *vt* **1** : to thaw **2** : to defrost **3** : to unfreeze (assets) — **descongelarse** *vr*
descongestionante *adj & nm* : decongestant
desconocer {18} *vt* **1** IGNORAR : to be unaware of **2** : to fail to recognize
desconocido[1], **-da** *adj* : unknown, unfamiliar
desconocido[2], **-da** *n* EXTRAÑO : stranger
desconocimiento *nm* : ignorance
desconsiderado, -da *adj* : inconsiderate, thoughtless — **desconsideradamente** *adj*
desconsolado, -da *adj* : disconsolate, heartbroken
desconsuelo *nm* AFLICCIÓN : grief, distress, despair
descontaminar *vt* : to decontaminate — **descontaminación** *nf*
descontar {19} *vt* **1** : to discount, to deduct **2** EXCEPTUAR : to except, to exclude
descontento[1], **-ta** *adj* : discontented, dissatisfied
descontento[2] *nm* : discontent, dissatisfaction
descontrol *nm* : lack of control, disorder, chaos
descontrolarse *vr* : to get out of control, to be out of hand
descorazonado, -da *adj* : disheartened, discouraged
descorrer *vt* : to draw back
descortés *adj, pl* **-teses** : discourteous, rude
descortesía *nf* : discourtesy, rudeness

descrédito *nm* DESPRESTIGIO **:** discredit
descremado, -da *adj* **:** nonfat, skim
describir {33} *vt* **:** to describe
descripción *nf, pl* **-ciones :** description
descriptivo, -va *adj* **:** descriptive
descrito *pp* → **describir**
descuartizar {21} *vt* **1 :** to cut up, to quarter **2 :** to tear to pieces
descubierto[1] *pp* → **descubrir**
descubierto[2]**, -ta** *adj* **1 :** exposed, revealed **2 al descubierto :** out in the open
descubridor, -dora *n* **:** discoverer, explorer
descubrimiento *nm* **:** discovery
descubrir {2} *vt* **1** HALLAR **:** to discover, to find out **2** REVELAR **:** to uncover, to reveal — **descubrirse** *vr*
descuento *nm* REBAJA **:** discount
descuidado, -da *adj* **1 :** neglectful, careless **2 :** neglected, unkempt
descuidar *vt* **:** to neglect, to overlook — *vi* **:** to be careless — **descuidarse** *vr* **1 :** to be careless, to drop one's guard **2 :** to let oneself go
descuido *nm* **1 :** carelessness, negligence **2 :** slip, oversight
desde *prep* **1 :** from **2 :** since **3 desde ahora :** from now on **4 desde entonces :** since then **5 desde hace :** for, since (a time) <ha estado nevando desde hace dos días : it's been snowing for two days> **6 desde luego :** of course **7 desde que :** since, ever since **8 desde ya :** right now, immediately
desdecir {11} *vi* **~ de 1 :** to be unworthy of **2 :** to clash with — **desdecirse** *vr* **1** CONTRADECIRSE **:** to contradict oneself **2** RETRACTARSE **:** to go back on one's word
desdén *nm, pl* **desdenes** DESPRECIO **:** disdain, scorn
desdentado, -da *adj* **:** toothless
desdeñar *vt* DESPRECIAR **:** to disdain, to scorn, to despise
desdeñoso, -sa *adj* **:** disdainful, scornful — **desdeñosamente** *adv*
desdibujar *vt* **:** to blur — **desdibujarse** *vr*
desdicha *nf* **1 :** misery **2 :** misfortune
desdichado[1]**, -da** *adj* **1 :** unfortunate **2 :** miserable, unhappy
desdichado[2]**, -da** *n* **:** wretch
desdicho *pp* → **desdecir**
desdiga, desdijo, etc. → **desdecir**
desdoblar *vt* DESPLEGAR **:** to unfold
deseable *adj* **:** desirable
desear *vt* **1 :** to wish <te deseo buena suerte : I wish you good luck> **2** QUERER **:** to want, to desire
desechable *adj* **:** disposable
desechar *vt* **1 :** to discard, to throw away **2** RECHAZAR **:** to reject
desecho *nm* **1 :** reject **2 desechos** *nmpl* RESIDUOS **:** rubbish, waste
desembarazarse {21} *vr* **~ de :** to get rid of
desembarcadero *nm* **:** jetty, landing pier
desembarcar {72} *vi* **:** to disembark — *vt* **:** to unload
desembarco *nm* **1 :** landing, arrival **2 :** unloading
desembarque *nm* → **desembarco**
desembocadura *nf* **1 :** mouth (of a river) **2 :** opening, end (of a street)
desembocar {72} *vi* **~ en** *or* **~ a 1 :** to flow into, to join **2 :** to lead to, to result in
desembolsar *vt* PAGAR **:** to disburse, to pay out
desembolso *nm* PAGO **:** disbursement, payment
desempacar {72} *v* **:** to unpack
desempate *nm* **:** tiebreaker, play-off
desempeñar *vt* **1 :** to play (a role) **2 :** to fulfill, to carry out **3 :** to redeem (from a pawnshop) — **desempeñarse** *vr* **:** to function, to act
desempeño *nm* **1 :** fulfillment, carrying out **2 :** performance
desempleado[1]**, -da** *adj* **:** unemployed
desempleado[2]**, -da** *n* **:** unemployed person
desempleo *nm* **:** unemployment
desempolvar *vt* **1 :** to dust off **2 :** to resurrect, to revive
desencadenar *vt* **1 :** to unchain **2 :** to trigger, to unleash — **desencadenarse** *vr*
desencajar *vt* **1 :** to dislocate **2 :** to disconnect, to disengage
desencantar *vt* **:** to disenchant, to disillusion — **desencantarse** *vr*
desencanto *nm* **:** disenchantment, disillusionment
desenchufar *vt* **:** to disconnect, to unplug
desenfadado, -da *adj* **1 :** uninhibited, carefree **2 :** confident, self-assured
desenfado *nm* **1** DESENVOLTURA **:** self-assurance, confidence **2 :** naturalness, ease
desenfrenadamente *adv* **:** wildly, with abandon
desenfrenado, -da *adj* **:** unbridled, unrestrained
desenfreno *nm* **:** abandon, unrestraint
desenganchar *vt* **:** to unhitch, to uncouple
desengañar *vt* **:** to disillusion, to disenchant — **desengañarse** *vr*
desengaño *nm* **:** disenchantment, disillusionment
desenlace *nm* **:** ending, outcome
desenlazar {21} *vt* **1 :** to untie **2 :** to clear up, to resolve
desenmarañar *vt* **:** to disentangle, to unravel
desenmascarar *vt* **:** to unmask, to expose
desenredar *vt* **:** to untangle, to disentangle
desenrollar *vt* **:** to unroll, to unwind
desentenderse {56} *vr* **~ de 1 :** to want nothing to do with, to be uninterested in **2 :** to pretend ignorance of

desenterrar {55} *vt* **1** EXHUMAR **:** to exhume **2 :** to unearth, to dig up

desentonar *vi* **1 :** to clash, to conflict **2 :** to be out of tune, to sing off-key

desentrañar *vt* **:** to get to the bottom of, to unravel

desenvainar *vt* **:** to draw, to unsheathe (a sword)

desenvoltura *nf* **1** DESENFADO **:** confidence, self-assurance **2** ELOCUENCIA **:** eloquence, fluency

desenvolver {89} *vt* **:** to unwrap, to open — **desenvolverse** *vr* **1 :** to unfold, to develop **2 :** to manage, to cope

desenvuelto[1] *pp* → **desenvolver**

desenvuelto[2]**, -ta** *adj* **:** confident, relaxed, self-assured

deseo *nm* **:** wish, desire

deseoso, -sa *adj* **:** eager, anxious

desequilibrar *vt* **:** to unbalance, to throw off balance — **desequilibrarse** *vr*

desequilibrio *nm* **:** imbalance

deserción *nf, pl* **-ciones :** desertion, defection

desertar *vi* **1 :** to desert, to defect **2 ~ de :** to abandon, to neglect

desertor, -tora *n* **:** deserter, defector

desesperación *nf, pl* **-ciones :** desperation, despair

desesperado, -da *adj* **:** desperate, despairing, hopeless — **desesperadamente** *adv*

desesperanza *nf* **:** despair, hopelessness

desesperar *vt* **:** to exasperate — *vi* **:** to despair, to lose hope — **desesperarse** *vr* **:** to become exasperated

desestimar *vt* **1 :** to reject, to disallow **2 :** to have a low opinion of

desfachatez *nf, pl* **-teces :** audacity, nerve, cheek

desfalcador, -dora *n* **:** embezzler

desfalcar {72} *vt* **:** to embezzle

desfalco *nm* **:** embezzlement

desfallecer {53} *vi* **1 :** to weaken **2 :** to faint

desfallecimiento *nm* **1 :** weakness **2 :** fainting

desfasado, -da *adj* **1 :** out of sync **2 :** out of step, behind the times

desfase *nm* **:** gap, lag <desfase horario : jet lag>

desfavorable *adj* **:** unfavorable, adverse — **desfavorablemente** *adv*

desfavorecido, -da *adj* **:** underprivileged

desfigurar *vt* **1 :** to disfigure, to mar **2 :** to distort, to misrepresent

desfiladero *nm* **:** narrow gorge, defile

desfilar *vi* **:** to parade, to march

desfile *nm* **:** parade, procession

desfogar {52} *vt* **1 :** to vent **2** *Mex* **:** to unclog, to unblock — **desfogarse** *vr* **:** to vent one's feelings, to let off steam

desforestación *nf, pl* **-ciones :** deforestation

desgajar *vt* **1 :** to tear off **2 :** to break apart — **desgajarse** *vr* **:** to come apart

desgana *nf* **1** INAPETENCIA **:** lack of appetite **2** APATÍA **:** apathy, unwillingness, reluctance

desgano *nm* → **desgana**

desgarbado, -da *adj* **:** ungainly

desgarrador, -dora *adj* **:** heartrending, heartbreaking

desgarradura *nf* **:** tear, rip

desgarrar *vt* **1 :** to tear, to rip **2 :** to break (one's heart) — **desgarrarse** *vr*

desgarre *nm* → **desgarro**

desgarro *nm* **:** tear

desgarrón *nm, pl* **-rrones :** rip, tear

desgastar *vt* **1 :** to use up **2 :** to wear away, to wear down

desgaste *nm* **:** deterioration, wear and tear

desglosar *vt* **:** to break down, to itemize

desglose *nm* **:** breakdown, itemization

desgobierno *nm* **:** anarchy, disorder

desgracia *nf* **1 :** misfortune **2 :** disgrace **3 por ~ :** unfortunately

desgraciadamente *adv* **:** unfortunately

desgraciado[1]**, -da** *adj* **1 :** unfortunate, unlucky **2 :** vile, wretched

desgraciado[2]**, -da** *n* **:** unfortunate person, wretch

desgranar *vt* **:** to shuck, to shell

deshabitado, -da *adj* **:** unoccupied, uninhabited

deshacer {40} *vt* **1 :** to destroy, to ruin **2** DESATAR **:** to undo, to untie **3 :** to break apart, to crumble **4 :** to dissolve, to melt **5 :** to break, to cancel — **deshacerse** *vr* **1 :** to fall apart, to come undone **2 ~ de :** to get rid of

deshecho[1] *pp* → **deshacer**

deshecho[2]**, -cha** *adj* **1 :** destroyed, ruined **2 :** devastated, shattered **3 :** undone, untied

desherbar {55} *vt* **:** to weed

desheredado, -da *adj* MARGINADO **:** dispossessed, destitute

desheredar *vt* **:** to disinherit

deshicieron, etc. → **deshacer**

deshidratar *vt* **:** to dehydrate — **deshidratación** *nf*

deshielo *nm* **:** thaw, thawing

deshilachar *vt* **:** to fray — **deshilacharse** *vr*

deshizo → **deshacer**

deshonestidad *nf* **:** dishonesty

deshonesto, -ta *adj* **:** dishonest

deshonra *nf* **:** dishonor, disgrace

deshonrar *vt* **:** to dishonor, to disgrace

deshonroso, -sa *adj* **:** dishonorable, disgraceful

deshuesar *vt* **1 :** to pit (a fruit, etc.) **2 :** to bone, to debone

deshumanizar {21} *vt* **:** to dehumanize — **deshumanización** *nf*

desidia *nf* **1** APATÍA **:** apathy, indolence **2** NEGLIGENCIA **:** negligence, sloppiness

desierto[1]**, -ta** *adj* **:** deserted, uninhabited

desierto[2] *nm* : desert
designación *nf, pl* **-ciones** NOMBRAMIENTO : appointment, naming (to an office, etc.)
designar *vt* NOMBRAR : to designate, to appoint, to name
designio *nm* : plan
desigual *adj* **1** : unequal **2** DISPAREJO : uneven
desigualdad *nf* **1** : inequality **2** : unevenness
desilusión *nf, pl* **-siones** DESENCANTO, DESENGAÑO : disillusionment, disenchantment
desilusionar *vt* DESENCANTAR, DESENGAÑAR : to disillusion, to disenchant — **desilusionarse** *vr*
desinfectante *adj & nm* : disinfectant
desinfectar *vt* : to disinfect — **desinfección** *nf*
desinflar *vt* : to deflate — **desinflarse** *vr*
desinhibido, -da *adj* : unihibited, unrestrained
desintegración *nf, pl* **-ciones** : disintegration
desintegrar *vt* : to disintegrate, to break up — **desintegrarse** *vr*
desinterés *nm* **1** : lack of interest, indifference **2** : unselfishness
desinteresado, -da *adj* GENEROSO : unselfish
desintoxicar {72} *vt* : to detoxify, to detox
desistir *vi* **1** : to desist, to stop **2** **~ de** : to give up, to relinquish
deslave *nm Mex* : landslide
desleal *adj* INFIEL : disloyal — **deslealmente** *adv*
deslealtad *nf* : disloyalty
desleír {66} *vt* : to dilute, to dissolve
desligar {52} *vt* **1** : to separate, to undo **2** : to free (from an obligation) — **desligarse** *vr* **~ de** : to extricate oneself from
deslindar *vt* **1** : to mark the limits of, to demarcate **2** : to define, to clarify
deslinde *nm* : demarcation
desliz *nm, pl* **deslices** : error, mistake, slip <desliz de la lengua : slip of the tongue>
deslizar {21} *vt* **1** : to slide, to slip **2** : to slip in — **deslizarse** *vr* **1** : to slide, to glide **2** : to slip away
deslucido, -da *adj* **1** : unimpressive, dull **2** : faded, dingy, tarnished
deslucir {45} *vt* **1** : to spoil **2** : to fade, to dull, to tarnish **3** : to discredit
deslumbrar *vt* : to dazzle — **deslumbrante** *adj*
deslustrado, -da *adj* : dull, lusterless
deslustrar *vt* : to tarnish, to dull
deslustre *nm* : tarnish
desmán *nm, pl* **desmanes** **1** : outrage, abuse **2** : misfortune
desmandarse *vr* : to behave badly, to get out of hand
desmantelar *vt* DESMONTAR : to dismantle
desmañado, -da *adj* : clumsy, awkward
desmayado, -da *adj* **1** : fainting, weak **2** : dull, pale
desmayar *vi* : to lose heart, to falter — **desmayarse** *vr* DESVANECERSE : to faint, to swoon
desmayo *nm* **1** : faint, fainting **2** **sufrir un desmayo** : to faint
desmedido, -da *adj* DESMESURADO : excessive, undue
desmejorar *vt* : to weaken, to make worse — *vi* : to decline (in health), to get worse
desmembramiento *nm* : dismemberment
desmembrar {55} *vt* **1** : to dismember **2** : to break up
desmemoriado, -da *adj* : absent-minded, forgetful
desmentido *nm* : denial
desmentir {76} *vt* **1** NEGAR : to deny, to refute **2** CONTRADECIR : to contradict
desmenuzar {21} *vt* **1** : to break down, to scrutinize **2** : to crumble, to shred — **desmenuzarse** *vr*
desmerecer {53} *vt* : to be unworthy of — *vi* **1** : to decline in value **2** **~ de** : to compare unfavorably with
desmesurado, -da *adj* DESMEDIDO : excessive, inordinate — **desmesuradamente** *adv*
desmigajar *vt* : to crumble — **desmigajarse** *vr*
desmilitarizado, -da *adj* : demilitarized
desmontar *vt* **1** : to clear, to level off **2** DESMANTELAR : to dismantle, to take apart — *vi* : to dismount
desmonte *nm* : clearing, leveling
desmoralizador, -dora *adj* : demoralizing
desmoralizar {21} *vt* DESALENTAR : to demoralize, to discourage
desmoronamiento *nm* : crumbling, falling apart
desmoronar *vt* : to wear away, to erode — **desmoronarse** *vr* : to crumble, to deteriorate, to fall apart
desmotadora *nf* : gin, cotton gin
desmovilizar {21} *vt* : to demobilize — **desmovilización** *nf*
desnaturalizar {21} *vt* **1** : to denature **2** : to distort, to alter
desnivel *nm* **1** : disparity, difference **2** : unevenness (of a surface) **3** **paso a desnivel** *Mex* : underpass
desnivelado, -da *adj* **1** : uneven **2** : unbalanced
desnudar *vt* **1** : to undress **2** : to strip, to lay bare — **desnudarse** *vr* : to undress, to strip off one's clothing
desnudez *nf, pl* **-deces** : nudity, nakedness
desnudismo *nm* → **nudismo**
desnudista → **nudista**
desnudo[1], **-da** *adj* : nude, naked, bare
desnudo[2] *nm* : nude

desnutrición *nf, pl* **-ciones :** MALNUTRICIÓN **:** malnutrition, undernourishment

desnutrido, -da *adj* MALNUTRIDO **:** malnourished, undernourished

desobedecer {53} *v* **:** to disobey

desobediencia *nf* **:** disobedience — **desobediente** *adj*

desocupación *nf, pl* **-ciones :** unemployment

desocupado, -da *adj* **1 :** vacant, empty **2 :** free, unoccupied **3 :** unemployed

desocupar *vt* **1 :** to empty **2 :** to vacate, to move out of — **desocuparse** *vr* **:** to leave, to quit (a job)

desodorante *adj & nm* **:** deodorant

desolación *nf, pl* **-ciones :** desolation

desolado, -da *adj* **1 :** desolate **2 :** devastated, distressed

desolador, -dora *adj* **1 :** devastating **2 :** bleak, desolate

desollar *vt* **:** to skin, to flay

desorbitado, -da *adj* **1 :** excessive, exorbitant **2 con los ojos desorbitados :** with eyes popping out of one's head

desorden *nm, pl* **desórdenes 1** DESBARAJUSTE **:** disorder, mess **2 :** disorder, disturbance, upset

desordenado, -da *adj* **1 :** untidy, messy **2 :** disorderly, unruly

desorganización *nf, pl* **-ciones :** disorganization

desorganizar {21} *vt* **:** to disrupt, to disorganize

desorientación *nf, pl* **-ciones :** disorientation, confusion

desorientar *vt* **:** to disorient, to mislead, to confuse — **desorientarse** *vr* **:** to become disoriented, to lose one's way

desovar *vi* **:** to spawn

despachar *vt* **1 :** to complete, to conclude **2 :** to deal with, to take care of, to handle **3 :** to dispatch, to send off **4** *fam* **:** to finish off, to kill — **despacharse** *vr fam* **:** to gulp down, to polish off

despacho *nm* **1 :** dispatch, shipment **2** OFICINA **:** office, study

despacio *adv* LENTAMENTE, LENTO **:** slowly, slow <¡despacio! : take it easy!, easy does it!>

desparasitar *vt* **:** to worm (an animal), to delouse

desparpajo *nm* **1** *fam* **:** self-confidence, nerve **2** *CA fam* **:** confusion, muddle

desparramar *vt* **1 :** to spill, to splatter **2 :** to spread, to scatter

despatarrarse *vr* **:** to sprawl (out)

despavorido, -da *adj* **:** terrified, horrified

despecho *nm* **1 :** spite **2 a despecho de :** despite, in spite of

despectivo, -va *adj* **1 :** contemptuous, disparaging **2 :** derogatory, pejorative

despedazar {21} *vt* **:** to cut to pieces, to tear apart

despedida *nf* **1 :** farewell, good-bye **2 despedida de soltera :** bridal shower

despedir {54} *vt* **1 :** to see off, to show out **2 :** to dismiss, to fire **3** EMITIR **:** to give off, to emit <despedir un olor : to give off an odor> — **despedirse** *vr* **:** to take one's leave, to say good-bye

despegado, -da *adj* **1 :** separated, detached **2 :** cold, distant

despegar {52} *vt* **:** to remove, to detach — *vi* **:** to take off, to lift off, to blast off

despegue *nm* **:** takeoff, liftoff

despeinado, -da *adj* **:** disheveled, tousled <estoy despeinada : my hair's a mess>

despejado, -da *adj* **1 :** clear, fair **2 :** alert, clear-headed **3 :** uncluttered, unobstructed

despejar *vt* **1 :** to clear, to free **2 :** to clarify — *vi* **1 :** to clear up **2 :** to punt (in sports)

despeje *nm* **1 :** clearing **2 :** punt (in sports)

despellejar *vt* **:** to skin (an animal)

despenalizar {21} *vt* **:** to legalize — **despenalización** *nf*

despensa *nf* **1 :** pantry, larder **2** PROVISIONES **:** provisions *pl,* supplies *pl*

despeñar *vt* **:** to hurl down

despepitar *vt* **:** to seed, to remove the seeds from

desperdiciar *vt* **1** DESAPROVECHAR, MALGASTAR **:** to waste **2 :** to miss, to miss out on

desperdicio *nm* **1 :** waste **2 desperdicios** *nmpl* RESIDUOS **:** refuse, scraps, rubbish

desperdigar {52} *vt* DISPERSAR **:** to disperse, to scatter

desperfecto *nm* **1** DEFECTO **:** flaw, defect **2 :** damage

despertador *nm* **:** alarm clock

despertar {55} *vi* **:** to awaken, to wake up — *vt* **1 :** to arouse, to wake **2** EVOCAR **:** to elicit, to evoke — **despertarse** *vr* **:** to wake (oneself) up

despiadado, -da *adj* CRUEL **:** cruel, merciless, pitiless — **despiadadamente** *adv*

despido *nm* **:** dismissal, layoff

despierto, -ta *adj* **1 :** awake, alert **2** LISTO **:** clever, sharp <con la mente despierta : with a sharp mind>

despilfarrador[1], -dora *adj* **:** extravagant, wasteful

despilfarrador[2], -dora *n* **:** spendthrift, prodigal

despilfarrar *vt* MALGASTAR **:** to squander, to waste

despilfarro *nm* **:** extravagance, wastefulness

despintar *vt* **:** to strip the paint from — **despintarse** *vr* **:** to fade, to wash off, to peel off

despistado[1], -da *adj* **1** DISTRAÍDO **:** absentminded, forgetful **2** CONFUSO **:** confused, bewildered

despistado², **-da** *n* : scatterbrain, absentminded person
despistar *vt* : to throw off the track, to confuse — **despistarse** *vr*
despiste *nm* **1** : absentmindedness **2** : mistake, slip
desplantador *nm* : garden trowel
desplante *nm* : insolence, rudeness
desplazamiento *nm* **1** : movement, displacement **2** : journey
desplazar {21} *vt* **1** : to replace, to displace **2** TRASLADAR : to move, to shift
desplegar {49} *vt* **1** : to display, to show, to manifest **2** DESDOBLAR : to unfold, to unfurl **3** : to spread (out) **4** : to deploy
despliegue *nm* **1** : display **2** : deployment
desplomarse *vr* **1** : to plummet, to fall **2** DERRUMBARSE : to collapse, to break down
desplome *nm* **1** : fall, drop **2** : collapse
desplumar *vt* : to pluck (a chicken, etc.)
despoblado¹, **-da** *adj* : uninhabited, deserted
despoblado² *nm* : open country, deserted area
despoblar {19} *vt* : to depopulate
despojar *vt* **1** : to strip, to clear **2** : to divest, to deprive — **despojarse** *vr* **1** ~ **de** : to remove (clothing) **2** ~ **de** : to relinquish, to renounce
despojos *nmpl* **1** : remains, scraps **2** : plunder, spoils
desportilladura *nf* : chip, nick
desportillar *vt* : to chip — **desportillarse** *vr*
desposeer {20} *vt* : to dispossess
déspota *nmf* : despot, tyrant
despotismo *nm* : despotism — **despótico, -ca** *adj*
despotricar {72} *vi* : to rant and rave, to complain excessively
despreciable *adj* **1** : despicable, contemptible **2** : negligible <nada despreciable : not inconsiderable, significant>
despreciar *vt* DESDEÑAR, MENOSPRECIAR : to despise, to scorn, to disdain
despreciativo, -va *adj* : scornful, disdainful
desprecio *nm* DESDÉN, MENOSPRECIO : disdain, contempt, scorn
desprender *vt* **1** SOLTAR : to detach, to loosen, to unfasten **2** EMITIR : to emit, to give off — **desprenderse** *vr* **1** : to come off, to come undone **2** : to be inferred, to follow **3** ~ **de** : to part with, to get rid of
desprendido, -da *adj* : generous, unselfish, disinterested
desprendimiento *nm* **1** : detachment **2** GENEROSIDAD : generosity **3 desprendimiento de tierras** : landslide
despreocupación *nf, pl* **-ciones** : indifference, lack of concern
despreocupado, -da *adj* : carefree, easygoing, unconcerned
desprestigiar *vt* DESACREDITAR : to discredit, to disgrace — **desprestigiarse** *vr* : to lose prestige
desprestigio *nm* DESCRÉDITO : discredit, disrepute
desprevenido, -da *adj* DESAPERCIBIDO : unprepared, off guard, unsuspecting
desproporción *nf, pl* **-ciones** : disproportion, disparity
desproporcionado, -da : out of proportion
despropósito *nm* : piece of nonsense, absurdity
desprotegido, -da *adj* : unprotected, vulnerable
desprovisto, -ta *adj* ~ **de** : devoid of, lacking in
después *adv* **1** : afterward, later **2** : then, next **3** ~ **de** : after, next after <después de comer : after eating> **4 después (de) que** : after <después que lo acabé : after I finished it> **5 después de todo** : after all **6 poco después** : shortly after, soon thereafter
despuntado, -da *adj* : blunt, dull
despuntar *vt* : to blunt — *vi* **1** : to dawn **2** : to sprout **3** : to excel, to stand out
desquiciar *vt* **1** : to unhinge (a door) **2** : to drive crazy — **desquiciarse** *vr* : to go crazy
desquitarse *vr* **1** : to get even, to retaliate **2** ~ **con** : to take it out on
desquite *nm* : revenge
desregulación *nf, pl* **-ciones** : deregulation
desregular *vt* : to deregulate
destacadamente *adv* : outstandingly, prominently
destacado, -da *adj* **1** : outstanding, prominent **2** : stationed, posted
destacar {72} *vt* **1** ENFATIZAR, SUBRAYAR : to emphasize, to highlight, to stress **2** : to station, to post — *vi* : to stand out
destajo *nm* **1** : piecework **2 a** ~ : by the item, by the job
destapador *nm* : bottle opener
destapar *vt* **1** : to open, to take the top off **2** DESCUBRIR : to reveal, to uncover **3** : to unblock, to unclog
destape *nm* : uncovering, revealing
destartalado, -da *adj* : dilapidated, tumbledown
destellar *vi* **1** : to sparkle, to flash, to glint **2** : to twinkle
destello *nm* **1** : flash, sparkle, twinkle **2** : glimmer, hint
destemplado, -da *adj* **1** : out of tune **2** : irritable, out of sorts **3** : unpleasant (of weather)
desteñir {67} *vi* : to run, to fade — **desteñirse** DESCOLORARSE : to fade
desterrado¹, **-da** *adj* : banished, exiled
desterrado², **-da** *n* : exile

desterrar {55} *vt* **1** EXILIAR : to banish, to exile **2** ERRADICAR : to eradicate, to do away with

destetar *vt* : to wean

destiempo *adv* **a ~** : at the wrong time

destierro *nm* EXILIO : exile

destilación *nf, pl* **-ciones** : distillation

destilador, -dora *n* : distiller

destilar *vt* **1** : to exude **2** : to distill

destilería *nf* : distillery

destinación *nf, pl* **-ciones** DESTINO : destination

destinado, -da *adj* : destined, bound

destinar *vt* **1** : to appoint, to assign **2** ASIGNAR : to earmark, to allot

destinatario, -ria *n* **1** : addressee **2** : payee

destino *nm* **1** : destiny, fate **2** DESTINACIÓN : destination **3** : use **4** : assignment, post

destitución *nf, pl* **-ciones** : dismissal, removal from office

destituir {41} *vt* : to dismiss, to remove from office

destorcer {14} *vt* : to untwist

destornillador *nm* : screwdriver

destornillar *vt* : to unscrew

destrabar *vt* **1** : to untie, to undo, to ease up **2** : to separate

destreza *nf* HABILIDAD : dexterity, skill

destronar *vt* : to depose, to dethrone

destrozado, -da *adj* **1** : ruined, destroyed **2** : devastated, brokenhearted

destrozar {21} *vt* **1** : to smash, to shatter **2** : to destroy, to wreck — **destrozarse** *vr*

destrozo *nm* **1** DAÑO : damage **2** : havoc, destruction

destrucción *nf, pl* **-ciones** : destruction

destructivo, -va *adj* : destructive

destructor[1], **-tora** *adj* : destructive

destructor[2] *nm* : destroyer (ship)

destruir {41} *vt* : to destroy — **destruirse** *vr*

desubicado, -da *adj* **1** : out of place **2** : confused, disoriented

desunión *nf, pl* **-niones** : disunity

desunir *vt* : to split, to divide

desusado, -da *adj* **1** INSÓLITO : unusual **2** OBSOLETO : obsolete, disused, antiquated

desuso *nm* : disuse, obsolescence <caer en desuso : to fall into disuse>

desvaído, -da *adj* **1** : pale, washed-out **2** : vague, blurred

desvainar *vt* : to shell

desvalido, -da *adj* DESAMPARADO : destitute, helpless

desvalijar *vt* **1** : to ransack **2** : to rob

desvalorización *nf, pl* **-ciones** **1** DEVALUACIÓN : devaluation **2** : depreciation

desvalorizar {21} *vt* : to devalue

desván *nm, pl* **desvanes** ÁTICO, BUHARDILLA : attic

desvanecer {53} *vt* **1** DISIPAR : to make disappear, to dispel **2** : to fade, to blur — **desvanecerse** *vr* **1** : to vanish, to disappear **2** : to fade **3** DESMAYARSE : to faint, to swoon

desvanecimiento *nm* **1** : disappearance **2** DESMAYO : faint **3** : fading

desvariar {85} *vi* **1** DELIRAR : to be delirious **2** : to rave, to talk nonsense

desvarío *nm* DELIRIO : delirium

desvelado, -da *adj* : sleepless

desvelar *vt* **1** : to keep awake **2** REVELAR : to reveal, to disclose — **desvelarse** *vr* **1** : to stay awake **2** : to do one's utmost

desvelo *nm* **1** : sleeplessness **2 desvelos** *nmpl* : efforts, pains

desvencijado, -da *adj* : dilapidated, rickety

desventaja *nf* : disadvantage, drawback

desventajoso, -sa *adj* : disadvantageous, unfavorable

desventura *nf* INFORTUNIO : misfortune

desventurado, -da *adj* : unfortunate, ill-fated

desvergonzado, -da *adj* : shameless, impudent

desvergüenza *nf* : shamelessness, impudence

desvestir {54} *vt* : to undress — **desvestirse** *vr* : to get undressed

desviación *nf, pl* **-ciones** **1** : deviation, departure **2** : detour, diversion

desviar {85} *vt* **1** : to change the course of, to divert **2** : to turn away, to deflect — **desviarse** *vr* **1** : to branch off **2** APARTARSE : to stray

desvinculación *nf, pl* **-ciones** : dissociation

desvincular *vt* **~ de** : to separate from, to dissociate from — **desvincularse** *vr*

desvío *nm* **1** : diversion, detour **2** : deviation

desvirtuar {3} *vt* **1** : to impair, to spoil **2** : to detract from **3** : to distort, to misrepresent

detalladamente *adv* : in detail, at great length

detallar *vt* : to detail

detalle *nm* **1** : detail **2 al detalle** : retail

detallista[1] *adj* **1** : meticulous **2** : retail

detallista[2] *nmf* **1** : perfectionist **2** : retailer

detección *nf, pl* **-ciones** : detection

detectar *vt* : to detect — **detectable** *adj*

detective *nmf* : detective

detector *nm* : detector <detector de mentiras : lie detector>

detención *nf, pl* **-ciones** **1** ARRESTO : detention, arrest **2** : stop, halt **3** : delay, holdup

detener {80} *vt* **1** ARRESTAR : to arrest, to detain **2** PARAR : to stop, to halt **3** : to keep, to hold back — **detenerse** *vr* **1** : to stop **2** : to delay, to linger

detenidamente *adv* : thoroughly, at length

detenimiento *nm* **con ~** : carefully, in detail

detentar *vt* : to hold, to retain
detergente *nm* : detergent
deteriorado, -da *adj* : damaged, worn
deteriorar *vt* ESTROPEAR : to damage, to spoil — **deteriorarse** *vr* **1** : to get damaged, to wear out **2** : to deteriorate, to worsen
deterioro *nm* **1** : deterioration, wear **2** : worsening, decline
determinación *nf, pl* **-ciones** **1** : determination, resolve **2 tomar una determinación** : to make a decision
determinado, -da *adj* **1** : certain, particular **2** : determined, resolute
determinante[1] *adj* : determining, deciding
determinante[2] *nm* : determinant
determinar *vt* **1** : to determine **2** : to cause, to bring about — **determinarse** *vr* : to make up one's mind, to decide
detestar *vt* : to detest — **detestable** *adj*
detonación *nf, pl* **-ciones** : detonation
detonador *nm* : detonator
detonante[1] *adj* : detonating, explosive
detonante[2] *nm* **1** → **detonador 2** : catalyst, cause
detonar *vi* : to detonate, to explode
detractor, -tora *n* : detractor, critic
detrás *adv* **1** : behind **2 ~ de** : in back of **3 por ~** : from behind
detuvo, etc. → **detener**
deuda *nf* **1** DÉBITO : debt **2 en deuda con** : indebted to
deudo, -da *n* : relative
deudor[1]**, -dora** *adj* : indebted
deudor[2]**, -dora** *n* : debtor
devaluación *nf, pl* **-ciones** DESVALORIZACIÓN : devaluation
devaluar {3} *vt* : to devalue — **devaluarse** *vr* : to depreciate
devanarse *vr* **devanarse los sesos** : to rack one's brains
devaneo *nm* **1** : flirtation, fling **2** : idle pursuit
devastador, -dora *adj* : devastating
devastar *vt* : to devastate — **devastación** *nf*
devenir {87} *vi* **1** : to come about **2 ~ en** : to become, to turn into
devoción *nf, pl* **-ciones** : devotion
devolución *nf, pl* **-ciones** REEMBOLSO : return, refund
devolver {89} *vt* **1** : to return, to give back **2** REEMBOLSAR : to refund, to pay back **3** : to vomit, to bring up — *vi* : to vomit, to throw up — **devolverse** *vr* : to return, to come back, to go back
devorar *vt* **1** : to devour **2** : to consume
devoto[1]**, -ta** *adj* : devout — **devotamente** *adv*
devoto[2]**, -ta** *n* : devotee, admirer
di → **dar, decir**
día *nm* **1** : day <todos los días : every day> **2** : daytime, daylight <de día : by day, in the daytime> <en pleno día : in broad daylight> **3 al día** : up-to-date **4 en su día** : in due time
diabetes *nf* : diabetes
diabético, -ca *adj & n* : diabetic
diablillo *nm* : little devil, imp
diablo *nm* DEMONIO : devil
diablura *nf* **1** : prank **2 diabluras** *nfpl* : mischief
diabólico, -ca *adj* : diabolical, diabolic, devilish
diaconisa *nf* : deaconess
diácono *nm* : deacon
diadema *nf* : diadem, crown
diáfano, -na *adj* : diaphanous
diafragma *nm* : diaphragm
diagnosticar {72} *vt* : to diagnose
diagnóstico[1]**, -ca** *adj* : diagnostic
diagnóstico[2] *nm* : diagnosis
diagonal *adj & nf* : diagonal — **diagonalmente** *adv*
diagrama *nm* **1** : diagram **2 diagrama de flujo** ORGANIGRAMA : flowchart
dialecto *nm* : dialect
dialogar {52} *vi* : to have a talk, to converse
diálogo *nm* : dialogue
diamante *nm* : diamond
diametral *adj* : diametric, diametrical — **diametralmente** *adv*
diámetro *nm* : diameter
diana *nf* **1** : target, bull's-eye **2** *or* **toque de diana** : reveille
diapositiva *nf* : slide, transparency
diario[1] *adv Mex* : every day, daily
diario[2]**, -ria** *adj* : daily, everyday — **diariamente** *adv*
diario[3] *nm* **1** : diary **2** PERIÓDICO : newspaper
diarrea *nf* : diarrhea
diatriba *nf* : diatribe, tirade
dibujante *nmf* **1** : draftsman *m,* draftswoman *f* **2** CARICATURISTA : cartoonist
dibujar *vt* **1** : to draw, to sketch **2** : to portray, to depict
dibujo *nm* **1** : drawing **2** : design, pattern **3 dibujos animados** : (animated) cartoons
dicción *nf, pl* **-ciones** : diction
diccionario *nm* : dictionary
dícese → **decir**
dicha *nf* **1** SUERTE : good luck **2** FELICIDAD : happiness, joy
dicho[1] *pp* → **decir**
dicho[2]**, -cha** *adj* : said, aforementioned
dicho[3] *nm* DECIR : saying, proverb
dichoso, -sa *adj* **1** : blessed **2** FELIZ : happy **3** AFORTUNADO : fortunate, lucky
diciembre *nm* : December
diciendo → **decir**
dictado *nm* : dictation
dictador, -dora *n* : dictator
dictadura *nf* : dictatorship
dictamen *nm, pl* **dictámenes** **1** : report **2** : judgment, opinion
dictaminar *vt* : to report — *vi* : to give an opinion, to pass judgment
dictar *vt* **1** : to dictate **2** : to pronounce (a judgment) **3** : to give, to deliver <dictar una conferencia : to give a lecture>
dictatorial *adj* : dictatorial

didáctico, -ca *adj* **:** didactic

diecinueve *adj & nm* **:** nineteen

diecinueveavo[1]**, -va** *adj* **:** nineteenth

diecinueveavo[2] *nm* **:** nineteenth (fraction)

dieciocho *adj & nm* **:** eighteen

dieciochoavo[1]**, -va** *or* **dieciochavo, -va** *adj* **:** eighteenth

dieciochoavo[2] *or* **dieciochavo** *nm* **:** eighteenth (fraction)

dieciséis *adj & nm* **:** sixteen

dieciseisavo[1]**, -va** *adj* **:** sixteenth

dieciseisavo[2] *nm* **:** sixteenth (fraction)

diecisietaeavo[1]**, -va** *adj* **:** seventeenth

diecisietaeavo[2] *nm* **:** seventeenth (fraction)

diecisiete *adj & nm* **:** seventeen

diecisieteavo[1]**, -va** *adj* **:** seventeenth

diecisieteavo[2] *nm* **:** seventeenth

diente *nm* **1 :** tooth <diente canino : eyetooth, canine tooth> **2 :** tusk, fang **3 :** prong, tine **4 diente de león :** dandelion

dieron, etc. → **dar**

diesel ['disɛl] *nm* **:** diesel

diestra *nf* **:** right hand

diestramente *adv* **:** skillfully, adroitly

diestro[1]**, -tra** *adj* **1 :** right **2 :** skillful, accomplished

diestro[2] *nm* **:** bullfighter, matador

dieta *nf* **:** diet

dietética *nf* **:** dietetics

dietético, -ca *adj* **:** dietetic

dietista *nmf* **:** dietitian

diez *adj & nm, pl* **dieces :** ten

difamación *nf, pl* **-ciones :** defamation, slander

difamar *vt* **:** to defame, to slander

difamatorio, -ria *adj* **:** slanderous, defamatory, libelous

diferencia *nf* **1 :** difference **2 a diferencia de :** unlike, in contrast to

diferenciación *nf, pl* **-ciones :** differentiation

diferenciar *vt* **:** to differentiate between, to distinguish — **diferenciarse** *vr* **:** to differ

diferendo *nm* **:** dispute, conflict

diferente *adj* DISTINTO **:** different — **diferentemente** *adv*

diferir {76} *vt* DILATAR, POSPONER **:** to postpone, to put off — *vi* **:** to differ

difícil *adj* **:** difficult, hard

difícilmente *adv* **1 :** with difficulty **2 :** hardly

dificultad *nf* **:** difficulty

dificultar *vt* **:** to make difficult, to obstruct

dificultoso, -sa *adj* **:** difficult, hard

difteria *nf* **:** diphtheria

difundir *vt* **1 :** to diffuse, to spread out **2 :** to broadcast, to spread

difunto, -ta *adj & n* FALLECIDO **:** deceased

difusión *nf, pl* **-siones 1 :** spreading **2 :** diffusion (of heat, etc.) **3 :** broadcast, broadcasting <los medios de difusión : the media>

difuso, -sa *adj* **:** diffuse, widespread

diga, etc. → **decir**

digerir {76} *vt* **:** to digest — **digerible** *adj*

digestión *nf, pl* **-tiones :** digestion

digestivo, -va *adj* **:** digestive

digital[1] *adj* **:** digital — **digitalmente** *adv*

digital[2] *nm* **1** DEDALERA **:** foxglove **2 :** digitalis

dígito *nm* **:** digit

dignarse *vr* **:** to deign, to condescend <no se dignó contestar : he didn't deign to answer>

dignatario, -ria *n* **:** dignitary

dignidad *nf* **1 :** dignity **2 :** dignitary

dignificar {72} *vt* **:** to dignify

digno, -na *adj* **1** HONORABLE **:** honorable **2 :** worthy — **dignamente** *adv*

digresión *nf, pl* **-ciones :** digression

dije *nm* **:** charm (on a bracelet)

dijo, etc. → **decir**

dilación *nf, pl* **-ciones :** delay

dilapidar *vt* **:** to waste, to squander

dilatar *vt* **1 :** to dilate, to widen, to expand **2** DIFERIR, POSPONER **:** to put off, to postpone — **dilatarse** *vr* **1 :** to expand (of gases, metals, etc.) **2** *Mex* **:** to take long, to be long

dilatorio, -ria *adj* **:** dilatory, delaying

dilema *nm* **:** dilemma

diligencia *nf* **1 :** diligence, care **2 :** promptness, speed **3 :** action, step **4 :** task, errand **5 :** stagecoach **6 diligencias** *nfpl* **:** judicial procedures, formalities

diligente *adj* **:** diligent — **diligentemente** *adv*

dilucidar *vt* **:** to elucidate, to clarify

diluir {41} *vt* **:** to dilute

diluviar *v impers* **:** to pour (with rain), to pour down

diluvio *nm* **1 :** flood **2 :** downpour

dimensión *nf, pl* **-siones :** dimension — **dimensional** *adj*

dimensionar *vt* **:** to measure, to gauge

diminuto, -ta *adj* **:** minute, tiny

dimisión *nf, pl* **-siones :** resignation

dimitir *vi* **:** to resign, to step down

dimos → **dar**

dinámica *nf* **:** dynamics

dinámico, -ca *adj* **:** dynamic — **dinámicamente** *adv*

dinamita *nf* **:** dynamite

dinamitar *vt* **:** to dynamite

dínamo *or* **dinamo** *nm* **:** dynamo

dinastía *nf* **:** dynasty

dineral *nm* **:** fortune, large sum of money

dinero *nm* **:** money

dinosaurio *nm* **:** dinosaur

dintel *nm* **:** lintel

dio, etc. → **dar**

diocesano, -na *adj* **:** diocesan

diócesis *nfs & pl* **:** diocese

dios, diosa *n* **:** god, goddess *f*

Dios *nm* **:** God

diploma *nm* **:** diploma

diplomacia *nf* **:** diplomacy

diplomado[1], **-da** *adj* : qualified, trained

diplomado[2] *nm Mex* : seminar

diplomático[1], **-ca** *adj* : diplomatic — **diplomáticamente** *adv*

diplomático[2], **-ca** *n* : diplomat

diputación *nf, pl* **-ciones** : deputation, delegation

diputado, -da *n* : delegate, representative

dique *nm* : dike

dirá, etc. → **decir**

dirección *nf, pl* **-ciones 1** : address **2** : direction **3** : management, leadership **4** : steering (of an automobile)

direccional[1] *adj* : directional

direccional[2] *nf* : directional, turn signal

directa *nf* : high gear

directamente *adv* : straight, directly

directiva *nf* **1** ORDEN : directive **2** DIRECTORIO, JUNTA : board of directors

directivo[1], **-va** *adj* : executive, managerial

directivo[2], **-va** *n* : executive, director

directo, -ta *adj* **1** : direct, straight, immediate **2 en ~** : live (in broadcasting)

director, -tora *n* **1** : director, manager, head **2** : conductor (of an orchestra)

directorial *adj* : managing, executive

directorio *nm* **1** : directory **2** DIRECTIVA, JUNTA : board of directors

directriz *nf, pl* **-trices** : guideline

dirigencia *nf* : leaders *pl*, leadership

dirigente[1] *adj* : directing, leading

dirigente[2] *nmf* : director, leader

dirigible *nm* : dirigible, blimp

dirigir {35} *vt* **1** : to direct, to lead **2** : to address **3** : to aim, to point **4** : to conduct (music) — **dirigirse** *vr* **~ a 1** : to go towards **2** : to speak to, to address

dirimir *vt* **1** : to resolve, to settle **2** : to annul, to dissolve (a marriage)

discapacidad *nf* MINUSVALÍA : disability, handicap

discapacitado[1], **-da** *adj* : disabled, handicapped

discapacitado[2], **-da** *n* : disabled person, handicapped person

discernimiento *nm* : discernment

discernir {25} *v* : to discern, to distinguish

disciplina *nf* : discipline

disciplinar *vt* : to discipline — **disciplinario, -ria** *adj*

discípulo, -la *n* : disciple, follower

disc jockey [ˌdiskˈjoke, -ˈdʒo-] *nmf* : disc jockey

disco *nm* **1** : phonograph record **2** : disc, disk <disco compacto : compact disc> **3** : discus

díscolo, -la *adj* : unruly, disobedient

disconforme *adj* : in disagreement

discontinuidad *nf* : discontinuity

discontinuo, -nua *adj* : discontinuous

discordancia *nf* DESAVENENCIA : conflict, disagreement

discordante *adj* **1** : discordant **2** : conflicting

discordia *nf* : discord

discoteca *nf* **1** : disco, discotheque **2** *CA, Mex* : record store

discreción *nf, pl* **-ciones** : discretion

discrecional *adj* : discretionary

discrepancia *nf* : discrepancy

discrepar *vi* **1** : to disagree **2** : to differ

discreto, -ta *adj* : discreet — **discretamente** *adv*

discriminación *nf, pl* **-ciones** : discrimination

discriminar *vt* **1** : to discriminate against **2** : to distinguish, to differentiate

discriminatorio, -ria *adj* : discriminatory

disculpa *nf* **1** : apology **2** : excuse

disculpable *adj* : excusable

disculpar *vt* : to excuse, to pardon — **disculparse** *vr* : to apologize

discurrir *vi* **1** : to flow **2** : to pass, to go by **3** : to ponder, to reflect

discurso *nm* **1** ORACIÓN : speech, address **2** : discourse, treatise

discusión *nf, pl* **-siones 1** : discussion **2** ALTERCADO, DISPUTA : argument

discutible *adj* : arguable, debatable

discutidor, -dora *adj* : argumentative

discutir *vt* **1** : to discuss **2** : to dispute — *vi* ALTERCAR : to argue, to quarrel

disecar {72} *vt* **1** : to dissect **2** : to stuff (for preservation)

disección *nf, pl* **-ciones** : dissection

diseminación *nf, pl* **-ciones** : dissemination, spreading

diseminar *vt* : to disseminate, to spread

disensión *nf, pl* **-siones** : dissension, disagreement

disentería *nf* : dysentery

disentir {76} *vi* : to dissent, to disagree

diseñador, -dora *n* : designer

diseñar *vt* **1** : to design, to plan **2** : to lay out, to outline

diseño *nm* : design

disertación *nf, pl* **-ciones 1** : lecture, talk **2** : dissertation

disertar *vi* : to lecture, to give a talk

disfraz *nm, pl* **disfraces 1** : disguise **2** : costume **3** : front, pretense

disfrazar {21} *vt* **1** : to disguise **2** : to mask, to conceal — **disfrazarse** *vr* : to wear a costume, to be in disguise

disfrutar *vt* : to enjoy — *vi* : to enjoy oneself, to have a good time

disfrute *nm* : enjoyment

disfunción *nf, pl* **-ciones** : dysfunction — **disfuncional** *adj*

disgresión *nf* → **digresión**

disgustar *vt* : to upset, to displease, to make angry — **disgustarse** *vr*

disgusto *nm* **1** : annoyance, displeasure **2** : argument, quarrel **3** : trouble, misfortune

disidencia *nf* : dissidence, dissent

disidente *adj & nmf* : dissident

disímbolo, -la *adj Mex* : dissimilar

disímil *adj* : dissimilar
disimulado, -da *adj* **1** : concealed, disguised **2** : furtive, sly
disimular *vi* : to dissemble, to pretend — *vt* : to conceal, to hide
disimulo *nm* **1** : dissembling, pretense **2** : slyness, furtiveness **3** : tolerance
disipar *vt* **1** : to dissipate **2** : to dispel — **disiparse** *vr*
diskette [diˈskɛt] *nm* : floppy disk, diskette
dislocar {72} *vt* : to dislocate — **dislocación** *nf*
disminución *nf, pl* **-ciones** : decrease, drop, fall
disminuir {41} *vt* REDUCIR : to reduce, to decrease, to lower — *vi* **1** : to lower **2** : to drop, to fall
disociación *nf, pl* **-ciones** : dissociation
disociar *vt* : to dissociate, to separate
disolución *nf, pl* **-ciones** **1** : dissolution, dissolving **2** : breaking up **3** : dissipation
disoluto, -ta *adj* : dissolute, dissipated
disolver {89} *vt* **1** : to dissolve **2** : to break up — **disolverse** *vr*
disonancia *nf* : dissonance — **disonante** *adj*
disparado, -da *adj* **salir disparado** *fam* : to take off in a hurry, to rush away
disparar *vi* **1** : to fire (a gun) **2** *Mex fam* : to pay — *vt* **1** : to shoot **2** : to rush off **3** *Mex fam* : to treat to, to buy — **dispararse** *vr* : to shoot up, to skyrocket
disparatado, -da *adj* ABSURDO, RIDÍCULO : absurd, ridiculous, crazy
disparate *nm* : silliness, stupidity <decir disparates : to talk nonsense>
disparejo, -ja *adj* DESIGUAL : uneven
disparidad *nf* : disparity
disparo *nm* TIRO : shot
dispendio *nm* : wastefulness, extravagance
dispendioso, -sa *adj* : wasteful, extravagant
dispensa *nf* : dispensation
dispensable *adj* **1** : dispensable **2** : excusable
dispensar *vt* **1** : to dispense, to give, to grant **2** EXCUSAR : to excuse, to forgive **3** EXIMIR : to exempt
dispensario *nm* **1** : dispensary, clinic **2** *Mex* : dispenser
dispersar *vt* DESPERDIGAR : to disperse, to scatter
dispersión *nf, pl* **-siones** : dispersion
disperso, -sa *adj* : dispersed, scattered
displicencia *nf* : indifference, coldness, disdain
displicente *adj* : indifferent, cold, disdainful
disponer {60} *vt* **1** : to arrange, to lay out **2** : to stipulate, to order **3** : to prepare — *vi* **~ de** : to have at one's disposal — **disponerse** *vr* **~ a** : to prepare to, to be about to
disponibilidad *nf* : availability
disponible *adj* : available
disposición *nf, pl* **-ciones** **1** : disposition **2** : aptitude, talent **3** : order, arrangement **4** : willingness, readiness **5** **última disposición** : last will and testament
dispositivo *nm* **1** APARATO, MECANISMO : device, mechanism **2** : force, detachment
dispuesto[1] *pp* → **disponer**
dispuesto[2]**, -ta** *adj* PREPARADO : ready, prepared, disposed
dispuso, etc. → **disponer**
disputa *nf* ALTERCADO, DISCUSIÓN : dispute, argument
disputar *vi* : to argue, to contend, to vie — *vt* : to dispute, to question — **disputarse** *vr* : to be in competition for <se disputan la corona : they're fighting for the crown>
disquera *nf* : record label, recording company
disquete *nm* → **diskette**
disquisición *nf, pl* **-ciones** **1** : formal discourse **2** **disquisiciones** *nfpl* : digressions
distancia *nf* : distance
distanciamiento *nm* **1** : distancing **2** : rift, estrangement
distanciar *vt* **1** : to space out **2** : to draw apart — **distanciarse** *vr* : to grow apart, to become estranged
distante *adj* **1** : distant, far-off **2** : aloof
distar *vi* **~ de** : to be far from <dista de ser perfecto : he is far from perfect>
diste → **dar**
distender {56} *vt* : to distend, to stretch
distensión *nf, pl* **-siones** : distension
distinción *nf, pl* **-ciones** : distinction
distinguido, -da *adj* : distinguished, refined
distinguir {26} *vt* **1** : to distinguish **2** : to honor — **distinguirse** *vr*
distintivo, -va *adj* : distinctive, distinguishing
distinto, -ta *adj* **1** DIFERENTE : different **2** CLARO : distinct, clear, evident
distorsión *nf, pl* **-siones** : distortion
distorsionar *vt* : to distort
distracción *nf, pl* **-ciones** **1** : distraction, amusement **2** : forgetfulness **3** : oversight
distraer {81} *vt* **1** : to distract **2** ENTRETENER : to entertain, to amuse — **distraerse** *vr* **1** : to get distracted **2** : to amuse oneself
distraídamente *adv* : absentmindedly
distraído[1] *pp* → **distraer**
distraído[2]**, -da** *adj* **1** : distracted, preoccupied **2** DESPISTADO : absentminded
distribución *nf, pl* **-ciones** : distribution
distribuidor, -dora *n* : distributor
distribuir {41} *vt* : to distribute
distrital *adj* : district, of the district

distrito *nm* : district
distrofia *nf* : dystrophy <distrofia muscular : muscular dystrophy>
disturbio *nm* : disturbance
disuadir *vt* : to dissuade, to discourage
disuasión *nf, pl* **-siones** : dissuasion
disuasorio, -ria *adj* : discouraging
disuelto *pp* → **disolver**
disyuntiva *nf* : dilemma
diurético[1], **-ca** *adj* : diuretic
diurético[2] *nm* : diuretic
diurno, -na *adj* : day, daytime
diva *nf* → **divo**
divagar {52} *vi* : to digress
diván *nm, pl* **divanes** : divan
divergencia *nf* : divergence, difference
divergente *adj* : divergent, differing
divergir {35} *vi* **1** : to diverge **2** : to differ, to disagree
diversidad *nf* : diversity, variety
diversificación *nf, pl* **-ciones** : diversification
diversificar {72} *vt* : to diversify
diversión *nf, pl* **-siones** ENTRETENIMIENTO : fun, amusement, diversion
diverso, -sa *adj* : diverse, various
divertido, -da *adj* **1** : amusing, funny **2** : entertaining, enjoyable
divertir {76} *vt* ENTRETENER : to amuse, to entertain — **divertirse** *vr* : to have fun, to have a good time
dividendo *nm* : dividend
dividir *vt* **1** : to divide, to split **2** : to distribute, to share out — **dividirse** *vr*
divieso *nm* : boil
divinidad *nf* : divinity
divino, -na *adj* : divine
divisa *nf* **1** : currency **2** LEMA : motto **3** : emblem, insignia
divisar *vt* : to discern, to make out
divisible *adj* : divisible
división *nf, pl* **-siones** : division
divisionismo *nm* : factionalism
divisivo, -va *adj* : divisive
divisor *nm* : denominator
divisorio, -ria *adj* : dividing
divo, -va *n* **1** : prima donna **2** : celebrity, star
divorciado[1], **-da** *adj* **1** : divorced **2** : split, divided
divorciado[2], **-da** *n* : divorcé *m*, divorcée *f*
divorciar *vt* : to divorce — **divorciarse** *vr* : to get a divorce
divorcio *nm* : divorce
divulgación *nf, pl* **-ciones** **1** : spreading, dissemination **2** : popularization
divulgar {52} *vt* **1** : to spread, to circulate **2** REVELAR : to divulge, to reveal **3** : to popularize — **divulgarse** *vr*
dizque *adv* : supposedly, apparently
dobladillar *vt* : to hem
dobladillo *nm* : hem
doblar *vt* **1** : to double **2** PLEGAR : to fold, to bend **3** : to turn <doblar la esquina : to turn the corner> **4** : to dub — *vi* **1** : to turn **2** : to toll, to ring — **doblarse** *vr* **1** : to fold up, to double over **2** : to give in, to yield
doble[1] *adj* : double — **doblemente** *adv*
doble[2] *nm* **1** : double **2** : toll (of a bell), knell
doble[3] *nmf* : stand-in, double
doblegar {52} *vt* **1** : to fold, to crease **2** : to force to yield — **doblegarse** *vr* : to yield, to bow
doblez[1] *nm, pl* **dobleces** : fold, crease
doblez[2] *nmf* : duplicity, deceitfulness
doce *adj & nm* : twelve
doceavo[1], **-va** *adj* : twelfth
doceavo[2] *nm* : twelfth (fraction)
docena *nf* **1** : dozen **2 docena de fraile** : baker's dozen
docencia *nf* : teaching
docente[1] *adj* : educational, teaching
docente[2] *n* : teacher, lecturer
dócil *adj* : docile — **dócilmente** *adv*
docilidad *nf* : docility
docto, -ta *adj* : learned, erudite
doctor, -tora *n* : doctor
doctorado *nm* : doctorate
doctrina *nf* : doctrine — **doctrinal** *adj*
documentación *nf, pl* **-ciones** : documentation
documental *adj & nm* : documentary
documentar *vt* : to document
documento *nm* : document
dogma *nm* : dogma
dogmático, -ca *adj* : dogmatic
dogmatismo *nm* : dogmatism
dólar *nm* : dollar
dolencia *nf* : ailment, malaise
doler {47} *vi* **1** : to hurt, to ache **2** : to grieve — **dolerse** *vr* **1** : to be distressed **2** : to complain
doliente *nmf* : mourner, bereaved
dolor *nm* **1** : pain, ache <dolor de cabeza : headache> **2** PENA, TRISTEZA : grief, sorrow
dolorido, -da *adj* **1** : sore, aching **2** : hurt, upset
doloroso, -sa *adj* **1** : painful **2** : distressing — **dolorosamente** *adv*
doloso, -sa *adj* : fraudulent — **dolosamente** *adv*
domador, -dora *n* : tamer
domar *vt* : to tame, to break in
domesticado, -da *adj* : domesticated, tame
domesticar {72} *vt* : to domesticate, to tame
doméstico, -ca *adj* : domestic, household
domiciliado, -da *adj* : residing
domiciliario, -ria *adj* **1** : home **2 arresto domiciliario** : house arrest
domiciliarse *vr* RESIDIR : to reside
domicilio *nm* : home, residence <cambio de domicilio : change of address>
dominación *nf, pl* **-ciones** : domination
dominancia *nf* : dominance
dominante *adj* **1** : dominant **2** : domineering

dominar *vt* **1** : to dominate **2** : to master, to be proficient at — *vi* : to predominate, to prevail — **dominarse** *vr* : to control oneself
domingo *nm* : Sunday
dominical *adj* : Sunday <periódico dominical : Sunday newspaper>
dominicano, -na *adj & n* : Dominican
dominio *nm* **1** : dominion, power **2** : mastery **3** : domain, field
dominó *nm, pl* **-nós** **1** : domino (tile) **2** : dominoes *pl* (game)
domo *nm* : dome
don[1] *nm* **1** : gift, present **2** : talent
don[2] *nm* **1** : title of courtesy preceding a man's first name **2** **don nadie** : nobody, insignificant person
dona *nf Mex* : doughnut, donut
donación *nf, pl* **-ciones** : donation
donador, -dora *n* : donor
donaire *nm* **1** GARBO : grace, poise **2** : witticism
donante *nf* → **donador**
donar *vt* : to donate
donativo *nm* : donation
doncella *nf* : maiden, damsel
doncellez *nf* : maidenhood
donde[1] *conj* : where, in which <el pueblo donde vivo : the town where I live>
donde[2] *prep* : over by <lo encontré donde la silla : I found it over by the chair>
dónde *adv* : where <¿dónde está su casa? : where is your house?>
dondequiera *adv* **1** : anywhere, no matter where **2** **dondequiera que** : wherever, everywhere
doña *nf* : title of courtesy preceding a woman's first name
doquier *adv* **por ~** : everywhere, all over
dorado[1], **-da** *adj* : gold, golden
dorado[2], **-da** *nm* : gilt
dorar *vt* **1** : to gild **2** : to brown
dormido, -da *adj* **1** : asleep **2** : numb <tiene el pie dormido : her foot's numb, her foot's gone to sleep>
dormilón, -lona *n* : sleepyhead, late riser
dormir {27} *vt* : to put to sleep — *vi* : to sleep — **dormirse** *vr* : to fall asleep
dormitar *vi* : to snooze, to doze
dormitorio *nm* **1** : bedroom **2** : dormitory
dorsal[1] *adj* : dorsal
dorsal[2] *nm* : number (worn in sports)
dorso *nm* **1** : back <el dorso de la mano : the back of the hand> **2** *Mex* : backstroke
dos *adj & nm* : two
doscientos[1], **-tas** *adj* : two hundred
doscientos[2] *nms & pl* : two hundred
dosel *nm* : canopy
dosificación *nf, pl* **-ciones** : dosage
dosis *nfs & pl* **1** : dose **2** : amount, quantity
dotación *nf, pl* **-ciones** **1** : endowment, funding **2** : staff, personnel
dotado, -da *adj* **1** : gifted **2** **~ de** : endowed with, equipped with
dotar *vt* **1** : to provide, to equip **2** : to endow
dote *nf* **1** : dowry **2** **dotes** *nfpl* : talent, gift
doy → **dar**
draga *nf* : dredge
dragado *nm* : dredging
dragar {52} *vt* : to dredge
dragón *nm, pl* **dragones** **1** : dragon **2** : snapdragon
drague, etc. → **dragar**
drama *nm* : drama
dramático, -ca *adj* : dramatic — **dramáticamente** *adv*
dramatizar {21} *vt* : to dramatize — **dramatización** *nf*
dramaturgo, -ga *n* : dramatist, playwright
drástico, -ca *adj* : drastic — **drásticamente** *adv*
drenaje *nm* : drainage
drenar *vt* : to drain
drene *nm Mex* : drain
driblar *vi* : to dribble (in basketball)
drible *nm* : dribble (in basketball)
droga *nf* : drug
drogadicción *nf, pl* **-ciones** : drug addiction
drogadicto, -ta *n* : drug addict
drogar {52} *vt* : to drug — **drogarse** *vr* : to take drugs
drogue, etc. → **drogar**
droguería *nf* FARMACIA : drugstore
dual *adj* : dual
dualidad *nf* : duality
dualismo *nm* : dualism
ducha *nf* : shower <darse una ducha : to take a shower>
ducharse *vr* : to take a shower
ducho, -cha *adj* : experienced, skilled, expert
ducto *nm* **1** : duct, shaft **2** : pipeline
duda *nf* : doubt <no cabe duda : there's no doubt about it>
dudar *vt* : to doubt — *vi* **~ en** : to hesitate to <no dudes en pedirme ayuda : don't hesitate to ask me for help>
dudoso, -sa *adj* **1** : doubtful **2** : dubious, questionable — **dudosamente** *adv*
duele, etc. → **doler**
duelo *nm* **1** : duel **2** LUTO : mourning
duende *nm* **1** : elf, goblin **2** ENCANTO : magic, charm <una bailarina que tiene duende : a dancer with a certain magic>
dueño, -na *nmf* **1** : owner, proprietor, proprietress *f* **2** : landlord, landlady *f*
duerme, etc. → **dormir**
dueto *nm* : duet
dulce[1] *adv* : sweetly, softly
dulce[2] *adj* **1** : sweet **2** : mild, gentle, mellow — **dulcemente** *adv*
dulce[3] *nm* : candy, sweet

dulcería *nf* **:** candy store
dulcificante *nm* **:** sweetener
dulzura *nf* **1 :** sweetness **2 :** gentleness, mellowness
duna *nf* **:** dune
dúo *nm* **:** duo, duet
duodécimo[1], -ma *adj* **:** twelfth
duodécimo[2], -ma *nm* **:** twelfth (in a series)
dúplex *nms & pl* **:** duplex apartment
duplicación *nf, pl* **-ciones :** duplication, copying
duplicado *nm* **:** duplicate, copy
duplicar {72} *vt* **1 :** to double **2 :** to duplicate, to copy
duplicidad *nf* **:** duplicity
duque *nm* **:** duke
duquesa *nf* **:** duchess
durabilidad *nf* **:** durability
durable → duradero
duración *nf, pl* **-ciones :** duration, length
duradero, -ra *adj* **:** durable, lasting
duramente *adv* **1 :** harshly, severely **2 :** hard
durante *prep* **:** during <durante todo el día : all day long> <trabajó durante tres horas : he worked for three hours>
durar *vi* **:** to last, to endure
durazno *nm* **1 :** peach **2 :** peach tree
dureza *nf* **1 :** hardness, toughness **2 :** severity, harshness
durmiente[1] *adj* **:** sleeping
durmiente[2] *nmf* **:** sleeper
durmió, etc. → dormir
duro[1] *adv* **:** hard <trabajé tan duro : I worked so hard>
duro[2], -ra *adj* **1 :** hard, tough **2 :** harsh, severe

E

e[1] *nf* **:** fifth letter of the Spanish alphabet
e[2] *conj* (*used instead of* **y** *before words beginning with i or hi*) **:** and
ebanista *nmf* **:** cabinetmaker
ebanistería *nf* **:** cabinetmaking
ébano *nm* **:** ebony
ebriedad *nf* EMBRIAGUEZ **:** inebriation, drunkenness
ebrio, -bria *adj* EMBRIAGADO **:** inebriated, drunk
ebullición *nf, pl* **-ciones :** boiling
eccéntrico → excéntrico
echar *vt* **1** LANZAR **:** to throw, to cast, to hurl **2** EXPULSAR **:** to throw out, to expel **3** EMITIR **:** to emit, give off **4** BROTAR **:** to sprout, to put forth **5** DESPEDIR **:** to fire, to dismiss **6 :** to put in, to add **7 echar a perder :** to spoil, to ruin **8 echar de menos :** to miss <echan de menos a su madre : they miss their mother> — *vi* **1 :** to start off **2 ~ a :** to begin to — **echarse** *vr* **1 :** to throw oneself **2 :** to lie down **3 :** to put on **4 ~ a :** to start to **5 echarse a perder :** to go bad, to spoil **6 echárselas de :** to pose as
ecléctico, -ca *adj* **:** eclectic
eclesiástico[1], -ca *adj* **:** ecclesiastical, ecclesiastic
eclesiástico[2] *nm* CLÉRIGO **:** cleric, clergyman
eclipsar *vt* **1 :** to eclipse **2 :** to outshine, to surpass
eclipse *nm* **:** eclipse
eco *nm* **:** echo
ecografía *nf* **:** ultrasound scanning
ecología *nf* **:** ecology
ecológico, -ca *adj* **:** ecological — **ecológicamente** *adv*
ecologista *nmf* **:** ecologist, environmentalist
ecólogo, -ga *n* **:** ecologist
economía *nf* **1 :** economy **2 :** economics
económicamente *adv* **:** financially
económico, -ca *adj* **:** economic, economical
economista *nmf* **:** economist
economizar {21} *vt* **:** to save, to economize on — *vi* **:** to save up, to be frugal
ecosistema *nm* **:** ecosystem
ecuación *nf, pl* **-ciones :** equation
ecuador *nm* **:** equator
ecuánime *adj* **1 :** even-tempered **2 :** impartial
ecuanimidad *nf* **1 :** equanimity **2 :** impartiality
ecuatorial *adj* **:** equatorial
ecuatoriano, -na *adj & n* **:** Ecuadorian
ecuestre *adj* **:** equestrian
ecuménico, -ca *adj* **:** ecumenical
eczema *nm* **:** eczema
edad *nf* **1 :** age <¿qué edad tiene? : how old is she?> **2** ÉPOCA, ERA **:** epoch, era
edema *nm* **:** edema
Edén *nm, pl* **Edenes :** Eden, paradise
edición *nf, pl* **-ciones 1 :** edition **2 :** publication, publishing
edicto *nm* **:** edict, proclamation
edificación *nf, pl* **-ciones 1 :** edification **2 :** construction, building
edificante *adj* **:** edifying
edificar {72} *vt* **1 :** to edify **2** CONSTRUIR **:** to build, to construct
edificio *nm* **:** building, edifice
editar *vt* **1 :** to edit **2** PUBLICAR **:** to publish
editor[1], -tora *adj* **:** publishing <casa editora : publishing house>
editor[2], -tora *n* **1 :** editor **2 :** publisher
editora *nf* **:** publisher, publishing company
editorial[1] *adj* **1 :** publishing **2 :** editorial
editorial[2] *nm* **:** editorial
editorial[3] *nf* **:** publishing house

editorializar {21} *vi* : to editorialize
edredón *nm, pl* **-dones** COBERTOR, COLCHA : comforter, eiderdown, quilt
educable *adj* : educable, teachable
educación *nf, pl* **-ciones 1** ENSEÑANZA : education **2** : manners *pl* — **educacional** *adj*
educado, -da *adj* : polite, well-mannered
educador, -dora *n* : educator
educando, -da *n* ALUMNO, PUPILO : pupil, student
educar {72} *vt* **1** : to educate **2** CRIAR : to bring up, to raise **3** : to train — **educarse** *vr* : to be educated
educativo, -va *adj* : educational
efectista *adj* : dramatic, sensational
efectivamente *adv* : really, actually
efectividad *nf* : effectiveness
efectivo[1], **-va** *adj* **1** : effective **2** : real, actual **3** : permanent, regular (of employment)
efectivo[2] *nm* : cash
efecto *nm* **1** : effect **2 en ~** : actually, in fact **3 efectos** *nmpl* : goods, property <efectos personales : personal effects>
efectuar {3} *vt* : to carry out, to bring about
efervescencia *nf* **1** : effervescence **2** : vivacity, high spirits *pl*
efervescente *adj* **1** : effervescent **2** : vivacious
eficacia *nf* **1** : effectiveness, efficacy **2** : efficiency
eficaz *adj, pl* **-caces 1** : effective **2** EFICIENTE : efficient — **eficazmente** *adv*
eficiencia *nf* : efficiency
eficiente *adj* EFICAZ : efficient — **eficientemente** *adv*
eficientizar {21} *vt Mex* : to streamline, to make more efficient
efigie *nf* : effigy
efímera *nf* : mayfly
efímero, -ra *adj* : ephemeral
efusión *nf, pl* **-siones 1** : effusion **2** : warmth, effusiveness **3 con ~** : effusively
efusivo, -va *adj* : effusive — **efusivamente** *adv*
egipcio, -cia *adj & n* : Egyptian
eglefino *nm* : haddock
ego *nm* : ego
egocéntrico, -ca *adj* : egocentric, self-centered
egoísmo *nm* : selfishness, egoism
egoísta[1] *adj* : selfish, egoistic
egoísta[2] *nmf* : egoist, selfish person
egotismo *nm* : egotism, conceit
egotista[1] *adj* : egotistic, egotistical, conceited
egotista[2] *nmf* : egotist, conceited person
egresado, -da *n* : graduate
egresar *vi* : to graduate
egreso *nm* **1** : graduation **2 ingresos y egresos** : income and expenditure
eje *nm* **1** : axle **2** : axis
ejecución *nf, pl* **-ciones** : execution
ejecutante *nmf* : performer
ejecutar *vt* **1** : to execute, to put to death **2** : to carry out, to perform
ejecutivo, -va *adj & n* : executive
ejecutor, -tora *n* : executor
ejemplar[1] *adj* : exemplary, model
ejemplar[2] *nm* **1** : copy (of a book, magazine, etc.) **2** : specimen, example
ejemplificar {72} *vt* : to exemplify, to illustrate
ejemplo *nm* **1** : example **2 por ~** : for example **3 dar ejemplo** : to set an example
ejercer {86} *vi* **~ de** : to practice as, to work as — *vt* **1** : to practice **2** : exercise (a right) **3** : to exert
ejercicio *nm* **1** : exercise **2** : practice
ejercitar *vt* **1** : to exercise **2** ADIESTRAR : to drill, to train
ejército *nm* : army
ejidal *adj Mex* : cooperative
ejido *nm* **1** : common land **2** *Mex* : cooperative
ejote *nm Mex* : green bean
el[1] *pron* (*referring to masculine nouns*) **1** : the one <tengo mi libro y el tuyo : I have my book and yours> <de los cantantes me gusta el de México : I prefer the singer from México> **2 el que** : he who, whoever, the one that <el que vino ayer : the one who came yesterday> <el que trabaja duro estará contento : he who works hard will be happy>
el[2], **la** *art, pl* **los, las** : the <los niños están en la casa : the boys are in the house> <me duele el pie : my foot hurts>
él *pron* : he, him <él es mi amigo : he's my friend> <hablaremos con él : we will speak with him>
elaboración *nf, pl* **-ciones 1** PRODUCCIÓN : production, making **2** : preparation, devising
elaborado, -da *adj* : elaborate
elaborar *vt* **1** : to make, to produce **2** : to devise, to draw up
elasticidad *nf* : elasticity
elástico[1], **-ca** *adj* **1** FLEXIBLE : flexible **2** : elastic
elástico[2] *nm* **1** : elastic (material) **2** : rubber band
elección *nf, pl* **-ciones 1** SELECCIÓN : choice, selection **2** : election
electivo, -va *adj* : elective
electo, -ta *adj* : elect <el presidente electo : the president-elect>
elector, -tora *n* : elector, voter
electorado *nm* : electorate
electoral *adj* : electoral, election
electricidad *nf* : electricity
electricista *nmf* : electrician
eléctrico, -ca *adj* : electric, electrical
electrificar {72} *vt* : to electrify — **electrificación** *nf*
electrizar {21} *vt* : to electrify, to thrill — **electrizante** *adj*

electrocardiógrafo *nm* : electrocardiograph
electrocardiograma *nm* : electrocardiogram
electrocutar *vt* : to electrocute — **electrocución** *nf*
electrodo *nm* : electrode
electrodoméstico *nm* : electric appliance
electroimán *nm, pl* **-manes** : electromagnet
electrólisis *nfs & pl* : electrolysis
electrolito *nm* : electrolyte
electromagnético, -ca *adj* : electromagnetic
electromagnetismo *nm* : electromagnetism
electrón *nm, pl* **-trones** : electron
electrónica *nf* : electronics
electrónico, -ca *adj* : electronic — **electrónicamente** *adv*
elefante, -ta *n* : elephant
elegancia *nf* : elegance
elegante *adj* : elegant, smart — **elegantemente** *adv*
elegía *nf* : elegy
elegíaco, -ca *adj* : elegiac
elegibilidad *nf* : eligibility
elegible *adj* : eligible
elegido, -da *adj* **1** : chosen, selected **2** : elected
elegir {28} *vt* **1** ESCOGER, SELECCIONAR : to choose, to select **2** : to elect
elemental *adj* **1** : elementary, basic **2** : fundamental, essential
elemento *nm* : element
elenco *nm* : cast (of actors)
elepé *nm* : long-playing record
elevación *nf, pl* **-ciones** : elevation, height
elevado, -da *adj* **1** : elevated, lofty **2** : high
elevador *nm* ASCENSOR : elevator
elevar *vt* **1** ALZAR : to raise, to lift **2** AUMENTAR : to raise, to increase **3** : to elevate (in a hierarchy), to promote **4** : to present, to submit — **elevarse** *vr* : to rise
elfo *nm* : elf
eliminación *nf, pl* **-ciones** : elimination, removal
eliminar *vt* **1** : to eliminate, to remove **2** : to do in, to kill
elipse *nf* : ellipse
elipsis *nf* : ellipsis
elíptico, -ca *adj* : elliptical, elliptic
elite *or* **élite** *nf* : elite
elixir *or* **elíxir** *nm* : elixir
ella *pron* : she, her <ella es mi amiga : she is my friend> <nos fuimos con ella : we left with her>
ello *pron* : it <es por ello que me voy : that's why I'm going>
ellos, ellas *pron pl* **1** : they, them **2 de ellos, de ellas** : theirs
elocución *nf, pl* **-ciones** : elocution
elocuencia *nf* : eloquence
elocuente *adj* : eloquent — **elocuentemente** *adv*
elogiar *vt* ENCOMIAR : to praise
elogio *nm* : praise
elote *nm* **1** *Mex* : corn, maize **2** *CA, Mex* : corncob
elucidación *nf, pl* **-ciones** ESCLARECIMIENTO : elucidation
elucidar *vt* ESCLARECER : to elucidate
eludir *vt* EVADIR : to evade, to avoid, to elude
emanación *nf, pl* **-ciones** : emanation
emanar *vi* **∼ de** : to emanate from — *vt* : to exude
emancipar *vt* : to emancipate — **emancipación** *nf*
embadurnar *vt* EMBARRAR : to smear, to daub
embajada *nf* : embassy
embajador, -dora *n* : ambassador
embalaje *nm* : packing, packaging
embalar *vt* EMPAQUETAR : to pack
embaldosar *vt* : to tile, to pave with tiles
embalsamar *vt* : to embalm
embalsar *vt* : to dam, to dam up
embalse *nm* : dam, reservoir
embarazada *adj* ENCINTA, PREÑADA : pregnant, expecting
embarazar {21} *vt* **1** : to obstruct, to hamper **2** PREÑAR : to make pregnant
embarazo *nm* : pregnancy
embarazoso, -sa *adj* : embarrassing, awkward
embarcación *nf, pl* **-ciones** : boat, craft
embarcadero *nm* : wharf, pier, jetty
embarcar {72} *vi* : to embark, to board — *vt* : to load
embarco *nm* : embarkation
embargar {52} *vt* **1** : to seize, to impound **2** : to overwhelm
embargo *nm* **1** : seizure **2** : embargo **3 sin ∼** : however, nevertheless
embarque *nm* **1** : embarkation **2** : shipment
embarrancar {72} *vi* **1** : to run aground **2** : to get bogged down
embarrar *vt* **1** : to cover with mud **2** EMBADURNAR : to smear
embarullar *vt fam* : to muddle, to confuse — **embarullarse** *vr fam* : to get mixed up
embate *nm* **1** : onslaught **2** : battering (of waves or wind)
embaucador, -dora *n* : swindler, deceiver
embaucar {72} *vt* : to trick, to swindle
embeber *vt* : to absorb, to soak up — *vi* : to shrink
embelesado, -da *adj* : spellbound
embelesar *vt* : to enchant, to captivate
embellecer {53} *vt* : to embellish, to beautify
embellecimiento *nm* : beautification, embellishment
embestida *nf* **1** : charge (of a bull) **2** ARREMETIDA : attack, onslaught
embestir {54} *vt* : to hit, to run into, to charge at — *vi* ARREMETER : to charge, to attack

emblanquecer {53} *vt* BLANQUEAR : to bleach, to whiten — **emblanquecerse** *vr* : to turn white
emblema *nm* : emblem
emblemático, -ca *adj* : emblematic
embolia *nf* : embolism
émbolo *nm* : piston
embolsarse *vr* **1** : to pocket (money) **2** : to collect (payment)
emborracharse *vr* EMBRIAGARSE : to get drunk
emborronar *vt* **1** : to blot, to smudge **2** GARABATEAR : to scribble
emboscada *nf* : ambush
emboscar {72} *vt* : to ambush — **emboscarse** *vr* : to lie in ambush
embotadura *nf* : bluntness, dullness
embotar *vt* **1** : to dull, to blunt **2** : to weaken, to enervate
embotellamiento *nm* ATASCO : traffic jam
embotellar *vt* ENVASAR : to bottle
embragar {52} *vi* : to engage the clutch
embrague *nm* : clutch
embravecerse {53} *vr* **1** : to get furious **2** : to get rough <el mar se embraveció : the sea became tempestuous>
embriagado, -da *adj* : inebriated, drunk
embriagador, -dora *adj* : intoxicating
embriagarse {52} *vr* EMBORRACHARSE : to get drunk
embriaguez *nf* EBRIEDAD : drunkenness, inebriation
embrión *nm, pl* **embriones** : embryo
embrionario, -ria *adj* : embryonic
embrollo *nm* ENREDO : imbroglio, confusion
embrujar *vt* HECHIZAR : to bewitch
embrujo *nm* : spell, curse
embudo *nm* : funnel
embuste *nm* **1** MENTIRA : lie, fib **2** ENGAÑO : trick, hoax
embustero[1], -ra *adj* : lying, deceitful
embustero[2], -ra *n* : liar, cheat
embutido *nm* **1** : sausage **2** : inlaid work
embutir *vt* **1** : to cram, to stuff, to jam **2** : to inlay
emergencia *nf* **1** : emergency **2** : emergence
emergente *adj* **1** : emergent **2** : consequent, resultant
emerger {15} *vi* : to emerge, to surface
emético[1], -ca *adj* : emetic
emético[2] *nm* : emetic
emigración *nf, pl* **-ciones** **1** : emigration **2** : migration
emigrante *adj & nmf* : emigrant
emigrar *vi* **1** : to emigrate **2** : to migrate
eminencia *nf* : eminence
eminente *adj* : eminent, distinguished
eminentemente *adv* : basically, essentially
emisario[1], -ria *n* : emissary
emisario[2] *nm* : outlet (of a body of water)
emisión *nf, pl* **-siones** **1** : emission **2** : broadcast **3** : issue <emisión de acciones : stock issue>
emisor *nm* TRANSMISOR : television or radio transmitter
emisora *nf* : radio station
emitir *vt* **1** : to emit, to give off **2** : to broadcast **3** : to issue **4** : to cast (a vote)
emoción *nf, pl* **-ciones** : emotion — **emocional** *adj* — **emocionalmente** *adv*
emocionado, -da *adj* **1** : moved, affected by emotion **2** ENTUSIASMADO : excited
emocionante *adj* **1** CONMOVEDOR : moving, touching **2** EXCITANTE : exciting, thrilling
emocionar *vt* **1** CONMOVER : to move, to touch **2** : to excite, to thrill — **emocionarse** *vr*
emotivo, -va *adj* : emotional, moving
empacador, -dora *n* : packer
empacar {72} *vt* **1** EMPAQUETAR : to pack **2** : to bale — *vi* : to pack — **empacarse** *vr* **1** : to balk, to refuse to budge **2** *Col, Mex fam* : to eat ravenously, to devour
empachar *vt* **1** ESTORBAR : to obstruct **2** : to give indigestion to **3** DISFRAZAR : to disguise, to mask — **empacharse** *vr* **1** INDIGESTARSE : to get indigestion **2** AVERGONZARSE : to be embarrassed
empacho *nm* **1** INDIGESTIÓN : indigestion **2** VERGÜENZA : embarrassment **3** **no tener empacho en** : to have no qualms about
empadronarse *vr* : to register to vote
empalagar {52} *vt* **1** : to cloy, to surfeit **2** FASTIDIAR : to annoy, to bother
empalagoso, -sa *adj* MELOSO : cloying, excessively sweet
empalar *vt* : to impale
empalizada *nf* : palisade (fence)
empalmar *vt* **1** : to splice, to link **2** : to combine — *vi* : to meet, to converge
empalme *nm* **1** CONEXIÓN : connection, link **2** : junction
empanada *nf* : pie, turnover
empanadilla *nf* : meat or seafood pie
empanar *vt* : to bread
empantanado, -da *adj* : bogged down, delayed
empañar *vt* **1** : to steam up **2** : to tarnish, to sully
empapado, -da *adj* : soggy, sodden
empapar *vt* MOJAR : to soak, to drench — **empaparse** *vr* **1** : to get soaking wet **2** **~ de** : to absorb, to be imbued with
empapelar *vt* : to wallpaper
empaque *nm fam* **1** : presence, bearing **2** : pomposity **3** DESCARO : impudence, nerve
empaquetar *vt* EMBALAR : to pack, to package — **empaquetarse** *vr fam* : to dress up

emparedado *nm* : sandwich
emparedar *vt* : to wall in, to confine
emparejar *vt* **1** : to pair, to match up **2** : to make even — *vi* : to catch up — **emparejarse** *vr* : to pair up
emparentado, -da *adj* : related
emparentar {55} *vi* : to become related by marriage
emparrillado *nm Mex* : gridiron (in football)
empastar *vt* **1** : to fill (a tooth) **2** : to bind (a book)
empaste *nm* : filling (of a tooth)
empatar *vt* : to tie, to connect — *vi* : to result in a draw, to be tied — **empatarse** *vr Ven* : to hook up, to link together
empate *nm* : draw, tie
empatía *nf* : empathy
empecinado, -da *adj* TERCO : stubborn
empecinarse *vr* OBSTINARSE : to be stubborn, to persist
empedernido, -da *adj* INCORREGIBLE : hardened, inveterate
empedrado *nm* : paving, pavement
empedrar {55} *vt* : to pave (with stones)
empeine *nm* : instep
empellón *nm, pl* **-llones** : shove, push
empelotado, -da *adj* **1** *Mex fam* : madly in love **2** *fam* : stark naked
empeñado, -da *adj* : determined, committed
empeñar *vt* **1** : to pawn **2** : to pledge, to give (one's word) — **empeñarse** *vr* **1** : to insist stubbornly **2** : to make an effort
empeño *nm* **1** : pledge, commitment **2** : insistence **3** ESFUERZO : effort, determination **4** : pawning <casa de empeños : pawnshop>
empeoramiento *nm* : worsening, deterioration
empeorar *vi* : to deteriorate, to get worse — *vt* : to make worse
empequeñecer {53} *vi* : to diminish, to become smaller — *vt* : to minimize, to make smaller
emperador *nm* : emperor
emperatriz *nf, pl* **-trices** : empress
empero *conj* : however, nevertheless
empezar {29} *v* COMENZAR : to start, to begin
empinado, -da *adj* : steep
empinar *vt* ELEVAR : to lift, to raise — **empinarse** *vr* : to stand on tiptoe
empírico, -ca *adj* : empirical — **empíricamente** *adv*
emplasto *nm* : poultice, dressing
emplazamiento *nm* **1** : location, site **2** CITACIÓN : summons, subpoena
emplazar {21} *vt* **1** CONVOCAR : to convene, to summon **2** : to subpoena **3** UBICAR : to place, to position
empleado, -da *n* : employee
empleador, -dora *n* PATRÓN : employer
emplear *vt* **1** : to employ **2** USAR : to use — **emplearse** *vr* **1** : to get a job **2** : to occupy oneself
empleo *nm* **1** OCUPACIÓN : employment, occupation, job **2** : use, usage
empobrecer {53} *vt* : to impoverish — *vi* : to become poor — **empobrecerse** *vr*
empobrecimiento *nm* : impoverishment
empollar *vi* : to brood eggs — *vt* : to incubate
empolvado, -da *adj* **1** : dusty **2** : powdered, powdery
empolvar *vt* **1** : to cover with dust **2** : to powder — **empolvarse** *vr* **1** : to gather dust **2** : to powder one's face
emporio *nm* **1** : center, capital, empire <un emporio cultural : a cultural center> <un emporio financiero : a financial empire> **2** : department store
empotrado, -da *adj* : built-in <armarios empotrados : built-in cabinets>
empotrar *vt* : to build into, to embed
emprendedor, -dora *adj* : enterprising
emprender *vt* : to undertake, to begin
empresa *nf* **1** COMPAÑÍA, FIRMA : company, corporation, firm **2** : undertaking, venture
empresariado *nm* **1** : business world **2** : management, managers *pl*
empresarial *adj* : business, managerial, corporate
empresario, -ria *n* **1** : manager **2** : businessman *m,* businesswoman *f* **3** : impresario
empujar *vi* : to push, to shove — *vt* **1** : to push **2** PRESIONAR : to spur on, to press
empuje *nm* : impetus, drive
empujón *nm, pl* **-jones** : push, shove
empuñadura *nf* MANGO : hilt, handle
empuñar *vt* **1** ASIR : to grasp **2 empuñar las armas** : to take up arms
emú *nm* : emu
emular *vt* IMITAR : to emulate — **emulación** *nf*
emulsión *nf, pl* **-siones** : emulsion
emulsionante *nm* : emulsifier
emulsionar *vt* : to emulsify
en *prep* **1** : in <en el bolsillo : in one's pocket> <en una semana : in a week> **2** : on <en la mesa : on the table> **3** : at <en casa : at home> <en el trabajo : at work> <en ese momento : at that moment>
enagua *nf* : petticoat, slip
enajenación *nf, pl* **-ciones 1** : transfer (of property) **2** : alienation **3** : absentmindedness
enajenado, -da *adj* : out of one's mind
enajenar *vt* **1** : to transfer (property) **2** : to alienate **3** : to enrapture — **enajenarse** *vr* **1** : to become estranged **2** : to go mad
enaltecer {53} *vt* : to praise, to extol
enamorado[1], -da *adj* : in love
enamorado[2], -da *n* : lover, sweetheart
enamoramiento *nm* : infatuation, crush

enamorar *vt* **:** to enamor, to win the love of — **enamorarse** *vr* **:** to fall in love
enamoriscarse {72} *vr fam* **:** to have a crush, to be infatuated
enamorizado, -da *adj* **:** amorous, passionate
enano[1], -na *adj* **:** tiny, minute
enano[2], -na *n* **:** dwarf, midget
enarbolar *vt* **1 :** to hoist, to raise **2 :** to brandish
enarcar {72} *vt* **:** to arch, to raise
enardecer {53} *vt* **1 :** to arouse (anger, passions) **2 :** to stir up, to excite — **enardecerse** *vr*
encabezado *nm Mex* **:** headline
encabezamiento *nm* **1 :** heading **2 :** salutation, opening
encabezar {21} *vt* **1 :** to head, to lead **2 :** to put a heading on
encabritarse *vr* **1 :** to rear up **2** *fam* **:** to get angry
encadenar *vt* **1 :** to chain **2 :** to connect, to link **3** INMOVILIZAR **:** to immobilize
encajar *vi* **:** to fit, to fit together, to fit in — *vt* **1 :** to insert, to stick **2 :** to take, to cope with <encajó el golpe : he withstood the blow>
encaje *nm* **1 :** lace **2 :** financial reserve
encajonar *vt* **1 :** to box, to crate **2 :** to cram in
encalar *vt* **:** to whitewash
encallar *vi* **1 :** to run aground **2 :** to get stuck
encallecido, -da *adj* **:** callused
encamar *vt* **:** to confine to a bed
encaminado, -da *adj* **1 :** on the right track **2 ~ a :** aimed at, designed to
encaminar *vt* **1 :** to direct, to channel **2 :** to head in the right direction — **encaminarse** *vr* **~ a :** to head for, to aim at
encandilar *vt* **:** to dazzle
encanecer {53} *vi* **:** to gray, to go gray
encantado, -da *adj* **1 :** charmed, bewitched **2 :** delighted
encantador[1], -dora *adj* **:** charming, delightful
encantador[2], -dora *n* **:** magician
encantamiento *nm* **:** enchantment, spell
encantar *vt* **1 :** to enchant, to bewitch **2 :** to charm, to delight <me encanta esta canción : I love this song>
encanto *nm* **1 :** charm, fascination **2** HECHIZO **:** spell **3 :** delightful person or thing
encañonar *vt* **:** to point (a gun) at, to hold up
encapotado, -da *adj* **:** cloudy, overcast
encapotarse *vr* **:** to cloud over, to become overcast
encaprichado, -da *adj* **:** infatuated
encaprichamiento *nm* **:** infatuation
encapuchado, -da *adj* **:** hooded
encarado, -da *adj* **estar mal encarado** *fam* **:** to be ugly-looking, to look mean
encaramar *vt* **:** to raise, to lift up — **encaramarse** *vr* **:** to perch
encarar *vt* CONFRONTAR **:** to face, to confront
encarcelación *nf* → **encarcelamiento**
encarcelamiento *nm* **:** incarceration, imprisonment
encarcelar *vt* **:** to incarcerate, to imprison
encarecer {53} *vt* **1 :** to increase, to raise (price, value) **2 :** to beseech, to entreat — **encarecerse** *vr* **:** to become more expensive
encarecidamente *adv* **:** insistently, urgently
encarecimiento *nm* **:** increase, rise (in price)
encargado[1], -da *adj* **:** in charge
encargado[2], -da *n* **:** manager, person in charge
encargar {52} *vt* **1 :** to put in charge of **2 :** to recommend, to advise **3 :** to order, to request — **encargarse** *vr* **~ de :** to take charge of
encargo *nm* **1 :** errand **2 :** job assignment **3 :** order <hecho de encargo : custom-made, made to order>
encariñarse *vr* **~ con :** to become fond of, to grow attached to
encarnación *nf, pl* **-ciones :** incarnation, embodiment
encarnado[1], -da *adj* **1 :** incarnate **2 :** flesh-colored **3 :** red **4 :** ingrown
encarnado[2] *nm* **:** red
encarnar *vt* **:** to incarnate, to embody — **encarnarse** *vr* **encarnarse una uña :** to have an ingrown nail
encarnizado, -da *adj* **1 :** bloodshot, inflamed **2 :** fierce, bloody
encarnizar {21} *vt* **:** to enrage, to infuriate — **encarnizarse** *vr* **:** to be brutal, to attack viciously
encarrilar *vt* **:** to guide, to put on the right track
encasillar *vt* CLASIFICAR **:** to classify, to pigeonhole, to categorize
encausar *vt* **:** to prosecute, to charge
encauzar {21} *vt* **:** to channel, to guide — **encauzarse** *vr*
encebollado, -da *adj* **:** cooked with onions
encefalitis *nms & pl* **:** encephalitis
encendedor *nm* **:** lighter
encender {56} *vi* **:** to light — *vt* **1 :** to light, to set fire to **2** PRENDER **:** to switch on **3 :** to start (a motor) **4 :** to arouse, to kindle — **encenderse** *vr* **1 :** to get excited **2 :** to blush
encendido[1], -da *adj* **1 :** burning **2 :** flushed **3 :** fiery, passionate
encendido[2] *nm* **:** ignition
encerado *nm* **1 :** waxing, polishing **2 :** blackboard
encerar *vt* **:** to wax, to polish
encerrar {55} *vt* **1 :** to lock up, to shut away **2 :** to contain, to include **3 :** to involve, to entail
encerrona *nf* **1** TRAMPA **:** trap, setup **2** **prepararle una encerrona a alguien**

: to set a trap for someone, to set someone up
encestar *vi* : to make a basket (in basketball)
enchapado *nm* : plating, coating (of metal)
encharcamiento *nm* : flood, flooding
encharcar {72} *vt* : to flood, to swamp — **encharcarse** *vr*
enchilada *nf* : enchilada
enchilar *vt Mex* : to season with chili
enchuecar {72} *vt Chile, Mex fam* : to make crooked, to twist
enchufar *vt* **1** : to plug in **2** : to connect, to fit together
enchufe *nm* **1** : connection **2** : plug, socket
encía *nf* : gum (tissue)
encíclica *nf* : encyclical
enciclopedia *nf* : encyclopedia
enciclopédico, -ca *adj* : encyclopedic
encierro *nm* **1** : confinement **2** : enclosure
encima *adv* **1** : on top, above **2** ADEMÁS : as well, besides **3 ~ de** : on, on top of, over **4 por encima de** : above, beyond <por encima de la ley : above the law> **5 echarse encima** : to take upon oneself **6 estar encima de** *fam* : to nag, to criticize **7 quitarse de encima** : to get rid of
encina *nf* : evergreen oak
encinta *adj* EMBARAZADA, PREÑADA : pregnant, expecting
enclaustrado, -da *adj* : cloistered, shut away
enclavado, -da *adj* : buried
enclenque *adj* : weak, sickly
encoger {15} *vt* **1** : to shrink, to make smaller **2** : to intimidate — *vi* : to shrink, to contract — **encogerse** *vr* **1** : to shrink **2** : to be intimidated, to cower, to cringe **3 encogerse de hombros** : to shrug <one's shoulders>
encogido, -da *adj* **1** : shriveled, shrunken **2** TÍMIDO : shy, inhibited
encogimiento *nm* **1** : shrinking, shrinkage **2** : shrug **3** TIMIDEZ : shyness
encolar *vt* : to paste, to glue
encolerizar {21} *vt* ENFURECER : to enrage, to infuriate — **encolerizarse** *vr*
encomendar {55} *vt* CONFIAR : to entrust, to commend — **encomendarse** *vr*
encomiable *adj* : commendable, praiseworthy
encomiar *vt* ELOGIAR : to praise, to pay tribute to
encomienda *nf* **1** : charge, mission **2** : royal land grant **3** : parcel
encomio *nm* : praise, eulogy
encomioso, -sa *adj* : eulogistic, laudatory
enconar *vt* **1** : to irritate, to anger **2** : to inflame — **enconarse** *vr* **1** : to become heated **2** : to fester
encono *nm* **1** RENCOR : animosity, rancor **2** : inflamation, infection
encontrado, -da *adj* : contrary, opposing
encontrar {19} *vt* **1** HALLAR : to find **2** : to encounter, to meet — **encontrarse** *vr* **1** REUNIRSE : to meet **2** : to clash, to conflict **3** : to be <su abuelo se encuentra mejor : her grandfather is doing better>
encorvar *vt* : to bend, to curve — **encorvarse** *vr* : to hunch over, to stoop
encrespar *vt* **1** : to curl, to ruffle, to ripple **2** : to annoy, to irritate — **encresparse** *vr* **1** : to curl one's hair **2** : to become choppy **3** : to get annoyed
encrucijada *nf* : crossroads
encuadernación *nf, pl* **-ciones** : bookbinding
encuadernar *vt* EMPASTAR : to bind (a book)
encuadrar *vt* **1** ENMARCAR : to frame **2** ENCAJAR : to fit, to insert **3** COMPRENDER : to contain, to include
encubierto *pp* → **encubrir**
encubrimiento *nm* : cover-up
encubrir {2} *vt* : to cover up, to conceal
encuentro *nm* **1** : meeting, encounter **2** : conference, congress
encuerado, -da *adj fam* : naked
encuerar *vt fam* : to undress
encuesta *nf* **1** INVESTIGACIÓN, PESQUISA : inquiry, investigation **2** SONDEO : survey
encuestador, -dora *n* : pollster
encuestar *vt* : to poll, to take a survey of
encumbrado, -da *adj* **1** : lofty, high **2** : eminent, distinguished
encumbrar *vt* **1** : to exalt, to elevate **2** : to extol — **encumbrarse** *vr* : to reach the top
encurtir *vt* ESCABECHAR : to pickle
ende *adv* **por ~** : therefore, consequently
endeble *adj* : feeble, weak
endeblez *nf* : weakness, frailty
endémico, -ca *adj* : endemic
endemoniado, -da *adj* : fiendish, diabolical
endentecer {53} *vi* : to teethe
enderezar {21} *vt* **1** : to straighten (out) **2** : to stand on end, to put upright
endeudado, -da *adj* : in debt, indebted
endeudamiento *nm* : indebtedness
endeudarse *vr* **1** : to go into debt **2** : to feel obliged
endiabladamente *adv* : extremely, diabolically
endiablado, -da *adj* **1** : devilish, diabolical **2** : complicated, difficult
endibia *or* **endivia** *nm* : endive
endilgar {52} *vt fam* : to spring, to foist <me endilgó la responsabilidad : he saddled me with the responsibility>
endocrino, -na *adj* : endocrine
endogamia *nf* : inbreeding

endosar *vt* **:** to endorse
endoso *nm* **:** endorsement
endulzante *nm* **:** sweetener
endulzar {21} *vt* **1 :** to sweeten **2 :** to soften, to mellow — **endulzarse** *vr*
endurecer {53} *vt* **:** to harden, to toughen — **endurecerse** *vr*
enebro *nm* **:** juniper
eneldo *nm* **:** dill
enema *nm* **:** enema
enemigo, -ga *adj & n* **:** enemy
enemistad *nf* **:** enmity, hostility
enemistar *vt* **:** to make enemies of — **enemistarse** *vr* **~ con :** to fall out with
energía *nf* **:** energy
enérgico, -ca *adj* **1 :** energetic, vigorous **2 :** forceful, emphatic — **enérgicamente** *adv*
energúmeno, -na *n fam* **:** lunatic, crazy person
enero *nm* **:** January
enervar *vt* **1 :** to enervate **2** *fam* **:** to annoy, to get on one's nerves — **enervante** *adj*
enésimo, -ma *adj* **:** umpteenth, nth
enfadar *vt* **1 :** to annoy, to make angry **2** *Mex fam* **:** to bore — **enfadarse** *vr* **:** to get angry, to get annoyed
enfado *nm* **:** anger, annoyance
enfadoso, -sa *adj* **:** irritating, annoying
enfardar *vt* **:** to bale
énfasis *nms & pl* **:** emphasis
enfático, -ca *adj* **:** emphatic — **enfáticamente** *adv*
enfatizar {21} *vt* DESTACAR, SUBRAYAR **:** to emphasize
enfermar *vt* **:** to make sick — *vi* **:** to fall ill, to get sick — **enfermarse** *vr*
enfermedad *nf* **1** INDISPOSICIÓN **:** sickness, illness **2 :** disease
enfermería *nf* **:** infirmary
enfermero, -ra *n* **:** nurse
enfermizo, -za *adj* **:** sickly
enfermo[1]**, -ma** *adj* **:** sick, ill
enfermo[2]**, -ma** *n* **1 :** sick person, invalid **2** PACIENTE **:** patient
enfilar *vt* **1 :** to take, to go along <enfiló la carretera de Montevideo : she went up the road to Montevideo> **2 :** to line up, to put in a row **3 :** to string, to thread **4 :** to aim, to direct — *vi* **:** to make one's way
enflaquecer {53} *vi* **:** to lose weight, to become thin — *vt* **:** to emaciate
enfocar {72} *vt* **1 :** to focus (on) **2 :** to consider, to look at
enfoque *nm* **:** focus
enfrascamiento *nm* **:** immersion, absorption
enfrascarse {72} *vr* **~ en :** to immerse oneself in, to get caught up in
enfrentamiento *nm* **:** clash, confrontation
enfrentar *vt* **:** to confront, to face — **enfrentarse** *vr* **1 ~ con :** to clash with **2 ~ a :** to face up to
enfrente *adv* **1** DELANTE **:** in front **2 :** opposite
enfriamiento *nm* **1** CATARRO **:** chill, cold **2 :** cooling off, damper
enfriar {85} *vt* **1 :** to chill, to cool **2 :** to cool down, to dampen — *vi* **:** to get cold — **enfriarse** *vr* **:** to get chilled, to catch a cold
enfundar *vt* **:** to sheathe, to encase
enfurecer {53} *vt* ENCOLERIZAR **:** to infuriate — **enfurecerse** *vr* **:** to fly into a rage
enfurecido, -da *adj* **:** furious, raging
enfurruñarse *vr fam* **:** to sulk
engalanar *vt* **:** to decorate, to deck out — **engalanarse** *vr* **:** to dress up
enganchar *vt* **1 :** to hook, to snag **2 :** to attach, to hitch up — **engancharse** *vr* **1 :** to get snagged, to get hooked **2 :** to enlist
enganche *nm* **1 :** hook **2 :** coupling, hitch **3** *Mex* **:** down payment
engañar *vt* **1** EMBAUCAR **:** to trick, to deceive, to mislead **2 :** to cheat on, to be unfaithful to — **engañarse** *vr* **1 :** to be mistaken **2 :** to deceive oneself
engaño *nm* **1 :** deception, trick **2 :** fake, feint (in sports)
engañoso, -sa *adj* **1 :** deceitful **2 :** misleading, deceptive
engarrotarse *vr* **:** to stiffen up, to go numb
engatusamiento *nm* **:** cajolery
engatusar *vt* **:** to coax, to cajole
engendrar *vt* **1 :** to beget, to father **2 :** to give rise to, to engender
engentarse *vr Mex* **:** to be in a daze
englobar *vt* **:** to include, to embrace
engomar *vt* **:** to glue
engordar *vt* **:** to fatten, to fatten up — *vi* **:** to gain weight
engorro *nm* **:** nuisance, bother
engorroso, -sa *adj* **:** bothersome
engranaje *nm* **:** gears *pl,* cogs *pl*
engranar *vt* **:** to mesh, to engage — *vi* **:** to mesh gears
engrandecer {53} *vt* **1 :** to enlarge **2 :** to exaggerate **3 :** to exalt
engrandecimiento *nm* **1 :** enlargement **2 :** exaggeration **3 :** exaltation
engrane *nm Mex* **:** cogwheel
engrapadora *nf* **:** stapler
engrapar *vt* **:** to staple
engrasar *vt* **:** to grease, to lubricate
engrase *nm* **:** greasing, lubrication
engreído, -da *adj* PRESUMIDO, VANIDOSO **:** vain, conceited, stuck-up
engreimiento *nm* ARROGANCIA **:** arrogance, conceit
engreír {66} *vt* ENVANECER **:** to make vain — **engreírse** *vr* **:** to become conceited
engrosar {19} *vt* **:** to enlarge, to increase, to swell — *vi* ENGORDAR **:** to gain weight
engrudo *nm* **:** paste
engullir {38} *vt* **:** to gulp down, to gobble up — **engullirse** *vr*
enharinar *vt* **:** to flour
enhebrar *vt* ENSARTAR **:** to string, to thread

enhiesto, -ta *adj* **1** : erect, upright **2** : lofty, towering
enhilar *vt* : to thread (a needle, etc.)
enhorabuena *nf* FELICIDADES : congratulations *pl*
enigma *nm* : enigma, mystery
enigmático, -ca *adj* : enigmatic — **enigmáticamente** *adv*
enjabonar *vt* : to soap up, to lather — **enjabonarse** *vr*
enjaezar {21} *vt* : to harness
enjalbegar {52} *vt* : to whitewash
enjambrar *vi* : to swarm
enjambre *nm* **1** : swarm **2** MUCHEDUMBRE : crowd, mob
enjaular *vt* **1** : to cage **2** *fam* : to jail, to lock up
enjuagar {52} *vt* : to rinse — **enjuagarse** *vr* : to rinse out
enjuague *nm* **1** : rinse **2 enjuague bucal** : mouthwash
enjugar {52} *vt* : to wipe away (tears)
enjuiciar *vt* **1** : to indict, to prosecute **2** JUZGAR : to try
enjundioso, -sa *adj* : substantial, weighty
enjuto, -ta *adj* : lean, gaunt
enlace *nm* **1** : bond, link, connection **2** : liaison
enladrillado *nm* : brick paving
enladrillar *vt* : to pave with bricks
enlatar *vt* ENVASAR : to can
enlazar {21} *v* : to join, to link, to fit together
enlistar *vt* : to list — **enlistarse** *vr* : to enlist
enlodado, -da *adj* BARROSO : muddy
enlodar *vt* **1** : to cover with mud **2** : to stain, to sully — **enlodarse** *vr*
enlodazar → **enlodar**
enloquecedor, -dora *adj* : maddening
enloquecer {53} *vt* ALOCAR : to drive crazy — **enloquecerse** *vr* : to go crazy
enlosado *nm* : flagstone pavement
enlosar *vt* : to pave with flagstone
enlutarse *vr* : to go into mourning
enmaderado *nm* **1** : wood paneling **2** : hardwood floor
enmarañar *vt* **1** : to tangle **2** : to complicate **3** : to confuse, to mix up — **enmarañarse** *vr*
enmarcar {72} *vt* **1** ENCUADRAR : to frame **2** : to provide the setting for
enmascarar *vt* : to mask, to disguise
enmasillar *vt* : to putty, to caulk
enmendar {55} *vt* **1** : to amend **2** CORREGIR : to emend, to correct **3** COMPENSAR : to compensate for — **enmendarse** *vr* : to mend one's ways
enmienda *nf* **1** : amendment **2** : correction, emendation
enmohecerse {53} *vr* **1** : to become moldy **2** OXIDARSE : to rust, to become rusty
enmudecer {53} *vt* : to mute, to silence — *vi* : to fall silent
enmugrar *vt* : to soil, to make dirty — **enmugrarse** *vr* : to get dirty
ennegrecer {53} *vt* : to blacken, to darken — **ennegrecerse** *vr*
ennoblecer {53} *vt* **1** : to ennoble **2** : to embellish
enojadizo, -za *adj* IRRITABLE : irritable, cranky
enojado, -da *adj* **1** : annoyed **2** : angry, mad
enojar *vt* **1** : to anger **2** : to annoy, to upset — **enojarse** *vr*
enojo *nm* **1** CÓLERA : anger **2** : annoyance
enojón, -jona *adj, pl* **-jones** *Chile, Mex fam* : irritable, cranky
enojoso, -sa *adj* FASTIDIOSO, MOLESTOSO : annoying, irritating
enorgullecer {53} *vt* : to make proud — **enorgullecerse** *vr* : to pride oneself
enorme *adj* INMENSO : enormous, huge — **enormemente** *adv*
enormidad *nf* **1** : enormity, seriousness **2** : immensity, hugeness
enraizado, -da *adj* : deep-seated, deeply rooted
enraizar {30} *vi* : to take root
enramada *nf* : arbor, bower
enramar *vt* : to cover with branches
enrarecer {53} *vt* : to rarefy — **enrarecerse** *vr*
enredadera *nf* : climbing plant, vine
enredar *vt* **1** : to tangle up, to entangle **2** : to confuse, to complicate **3** : to involve, to implicate — **enredarse** *vr*
enredo *nm* **1** EMBROLLO : muddle, confusion **2** MARAÑA : tangle
enredoso, -sa *adj* : complicated, tricky
enrejado *nm* **1** : railing **2** : grating, grille **3** : trellis, lattice
enrevesado, -da *adj* : complicated, involved
enriquecer {53} *vt* : to enrich — **enriquecerse** *vr* : to get rich
enriquecido, -da *adj* : enriched
enriquecimiento *nm* : enrichment
enrojecer {53} *vt* : to make red, to redden — **enrojecerse** *vr* : to blush
enrolar *vt* RECLUTAR : to recruit — **enrolarse** *vr* INSCRIBIRSE : to enlist, to sign up
enrollar *vt* : to roll up, to coil — **enrollarse** *vr*
enronquecerse {53} *vr* : to become hoarse
enroscar {72} *vt* TORCER : to twist — **enroscarse** *vr* : to coil, to twine
ensacar {72} *vt* : to bag (up)
ensalada *nf* : salad
ensaladera *nf* : salad bowl
ensalmo *nm* : incantation, spell
ensalzar {21} *vt* **1** : to praise, to extol **2** EXALTAR : to exalt
ensamblaje *nm* : assembly
ensamblar *vt* **1** : to assemble **2** : to join, to fit together
ensanchar *vt* **1** : to widen **2** : to expand, to extend — **ensancharse** *vr*
ensanche *nm* **1** : widening **2** : expansion, development

ensangrentado, -da *adj* : bloody, bloodstained
ensañarse *vr* : to act cruelly, to be merciless
ensartar *vt* **1** ENHEBRAR : to string, to thread **2** : to skewer, to pierce
ensayar *vi* : to rehearse — *vt* **1** : to try out, to test **2** : to assay
ensayista *nmf* : essayist
ensayo *nm* **1** : essay **2** : trial, test **3** : rehearsal **4** : assay (of metals)
enseguida *adv* INMEDIATAMENTE : right away, immediately, at once
ensenada *nf* : cove, inlet
enseña *nf* **1** INSIGNIA : emblem, insignia **2** : standard, banner
enseñanza *nf* **1** EDUCACIÓN : education **2** : teaching
enseñar *vt* **1** : to teach **2** MOSTRAR : to show, to display — **enseñarse** *vr* **~ a** : to learn to, to get used to
enseres *nmpl* : equipment, furnishings *pl* <enseres domésticos : household goods>
ensillar *vt* : to saddle (up)
ensimismado, -da *adj* : absorbed, engrossed
ensimismarse *vr* : to lose oneself in thought
ensoberbecerse {53} *vr* : to become haughty
ensombrecer {53} *vt* : to cast a shadow over, to darken — **ensombrecerse** *vr*
ensoñación *nf, pl* **-ciones** : fantasy
ensopar *vt* **1** : to drench **2** : to dunk, to dip
ensordecedor, -dora *adj* : deafening, thunderous
ensordecer {53} *vt* : to deafen — *vi* : to go deaf
ensuciar *vt* : to soil, to dirty — **ensuciarse** *vr*
ensueño *nm* **1** : daydream, revery **2** FANTASÍA : illusion, fantasy
entablar *vt* **1** : to cover with boards **2** : to initiate, to enter into, to start
entallar *vt* AJUSTAR : to tailor, to fit, to take in — *vi* QUEDAR : to fit
ente *nm* **1** : being, entity **2** : body, organization <ente rector : ruling body> **3** *fam* : eccentric, crackpot
enteco, -ca *adj* : gaunt, frail
entenado, -da *n Mex* : stepchild, stepson *m,* stepdaughter *f*
entender[1] {56} *vt* **1** COMPRENDER : to understand **2** OPINAR : to think, to believe **3** QUERER : to mean, to intend **4** DEDUCIR : to infer, to deduce — *vi* **1** : to understand <¡ya entiendo! : now I understand!> **2 ~ de** : to know about, to be good at **3 ~ en** : to be in charge of — **entenderse** *vr* **1** : to be understood **2** : to get along well, to understand each other **3 ~ con** : to deal with
entender[2] *nm* **a mi entender** : in my opinion
entendible *adj* : understandable
entendido[1], **-da** *adj* **1** : skilled, expert **2 tener entendido** : to understand, to be under the impression <teníamos entendido que vendrías : we were under the impression you would come> **3 darse por entendido** : to go without saying
entendido[2] *nm* : expert, authority, connoisseur
entendimiento *nm* **1** : intellect, mind **2** : understanding, agreement
enterado, -da *adj* : aware, well-informed <estar enterado de : to be privy to>
enteramente *adv* : entirely, completely
enterar *vt* INFORMAR : to inform — **enterarse** *vr* INFORMARSE : to find out, to learn
entereza *nf* **1** INTEGRIDAD : integrity **2** FORTALEZA : fortitude **3** FIRMEZA : resolve
enternecedor, -dora *adj* CONMOVEDOR : touching, moving
enternecer {53} *vt* CONMOVER : to move, to touch
entero[1], **-ra** *adj* **1** : entire, whole **2** : complete, absolute **3** : intact — **enteramente** *adv*
entero[2] *nm* **1** : integer, whole number **2** : point (in finance)
enterramiento *nm* : burial
enterrar {55} *vt* : to bury
entibiar *vt* : to cool (down) — **entibiarse** *vr* : to become lukewarm
entidad *nf* **1** ENTE : entity **2** : body, organization **3** : firm, company **4** : importance, significance
entierro *nm* **1** : burial **2** : funeral
entintar *vt* : to ink
entoldado *nm* : awning
entomología *nf* : entomology
entomólogo, -ga *n* : entomologist
entonación *nf, pl* **-ciones** : intonation
entonar *vi* : to be in tune — *vt* **1** : to intone **2** : to tone up
entonces *adv* **1** : then **2 desde ~** : since then **3 en aquel entonces** : in those days
entornado, -da *adj* ENTREABIERTO : half-closed, ajar
entornar *vt* ENTREABRIR : to leave ajar
entorno *nm* : surroundings *pl,* environment
entorpecer {53} *vt* **1** : to hinder, to obstruct **2** : to dull — **entorpecerse** *vr* : to dull the senses
entrada *nf* **1** : entrance, entry **2** : ticket, admission **3** : beginning, onset **4** : entrée **5** : cue (in music) **6 entradas** *nfpl* : income <entradas y salidas : income and expenditures> **7 tener entradas** : to have a receding hairline
entrado, -da *adj* **entrado en años** : elderly
entramado *nm* : framework
entrampar *vt* **1** ATRAPAR : to entrap, to ensnare **2** ENGAÑAR : to deceive, to trick

entrante *adj* **1 :** next, upcoming <el año entrante : next year> **2 :** incoming, new <el presidente entrante : the president elect>

entraña *nf* **1** MEOLLO **:** core, heart, crux **2 entrañas** *nfpl* VÍSCERAS **:** entrails

entrañable *adj* **:** close, intimate

entrañar *vt* **:** to entail, to involve

entrar *vi* **1 :** to enter, to go in, to come in **2 :** to begin — *vt* **1 :** to bring in, to introduce **2 :** to access

entre *prep* **1 :** between **2 :** among

entreabierto[1] *pp* → **entreabrir**

entreabierto[2], **-ta** *adj* ENTORNADO **:** half-open, ajar

entreabrir {2} *vt* ENTORNAR **:** to leave ajar

entreacto *nm* **:** intermission, interval

entrecano, -na *adj* **:** grayish, graying

entrecejo *nm* **fruncir el entrecejo :** to knit one's brows

entrecomillar *vt* **:** to place in quotation marks

entrecortado, -da *adj* **1 :** labored, difficult <respiración entrecortada : shortness of breath> **2 :** faltering, hesitant <con la voz entrecortada : with a catch in his voice>

entrecruzar {21} *vt* ENTRELAZAR **:** to interweave, to intertwine — **entrecruzarse** *vr*

entredicho *nm* **1** DUDA **:** doubt, question **2 :** prohibition

entrega *nf* **1 :** delivery **2 :** handing over, surrender **3 :** installment <entrega inicial : down payment>

entregar {52} *vt* **1 :** to deliver **2** DAR **:** to give, to present **3 :** to hand in, to hand over — **entregarse** *vr* **1 :** to surrender, to give in **2 :** to devote oneself

entrelazar {21} *vt* ENTRECRUZAR **:** to interweave, to intertwine

entremedias *adv* **1 :** in between, halfway **2 :** in the meantime

entremés *nm, pl* **-meses 1** APERITIVO **:** appetizer, hors d'oeuvre **2 :** interlude, short play

entremeterse → **entrometerse**

entremetido *nm* → **entrometido**

entremezclar *vt* **:** to intermingle

entrenador, -dora *n* **:** trainer, coach

entrenamiento *nm* **:** training, drill, practice

entrenar *vt* **:** to train, to drill, to practice — **entrenarse** *vr* **:** to train, to spar (in boxing)

entreoír {50} *vt* **:** to hear indistinctly

entrepierna *nf* **1 :** inner thigh **2 :** crotch **3 :** inseam

entrepiso *nm* ENTRESUELO **:** mezzanine

entresacar {72} *vt* **1** SELECCIONAR **:** to pick out, to select **2 :** to thin out

entresuelo *nm* ENTREPISO **:** mezzanine

entretanto[1] *adv* **:** meanwhile

entretanto[2] *nm* **en el entretanto :** in the meantime

entretejer *vt* **:** to interweave

entretela *nf* **:** facing (of a garment)

entretener {80} *vt* **1** DIVERTIR **:** to entertain, to amuse **2** DISTRAER **:** to distract **3** DEMORAR **:** to delay, to hold up — **entretenerse** *vr* **1 :** to amuse oneself **2 :** to dally

entretenido, -da *adj* DIVERTIDO **:** entertaining, amusing

entretenimiento *nm* **1 :** entertainment, pastime **2** DIVERSIÓN **:** fun, amusement

entrever {88} *vt* **1 :** to catch a glimpse of **2 :** to make out, to see indistinctly

entreverar *vt* **:** to mix, to intermingle

entrevero *nm* **:** confusion, disorder

entrevista *nf* **:** interview

entrevistador, -dora *n* **:** interviewer

entrevistar *vt* **:** to interview — **entrevistarse** *vr* REUNIRSE **~ con :** to meet with

entristecer {53} *vt* **:** to sadden

entrometerse *vr* **:** to interfere, to meddle

entrometido, -da *n* **:** meddler, busybody

entroncar {72} *vt* RELACIONAR **:** to establish a relationship between, to connect — *vi* **1 :** to be related **2 :** to link up, to be connected

entronque *nm* **1 :** kinship **2** VÍNCULO **:** link, connection

entuerto *nm* **:** wrong, injustice

entumecer {53} *vt* **:** to make numb, to be numb — **entumecerse** *vr* **:** to go numb, to fall asleep

entumecido, -da *adj* **1 :** numb **2 :** stiff (of muscles, joints, etc.)

entumecimiento *nm* **:** numbness

enturbiar *vt* **1 :** to cloud **2 :** to confuse — **enturbiarse** *vr*

entusiasmar *vt* **:** to excite, to fill with enthusiasm — **entusiasmarse** *vr* **:** to get excited

entusiasmo *nm* **:** enthusiasm

entusiasta[1] *adj* **:** enthusiastic

entusiasta[2] *nmf* AFICIONADO **:** enthusiast

enumerar *vt* **:** to enumerate — **enumeración** *nf*

enunciación *nf, pl* **-ciones :** enunciation, statement

enunciar *vt* **:** to enunciate, to state

envainar *vt* **:** to sheathe

envalentonar *vt* **:** to make bold, to encourage — **envalentonarse** *vr*

envanecer {53} *vt* ENGREÍR **:** to make vain — **envanecerse** *vr*

envasar *vt* **1** EMBOTELLAR **:** to bottle **2** ENLATAR **:** to can **3 :** to pack in a container

envase *nm* **1 :** packaging, packing **2 :** container **3** LATA **:** can **4 :** empty bottle

envejecer {53} *vt* **:** to age, to make look old — *vi* **:** to age, to grow old

envejecido, -da *adj* **:** aged, old-looking

envejecimiento *nm* **:** aging

envenenamiento *nm* **:** poisoning

envenenar *vt* **1 :** to poison **2 :** to embitter

envergadura *nf* **1 :** span, breadth, spread **2 :** importance, scope
envés *nm, pl* **enveses :** reverse, opposite side
enviado, -da *n* **:** envoy, correspondent
enviar {85} *vt* **1 :** to send **2 :** to ship
envidia *nf* **:** envy, jealousy
envidiar *vt* **:** to envy — **envidiable** *adj*
envidioso, -sa *adj* **:** envious, jealous
envilecer {53} *vt* **:** to degrade, to debase
envilecimiento *nm* **:** degradation, debasement
envío *nm* **1 :** shipment **2 :** remittance
enviudar *vi* **:** to be widowed, to become a widower
envoltorio *nm* **1 :** bundle, package **2 :** wrapping, wrapper
envoltura *nf* **:** wrapper, wrapping
envolver {89} *vt* **1 :** to wrap **2 :** to envelop, to surround **3 :** to entangle, to involve — **envolverse** *vr* **1 :** to become involved **2 :** to wrap oneself (up)
envuelto *pp* → **envolver**
enyerbar *vt Mex* **:** to bewitch
enyesar *vt* **1 :** to plaster **2** ESCAYOLAR **:** to put in a plaster cast
enzima *nf* **:** enzyme
éon *nm, pl* **eones :** aeon
eperlano *nm* **:** smelt (fish)
épico, -ca *adj* **:** epic
epicúreo[1]**, -rea** *adj* **:** epicurean
epicúreo[2]**, -rea** *n* **:** epicure
epidemia *nf* **:** epidemic
epidémico, -ca *adj* **:** epidemic
epidermis *nf* **:** epidermis
epifanía *nf* **:** feast of the Epiphany (January 6th)
epigrama *nm* **:** epigram
epilepsia *nf* **:** epilepsy
epiléptico, -ca *adj & n* **:** epileptic
epílogo *nm* **:** epilogue
episcopal *adj* **:** episcopal
episcopalista *adj & nmf* **:** Episcopalian
episódico, -ca *adj* **:** episodic
episodio *nm* **:** episode
epístola *nf* **:** epistle
epitafio *nm* **:** epitaph
epíteto *nm* **:** epithet, name
epítome *nm* **:** summary, abstract
época *nf* **1** EDAD, ERA, PERÍODO **:** epoch, age, period **2 :** time of year, season **3 de ~ :** vintage, antique
epopeya *nf* **:** epic poem
equidad *nf* JUSTICIA **:** equity, justice, fairness
equilátero, -ra *adj* **:** equilateral
equilibrado, -da *adj* **:** well-balanced
equilibrar *vt* **:** to balance — **equilibrarse** *vr*
equilibrio *nm* **1 :** balance, equilibrium <perder el equilibrio : to lose one's balance> <equilibrio político : balance of power> **2 :** poise, aplomb
equilibrista *nmf* ACRÓBATA, FUNÁMBULO **:** acrobat, tightrope walker
equino, -na *adj* **:** equine
equinoccio *nm* **:** equinox
equipaje *nm* BAGAJE **:** baggage, luggage
equipamiento *nm* **:** equipping, equipment
equipar *vt* **:** to equip — **equiparse** *vr*
equiparable *adj* **:** comparable
equiparar *vt* **1** IGUALAR **:** to put on a same level, to make equal **2** COMPARAR **:** to compare
equipo *nm* **1 :** team, crew **2 :** gear, equipment
equitación *nf, pl* **-ciones :** horseback riding, horsemanship
equitativo, -va *adj* JUSTO **:** equitable, fair, just — **equitativamente** *adv*
equivalencia *nf* **:** equivalence
equivalente *adj & nm* **:** equivalent
equivaler {84} *vi* **:** to be equivalent
equivocación *nf, pl* **-ciones** ERROR **:** error, mistake
equivocado, -da *adj* **:** mistaken, wrong — **equivocadamente** *adv*
equivocar {72} *vt* **:** to mistake, to confuse — **equivocarse** *vr* **:** to make a mistake, to be wrong
equívoco[1]**, -ca** *adj* AMBIGUO **:** ambiguous, equivocal
equívoco[2] *nm* **:** misunderstanding
era[1]**, etc.** → **ser**
era[2] *nf* EDAD, ÉPOCA **:** era, age
erario *nm* **:** public treasury
erección *nf, pl* **-ciones :** erection, raising
eremita *nmf* ERMITAÑO **:** hermit
ergonomía *nf* **:** ergonomic
erguido, -da *adj* **:** erect, upright
erguir {31} *vt* **:** to raise, to lift up — **erguirse** *vr* **:** to straighten up
erial *nm* **:** uncultivated land
erigir {35} *vt* **:** to build, to erect — **erigirse** *vr* **~ en :** to set oneself up as
erizado, -da : bristly
erizarse {21} *vr* **:** to bristle, to stand on end
erizo *nm* **1 :** hedgehog **2 erizo de mar :** sea urchin
ermitaño[1]**, -ña** *n* EREMITA **:** hermit, recluse
ermitaño[2] *nm* **:** hermit crab
erogación *nf, pl* **-ciones :** expenditure
erogar {52} *vt* **1 :** to pay out **2 :** to distribute
erosión *nf, pl* **-siones :** erosion
erosionar *vt* **:** to erode
erótico, -ca *adj* **:** erotic
erotismo *nm* **:** eroticism
errabundo, -da *adj* ERRANTE, VAGABUNDO **:** wandering
erradicar {72} *vt* **:** to eradicate — **erradicación** *nf*
errado, -da *adj* **:** wrong, mistaken
errante *adj* ERRABUNDO, VAGABUNDO **:** errant, wandering
errar {32} *vt* FALLAR **:** to miss — *vi* **1** DESACERTAR **:** to be wrong, to be mistaken **2** VAGAR **:** to wander
errata *nf* **:** misprint, error

errático, -ca *adj* : erratic — **erráticamente** *adv*
erróneo, -nea *adj* EQUIVOCADO : erroneous, wrong — **erróneamente** *adv*
error *nm* EQUIVOCACIÓN : error, mistake
eructar *vi* : to belch, to burp
eructo *nm* : belch, burp
erudición *nf, pl* **-ciones** : erudition, learning
erudito[1], -ta *adj* LETRADO : erudite, learned
erudito[2], -ta *n* : scholar
erupción *nf, pl* **-ciones 1** : eruption **2** SARPULLIDO : rash
eruptivo, -va *adj* : eruptive
es → **ser**
esbelto, -ta *adj* DELGADO : slender, slim
esbirro *nm* : henchman
esbozar {21} *vt* BOSQUEJAR : to sketch, to outline
esbozo *nm* **1** : sketch **2** : rough draft
escabechar *vt* **1** ENCURTIR : to pickle **2** *fam* : to kill, to rub out
escabeche *nm* : brine (for pickling)
escabechina *nf* MASACRE : massacre, bloodbath
escabel *nm* : footstool
escabroso, -sa *adj* **1** : rugged, rough **2** : difficult, tough **3** : risqué
escabullirse {38} *vr* : to slip away, to escape
escala *nf* **1** : scale **2** ESCALERA : ladder **3** : stopover
escalada *nf* : ascent, climb
escalador, -dora *n* ALPINISTA : mountain climber
escalafón *nm, pl* **-fones 1** : list of personnel **2** : salary scale, rank
escalar *vt* : to climb, to scale — *vi* **1** : to go climbing **2** : to escalate
escaldar *vt* : to scald
escalera *nf* **1** : ladder <escalera de tijera : stepladder> **2** : stairs *pl,* staircase **3 escalera mecánica** : escalator
escalfador *nm* : chafing dish
escalfar *vt* : to poach (eggs)
escalinata *nf* : flight of stairs
escalofriante *adj* : horrifying, bloodcurdling
escalofrío *nm* : shiver, chill, shudder
escalón *nm, pl* **-lones 1** : echelon **2** : step, rung
escalonado, -da *adj* GRADUAL : gradual, staggered
escalonar *vt* **1** : to terrace **2** : to stagger, to alternate
escalpelo *nm* BISTURÍ : scalpel
escama *nf* **1** : scale (of fish or reptiles) **2** : flake (of skin)
escamar *vt* **1** : to scale (fish) **2** : to make suspicious
escamocha *nf Mex* : fruit salad
escamoso, -sa *adj* : scaly
escamotear *vt* **1** : to palm, to conceal **2** *fam* : to lift, to swipe **3** : to hide, to cover up
escandalizar {21} *vt* : to shock, to scandalize — *vi* : to make a fuss — **escandalizarse** *vr* : to be shocked
escándalo *nm* **1** : scandal **2** : scene, commotion
escandaloso, -sa *adj* **1** : shocking, scandalous **2** RUIDOSO : noisy, rowdy **3** : flagrant, outrageous — **escandalosamente** *adv*
escandinavo, -va *adj & n* : Scandinavian
escandir *vt* : to scan (poetry)
escáner *nm* : scanner, scan
escaño *nm* **1** : seat (in a legislative body) **2** BANCO : bench
escapada *nf* HUIDA : flight, escape
escapar *vi* HUIR : to escape, to flee, to run away — **escaparse** *vr* : to escape notice, to leak out
escaparate *nm* **1** : shop window **2** : showcase
escapatoria *nf* **1** : loophole, excuse, pretext <no tener escapatoria : to have no way out> **2** ESCAPADA : escape, flight
escape *nm* **1** FUGA : escape **2** : exhaust (from a vehicle)
escapismo *nm* : escapism
escápula *nm* OMÓPLATO : scapula, shoulder blade
escapulario *nm* : scapular
escarabajo *nm* : beetle
escaramuza *nf* **1** : skirmish **2** : scrimmage
escaramuzar {21} *vi* : to skirmish
escarapela *nf* : rosette (ornament)
escarbar *vt* **1** : to dig, to scratch up **2** : to poke, to pick **3** ~ **en** : to investigate, to pry into
escarcha *nf* **1** : frost **2** *Mex, PRi* : glitter
escarchar *vt* **1** : to frost (a cake) **2** : to candy (fruit)
escardar *vt* **1** : to weed, to hoe **2** : to weed out
escariar *vt* : to ream
escarlata *adj & nf* : scarlet
escarlatina *nf* : scarlet fever
escarmentar {55} *vt* : to punish, to teach a lesson to — *vi* : to learn one's lesson
escarmiento *nm* **1** : lesson, warning **2** CASTIGO : punishment
escarnecer {53} *vt* RIDICULIZAR : to ridicule, to mock
escarnio *nm* : ridicule, mockery
escarola *nf* : escarole
escarpa *nf* : escarpment, steep slope
escarpado, -da *adj* : steep, sheer
escarpia *nf* : hook, spike
escasamente *adv* : scarcely, barely
escasear *vi* : to be scarce, to run short
escasez *nf, pl* **-seces** : shortage, scarcity
escaso, -sa *adj* **1** : scarce, scant **2** ~ **de** : short of
escatimar *vt* : to skimp on, to be sparing with <no escatimar esfuerzos : to spare no effort>
escayola *nf* **1** : plaster (for casts) **2** : plaster cast
escayolar *vt* : to put in a plaster cast

escena *nf* **1 :** scene **2 :** stage
escenario *nm* **1** ESCENA **:** stage **2 :** setting, scene <el escenario del crimen : the scene of the crime>
escénico, -ca *adj* **1 :** scenic **2 :** stage
escenificar {72} *vt* **:** to stage, to dramatize
escepticismo *nm* **:** skepticism
escéptico¹, -ca *adj* **:** skeptical
escéptico², -ca *n* **:** skeptic
escindirse *vr* **1 :** to split **2 :** to break away
escisión *nf, pl* **-siones 1 :** split, division **2 :** excision
esclarecer {53} *vt* **1** ELUCIDAR **:** to elucidate, to clarify **2** ILUMINAR **:** to illuminate, to light up
esclarecimiento *nm* ELUCIDACIÓN **:** elucidation, clarification
esclavitud *nf* **:** slavery
esclavización *nf, pl* **-ciones :** enslavement
esclavizar {21} *vt* **:** to enslave
esclavo, -va *n* **:** slave
esclerosis *nf* **esclerosis múltiple :** multiple sclerosis
esclusa *nf* **:** floodgate, lock (of a canal)
escoba *nf* **:** broom
escobilla *nf* **:** small broom, brush, whisk broom
escobillón *nm, pl* **-llones :** swab
escocer {14} *vi* ARDER **:** to smart, to sting — **escocerse** *vr* **:** to be sore
escocés¹, -cesa *adj, mpl* **-ceses 1 :** Scottish **2 :** tartan, plaid
escocés², -cesa *n, mpl* **-ceses :** Scottish person, Scot
escocés³ *nm* **1 :** Scots (language) **2** *pl* **-ceses :** Scotch (whiskey)
escofina *nf* **:** file, rasp
escoger {15} *vt* ELEGIR, SELECCIONAR **:** to choose, to select
escogido, -da *adj* **:** choice, select
escolar¹ *adj* **:** school
escolar² *nmf* **:** student, pupil
escolaridad *nf* **:** schooling <escolaridad obligatoria : compulsory education>
escolarización *nf, pl* **-ciones :** education, schooling
escollo *nm* **1 :** reef **2** OBSTÁCULO **:** obstacle
escolta *nmf* **:** escort
escoltar *vt* **:** to escort, to accompany
escombro *nm* **1 :** debris, rubbish **2 escombros** *nmpl* **:** ruins, rubble
esconder *vt* OCULTAR **:** to hide, to conceal
escondidas *nfpl* **1 :** hide-and-seek **2 a ~ :** secretly, in secret
escondimiento *nm* **:** concealment
escondite *nm* **1** ENCONDRIJO **:** hiding place **2** ESCONDIDAS **:** hide-and-seek
escondrijo *nm* ESCONDITE **:** hiding place
escopeta *nf* **:** shotgun
escoplear *vt* **:** to chisel (out)
escoplo *nm* **:** chisel
escora *nf* **:** list, heeling
escorar *vi* **:** to list, to heel (of a boat)
escorbuto *nm* **:** scurvy
escoria *nf* **1 :** slag, dross **2** HEZ **:** dregs *pl,* scum <la escoria de la sociedad : the dregs of society>
Escorpio *or* **Escorpión** *nmf* **:** Scorpio
escorpión *nm, pl* **-piones** ALACRÁN **:** scorpion
escote *nm* **1 :** low neckline **2 pagar a escote :** to go dutch
escotilla *nf* **:** hatch, hatchway
escotillón *nf, pl* **-llones :** trapdoor
escozor *nm* **:** smarting, stinging
escriba *nm* **:** scribe
escribano, -na *n* **1 :** court clerk **2** NOTARIO **:** notary public
escribir {33} *v* **1 :** to write **2 :** to spell — **escribirse** *vr* CARTEARSE **:** to write to one another, to correspond
escrito¹ *pp* → **escribir**
escrito², -ta *adj* **:** written
escrito³ *nm* **1 :** written document **2 escritos** *nmpl* **:** writings, works
escritor, -tora *n* **:** writer
escritorio *nm* **:** desk
escritorzuelo, -la *n* **:** hack (writer)
escritura *nf* **1 :** writing, handwriting **2 :** deed
escroto *nm* **:** scrotum
escrúpulo *nm* **:** scruple
escrupuloso, -sa *adj* **1 :** scrupulous **2** METICULOSO **:** exact, meticulous — **escrupulosamente** *adv*
escrutador, -dora *adj* **:** penetrating, searching
escrutar *vt* ESCUDRIÑAR **:** to scrutinize, to examine closely
escrutinio *nm* **:** scrutiny
escuadra *nf* **1 :** square (instrument) **2 :** fleet, squadron
escuadrilla *nf* **:** squadron, formation, flight
escuadrón *nm, pl* **-drones :** squadron
escuálido, -da *adj* **1 :** skinny, scrawny **2** INMUNDO **:** filthy, squalid
escuchar *vt* **1 :** to listen to **2 :** to hear — *vi* **:** to listen — **escucharse** *vr*
escudar *vt* **:** to shield — **escudarse** *vr* **~ en :** to hide behind
escudero *nm* **:** squire
escudo *nm* **1 :** shield **2 escudo de armas :** coat of arms
escudriñar *vt* **1** ESCRUTAR **:** to scrutinize **2 :** to inquire into, to investigate
escuela *nf* **:** school
escueto, -ta *adj* **1 :** plain, simple **2 :** succinct, concise — **escuetamente** *adv*
escuincle, -cla *n Mex fam* **:** child, kid
esculcar {72} *vt* **:** to search
esculpir *vt* **1 :** to sculpt **2 :** to carve, to engrave — *vi* **:** to sculpt
escultor, -tora *n* **:** sculptor
escultórico, -ca *adj* **:** sculptural
escultura *nf* **:** sculpture
escultural *adj* **:** statuesque
escupidera *nf* **:** spittoon, cuspidor
escupir *v* **:** to spit
escupitajo *nm* **:** spit
escurridizo, -za *adj* **:** slippery, elusive

escurridor *nm* **1 :** dish rack **2 :** colander
escurrir *vt* **1 :** to wring out **2 :** to drain — *vi* **1 :** to drain **2 :** to drip, to drip-dry — **escurrirse** *vr* **:** to slip away
ese, esa *adj, mpl* **esos :** that, those
ése, ésa *pron, mpl* **ésos :** that one, those ones *pl*
esencia *nf* **:** essence
esencial *adj* **:** essential — **esencialmente** *adv*
esfera *nf* **1 :** sphere **2 :** face, dial (of a watch)
esférico¹, -ca *adj* **:** spherical
esférico² *nm* **:** ball (in sports)
esfinge *nf* **:** sphinx
esforzado, -da *adj* **1 :** energetic, vigorous **2** VALIENTE **:** courageous, brave
esforzar {36} *vt* **:** to strain — **esforzarse** *vr* **:** to make an effort
esfuerzo *nm* **1 :** effort **2** ÁNIMO, VIGOR **:** spirit, vigor **3 sin ~ :** effortlessly
esfumar *vt* **:** to tone down, to soften — **esfumarse** *vr* **1 :** to fade away, to vanish **2** *fam* **:** to take off, to leave
esgrima *nf* **:** fencing (sport)
esgrimidor, -dora *n* **:** fencer
esgrimir *vt* **1 :** to brandish, to wield **2 :** to use, to resort to — *vi* **:** to fence
esguince *nm* **:** sprain, strain (of a muscle)
eslabón *nm, pl* **-bones :** link
eslabonar *vt* **:** to link, to connect, to join
eslavo¹, -va *adj* **:** Slavic
eslavo², -va *n* **:** Slav
eslogan *nm, pl* **-lóganes :** slogan
eslovaco, -ca *adj & n* **:** Slovakian, Slovak
esloveno, -na *adj & nm* **:** Slovene, Slovenian
esmaltar *vt* **:** to enamel
esmalte *nm* **1 :** enamel **2 esmalte de uñas :** nail polish
esmerado, -da *adj* **:** careful, painstaking
esmeralda *nf* **:** emerald
esmerarse *vr* **:** to take great pains, to do one's utmost
esmeril *nm* **:** emery
esmero *nm* **:** meticulousness, great care
esmoquin *nm, pl* **-quins :** tuxedo
esnob¹ *adj, pl* **esnobs :** snobbish
esnob² *nmf, pl* **esnobs :** snob
esnobismo *nm* **:** snobbery, snobbishness
eso *pron* (*neuter*) **1 :** that <eso no me gusta : I don't like that> **2 ¡eso es! :** that's it!, that's right! **3 a eso de :** around <a eso de las tres : around three o'clock> **4 en ~ :** at that point, just then
esófago *nm* **:** esophagus
esos → **ese**
ésos → **ése**
esotérico, -ca *adj* **:** esoteric — **esotéricamente** *adv*
espabilado, -da *adj* **:** bright, smart
espabilarse *vr* **1 :** to awaken **2 :** to get a move on **3 :** to get smart, to wise up
espacial *adj* **1 :** space **2 :** spatial
espaciar *vt* DISTANCIAR **:** to space out, to spread out
espacio *nm* **1 :** space, room **2 :** period, length (of time) **3 espacio exterior :** outer space
espacioso, -sa *adj* **:** spacious, roomy
espada¹ *nf* **1 :** sword **2 espadas** *nfpl* **:** spades (in playing cards)
espada² *nm* MATADOR, TORERO **:** bullfighter, matador
espadaña *nf* **1 :** belfry **2 :** cattail
espadilla *nf* **:** scull, oar
espagueti *nm or* **espaguetis** *nmpl* **:** spaghetti
espalda *nf* **1 :** back **2 espaldas** *nfpl* **:** shoulders, back **3 por la espalda :** from behind
espaldarazo *nm* **1 :** recognition, support **2 :** slap on the back
espaldera *nf* **:** trellis
espantajo *nm* **:** scarecrow
espantapájaros *nms & pl* **:** scarecrow
espantar *vt* ASUSTAR **:** to scare, to frighten — **espantarse** *vr*
espanto *nm* **:** fright, fear, horror
espantoso, -sa *adj* **1 :** frightening, terrifying **2 :** frightful, dreadful
español¹, -ñola *adj* **:** Spanish
español², -ñola *n* **:** Spaniard
español³ *nm* CASTELLANO **:** Spanish (language)
esparadrapo *nm* **:** adhesive bandage, Band-Aid™
esparcimiento *nm* **1** DIVERSIÓN, RECREO **:** entertainment, recreation **2** DESCANSO **:** relaxation **3** DISEMINACIÓN **:** dissemination, spreading
esparcir {83} *vt* DISPERSAR **:** to scatter, to spread — **esparcirse** *vr* **1 :** to spread out **2** DESCANSARSE **:** to take it easy **3** DIVERTIRSE **:** to amuse oneself
espárrago *nm* **:** asparagus
espartano, -na *adj* **:** severe, austere
espasmo *nm* **:** spasm
espasmódico, -ca *adj* **:** spasmodic
espástico, -ca *adj* **:** spastic
espátula *nf* **:** spatula
especia *nf* **:** spice
especial *adj & nm* **:** special
especialidad *nf* **:** specialty
especialista *nmf* **:** specialist, expert
especializarse {21} *vr* **:** to specialize
especialmente *adv* **:** especially, particularly
especie *nf* **1 :** species **2** CLASE, TIPO **:** type, kind, sort
especificación *nf, pl* **-ciones :** specification
especificar {72} *vt* **:** to specify
específico, -ca *adj* **:** specific — **específicamente** *adv*
espécimen *nm, pl* **especímenes :** specimen
especioso, -sa *adj* **:** specious
espectacular *adj* **:** spectacular — **espectacularmente** *adv*

espectáculo *nm* **1** : spectacle, sight **2** : show, performance
espectador, -dora *n* : spectator, onlooker
espectro *nm* **1** : ghost, specter **2** : spectrum
especulación *nf, pl* **-ciones** : speculation
especulador, -dora *n* : speculator
especular *vi* : to speculate
especulativo, -va *adj* : speculative
espejismo *nm* **1** : mirage **2** : illusion
espejo *nm* : mirror
espejuelos *nmpl* ANTEOJOS : spectacles, glasses
espeluznante *adj* : hair-raising, terrifying
espera *nf* : wait
esperanza *nf* : hope, expectation
esperanzado, -da *adj* : hopeful
esperanzador, -dora *adj* : encouraging, promising
esperanzar {21} *vt* : to give hope to
esperar *vt* **1** AGUARDAR : to wait for, to await **2** : to expect **3** : to hope <espero poder trabajar : I hope to be able to work> <espero que sí : I hope so> — *vi* : to wait — **esperarse** *vr* **1** : to expect, to be hoped <como podría esperarse : as would be expected> **2** : to hold on, to hang on <espérate un momento : hold on a minute>
esperma *nmf* : sperm
esperpéntico, -ca *adj* GROTESCO : grotesque
esperpento *nm fam* MAMARRACHO : sight, fright <voy hecha un esperpento : I really look a sight>
espesante *nm* : thickener
espesar *vt* : to thicken — **espesarse** *vr*
espeso, -sa *adj* : thick, heavy, dense
espesor *nm* : thickness, density
espesura *nf* **1** : thickness **2** : thicket
espetar *vt* **1** : to blurt out **2** : to skewer
espía *nmf* : spy
espiar {85} *vt* : to spy on, to observe — *vi* : to spy
espiga *nf* **1** : ear (of wheat) **2** : spike (of flowers)
espigado, -da *adj* : willowy, slender
espigar {52} *vt* : to glean, to gather — **espigarse** *vr* : to grow quickly, to shoot up
espigón *nm, pl* **-gones** : breakwater
espina *nf* **1** : thorn **2** : spine <espina dorsal : spinal column> **3** : fish bone
espinaca *nf* **1** : spinach (plant) **2 espinacas** *nfpl* : spinach (food)
espinal *adj* : spinal
espinazo *nm* : backbone
espineta *nf* : spinet
espinilla *nf* **1** BARRO, GRANO : pimple **2** : shin
espino *nm* : hawthorn
espinoso, -sa *adj* **1** : thorny, prickly **2** : bony (of fish) **3** : knotty, difficult
espionaje *nm* : espionage
espiración *nf, pl* **-ciones** : exhalation
espiral *adj & nf* : spiral
espirar *vt* EXHALAR : to breathe out, to give off — *vi* : to exhale
espiritismo *nm* : spiritualism
espiritista *nmf* : spiritualist
espíritu *nm* **1** : spirit **2** ÁNIMO : state of mind, spirits *pl* **3 el Espíritu Santo** : the Holy Ghost
espiritual *adj* : spiritual — **espiritualmente** *adv*
espiritualidad *nf* : spirituality
espita *nf* : spigot, tap
esplendidez *nf, pl* **-deces** ESPLENDOR : magnificence, splendor
espléndido, -da *adj* **1** : splendid, magnificent **2** : generous, lavish — **espléndidamente** *adv*
esplendor *nm* ESPLENDIDEZ : splendor
esplendoroso, -sa *adj* MAGNÍFICO : magnificent, grand
espliego *nm* LAVANDA : lavender
espolear *vt* : to spur on
espoleta *nf* **1** DETONADOR : detonator, fuse **2** : wishbone
espolón *nm, pl* **-lones** : spur (of poultry), fetlock (of a horse)
espolvorear *vt* : to sprinkle, to dust
esponja *nf* **1** : sponge **2 tirar la esponja** : to throw in the towel
esponjado, -da *adj* : spongy
esponjoso, -sa *adj* **1** : spongy **2** : soft, fluffy
esponsales *nmpl* : betrothal, engagement
espontaneidad *nf* : spontaneity
espontáneo, -nea *adj* : spontaneous — **espontáneamente** *adv*
espora *nf* : spore
esporádico, -ca *adj* : sporadic — **esporádicamente** *adv*
esposar *vt* : to handcuff
esposas *nfpl* : handcuffs
esposo, -sa *n* : spouse, wife *f*, husband *m*
esprint *nm* : sprint
esprintar *vi* : to sprint
esprinter *nmf* : sprinter
espuela *nf* : spur
espuerta *nf* : two-handled basket
espulgar {52} *vt* **1** : to delouse **2** : to scrutinize
espuma *nf* **1** : foam **2** : lather **3** : froth, head (on beer)
espumar *vi* : to foam, to froth — *vt* : to skim off
espumoso, -sa *adj* : foamy, frothy
espurio, -ria *adj* : spurious
esputar *v* : to expectorate, to spit
esputo *nm* : spit, sputum
esqueje *nm* : cutting (from a plant)
esquela *nf* **1** : note **2** : notice, announcement
esquelético, -ca *adj* : emaciated, skeletal
esqueleto *nm* **1** : skeleton **2** ARMAZÓN : framework
esquema *nf* BOSQUEJO : outline, sketch, plan
esquemático, -ca *adj* : schematic

esquí *nm* **1** : ski **2 esquí acuático** : water ski, waterskiing
esquiador, -dora *n* : skier
esquiar {85} *vi* : to ski
esquife *nm* : skiff
esquila *nf* **1** CENCERRO : cowbell **2** : shearing
esquilar *vt* TRASQUILAR : to shear
esquimal *adj & nmf* : Eskimo
esquina *nf* : corner
esquinazo *nm* **1** : corner **2 dar esquinazo a** *fam* : to stand up, to give the slip to
esquirla *nf* : splinter (of bone, glass, etc.)
esquirol *nm* ROMPEHUELGAS : strikebreaker, scab
esquisto *nm* : shale
esquivar *vt* **1** EVADIR : to dodge, to evade **2** EVITAR : to avoid
esquivez *nf, pl* **-veces 1** : aloofness **2** TIMIDEZ : shyness
esquivo, -va *adj* **1** HURAÑO : aloof, unsociable **2** : shy **3** : elusive, evasive
esquizofrenia *nf* : schizophrenia
esquizofrénico, -ca *adj & n* : schizophrenic
esta → **este**[1]
ésta → **éste**
estabilidad *nf* : stability
estabilización *nf, pl* **-ciones** : stabilization
estabilizador *nm* : stabilizer
estabilizar {21} *vt* : to stabilize — **estabilizarse** *vr*
estable *adj* : stable, steady
establecer {53} *vt* FUNDAR, INSTITUIR : to establish, to found, to set up — **establecerse** *vr* INSTALARSE : to settle, to establish oneself
establecimiento *nm* **1** : establishing **2** : establishment, institution, office
establo *nm* : stable
estaca *nf* : stake, picket, post
estacada *nf* **1** : picket fence **2** : stockade
estacar {72} *vt* **1** : to stake out **2** : to fasten down with stakes — **estacarse** *vr* : to remain rigid
estación *nf, pl* **-ciones 1** : station <estación de servicio : service station, gas station> **2** : season
estacional *adj* : seasonal
estacionamiento *nm* **1** : parking **2** : parking lot
estacionar *vt* **1** : to place, to station **2** : to park — **estacionarse** *vr* **1** : to park **2** : to remain stationary
estacionario, -ria *adj* **1** : stationary **2** : stable
estada *nf* : stay
estadía *nf* ESTANCIA : stay, sojourn
estadio *nm* **1** : stadium **2** : phase, stage
estadista *nmf* : statesman
estadística *nf* **1** : statistic, figure **2** : statistics
estadístico[1], **-ca** *adj* : statistical — **estadísticamente** *adv*
estadístico[2], **-ca** *n* : statistician
estado *nm* **1** : state **2** : status <estado civil : marital status> **3** CONDICIÓN : condition
estadounidense *adj & nmf* AMERICANO, NORTEAMERICANO : American
estafa *nf* : swindle, fraud
estafador, -dora *n* : cheat, swindler
estafar *vt* DEFRAUDAR : to swindle, to defraud
estalactita *nf* : stalactite
estalagmita *nf* : stalagmite
estallar *vi* **1** REVENTAR : to burst, to explode, to erupt **2** : to break out
estallido *nm* **1** EXPLOSIÓN : explosion **2** : report (of a gun) **3** : outbreak, outburst
estambre *nm* **1** : worsted (fabric) **2** : stamen
estampa *nf* **1** ILUSTRACIÓN, IMAGEN : printed image, illustration **2** ASPECTO : appearance, demeanor
estampado[1], **-da** *adj* : patterned, printed
estampado[2] *nm* : print, pattern
estampar *vt* : to stamp, to print, to engrave
estampida *nf* : stampede
estampilla *nf* **1** : rubber stamp **2** SELLO, TIMBRE : postage stamp
estancado, -da *adj* : stagnant
estancamiento *nm* : stagnation
estancar {72} *vt* **1** : to dam up, to hold back **2** : to bring to a halt, to deadlock — **estancarse** *vr* **1** : to stagnate **2** : to be brought to a standstill, to be deadlocked
estancia *nf* **1** ESTADÍA : stay, sojourn **2** : ranch, farm
estanciero, -ra *n* : rancher, farmer
estanco, -ca *adj* : watertight
estándar *adj & nm* : standard
estandarización *nf, pl* **-ciones** : standardization
estandarizar {21} *vt* : to standardize
estandarte *nm* : standard, banner
estanque *nm* **1** : pool, pond **2** : tank, reservoir
estante *nm* REPISA : shelf
estantería *nf* : shelves *pl,* bookcase
estaño *nm* : tin
estaquilla *nf* **1** : peg **2** ESPIGA : spike
estar {34} *v aux* : to be <estoy aprendiendo inglés : I'm learning English> <está terminado : it's finished> — *vi* **1** (*indicating a state or condition*) : to be <está muy alto : he's so tall, he's gotten very tall><¿ya estás mejor? : are you feeling better now?> <estoy casado : I'm married> **2** (*indicating location*) : to be <están en la mesa : they're on the table> <estamos en la página 2 : we're on page 2> **3** : to be at home <¿está María? : is Maria in?> **4** : to remain <estaré aquí 5 días : I'll be here for 5 days> **5** : to be ready, to be done <estará para las diez : it will be ready by ten o'clock> **6** : to agree <¿estamos? : are we in agreement?> <estoy contigo : I'm with you> **7**

¿**cómo estás?** : how are you? **8** ¡**está bien!** : all right!, that's fine! **9 ~ a** : to cost **10 ~ a** : to be <¿a qué dia estamos? : what's today's date?> **11 ~ con** to have <está con fiebre : she has a fever> **12 ~ de** : to be <estoy de vacaciones : I'm on vacation> <está de director hoy : he's acting as director today> **13 estar bien (mal)** : to be well (sick) **14 ~ para** : to be in the mood for **15 ~ por** : to be in favor of **16 ~ por** : to be about to <está por cerrar : it's on the verge of closing> **17 estar de más** : to be unnecessary **18 estar que** : to be (in a state or condition) <está que echa chispas : he's hopping mad> — **estarse** *vr* QUEDARSE : to stay, to remain <¡estáte quieto! : be still!>
estarcir {83} *vt* : to stencil
estatal *adj* : state, national
estática *nf* : static
estático, -ca *adj* : static
estatizar {21} *vt* : to nationalize — **estatización** *nf*
estatua *nf* : statue
estatuilla *nf* : statuette, figurine
estatura *nf* : height, stature <de mediana estatura : of medium height>
estatus *nm* : status, prestige
estatutario, -ria *adj* : statutory
estatuto *nm* : statute
este[1], **esta** *adj, mpl* **estos** : this, these
este[2] *adj* : eastern, east
este[3] *nm* **1** ORIENTE : east **2** : east wind **3 el Este** : the East, the Orient
éste, ésta *pron, mpl* **éstos 1** : this one, these ones *pl* **2** : the latter
estela *nf* **1** : wake (of a ship) **2** RASTRO : trail (of dust, smoke, etc.)
estelar *adj* : stellar
estelarizar {21} *vt Mex* : to star in, to be the star of
esténcil *nm* : stencil
estentóreo, -rea *adj* : loud, thundering
estepa *nf* : steppe
éster *nf* : ester
estera *nf* : mat
estercolero *nm* : dunghill
estéreo *adj & nm* : stereo
estereofónico, -ca *adj* : stereophonic
estereotipado, -da *adj* : stereotyped
estereotipar *vt* : to stereotype
estereotipo *nm* : stereotype
estéril *adj* **1** : sterile, germ-free **2** : infertile, barren **3** : futile, vain
esterilidad *nf* **1** : sterility **2** : infertility
esterilizar {21} *vt* **1** : to sterilize, to disinfect **2** : to sterilize (a person), to spay (an animal) — **esterilización** *nf*
esterlina *adj* : sterling
esternón *nm, pl* **-nones** : sternum
estero *nm* : estuary
estertor *nm* : death rattle
estética *nf* : aesthetics
estético, -ca *adj* : aesthetic — **estéticamente** *adv*
estetoscopio *nm* : stethoscope
estibador, -dora *n* : longshoreman, stevedore
estibar *vt* : to load (freight)
estiércol *nm* : dung, manure
estigma *nm* : stigma
estigmatizar {21} *vt* : to stigmatize, to brand
estilarse *vr* : to be in fashion
estilete *nm* : stiletto
estilista *nmf* : stylist
estilizar {21} *vt* : to stylize
estilo *nm* **1** : style **2** : fashion, manner **3** : stylus
estima *nf* ESTIMACIÓN : esteem, regard
estimable *adj* **1** : considerable **2** : estimable, esteemed
estimación *nf, pl* **-ciones 1** ESTIMA : esteem, regard **2** : estimate
estimado, -da *adj* : esteemed, dear <Estimado señor Ortiz : Dear Mr. Ortiz>
estimar *vt* **1** APRECIAR : to esteem, to respect **2** EVALUAR : to estimate, to appraise **3** OPINAR : to consider, to deem
estimulación *nf, pl* **-ciones** : stimulation
estimulante[1] *adj* : stimulating
estimulante[2] *nm* : stimulant
estimular *vt* **1** : to stimulate **2** : to encourage
estímulo *nm* **1** : stimulus **2** INCENTIVO : incentive, encouragement
estío *nm* : summertime
estipendio *nm* **1** : salary **2** : stipend, remuneration
estipular *vt* : to stipulate — **estipulación** *nf*
estirado, -da *adj* **1** : stretched, extended **2** PRESUMIDO : stuck-up, conceited
estiramiento *nm* **1** : stretching **2 estiramiento facial** : face-lift
estirar *vt* : to stretch (out), to extend — **estirarse** *vr*
estirón *nm, pl* **-rones 1** : pull, tug **2 dar un estirón** : to grow quickly, to shoot up
estirpe *nf* LINAJE : lineage, stock
estival *adj* VERANIEGO : summer
esto *pron* (*neuter*) **1** : this <¿qué es esto? : what is this?> **2 en ~** : at this point **3 por ~** : for this reason
estocada *nf* **1** : final thrust (in bullfighting) **2** : thrust, lunge (in fencing)
estofa *nf* CLASE : class, quality <de baja estofa : low-class, poor-quality>
estofado *nm* COCIDO, GUISADO : stew
estofar *vt* GUISAR : to stew
estoicismo *nm* : stoicism
estoico[1], **-ca** *adj* : stoic, stoical
estoico[2], **-ca** *n* : stoic
estola *nf* : stole
estomacal *adj* GÁSTRICO : stomach, gastric
estómago *nm* : stomach
estoniano, -na *adj & n* : Estonian
estopa *nf* **1** : tow (yarn or cloth) **2** : burlap

estopilla *nf* : cheesecloth

estoque *nm* : rapier, sword

estorbar *vt* OBSTRUIR : to obstruct, to hinder — *vi* : to get in the way

estorbo *nm* **1** : obstacle, hindrance **2** : nuisance

estornino *nm* : starling

estornudar *vi* : to sneeze

estornudo *nm* : sneeze

estos → **este**[1]

éstos → **éste**

estoy → **estar**

estrabismo *nm* : squint

estrado *nm* **1** : dais, platform, bench (of a judge) **2** ESTRADOS *nmpl* : courts of law

estrafalario, -ria *adj* ESTRAMBÓTICO, EXCÉNTRICO : eccentric, bizarre

estragar {52} *vt* DEVASTAR : to ruin, to devastate

estragón *nm* : tarragon

estragos *nmpl* **1** : ravages, destruction, devastation <los estragos de la guerra : the ravages of war> **2 hacer estragos en** *or* **causar estragos entre** : to play havoc with

estrambótico, -ca *adj* ESTRAFALARIO, EXCÉNTRICO : eccentric, bizarre

estrangulamiento *nm* : strangling, strangulation

estrangular *vt* AHOGAR : to strangle — **estrangulación** *nf*

estratagema *nf* ARTIMAÑA : stratagem, ruse

estratega *nmf* : strategist

estrategia *nf* : strategy

estratégico, -ca *adj* : strategic, tactical — **estratégicamente** *adv*

estratificación *nf, pl* **-ciones** : stratification

estratificado, -da *adj* : stratified

estrato *nm* : stratum, layer

estratosfera *nf* : stratosphere

estratosférico, -ca *adj* **1** : stratospheric **2** : astronomical, exorbitant

estrechamiento *nm* **1** : narrowing **2** : narrow point **3** : tightening, strengthening (of relations)

estrechar *vt* **1** : to narrow **2** : to tighten, to strengthen (a bond) **3** : to hug, to embrace **4 estrechar la mano de** : to shake hands with — **estrecharse** *vr*

estrechez *nf, pl* **-checes 1** : tightness, narrowness **2 estrecheces** *nfpl* : financial problems

estrecho[1], **-cha** *adj* **1** : tight, narrow **2** ÍNTIMO : close — **estrechamente** *adv*

estrecho[2] *nm* : strait, narrows

estrella *nf* **1** ASTRO : star <estrella fugaz : shooting star> **2** : destiny <tener buena estrella : to be born lucky> **3** : movie star **4 estrella de mar** : starfish

estrellado, -da *adj* **1** : starry **2** : star-shaped **3 huevos estrellados** : fried eggs

estrellamiento *nm* : crash, collision

estrellar *vt* : to smash, to crash — **estrellarse** *vr* : to crash, to collide

estrellato *nm* : stardom

estremecedor, -dora *adj* : horrifying

estremecer {53} *vt* : to cause to shake — *vi* : to tremble, to shake — **estremecerse** *vr* : to shudder, to shiver (with emotion)

estremecimiento *nm* : trembling, shaking, shivering

estrenar *vt* **1** : to use for the first time **2** : to premiere, to open — **estrenarse** *vr* : to make one's debut

estreno *nm* DEBUT : debut, premiere

estreñimiento *nm* : constipation

estreñirse {67} *vr* : to be constipated

estrépito *nm* ESTRUENDO : clamor, din

estrepitoso, -sa *adj* : clamorous, noisy — **estrepitosamente** *adv*

estrés *nm, pl* **estreses** : stress

estresante *adj* : stressful

estresar *vt* : to stress, to stress out

estría *nf* : fluting, groove

estribación *nf, pl* **-ciones 1** : spur, ridge **2 estribaciones** *nfpl* : foothills

estribar *vi* FUNDARSE **~ en** : to be due to, to stem from

estribillo *nm* : refrain, chorus

estribo *nm* **1** : stirrup **2** : abutment, buttress **3 perder los estribos** : to lose one's temper

estribor *nm* : starboard

estricnina *nf* : strychnine

estricto, -ta *adj* SEVERO : strict, severe — **estrictamente** *adv*

estridente *adj* : strident, shrill, loud — **estridentemente** *adv*

estrofa *nf* : stanza, verse

estrógeno *nm* : estrogen

estropajo *nm* : scouring pad

estropear *vt* **1** ARRUINAR : to ruin, to spoil **2** : to break, to damage — **estropearse** *vr* **1** : to spoil, to go bad **2** : to break down

estropicio *nm* DAÑO : damage, breakage

estructura *nf* : structure, framework

estructuración *nf, pl* **-ciones** : structuring, structure

estructural *adj* : structural — **estructuralmente** *adv*

estructurar *vt* : to structure, to organize

estruendo *nm* ESTRÉPITO : racket, din, roar

estruendoso, -sa *adj* : resounding, thunderous

estrujar *vt* APRETAR : to press, to squeeze

estuario *nm* : estuary

estuche *nm* : kit, case

estuco *nm* : stucco

estudiado, -da *adj* : affected, mannered

estudiantado *nm* : student body, students *pl*

estudiante *nmf* : student

estudiantil *adj* : student <la vida estudiantil : student life>

estudiar *v* : to study
estudio *nm* **1** : study **2** : studio **3 estudios** *nmpl* : studies, education
estudioso, -sa *adj* : studious
estufa *nf* **1** : stove, heater **2** *Col, Mex* : cooking stove, range
estupefacción *nf, pl* **-ciones** : stupefaction, astonishment
estupefaciente¹ *adj* : narcotic
estupefaciente² *nm* DROGA, NARCÓTICO : drug, narcotic
estupefacto, -ta *adj* : astonished, stunned
estupendo, -da *adj* MARAVILLOSO : stupendous, marvelous — **estupendamente** *adv*
estupidez *nf, pl* **-deces 1** : stupidity **2** : nonsense
estúpido¹, -da *adj* : stupid — **estúpidamente** *adj*
estúpido², -da *n* IDIOTA : idiot, fool
estupor *nm* **1** : stupor **2** : amazement
esturión *nm, pl* **-riones** : sturgeon
estuvo, etc. → **estar**
etano *nm* : ethane
etanol *nm* : ethanol
etapa *nf* FASE : stage, phase
etcétera¹ : et cetera, and so on
etcétera² *nmf* : etcetera
éter *nm* : ether
etéreo, -rea *adj* : ethereal, heavenly
eternidad *nf* : eternity
eternizar {21} *vt* PERPETUAR : to make eternal, to perpetuate — **eternizarse** *vr fam* : to take forever
eterno, -na *adj* : eternal, endless — **eternamente** *adv*
ética *nf* : ethics
ético, -ca *adj* : ethical — **éticamente** *adv*
etimología *nf* : etymology
etimológico, -ca *adj* : etymological
etimólogo, -ga *n* : etymologist
etíope *adj & nmf* : Ethiopian
etiqueta *nf* **1** : etiquette **2** : tag, label **3 de ~** : formal, dressy
etiquetar *vt* : to label
étnico, -ca *adj* : ethnic
etnología *nf* : ethnology
etnólogo, -ga *n* : ethnologist
eucalipto *nm* : eucalyptus
Eucaristía *nf* : Eucharist, communion
eucarístico, -ca *adj* : eucharistic
eufemismo *nm* : euphemism
eufemístico, -ca *adj* : euphemistic
eufonía *nf* : euphony
eufónico, -ca *adj* : euphonious
euforia *nf* : euphoria, joyousness
eufórico, -ca *adj* : euphoric, exuberant, joyous — **eufóricamente** *adv*
eunuco *nm* : eunuch
europeo, -pea *adj & n* : European
euskera *nm* : Basque (language)
eutanasia *nf* : euthanasia
evacuación *nf, pl* **-ciones** : evacuation
evacuar *vt* **1** : to evacuate, to vacate **2** : to carry out — *vi* : to have a bowel movement
evadir *vt* ELUDIR : to evade, to avoid — **evadirse** *vr* : to escape, to slip away
evaluación *nf, pl* **-ciones** : assessment, evaluation
evaluar {3} *vt* : to evaluate, to assess, to appraise
evangélico, -ca *adj* : evangelical — **evangélicamente** *adv*
evangelio *nm* : gospel
evangelismo *nm* : evangelism
evangelista *nm* : evangelist
evangelizador, -dora *n* : evangelist, missionary
evaporación *nf, pl* **-ciones** : evaporation
evaporar *vt* : to evaporate — **evaporarse** *vr* ESFUMARSE : to disappear, to vanish
evasión *nf, pl* **-siones 1** : escape, flight **2** : evasion, dodge
evasiva *nf* : excuse, pretext
evasivo, -va *adj* : evasive
evento *nm* : event
eventual *adj* **1** : possible **2** : temporary <trabajadores eventuales : temporary workers> — **eventualmente** *adv*
eventualidad *nf* : possibility, eventuality
evidencia *nf* **1** : evidence, proof **2 poner en evidencia** : to demonstrate, to make clear
evidenciar *vt* : to demonstrate, to show — **evidenciarse** *vr* : to be evident
evidente *adj* : evident, obvious, clear — **evidentemente** *adv*
eviscerar *vt* : to eviscerate
evitable *adj* : avoidable, preventable
evitar *vt* **1** : to avoid **2** PREVENIR : to prevent **3** ELUDIR : to escape, to elude
evocación *nf, pl* **-ciones** : evocation
evocador, -dora *adj* : evocative
evocar {72} *vt* **1** : to evoke **2** RECORDAR : to recall
evolución *nf, pl* **-ciones 1** : evolution **2** : development, progress
evolucionar *vi* **1** : to evolve **2** : to change, to develop
evolutivo, -va *adj* : evolutionary
exabrupto *nm* : pointed remark
exacción *nf, pl* **-ciones** : levying, exaction
exacerbar *vt* **1** : to exacerbate, to aggravate **2** : to irritate, to exasperate
exactamente *adv* : exactly
exactitud *nf* PRECISIÓN : accuracy, precision, exactitude
exacto, -ta *adj* PRECISO : accurate, precise, exact
exageración *nf, pl* **-ciones** : exaggeration
exagerado, -da *adj* **1** : exaggerated **2** : excessive — **exageradamente** *adv*
exagerar *v* : to exaggerate
exaltación *nf, pl* **-ciones 1** : exaltation **2** : excitement, agitation
exaltado¹, -da *adj* : excitable, hotheaded
exaltado², -da *n* : hothead

exaltar *vt* **1** ENSALZAR **:** to exalt, to extol **2 :** to excite, to agitate — **exaltarse** *vr* ACALORARSE **:** to get overexcited
ex–alumno → **alumno**
examen *nm, pl* **exámenes 1 :** examination, test **2 :** consideration, investigation
examinar *vt* **1 :** to examine **2** INSPECCIONAR **:** to inspect — **examinarse** *vr* **:** to take an exam
exánime *adj* **1 :** lifeless **2 :** exhausted
exasperar *vt* IRRITAR **:** to exasperate, to irritate — **exasperación** *nf*
excavación *nf, pl* **-ciones :** excavation
excavadora *nf* **:** excavator
excavar *v* **:** to excavate, to dig
excedente[1] *adj* **1 :** excessive **2 :** excess, surplus
excedente[2] *nm* **:** surplus, excess
exceder *vt* **:** to exceed, to surpass — **excederse** *vr* **:** to go too far
excelencia *nf* **1 :** excellence **2 :** excellency <Su Excelencia : His Excellency>
excelente *adj* **:** excellent — **excelentemente** *adv*
excelso, -sa *adj* **:** lofty, sublime
excentricidad *nf* **:** eccentricity
excéntrico, -ca *adj & n* **:** eccentric
excepción *nf, pl* **-ciones :** exception
excepcional *adj* EXTRAORDINARIO **:** exceptional, extraordinary, rare
excepto *prep* SALVO **:** except
exceptuar {3} *vt* EXCLUIR **:** to except, to exclude
excesivo, -va *adj* **:** excessive — **excesivamente** *adv*
exceso *nm* **1 :** excess **2 excesos** *nmpl* **:** excesses, abuses **3 exceso de velocidad :** speeding
excitabilidad *nf* **:** excitability
excitación *nf, pl* **-ciones :** excitement
excitante *adj* **:** exciting
excitar *vt* **:** to excite, to arouse — **excitarse** *vr*
exclamación *nf, pl* **-ciones :** exclamation
exclamar *v* **:** to exclaim
excluir {41} *vt* EXCEPTUAR **:** to exclude, to leave out
exclusión *nf, pl* **-siones :** exclusion
exclusividad *nf* **1 :** exclusiveness **2 :** exclusive rights *pl*
exclusivo, -va *adj* **:** exclusive — **exclusivamente** *adv*
excomulgar {52} *vt* **:** to excommunicate
excomunión *nf, pl* **-niones :** excommunication
excreción *nf, pl* **-ciones :** excretion
excremento *nm* **:** excrement
excretar *vt* **:** to excrete
exculpar *vt* **:** to exonerate, to exculpate — **exculpación** *nf*
excursión *nf, pl* **-siones :** excursion, outing
excursionista *nmf* **1 :** sightseer, tourist **2 :** hiker
excusa *nf* **1** PRETEXTO **:** excuse **2** DISCULPA **:** apology
excusar *vt* **1 :** to excuse **2 :** to exempt — **excusarse** *vr* **:** to apologize, to send one's regrets
execrable *adj* **:** detestable, abominable
exención *nf, pl* **-ciones :** exemption
exento, -ta *adj* **1 :** exempt, free **2 exento de impuestos :** tax-exempt
exequias *nfpl* FUNERALES **:** funeral rites
exhalar *vt* ESPIRAR **:** to exhale, to give off
exhaustivo, -va *adj* **:** exhaustive — **exhaustivamente** *adv*
exhausto, -ta *adj* AGOTADO **:** exhausted, worn-out
exhibición *nf, pl* **-ciones 1 :** exhibition, show **2 :** showing
exhibir *vt* **:** to exhibit, to show, to display — **exhibirse** *vr*
exhortación *nf, pl* **-ciones :** exhortation
exhortar *vt* **:** to exhort
exhumar *vt* DESENTERRAR **:** to exhume — **exhumación** *nf*
exigencia *nf* **:** demand, requirement
exigente *adj* **:** demanding, exacting
exigir {35} *vt* **1 :** to demand, to require **2 :** to exact, to levy
exiguo, -gua *adj* **:** meager
exiliado[1], **-da** *adj* **:** exiled, in exile
exiliado[2], **-da** *n* **:** exile
exiliar *vt* DESTERRAR **:** to exile, to banish — **exiliarse** *vr* **:** to go into exile
exilio *nm* DESTIERRO **:** exile
eximio, -mia *adj* **:** distinguished, eminent
eximir *vt* EXONERAR **:** to exempt
existencia *nf* **1 :** existence **2 existencias** *nfpl* MERCANCÍA **:** goods, stock
existente *adj* **1 :** existing, in existence **2 :** in stock
existir *vi* **:** to exist
éxito *nm* **1** TRIUNFO **:** success, hit **2 tener éxito :** to be successful
exitoso, -sa *adj* **:** successful — **exitosamente** *adv*
éxodo *nm* **:** exodus
exoneración *nf, pl* **-ciones** EXENCIÓN **:** exoneration, exemption
exonerar *vt* **1** EXIMIR **:** to exempt, to exonerate **2** DESPEDIR **:** to dismiss
exorbitante *adj* **:** exorbitant
exorcismo *nm* **:** exorcism — **exorcista** *nmf*
exorcizar {21} *vt* **:** to exorcize
exótico, -ca *adj* **:** exotic
expandir *vt* EXPANSIONAR **:** to expand — **expandirse** *vr* **:** to spread
expansión *nf, pl* **-siones 1 :** expansion, spread **2** DIVERSIÓN **:** recreation, relaxation
expansionar *vt* EXPANDIR **:** to expand — **expansionarse** *vr* **1 :** to expand **2** DIVERTIRSE **:** to amuse oneself, to relax
expansivo, -va *adj* **:** expansive
expatriado, -da *adj & n* **:** expatriate
expatriarse {85} *vr* **1** EMIGRAR **:** to emigrate **2 :** to go into exile

expectación *nf, pl* **-ciones** : expectation, anticipation
expectante *adj* : expectant
expectativa *nf* **1** : expectation, hope **2 expectativas** *nfpl* : prospects
expedición *nf, pl* **-ciones** : expedition
expediente *nm* **1** : expedient, means **2** ARCHIVO : file, dossier, record
expedir {54} *vt* **1** EMITIR : to issue **2** DESPACHAR : to dispatch, to send
expedito, -ta *adj* **1** : free, clear **2** : quick, easy
expeler *vt* : to expel, to eject
expendedor, -dora *n* : dealer, seller
expendio *nm* TIENDA : store, shop
expensas *nfpl* **1** : expenses, costs **2 a expensas de** : at the expense of
experiencia *nf* **1** : experience **2** EXPERIMENTO : experiment
experimentación *nf, pl* **-ciones** : experimentation
experimental *adj* : experimental
experimentar *vi* : to experiment — *vt* **1** : to experiment with, to test out **2** : to experience
experimento *nm* EXPERIENCIA : experiment
experto, -ta *adj & n* : expert
expiación *nf, pl* **-ciones** : expiation, atonement
expiar {85} *vt* : to expiate, to atone for
expiración *nf, pl* **-ciones** VENCIMIENTO : expiration
expirar *vi* **1** FALLECER, MORIR : to pass away, to die **2** : to expire
explanada *nf* : esplanade, promenade
explayar *vt* : to extend — **explayarse** *vr* : to expound, to speak at length
explicable *adj* : explicable, explainable
explicación *nf, pl* **-ciones** : explanation
explicar {72} *vt* : to explain — **explicarse** *vr* : to understand
explicativo, -va *adj* : explanatory
explicitar *vt* : to state explicitly, to specify
explícito, -ta *adj* : explicit — **explícitamente** *adv*
exploración *nf, pl* **-ciones** : exploration
explorador, -dora *n* : explorer, scout
explorar *vt* : to explore — **exploratorio, -ria** *adj*
explosión *nf, pl* **-siones 1** ESTALLIDO : explosion **2** : outburst <una explosión de ira : an outburst of anger>
explosivo, -va *adj* : explosive
explotación *nf, pl* **-ciones 1** : exploitation **2** : operation, running
explotar *vt* **1** : to exploit **2** : to operate, to run — *vi* ESTALLAR, REVENTAR : to explode
exponente *nm* : exponent
exponential *adj* : exponential — **exponentialmente** *adv*
exponer {60} *vt* **1** : to exhibit, to show, to display **2** : to explain, to present, to set forth **3** : to expose, to risk — *vi* : to exhibit
exportación *nf, pl* **-ciones 1** : exportation **2 exportaciones** *nfpl* : exports
exportador, -dora *n* : exporter
exportar *vt* : to export — **exportable** *adj*
exposición *nf, pl* **-ciones 1** EXHIBICIÓN : exposition, exhibition **2** : exposure **3** : presentation, statement
expositor, -tora *n* **1** : exhibitor **2** : exponent
exprés *nms & pl* **1** : express, express train **2** : espresso
expresamente *adv* : expressly, on purpose
expresar *vt* : to express — **expresarse** *vr*
expresión *nf, pl* **-siones** : expression
expresivo, -va *adj* **1** : expressive **2** CARIÑOSO : affectionate — **expresivamente** *adv*
expreso[1]**, -sa** *adj* : express, specific
expreso[2] *nm* : express train, express
exprimidor *nm* : squeezer, juicer
exprimir *vt* **1** : to squeeze **2** : to exploit
expropiar *vt* : to expropriate, to commandeer — **expropiación** *nf*
expuesto[1] *pp* → **exponer**
expuesto[2]**, -ta** *adj* **1** : exposed **2** : hazardous, risky
expulsar *vt* : to expel, to eject
expulsión *nf, pl* **-siones** : expulsion
expurgar {52} *vt* : to expurgate
expuso, etc. → **exponer**
exquisitez *nf, pl* **-teces 1** : exquisiteness, refinement **2** : delicacy, special dish
exquisito, -ta *adj* **1** : exquisite **2** : delicious
extasiarse {85} *vr* : to be in ecstasy, to be enraptured
éxtasis *nms & pl* : ecstasy, rapture
extático, -ta *adj* : ecstatic
extemporáneo, -nea *adj* **1** : unseasonable **2** : untimely
extender {56} *vt* **1** : to spread out, to stretch out **2** : to broaden, to expand <extender la influencia : to broaden one's influence> **3** : to draw up (a document), to write out (a check) — **extenderse** *vr* **1** : to spread **2** : to last
extendido, -da *adj* **1** : outstretched **2** : widespread
extensamente *adv* : extensively, at length
extensible *adj* : extensible, extendable
extensión *nf, pl* **-siones 1** : extension, stretching **2** : expanse, spread **3** : extent, range **4** : length, duration
extenso, -sa *adj* **1** : extensive, detailed **2** : spacious, vast
extenuar {3} *vt* : to exhaust, to tire out — **extenuarse** *vr* — **extenuante** *adj*
exterior[1] *adj* **1** : exterior, external **2** : foreign <asuntos exteriores : foreign affairs>
exterior[2] *nm* **1** : outside **2** : abroad
exteriorizar {21} *vt* : to express, to reveal
exteriormente *adv* : outwardly

exterminar *vt* : to exterminate — **exterminación** *nf*
exterminio *nm* : extermination
externar *vt Mex* : to express, to display
externo, -na *adj* : external, outward
extinción *nf, pl* **-ciones** : extinction
extinguidor *nm* : fire extinguisher
extinguir {26} *vt* **1** APAGAR : to extinguish, to put out **2** : to wipe out — **extinguirse** *vr* **1** APAGARSE : to go out, to fade out **2** : to die out, to become extinct
extinto, -ta *adj* : extinct
extintor *nm* : extinguisher
extirpación *n, pl* **-ciones** : removal, excision
extirpar *vt* : to eradicate, to remove, to excise — **extirparse** *vr*
extorsión *nf, pl* **-siones 1** : extortion **2** : harm, trouble
extorsionar *vt* : to extort
extra[1] *adv* : extra
extra[2] *adj* **1** : additional, extra **2** : superior, top-quality
extra[3] *nmf* : extra (in movies)
extra[4] *nm* : extra expense <paga extra : bonus>
extracción *nf, pl* **-ciones** : extraction
extracto *nm* **1** : extract <extracto de vainilla : vanilla extract> **2** : abstract, summary
extradición *nf, pl* **-ciones** : extradition
extraditar *vt* : to extradite
extraer {81} *vt* : to extract
extraído *pp* → **extraer**
extrajudicial *adj* : out-of-court
extramatrimonial *adj* : extramarital
extranjerizante *adj* : foreign-sounding, foreign-looking
extranjero[1], **-ra** *adj* : foreign
extranjero[2], **-ra** *n* : foreigner
extranjero[3] *nm* : foreign countries *pl* <viajó al extranjero : he traveled abroad> <trabajan en el extranjero : they work overseas>
extrañamente *adv* : strangely, oddly
extrañamiento *nm* ASOMBRO : amazement, surprise, wonder
extrañar *vt* : to miss (someone) — **extrañarse** *vr* : to be surprised
extrañeza *nf* **1** : strangeness, oddness **2** : surprise
extraño[1], **-ña** *adj* **1** RARO : strange, odd **2** EXTRANJERO : foreign
extraño[2], **-ña** *n* DESCONOCIDO : stranger
extraoficial *adj* OFICIOSO : unofficial — **extraoficialmente** *adv*
extraordinario, -ria *adj* EXCEPCIONAL : extraordinary — **extraordinariamente** *adv*
extrasensorial *adj* : extrasensory <percepción extrasensorial : extrasensory perception>
extraterrestre *adj & nmf* : extraterrestrial, alien
extravagancia *nf* : extravagance, outlandishness, flamboyance
extravagante *adj* : extravagant, outrageous, flamboyant
extraviar {85} *vt* **1** : to mislead, to lead astray **2** : to misplace, to lose — **extraviarse** *vr* : to get lost, to go astray
extravío *nm* **1** PÉRDIDA : loss, misplacement **2** : misconduct
extremado, -da *adj* : extreme — **extremadamente** *adv*
extremar *vt* : to carry to extremes — **extremarse** *vr* : to do one's utmost
extremidad *nf* **1** : extremity, tip, edge **2 extremidades** *nfpl* : extremities
extremista *adj & nmf* : extremist
extremo[1], **-ma** *adj* **1** : extreme, utmost **2** EXCESIVO : excessive **3 en caso extremo** : as a last resort
extremo[2] *nm* **1** : extreme, end **2 al extremo de** : to the point of **3 en ~** : in the extreme
extrovertido[1] **-da** *adj* : extroverted, outgoing
extrovertido[2], **-da** *n* : extrovert
extrudir *vt* : to extrude
exuberancia *nf* **1** : exuberance **2** : luxuriance, lushness
exuberante *adj* : exuberant, luxuriant — **exuberantemente** *adv*
exudar *vt* : to exude
exultación *nf, pl* **-ciones** : exultation, elation
exultante *adj* : exultant, elated — **exultantemente** *adv*
exultar *vi* : to exult, to rejoice
eyacular *vi* : to ejaculate — **eyaculación** *nf*
eyección *nf, pl* **-ciones** : ejection, expulsion
eyectar *vt* : to eject, to expel — **eyectarse** *vr*

F

f *nf* : sixth letter of the Spanish alphabet
fábrica *nf* FACTORÍA : factory
fabricación *nf, pl* **-ciones** : manufacture
fabricante *nmf* : manufacturer
fabricar {72} *vt* MANUFACTURAR : to manufacture, to make
fabril *adj* INDUSTRIAL : industrial, manufacturing
fábula *nf* **1** : fable **2** : fabrication, fib
fabuloso, -sa *adj* **1** : fabulous, fantastic **2** : mythical, fabled
facción *nf, pl* **facciones 1** : faction **2 facciones** *nfpl* RASGOS : features
faccioso, -sa *adj* : factious
faceta *nf* : facet
facha *nf* : appearance, look <estar hecho una facha : to look a sight>
fachada *nf* : facade

facial *adj* : facial
fácil *adj* 1 : easy 2 : likely, probable <es fácil que no pase : it probably won't happen>
facilidad *nf* 1 : facility, ease 2 **facilidades** *nfpl* : facilities, services 3 **facilidades** *nfpl* : opportunities
facilitar *vt* 1 : to facilitate 2 : to provide, to supply
fácilmente *adv* : easily, readily
facsímil *or* **facsímile** *nm* 1 : facsimile, copy 2 : fax
facsimilar *adj* : facsimile
factibilidad *nf* : feasibility
factible *adj* : feasible, practicable
facticio, -cia *adj* : artificial, factitious
factor[1], -tora *n* 1 : agent, factor 2 : baggage clerk
factor[2] *nm* ELEMENTO : factor, element
factoría *nf* FÁBRICA : factory
factótum *nm* : factotum
factura *nf* 1 : making, manufacturing 2 : bill, invoice
facturación *nf, pl* **-ciones** 1 : invoicing, billing 2 : check-in
facturar *vt* 1 : to bill, to invoice 2 : to register, to check in
facultad *nf* 1 : faculty, ability <facultades mentales : mental faculties> 2 : authority, power 3 : school (of a university) <facultad de derecho : law school>
facultar *vt* : to authorize, to empower
facultativo, -va *adj* 1 OPTATIVO : voluntary, optional 2 : medical <informe facultativo : medical report>
faena *nf* : task, job, work <faenas domésticas : housework>
faenar *vi* 1 : to work, to labor 2 PESCAR : to fish
fagot *nm* : bassoon
faisán *nm, pl* **faisanes** : pheasant
faja *nf* 1 : sash, belt 2 : girdle 3 : strip (of land)
fajar *vt* 1 : to wrap (a sash or girdle) around 2 : to hit, to thrash — **fajarse** *vr* 1 : to put on a sash or girdle 2 : to come to blows
fajo *nm* : bundle, sheaf <un fajo de billetes : a wad of cash>
falacia *nf* : fallacy
falaz, -laza *adj, mpl* **falaces** FALSO : fallacious, false
falda *nf* 1 : skirt <falda escocesa : kilt> 2 REGAZO : lap (of the body) 3 VERTIENTE : side, slope
falible *adj* : fallible
fálico, -ca *adj* : phallic
falla *nf* 1 : flaw, defect 2 : (geological) fault 3 : fault, failing
fallar *vi* 1 FRACASAR : to fail, to go wrong 2 : to rule (in a court of law) — *vt* 1 ERRAR : to miss (a target) 2 : to pronounce judgment on
fallecer {53} *vi* MORIR : to pass away, to die
fallecido, -da *adj & n* DIFUNTO : deceased
fallecimiento *nm* : demise, death
fallido, -da *adj* : failed, unsuccessful
fallo *nm* 1 SENTENCIA : sentence, judgment, verdict 2 : error, fault
falo *nm* : phallus, penis
falsamente *adv* : falsely
falsear *vt* 1 : to falsify, to fake 2 : to distort — *vi* 1 CEDER : to give way 2 : to be out of tune
falsedad *nf* 1 : falseness, hypocrisy 2 MENTIRA : falsehood, lie
falsete *nm* : falsetto
falsificación *nf, pl* **-ciones** 1 : counterfeit, forgery 2 : falsification
falsificador, -dora *n* : counterfeiter, forger
falsificar {72} *vt* 1 : to counterfeit, to forge 2 : to falsify
falso, -sa *adj* 1 FALAZ : false, untrue 2 : counterfeit, forged
falta *nf* 1 CARENCIA : lack <hacer falta : to be lacking, to be needed> 2 DEFECTO : defect, fault, error 3 : offense, misdemeanor 4 : foul (in basketball), fault (in tennis)
faltar *vi* 1 : to be lacking, to be needed <me falta ayuda : I need help> 2 : to be absent, to be missing 3 QUEDAR : to remain, to be left <faltan pocos días para la fiesta : the party is just a few days away> 4 **¡no faltaba más!** : don't mention it!, you're welcome!
falto, -ta *adj* **~ de** : lacking (in), short of
fama *nf* 1 : fame 2 REPUTACIÓN : reputation 3 **de mala fama** : disreputable
famélico, -ca *adj* HAMBRIENTO : starving, famished
familia *nf* 1 : family 2 **familia política** : in-laws
familiar[1] *adj* 1 CONOCIDO : familiar 2 : familial, family 3 INFORMAL : informal
familiar[2] *nmf* PARIENTE : relation, relative
familiaridad *nf* 1 : familiarity 2 : informality
familiarizarse {21} *vr* **~ con** : to familiarize oneself with
famoso[1], -sa *adj* CÉLEBRE : famous
famoso[2], -sa *n* : celebrity
fanal *nm* 1 : beacon, signal light 2 *Mex* : headlight
fanático, -ca *adj & n* : fanatic
fanatismo *nm* : fanaticism
fandango *nm* : fandango
fanfarria *nf* 1 : (musical) fanfare 2 : pomp, ceremony
fanfarrón[1], -rrona *adj, mpl* **-rrones** *fam* : bragging, boastful
fanfarrón[2], -rrona *n, mpl* **-rrones** *fam* : braggart
fanfarronada *nf* : boast, bluster
fanfarronear *vi* : to brag, to boast
fango *nm* LODO : mud, mire
fangosidad *nf* : muddiness
fangoso, -sa *adj* LODOSO : muddy
fantasear *vi* : to fantasize, to daydream
fantasía *nf* 1 : fantasy 2 : imagination

fantasma *nm* : ghost, phantom
fantasmal *adj* : ghostly
fantástico, -ca *adj* **1** : fantastic, imaginary, unreal **2** *fam* : great, fantastic
faquir *nm* : fakir
farándula *nf* : show business, theater
faraón *nm, pl* **faraones** : pharaoh
fardo *nm* **1** : bale **2** : bundle
farfulla *nf* : jabbering
farfullar *v* : to jabber, to gabble
faringe *nf* : pharynx
faríngeo, -gea *adj* : pharyngeal
fariña *nf* : coarse manioc flour
farmacéutico[1]**, -ca** *adj* : pharmaceutical
farmacéutico[2]**, -ca** *n* : pharmacist
farmacia *nf* : drugstore, pharmacy
fármaco *nm* : medicine, drug
farmacodependencia *nf* : drug addiction
farmacología *nf* : pharmacology
faro *nm* **1** : lighthouse **2** : headlight
farol *nm* **1** : streetlight **2** : lantern, lamp **3** *fam* : bluff **4** *Mex* : headlight
farola *nf* **1** : lamppost **2** : streetlight
farolero, -ra *n fam* : bluffer
farra *nf* : spree, revelry
fárrago *nm* REVOLTIJO : hodgepodge, jumble
farsa *nf* **1** : farce **2** : fake, sham
farsante *nmf* CHARLATÁN : charlatan, fraud, phony
fascículo *nm* : fascicle, part (of a publication)
fascinación *nf, pl* **-ciones** : fascination
fascinante *adj* : fascinating
fascinar *vt* **1** : to fascinate **2** : to charm, to captivate
fascismo *nm* : fascism
fascista *adj & nmf* : fascist
fase *nf* : phase, stage
fastidiar *vt* **1** MOLESTAR : to annoy, to bother, to hassle **2** ABURRIR : to bore — *vi* : to be annoying or bothersome
fastidio *nm* **1** MOLESTIA : annoyance, nuisance, hassle **2** ABURRIMIENTO : boredom
fastidioso, -sa *adj* **1** MOLESTO : annoying, bothersome **2** ABURRIDO : boring
fatal *adj* **1** MORTAL : fatal **2** *fam* : awful, terrible **3** : fateful, unavoidable
fatalidad *nf* **1** : fatality **2** DESGRACIA : misfortune, bad luck
fatalismo *nm* : fatalism
fatalista[1] *adj* : fatalistic
fatalista[2] *nmf* : fatalist
fatalmente *adv* **1** : unavoidably **2** : unfortunately
fatídico, -ca *adj* : fateful, momentous
fatiga *nf* CANSANCIO : fatigue
fatigado, -da *adj* AGOTADO : weary, tired
fatigar {52} *vt* CANSAR : to fatigue, to tire — **fatigarse** *vr* : to wear oneself out
fatigoso, -sa *adj* : fatiguing, tiring
fatuidad *nf* **1** : fatuousness **2** VANIDAD : vanity, conceit
fatuo, -tua *adj* **1** : fatuous **2** PRESUMIDO : vain
fauces *nfpl* : jaws *pl,* maw
faul *nm, pl* **fauls** : foul, foul ball
fauna *nf* : fauna
fausto *nm* : splendor, magnificence
favor *nm* **1** : favor **2 a favor de** : in favor of **3 por ~** : please
favorable *adj* : favorable — **favorablemente** *adv*
favorecedor, -dora *adj* : becoming, flattering
favorecer {53} *vt* **1** : to favor **2** : to look well on, to suit
favorecido, -da *adj* **1** : flattering **2** : fortunate
favoritismo *nm* : favoritism
favorito, -ta *adj & n* : favorite
fax *nm* : fax, facsimile
fayuca *nf Mex* **1** : contraband **2** : black market
fayuquero *nm Mex* : smuggler, black marketeer
faz *nf* **1** : face, countenance <la faz de la tierra : the face of the earth> **2** : side (of coins, fabric, etc.)
fe *nf* **1** : faith **2** : assurance, testimony <dar fe de : to bear witness to> **3** : intention, will <de buena fe : bona fide, in good faith>
fealdad *nf* : ugliness
febrero *nm* : February
febril *adj* : feverish — **febrilmente** *adv*
fecal *adj* : fecal
fecha *nf* **1** : date **2 fecha de caducidad** *or* **fecha de vencimiento** : expiration date **3 fecha límite** : deadline
fechar *vt* : to date, to put a date on
fechoría *nf* : misdeed
fécula *nf* : starch
fecundar *vt* : to fertilize (an egg) — **fecundación** *nf*
fecundidad *nf* **1** : fecundity, fertility **2** : productiveness
fecundo, -da *adj* FÉRTIL : fertile, fecund
federación *nf, pl* **-ciones** : federation
federal *adj* : federal
federalismo *nm* : federalism
federalista *adj & nmf* : federalist
federar *vt* : to federate
fehaciente *adj* : reliable, irrefutable — **fehacientemente** *adv*
feldespato *nm* : feldspar
felicidad *nf* **1** : happiness **2 ¡felicidades!** : best wishes!, congratulations!, happy birthday!
felicitación *nf, pl* **-ciones 1** : congratulation <¡felicitaciones! : congratulations!> **2** : greeting card
felicitar *vt* CONGRATULAR : to congratulate — **felicitarse** *vr* : to be glad about
feligrés, -gresa *n, mpl* **-greses** : parishioner
feligresía *nf* : parish
felino, -na *adj & n* : feline
feliz *adj, pl* **felices 1** : happy **2 Feliz Navidad** : Merry Christmas

felizmente *adv* **1** : happily **2** : fortunately, luckily
felonía *nf* : felony
felpa *nf* **1** : terry cloth **2** : plush
felpudo *nm* : doormat
femenil *adj* : women's, girls' <futbol femenil : women's soccer>
femenino, -na *adj* **1** : feminine **2** : women's <derechos femeninos : women's rights> **3** : female
femineidad *nf* : femininity
feminidad *nf* : femininity
feminismo *nm* : feminism
feminista *adj & nmf* : feminist
femoral *adj* : femoral
fémur *nm* : femur, thighbone
fenecer {53} *vi* **1** : to die, to pass away **2** : to come to an end, to cease
fénix *nm* : phoenix
fenomenal *adj* **1** : phenomenal **2** *fam* : fantastic, terrific — **fenomenalmente** *adv*
fenómeno *nm* **1** : phenomenon **2** : prodigy, genius
feo[1] *adv* : badly, bad
feo[2], fea *adj* **1** : ugly **2** : unpleasant, nasty
féretro *nm* ATAÚD : coffin, casket
feria *nf* **1** : fair, market **2** : festival, holiday **3** *Mex* : change (money)
feriado, -da *adj* **día feriado** : public holiday
ferial *nm* : fairground
fermentar *v* : to ferment — **fermentación** *nf*
fermento *nm* : ferment
ferocidad *nf* : ferocity, fierceness
feroz *adj, pl* **feroces** FIERO : ferocious, fierce — **ferozmente** *adv*
férreo, -rrea *adj* **1** : iron **2** : strong, steely <una voluntad férrea : an iron will> **3** : strict, severe **4 vía férrea** : railroad track
ferretería *nf* **1** : hardware store **2** : hardware **3** : foundry, ironworks
férrico, -ca *adj* : ferric
ferrocarril *nm* : railroad, railway
ferrocarrilero → **ferroviario**
ferroso, -sa *adj* : ferrous
ferroviario, -ria *adj* : rail, railroad
ferry *nm, pl* **ferrys** : ferry
fértil *adj* FECUNDO : fertile, fruitful
fertilidad *nf* : fertility
fertilizante[1] *adj* : fertilizing <droga fertilizante : fertility drug>
fertilizante[2] *nm* ABONO : fertilizer
fertilizar *vt* ABONAR : to fertilize — **fertilización** *nf*
ferviente *adj* FERVOROSO : fervent
fervor *nm* : fervor, zeal
fervoroso, -sa *adj* FERVIENTE : fervent, zealous
festejar *vt* **1** CELEBRAR : to celebrate **2** AGASAJAR : to entertain, to wine and dine **3** *Mex fam* : to thrash, to beat
festejo *nm* : celebration, festivity
festín *nm, pl* **festines** : banquet, feast
festinar *vt* : to hasten, to hurry up
festival *nm* : festival
festividad *nf* **1** : festivity **2** : (religious) feast, holiday
festivo, -va *adj* **1** : festive **2 día festivo** : holiday — **festivamente** *adv*
fetal *adj* : fetal
fetiche *nm* : fetish
fétido, -da *adj* : fetid, foul
feto *nm* : fetus
feudal *adj* : feudal — **feudalismo** *nm*
feudo *nm* **1** : fief **2** : domain, territory
fiabilidad *nf* : reliability, trustworthiness
fiable *adj* : trustworthy, reliable
fiado, -da *adj* : on credit
fiador, -dora *n* : bondsman, guarantor
fiambrería *nf* : delicatessen
fiambres *nfpl* : cold cuts
fianza *nf* **1** CAUCIÓN : bail, bond **2** : surety, deposit
fiar {85} *vt* **1** : to sell on credit **2** : to guarantee — **fiarse** *vr* **~ de** : to place trust in
fiasco *nm* FRACASO : fiasco, failure
fibra *nf* **1** : fiber **2 fibra de vidrio** : fiberglass
fibrilar *vi* : to fibrillate — **fibrilación** *nf*
fibroso, -sa *adj* : fibrous
ficción *nf, pl* **ficciones 1** : fiction **2** : fabrication, lie
ficha *nf* **1** : index card **2** : file, record **3** : token **4** : domino, checker, counter, poker chip
fichar *vt* **1** : to open a file on **2** : to sign up — *vi* : to punch in, to punch out
fichero *nm* **1** : card file **2** : filing cabinet
ficticio, -cia *adj* : fictitious
fidedigno, -na *adj* FIABLE : reliable, trustworthy
fideicomisario, -ria *n* : trustee
fideicomiso *nm* : trusteeship, trust <guardar en fideicomiso : to hold in trust>
fidelidad *nf* : fidelity, faithfulness
fideo *nm* : noodle
fiduciario[1], -ria *adj* : fiduciary
fiduciario[2], -ria *n* : trustee
fiebre *nf* **1** CALENTURA : fever, temperature <fiebre amarilla : yellow fever> <fiebre palúdica : malaria> **2** : fever, excitement
fiel[1] *adj* **1** : faithful, loyal **2** : accurate — **fielmente** *adv*
fiel[2] *nm* **1** : pointer (of a scale) **2 los fieles** : the faithful
fieltro *nm* : felt
fiera *nf* **1** : wild animal, beast **2** : fiend, demon <una fiera para el trabajo : a demon for work>
fiero, -ra *adj* FEROZ : fierce, ferocious
fierro *nm* HIERRO : iron
fiesta *nf* **1** : party, fiesta **2** : holiday, feast day
figura *nf* **1** : figure **2** : shape, form **3 figura retórica** : figure of speech
figurado, -da *adj* : figurative — **figuradamente** *adv*

figurar *vi* **1 :** to figure, to be included <Rivera figura entre los más grandes pintores de México : Rivera is among Mexico's greatest painters> **2 :** to be prominent, to stand out — *vt* **:** to represent <esta línea figura el horizonte : this line represents the horizon> — **figurarse** *vr* **:** to imagine, to think <¡figúrate el lío en que se metió! : imagine the mess she got into!>

fijación *nf, pl* **-ciones 1 :** fixation, obsession **2 :** fixing, establishing **3 :** fastening, securing

fijador *nm* **1 :** fixative **2 :** hair spray

fijamente *adv* **:** fixedly

fijar *vt* **1 :** to fasten, to affix **2** ESTABLECER **:** to establish, to set up **3** CONCRETAR **:** to set, to fix <fijar la fecha : to set the date> — **fijarse** *vr* **1 :** to settle, to become fixed **2 ~ en :** to notice, to pay attention to

fijeza *nf* **1 :** firmness (of convictions) **2 :** persistence, constancy <mirar con fijeza a : to stare at>

fijiano, -na *adj & n* **:** Fijian

fijo, -ja *adj* **1 :** fixed, firm, steady **2** PERMANENTE **:** permanent

fila *nf* **1** HILERA **:** line, file <ponerse en fila : to get in line> **2 :** rank, row **3 filas** *nfpl* **:** ranks <cerrar filas : to close ranks>

filamento *nm* **:** filament

filantropía *nf* **:** philanthropy

filantrópico, -ca *adj* **:** philanthropic

filántropo, -pa *n* **:** philanthropist

filatelia *nf* **:** philately, stamp collecting

filatelista *nmf* **:** stamp collector, philatelist

filete *nm* **1 :** fillet **2** SOLOMILLO **:** sirloin **3 :** thread (of a screw)

filiación *nf, pl* **-ciones 1 :** affiliation, connection **2 :** particulars *pl,* (police) description

filial[1] *adj* **:** filial

filial[2] *nf* **:** affiliate, subsidiary

filibustero *nm* **:** freebooter, pirate

filigrana *nf* **1 :** filigree **2 :** watermark (on paper)

filipino, -na *adj & n* **:** Filipino

filmación *nf, pl* **-ciones :** filming, shooting

filmar *vt* **:** to film, to shoot

filme *or* **film** *nm* PELÍCULA **:** film, movie

filmina *nf* **:** slide, transparency

filo *nm* **1 :** cutting edge, blade **2 :** edge <al filo del escritorio : at the edge of the desk> <al filo de la medianoche : at the stroke of midnight>

filología *nf* **:** philology

filólogo, -ga *n* **:** philologist

filón *nm, pl* **filones 1 :** seam, vein (of minerals) **2** *fam* **:** successful business, gold mine

filoso, -sa *adj* **:** sharp

filosofar *vi* **:** to philosophize

filosofía *nf* **:** philosophy

filosófico, -ca *adj* **:** philosophic, philosophical — **filosóficamente** *adv*

filósofo, -fa *n* **:** philosopher

filtración *nf* **:** seepage, leaking

filtrar *v* **:** to filter — **filtrarse** *vr* **:** to seep through, to leak

filtro *nm* **:** filter

filudo, -da *adj* **:** sharp

fin *nm* **1 :** end **2 :** purpose, aim, objective **3 en ~ :** in short **4 fin de semana :** weekend **5 por ~ :** finally, at last

finado, -da *adj & n* DIFUNTO **:** deceased

final[1] *adj* **:** final, ultimate — **finalmente** *adv*

final[2] *nm* **1 :** end, conclusion, finale **2 finales** *nmpl* **:** play-offs

finalidad *nf* **1 :** purpose, aim **2 :** finality

finalista *nmf* **:** finalist

finalización *nf* **:** completion, end

finalizar {21} *v* **:** to finish, to end

financiación *nf, pl* **-ciones :** financing, funding

financiamiento *nm* → **financiación**

financiar *vt* **:** to finance, to fund

financiero[1], **-ra** *adj* **:** financial

financiero[2], **-ra** *n* **:** financier

financista *nmf* **:** financier

finanzas *nfpl* **:** finances, finance <altas finanzas : high finance>

finca *nf* **1 :** farm, ranch **2 :** country house

fineza *nf* FINURA, REFINAMIENTO **:** refinement

fingido, -da *adj* **:** false, feigned

fingimiento *nm* **:** pretense

fingir {35} *v* **:** to feign, to pretend

finiquitar *vt* **1 :** to settle (an account) **2 :** to conclude, to bring to an end

finiquito *nm* **:** settlement (of an account)

finito, -ta *adj* **:** finite

finja, etc. → **fingir**

finlandés, -desa *adj & n* **:** Finnish

fino, -na *adj* **1 :** fine, excellent **2 :** delicate, slender **3** REFINADO **:** refined **4 :** sharp, acute <olfato fino : keen sense of smell> **5 :** subtle

finta *nf* **:** feint

fintar *or* **fintear** *vi* **:** to feint

finura *nf* **1 :** fineness, high quality **2** FINEZA, REFINAMIENTO **:** refinement

fiordo *nm* **:** fjord

fique *nm* **:** sisal

firma *nf* **1 :** signature **2 :** signing **3** EMPRESA **:** firm, company

firmamento *nm* **:** firmament, sky

firmante *nmf* **:** signer, signatory

firmar *v* **:** to sign

firme *adj* **1 :** firm, resolute **2 :** steady, stable

firmemente *adv* **:** firmly

firmeza *nf* **1 :** firmness, stability **2 :** strength, resolve

firuletes *nmpl* **:** frills, adornments

fiscal[1] *adj* **:** fiscal — **fiscalmente** *adv*

fiscal[2] *nmf* **:** district attorney, prosecutor

fiscalizar {21} *vt* **1 :** to audit, to inspect **2 :** to oversee **3 :** to criticize

fisco *nm* **:** national treasury, exchequer

fisgar {52} *vt* HUSMEAR : to pry into, to snoop on
fisgón, -gona *n, mpl* **fisgones** : snoop, busybody
fisgonear *vi* : to snoop, to pry
fisgue, etc. → **fisgar**
física *nf* : physics
físico[1], **-ca** *adj* : physical — **físicamente** *adv*
físico[2], **-ca** *n* : physicist
físico[3] *nm* : physique, figure
fisiología *nf* : physiology
fisiológico, -ca *adj* : physiological, physiologic
fisiólogo, -ga *n* : physiologist
fisión *nf, pl* **fisiones** : fission — **fisionable** *adj*
fisionomía *nf* → **fisonomía**
fisioterapeuta *nmf* : physical therapist
fisioterapia *nf* : physical therapy
fisonomía *nf* : physiognomy, features *pl*
fistol *nm Mex* : tie clip
fisura *nf* : fissure, crevasse
fláccido, -da *or* **flácido, -da** *adj* : flaccid, flabby
flaco, -ca *adj* **1** DELGADO : thin, skinny **2** : feeble, weak <una excusa flaca : a feeble excuse>
flagelar *vt* : to flagellate — **flagelación** *nf*
flagelo *nm* **1** : scourge, whip **2** : calamity
flagrante *adj* : flagrant, glaring, blatant — **flagrantemente** *adv*
flama *nf* LLAMA : flame
flamante *adj* **1** : bright, brilliant **2** : brand-new
flamear *vi* **1** LLAMEAR : to flame, to blaze **2** ONDEAR : to flap, to flutter
flamenco[1], **-ca** *adj* **1** : flamenco **2** : Flemish
flamenco[2], **-ca** *n* : Fleming, Flemish person
flamenco[3] *nm* **1** : Flemish (language) **2** : flamingo **3** : flamenco (music or dance)
flanco *nm* : flank, side
flanquear *vt* : to flank
flaquear *vi* DECAER : to flag, to weaken
flaqueza *nf* **1** DEBILIDAD : frailty, feebleness **2** : thinness **3** : weakness, failing
flato *nm* : gloom, melancholy
flatulento, -ta *adj* : flatulent — **flatulencia** *nf*
flauta *nf* **1** : flute **2** **flauta dulce** : recorder
flautín *nm, pl* **flautines** : piccolo
flautista *nmf* : flute player, flutist
flebitis *nf* : phlebitis
flecha *nf* : arrow
fleco *nm* **1** : bangs *pl* **2** : fringe
flema *nf* : phlegm
flemático, -ca *adj* : phlegmatic, stolid, impassive
flequillo *nm* : bangs *pl*
fletar *vt* **1** : to charter, to hire **2** : to load (freight)
flete *nm* **1** : charter fee **2** : shipping cost **3** : freight, cargo
fletero *nm* : shipper, carrier
flexibilidad *nf* : flexibility
flexibilizar {21} *vt* : to make more flexible
flexible[1] *adj* : flexible
flexible[2] *nm* **1** : flexible electrical cord **2** : soft hat
flirtear *vi* : to flirt
flojear *vi* **1** DEBILITARSE : to weaken, to flag **2** : to idle, to loaf around
flojedad *nf* : weakness
flojera *nf fam* **1** : lethargy, feeling of weakness **2** : laziness
flojo, -ja *adj* **1** SUELTO : loose, slack **2** : weak, poor <está flojo en las ciencias : he's weak in science> **3** PEREZOSO : lazy
flor *nf* **1** : flower **2** **flor de Pascua** : poinsettia
flora *nf* : flora
floración *nf* : flowering <en plena floración : in full bloom>
floral *adj* : floral
floreado, -da *adj* : flowered, flowery
florear *vi* FLORECER : to flower, to bloom — *vt* **1** : to adorn with flowers **2** *Mex* : to flatter, to compliment
florecer {53} *vi* **1** : to bloom, to blossom **2** : to flourish, to thrive
floreciente *adj* **1** : flowering **2** PROSPERO : flourishing, thriving
florecimiento *nm* : flowering
floreo *nm* : flourish
florería *nf* : flower shop, florist's
florero[1], **-ra** *n* : florist
florero[2] *nm* JARRÓN : vase
floresta *nf* **1** : glade, grove **2** BOSQUE : woods
florido, -da *adj* **1** : full of flowers **2** : florid, flowery <escritos floridos : flowery prose>
florista *nmf* : florist
floritura *nf* : frill, embellishment
flota *nf* : fleet
flotabilidad *nf* : buoyancy
flotación *nf, pl* **-ciones** : flotation
flotador *nm* **1** : float **2** : life preserver
flotante *adj* : floating, buoyant
flotar *vi* : to float
flote *nm* **a ~** : afloat
flotilla *nf* : flotilla, fleet
fluctuar {3} *vi* **1** : to fluctuate **2** VACILAR : to vacillate — **fluctuación** *nf* — **fluctuante** *adj*
fluidez *nf* **1** : fluency **2** : fluidity
fluido[1], **-da** *adj* **1** : flowing **2** : fluent **3** : fluid
fluido[2] *nm* : fluid
fluir {41} *vi* : to flow
flujo *nm* **1** : flow **2** : discharge
flúor *nm* : fluorine
fluoración *nf, pl* **-ciones** : fluoridation
fluorescencia *nf* : fluorescence — **fluorescente** *adj*
fluorizar {21} *vt* : to fluoridate
fluoruro *nm* : fluoride
fluvial *adj* : fluvial, river

fluye, etc. → **fluir**
fobia *nf* **:** phobia
foca *nf* **:** seal (animal)
focal *adj* **:** focal
focha *nf* **:** coot
foco *nm* **1 :** focus **2 :** center, pocket **3 :** lightbulb **4 :** spotlight **5 :** headlight
fofo, -fa *adj* **1** ESPONJOSO **:** soft, spongy **2 :** flabby
fogaje *nm* **1** FUEGO **:** skin eruption, cold sore **2** BOCHORNO **:** hot and humid weather
fogata *nf* **:** bonfire
fogón *nm, pl* **fogones :** bonfire
fogonazo *nm* **:** flash, explosion
fogonero, -ra *n* **:** stoker (of a furnace), fireman
fogoso, -sa *adj* ARDIENTE **:** ardent
foguear *vt* **:** to inure, to accustom
foja *nf* **:** sheet (of paper)
folículo *nm* **:** follicle
folio *nm* **:** folio, leaf
folklore *nm* **:** folklore
folklórico, -ca *adj* **:** folk, traditional
follaje *nm* **:** foliage
folleto *nm* **:** pamphlet, leaflet, circular
fomentar *vt* **1 :** to foment, to stir up **2** PROMOVER **:** to promote, to foster
fomento *nm* **:** promotion, encouragement
fonda *nf* **1** POSADA **:** inn **2 :** small restaurant
fondeado, -da *adj fam* **:** rich, in the money
fondear *vt* **1 :** to sound **2 :** to sound out, to examine **3** *Mex* **:** to fund, to finance — *vi* ANCLAR **:** to anchor — **fondearse** *vr fam* **:** to get rich
fondeo *nm* **1 :** anchoring **2** *Mex* **:** funding, financing
fondillos *mpl* **:** seat, bottom (of clothing)
fondo *nm* **1 :** bottom **2 :** rear, back, end **3 :** depth **4 :** background **5 :** sea bed **6 :** fund <fondo de inversiones : investment fund> **7** *Mex* **:** slip, petticoat **8 fondos** *nmpl* **:** funds, resources <cheque sin fondos : bounced check> **9 a ~ :** thoroughly, in depth **10 en ~ :** abreast
fonema *nm* **:** phoneme
fonética *nf* **:** phonetics
fonético, -ca *adj* **:** phonetic
fontanería *nf* PLOMERÍA **:** plumbing
fontanero, -ra *n* PLOMERO **:** plumber
footing [ˈfuˌtɪŋ] *nm* **:** jogging <hacer footing : to jog>
foque *nm* **:** jib
forajido, -da *n* **:** bandit, fugitive, outlaw
foráneo, -nea *adj* **:** foreign, strange
forastero, -ra *n* **:** stranger, outsider
forcejear *vi* **:** to struggle
forcejeo *nm* **:** struggle
fórceps *nms & pl* **:** forceps *pl*
forense *adj* **:** forensic, legal
forestal *adj* **:** forest
forja *nf* FRAGUA **:** forge
forjar *vt* **1 :** to forge **2 :** to shape, to create <forjar un compromiso : to hammer out a compromise> **3 :** to invent, to concoct
forma *nf* **1 :** form, shape **2** MANERA, MODO **:** manner, way **3 :** fitness <estar en forma : to be fit, to be in shape> **4 formas** *nfpl* **:** appearances, conventions
formación *nf, pl* **-ciones 1 :** formation **2 :** training <formación profesional : vocational training>
formal *adj* **1 :** formal **2 :** serious, dignified **3 :** dependable, reliable
formaldehído *nm* **:** formaldehyde
formalidad *nf* **1 :** formality **2 :** seriousness, dignity **3 :** dependability, reliability
formalizar {21} *vt* **:** to formalize, to make official
formalmente *adv* **:** formally
formar *vt* **1 :** to form, to make **2** CONSTITUIR **:** to constitute, to make up **3 :** to train, to educate — **formarse** *vr* **1** DESARROLLARSE **:** to develop, to take shape **2** EDUCARSE **:** to be educated
formatear *vt* **:** to format
formativo, -va *adj* **:** formative
formato *nm* **:** format
formidable *adj* **1 :** formidable, tremendous **2** *fam* **:** fantastic, terrific
formón *nm, pl* **formones :** chisel
fórmula *nf* **:** formula
formulación *nf, pl* **-ciones :** formulation
formular *vt* **1 :** to formulate, to draw up **2 :** to make, to lodge (a protest or complaint)
formulario *nm* **:** form <rellenar un formulario : to fill out a form>
fornicar {72} *vi* **:** to fornicate — **fornicación** *nf*
fornido, -da *adj* **:** well-built, burly, hefty
foro *nm* **1 :** forum **2 :** public assembly, open discussion
forraje *nm* **1 :** forage, fodder **2 :** foraging **3** *fam* **:** hodgepodge
forrajear *vi* **:** to forage
forrar *vt* **1 :** to line (a garment) **2 :** to cover (a book)
forro *nm* **1 :** lining **2** CUBIERTA **:** book cover
forsitia *nf* **:** forsythia
fortachón, -chona *adj, pl* **-chones** *fam* **:** brawny, strong, tough
fortalecer {53} *vt* **:** to strengthen, to fortify — **fortalecerse** *vr*
fortalecimiento *nm* **1 :** strengthening, fortifying **2 :** fortifications
fortaleza *nf* **1 :** fortress **2** FUERZA **:** strength **3 :** resolution, fortitude
fortificación *nf, pl* **-ciones :** fortification
fortificar {72} *vt* **1 :** to fortify **2 :** to strengthen
fortín *nm, pl* **fortines :** small fort
fortuito, -ta *adj* **:** fortuitous

fortuna *nf* **1** SUERTE **:** fortune, luck **2** RIQUEZA **:** wealth, fortune
forzar {36} *vt* **1** OBLIGAR **:** to force, to compel **2 :** to force open **3 :** to strain <forzar los ojos : to strain one's eyes>
forzosamente *adv* **1 :** forcibly, by force **2 :** necessarily, inevitably <forzosamente tendrán que pagar : they'll have no choice but to pay>
forzoso, -sa *adj* **1 :** forced, compulsory **2 :** necessary, inevitable
fosa *nf* **1 :** ditch, pit <fosa séptica : septic tank> **2** TUMBA **:** grave **3 :** cavity <fosas nasales : nasal cavities, nostrils>
fosfato *nm* **:** phosphate
fosforescencia *nf* **:** phosphorescence — **fosforescente** *adj*
fósforo *nm* **1** CERILLA **:** match **2 :** phosphorus
fósil[1] *adj* **:** fossilized, fossil
fósil[2] *nm* **:** fossil
fosilizarse {21} *vr* **:** to fossilize, to become fossilized
foso *nm* **1** FOSA, ZANJA **:** ditch **2 :** pit (of a theater) **3 :** moat
foto *nf* **:** photo, picture
fotocopia *nf* **:** photocopy — **fotocopiar** *vt*
fotocopiadora *nf* COPIADORA **:** photocopier
fotoeléctrico, -ca *adj* **:** photoelectric
fotogénico, -ca *adj* **:** photogenic
fotografía *nf* **1 :** photograph **2 :** photography
fotografiar {85} *vt* **:** to photograph
fotográfico, -ca *adj* **:** photographic — **fotográficamente** *adv*
fotógrafo, -fa *n* **:** photographer
fotosíntesis *nf* **:** photosynthesis
fotosintético, -ca *adj* **:** photosynthetic
fracasado[1]**, -da** *adj* **:** unsuccessful, failed
fracasado[2]**, -da** *n* **:** failure
fracasar *vi* **1** FALLAR **:** to fail **2 :** to fall through
fracaso *nm* FIASCO **:** failure
fracción *nf, pl* **fracciones 1 :** fraction **2 :** part, fragment **3 :** faction, splinter group
fraccionamiento *nm* **1 :** division, breaking up **2** *Mex* **:** residential area, housing development
fraccionar *vt* **:** to divide, to break up
fractura *nf* **1 :** fracture **2 fractura complicada :** compound fracture
fracturarse *vr* QUEBRARSE, ROMPERSE **:** to fracture, to break <fracturarse el brazo : to break one's arm>
fragancia *nf* **:** fragrance, scent
fragante *adj* **:** fragrant
fragata *nf* **:** frigate
frágil *adj* **1 :** fragile **2 :** frail, delicate
fragilidad *nf* **1 :** fragility **2 :** frailty, delicacy
fragmentar *vt* **:** to fragment — **fragmentación** *nf*
fragmentario, -ria *adj* **:** fragmentary, sketchy
fragmento *nm* **1 :** fragment, shard **2 :** bit, snippet **3 :** excerpt, passage
fragor *nm* **:** clamor, din, roar
fragoroso, -sa *adj* **:** thunderous, deafening
fragoso, -sa *adj* **1 :** rough, uneven **2 :** thick, dense
fragua *nf* FORJA **:** forge
fraguar {10} *vt* **1 :** to forge **2 :** to conceive, to concoct, to hatch — *vi* **:** to set, to solidify
fraile *nm* **:** friar, monk
frambuesa *nf* **:** raspberry
francamente *adv* **1 :** frankly, candidly **2** REALMENTE **:** really <es francamente admirable : it's really impressive>
francés[1]**, -cesa** *adj, mpl* **franceses :** French
francés[2]**, -cesa** *n, mpl* **franceses :** French person, Frenchman *m*, Frenchwoman *f*
francés[3] *nm* **:** French (language)
franciscano, -na *adj & n* **:** Franciscan
francmasón, -sona *n, mpl* **-sones :** Freemason — **francmasonería** *nf*
franco[1]**, -ca** *adj* **1** CÁNDIDO **:** frank, candid **2** PATENTE **:** clear, obvious **3 :** free <franco a bordo : free on board>
franco[2] *nm* **:** franc
francotirador, -dora *n* **:** sniper
franela *nf* **:** flannel
franja *nf* **1 :** stripe, band **2 :** border, fringe
franquear *vt* **1 :** to clear **2** ATRAVESAR **:** to cross, to go through **3 :** to pay the postage on
franqueo *nm* **:** postage
franqueza *nf* **:** frankness
franquicia *nf* **1** EXENCIÓN **:** exemption **2 :** franchise
frasco *nm* **:** small bottle, flask, vial
frase *nf* **1 :** phrase **2** ORACIÓN **:** sentence
frasear *vt* **:** to phrase
fraternal *adj* **:** fraternal, brotherly
fraternidad *nf* **1 :** brotherhood **2 :** fraternity
fraternizar {21} *vi* **:** to fraternize — **fraternización** *nf*
fraterno, -na *adj* **:** fraternal, brotherly
fratricida *adj* **:** fratricidal
fratricidio *nm* **:** fratricide
fraude *nm* **:** fraud
fraudulento, -ta *adj* **:** fraudulent — **fraudulentamente** *adv*
fray *nm* **:** brother (title of a friar) <Fray Bartolomé : Brother Bartholomew>
frazada *nf* COBIJA, MANTA **:** blanket
frecuencia *nf* **:** frequency
frecuentar *vt* **:** to frequent, to haunt
frecuente *adj* **:** frequent — **frecuentemente** *adv*
fregadera *nf fam* **:** hassle, pain in the neck
fregadero *nm* **:** kitchen sink
fregado[1]**, -da** *adj fam* **:** annoying, bothersome
fregado[2] *nm* **1 :** scrubbing, scouring **2** *fam* **:** mess, muddle

fregar {49} *vt* **1 :** to scrub, to scour, to wash <fregar los trastes : to do the dishes> <fregar el suelo : to scrub the floor> **2** *fam* **:** to annoy — *vi* **1 :** to wash the dishes **2 :** to clean, to scrub **3** *fam* **:** to be annoying

freidera *nf Mex* **:** frying pan

freír {37} *vt* **:** to fry — **freírse** *vr*

frenar *vt* **1 :** to brake **2** DETENER **:** to curb, to check — *vi* **:** to apply the brakes — **frenarse** *vr* **:** to restrain oneself

frenesí *nm* **:** frenzy

frenético, -ca *adj* **:** frantic, frenzied — **frenéticamente** *adv*

freno *nm* **1 :** brake **2 :** bit (of a bridle) **3 :** check, restraint **4 frenos** *nmpl Mex* **:** braces (for teeth)

frente[1] *nm* **1 :** front <al frente de : at the head of> <en frente : in front, opposite> **2 :** facade **3 :** front line, sphere of activity **4 :** front (in meteorology) <frente frío : cold front> **5 hacer frente a :** to face up to, to brave

frente[2] *nf* **1 :** forehead, brow **2 frente a frente :** face to face

fresa *nf* **1 :** strawberry **2 :** drill (in dentistry)

fresco[1], -ca *adj* **1 :** fresh **2 :** cool **3** *fam* **:** insolent, nervy

fresco[2] *nm* **1 :** coolness **2 :** fresh air <al fresco : in the open air, outdoors> **3 :** fresco

frescor *nm* **:** cool air <el frescor de la noche : the cool of the evening>

frescura *nf* **1 :** freshness **2 :** coolness **3 :** calmness **4** DESCARO **:** nerve, audacity

fresno *nm* **:** ash (tree)

freza *nf* **:** spawn, roe

frezar {21} *vi* DESOVAR **:** to spawn

friable *adj* **:** friable

frialdad *nf* **1 :** coldness **2** INDIFERENCIA **:** indifference, unconcern

fríamente *adv* **:** coldly, indifferently

fricasé *nm* **:** fricassee

fricción *nf, pl* **fricciones 1 :** friction **2 :** rubbing, massage **3 :** discord, disagreement <fricción entre los hermanos : friction between the brothers>

friccionar *vt* **1** FROTAR **:** to rub **2 :** to massage

friega[1], friegue, etc. → **fregar**

friega[2] *nf* **1** FRICCIÓN **:** rubdown, massage **2 :** annoyance, bother

frigidez *nf* **:** (sexual) frigidity

frigorífico *nm Spain* **:** refrigerator

frijol *nm* **:** bean <frijoles refritos : refried beans>

frío[1], fría *adj* **1 :** cold **2** INDIFERENTE **:** cool, indifferent

frío[2] *nm* **1 :** cold <hace mucho frío esta noche : it's very cold tonight> **2** INDIFERENCIA **:** coldness, indifference **3 tener frío :** to feel cold <tengo frío : I'm cold> **4 tomar frío** RESFRIARSE **:** to catch a cold

friolento, -ta *adj* **:** sensitive to cold

friolera *nf* (*used ironically or humorously*) **:** trifling amount <una friolera de mil dólares : a mere thousand dollars>

friso *nm* **:** frieze

fritar *vt* **:** to fry

frito[1] *pp* → **freír**

frito[2], -ta *adj* **1 :** fried **2** *fam* **:** worn-out, fed up <tener frito a alguien : to get on someone's nerves> **3** *fam* **:** fast asleep <se quedó frito en el sofá : she fell asleep on the couch>

fritura *nf* **1 :** frying **2 :** fried food

frivolidad *nf* **:** frivolity

frívolo, -la *adj* **:** frivolous — **frívolamente** *adv*

fronda *nf* **1 :** frond **2 frondas** *nfpl* **:** foliage

frondoso, -sa *adj* **:** leafy, luxuriant

frontal *adj* **:** frontal, head-on <un choque frontal : a head-on collision>

frontalmente *adv* **:** head-on

frontera *nf* **:** border, frontier

fronterizo, -za *adj* **:** border, on the border <estados fronterizos : neighboring states>

frotar *vt* **1 :** to rub **2 :** to strike (a match) — **frotarse** *vr* **:** to rub (together)

frote *nm* **:** rubbing, rub

fructífero, -ra *adj* **:** fruitful, productive

fructificar {72} *vi* **1 :** to bear or produce fruit **2 :** to be productive

fructuoso, -sa *adj* **:** fruitful

frugal *adj* **:** frugal, thrifty — **frugalmente** *adv*

frugalidad *adj* **:** frugality

frunce *nm* **:** gather (in cloth), pucker

fruncido *nm* **:** gathering, shirring

fruncir {83} *vt* **1 :** to gather, to shirr **2 fruncir el ceño :** to knit one's brow, to frown **3 fruncir la boca :** to pucker up, to purse one's lips

frunza, etc. → **fruncir**

frustración *nf, pl* **-ciones :** frustration

frustrado, -da *adj* **1 :** frustrated **2 :** failed, unsuccessful

frustrante *adj* **:** frustrating

frustrar *vt* **:** to frustrate, to thwart — **frustrarse** *vr* FRACASAR **:** to fail, to come to nothing <se frustraron sus esperanzas : his hopes were dashed>

fruta *nf* **:** fruit

frutal[1] *adj* **:** fruit, fruit-bearing

frutal[2] *nm* **:** fruit tree

frutilla *nf* **:** South American strawberry

fruto *nm* **1 :** fruit, agricultural product <los frutos de la tierra : the fruits of the earth> **2 :** result, consequence <los frutos de su trabajo : the fruits of his labor>

fucsia *adj & nm* **:** fuchsia

fue, etc. → **ir, ser**

fuego *nm* **1 :** fire **2 :** light <¿tienes fuego? : have you got a light?> **3 :** flame, burner (on a stove) **4 :** ardor, passion **5** FOGAJE **:** skin eruption, cold sore **6 fuegos artificiales** *nmpl* : fireworks

fuelle *nm* : bellows

fuente *nf* **1** MANANTIAL : spring **2** : fountain **3** ORIGEN : source <fuentes informativas : sources of information> **4** : platter, serving dish

fuera *adv* **1** : outside, out **2** : abroad, away **3 ~ de** : outside of, out of, beyond **4 ~ de** : besides, in addition to <fuera de eso : aside from that> **5 fuera de lugar** : out of place, amiss

fuerce, fuerza, etc. → **forzar**

fuero *nm* **1** JURISDICCIÓN : jurisdiction **2** : privilege, exemption **3 fuero interno** : conscience, heart of hearts

fuerte[1] *adv* **1** : strongly, tightly, hard **2** : loudly **3** : abundantly

fuerte[2] *adj* **1** : strong **2** : intense <un fuerte dolor : an intense pain> **3** : loud **4** : extreme, excessive

fuerte[3] *nm* **1** : fort, stronghold **2** : forte, strong point

fuerza *nf* **1** : strength, vigor <fuerza de voluntad : willpower> **2** : force <fuerza bruta : brute force> **3** : power, might <fuerza de brazos : manpower> **4 fuerzas** *nfpl* : forces <fuerzas armadas : armed forces> **5 a fuerza de** : by, by dint of

fuetazo *nm* : lash

fuga *nf* **1** HUIDA : flight, escape **2** : fugue **3** : leak <fuga de gas : gas leak>

fugarse {52} *vr* **1** : to escape **2** HUIR : to flee, to run away **3** : to elope

fugaz *adj, pl* **fugaces** : brief, fleeting

fugitivo, -va *adj & n* : fugitive

fulana *nf* : hooker, slut

fulano, -na *n* : so-and-so, what's-his-name, what's-her-name <fulano, mengano, y zutano : Tom, Dick, and Harry> <señora fulana de tal : Mrs. so-and-so>

fulcro *nm* : fulcrum

fulgor *nm* : brilliance, splendor

fulgurar *vi* : to shine brightly, to gleam, to glow

fulminante *adj* **1** : fulminating, explosive **2** : devastating, terrible <una mirada fulminante : a withering look>

fulminar *vt* **1** : to strike with lightning **2** : to strike down <fulminar a alguien con la mirada : to look daggers at someone>

fumador, -dora *n* : smoker

fumar *v* : to smoke

fumble *nm* : fumble (in football)

fumblear *vt* : to fumble (in football)

fumigante *nm* : fumigant

fumigar {52} *vt* : to fumigate — **fumigación** *nf*

funámbulo, -la *n* EQUILIBRISTA : tightrope walker

función *nf, pl* **funciones** **1** : function **2** : duty **3** : performance, show

funcional *adj* : functional — **funcionalmente** *adv*

funcionamiento *nm* **1** : functioning **2 en ~** : in operation

funcionar *vi* **1** : to function **2** : to run, to work

funcionario, -ria *n* : civil servant, official

funda *nf* **1** : case, cover, sheath **2** : pillowcase

fundación *nf, pl* **-ciones** : foundation, establishment

fundado, -da *adj* : well-founded, justified

fundador, -dora *n* : founder

fundamental *adj* BÁSICO : fundamental, basic — **fundamentalmente** *adv*

fundamentar *vt* **1** : to lay the foundations for **2** : to support, to back up **3** : to base, to found

fundamento *nm* : basis, foundation, groundwork

fundar *vt* **1** ESTABLECER, INSTITUIR : to found, to establish **2** BASAR : to base — **fundarse** *vr* **~ en** : to be based on, to stem from

fundición *nf, pl* **-ciones** **1** : founding, smelting **2** : foundry

fundir *vt* **1** : to melt down, to smelt **2** : to fuse, to merge **3** : to burn out (a lightbulb) — **fundirse** *vr* **1** : to fuse together, to blend, to merge **2** : to melt, to thaw **3** : to fade (in television or movies)

fúnebre *adj* **1** : funeral, funereal **2** LÚGUBRE : gloomy, mournful

funeral[1] *adj* : funeral, funerary

funeral[2] *nm* **1** : funeral **2 funerales** *nmpl* EXEQUIAS : funeral rites

funeraria *nf* **1** : funeral home, funeral parlor **2 director de funeraria** : funeral director, undertaker

funerario, -ria *adj* : funeral

funesto, -ta *adj* : terrible, disastrous <consecuencias funestas : disastrous consequences>

fungicida[1] *adj* : fungicidal

fungicida[2] *nm* : fungicide

fungir {35} *vi* : to act, to function <fungir de asesor : to act as a consultant>

fungoso, -sa *adj* : fungous

funja, etc. → **fungir**

furgón *nm, pl* **furgones** **1** : van, truck **2** : freight car, boxcar **3 furgón de cola** : caboose

furgoneta *nf* : van

furia *nf* **1** CÓLERA, IRA : fury, rage **2** : violence, fury <la furia de la tormenta : the fury of the storm>

furibundo, -da *adj* : furious

furiosamente *adv* : furiously, frantically

furioso, -sa *adj* **1** AIRADO : furious, irate **2** : intense, violent

furor *nm* **1** : fury, rage **2** : violence (of the elements) **3** : passion, frenzy **4** : enthusiasm <hacer furor : to be all the rage>

furtivo, -va *adj* : furtive — **furtivamente** *adv*

furúnculo *nm* DIVIESO : boil
fuselaje *nm* : fuselage
fusible *nm* : (electrical) fuse
fusil *nm* : rifle
fusilar *vt* **1** : to shoot, to execute (by firing squad) **2** *fam* : to plagiarize, to pirate
fusilería *nf* **1** : rifles *pl,* rifle fire **2 descarga de fusilería** : fusillade
fusión *nf, pl* **fusiones 1** : fusion **2** : union, merger
fusionar *vt* **1** : to fuse **2** : to merge, to amalgamate — **fusionarse** *vr*
fusta *nf* : riding crop
fustigar {52} *vt* **1** AZOTAR : to whip, to lash **2** : to upbraid, to berate
futbol *or* **fútbol** *nm* **1** : soccer **2 futbol americano** : football
futbolista *nmf* : soccer player
futesa *nf* **1** : small thing, trifle **2 futesas** *nfpl* : small talk
fútil *adj* : trifling, trivial
futurista *adj* : futuristic
futuro[1], **-ra** *adj* : future
futuro[2] *nm* PORVENIR : future

G

g *nf* : seventh letter of the Spanish alphabet
gabán *nm, pl* **gabanes** : topcoat, overcoat
gabardina *nf* **1** : gabardine **2** : trench coat, raincoat
gabarra *nf* : barge
gabinete *nm* **1** : cabinet (in government) **2** : study, office (in the home) **3** : (professional) office
gablete *nm* : gable
gabonés, -nesa *adj & n, mpl* **-neses** : Gabonese
gacela *nf* : gazelle
gaceta *nf* : gazette, newspaper
gachas *nfpl* : porridge
gacho, -cha *adj* **1** : drooping, turned downward **2** *Mex fam* : nasty, awful **3 ir a gachas** *fam* : to go on all fours
gaélico[1], **-ca** *adj* : Gaelic
gaélico[2] *nm* : Gaelic (language)
gafas *nfpl* ANTEOJOS : eyeglasses, glasses
gaita *nf* : bagpipes *pl*
gajes *nmpl* **gajes del oficio** : occupational hazards
gajo *nm* **1** : broken branch (of a tree) **2** : cluster, bunch (of fruit) **3** : segment (of citrus fruit)
gala *nf* **1** : gala <vestido de gala : formal dress> <tener algo a gala : to be proud of something> **2 galas** *nfpl* : finery, attire
galáctico, -ca *adj* : galactic
galán *nm, pl* **galanes 1** : ladies' man, gallant **2** : leading man, hero **3** : boyfriend, suitor
galano, -na *adj* **1** : elegant **2** *Mex* : mottled
galante *adj* : gallant, attentive — **galantemente** *adv*
galantear *vt* **1** CORTEJAR : to court, to woo **2** : to flirt with
galanteo *nm* **1** CORTEJO : courtship **2** : flirtation, flirting
galantería *nf* **1** : gallantry, attentiveness **2** : compliment
galápago *nm* : aquatic turtle
galardón *nm, pl* **-dones** : award, prize
galardonado, -da *adj* : prize-winning
galardonar *vt* : to give an award to
galaxia *nf* : galaxy
galeno *nm fam* : physician, doctor
galeón *nm, pl* **galeones** : galleon
galera *nf* : galley
galería *nf* **1** : gallery, balcony (in a theater) <galería comercial : shopping mall> **2** : corridor, passage
galerón *nm, pl* **-rones** *Mex* : large hall
galés[1], **-lesa** *adj* : Welsh
galés[2], **-lesa** *n, mpl* **galeses 1** : Welshman *m,* Welshwoman *f* **2 los galeses** : the Welsh
galés[3] *nm* : Welsh (language)
galgo *nm* : greyhound
galimatías *nms & pl* : gibberish, nonsense
galio *nm* : gallium
gallardete *nm* : pennant, streamer
gallardía *nf* **1** VALENTÍA : bravery **2** APOSTURA : elegance, gracefulness
gallardo, -da *adj* **1** VALIENTE : brave **2** APUESTO : elegant, graceful
gallear *vi* : to show off, to strut around
gallego[1], **-ga** *adj* **1** : Galician **2** *fam* : Spanish
gallego[2], **-ga** *n* **1** : Galician **2** *fam* : Spaniard
galleta *nf* **1** : cookie **2** : cracker
gallina *nf* **1** : hen **2 gallina de Guinea** : guinea fowl
gallinazo *nm* : vulture, buzzard
gallinero *nm* : chicken coop, henhouse
gallito, -ta *adj fam* : cocky, belligerent
gallo *nm* **1** : rooster, cock **2** *fam* : squeak or crack in the voice **3** *Mex* : serenade **4 gallo de pelea** : gamecock
galo[1], **-la** *adj* **1** : Gaulish **2** : French
galo[2], **-la** *n* : Frenchman *m,* Frenchwoman *f*
galocha *nf* : galosh
galón *nm, pl* **galones 1** : gallon **2** : stripe (military insignia)
galopada *nf* : gallop
galopante *adj* : galloping <inflación galopante : galloping inflation>
galopar *vi* : to gallop
galope *nm* : gallop

galpón *nm, pl* **galpones** : shed, storehouse

galvanizar {21} *vt* : to galvanize — **galvanización** *nf*

gama *nf* **1** : range, spectrum, gamut **2** → **gamo**

gamba *nf* : large shrimp, prawn

gameto *nm* : gamete

gamo, -ma *n* : fallow deer

gamuza *nf* **1** : suede **2** : chamois

gana *nf* **1** : desire, inclination **2 de buena gana** : willingly, readily, gladly **3 de mala gana** : reluctantly, half-heartedly **4 tener ganas de** : to feel like, to be in the mood for <tengo ganas de bailar : I feel like dancing> **5 ponerle ganas a algo** : to put effort into something

ganadería *nf* **1** : cattle raising, stockbreeding **2** : cattle ranch **3** GANADO : cattle *pl,* livestock

ganadero[1], -ra *adj* : cattle, ranching

ganadero[2], -ra *n* : rancher, stockbreeder

ganado *nm* **1** : cattle *pl,* livestock **2 ganado ovino** : sheep *pl* **3 ganado porcino** : swine *pl*

ganador[1], -dora *adj* : winning

ganador[2], -dora *n* : winner

ganancia *nf* **1** : profit **2 ganancias** *nfpl* : winnings, gains

ganancioso, -sa *adj* : profitable

ganar *vt* **1** : to win **2** : to gain <ganar tiempo : to buy time> **3** : to earn <ganar dinero : to make money> **4** : to acquire, to obtain — *vi* **1** : to win **2** : to profit <salir ganando : to come out ahead> — **ganarse** *vr* **1** : to gain, to win <ganarse a alguien : to win someone over> **2** : to earn <ganarse la vida : to make a living> **3** : to deserve

gancho *nm* **1** : hook **2** : clothes hanger **3** : hairpin, bobby pin **4** *Col* : safety pin

gandul[1] *nm CA, Car, Col* : pigeon pea

gandul[2], -dula *n fam* : idler, lazybones

gandulear *vi* : to idle, to loaf, to lounge about

ganga *nf* : bargain

ganglio *nm* **1** : ganglion **2** : gland

gangrena *nf* : gangrene — **gangrenoso, -sa** *adj*

gángster *nmf, pl* **gángsters** : gangster

gansada *nf* : silly thing, nonsense

ganso, -sa *n* **1** : goose, gander *m* **2** : idiot, fool

gañido *nm* : yelp (of a dog)

gañir {38} *vi* : to yelp

garabatear *v* : to scribble, to scrawl, to doodle

garabato *nm* **1** : doodle **2 garabatos** *nmpl* : scribble, scrawl

garaje *nm* : garage

garante *nmf* : guarantor

garantía *nf* **1** : guarantee, warranty **2** : security <garantía de trabajo : job security>

garantizar {21} *vt* : to guarantee

garapiña *nf* : pineapple drink

garapiñar *vt* : to candy

garbanzo *nm* : chickpea, garbanzo

garbo *nm* **1** DONAIRE : grace, poise **2** : jauntiness

garboso, -sa *adj* **1** : graceful **2** : elegant, stylish

garceta *nf* : egret

gardenia *nf* : gardenia

garfio *nm* : hook, gaff, grapnel

gargajo *nm* : phlegm

garganta *nf* **1** : throat **2** : neck (of a person or a bottle) **3** : ravine, narrow pass

gargantilla *nf* : choker, necklace

gárgara *nf* **1** : gargle, gargling **2 hacer gárgaras** : to gargle

gargarizar *vi* : to gargle

gárgola *nf* : gargoyle

garita *nf* **1** : cabin, hut **2** : sentry box, lookout post

garoso, -sa *adj Col, Ven* : gluttonous, greedy

garra *nf* **1** : claw **2** : hand, paw **3 garras** *nfpl* : claws, clutches <caer en las garras de alguien : to fall into someone's clutches>

garrafa *nf* : decanter, carafe

garrafal *adj* : terrible, monstrous

garrafón *nm, pl* **-fones** : large decanter, large bottle

garrapata *nf* : tick

garrobo *nm CA* : large lizard, iguana

garrocha *nf* **1** PICA : lance, pike **2** : pole <salto con garrocha : pole vault>

garrotazo *nm* : blow (with a club)

garrote *nm* **1** : club, stick **2** *Mex* : brake

garúa *nf* : drizzle

garuar {3} *v impers* LLOVIZNAR : to drizzle

garza *nf* : heron

gas *nm* : gas, vapor, fumes *pl* <gas lagrimógeno : tear gas>

gasa *nf* : gauze

gasear *vt* **1** : to gas **2** : to aerate (a liquid)

gaseosa *nf* REFRESCO : soda, soft drink

gaseoso, -sa *adj* **1** : gaseous **2** : carbonated, fizzy

gasoducto *nm* : gas pipeline

gasolina *nf* : gasoline, gas

gasolinera *nf* : gas station, service station

gastado, -da *adj* **1** : spent **2** : worn, worn-out

gastador[1], -dora *adj* : extravagant, spendthrift

gastador[2], -dora *n* : spendthrift

gastar *vt* **1** : to spend **2** CONSUMIR : to consume, to use up **3** : to squander, to waste **4** : to wear <gasta un bigote : he sports a mustache> — **gastarse** *vr* **1** : to spend, to expend **2** : to run down, to wear out

gasto *nm* **1** : expense, expenditure **2** DETERIORO : wear **3 gastos generales** *or* **gastos indirectos** : overhead

gástrico, -ca *adj* : gastric

gastritis *nf* : gastritis

gastronomía *nf* : gastronomy
gastronómico, -ca *adj* : gastronomic
gastrónomo, -ma *n* : gourmet
gatas *adv* **andar a gatas** : to crawl, to go on all fours
gatear *vi* **1** : to crawl **2** : to climb, to clamber (up)
gatillero *nm Mex* : gunman
gatillo *nm* : trigger
gatito, -ta *n* : kitten
gato[1], **-ta** *n* : cat
gato[2] *nm* : jack (for an automobile)
gauchada *nf Arg, Uru* : favor, kindness
gaucho *nm* : gaucho
gaveta *nf* **1** CAJÓN : drawer **2** : till
gavilla *nf* **1** : gang, band **2** : sheaf
gaviota *nf* : gull, seagull
gay [ˈge, ˈgai] *adj* : gay (homosexual)
gaza *nf* : loop
gazapo *nm* **1** : young rabbit **2** : misprint, error
gazmoñería *nf* MOJIGATERÍA : prudery, primness
gazmoño[1], **-ña** *adj* : prudish, prim
gazmoño[2], **-ña** *n* MOJIGATO : prude, prig
gaznate *nm* : throat, gullet
gazpacho *nm* : gazpacho
géiser *or* **géyser** *nm* : geyser
gel *nm* : gel
gelatina *nf* : gelatin
gélido, -da *adj* : icy, freezing cold
gelificarse *vr* : to jell
gema *nf* : gem
gemelo[1], **-la** *adj & n* MELLIZO : twin
gemelo[2] *nm* **1** : cuff link **2 gemelos** *nmpl* BINOCULARES : binoculars
gemido *nm* : moan, groan, wail
Géminis *nmf* : Gemini
gemir {54} *vi* : to moan, to groan, to wail
gen *or* **gene** *nm* : gene
gendarme *nmf* POLICÍA : police officer, policeman *m,* policewoman *f*
gendarmería *nf* : police
genealogía *nf* : genealogy
genealógico, -ca *adj* : genealogical
generación *nf, pl* **-ciones 1** : generation <tercera generación : third generation> **2** : generating, creating **3** : class <la generación del '97 : the class of '97>
generacional *adj* : generation, generational
generador *nm* : generator
general[1] *adj* **1** : general **2 en ~** *or* **por lo general** : in general, generally
general[2] *nmf* **1** : general **2 general de división** : major general
generalidad *nf* **1** : generality, generalization **2** : majority
generalización *nf, pl* **-ciones 1** : generalization **2** : escalation, spread
generalizado, -da *adj* : generalized, widespread
generalizar {21} *vi* : to generalize — *vt* : to spread, to spread out — **generalizarse** *vr* : to become widespread
generalmente *adv* : usually, generally
generar *vt* : to generate — **generarse** *vr*
genérico, -ca *adj* : generic
género *nm* **1** : genre, class, kind <el género humano : the human race, mankind> **2** : gender (in grammar) **3 géneros** *nmpl* : goods, commodities
generosidad *nf* : generosity
generoso, -sa *adj* **1** : generous, unselfish **2** : ample — **generosamente** *adv*
genética *nf* : genetics
genético, -ca *adj* : genetic — **genéticamente** *adv*
genetista *nmf* : geneticist
genial *adj* **1** AGRADABLE : genial, pleasant **2** : brilliant <una obra genial : a work of genius> **3** *fam* FORMIDABLE : fantastic, terrific
genialidad *nf* **1** : genius **2** : stroke of genius **3** : eccentricity
genio *nm* **1** : genius **2** : temper, disposition <de mal genio : bad-tempered> **3** : genie
genital *adj* : genital
genitales *nmpl* : genitals, genitalia
genocidio *nm* : genocide
genotipo *nm* : genotype
gente *nf* **1** : people **2** : relatives *pl,* folks *pl* **3 gente menuda** *fam* : children, kids *pl* **4 ser buena gente** : to be nice, to be kind
gentil[1] *adj* **1** AMABLE : kind **2** : gentile
gentil[2] *nmf* : gentile
gentileza *nf* **1** AMABILIDAD : kindness **2** CORTESÍA : courtesy
gentilicio, -cia *adj* **1** : national, tribal **2** : family
gentío *nm* MUCHEDUMBRE, MULTITUD : crowd, mob
gentuza *nf* CHUSMA : riffraff, rabble
genuflexión *nf, pl* **-xiones 1** : genuflection **2 hacer una genuflexión** : to genuflect
genuino, -na *adj* : genuine — **genuinamente** *adv*
geofísica *nf* : geophysics
geofísico, -ca *adj* : geophysical
geografía *nf* : geography
geográfico, -ca *adj* : geographic, geographical — **geográficamente** *adv*
geógrafo, -fa *n* : geographer
geología *nf* : geology
geológico, -ca *adj* : geologic, geological — **geológicamente** *adv*
geólogo, -ga *n* : geologist
geometría *nf* : geometry
geométrico, -ca *adj* : geometric, geometrical — **geométricamente** *adv*
geopolítica *nf* : geopolitics
geopolítico, -ca *adj* : geopolitical
georgiano, -na *adj & n* : Georgian
geranio *nm* : geranium
gerbo *nm* : gerbil
gerencia *nf* : management, administration
gerencial *adj* : managerial
gerente *nmf* : manager, director
geriatría *nf* : geriatrics

geriátrico, -ca *adj* : geriatric
germanio *nm* : germanium
germano, -na *adj* : Germanic, German
germen *nm, pl* **gérmenes** : germ
germicida *nf* : germicide
germinación *nf, pl* **-ciones** : germination
germinar *vi* : to germinate, to sprout
gerontología *nf* : gerontology
gerundio *nm* : gerund
gesta *nf* : deed, exploit
gestación *nf, pl* **-ciones** : gestation
gesticulación *nf, pl* **-ciones** : gesturing, gesticulation
gesticular *vi* : to gesticulate, to gesture
gestión *nf, pl* **gestiones 1** TRÁMITE : procedure, step **2** ADMINISTRACIÓN : management **3 gestiones** *nfpl* : negotiations
gestionar *vt* **1** : to negotiate, to work towards **2** ADMINISTRAR : to manage, to handle
gesto *nm* **1** ADEMÁN : gesture **2** : facial expression **3** MUECA : grimace
gestor[1], -tora *adj* : facilitating, negotiating, managing
gestor[2], -tora *n* : facilitator, manager
géyser *nm* → **géiser**
ghanés, -nesa *adj & n, mpl* **ghaneses** : Ghanaian
ghetto → **gueto**
giba *nf* **1** : hump (of an animal) **2** : hunchback (of a person)
gibón *nm, pl* **gibones** : gibbon
giboso[1], -sa *adj* : hunchbacked, humpbacked
giboso[2], -sa *n* : hunchback, humpback
gigante[1] *adj* : giant, gigantic
gigante[2], -ta *n* : giant
gigantesco, -ca *adj* : gigantic, huge
gime, etc. → **gemir**
gimnasia *nf* : gymnastics
gimnasio *nm* : gymnasium, gym
gimnasta *nmf* : gymnast
gimnástico, -ca *adj* : gymnastic
gimotear *vi* LLORIQUEAR : to whine, to whimper
gimoteo *nm* : whimpering
ginebra *nf* : gin
ginecología *nf* : gynecology
ginecológico, -ca *adj* : gynecologic, gynecological
ginecólogo, -ga *n* : gynecologist
gira *nf* : tour
giralda *nf* : weather vane
girar *vi* **1** : to turn around, to revolve **2** : to swing around, to swivel — *vt* **1** : to turn, to twist, to rotate **2** : to draft (checks) **3** : to transfer (funds)
girasol *nm* MIRASOL : sunflower
giratorio, -ria *adj* : revolving
giro *nm* **1** VUELTA : turn, rotation **2** : change of direction <giro de 180 grados : U-turn, about-face> **3 giro bancario** : bank draft **4 giro postal** : money order
giroscopio *or* **giróscopo** *nm* : gyroscope
gis *nm Mex* : chalk
gitano, -na *adj & n* : Gypsy
glacial *adj* : glacial, icy — **glacialmente** *adv*
glaciar *nm* : glacier
gladiador *nm* : gladiator
gladiolo *or* **gladíolo** *nm* : gladiolus
glándula *nf* : gland — **glandular** *adj*
glaseado *nm* : glaze, icing
glasear *vt* : to glaze
glaucoma *nm* : glaucoma
glicerina *nf* : glycerin, glycerol
glicinia *nf* : wisteria
global *adj* **1** : global, worldwide **2** : full, comprehensive **3** : total, overall
globalizar {21} *vt* **1** ABARCAR : to include, to encompass **2** : to extend worldwide
globalmente *adv* : globally, as a whole
globo *nm* **1** : globe, sphere **2** : balloon **3 globo ocular** : eyeball
glóbulo *nm* **1** : globule **2** : blood cell, corpuscle
gloria *nf* **1** : glory **2** : fame, renown **3** : delight, enjoyment **4** : star, legend <las glorias del cine : the great names in motion pictures>
glorieta *nf* **1** : rotary, traffic circle **2** : bower, arbor
glorificar {72} *vt* ALABAR : to glorify — **glorificación** *nf*
glorioso, -sa *adj* : glorious — **gloriosamente** *adv*
glosa *nf* **1** : gloss **2** : annotation, commentary
glosar *vt* **1** : to gloss **2** : to annotate, to comment on (a text)
glosario *nm* : glossary
glotis *nf* : glottis
glotón[1], -tona *adj, mpl* **glotones** : gluttonous
glotón[2], -tona *n, mpl* **glotones** : glutton
glotón[3] *nm, pl* **glotones** : wolverine
glotonería *nf* GULA : gluttony
glucosa *nf* : glucose
glutinoso, -sa *adj* : glutinous
gnomo *nm* : gnome
gobernación *nf, pl* **-ciones** : governing, government
gobernador, -dora *n* : governor
gobernante[1] *adj* : ruling, governing
gobernante[2] *nmf* : ruler, leader, governor
gobernar {55} *vt* **1** : to govern, to rule **2** : to steer, to sail (a ship) — *vi* **1** : to govern **2** : to steer
gobierno *nm* : government
goce[1], etc. → **gozar**
goce[2] *nm* **1** PLACER : enjoyment, pleasure **2** : use, possession
gol *nm* : goal (in soccer)
golear *vt* : to rout, to score many goals against (in soccer)
goleta *nf* : schooner
golf *nm* : golf
golfista *nmf* : golfer
golfo *nm* : gulf, bay
golondrina *nf* **1** : swallow (bird) **2 golondrina de mar** : tern

golosina *nf* **:** sweet, snack
goloso, -sa *adj* **:** fond of sweets <ser goloso : to have a sweet tooth>
golpazo *nm* **:** heavy blow, bang, thump
golpe *nm* **1 :** blow <caerle a golpes a alguien : to give someone a beating> **2 :** knock **3 de ~ :** suddenly **4 de un golpe :** all at once, in one fell swoop **5 golpe de estado :** coup, coup d'etat **6 golpe de suerte :** stroke of luck
golpeado, -da *adj* **1 :** beaten, hit **2 :** bruised (of fruit) **3 :** dented
golpear *vt* **1 :** to beat (up), to hit **2 :** to slam, to bang, to strike — *vi* **1 :** to knock (at a door) **2 :** to beat <la lluvia golpeaba contra el tejado : the rain beat against the roof> — **golpearse** *vr*
golpetear *v* **:** to knock, to rattle, to tap
golpeteo *nm* **:** banging, knocking, tapping
goma *nf* **1 :** gum <goma de mascar : chewing gum> **2** CAUCHO **:** rubber <goma espuma : foam rubber> **3** PEGAMENTO **:** glue **4 :** rubber band **5** *Arg* **:** tire **6** *or* **goma de borrar :** eraser
gomita *nf* **:** rubber band
gomoso, -sa *adj* **:** gummy, sticky
góndola *nf* **:** gondola
gong *nm* **:** gong
gonorrea *nf* **:** gonorrhea
gorda *nf Mex* **:** thick corn tortilla
gordinflón[1], -flona *adj, mpl* **-flones** *fam* **:** chubby, pudgy
gordinflón[2], -flona *n, mpl* **-flones** *fam* **:** chubby person
gordo[1], -da *adj* **1 :** fat **2 :** thick **3 :** fatty, greasy, oily **4 :** unpleasant <me cae gorda tu tía : I can't stand your aunt>
gordo[2], -da *n* **:** fat person
gordo[3] *nm* **1** GRASA **:** fat **2 :** jackpot
gordura *nf* **:** fatness, flab
gorgojo *nm* **:** weevil
gorgotear *vi* **:** to gurgle, to bubble
gorgoteo *nm* **:** gurgle
gorila *nm* **:** gorilla
gorjear *vi* **1 :** to chirp, to tweet, to warble **2 :** to gurgle
gorjeo *nm* **1 :** chirping, warbling **2 :** gurgling
gorra *nf* **1 :** bonnet **2 :** cap **3 de ~** *fam* **:** for free, at someone else's expense <vivir de gorra : to sponge, to freeload>
gorrear *vt fam* **:** to bum, to scrounge — *vi fam* **:** to freeload
gorrero, -ra *n fam* **:** freeloader, sponger
gorrión *nm, pl* **gorriones :** sparrow
gorro *nm* **1 :** cap **2 estar hasta el gorro :** to be fed up
gorrón, -rrona *n fam, mpl* **gorrones :** freeloader, scrounger
gorronear *vt fam* **:** to bum, to scrounge — *vi fam* **:** to freeload
gota *nf* **1 :** drop <una gota de sudor : a bead of sweat> <como dos gotas de agua : like two peas in a pod> <sudar la gota gorda : to sweat buckets, to work very hard> **2 :** gout
gotear *v* **1 :** to drip **2 :** to leak — *v impers* LLOVIZNAR **:** to drizzle
goteo *nm* **:** drip, dripping
gotera *nf* **1 :** leak **2 :** stain (from dripping water)
gotero *nm* **:** (medicine) dropper
gótico, -ca *adj* **:** Gothic
gourmet *nmf* **:** gourmet
gozar {21} *vi* **1 :** to enjoy oneself, to have a good time **2 ~ de :** to enjoy, to have, to possess <gozar de buena salud : to enjoy good health> **3 ~ con :** to take delight in
gozne *nm* BISAGRA **:** hinge
gozo *nm* **1 :** joy **2** PLACER **:** enjoyment, pleasure
gozoso, -sa *adj* **:** joyful
grabación *nf, pl* **-ciones :** recording
grabado *nm* **1 :** engraving **2 grabado al aguafuerte :** etching
grabador, -dora *n* **:** engraver
grabadora *nf* **:** tape recorder
grabar *vt* **1 :** to engrave **2 :** to record, to tape — *vi* **grabar al aguafuerte :** to etch — **grabarse** *vr* **grabársele a alguien en la memoria :** to become engraved on someone's mind
gracia *nf* **1 :** grace **2 :** favor, kindness **3 :** humor, wit <su comentario no me hizo gracia : I wasn't amused by his remark> **4 gracias** *nfpl* **:** thanks <¡gracias! : thank you!> <dar gracias : to give thanks>
grácil *adj* **1 :** graceful **2 :** delicate, slender, fine
gracilidad *nm* **:** gracefulness
gracioso, -sa *adj* **1** CHISTOSO **:** funny, amusing **2 :** cute, attractive
grada *nf* **1 :** harrow **2** PELDAÑO **:** step, stair **3 gradas** *nfpl* **:** bleachers, grandstand
gradación *nf, pl* **-ciones :** gradation, scale
gradar *vt* **:** to harrow, to hoe
gradería *nf* **:** tiers *pl,* stands *pl,* rows *pl* (in a theater)
gradiente *nf* **:** gradient, slope
grado *nm* **1 :** degree (in meteorology and mathematics) <grado centígrado : degree centigrade> **2 :** extent, level, degree <en grado sumo : greatly, to the highest degree> **3** RANGO **:** rank **4 :** year, class (in education) **5 de buen grado :** willingly, readily
graduable *adj* **:** adjustable
graduación *nf, pl* **-ciones 1 :** graduation (from a school) **2** GRADO **:** rank **3 :** alcohol content, proof
graduado[1], -da *adj* **1 :** graduated **2 lentes graduados :** prescription lenses
graduado[2], -da *n* **:** graduate
gradual *adj* **:** gradual — **gradualmente** *adv*
graduar {3} *v* **1 :** to regulate, to adjust **2** CALIBRAR **:** to calibrate, to gauge —

graduarse *vr* : to graduate (from a school)
gráfica *nf* → **gráfico**[2]
gráfico[1], **-ca** *adj* : graphic — **gráficamente** *adv*
gráfico[2] *nm* **1** : graph, chart **2** : graphic (for a computer, etc.) **3 gráfico de barras** : bar graph
grafismo *nm* : graphics *pl*
grafito *nm* : graphite
gragea *nf* **1** : coated pill or tablet **2 grageas** *nfpl* : sprinkles, jimmies
grajo *nm* : rook (bird)
grama *nf* : grass
gramática *nf* : grammar
gramatical *adj* : grammatical — **gramaticalmente** *adv*
gramo *nm* : gram
gran → **grande**
grana *nf* : scarlet, deep red
granada *nf* **1** : pomegranate **2** : grenade <granada de mano : hand grenade>
granadero *nm* **1** : grenadier **2 granaderos** *nmpl Mex* : riot squad
granadino, -na *adj & n* : Grenadian
granado, -da *adj* **1** DISTINGUIDO : distinguished **2** : choice, select
granate *nm* **1** : garnet **2** : deep red, maroon
grande *adj* (**gran** *before singular nouns*) **1** : large, big <un libro grande : a big book> **2** ALTO : tall **3** NOTABLE : great <un gran autor : a great writer> **4** (*indicating intensity*) : great <con gran placer : with great pleasure> **5** : old, grown-up <hijos grandes : grown children>
grandeza *nf* **1** MAGNITUD : greatness, size **2** : nobility **3** : generosity, graciousness **4** : grandeur, magnificence
grandilocuencia *nf* : grandiloquence — **grandilocuente** *adj*
grandiosidad *nf* : grandeur
grandioso, -sa *adj* **1** MAGNÍFICO : grand, magnificent **2** : grandiose
granel *adv* **1 a ~** : galore, in great quantities **2 a ~** : in bulk <vender a granel : to sell in bulk>
granero *nm* : barn, granary
granito *nm* : granite
granizada *nf* : hailstorm
granizar {21} *v impers* : to hail
granizo *nm* : hail
granja *nf* : farm
granjear *vt* : to earn, to win — **granjearse** *vr* : to gain, to earn
granjero, -ra *n* : farmer
grano *nm* **1** PARTÍCULA : grain, particle <un grano de arena : a grain of sand> **2** : grain (of rice, etc.), bean (of coffee), seed **3** : grain (of wood or rock) **4** BARRO, ESPINILLA : pimple **5 ir al grano** : to get to the point
granuja *nmf* PILLUELO : rascal, urchin
granular[1] *vt* : to granulate — **granularse** *vr* : to break out in spots
granular[2] *adj* : granular, grainy
granza *nf* : chaff
grapa *nf* **1** : staple **2** : clamp
grapadora *nf* ENGRAPADORA : stapler
grapar *vt* ENGRAPAR : to staple
grasa *nf* **1** : grease **2** : fat **3** *Mex* : shoe polish
grasiento, -ta *adj* : greasy, oily
graso, -sa *adj* **1** : fatty **2** : greasy, oily
grasoso, -sa *adj* GRASIENTO : greasy, oily
gratificación *nf, pl* **-ciones 1** SATISFACCIÓN : gratification **2** : bonus **3** RECOMPENSA : recompense, reward
gratificar {72} *vt* **1** SATISFACER : to satisfy, to gratify **2** RECOMPENSAR : to reward **3** : to give a bonus to
gratinado, -da *adj* : au gratin
gratis[1] *adv* GRATUITAMENTE : free, for free, gratis
gratis[2] *adj* GRATUITO : free, gratis
gratitud *nf* : gratitude
grato, -ta *adj* AGRADABLE, PLACENTERO : pleasant, agreeable — **gratamente** *adv*
gratuitamente *adv* **1** : gratuitously **2** GRATIS : free, for free, gratis
gratuito, -ta *adj* **1** : gratuitous, unwarranted **2** GRATIS : free, gratis
grava *nf* : gravel
gravamen *nm, pl* **-vámenes 1** : burden, obligation **2** : (property) tax
gravar *vt* **1** : to burden, to encumber **2** : to levy (a tax)
grave *adj* **1** : grave, important **2** : serious, somber **3** : serious (of an illness)
gravedad *nf* **1** : gravity <centro de gravedad : center of gravity> **2** : seriousness, severity
gravemente *adv* : gravely, seriously
gravilla *nf* : (fine) gravel
gravitación *nf, pl* **-ciones** : gravitation
gravitar *vi* **1** : to gravitate **2 ~ sobre** : to rest on **3 ~ sobre** : to loom over
gravoso, -sa *adj* **1** ONEROSO : burdensome, onerous **2** : costly
graznar *vi* : to caw, to honk, to quack, to squawk
graznido *nm* : cawing, honking, quacking, squawking
gregario, -ria *adj* : gregarious
gregoriano, -na *adj* : Gregorian
gremial *adj* SINDICAL : union, labor
gremio *nm* SINDICATO : union, guild
greña *nf* **1** : mat, tangle **2 greñas** *nfpl* MELENAS : shaggy hair, mop
greñudo, -da *n* HIPPIE, MELENUDO : longhair, hippie
grey *nf* : congregation, flock
griego[1], **-ga** *adj & n* : Greek
griego[2] *nm* : Greek (language)
grieta *nf* : crack, crevice
grifo *nm* **1** : faucet <agua del grifo : tap water> **2** : griffin
grillete *nm* : shackle
grillo *nm* **1** : cricket **2 grillos** *nmpl* : fetters, shackles
grima *nf* **1** : disgust, uneasiness **2 darle grima a alguien** : to get on someone's nerves

gringo, -ga *adj & n* YANQUI : Yankee, gringo
gripa *nf Col, Mex* : flu
gripe *nf* : flu
gris *adj* **1** : gray **2** : overcast, cloudy
grisáceo, -cea *adj* : grayish
gritar *v* : to shout, to scream, to cry
gritería *nf* : shouting, clamor
grito *nm* : shout, scream, cry <a grito pelado : at the top of one's voice>
groenlandés, -desa *adj & n* : Greenlander
grogui *adj fam* : dazed, groggy
grosella *nf* **1** : currant **2 grosella espinosa** : gooseberry
grosería *nf* **1** : insult, coarse language **2** : rudeness, discourtesy
grosero[1], -ra *adj* **1** : rude, fresh **2** : coarse, vulgar
grosero[2], -ra *n* : rude person
grosor *nm* : thickness
grosso *adj* **a grosso modo** : roughly, broadly, approximately
grotesco, -ca *adj* : grotesque, hideous
grúa *nf* **1** : crane (machine) **2** : tow truck
gruesa *nf* : gross
grueso[1], -sa *adj* **1** : thick, bulky **2** : heavy, big **3** : heavyset, stout
grueso[2] *nm* **1** : thickness **2** : main body, mass **3 en ~** : in bulk
grulla *nf* : crane (bird)
grumo *nm* : lump, glob
gruñido *nm* : growl, grunt
gruñir {38} *vi* **1** : to growl, to grunt **2** : to grumble
gruñón[1], -ñona *adj, mpl* **gruñones** *fam* : grumpy, crabby
gruñón[2], -ñona *n, mpl* **gruñones** *fam* : grumpy person, nag
grupa *nf* : rump, hindquarters *pl*
grupo *nm* : group
gruta *nf* : grotto, cave
guacal *nm Col, Mex, Ven* : crate
guacamayo *nm* : macaw
guacamole *or* **guacamol** *nm* : guacamole
guacamote *nm Mex* : yuca, cassava
guachinango → huachinango
guacho, -cha *adj* **1** *Arg, Col, Chile, Peru* : orphaned **2** *Chile, Peru* : odd, unmatched
guadaña *nf* : scythe
guagua *nf* **1** *Arg, Col, Chile, Peru* : baby **2** *Cuba, PRi* : bus
guaira *nf* **1** *CA* : traditional flute **2** *Peru* : smelting furnace
guajiro, -ra *n Cuba* : peasant
guajolote *nm Mex* : turkey
guanábana *nf* : guanabana, soursop (fruit)
guanaco *nm* : guanaco
guandú *nm CA, Car, Col* : pigeon pea
guango, -ga *adj Mex* **1** : loose-fitting, baggy **2** : slack, loose
guano *nm* : guano
guante *nm* **1** : glove <guante de boxeo : boxing glove> **2 arrojarle el guante (a alguien)** : to throw down the gauntlet (to someone)
guantelete *nm* : gauntlet
guapo, -pa *adj* **1** : handsome, good-looking, attractive **2** : elegant, smart **3** *fam* : bold, dashing
guapura *nf fam* : handsomeness, attractiveness, good looks *pl* <¡qué guapura! : what a vision!>
guarache → huarache
guarachear *vi Cuba, PRi fam* : to go on a spree, to go out on the town
guaraní[1] *adj & nmf* : Guarani
guaraní[2] *nm* : Guarani (language of Paraguay)
guarda *nmf* **1** GUARDIÁN : security guard **2** : keeper, custodian
guardabarros *nms & pl* : fender, mudguard
guardabosque *nmfs & pl* : forest ranger, gamekeeper
guardacostas[1] *nmfs & pl* : coastguardsman
guardacostas[2] *nms & pl* : coast guard vessel
guardaespaldas *nmfs & pl* : bodyguard
guardafangos *nms & pl* : fender, mudguard
guardameta *nmf* ARQUERO, PORTERO : goalkeeper, goalie
guardapelo *nm* : locket
guardapolvo *nm* **1** : dustcover **2** : duster, housecoat
guardar *vt* **1** : to guard **2** : to maintain, to preserve **3** CONSERVAR : to put away **4** RESERVAR : to save **5** : to keep (a secret or promise) — **guardarse** *vr* **1 ~ de** : to refrain from **2 ~ de** : to guard against, to be careful not to
guardarropa *nm* **1** : cloakroom, checkroom **2** ARMARIO : closet, wardrobe
guardería *nf* : nursery, day-care center
guardia[1] *nf* **1** : guard, defense **2** : guard duty, watch **3 en ~** : on guard
guardia[2] *nmf* **1** : sentry, guardsman, guard **2** : police officer, policeman *m*, policewoman *f*
guardián, -diana *n, mpl* **guardianes 1** GUARDA : security guard, watchman **2** : guardian, keeper **3 perro guardián** : watchdog
guarecer {53} *vt* : to shelter, to protect — **guarecerse** *vr* : to take shelter
guarida *nf* **1** : den, lair **2** : hideout
guarismo *nm* : figure, numeral
guarnecer {53} *vt* **1** : to adorn **2** : to garnish **3** : to garrison
guarnición *nf, pl* **-ciones 1** : garnish **2** : garrison **3** : decoration, trimming, setting (of a jewel)
guaro *nm CA* : liquor distilled from sugarcane
guasa *nf fam* **1** : joking, fooling around **2 de ~** : in jest, as a joke
guasón[1], -sona *adj, mpl* **guasones** *fam* : funny, witty

guasón[2], -sona *n, mpl* **guasones** *fam* : joker, clown
guatemalteco, -ca *adj & n* : Guatemalan
guau *interj* : wow!
guayaba *nf* : guava (fruit)
gubernamental *adj* : governmental
gubernativo, -va → **gubernamental**
gubernatura *nf Mex* : governing body
guepardo *nm* : cheetah
güero, -ra *adj Mex* : blond, fair
guerra *nf* **1** : war <declarar la guerra : to declare war> <guerra sin cuartel : all-out war> **2** : warfare **3** LUCHA : conflict, struggle
guerrear *vi* : to wage war
guerrero[1], -ra *adj* **1** : war, fighting **2** : warlike
guerrero[2], -ra *n* : warrior
guerrilla *nf* : guerrilla warfare
guerrillero, -ra *adj & n* : guerrilla
gueto *nm* : ghetto
guía[1] *nf* **1** : directory, guidebook **2** ORIENTACIÓN : guidance, direction <la conciencia me sirve como guía : conscience is my guide>
guía[2] *nmf* : guide, leader <guía de turismo : tour guide>
guiar {85} *vt* **1** : to guide, to lead **2** CONDUCIR : to manage — **guiarse** *vr* : to be guided by, to go by
guija *nf* : pebble
guijarro *nm* : pebble
guillotina *nf* : guillotine — **guillotinar** *vt*
guinda[1] *adj & nm Mex* : burgundy (color)
guinda[2] *nf* : morello (cherry)
guineo *nm Car* : banana
guinga *nf* : gingham
guiñada → **guiño**
guiñar *vi* : to wink
guiño *nm* : wink
guión *nm, pl* **guiones** **1** : script, screenplay **2** : hyphen, dash **3** ESTANDARTE : standard, banner
guirnalda *nf* : garland
guisa *nf* **1** : manner, fashion **2 a guisa de** : like, by way of **3 de tal guisa** : in such a way
guisado ESTOFADO *nm* : stew
guisante *nm* : pea
guisar *vt* **1** ESTOFAR : to stew **2** *Spain* : to cook
guiso *nm* **1** : stew **2** : casserole
güisqui → **whisky**
guita *nf* : string, twine
guitarra *nf* : guitar
guitarrista *nmf* : guitarist
gula *nf* GLOTONERÍA : gluttony, greed
gusano *nm* **1** LOMBRIZ : worm, earthworm <gusano de seda : silkworm> **2** : caterpillar, maggot, grub
gustar *vt* **1** : to taste **2** : to like <¿gustan pasar? : would you like to come in?> — *vi* **1** : to be pleasing <me gustan los dulces : I like sweets> <a María le gusta Carlos : Maria is attracted to Carlos> <no me gusta que me griten : I don't like to be yelled at> **2 ~ de** : to like, to enjoy <no gusta de chismes : she doesn't like gossip> **3 como guste** : as you wish, as you like
gustativo, -va *adj* : taste <papilas gustativas : taste buds>
gusto *nm* **1** : flavor, taste **2** : taste, style **3** : pleasure, liking **4** : whim, fancy <a gusto : at will> **5 a ~** : comfortable, at ease **6 al gusto** : to taste, as one likes **7 mucho gusto** : pleased to meet you
gustosamente *adv* : gladly
gustoso, -sa *adj* **1** : willing, glad <nuestra empresa participará gustosa : our company will be pleased to participate> **2** : zesty, tasty
gutural *adj* : guttural

H

h *nf* : eighth letter of the Spanish alphabet
ha → **haber**
haba *nf* : broad bean
habanero[1], -ra *adj* : of or from Havana
habanero[2], -ra *n* : native or resident of Havana
haber[1] {39} *v aux* **1** : have, has <no ha llegado el envío : the shipment hasn't arrived> **2 ~ de** : must <ha de ser tarde : it must be late> — *v impers* **1 hay** : there is, there are <hay dos mensajes : there are two messages> <¿qué hay de nuevo? : what's new?> **2 hay que** : it is necessary <hay que trabajar más rápido : you have to work faster>
haber[2] *nm* **1** : assets *pl* **2** : credit, credit side **3 haberes** *nmpl* : salary, income, remuneration
habichuela *nf* **1** : bean, kidney bean **2** : green bean
hábil *adj* **1** : able, skillful **2** : working <días hábiles : working days>
habilidad *nf* CAPACIDAD : ability, skill
habilidoso, -sa *adj* : skillful, clever
habilitación *nf, pl* **-ciones** **1** : authorization **2** : furnishing, equipping
habilitar *vt* **1** : to enable, to authorize, to empower **2** : to equip, to furnish
hábilmente *adv* : skillfully, expertly
habitable *adj* : habitable, inhabitable
habitación *nf, pl* **-ciones** **1** CUARTO : room **2** DORMITORIO : bedroom **3** : habitation, occupancy

habitante *nmf* **:** inhabitant, resident

habitar *vt* **:** to inhabit — *vi* **:** to reside, to dwell

hábitat *nm, pl* **-tats :** habitat

hábito *nm* **1 :** habit, custom **2 :** habit (of a monk or nun)

habitual *adj* **:** habitual, customary — **habitualmente** *adv*

habituar {3} *vt* **:** to accustom, to habituate — **habituarse** *vr* **~ a :** to get used to, to grow accustomed to

habla *nf* **1 :** speech **2 :** language, dialect **3 de ~ :** speaking <de habla inglesa : English-speaking>

hablado, -da *adj* **1 :** spoken **2 mal hablado :** foulmouthed

hablador[1], -dora *adj* **:** talkative

hablador[2], -dora *n* **:** chatterbox

habladuría *nf* **1 :** rumor **2 habladurías** *nfpl* **:** gossip, scandal

hablante *nmf* **:** speaker

hablar *vi* **1 :** to speak, to talk <hablar en broma : to be joking> **2 ~ de :** to mention, to talk about **3 dar que hablar :** to make people talk — *vt* **1 :** to speak (a language) **2 :** to talk about, to discuss <háblalo con tu jefe : discuss it with your boss> — **hablarse** *vr* **1 :** to speak to each other, to be on speaking terms **2 se habla inglés (etc.) :** English (etc.) spoken

habrá, etc. → **haber**

hacedor, -dora *n* **:** creator, maker, doer

hacendado, -da *n* **:** landowner

hacer {40} *vt* **1 :** to make **2 :** to do, to perform **3 :** to force, to oblige <los hice esperar : I made them wait> — *vi* **:** to act <haces bien : you're doing the right thing> — *v impers* **1** (*referring to weather*) <hacer frío : to be cold> <hace viento : it's windy> **2 hace :** ago <hace mucho tiempo : a long time ago, for a long time> **3 no le hace :** it doesn't matter, it makes no difference **4 hacer falta :** to be necessary, to be needed — **hacerse** *vr* **1 :** to become **2 :** to pretend, to act, to play <hacerse el tonto : to play dumb> **3 :** to seem <el examen se me hizo difícil : the exam seemed difficult to me> **4 :** to get, to grow <se hace tarde : it's growing late>

hacha *nf* **:** hatchet, ax

hachazo *nm* **:** blow, chop (with an ax)

hachís *nm* **:** hashish

hacia *prep* **1 :** toward, towards <hacia abajo : downward> <hacia adelante : forward> **2 :** near, around, about <hacia las seis : about six o'clock>

hacienda *nf* **1 :** estate, ranch, farm **2 :** property **3 :** livestock **4 la Hacienda :** department of revenue, tax office

hacinar *vt* **1 :** to pile up, to stack **2 :** to overcrowd — **hacinarse** *vr* **:** to crowd together

hada *nf* **:** fairy

hado *nm* **:** destiny, fate

haga, etc. → **hacer**

haitiano, -na *adj & n* **:** Haitian

halagador[1], -dora *adj* **:** flattering

halagador[2], -dora *n* **:** flatterer

halagar {52} *vt* **:** to flatter, to compliment

halago *nm* **:** flattery, praise

halagüeño, -ña *adj* **1 :** flattering **2 :** encouraging, promising

halcón *nm, pl* **halcones :** hawk, falcon

halibut *nm, pl* **-buts :** halibut

hálito *nm* **1 :** breath **2 :** gentle breeze

hallar *vt* **1** ENCONTRAR **:** to find **2** DESCUBRIR **:** to discover, to find out — **hallarse** *vr* **1 :** to be situated, to find oneself **2 :** to feel <no se halla bien : he doesn't feel comfortable, he feels out of place>

hallazgo *nm* **1 :** discovery **2 :** find <¡es un verdadero hallazgo! : it's a real find!>

halo *nm* **1 :** halo **2 :** aura

halógeno *nm* **:** halogen

hamaca *nf* **:** hammock

hambre *nf* **1 :** hunger **2 :** starvation **3 tener hambre :** to be hungry **4 dar hambre :** to make hungry

hambriento, -ta *adj* **:** hungry, starving

hambruna *nf* **:** famine

hamburguesa *nf* **:** hamburger

hampa *nf* **:** criminal underworld

hampón, -pona *n, mpl* **hampones :** criminal, thug

hámster *nm, pl* **hámsters :** hamster

han → **haber**

handicap *or* **hándicap** [ˈhandiˌkap] *nm, pl* **-caps :** handicap (in sports)

hangar *nm* **:** hangar

hará, etc. → **hacer**

haragán[1], -gana *adj, mpl* **-ganes :** lazy, idle

haragán[2], -gana *n, mpl* **-ganes** HOLGAZÁN **:** slacker, good-for-nothing

haraganear *vi* **:** to be lazy, to waste one's time

haraganería *nf* **:** laziness

harapiento, -ta *adj* **:** ragged, tattered

harapos *nmpl* ANDRAJOS **:** rags, tatters

hardware [ˈhardˌwɛr] *nm* **:** computer hardware

harén *nm, pl* **harenes :** harem

harina *nf* **1 :** flour **2 harina de maíz :** cornmeal

hartar *vt* **1 :** to glut, to satiate **2** FASTIDIAR **:** to tire, to irritate, to annoy — **hartarse** *vr* **:** to be weary, to get fed up

harto[1] *adv* **:** most, extremely, very

harto[2], -ta *adj* **1 :** full, satiated **2 :** fed up

hartura *nf* **1 :** surfeit **2 :** abundance, plenty

has → **haber**

hasta[1] *adv* **:** even

hasta[2] *prep* **1 :** until, up until <hasta entonces : until then> <¡hasta luego! : see you later!> **2 :** as far as <nos fuimos hasta Managua : we went all the way to Managua> **3 :** up to <hasta cierto punto : up to a certain point> **4 hasta que :** until

hastiar {85} *vt* **1** : to make weary, to bore **2** : to disgust, to sicken — **hastiarse** *vr* ~ **de** : to get tired of
hastío *nm* **1** TEDIO : tedium **2** REPUGNANCIA : disgust
hato *nm* **1** : flock, herd **2** : bundle (of possessions)
hawaiano, -na *adj & n* : Hawaiian
hay → **haber**
haya[1]**, etc.** → **haber**
haya[2] *nf* : beech (tree and wood)
hayuco *nm* : beechnut
haz[1] → **hacer**
haz[2] *nm, pl* **haces 1** FARDO : bundle **2** : beam (of light)
haz[3] *nf, pl* **haces 1** : face **2 haz de la tierra** : surface of the earth
hazaña *nf* PROEZA : feat, exploit
hazmerreír *nm fam* : laughingstock
he[1] {39} → **haber**
he[2] *v impers* **he aquí** : here is, here are, behold
hebilla *nf* : buckle, clasp
hebra *nf* : strand, thread
hebreo[1]**, -brea** *adj & n* : Hebrew
hebreo[2] *nm* : Hebrew (language)
hecatombe *nm* **1** MATANZA : massacre **2** : disaster
heces → **hez**
hechicería *nf* **1** BRUJERÍA : sorcery, witchcraft **2** : curse, spell
hechicero[1]**, -ra** *adj* : bewitching, enchanting
hechicero[2]**, -ra** *n* : sorcerer, sorceress *f*
hechizar {21} *vt* **1** EMBRUJAR : to bewitch **2** CAUTIVAR : to charm
hechizo *nm* **1** SORTILEGIO : spell, enchantment **2** ENCANTO : charm, fascination
hecho[1] *pp* → **hacer**
hecho[2]**, -cha** *adj* **1** : made, done **2** : ready-to-wear **3** : complete, finished <hecho y derecho : full-fledged>
hecho[3] *nm* **1** : fact **2** : event <hechos históricos : historic events> **3** : act, action **4 de** ~ : in fact, in reality
hechura *nf* **1** : style **2** : craftsmanship, workmanship **3** : product, creation
hectárea *nf* : hectare
heder {56} *vi* : to stink, to reek
hediondez *nf* : stink, stench
hediondo, -da *adj* MALOLIENTE : foul-smelling, stinking
hedor *nm* : stench, stink
hegemonía *nf* **1** : dominance **2** : hegemony (in politics)
helada *nf* : frost (in meteorology)
heladería *nf* : ice-cream parlor, ice-cream stand
helado[1]**, -da** *adj* **1** GÉLIDO : icy, freezing cold **2** CONGELADO : frozen
helado[2] *nm* : ice cream
heladora *nf* CONGELADOR : freezer
helar {55} *v* CONGELAR : to freeze — *v impers* : to produce frost <anoche heló : there was frost last night> — **helarse** *vr*
helecho *nm* : fern, bracken
hélice *nf* **1** : spiral, helix **2** : propeller
helicóptero *nm* : helicopter
helio *nm* : helium
helipuerto *nm* : heliport
hembra *adj & nf* : female
hemisférico, -ca *adj* : hemispheric, hemispherical
hemisferio *nm* : hemisphere
hemofilia *nf* : hemophilia
hemofílico, -ca *adj & n* : hemophiliac
hemoglobina *nf* : hemoglobin
hemorragia *nf* **1** : hemorrhage **2 hemorragia nasal** : nosebleed
hemorroides *nfpl* ALMORRANAS : hemorrhoids, piles
hemos → **haber**
henchido, -da *adj* : swollen, bloated
henchir {54} *vt* **1** : to stuff, to fill **2** : to swell, to swell up — **henchirse** *vr* : to stuff oneself **2** LLENARSE : to fill up, to be full
hender {56} *vt* : to cleave, to split
hendidura *nf* : crack, crevice, fissure
henequén *nm, pl* **-quenes** : sisal hemp
heno *nm* : hay
hepatitis *nf* : hepatitis
heráldica *nf* : heraldry
heráldico, -ca *adj* : heraldic
heraldo *nm* : herald
herbario, -ria *adj* : herbal
herbicida *nm* : herbicide, weed killer
herbívoro[1]**, -ra** *adj* : herbivorous
herbívoro[2] *nm* : herbivore
herbolario, -ria *n* : herbalist
hercúleo, -lea *adj* : herculean
heredar *vt* : to inherit
heredero, -ra *n* : heir, heiress *f*
hereditario, -ria *adj* : hereditary
hereje *nmf* : heretic
herejía *nf* : heresy
herencia *nf* **1** : inheritance **2** : heritage **3** : heredity
herético, -ca *adj* : heretical
herida *nf* : injury, wound
herido[1]**, -da** *adj* **1** : injured, wounded **2** : hurt, offended
herido[2]**, -da** *n* : injured person, casualty
herir {76} *vt* **1** : to injure, to wound **2** : to hurt, to offend
hermafrodita *nmf* : hermaphrodite
hermanar *vt* **1** : to unite, to bring together **2** : to match up, to twin (cities)
hermanastro, -tra *n* : half brother *m*, half sister *f*
hermandad *nf* **1** FRATERNIDAD : brotherhood <hermandad de mujeres : sisterhood, sorority> **2** : association
hermano, -na *n* : sibling, brother *m*, sister *f*
hermético, -ca *adj* : hermetic, watertight — **herméticamente** *adv*
hermoso, -sa *adj* BELLO : beautiful, lovely — **hermosamente** *adv*
hermosura *nf* BELLEZA : beauty, loveliness
hernia *nf* : hernia
héroe *nm* : hero
heroicidad *nf* : heroism, heroic deed

heroico, -ca *adj* : heroic — **heroicamente** *adv*
heroína *nf* **1** : heroine **2** : heroin
heroísmo *nm* : heroism
herpes *nms & pl* **1** : herpes **2** : shingles
herradura *nf* : horseshoe
herraje *nm* : ironwork
herramienta *nf* : tool
herrar {55} *vt* : to shoe (a horse)
herrería *nf* : blacksmith's shop
herrero, -ra *n* : blacksmith
herrumbre *nf* ORÍN : rust
herrumbroso, -sa *adj* OXIDADO : rusty
hertzio *nm* : hertz
hervidero *nm* **1** : mass, swarm **2** : hotbed (of crime, etc.)
hervidor *nm* : kettle
hervir {76} *vi* **1** BULLIR : to boil, to bubble **2 ~ de** : to teem with, to be swarming with — *vt* : to boil
hervor *nm* **1** : boiling **2** : fervor, ardor
heterogeneidad *nf* : heterogeneity
heterogéneo, -nea *adj* : heterogeneous
heterosexual *adj & nmf* : heterosexual
heterosexualidad *nf* : heterosexuality
hexágono *nm* : hexagon — **hexagonal** *adj*
hez *nf, pl* **heces 1** ESCORIA : scum, dregs *pl* **2** : sediment, lees *pl* **3 heces** *nfpl* : feces, excrement
hiato *nm* : hiatus
hibernar *vi* : to hibernate — **hibernación** *nf*
híbrido[1], -da *adj* : hybrid
híbrido[2] *nm* : hybrid
hicieron, etc. → **hacer**
hidalgo, -ga *n* : nobleman *m*, noblewoman *f*
hidrante *nm CA, Col* : hydrant
hidratar *vt* : to moisturize — **hidratante** *adj*
hidrato *nm* **1** : hydrate **2 hidrato de carbono** : carbohydrate
hidráulico, -ca *adj* : hydraulic
hidroavión *nm, pl* **-viones** : seaplane
hidrocarburo *nm* : hydrocarbon
hidroeléctrico, -ca *adj* : hydroelectric
hidrofobia *nf* RABIA : hydrophobia, rabies
hidrófugo, -ga *adj* : water-repellent
hidrógeno *nm* : hydrogen
hidroplano *nm* : hydroplane
hiede, etc. → **heder**
hiedra *nf* **1** : ivy **2 hiedra venenosa** : poison ivy
hiel *nf* **1** BILIS : bile **2** : bitterness
hiela, etc. → **helar**
hielo *nm* **1** : ice **2** : coldness, reserve <romper el hielo : to break the ice>
hiena *nf* : hyena
hiende, etc. → **hender**
hierba *nf* **1** : herb **2** : grass **3 mala hierba** : weed
hierbabuena *nf* : mint, spearmint
hiere, etc. → **herir**
hierra, etc. → **herrar**
hierro *nm* **1** : iron <hierro fundido : cast iron> **2** : branding iron
hierve, etc. → **hervir**
hígado *nm* : liver
higiene *nf* : hygiene
higiénico, -ca *adj* : hygienic — **higiénicamente** *adv*
higienista *nmf* : hygienist
higo *nm* **1** : fig **2 higo chumbo** : prickly pear (fruit)
higrómetro *nm* : hygrometer
higuera *nf* : fig tree
hijastro, -tra *n* : stepson *m*, stepdaughter *f*
hijo, -ja *n* **1** : son *m*, daughter *f* **2 hijos** *nmpl* : children, offspring
híjole *interj Mex* : wow!, good grief!
hilacha *nf* **1** : ravel, loose thread **2 mostrar la hilacha** : to show one's true colors
hilado *nm* **1** : spinning **2** HILO : yarn, thread
hilar *vt* **1** : to spin (thread) **2** : to consider, to string together (ideas) — *vi* **1** : to spin **2 hilar delgado** : to split hairs
hilarante *adj* **1** : humorous, hilarious **2 gas hilarante** : laughing gas
hilaridad *nf* : hilarity
hilera *nf* FILA : file, row, line
hilo *nm* **1** : thread <colgar de un hilo : to hang by a thread> <hilo dental : dental floss> **2** LINO : linen **3** : (electric) wire **4** : theme, thread (of a discourse) **5** : trickle (of water, etc.)
hilvanar *vt* **1** : to baste, to tack **2** : to piece together
himnario *nm* : hymnal
himno *nm* **1** : hymn **2 himno nacional** : national anthem
hincapié *nm* **hacer hincapié en** : to emphasize, to stress
hincar {72} *vt* CLAVAR : to stick, to plunge — **hincarse** *vr* **hincarse de rodillas** : to kneel down, to fall to one's knees
hinchado, -da *adj* **1** : swollen, inflated **2** : pompous, overblown
hinchar *vt* **1** INFLAR : to inflate **2** : to exaggerate — **hincharse** *vr* **1** : to swell up **2** : to become conceited, to swell with pride
hinchazón *nf, pl* **-zones** : swelling
hinche, etc. → **henchir**
hindú *adj & nmf* : Hindu
hinduismo *nm* : Hinduism
hiniesta *nf* : broom (plant)
hinojo *nm* **1** : fennel **2 de hinojos** : on bended knee
hinque, etc. → **hincar**
hipar *vi* : to hiccup
hiperactividad *nf* : hyperactivity
hiperactivo, -va *adj* : hyperactive, overactive
hipérbole *nf* : hyperbole
hiperbólico, -ca *adj* : hyperbolic, exaggerated
hipercrítico, -ca *adj* : hypercritical
hipermetropía *nf* : farsightedness
hipersensibilidad *nf* : hypersensitivity
hipersensible *adj* : hypersensitive

hipertensión *nf, pl* **-siones :** hypertension, high blood pressure

hípico, -ca *adj* **:** equestrian <concurso hípico : horse show>

hipil *nm* → **huipil**

hipnosis *nfs & pl* **:** hypnosis

hipnótico, -ca *adj* **:** hypnotic

hipnotismo *nm* **:** hypnotism

hipnotizador[1], **-dora** *adj* **1 :** hypnotic **2 :** spellbinding, mesmerizing

hipnotizador[2], **-dora** *n* **:** hypnotist

hipnotizar {21} *vt* **:** to hypnotize

hipo *nm* **:** hiccup, hiccups *pl*

hipocampo *nm* **:** sea horse

hipocondría *nf* **:** hypochondria

hipocondríaco, -ca *adj & n* **:** hypochondriac

hipocresía *nf* **:** hypocrisy

hipócrita[1] *adj* **:** hypocritical — **hipócritamente** *adv*

hipócrita[2] *nmf* **:** hypocrite

hipodérmico, -ca *adj* **aguja hipodérmica :** hypodermic needle

hipódromo *nm* **:** racetrack

hipopótamo *nm* **:** hippopotamus

hipoteca *nf* **:** mortgage

hipotecar {72} *vt* **1 :** to mortgage **2 :** to compromise, to jeopardize

hipotecario, -ria *adj* **:** mortgage

hipotensión *nf* **:** low blood pressure

hipotenusa *nf* **:** hypotenuse

hipótesis *nfs & pl* **:** hypothesis

hipotético, -ca *adj* **:** hypothetical — **hipotéticamente** *adv*

hippie *or* **hippy** [ˈhipi] *nmf, pl* **hippies** [-pis] **:** hippie

hiriente *adj* **:** hurtful, offensive

hirió, etc. → **herir**

hirsuto, -ta *adj* **1 :** hirsute, hairy **2 :** bristly, wiry

hirviente *adj* **:** boiling

hirvió, etc. → **hervir**

hisopo *nm* **1 :** hyssop **2 :** cotton swab

hispánico, -ca *adj & n* **:** Hispanic

hispano[1], **-na** *adj* **:** Hispanic <de habla hispana : Spanish-speaking>

hispano[2], **-na** *n* **:** Hispanic (person)

hispanoamericano[1], **-na** *adj* LATINOAMERICANO **:** Latin-American

hispanoamericano[2], **-na** *n* LATINOAMERICANO **:** Latin American

hispanohablante[1] *adj* **:** Spanish-speaking

hispanohablante[2] *nmf* **:** Spanish speaker

histerectomía *nf* **:** hysterectomy

histeria *nf* **1 :** hysteria **2 :** hysterics

histérico, -ca *adj* **:** hysterical — **histéricamente** *adv*

histerismo *nm* **1 :** hysteria **2 :** hysterics

historia *nf* **1 :** history **2** NARRACIÓN, RELATO **:** story

historiador, -dora *n* **:** historian

historial *nm* **1 :** record, document **2** CURRÍCULUM **:** résumé, curriculum vitae

histórico, -ca *adj* **1 :** historical **2 :** historic, important — **históricamente** *adv*

historieta *nf* **:** comic strip

histrionismo *nm* **:** histrionics, acting

hit [ˈhit] *nm, pl* **hits 1** ÉXITO **:** hit, popular song **2 :** hit (in baseball)

hito *nm* **:** milestone, landmark

hizo → **hacer**

hobby [ˈhɔbi] *nm, pl* **hobbies** [-bis] **:** hobby

hocico *nm* **:** snout, muzzle

hockey [ˈhɔke, -ki] *nm* **:** hockey

hogar *nm* **1 :** home **2 :** hearth, fireplace

hogareño, -ña *adj* **1 :** home-loving **2 :** domestic, homelike

hogaza *nf* **:** large loaf (of bread)

hoguera *nf* **1** FOGATA **:** bonfire **2 morir en la hoguera :** to burn at the stake

hoja *nf* **1 :** leaf, petal, blade (of grass) **2 :** sheet (of paper), page (of a book) <hoja de cálculo : spreadsheet> **3** FORMULARIO **:** form <hoja de pedido : order form> **4 :** blade (of a knife) <hoja de afeitar : razor blade>

hojalata *nf* **:** tinplate

hojaldra *or* **hojaldre** *nm* **:** puff pastry

hojarasca *nf* **:** fallen leaves *pl*

hojear *vt* **:** to leaf through (a book or magazine)

hojuela *nf* **1 :** leaflet, young leaf **2 :** flake

hola *interj* **:** hello!, hi!

holandés[1], **-desa** *adj, mpl* **-deses :** Dutch

holandés[2], **-desa** *n, mpl* **-deses :** Dutch person, Dutchman *m,* Dutchwoman *f* <los holandeses : the Dutch>

holandés[3] *nm* **:** Dutch (language)

holgadamente *adv* **:** comfortably, easily <vivir holgadamente : to be well-off>

holgado, -da *adj* **1 :** loose, baggy **2 :** at ease, comfortable

holganza *nf* **:** leisure, idleness

holgazán[1], **-zana** *adj, mpl* **-zanes :** lazy

holgazán[2], **-zana** *n, mpl* **-zanes** HARAGÁN **:** slacker, idler

holgazanear *vi* HARAGANEAR **:** to laze around, to loaf

holgazanería *nf* PEREZA **:** idleness, laziness

holgura *nf* **1 :** looseness **2** COMODIDAD **:** comfort, ease

holístico, -ca *adj* **:** holistic

hollar {19} *vt* **:** to tread on, to trample

hollín *nm, pl* **hollines** TIZNE **:** soot

holocausto *nm* **:** holocaust

holograma *nm* **:** hologram

hombre *nm* **1 :** man <el hombre : man, mankind> **2 hombre de estado :** statesman **3 hombre de negocios :** businessman **4 hombre lobo :** werewolf

hombrera *nf* **1 :** shoulder pad **2 :** epaulet

hombría *nf* **:** manliness

hombro *nm* **:** shoulder <encogerse de hombros : to shrug one's shoulders>

hombruno, -na *adj* **:** mannish

homenaje *nm* : homage, tribute <rendir homenaje a : to pay tribute to>

homenajear *vt* : to pay homage to, to honor

homeopatía *nf* : homeopathy

homicida[1] *adj* : homicidal, murderous

homicida[2] *nmf* ASESINO : murderer

homicidio *nm* ASESINATO : homicide, murder

homilía *nf* : homily, sermon

homófono *nm* : homophone

homogeneidad *nf* : homogeneity

homogeneización *nf* : homogenization

homogeneizar {21} *vt* : to homogenize

homogéneo, -nea *adj* : homogeneous

homógrafo *nm* : homograph

homologación *nf, pl* **-ciones 1** : sanctioning, approval **2** : parity

homologar {52} *vt* **1** : to sanction **2** : to bring into line

homólogo[1]**, -ga** *adj* : homologous, equivalent

homólogo[2]**, -ga** *n* : counterpart

homónimo[1]**, -ma** *n* TOCAYO : namesake

homónimo[2] *nm* : homonym

homosexual *adj & nmf* : homosexual

homosexualidad *nf* : homosexuality

honda *nf* : sling

hondo[1] *adv* : deeply

hondo[2]**, -da** *adj* PROFUNDO : deep <en lo más hondo de : in the depths of> — **hondamente** *adv*

hondonada *nf* **1** : hollow, depression **2** : ravine, gorge

hondura *nf* : depth

hondureño, -ña *adj & n* : Honduran

honestidad *nf* **1** : decency, modesty **2** : honesty, uprightness

honesto, -ta *adj* **1** : decent, virtuous **2** : honest, honorable — **honestamente** *adv*

hongo *nm* **1** : fungus **2** : mushroom

honor *nm* **1** : honor <en honor a la verdad : to be quite honest> **2 honores** *nmpl* : honors <hacer los honores : to do the honors>

honorable *adj* HONROSO : honorable — **honorablemente** *adv*

honorario, -ria *adj* : honorary

honorarios *nmpl* : payment, fees (for professional services)

honorífico, -ca *adj* : honorary <mención honorífica : honorable mention>

honra *nf* **1** : dignity, self-respect <tener a mucha honra : to take great pride in> **2** : good name, reputation

honradamente *adv* : honestly, decently

honradez *nf, pl* **-deces** : honesty, integrity, probity

honrado, -da *adj* **1** HONESTO : honest, upright **2** : honored

honrar *vt* **1** : to honor **2** : to be a credit to <su generosidad lo honra : his generosity does him credit>

honroso, -sa *adj* HONORABLE : honorable — **honrosamente** *adv*

hora *nf* **1** : hour <media hora : half an hour> <a la última hora : at the last minute> <a la hora en punto : on the dot> <horas de oficina : office hours> **2** : time <¿qué hora es? : what time is it?> **3** CITA : appointment

horario *nm* : schedule, timetable, hours *pl* <horario de visita : visiting hours>

horca *nf* **1** : gallows *pl* **2** : pitchfork

horcajadas *nfpl* **a ~** : astride, astraddle

horcón *nm, pl* **horcones** : wooden post, prop

horda *nf* : horde

horizontal *adj* : horizontal — **horizontalmente** *adv*

horizonte *nm* : horizon, skyline

horma *nf* **1** : shoe tree **2** : shoemaker's last

hormiga *nf* : ant

hormigón *nm, pl* **-gones** CONCRETO : concrete

hormigonera *nf* : cement mixer

hormigueo *nm* **1** : tingling, pins and needles *pl* **2** : uneasiness

hormiguero *nm* **1** : anthill **2** : swarm (of people)

hormona *nf* : hormone — **hormonal** *adj*

hornacina *nf* : niche, recess

hornada *nf* : batch

hornear *vt* : to bake

hornilla *nf* : burner (of a stove)

horno *nm* **1** : oven <horno crematorio : crematorium> <horno de microondas : microwave oven> **2** : kiln

horóscopo *nm* : horoscope

horqueta *nf* **1** : fork (in a river or road) **2** : crotch (in a tree) **3** : small pitchfork

horquilla *nf* **1** : hairpin, bobby pin **2** : pitchfork

horrendo, -da *adj* : horrendous, horrible

horrible *adj* : horrible, dreadful — **horriblemente** *adv*

horripilante *adj* : horrifying, hair-raising

horripilar *vt* : to horrify, to terrify

horror *nm* : horror, dread

horrorizado, -da *adj* : terrified

horrorizar {21} *vt* : to horrify, to terrify — **horrorizarse** *vr*

horroroso, -sa *adj* **1** : horrifying, terrifying **2** : dreadful, bad

hortaliza *nf* **1** : vegetable **2 hortalizas** *nfpl* : garden produce

hortera *adj Spain fam* : tacky, gaudy

hortícola *adj* : horticultural

horticultor, -ra *n* : horticulturist

horticultura *nf* : horticulture

hosco, -ca *adj* : sullen, gloomy

hospedaje *nm* : lodging, accomodations *pl*

hospedar *vt* : to provide with lodging, to put up — **hospedarse** *vr* : to stay, to lodge

hospicio *nm* **:** orphanage
hospital *nm* **:** hospital
hospitalario, -ria *adj* **:** hospitable
hospitalidad *nf* **:** hospitality
hospitalización *nf, pl* **-ciones :** hospitalization
hospitalizar {21} *vt* **:** to hospitalize — **hospitalizarse** *vr*
hostería *nf* POSADA **:** inn
hostia *nf* **:** host, Eucharist
hostigamiento *nm* **:** harassment
hostigar {52} *vt* ACOSAR, ASEDIAR **:** to harass, to pester
hostil *adj* **:** hostile
hostilidad *nf* **1 :** hostility, antagonism **2 hostilidades** *nfpl* **:** (military) hostilities
hostilizar {21} *vt* **:** to harass
hotel *nm* **:** hotel
hotelero[1], -ra *adj* **:** hotel <la industria hotelera **:** the hotel business>
hotelero[2], -ra *n* **:** hotel manager, hotelier
hoy *adv* **1 :** today <hoy mismo **:** right now, this very day> **2 :** now, nowadays <de hoy en adelante **:** from now on>
hoyo *nm* AGUJERO **:** hole
hoyuelo *nm* **:** dimple
hoz *nf, pl* **hoces :** sickle
hozar {21} *vi* **:** to root (of a pig)
huachinango *nm Mex* **:** red snapper
huarache *nm* **:** huarache sandal
hubo, etc. → **haber**
hueco[1], -ca *adj* **1 :** hollow, empty **2 :** soft, spongy **3 :** hollow-sounding, resonant **4 :** proud, conceited **5 :** superficial
hueco[2] *nm* **1 :** hole, hollow, cavity **2 :** gap, space **3 :** recess, alcove
huele, etc. → **oler**
huelga *nf* **1** PARO **:** strike **2 hacer huelga :** to strike, to go on strike
huelguista *nmf* **:** striker
huella[1], etc. → **hollar**
huella[2] *nf* **1 :** footprint <seguir las huellas de alguien **:** to follow in someone's footsteps> **2 :** mark, impact <dejar huella **:** to leave one's mark> <sin dejar huella **:** without a trace> **3 huella digital** *or* **huella dactilar :** fingerprint
huérfano[1], -na *adj* **1 :** orphan, orphaned **2 :** defenseless **3 ~ de :** lacking, devoid of
huérfano[2], -na *n* **:** orphan
huerta *nf* **1 :** large vegetable garden, truck farm **2 :** orchard **3 :** irrigated land
huerto *nm* **1 :** vegetable garden **2 :** orchard
hueso *nm* **1 :** bone **2 :** pit, stone (of a fruit)
huésped[1], -peda *n* INVITADO **:** guest
huésped[2] *nm* **:** host <organismo huésped **:** host organism>
huestes *nfpl* **1 :** followers **2 :** troops, army
huesudo, -da *adj* **:** bony
hueva *nf* **:** roe, spawn
huevo *nm* **:** egg <huevos revueltos **:** scrambled eggs>
huida *nf* **:** flight, escape
huidizo, -za *adj* **1** ESCURRIDIZO **:** elusive, slippery **2 :** shy, evasive
huipil *nm CA, Mex* **:** traditional sleeveless blouse or dress
huir {41} *vi* **1** ESCAPAR **:** to escape, to flee **2 ~ de :** to avoid
huiro *nm Chile, Peru* **:** seaweed
huizache *nm* **:** huisache, acacia
hule *nm* **1 :** oilcloth, oilskin **2** *Mex* **:** rubber **3 hule espuma** *Mex* **:** foam rubber
humanidad *nf* **1 :** humanity, mankind **2 :** humaneness **3 humanidades** *nfpl* **:** humanities *pl*
humanismo *nm* **:** humanism
humanista *nmf* **:** humanist
humanístico, -ca *adj* **:** humanistic
humanitario, -ria *adj & n* **:** humanitarian
humano[1], -na *adj* **1 :** human **2** BENÉVOLO **:** humane , benevolent — **humanamente** *adv*
humano[2] *nm* **:** human being, human
humareda *nf* **:** cloud of smoke
humeante *adj* **1 :** smoky **2 :** smoking, steaming
humear *vi* **1 :** to smoke **2 :** to steam
humectante[1] *adj* **:** moisturizing
humectante[2] *nm* **:** moisturizer
humedad *nf* **1 :** humidity **2 :** dampness, moistness
humedecer {53} *vt* **1 :** to humidify **2 :** to moisten, to dampen
húmedo, -da *adj* **1 :** humid **2 :** moist, damp
humidificador *nm* **:** humidifier
humidificar {72} *vt* **:** to humidify
humildad *nf* **1 :** humility **2 :** lowliness
humilde *adj* **1 :** humble **2 :** lowly <gente humilde **:** poor people>
humildemente *adv* **:** meekly, humbly
humillación *nf, pl* **-ciones :** humiliation
humillante *adj* **:** humiliating
humillar *vt* **:** to humiliate — **humillarse** *vr* **:** to humble oneself <humillarse a hacer algo **:** to stoop to doing something>
humo *nm* **1 :** smoke, steam, fumes **2 humos** *nmpl* **:** airs *pl,* conceit
humor *nm* **1 :** humor **2 :** mood, temper <está de buen humor **:** she's in a good mood>
humorada *nf* **1** BROMA **:** joke, witticism **2 :** whim, caprice
humorismo *nm* **:** humor, wit
humorista *nmf* **:** humorist, comedian, comedienne *f*
humorístico, -ca *adj* **:** humorous — **humorísticamente** *adv*
humoso, -sa *adj* **:** smoky, steamy
humus *nm* **:** humus
hundido, -da *adj* **1 :** sunken **2 :** depressed

hundimiento *nm* **1 :** sinking **2 :** collapse, ruin
hundir *vt* **1 :** to sink **2 :** to destroy, to ruin — **hundirse** *vr* **1 :** to sink down **2 :** to cave in **3 :** to break down, to go to pieces
húngaro[1], **-ra** *adj & n* **:** Hungarian
húngaro[2] *nm* **:** Hungarian (language)
huracán *nm, pl* **-canes :** hurricane
huraño, -ña *adj* **1 :** unsociable, aloof **2 :** timid, skittish (of an animal)
hurgar {52} *vt* **:** to poke, to jab, to rake (a fire) — *vi* **~ en :** to rummage in, to poke through
hurgue, etc. → **hurgar**
hurón *nm, pl* **hurones :** ferret
huronear *vi* **:** to pry, to snoop
hurra *interj* **:** hurrah!, hooray!
hurtadillas *nfpl* **a ~ :** stealthily, on the sly
hurtar *vt* ROBAR **:** to steal
hurto *nm* **1 :** theft, robbery **2 :** stolen property, loot
husmear *vt* **1 :** to follow the scent of, to track **2 :** to sniff out, to pry into — *vi* **1 :** to pry, to snoop **2 :** to sniff around (of an animal)
huso *nm* **1 :** spindle **2 huso horario :** time zone
huy *interj* **:** ow!, ouch!
huye, etc. → **huir**

I

i *nf* **:** ninth letter of the Spanish alphabet
iba, etc. → **ir**
ibérico, -ca *adj* **:** Iberian
ibero, -ra *or* **íbero, -ra** *adj & n* **:** Iberian
iberoamericano, -na *adj* HISPANOAMERICANO, LATINOAMERICANO **:** Latin-American
ibis *nfs & pl* **:** ibis
ice, etc. → **izar**
iceberg *nm, pl* **icebergs :** iceberg
icono *nm* **:** icon
iconoclasia *nf* **:** iconoclasm
iconoclasta *nmf* **:** iconoclast
ictericia *nf* **:** jaundice
ida *nf* **1 :** going, departure **2 ida y vuelta :** round-trip **3 idas y venidas :** comings and goings
idea *nf* **1 :** idea, notion **2 :** opinion, belief **3** PROPÓSITO **:** intention
ideal *adj & nm* **:** ideal — **idealmente** *adv*
idealismo *nm* **:** idealism
idealista[1] *adj* **:** idealistic
idealista[2] *nmf* **:** idealist
idealizar {21} *vt* **:** to idealize — **idealización** *nf*
idear *vt* **:** to devise, to think up
ideario *nm* **:** ideology
ídem *nm* **:** idem, the same, ditto
idéntico, -ca *adj* **:** identical, alike — **idénticamente** *adv*
identidad *nf* **:** identity
identificable *adj* **:** identifiable
identificación *nf, pl* **-ciones 1 :** identification, identifying **2 :** identification document, ID
identificar {72} *vt* **:** to identify — **identificarse** *vr* **1 :** to identify oneself **2 ~ con :** to identify with
ideología *nf* **:** ideology — **ideológicamente** *adv*
ideológico, -ca *adj* **:** ideological
idílico, -ca *adj* **:** idyllic
idilio *nm* **:** idyll
idioma *nm* **:** language <el idioma inglés : the English language>
idiomático, -ca *adj* **:** idiomatic — **idiomáticamente** *adv*
idiosincrasia *nf* **:** idiosyncrasy
idiosincrásico, -ca *adj* **:** idiosyncratic
idiota[1] *adj* **:** idiotic, stupid, foolish
idiota[2] *nmf* **:** idiot, foolish person
idiotez *nf, pl* **-teces 1 :** idiocy **2 :** idiotic act or remark <¡no digas idioteces! : don't talk nonsense!>
ido *pp* → **ir**
idólatra[1] *adj* **:** idolatrous
idólatra[2] *nmf* **:** idolater
idolatrar *vt* **:** to idolize
idolatría *nf* **:** idolatry
ídolo *nm* **:** idol
idoneidad *nf* **:** suitability
idóneo, -nea *adj* ADECUADO **:** suitable, fitting
iglesia *nf* **:** church
iglú *nm* **:** igloo
ignición *nf, pl* **-ciones :** ignition
ignífugo, -ga *adj* **:** fire-resistant, fireproof
ignominia *nf* **:** ignominy, disgrace
ignominioso, -sa *adj* **:** ignominious, shameful
ignorancia *nf* **:** ignorance
ignorante[1] *adj* **:** ignorant
ignorante[2] *nmf* **:** ignorant person, ignoramus
ignorar *vt* **1 :** to ignore **2** DESCONOCER **:** to be unaware of <lo ignoramos por absoluto : we have no idea>
ignoto, -ta *adj* **:** unknown
igual[1] *adv* **1 :** in the same way **2 por ~ :** equally
igual[2] *adj* **1 :** equal **2** IDÉNTICO **:** the same, alike **3 :** even, smooth **4** SEMEJANTE **:** similar **5** CONSTANTE **:** constant
igual[3] *nmf* **:** equal, peer
igualación *nf* **1 :** equalization **2 :** leveling, smoothing **3 :** equating (in mathematics)
igualado, -da *adj* **1 :** even (of a score) **2 :** level **3** *Mex* **:** disrespectful
igualar *vt* **1 :** to equalize **2 :** to tie <igualar el marcador : to even the score>

igualdad *nf* **1** : equality **2** UNIFORMIDAD : evenness, uniformity
igualmente *adv* **1** : equally **2** ASIMISMO : likewise
iguana *nf* : iguana
ijada *nf* : flank, loin, side
ijar *nm* → **ijada**
ilegal[1] *adj* : illegal, unlawful — **ilegalmente** *adv*
ilegal[2] *nmf CA, Mex* : illegal alien
ilegalidad *nf* : illegality, unlawfulness
ilegibilidad *nf* : illegibility
ilegible *adj* : illegible — **ilegiblemente** *adv*
ilegitimidad *nf* : illegitimacy
ilegítimo, -ma *adj* : illegitimate, unlawful
ileso, -sa *adj* : uninjured, unharmed
ilícito, -ta *adj* : illicit — **ilícitamente** *adv*
ilimitado, -da *adj* : unlimited
ilógico, -ca *adj* : illogical — **ilógicamente** *adv*
iluminación *nf, pl* **-ciones 1** : illumination **2** ALUMBRADO : lighting
iluminado, -da *adj* : illuminated, lighted
iluminar *vt* **1** : to illuminate, to light (up) **2** : to enlighten
ilusión *nf, pl* **-siones 1** : illusion, delusion **2** ESPERANZA : hope <hacerse ilusiones : to get one's hopes up>
ilusionado, -da *adj* ESPERANZADO : hopeful, eager
ilusionar *vt* : to build up hope, to excite — **ilusionarse** *vr* : to get one's hopes up
iluso[1], **-sa** *adj* : naive, gullible
iluso[2], **-sa** *n* SOÑADOR : dreamer, visionary
ilusorio, -ria *adj* ENGAÑOSO : illusory, misleading
ilustración *nf, pl* **-ciones 1** : illustration **2** : erudition, learning <la Ilustración : the Enlightenment>
ilustrado, -da *adj* **1** : illustrated **2** DOCTO : learned, erudite
ilustrador, -dora *n* : illustrator
ilustrar *vt* **1** : to illustrate **2** ACLARAR, CLARIFICAR : to explain
ilustrativo, -va *adj* : illustrative
ilustre *adj* : illustrious, eminent
imagen *nf, pl* **imágenes** : image, picture
imaginable *adj* : imaginable, conceivable
imaginación *nf, pl* **-ciones** : imagination
imaginar *vt* : to imagine — **imaginarse** *vr* **1** : to suppose, to imagine **2** : to picture
imaginario, -ria *adj* : imaginary
imaginativo, -va *adj* : imaginative — **imaginativamente** *adv*
imán *nm, pl* **imanes** : magnet
imantar *vt* : to magnetize
imbatible *adj* : unbeatable
imbécil[1] *adj* : stupid, idiotic
imbécil[2] *nmf* **1** : imbecile **2** *fam* : idiot, dope
imborrable *adj* : indelible
imbuir {41} *vt* : to imbue — **imbuirse** *vr*
imitación *nf, pl* **-ciones 1** : imitation **2** : mimicry, impersonation
imitador[1], **-dora** *adj* : imitative
imitador[2], **-dora** *n* **1** : imitator **2** : mimic
imitar *vt* **1** : to imitate, to copy **2** : to mimic, to impersonate
impaciencia *nf* : impatience
impacientar *vt* : to make impatient, to exasperate — **impacientarse** *vr*
impaciente *adj* : impatient — **impacientemente** *adv*
impactado, -da *adj* : shocked, stunned
impactante *adj* **1** : shocking **2** : impressive, powerful
impactar *vt* **1** GOLPEAR : to hit **2** IMPRESIONAR : to impact, to affect — **impactarse** *vr*
impacto *nm* **1** : impact, effect **2** : shock, collision
impagable *adj* **1** : unpayable **2** : priceless
impago *nm* : nonpayment
impalpable *adj* INTANGIBLE : impalpable, intangible
impar[1] *adj* : odd <números impares : odd numbers>
impar[2] *nm* : odd number
imparable *adj* : unstoppable
imparcial *adj* : impartial — **imparcialmente** *adv*
imparcialidad *nf* : impartiality
impartir *vt* : to impart, to give
impasible *adj* : impassive, unmoved — **impasiblemente** *adv*
impasse *nm* : impasse
impávido, -da *adj* : undaunted, unperturbed
impecable *adj* INTACHABLE : impeccable, faultless — **impecablemente** *adv*
impedido, -da *adj* : disabled, crippled
impedimento *nm* **1** : impediment, obstacle **2** : disability
impedir {54} *vt* **1** : to prevent, to block **2** : to impede, to hinder
impeler *vt* **1** : to drive, to propel **2** : to impel
impenetrable *adj* : impenetrable — **impenetrabilidad** *nf*
impenitente *adj* : unrepentant, impenitent
impensable *adj* : unthinkable
impensado, -da *adj* : unforeseen, unexpected
imperante *adj* : prevailing
imperar *vi* **1** : to reign, to rule **2** PREDOMINAR : to prevail
imperativo[1], **-va** *adj* : imperative
imperativo[2] *nm* : imperative
imperceptible *adj* : imperceptible — **imperceptiblemente** *adv*
imperdible *Spain nm* : safety pin

imperdonable *adj* : unpardonable, unforgivable

imperecedero, -ra *adj* **1** : imperishable **2** INMORTAL : immortal, everlasting

imperfección *nf, pl* **-ciones 1** : imperfection **2** DEFECTO : defect, flaw

imperfecto[1], -ta *adj* : imperfect, flawed

imperfecto[2] *nm* : imperfect tense

imperial *adj* : imperial

imperialismo *nm* : imperialism

imperialista *adj & nmf* : imperialist

impericia *nf* : lack of skill, incompetence

imperio *nm* : empire

imperioso, -sa *adj* **1** : imperious **2** : pressing, urgent — **imperiosamente** *adv*

impermeabilizante *adj* : water-repellent

impermeabilizar {21} *vt* : to waterproof

impermeable[1] *adj* **1** : impervious **2** : impermeable, waterproof

impermeable[2] *nm* : raincoat

impersonal *adj* : impersonal — **impersonalmente** *adv*

impertinencia *nf* INSOLENCIA : impertinence, insolence

impertinente *adj* **1** INSOLENTE : impertinent, insolent **2** INOPORTUNO : inappropriate, uncalled-for **3** IRRELEVANTE : irrelevant

imperturbable *adj* : imperturbable, impassive, stolid

ímpetu *nm* **1** : impetus, momentum **2** : vigor, energy **3** : force, violence

impetuoso, -sa *adj* : impetuous, impulsive — **impetuosamente** *adv*

impiedad *nf* : impiety

impío, -pía *adj* : impious, ungodly

implacable *adj* : implacable, relentless — **implacablemente** *adv*

implantación *nf, pl* **-ciones 1** : implantation **2** ESTABLECIMIENTO : establishment, introduction

implantado, -da *adj* : well-established

implantar *vt* **1** : to implant **2** ESTABLECER : to establish, to introduce — **implantarse** *vr*

implante *nm* : implant

implementar *vt* : to implement — **implementarse** *vr* — **implementación** *nf*

implemento *nm* : implement, tool

implicación *nf, pl* **-ciones** : implication

implicar {72} *vt* **1** ENREDAR, ENVOLVER : to involve, to implicate **2** : to imply

implícito, -ta *adj* : implied, implicit — **implícitamente** *adv*

implorar *vt* : to implore

implosión *nf, pl* **-siones** : implosion — **implosivo, -va** *adj*

implosionar *vi* : to implode

imponderable *adj & nm* : imponderable

imponente *adj* : imposing, impressive

imponer {60} *vt* **1** : to impose **2** : to confer — *vi* : to be impressive, to command respect — **imponerse** *vr* **1** : to take on (a duty) **2** : to assert oneself **3** : to prevail

imponible *adj* : taxable

impopular *adj* : unpopular — **impopularidad** *nf*

importación *nf, pl* **-ciones 1** : importation **2 importaciones** *nfpl* : imports

importado, -da *adj* : imported

importador[1], -dora *adj* : importing

importador[2], -dora *n* : importer

importancia *nf* : importance

importante *adj* : important — **importantemente** *adv*

importar *vi* : to matter, to be important <no le importa lo que piensen : she doesn't care what they think> — *vt* : to import

importe *nm* **1** : price, cost **2** : sum, amount

importunar *vt* : to bother, to inconvenience — *vi* : to be inconvenient

importuno, -na *adj* **1** : inopportune, inconvenient **2** : bothersome, annoying

imposibilidad *nf* : impossibility

imposibilitado, -da *adj* **1** : disabled, crippled **2 verse imposibilitado** : to be unable (to do something)

imposibilitar *vt* **1** : to make impossible **2** : to disable, to incapacitate — **imposibilitarse** *vr* : to become disabled

imposible *adj* : impossible

imposición *nf, pl* **-ciones 1** : imposition **2** EXIGENCIA : demand, requirement **3** : tax **4** : deposit

impositivo, -va *adj* : tax <tasa impositiva : tax rate>

impostor, -tora *n* : impostor

impotencia *nf* **1** : impotence, powerlessness **2** : impotence (in medicine)

impotente *adj* **1** : powerless **2** : impotent

impracticable *adj* : impracticable

imprecisión *nf, pl* **-siones 1** : imprecision, vagueness **2** : inaccuracy

impreciso, -sa *adj* **1** : imprecise, vague **2** : inaccurate

impredecible *adj* : unpredictable

impregnar *vt* : to impregnate

imprenta *nf* **1** : printing **2** : printing shop, press

imprescindible *adj* : essential, indispensable

impresentable *adj* : unpresentable, unfit

impresión *nf, pl* **-siones 1** : print, printing **2** : impression, feeling

impresionable *adj* : impressionable

impresionante *adj* : impressive, incredible, amazing — **impresionantemente** *adv*

impresionar *vt* **1** : to impress, to strike **2** : to affect, to move — *vi* : to make an impression — **impresionarse** *vr* : to be affected, to be removed

impresionismo *nm* : impressionism

impresionista[1] *adj* : impressionist, impressionistic
impresionista[2] *nmf* : impressionist
impreso[1] *pp* → **imprimir**
impreso[2], **-sa** *adj* : printed
impreso[3] *nm* PUBLICACIÓN : printed matter, publication
impresor, -sora *n* : printer
impresora *nf* : (computer) printer
imprevisible *adj* : unforeseeable
imprevisión *nf, pl* **-siones** : lack of foresight, thoughtlessness
imprevisto[1], **-ta** *adj* : unexpected, unforeseen
imprevisto[2] *nm* : unexpected occurrence, contingency
imprimir {42} *vt* **1** : to print **2** : to imprint, to stamp, to impress
improbabilidad *nf* : improbability
improbable *adj* : improbable, unlikely
improcedente *adj* **1** : inadmissible **2** : inappropriate, improper
improductivo, -va *adj* : unproductive
improperio *nm* : affront, insult
impropio, -pia *adj* **1** : improper, incorrect **2** INADECUADO : unsuitable, inappropriate
improvisación *nf, pl* **-ciones** : improvisation, ad-lib
improvisado, -da *adj* : improvised, ad-lib
improvisar *v* : to improvise, to ad-lib
improviso *adj* **de ~** : all of a sudden, unexpectedly
imprudencia *nf* INDISCRECIÓN : imprudence, indiscretion
imprudente *adj* INDISCRETO : imprudent, indiscreet — **imprudentemente** *adv*
impúdico, -ca *adj* : shameless, indecent
impuesto[1] *pp* → **imponer**
impuesto[2] *nm* : tax
impugnar *vt* : to challenge, to contest
impulsar *vt* : to propel, to drive
impulsividad *nf* : impulsiveness
impulsivo, -va *adj* : impulsive — **impulsivamente** *adv*
impulso *nm* **1** : drive, thrust **2** : impulse, urge
impune *adj* : unpunished
impunemente *adv* : with impunity
impunidad *nf* : impunity
impureza *nf* : impurity
impuro, -ra *adj* : impure
impuso, etc. → **imponer**
imputable *adj* ATRIBUIBLE : attributable
imputación *nf, pl* **-ciones 1** : attribution, imputation **2** : accusation
imputar *vt* ATRIBUIR : to impute, to attribute
inacabable *adj* : endless
inacabado, -da *adj* INCONCLUSO : unfinished
inaccesibilidad *nf* : inaccessibility
inaccesible *adj* **1** : inaccessible **2** : unattainable
inacción *nf, pl* **-ciones** : inactivity, inaction
inaceptable *adj* : unacceptable
inactividad *nf* : inactivity, idleness
inactivo, -va *adj* : inactive, idle
inadaptado[1], **-da** *adj* : maladjusted
inadaptado[2], **-da** *n* : misfit
inadecuación *nf, pl* **-ciones** : inadequacy
inadecuado, -da *adj* **1** : inadequate **2** IMPROPIO : inappropriate — **inadecuadamente** *adv*
inadmisible *adj* **1** : inadmissible **2** : unacceptable
inadvertencia *nf* : oversight
inadvertidamente *adv* : inadvertently
inadvertido, -da *adj* **1** : unnoticed <pasar inadvertido : to go unnoticed> **2** DESPISTADO, DISTRAÍDO : inattentive, distracted
inagotable *adj* : inexhaustible
inaguantable *adj* INSOPORTABLE : insufferable, unbearable
inalámbrico, -ca *adj* : wireless, cordless
inalcanzable *adj* : unreachable, unattainable
inalienable *adj* : inalienable
inalterable *adj* **1** : unalterable, unchangeable **2** : impassive **3** : colorfast
inamovible *adj* : immovable, fixed
inanición *nf, pl* **-ciones** : starvation
inanimado, -da *adj* : inanimate
inapelable *adj* : indisputable
inapetencia *nf* : lack of appetite
inaplicable *adj* : inapplicable
inapreciable *adj* **1** : imperceptible, negligible **2** : invaluable
inapropiado, -da *adj* : inappropriate, unsuitable
inarticulado, -da *adj* : inarticulate, unintelligible — **inarticuladamente** *adv*
inasequible *adj* : unattainable, inaccessible
inasistencia *nf* AUSENCIA : absence
inatacable *adj* : unassailable, indisputable
inaudible *adj* : inaudible
inaudito, -ta *adj* : unheard-of, unprecedented
inauguración *nf, pl* **-ciones** : inauguration
inaugural *adj* : inaugural, opening
inaugurar *vt* **1** : to inaugurate **2** : to open
inca *adj & nmf* : Inca
incalculable *adj* : incalculable
incalificable *adj* : indescribable
incandescencia *nf* : incandescence — **incandescente** *adj*
incansable *adj* INFATIGABLE : tireless — **incansablemente** *adv*
incapacidad *nf* **1** : inability, incapacity **2** : disability, handicap
incapacitado, -da *adj* **1** : disqualified **2** : disabled, handicapped
incapacitar *vt* **1** : to incapacitate, to disable **2** : to disqualify
incapaz *adj, pl* **-paces 1** : incapable, unable **2** : incompetent, inept

incautación *nf, pl* **-ciones** : seizure, confiscation

incautar *vt* CONFISCAR : to confiscate, to seize — **incautarse** *vr*

incauto, -ta *adj* : unwary, unsuspecting

incendiar *vt* : to set fire to, to burn (down) — **incendiarse** *vr* : to catch fire

incendiario[1], -ria *adj* : incendiary, inflammatory

incendiario[2], -ria *n* : arsonist

incendio *nm* **1** : fire **2 incendio premeditado** : arson

incentivar *vt* : to encourage, to stimulate

incentivo *nm* : incentive

incertidumbre *nf* : uncertainty, suspense

incesante *adj* : incessant — **incesantemente** *adv*

incesto *nm* : incest

incidencia *nf* **1** : incident **2** : effect, impact **3 por ~** : by chance, accidentally

incidental *adj* : incidental

incidentalmente *adv* : by chance

incidente *nm* : incident, occurrence

incidir *vi* **1 ~ en** : to fall into, to enter into <incidimos en el mismo error : we fell into the same mistake> **2 ~ en** : to affect, to influence, to have a bearing on

incienso *nm* : incense

incierto, -ta *adj* **1** : uncertain **2** : untrue **3** : unsteady, insecure

incineración *nf, pl* **-ciones 1** : incineration **2** : cremation

incinerador *nm* : incinerator

incinerar *vt* **1** : to incinerate **2** : to cremate

incipiente *adj* : incipient

incisión *nf, pl* **-siones** : incision

incisivo[1], -va *adj* : incisive

incisivo[2] *nm* : incisor

inciso *nm* : digression, aside

incitación *nf, pl* **-ciones** : incitement

incitante *adj* : provocative

incitar *vt* : to incite, to rouse

incivilizado, -da *adj* : uncivilized

inclemencia *nf* : inclemency, severity

inclemente *adj* : inclement

inclinación *nf, pl* **-ciones 1** PROPENSIÓN : inclination, tendency **2** : incline, slope

inclinado, -da *adj* **1** : sloping **2** : inclined, apt

inclinar *vt* : to tilt, to lean, to incline <inclinar la cabeza : to bow one's head> — **inclinarse** *vr* **1** : to lean, to lean over **2 ~ a** : to be inclined to

incluir {41} *vt* : to include

inclusión *nf, pl* **-siones** : inclusion

inclusive *adv* : inclusively, up to and including

inclusivo, -va *adj* : inclusive

incluso *adv* **1** AUN : even, in fact <es importante e incluso crucial : it is important and even crucial> **2** : inclusively

incógnita *nf* **1** : unknown quantity (in mathematics) **2** : mystery

incógnito, -ta *adj* **1** : unknown **2 de incógnito** : incognito

incoherencia *nf* : incoherence

incoherente *adj* : incoherent — **incoherentemente** *adv*

incoloro, -ra *adj* : colorless

incombustible *adj* : fireproof

incomible *adj* : inedible

incomodar *vt* **1** : to make uncomfortable **2** : to inconvenience — **incomodarse** *vr* : to put oneself out, to take the trouble

incomodidad *nf* **1** : discomfort, awkwardness **2** MOLESTIA : inconvenience, bother

incómodo, -da *adj* **1** : uncomfortable, awkward **2** INCONVENIENTE : inconvenient

incomparable *adj* : incomparable

incompatibilidad *nf* : incompatibility

incompatible *adj* : incompatible, uncongenial

incompetencia *nf* : incompetence

incompetente *adj & nmf* : incompetent

incompleto, -ta *adj* : incomplete

incomprendido, -da *adj* : misunderstood

incomprensible *adj* : incomprehensible

incomprensión *nf, pl* **-siones** : lack of understanding, incomprehension

incomunicación *nf, pl* **-ciones** : lack of communication

incomunicado, -da *adj* **1** : cut off, isolated **2** : in solitary confinement

inconcebible *adj* : inconceivable, unthinkable — **inconcebiblemente** *adv*

inconcluso, -sa *adj* INACABADO : unfinished

incondicional *adj* : unconditional — **incondicionalmente** *adv*

inconexo, -xa *adj* : unconnected, disconnected

inconfesable *adj* : unspeakable, shameful

inconforme *adj & nmf* : nonconformist

inconformidad *nf* : nonconformity

inconformista *adj & nmf* : nonconformist

inconfundible *adj* : unmistakable, obvious — **inconfundiblemente** *adv*

incongruencia *nf* : incongruity

incongruente *adj* : incongruous

inconmensurable *adj* : vast, immeasurable

inconquistable *adj* : unyielding

inconsciencia *nf* **1** : unconsciousness, unawareness **2** : irresponsibility

inconsciente[1] *adj* **1** : unconscious, unaware **2** : reckless, needless — **inconscientemente** *adv*

inconsciente[2] *n* **el inconsciente** : the unconscious

inconsecuente *adj* : inconsistent — **inconsecuencia** *nf*

inconsiderado, -da *adj* : inconsiderate, thoughtless

inconsistencia *nf* : inconsistency

inconsistente *adj* **1** : weak, flimsy **2** : watery, runny (of a sauce, etc.) **3** : inconsistent, weak (of an argument)

inconsolable *adj* : inconsolable — **inconsolablemente** *adv*

inconstancia *nf* : inconstancy

inconstante *adj* : inconstant, fickle, changeable

inconstitucional *adj* : unconstitutional

inconstitucionalidad *nf* : unconstitutionality

incontable *adj* INNUMERABLE : countless, innumerable

incontenible *adj* : uncontrollable, unstoppable

incontestable *adj* INCUESTIONABLE, INDISCUTIBLE : irrefutable, indisputable

incontinencia *nf* : incontinence — **incontinente** *adj*

incontrolable *adj* : uncontrollable

incontrolado, -da *adj* : uncontrolled, out of control

incontrovertible *adj* : indisputable

inconveniencia *nf* **1** : inconvenience, trouble **2** : unsuitability, inappropriateness **3** : tactless remark

inconveniente[1] *adj* **1** INCÓMODO : inconvenient **2** INAPROPIADO : improper, unsuitable

inconveniente[2] *nm* : obstacle, problem, snag <no tengo inconveniente en hacerlo : I don't mind doing it>

incorporación *nf, pl* **-ciones** : incorporation

incorporar *vt* **1** : to incorporate **2** : to add, to include — **incorporarse** *vr* **1** : to sit up **2 ~ a** : to join

incorpóreo, -rea *adj* : incorporeal, bodiless

incorrección *n, pl* **-ciones** : impropriety, improper word or action

incorrecto, -ta *adj* : incorrect — **incorrectamente** *adv*

incorregible *adj* : incorrigible — **incorregibilidad** *nf*

incorruptible *adj* : incorruptible

incredulidad *nf* : incredulity, skepticism

incrédulo[1], **-la** *adj* : incredulous, skeptical

incrédulo[2], **-la** *n* : skeptic

increíble *adj* : incredible, unbelievable — **increíblemente** *adv*

incrementar *vt* : to increase — **incrementarse** *vr*

incremento *nm* AUMENTO : increase

incriminar *vt* : to incriminate — **incriminación** *nf*

incruento, -ta *adj* : bloodless

incrustación *nf, pl* **-ciones** : inlay

incrustar *vt* **1** : to embed **2** : to inlay — **incrustarse** *vr* : to become embedded

incubación *nf, pl* **-ciones** : incubation

incubadora *nf* : incubator

incubar *v* : to incubate

incuestionable *adj* INCONTESTABLE, INDISCUTIBLE : unquestionable, indisputable — **incuestionablemente** *adv*

inculcar {72} *vt* : to inculcate, to instill

inculpar *vt* ACUSAR : to accuse, to charge

inculto, -ta *adj* **1** : uncultured, ignorant **2** : uncultivated, fallow

incumbencia *nf* : obligation, responsibility

incumbir *vi* (*3rd person only*) **~ a** : to be incumbent upon, to be of concern to <a mí no me incumbe : it's not my concern>

incumplido, -da *adj* : irresponsible, unreliable

incumplimiento *nm* **1** : nonfulfillment, neglect **2 incumplimiento de contrato** : breach of contract

incumplir *vt* : to fail to carry out, to break (a promise, a contract)

incurable *adj* : incurable

incurrir *vi* **1 ~ en** : to incur <incurrir en gastos : to incur expenses> **2 ~ en** : to fall into, to commit <incurrió en un error : he made a mistake>

incursión *nf, pl* **-siones** : incursion, raid

incursionar *vi* **1** : to raid **2 ~ en** : to go into, to enter <el actor incursionó en el baile : the actor worked in dance for a while>

indagación *nf, pl* **-ciones** : investigation, inquiry

indagar {52} *vt* : to inquire into, to investigate

indebido, -da *adj* : improper, undue — **indebidamente** *adv*

indecencia *nf* : indecency, obscenity

indecente *adj* : indecent, obscene

indecible *adj* : indescribable, inexpressible

indecisión *nf, pl* **-siones** : indecision

indeciso, -sa *adj* **1** IRRESOLUTO : indecisive **2** : undecided

indeclinable *adj* : unavoidable

indecoro *nm* : impropriety, indecorousness

indecoroso, -sa *adj* : indecorous, unseemly

indefectible *adj* : unfailing, sure

indefendible *adj* : indefensible

indefenso, -sa *adj* : defenseless, helpless

indefinido, -da *adj* **1** : undefined, vague **2** INDETERMINADO : indefinite — **indefinidamente** *adv*

indeleble *adj* : indelible — **indeleblemente** *adv*

indelicado, -da *adj* : indelicate, tactless

indemnización *nf, pl* **-ciones 1** : indemnity **2 indemnización por despido** : severance pay

indemnizar {21} *vt* : to indemnify, to compensate

independencia *nf* : independence

independiente *adj* : independent — **independientemente** *adv*

independizarse {21} *vr* : to become independent, to gain independence

indescifrable *adj* : indecipherable

indescriptible *adj* : indescribable — **indescriptiblemente** *adv*

indeseable *adj & nmf* : undesirable

indestructible *adj* : indestructible

indeterminación *nf, pl* **-ciones** : indeterminacy

indeterminado, -da *adj* **1** INDEFINIDO : indefinite **2** : indeterminate

indexar *vt* INDICIAR : to index (wages, prices, etc.)

indicación *nf, pl* **-ciones 1** : sign, signal **2** : direction, instruction **3** : suggestion, hint

indicado, -da *adj* **1** APROPIADO : appropriate, suitable **2** : specified, indicated <al día indicado : on the specified day>

indicador *nm* **1** : gauge, dial, meter **2** : indicator <indicadores económicos : economic indicators>

indicar {72} *vt* **1** SEÑALAR : to indicate **2** ENSEÑAR, MOSTRAR : to show

indicativo[1], -va *adj* : indicative

indicativo[2] *nm* : indicative (mood)

índice *nm* **1** : index **2** : index finger, forefinger **3** INDICIO : indication

indiciar *vt* : to index (prices, wages, etc.)

indicio *nm* : indication, sign

indiferencia *nf* : indifference

indiferente *adj* **1** : indifferent, unconcerned **2 ser indiferente** : to be of no concern <me es indiferente : it doesn't matter to me>

indígena[1] *adj* : indigenous, native

indígena[2] *nmf* : native

indigencia *nf* MISERIA : poverty, destitution

indigente *adj & nmf* : indigent

indigestarse *vr* **1** EMPACHARSE : to have indigestion **2** *fam* : to nauseate, to disgust <ese tipo se me indigesta : that guy makes me sick>

indigestión *nf, pl* **-tiones** EMPACHO : indigestion

indigesto, -ta *adj* : indigestible, difficult to digest

indignación *nf, pl* **-ciones** : indignation

indignado, -da *adj* : indignant

indignante *adj* : outrageous, infuriating

indignar *vt* : to outrage, to infuriate — **indignarse** *vr*

indignidad *nf* : indignity

indigno, -na *adj* : unworthy

indio[1], -dia *adj* **1** : American Indian, Indian, Amerindian **2** : Indian (from India)

indio[2], -dia *n* **1** : American Indian **2** : Indian (from India)

indirecta *nf* **1** : hint, innuendo **2 echar indirectas** *or* **lanzar indirectas** : to drop a hint, to insinuate

indirecto, -ta *adj* : indirect — **indirectamente** *adv*

indisciplina *nf* : indiscipline, unruliness

indisciplinado, -da *adj* : undisciplined, unruly

indiscreción *nf, pl* **-ciones 1** IMPRUDENCIA : indiscretion **2** : tactless remark

indiscreto, -ta *adj* IMPRUDENTE : indiscreet, imprudent — **indiscretamente** *adv*

indiscriminado, -da *adj* : indiscriminate — **indiscriminadamente** *adv*

indiscutible *adj* INCONTESTABLE, INCUESTIONABLE : indisputable, unquestionable — **indiscutiblemente** *adv*

indispensable *adj* : indispensable — **indispensablemente** *adv*

indisponer {60} *vt* **1** : to spoil, to upset **2** : to make ill — **indisponerse** *vr* **1** : to become ill **2 ~ con** : to fall out with

indisposición *nf, pl* **-ciones** : indisposition, illness

indispuesto, -ta *adj* : unwell, indisposed

indistinguible *adj* : indistinguishable

indistintamente *adv* **1** : indistinctly **2** : indiscriminately

indistinto, -ta *adj* : indistinct, vague, faint

individual *adj* : individual — **individualmente** *adv*

individualidad *nf* : individuality

individualismo *nm* : individualism

individualista[1] *adj* : individualistic

individualista[2] *nmf* : individualist

individualizar {21} *vt* : to individualize

individuo *nm* : individual, person

indivisible *adj* : indivisible — **indivisibilidad** *nf*

indocumentado, -da *n* : illegal immigrant

índole *nf* **1** : nature, character **2** CLASE, TIPO : sort, kind

indolencia *nf* : indolence, laziness

indolente *adj* : indolent, lazy

indoloro, -ra *adj* : painless

indomable *adj* **1** : indomitable **2** : unruly, unmanageable

indómito, -ta *adj* : indomitable

indonesio, -sia *adj & n* : Indonesian

inducción *nf, pl* **-ciones** : induction

inducir {61} *vt* **1** : to induce, to cause **2** : to infer, to deduce

inductivo, -va *adj* : inductive

indudable *adj* : unquestionable, beyond doubt

indudablemente *adv* : undoubtedly, unquestionably

indulgencia *nf* **1** : indulgence, leniency **2** : indulgence (in religion)

indulgente *adj* : indulgent, lenient

indultar *vt* : to pardon, to reprieve

indulto *nm* : pardon, reprieve

indumentaria *nf* : clothing, attire

industria *nf* : industry

industrial[1] *adj* : industrial

industrial[2] *nmf* : industrialist, manufacturer
industrialización *nf, pl* **-ciones** : industrialization
industrializar {21} *vt* : to industrialize
industrioso, -sa *adj* : industrious
inédito, -ta *adj* **1** : unpublished **2** : unprecedented
inefable *adj* : ineffable
ineficacia *nf* **1** : inefficiency **2** : ineffectiveness
ineficaz *adj, pl* **-caces 1** : inefficient **2** : ineffective — **ineficazmente** *adv*
ineficiencia *nf* : inefficiency
ineficiente *adj* : inefficient — **ineficientemente** *adv*
inelegancia *nf* : inelegance — **inelegante** *adj*
inelegible *adj* : ineligible — **inelegibilidad** *nf*
ineludible *adj* : inescapable, unavoidable — **ineludiblemente** *adv*
ineptitud *nf* : ineptitude, incompetence
inepto, -ta *adj* : inept, incompetent
inequidad *nf* : inequity
inequitativo, -va *adj* : inequitable
inequívoco, -ca *adj* : unequivocal, unmistakable — **inequívocamente** *adv*
inercia *nf* **1** : inertia **2** : apathy, passivity **3 por ~** : out of habit
inerme *adj* : unarmed, defenseless
inerte *adj* : inert
inescrupuloso, -sa *adj* : unscrupulous
inescrutable *adj* : inscrutable
inesperado, -da *adj* : unexpected — **inesperadamente** *adv*
inestabilidad *nf* : instability, unsteadiness
inestable *adj* : unstable, unsteady
inestimable *adj* : inestimable, invaluable
inevitabilidad *nf* : inevitability
inevitable *adj* : inevitable, unavoidable — **inevitablemente** *adv*
inexactitud *nf* : inaccuracy
inexacto, -ta *adj* : inexact, inaccurate
inexcusable *adj* : inexcusable, unforgivable
inexistencia *nf* : lack, nonexistence
inexistente *adj* : nonexistent
inexorable *adj* : inexorable — **inexorablemente** *adv*
inexperiencia *nf* : inexperience
inexperto, -ta *adj* : inexperienced, unskilled
inexplicable *adj* : inexplicable — **inexplicablemente** *adv*
inexplorado, -da *adj* : unexplored
inexpresable *adj* : inexpressible
inexpresivo, -va *adj* : inexpressive, expressionless
inextinguible *adj* **1** : inextinguishable **2** : unquenchable
inextricable *adj* : inextricable — **inextricablemente** *adv*
infalible *adj* : infallible — **infaliblemente** *adv*
infame *adj* **1** : infamous **2** : loathsome, vile <tiempo infame : terrible weather>
infamia *nf* : infamy, disgrace
infancia *nf* **1** NIÑEZ : infancy, childhood **2** : children *pl* **3** : beginnings *pl*
infante *nm* **1** : infante, prince **2** : infantryman
infantería *nf* : infantry
infantil *adj* **1** : childish, infantile **2** : child's, children's
infarto *nm* : heart attack
infatigable *adj* : indefatigable, tireless — **infatigablemente** *adv*
infección *nf, pl* **-ciones** : infection
infeccioso, -sa *adj* : infectious
infectar *vt* : to infect — **infectarse** *vr*
infecto, -ta *adj* **1** : infected **2** : repulsive, sickening
infecundidad *nf* : infertility
infecundo, -da *adj* : infertile, barren
infelicidad *nf* : unhappiness
infeliz[1] *adj, pl* **-lices 1** : unhappy **2** : hapless, unfortunate, wretched
infeliz[2] *nmf, pl* **-lices** : wretch
inferior[1] *adj* : inferior, lower
inferior[2] *nmf* : inferior, underling
inferioridad *nf* : inferiority
inferir {76} *vt* **1** DEDUCIR : to infer, to deduce **2** : to cause (harm or injury), to inflict
infernal *adj* : infernal, hellish
infestación *n, pl* **-ciones** : infestation
infestar *vt* **1** : to infest **2** : to overrun, to invade
infición *nf, pl* **-ciones** *Mex* : pollution
infidelidad *nf* : unfaithfulness, infidelity
infiel[1] *adj* : unfaithful, disloyal
infiel[2] *nmf* : infidel, heathen
infierno *nm* **1** : hell **2 el quinto infierno** : the middle of nowhere
infiltrar *vt* : to infiltrate — **infiltrarse** *vr* — **infiltración** *nf*
infinidad *nf* **1** : infinity **2** SINFÍN : great number, huge quantity <una infinidad de veces : countless times>
infinitesimal *adj* : infinitesimal
infinitivo *nm* : infinitive
infinito[1] *adv* : infinitely, vastly
infinito[2]**, -ta** *adj* **1** : infinite **2** : limitless, endless **3 hasta lo infinito** : ad infinitum — **infinitamente** *adv*
infinito[3] *nm* : infinity
inflable *adj* : inflatable
inflación *nf, pl* **-ciones** : inflation
inflacionario, -ria *adj* : inflationary
inflamable *adj* : flammable
inflamación *nf, pl* **-ciones** : inflammation
inflamar *vt* : to inflame
inflamatorio, -ria *adj* : inflammatory
inflar *vt* HINCHAR : to inflate — **inflarse** *vr* **1** : to swell **2** : to become conceited
inflexibilidad *nf* : inflexibility
inflexible *adj* : inflexible, unyielding
inflexión *nf, pl* **-xiones** : inflection
infligir {35} *vt* : to inflict
influencia *nf* INFLUJO : influence

influenciable *adj* : easily influenced, suggestible
influenciar *vt* : to influence
influenza *nf* : influenza
influir {41} *vt* : to influence — *vi* ~ **en** *or* ~ **sobre** : to have an influence on, to affect
influjo *nm* INFLUENCIA : influence
influyente *adj* : influential
información *nf, pl* **-ciones 1** : information **2** INFORME : report, inquiry **3** NOTICIAS : news
informado, -da *adj* : informed <bien informado : well-informed>
informador, -dora *n* : informer, informant
informal *adj* **1** : unreliable (of persons) **2** : informal, casual — **informalmente** *adv*
informalidad *nf* : informality
informante *nmf* : informant
informar *vt* ENTERAR : to inform — *vi* : to report — **informarse** *vr* ENTERARSE : to get information, to find out
informática *nf* : computer science, computing
informativo[1], **-va** *adj* : informative
informativo[2] *nm* : news program, news
informatización *nf, pl* **-ciones** : computerization
informatizar {21} *vt* : to computerize
informe[1] *adj* AMORFO : shapeless, formless
informe[2] *nm* **1** : report **2** : reference (for employment) **3** INFORMES *nmpl* : information, data
infortunado, -da *adj* : unfortunate, unlucky
infortunio *nm* **1** DESGRACIA : misfortune **2** CONTRATIEMPO : mishap
infracción *nf, pl* **-ciones** : violation, offense, infraction
infractor, -tora *n* : offender
infraestructura *nf* : infrastructure
infrahumano, -na *adj* : subhuman
infranqueable *adj* **1** : impassable **2** : insurmountable
infrarrojo, -ja *adj* : infrared
infrecuente *adj* : infrequent
infringir {35} *vt* : to infringe, to breach
infructuoso, -sa *adj* : fruitless — **infructuosamente** *adv*
ínfulas *nfpl* **1** : conceit **2 darse ínfulas** : to put on airs
infundado, -da *adj* : unfounded, baseless
infundio *nm* : false story, lie, tall tale <todo eso son infundios : that's a pack of lies>
infundir *vt* **1** : to instill **2 infundir ánimo a** : to encourage **3 infundir miedo a** : to intimidate
infusión *nf, pl* **-siones** : infusion
ingeniar *vt* : to devise, to think up — **ingeniarse** *vr* : to manage, to find a way
ingeniería *nf* : engineering
ingeniero, -ra *n* : engineer
ingenio *nm* **1** : ingenuity **2** CHISPA : wit, wits **3** : device, apparatus **4 ingenio azucarero** : sugar refinery
ingenioso, -sa *adj* **1** : ingenious **2** : clever, witty — **ingeniosamente** *adv*
ingente *adj* : huge, enormous
ingenuidad *nf* : naïveté, ingenuousness
ingenuo[1], **-nua** *adj* CÁNDIDO : naive — **ingenuamente** *adv*
ingenuo[2], **-nua** *n* : naive person
ingerencia → **injerencia**
ingerir {76} *vt* : to ingest, to consume
ingestión *nf, pl* **-tiones** : ingestion
ingle *nf* : groin
inglés[1], **-glesa** *adj, mpl* **ingleses** : English
inglés[2], **-glesa** *n, mpl* **ingleses** : Englishman *m,* Englishwoman *f*
inglés[3] *nm* : English (language)
inglete *nm* : miter joint
ingobernable *adj* : ungovernable, lawless
ingratitud *nf* : ingratitude
ingrato[1], **-ta** *adj* **1** : ungrateful **2** : thankless
ingrato[2], **-ta** *n* : ingrate
ingrediente *nm* : ingredient
ingresar *vt* **1** : to admit <ingresaron a Luis al hospital : Luis was admitted into the hospital> **2** : to deposit — *vi* **1** : to enter, to go in **2** ~ **en** : to join, to enroll in
ingreso *nm* **1** : entrance, entry **2** : admission **3 ingresos** *nmpl* : income, earnings *pl*
íngrimo, -ma *adj* : all alone, all by oneself
inhábil *adj* : unskillful, clumsy
inhabilidad *nf* **1** : unskillfulness **2** : unfitness
inhabilitar *vt* **1** : to disqualify, to bar **2** : to disable
inhabitable *adj* : uninhabitable
inhabituado, -da *adj* ~ **a** : unaccustomed to
inhalante *nm* : inhalant
inhalar *vt* : to inhale — **inhalación** *nf*
inherente *adj* : inherent
inhibición *nf, pl* **-ciones** COHIBICIÓN : inhibition
inhibir *vt* : to inhibit — **inhibirse** *vr*
inhóspito, -ta *adj* : inhospitable
inhumación *nf, pl* **-ciones** : interment, burial
inhumanidad *nf* : inhumanity
inhumano, -na *adj* : inhuman, cruel, inhumane
inhumar *vt* : to inter, to bury
iniciación *nf, pl* **-ciones 1** : initiation **2** : introduction
iniciado, -da *n* : initiate
iniciador[1], **-dora** *adj* : initiatory
iniciador[2], **-dora** *n* : initiator, originator
inicial[1] *adj* : initial, original — **inicialmente** *adv*
inicial[2] *nf* : initial (letter)

iniciar *vt* COMENZAR : to initiate, to begin — **iniciarse** *vr*
iniciativa *nf* : initiative
inicio *nm* COMIENZO : beginning
inicuo, -cua *adj* : iniquitous, wicked
inigualado, -da *adj* : unequaled
inimaginable *adj* : unimaginable
inimitable *adj* : inimitable
ininteligible *adj* : unintelligible
ininterrumpido, -da *adj* : uninterrupted, continuous — **ininterrumpidamente** *adv*
iniquidad *nf* : iniquity, wickedness
injerencia *nf* : interference
injerirse {76} *vr* ENTROMETERSE, INMISCUIRSE : to meddle, to interfere
injertar *vt* : to graft
injerto *nm* : graft <injerto de piel : skin graft>
injuria *nf* AGRAVIO : affront, insult
injuriar *vt* INSULTAR : to insult, to revile
injurioso, -sa *adj* : insulting, abusive
injusticia *nf* : injustice, unfairness
injustificable *adj* : unjustifiable
injustificadamente *adv* : unjustifiably, unfairly
injustificado, -da *adj* : unjustified, unwarranted
injusto, -ta *adj* : unfair, unjust — **injustamente** *adv*
inmaculado, -da *adj* : immaculate, spotless
inmadurez *nf, pl* **-reces** : immaturity
inmaduro, -ra *adj* **1** : immature **2** : unripe
inmediaciones *nfpl* : environs, surrounding area
inmediatamente *adv* ENSEGUIDA : immediately
inmediatez *nf, pl* **-teces** : immediacy
inmediato, -ta *adj* **1** : immediate **2** CONTIGUO : adjoining **3 de ∼** : immediately, right away **4 ∼ a** : next to, close to
inmejorable *adj* : excellent, unbeatable
inmensidad *nf* : immensity, vastness
inmenso, -sa *adj* ENORME : immense, huge, vast — **inmensamente** *adv*
inmensurable *adj* : boundless, immeasurable
inmerecido, -da *adj* : undeserved — **inmerecidamente** *adv*
inmersión *nf, pl* **-siones** : immersion
inmerso, -sa *adj* **1** : immersed **2** : involved, absorbed
inmigración *nf, pl* **-ciones** : immigration
inmigrado, -da *adj & n* : immigrant
inmigrante *adj & nmf* : immigrant
inmigrar *vi* : to immigrate
inminencia *nf* : imminence
inminente *adj* : imminent — **inminentemente** *adv*
inmiscuirse {41} *vr* ENTROMETERSE, INJERIRSE : to meddle, to interfere
inmobiliario, -ria *adj* : real estate, property
inmoderación *n, pl* **-ciones** : immoderation, intemperance
inmoderado, -da *adj* : immoderate, excessive — **inmoderamente** *adv*
inmodestia *nf* : immodesty — **inmodesto, -ta** *adj*
inmolar *vt* : to immolate — **inmolación** *nf*
inmoral *adj* : immoral
inmoralidad *nf* : immorality
inmortal *adj & nmf* : immortal
inmortalidad *nf* : immortality
inmortalizar {21} *vt* : to immortalize
inmotivado, -da *adj* **1** : unmotivated **2** : groundless
inmovible *adj* : immovable, fixed
inmóvil *adj* **1** : still, motionless **2** : steadfast
inmovilidad *nf* : immobility
inmovilizar {21} *vt* : to immobilize
inmueble *nm* : building, property
inmundicia *nf* : dirt, filth, trash
inmundo, -da *adj* : dirty, filthy, nasty
inmune *adj* : immune
inmunidad *nf* : immunity
inmunizar {21} *vt* : to immunize — **inmunización** *nf*
inmunología *nf* : immunology
inmunológico, -ca *adj* : immune <sistema inmunológico : immune system>
inmutabilidad *nf* : immutability
inmutable *adj* : immutable, unchangeable
innato, -ta *adj* : innate, inborn
innecesario, -ria *adj* : unnecessary — **innecesariamente** *adv*
innegable *adj* : undeniable
innoble *adj* : ignoble — **innoblemente** *adv*
innovación *nf, pl* **-ciones** : innovation
innovador, -dora *adj* : innovative
innovar *vt* : to introduce — *vi* : to innovate
innumerable *adj* INCONTABLE : innumerable, countless
inobjetable *adj* : indisputable, unobjectionable
inocencia *nf* : innocence
inocente[1] *adj* **1** : innocent **2** INGENUO : naive — **inocentemente** *adv*
inocente[2] *nmf* : innocent person
inocentón[1], **-tona** *adj, mpl* **-tones** : naive, gullible
inocentón[2], **-tona** *n, mpl* **-tones** : simpleton, dupe
inocuidad *nf* : harmlessness
inocular *vt* : to inoculate, to vaccinate — **inoculación** *nf*
inocuo, -cua *adj* : innocuous, harmless
inodoro[1], **-ra** *adj* : odorless
inodoro[2] *nm* : toilet
inofensivo, -va *adj* : inoffensive, harmless
inolvidable *adj* : unforgettable
inoperable *adj* : inoperable
inoperante *adj* : ineffective, inoperative

inopinado, -da *adj* : unexpected — **inopinadamente** *adv*
inoportuno, -na *adj* : untimely, inopportune, inappropriate
inorgánico, -ca *adj* : inorganic
inoxidable *adj* **1** : rustproof **2 acero inoxidable** : stainless steel
inquebrantable *adj* : unshakable, unwavering
inquietante *adj* : disturbing, worrisome
inquietar *vt* PREOCUPAR : to disturb, to upset, to worry — **inquietarse** *vr*
inquieto, -ta *adj* **1** : anxious, uneasy, worried **2** : restless
inquietud *nf* **1** : anxiety, uneasiness, worry **2** AGITACIÓN : restlessness
inquilinato *nm* : tenancy
inquilino, -na *n* : tenant, occupant
inquina *nf* **1** : aversion, dislike **2** : ill will <tener inquina a alguien : to have a grudge against someone>
inquirir {4} *vi* : to make inquiries — *vt* : to investigate
inquisición *nf, pl* **-ciones** : investigation, inquiry
inquisidor, -dora *adj* : inquisitive
inquisitivo, -va *adj* : inquisitive, curious — **inquisitivamente** *adv*
insaciable *adj* : insatiable
insalubre *adj* **1** : unhealthy **2** ANTIHIGIÉNICO : unsanitary
insalubridad *nf* : unhealthiness
insalvable *adj* : insuperable, insurmountable
insano, -na *adj* **1** LOCO : insane, mad **2** INSALUBRE : unhealthy
insatisfacción *nf, pl* **-ciones** : dissatisfaction
insatisfactorio *nm* : unsatisfactory
insatisfecho, -cha *adj* **1** : dissatisfied **2** : unsatisfied
inscribir {33} *vt* **1** MATRICULAR : to enroll, to register **2** GRABAR : to engrave — **inscribirse** *vr* : to register, to sign up
inscripción *nf, pl* **-ciones 1** MATRÍCULA : enrollment, registration **2** : inscription
inscrito *pp* → **inscribir**
insecticida[1] *adj* : insecticidal
insecticida[2] *nm* : insecticide
insecto *nm* : insect
inseguridad *nf* **1** : insecurity **2** : lack of safety **3** : uncertainty
inseguro, -ra *adj* **1** : insecure **2** : unsafe **3** : uncertain
inseminar *vt* : to inseminate — **inseminación** *nf*
insensatez *nf, pl* **-teces** : foolishness, stupidity
insensato[1], **-ta** *adj* : foolish, senseless
insensato[2], **-ta** *n* : fool
insensibilidad *nf* : insensitivity
insensible *adj* : insensitive, unfeeling
inseparable *adj* : inseparable — **inseparablemente** *adv*
inserción *nf, pl* **-ciones** : insertion
insertar *vt* : to insert
inservible *adj* INÚTIL : useless, unusable
insidia *nf* **1** : snare, trap **2** : malice
insidioso, -sa *adj* : insidious
insigne *adj* : noted, famous
insignia *nf* ENSEÑA : insignia, emblem, badge
insignificancia *nf* **1** : insignificance **2** NIMIEDAD : trifle, triviality
insignificante *adj* : insignificant
insincero, -ra *adj* : insincere — **insinceridad** *nf*
insinuación *nf, pl* **-ciones** : insinuation, hint
insinuante *adj* : suggestive
insinuar {3} *vt* : to insinuate, to hint at — **insinuarse** *vr* **1 ~ a** : to make advances to **2 ~ en** : to worm one's way into
insipidez *nf, pl* **-deces** : insipidness, blandness
insípido, -da *adj* : insipid, bland
insistencia *nf* : insistence
insistente *adj* : insistent — **insistentemente** *adv*
insistir *v* : to insist
insociable *adj* : unsociable
insolación *nf, pl* **-ciones** : sunstroke
insolencia *nf* IMPERTINENCIA : insolence
insolente *adj* IMPERTINENTE : insolent
insólito, -ta *adj* : rare, unusual
insoluble *adj* : insoluble — **insolubilidad** *nf*
insolvencia *nf* : insolvency, bankruptcy
insolvente *adj* : insolvent, bankrupt
insomne *adj & nmf* : insomniac
insomnio *nm* : insomnia
insondable *adj* : fathomless, deep
insonorizado, -da *adj* : soundproof
insoportable *adj* INAGUANTABLE : unbearable, intolerable
insoslayable *adj* : unavoidable, inescapable
insospechado, -da *adj* : unexpected, unforeseen
insostenible *adj* : untenable
inspección *nf, pl* **-ciones** : inspection
inspeccionar *vt* : to inspect
inspector, -tora *n* : inspector
inspiración *nf, pl* **-ciones 1** : inspiration **2** INHALACIÓN : inhalation
inspirador, -dora *adj* : inspiring
inspirar *vt* : to inspire — *vi* INHALAR : to inhale
instalación *nf, pl* **-ciones** : installation
instalar *vt* **1** : to install **2** : to instate — **instalarse** *vr* ESTABLECERSE : to settle, to establish oneself
instancia *nf* **1** : petition, request **2 en última instancia** : as a last resort
instantánea *nf* : snapshot
instantáneo, -nea *adj* : instantaneous — **instantáneamente** *adv*
instante *nm* **1** : instant, moment **2 al instante** : immediately **3 a cada instante** : frequently, all the time **4 por instantes** : constantly, incessantly

instar *vt* APREMIAR **:** to urge, to press — *vi* URGIR **:** to be urgent or pressing <insta que vayamos pronto : it is imperative that we leave soon>
instauración *nf, pl* **-ciones :** establishment
instaurar *vt* **:** to establish
instigador, -dora *n* **:** instigator
instigar {52} *vt* **:** to instigate, to incite
instintivo, -va *adj* **:** instinctive — **instintivamente** *adv*
instinto *nm* **:** instinct
institución *nf, pl* **-ciones :** institution
institucional *adj* **:** institutional — **institucionalmente** *adv*
institucionalización *nf, pl* **-ciones :** institutionalization
institucionalizar {21} *vt* **:** to institutionalize
instituir {41} *vt* ESTABLECER, FUNDAR **:** to institute, to establish, to found
instituto *nm* **:** institute
institutriz *nf, pl* **-trices :** governess *f*
instrucción *nf, pl* **-ciones 1** EDUCACIÓN **:** education **2 instrucciones** *nfpl* **:** instructions, directions
instructivo, -va *adj* **:** instructive, educational
instructor, -tora *n* **:** instructor
instruir {41} *vt* **1** ADIESTRAR **:** to instruct, to train **2** ENSEÑAR **:** to educate, to teach
instrumentación *nf, pl* **-ciones :** orchestration
instrumental *adj* **:** instrumental
instrumentar *vt* **:** to orchestrate
instrumentista *nmf* **:** instrumentalist
instrumento *nm* **:** instrument
insubordinado, -da *adj* **:** insubordinate — **insubordinación** *nf*
insubordinarse *vr* **:** to rebel
insuficiencia *nf* **1 :** insufficiency, inadequacy **2 insuficiencia cardíaca :** heart failure
insuficiente *adj* **:** insufficient, inadequate — **insuficientemente** *adv*
insufrible *adj* **:** insufferable
insular *adj* **:** insular
insulina *nf* **:** insulin
insulso, -sa *adj* **1** INSÍPIDO **:** insipid, bland **2 :** dull
insultante *adj* **:** insulting
insultar *vt* **:** to insult
insulto *nm* **:** insult
insumos *nmpl* **:** supplies <insumos agrícolas : agricultural supplies>
insuperable *adj* **:** insuperable, insurmountable
insurgente *adj & nmf* **:** insurgent — **insurgencia** *nf*
insurrección *nf, pl* **-ciones :** insurrection, uprising
insustancial *adj* **:** insubstantial, flimsy
insustituible *adj* **:** irreplaceable
intachable *adj* **:** irreproachable, faultless
intacto, -ta *adj* **:** intact
intangible *adj* IMPALPABLE **:** intangible, impalpable
integración *nf, pl* **-ciones :** integration
integral *adj* **1 :** integral, essential **2 pan integral :** whole grain bread
integrante[1] *adj* **:** integrating, integral
integrante[2] *nmf* **:** member
integrar *vt* **:** to make up, to compose — **integrarse** *vr* **:** to integrate, to fit in
integridad *nf* **1** RECTITUD **:** integrity, honesty **2 :** wholeness, completeness
integrismo *nm* **:** fundamentalism
integrista *adj & nmf* **:** fundamentalist
íntegro, -gra *adj* **1 :** honest, upright **2** ENTERO **:** whole, complete **3 :** unabridged
intelecto *nm* **:** intellect
intelectual *adj & nmf* **:** intellectual — **intelectualmente** *adv*
intelectualidad *nf* **:** intelligentsia
inteligencia *nf* **:** intelligence
inteligente *adj* **:** intelligent — **inteligentemente** *adv*
inteligible *adj* **:** intelligible — **inteligibilidad** *nf*
intemperancia *adj* **:** intemperance, excess
intemperie *nf* **1 :** bad weather, elements *pl* **2 a la intemperie :** in the open air, outside
intempestivo, -va *adj* **:** inopportune, untimely — **intempestivamente** *adv*
intención *nf, pl* **-ciones :** intention, plan
intencional *adj* **:** intentional — **intencionalmente** *adv*
intendencia *nf* **:** management, administration
intendente *nmf* **:** quartermaster
intensidad *nf* **:** intensity
intensificar {72} *vt* **:** to intensify — **intensificarse** *vr*
intensivo, -va *adj* **:** intensive — **intensivamente** *adv*
intenso, -sa *adj* **:** intense — **intensamente** *adv*
intentar *vt* **:** to attempt, to try
intento *nm* **1** PROPÓSITO **:** intent, intention **2** TENTATIVA **:** attempt, try
interacción *nf, pl* **-ciones :** interaction
interactivo, -va *adj* **:** interactive
interactuar {3} *vi* **:** to interact
intercalar *vt* **:** to intersperse, to insert
intercambiable *adj* **:** interchangeable
intercambiar *vt* CANJEAR **:** to exchange, to trade
intercambio *nm* CANJE **:** exchange, trade
interceder *vi* **:** to intercede
intercepción *nf, pl* **-ciones :** interception
interceptar *vt* **1 :** to intercept, to block **2 interceptar las líneas :** to wiretap
intercesión *nf, pl* **-siones :** intercession
intercomunicación *nf, pl* **-ciones :** intercommunication
interconexión *nf, pl* **-xiones :** interconnection
interconfesional *adj* **:** interdenominational

interdependencia *nf* **:** interdependence — **interdependiente** *adj*
interdicción *nf, pl* **-ciones :** interdiction, prohibition
interés *nm, pl* **-reses :** interest
interesado, -da *adj* **1 :** interested **2 :** selfish, self-seeking
interesante *adj* **:** interesting
interesar *vt* **:** to interest — *vi* **:** to be of interest, to be interesting — **interesarse** *vr*
interestatal *adj* **:** interstate <autopista interestatal : interstate highway>
interestelar *adj* **:** interstellar
interfaz *nf, pl* **-faces :** interface
interferencia *nf* **:** interference, static
interferir {76} *vi* **:** to interfere, to meddle — *vt* **:** to interfere with, to obstruct
interín¹ *or* **ínterin** *adv* **:** meanwhile
interín² *or* **ínterin** *nm, pl* **-rines :** meantime, interim <en el interín : in the meantime>
interinamente *adv* **:** temporarily
interino, -na *adj* **:** acting, temporary, interim
interior¹ *adj* **:** interior, inner
interior² *nm* **1 :** interior, inside **2 :** inland region
interiormente *adv* **:** inwardly
interjección *nf, pl* **-ciones :** interjection
interlocutor, -tora *n* **:** interlocutor, speaker
intermediario, -ria *adj & n* **:** intermediary, go-between
intermedio¹**, -dia** *adj* **:** intermediate
intermedio² *nm* **1 :** intermission **2 por intermedio de :** by means of
interminable *adj* **:** interminable, endless — **interminablemente** *adv*
intermisión *nf, pl* **-siones :** intermission, pause
intermitente¹ *adj* **1 :** intermittent **2 luz intermitente :** strobe light — **intermitentemente** *adv*
intermitente² *nm* **:** blinker, turn signal
internacional *adj* **:** international — **internacionalmente** *adv*
internacionalismo *nm* **:** internationalism
internacionalizar {21} *vt* **:** to internationalize
internado *nm* **:** boarding school
internar *vt* **:** to commit, to confine — **internarse** *vr* **1 :** to penetrate, to advance into **2 ~ en :** to go into, to enter
internista *nmf* **:** internist
interno¹**, -na** *adj* **:** internal — **internamente** *adv*
interno²**, -na** *n* **1 :** intern **2 :** inmate, internee
interpelación *nf, pl* **-ciones :** appeal, plea
interpelar *vt* **:** to question (formally)
interpolar *vt* **:** to insert, to interpolate
interponer {60} *vt* **:** to interpose — **interponerse** *vr* **:** to intervene
interpretación *nf, pl* **-ciones :** interpretation
interpretar *vt* **1 :** to interpret **2 :** to play, to perform
interpretativo, -va *adj* **:** interpretive
intérprete *nmf* **1** TRADUCTOR **:** interpreter **2 :** performer
interpuesto *pp* → **interponer**
interracial *adj* **:** interracial
interrelación *nf, pl* **-ciones :** interrelationship
interrelacionar *vi* **:** to interrelate
interrogación *nf, pl* **-ciones 1 :** interrogation, questioning **2 signo de interrogación :** question mark
interrogador, -dora *n* **:** interrogator, questioner
interrogante¹ *adj* **:** questioning
interrogante² *nm* **1 :** question mark **2 :** query
interrogar {52} *vt* **:** to interrogate, to question
interrogativo, -va *adj* **:** interrogative
interrogatorio *nm* **:** interrogation, questioning
interrumpir *v* **:** to interrupt
interrupción *nf, pl* **-ciones :** interruption
interruptor *nm* **1 :** (electrical) switch **2 :** circuit breaker
intersección *nf, pl* **-ciones :** intersection
intersticio *nm* **:** interstice — **intersticial** *adj*
intervalo *nm* **:** interval
intervención *nf, pl* **-ciones 1 :** intervention **2 :** audit **3 intervención quirúrgica :** operation
intervencionista *adj & nmf* **:** interventionist
intervenir {87} *vi* **1 :** to take part **2** INTERCEDER **:** to intervene, to intercede — *vt* **1 :** to control, to supervise **2 :** to audit **3 :** to operate on **4 :** to tap (a telephone)
interventor, -tora *n* **1 :** inspector **2 :** auditor, comptroller
intestado, -da *adj* **:** intestate
intestinal *adj* **:** intestinal
intestino *nm* **:** intestine
intimar *vi* **~ con :** to become friendly with — *vt* **:** to require, to call on
intimidación *nf, pl* **-ciones :** intimidation
intimidad *nf* **1 :** intimacy **2 :** privacy, private life
intimidar *vt* ACOBARDAR **:** to intimidate
íntimo, -ma *adj* **1 :** intimate, close **2** PRIVADO **:** private — **íntimamente** *adv*
intitular *vt* **:** to entitle, to title
intocable *adj* **:** untouchable
intolerable *adj* **:** intolerable, unbearable
intolerancia *nf* **:** intolerance
intolerante¹ *adj* **:** intolerant
intolerante² *nmf* **:** intolerant person, bigot
intoxicación *nf, pl* **-ciones :** poisoning
intoxicante *nm* **:** poison

intoxicar {72} *vt* : to poison
intranquilidad *nf* PREOCUPACIÓN : worry, anxiety
intranquilizar {21} *vt* : to upset, to make uneasy — **intranquilizarse** *vr* : to get worried, to be anxious
intranquilo, -la *adj* PREOCUPADO : uneasy, worried
intransigencia *nf* : intransigence
intransigente *adj* : intransigent, unyielding
intransitable *adj* : impassable
intransitivo, -va *adj* : intransitive
intrascendente *adj* : unimportant, insignificant
intratable *adj* **1** : intractable **2** : awkward **3** : unsociable
intravenoso, -sa *adj* : intravenous
intrepidez *nf* : fearlessness
intrépido, -da *adj* : intrepid, fearless
intriga *nf* : intrigue
intrigante *nmf* : schemer
intrigar {52} *v* : to intrigue — **intrigante** *adj*
intrincado, -da *adj* : intricate, involved
intrínseco, -ca *adj* : intrinsic — **intrínsecamente** *adv*
introducción *nf, pl* **-ciones** : introduction
introducir {61} *vt* **1** : to introduce **2** : to bring in **3** : to insert **4** : to input, to enter — **introducirse** *vr* : to penetrate, to get into
introductorio, -ria *adj* : introductory
intromisión *nf, pl* **-siones** : interference, meddling
introspección *nf, pl* **-ciones** : introspection
introspectivo, -va *adj* : introspective
introvertido¹, -da *adj* : introverted
introvertido², -da *n* : introvert
intrusión *nf, pl* **-siones** : intrusion
intruso¹, -sa *adj* : intrusive
intruso², -sa *n* : intruder
intuición *nf, pl* **-ciones** : intuition
intuir {41} *vt* : to intuit, to sense
intuitivo, -va *adj* : intuitive — **intuitivamente** *adv*
inundación *nf, pl* **-ciones** : flood, inundation
inundar *vt* : to flood, to inundate
inusitado, -da *adj* : unusual, uncommon — **inusitadamente** *adv*
inusual *adj* : unusual, uncommon — **inusualmente** *adv*
inútil¹ *adj* INSERVIBLE : useless — **inútilmente** *adv*
inútil² *nmf* : good-for-nothing
inutilidad *nf* : uselessness
inutilizar {21} *vt* **1** : to make useless **2** INCAPACITAR : to disable, to put out of commission
invadir *vt* : to invade
invalidar *vt* : to nullify, to invalidate
invalidez *nf, pl* **-deces 1** : invalidity **2** : disablement
inválido, -da *adj & n* : invalid
invariable *adj* : invariable — **invariablemente** *adv*
invasión *nf, pl* **-siones** : invasion
invasivo, -va *adj* : invasive
invasor¹, -sora *adj* : invading
invasor², -sora *n* : invader
invectiva *nf* : invective, abuse
invencible *adj* **1** : invincible **2** : insurmountable
invención *nf, pl* **-ciones 1** INVENTO : invention **2** MENTIRA : fabrication, lie
inventar *vt* **1** : to invent **2** : to fabricate, to make up
inventariar {85} *vt* : to inventory
inventario *nm* : inventory
inventiva *nf* : ingenuity, inventiveness
inventivo, -va *adj* : inventive
invento *nm* INVENCIÓN : invention
inventor, -tora *n* : inventor
invernadero *nm* : greenhouse, hothouse
invernal *adj* : winter, wintry
invernar {55} *vi* **1** : to spend the winter **2** HIBERNAR : to hibernate
inverosímil *adj* : unlikely, farfetched
inversión *nf, pl* **-siones 1** : inversion **2** : investment
inversionista *nmf* : investor
inverso¹, -sa *adj* **1** : inverse, inverted **2** CONTRARIO : opposite **3 a la inversa** : on the contrary, vice versa **4 en orden inverso** : in reverse order — **inversamente** *adv*
inverso² *n* : inverse
inversor, -sora *n* : investor
invertebrado¹, -da *adj* : invertebrate
invertebrado² *nm* : invertebrate
invertir {76} *vt* **1** : to invert, to reverse **2** : to invest — *vi* : to make an investment — **invertirse** *vr* : to be reversed
investidura *nf* : investiture, inauguration
investigación *nf, pl* **-ciones 1** ENCUESTA, INDAGACIÓN : investigation, inquiry **2** : research
investigador¹, -dora *adj* : investigative
investigador², -dora *n* **1** : investigator **2** : researcher
investigar {52} *vt* **1** INDAGAR : to investigate **2** : to research — *vi* **~ sobre** : to do research into
investir {54} *vt* **1** : to empower **2** : to swear in, to inaugurate
inveterado, -da *adj* : inveterate, deep-seated
invicto, -ta *adj* : undefeated
invidente¹ *adj* CIEGO : blind, sightless
invidente² *nmf* CIEGO : blind person
invierno *nm* : winter, wintertime
inviolable *adj* : inviolable — **inviolabilidad** *nf*
inviolado, -da *adj* : inviolate, pure
invisibilidad *nf* : invisibility
invisible *adj* : invisible — **invisiblemente** *adv*
invitación *nf, pl* **-ciones** : invitation
invitado, -da *n* : guest

invitar *vt* : to invite
invocación *nf, pl* **-ciones** : invocation
invocar {72} *vt* : to invoke, to call on
involucramiento *nm* : involvement
involucrar *vt* : to implicate, to involve — **involucrarse** *vr* : to get involved
involuntario, -ria *adj* : involuntary — **involuntariamente** *adv*
invulnerable *adj* : invulnerable
inyección *nf, pl* **-ciones** : injection, shot
inyectado, -da *adj* **ojos inyectados** : bloodshot eyes
inyectar *vt* : to inject
ion *nm* : ion
ionizar {21} *vt* : to ionize — **ionización** *nf*
ionosfera *nf* : ionosphere
ir {43} *vi* **1** : to go <ir a pie : to go on foot, to walk> <ir a caballo : to ride horseback> <ir a casa : to go home> **2** : to lead, to extend, to stretch <el camino va de Cali a Bogotá : the road goes from Cali to Bogotá> **3** FUNCIONAR : to work, to function <esta computadora ya no va : this computer doesn't work anymore> **4** : to get on, to get along <¿cómo te va? : how are you?, how's it going?> <el negocio no va bien : the business isn't doing well> **5** : to suit <ese vestido te va bien : that dress really suits you> **6 ~ con** : to be <ir con prisa : to be in a hurry> **7 ~ por** : to follow, to go along <fueron por la costa : they followed the shoreline> **8 dejarse ir** : to let oneself go **9 ir a parar** : to end up **10 vamos a ver** : let's see — *v aux* **1** (*with present participle*) <ir caminando : to walk> <¡voy corriendo! : I'll be right there!> **2 ~ a** : to be going to <voy a hacerlo : I'm going to do it> <el avión va a despegar : the plane is about to take off> — **irse** *vr* **1** : to leave, to go <¡vámonos! : let's go!> <todo el mundo se fue : everyone left> **2** ESCAPARSE : to leak **3** GASTARSE : to be used up, to be gone
ira *nf* CÓLERA, FURIA : wrath, anger
iracundo, -da *adj* : irate, angry
iraní *adj & nmf* : Iranian
iraquí *adj & nmf* : Iraqi
irascible *adj* : irascible, irritable — **irascibilidad** *nf*
irga, irgue, etc. → **erguir**
iridio *nm* : iridium
iridiscencia *nf* : iridescence — **iridiscente** *adj*
iris *nms & pl* **1** : iris **2 arco iris** : rainbow
irlandés[1], **-desa** *adj, mpl* **-deses** : Irish
irlandés[2], **-desa** *n, pl* **-deses** : Irish person, Irishman *m*, Irishwoman *f*
irlandés[3] *nm* : Irish (language)
ironía *nf* : irony
irónico, -ca *adj* : ironic, ironical — **irónicamente** *adv*
irracional *adj* : irrational — **irracionalmente** *adv*
irracionalidad *nf* : irrationality
irradiar *vt* : to radiate, to irradiate
irrazonable *adj* : unreasonable
irreal *adj* : unreal
irrebatible *adj* : unanswerable, irrefutable
irreconciliable *adj* : irreconcilable
irreconocible *adj* : unrecognizable
irrecuperable *adj* : irrecoverable, irretrievable
irredimible *adj* : irredeemable
irreductible *adj* : unyielding
irreemplazable *adj* : irreplaceable
irreflexión *nf, pl* **-xiones** : thoughtlessness, impetuosity
irreflexivo, -va *adj* : rash, unthinking — **irreflexivamente** *adv*
irrefrenable *adj* : uncontrollable, unstoppable <un impulso irrefrenable : an irresistable urge>
irrefutable *adj* : irrefutable
irregular *adj* : irregular — **irregularmente** *adv*
irregularidad *nf* : irregularity
irrelevante *adj* : irrelevant — **irrelevancia** *nf*
irreligioso, -sa *adj* : irreligious
irremediable *adj* : incurable — **irremediablemente** *adv*
irreparable *adj* : irreparable
irreprimible *adj* : irrepressible
irreprochable *adj* : irreproachable
irresistible adj : irresistible — **irresistiblemente** adv
irresolución *nf, pl* **-ciones** : indecision, hesitation
irresoluto, -ta *adj* INDECISO : undecided
irrespeto *nm* : disrespect
irrespetuoso, -sa *adj* : disrespectful — **irrespetuosamente** *adv*
irresponsabilidad *nf* : irresponsibility
irresponsable *adj* : irresponsible — **irresponsablemente** *adv*
irrestricto, -ta *adj* : unrestricted, unconditional <apoyo irrestricto : unconditional support>
irreverencia *nf* : disrespect
irreverente *adj* : disrespectful
irreversible *adj* : irreversible
irrevocable *adj* : irrevocable — **irrevocablemente** *adv*
irrigar {52} *vt* : to irrigate — **irrigación** *nf*
irrisible *adj* : laughable
irrisión *nf, pl* **-siones** : derision, ridicule
irrisorio, -ria *adj* RISIBLE : ridiculous, ludicrous
irritabilidad *nf* : irritability
irritable *adj* : irritable
irritación *nf, pl* **-ciones** : irritation
irritante *adj* : irritating
irritar *vt* : to irritate — **irritación** *nf*
irrompible *adj* : unbreakable
irrumpir *vi* **~ en** : to burst into
irrupción *nf, pl* **-ciones 1** : irruption **2** : invasion
isla *nf* : island

islámico, -ca *adj* : Islamic, Muslim
islandés[1], -desa *adj, mpl* **-deses** : Icelandic
islandés[2], -desa *n, mpl* **-deses** : Icelander
islandés[3] *nm* : Icelandic (language)
isleño, -ña *n* : islander
islote *nm* : islet
isometría *nfs & pl* : isometrics
isométrico, -ca *adj* : isometric
isósceles *adj* : isosceles <triángulo isósceles : isosceles triangle>
isótopo *nm* : isotope
israelí *adj & nmf* : Israeli
istmo *nm* : isthmus
itacate *nm Mex* : pack, provisions *pl*
italiano[1], -na *adj & n* : Italian
italiano[2] *nm* : Italian (language)
iterbio *nm* : ytterbium
itinerante *adj* AMBULANTE : traveling, itinerant
itinerario *nm* : itinerary, route
itrio *nm* : yttrium
izar {21} *vt* : to hoist, to raise <izar la bandera : to raise the flag>
izquierda *nf* : left
izquierdista *adj & nmf* : leftist
izquierdo, -da *adj* : left

J

j *nf* : tenth letter of the Spanish alphabet
jabalí *nm* : wild boar
jabalina *nf* : javelin
jabón *nm, pl* **jabones** : soap
jabonar *vt* ENJABONAR : to soap up, to lather — **jabonarse** *vr*
jabonera *nf* : soap dish
jabonoso, -sa *adj* : soapy
jaca *nf* **1** : pony **2** YEGUA : mare
jacal *nm Mex* : shack, hut
jacinto *nm* : hyacinth
jactancia *nf* **1** : boastfulness **2** : boasting, bragging
jactancioso[1], -sa *adj* : boastful
jactancioso[2], -sa *n* : boaster, braggart
jactarse *vr* : to boast, to brag
jade *nm* : jade
jadear *vi* : to pant, to gasp, to puff — **jadeante** *adj*
jadeo *nm* : panting, gasping, puffing
jaez *nm, pl* **jaeces 1** : harness **2** : kind, sort, ilk **3 jaeces** *nmpl* : trappings
jaguar *nm* : jaguar
jai alai *nm* : jai alai
jaiba *nf* CANGREJO : crab
jalapeño *nm Mex* : jalapeño pepper
jalar *vt* **1** : to pull, to tug **2** *fam* : to attract, to draw in <las ideas nuevas lo jalan : new ideas appeal to him> — *vi* **1** : to pull, to pull together **2** *fam* : to hurry up, to get going **3** *Mex fam* : to be in working order <esta máquina no jala : this machine doesn't work>
jalbegue *nm* : whitewash
jalea *nf* : jelly
jalear *vt* : to encourage, to urge on
jaleo *nm fam* **1** : uproar, ruckus, racket **2** *fam* : confusion, hassle **3** : cheering and clapping (for a dance)
jalón *nm, pl* **jalones 1** : milestone, landmark **2** TIRÓN : pull, tug
jalonar *vt* : to mark, to stake out
jalonear *vt Mex, Peru fam* : to tug at — *vi* **1** *fam* : to pull, to tug **2** *CA fam* : to haggle
jamaica *nf* : hibiscus
jamaicano, -na → **jamaiquino**
jamaiquino, -na *adj & n* : Jamaican
jamás *adv* **1** NUNCA : never **2 nunca jamás** *or* **jamás de los jamases** : never ever **3 para siempre jamás** : for ever and ever
jamba *nf* : jamb
jamelgo *nm* : nag (horse)
jamón *nm, pl* **jamones** : ham
Januká *nmf* : Hanukkah
japonés, -nesa *adj & n, mpl* **-neses** : Japanese
jaque *nm* **1** : check (in chess) <jaque mate : checkmate> **2 tener en jaque** : to intimidate, to bully
jaqueca *nf* : headache, migraine
jarabe *nm* **1** : syrup **2** : Mexican folk dance
jarana *nf* **1** *fam* : revelry, partying, spree **2** *fam* : joking, fooling around **3** : small guitar
jaranear *vi fam* : to go on a spree, to party
jarcia *nf* **1** : rigging **2** : fishing tackle
jardín *nm, pl* **jardines 1** : garden **2 jardín de niños** : kindergarten **3 los jardines** *nmpl* : the outfield
jardinería *nf* : gardening
jardinero, -ra *n* **1** : gardener **2** : outfielder (in baseball)
jarra *nf* **1** : pitcher, jug **2** : stein, mug **3 de jarras** *or* **en jarras** : akimbo
jarrete *nm* **1** : back of the knee **2** : hock (of an animal)
jarro *nm* **1** : pitcher, jug **2** : mug
jarrón *nm, pl* **jarrones** FLORERO : vase
jaspe *nm* : jasper
jaspeado, -da *adj* **1** VETEADO : streaked, veined **2** : speckled, mottled
jaula *nf* : cage
jauría *nf* : pack of hounds
javanés, -nesa *adj & n* : Javanese
jazmín *nm, pl* **jazmines** : jasmine
jazz [ˈjas, ˈdʒas] *nm* : jazz
jeans [ˈjins, ˈdʒins] *nmpl* : jeans
jeep [ˈjip, ˈdʒip] *nm, pl* **jeeps** : jeep
jefatura *nf* **1** : leadership **2** : headquarters <jefatura de policía : police headquarters>
jefe, -fa *n* **1** : chief, head, leader <jefe de bomberos : fire chief> **2** : boss
Jehová *nm* : Jehovah

jején *nm, pl* **jejenes** : gnat, small mosquito

jengibre *nm* : ginger

jeque *nm* : sheikh, sheik

jerarca *nmf* : leader, chief

jerarquía *nf* **1** : hierarchy **2** RANGO : rank

jerárquico, -ca *adj* : hierarchical

jerbo *nm* : gerbil

jerez *nm, pl* **jereces** : sherry

jerga *nf* **1** : jargon, slang **2** : coarse cloth

jerigonza *nf* GALIMATÍAS : mumbo jumbo, gibberish

jeringa *nf* : syringe

jeringar {52} *vt* **1** : to inject **2** *fam* JOROBAR : to annoy, to pester — *vi fam* JOROBAR : to be annoying, to be a nuisance

jeringuear → **jeringar**

jeringuilla *nf* → **jeringa**

jeroglífico *nm* : hieroglyphic

jersey *nm, pl* **jerseys 1** : jersey (fabric) **2** *Spain* : sweater

jesuita *adj & nm* : Jesuit

Jesús *nm* : Jesus

jeta *nf* **1** : snout **2** *fam* : face, mug

jíbaro, -ra *adj* **1** : Jivaro **2** : rustic, rural

jibia *nf* : cuttlefish

jícama *nf* : jicama

jícara *nf Mex* : calabash

jilguero *nm* : European goldfinch

jinete *nmf* : horseman, horsewoman *f,* rider

jinetear *vt* **1** : to ride, to perform (on horseback) **2** DOMAR : to break in (a horse) — *vi* CABALGAR : to ride horseback

jingoísmo [ˌjiŋgoˈizmo, ˌdʒɪŋ-] *nm* : jingoism

jingoísta *adj* : jingoist, jingoistic

jiote *nm Mex* : rash

jira *nf* : outing, picnic

jirafa *nf* **1** : giraffe **2** : boom microphone

jirón *nm, pl* **jirones** : shred, rag <hecho jirones : in tatters>

jitomate *nm Mex* : tomato

jockey [ˈjɔki, ˈdʒɔ-] *nmf, pl* **jockeys** [-kis] : jockey

jocosidad *nf* : humor, jocularity

jocoso, -sa *adj* : playful, jocular — **jocosamente** *adv*

jofaina *nf* : washbowl

jogging [ˈjɔgiŋ, ˈdʒɔ-] *nm* : jogging

jolgorio *nm* : merrymaking, fun

jonrón *nm, pl* **jonrones** : home run

jordano, -na *adj & n* : Jordanian

jornada *nf* **1** : expedition, day's journey **2 jornada de trabajo** : working day **3 jornadas** *nfpl* : conference, congress

jornal *nm* **1** : day's pay **2 a ~** : by the day

jornalero, -ra *n* : day laborer

joroba *nf* **1** GIBA : hump **2** *fam* : nuisance, pain in the neck

jorobado[1], -da *adj* GIBOSO : hunchbacked, humpbacked

jorobado[2], -da *n* GIBOSO : hunchback, humpback

jorobar *vt fam* JERINGAR : to bother, to annoy — *vi fam* JERINGAR : to be annoying, to be a nuisance

jorongo *nm Mex* : full-length poncho

jota *nf* **1** : jot, bit <no entiendo ni jota : I don't understand a word of it> <no se ve ni jota : you can't see a thing> **2** : jack (in playing cards)

joven[1] *adj, pl* **jóvenes 1** : young **2** : youthful

joven[2] *nmf, pl* **jóvenes** : young man *m,* young woman *f,* young person

jovial *adj* : jovial, cheerful — **jovialmente** *adv*

jovialidad *nf* : joviality, cheerfulness

joya *nf* **1** : jewel, piece of jewelry **2** : treasure, gem <la nueva empleada es una joya : the new employee is a real gem>

joyería *nf* **1** : jewelry store **2** : jewelry **3 joyería de fantasía** : costume jewelry

joyero, -ra *n* : jeweler

juanete *nm* : bunion

jubilación *nf, pl* **-ciones 1** : retirement **2** PENSIÓN : pension

jubilado[1], -da *adj* : retired, in retirement

jubilado[2], -da *nmf* : retired person, retiree

jubilar *vt* **1** : to retire, to pension off **2** *fam* : to get rid of, to discard — **jubilarse** *vr* : to retire

jubileo *nm* : jubilee

júbilo *nm* : jubilation, joy

jubiloso, -sa *adj* : jubilant, joyous

judaico, -ca *adj* : Judaic, Jewish

judaísmo *nm* : Judaism

judía *nf* **1** : bean **2** *or* **judía verde** : green bean, string bean

judicatura *nf* **1** : judiciary, judges *pl* **2** : office of judge

judicial *adj* : judicial — **judicialmente** *adv*

judío[1], -día *adj* : Jewish

judío[2], -día *n* : Jewish person, Jew

judo [ˈjuðo, ˈdʒu-] *nm* : judo

juega, juegue, etc. → **jugar**

juego *nm* **1** : play, playing <poner en juego : to bring into play> **2** : game, sport <juego de cartas : card game> <Juegos Olímpicos : Olympic Games> **3** : gaming, gambling <estar en juego : to be at stake> **4** : set <un juego de llaves : a set of keys> **5 hacer juego** : to go together, to match **6 juego de manos** : conjuring trick, sleight of hand

juerga *nf* : partying, binge <irse de juerga : to go on a spree>

juerguista *nmf* : reveler, carouser

jueves *nms & pl* : Thursday

juez *nmf, pl* **jueces 1** : judge **2** ÁRBITRO : umpire, referee

jugada *nf* **1** : play, move **2** : trick <hacer una mala jugada : to play a dirty trick>
jugador, -dora *n* **1** : player **2** : gambler
jugar {44} *vi* **1** : to play <jugar a la pelota : to play ball> **2** APOSTAR : to gamble, to bet **3** : to joke, to kid — *vt* **1** : to play <jugar un papel : to play a role> <jugar una carta : to play a card> **2** : to bet — **jugarse** *vr* **1** : to risk, to gamble away <jugarse la vida : to risk one's life> **2 jugarse el todo por el todo** : to risk everything
jugarreta *nf fam* : prank, dirty trick
juglar *nm* : minstrel
jugo *nm* **1** : juice **2** : substance, essence <sacarle el jugo a algo : to get the most out of something>
jugosidad *nf* : juiciness, succulence
jugoso, -sa *adj* : juicy
juguete *nm* : toy
juguetear *vi* **1** : to play, to cavort, to frolic **2** : to toy, to fiddle
juguetería *nf* : toy store
juguetón, -tona *adj, mpl* **-tones** : playful — **juguetonamente** *adv*
juicio *nm* **1** : good judgment, reason, sense **2** : opinion <a mi juicio : in my opinion> **3** : trial <llevar a juicio : to take to court>
juicioso, -sa *adj* : judicious, wise — **juiciosamente** *adv*
julio *nm* : July
juncia *nf* : sedge
junco *nm* **1** : reed, rush **2** : junk (boat)
jungla *nf* : jungle
junio *nm* : June
junquillo *nm* : jonquil
junta *nf* **1** : board, committee <junta directiva : board of directors> **2** REUNIÓN : meeting, session **3** : junta **4** : joint, gasket
juntamente *adv* **1** : jointly, together <juntamente con : together with> **2** : at the same time
juntar *vt* **1** UNIR : to unite, to combine, to put together **2** REUNIR : to collect, to gather together, to assemble **3** : to close partway <juntar la puerta : to leave the door ajar> — **juntarse** *vr* **1** : to join together **2** : to socialize, to get together
junto, -ta *adj* **1** UNIDO : joined, united **2** : close, adjacent <colgaron los dos retratos juntos : they hung the two paintings side by side> **3** (*used adverbially*) : together <llegamos juntos : we arrived together> **4 ~ a** : next to, alongside of **5 ~ con** : together with, along with
juntura *nf* : joint, coupling
Júpiter *nm* : Jupiter
jura *nf* : oath, pledge <jura de bandera : pledge of allegiance>
jurado[1] *nm* : jury
jurado[2], **-da** *n* : juror
juramento *nm* **1** : oath <juramento hipocrático : Hippocratic oath> **2** : swearword, oath
jurar *vt* **1** : to swear <jurar lealtad : to swear loyalty> **2** : to take an oath <el alcalde juró su cargo : the mayor took the oath of office> — *vi* : to curse, to swear
jurídico, -ca *adj* : legal
jurisdicción *nf, pl* **-ciones** : jurisdiction
jurisdiccional *adj* : jurisdictional, territorial
jurisprudencia *nf* : jurisprudence, law
justa *nf* **1** : joust **2** TORNEO : tournament, competition
justamente *adv* **1** PRECISAMENTE : precisely, exactly **2** : justly, fairly
justar *vi* : to joust
justicia *nf* **1** : justice, fairness <hacerle justicia a : to do justice to> <ser de justicia : to be only fair> **2 la justicia** : the law <tomarse la justicia por su mano : to take the law into one's own hands>
justiciero, -ra *adj* : righteous, avenging
justificable *adj* : justifiable
justificación *nf, pl* **-ciones** : justification
justificante *nm* **1** : justification **2** : proof, voucher
justificar {72} *vt* **1** : to justify **2** : to excuse, to vindicate
justo[1] *adv* **1** : justly **2** : right, exactly <justo a tiempo : just in time> **3** : tightly
justo[2], **-ta** *adj* **1** : just, fair **2** : right, exact **3** : tight <estos zapatos me quedan muy justos : these shoes are too tight>
justo[3], **-ta** *n* : just person <los justos : the just>
juvenil *adj* **1** : juvenile, young, youthful **2** ADOLESCENTE : teenage
juventud *nf* **1** : youth **2** : young people
juzgado *nm* TRIBUNAL : court, tribunal
juzgar {52} *vt* **1** : to try, to judge (a case in court) **2** : to pass judgment on **3** CONSIDERAR : to consider, to deem
juzgue, etc. → **juzgar**

K

k *nf* : eleventh letter of the Spanish alphabet
kaki *adj & nm* → **caqui**
kaleidoscopio *nm* → **caleidoscopio**
kamikaze *adj & nm* : kamikaze
kampucheano, -na *adj & n* : Kampuchean
kan *nm* : khan
karaoke *nm* : karaoke
karate *or* **kárate** *nm* : karate

kayac *or* **kayak** *nm, pl* **kayacs** *or* **kayaks** : kayak
keniano, -na *adj & n* : Kenyan
kepí *nm* : kepi
kermesse *or* **kermés** [kɛrˈmɛs] *nf, pl* **kermesses** *or* **kermeses** [-ˈmɛsɛs] : charity fair, bazaar
kerosene *or* **kerosén** *or* **keroseno** *nm* : kerosene, paraffin
kilo *nm* **1** : kilo, kilogram **2** *fam* : large amount
kilobyte [ˌkiloˈbait] *nm* : kilobyte
kilociclo *nm* : kilocycle
kilogramo *nm* : kilogram
kilohertzio *nm* : kilohertz
kilometraje *nm* : distance in kilometers, mileage
kilométrico, -ca *adj fam* : endless, very long
kilómetro *nm* : kilometer
kilovatio *nm* : kilowatt
kimono *nm* : kimono
kinder [ˈkɪndɛr] *nm* → **kindergarten**
kindergarten [ˌkɪndɛrˈgartɛn] *nm, pl* **kindergartens** [-tɛns] : kindergarten, nursery school
kinesiología *nf* : physical therapy
kinesiólogo, -ga *n* : physical therapist
kiosco *nm* → **quiosco**
kit *nm, pl* **kits** : kit
kiwi [ˈkiwi] *nm* **1** : kiwi (bird) **2** : kiwifruit
klaxon *nm* → **claxon**
knockout [nɔˈkaut] *nm* → **nocaut**
koala *nm* : koala bear
kriptón *nm* : krypton
kurdo[1], -da *adj* : Kurdish
kurdo[2], -da *n* : Kurd
kuwaiti [kuˌwaiˈti] *adj & nmf* : Kuwaiti

L

l *nf* : twelfth letter of the Spanish alphabet
la[1] *pron* **1** : her, it <llámala hoy : call her today> <sacó la botella y la abrió : he took out the bottle and opened it> **2** (*formal*) : you <no la vi a usted, Señora Díaz : I didn't see you, Mrs. Díaz> **3** : the one <mi casa y la de la puerta roja : my house and the one with the red door> **4 la que** : the one who
la[2] *art* → **el[2]**
laberíntico, -ca *adj* : labyrinthine
laberinto *nm* : labyrinth, maze
labia *nf fam* : gift of gab <tu amigo tiene labia : your friend has a way with words>
labial *adj* : labial, lip <lápiz labial : lipstick>
labio *nm* **1** : lip **2 labio leporino** : harelip
labor *nf* : work, labor
laborable *adj* **1** : arable **2 día laborable** : workday, business day
laboral *adj* **1** : work, labor <costos laborales : labor costs> **2 estancia laboral** : workstation
laborar *vi* : to work
laboratorio *nm* : laboratory, lab
laboriosidad *nf* : industriousness, diligence
laborioso, -sa *adj* **1** : laborious, hard **2** : industrious, hard-working
labrado[1], -da *adj* **1** : cultivated, tilled **2** : carved, wrought
labrado[2] *nm* : cultivated field
labrador, -dora *n* : farmer
labranza *nf* : farming
labrar *vt* **1** : to carve, to work (metal) **2** : to cultivate, to till **3** : to cause, to bring about
laca *nf* **1** : lacquer, shellac **2** : hair spray **3 laca de uñas** : nail polish
lacayo *nm* : lackey
lace, etc. → **lazar**
lacear *vt* : to lasso
laceración *nf, pl* **-ciones** : laceration
lacerante *adj* : hurtful, wounding
lacerar *vt* **1** : to lacerate, to cut **2** : to hurt, to wound (one's feelings)
lacio, -cia *adj* **1** : limp, lank **2 pelo lacio** : straight hair
lacónico, -ca *adj* : laconic — **lacónicamente** *adv*
lacra *nf* **1** : scar, mark (on the skin) **2** : stigma, blemish
lacrar *vt* : to seal (with wax)
lacrimógeno, -na *adj* **gas lacrimógeno** : tear gas
lacrimoso, -sa *adj* : tearful, moving
lactancia *nf* **1** : lactation **2** : breastfeeding
lactante *nmf* : nursing infant, suckling
lactar *v* : to breast-feed
lácteo, -tea *adj* **1** : dairy **2 Vía Láctea** : Milky Way
láctico, -ca *adj* : lactic
lactosa *nf* : lactose
ladeado, -da *adj* : crooked, tilted, lopsided
ladear *vt* : to tilt, to tip — **ladearse** *vr* : to bend (over)
ladera *nf* : slope, hillside
ladino[1], -na *adj* **1** : cunning, shrewd **2** *CA, Mex* : mestizo
ladino[2], -na *n* **1** : trickster **2** *CA, Mex* : Spanish-speaking Indian **3** *CA, Mex* : mestizo
lado *nm* **1** : side **2** PARTE : place <miró por todos lados : he looked everywhere> **3 al lado de** : next to, beside **4 de ~** : tilted, sideways <está de lado : it's lying on its side> **5 hacerse a un lado** : to step aside **6 lado a lado** : side by side **7 por otro lado** : on the other hand
ladrar *vi* : to bark
ladrido *nm* : bark (of a dog), barking

ladrillo *nm* **:** brick
ladrón, -drona *n, mpl* **ladrones :** robber, thief, burglar
lagartija *nf* **:** small lizard
lagarto *nm* **1 :** lizard **2 lagarto de Indias :** alligator
lago *nm* **:** lake
lágrima *nf* **:** tear, teardrop
lagrimear *vi* **1 :** to water (of eyes) **2 :** to weep easily
laguna *nf* **1 :** lagoon **2 :** lacuna, gap
laicado *nm* **:** laity
laico[1], -ca *adj* **:** lay, secular
laico[2], -ca *n* **:** layman *m,* laywoman *f*
laja *nf* **:** slab
lama[1] *nf* **:** slime, ooze
lama[2] *nm* **:** lama
lamber *vt* **:** to lick
lamentable *adj* **1 :** unfortunate, lamentable **2 :** pitiful, sad
lamentablemente *adv* **:** unfortunately, regrettably
lamentación *nf, pl* **-ciones :** lamentation, groaning, moaning
lamentar *vt* **1 :** to lament **2 :** to regret <lo lamento : I'm sorry> **— lamentarse** *vr* **:** to grumble, to complain
lamento *nm* **:** lament, groan, cry
lamer *vt* **1 :** to lick **2 :** to lap against
lamida *nf* **:** lick
lámina *nf* **1** PLANCHA **:** sheet, plate **2 :** plate, illustration
laminado[1], -da *adj* **:** laminated
laminado[2] *nm* **:** laminate
laminar *vt* **:** to laminate **— laminación** *nf*
lámpara *nf* **:** lamp
lampiño, -ña *adj* **:** hairless
lamprea *nf* **:** lamprey
lana *nf* **1 :** wool <lana de acero : steel wool> **2** *Mex fam* **:** money, dough
lance[1], etc. → lanzar
lance[2] *nm* **1** INCIDENTE **:** event, incident **2** RIÑA **:** quarrel **3 :** throw, cast (of a net, etc.) **4 :** move, play (in a game), throw (of dice)
lancear *vt* **:** to spear
lanceta *nf* **:** lancet
lancha *nf* **1 :** small boat, launch **2 lancha motora :** motorboat, speedboat
langosta *nf* **1 :** lobster **2 :** locust
langostino *nm* **:** prawn, crayfish
languidecer {53} *vi* **:** to languish
languidez *nf, pl* **-deces :** languor, listlessness
lánguido, -da *adj* **:** languid, listless **— lánguidamente** *adv*
lanolina *nf* **:** lanolin
lanudo, -da *adj* **:** woolly
lanza *nf* **:** spear, lance
lanzadera *nf* **1 :** shuttle (for weaving) **2 lanzadera espacial :** space shuttle
lanzado, -da *adj* **1 :** impulsive, brazen **2 :** forward, determined <ir lanzado : to hurtle along>
lanzador, -dora *n* **:** thrower, pitcher
lanzallamas *nms & pl* **:** flamethrower
lanzamiento *nm* **1 :** throw **2 :** pitch (in baseball) **3 :** launching, launch
lanzar {21} *vt* **1 :** to throw, to hurl **2 :** to pitch **3 :** to launch **— lanzarse** *vr* **1 :** to throw oneself (at, into) **2 ~ a :** to embark upon, to undertake
laosiano, -na *adj & n* **:** Laotian
lapicero *nm* **1 :** mechanical pencil **2** *CA, Peru* **:** ballpoint pen
lápida *nf* **:** marker, tombstone
lapidar *vt* APEDREAR **:** to stone
lapidario, -ria *adj & n* **:** lapidary
lápiz *nm, pl* **lápices 1 :** pencil **2 lápiz de labios** *or* **lápiz labial :** lipstick
lapón, -pona *adj & n, mpl* **lapones :** Lapp
lapso *nm* **:** lapse, space (of time)
lapsus *nms & pl* **:** error, slip
laquear *vt* **:** to lacquer, to varnish, to shellac
largamente *adv* **1 :** at length, extensively **2 :** easily, comfortably **3 :** generously
largar {52} *vt* **1** SOLTAR **:** to let loose, to release **2** AFLOJAR **:** to loosen, to slacken **3** *fam* **:** to give, to hand over **4** *fam* **:** to hurl, to let fly (insults, etc.) **— largarse** *vr fam* **:** to scram, to beat it
largo[1], -ga *adj* **1 :** long **2 a lo largo :** lengthwise **3 a lo largo de :** along **4 a la larga :** in the long run
largo[2] *nm* **:** length <tres metros de largo : three meters long>
largometraje *nm* **:** feature film
largue, etc. → largar
larguero *nm* **:** crossbeam
largueza *nf* **:** generosity, largesse
larguirucho, -cha *adj fam* **:** lanky
largura *nf* **:** length
laringe *nf* **:** larynx
laringitis *nfs & pl* **:** laryngitis
larva *nf* **:** larva **— larval** *adj*
las → el[2], los[1]
lasaña *nf* **:** lasagna
lasca *nf* **:** chip, chipping
lascivia *nf* **:** lasciviousness, lewdness
lascivo, -va *adj* **:** lascivious, lewd **— lascivamente** *adv*
láser *nm* **:** laser
lasitud *nf* **:** lassitude, weariness
laso, -sa *adj* **:** languid, weary
lástima *nf* **1 :** compassion, pity **2** PENA **:** shame, pity <¡qué lástima! : what a shame!>
lastimadura *nf* **:** injury, wound
lastimar *vt* **1** DAÑAR, HERIR **:** to hurt, to injure **2** AGRAVIAR **:** to offend **— lastimarse** *vr* **:** to hurt oneself
lastimero, -ra *adj* **:** pitiful, wretched
lastimoso, -sa *adj* **1 :** shameful **2 :** pitiful, terrible
lastrar *vt* **1 :** to ballast **2 :** to burden, to encumber
lastre *nm* **1 :** burden **2 :** ballast
lata *nf* **1 :** tinplate **2 :** tin can **3** *fam* **:** pest, bother, nuisance **4 dar lata** *fam* **:** to bother, to annoy
latencia *nf* **:** latency
latente *adj* **:** latent

lateral[1] *adj* **1 :** lateral, side **2 :** indirect — **lateralmente** *adv*
lateral[2] *nm* **:** end piece, side
látex *nms & pl* **:** latex
latido *nm* **:** beat, throb <latido del corazón : heartbeat>
latifundio *nm* **:** large estate
latigazo *nm* **:** lash (with a whip)
látigo *nm* AZOTE **:** whip
latín *nm* **:** Latin (language)
latino[1], **-na** *adj* **1 :** Latin **2** *fam* **:** Latin-American
latino[2], **-na** *n fam* **:** Latin American
latinoamericano[1], **-na** *adj* HISPANOAMERICANO **:** Latin American
latinoamericano, -na *n* **:** Latin American
latir *vi* **1 :** to beat, to throb **2 latirle a uno** *Mex fam* **:** to have a hunch <me late que no va a venir : I have a feeling he's not going to come>
latitud *nf* **1 :** latitude **2 :** breadth
lato, -ta *adj* **1 :** extended, lengthy **2 :** broad (in meaning)
latón *nm, pl* **latones :** brass
latoso[1], **-sa** *adj fam* **:** annoying, bothersome
latoso[2], **-sa** *n fam* **:** pest, nuisance
latrocinio *nm* **:** larceny
laúd *nm* **:** lute
laudable *adj* **:** laudable, praiseworthy
laudo *nm* **:** findings, decision
laureado, -da *adj & n* **:** laureate
laurear *vt* **:** to award, to honor
laurel *nm* **1 :** laurel **2 :** bay leaf **3 dormirse en sus laureles :** to rest on one's laurels
lava *nf* **:** lava
lavable *adj* **:** washable
lavabo *nm* **1** LAVAMANOS **:** sink, washbowl **2 :** lavatory, toilet
lavadero *nm* **:** laundry room
lavado *nm* **1 :** laundry, wash **2 :** laundering <lavado de dinero : money laundering>
lavadora *nf* **:** washing machine
lavamanos *nms & pl* LAVABO **:** sink, washbowl
lavanda *nf* ESPLIEGO **:** lavender
lavandería *nf* **:** laundry (service)
lavandero, -ra *n* **:** launderer, laundress *f*
lavaplatos *nms & pl* **1 :** dishwasher **2** *Chile, Col, Mex* **:** kitchen sink
lavar *vt* **1 :** to wash, to clean **2 :** to launder (money) **3 lavar en seco :** to dry-clean — **lavarse** *vr* **1 :** to wash oneself **2 lavarse las manos de :** to wash one's hands of
lavativa *nf* **:** enema
lavatorio *nm* **:** lavatory, washroom
lavavajillas *nms & pl* **:** dishwasher
laxante *adj & nm* **:** laxative
laxitud *nf* **:** laxity, slackness
laxo, -xa *adj* **:** lax, slack
lazada *nf* **:** bow, loop
lazar {21} *vt* **:** to rope, to lasso
lazo *nm* **1** VÍNCULO **:** link, bond **2 :** bow, ribbon **3 :** lasso, lariat
le *pron* **1 :** to her, to him, to it <¿qué le dijiste? : what did you tell him?> **2 :** from her, from him, from it <el ladrón le robó la cartera : the thief stole his wallet> **3 :** for her, for him, for it <cómprale flores a tu mamá : buy your mom some flowers> **4** (*formal*) **:** to you, for you <le traje un regalo : I brought you a gift>
leal *adj* **:** loyal, faithful — **lealmente** *adv*
lealtad *nf* **:** loyalty, allegiance
lebrel *nm* **:** hound
lección *nf, pl* **lecciones :** lesson
lechada *nf* **1 :** whitewash **2 :** grout
lechal *adj* **:** suckling, unweaned <cordero lechal : suckling lamb>
leche *nf* **1 :** milk <leche en polvo : powdered milk> <leche de magnesia : milk of magnesia> **2 :** milky sap
lechera *nf* **1 :** milk jug **2 :** dairymaid *f*
lechería *nf* **:** dairy store
lechero[1], **-ra** *adj* **:** dairy
lechero[2], **-ra** *n* **:** milkman *m,* milk dealer
lecho *nm* **1 :** bed <un lecho de rosas : a bed of roses> <lecho de muerte : deathbed> **2 :** riverbed **3 :** layer, stratum (in geology)
lechón, -chona *n, mpl* **lechones :** suckling pig
lechoso, -sa *adj* **:** milky
lechuga *nf* **:** lettuce
lechuza *nf* BÚHO **:** owl, barn owl
lectivo, -va *adj* **:** school <año lectivo : school year>
lector[1], **-tora** *adj* **:** reading <nivel lector : reading level>
lector[2], **-tora** *n* **:** reader
lector[3] *nm* **:** scanner, reader <lector óptico : optical scanner>
lectura *nf* **1 :** reading **2 :** reading matter
leer {20} *v* **:** to read
legación *nf, pl* **-ciones :** legation
legado *nm* **1 :** legacy, bequest **2 :** legate, emissary
legajo *nm* **:** dossier, file
legal *adj* **:** legal, lawful — **legalmente** *adv*
legalidad *nf* **:** legality, lawfulness
legalizar {21} *vt* **:** to legalize — **legalización** *nf*
legar {52} *vt* **1 :** to bequeath, to hand down **2** DELEGAR **:** to delegate
legendario, -ria *adj* **:** legendary
legible *adj* **:** legible
legión *nf, pl* **legiones :** legion
legionario, -ria *n* **:** legionnaire
legislación *nf* **1 :** legislation, lawmaking **2 :** laws *pl,* legislation
legislador[1], **-dora** *adj* **:** legislative
legislador[2], **-dora** *n* **:** legislator
legislar *vi* **:** to legislate
legislativo, -va *adj* **:** legislative
legislatura *nf* **1 :** legislature **2 :** term of office
legitimar *vt* **1 :** to legitimize **2 :** to authenticate — **legitimación** *nf*

legitimidad *nf* **:** legitimacy

legítimo, -ma *adj* **1 :** legitimate **2 :** genuine, authentic — **legítimamente** *adv*

lego[1], -ga *adj* **1 :** secular, lay **2 :** uniformed, ignorant

lego[2], -ga *n* **:** layperson, layman *m,* laywoman *f*

legua *nf* **1 :** league **2 notarse a leguas :** to be very obvious <se notaba a leguas : you could tell from a mile away>

legue, etc. → **legar**

legumbre *nf* **1** HORTALIZA **:** vegetable **2 :** legume

leíble *adj* **:** readable

leída *nf* **:** reading, read <de una leída : in one reading, at one go>

leído[1] *pp* → **leer**

leído[2], -da *adj* **:** well-read

lejanía *nf* **:** remoteness, distance

lejano, -na *adj* **:** remote, distant, far away

lejía *nf* **1 :** lye **2 :** bleach

lejos *adv* **1 :** far away, distant <a lo lejos : in the distance, far off> <desde lejos : from a distance> **2 :** long ago, a long way off <está lejos de los 50 años : he's a long way from 50 years old> **3 de ~ :** by far <esta decisión fue de lejos la más fácil : this decision was by far the easiest> **4 ~ de :** far from <lejos de ser reprobado, recibió una nota de B : far from failing, he got a B>

lelo, -la *adj* **:** silly, stupid

lema *nm* **:** motto, slogan

lencería *nf* **:** lingerie

lengua *nf* **1 :** tongue <morderse la lengua : to bite one's tongue> **2** IDIOMA **:** language <lengua materna : mother tongue, native language> <lengua muerta : dead language>

lenguado *nm* **:** sole, flounder

lenguaje *nm* **1 :** language, speech **2 lenguaje gestual** *or* **lenguaje de gestos :** sign language **3 lenguaje de programación :** programming language

lengüeta *nf* **1 :** tongue (of a shoe), tab, flap **2 :** reed (of a musical instrument) **3 :** barb, point

lengüetada *nf* **beber a lengüetadas :** to lap (up)

lenidad *nf* **:** leniency

lenitivo, -va *adj* **:** soothing

lente *nmf* **1 :** lens <lentes de contacto : contact lenses> **2 lentes** *nmpl* ANTEOJOS **:** eyeglasses <lentes de sol : sunglasses>

lenteja *nf* **:** lentil

lentejuela *nf* **:** sequin, spangle

lentitud *nf* **:** slowness

lento[1] *adv* DESPACIO **:** slowly

lento[2], -ta *adj* **1 :** slow **2 :** slow-witted, dull — **lentamente** *adv*

leña *nf* **:** wood, firewood

leñador, -dora *n* **:** lumberjack, woodcutter

leñera *nf* **:** woodshed

leño *nm* **:** log

leñoso, -sa *adj* **:** woody

Leo *nmf* **:** Leo

león, -ona *n, mpl* **leones 1 :** lion, lioness *f* **2** (*in various countries*) **:** puma, cougar

leonado, -da *adj* **:** tawny

leonino, -na *adj* **1 :** leonine **2 :** one-sided, unfair

leopardo *nm* **:** leopard

leotardo *nm* MALLA **:** leotard, tights *pl*

leperada *nf Mex* **:** obscenity

lépero, -ra *adj Mex* **:** vulgar, coarse

lepra *nf* **:** leprosy

leproso[1], -sa *adj* **:** leprous

leproso[2], -sa *n* **:** leper

lerdo, -da *adj* **1 :** clumsy **2 :** dull, oafish, slow-witted

les *pron* **1 :** to them <dales una propina : give them a tip> **2 :** from them <se les privó de su herencia : they were deprived of their inheritance> **3 :** for them <les hice sus tareas : I did their homework for them> **4 :** to you *pl*, for you *pl* <les compré un regalo : I bought you all a present>

lesbiana *nf* **:** lesbian — **lesbiano, -na** *adj*

lesbianismo *nm* **:** lesbianism

lesión *nf, pl* **lesiones** HERIDA **:** lesion, wound, injury <una lesión grave : a serious injury>

lesionado, -da *adj* HERIDO **:** injured, wounded

lesionar *vt* **:** to injure, to wound — **lesionarse** *vr* **:** to hurt oneself

lesivo, -va *adj* **:** harmful, damaging

letal *adj* MORTÍFERO **:** deadly, lethal — **letalmente** *adv*

letanía *nf* **1 :** litany **2** *fam* **:** spiel, song and dance

letárgico, -ca *adj* **:** lethargic

letargo *nm* **:** lethargy, torpor

letón[1], -tona *adj & n, mpl* **letones :** Latvian

letón[2] *nm* **:** Latvian (language)

letra *nf* **1 :** letter **2** CALIGRAFÍA **:** handwriting, lettering **3 :** lyrics *pl* **4 al pie de la letra :** word for word, by the book **5 letras** *nfpl* **:** arts (in education)

letrado[1], -da *adj* ERUDITO **:** learned, erudite

letrado[2], -da *n* **:** attorney-at-law, lawyer

letrero *nm* RÓTULO **:** sign, notice

letrina *nf* **:** latrine

letrista *nmf* **:** lyricist, songwriter

leucemia *nf* **:** leukemia

levadizo, -za *adj* **1 :** liftable **2 puente levadizo :** drawbridge

levadura *nf* **1 :** yeast, leavening **2 levadura en polvo :** baking powder

levantamiento *nm* **1** ALZAMIENTO **:** uprising **2 :** raising, lifting <levantamiento de pesas : weight lifting>

levantar *vt* **1** ALZAR **:** to lift, to raise **2 :** to put up, to erect **3 :** to call off, to adjourn **4 :** to give rise to, to arouse

<levantar sospechas : to arouse suspicion> — **levantarse** *vr* **1** : to rise, to stand up **2** : to get out of bed

levar *vt* **levar anclas** : to weigh anchor

leve *adj* **1** : light, slight **2** : trivial, unimportant — **levemente** *adv*

levedad *nf* : lightness

levemente *adv* LIGERAMENTE : lightly, softly

léxico[1], -ca *adj* : lexical

léxico[2] *nm* : lexicon, glossary

lexicografía *nf* : lexicography

lexicográfico, -ca *adj* : lexicographical, lexicographic

lexicógrafo, -fa *n* : lexicographer

ley *nf* **1** : law <fuera de la ley : outside the law> <la ley de gravedad : the law of gravity> **2** : purity (of metals) <oro de ley : pure gold>

leyenda *nf* **1** : legend **2** : caption, inscription

leyó, etc. → **leer**

liar {85} *vt* **1** ATAR : to bind, to tie (up) **2** : to roll (a cigarette) **3** : to confuse — **liarse** *vr* : to get mixed up

libanés, -nesa *adj & n, mpl* **-neses** : Lebanese

libar *vt* **1** : to suck (nectar) **2** : to sip, to swig (liquor, etc.)

libelo *nm* **1** : libel, lampoon **2** : petition (in court)

libélula *nf* : dragonfly

liberación *nf, pl* **-ciones** : liberation, deliverance <liberación de la mujer : women's liberation>

liberado, -da *adj* **1** : liberated <una mujer liberada : a liberated woman> **2** : freed, delivered

liberal *adj & nmf* : liberal

liberalidad *nf* : generosity, liberality

liberalismo *nm* : liberalism

liberalizar {21} *vt* : to liberalize — **liberalización** *nf*

liberar *vt* : to liberate, to free — **liberarse** *vr* : to get free of

liberiano, -na *adj & n* : Liberian

libertad *nf* **1** : freedom, liberty <tomarse la libertad de : to take the liberty of> **2 libertad bajo fianza** : bail **3 libertad condicional** : parole

libertador[1], -dora *adj* : liberating

libertador[2], -dora *n* : liberator

libertar *vt* LIBRAR : to set free

libertario, -ria *adj & n* : libertarian

libertinaje *nm* : licentiousness, dissipation

libertino[1], -na *adj* : licentious, dissolute

libertino[2], -na *n* : libertine

libidinoso, -sa *adj* : lustful, lewd

libido *nf* : libido

libio, -bia *adj & n* : Libyan

libra *nf* **1** : pound **2 libra esterlina** : pound sterling

Libra *nmf* : Libra

libramiento *nm* **1** : liberating, freeing **2** LIBRANZA : order of payment **3** *Mex* : beltway

libranza *nf* : order of payment

librar *vt* **1** LIBERTAR : to deliver, to set free **2** : to wage <librar batalla : to do battle> **3** : to issue <librar una orden : to issue an order> — **librarse** *vr* **~ de** : to free oneself from, to get out of

libre *adj* **1** : free <un país libre : a free country> <libre de : free from, exempt from> <libre albedrío : free will> **2** DESOCUPADO : vacant **3 día libre** : day off

librea *nf* : livery

librecambio *nm* : free trade

libremente *adv* : freely

librería *nf* : bookstore

librero[1], -ra *n* : bookseller

librero[2] *nm Mex* : bookcase

libresco, -ca *adj* : bookish

libreta *nf* CUADERNO : notebook

libreto *nm* : libretto, script

libro *nm* **1** : book <libro de texto : textbook> **2 libros** *nmpl* : books (in bookkeeping), accounts <llevar los libros : to keep the books>

licencia *nf* **1** : permission **2** : leave, leave of absence **3** : permit, license <licencia de conducir : driver's license>

licenciado, -da *n* **1** : university graduate **2** ABOGADO : lawyer

licenciar *vt* **1** : to license, to permit, to allow **2** : to discharge **3** : to grant a university degree to — **licenciarse** *vr* : to graduate

licenciatura *nf* **1** : college degree **2** : course of study (at a college or university)

licencioso, -sa *adj* : licentious, lewd

liceo *nm* : secondary school, high school

licitación *nf, pl* **-ciones** : bid, bidding

licitar *vt* : to bid on

lícito, -ta *adj* **1** : lawful, licit **2** JUSTO : just, fair

licor *nm* **1** : liquor **2** : liqueur

licorera *nf* : decanter

licuado *nm* BATIDO : milk shake

licuadora *nf* : blender

licuar {3} *vt* : to liquefy — **licuarse** *vr*

lid *nf* **1** : fight, combat **2** : argument, dispute **3 lides** *nfpl* : matters, affairs **4 en buena lid** : fair and square

líder[1] *adj* : leading, foremost

líder[2] *nmf* : leader

liderar *vt* DIRIGIR : to lead, to head

liderato *nm* : leadership, leading

liderazgo *nm* → **liderato**

lidiar *vt* : to fight — *vi* BATALLAR, LUCHAR : to struggle, to battle, to wrestle

liebre *nf* : hare

liendre *nf* : nit

lienzo *nm* **1** : linen **2** : canvas, painting **3** : stretch of wall or fencing

liga *nf* **1** ASOCIACIÓN : league **2** GOMITA : rubber band **3** : garter

ligado, -da *adj* : linked, connected

ligadura *nf* **1** ATADURA : tie, bond **2** : ligature

ligamento *nm* : ligament

ligar {52} *vt* : to bind, to tie (up)

ligeramente *adv* **1** : slightly **2** LEVEMENTE : lightly, gently **3** : casually, flippantly

ligereza *nf* **1** : lightness **2** : flippancy **3** : agility

ligero, -ra *adj* **1** : light, lightweight **2** : slight, minor **3** : agile, quick **4** : lighthearted, superficial

ligue, etc. → **ligar**

lija *nf or* **papel de lija** : sandpaper

lijar *vt* : to sand

lila[1] *adj* : lilac, light purple

lila[2] *nf* : lilac

lima *nf* **1** : lime (fruit) **2** : file <lima de uñas : nail file>

limadora *nf* : polisher

limar *vt* **1** : to file **2** : to polish, to put the final touch on **3** : to smooth over <limar las diferencias : to iron out differences>

limbo *nm* **1** : limbo **2** : limb (in botany and astronomy)

limeño[1], **-ña** *adj* : of or from Lima, Peru

limeño[2], **-ña** *n* : person from Lima, Peru

limero *nm* : lime tree

limitación *nf, pl* **-ciones 1** : limitation **2** : limit, restriction <sin limitación : unlimited>

limitado, -da *adj* **1** RESTRINGIDO : limited **2** : dull, slow-witted

limitar *vt* RESTRINGIR : to limit, to restrict — *vi* **~ con** : to border on — **limitarse** *vr* **~ a** : to limit oneself to

límite *nm* **1** : boundary, border **2** : limit <el límite de mi paciencia : the limit of my patience> <límite de velocidad : speed limit> **3 fecha límite** : deadline

limítrofe *adj* LINDANTE, LINDERO : bordering, adjoining

limo *nm* : slime, mud

limón *nm, pl* **limones 1** : lemon **2** : lemon tree **3 limón verde** *Mex* : lime

limonada *nf* : lemonade

limosna *nf* : alms, charity

limosnear *vi* : to beg (for alms)

limosnero, -ra *n* MENDIGO : beggar

limoso, -sa *adj* : slimy

limpiabotas *nmfs & pl* : bootblack

limpiador[1], **-dora** *adj* : cleaning

limpiador[2], **-dora** *n* : cleaning person, cleaner

limpiamente *adv* : cleanly, honestly, fairly

limpiaparabrisas *nms & pl* : windshield wiper

limpiar *vt* **1** : to clean, to cleanse **2** : to clean up, to remove defects **3** *fam* : to clean out (in a game) **4** *fam* : to swipe, to pinch — *vi* : to clean — **limpiarse** *vr*

limpiavidrios *nmfs & pl Mex* : windshield wiper

límpido, -da *adj* : limpid

limpieza *nf* **1** : cleanliness, tidiness **2** : cleaning **3** HONRADEZ : integrity, honesty **4** DESTREZA : skill, dexterity

limpio[1] *adv* : fairly

limpio[2], **-pia** *adj* **1** : clean, neat **2** : honest <un juego limpio : a fair game> **3** : free <limpio de impurezas : pure, free from impurities> **4** : clear, net <ganancia limpia : clear profit>

limusina *nf* : limousine

linaje *nm* ABOLENGO : lineage, ancestry

linaza *nf* : linseed

lince *nm* : lynx

linchamiento *nm* : lynching

linchar *vt* : to lynch

lindante *adj* LIMÍTROFE, LINDERO : bordering, adjoining

lindar *vi* **1 ~ con** : to border, to skirt **2 ~ con** BORDEAR : to border on, to verge on

linde *nmf* : boundary, limit

lindero[1], **-ra** *adj* LIMÍTROFE, LINDANTE : bordering, adjoining

lindero[2] *nm* : boundary, limit

lindeza *nf* **1** : prettiness **2** : clever remark **3 lindezas** *nfpl* (*used ironically*) : insults

lindo[1] *adv* **1** : beautifully, wonderfully <canta lindo tu mujer : your wife sings beautifully> **2 de lo lindo** : a lot, a great deal <los zancudos nos picaban de lo lindo : the mosquitoes were biting away at us>

lindo[2], **-da** *adj* **1** BONITO : pretty, lovely **2** MONO : cute

línea *nf* **1** : line <línea divisoria : dividing line> <línea de banda : sideline> **2** : line, course, position <línea de conducta : course of action> <en líneas generales : in general terms, along general lines> **3** : line, service <línea aérea : airline> <línea telefónica : telephone line>

lineal *adj* : linear

linfa *nf* : lymph

linfático, -ca *adj* : lymphatic

lingote *nm* : ingot

lingüista *nmf* : linguist

lingüística *nf* : linguistics

lingüístico, -ca *adj* : linguistic

linimento *nm* : liniment

lino *nm* **1** : linen **2** : flax

linóleo *nm* : linoleum

linterna *nf* **1** : lantern **2** : flashlight

lío *nm fam* **1** : confusion, mess **2** : hassle, trouble, jam <meterse en un lío : to get into a jam> **3** : affair, liason

liofilizar {21} *vt* : to freeze-dry

lioso, -sa *adj fam* **1** : confusing, muddled **2** : troublemaking

liquen *nm* : lichen

liquidación *nf, pl* **-ciones 1** : liquidation **2** : clearance sale **3** : settlement, payment

liquidar *vt* **1** : to liquefy **2** : to liquidate **3** : to settle, to pay off **4** *fam* : to rub out, to kill

liquidez *nf, pl* **-deces** : liquidity

líquido[1], -da *adj* **1 :** liquid, fluid **2 :** net <ingresos líquidos : net income>

líquido[2] *nm* **1 :** liquid, fluid <líquido de frenos : brake fluid> **2 :** ready cash, liquid assets

lira *nf* **:** lyre

lírica *nf* **:** lyric poetry

lírico, -ca *adj* **:** lyric, lyrical

lirio *nm* **1 :** iris **2 lirio de los valles** MUGUETE **:** lily of the valley

lirismo *nm* **:** lyricism

lirón *nm, pl* **lirones :** dormouse

lisiado[1], -da *adj* **:** disabled, crippled

lisiado[2], -da *n* **:** disabled person, cripple

lisiar *vt* **:** to cripple, to disable — **lisiarse** *vr*

liso, -sa *adj* **1 :** smooth **2 :** flat **3 :** straight <pelo liso : straight hair> **4 :** plain, unadorned <liso y llano : plain and simple>

lisonja *nf* **:** flattery

lisonjear *vt* ADULAR **:** to flatter

lista *nf* **1 :** list **2 :** roster, roll <pasar lista : to take attendance> **3 :** stripe, strip **4 :** menu

listado[1], -da *adj* **:** striped

listado[2] *nm* **:** listing

listar *vt* **:** to list

listeza *nf* **:** smartness, alertness

listo, -ta *adj* **1** DISPUESTO, PREPARADO **:** ready <¿estás listo? : are you ready?> **2 :** clever, smart

listón *nm, pl* **listones 1 :** ribbon **2 :** strip (of wood), lath **3 :** high bar (in sports)

lisura *nf* **:** smoothness

litera *nf* **:** bunk bed, berth

literal *adj* **:** literal — **literalmente** *adv*

literario, -ria *adj* **:** literary

literato, -ta *n* **:** writer, author

literatura *nf* **:** literature

litigante *adj & nmf* **:** litigant

litigar {52} *vi* **:** to litigate, to be in litigation

litigio *nm* **1 :** litigation, lawsuit **2 en ~ :** in dispute

litigioso, -sa *adj* **:** litigious

litio *nm* **:** lithium

litografía *nf* **1 :** lithography **2 :** lithograph

litógrafo, -fa *n* **:** lithographer

litoral[1] *adj* **:** coastal

litoral[2] *nm* **:** shore, seaboard

litosfera *nf* **:** lithosphere

litro *nm* **:** liter

lituano[1], -na *adj & n* **:** Lithuanian

lituano[2] *nm* **:** Lithuanian (language)

liturgia *nf* **:** liturgy

litúrgico, -ca *adj* **:** liturgical — **litúrgicamente** *adv*

liviandad *nf* LIGEREZA **:** lightness

liviano, -na *adj* **1 :** light, slight **2** INCONSTANTE **:** fickle

lividez *nf* PALIDEZ **:** pallor

lívido, -da *adj* **1** AMORATADO **:** livid **2** PÁLIDO **:** pallid, extremely pale

living *nm* **:** living room

llaga *nf* **:** sore, wound

llama *nf* **1 :** flame **2 :** llama

llamada *nf* **:** call <llamada a larga distancia : long-distance call> <llamada al orden : call to order>

llamado[1], -da *adj* **:** named, called <una mujer llamada Rosa : a woman called Rosa>

llamado[2] → **llamamiento**

llamador *nm* **:** door knocker

llamamiento *nm* **:** call, appeal

llamar *vt* **1 :** to name, to call **2 :** to call, to summon **3 :** to phone, to call up — **llamarse** *vr* **:** to be called, to be named <¿cómo te llamas? : what's your name?>

llamarada *nf* **1 :** flare-up, sudden blaze **2 :** flushing (of the face)

llamativo, -va *adj* **:** flashy, showy, striking

llameante *adj* **:** flaming, blazing

llamear *vi* **:** to flame, to blaze

llana *nf* **1 :** trowel **2** → **llano[2]**

llanamente *adv* **:** simply, plainly, straightforwardly

llaneza *nf* **:** simplicity, naturalness

llano[1], -na *adj* **1 :** even, flat **2 :** frank, open **3** LISO **:** plain, simple

llano[2] *nm* **:** plain

llanta *nf* **1** NEUMÁTICO **:** tire **2 :** rim

llantén *nm, pl* **llantenes :** plantain (weed)

llanto *nm* **:** crying, weeping

llanura *nf* **:** plain, prairie

llave *nf* **1 :** key **2 :** faucet **3** INTERRUPTOR **:** switch **4 :** brace (punctuation mark) **5 llave inglesa :** monkey wrench

llavero *nm* **:** key chain, key ring

llegada *nf* **:** arrival

llegar {52} *vi* **1 :** to arrive, to come **2 ~ a :** to arrive at, to reach, to amount to **3 ~ a :** to manage to <llegó a terminar la novela : she managed to finish the novel> **4 llegar a ser :** to become <llegó a ser un miembro permanente : he became a permanent member>

llegue, etc. → **llegar**

llenar *vt* **1 :** to fill, to fill up, to fill in **2 :** to meet, to fulfill <los regalos no llenaron sus expectativas : the gifts did not meet her expectations> — **llenarse** *vr* **:** to fill up, to become full

llenito, -ta *adj fam* REGORDETE **:** chubby, plump

lleno[1], -na *adj* **1 :** full, filled **2 de ~ :** completely, fully **3 estar lleno de sí mismo :** to be full of oneself

lleno[2] *nm* **1** *fam* **:** plenty, abundance **2 :** full house, sellout

llevadero, -ra *adj* **:** bearable

llevar *vt* **1 :** to take away, to carry <me gusta, me lo llevo : I like it, I'll take it> **2 :** to wear **3 :** to take, to lead <llevamos a Pedro al cine : we took Pedro to the movies> **4 llevar a cabo :** to carry out **5 llevar adelante :** to carry on, to keep going — *vi* **:** to lead <un problema lleva al otro : one problem leads to another> — *v aux* **:** to have <llevo mucho tiempo buscándolo : I've been looking for it for a long time> <lleva leído medio libro : he's halfway through the book> — **llevarse** *vr* **1** : to take away, to carry off **2** : to get along <siempre nos llevábamos bien : we always got along well>

llorar *vi* : to cry, to weep — *vt* : to mourn, to bewail

lloriquear *vi* : to whimper, to whine

lloriqueo *nm* : whimpering, whining

llorón, -rona *n, mpl* **llorones** : crybaby, whiner

lloroso, -sa *adj* : tearful, sad

llovedizo, -za *adj* : rain <agua llovediza : rainwater>

llover {47} *v impers* : to rain <está lloviendo : it's raining> <llover a cántaros : to rain cats and dogs> — *vi* : to rain down, to shower <le llovieron regalos : he was showered with gifts>

llovizna *nf* : drizzle, sprinkle

lloviznar *v impers* : to drizzle, to sprinkle

llueve, etc. → **llover**

lluvia *nf* **1** : rain, rainfall **2** : barrage, shower

lluvioso, -sa *adj* : rainy

lo[1] *pron* **1** : him, it <lo vi ayer : I saw him yesterday> <lo entiendo : I understand it> <no lo creo : I don't believe so> **2** (*formal, masculine*) : you <disculpe, señor, no lo oí : excuse me sir, I didn't hear you> **3 lo que** : what, that which <eso es lo que más le gusta : that's what he likes the most>

lo[2] *art* **1** : the <lo mejor : the best, the best thing> **2** : how <sé lo bueno que eres : I know how good you are>

loa *nf* : praise

loable *adj* : laudable, praiseworthy — **loablemente** *adv*

loar *vt* : to praise, to laud

lobato, -ta *n* : wolf cub

lobby *nm* : lobby, pressure group

lobo, -ba *n* : wolf

lóbrego, -ga *adj* SOMBRÍO : gloomy, dark

lobulado, -da *adj* : lobed

lóbulo *nm* : lobe <lóbulo de la oreja : earlobe>

locación *nf, pl* **-ciones 1** : location (in moviemaking) **2** *Mex* : place

local[1] *adj* : local — **localmente** *adv*

local[2] *nm* : premises *pl*

localidad *nf* : town, locality

localización *nf, pl* **-ciones 1** : locating, localization **2** : location

localizar {21} *vt* **1** UBICAR : to locate, to find **2** : to localize — **localizarse** *vr* UBICARSE : to be located <se localiza en el séptimo piso : it is located on the seventh floor>

locatario, -ria *n* : tenant

loción *nf, pl* **lociones** : lotion

lócker *nm, pl* **lóckers** : locker

loco[1]**, -ca** *adj* **1** DEMENTE : crazy, insane, mad **2 a lo loco** : wildly, recklessly **3 volverse loco** : to go mad

loco[2]**, -ca** *n* **1** : crazy person, lunatic **2 hacerse el loco** : to act the fool

locomoción *nf, pl* **-ciones** : locomotion

locomotor, -tora *adj* : locomotive

locomotora *nf* **1** : locomotive **2** : driving force

locuacidad *nf* : loquacity, talkativeness

locuaz *adj, pl* **locuaces** : loquacious, talkative

locución *nf, pl* **-ciones** : locution, phrase <locución adverbial : adverbial phrase>

locura *nf* **1** : insanity, madness **2** : crazy thing, folly

locutor, -tora *n* : announcer

lodazal *nm* : bog, quagmire

lodo *nm* BARRO : mud, mire

lodoso, -sa *adj* : muddy

logaritmo *nm* : logarithm

logia *nf* : lodge <logia masónica : Masonic lodge>

lógica *nf* : logic

lógico, -ca *adj* : logical — **lógicamente** *adv*

logística *nf* : logistics *pl*

logístico, -ca *adj* : logistic, logistical

logo *nm* → **logotipo**

logotipo *nm* : logo

logrado, -da *adj* : successful, well done

lograr *vt* **1** : to get, to obtain **2** : to achieve, to attain — **lograrse** *vr* : to be successful

logro *nm* : achievement, attainment

loma *nf* : hill, hillock

lombriz *nf, pl* **lombrices** : worm <lombriz de tierra : earthworm, night crawler> <lombriz solitaria : tapeworm> <tener lombrices : to have worms>

lomo *nm* **1** : back (of an animal) **2** : loin <lomo de cerdo : pork loin> **3** : spine (of a book) **4** : blunt edge (of a knife)

lona *nf* : canvas

loncha *nf* LONJA, REBANADA : slice

lonche *nm* **1** ALMUERZO : lunch **2** *Mex* : submarine sandwich

lonchería *nf Mex* : luncheonette

londinense[1] *adj* : of or from London

londinense[2] *nmf* : Londoner

longaniza *nf* : spicy pork sausage

longevidad *nf* : longevity

longevo, -va *adj* : long-lived

longitud *nf* **1** LARGO : length <longitud de onda : wavelength> **2** : longitude

longitudinal *adj* : longitudinal

lonja *nf* LONCHA, REBANADA : slice

lontananza *nf* : background <en lontananza : in the distance, far away>

lord *nm, pl* **lores** (*title in England*) : lord

loro *nm* : parrot

los[1]**, las** *pron* **1** : them <hice galletas y se las di a los nuevos vecinos : I made cookies and gave them to the

new neighbors> **2** : you <voy a llevarlos a los dos : I am going to take both of you> **3 los que, las que** : those, who, the ones <los que van a cantar deben venir temprano : those who are singing must come early> **4** (*used with* **haber**) <los hay en varios colores : they come in various colors>
los[2] → **el**[2]
losa *nf* : flagstone, paving stone
loseta *nf* BALDOSA : floor tile
lote *nm* **1** : part, share **2** : batch, lot **3** : plot of land, lot
lotería *nf* : lottery
loto *nm* : lotus
loza *nf* **1** : crockery, earthenware **2** : china
lozanía *nf* **1** : healthiness, robustness **2** : luxuriance, lushness
lozano, -na *adj* **1** : robust, healthy-looking <un rostro lozano : a smooth, fresh face> **2** : lush, luxuriant
lubricante[1] *adj* : lubricating
lubricante[2] *nm* : lubricant
lubricar {72} *vt* : to lubricate, to oil — **lubricación** *nf*
lucero *nm* : bright star <lucero del alba : morning star>
lucha *nf* **1** : struggle, fight **2** : wrestling
luchador, -dora *n* **1** : fighter **2** : wrestler
luchar *vi* **1** : to fight, to struggle **2** : to wrestle
luchón, -chona *adj, mpl* **luchones** *Mex* : industrious, hardworking
lucidez *nf, pl* **-deces** : lucidity, clarity
lucido, -da *adj* MAGNÍFICO : magnificent, splendid
lúcido, -da *adj* : lucid
luciérnaga *nf* : firefly, glowworm
lucimiento *nm* **1** : brilliance, splendor, sparkle **2** : triumph, success <salir con lucimiento : to succeed with flying colors>
lucio *nm* : pike (fish)
lucir {45} *vi* **1** : to shine **2** : to look good, to stand out **3** : to seem, to appear <ahora luce contento : he looks happy now> — *vt* **1** : to wear, to sport **2** : to flaunt, to show off — **lucirse** *vr* **1** : to distinguish oneself, to excel **2** : to show off
lucrarse *vr* : to make a profit
lucrativo, -va *adj* : lucrative, profitable — **lucrativamente** *adv*
lucro *nm* GANANCIA : profit, gain
luctuoso, -sa *adj* : mournful, tragic
luego[1] *adv* **1** DESPUÉS : then, afterwards **2** : later (on) **3 desde ~** : of course **4 ¡hasta luego!** : see you later! **5 luego que** : as soon as **6 luego luego** *Mex fam* : right away, immediately
luego[2] *conj* : therefore <pienso, luego existo : I think, therefore I am>
lugar *nm* **1** : place, position <se llevó el primer lugar en su división : she took first place in her division> **2** ESPACIO : space, room **3 dar lugar a** : to give rise to, to lead to **4 en lugar de** : instead of **5 lugar común** : cliché, platitude **6 tener lugar** : to take place
lugareño[1], **-ña** *adj* : village, rural
lugareño[2], **-ña** *n* : villager
lugarteniente *nmf* : lieutenant, deputy
lúgubre *adj* : gloomy, lugubrious
lujo *nm* **1** : luxury **2 de ~** : deluxe
lujoso, -sa *adj* : luxurious
lujuria *nf* : lust, lechery
lujurioso, -sa *adj* : lustful, lecherous
lumbar *adj* : lumbar
lumbre *nf* **1** FUEGO : fire **2** : brilliance, splendor **3 poner en la lumbre** : to put on the stove, to warm up
lumbrera *nf* **1** : skylight **2** : vent, port **3** : brilliant person, luminary
luminaria *nf* **1** : altar lamp **2** LUMBRERA : luminary, celebrity
luminiscencia *nf* : luminescence — **luminiscente** *adj*
luminosidad *nf* : luminosity, brightness
luminoso, -sa *adj* : shining, luminous
luna *nf* **1** : moon **2 luna de miel** : honeymoon
lunar[1] *adj* : lunar
lunar[2] *nm* **1** : mole, beauty spot **2** : defect, blemish **3** : polka dot
lunático, -ca *adj & n* : lunatic
lunes *nms & pl* : Monday
luneta *nf* **1** : lens (of eyeglasses) **2** : windshield (of an automobile) **3** : crescent
lupa *nf* : magnifying glass
lúpulo *nm* : hops (plant)
lustrar *vt* : to shine, to polish
lustre *nm* **1** BRILLO : luster, shine **2** : glory, distinction
lustroso, -sa *adj* BRILLOSO : lustrous, shiny
luto *nm* : mourning <estar de luto : to be in mourning>
luz *nf, pl* **luces 1** : light **2** : lighting **3** *fam* : electricity **4** : window, opening **5** : light, lamp **6** : span, spread (between supports) **7 a la luz de** : in light of **8 dar a luz** : to give birth **9 traje de luces** : matador's costume
luzca, etc. → **lucir**

M

m *nf* : thirteenth letter of the Spanish alphabet
macabro, -bra *adj* : macabre
macaco[1], **-ca** *adj* : ugly, misshapen
macaco[2], **-ca** *n* : macaque
macadán *nm, pl* **-danes** : macadam
macana *nf* **1** : club, cudgel **2** *fam* : nonsense, silliness **3** *fam* : lie, fib
macanudo, -da *adj fam* : great, fantastic

macarrón *nm, pl* **-rrones 1 :** macaroon **2 macarrones** *nmpl* **:** macaroni
maceta *nf* **1 :** flowerpot **2 :** mallet **3** *Mex fam* **:** head
machacar {72} *vt* **1 :** to crush, to grind **2 :** to beat, to pound — *vi* **:** to insist, to go on (about)
machacón, -cona *adj, mpl* **-cones :** insistent, tiresome
machete *nm* **:** machete
machetear *vt* **:** to hack with a machete — *vi Mex fam* **:** to plod, to work tirelessly
machismo *nm* **1 :** machismo **2 :** male chauvinism
machista *nm* **:** male chauvinist
macho[1] *adj* **1 :** male **2 :** macho, virile, tough
macho[2] *nm* **1 :** male **2 :** he-man
machote *nm* **1** *fam* **:** tough guy, he-man **2** *CA, Mex* **:** rough draft, model **3** *Mex* **:** blank form
machucar {72} *vt* **1 :** to pound, to beat, to crush **2 :** to bruise
machucón *nm, pl* **-cones 1** MORETÓN **:** bruise **2 :** smashing, pounding
macilento, -ta *adj* **:** gaunt, wan
macis *nm* **:** mace (spice)
macizo, -za *adj* **1 :** solid <oro macizo : solid gold> **2 :** strong, strapping **3 :** massive
macrocosmo *nm* **:** macrocosm
mácula *nf* **:** blemish, stain
madeja *nf* **1 :** skein, hank **2 :** tangle (of hair)
madera *nf* **1 :** wood **2 :** lumber, timber **3 madera dura** *or* **madera noble :** hardwood
maderero, -ra *adj* **:** timber, lumber
madero *nm* **:** piece of lumber, plank
madrastra *nf* **:** stepmother
madrazo *nm Mex fam* **:** punch, blow <se agarraron a madrazos : they beat each other up>
madre *nf* **1 :** mother **2 madre política :** mother-in-law **3 la Madre Patria :** the mother country (said of Spain)
madrear *vt Mex fam* **:** to beat up
madreperla *nf* NÁCAR **:** mother-of-pearl
madreselva *nf* **:** honeysuckle
madriguera *nf* **:** burrow, den, lair
madrileño[1], -ña *adj* **:** of or from Madrid
madrileño[2], -ña *n* **:** person from Madrid
madrina *nf* **1 :** godmother **2 :** bridesmaid **3 :** sponsor
madrugada *nf* **1 :** early morning, wee hours **2** ALBA **:** dawn, daybreak
madrugador, -dora *n* **:** early riser
madrugar {52} *vi* **1 :** to get up early **2 :** to get a head start
madurar *v* **1 :** to ripen **2 :** to mature
madurez *nf, pl* **-reces 1 :** maturity **2 :** ripeness
maduro, -ra *adj* **1 :** mature **2 :** ripe
maestría *nf* **1 :** mastery, skill **2 :** master's degree
maestro[1], -tra *adj* **1 :** masterly, skilled **2 :** chief, main **3 :** trained <un elefante maestro : a trained elephant>
maestro[2], -tra *n* **1 :** teacher (in grammar school) **2 :** expert, master **3 :** maestro
Mafia *nf* **:** Mafia
mafioso, -sa *n* **:** mafioso, gangster
magdalena *nf* **:** bun, muffin
magenta *adj & n* **:** magenta
magia *nf* **:** magic
mágico, -ca *adj* **:** magic, magical — **mágicamente** *adv*
magisterio *nm* **1 :** teaching **2 :** teachers *pl,* teaching profession
magistrado, -da *n* **:** magistrate, judge
magistral *adj* **1 :** masterful, skillful **2 :** magisterial
magistralmente *adv* **:** masterfully, brilliantly
magistratura *nf* **:** judgeship, magistracy
magma *nm* **:** magma
magnanimidad *nf* **:** magnanimity
magnánimo, -ma *adj* GENEROSO **:** magnanimous — **magnánimamente** *adv*
magnate *nmf* **:** magnate, tycoon
magnesia *nf* **:** magnesia
magnesio *nm* **:** magnesium
magnético, -ca *adj* **:** magnetic
magnetismo *nm* **:** magnetism
magnetizar {21} *vt* **:** to magnetize
magnetófono *nm* **:** tape recorder
magnetofónico, -ca *adj* **cinta magnetofónica :** magnetic tape
magnificar {72} *vt* **1 :** to magnify **2** EXAGERAR **:** to exaggerate **3** ENSALZAR **:** to exalt, to extol, to praise highly
magnificencia *nf* **:** magnificence, splendor
magnífico, -ca *adj* ESPLENDOROSO **:** magnificent, splendid — **magníficamente** *adv*
magnitud *nf* **:** magnitude
magnolia *nf* **:** magnolia (flower)
magnolio *nm* **:** magnolia (tree)
mago, -ga *n* **1 :** magician **2 :** wizard (in folk tales, etc.) **3 los Reyes Magos :** the Magi
magro, -gra *adj* **1 :** lean (of meat) **2 :** meager
maguey *nm* **:** maguey
magulladura *nf* MORETÓN **:** bruise
magullar *vt* **:** to bruise — **magullarse** *vr*
mahometano[1], -na *adj* ISLÁMICO **:** Islamic, Muslim
mahometano[2], -na *n* **:** Muslim
mahonesa *nf* → **mayonesa**
maicena *nf* **:** cornstarch
maíz *nm* **:** corn, maize
maizal *nm* **:** cornfield
maja *nf* **:** pestle
majadería *nf* **1** TONTERÍA **:** stupidity, foolishness **2** *Mex* LEPERADA **:** insult, obscenity
majadero[1], -ra *adj* **1 :** foolish, silly **2** *Mex* LÉPERO **:** crude, vulgar

majadero², **-ra** *n* **1** TONTO : fool **2** *Mex* : rude person, boor
majar *vt* : to crush, to mash
majestad *nf* : majesty <Su Majestad : Your Majesty>
majestuosamente *adv* : majestically
majestuosidad *nf* : majesty, grandeur
majestuoso, -sa *adj* : majestic, stately
majo, -ja *adj Spain* **1** : nice, likeable **2** GUAPO : attractive, good-looking
mal¹ *adv* **1** : badly, poorly <baila muy mal : he dances very badly> **2** : wrong, incorrectly <me entendió mal : she misunderstood me> **3** : with difficulty, hardly <mal puedo oírte : I can hardly hear you> **4 de mal en peor** : from bad to worse **5 menos mal** : it could have been worse
mal² *adj* → **malo**
mal³ *nm* **1** : evil, wrong **2** DAÑO : harm, damage **3** DESGRACIA : misfortune **4** ENFERMEDAD : illness, sickness
malabar *adj* **juegos malabares** : juggling
malabarista *nmf* : juggler
malaconsejado, -da *adj* : ill-advised
malacostumbrado, -da *adj* CONSENTIDO : spoiled, pampered
malacostumbrar *vt* : to spoil
malagradecido, -da *adj* INGRATO : ungrateful
malaisio → **malasio**
malaquita *nf* : malachite
malaria *nf* PALUDISMO : malaria
malasio, -sia *adj & n* : Malaysian
malaventura *nf* : misadventure, misfortune
malaventurado, -da *adj* MALHADADO : ill-fated, unfortunate
malayo, -ya *adj & n* : Malay, Malayan
malbaratar *vt* **1** MALGASTAR : to squander **2** : to undersell
malcriado¹, **-da** *adj* **1** : ill-bred, bad-mannered **2** : spoiled, pampered
malcriado², **-da** *n* : spoiled brat
maldad *nf* **1** : evil, wickedness **2** : evil deed
maldecir {11} *vt* : to curse, to damn — *vi* **1** : to curse, to swear **2 ~ de** : to speak ill of, to slander, to defame
maldición *nf, pl* **-ciones** : curse
maldiga, maldijo, etc. → **maldecir**
maldito, -ta *adj* **1** : cursed, damned <¡maldita sea! : damn it all!> **2** : wicked
maldoso, -sa *adj Mex* : mischievous
maleable *adj* : malleable
maleante *nmf* : crook, thug
malecón *nm, pl* **-cones** : jetty, breakwater
maleducado, -da *adj* : ill-mannered, rude
maleficio *nm* : curse, hex
maléfico, -ca *adj* : evil, harmful
malentender {56} *vt* : to misunderstand
malentendido *nm* : misunderstanding
malestar *nm* **1** : discomfort **2** IRRITACIÓN : annoyance **3** INQUIETUD : uneasiness, unrest
maleta *nf* : suitcase, bag <haz tus maletas : pack your bags>
maletero¹, **-ra** *n* : porter
maletero² *nm* : trunk (of an automobile)
maletín *nm, pl* **-tines** **1** PORTAFOLIO : briefcase **2** : overnight bag, satchel
malevolencia *nf* : malevolence, wickedness
malévolo, -la *adj* : malevolent, wicked
maleza *nf* **1** : thicket, underbrush **2** : weeds *pl*
malformación *nf, pl* **-ciones** : malformation
malgache *adj & nmf* : Madagascan
malgastar *vt* : to squander (resources), to waste (time, effort)
malhablado, -da *adj* : foul-mouthed
malhadado, -da *adj* MALAVENTURADO : ill-fated
malhechor, -chora *n* : criminal, delinquent, wrongdoer
malherir {76} *vt* : to injure seriously
malhumor *nm* : bad mood, sullenness
malhumorado, -da *adj* : bad-tempered, cross
malicia *nf* **1** : wickedness, malice **2** : mischief, naughtiness **3** : cunning, craftiness
malicioso, -sa *adj* **1** : malicious **2** PÍCARO : mischievous
malignidad *nf* **1** : malignancy **2** MALDAD : evil
maligno, -na *adj* **1** : malignant <un tumor maligno : a malignant tumor> **2** : evil, harmful, malign
malinchismo *nm Mex* : preference for foreign goods or people — **malinchista** *adj*
malintencionado, -da *adj* : malicious, spiteful
malinterpretar *vt* : to misinterpret
malla *nf* **1** : mesh **2** LEOTARDO : leotard, tights *pl* **3 malla de baño** : bathing suit
mallorquín, -quina *adj & n* : Majorcan
malnutrición *nf, pl* **-ciones** DESNUTRICIÓN : malnutrition
malnutrido, -da *adj* DESNUTRIDO : malnourished, undernourished
malo¹, **-la** *adj* (**mal** *before masculine singular nouns*) **1** : bad <mala suerte : bad luck> **2** : wicked, naughty **3** : cheap, poor (quality) **4** : harmful <malo para la salud : bad for one's health> **5** (*using the form* **mal**) : unwell <estar mal del corazón : to have heart trouble> **6 estar de malas** : to be in a bad mood
malo², **-la** *n* : villain, bad guy (in novels, movies, etc.)
malogrado, -da *adj* : failed, unsuccessful
malograr *vt* **1** : to spoil, to ruin **2** : to waste (an opportunity, time) — **mal-**

ograrse *vr* **1** FRACASAR **:** to fail **2 :** to die young

malogro *nm* **1 :** untimely death **2** FRACASO **:** failure

maloliente *adj* HEDIONDO **:** foul-smelling, smelly

malparado, -da *adj* **salir malparado** *or* **quedar malparado :** to come out of (something) badly, to end up in a bad state

malpensado, -da *adj* **:** distrustful, suspicious, nasty-minded

malquerencia *nf* AVERSIÓN **:** ill will, dislike

malquerer {64} *vt* **:** to dislike

malquiso, etc. → **malquerer**

malsano, -na *adj* **:** unhealthy

malsonante *adj* **:** rude, offensive <palabras malsonantes : foul language>

malta *nf* **:** malt

malteada *nf* **:** malted milk <malteada de chocolate : chocolate malt>

maltés, -tesa *adj & n, mpl* **malteses :** Maltese

maltratar *vt* **1 :** to mistreat, to abuse **2 :** to damage, to spoil

maltrato *nm* **:** mistreatment, abuse

maltrecho, -cha *adj* **:** battered, damaged

malucho, -cha *adj fam* **:** sick, under the weather

malva *adj & nm* **:** mauve

malvado[1], -da *adj* **:** evil, wicked

malvado[2], -da *n* **:** evildoer, wicked person

malvavisco *nm* **:** marshmallow

malvender *vt* **:** to sell at a loss

malversación *nf, pl* **-ciones :** misappropriation (of funds), embezzlement

malversador, -dora *n* **:** embezzler

malversar *vt* **:** to embezzle

malvivir *vi* **:** to live badly, to just scrape by

mamá *nf fam* **:** mom, mama

mamar *vi* **1 :** to suckle **2 darle de mamar a :** to breast-feed — *vt* **1 :** to suckle, to nurse **2 :** to learn from childhood, to grow up with — **mamarse** *vr fam* **:** to get drunk

mamario, -ria *adj* **:** mammary

mamarracho *nm fam* **1** ESPERPENTO **:** mess, sight **2 :** laughingstock, fool **3 :** rubbish, junk

mambo *nm* **:** mambo

mami *nf fam* **:** mommy

mamífero[1], -ra *adj* **:** mammalian

mamífero[2] *nm* **:** mammal

mamila *nf* **1 :** nipple **2** *Mex* **:** baby bottle, pacifier

mamografía *nf* **:** mammogram

mamola *nf* **:** pat, chuck under the chin

mamotreto *nm fam* **1 :** huge book, tome **2** ARMATOSTE **:** hulk, monstrosity

mampara *nf* BIOMBO **:** screen, room divider

mamparo *nm* **:** bulkhead

mampostería *nf* **:** masonry, stonemasonery

mampostero *nm* **:** mason, stonemason

mamut *nm, pl* **mamuts :** mammoth

maná *nm* **:** manna

manada *nf* **1 :** flock, herd, pack **2** *fam* **:** horde, mob <llegaron en manada : they came in droves>

manantial *nm* **1** FUENTE **:** spring **2 :** source

manar *vi* **1 :** to flow **2 :** to abound

manatí *nm* **:** manatee

mancha *nf* **1 :** stain, spot, mark <mancha de sangre : bloodstain> **2 :** blemish, blot <una mancha en su reputación : a blemish on his reputation> **3 :** patch

manchado, -da *adj* **:** stained

manchar *vt* **1** ENSUCIAR **:** to stain, to soil **2** DESHONRAR **:** to sully, to tarnish — **mancharse** *vr* **:** to get dirty

mancillar vt **:** to sully, to besmirch

manco, -ca *adj* **:** one-armed, one-handed

mancomunar *vt* **:** to combine, to pool — **mancomunarse** *vr* **:** to unite, to join together

mancomunidad *nf* **1 :** commonwealth **2 :** association, confederation

mancuernas *nfpl* **:** cuff links

mancuernillas *nf Mex* **:** cuff links

mandadero, -ra *n* **:** errand boy *m,* errand girl *f,* messenger

mandado *nm* **1 :** order, command **2 :** errand <hacer los mandados : to run errands, to go shopping>

mandamás *nmf, pl* **-mases** *fam* **:** boss, bigwig, honcho

mandamiento *nm* **1 :** commandment **2 :** command, order, warrant <mandamiento judicial : warrant, court order>

mandar *vt* **1** ORDENAR **:** to command, to order **2** ENVIAR **:** to send <te manda saludos : he sends you his regards> **3** ECHAR **:** to hurl, to throw **4 ¿mande?** *Mex* **:** yes?, pardon? — *vi* **:** to be the boss, to be in charge — **mandarse** *vr Mex* **:** to take liberties, to take advantage

mandarina *nf* **:** mandarin orange, tangerine

mandatario, -ria *n* **1 :** leader (in politics) <primer mandatario : head of state> **2 :** agent (in law)

mandato *nm* **1 :** term of office **2 :** mandate

mandíbula *nf* **1 :** jaw **2 :** mandible

mandil *nm* **1** DELANTAL **:** apron **2 :** horse blanket

mandilón *nm, pl* **-lones** *fam* **:** wimp, coward

mandioca *nf* **1 :** manioc, cassava **2 :** tapioca

mando *nm* **1 :** command, leadership **2 :** control (for a device) <mando a distancia : remote control> **3 al mando de :** in charge of **4 al mando de :** under the command of

mandolina *nf* **:** mandolin

mandón, -dona *adj, mpl* **mandones :** bossy, domineering

mandonear *vt fam* MANGONEAR : to boss around
mandrágora *nf* : mandrake
manecilla *nf* : hand (of a clock), pointer
manejable *adj* **1** : manageable **2** : docile, easily led
manejar *vt* **1** CONDUCIR : to drive (a car) **2** OPERAR : to handle, to operate **3** : to manage **4** : to manipulate (a person) — *vi* : to drive — **manejarse** *vr* **1** COMPORTARSE : to behave **2** : to get along, to manage
manejo *nm* **1** : handling, operation **2** : management
manera *nf* **1** MODO : way, manner, fashion **2 de cualquier manera** *or* **de todas maneras** : anyway, anyhow **3 de manera que** : so, in order that **4 de ninguna manera** : by no means, absolutely not **5 manera de ser** : personality, demeanor
manga *nf* **1** : sleeve **2** MANGUERA : hose
manganeso *nm* : manganese
mangle *nm* : mangrove
mango *nm* **1** : hilt, handle **2** : mango
mangonear *vt fam* : to boss around, to bully — *vi* **1** : to be bossy **2** : to loaf, to fool around
mangosta *nf* : mongoose
manguera *nf* : hose
maní *nm, pl* **maníes** : peanut
manía *nf* **1** OBSESIÓN : mania, obsession **2** : craze, fad **3** : odd habit, peculiarity **4** : dislike, aversion
maníaco¹, -ca *adj* : maniacal
maníaco², -ca *n* : maniac
maniatar *vt* : to tie the hands of, to manacle
maniático¹, -ca *adj* **1** MANÍACO : maniacal **2** : obsessive **3** : fussy, finicky
maniático², -ca *n* **1** MANÍACO : maniac, lunatic **2** : obsessive person, fanatic **3** : eccentric, crank
manicomio *nm* : insane asylum, madhouse
manicura *nf* : manicure
manicuro, -ra *n* : manicurist
manido, -da *adj* : hackneyed, stale, trite
manifestación *nf, pl* **-ciones 1** : manifestation, sign **2** : demonstration, rally
manifestante *nmf* : demonstrator
manifestar {55} *vt* **1** : to demonstrate, to show **2** : to declare — **manifestarse** *vr* **1** : to be or become evident **2** : to state one's position <se han manifestado a favor del acuerdo : they have declared their support for the agreement> **3** : to demonstrate, to rally
manifiesto¹, -ta *adj* : manifest, evident, clear — **manifiestamente** *adv*
manifiesto² *nm* : manifesto
manija *nf* MANGO : handle
manilla *nf* → **manecilla**
manillar *nm* : handlebars *pl*
maniobra *nf* : maneuver, stratagem
maniobrar *v* : to maneuver
manipulación *nf, pl* **-ciones** : manipulation
manipulador¹, -dora *adj* : manipulating, manipulative
manipulador², -dora *n* : manipulator
manipular *vt* **1** : to manipulate **2** MANEJAR : to handle
maniquí¹ *nmf, pl* **-quíes** : mannequin, model
maniquí² *nm, pl* **-quíes** : mannequin, dummy
manirroto¹, -ta *adj* : extravagant
manirroto², -ta *n* : spendthrift
manivela *nf* : crank
manjar *nm* : delicacy, special dish
mano¹ *nf* **1** : hand **2** : coat (of paint or varnish) **3 a ~** : by hand **4 a ~** *or* **a la mano** : handy, at hand, nearby **5 darse la mano** : to shake hands **6 de la mano** : hand in hand <la política y la economía van de la mano : politics and economics go hand in hand> **7 de primera mano** : firsthand, at firsthand **8 de segunda mano** : secondhand <ropa de segunda mano : secondhand clothing> **9 mano a mano** : one-on-one **10 mano de obra** : labor, manpower **11 mano de mortero** : pestle **12 echar una mano** : to lend a hand **13** *Mex fam* **mano negra** : shady dealings *pl*
mano², -na *n Mex fam* : buddy, pal <¡oye, mano! : hey man!>
manojo *nm* PUÑADO : handful, bunch
manopla *nf* **1** : mitten, mitt **2** : brass knuckles *pl*
manosear *vt* **1** : to handle or touch excessively **2** ACARICIAR : to fondle, to caress
manotazo *nm* : slap, smack, swipe
manotear *vi* : to wave one's hands, to gesticulate
mansalva *adv* **a ~** : at close range
mansarda *nf* BUHARDILLA : attic
mansedumbre *nf* **1** : gentleness, meekness **2** : tameness
mansión *nf, pl* **-siones** : mansion
manso, -sa *adj* **1** : gentle, meek **2** : tame — **mansamente** *adv*
manta *nf* **1** COBIJA, FRAZADA : blanket **2** : poncho **3** *Mex* : coarse cotton fabric
manteca *nf* **1** GRASA : lard, fat **2** : butter
mantecoso, -sa *adj* : buttery
mantel *nm* **1** : tablecloth **2** : altar cloth
mantelería *nf* : table linen
mantener {80} *vt* **1** SUSTENTAR : to support, to feed <mantener uno su familia : to support one's family> **2** CONSERVAR : to keep, to preserve **3** CONTINUAR : to keep up, to sustain <mantener una correspondencia : to keep up a correspondence> **4** AFIRMAR : to maintain, to affirm — **mantenerse** *vr* **1** : to support oneself, to subsist **2 mantenerse firme** : to hold one's ground
mantenimiento *nm* **1** : maintenance, upkeep **2** : sustenance, food **3** : preservation

mantequera *nf* **1** : churn **2** : butter dish
mantequería *nf* **1** : creamery, dairy **2** : grocery store
mantequilla *nf* : butter
mantilla *nf* : mantilla
manto *nm* **1** : cloak **2** : mantle (in geology)
mantón *nm, pl* **-tones** CHAL : shawl
mantuvo, etc. → **mantener**
manual[1] *adj* **1** : manual <trabajo manual : manual labor> **2** : handy, manageable — **manualmente** *adv*
manual[2] *nm* : manual, handbook
manualidades *nfpl* : handicrafts (in schools)
manubrio *nm* **1** : handle, crank **2** : handlebars *pl*
manufactura *nf* **1** FABRICACIÓN : manufacture **2** : manufactured item, product **3** FÁBRICA : factory
manufacturar *vt* FABRICAR : to manufacture
manufacturero[1], **-ra** *adj* : manufacturing
manufacturero[2], **-ra** *n* FABRICANTE : manufacturer
manuscrito[1], **-ta** *adj* : handwritten
manuscrito[2] *nm* : manuscript
manutención *nf, pl* **-ciones** : maintenance, support
manzana *nf* **1** : apple **2** CUADRA : block (enclosed by streets or buildings) **3** *or* **manzana de Adán** : Adam's apple
manzanal *nm* **1** : apple orchard **2** MANZANO : apple tree
manzanar *nm* : apple orchard
manzanilla *nf* **1** : chamomile **2** : chamomile tea
manzano *nm* : apple tree
maña *nf* **1** : dexterity, skill **2** : cunning, guile **3** **mañas** *or* **malas mañas** *nfpl* : bad habits, vices
mañana *nf* **1** : morning **2** : tomorrow
mañanero, -ra *adj* MATUTINO : morning <rocío mañanero : morning dew>
mañanitas *nfpl Mex* : birthday serenade
mañoso, -sa *adj* **1** HÁBIL : skillful **2** ASTUTO : cunning, crafty **3** : fussy, finicky
mapa *nm* CARTA : map
mapache *nm* : raccoon
mapamundi *nm* : map of the world
maqueta *nf* : model, mock-up
maquillador, -dora *n* : makeup artist
maquillaje *nm* : makeup
maquillarse *vr* : to put on makeup, to make oneself up
máquina *nf* **1** : machine <máquina de coser : sewing machine> <máquina de escribir : typewriter> **2** LOCOMOTORA : engine, locomotive **3** : machine (in politics) **4 a toda máquina** : at full speed
maquinación *nf, pl* **-ciones** : machination, scheme, plot
maquinal *adj* : mechanical, automatic — **maquinalmente** *adv*
maquinar *vt* : to plot, to scheme
maquinaria *nf* **1** : machinery **2** : mechanism, works *pl*
maquinilla *nf* **1** : small machine or device **2** *CA, Car* : typewriter
maquinista *nmf* **1** : machinist **2** : railroad engineer
mar *nmf* **1** : sea <un mar agitado : a rough sea> <hacerse a la mar : to set sail> **2 alta mar** : high seas
maraca *nf* : maraca
maraña *nf* **1** : thicket **2** ENREDO : tangle, mess
marasmo *nm* : paralysis, stagnation
maratón *nm, pl* **-tones** : marathon
maravilla *nf* **1** : wonder, marvel <a las mil maravillas : wonderfully, marvelously> <hacer maravillas : to work wonders> **2** : marigold
maravillar *vt* ASOMBRAR : to astonish, to amaze — **maravillarse** *vr* : to be amazed, to marvel
maravilloso, -sa *adj* ESTUPENDO : wonderful, marvelous — **maravillosamente** *adv*
marbete *nm* **1** ETIQUETA : label, tag **2** *PRi* : registration sticker (of a car)
marca *nf* **1** : mark **2** : brand, make **3** : trademark <marca registrada : registered trademark> **4** : record (in sports) <batir la marca : to beat the record>
marcado, -da *adj* : marked <un marcado contraste : a marked contrast>
marcador *nm* **1** TANTEADOR : scoreboard **2** : marker, felt-tipped pen **3 marcador de libros** : bookmark
marcaje *nm* **1** : scoring (in sports) **2** : guarding (in sports)
marcapasos *nms & pl* : pacemaker
marcar {72} *vt* **1** : to mark **2** : to brand (livestock) **3** : to indicate, to show **4** RESALTAR : to emphasize **5** : to dial (a telephone) **6** : to guard (an opponent) **7** ANOTAR : to score (a goal, a point) — *vi* **1** ANOTAR : to score **2** : to dial
marcha *nf* **1** : march **2** : hike, walk <ir de marcha : to go hiking> **3** : pace, speed <a toda marcha : at top speed> **4** : gear (of an automobile) <marcha atrás : reverse, reverse gear> **5 en ~** : in motion, in gear, under way
marchar *vi* **1** IR : to go, to travel **2** ANDAR : to walk **3** FUNCIONAR : to work, to go **4** : to march — **marcharse** *vr* : to leave
marchitar *vi* : to make wither, to wilt — **marchitarse** *vr* **1** : to wither, to shrivel up, to wilt **2** : to languish, to fade away
marchito, -ta *adj* : withered, faded
marcial *adj* : martial, military
marco *nm* **1** : frame, framework **2** : goalposts *pl* **3** AMBIENTE : setting, atmosphere **4** : mark (unit of currency)
marea *nf* : tide
mareado, -da *adj* **1** : dizzy, lightheaded **2** : queasy, nauseous **3** : seasick

marear *vt* **1 :** to make sick <los gases me marearon : the fumes made me sick> **2 :** to bother, to annoy — **marearse** *vr* **1 :** to get sick, to become nauseated **2 :** to feel dizzy **3 :** to get tipsy

marejada *nf* **1 :** surge, swell (of the sea) **2 :** undercurrent, ferment, unrest

maremoto *nm* **:** tidal wave

mareo *nm* **1 :** dizzy spell **2 :** nausea **3 :** seasickness, motion sickness **4 :** annoyance, vexation

marfil *nm* **:** ivory

margarina *nf* **:** margarine

margarita *nf* **1 :** daisy **2 :** margarita (cocktail)

margen[1] *nf, pl* **márgenes :** bank (of a river), side (of a street)

margen[2] *nm, pl* **márgenes 1 :** edge, border **2 :** margin <margen de ganancia : profit margin>

marginación *nf, pl* **-ciones :** marginalization, exclusion

marginado[1], **-da** *adj* **1** DESHEREDADO **:** outcast, alienated, dispossessed **2 clases marginadas :** underclass

marginado[2], **-da** *n* **:** outcast, misfit

marginal *adj* **:** marginal, fringe

marginalidad *nf* **:** marginality

marginar *vt* **:** to ostracize, to exclude

mariachi *nm* **:** mariachi musician or band

maridaje *nm* **:** marriage, union

maridar *vt* UNIR **:** to marry, to unite

marido *nm* ESPOSO **:** husband

marihuana *or* **mariguana** *or* **marijuana** *nf* **:** marihuana

marimacho *nmf fam* **1 :** mannish woman **2 :** tomboy

marimba *nf* **:** marimba

marina *nf* **1 :** coast, coastal area **2 :** navy, fleet <marina mercante : merchant marine>

marinada *nf* **:** marinade

marinar *vt* **:** to marinate

marinero[1], **-ra** *adj* **1 :** seaworthy **2 :** sea, marine

marinero[2] *nm* **:** sailor

marino[1], **-na** *adj* **:** marine, sea

marino[2] *nm* **:** sailor, seaman

marioneta *nf* TÍTERE **:** puppet, marionette

mariposa *nf* **1 :** butterfly **2 mariposa nocturna :** moth

mariquita[1] *nf* **:** ladybug

mariquita[2] *nm fam* **:** sissy, wimp

mariscal *nm* **1 :** marshal **2 mariscal de campo :** field marshal (in the military), quarterback (in football)

marisco *nm* **1 :** shellfish **2 mariscos** *nmpl* **:** seafood

marisma *nf* **:** marsh, salt marsh

marital *adj* **:** marital, married <la vida marital : married life>

marítimo, -ma *adj* **:** maritime, shipping <la industria marítima : the shipping industry>

marmita *nf* **:** (cooking) pot

mármol *nm* **:** marble

marmóreo, -rea *adj* **:** marble, marmoreal

marmota *nf* **1 :** marmot **2 marmota de América :** woodchuck, groundhog

maroma *nf* **1 :** rope **2 :** acrobatic stunt **3** *Mex* **:** somersault

marque, etc. → **marcar**

marqués, -quesa *n, mpl* **marqueses :** marquis *m,* marquess *m,* marquise *f,* marchioness *f*

marquesina *nf* **:** marquee, canopy

marqueta *nf Mex* **:** block (of chocolate), lump (of sugar or salt)

marranada *nf* **1 :** disgusting thing **2 :** dirty trick

marrano[1], **-na** *adj* **:** filthy, disgusting

marrano[2], **-na** *n* **1** CERDO **:** pig, hog **2 :** dirty pig, slob

marrar *vt* **:** to miss (a target) — *vi* **:** to fail, to go wrong

marras *adv* **1 :** long ago **2 de ~ :** said, aforementioned <el individuo de marras : the individual in question>

marrasquino *nm* **:** maraschino

marrón *adj & nm, pl* **marrones** CASTAÑO **:** brown

marroquí *adj & nmf, pl* **-quíes :** Moroccan

marsopa *nf* **:** porpoise

marsupial *nm* **:** marsupial

marta *nf* **1 :** marten **2 marta cebellina :** sable (animal)

Marte *nm* **:** Mars

martes *nms & pl* **:** Tuesday

martillar *v* **:** to hammer

martillazo *nm* **:** blow with a hammer

martillo *nm* **1 :** hammer **2 martillo neumático :** jackhammer

martinete *nm* **1 :** heron **2 :** pile driver

mártir *nmf* **:** martyr

martirio *nm* **1 :** martyrdom **2 :** ordeal, torment

martirizar {21} *vt* **1 :** to martyr **2** ATORMENTAR **:** to torment

marxismo *nm* **:** Marxism

marxista *adj & nmf* **:** Marxist

marzo *nm* **:** March

mas *conj* PERO **:** but

más[1] *adv* **1 :** more <¿hay algo más grande? : is there anything bigger?> **2 :** most <Luis es el más alto : Luis is the tallest> **3 :** longer <el sabor dura más : the flavor lasts longer> **4 :** rather <más querría andar : I would rather walk> **5 a ~ :** besides, in addition **6 más allá :** further **7 qué . . . más . . . :** what . . ., what a . . . <¡qué día más bonito! : what a beautiful day!>

más[2] *adj* **1 :** more <dáme dos kilos más : give me two more kilos> **2 :** most <la que ganó más dinero : the one who earned the most money> **3 :** else <¿quién más quiere vino? : who else wants wine?>

más[3] *n* **:** plus sign

más[4] *prep* **:** plus <tres más dos es igual a cinco : three plus two equals five>

más[5] *pron* **1 :** more <¿tienes más? : do you have more?> **2 a lo más :** at most **3 de ~ :** extra, excess **4 más o menos :** more or less, approximately **5 por más que :** no matter how much <por más que corras no llegarás a tiempo : no matter how fast you run you won't arrive on time>

masa *nf* **1 :** mass, volume <masa atómica : atomic mass> <producción en masa : mass production> **2 :** dough, batter **3 masas** *nfpl* **:** people, masses <las masas populares : the common people> **4 masa harina** *Mex* **:** corn flour (for tortillas, etc.)

masacrar *vt* **:** to massacre

masacre *nf* **:** massacre

masaje *nm* **:** massage

masajear *vt* **:** to massage

masajista *nmf* **:** masseur *m,* masseuse *f*

mascar {72} *v* MASTICAR **:** to chew

máscara *nf* **1** CARETA **:** mask **2 :** appearance, pretense

mascarada *nf* **:** masquerade

mascarilla *nf* **1 :** mask (in medicine) <mascarilla de oxígeno : oxygen mask> **2 :** facial mask (in cosmetology)

mascota *nf* **:** mascot

masculinidad *nf* **:** masculinity

masculino, -na *adj* **1 :** masculine, male **2 :** manly **3 :** masculine (in grammar)

mascullar *v* **:** to mumble, to mutter

masificado, -da *adj* **:** overcrowded

masilla *nf* **:** putty

masivamente *adv* **:** en masse

masivo, -va *adj* **:** mass <comunicación masiva : mass communication>

masón *nm, pl* **masones** FRANCMASÓN **:** Mason, Freemason

masonería *nf* FRANCMASONERÍA **:** Masonry, Freemasonry

masónico, -ca *adj* **:** Masonic

masoquismo *nm* **:** masochism

masoquista[1] *adj* **:** masochistic

masoquista[2] *nmf* **:** masochist

masque, etc. → **mascar**

masticar {72} *v* MASCAR **:** to chew, to masticate

mástil *nm* **1 :** mast **2** ASTA **:** flagpole **3 :** neck (of a stringed instrument)

mastín *nm, pl* **mastines :** mastiff

mástique *nm* **:** putty, filler

mastodonte *nm* **:** mastodon

masturbación *nf, pl* **-ciones :** masturbation

masturbarse *vr* **:** to masturbate

mata *nf* **1** ARBUSTO **:** bush, shrub **2 :** plant <mata de tomate : tomato plant> **3 :** sprig, tuft **4 mata de pelo :** mop of hair

matadero *nm* **:** slaughterhouse, abattoir

matado, -da *adj Mex* **:** strenuous, exhausting

matador *nm* TORERO **:** matador, bullfighter

matamoscas *nms & pl* **:** flyswatter

matanza *nf* MASACRE **:** slaughter, butchering

matar *vt* **1 :** to kill **2 :** to slaughter, to butcher **3** APAGAR **:** to extinguish, to put out (fire, light) **4 :** to tone down (colors) **5 :** to pass, to waste (time) **6 :** to trump (in card games) — *vi* **:** to kill — **matarse** *vr* **1 :** to be killed **2** SUICIDARSE **:** to commit suicide **3** *fam* **:** to exhaust oneself <se mató tratando de terminarlo : he knocked himself out trying to finish it>

matasanos *nms & pl fam* **:** quack

matasellar *vt* **:** to cancel (a stamp), to postmark

matasellos *nms & pl* **:** postmark

matatena *nf Mex* **:** jacks

mate[1] *adj* **:** matte, dull

mate[2] *nm* **1 :** maté **2 jaque mate :** checkmate <darle mate a *or* darle jaque mate a : to checkmate>

matemática → **matemáticas**

matemáticas *nfpl* **:** mathematics, math

matemático[1], **-ca** *adj* **:** mathematical — **matemáticamente** *adv*

matemático[2], **-ca** *n* **:** mathematician

materia *nf* **1 :** matter <materia gris : gray matter> **2 :** material <materia prima : raw material> **3 :** (academic) subject **4 en materia de :** on the subject of, concerning

material[1] *adj* **1 :** material, physical, real **2 daños materiales :** property damage

material[2] *nm* **1 :** material <material de construcción : building material> **2** EQUIPO **:** equipment, gear

materialismo *nm* **:** materialism

materialista[1] *adj* **:** materialistic

materialista[2] *nmf* **1 :** materialist **2** *Mex* **:** truck driver

materializar {21} *vt* **:** to bring to fruition, to realize — **materializarse** *vr* **:** to materialize, to come into being

materialmente *adv* **1 :** materially, physically <materialmente imposible : physically impossible> **2 :** really, absolutely

maternal *adj* **:** maternal, motherly

maternidad *nf* **1 :** maternity, motherhood **2 :** maternity hospital, maternity ward

materno, -na *adj* **:** maternal

matinal *adj* MATUTINO **:** morning <la pálida luz matinal : the pale morning light>

matinée *or* **matiné** *nf* **:** matinee

matiz *nm, pl* **matices 1 :** hue, shade **2 :** nuance

matización *nf, pl* **-ciones 1 :** tinting, toning, shading **2 :** clarification (of a statement)

matizar {21} *vt* **1 :** to tinge, to tint (colors) **2 :** to vary, to modulate (sounds) **3 :** to qualify (statements)

matón *nm, pl* **matones :** thug, bully

matorral *nm* **1 :** thicket **2 :** scrub, scrubland

matraca *nf* **1 :** rattle, noisemaker **2 dar la matraca a :** to pester, to nag
matriarca *nf* **:** matriarch
matriarcado *nm* **:** matriarchy
matrícula *nf* **1 :** list, roll, register **2** INSCRIPCIÓN **:** registration, enrollment **3 :** license plate, registration number
matriculación *nf, pl* **-ciones :** matriculation, registration
matricular *vt* **1** INSCRIBIR **:** to enroll, to register (a person) **2 :** to register (a vehicle) — **matricularse** *vr* **:** to matriculate
matrimonial *adj* **:** marital, matrimonial <la vida matrimonial : married life>
matrimonio *nm* **1 :** marriage, matrimony **2 :** married couple
matriz *nf, pl* **matrices 1 :** uterus, womb **2 :** original, master copy **3 :** main office, headquarters **4 :** stub (of a check) **5 :** matrix <matriz de puntos : dot matrix>
matrona *nf* **:** matron
matronal *adj* **:** matronly
matutino[1], -na *adj* **:** morning <la edición matutina : the morning edition>
matutino[2] *nm* **:** morning paper
maullar {8} *vi* **:** to meow
maullido *nm* **:** meow
mauritano, -na *adj & n* **:** Mauritanian
mausoleo *nm* **:** mausoleum
maxilar *nm* **:** jaw, jawbone
máxima *nf* **:** maxim
máxime *adv* ESPECIALMENTE **:** especially, principally
maximizar {21} *vt* **:** to maximize
máximo[1], -ma *adj* **:** maximum, greatest, highest
máximo[2] *nm* **1 :** maximum **2 al máximo :** to the utmost **3 como ~ :** at the most, at the latest
maya[1] *adj & nmf* **:** Mayan
maya[2] *nmf* **:** Maya, Mayan
mayo *nm* **:** May
mayonesa *nf* **:** mayonnaise
mayor[1] *adj* **1** (*comparative of* **grande**) **:** bigger, larger, greater, elder, older **2** (*superlative of* **grande**) **:** biggest, largest, greatest, eldest, oldest **3 :** grown-up, mature **4 :** main, major **5 mayor de edad :** of (legal) age **6 al por mayor** *or* **por ~ :** wholesale
mayor[2] *nmf* **1 :** major (in the military) **2 :** adult
mayoral *nm* CAPATAZ **:** foreman, overseer
mayordomo *nm* **:** butler, majordomo
mayoreo *nm* **:** wholesale
mayores *nmpl* **:** grown-ups, elders
mayoría *nf* **1 :** majority **2 en su mayoría :** on the whole
mayorista[1] *adj* ALMACENISTA **:** wholesale
mayorista[2] *nmf* **:** wholesaler
mayoritariamente *adv* **:** primarily, chiefly
mayoritario, -ria *adj & n* **:** majority <un consenso mayoritario : a majority consensus>
mayormente *adv* **:** primarily, chiefly
mayúscula *nf* **:** capital letter
mayúsculo, -la *adj* **1 :** capital, uppercase **2 :** huge, terrible <un problema mayúsculo : a huge problem>
maza *nf* **1 :** mace (weapon) **2 :** drumstick **3** *fam* **:** bore, pest
mazacote *nm* **1 :** concrete **2 :** lumpy mess (of food) **3 :** eyesore, crude work of art
mazapán *nm, pl* **-panes :** marzipan
mazmorra *nf* CALABOZO **:** dungeon
mazo *nm* **1 :** mallet **2 :** pestle **3** MANOJO **:** handful, bunch
mazorca *nf* **1** CHOCLO **:** cob, ear of corn **2 pelar la mazorca** *Mex fam* **:** to smile from ear to ear
me *pron* **1 :** me <me vieron : they saw me> **2 :** to me, for me, from me <dame el libro : give me the book> <me lo compró : he bought it for me> <me robaron la cartera : they stole my pocketbook> **3 :** myself, to myself, for myself, from myself <me preparé una buena comida : I cooked myself a good dinner> <me equivoqué : I made a mistake>
mecánica *nf* **:** mechanics
mecánico[1], -ca *adj* **:** mechanical — **mecánicamente** *adv*
mecánico[2], -ca *n* **1 :** mechanic **2 :** technician <mecánico dental : dental technician>
mecanismo *nm* **:** mechanism
mecanización *nf, pl* **-ciones :** mechanization
mecanizar {21} *vt* **:** to mechanize
mecanografía *nf* **:** typing
mecanografiar {85} *vt* **:** to type
mecanógrafo, -fa *n* **:** typist
mecate *nm CA, Mex, Ven* **:** rope, twine, cord
mecedor *nm* **:** glider (seat)
mecedora *nf* **:** rocking chair
mecenas *nmfs & pl* **:** patron (of the arts), sponsor
mecenazgo *nm* PATROCINIO **:** sponsorship, patronage
mecer {86} *vt* **1 :** to rock **2** COLUMPIAR **:** to push (on a swing) — **mecerse** *vr* **:** to rock, to swing, to sway
mecha *nf* **1 :** fuse **2 :** wick **3 mechas** *nfpl* **:** highlights (in hair)
mechero *nm* **1 :** burner **2** *Spain* **:** lighter
mechón *nm, pl* **mechones :** lock (of hair)
medalla *nf* **:** medal, medallion
medallista *nmf* **:** medalist
medallón *nm, pl* **-llones 1 :** medallion **2 :** locket
media *nf* **1** CALCETÍN **:** sock **2 :** average, mean **3 medias** *nfpl* **:** stockings, hose, tights **4 a medias :** by halves, half and half, halfway <ir a medias : to go

halves> <verdad a medias : half-truth>

mediación *nf, pl* **-ciones** : mediation

mediado, -da *adj* **1** : half full, half empty, half over **2** : halfway through <mediada la tarea : halfway through the job>

mediador, -dora *n* : mediator

mediados *nmpl* **a mediados de** : halfway through, in the middle of <a mediados del mes : towards the middle of the month, mid-month>

medialuna *nf* **1** : crescent **2** : croissant, crescent roll

medianamente *adv* : fairly, moderately

medianero, -ra *adj* **1** : dividing **2** : mediating

medianía *nf* **1** : middle position **2** : mediocre person, mediocrity

mediano, -na *adj* **1** : medium, average <la mediana edad : middle age> **2** : mediocre

medianoche *nf* : midnight

mediante *prep* : through, by means of <Dios mediante : God willing>

mediar *vi* **1** : to mediate **2** : to be in the middle, to be halfway through **3** : to elapse, to pass <mediaron cinco años entre el inicio de la guerra y el armisticio : five years passed between the start of the war and the armistice> **4** : to be a consideration <media el hecho de que cuesta mucho : one must take into account that it is costly> **5** : to come up, to happen <medió algo urgente : something pressing came up>

mediatizar {21} *vt* : to influence, to interfere with

medicación *nf, pl* **-ciones** : medication, treatment

medicamento *nm* : medication, medicine, drug

medicar {72} *vt* : to medicate — **medicarse** *vr* : to take medicine

medicina *nf* : medicine

medicinal *adj* **1** : medicinal **2** : medicated

medicinar *vt* : to give medication to, to dose

medición *nf, pl* **-ciones** : measuring, measurement

médico[1], -ca *adj* : medical <una receta médica : a doctor's prescription>

médico[2], -ca *n* DOCTOR : doctor, physician

medida *nf* **1** : measurement, measure <hecho a medida : custom-made> **2** : measure, step <tomar medidas : to take steps> **3** : moderation, prudence <sin medida : immoderately> **4** : extent, degree <en gran medida : to a great extent>

medidor *nm* : meter, gauge

medieval *adj* : medieval — **medievalista** *nmf*

medievo *nm* → **medioevo**

medio[1] *adv* **1** : half <está medio dormida : she's half asleep> **2** : rather, kind of <está medio aburrida esta fiesta : this party is rather boring>

medio[2], -dia *adj* **1** : half <una media hora : half an hour> <medio hermano : half brother> <a media luz : in the half-light> <son las tres y media : it's half past three, it's three-thirty> **2** : midway, halfway <a medio camino : halfway there> **3** : middle <la clase media : the middle class> **4** : average <la temperatura media : the average temperature>

medio[3] *nm* **1** CENTRO : middle, center <en medio de : in the middle of, amid> **2** AMBIENTE : milieu, environment **3** : medium, spiritualist **4** : means *pl,* way <por medio de : by means of> <los medios de comunicación : the media> **5 medios** *nmpl* : means, resources

mediocre *adj* : mediocre, average

mediocridad *nf* : mediocrity

mediodía *nm* : noon, midday

medioevo *nm* : Middle Ages

medir {54} *vt* **1** : to measure **2** : to weigh, to consider <medir los riesgos : to weigh the risks> — *vi* : to measure — **medirse** *vr* : to be moderate, to exercise restraint

meditabundo, -da *adj* PENSATIVO : pensive, thoughtful

meditación *nf, pl* **-ciones** : meditation, thought

meditar *vi* : to meditate, to think <meditar sobre la vida : to contemplate life> — *vt* **1** : to think over, to consider **2** : to plan, to work out

meditativo, -va *adj* : pensive

mediterráneo, -nea *adj* : Mediterranean

medrar *vi* **1** PROSPERAR : to prosper, to thrive **2** AUMENTAR : to increase, to grow

medro *nm* PROSPERIDAD : prosperity, growth

medroso, -sa *adj* : fainthearted, fearful

médula *nf* **1** : marrow, pith **2 médula espinal** : spinal cord

medular *adj* : fundamental, core <el punto medular : the crux of the matter>

medusa *nf* : jellyfish, medusa

megabyte *nm* : megabyte

megáfono *nm* : megaphone

megahertzio *nm* : megahertz

megatón *nm, pl* **-tones** : megaton

megavatio *nm* : megawatt

mejicano → **mexicano**

mejilla *nf* : cheek

mejillón *nm, pl* **-llones** : mussel

mejor[1] *adv* **1** : better <Carla cocina mejor que Ana : Carla cooks better than Ana> **2** : best <ella es la que lo hace mejor : she's the one who does it best> **3** : rather <mejor morir que rendirme : I'd rather die than give up> **4** : it's better that . . . <mejor te

vas : you'd better go> **5 a lo mejor** : maybe, perhaps

mejor[2] *adj* **1** (*comparative of* **bueno**) : better <a falta de algo mejor : for lack of something better> **2** (*comparative of* **bien**) : better <está mucho mejor : he's much better> **3** (*superlative of* **bueno**) : best, the better <mi mejor amigo : my best friend> **4** (*superlative of* **bien**) : best, the better <duermo mejor en un clima seco : I sleep best in a dry climate> **5** PREFERIBLE : preferable, better **6 lo mejor** : the best thing, the best part

mejor[3] *nmf* (*with definite article*) : the better (one), the best (one)

mejora *nf* : improvement

mejoramiento *nm* : improvement

mejorana *nf* : marjoram

mejorar *vt* : to improve, to make better — *vi* : to improve, to get better — **mejorarse** *vr*

mejoría *nf* : improvement, betterment

mejunje *nm* : concoction, brew

melancolía *nf* : melancholy, sadness

melancólico, -ca *adj* : melancholy, sad

melanoma *nm* : melanoma

melaza *nf* : molasses

maleficio *nm* : curse, spell

melena *nf* **1** : mane **2** : long hair **3 melenas** *nfpl* GREÑAS : shaggy hair, mop

melenudo[1], **-da** *adj fam* : longhaired

melenudo[2], **-da** *n* GREÑUDO : longhair, hippie

melindres *nmpl* **1** : affectation, airs *pl* **2** : finickiness

melindroso[1], **-sa** *adj* **1** : affected **2** : fussy, finicky

melindroso[2], **-sa** *n* : finicky person, fussbudget

melisa *nf* : lemon balm

mella *nf* **1** : dent, nick **2 hacer mella en** : to have an effect on, to make an impression on

mellado, -da *adj* **1** : chipped, dented **2** : gap-toothed

mellar *vt* : to dent, to nick

mellizo, -za *adj & n* GEMELO : twin

melocotón *nm, pl* **-tones** : peach

melodía *nf* : melody, tune

melódico, -ca *adj* : melodic

melodioso, -sa *adj* : melodious

melodrama *nm* : melodrama

melodramático, -ca *adj* : melodramatic

melón *nm, pl* **melones** : melon, cantaloupe

meloso, -sa *adj* **1** : honeyed, sweet **2** EMPALAGOSO : cloying, saccharine

membrana *nf* **1** : membrane **2 membrana interdigital** : web, webbing (of a bird's foot) — **membranoso, -sa** *adj*

membresía *nf* : membership, members *pl*

membrete *nm* : letterhead, heading

membrillo *nm* : quince

membrudo, -da *adj* FORNIDO : muscular, well-built

memez *nf, pl* **memeces** : stupid thing

memo, -ma *adj* : silly, stupid

memorabilia *nf* : memorabilia

memorable *adj* : memorable

memorándum *or* **memorando** *nm, pl* **-dums** *or* **-dos** **1** : memorandum, memo **2** : memo book, appointment book

memoria *nf* **1** : memory <de memoria : by heart> <hacer memoria : to try to remember> <traer a la memoria : to call to mind> **2** RECUERDO : remembrance, memory <su memoria perdurará para siempre : his memory will live forever> **3** : report <memoria annual : annual report> **4 memorias** *nfpl* : memoirs

memorizar {21} *vt* : to memorize — **memorización** *nf*

mena *nf* : ore

menaje *nm* : household goods *pl*, furnishings *pl*

mención *nf, pl* **-ciones** : mention

mencionar *vt* : to mention, to refer to

mendaz *adj, pl* **mendaces** : mendacious, lying

mendicidad *nf* : begging

mendigar {52} *vi* : to beg — *vt* : to beg for

mendigo, -ga *n* LIMOSNERO : beggar

mendrugo *nm* : crust (of bread)

menear *vt* **1** : to shake (one's head) **2** : to sway, to wiggle (one's hips) **3** : to wag (a tail) **4** : to stir (a liquid) — **menearse** *vr* **1** : to wiggle one's hips **2** : to fidget

meneo *nm* **1** : movement **2** : shake, toss **3** : swaying, wagging, wiggling **4** : stir, stirring

menester *nm* **1** : activity, occupation, duties *pl* **2 ser menester** : to be necessary <es menester que vengas : you must come>

mengano, -na *n* → **fulano**

mengua *nf* **1** : decrease, decline **2** : lack, want **3** : discredit, dishonor

menguar *vt* : to diminish, to lessen — *vi* **1** : to decline, to decrease **2** : to wane — **menguante** *adj*

meningitis *nf* : meningitis

menisco *nm* : meniscus, cartilage

menjurje *nm* → **mejunje**

menopausia *nf* : menopause

menor[1] *adj* **1** (*comparative of* **pequeño**) : smaller, lesser, younger **2** (*superlative of* **pequeño**) : smallest, least, youngest **3** : minor **4 al por menor** : retail **5 ser menor de edad** : to be a minor, to be underage

menor[2] *nmf* : minor, juvenile

menos[1] *adv* **1** : less <llueve menos en agosto : it rains less in August> **2** : least <el coche menos caro : the least expensive car> **3 ~ de** : less than, fewer than

menos[2] *adj* **1** : less, fewer <tengo más trabajo y menos tiempo : I have more

work and less time> **2** : least, fewest <la clase que tiene menos estudiantes : the class that has the fewest students>
menos[3] *prep* **1** SALVO, EXCEPTO : except **2** : minus <quince menos cuatro son once : fifteen minus four is eleven>
menos[4] *pron* **1** : less, fewer <no deberías aceptar menos : you shouldn't accept less> **2 al menos** *or* **por lo menos** : at least **3 a menos que** : unless
menoscabar *vt* **1** : to lessen, to diminish **2** : to disgrace, to discredit **3** PERJUDICAR : to harm, to damage
menoscabo *nm* **1** : lessening, diminishing **2** : disgrace, discredit **3** : harm, damage
menospreciar *vt* **1** DESPRECIAR : to scorn, to look down on **2** : to underestimate, to undervalue
menosprecio *nm* DESPRECIO : contempt, scorn
mensaje *nm* : message
mensajero, -ra *n* : messenger
menso, -sa *adj Mex fam* : foolish, stupid
menstrual *adj* : menstrual
menstruar {3} *vi* : to menstruate — **menstruación** *nf*
mensual *adj* : monthly
mensualidad *nf* **1** : monthly payment, installment **2** : monthly salary
mensualmente *adv* : every month, monthly
mensurable *adj* : measurable
menta *nf* **1** : mint, peppermint **2 menta verde** : spearmint
mentado, -da *adj* **1** : aforementioned **2** FAMOSO : renowned, famous
mental *adj* : mental, intellectual — **mentalmente** *adv*
mentalidad *nf* : mentality
mentar {55} *vt* **1** : to mention, to name **2 mentar la madre a** *fam* : to insult, to swear at
mente *nf* : mind <tener en mente : to have in mind>
mentecato[1], -ta *adj* : foolish, simple
mentecato[2], -ta *n* : fool, idiot
mentir {76} *vi* : to lie
mentira *nf* : lie
mentiroso[1], -sa *adj* EMBUSTERO : lying, untruthful
mentiroso[2], -sa *n* EMBUSTERO : liar
mentís *nm, pl* **mentises** : denial, repudiation <dar el mentís a : to deny, to refute>
mentol *nm* : menthol
mentón *nm, pl* **mentones** BARBILLA : chin
mentor *nm* : mentor, counselor
menú *nm, pl* **menús** : menu
menudear *vi* : to occur frequently — *vt* : to do repeatedly
menudencia *nf* **1** : trifle **2 menudencias** *nfpl* : giblets
menudeo *nm* : retail, retailing
menudillos *nmpl* : giblets
menudo[1], -da *adj* **1** : minute, small **2 a ~** FRECUENTEMENTE : often, frequently
menudo[2] *nm* **1** *Mex* : tripe stew **2 menudos** *nmpl* : giblets
meñique *nm or* **dedo meñique** : little finger, pinkie
meollo *nm* **1** MÉDULA : marrow **2** SESO : brains *pl* **3** ENTRAÑA : essence, core <el meollo del asunto : the heart of the matter>
mequetrefe *nm fam* : good-for-nothing
mercachifle *nm* : peddler, hawker
mercadeo *nm* : marketing
mercadería *nf* : merchandise, goods *pl*
mercado *nm* : market <mercado de trabajo *or* mercado laboral : labor market> <mercado de valores *or* mercado bursátil : stock market>
mercadotecnia *nf* : marketing
mercancía *nf* : merchandise, goods *pl*
mercante *nmf* : merchant, dealer
mercantil *adj* COMERCIAL : commercial, mercantile
merced *nf* **1** : favor **2 ~ a** : thanks to, due to **3 a merced de** : at the mercy of
mercenario, -ria *adj & n* : mercenary
mercería *nf* : notions store
mercurio *nm* : mercury
Mercurio *nm* : Mercury (planet)
merecedor, -dora *adj* : deserving, worthy
merecer {53} *vt* : to deserve, to merit — *vi* : to be worthy
merecidamente *adv* : rightfully, deservedly
merecido *nm* : something merited, due <recibieron su merecido : they got their just deserts>
merecimiento *nm* : merit, worth
merendar {55} *vi* : to have an afternoon snack — *vt* : to have as an afternoon snack
merendero *nm* **1** : lunchroom, snack bar **2** : picnic area
merengue *nm* **1** : meringue **2** : merengue (dance)
meridiano[1], -na *adj* **1** : midday **2** : crystal clear
meridiano[2] *nm* : meridian
meridional *adj* SUREÑO : southern
merienda *nf* : afternoon snack, tea
mérito *nm* : merit
meritorio[1], -ria *adj* : deserving, meritorious
meritorio[2], -ria *n* : intern, trainee
merluza *nf* : hake
merma *nf* **1** : decrease, cut **2** : waste, loss
mermar *vi* : to decrease, to diminish — *vt* : to reduce, to cut down
mermelada *nf* : marmalade, jam
mero[1], -ra *adv Mex fam* **1** : nearly, almost <ya mero me caí : I almost fell> **2** : just, exactly <aquí mero : right here>

mero², **-ra** *adj* **1** : mere, simple **2** *Mex fam* (*used as an intensifier*) : very <en el mero centro : in the very center of town>
mero³ *nm* : grouper
merodeador, **-dora** *n* **1** : marauder **2** : prowler
merodear *vi* **1** : to maraud, to pillage **2** : to prowl around, to skulk
mes *nm* : month
mesa *nf* **1** : table **2** : committee, board
mesada *nf* : allowance, pocket money
mesarse *vr* : to pull at <mesarse los cabellos : to tear one's hair>
mesero, **-ra** *n* CAMARERO : waiter, waitress *f*
meseta *nf* : plateau, tableland
Mesías *nm* : Messiah
mesón *nm, pl* **mesones** : inn
mesonero, **-ra** *nm* : innkeeper
mestizo¹, **-za** *adj* **1** : of mixed ancestry **2** HÍBRIDO : hybrid
mestizo², **-za** *n* : person of mixed ancestry
mesura *nf* **1** MODERACIÓN : moderation, discretion **2** CORTESÍA : courtesy **3** GRAVEDAD : seriousness, dignity
mesurado, **-da** *adj* COMEDIDO : moderate, restrained
mesurar *vt* : to moderate, to restrain, to temper — **mesurarse** *vr* : to restrain oneself
meta *nf* : goal, objective
metabólico, **-ca** *adj* : metabolic
metabolismo *nm* : metabolism
metabolizar {21} *vt* : to metabolize
metafísica *nf* : metaphysics
metafísico, **-ca** *adj* : metaphysical
metáfora *nf* : metaphor
metafórico, **-ca** *adj* : metaphoric, metaphorical
metal *nm* **1** : metal **2** : brass section (in an orchestra)
metálico, **-ca** *adj* : metallic, metal
metalistería *nf* : metalworking
metalurgia *nf* : metallurgy
metalúrgico¹, **-ca** *adj* : metallurgical
metalúrgico², **-ca** *n* : metallurgist
metamorfosis *nfs & pl* : metamorphosis
metano *nm* : methane
meteórico, **-ca** *adj* : meteoric
meteorito *nm* : meteorite
meteoro *nm* : meteor
meteorología *nf* : meteorology
meteorológico, **-ca** *adj* : meteorologic, meteorological
meteorólogo, **-ga** *n* : meteorologist
meter *vt* **1** : to put (in) <metieron su dinero en el banco : they put their money in the bank> **2** : to fit, to squeeze <puedes meter dos líneas más en esa página : you can fit two more lines on that page> **3** : to place (in a job) <lo metieron de barrendero : they got him a job as a street sweeper> **4** : to involve <lo metió en un buen lío : she got him in an awful mess> **5** : to make, to cause <meten demasiado ruido : they make too much noise> **6** : to spread (a rumor) **7** : to strike (a blow) **8** : to take up, to take in (clothing) **9 a todo meter** : at top speed — **meterse** *vr* **1** : to get into, to enter **2** *fam* : to meddle <no te metas en lo que no te importa : mind your own business> **3 ~ con** *fam* : to pick a fight with, to provoke <no te metas conmigo : don't mess with me>
metiche¹ *adj Mex fam* : nosy
metiche² *nmf Mex fam* : busybody
meticulosidad *nf* : thoroughness, meticulousness
meticuloso, **-sa** *adj* : meticulous, thorough — **meticulosamente** *adv*
metida *nf* **metida de pata** *fam* : blunder, gaffe, blooper
metódico, **-ca** *adj* : methodical — **metódicamente** *adv*
metodista *adj & nmf* : Methodist
método *nm* : method
metodología *nf* : methodology
metomentodo *nmf fam* : busybody
metralla *nf* : shrapnel
metralleta *nf* : submachine gun
métrico, **-ca** *adj* **1** : metric **2 cinta métrica** : tape measure
metro *nm* **1** : meter **2** : subway
metrónomo *nm* : metronome
metrópoli *nf or* **metrópolis** *nfs & pl* : metropolis
metropolitano, **-na** *adj* : metropolitan
mexicanismo *nm* : Mexican word or expression
mexicano, **-na** *adj & n* : Mexican
mexicoamericano, **-na** *adj & n* : Mexican-American
meza, **etc.** → **mecer**
mezcla *nf* **1** : mixing **2** : mixture, blend **3** : mortar (masonry material)
mezclar *vt* **1** : to mix, to blend **2** : to mix up, to muddle **3** INVOLUCRAR : to involve — **mezclarse** *vr* **1** : to get mixed up (in) **2** : to mix, to mingle (socially)
mezclilla *nf Chile, Mex* : denim <pantalones de mezclilla : jeans>
mezcolanza *nf* : jumble, hodgepodge
mezquindad *nf* **1** : meanness, stinginess **2** : petty deed, mean action
mezquino¹, **-na** *adj* **1** : mean, petty **2** : stingy **3** : paltry
mezquino² *nm Mex* : wart
mezquita *nf* : mosque
mezquite *nm* : mesquite
mi *adj* : my
mí *pron* **1** : me <es para mí : it's for me> <a mí no me importa : it doesn't matter to me> **2 mí mismo, mí misma** : myself
miasma *nm* : miasma
miau *nm* : meow
mica *nf* : mica
mico *nm* : monkey, long-tailed monkey
micra *nf* : micron
microbio *nm* : microbe, germ
microbiología *nf* : microbiology

microbiólogico, -ca *adj* : microbiological
microbús *nm, pl* **-buses** : minibus
microcomputadora *nf* : microcomputer
microcosmos *nms & pl* : microcosm
microficha *nf* : microfiche
microfilm *nm, pl* **-films** : microfilm
micrófono *nm* : microphone
micrómetro *nm* : micrometer
microonda *nf* : microwave
microondas *nms & pl* : microwave, microwave oven
microordenador *nm Spain* : microcomputer
microorganismo *nm* : microorganism
microprocesador *nm* : microprocessor
microscópico, -ca *adj* : microscopic
microscopio *nm* : microscope
mide, etc. → **medir**
miedo *nm* **1** TEMOR : fear <le tiene miedo al perro : he's scared of the dog> <tenían miedo de hablar : they were afraid to speak> **2 dar miedo** : to frighten
miedoso, -sa *adj* TEMEROSO : fearful
miel *nf* : honey
miembro *nm* **1** : member **2** EXTREMIDAD : limb, extremity
mienta, etc. → **mentar**
miente, etc. → **mentir**
mientras[1] *adv* **1** *or* **mientras tanto** : meanwhile, in the meantime **2 mientras más** : the more <mientras más como, más quiero : the more I eat, the more I want>
mientras[2] *conj* **1** : while, as <roncaba mientras dormía : he snored while he was sleeping> **2** : as long as <luchará mientras pueda : he will fight as long as he is able> **3 mientras que** : while, whereas <él es alto mientras que ella es muy baja : he is tall, whereas she is very short>
miércoles *nms & pl* : Wednesday
miga *nf* **1** : crumb **2 hacer buenas (malas) migas con** : to get along well (poorly) with
migaja *nf* **1** : crumb **2 migajas** *nfpl* SOBRAS : leftovers, scraps
migración *nf, pl* **-ciones** : migration
migrante *nmf* : migrant
migraña *nf* : migraine
migratorio, -ria *adj* : migratory
mijo *nm* : millet
mil[1] *adj* : thousand
mil[2] *nm* : one thousand, a thousand
milagro *nm* : miracle <de milagro : miraculously>
milagroso, -sa *adj* : miraculous, marvelous — **milagrosamente** *adv*
milenio *nm* : millennium
milésimo, -ma *adj* : thousandth — **milésimo** *n*
milicia *nf* **1** : militia **2** : military service
miligramo *nm* : milligram
mililitro *nm* : milliliter
milímetro *nm* : millimeter
militancia *nf* : militancy
militante[1] *adj* : militant
militante[2] *nmf* : militant, activist
militar[1] *vi* **1** : to serve (in the military) **2** : to be active (in politics)
militar[2] *adj* : military
militar[3] *nmf* SOLDADO : soldier
militarizar {21} *vt* : to militarize
milla *nf* : mile
millar *nm* : thousand
millón *nm, pl* **millones** : million
millonario, -ria *n* : millionaire
millonésimo[1], -ma *adj* : millionth
millonésimo[2] *nm* : millionth
mil millones *nms & pl* : billion
milpa *nf CA, Mex* : cornfield
milpiés *nms & pl* : millipede
mimar *vt* CONSENTIR : to pamper, to spoil
mimbre *nm* : wicker
mimeógrafo *nm* : mimeograph
mímica *nf* **1** : mime, sign language **2** IMITACIÓN : mimicry
mimo *nm* **1** : pampering, indulgence <hacerle mimos a alguien : to pamper someone> **2** : mime
mimoso, -sa *adj* **1** : fussy, finicky **2** : affectionate, clinging
mina *nf* **1** : mine **2** : lead (for pencils)
minar *vt* **1** : to mine **2** DEBILITAR : to undermine
minarete *nm* ALMINAR : minaret
mineral *adj & nm* : mineral
minería *nf* : mining
minero[1], -ra *adj* : mining
minero[2], -ra *n* : miner, mine worker
miniatura *nf* : miniature
minicomputadora *nf* : minicomputer
minifalda *nf* : miniskirt
minifundio *nm* : small farm
minimizar {21} *vt* : to minimize
mínimo[1], -ma *adj* **1** : minimum <salario mínimo : minimum wage> **2** : least, smallest **3** : very small, minute
mínimo[2] *nm* **1** : minimum, least amount **2** : modicum, small amount **3 como ~** : at least
minino, -na *n fam* : pussy, pussycat
miniserie *nf* : miniseries
ministerial *adj* : ministerial
ministerio *nm* : ministry, department
ministro, -tra *n* : minister, secretary <primer ministro : prime minister> <Ministro de Defensa : Secretary of Defense>
minivan [ˌminiˈban, -ˈvan] *nf, pl* **-vanes** : minivan
minoría *nf* : minority
minorista[1] *adj* : retail
minorista[2] *nmf* : retailer
minoritario, -ria *adj* : minority
mintió, etc. → **mentir**
minuciosamente *adv* **1** : minutely **2** : in great detail **3** : thoroughly, meticulously
minucioso, -sa *adj* **1** : minute **2** DETALLADO : detailed **3** : thorough, meticulous
minué *nm* : minuet

minúsculo, -la *adj* DIMINUTO : tiny, miniscule

minusvalía *nf* : disability, handicap

minusválido[1], -da *adj* : handicapped, disabled

minusválido[2], -da *n* : handicapped person

minuta *nf* **1** BORRADOR : rough draft **2** : bill, fee

minutero *nm* : minute hand

minuto *nm* : minute

mío[1], mía *adj* **1** : my, of mine <¡Dios mío! : my God!, good heavens!> <una amiga mía : a friend of mine> **2** : mine <es mío : it's mine>

mío[2], mía *pron* (*with definite article*) : mine, my own <tus zapatos son iguales a los míos : your shoes are just like mine>

miope *adj* : nearsighted, myopic

miopía *nf* : myopia, nearsightedness

mira *nf* **1** : sight (of a firearm or instrument) **2** : aim, objective <con miras a : with the intention of, with a view to> <de amplias miras : broad-minded> <poner la mira en : to aim at, to aspire to>

mirada *nf* **1** : look, glance, gaze **2** EXPRESIÓN : look, expression <una mirada de sorpresa : a look of surprise>

mirado, -da *adj* **1** : cautious, careful **2** : considerate **3 bien mirado** : well thought of **4 mal mirado** : disliked, disapproved of

mirador *nm* : balcony, lookout, vantage point

miramiento *nm* **1** CONSIDERACIÓN : consideration, respect **2 sin miramientos** : without due consideration, carelessly

mirar *vt* **1** : to look at **2** OBSERVAR : to watch **3** REFLEXIONAR : to consider, to think over — *vi* **1** : to look **2** : to face, to overlook **3 ~ por** : to look after, to look out for — **mirarse** *vr* **1** : to look at oneself **2** : to look at each other

mirasol *nm* GIRASOL : sunflower

miríada *nf* : myriad

mirlo *nm* : blackbird

mirra *nf* : myrrh

mirto *nm* ARRAYÁN : myrtle

misa *nf* : Mass

misantropía *nf* : misanthropy

misantrópico, -ca *adj* : misanthropic

misántropo, -pa *n* : misanthrope

miscelánea *nf* : miscellany

misceláneo, -nea *adj* : miscellaneous

miserable *adj* **1** LASTIMOSO : miserable, wretched **2** : paltry, meager **3** MEZQUINO : stingy, miserly **4** : despicable, vile

miseria *nf* **1** POBREZA : poverty **2** : misery, suffering **3** : pittance, meager amount

misericordia *nf* COMPASIÓN : mercy, compassion

misericordioso, -sa *adj* : merciful

mísero, -ra *adj* **1** : wretched, miserable **2** : stingy **3** : paltry, meager

misil *nm* : missile

misión *nf, pl* **misiones** : mission

misionero, -ra *adj & n* : missionary

misiva *nf* : missive, letter

mismísimo, -ma *adj* (*used as an intensifier*) : very, selfsame <el mismísimo día : that very same day>

mismo[1] *adv* (*used as an intensifier*) : right, exactly <hazlo ahora mismo : do it right now> <te llamará hoy mismo : he'll definitely call you today>

mismo[2], -ma *adj* **1** : same **2** (*used as an intensifier*) : very <en ese mismo momento : at that very moment> **3** : oneself <lo hizo ella misma : she made it herself> **4 por lo mismo** : for that reason

misoginia *nf* : misogyny

misógino *nm* : misogynist

misterio *nm* : mystery

misterioso, -sa *adj* : mysterious — **misteriosamente** *adv*

misticismo *nm* : mysticism

místico[1], -ca *adj* : mystic, mystical

místico[2], -ca *n* : mystic

mitad *nf* **1** : half <mitad y mitad : half and half> **2** MEDIO : middle <a mitad de : halfway through> <por la mitad : in half>

mítico, -ca *adj* : mythical, mythic

mitigar {52} *vt* ALIVIAR : to mitigate, to alleviate — **mitigación** *nf*

mitin *nm, pl* **mítines** : (political) meeting, rally

mito *nm* LEYENDA : myth, legend

mitología *nm* : mythology

mitológico, -ca *adj* : mythological

mitosis *nfs & pl* : mitosis

mitra *nf* : miter (bishop's hat)

mixto, -ta *adj* **1** : mixed, joint **2** : coeducational

mixtura *nf* : mixture, blend

mnemónico, -ca *adj* : mnemonic

mobiliario *nm* : furniture

mocasín *nm, pl* **-sines** : moccasin

mocedad *nf* **1** JUVENTUD : youth **2** : youthful prank

mochila *nf* MORRAL : backpack, knapsack

moción *nf, pl* **-ciones 1** MOVIMIENTO : motion, movement **2** : motion (to a court or assembly)

moco *nm* **1** : mucus **2** *fam* : snot <limpiarse los mocos : to wipe one's (runny) nose>

mocoso, -sa *n* : kid, brat

moda *nf* **1** : fashion, style **2 a la moda** *or* **de ~** : in style, fashionable **3 moda pasajera** : fad

modales *nmpl* : manners

modalidad *nf* **1** CLASE : kind, type **2** MANERA : way, manner

modelar *vt* : to model, to mold — **modelarse** *vr* : to model oneself after, to emulate

modelo[1] *adj* : model <una casa modelo : a model home>
modelo[2] *nm* : model, example, pattern
modelo[3] *nmf* : model, mannequin
módem *or* **modem** ['moðɛm] *nm* : modem
moderación *nf, pl* **-ciones** MESURA : moderation
moderado, -da *adj & n* : moderate — **moderadamente** *adv*
moderador, -dora *n* : moderator, chair
moderar *vt* **1** TEMPERAR : to temper, to moderate **2** : to curb, to reduce <moderar gastos : to curb spending> **3** PRESIDIR : to chair (a meeting) — **moderarse** *vr* **1** : to restrain oneself **2** : to diminish, to calm down
modernidad *nf* **1** : modernity, modernness **2** : modern age
modernismo *nm* : modernism
modernista[1] *adj* : modernist, modernistic
modernista[2] *nmf* : modernist
modernizar {21} *vt* : to modernize — **modernización** *nf*
moderno, -na *adj* : modern, up-to-date
modestia *nf* : modesty
modesto, -ta *adj* : modest — **modestamente** *adv*
modificación *nf, pl* **-ciones** : alteration
modificante *nm* : modifier
modificar {72} *vt* ALTERAR : to modify, to alter, to adapt
modismo *nm* : idiom
modista *nmf* **1** : dressmaker **2** : fashion designer
modo *nm* **1** MANERA : way, manner, mode <de un modo u otro : one way or another> <a mi modo de ver : to my way of thinking> **2** : mood (in grammar) **3** : mode (in music) **4 a modo de** : by way of, in the manner of, like <a modo de ejemplo : by way of example> **5 de cualquier modo** : in any case, anyway **6 de modo que** : so, in such a way that **7 de todos modos** : in any case, anyway **8 en cierto modo** : in a way, to a certain extent
modorra *nf* : drowsiness, lethargy
modular[1] *v* : to modulate — **modulación** *nf*
modular[2] *adj* : modular
módulo *nm* : module, unit
mofa *nf* **1** : mockery, ridicule **2 hacer mofa de** : to make fun of, to ridicule
mofarse *vr* **∼ de** : to scoff at, to make fun of
mofeta *nf* ZORRILLO : skunk
mofle *nm CA, Mex* : muffler (of a car)
moflete *nm fam* : fat cheek
mofletudo, -da *adj fam* : fat-cheeked, chubby
mohín *nm, pl* **mohines** : grimace, face
mohino, -na *adj* : gloomy, melancholy
moho *nm* **1** : mold, mildew **2** : rust
mohoso, -sa *adj* **1** : moldy **2** : rusty
moisés *nm, pl* **moiseses** : bassinet, cradle
mojado[1], **-da** *adj* : wet
mojado[2], **-da** *n Mex fam* : illegal immigrant
mojar *vt* **1** : to wet, to moisten **2** : to dunk — **mojarse** *vr* : to get wet
mojigatería *nf* **1** : hypocrisy **2** GAZMOÑERÍA : primness, prudery
mojigato[1], **-ta** *adj* : prudish, prim — **mojigatamente** *adv*
mojigato[2], **-ta** *n* : prude, prig
mojón *nm, pl* **mojones** : boundary stone, marker
molar *nm* MUELA : molar
molcajete *nm Mex* : mortar
molde *nm* **1** : mold, form **2 letras de molde** : printing, block lettering
moldear *vt* **1** FORMAR : to mold, to shape **2** : to cast
moldura *nf* : molding
mole[1] *nm Mex* **1** : spicy sauce made with chilies and usually chocolate **2** : meat served with mole sauce
mole[2] *nf* : mass, bulk
molécula *nf* : molecule — **molecular** *adj*
moler {47} *vt* **1** : to grind, to crush **2** CANSAR : to exhaust, to wear out
molestar *vt* **1** FASTIDIAR : to annoy, to bother **2** : to disturb, to disrupt — *vi* : to be a nuisance — **molestarse** *vr* **∼ en** : to take the trouble to
molestia *nf* **1** FASTIDIO : annoyance, bother, nuisance **2** : trouble <se tomó la molestia de investigar : she took the trouble to investigate> **3** MALESTAR : discomfort
molesto, -ta *adj* **1** ENOJADO : bothered, annoyed **2** FASTIDIOSO : bothersome, annoying
molestoso, -sa *adj* : bothersome, annoying
molido, -da *adj* **1** MACHACADO : ground, crushed **2 estar molido** : to be exhausted
molinero, -ra *n* : miller
molinillo *nm* : grinder, mill <molinillo de café : coffee grinder>
molino *nm* **1** : mill **2 molino de viento** : windmill
molla *nf* : soft fleshy part, flesh (of fruit), lean part (of meat)
molleja *nf* : gizzard
molusco *nm* : mollusk
momentáneamente *adv* : momentarily
momentáneo, -nea *adj* **1** : momentary **2** TEMPORARIO : temporary
momento *nm* **1** : moment, instant <espera un momentito : wait just a moment> **2** : time, period of time <momentos difíciles : hard times> **3** : present, moment <los atletas del momento : the athletes of the moment, today's popular athletes> **4** : momentum **5 al momento** : right away, at once **6 de ∼** : at the moment, for the moment **7 de un momento a otro** : any time now **8 por momentos** : at times

momia *nf* : mummy

monaguillo *nm* ACÓLITO : altar boy

monarca *nmf* : monarch

monarquía *nf* : monarchy

monárquico, -ca *n* : monarchist

monasterio *nm* : monastery

monástico, -ca *adj* : monastic

mondadientes *nms & pl* PALILLO : toothpick

mondar *vt* : to peel

mondongo *nm* ENTRAÑAS : innards *pl,* insides *pl,* guts *pl*

moneda *nf* **1** : coin **2** : money, currency

monedero *nm* : change purse

monetario, -ria *adj* : monetary, financial

mongol, -gola *adj & n* : Mongol, Mongolian

monitor[1]**, -tora** *n* : instructor (in sports)

monitor[2] *nm* : monitor <monitor de televisión : television monitor>

monitorear *vt* : to monitor

monja *nf* : nun

monje *nm* : monk

mono[1]**, -na** *adj fam* : lovely, pretty, cute, darling

mono[2]**, -na** *n* : monkey

monóculo *nm* : monocle

monogamia *nf* : monogamy

monógamo -ma *adj* : monogamous

monografía *nf* : monograph

monograma *nm* : monogram

monolingüe *adj* : monolingual

monolítico, -ca *adj* : monolithic

monolito *nm* : monolith

monólogo *nm* : monologue

monomanía *nf* : obsession

monopatín *nm, pl* **-tines** : scooter

monopolio *nm* : monopoly

monopolizar {21} *vt* : to monopolize — **monopolización** *nf*

monosilábico, -ca *adj* : monosyllabic

monosílabo *nm* : monosyllable

monoteísmo *nm* : monotheism

monoteísta[1] *adj* : monotheistic

monoteísta[2] *nmf* : monotheist

monotonía *nf* **1** : monotony **2** : monotone

monótono, -na *adj* : monotonous — **monótonamente** *adv*

monóxido *nm* : monoxide <monóxido de carbono : carbon monoxide>

monserga *nf* : gibberish, drivel

monstruo *nm* : monster

monstruosidad *nf* : monstrosity

monstruoso, -sa *adj* : monstrous — **monstruosamente** *adv*

monta *nf* **1** : sum, total **2** : importance, value <de poca monta : unimportant, insignificant>

montaje *nm* **1** : assembling, assembly **2** : montage

montante *nm* : transom, fanlight

montaña *nf* **1** MONTE : mountain **2** **montaña rusa** : roller coaster

montañero, -ra *n* : mountaineer, mountain climber

montañoso, -sa *adj* : mountainous

montar *vt* **1** : to mount **2** ESTABLECER : to set up, to establish **3** ARMAR : to assemble, to put together **4** : to edit (a film) **5** : to stage, to put on (a show) **6** : to cock (a gun) **7** **montar en bicicleta** : to get on a bicycle **8** **montar a caballo** CABALGAR : to ride horseback

monte *nm* **1** MONTAÑA : mountain, mount **2** : woodland, scrubland <monte bajo : underbrush> **3** : outskirts (of a town), surrounding country **4** **monte de piedad** : pawnshop

montés *adj, pl* **monteses** : wild (of animals or plants)

montículo *nm* **1** : mound, heap **2** : hillock, knoll

monto *nm* : amount, total

montón *nm, pl* **-tones** **1** : heap, pile **2** *fam* : ton, load <un montón de preguntas : a ton of questions> <montones de gente : loads of people>

montura *nf* **1** : mount (horse) **2** : saddle, tack **3** : setting, mounting (of jewelry) **4** : frame (of glasses)

monumental *adj fam* **1** : tremendous, terrific **2** : massive, huge

monumento *nm* : monument

monzón *nm, pl* **monzones** : monsoon

moño *nm* **1** : bun (chignon) **2** LAZO : bow, knot <corbata de moño : bow tie>

moquear *vi* : to snivel

moquillo *nm* : distemper

mora *nf* **1** : blackberry **2** : mulberry

morada *nf* RESIDENCIA : dwelling, abode

morado[1]**, -da** *adj* : purple

morado[2] *nm* : purple

morador, -dora *n* : dweller, inhabitant

moral[1] *adj* : moral — **moralmente** *adv*

moral[2] *nf* **1** MORALIDAD : ethics, morality, morals *pl* **2** ÁNIMO : morale, spirits *pl*

moraleja *nf* : moral (of a story)

moralidad *nf* : morality

moralista[1] *adj* : moralistic

moralista[2] *nmf* : moralist

morar *vi* : to dwell, to reside

moratoria *nf* : moratorium

morboso, -sa *adj* : morbid — **morbosidad** *nf*

morcilla *nf* : blood sausage, blood pudding

mordacidad *nf* : bite, sharpness

mordaz *adj* : caustic, scathing

mordaza *nf* **1** : gag **2** : clamp

mordedura *nf* : bite (of an animal)

morder {47} *v* : to bite

mordida *nf* **1** : bite **2** *CA, Mex* : bribe, payoff

mordisco *nm* : bite, nibble

mordisquear *vt* : to nibble (on), to bite

morena *nf* **1** : moraine **2** : moray (eel)

moreno[1]**, -na** *adj* **1** : brunette **2** : dark, dark-skinned

moreno[2]**, -na** *n* **1** : brunette **2** : dark-skinned person

moretón *nm, pl* **-tones** : bruise

morfina *nf* : morphine

morfología *nf* : morphology

morgue *nf* : morgue

moribundo[1], **-da** *adj* : dying, moribund

moribundo[2], **-da** *n* : dying person

morillo *nm* : andiron

morir {46} *vi* **1** FALLECER : to die **2** APAGARSE : to die out, to go out

mormón, -mona *adj & n, pl* **mormones** : Mormon

moro[1], **-ra** *adj* : Moorish

moro[2], **-ra** *n* **1** : Moor **2** : Muslim

morosidad *nf* **1** : delinquency (in payment) **2** : slowness

moroso, -sa *adj* **1** : delinquent, in arrears <cuentas morosas : delinquent accounts> **2** : slow, sluggish

morral *nm* MOCHILA : backpack, knapsack

morralla *nf* **1** : small fish **2** : trash, riffraff **3** *Mex* : small change

morriña *nf* : homesickness

morro *nm* HOCICO : snout

morsa *nf* : walrus

morse *nm* : Morse code

mortaja *nf* SUDARIO : shroud

mortal[1] *adj* **1** : mortal **2** FATAL : fatal, deadly — **mortalmente** *adv*

mortal[2] *nmf* : mortal

mortalidad *nf* : mortality

mortandad *nf* **1** : loss of life, death toll **2** : carnage, slaughter

mortero *nm* : mortar (bowl, cannon, or building material)

mortífero, -ra *adj* LETAL : deadly, fatal

mortificación *nf, pl* **-ciones 1** : mortification **2** TORMENTO : anguish, torment

mortificar {72} *vt* **1** : to mortify **2** TORTURAR : to trouble, to torment — **mortificarse** *vr* : to be mortified, to feel embarrassed

mosaico *nm* : mosaic

mosca *nf* **1** : fly **2 mosca común** : housefly

moscada *adj* **nuez moscada** : nutmeg

moscovita *adj & nmf* : Muscovite

mosquearse *vr* **1** : to become suspicious **2** : to take offense

mosquete *nm* : musket

mosquetero *nm* : musketeer

mosquitero *nm* : mosquito net

mosquito *nm* ZANCUDO : mosquito

mostachón *nm, pl* **-chones** : macaroon

mostaza *nf* : mustard

mostrador *nm* : counter (in a store)

mostrar {19} *vt* **1** : to show **2** EXHIBIR : to exhibit, to display — **mostrarse** *vr* : to show oneself, to appear

mota *nf* **1** : fleck, speck **2** : defect, blemish

mote *nm* SOBRENOMBRE : nickname

moteado, -da *adj* : dotted, spotted, dappled

motel *nm* : motel

motín *nm, pl* **motines 1** : riot **2** : rebellion, mutiny

motivación *nf, pl* **-ciones** : motivation — **motivacional** *adj*

motivar *vt* **1** CAUSAR : to cause **2** IMPULSAR : to motivate

motivo *nm* **1** MÓVIL : motive **2** CAUSA : cause, reason **3** TEMA : theme, motif

moto *nf* : motorcycle, motorbike

motocicleta *nf* : motorcycle

motociclismo *nm* : motorcycling

motociclista *nmf* : motorcyclist

motor[1], **-ra** *adj* MOTRIZ : motor

motor[2] *nm* **1** : motor, engine **2** : driving force, cause

motorista *nmf* : motorist

motriz *adj, pl* **motrices** : driving

motu proprio *adv* **de motu proprio** [de'motu'proprio] : voluntarily, of one's own accord

mousse ['mus] *nm* : mousse

mover {47} *vt* **1** TRASLADAR : to move, to shift **2** AGITAR : to shake, to nod (the head) **3** ACCIONAR : to power, to drive **4** INDUCIR : to provoke, to cause **5** : to excite, to stir — **moverse** *vr* **1** : to move, to move over **2** : to hurry, to get a move on **3** : to get moving, to make an effort

movible *adj* : movable

movida *nf* : move (in a game)

móvil[1] *adj* : mobile

móvil[2] *nm* **1** MOTIVO : motive **2** : mobile

movilidad *nf* : mobility

movilizar {21} *vt* : to mobilize — **movilización** *nf*

movimiento *nm* : movement, motion <movimiento del cuerpo : bodily movement> <movimiento sindicalista : labor movement>

mozo[1], **-za** *adj* : young, youthful

mozo[2], **-za** *n* **1** JOVEN : young man *m*, young woman *f*, youth **2** : helper, servant

mucamo, -ma *n* : servant, maid *f*

muchacha *nf* : maid

muchacho, -cha *n* **1** : kid, boy *m*, girl *f* **2** JOVEN : young man *m*, young woman *f*

muchedumbre *nf* MULTITUD : crowd, multitude

mucho[1] *adv* **1** : much, a lot <mucho más : much more> <le gusta mucho : he likes it a lot> **2** : long, a long time <tardó mucho en venir : he was a long time getting here> **3 por mucho que** : no matter how much

mucho[2], **-cha** *adj* **1** : a lot of, many, much <mucha gente : a lot of people> <hace mucho tiempo que no lo veo : I haven't seen him in ages> **2 muchas veces** : often

mucho[3], **-cha** *pron* **1** : a lot, many, much <hay mucho que hacer : there is a lot to do> <muchas no vinieron : many didn't come> **2 cuando ~** *or* **como ~** : at most **3 con ~** : by far **4 ni mucho menos** : not at all, far from it

mucílago *nm* : mucilage

mucosidad *nf* : mucus

mucoso, -sa *adj* : mucous, slimy

muda *nf* **1** : change <muda de ropa : change of clothes> **2** : molt, molting

mudanza *nf* **1** CAMBIO : change **2** TRASLADO : move, moving

mudar *v* **1** CAMBIAR : to change **2** : to molt, to shed — **mudarse** *vr* **1** TRASLADARSE : to move (one's residence) **2** : to change (clothes)

mudo[1], -da *adj* **1** SILENCIOSO : silent <el cine mudo : silent films> **2** : mute, dumb

mudo[2], -da *n* : mute

mueble *nm* **1** : piece of furniture **2** **muebles** *nmpl* : furniture, furnishings

mueblería *nf* : furniture store

mueca *nf* : grimace, face

muela *nf* **1** : tooth, molar <dolor de muelas : toothache> <muela de juicio : wisdom tooth> **2** : millstone **3** : whetstone

muele, etc. → **moler**

muelle[1] *adj* : soft, comfortable, easy

muelle[2] *nm* **1** : wharf, dock **2** RESORTE : spring

muérdago *nm* : mistletoe

muerde, etc. → **morder**

muere, etc. → **morir**

muerte *nf* : death

muerto[1] *pp* → **morir**

muerto[2], -ta *adj* **1** : dead **2** : lifeless, flat, dull **3** **~ de** : dying of <estoy muerto de hambre : I'm dying of hunger>

muerto[3], -ta *nm* DIFUNTO : dead person, deceased

muesca *nf* : nick, notch

muestra[1], etc. → **mostrar**

muestra[2] *nf* **1** : sample **2** SEÑAL : sign, show <una muestra de respeto : a show of respect> **3** EXPOSICIÓN : exhibition, exposition **4** : pattern, model

mueve, etc. → **mover**

mugido *nm* : moo, lowing, bellow

mugir {35} *vi* : to moo, to low, to bellow

mugre *nf* SUCIEDAD : grime, filth

mugriento, -ta *adj* : filthy

muguete *nm* : lily of the valley

muja, etc. → **mugir**

mujer *nf* **1** : woman **2** ESPOSA : wife

mulato, -ta *adj & n* : mulatto

muleta *nf* : crutch

mullido, -da *adj* **1** : soft, fluffy **2** : spongy, springy

mulo, -la *n* : mule

multa *nf* : fine

multicolor *adj* : multicolored

multicultural *adj* : multicultural

multidisciplinario, -ria *adj* : multidisciplinary

multifacético, -ca *adj* : multifaceted

multifamiliar *adj* : multifamily

multilateral *adj* : multilateral

multimedia *nf* : multimedia

multimillonario, -ria *n* : multimillionaire

multinacional *adj* : multinational

múltiple *adj* : multiple

multiplicación *nf, pl* **-ciones** : multiplication

multiplicar {72} *v* **1** : to multiply **2** : to increase — **multiplicarse** *vr* : to multiply, to reproduce

multiplicidad *nf* : multiplicity

múltiplo *nm* : multiple

multitud *nf* MUCHEDUMBRE : crowd, multitude

multiuso, -sa *adj* : multipurpose

multivitamínico, -ca *adj* : multivitamin

mundano, -na *adj* : worldly, earthly

mundial *adj* : world, worldwide

mundialmente *adv* : worldwide, all over the world

mundo *nm* **1** : world **2** **todo el mundo** : everyone, everybody

municiones *nfpl* : ammunition, munitions

municipal *adj* : municipal

municipio *nm* **1** : municipality **2** AYUNTAMIENTO : town council

muñeca *nf* **1** : doll **2** MANIQUÍ : mannequin **3** : wrist

muñeco *nm* **1** : doll, boy doll **2** MARIONETA : puppet

muñon *nm, pl* **muñones** : stump (of an arm or leg)

mural *adj & nm* : mural

muralista *nmf* : muralist

muralla *nf* : rampart, wall

murciélago *nm* : bat (animal)

murga *nf* : band of street musicians

murió, etc. → **morir**

murmullo *nm* **1** : murmur, murmuring **2** : rustling, rustle <el murmullo de las hojas : the rustling of the leaves>

murmurar *vt* **1** : to murmur, to mutter **2** : to whisper (gossip) — *vi* **1** : to murmur **2** CHISMEAR : to gossip

muro *nm* : wall

musa *nf* : muse

musaraña *nf* : shrew

muscular *adj* : muscular

musculatura *nf* : muscles *pl,* musculature

músculo *nm* : muscle

musculoso, -sa *adj* : muscular, brawny

muselina *nf* : muslin

museo *nm* : museum

musgo *nm* : moss

musgoso, -sa *adj* : mossy

música *nf* : music

musical *adj* : musical — **musicalmente** *adv*

músico[1], -ca *adj* : musical

músico[2], -ca *n* : musician

musitar *vt* : to mumble, to murmur

muslo *nm* : thigh

musulmán, -mana *adj & n, mpl* **-manes** : Muslim

mutación *nf, pl* **-ciones** : mutation

mutante *adj & nm* : mutant

mutar *v* : to mutate

mutilar *vt* : to mutilate — **mutilación** *nf*

mutis *nm* **1** : exit (in theater) **2** : silence

mutual *adj* : mutual

mutuo, -tua *adj* : mutual, reciprocal — **mutuamente** *adv*

muy *adv* **1** : very, quite <es muy inteligente : she's very intelligent> <muy bien : very well, fine> <eso es muy americano : that's typically American> **2** : too <es muy grande para él : it's too big for him>

N

n *nf* : fourteenth letter of the Spanish alphabet

nabo *nm* : turnip

nácar *nm* MADREPERLA : nacre, mother-of-pearl

nacarado, -da *adj* : pearly

nacer {48} *vi* **1** : to be born <nací en Guatemala : I was born in Guatemala> <no nació ayer : he wasn't born yesterday> **2** : to hatch **3** : to bud, to sprout **4** : to rise, to originate **5 nacer para algo** : to be born to be something **6 volver a nacer** : to have a lucky escape

nacido[1], -da *adj* **1** : born **2 recién nacido** : newborn

nacido[2], -da *n* **1 los nacidos** : those born (at a particular time) **2 recién nacido** : newborn baby

naciente *adj* **1** : newfound, growing **2** : rising <el sol naciente : the rising sun>

nacimiento *nm* **1** : birth **2** : source (of a river) **3** : beginning, origin **4** BELÉN : Nativity scene, crèche

nación *nf, pl* **naciones** : nation, country, people (of a country)

nacional[1] *adj* : national

nacional[2] *nmf* CIUDADANO : national, citizen

nacionalidad *nf* : nationality

nacionalismo *nm* : nationalism

nacionalista[1] *adj* : nationalist, nationalistic

nacionalista[2] *nmf* : nationalist

nacionalización *nf, pl* **-ciones 1** : nationalization **2** : naturalization

nacionalizar {21} *vt* **1** : to nationalize **2** : to naturalize (as a citizen) — **nacionalizarse** *vr*

naco, -ca *adj Mex* : trashy, vulgar, common

nada[1] *adv* : not at all, not in the least <no estamos nada cansados : we are not at all tired>

nada[2] *nf* **1** : nothingness **2** : smidgen, bit <una nada le disgusta : the slightest thing upsets him>

nada[3] *pron* **1** : nothing <no estoy haciendo nada : I'm not doing anything> **2 casi nada** : next to nothing **3 de ~** : you're welcome **4 dentro de nada** : very soon, in no time **5 nada más** : nothing else, nothing more

nadador, -dora *n* : swimmer

nadar *vi* **1** : to swim **2 ~ en** : to be swimming in, to be rolling in — *vt* : to swim

nadería *nf* : small thing, trifle

nadie *pron* : nobody, no one <no vi a nadie : I didn't see anyone>

nadir *nm* : nadir

nado *nm* **1** *Mex* : swimming **2 a ~** : swimming <cruzó el río a nado : he swam across the river>

nafta *nf* **1** : naphtha **2** (*in various countries*) : gasoline

naftalina *nf* : naphthalene, mothballs *pl*

náhuatl[1] *adj & nmf, pl* **nahuas** : Nahuatl

náhuatl[2] *nm* : Nahuatl (language)

nailon → **nilón**

naipe *nm* : playing card

nalga *nf* **1** : buttock **2 nalgas** *nfpl* : buttocks, bottom

nalgada *nf* : smack on the bottom, spanking

namibio, -bia *adj & n* : Namibian

nana *nf* **1** : lullaby **2** *fam* : grandma **3** *CA, Col, Mex, Ven* : nanny

nanay *interj fam* : no way!, not likely!

naranja[1] *adj & nm* : orange (color)

naranja[2] *nf* : orange (fruit)

naranjal *nm* : orange grove

naranjo *nm* : orange tree

narcisismo *nm* : narcissism

narcisista[1] *adj* : narcissistic

narcisista[2] *nmf* : narcissist

narciso *nm* : narcissus, daffodil

narcótico[1], -ca *adj* : narcotic

narcótico[2] *nm* : narcotic

narcotizar {21} *vt* : to drug, to dope

narcotraficante *nmf* : drug trafficker

narcotráfico *nm* : drug trafficking

narigón, -gona *adj, mpl* **-gones** : big-nosed

narigudo → **narigón**

nariz *nf, pl* **narices 1** : nose <sonar(se) la nariz : to blow one's nose> **2** : sense of smell

narración *nf, pl* **-ciones** : narration, account

narrador, -dora *n* : narrator

narrar *vt* : to narrate, to tell

narrativa *nf* : narrative, story

narrativo, -va *adj* : narrative

narval *nm* : narwhal

nasa *nf* : creel

nasal *adj* : nasal

nata *nf* **1** : cream <nata batida : whipped cream> **2** : skin (on boiled milk)

natación *nf, pl* **-ciones** : swimming

natal *adj* : native, natal

natalicio *nm* : birthday <el natalicio de George Washington : George Washington's birthday>

natalidad *nf* : birthrate

natillas *nfpl* : custard

natividad *nf* : birth, nativity

nativo, -va *adj & n* : native

natural[1] *adj* **1** : natural **2** : normal <como es natural : naturally, as expected> **3 ~ de** : native of, from **4 de tamaño natural** : life-size

natural[2] *nm* **1** CARÁCTER : disposition, temperament **2** : native <un natural de Venezuela : a native of Venezuela>

naturaleza *nf* **1** : nature <la madre naturaleza : mother nature> **2** ÍNDOLE : nature, disposition, constitution <la naturaleza humana : human nature> **3 naturaleza muerta** : still life

naturalidad *nf* : simplicity, naturalness

naturalismo *nm* : naturalism

naturalista[1] *adj* : naturalistic

naturalista[2] *nmf* : naturalist

naturalización *nf, pl* **-ciones** : naturalization

naturalizar {21} *vt* : to naturalize — **naturalizarse** *vr* NACIONALIZARSE : to become naturalized

naturalmente *adv* **1** : naturally, inherently **2** : of course

naufragar {52} *vi* **1** : to be shipwrecked **2** FRACASAR : to fail, to collapse

naufragio *nm* **1** : shipwreck **2** FRACASO : failure, collapse

náufrago[1], **-ga** *adj* : shipwrecked, castaway

náufrago[2], **-ga** *n* : shipwrecked person, castaway

náusea *nf* **1** : nausea **2 dar náuseas** : to nauseate, to disgust **3 náuseas matutinas** : morning sickness

nauseabundo, -da *adj* : nauseating, sickening

náutica *nf* : navigation

náutico, -ca *adj* : nautical

nautilo *nm* : nautilus

navaja *nf* **1** : pocketknife, penknife <navaja de muelle : switchblade> **2 navaja de afeitar** : straight razor, razor blade

navajo, -ja *adj & n* : Navajo

naval *adj* : naval

nave *nf* **1** : ship <nave capitana : flagship> <nave espacial : spaceship> **2** : nave <nave lateral : aisle> **3 quemar uno sus naves** : to burn one's bridges

navegabilidad *nf* : navigability

navegable *adj* : navigable

navegación *nf, pl* **-ciones** : navigation

navegante[1] *adj* : sailing, seafaring

navegante[2] *nmf* : navigator

navegar {52} *v* : to navigate, to sail

Navidad *nf* : Christmas, Christmastime <Feliz Navidad : Merry Christmas>

navideño, -ña *adj* : Christmas

naviero, -ra *adj* : shipping

náyade *nf* : naiad

nazca, etc. → **nacer**

nazi *adj & nmf* : Nazi

nazismo *nm* : Nazism

nébeda *nf* : catnip

neblina *nf* : light fog, mist

neblinoso, -sa *adj* : misty, foggy

nebulosa *nf* : nebula

nebulosidad *nf* : mistiness, haziness

nebuloso, -sa *adj* **1** : hazy, misty **2** : nebulous, vague

necedad *nf* : stupidity, foolishness <decir necedades : to talk nonsense>

necesariamente *adv* : necessarily

necesario, -ria *adj* **1** : necessary **2 si es necesario** : if need be **3 hacerse necesario** : to be required

neceser *nm* : toilet kit, vanity case

necesidad *nf* **1** : need, necessity **2** : poverty, want **3 necesidades** *nfpl* : hardships **4 hacer sus necesidades** : to relieve oneself

necesitado, -da *adj* : needy

necesitar *vt* **1** : to need **2** : to necessitate, to require — *vi* **~ de** : to have need of

necio[1], **-cia** *adj* **1** : foolish, silly, dumb **2** *fam* : naughty

necio[2], **-cia** *n* ESTÚPIDO : fool, idiot

necrología *nf* : obituary

necrópolis *nfs & pl* : cemetery

néctar *nm* : nectar

nectarina *nf* : nectarine

neerlandés[1], **-desa** *adj, mpl* **-deses** HOLANDÉS : Dutch

neerlandés[2], **-desa** *n, mpl* **-deses** HOLANDÉS : Dutch person, Dutchman *m*

nefando, -da *adj* : unspeakable, heinous

nefario, -ria *adj* : nefarious

nefasto, -ta *adj* **1** : ill-fated, unlucky **2** : disastrous, terrible

negación *nf, pl* **-ciones 1** : negation, denial **2** : negative (in grammar)

negar {49} *vt* **1** : to deny **2** REHUSAR : to refuse **3** : to disown — **negarse** *vr* **1** : to refuse **2** : to deny oneself

negativa *nf* **1** : denial **2** : refusal

negativo[1], **-va** *adj* : negative

negativo[2] *nm* : negative (of a photograph)

negligé *nm* : negligee

negligencia *nf* : negligence

negligente *adj* : neglectful, negligent — **negligentemente** *adv*

negociable *adj* : negotiable

negociación *nf, pl* **-ciones 1** : negotiation **2 negociación colectiva** : collective bargaining

negociador, -dora *n* : negotiator

negociante *nmf* : businessman *m*, businesswoman *f*

negociar *vt* : to negotiate — *vi* : to deal, to do business

negocio *nm* **1** : business, place of business **2** : deal, transaction **3 negocios** *nmpl* : commerce, trade, business

negrero, -ra *n* **1** : slave trader **2** *fam* : slave driver, brutal boss

negrita *nf* : boldface (type)

negro[1], **-gra** *adj* **1 :** black, dark **2** BRONCEADO **:** suntanned **3 :** gloomy, awful, desperate <la cosa se está poniendo negra : things are looking bad> **4 mercado negro :** black market

negro[2], **-gra** *n* **1 :** dark-skinned person, black person **2** *fam* **:** darling, dear

negro[3] *nm* **:** black (color)

negrura *nf* **:** blackness

negruzco, -ca *adj* **:** blackish

nene, -na *n* **:** baby, small child

nenúfar *nm* **:** water lily

neocelandés → **neozelandés**

neoclasicismo *nm* **:** neoclassicism

neoclásico, -ca *adj* **:** neoclassical

neófito, -ta *n* **:** neophyte, novice

neologismo *nm* **:** neologism

neón *nm, pl* **neones :** neon

neoyorquino[1], **-na** *adj* **:** of or from New York

neoyorquino[2], **-na** *n* **:** New Yorker

neozelandés[1], **-desa** *adj, mpl* **-deses :** of or from New Zealand

neozelandés[2], **-desa** *n, mpl* **-deses :** New Zealander

nepalés, -lesa *adj & n, mpl* **-leses :** Nepali

nepotismo *nm* **:** nepotism

neptunio *nm* **:** neptunium

Neptuno *nm* **:** Neptune

nervio *nm* **1 :** nerve **2 :** tendon, sinew, gristle (in meat) **3 :** energy, drive **4 :** rib (of a vault) **5 nervios** *nmpl* **:** nerves <estar mal de los nervios : to be a bundle of nerves> <ataque de nervios : nervous breakdown>

nerviosamente *adv* **:** nervously

nerviosidad *nf* → **nerviosismo**

nerviosismo *nf* **:** nervousness, anxiety

nervioso, -sa *adj* **1 :** nervous, nerve <sistema nervioso : nervous system> **2 :** high-strung, restless, anxious <ponerse nervioso : to get nervous> **3 :** vigorous, energetic

nervudo, -da *adj* **:** sinewy, wiry

neta *nf Mex fam* **:** truth <la neta es que me cae mal : the truth is, I don't like her>

netamente *adv* **:** clearly, obviously

neto, -ta *adj* **1 :** net <peso neto : net weight> **2 :** clear, distinct

neumático[1], **-ca** *adj* **:** pneumatic

neumático[2] *nm* LLANTA **:** tire

neumonía *nf* PULMONÍA **:** pneumonia

neural *adj* **:** neural

neuralgia *nf* **:** neuralgia

neuritis *nf* **:** neuritis

neurología *nf* **:** neurology

neurológico, -ca *adj* **:** neurological, neurologic

neurólogo, -ga *n* **:** neurologist

neurosis *nfs & pl* **:** neurosis

neurótico, -ca *adj & n* **:** neurotic

neutral *adj* **:** neutral

neutralidad *nf* **:** neutrality

neutralizar {21} *vt* **:** to neutralize — **neutralización** *nf*

neutro, -tra *adj* **1 :** neutral **2 :** neuter

neutrón *nm, pl* **neutrones :** neutron

nevada *nf* **:** snowfall

nevado, -da *adj* **1 :** snowcapped **2 :** snow-white

nevar {55} *v impers* **:** to snow

nevasca *nf* **:** snowstorm, blizzard

nevera *nf* REFRIGERADOR **:** refrigerator

nevería *nf Mex* **:** ice cream parlor

nevisca *nf* **:** light snowfall, flurry

nevoso, -sa *adj* **:** snowy

nexo *nm* VÍNCULO **:** link, connection, nexus

ni *conj* **1 :** neither, nor <afuera no hace ni frío ni calor : it's neither cold nor hot outside> **2 ni que :** not even if, not as if <ni que me pagaran : not even if they paid me> <ni que fuera (yo) su madre : it's not as if I were his mother> **3 ni siquiera :** not even <ni siquiera nos llamaron : they didn't even call us>

nicaragüense *adj & nmf* **:** Nicaraguan

nicho *nm* **:** niche

nicotina *nf* **:** nicotine

nido *nm* **1 :** nest **2 :** hiding place, den

niebla *nf* **:** fog, mist

niega, niegue, etc. → **negar**

nieto, -ta *n* **1 :** grandson *m,* granddaughter *f* **2 nietos** *nmpl* **:** grandchildren

nieva, etc. → **nevar**

nieve *nf* **1 :** snow **2** *Cuba, Mex, PRi* **:** sherbet

nigeriano, -na *adj & n* **:** Nigerian

nigua *nf* **:** sand flea, chigger

nihilismo *nm* **:** nihilism

nilón *or* **nilon** *nm, pl* **nilones :** nylon

nimbo *nm* **1 :** halo **2 :** nimbus

nimiedad *nf* INSIGNIFICANCIA **:** trifle, triviality

nimio, -mia *adj* INSIGNIFICANTE **:** insignificant, trivial

ninfa *nf* **:** nymph

ningunear *vt Mex fam* **:** to disrespect

ninguno[1], **-na** (**ningún** *before masculine singular nouns*) *adj, mpl* **ningunos :** no, none <no es ninguna tonta : she's no fool> <no debe hacerse en ningún momento : that should never be done>

ninguno[2], **-na** *pron* **1 :** neither, none <ninguno de los dos ha vuelto aún : neither one has returned yet> **2 :** no one, no other <te quiero más que a ninguna : I love you more than any other>

niña *nf* **1** PUPILA **:** pupil (of the eye) **2 la niña de los ojos :** the apple of one's eye

niñada *nf* **1 :** childishness **2 :** trifle, silly thing

niñería *nf* → **niñada**

niñero, -ra *n* **:** baby-sitter, nanny

niñez *nf, pl* **niñeces** INFANCIA **:** childhood

niño, -ña *n* **:** child, boy *m,* girl *f*

niobio *nm* **:** niobium

nipón, -pona *adj & n, mpl* **nipones** JAPONÉS **:** Japanese

níquel *nm* **:** nickel

nitidez *nf, pl* **-deces** CLARIDAD **:** clarity, vividness, sharpness
nítido, -da *adj* CLARO **:** clear, vivid, sharp
nitrato *nm* **:** nitrate
nítrico, -ca *adj* **ácido nítrico :** nitric acid
nitrito *nm* **:** nitrite
nitrógeno *nm* **:** nitrogen
nitroglicerina *nf* **:** nitroglycerin
nivel *nm* **1 :** level, height <nivel del mar : sea level> **2 :** level, standard <nivel de vida : standard of living>
nivelar *vt* **:** to level (out)
nixtamal *nm Mex* **:** limed corn used for tortillas
no *adv* **1 :** no <¿quieres ir al mercado? no, voy más tarde : do you want to go shopping? no, I'm going later> **2 :** not <¡no hagas eso! : don't do that!> <creo que no : I don't think so> **3 :** non- <no fumador : non-smoker> **4 ¡como no! :** of course! **5 no bien :** as soon as, no sooner
nobelio *nm* **:** nobelium
noble[1] *adj* **:** noble — **noblemente** *adv*
noble[2] *nmf* **:** nobleman *m,* noblewoman *f*
nobleza *nf* **1 :** nobility **2** HONRADEZ **:** honesty, integrity
nocaut *nm* **:** knockout, KO
noche *nf* **1 :** night, nighttime, evening **2 buenas noches :** good evening, good night **3 de noche** *or* **por la noche :** at night **4 hacerse de noche :** to get dark
Nochebuena *nf* **:** Christmas Eve
nochecita *nf* **:** dusk
Nochevieja *nf* **:** New Year's Eve
noción *nf, pl* **nociones 1** CONCEPTO **:** notion, concept **2 nociones** *nfpl* **:** smattering, rudiments *pl*
nocivo, -va *adj* DAÑINO **:** harmful, noxious
noctámbulo, -la *n* **1 :** sleepwalker **2 :** night owl
nocturno[1], **-na** *adj* **:** night, nocturnal
nocturno[2] *nm* **:** nocturne
nodriza *nf* **:** wet nurse
nódulo *nm* **:** nodule
nogal *nm* **1 :** walnut tree **2** *Mex* **:** pecan tree **3 nogal americano :** hickory
nómada[1] *adj* **:** nomadic
nómada[2] *nmf* **:** nomad
nomás *adv* **:** only, just <lo hice nomás porque sí : I did it just because> <nomás de recordarlo me enojo : I get angry just remembering it> <nomás faltan dos semanas para Navidad : there are only two weeks left till Christmas>
nombradía *nf* RENOMBRE **:** fame, renown
nombrado, -da *adj* **:** famous, well-known
nombramiento *nm* **:** appointment, nomination
nombrar *vt* **1 :** to appoint **2 :** to mention, to name
nombre *nm* **1 :** name <nombre de pluma : pseudonym, pen name> <en nombre : on behalf of> <sin nombre : nameless> **2 :** noun <nombre propio : proper noun> **3 :** fame, renown
nomenclatura *nf* **:** nomenclature
nomeolvides *nmfs & pl* **:** forget-me-not
nómina *nf* **:** payroll
nominación *nf, pl* **-ciones :** nomination
nominal *adj* **:** nominal — **nominalmente** *adv*
nominar *vt* **:** to nominate
nominativo[1], **-va** *adj* **:** nominative
nominativo[2] *nm* **:** nominative (case)
nomo *nm* **:** gnome
non[1] *adj* IMPAR **:** odd, not even
non[2] *nm* **:** odd number
nonagésimo[1], **-ma** *adj* **:** ninetieth, ninety-
nonagésimo[2], **-ma** *n* **:** ninetieth, ninety- (in a series)
nono, -na *adj* **:** ninth — **nono** *nm*
nopal *nm* **:** nopal, cactus
nopalitos *nmpl Mex* **:** pickled cactus leaves
noquear *vt* **:** to knock out, to KO
norcoreano, -na *adj & n* **:** North Korean
nordeste[1] *or* **noreste** *adj* **1 :** northeastern **2 :** northeasterly
nordeste[2] *or* **noreste** *nm* **:** northeast
nórdico, -ca *adj & n* ESCANDINAVO **:** Scandinavian
noreste → **nordeste**
noria *nf* **1 :** waterwheel **2 :** Ferris wheel
norirlandés[1], **-desa** *adj, mpl* **-deses :** Northern Irish
norirlandés[2], **-desa** *n, mpl* **-deses :** person from Northern Ireland
norma *nf* **1 :** rule, regulation **2 :** norm, standard
normal *adj* **1 :** normal, usual **2 :** standard **3 escuela normal :** teacher-training college
normalidad *nf* **:** normality, normalcy
normalización *nf, pl* **-ciones** *nf* **1** REGULARIZACIÓN **:** normalization **2** ESTANDARIZACIÓN **:** standardization
normalizar {21} *vt* **1** REGULARIZAR **:** to normalize **2** ESTANDARIZAR **:** to standardize — **normalizarse** *vr* **:** to return to normal
normalmente *adv* GENERALMENTE **:** ordinarily, generally
noroeste[1] *adj* **1 :** northwestern **2 :** northwesterly
noroeste[2] *nm* **:** northwest
norte[1] *adj* **:** north, northern
norte[2] *nm* **1 :** north **2 :** north wind **3** META **:** aim, objective
norteamericano, -na *adj & n* **1 :** North American **2** AMERICANO, ESTADOUNIDENSE **:** American, native or inhabitant of the United States
norteño[1], **-ña** *adj* **:** northern
norteño[2], **-ña** *n* **:** Northerner

noruego[1], **-ga** *adj & n* : Norwegian

noruego[2] *nm* : Norwegian (language)

nos *pron* **1** : us <nos enviaron a la frontera : they sent us to the border> **2** : ourselves <nos divertimos muchísimo : we enjoyed ourselves a great deal> **3** : each other, one another <nos vimos desde lejos : we saw each other from far away> **4** : to us, for us, from us <nos lo dio : he gave it to us> <nos lo compraron : they bought it from us>

nosotros, -tras *pron* **1** : we <nosotros llegamos ayer : we arrived yesterday> **2** : us <ven con nosotros : come with us> **3 nosotros mismos** : ourselves <lo arreglamos nosotros mismos : we fixed it ourselves>

nostalgia *nf* **1** : nostalgia, longing **2** : homesickness

nostálgico, -ca *adj* **1** : nostalgic **2** : homesick

nota *nf* **1** : note, message **2** : announcement <nota de prensa : press release> **3** : grade, mark (in school) **4** : characteristic, feature, touch **5** : note (in music) **6** : bill, check (in a restaraunt)

notable *adj* **1** : notable, noteworthy **2** : outstanding

notar *vt* **1** : to notice <hacer notar algo : to point out something> **2** : to tell <la diferencia se nota inmediatamente : you can tell the difference right away> — **notarse** *vr* **1** : to be evident, to show **2** : to feel, to seem

notario, -ria *n* : notary, notary public

noticia *nf* **1** : news item, piece of news **2 noticias** *nfpl* : news

noticiero *nm* : news program, newscast

noticioso, -sa *adj* : news <agencia noticiosa : news agency>

notificación *nf, pl* **-ciones** : notification

notificar {72} *vt* : to notify, to inform

notoriedad *nf* **1** : knowledge, obviousness **2** : fame, notoriety

notorio, -ria *adj* **1** OBVIO : obvious, evident **2** CONOCIDO : well-known

novato[1], **-ta** *adj* : inexperienced, new

novato[2], **-ta** *n* : beginner, novice

novecientos[1], **-tas** *adj* : nine hundred

novecientos[2] *nms & pl* : nine hundred

novedad *nf* **1** : newness, novelty **2** : innovation

novedoso, -sa *adj* : original, novel

novel *adj* NOVATO : inexperienced, new

novela *nf* **1** : novel **2** : soap opera

novelar *vt* : to fictionalize, to make a novel out of

novelesco, -ca *adj* **1** : fictional **2** : fantastic, fabulous

novelista *nmf* : novelist

novena *nf* : novena

noveno, -na *adj* : ninth — **noveno, -na** *n*

noventa *adj & nm* : ninety

noventavo[1], **-va** *adj* : ninetieth

noventavo[2] *nm* : ninetieth (fraction)

noviazgo *nm* **1** : courtship, relationship **2** : engagement, betrothal

novicio, -cia *n* **1** : novice (in religion) **2** PRINCIPIANTE : novice, beginner

noviembre *nm* : November

novilla *nf* : heifer

novillada *nf* : bullfight featuring young bulls

novillero, -ra *n* : apprentice bullfighter

novillo *nm* : young bull

novio, -via *n* **1** : boyfriend *m,* girlfriend *f* **2** PROMETIDO : fiancé *m,* fiancée *f* **3** : bridegroom *m,* bride *f*

novocaína *nf* : novocaine

nubarrón *nm, pl* **-rrones** : storm cloud

nube *nf* **1** : cloud <andar en las nubes : to have one's head in the clouds> <por las nubes : sky-high> **2** : cloud (of dust), swarm (of insects, etc.)

nublado[1], **-da** *adj* **1** NUBOSO : cloudy, overcast **2** : clouded, dim

nublado[2] *nm* **1** : storm cloud **2** AMENAZA : menace, threat

nublar *vt* **1** : to cloud **2** OSCURECER : to obscure — **nublarse** *vr* : to get cloudy

nubosidad *nf* : cloudiness

nuboso, -sa *adj* NUBLADO : cloudy

nuca *nf* : nape, back of the neck

nuclear *adj* : nuclear

núcleo *nm* **1** : nucleus **2** : center, heart, core

nudillo *nm* : knuckle

nudismo *nm* : nudism

nudista *adj & nmf* : nudist

nudo *nm* **1** : knot <square knot : nudo de rizo> <un nudo en la garganta : a lump in one's throat> **2** : node **3** : junction, hub <nudo de comunicaciones : communication center> **4** : crux, heart (of a problem, etc.)

nudoso, -sa *adj* : knotty, gnarled

nuera *nf* : daughter-in-law

nuestro[1], **-tra** *adj* : our

nuestro[2], **-tra** *pron* (*with definite article*) : ours, our own <el nuestro es más grande : ours is bigger> <es de los nuestros : it's one of ours>

nuevamente *adv* : again, anew

nuevas *nfpl* : tidings *pl*

nueve *adj & nm* : nine

nuevecito, -ta *adj* : brand-new

nuevo, -va *adj* **1** : new <una casa nueva : a new house> <¿qué hay de nuevo? : what's new?> **2 de ~** : again, once more

nuez *nf, pl* **nueces 1** : nut **2** : walnut **3** *Mex* : pecan **4 nuez de Adán** : Adam's apple **5 nuez moscada** : nutmeg

nulidad *nf* **1** : nullity **2** : incompetent person <¡es una nulidad! : he's hopeless!>

nulo, -la *adj* **1** : null, null and void **2** INEPTO : useless, inept <es nula para la cocina : she's hopeless at cooking>

numen *nm* : poetic muse, inspiration

numerable *adj* : countable

numeración *nf, pl* **-ciones 1 :** numbering **2 :** numbers *pl,* numerals *pl* <numeración romana : Roman numerals>
numerador *nm* **:** numerator
numeral *adj* **:** numeral
numerar *vt* **:** to number
numerario, -ria *adj* **:** long-standing, permanent <profesor numerario : tenured professor>
numérico, -ca *adj* **:** numerical **— numéricamente** *adv*
número *nm* **1 :** number <número impar : odd number> <número ordinal : ordinal number> <número arábico : Arabic numeral> <número quebrado : fraction> **2 :** issue (of a publication) **3 sin ~ :** countless
numeroso, -sa *adj* **:** numerous
numismática *nf* **:** numismatics
nunca *adv* **1 :** never, ever <nunca es tarde : it's never too late> <no trabaja casi nunca : he hardly ever works> **2 nunca más :** never again **3 nunca jamás :** never ever
nuncio *nm* **:** harbinger, herald
nupcial *adj* **:** nuptial, wedding
nupcias *nfpl* **:** nuptials *pl,* wedding
nutria *nf* **1 :** otter **2 :** nutria
nutrición *nf, pl* **-ciones :** nutrition, nourishment
nutrido, -da *adj* **1 :** nourished <mal nutrido : undernourished, malnourished> **2 :** considerable, abundant <de nutrido : full of, abounding in>
nutriente *nm* **:** nutrient
nutrimento *nm* **:** nutriment
nutrir *vt* **1** ALIMENTAR **:** to feed, to nourish **2 :** to foster, to provide
nutritivo, -va *adj* **:** nourishing, nutritious
nylon *nm* → **nilón**

ñ *nf* **:** fifteenth letter of the Spanish alphabet
ñame *nm* **:** yam
ñandú *nm* **:** rhea
ñapa *nf* **:** extra amount <de ñapa : for good measure>
ñoñear *vi fam* **:** to whine
ñoño, -ña *adj fam* **:** whiny, fussy <no seas tan ñoño : don't be such a wimp>
ñoquis *nmpl* **:** gnocchi *pl*
ñu *nm* **:** gnu, wildebeest

O

o[1] *nf* **:** sixteenth letter of the Spanish alphabet
o[2] *conj* (**u** *before words beginning with o- or ho-*) **1 :** or <¿vienes con nosotros o te quedas? : are you coming with us or staying?> **2 :** either <o vienes con nosotros o te quedas : either you come with us or you stay> **3 o sea :** that is to say, in other words
oasis *nms & pl* **:** oasis
obcecado, -da *adj* **1 :** blinded <obcecado por la ira : blinded by rage> **2 :** stubborn, obstinate
obcecar {72} *vt* **:** to blind (by emotions) **— obcecarse** *vr* **:** to become stubborn
obedecer {53} *vt* **:** to obey <obedecer órdenes : to obey orders> <obedece a tus padres : obey your parents> **—** *vi* **1 :** to obey **2 ~ a :** to respond to **3 ~ a :** to be due to, to result from
obediencia *nf* **:** obedience
obediente *adj* **:** obedient **— obedientemente** *adv*
obelisco *nm* **:** obelisk
obertura *nf* **:** overture
obesidad *nf* **:** obesity
obeso, -sa *adj* **:** obese
óbice *nm* **:** obstacle, impediment
obispado *nm* DIÓCESIS **:** bishopric, diocese
obispo *nm* **:** bishop
obituario *nm* **:** obituary
objeción *nf, pl* **-ciones :** objection <ponerle objeciones a algo : to object to something>
objetar *v* **:** to object <no tengo nada que objetar : I have no objections>
objetividad *nf* **:** objectivity
objetivo[1]**, -va** *adj* **:** objective **— objetivamente** *adv*
objetivo[2] *nm* **1** META **:** objective, goal, target **2 :** lens
objeto *nm* **1** COSA **:** object, thing **2** OBJETIVO **:** objective, purpose <con objeto de : in order to, with the aim of> **3 objeto volador no identificado :** unidentified flying object
objetor, -tora *n* **:** objector <objetor de conciencia : conscientious objector>
oblea *nf* **1 :** wafer **2 hecho una oblea** *fam* **:** skinny as a rail
oblicuo, -cua *adj* **:** oblique **— oblicuamente** *adv*
obligación *nf, pl* **-ciones 1** DEBER **:** obligation, duty **2 :** bond, debenture
obligado, -da *adj* **1 :** obliged **2 :** obligatory, compulsory **3 :** customary
obligar {52} *vt* **:** to force, to require, to oblige **— obligarse** *vr* **:** to commit

oneself, to undertake (to do something)

obligatorio, -ria *adj* : mandatory, required, compulsory

obliterar *vt* : to obliterate, to destroy — **obliteración** *nf*

oblongo, -ga *adj* : oblong

obnubilación *nf, pl* **-ciones** : bewilderment, confusion

obnubilar *vt* : to daze, to bewilder

oboe[1] *nm* : oboe

oboe[2] *nmf* : oboist

obra *nf* **1** : work <obra de arte : work of art> <obra de teatro : play> <obra de consulta : reference work> **2** : deed <una buena obra : a good deed> **3** : construction work **4 obra maestra** : masterpiece **5 obras públicas** : public works **6 por obra de** : thanks to, because of

obrar *vt* : to work, to produce <obrar milagros : to work miracles> — *vi* **1** : to act, to behave <obrar con cautela : to act with caution> **2 obrar en poder de** : to be in possession of

obrero[1]**, -ra** *adj* : working <la clase obrera : the working class>

obrero[2]**, -ra** *n* : worker, laborer

obscenidad *nf* : obscenity

obsceno, -na *adj* : obscene

obscurecer, obscuridad, obscuro → **oscurecer, oscuridad, oscuro**

obsequiar *vt* REGALAR : to give, to present <lo obsequiaron con una placa : they presented him with a plaque>

obsequio *nm* REGALO : gift, present

obsequiosidad *nf* : attentiveness, deference

obsequioso, -sa *adj* : obliging, attentive

observación *nf, pl* **-ciones 1** : observation, watching **2** : remark, comment

observador[1]**, -dora** *adj* : observant

observador[2]**, -dora** *n* : observer, watcher

observancia *nf* : observance

observar *vt* **1** : to observe, to watch <estábamos observando a los niños : we were watching the children> **2** NOTAR : to notice **3** ACATAR : to obey, to abide by **4** COMENTAR : to remark, to comment

observatorio *nm* : observatory

obsesión *nf, pl* **-siones** : obsession

obsesionar *vt* : to obsess, to preoccupy excessively — **obsesionarse** *vr*

obsesivo, -va *adj* : obsessive

obseso, -sa *adj* : obsessed

obsolescencia *nf* DESUSO : obsolescence — **obsolescente** *adj*

obsoleto, -ta *adj* DESUSADO : obsolete

obstaculizar {21} *vt* IMPEDIR : to obstruct, to hinder

obstáculo *nm* IMPEDIMENTO : obstacle

obstante[1] *conj* **no obstante** : nevertheless, however

obstante[2] *prep* **no obstante** : in spite of, despite <mantuvo su inocencia no obstante la evidencia : he maintained his innocence in spite of the evidence>

obstar *v impers* **~ a** *or* **~ para** : to hinder, to prevent <eso no obsta para que me vaya : that doesn't prevent me from leaving>

obstetra *nmf* TOCÓLOGO : obstetrician

obstetricia *nf* : obstetrics

obstétrico, -ca *adj* : obstetric, obstetrical

obstinación *nf, pl* **-ciones 1** TERQUEDAD : obstinacy, stubbornness **2** : perseverance, tenacity

obstinado, -da *adj* **1** TERCO : obstinate, stubborn **2** : persistent — **obstinadamente** *adv*

obstinarse *vr* EMPECINARSE : to be obstinate, to be stubborn

obstrucción *nf, pl* **-ciones** : obstruction, blockage

obstruccionismo *nm* : obstructionism, filibustering

obstructor, -tora *adj* : obstructive

obstruir {41} *vt* BLOQUEAR : to obstruct, to block, to clog — **obstruirse** *vr*

obtención *nf* : obtaining, procurement

obtener {80} *vt* : to obtain, to secure, to get — **obtenible** *adj*

obturador *nm* : shutter (of a camera)

obtuso, -sa *adj* : obtuse

obtuvo, etc. → **obtener**

obviar *vt* : to get around (a difficulty), to avoid

obvio, -via *adj* : obvious — **obviamente** *adv*

oca *nf* : goose

ocasión *nf, pl* **-siones 1** : occasion, time **2** : opportunity, chance **3** : bargain **4 de ~** : secondhand **5 aviso de ocasión** *Mex* : classified ad

ocasional *adj* **1** : occasional **2** : chance, fortuitous

ocasionalmente *adv* **1** : occasionally **2** : by chance

ocasionar *vt* CAUSAR : to cause, to occasion

ocaso *nm* **1** ANOCHECER : sunset, sundown **2** DECADENCIA : decline, fall

occidental *adj* : western, occidental

occidente *nm* **1** OESTE, PONIENTE : west **2 el Occidente** : the West

oceánico, -ca *adj* : oceanic

océano *nm* : ocean

oceanografía *nf* : oceanography

oceanográfico, -ca *adj* : oceanographic

ocelote *nm* : ocelot

ochenta *adj & nm* : eighty

ochentavo[1]**, -va** *adj* : eightieth

ochentavo[2] *nm* : eightieth (fraction)

ocho *adj & nm* : eight

ochocientos[1]**, -tas** *adj* : eight hundred

ochocientos[2] *nms & pl* : eight hundred

ocio *nm* **1** : free time, leisure **2** : idleness

ociosidad *nf* : idleness, inactivity

ocioso, -sa *adj* **1** INACTIVO : idle, inactive **2** INÚTIL : pointless, useless
ocre *nm* : ocher
octágono *nm* : octagon — **octagonal** *adj*
octava *nf* : octave
octavo, -va *adj* : eighth — **octavo, -va** *n*
octeto *nm* **1** : octet **2** : byte
octogésimo[1], -ma *adj* : eightieth, eighty-
octogésimo[2], -ma *n* : eightieth, eighty- (in a series)
octubre *nm* : October
ocular *adj* **1** : ocular, eye <músculos oculares : eye muscles> **2 testigo ocular** : eyewitness
oculista *nmf* : oculist, opthalmologist
ocultación *nf, pl* **-ciones** : concealment
ocultar *vt* ESCONDER : to conceal, to hide — **ocultarse** *vr*
oculto, -ta *adj* **1** ESCONDIDO : hidden, concealed **2** : occult
ocupación *nf, pl* **-ciones 1** : occupation, activity **2** : occupancy **3** EMPLEO : employment, job
ocupacional *adj* : occupational, job-related
ocupado, -da *adj* **1** : busy **2** : taken <este asiento está ocupado : this seat is taken> **3** : occupied <territorios ocupados : occupied territories> **4 señal de ocupado** : busy signal
ocupante *nmf* : occupant
ocupar *vt* **1** : to occupy, to take possession of **2** : to hold (a position) **3** : to employ, to keep busy **4** : to fill (space, time) **5** : to inhabit (a dwelling) **6** : to bother, to concern — **ocuparse** *vr* **~ de 1** : to be concerned with **2** : to take care of
ocurrencia *nf* **1** : occurrence, event **2** : witticism **3** : bright idea
ocurrente *adj* **1** : witty **2** : clever, sharp
ocurrir *vi* : to occur, to happen — **ocurrirse** *vr* **~ a** : to occur to, to strike <se me ocurrió una mejor idea : a better idea occurred to me>
oda *nf* : ode
odiar *vt* ABOMINAR, ABORRECER : to hate
odio *nm* : hate, hatred
odioso, -sa *adj* ABOMINABLE, ABORRECIBLE : hateful, detestable
odisea *nf* : odyssey
odontología *nf* : dentistry, dental surgery
odontólogo, -ga *n* : dentist, dental surgeon
oeste[1] *adj* **1** : west, western <la región oeste : the western region> **2** : westerly
oeste[2] *nm* **1** : west, West **2** : west wind
ofender *vt* AGRAVIAR : to offend, to insult — *vi* : to offend, to be insulting — **ofenderse** *vr* : to take offense
ofensa *nf* : offense, insult
ofensiva *nf* : offensive <pasar a la ofensiva : to go on the offensive>
ofensivo, -va *adj* : offensive, insulting
ofensor, -sora *n* : offender
oferente *nmf* **1** : supplier **2** FUENTE : source <un oferente no identificado : an unidentified source>
oferta *nf* **1** : offer **2** : sale, bargain <las camisas están en oferta : the shirts are on sale> **3 oferta y demanda** : supply and demand
ofertar *vt* OFRECER : to offer
oficial[1] *adj* : official — **oficialmente** *adv*
oficial[2] *nmf* **1** : officer, police officer, commissioned officer (in the military) **2** : skilled worker
oficializar {21} *vt* : to make official
oficiante *nmf* : celebrant
oficiar *vt* **1** : to inform officially **2** : to officiate at, to celebrate (Mass) — *vi* **~ de** : to act as
oficina *nf* : office
oficinista *nmf* : office worker
oficio *nm* **1** : trade, profession <es electricista de oficio : he's an electrician by trade> **2** : function, role **3** : official communication **4** : experience <tener oficio : to be experienced> **5** : religious ceremony
oficioso, -sa *adj* **1** EXTRAOFICIAL : unofficial **2** : officious — **oficiosamente** *adv*
ofrecer {53} *vt* **1** : to offer **2** : to provide, to give **3** : to present (an appearance, etc.) — **ofrecerse** *vr* **1** : to offer oneself, to volunteer **2** : to open up, to present itself
ofrecimiento *nm* : offer, offering
ofrenda *nf* : offering
oftalmología *nf* : ophthalmology
oftalmólogo, -ga *n* : ophthalmologist
ofuscación *nf, pl* **-ciones** : blindness, confusion
ofuscar {72} *vt* **1** : to blind, to dazzle **2** CONFUNDIR : to bewilder, to confuse — **ofuscarse** *vr* **~ con** : to be blinded by
ogro *nm* : ogre
ohm *nm, pl* **ohms** : ohm
ohmio *nm* → **ohm**
oídas *nfpl* **de ~** : by hearsay
oído *nm* **1** : ear <oído interno : inner ear> **2** : hearing <duro de oído : hard of hearing> **3 tocar de oído** : to play by ear
oiga, etc. → **oír**
oír {50} *vi* : to hear — *vt* **1** : to hear **2** ESCUCHAR : to listen to **3** : to pay attention to, to heed **4 ¡oye!** *or* **¡oiga!** : listen!, excuse me!, look here!
ojal *nm* : buttonhole
ojalá *interj* **1** : I hope so!, if only!, God willing! **2** : I hope, I wish, hopefully <¡ojalá que le vaya bien! : I hope things go well for her!> <¡ojalá no llueva! : hopefully it won't rain!>
ojeada *nf* : glimpse, glance <echar una ojeada : to have a quick look>
ojear *vt* : to eye, to have a look at
ojete *nm* : eyelet

ojiva *nf* **:** warhead

ojo *nm* **1 :** eye **2 :** judgment, sharpness <tener buen ojo para : to be a good judge of, to have a good eye for> **3 :** hole (in cheese), eye (in a needle), center (of a storm) **4 :** span (of a bridge) **5 a ojos vistas :** openly, publicly **6 andar con ojo :** to be careful **7 ojo de agua** *Mex* **:** spring, source **8 ¡ojo! :** look out!, pay attention!

ola *nf* **1 :** wave **2 ola de calor :** heat wave

oleada *nf* **:** swell, wave <una oleada de protestas : a wave of protests>

oleaje *nm* **:** waves *pl*, surf

óleo *nm* **1 :** oil **2 :** oil painting

oleoducto *nm* **:** oil pipeline

oleoso, -sa *adj* **:** oily

oler {51} *vt* **1 :** to smell **2** INQUIRIR **:** to pry into, to investigate **3** AVERIGUAR **:** to smell out, to uncover — *vi* **1 :** to smell <huele mal : it smells bad> **2 ~ a :** to smell like, to smell of <huele a pino : it smells like pine> — **olerse** *vr* **:** to have a hunch, to suspect

olfatear *vt* **1 :** to sniff **2 :** to sense, to sniff out

olfativo, -va *adj* **:** olfactory

olfato *nm* **1 :** sense of smell **2 :** nose, instinct

oligarquía *nf* **:** oligarchy

olimpiada *or* **olimpíada** *nf* **:** Olympics *pl*, Olympic Games *pl*

olímpico, -ca *adj* **:** Olympic

olisquear *vt* **:** to sniff at

oliva *nf* ACEITUNA **:** olive <aceite de oliva : olive oil>

olivo *nm* **:** olive tree

olla *nf* **1 :** pot <olla de presión : pressure cooker> **2 olla podrida :** Spanish stew

olmeca *adj & nmf* **:** Olmec

olmo *nm* **:** elm

olor *nm* **:** smell, odor

oloroso, -sa *adj* **:** scented, fragrant

olote *nm Mex* **:** cob, corncob

olvidadizo, -za *adj* **:** forgetful, absent-minded

olvidar *vt* **1 :** to forget, to forget about <olvida lo que pasó : forget about what happened> **2 :** to leave behind <olvidé mi chequera en la casa : I left my checkbook at home> — **olvidarse** *vr* **:** to forget <se me olvidó mi cuaderno : I forgot my notebook> <se le olvidó llamarme : he forgot to call me>

olvido *nm* **1 :** forgetfulness **2 :** oblivion **3** DESCUIDO **:** oversight

omaní *adj & nmf* **:** Omani

ombligo *nm* **:** navel, belly button

ombudsman *nmfs & pl* **:** ombudsman

omelette *nmf* **:** omelet

ominoso, -sa *adj* **:** ominous — **ominosamente** *adv*

omisión *nf, pl* **-siones :** omission, neglect

omiso, -sa *adj* **1** NEGLIGENTE **:** neglectful **2 hacer caso omiso de :** to ignore

omitir *vt* **1 :** to omit, to leave out **2 :** to fail to <omitió dar su nombre : he failed to give his name>

ómnibus *n, pl* **-bus** *or* **-buses :** bus, coach

omnipotencia *nf* **:** omnipotence

omnipotente *adj* TODOPODEROSO **:** omnipotent, almighty

omnipresencia *nf* **:** ubiquity, omnipresence

omnipresente *adj* **:** ubiquitous, omnipresent

omnisciente *adj* **:** omniscient — **omnisciencia** *nf*

omnívoro, -ra *adj* **:** omnivorous

omóplato *or* **omoplato** *nm* **:** shoulder blade

once *adj & nm* **:** eleven

onceavo[1], -va *adj* **:** eleventh

onceavo[2] *nm* **:** eleventh (fraction)

onda *nf* **1 :** wave, ripple, undulation <onda sonora : sound wave> **2 :** wave (in hair) **3 :** scallop (on clothing) **4** *fam* **:** wavelength, understanding <agarrar la onda : to get the point> <en la onda : on the ball, with it> **5 ¿qué onda?** *fam* **:** what's happening?, what's up?

ondear *vi* **:** to ripple, to undulate, to flutter

ondulación *nf, pl* **-ciones :** undulation

ondulado, -da *adj* **1 :** wavy <pelo ondulado : wavy hair> **2 :** undulating

ondular *vt* **:** to wave (hair) — *vi* **:** to undulate, to ripple

oneroso, -sa *adj* GRAVOSO **:** onerous, burdensome

ónix *nm* **:** onyx

onza *nf* **:** ounce

opacar {72} *vt* **1 :** to make opaque or dull **2 :** to outshine, to overshadow

opacidad *nf* **1 :** opacity **2 :** dullness

opaco, -ca *adj* **1 :** opaque **2 :** dull

ópalo *nm* **:** opal

opción *nf, pl* **opciones 1** ALTERNATIVA **:** option, choice **2 :** right, chance <tener opción a : to be eligible for>

opcional *adj* **:** optional — **opcionalmente** *adv*

ópera *nf* **:** opera

operación *nf, pl* **-ciones 1 :** operation **2 :** transaction, deal

operacional *adj* **:** operational

operador, -dora *n* **1 :** operator **2 :** cameraman, projectionist

operante *adj* **:** operating, working

operar *vt* **1 :** to produce, to bring about **2** INTERVENIR **:** to operate on **3** *Mex* **:** to operate, to run (a machine) — *vi* **1 :** to operate, to function **2 :** to deal, to do business — **operarse** *vr* **1 :** to come about, to take place **2 :** to have an operation

operario, -ria *n* **:** laborer, worker

operático, -ca → **operístico**

operativo[1], -va *adj* **1 :** operating <capacidad operativa : operating capacity> **2 :** operative

operativo[2] *nm* : operation <operativo militar : military operation>
opereta *nf* : operetta
operístico, -ca *adj* : operatic
opiato *nm* : opiate
opinable *adj* : arguable
opinar *vi* **1** : to think, to have an opinion **2** : to express an opinion **3 opinar bien de** : to think highly of — *vt* : to think <opinamos lo mismo : we're of the same opinion, we're in agreement>
opinión *nf, pl* **-niones** : opinion, belief
opio *nm* : opium
oponente *nmf* : opponent
oponer {60} *vt* **1** CONTRAPONER : to oppose, to place against **2 oponer resistencia** : to resist, to put up a fight — **oponerse** *vr* **~ a** : to object to, to be against
oporto *nm* : port (wine)
oportunamente *adv* **1** : at the right time, opportunely **2** : appropriately
oportunidad *nf* : opportunity, chance
oportunismo *nm* : opportunism
oportunista[1] *adj* : opportunistic
oportunista[2] *nmf* : opportunist
oportuno, -na *adj* **1** : opportune, timely **2** : suitable, appropriate
oposición *nf, pl* **-ciones** : opposition
opositor, -tora *n* ADVERSARIO : opponent
oposum *nm* ZARIGÜEYA : opossum
opresión *nf, pl* **-siones 1** : oppression **2 opresión de pecho** : tightness in the chest
opresivo, -va *adj* : oppressive
opresor[1], **-sora** *adj* : oppressive
opresor[2], **-sora** *n* : oppressor
oprimir *vt* **1** : to oppress **2** : to press, to squeeze <oprima el botón : push the button>
oprobio *nm* : opprobrium, shame
optar *vi* **1 ~ por** : to opt for, to choose **2 ~ a** : to aspire to, to apply for <dos candidatos optan a la presidencia : two candidates are running for president>
optativo, -va *adj* FACULTATIVO : optional
óptica *nf* **1** : optics **2** : optician's shop **3** : viewpoint
óptico[1], **-ca** *adj* : optical, optic
óptico[2], **-ca** *n* : optician
optimismo *nm* : optimism
optimista[1] *adj* : optimistic
optimista[2] *nmf* : optimist
óptimo, -ma *adj* : optimum, optimal
optometría *nf* : optometry — **optometrista** *nmf*
opuesto[1] *pp* → **oponer**
opuesto[2] *adj* **1** : opposite, contrary **2** : opposed
opulencia *nf* : opulence — **opulento, -ta** *adj*
opus *nm* : opus
opuso, etc. → **oponer**
ora *conj* : now <los matices eran variados, ora verdes, ora ocres : the hues were varied, now green, now ocher>
oración *nf, pl* **-ciones 1** DISCURSO : oration, speech **2** PLEGARIA : prayer **3** FRASE : sentence, clause
oráculo *nm* : oracle
orador, -dora *n* : speaker, orator
oral *adj* : oral — **oralmente** *adv*
órale *interj Mex fam* **1** : sure!, OK! <¿los dos por cinco pesos? ¡órale! : both for five pesos? you've got a deal!> **2** : come on! <¡órale, vámonos! : come on, let's go!>
orangután *nm, pl* **-tanes** : orangutan
orar *vi* REZAR : to pray
oratoria *nf* : oratory
oratorio *nm* **1** CAPILLA : oratory, chapel **2** : oratorio
orbe *nm* **1** : orb, sphere **2** GLOBO : globe, world
órbita *nf* **1** : orbit **2** : eye socket **3** ÁMBITO : sphere, field
orbitador *nm* : space shuttle, orbiter
orbital *adj* : orbital
orden[1] *nm, pl* **órdenes 1** : order <todo está en orden : everything's in order> <por orden cronológico : in chronological order> **2 orden del día** : agenda (at a meeting) **3 orden público** : law and order
orden[2] *nf, pl* **órdenes 1** : order <una orden religiosa : a religious order> <una orden de tacos : an order of tacos> **2 orden de compra** : purchase order **3 estar a la orden del día** : to be the order of the day, to be prevalent
ordenación *nf, pl* **-ciones 1** : ordination **2** : ordering, organizing
ordenadamente *adv* : in an orderly fashion, neatly
ordenado, -da *adj* : orderly, neat
ordenador *nm Spain* : computer
ordenamiento *nm* **1** : ordering, organizing **2** : code (of laws)
ordenanza[1] *nf* REGLAMENTO : ordinance, regulation
ordenanza[2] *nm* : orderly (in the armed forces)
ordenar *vt* **1** MANDAR : to order, to command **2** ARREGLAR : to put in order, to arrange **3** : to ordain (a priest)
ordeñar *vt* : to milk
ordeño *nm* : milking
ordinal *nm* : ordinal (number)
ordinariamente *adv* **1** : usually **2** : coarsely
ordinariez *nf* : coarseness, vulgarity
ordinario, -ria *adj* **1** : ordinary **2** : coarse, common, vulgar **3 de ~** : usually
orear *vt* : to air
orégano *nm* : oregano
oreja *nf* : ear
orfanato *nm* : orphanage
orfanatorio *nm Mex* : orphanage
orfebre *nmf* : goldsmith, silversmith
orfebrería *nf* : articles of gold or silver

orfelinato *nm* : orphanage
orgánico, -ca *adj* : organic — **orgánicamente** *adv*
organigrama *nm* : organization chart, flowchart
organismo *nm* **1** : organism **2** : agency, organization
organista *nmf* : organist
organización *nf, pl* **-ciones** : organization
organizador¹, -dora *adj* : organizing
organizador², -dora *n* : organizer
organizar {21} *vt* : to organize, to arrange — **organizarse** *vr* : to get organized
organizativo, -va *adj* : organizational
órgano *nm* : organ
orgasmo *nm* : orgasm
orgía *nf* : orgy
orgullo *nm* : pride
orgulloso, -sa *adj* : proud — **orgullosamente** *adv*
orientación *nf, pl* **-ciones 1** : orientation **2** DIRECCIÓN : direction, course **3** GUÍA : guidance, direction
oriental¹ *adj* **1** : eastern **2** : oriental **3** *Arg, Uru* : Uruguayan
oriental² *nmf* **1** : Easterner **2** : Oriental **3** *Arg, Uru* : Uruguayan
orientar *vt* **1** : to orient, to position **2** : to guide, to direct — **orientarse** *vr* **1** : to orient oneself, to get one's bearings **2** ~ **hacia** : to turn towards, to lean towards
oriente *nm* **1** : east, East **2 el Oriente** : the Orient
orífice *nmf* : goldsmith
orificio *nm* : orifice, opening
origen *nm, pl* **orígenes 1** : origin **2** : lineage, birth **3 dar origen a** : to give rise to **4 en su origen** : originally
original *adj & nm* : original — **originalmente** *adv*
originalidad *nf* : originality
originar *vt* : to originate, to give rise to — **originarse** *vr* : to originate, to begin
originario, -ria *adj* ~ **de** : native of
originariamente *adv* : originally
orilla *nf* **1** BORDE : border, edge **2** : bank (of a river) **3** : shore
orillar *vt* **1** : to skirt, to go around **2** : to trim, to edge (cloth) **3** : to settle, to wind up **4** *Mex* : to pull over (a vehicle)
orín *nm* **1** HERRUMBRE : rust **2 orines** *nmpl* : urine
orina *nf* : urine
orinación *nf* : urination
orinal *nm* : urinal (vessel)
orinar *vi* : to urinate — **orinarse** *vr* : to wet oneself
oriol *nm* OROPÉNDOLA : oriole
oriundo, -da *adj* ~ **de** : native of
orla *nf* : border, edging
orlar *vt* : to edge, to trim
ornamentación *nf, pl* **-ciones** : ornamentation
ornamental *adj* : ornamental
ornamentar *vt* ADORNAR : to ornament, to adorn
ornamento *nm* : ornament, adornment
ornar *vt* : to adorn, to decorate
ornitología *nf* : ornithology
ornitólogo, -ga *n* : ornithologist
ornitorrinco *nm* : platypus
oro *nm* : gold
orondo, -da *adj* **1** : rounded, potbellied (of a container) **2** *fam* : smug, self-satisfied
oropel *nm* : glitz, glitter, tinsel
oropéndola *nf* : oriole
orquesta *nf* : orchestra — **orquestal** *adj*
orquestar *vt* : to orchestrate — **orquestación** *nf*
orquídea *nf* : orchid
ortiga *nf* : nettle
ortodoncia *nf* : orthodontics
ortodoncista *nmf* : orthodontist
ortodoxia *nf* : orthodoxy
ortodoxo, -xa *adj* : orthodox
ortografía *nf* : orthography, spelling
ortográfico, -ca *adj* : orthographic, spelling
ortopedia *nf* : orthopedics
ortopedista *nmf* : orthopedist
oruga *nf* **1** : caterpillar **2** : track (of a tank, etc.)
orzuelo *nm* : sty, stye (in the eye)
os *pron pl* (*objective form of* **vosotros**) *Spain* **1** : you, to you **2** : yourselves, to yourselves **3** : each other, to each other
osa *nf* → **oso**
osadía *nf* **1** VALOR : boldness, daring **2** AUDACIA : audacity, nerve
osado, -da *adj* **1** : bold, daring **2** : audacious, impudent — **osadamente** *adv*
osamenta *nf* : skeletal remains *pl*, bones *pl*
osar *vi* : to dare
oscilación *nf, pl* **-ciones 1** : oscillation **2** : fluctuation **3** : vacillation, wavering
oscilar *vi* **1** BALANCEARSE : to swing, to sway, to oscillate **2** FLUCTUAR : to fluctuate **3** : to vacillate, to waver
oscuramente *adv* : obscurely
oscurecer {53} *vt* **1** : to darken **2** : to obscure, to confuse, to cloud **3 al oscurecer** : at dusk, at nightfall — *v impers* : to grow dark, to get dark — **oscurecerse** *vr* : to darken, to dim
oscuridad *nf* **1** : darkness **2** : obscurity
oscuro, -ra *adj* **1** : dark **2** : obscure **3 a oscuras** : in the dark, in darkness
óseo, ósea *adj* : skeletal, bony
ósmosis *or* **osmosis** *nf* : osmosis
oso, osa *n* **1** : bear **2 Osa Mayor** : Big Dipper **3 Osa Menor** : Little Dipper **4 oso blanco** : polar bear **5 oso hormiguero** : anteater **6 oso de peluche** : teddy bear
ostensible *adj* : ostensible, apparent — **ostensiblemente** *adv*
ostentación *nf, pl* **-ciones** : ostentation, display

ostentar *vt* **1** : to display, to flaunt **2** POSEER : to have, to hold <ostenta el récord mundial : he holds the world record>
ostentoso, -sa *adj* : ostentatious, showy — **ostentosamente** *adv*
osteópata *nmf* : osteopath
osteopatía *n* : osteopathy
osteoporosis *nf* : osteoporosis
ostión *nm, pl* **ostiones 1** *Mex* : oyster **2** *Chile* : scallop
ostra *nf* : oyster
ostracismo *nm* : ostracism
otear *vt* : to scan, to survey, to look over
otero *nm* : knoll, hillock
otomana *nf* : ottoman
otoñal *adj* : autumn, autumnal
otoño *nm* : autumn, fall
otorgamiento *nm* : granting, awarding
otorgar {52} *vt* **1** : to grant, to award **2** : to draw up, to frame (a legal document)
otro[1]**, otra** *adj* **1** : other **2** : another <en otro juego, ellos ganaron : in another game, they won> **3 otra vez** : again **4 de otra manera** : otherwise **5 otra parte** : elsewhere **6 en otro tiempo** : once, formerly
otro[2]**, otra** *pron* **1** : another one <dame otro : give me another> **2** : other one <el uno o el otro : one or the other> **3 los otros, las otras** : the others, the rest <me dio una y se quedó con las otras : he gave me one and kept the rest>
ovación *nf, pl* **-ciones** : ovation
ovacionar *vt* : to cheer, to applaud
oval → **ovalado**
ovalado, -da *adj* : oval
óvalo *nm* : oval
ovárico, -ca *adj* : ovarian
ovario *nm* : ovary
oveja *nf* **1** : sheep, ewe **2 oveja negra** : black sheep
overol *nm* : overalls *pl*
ovillar *vt* : to roll into a ball
ovillo *nm* **1** : ball (of yarn) **2** : tangle
ovni *or* **OVNI** *nm* (*objeto volador no identificado*) : UFO
ovoide *adj* : ovoid, ovoidal
ovulación *nf, pl* **-ciones** : ovulation
ovular *vi* : to ovulate
óvulo *nm* : ovum
oxidación *nf, pl* **-ciones 1** : oxidation **2** : rusting
oxidado, -da *adj* : rusty
oxidar *vt* **1** : to cause to rust **2** : to oxidize — **oxidarse** *vr* : to rust, to become rusty
óxido *nm* **1** HERRUMBRE, ORÍN : rust **2** : oxide
oxigenar *vt* **1** : to oxygenate **2** : to bleach (hair)
oxígeno *nm* : oxygen
oxiuro *nm* : pinworm
oye, etc. → **oír**
oyente *nmf* **1** : listener **2** : auditor, auditing student
ozono *nm* : ozone

P

p *nf* : seventeenth letter of the Spanish alphabet
pabellón *nm, pl* **-llones 1** : pavilion **2** : summerhouse, lodge **3** : flag (of a vessel)
pabilo *nm* MECHA : wick
paca *nf* FARDO : bale
pacana *nf* : pecan
pacer {48} *v* : to graze, to pasture
paces → **paz**
pachanga *nf fam* : party, bash
paciencia *nf* : patience
paciente *adj & nmf* : patient — **pacientemente** *adv*
pacificación *nf, pl* **-ciones** : pacification
pacíficamente *adv* : peacefully, peaceably
pacificar {72} *vt* : to pacify, to calm — **pacificarse** *vr* : to calm down, to abate
pacífico, -ca *adj* : peaceful, pacific
pacifismo *nm* : pacifism
pacifista *adj & nmf* : pacifist
pacotilla *nf* **de ~** : shoddy, trashy
pactar *vt* : to agree on — *vi* : to come to an agreement
pacto *nm* CONVENIO : pact, agreement
padecer {53} *vt* : to suffer, to endure — *vi* ADOLECER **~ de** : to suffer from
padecimiento *nm* **1** : suffering **2** : ailment, condition
padrastro *nm* **1** : stepfather **2** : hangnail
padre[1] *adj Mex fam* : fantastic, great
padre[2] *nm* **1** : father **2 padres** *nmpl* : parents
padrenuestro *nm* : Lord's Prayer, paternoster
padrino *nm* **1** : godfather **2** : best man **3** : sponsor, patron
padrón *nm, pl* **padrones** : register, roll <padrón municipal : city register>
paella *nf* : paella
paga *nf* **1** : payment **2** : pay, wages *pl*
pagadero, -ra *adj* : payable
pagado, -da *adj* **1** : paid **2 pagado de sí mismo** : self-satisfied, smug
pagador, -dora *n* : payer
paganismo *nm* : paganism
pagano, -na *adj & n* : pagan
pagar {52} *vt* : to pay, to pay for, to repay — *vi* : to pay
pagaré *nm* VALE : promissory note, IOU
página *nf* : page

pago *nm* **1 :** payment **2 en pago de :** in return for

pagoda *nf* **:** pagoda

pague, etc. → **pagar**

país *nm* **1** NACIÓN **:** country, nation **2** REGIÓN **:** region, territory

paisaje *nm* **:** scenery, landscape

paisano, -na *n* COMPATRIOTA **:** compatriot, fellow countryman

paja *nf* **1 :** straw **2** *fam* **:** trash, tripe

pajar *nm* **:** hayloft, haystack

pajarera *nf* **:** aviary

pájaro *nm* **:** bird <pájaro cantor : songbird> <pájaro bobo : penguin> <pájaro carpintero : woodpecker>

pajita *nf* **:** (drinking) straw

pajote *nm* **:** straw, mulch

pala *nf* **1 :** shovel, spade **2 :** blade (of an oar or a rotor) **3 :** paddle, racket

palabra *nf* **1** VOCABLO **:** word **2** PROMESA **:** word, promise <un hombre de palabra : a man of his word> **3** HABLA **:** speech **4 :** right to speak <tener la palabra : to have the floor>

palabrería *nf* **:** empty talk

palabrota *nf* **:** swearword

palacio *nm* **1 :** palace, mansion **2 palacio de justicia :** courthouse

paladar *nm* **1 :** palate **2** GUSTO **:** taste

paladear *vt* SABOREAR **:** to savor

paladín *nm, pl* **-dines :** champion, defender

palanca *nf* **1 :** lever, crowbar **2** *fam* **:** leverage, influence **3 palanca de cambio** *or* **palanca de velocidad :** gearshift

palangana *nf* **:** washbowl

palanqueta *nf* **:** jimmy, small crowbar

palco *nm* **:** box (in a theater or stadium)

palear *vt* **1 :** to shovel **2 :** to paddle

palenque *nm* **1** ESTACADA **:** stockade, palisade **2 :** arena, ring

paleontología *nf* **:** paleontology

paleontólogo, -ga *n* **:** paleontologist

palestino, -na *adj & n* **:** Palestinian

palestra *nf* **:** arena <salir a la palestra : to join the fray>

paleta *nf* **1 :** palette **2 :** trowel **3 :** spatula **4 :** blade, vane **5 :** paddle **6** *CA, Mex* **:** lollipop, Popsicle—

paletilla *nf* **:** shoulder blade

paliar *vt* MITIGAR **:** to alleviate, to palliate

paliativo[1], -va *adj* **:** palliative

paliativo[2] *nm* **:** palliative

palidecer {53} *vi* **:** to turn pale

palidez *nf, pl* **-deces :** paleness, pallor

pálido, -da *adj* **:** pale

palillo *nm* **1** MONDADIENTES **:** toothpick **2 palillos** *nmpl* **:** chopsticks **3 palillo de tambor :** drumstick

paliza *nf* **:** beating, pummeling <darle una paliza a : to beat, to thrash>

palma *nf* **1 :** palm (of the hand) **2 :** palm (tree or leaf) **3 batir palmas :** to clap, to applaud **4 llevarse la palma** *fam* **:** to take the cake

palmada *nf* **1 :** pat **2 :** slap **3 :** clap

palmarés *nm* **:** record (of achievements)

palmario, -ria *adj* MANIFIESTO **:** clear, manifest

palmeado, -da *adj* **:** webbed

palmear *vt* **:** to slap on the back — *vi* **:** to clap, to applaud

palmera *nf* **:** palm tree

palmo *nm* **1 :** span, small amount **2 palmo a palmo :** bit by bit, inch by inch **3 dejar con un palmo de narices :** to disappoint

palmotear *vi* **:** to applaud

palmoteo *nm* **:** clapping, applause

palo *nm* **1 :** stick, pole, post **2 :** shaft, handle <palo de escoba : broomstick> **3 :** mast, spar **4 :** wood **5 :** blow (with a stick) **6 :** suit (of cards)

paloma *nf* **1 :** pigeon, dove **2 paloma mensajera :** carrier pigeon

palomilla *nf* **:** moth

palomitas *nfpl* **:** popcorn

palpable *adj* **:** palpable, tangible

palpar *vt* **:** to feel, to touch

palpitación *nf, pl* **-ciones :** palpitation

palpitar *vi* **:** to palpitate, to throb — **palpitante** *adj*

palta *nf* **:** avocado

paludismo *nm* MALARIA **:** malaria

palurdo, -da *n* **:** boor, yokel, bumpkin

pampa *nf* **:** pampa

pampeano, -na *adj* **:** pampean, pampas

pampero → **pampeano**

pan *nm* **1 :** bread **2 :** loaf of bread **3 :** cake, bar <pan de jabón : bar of soap> **4 pan dulce** *CA, Mex* **:** traditional pastry **5 pan tostado :** toast **6 ser pan comido** *fam* **:** to be a piece of cake, to be a cinch

pana *nf* **:** corduroy

panacea *nf* **:** panacea

panadería *nf* **:** bakery, bread shop

panadero, -ra *n* **:** baker

panal *nm* **:** honeycomb

panameño, -ña *adj & n* **:** Panamanian

pancarta *nf* **:** placard, sign

pancita *nf Mex* **:** tripe

páncreas *nms & pl* **:** pancreas

panda *nmf* **:** panda

pandeado, -da *adj* **:** warped

pandearse *vr* **1 :** to warp **2 :** to bulge, to sag

pandemonio *or* **pandemónium** *nm* **:** pandemonium

pandereta *nf* **:** tambourine

pandero *nm* **:** tambourine

pandilla *nf* **1 :** group, clique **2 :** gang

panecito *nm* **:** roll, bread roll

panegírico[1], -ca *adj* **:** eulogistic, panegyrical

panegírico[2] *nm* **:** eulogy, panegyric

panel *nm* **:** panel — **panelista** *nmf*

panera *nf* **:** bread box

panfleto *nm* **:** pamphlet

pánico *nm* **:** panic

panorama *nm* **1** VISTA **:** panorama, view **2 :** scene, situation <el pa-

norama nacional : the national scene> **3** PERSPECTIVA : outlook

panorámico, -ca *adj* : panoramic

panqueque *nm* : pancake

pantaletas *nfpl* : panties

pantalla *nf* **1** : screen, monitor **2** : lampshade **3** : fan

pantalón *nm, pl* **-lones 1** : pants *pl,* trousers *pl* **2 pantalones vaqueros** : jeans **3 pantalones de mezclilla** *Chile, Mex* : jeans **4 pantalones de montar** : jodhpurs

pantano *nm* **1** : swamp, marsh, bayou **2** : reservoir **3** : obstacle, difficulty

pantanoso, -sa *adj* **1** : marshy, swampy **2** : difficult, thorny

panteón *nm, pl* **-teones 1** CEMENTERIO : cemetery **2** : pantheon, mausoleum

pantera *nf* : panther

pantimedias *nfpl Mex* : panty hose

pantomima *nf* : pantomime

pantorrilla *nf* : calf (of the leg)

pantufla *nf* ZAPATILLA : slipper

panza *nf* BARRIGA : belly, paunch

panzón, -zona *adj, mpl* **panzones** : potbellied, paunchy

pañal *nm* : diaper

pañería *nf* **1** : cloth, material **2** : fabric store

pañito *nm* : doily

paño *nm* **1** : cloth **2** : rag, dust cloth **3 paño de cocina** : dishcloth **4 paño higiénico** : sanitary napkin

pañuelo *nm* **1** : handkerchief **2** : scarf

papa[1] *nm* : pope

papa[2] *nf* **1** : potato **2 papa dulce** : sweet potato **3 papas fritas** : potato chips, french fries **4 papas a la francesa** *Mex* : french fries

papá *nm fam* **1** : dad, pop **2 papás** *nmpl* : parents, folks

papada *nf* **1** : double chin, jowl **2** : dewlap

papagayo *nm* LORO : parrot

papal *adj* : papal

papalote *nm Mex* : kite

papaya *nf* : papaya

papel *nm* **1** : paper, piece of paper **2** : role, part **3 papel de estaño** : tinfoil **4 papel de empapelar** *or* **papel pintado** : wallpaper **5 papel higiénico** : toilet paper **6 papel de lija** : sandpaper

papeleo *nm* : paperwork, red tape

papelera *nf* : wastebasket

papelería *nf* : stationery store

papelero, -ra *adj* : paper

papeleta *nf* **1** : ballot **2** : ticket, slip

paperas *nfpl* : mumps

papi *nm fam* : daddy, papa

papilla *nf* **1** : pap, mash **2 hacer papilla** : to beat to a pulp

papiro *nm* : papyrus

paquete *nm* BULTO : package, parcel

paquistaní *adj & nmf* : Pakistani

par[1] *adj* : even (in number)

par[2] *nm* **1** : pair, couple **2** : equal, peer <sin par : matchless, peerless> **3** : par (in golf) **4** : rafter **5 de par en par** : wide open

par[3] *nf* **1** : par <por encima de la par : above par> **2 a la par que** : at the same time as, as well as <interesante a la par que instructivo : both interesting and informative>

para *prep* **1** : for <para ti : for you> <alta para su edad : tall for her age> <una cita para el lunes : an appointment for Monday> **2** : to, towards <para la derecha : to the right> <van para el río : they're heading towards the river> **3** : to, in order to <lo hace para molestarte : he does it to annoy you> **4** : around, by (a time) <para mañana estarán listos : they'll be ready by tomorrow> **5 para adelante** : forwards **6 para atrás** : backwards **7 para que** : so, so that, in order that <te lo digo para que sepas : I'm telling you so you'll know>

parabién *nm, pl* **-bienes** : congratulations *pl*

parábola *nf* **1** : parable **2** : parabola

parabrisas *nms & pl* : windshield

paracaídas *nms & pl* : parachute

paracaidista *nmf* **1** : parachutist **2** : paratrooper

parachoques *nms & pl* : bumper

parada *nf* **1** : stop <parada de autobús : bus stop> **2** : catch, save, parry (in sports) **3** DESFILE : parade

paradero *nm* : whereabouts

paradigma *nm* : paradigm

parado, -da *adj* **1** : motionless, idle, stopped **2** : standing (up) **3** : confused, bewildered **4 bien (mal) parado** : in good (bad) shape <salió bien parado : it turned out well for him>

paradoja *nf* : paradox

paradójico, -ca *adj* : paradoxical

parafernalia *nf* : paraphernalia

parafina *nf* : paraffin

parafrasear *vt* : to paraphrase

paráfrasis *nfs & pl* : paraphrase

paraguas *nms & pl* : umbrella

paraguayo, -ya *adj & n* : Paraguayan

paraíso *nm* **1** : paradise, heaven **2 paraíso fiscal** : tax shelter

paraje *nm* : spot, place

paralelismo *nm* : parallelism, similarity

paralelo[1]**, -la** *adj* : parallel

paralelo[2] *nm* : parallel

paralelogramo *nm* : parallelogram

parálisis *nfs & pl* **1** : paralysis **2** : standstill **3 parálisis cerebral** : cerebral palsy

paralítico, -ca *adj & n* : paralytic

paralizar {21} *vt* **1** : to paralyze **2** : to bring to a standstill — **paralizarse** *vr*

parámetro *nm* : parameter

páramo *nm* : barren plateau, moor

parangón *nm, pl* **-gones 1** : comparison **2 sin ~** : incomparable

paraninfo *nm* : auditorium, assembly hall

paranoia *nf* : paranoia

paranoico, -ca *adj & n* : paranoid

parapeto *nm* : parapet, rampart

parapléjico, -ca *adj & n* : paraplegic

parar *vt* **1** DETENER : to stop **2** : to stand, to prop — *vi* **1** CESAR : to stop **2** : to stay, to put up **3 ir a parar** : to end up, to wind up — **pararse** *vr* **1** : to stop **2** ATASCARSE : to stall (out) **3** : to stand up, to get up

pararrayos *nms & pl* : lightning rod

parasitario, -ria *adj* : parasitic

parasitismo *nm* : parasitism

parásito *nm* : parasite

parasol *nm* SOMBRILLA : parasol

parcela *nf* : parcel, tract of land

parcelar *vt* : to parcel (land)

parchar *vt* : to patch, to patch up

parche *nm* : patch

parcial *adj* : partial — **parcialmente** *adv*

parcialidad *nf* : partiality, bias

parco, -ca *adj* **1** : sparing, frugal **2** : moderate, temperate

pardo, -da *adj* : brownish grey

pardusco → **pardo**

parecer[1] {53} *vi* **1** : to seem, to look, to appear to be <parece bien fácil : it looks very easy> <así parece : so it seems> <pareces una princesa : you look like a princess> **2** : to think, to have an opinion <me parece que sí : I think so> **3** : to like, to be in agreement <si te parece : if you like, if it's all right with you> — **parecerse** *vr* **~ a** : to resemble

parecer[2] *nm* **1** OPINIÓN : opinion **2** ASPECTO : appearance <al parecer : apparently>

parecido[1], **-da** *adj* **1** : similar, alike **2 bien parecido** : good-looking

parecido[2] *nm* : resemblance, similarity

pared *nf* : wall

pareja *nf* **1** : couple, pair **2** : partner, mate

parejo, -ja *adj* **1** : even, smooth, level **2** : equal, similar

parentela *nf* : relations *pl*, kinfolk

parentesco *nm* : relationship, kinship

paréntesis *nms & pl* **1** : parenthesis **2** : digression

parentético, -ca *adj* : parenthetic, parenthetical

paria *nmf* : pariah, outcast

paridad *nf* : parity, equality

pariente *nmf* : relative, relation

parir *vi* : to give birth — *vt* : to give birth to, to bear

parking *nm* : parking lot

parlamentar *vi* : to talk, to parley

parlamentario[1], **-ria** *adj* : parliamentary

parlamentario[2], **-ria** *n* : member of parliament

parlamento *nm* **1** : parliament **2** : negotiations *pl*, talks *pl*

parlanchín[1], **-china** *adj, mpl* **-chines** : chatty, talkative

parlanchín[2], **-china** *n, mpl* **-chines** : chatterbox

parlante *nm* ALTOPARLANTE : loudspeaker

parlotear *vi fam* : to gab, to chat, to prattle

parloteo *nm fam* : prattle, chatter

paro *nm* **1** HUELGA : strike **2** : stoppage, stopping **3 paro forzoso** : layoff

parodia *nf* : parody

parodiar *vt* : to parody

parpadear *vi* **1** : to blink **2** : to flicker

parpadeo *nm* **1** : blink, blinking **2** : flickering

párpado *nm* : eyelid

parque *nm* **1** : park **2 parque de atracciones** : amusement park

parquear *vt* : to park — **parquearse** *vr*

parqueo *nm* : parking

parquet *or* **parqué** *nm* : parquet

parquímetro *nm* : parking meter

parra *nf* : vine, grapevine

párrafo *nm* : paragraph

parranda *nf fam* : party, spree

parrilla *nf* **1** : broiler, grill **2** : grate

parrillada *nf* BARBACOA : barbecue

párroco *nm* : parish priest

parroquia *nf* **1** : parish **2** : parish church **3** : customers *pl*, clientele

parroquial *adj* : parochial

parroquiano, -na *nm* **1** : parishioner **2** : customer, patron

parsimonia *nf* **1** : calm **2** : parsimony, thrift

parsimonioso, -sa *adj* **1** : calm, unhurried **2** : parsimonious, thrifty

parte[1] *nm* : report, dispatch

parte[2] *nf* **1** : part, share **2** : part, place <en alguna parte : somewhere> <por todas partes : everywhere> **3** : party (in negotiations, etc.) **4 de parte de** : on behalf of **5 ¿de parte de quién?** : may I ask who's calling? **6 tomar parte** : to take part

partero, -ra *n* : midwife

partición *nf, pl* **-ciones** : division, sharing

participación *nf, pl* **-ciones 1** : participation **2** : share, interest **3** : announcement, notice

participante *nmf* **1** : participant **2** : competitor, entrant

participar *vi* **1** : to participate, to take part **2 ~ en** : to have a share in — *vt* : to announce, to notify

partícipe *nmf* : participant

participio *nm* : participle

partícula *nf* : particle

particular[1] *adj* **1** : particular, specific **2** : private, personal **3** : special, unique

particular[2] *nm* **1** : matter, detail **2** : individual

particularidad *nf* : characteristic, peculiarity

particularizar {21} *vt* **1** : to distinguish, to characterize **2** : to specify

partida *nf* **1 :** departure **2 :** item, entry **3 :** certificate <partida de nacimiento : birth certificate> **4 :** game, match, hand **5 :** party, group

partidario, -ria *n* **:** follower, supporter

partido *nm* **1 :** (political) party **2 :** game, match <partido de futbol : soccer game> **3** APOYO **:** support, following **4** PROVECHO **:** profit, advantage <sacar partido de : to profit from>

partir *vt* **1 :** to cut, to split **2 :** to break, to crack **3 :** to share (out), to divide — *vi* **1 :** to leave, to depart **2 ~ de :** to start from **3 a partir de :** as of, from <a partir de hoy : as of today> — **partirse** *vr* **1 :** to smash, to split open **2 :** to chap

partisano, -na *adj & n* **:** partisan

partitura *nf* **:** (musical) score

parto *nm* **1 :** childbirth, delivery, labor <estar de parto : to be in labor> **2 :** product, creation, brainchild

parvulario *nm* **:** nursery school

párvulo, -la *n* **:** toddler, preschooler

pasa *nf* **1 :** raisin **2 pasa de Corinto :** currant

pasable *adj* **:** passable, tolerable — **pasablemente** *adv*

pasada *nf* **1 :** passage, passing **2 :** pass, wipe, coat (of paint) **3 de ~ :** in passing **4 mala pasada :** dirty trick

pasadizo *nm* **:** passageway, corridor

pasado[1], -da *adj* **1 :** past <el año pasado : last year> <pasado mañana : the day after tomorrow> <pasadas las siete : after seven o'clock> **2 :** stale, bad, overripe **3 :** old-fashioned, out-of-date **4 :** overripe, slightly spoiled

pasado[2] *nm* **:** past

pasador *nm* **1 :** bolt, latch **2 :** barrette **3** *Mex* **:** bobby pin

pasaje *nm* **1 :** ticket (for travel) **2** TARIFA **:** fare **3 :** passageway **4 :** passengers *pl*

pasajero[1], -ra *adj* **:** passing, fleeting

pasajero[2], -ra *n* **:** passenger

pasamanos *nms & pl* **1 :** handrail **2 :** banister

pasante *nmf* **:** assistant

pasaporte *nm* **:** passport

pasar *vi* **1 :** to pass, to go by, to come by **2 :** to come in, to enter <¿se puede pasar? : may we come in?> **3 :** to happen <¿qué pasa? : what's happening?, what's going on?> **4 :** to manage, to get by **5 :** to be over, to end **6 ~ de :** to exceed, to go beyond **7 ~ por :** to pretend to be — *vt* **1 :** to pass, to give <¿me pasas la sal? : would you pass me the salt?> **2 :** to pass (a test) **3 :** to go over, to cross **4 :** to spend (time) **5 :** to tolerate **6 :** to go through, to suffer **7 :** to show (a movie, etc.) **8 :** to overtake, to pass, to surpass **9 :** to pass over, to wipe up **10 pasarlo bien** *or* **pasarla bien :** to have a good time **11 pasarlo mal** *or* **pasarla mal :** to have a bad time, to have a hard time **12 pasar por alto :** to overlook, to omit — **pasarse** *vr* **1 :** to move, to pass, to go away **2 :** to slip one's mind, to forget **3 :** to go too far

pasarela *nf* **1 :** gangplank **2 :** footbridge **3 :** runway, catwalk

pasatiempo *nm* **:** pastime, hobby

Pascua *nf* **1 :** Easter **2 :** Passover **3 :** Christmas **4 Pascuas** *nfpl* **:** Christmas season

pase *nm* **1** PERMISO **:** pass, permit **2 pase de abordar** *Mex* **:** boarding pass

pasear *vi* **:** to take a walk, to go for a ride — *vt* **1 :** to take for a walk **2 :** to parade around, to show off — **pasearse** *vr* **:** to walk around

paseo *nm* **1 :** walk, stroll **2 :** ride **3** EXCURSIÓN **:** outing, trip

pasiflora *nf* **:** passionflower

pasillo *nm* CORREDOR **:** hallway, corridor, aisle

pasión *nf, pl* **pasiones :** passion

pasional *adj* **:** passionate <crimen pasional : crime of passion>

pasionaria *nf* → **pasiflora**

pasivo[1], -va *adj* **:** passive — **pasivamente** *adv*

pasivo[2] *nm* **1 :** liability <activos y pasivos : assets and liabilities> **2 :** debit side (of an account)

pasmado, -da *adj* **:** stunned, flabbergasted

pasmar *vt* **:** to amaze, to stun — **pasmarse** *vr*

pasmo *nm* **1 :** shock, astonishment **2 :** wonder, marvel

pasmoso, -sa *adj* **:** incredible, amazing — **pasmosamente** *adv*

paso[1], -sa *adj* **:** dried <ciruela pasa : prune>

paso[2] *nm* **1 :** passage, passing <de paso : in passing, on the way> **2 :** way, path <abrirse paso : to make one's way> **3 :** crossing <paso de peatones : crosswalk> <paso a desnivel : underpass> <paso elevado : overpass> **4 :** step <paso a paso : step by step> **5 :** pace, gait <a buen paso : quickly, at a good rate>

pasta *nf* **1 :** paste <pasta de dientes *or* pasta dental : toothpaste> **2 :** pasta **3 :** pastry dough **4 libro en pasta dura :** hardcover book **5 tener pasta de :** to have the makings of

pastar *vi* **:** to graze — *vt* **:** to put to pasture

pastel[1] *adj* **:** pastel

pastel[2] *nm* **1 :** cake <pastel de cumpleaños : birthday cake> **2 :** pie, turnover **3 :** pastel

pastelería *nf* **:** pastry shop

pasteurización *nf, pl* **-ciones :** pasteurization

pasteurizar {21} *vt* **:** to pasteurize

pastilla *nf* **1** COMPRIMIDO, PÍLDORA **:** pill, tablet **2 :** lozenge <pastilla para la tos

: cough drop> **3** : cake (of soap), bar (of chocolate)

pastizal *nm* : pasture, grazing land

pasto *nm* **1** : pasture **2** HIERBA : grass, lawn

pastor, -tora *n* **1** : shepherd, shepherdess *f* **2** : minister, pastor

pastoral *adj & nf* : pastoral

pastorear *vt* : to shepherd, to tend

pastorela *nf* **1** : pastoral, pastourelle **2** *Mex* : a traditional Christmas play

pastoso, -sa *adj* **1** : pasty, doughy **2** : smooth, mellow (of sounds)

pata *nf* **1** : paw, leg (of an animal) **2** : foot, leg (of furniture) **3 patas de gallo** : crow's-feet **4 meter la pata** *fam* : to put one's foot in it, to make a blunder

patada *nf* **1** PUNTAPIÉ : kick **2** : stamp (of the foot)

patalear *vi* **1** : to kick **2** : to stamp one's feet

pataleta *nf fam* : tantrum

patán[1] *adj, pl* **patanes** : boorish, crude

patán[2] *nm, pl* **patanes** : boor, lout

patata *nf Spain* : potato

patear *vt* : to kick — *vi* : to stamp one's foot

patentar *vt* : to patent

patente[1] *adj* EVIDENTE : obvious, patent — **patentemente** *adv*

patente[2] *nf* : patent

paternal *adj* : fatherly, paternal

paternidad *nf* **1** : fatherhood, paternity **2** : parenthood **3** : authorship

paterno, -na *adj* : paternal <abuela paterna : paternal grandmother>

patético, -ca *adj* : pathetic, moving

patetismo *nm* : pathos

patíbulo *nm* : gallows, scaffold

patillas *nfpl* : sideburns

patín *nm, pl* **patines** : skate <patín de ruedas : roller skate>

patinador, -dora *n* : skater

patinaje *nm* : skating

patinar *vi* **1** : to skate **2** : to skid, to slip **3** *fam* : to slip up, to blunder

patinazo *nm* **1** : skid **2** *fam* : blunder, slipup

patineta *nf* **1** : scooter **2** : skateboard

patinete *nm* : scooter

patio *nm* **1** : courtyard, patio **2 patio de recreo** : playground

patito, -ta *n* : duckling

pato, -ta *n* **1** : duck **2 pato real** : mallard **3 pagar el pato** *fam* : to take the blame

patología *nf* : pathology

patológico, -ca *adj* : pathological

patólogo, -ga *n* : pathologist

patraña *nf* : tall tale, humbug, nonsense

patria *nf* : native land

patriarca *nm* : patriarch — **patriarcal** *adj*

patriarcado *nm* : patriarchy

patrimonio *nm* : patrimony, legacy

patrio, -tria *adj* **1** : native, home <suelo patrio : native soil> **2** : paternal

patriota[1] *adj* : patriotic

patriota[2] *nmf* : patriot

patriotería *nf* : jingoism, chauvinism

patriotero[1]**, -ra** *adj* : jingoistic, chauvinistic

patriotero[2]**, -ra** *n* : jingoist, chauvinist

patriótico, -ca *adj* : patriotic

patriotismo *nm* : patriotism

patrocinador, -dora *n* : sponsor, patron

patrocinar *vt* : to sponsor

patrocinio *nm* : sponsorship, patronage

patrón[1]**, -trona** *n, mpl* **patrones 1** JEFE : boss **2** : patron saint

patrón[2] *nm, pl* **patrones 1** : standard **2** : pattern (in sewing)

patronal *adj* **1** : management, employers' <sindicato patronal : employers' association> **2** : pertaining to a patron saint <fiesta patronal : patron saint's day>

patronato *nm* **1** : board, council **2** : foundation, trust

patrono, -na *n* **1** : employer **2** : patron saint

patrulla *nf* **1** : patrol **2** : police car, cruiser

patrullar *v* : to patrol

patrullero *nm* **1** : police car **2** : patrol boat

paulatino, -na *adj* : gradual

paupérrimo, -ma *adj* : destitute, poverty-stricken

pausa *nf* : pause, break

pausado[1] *adv* : slowly, deliberately <habla más pausado : speak more slowly>

pausado[2]**, -da** *adj* : slow, deliberate — **pausadamente** *adv*

pauta *nf* **1** : rule, guideline **2** : lines *pl* (on paper)

pava *nf Arg, Bol, Chile* : kettle

pavimentar *vt* : pave

pavimento *nm* : pavement

pavo, -va *n* **1** : turkey **2 pavo real** : peacock **3 comer pavo** : to be a wallflower

pavón *nm, pl* **pavones** : peacock

pavonearse *vr* : to strut, to swagger

pavoneo *nm* : strut, swagger

pavor *nm* TERROR : dread, terror

pavoroso, -sa *adj* ATERRADOR : dreadful, terrifying

payasada *nf* BUFONADA : antic, buffoonery

payasear *vi* : to clown around

payaso, -sa *n* : clown

paz *nf, pl* **paces 1** : peace **2 dejar en paz** : to leave alone **3 hacer las paces** : to make up, to reconcile

pazca, etc. → **pacer**

PC *nmf* : PC, personal computer

peaje *nm* : toll

peatón *nm, pl* **-tones** : pedestrian

peca *nf* : freckle

pecado *nm* : sin
pecador[1], **-dora** *adj* : sinful, sinning
pecador[2], **-dora** *n* : sinner
pecaminoso, -sa *adj* : sinful
pecar {72} *vi* **1** : to sin **2 ~ de** : to be too much (something) <no pecan de amabilidad : they're not overly friendly>
pécari *or* **pecarí** *nm* : peccary
pececillo *nm* : small fish
pecera *nf* : fishbowl, fish tank
pecho *nm* **1** : chest **2** SENO : breast, bosom **3** : heart, courage **4 dar el pecho** : to breast-feed **5 tomar a pecho** : to take to heart
pechuga *nf* : breast (of fowl)
pecoso, -sa *adj* : freckled
pectoral *adj* : pectoral
peculado *nm* : embezzlement
peculiar *adj* **1** CARACTERÍSTICO : particular, characteristic **2** RARO : peculiar, uncommon
peculiaridad *nf* : peculiarity
pecuniario, -ria *adj* : pecuniary
pedagogía *nf* : pedagogy
pedagógico, -ca *adj* : pedagogic, pedagogical
pedagogo, -ga *n* : educator, pedagogue
pedal *nm* : pedal
pedalear *vi* : to pedal
pedante[1] *adj* : pedantic
pedante[2] *nmf* : pedant
pedantería *nf* : pedantry
pedazo *nm* TROZO : piece, bit, chunk <caerse a pedazos : to fall to pieces> <hacer pedazos : to tear into shreds, to smash to pieces>
pedernal *nm* : flint
pedestal *nm* : pedestal
pedestre *adj* : commonplace, pedestrian
pediatra *nmf* : pediatrician
pediatría *nf* : pediatrics
pediátrico, -ca *adj* : pediatric
pedido *nm* **1** : order (of merchandise) **2** : request
pedigrí *nm* : pedigree
pedir {54} *vt* **1** : to ask for, to request <le pedí un préstamo a Claudia : I asked Claudia for a loan> **2** : to order (food, merchandise) **3 pedir disculpas** *or* **pedir perdón** : to apologize — *vi* **1** : to order **2** : to beg
pedrada *nf* **1** : blow (with a rock or stone) <la ventana se quebró de una pedrada : the window was broken by a rock> **2** *fam* : cutting remark, dig
pedregal *nm* : rocky ground
pedregoso, -sa *adj* : rocky, stony
pedrera *nf* CANTERA : quarry
pedrería *nf* : precious stones *pl*, gems *pl*
pegado, -da *adj* **1** : glued, stuck, stuck together **2 ~ a** : right next to
pegajoso, -sa *adj* **1** : sticky, gluey **2** : catchy <una tonada pegajosa : a catchy tune>
pegamento *nm* : adhesive, glue
pegar {52} *vt* **1** : to glue, to stick, to paste **2** : to attach, to sew on **3** : to infect with, to give <me pegó el resfriado : he gave me his cold> **4** GOLPEAR : to hit, to deal, to strike <me pegaron un puntapié : they gave me a kick> **5** : to give (out with) <pegó un grito : she let out a yell> — *vi* **1** : to adhere, to stick **2 ~ en** : to hit, to strike (against) **3 ~ con** : to match, to go with — **pegarse** *vr* **1** GOLPEARSE : to hit oneself, to hit each other **2** : to stick, to take hold **3** : to be contagious **4** *fam* : to tag along, to stick around
pegote *nm* **1** : sticky mess **2** *Mex* : sticker, adhesive label
pegue, etc. → **pegar**
peinado *nm* : hairstyle, hairdo
peinador, -dora *n* : hairdresser
peinar *vt* : to comb — **peinarse** *vr*
peine *nm* : comb
peineta *nf* : ornamental comb
peladez *nf, pl* **-deces** *Mex fam* : obscenity, bad language
pelado, -da *adj* **1** : bald, hairless **2** : peeled **3** : bare, barren **4** : broke, penniless **5** *Mex fam* : coarse, crude
pelador *nm* : peeler
pelagra *nf* : pellagra
pelaje *nm* : coat (of an animal), fur
pelar *vt* **1** : to peel, to shell **2** : to skin **3** : to pluck **4** : to remove hair from **5** *fam* : to clean out (of money) — **pelarse** *vr* **1** : to peel **2** *fam* : to get a haircut **3** *Mex fam* : to split, to leave
peldaño *nm* **1** : step, stair **2** : rung
pelea *nf* **1** LUCHA : fight **2** : quarrel
pelear *vi* **1** LUCHAR : to fight **2** DISPUTAR : to quarrel — **pelearse** *vr*
peleón, -ona *adj, mpl* **-ones** *Spain* : quarrelsome, argumentative
peleonero, -ra *adj Mex* : quarrelsome
peletería *nf* **1** : fur shop **2** : fur trade
peletero, -ra *n* : furrier
peliagudo, -da *adj* : tricky, difficult, ticklish
pelícano *nm* : pelican
película *nf* **1** : movie, film **2** : (photographic) film **3** : thin covering, layer
peligrar *vi* : to be in danger
peligro *nm* **1** : danger, peril **2** : risk <correr peligro de : to run the risk of>
peligroso, -sa *adj* : dangerous, hazardous
pelirrojo[1], **-ja** *adj* : red-haired, redheaded
pelirrojo[2], **-ja** *n* : redhead
pellejo *nm* **1** : hide, skin **2 salvar el pellejo** : to save one's neck
pellizcar {72} *vt* **1** : to pinch **2** : to nibble on
pellizco *nm* : pinch
pelo *nm* **1** : hair **2** : fur **3** : pile, nap **4 a pelo** : bareback **5 con pelos y señales** : in great detail **6 no tener pelos en la lengua** : to not mince words, to be blunt **7 tomarle el pelo a alguien** : to tease someone, to pull someone's leg

pelón, -lona *adj, mpl* **pelones 1 :** bald **2** *fam* **:** broke **3** *Mex fam* **:** tough, difficult

pelota *nf* **1 :** ball **2** *fam* **:** head **3 en pelotas** *fam* **:** naked **4 pelota vasca :** jai alai **5 pasar la pelota** *fam* **:** to pass the buck

pelotón *nm, pl* **-tones :** squad, detachment

peltre *nm* **:** pewter

peluca *nf* **:** wig

peluche *nm* **:** plush (fabric)

peludo, -da *adj* **:** hairy, shaggy, bushy

peluquería *nf* **1 :** hairdresser's, barber shop **2 :** hairdressing

peluquero, -ra *n* **:** barber, hairdresser

peluquín *nm, pl* **-quines** TUPÉ **:** hairpiece, toupee

pelusa *nf* **:** lint, fuzz

pélvico, -ca *adj* **:** pelvic

pelvis *nfs & pl* **:** pelvis

pena *nf* **1** CASTIGO **:** punishment, penalty <pena de muerte : death penalty> **2** AFLICCIÓN **:** sorrow, grief <morir de pena : to die of a broken heart> <¡que pena! : what a shame!, how sad!> **3** DOLOR **:** pain, suffering **4** DIFICULTAD **:** difficulty, trouble <a duras penas : with great difficulty> **5** VERGÜENZA **:** shame, embarrassment **6 valer la pena :** to be worthwhile

penacho *nm* **1 :** crest, tuft **2 :** plume (of feathers)

penal[1] *adj* **:** penal

penal[2] *nm* CÁRCEL **:** prison, penitentiary

penalidad *nf* **1 :** hardship **2 :** penalty, punishment

penalizar {21} *vt* **:** to penalize

penalty *nm* **:** penalty (in sports)

penar *vt* **:** to punish, to penalize — *vi* **:** to suffer, to grieve

pendenciero, -ra *adj* **:** argumentative, quarrelsome

pender *vi* **1 :** to hang **2 :** to be pending

pendiente[1] *adj* **1 :** pending **2 estar pendiente de :** to be watchful of, to be on the lookout for

pendiente[2] *nm Spain* **:** earring

pendiente[3] *nf* **:** slope, incline

pendón *nm, pl* **pendones :** banner

péndulo *nm* **:** pendulum

pene *nm* **:** penis

penetración *nf, pl* **-ciones 1 :** penetration **2 :** insight

penetrante *adj* **1 :** penetrating, piercing **2 :** sharp, acute **3 :** deep (of a wound)

penetrar *vi* **1 :** to penetrate, to sink in **2 ~ por** *or* **~ en :** to pierce, to go in, to enter into <el frío penetra por la ventana : the cold comes right in through the window> — *vt* **1 :** to penetrate, to permeate **2 :** to pierce <el dolor penetró su corazón : sorrow pierced her heart> **3 :** to fathom, to understand

penicilina *nf* **:** penicillin

península *nf* **:** peninsula — **peninsular** *adj*

penitencia *nf* **:** penance, penitence

penitenciaría *nf* **:** penitentiary

penitente *adj & nmf* **:** penitent

penol *nm* **:** yardarm

penoso, -sa *adj* **1 :** painful, distressing **2 :** difficult, arduous **3 :** shy, bashful

pensado, -da *adj* **1 bien pensado :** well thought-out **2 en el momento menos pensado :** when least expected **3 poco pensado :** badly thought-out **4 mal pensado :** evil-minded

pensador, -dora *n* **:** thinker

pensamiento *nm* **1 :** thought **2 :** thinking **3 :** pansy

pensar {55} *vi* **1 :** to think **2 ~ en :** to think about — *vt* **1 :** to think **2 :** to think about **3 :** to intend, to plan on — **pensarse** *vr* **:** to think over

pensativo, -va *adj* **:** pensive, thoughtful

pensión *nf, pl* **pensiones 1** JUBILACIÓN **:** pension **2 :** boarding house **3 pensión alimenticia :** alimony

pensionado, -da *n* → **pensionista**

pensionista *nmf* **1** JUBILADO **:** pensioner, retiree **2 :** boarder, lodger

pentágono *nm* **:** pentagon — **pentagonal** *adj*

pentagrama *nm* **:** staff (in music)

penúltimo, -ma *adj* **:** next to last, penultimate

penumbra *nf* **:** semidarkness

penuria *nf* **1** ESCASEZ **:** shortage, scarcity **2 :** poverty

peña *nf* **:** rock, crag

peñasco *nm* **:** crag, large rock

peñón *nm* → **peñasco**

peón *nm, pl* **peones 1 :** laborer, peon **2 :** pawn (in chess)

peonía *nf* **:** peony

peor[1] *adv* **1** (*comparative of* **mal**) **:** worse <se llevan peor que antes : they get along worse than before> **2** (*superlative of* **mal**) **:** worst <me fue peor que a nadie : I did the worst of all>

peor[2] *adj* **1** (*comparative of* **malo**) **:** worse <es peor que el original : it's worse than the original> **2** (*superlative of* **malo**) **:** worst <el peor de todos : the worst of all>

pepa *nf* **:** seed, pit (of a fruit)

pepenador, -dora *n CA, Mex* **:** scavenger

pepenar *vt CA, Mex* **:** to scavenge, to scrounge

pepinillo *nm* **:** pickle, gherkin

pepino *nm* **:** cucumber

pepita *nf* **1 :** seed, pip **2 :** nugget **3** *Mex* **:** dried pumpkin seed

peque, etc. → **pecar**

pequeñez *nf, pl* **-ñeces 1 :** smallness **2 :** trifle, triviality **3 pequeñez de espíritu :** pettiness

pequeño[1], **-ña** *adj* **1 :** small, little <un libro pequeño : a small book> **2 :** young **3** BAJO **:** short

pequeño[2], **-ña** *n* **:** child, little one

pera *nf* : pear

peraltar *vt* : to bank (a road)

perca *nf* : perch (fish)

percal *nm* : percale

percance *nm* : mishap, misfortune

percatarse *vr* **~ de** : to notice, to become aware of

percebe *nm* : barnacle

percepción *nf, pl* **-ciones 1** : perception **2** : idea, notion **3** COBRO : receipt (of payment), collection

perceptible *adj* : perceptible, noticeable — **perceptiblemente** *adv*

percha *nf* **1** : perch **2** : coat hanger **3** : coatrack, coat hook

perchero *nm* : coatrack

percibir *vt* **1** : to perceive, to notice, to sense **2** : to earn, to draw (a salary)

percudido, -da *adj* : grimy

percudir *vt* : to make grimy — **percudirse** *vr*

percusión *nf, pl* **-siones** : percussion

percusor *or* **percutor** *nm* : hammer (of a firearm)

perdedor[1], -dora *adj* : losing

perdedor[2], -dora *n* : loser

perder {56} *vt* **1** : to lose **2** : to miss <perdimos la oportunidad : we missed the opportunity> **3** : to waste (time) — *vi* : to lose — **perderse** *vr* EXTRAVIARSE : to get lost, to stray

perdición *nf, pl* **-ciones** : perdition, damnation

pérdida *nf* **1** : loss **2 pérdida de tiempo** : waste of time

perdidamente *adv* : hopelessly

perdido, -da *adj* **1** : lost **2** : inveterate, incorrigible <es un caso perdido : he's a hopeless case> **3** : in trouble, done for **4 de ~** *Mex fam* : at least

perdigón *nm, pl* **-gones** : shot, pellet

perdiz *nf, pl* **perdices** : partridge

perdón[1] *nm, pl* **perdones** : forgiveness, pardon

perdón[2] *interj* : excuse me!, sorry!

perdonable *adj* : forgivable

perdonar *vt* **1** DISCULPAR : to forgive, to pardon **2** : to exempt, to excuse

perdurable *adj* : lasting

perdurar *vi* : to last, to endure, to survive

perecedero, -ra *adj* : perishable

perecer {53} *vi* : to perish, to die

peregrinación *nf, pl* **-ciones** : pilgrimage

peregrinaje *nm* → **peregrinación**

peregrino[1], -na *adj* **1** : unusual, odd **2** MIGRATORIO : migratory

peregrino[2], -na *n* : pilgrim

perejil *nm* : parsley

perenne *adj* : perennial

pereza *nf* FLOJERA, HOLGAZANERÍA : laziness, idleness

perezoso[1], -sa *adj* FLOJO, HOLGAZÁN : lazy

perezoso[2] *nm* : sloth (animal)

perfección *nf, pl* **-ciones** : perfection

perfeccionamiento *nm* : perfecting, refinement

perfeccionar *vt* : to perfect, to refine

perfeccionismo *nm* : perfectionism

perfeccionista *nmf* : perfectionist

perfecto, -ta *adj* : perfect — **perfectamente** *adv*

perfidia *nf* : perfidy, treachery

pérfido, -da *adj* : perfidious

perfil *nm* **1** : profile **2 de ~** : sideways, from the side **3 perfiles** *nmpl* RASGOS : features, characteristics

perfilar *vt* : to outline, to define — **perfilarse** *vr* **1** : to be outlined, to be silhouetted **2** : to take shape

perforación *nf, pl* **-ciones 1** : perforation **2** : drilling

perforar *vt* **1** : to perforate, to pierce **2** : to drill, to bore

perfumar *vt* : to perfume, to scent — **perfumarse** *vr*

perfume *nm* : perfume, scent

pergamino *nm* : parchment

pérgola *nf* : pergola, arbor

pericia *nf* : skill, expertise

pericial *adj* : expert <testigo pericial : expert witness>

perico *nm* COTORRA : small parrot

periferia *nf* : periphery

periférico[1], -ca *adj* : peripheral

periférico[2] *nm* **1** *CA, Mex* : beltway **2** : peripheral

perilla *nf* **1** : goatee **2** : pommel (on a saddle) **3** *Col, Mex* : knob, handle **4 perilla de la oreja** : earlobe **5 de perillas** *fam* : handy, just right

perímetro *nm* : perimeter

periódico[1], -ca *adj* : periodic — **periódicamente** *adv*

periódico[2] *nm* DIARIO : newspaper

periodismo *nm* : journalism

periodista *nmf* : journalist

periodístico, -ca *adj* : journalistic, news

período *or* **periodo** *nm* : period

peripecia *nf* VICISITUD : vicissitude, reversal <las peripecias de su carrera : the ups and downs of her career>

periquito *nm* **1** : parakeet **2 periquito australiano** : budgerigar

periscopio *nm* : periscope

perito, -ta *adj & n* : expert

perjudicar {72} *vt* : to harm, to be detrimental to

perjudicial *adj* : harmful, detrimental

perjuicio *nm* **1** : harm, damage **2 en perjuicio de** : to the detriment of

perjurar *vi* : to perjure oneself

perjurio *nm* : perjury

perjuro, -ra *n* : perjurer

perla *nf* **1** : pearl **2 de perlas** *fam* : wonderfully <me viene de perlas : it suits me just fine>

permanecer {53} *vi* **1** QUEDARSE : to remain, to stay **2** SEGUIR : to remain, to continue to be

permanencia *nf* **1** : permanence, continuance **2** ESTANCIA : stay

permanente[1] *adj* **1** : permanent **2** : constant — **permanentemente** *adv*

permanente[2] *nf* : permanent (wave)

permeabilidad *nf* : permeability

permeable *adj* : permeable

permisible *adj* : permissible, allowable

permisividad *nf* : permissiveness

permisivo, -va *adv* : permissive

permiso *nm* **1 :** permission **2 :** permit, license **3 :** leave, furlough **4 con ~** : excuse me, pardon me

permitir *vt* : to permit, to allow — **permitirse** *vr*

permuta *nf* : exchange

permutar *vt* INTERCAMBIAR : to exchange

pernicioso, -sa *adj* : pernicious, destructive

pernil *nm* **1 :** haunch (of an animal) **2 :** leg (of meat), ham **3 :** trouser leg

perno *nm* : bolt, pin

pernoctar *vi* : to stay overnight, to spend the night

pero[1] *nm* **1 :** fault, defect <ponerle peros a : to find fault with> **2 :** objection

pero[2] *conj* : but

perogrullada *nf* : truism, platitude, cliché

peroné *nm* : fibula

perorar *vi* : to deliver a speech

perorata *nf* : oration, long-winded speech

peróxido *nm* : peroxide

perpendicular *adj & nf* : perpendicular

perpetrar *vt* : to perpetrate

perpetuar {3} *vt* ETERNIZAR : to perpetuate

perpetuidad *nf* : perpetuity

perpetuo, -tua *adj* : perpetual — **perpetuamente** *adv*

perplejidad *nf* : perplexity

perplejo, -ja *adj* : perplexed, puzzled

perrada *nf fam* : dirty trick

perrera *nf* : kennel, dog pound

perrero, -ra *n* : dogcatcher

perrito, -ta *n* CACHORRO : puppy, small dog

perro, -rra *n* **1 :** dog, bitch *f* **2 perro caliente :** hot dog **3 perro salchicha :** dachshund **4 perro faldero :** lapdog **5 perro cobrador :** retriever

persa *adj & nmf* : Persian

persecución *nf, pl* **-ciones 1 :** pursuit, chase **2 :** persecution

perseguidor, -dora *n* **1 :** pursuer **2 :** persecutor

perseguir {75} *vt* **1 :** to pursue, to chase **2 :** to persecute **3 :** to pester, to annoy

perseverancia *nf* : perseverance

perseverar *vi* : to persevere

persiana *nf* : blind, venetian blind

persignarse *vr* SANTIGUARSE : to cross oneself, to make the sign of the cross

persistir *vi* : to persist — **persistencia** *nf* — **persistente** *adj*

persona *nf* : person

personaje *nm* **1 :** character (in drama or literature) **2 :** personage, celebrity

personal[1] *adj* : personal — **personalmente** *adv*

personal[2] *nm* : personnel, staff

personalidad *nf* : personality

personalizar {21} *vt* : to personalize

personificar {72} *vi* : to personify — **personificación** *nf*

perspectiva *nf* **1 :** perspective, view **2 :** prospect, outlook

perspicacia *nf* : shrewdness, perspicacity, insight

perspicaz *adj, pl* **-caces :** shrewd, perspicacious

persuadir *vt* : to persuade — **persuadirse** *vr* : to become convinced

persuasión *nf, pl* **-siones :** persuasion

persuasivo, -va *adj* : persuasive

pertenecer {53} *vi* : to belong

perteneciente *adj* **~ a :** belonging to

pertenencia *nf* **1 :** membership **2 :** ownership **3 pertenencias** *nfpl* : belongings, possessions

pértiga *nf* GARROCHA : pole <salto de pértiga : pole vault>

pertinaz *adj, pl* **-naces 1** OBSTINADO : obstinate **2** PERSISTENTE : persistent

pertinencia *nf* : pertinence, relevance — **pertinente** *adj*

pertrechos *nmpl* : equipment, gear

perturbación *nf, pl* **-ciones :** disturbance, disruption

perturbador, -dora *adj* **1** INQUIETANTE : disturbing, troubling **2 :** disruptive

perturbar *vt* **1 :** to disturb, to trouble **2 :** to disrupt

peruano, -na *adj & n* : Peruvian

perversidad *nf* : perversity, depravity

perversión *nf, pl* **-siones :** perversion

perverso, -sa *adj* : wicked, depraved

pervertido[1]**, -da** *adj* DEPRAVADO : perverted, depraved

pervertido[2]**, -da** *n* : pervert

pervertir {76} *vt* : to pervert, to corrupt

pesa *nf* **1 :** weight **2 levantamiento de pesas :** weightlifting

pesadamente *adv* **1 :** heavily **2 :** slowly, clumsily

pesadez *nf, pl* **-deces 1 :** heaviness **2 :** slowness **3 :** tediousness

pesadilla *nf* : nightmare

pesado[1]**, -da** *adj* **1 :** heavy **2 :** slow **3 :** irritating, annoying **4 :** tedious, boring **5 :** tough, difficult

pesado[2]**, -da** *n fam* : bore, pest

pesadumbre *nf* AFLICCIÓN : grief, sorrow, sadness

pésame *nm* : condolences *pl* <mi más sentido pésame : my heartfelt condolences>

pesar[1] *vt* **1 :** to weigh **2** EXAMINAR : to consider, to think over — *vi* **1 :** to weigh <¿cuánto pesa? : how much does it weigh?> **2 :** to be heavy **3 :** to weigh heavily, to be a burden <no le pesa : it's not a burden on him> <pesa sobre mi corazón : it weighs upon my heart> **4** INFLUIR : to carry weight, to have bearing **5** (*with personal pro-*

nouns) : to grieve, to sadden <me pesa mucho : I'm very sorry> **6 pese a** : in spite of, despite

pesar[2] *nm* **1** AFLICCIÓN, PENA : sorrow, grief **2** REMORDIMIENTO : remorse **3 a pesar de** : in spite of, despite

pesaroso, -sa *adj* **1** : sad, mournful **2** ARREPENTIDO : sorry, regretful

pesca *nf* : fishing

pescadería *nf* : fish market

pescado *nm* : fish (as food)

pescador, -dora *n* : fisherman *m*, fisherwoman *f*

pescar {72} *vt* **1** : to fish for **2** : to catch **3** *fam* : to get a hold of, to land — *vi* : to fish, to go fishing

pescuezo *nm* : neck

pesebre *nm* : manger

pesera *nf Mex* : minibus

peseta *nf* : peseta (Spanish unit of currency)

pesimismo *nm* : pessimism

pesimista[1] *adj* : pessimistic

pesimista[2] *nmf* : pessimist

pésimo, -ma *adj* : dreadful, abominable

peso *nm* **1** : weight, heaviness **2** : burden, responsibility **3** : weight (in sports) **4** BÁSCULA : scales *pl* **5** : peso

pesque, etc. → **pescar**

pesquería *nf* : fishery

pesquero[1], **-ra** *adj* : fishing <pueblo pesquero : fishing village>

pesquero[2] *nm* : fishing boat

pesquisa *nf* INVESTIGACIÓN : inquiry, investigation

pestaña *nf* **1** : eyelash **2** : flange, rim

pestañear *vi* : to blink

pestañeo *nm* : blink

peste *nf* **1** : plague, pestilence **2** : stench, stink **3** : nuisance, pest

pesticida *nm* : pesticide

pestilencia *nf* **1** : stench, foul odor **2** : pestilence

pestilente *adj* **1** : foul, smelly **2** : pestilent

pestillo *nm* CERROJO : bolt, latch

petaca *nf* **1** *Mex* : suitcase **2 petacas** *nfpl Mex fam* : bottom, behind

pétalo *nm* : petal

petardear *vi* : to backfire

petardeo *nm* : backfiring

petardo *nm* : firecracker

petate *nm Mex* : mat

petición *nf, pl* **-ciones** : petition, request

peticionar *vt* : to petition

peticionario, -ria *n* : petitioner

petirrojo *nm* : robin

peto *nm* : bib (of clothing)

pétreo, -trea *adj* : stone, stony

petrificar {72} *vt* : to petrify

petróleo *nm* : oil, petroleum

petrolero[1], **-ra** *adj* : oil <industria petrolera : oil industry>

petrolero[2] *nm* : oil tanker

petulancia *nf* INSOLENCIA : insolence, petulance

petulante *adj* INSOLENTE : insolent, petulant — **petulantemente** *adv*

petunia *nf* : petunia

peyorativo, -va *adj* : pejorative

pez[1] *nm, pl* **peces 1** : fish **2 pez de colores** : goldfish **3 pez espada** : swordfish **4 pez gordo** : big shot

pez[2] *nf, pl* **peces** : pitch, tar

pezón *nm, pl* **pezones** : nipple

pezuña *nf* : hoof <pezuña hendida : cloven hoof>

pi *nf* : pi

piadoso, -sa *adj* **1** : compassionate, merciful **2** DEVOTO : pious, devout

pianista *nmf* : pianist, piano player

piano *nm* : piano

piar {85} *vi* : to chirp, to cheep, to tweet

pibe, -ba *n Arg, Uru fam* : kid, child

pica *nf* **1** : pike, lance **2** : goad (in bullfighting) **3** : spade (in playing cards)

picada *nf* **1** : bite, sting (of an insect) **2** : sharp descent

picadillo *nm* **1** : minced meat, hash **2 hacer picadillo a** : to beat to a pulp

picado, -da *adj* **1** : perforated **2** : minced, chopped **3** : decayed (of teeth) **4** : choppy, rough **5** *fam* : annoyed, miffed

picador *nm* : picador

picadura *nf* **1** : sting, bite **2** : prick, puncture **3** : decay, cavity

picaflor *nm* COLIBRÍ : hummingbird

picana *nf* : goad, prod

picante[1] *adj* **1** : hot, spicy **2** : sharp, cutting **3** : racy, risqué

picante[2] *nm* **1** : spiciness **2** : hot spices *pl*, hot sauce

picaporte *nm* **1** : latch **2** : door handle **3** ALDABA : door knocker

picar {72} *vt* **1** : to sting, to bite **2** : to peck at **3** : to nibble on **4** : to prick, to puncture, to punch (a ticket) **5** : to grind, to chop **6** : to goad, to incite **7** : to pique, to provoke — *vi* **1** : to itch **2** : to sting **3** : to be spicy **4** : to nibble **5** : to take the bait **6 ~ en** : to dabble in **7 picar muy alto** : to aim too high — **picarse** *vr* **1** : to get a cavity, to decay **2** : to get annoyed, to take offense

picardía *nf* **1** : cunning, craftiness **2** : prank, dirty trick

picaresco, -ca *adj* **1** : picaresque **2** : rascally, roguish

pícaro[1], **-ra** *adj* **1** : mischievous **2** : cunning, sly **3** : off-color, risqué

pícaro[2], **-ra** *n* **1** : rogue, scoundrel **2** : rascal

picazón *nf, pl* **-zones** COMEZÓN : itch

picea *nf* : spruce (tree)

pichel *nm* : pitcher, jug

pichón, -chona *n, mpl* **pichones 1** : young pigeon, squab **2** *Mex fam* : novice, greenhorn

picnic *nm* : picnic

pico *nm* **1** : peak **2** : point, spike **3** : beak, bill **4** : pick, pickax **5 y pico**

: and a little, and a bit <las siete y pico : a little after seven> <dos metros y pico : a bit over two meters>

picor *nm* : itch, irritation

picoso, -sa *adj Mex* : very hot, spicy

picota *nf* **1** : pillory, stock **2 poner a alguien en la picota** : to put someone on the spot

picotada *nf* → **picotazo**

picotazo *nm* : peck (of a bird)

picotear *vt* : to peck — *vi* : to nibble, to pick

pictórico, -ca *adj* : pictorial

picudo, -da *adj* **1** : pointy, sharp **2 ~ para** *Mex fam* : clever at, good at

pide, etc. → **pedir**

pie *nm* **1** : foot <a pie : on foot> <de pie : on one's feet, standing> **2** : base, bottom, stem, foot <pie de la cama : foot of the bed> <pie de una lámpera : base of a lamp> <pie de la escalera : bottom of the stairs> <pie de una copa : stem of a glass> **3** : foot (in measurement) <pie cuadrado : square foot> **4** : cue (in theater) **5 dar pie a** : to give cause for, to give rise to **6 en pie de igualidad** : on equal footing

piedad *nf* **1** COMPASIÓN : mercy, pity **2** DEVOCIÓN : piety, devotion

piedra *nf* **1** : stone **2** : flint (of a lighter) **3** : hailstone **4 piedra de afilar** : whetstone, grindstone **5 piedra angular** : cornerstone **6 piedra arenisca** : sandstone **7 piedra caliza** : limestone **8 piedra imán** : lodestone **9 piedra de molino** : millstone **10 piedra de toque** : touchstone

piel *nf* **1** : skin **2** CUERO : leather, hide <piel de venado : deerskin> **3** : fur, pelt **4** CÁSCARA : peel, skin **5 piel de gallina** : goose bumps *pl* <me pone la piel de gallina : it gives me goose bumps>

piélago *nm* **el piélago** : the deep, the ocean

piensa, etc. → **pensar**

pienso *nm* : feed, fodder

pierde, etc. → **perder**

pierna *nf* : leg

pieza *nf* **1** ELEMENTO : piece, part, component <vestido de dos piezas : two-piece dress> <pieza de recambio : spare part> <pieza clave : key element> **2** : piece (in chess) **3** OBRA : piece, work <pieza de teatro : play> **4** : room, bedroom

pifia *nf fam* : goof, blunder

pigargo *nm* : osprey

pigmentación *nf, pl* **-ciones** : pigmentation

pigmento *nm* : pigment

pigmeo, -mea *adj & n* : pygmy, Pygmy

pijama *nm* : pajamas *pl*

pila *nf* **1** BATERÍA : battery <pila de linterna : flashlight battery> **2** MONTÓN : pile, heap **3** : sink, basin, font <pila bautismal : baptismal font> <pila para pájaros : birdbath>

pilar *nm* **1** : pillar, column **2** : support, mainstay

píldora *nf* PASTILLA : pill

pillaje *nm* : pillage, plunder

pillar *vt fam* **1** : to catch <¡cuidado! ¡nos pillarán! : watch out! they'll catch us!> **2** : to grasp, to catch on <¿no lo pillas? : don't you get it?>

pillo[1], -lla *adj* : cunning, crafty

pillo[2], -lla *n* **1** : rascal, brat **2** : rogue, scoundrel

pilluelo, -la *n* : urchin

pilotar *vt* : to pilot, to drive

pilote *nm* : pile (stake)

pilotear → **pilotar**

piloto *nm* **1** : pilot, driver **2** : pilot light

piltrafa *nf* **1** : poor quality meat **2** : wretch **3 piltrafas** *nfpl* : food scraps

pimentero *nm* : pepper shaker

pimentón *nm, pl* **-tones 1** : paprika **2** : cayenne pepper

pimienta *nf* **1** : pepper (condiment) **2 pimienta de Jamaica** : allspice

pimiento *nm* : pepper (fruit) <pimiento verde : green pepper>

pináculo *nm* **1** : pinnacle (of a building) **2** : peak, acme

pincel *nm* : paintbrush

pincelada *nf* **1** : brushstroke **2 últimas pinceladas** : final touches

pinchar *vt* **1** PICAR : to puncture (a tire) **2** : to prick, to stick **3** : to goad, to tease, to needle — *vi* **1** : to be prickly **2** : to get a flat tire **3** *fam* : to get beaten, to lose out — **pincharse** *vr* : to give oneself an injection

pinchazo *nm* **1** : prick, jab **2** : puncture, flat tire

pingüe *adj* **1** : rich, huge (of profits) **2** : lucrative

pingüino *nm* : penguin

pininos *or* **pinitos** *nmpl* : first steps <hacer pininos : to take one's first steps, to toddle>

pino *nm* : pine, pine tree

pinta *nf* **1** : dot, spot **2** : pint **3** *fam* : aspect, appearance <las peras tienen buena pinta : the pears look good> **4 pintas** *nfpl Mex* : graffiti

pintadas *nfpl* : graffiti

pintar *vt* **1** : to paint **2** : to draw, to mark **3** : to describe, to depict — *vi* **1** : to paint, to draw **2** : to look <no pinta bien : it doesn't look good> **3** *fam* : to count <aquí no pinta nada : he has no say here> — **pintarse** *vr* **1** MAQUILLARSE : to put on makeup **2 pintárselas solo** *fam* : to manage by oneself, to know it all

pintarrajear *vt* : to daub (with paint)

pinto, -ta *adj* : speckled, spotted

pintor, -tora *n* **1** : painter **2 pintor de brocha gorda** : housepainter, dauber

pintoresco, -ca *adj* : picturesque, quaint

pintura *nf* **1** : paint **2** : painting (art, work of art)

pinza *nf* **1 :** clothespin **2 :** claw, pincer **3 :** pleat, dart **4 pinzas** *nfpl* **:** tweezers **5 pinzas** *nfpl* ALICATES **:** pliers, pincers

pinzón *nm, pl* **pinzones :** finch

piña *nf* **1 :** pineapple **2 :** pine cone

piñata *nf* **:** piñata

piñón *nm, pl* **piñones 1 :** pine nut **2 :** pinion

pío[1], pía *adj* **1** DEVOTO **:** pious, devout **2 :** piebald, pied, dappled

pío[2] *nm* **:** peep, tweet, cheep

piocha *nf* **1 :** pickax **2** *Mex* **:** goatee

piojo *nm* **:** louse

piojoso, -sa *adj* **1 :** lousy **2 :** filthy

pionero[1], -ra *adj* **:** pioneering

pionero[2], -ra *n* **:** pioneer

pipa *nf* **:** pipe (for smoking)

pipián *nm, pl* **pipianes** *Mex* **:** a spicy sauce or stew

pipiolo, -la *n fam* **1 :** greenhorn, novice **2 :** kid, youngster

pique[1], etc. → **picar**

pique[2] *nm* **1 :** pique, resentment **2 :** rivalry, competition **3 a pique de :** about to, on the verge of **4 irse a pique :** to sink, to founder

piqueta *nf* **:** pickax

piquete *nm* **1 :** picketers *pl*, picket line **2 :** squad, detachment **3** *Mex* **:** prick, jab

piquetear *vt* **1 :** to picket **2** *Mex* **:** to prick, to jab

pira *nf* **:** pyre

piragua *nf* **:** canoe — **piragüista** *nmf*

pirámide *nf* **:** pyramid

piraña *nf* **:** piranha

pirata[1] *adj* **:** bootleg, pirated

pirata[2] *nmf* **1 :** pirate **2 :** bootlegger **3 pirata aéreo :** hijacker

piratear *vt* **1 :** to hijack, to commandeer **2 :** to bootleg, to pirate

piratería *nf* **:** piracy, bootlegging

piromanía *nf* **:** pyromania

pirómano, -na *n* **:** pyromaniac

piropo *nm* **:** flirtatious compliment

pirotecnia *nf* **:** fireworks *pl*, pyrotechnics *pl*

pirotécnico, -ca *adj* **:** fireworks, pyrotechnic

pírrico, -ca *adj* **:** Pyrrhic

pirueta *nf* **:** pirouette

pirulí *nm* **:** cone-shaped lollipop

pisada *nf* **1 :** footstep **2** HUELLA **:** footprint

pisapapeles *nms & pl* **:** paperweight

pisar *vt* **1 :** to step on, to set foot in **2 :** to walk all over, to mistreat — *vi* **:** to step, to walk, to tread

piscina *nf* **1 :** swimming pool **2 :** fish pond

Piscis *nmf* **:** Pisces

piso *nm* **1** PLANTA **:** floor, story **2** SUELO **:** floor **3** *Spain* **:** apartment

pisotear *vt* **1 :** to stamp on, to trample **2** PISAR **:** to walk all over **3 :** to flout, to disregard

pisotón *nm, pl* **-tones :** stamp, step <sufrieron empujones y pisotones : they were pushed and stepped on>

pista *nf* **1** RASTRO **:** trail, track <siguen la pista de los sospechosos : they're on the trail of the suspects> **2 :** clue **3** CAMINO **:** road, trail **4 :** track, racetrack **5 :** ring, arena, rink **6 pista de aterrizaje :** runway, airstrip **7 pista de baile :** dance floor

pistacho *nm* **:** pistachio

pistilo *nm* **:** pistil

pistola *nf* **1 :** pistol, handgun **2 :** spray gun

pistolera *nf* **:** holster

pistolero *nm* **:** gunman

pistón *nm, pl* **pistones :** piston

pita *nf* **1 :** agave **2 :** pita fiber **3 :** twine

pitar *vi* **1 :** to blow a whistle **2 :** to whistle, to boo **3 :** to beep, to honk, to toot — *vt* **:** to whistle at, to boo

pitido *nm* **1 :** whistle, whistling **2 :** beep, honk, toot

pito *nm* **1** SILBATO **:** whistle **2 no me importa un pito** *fam* **:** I don't give a damn

pitón *nm, pl* **pitones** *nm* **1 :** python **2 :** point of a bull's horn

pituitario, -ria *adj* **:** pituitary

pívot *nmf, pl* **pívots :** center (in basketball)

pivote *nm* **:** pivot

piyama *nmf* **:** pajamas *pl*

pizarra *nf* **1 :** slate **2 :** blackboard **3 :** scoreboard

pizarrón *nm, pl* **-rrones :** blackboard, chalkboard

pizca *nf* **1 :** pinch <una pizca de canela : a pinch of cinnamon> **2 :** speck, trace <ni pizca : not a bit> **3** *Mex* **:** harvest

pizcar {72} *vt Mex* **:** to harvest

pizque, etc. → **pizcar**

pizza ['pitsa, 'pisa] *nf* **:** pizza

pizzería *nf* **:** pizzeria, pizza parlor

placa *nf* **1 :** sheet, plate **2 :** plaque, nameplate **3 :** plate (in photography) **4 :** badge, insignia **5 placa de matrícula :** license plate, tag **6 placa dental :** plaque, tartar

placebo *nm* **:** placebo

placenta *nf* **:** placenta, afterbirth

placentero, -ra *adj* AGRADABLE, GRATO **:** pleasant, agreeable

placer[1] {57} *vi* GUSTAR **:** to be pleasing <hazlo como te plazca : do it however you please>

placer[2] *nm* **1 :** pleasure, enjoyment **2 a ~ :** as much as one wants

plácido, -da *adj* TRANQUILO **:** placid, calm

plaga *nf* **1 :** plague, infestation, blight **2** CALAMIDAD **:** disaster, scourge

plagado, -da *adj* **~ de :** filled with, covered with

plagar {52} *vt* **:** to plague

plagiar *vt* **1 :** to plagiarize **2** SECUESTRAR **:** to kidnap, to abduct

plagiario, -ria *n* **1 :** plagiarist **2** SECUESTRADOR **:** kidnapper, abductor

plagio *nm* **1 :** plagiarism **2** SECUESTRO **:** kidnapping, abduction

plague, etc. → **plagar**

plan *nm* **1 :** plan, strategy, program <plan de inversiones : investment plan> <plan de estudios : curriculum> **2** PLANO **:** plan, diagram **3 :** attitude, intent, purpose <ponte en plan serio : be serious> <estamos en plan de divertirnos : we're looking to have some fun>

plana *nf* **1 :** page <noticias en primera plana : front-page news> **2 plana mayor :** staff (in the military)

plancha *nf* **1 :** iron, ironing **2 :** grill, griddle <a la plancha : grilled> **3 :** sheet, plate <plancha para hornear : baking sheet> **4** *fam* **:** blunder, blooper

planchada *nf* **:** ironing, pressing

planchado *nm* → **planchada**

planchar *v* **:** to iron

planchazo *nm fam* **:** goof, blunder

plancton *nm* **:** plankton

planeación *nf* → **planeamiento**

planeador *nm* **:** glider (aircraft)

planeamiento *nm* **:** plan, planning

planear *vt* **:** to plan — *vi* **:** to glide (in the air)

planeo *nm* **:** gliding, soaring

planeta *nm* **:** planet

planetario[1], -ria *adj* **1 :** planetary **2 :** global, worldwide

planetario[2] *nm* **:** planetarium

planicie *nf* **:** plain

planificación *nf* **:** planning <planificación familiar : family planning>

planificar {72} *vt* **:** to plan

planilla *nf* **1** LISTA **:** list **2** NÓMINA **:** payroll **3** TABLA **:** chart, table **4** *Mex* **:** slate, ticket (of candidates) **5 planilla de cálculo** *Arg, Chile* **:** spreadsheet

plano[1], -na *adj* **:** flat, level, plane

plano[2] *nm* **1** PLAN **:** map, plan **2 :** plane (surface) **3** NIVEL **:** level <en un plano personal : on a personal level> **4 :** shot (in photography) **5 de ~ :** flatly, outright, directly <se negó de plano : he flatly refused>

planta *nf* **1 :** plant <planta de interior : houseplant> **2** FÁBRICA **:** plant, factory **3** PISO **:** floor, story **4 :** staff, employees *pl* **5 :** sole (of the foot)

plantación *nf, pl* **-ciones 1 :** plantation **2 :** planting

plantar *vt* **1 :** to plant, to sow **2 :** to put in, to place **3** *fam* **:** to plant, to land <plantar un beso : to plant a kiss> **4** *fam* **:** to leave, to jilt — **plantarse** *vr* **1 :** to stand firm **2** *fam* **:** to arrive, to show up **3** *fam* **:** to balk

planteamiento *nm* **1 :** approach, position <el planteamiento feminista : the feminist viewpoint> **2 :** explanation, exposition **3 :** proposal, suggestion, plan

plantear *vt* **1 :** to set forth, to bring up, to suggest **2 :** to establish, to set up **3 :** to create, to pose (a problem) — **plantearse** *vr* **1 :** to think about **2 :** to arise

plantel *nm* **1 :** educational institution **2 :** staff, team

planteo *nm* → **planteamiento**

plantilla *nf* **1 :** insole **2 :** pattern, template, stencil **3** *Mex, Spain* **:** staff, roster of employees

plantío *nm* **:** field (planted with a crop)

plantón *nm, pl* **plantones 1 :** seedling **2 :** long wait <darle a alguien un plantón : to stand someone up>

plañidero[1], -ra *adj* **:** mournful

plañidero[2], -ra *nf* **:** hired mourner

plañir {38} *v* **:** to mourn, to lament

plasma *nm* **:** plasma

plasmar *vt* **:** to express, to give form to — **plasmarse** *vr*

plasta *nf* **:** soft mass, lump

plástica *nf* **:** modeling, sculpture

plasticidad *nf* **:** plasticity

plástico[1], -ca *adj* **:** plastic

plástico[2] *nm* **:** plastic

plastificar {72} *vt* **:** to laminate

plata *nf* **1 :** silver **2 :** money

plataforma *nf* **1** ESTRADO, TARIMA **:** platform, dais **2 :** platform (in politics) **3 :** springboard, stepping stone **4 plataforma continental :** continental shelf **5 plataforma de lanzamiento :** launchpad **6 plataforma petrolífera :** oil rig (at sea)

platal *nm* **:** large sum of money, fortune

platanal *nm* **:** banana plantation

platanero[1], -ra *adj* **:** banana, banana-producing

platanero[2], -ra *n* **:** banana grower

plátano *nm* **1 :** banana **2 :** plantain **3 plátano macho** *Mex* **:** plantain

platea *nf* **:** orchestra, pit (in a theater)

plateado, -da *adj* **1 :** silver, silvery **2 :** silver-plated

plática *nf* **1 :** talk, lecture **2 :** chat, conversation

platicar {72} *vi* **:** to talk, to chat — *vt Mex* **:** to tell, to say

platija *nf* **:** flatfish, flounder

platillo *nm* **1 :** saucer <platillo volador : flying saucer> **2 :** cymbal **3** *Mex* **:** dish <platillos típicos : local dishes>

platino *nm* **:** platinum

plato *nm* **1 :** plate, dish <lavar los platos : to do the dishes> **2 :** serving, helping **3 :** course (of a meal) **4 :** dish <plato típico : typical dish> **5 :** home plate (in baseball) **6 plato hondo :** soup bowl

plató *nm* **:** set (in the movies)

platónico, -ca *adj* **:** platonic

playa *nf* **:** beach, seashore

playera *nf* **1 :** canvas sneaker **2** *CA, Mex* **:** T-shirt

plaza *nf* **1 :** square, plaza **2 :** marketplace **3 :** room, space, seat (in a vehicle) **4 :** post, position **5 plaza fuerte**

: stronghold, fortified city **6 plaza de toros** : bullring
plazca, etc. → **placer**
plazo *nm* **1** : period, term <un plazo de cinco días : a period of five days> <a largo plazo : long-term> **2** ABONO : installment <pagar a plazos : to pay in installments>
pleamar *nf* : high tide
plebe *nf* : common people, masses *pl*
plebeyo[1], -ya *adj* : plebeian
plebeyo[2], -ya *n* : plebeian, commoner
plegable *adj* : folding, collapsible
plegadizo → **plegable**
plegar {49} *vt* DOBLAR : to fold, to bend — **plegarse** *vr* : to give in, to yield
plegaria *nf* ORACIÓN : prayer
pleito *nm* **1** : lawsuit **2** : fight, argument, dispute
plenamente *adv* COMPLETAMENTE : fully, completely
plenario, -ria *adj* : plenary, full
plenilunio *nm* : full moon
plenipotenciario, -ria *n* : plenipotentiary
plenitud *nf* : fullness, abundance
pleno, -na *adj* COMPLETO (*often used as an intensifier*) : full, complete <en pleno uso de sus facultades : in full command of his faculties> <en plena noche : in the middle of the night> <en pleno corazón de la ciudad : right in the heart of the city>
plétora *nf* : plethora
pleuresía *nf* : pleurisy
pliega, pliegue, etc. → **plegar**
pliego *nm* **1** HOJA : sheet of paper **2** : sealed document
pliegue *nm* **1** DOBLEZ : crease, fold **2** : pleat
plisar *vt* : to pleat
plomada *nf* **1** : plumb line **2** : sinker
plomería *nf* FONTANERÍA : plumbing
plomero, -ra *n* FONTANERO : plumber
plomizo, -za *adj* : leaden
plomo *nm* **1** : lead **2** : plumb line **3** : fuse **4** *fam* : bore, drag **5 a ~** : plumb, straight
plugo, etc. → **placer**
pluma *nf* **1** : feather **2** : pen **3 pluma fuente** : fountain pen
plumaje *nm* : plumage
plumero *nm* : feather duster
plumilla *nf* : nib
plumón *nm, pl* **plumones** : down
plumoso, -sa *adj* : feathery, downy
plural *adj & nm* : plural
pluralidad *nf* : plurality
pluralizar {21} *vt* : to pluralize
pluriempleado, -da *adj* : holding more than one job
pluriempleo *nm* : moonlighting
plus *nm* : bonus
plusvalía *nf* : appreciation, capital gain
Plutón *nm* : Pluto
plutocracia *nf* : plutocracy
plutonio *nm* : plutonium
población *nf, pl* **-ciones 1** : population **2** : city, town, village
poblado[1], -da *adj* **1** : inhabited, populated **2** : full, thick <cejas pobladas : bushy eyebrows>
poblado[2] *nm* : village, settlement
poblador, -dora *n* : settler
poblar {19} *vt* **1** : to populate, to inhabit **2** : to settle, to colonize **3 ~ de** : to stock with, to plant with — **poblarse** *vr* : to fill up, to become crowded
pobre[1] *adj* **1** : poor, impoverished **2** : unfortunate <¡pobre de mí! : poor me!> **3** : weak, deficient <una dieta pobre : a poor diet>
pobre[2] *nmf* : poor person <los pobres : the poor> <¡pobre! : poor thing!>
pobremente *adv* : poorly
pobreza *nf* : poverty
pocilga *nf* CHIQUERO : pigsty, pigpen
pocillo *nm* : small coffee cup, demitasse
poción *nf, pl* **pociones** : potion
poco[1] *adv* **1** : little, not much <poco probable : not very likely> <come poco : he doesn't eat much> **2** : a short time, a while <tardaremos poco : we won't be very long> **3 poco antes** : shortly before **4 poco después** : shortly after
poco[2], -ca *adj* **1** : little, not much, (a) few <tengo poco dinero : I don't have much money> <en no pocas ocasiones : on more than a few occasions> <poca gente : few people> **2 pocas veces** : rarely
poco[3], -ca *pron* **1** : little, few <le falta poco para terminar : he's almost finished> <uno de los pocos que quedan : one of the remaining few> **2 un poco** : a little, a bit <un poco de vino : a little wine> <un poco extraño : a bit strange> **3 a ~** *Mex* (*used to express disbelief*) <¿a poco no se te hizo difícil? : you mean you didn't find it difficult?> **4 de a poco** : little by little **5 hace poco** : not long ago **6 poco a poco** : little by little **7 dentro de poco** : shortly, in a little while **8 por ~** : nearly, almost
podar *vt* : to prune, to trim
poder[1] {58} *v aux* **1** : to be able to, can <no puede hablar : he can't speak> **2** (*expressing possibility*) : might, may <puede llover : it may rain at any moment> <¿cómo puede ser? : how can that be?> **3** (*expressing permission*) : can, may <¿puedo ir a la fiesta? : can I go to the party?> <¿se puede? : may I come in?> — *vi* **1** : to beat, to defeat <cree que le puede a cualquiera : he thinks he can beat anyone> **2** : to be possible <¿crees que vendrán? — puede (que sí) : do you think they'll come? — maybe> **3 ~ con** : to cope with, to manage <¡no puedo con estos niños! : I can't handle these children!> **4 no poder más** : to have had enough <no puede más : she can't take anymore> **5 no poder menos**

que : to not be able to help <no pudo menos que asombrarse : she couldn't help but be amazed>
poder[2] *nm* **1** : control, power <poder adquisitivo : purchasing power> **2** : authority <el poder legislativo : the legislature> **3** : possession <está en mi poder : it's in my hands> **4** : strength, force <poder militar : military might>
poderío *nm* **1** : power **2** : wealth, influence
poderoso, -sa *adj* **1** : powerful **2** : wealthy, influential **3** : effective
podiatría *nf* : podiatry
podio *nm* : podium
pódium *nm* → **podio**
podología *nf* : podiatry, chiropody
podólogo, -ga *n* : podiatrist, chiropodist
podrá, etc. → **poder**
podredumbre *nf* **1** : decay, rottenness **2** : corruption
podrido, -da *adj* **1** : rotten, decayed **2** : corrupt
podrir → **pudrir**
poema *nm* : poem
poesía *nf* **1** : poetry **2** POEMA : poem
poeta *nmf* : poet
poético, -ca *adj* : poetic, poetical
pogrom *nm* : pogrom
póker *or* **poker** *nm* : poker (card game)
polaco[1], **-ca** *adj* : Polish
polaco[2], **-ca** *n* : Pole, Polish person
polaco[3] *nm* : Polish (language)
polar *adj* : polar
polarizar {21} *vt* : to polarize — **polarizarse** *vr* — **polarización** *nf*
polea *nf* : pulley
polémica *nf* CONTROVERSIA : controversy, polemics
polémico, -ca *adj* CONTROVERTIDO : controversial, polemical
polen *nm, pl* **pólenes** : pollen
policía[1] *nf* : police
policía[2] *nmf* : police officer, policeman *m*, policewoman *f*
policíaco, -ca *or* **policiaco, -ca** *adj* : police <novela policíaca : detective story>
policial *adj* : police
poliéster *nm* : polyester
poligamia *nf* : polygamy
polígamo[1], **-ma** *adj* : polygamous
polígamo[2], **-ma** *n* : polygamist
polígono *nm* : polygon — **polígonal** *adj*
poliinsaturado, -da *adj* : polyunsaturated
polilla *nf* : moth
polimerizar {21} *vt* : to polymerize
polímero *nm* : polymer
polinesio, -sia *adj & n* : Polynesian
polinizar {21} *vt* : to pollinate — **polinización** *nf*
polio *nf* : polio
poliomielitis *nf* : poliomyelitis, polio
polisón *nm, pl* **-sones** : bustle (on clothing)
politécnico, -ca *adj* : polytechnic
politeísmo *nm* : polytheism — **politeísta** *adj & nmf*
política *nf* **1** : politics **2** : policy
políticamente *adv* : politically
político[1], **-ca** *adj* **1** : political **2** : tactful, politic **3** : by marriage <padre político : father-in-law>
político[2], **-ca** *n* : politician
póliza *nf* : policy <póliza de seguros : insurance policy>
polizón *nm, pl* **-zones** : stowaway <viajar de polizón : to stow away>
polla *nf* APUESTA : bet
pollera *nf* **1** : chicken coop **2** : skirt
pollero, -ra *n* **1** : poulterer **2** : poultry farm **3** *Mex fam* COYOTE : smuggler of illegal immigrants
pollito, -ta *n* : chick, young bird, fledgling
pollo, -lla *n* **1** : chicken **2** POLLITO : chick **3** JOVEN : young man *m*, young lady *f*
polluelo *nm* → **pollito**
polo *nm* **1** : pole <el Polo Norte : the North Pole> <polo negativo : negative pole> **2** : polo (sport) **3** : polo shirt **4** : focal point, center **5 polo opuesto** : exact opposite
polución *nf, pl* **-ciones** CONTAMINACIÓN : pollution
polvareda *nf* **1** : cloud of dust **2** : uproar, fuss
polvera *nf* : compact (for face powder)
polvo *nm* **1** : dust **2** : powder **3 polvos** *nmpl* : face powder **4 polvos de hornear** : baking powder **5 hacer polvo** *fam* : to crush, to shatter <vas a hacer polvo el reloj : you're going to destroy your watch>
pólvora *nf* **1** : gunpowder **2** : fireworks *pl*
polvoriento, -ta *adj* : dusty, powdery
polvorín *nm, pl* **-rines** : magazine, storehouse (for explosives)
pomada *nf* : ointment, cream
pomelo *nm* : grapefruit
pómez *nm or* **piedra pómez** : pumice
pomo *nm* **1** : pommel (on a sword) **2** : knob, handle **3** : perfume bottle
pompa *nf* **1** : bubble **2** : pomp, splendor **3 pompas fúnebres** : funeral
pompón *nm, pl* **pompones** BORLA : pom-pom
pomposidad *nf* **1** : pomp, splendor **2** : pomposity, ostentation
pomposo, -sa *adj* : pompous — **pomposamente** *adv*
pómulo *nm* : cheekbone
pon → **poner**
ponchadura *nf Mex* : puncture, flat (tire)
ponchar *vt* **1** : to strike out (in baseball) **2** *Mex* : to puncture — **poncharse** *vr* **1** *Col, Ven* : to strike out (in baseball) **2** *Mex* : to blow out (of a tire)

ponche *nm* **1** : punch (drink) **2 ponche de huevo** : eggnog
poncho *nm* : poncho
ponderación *nf, pl* **-ciones 1** : consideration, deliberation **2** : high praise
ponderar *vt* **1** : to weigh, to consider **2** : to speak highly of
pondrá, etc. → **poner**
ponencia *nf* **1** DISCURSO : paper, presentation, address **2** INFORME : report
ponente *nmf* : speaker, presenter
poner {60} *vt* **1** COLOCAR : to put, to place <pon el libro en la mesa : put the book on the table> **2** AGREGAR, AÑADIR : to put in, to add **3** : to put on (clothes) **4** CONTRIBUIR : to contribute **5** ESCRIBIR : to put in writing <no le puso su nombre : he didn't put his name on it> **6** IMPONER : to set, to impose **7** EXPONER : to put, to expose <lo puso en peligro : she put him in danger> **8** : to prepare, to arrange <poner la mesa : to set the table> **9** : to name <le pusimos Ana : we called her Ana> **10** ESTABLECER : to set up, to establish <puso un restaurante : he opened up a restaurant> **11** INSTALAR : to install, to put in **12** (*with an adjective or adverb*) : to make <siempre lo pones de mal humor : you always put him in a bad mood> **13** : to turn on, to switch on **14** SUPONER : to suppose <pongamos que no viene : supposing he doesn't come> **15** : to lay (eggs) **16 ~ a** : to start (someone doing something) <lo puse a trabajar : I put him to work> **17 ~ de** : to place as <la pusieron de directora : they made her director> **18 ~ en** : to put in (a state or condition) <poner en duda : to call into question — *vi* **1** : to contribute **2** : to lay eggs — **ponerse** *vr* **1** : to move (into a position) <ponerse de pie : to stand up> **2** : to put on, to wear **3** : to become, to turn <se puso colorado : he turned red> **4** : to set (of the sun or moon)
poni *or* **poney** *nm* : pony
ponga, etc. → **poner**
poniente *nm* **1** OCCIDENTE : west **2** : west wind
ponqué *nm Col, Ven* : cake
pontifical *adj* : pontifical
pontificar {72} *vi* : to pontificate
pontífice *nm* : pontiff, pope
pontón *nm, pl* **pontones** : pontoon
ponzoña *nf* VENENO : poison — **ponzoñoso, -sa** *adj*
popa *nf* **1** : stern **2 a ~** : astern, abaft, aft
popelín *nm, pl* **-lines** : poplin
popelina *nf* : poplin
popote *nm Mex* : (drinking) straw
populachero, -ra *adj* : common, popular, vulgar
populacho *nm* : rabble, masses *pl*
popular *adj* **1** : popular **2** : traditional **3** : colloquial
popularidad *nf* : popularity
popularizar {21} *vt* : to popularize — **popularizarse** *vr*
populista *adj & nmf* : populist — **populismo** *nm*
populoso, -sa *adj* : populous
popurrí *nm* : potpourri
por *prep* **1** : for, during <se quedaron allí por la semana : they stayed there during the week> <por el momento : for now, at the moment> **2** : around, during <por noviembre empieza a nevar : around November it starts to snow> <por la mañana : in the morning> **3** : around (a place) <debe estar por allí : it must be over there> <por todas partes : everywhere> **4** : by, through, along <por la puerta : through the door> <pasé por tu casa : I stopped by your house> <por la costa : along the coast> **5** : for, for the sake of <lo hizo por su madre : he did it for his mother> <¡por Dios! : for heaven's sake!> **6** : because of, on account of <llegué tarde por el tráfico : I arrived late because of the traffic> <dejar por imposible : to give up as impossible> **7** : per <60 millas por hora : 60 miles per hour> <por docena : by the dozen> **8** : for, in exchange for, instead of <su hermana habló por él : his sister spoke on his behalf> **9** : by means of <hablar por teléfono : to talk on the phone> <por escrito : in writing> **10** : as for <por mí : as far as I'm concerned> **11** : times <tres por dos son seis : three times two is six> **12** SEGÚN : from, according to <por lo que dices : judging from what you're telling me> **13** : as, for <por ejemplo : for example> **14** : by <hecho por mi abuela : made by my grandmother> <por correo : by mail> **15** : for, in order to <lucha por ganar su respeto : he struggles to win her respect> **16 estar por** : to be about to **17 por ciento** : percent **18 por favor** : please **19 por lo tanto** : therefore, consequently **20 ¿por qué?** : why? **21 por que** → **porque 22 por . . . que** : no matter how <por mucho que intente : no matter how hard I try> **23 por si** *or* **por si acaso** : just in case
porcelana *nf* : china, porcelain
porcentaje *nm* : percentage
porche *nm* : porch
porción *nf, pl* **porciones 1** : portion **2** PARTE : part, share **3** RACIÓN : serving, helping
pordiosear *vi* MENDIGAR : beg
pordiosero, -ra *n* MENDIGO : beggar
porfiado, -da *adj* OBSTINADO, TERCO : obstinate, stubborn — : **porfiadamente** *adv*
porfiar {85} *vi* : to insist, to persist
pormenor *nm* DETALLE : detail
pormenorizar {21} *vi* : to go into detail — *vt* : to tell in detail
pornografía *nf* : pornography

pornográfico, -ca *adj* : pornographic
poro *nm* : pore
poroso, -sa *adj* : porous — **porosidad** *nf*
poroto *nm Arg, Chile, Uru* : bean
porque *conj* **1** : because **2** *or* **por que** : in order that
porqué *nm* : reason, cause
porquería *nf* **1** SUCIEDAD : dirt, filth **2** : nastiness, vulgarity **3** : worthless thing, trifle **4** : junk food
porra *nf* **1** : nightstick, club **2** *Mex* : cheer, yell <los aficionados le echaban porras : the fans cheered him on>
porrazo *nm* **1** : blow, whack **2 de golpe y porrazo** : suddenly
porrista *nmf* **1** : cheerleader **2** : fan, supporter
portaaviones *nms & pl* : aircraft carrier
portada *nf* **1** : title page **2** : cover **3** : facade, front
portador, -dora *n* : carrier, bearer
portafolio *or* **portafolios** *nm, pl* **-lios 1** MALETÍN : briefcase **2** : portfolio (of investments)
portal *nm* **1** : portal, doorway **2** VESTÍBULO : vestibule, hall
portar *vt* **1** : to carry, to bear **2** : to wear — **portarse** *vr* CONDUCIRSE : to behave <pórtate bien : behave yourself>
portátil *adj* : portable
portaviandas *nms & pl* : lunch box
portaviones *nm* → **portaaviones**
portavoz *nmf, pl* **-voces** : spokesperson, spokesman *m,* spokeswoman *f*
portazo *nm* : slam (of a door)
porte *nm* **1** ASPECTO : bearing, demeanor **2** TRANSPORTE : transport, carrying <porte pagado : postage paid>
portento *nm* MARAVILLA : marvel, wonder
portentoso, -sa *adj* MARAVILLOSO : marvelous, wonderful
porteño, -ña *adj* : of or from Buenos Aires
portería *nf* **1** ARCO : goal, goalposts *pl* **2** : superintendent's office
portero, -ra *n* **1** ARQUERO : goalkeeper, goalie **2** : doorman *m* **3** : janitor, superintendent
pórtico *nm* : portico
portilla *nf* : porthole
portón *nm, pl* **portones 1** : main door **2** : gate
portugués[1], -guesa *adj & n, mpl* **-gueses** : Portuguese
portugués[2] *nm* : Portuguese (language)
porvenir *nm* FUTURO : future
pos *adv* **en pos de** : in pursuit of
posada *nf* **1** : inn **2** *Mex* : Advent celebration
posadero, -ra *n* : innkeeper
posar *vi* : to pose — *vt* : to place, to lay — **posarse** *vr* **1** : to land, to light, to perch **2** : to settle, to rest
posavasos *nms & pl* : coaster (for drinks)
posdata *nf* → **postdata**
pose *nf* : pose
poseedor, -dora *n* : possessor, holder
poseer {20} *vt* : to possess, to hold, to have
poseído, -da *adj* : possessed
posesión *nf, pl* **-siones** : possession
posesionarse *vr* **~ de** : to take possession of, to take over
posesivo[1], -va *adj* : possessive
posesivo[2] *nm* : possessive case
posguerra *nf* : postwar period
posibilidad *nf* **1** : possibility **2 posibilidades** *nfpl* : means, income
posibilitar *vt* : to make possible, to permit
posible *adj* : possible — **posiblemente** *adv*
posición *nf, pl* **-ciones 1** : position, place **2** : status, standing **3** : attitude, stance
posicionar *vt* **1** : to position, to place **2** : to establish — **posicionarse** *vr*
positivo[1], -va *adj* : positive
positivo[2] *nm* : print (in photography)
poso *nm* **1** : sediment, dregs *pl* **2** : grounds *pl* (of coffee)
posoperatorio, -ria *adj* : postoperative
posponer {60} *vt* **1** : to postpone **2** : to put behind, to subordinate
pospuso, etc. → **posponer**
posta *nf* : relay race
postal[1] *adj* : postal
postal[2] *nm* : postcard
postdata *nf* : postscript
poste *nm* : post, pole <poste de teléfonos : telephone pole>
póster *or* **poster** *nm, pl* **pósters** *or* **posters** : poster, placard
postergación *nf, pl* **-ciones** : postponement, deferring
postergar {52} *vt* **1** : to delay, to postpone **2** : to pass over (an employee)
posteridad *nf* : posterity
posterior *adj* **1** ULTERIOR : later, subsequent **2** TRASERO : back, rear
postgrado *nm* : graduate course
postgraduado, -da *n* : graduate student, postgraduate
postigo *nm* **1** CONTRAVENTANA : shutter **2** : small door, wicket gate
postilla *nf* : scab
postizo, -za *adj* : artificial, false <dentadura postiza : dentures>
postnatal *adj* : postnatal
postor, -tora *n* : bidder <mejor postor : highest bidder>
postración *nf, pl* **-ciones 1** : prostration **2** ABATIMIENTO : depression
postrado, -da *adj* **1** : prostrate **2 postrado en cama** : bedridden
postrar *vt* DEBILITAR : to debilitate, to weaken — **postrarse** *vr* : to prostrate oneself
postre *nm* : dessert

postrero, -ra *adj* (**postrer** *before masculine singular nouns*) ÚLTIMO : last

postulación *nf, pl* **-ciones 1 :** collection **2 :** nomination (of a candidate)

postulado *nm* **:** postulate, assumption

postulante, -ta *n* **1 :** postulant **2 :** candidate, applicant

postular *vt* **1 :** to postulate **2 :** to nominate **3 :** to propose — **postularse** *vr* **:** to run, to be a candidate

póstumo, -ma *adj* **:** posthumous — **póstumamente** *adv*

postura *nf* **1 :** posture, position (of the body) **2** ACTITUD, POSICIÓN **:** position, stance

potable *adj* **:** drinkable, potable

potaje *nm* **:** thick vegetable soup, pottage

potasa *nf* **:** potash

potasio *nm* **:** potassium

pote *nm* **1** OLLA **:** pot **2 :** jar, container

potencia *nf* **1 :** power <potencias extranjeras : foreign powers> <elevado a la tercera potencia : raised to the third power> **2 :** capacity, potency

potencial *adj & nm* **:** potential

potenciar *vt* **:** to promote, to foster

potenciómetro *nm* **:** dimmer, dimmer switch

potentado, -da *n* **1** SOBERANO **:** potentate, sovereign **2** MAGNATE **:** tycoon, magnate

potente *adj* **1 :** powerful, strong **2 :** potent, virile

potestad *nf* **1** AUTORIDAD **:** authority, jurisdiction **2 patria potestad :** custody, guardianship

potrero *nm* **1 :** field, pasture **2 :** cattle ranch

potro[1], -tra *n* **:** colt *m,* filly *f*

potro[2] *nm* **1 :** rack (for torture) **2 :** horse (in gymnastics)

pozo *nm* **1 :** well <pozo de petróleo : oil well> **2 :** deep pool (in a river) **3 :** mine shaft **4** *Arg, Par, Uru* **:** pothole **5 pozo séptico :** cesspool

pozole *nm Mex* **:** spicy stew made with pork and hominy

práctica *nf* **1 :** practice, experience **2** EJERCICIO **:** exercising <la práctica de la medicina : the practice of medicine> **3** APLICACIÓN **:** application, practice <poner en práctica : to put into practice> **4 prácticas** *nfpl* **:** training

practicable *adj* **:** practicable, feasible

prácticamente *adv* **:** practically

practicante[1] *adj* **:** practicing <católicos practicantes : practicing Catholics>

practicante[2] *nmf* **:** practicer, practitioner

practicar {72} *vt* **1 :** to practice **2 :** to perform, to carry out **3 :** to exercise (a profession) — *vi* **:** to practice

práctico, -ca *adj* **:** practical, useful

pradera *nf* **:** grassland, prairie

prado *nm* **1** CAMPO **:** field, meadow **2 :** park

pragmático, -ca *adj* **:** pragmatic — **pragmáticamente** *adv*

pragmatismo *nm* **:** pragmatism

preámbulo *nm* **1** INTRODUCCIÓN **:** preamble, introduction **2** RODEO **:** evasion <gastar preámbulos : to beat around the bush>

prebélico, -ca *adj* **:** antebellum

prebenda *nf* **:** privilege, perquisite

precalentar {55} *vt* **:** to preheat

precariedad *nf* **:** precariousness

precario, -ria *adj* **:** precarious — **precariamente** *adv*

precaución *nf, pl* **-ciones 1 :** precaution <medidas de precaución : precautionary measures> **2** PRUDENCIA **:** caution, care <con precaución : cautiously>

precautorio, -ria *adj* **:** precautionary

precaver *vt* PREVENIR **:** to prevent, to guard against — **precaverse** *vr* PREVENIRSE **:** to take precautions, to be on guard

precavido, -da *adj* CAUTELOSO **:** cautious, prudent

precedencia *nf* **:** precedence, priority

precedente[1] *adj* **:** preceding, previous

precedente[2] *nm* **:** precedent

preceder *v* **:** to precede

precepto *nm* **:** rule, precept

preciado, -da *adj* **:** esteemed, prized, valuable

preciarse *vr* **1** JACTARSE **:** to boast, to brag **2 ~ de :** to pride oneself on

precinto *nm* **:** seal

precio *nm* **1 :** price **2 :** cost, sacrifice <a cualquier precio : whatever the cost>

preciosidad *nf* **:** beautiful thing <este vestido es una preciosidad : this dress is lovely>

precioso, -sa *adj* **1** HERMOSO **:** beautiful, exquisite **2** VALIOSO **:** precious, valuable

precipicio *nm* **1 :** precipice **2** RUINA **:** ruin

precipitación *nf, pl* **-ciones 1** PRISA **:** haste, hurry, rush **2 :** precipitation, rain, snow

precipitado, -da *adj* **1 :** hasty, sudden **2 :** rash — **precipitadamente** *adv*

precipitar *vt* **1** APRESURAR **:** to hasten, to speed up **2** ARROJAR **:** to hurl, to throw — **precipitarse** *vr* **1** APRESURARSE **:** to rush **2 :** to act rashly **3** ARROJARSE **:** to throw oneself

precisamente *adv* JUSTAMENTE **:** precisely, exactly

precisar *vt* **1 :** to specify, to determine exactly **2** NECESITAR **:** to need, to require — *vi* **:** to be necessary

precisión *nf, pl* **-siones 1** EXACTITUD **:** precision, accuracy **2** CLARIDAD **:** clarity (of style, etc.) **3** NECESIDAD **:** necessity <tener precisión de : to have need of>

preciso, -sa *adj* **1** EXACTO **:** precise **2 :** very, exact <en ese preciso instante : at that very instant> **3** NECESARIO **:** necessary

precocidad *nf* **:** precocity
precocinar *vt* **:** to precook
preconcebir {54} *vt* **:** to preconceive
precondición *nf, pl* **-ciones :** precondition
preconizar {21} *vt* **1 :** to recommend, to advocate **2 :** to extol
precoz *adj, pl* **precoces 1 :** precocious **2 :** early, premature — **precozmente** *adv*
precursor, -sora *n* **:** forerunner, precursor
predecesor, -sora *n* ANTECESOR **:** predecessor
predecir {11} *vt* **:** to foretell, to predict
predestinado, -da *adj* **:** predestined, fated
predestinar *vt* **:** to predestine — **predestinación** *nf*
predeterminar *vt* **:** to predetermine
prédica *nf* SERMÓN **:** sermon
predicado *nm* **:** predicate
predicador, -dora *n* **:** preacher
predicar {72} *v* **:** to preach
predicción *nf, pl* **-ciones 1 :** prediction **2** PRONÓSTICO **:** forecast <predicción del tiempo : weather forecast>
prediga, predijo, etc. → **predecir**
predilección *nf, pl* **-ciones :** predilection, preference
predilecto, -ta *adj* **:** favorite
predio *nm* **:** property, piece of land
predisponer {60} *vt* **1 :** to predispose, to incline **2 :** to prejudice, to bias
predisposición *nf, pl* **-ciones 1 :** predisposition, tendency **2 :** prejudice, bias
predominante *adj* **:** predominant — **predominantemente** *adv*
predominar *vi* PREVALECER **:** to predominate, to prevail
predominio *nm* **:** predominance, prevalence
preeminente *adj* **:** preeminent — **preeminencia** *nf*
preescolar *adj & nm* **:** preschool
preestreno *nm* **:** preview
prefabricado, -da *adj* **:** prefabricated
prefacio *nm* **:** preface
prefecto *nm* **:** prefect
preferencia *nf* **1 :** preference **2** PRIORIDAD **:** priority **3 de ~ :** preferably
preferencial *adj* **:** preferential
preferente *adj* **:** preferential, special <trato preferente : special treatment>
preferentemente *adv* **:** preferably
preferible *adj* **:** preferable
preferido, -da *adj & n* **:** favorite
preferir {76} *vt* **:** to prefer
prefijo *nm* **:** prefix
pregonar *vt* **1 :** to proclaim, to announce **2 :** to hawk (merchandise) **3 :** to extol **4 :** to reveal, to disclose
pregunta *nf* **1 :** question **2 hacer una pregunta :** to ask a question
preguntar *vt* **:** to ask, to question — *vi* **:** to ask, to inquire — **preguntarse** *vr* **:** to wonder
preguntón, -tona *adj, mpl* **-tones :** inquisitive
prehistórico, -ca *adj* **:** prehistoric
prejuicio *nm* **:** prejudice
prejuzgar {52} *vt* **:** to prejudge
prelado *nm* **:** prelate
preliminar *adj & nm* **:** preliminary
preludio *nm* **:** prelude
prematrimonial *adj* **:** premarital
prematuro, -ra *adj* **:** premature
premeditación *nf, pl* **-ciones :** premeditation
premeditar *vt* **:** to premeditate, to plan
premenstrual *adj* **:** premenstrual
premiado, -da *adj* **:** winning, prizewinning
premiar *vt* **1 :** to award a prize to **2 :** to reward
premier *nmf* **:** premier, prime minister
premio *nm* **1 :** prize <premio gordo : grand prize, jackpot> **2 :** reward **3 :** premium
premisa *nf* **:** premise, basis
premolar *nm* **:** bicuspid (tooth)
premonición *nf, pl* **-ciones :** premonition
premura *nf* **:** haste, urgency
prenatal *adj* **:** prenatal
prenda *nf* **1 :** piece of clothing **2 :** security, pledge
prendar *vt* **1 :** to charm, to captivate **2 :** to pawn, to pledge — **prendarse** *vr* **~ de :** to fall in love with
prendedor *nm* **:** brooch, pin
prender *vt* **1** SUJETAR **:** to pin, to fasten **2** APRESAR **:** to catch, to apprehend **3 :** to light (a cigarette, a match) **4 :** to turn on <prende la luz : turn on the light> **5 prender fuego a :** to set fire to — *vi* **1 :** to take root **2 :** to catch fire **3 :** to catch on
prensa *nf* **1 :** printing press **2 :** press <conferencia de prensa : press conference>
prensar *vt* **:** to press
prensil *adj* **:** prehensile
preñado, -da *adj* **1 :** pregnant **2 ~ de :** filled with
preñar *vt* EMBARAZAR **:** to make pregnant
preñez *nf, pl* **preñeces :** pregnancy
preocupación *nf, pl* **-ciones** INQUIETUD **:** worry, concern
preocupante *adj* **:** worrisome
preocupar *vt* INQUIETAR **:** to worry, to concern — **preocuparse** *vr* APURARSE **:** to worry, to be concerned
preparación *nf, pl* **-ciones 1 :** preparation, readiness **2 :** education, training **3 :** (medicinal) preparation
preparado[1], **-da** *adj* **1 :** ready, prepared **2 :** trained
preparado[2] *nm* **:** preparation, mixture
preparar *vt* **1 :** to prepare, to make ready **2 :** to teach, to train, to coach — **prepararse** *vr*
preparativos *nmpl* **:** preparations
preparatoria *nf Mex* **:** high school
preparatorio, -ria *adj* **:** preparatory

preponderante *adj* : preponderant, predominant — **preponderancia** *nf* — **preponderantemente** *adv*

preposición *nf, pl* **-ciones** : preposition — **preposicional** *adj*

prepotente *adj* : arrogant, domineering, overbearing — **prepotencia** *nf*

prerrogativa *nf* : prerogative, privilege

presa *nf* **1** : capture, seizure <hacer presa de : to seize> **2** : catch, prey <presa de : prey to, seized with> **3** : claw, fang **4** DIQUE : dam **5** : morsel, piece (of food)

presagiar *vt* : to presage, to portend

presagio *nm* : omen, portent

presbiterio *nm* : presbytery, sanctuary (of a church)

presbítero *nm* : presbyter

presciencia *nf* : prescience

prescindir *vi* **~ de 1** : to do without, to dispense with **2** DESATENDER : to ignore, to disregard **3** OMITIR : to omit, to skip

prescribir {33} *vt* : to prescribe

prescripción *nf, pl* **-ciones** : prescription

prescrito *pp* → **prescribir**

presencia *nf* **1** : presence **2** ASPECTO : appearance

presenciar *vt* : to be present at, to witness

presentación *nf, pl* **-ciones 1** : presentation **2** : introduction **3** : appearance

presentador, -dora *n* : newscaster, anchorman *m,* anchorwoman *f*

presentar *vt* **1** : to present, to show **2** : to offer, to give **3** : to submit (a document), to launch (a product) **4** : to introduce (a person) — **presentarse** *vr* **1** : to show up, to appear **2** : to arise, to come up **3** : to introduce oneself

presente[1] *adj* **1** : present, in attendance **2** : present, current **3 tener presente** : to keep in mind

presente[2] *nm* **1** : present (time, tense) **2** : one present <entre los presentes se encontraban . . . : those present included . . .>

presentimiento *nm* : premonition, hunch, feeling

presentir {76} *vt* : to sense, to intuit <presentía lo que iba a pasar : he sensed what was going to happen>

preservación *nf, pl* **-ciones** : preservation

preservar *vt* **1** : to preserve **2** : to protect

preservativo *nm* CONDÓN : condom

presidencia *nf* **1** : presidency **2** : chairmanship

presidencial *adj* : presidential

presidente, -ta *n* **1** : president **2** : chair, chairperson **3** : presiding judge

presidiario, -ria *n* : convict, prisoner

presidio *nm* : prison, penitentiary

presidir *vt* **1** MODERAR : to preside over, to chair **2** : to dominate, to rule over

presilla *nf* : eye, loop, fastener

presión *nf, pl* **presiones 1** : pressure **2 presión arterial** : blood pressure

presionar *vt* **1** : to pressure **2** : to press, to push — *vi* : to put on the pressure

preso[1], -sa *adj* : imprisoned

preso[2], -sa *n* : prisoner

prestado, -da *adj* **1** : borrowed, on loan **2 pedir prestado** : to borrow

prestamista *nmf* : moneylender, pawnbroker

préstamo *nm* : loan

prestar *vt* **1** : to lend, to loan **2** : to render (a service), to give (aid) **3 prestar atención** : to pay attention **4 prestar juramento** : to take an oath — **prestarse** *vr* : to lend oneself <se presta a confusiones : it lends itself to confusion>

prestatario, -ria *n* : borrower

presteza *nf* : promptness, speed

prestidigitación *nf, pl* **-ciones** : sleight of hand, prestidigitation

prestidigitador, -dora *n* : conjurer, magician

prestigio *nm* : prestige — **prestigioso, -sa** *adj*

presto[1] *adv* : promptly, at once

presto[2], -ta *adj* **1** : quick, prompt **2** DISPUESTO, PREPARADO : ready

presumido, -da *adj* VANIDOSO : conceited, vain

presumir *vt* SUPONER : to presume, to suppose — *vi* **1** ALARDEAR : to boast, to show off **2 ~ de** : to consider oneself <presume de inteligente : he thinks he's intelligent>

presunción *nf, pl* **-ciones 1** SUPOSICIÓN : presumption, supposition **2** VANIDAD : conceit, vanity

presunto, -ta *adj* : presumed, supposed, alleged — **presuntamente** *adv*

presuntuoso, -sa *adj* : conceited

presuponer {60} *vt* : to presuppose

presupuestal *adj* : budget, budgetary

presupuestar *vi* : to budget — *vt* : to budget for

presupuestario, -ria *adj* : budget, budgetary

presupuesto *nm* **1** : budget, estimate **2** : assumption, supposition

presurizar {21} *vt* : to pressurize

presuroso, -sa *adj* : hasty, quick

pretencioso, -sa *adj* : pretentious

pretender *vt* **1** INTENTAR : to attempt, to try <pretendo estudiar : I'm trying to study> **2** AFIRMAR : to claim <pretende ser pobre : he claims he's poor> **3** : to seek, to aspire to <¿qué pretendes tú? : what are you after?> **4** CORTEJAR : to court **5 pretender que** : to expect <¿pretendes que lo crea? : do you expect me to believe you?>

pretendiente[1] *nmf* **1** : candidate, applicant **2** : pretender, claimant (to a throne, etc.)

pretendiente[2] *nm* : suitor

pretensión *nf, pl* **-siones 1 :** intention, hope, plan **2 :** pretension <sin pretensiones : unpretentious>
pretexto *nm* EXCUSA **:** pretext, excuse
pretil *nm* **:** parapet, railing
prevalecer {53} *vi* **:** to prevail, to triumph
prevaleciente *adj* **:** prevailing, prevalent
prevalerse {84} *vr* **~ de :** to avail oneself of, to take advantage of
prevención *nf, pl* **-ciones 1 :** prevention **2 :** preparation, readiness **3 :** precautionary measure **4 :** prejudice, bias
prevenido, -da *adj* **1** PREPARADO **:** prepared, ready **2** ADVERTIDO **:** forewarned **3** CAUTELOSO **:** cautious
prevenir {87} *vt* **1 :** to prevent **2 :** to warn — **prevenirse** *vr* **~ contra** *or* **~ de :** to take precautions against
preventivo, -va *adj* **:** preventive, precautionary
prever {88} *vt* ANTICIPAR **:** to foresee, to anticipate
previo, -via *adj* **1 :** previous, prior **2 :** after, upon <previo pago : after paying, upon payment>
previsible *adj* **:** foreseeable
previsión *nf, pl* **-siones 1 :** foresight **2 :** prediction, forecast **3 :** precaution
previsor, -sora *adj* **:** farsighted, prudent
prieto, -ta *adj* **1 :** blackish, dark **2 :** dark-skinned, swarthy **3 :** tight, compressed
prima *nf* **1 :** premium **2 :** bonus **3** → **primo**
primacía *nf* **1 :** precedence, priority **2 :** superiority, supremacy
primado *nm* **:** primate (bishop)
primario, -ria *adj* **:** primary
primate *nm* **:** primate
primavera *nf* **1 :** spring (season) **2** PRÍMULA **:** primrose
primaveral *adj* **:** spring, springlike
primero[1] *adv* **1 :** first **2 :** rather, sooner
primero[2]**, -ra** *adj* (**primer** *before masculine singular nouns*) **1 :** first **2 :** top, leading **3 :** fundamental, basic **4 de primera :** first-rate
primero[3]**, -ra** *n* **:** first
primicia *nf* **1 :** first fruits **2 :** scoop, exclusive
primigenio, -nia *adj* **:** original, primary
primitivo, -va *adj* **1 :** primitive **2** ORIGINAL **:** original
primo, -ma *n* **:** cousin
primogénito, -ta *adj & n* **:** firstborn
primor *nm* **1 :** skill, care **2 :** beauty, elegance
primordial *adj* **1 :** primordial **2 :** basic, fundamental
primoroso, -sa *adj* **1 :** exquisite, fine, delicate **2 :** skillful
prímula *nf* **:** primrose
princesa *nf* **:** princess
principado *nm* **:** principality
principal[1] *adj* **1 :** main, principal **2 :** foremost, leading
principal[2] *nm* **:** capital, principal
príncipe *nm* **:** prince
prinipesco, -ca *adj* **:** princely
principiante[1] *adj* **:** beginning
principiante[2] *nmf* **:** beginner, novice
principiar *vt* EMPEZAR **:** to begin
principio *nm* **1** COMIENZO **:** beginning **2 :** principle **3 al principio :** at first **4 a principios de :** at the beginning of <a principios de agosto : at the beginning of August> **5 en ~ :** in principle
pringar {52} *vt* **1 :** to dip (in grease) **2 :** to soil, to spatter (with grease) — **pringarse** *vr*
pringoso, -sa *adj* **:** greasy
pringue[1]**, etc.** → **pringar**
pringue[2] *nm* **:** grease, drippings *pl*
prior, priora *n* **:** prior *m,* prioress *f*
priorato *nm* **:** priory
prioridad *nf* **:** priority, precedence
prisa *nf* **1 :** hurry, rush **2 a ~** *or* **de ~ :** quickly, fast **3 a toda prisa :** as fast as possible **4 darse prisa :** to hurry **5 tener prisa :** to be in a hurry
prisión *nf, pl* **prisiones 1** CÁRCEL **:** prison, jail **2** ENCARCELAMIENTO **:** imprisonment
prisionero, -ra *n* **:** prisoner
prisma *nf* **:** prism
prismáticos *nmpl* **:** binoculars
prístino, -na *adj* **:** pristine
privacidad *nf* **:** privacy
privación *nf, pl* **-ciones 1 :** deprivation **2 :** privation, want
privado, -da *adj* **:** private — **privadamente** *adv*
privar *vt* **1** DESPOJAR **:** to deprive **2 :** to stun, to knock out — **privarse** *vr* **:** to deprive oneself
privativo, -va *adj* **:** exclusive, particular
privilegiado, -da *adj* **:** privileged
privilegiar *vt* **:** to grant a privilege to, to favor
privilegio *nm* **:** privilege
pro[1] *nm* **1 :** pro, advantage <los pros y contras : the pros and cons> **2 en pro de :** for, in favor of
pro[2] *prep* **:** for, in favor of <grupos pro derechos humanos : groups supporting human rights>
proa *nf* **:** bow, prow
probabilidad *nf* **:** probability
probable *adj* **:** probable, likely
probablemente *adv* **:** probably
probar {19} *vt* **1 :** to demonstrate, to prove **2 :** to test, to try out **3 :** to try on (clothing) **4 :** to taste, to sample — *vi* **:** to try — **probarse** *vr* **:** to try on (clothing)
probeta *nf* **:** test tube
probidad *nf* **:** probity
problema *nm* **:** problem
problemática *nf* **:** set of problems <la problemática que debemos enfrentar : the problems we must face>
probóscide *nf* **:** proboscis

problemático, -ca *adj* : problematic
procaz *adj, pl* **procaces 1** : insolent, impudent **2** : indecent
procedencia *nf* : origin, source
procedente *adj* **1** : proper, fitting **2** ~ **de** : coming from
proceder *vi* **1** AVANZAR : to proceed **2** : to act, to behave **3** : to be appropriate, to be fitting **4** ~ **de** : to originate from, to come from
procedimiento *nm* : procedure, process
prócer *nmf* : eminent person, leader
procesado, -da *n* : accused, defendant
procesador *nm* : processor <procesador de textos : word processor>
procesamiento *nm* : processing <procesamiento de datos : data processing>
procesar *vt* **1** : to prosecute, to try **2** : to process
procesión *nf, pl* **-siones** : procession
proceso *nm* **1** : process **2** : trial, proceedings *pl*
proclama *nf* : proclamation
proclamación *nf, pl* **-ciones** : proclamation
proclamar *vt* : to proclaim — **proclamarse** *vr*
proclive *adj* ~ **a** : inclined to, prone to
proclividad *nf* : proclivity, inclination
procrear *vi* : to procreate — **procreación** *nf*
procurador, -dora *n* ABOGADO : attorney
procurar *vt* **1** INTENTAR : to try, to endeavor **2** CONSEGUIR : to obtain, to procure **3 procurar hacer** : to manage to do
prodigar {52} *vt* : to lavish, to be generous with
prodigio *nm* : wonder, marvel
prodigioso, -sa *adj* : prodigious, marvelous
pródigo[1], -ga *adj* **1** : generous, lavish **2** : wasteful, prodigal
pródigo[2], -ga *n* : spendthrift, prodigal
producción *nf, pl* **-ciones 1** : production **2 producción en serie** : mass production
producir {61} *vt* **1** : to produce, to make, to manufacture **2** : to cause, to bring about **3** : to bear (interest) — **producirse** *vr* : to take place, to occur
productividad *nf* : productivity
productivo, -va *adj* **1** : productive **2** LUCRATIVO : profitable
producto *nm* **1** : product **2** : proceeds *pl*, yield
productor, -tora *n* : producer
proeza *nf* HAZAÑA : feat, exploit
profanar *vt* : to profane, to desecrate — **profanación** *nf*
profano[1], -na *adj* **1** : profane **2** : worldly, secular
profano[2], -na *n* : nonspecialist
profecía *nf* : prophecy
proferir {76} *vt* **1** : to utter **2** : to hurl (insults)
profesar *vt* **1** : to profess, to declare **2** : to practice, to exercise
profesión *nf, pl* **-siones** : profession
profesional *adj & nmf* : professional — **profesionalmente** *adv*
profesionalismo *nm* : professionalism
profesionalizar {21} *vt* : to professionalize
profesionista *nmf Mex* : professional
profesor, -sora *n* **1** MAESTRO : teacher **2** : professor
profesorado *nm* **1** : faculty **2** : teaching profession
profeta *nm* : prophet
profético, -ca *adj* : prophetic
profetisa *nf* : prophetess, prophet
profetizar {21} *vt* : to prophesy
prófugo, -ga *adj & n* : fugitive
profundidad *nf* : depth, profundity
profundizar {21} *vt* **1** : to deepen **2** : to study in depth — *vi* ~ **en** : to go deeply into, to study in depth
profundo, -da *adj* **1** HONDO : deep **2** : profound — **profundamente** *adv*
profusión *nf, pl* **-siones** : abundance, profusion
profuso, -sa *adj* : profuse, abundant, extensive
progenie *nf* : progeny, offspring
progenitor, -tora *n* ANTEPASADO : ancestor, progenitor
prognóstico *nm* : prognosis
programa *nm* **1** : program **2** : plan **3 programa de estudios** : curriculum
programable *adj* : programmable
programación *nf, pl* **-ciones 1** : programming **2** : planning
programador, -dora *n* : programmer
programar *vt* **1** : to schedule, to plan **2** : to program (a computer, etc.)
progresar *vi* : to progress, to make progress
progresista *adj & nmf* : progressive
progresivo, -va *adj* : progressive, gradual
progreso *nm* : progress
prohibición *nf, pl* **-ciones** : ban, prohibition
prohibir {62} *vt* : to prohibit, to ban, to forbid
prohibitivo, -va *adj* : prohibitive
prohijar {5} *vt* ADOPTAR : to adopt
prójimo *nm* : neighbor, fellow man
prole *nf* : offspring, progeny
proletariado *nm* : proletariat, working class
proletario, -ria *adj & n* : proletarian
proliferar *vi* : to proliferate — **proliferación** *nf*
prolífico, -ca *adj* : prolific
prolijo, -ja *adj* : wordy, long-winded
prólogo *nm* : prologue, preface, foreword
prolongación *nf, pl* **-ciones** : extension, lengthening

prolongar {52} *vt* **1 :** to prolong **2 :** to extend, to lengthen — **prolongarse** *vr* CONTINUAR **:** to last, to continue

promediar *vt* **1 :** to average **2 :** to divide in half — *vi* **:** to be half over

promedio *nm* **1 :** average **2 :** middle, mid-point

promesa *nf* **:** promise

prometedor, -dora *adj* **:** promising, hopeful

prometer *vt* **:** to promise — *vi* **:** to show promise — **prometerse** *vr* COMPROMETERSE **:** to get engaged

prometido[1]**, -da** *adj* **:** engaged

prometido[2]**, -da** *n* NOVIO **:** fiancé *m,* fiancée *f*

prominente *adj* **:** prominent — **prominencia** *nf*

promiscuo, -cua *adj* **:** promiscuous — **promiscuidad** *nf*

promisorio, -ria *adj* **1 :** promising **2 :** promissory

promoción *nf, pl* **-ciones 1 :** promotion **2 :** class, year **3 :** play-off (in soccer)

promocionar *vt* **:** to promote — **promocional** *adj*

promontorio *nm* **:** promontory, headland

promotor, -tora *n* **:** promoter

promover {47} *vt* **1 :** to promote, to advance **2** FOMENTAR **:** to foster, to encourage **3** PROVOCAR **:** to provoke, to cause

promulgación *nf, pl* **-ciones 1 :** enactment **2 :** proclamation, enactment

promulgar {52} *vt* **1 :** to promulgate, to proclaim **2 :** to enact (a law or decree)

prono, -na *adj* **:** prone

pronombre *nm* **:** pronoun

pronosticar {72} *vt* **:** to predict, to forecast

pronóstico *nm* **1** PREDICCIÓN **:** forecast, prediction **2 :** prognosis

prontitud *nf* **1** PRESTEZA **:** promptness, speed **2 con ~ :** promptly, quickly

pronto[1] *adv* **1 :** quickly, promptly **2 :** soon **3 de ~ :** suddenly **4 lo más pronto posible :** as soon as possible **5 tan pronto como :** as soon as

pronto[2]**, -ta** *adj* **1** RÁPIDO **:** quick, speedy, prompt **2** PREPARADO **:** ready

pronunciación *nf, pl* **-ciones :** pronunciation

pronunciado, -da *adj* **1 :** pronounced, sharp, steep **2 :** marked, noticeable

pronunciar *vt* **1 :** to pronounce, to say **2 :** to give, to deliver (a speech) **3 pronunciar un fallo :** to pronounce sentence — **pronunciarse** *vr* **:** to declare oneself

propagación *nf, pl* **-ciones :** propagation, spreading

propaganda *nf* **1 :** propaganda **2** PUBLICIDAD **:** advertising

propagar {52} *vt* **1 :** to propagate **2 :** to spread, to disseminate — **propagarse** *vr*

propalar *vt* **1 :** to divulge **2 :** to spread

propano *nm* **:** propane

propasarse *vr* **:** to go too far, to overstep one's bounds

propensión *nf, pl* **-siones** INCLINACIÓN **:** inclination, propensity

propenso, -sa *adj* **:** prone, susceptible

propiamente *adv* **1 :** properly, correctly **2 :** exactly, precisely <propiamente dicho **:** strictly speaking>

propiciar *vt* **1 :** to propitiate **2 :** to favor, to foster

propicio, -cia *adj* **:** favorable, propitious

propiedad *nf* **1 :** property <propiedad privada **:** private property> **2 :** ownership **3** CUALIDAD **:** property, quality **4 :** suitability, appropriateness

propietario[1]**, -ria** *adj* **:** proprietary

propietario[2]**, -ria** *n* DUEÑO **:** owner, proprietor

propina *nf* **:** tip, gratuity

propinar *vt* **:** to give, to strike <propinar una paliza **:** to give a beating>

propio, -pia *adj* **1 :** own <su propia casa **:** his own house> <sus recursos propios **:** their own resources> **2** APROPIADO **:** appropriate, suitable **3** CARACTERÍSTICO **:** characteristic, typical **4** MISMO **:** oneself <el propio director **:** the director himself>

proponer {60} *vt* **1 :** to propose, to suggest **2 :** to nominate — **proponerse** *vr* **:** to intend, to plan, to set out <lo que se propone lo cumple **:** he does what he sets out to do>

proporción *nf, pl* **-ciones 1 :** proportion **2 :** ratio (in mathematics) **3 proporciones** *nfpl* **:** proportions, size <de grandes proporciones **:** very large>

proporcionado, -da *adj* **1 :** proportionate **2 :** proportioned <bien proporcionado **:** well-proportioned> — **proporcionadamente** *adv*

proporcional *adj* **:** proportional — **proporcionalmente** *adv*

proporcionar *vt* **1 :** to provide, to give **2 :** to proportion, to adapt

proposición *nf, pl* **-ciones :** proposal, proposition

propósito *nm* **1** INTENCIÓN **:** purpose, intention **2 a ~ :** by the way **3 a ~ :** on purpose, intentionally

propuesta *nf* PROPOSICIÓN **:** proposal

propulsar *vt* **1** IMPULSAR **:** to propel, to drive **2** PROMOVER **:** to promote, to encourage

propulsión *nf, pl* **-siones :** propulsion

propulsor *nm* **:** propellant

propuso, etc. → **proponer**

prorrata *nf* **1 :** share, quota **2 a ~ :** pro rata, proportionately

prórroga *nf* **1 :** extension, deferment **2 :** overtime (in sports)

prorrogar {52} *vt* **1 :** to extend (a deadline) **2 :** to postpone

prorrumpir *vi* **:** to burst forth, to break out <prorrumpí en lágrimas **:** I burst into tears>

prosa *nf* **:** prose

prosaico, -ca *adj* : prosaic, mundane

proscribir {33} *v* **1** PROHIBIR : to prohibit, to ban, to proscribe **2** DESTERRAR : to banish, to exile

proscripción *nf, pl* **-ciones 1** PROHIBICIÓN : ban, proscription **2** DESTIERRO : banishment

proscrito[1] *pp* → **proscribir**

proscrito[2], -ta *n* **1** DESTERRADO : exile **2** : outlaw

prosecución *nf, pl* **-ciones 1** : continuation **2** : pursuit

proseguir {75} *vt* **1** CONTINUAR : to continue **2** : to pursue (studies, goals) — *vi* : to continue, to go on

prosélito, -ta *n* : proselyte

prospección *nf, pl* **-ciones** : prospecting, exploration

prospectar *vi* : to prospect

prospecto *nm* : prospectus, leaflet, brochure

prosperar *vi* : to prosper, to thrive

prosperidad *nf* : prosperity

próspero, -ra *adj* : prosperous, flourishing

próstata *nf* : prostate

prostitución *nf, pl* **-ciones** : prostitution

prostituir {41} *vt* : to prostitute — **prostituirse** *vr* : to prostitute oneself

prostituto, -ta *n* : prostitute

protagonista *nmf* **1** : protagonist, main character **2** : leader

protagonizar {21} *vt* : to star in

protección *nf, pl* **-ciones** : protection

protector[1], -tora *adj* : protective

protector[2], -tora *n* **1** : protector, guardian **2** : patron

protector[3] *nm* : protector, guard <chaleco protector : chest protector>

protectorado *nm* : protectorate

proteger {15} *vt* : to protect, to defend — **protegerse** *vr*

protegido, -da *n* : protégé

proteína *nf* : protein

prótesis *nfs & pl* : prosthesis

protesta *nf* **1** : protest **2** *Mex* : promise, oath

protestante *adj & nmf* : Protestant

protestantismo *nm* : Protestantism

protestar *vi* : to protest, to object — *vt* **1** : to protest, to object to **2** : to declare, to profess

protocolo *nm* : protocol

protón *nm, pl* **protones** : proton

protoplasma *nm* : protoplasm

prototipo *nm* : prototype

protozoario *or* **protozoo** *nm* : protozoan

protuberancia *nf* : protuberance — **protuberante** *adj*

provecho *nm* : benefit, advantage

provechoso, -sa *adj* BENEFICIOSO : beneficial, profitable, useful — **provechosamente** *adv*

proveedor, -dora *n* : provider, supplier

proveer {63} *vt* : to provide, to supply — **proveerse** *vr* ~ **de** : to obtain, to supply oneself with

provenir {87} *vi* ~ **de** : to come from

provenzal[1] *adj* : Provençal

provenzal[2] *nmf* : Provençal

provenzal[3] *nm* : Provençal (language)

proverbio *nm* REFRÁN : proverb — **proverbial** *adj*

providencia *nf* **1** : providence, foresight **2** : Providence, God **3 providencias** *nfpl* : steps, measures

providencial *adj* : providential

provincia *nf* : province — **provincial** *adj*

provinciano, -na *adj* : provincial, unsophisticated

provisión *nf, pl* **-siones** : provision

provisional *adj* : provisional, temporary

provisionalmente *adv* : provisionally, tentatively

provisorio, -ria *adj* : provisional, temporary

provisto *pp* → **proveer**

provocación *nf, pl* **-ciones** : provocation

provocador[1], -dora *adj* : provocative, provoking

provocador[2], -dora *n* AGITADOR : agitator

provocar {72} *vt* **1** CAUSAR : to provoke, to cause **2** IRRITAR : to provoke, to pique

provocativo, -va *adj* : provocative

proxeneta *nmf* : pimp *m*

próximamente *adv* : shortly, soon

proximidad *nf* **1** : nearness, proximity **2 proximidades** *nfpl* : vicinity

próximo, -ma *adj* **1** : near, close <la Navidad está próxima : Christmas is almost here> **2** SIGUIENTE : next, following <la próxima semana : the following week>

proyección *nf, pl* **-ciones 1** : projection **2** : showing, screening (of a film) **3** : range, influence, diffusion

proyectar *vt* **1** : to plan **2** LANZAR : to throw, to hurl **3** : to project, to cast (light or shadow) **4** : to show, to screen (a film)

proyectil *nm* : projectile, missile

proyecto *nm* **1** : plan, project **2 proyecto de ley** : bill

proyector *nm* **1** : projector **2** : spotlight

prudencia *nf* : prudence, care, discretion

prudente *adj* : prudent, sensible, reasonable

prueba[1], etc. → **probar**

prueba[2] *nf* **1** : proof, evidence **2** : trial, test **3** : proof (in printing or photography) **4** : event, qualifying round (in sports) **5 a prueba de agua** : waterproof **6 prueba de fuego** : acid test **7 poner a prueba** : to put to the test

prurito *nm* **1** : itching **2** : desire, urge

psicoanálisis *nm* : psychoanalysis — **psicoanalista** *nmf*

psicoanalítico, -ca *adj* : psychoanalytic

psicoanalizar {21} *vt* : to psychoanalyze

psicología *nf* : psychology

psicológico, -ca *adj* : psychological — **psicológicamente** *adv*

psicólogo, -ga *n* : psychologist

psicópata *nmf* : psychopath

psicopático, -ca *adj* : psycopathic

psicosis *nfs & pl* : psychosis

psicosomático, -ca *adj* : psychosomatic

psicoterapeuta *nmf* : psychotherapist

psicoterapia *nf* : psychotherapy

psicótico, -ca *adj & n* : psychotic

psique *nf* : psyche

psiquiatra *nmf* : psychiatrist

psiquiatría *nf* : psychiatry

psiquiátrico[1], -ca *adj* : psychiatric

psiquiátrico[2] *nm* : mental hospital

psíquico, -ca *adj* : psychic

psiquis *nfs & pl* : psyche

psoriasis *nf* : psoriasis

ptomaína *nf* : ptomaine

púa *nf* **1** : barb <alambre de púas : barbed wire> **2** : tooth (of a comb) **3** : quill, spine

pubertad *nf* : puberty

pubiano → **púbico**

púbico, -ca *adj* : pubic

publicación *nf, pl* **-ciones** : publication

publicar {72} *vt* **1** : to publish **2** DIVULGAR : to divulge, to disclose

publicidad *nf* **1** : publicity **2** : advertising

publicista *nmf* : publicist

publicitar *vt* **1** : to publicize **2** : to advertise

publicitario, -ria *adj* : advertising, publicity <agencia publicitaria : advertising agency>

público[1], -ca *adj* : public — **públicamente** *adv*

público[2] *nm* **1** : public **2** : audience, spectators *pl*

puchero *nm* **1** : pot **2** : stew **3** : pout <hacer pucheros : to pout>

pucho *nm* **1** : waste, residue **2** : cigarette butt **3 a puchos** : little by little, bit by bit

púdico, -ca *adj* : chaste, modest

pudiente *adj* **1** : powerful **2** : rich, wealthy

pudín *nm, pl* **pudines** BUDÍN : pudding

pudo, etc. → **poder**

pudor *nm* : modesty, reserve

pudoroso, -sa *adj* : modest, reserved, shy

pudrir {59} *vt* **1** : to rot **2** *fam* : to annoy, to upset — **pudrirse** *vr* **1** : to rot **2** : to languish

pueblerino, -na *adj* : provincial, countrified

puebla, etc. → **poblar**

pueblo *nm* **1** NACIÓN : people **2** : common people **3** ALDEA, POBLADO : town, village

puede, etc. → **poder**

puente *nm* **1** : bridge <puente levadizo : drawbridge> **2** : denture, bridge **3 puente aéreo** : airlift

puerco[1], -ca *adj* : dirty, filthy

puerco[2], -ca *n* **1** CERDO, MARRANO : pig, hog **2** : pig, dirty or greedy person **3 puerco espín** : porcupine

pueril *adj* : childish, puerile

puerro *nm* : leek

puerta *nf* **1** : door, entrance, gate **2 a puerta cerrada** : behind closed doors

puerto *nm* **1** : port, harbor **2** : mountain pass **3 puerto marítimo** : seaport

puertorriqueño, -ña *adj & n* : Puerto Rican

pues *conj* **1** : since, because, for <no puedo ir, pues no tengo plata : I can't go, since I don't have any money> <lo hace, pues a él le gusta : he does it because he likes to> **2** (*used interjectionally*) : well, then <¡pues claro que sí! : well, of course!> <¡pues no voy! : well then, I'm not going!>

puesta *nf* **1** : setting <puesta del sol : sunset> **2** : laying (of eggs) **3 puesta a punto** : tune-up **4 puesta en marcha** : start, starting up

puestero, -ra *n* : seller, vendor

puesto[1] *pp* → **poner**

puesto[2], -ta *adj* : dressed <bien puesto : well-dressed>

puesto[3] *nm* **1** LUGAR, SITIO : place, position **2** : position, job **3** : kiosk, stand, stall **4 puesto que** : since, given that

pugilato *nm* BOXEO : boxing, pugilism

pugilista *nm* BOXEADOR : boxer, pugilist

pugna *nf* **1** CONFLICTO, LUCHA : conflict, struggle **2 en ∼** : at odds, in conflict

pugnar *vi* LUCHAR : to fight, to strive, to struggle

pugnaz *adj* : pugnacious

pujante *adj* : mighty, powerful

pujanza *nf* : strength, vigor <pujanza económica : economic strength>

pulcritud *nf* **1** : neatness, tidiness **2** ESMERO : meticulousness

pulcro, -cra *adj* **1** : clean, neat **2** : exquisite, delicate, refined

pulga *nf* **1** : flea **2 tener malas pulgas** : to be bad-tempered

pulgada *nf* : inch

pulgar *nm* **1** : thumb **2** : big toe

pulir *vt* **1** : to polish, to shine **2** REFINAR : to refine, to perfect

pulla *nf* **1** : cutting remark, dig, gibe **2** : obscenity

pulmón *nm, pl* **pulmones** : lung

pulmonar *adj* : pulmonary

pulmonía *nf* NEUMONÍA : pneumonia

pulpa *nf* : pulp, flesh

pulpería *nf* : small grocery store

púlpito *nm* : pulpit

pulpo *nm* : octopus

pulsación *nf, pl* **-ciones 1** : beat, pulsation, throb **2** : keystroke

pulsar *vt* **1** APRETAR : to press, to push **2** : to strike (a key) **3** : to assess — *vi* : to beat, to throb

pulsera *nf* : bracelet

pulso *nm* **1 :** pulse <tomarle el pulso a alguien : to take someone's pulse> <tomarle el pulso a la opinión : to sound out opinion> **2 :** steadiness (of hand) <dibujo a pulso : freehand sketch>

pulular *vi* ABUNDAR : to abound, to swarm <en el río pululan los peces : the river is teeming with fish>

pulverizador *nm* **1 :** atomizer, spray **2 :** spray gun

pulverizar {21} *vt* **1 :** to pulverize, to crush **2 :** to spray

puma *nf* : cougar, puma

puna *nf* : bleak Andean tableland

punción *nf, pl* **punciones :** puncture

punible *adj* : punishable

punitivo, -va *adj* : punitive

punce, etc. → **punzar**

punta *nf* **1 :** tip, end <punta del dedo : fingertip> <en la punta de la lengua : at the tip of one's tongue> **2 :** point (of a weapon or pencil) <punta de lanza : spearhead> **3 :** point, headland **4 :** bunch, lot <una punta de ladrones : a bunch of thieves> **5 a punta de :** by, by dint of

puntada *nf* **1 :** stitch (in sewing) **2** PUNZADA : sharp pain, stitch, twinge **3** *Mex* : witticism, quip

puntal *nm* **1 :** prop, support **2 :** stanchion

puntapié *nm* PATADA : kick

puntazo *nm* CORNADA : wound (from a goring)

puntear *vt* **1 :** to pluck (a guitar) **2 :** to lead (in sports)

puntería *nf* : aim, marksmanship

puntero *nm* **1 :** pointer **2 :** leader

puntiagudo, -da *adj* : sharp, pointed

puntilla *nf* **1 :** lace edging **2 :** dagger (in bullfighting) **3 de puntillas :** on tiptoe

puntilloso, -sa *adj* : punctilious

punto *nm* **1 :** dot, point **2 :** period (in punctuation) **3 :** item, question **4 :** spot, place **5 :** moment, stage, degree **6 :** point (in a score) **7 :** stitch **8 en ~ :** on the dot, sharp <a las dos en punto : at two o'clock sharp> **9 al punto :** at once **10 a punto fijo :** exactly, certainly **11 dos puntos :** colon **12 hasta cierto punto :** up to a point **13 punto decimal :** decimal point **14 punto de vista :** point of view **15 punto y coma :** semicolon **16 y punto :** period <es el mejor que hay y punto : it's the best there is, period> **17 puntos cardinales :** points of the compass

puntuación *nf, pl* **-ciones 1 :** punctuation **2 :** scoring, score, grade

puntual *adj* **1 :** prompt, punctual **2 :** exact, accurate — **puntualmente** *adv*

puntualidad *nf* **1 :** promptness, punctuality **2 :** exactness, accuracy

puntualizar {21} *vt* **1 :** to specify, to state **2 :** to point out

puntuar {3} *vt* : to punctuate — *vi* : to score points

punzada *nf* : sharp pain, twinge, stitch

punzante *adj* **1 :** sharp **2** CÁUSTICO : biting, caustic

punzar {21} *vt* : to pierce, to puncture

punzón *nm, pl* **punzones 1 :** awl **2 :** hole punch

puñado *nm* **1 :** handful **2 a puñados :** lots of, by the handful

puñal *nm* DAGA : dagger

puñalada *nf* : stab, stab wound

puñetazo *nm* : punch (with the fist)

puño *nm* **1 :** fist **2 :** handful, fistful **3 :** cuff (of a shirt) **4 :** handle, hilt

pupila *nf* : pupil (of the eye)

pupilo, -la *n* **1 :** pupil, student **2 :** ward, charge

pupitre *nm* : writing desk

puré *nm* : purée <puré de papas : mashed potatoes>

pureza *nf* : purity

purga *nf* **1 :** laxative **2 :** purge

purgante *adj & nm* : laxative, purgative

purgar {52} *vt* **1 :** to purge, to cleanse **2 :** to liquidate (in politics) **3 :** to give a laxative to — **purgarse** *vr* **1 :** to take a laxative **2 ~ de :** to purge oneself of

purgatorio *nm* : purgatory

purgue, etc. → **purgar**

purificador *nm* : purifier

purificar {72} *vt* : to purify — **purificación** *nf*

puritano[1]**, -na** *adj* : puritanical, puritan

puritano[2]**, -na** *n* **1 :** Puritan **2 :** puritan

puro[1] *adv* : sheer, much <de puro terco : out of sheer stubbornness>

puro[2]**, -ra** *adj* **1 :** pure <aire puro : fresh air> **2 :** plain, simple, sheer <por pura curiosidad : from sheer curiosity> **3 :** only, just <emplean puras mujeres : they only employ women> **4 pura sangre :** Thoroughbred horse

puro[3] *nm* : cigar

púrpura *nf* : purple

purpúreo, -rea *adj* : purple

purpurina *nf* : glitter (for decoration)

pus *nm* : pus

pusilánime *adj* COBARDE : pusillanimous, cowardly

puso, etc. → **poner**

pústula *nf* : pustule, pimple

puta *nf* : whore, slut

putrefacción *nf, pl* **-ciones :** putrefaction

putrefacto, -ta *adj* **1** PODRIDO : putrid, rotten **2 :** decayed

pútrido, -da *adj* : putrid, rotten

puya *nf* **1 :** point (of a lance) **2 lanzar una puya :** to gibe, to taunt

Q

q *nf* : eighteenth letter of the Spanish alphabet

que[1] *conj* **1** : that <dice que está listo : he says that he's ready> <espero que lo haga : I hope that he does it> **2** : than <más que nada : more than anything> **3** (*implying permission or desire*) <¡que entre! : send him in!> <¡que te vaya bien! : I wish you well!> **4** (*indicating a reason or cause*) <¡cuidado, que te caes! : be careful, you're about to fall!> <no provoques al perro, que te va a morder : don't provoke the dog or (else) he'll bite> **5 es que** : the thing is that, I'm afraid that **6 yo que tú** : if I were you

que[2] *pron* **1** : who, that <la niña que viene : the girl who is coming> **2** : whom, that <los alumnos que enseñé : the students that I taught> **3** : that, which <el carro que me gusta : the car that I like> **4 el (la, lo, las, los) que** → **el[1], la[1], lo[1], los[1]**

qué[1] *adv* : how, what <¡qué bonito! : how pretty!>

qué[2] *adj* : what, which <¿qué hora es? : what time is it?>

qué[3] *pron* : what <¿qué quieres? : what do you want?>

quebracho *nm* : quebracho (tree)

quebrada *nf* DESFILADERO : ravine, gorge

quebradizo, -za *adj* FRÁGIL : breakable, delicate, fragile

quebrado[1], -da *adj* **1** : bankrupt **2** : rough, uneven **3** ROTO : broken

quebrado[2] *nm* : fraction

quebrantamiento *nm* **1** : breaking **2** : deterioration, weakening

quebrantar *vt* **1** : to break, to split, to crack **2** : to weaken **3** : to violate (a law or contract)

quebranto *nm* **1** : break, breaking **2** AFLICCIÓN : affliction, grief **3** PÉRDIDA : loss

quebrar {55} *vt* **1** ROMPER : to break **2** DOBLAR : to bend, to twist — *vi* **1** : to go bankrupt **2** : to fall out, to break up — **quebrarse** *vr*

queda *nf* : curfew

quedar *vi* **1** PERMANECER : to remain, to stay **2** : to be <quedamos contentos con las mejoras : we were pleased with the improvements> **3** : to be situated <queda muy lejos : it's very far, it's too far away> **4** : to be left <quedan sólo dos alternativas : there are only two options left> **5** : to fit, to suit <estos zapatos no me quedan : these shoes don't fit> **6 quedar bien (mal)** : to turn out well (badly) **7 ~ en** : to agree, to arrange <¿en qué quedamos? : what's the arrangement, then?> — **quedarse** *vr* **1** : to stay <se quedó en casa : she stayed at home> **2** : to keep on <se quedó esperando : he kept on waiting> **3 quedarse atrás** : to stay behind <no quedarse atrás : to be no slouch> **4 ~ con** : to remain <me quedé con hambre después de comer : I was still hungry after I ate>

quedo[1] *adv* : softly, quietly

quedo[2], -da *adj* : quiet, still

quehacer *nm* **1** : work **2 quehaceres** *nmpl* : chores

queja *nf* : complaint

quejarse *vr* **1** : to complain **2** : to groan, to moan

quejido *nm* **1** : groan, moan **2** : whine, whimper

quejoso, -sa *adj* : complaining, whining

quejumbroso, -sa *adj* : querulous, whining

quema *nf* **1** FUEGO : fire **2** : burning

quemado, -da *adj* **1** : burned, burnt **2** : annoyed **3** : burned-out

quemador *nm* : burner

quemadura *nf* : burn

quemar *vt* : to burn, to set fire to — *vi* : to be burning hot — **quemarse** *vr*

quemarropa *nf* **a ~** : point-blank

quemazón *nf, pl* **-zones 1** : burning **2** : intense heat **3** : itch **4** : cutting remark

quena *nf* : Peruvian reed flute

quepa, etc. → **caber**

querella *nf* **1** : complaint **2** : lawsuit

querellante *nmf* : plaintiff

querellarse *vr* **~ contra** : to bring suit against, to sue

querer[1] {64} *vt* **1** DESEAR : to want, to desire <quiere ser profesor : he wants to be a teacher> <¿cuánto quieres por esta computadora? : how much do you want for this computer?> **2** : to love, to like, to be fond of <te quiero : I love you> **3** (*indicating a request*) <¿quieres pasarme la leche? : please pass the milk> **4 querer decir** : to mean **5 sin ~** : unintentionally — *vi* : like, want <si quieras : if you like>

querer[2] *nm* : love, affection

querido[1], -da *adj* : dear, beloved

querido[2], -da *n* : dear, sweetheart

queroseno *nm* : kerosene

querúbico, -ca *adj* : cherubic

querrá, etc. → **querer**

querubín *nm, pl* **-bines** : cherub

quesadilla *nf* : quesadilla

quesería *nf* : cheese shop

queso *nm* : cheese

quetzal *nm* **1** : quetzal (bird) **2** : monetary unit of Guatemala

quicio *nm* **1 estar fuera de quicio** : to be beside oneself **2 sacar de quicio** : to exasperate, to drive crazy

quid *nm* : crux, gist <el quid de la cuestión : the crux of the matter>

quiebra[1], etc. → **quebrar**

quiebra[2] *nf* **1 :** break, crack **2** BANCARROTA **:** failure, bankruptcy

quien *pron, pl* **quienes 1 :** who, whom <no sé quien ganará : I don't know who will win> <las personas con quienes trabajo : the people with whom I work> **2 :** whoever, whomever <quien quiere salir que salga : whoever wants to can leave> **3 :** anyone, some people <hay quienes no están de acuerdo : some people don't agree>

quién *pron, pl* **quiénes 1 :** who, whom <¿quién sabe? : who knows?> <¿con quién hablo? : with whom am I speaking?> **2 de ~ :** whose <¿de quién es este libro? : whose book is this?>

quienquiera *pron, pl* **quienesquiera :** whoever, whomever

quiere, etc. → **querer**

quieto, -ta *adj* **1 :** calm, quiet **2** INMÓVIL **:** still

quietud *nf* **1 :** calm, tranquility **2** INMOVILIDAD **:** stillness

quijada *nf* **:** jaw, jawbone

quijotesco, -ca *adj* **:** quixotic

quilate *nm* **:** karat

quilla *nf* **:** keel

quimera *nf* **:** chimera, illusion

quimérico, -ca *adj* **:** chimeric, fanciful

química *nf* **:** chemistry

químico[1], -ca *adj* **:** chemical

químico[2], -ca *n* **:** chemist

quimioterapia *nf* **:** chemotherapy

quimono *nm* **:** kimono

quince *adj & nm* **:** fifteen

quinceañero, -ra *n* **:** fifteen-year-old, teenager

quinceavo[1], -va *adj* **:** fifteenth

quinceavo[2] *nm* **:** fifteenth (fraction)

quincena *nf* **:** two week period, fortnight

quincenal *adj* **:** bimonthly, twice a month

quingombó *nm* **:** okra

quincuagésimo[1], -ma *adj* **:** fiftieth, fifty-

quincuagésimo[2], -ma *n* **:** fiftieth, fifty- (in a series)

quiniela *nf* **:** sports lottery

quinientos[1], -tas *adj* **:** five hundred

quinientos[2] *nms & pl* **:** five hundred

quinina *nf* **:** quinine

quino *nm* **:** cinchona

quinqué *nm* **:** oil lamp

quinquenal *adj* **:** five-year <un plan quinquenal : a five-year plan>

quinta *nf* **:** country house, villa

quintaesencia *nf* **:** quintessence — **quintaesencial** *adj*

quintal *nm* **:** hundredweight

quinteto *nm* **:** quintet

quintillizo, -za *n* **:** quintuplet

quinto, -ta *adj* **:** fifth — **quinto, -ta** *n*

quíntuplo, -la *adj* **:** quintuple, fivefold

quiosco *nm* **1 :** kiosk **2 :** newsstand **3 quiosco de música :** bandstand

quirófano *nm* **:** operating room

quiromancia *nf* **:** palmistry

quiropráctica *nf* **:** chiropractic

quiropráctico, -ca *n* **:** chiropractor

quirúrgico, -ca *adj* **:** surgical — **quirúrgicamente** *adv*

quiso, etc. → **querer**

quisquilloso[1], -sa *adj* **:** fastidious, fussy

quisquilloso[2], -sa *n* **:** fussy person, fussbudget

quiste *nm* **:** cyst

quitaesmalte *nm* **:** nail polish remover

quitamanchas *nms & pl* **:** stain remover

quitanieves *nms & pl* **:** snowplow

quitar *vt* **1 :** to remove, to take away **2 :** to take off (clothes) **3 :** to get rid of, to relieve — **quitarse** *vr* **1 :** to withdraw, to leave **2 :** to take off (one's clothes) **3 ~ de :** to give up (a habit) **4 quitar de encima :** to get rid of

quitasol *nm* **:** parasol

quiteño[1], -ña *adj* **:** of or from Quito

quiteño[2], -ña *n* **:** person from Quito

quizá *or* **quizás** *adv* **:** maybe, perhaps

quórum *nm, pl* **quórums :** quorum

R

r *nf* **:** nineteenth letter of the Spanish alphabet

rábano *nm* **1 :** radish **2 rábano picante :** horseradish

rabí *nmf, pl* **rabíes :** rabbi

rabia *nf* **1** HIDROFOBIA **:** rabies, hydrophobia **2 :** rage, anger

rabiar *vi* **1 :** to rage, to be furious **2 :** to be in great pain **3 a ~** *fam* **:** like crazy, like mad

rabieta *nf* BERRINCHE **:** tantrum

rabino, -na *n* **:** rabbi

rabioso, -sa *adj* **1 :** enraged, furious **2 :** rabid

rabo *nm* **1** COLA **:** tail **2 el rabo del ojo :** the corner of one's eye

racha *nf* **1 :** gust of wind **2 :** run, series, string <racha perdedora : losing streak>

racheado, -da *adj* **:** gusty, windy

racial *adj* **:** racial

racimo *nm* **:** bunch, cluster <un racimo de uvas : a bunch of grapes>

raciocinio *nm* **:** reason, reasoning

ración *nf, pl* **raciones 1 :** share, ration **2** PORCIÓN **:** portion, helping

racional *adj* **:** rational, reasonable — **racionalmente** *adv*

racionalidad *nf* **:** rationality

racionalización *nf, pl* **-ciones** : rationalization
racionalizar {21} *vt* **1** : to rationalize **2** : to streamline
racionamiento *nm* : rationing
racionar *vt* : to ration
racismo *nm* : racism
racista *adj & nmf* : racist
radar *nm* : radar
radiación *nf, pl* **-ciones** : radiation, irradiation
radiactividad *nf* : radioactivity
radiactivo, -va *adj* : radioactive
radiador *nm* : radiator
radial *adj* **1** : radial **2** : radio, broadcasting <emisora radial : radio transmitter>
radiante *adj* : radiant
radiar *vt* **1** : to radiate **2** : to irradiate **3** : to broadcast (on the radio)
radical[1] *adj* : radical, extreme — **radicalmente** *adv*
radical[2] *nmf* : radical
radicalismo *nm* : radicalism
radicar {72} *vi* **1** : to be found, to lie **2** ARRAIGAR : to take root — **radicarse** *vr* : to settle, to establish oneself
radio[1] *nm* **1** : radius **2** : radium
radio[2] *nmf* : radio
radioactividad *nf* : radioactivity
radioactivo, -va *adj* : radioactive
radioaficionado, -da *n* : ham radio operator
radiodifusión *nf, pl* **-siones** : radio broadcasting
radiodifusora *nf* : radio station
radioemisora *nf* : radio station
radiofaro *nm* : radio beacon
radiofónico, -ca *adj* : radio <estación radiofónica pública : public radio station>
radiofrecuencia *nf* : radio frequency
radiografía *nf* : X ray (photograph)
radiografiar {85} *vt* : to x-ray
radiología *nf* : radiology
radiólogo, -ga *n* : radiologist
radón *nm* : radon
raer {65} *vt* RASPAR : to scrape, to scrape off
ráfaga *nf* **1** : gust (of wind) **2** : flash, burst <una ráfaga de luz : a flash of light>
raid *nm CA, Mex fam* : lift, ride
raído, -da *adj* : worn, shabby
raiga, etc. → **raer**
raíz *nf, pl* **raíces** **1** : root **2** : origin, source **3** **a raíz de** : following, as a result of **4** **echar raíces** : to take root
raja *nf* **1** : crack, slit **2** : slice, wedge
rajá *nm* : raja
rajadura *nf* : crack, split
rajar *vt* HENDER : to crack, to split — *vi* **1** *fam* : to chatter **2** *fam* : to boast, to brag — **rajarse** *vr* **1** : to crack, to split open **2** *fam* : to back out
rajatabla *adv* **a ~** : strictly, to the letter
ralea *nf* : kind, sort, ilk <son de la misma valea : they're two of a kind>
ralentí *nm* **dejar al ralentí** : to leave (a motor) idling
rallado, -da *adj* **1** : grated **2** **pan rallado** : bread crumbs *pl*
rallador *nm* : grater
rallar *vt* : to grate
ralo, -la *adj* : sparse, thin
rama *nf* : branch
ramaje *nm* : branches *pl*
ramal *nm* **1** : branchline **2** : halter, strap
ramera *nf* : harlot, prostitute
ramificación *nf, pl* **-ciones** : ramification
ramificarse {72} *vr* : to branch out, to divide into branches
ramillete *nm* **1** RAMO : bouquet **2** : select group, cluster
ramo *nm* **1** : branch **2** RAMILLETE : bouquet **3** : division (of science or industry) **4** **Domingo de Ramos** : Palm Sunday
rampa *nf* : ramp, incline
rana *nf* **1** : frog **2** **rana toro** : bullfrog
ranchera *nf Mex* : traditional folk song
ranchería *nf* : settlement
ranchero, -ra *n* : rancher, farmer
rancho *nm* **1** : ranch, farm **2** : hut **3** : settlement, camp **4** : food, mess (for soldiers, etc.)
rancio, -cia *adj* **1** : aged, mellow (of wine) **2** : ancient, old **3** : rancid
rango *nm* **1** : rank, status **2** : high social standing **3** : pomp, splendor
ranúnculo *nm* : buttercup
ranura *nf* : groove, slot
rapacidad *nf* : rapacity
rapar *vt* **1** : to crop **2** : to shave
rapaz[1] *adj, pl* **rapaces** : rapacious, predatory
rapaz[2]**, -paza** *n, mpl* **rapaces** : youngster, child
rape *nm* : close haircut
rapé *nm* : snuff
rapidez *nf* : rapidity, speed
rápido[1] *adv* : quickly, fast <¡manejas tan rápido! : you drive so fast!>
rápido[2]**, -da** *adj* : rapid, quick — **rápidamente** *adv*
rápido[3] *nm* **1** : express train **2** **rápidos** *nmpl* : rapids
rapiña *nf* **1** : plunder, pillage **2** **ave de rapiña** : bird of prey
raposa *nf* : vixen (fox)
rapsodia *nf* : rhapsody
raptar *vt* SEQUESTRAR : to abduct, to kidnap
rapto *nm* **1** SECUESTRO : kidnapping, abduction **2** ARREBATO : fit, outburst
raptor, -tora *n* SECUESTRADOR : kidnapper
raque *nm* : beachcombing
raquero, -ra *n* : beachcomber
raqueta *nf* **1** : racket (in sports) **2** : snowshoe
raquítico, -ca *adj* **1** : scrawny, weak **2** : measly, skimpy
raquitismo *nm* : rickets
raramente *adv* : seldom, rarely

rareza *nf* **1** : rarity **2** : peculiarity, oddity

raro, -ra *adj* **1** EXTRAÑO : odd, strange, peculiar **2** : unusual, rare **3** : exceptional **4 rara vez** : seldom, rarely

ras *nm* **a ras de** : level with

rasar *vt* **1** : to skim, to graze **2** : to level

rascacielos *nms & pl* : skyscraper

rascar {72} *vt* **1** : to scratch **2** : to scrape — **rascarse** *vr* : to scratch an itch

rasgadura *nf* : tear, rip

rasgar {52} *vt* : to rip, to tear — **rasgarse** *vr*

rasgo *nm* **1** : stroke (of a pen) <a grandes rasgos : in broad outlines> **2** CARACTERÍSTICA : trait, characteristic **3** : gesture, deed **4 rasgos** *nmpl* FACCIONES : features

rasgón *nm, pl* **rasgones** : rip, tear

rasgue, etc. → **rasgar**

rasguear *vt* : to strum

rasguñar *vt* **1** : to scratch **2** : to sketch, to outline

rasguño *nm* **1** : scratch **2** : sketch

raso[1], -sa *adj* **1** : level, flat **2 soldado raso** : private (in the army) <los soldados rasos : the ranks>

raso[2] *nm* : satin

raspadura *nf* **1** : scratching, scraping **2 raspaduras** *nfpl* : scrapings

raspar *vt* **1** : to scrape **2** : to file down, to smooth — *vi* : to be rough

rasque, etc. → **rascar**

rastra *nf* **1** : harrow **2 a rastras** : by dragging, unwillingly

rastrear *vt* **1** : to track, to trace **2** : to comb, to search **3** : to trawl

rastrero, -ra *adj* **1** : creeping, crawling **2** : vile, despicable

rastrillar *vt* : to rake, to harrow

rastrillo *nm* **1** : rake **2** *Mex* : razor

rastro *nm* **1** PISTA : trail, track **2** VESTIGIO : trace, sign

rastrojo *nm* : stubble (of plants)

rasurar *vt* AFEITAR : to shave — **rasurarse** *vr*

rata[1] *nm fam* : pickpocket, thief

rata[2] *nf* **1** : rat **2** *Col, Pan, Peru* : rate, percentage

ratear *vt* : to pilfer, to steal

ratero, -ra *n* : petty thief

ratificación *nf, pl* **-ciones** : ratification

ratificar {72} *vt* **1** : to ratify **2** : to confirm

rato *nm* **1** : while **2 pasar el rato** : to pass the time **3 a cada rato** : all the time, constantly <les sacaba dinero a cada rato : he was always taking money from them> **4 al poco rato** : later, shortly after

ratón[1], -tona *n, mpl* **ratones 1** : mouse **2 ratón de biblioteca** *fam* : bookworm

ratón[2] *nm, pl* **ratones 1** : (computer) mouse **2** *CoRi* : biceps

ratonera *nf* : mousetrap

raudal *nm* **1** : torrent **2 a raudales** : in abundance

raya[1], etc. → **raer**

raya[2] *nf* **1** : line **2** : stripe **3** : skate, ray **4** : part (in the hair) **5** : crease (in clothing)

rayar *vt* **1** ARAÑAR : to scratch **2** : to scrawl on, to mark up <rayaron las paredes : they covered the walls with graffiti> — *vi* **1** : to scratch **2** AMANECER : to dawn, to break <al rayar el alba : at break of day> **3 ~ con** : to be adjacent to, to be next to **4 ~ en** : to border on, to verge on <su respuesta raya en lo ridículo : his answer borders on the ridiculous> — **rayarse** *vr*

rayo *nm* **1** : ray, beam <rayo láser : laser beam> <rayo de gamma : gamma ray> <rayo de sol : sunbeam> **2** RELÁMPAGO : lightning bolt **3 rayo X** : X ray

rayón *nm, pl* **rayones** : rayon

raza *nf* **1** : race <raza humana : human race> **2** : breed, strain **3 de ~** : thoroughbred, pedigreed

razón *nf, pl* **razones 1** MOTIVO : reason, motive <en razón de : by reason of, because of> **2** JUSTICIA : rightness, justice <tener razón : to be right> **3** : reasoning, sense <perder la razón : to lose one's mind> **4** : ratio, proportion

razonable *adj* : reasonable — **razonablemente** *adv*

razonado, -da *adj* : itemized, detailed

razonamiento *nm* : reasoning

razonar *v* : to reason, to think

reabastecimiento *nm* : replenishment

reabierto *pp* → **reabrir**

reabrir {2} *vt* : to reopen — **reabrirse** *vr*

reacción *nf, pl* **-ciones 1** : reaction **2 motor a reacción** : jet engine

reaccionar *vi* : to react, to respond

reaccionario, -ria *adj & n* : reactionary

reacio, -cia *adj* : resistant, opposed

reacondicionar *vt* : to recondition

reactor *nm* **1** : reactor <reactor nuclear : nuclear reactor> **2** : jet engine **3** : jet airplane, jet

reafirmar *vt* : to reaffirm, to assert, to strengthen

reajustar *vt* : to readjust, to adjust

reajuste *nm* : readjustment <reajuste de precios : price increase>

real *adj* **1** : real, true **2** : royal

realce *nm* **1** : embossing, relief **2 dar realce** : to highlight, to bring out

realeza *nf* : royalty

realidad *nf* **1** : reality **2 en ~** : in truth, actually

realinear *vt* : to realign

realismo *nm* **1** : realism **2** : royalism

realista[1] *adj* **1** : realistic **2** : realist **3** : royalist

realista[2] *nmf* **1** : realist **2** : royalist

realización *nf, pl* **-ciones** : execution, realization

realizar {21} *vt* **1** : to carry out, to execute **2** : to produce, to direct (a film or play) **3 :** to fulfill, to achieve **4 :** to realize (a profit) — **realizarse** *vr* **1 :** to come true **2 :** to fulfill oneself

realmente *adv* **:** really, in reality

realzar {21} *vt* **1 :** to heighten, to raise **2 :** to highlight, to enhance

reanimación *nf, pl* **-ciones :** revival, resuscitation

reanimar *vt* **1 :** to revive, to restore **2 :** to resuscitate — **reanimarse** *vr* **:** to come around, to recover

reanudar *vt* **:** to resume, to renew — **reanadarse** *vr* **:** to resume, to continue

reaparecer {53} *vi* **1 :** to reappear **2 :** to make a comeback

reaparición *nf, pl* **-ciones :** reappearance

reapertura *nf* **:** reopening

reata *nf* **1 :** rope **2** *Mex* **:** lasso, lariat **3 de ~ :** single file

reavivar *vt* **:** to revive, to reawaken

rebaja *nf* **1 :** reduction **2** DESCUENTO **:** discount **3 rebajas** *nfpl* **:** sale

rebajar *vt* **1 :** to reduce, to lower **2 :** to lessen, to diminish **3 :** to humiliate — **rebajarse** *vr* **: 1 :** to humble oneself **2 rebajarse a :** to stoop to

rebanada *nf* **:** slice

rebañar *vt* **:** to mop up, to sop up

rebaño *nm* **1 :** flock **2 :** herd

rebasar *vt* **1 :** to surpass, to exceed **2** *Mex* **:** to pass, to overtake

rebatiña *nf* **:** scramble, fight (over something)

rebatir *vt* REFUTAR **:** to refute

rebato *nm* **1 :** surprise attack **2 tocar a rebato :** to sound the alarm

rebelarse *vr* **:** to rebel

rebelde[1] *adj* **:** rebellious, unruly

rebelde[2] *nmf* **1 :** rebel **2 :** defaulter

rebeldía *nf* **1 :** rebelliousness **2 en ~ :** in default

rebelión *nf, pl* **-liones :** rebellion

rebobinar *vt* **:** to rewind

reborde *nm* **:** border, flange, rim

rebosante *adj* **:** brimming, overflowing <rebosante de salud : brimming with health>

rebosar *vi* **1 :** to overflow **2 ~ de :** to abound in, to be bursting with — *vt* **:** to radiate

rebotar *vi* **1 :** to bounce **2 :** to ricochet, to rebound

rebote *nm* **1 :** bounce **2 :** rebound, ricochet

rebozar {21} *vt* **:** to coat in batter

rebozo *nm* **1 :** shawl, wrap **2 sin ~ :** frankly, openly

rebullir {38} *v* **:** to move, to stir — **rebullirse** *vr*

rebuscado, -da *adj* **:** affected, pretentious

rebuscar {72} *vi* **:** to search thoroughly

rebuznar *vi* **:** to bray

rebuzno *nm* **:** bray, braying

recabar *vt* **1 :** to gather, to obtain, to collect **2 recabar fondos :** to raise money

recado *nm* **1 :** message <mandar recado : to send word> **2** *Spain* **:** errand

recaer {13} *vi* **1 :** to relapse **2 ~ en** *or* **~ sobre :** to fall on, to fall to

recaída *nf* **:** relapse

recaiga, etc. → **recaer**

recalar *vi* **:** to arrive

recalcar {72} *vt* **:** to emphasize, to stress

recalcitrante *adj* **:** recalcitrant

recalentar {55} *vt* **1 :** to reheat, to warm up **2 :** to overheat

recámara *nf* **1** *Col, Mex, Pan* **:** bedroom **2 :** chamber (of a firearm)

recamarera *nf Mex* **:** chambermaid

recambio *nm* **1 :** spare part **2 :** refill (for a pen, etc.)

recapacitar *vi* **1 :** to reconsider **2 ~ en :** to reflect on, to weigh

recapitular *v* **:** to recapitulate — **recapitulación** *nf*

recargable *adj* **:** rechargeable

recargado, -da *adj* **:** overly elaborate or ornate

recargar {52} *vt* **1 :** to recharge **2 :** to overload

recargo *nm* **:** surcharge

recatado, -da *adj* MODESTO **:** modest, demure

recato *nm* PUDOR **:** modesty

recaudación *nf, pl* **-ciones 1 :** collection **2 :** earnings *pl*, takings *pl*

recaudador, -dora *n* **recaudador de impuestos :** tax collector

recaudar *vt* **:** to collect

recaudo *nm* **:** safe place <a (buen) recaudo : in safe keeping>

recayó, etc. → **recaer**

rece, etc. → **rezar**

recelo *nm* **:** distrust, suspicion

receloso, -sa *adj* **:** distrustful, suspicious

recepción *nf, pl* **-ciones :** reception

recepcionista *nmf* **:** receptionist

receptáculo *nm* **:** receptacle

receptividad *nf* **:** receptivity, receptiveness

receptivo, -va *adj* **:** receptive

receptor[1]**, -tora** *adj* **:** receiving

receptor[2]**, -tora** *n* **1 :** recipient **2 :** catcher (in baseball), receiver (in football)

receptor[3] *nm* **:** receiver <receptor de televisión : television set>

recesión *nf, pl* **-siones :** recession

recesivo, -va *adj* **:** recessive

receso *nm* **:** recess, adjournment

receta *nf* **1 :** recipe **2 :** prescription

recetar *vt* **:** to prescribe (medications)

rechazar {21} *vt* **1 :** to reject **2 :** to turn down, to refuse

rechazo *nm* **:** rejection, refusal

rechifla *nf* **:** booing, jeering

rechinar *vi* **1 :** to squeak **2 :** to grind, to gnash <hacer rechinar los dientes : to grind one's teeth>
rechoncho, -cha *adj fam* **:** chubby, squat
recibidor *nm* **:** vestibule, entrance hall
recibimiento *nm* **:** reception, welcome
recibir *vt* **1 :** to receive, to get **2 :** to welcome — *vi* **:** to receive visitors — **recibirse** *vr* **~ de :** to qualify as
recibo *nm* **:** receipt
reciclable *adj* **:** recyclable
reciclado *nm* → **reciclaje**
reciclaje *nm* **1 :** recycling **2 :** retraining
reciclar *vt* **1 :** to recycle **2 :** to retrain
recién *adv* **1 :** newly, recently <recién nacido : newborn> <recién casados : newlyweds> <recién llegado : newcomer> **2 :** just, only just <recién ahora me acordé : I just now remembered>
reciente *adj* **:** recent — **recientemente** *adv*
recinto *nm* **1 :** enclosure **2 :** site, premises *pl*
recio[1] *adv* **1 :** strongly, hard **2 :** loudly, loud
recio[2], **-cia** *adj* **1 :** severe, harsh **2 :** tough, strong
recipiente[1] *nm* **:** container, receptacle
recipiente[2] *nmf* **:** recipient
reciprocar {72} *vi* **:** to reciprocate
reciprocidad *nf* **:** reciprocity
recíproco, -ca *adj* **:** reciprocal, mutual
recitación *nf, pl* **-ciones :** recitation, recital
recital *nm* **:** recital
recitar *vt* **:** to recite
reclamación *nf, pl* **-ciones 1 :** claim, demand **2** QUEJA **:** complaint
reclamar *vt* **1** EXIGIR **:** to demand, to require **2 :** to claim — *vi* **:** to complain
reclamo *nm* **1 :** bird call, lure **2 :** lure, decoy **3 :** inducement, attraction **4 :** advertisement **5 :** complaint
reclinar *vt* **:** to rest, to lean — **reclinarse** *vr* **:** to recline, to lean back
recluir {41} *vt* **:** to confine, to lock up — **recluirse** *vr* **:** to shut oneself up, to withdraw
reclusión *nf, pl* **-siones :** imprisonment
recluso, -sa *n* **1 :** inmate, prisoner **2** SOLITARIO **:** recluse
recluta *nmf* **:** recruit, draftee
reclutamiento *nm* **:** recruitment, recruiting
reclutar *vt* ENROLAR **:** to recruit, to enlist
recobrar *vt* **:** to recover, to regain — **recobrarse** *vr* **:** to recover, to recuperate
recocer {14} *vt* **:** to overcook, to cook again
recodo *nm* **:** bend
recogedor *nm* **:** dustpan
recoger {15} *vt* **1 :** to collect, to gather **2 :** to get, to retrieve, to pick up **3 :** to clean up, to tidy (up)
recogido, -da *adj* **:** quiet, secluded
recogimiento *nm* **1 :** collecting, gathering **2 :** withdrawal **3 :** absorption, concentration
recolección *nf, pl* **-ciones 1 :** collection <recolección de basura : trash pickup> **2 :** harvest
recolectar *vt* **1 :** to gather, to collect **2 :** to harvest, to pick
recomendable *adj* **:** advisable, recommended
recomendación *nf, pl* **-ciones :** recommendation
recomendar {55} *vt* **1 :** to recommend **2** ACONSEJAR **:** to advise
recompensa *nf* **:** reward, recompense
recompensar *vt* **1** PREMIAR **:** to reward **2 :** to compensate
reconciliación *nf, pl* **-ciones :** reconciliation
reconciliar *vt* **:** to reconcile — **reconciliarse** *vr*
recóndito, -ta *adj* **1 :** remote, isolated **2 :** hidden, recondite **3 en lo más recóndito de :** in the depths of
reconfortar *vt* **:** to comfort — **reconfortante** *adj*
reconocer {18} *vt* **1 :** to recognize **2 :** to admit **3 :** to examine
reconocible *adj* **:** recognizable
reconocido, -da *adj* **1 :** recognized, accepted **2 :** grateful
reconocimiento *nm* **1 :** acknowledgment, recognition, avowal **2 :** (medical) examination **3 :** reconnaissance
reconsiderar *vt* **:** to reconsider — **reconsideración** *nf*
reconstrucción *nf, pl* **-ciones :** reconstruction
reconstruir {41} *vt* **:** to rebuild, to reconstruct
reconversión *nf, pl* **-siones :** restructuring
reconvertir {76} *vt* **1 :** to restructure **2 :** to retrain
recopilación *nf, pl* **-ciones 1 :** summary **2 :** collection, compilation
recopilar *vt* **:** to compile, to collect
récord *or* **record** [ˈrɛkɔr] *nm, pl* **récords** *or* **records** [-kɔrs] **:** record <record mundial : world record> — **récord** *or* **record** *adj*
recordar {19} *vt* **1 :** to recall, to remember **2 :** to remind — *vi* **1** ACORDARSE **:** to remember **2** DESPERTAR **:** to wake up
recordatorio[1], **-ria** *adj* **:** commemorative
recordatorio[2] *nm* **:** reminder
recorrer *vt* **1 :** to travel through, to tour **2 :** to cover (a distance) **3 :** to go over, to look over
recorrido *nm* **1 :** journey, trip **2 :** path, route, course **3 :** round (in golf)
recortar *vt* **1 :** to cut, to reduce **2 :** to cut out **3 :** to trim, to cut off **4 :** to outline — **recortarse** *vr* **:** to stand out <los árboles se recortaban en el horizonte : the trees were silhouetted against the horizon>

recorte *nm* **1** : cut, reduction **2** : clipping <recortes de periódicos : newspaper clippings>

recostar {19} *vt* : to lean, to rest — **recostarse** *vr* : to lie down, recline

recoveco *nm* **1** VUELTA : bend, turn **2** : nook, corner **3 recovecos** *nmpl* : intricacies, ins and outs

recreación *nf, pl* **-ciones 1** : re-creation **2** DIVERSIÓN : recreation, entertainment

recrear *vt* **1** : to re-create **2** : to entertain, to amuse — **recrearse** *vr* : to enjoy oneself

recreativo, -va *adj* : recreational

recreo *nm* **1** DIVERSIÓN : entertainment, amusement **2** : recess, break

recriminación *nf, pl* **-ciones** : reproach, recrimination

recriminar *vt* : to reproach — *vi* : to recriminate — **recriminarse** *vr*

recrudecer {53} *v* : to intensify, to worsen — **recrudecerse** *vr*

rectal *adj* : rectal

rectangular *adj* : rectangular

rectángulo *nm* : rectangle

rectificación *nf, pl* **-ciones** : rectification, correction

rectificar {72} *vt* **1** : to rectify, to correct **2** : to straighten (out)

rectitud *nf* **1** : straightness **2** : honesty, rectitude

recto[1] *adv* : straight

recto[2], **-ta** *adj* **1** : straight **2** : upright, honorable **3** : sound

recto[3] *nm* : rectum

rector[1], **-tora** *adj* : governing, managing

rector[2], **-tora** *n* : rector

rectoría *nf* : rectory

recubierto *pp* → **recubrir**

recubrir {2} *vt* : to cover, to coat

recuento *nm* : recount, count <un recuento de los votos : a recount of the votes>

recuerdo *nm* **1** : memory **2** : souvenir, memento **3 recuerdos** *nmpl* : regards

recuperación *nf, pl* **-ciones 1** : recovery, recuperation **2 recuperación de datos** : data retrieval

recuperar *vt* **1** : to recover, to get back, to retrieve **2** : to recuperate **3** : to make up for <recuperar el tiempo perdido : to make up for lost time> — **recuperarse** *vr* **~ de** : to recover from, to get over

recurrente *adj* : recurrent, recurring

recurrir *vi* **1 ~ a** : to turn to, to appeal to **2 ~ a** : to resort to **3** : to appeal (in law)

recurso *nm* **1** : recourse <el último recurso : the last resort> **2** : appeal (in law) **3 recursos** *nmpl* : resources, means <recursos naturales : natural resources>

red *nf* **1** : net, mesh **2** : network, system, chain **3** : trap, snare

redacción *nf, pl* **-ciones 1** : writing, composition **2** : editing

redactar *vt* **1** : to write, to draft **2** : to edit

redactor, -tora *n* : editor

redada *nf* **1** : raid **2** : catch, haul

redefinir *vt* : to redefine — **redefinición** *nf*

redención *nf, pl* **-ciones** : redemption

redentor[1], **-tora** *adj* : redeeming

redentor[2], **-tora** *n* : redeemer

redescubierto *pp* → **redescubrir**

redescubrir {2} *vt* : to rediscover

redicho, -cha *adj fam* : affected, pretentious

redil *nm* **1** : sheepfold **2 volver al redil** : to return to the fold

redimir *vt* : to redeem, to deliver (from sin)

rediseñar *vt* : to redesign

redistribuir {41} *vt* : to redistribute — **redistribución** *nf*

rédito *nm* : return, yield

redituar {3} *vt* : to produce, to yield

redoblar *vt* : to redouble, to strengthen — **redoblado, -da** *adj*

redomado, -da *adj* **1** : sly, crafty **2** : utter, out-and-out

redonda *nf* **1** : region, surrounding area **2 a la redonda** ALREDEDOR : around <de diez millas a la redonda : for ten miles around>

redondear *vt* : to round off, to round out

redondel *nm* **1** : ring, circle **2** : bullring, arena

redondez *nf* : roundness

redondo, -da *adj* **1** : round <mesa redonda : round table> **2** : great, perfect <un negocio redondo : an excellent deal> **3** : straightforward, flat <un rechazo redondo : a flat refusal> **4** *Mex* : round-trip **5 en ~** : around

reducción *nf, pl* **-ciones** : reduction, decrease

reducido, -da *adj* **1** : reduced, limited **2** : small

reducir {61} *vt* **1** DISMINUIR : to reduce, to decrease, to cut **2** : to subdue **3** : to boil down — **reducirse** *vr* **~ a** : to come down to, to be nothing more than

redundancia *nf* : reduncancy

redundante *adj* : redundant

reedición *nf, pl* **-ciones** : reprint

reelegir {28} *vt* : to reelect — **reelección** *nf*

reembolsable *adj* : refundable

reembolsar *vt* **1** : to refund, to reimburse **2** : to repay

reembolso *nm* : refund, reimbursement

reemplazable *adj* : replaceable

reemplazar {21} *vt* : to replace, to substitute

reemplazo *nm* : replacement, substitution

reencarnación *nf, pl* **-ciones** : reincarnation

reencuentro *nm* : reunion

reestablecer {53} *vt* : to reestablish

reestructurar *vt* **:** to restructure
reexaminar *vt* **:** to reexamine
refaccionar *vt* **:** to repair, to renovate
refacciones *nfpl* **:** repairs, renovations
referencia *nf* **1 :** reference **2 hacer referencia a :** to refer to
referendo *nm* → **referéndum**
referéndum *nm, pl* **-dums :** referendum
referente *adj* **~ a :** concerning
réferi *or* **referi** [ˈrɛfɛri] *nmf* **:** referee
referir {76} *vt* **1 :** to relate, to tell **2 :** to refer <nos refirió al diccionario : she referred us to the dictionary> — **referirse** *vr* **1 ~ a :** to refer to **2 ~ a :** to be concerned, to be in reference to <en lo que se refiere a la educación : as far as education is concerned>
refinado[1], **-da** *adj* **:** refined
refinado[2] *nm* **:** refining
refinamiento *nm* **1 :** refining **2** FINURA **:** refinement
refinanciar *vt* **:** to refinance
refinar *vt* **:** to refine
refinería *nf* **:** refinery
reflectante *adj* **:** reflective, reflecting
reflector[1], **-tora** *adj* **:** reflecting
reflector[2] *nm* **1 :** spotlight, searchlight **2 :** reflector
reflejar *vt* **:** to reflect — **reflejarse** *vr* **:** to be reflected <la decepción se refleja en su rostro : the disappointment shows on her face>
reflejo *nm* **1 :** reflection **2 :** reflex **3 reflejos** *nmpl* **:** highlights, streaks (in hair)
reflexión *nf, pl* **-xiones :** reflection, thought
reflexionar *vi* **:** to reflect, to think
reflexivo, -va *adj* **1 :** reflective, thoughtful **2 :** reflexive
reflujo *nm* **:** ebb, ebb tide
reforma *nf* **1 :** reform **2 :** alteration, renovation
reformador, -dora *n* **:** reformer
reformar *vt* **1 :** to reform **2 :** to change, to alter **3 :** to renovate, to repair — **reformarse** *vr* **:** to mend one's ways
reformatorio *nm* **:** reformatory
reformular *vt* **:** to reformulate — **reformulación** *nf*
reforzar {36} *vt* **1 :** to reinforce, to strengthen **2 :** to encourage, to support
refracción *nf, pl* **-ciones :** refraction
refractar *vt* **:** to refract — **refractarse** *vr*
refractario, -ria *adj* **:** refractory, obstinate
refrán *nm, pl* **refranes** ADAGIO **:** proverb, saying
refregar {49} *vt* **:** to scrub
refrenar *vt* **1 :** to rein in (a horse) **2 :** to restrain, to check — **refrenarse** *vr* **:** to restrain oneself
refrendar *vt* **1 :** to countersign, to endorse **2 :** to stamp (a passport)
refrescante *adj* **:** refreshing
refrescar {72} *vt* **1 :** to refresh, to cool **2 :** to brush up (on) **3 refrescar la memoria :** to refresh one's memory — *vi* **:** to turn cooler
refresco *nm* **:** refreshment, soft drink
refriega *nf* **:** skirmish, scuffle
refrigeración *nf, pl* **-ciones 1 :** refrigeration **2 :** air-conditioning
refrigerador *nmf* NEVERA **:** refrigerator
refrigeradora *nf Col, Peru* **:** refrigerator
refrigerante *nm* **:** coolant
refrigerar *vt* **1 :** to refrigerate **2 :** to air-condition
refrigerio *nm* **:** snack, refreshments *pl*
refrito[1], **-ta** *adj* **:** refried
refrito[2] *nm* **:** rehash
refuerzo *nm* **:** reinforcement, support
refugiado, -da *n* **:** refugee
refugiar *vt* **:** to shelter — **refugiarse** *vr* ACOGERSE **:** to take refuge
refugio *nm* **:** refuge, shelter
refulgencia *nf* **:** brilliance, splendor
refulgir {35} *vi* **:** to shine brightly
refundir *vt* **1 :** to recast (metals) **2 :** to revise, to rewrite
refunfuñar *vi* **:** to grumble, to groan
refutar *vt* **:** to refute — **refutación** *nf*
regadera *nf* **1 :** watering can **2 :** shower head, shower **3 :** sprinkler
regaderazo *nm Mex* **:** shower
regalar *vt* **1** OBSEQUIAR **:** to present (as a gift), to give away **2 :** to regale, to entertain **3 :** to flatter, to make a fuss over — **regalarse** *vr* **:** to pamper oneself
regalía *nf* **:** royalty, payment
regaliz *nm, pl* **-lices :** licorice
regalo *nm* **1** OBSEQUIO **:** gift, present **2 :** pleasure, comfort **3 :** treat
regañadientes *mpl* **a ~ :** reluctantly, unwillingly
regañar *vt* **:** to scold, to give a talking to — *vi* **1** QUEJARSE **:** to grumble, to complain **2** REÑIR **:** to quarrel, to argue
regaño *nm fam* **:** scolding
regañon, -ñona *adj, mpl* **-ñones** *fam* **:** grumpy, irritable
regar {49} *vt* **1 :** to irrigate **2 :** to water **3 :** to wash, to hose down **4 :** to spill, to scatter
regata *nf* **:** regatta, yacht race
regate *nm* **:** dodge, feint
regatear *vt* **1 :** to haggle over **2** ESCATIMAR **:** to skimp on, to be sparing with — *vi* **:** to bargain, to haggle
regateo *nm* **:** bargaining, haggling
regatón *nm, pl* **-tones :** ferrule, tip
regazo *nm* **:** lap (of a person)
regencia *nf* **:** regency
regenerar *vt* **:** to regenerate — **regenerarse** *vr* — **regeneración** *nf*
regentar *vt* **:** to run, to manage
regente *nmf* **:** regent
regidor, -dora *n* **:** town councillor
régimen *nm, pl* **regímenes 1 :** regime **2 :** diet **3 :** regimen, rules *pl* <régimen de vida : lifestyle>
regimiento *nm* **:** regiment

regio, -gia *adj* **1 :** great, magnificent **2 :** regal, royal

región *nf, pl* **regiones :** region, area

regional *adj* **:** regional — **regionalmente** *adv*

regir {28} *vt* **1 :** to rule **2 :** to manage, to run **3 :** to control, to govern <las costumbres que rigen la conducta : the customs which govern behavior> — *vi* **:** to apply, to be in force <las leyes rigen en los tres países : the laws apply in all three countries> — **regirse** *vr* **~ por :** to go by, to be guided by

registrador[1], -dora *adj* **caja registradora :** cash register

registrador[2], -dora *n* **:** registrar, recorder

registrar *vt* **1 :** to register, to record **2** GRABAR **:** to record, to tape **3 :** to search, to examine — **registrarse** *vr* **1** INSCRIBIRSE **:** to register **2** OCURRIR **:** to happen, to occur

registro *nm* **1 :** register **2 :** registration **3 :** registry, record office **4 :** range (of a voice or musical instrument) **5 :** search

regla *nf* **1** NORMA **:** rule, regulation **2 :** ruler <regla de cálculo : slide rule> **3** MENSTRUACIÓN **:** period, menstruation

reglamentación *nf, pl* **-ciones 1 :** regulation **2 :** rules *pl*

reglamentar *vt* **:** to regulate, to set rules for

reglamentario, -ria *adj* **:** regulation, official <equipo reglamentario : standard equipment>

reglamento *nm* **:** regulations *pl*, rules *pl* <reglamento de tráfico : traffic regulations>

regocijar *vt* **:** to gladden, to delight — **regocijarse** *vr* **:** to rejoice

regocijo *nm* **:** delight, rejoicing

regordete *adj fam* LLENITO **:** chubby

regresar *vt* DEVOLVER **:** to give back — *vi* **:** to return, to come back, to go back

regresión *nf, pl* **-siones :** regression, return

regresivo, -va *adj* **:** regressive

regreso *nm* **1 :** return **2 estar de regreso :** to be back, to be home

reguero *nm* **1 :** irrigation ditch **2 :** trail, trace **3 propagarse como reguero de pólvora :** to spread like wildfire

regulable *adj* **:** adjustable

regulación *nf, pl* **-ciones :** regulation, control

regulador[1], -dora *adj* **:** regulating, regulatory

regulador[2] *nm* **1 :** regulator, governor **2 regulador de tiro :** damper (in a chimney)

regular[1] *vt* **:** to regulate, to control

regular[2] *adj* **1 :** regular **2 :** fair, OK, so-so **3 :** medium, average **4 por lo regular :** in general, generally

regularidad *nf* **:** regularity

regularización *nf, pl* **-ciones** NORMALIZACIÓN **:** normalization

regularizar {21} *vt* NORMALIZAR **:** to normalize, to make regular

regularmente *adv* **:** regularly

rehabilitar *vt* **1 :** to rehabilitate **2 :** to reinstate **3 :** renovate, to restore — **rehabilitación** *nf*

rehacer {40} *vt* **1 :** to redo **2 :** to remake, to repair, to renew — **rehacerse** *vr* **1 :** to recover **2 ~ de :** to get over

rehecho *pp* → **rehacer**

rehén *nm, pl* **rehenes :** hostage

rehicieron, etc. → **rehacer**

rehizo → **rehacer**

rehuir {41} *vt* **:** to avoid, to shun

rehusar {8} *v* **:** to refuse

reimprimir *vt* **:** to reprint

reina *nf* **:** queen

reinado *nm* **:** reign

reinante *adj* **1 :** reigning **2 :** prevailing, current

reinar *vi* **1 :** to reign **2 :** to prevail

reincidencia *nf* **:** recidivism, relapse

reincidente *nmf* **:** backslider, recidivist

reincidir *vi* **:** to backslide, to retrogress

reincorporar *vt* **:** to reinstate — **reincorporarse** *vr* **~ a :** to return to, to rejoin

reino *nm* **:** kingdom, realm <reino animal : animal kingdom>

reinstalar *vt* **1 :** to reinstall **2 :** to reinstate

reintegrar *vt* **1 :** to reintegrate, reinstate **2 :** to refund, to reimburse — **reintegrarse** *vr* **~ a :** to return to, to rejoin

reír {66} *vi* **:** to laugh — *vt* **:** to laugh at — **reírse** *vr*

reiteración *nf, pl* **-ciones :** reiteration, repetition

reiterado, -da *adj* **:** repeated <lo explicó en reiteradas ocasiones : he explained it repeatedly> — **reiteradamente** *adv*

reiterar *vt* **:** to reiterate, to repeat

reiterativo, -va *adj* **:** repetitive, repetitious

reivindicación *nf, pl* **-ciones 1 :** demand, claim **2 :** vindication

reivindicar {72} *vt* **1 :** to vindicate **2 :** to demand, to claim **3 :** to restore

reja *nf* **1 :** grill, grating <entre rejas : behind bars> **2 :** plowshare

rejilla *nf* **:** grille, grate, screen

rejuvenecer {53} *vt* **:** to rejuvenate — *vi* **:** to be rejuvenated — **rejuvenecerse** *vr*

rejuvencimiento *m* **:** rejuvenation

relación *nf, pl* **-ciones 1 :** relation, connection, relevance **2 :** relationship **3** RELATO **:** account **4** LISTA **:** list **5 con relación a** *or* **en relación con :** in relation to, concerning **6 relaciones públicas :** public relations

relacionar *vt* **:** to relate, to connect — **relacionarse** *vr* **~ con :** to be connected to, to be linked with

relajación *nf, pl* **-ciones :** relaxation
relajado, -da *adj* **1 :** relaxed, loose **2 :** dissolute, depraved
relajar *vt* **:** to relax, to slacken — *vi* **:** to be relaxing — **relajarse** *vr*
relajo *nm* **1 :** commotion, ruckus **2 :** joke, laugh <lo hizo de relajo : he did it for a laugh>
relamerse *vr* **:** to smack one's lips, to lick one's chops
relámpago *nm* **:** flash of lightning
relampaguear *vi* **:** to flash
relanzar {21} *vt* **:** to relaunch
relatar *vt* **:** to relate, to tell
relativo, -va *adj* **1 :** relative **2 en lo relativo a :** with regard to, concerning — **relativamente** *adv*
relato *nm* **1 :** story, tale **2 :** account
releer {20} *vt* **:** to reread
relegar {52} *vt* **1 :** to relegate **2 relegar al olvido :** to consign to oblivion
relevante *adj* **:** outstanding, important
relevar *vt* **1 :** to relieve, to take over from **2 ~ de :** to exempt from — **relevarse** *vr* **:** to take turns
relevo *nm* **1 :** relief, replacement **2 :** relay <carrera de relevos : relay race>
relicario *nm* **1 :** reliquary **2 :** locket
relieve *nm* **1 :** relief, projection <mapa en relieve : relief map> <letras en relieve : embossed letters> **2 :** prominence, importance **3 poner en relieve :** to highlight, to emphasize
religión *nf, pl* **-giones :** religion
religiosamente *adv* **:** religiously, faithfully
religioso[1], -sa *adj* **:** religious
religioso[2], -sa *n* **:** monk *m,* nun *f*
relinchar *vi* **:** to neigh, to whinny
relincho *nm* **:** neigh, whinny
reliquia *nf* **1 :** relic **2 reliquia de familia :** family heirloom
rellenar *vt* **1 :** to refill **2 :** to stuff, to fill **3 :** to fill out
relleno[1], -na *adj* **:** stuffed, filled
relleno[2] *nm* **:** stuffing, filling
reloj *nm* **1 :** clock **2 :** watch **3 reloj de arena :** hourglass **4 reloj de pulsera :** wristwatch **5 como un reloj :** like clockwork
relojería *nf* **1 :** watchmaker's shop **2 :** watchmaking, clockmaking
reluciente *adj* **:** brilliant, shining
relucir {45} *vi* **1 :** to glitter, to shine **2 salir a relucir :** to come to the surface **3 sacar a relucir :** to bring up, to mention
relumbrante *adj* **:** dazzling
relumbrar *vi* **:** to shine brightly
relumbrón *nm, pl* **-brones 1 :** flash, glare **2 de ~ :** flashy, showy
remachar *vt* **1 :** to rivet **2 :** to clinch (a nail) **3 :** to stress, to drive home — *vi* **:** to smash, to spike (a ball)
remache *nm* **1 :** rivet **2 :** smash, spike (in sports)
remanente *nm* **1 :** remainder, balance **2 :** surplus
remanso *nm* **:** pool
remar *vi* **1 :** to row, to paddle **2 :** to struggle, to toil
remarcar {72} *vt* **:** to emphasize, to stress
rematado, -da *adj* **:** utter, complete
rematador, -dora *n* **:** auctioneer
rematar *vt* **1 :** to finish off **2 :** to auction — *vi* **1 :** to shoot **2 :** to end
remate *nm* **1 :** shot (in sports) **2 :** auction **3 :** end, conclusion **4 como ~ :** to top it off **5 de ~ :** completely, utterly
remecer {86} *vt* **:** to sway, to swing
remedar *vt* **1** IMITAR **:** to imitate, to copy **2 :** to mimic, to ape
remediar *vt* **1 :** to remedy, to repair **2 :** to help out, to assist **3** EVITAR **:** to prevent, to avoid
remedio *nm* **1 :** remedy, cure **2 :** solution **3 :** option <no me quedó más remedio : I had no other choice> <no hay remedio : it can't be helped> **4 poner remedio a :** to put a stop to **5 sin ~ :** unavoidable, inevitable
remedo *nm* **:** imitation
rememorar *vi* **:** to recall <rememorar los viejos tiempos : to reminisce>
remendar {55} *vt* **1 :** to mend, to patch, to darn **2 :** to correct
remero, -ra *n* **:** rower
remesa *nf* **1 :** remittance **2 :** shipment
remezón *nm, pl* **-zones :** mild earthquake, tremor
remiendo *nm* **1 :** patch **2 :** correction
remilgado, -da *adj* **1 :** prim, prudish **2 :** affected
remilgo *nm* **:** primness, affectation
reminiscencia *nf* **:** reminiscence
remisión *nf, pl* **-siones 1** ENVÍO **:** sending, delivery **2 :** remission **3 :** reference, cross-reference
remiso, -sa *adj* **1 :** lax, remiss **2 :** reluctant
remitente[1] *nm* **:** return address
remitente[2] *nmf* **:** sender (of a letter, etc.)
remitir *vt* **1 :** to send, to remit **2 ~ a :** to refer to, to direct to <nos remitió al diccionario : he referred us to the dictionary> — *vi* **:** to subside, to let up
remo *nm* **1 :** paddle, oar **2 :** rowing (sport)
remoción *nf, pl* **-ciones 1 :** removal **2 :** dismissal
remodelación *nf, pl* **-ciones 1 :** remodeling **2 :** reorganization, restructuring
remodelar *vt* **1 :** to remodel **2 :** to restructure
remojar *vt* **1 :** to soak, to steep **2 :** to dip, to dunk **3 :** to celebrate with a drink
remojo *nm* **1 :** soaking, steeping **2 poner en remojo :** to soak, to leave soaking
remolacha *nf* **:** beet
remolcador *nm* **:** tugboat
remolcar {72} *vt* **:** to tow, to haul

remolino *nm* **1 :** whirlwind **2 :** eddy, whirlpool **3 :** crowd, throng **4 :** cowlick

remolque *nm* **1 :** towing, tow **2 :** trailer **3 a ~ :** in tow

remontar *vt* **1 :** to overcome **2** SUBIR **:** to go up — **remontarse** *vr* **1 :** to soar **2 ~ a :** to date from, to go back to

rémora *nf* **:** obstacle, hindrance

remorder {47} *vt* INQUIETAR **:** to trouble, to distress

remordimiento *nm* **:** remorse

remotamente *adv* **:** remotely, vaguely

remoto, -ta *adj* **1 :** remote, unlikely <hay una posibilidad remota : there is a slim possibility> **2 :** distant, far-off

remover {47} *vt* **1 :** to stir **2 :** to move around, to turn over **3 :** to stir up **4 :** to remove **5 :** to dismiss

remozamiento *nm* **:** renovation

remozar {21} *vt* **1 :** to renew, to brighten up **2 :** to redo, to renovate

remuneración *nf, pl* **-ciones :** remuneration, pay

remunerar *vt* **:** to pay, to remunerate

remunerativo, -va *adj* **:** remunerative

renacer {48} *vi* **:** to be reborn, to revive

renacimiento *nm* **1 :** rebirth, revival **2 el Renacimiento :** the Renaissance

renacuajo *nm* **:** tadpole, pollywog

renal *adj* **:** renal, kidney

rencilla *nf* **:** quarrel

renco, -ca *adj* **:** lame

rencor *nm* **1 :** rancor, enmity, hostility **2 guardar rencor :** to hold a grudge

rencoroso, -sa *adj* **:** resentful, rancorous

rendición *nf, pl* **-ciones 1 :** surrender, submission **2 :** yield, return

rendido, -da *adj* **1 :** submissive **2 :** worn-out, exhausted **3 :** devoted

rendija *nf* GRIETA **:** crack, split

rendimiento *nm* **1 :** performance **2 :** yield

rendir {54} *vt* **1 :** to render, to give <rendir las gracias : to give thanks> <rendir homenaje a : to pay homage to> **2 :** to yield **3** CANSAR **:** to exhaust — *vi* **1** CUNDIR **:** to progress, to make headway **2 :** to last, to go a long way — **rendirse** *vr* **:** to surrender, to give up

renegado, -da *n* **:** renegade

renegar {49} *vi* **1 ~ de :** to renounce, to disown, to give up **2 ~ de :** to complain about — *vt* **1 :** to deny vigorously **2 :** to abhor, to hate

renegociar *vt* **:** to renegotiate — **renegociación** *nf*

renglón *nm, pl* **renglones 1 :** line (of writing) **2 :** merchandise, line (of products)

rengo, -ga *adj* **:** lame

renguear *vi* **:** to limp

reno *nm* **:** reindeer

renombrado, -da *adj* **:** renowned, famous

renombre *nm* NOMBRADÍA **:** renown, fame

renovable *adj* **:** renewable

renovación *nf, pl* **-ciones 1 :** renewal <renovación de un contrato : renewal of a contract> **2 :** change, renovation

renovar {19} *vt* **1 :** to renew, to restore **2 :** to renovate

renquear *vi* **:** to limp, to hobble

renquera *nf* COJERA **:** limp, lameness

renta *nf* **1 :** income **2 :** rent **3 impuesto sobre la renta :** income tax

rentable *adj* **:** profitable

rentar *vt* **1 :** to produce, to yield **2** ALQUILAR **:** to rent

renuencia *nf* **:** reluctance, unwillingness

renuente *adj* **:** reluctant, unwilling

renuncia *nf* **1 :** resignation **2 :** renunciation **3 :** waiver

renunciar *vi* **1 :** to resign **2 ~ a :** to renounce, to relinquish <renunció al título : he relinquished the title>

reñido, -da *adj* **1 :** tough, hard-fought **2 :** at odds, on bad terms

reñir {67} *vi* **1 :** to argue **2 ~ con :** to fall out with, to go up against — *vt* **:** to scold, to reprimand

reo, rea *n* **1 :** accused, defendant **2 :** offender, culprit

reojo *nm* **de ~ :** out of the corner of one's eye <una mirada de reojo : a sidelong glance>

reorganizar {21} *vt* **:** to reorganize — **reorganización** *nf*

repantigarse {52} *vr* **:** to slouch, to loll about

reparación *nf, pl* **-ciones 1 :** reparation, amends **2 :** repair

reparar *vt* **1 :** to repair, to fix, to mend **2 :** to make amends for **3 :** to correct **4 :** to restore, to refresh — *vi* **1 ~ en :** to observe, to take notice of **2 ~ en :** to consider, to think about

reparo *nm* **1 :** repair, restoration **2 :** reservation, qualm <no tuvieron reparos en decírmelo : they didn't hesitate to tell me> **3 poner reparos a :** to find fault with, to object to

repartición *nf, pl* **-ciones 1 :** distribution **2 :** department, division

repartidor[1], -dora *adj* **:** delivery <camión repartidor : delivery truck>

repartidor[2], -dora *n* **:** delivery person, distributor

repartimiento *nm* → **repartición**

repartir *vt* **1 :** to allocate **2** DISTRIBUIR **:** to distribute, to hand out **3 :** to spread

reparto *nm* **1 :** allocation **2 :** distribution **3 :** cast (of characters)

repasar *vt* **1 :** to pass by again **2 :** to review, to go over **3 :** to mend

repaso *nm* **1 :** review **2 :** mending **3 :** checkup, overhaul

repatriar {85} *vt* **:** to repatriate — **repatriación** *nf*

repavimentar *vt* **:** to resurface

repelente[1] *adj* **:** repellent, repulsive

repelente[2] *nm* : repellent <repelente de insectos : insect repellent>
repeler *vt* **1** : to repel, to resist, to repulse **2** : to reject **3** : to disgust <el sabor me repele : I find the taste repulsive>
repensar {55} *v* : to rethink, to reconsider
repente *nm* **1** : sudden movement, start <de repente : suddenly> **2** : fit, outburst <un repente de ira : a fit of anger>
repentino, -na *adj* : sudden — **repentinamente** *adv*
repercusión *nf, pl* **-siones** : repercussion
repercutir *vi* **1** : to reverberate, to echo **2 ~ en** : to have effects on, to have repercussions on
repertorio *nm* : repertoire
repetición *nf, pl* **-ciones 1** : repetition **2** : rerun, repeat
repetidamente *adv* : repeatedly
repetido, -da *adj* **1** : repeated, numerous **2 repetidas veces** : repeatedly, time and again
repetir {54} *vt* **1** : to repeat **2** : to have a second helping of — **repetirse** *vr* **1** : to repeat oneself **2** : to recur
repetitivo, -va *adj* : repetitive, repetitious
repicar {72} *vt* : to ring — *vi* : to ring out, to peal
repique *nm* : ringing, pealing
repisa *nf* : shelf, ledge <repisa de chimenea : mantelpiece> <repisa de ventana : windowsill>
replantear *vt* : to redefine, to restate — **replantearse** *vr* : to reconsider
replegar {49} *vt* : to fold — **replegarse** *vr* RETIRARSE : to retreat, to withdraw
repleto, -ta *adj* **1** : replete, full **2 ~ de** : packed with, crammed with
réplica *nf* **1** : reply **2** : replica, reproduction **3** *Chile, Mex* : aftershock
replicación *nf, pl* **-ciones** : replication
replicar {72} *vi* **1** : to reply, to retort **2** : to argue, to answer back
repliegue *nm* **1** : fold **2** : retreat, withdrawal
repollo *nm* COL : cabbage
reponer {60} *vt* **1** : to replace, to put back **2** : to reinstate **3** : to reply — **reponerse** *vr* : to recover
reportaje *nm* : article, story, report
reportar *vt* **1** : to check, to restrain **2** : to bring, to carry, to yield <me reportó numerosos beneficios : it brought me many benefits> **3** : to report — **reportarse** *vr* **1** CONTENERSE : to control oneself **2** PRESENTARSE : to report, to show up
reporte *nm* : report
reportear *vt* : to report on, to cover
reportero, -ra *n* **1** : reporter **2 reportero gráfico** : photojournalist
reposado, -da *adj* : calm
reposar *vi* **1** : to rest, to repose **2** : to stand, to settle <deje reposar la masa media hora : let the dough stand for half an hour> **3** : to lie, to be buried — **reposarse** *vr* : to settle
reposición *nf, pl* **-ciones 1** : replacement **2** : reinstatement **3** : revival
repositorio *nm* : repository
reposo *nm* : repose, rest
repostar *vi* **1** : to stock up **2** : to refuel
repostería *nf* **1** : confectioner's shop **2** : pastry-making
repostero, -ra *n* : confectioner
repreguntar *vt* : to cross-examine
repreguntas *nfpl* : cross-examination
reprender *vt* : to reprimand, to scold
reprensible *adj* : reprehensible
represa *nf* : dam
represalia *nf* **1** : reprisal, retaliation **2 tomar represalias** : to retaliate
represar *vt* : to dam
representación *nf, pl* **-ciones 1** : representation **2** : performance **3 en representación de** : on behalf of
representante *nmf* **1** : representative **2** : performer
representar *vt* **1** : to represent, to act for **2** : to perform **3** : to look, to appear as **4** : to symbolize, to stand for **5** : to signify, to mean — **representarse** *vr* : to imagine, to picture
representativo, -va *adj* : representative
represión *nf, pl* **-siones** : repression
represivo, -va *adj* : repressive
reprimenda *nf* : reprimand
reprimir *vt* **1** : to repress **2** : to suppress, to stifle
reprobable *adj* : reprehensible, culpable
reprobación *nf* : disapproval
reprobar {19} *vt* **1** DESAPROBAR : to condemn, to disapprove of **2** : to fail (a course)
reprobatorio, -ria *adj* : disapproving, admonitory
reprochar *vt* : to reproach — **reprocharse** *vr*
reproche *nm* : reproach
reproducción *nf, pl* **-ciones** : reproduction
reproducir {61} *vt* : to reproduce — **reproducirse** *vr* **1** : to breed, to reproduce **2** : to recur
reproductor, -tora *adj* : reproductive
reptar *vi* : to crawl, to slither
reptil[1] *adj* : reptilian
reptil[2] *nm* : reptile
república *nf* : republic
republicanismo *nm* : republicanism
republicano, -na *adj & n* : republican
repudiar *vt* : to repudiate — **repudiación** *nf*
repudio *nm* : repudiation
repuesto[1] *pp* → **reponer**
repuesto[2] *nm* **1** : spare part **2 de ~** : spare <rueda de repuesto : spare wheel>
repugnancia *nf* : repugnance

repugnante *adj* : repulsive, repugnant, revolting
repugnar *vt* : to cause repugnance, to disgust — **repugnarse** *vr*
repujar *vt* : to emboss
repulsivo, -va *adj* : repulsive
repuntar *vt Arg, Chile* : to round up (cattle) — *vi* : to begin to appear — **repuntarse** *vr* : to fall out, to quarrel
repuso, etc. → **reponer**
reputación *nf, pl* **-ciones** : reputation
reputar *vt* : to consider, to deem
requerir {76} *vt* **1** : to require, to call for **2** : to summon, to send for
requesón *nm, pl* **-sones** : curd cheese, cottage cheese
réquiem *nm* : requiem
requisa *nf* **1** : requisition **2** : seizure **3** : inspection
requisar *vt* **1** : to requisition **2** : to seize **3** INSPECCIONAR : to inspect
requisito *nm* **1** : requirement **2 requisito previo** : prerequisite
res *nf* **1** : beast, animal **2** *CA, Mex* : beef **3 reses** *nfpl* : cattle <60 reses : 60 head of cattle>
resabio *nm* **1** VICIO : bad habit, vice **2** DEJO : aftertaste
resaca *nf* **1** : undertow **2** : hangover
resaltar *vi* **1** SOBRESALIR : to stand out **2 hacer resaltar** : to bring out, to highlight — *vt* : to stress, to emphasize
resarcimiento *nm* **1** : compensation **2** : reimbursement
resarcir {83} *vt* : to compensate, to indemnify — **resarcirse** *vr* **~ de** : to make up for
resbaladizo, -za *adj* **1** RESBALOSO : slippery **2** : tricky, ticklish, delicate
resbalar *vi* **1** : to slip, to slide **2** : to slip up, to make a mistake **3** : to skid — **resbalarse** *vr*
resbalón *nm, pl* **-lones** : slip
resbaloso, -sa *adj* : slippery
rescatar *vt* **1** : to rescue, to save **2** : to recover, to get back
rescate *nm* **1** : rescue **2** : recovery **3** : ransom
rescindir *vt* : to rescind, to annul, to cancel
rescisión *nf, pl* **-siones** : annulment, cancelation
rescoldo *nm* : embers *pl*
resecar {72} *vt* : to make dry, to dry up — **resecarse** *vr* : to dry up
reseco, -ca *adj* : dry, dried-up
resentido, -da *adj* : resentful
resentimiento *nm* : resentment
resentirse {76} *vr* **1** : to suffer, to be weakened **2** OFENDERSE : to be upset <se resintió porque la insultaron : she got upset when they insulted her, she resented being insulted> **3 ~ de** : to feel the effects of
reseña *nf* **1** : report, summary, review **2** : description
reseñar *vt* **1** : to review **2** DESCRIBIR : to describe
reserva *nf* **1** : reservation **2** : reserve **3** : confidence, privacy <con la mayor reserva : in strictest confidence> **4 de ~** : spare, in reserve **5 reservas** *nfpl* : reservations, doubts
reservación *nf, pl* **-ciones** : reservation
reservado, -da *adj* **1** : reserved, reticent **2** : confidential
reservar *vt* : to reserve — **reservarse** *vr* **1** : to save oneself **2** : to conceal, to keep to oneself
reservorio *nm* : reservoir, reserve
resfriado *nm* CATARRO : cold
resfriar {85} *vt* : to cool — **resfriarse** *vr* **1** : to cool off **2** : to catch a cold
resfrío *nm* : cold
resguardar *vt* : to safeguard, to protect — **resguardarse** *vr*
resguardo *nm* **1** : safeguard, protection **2** : receipt, voucher **3** : border guard, coast guard
residencia *nf* **1** : residence **2** : boarding house
residencial *adj* : residential
residente *adj & nmf* : resident
residir *vi* **1** VIVIR : to reside, to dwell **2 ~ en** : to lie in, to consist of
residual *adj* : residual
residuo *nm* **1** : residue **2** : remainder **3 residuos** *nmpl* : waste <residuos nucleares : nuclear waste>
resignación *nf, pl* **-ciones** : resignation
resignar *vt* : to resign — **resignarse** *vr* **~ a** : to resign oneself to
resina *nf* **1** : resin **2 resina epoxídica** : epoxy
resistencia *nf* **1** : resistance **2** AGUANTE : endurance, strength, stamina
resistente *adj* **1** : resistant **2** : strong, tough
resistir *vt* **1** : to stand, to bear, to tolerate **2** : to withstand — *vi* : to resist <resistió hasta el último minuto : he held out until the last minute> — **resistirse** *vr* **~ a** : to be resistent to, to be reluctant
resollar {19} *vi* : to breathe heavily, to wheeze
resolución *nf, pl* **-ciones 1** : resolution, settlement **2** : decision **3** : determination, resolve
resolver {89} *vt* **1** : to resolve, to settle **2** : to decide — **resolverse** *vr* : to make up one's mind
resonancia *nf* **1** : resonance **2** : impact, repercussions *pl*
resonante *adj* **1** : resonant **2** : tremendous, resounding <un éxito resonante : a resounding success>
resonar {19} *vi* : to resound, to ring
resoplar *vi* **1** : to puff, to pant **2** : to snort
resoplo *nm* **1** : puffing, panting **2** : snort
resorte *nm* **1** MUELLE : spring **2** : elasticity **3** : influence, means *pl* <tocar resortes : to pull strings>
resortera *nf Mex* : slingshot

respaldar *vt* **:** to back, to support, to endorse — **respaldarse** *vr* **:** to lean back
respaldo *nm* **1 :** back (of an object) **2 :** support, backing
respectar *vt* **:** to concern, to relate to <por lo que a mí respecta : as far as I'm concerned>
respectivo, -va *adj* **:** respective — **respectivamente** *adv*
respecto *nm* **1 ~ a :** in regard to, concerning **2 al respecto :** on this matter, in this respect
respetable *adj* **:** respectable — **respetabilidad** *nf*
respetar *vt* **:** to respect
respeto *nm* **1 :** respect, consideration **2 respetos** *nmpl* **:** respects <presentar sus respetos : to pay one's respects>
respetuosidad *nf* **:** respectfulness
respetuoso, -sa *adj* **:** respectful — **respetuosamente** *adv*
respingo *nm* **:** start, jump
respiración *nf, pl* **-ciones :** respiration, breathing
respiradero *nm* **:** vent, ventilation shaft
respirador *nm* **:** respirator
respirar *v* **:** to breathe
respiratorio, -ria *adj* **:** respiratory
respiro *nm* **1 :** breath **2 :** respite, break
resplandecer {53} *vi* **1 :** to shine **2 :** to stand out
resplandeciente *adj* **1 :** resplendent, shining **2 :** radiant
resplandor *nm* **1 :** brightness, brilliance, radiance **2 :** flash
responder *vt* **:** to answer — *vi* **1 :** to answer, to reply, to respond **2 ~ a :** to respond to <responder al tratamiento : to respond to treatment> **3 ~ de :** to answer for, to vouch for (something) **4 ~ por :** to vouch for (someone)
responsabilidad *nf* **:** responsibility
responsable *adj* **:** responsible — **responsablemente** *adv*
respuesta *nf* **:** answer, response
resquebrajar *vt* **:** to split, to crack — **resquebrajarse** *vr*
resquemor *nm* **:** resentment, bitterness
resquicio *nm* **1 :** crack **2 :** opportunity, chance **3 :** trace <sin un resquicio de remordimiento : without a trace of remorse> **4 resquicio legal :** loophole
resta *nf* SUSTRACCIÓN **:** subtraction
restablecer {53} *vt* **:** to reestablish, to restore — **restablecerse** *vr* **:** to recover
restablecimiento *nm* **1 :** reestablishment, restoration **2 :** recovery
restallar *vi* **:** to crack, to crackle, to click
restallido *nm* **:** crack, crackle
restante *adj* **1 :** remaining **2 lo restante, los restantes :** the rest
restañar *vt* **:** to stanch
restar *vt* **1 :** to deduct, to subtract <restar un punto : to deduct a point> **2 :** to minimize, to play down — *vi* **:** to remain, to be left
restauración *nf, pl* **-ciones 1 :** restoration **2 :** catering, food service
restaurante *nm* **:** restaurant
restaurar *vt* **:** to restore
restitución *nf, pl* **-ciones :** restitution, return
restituir {41} *vt* **:** to return, to restore, to reinstate
resto *nm* **1 :** rest, remainder **2 restos** *nmpl* **:** remains <restos de comida : leftovers> <restos arqueológicos : archeological ruins> **3 restos mortales :** mortal remains
restorán *nm, pl* **-ranes :** restaurant
restregadura *nf* **:** scrub, scrubbing
restregar {49} *vt* **1 :** to rub **2 :** to scrub — **restregarse** *vr*
restricción *nf, pl* **-ciones :** restriction, limitation
restrictivo, -va *adj* **:** restrictive
restringido, -da *adj* LIMITADO **:** limited, restricted
restringir {35} *vt* LIMITAR **:** to restrict, to limit
restructuración *nf* **:** restructuring
restructurar *vt* **:** to restructure
resucitación *nf* **:** resuscitation <resucitación cardiopulmonar : CPR, cardiopulmonary resuscitation>
resucitar *vt* **1 :** to resuscitate, to revive, to resurrect **2 :** to revitalize
resuello *nm* **1 :** puffing, heavy breathing, wheezing **2 :** break, breather
resuelto[1] *pp* → **resolver**
resuelto[2], -ta *adj* **:** determined, resolved, resolute
resulta *nf* **1 :** consequence, result **2 a resultas de** *or* **de resultas de :** as a result of
resultado *nm* **:** result, outcome
resultante *adj & nf* **:** resultant
resultar *vi* **1 :** to work, to work out <mi idea no resultó : my idea didn't work out> **2 :** to prove, to turn out to be <resultó bien simpático : he turned out to be very nice> **3 ~ en :** to lead to, to result in **4 ~ de :** to be the result of
resumen *nm, pl* **-súmenes 1 :** summary, summation **2 en ~ :** in summary, in short
resumidero *nm* **:** drain
resumir *v* **:** to summarize, to sum up
resurgimiento *nm* **:** resurgence
resurgir {35} *vi* **:** to reappear, to revive
resurrección *nf, pl* **-ciones :** resurrection
retablo *nm* **1 :** tableau **2 :** altarpiece
retador, -dora *n* **:** challenger (in sports)
retaguardia *nf* **:** rear guard
retahíla *nf* **:** string, series <una retahíla de insultos : a volley of insults>
retaliación *nf, pl* **-ciones :** retaliation
retama *nf* **:** broom (plant)
retar *vt* DESAFIAR **:** to challenge, to defy
retardante *adj* **:** retardant

retardar *vt* **1** RETRASAR **:** to delay, to retard **2 :** to postpone

retazo *nm* **1 :** remnant, scrap **2 :** fragment, piece <retazos de su obra : bits and pieces from his writings>

retención *nf, pl* **-ciones 1 :** retention **2 :** deduction, withholding

retener {80} *vt* **1 :** to retain, to keep **2 :** to withhold **3 :** to detain

retentivo, -va *adj* **:** retentive

reticencia *nf* **1 :** reluctance, reticence **2 :** insinuation

reticente *adj* **1 :** reluctant, reticent **2 :** insinuating, misleading

retina *nf* **:** retina

retintín *nm, pl* **-tines 1 :** jingle, jangle **2 con ~ :** sarcastically

retirada *nf* **1 :** retreat <batirse en retirada : to withdraw, to beat a retreat> **2 :** withdrawl (of funds) **3 :** retirement **4 :** refuge, haven

retirado, -da *adj* **1 :** remote, distant, far off **2 :** secluded, quiet

retirar *vt* **1 :** to remove, to take away, to recall **2 :** to withdraw, to take out — **retirarse** *vr* **1** REPLEGARSE **:** to retreat, to withdraw **2** JUBILARSE **:** to retire

retiro *nm* **1** JUBILACIÓN **:** retirement **2 :** withdrawal, retreat **3 :** seclusion

reto *nm* DESAFÍO **:** challenge, dare

retocar {72} *vt* **:** to touch up

retoñar *vi* **:** to sprout

retoño *nm* **:** sprout, shoot

retoque *nm* **:** retouching

retorcer {14} *vt* **1 :** to twist **2 :** to wring — **retorcerse** *vr* **1 :** to get twisted, to get tangled up **2 :** to squirm, to writhe, to wiggle about

retorcijón *nm, pl* **-jones :** cramp, sharp pain

retorcimiento *nm* **1 :** twisting, wringing **2 :** deviousness

retórica *nf* **:** rhetoric

retórico, -ca *adj* **:** rhetorical — **retóricamente** *adv*

retornar *v* **:** to return

retorno *nm* **:** return

retozar {21} *vi* **:** to frolic, to romp

retozo *nm* **:** frolicking

retozón, -zona *adj, mpl* **-zones :** playful

retracción *nf, pl* **-ciones :** retraction, withdrawal

retractable *adj* **:** retractable

retractación *nf, pl* **-ciones :** retraction (of a statement, etc.)

retractarse *vr* **1 :** to withdraw, to back down **2 ~ de :** to take back, to retract

retraer {81} *vt* **1 :** to bring back **2 :** to dissuade — **retraerse** *vr* **1** RETIRARSE **:** to withdraw, to retire **2** REFUGIARSE **:** to take refuge

retraído, -da *adj* **:** withdrawn, retiring, shy

retraimiento *nm* **1 :** shyness, timidity **2 :** withdrawal

retrasado, -da *adj* **1 :** retarded, mentally slow **2 :** behind, in arrears **3 :** backward (of a country) **4 :** slow (of a watch)

retrasar *vt* **1** DEMORAR, RETARDAR **:** to delay, to hold up **2 :** to put off, to postpone — **retrasarse** *vr* **1 :** to be late **2 :** to fall behind

retraso *nm* **1** ATRASO **:** delay, lateness **2 retraso mental :** mental retardation

retratar *vt* **1 :** to portray, to depict **2 :** to photograph **3 :** to paint a portrait of

retrato *nm* **1 :** depiction, portrayal **2 :** portrait, photograph

retrete *nm* **:** restroom, toilet

retribución *nf, pl* **-ciones 1 :** pay, payment **2 :** reward

retribuir {41} *vt* **1 :** to pay **2 :** to reward

retroactivo, -va *adj* **:** retroactive — **retroactivamente** *adv*

retroalimentación *nf, pl* **-ciones :** feedback

retroceder *vi* **1 :** to move back, to turn back **2 :** to back off, to back down **3 :** to recoil (of a firearm)

retroceso *nm* **1 :** backward movement **2 :** backing down **3 :** setback, relapse **4 :** recoil

retrógrado, -da *adj* **1 :** reactionary **2 :** retrograde

retropropulsión *nf* **:** jet propulsion

retrospectiva *nf* **:** retrospective, hindsight

retrospectivo, -va *adj* **1 :** retrospective **2 mirada retrospectiva :** backward glance

retrovisor *nm* **:** rearview mirror

retruécano *nm* **:** pun, play on words

retumbar *vi* **1 :** to boom, to thunder **2 :** to resound, to reverberate

retumbo *nm* **:** booming, thundering, roll

retuvo, etc. → **retener**

reubicar {72} *vt* **:** to relocate — **reubicación** *nf*

reuma *or* **reúma** *nmf* → **reumatismo**

reumático, -ca *adj* **:** rheumatic

reumatismo *nm* **:** rheumatism

reunión *nf, pl* **-niones 1 :** meeting **2 :** gathering, reunion

reunir {68} *vt* **1 :** to unite, to join, to bring together **2 :** to have, to possess <reunieron los requisitos necesarios : they fulfilled the necessary requirements> **3 :** to gather, to collect, to raise (funds) — **reunirse** *vr* **:** to meet

reutilizable *adj* **:** reusable

reutilizar {21} *vt* **:** to recycle, to reuse

revalidar *vt* **1 :** to confirm, to ratify **2 :** to defend (a title)

revaluar {3} *vt* **:** to reevaluate — **revaluación** *n*

revancha *nf* **1** DESQUITE **:** revenge, requital **2 :** rematch

revelación *nf, pl* **-ciones :** revelation

revelado *nm* **:** developing (of film)

revelador[1], **-dora** *adj* **:** revealing

revelador[2] *nm* **:** developer

revelar *vt* **1** : to reveal, to disclose **2** : to develop (film)
revendedor, -dora *n* **1** : scalper **2** DETALLISTA : retailer
revender *vt* **1** : to resell **2** : to scalp
reventa *nf* **1** : resale **2** : scalping
reventar {55} *vi* **1** ESTALLAR, EXPLOTAR : to burst, to blow up **2 ~ de** : to be bursting with — *vt* **1** : to burst **2** *fam* : to annoy, to rile
reventón *nm, pl* **-tones 1** : burst, bursting **2** : blowout, flat tire **3** *Mex fam* : bash, party
reverberar *vi* : to reverberate — **reverberación** *nf*
reverdecer {53} *vi* **1** : to grow green again **2** : to revive
reverencia *nf* **1** : reverence **2** : bow, curtsy
reverenciar *vt* : to revere, to venerate
reverendo[1], **-da** *adj* **1** : reverend **2** *fam* : total, absolute <es un reverendo imbécil : he is a complete idiot>
reverendo[2], **-da** *n* : reverend
reverente *adj* : reverent
reversa *nf Col, Mex* : reverse (gear)
reversible *adj* : reversible
reversión *nf, pl* **-siones** : reversion
reverso *nm* **1** : back, other side **2 el reverso de la medalla** : the complete opposite
revertir {76} *vi* **1** : to revert, to go back **2 ~ en** : to result in, to end up as
revés *nm, pl* **reveses 1** : back, wrong side **2** : setback, reversal **3** : backhand (in sports) **4 al revés** : the other way around, upside down, inside out **5 al revés de** : contrary to
revestimiento *nm* : covering, facing (of a building)
revestir {54} *vt* **1** : to coat, to cover, to surface **2** : to conceal, to disguise **3** : to take on, to assume <la reunión revistió gravedad : the meeting took on a serious note>
revisar *vt* **1** : to examine, to inspect, to check **2** : to check over, to overhaul (machinery) **3** : to revise
revisión *nf, pl* **-siones 1** : revision **2** : inspection, check
revisor, -sora *n* **1** : inspector **2** : conductor (on a train)
revista *nf* **1** : magazine, journal **2** : revue **3 pasar revista** : to review, to inspect
revistar *vt* : to review, to inspect
revitalizar {21} *vt* : to revitalize — **revitalización** *nf*
revivir *vi* : to revive, to come alive again — *vt* : to relive
revocación *nf, pl* **-ciones** : revocation, repeal
revocar {72} *vt* **1** : to revoke, to repeal **2** : to plaster (a wall)
revolcar {82} *vt* : to knock over, to knock down — **revolcarse** *vr* : to roll around, to wallow
revolcón *nm, pl* **-cones** *fam* : tumble, fall
revolotear *vi* : to flutter around, to flit
revoloteo *nm* : fluttering, flitting
revoltijo *nm* **1** FÁRRAGO : mess, jumble **2** *Mex* : traditional seafood dish
revoltoso, -sa *adj* : unruly, rebellious
revolución *nf, pl* **-ciones** : revolution
revolucionar *vt* : to revolutionize
revolucionario, -ria *adj & n* : revolutionary
revolver {89} *vt* **1** : to move about, to mix, to shake, to stir **2** : to upset (one's stomach) **3** : to mess up, to rummage through <revolver la casa : to turn the house upside down> — **revolverse** *vr* **1** : to toss and turn **2** VOLVERSE : to turn around
revólver *nm* : revolver
revoque *nm* : plaster
revuelo *nm* **1** : fluttering **2** : commotion, stir
revuelta *nf* : uprising, revolt
revuelto[1] *pp* → **revolver**
revuelto[2], **-ta** *adj* **1** : choppy, rough <mar revuelto : rough sea> **2** : untidy **3 huevos revueltos** : scrambled eggs
rey *nm* : king
reyerta *nf* : brawl, fight
rezagado, -da *n* : straggler, latecomer
rezagar {52} *vt* **1** : to leave behind **2** : to postpone — **rezagarse** *vr* : to fall behind, to lag
rezar {21} *vi* **1** : to pray **2** : to say <como reza el refrán : as the saying goes> **3 ~ con** : to concern, to have to do with — *vt* : to say, to recite <rezar un Ave María : to say a Hail Mary>
rezo *nm* : prayer, praying
rezongar {52} *vi* : to gripe, to grumble
rezumar *v* : to ooze, to leak
ría[1], **etc.** → **reír**
ría[2] *nf* : estuary
riachuelo *nm* ARROYO : brook, stream
riada *nf* : flood
ribera *nf* : bank, shore
ribete *nm* **1** : border, trim **2** : frill, adornment **3 ribetes** *nmpl* : hint, touch <tiene sus ribetes de genio : there's a touch of genius in him>
ribetear *vt* : to border, to edge, to trim
ricamente *adv* : richly, splendidly
rice, etc. → **rizar**
rico[1], **-ca** *adj* **1** : rich, wealthy **2** : fertile **3** : luxurious, valuable **4** : delicious **5** : adorable, lovely **6** : great, wonderful
rico[2], **-ca** *n* : rich person
ridiculez *nf, pl* **-leces** : ridiculousness, absurdity
ridiculizar {21} *vt* : to ridicule
ridículo[1], **-la** *adj* ABSURDO, DISPARATADO : ridiculous, ludicrous — **ridículamente** *adv*
ridículo[2], **-la** *n* **1 hacer el ridículo** : to make a fool of oneself **2 poner en ridículo** : to ridicule
ríe, etc. → **reír**
riega, riegue, etc. → **regar**
riego *nm* : irrigation

riel *nm* **:** rail, track

rienda *nf* **1 :** rein **2 dar rienda suelta a :** to give free rein to **3 llevar las riendas :** to be in charge **4 tomar las riendas :** to take control

riesgo *nm* **:** risk

riesgoso, -sa *adj* **:** risky

rifa *nf* **:** raffle

rifar *vt* **:** to raffle — *vi* **:** to quarrel, to fight

rifle *nm* **:** rifle

rige, rija, etc. → **regir**

rigidez *nf, pl* **-deces 1 :** rigidity, stiffness <rigidez cadavérica : rigor mortis> **2 :** inflexibility

rígido, -da *adj* **1 :** rigid, stiff **2 :** strict — **rígidamente** *adv*

rigor *nm* **1 :** rigor, harshness **2 :** precision, meticulousness **3 de ~ :** usual <la respuesta de rigor : the standard reply> **4 de ~ :** essential, obligatory **5 en ~ :** strictly speaking, in reality

riguroso, -sa *adj* **:** rigorous — **rigurosamente** *adv*

rima *nf* **1 :** rhyme **2 rimas** *nfpl* **:** verse, poetry

rimar *vi* **:** to rhyme

rimbombante *adj* **1 :** grandiose, showy **2 :** bombastic, pompous

rímel *or* **rimel** *nm* **:** mascara

rin *nm Col, Mex* **:** wheel, rim (of a tire)

rincón *nm, pl* **rincones :** corner, nook

rinde, etc. → **rendir**

rinoceronte *nm* **:** rhinoceros

riña *nf* **1 :** fight, brawl **2 :** dispute, quarrel

riñe, etc. → **reñir**

riñón *nm, pl* **riñones :** kidney

río[1] → **reír**

río[2] *nm* **1 :** river **2 :** torrent, stream <un río de lágrimas : a flood of tears>

ripio *nm* **1 :** debris, rubble **2 :** gravel

riqueza *nf* **1 :** wealth, riches *pl* **2 :** richness **3 riquezas naturales :** natural resources

risa *nf* **1 :** laughter, laugh **2 dar risa :** to make laugh <me dio mucha risa : I found it very funny> **3** *fam* **morirse de la risa :** to die laughing, to crack up

risco *nm* **:** crag, cliff

risible *adj* IRRISORIO **:** ludicrous, laughable

risita *nf* **:** giggle, titter, snicker

risotada *nf* **:** guffaw

ristra *nf* **:** string, series *pl*

risueño, -ña *adj* **1 :** cheerful, pleasant **2 :** promising

rítmico, -ca *adj* **:** rhythmical, rhythmic — **rítmicamente** *adv*

ritmo *nm* **1 :** rhythm **2 :** pace, tempo <trabajó a ritmo lento : she worked at a slow pace>

rito *nm* **:** rite, ritual

ritual *adj & nm* **:** ritual — **ritualmente** *adv*

rival *adj & nmf* COMPETIDOR **:** rival

rivalidad *nf* **:** rivalry, competition

rivalizar {21} *vi* **~ con :** to rival, to compete with

rizado, -da *adj* **1 :** curly **2 :** ridged **3 :** ripply, undulating

rizar {21} *vt* **1 :** to curl **2 :** to ripple, to ruffle (a surface) **3 :** to crumple, to fold — **rizarse** *vr* **1 :** to frizz **2 :** to ripple

rizo *nm* **1 :** curl **2 :** loop (in aviation)

robalo *or* **róbalo** *nm* **:** sea bass

robar *vt* **1 :** to steal **2 :** to rob, to burglarize **3** SECUESTRAR **:** to abduct, to kidnap **4 :** to captivate — *vi* **~ en :** to break into

roble *nm* **:** oak

robo *nm* **:** robbery, theft

robot *nm, pl* **robots :** robot

robótica *nf* **:** robotics

robustecer {53} *vt* **:** to grow stronger, to strengthen

robustez *nf* **:** sturdiness, robustness

robusto, -ta *adj* **:** robust, sturdy

roca *nf* **:** rock, boulder

roce[1], **etc.** → **rozar**

roce[2] *nm* **1 :** rubbing, chafing **2 :** brush, graze, touch **3 :** close contact, familiarity **4 :** friction, disagreement

rociador *nm* **:** sprinkler

rociar {85} *vt* **:** to spray, to sprinkle

rocío *nm* **1 :** dew **2 :** shower, light rain

rocola *nf* **:** jukebox

rocoso, -sa *adj* **:** rocky

rodada *nf* **:** track (of a tire), rut

rodado, -da *adj* **1 :** wheeled **2 :** dappled (of a horse)

rodaja *nf* **:** round, slice

rodaje *nm* **1 :** filming, shooting **2 :** breaking in (of a vehicle)

rodamiento *nm* **1 :** bearing <rodamiento de bolas : ball bearings> **2 :** rolling

rodar {19} *vi* **1 :** to roll, to roll down, to roll along <rodé por la escalera : I tumbled down the stairs> <todo rodaba bien : everthing was going along well> **2** GIRAR **:** to turn, to go around **3 :** to move about, to travel <andábamos rodando por todas partes : we drifted along from place to place> — *vt* **1 :** to film, to shoot **2 :** to break in (a new vehicle)

rodear *vt* **1 :** to surround **2 :** to round up (cattle) — *vi* **1 :** to go around **2 :** to beat around the bush — **rodearse** *vr* **~ de :** to surround oneself with

rodeo *nm* **1 :** rodeo, roundup **2** DESVÍO **:** detour **3 :** evasion <andar con rodeos : to beat around the bush> <sin rodeos : without reservations>

rodilla *nf* **:** knee

rodillo *nm* **1 :** roller **2 :** rolling pin

rododendro *nm* **:** rhododendron

roedor[1], **-dora** *adj* **:** gnawing

roedor[2] *nm* **:** rodent

roer {69} *vt* **1 :** to gnaw **2 :** to eat away at, to torment

rogar {16} *vt* **:** to beg, to request — *vi* **1 :** to beg, to plead **2 :** to pray

rojez *nf* **:** redness

roiga, etc. → **roer**

rojizo, -za *adj* : reddish

rojo[1], -ja *adj* **1** : red **2 ponerse rojo** : to blush

rojo[2] *nm* : red

rol *nm* **1** : role **2** : list, roll

rollo *nm* **1** : roll, coil <un rollo de cinta : a roll of tape> <en rollo : rolled up> **2** *fam* : roll of fat **3** *fam* : boring speech, lecture

romance *nm* **1** : Romance language **2** : ballad **3** : romance **4 en buen romance** : simply stated, simply put

romano, -na *adj & n* : Roman

romanticismo *nm* : romanticism

romántico, -ca *adj* : romantic — **románticamente** *adv*

rombo *nm* : rhombus

romería *nf* **1** : pilgrimage, procession **2** : crowd, gathering

romero[1], -ra *n* PEREGRINO : pilgrim

romero[2] *nm* : rosemary

romo, -ma *adj* : blunt, dull

rompecabezas *nms & pl* : puzzle, riddle

rompehielos *nms & pl* : icebreaker (ship)

rompehuelgas *nmfs & pl* ESQUIROL : strikebreaker, scab

rompenueces *nms & pl* : nutcracker

rompeolas *ns & pl* : breakwater, jetty

romper {70} *vt* **1** : to break, to smash **2** : to rip, to tear **3** : to break off (relations), to break (a contract) **4** : to break through, to break down **5** GASTAR : to wear out — *vi* **1** : to break <al romper del día : at the break of day> **2 ~ a** : to begin to, to burst out with <romper a llorar : to burst into tears> **3 ~ con** : to break off with

rompope *nm CA, Mex* : drink similar to eggnog

ron *nm* : rum

roncar {72} *vi* **1** : to snore **2** : to roar

ronco, -ca *adj* **1** : hoarse **2** : husky (of the voice) — **roncamente** *adv*

ronda *nf* **1** : beat, patrol **2** : round (of drinks, of negotiations, of a game)

rondar *vt* **1** : to patrol **2** : to hang around <siempre está rondando la calle : he's always hanging around the street> **3** : to be approximately <debe rondar los cincuenta : he must be about 50> — *vi* **1** : to be on patrol **2** : to prowl around, to roam about

ronque, etc. → **roncar**

ronquera *nf* : hoarseness

ronquido *nm* **1** : snore **2** : roar

ronronear *vi* : to purr

ronroneo *nm* : purr, purring

ronzal *nm* : halter (for an animal)

ronzar {21} *v* : to munch, to crunch

roña *nf* **1** : mange **2** : dirt, filth **3** *fam* : stinginess

roñoso, -sa *adj* **1** : mangy **2** : dirty **3** *fam* : stingy

ropa *nf* **1** : clothes *pl,* clothing **2 ropa interior** : underwear

ropaje *nm* : apparel, garments *pl,* regalia

ropero *nm* ARMARIO, CLÓSET : wardrobe, closet

rosa[1] *adj* : rose-colored, pink

rosa[2] *nm* : rose, pink (color)

rosa[3] *nf* : rose (flower)

rosáceo, -cea *adj* : pinkish

rosado[1], -da *adj* **1** : pink **2 vino rosado** : rosé

rosado[2] *nm* : pink (color)

rosal *nm* : rosebush

rosario *nm* **1** : rosary **2** : series <un rosario de islas : a string of islands>

rosbif *nm* : roast beef

rosca *nf* **1** : thread (of a screw) <una tapa a rosca : a screw top> **2** : ring, coil

roseta *nf* : rosette

rosquilla *nf* : ring-shaped pastry, doughnut

rostro *nm* : face, countenance

rotación *nf, pl* **-ciones** : rotation

rotar *vt* : to rotate, to turn — *vi* : to turn, to spin

rotativo[1], -va *adj* : rotary

rotativo[2] *nm* : newspaper

rotatorio, -ria → **rotativo[1]**

roto[1] *pp* → **romper**

roto[2], -ta *adj* **1** : broken **2** : ripped, torn

rotonda *nf* **1** : traffic circle, rotary **2** : rotunda

rotor *nm* : rotor

rótula *nf* : kneecap

rotular *vt* **1** : to head, to entitle **2** : to label

rótulo *nm* **1** : heading, title **2** : label, sign

rotundo, -da *adj* **1** REDONDO : round **2** : categorical, absolute <un éxito rotundo : a resounding success> — **rotundamente** *adv*

rotura *nf* : break, tear, fracture

roya *nf* : plant rust

roya, etc. → **roer**

rozado, -da *adj* GASTADO : worn

rozadura *nf* **1** : scratch, abrasion **2** : rubbed spot, sore

rozar {21} *vt* **1** : to chafe, to rub against **2** : to border on, to touch on **3** : to graze, to touch lightly — **rozarse** *vr* **~ con** *fam* : to rub shoulders with

ruandés, -desa *adj & n* : Rwandan

ruano, -na *adj* : roan

rubí *nm, pl* **rubíes** : ruby

rubio, -bia *adj & n* : blond

rublo *nm* : ruble

rubor *nm* **1** : flush, blush **2** : rouge, blusher

ruborizarse {21} *vr* : to blush

rubrica *nf* : title, heading

rubricar {72} *vt* **1** : sign with a flourish <firmado y rubricado : signed and sealed> **2** : to endorse, to sanction

rubro *nm* **1** : heading, title **2** : line, area (in business)

rudeza *nf* ASPEREZA : roughness, coarseness

rudimentario, -ria *adj* **:** rudimentary **— rudimentariamente** *adv*

rudimento *nm* **:** rudiment, basics *pl*

rudo, -da *adj* **1 :** rough, harsh **2 :** coarse, unpolished **— rudamente** *adv*

rueda[1], etc. → rodar

rueda[2] *nf* **1 :** wheel **2** RODAJA **:** round slice **3 :** circle, ring **4 rueda de andar :** treadmill **5 rueda de prensa :** press conference **6 ir sobre ruedas :** to go smoothly

ruedita *nf* **:** caster (on furniture)

ruedo *nm* **1 :** bullring, arena **2 :** rotation, turn **3 :** hem

ruega, ruegue, etc. → rogar

ruego *nm* **:** request, appeal, plea

rugido *nm* **:** roar

rugir {35} *vi* **:** to roar

ruibarbo *nm* **:** rhubarb

ruido *nm* **:** noise, sound

ruidoso, -sa *adj* **:** loud, noisy **— ruidosamente** *adv*

ruin *adj* **1 :** base, despicable **2 :** mean, stingy

ruina *nf* **1 :** ruin, destruction **2 :** downfall, collapse **3 ruinas** *nfpl* **:** ruins, remains

ruinoso, -sa *adj* **1 :** run-down, dilapidated **2 :** ruinous, disasterous

ruiseñor *nm* **:** nightingale

ruja, etc. → rugir

ruleta *nf* **:** roulette

rulo *nm* **:** curler, roller

rumano, -na *n* **:** Romanian, Rumanian

rumbo *nm* **1 :** direction, course <con rumbo a : bound for, heading for> <perder el rumbo : to go off course, to lose one's bearings> <sin rumbo : aimless, aimlessly> **2 :** ostentation, pomp **3 :** lavishness, generosity

rumiante *adj & nm* **:** ruminant

rumiar *vt* **:** to ponder, to mull over — *vi* **1 :** to chew the cud **2 :** to ruminate, to ponder

rumor *nm* **1 :** rumor **2 :** murmur

rumorearse *or* **rumorarse** *vr* **:** to be rumored <se rumorea que se va : rumor has it that she's leaving>

rumoroso, -sa *adj* **:** murmuring, babbling <un arroyo rumoroso : a babbling brook>

rupia *nf* **:** rupee

ruptura *nf* **1 :** break **2 :** breaking, breach (of a contract) **3 :** breaking off, breakup

rural *adj* **:** rural

ruso[1], -sa *adj & n* **:** Russian

ruso[2] *nm* **:** Russian (language)

rústico[1], -ca *adj* **:** rural, rustic

rústico[2], -ca *n* **:** rustic, country dweller

ruta *nf* **:** route

rutina *nf* **:** routine, habit

rutinario, -ria *adj* **:** routine, ordinary <visita rutinaria : routine visit> **— rutinariamente** *adv*

S

s *nf* **:** twentieth letter of the Spanish alphabet

sábado *nm* **1 :** Saturday **2 :** Sabbath

sábalo *nm* **:** shad

sabana *nf* **:** savanna

sábana *nf* **:** sheet, bedsheet

sabandija *nf* BICHO **:** bug, small reptile, pesky creature

sabático, -ca *adj* **:** sabbatical

sabedor, -dora *adj* **:** aware, informed

sabelotodo *nmf fam* **:** know-it-all

saber[1] {71} *vt* **1 :** to know **2 :** to know how to, to be able to <sabe tocar el violín : she can play the violin> **3 :** to learn, to find out **4 a ~ :** to wit, namely — *vi* **1 :** to know, to suppose **2 :** to be informed <supimos del desastre : we heard about the disaster> **3 :** to taste <esto no sabe bien : this doesn't taste right> **4 ~ a :** to taste like <sabe a naranja : it tastes like orange> **— saberse** *vr* **:** to know <ese chiste no me lo sé : I don't know that joke>

saber[2] *nm* **:** knowledge, learning

sabiamente *adv* **:** wisely

sabido, -da *adj* **:** well-known

sabiduría *nf* **1 :** wisdom **2 :** learning, knowledge

sabiendas *adv* **1 a ~ :** knowingly **2 a sabiendas de que :** knowing full well that

sabio[1], -bia *adj* **1** PRUDENTE **:** wise, sensible **2** DOCTO **:** learned

sabio[2], -bia *n* **1 :** wise person **2 :** savant, learned person

sable *nm* **:** saber, cutlass

sablear *vt fam* **:** to scrounge, to cadge

sabor *nm* **1 :** flavor, taste **2 sin ~ :** flavorless

saborear *vt* **1 :** to taste, to savor **2 :** to enjoy, to relish

sabotaje *nm* **:** sabotage

saboteador, -dora *n* **:** saboteur

sabotear *vt* **:** to sabotage

sabrá, etc. → saber

sabroso, -sa *adj* **1** RICO **:** delicious, tasty **2** AGRADABLE **:** pleasant, nice, lovely

sabueso *nm* **1 :** bloodhound **2** *fam* **:** detective, sleuth

sacacorchos *nms & pl* **:** corkscrew

sacapuntas *nms & pl* **:** pencil sharpener

sacar {72} *vt* **1 :** to pull out, to take out <saca el pollo del congelador : take the chicken out of the freezer> **2 :** to get, to obtain <saqué un 100 en el examen : I got 100 on the exam> **3 :** to get out, to extract <le saqué la infor-

mación : I got the information from him> **4 :** to stick out <sacar la lengua : to stick out one's tongue> **5 :** to bring out, to introduce <sacar un libro : to publish a book> <sacaron una moda nueva : they introduced a new style> **6 :** to take (photos) **7 :** to make (copies) — *vi* **1 :** to kick off (in soccer or football) **2 :** to serve (in sports)

sacarina *nf* **:** saccharin

sacarosa *nf* **:** sucrose

sacerdocio *nm* **:** priesthood

sacerdotal *adj* **:** priestly

sacerdote, -tisa *n* **:** priest *m,* priestess *f*

saciar *vt* **1** HARTAR **:** to sate, to satiate **2** SATISFACER **:** to satisfy

saciedad *nf* **:** satiety

saco *nm* **1 :** bag, sack **2 :** sac **3 :** jacket, sport coat

sacramento *nm* **:** sacrament — **sacramental** *adj*

sacrificar {72} *vt* **:** to sacrifice — **sacrificarse** *vr* **:** to sacrifice oneself, to make sacrifices

sacrificio *nm* **:** sacrifice

sacrilegio *nm* **:** sacrilege

sacrílego, -ga *adj* **:** sacrilegious

sacristán *nm, pl* **-tanes :** sexton, sacristan

sacristía *nf* **:** sacristy, vestry

sacro, -cra *adj* SAGRADO **:** sacred <arte sacro : sacred art>

sacrosanto, -ta *adj* **:** sacrosanct

sacudida *nf* **1 :** shaking **2 :** jerk, jolt, shock **3 :** shake-up, upheaval

sacudir *vt* **1 :** to shake, to beat **2 :** to jerk, to jolt **3 :** to dust off **4** CONMOVER **:** to shake up, to shock — **sacudirse** *vr* **:** to shake off

sacudón *nm, pl* **-dones :** intense jolt or shake-up

sádico[1], -ca *adj* **:** sadistic

sádico[2], -ca *n* **:** sadist

sadismo *nm* **:** sadism

safari *nm* **:** safari

saga *nf* **:** saga

sagacidad *nf* **:** sagacity, shrewdness

sagaz *adj, pl* **sagaces** PERSPICAZ **:** shrewd, discerning, sagacious

Sagitario *nmf* **:** Sagittarius, Sagittarian

sagrado, -da *adj* **:** sacred, holy

sainete *nm* **:** comedy sketch, one-act farce <este proceso es un sainete : these proceedings are a farce>

sajar *vt* **:** to lance, to cut open

sal[1] → **salir**

sal[2] *nf* **1 :** salt **2** *CA, Mex* **:** misfortune, bad luck

sala *nf* **1 :** living room **2 :** room, hall <sala de conferencias : lecture hall> <sala de urgencias : emergency room> <sala de baile : ballroom>

salado, -da *adj* **1 :** salty **2 agua salada :** salt water

salamandra *nf* **:** salamander

salami *nm* **:** salami

salar *vt* **1 :** to salt **2 :** to spoil, to ruin **3** *CoRi, Mex* **:** to jinx, to bring bad luck

salarial *adj* **:** salary, salary-related

salario *nm* **1 :** salary **2 salario mínimo :** minimum wage

salaz *adj, pl* **salaces :** salacious, lecherous

salchicha *nf* **1 :** sausage **2 :** frankfurter, wiener

salchichón *nf, pl* **-chones :** a type of deli meat

salchichonería *nf Mex* **1 :** delicatessen **2 :** cold cuts *pl*

saldar *vt* **:** to settle, to pay off <saldar una cuenta : to settle an account>

saldo *nm* **1 :** settlement, payment **2 :** balance <saldo de cuenta : account balance> **3 :** remainder, leftover merchandise

saldrá, etc. → **salir**

salero *nm* **1 :** saltshaker **2 :** wit, charm

salga, etc. → **salir**

salida *nf* **1 :** exit <salida de emergencia : emergency exit> **2 :** leaving, departure **3** SOLUCIÓN **:** way out, solution **4 :** start (of a race) **5** OCURRENCIA **:** wisecrack, joke **6 salida del sol :** sunrise

saliente[1] *adj* **1 :** departing, outgoing **2 :** projecting **3** DESTACADO **:** salient, prominent

saliente[2] *nm* **1 :** projection, protrusion **2 ventana en saliente :** bay window

salinidad *nf* **:** salinity, saltiness

salino, -na *adj* **:** saline <solución salina : saline solution>

salir {73} *vi* **1 :** to go out, to come out, to get out <salimos todas las noches : we go out every night> <su libro acaba de salir : her book just came out> **2** PARTIR **:** to leave, to depart **3** APARECER **:** to appear <salió en todos los diarios : it came out in all the papers> **4 :** to project, to stick out **5 :** to cost, to come to **6** RESULTAR **:** to turn out, to prove **7 :** to come up, to occur <salga lo que salga : whatever happens> <salió una oportunidad : an opportunity came up> **8 ~ a :** to take after, to look like, to resemble **9 ~ con :** to go out with, to date — **salirse** *vr* **1 :** to escape, to get out, to leak out **2 :** to come loose, to come off **3 salirse con la suya :** to get one's own way

saliva *nf* **:** saliva

salivar *vi* **:** to salivate

salmo *nm* **:** psalm

salmón[1] *adj* **:** salmon-colored

salmón[2] *nm, pl* **salmones :** salmon

salmuera *nf* **:** brine

salobre *adj* **:** brackish, briny

salón *nm, pl* **salones 1 :** hall, large room <salón de clase : classroom> <salón de baile : ballroom> **2 :** salon <salón de belleza : beauty salon> **3 :** parlor, sitting room

salpicadera *nf Mex* **:** fender

salpicadura *nf* **:** spatter, splash

salpicar {72} *vt* **1 :** to spatter, to splash **2 :** to sprinkle, to scatter about

salpimentar {55} *vt* **1 :** to season (with salt and pepper) **2 :** to spice up

salsa *nf* **1 :** sauce <salsa picante : hot sauce> <salsa inglesa : Worcestershire sauce> <salsa tártara : tartar sauce> **2 :** gravy **3 :** salsa (music) **4 salsa mexicana :** salsa (sauce)

salsero, -ra *n* **:** salsa musician

saltador, -dora *n* **:** jumper

saltamontes *nms & pl* **:** grasshopper

saltar *vi* **1** BRINCAR **:** to jump, to leap **2 :** to bounce **3 :** to come off, to pop out **4 :** to shatter, to break **5 :** to explode, to blow up — *vt* **1 :** to jump, to jump over **2 :** to skip, to miss — **saltarse** *vr* OMITIR **:** to skip, to omit <me salté ese capítulo : I skipped that chapter>

saltarín, -rina *adj, mpl* **-rines :** leaping, hopping <frijol saltarín : jumping bean>

salteado, -da *adj* **1 :** sautéed **2 :** jumbled up <los episodios se transmitieron salteados : the episodes were broadcast in random order>

salteador *nm* **:** highwayman

saltear *vt* **1** SOFREÍR **:** to sauté **2 :** to skip around, to skip over

saltimbanqui *nmf* **:** acrobat

salto *nm* **1** BRINCO **:** jump, leap, skip **2 :** jump, dive (in sports) **3 :** gap, omission **4 dar saltos :** to jump up and down **5** *or* **salto de agua** CATARATA **:** waterfall

saltón, -tona *adj, mpl* **saltones :** bulging, protruding

salubre *adj* **:** healthful, salubrious

salubridad *nf* **:** healthfulness, health

salud *nf* **1 :** health <buena salud : good health> **2 ¡salud! :** bless you! (when someone sneezes) **3 ¡salud! :** cheers!, to your health!

saludable *adj* **1** SALUBRE **:** healthful **2** SANO **:** healthy, well

saludar *vt* **1 :** to greet, to say hello to **2 :** to salute — **saludarse** *vr*

saludo *nm* **1 :** greeting, regards *pl* **2 :** salute

salutación *nf, pl* **-ciones :** salutation

salva *nf* **1 :** salvo, volley **2 salva de aplausos :** round of applause

salvación *nf, pl* **-ciones 1 :** salvation **2** RESCATE **:** rescue

salvado *nm* **:** bran

salvador, -dora *n* **1 :** savior, rescuer **2 el Salvador :** the Savior

salvadoreño, -ña *adj & n* **:** Salvadoran, El Salvadoran

salvaguardar *vt* **:** to safeguard

salvaguardia *or* **salvaguarda** *nf* **:** safeguard, defense

salvajada *nf* ATROCIDAD **:** atrocity, act of savagery

salvaje[1] *adj* **1 :** wild <animales salvajes : wild animals> **2 :** savage, cruel **3 :** primitive, uncivilized

salvaje[2] *nmf* **:** savage

salvajismo *nm* **:** savagery

salvamento *nm* **1 :** rescuing, lifesaving **2 :** salvation **3 :** refuge

salvar *vt* **1 :** to save, to rescue **2 :** to cover (a distance) **3 :** to get around (an obstacle), to overcome (a difficulty) **4 :** to cross, to jump across **5 salvando :** except for, excluding — **salvarse** *vr* **1 :** to survive, to escape **2 :** to save one's soul

salvavidas[1] *nms & pl* **1 :** life preserver **2 bote salvavidas :** lifeboat

salvavidas[2] *nmf* **:** lifeguard

salvedad *nf* **1** EXCEPCIÓN **:** exception **2 :** proviso, stipulation

salvia *nf* **:** sage (plant)

salvo[1]**, -va** *adj* **1 :** unharmed, sound <sano y salvo : safe and sound> **2 a ~ :** safe from danger

salvo[2] *prep* **1** EXCEPTO **:** except (for), save <todos asistirán salvo Jaime : all will attend except for Jaime> **2 salvo que :** unless <salvo que llueva : unless it rains>

salvoconducto *nm* **:** safe-conduct

samba *nf* **:** samba

San → **santo**[1]

sanar *vt* **:** to heal, to cure — *vi* **:** to get well, to recover

sanatorio *nm* **1 :** sanatorium **2 :** clinic, private hospital

sanción *nf, pl* **sanciones :** sanction

sancionar *vt* **1 :** to penalize, to impose a sanction on **2 :** to sanction, to approve

sancochar *vt* **:** to parboil

sandalia *nf* **:** sandal

sándalo *nm* **:** sandalwood

sandez *nf, pl* **sandeces** ESTUPIDEZ **:** nonsense, silly thing to say

sandía *nf* **:** watermelon

sandwich [ˈsandwitʃ, ˈsaŋgwitʃ] *nm, pl* **sandwiches** [-dwitʃɛs, -gwi-] EMPAREDADO **:** sandwich

saneamiento *nm* **1 :** cleaning up, sanitation **2 :** reorganizing, streamlining

sanear *vt* **1 :** to clean up, to sanitize **2 :** to reorganize, to streamline

sangrante *adj* **1 :** bleeding **2 :** flagrant, blatant

sangrar *vi* **:** to bleed — *vt* **:** to indent (a paragraph, etc.)

sangre *nf* **1 :** blood **2 a sangre fría :** in cold blood **3 a sangre y fuego :** by violent force **4 pura sangre :** thoroughbred

sangría *nf* **1 :** bloodletting **2 :** sangria (wine punch) **3 :** drain, draining <una sangría fiscal : a financial drain> **4 :** indentation, indenting

sangriento, -ta *adj* **1 :** bloody **2 :** cruel

sanguijuela *nf* **1 :** leech, bloodsucker **2 :** sponger, leech

sanguinario, -ria *adj* **:** bloodthirsty

sanguíneo, -nea *adj* **1 :** blood <vaso sanguíneo : blood vessel> **2 :** sanguine, ruddy

sanidad *nf* **1 :** health **2 :** public health, sanitation

sanitario[1], -ria *adj* **1 :** sanitary **2 :** health <centro sanitario : health center>

sanitario[2], -ria *n* **:** sanitation worker

sanitario[3] *nm Col, Mex, Ven* **:** toilet <los sanitarios : the toilets, the restroom>

sano, -na *adj* **1** SALUDABLE **:** healthy **2 :** wholesome **3 :** whole, intact

santiaguino, -na *adj* **:** of or from Santiago, Chile

santiamén *nm* **en un santiamén :** in no time at all

santidad *nf* **:** holiness, sanctity

santificar {72} *vt* **:** to sanctify, to consecrate, to hallow

santiguarse {10} *vr* PERSIGNARSE **:** to cross oneself

santo[1], -ta *adj* **1 :** holy, saintly <el Santo Padre : the Holy Father> <una vida santa : a saintly life> **2 Santo, Santa** (**San** *before names of masculine saints except those beginning with D or T*) **:** Saint <Santa Clara : Saint Claire> <Santo Tomás : Saint Thomas> <San Francisco : Saint Francis>

santo[2], -ta *n* **:** saint

santo[3] *nm* **1 :** saint's day **2** CUMPLEAÑOS **:** birthday

santuario *nm* **:** sanctuary

santurrón, -rrona *adj, mpl* **-rrones :** overly pious, sanctimonious — **santurronamente** *adv*

saña *nf* **1 :** fury, rage **2 :** viciousness <con saña : viciously>

sapo *nm* **:** toad

saque[1], etc. → sacar

saque[2] *nm* **1 :** kick-off (in soccer or football) **2 :** serve, service (in sports)

saqueador, -dora *n* DEPREDADOR **:** plunderer, looter

saquear *vt* **:** to sack, to plunder, to loot

saqueo *nm* DEPREDACIÓN **:** sacking, plunder, looting

sarampión *nm* **:** measles *pl*

sarape *nm CA, Mex* **:** serape, blanket

sarcasmo *nm* **:** sarcasm

sarcástico, -ca *adj* **:** sarcastic

sarcófago *nm* **:** sarcophagus

sardina *nf* **:** sardine

sardónico, -ca *adj* **:** sardonic

sarga *nf* **:** serge

sargento *nmf* **:** sergeant

sarna *nf* **:** mange

sarnoso, -sa *adj* **:** mangy

sarpullido *nm* ERUPCIÓN **:** rash

sarro *nm* **1 :** deposit, coating **2 :** tartar, plaque

sartén *nmf, pl* **sartenes 1 :** frying pan **2 tener la sartén por el mango :** to call the shots, to be in control

sasafrás *nm* **:** sassafras

sastre, -tra *n* **:** tailor

sastrería *nf* **1 :** tailoring **2 :** tailor's shop

Satanás *or* **Satán** *nm* **:** Satan, the devil

satánico, -ca *adj* **:** satanic

satélite *nm* **:** satellite

satín *or* **satén** *nm, pl* **satines** *or* **satenes :** satin

satinado, -da *adj* **:** satiny, glossy

sátira *nf* **:** satire

satírico, -ca *adj* **:** satirical, satiric

satirizar {21} *vt* **:** to satirize

sátiro *nm* **:** satyr

satisfacción *nf, pl* **-ciones :** satisfaction

satisfacer {74} *vt* **1 :** to satisfy **2 :** to fulfill, to meet **3 :** to pay, to settle — **satisfacerse** *vr* **1 :** to be satisfied **2 :** to take revenge

satisfactorio, -ria *adj* **:** satisfactory — **satisfactoriamente** *adv*

satisfecho, -cha *adj* **:** satisfied, content, pleased

saturación *nf, pl* **-ciones :** saturation

saturar *vt* **1 :** to saturate, to fill up **2 :** to satiate, to surfeit

saturnismo *nm* **:** lead poisoning

Saturno *nm* **:** Saturn

sauce *nm* **:** willow

saúco *nm* **:** elder (tree)

saudí *or* **saudita** *adj & nmf* **:** Saudi, Saudi Arabian

sauna *nmf* **:** sauna

savia *nf* **:** sap

saxofón *nm, pl* **-fones :** saxophone

sazón[1] *nf, pl* **sazones 1 :** flavor, seasoning **2 :** ripeness, maturity <en sazón : in season, ripe> **3 a la sazón :** at that time, then

sazón[2] *nmf, pl* **sazones** *Mex* **:** flavor, seasoning

sazonar *vt* CONDIMENTAR **:** to season, to spice

sé → saber, ser

se *pron* **1 :** to him, to her, to you, to them <se los daré a ella : I'll give them to her> **2 :** each other, one another <se abrazaron : they hugged each other> **3 :** himself, herself, itself, yourself, yourselves, themselves <se afeitó antes de salir : he shaved before leaving> **4** (*used in passive constructions*) <se dice que es hermosa : they say she's beautiful> <se habla inglés : English spoken>

sea, etc. → ser

sebo *nm* **1 :** grease, fat **2 :** tallow **3 :** suet

secado *nm* **:** drying

secador *nm* **:** hair dryer

secadora *nf* **1 :** dryer, clothes dryer **2** *Mex* **:** hair dryer

secante *nm* **:** blotting paper, blotter

secar {72} *v* **:** to dry — **secarse** *vr* **1 :** to get dry **2 :** to dry up

sección *nf, pl* **secciones 1 :** section <sección transversal : cross section> **2 :** department, division

seco, -ca *adj* **1 :** dry **2** DISECADO **:** dried <fruta seca : dried fruit> **3 :** thin, lean **4 :** curt, brusque **5 :** sharp <un golpe seco : a sharp blow> **6 a secas :** simply, just <se llama Chico, a secas : he's just called Chico> **7 en ~**

: abruptly, suddenly <frenar en seco : to make a sudden stop>
secoya *nf* : sequoia, redwood
secreción *nf, pl* **-ciones** : secretion
secretar *vt* : to secrete
secretaría *nf* **1** : secretariat, administrative department **2** *Mex* : ministry, cabinet office
secretariado *nm* **1** : secretariat **2** : secretarial profession
secretario, -ria *n* : secretary — **secretarial** *adj*
secreto[1], -ta *adj* **1** : secret **2** : secretive — **secretamente** *adv*
secreto[2] *nm* **1** : secret **2** : secrecy
secta *nf* : sect
sectario, -ria *adj & n* : sectarian
sector *nm* : sector
secuaz *nmf, pl* **secuaces** : follower, henchman, underling
secuela *nf* : consequence, sequel <las secuelas de la guerra : the aftermath of the war>
secuencia *nf* : sequence
secuestrador, -dora *n* **1** : kidnapper, abductor **2** : hijacker
secuestrar *vt* **1** RAPTAR : to kidnap, to abduct **2** : to hijack, to commandeer **3** CONFISCAR : to confiscate, to seize
secuestro *nm* **1** RAPTO : kidnapping, abduction **2** : hijacking **3** : seizure, confiscation
secular *adj* : secular — **secularismo** *nm* — **secularización** *nf*
secundar *vt* : to support, to second
secundaria *nf* **1** : secondary education, high school **2** *Mex* : junior high school, middle school
secundario, -ria *adj* : secondary
secuoya *nf* : sequoia
sed *nf* **1** : thirst <tener sed : to be thirsty> **2 tener sed de** : to hunger for, to thirst for
seda *nf* : silk
sedación *nf, pl* **-ciones** : sedation
sedal *nm* : fishing line
sedán *nm, pl* **sedanes** : sedan
sedante *adj & nm* CALMANTE : sedative
sedar *vt* : to sedate
sede *nf* **1** : seat, headquarters **2** : venue, site **3 la Santa Sede** : the Holy See
sedentario, -ria *adj* : sedentary
sedición *nf, pl* **-ciones** : sedition — **sedicioso, -sa** *adj*
sediento, -ta *adj* : thirsty, thirsting
sedimentación *nf, pl* **-ciones** : sedimentation
sedimentario, -ria *adj* : sedimentary
sedimento *nm* : sediment
sedoso, -sa *adj* : silky, silken
seducción *nf, pl* **-ciones** : seduction
seducir {61} *vt* **1** : to seduce **2** : to captivate, to charm
seductivo, -va *adj* : seductive
seductor[1], -tora *adj* **1** SEDUCTIVO : seductive **2** ENCANTADOR : charming, alluring
seductor[2], -tora *n* : seducer
segar {49} *vt* **1** : to reap, to harvest, to cut **2** : to sever abruptly <una vida segada por la enfermedad : a life cut short by illness>
seglar[1] *adj* LAICO : lay, secular
seglar[2] *nm* LAICO : layperson, layman *m,* laywoman *f*
segmentación *nm, pl* **-ciones** : segmentation
segmentado, -da *adj* : segmented
segmento *nm* : segment
segregar {52} *vt* **1** : to segregate **2** SECRETAR : to secrete
seguida *nf* **en ~** : right away, immediately <vuelvo en seguida : I'll be right back>
seguidamente *adv* **1** : next, immediately after **2** : without a break, continuously
seguido[1] *adv* **1** RECTO : straight, straight ahead **2** : often, frequently
seguido[2], -da *adj* **1** CONSECUTIVO : consecutive, successive <tres días seguidos : three days in a row> **2** : straight, unbroken **3 ~ por** *or* **~ de** : followed by
seguidor, -dora *n* : follower, supporter
seguimiento *nm* **1** : following, pursuit **2** : continuation **3** : tracking, monitoring
seguir {75} *vt* **1** : to follow <el sol sigue la lluvia : sunshine follows the rain> <seguiré tu consejo : I'll follow your advice> <me siguieron con la mirada : they followed me with their eyes> **2** : to go along, to keep on <seguimos toda la carretera panamericana : we continued along the Pan-American Highway> <siguió hablando : he kept on talking> <seguir el curso : to stay on course> **3** : to take (a course, a treatment) — *vi* **1** : to go on, to keep going <sigue adelante : keep going, carry on> **2** : to remain, to continue to be <¿todavía sigues aquí? : you're still here?> <sigue con vida : she's still alive> **3** : to follow, to come after <la frase que sigue : the following sentence>
según[1] *adv* : it depends <según y como : it all depends on>
según[2] *conj* **1** COMO, CONFORME : as, just as <según lo dejé : just as I left it> **2** : depending on how <según se vea : depending on how one sees it>
según[3] *prep* **1** : according to <según los rumores : according to the rumors> **2** : depending on <según los resultados : depending on the results>
segundo[1], -da *adj* : second <el segundo lugar : second place>
segundo[2], -da *n* **1** : second (in a series) **2** : second (person), second-in-command
segundo[3] *nm* : second <sesenta segundos : sixty seconds>
seguramente *adv* **1** : for sure, surely **2** : probably

seguridad *nf* **1** : safety, security **2** : (financial) security <seguridad social : Social Security> **3** CERTEZA : certainty, assurance <con toda seguridad : with complete certainty> **4** : confidence, self-confidence
seguro[1] *adv* : certainly, definitely <va a llover, seguro : it's going to rain for sure> <¡seguro que sí! : of course!>
seguro[2], **-ra** *adj* **1** : safe, secure **2** : sure, certain <estoy segura que es él : I'm sure that's him> **3** : reliable, trustworthy **4** : self-assured
seguro[3] *nm* **1** : insurance <seguro de vida : life insurance> **2** : fastener, clasp **3** *Mex* : safety pin
seis *adj & nm* : six
seiscientos[1], **-tas** *adj* : six hundred
seiscientos[2] *nms & pl* : six hundred
selección *nf, pl* **-ciones 1** ELECCIÓN : selection, choice **2 selección natural** : natural selection
seleccionar *vt* ELEGIR : to select, to choose
selectivo, -va *adj* : selective — **selectivamente** *adv*
selecto, -ta *adj* **1** : choice, select **2** EXCLUSIVO : exclusive
selenio *nm* : selenium
sellar *vt* **1** : to seal **2** : to stamp
sello *nm* **1** : seal **2** ESTAMPILLA, TIMBRE : postage stamp **3** : hallmark, characteristic
selva *nf* **1** BOSQUE : woods *pl,* forest <selva húmeda : rain forest> **2** JUNGLA : jungle
selvático, -ca *adj* **1** : forest, jungle <sendero selvático : jungle path> **2** : wild
semáforo *nm* **1** : traffic light **2** : stop signal
semana *nf* : week
semanal *adj* : weekly — **semanalmente** *adv*
semanario *nm* : weekly (publication)
semántica *nf* : semantics
semántico, -ca *adj* : semantic
semblante *nm* **1** : countenance, face **2** : appearance, look
semblanza *nf* : biographical sketch, profile
sembrado *nm* : cultivated field
sembrador, -dora *n* : planter, sower
sembradora *nf* : seeder (machine)
sembrar {55} *vt* **1** : to plant, to sow **2** : to scatter, to strew <sembrar el pánico : to spread panic>
semejante[1] *adj* **1** PARECIDO : similar, alike **2** TAL : such <nunca he visto cosa semejante : I have never seen such a thing>
semejante[2] *nm* PRÓJIMO : fellowman
semejanza *nf* PARECIDO : similarity, resemblance
semejar *vi* : to resemble, to look like — **semejarse** *vr* : to be similar, to look alike
semen *nm* : semen
semental *nm* : stud (animal) <caballo semental : stallion>
semestre *nm* : semester
semicírculo *nm* : semicircle, half circle
semiconductor *nm* : semiconductor
semidiós *nm, pl* **-dioses** : demigod *m*
semifinal *nf* : semifinal
semifinalista[1] *adj* : semifinal
semifinalista[2] *nmf* : semifinalist
semiformal *adj* : semiformal
semilla *nf* : seed
semillero *nm* **1** : seedbed **2** : hotbed, breeding ground
seminario *nm* **1** : seminary **2** : seminar, graduate course
seminarista *nm* : seminarian
semiprecioso, -sa *adj* : semiprecious
semita[1] *adj* : Semitic
semita[2] *nmf* : Semite
sémola *nf* : semolina
sempiterno, -na *adj* ETERNO : eternal, everlasting
senado *nm* : senate
senador, -dora *n* : senator
sencillamente *adv* : simply, plainly
sencillez *nf* : simplicity
sencillo[1], **-lla** *adj* **1** : simple, easy **2** : plain, unaffected **3** : single
sencillo[2] *nm* **1** : single (recording) **2** : small change (coins) **3** : one-way ticket
senda *nf* CAMINO, SENDERO : path, way
sendero *nm* CAMINO, SENDA : path, way
sendos, -das *adj pl* : each, both <llevaban sendos vestidos nuevos : they were each wearing a new dress>
senectud *nf* ANCIANIDAD : old age
senegalés, -lesa *adj & n, mpl* **-leses** : Senegalese
senil *adj* : senile — **senilidad** *nf*
seno *nm* **1** : breast, bosom <los senos : the breasts> <el seno de la familia : the bosom of the family> **2** : sinus **3 seno materno** : womb
sensación *nf, pl* **-ciones 1** IMPRESIÓN : feeling <tener la sensación : to have a feeling> **2** : sensation <causar sensación : to cause a sensation>
sensacional *adj* : sensational
sensacionalista *adj* : sensationalistic, lurid
sensatez *nf* **1** : good sense **2 con ~** : sensibly
sensato, -ta *n* : sensible, sound — **sensatamente** *adv*
sensibilidad *nf* **1** : sensitivity, sensibility **2** SENSACIÓN : feeling
sensibilizar {21} *vt* : to sensitize
sensible *adj* **1** : sensitive **2** APRECIABLE : considerable, significant
sensiblemente *adv* : considerably, significantly
sensiblería *nf* : sentimentality, mush
sensiblero, -ra *adj* : mawkish, sentimental, mushy
sensitivo, -va *adj* **1** : sense <órganos sensitivos : sense organs> **2** : sentient, capable of feeling
sensor *nm* : sensor

sensorial *adj* **:** sensory

sensual *adj* **:** sensual, sensuous — **sensualmente** *adv*

sensualidad *nf* **:** sensuality

sentado, -da *adj* **1 :** sitting, seated **2 :** established, settled <dar por sentado : to take for granted> <dejar sentado : to make clear> **3 :** sensible, steady, judicious

sentar {55} *vt* **1 :** to seat, to sit **2 :** to establish, to set — *vi* **1 :** to suit <ese color te sienta : that color suits you> **2 :** to agree with (of food or drink) <las cebollas no me sientan : onions don't agree with me> **3 :** to please <le sentó mal el paseo : she didn't enjoy the trip> — **sentarse** *vr* **:** to sit, to sit down <siéntese, por favor : please have a seat>

sentencia *nf* **1 :** sentence, judgment **2 :** maxim, saying

sentenciar *vt* **:** to sentence

sentido[1], -da *adj* **1 :** heartfelt, sincere <mi más sentido pésame : my sincerest condolences> **2 :** touchy, sensitive **3 :** offended, hurt

sentido[2] *nm* **1 :** sense <sentido común : common sense> <los cinco sentidos : the five senses> <sin sentido : senseless> **2** CONOCIMIENTO **:** consciousness **3** SIGNIFICADO **:** meaning, sense <doble sentido : double entendre> **4 :** direction <calle de sentido único : one-way street>

sentimental[1] *adj* **1 :** sentimental **2 :** love, romantic <vida sentimental : love life>

sentimental[2] *nmf* **:** sentimentalist

sentimentalismo *nm* **:** sentimentality, sentimentalism

sentimiento *nm* **1 :** feeling, emotion **2** PESAR **:** regret, sorrow

sentir {76} *vt* **1 :** to feel, to experience <no siento nada de dolor : I don't feel any pain> <sentía sed : he was feeling thirsty> <sentir amor : to feel love> **2** PERCIBIR **:** to perceive, to sense <sentir un ruido : to hear a noise> **3** LAMENTAR **:** to regret, to feel sorry for <lo siento mucho : I'm very sorry> — *vi* **1 :** to have feeling, to feel **2 sin ~ :** without noticing, inadvertently — **sentirse** *vr* **1 :** to feel <¿te sientes mejor? : are you feeling better?> **2** *Chile, Mex* **:** to take offense

seña *nf* **1 :** sign, signal **2 dar señas de :** to show signs of

señal *nf* **1 :** signal **2 :** sign <señal de tráfico : traffic sign> **3** INDICIO **:** indication <en señal de : as a token of> **4** VESTIGIO **:** trace, vestige **5 :** scar, mark **6 :** deposit, down payment

señalado, -da *adj* **:** distinguished, notable

señalador *nm* **:** marker <señalador de libros : bookmark>

señalar *vt* **1** INDICAR **:** to indicate, to show **2 :** to mark **3 :** to point out, to stress **4 :** to fix, to set — **señalarse** *vr* **:** to distinguish oneself

señor, -ñora *n* **1 :** gentleman *m,* man *m,* lady *f,* woman *f,* wife *f* **2 :** Sir *m,* Madam *f* <estimados señores : Dear Sirs> **3 :** Mr. *m,* Mrs. *f* **4 :** lord *m,* lady *f* <el Señor : the Lord>

señoría *nf* **1 :** lordship **2 Su Señoría :** Your Honor

señorial *adj* **:** stately, regal

señorío *nm* **1 :** manor, estate **2 :** dominion, power **3 :** elegance, class

señorita *nf* **1 :** young lady, young woman **2 :** Miss

señuelo *nm* **1 :** decoy **2 :** bait

sépalo *nm* **:** sepal

sepa, etc. → **saber**

separación *nf, pl* **-ciones 1 :** separation, division **2 :** gap, space

separadamente *adv* **:** separately, apart

separado, -da *adj* **1 :** separated **2 :** separate <vidas separadas : separate lives> **3 por ~ :** separately

separar *vt* **1 :** to separate, to divide **2 :** to split up, to pull apart — **separarse** *vr*

sepelio *nm* **:** interment, burial

sepia[1] *adj & nm* **:** sepia

sepia[2] *nf* **:** cuttlefish

septentrional *adj* **:** northern

séptico, -ca *adj* **:** septic

septiembre *nm* **:** September

séptimo[1], -ma *adj* **:** seventh

séptimo[2] *nm* **:** seventh

septuagésimo[1], -ma *adj* **:** seventieth

septuagésimo[2] *nm* **:** seventieth

sepulcral *adj* **1 :** sepulcral **2 :** dismal, gloomy

sepulcro *nm* TUMBA **:** tomb, sepulchre

sepultar *vt* ENTERRAR **:** to bury

sepultura *nf* **1 :** burial **2** TUMBA **:** grave, tomb

seque, etc. → **secar**

sequedad *nf* **1 :** dryness **2 :** brusqueness, curtness

sequía *nf* **:** drought

séquito *nm* **:** retinue, entourage

ser[1] {77} *vi* **1 :** to be <él es mi hermano : he is my brother> <Camila es linda : Camila is pretty> **2 :** to exist, to live <ser, o no ser : to be or not to be> **3 :** to take place, to occur <el concierto es el domingo : the concert is on Sunday> **4** (*used with expressions of time, date, season*) <son las diez : it's ten o'clock> <hoy es el 9 : today's the 9th> **5 :** to cost, to come to <¿cuánto es? : how much is it?> **6** (*with the future tense*) **:** to be able to be <¿será posible? : can it be possible?> **7 ~ de :** to come from <somos de Managua : we're from Managua> **8 ~ de :** to belong to <ese lápiz es de Juan : that's Juan's pencil> **9 es que :** the thing is that <es que no lo conozco : it's just that I don't know him> **10 ¡sea! :** agreed!, all right! **11 sea . . . sea :** either . . . or — *v aux* (*used in passive constructions*) **:** to be <la cuenta

ha sido pagada : the bill has been paid> <él fue asesinado : he was murdered>
ser² *nm* : being <ser humano : human being>
seráfico, -ca *adj* : angelic, seraphic
serbio¹, -bia *adj & n* : Serb, Serbian
serbio² *nm* : Serbian (language)
serbocroata¹ *adj* : Serbo-Croatian
serbocroata² *nm* : Serbo-Croatian (language)
serenar *vt* : to calm, to soothe — **serenarse** *vr* CALMARSE : to calm down
serenata *nf* : serenade
serendipia *nf* : serendipity
serenidad *nf* : serenity, calmness
sereno¹, -na *adj* **1** SOSEGADO : serene, calm, composed **2** : fair, clear (of weather) **3** : calm, still (of the sea) — **serenamente** *adv*
sereno² *nm* : night watchman
seriado, -da *adj* : serial
serial *nm* : serial (on radio or television)
seriamente *adv* : seriously
serie *nf* **1** : series **2** SERIAL : serial **3 fabricación en serie** : mass production **4 fuera de serie** : extraordinary, amazing
seriedad *nf* **1** : seriousness, earnestness **2** : gravity, importance
serio, -ria *adj* **1** : serious, earnest **2** : reliable, responsible **3** : important **4 en ~** : seriously, in earnest — **seriamente** *adv*
sermón *nm, pl* **sermones 1** : sermon **2** *fam* : harangue, lecture
sermonear *vt fam* : to harangue, to lecture
serpentear *vi* : to twist, to wind — **serpenteante** *adj*
serpentina *nf* : paper streamer
serpiente *nf* : serpent, snake
serrado, -da *adj* DENTADO : serrated
serranía *nf* : mountainous area
serrano, -na *adj* : from the mountains
serrar {55} *vt* : to saw
serrín *nm, pl* **serrines** : sawdust
serruchar *vt* : to saw up
serrucho *nm* : saw, handsaw
servicentro *nm Peru* : gas station
servicial *adj* : obliging, helpful
servicio *nm* **1** : service **2** SAQUE : serve (in sports) **3 servicios** *nmpl* : restroom
servidor, -dora *n* **1** : servant **2 su seguro servidor** : yours truly (in correspondence)
servidumbre *nf* **1** : servitude **2** : help, servants *pl*
servil *adj* **1** : servile, subservient **2** : menial
servilismo *nm* : servility, subservience
servilleta *nf* : napkin
servir {54} *vt* **1** : to serve, to be of use to **2** : to serve, to wait **3** SURTIR : to fill (an order) — *vi* **1** : to work <mi radio no sirve : my radio isn't working> **2** : to be of use, to be helpful <esa computadora no sirve para nada : that computer's perfectly useless> — **servirse** *vr* **1** : to help oneself to **2** : to be kind enough <sírvase enviarnos un catálogo : please send us a catalog>
sésamo *nm* AJONJOLÍ : sesame, sesame seeds *pl*
sesenta *adj & nm* : sixty
sesentavo¹, -va *adj* : sixtieth
sesentavo² *n* : sixtieth (fraction)
sesgado, -da *adj* **1** : inclined, tilted **2** : slanted, biased
sesgar {52} *vt* **1** : to cut on the bias **2** : to tilt **3** : to bias, to slant
sesgo *nm* : bias
sesgue, etc. → **sesgar**
sesión *nf, pl* **sesiones 1** : session **2** : showing, performance
sesionar *vi* REUNIRSE : to meet, to be in session
seso *nm* **1** : brains, intelligence **2 sesos** *nmpl* : brains (as food)
sesudo, -da *adj* **1** : prudent, sensible **2** : brainy
set *nm, pl* **sets** : set (in tennis)
seta *nf* : mushroom
setecientos¹, -tas *adj* : seven hundred
setecientos² *nms & pl* : seven hundred
setenta *adj & nm* : seventy
setentavo¹, -va *adj* : seventieth
setentavo² *nm* : seventieth
setiembre *nm* → **septiembre**
seto *nm* **1** : fence, enclosure **2 seto vivo** : hedge
seudónimo *nm* : pseudonym
severidad *nf* **1** : harshness, severity **2** : strictness
severo, -ra *adj* **1** : harsh, severe **2** ESTRICTO : strict — **severamente** *adv*
sexagésimo¹, -ma *adj* : sixtieth, sixty-
sexagésimo², -ma *n* : sixtieth, sixty- (in a series)
sexismo *nm* : sexism — **sexista** *adj & nmf*
sexo *nm* : sex
sextante *nm* : sextant
sexteto *nm* : sextet
sexto, -ta *adj* : sixth — **sexto, -ta** *n*
sexual *adj* : sexual, sex <educación sexual : sex education> — **sexualmente** *adv*
sexualidad *nf* : sexuality
sexy *adj, pl* **sexy** *or* **sexys** : sexy
shock [ˈʃɔk, ˈtʃɔk] *nm* : shock <estado de shock : state of shock>
short *nm, pl* **shorts** : shorts *pl*
show *nm, pl* **shows** : show
si *conj* **1** : if <lo haré si me pagan : I'll do it if they pay me> <si lo supiera te lo diría : if I knew it I would tell you> **2** : whether, if <no importa si funciona o no : it doesn't matter whether it works (or not)> **3** (*expressing desire, protest, or surprise*) <si supiera la verdad : if only I knew the truth> <¡si no quiero! : but I don't want to!> **4 si bien** : although <si bien se ha progresado : although progress has been made> **5 si no** : otherwise, or

else <si no, no voy : otherwise I won't go>

sí[1] *adv* **1 :** yes <sí, gracias : yes, please> <creo que sí : I think so> **2 sí que :** indeed, absolutely <esta vez sí que ganaré : this time I'm sure to win> **3 porque sí** *fam* **:** because, just because <lo hizo porque sí : she did it just because>

sí[2] *nm* **:** yes <dar el sí : to say yes, to express consent>

sí[3] *pron* **1 de por sí** *or* **en sí :** by itself, in itself, per se **2 fuera de sí :** beside oneself **3 para sí (mismo) :** to himself, to herself, for himself, for herself **4 entre ~ :** among themselves

siamés, -mesa *adj & n, mpl* **siameses :** Siamese

sibilante *adj & nf* **:** sibilant

siciliano, -na *adj & n* **:** Sicilian

sico- → **psico-**

sicomoro *or* **sicómoro** *nm* **:** sycamore

SIDA *or* **sida** *nm* **:** AIDS

siderurgia *nf* **:** iron and steel industry

siderúrgico, -ca *adj* **:** steel, iron <the steel industry : la industria siderúrgica>

sidra *nf* **:** hard cider

siega[1], **siegue, etc.** → **segar**

siega[2] *nf* **1 :** harvesting **2 :** harvest time **3 :** harvested crop

siembra[1], **etc.** → **sembrar**

siembra[2] *nf* **1 :** sowing **2 :** sowing season **3** SEMBRADO **:** cultivated field

siempre *adv* **1 :** always <siempre tienes hambre : you're always hungry> **2 :** still <¿siempre te vas? : are you still going?> **3** *Mex* **:** after all <siempre no fui : I didn't go after all> **4 siempre que :** whenever, every time <siempre que pasa : every time he walks by> **5 para ~ :** forever, for good **6 siempre y cuando :** provided that

sien *nf* **:** temple (on the forehead)

sienta, etc. → **sentar**

siente, etc. → **sentir**

sierpe *nf* **:** serpent, snake

sierra[1], **etc.** → **serrar**

sierra[2] *nf* **1 :** saw <sierra de vaivén : jigsaw> **2** CORDILLERA **:** mountain range **3 :** mountains *pl* <viven en la sierra : they live in the mountains>

siervo, -va *n* **1 :** slave **2 :** serf

siesta *nf* **:** nap, siesta

siete *adj & nm* **:** seven

sífilis *nf* **:** syphilis

sifón *nm, pl* **sifones :** siphon

siga, sigue, etc. → **seguir**

sigilo *nm* **:** secrecy, stealth

sigiloso, -sa *adj* FURTIVO **:** furtive, stealthy — **sigilosamente** *adv*

sigla *nf* **:** acronym, abbreviation

siglo *nm* **1 :** century **2 :** age <el Siglo de Oro : the Golden Age> <hace siglos que no te veo : I haven't seen you in ages> **3 :** world, secular life

signar *vt* **:** to sign (a treaty or agreement)

signatario, -ria *n* **:** signatory

significación *nf, pl* **-ciones 1 :** significance, importance **2 :** signification, meaning

significado *nm* **1 :** sense, meaning **2 :** significance

significante *adj* **:** significant

significar {72} *vt* **1 :** to mean, to signify **2 :** to express, to make known — **significarse** *vr* **1 :** to draw attention, to become known **2 :** to take a stance

significativo, -va *adj* **1 :** significant, important **2 :** meaningful — **significativamente** *adv*

signo *nm* **1 :** sign <signo de igual : equal sign> <un signo de alegría : a sign of happiness> **2 :** (punctuation) mark <signo de interrogación : question mark> <signo de admiración : exclamation point> <signo de intercalación : caret>

siguiente *adj* **:** next, following

sílaba *nf* **:** syllable

silábico, -ca *adj* **:** syllabic

silbar *v* **:** to whistle

silbato *nm* PITO **:** whistle

silbido *nm* **:** whistle, whistling

silenciador *nm* **1 :** muffler (of an automobile) **2 :** silencer

silenciar *vt* **1 :** to silence **2 :** to muffle

silencio *nm* **1 :** silence, quiet <¡silencio! : be quiet!> **2 :** rest (in music)

silencioso, -sa *adj* **:** silent, quiet — **silenciosamente** *adv*

sílice *nf* **:** silica

silicio *nm* **:** silicon

silla *nf* **1 :** chair **2 silla de ruedas :** wheelchair

sillón *nm, pl* **sillones :** armchair, easy chair

silo *nm* **:** silo

silueta *nf* **1 :** silhouette **2 :** figure, shape

silvestre *adj* **:** wild <flor silvestre : wildflower>

silvicultor, -tora *n* **:** forester

silvicultura *nf* **:** forestry

sima *nf* ABISMO **:** chasm, abyss

simbólico, -ca *adj* **:** symbolic — **simbólicamente** *adj*

simbolismo *nm* **:** symbolism

simbolizar {21} *vt* **:** to symbolize

símbolo *nm* **:** symbol

simetría *nf* **:** symmetry

simétrico, -ca *adj* **:** symmetrical, symmetric

simiente *nf* **:** seed

símil *nm* **1 :** simile **2 :** analogy, comparison

similar *adj* SEMEJANTE **:** similar, alike

similitud *nf* **:** similarity, resemblance

simio *nm* **:** ape

simpatía *nf* **1 :** liking, affection <tomarle simpatía a : to take a liking to> **2 :** warmth, friendliness **3 :** support, solidarity

simpático, -ca *adj* **:** nice, friendly, likeable

simpatizante *nf* **:** sympathizer, supporter

simpatizar {21} *vi* **1 :** to get along, to hit it off <simpaticé mucho con él : I really liked him> **2 ~ con :** to sympathize with, to support

simple[1] *adj* **1** SENCILLO **:** plain, simple, easy **2 :** pure, mere <por simple vanidad : out of pure vanity> **3 :** simpleminded, foolish

simple[2] *n* **:** fool, simpleton

simplemente *adv* **:** simply, merely, just

simpleza *nf* **1 :** foolishness, simpleness **2** NECEDAD **:** nonsense

simplicidad *nf* **:** simplicity

simplificar {72} *vt* **:** to simplify — **simplificación** *nf*

simposio *or* **simposium** *nm* **:** symposium

simulación *nf, pl* **-ciones :** simulation

simulacro *nm* **:** imitation, sham <simulacro de juicio : mock trial>

simular *vt* **1 :** to simulate **2 :** to feign, to pretend

simultáneo, -nea *adj* **:** simultaneous — **simultáneamente** *adv*

sin *prep* **1 :** without <sin querer : unintentionally> <sin refinar : unrefined> **2 sin que :** without <lo hicimos sin que él se diera cuenta : we did it without him noticing>

sinagoga *nf* **:** synagogue

sinceridad *nf* **:** sincerity

sincero, -ra *adj* **:** sincere, honest, true — **sinceramente** *adv*

síncopa *nf* **:** syncopation

sincopar *vt* **:** to syncopate

sincronizar {21} *vt* **:** to synchronize — **sincronización** *nf*

sindical *adj* GREMIAL **:** union, labor <representante sindical : union representative>

sindicalización *nf, pl* **-ciones :** unionizing, unionization

sindicalizar {21} *vt* **:** to unionize — **sindicalizarse** *vr* **1 :** to form a union **2 :** to join a union

sindicar → **sindicalizar**

sindicato *nm* GREMIO **:** union, guild

síndrome *nm* **:** syndrome

sinecura *nf* **:** sinecure

sinfín *nm* **:** endless number <un sinfín de problemas : no end of problems>

sinfonía *nf* **:** symphony

sinfónica *nf* **:** symphony orchestra

sinfónico, -ca *adj* **:** symphonic, symphony

singular[1] *adj* **1 :** singular, unique **2** PARTICULAR **:** peculiar, odd **3 :** singular (in grammar) — **singularmente** *adv*

singular[2] *nm* **:** singular

singularidad *nf* **:** uniqueness, singularity

singularizar {21} *vt* **:** to make unique or distinct — **singularizarse** *vr* **:** to stand out, to distinguish oneself

siniestrado, -da *adj* **:** damaged, wrecked <zona siniestrada : disaster zone>

siniestro[1]**, -tra** *adj* **1** IZQUIERDO **:** left, left-hand **2** MALVADO **:** sinister, evil

siniestro[2] *nm* **:** accident, disaster

sinnúmero → **sinfín**

sino *conj* **1 :** but, rather <no será hoy, sino mañana : it won't be today, but tomorrow> **2** EXCEPTO **:** but, except <no hace sino despertar suspicacias : it does nothing but arouse suspicion>

sinónimo[1]**, -ma** *adj* **:** synonymous

sinónimo[2] *nm* **:** synonym

sinopsis *nfs & pl* RESUMEN **:** synopsis, summary

sinrazón *nf, pl* **-zones :** wrong, injustice

sinsabores *nmpl* **:** woes, troubles

sinsonte *nm* **:** mockingbird

sintáctico, -ca *adj* **:** syntactic, syntactical

sintaxis *nfs & pl* **:** syntax

síntesis *nfs & pl* **1 :** synthesis, fusion **2** SINOPSIS **:** synopsis, summary

sintético, -ca *adj* **:** synthetic — **sintéticamente** *adv*

sintetizar {21} *vt* **1 :** to synthesize **2** RESUMIR **:** to summarize

sintió, etc. → **sentir**

síntoma *nm* **:** symptom

sintomático, -ca *adj* **:** symptomatic

sintonía *nf* **1 :** tuning in (of a radio) **2 en sintonía con :** in tune with, attuned to

sintonizador *nm* **:** tuner, knob for tuning (of a radio, etc.)

sintonizar {21} *vt* **:** to tune (in) to — *vi* **1 :** to tune in **2 ~ con :** to be in tune with, to empathize with

sinuosidad *nf* **:** sinuosity

sinuoso, -sa *adj* **1 :** winding, sinuous **2 :** devious

sinvergüenza[1] *adj* **1** DESCARADO **:** shameless, brazen, impudent **2** TRAVIESO **:** naughty

sinvergüenza[2] *nmf* **1 :** rogue, scoundrel **2 :** brat, rascal

sionista *adj & nmf* **:** Zionist — **sionismo** *nm*

siqui- → **psiqui-**

siquiera *adv* **1 :** at least <dame siquiera un poquito : at least give me a little bit> **2** (*in negative constructions*) **:** not even <ni siquiera nos saludaron : they didn't even say hello to us>

sirena *nf* **1 :** mermaid **2 :** siren <sirena de niebla : foghorn>

sirio, -ria *adj & n* **:** Syrian

sirope *nm* **:** syrup

sirve, etc. → **servir**

sirviente, -ta *n* **:** servant, maid *f*

sisal *nm* **:** sisal

sisear *vi* **:** to hiss

siseo *nm* **:** hiss

sísmico, -ca *adj* **:** seismic

sismo *nm* **1** TERREMOTO **:** earthquake **2** TEMBLOR **:** tremor

sismógrafo *nm* **:** seismograph

sistema *nm* **:** system

sistemático, -ca *adj* **:** systematic — **sistemáticamente** *adv*
sistematizar {21} *vt* **:** to systematize
sistémico, -ca *adj* **:** systemic
sitiar *vt* ASEDIAR **:** to besiege
sitio *nm* **1** LUGAR **:** place, site <vámonos a otro sitio **:** let's go somewhere else> **2** ESPACIO **:** room, space <hacer sitio a **:** to make room for> **3 :** siege <estado de sitio **:** state of siege> **4** *Mex* **:** taxi stand
situación *nf, pl* **-ciones :** situation
situado, -da *adj* **:** situated, placed
situar {3} *vt* UBICAR **:** to situate, to place, to locate — **situarse** *vr* **1 :** to be placed, to be located **2 :** to make a place for oneself, to do well
sketch *nm* **:** sketch, skit
slip *nm* **:** briefs *pl*, underpants *pl*
smog *nm* **:** smog
smoking *nm* ESMOQUIN **:** tuxedo
snob → **esnob**
so *prep* **:** under <so pena de **:** under penalty of>
sobaco *nm* **:** armpit
sobado, -da *adj* **1 :** worn, shabby **2 :** well-worn, hackneyed
sobar *vt* **1 :** to finger, to handle **2 :** to knead **3 :** to rub, to massage **4** *fam* **:** to beat, to pummel
soberanía *nf* **:** sovereignty
soberano, -na *adj & n* **:** sovereign
soberbia *nf* **1** ORGULLO **:** pride, arrogance **2** MAGNIFICENCIA **:** magnificence
soberbio, -bia *adj* **1 :** proud, arrogant **2 :** grand, magnificent
sobornable *adv* **:** venal, bribable
sobornar *vt* **:** to bribe
soborno *nm* **1 :** bribery **2 :** bribe
sobra *nf* **1 :** excess, surplus **2 de ~ :** extra, to spare **3 sobras** *nfpl* **:** leftovers, scraps
sobrado, -da *adj* **:** abundant, excessive, more than enough
sobrante[1] *adj* **:** remaining, superfluous
sobrante[2] *nm* **:** remainder, surplus
sobrar *vi* **:** to be in excess, to be superfluous <más vale que sobre a que falte **:** it's better to have too much than not enough>
sobre[1] *nm* **1 :** envelope **2 :** packet <un sobre de sazón **:** a packet of seasoning>
sobre[2] *prep* **1 :** on, on top of <sobre la mesa **:** on the table> **2 :** over, above **3 :** about <¿tiene libros sobre Bolivia? **:** do you have books on Bolivia?> **4 sobre todo :** especially, above all
sobrealimentar *vt* **:** to overfeed
sobrecalentar {55} *vt* **:** to overheat — **sobrecalentarse** *vr*
sobrecama *nmf* **:** bedspread
sobrecargar {52} *vt* **:** to overload, to overburden, to weigh down
sobrecoger {15} *vt* **1 :** to surprise, to startle **2 :** to scare — **sobrecogerse** *vr*
sobrecubierta *nf* **:** dust jacket
sobredosis *nfs & pl* **:** overdose
sobreentender {56} *vt* **:** to infer, to understand
sobreestimar *vt* **:** to overestimate, to overrate
sobreexitado, -da *adj* **:** overexcited
sobreexponer {60} *vt* **:** to overexpose
sobregirar *vt* **:** to overdraw
sobregiro *nm* **:** overdraft
sobrehumano, -na *adj* **:** superhuman
sobrellevar *vt* **:** to endure, to bear
sobremanera *adv* **:** exceedingly
sobremesa *nf* **:** after-dinner conversation
sobrenatural *adj* **:** supernatural
sobrenombre *nm* APODO **:** nickname
sobrentender → **sobreentender**
sobrepasar *vt* **:** to exceed, to surpass — **sobrepasarse** *vr* PASARSE **:** to go too far
sobrepelliz *nf, pl* **-pellices :** surplice
sobrepeso *nm* **1 :** excess weight **2 :** overweight, obesity
sobrepoblación, sobrepoblado → **superpoblación, superpoblado**
sobreponer {60} *vt* **1** SUPERPONER **:** to superimpose **2** ANTEPONER **:** to put first, to give priority to — **sobreponerse** *vr* **1 :** to pull oneself together **2 ~ a :** to overcome
sobreprecio *nm* **:** surcharge
sobreproducción *nf, pl* **-ciones :** overproduction
sobreproducir {61} *vt* **:** to overproduce
sobreprotector, -tora *adj* **:** overprotective
sobreproteger {15} *vt* **:** to overprotect
sobresaliente[1] *adj* **1 :** protruding, projecting **2 :** outstanding, noteworthy **3 :** significant, salient
sobresaliente[2] *nmf* **:** understudy
sobresalir {73} *vi* **1 :** to protrude, to jut out, to project **2 :** to stand out, to excel
sobresaltar *vt* **:** to startle, to frighten — **sobresaltarse** *vr*
sobresalto *nm* **:** start, fright
sobresueldo *nm* **:** bonus, additional pay
sobretasa *nf* **:** surcharge <sobretasa a la gasolina **:** gas tax>
sobretodo *nm* **:** overcoat
sobrevalorar *or* **sobrevaluar** {3} *vt* **:** to overvalue, to overrate
sobrevender *vt* **:** to oversell
sobrevenir {87} *vi* ACAECER **:** to take place, to come about <podrían sobrevenir complicaciones **:** complications could occur>
sobrevivencia *nf* → **supervivencia**
sobreviviente → **superviviente**
sobrevivir *vi* **:** to survive — *vt* **:** to outlive, to outlast
sobrevolar {19} *vt* **:** to fly over, to overfly
sobriedad *nf* **:** sobriety, moderation
sobrino, -na *n* **:** nephew *m*, niece *f*
sobrio, -bria *adj* **:** sober — **sobriamente** *adv*

socarrón, -rrona *adj, mpl* **-rrones 1** : sly, cunning **2** : sarcastic

socavar *vt* : to undermine

sociabilidad *nf* : sociability

sociable *adj* : sociable

social *adj* : social — **socialmente** *adv*

socialista *adj & nmf* : socialist — **socialismo** *nm*

sociedad *nf* **1** : society **2** : company, enterprise **3 sociedad anónima** : incorporated company

socio, -cia *n* **1** : member **2** : partner

socioeconómico, -ca *adj* : socioeconomic

sociología *nf* : sociology

sociológico, -ca *adj* : sociological — **sociológicamente** *adv*

sociólogo, -ga *n* : sociologist

socorrer *vt* : to assist, to come to the aid of

socorrido, -da *adj* ÚTIL : handy, practical

socorrista *nmf* **1** : rescue worker **2** : lifeguard

socorro *nm* AUXILIO **1** : aid, help <equipo de socorro : rescue team> **2 ¡socorro!** : help!

soda *nf* : soda, soda water

sodio *nf* : sodium

soez *adj, pl* **soeces** GROSERO : rude, vulgar — **soezmente** *adv*

sofá *nm* : couch, sofa

sofistería *nf* : sophistry — **sofista** *nmf*

sofisticación *nf, pl* **-ciones** : sophistication

sofisticado, -da *adj* : sophisticated

sofocante *adj* : suffocating, stifling

sofocar {72} *vt* **1** AHOGAR : to suffocate, to smother **2** EXTINGUIR : to extinguish, to put out (a fire) **3** APLASTAR : to crush, to put down <sofocar una rebelión : to crush a rebellion> — **sofocarse** *vr* **1** : to suffocate **2** *fam* : to get upset, to get mad

sofreír {66} *vt* : to sauté

sofrito[1], -ta *adj* : sautéed

sofrito[2] *nm* : seasoning sauce

softbol *nm* : softball

software *nm* : software

soga *nf* : rope

soja *nf* → **soya**

sojuzgar *vt* : to subdue, to conquer, to subjugate

sol *nm* **1** : sun **2** : Peruvian unit of currency

solamente *adv* SÓLO : only, just

solapa *nf* **1** : lapel (of a jacket) **2** : flap (of an envelope)

solapado, -da *adj* : secret, underhanded

solapar *vt* : to cover up, to keep secret — **solaparse** *vr* : to overlap

solar[1] {19} *vt* : to floor, to tile

solar[2] *adj* : solar, sun

solar[3] *nm* **1** TERRENO : lot, piece of land, site **2** *Cuba, Peru* : tenement building

solariego, -ga *adj* : ancestral

solaz *nm, pl* **solaces 1** CONSUELO : solace, comfort **2** DESCANSO : relaxation, recreation

solazarse {21} *vr* : to relax, to enjoy oneself

soldado *nm* **1** : soldier **2 soldado raso** : private, enlisted man

soldador[1], -dora *n* : welder

soldador[2] *nm* : soldering iron

soldadura *nf* **1** : welding **2** : soldering, solder

soldar {19} *vt* **1** : to weld **2** : to solder

soleado, -da *adj* : sunny

soledad *nf* : loneliness, solitude

solemne *adj* : solemn — **solemnemente** *adv*

solemnidad *nf* : solemnity

soler {78} *vi* : to be in the habit of, to tend to <solía tomar café por la tarde : she usually drank coffee in the afternoon> <eso suele ocurrir : that frequently happens>

solera *nf* **1** : prop, support **2** : tradition

solicitante *nmf* : applicant

solicitar *vt* **1** : to request, to solicit **2** : to apply for <solicitar empleo : to apply for employment>

solícito, -ta *adj* : solicitous, attentive, obliging

solicitud *nf* **1** : solicitude, concern **2** : request **3** : application

solidaridad *nf* : solidarity

solidario, -ria *adj* : supportive, united in support <se declararon solidarios con la nueva ley : they declared their support for the new law> <espíritu solidario : spirit of solidarity>

solidarizar {21} *vi* : to be in solidarity <solidarizamos con la huelga : we support the strike>

solidez *nf* **1** : solidity, firmness **2** : soundness (of an argument, etc.)

solidificar {72} *vt* : to solidify, to make solid — **solidificarse** *vr* — **solidificación** *nf*

sólido[1], -da *adj* **1** : solid, firm **2** : sturdy, well-made **3** : sound, well-founded — **sólidamente** *adv*

sólido[2] *nm* : solid

soliloquio *nm* : soliloquy

solista *nmf* : soloist

solitaria *nf* TENIA : tapeworm

solitario[1], -ria *adj* **1** : lonely **2** : lone, solitary **3** DESIERTO : deserted, lonely <una calle solitaria : a deserted street>

solitario[2], -ria *n* : recluse, loner

solitario[3] *nm* : solitaire

sollozar {21} *vi* : to sob

sollozo *nm* : sob

solo[1], -la *adj* **1** : alone, by oneself **2** : lonely **3** ÚNICO : only, sole, unique <hay un solo problema : there's only one problem> **4 a solas** : alone

solo[2] *nm* : solo

sólo *adv* SOLAMENTE : just, only <sólo quieren comer : they just want to eat>

solomillo *nm* : sirloin, loin

solsticio *nm* : solstice

soltar {19} *vt* **1 :** to let go of, to drop **2 :** to release, to set free **3** AFLOJAR **:** to loosen, to slacken
soltería *nf* **:** bachelorhood, spinsterhood
soltero[1], -ra *adj* **:** single, unmarried
soltero[2], -ra *n* **1 :** bachelor *m,* single man *m,* single woman *f* **2 apellido de soltera :** maiden name
soltura *nf* **1 :** looseness, slackness **2 :** fluency (of language) **3 :** agility, ease of movement
soluble *adj* **:** soluble — **solubilidad** *nf*
solución *nf, pl* **-ciones 1 :** solution (in a liquid) **2 :** answer, solution
solucionar *vt* RESOLVER **:** to solve, to resolve — **solucionarse** *vr*
solvencia *nf* **1 :** solvency **2 :** settling, payment (of debts) **3 :** reliability <solvencia moral : trustworthiness>
solvente[1] *adj* **1 :** solvent **2 :** reliable, trustworthy
solvente[2] *nm* **:** solvent
somalí *adj & nmf* **:** Somalian
sombra *nf* **1 :** shadow **2 :** shade **3 sombras** *nfpl* **:** darkness, shadows *pl* **4 sin sombra de duda :** without a shadow of a doubt
sombreado, -da *adj* **1 :** shady **2 :** shaded, darkened
sombrear *vt* **:** to shade
sombrerero, -ra *n* **:** milliner, hatter
sombrero *nm* **1 :** hat **2 sin ~ :** bareheaded **3 sombrero hongo :** derby
sombrilla *nf* **:** parasol, umbrella
sombrío, -bría *adj* LÓBREGO **:** dark, somber, gloomy — **sombríamente** *adv*
someramente *adv* **:** cursorily, summarily
somero, -ra *adj* **:** superficial, cursory, shallow
someter *vt* **1 :** to subjugate, to conquer **2 :** to subordinate **3 :** to subject (to treatment or testing) **4 :** to submit, to present — **someterse** *vr* **1 :** to submit, to yield **2 :** to undergo
sometimiento *nm* **1 :** submission, subjection **2 :** presentation
somnífero[1], -ra *adj* **:** soporific
somnífero[2] *nm* **:** sleeping pill
somnolencia *nf* **:** drowsiness, sleepiness
somnoliento, -ta *adj* **:** drowsy, sleepy
somorgujo *or* **somormujo** *nm* **:** loon, grebe
somos → **ser**
son[1] → **ser**
son[2] *nm* **1 :** sound <al son de la trompeta : at the sound of the trumpet> **2 :** news, rumor **3 en son de :** as, in the manner of, by way of <en son de broma : as a joke> <en son de paz : in peace>
sonado, -da *adj* **:** celebrated, famous, much-discussed
sonaja *nf* **:** rattle
sonajero *nm* **:** rattle (toy)
sonámbulo, -la *n* **:** sleepwalker
sonar[1] {19} *vi* **1 :** to sound <suena bien : it sounds good> **2 :** to ring (bells) **3 :** to look or sound familiar <me suena ese nombre : that name rings a bell> **4 ~ a :** to sound like — *vt* **1 :** to ring **2 :** to blow (a trumpet, a nose) — **sonarse** *vr* **:** to blow one's nose
sonar[2] *nm* **:** sonar
sonata *nf* **:** sonata
sonda *nf* **1 :** sounding line **2 :** probe **3** CATÉTER **:** catheter
sondar *vt* **1 :** to sound, to probe (in medicine, drilling, etc.) **2 :** to probe, to explore (outer space)
sondear *vt* **1 :** to sound **2 :** to probe **3 :** to sound out, to test (opinions, markets)
sondeo *nm* **1 :** sounding, probing **2 :** drilling **3** ENCUESTA **:** survey, poll
soneto *nm* **:** sonnet
sónico, -ca *adj* **:** sonic
sonido *nm* **:** sound
sonoridad *nf* **:** sonority, resonance
sonoro, -ra *adj* **1 :** resonant, sonorous, voiced (in linguistics) **2 :** resounding, loud **3 banda sonora :** soundtrack
sonreír {66} *vi* **:** to smile
sonriente *adj* **:** smiling
sonrisa *nf* **:** smile
sonrojar *vt* **:** to cause to blush — **sonrojarse** *vr* **:** to blush
sonrojo *nm* RUBOR **:** blush
sonrosado, -da *adj* **:** rosy, pink
sonsacar {72} *vt* **:** to wheedle, to extract
sonsonete *nm* **1 :** tapping **2 :** drone **3 :** mocking tone
soñador[1], -dora *adj* **:** dreamy
soñador[2], -dora *n* **:** dreamer
soñar {19} *v* **1 :** to dream **2 ~ con :** to dream about **3 soñar despierto :** to daydream
soñoliento, -ta *adj* **:** sleepy, drowsy
sopa *nf* **1 :** soup **2 estar hecho una sopa :** to be soaked to the bone
sopera *nf* **:** soup tureen
sopesar *vt* **:** to weigh, to evaluate
soplar *vi* **:** to blow — *vt* **:** to blow on, to blow out, to blow off
soplete *nm* **:** blowtorch
soplido *nm* **:** puff
soplo *nm* **:** puff, gust
soplón, -plona *n, mpl* **soplones** *fam* **:** tattletale, sneak
sopor *nm* SOMNOLENCIA **:** drowsiness, sleepiness
soporífero, -ra *adj* **:** soporific
soportable *adj* **:** bearable, tolerable
soportar *vt* **1** SOSTENER **:** to support, to hold up **2** RESISTIR **:** to withstand, to resist **3** AGUANTAR **:** to bear, to tolerate
soporte *nm* **:** base, stand, support
soprano *nmf* **:** soprano
sor *nf* **:** Sister (religious title)
sorber *vt* **1 :** to sip, to suck in **2 :** to absorb, to soak up
sorbete *nm* **:** sherbet
sorbo *nm* **1 :** sip, gulp, swallow **2 beber a sorbos :** to sip

sordera *nf* : deafness
sordidez *nf, pl* **-deces** : sordidness, squalor
sórdido, -da *adj* : sordid, dirty, squalid
sordina *nf* : mute (for a musical instrument)
sordo, -da *adj* **1** : deaf **2** : muted, muffled
sordomudo, -da *n* : deaf-mute
sorgo *nm* : sorghum
soriasis *nfs & pl* : psoriasis
sorna *nf* : sarcasm, mocking tone
sorprendente *adj* : surprising — **sorprendentemente** *adv*
sorprender *vt* : to surprise — **sorprenderse** *vr*
sorpresa *nf* : surprise
sorpresivo, -va *adj* **1** : surprising, surprise **2** IMPREVISTO : sudden, unexpected
sortear *vt* **1** RIFAR : to raffle, to draw lots for **2** : to dodge, to avoid
sorteo *nm* : drawing, raffle
sortija *nf* **1** ANILLO : ring **2** : curl, ringlet
sortilegio *nm* **1** HECHIZO : spell, charm **2** HECHICERÍA : sorcery
SOS *nm* : SOS
sosegado, -da *adj* SERENO : calm, tranquil, serene
sosegar {49} *vt* : to calm, to pacify — **sosegarse** *vr*
sosiego *nm* : tranquillity, serenity, calm
soslayar *vt* ESQUIVAR : to dodge, to evade
soslayo *nm* **de ~** : obliquely, sideways <mirar de soslayo : to look askance>
soso, -sa *adj* **1** INSÍPIDO : bland, flavorless **2** ABURRIDO : dull, boring
sospecha *nf* : suspicion
sospechar *vt* : to suspect — *vi* : to be suspicious
sospechosamente *adv* : suspiciously
sospechoso[1], -sa *adj* : suspicious, suspect
sospechoso[2], -sa *n* : suspect
sostén *nm, pl* **sostenes 1** APOYO : support **2** : sustenance **3** : brassiere, bra
sostener {80} *vt* **1** : to support, to hold up **2** : to hold <sostenme la puerta : hold the door for me> <sostener una conversación : to hold a conversation> **3** : to sustain, to maintain — **sostenerse** *vr* **1** : to stand, to hold oneself up **2** : to continue, to remain
sostenible *adj* : sustainable, tenable
sostenido[1], -da *adj* **1** : sustained, prolonged **2** : sharp (in music)
sostenido[2] *nm* : sharp (in music)
sostuvo, etc. → **sostener**
sotana *nf* : cassock
sótano *nm* : basement
sotavento *nm* : lee <a sotavento : leeward>
soterrar {55} *vt* **1** : to bury **2** : to conceal, to hide away
soto *nm* : grove, copse
souvenir *nm, pl* **-nirs** RECUERDO : souvenir, memento
soviético, -ca *adj* : Soviet
soy → **ser**
soya *nf* : soy, soybean
spaghetti *nm* → **espagueti**
sport [ɛ'spor] *adj* : sport, casual
sprint [ɛ'sprin, -'sprint] *nm* : sprint — **sprinter** *nmf*
squash [ɛ'skwaʃ, -'skwatʃ] *nm* : squash (sport)
Sr. *nm* : Mr.
Sra. *nf* : Mrs., Ms.
Srta. *or* **Srita.** *nf* : Miss, Ms.
standard → **estándar**
stress *nm* → **estrés**
su *adj* **1** : his, her, its, their, one's <su libro : her book> <sus consecuencias : its consequences> **2** (*formal*) : your <tómese su medicina, señor : take your medicine, sir>
suave *adj* **1** BLANDO : soft **2** LISO : smooth **3** : gentle, mild **4** *Mex fam* : great, fantastic
suavemente *adj* : smoothly, gently, softly
suavidad *nf* : softness, smoothness, mellowness
suavizante *nm* : softener, fabric softener
suavizar {21} *vt* **1** : to soften, to smooth out **2** : to tone down — **suavizarse** *vr*
subacuático, -ca *adj* : underwater
subalterno[1], -na *adj* **1** SUBORDINADO : subordinate **2** SECUNDARIO : secondary
subalterno[2], -na *n* SUBORDINADO : subordinate
subarrendar {55} *vt* : to sublet
subasta *nf* : auction
subastador, -dora *n* : auctioneer
subastar *vt* : to auction, to auction off
subcampeón, -peona *n, mpl* **-peones** : runner-up
subcomité *nm* : subcommittee
subconsciente *adj & nm* : subconscious — **subconscientemente** *adv*
subcontratar *vt* : to subcontract
subcontratista *nmf* : subcontractor
subcultura *nf* : subculture
subdesarrollado, -da *adj* : underdeveloped
subdirector, -tora *n* : assistant manager
súbdito, -ta *n* : subject (of a monarch)
subdividir *vt* : to subdivide
subdivisión *nf, pl* **-siones** : subdivision
subestimar *vt* : to underestimate, to undervalue
subexponer {60} *vt* : to underexpose
subexposición *nf, pl* **-ciones** : underexposure
subgrupo *nm* : subgroup
subibaja *nm* : seesaw
subida *nf* **1** : ascent, climb **2** : rise, increase **3** : slope, hill <ir de subida : to go uphill>

subido, -da *adj* **1 :** intense, strong <amarillo subido : bright yellow> **2 subido de tono :** risqué
subir *vt* **1 :** to bring up, to take up **2 :** to climb, to go up **3 :** to raise — *vi* **1 :** to go up, to come up **2 :** to rise, to increase **3 :** to be promoted **4 ~ a :** to get on, to mount <subir a un tren : to get on a train> — **subirse** *vr* **1 :** to climb (up) **2 :** to pull up (clothing) **3 subirse a la cabeza :** to go to one's head
súbito, -ta *adj* **1** REPENTINO **:** sudden **2 de ~ :** all of a sudden, suddenly — **súbitamente** *adv*
subjetivo, -va *adj* **:** subjective — **subjetivamente** *adv* — **subjetividad** *nf*
subjuntivo[1], -va *adj* **:** subjunctive
subjuntivo[2] *nm* **:** subjunctive
sublevación *nf, pl* **-ciones** ALZAMIENTO **:** uprising, rebellion
sublevar *vt* **:** to incite to rebellion — **sublevarse** *vr* **:** to rebel, to rise up
sublimar *vt* **:** to sublimate — **sublimación** *nf*
sublime *adj* **:** sublime
submarinismo *nm* **:** scuba diving
submarinista *nmf* **:** scuba diver
submarino[1], -na *adj* **:** submarine, undersea
submarino[2] *nm* **:** submarine
suboficial *nmf* **:** noncommissioned officer, petty officer
subordinado, -da *adj & n* **:** subordinate
subordinar *vt* **:** to subordinate — **subordinarse** *vr* — **subordinación** *nf*
subproducto *nm* **:** by-product
subrayar *vt* **1 :** to underline, to underscore **2** ENFATIZAR **:** to highlight, to emphasize
subrepticio, -cia *adj* **:** surreptitious — **subrepticiamente** *adv*
subsahariano, -na *adj* **:** sub-Saharan
subsanar *vt* **1** RECTIFICAR **:** to rectify, to correct **2 :** to overlook, to excuse **3 :** to make up for
subscribir → suscribir
subsecretario, -ria *n* **:** undersecretary
subsecuente *adj* **:** subsequent — **subsecuentemente** *adv*
subsidiar *vt* **:** to subsidize
subsidiaria *nf* **:** subsidiary
subsidio *nm* **:** subsidy
subsiguiente *adj* **:** subsequent
subsistencia *nf* **1 :** subsistence **2 :** sustenance
subsistir *vi* **1 :** to subsist, to live **2 :** to endure, to survive
substancia *nf* **→ sustancia**
subteniente *nmf* **:** second lieutenant
subterfugio *nm* **:** subterfuge
subterráneo[1], -nea *adj* **:** underground, subterranean
subterráneo[2] *nm* **1 :** underground passage, tunnel **2** *Arg, Uru* **:** subway
subtítulo *nm* **:** subtitle, subheading
subtotal *nm* **:** subtotal
suburbano, -na *adj* **:** suburban
suburbio *nm* **1 :** suburb **2 :** slum (outside a city)
subvención *nf, pl* **-ciones :** subsidy, grant
subvencionar *vt* **:** to subsidize
subversivo, -va *adj & n* **:** subversive — **subversión** *nf*
subvertir {76} *vt* **:** to subvert
subyacente *adj* **:** underlying
subyugar {52} *vt* **:** to subjugate — **subyugación** *nf*
succión *nf, pl* **succiones :** suction
succionar *vt* **:** to suck up, to draw in
sucedáneo *nm* **:** substitute <sucedáneo de azucar : sugar substitute>
suceder *vi* **1** OCURRIR **:** to happen, to occur <¿qué sucede? : what's going on?> <suceda lo que suceda : come what may> **2 ~ a :** to follow, to succeed <suceder al trono : to succeed to the throne> <a la primavera sucede el verano : summer follows sping>
sucesión *nf, pl* **-siones 1 :** succession **2 :** sequence, series **3 :** issue, heirs *pl*
sucesivamente *adv* **:** successively, consecutively <y así sucesivamente : and so on>
sucesivo, -va *adj* **:** successive <en los días sucesivos : in the days that followed>
suceso *nm* **1 :** event, happening, occurrence **2 :** incident, crime
sucesor, -sora *n* **:** successor
suciedad *nf* **1 :** dirtiness, filthiness **2** MUGRE **:** dirt, filth
sucinto, -ta *adj* CONCISO **:** succinct, concise — **sucintamente** *adv*
sucio, -cia *adj* **:** dirty, filthy
sucre *nm* **:** Ecuadoran unit of currency
suculento, -ta *adj* **:** succulent
sucumbir *vi* **:** to succumb
sucursal *nf* **:** branch (of a business)
sudadera *nf* **:** sweatshirt
sudado, -da → sudoroso
sudafricano, -na *adj & n* **:** South African
sudamericano, -na *adj & n* **:** South American
sudanés, -nesa *adj & n, mpl* **-neses :** Sudanese
sudar *vi* TRANSPIRAR **:** to sweat, to perspire
sudario *nm* **:** shroud
sudeste → sureste
sudoeste → suroeste
sudor *nm* TRANSPIRACIÓN **:** sweat, perspiration
sudoroso, -sa *adj* **:** sweaty
sueco[1], -ca *adj* **:** Swedish
sueco[2], -ca *n* **:** Swede
sueco[3] *nm* **:** Swedish (language)
suegro, -gra *n* **1 :** father-in-law *m,* mother-in-law *f* **2 suegros** *nmpl* **:** in-laws
suela *nf* **:** sole (of a shoe)
suelda, etc. → soldar
sueldo *nm* **:** salary, wage
suele, etc. → soler

suelo *nm* **1 :** ground <caerse al suelo : to fall down, to hit the ground> **2 :** floor, flooring **3** TIERRA **:** soil, land
suelta, etc. → **soltar**
suelto[1], **-ta** *adj* **:** loose, free, unattached
suelto[2] *nm* **:** loose change
suena, etc. → **sonar**
sueña, etc. → **soñar**
sueño *nm* **1 :** dream **2 :** sleep <perder el sueño : to lose sleep> **3 :** sleepiness <tener sueño : to be sleepy>
suero *nm* **1 :** serum **2 :** whey
suerte *nf* **1** FORTUNA **:** luck, fortune <tener suerte : to be lucky> <por suerte : luckily> **2** DESTINO **:** fate, destiny, lot **3** CLASE, GÉNERO **:** sort, kind <toda suerte de cosas : all kinds of things>
suertudo, -da *adj fam* **:** lucky
suéter *nm* **:** sweater
suficiencia *nf* **1 :** adequacy, sufficiency **2 :** competence, fitness **3 :** smugness, self-satisfaction
suficiente *adj* **1** BASTANTE **:** enough, sufficient <tener suficiente : to have enough> **2 :** suitable, fit **3 :** smug, complacent
suficientemente *adv* **:** sufficiently, enough
sufijo *nm* **:** suffix
suflé *nm* **:** soufflé
sufragar {52} *vt* **1** AYUDAR **:** to help out, to support **2 :** to defray (costs) — *vi* **:** to vote
sufragio *nm* **:** suffrage, vote
sufrido, -da *adj* **1 :** long-suffering, patient **2 :** sturdy, serviceable (of clothing)
sufrimiento *nm* **:** suffering
sufrir *vt* **1 :** to suffer <sufrir una pérdida : to suffer a loss> **2 :** to tolerate, to put up with <ella no lo puede sufrir : she can't stand him> — *vi* **:** to suffer
sugerencia *nf* **:** suggestion
sugerir {76} *vt* **1** PROPONER, RECOMENDAR **:** to suggest, to recommend, to propose **2 :** to suggest, to bring to mind
sugestión *nf, pl* **-tiones :** suggestion, prompting <poder de sugestión : power of suggestion>
sugestionable *adj* **:** suggestible, impressionable
sugestionar *vt* **:** to influence, to sway — **sugestionarse** *vr* **~ con :** to talk oneself into, to become convinced of
sugestivo, -va *adj* **1 :** suggestive **2 :** interesting, stimulating
suicida[1] *adj* **:** suicidal
suicida[2] *nmf* **:** suicide victim, suicide
suicidarse *vr* **:** to commit suicide
suicidio *nm* **:** suicide
suite *nf* **:** suite
suizo, -za *adj & n* **:** Swiss
sujeción *nf, pl* **-ciones 1 :** holding, fastening **2 :** subjection
sujetador *nm* **1 :** fastener **2 :** holder <sujetador de tazas : cup holder>
sujetalibros *nms & pl* **:** bookend
sujetapapeles *nms & pl* CLIP **:** paper clip
sujetar *vt* **1 :** to hold on to, to steady, to hold down **2** FIJAR **:** to fasten, to attach **3** DOMINAR **:** to subdue, to conquer — **sujetarse** *vr* **1 :** to hold on, to hang on **2 ~ a :** to abide by
sujeto[1], **-ta** *adj* **1 :** secure, fastened **2 ~ a :** subject to
sujeto[2] *nm* **1** INDIVIDUO **:** individual, character **2 :** subject (in grammar)
sulfúrico, -ca *adj* **:** sulfuric
sulfuro *nm* **:** sulfur
sultán *nm, pl* **sultanes :** sultan
suma *nf* **1** CANTIDAD **:** sum, quantity **2 :** addition
sumamente *adv* **:** extremely, exceedingly
sumar *vt* **1 :** to add, to add up **2 :** to add up to, to total — *vi* **:** to add up — **sumarse** *vr* **~ a :** to join
sumario[1], **-ria** *adj* SUCINTO **:** succinct, summary — **sumariamente** *adv*
sumario[2] *nm* **:** summary
sumergir {35} *vt* **:** to submerge, to immerse, to plunge — **sumergirse** *vr*
sumersión *nf, pl* **-siones :** submersion, immersion
sumidero *nm* **:** drain, sewer
suministrar *vt* **:** to supply, to provide
suministro *nm* **:** supply, provision
sumir *vt* SUMERGIR **:** to plunge, to immerse, to sink — **sumirse** *vr*
sumisión *nf, pl* **-siones 1 :** submission **2 :** submissiveness
sumiso, -sa *adj* **:** submissive, acquiescent, docile
sumo, -ma *adj* **1 :** extreme, great, high <la suma autoridad : the highest authority> **2 a lo sumo :** at the most — **sumamente** *adv*
suntuoso, -sa *adj* **:** sumptuous, lavish — **suntuosamente** *adv*
supeditar *vt* SUBORDINAR **:** to subordinate — **supeditación** *nf*
super[1] *or* **súper** *adj fam* **:** super, great
super[2] *nm* SUPERMERCADO **:** market, supermarket
superable *adj* **:** surmountable
superabundancia *nf* **:** overabundance, superabundance — **superabundante** *adj*
superar *vt* **1 :** to surpass, to exceed **2 :** to overcome, to surmount — **superarse** *vr* **:** to improve oneself
superávit *nm, pl* **-vit** *or* **-vits :** surplus
superchería *nf* **:** trickery, fraud
superestructura *nf* **:** superstructure
superficial *adj* **:** superficial — **superficialmente** *adv*
superficialidad *nf* **:** superficiality
superficie *nf* **1 :** surface **2 :** area <el superficie de un triángulo : the area of a triangle>
superfluidad *nf* **:** superfluity
superfluo, -flua *adj* **:** superfluous
superintendente *nmf* **:** supervisor, superintendent

superior[1] *adj* **1 :** superior **2 :** upper <nivel superior : upper level> **3 :** higher <educación superior : higher education> **4 ~ a :** above, higher than, in excess of

superior[2] *nm* **:** superior

superioridad *nf* **:** superiority

superlativo[1], **-va** *adj* **:** superlative

superlativo[2] *nm* **:** superlative

supermercado *nm* **:** supermarket

superpoblación *nf, pl* **-ciones :** overpopulation

superpoblado, -da *adj* **:** overpopulated

superponer {60} *vt* **:** to superimpose

superpotencia *nf* **:** superpower

superproducción *nf* → **sobreproducción**

supersónico, -ca *adj* **:** supersonic

superstición *nf, pl* **-ciones :** superstition

supersticioso, -sa *adj* **:** superstitious

supervisar *vt* **:** to supervise, to oversee

supervisión *nf, pl* **-siones :** supervision

supervisor, -sora *n* **:** supervisor, overseer

supervivencia *nf* **:** survival

superviviente *nmf* **:** survivor

supino, -na *adj* **:** supine

suplantar *vt* **:** to supplant, to replace

suplemental → **suplementario**

suplementario, -ria *adj* **:** supplementary, additional, extra

suplemento *nm* **:** supplement

suplencia *nf* **:** substitution, replacement

suplente *adj & nmf* **:** substitute <equipo suplente : replacement team>

supletorio, -ria *adj* **:** extra, additional <teléfono supletorio : extension phone> <cama supletoria : spare bed>

súplica *nf* **:** plea, entreaty

suplicar {72} *vt* IMPLORAR, ROGAR **:** to entreat, to implore, to supplicate

suplicio *nm* TORMENTO **:** ordeal, torture

suplir *vt* **1** COMPENSAR **:** to make up for, to compensate for **2** REEMPLAZAR **:** to replace, to substitute

supo, etc. → **saber**

suponer {60} *vt* **1** PRESUMIR **:** to suppose, to assume <supongo que sí : I guess so, I suppose so> <se supone que van a llegar mañana : they're supposed to arrive tomorrow> **2 :** to imply, to suggest **3 :** to involve, to entail <el éxito supone mucho trabajo : success involves a lot of work>

suposición *nf, pl* **-ciones** PRESUNCIÓN **:** supposition, assumption

supositorio *nm* **:** suppository

supremacía *nf* **:** supremacy

supremo, -ma *adj* **:** supreme

supresión *nf, pl* **-siones 1 :** suppression, elimination **2 :** deletion

suprimir *vt* **1 :** to suppress, to eliminate **2 :** to delete

supuestamente *adv* **:** supposedly, allegedly

supuesto, -ta *adj* **1 :** supposed, alleged **2 por ~ :** of course, absolutely

supurar *vi* **:** to ooze, to discharge

supuso, etc. → **suponer**

sur[1] *adj* **:** southern, southerly, south

sur[2] *nm* **1 :** south, South **2 :** south wind

surafricano, -na → **sudafricano**

suramericano, -na → **sudamericano**

surcar {72} *vt* **1 :** to plow (through) **2 :** to groove, to score, to furrow

surco *nm* **:** groove, furrow, rut

sureño[1], **-ña** *adj* **:** southern, Southern

sureño[2], **-ña** *n* **:** Southerner

sureste[1] *adj* **1 :** southeast, southeastern **2 :** southeasterly

sureste[2] *nm* **:** southeast, Southeast

surf *nm* **:** surfing

surfear *vi* **:** to surf

surfing *nm* → **surf**

surfista *nmf* **:** surfer

surgimiento *nm* **:** rise, emergence

surgir {35} *vi* **:** to rise, to arise, to emerge

suroeste[1] *adj* **1 :** southwest, southwestern **2 :** southwesterly

suroeste[2] *nm* **:** southwest, Southwest

surtido[1], **-da** *adj* **1 :** assorted, varied **2 :** stocked, provisioned

surtido[2] *nm* **:** assortment, selection

surtidor *nm* **1 :** jet, spout **2** *Arg, Chile, Spain* **:** gas pump

surtir *vt* **1 :** to supply, to provide <surtir un pedido : to fill an order> **2 surtir efecto :** to have an effect — *vi* **:** to spout, to spurt up — **surtirse** vr **:** to stock up

susceptible *adj* **:** susceptible, sensitive — **susceptibilidad** *nf*

suscitar *vt* **:** to provoke, to give rise to

suscribir {33} *vt* **1 :** to sign (a formal document) **2 :** to endorse, to sanction — **suscribirse** *vr* **~ a :** to subscribe to

suscripción *nf, pl* **-ciones 1 :** subscription **2 :** endorsement, sanction **3 :** signing

suscriptor, -tora *n* **:** subscriber

susodicho, -cha *adj* **:** aforementioned, aforesaid

suspender *vt* **1** COLGAR **:** to suspend, to hang **2 :** to suspend, to discontinue **3 :** to suspend, to dismiss

suspensión *nf, pl* **-siones :** suspension

suspenso *nm* **:** suspense

suspicacia *nf* **:** suspicion, mistrust

suspicaz *adj, pl* **-caces** DESCONFIADO **:** suspicious, wary

suspirar *vi* **:** to sigh

suspiro *nm* **:** sigh

surque, etc. → **surcar**

suscrito *pp* → **suscribir**

sustancia *nf* **1 :** substance **2 sin ~ :** shallow, lacking substance

sustancial *adj* **1 :** substantial **2** ESENCIAL, FUNDAMENTAL **:** essential, fundamental — **sustancialmente** *adv*

sustancioso, -sa *adj* **1** NUTRITIVO **:** hearty, nutritious **2 :** substantial, solid
sustantivo *nm* **:** noun
sustentación *nf, pl* **-ciones** SOSTÉN **:** support
sustentar *vt* **1 :** to support, to hold up **2 :** to sustain, to nourish **3 :** to maintain, to hold (an opinion) — **sustentarse** *vr* **:** to support oneself
sustento *nm* **1 :** means of support, livelihood **2 :** sustenance, food
sustitución *nf, pl* **-ciones :** replacement, substitution
sustituir {41} *vt* **1 :** to replace, to substitute for **2 :** to stand in for
sustituto, -ta *n* **:** substitute, stand-in
susto *nm* **:** fright, scare
sustracción *nf, pl* **-ciones 1** RESTA **:** subtraction **2 :** theft
sustraer {81} *vt* **1 :** to remove, to take away **2** RESTAR **:** to subtract **3 :** to steal — **sustraerse** *vr* **~ a :** to avoid, to evade
susurrar *vi* **1 :** to whisper **2 :** to murmur **3 :** to rustle (leaves, etc.) — *vt* **:** to whisper
susurro *nm* **1 :** whisper **2 :** murmur **3 :** rustle, rustling
sutil *adj* **1 :** delicate, thin, fine **2 :** subtle
sutileza *nf* **1 :** delicacy **2 :** subtlety
sutura *nf* **:** suture
suturar *vt* **:** to suture
suyo[1], -ya *adj* **1 :** his, her, its, theirs <los libros suyos : his books> <un amigo suyo : a friend of hers> <esta casa es suya : this house is theirs> **2** (*formal*) **:** yours <¿este abrigo es suyo, señor? : is this your coat, sir?>
suyo[2], -ya *pron* **1 :** his, hers, theirs <mi guitarra y la suya : my guitar and hers> <ellos trajeron las suyas : they brought theirs, they brought their own> **2** (*formal*) **:** yours <usted olvidó la suya : you forgot yours>
switch *nm* **:** switch

T

t *nf* **:** twenty-first letter of the Spanish alphabet
taba *nf* **:** anklebone
tabacalero[1], -ra *adj* **:** tobacco <industria tabacalera : tobacco industry>
tabacalero[2], -ra *n* **:** tobacco grower
tabaco *nm* **:** tobacco
tábano *nm* **:** horsefly
taberna *nf* **:** tavern, bar
tabernáculo *nm* **:** tabernacle
tabicar {72} *vt* **:** to wall up
tabique *nm* **:** thin wall, partition
tabla *nf* **1 :** table, list <tabla de multiplicar : multiplication table> **2 :** board, plank, slab <tabla de planchar : ironing board> **3 :** plot, strip (of land) **4 tablas** *nfpl* **:** stage, boards *pl*
tablado *nm* **1 :** flooring, floorboards **2 :** platform, scaffold **3 :** stage
tablero *nm* **1 :** bulletin board **2 :** board (in games) <tablero de ajedrez : chessboard> <tablero de damas : checkerboard> **3** PIZARRA **:** blackboard **4 :** switchboard **5 tablero de instrumentos :** dashboard, instrument panel
tableta *nf* **1** COMPRIMIDO, PÍLDORA **:** tablet, pill **2 :** bar (of chocolate)
tabletear *vi* **:** to rattle, to clack
tableteo *nm* **:** clack, rattling
tablilla *nf* **1 :** small board or tablet **2 :** bulletin board **3 :** splint
tabloide *nm* **:** tabloid
tablón *nm, pl* **tablones 1 :** plank, beam **2 tablón de anuncios :** bulletin board
tabú[1] *adj* **:** taboo
tabú[2] *nm, pl* **tabúes** or **tabús :** taboo
tabulador *nm* **:** tabulator
tabular[1] *vt* **:** to tabulate
tabular[2] *adj* **:** tabular
taburete *nm* **:** footstool, stool
tacañería *nf* **:** miserliness, stinginess
tacaño[1], -ña *adj* MEZQUINO **:** stingy, miserly
tacaño[2], -ña *n* **:** miser, tightwad
tacha *nf* **1 :** flaw, blemish, defect **2 poner tacha a :** to find fault with **3 sin ~ :** flawless
tachadura *nf* **:** erasure, correction
tachar *vt* **1 :** to cross out, to delete **2 ~ de :** to accuse of, to label as <lo tacharon de mentiroso : they accused him of being a liar>
tachón *nm, pl* **tachones :** stud, hobnail
tachonar *vt* **:** to stud
tachuela *nf* **:** tack, hobnail, stud
tácito, -ta *adj* **:** tacit, implicit — **tácitamente** *adv*
taciturno, -na *adj* **1 :** taciturn **2 :** sullen, gloomy
tacle *nm* **:** tackle
taclear *vt* **:** to tackle (in football)
taco *nm* **1 :** wad, stopper, plug **2 :** pad (of paper) **3 :** cleat **4 :** heel (of a shoe) **5 :** cue (in billiards) **6 :** light snack, bite **7 :** taco
tacón *nm, pl* **tacones :** heel (of a shoe) <de tacón alto : high-heeled>
táctica *nf* **:** tactic, tactics *pl*
táctico[1], -ca *adj* **:** tactical
táctico[2], -ca *n* **:** tactician
táctil *adj* **:** tactile
tacto *nm* **1 :** touch, touching, feel **2** DELICADEZA **:** tact
tafetán *nm, pl* **-tanes :** taffeta
tahúr *nm, pl* **tahúres :** gambler
tailandés[1], -desa *adj & n, pl* **-deses :** Thai
tailandés[2] *nm* **:** Thai (language)

taimado, -da *adj* **1 :** crafty, sly **2** *Chile* **:** sullen, sulky
tajada *nf* **1 :** slice **2 sacar tajada** *fam* **:** to get one's share
tajante *adj* **1 :** cutting, sharp **2 :** decisive, categorical
tajantemente *adj* **:** emphatically, categorically
tajar *vt* **:** to cut, to slice
tajo *nm* **1 :** cut, slash, gash **2** ESCARPA **:** steep cliff
tal[1] *adv* **1 :** so, in such a way **2 tal como :** just as <tal como lo hice : just the way I did it> **3 con tal que :** provided that, as long as **4 ¿qué tal? :** how are you?, how's it going?
tal[2] *adj* **1 :** such, such a **2 tal vez :** maybe, perhaps
tal[3] *pron* **1 :** such a one, someone **2 :** such a thing, something **3 tal para cual :** two of a kind
tala *nf* **:** felling (of trees)
taladrar *vt* **:** to drill
taladro *nm* **:** drill, auger <taladro eléctrico : power drill>
talante *nm* **1** HUMOR **:** mood, disposition **2** VOLUNTAD **:** will, willingness
talar *vt* **1 :** to cut down, to fell **2** DEVASTAR **:** to devastate, to destroy
talco *nm* **1 :** talc **2 :** talcum powder
talego *nm* **:** sack
talento *nm* **:** talent, ability
talentoso, -sa *adj* **:** talented, gifted
talismán *nm, pl* **-manes** AMULETO **:** talisman, charm
talla *nf* **1** ESTATURA **:** height **2 :** size (in clothing) **3 :** stature, status **4 :** sculpture, carving
tallar *vt* **1 :** to sculpt, to carve **2 :** to measure (someone's height) **3 :** to deal (cards)
tallarín *nf, pl* **-rines :** noodle
talle *nm* **1 :** size **2 :** waist, waistline **3 :** figure, shape
taller *nm* **1 :** shop, workshop **2 :** studio (of an artist)
tallo *nm* **:** stalk, stem <tallo de maíz : cornstalk>
talón *nm, pl* **talones 1 :** heel (of the foot) **2 :** stub (of a check) **3 talón de Aquiles :** Achilles' heel
talud *nm* **:** slope, incline
tamal *nm* **:** tamale
tamaño[1], **-ña** *adj* **:** such a big <¿crees tamaña mentira? : do you believe such a lie?>
tamaño[2] *nm* **1 :** size **2 de tamaño natural :** life-size
tamarindo *nm* **:** tamarind
tambalearse *vr* **1 :** to teeter **2 :** to totter, to stagger, to sway — **tambaleante** *adj*
tambaleo *nm* **:** staggering, lurching, swaying
también *adv* **:** too, as well, also
tambor *nm* **:** drum
tamborilear *vi* **:** to drum, to tap
tamborileo *nm* **:** tapping, drumming
tamiz *nm* **:** sieve
tamizar {21} *vt* **:** to sift
tampoco *adv* **:** neither, not either <ni yo tampoco : me neither>
tampón *nm, pl* **tampones 1 :** ink pad **2 :** tampon
tam–tam *nm* **:** tom-tom
tan *adv* **1 :** so, so very <no es tan difícil : it is not that difficult> **2 :** as <tan pronto como : as soon as> **3 tan siquiera :** at least, at the least **4 tan sólo :** only, merely
tanda *nf* **1 :** turn, shift **2 :** batch, lot, series
tándem *nm* **1 :** tandem (bicycle) **2 :** duo, pair
tangente *adj* & *nf* **:** tangent — **tangencial** *adj*
tangible *adj* **:** tangible
tango *nm* **:** tango
tanino *nm* **:** tannin
tanque *nm* **1 :** tank, reservoir **2 :** tanker, tank (vehicle)
tanteador *nm* MARCADOR **:** scoreboard
tantear *vt* **1 :** to feel, to grope **2 :** to size up, to weigh — *vi* **1 :** to keep score **2 :** to feel one's way
tanteo *nm* **1 :** estimate, rough calculation **2 :** testing, sizing up **3 :** scoring
tanto[1] *adv* **1 :** so much <tanto mejor : so much the better> **2 :** so long <¿por qué te tardaste tanto? : why did you take so long?>
tanto[2], **-ta** *adj* **1 :** so much, so many, such <no hagas tantas preguntas : don't ask so many questions> <tiene tanto encanto : he has such charm, he's so charming> **2 :** as much, as many <come tantos dulces como yo : she eats as many sweets as I do> **3 :** odd, however many <cuarenta y tantos años : forty-odd years>
tanto[3] *nm* **1 :** certain amount **2 :** goal, point (in sports) **3 al tanto :** abreast, in the picture **4 un tanto :** somewhat, rather <un tanto cansado : rather tired>
tanto[4], **-ta** *pron* **1 :** so much, so many <tiene tanto que hacer : she has so much to do> <¡no me des tantos! : don't give me so many!> **2 entre ~ :** meanwhile **3 por lo tanto :** therefore
tañer {79} *vt* **1 :** to ring (a bell) **2 :** to play (a musical instrument)
tañido *nm* **1** CAMPANADA **:** ring, peal, toll **2 :** sound (of an instrument)
tapa *nf* **1 :** cover, top, lid **2** *Spain* **:** bar snack
tapacubos *nms & pl* **:** hubcap
tapadera *nf* **1 :** cover, lid **2 :** front, cover (for an organization or person)
tapar *vt* **1** CUBRIR **:** to cover, to cover up **2** OBSTRUIR **:** to block, to obstruct — **taparse** *vr*
tapete *nm* **1 :** small rug, mat **2 :** table cover **3 poner sobre el tapete :** to bring up for discussion
tapia *nf* **:** (adobe) wall, garden wall
tapiar *vt* **1 :** to wall in **2 :** to enclose, to block off

tapicería *nf* **1** : upholstery **2** TAPIZ : tapestry
tapicero, -ra *n* : upholsterer
tapioca *nf* : tapioca
tapir *nm* : tapir
tapiz *nm, pl* **tapices** : tapestry
tapizar {21} *vt* **1** : to upholster **2** : to cover, to carpet
tapón *nm, pl* **tapones** **1** : cork **2** : bottle cap **3** : plug, stopper
tapujo *nm* **1** : deceit, pretension **2 sin tapujos** : openly, frankly
taquigrafía *nf* : stenography, shorthand
taquigráfico, -ca *adj* : stenographic
taquígrafo, -fa *n* : stenographer
taquilla *nf* **1** : box office, ticket office **2** : earnings *pl*, take
taquillero, -ra *adj* : box-office, popular <un éxito taquillero : a box-office success>
tarántula *nf* : tarantula
tararear *vt* : to hum
tardanza *nf* : lateness, delay
tardar *vi* **1** : to delay, to take a long time **2** : to be late **3 a más tardar** : at the latest — *vt* DEMORAR : to take (time) <tarda una hora : it takes an hour>
tarde[1] *adv* **1** : late **2 tarde o temprano** : sooner or later
tarde[2] *nf* **1** : afternoon, evening **2 ¡buenas tardes!** : good afternoon!, good evening! **3 en la tarde** *or* **por la tarde** : in the afternoon, in the evening
tardío, -día *adj* : late, tardy
tardo, -da *adj* : slow
tarea *nf* **1** : task, job **2** : homework
tarifa *nf* **1** : rate <tarifas postales : postal rates> **2** : fare (for transportation) **3** : price list **4** ARANCEL : duty
tarima *nf* PLATAFORMA : dais, platform, stage
tarjeta *nf* : card <tarjeta de crédito : credit card> <tarjeta postal : postcard>
tarro *nm* **1** : jar, pot **2** *Arg, Chile* : can, tin
tarta *nf* **1** : tart **2** : cake
tartaleta *nf* : tart
tartamudear *vi* : to stammer, to stutter
tartamudeo *nm* : stutter, stammer
tartán *nm, pl* **tartanes** : tartan, plaid
tártaro *nm* : tartar <cream of tartar : crémor, tártaro>
tasa *nf* **1** : rate <tasa de desempleo : unemployment rate> **2** : tax, fee **3** : appraisal, valuation
tasación *nf, pl* **-ciones** : appraisal, assessment
tasador, -dora *n* : assessor, appraiser
tasar *vt* **1** VALORAR : to appraise, to value **2** : to set the price of **3** : to ration, to limit
tasca *nf* : cheap bar, dive
tatuaje *nm* : tattoo, tattooing
tatuar {3} *vt* : to tattoo
taurino, -na *adj* : bull, bullfighting
Tauro *nmf* : Taurus
tauromaquia *nf* : (art of) bullfighting
taxi *nm, pl* **taxis** : taxi, taxicab
taxidermia *nf* : taxidermy
taxidermista *nmf* : taxidermist
taxímetro *nm* : taximeter
taxista *nmf* : taxi driver
taza *nf* **1** : cup **2** : cupful **3** : (toilet) bowl **4** : basin (of a fountain)
tazón *nm, pl* **tazones** **1** : bowl **2** : large cup, mug
te *pron* **1** : you <te quiero : I love you> **2** : for you, to you, from you <me gustaría dártelo : I would like to give it to you> **3** : yourself, for yourself, to yourself, from yourself <¡cálmate! : calm yourself!> <¿te guardaste uno? : did you keep one for yourself?> **4** : thee
té *nm* **1** : tea **2** : tea party
tea *nf* : torch
teatral *adj* : theatrical — **teatralmente** *adv*
teatro *nm* **1** : theater **2 hacer teatro** : to put on an act, to exaggerate
teca *nf* : teak
techado *nm* **1** : roof **2 bajo techado** : under cover, indoors
techar *vt* : to roof, to shingle
techo *nm* **1** TEJADO : roof **2** : ceiling **3** : upper limit, ceiling
techumbre *nf* : roofing
tecla *nf* **1** : key (of a musical instrument or a machine) **2 dar en la tecla** : to hit the nail on the head
teclado *nm* : keyboard
teclear *vt* : to type in, to enter
técnica *nf* **1** : technique, skill **2** : technology
técnico[1], **-ca** *adj* : technical — **técnicamente** *adv*
técnico[2], **-ca** *n* : technician, expert, engineer
tecnología *nf* : technology
tecnológico, -ca *adj* : technological — **tecnológicamente** *adv*
tecolote *nm Mex* : owl
tedio *nm* : tedium, boredom
tedioso, -sa *adj* : tedious, boring — **tediosamente** *adv*
teja *nf* : tile
tejado *nm* TECHO : roof
tejedor, -dora *n* : weaver
tejer *vt* **1** : to knit, to crochet **2** : to weave **3** FABRICAR : to concoct, to make up, to fabricate
tejido *nm* **1** TELA : fabric, cloth **2** : weave, texture **3** : tissue <tejido muscular : muscle tissue>
tejo *nm* : yew
tejón *nm, pl* **tejones** : badger
tela *nf* **1** : fabric, cloth, material **2 tela de araña** : spiderweb **3 poner en tela de juicio** : to call into question, to doubt
telar *nm* : loom
telaraña *nf* : spiderweb, cobweb
tele *nf fam* : TV, television
telecomunicación *nf, pl* **-ciones** : telecommunication

teleconferencia *nf* : teleconference

teledifusión *nf, pl* **-siones** : television broadcasting

teledirigido, -da *adj* : remote-controlled

telefonear *v* : to telephone, to call

telefónico, -ca *adj* : phone, telephone <llamada telefónica : phone call>

telefonista *nmf* : telephone operator

teléfono *nm* **1** : telephone **2 llamar por teléfono** : to telephone, to make a phone call

telegrafiar {85} *v* : to telegraph

telegráfico, -ca *adj* : telegraphic

telégrafo *nm* : telegaph

telegrama *nm* : telegram

telenovela *nf* : soap opera

telepatía *nf* : telepathy

telepático, -ca *adj* : telepathic — **telepáticamente** *adv*

telescópico, -ca *adj* : telescopic

telescopio *nm* : telescope

telespectador, -dora *n* : television viewer

telesquí *nm, pl* **-squís** : ski lift

televidente *nmf* : television viewer

televisar *vt* : to televise

televisión *nf, pl* **-siones** : television, TV

televisivo, -va *adj* : television <serie televisiva : television series>

televisor *nm* : television set

telón *nm, pl* **telones 1** : curtain (in theater) **2 telón de fondo** : backdrop, background

tema *nm* **1** ASUNTO : theme, topic, subject **2** MOTIVO : motif, central theme

temario *nm* **1** : set of topics (for study) **2** : agenda

temática *nf* : subject matter

temático, -ca *adj* : thematic

temblar {55} *vi* **1** : to tremble, to shake, to shiver <le temblaban las rodillas : his knees were shaking> **2** : to shudder, to be afraid <tiemblo con sólo pensarlo : I shudder to think of it>

temblor *nm* **1** : shaking, trembling **2** : tremor, earthquake

tembloroso, -sa *adj* : tremulous, trembling, shaking <con la voz temblorosa : with a shaky voice>

temer *vt* : to fear, to dread — *vi* : to be afraid

temerario, -ria *adj* : reckless, rash — **temerariamente** *adv*

temeridad *nf* **1** : temerity, recklessness, rashness **2** : rash act

temeroso, -sa *adj* MIEDOSO : fearful, frightened

temible *adj* : fearsome, dreadful

temor *nm* MIEDO : fear, dread

témpano *nm* : ice floe

temperamento *nm* : temperament — **temperamental** *adj*

temperancia *nf* : temperance

temperar *vt* MODERAR : to temper, to moderate — *vi* : to have a change of air

temperatura *nf* : temperature

tempestad *nf* **1** : storm, tempest **2 tempestad de arena** : sandstorm

tempestuoso, -sa *adj* : tempestuous, stormy

templado, -da *adj* **1** : temperate, mild **2** : moderate, restrained **3** : warm, lukewarm **4** VALIENTE : courageous, bold

templanza *nf* **1** : temperance, moderation **2** : mildness (of weather)

templar *vt* **1** : to temper (steel) **2** : to restrain, to moderate **3** : to tune (a musical instrument) **4** : to warm up, to cool down — **templarse** *vr* **1** : to be moderate **2** : to warm up, to cool down

temple *nm* **1** : temper (of steel, etc.) **2** HUMOR : mood <de buen temple : in a good mood> **3** : tuning **4** VALOR : courage

templo *nm* **1** : temple **2** : church, chapel

tempo *nm* : tempo (in music)

temporada *nf* **1** : season, time <temporada de béisbol : baseball season> **2** : period, spell <por temporadas : on and off>

temporal[1] *adj* **1** : temporal **2** : temporary

temporal[2] *nm* **1** : storm **2 capear el temporal** : to weather the storm

temporalmente *adv* : temporarily

temporario, -ria *adj* : temporary — **temporariamente** *adv*

temporero[1], **-ra** *adj* : temporary, seasonal

temporero[2], **-ra** *n* : temporary or seasonal worker

temporizador *nm* : timer

tempranero, -ra *adj* **1** : early **2** : early-rising

temprano[1] *adv* : early <lo más temprano posible : as soon as possible>

temprano[2], **-na** *adj* : early <la parte temprana del siglo : the early part of the century>

ten → **tener**

tenacidad *nf* : tenacity, perseverance

tenaz *adj, pl* **tenaces 1** : tenacious, persistent **2** : strong, tough

tenaza *nf or* **tenazas** *nfpl* **1** : pliers, pincers **2** : tongs **3** : claw (of a crustacean)

tenazmente *adv* : tenaciously

tendedero *nm* : clothesline

tendencia *nf* **1** PROPENSIÓN : tendency, inclination **2** : trend

tendencioso, -sa *adj* : tendencious, biased

tendente → **tendiente**

tender {56} *vt* **1** EXTENDER : to spread out, to lay out **2** : to hang out (clothes) **3** : to lay (cables, etc.) **4** : to set (a trap) — *vi* **~ a** : to tend to, to have a tendency towards — **tenderse** *vr* : to stretch out, to lie down

tendero, -ra *n* : shopkeeper, storekeeper

tendido *nm* **1 :** laying (of cables, etc.) **2 :** seats *pl,* section (at a bullfight)

tendiente *adj* **~ a :** aimed at, designed to

tendón *nm, pl* **tendones :** tendon

tenebrosidad *nf* **:** darkness, gloom

tendrá, etc. → **tener**

tenebroso, -sa *adj* **1** OSCURO **:** gloomy, dark **2** SINIESTRO **:** sinister

tenedor[1], -dora *n* **1 :** holder **2 tenedor de libros, tenedora de libros :** bookkeeper

tenedor[2] *nm* **:** table fork

tenencia *nf* **1 :** possession, holding **2 :** tenancy **3 :** tenure

tener {80} *vt* **1 :** to have <tiene ojos verdes : she has green eyes> <tengo mucho que hacer : I have a lot to do> <tiene veinte años : he's twenty years old> <tiene un metro de largo : it's one meter long> **2 :** to hold <ten esto un momento : hold this for a moment> **3 :** to feel, to make <tengo frío : I'm cold> <eso nos tiene contentos : that makes us happy> **4 ~ por :** to think, to consider <me tienes por loco : you think I'm crazy> — *v aux* **1 tener que :** to have to <tengo que salir : I have to leave> <tiene que estar aquí : it has to be here, it must be here> **2** (*with past participle*) <tenía pensado escribirte : I've been thinking of writing to you> — **tenerse** *vr* **1 :** to stand up **2 ~ por :** to consider oneself <me tengo por afortunado : I consider myself lucky>

tenería *nf* CURTIDURÍA **:** tannery

tenga, etc. → **tener**

tenia *nf* SOLITARIA **:** tapeworm

teniente *nmf* **1 :** lieutenant **2 teniente coronel :** lieutenant colonel

tenis *nms & pl* **1 :** tennis **2 tenis** *nmpl* **:** sneakers *pl*

tenista *nmf* **:** tennis player

tenor *nm* **1 :** tenor **2 :** tone, sense

tensar *vt* **1 :** to tense, to make taut **2 :** to draw (a bow) — **tensarse** *vr* **:** to become tense

tensión *nf, pl* **tensiones 1 :** tension, tautness **2 :** stress, strain **3 tensión arterial :** blood pressure

tenso, -sa *adj* **:** tense

tentación *nf, pl* **-ciones :** temptation

tentáculo *nm* **:** tentacle, feeler

tentador[1], -dora *adj* **:** tempting

tentador[2], -dora *n* **:** tempter, temptress *f*

tentar {55} *vt* **1** TOCAR **:** to feel, to touch **2** PROBAR **:** to test, to try **3** ATRAER **:** to tempt, to entice

tentativa *nf* **:** attempt, try

tentempié *nm fam* **:** snack, bite

tenue *adj* **1 :** tenuous **2 :** faint, weak, dim **3 :** light, fine **4 :** thin, slender

teñir {67} *vt* **1 :** to dye **2 :** to stain

teodolito *nm* **:** theodolite, transit (for surveying)

teología *nf* **:** theology

teológico, -ca *adj* **:** theological

teólogo, -ga *n* **:** theologian

teorema *nm* **:** theorem

teoría *nf* **:** theory

teórico[1], -ca *adj* **:** theoretical — **teóricamente** *adv*

teórico[2], -ca *n* **:** theorist

teorizar {21} *vi* **:** to theorize

tepe *nm* **:** sod, turf

teponaztle *nm Mex* **:** traditional drum

tequila *nm* **:** tequila

terapeuta *nmf* **:** therapist

terapéutica *nf* **:** therapeutics

terapéutico, -ca *adj* **:** therapeutic

terapia *nf* **1 :** therapy **2 terapia intensiva :** intensive care

tercer → **tercero**

tercermundista *adj* **:** third-world

tercero[1], -ra *adj* (**tercer** *before masculine singular nouns*) **1 :** third **2 el Tercer Mundo :** the Third World

tercero[2], -ra *n* **:** third (in a series)

terciar *vt* **1 :** to place diagonally **2 :** to divide into three parts — *vi* **1 :** to mediate **2 ~ en :** to take part in

terciario, -ria *adj* **:** tertiary

tercio[1], -cia → **tercero**

tercio[2] *nm* **:** third <dos tercios : two thirds>

terciopelo *nm* **:** velvet

terco, -ca *adj* OBSTINADO **:** obstinate, stubborn

tergiversación *nf, pl* **-ciones :** distortion

tergiversar *vt* **:** to distort, to twist

termal *adj* **:** thermal, hot

termas *nfpl* **:** hot springs

térmico, -ca *adj* **:** thermal, heat <energía térmica : thermal energy>

terminación *nf, pl* **-ciones :** termination, conclusion

terminal[1] *adj* **:** terminal — **terminalmente** *adv*

terminal[2] *nm* (*in some regions f*) **:** (electric or electronic) terminal

terminal[3] *nf* (*in some regions m*) **:** terminal, station

terminante *adj* **:** final, definitive, categorical — **terminantemente** *adv*

terminar *vt* **1** CONCLUIR **:** to end, to conclude **2** ACABAR **:** to complete, to finish off — *vi* **1 :** to finish **2 :** to stop, to end — **terminarse** *vr* **1 :** to run out **2 :** to come to an end

término *nm* **1** CONCLUSIÓN **:** end, conclusion **2 :** term, expression **3 :** period, term of office **4 término medio :** happy medium **5 términos** *nmpl* **:** terms, specifications <los términos del acuerdo : the terms of the agreement>

terminología *nf* **:** terminology

termita *nf* **:** termite

termo *nm* **:** thermos

termodinámica *nf* **:** thermodynamics

termómetro *nm* **:** thermometer

termóstato *nm* **:** thermostat

ternera *nf* **:** veal

ternero, -ra *n* **:** calf

terno *nm* **1 :** set of three **2 :** three-piece suit

ternura *nf* **:** tenderness

terquedad *nf* OBSTINACIÓN **:** obstinacy, stubbornness

terracota *nf* **:** terra-cotta

terraplén *nm, pl* **-plenes :** terrace, embankment

terráqueo, -quea *adj* **1 :** earth **2 globo terráqueo :** the earth, globe (of the earth)

terrateniente *nmf* **:** landowner

terraza *nf* **1 :** terrace, veranda **2 :** balcony (in a theater) **3 :** terrace (in agriculture)

terremoto *nm* **:** earthquake

terrenal *adj* **:** worldly, earthly

terreno *nm* **1 :** terrain **2** SUELO **:** earth, ground **3 :** plot, tract of land **4 perder terreno :** to lose ground **5 preparar el terreno :** to pave the way

terrestre *adj* **:** terrestrial

terrible *adj* **:** terrible, horrible — **terriblemente** *adv*

terrier *nmf* **:** terrier

territorial *adj* **:** territorial

territorio *nm* **:** territory

terrón *nm, pl* **terrones 1 :** clod (of earth) **2 terrón de azúcar :** lump of sugar

terror *nm* **:** terror

terrorífico, -ca *adj* **:** horrific, terrifying

terrorismo *nm* **:** terrorism

terrorista *adj & nmf* **:** terrorist

terroso, -sa *adj* **:** earthy <colores terrosos : earthy colors>

terruño *nm* **:** native land, homeland

terso, -sa *adj* **1 :** smooth **2 :** glossy, shiny **3 :** polished, flowing (of a style)

tersura *nf* **1 :** smoothness **2 :** shine

tertulia *nf* **:** gathering, group <tertulia literaria : literary circle>

tesauro *nm* **:** thesaurus

tesis *nfs & pl* **:** thesis

tesón *nm* **:** persistence, tenacity

tesonero, -ra *adj* **:** persistent, tenacious

tesorería *nf* **:** treasurer's office

tesorero, -ra *n* **:** treasurer

tesoro *nm* **1 :** treasure **2 :** thesaurus

testaferro *nm* **:** figurehead

testamentario[1], -ria *adj* **:** testamentary

testamentario[2], -ria *n* ALBACEA **:** executor, executrix *f*

testamento *nm* **:** testament, will

testar *vi* **:** to draw up a will

testarudo, -da *adj* **:** stubborn, pigheaded

testículo *nm* **:** testicle

testificar {72} *v* **:** to testify

testigo *nmf* **:** witness

testimonial *adj* **1 :** testimonial **2 :** token

testimoniar *vi* **:** to testify

testimonio *nm* **:** testimony, statement

teta *nf* **:** teat

tétano *or* **tétanos** *nm* **:** tetanus, lockjaw

tetera *nf* **1 :** teapot **2 :** teakettle

tetilla *nf* **1 :** teat **2 :** nipple

tetina *nf* **:** nipple (on a bottle)

tétrico, -ca *adj* **:** somber, gloomy

textil *adj & nm* **:** textile

texto *nm* **:** text

textual *adj* **:** literal, exact — **textualmente** *adv*

textura *nf* **:** texture

tez *nf, pl* **teces :** complexion, coloring

ti *pron* **1 :** you <es para ti : it's for you> **2 ti mismo, ti misma :** yourself **3 :** thee

tía → **tío**

tiamina *nf* **:** thiamine

tianguis *nm Mex* **:** open-air market

tibetano, -na *adj & n* **:** Tibetan

tibia *nf* **:** tibia

tibieza *nf* **1 :** tepidness **2 :** halfheartedness

tibio, -bia *adj* **1 :** lukewarm, tepid **2 :** cool, unenthusiastic

tiburón *nm, pl* **-rones 1 :** shark **2 :** raider (in finance)

tic *nm* **1 :** click, tick **2 tic nervioso :** tic

tico, -ca *adj & n fam* **:** Costa Rican

tiembla, etc. → **temblar**

tiempo *nm* **1 :** time <justo a tiempo : just in time> <perder tiempo : to waste time> <tiempo libre : spare time> **2 :** period, age <en los tiempos que corren : nowadays> **3 :** season, moment <antes de tiempo : prematurely> **4 :** weather <hace buen tiempo : the weather is fine, it's nice outside> **5 :** tempo (in music) **6 :** half (in sports) **7 :** tense (in grammar)

tienda *nf* **1 :** store, shop **2** *or* **tienda de campaña :** tent

tiende, etc. → **tender**

tiene, etc. → **tener**

tienta[1], etc. → **tentar**

tienta[2] *nf* **andar a tientas :** to feel one's way, to grope around

tiernamente *adv* **:** tenderly

tierno, -na *adj* **1 :** affectionate, tender **2 :** tender, young

tierra *nf* **1 :** land **2** SUELO **:** ground, earth **3 :** country, homeland, soil **4 tierra natal :** native land **5 la Tierra :** the Earth

tieso, -sa *adj* **1 :** stiff, rigid **2 :** upright, erect

tiesto *nm* **1 :** potsherd **2** MACETA **:** flowerpot

tiesura *nf* **:** stiffness, rigidity

tifoidea *nf* **:** typhoid

tifoideo, -dea *adj* **:** typhoid <fiebre tifoidea : typhoid fever>

tifón *nm, pl* **tifones :** typhoon

tifus *nm* **:** typhus

tigre, -gresa *n* **1 :** tiger, tigress *f* **2 :** jaguar

tijera *nf* **1** *or* **tijeras** *nfpl* **:** scissors **2 de ~ :** folding <escalera de tijera : stepladder>

tijereta *nf* **:** earwig

tijeretada *nf or* **tijeretazo** *nm* **:** cut, snip

tildar *vt* **~ de :** to brand as, to call <lo tildaron de traidor : they branded him as a traitor>
tilde *nf* **1 :** accent mark **2 :** tilde (accent over *ñ*)
tilo *nm* **:** linden (tree)
timador, -dora *n* **:** swindler
timar *vt* **:** to swindle, to cheat
timbal *nm* **1 :** kettledrum **2 timbales** *nmpl* **:** timpani
timbre *nm* **1 :** bell <tocar el timbre : to ring the doorbell> **2 :** tone, timbre **3** SELLO **:** seal, stamp **4** *CA, Mex* **:** postage stamp
timidez *nf* **:** timidity, shyness
tímido, -da *adj* **:** timid, shy — **tímidamente** *adv*
timo *nm fam* **:** swindle, trick, hoax
timón *nm, pl* **timones :** rudder <estar al timón : to beat the helm>
timonel *nm* **:** helmsman, coxwain
timorato, -ta *adj* **1 :** timorous **2 :** sanctimonious
tímpano *nm* **1 :** eardrum **2 tímpanos** *nmpl* **:** timpani, kettledrums
tina *nf* **1** BAÑERA **:** tub, bathtub **2 :** vat
tinaco *nm Mex* **:** water tank
tinieblas *nfpl* **1** OSCURIDAD **:** darkness **2 :** ignorance
tino *nm* **1 :** good judgment, sense **2 :** tact, sensitivity, insight
tinta *nf* **:** ink
tinte *nm* **1 :** dye, coloring **2 :** overtone <tintes raciales : racial overtones>
tintero *nm* **1 :** inkwell **2 quedarse en el tintero :** to remain unsaid
tintinear *vt* **:** to jingle, to clink, to tinkle
tintineo *nm* **:** clink, jingle, tinkle
tinto, -ta *adj* **1 :** dyed, stained <tinto en sangre : bloodstained> **2 :** red (of wine)
tintorería *nf* **:** dry cleaner (service)
tintura *nf* **1 :** dye, tint **2 :** tincture <tintura de yodo : tincture of iodine>
tiña *nf* **:** ringworm
tiñe, etc. → **teñir**
tío, tía *n* **:** uncle *m,* aunt *f*
tiovivo *nm* **:** merry-go-round
tipi *nm* **:** tepee
típico, -ca *adj* **:** typical — **típicamente** *adv*
tipificar {72} *vt* **1 :** to classify, to categorize **2 :** to typify
tiple *nm* **:** soprano
tipo[1] *nm* **1** CLASE **:** type, kind, sort **2 :** figure, build, appearance **3 :** rate <tipo de interés : interest rate> **4 :** (printing) type, typeface **5 :** style, model <un vestido tipo 60's : a 60's-style dress>
tipo[2]**, -pa** *n fam* **:** guy *m,* gal *f,* character
tipografía *nf* **:** typography, printing
tipográfico, -ca *adj* **:** typographic, typographical
tipográfo, -fa *n* **:** printer, typographer
tique *or* **tiquet** *nm* **1 :** ticket **2 :** receipt
tira *nf* **1 :** strip, strap **2 tira cómica :** comic, comic strip
tirabuzón *nf, pl* **-zones :** corkscrew
tirada *nf* **1 :** throw **2 :** distance, stretch **3** IMPRESIÓN **:** printing, issue
tiradero *nm Mex* **1 :** dump **2 :** mess, clutter
tirador[1] *nm* **:** handle, knob
tirador[2]**, -dora** *n* **:** marksman *m,* markswoman *f*
tiragomas *nms & pl* **:** slingshot
tiranía *nf* **:** tyranny
tiránico, -ca *adj* **:** tyrannical
tiranizar {21} *vt* **:** to tyrannize
tirano[1]**, -na** *adj* **:** tyrannical, despotic
tirano[2]**, -na** *n* **:** tyrant
tirante[1] *adj* **1 :** tense, strained **2 :** taut
tirante[2] *nm* **1 :** shoulder strap **2 tirantes** *nmpl* **:** suspenders
tirantez *nf* **1 :** tautness **2 :** tension, friction, strain
tirar *vt* **1 :** to throw, to hurl, to toss **2** BOTAR **:** to throw away, to throw out, to waste **3** DERRIBAR **:** to knock down **4 :** to shoot, to fire, to launch **5 :** to take (a photo) **6 :** to print, to run off — *vi* **1 :** to pull, to draw **2 :** to shoot **3 :** to attract **4 :** to get by, to manage <va tirando : he's getting along, he's managing> **5 ~ a :** to tend towards, to be rather <tira a picante : it's a bit spicy> — **tirarse** *vr* **1 :** to throw oneself **2** *fam* **:** to spend (time)
tiritar *vi* **:** to shiver, to tremble
tiro *nm* **1** BALAZO, DISPARO **:** shot, gunshot **2 :** shot, kick (in sports) **3 :** flue **4 :** team (of horses, etc.) **5 a ~ :** within range **6 al tiro :** right away **7 tiro de gracia :** coup de grace, death blow
tiroideo, -dea *adj* **:** thyroid
tiroides *nmf* **:** thyroid, thyroid gland — **tiroides** *adj*
tirolés, -lesa *adj* **:** Tyrolean
tirón *nm, pl* **tirones 1 :** pull, tug, yank **2 de un tirón :** all at once, in one go
tiroteo *nm* **1 :** shooting **2 :** gunfight, shoot-out
tirria *nf fam* **tener tirria a :** to have a grudge against
titánico, -ca *adj* **:** titanic, huge
titanio *nm* **:** titanium
títere *nm* **:** puppet
tití *nm* **:** marmoset
titilar *vi* **:** to twinkle, to flicker
titileo *nm* **:** twinkle, flickering
titiritero, -ra *n* **1 :** puppeteer **2 :** acrobat
titubear *vi* **1 :** to hesitate **2 :** to stutter, to stammer — **titubeante** *adj*
titubeo *nm* **1 :** hesitation **2 :** stammering
titulado, -da *adj* **1 :** titled, entitled **2 :** qualified
titular[1] *vt* **:** to title, to entitle — **titularse** *vr* **1 :** to be called, to be entitled **2 :** to receive a degree
titular[2] *adj* **:** titular, official

titular[3] *nm* : headline
titular[4] *nmf* **1** : owner, holder **2** : officeholder, incumbent
título *nm* **1** : title **2** : degree, qualification **3** : security, bond **4 a título de** : by way of, in the capacity of
tiza *nf* : chalk
tiznar *vt* : to blacken (with soot, etc.)
tizne *nm* HOLLÍN : soot
tiznón *nm, pl* **tiznones** : stain, smudge
tlapalería *nf Mex* : hardware store
TNT *nm* : TNT
toalla *nf* : towel
toallita *nf* : washcloth
tobillo *nm* : ankle
tobogán *nm, pl* **-ganes 1** : toboggan, sled **2** : slide, chute
tocadiscos *nms & pl* : record player, phonograph
tocado[1], **-da** *adj* **1** : bad, bruised (of fruit) **2** *fam* : touched, not all there
tocado[2] *nm* : headdress
tocador[1] *nm* **1** : dressing table, vanity table **2 artículos de tocador** : toiletries
tocador[2], **-dora** *n* : player (of music)
tocante *adj* **~ a** : with regard to, regarding
tocar {72} *vt* **1** : to touch, to feel, to handle **2** : to touch on, to refer to **3** : to concern, to affect **4** : to play (a musical instrument) — *vi* **1** : to knock, to ring <tocar a la puerta : to rap on the door> **2 ~ en** : to touch on, to border on <eso toca en lo ridículo : that's almost ludicrous> **3 tocarle a** : to fall to, to be up to, to be one's turn <¿a quién le toca manejar? : whose turn is it to drive?>
tocayo, -ya *n* : namesake
tocineta *nf Col, Ven* : bacon
tocino *nm* **1** : bacon **2** : salt pork
tocología *nf* OBSTETRICIA : obstetrics
tocólogo, -ga *n* OBSTETRA : obstetrician
tocón *nm, pl* **tocones** CEPA : stump (of a tree)
todavía *adv* **1** AÚN : still, yet <todavía puedes verlo : you can still see it> **2** : even <todavía más rápido : even faster> **3 todavía no** : not yet
todo[1], **-da** *adj* **1** : all, whole, entire <con toda sinceridad : with all sincerity> <toda la comunidad : the whole community> **2** : every, each <a todo nivel : at every level> **3** : maximum <a toda velocidad : at top speed> **4 todo el mundo** : everyone, everybody
todo[2] *nm* : whole
todo[3], **-da** *pron* **1** : everything, all, every bit <lo sabe todo : he knows it all> <es todo un soldado : he's every inch a soldier> **2 todos, -das** *pl* : everybody, everyone, all
todopoderoso, -sa *adj* OMNIPOTENTE : almighty, all-powerful
toga *nf* **1** : toga **2** : gown, robe (for magistrates, etc.)
toldo *nm* : awning, canopy
tolerable *adj* : tolerable — **tolerablemente** *adv*
tolerancia *nf* : tolerance, toleration
tolerante *adj* : tolerant — **tolerantemente** *adv*
tolerar *vt* : to tolerate
tolete *nm* : oarlock
tolva *nf* : hopper (container)
toma *nf* **1** : taking, seizure, capture **2** DOSIS : dose **3** : take, shot **4 toma de corriente** : wall socket, outlet **5 toma y daca** : give-and-take
tomar *vt* **1** : to take <tomé el libro : I took the book> <tomar un taxi : to take a taxi> <tomar una foto : to take a photo> <toma dos años : it takes two years> <tomaron medidas drásticas : they took drastic measures> **2** BEBER : to drink **3** CAPTURAR : to capture, to seize **4 tomar el sol** : to sunbathe **5 tomar tierra** : to land — *vi* : to drink (alcohol) — **tomarse** *vr* **1** : to take <tomarse la molestia de : to take the trouble to> **2** : to drink, to eat, to have
tomate *nm* : tomato
tomillo *nm* : thyme
tomo *nm* : volume, tome
ton *nm* **sin ton ni son** : without rhyme or reason
tonada *nf* **1** : tune, song **2** : accent
tonalidad *nf* : tonality
tonel *nm* BARRICA : barrel, cask
tonelada *nf* : ton
tonelaje *nm* : tonnage
tónica *nf* **1** : tonic (water) **2** : tonic (in music) **3** : trend, tone <dar la tónica : to set the tone>
tónico[1], **-ca** *adj* : tonic
tónico[2] *nm* : tonic <tónico capilar : hair tonic>
tono *nm* **1** : tone <tono muscular : muscle tone> **2** : shade (of colors) **3** : key (in music)
tontamente *adv* : foolishly, stupidly
tontear *vi* **1** : to fool around, to play the fool **2** : to flirt
tontería *nf* **1** : foolishness **2** : stupid remark or action **3 decir tonterías** : to talk nonsense
tonto[1], **-ta** *adj* **1** : dumb, stupid **2** : silly **3 a tontas y a locas** : without thinking, haphazardly
tonto[2], **-ta** *n* : fool, idiot
topacio *nm* : topaz
toparse *vr* **~ con** : to bump into, to run into, to come across <me topé con algunas dificultades : I ran into some problems>
tope *nm* **1** : limit, end <hasta el tope : to the limit, to the brim> **2** : stop, check, buffer <tope de puerta : doorstop> **3** : bump, collision **4** *Mex* : speed bump
tópico[1], **-ca** *adj* **1** : topical, external **2** : trite, commonplace
tópico[2] *nm* **1** : topic, subject **2** : cliché, trite expression

topo *nm* **1 :** mole (animal) **2** *fam* **:** clumsy person, blunderer
topografía *nf* **:** topography
topográfico, -ca *adj* **:** topographic, topographical
topógrafo, -fa *n* **:** topographer
toque[1]**, etc. → tocar**
toque[2] *nm* **1 :** touch <el último toque : the finishing touch> <un toque de color : a touch of color> **2 :** ringing, peal, chime **3** *Mex* **:** shock, jolt **4 toque de queda :** curfew **5 toque de diana :** reveille
toquetear *vt* **:** to touch, to handle, to finger
tórax *nm* **:** thorax
torbellino *nm* **:** whirlwind
torcedura *nf* **1 :** twisting, buckling **2 :** sprain
torcer {14} *vt* **1 :** to bend, to twist **2 :** to sprain **3 :** to turn (a corner) **4 :** to wring, to wring out **5 :** to distort — *vi* **:** to turn — **torcerse** *vr*
torcido, -da *adj* **1 :** twisted, crooked **2 :** devious
tordo *nm* ZORZAL **:** thrush
torear *vt* **1 :** to fight (bulls) **2 :** to dodge, to sidestep
toreo *nm* **:** bullfighting
torero, -ra *n* MATADOR **:** bullfighter, matador
tormenta *nf* **1 :** storm <tormenta de nieve : snowstorm> **2 :** turmoil, frenzy
tormento *nm* **1 :** torment, anguish **2 :** torture
tormentoso, -sa *adj* **:** stormy, turbulent
tornado *nm* **:** tornado
tornamesa *nmf* **:** turntable
tornar *vt* **1 :** to return, to give back **2 :** to make, to render — *vi* **:** to go back — **tornarse** *vr* **:** to become, to turn into
tornasol *nm* **1 :** reflected light **2 :** sunflower **3 :** litmus
tornear *vt* **:** to turn (in carpentry)
torneo *nm* **:** tournament
tornillo *nm* **1 :** screw **2 tornillo de banco :** vise
torniquete *nm* **1 :** tourniquet **2 :** turnstile
torno *nm* **1 :** lathe **2 :** winch **3 torno de banco :** vise **4 en torno a :** around, about <en torno a este asunto : about this issue> <en torno suyo : around him>
toro *nm* **:** bull
toronja *nf* **:** grapefruit
toronjil *nm* **:** balm, lemon balm
torpe *adj* **1** DESMAÑADO **:** clumsy, awkward **2 :** stupid, dull — **torpemente** *adv*
torpedear *vt* **:** to torpedo
torpedo *nm* **:** torpedo
torpeza *nf* **1 :** clumsiness, awkwardness **2 :** stupidity **3 :** blunder
torre *nf* **1 :** tower <torre de perforación : oil rig> **2 :** turret **3 :** rook, castle (in chess)
torrencial *adj* **:** torrential — **torrencialmente** *adv*
torrente *nm* **1 :** torrent **2 torrente sanguíneo :** bloodstream
torreón *nm, pl* **-rreones :** tower (of a castle)
torreta *nf* **:** turret (of a tank, ship, etc.)
tórrido, -da *adj* **:** torrid
torsión *nf, pl* **torsiones :** torsion — **torsional** *adj*
torso *nm* **:** torso, trunk
torta *nf* **1 :** torte, cake **2** *Mex* **:** sandwich
tortazo *nm fam* **:** blow, wallop
tortilla *nf* **1 :** tortilla **2** *or* **tortilla de huevo :** omelet
tórtola *nf* **:** turtledove
tortuga *nf* **1 :** turtle, tortoise **2 tortuga de agua dulce :** terrapin **3 tortuga boba :** loggerhead
tortuoso, -sa *adj* **:** tortuous, winding
tortura *nf* **:** torture
torturador, -dora *n* **:** torturer
torturar *vt* **:** to torture, to torment
torvo, -va *adj* **:** grim, stern, baleful
torzamos, etc. → torcer
tos *nf* **1 :** cough **2 tos ferina :** whooping cough
tosco, -ca *adj* **:** rough, coarse
toser *vi* **:** to cough
tosquedad *nf* **:** crudeness, coarseness, roughness
tostada *nf* **1 :** piece of toast **2 :** tostada
tostador *nm* **1 :** toaster **2 :** roaster (for coffee)
tostar {19} *vt* **1 :** to toast **2 :** to roast (coffee) **3 :** to tan — **tostarse** *vr* **:** to get a tan
tostón *nm, pl* **tostones** *Car* **:** fried plantain chip
total[1] *adv* **:** in the end, so <total, que no fui : in short, I didn't go>
total[2] *adj & nm* **:** total — **totalmente** *adv*
totalidad *nf* **:** totality, whole
totalitario, -ria *adj & n* **:** totalitarian
totalitarismo *nm* **:** totalitarianism
totalizar {21} *vt* **:** total, to add up to
tótem *nm, pl* **tótems :** totem
totopo *nm CA, Mex* **:** tortilla chip
totuma *nf* **:** calabash
tour [ˈtur] *nm, pl* **tours :** tour, excursion
toxicidad *nf* **:** toxicity
tóxico[1]**, -ca** *adj* **:** toxic, poisonous
tóxico[2] *nm* **:** poison
toxicomanía *nf* **:** drug addiction
toxicómano, -na *n* **:** drug addict
toxina *nf* **:** toxin
tozudez *nf* **:** stubbornness, obstinancy
tozudo, -da *adj* **:** stubborn, obstinate — **tozudamente** *adv*
traba *nf* **1 :** tie, bond **2 :** obstacle, hinderance
trabajador[1]**, -dora** *adj* **:** hard-working
trabajador[2]**, -dora** *n* **:** worker

trabajar *vi* **1 :** to work <trabaja mucho : he works hard> <trabajo de secretaria : I work as a secretary> **2 :** to strive <trabajan por mejores oportunidades : they're striving for better opportunities> **3 :** to act, to perform <trabajar en una película : to be in a movie> — *vt* **1 :** to work (metal) **2 :** to knead **3 :** to till **4 :** to work on <tienes que trabajar el español : you need to work on your Spanish>

trabajo *nm* **1 :** work, job **2** LABOR **:** labor, work <tengo mucho trabajo : I have a lot of work to do> **3** TAREA **:** task **4** ESFUERZA **:** effort **5 costar trabajo :** to be difficult **6 tomarse el trabajo :** to take the trouble **7 trabajo en equipo :** teamwork **8 trabajos** *nmpl* **:** hardships, difficulties

trabajoso, -sa *adj* LABORIOSO **:** laborious — **trabajosamente** *adv*

trabalenguas *nms & pl* **:** tongue twister

trabar *vt* **1 :** to join, to connect **2 :** to impede, to hold back **3 :** to strike up (a conversation), to form (a friendship) **4 :** to thicken (sauces) — **trabarse** *vr* **1 :** to jam **2 :** to become entangled **3 :** to be tongue-tied, to stammer

trabucar {72} *vt* **:** to confuse, to mix up

trabuco *nm* **:** blunderbuss

tracalero, -ra *adj Mex* **:** dishonest, tricky

tracción *nf* **:** traction

trace, etc. → **trazar**

tracto *nm* **:** tract

tractor *nm* **:** tractor

tradición *nf, pl* **-ciones :** tradition

tradicional *adj* **:** traditional — **tradicionalmente** *adv*

traducción *nf, pl* **-ciones :** translation

traducible *adj* **:** translatable

traducir {61} *vt* **1 :** to translate **2 :** to convey, to express — **traducirse** *vr* **~ en :** to result in

traductor, -dora *n* **:** translator

traer {81} *vt* **1 :** to bring <trae una ensalada : bring a salad> **2** CAUSAR **:** to cause, to bring about <el problema puede traer graves consecuencias : the problem could have serious consequences> **3 :** to carry, to have <todos los periódicos traían las mismas noticias : all of the newspapers carried the same news> **4** LLEVAR **:** to wear — **traerse** *vr* **1 :** to bring along **2 traérselas :** to be difficult

traficante *nmf* **:** dealer, trafficker

traficar {72} *vi* **1 :** to trade, to deal **2 ~ en :** to traffic in

tráfico *nm* **1 :** trade **2 :** traffic

tragaluz *nf, pl* **-luces :** skylight, fanlight

tragar {52} *v* **:** to swallow — **tragarse**

tragedia *nf* **:** tragedy

trágico, -ca *adj* **:** tragic — **trágicamente** *adv*

trago *nm* **1 :** swallow, swig **2 :** drink, liquor **3 trago amargo :** hard time

trague, etc. → **tragar**

traición *nf, pl* **traiciones 1 :** treason **2 :** betrayal, treachery

traicionar *vt* **:** to betray

traicionero, -ra → **traidor**

traidor[1], -dora *adj* **:** traitorous, treasonous

traidor[2], -dora *n* **:** traitor

traiga, etc. → **traer**

tráiler *or* **trailer** *nm* **:** trailer

traílla *nf* **1 :** leash **2 :** harrow

traje *nm* **1 :** suit **2 :** dress **3 :** costume **4 traje de baño :** bathing suit

trajín *nm, pl* **trajines 1 :** transport **2** *fam* **:** hustle and bustle

trajinar *vt* **:** to transport, to carry — *vi* **:** to rush around

trajo, etc. → **traer**

trama *nf* **1 :** plot **2 :** weave, weft (fabric)

tramar *vt* **1 :** to plot, to plan **2 :** to weave

tramitar *vt* **:** to transact, to negotiate, to handle

trámite *nm* **:** procedure, step

tramo *nm* **1 :** stretch, section **2 :** flight (of stairs)

trampa *nf* **1 :** trap **2 hacer trampas :** to cheat

trampear *vt* **:** to cheat

trampero, -ra *n* **:** trapper

trampilla *nf* **:** trapdoor

trampolín *nm, pl* **-lines 1 :** diving board **2 :** trampoline **3 :** springboard <un trampolín al éxito : a springboard to success>

tramposo[1], -sa *adj* **:** crooked, cheating

tramposo[2], -sa *n* **:** cheat, swindler

tranca *nf* **1 :** stick, club **2 :** bar, crossbar

trancar {72} *vt* **:** to bar (a door or window)

trancazo *nm* GOLPE **:** blow, hit

trance *nm* **1 :** critical juncture, tough time **2 :** trance **3 en trance de :** in the process of <en trance de extinción : on the verge of extinction>

tranco *nm* **1 :** stride **2** UMBRAL **:** threshold

tranque, etc. → **trancar**

tranquilidad *nf* **:** tranquility, peace

tranquilizador, -dora *adj* **1 :** soothing **2 :** reassuring

tranquilizante[1] *adj* **1 :** reassuring **2 :** tranquilizing

tranquilizante[2] *nm* **:** tranquilizer

tranquilizar {21} *vt* CALMAR **:** to calm down, to soothe <tranquilizar la conciencia : to ease the conscience> — **tranquilizarse** *vr*

tranquilo, -la *adj* CALMO **:** calm, tranquil <una vida tranquila : a quiet life> — **tranquilamente** *adv*

transacción *nf, pl* **-ciones :** transaction

transar *vi* TRANSIGIR **:** to give way, to compromise — *vt* **:** to buy and sell

transatlántico[1], -ca *adj* **:** transatlantic

transatlántico[2] *nm* : ocean liner
transbordador *nm* **1** : ferry **2 transbordador espacial** : space shuttle
transbordar *v* : to transfer
transbordo *nm* : transfer
transcendencia *nf* → **trascendencia**
transcender → **trascender**
transcribir {33} *vt* : to transcribe
transcrito *pp* → **transcribir**
transcripción *nf, pl* **-ciones** : transcription
transcurrir *vi* : to elapse, to pass
transcurso *nm* : course, progression <en el transcurso de cien años : over the course of a hundred years>
transeúnte *nmf* **1** : passerby **2** : transient
transferencia *nf* : transfer, transference
transferir {76} *vt* TRASLADAR : to transfer — **transferible** *adj*
transfigurar *vt* : to transfigure, to transform — **transfiguración** *nf*
transformación *nf, pl* **-ciones** : transformation, conversion
transformador *nm* : transformer
transformar *vt* **1** CONVERTIR : to convert **2** : to transform, to change, to alter — **transformarse** *vr*
transfusión *nf, pl* **-siones** : transfusion
transgredir {1} *vt* : to transgress — **transgresión** *nf*
transgresor, -sora *n* : transgressor
transición *nf, pl* **-ciones** : transition <período de transición : transition period>
transido, -da *adj* : overcome, beset <transido de dolor : racked with pain>
transigir {35} *vi* **1** : to give in, to compromise **2 ~ con** : to tolerate, to put up with
transistor *nm* : transistor
transitable *adj* : passable
transitar *vi* : to go, to pass, to travel <transitar por la ciudad : to travel through the city>
transitivo, -va *adj* : transitive
tránsito *nm* **1** TRÁFICO : traffic <hora de máximo tránsito : rush hour> **2** : transit, passage, movement **3** : death, passing
transitorio, -ria *adj* **1** : transitory **2** : provisional, temporary — **transitoriamente** *adv*
translúcido, -da *adj* : translucent
translucir → **traslucir**
transmisión *nf, pl* **-siones 1** : transmission, broadcast **2** : transfer **3** : transmission (of an automobile)
transmisor *nm* : transmitter
transmitir *vt* **1** : to transmit, to broadcast **2** : to pass on, to transfer — *vi* : to transmit, to broadcast
transparencia *nf* : transparency
transparentar *vt* : to reveal, to betray — **transparentarse** *vr* **1** : to be transparent **2** : to show through
transparente[1] *adj* : transparent — **transparentemente** *adv*
transparente[2] *nm* : shade, blind
transpiración *nf, pl* **-ciones** SUDOR : perspiration, sweat
transpirado, -da *adj* : sweaty
transpirar *vi* **1** SUDAR : to perspire, to sweat **2** : to transpire
transplantar, transplante → **trasplantar, trasplante**
transponer {60} *vt* **1** : to transpose, to move about **2** TRASPLANTAR : to transplant — **transponerse** *vr* **1** OCULTARSE : to hide **2** PONERSE : to set, to go down (of the sun or moon) **3** DORMITAR : to doze off
transportación *nf, pl* **-ciones** : transportation
transportador *nm* **1** : protractor **2** : conveyor
transportar *vt* **1** : to transport, to carry **2** : to transmit **3** : to transpose (music) — **transportarse** *vr* : to get carried away
transporte *nm* : transport, transportation
transportista *nmf* : hauler, carrier, trucker
transpuso, etc. → **transponer**
transversal *adj* : transverse, cross <corte transversal : cross section>
transversalmente *adv* : obliquely
transverso, -sa *adj* : transverse
tranvía *nm* : streetcar, trolley
trapeador *nm* : mop
trapear *vt* : to mop
trapecio *nm* **1** : trapezoid **2** : trapeze
trapezoide *nm* : trapezoid
trapo *nm* **1** : cloth, rag <trapo de polvo : dust cloth> **2 soltar el trapo** : to burst into tears **3 trapos** *nmpl fam* : clothes
tráquea *nf* : trachea, windpipe
traquetear *vi* : to clatter, to jolt
traqueteo *nm* **1** : jolting **2** : clattering, clatter
tras *prep* **1** : after <día tras día : day after day> <uno tras otro : one after another> **2** : behind <tras la puerta : behind the door>
trasbordar, trasbordo → **transbordar, transbordo**
trascendencia *nf* **1** : importance, significance **2** : transcendence
trascendental *adj* **1** : transcendental **2** : important, momentous
trascendente *adj* **1** : important, significant **2** : transcendent
trascender {56} *vi* **1** : to leak out, to become known **2** : to spread, to have a wide effect **3 ~ a** : to smell of <la casa trascendía a flores : the house smelled of flowers> **4 ~ de** : to transcend, to go beyond — *vt* : to transcend
trasero[1], **-sa** *adj* POSTERIOR : rear, back
trasero[2] *nm* : buttocks
trasfondo *nm* **1** : background, backdrop **2** : undertone, undercurrent
trasformación *nf* → **transformación**
trasgo *nm* : goblin, imp

trasgredir → **transgredir**

trasladar *vt* **1** TRANSFERIR : to transfer, to move **2** POSPONER : to postpone **3** TRADUCIR : to translate **4** COPIAR : to copy, to transcribe — **trasladarse** *vr* MUDARSE : to move, to relocate

traslado *nm* **1** : transfer, move **2** : copy

traslapar *vt* : to overlap — **traslaparse** *vr*

traslapo *nm* : overlap

traslúcido, -da → **translúcido**

traslucir {45} *vi* : to reveal, to show — **traslucirse** *vr* : to show through

trasmano *nm* **a ~** : out of the way, out of reach

trasmisión, trasmitir → **transmisión, transmitir**

trasnochar *vi* : to stay up all night

trasparencia *nf,* **trasparente** → **transparencia, transparente**

traspasar *vt* **1** PERFORAR : to pierce, to go through **2** : to go beyond <traspasar los límites : to overstep the limits> **3** ATRAVESAR : to cross, to go across **4** : to sell, to transfer

traspaso *nm* : transfer, sale

traspié *nm* **1** : stumble **2** : blunder

traspiración *nf* → **transpiración**

trasplantar *vt* : to transplant

trasplante *nm* : transplant

trasponer → **transponer**

trasportar → **transportar**

trasquilar *vt* ESQUILAR : to shear

traste *nm* **1** : fret (on a guitar) **2** *CA, Mex, PRi* : kitchen utensil <lavar los trastes : to do the dishes> **3 dar al traste con** : to ruin, to destroy **4 irse al traste** : to fall through

trastornar *vt* : to disturb, to upset, to disrupt — **trastornarse** *vr*

trastorno *nm* **1** : disorder <trastorno mental : mental disorder> **2** : disturbance, upset

trastos *nmpl* **1** : implements, utensils **2** *fam* : pieces of junk, stuff

trasunto *nm* : image, likeness

tratable *adj* **1** : friendly, sociable **2** : treatable

tratado *nm* **1** : treatise **2** : treaty

tratamiento *nm* : treatment

tratante *nmf* : dealer, trader

tratar *vi* **1 ~ con** : to deal with, to have contact with <no trato mucho con los clientes : I don't have much contact with customers> **2 ~ de** : to try to <estoy tratando de comer : I am trying to eat> **3 ~ de** *or* **~ sobre** : to be about, to concern <el libro trata de las plantas : the book is about plants> **4 ~ en** : to deal in <trata en herramientas : he deals in tools> — *vt* **1** : to treat <tratan bien a sus empleados : they treat their employees well> **2** : to handle <trató el tema con delicadeza : he handled the subject tactfully> — **tratarse** *vr* **~ de** : to be about, to concern

trato *nm* **1** : deal, agreement **2** : relationship, dealings *pl* **3** : treatment <malos tratos : ill-treatment>

trauma *nm* : trauma

traumático, -ca *adj* : traumatic — **traumáticamente** *adv*

traumatismo *nm* : injury <traumatismo cervical : whiplash>

través *nm* **1 a través de** : across, through **2 al través** : crosswise, across **3 de través** : sideways

travesaño *nm* **1** : crossbar **2** : crossbeam, crosspiece, transom (of a window)

travesía *nf* : voyage, crossing (of the sea)

travesura *nf* **1** : prank, mischievous act **2 travesuras** *nfpl* : mischief

travieso, -sa *adj* : mischievous, naughty — **traviesamente** *adv*

trayecto *nm* **1** : journey **2** : route **3** : trajectory, path

trayectoria *nf* : course, path, trajectory

trayendo → **traer**

traza *nf* **1** DISEÑO : design, plan **2** : appearance

trazado *nm* **1** BOSQUEJO : outline, sketch **2** PLAN : plan, layout

trazar {21} *vt* **1** : to trace **2** : to draw up, to devise **3** : to outline, to sketch

trazo *nm* **1** : stroke, line **2** : sketch, outline

trébol *nm* **1** : clover, shamrock **2** : club (playing card)

trece *adj & nm* : thirteen

treceavo[1]**, -va** *adj* : thirteenth

treceavo[2] *nm* : thirteenth (fraction)

trecho *nm* **1** : stretch, period <de trecho en trecho : at intervals> **2** : distance, space

tregua *nf* **1** : truce **2** : lull, respite **3 sin ~** : relentless, unrelenting

treinta *adj & nm* : thirty

treintavo[1]**, -va** *adj* : thirtieth

treintavo[2] *nm* : thirtieth (fraction)

tremendo, -da *adj* **1** : tremendous, enormous **2** : terrible, dreadful **3** *fam* : great, super

trementina *nf* AGUARRÁS : turpentine

trémulo, -la *adj* **1** : trembling, shaky **2** : flickering

tren *nm* **1** : train **2** : set, assembly <tren de aterrizaje : landing gear> **3** : speed, pace <a todo tren : at top speed>

trence, etc. → **trenzar**

trenza *nf* : braid, pigtail

trenzar {21} *vt* : to braid — **trenzarse** *vr* : to get involved

trepador, -dora *adj* : climbing <rosal trepador : rambling rose>

trepadora *nf* **1** : climbing plant, climber **2** : nuthatch

trepar *vi* **1** : to climb <trepar a un árbol : to climb up a tree> **2** : to creep, to spread (of a plant)

trepidación *nf, pl* **-ciones** : vibration

trepidante *adj* **1** : vibrating **2** : fast, frantic

trepidar *vi* **1 :** to shake, to vibrate **2 :** to hesitate, to waver

tres *adj & nm* **:** three

trescientos[1], **-tas** *adj* **:** two hundred

trescientos[2] *nms & pl* **:** three hundred

treta *nf* **:** trick, ruse

tríada *nf* **:** triad

triángulo *nm* **:** triangle — **triangular** *adj*

tribal *adj* **:** tribal

tribu *nf* **:** tribe

tribulación *nf, pl* **-ciones :** tribulation

tribuna *nf* **1 :** dais, platform **2 :** stands *pl*, bleachers *pl*, grandstand

tribunal *nm* **:** court, tribunal

tributar *vt* **:** to pay, to render — *vi* **:** to pay taxes

tributario[1], **-ria** *adj* **:** tax <evasión tributaria : tax evasion>

tributario[2] *nm* **:** tributary

tributo *nm* **1 :** tax **2 :** tribute

triciclo *nm* **:** tricycle

tricolor *adj* **:** tricolor, tricolored

tridente *nm* **:** trident

tridimensional *adj* **:** three-dimensional, 3-D

trienal *adj* **:** triennial

trifulca *nf fam* **:** row, ruckus

trigésimo[1], **-ma** *adj* **:** thirtieth, thirty-

trigésimo[2], **-ma** *n* **:** thirtieth, thirty- (in a series)

trigo *nm* **1 :** wheat **2 trigo rubión :** buckwheat

trigonometría *nf* **:** trigonometry

trigueño, -ña *adj* **1 :** light brown (of hair) **2** MORENO **:** dark, olive-skinned

trillado, -da *adj* **:** trite, hackneyed

trilladora *nf* **:** thresher, threshing machine

trillar *vt* **:** to thresh

trillizo, -za *n* **:** triplet

trilogía *nf* **:** trilogy

trimestral *adj* **:** quarterly — **trimestralmente** *adv*

trinar *vi* **1 :** to thrill **2 :** to warble

trinchar *vt* **:** to carve, to cut up

trinchera *nf* **1 :** trench, ditch **2 :** trench coat

tridente *nm* **:** trident

trineo *nm* **:** sled, sleigh

trinidad *nf* **la Trinidad :** the Trinity

trino *nm* **:** trill, warble

trinquete *nm* **:** ratchet

trío *nm* **:** trio

tripa *nf* **1** INTESTINO **:** gut, intestine **2 tripas** *nfpl fam* **:** belly, tummy, insides *pl* <dolerle a uno las tripas : to have a stomach ache>

tripartito, -ta *adj* **:** tripartite

triple *adj & nm* **:** triple

triplicado *nm* **:** triplicate

triplicar {72} *vt* **:** to triple, to treble

trípode *nm* **:** tripod

tripulación *nf, pl* **-ciones :** crew

tripulante *nmf* **:** crew member

tripular *vt* **:** to man

tris *nm* **estar en un tris de :** to be within an inch of, to be very close to

triste *adj* **1 :** sad, gloomy <ponerse triste : to become sad> **2 :** desolate, dismal <una perspectiva triste : a dismal outlook> **3 :** sorry, sorry-looking <la triste verdad : the sorry truth>

tristeza *nf* DOLOR **:** sadness, grief

tristón, -tona *adj, mpl* **-tones :** melancholy, downhearted

tritón *nm, pl* **tritones :** newt

triturar *vt* **:** to crush, to grind

triunfal *adj* **:** triumphal, triumphant — **triunfalmente** *adv*

triunfante *adj* **:** triumphant, victorious

triunfar *vi* **:** to triumph, to win

triunfo *nm* **1 :** triumph, victory **2** ÉXITO **:** success **3 :** trump (in card games)

triunvirato *nm* **:** triumvirate

trivial *adj* **1 :** trivial **2 :** trite, commonplace

trivialidad *nf* **:** triviality

triza *nf* **1 :** shred, bit **2 hacer trizas :** to tear into shreds, to smash to pieces

trocar {82} *vt* **1** CAMBIAR **:** to exchange, to trade **2** CAMBIAR **:** to change, to alter, to transform **3** CONFUNDIR **:** to confuse, to mix up

trocha *nf* **:** path, trail

troce, etc. → **trozar**

trofeo *nm* **:** trophy

tromba *nf* **1 :** whirlwind **2 tromba de agua :** downpour, cloudburst

trombón *nm, pl* **trombones 1 :** trombone **2 :** trombonist — **trombonista** *nmf*

trombosis *nf* **:** thrombosis

trompa *nf* **1 :** trunk (of an elephant), proboscis (of an insect) **2 :** horn <trompa de caza : hunting horn> **3 :** tube, duct (in the body)

trompada *nf fam* **1 :** punch, blow **2 :** bump, collision (of persons)

trompeta *nf* **:** trumpet

trompetista *nmf* **:** trumpet player, trumpeter

trompo *nm* **:** spinning top

tronada *nf* **:** thunderstorm

tronar {19} *vi* **1 :** to thunder, to roar **2 :** to be furious, to rage **3** *CA, Mex fam* **:** to shoot — *v impers* **:** to thunder <está tronando : it's thundering>

tronchar *vt* **1 :** to snap, to break off **2 :** to cut off (relations)

tronco *nm* **1 :** trunk (of a tree) **2 :** log **3 :** torso

trono *nm* **1 :** throne **2** *fam* **:** toilet

tropa *nf* **1 :** troop, soldiers *pl* **2 :** crowd, mob **3 :** herd (of livestock)

tropel *nm* **:** mob, swarm

tropezar {29} *vi* **1 :** to trip, to stumble **2 :** to slip up, to blunder **3 ~ con :** to run into, to bump into **4 ~ con :** to come up against (a problem)

tropezón *nm, pl* **-zones 1 :** stumble **2 :** mistake, slip

tropical *adj* **:** tropical

trópico *nm* **1 :** tropic <trópico de Cáncer : tropic of Cancer> **2 el trópico :** the tropics

tropiezo *nm* **1** CONTRATIEMPO : snag, setback **2** EQUIVOCACIÓN : mistake, slip
troqué, etc. → **trocar**
troquel *nm* : die (for stamping)
trotamundos *nmf* : globe-trotter
trotar *vi* **1** : to trot **2** : to jog **3** *fam* : to rush about
trote *nm* **1** : trot **2** *fam* : rush, bustle **3 de ~** : durable, for everyday use
trovador, -dora *n* : troubadour
trozar {21} *vt* : to cut up, to dice
trozo *nm* **1** PEDAZO : piece, bit, chunk **2** : passage, extract
trucha *nf* : trout
truco *nm* **1** : trick **2** : knack
truculento, -ta *adj* : horrifying, gruesome
trueca, trueque, etc. → **trocar**
truena, etc. → **tronar**
trueno *nm* : thunder
trueque *nm* : barter, exchange
trufa *nf* : truffle
truncar {72} *vt* **1** : to truncate, to cut short **2** : to thwart, to frustrate <truncó sus esperanzas : she shattered their hopes>
trunco, -ca *adj* **1** : truncated **2** : unfinished, incomplete
trunque, etc. → **truncar**
tu *adj* **1** : your <tu vestido : your dress> <toma tus vitaminas : take your vitamins> **2** : thy
tú *pron* **1** : you <tú eres mi hijo : you are my son> **2** : thou
tuba *nf* : tuba
tubérculo *nm* : tuber
tuberculosis *nf* : tuberculosis
tuberculoso, -sa *adj* : tuberculous, tubercular
tubería *nf* : pipes *pl*, tubing
tuberoso, -sa *adj* : tuberous
tubo *nm* **1** : tube <tubo de ensayo : test tube> **2** : pipe <tubo de desagüe : drainpipe> **3 tubo digestivo** : alimentary canal
tubular *adj* : tubular
tuerca *nf* : nut <tuercas y tornillos : nuts and bolts>
tuerce, etc. → **torcer**
tuerto, -ta *adj* : one-eyed, blind in one eye
tuerza, etc. → **torcer**
tuesta, etc. → **tostar**
tuétano *nm* : marrow
tufo *nm* **1** : fume, vapor **2** *fam* : stench, stink
tugurio *nm* : hovel
tulipán *nm, pl* **-panes** : tulip
tumba *nf* **1** SEPULCRO : tomb **2** FOSA : grave **3** : felling of trees
tumbar *vt* **1** : to knock down **2** : to fell, to cut down — *vi* : to fall down — **tumbarse** *vr* ACOSTARSE : to lie down
tumbo *nm* **1** : tumble, fall **2 dar tumbos** : to jolt, to bump around
tumor *nm* : tumor
túmulo *nm* : burial mound
tumulto *nm* **1** ALBOROTO : commotion, tumult **2** MOTÍN : riot **3** MULTITUD : crowd
tumultuoso, -sa *adj* : tumultuous
tuna *nf* : prickly pear (fruit)
tundra *nf* : tundra
tunecino, -na *adj & n* : Tunisian
túnel *nm* : tunnel
tungsteno *nm* : tungsten
túnica *nf* : tunic
tupé *nm* PELUQUÍN : toupee
tupido, -da *adj* **1** DENSO : dense, thick **2** OBSTRUIDO : obstructed, blocked up
turba *nf* **1** : peat **2** : mob, throng
turbación *nf, pl* **-ciones 1** : disturbance **2** : alarm, concern **3** : confusion
turbante *nm* : turban
turbar *vt* **1** : to disturb, to disrupt **2** : to worry, to upset **3** : to confuse
turbina *nf* : turbine
turbio, -bia *adj* **1** : cloudy, murky, turbid **2** : dim, blurred **3** : shady, crooked
turbopropulsor *nm* : turboprop
turborreactor *nm* : turbojet
turbulencia *nf* : turbulence
turbulento, -ta *adj* : turbulent
turco[1], -ca *adj* : Turkish
turco[2], -ca *n* : Turk
turgente *adj* : turgid, swollen
turismo *nm* : tourism, tourist industry
turista *nmf* : tourist, vacationer
turístico, -ca *adj* : tourist, travel
turnar *vi* : to take turns, to alternate
turno *nm* **1** : turn <ya te tocará tu turno : you'll get your turn> **2** : shift, duty <turno de noche : night shift> **3 por turno** : alternately
turón *nm, pl* **turones** : polecat
turquesa *nf* : turquoise
turrón *nm, pl* **turrones** : nougat
tusa *nf* : corn husk
tutear *vt* : to address as *tú*
tutela *nf* **1** : guardianship **2** : tutelage, protection
tuteo *nm* : addressing as *tú*
tutor, -tora *n* **1** : tutor **2** : guardian
tuvo, etc. → **tener**
tuyo[1], -ya *adj* : yours, of yours <un amigo tuyo : a friend of yours> <¿es tuya esta casa? : is this house yours?>
tuyo[2], -ya *pron* **1** : yours <ése es el tuyo : that one is yours> <trae la tuya : bring your own> **2 los tuyos** : your relations, your friends <¿vendrán los tuyos? : are your folks coming?>
tweed [ˈtwið] *nm* : tweed

U

u[1] *nf* : twenty-second letter of the Spanish alphabet
u[2] *conj* (*used instead of* **o** *before words beginning with o- or ho-*) : or
ualabí *nm* : wallaby
uapití *nm* : American elk, wapiti
ubicación *nf, pl* **-ciones** : location, position
ubicar {72} *vt* **1** SITUAR : to place, to put, to position **2** LOCALIZAR : to locate, to find — **ubicarse** *vr* **1** LOCALIZARSE : to be placed, to be located **2** SITUARSE : to position oneself
ubicuidad *nf* OMNIPRESENCIA : ubiquity
ubicuo, -cua *adj* OMNIPRESENTE : ubiquitous
ubre *nf* : udder
ucraniano, -na *adj & n* : Ukranian
Ud., Uds. → **usted**
ufanarse *vr* **~ de** : to boast about, to pride oneself on
ufano, -na *adj* **1** ORGULLOSO : proud **2** : self-satisfied, smug
ugandés, -desa *adj & n, mpl* **-deses** : Ugandan
ukelele *nm* : ukulele
úlcera *nf* : ulcer — **ulceroso, -sa** *adj*
ulcerar *vt* : to ulcerate — **ulcerarse** *vr* — **ulceración** *nf*
ulceroso, -sa *adj* : ulcerous
ulterior *adj* : later, subsequent — **ulteriormente** *adv*
últimamente *adv* : lately, recently
ultimar *vt* **1** CONCLUIR : to complete, to finish, to finalize **2** MATAR : to kill
ultimátum *nm, pl* **-tums** : ultimatum
último, -ma *adj* **1** : last, final <la última galleta : the last cookie> <en último caso : as a last resort> **2** : last, latest, most recent <su último viaje a España : her last trip to Spain> <en los últimos años : in recent years> **3 por ~** : finally
ultrajar *vt* INSULTAR : to offend, to outrage, to insult
ultraje *nm* INSULTO : outrage, insult
ultramar *nm* **de ~** *or* **en ~** : overseas, abroad
ultranza *nf* **a ~ 1** : to the extreme <lo defendió a ultranza : she defended him fiercely> **2** : extreme, out-and-out <perfeccionismo a ultranza : rabid perfectionism>
ultrarrojo, -ja *adj* : infrared
ultravioleta *adj* : ultraviolet
ulular *vi* **1** : to hoot **2** : to howl, to wail
ululato *nm* : hoot (of an owl), wail (of a person)
umbilical *adj* : umbilical <cordón umbilical : umbilical cord>
umbral *nm* : threshold, doorstep
un[1] → **uno**[1]
un[2], **una** *art, mpl* **unos 1** : a, an **2 unos** *or* **unas** *pl* : some, a few <hace unas semanas : a few weeks ago> **3 unos** *or* **unas** *pl* : about, approximately <unos veinte años antes : about twenty years before>
unánime *adj* : unanimous — **unánimemente** *adv*
unanimidad *nf* **1** : unanimity **2 por ~** : unanimously
unción *nf, pl* **-ciones** : unction
uncir {83} *vt* : to yoke
undécimo[1], **-ma** *adj* : eleventh
undécimo[2], **-ma** *n* : eleventh (in a series)
ungir {35} *vt* : to anoint
ungüento *nm* : ointment, salve
únicamente *adv* : only, solely
unicelular *adj* : unicellular
único[1], **-ca** *adj* **1** : only, sole **2** : unique, extraordinary
único[2], **-ca** *n* : only one <los únicos que vinieron : the only ones who showed up>
unicornio *nm* : unicorn
unidad *nf* **1** : unity **2** : unit
unidireccional *adj* : unidirectional
unido, -da *adj* **1** : joined, united **2** : close <unos amigos muy unidos : very close friends>
unificar {72} *vt* : to unify — **unificación** *nf*
uniformado, -da *adj* : uniformed
uniformar *vt* ESTANDARIZAR : to standardize, to make uniform
uniforme[1] *adj* : uniform — **uniformemente** *adv*
uniforme[2] *nm* : uniform
uniformidad *nf* : uniformity
unilateral *adj* : unilateral — **unilateralmente** *adv*
unión *nf, pl* **uniones 1** : union **2** JUNTURA : joint, coupling
unir *vt* **1** JUNTAR : to unite, to join, to link **2** COMBINAR : to combine, to blend — **unirse** *vr* **1** : to join together **2** : to combine, to mix together **3 ~ a** : to join <se unieron al grupo : they joined the group>
unísono *nm* : unison <al unísono : in unison>
unitario, -ria *adj* : unitary, unit <precio unitario : unit price>
universal *adj* : universal — **universalmente** *adv*
universidad *nf* : university
universitario[1], **-ria** *adj* : university, college
universitario[2], **-ria** *n* : university student, college student
universo *nm* : universe
unja, etc. → **ungir**
uno[1], **una** *adj* (**un** *before masculine singular nouns*) : one <una silla : one chair> <tiene treinta y un años : he's thirty-one years old> <el tomo uno : volume one>
uno[2] *nm* : one, number one
uno[3], **una** *pron* **1** : one (number) <uno por uno : one by one> <es la una : it's

one o'clock> **2 :** one (person or thing) <una es mejor que las otras : one (of them) is better than the others> <hacerlo uno mismo : to do it oneself> **3 unos, unas** *pl* **:** some (ones), some people **4 uno y otro :** both **5 unos y otros :** all of them **6 el uno al otro :** one another, each other <se enseñaron los unos a los otros : they taught each other>

untar *vt* **1 :** to anoint **2 :** to smear, to grease **3 :** to bribe

unza, etc. → **uncir**

uña *nf* **1 :** fingernail, toenail **2 :** claw, hoof, stinger

uranio *nm* **:** uranium

Urano *nm* **:** Uranus

urbanidad *nf* **:** urbanity, courtesy

urbanización *nf, pl* **-ciones :** housing development, residential area

urbano, -na *adj* **1 :** urban **2** CORTÉS **:** urbane, polite

urbe *nf* **:** large city, metropolis

urdimbre *nf* **:** warp (in a loom)

uretra *nf* **:** urethra

urgencia *nf* **1 :** urgency **2** EMERGENCIA **:** emergency

urgente *adj* **:** urgent — **urgentemente** *adv*

urgir {35} *v impers* **:** to be urgent, to be pressing <me urge localizarlo : I urgently need to find him> <el tiempo urge : time is running out>

urinario[1]**, -ria** *adj* **:** urinary

urinario[2] *nm* **:** urinal (place)

urja, etc. → **urgir**

urna *nf* **1 :** urn **2 :** ballot box <acudir a las urnas : to go to the polls>

urogallo *nm* **:** grouse (bird)

urraca *nf* **1 :** magpie **2 urraca de América :** blue jay

urticaria *nf* **:** hives

uruguayo, -ya *adj & n* **:** Uruguayan

usado, -da *adj* **1 :** used, secondhand **2 :** worn, worn-out

usanza *nf* **:** custom, usage

usar *vt* **1** EMPLEAR, UTILIZAR **:** to use, to make use of **2** CONSUMIR **:** to consume, to use (up) **3** LLEVAR **:** to wear **4 de usar y tirar :** disposable — **usarse 1 :** to be used **2 :** to be in fashion

uso *nm* **1** EMPLEO, UTILIZACIÓN **:** use <de uso personal : for personal use> <hacer uso de : to make use of> **2 :** wear <uso y desgaste : wear and tear> **3** USANZA **:** custom, usage, habit <al uso de : in the manner of, in the style of>

usted *pron* **1** (*formal form of address in most countries; often written as* **Ud.** *or* **Vd.**) **:** you **2 ustedes** *pl* (*often written as* **Uds.** *or* **Vds.**) **:** you, all of you

usual *adj* **:** usual, common, normal <poco usual : not very common> — **usualmente** *adv*

usuario, -ria *n* **:** user

usura *nf* **:** usury — **usurario, -ria** *adj*

usurero, -ra *n* **:** usurer

usurpador, -dora *n* **:** usurper

usurpar *vt* **:** to usurp — **usurpación** *nf*

utensilio *nm* **:** utensil, tool

uterino, -na *adj* **:** uterine

útero *nm* **:** uterus, womb

útil *adj* **:** useful, handy, helpful

útiles *nmpl* **:** implements, tools

utilidad *nf* **1 :** utility, usefulness **2 utilidades** *nfpl* **:** profits

utilitario, -ria *adj* **:** utilitarian

utilizable *adj* **:** usable, fit for use

utilización *nf, pl* **-ciones :** utilization, use

utilizar {21} *vt* **:** to use, to utilize

útilmente *adv* **:** usefully

utopía *nf* **:** utopia

utópico, -ca *adj* **:** utopian

uva *nf* **:** grape

uvular *adj* **:** uvular

V

v *nf* **:** twenty-third letter of the Spanish alphabet

va → **ir**

vaca *nf* **:** cow

vacación *nf, pl* **-ciones 1 :** vacation <dos semanas de vacaciones : two weeks of vacation> **2 estar de vacaciones :** to be on vacation **3 irse de vacaciones :** to go on vacation

vacacionar *vi Mex* **:** to vacation

vacacionista *nmf CA, Mex* **:** vacationer

vacante[1] *adj* **:** vacant, empty

vacante[2] *nf* **:** vacancy (for a job)

vaciado *nm* **:** cast, casting <vaciado de yeso : plaster cast>

vaciar {85} *vt* **1 :** to empty, to empty out, to drain **2** AHUECAR **:** to hollow out **3 :** to cast (in a mold) — *vi* **~ en :** to flow into, to empty into

vacilación *nf, pl* **-ciones :** hesitation, vacillation

vacilante *adj* **1 :** hesitant, unsure **2 :** shaky, unsteady **3 :** flickering

vacilar *vi* **1 :** to hesitate, to vacillate, to waver **2 :** to be unsteady, to wobble **3 :** to flicker **4** *fam* **:** to joke, to fool around

vacío[1]**, -cía** *adj* **1 :** vacant **2 :** empty **3 :** meaningless

vacío[2] *nm* **1 :** emptiness, void **2 :** space, gap **3 :** vacuum **4 hacerle el vacío a alguien :** to ostracize someone, to give someone the cold shoulder

vacuidad *nf* **:** vacuity, vacuousness

vacuna *nf* **:** vaccine

vacunación *nf, pl* **-ciones** INOCULACIÓN **:** vaccination, inoculation

vacunar *vt* INOCULAR : to vaccinate, to inoculate

vacuno[1], -na *adj* : bovine <ganado vacuno : beef cattle>

vacuno[2] *nm* : bovine

vacuo, -cua *adj* : empty, shallow, inane

vadear *vt* : to ford, to wade across

vado *nm* : ford

vagabundear *vi* : to wander, to roam about

vagabundo[1], -da *adj* **1** ERRANTE : wandering **2** : stray

vagabundo[2], -da *n* : vagrant, bum, vagabond

vagamente *adv* : vaguely

vagancia *nf* **1** : vagrancy **2** PEREZA : laziness, idleness

vagar {52} *vi* ERRAR : to roam, to wander

vagina *nf* : vagina — **vaginal** *adj*

vago[1], -ga *adj* **1** : vague **2** PEREZOSO : lazy, idle

vago[2], -ga *n* **1** : idler, loafer **2** VAGABUNDO : vagrant, bum

vagón *nm, pl* **vagones** : car (of a train)

vague, etc. → **vagar**

vaguear *vi* **1** : to loaf, to lounge around **2** VAGAR : to wander

vaguedad *nf* : vagueness

vahído *nm* : dizzy spell

vaho *nm* **1** : breath **2** : vapor, steam (on glass, etc.)

vaina *nf* **1** : sheath, scabbard **2** : pod (of a pea or bean) **3** *fam* : nuisance, bother

vainilla *nf* : vanilla

vaivén *nm, pl* **vaivenes 1** : swinging, swaying, rocking **2** : change, fluctuation <los vaivenes de la vida : life's ups and downs>

vajilla *nf* : dishes *pl*, set of dishes

valdrá, etc. → **valer**

vale *nm* **1** : voucher **2** PAGARÉ : promissary note, IOU

valedero, -ra *adj* : valid

valentía *nf* : courage, valor

valer {84} *vt* **1** : to be worth <valen una fortuna : they're worth a fortune> <no vale protestar : there's no point in protesting> <valer la pena : to be worth the trouble> **2** : to cost <¿cuánto vale? : how much does it cost?> **3** : to earn, to gain <le valió una reprimenda : it earned him a reprimand> **4** : to protect, to aid <¡válgame Dios! : God help me!> **5** : to be equal to — *vi* **1** : to have value <sus consejos no valen para nada : his advice is worthless> **2** : to be valid, to count <¡eso no vale! : that doesn't count!> **3 hacerse valer** : to assert oneself **4 más vale** : it's better <más vale que te vayas : you'd better go> — **valerse** *vr* **1 ~ de** : to take advantage of **2 valerse solo** *or* **valerse por sí mismo** : to look after oneself **3** *Mex* : to be fair <no se vale : it's not fair>

valeroso, -sa *adj* : brave, valiant

valet [ˈbalɛt, -ˈlɛ] *nm* : jack (in playing cards)

valga, etc. → **valer**

valía *nf* : value, worth

validar *vt* : to validate — **validación** *nf*

validez *nf* : validity

válido, -da *adj* : valid

valiente *adj* **1** : brave, valiant **2** (*used ironically*) : fine, great <¡valiente amiga! : what a fine friend!> — **valientemente** *adv*

valija *nf* : suitcase, valise

valioso, -sa *adj* PRECIOSO : valuable, precious

valla *nf* **1** : fence, barricade **2** : hurdle (in sports) **3** : obstacle, hindrance

vallar *vt* : to fence, to put a fence around

valle *nm* : valley, vale

valor *nm* **1** : value, worth, importance **2** CORAJE : courage, valor **3 valores** *nmpl* : values, principles **4 valores** *nmpl* : securities, bonds **5 sin ~** : worthless

valoración *nf, pl* **-ciones 1** EVALUACIÓN : valuation, appraisal, assessment **2** APRECIACIÓN : appreciation

valorar *vt* **1** EVALUAR : to evaluate, to appraise, to assess **2** APRECIAR : to value, to appreciate

valorizarse {21} *vr* : to appreciate, to increase in value — **valorización** *nf*

vals *nm* : waltz

valsar *vi* : to waltz

valuación *nf, pl* **-ciones** : valuation, appraisal

valuar {3} *vt* : to value, to appraise, to assess

válvula *nf* **1** : valve **2 válvula reguladora** : throttle

vamos → **ir**

vampiro *nm* : vampire

van → **ir**

vanadio *nm* : vanadium

vanagloriarse *vr* : to boast, to brag

vanamente *adv* : vainly, in vain

vandalismo : vandalism

vándalo *nm* : vandal — **vandalismo** *nm*

vanguardia *nf* **1** : vanguard **2** : avante-garde **3 a la vanguardia** : at the forefront

vanidad *nf* : vanity

vanidoso, -sa *adj* PRESUMIDO : vain, conceited

vano, -na *adj* **1** INÚTIL : vain, useless **2** : vain, worthless <vanas promesas : empty promises> **3 en ~** : in vain, of no avail

vapor *nm* **1** : vapor, steam **2** : steamer, steamship **3 al vapor** : steamed

vaporizador *nm* : vaporizer

vaporizar {21} *vt* : to vaporize — **vaporizarse** *vr* — **vaporización** *nf*

vaporoso, -sa *adj* **1** : vaporous **2** : sheer, airy

vapulear *vt* : to beat, to thrash

vaquero[1], -ra *adj* : cowboy <pantalón vaquero : jeans>
vaquero[2], -ra *n* : cowboy *m,* cowgirl *f*
vaqueros *nmpl* JEANS : jeans
vaquilla *nf* : heifer
vara *nf* **1 :** pole, stick, rod **2 :** staff (of office) **3 :** lance, pike (in bullfighting) **4 :** yardstick **5 vara de oro :** goldenrod
varado, -da *adj* **1 :** beached, aground **2 :** stranded
varar *vt* : to beach (a ship), to strand — *vi* : to run aground
variable *adj & nf* : variable — **variabilidad** *nf*
variación *nf, pl* **-ciones** : variation
variado, -da *adj* : varied, diverse
variante *adj & nf* : variant
varianza *nf* : variance
variar {85} *vt* **1 :** to change, to alter **2 :** to diversify — *vi* **1 :** to vary, to change **2 variar de opinión :** to change one's mind
varicela *nf* : chicken pox
varices *or* **várices** *nfpl* : varicose veins
varicoso, -sa *adj* : varicose
variedad *nf* DIVERSIDAD : variety, diversity
varilla *nf* **1 :** rod, bar **2 :** spoke (of a wheel) **3 :** rib (of an umbrella)
vario, -ria *adj* **1 :** varied, diverse **2 :** variegated, motley **3 :** changeable **4 varios, varias** *pl* : various, several
variopinto, -ta *adj* : diverse, assorted, motley
varita *nf* : wand <varita mágica : magic wand>
varón *nm, pl* **varones 1** HOMBRE : man, male **2** NIÑO : boy
varonil *adj* **1 :** masculine, manly **2 :** mannish
vas → **ir**
vasallo *nm* : vassal — **vasallaje** *nm*
vasco[1], -ca *adj & n* : Basque
vasco[2] *nm* : Basque (language)
vascular *adj* : vascular
vasija *nf* : container, vessel
vaso *nm* **1 :** glass, tumbler **2 :** glassful **3 :** vessel <vaso sanguíneo : blood vessel>
vástago *nm* **1 :** offspring, descendent **2 :** shoot (of a plant)
vastedad *nf* : vastness, immensity
vasto, -ta *adj* : vast, immense
vataje *nm* : wattage
vaticinar *vt* : to predict, to foretell
vaticinio *nm* : prediction, prophecy
vatio *nm* : watt
vaya, etc. → **ir**
Vd., Vds. → **usted**
ve, etc. → **ir, ver**
vea, etc. → **ver**
vecinal *adj* : local
vecindad *nf* **1 :** neighborhood, vicinity **2 casa de vecindad :** tenement
vecindario *nm* **1 :** neighborhood, area **2 :** residents *pl*
vecino, -na *n* **1 :** neighbor **2 :** resident, inhabitant
veda *nf* **1** PROHIBICIÓN : prohibition **2 :** closed season (for hunting or fishing)
vedar *vt* **1 :** to prohibit, to ban **2** IMPEDIR : to impede, to prevent
vega *nf* : fertile lowland
vegetación *nf, pl* **-ciones 1 :** vegetation **2 vegetaciones** *nfpl* : adenoids
vegetal *adj & nm* : vegetable, plant
vegetar *vi* : to vegetate
vegetarianismo *nm* : vegetarianism
vegetariano, -na *adj & n* : vegetarian
vegetativo, -va *adj* : vegetative
vehemente *adj* : vehement — **vehemencia** *nf*
vehículo *nm* : vehicle — **vehicular** *adj*
veía, etc. → **ver**
veinte *adj & nm* : twenty
veinteavo[1], -va *adj* : twentieth
veinteavo[2] *nm* : twentieth (fraction)
veintena *nf* : group of twenty, score <una veintena de participantes : about twenty participants>
vejación *nf, pl* **-ciones** : ill-treatment, humiliation
vejar *vt* : to mistreat, to ridicule, to harass
vejete *nm* : old fellow, codger
vejez *nf* : old age
vejiga *nf* **1 :** bladder **2** AMPOLLA : blister
vela *nf* **1** VIGILIA : wakefulness <pasé la noche en vela : I stayed awake all night> **2 :** watch, vigil, wake **3 :** candle **4 :** sail
velada *nf* : evening party, soirée
velado, -da *adj* **1 :** veiled, hidden **2 :** blurred **3 :** muffled
velador[1], -dora *n* : guard, night watchman
velador[2] *nm* **1 :** candlestick **2 :** night table
velar *vt* **1 :** to hold a wake over **2 :** to watch over, to sit up with **3 :** to blur, to expose (a photo) **4 :** to veil, to conceal — *vi* **1 :** to stay awake **2 ~ por :** to watch over, to look after
velatorio *nm* VELORIO : wake (for the dead)
veleidad *nf* **1 :** fickleness **2 :** whim, caprice
veleidoso, -sa : fickle, capricious
velero *nm* **1 :** sailing ship **2 :** sailboat
veleta *nf* : weather vane
vello *nm* **1 :** body hair **2 :** down, fuzz
vellocino *nm* : fleece
vellón *nm, pl* **vellones 1 :** fleece, sheepskin **2** *PRi* : nickel (coin)
vellosidad *nf* : downiness, hairiness
velloso, -sa *adj* : downy, fluffy, hairy
velo *nm* : veil
velocidad *nf* **1 :** speed, velocity <velocidad máxima : speed limit> **2** MARCHA : gear (of an automobile)
velocímetro *nm* : speedometer
velocista *nmf* : sprinter
velorio *nm* VELATORIO : wake (for the dead)
velour *nm* : velour, velours

veloz *adj, pl* **veloces** : fast, quick, swift — **velozmente** *adv*
ven → **venir**
vena *nf* **1** : vein <vena yugular : jugular vein> **2** : vein, seam, lode **3** : grain (of wood) **4** : style <en vena lírica : in a lyrical vein> **5** : strain, touch <una vena de humor : a touch of humor> **6** : mood
venado *nm* **1** : deer **2** : venison
venal *adj* : venal — **venalidad** *nf*
vencedor, -dora *n* : winner, victor
vencejo *nm* : swift (bird)
vencer {86} *vt* **1** DERROTAR : to vanquish, to defeat **2** SUPERAR : to overcome, to surmount — *vi* **1** GANAR : to win, to triumph **2** CADUCAR : to expire <el plazo vence el jueves : the deadline is Thursday> **3** : to fall due, to mature — **vencerse** *vr* **1** DOMINARSE : to control oneself **2** : to break, to collapse
vencido, -da *adj* **1** : defeated **2** : expired **3** : due, payable **4 darse por vencido** : to give up
vencimiento *nm* **1** : defeat **2** : expiration **3** : maturity (of a loan)
venda *nf* : bandage
vendaje *nm* : bandage, dressing
vendar *vt* **1** : to bandage **2 vendar los ojos** : to blindfold
vendaval *nm* : gale, strong wind
vendedor, -dora *n* : salesperson, salesman *m,* saleswoman *f*
vender *vt* **1** : to sell **2** : to sell out, to betray — **venderse 1** : to be sold <se vende : for sale> **2** : to sell out
vendetta *nf* : vendetta
vendible *adj* : salable, marketable
vendimia *nf* : grape harvest
vendrá, etc. → **venir**
veneno *nm* **1** : poison **2** : venom
venenoso, -sa *adj* : poisonous, venomous
venerable *adj* : venerable
veneración *nf, pl* **-ciones** : veneration, reverence
venerar *vt* : to venerate, to revere
venéreo, -rea *adj* : venereal
venero *nm* **1** VENA : seam, lode, vein **2** MANANTIAL : spring **3** FUENTE : origin, source
venezolano, -na *adj & n* : Venezuelan
venga, etc. → **venir**
vengador, -dora *n* : avenger
venganza *nf* : vengeance, revenge
vengar {52} *vt* : to avenge — **vengarse** *vr* : to get even, to revenge oneself
vengativo, -va *adj* : vindictive, vengeful
vengue, etc. → **vengar**
venia *nf* **1** PERMISO : permission, leave **2** PERDÓN : pardon **3** : bow (of the head)
venial *adj* : venial
venida *nf* **1** LLEGADA : arrival, coming **2** REGRESO : return **3 idas y venidas** : comings and goings
venidero, -ra *adj* : coming, future
venir {87} *vi* **1** : to come <lo vi venir : I saw him coming> <¡venga! : come on!> **2** : to arrive <vinieron en coche : they came by car> **3** : to come, to originate <sus zapatos vienen de Italia : her shoes are from Italy> **4** : to come, to be available <viene envuelto en plástico : it comes wrapped in plastic> **5** : to come back, to return **6** : to affect, to overcome <me vino un vahído : a dizzy spell came over me> **7** : to fit <te viene un poco grande : it's a little big for you> **8** (*with the present participle*) : to have been <viene entrenando diariamente : he's been training daily> **9 ~ a** (*with the infinitive*) : to end up, to turn out <viene a ser lo mismo : it comes out the same> **10 que viene** : coming, next <el año que viene : next year> **11 venir bien** : to be suitable, to be just right — **venirse** *vr* **1** : to come, to arrive **2** : to come back **3 venirse abajo** : to fall apart, to collapse
venta *nf* **1** : sale **2 venta al por menor** *or* **venta al detalle** : retail sales
ventaja *nf* **1** : advantage **2** : lead, head start **3 ventajas** *nfpl* : perks, extras
ventajoso, -sa *adj* **1** : advantageous **2** : profitable — **ventajosamente** *adv*
ventana *nf* **1** : window (of a building) **2 ventana de la nariz** : nostril
ventanal *nm* : large window
ventanilla *nf* **1** : window (of a vehicle or airplane) **2** : ticket window, box office
ventero, -ra *n* : innkeeper
ventilación *nf, pl* **-ciones** : ventilation
ventilador *nm* **1** : ventilator **2** : fan
ventilar *vt* **1** : to ventilate, to air out **2** : to air, to discuss **3** : to make public, to reveal — **ventilarse** *vr* : to get some air
ventisca *nf* : snowstorm, blizzard
ventisquero *nm* : snowdrift
ventosear *vi* : to break wind
ventosidad *nf* : wind, flatulence
ventoso, -sa *adj* : windy
ventrículo *nm* : ventricle
ventrílocuo, -cua *n* : ventriloquist
ventriloquia *nf* : ventriloquism
ventura *nf* **1** : fortune, luck, chance **2** : happiness **3 a la ventura** : at random, as it comes
venturoso, -sa *adj* **1** AFORTUNADO : fortunate, lucky **2** : successful
Venus *nm* : Venus
venza, etc. → **vencer**
ver[1] {88} *vt* **1** : to see <vimos la película : we saw the movie> **2** ENTENDER : to understand <ya lo veo : now I get it> **3** EXAMINAR : to examine, to look into <lo veré : I'll take a look at it> **4** JUZGAR : to see, to judge <a mi manera de ver : to my way of thinking> **5** VISITAR : to meet with, to visit **6** AVERIGUAR : to find out **7 a ver** *or* **vamos a ver** : let's see — *vi* **1** : to see **2** ENTERARSE : to learn, to find out **3**

ENTENDER : to understand — **verse** *vr* **1** HALLARSE : to find oneself **2** PARECER : to look, to appear **3** ENCONTRARSE : to see each other, to meet

ver[2] *nm* **1** : looks *pl*, appearance **2** : opinion <a mi ver : in my view>

vera *nf* : side <a la vera del camino : alongside the road>

veracidad *nf* : truthfulness, veracity

veranda *nf* : veranda

veraneante *nmf* : summer vacationer

veranear *vi* : to spend the summer

veraniego, -ga *adj* **1** ESTIVAL : summer <el sol veraniego : the summer sun> **2** : summery

verano *nm* : summer

veras *nfpl* **de ~** : really, truly

veraz *adj, pl* **veraces** : truthful, veracious

verbal *adj* : verbal — **verbalmente** *adv*

verbalizar {21} *vt* : to verbalize, to express

verbena *nf* **1** FIESTA : festival, fair **2** : verbena, vervain

verbigracia *adv* : for example

verbo *nm* : verb

verborrea *nf* : verbiage

verbosidad *nf* : verbosity, wordiness

verboso, -sa *adj* : verbose, wordy

verdad *nf* **1** : truth **2 de ~** : really, truly **3 ¿verdad?** : right?, isn't that so?

verdaderamente *adv* : really, truly

verdadero, -dera *adj* **1** REAL, VERÍDICO : true, real **2** AUTÉNTICO : genuine

verde[1] *adj* **1** : green (in color) **2** : green, unripe **3** : inexperienced, green **4** : dirty, risqué

verde[2] *nm* : green

verdear *vi* : to turn green, to become verdant

verdín *nm, pl* **verdines** : slime, scum

verdor *nm* **1** : greenness **2** : verdure

verdoso, -sa *adj* : greenish

verdugo *nm* **1** : executioner, hangman **2** : tyrant

verdugón *nm, pl* **-gones** : welt, wheal

verdura *nf* : vegetable(s), green(s)

vereda *nf* **1** SENDA : path, trail **2** : sidewalk, pavement

veredicto *nm* : verdict

verga *nf* : spar, yard (of a ship)

vergonzoso, -sa *adj* **1** : disgraceful, shameful **2** : bashful, shy — **vergonzosamente** *adv*

vergüenza *nf* **1** : disgrace, shame **2** : embarrassment **3** : bashfulness, shyness

vericueto *nm* : rough terrain

verídico, -ca *adj* **1** REAL, VERDADERO : true, real **2** VERAZ : truthful

verificación *nf, pl* **-ciones 1** : verification **2** : testing, checking

verificador, -dora *n* : inspector, tester

verificar {72} *vt* **1** : to verify, to confirm **2** : to test, to check **3** : to carry out, to conduct — **verificarse** *vr* **1** : to take place, to occur **2** : to come true

verja *nf* **1** : rails *pl* (of a fence) **2** : grating, grille **3** : gate

vermut *nm, pl* **vermuts** : vermouth

vernáculo, -la *adj* : vernacular

vernal *adj* : vernal, spring

verosímil *adj* **1** : probable, likely **2** : credible, realistic

verosimilitud *nf* **1** : probability, likeliness **2** : verisimilitude

verraco *nm* : boar

verruga *nf* : wart

versado, -da *adj* **~ en** : versed in, knowledgeable about

versar *vi* **~ sobre** : to deal with, to be about

versátil *adj* **1** : versatile **2** : fickle

versatilidad *nf* **1** : versatility **2** : fickleness

versículo *nm* : verse (in the Bible)

versión *nf, pl* **versiones 1** : version **2** : translation

verso *nm* : verse

versus *prep* : versus, against

vértebra *nf* : vertebra — **vertebral** *adj*

vertebrado[1], **-da** *adj* : vertebrate

vertebrado[2] *nm* : vertebrate

vertedero *nm* **1** : garbage dump **2** DESAGÜE : drain, outlet

verter {56} *vt* **1** : to pour **2** : to spill, to shed **3** : to empty out **4** : to express, to voice **5** : to translate, to render — *vi* : to flow

vertical *adj & nf* : vertical — **verticalmente** *adv*

vértice *nm* : vertex, apex

vertido *nm* : spilling, spill

vertiente *nf* **1** : slope **2** : aspect, side, element

vertiginoso, -sa *adj* : vertiginous — **vertiginosamente** *adv*

vértigo *nm* : vertigo, dizziness

vesícula *nf* **1** : vesicle **2 vesícula biliar** : gallbladder

vesicular *adj* : vesicular

vestíbulo *nm* : vestibule, hall, lobby, foyer

vestido *nm* **1** : dress, costume, clothes *pl* **2** : dress (garment)

vestidor *nm* : dressing room

vestiduras *nfpl* **1** : clothing, raiment, regalia **2** *or* **vestiduras sacerdotales** : vestments

vestigio *nm* : vestige, sign, trace

vestimenta *nf* ROPA : clothing, clothes *pl*

vestir {54} *vt* **1** : to dress, to clothe **2** LLEVAR : to wear **3** ADORNAR : to decorate, to dress up — *vi* **1** : to dress <vestir bien : to dress well> **2** : to look good, to suit the occasion — **vestirse** *vr* **1** : to get dressed **2 ~ de** : to dress up as <se vistieron de soldados : they dressed up as soldiers> **3 ~ de** : to wear, to dress in

vestuario *nm* **1** : wardrobe **2** : dressing room, locker room

veta *nf* **1** : grain (in wood) **2** : vein, seam, lode **3** : trace, streak <una veta de terco : a stubborn streak>

vetar *vt* **:** to veto

veteado, -da *adj* **:** streaked, veined

veterano, -na *adj & n* **:** veteran

veterinaria *nf* **:** veterinary medicine

veterinario[1], **-ria** *adj* **:** veterinary

veterinario[2], **-ria** *n* **:** veterinarian

veto *nm* **:** veto

vetusto, -ta *adj* ANTIGUO **:** ancient, very old

vez *nf, pl* **veces 1 :** time, occasion <a la vez : at the same time> <a veces : at times, occasionally> <de vez en cuando : from time to time> **2** (*with numbers*) **:** time <una vez : once> <de una vez : all at once> <de una vez para siempre : once and for all> <dos veces : twice> **3 :** turn <a su vez : in turn> <en vez de : instead of> <hacer las veces de : to act as, to stand in for>

vía[1] *nf* **1** RUTA, CAMINO **:** road, route, way <Vía Láctea : Milky Way> **2** MEDIO **:** means, way <por vía oficial : through official channels> **3 :** track, line (of a railroad) **4 :** tract, passage <por vía oral : orally> **5 en vías de :** in the process of <en vías de solución : on the road to a solution> **6 por ~ :** by (in transportation) <por vía aérea : by air, airmail>

vía[2] *prep* **:** via

viable *adj* **:** viable, feasible — **viabilidad** *nf*

viaducto *nm* **:** viaduct

viajante *mf* **:** traveling salesman, traveling saleswoman

viajar *vi* **:** to travel, to journey

viaje *nm* **:** trip, journey <viaje de negocios : business trip>

viajero[1], **-ra** *adj* **:** traveling

viajero[2], **-ra** *n* **1 :** traveler **2** PASAJERO **:** passenger

vial *adj* **:** road, traffic

viático *nm* **:** travel allowance, travel expenses *pl*

víbora *nf* **:** viper

vibración *nf, pl* **-ciones :** vibration

vibrador *nm* **:** vibrator

vibrante *adj* **1 :** vibrant **2 :** vibrating

vibrar *vi* **:** to vibrate

vibratorio, -ria *adj* **:** vibratory

vicario, -ria *n* **:** vicar

vicealmirante *nmf* **:** vice admiral

vicepresidente, -ta *n* **:** vice president — **vicepresidencia** *nf*

viceversa *adv* **:** vice versa, conversely

viciado, -da *adj* **:** stuffy, close

viciar *vt* **1 :** to corrupt **2 :** to invalidate **3** FALSEAR **:** to distort **4 :** to pollute, to adulterate

vicio *nm* **1 :** vice, depravity **2 :** bad habit **3 :** defect, blemish

vicioso, -sa *adj* **:** depraved, corrupt

vicisitud *nf* **:** vicissitude

víctima *nf* **:** victim

victimario, -ria *n* ASESINO **:** killer, murderer

victimizar {21} *vt Arg, Mex* **:** to victimize

victoria *nf* **:** victory — **victorioso, -sa** *adj* — **victoriosamente** *adv*

victoriano, -na *adj* **:** Victorian

vid *nf* **:** vine, grapevine

vida *nf* **1 :** life <la vida cotidiana : everyday life> **2 :** life span, lifetime **3** BIOGRAFÍA **:** biography, life **4 :** way of life, lifestyle **5 :** livelihood <ganarse la vida : to earn one's living> **6** VIVEZA **:** liveliness **7 media vida :** half-life

vidente *nmf* **1 :** psychic, clairvoyant **2 :** sighted person

video *or* **vídeo** *nm* **:** video

videocasete *or* **videocasette** *nm* **:** videocassette

videocasetera *or* **videocasettera** *nf* **:** videocassette recorder, VCR

videocinta *nf* **:** videotape

videograbar *vt* **:** to videotape

vidriado *nm* **:** glaze

vidriar *vt* **:** to glaze (pottery, tile, etc.)

vidriera *nf* **1 :** stained-glass window **2 :** glass door or window **3 :** store window

vidriero, -ra *n* **:** glazier

vidrio *nm* **1 :** glass, piece of glass **2 :** windowpane

vidrioso, -sa *adj* **1 :** brittle, fragile **2 :** slippery **3 :** glassy, glazed (of eyes) **4 :** touchy, delicate

vieira *nf* **1 :** scallop **2 :** scallop shell

viejo[1], **-ja** *adj* **1** ANCIANO **:** old, elderly **2** ANTIGUO **:** former, longstanding <viejas tradiciones : old traditions> <viejos amigos : old friends> **3** GASTADO **:** old, worn, worn-out

viejo[2], **-ja** *n* ANCIANO **:** old man *m,* old woman *f*

viene, etc. → **venir**

viento *nm* **1 :** wind **2 hacer viento :** to be windy **3 contra viento y marea :** against all odds **4 viento en popa :** splendidly, successfully

vientre *nm* **1 :** abdomen, belly **2 :** womb **3 :** bowels *pl*

viernes *nms & pl* **:** Friday

vierte, etc. → **verter**

vietnamita *adj & nmf* **:** Vietnamese

viga *nf* **1 :** beam, rafter, girder **2 viga voladiza :** cantilever

vigencia *nf* **1 :** validity **2 :** force, effect <entrar en vigencia : to go into effect>

vigente *adj* **:** valid, in force

vigésimo[1], **-ma** *adj* **:** twentieth, twenty- <la vigésima segunda edición : the twenty-second edition>

vigésimo[2], **-ma** *n* **:** twentieth, twenty- (in a series)

vigía *nmf* **:** lookout

vigilancia *nf* **:** vigilance, watchfulness <bajo vigilancia : under surveillance>

vigilante[1] *adj* **:** vigilant, watchful

vigilante[2] *nmf* **:** watchman, guard

vigilar *vt* **1** CUIDAR **:** to look after, to keep an eye on **2** GUARDAR **:** to watch over, to guard — *vi* **1 :** to be watchful **2 :** to keep watch

vigilia *nf* **1** VELA **:** wakefulness **2 :** night work **3 :** vigil (in religion)
vigor *nm* **1 :** vigor, energy, strength **2** VIGENCIA **:** force, effect
vigorizante *adj* **:** envigorating
vigorizar {21} *vt* **:** to strengthen, to invigorate
vigoroso, -sa *adj* **:** vigorous — **vigorosamente** *adv*
VIH *nm* **:** HIV
vil *adj* **:** vile, dispicable
vileza *nf* **1 :** vileness **2 :** despicable action, villainy
vilipendiar *vt* **:** to vilify, to revile
villa *nf* **1 :** town, village **2 :** villa
villancico *nm* **:** carol, Christmas carol
villano, -na *n* **1 :** villain **2 :** peasant
vilo *nm* **en ~ 1 :** in the air **2 :** uncertain, in suspense
vinagre *nm* **:** vinegar
vinagrera *nf* **:** cruet (for vinegar)
vinatería *nf* **:** wine shop
vinculación *nf, pl* **-ciones 1 :** linking **2** RELACIÓN **:** bond, link, connection
vincular *vt* CONECTAR, RELACIONAR **:** to tie, to link, to connect
vínculo *nm* LAZO **:** tie, link, bond
vindicación *nf, pl* **-ciones :** vindication
vindicar *vt* **1 :** to vindicate **2 :** to avenge
vinilo *nm* **:** vinyl
vino[1], etc. → venir
vino[2] *nm* **:** wine
viña *nf* **:** vineyard
viñedo *nm* **:** vineyard
vio, etc. → ver
viola *nf* **:** viola
violación *nf, pl* **-ciones 1 :** violation, offense **2 :** rape
violador[1], -dora *n* **:** violator, offender
violador[2] *nm* **:** rapist
violar *vt* **1 :** to rape **2 :** to violate (a law or right) **3** PROFANAR **:** to desecrate
violencia *nf* **:** violence
violentamente *adv* **:** by force, violently
violentar *vt* **1** FORZAR **:** to break open, to force **2 :** to distort (words or ideas) — **violentarse** *vr* **:** to force oneself
violento, -ta *adj* **1 :** violent **2** EMBARAZOSO, INCÓMODO **:** awkward, embarassing
violeta[1] *adj & nm* **:** violet (color)
violeta[2] *nf* **:** violet (flower)
violín *nm, pl* **-lines :** violin
violinista *nmf* **:** violinist
violonchelista *nmf* **:** cellist
violonchelo *nm* **:** cello, violoncello
VIP *nmf, pl* **VIPs :** VIP
vira *nf* **:** welt (of a shoe)
virago *nf* **:** virago, shrew
viraje *nm* **1 :** turn, swerve **2 :** change
viral *adj* **:** viral
virar *vi* **:** to tack, to turn, to veer
virgen[1] *adj* **:** virgin <lana virgen : virgin wool>
virgen[2] *nmf, pl* **vírgenes :** virgin <la Santísima Virgen : the Blessed Virgin>
virginal *adj* **:** virginal, chaste
virginidad *nf* **:** virginity
Virgo *nmf* **:** Virgo
vírico, -ca *adj* **:** viral
viril *adj* **:** virile — **virilidad** *nf*
virrey, -rreina *n* **:** viceroy *m,* vicereine *f*
virtual *adj* **:** virtual — **virtualmente** *adv*
virtud *nf* **1 :** virtue **2 en virtud de :** by virtue of
virtuosismo *nm* **:** virtuosity
virtuoso[1], -sa *adj* **:** virtuous — **virtuosamente** *adv*
virtuoso[2], -sa *n* **:** virtuoso
viruela *nf* **1 :** smallpox **2 :** pockmark
virulencia *nf* **:** virulence
virulento, -ta *adj* **:** virulent
virus *nm* **:** virus
viruta *nf* **:** shaving
visa *nf* **:** visa
visado *nm Spain* **:** visa
visaje *nm* **:** face, grimace <hacer visajes : to make faces>
visceral *adj* **:** visceral
vísceras *nfpl* **:** viscera, entrails
visconde, -desa *n* **:** viscount *m,* viscountess *f*
viscosidad *nf* **:** viscosity
viscoso, -sa *adj* **:** viscous
visera *nf* **:** visor
visibilidad *nf* **:** visibility
visible *adj* **:** visible — **visiblemente** *adv*
visión *nf, pl* **visiones 1 :** vision, eyesight **2 :** view, perspective **3 :** vision, illusion <ver visiones : to be seeing things>
visionario, -ria *adj & n* **:** visionary
visita *nf* **1 :** visit, call **2 :** visitor **3 ir de visita :** to go visiting
visitador, -dora *n* **:** visitor, frequent caller
visitante[1] *adj* **:** visiting
visitante[2] *nmf* **:** visitor
visitar *vt* **:** to visit
vislumbrar *vt* **1 :** to discern, to make out **2 :** to begin to see, to have an inkling of
vislumbre *nf* **:** glimmer, gleam
viso *nm* **1** APARIENCIA **:** appearance <tener visos de : to seem, to show signs of> **2** DESTELLO **:** glint, gleam **3 :** sheen, iridescence
visón *nm, pl* **visones :** mink
víspera *nf* **1 :** eve, day before **2 vísperas** *nfpl* **:** vespers
vista *nf* **1** VISIÓN **:** vision, eyesight **2** MIRADA **:** look, gaze, glance **3** PANORAMA **:** view, vista, panorama **4 :** hearing (in court) **5 a primera vista :** at first sight **6 en vista de :** in view of **7 hacer la vista gorda :** to turn a blind eye **8 ¡hasta la vista! :** so long!, see you! **9 perder de vista :** to lose sight of **10 punto de vista :** point of view
vistazo *nm* **:** glance, look
viste, etc. → ver, vestir

visto[1] *pp* → **ver**
visto[2], **-ta** *adj* **1 :** obvious, clear **2 :** in view of, considering **3 estar bien visto :** to be approved of **4 estar mal visto :** to be frowned upon **5 por lo visto :** apparently **6 nunca visto :** unheard-of **7 visto que :** since, given that
visto[3] *nm* **visto bueno :** approval
vistoso, -sa *adj* **:** colorful, bright
visual *adj* **:** visual — **visualmente** *adv*
visualización *nf, pl* **-ciones :** visualization
visualizar {21} *vt* **1 :** to visualize **2 :** to display (on a screen)
vital *adj* **1 :** vital **2 :** lively, dynamic
vitalicio, -cia *adj* **:** life, lifetime
vitalidad *nf* **:** vitality
vitamina *nf* **:** vitamin
vitamínico, -ca *adj* **:** vitamin <complejos vitamínicos : vitamin compounds>
vitorear *vt* **:** to cheer, to acclaim
vitral *nm* **:** stained-glass window
vítreo, -rea *adj* **:** vitreous, glassy
vitrina *nf* **1 :** showcase, display case **2 :** store window
vitriolo *nm* **:** vitriol
vituperar *vt* **:** to condemn, to vituperate against
vituperio *nm* **:** vituperation, censure
viudez *nf* **:** widowerhood, widowhood
viudo, -da *n* **:** widower *m,* widow *f*
vivacidad *nf* VIVEZA **:** vivacity, liveliness
vivamente *adv* **1 :** in a lively manner **2 :** vividly **3 :** strongly, acutely <lo recomendamos vivamente : we strongly recommend it>
vivaque *nm* **:** bivouac
vivaquear *vi* **:** to bivouac
vivar *vi* **:** to cheer
vivaz *adj, pl* **vivaces 1 :** lively, vivacious **2 :** clever, sharp **3 :** perennial
víveres *nmpl* **:** provisions, supplies, food
vivero *nm* **1 :** nursery (for plants) **2 :** hatchery, fish farm
viveza *nf* **1** VIVACIDAD **:** liveliness **2** BRILLO **:** vividness, brightness **3** ASTUCIA **:** cleverness, sharpness
vívido, -da *adj* **:** vivid, lively
vividor, -dora *n* **:** sponger, parasite
vivienda *nf* **1 :** housing **2** MORADA **:** dwelling, home
viviente *adj* **:** living
vivificar {72} *vt* **:** to vivify, to give life to
vivir[1] *vi* **1 :** to live, to be alive **2** SUBSISTIR **:** to subsist, to make a living **3** RESIDIR **:** to reside **4 :** to spend one's life <vive para trabajar : she lives to work> **5 ~ de :** to live on — *vt* **1 :** to live <vivir su vida : to live one's life> **2** EXPERIMENTAR **:** to go through, to experience
vivir[2] *nm* **1 :** life, lifestyle **2 de mal vivir :** disreputable
vivisección *nf, pl* **-ciones :** vivisection
vivo, -va *adj* **1 :** alive **2** INTENSO **:** vivid, bright, intense **3** ANIMADO **:** lively, vivacious **4** ASTUTO **:** sharp, clever **5 en ~ :** live <transmisión en vivo : live broadcast> **6 al rojo vivo :** red-hot
vizconde, -desa *n* **:** viscount *m,* viscountess *f*
vocablo *nm* PALABRA **:** word
vocabulario *nm* **:** vocabulary
vocación *nf, pl* **-ciones :** vocation
vocacional *adj* **:** vocational
vocal[1] *adj* **:** vocal
vocal[2] *nmf* **:** member (of a committee, board, etc.)
vocal[3] *nf* **:** vowel
vocalista *nmf* CANTANTE **:** singer, vocalist
vocalizar {21} *vi* **:** to vocalize
vocear *v* **:** to shout
vocerío *nm* **:** clamor, shouting
vocero, -ra *n* PORTAVOZ **:** spokesperson, spokesman *m,* spokeswoman *f*
vociferante *adj* **:** vociferous
vociferar *vi* GRITAR **:** to shout, to yell
vodevil *nm* **:** vaudeville
vodka *nm* **:** vodka
voladizo[1], **-za** *adj* **:** projecting
voladizo[2] *nm* **:** projection
volador, -dora *adj* **:** flying
volando *adv* **:** quickly, in a hurry
volante[1] *adj* **:** flying
volante[2] *nm* **1 :** steering wheel **2** FOLLETO **:** flier, circular **3 :** shuttlecock **4 :** flywheel **5 :** balance wheel (of a watch) **6 :** ruffle, flounce
volar {19} *vi* **1 :** to fly **2** CORRER **:** to hurry, to rush <el tiempo vuela : time flies> <pasar volando : to fly past> **3** DIVULGARSE **:** to spread <unos rumores volaban : rumors were spreading around> **4** DESAPARECER **:** to disappear <el dinero ya voló : the money's already gone> — *vt* **1 :** to blow up, to demolish **2 :** to irritate
volátil *adj* **:** volatile — **volatilidad** *nf*
volatilizar {21} *vt* **:** to volatize — **volatilizarse** *vr*
volcán *nm, pl* **volcanes :** volcano
volcánico, -ca *adj* **:** volcanic
volcar {82} *vt, pl* **volcanes 1 :** to upset, to knock over, to turn over **2 :** to empty out **3 :** to make dizzy **4 :** to cause a change of mind in **5 :** to irritate — *vi* **1 :** to overturn, to tip over **2 :** to capsize — **volcarse** *vr* **1 :** to overturn **2 :** to do one's utmost
volea *nf* **:** volley (in sports)
volear *vi* **:** to volley (in sports)
voleibol *nm* **:** volleyball
voleo *nm* **al voleo :** haphazardly, at random
volframio *nm* **:** wolfram, tungsten
volición *nf, pl* **-ciones :** volition
volqué, etc. → **volcar**
voltaje *nm* **:** voltage
voltear *vt* **1 :** to turn over, to turn upside down **2 :** to reverse, to turn inside out **3 :** to turn <voltear la cara : to turn one's head> **4 :** to knock

down — *vi* **1** : to roll over, to do somersaults **2** : to turn <volteó a la izquierda : he turned left> — **voltearse** *vr* **1** : to turn around **2** : to change one's allegiance

voltereta *nf* : somersault, tumble

voltio *nm* : volt

volubilidad *nf* : fickleness, changeableness

voluble *adj* : fickle, changeable

volumen *nm, pl* **-lúmenes 1** TOMO : volume, book **2** : capacity, size, bulk **3** CANTIDAD : amount <el volumen de ventas : the volume of sales> **4** : volume, loudness

voluminoso, -sa *adj* : voluminous, massive, bulky

voluntad *nf* **1** : will, volition **2** DESEO : desire, wish **3** INTENCIÓN : intention **4 a voluntad** : at will **5 buena voluntad** : good will **6 mala voluntad** : ill will **7 fuerza de voluntad** : willpower

voluntario[1], **-ria** *adj* : voluntary — **voluntariamente** *adv*

voluntario[2], **-ria** *n* : volunteer

voluntarioso, -sa *adj* **1** : stubborn **2** : willing, eager

voluptuosidad *nf* : voluptuousness

voluptuoso, -sa *adj* : voluptuous — **voluptuosamente** *adv*

voluta *nf* : spiral, column (of smoke)

volver {89} *vi* **1** : to return, to come or go back <volver a casa : to return home> **2** : to revert <volver al tema : to get back to the subject> **3 ~ a** : to do again <volvieron a llamar : they called again> **4 volver en sí** : to come to, to regain consciousness — *vt* **1** : to turn, to turn over, to turn inside out **2** : to return, to repay, to restore **3** : to cause, to make <la volvía loca : it was driving her crazy> — **volverse** *vr* **1** : to become <se volvió deprimido : he became depressed> **2** : to turn around

vomitar *vi* : to vomit — *vt* **1** : to vomit **2** : to spew out (lava, etc.)

vómito *nm* **1** : vomiting **2** : vomit

voracidad *nf* : voracity

vorágine *nf* : whirlpool, maelstrom

voraz *adj, pl* **voraces** : voracious — **vorazmente** *adv*

vórtice *nm* **1** : whirlpool, vortex **2** TORBELLINO : whirlwind

vos *pron* (*in some regions of Latin America*) : you

vosear *vt* : to address as *vos*

vosotros, -tras *pron pl Spain* **1** : you, yourselves **2** : ye

votación *nf, pl* **-ciones** : vote, voting

votante *nmf* : voter

votar *vi* : to vote — *vt* : to vote for

votivo, -va *adj* : votive

voto *nm* **1** : vote **2** : vow (in religion) **3 votos** *nmpl* : good wishes

voy → **ir**

voz *nf, pl* **voces 1** : voice **2** : opinion, say **3** GRITO : shout, yell **4** : sound **5** VOCABLO : word, term **6** : rumor **7 a voz en cuello** : at the top of one's lungs **8 dar voces** : to shout **9 en voz alta** : aloud, in a loud voice **10 en voz baja** : softly, in a low voice

vudú *nm* : voodoo

vuelco *nm* : upset, overturning <me dio un vuelco el corazón : my heart skipped a beat>

vuela, etc. → **volar**

vuelca, vuelque, etc. → **volcar**

vuelo *nm* **1** : flight, flying <alzar el vuelo : to take flight> **2** : flight (of an aircraft) <vuelo espacial : space flight> **3** : flare, fullness (of clothing) **4 al vuelo** : on the wing

vuelta *nf* **1** GIRO : turn <se dio la vuelta : he turned around> **2** REVOLUCIÓN : circle, revolution <dio la vuelta al mundo : she went around the world> <las ruedas daban vueltas : the wheels were spinning> **3** : flip, turn <le dio la vuelta : she flipped it over> **4** : bend, curve <a la vuelta de la esquina : around the corner> **5** REGRESO : return <de ida y vuelta : round trip> <a vuelta de correo : return mail> **6** : round, lap (in sports or games) **7** PASEO : walk, drive, ride <dio una vuelta : he went for a walk> **8** DORSO, REVÉS : back, other side <a la vuelta : on the back> **9** : cuff (of pants) **10 darle vueltas** : to think over **11 estar de vuelta** : to be back

vuelto *pp* → **volver**

vuelve, etc. → **volver**

vuestro[1], **-stra** *adj Spain* : your, of yours <vuestros coches : your cars> <una amiga vuestra : a friend of yours>

vuestro[2], **-stra** *pron Spain* (*with definite article*) : yours <la vuestra es más grande : yours is bigger> <esos son los vuestros : those are yours>

vulcanizar {21} *vt* : to vulcanize

vulgar *adj* **1** : common **2** : vulgar

vulgaridad *nf* : vulgarity

vulgarismo *nm* : vulgarism

vulgarizar {21} *vt* : to vulgarize, to popularize

vulgarmente *adv* : vulgarly, popularly

vulgo *nm* **el vulgo** : the masses, common people

vulnerable *adj* : vulnerable — **vulnerabilidad** *nf*

vulnerar *vt* **1** : to injure, to damage (one's reputation or honor) **2** : to violate, to break (a law or contract)

W

w *nf* **:** twenty-fourth letter of the Spanish alphabet
wafle *nm* **:** waffle
waflera *nf* **:** waffle iron
wapití *nm* **:** wapiti, elk
whisky *nm, pl* **whiskys** *or* **whiskies :** whiskey
wigwam *nm* **:** wigwam

X

x *nf* **:** twenty-fifth letter of the Spanish alphabet
xenofobia *nf* **:** xenophobia
xenófobo[1], -ba *adj* **:** xenophobic
xenófobo[2], -ba *n* **:** xenophobe
xenón *nm* **:** xenon
xerocopiar *vt* **:** to photocopy, to xerox
xilófono *nm* **:** xylophone

Y

y[1] *nf* **:** twenty-sixth letter of the Spanish alphabet
y[2] *conj* **1 :** and <mi hermano y yo : my brother and I> <¿y los demás? : and (what about) the others?> **2** (*used in numbers*) <cincuenta y cinco : fifty-five> **3** *fam* **:** well <y por supuesto : well, of course>
ya[1] *adv* **1 :** already <ya terminó : she's finished already> **2 :** now, right now <¡hazlo ya! : do it now!> <ya mismo : right away> **3 :** later, soon <ya iremos : we'll go later on> **4 :** no longer, anymore <ya no fuma : he no longer smokes> **5** (*used for emphasis*) **:** <¡ya lo sé! : I know!> <ya lo creo : of course> **6 no ya :** not only <no ya lloran sino gritan : they're not only crying but screaming> **7 ya que :** now that, since <ya que sabe la verdad : now that she knows the truth>
ya[2] *conj* **ya . . . ya :** whether . . . or, first . . . then <ya le gusta, ya no : first he likes it, then he doesn't>
yac *nm* **:** yak
yacer {90} *vi* **:** to lie <en esta tumba yacen sus abuelos : his grandparents lie in this grave>
yacimiento *nm* **:** bed, deposit <yacimiento petrolífero : oil field>
yaga, etc. → yacer
yanqui *adj & nmf* **:** Yankee
yarda *nf* **:** yard
yate *nm* **:** yacht
yaz, yazca, yazga, etc. → yacer
yedra *nf* **:** ivy
yegua *nf* **:** mare
yelmo *nm* **:** helmet
yema *nf* **1 :** bud, shoot **2 :** yolk (of an egg) **3 yema del dedo :** fingertip
yemenita *adj & nmf* **:** Yemenite
yendo → ir
yerba *nf* **1** *or* **yerba mate :** maté **2 → hierba**
yerga, yergue, etc. → erguir
yermo[1], -ma *adj* **:** barren, deserted
yermo[2] *nm* **:** wasteland
yerno *nm* **:** son-in-law
yerra, etc. → errar
yerro *nm* **:** blunder, mistake
yerto, -ta *adj* **:** rigid, stiff
yesca *nf* **:** tinder
yeso *nm* **1 :** plaster **2 :** gypsum
yo[1] *nm* **:** ego, self
yo[2] *pron* **1 :** I **2 :** me <todos menos yo : everyone except me> <tan bajo como yo : as short as me> **3 soy yo :** it is I, it's me
yodado, -da *adj* **:** iodized
yodo *nm* **:** iodine
yoduro *nm* **:** iodide
yoga *nm* **:** yoga
yogui *nm* **:** yogi
yogurt *or* **yogur** *nm* **:** yogurt
yola *nf* **:** yawl
yoyo *or* **yoyó** *nm* **:** yo-yo
yuca *nf* **1 :** yucca (plant) **2 :** cassava, manioc
yucateco[1], -ca *adj* **:** of or from the Yucatán
yucateco[2], -ca *n* **:** person from the Yucatán
yudo → judo
yugo *nm* **:** yoke
yugoslavo, -va *adj & n* **:** Yugoslavian
yugular *adj* **:** jugular <vena yugular : jugular vein>
yungas *nfpl Bol, Chile, Peru* **:** warm tropical valleys
yunque *nm* **:** anvil
yunta *nf* **:** yoke, team (of oxen)
yute *nm* **:** jute
yuxtaponer {60} *vt* **:** to juxtapose — **yuxtaposición** *nf*

Z

z *nf* : twenty-seventh letter of the Spanish alphabet
zacate *nm CA, Mex* **1** : grass, forage **2** : hay
zafacón *nm, pl* **-cones** : wastebasket
zafar *vt* : to loosen, to untie — **zafarse** *vr* **1** : to loosen up, to come undone **2** : to get free of
zafio, -fia *adj* : coarse, crude
zafiro *nm* : sapphire
zaga *nf* **1** : defense (in sports) **2 a la zaga** *or* **en ~** : behind, in the rear
zagual *nm* : paddle (of a canoe)
zaguán *nm, pl* **zaguanes** : front hall, vestibule
zaherir {76} *vt* **1** : to criticize sharply **2** : to wound, to mortify
zahones *nmpl* : chaps
zaino, -na *adj* : chestnut (color)
zalamería *nf* : flattery, sweet talk
zalamero[1], **-ra** *adj* : flattering, fawning
zalamero[2], **-ra** *n* : flatterer
zambiano, -na *adj & nmf* : Zambian
zambullida *nf* : dive, plunge
zambullirse {38} *vr* : to dive, to plunge
zanahoria *nf* : carrot
zancada *nf* : stride, step
zancadilla *nf* **1** : trip, stumble **2** *fam* : trick, ruse
zancos *nmpl* : stilts
zancuda *nf* : wading bird
zancudo *nm* MOSQUITO : mosquito
zángano *nm* : drone, male bee
zanja *nf* : ditch, trench
zanjar *vt* ACLARAR : to settle, to clear up, to resolve
zapallo *nm Arg, Chile, Peru, Uru* : pumpkin
zapapico *nm* : pickax
zapata *nf* : brake shoe
zapatería *nf* **1** : shoemaker's, shoe factory **2** : shoe store
zapatero[1], **-ra** *adj* : dry, tough, poorly cooked
zapatero[2], **-ra** *n* : shoemaker, cobbler
zapatilla *nf* **1** PANTUFLA : slipper **2** *or* **zapatilla de deporte** : sneaker
zapato *nm* : shoe
zar, zarina *n* : czar *m*, czarina *f*
zarandear *vt* **1** : to sift, to sieve **2** : to shake, to jostle, to jiggle
zarapito *nm* : curlew
zarcillo *nm* **1** : earring **2** : tendril (of a plant)
zarigüeya *nf* : opossum
zarista *adj & nmf* : czarist
zarpa *nf* : paw
zarpar *vi* : to set sail, to raise anchor
zarza *nf* : bramble, blackberry bush
zarzamora *nf* **1** : blackberry **2** : bramble, blackberry bush
zarzaparrilla *nf* : sarsaparilla
zepelín *nm, pl* **-lines** : zeppelin
zigoto *nm* : zygote
zigzag *nm, pl* **zigzags** *or* **zigzagues** : zigzag
zigzaguear *vi* : to zigzag
zimbabuense *adj & nmf* : Zimbabwean
zinc *nm* : zinc
zinnia *nf* : zinnia
zíper *nm CA, Mex* : zipper
zircón *nm, pl* **zircones** : zircon
zócalo *nm Mex* : main square
zodíaco *nm* : zodiac — **zodíacal** *adj*
zombi *or* **zombie** *nmf* : zombie
zona *nf* : zone, district, area
zonzo[1], **-za** *adj* : stupid, silly
zonzo[2], **-za** *n* : idiot, nitwit
zoo *nm* : zoo
zoología *nf* : zoology
zoológico[1], **-ca** *adj* : zoological
zoológico[2] *nm* : zoo
zoólogo, -ga *n* : zoologist
zoom *nm* : zoom lens
zopilote *nm CA, Mex* : buzzard
zoquete *nmf fam* : oaf, blockhead
zorrillo *nm* MOFETA : skunk
zorro[1], **-rra** *adj* : sly, crafty
zorro[2], **-rra** *n* **1** : fox, vixen **2** : sly crafty person
zorzal *nm* : thrush
zozobra *nf* : anxiety, worry
zozobrar *vi* : to capsize
zueco *nm* : clog (shoe)
zulú[1] *adj & nmf* : Zulu
zulú[2] *nm* : Zulu (language)
zumaque *nm* : sumac
zumbar *vi* : to buzz, to hum — *vt fam* **1** : to hit, to thrash **2** : to make fun of
zumbido *nm* : buzzing, humming
zumo *nf* JUGO : juice
zurcir {83} *vt* : to darn, to mend
zurdo[1], **-da** *adj* : left-handed
zurdo[2], **-da** *n* : left-handed person
zurza, etc. → **zurcir**
zutano, -na → **fulano**

English–Spanish Dictionary

A

a[1] [ˈeɪ] *n, pl* **a's** *or* **as** [ˈeɪz] **:** primera letra del alfabeto inglés

a[2] [ə, ˈeɪ] *art* (**an** [ən, ˈæn] *before vowel or silent h*) **1 :** un *m,* una *f* <a house : una casa> <half an hour : media hora> <what a surprise! : ¡qué sorpresa!> **2** PER **:** por, a la, al <30 kilometers an hour : 30 kilómetros por hora> <twice a month : dos veces al mes>

aardvark [ˈɑrdˌvɑrk] *n* **:** oso *m* hormiguero

aback [əˈbæk] *adv* **1 :** por sorpresa **2 to be taken aback :** quedarse desconcertado

abacus [ˈæbəkəs] *n, pl* **abaci** [ˈæbəˌsaɪ, -ˌkiː] *or* **abacuses :** ábaco *m*

abaft [əˈbæft] *adv* **:** a popa

abalone [ˌæbəˈloːni] *n* **:** abulón *m,* oreja *f* marina

abandon[1] [əˈbændən] *vt* **1** DESERT, FORSAKE **:** abandonar, desamparar (a alguien), desertar de (algo) **2** GIVE UP, SUSPEND **:** renunciar a, suspender <he abandoned the search : suspendió la búsqueda> **3** EVACUATE, LEAVE **:** abandonar, evacuar, dejar <to abandon ship : abandonar el buque> **4 to abandon oneself :** entregarse, abandonarse

abandon[2] *n* **:** desenfreno *m* <with wild abandon : desenfrenadamente>

abandoned [əˈbændənd] *adj* **1** DESERTED **:** abandonado **2** UNRESTRAINED **:** desenfrenado, desinhibido

abandonment [əˈbændənmənt] *n* **:** abandono *m,* desamparo *m*

abase [əˈbeɪs] *vt* **abased; abasing :** degradar, humillar, rebajar

abash [əˈbæʃ] *vt* **:** avergonzar, abochornar

abashed [əˈbæʃt] *adj* **:** avergonzado

abate [əˈbeɪt] *vi* **abated; abating :** amainar, menguar, disminuir

abattoir [ˈæbəˌtwɑr] *n* **:** matadero *m*

abbess [ˈæbɪs, -ˌbɛs, -bəs] *n* **:** abadesa *f*

abbey [ˈæbi] *n, pl* **-beys :** abadía *f*

abbot [ˈæbət] *n* **:** abad *m*

abbreviate [əˈbriːviˌeɪt] *vt* **-ated; -ating :** abreviar

abbreviation [əˌbriːviˈeɪʃən] *n* **:** abreviación *f,* abreviatura *f*

abdicate [ˈæbdɪˌkeɪt] *v* **-cated; -cating :** abdicar

abdication [ˌæbdɪˈkeɪʃən] *n* **:** abdicación *f*

abdomen [ˈæbdəmən, æbˈdoːmən] *n* **:** abdomen *m,* vientre *m*

abdominal [æbˈdɑmənəl] *adj* **:** abdominal **— abdominally** *adv*

abduct [æbˈdʌkt] *vt* **:** raptar, secuestrar

abduction [æbˈdʌkʃən] *n* **:** rapto *m,* secuestro *m*

abductor [æbˈdʌktər] *n* **:** raptor *m,* -tora *f;* secuestrador *m,* -dora *f*

abed [əˈbɛd] *adv & adj* **:** en cama

aberrant [æˈbɛrənt, ˈæbərənt] *adj* **1** ABNORMAL **:** anormal, aberrante **2** ATYPICAL **:** anómalo, atípico

aberration [ˌæbəˈreɪʃən] *n* **1 :** aberración *f* **2** DERANGEMENT **:** perturbación *f* mental

abet [əˈbɛt] *vt* **abetted; abetting** ASSIST **:** ayudar <to aid and abet : ser cómplice de>

abeyance [əˈbeɪənts] *n* **:** desuso *m,* suspensión *f*

abhor [əbˈhɔr, æb-] *vt* **-horred; -horring :** abominar, aborrecer

abhorrence [əbˈhɔrənts, æb-] *n* **:** aborrecimiento *m,* odio *m*

abhorrent [əbˈhɔrənt, æb-] *adj* **:** abominable, aborrecible, odioso

abide [əˈbaɪd] *v* **abode** [əˈboːd] *or* **abided; abiding** *vt* STAND **:** soportar, tolerar <I can't abide them : no los puedo ver> **—** *vi* **1** ENDURE **:** quedar, permanecer **2** DWELL **:** morar, residir **3 to abide by :** atenerse a

ability [əˈbɪləti] *n, pl* **-ties 1** CAPABILITY **:** aptitud *f,* capacidad *f,* facultad *f* **2** COMPETENCE **:** competencia *f* **3** TALENT **:** talento *m,* don *m,* habilidad *f*

abject [ˈæbˌdʒɛkt, æbˈ-] *adj* **1** WRETCHED **:** miserable, desdichado **2** HOPELESS **:** abatido, desesperado **3** SERVILE **:** servil <abject flattery : halagos serviles> **— abjectly** *adv*

ablaze [əˈbleɪz] *adj* **1** BURNING **:** ardiendo, en llamas **2** RADIANT **:** resplandeciente, radiante

able [ˈeɪbəl] *adj* **abler; ablest 1** CAPABLE **:** capaz, hábil **2** COMPETENT **:** competente

ablution [əˈbluːʃən] *n* **:** ablución *f* <to perform one's ablutions : lavarse>

ably [ˈeɪbəli] *adv* **:** hábilmente, eficientemente

abnormal [æbˈnɔrməl] *adj* **:** anormal **— abnormally** *adv*

abnormality [ˌæbnərˈmæləti, -nɔr-] *n, pl* **-ties :** anormalidad *f*

aboard[1] [əˈbord] *adv* **:** a bordo

aboard[2] *prep* **:** a bordo de

abode[1] **→ abide**

abode[2] [əˈboːd] *n* **:** morada *f,* residencia *f,* vivienda *f*

abolish [əˈbɑlɪʃ] *vt* **:** abolir, suprimir

abolition [ˌæbəˈlɪʃən] *n* **:** abolición *f,* supresión *f*

abominable [əˈbɑmənəbəl] *adj* DETESTABLE **:** abominable, aborrecible, espantoso

abominate [əˈbɑməˌneɪt] *vt* **-nated; -nating :** abominar, aborrecer

abomination [əˌbɑməˈneɪʃən] *n* **:** abominación *f*

aboriginal [ˌæbəˈrɪdʒənəl] *adj* **:** aborigen, indígena

aborigine [ˌæbəˈrɪdʒəni] *n* NATIVE : aborigen *mf,* indígena *mf*

abort [əˈbɔrt] *vt* **1** : abortar (en medicina) **2** CALL OFF : suspender, abandonar — *vi* : abortar, hacerse un aborto

abortion [əˈbɔrʃən] *n* : aborto *m*

abortive [əˈbɔrtɪv] *adj* UNSUCCESSFUL : fracasado, frustrado, malogrado

abound [əˈbaʊnd] *vi* **to abound in** : abundar en, estar lleno de

about[1] [əˈbaʊt] *adv* **1** APPROXIMATELY : aproximadamente, casi, más o menos **2** AROUND : por todas partes, alrededor <the children are running about : los niños están corriendo por todas partes> **3 to be about to** : estar a punto de **4 to be up and about** : estar levantado

about[2] *prep* **1** AROUND : alrededor de **2** CONCERNING : de, acerca de, sobre <he always talks about politics : siempre habla de política>

above[1] [əˈbʌv] *adv* **1** OVERHEAD : por encima, arriba **2** : más arriba <as stated above : como se indica más arriba>

above[2] *adj* : anterior, antedicho <for the above reasons : por las razones antedichas>

above[3] *prep* **1** OVER : encima de, arriba de, sobre **2** : superior a, por encima de <he's above those things : él está por encima de esas cosas> **3** : más de, superior a <he earns above $50,000 : gana más de $50,000> <a number above 10 : un número superior a 10> **4 above all** : sobre todo

aboveboard[1] [əˈbʌvˈbord, -ˌbord] *adv* **open and aboveboard** : sin tapujos

aboveboard[2] *adj* : legítimo, sincero

abrade [əˈbreɪd] *vt* **abraded; abrading 1** ERODE : erosionar, corroer **2** SCRAPE : escoriar, raspar

abrasion [əˈbreɪʒən] *n* **1** SCRAPE, SCRATCH : raspadura *f,* rasguño *m* **2** EROSION : erosión *f*

abrasive[1] [əˈbreɪsɪv] *adj* **1** ROUGH : abrasivo, áspero **2** BRUSQUE, IRRITATING : brusco, irritante

abrasive[2] *n* : abrasivo *m*

abreast [əˈbrɛst] *adv* **1** : en fondo, al lado <to march three abreast : marchar de tres en fondo> **2 to keep abreast** : mantenerse al día

abridge [əˈbrɪdʒ] *vt* **abridged; abridging** : compendiar, resumir

abridgment *or* **abridgement** [əˈbrɪdʒmənt] *n* : compendio *m,* resumen *m*

abroad [əˈbrɔd] *adv* **1** ABOUT, WIDELY : por todas partes, en todas direcciones <the news spread abroad : la noticia corrió por todas partes> **2** OVERSEAS : en el extranjero, en el exterior

abrupt [əˈbrʌpt] *adj* **1** SUDDEN : abrupto, repentino, súbito **2** BRUSQUE, CURT : brusco, cortante — **abruptly** *adv*

abscess [ˈæbˌsɛs] *n* : absceso *m*

abscond [æbˈskɑnd] *vi* : huir, fugarse

absence [ˈæbsənts] *n* **1** : ausencia *f* (de una persona) **2** LACK : falta *f,* carencia *f*

absent[1] [æbˈsɛnt] *vt* **to absent oneself** : ausentarse

absent[2] [ˈæbsənt] *adj* : ausente

absentee [ˌæbsənˈtiː] *n* : ausente *mf*

absentminded [ˌæbsəntˈmaɪndəd] *adj* : distraído, despistado

absentmindedly [ˌæbsəntˈmaɪndədli] *adv* : distraídamente

absentmindedness [ˌæbsəntˈmaɪndədnəs] *n* : distracción *f,* despiste *m*

absolute [ˈæbsəˌluːt, ˌæbsəˈluːt] *adj* **1** COMPLETE, PERFECT : completo, pleno, perfecto **2** UNCONDITIONAL : absoluto, incondicional **3** DEFINITE : categórico, definitivo

absolutely [ˈæbsəˌluːtli, ˌæbsəˈluːtli] *adv* **1** COMPLETELY : completamente, absolutamente **2** CERTAINLY : desde luego <do you agree? absolutely! : ¿estás de acuerdo? ¡desde luego!>

absolution [ˌæbsəˈluːʃən] *n* : absolución *f*

absolve [əbˈzɑlv, æb-, -ˈsɑlv] *vt* **-solved; -solving** : absolver, perdonar

absorb [əbˈzɔrb, æb-, -ˈsɔrb] *vt* **1** : absorber, embeber (un líquido), amortiguar (un golpe, la luz) **2** ENGROSS : absorber **3** ASSIMILATE : asimilar

absorbed [əbˈzɔrbd, æb-, -ˈsɔrbd] *adj* ENGROSSED : absorto, ensimismado

absorbency [əbˈzɔrbəntsi, æb-, -ˈsɔr-] *n* : absorbencia *f*

absorbent [əbˈzɔrbənt, æb-, -ˈsɔr-] *adj* : absorbente

absorbing [əbˈzɔrbɪŋ, æb-, -ˈsɔr-] *adj* : absorbente, fascinante

absorption [əbˈzɔrpʃən, æb-, -ˈsɔrp-] *n* **1** : absorción *f* **2** CONCENTRATION : concentración *f*

abstain [əbˈsteɪn, æb-] *vi* : abstenerse

abstainer [əbˈsteɪnər, æb-] *n* : abstemio *m,* -mia *f*

abstemious [æbˈstiːmiəs] *adj* : abstemio, sobrio — **abstemiously** *adv*

abstention [əbˈstɛntʃən, æb-] *n* : abstención *f*

abstinence [ˈæbstənənts] *n* : abstinencia *f*

abstract[1] [æbˈstrækt, ˈæbˌ-] *vt* **1** EXTRACT : abstraer, extraer **2** SUMMARIZE : compendiar, resumir

abstract[2] *adj* : abstracto — **abstractly** [æbˈstræktli, ˈæbˌ-] *adv*

abstract[3] [ˈæbˌstrækt] *n* : resumen *m,* compendio *m,* sumario *m*

abstraction [æbˈstrækʃən] *n* **1** : abstracción *f,* idea *f* abstracta **2** ABSENTMINDEDNESS : distracción *f*

abstruse [əbˈstruːs, æb-] *adj* : abstruso, recóndito — **abstrusely** *adv*

absurd [əbˈsərd, -ˈzərd] *adj* : absurdo, ridículo, disparatado — **absurdly** *adv*

absurdity [əbˈsərdəti, -ˈzər-] *n, pl* **-ties 1** : absurdo *m* **2** NONSENSE : disparate *m,* despropósito *m*

abundance [ə'bʌndənts] *n* : abundancia *f*
abundant [ə'bʌndənt] *adj* : abundante, cuantioso, copioso
abundantly [ə'bʌndəntli] *adv* : abundantemente, en abundancia
abuse¹ [ə'bjuːz] *vt* **abused; abusing 1** MISUSE : abusar de **2** MISTREAT : maltratar **3** REVILE : insultar, injuriar, denostar
abuse² [ə'bjuːs] *n* **1** MISUSE : abuso *m* **2** MISTREATMENT : abuso *m,* maltrato *m* **3** INSULTS : insultos *mpl,* improperios *mpl* <a string of abuse : una serie de improperios>
abuser [ə'bjuːzər] *n* : abusador *m,* -dora *f*
abusive [ə'bjuːsɪv] *adj* **1** ABUSING : abusivo **2** INSULTING : ofensivo, injurioso, insultante — **abusively** *adv*
abut [ə'bʌt] *v* **abutted; abutting** *vt* : bordear — *vi* **to abut on** : colindar con
abutment [ə'bʌtmənt] *n* **1** BUTTRESS : contrafuerte *m,* estribo *m* **2** CLOSENESS : contigüidad *f*
abysmal [ə'bɪzməl] *adj* **1** DEEP : abismal, insondable **2** TERRIBLE : atroz, desastroso
abysmally [ə'bɪzməli] *adv* : desastrosamente, terriblemente
abyss [ə'bɪs, 'æbɪs] *n* : abismo *m,* sima *f*
acacia [ə'keɪʃə] *n* : acacia *f*
academic¹ [ˌækə'dɛmɪk] *adj* **1** : académico **2** THEORETICAL : teórico — **academically** [-mɪkli] *adv*
academic² *n* : académico *m,* -ca *f*
academy [ə'kædəmi] *n, pl* **-mies** : academia *f*
accede [æk'siːd] *vi* **-ceded; -ceding 1** AGREE : acceder, consentir **2** ASCEND : subir, acceder <he acceded to the throne : subió al trono>
accelerate [ɪk'sɛləˌreɪt, æk-] *v* **-ated; -ating** *vt* : acelerar, apresurar — *vi* : acelerar (dícese de un carro)
acceleration [ɪkˌsɛlə'reɪʃən, æk-] *n* : aceleración *f*
accelerator [ɪk'sɛləˌreɪt̬ər, æk-] *n* : acelerador *m*
accent¹ ['ækˌsɛnt, æk'sɛnt] *vt* : acentuar
accent² ['ækˌsɛnt, -sənt] *n* **1** : acento *m* **2** EMPHASIS, STRESS : énfasis *m,* acento *m*
accentuate [ɪk'sɛntʃʊˌeɪt, æk-] *vt* **-ated; -ating** : acentuar, poner énfasis en
accept [ɪk'sɛpt, æk-] *vt* **1** : aceptar **2** ACKNOWLEDGE : admitir, reconocer
acceptability [ɪkˌsɛptə'bɪlət̬i, æk-] *n* : aceptabilidad *f*
acceptable [ɪk'sɛptəbəl, æk-] *adj* : aceptable, admisible — **acceptably** [-bli] *adv*
acceptance [ɪk'sɛptənts, æk-] *n* : aceptación *f,* aprobación *f*
access¹ ['ækˌsɛs] *vt* : obtener acceso a, entrar a
access² *n* : acceso *m*
accessible [ɪk'sɛsəbəl, æk-] *adj* : accesible, asequible
accession [ɪk'sɛʃən, æk-] *n* **1** : ascenso *f,* subida *f* (al trono, etc.) **2** ACQUISITION : adquisición *f*
accessory¹ [ɪk'sɛsəri, æk-] *adj* : auxiliar
accessory² *n, pl* **-ries 1** : accesorio *m,* complemento *m* **2** ACCOMPLICE : cómplice *mf*
accident ['æksədənt] *n* **1** MISHAP : accidente *m* **2** CHANCE : casualidad *f*
accidental [ˌæksə'dɛntəl] *adj* : accidental, casual, imprevisto, fortuito
accidentally [ˌæksə'dɛntəli, -'dɛntli] *adv* **1** BY CHANCE : por casualidad **2** UNINTENTIONALLY : sin querer, involuntariamente
acclaim¹ [ə'kleɪm] *vt* : aclamar, elogiar
acclaim² *n* : aclamación *f,* elogio *m*
acclamation [ˌæklə'meɪʃən] *n* : aclamación *f*
acclimate ['ækləˌmeɪt, ə'klaɪmət] → **acclimatize**
acclimatize [ə'klaɪməˌtaɪz] *v* **-tized; -tizing** *vt* **1** : aclimatar **2 to acclimatize oneself** : aclimatarse
accolade ['ækəˌleɪd, -ˌlɑd] *n* **1** PRAISE : elogio *m* **2** AWARD : galardón *m*
accommodate [ə'kɑməˌdeɪt] *vt* **-dated; -dating 1** ADAPT : acomodar, adaptar **2** SATISFY : tener en cuenta, satisfacer **3** HOLD : dar cabida a, tener cabida para
accommodation [əˌkɑmə'deɪʃən] *n* **1** : adaptación *f,* adecuación *f* **2 accommodations** *npl* LODGING : alojamiento *m,* hospedaje *m*
accompaniment [ə'kʌmpənəmənt, -'kɑm-] *n* : acompañamiento *m*
accompanist [ə'kʌmpənɪst, -'kɑm-] *n* : acompañante *mf*
accompany [ə'kʌmpəni, -'kɑm-] *vt* **-nied; -nying** : acompañar
accomplice [ə'kɑmpləs, -'kʌm-] *n* : cómplice *mf*
accomplish [ə'kɑmplɪʃ, -'kʌm-] *vt* : efectuar, realizar, lograr, llevar a cabo
accomplished [ə'kɑmplɪʃt, -'kʌm-] *adj* : consumado, logrado
accomplishment [ə'kɑmplɪʃmənt, -'kʌm-] *n* **1** ACHIEVEMENT : logro *m,* éxito *m* **2** SKILL : destreza *f,* habilidad *f*
accord¹ [ə'kɔrd] *vt* GRANT : conceder, otorgar — *vi* **to accord with** : concordar con, conformarse con
accord² *n* **1** AGREEMENT : acuerdo *m,* convenio *m* **2** VOLITION : voluntad *f* <on one's own accord : voluntariamente, de motu proprio>
accordance [ə'kɔrdənts] *n* **1** ACCORD : acuerdo *m,* conformidad *f* **2 in ac-**

cordance with : conforme a, según, de acuerdo con
accordingly [əˈkɔrdɪŋli] *adv* **1** CORRESPONDINGLY : en consecuencia **2** CONSEQUENTLY : por consiguiente, por lo tanto
according to [əˈkɔrdɪŋ] *prep* : según, de acuerdo con, conforme a
accordion [əˈkɔrdiən] *n* : acordeón *m*
accordionist [əˈkɔrdiənɪst] *n* : acordeonista *mf*
accost [əˈkɔst] *vt* : abordar, dirigirse a
account[1] [əˈkaʊnt] *vt* : considerar, estimar <he accounts himself lucky : se considera afortunado> — *vi* **to account for :** dar cuenta de, explicar
account[2] *n* **1 :** cuenta *f* <savings account : cuenta de ahorros> **2** EXPLANATION : versión *f,* explicación *f* **3** REPORT : relato *m,* informe *m* **4** IMPORTANCE : importancia *f* <to be of no account : no tener importancia> **5 on account of** BECAUSE OF : a causa de, debido a, por **6 on no account :** de ninguna manera
accountability [əˌkaʊntəˈbɪləti] *n* : responsabilidad *f*
accountable [əˈkaʊntəbəl] *adj* : responsable
accountant [əˈkaʊntənt] *n* : contador *m,* -dora *f;* contable *mf Spain*
accounting [əˈkaʊntɪŋ] *n* : contabilidad *f*
accoutrements *or* **accouterments** [əˈkuːtrəmənts, -ˈkuːtər-] *npl* **1** EQUIPMENT : equipo *m,* avíos *mpl* **2** ACCESSORIES : accesorios *mpl* **3** TRAPPINGS : símbolos *mpl* <the accoutrements of power : los símbolos del poder>
accredit [əˈkrɛdət] *vt* : acreditar, autorizar
accreditation [əˌkrɛdəˈteɪʃən] *n* : acreditación *f,* homologación *f*
accrual [əˈkruːəl] *n* : incremento *m,* acumulación *f*
accrue [əˈkruː] *vi* **-crued; -cruing** : acumularse, aumentarse
accumulate [əˈkjuːmjəˌleɪt] *v* **-lated; -lating** *vt* : acumular, amontonar — *vi* : acumularse, amontonarse
accumulation [əˌkjuːmjəˈleɪʃən] *n* : acumulación *f,* amontonamiento *m*
accuracy [ˈækjərəsi] *n* : exactitud *f,* precisión *f*
accurate [ˈækjərət] *adj* : exacto, correcto, fiel, preciso — **accurately** *adv*
accusation [ˌækjəˈzeɪʃən] *n* : acusación *f*
accuse [əˈkjuːz] *vt* **-cused; -cusing** : acusar, delatar, denunciar
accused [əˈkjuːzd] *ns & pl* DEFENDANT : acusado *m,* -da *f*
accuser [əˈkjuːzər] *n* : acusador *m,* -dora *f*
accustom [əˈkʌstəm] *vt* : acostumbrar, habituar
ace [ˈeɪs] *n* : as *m*
acerbic [əˈsərbɪk, æ-] *adj* : acerbo, mordaz
acetate [ˈæsəˌteɪt] *n* : acetato *m*
acetylene [əˈsɛtələn, -təˌliːn] *n* : acetileno *m*
ache[1] [ˈeɪk] *vi* **ached; aching 1 :** doler **2 to ache for :** anhelar, ansiar
ache[2] *n* : dolor *m*
achieve [əˈtʃiːv] *vt* **achieved; achieving** : lograr, alcanzar, conseguir, realizar
achievement [əˈtʃiːvmənt] *n* : logro *m,* éxito *m,* realización *f*
acid[1] [ˈæsəd] *adj* **1** SOUR : ácido, agrio **2** CAUSTIC, SHARP : acerbo, mordaz — **acidly** *adv*
acid[2] *n* : ácido *m*
acidic [əˈsɪdɪk, æ-] *adj* : ácido
acidity [əˈsɪdəti, æ-] *n, pl* **-ties** : acidez *f*
acknowledge [ɪkˈnɑlɪdʒ, æk-] *vt* **-edged; -edging 1** ADMIT : reconocer, admitir **2** RECOGNIZE : reconocer **3 to acknowledge receipt of :** acusar recibo de
acknowledgment [ɪkˈnɑlɪdʒmənt, æk-] *n* **1** RECOGNITION : reconocimiento *m* **2** THANKS : agradecimiento *m*
acme [ˈækmi] *n* : colmo *m,* apogeo *m,* cúspide *f*
acne [ˈækni] *n* : acné *m*
acorn [ˈeɪˌkɔrn, -kərn] *n* : bellota *f*
acoustic [əˈkuːstɪk] *or* **acoustical** [-stɪkəl] *adj* : acústico — **acoustically** *adv*
acoustics [əˈkuːstɪks] *ns & pl* : acústica *f*
acquaint [əˈkweɪnt] *vt* **1** INFORM : enterar, informar **2** FAMILIARIZE : familiarizar **3 to be acquainted with** : conocer a (una persona), estar al tanto de (un hecho)
acquaintance [əˈkweɪntənts] *n* **1** KNOWLEDGE : conocimiento *m* **2** : conocido *m,* -da *f* <friends and acquaintances : amigos y conocidos>
acquiesce [ˌækwiˈɛs] *vi* **-esced; -escing** : consentir, conformarse
acquiescence [ˌækwiˈɛsənts] *n* : consentimiento *m,* aquiescencia *f*
acquire [əˈkwaɪr] *vt* **-quired; -quiring** : adquirir, obtener
acquisition [ˌækwəˈzɪʃən] *n* : adquisición *f*
acquisitive [əˈkwɪzətɪv] *adj* : adquisitivo, codicioso
acquit [əˈkwɪt] *vt* **-quitted; -quitting 1 :** absolver, exculpar **2 to acquit oneself :** comportarse, defenderse
acquittal [əˈkwɪtəl] *n* : absolución *f,* exculpación *f*
acre [ˈeɪkər] *n* : acre *m*
acreage [ˈeɪkərɪdʒ] *n* : superficie *f* en acres
acrid [ˈækrəd] *adj* **1** BITTER : acre **2** CAUSTIC : acre, mordaz — **acridly** *adv*
acrimonious [ˌækrəˈmoːniəs] *adj* : áspero, cáustico, sarcástico
acrimony [ˈækrəˌmoːni] *n, pl* **-nies** : acrimonia *f*

acrobat [ˈækrəˌbæt] *n* **:** acróbata *mf,* satimbanqui *mf*
acrobatic [ˌækrəˈbæt̬ɪk] *adj* **:** acrobático
acronym [ˈækrəˌnɪm] *n* **:** acrónimo *m*
across[1] [əˈkrɔs] *adv* **1** CROSSWISE **:** al través **2 :** a través, del otro lado <he's already across **:** ya está del otro lado> **3 :** de ancho <40 feet across **:** 40 pies de ancho>
across[2] *prep* **1 :** al otro lado de <across the street **:** al otro lado de la calle> **2 :** a través de <a log across the road **:** un tronco a través del camino>
acrylic [əˈkrɪlɪk] *n* **:** acrílico *m*
act[1] [ˈækt] *vi* **1** PERFORM **:** actuar, interpretar **2** FEIGN, PRETEND **:** fingir, simular **3** BEHAVE **:** comportarse **4** FUNCTION **:** actuar, servir, funcionar **5 :** tomar medidas <he acted to save the business **:** tomó medidas para salvar el negocio> **6 to act as :** servir de, hacer de
act[2] *n* **1** DEED **:** acto *m,* hecho *m,* acción *f* **2** DECREE **:** ley *f,* decreto *m* **3 :** acto *m* (en una obra de teatro), número *m* (en un espectáculo) **4** PRETENSE **:** fingimiento *m*
action [ˈækʃən] *n* **1** DEED **:** acción *f,* acto *m,* hecho *m* **2** BEHAVIOR **:** actuación *f,* comportamiento *m* **3** LAWSUIT **:** demanda *f* **4** MOVEMENT **:** movimiento *m* **5** COMBAT **:** combate *m* **6** PLOT **:** acción *f,* trama *f* **7** MECHANISM **:** mecanismo *m*
activate [ˈæktəˌveɪt] *vt* **-vated; -vating :** activar
active [ˈæktɪv] *adj* **1** MOVING **:** activo, en movimiento **2** LIVELY **:** vigoroso, enérgico **3 :** en actividad <an active volcano **:** un volcán en actividad> **4** OPERATIVE **:** vigente
actively [ˈæktɪvli] *adv* **:** activamente, enérgicamente
activity [ækˈtɪvət̬i] *n, pl* **-ties 1** MOVEMENT **:** actividad *f,* movimiento *m* **2** VIGOR **:** vigor *m,* energía *f* **3** OCCUPATION **:** actividad *f,* ocupación *f*
actor [ˈæktər] *n* **:** actor *m,* artista *mf*
actress [ˈæktrəs] *n* **:** actriz *f*
actual [ˈækʧʊəl] *adj* **:** real, verdadero
actuality [ˌækʧʊˈæləti] *n, pl* **-ties :** realidad *f*
actually [ˈækʧʊəli, -ʃəli] *adv* **:** realmente, en realidad
actuary [ˈækʧʊˌɛri] *n, pl* **-aries :** actuario *m,* -ria *f* de seguros
acumen [əˈkjuːmən] *n* **:** perspicacia *f*
acupuncture [ˈækjʊˌpʌŋkʧər] *n* **:** acupuntura *f*
acute [əˈkjuːt] *adj* **acuter; acutest 1** SHARP **:** agudo **2** PERCEPTIVE **:** perspicaz, sagaz **3** KEEN **:** fino, muy desarrollado, agudo <an acute sense of smell **:** un fino olfato> **4** SEVERE **:** grave **5 acute angle :** ángulo *m* agudo
acutely [əˈkjuːtli] *adv* **:** intensamente <to be acutely aware **:** estar perfectamente consciente>
acuteness [əˈkjuːtnəs] *n* **:** agudeza *f*
ad [ˈæd] → **advertisement**
adage [ˈædɪdʒ] *n* **:** adagio *m,* refrán *m,* dicho *m*
adamant [ˈædəmənt, -ˌmænt] *adj* **:** firme, categórico, inflexible — **adamantly** *adv*
Adam's apple [ˈædəmz] *n* **:** nuez *f* de Adán
adapt [əˈdæpt] *vt* **:** adaptar, ajustar — *vi* **:** adaptarse
adaptability [əˌdæptəˈbɪlət̬i] *n* **:** adaptabilidad *f,* flexibilidad *f*
adaptable [əˈdæptəbəl] *adj* **:** adaptable, amoldable
adaptation [ˌæˌdæpˈteɪʃən, -dəp-] *n* **1 :** adaptación *f,* modificación *f* **2** VERSION **:** versión *f*
adapter [əˈdæptər] *n* **:** adaptador *m*
add [ˈæd] *vt* **1 :** añadir, agregar <to add a comment **:** añadir una observación> **2 :** sumar <add these numbers **:** suma estos números> — *vi* **:** sumar (en total)
adder [ˈædər] *n* **:** víbora *f*
addict[1] [əˈdɪkt] *vt* **:** causar adicción en
addict[2] [ˈædɪkt] *n* **1 :** adicto *m,* -ta *f* **2 drug addict :** drogadicto *m,* -ta *f;* toxicómano *m,* -na *f*
addiction [əˈdɪkʃən] *n* **1 :** adicción *f,* dependencia *f* **2 drug addiction :** drogadicción *f*
addictive [əˈdɪktɪv] *adj* **:** adictivo
addition [əˈdɪʃən] *n* **1 :** adición *f,* añadidura *f* **2 in ~ :** además, también
additional [əˈdɪʃənəl] *adj* **:** extra, adicional, de más
additionally [əˈdɪʃənəli] *adv* **:** además, adicionalmente
additive [ˈædət̬ɪv] *n* **:** aditivo *m*
addle [ˈædəl] *vt* **-dled; -dling :** confundir, enturbiar
address[1] [əˈdrɛs] *vt* **1 :** dirigirse a, pronunciar un discurso ante <to address a jury **:** dirigirse a un jurado> **2 :** dirigir, ponerle la dirección a <to address a letter **:** dirigir una carta>
address[2] [əˈdrɛs, ˈæˌdrɛs] *n* **1** SPEECH **:** discurso *m,* alocución *f* **2 :** dirección *f* (de una residencia, etc.)
adenoids [ˈædˌnɔɪd, -dənˌɔɪd] *npl* **:** adenoides *fpl*
adept [əˈdɛpt] *adj* **:** experto, hábil — **adeptly** *adv*
adequacy [ˈædɪkwəsi] *n, pl* **-cies :** cantidad *f* suficiente
adequate [ˈædɪkwət] *adj* **1** SUFFICIENT **:** adecuado, suficiente **2** ACCEPTABLE, PASSABLE **:** adecuado, aceptable
adequately [ˈædɪkwətli] *adv* **:** suficientemente, apropiadamente
adhere [ædˈhɪr, əd-] *vi* **-hered; -hering 1** STICK **:** pegarse, adherirse **2 to adhere to :** adherirse a (una política, etc.), cumplir con (una promesa)

adherence [æd'hɪrənts, əd-] *n* : adhesión *f,* adherencia *f,* observancia *f* (de una ley, etc.)
adherent[1] [æd'hɪrənt, əd-] *adj* : adherente, adhesivo, pegajoso
adherent[2] *n* : adepto *m,* -ta *f;* partidario *m,* -ria *f*
adhesive[1] [æd'hiːsɪv, əd-, -zɪv] *adj* : adhesivo
adhesive[2] *n* : adhesivo *m,* pegamento *m*
adjacent [ə'dʒeɪsənt] *adj* : adyacente, colindante, contiguo
adjective ['ædʒɪktɪv] *n* : adjetivo *m* — **adjectival** [ˌædʒɪk'taɪvəl] *adj*
adjoin [ə'dʒɔɪn] *vt* : lindar con, colindar con
adjoining [ə'dʒɔɪnɪŋ] *adj* : contiguo, colindante
adjourn [ə'dʒərn] *vt* : levantar, suspender <the meeting is adjourned : se levanta la sesión> — *vi* : aplazarse
adjournment [ə'dʒərnmənt] *n* : suspensión *f,* aplazamiento *m*
adjudicate [ə'dʒuːdɪˌkeɪt] *vt* **-cated; -cating** : juzgar, arbitrar
adjunct ['æˌdʒʌŋkt] *n* : adjunto *m,* complemento *m*
adjust [ə'dʒʌst] *vt* : ajustar, arreglar, regular — *vi* **to adjust to** : adaptarse a
adjustable [ə'dʒʌstəbəl] *adj* : ajustable, regulable, graduable
adjustment [ə'dʒʌstmənt] *n* : ajuste *m,* modificación *f*
ad–lib[1] ['æd'lɪb] *v* **-libbed; -libbing** : improvisar
ad–lib[2] *adj* : improvisado
administer [æd'mɪnəstər, əd-] *vt* : administrar
administration [ædˌmɪnə'streɪʃən, əd-] *n* **1** MANAGING : administración *f,* dirección *f* **2** GOVERNMENT, MANAGEMENT : administración *f,* gobierno *m*
administrative [æd'mɪnəˌstreɪt̬ɪv, əd-] *adj* : administrativo — **administratively** *adv*
administrator [æd'mɪnəˌstreɪt̬ər, əd-] *n* : administrador *m,* -dora *f*
admirable ['ædmərəbəl] *adj* : admirable, loable — **admirably** *adv*
admiral ['ædmərəl] *n* : almirante *mf*
admiration [ˌædmə'reɪʃən] *n* : admiración *f*
admire [æd'maɪr] *vt* **-mired; -miring** : admirar
admirer [æd'maɪrər] *n* : admirador *m,* -dora *f*
admiring [æd'maɪrɪŋ] *adj* : admirativo, de admiración
admiringly [æd'maɪrɪŋli] *adv* : con admiración
admissible [æd'mɪsəbəl] *adj* : admisible, aceptable
admission [æd'mɪʃən] *n* **1** ADMITTANCE : entrada *f,* admisión *f* **2** ACKNOWLEDGMENT : reconocimiento *m,* admisión *f*
admit [æd'mɪt, əd-] *vt* **-mitted; -mitting 1** : admitir, dejar entrar <the museum admits children : el museo deja entrar a los niños> **2** ACKNOWLEDGE : reconocer, admitir
admittance [æd'mɪtənts, əd-] *n* : admisión *f,* entrada *f,* acceso *m*
admittedly [æd'mɪt̬ədli, əd-] *adv* : la verdad es que, lo cierto es que <admittedly we went too fast : la verdad es que fuimos demasiado de prisa>
admonish [æd'mɑnɪʃ, əd-] *vt* : amonestar, reprender
admonition [ˌædmə'nɪʃən] *n* : admonición *f*
ado [ə'duː] *n* **1** FUSS : ruido *m,* alboroto *m* **2** TROUBLE : dificultad *f,* lío *m* **3** **without further ado** : sin más preámbulos
adobe [ə'doːbi] *n* : adobe *m*
adolescence [ˌædəl'ɛsənts] *n* : adolescencia *f*
adolescent[1] [ˌædəl'ɛsənt] *adj* : adolescente, de adolescencia
adolescent[2] *n* : adolescente *mf*
adopt [ə'dɑpt] *vt* : adoptar
adoption [ə'dɑpʃən] *n* : adopción *f*
adorable [ə'dorəbəl] *adj* : adorable, encantador
adorably [ə'dorəbli] *adv* : de manera adorable
adoration [ˌædə'reɪʃən] *n* : adoración *f*
adore [ə'dor] *vt* **adored; adoring 1** WORSHIP : adorar **2** LOVE : querer, adorar **3** LIKE : encantarle (algo a uno), gustarle mucho (algo a uno) <I adore your new dress : me encanta tu vestido nuevo>
adorn [ə'dɔrn] *vt* : adornar, ornar, engalanar
adornment [ə'dɔrnmənt] *n* : adorno *m,* decoración *f*
adrift [ə'drɪft] *adj & adv* : a la deriva
adroit [ə'drɔɪt] *adj* : diestro, hábil — **adroitly** *adv*
adroitness [ə'drɔɪtnəs] *n* : destreza *f,* habilidad *f*
adult[1] [ə'dʌlt, 'æˌdʌlt] *adj* : adulto
adult[2] *n* : adulto *m,* -ta *f*
adulterate [ə'dʌltəˌreɪt] *vt* **-ated; -ating** : adulterar
adulterous [ə'dʌltərəs] *adj* : adúltero
adultery [ə'dʌltəri] *n, pl* **-teries** : adulterio *m*
adulthood [ə'dʌltˌhʊd] *n* : adultez *f,* edad *f* adulta
advance[1] [æd'vænts, əd-] *v* **-vanced; -vancing** *vt* **1** : avanzar, adelantar <to advance troops : avanzar las tropas> **2** PROMOTE : ascender, promover **3** PROPOSE : proponer, presentar **4** : adelantar, anticipar <they advanced me next month's salary : me adelantaron el sueldo del próximo mes> — *vi* **1** PROCEED : avanzar, adelantarse **2** PROGRESS : progresar
advance[2] *adj* : anticipado <advance notice : previo aviso>
advance[3] *n* **1** PROGRESSION : avance *m* **2** PROGRESS : adelanto *m,* mejora *f,* pro-

greso *m* **3** RISE : aumento *m,* alza *f* **4** LOAN : anticipo *m,* préstamo *m* **5 in ~** : por adelantado

advanced [æd'væntst, əd-] *adj* **1** DEVELOPED : avanzado, desarrollado **2** PRECOCIOUS : adelantado, precoz **3** HIGHER : superior

advancement [æd'væntsmənt, əd-] *n* **1** FURTHERANCE : fomento *m,* adelantamiento *m,* progreso *m* **2** PROMOTION : ascenso *m*

advantage [əd'væntɪdʒ, æd-] *n* **1** SUPERIORITY : ventaja *f,* superioridad *f* **2** GAIN : provecho *m,* partido *m* **3 to take advantage of** : aprovecharse de

advantageous [ˌædˌvæn'teɪdʒəs, -vən-] *adj* : ventajoso, provechoso — **advantageously** *adv*

advent ['ædˌvɛnt] *n* **1 Advent** : Adviento *m* **2** ARRIVAL : advenimiento *m,* venida *f*

adventure [æd'vɛntʃər, əd-] *n* : aventura *f*

adventurer [æd'vɛntʃərər, əd-] *n* : aventurero *m,* -ra *f*

adventurous [æd'vɛntʃərəs, əd-] *adj* **1** : intrépido, aventurero <an adventurous traveler : un viajero intrépido> **2** RISKY : arriesgado, aventurado

adverb ['ædˌvərb] *n* : adverbio *m* — **adverbial** [æd'vərbiəl] *adj*

adversary ['ædvərˌsɛri] *n, pl* **-saries** : adversario *m,* -ria *f*

adverse [æd'vərs, 'æd-ˌ] *adj* **1** OPPOSING : opuesto, contrario **2** UNFAVORABLE : adverso, desfavorable — **adversely** *adv*

adversity [æd'vərsət̬i, əd-] *n, pl* **-ties** : adversidad *f*

advertise ['ædvərˌtaɪz] *v* **-tised; -tising** *vt* : anunciar, hacerle publicidad a — *vi* : hacer publicidad, hacer propaganda

advertisement ['ædvərˌtaɪzmənt; æd'vərt̬əzmənt] *n* : anuncio *m*

advertiser ['ædvərˌtaɪzər] *n* : anunciante *mf*

advertising ['ædvərˌtaɪzɪŋ] *n* : publicidad *f,* propaganda *f*

advice [æd'vaɪs] *n* : consejo *m,* recomendación *f* <take my advice : sigue mis consejos>

advisability [ædˌvaɪzə'bɪlət̬i, əd-] *n* : conveniencia *f*

advisable [æd'vaɪzəbəl, əd-] *adj* : aconsejable, recomendable, conveniente

advise [æd'vaɪz, əd-] *v* **-vised; -vising** *vt* **1** COUNSEL : aconsejar, asesorar **2** RECOMMEND : recomendar **3** INFORM : informar, notificar — *vi* : dar consejo

adviser *or* **advisor** [æd'vaɪzər, əd-] *n* : consejero *m,* -ra *f;* asesor *m,* -sora *f*

advisory [æd'vaɪzəri, əd-] *adj* **1** : consultivo **2 in an advisory capacity** : como asesor

advocacy ['ædvəkəsi] *n* : promoción *f,* apoyo *m*

advocate¹ ['ædvəˌkeɪt] *vt* **-cated; -cating** : recomendar, abogar por, ser partidario de

advocate² ['ædvəkət] *n* : defensor *m,* -sora *f;* partidario *m,* -ria *f*

adze ['ædz] *n* : azuela *f*

aeon ['iːən, 'iːˌɑn] *n* : eón *m,* siglo *m,* eternidad *f*

aerate ['ærˌeɪt] *vt* **-ated; -ating** : gasear (un líquido), oxigenar (la sangre)

aerial¹ ['æriəl] *adj* : aéreo

aerial² *n* : antena *f*

aerie ['æri, 'ɪri, 'eɪəri] *n* : aguilera *f*

aerobic [ˌær'oːbɪk] *adj* : aerobio, aeróbico <aerobic exercises : ejercicios aeróbicos>

aerobics [ˌær'oːbɪks] *ns & pl* : aeróbic *m*

aerodynamic [ˌæroːdaɪ'næmɪk] *adj* : aerodinámico — **aerodynamically** [-mikli] *adv*

aerodynamics [ˌæroːdaɪ'næmɪks] *n* : aerodinámica *f*

aeronautical [ˌærə'nɔ̌t̬ɪkəl] *adj* : aeronáutico

aeronautics [ˌærə'nɔ̌tɪks] *n* : aeronáutica *f*

aerosol ['ærəˌsɔl] *n* : aerosol *m*

aerospace¹ ['æroˌspeɪs] *adj* : aeroespacial

aerospace² *n* : espacio *m*

aesthetic [ɛs'θɛt̬ɪk] *adj* : estético — **aesthetically** [-tɪkli] *adv*

aesthetics [ɛs'θɛt̬ɪks] *n* : estética *f*

afar [ə'fɑr] *adv* : lejos, a lo lejos

affability [ˌæfə'bɪlət̬i] *n* : afabilidad *f*

affable ['æfəbəl] *adj* : afable — **affably** *adv*

affair [ə'fær] *n* **1** MATTER : asunto *m,* cuestión *f,* caso *m* **2** EVENT : ocasión *f,* acontecimiento *m* **3** LIAISON : amorío *m,* aventura *f* **4 business affairs** : negocios *mpl* **5 current affairs** : actualidades *fpl*

affect [ə'fɛkt, æ-] *vt* **1** INFLUENCE, TOUCH : afectar, tocar **2** FEIGN : fingir

affectation [ˌæˌfɛk'teɪʃən] *n* : afectación *f*

affected [ə'fɛktəd, æ-] *adj* **1** FEIGNED : afectado, fingido **2** MOVED : conmovido

affecting [ə'fɛktɪŋ, æ-] *adj* : conmovedor

affection [ə'fɛkʃən] *n* : afecto *m,* cariño *m*

affectionate [ə'fɛkʃənət] *adj* : afectuoso, cariñoso — **affectionately** *adv*

affidavit [ˌæfə'deɪvət, 'æfəˌ-] *n* : declaración *f* jurada, affidávit *m*

affiliate¹ [ə'fɪliˌeɪt] *v* **-ated; -ating** *vt* : afiliar, asociar <to be affiliated with : estar afiliado a>

affiliate² [ə'fɪliət] *n* : afiliado *m,* -da *f* (persona), filial *f* (organización)

affiliation [əˌfɪli'eɪʃən] *n* : afiliación *f,* filiación *f*

affinity [ə'fɪnət̬i] *n, pl* **-ties** : afinidad *f*

affirm [ə'fərm] *vt* : afirmar, aseverar, declarar
affirmation [ˌæfər'meɪʃən] *n* : afirmación *f,* aserto *m,* declaración *f*
affirmative[1] [ə'fərmət̬ɪv] *adj* : afirmativo <affirmative action : acción afirmativa>
affirmative[2] *n* **1** : afirmativa *f* **2 to answer in the affirmative** : responder afirmativamente, dar una respuesta afirmativa
affix [ə'fɪks] *vt* : fijar, poner, pegar
afflict [ə'flɪkt] *vt* **1** : afligir, aquejar **2 to be afflicted with** : padecer de, sufrir de
affliction [ə'flɪkʃən] *n* **1** TRIBULATION : aflicción *f,* tribulación *f* **2** AILMENT : enfermedad *f,* padecimiento *m*
affluence ['æˌfluːən*t*s; æ'fluː-, ə-] *n* : afluencia *f,* abundancia *f,* prosperidad *f*
affluent ['æˌfluːənt; æ'fluː-, ə-] *adj* : próspero, adinerado
afford [ə'ford] *vt* **1** : tener los recursos para, permitirse el lujo de <I can afford it : puedo permitírmelo, tengo con que comprarlo> **2** PROVIDE : ofrecer, proporcionar, dar
affront[1] [ə'frʌnt] *vt* : afrentar, insultar, ofender
affront[2] *n* : afrenta *f,* insulto *m,* ofensa *f*
Afghan ['æfˌgæn, -gən] *n* : afgano *m,* -na *f* — **Afghan** *adj*
afire [ə'faɪr] *adj* : ardiendo, en llamas
aflame [ə'fleɪm] *adj* : llameante, en llamas
afloat [ə'floːt] *adv & adj* : a flote
afoot [ə'fʊt] *adj* **1** WALKING : a pie, andando **2** UNDER WAY : en marcha <something suspicious is afoot : algo sospechoso se está tramando>
aforesaid [ə'forˌsɛd] *adj* : antes mencionado, antedicho
afraid [ə'freɪd] *adj* **1 to be afraid** : tener miedo **2 to be afraid that** : temerse que <I'm afraid not : me temo que no>
afresh [ə'frɛʃ] *adv* **1** : de nuevo, otra vez **2 to start afresh** : volver a empezar
African ['æfrɪkən] *n* : africano *m,* -na *f* — **African** *adj*
Afro–American[1] [ˌæfroə'mɛrɪkən] *adj* : afroamericano *m,* -na *f*
Afro–American[2] *n* : afroamericano
aft ['æft] *adv* : a popa
after[1] ['æftər] *adv* **1** AFTERWARD : después **2** BEHIND : detrás, atrás
after[2] *adj* : posterior, siguiente <in after years : en los años posteriores>
after[3] *conj* : después de, después de que <after we ate : después de que comimos, después de comer>
after[4] *prep* **1** FOLLOWING : después de, tras <after Saturday : después del sábado> <day after day : día tras día> **2** BEHIND : tras de, después de <I ran after the dog : corrí tras del perro> **3** CONCERNING : por <they asked after you : preguntaron por ti> **4 after all** : después de todo
aftereffect ['æftərɪˌfɛkt] *n* : efecto *m* secundario
afterlife ['æftərˌlaɪf] *n* : vida *f* venidera, vida *f* después de la muerte
aftermath ['æftərˌmæθ] *n* : consecuencias *fpl,* resultados *mpl*
afternoon [ˌæftər'nuːn] *n* : tarde *f*
afterthought ['æftərˌθɔt] *n* : ocurrencia *f* tardía, idea *f* tardía
afterward ['æftərwərd] *or* **afterwards** [-wərdz] *adv* : después, luego <soon afterward : poco después>
again [ə'gɛn, -'gɪn] *adv* **1** ANEW, OVER : de nuevo, otra vez **2** BESIDES : además **3 then again** : por otra parte <I may stay, then again I may not : puede ser que me quede, por otra parte, puede que no>
against [ə'gɛn*t*st, -'gɪn*t*st] *prep* **1** TOUCHING : contra <against the wall : contra la pared> **2** OPPOSING : contra, en contra de <I will vote against the proposal : votaré en contra de la propuesta> <against the grain : a contrapelo>
agape [ə'geɪp] *adj* : boquiabierto
agate ['ægət] *n* : ágata *f*
age[1] ['eɪdʒ] *vi* **aged; aging** : envejecer, madurar
age[2] *n* **1** : edad *f* <ten years of age : diez años de edad> <to be of age : ser mayor de edad> **2** PERIOD : era *f,* siglo *m,* época *f* **3 old age** : vejez *f* **4 ages** *npl* : siglos *mpl,* eternidad *f*
aged *adj* **1** ['eɪdʒəd, 'eɪdʒd] OLD : anciano, viejo, vetusto **2** ['eɪdʒd] (*indicating a specified age*) <a girl aged 10 : una niña de 10 años de edad>
ageless ['eɪdʒləs] *adj* **1** YOUTHFUL : eternamente joven **2** TIMELESS : eterno, perenne
agency ['eɪdʒən*t*si] *n, pl* **-cies 1** : agencia *f,* oficina *f* <travel agency : agencia de viajes> **2 through the agency of** : a través de, por medio de
agenda [ə'dʒɛndə] *n* : agenda *f,* orden *m* del día
agent ['eɪdʒənt] *n* **1** MEANS : agente *m,* medio *m,* instrumento *m* **2** REPRESENTATIVE : agente *mf,* representante *mf*
aggravate ['ægrəˌveɪt] *vt* **-vated; -vating 1** WORSEN : agravar, empeorar **2** ANNOY : irritar, exasperar
aggravation [ˌægrə'veɪʃən] *n* **1** WORSENING : empeoramiento *m* **2** ANNOYANCE : molestia *f,* irritación *f,* exasperación *f*
aggregate[1] ['ægrɪˌgeɪt] *vt* **-gated; -gating** : juntar, sumar
aggregate[2] ['ægrɪgət] *adj* : total, global, conjunto
aggregate[3] ['ægrɪgət] *n* **1** CONGLOMERATE : agregado *m,* conglomerado *m* **2** WHOLE : total *m,* conjunto *m*

aggression [ə'grɛʃən] *n* **1** ATTACK : agresión *f* **2** AGGRESSIVENESS : agresividad *f*

aggressive [ə'grɛsɪv] *adj* : agresivo — **aggressively** *adv*

aggressiveness [ə'grɛsɪvnəs] *n* : agresividad *f*

aggressor [ə'grɛsər] *n* : agresor *m*, -sora *f*

aggrieved [ə'gri:vd] *adj* : ofendido, herido

aghast [ə'gæst] *adj* : espantado, aterrado, horrorizado

agile ['ædʒəl] *adj* : ágil

agility [ə'dʒɪləṱi] *n, pl* **-ties** : agilidad *f*

agitate ['ædʒə,teɪt] *v* **-tated; -tating** *vt* **1** SHAKE : agitar **2** UPSET : inquietar, perturbar — *vi* **to agitate against** : hacer campaña en contra de

agitation [,ædʒə'teɪʃən] *n* : agitación *f*, inquietud *f*

agitator ['ædʒə,teɪṱər] *n* : agitador *m*, -dora *f*

agnostic [æg'nɑstɪk] *n* : agnóstico *m*, -ca *f*

ago [ə'go:] *adv* : hace <two years ago : hace dos años> <long ago : hace tiempo, hace mucho tiempo>

agog [ə'gɑg] *adj* : ansioso, curioso

agonize ['ægə,naɪz] *vi* **-nized; -nizing** : tormentarse, angustiarse

agonizing ['ægə,naɪzɪŋ] *adj* : angustioso, terrible — **agonizingly** [-zɪŋli] *adv*

agony ['ægəni] *n, pl* **-nies 1** PAIN : dolor *m* **2** ANGUISH : angustia *f*

agrarian [ə'grɛriən] *adj* : agrario

agree [ə'gri:] *v* **agreed; agreeing** *vt* ACKNOWLEDGE : estar de acuerdo <he agreed that I was right : estuvo de acuerdo en que tenía razón> — *vi* **1** CONCUR : estar de acuerdo **2** CONSENT : ponerse de acuerdo **3** TALLY : concordar **4 to agree with** : sentarle bien (a alguien) <this climate agrees with me : este clima me sienta bien>

agreeable [ə'gri:əbəl] *adj* **1** PLEASING : agradable, simpático **2** WILLING : dispuesto **3** AGREEING : de acuerdo, conforme

agreeably [ə'gri:əbli] *adv* : agradablemente

agreement [ə'gri:mənt] *n* **1** : acuerdo *m*, conformidad *f* <in agreement with : de acuerdo con> **2** CONTRACT, PACT : acuerdo *m*, pacto *m*, convenio *m* **3** CONCORD, HARMONY : concordia *f*

agriculture ['ægrɪ,kʌltʃər] *n* : agricultura *f* — **agricultural** [,ægrɪ'kʌltʃərəl] *adj*

aground [ə'graʊnd] *adj* : encallado, varado

ahead [ə'hɛd] *adv* **1** : al frente, delante, adelante <he walked ahead : caminó delante> **2** BEFOREHAND : por adelantado, con antelación **3** LEADING : a la delantera **4 to get ahead** : adelantar, progresar

ahead of *prep* **1** : al frente de, delante de, antes de **2 to get ahead of** : adelantarse a

ahoy [ə'hɔɪ] *interj* **ship ahoy!** : ¡barco a la vista!

aid[1] ['eɪd] *vt* : ayudar, auxiliar

aid[2] *n* **1** HELP : ayuda *f*, asistencia *f* **2** ASSISTANT : asistente *mf*

aide ['eɪd] *n* : ayudante *mf*

AIDS ['eɪdz] *n* : SIDA *m*, sida *m*

ail ['eɪl] *vt* : molestar, afligir — *vi* : sufrir, estar enfermo

aileron ['eɪlə,rɑn] *n* : alerón *m*

ailment ['eɪlmənt] *n* : enfermedad *f*, dolencia *f*, achaque *m*

aim[1] ['eɪm] *vt* **1** : apuntar (un arma), dirigir (una observación) **2** INTEND : proponerse, querer <he aims to do it tonight : se propone hacerlo esta noche> — *vi* **1** POINT : apuntar **2 to aim at** : aspirar a

aim[2] *n* **1** MARKSMANSHIP : puntería *f* **2** GOAL : propósito *m*, objetivo *m*, fin *m*

aimless ['eɪmləs] *adj* : sin rumbo, sin objeto

aimlessly ['eɪmləsli] *adv* : sin rumbo, sin objeto

air[1] ['ær] *vt* **1** : airear, ventilar <to air out a mattress : airear un colchón> **2** EXPRESS : airear, manifestar, comunicar **3** BROADCAST : transmitir, emitir

air[2] *n* **1** : aire *m* **2** MELODY : aire *m* **3** APPEARANCE : aire *m*, aspecto *m* **4 airs** *npl* : aires *mpl*, afectación *f* **5 by ~** : por avión (dícese de una carta), en avión (dícese de una persona) **6 to be on the air** : estar en el aire, estar emitiendo

airborne ['ær,born] *adj* **1** : aerotransportado <airborne troops : tropas aerotransportadas> **2** FLYING : volando, en el aire

air–condition [,ærkən'dɪʃən] *vt* : climatizar, condicionar con el aire

air conditioner [,ærkən'dɪʃənər] *n* : acondicionador *m* de aire

air–conditioning [,ærkən'dɪʃənɪŋ] *n* : aire *m* acondicionado

aircraft ['ær,kræft] *ns & pl* **1** : avión *m*, aeronave *f* **2 aircraft carrier** : portaaviones *m*

airfield ['ær,fi:ld] *n* : aeródromo *m*, campo *m* de aviación

air force *n* : fuerza *f* aérea

airlift ['ær,lɪft] *n* : puente *m* aéreo, transporte *m* aéreo

airline ['ær,laɪn] *n* : aerolínea *f*, línea *f* aérea

airliner ['ær,laɪnər] *n* : avión *m* de pasajeros

airmail[1] ['ær,meɪl] *vt* : enviar por vía aérea

airmail[2] *n* : correo *m* aéreo

airman ['ærmən] *n, pl* **-men** [-mən, -,mɛn] **1** AVIATOR : aviador *m*, -dora *f* **2** : soldado *m* de la fuerza aérea

airplane ['ær,pleɪn] *n* : avión *m*

airport ['ær,port] *n* : aeropuerto *m*

airship [ˈær,ʃɪp] *n* : dirigible *m,* zepelín *m*
airstrip [ˈær,strɪp] *n* : pista *f* de aterrizaje
airtight [ˈærˈtaɪt] *adj* : hermético, herméticamente cerrado
airwaves [ˈær,weɪvz] *npl* : radio *m,* televisión *f*
airy [ˈæri] *adj* **airier** [-iər]; **-est 1** DELICATE, LIGHT : delicado, ligero **2** BREEZY : aireado, bien ventilado
aisle [ˈaɪl] *n* : pasillo *m,* nave *f* lateral (de una iglesia)
ajar [əˈdʒɑr] *adj* : entreabierto, entornado
akimbo [əˈkɪmbo] *adj & adv* : en jarras
akin [əˈkɪn] *adj* **1** RELATED : emparentado **2** SIMILAR : semejante, parecido
alabaster [ˈælə,bæstər] *n* : alabastro *m*
alacrity [əˈlækrəṭi] *n* : presteza *f,* prontitud *f*
alarm¹ [əˈlɑrm] *vt* **1** WARN : alarmar, alertar **2** FRIGHTEN : asustar
alarm² *n* **1** WARNING : alarma *f,* alerta *f* **2** APPREHENSION, FEAR : aprensión *f,* inquietud *f,* temor *m* **3 alarm clock** : despertador *m*
alas [əˈlæs] *interj* : ¡ay!
Albanian [ælˈbeɪniən] *n* : albanés *m,* -nesa *f* — **Albanian** *adj*
albatross [ˈælbə,trɔs] *n, pl* **-tross** *or* **-trosses** : albatros *m*
albeit [ɔlˈbiːət, æl-] *conj* : aunque
albino [ælˈbaɪno] *n, pl* **-nos** : albino *m,* -na *f*
album [ˈælbəm] *n* : álbum *m*
albumen [ælˈbjuːmən] *n* **1** : clara *f* de huevo **2** → **albumin**
albumin [ælˈbjuːmən] *n* : albúmina *f*
alcohol [ˈælkə,hɔl] *n* **1** ETHANOL : alcohol *m,* etanol *m* **2** LIQUOR : alcohol *m,* bebidas *fpl* alcohólicas
alcoholic¹ [,ælkəˈhɔlɪk] *adj* : alcohólico
alcoholic² *n* : alcohólico *m,* -ca *f*
alcoholism [ˈælkəhɔ,lɪzəm] *n* : alcoholismo *m*
alcove [ˈæl,koːv] *n* : nicho *m,* hueco *m*
alderman [ˈɔldərmən] *n, pl* **-men** [-mən, -,mɛn] : concejal *mf*
ale [ˈeɪl] *n* : cerveza *f*
alert¹ [əˈlərt] *vt* : alertar, poner sobre aviso
alert² *adj* **1** WATCHFUL : alerta, vigilante **2** QUICK : listo, vivo
alert³ *n* : alerta *f,* alarma *f*
alertly [əˈlərtli] *adv* : con listeza
alertness [əˈlərtnəs] *n* **1** WATCHFULNESS : vigilancia *f* **2** ASTUTENESS : listeza *f,* viveza *f*
alfalfa [ælˈfælfə] *n* : alfalfa *f*
alga [ˈælgə] *n, pl* **-gae** [ˈæl,dʒiː] : alga *f*
algebra [ˈældʒəbrə] *n* : álgebra *m*
algebraic [,ældʒəˈbreɪɪk] *adj* : algebraico — **algebraically** [-ɪkli] *adv*
Algerian [ælˈdʒɪriən] *n* : argelino *m,* -na *f* — **Algerian** *adj*
alias¹ [ˈeɪliəs] *adv* : alias
alias² *n* : alias *m*
alibi¹ [ˈælə,baɪ] *vi* : ofrecer una coartada
alibi² *n* **1** : coartada *f* **2** EXCUSE : pretexto *m,* excusa *f*
alien¹ [ˈeɪliən] *adj* **1** STRANGE : ajeno, extraño **2** FOREIGN : extranjero, foráneo **3** EXTRATERRESTRIAL : extraterrestre
alien² *n* **1** FOREIGNER : extranjero *m,* -ra *f;* forastero *m,* -ra *f* **2** EXTRATERRESTRIAL : extraterrestre *mf*
alienate [ˈeɪliə,neɪt] *vt* **-ated; -ating 1** ESTRANGE : alienar, enajenar **2 to alienate oneself** : alejarse, distanciarse
alienation [,eɪliəˈneɪʃən] *n* : alienación *f,* enajenación *f*
alight [əˈlaɪt] *vi* **1** DISMOUNT : bajarse, apearse **2** LAND : posarse, aterrizar
align [əˈlaɪn] *vt* : alinear
alignment [əˈlaɪnmənt] *n* : alineación *f,* alineamiento *m*
alike¹ [əˈlaɪk] *adv* : igual, del mismo modo
alike² *adj* : igual, semejante, parecido
alimentary [,æləˈmɛntəri] *adj* **1** : alimenticio **2 alimentary canal** : tubo *m* digestivo
alimony [ˈælə,moːni] *n, pl* **-nies** : pensión *f* alimenticia
alive [əˈlaɪv] *adj* **1** LIVING : vivo, viviente **2** LIVELY : animado, activo **3** ACTIVE : vigente, en uso **4** AWARE : consciente <alive to the danger : consciente del peligro>
alkali [ˈælkə,laɪ] *n, pl* **-lies** [-,laɪz] *or* **-lis** [-,laɪz] : álcali *m*
alkaline [ˈælkələn, -,laɪn] *adj* : alcalino
all¹ [ˈɔl] *adv* **1** COMPLETELY : todo, completamente **2** : igual <the score is 14 all : es 14 iguales, están empatados a 14> **3 all the better** : tanto mejor **4 all the more** : aún más, todavía más
all² *adj* : todo <all the children : todos los niños> <in all likelihood : con toda probabilidad, con la mayor probabilidad>
all³ *pron* **1** : todo, -da <they ate it all : lo comieron todo> <that's all : eso es todo> <enough for all : suficiente para todos> **2 all in all** : en general **3 not at all** (*in negative constructions*) : en absoluto, para nada
Allah [ˈɑlɑ, ɑˈlɑ] *n* : Alá *m*
all–around [,ɔləˈraʊnd] *adj* : completo, amplio
allay [əˈleɪ] *vt* **1** ALLEVIATE : aliviar, mitigar **2** CALM : aquietar, calmar
allegation [,ælɪˈgeɪʃən] *n* : alegato *m,* acusación *f*
allege [əˈlɛdʒ] *vt* **-leged; -leging 1** : alegar, afirmar **2 to be alleged** : decirse, pretenderse <she is alleged

to be wealthy : se dice que es adinerada>

alleged [ə'lɛdʒd, ə'lɛdʒəd] *adj* : presunto, supuesto

allegedly [ə'lɛdʒədli] : *adv* : supuestamente, según se alega

allegiance [ə'liːdʒənts] *n* : lealtad *f,* fidelidad *f*

allegorical [ˌælə'gɔrɪkəl] *adj* : alegórico

allegory ['æləˌgori] *n, pl* **-ries** : alegoría *f*

alleluia [ˌɑlə'luːjə, ˌæ-] → **hallelujah**

allergic [ə'lərdʒɪk] *adj* : alérgico

allergy ['ælərdʒi] *n, pl* **-gies** : alergia *f*

alleviate [ə'liːviˌeɪt] *vt* **-ated; -ating** : aliviar, mitigar, paliar

alleviation [əˌliːvi'eɪʃən] *n* : alivio *m*

alley ['æli] *n, pl* **-leys 1** : callejón *m* **2 bowling alley** : bolera *f*

alliance [ə'laɪənts] *n* : alianza *f,* coalición *f*

alligator ['æləˌgeɪt̬ər] *n* : caimán *m*

alliteration [əˌlɪt̬ə'reɪʃən] *n* : aliteración *f*

allocate ['æləˌkeɪt] *vt* **-cated; -cating** : asignar, adjudicar

allocation [ˌælə'keɪʃən] *n* : asignación *f,* reparto *m,* distribución *f*

allot [ə'lɑt] *vt* **-lotted; -lotting** : repartir, distribuir, asignar

allotment [ə'lɑtmənt] *n* : reparto *m,* asignación *f,* distribución *f*

allow [ə'laʊ] *vt* **1** PERMIT : permitir, dejar **2** ALLOT : conceder, dar **3** ADMIT, CONCEDE : admitir, conceder — *vi* **to allow for** : tener en cuenta

allowable [ə'laʊəbəl] *adj* **1** PERMISSIBLE : permisible, lícito **2** : deducible <allowable expenditure : gasto deducible>

allowance [ə'laʊənts] *n* **1** : complemento *m* (para gastos, etc.), mesada *f* (para niños) **2 to make allowance(s)** : tener en cuenta, disculpar

alloy ['æˌlɔɪ] *n* : aleación *f*

all right[1] *adv* **1** YES : sí, por supuesto **2** WELL : bien <I did all right : me fue bien> **3** DEFINITELY : bien, ciertamente, sin duda <he's sick all right : está bien enfermo>

all right[2] *adj* **1** OK : bien <are you all right? : ¿estás bien?> **2** SATISFACTORY : bien, bueno <your work is all right : tu trabajo es bueno>

all–round [ˌɔl'raʊnd] → **all–around**

allspice ['ɔlspaɪs] *n* : pimienta *f* de Jamaica

allude [ə'luːd] *vi* **-luded; -luding** : aludir, referirse

allure[1] [ə'lʊr] *vt* **-lured; -luring** : cautivar, atraer

allure[2] *n* : atractivo *m,* encanto *m*

allusion [ə'luːʒən] *n* : alusión *f*

ally[1] [ə'laɪ, 'æˌlaɪ] *vi* **-lied; -lying** : aliarse

ally[2] ['æˌlaɪ, ə'laɪ] *n* : aliado *m,* -da *f*

almanac ['ɔlməˌnæk, 'æl-] *n* : almanaque *m*

almighty [ɔl'maɪt̬i] *adj* : omnipotente, todopoderoso

almond ['ɑmənd, 'ɑl-, 'æ-, 'æl-] *n* : almendra *f*

almost ['ɔlˌmoːst, ɔl'moːst] *adv* : casi, prácticamente

alms ['ɑmz, 'ɑlmz, 'ælmz] *ns & pl* : limosna *f,* caridad *f*

aloft [ə'lɔft] *adv* : en alto, en el aire

alone[1] [ə'loːn] *adv* : sólo, solamente, únicamente

alone[2] *adj* : solo <they're alone in the house : están solos en la casa>

along[1] [ə'lɔŋ] *adv* **1** FORWARD : adelante <farther along : más adelante> <move along! : ¡circulen, por favor!> **2 to bring along** : traer **3 ~ with** : con, junto con **4 all along** : desde el principio

along[2] *prep* **1** : por, a lo largo de <along the coast : a lo largo de la costa> **2** : en, en el curso de, por <along the way : en el curso del viaje>

alongside[1] [əˌlɔŋ'saɪd] *adv* : al costado, al lado

alongside[2] *or* **alongside of** *prep* : junto a, al lado de

aloof [ə'luːf] *adj* : distante, reservado

aloofness [ə'luːfnəs] *n* : reserva *f,* actitud *f* distante

aloud [ə'laʊd] *adv* : en voz alta

alpaca [æl'pækə] *n* : alpaca *f*

alphabet ['ælfəˌbɛt] *n* : alfabeto *m*

alphabetical [ˌælfə'bɛt̬ɪkəl] *or* **alphabetic** [-'bɛt̬ɪk] *adj* : alfabético — **alphabetically** [-t̬ɪkli] *adv*

alphabetize ['ælfəbəˌtaɪz] *vt* **-ized; -izing** : alfabetizar, poner en orden alfabético

already [ɔl'rɛdi] *adv* : ya

also ['ɔlˌsoː] *adv* : también, además

altar ['ɔltər] *n* : altar *m*

alter ['ɔltər] *vt* : alterar, cambiar, modificar

alteration [ˌɔltə'reɪʃən] *n* : alteración *f,* cambio *m,* modificación *f*

altercation [ˌɔltər'keɪʃən] *n* : altercado *m,* disputa *f*

alternate[1] ['ɔltərˌneɪt] *v* **-nated; -nating** : alternar

alternate[2] ['ɔltərnət] *adj* **1** : alterno <alternate cycles of inflation and depression : ciclos alternos de inflación y depresión> **2** : uno sí y uno no <he cooks on alternate days : cocina un día sí y otro no>

alternate[3] ['ɔltərnət] *n* : suplente *mf;* sustituto *m,* -ta *f*

alternately ['ɔltərnətli] *adv* : alternativamente, por turno

alternating current ['ɔltərˌneɪt̬ɪŋ] *n* : corriente *f* alterna

alternation [ˌɔltər'neɪʃən] *n* : alternancia *f,* rotación *f*

alternative[1] [ɔl'tərnət̬ɪv] *adj* : alternativo

alternative[2] *n* **:** alternativa *f*
alternator ['ɔltər,neɪṭər] *n* **:** alternador *m*
although [ɔl'ðo:] *conj* **:** aunque, a pesar de que
altitude ['æltə,tu:d, -,tju:d] *n* **:** altitud *f,* altura *f*
alto ['æl,to:] *n, pl* **-tos :** alto *mf,* contralto *mf*
altogether [,ɔltə'gɛðər] *adv* **1** COMPLETELY **:** completamente, totalmente, del todo **2** ON THE WHOLE **:** en suma, en general
altruism ['æltrʊ,ɪzəm] *n* **:** altruismo *m*
altruistic [,æltrʊ'ɪstɪk] *adj* **:** altruista — **altruistically** [-tɪkli] *adv*
alum ['æləm] *n* **:** alumbre *m*
aluminum [ə'lu:mənəm] *n* **:** aluminio *m*
alumna [ə'lʌmnə] *n, pl* **-nae** [-,ni:] **:** ex-alumna *f*
alumnus [ə'lʌmnəs] *n, pl* **-ni** [-,naɪ] **:** ex-alumno *m*
always ['ɔlwiz, -,weɪz] *adv* **1** INVARIABLY **:** siempre, invariablemente **2** FOREVER **:** para siempre
am → be
amalgam [ə'mælgəm] *n* **:** amalgama *f*
amalgamate [ə'mælgə,meɪt] *vt* **-ated; -ating :** amalgamar, unir, fusionar
amalgamation [ə,mælgə'meɪʃən] *n* **:** fusión *f,* unión *f*
amaryllis [,æmə'rɪləs] *n* **:** amarilis *f*
amass [ə'mæs] *vt* **:** amasar, acumular
amateur ['æmətʃər, -tər, -,tʊr, -,tjʊr] *n* **1 :** amateur *mf* **2** BEGINNER **:** principiante *mf;* aficionado *m,* -da *f*
amateurish ['æmə,tʃərɪʃ, -,tər-, -,tʊr-, -,tjʊr-] *adj* **:** amateur, inexperto
amaze [ə'meɪz] *vt* **amazed; amazing :** asombrar, maravillar, pasmar
amazement [ə'meɪzmənt] *n* **:** asombro *m,* sorpresa *f*
amazing [ə'meɪzɪŋ] *adj* **:** asombroso, sorprendente — **amazingly** [-zɪŋli] *adv*
ambassador [æm'bæsədər] *n* **:** embajador *m,* -dora *f*
amber ['æmbər] *n* **:** ámbar *m*
ambergris ['æmbər,grɪs, -,gri:s] *n* **:** ámbar *m* gris
ambidextrous [,æmbɪ'dɛkstrəs] *adj* **:** ambidextro — **ambidextrously** *adv*
ambience *or* **ambiance** ['æmbiənts, 'ɑmbi,ɑnts] *n* **:** ambiente *m,* atmósfera *f*
ambiguity [,æmbə'gju:əṭi] *n, pl* **-ties :** ambigüedad *f*
ambiguous [æm'bɪgjʊəs] *adj* **:** ambiguo
ambition [æm'bɪʃən] *n* **:** ambición *f*
ambitious [æm'bɪʃəs] *adj* **:** ambicioso — **ambitiously** *adv*
ambivalence [æm'bɪvələnts] *n* **:** ambivalencia *f*
ambivalent [æm'bɪvələnt] *adj* **:** ambivalente
amble[1] ['æmbəl] *vi* **-bled; -bling :** ir tranquilamente, pasearse despreocupadamente
amble[2] *n* **:** paseo *m* tranquilo
ambulance ['æmbjələnts] *n* **:** ambulancia *f*
ambush[1] ['æm,bʊʃ] *vt* **:** emboscar
ambush[2] *n* **:** emboscada *f,* celada *f*
ameliorate [ə'mi:ljə,reɪt] *v* **-rated; -rating** IMPROVE **:** mejorar
amelioration [ə,mi:ljə'reɪʃən] *n* **:** mejora *f*
amen ['eɪ'mɛn, 'ɑ-] *interj* **:** amén
amenable [ə'mi:nəbəl, -'mɛ-] *adj* RESPONSIVE **:** susceptible, receptivo, sensible
amend [ə'mɛnd] *vt* **1** IMPROVE **:** mejorar, enmendar **2** CORRECT **:** enmendar, corregir
amendment [ə'mɛndmənt] *n* **:** enmienda *f*
amends [ə'mɛndz] *ns & pl* **:** compensación *f,* reparación *f,* desagravio *m*
amenity [ə'mɛnəṭi, -'mi:-] *n, pl* **-ties 1** PLEASANTNESS **:** lo agradable, amenidad *f* **2 amenities** *npl* **:** servicios *mpl*, comodidades *fpl*
American [ə'mɛrɪkən] *n* **:** americano *m,* -na *f* — **American** *adj*
American Indian *n* **:** indio *m* (americano), india *f* (americana)
amethyst ['æməθəst] *n* **:** amatista *f*
amiability [,eɪmi:ə'bɪləṭi] *n* **:** amabilidad *f,* afabilidad *f*
amiable ['eɪmi:əbəl] *adj* **:** amable, afable — **amiably** [-bli] *adv*
amicable ['æmɪkəbəl] *adj* **:** amigable, amistoso, cordial — **amicably** [-bli] *adv*
amid [ə'mɪd] *or* **amidst** [ə'mɪdst] *prep* **:** en medio de, entre
amino acid [ə'mi:no] *n* **:** aminoácido *m*
amiss[1] [ə'mɪs] *adv* **:** mal, fuera de lugar <to take amiss : tomar a mal, llevar a mal>
amiss[2] *adj* **1** WRONG **:** malo, inoportuno **2 there's something amiss :** pasa algo, algo anda mal
ammeter ['æ,mi:ṭər] *n* **:** amperímetro *m*
ammonia [ə'mo:njə] *n* **:** amoníaco *m*
ammunition [,æmjə'nɪʃən] *n* **1 :** municiones *fpl* **2** ARGUMENTS **:** argumentos *mpl*
amnesia [æm'ni:ʒə] *n* **:** amnesia *f*
amnesty ['æmnəsti] *n, pl* **-ties :** amnistía *f*
amoeba [ə'mi:bə] *n, pl* **-bas** *or* **-bae** [-,bi:] **:** ameba *f*
amoebic [ə'mi:bɪk] *adj* **:** amébico
amok [ə'mʌk, -'mɑk] *adv* **to run amok :** correr a ciegas, enloquecerse, desbocarse (dícese de la economía, etc.)
among [ə'mʌŋ] *prep* **:** entre
amorous ['æmərəs] *adj* **1** PASSIONATE **:** enamoradizo, apasionado **2** ENAM-

ORED : enamorado **3** LOVING : amoroso, cariñoso

amorously [ˈæmərəsli] *adv* : con cariño

amorphous [əˈmɔrfəs] *adj* : amorfo, informe

amortize [ˈæmərˌtaɪz, əˈmɔr-] *vt* **-tized; -tizing** : amortizar

amount[1] [əˈmaʊnt] *vi* **to amount to 1** : equivaler a, significar <that amounts to treason : eso equivale a la traición> **2** : ascender (a) <my debts amount to $2000 : mis deudas ascienden a $2000>

amount[2] *n* : cantidad *f,* suma *f*

ampere [ˈæmˌpɪr] *n* : amperio *m*

ampersand [ˈæmpərˌsænd] *n* : el signo *&*

amphibian [æmˈfɪbiən] *n* : anfibio *m*

amphibious [æmˈfɪbiəs] *adj* : anfibio

amphitheater [ˈæmfəˌθiːət̬ər] *n* : anfiteatro *m*

ample [ˈæmpəl] *adj* **-pler; -plest 1** LARGE, SPACIOUS : amplio, extenso, grande **2** ABUNDANT : abundante, generoso

amplifier [ˈæmpləˌfaɪər] *n* : amplificador *m*

amplify [ˈæmpləˌfaɪ] *vt* **-fied; -fying** : amplificar

amply [ˈæmpli] *adv* : ampliamente, abundantemente, suficientemente

amputate [ˈæmpjəˌteɪt] *vt* **-tated; -tating** : amputar

amputation [ˌæmpjəˈteɪʃən] *n* : amputación *f*

amuck [əˈmʌk] → **amok**

amulet [ˈæmjələt] *n* : amuleto *m,* talismán *m*

amuse [əˈmjuːz] *vt* **amused; amusing 1** ENTERTAIN : entretener, distraer **2** : hacer reír, divertir <the joke amused us : la broma nos hizo reír>

amusement [əˈmjuːzmənt] *n* **1** ENTERTAINMENT : diversión *f,* entretenimiento *m,* pasatiempo *m* **2** LAUGHTER : risa *f*

an → **a**[2]

anachronism [əˈnækrəˌnɪzəm] *n* : anacronismo *m*

anachronistic [əˌnækrəˈnɪstɪk] *adj* : anacrónico

anaconda [ˌænəˈkɑndə] *n* : anaconda *f*

anagram [ˈænəˌgræm] *n* : anagrama *m*

anal [ˈeɪnəl] *adj* : anal

analgesic [ˌænəlˈdʒiːzɪk, -sɪk] *n* : analgésico *m*

analogical [ˌænəˈlɑdʒɪkəl] *adj* : analógico — **analogically** [-kli] *adv*

analogous [əˈnæləgəs] *adj* : análogo

analogy [əˈnælədʒi] *n, pl* **-gies** : analogía *f*

analysis [əˈnæləsəs] *n, pl* **-yses** [-ˌsiːz] **1** : análisis *m* **2** PSYCHOANALYSIS : psicoanálisis *m*

analyst [ˈænəlɪst] *n* **1** : analista *mf* **2** PSYCHOANALYST : psicoanalista *mf*

analytic [ˌænəˈlɪt̬ɪk] *or* **analytical** [-t̬ɪkəl] *adj* : analítico — **analytically** [-t̬ɪkli] *adv*

analyze [ˈænəˌlaɪz] *vt* **-lyzed; -lyzing** : analizar

anarchic [æˈnɑrkɪk] *adj* : anárquico — **anarchically** [-kɪkli] *adv*

anarchism [ˈænərˌkɪzəm, -nɑr-] *n* : anarquismo *m*

anarchist [ˈænərkɪst, -nɑr-] *n* : anarquista *mf*

anarchy [ˈænərki, -nɑr-] *n* : anarquía *f*

anathema [əˈnæθəmə] *n* : anatema *m*

anatomic [ˌænəˈtɑmɪk] *or* **anatomical** [-mɪkəl] *adj* : anatómico — **anatomically** [-mɪkli] *adv*

anatomy [əˈnæt̬əmi] *n, pl* **-mies** : anatomía *f*

ancestor [ˈænˌsɛstər] *n* : antepasado *m,* -da *f;* antecesor *m,* -sora *f*

ancestral [ænˈsɛstrəl] *adj* : ancestral, de los antepasados

ancestry [ˈænˌsɛstri] *n* **1** DESCENT : ascendencia *f,* linaje *m,* abolengo *m* **2** ANCESTORS : antepasados *mpl*, -das *fpl*

anchor[1] [ˈæŋkər] *vt* **1** MOOR : anclar, fondear **2** FASTEN : sujetar, asegurar, fijar

anchor[2] *n* **1** : ancla *f* **2** : presentador *m,* -dora *f* (en televisión)

anchorage [ˈæŋkərɪdʒ] *n* : anclaje *m*

anchovy [ˈænˌtʃoːvi, ænˈtʃoː-] *n, pl* **-vies** *or* **-vy** : anchoa *f*

ancient [ˈeɪntʃənt] *adj* **1** : antiguo <ancient history : historia antigua> **2** OLD : viejo

ancients [ˈeɪntʃənts] *npl* : los antiguos *mpl*

and [ˈænd] *conj* **1** : y (e *before words beginning with i- or hi-*) **2** : con <ham and eggs : huevos con jamón> **3** : a <go and see : ve a ver> **4** : de <try and finish it soon : trata de terminarlo pronto>

andiron [ˈænˌdaɪərn] *n* : morillo *m*

Andorran [ænˈdɔrən] *n* : andorrano *m,* -na *f* — **Andorran** *adj*

androgynous [ænˈdrɑdʒənəs] *adj* : andrógino

anecdotal [ˌænɪkˈdoːt̬əl] *adj* : anecdótico

anecdote [ˈænɪkˌdoːt] *n* : anécdota *f*

anemia [əˈniːmiə] *n* : anemia *f*

anemic [əˈniːmɪk] *adj* : anémico

anemone [əˈnɛməni] *n* : anémona *f*

anesthesia [ˌænəsˈθiːʒə] *n* : anestesia *f*

anesthetic[1] [ˌænəsˈθɛt̬ɪk] *adj* : anestésico

anesthetic[2] *n* : anestésico *m*

anesthetist [əˈnɛsθətɪst] *n* : anestesista *mf*

anesthetize [əˈnɛsθəˌtaɪz] *vt* **-tize; -tized** : anestesiar

anew [əˈnuː, -ˈnjuː] *adv* : de nuevo, otra vez, nuevamente

angel [ˈeɪndʒəl] *n* : ángel *m*

angelic [æn'dʒɛlɪk] *or* **angelical** [-lɪkəl] *adj* : angélico — **angelically** [-lɪkli] *adv*
anger¹ ['æŋgər] *vt* : enojar, enfadar
anger² *n* : enojo *m,* enfado *m,* ira *f,* cólera *f,* rabia *f*
angina [æn'dʒaɪnə] *n* : angina *f*
angle¹ ['æŋgəl] *v* **angled; angling** *vt* DIRECT, SLANT : orientar, dirigir — *vi* FISH : pescar (con caña)
angle² *n* **1** : ángulo *m* **2** POINT OF VIEW : perspectiva *f,* punto *m* de vista
angler ['æŋglər] *n* : pescador *m,* -dora *f*
Anglo–Saxon¹ [,æŋglo'sæksən] *adj* : anglosajón
Anglo–Saxon² *n* : anglosajón *m,* -jona *f*
Angolan [æŋ'go:lən, æn-] *n* : angoleño *m,* -ña *f* — **Angolan** *adj*
angora [æŋ'gorə, æn-] *n* : angora *f*
angrily ['æŋgrəli] *adv* : furiosamente, con ira
angry ['æŋgri] *adj* **-grier; -est** : enojado, enfadado, furioso
anguish ['æŋgwɪʃ] *n* : angustia *f,* congoja *f*
anguished ['æŋgwɪʃt] *adj* : angustiado, acongojado
angular ['æŋgjələr] *adj* : angular (dícese de las formas), anguloso (dícese de las caras)
animal ['ænəməl] *n* **1** : animal *m* **2** BRUTE : bruto *m,* -ta *f*
animate¹ ['ænə,meɪt] *vt* **-mated; -mating** : animar
animate² ['ænəmət] *adj* : animado
animated ['ænə,meɪtəd] *adj* **1** LIVELY : animado, vivo, vivaz **2 animated cartoon** : dibujos *mpl* animados
animation [,ænə'meɪʃən] *n* : animación *f*
animosity [,ænə'mɑsəṭi] *n, pl* **-ties** : animosidad *f,* animadversión *f*
anise ['ænəs] *n* : anís *m*
aniseed ['ænəs,si:d] *n* : anís *m,* semilla *f* de anís
ankle ['æŋkəl] *n* : tobillo *m*
anklebone ['æŋkəl,bo:n] *n* : taba *f*
annals ['ænəlz] *npl* : anales *mpl,* crónica *f*
anneal [ə'ni:l] *vt* **1** TEMPER : templar **2** STRENGTHEN : fortalecer
annex¹ [ə'nɛks, 'æ,nɛks] *vt* : anexar
annex² ['æ,nɛks, -nɪks] *n* : anexo *m,* anejo *m*
annexation [,æ,nɛk'seɪʃən] *n* : anexión *f*
annihilate [ə'naɪə,leɪt] *vt* **-lated; -lating** : aniquilar
annihilation [ə,naɪə'leɪʃən] *n* : aniquilación *f,* aniquilamiento *m*
anniversary [,ænə'vərsəri] *n, pl* **-ries** : aniversario *m*
annotate ['ænə,teɪt] *vt* **-tated; -tating** : anotar
annotation [,ænə'teɪʃən] *n* : anotación *f*
announce [ə'naʊnts] *vt* **-nounced; -nouncing** : anunciar
announcement [ə'naʊntsmənt] *n* : anuncio *m*
announcer [ə'naʊntsər] *n* : anunciador *m,* -dora *f;* comentarista *mf;* locutor *m,* -tora *f*
annoy [ə'nɔɪ] *vt* : molestar, fastidiar, irritar
annoyance [ə'nɔɪənts] *n* **1** IRRITATION : irritación *f,* fastidio *m* **2** NUISANCE : molestia *f,* fastidio *m*
annoying [ə'nɔɪɪŋ] *adj* : molesto, fastidioso, engorroso — **annoyingly** [-ɪŋli] *adv*
annual¹ ['ænjʊəl] *adj* : anual — **annually** *adv*
annual² *n* **1** : planta *f* anual **2** YEARBOOK : anuario *m*
annuity [ə'nu:əṭi] *n, pl* **-ties** : anualidad *f*
annul [ə'nʌl] *vt* **anulled; anulling** : anular, invalidar
annulment [ə'nʌlmənt] *n* : anulación *f*
anode ['æ,no:d] *n* : ánodo
anoint [ə'nɔɪnt] *vt* : ungir
anomalous [ə'nɑmələs] *adj* : anómalo
anomaly [ə'nɑməli] *n, pl* **-lies** : anomalía *f*
anonymity [,ænə'nɪməṭi] *n* : anonimato *m*
anonymous [ə'nɑnəməs] *adj* : anónimo — **anonymously** *adv*
another¹ [ə'nʌðər] *adj* : otro
another² *pron* : otro, otra
answer¹ ['æntsər] *vt* **1** : contestar (a), responder (a) <to answer the telephone : contestar el teléfono> **2** FULFILL : satisfacer **3 to answer for** : ser responsable de, pagar por <she'll answer for that mistake : pagará por ese error> — *vi* : contestar, responder
answer² *n* **1** REPLY : respuesta *f,* contestación *f* **2** SOLUTION : solución *f*
answerable ['æntsərəbəl] *adj* : responsable
ant ['ænt] *n* : hormiga *f*
antagonism [æn'tægə,nɪzəm] *n* : antagonismo *m,* hostilidad *f*
antagonist [æn'tægənɪst] *n* : antagonista *mf*
antagonistic [æn,tægə'nɪstɪk] *adj* : antagonista, hostil
antagonize [æn'tægə,naɪz] *vt* **-nized; -nizing** : antagonizar
antarctic [ænt'ɑrktɪk, -'ɑrṭɪk] *adj* : antártico
antarctic circle *n* : círculo *m* antártico
antebellum [,æntɪ'bɛləm] *adj* : prebélico
antecedent¹ [,æntə'si:dənt] *adj* : antecedente, precedente
antecedent² *n* : antecedente *mf;* precursor *m,* -sora *f*
antelope ['æntəl,o:p] *n, pl* **-lope** *or* **-lopes** : antílope *m*
antenna [æn'tɛnə] *n, pl* **-nae** [-,ni:, -,naɪ] *or* **-nas** : antena *f*
anterior [æn'tɪriər] *adj* : anterior
anthem ['ænθəm] *n* : himno *m* <national anthem : himno nacional>

anther ['ænθər] *n* : antera *f*
anthill ['ænt,hɪl] *n* : hormiguero *m*
anthology [æn'θɑləd͡ʒi] *n, pl* **-gies** : antología *f*
anthracite ['ænθrə,saɪt] *n* : antracita *f*
anthropoid[1] ['ænθrə,pɔɪd] *adj* : antropoide
anthropoid[2] *n* : antropoide *mf*
anthropological [,ænθrəpə'lɑd͡ʒɪkəl] *adj* : antropológico
anthropologist [,ænθrə'pɑləd͡ʒɪst] *n* : antropólogo *m,* -ga *f*
anthropology [,ænθrə'pɑləd͡ʒi] *n* : antropología *f*
antiabortion [,æntiə'bɔrʃən, ,æntaɪ-] *adj* : antiaborto
antiaircraft [,ænti'ær,kræft, ,æntaɪ-] *adj* : antiaéreo
anti–American [,æntiə'mɛrɪkən, ,æntaɪ-] *adj* : antiamericano
antibiotic[1] [,æntibaɪ'ɑt̬ɪk, ,æntaɪ-, -bi-] *adj* : antibiótico
antibiotic[2] *n* : antibiótico *m*
antibody ['ænti,bɑdi] *n, pl* **-bodies** : anticuerpo *m*
antic[1] ['æntɪk] *adj* : extravagante, juguetón
antic[2] *n* : payasada *f,* travesura *f*
anticipate [æn'tɪsə,peɪt] *vt* **-pated; -pating 1** FORESEE : anticipar, prever **2** EXPECT : esperar, contar con
anticipation [æn,tɪsə'peɪʃən] *n* **1** FORESIGHT : previsión *f* **2** EXPECTATION : anticipación *f,* expectación *f,* esperanza *f*
anticipatory [æn'tɪsəpə,tori] *adj* : en anticipación, en previsión
anticlimactic [,æntiklaɪ'mæktɪk] *adj* : anticlimático, decepcionante
anticlimax [,ænti'klaɪ,mæks] *n* : anticlímax *m*
anticommunism [,ænti'kɑmjə,nɪzəm, ,æntaɪ-] *n* : anticomunismo *m*
anticommunist[1] [,ænti'kɑmjənɪst, ,æntaɪ-] *adj* : anticomunista
anticommunist[2] *n* : anticomunista *mf*
antidemocratic [,ænti,dɛmə'kræt̬ɪk, ,æntaɪ-] *adj* : antidemocrático
antidote ['æntɪ,doːt] *n* : antídoto *m*
antidrug [,ænti'drʌg, ,æntaɪ-; 'ænti,drʌg, 'æntaɪ-] *adj* : antidrogas
antifascist [,ænti'fæʃɪst, ,æntaɪ-] *adj* : antifascista
antifeminist [,ænti'fɛmənɪst, ,æntaɪ-] *adj* : antifeminista
antifreeze ['ænti,friːz] *n* : anticongelante *m*
anti–imperialism [,æntiɪm'pɪriə,lɪzəm, ,æntaɪ-] *n* : antiimperialismo *m*
anti–imperialist [,æntiɪm'pɪriəlɪst, ,æntaɪ-] *adj* : antiimperialista
anti–inflationary [,æntiɪn'fleɪʃə,nɛri, ,æntaɪ-] *adj* : antiinflacionario
antimony ['æntə,moːni] *n* : antimonio *m*
antipathy [æn'tɪpəθi] *n, pl* **-thies** : antipatía *f,* aversión *f*
antiperspirant [,ænti'pərspərənt, ,æntaɪ-] *n* : antitranspirante *m*
antiquarian[1] [,æntə'kwɛriən] *adj* : antiguo, anticuario <an antiquarian book : un libro antiguo>
antiquarian[2] *n* : anticuario *m,* -ria *f*
antiquary ['æntə,kwɛri] → **antiquarian**[2]
antiquated ['æntə,kweɪt̬əd] *adj* : anticuado, pasado de moda
antique[1] [æn'tiːk] *adj* **1** OLD : antiguo, de época <an antique mirror : un espejo antiguo> **2** OLD-FASHIONED : anticuado, pasado de moda
antique[2] *n* : antigüedad *f*
antiquity [æn'tɪkwət̬i] *n, pl* **-ties** : antigüedad
antirevolutionary [,ænti,rɛvə'luːʃə,nɛri, ,æntaɪ-] *adj* : antirrevolucionario
anti–Semitic [,æntisə'mɪt̬ɪk, ,æntaɪ-] *adj* : antisemita
anti–Semitism [,ænti'sɛmə,tɪzəm, ,æntaɪ-] *n* : antisemitismo *m*
antiseptic[1] [,æntə'sɛptɪk] *adj* : antiséptico — **antiseptically** [-tɪkli] *adv*
antiseptic[2] *n* : antiséptico *m*
antismoking [,ænti'smoːkɪŋ, ,æntaɪ-] *adj* : antitabaco
antisocial [,ænti'soːʃəl, ,æntaɪ-] *adj* **1** : antisocial **2** UNSOCIABLE : poco sociable
antitheft [,ænti'θɛft, ,æntaɪ-] *adj* : antirrobo
antithesis [æn'tɪθəsɪs] *n, pl* **-eses** [-,siːz] : antítesis *f*
antitoxin [,ænti'tɑksən, ,æntaɪ-] *n* : antitoxina *f*
antitrust [,ænti'trʌst, ,æntaɪ-] *adj* : antimonopolista
antler ['æntlər] *n* : asta *f,* cuerno *m*
antonym ['æntə,nɪm] *n* : antónimo *m*
anus ['eɪnəs] *n* : ano *m*
anvil ['ænvəl, -vɪl] *n* : yunque *m*
anxiety [æŋk'zaɪət̬i] *n, pl* **-eties 1** UNEASINESS : inquietud *f,* preocupación *f,* ansiedad *f* **2** APPREHENSION : ansiedad *f,* angustia *f*
anxious ['æŋkʃəs] *adj* **1** WORRIED : inquieto, preocupado, ansioso **2** WORRISOME : preocupante, inquietante **3** EAGER : ansioso, deseoso
anxiously ['æŋkʃəsli] *adv* : con inquietud, con ansiedad
any[1] ['ɛni] *adv* **1** : algo <is it any better? : ¿está (algo) mejor?> **2** : para nada <it is not any good : no sirve para nada>
any[2] *adj* **1** : alguno <is there any doubt? : ¿hay alguna duda?> <call me if you have any questions : llámeme si tiene alguna pregunta> **2** : cualquier <I can answer any question : puedo responder a cualquier pregunta> **3** : todo <in any case : en todo caso> **4** : ningún <he would not accept it under any circumstances : no lo aceptaría bajo ninguna circunstancia>
any[3] *pron* **1** : alguno *m,* -na *f* <are there any left? : ¿queda alguno?> **2** : nin-

guno *m*, -na *f* <I don't want any : no quiero ninguno>
anybody [ˈɛni͵bʌdi, -͵bɑ-] → **anyone**
anyhow [ˈɛni͵haʊ] *adv* **1** HAPHAZARDLY : de cualquier manera **2** IN ANY CASE : de todos modos, en todo caso
anymore [͵ɛniˈmor] *adv* **1** : ya, ya más <he doesn't dance anymore : ya no baila más> **2** : todavía <do they sing anymore? : ¿cantan todavía?>
anyone [ˈɛni͵wʌn] *pron* **1** : alguien <is anyone here? : ¿hay alguien aquí?> <if anyone wants to come : si alguno quiere venir> **2** : cualquiera <anyone can play : cualquiera puede jugar> **3** : nadie <I don't want anyone here : no quiero a nadie aquí>
anyplace [ˈɛni͵pleɪs] → **anywhere**
anything [ˈɛni͵θɪŋ] *pron* **1** : algo, alguna cosa <do you want anything? : ¿quieres algo?, ¿quieres alguna cosa?> **2** : nada <hardly anything : casi nada> **3** : cualquier cosa <I eat anything : como de todo>
anytime [ˈɛni͵taɪm] *adv* : en cualquier momento, a cualquier hora, cuando sea
anyway [ˈɛni͵weɪ] → **anyhow**
anywhere [ˈɛni͵*h*wɛr] *adv* **1** : en algún sitio, en alguna parte <do you see it anywhere? : ¿lo ves en alguna parte?> **2** : en ningún sitio, por ninguna parte <I can't find it anywhere : no puedo encontrarlo por ninguna parte> **3** : en cualquier parte, dondequiera, donde sea <put it anywhere : ponlo dondequiera>
aorta [eɪˈɔrṭə] *n, pl* **-tas** *or* **-tae** [-ṭi, -ṭaɪ] : aorta *f*
apart [əˈpɑrt] *adv* **1** SEPARATELY : aparte, separadamente **2** ASIDE : aparte, a un lado **3 to fall apart** : deshacerse, hacerse pedazos **4 to take apart** : desmontar, desmantelar
apartheid [əˈpɑr͵teɪt, -͵taɪt] *n* : apartheid *m*
apartment [əˈpɑrtmənt] *n* : apartamento *m*, departamento *m*, piso *m Spain*
apathetic [͵æpəˈθɛṭɪk] *adj* : apático, indiferente — **apathetically** [-ṭɪkli] *adv*
apathy [ˈæpəθi] *n* : apatía *f*, indiferencia *f*
ape[1] [ˈeɪp] *vt* **aped; aping** : imitar, remedar
ape[2] *n* : simio *m;* mono *m*, -na *f*
aperture [ˈæpərtʃər, -͵tʃʊr] *n* : abertura *f*, rendija *f*, apertura *f* (en fotografía)
apex [ˈeɪ͵pɛks] *n, pl* **apexes** *or* **apices** [ˈeɪpə͵siːz, ˈæ-] : ápice *m*, cúspide *f*, cima *f*
aphid [ˈeɪfɪd, ˈæ-] *n* : áfido *m*
aphorism [ˈæfə͵rɪzəm] *n* : aforismo *m*
aphoristic [͵æfəˈrɪstɪk] *adj* : aforístico
aphrodisiac [͵æfrəˈdiːzi͵æk, -ˈdɪ-] *n* : afrodisíaco *m*
apiary [ˈeɪpi͵ɛri] *n, pl* **-aries** : apiario *m*, colmenar *m*
apiece [əˈpiːs] *adv* : cada uno
aplenty [əˈplɛnti] *adj* : en abundancia
aplomb [əˈplɑm, -ˈplʌm] *n* : aplomo *m*
apocalypse [əˈpɑkə͵lɪps] *n* : apocalipsis *m*
apocalyptic [ə͵pɑkəˈlɪptɪk] *adj* : apocalíptico
apocrypha [əˈpɑkrəfə] *n* : textos *mpl* apócrifos
apocryphal [əˈpɑkrəfəl] *adj* : apócrifo
apologetic [ə͵pɑləˈdʒɛṭɪk] *adj* : lleno de disculpas
apologetically [ə͵pɑləˈdʒɛṭɪkli] *adv* : disculpándose, con aire de disculpas
apologize [əˈpɑlə͵dʒaɪz] *vi* **-gized; -gizing** : disculparse, pedir perdón
apology [əˈpɑlədʒi] *n, pl* **-gies** : disculpa *f*, excusa *f*
apoplectic [͵æpəˈplɛktɪk] *adj* : apoplético
apoplexy [ˈæpə͵plɛksi] *n* : apoplejía *f*
apostasy [əˈpɑstəsi] *n, pl* **-sies** : apostasía *f*
apostate [əˈpɑs͵teɪt] *n* : apóstata *mf*
apostle [əˈpɑsəl] *n* : apóstol *m*
apostleship [əˈpɑsəlʃɪp] *n* : apostolado *m*
apostolic [͵æpəˈstɑlɪk] *adj* : apostólico
apostrophe [əˈpɑstrə͵fiː] *n* : apóstrofo *m*
apothecary [əˈpɑθə͵kɛri] *n, pl* **-caries** : boticario *m*, -ria *f*
appall [əˈpɔl] *vt* : consternar, horrorizar
apparatus [͵æpəˈræṭəs, -ˈreɪ-] *n, pl* **-tuses** *or* **-tus** : aparato *m*, equipo *m*
apparel [əˈpærəl] *n* : atavío *m*, ropa *f*
apparent [əˈpærənt] *adj* **1** VISIBLE : visible **2** OBVIOUS : claro, evidente, manifiesto **3** SEEMING : aparente, ostensible
apparently [əˈpærəntli] *adv* : aparentemente, al parecer
apparition [͵æpəˈrɪʃən] *n* : aparición *f*, visión *f*
appeal[1] [əˈpiːl] *vt* **1** : apelar <to appeal a decision : apelar contra una decisión> — *vi* **1 to appeal for** : pedir, solicitar **2 to appeal to** : atraer a <that doesn't appeal to me : eso no me atrae>
appeal[2] *n* **1** : apelación *f* (en derecho) **2** PLEA : ruego *m*, súplica *f* **3** ATTRACTION : atracción *f*, atractivo *m*, interés *m*
appear [əˈpɪr] *vi* **1** : aparecer, aparecerse, presentarse <he suddenly appeared : apareció de repente> **2** COME OUT : aparecer, salir, publicarse **3** : comparecer (ante el tribunal), actuar (en el teatro) **4** SEEM : parecer
appearance [əˈpɪrən*t*s] *n* **1** APPEARING : aparición *f*, presentación *f*, comparecencia *f* (ante un tribunal), publicación *f* (de un libro) **2** LOOK : apariencia *f*, aspecto *m*

appease [ə'pi:z] *vt* **-peased; -peasing 1** CALM, PACIFY **:** aplacar, apaciguar, sosegar **2** SATISFY **:** satisfacer, mitigar
appeasement [ə'pi:zmənt] *n* **:** aplacamiento *m,* apaciguamiento *m*
append [ə'pɛnd] *vt* **:** agregar, añadir, adjuntar
appendage [ə'pɛndɪdʒ] *n* **1** ADDITION **:** apéndice *m,* añadidura *f* **2** LIMB **:** miembro *m,* extremidad *f*
appendectomy [ˌæpən'dɛktəmi] *n, pl* **-mies :** apendicectomía *f*
appendicitis [əˌpɛndə'saɪt̬əs] *n* **:** apendicitis *f*
appendix [ə'pɛndɪks] *n, pl* **-dixes** *or* **-dices** [-dəˌsi:z] **:** apéndice *m*
appetite ['æpəˌtaɪt] *n* **1** CRAVING **:** apetito *m,* deseo *m,* ganas *fpl* **2** PREFERENCE **:** gusto *m,* preferencia *f* <the cultural appetites of today : los gustos culturales de hoy>
appetizer ['æpəˌtaɪzər] *n* **:** aperitivo *m,* entremés *m,* botana *f Mex,* tapa *f Spain*
appetizing ['æpəˌtaɪzɪŋ] *adj* **:** apetecible, apetitoso — **appetizingly** [-zɪŋli] *adv*
applaud [ə'plɔd] *v* **:** aplaudir
applause [ə'plɔz] *n* **:** aplauso *m*
apple ['æpəl] *n* **:** manzana *f*
appliance [ə'plaɪənts] *n* **1 :** aparato *m* **2 household appliance :** electrodoméstico *m,* aparato *m* electrodoméstico
applicability [ˌæplɪkə'bɪlət̬i, əˌplɪkə-] *n* **:** aplicabilidad *f*
applicable ['æplɪkəbəl, ə'plɪkə-] *adj* **:** aplicable, pertinente
applicant ['æplɪkənt] *n* **:** solicitante *mf,* aspirante *mf,* postulante *mf;* candidato *m,* -ta *f*
application [ˌæplə'keɪʃən] *n* **1** USE **:** aplicación *f,* empleo *m,* uso *m* **2** DILIGENCE **:** aplicación *f,* diligencia *f,* dedicación *f* **3** REQUEST **:** solicitud *f,* petición *f,* demanda *f*
applicator ['æpləˌkeɪt̬ər] *n* **:** aplicador *m*
appliqué¹ [ˌæplə'keɪ] *vt* **:** decorar con apliques
appliqué² *n* **:** aplique *m*
apply [ə'plaɪ] *v* **-plied; -plying** *vt* **1 :** aplicar (una sustancia, los frenos, el conocimiento) **2 to apply oneself :** dedicarse, aplicarse — *vi* **1 :** aplicarse, referirse <the rules apply to everyone : las reglas se aplican a todos> **2 to apply for :** solicitar, pedir
appoint [ə'pɔɪnt] *vt* **1** NAME **:** nombrar, designar **2** FIX, SET **:** fijar, señalar, designar <to appoint a date : fijar una fecha> **3** EQUIP **:** equipar <a well-appointed office : una oficina bien equipada>
appointee [əˌpɔɪn'ti:, ˌæ-] *n* **:** persona *f* designada
appointment [ə'pɔɪntmənt] *n* **1** APPOINTING **:** nombramiento *m,* designación *f* **2** ENGAGEMENT **:** cita *f,* hora *f* **3** POST **:** puesto *m*
apportion [ə'porʃən] *vt* **:** distribuir, repartir
apportionment [ə'porʃənmənt] *n* **:** distribución *f,* repartición *f,* reparto *m*
apposite ['æpəzət] *adj* **:** apropiado, oportuno, pertinente — **appositely** *adv*
appraisal [ə'preɪzəl] *n* **:** evaluación *f,* valoración *f,* tasación *f,* apreciación *f*
appraise [ə'preɪz] *vt* **-praised; -praising :** evaluar, valorar, tasar, apreciar
appraiser [ə'preɪzər] *n* **:** tasador *m,* -dora *f*
appreciable [ə'pri:ʃəbəl, -'prɪʃiə-] *adj* **:** apreciable, sensible, considerable — **appreciably** [-bli] *adv*
appreciate [ə'pri:ʃiˌeɪt, -'prɪ-] *v* **-ated; -ating** *vt* **1** VALUE **:** apreciar, valorar **2 :** agradecer <we appreciate his frankness : agradecemos su franqueza> **3** UNDERSTAND **:** darse cuenta de, entender — *vi* **:** apreciarse, valorizarse
appreciation [əˌpri:ʃi'eɪʃən, -ˌprɪ-] *n* **1** GRATITUDE **:** agradecimiento *m,* reconocimiento *m* **2** VALUING **:** apreciación *f,* valoración *f,* estimación *f* <art appreciation : apreciación artística> **3** UNDERSTANDING **:** comprensión *f,* entendimiento *m*
appreciative [ə'pri:ʃət̬ɪv, -'prɪ-; ə'pri:ʃiˌeɪ-] *adj* **1 :** apreciativo <an appreciative audience : un público apreciativo> **2** GRATEFUL **:** agradecido **3** ADMIRING **:** de admiración
apprehend [ˌæprɪ'hɛnd] *vt* **1** ARREST **:** aprehender, detener, arrestar **2** DREAD **:** temer **3** COMPREHEND **:** comprender, entender
apprehension [ˌæprɪ'hɛntʃən] *n* **1** ARREST **:** arresto *m,* detención *f,* aprehensión *f* **2** ANXIETY **:** aprensión *f,* ansiedad *f,* temor *m* **3** UNDERSTANDING **:** comprensión *f,* percepción *f*
apprehensive [ˌæprɪ'hɛntsɪv] *adj* **:** aprensivo, inquieto — **apprehensively** *adv*
apprentice¹ [ə'prɛntɪs] *vt* **-ticed; -ticing :** colocar de aprendiz
apprentice² *n* **:** aprendiz *m,* -diza *f*
apprenticeship [ə'prɛntɪsˌʃɪp] *n* **:** aprendizaje *f*
apprise [ə'praɪz] *vt* **-prised; -prising :** informar, avisar
approach¹ [ə'pro:tʃ] *vt* **1** NEAR **:** acercarse a **2** APPROXIMATE **:** aproximarse a **3 :** abordar, dirigirse a <I approached my boss with the proposal : me dirigí a mi jefe con la propuesta> **4** TACKLE **:** abordar, enfocar, considerar — *vi* **:** acercarse, aproximarse
approach² *n* **1** NEARING **:** acercamiento *m,* aproximación *f* **2** POSITION **:** enfoque *m,* planteamiento *m* **3** OFFER **:** propuesta *f,* oferta *f* **4** ACCESS **:** acceso *m,* vía *f* de acceso
approachable [ə'pro:tʃəbəl] *adj* **:** accesible, asequible

approbation [ˌæprəˈbeɪʃən] *n* : aprobación *f*
appropriate[1] [əˈproːpriˌeɪt] *vt* **-ated; -ating 1** SEIZE : apropiarse de **2** ALLOCATE : destinar, asignar
appropriate[2] [əˈproːpriət] *adj* : apropiado, adecuado, idóneo — **appropriately** *adv*
appropriateness [əˈproːpriətnəs] *n* : idoneidad *f,* propiedad *f*
appropriation [əˌproːpriˈeɪʃən] *n* **1** SEIZURE : apropiación *f* **2** ALLOCATION : asignación *f*
approval [əˈpruːvəl] *n* **1** : aprobación *f,* visto *m* bueno **2 on approval** : a prueba
approve [əˈpruːv] *vt* **-proved; -proving 1** : aprobar, sancionar, darle el visto bueno a **2 to approve of** : consentir en, aprobar <he doesn't approve of smoking : está en contra del tabaco>
approximate[1] [əˈprɑksəˌmeɪt] *vt* **-mated; -mating** : aproximarse a, acercarse a
approximate[2] [əˈprɑksəmət] *adj* : aproximado
approximately [əˈprɑksəmətli] *adv* : aproximadamente, más o menos
approximation [əˌprɑksəˈmeɪʃən] *n* : aproximación *f*
appurtenance [əˈpərtənənts] *n* : accesorio *m*
apricot [ˈæprəˌkɑt, ˈeɪ-] *n* : albaricoque *m,* chabacano *m Mex*
April [ˈeɪprəl] *n* : abril *m*
apron [ˈeɪprən] *n* : delantal *m,* mandil *m*
apropos[1] [ˌæprəˈpoː, ˈæprəˌpoː] *adv* : a propósito
apropos[2] *adj* : pertinente, oportuno, acertado
apropos of *prep* : a propósito de
apt [ˈæpt] *adj* **1** FITTING : apto, apropiado, acertado, oportuno **2** LIABLE : propenso, inclinado **3** CLEVER, QUICK : listo, despierto
aptitude [ˈæptəˌtuːd, -ˌtjuːd] *n* **1** : aptitud *f,* capacidad *f* <aptitude test : prueba de aptitud> **2** TALENT : talento *m,* facilidad *f*
aptly [ˈæptli] *adv* : acertadamente
aqua [ˈækwə, ˈɑ-] *n* : color *m* aguamarina
aquarium [əˈkwæriəm] *n, pl* **-iums** *or* **-ia** [-iə] : acuario *m*
Aquarius [əˈkwæriəs] *n* : Acuario *mf*
aquatic [əˈkwɑt̬ɪk, -ˈkwæ-] *adj* : acuático
aqueduct [ˈækwəˌdʌkt] *n* : acueducto *m*
aquiline [ˈækwəˌlaɪn, -lən] *adj* : aguileño
Arab[1] [ˈærəb] *adj* : árabe
Arab[2] *n* : árabe *mf*
arabesque [ˌærəˈbɛsk] *n* : arabesco *m*
Arabian[1] [əˈreɪbiən] *adj* : árabe
Arabian[2] *n* → **Arab**[2]
Arabic[1] [ˈærəbɪk] *adj* : árabe
Arabic[2] *n* : árabe *m* (idioma)
arable [ˈærəbəl] *adj* : arable, cultivable
arbiter [ˈɑrbət̬ər] *n* : árbitro *m,* -tra *f*
arbitrary [ˈɑrbəˌtrɛri] *adj* : arbitrario — **arbitrarily** [ˌɑrbəˈtrɛrəli] *adv*
arbitrate [ˈɑrbəˌtreɪt] *v* **-trated; -trating** : arbitrar
arbitration [ˌɑrbəˈtreɪʃən] *n* : arbitraje *m*
arbitrator [ˈɑrbəˌtreɪt̬ər] *n* : árbitro *m,* -tra *f*
arbor [ˈɑrbər] *n* : cenador *m,* pérgola *f*
arboreal [ɑrˈboriəl] *adj* : arbóreo
arc[1] [ˈɑrk] *vi* **arced; arcing** : formar un arco
arc[2] *n* : arco *m*
arcade [ɑrˈkeɪd] *n* **1** ARCHES : arcada *f* **2** MALL : galería *f* comercial
arcane [ɑrˈkeɪn] *adj* : arcano, secreto, misterioso
arch[1] [ˈɑrtʃ] *vt* : arquear, enarcar — *vi* : formar un arco, arquearse
arch[2] *adj* **1** CHIEF : principal **2** MISCHIEVOUS : malicioso, pícaro
arch[3] *n* : arco *m*
archaeological [ˌɑrkiəˈlɑdʒɪkəl] *adj* : arqueológico
archaeologist [ˌɑrkiˈɑlədʒɪst] *n* : arqueólogo *m,* -ga *f*
archaeology *or* **archeology** [ˌɑrkiˈɑlədʒi] *n* : arqueología *f*
archaic [ɑrˈkeɪɪk] *adj* : arcaico — **archaically** [-ɪkli] *adv*
archangel [ˈɑrkˌeɪndʒəl] *n* : arcángel *m*
archbishop [ɑrtʃˈbɪʃəp] *n* : arzobispo *m*
archdiocese [ɑrtʃˈdaɪəsəs, -ˌsiːz, -ˌsiːs] *n* : archidiócesis *f*
archer [ˈɑrtʃər] *n* : arquero *m,* -ra *f*
archery [ˈɑrtʃəri] *n* : tiro *m* al arco
archetype [ˈɑrkɪˌtaɪp] *n* : arquetipo *m*
archipelago [ˌɑrkəˈpɛləˌgoː, ˌɑrtʃə-] *n, pl* **-goes** *or* **-gos** [-goːz] : archipiélago *m*
architect [ˈɑrkəˌtɛkt] *n* : arquitecto *m,* -ta *f*
architectural [ˌɑrkəˈtɛktʃərəl] *adj* : arquitectónico — **architecturally** *adv*
architecture [ˈɑrkəˌtɛktʃər] *n* : arquitectura *f*
archives [ˈɑrˌkaɪvz] *npl* : archivo *m*
archivist [ˈɑrkəvɪst, -ˌkaɪ-] *n* : archivero *m,* -ra *f;* archivista *mf*
archway [ˈɑrtʃˌweɪ] *n* : arco *m,* pasadizo *m* abovedado
arctic [ˈɑrktɪk, ˈɑrt-] *adj* **1** : ártico <arctic regions : zonas árticas> **2** FRIGID : glacial
arctic circle *n* : círculo *m* ártico
ardent [ˈɑrdənt] *adj* **1** PASSIONATE : ardiente, fogoso, apasionado **2** FERVENT : ferviente, fervoroso — **ardently** *adv*
ardor [ˈɑrdər] *n* : ardor *m,* pasión *f,* fervor *m*
arduous [ˈɑrdʒʊəs] *adj* : arduo, duro, riguroso — **arduously** *adv*

arduousness [ˈɑrdʒʊəsnəs] *n* **:** dureza *f,* rigor *m*
are → **be**
area [ˈæriə] *n* **1** SURFACE **:** área *f,* superficie *f* **2** REGION **:** área *f,* región *f,* zona *f* **3** FIELD **:** área *f,* terreno *m,* campo *m* (de conocimiento)
area code *n* **:** código *m* de la zona, prefijo *m Spain*
arena [əˈriːnə] *n* **1 :** arena *f,* estadio *m* <sports arena : estadio deportivo> **2 :** arena *f,* ruedo *m* <the political arena : el ruedo político>
Argentine [ˈɑrdʒənˌtaɪn, -ˌtiːn] *or* **Argentinean** *or* **Argentinian** [ˌɑrdʒənˈtɪniən] *n* **:** argentino *m,* -na *f* — **Argentine** *or* **Argentinean** *or* **Argentinian** *adj*
argon [ˈɑrˌgɑn] *n* **:** argón *m*
argot [ˈɑrgət, -ˌgoː] *n* **:** argot *m*
arguable [ˈɑrgjʊəbəl] *adj* **:** discutible
argue [ˈɑrˌgjuː] *v* **-gued; -guing** *vi* **1** REASON **:** argüir, argumentar, razonar **2** DISPUTE **:** discutir, pelear(se), alegar — *vt* **1** SUGGEST **:** sugerir **2** MAINTAIN **:** alegar, argüir, sostener **3** DISCUSS **:** discutir, debatir
argument [ˈɑrgjəmənt] *n* **1** REASONING **:** argumento *m,* razonamiento *m* **2** DISCUSSION **:** discusión *f,* debate *m* **3** QUARREL **:** pelea *f,* riña *f,* disputa *f*
argumentative [ˌɑrgjəˈmɛntəṭɪv] *adj* **:** discutidor
argyle [ˈɑrˌgaɪl] *n* **:** diseño *m* de rombos
aria [ˈɑriə] *n* **:** aria *f*
arid [ˈærəd] *adj* **:** árido
aridity [əˈrɪdəṭi, æ-] *n* **:** aridez *f*
Aries [ˈɛriːz, -iˌiːz] *n* **:** Aries *mf*
arise [əˈraɪz] *vi* **arose** [əˈroːz]; **arisen** [əˈrɪzən]; **arising 1** ASCEND **:** ascender, subir, elevarse **2** ORIGINATE **:** originarse, surgir, presentarse **3** GET UP **:** levantarse
aristocracy [ˌærəˈstɑkrəsi] *n, pl* **-cies :** aristocracia *f*
aristocrat [əˈrɪstəˌkræt] *n* **:** aristócrata *mf*
aristocratic [əˌrɪstəˈkræṭɪk] *adj* **:** aristocrático, noble
arithmetic¹ [ˌærɪθˈmɛṭɪk] *or* **arithmetical** [-ṭɪkəl] *adj* **:** aritmético
arithmetic² [əˈrɪθməˌtɪk] *n* **:** aritmética
ark [ˈɑrk] *n* **:** arca *f*
arm¹ [ˈɑrm] *vt* **:** armar — *vi* **:** armarse
arm² *n* **1 :** brazo *m* (del cuerpo o de un sillón), manga *f* (de una prenda) **2** BRANCH **:** rama *f,* sección *f* **3** WEAPON **:** arma *f* <to take up arms : tomar las armas> **4 coat of arms :** escudo *m* de armas
armada [ɑrˈmɑdə, -ˈmeɪ-] *n* **:** armada *f,* flota *f*
armadillo [ˌɑrməˈdɪlo] *n, pl* **-los :** armadillo *m*
armament [ˈɑrməmənt] *n* **:** armamento *m*
armed [ˈɑrmd] *adj* **1 :** armado <armed robbery : robo a mano armada> **2 armed forces :** fuerzas *fpl* armadas
Armenian [ɑrˈmiːniən] *n* **:** armenio *m,* -nia *f* — **Armenian** *adj*
armistice [ˈɑrməstɪs] *n* **:** armisticio *m*
armor [ˈɑrmər] *n* **:** armadura *f,* coraza *f*
armored [ˈɑrmərd] *adj* **:** blindado, acorazado
armory [ˈɑrməri] *n, pl* **-mories :** arsenal *m* (almacén), armería *f* (museo), fábrica *f* de armas
armpit [ˈɑrmˌpɪt] *n* **:** axila *f,* sobaco *m*
army [ˈɑrmi] *n, pl* **-mies 1 :** ejército *m* (militar) **2** MULTITUDE **:** legión *f,* multitud *f,* ejército *m*
aroma [əˈroːmə] *n* **:** aroma *f*
aromatic [ˌærəˈmæṭɪk] *adj* **:** aromático
around¹ [əˈraʊnd] *adv* **1 :** de circunferencia <a tree three feet around : un árbol de tres pies de circunferencia> **2 :** alrededor, a la redonda <for miles around : por millas a la redonda> <all around : por todos lados, todo alrededor> **3 :** por ahí <they're somewhere around : deben estar por ahí> **4** APPROXIMATELY **:** más o menos, aproximadamente <around 5 o'clock : a eso de las 5> **5 to turn around :** darse la vuelta, voltearse
around² *prep* **1** SURROUNDING **:** alrededor de, en torno a **2** THROUGH **:** por, en <he traveled around Mexico : viajó por México> <around the house : en casa> **3 :** a la vuelta de <around the corner : a la vuelta de la esquina> **4** NEAR **:** alrededor de, cerca de
arousal [əˈraʊzəl] *n* **:** excitación *f*
arouse [əˈraʊz] *vt* **aroused; arousing 1** AWAKE **:** despertar **2** EXCITE **:** despertar, suscitar, excitar
arraign [əˈreɪn] *vt* **:** hacer comparecer (ante un tribunal)
arraignment [əˈreɪnmənt] *n* **:** orden *m* de comparecencia, acusación *f*
arrange [əˈreɪndʒ] *vt* **-ranged; -ranging 1** ORDER **:** arreglar, poner en orden, disponer **2** SETTLE **:** arreglar, fijar, concertar **3** ADAPT **:** arreglar, adaptar
arrangement [əˈreɪndʒmənt] *n* **1** ORDER **:** arreglo *m,* orden *m* **2** ARRANGING **:** disposición *f* <floral arrangement : arreglo floral> **3** AGREEMENT **:** arreglo *m,* acuerdo *m,* convenio *m* **4 arrangements** *npl* **:** preparativos *mpl,* planes *mpl*
array¹ [əˈreɪ] *vt* **1** ORDER **:** poner en orden, presentar, formar **2** GARB **:** vestir, ataviar, engalanar
array² *n* **1** ORDER **:** orden *m,* formación *f* **2** ATTIRE **:** atavío *m,* galas *mpl* **3** RANGE, SELECTION **:** selección *f,* serie *f,* gama *f* <an array of problems : una serie de problemas>
arrears [əˈrɪrz] *npl* **:** atrasos *mpl* <to be in arrears : estar atrasado en los pagos>

arrest[1] [ə'rɛst] *vt* **1** APPREHEND : arrestar, detener **2** CHECK, STOP : detener, parar
arrest[2] *n* **1** APPREHENSION : arresto *m,* detención *f* <under arrest : detenido> **2** STOPPING : paro *m*
arrival [ə'raɪvəl] *n* : llegada *f,* venida *f,* arribo *m*
arrive [ə'raɪv] *vi* **-rived; -riving 1** COME : llegar, arribar **2** SUCCEED : triunfar, tener éxito
arrogance ['ærəgən*t*s] *n* : arrogancia *f,* soberbia *f,* altanería *f,* altivez *f*
arrogant ['ærəgənt] *adj* : arrogante, soberbio, altanero, altivo — **arrogantly** *adv*
arrogate ['ærə,geɪt] *vt* **-gated; -gating to arrogate to oneself** : arrogarse
arrow ['æro] *n* : flecha *f*
arrowhead ['æro,hɛd] *n* : punta *f* de flecha
arroyo [ə'rɔɪo] *n* : arroyo *m*
arsenal ['ɑrsənəl] *n* : arsenal *m*
arsenic ['ɑrsənɪk] *n* : arsénico *m*
arson ['ɑrsən] *n* : incendio *m* premeditado
arsonist *n* ['ɑrsənɪst] : incendiario *m,* -ria *f;* pirómano *m,* -na *f*
art ['ɑrt] *n* **1** : arte *m* **2** SKILL : destreza *f,* habilidad *f,* maña *f* **3 arts** *npl* : letras *fpl* (en la educación) **4 fine arts** : bellas artes *fpl*
arterial [ɑr'tɪriəl] *adj* : arterial
arteriosclerosis [ɑr,tɪriosklə'ro:sɪs] *n* : arteriosclerosis *f*
artery ['ɑrtəri] *n, pl* **-teries 1** : arteria *f* **2** THOROUGHFARE : carretera *f* principal, arteria *f*
artesian well [ɑr'ti:ʒən] *n* : pozo *m* artesiano
artful ['ɑrtfəl] *adj* **1** INGENIOUS : ingenioso, diestro **2** CRAFTY : astuto, taimado, ladino, artero — **artfully** *adv*
arthritic [ɑr'θrɪtɪk] *adj* : artrítico
arthritis [ɑr'θraɪtəs] *n, pl* **-tides** [ɑr'θrɪtə,di:z] : artritis *f*
arthropod ['ɑrθrə,pɑd] *n* : artrópodo *m*
artichoke ['ɑrtə,tʃo:k] *n* : alcachofa *f*
article ['ɑrtɪkəl] *n* **1** ITEM : artículo *m,* objeto *m* **2** ESSAY : artículo *m* **3** CLAUSE : artículo *m,* cláusula *f* **4** : artículo *m* <definite article : artículo determinado>
articulate[1] [ɑr'tɪkjə,leɪt] *vt* **-lated; -lating 1** UTTER : articular, enunciar, expresar **2** CONNECT : articular (en anatomía)
articulate[2] [ɑr'tɪkjələt] *adj* **to be articulate** : poder articular palabras, expresarse bien
articulately [ɑr'tɪkjələtli] *adv* : elocuentemente, con fluidez
articulateness [ɑr'tɪkjələtnəs] *n* : elocuencia *f,* fluidez *f*
articulation [ɑr,tɪkjə'leɪʃən] *n* **1** JOINT : articulación *f* **2** UTTERANCE : articulación *f,* declaración *f* **3** ENUNCIATION : articulación *f,* pronunciación *f*
artifact ['ɑrtə,fækt] *n* : artefacto *m*
artifice ['ɑrtəfəs] *n* : artificio *m*
artificial [,ɑrtə'fɪʃəl] *adj* **1** SYNTHETIC : artificial, sintético **2** FEIGNED : artificial, falso, afectado
artificially [,ɑrtə'fɪʃəli] *adv* : artificialmente, con afectación
artillery [ɑr'tɪləri] *n, pl* **-leries** : artillería *f*
artisan ['ɑrtəzən, -sən] *n* : artesano *m,* -na *f*
artist ['ɑrtɪst] *n* : artista *mf*
artistic [ɑr'tɪstɪk] *adj* : artístico — **artistically** [-tɪkli] *adv*
artistry ['ɑrtəstri] *n* : maestría *f,* arte *m*
artless ['ɑrtləs] *adj* : sencillo, natural, ingenuo, cándido — **artlessly** *adv*
artlessness ['ɑrtləsnəs] *n* : ingenuidad *f,* candidez *f*
arty ['ɑrti] *adj* **artier; -est** : pretenciosamente artístico
as[1] ['æz] *adv* **1** : tan, tanto <this one's not as difficult : éste no es tan difícil> **2** : como <some trees, as oak and pine : algunos árboles, como el roble y el pino>
as[2] *conj* **1** LIKE : como, igual que **2** WHEN, WHILE : cuando, mientras, a la vez que **3** BECAUSE : porque **4** THOUGH : aunque, por más que <strange as it may appear : por extraño que parezca> **5 as is** : tal como está
as[3] *prep* **1** : de <I met her as a child : la conocí de pequeña> **2** LIKE : como <behave as a man : compórtate como un hombre>
as[4] *pron* : que <in the same building as my brother : en el mismo edificio que mi hermano>
asbestos [æz'bɛstəs, æs-] *n* : asbesto *m,* amianto *m*
ascend [ə'sɛnd] *vi* : ascender, subir — *vt* : subir, subir a, escalar
ascendancy [ə'sɛndən*t*si] *n* : ascendiente *m,* predominio *m*
ascendant[1] [ə'sɛndənt] *adj* **1** RISING : ascendente **2** DOMINANT : superior, dominante
ascendant[2] *n* **to be in the ascendant** : estar en alza, ir ganando predominio
ascension [ə'sɛntʃən] *n* : ascensión *f*
ascent [ə'sɛnt] *n* **1** RISE : ascensión, *f,* subida *f,* ascenso *m* **2** SLOPE : cuesta *f,* pendiente *f*
ascertain [,æsər'teɪn] *vt* : determinar, establecer, averiguar
ascertainable [,æsər'teɪnəbəl] *adj* : determinable, averiguable
ascetic[1] [ə'sɛtɪk] *adj* : ascético
ascetic[2] *n* : asceta *mf*
asceticism [ə'sɛtə,sɪzəm] *n* : ascetismo *m*
ascribable [ə'skraɪbəbəl] *adj* : atribuible, imputable
ascribe [ə'skraɪb] *vt* **-cribed; -cribing** : atribuir, imputar
aseptic [eɪ'sɛptɪk] *adj* : aséptico
as for *prep* CONCERNING : en cuanto a, respecto a, para

ash [ˈæʃ] *n* **1 :** ceniza *f* <to reduce to ashes : reducir a cenizas> **2 :** fresno *m* (árbol)

ashamed [əˈʃeɪmd] *adj* **:** avergonzado, abochornado, apenado **— ashamedly** [əˈʃeɪmədli] *adv*

ashen [ˈæʃən] *adj* **:** lívido, ceniciento, pálido

ashore [əˈʃor] *adv* **1 :** en tierra **2 to go ashore :** desembarcar

ashtray [ˈæʃˌtreɪ] *n* **:** cenicero *m*

Asian[1] [ˈeɪʒən, -ʃən] *adj* **:** asiático

Asian[2] *n* **:** asiático *m,* -ca *f*

aside [əˈsaɪd] *adv* **1 :** a un lado <to step aside : hacerse a un lado> **2 :** de lado, aparte <jesting aside : bromas aparte> **3 to set aside :** guardar, apartar, reservar

aside from *prep* **1** BESIDES **:** además de **2** EXCEPT **:** aparte de, menos

as if *conj* **:** como si

asinine [ˈæsənˌaɪn] *adj* **:** necio, estúpido

ask [ˈæsk] *vt* **1 :** preguntar <ask him if he's coming : pregúntale si viene> **2** REQUEST **:** pedir, solicitar <to ask a favor : pedir un favor> **3** INVITE **:** invitar **—** *vi* **1** INQUIRE **:** preguntar <I asked about her children : pregunté por sus niños> **2** REQUEST **:** pedir <we asked for help : pedimos ayuda>

askance [əˈskæn*t*s] *adv* **1** SIDELONG **:** de reojo, de soslayo **2** SUSPICIOUSLY **:** con recelo, con desconfianza

askew [əˈskjuː] *adj* **:** torcido, ladeado

asleep [əˈsliːp] *adj* **1 :** dormido, durmiendo **2 to fall asleep :** quedarse dormido

as of *prep* **:** desde, a partir de

asparagus [əˈspærəgəs] *n* **:** espárrago *m*

aspect [ˈæˌspɛkt] *n* **:** aspecto *m*

aspen [ˈæspən] *n* **:** álamo *m* temblón

asperity [æˈspɛrəṭi, ə-] *n, pl* **-ties :** aspereza *f*

aspersion [əˈspərʒən] *n* **:** difamación *f,* calumnia *f*

asphalt [ˈæsˌfɔlt] *n* **:** asfalto *m*

asphyxia [æˈsfɪksiə, ə-] *n* **:** asfixia *f*

asphyxiate [æˈsfɪksiˌeɪt] *v* **-ated; -ating** *vt* **:** asfixiar **—** *vi* **:** asfixiarse

asphyxiation [æˌsfɪksiˈeɪʃən] *n* **:** asfixia *f*

aspirant [ˈæspərənt, əˈspaɪrənt] *n* **:** aspirante *mf,* pretendiente *mf*

aspiration [ˌæspəˈreɪʃən] *n* **1** DESIRE **:** aspiración *f,* anhelo *m,* ambición *f* **2** BREATHING **:** aspiración *f*

aspire [əˈspaɪr] *vi* **-pired; -piring :** aspirar

aspirin [ˈæsprən, ˈæspə-] *n, pl* **aspirin** *or* **aspirins :** aspirina *f*

ass [ˈæs] *n* **1 :** asno *m* **2** IDIOT **:** imbécil *mf,* idiota *mf*

assail [əˈseɪl] *vt* **:** atacar, asaltar

assailant [əˈseɪlənt] *n* **:** asaltante *mf,* atacante *mf*

assassin [əˈsæsən] *n* **:** asesino *m,* -na *f*

assassinate [əˈsæsənˌeɪt] *vt* **-nated; -nating :** asesinar

assassination [əˌsæsənˈeɪʃən] *n* **:** asesinato *m*

assault[1] [əˈsɔlt] *vt* **:** atacar, asaltar, agredir

assault[2] *n* **:** ataque *m,* asalto *m,* agresión *f*

assay[1] [æˈseɪ, ˈæˌseɪ] *vt* **:** ensayar

assay[2] [ˈæˌseɪ, æˈseɪ] *n* **:** ensayo *m*

assemble [əˈsɛmbəl] *v* **-bled; -bling** *vt* **1** GATHER **:** reunir, recoger, juntar **2** CONSTRUCT **:** ensamblar, montar, construir **—** *vi* **:** reunirse, congregarse

assembly [əˈsɛmbli] *n, pl* **-blies 1** MEETING **:** reunión *f* **2** CONSTRUCTING **:** ensamblaje *m,* montaje *m*

assemblyman [əˈsɛmblimən] *n, pl* **-men** [-mən, -ˌmɛn] **:** asambleísta *m*

assemblywoman [əˈsɛmbliˌwʊmən] *n, pl* **-women** [-ˌwɪmən] **:** asambleísta *f*

assent[1] [əˈsɛnt] *vi* **:** asentir, consentir

assent[2] *n* **:** asentimiento *m,* aprobación *f*

assert [əˈsərt] *vt* **1** AFFIRM **:** afirmar, aseverar, mantener **2 to assert oneself :** imponerse, hacerse valer

assertion [əˈsərʃən] *n* **:** afirmación *f,* aseveración *f,* aserto *m*

assertive [əˈsərṭɪv] *adj* **:** firme, enérgico

assertiveness [əˈsərṭɪvnəs] *n* **:** seguridad *f* en sí mismo

assess [əˈsɛs] *vt* **1** IMPOSE **:** gravar (un impuesto), imponer **2** EVALUATE **:** evaluar, valorar, aquilatar

assessment [əˈsɛsmənt] *n* **:** evaluación *f,* valoración *f*

assessor [əˈsɛsər] *n* **:** evaluador *m,* -dora *f;* tasador *m,* -dora *f*

asset [ˈæˌsɛt] *n* **1 :** ventaja *f,* recurso *m* **2 assets** *npl* **:** bienes *mpl,* activo *m* <assets and liabilities : activo y pasivo>

assiduous [əˈsɪdʒʊəs] *adj* **:** diligente, aplicado, asiduo **— assiduously** *adv*

assign [əˈsaɪn] *vt* **1** APPOINT **:** designar, nombrar **2** ALLOT **:** asignar, señalar **3** ATTRIBUTE **:** atribuir, dar, conceder

assignment [əˈsaɪnmənt] *n* **1** TASK **:** función *f,* tarea *f,* misión *f* **2** HOMEWORK **:** tarea *f,* asignación *f PRi,* deberes *mpl Spain* **3** APPOINTMENT **:** nombramiento *m* **4** ALLOCATION **:** asignación *f*

assimilate [əˈsɪməˌleɪt] *v* **-lated; -lating** *vt* **:** asimilar **—** *vi* **:** adaptarse, integrarse

assimilation [əˌsɪməˈleɪʃən] *n* **:** asimilación *f*

assist[1] [əˈsɪst] *vt* **:** asistir, ayudar

assist[2] *n* **:** asistencia *f,* contribución *f*

assistance [əˈsɪstən*t*s] *n* **:** asistencia *f,* ayuda *f,* auxilio *m*

assistant [əˈsɪstənt] *n* **:** ayudante *mf,* asistente *mf*

associate[1] [əˈsoːʃiˌeɪt, -si-] *v* **-ated; -ating** *vt* **1** CONNECT, RELATE **:** asociar, relacionar **2 to be associated with**

: estar relacionado con, estar vinculado a — *vi* **to associate with** : relacionarse con, frecuentar

associate² [ə'soːʃiət, -siət] *n* : asociado *m,* -da *f;* colega *mf;* socio *m,* -cia *f*

association [ə,soːʃi'eɪʃən, -si-] *n* **1** ORGANIZATION : asociación *f,* sociedad *f* **2** RELATIONSHIP : asociación *f,* relación *f*

as soon as *conj* : en cuanto, tan pronto como

assorted [ə'sɔrt̬əd] *adj* : surtido

assortment [ə'sɔrtmənt] *n* : surtido *m,* variedad *f,* colección *f*

assuage [ə'sweɪdʒ] *vt* **-suaged; -suaging 1** EASE : aliviar, mitigar **2** CALM : calmar, aplacar **3** SATISFY : saciar, satisfacer

assume [ə'suːm] *vt* **-sumed; -suming 1** SUPPOSE : suponer, asumir **2** UNDERTAKE : asumir, encargarse de **3** TAKE ON : adquirir, adoptar, tomar <to assume importance : tomar importancia> **4** FEIGN : adoptar, afectar, simular

assumption [ə'sʌmpʃən] *n* : asunción *f,* presunción *f*

assurance [ə'ʃʊrənts] *n* **1** CERTAINTY : certidumbre *f,* certeza *f* **2** CONFIDENCE : confianza *f,* aplomo *m,* seguridad *f*

assure [ə'ʃʊr] *vt* **-sured; -suring** : asegurar, garantizar <I assure you that I'll do it : te aseguro que lo haré>

assured [ə'ʃʊrd] *adj* **1** CERTAIN : seguro, asegurado **2** CONFIDENT : confiado, seguro de sí mismo

aster ['æstər] *n* : áster *m*

asterisk ['æstə,rɪsk] *n* : asterisco *m*

astern [ə'stərn] *adv* **1** BEHIND : detrás, a popa **2** BACKWARDS : hacia atrás

asteroid ['æstə,rɔɪd] *n* : asteroide *m*

asthma ['æzmə] *n* : asma *m*

asthmatic [æz'mæt̬ɪk] *adj* : asmático

as though → **as if**

astigmatism [ə'stɪgmə,tɪzəm] *n* : astigmatismo *m*

as to *prep* **1** ABOUT : sobre, acerca de **2** → **according to**

astonish [ə'stɑnɪʃ] *vt* : asombrar, sorprender, pasmar

astonishing [ə'stɑnɪʃɪŋ] *adj* : asombroso, sorprendente, increíble — **astonishingly** *adv*

astonishment [ə'stɑnɪʃmənt] *n* : asombro *m,* estupefacción *f,* sorpresa *f*

astound [ə'staʊnd] *vt* : asombrar, pasmar, dejar estupefacto

astounding [ə'staʊndɪŋ] *adj* : asombroso, pasmoso — **astoundingly** *adv*

astraddle [ə'strædəl] *adv* : a horcajadas

astral ['æstrəl] *adj* : astral

astray [ə'streɪ] *adv & adj* : perdido, extraviado, descarriado

astride [ə'straɪd] *adv* : a horcajadas

astringency [ə'strɪndʒəntsi] *n* : astringencia *f*

astringent¹ [ə'strɪndʒənt] *adj* : astringente

astringent² *n* : astringente *m*

astrologer [ə'strɑlədʒər] *n* : astrólogo *m,* -ga *f*

astrological [,æstrə'lɑdʒɪkəl] *adj* : astrológico

astrology [ə'strɑlədʒi] *n* : astrología *f*

astronaut ['æstrə,nɔt] *n* : astronauta *mf*

astronautic [,æstrə'nɔt̬ɪk] *or* **astronautical** [-t̬ɪkəl] *adj* : astronáutico

astronautics [,æstrə'nɔt̬ɪks] *ns & pl* : astronáutica *f*

astronomer [ə'strɑnəmər] *n* : astrónomo *m,* -ma *f*

astronomical [,æstrə'nɑmɪkəl] *adj* **1** : astronómico **2** ENORMOUS : astronómico, enorme, gigantesco

astronomy [ə'strɑnəmi] *n, pl* **-mies** : astronomía *f*

astute [ə'stuːt, -'stjuːt] *adj* : astuto, sagaz, perspicaz — **astutely** *adv*

astuteness [ə'stuːtnəs, -'stjuːt-] *n* : astucia *f,* sagacidad *f,* perspicacia *f*

asunder [ə'sʌndər] *adv* : en dos, en pedazos <to tear asunder : hacer pedazos>

as well as¹ *conj* : tanto como

as well as² *prep* BESIDES : además de, aparte de

as yet *adv* : aún, todavía

asylum [ə'saɪləm] *n* **1** REFUGE : refugio *m,* santuario *m,* asilo *m* **2 insane asylum** : manicomio *m*

asymmetrical [,eɪsə'mɛtrɪkəl] *or* **asymmetric** [-'mɛtrɪk] *adj* : asimétrico

asymmetry [,eɪ'sɪmətri] *n* : asimetría *f*

at ['æt] *prep* **1** : en <at the top : en lo alto> <at peace : en paz> <at Ana's house : en casa de Ana> **2** : a <at the rear : al fondo> <at 10 o'clock : a las diez> **3** : por <at last : por fin> <to be surprised at something : sorprenderse por algo> **4** : de <he's laughing at you : está riéndose de ti> **5** : para <you're good at this : eres bueno para esto>

at all *adv* : en absoluto, para nada

ate → **eat**

atheism *n* ['eɪθi,ɪzəm] : ateísmo *m*

atheist ['eɪθiɪst] *n* : ateo *m,* atea *f*

atheistic [,eɪθi'ɪstɪk] *adj* : ateo

athlete ['æθ,liːt] *n* : atleta *mf*

athletic [æθ'lɛt̬ɪk] *adj* : atlético

athletics [æθ'lɛt̬ɪks] *ns & pl* : atletismo *m*

atlas ['ætləs] *n* : atlas *m*

atmosphere ['ætmə,sfɪr] *n* **1** AIR : atmósfera *f,* aire *m* **2** AMBIENCE : ambiente *m,* atmósfera *f,* clima *m*

atmospheric [,ætmə'sfɪrɪk, -'sfɛr-] *adj* : atmosférico — **atmospherically** [-ɪkli] *adv*

atoll ['æ,tɔl, 'eɪ-, -,tɑl] *n* : atolón *m*

atom ['æt̬əm] *n* **1** : átomo *m* **2** SPECK : ápice *m,* pizca *f*

atomic [ə'tɑmɪk] *adj* : atómico

atomic bomb *n* : bomba *f* atómica
atomizer ['æt̬ə,maɪzər] *n* : atomizador *m,* pulverizador *m*
atone [ə'to:n] *vt* **atoned; atoning to atone for** : expiar
atonement [ə'to:nmənt] *n* : expiación *f,* desagravio *m*
atop[1] [ə'tɑp] *adj* : encima
atop[2] *prep* : encima de, sobre
atrium ['eɪtriəm] *n, pl* **atria** [-triə] *or* **atriums 1** : atrio *m* **2** : aurícula *f* (del corazón)
atrocious [ə'tro:ʃəs] *adj* : atroz — **atrociously** *adv*
atrocity [ə'trɑsət̬i] *n, pl* **-ties** : atrocidad *f*
atrophy[1] ['ætrəfi] *vt* **-phied; -phying** : atrofiar
atrophy[2] *n, pl* **-phies** : atrofia *f*
atropine ['ætrə,pi:n] *n* : atropina *f*
attach [ə'tætʃ] *vt* **1** FASTEN : sujetar, atar, amarrar, pegar **2** JOIN : juntar, adjuntar **3** ATTRIBUTE : dar, atribuir <I attached little importance to it : le di poca importancia> **4** SEIZE : embargar **5 to become attached to someone** : encariñarse con alguien
attaché [,æt̬ə'ʃeɪ, ,æ,tæ-, ə,tæ-] *n* : agregado *m,* -da *f*
attachment [ə'tætʃmənt] *n* **1** ACCESSORY : accesorio *m* **2** CONNECTION : conexión *f,* acoplamiento *m* **3** FONDNESS : apego *m,* cariño *m,* afición *f*
attack[1] [ə'tæk] *vt* **1** ASSAULT : atacar, asaltar, agredir **2** TACKLE : acometer, combatir, enfrentarse con
attack[2] *n* **1** : ataque *m,* asalto *m,* acometida *f* <to launch an attack : lanzar un ataque> **2** : ataque *m,* crisis *f* <heart attack : ataque cardíaco, infarto> <attack of nerves : crisis nerviosa>
attacker [ə'tækər] *n* : asaltante *mf*
attain [ə'teɪn] *vt* **1** ACHIEVE : lograr, conseguir, alcanzar, realizar **2** REACH : alcanzar, llegar a
attainable [ə'teɪnəbəl] *adj* : alcanzable, realizable, asequible
attainment [ə'teɪnmənt] *n* : logro *m,* consecución *f,* realización *f*
attempt[1] [ə'tɛmpt] *vt* : intentar, tratar de
attempt[2] *n* : intento *m,* tentativa *f*
attend [ə'tɛnd] *vt* **1** : asistir a <to attend a meeting : asistir a una reunión> **2** : atender, ocuparse de, cuidar <to attend a patient : atender a un paciente> **3** HEED : atender a, hacer caso de **4** ACCOMPANY : acompañar
attendance [ə'tɛndənts] *n* **1** ATTENDING : asistencia *f* **2** TURNOUT : concurrencia *f*
attendant[1] [ə'tɛndənt] *adj* : concomitante, inherente
attendant[2] *n* : asistente *mf,* acompañante *mf,* guarda *mf*
attention [ə'tɛntʃən] *n* **1** : atención *f* **2 to pay attention** : prestar atención, hacer caso **3 to stand at attention** : estar firme
attentive [ə'tɛntɪv] *adj* : atento — **attentively** *adv*
attentiveness [ə'tɛntɪvnəs] *n* **1** THOUGHTFULNESS : cortesía *f,* consideración *f* **2** CONCENTRATION : atención *f,* concentración *f*
attest [ə'tɛst] *vt* : atestiguar, dar fe de
attestation [,æ,tɛs'teɪʃən] *n* : testimonio *m*
attic ['ætɪk] *n* : ático *m,* desván *m,* buhardilla *f*
attire[1] [ə'taɪr] *vt* **-tired; -tiring** : ataviar
attire[2] *n* : atuendo *m,* atavío *m*
attitude ['æt̬ə,tu:d, -,tju:d] *n* **1** FEELING : actitud *f* **2** POSTURE : postura *f*
attorney [ə'tərni] *n, pl* **-neys** : abogado *m,* -da *f*
attract [ə'trækt] *vt* **1** : atraer **2 to attract attention** : llamar la atención
attraction [ə'trækʃən] *n* : atracción *f,* atractivo *m*
attractive [ə'træktɪv] *adj* : atractivo, atrayente
attractively [ə'træktɪvli] *adv* : de manera atractiva, de buen gusto, hermosamente
attractiveness [ə'træktɪvnəs] *n* : atractivo *m*
attributable [ə'trɪbjʊt̬əbəl] *adj* : atribuible, imputable
attribute[1] [ə'trɪ,bju:t] *vt* **-tributed; -tributing** : atribuir
attribute[2] ['ætrə,bju:t] *n* : atributo *m,* cualidad *f*
attribution [,ætrə'bju:ʃən] *n* : atribución *f*
attune [ə'tu:n, -'tju:n] *vt* **-tuned; -tuning 1** ADAPT : adaptar, adecuar **2 to be attuned to** : estar en armonía con
auburn ['ɔbərn] *adj* : castaño rojizo
auction[1] ['ɔkʃən] *vt* : subastar, rematar
auction[2] *n* : subasta *f,* remate *m*
auctioneer [,ɔkʃə'nɪr] *n* : subastador *m,* -dora *f;* rematador *m,* -dora *f*
audacious [ɔ'deɪʃəs] *adj* : audaz, atrevido
audacity [ɔ'dæsət̬i] *n, pl* **-ties** : audacia *f,* atrevimiento *m,* descaro *m*
audible ['ɔdəbəl] *adj* : audible — **audibly** [-bli] *adv*
audience ['ɔdiənts] *n* **1** INTERVIEW : audiencia *f* **2** PUBLIC : audiencia *f,* público *m,* auditorio *m,* espectadores *mpl*
audio[1] ['ɔdi,o:] *adj* : de sonido, de audio
audio[2] *n* : audio *m*
audiovisual [,ɔdio'vɪʒʊəl] *adj* : audiovisual
audit[1] ['ɔdət] *vt* **1** : auditar (finanzas) **2** : asistir como oyente a (una clase o un curso)
audit[2] *n* : auditoría *f*
audition[1] [ɔ'dɪʃən] *vi* : hacer una audición
audition[2] *n* : audición *f*

auditor [ˈɔdət̬ər] *n* **1** : auditor *m,* -tora *f* (de finanzas) **2** STUDENT : oyente *mf*
auditorium [ˌɔdəˈtoriəm] *n, pl* **-riums** *or* **-ria** [-riə] : auditorio *m,* sala *f*
auditory [ˈɔdəˌtori] *adj* : auditivo
auger [ˈɔgər] *n* : taladro *m,* barrena *f*
augment [ɔgˈmɛnt] *vt* : aumentar, incrementar
augmentation [ˌɔgmənˈteɪʃən] *n* : aumento *m,* incremento *m*
augur[1] [ˈɔgər] *vt* : augurar, presagiar — *vi* **to augur well** : ser de buen agüero
augur[2] *n* : augur *m*
augury [ˈɔgjʊri, -gər-] *n, pl* **-ries** : augurio *m,* presagio *m,* agüero *m*
august [ɔˈgʌst] *adj* : augusto
August [ˈɔgəst] *n* : agosto *m*
auk [ˈɔk] *n* : alca *f*
aunt [ˈænt, ˈant] *n* : tía *f*
aura [ˈɔrə] *n* : aura *f*
aural [ˈɔrəl] *adj* : auditivo
auricle [ˈɔrɪkəl] *n* : aurícula *f*
aurora borealis [əˈrorəˌboriˈæləs] *n* : aurora *f* boreal
auspices [ˈɔspəsəz, -ˌsiːz] *npl* : auspicios *mpl*
auspicious [ɔˈspɪʃəs] *adj* : prometedor, propicio, de buen augurio
austere [ɔˈstɪr] *adj* : austero, severo, adusto — **austerely** *adv*
austerity [ɔˈstɛrət̬i] *n, pl* **-ties** : austeridad *f*
Australian [ɔˈstreɪljən] *n* : australiano *m,* -na *f* — **Australian** *adj*
Austrian [ˈɔstriən] *n* : austriaco *m,* -ca *f* — **Austrian** *adj*
authentic [əˈθɛntɪk, ɔ-] *adj* : auténtico, genuino — **authentically** [-tɪkli] *adv*
authenticate [əˈθɛntɪˌkeɪt, ɔ-] *vt* **-cated; -cating** : autenticar, autentificar
authenticity [ɔˌθɛnˈtɪsət̬i] *n* : autenticidad *f*
author [ˈɔθər] *n* **1** WRITER : escritor *m,* -tora *f;* autor *m,* -tora *f* **2** CREATOR : autor *m,* -tora *f;* creador *m,* -dora *f;* artífice *mf*
authoritarian [ɔˌθɔrəˈtɛriən, ə-] *adj* : autoritario
authoritative [əˈθɔrəˌteɪt̬ɪv, ɔ-] *adj* **1** RELIABLE : fidedigno, autorizado **2** DICTATORIAL : autoritario, dictatorial, imperioso
authoritatively [əˈθɔrəˌteɪt̬ɪvli, ɔ-] *adv* **1** RELIABLY : con autoridad **2** DICTATORIALLY : de manera autoritaria
authority [əˈθɔrət̬i, ɔ-] *n, pl* **-ties 1** EXPERT : autoridad *f;* experto *m,* -ta *f* **2** POWER : autoridad *f,* poder *m* **3** AUTHORIZATION : autorización *f,* licencia *f* **4 the authorities** : las autoridades *fpl* **5 on good authority** : de buena fuente
authorization [ˌɔθərəˈzeɪʃən] *n* : autorización *f*
authorize [ˈɔθəˌraɪz] *vt* **-rized; -rizing** : autorizar, facultar
authorship [ˈɔθərˌʃɪp] *n* : autoría *f*
auto [ˈɔt̬o] → **automobile**
autobiographical [ˌɔt̬oˌbaɪəˈgræfɪkəl] *adj* : autobiográfico
autobiography [ˌɔt̬obaɪˈɑgrəfi] *n, pl* **-phies** : autobiografía *f*
autocracy [ɔˈtɑkrəsi] *n, pl* **-cies** : autocracia *f*
autocrat [ˈɔt̬əˌkræt] *n* : autócrata *mf*
autocratic [ˌɔt̬əˈkræt̬ɪk] *adj* : autocrático — **autocratically** [-t̬ɪkli] *adv*
autograph[1] [ˈɔt̬əˌgræf] *vt* : autografiar
autograph[2] *n* : autógrafo *m*
automate [ˈɔt̬əˌmeɪt] *vt* **-mated; -mating** : automatizar
automatic [ˌɔt̬əˈmæt̬ɪk] *adj* : automático — **automatically** [-t̬ɪkli] *adv*
automation [ˌɔt̬əˈmeɪʃən] *n* : automatización *f*
automaton [ɔˈtɑməˌtɑn] *n, pl* **-atons** *or* **-ata** [-tə, -ˌtɑ] : autómata *m*
automobile [ˌɔt̬əmoˈbiːl, -ˈmoːˌbiːl] *n* : automóvil *m,* auto *m,* carro *m,* coche *m*
automotive [ˌɔt̬əˈmoːt̬ɪv] *adj* : automotor
autonomous [ɔˈtɑnəməs] *adj* : autónomo — **autonomously** *adv*
autonomy [ɔˈtɑnəmi] *n, pl* **-mies** : autonomía *f*
autopsy [ˈɔˌtɑpsi, -təp-] *n, pl* **-sies** : autopsia *f*
autumn [ˈɔt̬əm] *n* : otoño *m*
autumnal [ɔˈtʌmnəl] *adj* : otoñal
auxiliary[1] [ɔgˈzɪljəri, -ˈzɪləri] *adj* : auxiliar
auxiliary[2] *n, pl* **-ries** : auxiliar *mf,* ayudante *mf*
avail[1] [əˈveɪl] *vt* **to avail oneself** : aprovecharse, valerse
avail[2] *n* **1** : provecho *m,* utilidad *f* **2 to no avail** : en vano **3 to be of no avail** : no servir de nada, ser inútil
availability [əˌveɪləˈbɪlət̬i] *n, pl* **-ties** : disponibilidad *f*
available [əˈveɪləbəl] *adj* : disponible
avalanche [ˈævəˌlæntʃ] *n* : avalancha *f,* alud *m*
avarice [ˈævərəs] *n* : avaricia *f,* codicia *f*
avaricious [ˌævəˈrɪʃəs] *adj* : avaricioso, codicioso
avenge [əˈvɛndʒ] *vt* **avenged; avenging** : vengar
avenger [əˈvɛndʒər] *n* : vengador *m,* -dora *f*
avenue [ˈævəˌnuː, -ˌnjuː] *n* **1** : avenida *f* **2** MEANS : vía *f,* camino *m*
average[1] [ˈævrɪdʒ, ˈævə-] *vt* **-aged; -aging 1** : hacer un promedio de <he averages 8 hours a day : hace un promedio de 8 horas diarias> **2** : calcular el promedio de, promediar (en matemáticas)
average[2] *adj* **1** MEAN : medio <the average temperature : la temperatura media> **2** ORDINARY : común, ordinario <the average man : el hombre común>

average[3] *n* : promedio *m*
averse [ə'vərs] *adj* : reacio, opuesto
aversion [ə'vərʒən] *n* : aversión *f*
avert [ə'vərt] *vt* **1** : apartar, desviar <he averted his eyes from the scene : apartó los ojos de la escena> **2** AVOID, PREVENT : evitar, prevenir
aviary ['eɪvi,ɛri] *n, pl* **-aries** : pajarera *f*
aviation [,eɪvi'eɪʃən] *n* : aviación *f*
aviator ['eɪvi,eɪt̬ər] *n* : aviador *m,* -dora *f*
avid ['ævɪd] *adj* **1** GREEDY : ávido, codicioso **2** ENTHUSIASTIC : ávido, entusiasta, ferviente — **avidly** *adv*
avocado [,ævə'kɑdo, ,ɑvə-] *n, pl* **-dos** : aguacate *m,* palta *f*
avocation [,ævə'keɪʃən] *n* : pasatiempo *m,* afición *f*
avoid [ə'vɔɪd] *vt* **1** SHUN : evitar, eludir **2** FORGO : evitar, abstenerse de <I always avoided gossip : siempre evitaba los chismes> **3** EVADE : evitar <if I can avoid it : si puedo evitarlo>
avoidable [ə'vɔɪdəbəl] *adj* : evitable
avoidance [ə'vɔɪdənts] *n* : el evitar
avoirdupois [,ævərdə'pɔɪz] *n* : sistema *m* inglés de pesos y medidas
avow [ə'vaʊ] *vt* : reconocer, confesar
avowal [ə'vaʊəl] *n* : reconocimiento *m,* confesión *f*
await [ə'weɪt] *vt* : esperar
awake[1] [ə'weɪk] *v* **awoke** [ə'wo:k]; **awoken** [ə'wo:kən] *or* **awaked; awaking** : despertar
awake[2] *adj* : despierto
awaken [ə'weɪkən] → **awake**[1]
award[1] [ə'wɔrd] *vt* : otorgar, conceder, conferir
award[2] *n* **1** PRIZE : premio *m,* galardón *m* **2** MEDAL : condecoración *f*
aware [ə'wær] *adj* : consciente <to be aware of : darse cuenta de, estar consciente de>
awareness [ə'wærnəs] *n* : conciencia *f,* conocimiento *m*
awash [ə'wɔʃ] *adj* : inundado
away[1] [ə'weɪ] *adv* **1** : de aquí <go away! : ¡fuera de aquí!, ¡vete!> **2** : de distancia <10 miles away : 10 millas de distancia, queda a 10 millas> **3 far away** : lejos, a lo lejos **4 right away** : en seguida, ahora mismo **5 to be away** : estar ausente, estar de viaje **6 to give away** : regalar (una posesión), revelar (un secreto) **7 to go away** : irse, largarse **8 to put away** : guardar **9 to turn away** : volver la cara
away[2] *adj* **1** ABSENT : ausente <away for the week : ausente por la semana> **2 away game** : partido *m* que se juega fuera
awe[1] ['ɔ] *vt* **awed; awing** : abrumar, asombrar, impresionar
awe[2] *n* : asombro *m*
awesome ['ɔsəm] *adj* **1** IMPOSING : imponente, formidable **2** AMAZING : asombroso
awestruck ['ɔ,strʌk] *adj* : asombrado
awful ['ɔfəl] *adj* **1** AWESOME : asombroso **2** DREADFUL : horrible, terrible, atroz **3** ENORMOUS : enorme, tremendo <an awful lot of people : muchísima gente, la mar de gente>
awfully ['ɔfəli] *adv* **1** EXTREMELY : terriblemente, extremadamente **2** BADLY : muy mal, espantosamente
awhile [ə'*h*waɪl] *adv* : un rato, algún tiempo
awkward ['ɔkwərd] *adj* **1** CLUMSY : torpe, desmañado **2** EMBARRASSING : embarazoso, delicado — **awkwardly** *adv*
awkwardness ['ɔkwərdnəs] *n* **1** CLUMSINESS : torpeza *f* **2** INCONVENIENCE : incomodidad *f*
awl ['ɔl] *n* : punzón *m*
awning ['ɔnɪŋ] *n* : toldo *m*
awry [ə'raɪ] *adj* 1 ASKEW : torcido **2 to go awry** : salir mal, fracasar
ax *or* **axe** ['æks] *n* : hacha *m*
axiom ['æksiəm] *n* : axioma *m*
axiomatic [,æksiə'mæt̬ɪk] *adj* : axiomático
axis ['æksɪs] *n, pl* **axes** [-,si:z] : eje *m*
axle ['æksəl] *n* : eje *m*
aye[1] ['aɪ] *adv* : sí
aye[2] *n* : sí *m*
azalea [ə'zeɪljə] *n* : azalea *f*
azimuth ['æzəməθ] *n* : azimut *m,* acimut *m*
azure[1] ['æʒər] *adj* : azur, celeste
azure[2] *n* : azur *m*

B

b ['bi:] *n, pl* **b's** *or* **bs** ['bi:z] : segunda letra del alfabeto inglés
babble[1] ['bæbəl] *vi* **-bled; -bling 1** PRATTLE : balbucear **2** CHATTER : charlatanear, parlotear *fam* **3** MURMUR : murmurar
babble[2] *n* : balbuceo *m* (de bebé), parloteo *m* (de adultos), murmullo *m* (de voces, de un arroyo)
babe ['beɪb] → **baby**[3]
babel ['beɪbəl, 'bæ-] *n* : babel *f,* caos *m*
baboon [bæ'bu:n] *n* : babuino *m*
baby[1] ['beɪbi] *vt* **-bied; -bying** : mimar, consentir
baby[2] *adj* **1** : de niño <a baby carriage : un cochecito> <baby talk : habla infantil> **2** TINY : pequeño, minúsculo
baby[3] *n, pl* **-bies** : bebé *m;* niño *m,* -ña *f*
babyhood ['beɪbi,hʊd] *n* : niñez *f,* primera infancia *f*
babyish ['beɪbiɪʃ] *adj* : infantil, pueril

baby–sit ['beɪbi,sɪt] *vi* **-sat** [-,sæt]; **-sitting** : cuidar niños, hacer de canguro *Spain*

baby–sitter ['beɪbi,sɪt̬ər] *n* : niñero *m,* -ra *f;* canguro *mf Spain*

baccalaureate [,bækə'lɔriət] *n* : licenciatura *f*

bachelor ['bætʃələr] *n* **1** : soltero *m* **2** : licenciado *m,* -da *f* <bachelor of arts degree : licenciatura en filosofía y letras>

bacillus [bə'sɪləs] *n, pl* **-li** [-,laɪ] : bacilo *m*

back[1] ['bæk] *vt* **1** *or* **to back up** SUPPORT : apoyar, respaldar **2** *or* **to back up** REVERSE : darle marcha atrás a (un vehículo) **3** : estar detrás de, formar el fondo de <trees back the garden : unos árboles están detrás del jardín> — *vi* **1** *or* **to back up** : retroceder **2** **to back away** : echarse atrás **3** **to back down** *or* **to back out** : volverse atrás, echarse para atrás

back[2] *adv* **1** : atrás, hacia atrás, detrás <to move back : moverse atrás> <back and forth : de acá para allá> **2** AGO : atrás, antes, ya <some years back : unos años atrás, ya unos años> <10 months back : hace diez meses> **3** : de vuelta, de regreso <we're back : estamos de vuelta> <she ran back : volvió corriendo> <to call back : llamar de nuevo>

back[3] *adj* **1** REAR : de atrás, posterior, trasero **2** OVERDUE : atrasado **3** **back pay** : atrasos *mpl*

back[4] *n* **1** : espalda *f* (de un ser humano), lomo *m* (de un animal) **2** : respaldo *m* (de una silla), espalda *f* (de ropa) **3** REVERSE : reverso *m,* dorso *m,* revés *m* **4** REAR : fondo *m,* parte *f* de atrás **5** : defensa *mf* (en deportes)

backache ['bæk,eɪk] *n* : dolor *m* de espalda

backbite ['bæk,baɪt] *v* **-bit** [-,bɪt]; **-bitten** [-,bɪtən]; **-biting** *vt* : calumniar, hablar mal de — *vi* : murmurar

backbiter ['bæk,baɪt̬ər] *n* : calumniador *m,* -dora *f*

backbone ['bæk,bo:n] *n* **1** : columna *f* vertebral **2** FIRMNESS : firmeza *f,* carácter *m*

backdrop ['bæk,drɑp] *n* : telón *m* de fondo

backer ['bækər] *n* **1** SUPPORTER : partidario *m,* -ria *f* **2** SPONSOR : patrocinador *m,* -dora *f*

backfire[1] ['bæk,faɪr] *vi* **-fired; -firing** **1** : petardear (dícese de un automóvil) **2** FAIL : fallar, salir el tiro por la culata

backfire[2] *n* : petardeo *m,* explosión *f*

background ['bæk,graʊnd] *n* **1** : fondo *m* (de un cuadro, etc.), antecedentes *mpl* (de una situación) **2** EXPERIENCE, TRAINING : experiencia *f* profesional, formación *f*

backhand[1] ['bæk,hænd] *adv* : de revés, con el revés

backhand[2] *n* : revés *m*

backhanded ['bæk,hændəd] *adj* **1** : dado con el revés, de revés **2** INDIRECT : indirecto, ambiguo

backing ['bækɪŋ] *n* **1** SUPPORT : apoyo *m,* respaldo *m* **2** REINFORCEMENT : refuerzo *m* **3** SUPPORTERS : partidarios *mpl,* -rias *fpl*

backlash ['bæk,læʃ] *n* : reacción *f* violenta

backlog ['bæk,lɔg] *n* : atraso *m,* trabajo *m* acumulado

backpack[1] ['bæk,pæk] *vi* : viajar con mochila

backpack[2] *n* : mochila *f*

backrest ['bæk,rɛst] *n* : respaldo *m*

backslide ['bæk,slaɪd] *vi* **-slid** [-,slɪd]; **-slid** *or* **-slidden** [-,slɪdən]; **-sliding** : recaer, reincidir

backstage [,bæk'steɪdʒ, 'bæk,-] *adv & adj* : entre bastidores

backtrack ['bæk,træk] *vi* : dar marcha atrás, volverse atrás

backup ['bæk,ʌp] *n* **1** SUPPORT : respaldo *m,* apoyo *m* **2** : copia *f* de seguridad (para computadoras)

backward[1] ['bækwərd] *or* **backwards** [-wərdz] *adv* **1** : hacia atrás **2** : de espaldas <he fell backwards : se cayó de espaldas> **3** : al revés <you're doing it backwards : lo estás haciendo al revés> **4** **to bend over backwards** : hacer todo lo posible

backward[2] *adj* **1** : hacia atrás <a backward glance : una mirada hacia atrás> **2** RETARDED : retrasado **3** SHY : tímido **4** UNDERDEVELOPED : atrasado

backwardness ['bækwərdnəs] *n* : atraso *m* (dícese de una región), retraso *m* (dícese de una persona)

backwoods [,bæk'wʊdz] *npl* : monte *m,* región *f* alejada

bacon ['beɪkən] *n* : tocino *m,* tocineta *f Col, Ven,* bacon *m Spain*

bacterial [bæk'tɪriəl] *adj* : bacteriano

bacteriologist [bæk,tɪri'ɑlədʒɪst] *n* : bacteriólogo *m,* -ga *f*

bacteriology [bæk,tɪri'ɑlədʒi] *n* : bacteriología *f*

bacterium [bæk'tɪriəm] *n, pl* **-ria** [-iə] : bacteria *f*

bad[1] ['bæd] *adv* → **badly**

bad[2] *adj* **1** : malo **2** ROTTEN : podrido **3** SERIOUS, SEVERE : grave **4** DEFECTIVE : defectuoso <a bad check : un cheque sin fondos> **5** HARMFUL : perjudicial **6** CORRUPT, EVIL : malo, corrompido **7** NAUGHTY : travieso **8** **from bad to worse** : de mal en peor **9** **too bad!** : ¡qué lástima!

bad[3] *n* : lo malo <the good and the bad : lo bueno y lo malo>

bade → **bid**

badge ['bædʒ] *n* : insignia *f,* botón *m,* chapa *f*

badger[1] ['bædʒər] *vt* : fastidiar, acosar, importunar

badger[2] *n* : tejón *m*

badly ['bædli] *adv* **1 :** mal **2** URGENTLY **:** mucho, con urgencia **3** SEVERELY **:** gravemente

badminton ['bæd,mɪntən, -,mɪt-] *n* **:** bádminton *m*

badness ['bædnəs] *n* **:** maldad *f*

baffle[1] ['bæfəl] *vi* **-fled; -fling 1** PERPLEX **:** desconcertar, confundir **2** FRUSTRATE **:** frustrar

baffle[2] *n* **:** deflector *m,* bafle *m* (acústico)

bafflement ['bæfəlmənt] *n* **:** desconcierto *m,* confusión *f*

bag[1] ['bæg] *v* **bagged; bagging** *vi* SAG **:** formar bolsas — *vt* **1 :** ensacar, poner en una bolsa **2 :** cobrar (en la caza), cazar

bag[2] *n* **1 :** bolsa *f,* saco *m* **2** HANDBAG **:** cartera *f,* bolso *m,* bolsa *f Mex* **3** SUITCASE **:** maleta *f,* valija *f*

bagatelle [,bægə'tɛl] *n* **:** bagatela *f*

bagel ['beɪgəl] *n* **:** rosquilla *f* de pan

baggage ['bægɪdʒ] *n* **:** equipaje *m*

baggy ['bægi] *adj* **-gier; -est :** holgado, ancho

bagpipe ['bæg,paɪp] *n* **:** gaita *f*

bail[1] ['beɪl] *vt* **1 :** achicar (agua de un bote) **2 to bail out :** poner en libertad (de una cárcel) bajo fianza **3 to bail out** EXTRICATE **:** sacar de apuros

bail[2] *n* **:** fianza *f,* caución *f*

bailiff ['beɪləf] *n* **:** aguacil *mf*

bailiwick ['beɪli,wɪk] *n* **:** dominio *m*

bailout ['beɪl,aʊt] *n* **:** rescate *m* (financial)

bait[1] ['beɪt] *vt* **1 :** cebar (un anzuelo o cepo) **2** HARASS **:** acosar

bait[2] *n* **:** cebo *m,* carnada *f*

bake[1] ['beɪk] *vt* **baked; baking :** hornear, hacer al horno

bake[2] *n* **:** fiesta con platos hechos al horno

baker ['beɪkər] *n* **:** panadero *m,* -ra *f*

baker's dozen *n* **:** docena *f* de fraile

bakery ['beɪkəri] *n, pl* **-ries :** panadería *f*

bakeshop ['beɪk,ʃɑp] *n* **:** pastelería *f,* panadería *f*

baking powder *n* **:** levadura *f* en polvo

baking soda → **sodium bicarbonate**

balance[1] ['bæləntS] *v* **-anced; -ancing** *vt* **1 :** hacer el balance de (una cuenta) <to balance the books : cuadrar las cuentas> **2** EQUALIZE **:** balancear, equilibrar **3** HARMONIZE **:** armonizar — *vi* **:** balancearse

balance[2] *n* **1** SCALES **:** balanza *f,* báscula *f* **2** COUNTERBALANCE **:** contrapeso *m* **3** EQUILIBRIUM **:** equilibrio *m* **4** REMAINDER **:** balance *m,* resto *m*

balanced ['bæləntst] *adj* **:** equilibrado, balanceado

balcony ['bælkəni] *n, pl* **-nies 1 :** balcón *m,* terraza *f* (de un edificio) **2 :** galería *f* (de un teatro)

bald ['bɔld] *adj* **1 :** calvo, pelado, pelón **2** PLAIN **:** simple, puro <the bald truth : la pura verdad>

balding ['bɔldɪŋ] *adj* **:** quedándose calvo

baldly ['bɔldli] *adv* **:** sin reparos, sin rodeos, francamente

baldness ['bɔldnəs] *n* **:** calvicie *f*

bale[1] ['beɪl] *vt* **baled; baling :** empacar, hacer balas de

bale[2] *n* **:** bala *f,* fardo *m,* paca *f*

baleful ['beɪlfəl] *adj* **1** DEADLY **:** mortífero **2** SINISTER **:** siniestro, funesto, torvo <a baleful glance : una mirada torva>

balk[1] ['bɔk] *vt* **:** obstaculizar, impedir — *vi* **1 :** plantarse *fam* (dícese de un caballo, etc.) **2 to balk at :** resistarse a, mostrarse reacio a

balk[2] *n* **:** obstáculo *m*

Balkan ['bɔlkən] *adj* **:** balcánico

balky ['bɔki] *adj* **balkier; -est :** reacio, obstinado, terco

ball[1] ['bɔl] *vt* **:** apelotonar, ovillar

ball[2] *n* **1 :** pelota *f,* bola *f,* balón *m,* ovillo *m* (de lana) **2 :** juego *m* con pelota o bola **3** DANCE **:** baile *m,* baile *m* de etiqueta

ballad ['bæləd] *n* **:** romance *m,* balada *f*

balladeer [,bælə'dɪr] *n* **:** cantante *mf* de baladas

ballast[1] ['bæləst] *vt* **:** lastrear

ballast[2] *n* **:** lastre *m*

ball bearing *n* **:** cojinete *m* de bola

ballerina [,bælə'ri:nə] *n* **:** bailarina *f*

ballet [bæ'leɪ, 'bæ,leɪ] *n* **:** ballet *m*

ballistic [bə'lɪstɪk] *adj* **:** balístico

ballistics [bə'lɪstɪks] *ns & pl* **:** balística *f*

balloon[1] [bə'lu:n] *vi* **1 :** viajar en globo **2** SWELL **:** hincharse, inflarse

balloon[2] *n* **:** globo *m*

balloonist [bə'lu:nɪst] *n* **:** aeróstata *mf*

ballot[1] ['bælət] *vi* **:** votar

ballot[2] *n* **1 :** papeleta *f* (de voto) **2** BALLOTING **:** votación *f* **3** VOTE **:** voto *m*

ballpoint pen ['bɔl,pɔɪnt] *n* **:** bolígrafo *m*

ballroom ['bɔl,ru:m, -,rʊm] *n* **:** sala *f* de baile

ballyhoo ['bæli,hu:] *n* **:** propaganda *f,* publicidad *f,* bombo *m fam*

balm ['bɑm, 'bɑlm] *n* **:** bálsamo *m,* ungüento *m*

balmy ['bɑmi, 'bɑl-] *adj* **balmier; -est 1** MILD **:** templado, agradable **2** SOOTHING **:** balsámico **3** CRAZY **:** chiflado *fam,* chalado *fam*

baloney [bə'lo:ni] *n* NONSENSE **:** tonterías *fpl,* estupideces *fpl*

balsa ['bɔlsə] *n* **:** balsa *f*

balsam ['bɔlsəm] *n* **1 :** bálsamo *m* **2** *or* **balsam fir :** abeto *m* balsámico

baluster ['bæləstər] *n* **:** balaustre *m*

balustrade ['bælə,streɪd] *n* **:** balaustrada *f*

bamboo [bæm'bu:] *n* **:** bambú *m*

bamboozle [bæm'bu:zəl] *vt* **-zled; -zling :** engañar, embaucar

ban[1] ['bæn] *vt* **banned; banning :** prohibir, proscribir

ban[2] *n* : prohibición *f,* proscripción *f*
banal [bə'nɑl, bə'næl, 'beɪnəl] *adj* : banal, trivial
banality [bə'næləti] *n, pl* **-ties** : banalidad *f,* trivialidad *f*
banana [bə'nænə] *n* : banano *m,* plátano *m,* banana *f,* cambur *m Ven,* guineo *m Car*
band[1] ['bænd] *vt* **1** BIND : fajar, atar **2 to band together** : unirse, juntarse
band[2] *n* **1** STRIP : banda *f,* cinta *f* (de un sombrero, etc.) **2** STRIPE : franja *f* **3** : banda *f* (de radiofrecuencia) **4** RING : anillo *m* **5** GROUP : banda *f,* grupo *m,* conjunto *m* <jazz band : conjunto de jazz>
bandage[1] ['bændɪdʒ] *vt* **-daged; -daging** : vendar
bandage[2] *n* : vendaje *m,* venda *f*
bandanna *or* **bandana** [bæn'dænə] *n* : pañuelo *m* (de colores)
bandit ['bændət] *n* : bandido *m,* -da *f;* bandolero *m,* -ra *f*
banditry ['bændətri] *n* : bandolerismo *m,* bandidaje *m*
bandstand ['bænd,stænd] *n* : quiosco *m* de música
bandwagon ['bænd,wægən] *n* **1** : carroza *f* de músicos **2 to jump on the bandwagon** : subirse al carro, seguir la moda
bandy[1] ['bændi] *vt* **-died; -dying 1** EXCHANGE : intercambiar **2 to bandy about** : circular, propagar
bandy[2] *adj* : arqueado, torcido <bandy-legged : de piernas arqueadas>
bane ['beɪn] *n* **1** POISON : veneno *m* **2** RUIN : ruina *f,* pesadilla *f*
baneful ['beɪnfəl] *adj* : nefasto, funesto
bang[1] ['bæŋ] *vt* **1** STRIKE : golpear, darse <he banged his elbow against the door : se dio con el codo en la puerta> **2** SLAM : cerrar (la puerta) con un portazo — *vi* **1** SLAM : cerrarse de un golpe **2 to bang on** : aporrear, golpear <she was banging on the table : aporreaba la mesa>
bang[2] *adv* : directamente, exactamente
bang[3] *n* **1** BLOW : golpe *m,* porrazo *m,* trancazo *m* **2** EXPLOSION : explosión *f,* estallido *m* **3** SLAM : portazo *m* **4 bangs** *npl* : flequilla *f,* fleco *m*
Bangladeshi [,bɑŋglə'dɛʃi, ,bæŋ-, ,bʌŋ-, -'deɪ-] *n* : bangladesí *mf* — **Bangladeshi** *adj*
bangle ['bæŋgəl] *n* : brazalete *m,* pulsera *f*
banish ['bænɪʃ] *vt* **1** EXILE : desterrar, exiliar **2** EXPEL : expulsar
banishment ['bænɪʃmənt] *n* **1** EXILE : destierro *m,* exilio *m* **2** EXPULSION : expulsión *f*
banister ['bænəstər] *n* **1** BALUSTER : balaustre *m* **2** HANDRAIL : pasamanos *m,* barandilla *f,* barandal *m*
banjo ['bæn,dʒoː] *n, pl* **-jos** : banjo *m*
bank[1] ['bæŋk] *vt* **1** TILT : peraltar (una carretera), ladear (un avión) **2** HEAP : amontonar **3** : cubrir (un fuego) **4** : depositar (dinero en un banco) — *vi* **1** : ladearse (dícese de un avión) **2** : tener una cuenta (en un banco) **3 to bank on** : contar con
bank[2] *n* **1** MASS : montón *m,* montículo *m,* masa *f* **2** : orilla *f,* ribera *f* (de un río) **3** : peralte *m* (de una carretera) **4** : banco *m* <World Bank : Banco Mundial> <banco de sangre : blood bank>
bankbook ['bæŋk,bʊk] *n* : libreta *f* bancaria, libreta *f* de ahorros
banker ['bæŋkər] *n* : banquero *m,* -ra *f*
bankrupt[1] ['bæŋ,krʌpt] *vt* : hacer quebrar, llevar a la quiebra, arruinar
bankrupt[2] *adj* **1** : en bancarrota, en quiebra **2 ~ of** LACKING : carente de, falto de
bankrupt[3] *n* : fallido *m,* -da *f;* quebrado *m,* -da *f*
bankruptcy ['bæŋ,krʌptsi] *n, pl* **-cies** : ruina *f,* quiebra *f,* bancarrota *f*
banner[1] ['bænər] *adj* : excelente
banner[2] *n* : estandarte *m,* bandera *f*
banns ['bænz] *npl* : amonestaciones *fpl*
banquet[1] ['bæŋkwət] *vi* : celebrar un banquete
banquet[2] *n* : banquete *m*
banter[1] ['bæntər] *vi* : bromear, hacer bromas
banter[2] *n* : bromas *fpl*
baptism ['bæp,tɪzəm] *n* : bautismo *m*
baptismal [bæp'tɪzməl] *adj* : bautismal
baptize [bæp'taɪz, 'bæp,taɪz] *vt* **-tized; -tizing** : bautizar
bar[1] ['bɑr] *vt* **barred; barring 1** OBSTRUCT : obstruir, bloquear **2** EXCLUDE : excluir **3** PROHIBIT : prohibir **4** SECURE : atrancar, asegurar <bar the door! : ¡atranca la puerta!>
bar[2] *n* **1** : barra *f,* barrote *m* (de una ventana), tranca *f* (de una puerta) **2** BARRIER : barrera *f,* obstáculo *m* **3** LAW : abogacía *f* **4** STRIPE : franja *f* **5** COUNTER : mostrador *m,* barra *f* **6** TAVERN : bar *m,* taberna *f*
bar[3] *prep* **1** : excepto, con excepción de **2 bar none** : sin excepción
barb ['bɑrb] *n* **1** POINT : púa *f,* lengüeta *f* **2** GIBE : pulla *f*
barbarian[1] [bɑr'bæriən] *adj* **1** : bárbaro **2** CRUDE : tosco, bruto
barbarian[2] *n* : bárbaro *m,* -ra *f*
barbaric [bɑr'bærɪk] *adj* **1** PRIMITIVE : primitivo **2** CRUEL : brutal, cruel
barbarity [bɑr'bærəti] *n, pl* **-ties** : barbaridad *f*
barbarous ['bɑrbərəs] *adj* **1** UNCIVILIZED : bárbaro **2** MERCILESS : despiadado, cruel
barbarously ['bɑrbərəsli] *adv* : bárbaramente

barbecue[1] [ˈbɑrbɪˌkjuː] *vt* **-cued; -cuing :** asar a la parrilla
barbecue[2] *n* **:** barbacoa *f,* parrillada *f*
barber [ˈbɑrbər] *n* **:** barbero *m,* -ra *f*
barbiturate [bɑrˈbɪtʃərət] *n* **:** barbitúrico *m*
bard [ˈbɑrd] *n* **:** bardo *m*
bare[1] [ˈbær] *vt* **bared; baring :** desnudar
bare[2] *adj* **1** NAKED **:** desnudo **2** EXPOSED **:** descubierto, sin protección **3** EMPTY **:** desprovisto, vacío **4** MINIMUM **:** mero, mínimo <the bare necessities : las necesidades mínimas> **5** PLAIN **:** puro, sencillo
bareback [ˈbærˌbæk] *or* **barebacked** [-ˌbækt] *adv & adj* **:** a pelo
barefaced [ˈbærˌfeɪst] *adj* **:** descarado
barefoot [ˈbærˌfʊt] *or* **barefooted** [-ˌfʊt̬əd] *adv & adj* **:** descalzo
bareheaded [ˈbærˈhɛdəd] *adv & adj* **:** sin sombrero, con la cabeza descubierta
barely [ˈbærli] *adv* **:** apenas, por poco
bareness [ˈbærnəs] *n* **:** desnudez *f*
bargain[1] [ˈbɑrgən] *vi* HAGGLE **:** regatear, negociar — *vt* BARTER **:** trocar, cambiar
bargain[2] *n* **1** AGREEMENT **:** acuerdo *m,* convenio *m* <to strike a bargain : cerrar un trato> **2 :** ganga *f* <bargain price : precio de ganga>
barge[1] [ˈbɑrdʒ] *vi* **barged; barging 1 :** mover con torpeza **2 to barge in :** entrometerse, interrumpir
barge[2] *n* **:** barcaza *f,* gabarra *f*
bar graph *n* **:** gráfico *m* de barras
baritone [ˈbærəˌtoːn] *n* **:** barítono *m*
barium [ˈbæriəm] *n* **:** bario *m*
bark[1] [ˈbɑrk] *vi* **:** ladrar — *vt or* **to bark out :** gritar <to bark out an order : dar una orden a gritos>
bark[2] *n* **1 :** ladrido *m* (de un perro) **2 :** corteza *f* (de un árbol) **3** *or* **barque :** tipo de embarcación con velas de proa y popa
barley [ˈbɑrli] *n* **:** cebada *f*
barn [ˈbɑrn] *n* **:** granero *m* (para cosechas), establo *m* (para ganado)
barnacle [ˈbɑrnɪkəl] *n* **:** percebe *m*
barnyard [ˈbɑrnˌjɑrd] *n* **:** corral *m*
barometer [bəˈrɑmət̬ər] *n* **:** barómetro *m*
barometric [ˌbærəˈmɛtrɪk] *adj* **:** barométrico
baron [ˈbærən] *n* **1 :** barón *m* **2** TYCOON **:** magnate *mf*
baroness [ˈbærənɪs, -nəs, -ˌnɛs] *n* **:** baronesa *f*
baronet [ˌbærəˈnɛt, ˈbærənət] *n* **:** baronet *m*
baronial [bəˈroːniəl] *adj* **1 :** de barón **2** STATELY **:** señorial, majestuoso
baroque [bəˈroːk, -ˈrɑk] *adj* **:** barroco
barracks [ˈbærəks] *ns & pl* **:** cuartel *m*
barracuda [ˌbærəˈkuːdə] *n, pl* **-da** *or* **-das :** barracuda *f*
barrage [bəˈrɑʒ, -ˈrɑdʒ] *n* **1 :** descarga *f* (de artillería) **2** DELUGE **:** aluvión *m* <a barrage of questions : un aluvión de preguntas>
barred [ˈbɑrd] *adj* **:** excluido, prohibido
barrel[1] [ˈbærəl] *v* **-reled** *or* **-relled; -reling** *or* **-relling** *vt* **:** embarrilar — *vi* **:** ir disparado
barrel[2] *n* **1 :** barril *m,* tonel *m* **2 :** cañón *m* (de un arma de fuego), cilindro *m* (de una cerradura)
barren [ˈbærən] *adj* **1** STERILE **:** estéril (dícese de las plantas o la mujer), árido (dícese del suelo) **2** DESERTED **:** yermo, desierto
barrette [bɑˈrɛt, bə-] *n* **:** pasador *m,* broche *m* para el cabello
barricade[1] [ˈbærəˌkeɪd, ˌbærəˈ-] *vt* **-caded; -cading :** cerrar con barricadas
barricade[2] *n* **:** barricada *f*
barrier [ˈbæriər] *n* **1 :** barrera *f* **2** OBSTACLE **:** obstáculo *m,* impedimento *m*
barring [ˈbɑrɪŋ] *prep* **:** excepto, salvo, a excepción de
barrio [ˈbɑrio, ˈbær-] *n* **:** barrio *m*
barroom [ˈbɑrˌruːm, -ˌrʊm] *n* **:** bar *m*
barrow [ˈbærˌoː] → **wheelbarrow**
bartender [ˈbɑrˌtɛndər] *n* **:** camarero *m,* -ra *f;* barman *m*
barter[1] [ˈbɑrt̬ər] *vt* **:** cambiar, trocar
barter[2] *n* **:** trueque *m,* permuta *f*
basalt [bəˈsɔlt, ˈbeɪˌ-] *n* **:** basalto *m*
base[1] [ˈbeɪs] *vt* **based; basing :** basar, fundamentar, establecer
base[2] *adj* **baser; basest 1 :** de baja ley (dícese de un metal) **2** CONTEMPTIBLE **:** vil, despreciable
base[3] *n, pl* **bases :** base *f*
baseball [ˈbeɪsˌbɔl] *n* **:** beisbol *m,* béisbol *m*
baseless [ˈbeɪsləs] *adj* **:** infundado
basely [ˈbeɪsli] *adv* **:** vilmente
basement [ˈbeɪsmənt] *n* **:** sótano *m*
baseness [ˈbeɪsnəs] *n* **:** vileza *f,* bajeza *f*
bash[1] [ˈbæʃ] *vt* **:** golpear violentamente
bash[2] *n* **1** BLOW **:** golpe *m,* porrazo *m,* madrazo *m Mex fam* **2** PARTY**:** fiesta *f,* juerga *f fam*
bashful [ˈbæʃfəl] *adj* **:** tímido, vergonzoso, penoso
bashfulness [ˈbæʃfəlnəs] *n* **:** timidez *f*
basic [ˈbeɪsɪk] *adj* **1** FUNDAMENTAL **:** básico, fundamental **2** RUDIMENTARY **:** básico, elemental **3 :** básico (en química)
basically [ˈbeɪsɪkli] *adv* **:** fundamentalmente
basil [ˈbeɪzəl, ˈbæzəl] *n* **:** albahaca *f*
basilica [bəˈsɪlɪkə] *n* **:** basílica *f*
basin [ˈbeɪsən] *n* **1** WASHBOWL **:** palangana *f,* lavamanos *m,* lavabo *m* **2 :** cuenca *f* (de un río)
basis [ˈbeɪsəs] *n, pl* **bases** [-ˌsiːz] **1** BASE **:** base *f,* pilar *m* **2** FOUNDATION **:** fundamento *m,* base *f* **3 on a weekly basis :** semanalmente

bask [ˈbæsk] *vi* **:** disfrutar, deleitarse <to bask in the sun : disfrutar del sol>

basket [ˈbæskət] *n* **:** cesta *f,* cesto *m,* canasta *f*

basketball [ˈbæskətˌbɔl] *n* **:** baloncesto *m,* basquetbol *m*

bas–relief [ˌbɑrɪˈliːf] *n* **:** bajorrelieve *m*

bass[1] [ˈbæs] *n, pl* **bass** *or* **basses** **:** róbalo *m* (pesca)

bass[2] [ˈbeɪs] *n* **:** bajo *m* (tono, voz, cantante)

bass drum *n* **:** bombo *m*

basset hound [ˈbæsətˌhaʊnd] *n* **:** basset *m*

bassinet [ˌbæsəˈnɛt] *n* **:** moisés *m,* cuna *f*

bassoon [bəˈsuːn, bæ-] *n* **:** fagot *m*

bass viol [ˈbeɪsˈvaɪəl, -ˌoːl] → **double bass**

bastard[1] [ˈbæstərd] *adj* **:** bastardo

bastard[2] *n* **:** bastardo *m,* -da *f*

bastardize [ˈbæstərˌdaɪz] *vt* **-ized; -izing** DEBASE **:** degradar, envilecer

baste [ˈbeɪst] *vt* **basted; basting 1** STITCH **:** hilvanar **2 :** bañar (con su jugo durante la cocción)

bastion [ˈbæstʃən] *n* **:** bastión *m,* baluarte *m*

bat[1] [ˈbæt] *vt* **batted; batting 1** HIT **:** batear **2 without batting an eye :** sin pestañear

bat[2] *n* **1 :** murciélago *m* (animal) **2 :** bate *m* <baseball bat : bate de beisbol>

batch [ˈbætʃ] *n* **:** hornada *f,* tanda *f,* grupo *m,* cantidad *f*

bate [ˈbeɪt] *vt* **bated; bating 1 :** aminorar, reducir **2 with bated breath :** con ansiedad, aguantando la respiración

bath [ˈbæθ, ˈbaθ] *n, pl* **baths** [ˈbæðz, ˈbæθs, ˈbaðz, ˈbaθs] **1** BATHING **:** baño *m* <to take a bath : bañarse> **2 :** baño *m* (en fotografía, etc.) **3** BATHROOM **:** baño *m,* cuarto *m* de baño **4** SPA **:** balneario *m* **5** LOSS **:** pérdida *f*

bathe [ˈbeɪð] *v* **bathed; bathing** *vt* **1** WASH **:** bañar, lavar **2** SOAK **:** poner en remojo **3** FLOOD **:** inundar <to bathe with light : inundar de luz> — *vi* **:** bañarse, ducharse

bather [ˈbeɪðər] *n* **:** bañista *mf*

bathrobe [ˈbæθˌroːb] *n* **:** bata *f* (de baño)

bathroom [ˈbæθˌruːm, -ˌrʊm] *n* **:** baño *m,* cuarto *m* de baño

bathtub [ˈbæθˌtʌb] *n* **:** bañera *f,* tina *f* (de baño)

batiste [bəˈtiːst] *n* **:** batista *f*

baton [bəˈtɑn] *n* **:** batuta *f,* bastón *m*

battalion [bəˈtæljən] *n* **:** batallón *m*

batten [ˈbætən] *vt* **to batten down the hatches :** cerrar las escotillas

batter[1] [ˈbæt̬ər] *vt* **1** BEAT **:** aporrear, golpear **2** MISTREAT **:** maltratar

batter[2] *n* **1 :** masa *f* para rebozar **2** HITTER **:** bateador *m,* -dora *f*

battering ram *n* **:** ariete *m*

battery [ˈbæt̬əri] *n, pl* **-teries 1 :** lesiones *fpl* <assault and battery : agresión con lesiones> **2** ARTILLERY **:** batería *f* **3 :** batería *f,* pila *f* (de electricidad) **4** SERIES **:** serie *f*

batting [ˈbæt̬ɪŋ] *n* **1** *or* **cotton batting :** algodón *m* en láminas **2 :** bateo *m* (en beisbol)

battle[1] [ˈbæt̬əl] *vi* **-tled; -tling :** luchar, pelear

battle[2] *n* **:** batalla *f,* lucha *f,* pelea *f*

battle–ax [ˈbæt̬əlˌæks] *n* **:** hacha *f* de guerra

battlefield [ˈbæt̬əlˌfɪːld] *n* **:** campo *m* de batalla

battlements [ˈbæt̬əlmənts] *npl* **:** almenas *fpl*

battleship [ˈbæt̬əlˌʃɪp] *n* **:** acorazado *m*

batty [ˈbæt̬i] *adj* **-tier; -est :** chiflado *fam,* chalado *fam*

bauble [ˈbɔbəl] *n* **:** chuchería *f,* baratija *f*

bawdiness [ˈbɔdinəs] *n* **:** picardía *f*

bawdy [ˈbɔdi] *adj* **bawdier; -est :** subido de tono, verde, colorado *Mex*

bawl[1] [ˈbɔl] *vi* **:** llorar a gritos

bawl[2] *n* **:** grito *m,* alarido *m*

bawl out *vt* SCOLD **:** regañar

bay[1] [ˈbeɪ] *vi* HOWL **:** aullar

bay[2] *adj* **:** castaño, zaino (dícese de los caballos)

bay[3] *n* **1 :** bahía *f* <Bay of Campeche : Bahía de Campeche> **2** *or* **bay horse :** caballo *m* castaño **3** LAUREL **:** laurel *m* **4** HOWL **:** aullido *m* **5 :** saliente *m* <bay window : ventana en saliente> **6** COMPARTMENT **:** área *f,* compartimento *m* **7 at ~ :** acorralado

bayberry [ˈbeɪˌbɛri] *n, pl* **-ries :** arrayán *m* brabántico

bayonet[1] [ˌbeɪəˈnɛt, ˈbeɪəˌnɛt] *vt* **-neted; -neting :** herir (*o* matar) con bayoneta

bayonet[2] *n* **:** bayoneta *f*

bayou [ˈbaɪˌuː, -ˌoː] *n* **:** pantano *m*

bazaar [bəˈzɑr] *n* **1 :** bazar *m* **2** SALE **:** venta *f* benéfica

bazooka [bəˈzuːkə] *n* **:** bazuca *f*

BB [ˈbiːbi] *n* **:** balín *m*

be [ˈbiː] *v* **was** [ˈwəz, ˈwɑz], **were** [ˈwər]; **been** [ˈbɪn]; **being; am** [ˈæm], **is** [ˈɪz], **are** [ˈɑr] *vi* **1** (*expressing equality*) **:** ser <José is a doctor : José es doctor> <I'm Ana's sister : soy la hermana de Ana> **2** (*expressing quality*) **:** ser <the tree is tall : el árbol es alto> <you're silly! : ¡eres tonto!> **3** (*expressing origin or possession*) **:** ser <she's from Managua : es de Managua> <it's mine : es mío> **4** (*expressing location*) **:** estar <my mother is at home : mi madre está en casa> <the cups are on the table : las tazas están en la mesa> **5** (*expressing existence*) **:** ser, existir <to be or not to be : ser, o no ser> <I think, therefore I am : pienso, luego existo> **6** (*expressing a state of being*)

: estar, tener <how are you? : ¿cómo estás?> <I'm cold : tengo frío> <she's 10 years old : tiene 10 años> <they're both sick : están enfermos los dos> — *v impers* **1** (*indicating time*) : ser <it's eight o'clock : son las ocho> <it's Friday : hoy es viernes> **2** (*indicating a condition*) : hacer, estar <it's sunny : hace sol> <it's very dark outside : está bien oscuro afuera> — *v aux* **1** (*expressing progression*) : estar <what are you doing? —I'm working : ¿qué haces? —estoy trabajando> **2** (*expressing occurrence*) : ser <it was finished yesterday : fue acabado ayer, se acabó ayer> <it was cooked in the oven : se cocinó en el horno> **3** (*expressing possibility*) : poderse <can she be trusted? : ¿se puede confiar en ella?> **4** (*expressing obligation*) : deber <you are to stay here : debes quedarte aquí> <he was to come yesterday : se esperaba que viniese ayer>

beach[1] [ˈbiːtʃ] *vt* : hacer embarrancar, hacer varar, hacer encallar

beach[2] *n* : playa *f*

beachcomber [ˈbiːtʃˌkoːmər] *n* : raquero *m,* -ra *f*

beachhead [ˈbiːtʃˌhɛd] *n* : cabeza *f* de playa

beacon [ˈbiːkən] *n* : faro *m*

bead[1] [ˈbiːd] *vi* : formarse en gotas

bead[2] *n* **1** : cuenta *f* **2** DROP : gota *f* **3 beads** *npl* NECKLACE : collar *m*

beady [ˈbiːdi] *adj* **beadier; -est 1** : de forma de cuenta **2 beady eyes** : ojos *mpl* pequeños y brillantes

beagle [ˈbiːgəl] *n* : beagle *m*

beak [ˈbiːk] *n* : pico *m*

beaker [ˈbiːkər] *n* **1** CUP : taza *f* alta **2** : vaso *m* de precipitados (en un laboratorio)

beam[1] [ˈbiːm] *vi* **1** SHINE : brillar **2** SMILE : sonreír radiantemente — *vt* BROADCAST : transmitir, emitir

beam[2] *n* **1** : viga *f,* barra *f* **2** RAY : rayo *m,* haz *m* de luz **3** : haz *m* de radiofaro (para guiar pilotos, etc.)

bean [ˈbiːn] *n* **1** : habichuela *f,* frijol *m* **2 broad bean** : haba *f* **3 string bean** : judía *f*

bear[1] [ˈbær] *v* **bore** [ˈbor]; **borne** [ˈbɔrn]; **bearing** *vt* **1** CARRY : llevar, portar **2** : dar a luz a (un niño) **3** PRODUCE : dar (frutas, cosechas) **4** ENDURE, SUPPORT : soportar, resistir, aguantar — *vi* **1** TURN : doblar, dar la vuelta <bear right : doble a la derecha> **2 to bear up** : resistir

bear[2] *n, pl* **bears** *or* **bear** : oso *m,* osa *f*

bearable [ˈbærəbəl] *adj* : soportable

beard [ˈbɪrd] *n* **1** : barba *f* **2** : arista *f* (de plantas)

bearded [ˈbɪrdəd] *adj* : barbudo, de barba

bearer [ˈbærər] *n* : portador *m,* -dora *f*

bearing [ˈbærɪŋ] *n* **1** CONDUCT, MANNERS : comportamiento *m,* modales *mpl* **2** SUPPORT : soporte *f* **3** SIGNIFICANCE : relacíon *f,* importancia *f* <to have no bearing on : no tener nada que ver con> **4** : cojinete *m,* rodamiento *m* (de una máquina) **5** COURSE, DIRECTION : dirección *f,* rumbo *m* <to get one's bearings : orientarse>

beast [ˈbiːst] *n* **1** : bestia *f,* fiera *f* <beast of burden : animal de carga> **2** BRUTE : bruto *m,* -ta *f;* bestia *mf*

beastly [ˈbiːstli] *adj* : detestable, repugnante

beat[1] [ˈbiːt] *v* **beat; beaten** [ˈbiːtən] *or* **beat; beating** *vt* **1** STRIKE : golpear, pegar, darle una paliza (a alguien) **2** DEFEAT : vencer, derrotar **3** AVOID : anticiparse a, evitar <to beat the crowd : evitar el gentío> **4** MASH, WHIP : batir — *vi* THROB : palpitar, latir

beat[2] *adj* EXHAUSTED : derrengado, muy cansado <I'm beat! : ¡estoy molido!>

beat[3] *n* **1** : golpe *m,* redoble *m* (de un tambor), latido *m* (del corazón) **2** RHYTHM : ritmo *m,* tiempo *m*

beater [ˈbiːtər] *n* **1** : batidor *m,* -dora *f* **2** EGGBEATER : batidor *m*

beatific [ˌbiːəˈtɪfɪk] *adj* : beatífico

beatitude [biˈætəˌtuːd] *n* **1** : beatitud *f* **2 the Beatitudes** : las bienaventuranzas

beau [ˈboː] *n, pl* **beaux** *or* **beaus** : pretendiente *m,* galán *m*

beautification [ˌbjuːtəfəˈkeɪʃən] *n* : embellecimiento *m*

beautiful [ˈbjuːtɪfəl] *adj* : hermoso, bello, lindo, precioso

beautifully [ˈbjuːtɪfəli] *adv* **1** ATTRACTIVELY : hermosamente **2** EXCELLENTLY : maravillosamente, excelentemente

beauty [ˈbjuːti] *n, pl* **-ties** : belleza *f,* hermosura *f,* beldad *f*

beauty shop *or* **beauty salon** *n* : salón *m* de belleza

beaver [ˈbiːvər] *n* : castor *m*

because [bɪˈkʌz, -ˈkɔz] *conj* : porque

because of *prep* : por, a causa de, debido a

beck [ˈbɛk] *n* **to be at the beck and call of** : estar a la entera disposición de, estar sometido a la voluntad de

beckon [ˈbɛkən] *vi* **to beckon to someone** : hacerle señas a alguien

become [bɪˈkʌm] *v* **-came** [-ˈkeɪm]; **-come; -coming** *vi* : hacerse, volverse, ponerse <he became famous : se hizo famoso> <to become sad : ponerse triste> <to become accustomed to : acostumbrarse a> — *vt* **1** BEFIT : ser apropiado para **2** SUIT : favorecer, quedarle bien (a alguien) <that dress becomes you : ese vestido te favorece>

becoming [bɪˈkʌmɪŋ] *adj* **1** SUITABLE : apropiado **2** FLATTERING : favorecedor

bed[1] [ˈbɛd] *v* **bedded; bedding** *vt* : acostar — *vi* : acostarse

bed[2] *n* **1** : cama *f,* lecho *m* **2** : cauce *m* (de un río), fondo *m* (del mar) **3**

: arriate *m* (para plantas) **4** LAYER, STRATUM : estrato *m,* capa *f*

bedbug ['bɛd,bʌg] *n* : chinche *f*

bedclothes ['bɛd,klo:ðz, -,klo:z] *npl* : ropa *f* de cama, sábanas *fpl*

bedding ['bɛdɪŋ] *n* **1** → **bedclothes 2** : cama *f* (para animales)

bedeck [bɪ'dɛk] *vt* : adornar, engalanar

bedevil [bɪ'dɛvəl] *vt* **-iled** *or* **-illed; -iling** *or* **-illing** : acosar, plagar

bedlam ['bɛdləm] *n* : locura *f,* caos *m,* alboroto *m*

bedraggled [bɪ'drægəld] *adj* : desaliñado, despeinado

bedridden ['bɛd,rɪdən] *adj* : postrado en cama

bedrock ['bɛd,rɑk] *n* : lecho *m* de roca

bedroom ['bɛd,ru:m, -,rʊm] *n* : dormitorio *m,* habitación *f,* pieza *f,* recámara *f Col, Mex, Pan*

bedspread ['bɛd,sprɛd] *n* : cubrecama *m,* colcha *f,* cobertor *m*

bee ['bi:] *n* **1** : abeja *f* (insecto) **2** GATHERING : círculo *m,* reunión *f*

beech ['bi:tʃ] *n, pl* **beeches** *or* **beech** : haya *f*

beechnut ['bi:tʃ,nʌt] *n* : hayuco *m*

beef[1] ['bi:f] *vt* **to beef up** : fortalecer, reforzar — *vi* COMPLAIN : quejarse

beef[2] *n, pl* **beefs** ['bi:fs] *or* **beeves** ['bi:vz] : carne *f* de vaca, carne *f* de res *CA, Mex*

beefsteak ['bi:f,steɪk] *n* : filete *m,* bistec *m*

beehive ['bi:,haɪv] *n* : colmena *f*

beekeeper ['bi:,ki:pər] *n* : apicultor *m,* -tora *f*

beeline ['bi:,laɪn] *n* **to make a beeline for** : ir derecho a, ir directo hacia

been → **be**

beep[1] ['bi:p] *v* : pitar

beep[2] *n* : pitido *m*

beeper ['bi:pər] *n* : busca *m,* buscapersonas *m*

beer ['bɪr] *n* : cerveza *f*

beeswax ['bi:z,wæks] *n* : cera *f* de abejas

beet ['bi:t] *n* : remolacha *f,* betabel *m Mex*

beetle ['bi:təl] *n* : escarabajo *m*

befall [bɪ'fɔl] *v* **-fell** [-'fɛl]; **-fallen** [-'fɔlən] *vt* : sucederle a, acontecerle a — *vi* : acontecer

befit [bɪ'fɪt] *vt* **-fitted; -fitting** : convenir a, ser apropiado para

before[1] [bɪ'for] *adv* **1** : antes <before and after : antes y después> **2** : anterior <the month before : el mes anterior>

before[2] *conj* : antes que <he would die before surrendering : moriría antes que rendirse>

before[3] *prep* **1** : antes de <before eating : antes de comer> **2** : delante de, ante <I stood before the house : estaba parada delante de la casa> <before the judge : ante el juez>

beforehand [bɪ'for,hænd] *adv* : antes, por adelantado, de antemano, con anticipación

befriend [bɪ'frɛnd] *vt* : hacerse amigo de

befuddle [bɪ'fʌdəl] *vt* **-dled; -dling** : aturdir, ofuscar, confundir

beg ['bɛg] *v* **begged; begging** *vt* : pedir, mendigar, suplicar <I begged him to go : le supliqué que fuera> — *vi* : mendigar, pedir limosna

beget [bɪ'gɛt] *vt* **-got** [-'gɑt]; **-gotten** [-'gɑtən] *or* **-got; -getting** : engendrar

beggar ['bɛgər] *n* : mendigo *m,* -ga *f;* pordiosero *m,* -ra *f*

begin [bɪ'gɪn] *v* **-gan** [-'gæn]; **-gun** [-'gʌn]; **-ginning** *vt* : empezar, comenzar, iniciar — *vi* **1** START : empezar, comenzar, iniciarse **2** ORIGINATE : nacer, originarse **3 to begin with** : en primer lugar, para empezar

beginner [bɪ'gɪnər] *n* : principiante *mf*

beginning [bɪ'gɪnɪŋ] *n* : principio *m,* comienzo *m*

begone [bi'gɔn] *interj* : ¡fuera de aquí!

begonia [bɪ'go:njə] *n* : begonia *f*

begrudge [bɪ'grʌdʒ] *vt* **-grudged; -grudging 1** : dar de mala gana **2** ENVY : envidiar, resentir

beguile [bɪ'gaɪl] *vt* **-guiled; -guiling 1** DECEIVE : engañar **2** AMUSE : divertir, entretener

behalf [bɪ'hæf, -'haf] *n* **1** : favor *m,* beneficio *m,* parte *f* **2 on behalf of** *or* **in behalf of** : de parte de, en nombre de

behave [bɪ'heɪv] *vi* **-haved; -having** : comportarse, portarse

behavior [bɪ'heɪvjər] *n* : comportamiento *m,* conducta *f*

behead [bɪ'hɛd] *vt* : decapitar

behest [bɪ'hɛst] *n* **1** : mandato *m,* orden *f* **2 at the behest of** : a instancia de

behind[1] [bɪ'haɪnd] *adv* : atrás, detrás <to fall behind : quedarse atrás>

behind[2] *prep* **1** : atrás de, detrás de, tras <behind the house : detrás de la casa> <one behind another : uno tras otro> **2** : atrasado con, después de <behind schedule : atrasado con el trabajo> <I arrived behind the others : llegué después de los otros> **3** SUPPORTING : en apoyo de, detrás

behold [bɪ'ho:ld] *vt* **-held; -holding** : contemplar

beholder [bɪ'ho:ldər] *n* : observador *m,* -dora *f*

behoove [bɪ'hu:v] *vt* **-hooved; -hooving** : convenirle a, corresponderle a <it behooves us to help him : nos conviene ayudarlo>

beige[1] ['beɪʒ] *adj* : beige

beige[2] *n* : beige *m*

being ['bi:ɪŋ] *n* **1** EXISTENCE : ser *m,* existencia *f* **2** CREATURE : ser *m,* ente *m*

belabor [bɪ'leɪbər] *vt* **to belabor the point** : extenderse sobre el tema

belated [bɪˈleɪt̬əd] *adj* : tardío, retrasado

belch[1] [ˈbɛltʃ] *vi* **1** BURP : eructar **2** EXPEL : expulsar, arrojar

belch[2] *n* : eructo *m*

beleaguer [bɪˈliːgər] *vt* **1** BESIEGE : asediar, sitiar **2** HARASS : fastidiar, molestar

belfry [ˈbɛlfri] *n, pl* **-fries** : campanario *m*

Belgian [ˈbɛldʒən] *n* : belga *mf* — **Belgian** *adj*

belie [bɪˈlaɪ] *vt* **-lied; -lying 1** MISREPRESENT : falsear, ocultar **2** CONTRADICT : contradecir, desmentir

belief [bəˈliːf] *n* **1** TRUST : confianza *f* **2** CONVICTION : creencia *f,* convicción *f* **3** FAITH : fe *f*

believable [bəˈliːvəbəl] *adj* : verosímil, creíble

believe [bəˈliːv] *v* **-lieved; -lieving** : creer

believer [bəˈliːvər] *n* **1** : creyente *mf* **2** : partidario *m,* -ria *f;* entusiasta *mf* <she's a great believer in vitamins : ella es una gran partidaria de las vitaminas>

belittle [bɪˈlɪt̬əl] *vt* **-littled; -littling 1** DISPARAGE : menospreciar, denigrar, rebajar **2** MINIMIZE : minimizar, quitar importancia a

Belizean [bəˈliːziən] *n* : beliceño *m,* -ña *f* — **Belizean** *adj*

bell[1] [ˈbɛl] *vt* : ponerle un cascabel a

bell[2] *n* : campana *f,* cencerro *m* (para una vaca o cabra), cascabel *m* (para un gato), timbre *m* (de teléfono, de la puerta)

belladonna [ˌbɛləˈdɑnə] *n* : belladona *f*

belle [ˈbɛl] *n* : belleza *f,* beldad *f*

bellhop [ˈbɛlˌhɑp] *n* : botones *m*

bellicose [ˈbɛlɪˌkoːs] *adj* : belicoso *m* — **bellicosity** [ˌbɛlɪˈkɑsət̬i] *n*

belligerence [bəˈlɪdʒərənts] *n* : agresividad *f,* beligerancia *f*

belligerent[1] [bəˈlɪdʒərənt] *adj* : agresivo, beligerante

belligerent[2] *n* : beligerante *mf*

bellow[1] [ˈbɛˌloː] *vi* : bramar, mugir — *vt* : gritar

bellow[2] *n* : bramido *m,* grito *m*

bellows [ˈbɛˌloːz] *ns & pl* : fuelle *m*

bellwether [ˈbɛlˌwɛðər] *n* : líder *mf*

belly[1] [ˈbɛli] *vi* **-lied; -lying** SWELL : hincharse, inflarse

belly[2] *n, pl* **-lies** : abdomen *m,* vientre *m,* barriga *f,* panza *f*

belong [bɪˈlɔŋ] *vi* **1** : pertenecer (a), ser propiedad (de) <it belongs to her : pertenece a ella, es suyo, es de ella> **2** : ser parte (de), ser miembro (de) <he belongs to the club : es miembro del club> **3** : deber estar, ir <your coat belongs in the closet : tu abrigo va en el ropero>

belongings [bɪˈlɔŋɪŋz] *npl* : pertenencias *fpl,* efectos *mpl* personales

beloved[1] [bɪˈlʌvəd, -ˈlʌvd] *adj* : querido, amado

beloved[2] *n* : amado *m,* -da *f;* enamorado *m,* -da *f;* amor *m*

below[1] [bɪˈloː] *adv* : abajo

below[2] *prep* **1** : abajo de, debajo de <below the window : debajo de la ventana> **2** : por debajo de, bajo <below average : por debajo del promedio> <5 degrees below zero : 5 grados bajo cero>

belt[1] [ˈbɛlt] *vt* **1** : ceñir con un cinturón, ponerle un cinturón a **2** THRASH : darle una paliza a, darle un trancazo a

belt[2] *n* **1** : cinturón *m,* cinto *m* (para el talle) **2** BAND, STRAP : cinta *f,* correa *f,* banda *f Mex* **3** AREA : frente *m,* zona *f*

bemoan [bɪˈmoːn] *vt* : lamentarse de

bemuse [bɪˈmjuːz] *vt* **-mused; -musing 1** BEWILDER : confundir, desconcertar **2** ENGROSS : absorber

bench [ˈbɛntʃ] *n* **1** SEAT : banco *m,* escaño *m,* banca *f* **2** : estrado *m* (de un juez) **3** COURT : tribunal *m*

bend[1] [ˈbɛnd] *v* **bent** [ˈbɛnt]; **bending** *vt* : torcer, doblar, curvar, flexionar — *vi* **1** : torcerse, agacharse <to bend over : inclinarse> **2** TURN : torcer, hacer una curva

bend[2] *n* **1** TURN : vuelta *f,* recodo *m* **2** CURVE : curva *f,* ángulo *m,* codo *m*

beneath[1] [bɪˈniːθ] *adv* : bajo, abajo, debajo

beneath[2] *prep* : bajo de, abajo de, por debajo de

benediction [ˌbɛnəˈdɪkʃən] *n* : bendición *f*

benefactor [ˈbɛnəˌfæktər] *n* : benefactor *m,* -tora *f*

beneficence [bəˈnɛfəsənts] *n* : beneficencia *f*

beneficent [bəˈnɛfəsənt] *adj* : benéfico, caritativo

beneficial [ˌbɛnəˈfɪʃəl] *adj* : beneficioso, provechoso — **beneficially** *adv*

beneficiary [ˌbɛnəˈfɪʃiˌɛri, -ˈfɪʃəri] *n, pl* **-ries** : beneficiario *m,* -ria *f*

benefit[1] [ˈbɛnəfɪt] *vt* : beneficiar — *vi* : beneficiarse

benefit[2] *n* **1** ADVANTAGE : beneficio *m,* ventaja *f,* provecho *m* **2** AID : asistencia *f,* beneficio *m* **3** : función *f* benéfica (para recaudar fondos)

benevolence [bəˈnɛvələnts] *n* : bondad *f,* benevolencia *f*

benevolent [bəˈnɛvələnt] *adj* : benévolo, bondadoso — **benevolently** *adv*

Bengali [bɛnˈgɔli, bɛŋ-] *n* **1** : bengalí *mf* **2** : bengalí *m* (idioma) — **Bengali** *adj*

benign [bɪˈnaɪn] *adj* **1** GENTLE, KIND : benévolo, amable **2** FAVORABLE : propicio, favorable **3** MILD : benigno <a benign tumor : un tumor benigno>

Beninese [bəˌniˈniːz, -ˌniː-, -ˈniːs; ˌbɛniˈ-] *n* : beninés *m*, -nesa *f* — **Beninese** *adj*

bent [ˈbɛnt] *n* : aptitud *f*, inclinación *f*

benumb [biˈnʌm] *vt* : entumecer

benzene [ˈbɛnˌziːn] *n* : benceno *m*

bequeath [biˈkwiːθ, -ˈkwiːð] *vt* : legar, dejar en testamento

bequest [biˈkwɛst] *n* : legado *m*

berate [biˈreit] *vt* **-rated; -rating** : reprender, regañar

bereaved[1] [biˈriːvd] *adj* : que está de luto, afligido (por la muerte de alguien)

bereaved[2] *n* **the bereaved** : los deudos del difunto (o de la difunta)

bereavement [biˈriːvmənt] *n* **1** SORROW : dolor *m*, pesar *m* **2** LOSS : pérdida *f*

bereft [biˈrɛft] *adj* : privado, desprovisto

beret [bəˈrei] *n* : boina *f*

beriberi [ˌbɛriˈbɛri] *n* : beriberi *m*

berm [ˈbərm] *n* : arcén *m*

berry [ˈbɛri] *n*, *pl* **-ries** : baya *f*

berserk [bərˈsərk, -ˈzərk] *adj* **1** : enloquecido **2 to go beserk** : volverse loco

berth[1] [ˈbərθ] *vi* : atracar

berth[2] *n* **1** DOCK : atracadero *m* **2** ACCOMMODATION : litera *f*, camarote *m* **3** POSITION : trabajo *m*, puesto *m*

beryl [ˈbɛrəl] *n* : berilo *m*

beseech [biˈsiːtʃ] *vt* **-sought** [-ˈsɔt] *or* **-seeched; -seeching** : suplicar, implorar, rogar

beset [biˈsɛt] *vt* **-set; -setting 1** HARASS : acosar **2** SURROUND : rodear

beside [biˈsaid] *prep* : al lado de, junto a

besides[1] [biˈsaidz] *adv* **1** ALSO : además, también, aparte **2** MOREOVER : además, por otra parte

besides[2] *prep* **1** : además de, aparte de <six others besides you : seis otros además de ti> **2** EXCEPT : excepto, fuera de, aparte de

besiege [biˈsiːdʒ] *vt* **-sieged; -sieging** : asediar, sitiar, cercar

besmirch [biˈsmərtʃ] *vt* : ensuciar, mancillar

best[1] [ˈbɛst] *vt* : superar, ganar a

best[2] *adv* (*superlative of* **well**) : mejor <as best I can : lo mejor que puedo>

best[3] *adj* (*superlative of* **good**) : mejor <my best friend : mi mejor amigo>

best[4] *n* **1 the best** : lo mejor, el mejor, la mejor, los mejores, las mejores **2 at ~** : a lo más **3 to do one's best** : hacer todo lo posible

bestial [ˈbɛstʃəl, ˈbiːs-] *adj* **1** : bestial **2** BRUTISH : brutal, salvaje

best man *n* : padrino *m*

bestow [biˈstoː] *vt* : conferir, otorgar, conceder

bestowal [biˈstoːəl] *n* : concesión *f*, otorgamiento *m*

bet[1] [ˈbɛt] *v* **bet; betting** *vt* : apostar — *vi* **to bet on** : apostarle a

bet[2] *n* : apuesta *f*

betoken [biˈtoːkən] *vt* : denotar, ser indicio de

betray [biˈtrei] *vt* **1** : traicionar <to betray one's country : traicionar uno a su patria> **2** DIVULGE, REVEAL : delatar, revelar <to betray a secret : revelar un secreto>

betrayal [biˈtreiəl] *n* : traición *f*, delación *f*, revelación *f* <betrayal of trust : abuso de confianza>

betrothal [biˈtroːðəl, -ˈtrɔ-] *n* : esponsales *mpl*, compromiso *m*

betrothed [biˈtroːðd, -ˈtrɔθt] *n* FIANCÉ : prometido *m*, -da *f*

better[1] [ˈbɛtər] *vt* **1** IMPROVE : mejorar **2** SURPASS : superar

better[2] *adv* (*comparative of* **well**) **1** : mejor **2** MORE : más <better than 50 miles : más de 50 millas>

better[3] *adj* (*comparative of* **good**) **1** : mejor <the weather is better today : hace mejor tiempo hoy> <I was sick, but now I'm better : estuve enfermo, pero ahora estoy mejor> **2** : mayor <the better part of a month : la mayor parte de un mes>

better[4] *n* **1** : el mejor, la mejor <the better of the two : el mejor de los dos> **2 to get the better of** : vencer a, quedar por encima de, superar

betterment [ˈbɛtərmənt] *n* : mejoramiento *m*, mejora *f*

bettor *or* **better** [ˈbɛtər] *n* : apostador *m*, -dora *f*

between[1] [biˈtwiːn] *adv* **1** : en medio, por lo medio **2 in ~** : intermedio

between[2] *prep* : entre

bevel[1] [ˈbɛvəl] *v* **-eled** *or* **-elled; -eling** *or* **-elling** *vt* : biselar — *vi* INCLINE : inclinarse

bevel[2] *n* : bisel *m*

beverage [ˈbɛvridʒ, ˈbɛvə-] *n* : bebida *f*

bevy [ˈbɛvi] *n*, *pl* **bevies** : grupo *m* (de personas), bandada *f* (de pájaros)

bewail [biˈweil] *vt* : lamentarse de, llorar

beware [biˈwær] *vi* **to beware of** : tener cuidado con <beware of the dog! : ¡cuidado con el perro!> — *vt* : guardarse de, cuidarse de

bewilder [biˈwildər] *vt* : desconcertar, dejar perplejo

bewilderment [biˈwildərmənt] *n* : desconcierto *m*, perplejidad *f*

bewitch [biˈwitʃ] *vt* **1** : hechizar, embrujar **2** CHARM : cautivar, encantar

bewitchment [biˈwitʃmənt] *n* : hechizo *m*

beyond[1] [biˈjɑnd] *adv* **1** FARTHER, LATER : más allá, más lejos (en el espacio), más adelante (en el tiempo) **2** MORE : más <$50 and beyond : $50 o más>

beyond[2] *n* **the beyond** : el más allá, lo desconocido

beyond[3] *prep* **1** : más allá de <beyond the frontier : más allá de la frontera>

2 : fuera de <beyond one's reach : fuera de su alcance> 3 BESIDES : además de

biannual [ˌbaɪˈænjʊəl] *adj* : bianual — **biannually** *adv*

bias[1] [ˈbaɪəs] *vt* **-ased** *or* **-assed; -asing** *or* **-assing 1** : predisponer, sesgar, influir en, afectar **2 to be biased against** : tener prejuicio contra

bias[2] *n* **1** : sesgo *m,* bies *m* (en la costura) **2** PREJUDICE : prejuicio *m* **3** TENDENCY : inclinación *f,* tendencia *f*

biased [ˈbaɪəst] *adj* : tendencioso, parcial

bib [ˈbɪb] *n* **1** : peto *m* **2** : babero *m* (para niños)

Bible [ˈbaɪbəl] *n* : Biblia *f*

biblical [ˈbɪblɪkəl] *adj* : bíblico

bibliographer [ˌbɪbliˈɑgrəfər] *n* : bibliógrafo *m,* -fa *f*

bibliographic [ˌbɪbliəˈgræfɪk] *adj* : bibliográfico

bibliography [ˌbɪbliˈɑgrəfi] *n, pl* **-phies** : bibliografía *f*

bicameral [ˌbaɪˈkæmərəl] *adj* : bicameral

bicarbonate [ˌbaɪˈkɑrbənət, -ˌneɪt] *n* : bicarbonato *m*

bicentennial [ˌbaɪsɛnˈtɛniəl] *n* : bicentenario *m*

biceps [ˈbaɪˌsɛps] *ns & pl* : bíceps *m*

bicker[1] [ˈbɪkər] *vi* : pelear, discutir, reñir

bicker[2] *n* : pelea *f,* riña *f,* discusión *f*

bicuspid [baɪˈkʌspɪd] *n* : premolar *m,* diente *m* bicúspide

bicycle[1] [ˈbaɪsɪkəl, -ˌsɪ-] *vi* **-cled; -cling** : ir en bicicleta

bicycle[2] *n* : bicicleta *f*

bicycling [ˈbaɪsɪkəlɪŋ] *n* : ciclismo *m*

bicyclist [ˈbaɪsɪkəlɪst] *n* : ciclista *mf*

bid[1] [ˈbɪd] *vt* **bade** [ˈbæd, ˈbeɪd] *or* **bid; bidden** [ˈbɪdən] *or* **bid; bidding 1** ORDER : pedir, mandar **2** INVITE : invitar **3** SAY : dar, decir <to bid good evening : dar las buenas noches> <to bid farewell to : decir adiós a> **4** : ofrecer (en una subasta), declarar (en juegos de cartas)

bid[2] *n* **1** OFFER : oferta *f* (en una subasta), declaración *f* (en juegos de cartas) **2** INVITATION : invitación *f* **3** ATTEMPT : intento *m,* tentativa *f*

bidder [ˈbɪdər] *n* : postor *m,* -tora *f*

bide [ˈbaɪd] *v* **bode** [ˈboːd] *or* **bided; bided; biding** *vt* : esperar, aguardar <to bide one's time : esperar el momento oportuno> — *vi* DWELL : morar, vivir

biennial [baɪˈɛniəl] *adj* : bienal — **biennially** *adv*

bier [ˈbɪr] *n* **1** STAND : andas *fpl* **2** COFFIN : ataúd *m,* féretro *m*

bifocals [ˈbaɪˌfoːkəlz] *npl* : lentes *mpl* bifocales, bifocales *mpl*

big [ˈbɪg] *adj* **bigger; biggest 1** LARGE : grande **2** PREGNANT : embarazada **3** IMPORTANT, MAJOR : importante, grande <a big decision : una gran decisión> **4** POPULAR : popular, famoso, conocido

bigamist [ˈbɪgəmɪst] *n* : bígamo *m,* -ma *f*

bigamous [ˈbɪgəməs] *adj* : bígamo

bigamy [ˈbɪgəmi] *n* : bigamia *f*

Big Dipper → **dipper**

bighorn [ˈbɪgˌhɔrn] *n, pl* **-horn** *or* **-horns** *or* **bighorn sheep** : oveja *f* salvaje de las montañas

bight [ˈbaɪt] *n* : bahía *f,* ensenada *f,* golfo *m*

bigot [ˈbɪgət] *n* : intolerante *mf*

bigoted [ˈbɪgət̬əd] *adj* : intolerante, prejuiciado, fanático

bigotry [ˈbɪgətri] *n, pl* **-tries** : intolerancia *f,* fanaticismo *m*

big shot *n* : pez *m* gordo *fam,* mandamás *mf*

bigwig [ˈbɪgˌwɪg] → **big shot**

bike [ˈbaɪk] *n* **1** : bicicleta *f,* bici *f fam* **2** : motocicleta *f,* moto *f*

bikini [bəˈkiːni] *n* : bikini *m*

bilateral [baɪˈlæt̬ərəl] *adj* : bilateral — **bilaterally** *adv*

bile [ˈbaɪl] *n* **1** : bilis *f* **2** IRRITABILITY : mal genio *m*

bilingual [baɪˈlɪŋgwəl] *adj* : bilingüe

bilious [ˈbɪliəs] *adj* **1** : bilioso **2** IRRITABLE : bilioso, colérico

bilk [ˈbɪlk] *vt* : burlar, estafar, defraudar

bill[1] [ˈbɪl] *vt* : pasarle la cuenta a — *vi* : acariciar <to bill and coo : acariciarse>

bill[2] *n* **1** LAW : proyecto *m* de ley, ley *f* **2** INVOICE : cuenta *f,* factura *f* **3** POSTER : cartel *m* **4** PROGRAM : programa *m* (del teatro) **5** : billete *m* <a five-dollar bill : un billete de cinco dólares> **6** BEAK : pico *m*

billboard [ˈbɪlˌbɔrd] *n* : cartelera *f*

billet[1] [ˈbɪlət] *vt* : acuartelar, alojar

billet[2] *n* : alojamiento *m*

billfold [ˈbɪlˌfoːld] *n* : billetera *f,* cartera *f*

billiards [ˈbɪljərdz] *n* : billar *m*

billion [ˈbɪljən] *n, pl* **billions** *or* **billion** : mil millones *mpl*

billow[1] [ˈbɪlo] *vi* : hincharse, inflarse

billow[2] *n* **1** WAVE : ola *f* **2** CLOUD : nube *f* <a billow of smoke : un nube de humo>

billowy [ˈbɪlowi] *adj* : ondulante

billy goat [ˈbɪliˌgoːt] *n* : macho *m* cabrío

bin [ˈbɪn] *n* : cubo *m,* cajón *m*

binary [ˈbaɪnəri, -ˌnɛri] *adj* : binario *m*

bind [ˈbaɪnd] *vt* **bound** [ˈbaʊnd]; **binding 1** TIE : atar, amarrar **2** OBLIGATE : obligar **3** UNITE : aglutinar, ligar, unir **4** BANDAGE : vendar **5** : encuadernar (un libro)

binder [ˈbaɪndər] *n* **1** FOLDER : carpeta *f* **2** : encuadernador *m,* -dora *f* (de libros)

binding [ˈbaɪndɪŋ] *n* **1** : encuadernación *f* (de libros) **2** COVER : cubierta *f,* forro *m*

binge [ˈbɪndʒ] *n* : juerga *f,* parranda *f fam*
bingo [ˈbɪŋˌgoː] *n, pl* **-gos** : bingo *m*
binocular [baɪˈnɑkjələr, bə-] *adj* : binocular
binoculars [bəˈnɑkjələrz, baɪ-] *npl* : binoculares *mpl*
biochemical¹ [ˌbaɪoˈkɛmɪkəl] *adj* : bioquímico
biochemical² *n* : bioquímico *m*
biochemist [ˌbaɪoˈkɛmɪst] *n* : bioquímico *m,* -ca *f*
biochemistry [ˌbaɪoˈkɛməstri] *n* : bioquímica *f*
biodegradable [ˌbaɪodɪˈgreɪdəbəl] *adj* : biodegradable
biodegradation [ˌbaɪodɛgrəˈdeɪʃən] *n* : biodegradación *f*
biodegrade [ˌbaɪodɪˈgreɪd] *vi* **-graded; -grading** : biodegradarse
biographer [baɪˈɑgrəfər] *n* : biógrafo *m,* -fa *f*
biographical [ˌbaɪəˈgræfɪkəl] *adj* : biográfico
biography [baɪˈɑgrəfi, biː-] *n, pl* **-phies** : biografía *f*
biologic [ˌbaɪəˈlɑdʒɪk] *or* **biological** [-dʒɪkəl] *adj* : biológico
biologist [baɪˈɑlədʒɪst] *n* : biólogo *m,* -ga *f*
biology [baɪˈɑlədʒi] *n* : biología *f*
biophysical [ˌbaɪoˈfɪzɪkəl] *adj* : biofísico
biophysicist [ˌbaɪoˈfɪzəsɪst] *n* : biofísico *m,* -ca *f*
biophysics [ˌbaɪoˈfɪzɪks] *ns & pl* : biofísica *f*
biopsy [ˈbaɪˌɑpsi] *n, pl* **-sies** : biopsia *f*
biotechnology [ˌbaɪotɛkˈnɑlədʒi] *n* : biotecnología *f*
biotic [baɪˈɑtɪk] *adj* : biótico
bipartisan [baɪˈpɑrtəzən, -sən] *adj* : bipartidista, de dos partidas
biped [ˈbaɪˌpɛd] *n* : bípedo *m*
birch [ˈbərtʃ] *n* : abedul *m*
bird [ˈbərd] *n* : pájaro *m* (pequeño), ave *f* (grande)
birdbath [ˈbərdˌbæθ, -ˌbaθ] *n* : pila *f* para pájaros
bird dog *n* : perro *m,* -rra *f* de caza
bird of prey *n* : ave *f* rapaz, ave *f* de presa
birdseed [ˈbərdˌsiːd] *n* : alpiste *m*
bird's–eye [ˈbərdzˌaɪ] *adj* **1** : visto desde arriba <bird's-eye view : vista aérea> **2** CURSORY : rápido, somero
birth [ˈbərθ] *n* **1** : nacimiento *m,* parto *m* **2** ORIGIN : origen *m,* nacimiento *m*
birthday [ˈbərθˌdeɪ] *n* : cumpleaños *m,* aniversario *m*
birthmark [ˈbərθˌmɑrk] *n* : mancha *f* de nacimiento
birthplace [ˈbərθˌpleɪs] *n* : lugar *m* de nacimiento
birthrate [ˈbərθˌreɪt] *n* : índice *m* de natalidad
birthright [ˈbərθˌraɪt] *n* : derecho *m* de nacimiento
biscuit [ˈbɪskət] *n* : bizcocho *m*
bisect [ˈbaɪˌsɛkt, ˌbaɪˈ-] *vt* : bisecar
bisector [ˈbaɪˌsɛktər, ˌbaɪˈ-] *n* : bisectriz *f*
bishop [ˈbɪʃəp] *n* : obispo *m*
bismuth [ˈbɪzməθ] *n* : bismuto *m*
bison [ˈbaɪzən, -sən] *ns & pl* : bisonte *m*
bistro [ˈbiːstro, ˈbɪs-] *n, pl* **-tros** : bar *m,* restaurante *m* pequeño
bit [ˈbɪt] *n* **1** FRAGMENT, PIECE : pedazo *m,* trozo *m* <a bit of luck : un poco de suerte> **2** : freno *m,* bocado *m* (de una brida) **3** : broca *f* (de un taladro) **4** : bit *m* (de información)
bitch¹ [ˈbɪtʃ] *vi* COMPLAIN : quejarse, reclamar
bitch² *n* : perra *f*
bite¹ [ˈbaɪt] *v* **bit** [ˈbɪt]; **bitten** [ˈbɪtən]; **biting** *vt* **1** : morder **2** STING : picar **3** PUNCTURE : punzar, pinchar **4** GRIP : agarrar — *vi* **1** : morder <that dog bites : ese perro muerde> **2** STING : picar (dícese de un insecto), cortar (dícese del viento) **3** : picar <the fish are biting now : ya están picando los peces> **4** GRAB : agarrarse
bite² *n* **1** BITING : mordisco *m,* dentellada *f* **2** SNACK : bocado *m* <a bite to eat : algo de comer> **3** : picadura *f* (de un insecto), mordedura *f* (de un animal) **4** SHARPNESS : mordacidad *f,* penetración *f*
biting *adj* **1** PENETRATING : cortante, penetrante **2** CAUSTIC : mordaz, sarcástico
bitter [ˈbɪtər] *adj* **1** ACRID : amargo, acre **2** PENETRATING : cortante, penetrante <bitter cold : frío glacial> **3** HARSH : duro, amargo <to the bitter end : hasta el final> **4** INTENSE, RELENTLESS : intenso, extremo, implacable <bitter hatred : odio implacable>
bitterly [ˈbɪtərli] *adv* : amargamente
bittern [ˈbɪtərn] *n* : avetoro *m* común
bitterness [ˈbɪtərnəs] *n* : amargura *f*
bituminous coal [bəˈtuːmənəs, -ˈtjuː-] *n* : carbón *m* bituminoso
bivalve [ˈbaɪˌvælv] *n* : bivalvo *m* — **bivalve** *adj*
bivouac¹ [ˈbɪvəˌwæk, ˈbɪvˌwæk] *vi* **-ouacked; -ouacking** : acampar, vivaquear
bivouac² *n* : vivaque *m*
bizarre [bəˈzɑr] *adj* : extraño, singular, estrafalario, estrambótico — **bizarrely** *adv*
blab [ˈblæb] *vi* **blabbed; blabbing** : parlotear *fam,* cotorrear *fam*
black¹ [ˈblæk] *vt* : ennegrecer
black² *adj* **1** : negro (color, raza) **2** SOILED : sucio **3** DARK : oscuro, negro **4** WICKED : malvado, perverso, malo **5** GLOOMY : negro, sombrío, deprimente
black³ *n* **1** : negro *m* (color) **2** : negro *m,* -gra *f* (persona)
black–and–blue [ˌblækənˈbluː] *adj* : amoratado

blackball [ˈblæk,bɔl] *vt* **1** OSTRACIZE : hacerle el vacío a, aislar **2** BOYCOTT : boicotear

blackberry [ˈblæk,bɛri] *n, pl* **-ries** : mora *f*

blackbird [ˈblæk,bərd] *n* : mirlo *m*

blackboard [ˈblæk,bɔrd] *n* : pizarra *f,* pizarrón *m*

blacken [ˈblækən] *vt* **1** BLACK : ennegrecer **2** DEFAME : deshonrar, difamar, manchar

blackhead [ˈblæk,hɛd] *n* : espinilla *f,* punto *m* negro

black hole *n* : agujero *m* negro

blackjack [ˈblæk,jæk] *n* **1** : cachiporra *f* (arma) **2** : veintiuna *f* (juego de cartas)

blacklist[1] [ˈblæk,lɪst] *vt* : poner en la lista negra

blacklist[2] *n* : lista *f* negra

blackmail[1] [ˈblæk,meɪl] *vt* : chantajear, hacer chantaje a

blackmail[2] *n* : chantaje *m*

blackmailer [ˈblæk,meɪlər] *n* : chantajista *mf*

blackout [ˈblæk,aʊt] *n* **1** : apagón *m* (de poder eléctrico) **2** FAINT : desmayo *m,* desvanecimiento *m*

black out *vt* : dejar sin luz — *vi* FAINT : perder el conocimiento, desmayarse

blacksmith [ˈblæk,smɪθ] *n* : herrero *m*

blacktop [ˈblæk,tɑp] *n* : asfalto *m*

bladder [ˈblædər] *n* : vejiga *f*

blade [ˈbleɪd] *n* : hoja *f* (de un cuchillo), cuchilla *f* (de un patín), pala *f* (de un remo o una hélice), brizna *f* (de hierba)

blamable [ˈbleɪməbəl] *adj* : culpable

blame[1] [ˈbleɪm] *vt* **blamed; blaming** : culpar, echar la culpa a

blame[2] *n* : culpa *f*

blameless [ˈbleɪmləs] *adj* : intachable, sin culpa, inocente — **blamelessly** *adv*

blameworthiness [ˈbleɪm,wərðinəs] *n* : culpa *f,* culpabilidad *f*

blameworthy [ˈbleɪm,wərði] *adj* : culpable, reprochable, censurable

blanch [ˈblæntʃ] *vt* WHITEN : blanquear — *vi* PALE : palidecer

bland [ˈblænd] *adj* : soso, insulso, desabrido <a bland smile : una sonrisa insulsa> <a bland diet : una dieta fácil de digerir>

blandishments [ˈblændɪʃmənts] *npl* : lisonjas *fpl,* halagos *mpl*

blandly [ˈblændli] *adv* : de manera insulsa

blandness [ˈblændnəs] *n* : lo insulso, lo desabrido

blank[1] [ˈblæŋk] *vt* OBLITERATE : borrar

blank[2] *adj* **1** DAZED : perplejo, desconcertado **2** EXPRESSIONLESS : sin expresión, inexpresivo **3** : en blanco (dícese de un papel), liso (dícese de una pared) **4** EMPTY : vacío, en blanco <a blank stare : una mirada vacía> <his mind went blank : se quedó en blanco>

blank[3] *n* **1** SPACE : espacio *m* en blanco **2** FORM : formulario *m* **3** CARTRIDGE : cartucho *m* de fogueo **4** *or* **blank key** : llave *f* ciega

blanket[1] [blæŋkət] *vt* : cubrir

blanket[2] *adj* : global

blanket[3] *n* : manta *f,* cobija *f,* frazada *f*

blankly [ˈblænkli] *adv* : sin comprender

blankness [ˈblænknəs] *n* **1** PERPLEXITY : desconcierto *m,* perplejidad *f* **2** EMPTINESS : vacío *m,* vacuidad *f*

blare[1] [ˈblær] *vi* **blared; blaring** : resonar

blare[2] *n* : estruendo *m*

blarney [ˈblɑrni] *n* : labia *f fam*

blasé [blɑˈzeɪ] *adj* : displicente, indiferente

blaspheme [blæsˈfiːm, ˈblæs,-] *vi* **-phemed; -pheming** : blasfemar

blasphemer [blæsˈfiːmər, ˈblæs,-] *n* : blasfemo *m,* -ma *f*

blasphemous [ˈblæsfəməs] *adj* : blasfemo

blasphemy [ˈblæsfəmi] *n, pl* **-mies** : blasfemia *f*

blast[1] [ˈblæst] *vt* **1** BLOW UP : volar, hacer volar **2** ATTACK : atacar, arremeter contra

blast[2] *n* **1** GUST : ráfaga *f* **2** EXPLOSION : explosión *f*

blast-off [ˈblæst,ɔf] *n* : despegue *m*

blast off *vi* : despegar

blatant [ˈbleɪtənt] *adj* : descarado — **blatantly** [ˈbleɪtəntli] *adv*

blaze[1] [ˈbleɪz] *v* **blazed; blazing** *vi* SHINE : arder, brillar, resplandecer — *vt* MARK : marcar, señalar <to blaze a trail : abrir un camino>

blaze[2] *n* **1** FIRE : fuego *m* **2** BRIGHTNESS : resplandor *m,* brillantez *f* **3** OUTBURST : arranque *m* <a blaze of anger : un arranque de cólera> **4** DISPLAY : alarde *m,* llamarada *f* <a blaze of color : un derroche de color>

blazer [ˈbleɪzər] *n* : chaqueta *f* deportiva, blazer *m*

bleach[1] [ˈbliːtʃ] *vt* : blanquear, decolorar

bleach[2] *n* : lejía *f,* blanqueador *m*

bleachers [ˈbliːtʃərz] *ns & pl* : gradas *fpl,* tribuna *f* descubierta

bleak [ˈbliːk] *adj* **1** DESOLATE : inhóspito, sombrío, desolado **2** DEPRESSING : deprimente, triste, sombrío

bleakly [ˈbliːkli] *adv* : sombríamente

bleakness [ˈbliːknəs] *n* : lo inhóspito, lo sombrío

blear [ˈblɪr] *adj* : empañado, nublado

bleary [ˈblɪri] *adj* **1** : adormilado, fatigado **2** **bleary–eyed** : con los ojos nublados

bleat[1] [ˈbliːt] *vi* : balar

bleat[2] *n* : balido *m*

bleed [ˈbliːd] *v* **bled** [ˈblɛd]; **bleeding** *vi* **1** : sangrar **2** GRIEVE : sufrir, afligirse **3** EXUDE : exudar (dícese de una planta), correrse (dícese de los colores) — *vt* **1** : sangrar (a una persona), purgar (frenos) **2 to bleed someone dry** : sacarle todo el dinero a alguien

blemish[1] ['blɛmɪʃ] *vt* : manchar, marcar

blemish[2] *n* : imperfección *f,* mancha *f,* marca *f*

blend[1] ['blɛnd] *vt* **1** MIX : mezclar **2** COMBINE : combinar, aunar

blend[2] *n* : mezcla *f,* combinación *f*

blender ['blɛndər] *n* : licuadora *f*

bless ['blɛs] *vt* **blessed** ['blɛst]; **blessing 1** CONSECRATE : bendecir, consagrar **2** : bendecir <may God bless you! : ¡que Dios te bendiga!> **3 to bless with** : dotar de **4 to bless oneself** : santiguarse

blessed ['blɛsəd] *or* **blest** ['blɛst] *adj* : bienaventurado, bendito, dichoso

blessedly ['blɛsədli] *adv* : felizmente, alegremente, afortunadamente

blessing ['blɛsɪŋ] *n* **1** : bendición *f* **2** APPROVAL : aprobación *f,* consentimiento *m*

blew → **blow**

blight[1] ['blaɪt] *vt* : arruinar, infestar

blight[2] *n* **1** : añublo *m* **2** PLAGUE : peste *f,* plaga *f* **3** DECAY : deterioro *m,* ruina *f*

blimp ['blɪmp] *n* : dirigible *m*

blind[1] ['blaɪnd] *vt* **1** : cegar, dejar ciego **2** DAZZLE : deslumbrar

blind[2] *adj* **1** SIGHTLESS : ciego **2** INSENSITIVE : ciego, insensible, sin razón **3** CLOSED : sin salida <blind alley : callejón sin salida>

blind[3] *n* **1** : persiana *f* (para una ventana) **2** COVER : escondite *m,* escondrijo *m*

blindfold[1] ['blaɪnd,fo:ld] *vt* : vendar los ojos

blindfold[2] *n* : venda *f* (para los ojos)

blindly ['blaɪndli] *adv* : a ciegas, ciegamente

blindness ['blaɪndnəs] *n* : ceguera *f*

blink[1] ['blɪŋk] *vi* **1** WINK : pestañear, parpadear **2** : brillar intermitentemente

blink[2] *n* : pestañeo *m,* parpadeo *m*

blinker ['blɪŋkər] *n* : intermitente *m,* direccional *f*

bliss ['blɪs] *n* **1** HAPPINESS : dicha *f,* felicidad *f* absoluta **2** PARADISE : paraíso *m*

blissful ['blɪsfəl] *adj* : dichoso, feliz — **blissfully** *adv*

blister[1] ['blɪstər] *vi* : ampollarse

blister[2] *n* : ampolla *f* (en la piel o una superficie), burbuja *f* (en una superficie)

blithe ['blaɪθ, 'blaɪð] *adj* **blither; blithest 1** CAREFREE : despreocupado **2** CHEERFUL : alegre, risueño — **blithely** *adv*

blitz[1] ['blɪts] *vt* **1** BOMBARD : bombardear **2** : atacar con rapidez

blitz[2] *n* **1** : bombardeo *m* aéreo **2** CAMPAIGN : ataque *m,* acometida *f*

blizzard ['blɪzərd] *n* : tormenta *f* de nieve, ventisca *f*

bloat ['blo:t] *vi* : hincharse, inflarse

blob ['blɑb] *n* : gota *f,* mancha *f,* borrón *m*

bloc ['blɑk] *n* : bloque *m*

block[1] ['blɑk] *vt* **1** OBSTRUCT : obstruir, bloquear **2** CLOG : atascar, atorar

block[2] *n* **1** PIECE : bloque *m* <building blocks : cubos de construcción> <auction block : plataforma de subastas> <starting block : taco de salida> **2** OBSTRUCTION : obstrucción *f,* bloqueo *m* **3** : cuadra *f,* manzana *f* (de edificios) <to go around the block : dar la vuelta a la cuadra> **4** BUILDING : edificio *m* (de apartamentos, oficinas, etc.) **5** GROUP, SERIES : serie *f,* grupo *m* <a block of tickets : una serie de entradas> **6 block and tackle** : aparejo *m* de poleas

blockade[1] [blɑ'keɪd] *vt* **-aded; -ading** : bloquear

blockade[2] *n* : bloqueo *m*

blockage ['blɑkɪdʒ] *n* : bloqueo *m,* obstrucción *f*

blockhead ['blɑk,hɛd] *n* : bruto *m,* -ta *f;* estúpido *m,* -da *f*

blond[1] *or* **blonde** ['blɑnd] *adj* : rubio, güero *Mex,* claro (dícese de la madera)

blond[2] *or* **blonde** *n* : rubio *m,* -bia *f;* güero *m,* -ra *f Mex*

blood ['blʌd] *n* **1** : sangre *f* **2** LIFEBLOOD : vida *f,* alma *f* **3** LINEAGE : linaje *m,* sangre *f*

blood bank *n* : banco *m* de sangre

bloodcurdling ['blʌd,kərdəlɪŋ] *adj* : espeluznante, aterrador

blooded ['blʌdəd] *adj* : de sangre <cold-blooded animal : animal de sangre fría>

bloodhound ['blʌd,haʊnd] *n* : sabueso *m*

bloodless ['blʌdləs] *adj* **1** : incruento, sin derramamiento de sangre **2** LIFELESS : desanimado, insípido, sin vida

bloodmobile ['blʌdmo,bi:l] *n* : unidad *f* móvil para donantes de sangre

blood pressure *n* : tensión *f,* presión *f* (arterial)

bloodshed ['blʌd,ʃɛd] *n* : derramamiento *m* de sangre

bloodshot ['blʌd,ʃɑt] *adj* : inyectado de sangre

bloodstain ['blʌd,steɪn] *n* : mancha *f* de sangre

bloodstained ['blʌd,steɪnd] *adj* : manchado de sangre

bloodstream ['blʌd,stri:m] *n* : torrente *m* sanguíneo, corriente *f* sanguínea

bloodsucker ['blʌd,sʌkər] *n* : sanguijuela *f*

bloodthirsty ['blʌd,θərsti] *adj* : sanguinario

blood vessel *n* : vaso *m* sanguíneo

bloody ['blʌdi] *adj* **bloodier; -est** : ensangrentado, sangriento

bloom[1] [ˈbluːm] *vi* **1** FLOWER : florecer **2** MATURE : madurar

bloom[2] *n* **1** FLOWER : flor *f* <to be in bloom : estar en flor> **2** FLOWERING : floración *f* <in full bloom : en plena floración> **3** : rubor *m* (de la tez) <in the bloom of youth : en plena juventud, en la flor de la vida>

bloomers [ˈbluːmərz] *npl* : bombachos *mpl*

blooper [ˈbluːpər] *n* : metedura *f* de pata *fam*

blossom[1] [ˈblɑsəm] *vi* : florecer, dar flor

blossom[2] *n* : flor *f*

blot[1] [ˈblɑt] *vt* **blotted; blotting 1** SPOT : emborronar, borronear **2** DRY : secar

blot[2] *n* **1** STAIN : mancha *f,* borrón *m* **2** BLEMISH : mancha *f,* tacha *f*

blotch[1] [ˈblɑtʃ] *vt* : emborronar, borronear

blotch[2] *n* : mancha *f,* borrón *m*

blotchy [ˈblɑtʃi] *adj* **blotchier; -est** : lleno de manchas

blotter [ˈblɑṭər] *n* : hoja *f* de papel secante, secante *m*

blouse [ˈblaʊs, ˈblaʊz] *n* : blusa *f*

blow[1] [ˈbloː] *v* **blew** [ˈbluː]; **blown** [ˈbloːn]; **blowing** *vi* **1** : soplar, volar <the wind is blowing hard : el viento está soplando con fuerza> <it blew out the door : voló por la puerta> <the window blew shut : se cerró la ventana> **2** SOUND : sonar <the whistle blew : sonó el silbato> **3 to blow out** : fundirse (dícese de un fusible eléctrico), reventarse (dícese de una llanta) — *vt* **1** : soplar, echar <to blow smoke : echar humo> **2** SOUND : tocar, sonar **3** SHAPE : soplar, dar forma a <to blow glass : soplar vidrio> **4** BUNGLE : echar a perder

blow[2] *n* **1** PUFF : soplo *m,* soplido *m* **2** GALE : vendaval *f* **3** HIT, STROKE : golpe *m* **4** CALAMITY : golpe *m,* desastre *m* **5 to come to blows** : llegar a las manos

blower [ˈbloːər] *n* FAN : ventilador *m*

blowout [ˈbloːˌaʊt] *n* : reventón *m*

blowtorch [ˈbloːˌtɔrtʃ] *n* : soplete *m*

blow up *vi* EXPLODE : estallar, hacer explosión — *vt* BLAST : volar, hacer volar

blubber[1] [ˈblʌbər] *vi* : lloriquear

blubber[2] *n* : esperma *f* de ballena

bludgeon [ˈblʌdʒən] *vt* : aporrear

blue[1] [ˈbluː] *adj* **bluer; bluest 1** : azul **2** MELANCHOLY : melancólico, triste

blue[2] *n* : azul *m*

blueberry [ˈbluːˌbɛri] *n, pl* **-ries** : arándano *m*

bluebird [ˈbluːˌbərd] *n* : azulejo *m*

blue cheese *n* : queso *m* azul

blueprint [ˈbluːˌprɪnt] *n* **1** : plano *m,* proyecto *m,* cianotipo *m* **2** PLAN : anteproyecto *m,* programa *m*

blues [ˈbluːz] *npl* **1** DEPRESSION : depresión *f,* melancolía *f* **2** : blues *m* <to sing the blues : cantar blues>

bluff[1] [ˈblʌf] *vi* : hacer un farol, blofear *Col, Mex*

bluff[2] *adj* **1** STEEP : escarpado **2** FRANK : campechano, franco, directo

bluff[3] *n* **1** : farol *m,* blof *m Col, Mex* **2** CLIFF : acantilado *m,* risco *m*

bluffer [ˈblʌfər] *n* : farolero *m,* -ra *f fam;* blofeador *m,* -dora *f Col, Mex*

bluing *or* **blueing** [ˈbluːɪŋ] *n* : añil *m,* azulete *m*

bluish [ˈbluːɪʃ] *adj* : azulado

blunder[1] [ˈblʌndər] *vi* **1** STUMBLE : tropezar, dar traspiés **2** ERR : cometer un error, tropezar, meter la pata *fam*

blunder[2] *n* : error *m,* fallo *m* garrafal, metedura *f* de pata *fam*

blunderbuss [ˈblʌndərˌbʌs] *n* : trabuco *m*

blunt[1] [ˈblʌnt] *vt* : despuntar (aguja o lápiz), desafilar (cuchillo o tijeras), suavizar (crítica)

blunt[2] *adj* **1** DULL : desafilado, despuntado **2** DIRECT : directo, franco, categórico

bluntly [ˈblʌntli] *adv* : sin rodeos, francamente, bruscamente

bluntness [ˈblʌntnəs] *n* **1** DULLNESS : falta *f* de filo, embotadura *f* **2** FRANKNESS : franqueza *f*

blur[1] [ˈblər] *vt* **blurred; blurring** : desdibujar, hacer borroso

blur[2] *n* **1** SMEAR : mancha *f,* borrón *m* **2** : aspecto *m* borroso <everything was just a blur : todo se volvió borroso>

blurb [ˈblərb] *n* : propaganda *f,* nota *f* publicitaria

blurt [ˈblərt] *vt* : espetar, decir impulsivamente

blush[1] [ˈblʌʃ] *vi* : ruborizarse, sonrojarse, hacerse colorado

blush[2] *n* : rubor *m,* sonrojo *m*

bluster[1] [ˈblʌstər] *vi* **1** BLOW : soplar con fuerza **2** BOAST : fanfarronear, echar bravatas

bluster[2] *n* : fanfarronada *f,* bravata *f*

blustery [ˈblʌstəri] *adj* : borrascoso, tempestuoso

boa [ˈboːə] *n* : boa *f*

boar [ˈbor] *n* : cerdo *m* macho, verraco *m*

board[1] [ˈbord] *vt* **1** : embarcarse en, subir a bordo de (una nave o un avión), subir a (un tren o carro) **2** LODGE : hospedar, dar hospedaje con comidas a **3 to board up** : cerrar con tablas

board[2] *n* **1** PLANK : tabla *f,* tablón *m* **2** : tablero *m* <chessboard : tablero de ajedrez> **3** MEALS : comida *f* <board and lodging : comida y alojamiento> **4** COMMITTEE, COUNCIL : junta *f,* consejo *m*

boarder [ˈbordər] *n* LODGER : huésped *m,* -peda *f*

boardinghouse [ˈbordɪŋˌhaʊs] *n* : casa *f* de huéspedes

boarding school *n* : internado *m*

boardwalk [ˈbordˌwɔk] *n* **:** paseo *m* marítimo entablado
boast[1] [ˈboːst] *vi* **:** alardear, presumir, jactarse
boast[2] *n* **:** jactancia *f,* alarde *m*
boaster [ˈboːstər] *n* **:** presumido *m,* -da *f;* fanfarrón *m,* -rrona *f fam*
boastful [ˈboːstfəl] *adj* **:** jactancioso, fanfarrón *fam*
boastfully [ˈboːstfəli] *adv* **:** de manera jactanciosa
boat[1] [ˈboːt] *vt* **:** transportar en barco, poner a bordo
boat[2] *n* **:** barco *m,* embarcación *f,* bote *m,* barca *f*
boatman [ˈboːtmən] *n, pl* **-men** [-mən, -ˌmɛn] **:** barquero *m*
boatswain [ˈboːsən] *n* **:** contramaestre *m*
bob[1] [ˈbɑb] *v* **bobbed; bobbing** *vi* **1 :** balancearse, mecerse <to bob up and down : subir y bajar> **2** *or* **to bob up** APPEAR **:** presentarse, surgir — *vt* **1 :** inclinar (la cabeza o el cuerpo) **2** CUT **:** cortar, recortar <she bobbed her hair : se cortó el pelo>
bob[2] *n* **1 :** inclinación *f* (de la cabeza, del cuerpo), sacudida *f* **2** FLOAT **:** flotador *m,* corcho *m* (de pesca) **3 :** pelo *m* corto
bobbin [ˈbɑbən] *n* **:** bobina *f,* carrete *m*
bobby pin [ˈbɑbiˌpɪn] *n* **:** horquilla *f*
bobcat [ˈbɑbˌkæt] *n* **:** lince *m* rojo
bobolink [ˈbɑbəˌlɪŋk] *n* **:** tordo *m* arrocero
bobsled [ˈbɑbˌslɛd] *n* **:** bobsleigh *m*
bobwhite [ˈbɑbˈhwaɪt] *n* **:** codorniz *m* (del Nuevo Mundo)
bode[1] [ˈboːd] *v* **boded; boding** *vt* **:** presagiar, augurar — *vi* **to bode well :** ser de buen agüero
bode[2] → **bide**
bodice [ˈbɑdəs] *n* **:** corpiño *m*
bodied [ˈbɑdid] *adj* **:** de cuerpo <lean-bodied : de cuerpo delgado> <able-bodied : no discapacitado>
bodiless [ˈbɑdiləs, ˈbɑdələs] *adj* **:** incorpóreo
bodily[1] [ˈbɑdəli] *adv* **:** en peso <to lift someone bodily : levantar a alguien en peso>
bodily[2] *adj* **:** corporal, del cuerpo <bodily harm : daños corporales>
body [ˈbɑdi] *n, pl* **bodies 1 :** cuerpo *m,* organismo *m* **2** CORPSE **:** cadáver *m* **3** PERSON **:** persona *f,* ser *m* humano **4 :** nave *f* (de una iglesia), carrocería (de un automóvil), fuselaje *m* (de un avión), casco *m* (de una nave) **5** COLLECTION, MASS **:** conjunto *m,* grupo *m,* masa *f* <in a body : todos juntos, en masa> **6** ORGANIZATION **:** organismo *m,* organización *f*
bodyguard [ˈbɑdiˌgɑrd] *n* **:** guardaespaldas *mf*
bog[1] [ˈbɑg, ˈbɔg] *vt* **bogged; bogging :** empantanar, inundar <to get bogged down : empantanarse>
bog[2] *n* **:** lodazal *m,* ciénaga *f,* cenagal *m*
bogey [ˈbʊgi, ˈboː-] *n, pl* **-geys :** terror *m,* coco *m fam*
boggle [ˈbɑgəl] *vi* **-gled; -gling :** quedarse atónito, quedarse pasmado <the mind boggles! : ¡es increíble!>
boggy [ˈbɑgi, ˈbɔ-] *adj* **boggier; -est :** cenagoso
bogus [ˈboːgəs] *adj* **:** falso, fingido, falaz
bohemian [boːˈhiːmiən] *n* **:** bohemio *m,* -mia *f* — **bohemian** *adj*
boil[1] [ˈbɔɪl] *vi* **1 :** hervir **2 to make one's blood boil :** hervirle la sangre a uno — *vt* **1 :** hervir, hacer hervir <to boil water : hervir agua> **2 :** cocer, hervir <to boil potatoes : cocer papas>
boil[2] *n* **1** BOILING **:** hervor *m* **2 :** furúnculo *m,* divieso *m* (in medicine)
boiler [ˈbɔɪlər] *n* **:** caldera *f*
boisterous [ˈbɔɪstərəs] *adj* **:** bullicioso, escandaloso — **boisterously** *adv*
bold [ˈboːld] *adj* **1** COURAGEOUS **:** valiente **2** INSOLENT **:** insolente, descarado **3** DARING **:** atrevido, andaz — **boldly** *adv*
boldface [ˈboːldˌfeɪs] *n or* **boldface type :** negrita *f*
boldness [ˈboːldnəs] *n* **1** COURAGE **:** valor *m,* coraje *m* **2** INSOLENCE **:** atrevimiento *m,* insolencia *f,* descaro *m* **3** DARING **:** audacia *f*
bolero [bəˈlɛro] *n, pl* **-ros :** bolero *m*
Bolivian [bəˈlɪviən] *n* **:** boliviano *m,* -na *f* — **Bolivian** *adj*
boll [ˈboːl] *n* **:** cápsula *f* (del algodón)
boll weevil *n* **:** gorgojo *m* del algodón
bologna [bəˈloːni] *n* **:** salchicha *f* ahumada
bolster[1] [ˈboːlstər] *vt* **-stered; -stering :** reforzar, reafirmar <to bolster morale : levantar la moral>
bolster[2] *n* **:** cabezal *m,* almohadón *m*
bolt[1] [ˈboːlt] *vt* **1** atornillar, sujetar con pernos <bolted to the floor : sujetado con pernos al suelo> **2 :** cerrar con pestillo, echar el cerrojo a <to bolt the door : echar el cerrojo a la puerta> **3 to bolt down :** engullir <she bolted down her dinner : engulló su comida> — *vi* **:** echar a correr, salir corriendo <he bolted from the room : salió corriendo de la sala>
bolt[2] *n* **1** LATCH **:** pestillo *m,* cerrojo *m* **2 :** tornillo *m,* perno *m* <nuts and bolts : tuercas y tornillos> **3 :** rollo *m* <a bolt of cloth : un rollo de tela> **4 lightning bolt :** relámpago *m,* rayo *m*
bomb[1] [ˈbɑm] *vt* **:** bombardear
bomb[2] *n* **:** bomba *f*
bombard [bɑmˈbɑrd, bəm-] *vt* **:** bombardear
bombardier [ˌbɑmbəˈdɪr] *n* **:** bombardero *m,* -ra *f*
bombardment [bɑmˈbɑrdmənt] *n* **:** bombardeo *m*

bombast [ˈbɑmˌbæst] *n* : grandilocuencia *f,* ampulosidad *f*

bombastic [bɑmˈbæstɪk] *adj* : grandilocuente, ampuloso, bombástico

bomber [ˈbɑmər] *n* : bombardero *m*

bombproof [ˈbɑmˌpruːf] *adj* : a prueba de bombas

bombshell [ˈbɑmˌʃɛl] *n* : bomba *f* <a political bombshell : una bomba política>

bona fide [ˈboːnəˌfaɪd, ˈbɑ-; ˌboːnəˈfaɪdi] *adj* **1** : de buena fe <a bona fide offer : una oferta de buena fe> **2** GENUINE : genuino, auténtico

bonanza [bəˈnænzə] *n* : bonanza *f*

bonbon [ˈbɑnˌbɑn] *n* : bombón *m*

bond[1] [ˈbɑnd] *vt* **1** INSURE : dar fianza a, asegurar **2** STICK : adherir, pegar — *vi* : adherirse, pegarse

bond[2] *n* **1** LINK, TIE : vínculo *m,* lazo *m* **2** BAIL : fianza *f,* caución *f* **3** : bono *m* <stocks and bonds : acciones y bonos> **4 bonds** *npl* FETTERS : cadenas *fpl*

bondage [ˈbɑndɪdʒ] *n* : esclavitud *f*

bondholder [ˈbɑndˌhoːldər] *n* : tenedor *m,* -dora *f* de bonos

bondsman [ˈbɑndzmən] *n, pl* **-men** [-mən, -ˌmɛn] **1** SLAVE : esclavo *m* **2** SURETY : fiador *m,* -dora *f*

bone[1] [ˈboːn] *vt* **boned; boning** : deshuesar

bone[2] *n* : hueso *m*

boneless [ˈboːnləs] *adj* : sin huesos, sin espinas

boner [ˈboːnər] *n* : metedura *f* de pata, metida *f* de pata

bonfire [ˈbɑnˌfaɪr] *n* : hoguera *f,* fogata *f,* fogón *m*

bonito [bəˈniːt̬o] *n, pl* **-tos** *or* **-to** : bonito *m*

bonnet [ˈbɑnət] *n* : sombrero *m* (de mujer), gorra *f* (de niño)

bonus [ˈboːnəs] *n* **1** : prima *f,* bonificación *f* (pagado al empleado) **2** ADVANTAGE, BENEFIT : beneficio *m,* provecho *m*

bony [ˈboːni] *adj* **bonier; -est** : huesudo, osudo

boo[1] [ˈbuː] *vt* : abuchear

boo[2] *n, pl* **boos** : abucheo *m*

booby [ˈbuːbi] *n, pl* **-bies** : bobo *m,* -ba *f;* tonto *m,* -ta *f*

book[1] [ˈbʊk] *vt* : reservar <to book a flight : reservar un vuelo>

book[2] *n* **1** : libro *m* **2 the Book** : la Biblia **3 by the book** : según las reglas

bookcase [ˈbʊkˌkeɪs] *n* : estantería *f,* librero *m Mex*

bookend [ˈbʊkˌɛnd] *n* : sujetalibros *m*

bookie [ˈbʊki] → **bookmaker**

bookish [ˈbʊkɪʃ] *adj* : libresco

bookkeeper [ˈbʊkˌkiːpər] *n* : tenedor *m,* -dora *f* de libros; contable *mf Spain*

bookkeeping [ˈbʊkˌkiːpɪŋ] *n* : contabilidad *f,* teneduría *f* de libros

booklet [ˈbʊklət] *n* : folleto *m*

bookmaker [ˈbʊkˌmeɪkər] *n* : corredor *m,* -dora *f* de apuestas

bookmark [ˈbʊkˌmɑrk] *n* : señalador *m* de libros, marcador *m* de libros

bookseller [ˈbʊkˌsɛlər] *n* : librero *m,* -ra *f*

bookshelf [ˈbʊkˌʃɛlf] *n, pl* **-shelves 1** : estante *m* **2 bookshelves** *npl* : estantería *f*

bookstore [ˈbʊkˌstor] *n* : librería *f*

bookworm [ˈbʊkˌwərm] *n* : ratón *m* de biblioteca *fam*

boom[1] [ˈbuːm] *vi* **1** THUNDER : tronar, resonar **2** FLOURISH, PROSPER : estar en auge, prosperar

boom[2] *n* **1** BOOMING : bramido *m,* estruendo *m* **2** FLOURISHING : auge *m* <population boom : auge de población>

boomerang [ˈbuːməˌræŋ] *n* : bumerán *m*

boon[1] [ˈbuːn] *adj* **boon companion** : amigo *m,* -ga *f* del alma

boon[2] *n* : ayuda *f,* beneficio *m,* adelanto *m*

boondocks [ˈbuːnˌdɑks] *npl* : area *f* rural remota, región *f* alejada

boor [ˈbʊr] *n* : grosero *m,* -ra *f*

boorish [ˈbʊrɪʃ] *adj* : grosero

boost[1] [ˈbuːst] *vt* **1** LIFT : levantar, alzar **2** INCREASE : aumentar, incrementar **3** PROMOTE : promover, fomentar, hacer publicidad por

boost[2] *n* **1** THRUST : impulso *m,* empujón *m* **2** ENCOURAGEMENT : estímulo *m,* aliento *m* **3** INCREASE : aumento *m,* incremento *m*

booster [ˈbuːstər] *n* **1** SUPPORTER : partidario *m,* -ria *f* **2 booster rocket** : cohete *m* propulsor **3 booster shot** : vacuna *f* de refuerzo

boot[1] [ˈbuːt] *vt* KICK : dar una patada a, patear

boot[2] *n* **1** : bota *f,* botín *m* **2** KICK : puntapié *m,* patada *f*

bootee *or* **bootie** [ˈbuːt̬i] *n* : botita *f,* botín *m*

booth [ˈbuːθ] *n, pl* **booths** [ˈbuːðz, ˈbuːθs] : cabina *f* (de teléfono, de votar), caseta *f* (de información), barraca *f* (a una feria)

bootlegger [ˈbuːtˌlɛgər] *n* : contrabandista *mf* del alcohol

booty [ˈbuːt̬i] *n, pl* **-ties** : botín *m*

booze [ˈbuːz] *n* : trago *m,* bebida *f* (alcohólica)

borax [ˈbɔrˌæks] *n* : bórax *m*

border[1] [ˈbɔrdər] *vt* **1** EDGE : ribetear, bordear **2** BOUND : limitar con, lindar con — *vi* VERGE : rayar, lindar <that borders on absurdity : eso raya en el absurdo>

border[2] *n* **1** EDGE : borde *m,* orilla *f* **2** TRIM : ribete *m* **3** FRONTIER : frontera *f*

bore[1] [ˈbor] *vt* **bored; boring 1** PIERCE : taladrar, perforar <to bore metals : taladrar metales> **2** OPEN : hacer, abrir <to bore a tunnel : abrir un túnel> **3** WEARY : aburrir

bore[2] → **bear**[1]
bore[3] *n* **1 :** pesado *m,* -da *f* (persona aburrida) **2** TEDIOUSNESS **:** pesadez *f,* lo aburrido **3** DIAMETER **:** calibre *m*
boredom [ˈbordəm] *n* **:** aburrimiento *m*
boring [ˈborɪŋ] *adj* **:** aburrido, pesado
born [ˈbɔrn] *adj* **1 :** nacido **2 :** nato <she's a born singer : es una cantante nata> <he's a born leader : nació para mandar>
borne → **bear**[1]
boron [ˈborˌɑn] *n* **:** boro *m*
borough [ˈbəro] *n* **:** distrito *m* municipal
borrow [ˈbɑro] *vt* **1 :** pedir prestado, tomar prestado **2** APPROPRIATE **:** apropiarse de, adoptar
Bosnian [ˈbɑzniən, ˈbɔz-] *n* **:** bosnio *m,* -nia *f* — **Bosnian** *adj*
bosom[1] [ˈbʊzəm, ˈbuː-] *adj* **:** íntimo
bosom[2] *n* **1** CHEST **:** pecho *m* **2** BREAST **:** pecho *m,* seno *m* **3** CLOSENESS **:** seno *m* <in the bosom of her family : en el seno de su familia>
bosomed [ˈbʊzəmd, ˈbuː-] *adj* **:** con busto <big-bosomed : con mucho busto>
boss[1] [ˈbɔs] *vt* **1** SUPERVISE **:** dirigir, supervisar **2 to boss around :** mandonear *fam,* mangonear *fam*
boss[2] *n* **:** jefe *m,* -fa *f;* patrón *m,* -trona *f*
bossy [ˈbɔsi] *adj* **bossier; -est :** mandón *fam,* autoritario, dominante
botanist [ˈbɑtənɪst] *n* **:** botánico *m,* -ca *f*
botany [ˈbɑtəni] *n* **:** botánica *f* — **botanical** [bəˈtænɪkəl] *adj*
botch[1] [ˈbɑtʃ] *vt* **:** hacer una chapuza de, estropear
botch[2] *n* **:** chapuza *f*
both[1] [ˈboːθ] *adj* **:** ambos, los dos, las dos <both books : ambos libros, los dos libros>
both[2] *conj* **:** tanto como <both Ana and her mother are tall : tanto Ana como su madre son altas>
both[3] *pron* **:** ambos *m,* -bas *f;* los dos, las dos
bother[1] [ˈbɑðər] *vt* **1** IRK **:** preocupar <nothing's bothering me : nada me preocupa> <what's bothering him? : ¿qué le pasa?> **2** PESTER **:** molestar, fastidiar — *vi* **to bother to :** molestarse en, tomar la molestia de
bother[2] *n* **1** TROUBLE **:** molestia *f,* problemas *mpl* **2** ANNOYANCE **:** molestia *f,* fastidio *m*
bothersome [ˈbɑðərsəm] *adj* **:** molesto, fastidioso
bottle[1] [ˈbɑtəl] *vt* **bottled; bottling :** embotellar, envasar
bottle[2] *n* **:** botella *f,* frasco *m*
bottleneck [ˈbɑtəlˌnɛk] *n* **1 :** cuello *m* de botello (en un camino) **2 :** embotellamiento *m,* atasco *m* (de tráfico) **3** OBSTACLE **:** obstáculo *m*
bottom[1] [ˈbɑtəm] *adj* **:** más bajo, inferior, de abajo
bottom[2] *n* **1 :** fondo *m* (de una caja, de una taza, del mar), pie *m* (de una escalera, una página, una montaña), asiento *m* (de una silla), parte *f* de abajo (de una pila) **2** CAUSE **:** origen *m,* causa *f* <to get to the bottom of : llegar al fondo de> **3** BUTTOCKS **:** trasero *m,* nalgas *fpl*
bottomless [ˈbɑtəmləs] *adj* **:** sin fondo, sin límites
botulism [ˈbɑtʃəˌlɪzəm] *n* **:** botulismo *m*
boudoir [bəˈdwɑr, bʊ-; ˈbuːˌ-, ˈbʊ-] *n* **:** tocador *m*
bough [ˈbaʊ] *n* **:** rama *f*
bought → **buy**[1]
bouillon [ˈbuːˌjɑn; ˈbʊlˌjɑn, -jən] *n* **:** caldo *m*
boulder [ˈboːldər] *n* **:** canto *m* rodado, roca *f* grande
boulevard [ˈbʊləˌvɑrd, ˈbuː-] *n* **:** bulevar *m,* boulevard *m*
bounce[1] [ˈbaʊnts] *v* **bounced; bouncing** *vt* **:** hacer rebotar — *vi* **:** rebotar
bounce[2] *n* **:** rebote *m*
bouncy [ˈbaʊntsi] *adj* **bouncier; -est 1** LIVELY **:** vivo, exuberante, animado **2** RESILIENT **:** elástico, flexible **3 :** que rebota (dícese de una pelota)
bound[1] [ˈbaʊnd] *vt* **:** delimitar, rodear — *vi* LEAP **:** saltar, dar brincos
bound[2] *adj* **1** OBLIGED **:** obligado **2 :** encuadernado, empastado <a book bound in leather : un libro encuadernado en cuero> **3** DETERMINED **:** decidido, empeñado **4 to be bound to :** ser seguro que, tener que, no caber duda que <it was bound to happen : tenía que suceder> **5 bound for :** con rumbo a <bound for Chicago : con rumbo a Chicago> <to be homeward bound : ir camino a casa>
bound[3] *n* **1** LIMIT **:** límite *m* **2** LEAP **:** salto *m,* brinco *m*
boundary [ˈbaʊndri, -dəri] *n, pl* **-aries :** límite *m,* línea *f* divisoria, linde *mf*
boundless [ˈbaʊndləs] *adj* **:** sin límites, infinito
bounteous [ˈbaʊntiəs] *adj* **1** GENEROUS **:** generoso **2** ABUNDANT **:** copioso, abundante — **bounteously** *adv*
bountiful [ˈbaʊntɪfəl] *adj* **1** GENEROUS, LIBERAL **:** munificente, pródigo, generoso **2** ABUNDANT **:** copioso, abundante
bounty [ˈbaʊnti] *n, pl* **-ties 1** GENEROSITY **:** generosidad *f,* munificiencia *f* **2** REWARD **:** recompensa *f*
bouquet [boːˈkeɪ, buː-] *n* **1 :** ramo *m,* ramillete *m* **2** FRAGRANCE **:** bouquet *m,* aroma *m*
bourbon [ˈbərbən, ˈbʊr-] *n* **:** bourbon *m,* whiskey *m* americano
bourgeois[1] [ˈbʊrʒˌwɑ, bʊrʒˈwɑ] *adj* **:** burgués
bourgeois[2] *n* **:** burgués *m,* -guesa *f*
bourgeoisie [ˌbʊrʒˌwɑˈzi] *n* **:** burguesía *f*

bout [ˈbaʊt] *n* **1** : encuentro *m,* combate *m* (en deportes) **2** ATTACK : ataque *m* (de una enfermedad) **3** PERIOD, SPELL : período *m* (de actividad)

boutique [buːˈtiːk] *n* : boutique *f*

bovine[1] [ˈboːˌvaɪn, -ˌviːn] *adj* : bovino, vacuno

bovine[2] *n* : bovino *m*

bow[1] [ˈbaʊ] *vi* **1** : hacer una reverencia, inclinarse **2** SUBMIT : ceder, resignarse, someterse — *vt* **1** LOWER : inclinar, bajar **2** BEND : doblar

bow[2] [ˈbaʊː] *n* **1** BOWING : reverencia *f,* inclinación *f* **2** : proa *f* (de un barco)

bow[3] [ˈboː] *vi* CURVE : arquearse, doblarse

bow[4] [ˈboː] *n* **1** ARCH, CURVE : arco *m,* curva *f* **2** : arco *m* (arma o vara para tocar varios instrumentos de música) **3** : lazo *m,* moño *m* <to tie a bow : hacer un moño>

bowels [ˈbaʊəls] *npl* **1** INTESTINES : intestinos *mpl* **2** : entrañas *fpl* <in the bowels of the earth : en las entrañas de la tierra>

bower [ˈbaʊər] *n* : enramada *f*

bowl[1] [ˈboːl] *vi* : jugar a los bolos

bowl[2] *n* : tazón *m,* cuenco *m*

bowler [ˈboːlər] *n* : jugador *m,* -dora *f* de bolos

bowling [ˈboːlɪŋ] *n* : bolos *mpl*

box[1] [ˈbɑks] *vt* **1** PACK : empaquetar, embalar, encajonar **2** SLAP : bofetear, cachetear — *vi* : boxear

box[2] *n* **1** CONTAINER : caja *f,* cajón *m* **2** COMPARTMENT : compartimento *m,* palco *m* (en el teatro) **3** SLAP : bofetada *f,* cachetada *f* **4** : boj *m* (planta)

boxcar [ˈbɑksˌkɑr] *n* : vagón *m* de carga, furgón *m*

boxer [ˈbɑksər] *n* : boxeador *m,* -dora *f*

boxing [ˈbɑksɪŋ] *n* : boxeo *m*

box office *n* : taquilla *f,* boletería *f*

boxwood [ˈbɑksˌwʊd] *n* : boj *m*

boy [ˈbɔɪ] *n* : niño *m,* chico *m*

boycott[1] [ˈbɔɪˌkɑt] *vt* : boicotear

boycott[2] *n* : boicot *m*

boyfriend [ˈbɔɪˌfrɛnd] *n* **1** FRIEND : amigo *m* **2** SWEETHEART : novio *m*

boyhood [ˈbɔɪˌhʊd] *n* : niñez *f*

boyish [ˈbɔɪɪʃ] *adj* : de niño, juvenil

bra [ˈbrɑ] → **brassiere**

brace[1] [ˈbreɪs] *v* **braced; bracing** *vt* **1** PROP UP, SUPPORT : apuntalar, apoyar, sostener **2** INVIGORATE : vigorizar **3** REINFORCE : reforzar — *vi* **to brace oneself** PREPARE : prepararse

brace[2] *n* **1** : berbiquí *m* <brace and bit : berbiquí y barrena> **2** CLAMP, REINFORCEMENT : abrazadera *f,* refuerzo *m* **3** : llave *f* (signo de puntuación) **4** **braces** *npl* : aparatos *mpl* (de ortodoncia), frenos *mpl Mex*

bracelet [ˈbreɪslət] *n* : brazalete *m,* pulsera *f*

bracken [ˈbrækən] *n* : helecho *m*

bracket[1] [ˈbrækət] *vt* **1** SUPPORT : asegurar, apuntalar **2** : poner entre corchetes **3** CATEGORIZE, GROUP : catalogar, agrupar

bracket[2] *n* **1** SUPPORT : soporte *m* **2** : corchete *m* (marca de puntuación) **3** CATEGORY, CLASS : clase *f,* categoría *f*

brackish [ˈbrækɪʃ] *adj* : salobre

brad [ˈbræd] *n* : clavo *m* con cabeza pequeña, clavito *m*

brag[1] [ˈbræg] *vi* **bragged; bragging** : alardear, fanfarronear, jactarse

brag[2] *n* : alarde *m,* jactancia *f,* fanfarronada *f*

braggart [ˈbrægərt] *n* : fanfarrón *m,* -rrona *f fam;* jactancioso *m,* -sa *f*

braid[1] [ˈbreɪd] *vt* : trenzar

braid[2] *n* : trenza *f*

braille [ˈbreɪl] *n* : braille *m*

brain[1] [ˈbreɪn] *vt* : romper la crisma a, aplastar el cráneo a

brain[2] *n* **1** : cerebro *m* **2** **brains** *npl* INTELLECT : inteligencia *f,* sesos *mpl*

brainless [ˈbreɪnləs] *adj* : estúpido, tonto

brainstorm [ˈbreɪnˌstɔrm] *n* : idea *f* brillante, idea *f* genial

brainy [ˈbreɪni] *adj* **brainier; -est** : inteligente, listo

braise [ˈbreɪz] *vt* **braised; braising** : cocer a fuego lento, estofar

brake[1] [ˈbreɪk] *v* **braked; braking** : frenar

brake[2] *n* : freno *m*

bramble [ˈbræmbəl] *n* : zarza *f,* zarzamora *f*

bran [ˈbræn] *n* : salvado *m*

branch[1] [ˈbræntʃ] *vi* **1** : echar ramas (dícese de una planta) **2** DIVERGE : ramificarse, separarse

branch[2] *n* **1** : rama *f* (de una planta) **2** EXTENSION : ramal *m* (de un camino, un ferrocarril, un río), rama *f* (de una familia o un campo de estudiar), sucursal *f* (de una empresa), agencia *f* (del gobierno)

brand[1] [ˈbrænd] *vt* **1** : marcar (ganado) **2** LABEL : tachar, tildar <they branded him as a liar : lo tacharon de mentiroso>

brand[2] *n* **1** : marca *f* (de ganado) **2** STIGMA : estigma *m* **3** MAKE : marca *f* <brand name : marca de fábrica>

brandish [ˈbrændɪʃ] *vt* : blandir

brand–new [ˈbrændˈnuː, -ˈnjuː] *adj* : nuevo, flamante

brandy [ˈbrændi] *n, pl* **-dies** : brandy *m*

brash [ˈbræʃ] *adj* **1** IMPULSIVE : impulsivo, impetuoso **2** BRAZEN : excesivamente desenvuelto, descarado

brass [ˈbræs] *n* **1** : latón *m* **2** GALL, NERVE : descaro *m,* cara *f fam* **3** OFFICERS : mandamases *mpl fam*

brassiere [brəˈzɪr, brɑ-] *n* : sostén *m,* brasier *m Col, Mex*

brassy [ˈbræsi] *adj* **brassier; -est** : dorado

brat [ˈbræt] *n* : mocoso *m,* -sa *f;* niño *m* mimado, niña *f* mimada

bravado [brəˈvɑdo] *n, pl* **-does** *or* **-dos** : bravuconadas *fpl,* bravatas *fpl*

brave[1] [ˈbreɪv] *vt* **braved; braving** : afrontar, hacer frente a

brave[2] *adj* **braver; bravest** : valiente, valeroso — **bravely** *adv*

brave[3] *n* : guerrero *m* indio

bravery [ˈbreɪvəri] *n* : valor *m,* valentía *f*

bravo [ˈbrɑˌvoː] *n, pl* **-vos** : bravo *m*

brawl[1] [ˈbrɔl] *vi* : pelearse, pegarse

brawl[2] *n* : pelea *f,* reyerta *f*

brawn [ˈbrɔn] *n* : fuerza *f* muscular

brawny [ˈbrɔni] *adj* **brawnier; -est** : musculoso

bray[1] [ˈbreɪ] *vi* : rebuznar

bray[2] *n* : rebuzno *m*

brazen [ˈbreɪzən] *adj* **1** : de latón **2** BOLD : descarado, directo

brazenly [ˈbreɪzənli] *adv* : descaradamente, insolentemente

brazenness [ˈbreɪzənnəs] *n* : descaro *m,* atrevimiento *m*

brazier [ˈbreɪʒər] *n* : brasero *m*

Brazilian [brəˈzɪljən] *n* : brasileño *m,* -ña *f* — **Brazilian** *adj*

Brazil nut [brəˈzɪlˌnʌt] *n* : nuez *f* de Brasil

breach[1] [ˈbriːtʃ] *vt* **1** PENETRATE : abrir una brecha en, penetrar **2** VIOLATE : infringir, violar

breach[2] *n* **1** VIOLATION : infracción *f,* violación *f* <breach of trust : abuso de confianza> **2** GAP, OPENING : brecha *f*

bread[1] [ˈbrɛd] *vt* : empanar

bread[2] *n* : pan *m*

breadth [ˈbrɛtθ] *n* : ancho *m,* anchura *f*

breadwinner [ˈbrɛdˌwɪnər] *n* : sostén *m* de la familia

break[1] [ˈbreɪk] *v* **broke** [ˈbroːk]; **broken** [ˈbroːkən]; **breaking** *vt* **1** SMASH : romper, quebrar **2** VIOLATE : infringir, violar, romper **3** SURPASS : batir, superar **4** CRUSH, RUIN : arruinar, deshacer, destrozar <to break one's spirit : quebrantar su espíritu> **5** : dar, comunicar <to break the news : dar las noticias> **6** INTERRUPT : cortar, interrumpir — *vi* **1** : romperse, quebrarse <my calculator broke : se me rompió la calculadora> **2** DISPERSE : dispersarse, despejarse **3** : estallar (dícese de una tormenta), romper (dícese del día) **4** CHANGE : cambiar (dícese del tiempo o de la voz) **5** DECREASE : bajar <my fever broke : me bajó la fiebre> **6** : divulgarse, revelarse <the news broke : la noticia se divulgó> **7 to break into** : forzar, abrir **8 to break out of** : escaparse de **9 to break through** : penetrar

break[2] *n* **1** : ruptura *f,* rotura *f,* fractura *f* (de un hueso), claro *m* (entre las nubes), cambio *m* (del tiempo) **2** CHANCE : oportunidad *f* <a lucky break : un golpe de suerte> **3** REST : descanso *m* <to take a break : tomar(se) un descanso>

breakable [ˈbreɪkəbəl] *adj* : quebradizo, frágil

breakage [ˈbreɪkɪdʒ] *n* **1** BREAKING : rotura *f* **2** DAMAGE : destrozos *mpl,* daños *mpl*

breakdown [ˈbreɪkˌdaʊn] *n* **1** : avería *f* (de máquinas), interrupción *f* (de comunicaciones), fracaso *m* (de negociaciones) **2** ANALYSIS : análisis *m,* desglose *m* **3** *or* **nervous breakdown** : crisis *f* nerviosa

break down *vi* **1** : estropearse, descomponerse <the machine broke down : la máquina se descompuso> **2** FAIL : fracasar **3** CRY : echarse a llorar — *vt* **1** DESTROY : derribar, echar abajo **2** OVERCOME : vencer (la resistencia), disipar (sospechas) **3** ANALYZE : analizar, descomponer

breaker [ˈbreɪkər] *n* **1** WAVE : ola *f* grande **2** : interruptor *m* automático (de electricidad)

breakfast[1] [ˈbrɛkfəst] *vi* : desayunar

breakfast[2] *n* : desayuno *m*

breakneck [ˈbreɪkˌnɛk] *adj* **at breakneck speed** : a una velocidad vertiginosa

break out *vi* **1** : salirse <she broke out in spots : le salieron granos> **2** ERUPT : estallar (dícese de una guerra, la violencia, etc.) **3** ESCAPE : fugarse, escaparse

break up *vt* **1** DIVIDE : dividir **2** : disolver (una muchedumbre, una pelea, etc.) — *vi* **1** BREAK : romperse **2** SEPARATE : deshacerse, separarse <I broke up with him : terminé con él>

breast [ˈbrɛst] *n* **1** : pecho *m,* seno *m* (de una mujer) **2** CHEST : pecho *m*

breastbone [ˈbrɛstˌboːn] *n* : esternón *m*

breast–feed [ˈbrɛstˌfiːd] *vt* **-fed** [-ˌfɛd]; **-feeding** : amamantar, darle de mamar (a un niño)

breath [ˈbrɛθ] *n* **1** BREATHING : aliento *m* <to hold one's breath : aguantar la respiración>**2** BREEZE : soplo *m* <a breath of fresh air : un soplo de aire freso>

breathe [ˈbriːð] *v* **breathed; breathing** *vi* **1** : respirar **2** LIVE : vivir, respirar — *vt* **1** : respirar, aspirar <to breathe fresh air : respirar el aire fresco> **2** UTTER : decir <I won't breathe a word of this : no diré nada de esto>

breathless [ˈbrɛθləs] *adj* : sin aliento, jadeante

breathlessly [ˈbrɛθləsli] *adv* : entrecortadamente, jadeando

breathlessness [ˈbrɛθləsnəs] *n* : dificultad *f* al respirar

breathtaking [ˈbrɛθˌteɪkɪŋ] *adj* IMPRESSIVE : impresionante, imponente

breeches [ˈbrɪtʃəz, ˈbriː-] *npl* : pantalones *mpl,* calzones *mpl,* bombachos *mpl*

breed[1] [ˈbriːd] *v* **bred** [ˈbrɛd]; **breeding** *vt* **1** : criar (animales) **2** ENGENDER

: engendrar, producir <familiarity breeds contempt : la confianza hace perder el respeto> **3** RAISE, REAR : criar, educar — *vi* REPRODUCE : reproducirse

breed[2] *n* **1** : variedad *f* (de plantas), raza *f* (de animales) **2** CLASS : clase *f,* tipo *m*

breeder [ˈbriːdər] *n* : criador *m,* -dora *f* (de animales); cultivador *m,* -dora *f* (de plantas)

breeze[1] [ˈbriːz] *vi* **breezed; breezing** : pasar con ligereza <to breeze in : entrar como si nada>

breeze[2] *n* : brisa *f,* soplo *m* (de aire)

breezy [ˈbriːzi] *adj* **breezier; -est 1** AIRY, WINDY : aireado, ventoso **2** LIVELY : animado, alegre **3** NONCHALANT : despreocupado

brethren → **brother**

brevity [ˈbrɛvəti] *n, pl* **-ties** : brevedad *f,* concisión *f*

brew[1] [ˈbruː] *vt* **1** : fabricar, elaborar (cerveza) **2** FOMENT : tramar, maquinar, fomentar — *vi* **1** : fabricar cerveza **2** : amenazar <a storm is brewing : una tormenta amenaza>

brew[2] *n* **1** BEER : cerveza *f* **2** POTION : brebaje *m*

brewer [ˈbruːər] *n* : cervecero *m,* -ra *f*

brewery [ˈbruːəri, ˈbrʊri] *n, pl* **-eries** : cervecería *f*

briar [ˈbraɪər] → **brier**

bribe[1] [ˈbraɪb] *vt* **bribed; bribing** : sobornar, cohechar, coimear *Arg, Chile, Peru*

bribe[2] *n* : soborno *m,* cohecho *m,* coima *f Arg, Chile, Peru,* mordida *f CA, Mex*

bribery [ˈbraɪbəri] *n, pl* **-eries** : soborno *m,* cohecho *m,* coima *f,* mordida *f CA, Mex*

bric–a–brac [ˈbrɪkəˌbræk] *npl* : baratijas *fpl,* chucherías *fpl*

brick[1] [ˈbrɪk] *vt* **to brick up** : tabicar, tapiar

brick[2] *n* : ladrillo *m*

bricklayer [ˈbrɪkˌleɪər] *n* : albañil *mf*

bricklaying [ˈbrɪkˌleɪɪŋ] *n* : albañilería *f*

bridal [ˈbraɪdəl] *adj* : nupcial, de novia

bride [ˈbraɪd] *n* : novia *f*

bridegroom [ˈbraɪdˌgruːm] *n* : novio *m*

bridesmaid [ˈbraɪdzˌmeɪd] *n* : dama *f* de honor

bridge[1] [ˈbrɪdʒ] *vt* **bridged; bridging 1** : tender un puente sobre **2 to bridge the gap** : salvar las diferencias

bridge[2] *n* **1** : puente *m* **2** : caballete *m* (de la nariz) **3** : puente *m* de mando (de un barco) **4** DENTURE : puente *m* (dental) **5** : bridge *m* (juego de naipes)

bridle[1] [ˈbraɪdəl] *v* **-dled; -dling** *vt* **1** : embridar (un caballo) **2** RESTRAIN : refrenar, dominar, contener — *vi* **to bridle at** : molestarse por, picarse por

bridle[2] *n* : brida *f*

brief[1] [ˈbriːf] *vt* : dar órdenes a, instruir

brief[2] *adj* : breve, sucinto, conciso

brief[3] *n* : resumen *m,* sumario *m*

briefcase [ˈbriːfˌkeɪs] *n* : portafolio *m,* maletín *m*

briefly [ˈbriːfli] *adv* : brevemente, por poco tiempo <to speak briefly : discursar en pocas palabras>

brier [ˈbraɪər] *n* **1** BRAMBLE : zarza *f,* rosal *m* silvestre **2** HEATH : brezo *m* veteado

brig [ˈbrɪg] *n* **1** : bergantín *m* (barco) **2** : calabozo *m* (en un barco)

brigade [brɪˈgeɪd] *n* : brigada *f*

brigadier general [ˌbrɪgəˈdɪr] *n* : general *m* de brigada

brigand [ˈbrɪgənd] *n* : bandolero *m,* -ra *f;* forajido *m,* -da *f*

bright [ˈbraɪt] *adj* **1** : brillante (dícese del sol, de los ojos), vivo (dícese de un color), claro, fuerte **2** CHEERFUL : alegre, animado <bright and early : muy temprano> **3** INTELLIGENT : listo, inteligente <a bright idea : una idea luminosa>

brighten [ˈbraɪtən] *vt* **1** ILLUMINATE : iluminar **2** ENLIVEN : alegrar, animar — *vi* **1** : hacerse más brillante **2 to brighten up** : animarse, alegrarse, mejorar

brightly [ˈbraɪtli] *adv* : vivamente, intensamente, alegremente

brightness [ˈbraɪtnəs] *n* **1** LUMINOSITY : luminosidad *f,* brillantez *f,* resplandor *m,* brillo *m* **2** CHEERFULNESS : alegría *f,* ánimo *m*

brilliance [ˈbrɪljənts] *n* **1** BRIGHTNESS : resplandor *m,* fulgor *m,* brillo *m,* brillantez *f* **2** INTELLIGENCE : inteligencia *f,* brillantez *f*

brilliancy [ˈbrɪljəntsi] → **brilliance**

brilliant [ˈbrɪljənt] *adj* : brillante

brilliantly [ˈbrɪljəntli] *adv* : brillantemente, con brillantez

brim[1] [ˈbrɪm] *vi* **brimmed; brimming 1** *or* **to brim over** : desbordarse, rebosar **2 to brim with tears** : llenarse de lágrimas

brim[2] *n* **1** : ala *f* (de un sombrero) **2** : borde *m* (de una taza o un vaso)

brimful [ˈbrɪmˈfʊl] *adj* : lleno hasta el borde, repleto, rebosante

brimless [ˈbrɪmləs] *adj* : sin ala

brimstone [ˈbrɪmˌstoːn] *n* : azufre *m*

brindled [ˈbrɪndəld] *adj* : manchado, pinto

brine [ˈbraɪn] *n* **1** : salmuera *f,* escabeche *m* (para encurtir) **2** OCEAN : océano *m,* mar *m*

bring [ˈbrɪŋ] *vt* **brought** [ˈbrɔt]; **bringing 1** CARRY : traer <bring me some coffee : tráigame un café> **2** PRODUCE : traer, producir, conseguir <his efforts will bring him success : sus esfuerzos le conseguirán el éxito> **3** PERSUADE : convencer, persuadir **4** YIELD : rendir, alcanzar, venderse por <to bring a good price : alcanzar un

precio alto> **5 to bring to an end** : terminar (con) **6 to bring to light** : sacar a la luz
bring about *vt* : ocasionar, provocar, determinar
bring forth *vt* PRODUCE : producir
bring out *vt* : sacar, publicar (un libro, etc.)
bring to *vt* REVIVE : resucitar
bring up *vt* **1** REAR : criar **2** MENTION : sacar, mencionar
brininess [ˈbraɪninəs] *n* : salinidad *f*
brink [ˈbrɪŋk] *n* : borde *m*
briny [ˈbraɪni] *adj* **brinier; -est** : salobre
briquette *or* **briquet** [brɪˈkɛt] *n* : briqueta *f*
brisk [ˈbrɪsk] *adj* **1** LIVELY : rápido, enérgico, brioso **2** INVIGORATING : fresco, estimulante
brisket [ˈbrɪskət] *n* : falda *f*
briskly [ˈbrɪskli] *adv* : rápidamente, enérgicamente, con brío
briskness [ˈbrɪsknəs] *n* : brío *m*, rapidez *f*
bristle[1] [ˈbrɪsəl] *vi* **-tled; -tling 1** : erizarse, ponerse de punta **2** : enfurecerse, enojarse <she bristled at the suggestion : se enfureció ante tal sugerencia> **3** : estar plagado, estar repleto <a city bristling with tourists : una ciudad repleta de turistas>
bristle[2] *n* : cerda *f* (de un animal), pelo *m* (de una planta)
bristly [ˈbrɪsəli] *adj* **bristlier; -est** : erizado, cerdoso, hirsuto
British[1] [ˈbrɪt̬ɪʃ] *adj* : británico
British[2] *n* **the British** *npl* : los británicos
brittle [ˈbrɪtəl] *adj* **-tler; -tlest** : frágil, quebradizo
brittleness [ˈbrɪtəlnəs] *n* : fragilidad *f*
broach [ˈbroːtʃ] *vt* BRING UP : mencionar, abordar, sacar
broad [ˈbrɔd] *adj* **1** WIDE : ancho **2** SPACIOUS : amplio, extenso **3** FULL : pleno <in broad daylight : en pleno día> **4** OBVIOUS : claro, evidente **5** TOLERANT : tolerante, liberal **6** GENERAL : general **7** ESSENTIAL : principal, esencial <the broad outline : los rasgos esenciales>
broadcast[1] [ˈbrɔdˌkæst] *vt* **-cast; -casting 1** SCATTER : esparcir, diseminar **2** CIRCULATE, SPREAD : divulgar, difundir, propagar **3** TRANSMIT : transmitir, emitir
broadcast[2] *n* **1** TRANSMISSION : transmisión *f*, emisión *f* **2** PROGRAM : programa *m*, emisión *f*
broadcaster [ˈbrɔdˌkæstər] *n* : presentador *m*, -dora *f*; locutor *m*, -tora *f*
broadcloth [ˈbrɔdˌklɔθ] *n* : paño *m* fino
broaden [ˈbrɔdən] *vt* : ampliar, ensanchar — *vi* : ampliarse, ensancharse
broadloom [ˈbrɔdˌluːm] *adj* : tejido en telar ancho
broadly [ˈbrɔdli] *adv* **1** GENERALLY : en general, aproximadamente **2** WIDELY : extensivamente
broad–minded [ˈbrɔdˈmaɪndəd] *adj* : tolerante, de amplias miras
broad–mindedness [brɔdˈmaɪndədnəs] *n* : tolerancia *f*
broadside [ˈbrɔdˌsaɪd] *n* **1** VOLLEY : andanada *f* **2** ATTACK : ataque *m*, invectiva *f*, andanada *f*
brocade [broˈkeɪd] *n* : brocado *m*
broccoli [ˈbrɑkəli] *n* : brócoli *m*, brécol *m*
brochure [broˈʃʊr] *n* : folleto *m*
brogue [ˈbroːg] *n* : acento *m* irlandés
broil[1] [ˈbrɔɪl] *vt* : asar a la parrilla
broil[2] *n* : asado *m*
broiler [ˈbrɔɪlər] *n* **1** GRILL : parrilla *f* **2** : pollo *m* para asar
broke[1] [ˈbroːk] → **break**[1]
broke[2] *adj* : pelado, arruinado <to go broke : arruinarse, quebrar>
broken [ˈbroːkən] *adj* **1** DAMAGED, SHATTERED : roto, quebrado, fracturado **2** IRREGULAR, UNEVEN : accidentado, irregular, recortado **3** VIOLATED : roto, quebrantado **4** INTERRUPTED : interrumpido, descontinuo **5** CRUSHED : abatido, quebrantado <a broken man : un hombre destrozado> **6** IMPERFECT : mal <to speak broken English : hablar el inglés con dificultad>
brokenhearted [ˌbroːkənˈhɑrt̬əd] *adj* : descorazonado, desconsolado
broker[1] [ˈbroːkər] *vt* : hacer corretaje de
broker[2] *n* **1** : agente *mf;* corredor *m*, -dora *f* **2** → **stockbroker**
brokerage [ˈbroːkərɪdʒ] *n* : corretage *m*, agencia *f* de corredores
bromine [ˈbroːˌmiːn] *n* : bromo *m*
bronchitis [brɑnˈkaɪt̬əs, brɑŋ-] *n* : bronquitis *f*
bronze[1] [ˈbrɑnz] *vt* **bronzed; bronzing** : broncear
bronze[2] *n* : bronce *m*
brooch [ˈbroːtʃ, ˈbruːtʃ] *n* : broche *m*, prendedor *m*
brood[1] [ˈbruːd] *vt* **1** INCUBATE : empollar, incubar **2** PONDER : sopesar, considerar — *vi* **1** INCUBATE : empollar **2** REFLECT : rumiar, reflexionar **3** WORRY : ponerse melancólico, inquietarse
brood[2] *adj* : de cría
brood[3] *n* : nidada *f* (de pájaros), camada *f* (de mamíferos)
brooder [ˈbruːdər] *n* **1** THINKER : pensador *m*, -dora *f* **2** INCUBATOR : incubadora *f*
brook[1] [ˈbrʊk] *vt* TOLERATE : tolerar, admitir
brook[2] *n* : arroyo *m*
broom [ˈbruːm, ˈbrʊm] *n* **1** : retama *f*, hiniesta *f* **2** : escoba *f* (para barrer)
broomstick [ˈbruːmˌstɪk, ˈbrʊm-] *n* : palo *m* de escoba
broth [ˈbrɔθ] *n, pl* **broths** [ˈbrɔθs, ˈbrɔðz] : caldo *m*

brothel [ˈbrɑθəl, ˈbrɔ-] *n* : burdel *m*

brother [ˈbrʌðər] *n, pl* **brothers** *also* **brethren** [ˈbrɛðrən, -ðərn] **1** : hermano *m* **2** KINSMAN : pariente *m*, familiar *m*

brotherhood [ˈbrʌðər,hʊd] *n* **1** FELLOWSHIP : fraternidad *f* **2** ASSOCIATION : hermandad *f*

brother–in–law [ˈbrʌðərɪn,lɔ] *n, pl* **brothers–in–law:** cuñado *m*

brotherly [ˈbrʌðərli] *adj* : fraternal

brought → **bring**

brow [ˈbraʊ] *n* **1** EYEBROW : ceja *f* **2** FOREHEAD : frente *f* **3** : cima *f* <the brow of a hill : la cima de una colina>

browbeat [ˈbraʊ,biːt] *vt* **-beat; -beaten** [-,biːtən] *or* **-beat; -beating** : intimidar

brown[1] [ˈbraʊn] *vt* **1** : dorar (en cocinar) **2** TAN : broncear — *vi* **1** : dorarse (en cocinar) **2** TAN : broncearse

brown[2] *adj* : marrón, café, castaño (dícese del pelo), moreno (dícese de la piel)

brown[3] *n* : marrón *m*, café *m*

brownish [ˈbraʊnɪʃ] *adj* : pardo

browse [ˈbraʊz] *vi* **browsed; browsing** **1** GRAZE : pacer **2** LOOK : mirar, echar un vistazo

bruin [ˈbruːɪn] *n* BEAR : oso *m*

bruise[1] [ˈbruːz] *vt* **bruised; bruising** **1** : contusionar, machucar, magullar (a una persona) **2** DAMAGE : magullar, dañar (frutas) **3** CRUSH : majar **4** HURT : herir (los sentimientos)

bruise[2] *n* : moretón *m*, cardenal *m*, magulladura *f* (dícese de frutas)

brunch [ˈbrʌntʃ] *n* : combinación *f* de desayuno y almuerzo

brunet[1] *or* **brunette** [bruːˈnɛt] *adj* : moreno

brunet[2] *or* **brunette** *n* : moreno *m*, -na *f*

brunt [ˈbrʌnt] *n* **to bear the brunt of** : llevar el peso de, aguantar el mayor impacto de

brush[1] [ˈbrʌʃ] *vt* **1** : cepillar <to brush one's teeth : cepillarse uno los dientes> **2** SWEEP : barrer, quitar con un cepillo **3** GRAZE : rozar **4 to brush off** DISREGARD : hacer caso omiso de, ignorar — *vi* **to brush up on** : repasar, refrescar, dar un repaso a

brush[2] *n* **1** *or* **brushwood** [ˈbrʌʃ-,wʊd] : broza *f* **2** SCRUB, UNDERBRUSH : maleza *f* **3** : cepillo *m*, pincel *m* (de artista), brocha *f* (de pintor) **4** TOUCH : roce *m* **5** SKIRMISH : escaramuza *f*

brush–off [ˈbrʌʃ,ɔf] *n* **to give the brush–off to** : dar calabazas a

brusque [ˈbrʌsk] *adj* : brusco — **brusquely** *adv*

brussels sprout [ˈbrʌsəlz,spraʊt] *n* : col *f* de Bruselas

brutal [ˈbruːtəl] *adj* : brutal, cruel, salvaje — **brutally** *adv*

brutality [bruːˈtæləṯi] *n, pl* **-ties** : brutalidad *f*

brutalize [ˈbruːtəl,aɪz] *vt* **-ized; -izing** : brutalizar, maltratar

brute[1] [ˈbruːt] *adj* : bruto <brute force : fuerza bruta>

brute[2] *n* **1** BEAST : bestia *f*, animal *m* **2** : bruto *m*, -ta *f*; bestia *mf* (persona)

brutish [ˈbruːtɪʃ] *adj* **1** : de animal **2** CRUEL : brutal, salvaje **3** STUPID : bruto, estúpido

bubble[1] [ˈbʌbəl] *vi* **-bled; -bling** : burbujear <to bubble over with joy : rebosar de alegría>

bubble[2] *n* : burbuja *f*

bubbly [ˈbʌbəli] *adj* **bubblier; -est** **1** BUBBLING : burbujeante **2** LIVELY : vivaz, lleno de vida

bubonic plague [buːˈbɑnɪk, ˈbjuː-] *n* : peste *f* bubónica

buccaneer [,bʌkəˈnɪr] *n* : bucanero *m*

buck[1] [ˈbʌk] *vi* **1** : corcovear (dícese de un caballo o un burro) **2** JOLT : dar sacudidas **3 to buck against** : resistirse a, rebelarse contra **4 to buck up** : animarse, levantar el ánimo — *vt* OPPOSE : oponerse a, ir en contra de

buck[2] *n, pl* **buck** *or* **bucks** **1** : animal *m* macho, ciervo *m* (macho) **2** DOLLAR : dólar *m* **3 to pass the buck** *fam* : pasar la pelota *fam*

bucket [ˈbʌkət] *n* : balde *m*, cubo *m*, cubeta *f Mex*

bucketful [ˈbʌkət,fʊl] *n* : balde *m* lleno

buckle[1] [ˈbʌkəl] *v* **-led; -ling** *vt* **1** FASTEN : abrochar **2** BEND, TWIST : combar, torcer — *vi* **1** BEND, TWIST : combarse, torcerse, doblarse (dícese de las rodillas) **2 to buckle down** : ponerse a trabajar con esmero **3 to buckle up** : abrocharse

buckle[2] *n* **1** : hebilla *f* **2** TWISTING : torcedura *f*

buckshot [ˈbʌk,ʃɑt] *n* : perdigón *m*

buckskin [ˈbʌk,skɪn] *n* : gamuza *f*

bucktooth [ˈbʌk,tuːθ] *n* : diente *m* saliente, diente *m* salido

buckwheat [ˈbʌk,*h*wiːt] *n* : trigo *m* rubión, alforfón *m*

bucolic [bjuːˈkɑlɪk] *adj* : bucólico

bud[1] [ˈbʌd] *v* **budded; budding** *vt* GRAFT : injertar — *vi* : brotar, hacer brotes

bud[2] *n* : brote *m*, yema *f*, capullo *m* (de una flor)

Buddhism [ˈbuː,dɪzəm, ˈbʊ-] *n* : Budismo *m*

Buddhist [ˈbuːdɪst, ˈbʊ-] *n* : budista *mf* — **Buddhist** *adj*

buddy [ˈbʌdi] *n, pl* **-dies** : amigo *m*, -ga *f*; compinche *mf fam*; cuate *m*, -ta *f Mex fam*

budge [ˈbʌdʒ] *vi* **budged; budging** **1** MOVE : moverse, desplazarse **2** YIELD : ceder

budget[1] [ˈbʌdʒət] *vt* : presupuestar (gastos), asignar (dinero) — *vi* : presupuestar, planear el presupuesto

budget[2] *n* : presupuesto

budgetary [ˈbʌdʒəˌtɛri] *adj* : presupuestario
buff[1] [ˈbʌf] *vt* POLISH : pulir, sacar brillo a, lustrar
buff[2] *adj* : beige, amarillento
buff[3] *n* **1** : beige *m,* amarillento *m* **2** ENTHUSIAST : aficionado *m,* -da *f;* entusiasta *mf*
buffalo [ˈbʌfəˌloː] *n, pl* **-lo** *or* **-loes 1** : búfalo *m* **2** BISON : bisonte *m*
buffer [ˈbʌfər] *n* **1** BARRIER : barrera *f* <buffer state : estado tapón> **2** SHOCK ABSORBER : amortiguador *m*
buffet[1] [ˈbʌfət] *vt* : golpear, zarandear, sacudir
buffet[2] *n* BLOW : golpe *m*
buffet[3] [ˌbʌˈfeɪ, ˌbuː-] *n* **1** : bufete *m,* bufé *m* (comida) **2** SIDEBOARD : aparador *m*
buffoon [ˌbʌˈfuːn] *n* : bufón *m,* -fona *f;* payaso *m,* -sa *f*
buffoonery [ˌbʌˈfuːnəri] *n, pl* **-eries** : bufonada *f,* payasada *f*
bug[1] [ˈbʌg] *vt* **bugged; bugging 1** PESTER : fastidiar, molestar **2** : ocultar micrófonos en
bug[2] *n* **1** INSECT : bicho *m,* insecto *m* **2** DEFECT : defecto *m,* falla *f,* problema *m* **3** GERM : microbio *m,* virus *m* **4** MICROPHONE : micrófono *m*
bugaboo [ˈbʌgəˌbuː] → **bogey**
bugbear [ˈbʌgˌbær] *n* : pesadilla *f,* coco *m*
buggy [ˈbʌgi] *n, pl* **-gies** : calesa *f* (tirada por caballos), cochecito *m* (para niños)
bugle [ˈbjuːgəl] *n* : clarín *m,* corneta *f*
bugler [ˈbjuːgələr] *n* : corneta *mf*
build[1] [ˈbɪld] *v* **built** [ˈbɪlt]; **building** *vt* **1** CONSTRUCT : construir, edificar, ensamblar, levantar **2** DEVELOP : desarrollar, elaborar, forjar **3** INCREASE : incrementar, aumentar — *vi* **to build up** : aumentar, intensificar
build[2] *n* PHYSIQUE : físico *m,* complexión *f*
builder [ˈbɪldər] *n* : constructor *m,* -tora *f;* contratista *mf*
building [ˈbɪldɪŋ] *n* **1** EDIFICE : edificio *m* **2** CONSTRUCTION : construcción *f*
built-in [ˈbɪltˈɪn] *adj* **1** : empotrado <built-in cabinets : armarios empotrados> **2** INHERENT : incorporado, intrínseco
bulb [ˈbʌlb] *n* **1** : bulbo *m* (de una planta), cabeza *f* (de ajo), cubeta *f* (de un termómetro) **2** LIGHTBULB : bombilla *f,* foco *m,* bombillo *m CA, Col, Ven*
bulbous [ˈbʌlbəs] *adj* : bulboso
Bulgarian [bʌlˈgæriən, bʊl-] *n* **1** : búlgaro *m,* -ra *f* **2** : búlgaro *m* (idioma) — **Bulgarian**
bulge[1] [ˈbʌldʒ] *vi* **bulged; bulging** : abultar, sobresalir
bulge[2] *n* : bulto *m,* protuberancia *f*
bulk[1] [ˈbʌlk] *vt* : hinchar — *vi* EXPAND, SWELL : ampliarse, hincharse
bulk[2] *n* **1** SIZE, VOLUME : volumen *m,* tamaño *m* **2** FIBER : fibra *f* **3** MASS : mole *f* **4 the bulk of** : la mayor parte de **5 in ~** : en grandes cantidades
bulkhead [ˈbʌlkˌhɛd] *n* : mamparo *m*
bulky [ˈbʌlki] *adj* **bulkier; -est** : voluminoso, grande
bull[1] [ˈbʊl] *adj* : macho
bull[2] *n* **1** : toro *m,* macho *m* (de ciertas especies) **2** : bula *f* (papal) **3** DECREE : decreto *m,* edicto *m*
bulldog [ˈbʊlˌdɔg] *n* : buldog *m*
bulldoze [ˈbʊlˌdoːz] *vt* **-dozed; -dozing 1** LEVEL : nivelar (el terreno), derribar (un edificio) **2** FORCE : forzar <he bulldozed his way through : se abrió paso a codazos>
bulldozer [ˈbʊlˌdoːzər] *n* : bulldozer *m*
bullet [ˈbʊlət] *n* : bala *f*
bulletin [ˈbʊlətən, -lətən] *n* **1** NOTICE : comunicado *m,* anuncio *m,* boletín *m* **2** NEWSLETTER : boletín *m* (informativo)
bulletin board *n* : tablón *m* de anuncios
bulletproof [ˈbʊlətˌpruːf] *adj* : antibalas, a prueba de balas
bullfight [ˈbʊlˌfaɪt] *n* : corrida *f* (de toros)
bullfighter [ˈbʊlˌfaɪtər] *n* : torero *m,* -ra *f;* matador *m*
bullfrog [ˈbʊlˌfrɔg] *n* : rana *f* toro
bullheaded [ˈbʊlˈhɛdəd] *adj* : testarudo
bullion [ˈbʊljən] *n* : oro *m* en lingotes, plata *f* en lingotes
bullock [ˈbʊlək] *n* **1** STEER : buey *m,* toro *m* castrado **2** : toro *m* joven, novillo *m*
bull's–eye [ˈbʊlzˌaɪ] *n, pl* **bull's–eyes** : diana *f,* blanco *m*
bully[1] [ˈbʊli] *vt* **-lied; -lying** : intimidar, amendrentar, mangonear
bully[2] *n, pl* **-lies** : matón *m;* bravucón *m,* -cona *f*
bulrush [ˈbʊlˌrʌʃ] *n* : especie *f* de junco
bulwark [ˈbʊlˌwərk, -ˌwɔrk; ˈbʌlˌwərk] *n* : baluarte *m,* bastión *f*
bum[1] [ˈbʌm] *v* **bummed; bumming** *vi* **to bum around** : vagabundear, vagar — *vt* : gorronear *fam,* sablear *fam*
bum[2] *adj* : inútil, malo <a bum rap : una acusación falsa>
bum[3] *n* **1** LOAFER : vago *m,* -ga *f* **2** HOBO, TRAMP : vagabundo *m,* -da *f*
bumblebee [ˈbʌmbəlˌbiː] *n* : abejorro *m*
bump[1] [ˈbʌmp] *vt* : chocar contra, golpear contra, dar <to bump one's head : darse (un golpe) en la cabeza> — *vi* **to bump into** MEET : encontrarse con, tropezarse con
bump[2] *n* **1** BULGE : bulto *m,* protuberancia *f* **2** IMPACT : golpe *m,* choque *m* **3** JOLT : sacudida *f*
bumper[1] [ˈbʌmpər] *adj* : extraordinario, récord <a bumper crop : una cosecha abundante>

bumper[2] *n* : parachoques *mpl*

bumpkin [ˈbʌmpkən] *n* : palurdo *m*, -da *f*

bumpy [ˈbʌmpi] *adj* **bumpier; -est** : desigual, lleno de baches (dícese de un camino), agitado (dícese de un vuelo en avión)

bun [ˈbʌn] *n* : bollo *m*

bunch[1] [ˈbʌntʃ] *vt* : agrupar, amontonar — *vi* **to bunch up** : amontarse, agruparse, fruncirse (dícese de una tela)

bunch[2] *n* : grupo *m*, montón *m*, ramo *m* (de flores)

bundle[1] [ˈbʌndəl] *vt* **-dled; -dling** : liar, atar

bundle[2] *n* **1** : fardo *m*, atado *m*, bulto *m*, haz *m* (de palos) **2** PARCEL : paquete *m* **3** LOAD : montón *m* <a bundle of money : un montón de dinero>

bungalow [ˈbʌŋgəˌloː] *n* : tipo de casa de un solo piso

bungle[1] [ˈbʌŋgəl] *vt* **-gled; -gling** : echar a perder, malograr

bungle[2] *n* : chapuza *f*, desatino *m*

bungler [ˈbʌŋgələr] *n* : chapucero *m*, -ra *f*; inepto *m*, -ta *f*

bunion [ˈbʌnjən] *n* : juanete *m*

bunk[1] [ˈbʌŋk] *vi* : dormir (en una litera)

bunk[2] *n* **1** *or* **bunk bed** : litera *f* **2** NONSENSE : tonterías *fpl*, bobadas *fpl*

bunker [ˈbʌŋkər] *n* **1** : carbonera *f* (en un barco) **2** SHELTER : búnker *m*

bunny [ˈbʌni] *n, pl* **-nies** : conejo *m*, -ja *f*

buoy[1] [ˈbuːi, ˈbɔɪ] *vt* **to buoy up 1** : mantener a flote **2** CHEER, HEARTEN : animar, levantar el ánimo a

buoy[2] *n* : boya *f*

buoyancy [ˈbɔɪəntsi, ˈbuːjən-] *n* **1** : flotabilidad *f* **2** OPTIMISM : confianza *f*, optimismo *m*

buoyant [ˈbɔɪənt, ˈbuːjənt] *adj* : boyante, flotante

bur *or* **burr** [ˈbər] *n* : abrojo *m* (de una planta)

burden[1] [ˈbərdən] *vt* : cargar, oprimir

burden[2] *n* : carga *f*, peso *m*

burdensome [ˈbərdənsəm] *adj* : oneroso

burdock [ˈbərˌdɑk] *n* : bardana *f*

bureau [ˈbjʊro] *n* **1** CHEST OF DRAWERS : cómoda *f* **2** DEPARTMENT : departamento *m* (del gobierno) **3** AGENCY : agencia *f* <travel bureau : agencia de viajes>

bureaucracy [bjʊˈrɑkrəsi] *n, pl* **-cies** : burocracia *f*

bureaucrat [ˈbjʊrəˌkræt] *n* : burócrata *mf*

bureaucratic [ˌbjʊrəˈkræṭɪk] *adj* : burocrático

burgeon [ˈbərdʒən] *vi* : florecer, retoñar, crecer

burglar [ˈbərglər] *n* : ladrón *m*, -drona *f*

burglarize [ˈbərgləˌraɪz] *vt* **-ized; -izing** : robar

burglary [ˈbərgləri] *n, pl* **-glaries** : robo *m*

burgle [ˈbərgəl] *vt* **-gled; -gling** : robar

burgundy [ˈbərgəndi] *n, pl* **-dies** : borgoña *m*, vino *m* de Borgoña

burial [ˈbɛriəl] *n* : entierro *m*, sepelio *m*

burlap [ˈbərˌlæp] *n* : arpillera *f*

burlesque[1] [bərˈlɛsk] *vt* **-lesqued; -lesquing** : parodiar

burlesque[2] *n* **1** PARODY : parodia *f* **2** REVUE : revista *f* (musical)

burly [ˈbərli] *adj* **-lier; -liest** : fornido, corpulento, musculoso

burn[1] [ˈbərn] *v* **burned** [ˈbərnd, ˈbərnt] *or* **burnt** [ˈbərnt]; **burning** *vt* **1** : quemar, incendiar <to burn a building : incendiar un edificio> <I burned my hand : me quemé la mano> **2** CONSUME : usar, gastar, consumir — *vi* **1** : arder (dícese de un fuego o un edificio), quemarse (dícese de la comida, etc.) **2** : estar prendido, estar encendido <we left the lights burning : dejamos las luces encendidas> **3 to burn out** : consumirse, apagarse **4 to burn with** : arder de <he was burning with jealousy : ardía de celos>

burn[2] *n* : quemadura *f*

burner [ˈbərnər] *n* : quemador *m*

burnish [ˈbərnɪʃ] *vt* : bruñir

burp[1] [ˈbərp] *vi* : eructar — *vt* : hacer eructar

burp[2] *n* : eructo *m*

burr → **bur**

burro [ˈbəro, ˈbʊr-] *n, pl* **-os** : burro *m*

burrow[1] [ˈbəro] *vi* **1** : cavar, hacer una madriguera **2 to burrow into** : hurgar en — *vt* : cavar, excavar

burrow[2] *n* : madriguera *f*, conejera *f* (de un conejo)

bursar [ˈbərsər] *n* : administrador *m*, -dora *f*

bursitis [bərˈsaɪṭəs] *n* : bursitis *f*

burst[1] [ˈbərst] *v* **burst** *or* **bursted; bursting** *vi* **1** : reventarse (dícese de una llanta o un globo), estallar (dícese de obuses o fuegos artificiales), romperse (dícese de un dique) **2 to burst in** : irrumpir en **3 to burst into** : empezar a, echar a <to burst into tears : echarse a llorar> — *vt* : reventar

burst[2] *n* **1** EXPLOSION : estallido *m*, explosión *f*, reventón *m* (de una llanta) **2** OUTBURST : arranque *m* (de actividad, de velocidad), arrebato *m* (de ira), salva *f* (de aplausos)

Burundian [bʊˈruːndiən, -ˈrʊn-] *n* : burundés *m*, -desa *f* — **Burundian** *adj*

bury [ˈbɛri] *vt* **buried; burying 1** INTER : enterrar, sepultar **2** HIDE : esconder, ocultar **3 to bury oneself in** : enfrascarse en

bus[1] [ˈbʌs] *v* **bused** *or* **bussed** [ˈbʌst]; **busing** *or* **bussing** [ˈbʌsɪŋ] *vt* : transportar en autobús — *vi* : viajar en autobús

bus[2] *n* : autobús *m,* bus *m,* camión *m Mex,* colectivo *m Arg, Bol, Peru*

busboy ['bʌs,bɔɪ] *n* : ayudante *mf* de camarero

bush ['bʊʃ] *n* **1** SHRUB : arbusto *m,* mata *f* **2** THICKET : maleza *f,* matorral *m*

bushel ['bʊʃəl] *n* : medida de áridos igual a 35.24 litros

bushing ['bʊʃɪŋ] *n* : cojinete *m*

bushy ['bʊʃi] *adj* **bushier; -est** : espeso, poblado <bushy eyebrows : cejas pobladas>

busily ['bɪzəli] *adv* : afanosamente, diligentemente

business ['bɪznəs, -nəz] *n* **1** OCCUPATION : ocupación *f,* oficio *m* **2** DUTY, MISSION : misión *f,* deber *m,* responsabilidad *f* **3** ESTABLISHMENT, FIRM : empresa *f,* firma *f,* negocio *m,* comercio *m* **4** COMMERCE : negocios *mpl,* comercio *m* **5** AFFAIR, MATTER : asunto *m,* cuestión *f,* cosa *f* <it's none of your business : no es asunto tuyo>

businessman ['bɪznəs,mæn, -nəz-] *n, pl* **-men** [-mən, -,mɛn] : empresario *m,* hombre *m* de negocios

businesswoman ['bɪznəs,wʊmən, -nəz-] *n, pl* **-women** [-,wɪmən] : empresaria *f,* mujer *f* de negocios

bust[1] ['bʌst] *vt* **1** BREAK, SMASH : romper, estropear, destrozar **2** TAME : domar, amansar (un caballo) — *vi* : romperse, estropearse

bust[2] *n* **1** : busto *m* (en la escultura) **2** BREASTS : pecho *m,* senos *mpl,* busto *m*

bustle[1] ['bʌsəl] *vi* **-tled; -tling to bustle about** : ir y venir, trajinar, ajetrearse

bustle[2] *n* **1** *or* **hustle and bustle** : bullicio *m,* ajetreo *m* **2** : polisón *m* (en la ropa femenina)

busy[1] ['bɪzi] *vt* **busied; busying to busy oneself with** : ocuparse con, ponerse a, entretenerse con

busy[2] *adj* **busier; -est 1** OCCUPIED : ocupado, atareado <he's busy working : está ocupado en su trabajo> <the telephone was busy : el teléfono estaba ocupado> **2** BUSTLING : concurrido, animado <a busy street : una calle concurrida, una calle con mucho tránsito>

busybody ['bɪzi,bɑdi] *n, pl* **-bodies** : entrometido *m,* -da *f;* metiche *mf fam;* metomentodo *mf*

but[1] ['bʌt] *conj* **1** THAT : que <there is no doubt but he is lazy : no cabe duda que sea perezoso> **2** WITHOUT : sin que **3** NEVERTHELESS : pero, no obstante, sin embargo <I called her but she didn't answer : la llamé pero no contestó> **4** YET : pero <he was poor but proud : era pobre pero orgulloso>

but[2] *prep* EXCEPT : excepto, menos <everyone but Carlos : todos menos Carlos> <the last but one : el penúltimo>

butcher[1] ['bʊtʃər] *vt* **1** SLAUGHTER : matar (animales) **2** KILL : matar, asesinar, masacrar **3** BOTCH : estropear, hacer una chapuza

butcher[2] *n* **1** : carnicero *m,* -ra *f* **2** KILLER : asesino *m,* -na *f* **3** BUNGLER : chapucero *m,* -ra *f*

butler ['bʌtlər] *n* : mayordomo *m*

butt[1] ['bʌt] *vt* **1** : embestir (con los cuernos), darle un cabezazo a **2** ABUT : colindar con, bordear — *vi* **to butt in 1** INTERRUPT : interrumpir **2** MEDDLE : entrometerse, meterse

butt[2] *n* **1** BUTTING : embestida *f* (de cuernos), cabezazo *m* **2** TARGET : blanco *m* <the butt of their jokes : el blanco de sus bromas> **3** BOTTOM, END : extremo *m,* culata *f* (de un rifle), colilla *f* (de un cigarillo)

butte ['bjuːt] *n* : colina *f* empinada y aislada

butter[1] ['bʌt̬ər] *vt* **1** : untar con mantequilla **2 to butter up** : halagar

butter[2] *n* : mantequilla *f*

buttercup ['bʌt̬ər,kʌp] *n* : ranúnculo *m*

butterfat ['bʌt̬ər,fæt] *n* : grasa *f* de la leche

butterfly ['bʌt̬ər,flaɪ] *n, pl* **-flies** : mariposa *f*

buttermilk ['bʌt̬ər,mɪlk] *n* : suero *m* de la leche

butternut ['bʌt̬ər,nʌt] *n* : nogal *m* ceniciento (árbol)

butterscotch ['bʌt̬ər,skɑtʃ] *n* : caramelo *m* duro hecho con mantequilla

buttery ['bʌt̬əri] *adj* : mantecoso

buttocks ['bʌt̬əks, -,tɑks] *npl* : nalgas *fpl,* trasero *m*

button[1] ['bʌtən] *vt* : abrochar, abotonar — *vi* : abrocharse, abotonarse

button[2] *n* : botón *m*

buttonhole[1] ['bʌtən,hoːl] *vt* **-holed; -holing** : acorralar

buttonhole [2] *n* : ojal *m*

buttress[1] ['bʌtrəs] *vt* : apoyar, reforzar

buttress[2] *n* **1** : contrafuerte *m* (en la arquitectura) **2** SUPPORT : apoyo *m,* sostén *m*

buxom ['bʌksəm] *adj* : con mucho busto, con mucho pecho

buy[1] ['baɪ] *vt* **bought** ['bɔt]; **buying** : comprar

buy[2] *n* BARGAIN : compra *f,* ganga *f*

buyer ['baɪər] *n* : comprador *m,* -dora *f*

buzz[1] ['bʌz] *vi* : zumbar (dícese de un insecto), sonar (dícese de un teléfono o un despertador)

buzz[2] *n* **1** : zumbido *m* (de insectos) **2** : murmullo *m,* rumor *m* (de voces)

buzzard ['bʌzərd] *n* VULTURE : buitre *m,* zopilote *m CA, Mex*

buzzer ['bʌzər] *n* : timbre *m,* chicharra *f*

buzzword ['bʌz,wərd] *n* : palabra *f* de moda

by[1] ['baɪ] *adv* **1** NEAR : cerca <he lives close by : vive muy cerca> **2 to stop**

by : pasar por casa, hacer una visita **3 to go by** : pasar <they rushed by : pasaron corriendo> **4 to put by** : reservar, poner a un lado **5 by and by** : poco después, dentro de poco **6 by and large** : en general

by[2] *prep* **1** NEAR : cerca de, al lado de, junto a **2** VIA : por <she left by the door : salió por la puerta> **3** PAST : por, por delante de <they walked by him : pasaron por delante de él> **4** DURING : de, durante <by night : de noche> **5** (*in expressions of time*) : para <we'll be there by ten : estaremos allí para las diez> <by then : para entonces> **6** (*indicating cause or agent*) : por, de, a <built by the Romans : construido por los romanos> <a book by Borges : un libro de Borges> <made by hand : hecho a mano>

by and by *adv* : dentro de poco

bygone[1] [ˈbaɪˌgɔn] *adj* : pasado

bygone[2] *n* **let bygones be bygones** : lo pasado, pasado está

bylaw *or* **byelaw** [ˈbaɪˌlɔ] *n* : norma *f*, reglamento *m*

by–line [ˈbaɪˌlaɪn] *n* : data *f*

bypass[1] [ˈbaɪˌpæs] *vt* : evitar

bypass[2] *n* : carretera *f* de circunvalación, desvío *m*

by–product [ˈbaɪˌprɑdəkt] *n* : subproducto *m*, producto *m* derivado

bystander [ˈbaɪˌstændər] *n* : espectador *m*, -dora *f*

byway [ˈbaɪˌweɪ] *n* : camino *m* (apartado), carretera *f* secundaria

byword [ˈbaɪˌwərd] *n* **1** PROVERB : proverbio *m*, refrán *m* **2 to be a byword for** : estar sinónimo de

C

c [ˈsiː] *n*, *pl* **c's** *or* **cs** : tercera letra del alfabeto inglés

cab [ˈkæb] *n* **1** TAXI : taxi *m* **2** : cabina *f* (de un camión o una locomotora) **3** CARRIAGE : coche *m* de caballos

cabal [kəˈbɑl, -ˈbæl] *n* **1** INTRIGUE, PLOT : conspiración *f*, complot *m*, intriga *f* **2** : grupo *m* de conspiradores

cabaret [ˌkæbəˈreɪ] *n* : cabaret *m*

cabbage [ˈkæbɪdʒ] *n* : col *f*, repollo *m*

cabbie *or* **cabby** [ˈkæbi] *n* : taxista *mf*

cabin [ˈkæbən] *n* **1** HUT : cabaña *f*, choza *f*, barraca *f* **2** STATEROOM : camarote *m* **3** : cabina *f* (de un automóvil o avión)

cabinet [ˈkæbnət] *n* **1** CUPBOARD : armario *m* **2** : gabinete *m*, consejo *m* de ministros **3 medicine cabinet** : botiquín *m*

cabinetmaker [ˈkæbnətˌmeɪkər] *n* : ebanista *mf*

cabinetmaking [ˈkæbnətˌmeɪkɪŋ] *n* : ebanistería *f*

cable[1] [ˈkeɪbəl] *vt* **-bled; -bling** : enviar un cable, telegrafiar

cable[2] *n* **1** : cable *m* (para colgar o sostener algo) **2** : cable *m* eléctrico **3** → **cablegram**

cablegram [ˈkeɪbəlˌgræm] *n* : telegrama *m*, cable *m*

caboose [kəˈbuːs] *n* : furgón *m* de cola, cabús *m Mex*

cabstand [ˈkæbˌstænd] *n* : parada *f* de taxis

cacao [kəˈkaʊ, -ˈkeɪo] *n*, *pl* **cacaos** : cacao *m*

cache[1] [ˈkæʃ] *vt* **cached; caching** : esconder, guardar en un escondrijo

cache[2] *n* **1** : escondite *m*, escondrijo *m* <cache of weapons : escondite de armas> **2** : cache *m* <cache memory : memoria cache>

cachet [kæˈʃeɪ] *n* : caché *m*, prestigio *m*

cackle[1] [ˈkækəl] *vi* **-led; -ling 1** CLUCK : cacarear **2** : reírse o carcajearse estridentemente <he was cackling with delight : estaba carcajeándose de gusto>

cackle[2] *n* **1** : cacareo *m* (de una polla) **2** LAUGH : risa *f* estridente

cacophony [kæˈkɑfəni, -ˈkɔ-] *n*, *pl* **-nies** : cacofonía *f*

cactus [ˈkæktəs] *n*, *pl* **cacti** [-ˌtaɪ] *or* **-tuses** : cacto *m*, cactus *m*

cadaver [kəˈdævər] *n* : cadáver *m*

cadaverous [kəˈdævərəs] *adj* : cadavérico

caddie[1] *or* **caddy** [ˈkædi] *vi* **caddied; caddying** : trabajar de caddie, hacer de caddie

caddie[2] *or* **caddy** *n*, *pl* **-dies** : caddie *mf*

caddy [ˈkædi] *n*, *pl* **-dies** : cajita *f* para té

cadence [ˈkeɪdənts] *n* : cadencia *f*, ritmo *m*

cadenced [ˈkeɪdəntst] *adj* : cadencioso, rítmico

cadet [kəˈdɛt] *n* : cadete *mf*

cadmium [ˈkædmiəm] *n* : cadmio *m*

cadre [ˈkæˌdreɪ, ˈkɑ-, -ˌdriː] *n* : cuadro *m* (de expertos)

café [kæˈfeɪ, kə-] *n* : café *m*, cafetería *f*

cafeteria [ˌkæfəˈtɪriə] *n* : cafetería *f*, restaurante *m* de autoservicio

caffeine [kæˈfiːn] *n* : cafeína *f*

cage[1] [ˈkeɪdʒ] *vt* **caged; caging** : enjaular

cage[2] *n* : jaula *f*

cagey [ˈkeɪdʒi] *adj* **-gier; -est 1** CAUTIOUS : cauteloso, reservado **2** SHREWD : astuto, vivo — **cagily** [-dʒəli] *adv*

caisson [ˈkeɪˌsɑn, -sən] *n* **1 :** cajón *m* de municiones **2 :** cajón *m* hidráulico
cajole [kəˈdʒoːl] *vt* **-joled; -joling :** engatusar
cajolery [kəˈdʒoːləri] *n* **:** engatusamiento *m*
cake[1] [ˈkeɪk] *v* **caked; caking** *vt* **:** cubrir <caked with mud : cubierto de barro> — *vi* **:** endurecerse
cake[2] *n* **1 :** torta *f,* bizcocho *m,* pastel *m* **2 :** pastilla *f* (de jabón) **3 to take the cake :** llevarse la palma, ser el colmo
calabash [ˈkæləˌbæʃ] *n* **:** calabaza *f*
calamine [ˈkæləˌmaɪn] *n* **:** calamina *f* <calamine lotion : loción de calamina>
calamitous [kəˈlæmət̬əs] *adj* **:** desastroso, catastrófico, calamitoso — **calamitously** *adv*
calamity [kəˈlæmət̬i] *n, pl* **-ties :** desastre *m,* desgracia *f,* calamidad *f*
calcium [ˈkælsiəm] *n* **:** calcio *m*
calcium carbonate [ˈkɑrbəˌneɪt, -nət] *n* **:** carbonato *m* de calcio
calculable [ˈkælkjələbəl] *adj* **:** calculable, computable
calculate [ˈkælkjəˌleɪt] *v* **-lated; -lating** *vt* **1** COMPUTE **:** calcular, computar **2** ESTIMATE **:** calcular, creer **3** INTEND **:** planear, tener la intención de <I calculated on spending $100 : planeaba gastar $100> — *vi* **:** calcular, hacer cálculos
calculated [ˈkælkjəˌleɪt̬əd] *adj* **1** ESTIMATED **:** calculado **2** DELIBERATE **:** intencional, premeditado, deliberado
calculating [ˈkælkjəˌleɪt̬ɪŋ] *adj* SHREWD **:** calculador, astuto
calculation [ˌkælkjəˈleɪʃən] *n* **:** cálculo *m*
calculator [ˈkælkjəˌleɪt̬ər] *n* **:** calculadora *f*
calculus [ˈkælkjələs] *n, pl* **-li** [-ˌlaɪ] **1 :** cálculo *m* <differential calculus : cálculo diferencial> **2** TARTAR **:** sarro *m* (dental)
caldron [ˈkɔldrən] → **cauldron**
calendar [ˈkæləndər] *n* **1 :** calendario *m* **2** SCHEDULE **:** calendario *m,* programa *m,* agenda *f*
calf [ˈkæf, ˈkɑf] *n, pl* **calves** [ˈkævz, ˈkɑvz] **1 :** becerro *m,* -rra *f;* ternero *m,* -ra *f* (de vacunos) **2 :** cría *f* (de otros mamíferos) **3 :** pantorrilla *f* (de la pierna)
calfskin [ˈkæfˌskɪn] *n* **:** piel *f* de becerro
caliber *or* **calibre** [ˈkæləbər] *n* **1 :** calibre *m* <a .38 caliber gun : una pistola de calibre .38> **2** ABILITY **:** calibre *m,* valor *m,* capacidad *f*
calibrate [ˈkæləˌbreɪt] *vt* **-brated; -brating :** calibrar (armas), graduar (termómetros)
calibration [ˌkæləˈbreɪʃən] *n* **:** calibrado *m,* calibración *f*
calico [ˈkælɪˌkoː] *n, pl* **-coes** *or* **-cos 1 :** calicó *m,* percal *m* **2** *or* **calico cat :** gato *m* manchado
calipers [ˈkæləpərz] *npl* **:** calibrador *m*
caliph *or* **calif** [ˈkeɪləf, ˈkæ-] *n* **:** califa *m*
calisthenics [ˌkæləsˈθɛnɪks] *ns & pl* **:** calistenia *f*
calk [ˈkɔk] → **caulk**
call[1] [ˈkɔl] *vi* **1** CRY, SHOUT **:** gritar, vociferar **2** VISIT **:** hacer (una) visita, visitar **3 to call for :** exigir, requerir, necesitar <it calls for patience : requiere mucha paciencia> — *vt* **1** SUMMON **:** llamar, convocar **2** TELEPHONE **:** llamar por teléfono, telefonear **3** NAME **:** llamar, apodar
call[2] *n* **1** SHOUT **:** grito *m,* llamada *f* **2 :** grito *m* (de un animal), reclamo *m* (de un pájaro) **3** SUMMONS **:** llamada *f* **4** DEMAND **:** llamado *m,* petición *f* **5** VISIT **:** visita *f* **6** DECISION **:** decisión *f* (en deportes) **7** *or* **telephone call :** llamada *f* (telefónica)
call down *vt* REPRIMAND **:** reprender, reñir
caller [ˈkɔlər] *n* **1** VISITOR **:** visita *f* **2 :** persona *f* que llama (por teléfono)
calling [ˈkɔlɪŋ] *n* **:** vocación *f,* profesión *f*
calliope [kəˈlaɪəˌpiː, ˈkæliˌoːp] *n* **:** órgano *m* de vapor
call off *vt* CANCEL **:** cancelar, suspender
callous[1] [ˈkæləs] *vt* **:** encallecer
callous[2] *adj* **1** CALLUSED **:** calloso, encallecido **2** UNFEELING **:** insensible, desalmado, cruel
callously [ˈkæləsli] *adv* **:** cruelmente, insensiblemente
callousness [ˈkæləsnəs] *n* **:** insensibilidad *f,* crueldad *f*
callow [ˈkælo] *adj* **:** inexperto, inmaduro
callus [ˈkæləs] *n* **:** callo m
callused [ˈkæləst] *adj* **:** encallecido, calloso
calm[1] [ˈkɑm, ˈkɑlm] *vt* **:** tranquilizar, calmar, sosegar — *vi* **:** tranquilizarse, calmarse <calm down! : ¡tranquilízate!>
calm[2] *adj* **1** TRANQUIL **:** calmo, tranquilo, sereno, ecuánime **2** STILL **:** en calma (dícese del mar), sin viento (dícese del aire)
calm[3] *n* **:** tranquilidad *f,* calma *f*
calmly [ˈkɑmli, ˈkɑlm-] *adv* **:** con calma, tranquilamente
calmness [ˈkɑmnəs, ˈkɑlm-] *n* **:** calma *f,* tranquilidad *f*
caloric [kəˈlɔrɪk] *adj* **:** calórico (dícese de los alimentos), calorífico (dícese de la energía)
calorie [ˈkæləri] *n* **:** caloría *f*
calumniate [kəˈlʌmniˌeɪt] *vt* **-ated; -ating :** calumniar, difamar
calumny [ˈkæləmni] *n, pl* **-nies :** calumnia *f,* difamación *f*
calve [ˈkæv, ˈkɑv] *vi* **calved; calving :** parir (dícese de los mamíferos)
calves → **calf**
calypso [kəˈlɪpˌsoː] *n, pl* **-sos :** calipso *m*

calyx ['keɪlɪks, 'kæ-] *n, pl* **-lyxes** *or* **-lyces** [-lə,si:z] **:** cáliz *m*

cam ['kæm] *n* **:** leva *f*

camaraderie [,kɑm'rɑdəri, ,kæm-; ,kɑmə'rɑ-] *n* **:** compañerismo *m,* camaradería *f*

Cambodian [kæm'bo:diən] *n* **:** camboyano *m,* -na *f* **— Cambodian** *adj*

came → **come**

camel ['kæməl] *n* **:** camello *m*

camellia [kə'mi:ljə] *n* **:** camelia *f*

cameo ['kæmi,o:] *n, pl* **-eos 1 :** camafeo *m* **2** *or* **cameo performance :** actuación *f* especial

camera ['kæmrə, 'kæmərə] *n* **:** cámara *f,* máquina *f* fotográfica

Cameroonian [,kæmə'ru:niən] *n* **:** camerunés *m,* -nesa *f*

camouflage[1] ['kæmə,flɑʒ, -,flɑdʒ] *vt* **-flaged; -flaging :** camuflajear, camuflar

camouflage[2] *n* **:** camuflaje *m*

camp[1] ['kæmp] *vi* **:** acampar, ir de camping

camp[2] *n* **1 :** campamento *m* **2** FACTION **:** campo *m,* bando *m* <in the same camp : del mismo bando> **3 to pitch camp :** acampar, poner el campamento **4 to break camp :** levantar el campamento

campaign[1] [kæm'peɪn] *vi* **:** hacer (una) campaña

campaign[2] *n* **:** campaña *f*

campanile [,kæmpə'ni:,li:, -'ni:l] *n, pl* **-niles** *or* **-nili** [-'ni:,li:] **:** campanario *m*

camper ['kæmpər] *n* **1 :** campista *mf* (persona) **2 :** cámper *m* (vehículo)

campground ['kæmp,graʊnd] *n* **:** campamento *m,* camping *m*

camphor ['kæmpfər] *n* **:** alcanfor *m*

campsite ['kæmp,saɪt] *n* **:** campamento *m,* camping *m*

campus ['kæmpəs] *n* **:** campus *m,* recinto *m* universitario

can[1] ['kæn] *v aux, past* **could** ['kʊd]; *present s & pl* **can 1 :** poder <could you help me? : ¿podría ayudarme?> **2 :** saber <she can't drive yet : todavía no sabe manejar> **3** MAY **:** poder, tener permiso para <can I sit down? : ¿puedo sentarme?> **4 :** poder <it can't be! : ¡no puede ser!> <where can they be? : ¿dónde estarán?>

can[2] ['kæn] *vt* **canned; canning 1 :** enlatar, envasar <to can tomatoes : enlatar tomates> **2** DISMISS, FIRE **:** despedir, echar

can[3] *n* **:** lata *f,* envase *m,* cubo *m* <a can of beer : una lata de cerveza> <garbage can : cubo de basura>

Canadian [kə'neɪdiən] *n* **:** canadiense *mf* **— Canadian** *adj*

canal [kə'næl] *n* **1 :** canal *m,* tubo *m* <alimentary canal : tubo digestivo> **2 :** canal *m* <Panama Canal : Canal de Panamá>

canapé ['kænəpi, -,peɪ] *n* **:** canapé *m*

canary [kə'nɛri] *n, pl* **-naries :** canario *m*

cancel ['kæntsəl] *vt* **-celed** *or* **-celled; -celing** *or* **-celling :** cancelar

cancellation [,kæntsə'leɪʃən] *n* **:** cancelación *f*

cancer ['kæntsər] *n* **:** cáncer *m*

Cancer *n* **:** Cáncer *mf*

cancerous ['kæntsərəs] *adj* **:** canceroso

candelabrum [,kændə'lɑbrəm, -'læ-] *or* **candelabra** [-brə] *n, pl* **-bra** *or* **-bras :** candelabro *m*

candid ['kændɪd] *adj* **1** FRANK **:** franco, sincero, abierto **2 :** natural, espontáneo (en la fotografía)

candidacy ['kændədəsi] *n, pl* **-cies :** candidatura *f*

candidate ['kændə,deɪt, -dət] *n* **:** candidato *m,* -ta *f*

candidly ['kændɪdli] *adv* **:** con franqueza

candied ['kændid] *adj* **:** confitado

candle ['kændəl] *n* **:** vela *f,* candela *f,* cirio *m* (ceremonial)

candlestick ['kændəl,stɪk] *n* **:** candelero *m*

candor ['kændər] *n* **:** franqueza *f*

candy ['kændi] *n, pl* **-dies :** dulce *m,* caramelo *m*

cane[1] ['keɪn] *vt* **caned; caning 1 :** tapizar (muebles) con mimbre **2** FLOG **:** azotar con una vara

cane[2] *n* **1 :** bastón *m* (para andar), vara *f* (para castigar) **2** REED **:** caña *f,* mimbre *m* (para muebles)

canine[1] ['keɪ,naɪn] *adj* **:** canino

canine[2] *n* **1** DOG **:** canino *m;* perro *m,* -rra *f* **2** *or* **canine tooth :** colmillo *m,* diente *m* canino

canister ['kænəstər] *n* **:** lata *f,* bote *m*

canker ['kæŋkər] *n* **:** úlcera *f* bucal

cannery ['kænəri] *n, pl* **-ries :** fábrica *f* de conservas

cannibal ['kænəbəl] *n* **:** caníbal *mf;* antropófago *m,* -ga *f*

cannibalism ['kænəbə,lɪzəm] *n* **:** canibalismo *m,* antropofagia *f*

cannily ['kænəbə,laɪz] *adv* **:** astutamente, sagazmente

cannon ['kænən] *n, pl* **-nons** *or* **-non :** cañón *m*

cannot (can not) ['kæn,ɑt, kə'nɑt] → **can**[1]

canny ['kæni] *adj* **-nier; -est** SHREWD **:** astuto, sagaz

canoe[1] [kə'nu:] *vt* **-noed; -noeing :** ir en canoa

canoe[2] *n* **:** canoa *f,* piragua *f*

canon ['kænən] *n* **1 :** canon *m* <canon law : derecho canónico> **2** WORKS **:** canon *m* <the canon of American literature : el canon de la literatura americana> **3 :** canónigo *m* (de una catedral) **4** STANDARD **:** canon *m,* norma *f*

canonize ['kænə,naɪz] *vt* **-ized; -izing :** canonizar

canopy [ˈkænəpi] *n, pl* **-pies** : dosel *m,* toldo *m*

cant[1] [ˈkænt] *vt* TILT : ladear, inclinar — *vi* **1** SLANT : ladearse, inclinarse, escorar (dícese de un barco) **2** : hablar insinceramente

cant[2] *n* **1** SLANT : plano *m* inclinado **2** JARGON : jerga *f* **3** : palabras *fpl* insinceras

can't [ˈkænt, ˈkant] (*contraction of* **can not**) → **can**[1]

cantaloupe [ˈkæntəlˌoːp] *n* : melón *m,* cantalupo *m*

cantankerous [kænˈtæŋkərəs] *adj* : irritable, irascible — **cantankerously** *adv*

cantankerousness [kænˈtæŋkərəsnəs] *n* : irritabilidad *f,* irascibilidad *f*

cantata [kənˈtɑt̬ə] *n* : cantata *f*

canteen [kænˈtiːn] *n* **1** FLASK : cantimplora *f* **2** CAFETERIA : cantina *f,* comedor *m* **3** : club *m* para actividades sociales y recreativas

canter[1] [ˈkæntər] *vi* : ir a medio galope

canter[2] *n* : medio galope *m*

cantilever [ˈkæntəˌliːvər, -ˌlɛvər] *n* **1** : viga *f* voladiza **2 cantilever bridge** : puente *m* voladizo

canto [ˈkænˌtoː] *n, pl* **-tos** : canto *m*

cantor [ˈkæntər] *n* : solista *mf*

canvas [ˈkænvəs] *n* **1** : lona *f* **2** SAILS : velas *fpl* (de un barco) **3** : lienzo *m,* tela *f* (de pintar) **4** PAINTING : pintura *f,* óleo *m,* cuadro *m*

canvass[1] [ˈkænvəs] *vt* **1** SOLICIT : solicitar votos o pedidos de, hacer campaña entre **2** SOUND OUT : sondear (opiniones, etc.)

canvass[2] *n* SURVEY : sondeo *m,* encuesta *f*

canyon [ˈkænjən] *n* : cañón *m*

cap[1] [ˈkæp] *vt* **capped; capping 1** COVER : tapar (un recipiente), enfundar (un diente), cubrir (una montaña) **2** CLIMAX : coronar, ser el punto culminante de <to cap it all off : para colmo> **3** LIMIT : limitar, poner un tope a

cap[2] *n* **1** : gorra *f,* gorro *m,* cachucha *f Mex* <baseball cap : gorra de béisbol> **2** COVER, TOP : tapa *f,* tapón *m* (de botellas), corcholata *f Mex* **3** LIMIT : tope *m,* límite *m*

capability [ˌkeɪpəˈbɪlət̬i] *n, pl* **-ties** : capacidad *f,* habilidad *f,* competencia *f*

capable [ˈkeɪpəbəl] *adj* : competente, capaz, hábil — **capably** [-bli] *adv*

capacious [kəˈpeɪʃəs] *adj* : amplio, espacioso, de gran capacidad *f*

capacity[1] [kəˈpæsət̬i] *adj* : completo, total <a capacity crowd : un lleno completo>

capacity[2] *n, pl* **-ties 1** ROOM, SPACE : capacidad *f,* cabida *f,* espacio *m* **2** CAPABILITY : habilidad *f,* competencia *f* **3** FUNCTION, ROLE : calidad *f,* función *f* <in his capacity as ambassador : en su calidad de embajador>

cape [ˈkeɪp] *n* **1** : capa *f* **2** : cabo *m* <Cape Horn : el Cabo de Hornos>

caper[1] [ˈkeɪpər] *vi* : dar saltos, correr y brincar

caper[2] *n* **1** : alcaparra *f* <olives and capers : aceitunas y alcaparras> **2** ANTIC, PRANK : broma *f,* travesura *f* **3** LEAP : brinco *m,* salto *m*

Cape Verdean [ˈkeɪpˈvərdiən] *n* : caboverdiano *m,* -na *f* — **Cape Verdean** *adj*

capful [ˈkæpˌfʊl] *n* : tapa *f,* tapita *f*

capillary[1] [ˈkæpəˌlɛri] *adj* : capilar

capillary[2] *n, pl* **-ries** : capilar *m*

capital[1] [ˈkæpət̬əl] *adj* **1** : capital <capital punishment : pena capital> **2** : mayúsculo (dícese de las letras) **3** : de capital <capital assets : activo fijo> <capital gain : ganancia de capital, plusvalía> **4** EXCELLENT : excelente, estupendo

capital[2] *n* **1** *or* **capital city** : capital *f,* sede *f* del gobierno **2** WEALTH : capital *m* **3** *or* **capital letter** : mayúscula *f* **4** : capitel *m* (de una columna)

capitalism [ˈkæpət̬əlˌɪzəm] *n* : capitalismo *m*

capitalist[1] [ˈkæpət̬əlɪst] *or* **capitalistic** [ˌkæpət̬əlˈɪstɪk] *adj* : capitalista

capitalist[2] *n* : capitalista *mf*

capitalization [ˌkæpət̬ələˈzeɪʃən] *n* : capitalización *f*

capitalize [ˈkæpət̬əlˌaɪz] *v* **-ized; -izing** *vt* **1** FINANCE : capitalizar, financiar **2** : escribir con mayúscula — *vi* **to capitalize on** : sacar partido de, aprovechar

capitol [ˈkæpət̬əl] *n* : capitolio *m*

capitulate [kəˈpɪtʃəˌleɪt] *vi* **-lated; -lating** : capitular

capitulation [kəˌpɪtʃəˈleɪʃən] *n* : capitulación *f*

capon [ˈkeɪˌpɑn, -pən] *n* : capón *m*

caprice [kəˈpriːs] *n* : capricho *m,* antojo *m*

capricious [kəˈprɪʃəs, -ˈpriː-] *adj* : caprichoso — **capriciously** *adv*

Capricorn [ˈkæprɪˌkɔrn] *n* : Capricornio *mf*

capsize [ˈkæpˌsaɪz, kæpˈsaɪz] *v* **-sized; -sizing** *vi* : volcar, volcarse — *vt* : hacer volcar

capstan [ˈkæpstən, -ˌstæn] *n* : cabrestante *m*

capsule [ˈkæpsəl, -ˌsuːl] *n* **1** : cápsula *f* (en la farmacéutica y botánica) **2 space capsule** : cápsula *f* espacial

captain[1] [ˈkæptən] *vt* : capitanear

captain[2] *n* **1** : capitán *m,* -tana *f* **2** HEADWAITER : jefe *m,* -fa *f* de comedor **3 captain of industry** : magnate *mf*

caption[1] [ˈkæpʃən] *vt* : ponerle una leyenda a (una ilustración), titular (un artículo), subtitular (una película)

caption[2] *n* **1** HEADING : titular *m,* encabezamiento *m* **2** : leyenda *f* (al pie de una ilustración) **3** SUBTITLE : subtítulo *m*

captivate ['kæptə,veɪt] *vt* **-vated; -vating** CHARM : cautivar, hechizar, encantar

captivating ['kæptə,veɪt̬ɪŋ] *adj* : cautivador, hechicero, encantador

captive[1] ['kæptɪv] *adj* : cautivo

captive[2] *n* : cautivo *m,* -va *f*

captivity [kæp'tɪvət̬i] *n* : cautiverio *m*

captor ['kæptər] *n* : captor *m,* -tora *f*

capture[1] ['kæpʃər] *vt* **-tured; -turing** **1** SEIZE : capturar, apresar **2** CATCH : captar <to capture one's interest : captar el interés de uno>

capture[2] *n* : captura *f,* apresamiento *m*

car ['kɑr] *n* **1** AUTOMOBILE : automóvil *m,* coche *m,* carro *m* **2** : vagón *m,* coche *m* (de un tren) **3** : cabina *f* (de un ascensor)

carafe [kə'ræf, -'rɑf] *n* : garrafa *f*

caramel ['kɑrməl; 'kærəməl, -,mɛl] *n* **1** : caramelo *m,* azúcar *f* quemada **2** *or* **caramel candy** : caramelo *m,* dulce *m* de leche

carat ['kærət] *n* : quilate *m*

caravan ['kærə,væn] *n* : caravana *f*

caraway ['kærə,weɪ] *n* : alcaravea *f*

carbine ['kɑr,baɪn, -,biːn] *n* : carabina *f*

carbohydrate [,kɑrbo'haɪ,dreɪt, -drət] *n* : carbohidrato *m,* hidrato *m* de carbono

carbon ['kɑrbən] *n* **1** : carbono *m* **2** → **carbon paper** **3** → **carbon copy**

carbonated ['kɑrbə,neɪt̬əd] *adj* : carbonatado (dícese del agua), gaseoso (dícese de las bebidas)

carbon copy *n* **1** : copia *f* al carbón **2** DUPLICATE : duplicado *m,* copia *f* exacta

carbon paper *n* : papel *m* carbón

carbuncle ['kɑr,bʌŋkəl] *n* : carbunco *m*

carburetor ['kɑrbə,reɪt̬ər, -bjə-] *n* : carburador *m*

carcass ['kɑrkəs] *n* : cuerpo *m* (de un animal muerto)

carcinogen [kɑr'sɪnədʒən, 'kɑrsənə-,dʒɛn] *n* : carcinógeno *m,* cancerígeno *m*

carcinogenic [,kɑrsəno'dʒɛnɪk] *adj* : carcinogénico

card[1] ['kɑrd] *vt* : cardar (fibras)

card[2] *n* **1** : carta *f,* naipe *m* <to play cards : jugar a las cartas> <a deck of cards : una baraja> **2** : tarjeta *f* <birthday card : tarjeta de cumpleaños> <business card : tarjeta (de visita)> **3** : carda *f* (para cardar fibras)

cardboard ['kɑrd,bord] *n* : cartón *m,* cartulina *f*

cardiac ['kɑrdi,æk] *adj* : cardíaco, cardiaco

cardigan ['kɑrdɪgən] *n* : cárdigan *m,* chaqueta *f* de punto

cardinal[1] ['kɑrdənəl] *adj* FUNDAMENTAL : cardinal, fundamental

cardinal[2] *n* : cardenal *m*

cardinal number *n* : número *m* cardinal

cardinal point *n* : punto *m* cardinal

cardiologist [,kɑrdi'ɑlədʒɪst] *n* : cardiólogo *m,* -ga *f*

cardiology [,kɑrdi'ɑlədʒi] *n* : cardiología *f*

cardiovascular [,kɑrdio'væskjələr] *adj* : cardiovascular

care[1] ['kær] *v* **cared; caring** *vi* **1** : importarle a uno <they don't care : no les importa> **2** : preocuparse, inquietarse <she cares about the poor : se preocupa por los pobres> **3 to care for** TEND : cuidar (de), atender, encargarse de **4 to care for** CHERISH : querer, sentir cariño por **5 to care for** LIKE : gustarle (algo a uno) <I don't care for your attitude : tu actitud no me agrada> — *vt* WISH : desear, querer <if you care to go : si deseas ir>

care[2] *n* **1** ANXIETY : inquietud *f,* preocupación *f* **2** CAREFULNESS : cuidado *m,* atención *f* <handle with care : manejar con cuidado> **3** CHARGE : cargo *m,* cuidado *m* **4 to take care of** : cuidar (de), atender, encargarse de

careen [kə'riːn] *vi* **1** SWAY : oscilar, balancearse **2** CAREER : ir a toda velocidad

career[1] [kə'rɪr] *vi* : ir a toda velocidad

career[2] *n* VOCATION : vocación *f,* profesión *f,* carrera *f*

carefree ['kær,friː, ,kær'-] *adj* : despreocupado

careful ['kærfəl] *adj* **1** CAUTIOUS : cuidadoso, cauteloso **2** PAINSTAKING : cuidadoso, esmerado, meticuloso

carefully ['kærfəli] *adv* : con cuidado, cuidadosamente

carefulness ['kærfəlnəs] *n* **1** CAUTION : cuidado *m,* cautela *f* **2** METICULOUSNESS : esmero *m,* meticulosidad *f*

caregiver ['kær,gɪvər] *n* : persona *f* que cuida a niños o enfermos

careless ['kærləs] *adj* : descuidado, negligente — **carelessly** *adv*

carelessness ['kærləsnəs] *n* : descuido *m,* negligencia *f*

caress[1] [kə'rɛs] *vt* : acariciar

caress[2] *n* : caricia *f*

caret ['kærət] *n* : signo *m* de intercalación

caretaker ['kɛr,teɪkər] *n* : conserje *mf;* velador *m,* -dora *f*

cargo ['kɑr,goː] *n, pl* **-goes** *or* **-gos** : cargamento *m,* carga *f*

caribou ['kærə,buː] *n, pl* **-bou** *or* **-bous** : caribú *m*

caricature[1] ['kærɪkə,tʃʊr] *vt* **-tured; -turing** : caricaturizar

caricature[2] *n* : caricatura *f*

caricaturist ['kærɪkə,tʃʊrɪst] *n* : caricaturista *mf*

caries ['kær,iːz] *n, pl* **caries** : caries *f*

carillon ['kærə,lɑn] *n* : carillón *m*

carmine ['kɑrmən, -,maɪn] *n* : carmín *m*

carnage ['kɑrnɪdʒ] *n* : matanza *f,* carnicería *f*

carnal [ˈkɑrnəl] *adj* : carnal
carnation [kɑrˈneɪʃən] *n* : clavel *m*
carnival [ˈkɑrnəvəl] *n* : carnaval *m,* feria *f*
carnivore [ˈkɑrnəˌvor] *n* : carnívoro *m*
carnivorous [kɑrˈnɪvərəs] *adj* : carnívoro
carol[1] [ˈkærəl] *vi* **-oled** *or* **-olled; -oling** *or* **-olling** : cantar villancicos
carol[2] *n* : villancico *m*
caroler *or* **caroller** [ˈkærələr] *n* : persona *f* que canta villancicos
carom[1] [ˈkærəm] *vi* **1** REBOUND : rebotar <the bullet caromed off the wall : la bala rebotó contra el muro> **2** : hacer carambola (en billar)
carom[2] *n* : carambola *f*
carouse [kəˈraʊz] *vt* **-roused; -rousing** : irse de parranda, irse de juerga
carousel *or* **carrousel** [ˌkærəˈsɛl, ˈkærəˌ-] *n* : carrusel *m,* tiovivo *m*
carouser [kəˈraʊzər] *n* : juerguista *mf*
carp[1] [ˈkɑrp] *vi* **1** COMPLAIN : quejarse **2 to carp at** : criticar
carp[2] *n, pl* **carp** *or* **carps** : carpa *f*
carpel [ˈkɑrpəl] *n* : carpelo *m*
carpenter [ˈkɑrpəntər] *n* : carpintero *m,* -ra *f*
carpentry [ˈkɑrpəntri] *n* : carpintería *f*
carpet[1] [ˈkɑrpət] *vt* : alfombrar
carpet[2] *n* : alfombra *f*
carpeting [ˈkɑrpət̬ɪŋ] *n* : alfombrado *m*
carport [ˈkɑrˌpɔrt] *n* : cochera *f,* garaje *m* abierto
carriage [ˈkærɪdʒ] *n* **1** TRANSPORT : transporte *m* **2** POSTURE : porte *m,* postura *f* **3 horse–drawn carriage** : carruaje *m,* coche *m* **4 baby carriage** : cochecito *m*
carrier [ˈkæriər] *n* **1** : transportista *mf,* empresa *f* de transportes **2** : portador *m,* -dora *f* (de una enfermedad) **3 aircraft carrier** : portaaviones *m*
carrier pigeon : paloma *f* mensajera
carrion [ˈkæriən] *n* : carroña *f*
carrot [ˈkærət] *n* : zanahoria *f*
carry [ˈkæri] *v* **-ried; -rying** *vt* **1** TRANSPORT : llevar, cargar, transportar (cargamento), conducir (electricidad), portar (un virus) <to carry a bag : cargar una bolsa> <to carry money : llevar dinero encima, traer dinero consigo> **2** BEAR : soportar, aguantar, resistir (peso) **3** STOCK : vender, tener en abasto **4** ENTAIL : llevar, implicar, acarrear **5** WIN : ganar (una elección o competición), aprobar (una moción) **6 to carry oneself** : portarse, comportarse <he carried himself honorably : se comportó dignamente> — *vi* : oírse, proyectarse <her voice carries well : su voz se puede oír desde lejos>
carryall [ˈkæriˌɔl] *n* : bolsa *f* de viaje
carry away *vt* **to get carried away** : exaltarse, entusiasmarse
carry on *vt* CONDUCT : realizar, ejercer, mantener <to carry on research : realizar investigaciones> <to carry on a correspondence : mantener una correspondencia> — *vi* **1** : portarse de manera escandalosa o inapropiada <it's embarrassing how he carries on : su manera de comportarse da vergüenza> **2** CONTINUE : seguir, continuar
carry out *vt* **1** PERFORM : llevar a cabo, realizar **2** FULFILL : cumplir
cart[1] [ˈkɑrt] *vt* : acarrear, llevar
cart[2] *n* : carreta *f,* carro *m*
cartel [kɑrˈtɛl] *n* : cártel *m*
cartilage [ˈkɑrt̬əlɪdʒ] *n* : cartílago *m*
cartilaginous [ˌkɑrt̬əlˈædʒənəs] *adj* : cartilaginoso
cartographer [kɑrˈtɑgrəfər] *n* : cartógrafo *m,* -fa *f*
cartography [kɑrˈtɑgrəfi] *n* : cartografía *f*
carton [ˈkɑrtən] *n* : caja *f* de cartón
cartoon [kɑrˈtuːn] *n* **1** : chiste *m* (gráfico), caricatura *f* <a political cartoon : un chiste político> **2** COMIC STRIP : tira *f* cómica, historieta *f* **3** *or* **animated cartoon** : dibujo *m* animado
cartoonist [kɑrˈtuːnɪst] *n* : caricaturista *mf,* dibujante *mf* (de chistes)
cartridge [ˈkɑrtrɪdʒ] *n* : cartucho *m*
carve [ˈkɑrv] *vt* **carved; carving 1** : tallar (madera), esculpir (piedra), grabar <he carved his name in the bark : grabó su nombre en la corteza> **2** SLICE : cortar, trinchar (carne)
cascade[1] [kæsˈkeɪd] *vi* **-caded; -cading** : caer en cascada
cascade[2] *n* : cascada *f,* salto *m* de agua
case[1] [ˈkeɪs] *vt* **cased; casing 1** BOX, PACK : embalar, encajonar **2** INSPECT : observar, inspeccionar (antes de cometer un delito)
case[2] *n* **1** : caso *m* <an unusual case : un caso insólito> <ablative case : caso ablativo> <a case of the flu : un caso de gripe> **2** BOX : caja *f* **3** CONTAINER : funda *f,* estuche *m* **4 in any case** : de todos modos, en cualquier caso **5 in case** : como precaución <just in case : por si acaso> **6 in case of** : en caso de
casement [ˈkeɪsmənt] *n* : ventana *f* con bisagras
cash[1] [ˈkæʃ] *vt* : convertir en efectivo, cobrar, cambiar (un cheque)
cash[2] *n* : efectivo *m,* dinero *m* en efectivo
cashew [ˈkæˌʃuː, kəˈʃuː] *n* : anacardo *m*
cashier[1] [kæˈʃɪr] *vt* : destituir, despedir
cashier[2] *n* : cajero *m,* -ra *f*
cashmere [ˈkæʒˌmɪr, ˈkæʃ-] *n* : cachemir *m*
casino [kəˈsiːˌnoː] *n, pl* **-nos** : casino *m*
cask [ˈkæsk] *n* : tonel *m,* barrica *f,* barril *m*
casket [ˈkæskət] *n* COFFIN : ataúd *m,* féretro *m*

casserole [ˈkæsəˌroːl] *n* **1** : cazuela *f* **2** : guiso *m,* guisado *m* <tuna casserole : guiso de atún>

cassette [kəˈsɛt, kæ-] *n* : cassette *mf*

cassock [ˈkæsək] *n* : sotana *f*

cast[1] [ˈkæst] *vt* **cast; casting 1** THROW : tirar, echar, arrojar <the die is cast : la suerte está echada> **2** : depositar (un voto) **3** : asignar (papeles en una obra de teatro) **4** MOLD : moldear, fundir, vaciar **5 to cast off** ABANDON : desamparar, abandonar

cast[2] *n* **1** THROW : lance *m,* lanzamiento *m* **2** APPEARANCE : aspecto *m,* forma *f* **3** : elenco *m,* reparto *m* (de una obra de teatro) **4 plaster cast** : molde *m* de yeso, escayola *f*

castanets [ˌkæstəˈnɛts] *npl* : castañuelas *fpl*

castaway[1] [ˈkæstəˌweɪ] *adj* : náufrago

castaway[2] *n* : náufrago *m,* -ga *f*

caste [ˈkæst] *n* : casta *f*

caster [ˈkæstər] *n* : ruedita *f* (de un mueble)

castigate [ˈkæstəˌgeɪt] *vt* **-gated; -gating** : castigar severamente, censurar, reprobar

cast iron *n* : hierro *m* fundido

castle [ˈkæsəl] *n* **1** : castillo *m* **2** : torre *f* (en ajedrez)

cast–off [ˈkæstˌɔf] *adj* : desechado

castoff [ˈkæstˌɔf] *n* : desecho *m*

castrate [ˈkæsˌtreɪt] *vt* **-trated; -trating** : castrar

castration [kæˈstreɪʃən] *n* : castración *f*

casual [ˈkæʒʊəl] *adj* **1** FORTUITOUS : casual, fortuito **2** INDIFFERENT : indiferente, despreocupado **3** INFORMAL : informal — **casually** [ˈkæʒʊəli, ˈkæʒəli] *adv*

casualness [ˈkæʒʊəlnəs] *n* **1** FORTUITOUSNESS : casualidad *f* **2** INDIFFERENCE : indiferencia *f,* despreocupación *f* **3** INFORMALITY : informalidad *f*

casualty [ˈkæʒʊəlti, ˈkæʒəl-] *n, pl* **-ties 1** ACCIDENT : accidente *m* serio, desastre *m* **2** VICTIM : víctima *f;* baja *f;* herido *m,* -da *f*

cat [ˈkæt] *n* : gato *m,* -ta *f*

cataclysm [ˈkæt̬əˌklɪzəm] *n* : cataclismo *m*

cataclysmal [ˌkæt̬əˈklɪzməl] *or* **cataclysmic** [ˌkæt̬əˈklɪzmɪk] *adj* : catastrófico

catacombs [ˈkæt̬əˌkoːmz] *npl* : catacumbas *fpl*

catalog[1] *or* **catalogue** [ˈkæt̬əˌlɔg] *vt* **-loged** *or* **-logued; -loging** *or* **-loguing** : catalogar

catalog[2] *n* : catálogo *m*

catalpa [kəˈtælpə, -ˈtɔl-] *n* : catalpa *f*

catalyst [ˈkæt̬əl̬əst] *n* : catalizador *m*

catalytic [ˌkæt̬əlˈɪtɪk] *adj* : catalítico

catamaran [ˌkæt̬əməˈræn, ˈkæt̬əməˌræn] *n* : catamarán *m*

catapult[1] [ˈkæt̬əˌpʌlt, -ˌpʊlt] *vt* : catapultar

catapult[2] *n* : catapulta *f*

cataract [ˈkæt̬əˌrækt] *n* : catarata *f*

catarrh [kəˈtɑr] *n* : catarro *m*

catastrophe [kəˈtæstrəˌfiː] *n* : catástrofe *f*

catastrophic [ˌkæt̬əˈstrɑfɪk] *adj* : catastrófico — **catastrophically** [-fɪkli] *adv*

catcall [ˈkætˌkɔl] *n* : rechifla *f,* abucheo *m*

catch[1] [ˈkætʃ, ˈkɛtʃ] *v* **caught** [ˈkɔt]; **catching** *vt* **1** CAPTURE, TRAP : capturar, agarrar, atrapar, coger **2** : agarrar, pillar *fam,* tomar de sorpresa <they caught him red-handed : lo pillaron con las manos en la masa> **3** GRASP : agarrar, captar **4** ENTANGLE : enganchar, enredar **5** : tomar (un tren, etc.) **6** : contagiarse de <to catch a cold : contagiarse de un resfriado, resfriarse> — *vi* **1** GRASP : agarrar **2** HOOK : engancharse **3** IGNITE : prender, agarrar

catch[2] *n* **1** CATCHING : captura *f,* atrapada *f,* parada *f* (de una pelota) **2** : redada *f* (de pescado), presa *f* (de caza) <he's a good catch : es un buen partido> **3** LATCH : pestillo *m,* pasador *m* **4** DIFFICULTY, TRICK : problema *m,* trampa *f,* truco *m*

catcher [ˈkætʃər, ˈkɛ-] *n* : catcher *mf;* receptor *m* , -tora *f* (en béisbol)

catching [ˈkætʃɪŋ, ˈkɛ-] *adj* : contagioso

catchup [ˈkætʃəp, ˈkɛ-] → **ketchup**

catchword [ˈkætʃˌwərd, ˈkɛtʃ-] *n* : eslogan *m,* lema *m*

catchy [ˈkætʃi, ˈkɛ-] *adj* **catchier; -est** : pegajoso <a catchy song : una canción pegajosa>

catechism [ˈkæt̬əˌkɪzəm] *n* : catecismo *m*

categorical [ˌkæt̬əˈgɔrɪkəl] *adj* : categórico, absoluto, rotundo — **categorically** [-kli] *adv*

categorize [ˈkætɪgəˌraɪz] *vt* **-rized; -rizing** : clasificar, catalogar

category [ˈkæt̬əˌgori] *n, pl* **-ries** : categoría *f,* género *m,* clase *f*

cater [ˈkeɪt̬ər] *vi* **1** : proveer alimentos (para fiestas, bodas, etc.) **2 to cater to** : atender a <to cater to all tastes : atender a todos los gustos>

catercorner[1] [ˈkæt̬iˌkɔrnər, ˈkæt̬ə-, ˈkɪt̬i-] *or* **cater–cornered** [-ˌkɔrnərd] *adv* : diagonalmente, en diagonal

catercorner[2] *or* **cater–cornered** *adj* : diagonal

caterer [ˈkeɪt̬ərər] *n* : proveedor *m,* -dora *f* de comida

caterpillar [ˈkæt̬ərˌpɪlər] *n* : oruga *f*

catfish [ˈkætˌfɪʃ] *n* : bagre *m*

catgut [ˈkætˌgʌt] *n* : cuerda *f* de tripa

catharsis [kəˈθɑrsɪs] *n, pl* **catharses** [-ˌsiːz] : catarsis *f*

cathartic[1] [kəˈθɑrt̬ɪk] *adj* : catártico

cathartic[2] *n* : purgante *m*

cathedral [kəˈθiːdrəl] *n* : catedral *f*

catheter [ˈkæθət̬ər] *n* : catéter *m,* sonda *f*

cathode ['kæ,θo:d] *n* **:** cátodo *m*
catholic ['kæθəlɪk] *adj* **1** BROAD, UNIVERSAL **:** liberal, universal **2 Catholic :** católico
Catholic *n* **:** católico *m*, -ca *f*
Catholicism [kə'θαlə,sɪzəm] *n* **:** catolicismo *m*
catkin ['kætkɪn] *n* **:** amento *m*, candelilla *f*
catlike ['kæt,laɪk] *adj* **:** gatuno, felino
catnap[1] ['kæt,næp] *vi* **-napped; -napping :** tomarse una siestecita
catnap[2] *n* **:** siesta *f* breve, siestecita *f*
catnip ['kæt,nɪp] *n* **:** nébeda *f*
catsup ['kɛtʃəp, 'kætsəp] → **ketchup**
cattail ['kæt,teɪl] *n* **:** espadaña *f*, anea *f*
cattiness ['kætinəs] *n* **:** malicia *f*
cattle ['kæţəl] *npl* **:** ganado *m*, reses *mpl*
cattleman ['kæţəlmən, -,mæn] *n, pl* **-men** [-mən, -,mɛn] **:** ganadero *m*
catty ['kæţi] *adj* **-tier; -est :** malicioso, malintencionado
catwalk ['kæt,wɔk] *n* **:** pasarela *f*
Caucasian[1] [kɔ'keɪʒən] *adj* **:** caucásico
Caucasian[2] *n* **:** caucásico *m*, -ca *f*
caucus ['kɔkəs] *n* **:** junta *f* de políticos
caught → **catch**
cauldron ['kɔldrən] *n* **:** caldera *f*
cauliflower ['kαlɪ,flaʊər, 'kɔ-] *n* **:** coliflor *f*
caulk[1] ['kɔk] *vt* **:** calafatear (un barco), enmasillar (una grieta)
caulk[2] *n* **:** masilla *f*
causal ['kɔzəl] *adj* **:** causal
cause[1] ['kɔz] *vt* **caused; causing :** causar, provocar, ocasionar
cause[2] *n* **1** ORIGIN **:** causa *f*, origen *m* **2** REASON **:** causa *f*, razón *f*, motivo *m* **3** LAWSUIT **:** litigio *m*, pleito *m* **4** MOVEMENT **:** causa *f*, movimiento *m*
causeless ['kɔzləs] *adj* **:** sin causa
causeway ['kɔz,weɪ] *n* **:** camino *m* elevado
caustic ['kɔstɪk] *adj* **1** CORROSIVE **:** cáustico, corrosivo **2** BITING **:** mordaz, sarcástico
cauterize ['kɔţə,raɪz] *vt* **-ized; -izing :** cauterizar
caution[1] ['kɔʃən] *vt* **:** advertir
caution[2] *n* **1** WARNING **:** advertencia *f*, aviso *m* **2** CARE, PRUDENCE **:** precaución *f*, cuidado *m*, cautela *f*
cautionary ['kɔʃə,nɛri] *adv* **:** admonitorio <cautionary tale : cuento moral>
cautious ['kɔʃəs] *adj* **:** cauteloso, cuidadoso, precavido
cautiously ['kɔʃəsli] *adv* **:** cautelosamente, con precaución
cautiousness ['kɔʃəsnəs] *n* **:** cautela *f*, precaución *f*
cavalcade [,kævəl'keɪd, 'kævəl,-] *n* **1 :** cabalgata *f* **2** SERIES **:** serie *f*
cavalier[1] [,kævə'lɪr] *adj* **:** altivo, desdeñoso — **cavalierly** *adv*
cavalier[2] *n* **:** caballero *m*
cavalry ['kævəlri] *n, pl* **-ries :** caballería *f*
cave[1] ['keɪv] *vi* **caved; caving** *or* **to cave in :** derrumbarse
cave[2] *n* **:** cueva *f*
cavern ['kævərn] *n* **:** caverna *f*
cavernous ['kævərnəs] *adj* **:** cavernoso — **cavernously** *adv*
caviar *or* **caviare** ['kævi,αr, 'kα-] *n* **:** caviar *m*
cavity ['kævəţi] *n, pl* **-ties 1** HOLE **:** cavidad *f*, hueco *m* **2** CARIES **:** caries *f*
cavort [kə'vɔrt] *vi* **:** brincar, hacer cabriolas
caw[1] ['kɔ] *vi* **:** graznar
caw[2] *n* **:** graznido *m*
cayenne pepper [,kaɪ'ɛn, ,keɪ-] *n* **:** pimienta *f* cayena, pimentón *m*
CD [,si:'di:] *n* **:** CD *m*, disco *m* compacto
cease ['si:s] *v* **ceased; ceasing** *vt* **:** dejar de <they ceased bickering : dejaron de discutir> — *vi* **:** cesar, pasarse
ceaseless ['si:sləs] *adj* **:** incesante, continuo
cedar ['si:dər] *n* **:** cedro *m*
cede ['si:d] *vt* **ceded; ceding :** ceder, conceder
ceiling ['si:lɪŋ] *n* **1 :** techo *m*, cielo *m* **2** LIMIT **:** límite *m*, tope *m*
celebrant ['sɛləbrənt] *n* **:** celebrante *mf*, oficiante *mf*
celebrate ['sɛlə,breɪt] *v* **-brated; -brating** *vt* **1 :** celebrar, oficiar <to celebrate Mass : celebrar la misa> **2 :** celebrar, festejar <we're celebrating our anniversary : estamos celebrando nuestro aniversario> **3** EXTOL **:** alabar, ensalzar, exaltar — *vi* **:** estar de fiesta, divertirse
celebrated ['sɛlə,breɪţəd] *adj* **:** célebre, famoso, renombrado
celebration [,sɛlə'breɪʃən] *n* **:** celebración *f*, festejos *mpl*
celebrity [sə'lɛbrəţi] *n, pl* **-ties 1** RENOWN **:** fama *f*, renombre *m*, celebridad *f* **2** PERSONALITY **:** celebridad *f*, personaje *m*
celery ['sɛləri] *n, pl* **-eries :** apio *m*
celestial [sə'lɛstʃəl, -'lɛstiəl] *adj* **1 :** celeste **2** HEAVENLY **:** celestial, paradisiaco
celibacy ['sɛləbəsi] *n* **:** celibato *m*
celibate[1] ['sɛləbət] *adj* **:** célibe
celibate[2] *n* **:** célibe *mf*
cell ['sɛl] *n* **1 :** célula *f* (de un organismo) **2 :** celda *f* (en una cárcel, etc.) **3 :** elemento *m* (de una pila)
cellar ['sɛlər] *n* **1** BASEMENT **:** sótano *m* **2 :** bodega *f* (de vinos)
cellist ['tʃɛlɪst] *n* **:** violonchelista *mf*
cello ['tʃɛ,lo:] *n, pl* **-los :** violonchelo *m*
cellophane ['sɛlə,feɪn] *n* **:** celofán *m*
cellular ['sɛljələr] *adj* **:** celular
cellulose ['sɛljə,lo:s] *n* **:** celulosa *f*

Celsius ['sɛlsiəs] *adj* : centígrado <100 degrees Celsius : 100 grados centígrados>

Celt ['kɛlt, 'sɛlt] *n* : celta *mf*

Celtic[1] ['kɛltɪk, 'sɛl-] *adj* : celta

Celtic[2] *n* : celta *m* (idioma)

cement[1] [sɪ'mɛnt] *vi* : unir o cubrir algo con cemento, cementar

cement[2] *n* **1** : cemento *m* **2** GLUE : pegamento *m*

cemetery ['sɛmə,tɛri] *n, pl* **-teries** : cementerio *m,* panteón *m*

censer ['sɛntsər] *n* : incensario *m*

censor[1] ['sɛntsər] *vt* : censurar

censor[2] *n* : censor *m,* -sora *f*

censorious [sɛn'soriəs] *adj* : de censura, crítico

censorship ['sɛntsər,ʃɪp] *n* : censura *f*

censure[1] ['sɛntʃər] *vt* **-sured; -suring** : censurar, criticar, reprobar — **censurable** [-tʃərəbəl] *adj*

censure[2] *n* : censura *f,* reproche *f* oficial

census ['sɛntsəs] *n* : censo *m*

cent ['sɛnt] *n* : centavo *m*

centaur ['sɛn,tɔr] *n* : centauro *m*

centennial[1] [sɛn'tɛniəl] *adj* : del centenario

centennial[2] *n* : centenario *m*

center[1] ['sɛntər] *vt* **1** : centrar **2** CONCENTRATE : concentrar, fijar, enfocar — *vi* : centrarse, enfocarse

center[2] *n* **1** : centro *m* <center of gravity : centro de gravedad> **2** : centro *mf* (en futbol americano), pívot *mf* (en basquetbol)

centerpiece ['sɛntər,pi:s] *n* : centro *m* de mesa

centigrade ['sɛntə,greɪd, 'sɑn-] *adj* : centígrado

centigram ['sɛntə,græm, 'sɑn-] *n* : centigramo *m*

centimeter ['sɛntə,mi:t̬ər, 'sɑn-] *n* : centímetro *m*

centipede ['sɛntə,pi:d] *n* : ciempiés *m*

central ['sɛntrəl] *adj* **1** : céntrico, central <in a central location : en un lugar céntrico> **2** MAIN, PRINCIPAL : central, fundamental, principal

Central American[1] *adj* : centroamericano

Central American[2] *n* : centroamericano *m,* -na *f*

centralization [,sɛntrələ'zeɪʃən] *n* : centralización *f*

centralize ['sɛntrə,laɪz] *vt* **-ized; -izing** : centralizar

centrally ['sɛntrəli] *adv* **1 centrally heated** : con calefacción central **2 centrally located** : céntrico, en un lugar céntrico

centre ['sɛntər] → **center**

centrifugal force [sɛn'trɪfjəgəl, -'trɪfɪgəl] *n* : fuerza *f* centrífuga

century ['sɛntʃəri] *n, pl* **-ries** : siglo *m*

ceramic[1] [sə'ræmɪk] *adj* : de cerámica

ceramic[2] *n* **1** : objeto *m* de cerámica, cerámica *f* **2 ceramics** *npl* : cerámica *f*

cereal[1] ['sɪriəl] *adj* : cereal

cereal[2] *n* : cereal *m*

cerebellum [,sɛrə'bɛləm] *n, pl* **-bellums** *or* **-bella** [-'bɛlə] : cerebelo *m*

cerebral [sə'ri:brəl, 'sɛrə-] *adj* : cerebral

cerebral palsy *n* : parálisis *f* cerebral

cerebrum [sə'ri:brəm, 'sɛrə-] *n, pl* **-brums** *or* **-bra** [-brə] : cerebro *m*

ceremonial[1] [,sɛrə'mo:niəl] *adj* : ceremonial

ceremonial[2] *n* : ceremonial *m*

ceremonious [,sɛrə'mo:niəs] *adj* **1** FORMAL : ceremonioso, formal **2** CEREMONIAL : ceremonial

ceremony ['sɛrə,mo:ni] *n, pl* **-nies** : ceremonia *f*

cerise [sə'ri:s] *n* : rojo *m* cereza

certain[1] ['sərtən] *adj* **1** DEFINITE : cierto, determinado <a certain percentage : un porcentaje determinado> **2** TRUE : cierto, con certeza <I don't know for certain : no sé exactamente> **3** : cierto, alguno <it has a certain charm : tiene cierta gracia> **4** INEVITABLE : seguro, inevitable **5** ASSURED : seguro, asegurado <she's certain to do well : seguro que le irá bien>

certain[2] *pron* : ciertos *pl,* algunos *pl* <certain of my friends : algunos de mis amigos>

certainly ['sərtənli] *adv* **1** DEFINITELY : ciertamente, seguramente **2** OF COURSE : por supuesto

certainty ['sərtənti] *n, pl* **-ties** : certeza *f,* certidumbre *f,* seguridad *f*

certifiable [,sərt̬ə'faɪəbəl] *adj* : certificable

certificate [sər'tɪfɪkət] *n* : certificado *m,* acta *f* <birth certificate : acta de nacimiento>

certification [,sərt̬əfə'keɪʃən] *n* : certificación *f*

certify ['sərt̬ə,faɪ] *vt* **-fied; -fying** **1** VERIFY : certificar, verificar, confirmar **2** ENDORSE : endosar, aprobar oficialmente

certitude ['sərt̬ə,tu:d, -,tju:d] *n* : certeza *f,* certidumbre *f*

cervical ['sərvɪkəl] *adj* **1** : cervical (dícese del cuello) **2** : del cuello del útero

cervix ['sərvɪks] *n, pl* **-vices** [-və-,si:z] *or* **-vixes** **1** NECK : cerviz *f* **2** *or* **uterine cervix** : cuello *m* del útero

cesarean[1] [sɪ'zæriən] *adj* : cesáreo

cesarean[2] *n* : cesárea *f*

cesium ['si:ziəm] *n* : cesio *m*

cessation [sɛ'seɪʃən] *n* : cesación *f,* cese *m*

cesspool ['sɛs,pu:l] *n* : pozo *m* séptico

Chadian ['tʃædiən] *n* : chadiano *m,* -na *f* — **Chadian** *adj*

chafe ['tʃeɪf] *v* **chafed; chafing** *vi* : enojarse, irritarse — *vt* : rozar

chaff ['tʃæf] *n* **1** : barcia *f,* granzas *fpl* **2 to separate the wheat from the chaff** : separar el grano de la paja

chafing dish [ˈtʃeɪfɪŋˌdɪʃ] *n* : escalfador *m*

chagrin[1] [ʃəˈgrɪn] *vt* : desilusionar, avergonzar

chagrin[2] *n* : desilusión *f,* disgusto *m*

chain[1] [ˈtʃeɪn] *vt* : encadenar

chain[2] *n* **1** : cadena *f* <steel chain : cadena de acero> <restaurant chain : cadena de restaurantes> **2** SERIES : serie *f* <chain of events : serie de eventos> **3 chains** *npl* FETTERS : grillos *mpl*

chair[1] [ˈtʃɛr] *vt* : presidir, moderar

chair[2] *n* **1** : silla *f* **2** CHAIRMANSHIP : presidencia *f* **3** → **chairman, chairwoman**

chairman [ˈtʃɛrmən] *n, pl* **-men** [-mən, -ˌmɛn] : presidente *m*

chairmanship [ˈtʃɛrmənˌʃɪp] *n* : presidencia *f*

chairwoman [ˈtʃɛrˌwʊmən] *n, pl* **-women** [-ˌwɪmən] : presidenta *f*

chaise longue [ˈʃeɪzˈlɔŋ] *n, pl* **chaise longues** [-lɔŋ, -ˈlɔŋz] : chaise longue *f*

chalet [ʃæˈleɪ] *n* : chalet *m,* chalé *m*

chalice [ˈtʃælɪs] *n* : cáliz *m*

chalk[1] [ˈtʃɔk] *vt* : escribir con tiza

chalk[2] *n* **1** LIMESTONE : creta *f,* caliza *f* **2** : tiza *f,* gis *m Mex* (para escribir)

chalkboard [ˈtʃɔkˌbord] → **blackboard**

chalk up *vt* **1** ASCRIBE : atribuir, adscribir **2** SCORE : apuntarse, anotarse (una victoria, etc.)

chalky [ˈtʃɔki] *adj* **chalkier; -est** : calcáreo

challenge[1] [ˈtʃælɪndʒ] *vt* **-lenged; -lenging 1** DISPUTE : disputar, cuestionar, poner en duda **2** DARE : desafiar, retar **3** STIMULATE : estimular, incentivar

challenge[2] *n* : reto *m,* desafío *m*

challenger [ˈtʃælɪndʒər] *n* : retador *m,* -dora *f;* contendiente *mf*

chamber [ˈtʃeɪmbər] *n* **1** ROOM : cámara *f,* sala *f* <the senate chamber : la cámara del senado> **2** : recámara *f* (de un arma de fuego), cámara *f* (de combustión) **3** : cámara *f* <chamber of commerce : cámara de comercio> **4 chambers** *npl or* **judge's chambers** : despacho *m* del juez

chambermaid [ˈtʃeɪmbərˌmeɪd] *n* : camarera *f*

chamber music *n* : música *f* de cámara

chameleon [kəˈmiːljən, -liən] *n* : camaleón *m*

chamois [ˈʃæmi] *n, pl* **chamois** [-mi, -miz] : gamuza *f*

champ[1] [ˈtʃæmp, ˈtʃɑmp] *vi* **1** : masticar ruidosamente **2 to champ at the bit** : impacientarse, comerle a uno la impaciencia

champ[2] [ˈtʃæmp] *n* : campeón *m,* -peona *f*

champagne [ʃæmˈpeɪn] *n* : champaña *m,* champán *m*

champion[1] [ˈtʃæmpiən] *vt* : defender, luchar por (una causa)

champion[2] *n* **1** ADVOCATE, DEFENDER : paladín *m;* campeón *m,* -peona *f;* defensor *m,* -sora *f* **2** WINNER : campeón *m,* -peona *f* <world champion : campeón mundial>

championship [ˈtʃæmpiənˌʃɪp] *n* : campeonato *m*

chance[1] [ˈtʃænts] *v* **chanced; chancing** *vi* **1** HAPPEN : ocurrir por casualidad **2 to chance upon** : encontrar por casualidad — *vt* RISK : arriesgar

chance[2] *adj* : fortuito, casual <a chance encounter : un encuentro casual>

chance[3] *n* **1** FATE, LUCK : azar *m,* suerte *f,* fortuna *f* **2** OPPORTUNITY : oportunidad *f,* ocasión *f* **3** PROBABILITY : probabilidad *f,* posibilidad *f* **4** RISK : riesgo *m* **5** : boleto *m* (de una rifa o lotería) **6 by chance** : por casualidad

chancellor [ˈtʃæntsələr] *n* **1** : canciller *m* **2** : rector *m,* -tora *f* (de una universidad)

chancre [ˈʃæŋkər] *n* : chancro *m*

chancy [ˈtʃæntsi] *adj* **chancier; -est** : riesgoso, arriesgado

chandelier [ˌʃændəˈlɪr] *n* : araña *f* de luces

change[1] [ˈtʃeɪndʒ] *v* **changed; changing** *vt* **1** ALTER : cambiar, alterar, modificar **2** EXCHANGE : cambiar de, intercambiar <to change places : cambiar de sitio> — *vi* **1** VARY : cambiar, variar, transformarse <you haven't changed : no has cambiado> **2** *or* **to change clothes** : cambiarse (de ropa)

change[2] *n* **1** ALTERATION : cambio *m* **2** : cambio *m,* vuelto *m* <two dollars change : dos dólares de vuelto> **3** COINS : cambio *m,* monedas *fpl*

changeable [ˈtʃeɪndʒəbəl] *adj* : cambiante, variable

changeless [ˈtʃeɪndʒləs] *adj* : invariable, constante

changer [ˈtʃeɪndʒər] *n* **1** : cambiador *m* <record changer : cambiador de discos> **2** *or* **money changer** : cambista *mf* (de dinero)

channel[1] [ˈtʃænəl] *vt* **-neled** *or* **-nelled; -neling** *or* **-nelling** : encauzar, canalizar

channel[2] *n* **1** RIVERBED : cauce *m* **2** STRAIT : canal *m,* estrecho *m* <English Channel : Canal de la Mancha> **3** COURSE, MEANS : vía *f,* conducto *m* <the usual channels : las vías normales> **4** : canal *m* (de televisión)

chant[1] [ˈtʃænt] *v* : salmodiar, cantar

chant[2] *n* : **1** : salmodia *f* **2 Gregorian chant** : canto *m* gregoriano

Chanukah [ˈxɑnəkə, ˈhɑ-] → **Hanukkah**

chaos [ˈkeɪˌɑs] *n* : caos *m*

chaotic [keɪˈɑtɪk] *adj* : caótico — **chaotically** [-tɪkli] *adv*

chap[1] [ˈtʃæp] *vi* **chapped; chapping** : partirse, agrietarse

chap[2] *n* FELLOW : tipo *m,* hombre *m*

chapel [ˈtʃæpəl] *n* : capilla *f*

chaperon[1] *or* **chaperone** [ˈʃæpəˌroːn] *vt* **-oned; -oning :** ir de chaperón, acompañar
chaperon[2] *or* **chaperone** *n* **:** chaperón *m,* -rona *f;* acompañante *mf*
chaplain [ˈtʃæplɪn] *n* **:** capellán *m*
chapter [ˈtʃæptər] *n* **1 :** capítulo *m* (de un libro) **2** BRANCH **:** sección *f,* división *f* (de una organización)
char [ˈtʃɑr] *vt* **charred; charring 1** BURN **:** carbonizar **2** SCORCH **:** chamuscar
character [ˈkærɪktər] *n* **1** LETTER, SYMBOL **:** carácter *m* <Chinese characters : caracteres chinos> **2** DISPOSITION **:** carácter *m,* personalidad *f* <of good character : de buena reputación> **3 :** tipo *m,* personaje *m* peculiar <he's quite a character! : ¡él es algo serio!> **4 :** personaje *m* (ficticio)
characteristic[1] [ˌkærɪktəˈrɪstɪk] *adj* **:** característico, típico — **characteristically** [-tɪkli] *adv*
characteristic[2] *n* **:** característica *f*
characterization [ˌkærɪktərəˈzeɪʃən] *n* **:** caracterización *f*
characterize [ˈkærɪktəˌraɪz] *vt* **-ized; -izing :** caracterizar
charades [ʃəˈreɪdz] *ns & pl* **:** charada *f*
charcoal [ˈtʃɑrˌkoːl] *n* **:** carbón *m*
chard [ˈtʃɑrd] → **Swiss chard**
charge[1] [ˈtʃɑrdʒ] *v* **charged; charging** *vt* **1 :** cargar <to charge the batteries : cargar las pilas> **2** ENTRUST **:** encomendar, encargar **3** COMMAND **:** ordenar, mandar **4** ACCUSE **:** acusar <charged with robbery : acusado de robo> **5 :** cargar a una cuenta, comprar a crédito — *vi* **1 :** cargar (contra el enemigo) <charge! : ¡a la carga!> **2 :** cobrar <they charge too much : cobran demasiado>
charge[2] *n* **1 :** carga *f* (eléctrica) **2** BURDEN **:** carga *f,* peso *m* **3** RESPONSIBILITY **:** cargo *m,* responsabilidad *f* <to take charge of : hacerse cargo de> **4** ACCUSATION **:** cargo *m,* acusación *f* **5** COST **:** costo *m,* cargo *m,* precio *m* **6** ATTACK **:** carga *f,* ataque *m*
charge card → **credit card**
chargeable [ˈtʃɑrdʒəbəl] *adj* **1 :** acusable, perseguible (dícese de un delito) **2 ~ to :** a cargo de (una cuenta)
charger [ˈtʃɑrdʒər] *n* **:** corcel *m,* caballo *m* (de guerra)
chariot [ˈtʃæriət] *n* **:** carro *m* (de guerra)
charisma [kəˈrɪzmə] *n* **:** carisma *m*
charismatic [ˌkærəzˈmætɪk] *adj* **:** carismático
charitable [ˈtʃærət̬əbəl] *adj* **1** GENEROUS **:** caritativo <a charitable organization : una organización benéfica> **2** KIND, UNDERSTANDING **:** generoso, benévolo, comprensivo — **charitably** [-bli] *adv*
charitableness [ˈtʃærət̬əbəlnəs] *n* **:** caridad *f*
charity [ˈtʃærət̬i] *n, pl* **-ties 1** GENEROSITY **:** caridad *f* **2** ALMS **:** caridad *f,* limosna *f* **3 :** organización *f* benéfica, obra *f* de beneficencia
charlatan [ˈʃɑrlətən] *n* **:** charlatán *m,* -tana *f;* farsante *mf*
charley horse [ˈtʃɑrliˌhɔrs] *n* **:** calambre *m*
charm[1] [ˈtʃɑrm] *vt* **:** encantar, cautivar, fascinar
charm[2] *n* **1** AMULET **:** amuleto *m,* talismán *m* **2** ATTRACTION **:** encanto *m,* atractivo *m* <it has a certain charm : tiene cierto atractivo> **3 :** dije *m,* colgante *m* <charm bracelet : pulsera de dijes>
charmer [ˈtʃɑrmər] *n* **:** persona *f* encantadora
charming [ˈtʃɑrmɪŋ] *adj* **:** encantador, fascinante
chart[1] [ˈtʃɑrt] *vt* **1 :** trazar un mapa de, hacer un gráfico de **2** PLAN **:** trazar, planear <to chart a course : trazar un derrotero>
chart[2] *n* **1** MAP **:** carta *f,* mapa *m* **2** DIAGRAM **:** gráfico *m,* cuadro *m,* tabla *f*
charter[1] [ˈtʃɑrt̬ər] *vt* **1 :** establecer los estatutos de (una organización) **2** RENT **:** alquilar, fletar
charter[2] *n* **1** STATUTES **:** estatutos *mpl* **2** CONSTITUTION **:** carta *f,* constitución *f*
chartreuse [ʃɑrˈtruːz, -ˈtruːs] *n* **:** color *m* verde-amarillo intenso
chary [ˈtʃæri] *adj* **charier; -est 1** WARY **:** cauteloso, precavido **2** SPARING **:** parco
chase[1] [ˈtʃeɪs] *vt* **chased; chasing 1** PURSUE **:** perseguir, ir a la caza de **2** DRIVE **:** ahuyentar, echar <he chased the dog from the garden : ahuyentó al perro del jardín> **3 :** grabar (metales)
chase[2] *n* **1** PURSUIT **:** persecución *f,* caza *f* **2 the chase** HUNTING **:** caza *f*
chaser [ˈtʃeɪsər] *n* **1** PURSUER **:** perseguidor *m,* -dora *f* **2 :** bebida *f* que se toma después de un trago de licor
chasm [ˈkæzəm] *n* **:** abismo *m,* sima *f*
chassis [ˈtʃæsi, ˈʃæsi] *n, pl* **chassis** [-siz] **:** chasis *m,* armazón *m*
chaste [ˈtʃeɪst] *adj* **chaster; -est 1 :** casto **2** MODEST **:** modesto, puro **3** AUSTERE **:** austero, sobrio
chastely [ˈtʃeɪstli] *adv* **:** castamente
chasten [ˈtʃeɪsən] *vt* **:** castigar, sancionar
chasteness [ˈtʃeɪstnəs] *n* **1** MODESTY **:** modestia *f,* castidad *f* **2** AUSTERITY **:** sobriedad *f,* austeridad *f*
chastise [ˈtʃæsˌtaɪz, tʃæsˈ-] *vt* **-tised; -tising 1** REPRIMAND **:** reprender, corregir, reprobar **2** PUNISH **:** castigar
chastisement [ˈtʃæsˌtaɪzmənt, tʃæsˈtaɪz-, ˈtʃæstəz-] *n* **:** castigo *m,* corrección *f*
chastity [ˈtʃæstət̬i] *n* **:** castidad *f,* decencia *f,* modestia *f*
chat[1] [ˈtʃæt] *vi* **chatted; chatting :** charlar, platicar

chat[2] *n* : charla *f,* plática *f*

château [ʃæˈtoː] *n, pl* **-teaus** [-ˈtoː, -ˈtoːz] *or* **-teaux** [-ˈtoːz] : mansión *f* campestre

chattel [ˈtʃætəl] *n* : bienes *fpl* muebles, enseres *mpl*

chatter[1] [ˈtʃætər] *vi* **1** : castañetear (dícese de los dientes) **2** GAB : parlotear *fam,* cotorrear *fam*

chatter[2] *n* **1** CHATTERING : castañeteo *m* (de dientes) **2** GABBING : parloteo *m fam,* cotorreo *m fam,* cháchara *f fam*

chatterbox [ˈtʃætərˌbɑks] *n* : parlanchín *m,* -china *f;* charlatán *m,* -tana *f;* hablador *m,* -dora *f*

chatty [ˈtʃæti] *adj* **chattier; chattiest** **1** TALKATIVE : parlanchín, charlatán **2** CONVERSATIONAL : familiar, conversador <a chatty letter : una carta llena de noticias>

chauffeur[1] [ˈʃoːfər, ʃoˈfər] *vi* : trabajar de chofer privado — *vt* : hacer de chofer para

chauffeur[2] *n* : chofer *m* privado

chauvinism [ˈʃoːvəˌnɪzəm] *n* : chauvinismo *m,* patriotería *f*

chauvinist [ˈʃoːvənɪst] *n* : chauvinista *mf;* patriotero *m,* -ta *f*

chauvinistic [ˌʃoːvəˈnɪstɪk] *adj* : chauvinista, patriotero

cheap[1] [ˈtʃiːp] *adv* : barato <to sell cheap : vender barato>

cheap[2] *adj* **1** INEXPENSIVE : barato, económico **2** SHODDY : barato, mal hecho **3** STINGY : tacaño, agarrado *fam,* codo *Mex*

cheapen [ˈtʃiːpən] *vt* : degradar, rebajar

cheaply [ˈtʃiːpli] *adv* : barato, a precio bajo

cheapness [ˈtʃiːpnəs] *n* **1** : baratura *f,* precio *m* bajo **2** STINGINESS : tacañería *f*

cheapskate [ˈtʃiːpˌskeɪt] *n* : tacaño *m,* -ña *f;* codo *m,* -da *f Mex*

cheat[1] [ˈtʃiːt] *vt* : defraudar, estafar, engañar — *vi* : hacer trampa

cheat[2] *n* **1** CHEATING : engaño *m,* fraude *m,* trampa *f* **2** → **cheater**

cheater [ˈtʃiːtər] *n* : estafador *m,* -dora *f;* tramposo *m,* -sa *f*

check[1] [ˈtʃɛk] *vt* **1** HALT : frenar, parar, detener **2** RESTRAIN : refrenar, contener, reprimir **3** VERIFY : verificar, comprobar **4** INSPECT : revisar, chequear, inspeccionar **5** MARK : marcar, señalar **6** : chequear, facturar (maletas, equipaje) **7** CHECKER : marcar con cuadros **8 to check in** : registrarse en un hotel **9 to check out** : irse de un hotel

check[2] *n* **1** HALT : detención *f* súbita, parada *f* **2** RESTRAINT : control *m,* freno *m* **3** INSPECTION : inspección *f,* verificación *f,* chequeo *m* **4** : cheque *m* <to pay by check : pagar con cheque> **5** VOUCHER : resguardo *m,* comprobante *m* **6** BILL : cuenta *f* (en un restaurante) **7** SQUARE : cuadro *m* **8** MARK : marca *f* **9** : jaque *m* (en ajedrez)

checker[1] [ˈtʃɛkər] *vt* : marcar con cuadros

checker[2] *n* **1** : pieza *f* (en el juego de damas) **2** : verificador *m,* -dora *f;* revisador *m,* -dora *f*

checkerboard [ˈtʃɛkərˌbord] *n* : tablero *m* de damas

checkers [ˈtʃɛkərz] *n* : damas *fpl*

checkmate[1] [ˈtʃɛkˌmeɪt] *vt* **-mated; -mating** **1** : dar jaque mate a (en ajedrez) **2** THWART : frustrar, arruinar

checkmate[2] *n* : jaque mate *m*

checkpoint [ˈtʃɛkˌpɔɪnt] *n* : puesto *m* de control

checkup [ˈtʃɛkˌʌp] *n* : examen *m* médico, chequeo *m*

cheddar [ˈtʃɛdər] *n* : queso *m* Cheddar

cheek [ˈtʃiːk] *n* **1** : mejilla *f,* cachete *m* **2** IMPUDENCE : insolencia *f,* descaro *m*

cheeky [ˈtʃiːki] *adj* **cheekier; -est** : descarado, insolente, atrevido

cheep[1] [ˈtʃiːp] *vi* : piar

cheep[2] *n* : pío *m*

cheer[1] [ˈtʃɪr] *vt* **1** ENCOURAGE : alentar, animar **2** GLADDEN : alegrar, levantar el ánimo a **3** ACCLAIM : aclamar, vitorear, echar porras a

cheer[2] *n* **1** CHEERFULNESS : alegría *f,* buen humor *m,* jovialidad *f* **2** APPLAUSE : aclamación *f,* ovación *f,* aplausos *mpl* <three cheers for the chief! : ¡viva el jefe!> **3 cheers!** : ¡salud!

cheerful [ˈtʃɪrfəl] *adj* : alegre, de buen humor

cheerfully [ˈtʃɪrfəli] *adv* : alegremente, jovialmente

cheerfulness [ˈtʃɪrfəlnəs] *n* : buen humor *m,* alegría *f*

cheerily [ˈtʃɪrəli] *adv* : alegremente

cheeriness [ˈtʃɪrinəs] *n* : buen humor *m,* alegría *f*

cheerleader [ˈtʃɪrˌliːdər] *n* : porrista *mf*

cheerless [ˈtʃɪrləs] *adj* BLEAK : triste, sombrío

cheerlessly [ˈtʃɪrləsli] *adv* : desanimadamente

cheery [ˈtʃɪri] *adj* **cheerier; -est** : alegre, de buen humor

cheese [ˈtʃiːz] *n* : queso *m*

cheesecloth [ˈtʃiːzˌklɔθ] *n* : estopilla *f*

cheesy [ˈtʃiːzi] *adj* **cheesier; -est** **1** : a queso **2** : que contiene queso **3** CHEAP : barato, de mala calidad

cheetah [ˈtʃiːtə] *n* : guepardo *m*

chef [ˈʃɛf] *n* : chef *m*

chemical[1] [ˈkɛmɪkəl] *adj* : químico — **chemically** [-mɪkli] *adv*

chemical[2] *n* : sustancia *f* química

chemise [ʃəˈmiːz] *n* **1** : camiseta *f,* prenda *f* interior de una pieza **2** : vestido *m* holgado

chemist [ˈkɛmɪst] *n* : químico *m,* -ca *f*

chemistry [ˈkɛmɪstri] *n, pl* **-tries** : química *f*

chemotherapy [ˌkiːmoˈθɛrəpi, ˌkɛmo-] *n, pl* **-pies** : quimioterapia *f*

chenille [ʃə'niːl] *n* **:** felpilla *f*

cherish ['tʃɛrɪʃ] *vt* **1** VALUE **:** apreciar, valorar **2** HARBOR **:** abrigar, albergar

cherry ['tʃɛri] *n, pl* **-ries 1 :** cereza *f* (fruta) **2 :** cerezo *m* (árbol)

cherub ['tʃɛrəb] *n* **1** *pl* **-ubim** ['tʃɛrə,bɪm, 'tʃɛrjə-] ANGEL **:** ángel *m,* querubín *m* **2** *pl* **-ubs :** niño *m* regordete, niña *f* regordeta

cherubic [tʃə'ruːbɪk] *adj* **:** querúbico, angelical

chess ['tʃɛs] *n* **:** ajedrez *m*

chessboard ['tʃɛs,bord] *n* **:** tablero *m* de ajedrez

chessman ['tʃɛsmən, -,mæn] *n, pl* **-men** [-mən, -,mɛn] **:** pieza *f* de ajedrez

chest ['tʃɛst] *n* **1 :** cofre *m,* baúl *m* **2 :** pecho *m* <chest pains : dolores de pecho>

chestnut ['tʃɛst,nʌt] *n* **1 :** castaña *f* (fruto) **2 :** castaño *m* (árbol)

chest of drawers *n* **:** cómoda *f*

chevron ['ʃɛvrən] *n* **:** galón *m* (de un oficial militar)

chew[1] ['tʃuː] *vt* **:** masticar, mascar

chew[2] *n* **:** algo que se masca (como tabaco)

chewable ['tʃuːəbəl] *adj* **:** masticable

chewing gum *n* **:** goma *f* de mascar, chicle *m*

chewy ['tʃuːi] *adj* **chewier; -est 1 :** fibroso (dícese de las carnes o los vegetales) **2 :** pegajoso, chicloso (dícese de los los dulces)

chic[1] ['ʃiːk] *adj* **:** chic, elegante, de moda

chic[2] *n* **:** chic *m,* elegancia *f*

Chicano [tʃɪ'kɑno] *n* **:** chicano *m,* -na *f* — **Chicano** *adj*

chick ['tʃɪk] *n* **:** pollito *m,* -ta *f;* polluelo *m,* -la *f*

chicken ['tʃɪkən] *n* **1** FOWL **:** pollo *m* **2** COWARD **:** cobarde *mf*

chickenhearted ['tʃɪkən,hɑrtəd] *n* **:** miedoso, cobarde

chicken pox *n* **:** varicela *f*

chicle ['tʃɪkəl] *n* **:** chicle *m* (resina)

chicory ['tʃɪkəri] *n, pl* **-ries 1 :** endibia *f* (para ensaladas) **2 :** achicoria *f* (aditivo de café)

chide ['tʃaɪd] *vt* **chid** ['tʃɪd] *or* **chided; chid** *or* **chidden** ['tʃɪdən] *or* **chided; chiding** ['tʃaɪdɪŋ] **:** regañar, reprender

chief[1] ['tʃiːf] *adj* **:** principal, capital <chief negotiator : negociador en jefe> — **chiefly** *adv*

chief[2] *n* **:** jefe *m,* -fa *f*

chieftain ['tʃiːftən] *n* **:** jefe *m,* -fa *f* (de una tribu)

chiffon [ʃɪ'fɑn, 'ʃɪ,-] *n* **:** chifón *m*

chigger ['tʃɪgər] *n* **:** nigua *f*

chignon ['ʃiːn,jɑn, -,jɔn] *n* **:** moño *m,* chongo *m Mex*

chilblain ['tʃɪl,bleɪn] *n* **:** sabañón *m*

child ['tʃaɪld] *n, pl* **children** ['tʃɪldrən] **1** BABY, YOUNGSTER **:** niño *m,* -ña *f;* criatura *f* **2** OFFSPRING **:** hijo *m,* -ja *f;* progenie *f*

childbearing[1] ['tʃaɪlbɛrɪŋ] *adj* **:** relativo al parto <of childbearing age : en edad fértil>

childbearing[2] → **childbirth**

childbirth ['tʃaɪld,bərθ] *n* **:** parto *m*

childhood ['tʃaɪld,hʊd] *n* **:** infancia *f,* niñez *f*

childish ['tʃaɪldɪʃ] *adj* **:** infantil, inmaduro — **childishly** *adv*

childishness ['tʃaɪldɪʃnəs] *n* **:** infantilismo *m,* inmadurez *f*

childless ['tʃaɪldləs] *adj* **:** sin hijos

childlike ['tʃaɪld,laɪk] *adj* **:** infantil, inocente <a childlike imagination : una imaginación infantil>

childproof ['tʃaɪld,pruːf] *adj* **:** a prueba de niños

Chilean ['tʃɪliən, tʃɪ'leɪən] **:** chileno *m,* -na *f* — **Chilean** *adj*

chili *or* **chile** *or* **chilli** ['tʃɪli] *n, pl* **chilies** *or* **chiles** *or* **chillies 1** *or* **chili pepper :** chile *m,* ají *m* **2 :** chile *m* con carne

chill[1] ['tʃɪl] *v* **:** enfriar

chill[2] *adj* **:** frío, gélido <a chill wind : un viento frío>

chill[3] *n* **1** CHILLINESS **:** fresco *m,* frío *m* **2** SHIVER **:** escalofrío *m* **3** DAMPER **:** enfriamiento *m,* frío *m* <to cast a chill over : enfriar>

chilliness ['tʃɪlinəs] *n* **:** frío *m,* fresco *m*

chilly ['tʃɪli] *adj* **chillier; -est :** frío <it's chilly tonight : hace frío esta noche>

chime[1] ['tʃaɪm] *v* **chimed; chiming** *vt* **:** hacer sonar (una campana) — *vi* **:** sonar una campana, dar campanadas

chime[2] *n* **1** BELLS **:** juego *m* de campanitas sintonizadas, carillón *m* **2** PEAL **:** tañido *m,* campanada *f*

chime in *vi* **:** meterse en una conversación

chimera *or* **chimaera** [kaɪ'mɪrə, kə-] *n* **:** quimera *f*

chimney ['tʃɪmni] *n, pl* **-neys :** chimenea *f*

chimney sweep *n* **:** deshollinador *m,* -dora *f*

chimp ['tʃɪmp, 'ʃɪmp] → **chimpanzee**

chimpanzee [,tʃɪm,pæn'ziː, ,ʃɪm-; tʃɪm'pænzi, ʃɪm-] *n* **:** chimpancé *m*

chin ['tʃɪn] *n* **:** barbilla *f,* mentón *m,* barba *f*

china ['tʃaɪnə] *n* **1** PORCELAIN **:** porcelana *f,* loza *f* **2** CROCKERY, TABLEWARE **:** loza *f,* vajilla *f*

chinchilla [tʃɪn'tʃɪlə] *n* **:** chinchilla *f*

Chinese ['tʃaɪ'niːz, -'niːs] *n* **1 :** chino *m,* -na *f* **2 :** chino *m* (idioma) — **Chinese** *adj*

chink ['tʃɪŋk] *n* **:** grieta *f,* abertura *f*

chintz ['tʃɪnts] *n* **:** chintz *m,* chinz *m*

chip[1] ['tʃɪp] *v* **chipped; chipping** *vt* **:** desportillar, desconchar, astillar (madera) — *vi* **:** desportillarse, desconcharse, descascararse (dícese de la pintura, etc.)

chip[2] *n* **1 :** astilla *f* (de madera o vidrio), lasca *f* (de piedra) <he's a chip

off the old block : de tal palo, tal astilla> **2** : bocado *m* pequeño (en rodajas o rebanadas) <tortilla chips : totopos, tortillitas tostadas> **3** : ficha *f* (de póker, etc.) **4** NICK : desportilladura *f,* mella *f* **5** : chip *m* <memory chip : chip de memoria>

chip in *v* CONTRIBUTE : contribuir

chipmunk ['tʃɪp,mʌŋk] *n* : ardilla *f* listada

chipper ['tʃɪpər] *adj* : alegre y vivaz

chiropodist [kə'rɑpədɪst, ʃə-] *n* : podólogo *m,* -ga *f*

chiropody [kə'rɑpədi, ʃə-] *n* : podología *f*

chiropractic ['kaɪrə,præktɪk] *n* : quiropráctica *f*

chiropractor ['kaɪrə,præktər] *n* : quiropráctico *m,* -ca *f*

chirp[1] ['tʃərp] *vi* : gorjear (dícese de los pájaros), chirriar (dícese de los grillos)

chirp[2] *n* : gorjeo *m* (de un pájaro), chirrido *m* (de un grillo)

chisel[1] ['tʃɪzəl] *vt* **-eled** *or* **-elled; -eling** *or* **-elling 1** : cincelar, tallar, labrar **2** CHEAT : estafar, defraudar

chisel[2] *n* : cincel *m* (para piedras y metales), escoplo *m* (para madera), formón *m*

chiseler ['tʃɪzələr] *n* SWINDLER : estafador *m,* -dora *f;* fraude *mf*

chit ['tʃɪt] *n* : resguardo *m,* recibo *m*

chitchat ['tʃɪt,tʃæt] *n* : cotorreo *m,* charla *f*

chivalric [ʃə'vælrɪk] → **chivalrous**

chivalrous ['ʃɪvəlrəs] *adj* **1** KNIGHTLY : caballeresco, relativo a la caballería **2** GENTLEMANLY : caballeroso, honesto, cortés

chivalrousness ['ʃɪvəlrəsnəs] *n* : caballerosidad *f,* cortesía *f*

chivalry ['ʃɪvəlri] *n, pl* **-ries 1** KNIGHTHOOD : caballería *f* **2** CHIVALROUSNESS : caballerosidad *f,* nobleza *f,* cortesía *f*

chive ['tʃaɪv] *n* : cebollino *m*

chloride ['klor,aɪd] *n* : cloruro *m*

chlorinate ['klorə,neɪt] *vt* **-nated; -nating** : clorar

chlorination [,klorə'neɪʃən] *n* : cloración *f*

chlorine ['klor,iːn] *n* : cloro *m*

chloroform[1] ['klorə,fɔrm] *vt* : cloroformizar

chloroform[2] *n* : cloroformo *m*

chlorophyll ['klorə,fɪl] *n* : clorofila *f*

chock–full ['tʃɑk'fʊl, 'tʃʌk-] *adj* : colmado, repleto

chocolate ['tʃɑkələt, 'tʃɔk-] *n* **1** : chocolate *m* **2** BONBON : bombón *m* **3** : color *m* chocolate, marrón *m*

choice[1] ['tʃɔɪs] *adj* **choicer; -est** : selecto, escogido, de primera calidad

choice[2] *n* **1** CHOOSING : elección *f,* selección *f* **2** OPTION : elección *f,* opción *f* <I have no choice : no tengo alternativa> **3** PREFERENCE : preferencia *f,* elección *f* **4** VARIETY : surtido *m,* selección *f* <a wide choice : un gran surtido>

choir ['kwaɪr] *n* : coro *m*

choirboy ['kwaɪr,bɔɪ] *n* : niño *m* de coro

choke[1] ['tʃoːk] *v* **choked; choking** *vt* **1** ASPHYXIATE, STRANGLE : sofocar, asfixiar, ahogar, estrangular **2** BLOCK : tapar, obstruir — *vi* **1** SUFFOCATE : asfixiarse, sofocarse, ahogarse, atragantarse (con comida) **2** CLOG : taparse, obstruirse

choke[2] *n* **1** CHOKING : estrangulación *f* **2** : choke *m* (de un motor)

choker ['tʃoːkər] *n* : gargantilla *f*

cholera ['kɑlərə] *n* : cólera *m*

cholesterol [kə'lɛstə,rɔl] *n* : colesterol *m*

choose ['tʃuːz] *v* **chose** ['tʃoːz]; **chosen** ['tʃoːzən]; **choosing** *vt* **1** SELECT : escoger, elegir <choose only one : escoja sólo uno> **2** DECIDE : decidir <he chose to leave : decidió irse> **3** PREFER : preferir <which one do you choose? : ¿cuál prefiere?> — *vi* : escoger <much to choose from : mucho de donde escoger>

choosy *or* **choosey** ['tʃuːzi] *adj* **choosier; -est** : exigente, remilgado

chop[1] ['tʃɑp] *vt* **chopped; chopping 1** MINCE : picar, cortar, moler (carne) **2 to chop down** : cortar, talar (un árbol)

chop[2] *n* **1** CUT : hachazo *m* (con una hacha), tajo *m* (con una cuchilla) **2** BLOW : golpe *m* (penetrante) <karate chop : golpe de karate> **3** : chuleta *f* <pork chops : chuletas de cerdo>

chopper ['tʃɑpər] → **helicopter**

choppy ['tʃɑpi] *adj* **choppier; -est 1** : agitado, picado (dícese del mar) **2** DISCONNECTED : incoherente, inconexo

chops ['tʃɑps] *npl* **1** : quijada *f,* mandíbula *f,* boca *f* (de una persona) **2 to lick one's chops** : relamerse

chopsticks ['tʃɑp,stɪks] *npl* : palillos *mpl*

choral ['korəl] *adj* : coral

chorale [kə'ræl, -'rɑl] *n* **1** : coral *f* (composición musical vocal) **2** CHOIR, CHORUS : coral *f,* coro *m*

chord ['kɔrd] *n* **1** : acorde *m* (en música) **2** : cuerda *f* (en anatomía o geometría)

chore ['tʃor] *n* **1** TASK : tarea *f* rutinaria **2** BOTHER, NUISANCE : lata *f fam,* fastidio *m* **3 chores** *npl* WORK : quehaceres *mpl,* faenas *fpl*

choreograph ['koriə,græf] *vt* : coreografiar

choreographer [,kori'ɑgrəfər] *n* : coreógrafo *m,* -fa *f*

choreographic [,koriə'græfɪk] *adj* : coreográfico

choreography [,kori'ɑgrəfi] *n, pl* **-phies** : coreografía *f*

chorister ['korəstər] *n* : corista *mf*

chortle[1] ['tʃɔrtəl] *vi* **-tled; -tling** : reírse (con satisfacción o júbilo)

chortle[2] *n* : risa *f* (de satisfacción o júbilo)
chorus[1] [ˈkorəs] *vt* : corear
chorus[2] *n* **1** : coro *m* (grupo o composición musical) **2** REFRAIN : coro *m,* estribillo *m*
chose *pp* → **choose**
chosen [ˈtʃoːzən] *adj* : elegido, selecto
chow [ˈtʃaʊ] *n* **1** FOOD : comida *f* **2** : chow-chow *m* (perro)
chowder [ˈtʃaʊdər] *n* : sopa *f* de pescado
christen [ˈkrɪsən] *vt* **1** BAPTIZE : bautizar **2** NAME : bautizar con el nombre de
Christendom [ˈkrɪsəndəm] *n* : cristiandad *f*
christening [ˈkrɪsənɪŋ] *n* : bautismo *m,* bautizo *m*
Christian[1] [ˈkrɪstʃən] *adj* : cristiano
Christian[2] *n* : cristiano *m,* -na *f*
Christianity [ˌkrɪstʃiˈænəṭi, ˌkrɪsˈtʃæ-] *n* : cristianismo *m*
Christian name *n* : nombre *m* de pila
Christmas [ˈkrɪsməs] *n* : Navidad *f* <Christmas season : las Navidades>
chromatic [kroːˈmæṭɪk] *adj* : cromático <chromatic scale : escala cromática>
chrome [ˈkroːm] *n* : cromo *m* (metal)
chromium [ˈkroːmiəm] *n* : cromo *m* (elemento)
chromosome [ˈkroːməˌsoːm, -ˌzoːm] *n* : cromosoma *m*
chronic [ˈkrɑnɪk] *adj* : crónico — **chronically** [-nɪkli] *adv*
chronicle[1] [ˈkrɑnɪkəl] *vt* **-cled; -cling** : escribir (una crónica o historia)
chronicle[2] *n* : crónica *f,* historia *f*
chronicler [ˈkrɑnɪklər] *n* : historiador *m,* -dora *f;* cronista *mf*
chronological [ˌkrɑnəlˈɑdʒɪkəl] *adj* : cronológico — **chronologically** [-kli] *adv*
chronology [krəˈnɑlədʒi] *n, pl* **-gies** : cronología *f*
chronometer [krəˈnɑməṭər] *n* : cronómetro *m*
chrysalis [ˈkrɪsələs] *n, pl* **chrysalides** [krɪˈsæləˌdiːz] *or* **chrysalises** : crisálida *f*
chrysanthemum [krɪˈsæntθəməm] *n* : crisantemo *m*
chubbiness [ˈtʃʌbinəs] *n* : gordura *f*
chubby [ˈtʃʌbi] *adj* **-bier; -est** : gordito, regordete, rechoncho
chuck[1] [ˈtʃʌk] *vt* **1** TOSS : tirar, lanzar, aventar *Col, Mex* **2 to chuck under the chin** : hacer la mamola
chuck[2] *n* **1** PAT : mamola *f,* palmada *f* **2** TOSS : lanzamiento *m* **3** *or* **chuck steak** : corte *m* de carne de res
chuckle[1] [ˈtʃʌkəl] *vi* **-led; -ling** : reírse entre dientes
chuckle[2] *n* : risita *f,* risa *f* ahogada
chug[1] [ˈtʃʌg] *vi* **chugged; chugging** : resoplar, traquetear
chug[2] *n* : resoplido *m,* traqueteo *m*
chum[1] [ˈtʃʌm] *vi* **chummed; chumming** : ser camaradas, ser cuates *Mex fam*
chum[2] *n* : amigo *m,* -ga *f;* camarada *mf;* compinche *mf fam*
chummy [ˈtʃʌmi] *adj* **-mier; -est** : amistoso <they're very chummy : son muy amigos>
chump [ˈtʃʌmp] *n* : tonto *m,* -ta *f;* idiota *mf*
chunk [ˈtʃʌnk] *n* **1** PIECE : cacho *m,* pedazo *m,* trozo *m* **2** : cantidad *f* grande <a chunk of money : mucho dinero>
chunky [ˈtʃʌnki] *adj* **chunkier; -est 1** STOCKY : fornido, robusto **2** : que contiene pedazos
church [ˈtʃərtʃ] *n* **1** : iglesia *f* <to go to church : ir a la iglesia> **2** CHRISTIANS : iglesia *f,* conjunto *m* de fieles cristianos **3** DENOMINATION : confesión *f,* secta *f* **4** CONGREGATION : feligreses *mpl,* fieles *mpl*
churchgoer [ˈtʃərtʃˌgoːər] *n* : practicante *mf*
churchyard [ˈtʃərtʃˌjɑrd] *n* : cementerio *m* (junto a una iglesia)
churn[1] [ˈtʃərn] *vt* **1** : batir (crema), hacer (mantequilla) **2** : agitar con fuerza, revolver — *vi* : agitarse, arremolinarse
churn[2] *n* : mantequera *f*
chute [ˈʃuːt] *n* : conducto *m* inclinado, vertedero *m* (para basuras)
chutney [ˈtʃʌtni] *n, pl* **-neys** : chutney *m*
chutzpah [ˈhʊtspə, ˈxʊt-, -ˌspɑ] *n* : descaro *m,* frescura *f,* cara *f fam*
cicada [səˈkeɪdə, -ˈkɑ-] *n* : cigarra *f,* chicharra *f*
cider [ˈsaɪdər] *n* **1** : jugo *m* (de manzana, etc.) **2 hard cider** : sidra *f*
cigar [sɪˈgɑr] *n* : puro *m,* cigarro *m*
cigarette [ˌsɪgəˈrɛt, ˈsɪgəˌrɛt] *n* : cigarrillo *m,* cigarro *m*
cinch[1] [ˈsɪntʃ] *vt* **1** : cinchar (un caballo) **2** ASSURE : asegurar
cinch[2] *n* **1** : cincha *f* (para caballos) **2** : algo fácil o seguro <it's a cinch : es bien fácil, es pan comido>
cinchona [sɪŋˈkoːnə] *n* : quino *m*
cinder [ˈsɪndər] *n* **1** EMBER : brasa *f,* ascua *f* **2 cinders** *npl* ASHES : cenizas *fpl*
cinema [ˈsɪnəmə] *n* : cine *m*
cinematic [ˌsɪnəˈmæṭɪk] *adj* : cinematográfico
cinnamon [ˈsɪnəmən] *n* : canela *f*
cipher [ˈsaɪfər] *n* **1** ZERO : cero *m* **2** CODE : cifra *f,* clave *f*
circa [ˈsərkə] *prep* : alrededor de, hacia <circa 1800 : hacia el año 1800>
circle[1] [ˈsərkəl] *v* **-cled; -cling** *vt* **1** : encerrar en un círculo, poner un círculo alrededor de **2** : girar alrededor de, dar vueltas a <we circled the building twice : le dimos vueltas al edificio dos veces> — *vi* : dar vueltas

circle² *n* **1 :** círculo *m* **2** CYCLE **:** ciclo *m* <to come full circle : volver al punto de partida> **3** GROUP **:** círculo *m,* grupo *m* (social)
circuit [ˈsərkət] *n* **1** BOUNDARY **:** circuito *m,* perímetro *m* (de una zona o un territorio) **2** TOUR **:** circuito *m,* recorrido *m,* tour *m* **3 :** circuito *m* (eléctrico) <a short circuit : un cortocircuito>
circuitous [ˌsərˈkjuːət̮əs] *adj* **:** sinuoso, tortuoso
circuitry [ˈsərkətri] *n, pl* **-ries :** sistema *m* de circuitos
circular¹ [ˈsərkjələr] *adj* ROUND **:** circular, redondo
circular² *n* **:** circular *f*
circulate [ˈsərkjəˌleɪt] *v* **-lated; -lating** *vi* **:** circular — *vt* **1 :** circular (noticias, etc.) **2** DISSEMINATE **:** hacer circular, divulgar
circulation [ˌsərkjəˈleɪʃən] *n* **:** circulación *f*
circulatory [ˈsərkjələˌtori] *adj* **:** circulatorio
circumcise [ˈsərkəmˌsaɪz] *vt* **-cised; -cising :** circuncidar
circumcision [ˌsərkəmˈsɪʒən, ˈsərkəmˌ-] *n* **:** circuncisión *f*
circumference [sərˈkʌmpfrənts] *n* **:** circunferencia *f*
circumflex [ˈsərkəmˌflɛks] *n* **:** acento *m* circunflejo
circumlocution [ˌsərkəmloˈkjuːʃən] *n* **:** circunlocución *f*
circumnavigate [ˌsərkəmˈnævəˌgeɪt] *vt* **-gated; -gating :** circunnavegar
circumscribe [ˈsərkəmˌskraɪb] *vt* **-scribed; -scribing 1 :** circunscribir, trazar una figura alrededor de **2** LIMIT **:** circunscribir, limitar
circumspect [ˈsərkəmˌspɛkt] *adj* **:** circunspecto, prudente, cauto
circumspection [ˌsərkəmˈspɛkʃən] *n* **:** circunspección *f,* cautela *f*
circumstance [ˈsərkəmˌstænts] *n* **1** EVENT **:** circunstancia *f,* acontecimiento *m* **2 circumstances** *npl* SITUATION **:** circunstancias *fpl,* situación *f* <under the circumstances : dadas las circunstancias> <under no circumstances : de ninguna manera, bajo ningún concepto> **3 circumstances** *npl* **:** situación *f* económica
circumstantial [ˌsərkəmˈstæntʃəl] *adj* **:** circunstancial
circumvent [ˌsərkəmˈvɛnt] *vt* **:** evadir, burlar (una ley o regla), sortear (una responsabilidad o dificultad)
circumvention [ˌsərkəmˈvɛntʃən] *n* **:** evasión *f*
circus [ˈsərkəs] *n* **:** circo *m*
cirrhosis [səˈroːsɪs] *n* **:** cirrosis *f*
cirrus [ˈsɪrəs] *n, pl* **-ri** [ˈsɪrˌaɪ] **:** cirro *m*
cistern [ˈsɪstərn] *n* **:** cisterna *f,* aljibe *m*
citadel [ˈsɪt̮ədəl, -ˌdɛl] *n* FORTRESS **:** ciudadela *f,* fortaleza *f*
citation [saɪˈteɪʃən] *n* **1** SUMMONS **:** emplazamiento *m,* citación *f,* convocatoria *f* (judicial) **2** QUOTATION **:** cita *f* **3** COMMENDATION **:** elogio *m,* mención *f* (de honor)
cite [ˈsaɪt] *vt* **cited; citing 1** ARRAIGN, SUBPOENA **:** emplazar, citar, hacer comparecer (ante un tribunal) **2** QUOTE **:** citar **3** COMMEND **:** elogiar, honrar (oficialmente)
citizen [ˈsɪt̮əzən] *n* **:** ciudadano *m,* -na *f*
citizenry [ˈsɪt̮əzənri] *n, pl* **-ries :** ciudadanía *f,* conjunto *m* de ciudadanos
citizenship [ˈsɪtəzənˌʃɪp] *n* **:** ciudadanía *f* <Nicaraguan citizenship : ciudadanía nicaragüense>
citron [ˈsɪtrən] *n* **:** cidra *f*
citrus [ˈsɪtrəs] *n, pl* **-rus** *or* **-ruses :** cítrico *m*
city [ˈsɪt̮i] *n, pl* **cities :** ciudad *f*
civic [ˈsɪvɪk] *adj* **:** cívico
civics [ˈsɪvɪks] *ns & pl* **:** civismo *m*
civil [ˈsɪvəl] *adj* **1 :** civil <civil law : derecho civil> **2** POLITE **:** civil, cortés
civilian [səˈvɪljən] *n* **:** civil *mf* <soldiers and civilians : soldados y civiles>
civility [səˈvɪlət̮i] *n, pl* **-ties :** cortesía *f,* educación *f*
civilization [ˌsɪvələˈzeɪʃən] *n* **:** civilización *f*
civilize [ˈsɪvəˌlaɪz] *vt* **-lized; -lizing :** civilizar — **civilized** *adj*
civil liberties *npl* **:** derechos *mpl* civiles
civilly [ˈsɪvəli] *adv* **:** cortésmente
civil rights *npl* **:** derechos *mpl* civiles
civil service *n* **:** administración *f* pública
civil war *n* **:** guerra *f* civil
clack¹ [ˈklæk] *vi* **:** tabletear
clack² *n* **:** tableteo *m*
clad [ˈklæd] *adj* **1** CLOTHED **:** vestido **2** COVERED **:** cubierto
claim¹ [ˈkleɪm] *vt* **1** DEMAND **:** reclamar, reivindicar <she claimed her rights : reclamó sus derechos> **2** MAINTAIN **:** afirmar, sostener <they claim it's theirs : sostienen que es suyo>
claim² *n* **1** DEMAND **:** demanda *f,* reclamación *f* **2** DECLARATION **:** declaración *f,* afirmación *f* **3 to stake a claim :** reclamar, reivindicar
claimant [ˈkleɪmənt] *n* **:** demandante *mf* (ante un juez), pretendiente *mf* (al trono, etc.)
clairvoyance [klærˈvɔɪənts] *n* **:** clarividencia *f*
clairvoyant¹ [klærˈvɔɪənt] *adj* **:** clarividente
clairvoyant² *n* **:** clarividente *mf*
clam [ˈklæm] *n* **:** almeja *f*
clamber [ˈklæmbər] *vi* **:** treparse o subirse torpemente
clammy [ˈklæmi] *adj* **-mier; -est :** húmedo y algo frío
clamor¹ [ˈklæmər] *vi* **:** gritar, clamar

clamor[2] *n* : clamor *m*

clamorous ['klæmərəs] *adj* : clamoroso, ruidoso, estrepitoso

clamp[1] ['klæmp] *vt* : sujetar con abrazaderas

clamp[2] *n* : abrazadera *f*

clan ['klæn] *n* : clan *m*

clandestine [klæn'dɛstɪn] *adj* : clandestino, secreto

clang[1] ['klæŋ] *vi* : hacer resonar (dícese de un objeto metálico)

clang[2] *n* : ruido *m* metálico fuerte

clangor ['klæŋər, -gər] *n* : estruendo *m* metálico

clank[1] ['klæŋk] *vi* : producir un ruido metálico seco

clank[2] *n* : ruido *m* metálico seco

clannish ['klænɪʃ] *adj* : exclusivista

clap[1] ['klæp] *v* **clapped; clapping** *vt* **1** SLAP, STRIKE : golpear ruidosamente, dar una palmada <to clap one's hands : batir palmas, dar palmadas> **2** APPLAUD : aplaudir — *vi* APPLAUD : aplaudir

clap[2] *n* **1** SLAP : palmada *f,* golpecito *m* **2** NOISE : ruido *m* seco <a clap of thunder : un trueno>

clapboard ['klæbərd, 'klæp,bord] *n* : tabla *f* de madera (para revestir muros)

clapper ['klæpər] *n* : badajo *m* (de una campana)

clarification [,klærəfə'keɪʃən] *n* : clarificación *f*

clarify ['klærə,faɪ] *vt* **-fied; -fying 1** EXPLAIN : aclarar **2** : clarificar (un líquido)

clarinet [,klærə'nɛt] *n* : clarinete *m*

clarinetist *or* **clarinettist** [,klærə'nɛtɪst] *n* : clarinetista *mf*

clarion ['klæriən] *adj* : claro y sonoro

clarity ['klærət̬i] *n* : claridad *f,* nitidez *f*

clash[1] ['klæʃ] *vi* **1** : sonar, chocarse <the cymbals clashed : los platillos sonaron> **2** : chocar, enfrentarse <the students clashed with the police : los estudiantes se enfrentaron con la policía> **3** CONFLICT : estar en conflicto, oponerse **4** : desentonar (dícese de los colores), coincidir (dícese de los datos)

clash[2] *n* **1** : ruido *m* (producido por un choque) **2** CONFLICT, CONFRONTATION : enfrentamiento *m,* conflicto *m,* choque *m* **3** : desentono *m* (de colores), coincidencia *f* (de datos)

clasp[1] ['klæsp] *vt* **1** FASTEN : sujetar, abrochar **2** EMBRACE, GRASP : agarrar, sujetar, abrazar

clasp[2] *n* **1** FASTENING : broche *m,* cierre *m* **2** EMBRACE, SQUEEZE : apretón *m,* abrazo *m*

class[1] ['klæs] *vt* : clasificar, catalogar

class[2] *n* **1** KIND, TYPE : clase *f,* tipo *m,* especie *f* **2** : clase *f,* rango *m* social <the working class : la clase obrera> **3** LESSON : clase *f,* curso *m* <English class : clase de inglés> **4** : conjunto *m* de estudiantes, clase *f* <the class of '97 : la promoción del 97>

classic[1] ['klæsɪk] *adj* : clásico

classic[2] *n* : clásico *m,* obra *f* clásica

classical ['klæsɪkəl] *adj* : clásico — **classically** [-kli] *adv*

classicism ['klæsə,sɪzəm] *n* : clasicismo *m*

classification [,klæsəfə'keɪʃən] *n* : clasificación *f*

classified ['klæsə,faɪd] *adj* **1** : clasificado <classified ads : avisos clasificados> **2** RESTRICTED : confidencial, secreto <classified documents : documentos secretos>

classify ['klæsə,faɪ] *vt* **-fied; -fying** : clasificar, catalogar

classless ['klæsləs] *adj* : sin clases

classmate ['klæs,meɪt] *n* : compañero *m,* -ra *f* de clase

classroom ['klæs,ru:m] *n* : aula *f,* salón *m* de clase

clatter[1] ['klæt̬ər] *vi* : traquetear, hacer ruido

clatter[2] *n* : traqueteo *m,* ruido *m,* estrépito *m*

clause ['klɔz] *n* : cláusula *f*

claustrophobia [,klɔstrə'fo:biə] *n* : claustrofobia *f*

clavicle ['klævɪkəl] *n* : clavícula *f*

claw[1] ['klɔ] *v* : arañar

claw[2] *n* : garra *f,* uña *f* (de un gato), pinza *f* (de un crustáceo)

clay ['kleɪ] *n* : arcilla *f,* barro *m*

clayey ['kleɪi] *adj* : arcilloso

clean[1] ['kli:n] *vt* : limpiar, lavar, asear

clean[2] *adv* : limpio, limpiamente <to play clean : jugar limpio>

clean[3] *adj* **1** : limpio **2** UNADULTERATED : puro **3** IRREPROACHABLE : intachable, sin mancha <to have a clean record : no tener antecedentes penales> **4** DECENT : decente **5** COMPLETE : completo, absoluto <a clean break with the past : un corte radical con el pasado>

cleaner ['kli:nər] *n* **1** : limpiador *m,* -dora *f* **2** : producto *m* de limpieza **3** DRY CLEANER : tintorería *f* (servicio)

cleanliness ['klɛnlinəs] *n* : limpieza *f,* aseo *m*

cleanly[1] ['kli:nli] *adv* : limpiamente, con limpieza

cleanly[2] ['klɛnli] *adj* **-lier; -est** : limpio, pulcro

cleanness ['kli:nnəs] *n* : limpieza *f*

cleanse ['klɛnz] *vt* **cleansed; cleansing** : limpiar, purificar

cleanser ['klɛnzər] *n* : limpiador *m,* purificador *m*

clear[1] ['klɪr] *vt* **1** CLARIFY : aclarar, clarificar (un líquido) **2** : despejar (una superficie), desatascar (un tubo), desmontar (una selva) <to clear the table : levantar la mesa> <to clear one's throat : carraspear, aclararse la voz> **3** EXONERATE : absolver, limpiar el nombre de **4** EARN : ganar, sacar (una ganancia de) **5** : pasar sin tocar

<he cleared the hurdle : saltó por encima de la valla> **6 to clear up** RESOLVE : aclarar, resolver, esclarecer — *vi* **1** DISPERSE : irse, despejarse, disiparse **2** : ser compensado (dícese de un cheque) **3 to clear up** : despejar (dícese del tiempo), mejorarse (dícese de una enfermedad)

clear[2] *adv* : claro, claramente

clear[3] *adj* **1** BRIGHT : claro, lúcido **2** FAIR : claro, despejado **3** TRANSPARENT : transparente, translúcido **4** EVIDENT, UNMISTAKABLE : evidente, claro, obvio **5** CERTAIN : seguro **6** UNOBSTRUCTED : despejado, libre

clear[4] *n* **1 in the clear** : inocente, libre de toda sospecha **2 in the clear** SAFE : fuera de peligro

clearance [ˈklɪrənts] *n* **1** CLEARING : despeje *m* **2** SPACE : espacio *m* (libre), margen *m* **3** AUTHORIZATION : autorización *f*, despacho *m* (de la aduana)

clearing [ˈklɪrɪŋ] *n* : claro *m* (de un bosque)

clearly [ˈklɪrli] *adv* **1** DISTINCTLY : claramente, directamente **2** OBVIOUSLY : obviamente, evidentemente

cleat [ˈkliːt] *n* **1** : taco *m* **2 cleats** *npl* : zapatos *mpl* deportivos (con tacos)

cleavage [ˈkliːvɪdʒ] *n* **1** CLEFT : hendidura *f*, raja *f* **2** : escote *m* (del busto)

cleave[1] [ˈkliːv] *vi* **cleaved** [ˈkliːvd] *or* **clove** [ˈkloːv]; **cleaving** ADHERE : adherirse, unirse

cleave[2] *vt* **cleaved; cleaving** SPLIT : hender, dividir, partir

cleaver [ˈkliːvər] *n* : cuchilla *f* de carnicero

clef [ˈklɛf] *n* : clave *f*

cleft [ˈklɛft] *n* : hendidura *f*, raja *f*, grieta *f*

clemency [ˈklɛməntsi] *n* : clemencia *f*

clement [ˈklɛmənt] *adj* **1** MERCIFUL : clemente, piadoso **2** MILD : clemente, apacible

clench [ˈklɛntʃ] *vt* **1** CLUTCH : agarrar **2** TIGHTEN : apretar (el puño, los dientes)

clergy [ˈklərdʒi] *n, pl* **-gies** : clero *m*

clergyman [ˈklərdʒimən] *n, pl* **-men** [-mən, -ˌmɛn] : clérigo *m*

cleric [ˈklɛrɪk] *n* : clérigo *m*, -ga *f*

clerical [ˈklɛrɪkəl] *adj* **1** : clerical <clerical collar : un alzacuello> **2** : de oficina <clerical staff : personal de oficina>

clerk[1] [ˈklərk, *Brit* ˈklɑrk] *vi* : trabajar de oficinista, trabajar de dependiente

clerk[2] *n* **1** : funcionario *m*, -ria *f* (de una oficina gubernamental) **2** : oficinista *mf*, empleado *m*, -da *f* de oficina **3** SALESPERSON : dependiente *m*, -ta *f*

clever [ˈklɛvər] *adj* **1** SKILLFUL : ingenioso, hábil **2** SMART : listo, inteligente, astuto

cleverly [ˈklɛvərli] *adv* **1** SKILLFULLY : ingeniosamente, hábilmente **2** INTELLIGENTLY : inteligentemente

cleverness [ˈklɛvərnəs] *n* **1** SKILL : ingenio *m*, habilidad *f* **2** INTELLIGENCE : inteligencia *f*

clew [ˈkluː] → **clue**

cliché [kliˈʃeɪ] *n* : cliché *m*, tópico *m*

click[1] [ˈklɪk] *vt* : chasquear (la lengua, los dedos) — *vi* **1** : chasquear **2** SUCCEED : tener éxito **3** GET ALONG : congeniar, llevarse bien

click[2] *n* : chasquido *m*

client [ˈklaɪənt] *n* : cliente *m*, -ta *f*

clientele [ˌklaɪənˈtɛl, ˌkliː-] *n* : clientela *f*

cliff [ˈklɪf] *n* : acantilado *m*, precipicio *m*, risco *m*

climate [ˈklaɪmət] *n* : clima *m*

climax[1] [ˈklaɪˌmæks] *vi* : llegar al punto culminante, culminar — *vt* : ser el punto culminante de

climax[2] *n* : clímax *m*, punto *m* culminante

climb[1] [ˈklaɪm] *vt* : escalar, trepar a, subir a <to climb a mountain : escalar una montaña> — *vi* **1** RISE : subir, ascender <prices are climbing : los precios están subiendo> **2** subirse, treparse <to climb up a tree : treparse a un árbol>

climb[2] *n* : ascenso *m*, subida *f*

climber [ˈklaɪmər] *n* **1** : escalador *m*, -dora *f* <a mountain climber : un alpinista> **2** : trepadora *f* (planta)

clinch[1] [ˈklɪntʃ] *vt* **1** FASTEN, SECURE : remachar (un clavo), afianzar, abrochar **2** SETTLE : decidir, cerrar <to clinch the title : ganar el título>

clinch[2] *n* : abrazo *m*, clinch *m* (en el boxeo)

clincher [ˈklɪntʃər] *n* : argumento *m* decisivo

cling [ˈklɪŋ] *vi* **clung** [ˈklʌŋ]; **clinging** **1** STICK : adherirse, pegarse **2** : aferrarse, agarrarse <he clung to the railing : se aferró a la barandilla>

clinic [ˈklɪnɪk] *n* : clínica *f*

clinical [ˈklɪnɪkəl] *adj* : clínico — **clinically** [-kli] *adv*

clink[1] [ˈklɪŋk] *vi* : tintinear

clink[2] *n* : tintineo *m*

clip[1] [ˈklɪp] *vt* **clipped; clipping** **1** CUT : cortar, recortar **2** HIT : golpear, dar un puñetazo a **3** FASTEN : sujetar (con un clip)

clip[2] *n* **1** → **clippers** **2** BLOW : golpe *m*, puñetazo *m* **3** PACE : paso *m* rápido **4** FASTENER : clip *m* <a paper clip : un sujetapapeles>

clipper [ˈklɪpər] *n* **1** : clíper *m* (buque de vela) **2 clippers** *npl* : tijeras *fpl* <nail clippers : cortaúñas>

clique [ˈkliːk, ˈklɪk] *n* : grupo *m* exclusivo, camarilla *f* (de políticos)

clitoris [ˈklɪtərəs, klɪˈtɔrəs] *n, pl* **clitorides** [-ˈtɔrəˌdiːz] : clítoris *m*

cloak[1] [ˈkloːk] *vt* : encubrir, envolver (en un manto de)

cloak[2] *n* : capa *f*, capote *m*, manto *m* <under the cloak of darkness : al amparo de la oscuridad>

clobber [ˈklɑbər] *vt* **:** dar una paliza a

clock[1] [ˈklɑk] *vt* **:** cronometrar

clock[2] *n* **1 :** reloj *m* (de pared), cronómetro *m* (en deportes o competencias) **2 around the clock :** las veinticuatro horas

clockwise [ˈklɑkˌwaɪz] *adv & adj* **:** en la dirección de las manecillas del reloj

clockwork [ˈklɑkˌwərk] *n* **:** mecanismo *m* de relojería

clod [ˈklɑd] *n* **1 :** terrón *m* **2** OAF **:** zoquete *mf*

clog[1] [ˈklɑg] *v* **clogged; clogging** *vt* **1** HINDER **:** estorbar, impedir **2** BLOCK **:** atascar, tapar — *vi* **:** atascarse, taparse

clog[2] *n* **1** OBSTACLE **:** traba *f,* impedimento *m,* estorbo *m* **2 :** zueco *m* (zapato)

cloister[1] [ˈklɔɪstər] *vt* **:** enclaustrar

cloister[2] *n* **:** claustro *m*

clone [ˈkloːn] *n* **1 :** clon *m* (de un organismo) **2** COPY **:** copia *f,* reproducción *f*

close[1] [ˈkloːz] *v* **closed; closing** *vt* **:** cerrar — *vi* **1 :** cerrarse, cerrar **2** TERMINATE **:** concluirse, terminar **3 to close in** APPROACH **:** acercarse, aproximarse

close[2] [ˈkloːs] *adv* **:** cerca, de cerca

close[3] *adj* **closer; closest 1** CONFINING **:** restrictivo, estrecho **2** SECRETIVE **:** reservado **3** STRICT **:** estricto, detallado **4** STUFFY **:** cargado, bochornoso (dícese del tiempo) **5** TIGHT **:** apretado, entallado, ceñido <it's a close fit : es muy apretado> **6** NEAR **:** cercano, próximo **7** INTIMATE **:** íntimo <close friends : amigos íntimos> **8** ACCURATE **:** fiel, exacto **9 :** reñido <a close election : una elección muy reñida>

close[4] [ˈkloːz] *n* **:** fin *m,* final *m,* conclusión *f*

closely [ˈkloːsli] *adv* **:** cerca, de cerca

closeness [ˈkloːsnəs] *n* **1** NEARNESS **:** cercanía *f,* proximidad *f* **2** INTIMACY **:** intimidad *f*

closet[1] [ˈklɑzət] *vt* **to be closeted with :** estar encerrado con

closet[2] *n* **:** armario *m,* guardarropa *f,* clóset *m*

closure [ˈkloːʒər] *n* **1** CLOSING, END **:** cierre *m,* clausura *f,* fin *m* **2** FASTENER **:** cierre *m*

clot[1] [ˈklɑt] *v* **clotted; clotting** *vt* **:** coagular, cuajar — *vi* **:** cuajarse, coagularse

clot[2] *n* **:** coágulo *m*

cloth [ˈklɔθ] *n, pl* **cloths** [ˈklɔðz, ˈklɔθs] **1** FABRIC **:** tela *f* **2** RAG **:** trapo *m* **3** TABLECLOTH **:** mantel *m*

clothe [ˈkloːð] *vt* **clothed** *or* **clad** [ˈklæd]; **clothing** DRESS **:** vestir, arropar, ataviar

clothes [ˈkloːz, ˈkloːðz] *npl* **1** CLOTHING **:** ropa *f* **2** BEDCLOTHES **:** ropa *f* de cama

clothespin [ˈkloːzˌpɪn] *n* **:** pinza *f* (para la ropa)

clothing [ˈkloːðɪŋ] *n* **:** ropa *f,* indumentaria *f*

cloud[1] [ˈklaʊd] *vt* **:** nublar, oscurecer — *vi* **to cloud over :** nublarse

cloud[2] *n* **:** nube *f*

cloudburst [ˈklaʊdˌbərst] *n* **:** chaparrón *m,* aguacero *m*

cloudless [ˈklaʊdləs] *adj* **:** despejado, claro

cloudy [ˈklaʊdi] *adj* **cloudier; -est :** nublado, nuboso

clout[1] [ˈklaʊt] *vt* **:** bofetear, dar un tortazo a

clout[2] *n* **1** BLOW **:** golpe *m,* tortazo *m fam* **2** INFLUENCE **:** influencia *f,* palanca *f fam*

clove[1] [ˈkloːv] *n* **1 :** diente *m* (de ajo) **2 :** clavo *m* (especia)

clove[2] → **cleave**

cloven hoof [ˈkloːvən] **:** pezuña *f* hendida

clover [ˈkloːvər] *n* **:** trébol *m*

cloverleaf [ˈkloːvərˌliːf] *n, pl* **-leafs** *or* **-leaves** [-ˌliːvz] **:** intersección *f* en trébol

clown[1] [ˈklaʊn] *vi* **:** payasear, bromear <stop clowning around : déjate de payasadas>

clown[2] *n* **:** payaso *m,* -sa *f*

clownish [ˈklaʊnɪʃ] *adj* **1 :** de payaso **2** BOORISH **:** grosero — **clownishly** *adv*

cloying [ˈklɔɪɪŋ] *adj* **:** empalagoso, meloso

club[1] [ˈklʌb] *vt* **clubbed; clubbing :** aporrear, dar garrotazos a

club[2] *n* **1** CUDGEL **:** garrote *m,* porra *f* **2 :** palo *m* <golf club : palo de golf> **3 :** trébol *m* (naipe) **4** ASSOCIATION **:** club *m*

clubfoot [ˈklʌbˌfʊt] *n, pl* **-feet :** pie *m* deforme

clubhouse [ˈklʌbˌhaʊs] *n* **:** sede *f* de un club

cluck[1] [ˈklʌk] *vi* **:** cloquear, cacarear

cluck[2] *n* **:** cloqueo *m,* cacareo *m*

clue[1] [ˈkluː] *vt* **clued; clueing** *or* **cluing** *or* **to clue in :** dar una pista a, informar

clue[2] *n* **:** pista *f,* indicio *m*

clump[1] [ˈklʌmp] *vi* **1 :** caminar con pisadas fuertes **2** LUMP **:** agruparse, aglutinarse — *vt* **:** amontonar

clump[2] *n* **1 :** grupo *m* (de arbustos o árboles), terrón *m* (de tierra) **2 :** pisada *f* fuerte

clumsily [ˈklʌmzəli] *adv* **:** torpemente, sin gracia

clumsiness [ˈklʌmzinəs] *n* **:** torpeza *f*

clumsy [ˈklʌmzi] *adj* **-sier; -est 1** AWKWARD **:** torpe, desmañado **2** TACTLESS **:** carente de tacto, poco delicado

clung → **cling**

cluster[1] [ˈklʌstər] *vt* **:** agrupar, juntar — *vi* **:** agruparse, apiñarse, arracimarse

cluster[2] *n* **:** grupo *m,* conjunto *m,* racimo *m* (de uvas)

clutch[1] [ˈklʌtʃ] *vt* **:** agarrar, asir — *vi* **to clutch at :** tratar de agarrar

clutch² *n* **1** GRASP, GRIP : agarre *m,* apretón *m* **2** : embrague *m,* clutch *m* (de una máquina) **3 clutches** *npl* : garras *fpl* <he fell into their clutches : cayó en sus garras>
clutter¹ [ˈklʌtər] *vt* : atiborrar o atestar de cosas, llenar desordenadamente
clutter² *n* : desorden *m,* revoltijo *m*
coach¹ [ˈkoːtʃ] *vt* : entrenar (atletas, artistas), preparar (alumnos)
coach² *n* **1** CARRIAGE : coche *m,* carruaje *m,* carroza *f* **2** : vagón *m* de pasajeros (de un tren) **3** BUS : autobús *m,* ómnibus *m* **4** : pasaje *m* aéreo de segunda clase **5** TRAINER : entrenador *m,* -dora *f*
coagulate [koˈægjəˌleɪt] *v* **-lated; -lating** *vt* : coagular, cuajar — *vi* : coagularse, cuajarse
coal [ˈkoːl] *n* **1** EMBER : ascua *f,* brasa *f* **2** : carbón *m* <a coal mine : una mina de carbón>
coalesce [ˌkoːəˈlɛs] *vi* **-alesced; -alescing** : unirse
coalition [ˌkoːəˈlɪʃən] *n* : coalición *f*
coarse [ˈkors] *adj* **coarser; -est 1** : grueso (dícese de la arena o la sal), basto (dícese de las telas), áspero (dícese de la piel) **2** CRUDE, ROUGH : basto, tosco, ordinario **3** VULGAR : grosero — **coarsely** *adv*
coarsen [ˈkorsən] *vt* : hacer áspero o basto — *vi* : volverse áspero o basto
coarseness [ˈkorsnəs] *n* : aspereza *f,* tosquedad *f*
coast¹ [ˈkoːst] *vi* : deslizarse, rodar sin impulso
coast² *n* : costa *f,* litoral *m*
coastal [ˈkoːstəl] *adj* : costero
coaster [ˈkoːstər] *n* : posavasos *m*
coast guard *n* : guardia *f* costera, guardacostas *mpl*
coastline [ˈkoːstˌlaɪn] *n* : costa *f*
coat¹ [ˈkoːt] *vt* : cubrir, revestir, bañar (en un líquido)
coat² *n* **1** : abrigo *m* <a sport coat : una chaqueta, un saco> **2** : pelaje *m* (de animales) **3** LAYER : capa *f,* mano *f* (de pintura)
coating [ˈkoːt̬ɪŋ] *n* : capa *f*
coat of arms *n* : escudo *m* de armas
coax [ˈkoːks] *vt* : engatusar, persuadir
cob [ˈkɑb] → **corncob**
cobalt [ˈkoːˌbɔlt] *n* : cobalto *m*
cobble [ˈkɑbəl] *vt* **cobbled; cobbling 1** : fabricar o remendar (zapatos) **2 to cobble together** : improvisar, hacer apresuradamente
cobbler [ˈkɑblər] *n* **1** SHOEMAKER : zapatero *m,* -ra *f* **2 fruit cobbler** : tarta *f* de fruta
cobblestone [ˈkɑbəlˌstoːn] *n* : adoquín *m*
cobra [ˈkoːbrə] *n* : cobra *f*
cobweb [ˈkɑbˌwɛb] *n* : telaraña *f*
cocaine [koːˈkeɪn, ˈkoːˌkeɪn] *n* : cocaína *f*
cock¹ [ˈkɑk] *vt* **1** : ladear <to cock one's head : ladear la cabeza> **2** : montar, amartillar (un arma de fuego)
cock² *n* **1** ROOSTER : gallo *m* **2** FAUCET : grifo *m,* llave *f* **3** : martillo *m* (de un arma de fuego)
cockatoo [ˈkɑkəˌtuː] *n, pl* **-toos** : cacatúa *f*
cockeyed [ˈkɑkˌaɪd] *adj* **1** ASKEW : ladeado, torcido, chueco **2** ABSURD : disparatado, absurdo
cockfight [ˈkɑkˌfaɪt] *n* : pelea *f* de gallos
cockiness [ˈkɑkinəs] *n* : arrogancia *f*
cockle [ˈkɑkəl] *n* : berberecho *m*
cockpit [ˈkɑkˌpɪt] *n* : cabina *f*
cockroach [ˈkɑkˌroːtʃ] *n* : cucaracha *f*
cocktail [ˈkɑkˌteɪl] *n* **1** : coctel *m,* cóctel *m* **2** APPETIZER : aperitivo *m*
cocky [ˈkɑki] *adj* **cockier; -est** : creído, engreído
cocoa [ˈkoːˌkoː] *n* **1** CACAO : cacao *m* **2** : cocoa *f,* chocolate *m* (bebida)
coconut [ˈkoːkəˌnʌt] *n* : coco *m*
cocoon [kəˈkuːn] *n* : capullo *m*
cod [ˈkɑd] *n, pl* **cod** : bacalao *m*
coddle [ˈkɑdəl] *vt* **-dled; -dling** : mimar, consentir
code [ˈkoːd] *n* **1** : código *m* <civil code : código civil> **2** : código *m,* clave *f* <secret code : clave secreta>
codeine [ˈkoːˌdiːn] *n* : codeína *f*
codger [ˈkɑdʒər] *n* : viejo *m,* vejete *m*
codify [ˈkɑdəˌfaɪ, ˈkoː-] *vt* **-fied; -fying** : codificar
coeducation [ˌkoːˌɛdʒəˈkeɪʃən] *n* : coeducación *f,* enseñanza *f* mixta
coeducational [ˌkoːˌɛdʒəˈkeɪʃənəl] *adj* : mixto
coefficient [ˌkoːəˈfɪʃənt] *n* : coeficiente *m*
coerce [koˈərs] *vt* **-erced; -ercing** : coaccionar, forzar, obligar
coercion [koˈərʒən, -ʃən] *n* : coacción *f*
coercive [koˈərsɪv] *adj* : coactivo
coexist [ˌkoːɪgˈzɪst] *vi* : coexistir
coexistence [ˌkoːɪgˈzɪstənts] *n* : coexistencia *f*
coffee [ˈkɔfi] *n* : café *m*
coffeepot [ˈkɔfiˌpɑt] *n* : cafetera *f*
coffer [ˈkɔfər] *n* : cofre *m*
coffin [ˈkɔfən] *n* : ataúd *m,* féretro *m*
cog [ˈkɑg] *n* : diente *m* (de una rueda dentada)
cogent [ˈkoːdʒənt] *adj* : convincente, persuasivo
cogitate [ˈkɑdʒəˌteɪt] *vi* **-tated; -tating** : reflexionar, meditar, discurrir
cogitation [ˌkɑdʒəˈteɪʃən] *n* : reflexión *f,* meditación *f*
cognac [ˈkoːnˌjæk] *n* : coñac *m*
cognate [ˈkɑgˌneɪt] *adj* : relacionado, afín
cogwheel [ˈkɑgˌhwiːl] *n* : rueda *f* dentada
cohabit [ˌkoːˈhæbət] *vi* : cohabitar
cohere [koˈhɪr] *vi* **-hered; -hering 1** ADHERE : adherirse, pegarse **2** : ser coherente o congruente

coherence [ko'hɪrənts] *n* **:** coherencia *f,* congruencia *f*

coherent [ko'hɪrənt] *adj* **:** coherente, congruente — **coherently** *adv*

cohesion [ko'hiːʒən] *n* **:** cohesión *f*

cohort ['koːˌhɔrt] *n* **1 :** cohorte *f* (de soldados) **2** COMPANION **:** compañero *m,* -ra *f;* colega *mf*

coiffure [kwɑ'fjʊr] *n* **:** peinado *m*

coil[1] ['kɔɪl] *vt* **:** enrollar — *vi* **:** enrollarse, enroscarse

coil[2] *n* **:** rollo *m* (de cuerda, etc.), espiral *f* (de humo)

coin[1] ['kɔɪn] *vt* **1** MINT **:** acuñar (moneda) **2** INVENT **:** acuñar, crear, inventar <to coin a phrase : como se suele decir>

coin[2] *n* **:** moneda *f*

coincide [ˌkoːɪn'saɪd, 'koːɪnˌsaɪd] *vi* **-cided; -ciding :** coincidir

coincidence [ko'ɪn*t*sədən*t*s] *n* **:** coincidencia *f,* casualidad *f* <what a coincidence! : ¡qué casualidad!>

coincident [ko'ɪn*t*sədənt] *adj* **:** coincidente, concurrente

coincidental [koˌɪn*t*sə'dɛntəl] *adj* **:** casual, accidental, fortuito

coitus ['koːət̬əs] *n* **:** coito *m*

coke ['koːk] *n* **:** coque *m*

colander ['kɑləndər, 'kʌ-] *n* **:** colador *m*

cold[1] ['koːld] *adj* **:** frío <it's cold out : hace frío> <a cold reception : una fría recepción> <in cold blood : a sangre fría>

cold[2] *n* **1 :** frío *m* <to feel the cold : sentir frío> **2 :** resfriado *m,* catarro *m* <to catch a cold : resfriarse>

cold–blooded ['koːld'blʌdəd] *adj* **1** CRUEL **:** cruel, despiadado **2 :** de sangre fría (dícese de los reptiles, etc.)

coldly ['koːldli] *adv* **:** fríamente, con frialdad

coldness ['koːldnəs] *n* **:** frialdad *f* (de una persona o una actitud), frío *m* (de la temperatura)

coleslaw ['koːlˌslɔ] *n* **:** ensalada *f* de col

colic ['kɑlɪk] *n* **:** cólico *m*

coliseum [ˌkɑlə'siːəm] *n* **:** coliseo *m,* arena *f*

collaborate [kə'læbəˌreɪt] *vi* **-rated; -rating :** colaborar

collaboration [kəˌlæbə'reɪʃən] *n* **:** colaboración *f*

collaborator [kə'læbəˌreɪt̬ər] *n* **1** COLLEAGUE **:** colaborador *m,* -dora *f* **2** TRAITOR **:** colaboracionista *mf*

collapse[1] [kə'læps] *vi* **-lapsed; -lapsing 1 :** derrumbarse, desplomarse, hundirse <the building collapsed : el edificio se derrumbó> **2** FALL **:** desplomarse, caerse <he collapsed on the bed : se desplomó en la cama> <to collapse with laughter : morirse de risa> **3** FAIL **:** fracasar, quebrar, arruinarse **4** FOLD **:** plegarse

collapse[2] *n* **1** FALL **:** derrumbe *m,* desplome *m* **2** BREAKDOWN, FAILURE **:** fracaso *m,* colapso *m* (físico), quiebra *f* (económica)

collapsible [kə'læpsəbəl] *adj* **:** plegable

collar[1] ['kɑlər] *vt* **:** agarrar, atrapar

collar[2] *n* **:** cuello *m*

collarbone ['kɑlərˌboːn] *n* **:** clavícula *f*

collate [kə'leɪt; 'kɑˌleɪt, 'koː-] *vt* **-lated; -lating 1** COMPARE **:** cotejar, comparar **2 :** ordenar, recopilar (páginas)

collateral[1] [kə'læt̬ərəl] *adj* **:** colateral

collateral[2] *n* **:** garantía *f,* fianza *f,* prenda *f*

colleague ['kɑˌliːg] *n* **:** colega *mf;* compañero *m,* -ra *f*

collect[1] [kə'lɛkt] *vt* **1** GATHER **:** recopilar, reunir, recoger <she collected her thoughts : puso en orden sus ideas> **2 :** coleccionar, juntar <to collect stamps : coleccionar timbres> **3 :** cobrar (una deuda), recaudar (un impuesto) **4** DRAW **:** cobrar, percibir (un sueldo, etc.) — *vi* **1** ACCUMULATE **:** acumularse, juntarse **2** CONGREGATE **:** congregarse, reunirse

collect[2] *adv & adj* **:** por cobrar, a cobro revertido

collectible *or* **collectable** [kə'lɛktəbəl] *adj* **:** coleccionable

collection [kə'lɛkʃən] *n* **1** COLLECTING **:** colecta *f* (de contribuciones), cobro *m* (de deudas), recaudación *f* (de impuestos) **2** GROUP **:** colección *f* (de objetos), grupo *m* (de personas)

collective[1] [kə'lɛktɪv] *adj* **:** colectivo — **collectively** *adv*

collective[2] *n* **:** colectivo *m*

collector [kə'lɛktər] *n* **1 :** coleccionista *mf* (de objetos) **2 :** cobrador *m,* -dora *f* (de deudas)

college ['kɑlɪdʒ] *n* **1 :** universidad *f* **2 :** colegio *m* (de electores o profesionales)

collegiate [kə'liːdʒət] *adj* **:** universitario

collide [kə'laɪd] *vi* **-lided; -liding :** chocar, colisionar, estrellarse

collie ['kɑli] *n* **:** collie *mf*

collision [kə'lɪʒən] *n* **:** choque *m,* colisión *f*

colloquial [kə'loːkwiəl] *adj* **:** coloquial

colloquialism [kə'loːkwiəˌlɪzəm] *n* **:** expresión *f* coloquial

collusion [kə'luːʒən] *n* **:** colusión *f*

cologne [kə'loːn] *n* **:** colonia *f*

Colombian [kə'lʌmbiən] *n* **:** colombiano *m,* -na *f* — **Colombian** *adj*

colon[1] ['koːlən] *n, pl* **colons** *or* **cola** [-lə] **:** colon *m* (de los intestinos)

colon[2] *n, pl* **colons :** dos puntos *mpl* (signo ortográfico)

colonel ['kərnəl] *n* **:** coronel *m*

colonial[1] [kə'loːniəl] *adj* **:** colonial

colonial[2] *n* **:** colono *m,* -na *f*

colonist ['kɑlənɪst] *n* **:** colono *m,* -na *f;* colonizador *m,* -dora *f*

colonization [ˌkɑlənəˈzeɪʃən] *n* : colonización *f*

colonize [ˈkɑləˌnaɪz] *vt* **-nized; -nizing** **1** : establecer una colonia en **2** SETTLE : colonizar

colonnade [ˌkɑləˈneɪd] *n* : columnata *f*

colony [ˈkɑləni] *n, pl* **-nies** : colonia *f*

color[1] [ˈkʌlər] *vt* **1** : colorear, pintar **2** INFLUENCE : influir en, influenciar — *vi* BLUSH : sonrojarse, ruborizarse

color[2] *n* **1** : color *m* <primary colors : colores primarios> **2** INTEREST, VIVIDNESS : color *m,* colorido *m* <local color : color local>

color–blind [ˈkʌlərˌblaɪnd] *adj* : daltónico

color blindness *n* : daltonismo *m*

colored [ˈkʌlərd] *adj* **1** : de color (dícese de los objetos) **2** : de color, negro (dícese de las personas)

colorfast [ˈkʌlərˌfæst] *adj* : que no se destiñe

colorful [ˈkʌlərfəl] *adj* **1** : lleno de colorido, de colores vivos **2** PICTURESQUE, STRIKING : pintoresco, llamativo

colorless [ˈkʌlərləs] *adj* **1** : incoloro, sin color **2** DULL : soso, aburrido

colossal [kəˈlɑsəl] *adj* : colosal

colossus [kəˈlɑsəs] *n, pl* **-si** [-ˌsaɪ] : coloso *m*

colt [ˈkoːlt] *n* : potro *m*

column [ˈkɑləm] *n* : columna *f*

columnist [ˈkɑləmnɪst, -ləmɪst] *n* : columnista *mf*

coma [ˈkoːmə] *n* : coma *m,* estado *m* de coma

comatose [ˈkoːməˌtoːs, ˈkɑ-] *adj* : comatoso, en estado de coma

comb[1] [ˈkoːm] *vt* **1** : peinar (el pelo) **2** SEARCH : peinar, rastrear, registrar a fondo

comb[2] *n* **1** : peine *m* **2** : cresta *f* (de un gallo)

combat[1] [kəmˈbæt, ˈkɑmˌbæt] *vt* **-bated** *or* **-batted; -bating** *or* **-batting** : combatir, luchar contra

combat[2] [ˈkɑmˌbæt] *n* : combate *m,* lucha *f*

combatant [kəmˈbætənt] *n* : combatiente *mf*

combative [kəmˈbæt̬ɪv] *adj* : combativo

combination [ˌkɑmbəˈneɪʃən] *n* : combinación *f*

combine[1] [kəmˈbaɪn] *v* **-bined; -bining** *vt* : combinar, aunar — *vi* : combinarse, mezclarse

combine[2] [ˈkɑmˌbaɪn] *n* **1** ALLIANCE : alianza *f* comercial o política **2** HARVESTER : cosechadora *f*

combustible [kəmˈbʌstəbəl] *adj* : inflamable, combustible

combustion [kəmˈbʌstʃən] *n* : combustión *f*

come [ˈkʌm] *vi* **came** [ˈkeɪm]; **come; coming** **1** APPROACH : venir, aproximarse <here they come : acá vienen> **2** ARRIVE : venir, llegar, alcanzar <they came yesterday : vinieron ayer> **3** ORIGINATE : venir, provenir <this wine comes from France : este vino viene de Francia> **4** AMOUNT : llegar, ascender <the investment came to two million : la inversión llegó a dos millones> **5 to come clean** : confesar, desahogar la conciencia **6 to come into** ACQUIRE : adquirir <to come into a fortune : heredar una fortuna> **7 to come off** SUCCEED : tener éxito, ser un éxito **8 to come out** : salir, aparecer, publicarse **9 to come to** REVIVE : recobrar el conocimiento, volver en sí **10 to come to pass** HAPPEN : acontecer **11 to come to terms** : llegar a un acuerdo

comeback [ˈkʌmˌbæk] *n* **1** RETORT : réplica *f,* respuesta *f* **2** RETURN : retorno *m,* regreso *m* <the champion announced his comeback : el campeón anunció su regreso>

come back *vi* **1** RETORT : replicar, contestar **2** RETURN : volver <come back here! : ¡vuelve acá!> <that style's coming back : ese estilo está volviendo>

comedian [kəˈmiːdiən] *n* : cómico *m,* -ca *f;* humorista *mf*

comedienne [kəˌmiːdiˈɛn] *n* : cómica *f,* humorista *f*

comedy [ˈkɑmədi] *n, pl* **-dies** : comedia *f*

comely [ˈkʌmli] *adj* **-lier; -est** : bello, bonito

comet [ˈkɑmət] *n* : cometa *m*

comfort[1] [ˈkʌmpfərt] *vt* **1** CHEER : confortar, alentar **2** CONSOLE : consolar

comfort[2] *n* **1** CONSOLATION : consuelo *m* **2** WELL-BEING : confort *m,* bienestar *m* **3** CONVENIENCE : comodidad *f* <the comforts of home : las comodidades del hogar>

comfortable [ˈkʌmpfərt̬əbəl, ˈkʌmpftə-] *adj* : cómodo, confortable — **comfortably** [ˈkʌmpfərt̬əbli, ˈkʌmpftə-] *adv*

comforter [ˈkʌmpfərt̬ər] *n* **1** : confortador *m,* -dora *f* **2** QUILT : edredón *m,* cobertor *m*

comic[1] [ˈkɑmɪk] *adj* : cómico, humorístico

comic[2] *n* **1** COMEDIAN : cómico *m,* -ca *f;* humorista *mf* **2** *or* **comic book** : historieta *f,* cómic *m*

comical [ˈkɑmɪkəl] *adj* : cómico, gracioso, chistoso

comic strip *n* : tira *f* cómica, historieta *f*

coming [ˈkʌmɪŋ] *adj* : siguiente, próximo, que viene

comma [ˈkɑmə] *n* : coma *f*

command[1] [kəˈmænd] *vt* **1** ORDER : ordenar, mandar **2** CONTROL, DIRECT : comandar, tener el mando de — *vi* **1** : dar órdenes **2** GOVERN : estar al mando *m,* gobernar

command[2] *n* **1** CONTROL, LEADERSHIP : mando *m,* control *m,* dirección *f* **2** ORDER : orden *f,* mandato *m* **3** MASTERY : maestría *f,* destreza *f,* dominio *m* **4** : tropa *f* asignada a un comandante

commandant [ˈkɑmən͵dɑnt, -͵dænt] *n* : comandante *mf*

commandeer [͵kɑmənˈdɪr] *vt* : piratear, secuestrar (un vehículo, etc.)

commander [kəˈmændər] *n* : comandante *mf*

commandment [kəˈmændmənt] *n* : mandamiento *m,* orden *f* <the Ten Commandments : los diez mandamientos>

commemorate [kəˈmɛmə͵reɪt] *vt* **-rated; -rating** : conmemorar

commemoration [kə͵mɛməˈreɪʃən] *n* : conmemoración *f*

commemorative [kəˈmɛmrət̮ɪv, -ˈmɛmə͵reɪt̮ɪv] *adj* : conmemorativo

commence [kəˈmɛnts] *v* **-menced; -mencing** *vt* : iniciar, comenzar — *vi* : iniciarse, comenzar

commencement [kəˈmɛntsmənt] *n* **1** BEGINNING : inicio *m,* comienzo *m* **2** : ceremonia *f* de graduación

commend [kəˈmɛnd] *vt* **1** ENTRUST : encomendar **2** RECOMMEND : recomendar **3** PRAISE : elogiar, alabar

commendable [kəˈmɛndəbəl] *adj* : loable, meritorio, encomiable

commendation [͵kɑmənˈdeɪʃən, -͵mɛn-] *n* : elogio *m,* encomio *m*

commensurate [kəˈmɛntsərət, -ˈmɛntʃʊrət] *adj* : proporcionado <commensurate with : en proporción a>

comment[1] [ˈkɑ͵mɛnt] *vi* **1** : hacer comentarios **2 to comment on** : comentar, hacer observaciones sobre

comment[2] *n* : comentario *m,* observación *f*

commentary [ˈkɑmən͵tɛri] *n, pl* **-taries** : comentario *m,* crónica *f* (deportiva)

commentator [ˈkɑmən͵teɪt̮ər] *n* : comentarista *mf,* cronista *mf* (de deportes)

commerce [ˈkɑmərs] *n* : comercio *m*

commercial[1] [kəˈmərʃəl] *adj* : comercial — **commercially** *adv*

commercial[2] *n* : comercial *m*

commercialize [kəˈmərʃə͵laɪz] *vt* **-ized; -izing** : comercializar

commiserate [kəˈmɪzə͵reɪt] *vi* **-ated; -ating** : compadecerse, consolarse

commiseration [kə͵mɪzəˈreɪʃən] *n* : conmiseración *f*

commission[1] [kəˈmɪʃən] *vt* **1** : nombrar (un oficial) **2** : comisionar, encargar <to commission a painting : encargar una pintura>

commission[2] *n* **1** : nombramiento *m* (al grado de oficial) **2** COMMITTEE : comisión *f,* comité *m* **3** COMMITTING : comisión *f,* realización *f* (de un acto) **4** PERCENTAGE : comisión *f* <sales commissions : comisiones de venta>

commissioned officer *n* : oficial *mf*

commissioner [kəˈmɪʃənər] *n* **1** : comisionado *m,* -da *f;* miembro *m* de una comisión **2** : comisario *m,* -ria *f* (de policía, etc.)

commit [kəˈmɪt] *vt* **-mitted; -mitting** **1** ENTRUST : encomendar, confiar **2** CONFINE : internar (en un hospital), encarcelar (en una prisión) **3** PERPETRATE : cometer <to commit a crime : cometer un crimen> **4 to commit oneself** : comprometerse

commitment [kəˈmɪtmənt] *n* **1** RESPONSIBILITY : compromiso *m,* responsabilidad *f* **2** DEDICATION : dedicación *f,* devoción *f* <commitment to the cause : devoción a la causa>

committee [kəˈmɪt̮i] *n* : comité *m*

commodious [kəˈmoːdiəs] *adj* SPACIOUS : amplio, espacioso

commodity [kəˈmɑdət̮i] *n, pl* **-ties** : artículo *m* de comercio, mercancía *f,* mercadería *f*

commodore [ˈkɑmə͵dor] *n* : comodoro *m*

common[1] [ˈkɑmən] *adj* **1** PUBLIC : común, público <the common good : el bien común> **2** SHARED : común <a common interest : un interés común> **3** GENERAL : común, general <it's common knowledge : todo el mundo lo sabe> **4** ORDINARY : ordinario, común y corriente <the common man : el hombre medio, el hombre de la calle>

common[2] *n* **1** : tierra *f* comunal **2 in ~** : en común

common cold *n* : resfriado *m* común

common denominator *n* : denominador *m* común

commoner [ˈkɑmənər] *n* : plebeyo *m,* -ya *f*

commonly [ˈkɑmənli] *adv* **1** FREQUENTLY : comúnmente, frecuentemente **2** USUALLY : normalmente

common noun *n* : nombre *m* común

commonplace[1] [ˈkɑmən͵pleɪs] *adj* : común, ordinario

commonplace[2] *n* : cliché *m,* tópico *m*

common sense *n* : sentido *m* común

commonwealth [ˈkɑmən͵wɛlθ] *n* : entidad *f* política <the British Commonwealth : la Mancomunidad Británica>

commotion [kəˈmoːʃən] *n* **1** RUCKUS : alboroto *m,* jaleo *m,* escándalo *m* **2** STIR, UPSET : revuelo *m,* conmoción *f*

communal [kəˈmjuːnəl] *adj* : communal

commune[1] [kəˈmjuːn] *vi* **-muned; -muning** : estar en comunión *f*

commune[2] [ˈkɑ͵mjuːn, kəˈmjuːn] *n* : comuna *f*

communicable [kəˈmjuːnɪkəbəl] *adj* CONTAGIOUS : transmisible, contagioso

communicate [kəˈmjuːnə͵keɪt] *v* **-cated; -cating** *vt* **1** CONVEY : comunicar, expresar, hacer saber **2** TRANSMIT : transmitir (una enfermedad), contagiar — *vi* : comunicarse, expresarse

communication [kə,mjuːnə'keɪʃən] *n* : comunicación *f*

communicative [kə'mjuːnɪ,keɪt̬ɪv, -kət̬ɪv] *adj* : comunicativo

communion [kə'mjuːnjən] *n* **1** SHARING : comunión *f* **2 Communion** : comunión *f*, eucaristía *f*

communiqué [kə'mjuːnə,keɪ, -,mjuːnə'keɪ] *n* : comunicado *m*

communism *or* **Communism** ['kɑmjə,nɪzəm] *n* : comunismo *m*

communist[1] *or* **Communist** ['kɑmjə,nɪst] *adj* : comunista <the Communist Party : el Partido Comunista>

communist[2] *or* **Communist** *n* : comunista *mf*

communistic *or* **Communistic** [,kɑmjə'nɪstɪk] *adj* : comunista

community [kə'mjuːnət̬i] *n, pl* **-ties** : comunidad *f*

commute [kə'mjuːt] *v* **-muted; -muting** *vt* REDUCE : conmutar, reducir (una sentencia) — *vi* : viajar de la residencia al trabajo

commuter [kə'mjuːt̬ər] *n* : persona *f* que viaja diariamente al trabajo

compact[1] [kəm'pækt, 'kɑm,pækt] *vt* : compactar, consolidar, comprimir

compact[2] [kəm'pækt, 'kɑm,pækt] *adj* **1** DENSE, SOLID : compacto, macizo, denso **2** CONCISE : breve, conciso

compact[3] ['kɑm,pækt] *n* **1** AGREEMENT : acuerdo *m*, pacto *m* **2** : polvera *f*, estuche *m* de maquillaje **3** *or* **compact car** : auto *m* compacto

compact disc ['kɑm,pækt'dɪsk] *n* : disco *m* compacto, compact disc *m*

compactly [kəm'pæktli, 'kɑm,pækt-] *adv* **1** DENSELY : densamente, macizamente **2** CONCISELY : concisamente, brevemente

companion [kəm'pænjən] *n* **1** COMRADE : compañero *m*, -ra *f*; acompañante *mf* **2** MATE : pareja *f* (de un zapato, etc.)

companionable [kəm'pænjənəbəl] *adj* : sociable, amigable

companionship [kəm'pænjən,ʃɪp] *n* : compañerismo *m*, camaradería *f*

company ['kʌmpəni] *n, pl* **-nies 1** FIRM : compañía *f*, empresa *f* **2** GROUP : compañía *f* (de actores o soldados) **3** GUESTS : visita *f* <we have company : tenemos visita>

comparable ['kɑmpərəbəl] *adj* : comparable, parecido

comparative[1] [kəm'pærət̬iv] *adj* RELATIVE : comparativo, relativo — **comparatively** *adv*

comparative[2] *n* : comparativo *m*

compare[1] [kəm'pær] *v* **-pared; -paring** *vt* : comparar — *vi* **to compare with** : poder comparar con, tener comparación con

compare[2] *n* : comparación *f* <beyond compare : sin igual, sin par>

comparison [kəm'pærəsən] *n* : comparación *f*

compartment [kəm'pɑrtmənt] *n* : compartimento *m*, compartimiento *m*

compass ['kʌmpəs, 'kɑm-] *n* **1** RANGE, SCOPE : alcance *m*, extensión *f*, límites *mpl* **2** : compás *m* (para trazar circunferencias) **3** : compás *m*, brújula *f* <the points of the compass : los puntos cardinales>

compassion [kəm'pæʃən] *n* : compasión *f*, piedad *f*, misericordia *f*

compassionate [kəm'pæʃənət] *adj* : compasivo

compatibility [kəm,pæt̬ə'bɪlət̬i] *n* : compatibilidad *f*

compatible [kəm'pæt̬əbəl] *adj* : compatible, afín

compatriot [kəm'peɪtriət, -'pæ-] *n* : compatriota *mf*; paisano *m*, -na *f*

compel [kəm'pɛl] *vt* **-pelled; -pelling** : obligar, compeler

compendium [kəm'pɛndiəm] *n, pl* **-diums** *or* **-dia** [-diə] : compendio *m*

compensate ['kɑmpən,seɪt] *v* **-sated; -sating** *vi* **to compensate for** : compensar — *vt* : indemnizar, compensar

compensation [,kɑmpən'seɪʃən] *n* : compensación *f*, indemnización *f*

compensatory [kəm'pɛntsə,tori] *adj* : compensatorio

compete [kəm'piːt] *vi* **-peted; -peting** : competir, contender, rivalizar

competence ['kɑmpətənts] *n* : competencia *f*, aptitud *f*

competency ['kɑmpətəntsi] → **competence**

competent ['kɑmpətənt] *adj* : competente, capaz

competition [,kɑmpə'tɪʃən] *n* : competencia *f*, concurso *m*

competitive [kəm'pɛt̬ət̬iv] *adj* : competitivo

competitor [kəm'pɛt̬ət̬ər] *n* : competidor *m*, -dora *f*

compile [kəm'paɪl] *vt* **-piled; -piling** : compilar, recopilar

complacency [kəm'pleɪsəntsi] *n* : satisfacción *f* consigo mismo, suficiencia *f*

complacent [kəm'pleɪsənt] *adj* : satisfecho de sí mismo, suficiente

complain [kəm'pleɪn] *vi* **1** GRIPE : quejarse, regañar, rezongar **2** PROTEST : reclamar, protestar

complaint [kəm'pleɪnt] *n* **1** GRIPE : queja *f* **2** AILMENT : afección *f*, dolencia *f* **3** ACCUSATION : reclamo *m*, acusación *f*

complement[1] ['kɑmplə,mɛnt] *vt* : complementar

complement[2] ['kɑmpləmənt] *n* : complemento *m*

complementary [,kɑmplə'mɛntəri] *adj* : complementario

complete[1] [kəm'pliːt] *vt* **-pleted; -pleting 1** : completar, hacer entero <this piece completes the collection : esta pieza completa la colección> **2** FINISH : completar, acabar, terminar

<she completed her studies : completó sus estudios>
complete[2] *adj* **-pleter; -est 1** WHOLE : completo, entero, íntegro **2** FINISHED : terminado, acabado **3** TOTAL : completo, total, absoluto
completely [kəmˈpliːtli] *adv* : completamente, totalmente
completion [kəmˈpliːʃən] *n* : finalización *f,* cumplimiento *m*
complex[1] [kɑmˈplɛks, kəm-; ˈkɑmˌplɛks] *adj* : complejo, complicado
complex[2] [ˈkɑmˌplɛks] *n* : complejo *m*
complexion [kəmˈplɛkʃən] *n* : cutis *m,* tez *f* <of dark complexion : de tez morena>
complexity [kəmˈplɛksət̬i, kɑm-] *n, pl* **-ties** : complejidad *f*
compliance [kəmˈplaɪən*t*s] *n* : conformidad *f* <in compliance with the law : conforme a la ley>
compliant [kəmˈplaɪənt] *adj* : dócil, sumiso
complicate [ˈkɑmpləˌkeɪt] *vt* **-cated; -cating** : complicar
complicated [ˈkɑmpləˌkeɪt̬əd] *adj* : complicado
complication [ˌkɑmpləˈkeɪʃən] *n* : complicación *f*
complicity [kəmˈplɪsət̬i] *n, pl* **-ties** : complicidad *f*
compliment[1] [ˈkɑmpləˌmɛnt] *vt* : halagar, florear *Mex*
compliment[2] [ˈkɑmpləmənt] *n* **1** : halago *m,* cumplido *m* **2 compliments** *npl* : saludos *mpl* <give them my compliments : déles saludos de mi parte>
complimentary [ˌkɑmpləˈmɛntəri] *adj* **1** FLATTERING : halagador, halagüeño **2** FREE : de cortesía, gratis
comply [kəmˈplaɪ] *vi* **-plied; -plying** : cumplir, acceder, obedecer
component[1] [kəmˈpoːnənt, ˈkɑmˌpoː-] *adj* : componente
component[2] *n* : componente *m,* elemento *m,* pieza *f*
compose [kəmˈpoːz] *vt* **-posed; -posing 1** : componer, crear <to compose a melody : componer una melodía > **2** CALM : calmar, serenar <to compose oneself : serenarse> **3** CONSTITUTE : constar, componer <to be composed of : constar de> **4** : componer (un texto a imprimirse)
composer [kəmˈpoːzər] *n* : compositor *m,* -tora *f*
composite[1] [kɑmˈpɑzət, kəm-; ˈkɑmpəzət] *adj* : compuesto (de varias partes)
composite[2] *n* : compuesto *m,* mezcla *f*
composition [ˌkɑmpəˈzɪʃən] *n* **1** MAKEUP : composición *f* **2** ESSAY : ensayo *m,* trabajo *m*
compost [ˈkɑmˌpoːst] *n* : abono *m* vegetal
composure [kəmˈpoːʒər] *n* : compostura *f,* serenidad *f*
compound[1] [kɑmˈpaʊnd, kəm-; ˈkɑmˌpaʊnd] *vt* **1** COMBINE, COMPOSE : combinar, componer **2** AUGMENT : agravar, aumentar <to compound a problem : agravar un problema>
compound[2] [ˈkɑmˌpaʊnd; kɑmˈpaʊnd, kəm-] *adj* : compuesto <compound interest : interés compuesto>
compound[3] [ˈkɑmˌpaʊnd] *n* **1** MIXTURE : compuesto *m,* mezcla *f* **2** ENCLOSURE : recinto *m* (de residencias, etc.)
compound fracture *n* : fractura *f* complicada
comprehend [ˌkɑmprɪˈhɛnd] *vt* **1** UNDERSTAND : comprender, entender **2** INCLUDE : comprender, incluir, abarcar
comprehensible [ˌkɑmprɪˈhɛn*t*səbəl] *adj* : comprensible
comprehension [ˌkɑmprɪˈhɛntʃən] *n* : comprensión *f*
comprehensive [ˌkɑmprɪˈhɛn*t*sɪv] *adj* **1** INCLUSIVE : inclusivo, exhaustivo **2** BROAD : extenso, amplio
compress[1] [kəmˈprɛs] *vt* : comprimir
compress[2] [ˈkɑmˌprɛs] *n* : compresa *f*
compression [kəmˈprɛʃən] *n* : compresión *f*
comprise [kəmˈpraɪz] *vt* **-prised; -prising 1** INCLUDE : comprender, incluir **2** : componerse de, constar de <the installation comprises several buildings : la instalación está compuesta de varios edificios>
compromise[1] [ˈkɑmprəˌmaɪz] *v* **-mised; -mising** *vi* : transigir, avenirse — *vt* JEOPARDIZE : comprometer, poner en peligro
compromise[2] *n* : acuerdo *m* mutuo, compromiso *m*
comptroller [kənˈtroːlər, ˈkɑmpˌtroː-] *n* : contralor *m,* -lora *f;* interventor *m,* -tora *f*
compulsion [kəmˈpʌlʃən] *n* **1** COERCION : coacción *f* **2** URGE : compulsión *f,* impulso *m*
compulsive [kəmˈpʌlsɪv] *adj* : compulsivo
compulsory [kəmˈpʌlsəri] *adj* : obligatorio
compunction [kəmˈpʌŋkʃən] *n* **1** QUALM : reparo *m,* escrúpulo *m* **2** REMORSE : remordimiento *m*
computation [ˌkɑmpjʊˈteɪʃən] *n* : cálculo *m,* cómputo *m*
compute [kəmˈpjuːt] *vt* **-puted; -puting** : computar, calcular
computer [kəmˈpjuːt̬ər] *n* : computadora *f,* computador *m,* ordenador *m Spain*
computerize [kəmˈpjuːt̬əˌraɪz] *vt* **-ized; -izing** : computarizar, informatizar
comrade [ˈkɑmˌræd] *n* : camarada *mf;* compañero *m,* -ra *f*
con[1] [ˈkɑn] *vt* **conned; conning** SWINDLE : estafar, timar
con[2] *adv* : contra

con[3] *n* : contra *m* <the pros and cons : los pros y los contras>
concave [kɑn'keɪv, 'kɑn,keɪv] *adj* : cóncavo
conceal [kən'siːl] *vt* : esconder, ocultar, disimular
concealment [kən'siːlmənt] *n* : escondimiento *m,* ocultación *f*
concede [kən'siːd] *vt* **-ceded; -ceding** **1** ALLOW, GRANT : conceder **2** ADMIT : conceder, reconocer <to concede defeat : reconocer la derrota>
conceit [kən'siːt] *n* : engreimiento *m,* presunción *f*
conceited [kən'siːt̬əd] *adj* : presumido, engreído, presuntuoso
conceivable [kən'siːvəbəl] *adj* : concebible, imaginable
conceivably [kən'siːvəbli] *adv* : posiblemente, de manera concebible
conceive [kən'siːv] *v* **-ceived; -ceiving** *vi* : concebir, embarazarse — *vt* IMAGINE : concebir, imaginar
concentrate[1] ['kɑn*t*sən,treɪt] *v* **-trated; -trating** *vt* : concentrar — *vi* : concentrarse
concentrate[2] *n* : concentrado *m*
concentration [,kɑn*t*sən'treɪʃən] *n* : concentración *f*
concentric [kən'sɛntrɪk] *adj* : concéntrico
concept ['kɑn,sɛpt] *n* : concepto *m,* idea *f*
conception [kən'sɛpʃən] *n* **1** : concepción *f* (de un bebé) **2** IDEA : concepto *m,* idea *f*
concern[1] [kən'sərn] *vt* **1** : tratarse de, tener que ver con <the novel concerns a sailor : la novela se trata de un marinero> **2** INVOLVE : concernir, incumbir a, afectar <that does not concern me : eso no me incumbe>
concern[2] *n* **1** AFFAIR : asunto *m* **2** WORRY : inquietud *f,* preocupación *f* **3** BUSINESS : negocio *m*
concerned [kən'sərnd] *adj* **1** ANXIOUS : preocupado, ansioso **2** INTERESTED, INVOLVED : interesado, afectado
concerning [kən'sərnɪŋ] *prep* REGARDING : con respecto a, acerca de, sobre
concert ['kɑn,sərt] *n* **1** AGREEMENT : concierto *m,* acuerdo *m* **2** : concierto *m* (musical)
concerted [kən'sərt̬əd] *adj* : concertado, coordinado <to make a concerted effort : coordinar los esfuerzos>
concertina [,kɑn*t*sər'tiːnə] *n* : concertina *f*
concerto [kən'tʃɛrt̬oː] *n, pl* **-ti** [-t̬i, -,tiː] *or* **-tos** : concierto *m* <violin concerto : concierto para violín>
concession [kən'sɛʃən] *n* : concesión *f*
conch ['kɑŋk, 'kɑntʃ] *n, pl* **conchs** ['kɑŋks] *or* **conches** ['kɑntʃəz] : caracol *m* (animal), caracola *f* (concha)
conciliatory [kən'sɪliə,tori] *adj* : conciliador, conciliatorio
concise [kən'saɪs] *adj* : conciso, breve — **concisely** *adv*
conclave ['kɑn,kleɪv] *n* : cónclave *m*
conclude [kən'kluːd] *v* **-cluded; -cluding** *vt* **1** END : concluir, finalizar <to conclude a meeting : concluir una reunión> **2** DECIDE : concluir, llegar a la conclusión de — *vi* END : concluir, terminar
conclusion [kən'kluːʒən] *n* **1** INFERENCE : conclusión *f* **2** END : fin *m,* final *m*
conclusive [kən'kluːsɪv] *adj* : concluyente, decisivo — **conclusively** *adv*
concoct [kən'kɑkt, kɑn-] *vt* **1** PREPARE : preparar, confeccionar **2** DEVISE : inventar, tramar
concoction [kən'kɑkʃən] *n* : invención *f,* mejunje *m,* brebaje *m*
concord ['kɑn,kɔrd, 'kɑŋ-] *n* **1** HARMONY : concordia *f,* armonía *f* **2** AGREEMENT : acuerdo *m*
concordance [kən'kɔrdən*t*s] *n* : concordancia *f*
concourse ['kɑn,kors] *n* : explanada *f,* salón *m* (para pasajeros)
concrete[1] [kɑn'kriːt, 'kɑn,kriːt] *adj* **1** REAL : concreto <concrete objects : objetos concretos> **2** SPECIFIC : determinado, específico **3** : de concreto, de hormigón <concrete walls : paredes de concreto>
concrete[2] ['kɑn,kriːt, kɑn'kriːt] *n* : concreto *m,* hormigón *m*
concur [kən'kər] *vi* **concurred; concurring** **1** COINCIDE : concurrir, coincidir **2** AGREE : concurrir, estar de acuerdo
concurrent [kən'kərənt] *adj* : concurrente, simultáneo
concussion [kən'kʌʃən] *n* : conmoción *f* cerebral
condemn [kən'dɛm] *vt* **1** CENSURE : condenar, reprobar, censurar **2** : declarar insalubre (alimentos), declarar ruinoso (un edificio) **3** SENTENCE : condenar <condemned to death : condenado a muerte>
condemnation [,kɑn,dɛm'neɪʃən] *n* : condena *f,* reprobación *f*
condensation [,kɑn,dɛn'seɪʃən, -dən-] *n* : condensación *f*
condense [kən'dɛn*t*s] *v* **-densed; -densing** *vt* **1** ABRIDGE : condensar, resumir **2** : condensar (vapor, etc.) — *vi* : condensarse
condescend [,kɑndɪ'sɛnd] *vi* **1** DEIGN : condescender, dignarse **2 to condescend to someone** : tratar a alguien con condescendencia
condescension [,kɑndɪ'sɛntʃən] *n* : condescendencia *f*
condiment ['kɑndəmənt] *n* : condimento *m*
condition[1] [kən'dɪʃən] *vt* **1** DETERMINE : condicionar, determinar **2** : acondicionar (el pelo o el aire), poner en forma (el cuerpo)

condition[2] *n* **1** STIPULATION **:** condición *f,* estipulación *f* <on the condition that : a condición de que> **2** STATE **:** condición *f,* estado *m* <in poor condition : en malas condiciones> **3 conditions** *npl* **:** condiciones *fpl,* situación *f* <working conditions : condiciones del trabajo>

conditional [kən'dɪʃənəl] *adj* **:** condicional — **conditionally** *adv*

condolence [kən'do:lənts] *n* **1** SYMPATHY **:** condolencia *f* **2 condolences** *npl* **:** pésame *m*

condominium [ˌkɑndə'mɪniəm] *n, pl* **-ums :** condominio *m*

condone [kən'do:n] *vt* **-doned; -doning :** aprobar, perdonar, tolerar

condor ['kɑndər, -ˌdɔr] *n* **:** cóndor *m*

conducive [kən'du:sɪv, -'dju:-] *adj* **:** propicio, favorable

conduct[1] [kən'dʌkt] *vt* **1** GUIDE **:** guiar, conducir <to conduct a tour : guiar una visita> **2** DIRECT **:** conducir, dirigir <to conduct an orchestra : dirigir una orquesta> **3** CARRY OUT **:** realizar, llevar a cabo <to conduct an investigation : llevar a cabo una investigación> **4** TRANSMIT **:** conducir, transmitir (calor, electricidad, etc.) **5 to conduct oneself** BEHAVE **:** conducirse, comportarse

conduct[2] ['kɑnˌdʌkt] *n* **1** MANAGEMENT **:** conducción *f,* dirección *f,* manejo *m* <the conduct of foreign affairs : la conducción de asuntos exteriores> **2** BEHAVIOR **:** conducta *f,* comportamiento *m*

conduction [kən'dʌkʃən] *n* **:** conducción *f*

conductivity [ˌkɑnˌdʌk'tɪvəṭi] *n, pl* **-ties :** conductividad *f*

conductor [kən'dʌktər] *n* **1 :** conductor *m,* -tora *f;* revisor *m,* -sora *f* (en un tren); cobrador *m,* -dora *f* (en un bus); director *m,* -tora *f* (de una orquesta) **2 :** conductor *m* (de electricidad, etc.)

conduit ['kɑnˌdu:ət, -ˌdju:-] *n* **:** conducto *m,* canal *m,* vía *f*

cone ['ko:n] *n* **1 :** piña *f* (fruto de las coníferas) **2 :** cono *m* (en geometría) **3 ice–cream cone :** cono *m,* barquillo *m,* cucurucho *m*

confection [kən'fɛkʃən] *n* **:** dulce *m*

confectioner [kən'fɛkʃənər] *n* **:** confitero *m,* -ra *f*

confederacy [kən'fɛdərəsi] *n, pl* **-cies :** confederación *f*

confederate[1] [kən'fɛdəˌreɪt] *v* **-ated; -ating** *vt* **:** unir, confederar — *vi* **:** confederarse, aliarse

confederate[2] [kən'fɛdərət] *adj* **:** confederado

confederate[3] *n* **:** cómplice *mf;* aliado *m,* -da *f*

confederation [kənˌfɛdə'reɪʃən] *n* **:** confederación *f,* alianza *f*

confer [kən'fər] *v* **-ferred; -ferring** *vt* **:** conferir, otorgar — *vi* **to confer with :** consultar

conference ['kɑnfrənts, -fərənts] *n* **:** conferencia *f* <press conference : conferencia de prensa>

confess [kən'fɛs] *vt* **:** confesar — *vi* **1 :** confesar <the prisoner confessed : el detenido confesó> **2 :** confesarse (en religión)

confession [kən'fɛʃən] *n* **:** confesión *f*

confessional [kən'fɛʃənəl] *n* **:** confesionario *m*

confetti [kən'fɛṭi] *n* **:** confeti *m*

confidant ['kɑnfəˌdɑnt, -ˌdænt] *n* **:** confidente *mf*

confide [kən'faɪd] *v* **-fided; -fiding :** confiar

confidence ['kɑnfədənts] *n* **1** TRUST **:** confianza *f* **2** SELF-ASSURANCE **:** confianza *f* en sí mismo, seguridad *f* en sí mismo **3** SECRET **:** confidencia *f,* secreto *m*

confident ['kɑnfədənt] *adj* **1** SURE **:** seguro **2** SELF-ASSURED **:** confiado, seguro de sí mismo

confidential [ˌkɑnfə'dɛntʃəl] *adj* **:** confidencial — **confidentially** [ˌkɑnfə'dɛntʃəli] *adv*

confidently ['kɑnfədəntli] *adv* **:** con seguridad, con confianza

configuration [kənˌfɪgjə'reɪʃən] *n* **:** configuración *f*

confine [kən'faɪn] *vt* **-fined; -fining 1** LIMIT **:** confinar, restringir, limitar **2** IMPRISON **:** recluir, encarcelar, encerrar

confinement [kən'faɪnmənt] *n* **:** confinamiento *m,* reclusión *f,* encierro *m*

confines ['kɑnˌfaɪnz] *npl* **:** límites *mpl,* confines *mpl*

confirm [kən'fərm] *vt* **1** RATIFY **:** ratificar **2** VERIFY **:** confirmar, verificar **3 :** confirmar (en religión)

confirmation [ˌkɑnfər'meɪʃən] *n* **:** confirmación *f*

confiscate ['kɑnfəˌskeɪt] *vt* **-cated; -cating :** confiscar, incautar, decomisar

confiscation [ˌkɑnfə'skeɪʃən] *n* **:** confiscación *f,* incautación *f,* decomiso *m*

conflagration [ˌkɑnflə'greɪʃən] *n* **:** conflagración *f*

conflict[1] [kən'flɪkt] *vi* **:** estar en conflicto, oponerse

conflict[2] ['kɑnˌflɪkt] *n* **:** conflicto *m* <to be in conflict : estar en desacuerdo>

conform [kən'fɔrm] *vi* **1** ACCORD, COMPLY **:** ajustarse, adaptarse, conformarse <it conforms with our standards : se ajusta a nuestras normas> **2** CORRESPOND **:** corresponder, encajar <to conform to the truth : corresponder a la verdad>

conformity [kən'fɔrməṭi] *n, pl* **-ties :** conformidad *f*

confound [kən'faʊnd, kɑn-] *vt* **:** confundir, desconcertar

confront [kən'frʌnt] *vt* **:** afrontar, enfrentarse a, encarar

confrontation [ˌkɑnfrən'teɪʃən] *n* **:** enfrentamiento *m,* confrontación *f*

confuse [kən'fjuːz] *vt* **-fused; -fusing 1** PUZZLE : confundir, enturbiar **2** COMPLICATE : confundir, enredar, complicar <to confuse the issue : complicar las cosas>
confusion [kən'fjuːʒən] *n* **1** PERPLEXITY : confusión *f* **2** MESS, TURMOIL : confusión *f*, embrollo *m*, lío *m fam*
congeal [kən'dʒiːl] *vi* **1** FREEZE : congelarse **2** COAGULATE, CURDLE : coagularse, cuajarse
congenial [kən'dʒiːniəl] *adj* : agradable, simpático
congenital [kən'dʒɛnət̬əl] *adj* : congénito
congest [kən'dʒɛst] *vt* **1** : congestionar (en la medicina) **2** OVERCROWD : abarrotar, atestar, congestionar (el tráfico) — *vi* : congestionarse
congestion [kən'dʒɛstʃən] *n* : congestión *f*
conglomerate¹ [kən'glɑmərət] *adj* : conglomerado
conglomerate² [kən'glɑmərət] *n* : conglomerado *m*
conglomeration [kən,glɑmə'reɪʃən] *n* : conglomerado *m*, acumulación *f*
Congolese [,kɑŋgə'liːz, -'liːs] *n* : congoleño *m*, -ña *f* — **Congolese** *adj*
congratulate [kən'grædʒə,leɪt, -'grætʃə-] *vt* **-lated; -lating** : felicitar
congratulation [kən,grædʒə'leɪʃən, -,grætʃə-] *n* : felicitación *f* <congratulations! : ¡felicidades!, ¡enhorabuena!>
congregate ['kɑŋgrɪ,geɪt] *v* **-gated; -gating** *vt* : congregar, reunir — *vi* : congregarse, reunirse
congregation [,kɑŋgrɪ'geɪʃən] *n* **1** GATHERING : congregación *f*, fieles *mpl* (a un servicio religioso) **2** PARISHIONERS : feligreses *mpl*
congress ['kɑŋgrəs] *n* : congreso *m*
congressional [kən'grɛʃənəl, kɑn-] *adj* : del congreso
congressman ['kɑŋgrəsmən] *n, pl* **-men** [-mən, -,mɛn] : congresista *m*, diputado *m*
congresswoman ['kɑŋgrəs,wʊmən] *n, pl* **-women** [-,wɪmən] : congresista *f*, diputada *f*
congruence [kən'gruːənts, 'kɑŋgrʊənts] *n* : congruencia *f*
congruent [kən'gruːənt, 'kɑŋgrʊənt] *adj* : congruente
conic ['kɑnɪk] → **conical**
conical ['kɑnɪkəl] *adj* : cónico
conifer ['kɑnəfər, 'koː-] *n* : conífera *f*
coniferous [koː'nɪfərəs, kə-] *adj* : conífero
conjecture¹ [kən'dʒɛktʃər] *v* **-tured; -turing** : conjeturar
conjecture² *n* : conjetura *f*, presunción *f*
conjugal ['kɑndʒɪgəl, kən'dʒuː-] *adj* : conyugal
conjugate ['kɑndʒə,geɪt] *vt* **-gated; -gating** : conjugar
conjugation [,kɑndʒə'geɪʃən] *n* : conjugación *f*
conjunction [kən'dʒʌŋkʃən] *n* : conjunción *f* <in conjunction with : en combinación con>
conjure ['kɑndʒər, 'kʌn-] *v* **-jured; -juring** *vt* **1** ENTREAT : rogar, suplicar **2 to conjure up** : hacer aparecer (apariciones), evocar (memorias, etc.) — *vi* : practicar la magia
conjurer *or* **conjuror** ['kɑndʒərər, 'kʌn-] *n* : mago *m*, -ga *f*; prestidigitador *m*, -dora *f*
connect [kə'nɛkt] *vi* : conectar, enlazar, empalmar, comunicarse — *vt* **1** JOIN, LINK : conectar, unir, juntar, vincular **2** RELATE : relacionar, asociar (ideas)
connection [kə'nɛkʃən] *n* : conexión *f*, enlace *m* <professional connections : relaciones profesionales>
connective [kə'nɛktɪv] *adj* : conectivo, conjuntivo <connective tissue : tejido conjuntivo>
connector [kə'nɛktər] *n* : conector *m*
connivance [kə'naɪvənts] *n* : connivencia *f*, complicidad *f*
connive [kə'naɪv] *vi* **-nived; -niving** CONSPIRE, PLOT : actuar en connivencia, confabularse, conspirar
connoisseur [,kɑnə'sər, -'sʊr] *n* : conocedor *m*, -dora *f*; entendido *m*, -da *f*
connotation [,kɑnə'teɪʃən] *n* : connotación *f*
connote [kə'noːt] *vt* **-noted; -noting** : connotar
conquer ['kɑŋkər] *vt* : conquistar, vencer
conqueror ['kɑŋkərər] *n* : conquistador *m*, -dora *f*
conquest ['kɑn,kwɛst, 'kɑŋ-] *n* : conquista *f*
conscience ['kɑntʃənts] *n* : conciencia *f*, consciencia *f* <to have a clear conscience : tener la conciencia limpia>
conscientious [,kɑntʃi'ɛntʃəs] *adj* : concienzudo — **conscientiously** *adv*
conscious ['kɑntʃəs] *adj* **1** AWARE : consciente <to become conscious of : darse cuenta de> **2** ALERT, AWAKE : consciente **3** INTENTIONAL : intencional, deliberado
consciously ['kɑntʃəsli] *adv* INTENTIONALLY : intencionalmente, deliberadamente, a propósito
consciousness ['kɑntʃəsnəs] *n* **1** AWARENESS : conciencia *f*, consciencia *f* **2** conocimiento *m* <to lose consciousness : perder el conocimiento>
conscript¹ [kən'skrɪpt] *vt* : reclutar, alistar, enrolar
conscript² ['kɑn,skrɪpt] *n* : conscripto *m*, -ta *f*; recluta *mf*
consecrate ['kɑntsə,kreɪt] *vt* **-crated; -crating** : consagrar
consecration [,kɑntsə'kreɪʃən] *n* : consagración *f*, dedicación *f*

consecutive [kən'sɛkjət̬iv] *adj* **:** consecutivo, seguido <on five consecutive days **:** cinco días seguidos>

consecutively [kən'sɛkjət̬ivli] *adv* **:** consecutivamente

consensus [kən'sɛntsəs] *n* **:** consenso *m*

consent[1] [kən'sɛnt] *vi* **1** AGREE **:** acceder, ponerse de acuerdo **2 to consent to do something :** consentir en hacer algo

consent[2] *n* **:** consentimiento *m,* permiso *m* <by common consent **:** de común acuerdo>

consequence ['kantsə,kwɛnts, -kwənts] *n* **1** RESULT **:** consecuencia *f,* secuela *f* **2** IMPORTANCE **:** importancia *f,* trascendencia *f*

consequent ['kantsəkwənt, -,kwɛnt] *adj* **:** consiguiente

consequential [,kantsə'kwɛntʃəl] *adj* **1** CONSEQUENT **:** consiguiente **2** IMPORTANT **:** importante, trascendente, trascendental

consequently ['kantsəkwəntli, -,kwɛnt-] *adv* **:** por consiguiente, por ende, por lo tanto

conservation [,kantsər'veɪʃən] *n* **:** conservación *f,* protección *f*

conservationist [,kantsər'veɪʃənɪst] *n* **:** conservacionista *mf*

conservatism [kən'sərvə,tɪzəm] *n* **:** conservadurismo *m*

conservative[1] [kən'sərvət̬iv] *adj* **1 :** conservador **2** CAUTIOUS **:** moderado, cauteloso <a conservative estimate **:** un cálculo moderado>

conservative[2] *n* **:** conservador *m,* -dora *f*

conservatory [kən'sərvə,tori] *n, pl* **-ries :** conservatorio *m*

conserve[1] [kən'sərv] *vt* **-served; -serving :** conservar, preservar

conserve[2] ['kan,sərv] *n* PRESERVES **:** confitura *f*

consider [kən'sɪdər] *vt* **1** CONTEMPLATE **:** considerar, pensar en <we'd considered attending **:** habíamos pensado en asistir> **2 :** considerar, tener en cuenta <consider the consequences **:** considera las consecuencias> **3** JUDGE, REGARD **:** considerar, estimar

considerable [kən'sɪdərəbəl] *adj* **:** considerable — **considerably** [-bli] *adv*

considerate [kən'sɪdərət] *adj* **:** considerado, atento

consideration [kən,sɪdə'reɪʃən] *n* **:** consideración *f* <to take into consideration **:** tener en cuenta>

considering [kən'sɪdərɪŋ] *prep* **:** teniendo en cuenta, visto

consign [kən'saɪn] *vt* **1** COMMIT, ENTRUST **:** confiar, encomendar **2** TRANSFER **:** consignar, transferir **3** SEND **:** consignar, enviar (mercancía)

consignment [kən'saɪnmənt] *n* **1 :** envío *m,* remesa *f* **2 on ~ :** en consignación

consist [kən'sɪst] *vi* **1** LIE **:** consistir <success consists in hard work **:** el éxito consiste en trabajar duro> **2 :** constar, componerse <the set consists of 5 pieces **:** el juego se compone de 5 piezas>

consistency [kən'sɪstəntsi] *n, pl* **-cies 1 :** consistencia *f* (de una mezcla o sustancia) **2** COHERENCE **:** coherencia *f* **3** UNIFORMITY **:** regularidad *f,* uniformidad *f*

consistent [kən'sɪstənt] *adj* **1** COMPATIBLE **:** compatible, coincidente <consistent with policy **:** coincidente con la política> **2** UNIFORM **:** uniforme, constante, regular — **consistently** [kən'sɪstəntli] *adv*

consolation [,kantsə'leɪʃən] *n* **1 :** consuelo *m* **2 consolation prize :** premio *m* de consolación

console[1] [kən'so:l] *vt* **-soled; -soling :** consolar

console[2] ['kan,so:l] *n* **:** consola *f*

consolidate [kən'salə,deɪt] *vt* **-dated; -dating :** consolidar, unir

consolidation [kən,salə'deɪʃən] *n* **:** consolidación *f*

consommé [,kantsə'meɪ] *n* **:** consomé *m*

consonant ['kantsənənt] *n* **:** consonante *m*

consort[1] [kən'sɔrt] *vi* **:** asociarse, relacionarse, tener trato <to consort with criminals **:** tener trato con criminales>

consort[2] ['kan,sɔrt] *n* **:** consorte *mf*

conspicuous [kən'spɪkjuəs] *adj* **1** OBVIOUS **:** visible, evidente **2** STRIKING **:** llamativo

conspicuously [kən'spɪkjuəsli] *adv* **:** de manera llamativa

conspiracy [kən'spɪrəsi] *n, pl* **-cies :** conspiración *f,* complot *m,* confabulación *f*

conspirator [kən'spɪrət̬ər] *n* **:** conspirador *m,* -dora *f*

conspire [kən'spaɪr] *vi* **-spired; -spiring :** conspirar, confabularse

constable ['kantstəbəl, 'kʌntstə-] *n* **:** agente *mf* de policía (en un pueblo)

constancy ['kantstəntsi] *n, pl* **-cies :** constancia *f*

constant[1] ['kantstənt] *adj* **1** FAITHFUL **:** leal, fiel **2** INVARIABLE **:** constante, invariable **3** CONTINUAL **:** constante, continuo

constant[2] *n* **:** constante *f*

constantly ['kantstəntli] *adv* **:** constantemente, continuamente

constellation [,kantstə'leɪʃən] *n* **:** constelación *f*

consternation [,kantstər'neɪʃən] *n* **:** consternación *f*

constipate ['kantstə,peɪt] *vt* **-pated; -pating :** estreñir

constipation [,kantstə'peɪʃən] *n* **:** estreñimiento *m,* constipación *f* (de vientre)

constituency [kən'stɪtʃʊəntsi] *n, pl* **-cies 1 :** distrito *m* electoral **2 :** residentes *mpl* de un distrito electoral
constituent[1] [kən'stɪtʃʊənt] *adj* **1** COMPONENT **:** constituyente, componente **2 :** constituyente, constitutivo <a constituent assembly : una asamblea constituyente>
constituent[2] *n* **1** COMPONENT **:** componente *m* **2** ELECTOR, VOTER **:** elector *m*, -tora *f;* votante *mf*
constitute ['kantstə,tu:t, -,tju:t] *vt* **-tuted; -tuting 1** ESTABLISH **:** constituir, establecer **2** COMPOSE, FORM **:** constituir, componer
constitution [,kantstə'tu:ʃən, -'tju:-] *n* **:** constitución *f*
constitutional [,kantstə'tu:ʃənəl, -'tju:-] *adj* **:** constitucional
constitutionality [,kantstə,tu:ʃə'næləṱi, -,tju:-] *n* **:** constitucionalidad *f*
constrain [kən'streɪn] *vt* **1** COMPEL **:** constreñir, obligar **2** CONFINE **:** constreñir, limitar, restringir **3** RESTRAIN **:** contener, refrenar
constraint [kən'streɪnt] *n* **:** restricción *f*, limitación *f*
constrict [kən'strɪkt] *vt* **:** estrechar, apretar, comprimir
constriction [kən'strɪkʃən] *n* **:** estrechamiento *m*, compresión *f*
construct [kən'strʌkt] *vt* **:** construir
construction [kən'strʌkʃən] *n* **:** construcción *f*
constructive [kən'strʌktɪv] *adj* **:** constructivo
construe [kən'stru:] *vt* **-strued; -struing :** interpretar
consul ['kantsəl] *n* **:** cónsul *mf*
consular ['kantsələr] *adj* **:** consular
consulate ['kantsələt] *n* **:** consulado *m*
consult [kən'sʌlt] *vt* **:** consultar — *vi* **to consult with :** consultar con, solicitar la opinión de
consultant [kən'sʌltənt] *n* **:** consultor *m*, -tora *f;* asesor *m*, -sora *f*
consultation [,kantsəl'teɪʃən] *n* **:** consulta *f*
consumable [kən'su:məbəl] *adj* **:** consumible
consume [kən'su:m] *vt* **-sumed; -suming :** consumir, usar, gastar
consumer [kən'su:mər] *n* **:** consumidor *m*, -dora *f*
consummate[1] ['kantsə,meɪt] *vt* **-mated; -mating :** consumar
consummate[2] [kən'sʌmət, 'kantsəmət] *adj* **:** consumado, perfecto
consummation [,kantsə'meɪʃən] *n* **:** consumación *f*
consumption [kən'sʌmpʃən] *n* **1** USE **:** consumo *m*, uso *m* <consumption of electricity : consumo de electricidad> **2** TUBERCULOSIS **:** tisis *f*, consunción *f*
contact[1] ['kan,tækt, kən'-] *vt* **:** ponerse en contacto con, contactar (con)
contact[2] ['kan,tækt] *n* **1** TOUCHING **:** contacto *m*, tocamiento *m* <to come into contact with : entrar en contacto con> **2** TOUCH **:** contacto *m*, comunicación *f* <to lose contact with : perder contacto con> **3** CONNECTION **:** contacto *m* (en negocios) **4 →** **contact lens**
contact lens ['kan,tækt'lɛnz] *n* **:** lente *mf* de contacto, pupilente *m Mex*
contagion [kən'teɪdʒən] *n* **:** contagio *m*
contagious [kən'teɪdʒəs] *adj* **:** contagioso
contain [kən'teɪn] *vt* **1 :** contener **2 to contain oneself :** contenerse
container [kən'teɪnər] *n* **:** recipiente *m*, envase *m*
contaminate [kən'tæmə,neɪt] *vt* **-nated; -nating :** contaminar
contamination [kən,tæmə'neɪʃən] *n* **:** contaminación *f*
contemplate ['kantəm,pleɪt] *v* **-plated; -plating** *vt* **1** VIEW **:** contemplar **2** PONDER **:** contemplar, considerar **3** CONSIDER, PROPOSE **:** proponerse, proyectar, pensar en <to contemplate a trip : pensar en viajar> — *vi* MEDITATE **:** meditar
contemplation [,kantəm'pleɪʃən] *n* **:** contemplación *f*
contemplative [kən'tɛmpləṱɪv, 'kantəm,pleɪṱɪv] *adj* **:** contemplativo
contemporaneous [kən,tɛmpə'reɪniəs] **→** **contemporary**[1]
contemporary[1] [kən'tɛmpə,rɛri] *adj* **:** contemporáneo
contemporary[2] *n, pl* **-raries :** contemporáneo *m*, -nea *f*
contempt [kən'tɛmpt] *n* **1** DISDAIN **:** desprecio *m*, desdén *m* <to hold in contempt : despreciar> **2 :** desacato *m* (ante un tribunal)
contemptible [kən'tɛmptəbəl] *adj* **:** despreciable, vil
contemptuous [kən'tɛmptʃʊəs] *adj* **:** despectivo, despreciativo, desdeñoso
contemptuously [kən'tɛmptʃʊəsli] *adv* **:** despectivamente, con desprecio
contend [kən'tɛnd] *vi* **1** STRUGGLE **:** luchar, lidiar, contender <to contend with a problem : lidiar con un problema> **2** COMPETE **:** competir <to contend for a position : competir por un puesto> — *vt* **1** ARGUE, MAINTAIN **:** argüir, sostener, afirmar <he contended that he was right : afirmó que tenía razón> **2** CONTEST **:** protestar contra (una decisión, etc.), disputar
contender [kən'tɛndər] *n* **:** contendiente *mf;* aspirante *mf;* competidor *m*, -dora *f*
content[1] [kən'tɛnt] *vt* SATISFY **:** contentar, satisfacer
content[2] *adj* **:** conforme, contento, satisfecho
content[3] *n* CONTENTMENT **:** contento *m*, satisfacción *f* <to one's heart's content : hasta quedar satisfecho, a más no poder>

content[4] [ˈkɑn,tɛnt] *n* **1** MEANING : contenido *m,* significado *m* **2** PROPORTION : contenido *m,* proporción *f* <fat content : contenido de grasa> **3 contents** *npl* : contenido *m,* sumario *m* (de un libro) <table of contents : índice de materias>
contented [kənˈtɛntəd] *adj* : conforme, satisfecho <a contented smile : una sonrisa de satisfacción>
contentedly [kənˈtɛntədli] *adv* : con satisfacción
contention [kənˈtɛntʃən] *n* **1** DISPUTE : disputa *f,* discusión *f* **2** COMPETITION : competencia *f,* contienda *f* **3** OPINION : argumento *m,* opinión *f*
contentious [kənˈtɛntʃəs] *adj* : disputador, pugnaz, combativo
contentment [kənˈtɛntmənt] *n* : satisfacción *f,* contento *m*
contest[1] [kənˈtɛst] *vt* : disputar, cuestionar, impugnar <to contest a will : impugnar un testamento>
contest[2] [ˈkɑn,tɛst] *n* **1** STRUGGLE : lucha *f,* contienda *f* **2** GAME : concurso *m,* competencia *f*
contestable [kənˈtɛstəbəl] *adj* : discutible, cuestionable
contestant [kənˈtɛstənt] *n* : concursante *mf;* competidor *m,* -dora *f*
context [ˈkɑn,tɛkst] *n* : contexto *m*
contiguous [kənˈtɪgjʊəs] *adj* : contiguo
continence [ˈkɑntənənts] *n* : continencia *f*
continent[1] [ˈkɑntənənt] *adj* : continente
continent[2] *n* : continente *m* — **continental** [,kɑntənˈɛntəl] *adj*
contingency [kənˈtɪndʒəntsi] *n, pl* **-cies** : contingencia *f,* eventualidad *f*
contingent[1] [kənˈtɪndʒənt] *adj* **1** POSSIBLE : contingente, eventual **2** ACCIDENTAL : fortuito, accidental **3 to be contingent on** : depender de, estar sujeto a
contingent[2] *n* : contingente *m*
continual [kənˈtɪnjʊəl] *adj* : continuo, constante — **continually** [kənˈtɪnjʊəli, -ˈtɪnjəli] *adv*
continuance [kənˈtɪnjʊənts] *n* **1** CONTINUATION : continuación *f* **2** DURATION : duración *f* **3** : aplazamiento *m* (de un proceso)
continuation [kən,tɪnjʊˈeɪʃən] *n* : continuación *f,* prolongación *f*
continue [kənˈtɪnju:] *v* **-tinued; -tinuing** *vi* **1** CARRY ON : continuar, seguir, proseguir <please continue : continúe, por favor> **2** ENDURE, LAST : continuar, prolongarse, durar **3** RESUME : continuar, reanudarse — *vt* **1** : continuar, seguir <she continued writing : continuó escribiendo> **2** RESUME : continuar, reanudar **3** EXTEND, PROLONG : continuar, prolongar
continuity [,kɑntənˈu:əti, -ˈju:-] *n, pl* **-ties** : continuidad *f*
continuous [kənˈtɪnjʊəs] *adj* : continuo — **continuously** *adv*
contort [kənˈtɔrt] *vt* : torcer, retorcer, contraer (el rostro) — *vi* : contraerse, demudarse
contortion [kənˈtɔrʃən] *n* : contorsión *f*
contour [ˈkɑn,tʊr] *n* **1** OUTLINE : contorno *m* **2 contours** *npl* SHAPE : forma *f,* curvas *fpl* **3 contour map** : mapa *m* topográfico
contraband [ˈkɑntrə,bænd] *n* : contrabando *m*
contraception [,kɑntrəˈsɛpʃən] *n* : anticoncepción *f,* contracepción *f*
contraceptive[1] [,kɑntrəˈsɛptɪv] *adj* : anticonceptivo, contraceptivo
contraceptive[2] *n* : anticonceptivo *m,* contraceptivo *m*
contract[1] [kənˈtrækt, 1 *usu* ˈkɑn,trækt] *vt* **1** : contratar (servicios profesionales) **2** : contraer (una enfermedad, una deuda) **3** TIGHTEN : contraer (un músculo) **4** SHORTEN : contraer (una palabra) — *vi* : contraerse, reducirse
contract[2] [ˈkɑn,trækt] *n* : contrato *m*
contraction [kənˈtrækʃən] *n* : contracción *f*
contractor [ˈkɑn,træktər, kənˈtræk-] *n* : contratista *mf*
contractual [kənˈtræktʃʊəl] *adj* : contractual — **contractually** *adv*
contradict [,kɑntrəˈdɪkt] *vt* : contradecir, desmentir
contradiction [,kɑntrəˈdɪkʃən] *n* : contradicción *f*
contradictory [,kɑntrəˈdɪktəri] *adj* : contradictorio
contralto [kənˈtræl,to:] *n, pl* **-tos** : contralto *m* (voz), contralto *mf* (vocalista)
contraption [kənˈtræpʃən] *n* DEVICE : aparato *m,* artefacto *m*
contrary[1] [ˈkɑn,trɛri, *2 often* kənˈtrɛri] *adj* **1** OPPOSITE : contrario, opuesto **2** BALKY, STUBBORN : terco, testarudo **3 contrary to** : al contrario de, en contra de <contrary to the facts : en contra de los hechos>
contrary[2] [ˈkɑn,trɛri] *n, pl* **-traries 1** OPPOSITE : lo contrario, lo opuesto **2 on the contrary** : al contrario, todo lo contrario
contrast[1] [kənˈtræst] *vi* DIFFER : contrastar, diferir — *vt* COMPARE : contrastar, comparar
contrast[2] [ˈkɑn,træst] *n* : contraste *m*
contravene [,kɑntrəˈvi:n] *vt* **-vened; -vening** : contravenir, infringir
contribute [kənˈtrɪbjət] *v* **-uted; -uting** *vt* : contribuir, aportar (dinero, bienes, etc.) — *vi* : contribuir
contribution [,kɑntrəˈbju:ʃən] *n* : contribución *f*
contributor [kənˈtrɪbjətər] *n* : contribuidor *m,* -dora *f;* colaborador *m,* -dora *f* (en periodismo)

contrite [ˈkɑnˌtraɪt, kənˈtraɪt] *adj* REPENTANT : contrito, arrepentido

contrition [kənˈtrɪʃən] *n* : contrición *f,* arrepentimiento *m*

contrivance [kənˈtraɪvənts] *n* **1** DEVICE : aparato *m,* artefacto *m* **2** SCHEME : artimaña *f,* treta *f,* ardid *m*

contrive [kənˈtraɪv] *vt* **-trived; -triving 1** DEVISE : idear, ingeniar, maquinar **2** MANAGE : lograr, ingeniárselas para <she contrived a way out of the mess : se las ingenió para salir del enredo>

control[1] [kənˈtroːl] *vt* **-trolled; -trolling** : controlar, dominar

control[2] *n* **1** : control *m,* dominio *m,* mando *m* <to be under control : estar bajo control> **2** RESTRAINT : control *m,* limitación *f* <birth control : control natal> **3** : control *m,* dispositivo *m* de mando <remote control : control remoto>

controllable [kənˈtroːləbəl] *adj* : controlable

controller [kənˈtroːlər, ˈkɑn,-] *n* **1** → **comptroller 2** : controlador *m,* -dora *f* <air traffic controller : controlador aéreo>

controversial [ˌkɑntrəˈvərʃəl, -siəl] *adj* : controvertido <a controversial decision : una decisión controvertida>

controversy [ˈkɑntrəˌvərsi] *n, pl* **-sies** : controversia *f*

controvert [ˈkɑntrəˌvərt, ˌkɑntrəˈ-] *vt* : controvertir, contradecir

contusion [kənˈtuːʒən, -tjuː-] *n* BRUISE : contusión *f,* moretón *m*

conundrum [kəˈnʌndrəm] *n* RIDDLE : acertijo *m,* adivinanza *f*

convalesce [ˌkɑnvəˈlɛs] *vi* **-lesced; -lescing** : convalecer

convalescence [ˌkɑnvəˈlɛsənts] *n* : convalecencia *f*

convalescent[1] [ˌkɑnvəˈlɛsənt] *adj* : convaleciente

convalescent[2] *n* : convaleciente *mf*

convection [kənˈvɛkʃən] *n* : convección *f*

convene [kənˈviːn] *v* **-vened; -vening** *vt* : convocar — *vi* : reunirse

convenience [kənˈviːnjənts] *n* **1** : conveniencia *f* <at your convenience : cuando le resulte conveniente> **2** AMENITY : comodidad *f* <modern conveniences : comodidades modernas>

convenient [kənˈviːnjənt] *adj* : conveniente, cómodo — **conveniently** *adv*

convent [ˈkɑnvənt, -ˌvɛnt] *n* : convento *m*

convention [kənˈvɛntʃən] *n* **1** PACT : convención *f,* convenio *m,* pacto *m* <the Geneva Convention : la Convención de Ginebra> **2** MEETING : convención *f,* congreso *m* **3** CUSTOM : convención *f,* convencionalismo *m*

conventional [kənˈvɛntʃənəl] *adj* : convencional — **conventionally** *adv*

converge [kənˈvərdʒ] *vi* **-verged; -verging** : converger, convergir

conversant [kənˈvərsənt] *adj* **conversant with** : versado con, experto en

conversation [ˌkɑnvərˈseɪʃən] *n* : conversación *f*

conversational [ˌkɑnvərˈseɪʃənəl] *adj* : familiar <a conversational style : un estilo familiar>

converse[1] [kənˈvərs] *vi* **-versed; -versing** : conversar

converse[2] [kənˈvərs, ˈkɑnˌvɛrs] *adj* : contrario, opuesto, inverso

conversely [kənˈvərsli, ˈkɑnˌvɛrs-] *adv* : a la inversa

conversion [kənˈvərʒən] *n* **1** CHANGE : conversión *f,* transformación *f,* cambio *m* **2** : conversión *f* (a una religión)

convert[1] [kənˈvərt] *vt* **1** : convertir (a una religión o un partido) **2** CHANGE : convertir, cambiar — *vi* : convertirse

convert[2] [ˈkɑnˌvərt] *n* : converso *m,* -sa *f*

converter *or* **convertor** [kənˈvərt̬ər] *n* : convertidor *m*

convertible[1] [kənˈvərt̬əbəl] *adj* : convertible

convertible[2] *n* : convertible *m,* descapotable *m*

convex [kɑnˈvɛks, ˈkɑn,-, kənˈ-] *adj* : convexo

convey [kənˈveɪ] *vt* **1** TRANSPORT : transportar, conducir **2** TRANSMIT : transmitir, comunicar, expresar (noticias, ideas, etc.)

conveyance [kənˈveɪənts] *n* **1** TRANSPORT : transporte *m,* transportación *f* **2** COMMUNICATION : transmisión *f,* comunicación *f* **3** TRANSFER : transferencia *f,* traspaso *m* (de una propiedad)

conveyor [kənˈveɪər] *n* : transportador *m,* -dora *f* <conveyor belt : cinta transportadora>

convict[1] [kənˈvɪkt] *vt* : declarar culpable

convict[2] [ˈkɑnˌvɪkt] *n* : preso *m,* -sa *f;* presidiario *m,* -ria *f;* recluso *m,* -sa *f*

conviction [kənˈvɪkʃən] *n* **1** : condena *f* (de un acusado) **2** BELIEF : convicción *f,* creencia *f*

convince [kənˈvɪnts] *vt* **-vinced; -vincing** : convencer

convincing [kənˈvɪntsɪŋ] *adj* : convincente, persuasivo

convincingly [kənˈvɪntsɪŋli] *adv* : de forma convincente

convivial [kənˈvɪvjəl, -ˈvɪviəl] *adj* : jovial, festivo, alegre

conviviality [kənˌvɪviˈæləṱi] *n, pl* **-ties** : jovialidad *f*

convoke [kənˈvoːk] *vt* **-voked; -voking** : convocar

convoluted [ˈkɑnvəˌluːṱəd] *adj* : intrincado, complicado

convoy [ˈkɑnˌvɔɪ] *n* : convoy *m*

convulse [kənˈvʌls] *v* **-vulsed; -vulsing** *vt* : convulsionar <convulsed with laughter : muerto de risa> — *vi* : sufrir convulsiones

convulsion [kən'vʌlʃən] *n* : convulsión *f*

convulsive [kən'vʌlsɪv] *adj* : convulsivo — **convulsively** *adv*

coo[1] ['kuː] *vi* : arrullar

coo[2] *n* : arrullo *m* (de una paloma)

cook[1] ['kʊk] *vi* : cocinar — *vt* **1** : preparar (comida) **2 to cook up** CONCOCT : inventar, tramar

cook[2] *n* : cocinero *m*, -ra *f*

cookbook ['kʊk,bʊk] *n* : libro *m* de cocina

cookery ['kʊkəri] *n, pl* **-eries** : cocina *f*

cookie *or* **cooky** ['kʊki] *n, pl* **-ies** : galleta *f* (dulce)

cookout ['kʊk,aʊt] *n* : comida *f* al aire libre

cool[1] ['kuːl] *vt* : refrescar, enfriar — *vi* **1** : refrescarse, enfriarse <the pie is cooling : el pastel se está enfriando> **2** : calmarse, tranquilizarse <his anger cooled : su ira se calmó>

cool[2] *adj* **1** : fresco, frío <cool weather : tiempo fresco> **2** CALM : tranquilo, sereno **3** ALOOF : frío, distante

cool[3] *n* **1** : fresco *m* <the cool of the evening : el fresco de la tarde> **2** COMPOSURE : calma *f*, serenidad *f*

coolant ['kuːlənt] *n* : refrigerante *m*

cooler ['kuːlər] *n* : nevera *f* portátil

coolie ['kuːli] *n* : culi *m*

coolly ['kuːlli] *adv* **1** CALMLY : con calma, tranquilamente **2** COLDLY : fríamente, con frialdad

coolness ['kuːlnəs] *n* **1** : frescura *f*, frescor *m* <the coolness of the evening : el frescor de la noche> **2** CALMNESS : tranquilidad *f*, serenidad *f* **3** COLDNESS, INDIFFERENCE : frialdad *f*, indiferencia

coop[1] ['kuːp, 'kʊp] *vt or* **to coop up** : encerrar <cooped up in the house : encerrado en la casa>

coop[2] *n* : gallinero *m*

co–op ['koː,ɑp] → **cooperative**[2]

cooperate [ko'ɑpə,reɪt] *vi* **-ated; -ating** : cooperar, colaborar

cooperation [ko,ɑpə'reɪʃən] *n* : cooperación *f*, colaboración *f*

cooperative[1] [ko'ɑpərətɪv, -'ɑpə,reɪtɪv] *adj* : cooperativo

cooperative[2] [ko'ɑpərətɪv] *n* : cooperativa *f*

co–opt [ko'ɑpt] *vt* **1** : nombrar como miembro, cooptar **2** APPROPRIATE : apropiarse de

coordinate[1] [ko'ɔrdən,eɪt] *v* **-nated; -nating** *vt* : coordinar — *vi* : coordinarse, combinar, acordar

coordinate[2] [ko'ɔrdənət] *adj* **1** COORDINATED : coordinado **2** EQUAL : igual, semejante

coordinate[3] [ko'ɔrdənət] *n* : coordenada *f*

coordination [ko,ɔrdən'eɪʃən] *n* : coordinación *f*

coordinator [ko'ɔrdən,eɪtər] *n* : coordinador *m*, -dora *f*

cop ['kɑp] → **police officer**

cope ['koːp] *vi* **coped; coping 1** : arreglárselas **2 to cope with** : hacer frente a, poder con <I can't cope with all this! : ¡no puedo con todo esto!>

copier ['kɑpiər] *n* : copiadora *f*, fotocopiadora *f*

copilot ['koː,paɪlət] *n* : copiloto *m*

copious ['koːpiəs] *adj* : copioso, abundante — **copiously** *adv*

copiousness ['koːpiəsnəs] *n* : abundancia *f*

copper ['kɑpər] *n* : cobre *m*

coppery ['kɑpəri] *adj* : cobrizo

copra ['koːprə, 'kɑ-] *n* : copra *f*

copse ['kɑps] *n* THICKET : soto *m*, matorral *m*

copulate ['kɑpjə,leɪt] *vi* **-lated; -lating** : copular

copulation [,kɑpjə'leɪʃən] *n* : cópula *f*, relaciones *fpl* sexuales

copy[1] ['kɑpi] *vt* **copied; copying 1** DUPLICATE : hacer una copia de, duplicar, reproducir **2** IMITATE : copiar, imitar

copy[2] *n, pl* **copies 1** : copia *f*, duplicado *m* (de un documento), reproducción *f* (de una obra de arte) **2** : ejemplar *m* (de un libro), número *m* (de una revista) **3** TEXT : manuscrito *m*, texto *m*

copyright[1] ['kɑpi,raɪt] *vt* : registrar los derechos de

copyright[2] *n* : derechos *mpl* de autor

coral[1] ['kɔrəl] *adj* : de coral <a coral reef : un arrecife de coral>

coral[2] *n* : coral *m*

coral snake *n* : serpiente *f* de coral

cord ['kɔrd] *n* **1** ROPE, STRING : cuerda *f*, cordón *m*, cordel *m* **2** : cuerda *f*, cordón *m*, médula *f* (en la anatomía) <vocal cords : cuerdas vocales> **3** : cuerda *f* <a cord of firewood : una cuerda de leña> **4** *or* **electric cord** : cable *m* eléctrico

cordial[1] ['kɔrdʒəl] *adj* : cordial — **cordially** *adv*

cordial[2] *n* : cordial *m*

cordiality [,kɔrdʒi'æləti] *n* : cordialidad *f*

cordon[1] ['kɔrdən] *vt* **to cordon off** : acordonar

cordon[2] *n* : cordón *m*

corduroy ['kɔrdə,rɔɪ] *n* **1** : pana *f* **2 corduroys** *npl* : pantalones *mpl* de pana

core[1] ['kor] *vt* **cored; coring** : quitar el corazón a (una fruta)

core[2] *n* **1** : corazón *m*, centro *m* (de algunas frutas) **2** CENTER : núcleo *m*, centro *m* **3** ESSENCE : núcleo *m*, meollo *m* <to the core : hasta la médula>

cork[1] ['kɔrk] *vt* : ponerle un corcho a

cork[2] *n* : corcho *m*

corkscrew ['kɔrk,skruː] *n* : tirabuzón *m*, sacacorchos *m*

cormorant ['kɔrmərənt, -,rænt] *n* : cormorán *m*

corn[1] ['kɔrn] *vt* : conservar en salmuera <corned beef : carne en conserva>

corn[2] *n* **1** GRAIN : grano *m* **2** : maíz *m,* elote *m Mex* <corn tortillas : tortillas de maíz> **3** : callo *m* <corn plaster : emplasto para callos>
corncob [ˈkɔrn,kɑb] *n* : mazorca *f* (de maíz), choclo *m,* elote *m CA, Mex*
cornea [ˈkɔrniə] *n* : córnea *f*
corner[1] [ˈkɔrnər] *vt* **1** TRAP : acorralar, arrinconar **2** MONOPOLIZE : monopolizar, acaparar (un mercado) — *vi* : tomar una curva, doblar una esquina (en un automóvil)
corner[2] *n* **1** ANGLE : rincón *m,* esquina *f,* ángulo *m* <the corner of a room : el rincón de una sala> <all corners of the world : todos los rincones del mundo> <to cut corners : atajar, economizar esfuerzos> **2** INTERSECTION : esquina *f* **3** IMPASSE, PREDICAMENT : aprieto *m,* impasse *m* <to be backed into a corner : estar acorralado>
cornerstone [ˈkɔrnər,stoːn] *n* : piedra *f* angular
cornet [kɔrˈnɛt] *n* : corneta *f*
cornice [ˈkɔrnɪs] *n* : cornisa *f*
cornmeal [ˈkɔrn,miːl] *n* : harina *f* de maíz
cornstalk [ˈkɔrn,stɔk] *n* : tallo *m* del maíz
cornstarch [ˈkɔrn,stɑrtʃ] *n* : maicena *f,* almidón *m* de maíz
cornucopia [,kɔrnəˈkoːpiə, -njə-] *n* : cornucopia *f*
corolla [kəˈrɑlə] *n* : corola *f*
corollary [ˈkɔrə,lɛri] *n, pl* **-laries** : corolario *m*
corona [kəˈroːnə] *n* : corona *f* (del sol)
coronary[1] [ˈkɔrə,nɛri] *adj* : coronario
coronary[2] *n, pl* **-naries 1** : trombosis *f* coronaria **2** HEART ATTACK : infarto *m,* ataque *m* al corazón
coronation [,kɔrəˈneɪʃən] *n* : coronación *f*
coroner [ˈkɔrənər] *n* : médico *m* forense
corporal[1] [ˈkɔrpərəl] *adj* : corporal <corporal punishment : castigos corporales>
corporal[2] *n* : cabo *m*
corporate [ˈkɔrpərət] *adj* : corporativo, empresarial
corporation [,kɔrpəˈreɪʃən] *n* : sociedad *f* anónima, corporación *f,* empresa *f*
corporeal [kɔrˈporiəl] *adj* **1** PHYSICAL : corpóreo **2** MATERIAL : material, tangible — **corporeally** *adv*
corps [ˈkor] *n, pl* **corps** [ˈkorz] : cuerpo *m* <medical corps : cuerpo médico> <diplomatic corps : cuerpo diplomático>
corpse [ˈkɔrps] *n* : cadáver *m*
corpulence [ˈkɔrpjələnts] *n* : obesidad *f,* gordura *f*
corpulent [ˈkɔrpjələnt] *adj* : obeso, gordo
corpuscle [ˈkɔr,pʌsəl] *n* : corpúsculo *m,* glóbulo *m* (sanguíneo)
corral[1] [kəˈræl] *vt* **-ralled; -ralling** : acorralar, encorralar (ganado)
corral[2] *n* : corral *m*
correct[1] [kəˈrɛkt] *vt* **1** RECTIFY : corregir, rectificar **2** REPRIMAND : corregir, reprender
correct[2] *adj* **1** ACCURATE, RIGHT : correcto, exacto <to be correct : estar en lo cierto> **2** PROPER : correcto, apropiado
correction [kəˈrɛkʃən] *n* : corrección *f*
corrective [kəˈrɛktɪv] *adj* : correctivo
correctly [kəˈrɛktli] *adv* : correctamente
correlate [ˈkɔrə,leɪt] *vt* **-lated; -lating** : relacionar, poner en correlación
correlation [,kɔrəˈleɪʃən] *n* : correlación *f*
correspond [,kɔrəˈspɑnd] *vi* **1** MATCH : corresponder, concordar, coincidir **2** WRITE : corresponderse, escribirse
correspondence [,kɔrəˈspɑndənts] *n* : correspondencia *f*
correspondent [,kɔrəˈspɑndənt] *n* : corresponsal *mf*
correspondingly [,kɔrəˈspɑndɪŋli] *adv* : en consecuencia, de la misma manera
corridor [ˈkɔrədər, -,dɔr] *n* : corredor *m,* pasillo *m*
corroborate [kəˈrɑbə,reɪt] *vt* **-rated; -rating** : corroborar
corroboration [kə,rɑbəˈreɪʃən] *n* : corroboración *f*
corrode [kəˈroːd] *v* **-roded; -roding** *vt* : corroer — *vi* : corroerse
corrosion [kəˈroːʒən] *n* : corrosión *f*
corrosive [kəˈroːsɪv] *adj* : corrosivo
corrugate [ˈkɔrə,geɪt] *vt* **-gated; -gating** : ondular, acanalar, corrugar
corrugated [ˈkɔrə,geɪtəd] *adj* : ondulado, acanalado <corrugated cardboard : cartón ondulado>
corrupt[1] [kəˈrʌpt] *vt* **1** PERVERT : corromper, pervertir, degradar (información) **2** BRIBE : sobornar
corrupt[2] *adj* : corrupto, corrompido
corruptible [kəˈrʌptəbəl] *adj* : corruptible
corruption [kəˈrʌpʃən] *n* : corrupción *f*
corsage [kɔrˈsɑʒ, -ˈsɑdʒ] *n* : ramillete *m* que se lleva como adorno
corset [ˈkɔrsət] *n* : corsé *m*
cortex [ˈkɔr,tɛks] *n, pl* **-tices** [ˈkɔrtə,siːz] *or* **-texes** : corteza *f* <cerebral cortex : corteza cerebral>
cortisone [ˈkɔrtə,soːn, -zoːn] *n* : cortisona *f*
cosmetic[1] [kɑzˈmɛtɪk] *adj* : cosmético
cosmetic[2] *n* : cosmético *m*
cosmic [ˈkɑzmɪk] *adj* **1** : cósmico <cosmic ray : rayo cósmico> **2** VAST : grandioso, inmenso, vasto
cosmonaut [ˈkɑzmə,nɔt] *n* : cosmonauta *mf*
cosmopolitan[1] [,kɑzməˈpɑlətən] *adj* : cosmopolita
cosmopolitan[2] *n* : cosmopolita *mf*

cosmos [ˈkɑzməs, -ˌmoːs, -ˌmɑs] *n* : cosmos *m,* universo *m*

cost[1] [ˈkɔst] *v* **cost; costing** *vt* : costar <how much does it cost? : ¿cuánto cuesta?, ¿cuánto vale?> — *vi* : costar <these cost more : éstos cuestan más>

cost[2] *n* : costo *m,* precio *m,* coste *m* <cost of living : costo de vida> <victory at all costs : victoria a toda costa>

Costa Rican[1] [ˌkɔstəˈriːkən] *adj* : costarricense

Costa Rican[2] *n* : costarricense *mf*

costly [ˈkɔstli] *adj* : costoso, caro

costume [ˈkɑsˌtuːm, -ˌtjuːm] *n* **1** : traje *m* <national costume : traje típico> **2** : disfraz *m* <costume party : fiesta de disfraces> **3** OUTFIT : vestimenta *f,* traje *m,* conjunto *m*

cosy [ˈkoːzi] → **cozy**

cot [ˈkɑt] *n* : catre *m*

coterie [ˈkoːt̬əˌri, ˌkoːt̬əˈ-] *n* : tertulia *f,* círculo *m* (social)

cottage [ˈkɑt̬ɪdʒ] *n* : casita *f* (de campo)

cottage cheese *n* : requesón *m*

cotton [ˈkɑtən] *n* : algodón *m*

cottonmouth [ˈkɑtənˌmaʊθ] → **moccasin**

cottonseed [ˈkɑtənˌsiːd] *n* : semilla *f* de algodón

cotton swab → **swab**

cottontail [ˈkɑtənˌteɪl] *n* : conejo *m* de cola blanca

couch[1] [ˈkaʊtʃ] *vt* : expresar, formular <couched in strong language : expresado en lenguaje enérgico>

couch[2] *n* SOFA : sofá *m*

cougar [ˈkuːgər] *n* : puma *m*

cough[1] [ˈkɔf] *vi* : toser

cough[2] *n* : tos *f*

could [ˈkʊd] → **can**

council [ˈkaʊntsəl] *n* **1** : concejo *m* <city council : concejo municipal, ayuntamiento> **2** MEETING : concejo *m,* junta *f* **3** BOARD : consejo *m* **4** : concilio *m* (eclesiástico)

councillor *or* **councilor** [ˈkaʊntsələr] *n* : concejal *m,* -jala *f*

councilman [ˈkaʊntsəlmən] *n, pl* **-men** [-mən, -ˌmɛn] : concejal *m*

councilwoman [ˈkaʊntsəlˌwʊmən] *n, pl* **-women** [-ˌwɪmən] : concejala *f*

counsel[1] [ˈkaʊntsəl] *v* **-seled** *or* **-selled; -seling** *or* **-selling** *vt* ADVISE : aconsejar, asesorar, recomendar — *vi* CONSULT : consultar

counsel[2] *n* **1** ADVICE : consejo *m,* recomendación *f* **2** CONSULTATION : consulta *f* **3 counsel** *ns & pl* LAWYER : abogado *m,* -da *f*

counselor *or* **counsellor** [ˈkaʊntsələr] *n* : consejero *m,* -ra *f;* consultor *m,* -tora *f;* asesor *m,* -sora *f*

count[1] [ˈkaʊnt] *vt* : contar, enumerar — *vi* **1** : contar <to count out loud : contar en voz alta> **2** MATTER : contar, valer, importar <that's what counts : eso es lo que cuenta> **3 to count on** : contar con

count[2] *n* **1** COMPUTATION : cómputo *m,* recuento *m,* cuenta *f* <to lose count : perder la cuenta> **2** CHARGE : cargo *m* <two counts of robbery : dos cargos de robo> **3** : conde *m* (noble)

countable [ˈkaʊntəbəl] *adj* : numerable

countdown [ˈkaʊntˌdaʊn] *n* : cuenta *f* atrás

countenance[1] [ˈkaʊntənənts] *vt* **-nanced; -nancing** : permitir, tolerar

countenance[2] *n* FACE : semblante *m,* rostro *m*

counter[1] [ˈkaʊntər] *vt* **1** → **counteract** **2** OPPOSE : oponerse a, resistir — *vi* RETALIATE : responder, contraatacar

counter[2] *adv* **counter to** : contrario a, en contra de

counter[3] *adj* : contrario, opuesto

counter[4] *n* **1** PIECE : ficha *f* (de un juego) **2** : mostrador *m* (de un negocio), ventanilla *f* (en un banco) **3** : contador *m* (aparato) **4** COUNTERBALANCE : fuerza *f* opuesta, contrapeso *m*

counteract [ˌkaʊntərˈækt] *vt* : contrarrestar

counterattack [ˈkaʊntərəˌtæk] *n* : contraataque *m*

counterbalance[1] [ˌkaʊntərˈbæləntս] *vt* **-anced; -ancing** : contrapesar

counterbalance[2] [ˈkaʊntərˌbæləntս] *n* : contrapeso *m*

counterclockwise [ˌkaʊntərˈklɑkˌwaɪz] *adv & adj* : en el sentido opuesto al de las manecillas del reloj

counterfeit[1] [ˈkaʊntərˌfɪt] *vt* **1** : falsificar (dinero) **2** PRETEND : fingir, aparentar

counterfeit[2] *adj* : falso, inauténtico

counterfeit[3] *n* : falsificación *f*

counterfeiter [ˈkaʊntərˌfɪt̬ər] *n* : falsificador *m,* -dora *f*

countermand [ˈkaʊntərˌmænd, ˌkaʊntərˈ-] *vt* : contramandar

countermeasure [ˈkaʊntərˌmɛʒər] *n* : contramedida *f*

counterpart [ˈkaʊntərˌpɑrt] *n* : homólogo *m,* contraparte *f Mex*

counterpoint [ˈkaʊntərˌpɔɪnt] *n* : contrapunto *m*

counterproductive [ˌkaʊntərprəˈdʌktɪv] *adj* : contraproducente

counterrevolution [ˌkaʊntərˌrɛvəˈluːʃən] *n* : contrarrevolución *f*

counterrevolutionary[1] [ˌkaʊntərˌrɛvəˈluːʃənˌɛri] *adj* : contrarrevolucionario

counterrevolutionary[2] *n, pl* **-ries** : contrarrevolucionario *m,* -ria *f*

countersign [ˈkaʊntərˌsaɪn] *n* : contraseña *f*

countess [ˈkaʊntɪs] *n* : condesa *f*

countless [ˈkaʊntləs] *adj* : incontable, innumerable

country[1] [ˈkʌntri] *adj* : campestre, rural

country[2] *n, pl* **-tries** **1** NATION : país *m,* nación *f,* patria *f* <country of origin : país de origen> <love of one's country : amor a la patria> **2** : campo *m*

<they left the city for the country : se fueron de la ciudad al campo>
countryman [ˈkʌntrimən] *n, pl* **-men** [-mən, -ˌmɛn] : compatriota *mf;* paisano *m,* -na *f*
countryside [ˈkʌntriˌsaɪd] *n* : campo *m,* campiña *f*
county [ˈkaʊnti] *n, pl* **-ties** : condado *m*
coup [ˈkuː] *n, pl* **coups** [ˈkuːz] **1** : golpe *m* maestro **2** *or* **coup d'etat** : golpe *m* (de estado), cuartelazo *m*
coupe [ˈkuːp] *n* : cupé *m*
couple[1] [ˈkʌpəl] *vt* **-pled; -pling** : acoplar, enganchar, conectar
couple[2] *n* **1** PAIR : par *m* <a couple of hours : un par de horas, unas dos horas> **2** : pareja *f* <a young couple : una pareja joven>
coupling [ˈkʌplɪŋ] *n* : acoplamiento *m*
coupon [ˈkuːˌpɑn, ˈkjuː-] *n* : cupón *m*
courage [ˈkərɪdʒ] *n* : valor *m,* valentía *f,* coraje *m*
courageous [kəˈreɪdʒəs] *adj* : valiente, valeroso
courier [ˈkʊriər, ˈkəriər] *n* : mensajero *m,* -ra *f*
course[1] [ˈkors] *vi* **coursed; coursing** : correr (a toda velocidad)
course[2] *n* **1** PROGRESS : curso *m,* transcurso *m* <to run its course : seguir su curso> **2** DIRECTION : rumbo *m* (de un avión), derrota *f,* derrotero *m* (de un barco) **3** PATH, WAY : camino *m,* vía *f* <course of action : línea de conducta> **4** : plato *m* (de una cena) <the main course : el plato principal> **5** : curso *m* (académico) **6 of course** : desde luego, por supuesto <yes, of course! : ¡claro que sí!>
court[1] [ˈkort] *vt* WOO : cortejar, galantear
court[2] *n* **1** PALACE : palacio *m* **2** RETINUE : corte *f,* séquito *m* **3** COURTYARD : patio *m* **4** : cancha *f* (de tenis, baloncesto, etc.) **5** TRIBUNAL : corte *f,* tribunal *m* <the Supreme Court : la Corte Suprema>
courteous [ˈkərt̬iəs] *adj* : cortés, atento, educado — **courteously** *adv*
courtesan [ˈkort̬əzən, ˈkər-] *n* : cortesana *f*
courtesy [ˈkərt̬əsi] *n, pl* **-sies** : cortesía *f*
courthouse [ˈkortˌhaʊs] *n* : palacio *m* de justicia, juzgado *m*
courtier [ˈkort̬iər, ˈkortjər] *n* : cortesano *m,* -na *f*
courtly [ˈkortli] *adj* **-lier; -est** : distinguido, elegante, cortés
court–martial[1] [ˈkortˌmɑrʃəl] *vt* : someter a consejo de guerra
court–martial[2] *n, pl* **courts–martial** [ˈkortsˌmɑrʃəl] : consejo *m* de guerra
court order *n* : mandamiento *m* judicial
courtroom [ˈkortˌruːm] *n* : tribunal *m,* corte *f*
courtship [ˈkortˌʃɪp] *n* : cortejo *m,* noviazgo *m*
courtyard [ˈkortˌjɑrd] *n* : patio *m*
cousin [ˈkʌzən] *n* : primo *m,* -ma *f*
cove [ˈkoːv] *n* : ensenada *f,* cala *f*
covenant [ˈkʌvənənt] *n* : pacto *m,* contrato *m*
cover[1] [ˈkʌvər] *vt* **1** : cubrir, tapar <cover your head : tápate la cabeza> <covered with mud : cubierto de lodo> **2** HIDE, PROTECT : encubrir, proteger **3** TREAT : tratar **4** INSURE : asegurar, cubrir
cover[2] *n* **1** SHELTER : cubierta *f,* abrigo *m,* refugio *m* <to take cover : ponerse a cubierto> <under cover of darkness : al amparo de la oscuridad> **2** LID, TOP : cubierta *f,* tapa *f* **3** : cubierta *f* (de un libro), portada *f* (de una revista) **4 covers** *npl* BEDCLOTHES : ropa *f* de cama, cobijas *fpl,* mantas *fpl*
coverage [ˈkʌvərɪdʒ] *n* : cobertura *f*
coverlet [ˈkʌvərlət] *n* : cobertor *m*
covert[1] [ˈkoːˌvərt, ˈkʌvərt] *adj* : encubierto, secreto <covert operations : operaciones encubiertas>
covert[2] [ˈkʌvərt, ˈkoː-] *n* THICKET : espesura *f,* maleza *f*
cover–up [ˈkʌvərˌʌp] *n* : encubrimiento
covet [ˈkʌvət] *vt* : codiciar
covetous [ˈkʌvət̬əs] *adj* : codicioso
covey [ˈkʌvi] *n, pl* **-eys 1** : bandada *f* pequeña (de codornices, etc.) **2** GROUP : grupo *m*
cow[1] [ˈkaʊ] *vt* : intimidar, acobardar
cow[2] *n* : vaca *f,* hembra *f* (de ciertas especies)
coward [ˈkaʊərd] *n* : cobarde *mf*
cowardice [ˈkaʊərdɪs] *n* : cobardía *f*
cowardly [ˈkaʊərdli] *adj* : cobarde
cowboy [ˈkaʊˌbɔɪ] *n* : vaquero *m,* cowboy *m*
cower [ˈkaʊər] *vi* : encogerse (de miedo), acobardarse
cowgirl [ˈkaʊˌgərl] *n* : vaquera *f*
cowherd [ˈkaʊˌhərd] *n* : vaquero *m,* -ra *f*
cowhide [ˈkaʊˌhaɪd] *n* : cuero *m,* piel *f* de vaca
cowl [ˈkaʊl] *n* : capucha *f* (de un monje)
cowlick [ˈkaʊˌlɪk] *n* : remolino *m*
cowpuncher [ˈkaʊˌpʌntʃər] → **cowboy**
cowslip [ˈkaʊˌslɪp] *n* : prímula *f,* primavera *f*
coxswain [ˈkɑksən, -ˌsweɪn] *n* : timonel *m*
coy [ˈkɔɪ] *adj* **1** SHY : tímido, cohibido **2** COQUETTISH : coqueto
coyote [kaɪˈoːt̬i, ˈkaɪˌoːt] *n, pl* **coyotes** *or* **coyote** : coyote *m*
cozy [ˈkoːzi] *adj* **-zier; -est** : acogedor, cómodo
crab [ˈkræb] *n* : cangrejo *m,* jaiba *f*
crabby [ˈkræbi] *adj* **-bier; -est** : gruñón, malhumorado
crabgrass [ˈkræbˌgræs] *n* : garranchuelo *m*

crack[1] [ˈkræk] *vi* **1 :** chasquear, restallar <the whip cracked : el látigo restalló> **2** SPLIT **:** rajarse, resquebrajarse, agrietarse **3 :** quebrarse (dícese de la voz) — *vt* **1 :** restallar, chasquear (un látigo, etc.) **2** SPLIT **:** rajar, agrietar, resquebrajar **3** BREAK **:** romper (un huevo), cascar (nueces), forzar (una caja fuerte) **4** SOLVE **:** resolver, descifrar (un código)

crack[2] *adj* FIRST-RATE **:** buenísimo, de primera

crack[3] *n* **1 :** chasquido *m,* restallido *m,* estallido *m* (de un arma de fuego), crujido *m* (de huesos) <a crack of thunder : un trueno> **2** WISECRACK **:** chiste *m,* ocurrencia *f,* salida *f* **3** CREVICE **:** raja *f,* grieta *f,* fisura *f* **4** BLOW **:** golpe *m* **5** ATTEMPT **:** intento *m*

crackdown [ˈkrækˌdaʊn] *n* **:** medidas *fpl* enérgicas

crack down *vt* **:** tomar medidas enérgicas

cracker [ˈkrækər] *n* **:** galleta *f* (de soda, etc.)

crackle[1] [ˈkrækəl] *vi* **-led; -ling :** crepitar, chisporrotear

crackle[2] *n* **:** crujido *m,* chisporroteo *m*

crackpot [ˈkrækˌpɑt] *n* **:** excéntrico *m,* -ca *f;* chiflado *m,* -da *f*

crack–up [ˈkrækˌʌp] *n* **1** CRASH **:** choque *m,* estrellamiento *m* **2** BREAKDOWN **:** crisis *f* nerviosa

crack up *vt* WRECK **:** estrellar (un vehículo) — *vi* **:** sufrir una crisis nerviosa

cradle[1] [ˈkreɪdəl] *vt* **-dled; -dling :** acunar, mecer (a un niño)

cradle[2] *n* **:** cuna *f*

craft [ˈkræft] *n* **1** TRADE **:** oficio *m* <the craft of carpentry : el oficio de carpintero> **2** CRAFTSMANSHIP, SKILL **:** arte *m,* artesanía *f,* destreza *f* **3** CRAFTINESS **:** astucia *f,* maña *f* **4** *pl usually* **craft** BOAT **:** barco *m,* embarcación *f* **5** *pl usually* **craft** AIRCRAFT **:** avión *m,* aeronave *f*

craftiness [ˈkræftinəs] *n* **:** astucia *f,* maña *f*

craftsman [ˈkræftsmən] *n, pl* **-men** [-mən, -ˌmɛn] **:** artesano *m,* -na *f*

craftsmanship [ˈkræftsmənˌʃɪp] *n* **:** artesanía *f,* destreza *f*

crafty [ˈkræfti] *adj* **craftier; -est :** astuto, taimado

crag [ˈkræg] *n* **:** peñasco *m*

craggy [ˈkrægi] *adj* **-gier; -est :** peñascoso

cram [ˈkræm] *v* **crammed; cramming** *vt* **1** JAM **:** embutir, meter **2** STUFF **:** atiborrar, abarrotar <crammed with people : atiborrado de gente> — *vi* **:** estudiar a última hora, memorizar (para un examen)

cramp[1] [ˈkræmp] *vt* **1 :** dar calambre en **2** RESTRICT **:** limitar, restringir, entorpecer <to cramp someone's style : cortarle el vuelo a alguien> — *vi or* **to cramp up :** acalambrarse

cramp[2] *n* **1** SPASM **:** calambre *m,* espasmo *m* (de los músculos) **2 cramps** *npl* **:** retorcijones *mpl* <stomach cramps : retorcijones de estómago>

cranberry [ˈkrænˌbɛri] *n, pl* **-berries :** arándano *m* (rojo y agrio)

crane[1] [ˈkreɪn] *vi* **craned; craning :** estirar <to crane one's neck : estirar el cuello>

crane[2] *n* **1 :** grulla *f* (ave) **2 :** grúa *f* (máquina)

cranial [ˈkreɪniəl] *adj* **:** craneal, craneano

cranium [ˈkreɪniəm] *n, pl* **-niums** *or* **-nia** [-niə]**:** cráneo *m*

crank[1] [ˈkræŋk] *vt or* **to crank up :** arrancar (con una manivela)

crank[2] *n* **1 :** manivela *f,* manubrio *m* **2** ECCENTRIC **:** excéntrico *m,* -ca *f*

cranky [ˈkræŋki] *adj* **crankier; -est :** irritable, malhumorado, enojadizo

cranny [ˈkræni] *n, pl* **-nies :** grieta *f* <every nook and cranny : todos los rincones>

crash[1] [ˈkræʃ] *vi* **1** SMASH **:** caerse con estrépito, estrellarse **2** COLLIDE **:** estrellarse, chocar **3** BOOM, RESOUND **:** retumbar, resonar — *vt* **1** SMASH **:** estrellar **2 to crash one's car :** tener un accidente

crash[2] *n* **1** DIN **:** estrépito *m* **2** COLLISION **:** choque *m,* colisión *f* <car crash : accidente automovilístico> **3** FAILURE **:** quiebra *f* (de un negocio), crac *m* (de la bolsa)

crass [ˈkræs] *adj* **:** grosero, de mal gusto

crate[1] [ˈkreɪt] *vt* **crated; crating :** empacar en un cajón

crate[2] *n* **:** cajón *m* (de madera)

crater [ˈkreɪt̬ər] *n* **:** cráter *m*

cravat [krəˈvæt] *n* **:** corbata *f*

crave [ˈkreɪv] *vt* **craved; craving :** ansiar, apetecer, tener muchas ganas de

craven [ˈkreɪvən] *adj* **:** cobarde, pusilánime

craving [ˈkreɪvɪŋ] *n* **:** ansia *f,* antojo *m,* deseo *m*

crawfish [ˈkrɔˌfɪʃ] → **crayfish**

crawl[1] [ˈkrɔl] *vi* **1** CREEP **:** arrastrarse, gatear (dícese de un bebé) **2** TEEM **:** estar plagado

crawl[2] *n* **:** paso *m* lento

crayfish [ˈkreɪˌfɪʃ] *n* **1 :** ástaco *m* (de agua dulce) **2 :** langostino *m* (de mar)

crayon [ˈkreɪˌɑn, -ən] *n* **:** crayón *m*

craze [ˈkreɪz] *n* **:** moda *f* pasajera, manía *f*

crazed [ˈkreɪzd] *adj* **:** enloquecido

crazily [ˈkreɪzəli] *adv* **:** locamente, erráticamente, insensatamente

craziness [ˈkreɪzinəs] *n* **:** locura *f,* demencia *f*

crazy [ˈkreɪzi] *adj* **-zier; -est 1** INSANE **:** loco, demente <to go crazy : volverse loco> **2** ABSURD, FOOLISH **:** loco, insensato, absurdo **3 to be crazy about :** estar loco por

creak[1] [ˈkriːk] *vi* : chirriar, rechinar, crujir
creak[2] *n* : chirrido *m,* crujido *m*
creaky [ˈkriːki] *adj* **creakier; -est** : chirriante, que cruje
cream[1] [ˈkriːm] *vt* **1** BEAT, MIX : batir, mezclar (azúcar y mantequilla, etc.) **2** : preparar (alimentos) con crema
cream[2] *n* **1** : crema *f* (de leche) **2** LOTION : crema *f,* loción *f* **3** ELITE : crema *f,* elite *f* <the cream of the crop : la crema y nata, lo mejor>
creamery [ˈkriːməri] *n, pl* **-eries** : fábrica *f* de productos lácteos
creamy [ˈkriːmi] *adj* **creamier; -est** : cremoso
crease[1] [ˈkriːs] *vt* **creased; creasing 1** : plegar, poner una raya en (pantalones) **2** WRINKLE : arrugar
crease[2] *n* : pliegue *m,* doblez *m,* raya *f* (de pantalones)
create [kriˈeɪt] *vt* **-ated; -ating** : crear, hacer
creation [kriˈeɪʃən] *n* : creación *f*
creative [kriˈeɪt̬ɪv] *adj* : creativo, original <creative people : personas creativas> <a creative work : un obra original>
creatively [kriˈeɪt̬ɪvli] *adv* : creativamente, con originalidad
creativity [ˌkriːeɪˈtɪvət̬i] *n* : creatividad *f*
creator [kriˈeɪt̬ər] *n* : creador *m,* -dora *f*
creature [ˈkriːtʃər] *n* : ser *m* viviente, criatura *f,* animal *m*
credence [ˈkriːdənts] *n* : crédito *m*
credentials [krɪˈdɛntʃəlz] *npl* : referencias *fpl* oficiales, cartas *fpl* credenciales
credibility [ˌkrɛdəˈbɪlət̬i] *n* : credibilidad *f*
credible [ˈkrɛdəbəl] *adj* : creíble
credit[1] [ˈkrɛdɪt] *vt* **1** BELIEVE : creer, dar crédito a **2** : ingresar, abonar <to credit $100 to an account : ingresar $100 en (una) cuenta> **3** ATTRIBUTE : atribuir <they credit the invention to him : a él se le atribuye el invento>
credit[2] *n* **1** : saldo *m* positivo, saldo *m* a favor (de una cuenta) **2** : crédito *m* <to buy on credit : comprar a crédito> <credit card : tarjeta de crédito> **3** CREDENCE : crédito *m* <I gave credit to everything he said : di crédito a todo lo que dijo> **4** RECOGNITION : reconocimiento *m* **5** : orgullo *m,* honor *m* <she's a credit to the school : ella es el orgullo de la escuela>
creditable [ˈkrɛdɪt̬əbəl] *adj* : encomiable, loable — **creditably** [-bli] *adv*
credit card *n* : tarjeta de crédito
creditor [ˈkrɛdɪt̬ər] *n* : acreedor *m,* -dora *f*
credulity [krɪˈduːlət̬i, -ˈdjuː-] *n* : credulidad *f*
credulous [ˈkrɛdʒələs] *adj* : crédulo
creed [ˈkriːd] *n* : credo *m*
creek [ˈkriːk, ˈkrɪk] *n* : arroyo *m,* riachuelo *m*
creel [ˈkriːl] *n* : nasa *f,* cesta *f* (de pescador)
creep[1] [ˈkriːp] *vi* **crept** [ˈkrɛpt]; **creeping 1** CRAWL : arrastrarse, gatear **2** : moverse lentamente o sigilosamente <he crept out of the house : salió sigilosamente de la casa> **3** SPREAD : trepar (dícese de una planta)
creep[2] *n* **1** CRAWL : paso *m* lento **2 creeps** *npl* : escalofríos *mpl* <that gives me the creeps : eso me da escalofríos>
creeper [ˈkriːpər] *n* : planta *f* trepadora, trepadora *f*
cremate [ˈkriːˌmeɪt] *vt* **-mated; -mating** : cremar
cremation [krɪˈmeɪʃən] *n* : cremación *f*
creosote [ˈkriːəˌsoːt] *n* : creosota *f*
crepe *or* **crêpe** [ˈkreɪp] *n* **1** : crespón *m* (tela) **2** PANCAKE : crepe *mf,* crepa *f Mex*
crescendo [krɪˈʃɛnˌdoː] *n, pl* **-dos** *or* **-does** : crescendo *m*
crescent [ˈkrɛsənt] *n* : creciente *m*
crest [ˈkrɛst] *n* **1** : cresta *f,* penacho *m* (de un ave) **2** PEAK, TOP : cresta *f* (de una ola), cima *f* (de una colina) **3** : emblema *m* (sobre un escudo de armas)
crestfallen [ˈkrɛstˌfɔlən] *adj* : alicaído, abatido
cretin [ˈkriːtən] *n* : cretino *m,* -na *f*
crevasse [krɪˈvæs] *n* : grieta *f,* fisura *f*
crevice [ˈkrɛvɪs] *n* : grieta *f,* hendidura *f*
crew [ˈkruː] *n* **1** : tripulación *f* (de una nave) **2** TEAM : equipo *m* (de trabajadores o atletas)
crib [ˈkrɪb] *n* **1** MANGER : pesebre *m* **2** GRANARY : granero *m* **3** : cuna *f* (de un bebé)
crick [ˈkrɪk] *n* : calambre *m,* espasmo *m* muscular
cricket [ˈkrɪkət] *n* **1** : grillo *m* (insecto) **2** : críquet *m* (juego)
crime [ˈkraɪm] *n* **1** : crimen *m,* delito *m* <to commit a crime : cometer un delito> **2** : crimen *m,* delincuencia *f* <organized crime : crimen organizado>
criminal[1] [ˈkrɪmənəl] *adj* : criminal
criminal[2] *n* : criminal *mf,* delincuente *mf*
crimp [ˈkrɪmp] *vt* : ondular, rizar (el pelo), arrugar (una tela, etc.)
crimson [ˈkrɪmzən] *n* : carmesí *m*
cringe [ˈkrɪndʒ] *vi* **cringed; cringing** : encogerse
crinkle[1] [ˈkrɪŋkəl] *v* **-kled; -kling** *vt* : arrugar — *vi* : arrugarse
crinkle[2] *n* : arruga *f*
crinkly [ˈkrɪŋkəli] *adj* : arrugado
cripple[1] [ˈkrɪpəl] *vt* **-pled; -pling 1** DISABLE : lisiar, dejar inválido **2** INCAPACITATE : inutilizar, incapacitar
cripple[2] *n* : lisiado *m,* -da *f*

crisis [ˈkraɪsɪs] *n, pl* **crises** [-ˌsiːz] : crisis *f*

crisp[1] [ˈkrɪsp] *vt* : tostar, hacer crujiente

crisp[2] *adj* **1** CRUNCHY : crujiente, crocante **2** FIRM, FRESH : firme, fresco <crisp lettuce : lechuga fresca> **3** LIVELY : vivaz, alegre <a crisp tempo : un ritmo alegre> **4** INVIGORATING : fresco, vigorizante <the crisp autumn air : el fresco aire otoñal> — **crisply** *adv*

crispy [ˈkrɪspi] *adj* **crispier; -est** : crujiente <crispy potato chips : papitas crujientes>

crisscross [ˈkrɪsˌkrɔs] *vt* : entrecruzar

criterion [kraɪˈtɪriən] *n, pl* **-ria** [-iə] : criterio *m*

critic [ˈkrɪt̬ɪk] *n* **1** : crítico *m*, -ca *f* (de las artes) **2** FAULTFINDER : detractor *m*, -tora *f;* criticón *m*, -cona *f*

critical [ˈkrɪtɪkəl] *adj* : crítico

critically [ˈkrɪtɪkli] *adv* : críticamente <critically ill : gravemente enfermo>

criticism [ˈkrɪt̬əˌsɪzəm] *n* : crítica *f*

criticize [ˈkrɪt̬əˌsaɪz] *vt* **-cized; -cizing** **1** EVALUATE, JUDGE : criticar, analizar, evaluar **2** CENSURE : criticar, reprobar

critique [krɪˈtiːk] *n* : crítica *f*, evaluación *f*

croak[1] [ˈkroːk] *vi* : croar

croak[2] *n* : croar *m*, canto *m* (de la rana)

Croatian [kroˈeɪʃən] *n* : croata *mf* — **Croatian** *adj*

crochet[1] [kroːˈʃeɪ] *v* : tejer al croché

crochet[2] *n* : croché *m*, crochet *m*

crock [ˈkrɑk] *n* : vasija *f* de barro

crockery [ˈkrɑkəri] *n* : vajilla *f* (de barro)

crocodile [ˈkrɑkəˌdaɪl] *n* : cocodrilo *m*

crocus [ˈkroːkəs] *n, pl* **-cuses** : azafrán *m*

crone [ˈkroːn] *n* : vieja *f* arpía, vieja *f* bruja

crony [ˈkroːni] *n, pl* **-nies** : amigote *m fam;* compinche *mf fam*

crook[1] [ˈkrʊk] *vt* : doblar (el brazo o el dedo)

crook[2] *n* **1** STAFF : cayado *m* (de pastor), báculo *m* (de obispo) **2** THIEF : ratero *m*, -ra *f;* ladrón *m*, -drona *f*

crooked [ˈkrʊkəd] *adj* **1** BENT : chueco, torcido **2** DISHONEST : deshonesto

crookedness [ˈkrʊkədnəs] *n* **1** : lo torcido, lo chueco **2** DISHONESTY : falta *f* de honradez

croon [ˈkruːn] *v* : cantar suavemente

crop[1] [ˈkrɑp] *v* **cropped; cropping** *vt* TRIM : recortar, cortar — *vi* **to crop up** : aparecer, surgir <these problems keep cropping up : estos problemas no cesan de surgir>

crop[2] *n* **1** : buche *m* (de un ave o insecto) **2** WHIP : fusta *f* (de jinete) **3** HARVEST : cosecha *f*, cultivo *m*

croquet [ˌkroːˈkeɪ] *n* : croquet *m*

croquette [ˌkroːˈkɛt] *n* : croqueta *f*

cross[1] [ˈkrɔs] *vt* **1** : cruzar, atravesar <to cross the street : cruzar la calle> <several canals cross the city : varios canales atraviesan la ciudad> **2** CANCEL : tachar, cancelar <he crossed his name off the list : tachó su nombre de la planilla> **3** INTERBREED : cruzar (en genética)

cross[2] *adj* **1** : que atraviesa <cross ventilation : ventilación que atraviesa un cuarto> **2** CONTRARY : contrario, opuesto <cross purposes : objetivos opuestos> **3** ANGRY : enojado, de mal humor

cross[3] *n* **1** : cruz *f* <the sign of the cross : la señal de la cruz> **2** : cruza *f* (en biología)

crossbones [ˈkrɔsˌboːnz] *npl* **1** : huesos *mpl* cruzados **2** → **skull**

crossbow [ˈkrɔsˌboː] *n* : ballesta *f*

crossbreed [ˈkrɔsˌbriːd] *vt* **-bred** [-+bred]; **-breeding** : cruzar

cross–examination [ˌkrɔsɪgˌzæməˈneɪʃən] *n* : repreguntas *fpl*, interrogatorio *m*

cross–examine [ˌkrɔsɪgˈzæmən] *vt* **-ined; -ining** : repreguntar

cross–eyed [ˈkrɔsˌaɪd] *adj* : bizco

crossing [ˈkrɔsɪŋ] *n* **1** INTERSECTION : cruce *m*, paso *m* <pedestrian crossing : paso de peatones> **2** VOYAGE : travesía *f* (del mar)

crossly [ˈkrɔsli] *adv* : con enojo, con enfado

cross–reference [ˌkrɔsˈrɛfrənts, -ˈrɛfərənts] *n* : referencia *f*, remisión *f*

crossroads [ˈkrɔsˌroːdz] *n* : cruce *m*, encrucijada *f*, crucero *m Mex*

cross section *n* **1** SECTION : corte *m* transversal **2** SAMPLE : muestra *f* representativa <a cross section of the population : una muestra representativa de la población>

crosswalk [ˈkrɔsˌwɔk] *n* : cruce *m* peatonal, paso *m* de peatones

crossways [ˈkrɔsˌweɪz] → **crosswise**

crosswise[1] [ˈkrɔsˌwaɪz] *adv* : transversalmente, diagonalmente

crosswise[2] *adj* : transversal, diagonal

crossword puzzle [ˈkrɔsˌwərd] *n* : crucigrama *m*

crotch [ˈkrɑtʃ] *n* : entrepierna *f*

crotchety [ˈkrɑtʃət̬i] *adj* CRANKY : malhumorado, irritable, enojadizo

crouch [ˈkraʊtʃ] *vi* : agacharse, ponerse de cuclillas

croup [ˈkruːp] *n* : crup *m*

crouton [ˈkruːˌtɑn] *n* : crutón *m*

crow[1] [ˈkroː] *vi* **1** : cacarear, cantar (como un cuervo) **2** BRAG : alardear, presumir

crow[2] *n* **1** : cuervo *m* (ave) **2** : cantar *m* (del gallo)

crowbar [ˈkroːˌbɑr] *n* : palanca *f*

crowd[1] [ˈkraʊd] *vi* : aglomerarse, amontonarse — *vt* : atestar, atiborrar, llenar

crowd[2] *n* : multitud *f*, muchedumbre *f*, gentío *m*

crown[1] [ˈkraʊn] *vt* : coronar

crown[2] *n* : corona *f*

crow's nest *n* : cofa *f*
crucial [ˈkruːʃəl] *adj* : crucial, decisivo
crucible [ˈkruːsəbəl] *n* : crisol *m*
crucifix [ˈkruːsəˌfɪks] *n* : crucifijo *m*
crucifixion [ˌkruːsəˈfɪkʃən] *n* : crucifixión *f*
crucify [ˈkruːsəˌfaɪ] *vt* **-fied; -fying** : crucificar
crude [ˈkruːd] *adj* **cruder; -est 1** RAW, UNREFINED : crudo, sin refinar <crude oil : petróleo crudo> **2** VULGAR : grosero, de mal gusto **3** ROUGH : tosco, burdo, rudo
crudely [ˈkruːdli] *adv* **1** VULGARLY : groseramente **2** ROUGHLY : burdamente, de manera rudimentaria
crudity [ˈkruːdət̬i] *n, pl* **-ties 1** VULGARITY : grosería *f* **2** COARSENESS, ROUGHNESS : tosquedad *f,* rudeza *f*
cruel [ˈkruːəl] *adj* **-eler** *or* **-eller; -elest** *or* **-ellest** : cruel
cruelly [ˈkruːəli] *adv* : cruelmente
cruelty [ˈkruːəlti] *n, pl* **-ties** : crueldad *f*
cruet [ˈkruːɪt] *n* : vinagrera *f,* aceitera *f*
cruise[1] [ˈkruːz] *vi* **cruised; cruising 1** : hacer un crucero **2** : navegar o conducir a una velocidad constante <cruising speed : velocidad de crucero>
cruise[2] *n* : crucero *m*
cruiser [ˈkruːzər] *n* **1** WARSHIP : crucero *m,* buque *m* de guerra **2** : patrulla *f* (de policía)
crumb [ˈkrʌm] *n* : miga *f,* migaja *f*
crumble [ˈkrʌmbəl] *v* **-bled; -bling** *vt* : desmigajar, desmenuzar — *vi* : desmigajarse, desmoronarse, desmenuzarse
crumbly [ˈkrʌmbli] *adj* : que se desmenuza fácilmente, friable
crumple [ˈkrʌmpəl] *v* **-pled; -pling** *vt* RUMPLE : arrugar — *vi* **1** WRINKLE : arrugarse **2** COLLAPSE : desplomarse
crunch[1] [ˈkrʌntʃ] *vt* **1** : ronzar (con los dientes) **2** : hacer crujir (con los pies, etc.) — *vi* : crujir
crunch[2] *n* : crujido *m*
crunchy [ˈkrʌntʃi] *adj* **crunchier; -est** : crujiente
crusade[1] [kruːˈseɪd] *vi* **-saded; -sading** : hacer una campaña (a favor de o contra algo)
crusade[2] *n* **1** : campaña *f* (de reforma, etc.) **2 Crusade** : cruzada *f*
crusader [kruːˈseɪdər] *n* **1** : cruzado *m* (en la Edad Media) **2** : campeón *m,* -peona *f* (de una causa)
crush[1] [ˈkrʌʃ] *vt* **1** SQUASH : aplastar, apachurrar **2** GRIND, PULVERIZE : triturar, machacar **3** SUPPRESS : aplastar, suprimir
crush[2] *n* **1** CROWD, MOB : gentío *m,* multitud *f,* aglomeración *f* **2** INFATUATION : enamoramiento *m*
crushing [ˈkrʌʃɪŋ] *adj* : aplastante, abrumador
crust [ˈkrʌst] *n* **1** : corteza *f,* costra *f* (de pan) **2** : tapa *f* de masa, pasta *f* (de un pastel) **3** LAYER : capa *f,* corteza *f* <the earth's crust : la corteza terrestre>
crustacean [ˌkrʌsˈteɪʃən] *n* : crustáceo *m*
crusty [ˈkrʌsti] *adj* **crustier; -est 1** : de corteza dura **2** CROSS, GRUMPY : enojado, malhumorado
crutch [ˈkrʌtʃ] *n* : muleta *f*
crux [ˈkrʌks, ˈkrʊks] *n, pl* **cruxes** : quid *m,* esencia *f,* meollo *m* <the crux of the problem : el quid del problema>
cry[1] [ˈkraɪ] *vi* **cried; crying 1** SHOUT : gritar <they cried for more : a gritos pidieron más> **2** WEEP : llorar
cry[2] *n, pl* **cries 1** SHOUT : grito *m* **2** WEEPING : llanto *m* **3** : chillido *m* (de un animal)
crybaby [ˈkraɪˌbeɪbi] *n, pl* **-bies** : llorón *m,* -rona *f*
crypt [ˈkrɪpt] *n* : cripta *f*
cryptic [ˈkrɪptɪk] *adj* : enigmático, críptico
crystal [ˈkrɪstəl] *n* : cristal *m*
crystalline [ˈkrɪstəlɪn] *adj* : cristalino
crystallize [ˈkrɪstəˌlaɪz] *v* **-lized; -lizing** *vt* : cristalizar, materializar <to crystallize one's thoughts : cristalizar uno sus pensamientos> — *vi* : cristalizarse
cub [ˈkʌb] *n* : cachorro *m*
Cuban [ˈkjuːbən] *n* : cubano *m,* -na *f* — **Cuban** *adj*
cubbyhole [ˈkʌbiˌhoːl] *n* : chiribitil *m*
cube[1] [ˈkjuːb] *vt* **cubed; cubing 1** : elevar (un número) al cubo **2** : cortar en cubos
cube[2] *n* **1** : cubo *m* **2 ice cube** : cubito *m* de hielo **3 sugar cube** : terrón *m* de azúcar
cubic [ˈkjuːbɪk] *adj* : cúbico
cubicle [ˈkjuːbɪkəl] *n* : cubículo *m*
cuckoo[1] [ˈkuːˌkuː, ˈkʊ-] *adj* : loco, chiflado
cuckoo[2] *n, pl* **-oos** : cuco *m,* cuclillo *m*
cucumber [ˈkjuːˌkʌmbər] *n* : pepino *m*
cud [ˈkʌd] *n* **to chew the cud** : rumiar
cuddle [ˈkʌdəl] *v* **-dled; -dling** *vi* : abrazarse tiernamente, acurrucarse — *vt* : abrazar
cudgel[1] [ˈkʌdʒəl] *vt* **-geled** *or* **-gelled; -geling** *or* **-gelling** : apalear, aporrear
cudgel[2] *n* : garrote *m,* porra *f*
cue[1] [ˈkjuː] *vt* **cued; cuing** *or* **cueing** : darle el pie a, darle la señal a
cue[2] *n* **1** SIGNAL : señal *f,* pie *m* (en teatro), entrada *f* (en música) **2** : taco *m* (de billar)
cuff[1] [ˈkʌf] *vt* : bofetear, cachetear
cuff[2] *n* **1** : puño *m* (de una camisa), vuelta *f* (de pantalones) **2** SLAP : bofetada *f,* cachetada *f* **3 cuffs** *npl* HANDCUFFS : esposas *fpl*
cuisine [kwɪˈziːn] *n* : cocina *f* <Mexican cuisine : la cocina mexicana>

culinary [ˈkʌləˌnɛri, ˈkjuːlə-] *adj* : culinario
cull [ˈkʌl] *vt* : seleccionar, entresacar
culminate [ˈkʌlməˌneɪt] *vi* **-nated; -nating** : culminar
culmination [ˌkʌlməˈneɪʃən] *n* : culminación *f*, punto *m* culminante
culpable [ˈkʌlpəbəl] *adj* : culpable
culprit [ˈkʌlprɪt] *n* : culpable *mf*
cult [ˈkʌlt] *n* : culto *m*
cultivate [ˈkʌltəˌveɪt] *vt* **-vated; -vating 1** TILL : cultivar, labrar **2** FOSTER : cultivar, fomentar **3** REFINE : cultivar, refinar <to cultivate the mind : cultivar la mente>
cultivation [ˌkʌltəˈveɪʃən] *n* **1** : cultivo *m* <under cultivation : en cultivo> **2** CULTURE, REFINEMENT : cultura *f*, refinamiento *m*
cultural [ˈkʌltʃərəl] *adj* : cultural — **culturally** *adv*
culture [ˈkʌltʃər] *n* **1** CULTIVATION : cultivo *m* **2** REFINEMENT : cultura *f*, educación *f*, refinamiento *m* **3** CIVILIZATION : cultura *f*, civilización *f* <the Incan culture : la cultura inca>
cultured [ˈkʌltʃərd] *adj* **1** EDUCATED, REFINED : culto, educado, refinado **2** : de cultivo, cultivado <cultured pearls : perlas de cultivo>
culvert [ˈkʌlvərt] *n* : alcantarilla *f*
cumbersome [ˈkʌmbərsəm] *adj* : torpe y pesado, difícil de manejar
cumulative [ˈkjuːmjələt̬ɪv, -ˌleɪt̬ɪv] *adj* : acumulativo
cumulus [ˈkjuːmjələs] *n, pl* **-li** [-ˌlaɪ, -ˌliː] : cúmulo *n*
cunning[1] [ˈkʌnɪŋ] *adj* **1** CRAFTY : astuto, taimado **2** CLEVER : ingenioso, hábil **3** CUTE : mono, gracioso, lindo
cunning[2] *n* **1** SKILL : habilidad *f* **2** CRAFTINESS : astucia *f*, maña *f*
cup[1] [ˈkʌp] *vt* **cupped; cupping** : ahuecar (las manos)
cup[2] *n* **1** : taza *f* <a cup of coffee : una taza de café> **2** CUPFUL : taza *f* **3** : media pinta *f* (unidad de medida) **4** GOBLET : copa *f* **5** TROPHY : copa *f*, trofeo *m*
cupboard [ˈkʌbərd] *n* : alacena *f*, armario *m*
cupcake [ˈkʌpˌkeɪk] *n* : pastelito *m*
cupful [ˈkʌpˌfʊl] *n* : taza *f*
cupola [ˈkjuːpələ, -ˌloː] *n* : cúpula *f*
cur [ˈkər] *n* : perro *m* callejero, perro *m* corriente *Mex*
curate [ˈkjʊrət] *n* : cura *m*, párroco *m*
curator [ˈkjʊrˌeɪt̬ər, kjʊˈreɪt̬ər] *n* : conservador *m*, -dora *f* (de un museo); director *m*, -tora *f* (de un zoológico)
curb[1] [ˈkərb] *vt* : refrenar, restringir, controlar
curb[2] *n* **1** RESTRAINT : freno *m*, control *m* **2** : borde *m* de la acera
curd [ˈkərd] *n* : cuajada *f*
curdle [ˈkərdəl] *v* **-dled; -dling** *vi* : cuajarse — *vt* : cuajar <to curdle one's blood : helarle la sangre a uno>
cure[1] [ˈkjʊr] *vt* **cured; curing 1** HEAL : curar, sanar **2** REMEDY : remediar **3** PROCESS : curar (alimentos, etc.)
cure[2] *n* **1** RECOVERY : curación *f*, recuperación *f* **2** REMEDY : cura *f*, remedio *m*
curfew [ˈkərˌfjuː] *n* : toque *m* de queda
curio [ˈkjʊriˌoː] *n, pl* **-rios** : curiosidad *f*, objeto *m* curioso
curiosity [ˌkjʊriˈɑsət̬i] *n, pl* **-ties** : curiosidad *f*
curious [ˈkjʊriəs] *adj* **1** INQUISITIVE : curioso **2** STRANGE : curioso, raro
curl[1] [ˈkərl] *vt* **1** : rizar, ondular (el pelo) **2** COIL : enrollar **3** TWIST : torcer <to curl one's lip : hacer una mueca> — *vi* **1** : rizarse, ondularse **2 to curl up** : acurrucarse (con un libro, etc.)
curl[2] *n* **1** RINGLET : rizo *m* **2** COIL : espiral *f*, rosca *f*
curler [ˈkərlər] *n* : rulo *m*
curlew [ˈkərˌluː, ˈkərlˌjuː] *n, pl* **-lews** *or* **-lew** : zarapito *m*
curly [ˈkərli] *adj* **curlier; -est** : rizado, crespo
currant [ˈkərənt] *n* **1** : grosella *f* (fruta) **2** RAISIN : pasa *f* de Corinto
currency [ˈkərəntsi] *n, pl* **-cies 1** PREVALENCE, USE : uso *m*, aceptación *f*, difusión *f* <to be in currency : estar en uso> **2** MONEY : moneda *f*, dinero *m*
current[1] [ˈkərənt] *adj* **1** PRESENT : actual <current events : actualidades> **2** PREVALENT : corriente, común — **currently** *adv*
current[2] *n* : corriente *f*
curriculum [kəˈrɪkjələm] *n, pl* **-la** [-lə] : currículum *m*, currículo *m*, programa *m* de estudio
curriculum vitae [ˈviːˌtaɪ, ˈvaɪt̬i] *n, pl* **curricula vitae** : currículum *m*, currículo *m*
curry[1] [ˈkəri] *vt* **-ried; -rying 1** GROOM : almohazar (un caballo) **2** : condimentar con curry **3 to curry favor** : congraciarse (con alguien)
curry[2] *n, pl* **-ries** : curry *m*
curse[1] [ˈkərs] *v* **cursed; cursing** *vt* **1** DAMN : maldecir **2** INSULT : injuriar, insultar, decir malas palabras a **3** AFFLICT : afligir — *vi* : maldecir, decir malas palabras
curse[2] *n* **1** : maldición *f* <to put a curse on someone : echarle una maldición a alguien> **2** AFFLICTION : maldición *f*, aflicción *f*, cruz *f*
cursor [ˈkərsər] *n* : cursor *m*
cursory [ˈkərsəri] *adj* : rápido, superficial, somero
curt [ˈkərt] *adj* : cortante, brusco, seco — **curtly** *adv*
curtail [kərˈteɪl] *vt* : acortar, limitar, restringir
curtailment [kərˈteɪlmənt] *n* : restricción *f*, limitación *f*
curtain [ˈkərtən] *n* : cortina *f* (de una ventana), telón *m* (en un teatro)
curtness [ˈkərtnəs] *n* : brusquedad *f*, sequedad *f*

curtsy[1] *or* **curtsey** [ˈkərtsi] *vt* **-sied** *or* **-seyed; -sying** *or* **-seying :** hacer una reverencia
curtsy[2] *or* **curtsey** *n, pl* **-sies** *or* **-seys :** reverencia *f*
curvature [ˈkərvəˌtʃʊr] *n* **:** curvatura *f*
curve[1] [ˈkərv] *v* **curved; curving** *vi* **:** torcerse, describir una curva — *vt* **:** encorvar
curve[2] *n* **:** curva *f*
cushion[1] [ˈkʊʃən] *vt* **1 :** poner cojines o almohadones a **2** SOFTEN **:** amortiguar, mitigar, suavizar <to cushion a blow : amortiguar un golpe>
cushion[2] *n* **1 :** cojín *m,* almohadón *m* **2** PROTECTION **:** colchón *m,* protección *f*
cusp [ˈkʌsp] *n* **:** cúspide *f* (de un diente), cuerno *m* (de la luna)
cuspid [ˈkʌspɪd] *n* **:** diente *m* canino, colmillo *m*
custard [ˈkʌstərd] *n* **:** natillas *fpl*
custodian [ˌkʌˈstoːdiən] *n* **:** custodio *m,* -dia *f;* guardián, -diana *f*
custody [ˈkʌstədi] *n, pl* **-dies :** custodia *f,* cuidado *m* <to be in custody : estar detenido>
custom[1] [ˈkʌstəm] *adj* **:** a la medida, a la orden
custom[2] *n* **1 :** costumbre *f,* tradición *f* **2 customs** *npl* **:** aduana *f*
customarily [ˌkʌstəˈmɛrəli] *adv* **:** habitualmente, normalmente, de costumbre
customary [ˈkʌstəˌmɛri] *adj* **1** TRADITIONAL **:** tradicional **2** USUAL **:** habitual, de costumbre
customer [ˈkʌstəmər] *n* **:** cliente *m,* -ta *f*
custom–made [ˈkʌstəmˈmeɪd] *adj* **:** hecho a la medida
cut[1] [ˈkʌt] *v* **cut; cutting** *vt* **1 :** cortar <to cut paper : cortar papel> **2 :** cortarse <to cut one's finger : cortarse uno el dedo> **3** TRIM **:** cortar, recortar <to have one's hair cut : cortarse el pelo> **4** INTERSECT **:** cruzar, atravesar **5** SHORTEN **:** acortar, abreviar **6** REDUCE **:** reducir, rebajar <to cut prices : rebajar los precios> **7 to cut one's teeth :** salirle los dientes a uno — *vi* **1 :** cortar, cortarse **2 to cut in :** entrometerse
cut[2] *n* **1 :** corte *m* <a cut of meat : un corte de carne> **2** SLASH **:** tajo *m,* corte *m,* cortadura *f* **3** REDUCTION **:** rebaja *f,* reducción *f* <a cut in the rates : una rebaja en las tarifas>
cute [ˈkjuːt] *adj* **cuter; -est :** mono *fam,* lindo
cuticle [ˈkjuːtɪkəl] *n* **:** cutícula *f*
cutlass [ˈkʌtləs] *n* **:** alfanje *m*
cutlery [ˈkʌtləri] *n* **:** cubiertos *mpl*
cutlet [ˈkʌtlət] *n* **:** chuleta *f*
cutter [ˈkʌt̬ər] *n* **1 :** cortadora *f* (implemento) **2 :** cortador *m,* -dora *f* (persona) **3 :** cúter *m* (embarcación)
cutthroat [ˈkʌtˌθroːt] *adj* **:** despiadado, desalmado <cutthroat competition : competencia feroz>
cutting[1] [ˈkʌt̬ɪŋ] *adj* **1 :** cortante <a cutting wind : un viento cortante> **2** CAUSTIC **:** mordaz
cutting[2] *n* **:** esqueje *m* (de una planta)
cuttlefish [ˈkʌt̬əlˌfɪʃ] *n, pl* **-fish** *or* **-fishes :** jibia *f,* sepia *f*
cyanide [ˈsaɪəˌnaɪd, -nɪd] *n* **:** cianuro *m*
cycle[1] [ˈsaɪkəl] *vi* **-cled; -cling :** andar en bicicleta, ir en bicicleta
cycle[2] *n* **1 :** ciclo *m* <life cycle : ciclo de vida, ciclo vital> **2** BICYCLE **:** bicicleta *f* **3** MOTORCYCLE **:** motocicleta *f*
cyclic [ˈsaɪklɪk, ˈsɪ-] *or* **cyclical** [-klɪkəl] *adj* **:** cíclico
cyclist [ˈsaɪklɪst] *n* **:** ciclista *mf*
cyclone [ˈsaɪˌkloːn] *n* **1 :** ciclón *m* **2** TORNADO **:** tornado *m*
cyclopedia *or* **cyclopaedia** [ˌsaɪkləˈpiːdiə] → **encyclopedia**
cylinder [ˈsɪləndər] *n* **:** cilindro *m*
cylindrical [səˈlɪndrɪkəl] *adj* **:** cilíndrico
cymbal [ˈsɪmbəl] *n* **:** platillo *m,* címbalo *m*
cynic [ˈsɪnɪk] *n* **:** cínico *m,* -ca *f*
cynical [ˈsɪnɪkəl] *adj* **:** cínico
cynicism [ˈsɪnəˌsɪzəm] *n* **:** cinismo *m*
cypress [ˈsaɪprəs] *n* **:** ciprés *m*
Cypriot [ˈsɪpriət, -ˌɑt] *n* **:** chipriota *mf* — **Cypriot** *adj*
cyst [ˈsɪst] *n* **:** quiste *m*
cytoplasm [ˈsaɪt̬oˌplæzəm] *n* **:** citoplasma *m*
czar [ˈzɑr, ˈsɑr] *n* **:** zar *m*
czarina [zɑˈriːnə, sɑ-] *n* **:** zarina *f*
Czech [ˈtʃɛk] *n* **1 :** checo *m,* -ca *f* **2 :** checo *m* (idioma) — **Czech** *adj*
Czechoslovak [ˌtʃɛkoˈsloːˌvɑk, -ˌvæk] *or* **Czechoslovakian** [-sloˈvɑkiən, -ˈvæ-] *n* **:** checoslovaco *m,* -ca *f* — **Czechoslovak** *or* **Czechoslovakian** *adj*

D

d [ˈdiː] *n, pl* **d's** *or* **ds** [ˈdiːz] **:** cuarta letra del alfabeto inglés
dab[1] [ˈdæb] *vt* **dabbed; dabbing :** darle toques ligeros a, aplicar suavemente
dab[2] *n* **1** BIT **:** toque *m,* pizca *f,* poco *m* <a dab of ointment : un toque de ungüento> **2** PAT **:** toque *m* ligero, golpecito *m*
dabble [ˈdæbəl] *v* **-bled; -bling** *vt* SPATTER **:** salpicar — *vi* **1** SPLASH **:** chapotear **2** TRIFLE **:** jugar, interesarse superficialmente

dabbler ['dæbələr] *n* : diletante *mf*
dachshund ['dɑks,hʊnt, -,hʊnd; 'dɑksənt, -sənd] *n* : perro *m* salchicha
dad ['dæd] *n* : papá *m fam*
daddy ['dædi] *n, pl* **-dies** : papi *m fam*
daffodil ['dæfə,dɪl] *n* : narciso *m*
daft ['dæft] *adj* : tonto, bobo
dagger ['dægər] *n* : daga *f,* puñal *m*
dahlia ['dæljə, 'dɑl-, 'deɪl-] *n* : dalia *f*
daily[1] ['deɪli] *adv* : a diario, diariamente
daily[2] *adj* : diario, cotidiano
daily[3] *n, pl* **-lies** : diario *m,* periódico *m*
daintily ['deɪntəli] *adv* : delicadamente, con delicadeza
daintiness ['deɪntinəs] *n* : delicadeza *f,* finura *f*
dainty[1] ['deɪnti] *adj* **-tier; -est 1** DELICATE : delicado **2** FASTIDIOUS : remilgado, melindroso **3** DELICIOUS : exquisito, sabroso
dainty[2] *n, pl* **-ties** DELICACY : exquisitez *f,* manjar *m*
dairy ['dæri] *n, pl* **-ies 1** *or* **dairy store** : lechería *f* **2** *or* **dairy farm** : granja *f* lechera
dairymaid ['dæri,meɪd] *n* : lechera *f*
dairyman ['dærimən, -,mæn] *n, pl* **-men** [-mən, -,mɛn] : lechero *m*
dais ['deɪəs] *n* : tarima *f,* estrado *m*
daisy ['deɪzi] *n, pl* **-sies** : margarita *f*
dale ['deɪl] *n* : valle *m*
dally ['dæli] *vi* **-lied; -lying 1** TRIFLE : juguetear **2** DAWDLE : entretenerse, perder tiempo
dalmatian [dæl'meɪʃən, dɔl-] *n* : dálmata *m*
dam[1] ['dæm] *vt* **dammed; damming** : represar, embalsar
dam[2] *n* **1** : represa *f,* dique *m* **2** : madre *f* (de animales domésticos)
damage[1] ['dæmɪdʒ] *vt* **-aged; -aging** : dañar (un objeto o una máquina), perjudicar (la salud o una reputación)
damage[2] *n* **1** : daño *m,* perjuicio *m* **2** **damages** *npl* : daños y perjuicios *mpl*
damask ['dæməsk] *n* : damasco *m*
dame ['deɪm] *n* LADY : dama *f,* señora *f*
damn[1] ['dæm] *vt* **1** CONDEMN : condenar **2** CURSE : maldecir
damn[2] *or* **damned** ['dæmd] *adj* : condenado *fam,* maldito *fam*
damn[3] *n* : pito *m,* bledo *m,* comino *m* <it's not worth a damn : no vale un pito> <I don't give a damn : me importa un comino>
damnable ['dæmnəbəl] *adj* : condenable, detestable
damnation [dæm'neɪʃən] *n* : condenación *f*
damned[1] ['dæmd] *adv* VERY : muy
damned[2] *adj* **1** → **damnable 2** REMARKABLE : extraordinario
damp[1] ['dæmp] *vt* → **dampen**
damp[2] *adj* : húmedo
damp[3] *n* MOISTURE : humedad *f*
dampen ['dæmpən] *vt* **1** MOISTEN : humedecer **2** DISCOURAGE : desalentar, desanimar
damper ['dæmpər] *n* **1** : regulador *m* de tiro (de una chimenea) **2** : sordina *f* (de un piano) **3 to put a damper on** : desanimar, apagar (el entusiasmo), enfriar
dampness ['dæmpnəs] *n* : humedad *f*
damsel ['dæmzəl] *n* : damisela *f*
dance[1] ['dænts] *v* **danced; dancing** : bailar
dance[2] *n* : baile *m*
dancer ['dæntsər] *n* : bailarín *m,* -rina *f*
dandelion ['dændəl,aɪən] *n* : diente *m* de león
dandruff ['dændrəf] *n* : caspa *f*
dandy[1] ['dændi] *adj* **-dier; -est** : excelente, magnífico, macanudo *fam*
dandy[2] *n, pl* **-dies 1** FOP : dandi *m* **2** : algo *m* excelente <this new program is a dandy : este programa nuevo es algo excelente>
Dane ['deɪn] *n* : danés *m,* -nesa *f*
Danish[1] ['deɪnɪʃ] *adj* : danés
Danish[2] *n* : danés *m* (idioma)
danger ['deɪndʒər] *n* : peligro *m*
dangerous ['deɪndʒərəs] *adj* : peligroso
dangle ['dæŋgəl] *v* **-gled; -gling** *vi* HANG : colgar, pender — *vt* **1** SWING : hacer oscilar **2** PROFFER : ofrecer (como incentivo) **3 to keep someone dangling** : dejar a alguien en suspenso
dank ['dæŋk] *adj* : frío y húmedo
dapper ['dæpər] *adj* : pulcro, atildado
dappled ['dæpəld] *adj* : moteado <a dappled horse : un caballo rodado>
dare[1] ['dær] *v* **dared; daring** *vi* : osar, atreverse <how dare you! : ¡cómo te atreves!> — *vt* **1** CHALLENGE : desafiar, retar **2 to dare to do something** : atreverse a hacer algo, osar hacer algo
dare[2] *n* : desafío *m,* reto *m*
daredevil ['dær,dɛvəl] *n* : persona *f* temeraria
daring[1] ['dærɪŋ] *adj* : osado, atrevido, audaz
daring[2] *n* : arrojo *m,* coraje *m,* audacia *f*
dark ['dɑrk] *adj* **1** : oscuro (dícese del ambiente o de los colores), moreno (dícese del pelo o de la piel) **2** SOMBER : sombrío, triste
darken ['dɑrkən] *vt* **1** DIM : oscurecer **2** SADDEN : entristecer — *vi* : ensombrecerse, nublarse
darkly ['dɑrkli] *adv* **1** DIMLY : oscuramente **2** GLOOMILY : tristemente **3** MYSTERIOUSLY : misteriosamente, enigmáticamente
darkness ['dɑrknəs] *n* : oscuridad *f,* tinieblas *f*
darling[1] ['dɑrlɪŋ] *adj* **1** BELOVED : querido, amado **2** CHARMING : encantador, mono *fam*

darling[2] *n* **1** BELOVED **:** querido *m,* -da *f;* amado *m,* -da *f;* cariño *m,* -ña *f* **2** FAVORITE **:** preferido *m,* -da *f;* favorito *m,* -ta *f*
darn[1] [ˈdɑrn] *vt* **:** zurcir
darn[2] *n* **1 :** zurcido *m* **2** → **damn**[3]
dart[1] [ˈdɑrt] *vt* THROW **:** lanzar, tirar — *vi* DASH **:** lanzarse, precipitarse
dart[2] *n* **1 :** dardo *m* **2 darts** *npl* **:** juego *m* de dardos
dash[1] [ˈdæʃ] *vt* **1** SMASH **:** romper, estrellar **2** HURL **:** arrojar, lanzar **3** SPLASH **:** salpicar **4** FRUSTRATE **:** frustrar **5 to dash off :** hacer (algo) rápidamente — *vi* **1** SMASH **:** romperse, estrellarse **2** DART **:** lanzarse, irse apresuradamente
dash[2] *n* **1** BURST, SPLASH **:** arranque *m,* salpicadura *f* (de aguas) **2 :** guión *m* largo (signo de puntuación) **3** DROP **:** gota *f,* pizca *f* **4** VERVE **:** brío *m* **5** RACE **:** carrera *f* <a 100-meter dash : una carrera de 100 metros> **6 to make a dash for it :** precipitarse (hacia), echarse a correr **7** → **dashboard**
dashboard [ˈdæʃˌbord] *n* **:** tablero *m* de instrumentos
dashing [ˈdæʃɪŋ] *adj* **:** gallardo, apuesto
data [ˈdeɪt̬ə, ˈdæ-, ˈdɑ-] *ns & pl* **:** datos *mpl,* información *f*
database [ˈdeɪt̬əˌbeɪs, ˈdæ-, ˈdɑ-] *n* **:** base *f* de datos
date[1] [ˈdeɪt] *v* **dated; dating** *vt* **1 :** fechar (una carta, etc.), datar (un objeto) <it was dated June 9 : estaba fechada el 9 de junio> **2 :** salir con <she's dating my brother : sale con mi hermano> — *vi* **:** datar
date[2] *n* **1 :** fecha *f* <to date : hasta la fecha> **2** EPOCH, PERIOD **:** época *f,* período *m* **3** APPOINTMENT **:** cita *f* **4** COMPANION **:** acompañante *mf* **5 :** dátil *m* (fruta)
dated [ˈdeɪt̬əd] *adj* OUT-OF-DATE **:** anticuado, pasado de moda
datum [ˈdeɪt̬əm, ˈdæ-, ˈdɑ-] *n, pl* **-ta** [-t̬ə] *or* **-tums :** dato *m*
daub[1] [ˈdɔb] *vt* **:** embadurnar
daub[2] *n* **:** mancha *f*
daughter [ˈdɔt̬ər] *n* **:** hija *f*
daughter–in–law [ˈdɔt̬ərɪnˌlɔ] *n, pl* **daughters–in–law :** nuera *f,* hija *f* política
daunt [ˈdɔnt] *vt* **:** amilanar, acobardar, intimidar
dauntless [ˈdɔntləs] *adj* **:** intrépido, impávido
davenport [ˈdævənˌport] *n* **:** sofá *m*
dawdle [ˈdɔdəl] *vi* **-dled; -dling 1** DALLY **:** demorarse, entretenerse, perder tiempo **2** LOITER **:** vagar, holgazanear, haraganear
dawn[1] [ˈdɔn] *vi* **1 :** amanecer, alborear, despuntar <Saturday dawned clear and bright : el sábado amaneció claro y luminoso> **2 to dawn on :** hacerse obvio <it dawned on me that she was right : me di cuenta de que tenía razón>
dawn[2] *n* **1** DAYBREAK **:** amanecer *m,* alba *f* **2** BEGINNING **:** albor *m,* comienzo *m* <the dawn of history : los albores de la historia> **3 from dawn to dusk :** de sol a sol
day [ˈdeɪ] *n* **1 :** día *m* **2** DATE **:** fecha *f* **3** TIME **:** día *m,* tiempo *m* <in olden days : antaño> **4** WORKDAY **:** jornada *f* laboral
daybreak [ˈdeɪˌbreɪk] *n* **:** alba *f,* amanecer *m*
day care *n* **:** servicio *m* de guardería infantil
daydream[1] [ˈdeɪˌdriːm] *vi* **:** soñar despierto, fantasear
daydream[2] *n* **:** ensueño *m,* ensoñación *f,* fantasía *f*
daylight [ˈdeɪˌlaɪt] *n* **1 :** luz *f* del día <in broad daylight : a plena luz del día> **2** → **daybreak 3** → **daytime**
daylight saving time *n* **:** hora *f* de verano
daytime [ˈdeɪˌtaɪm] *n* **:** horas *fpl* diurnas, día *m*
daze[1] [ˈdeɪz] *vt* **dazed; dazing 1** STUN **:** aturdir **2** DAZZLE **:** deslumbrar, ofuscar
daze[2] *n* **1 :** aturdimiento *m* **2 in a daze :** aturdido, atonado
dazzle[1] [ˈdæzəl] *vt* **-zled; -zling :** deslumbrar, ofuscar
dazzle[2] *n* **:** resplandor *m,* brillo *m*
DDT [ˌdiːˌdiːˈtiː] *n* **:** DDT *m*
deacon [ˈdiːkən] *n* **:** diácono *m*
dead[1] [ˈdɛd] *adv* **1** ABRUPTLY **:** repentinamente, súbitamente <to stop dead : parar en seco> **2** ABSOLUTELY **:** absolutamente <I'm dead certain : estoy absolutamente seguro> **3** DIRECTLY **:** justo <dead ahead : justo adelante>
dead[2] *adj* **1** LIFELESS **:** muerto **2** NUMB **:** entumecido **3** INDIFFERENT **:** indiferente, frío **4** INACTIVE **:** inactivo <a dead volcano : un volcán inactivo> **5 :** desconectado (dícese del teléfono), descargado (dícese de una batería) **6** EXHAUSTED **:** agotado, derrengado, muerto **7** OBSOLETE **:** obsoleto, muerto <a dead language : una lengua muerta> **8** EXACT **:** exacto <in the dead center : justo en el blanco>
dead[3] *n* **1 the dead :** los muertos **2 in the dead of night :** a las altas horas de la noche **3 in the dead of winter :** en pleno invierno
deadbeat [ˈdɛdˌbiːt] *n* **1** LOAFER **:** vago *m,* -ga *f;* holgazán *m,* -zana *f* **2** FREELOADER **:** gorrón *m,* -rrona *f fam;* gorrero *m,* -ra *f fam*
deaden [ˈdɛdən] *vt* **1 :** atenuar (un dolor), entorpecer (sensaciones) **2** DULL **:** deslustrar **3** DISPIRIT **:** desanimar **4** MUFFLE **:** amortiguar, reducir (sonidos)
dead–end [ˈdɛdˈɛnd] *adj* **1 :** sin salida <dead-end street : calle sin salida> **2 :** sin futuro <a dead-end job : un trabajo sin porvenir>
dead end *n* **:** callejón *m* sin salida

dead heat *n* : empate *m*

deadline [ˈdɛd,laɪn] *n* : fecha *f* límite, fecha *f* tope, plazo *m* (determinado)

deadlock[1] [ˈdɛd,lɑk] *vt* : estancar — *vi* : estancarse, llegar a punto muerto

deadlock[2] *n* : punto *m* muerto, impasse *m*

deadly[1] [ˈdɛdli] *adv* : extremadamente, sumamente <deadly serious : muy en serio>

deadly[2] *adj* **-lier; -est 1** LETHAL : mortal, letal, mortífero **2** ACCURATE : certero, preciso <a deadly aim : una puntería infalible> **3** CAPITAL : capital <the seven deadly sins : los siete pecados capitales> **4** DULL : funesto, aburrido **5** EXTREME : extremo, absoluto <a deadly calm : una calma absoluta>

deadpan[1] [ˈdɛd,pæn] *adv* : de manera inexpresiva, sin expresión

deadpan[2] *adj* : inexpresivo, impasible

deaf [ˈdɛf] *adj* : sordo

deafen [ˈdɛfən] *vt* **-ened; -ening** : ensordecer

deaf–mute [ˈdɛfˈmjuːt] *n* : sordomudo *m*, -da *f*

deafness [ˈdɛfnəs] *n* : sordera *f*

deal[1] [ˈdiːl] *v* **dealt; dealing** *vt* **1** APPORTION : repartir <to deal justice : repartir la justicia> **2** DISTRIBUTE : repartir, dar (naipes) **3** DELIVER : asestar, propinar <to deal a blow : asestar un golpe> — *vi* **1** : dar, repartir (en juegos de naipes) **2 to deal in** : comerciar en, traficar con (drogas) **3 to deal with** CONCERN : tratar de, tener que ver con <the book deals with poverty : el libro trata de la pobreza> **4 to deal with** HANDLE : tratar (con), encargarse de **5 to deal with** TREAT : tratar <the judge dealt with him severely : el juez lo trató con severidad> **6 to deal with** ACCEPT : aceptar (una situación o desgracia)

deal[2] *n* **1** : reparto *m* (de naipes) **2** AGREEMENT, TRANSACTION : trato *m*, acuerdo *m*, transacción *f* **3** TREATMENT : trato *m* <he got a raw deal : le hicieron una injusticia> **4** BARGAIN : ganga *f*, oferta *f* **5 a good deal** *or* **a great deal** : mucho, una gran cantidad

dealer [ˈdiːlər] *n* : comerciante *mf*, traficante *mf*

dealings [ˈdiːlɪŋz] *npl* **1** : relaciones *fpl* (personales) **2** TRANSACTIONS : negocios *mpl*, transacciones *fpl*

dean [ˈdiːn] *n* **1** : deán *m* (del clero) **2** : decano *m*, -na *f* (de una facultad o profesión)

dear[1] [ˈdɪr] *adj* **1** ESTEEMED, LOVED : querido, estimado <a dear friend : un amigo querido> <Dear Sir : Estimado Señor> **2** COSTLY : caro, costoso

dear[2] *n* : querido *m*, -da *f*; amado *m*, -da *f*

dearly [ˈdɪrli] *adv* **1** : mucho <I love them dearly : los quiero mucho> **2** : caro <to pay dearly : pagar caro>

dearth [ˈdərθ] *n* : escasez *f*, carestía *f*

death [ˈdɛθ] *n* **1** : muerte *f*, fallecimiento *m* <to be the death of : matar> **2** FATALITY : víctima *f* (mortal); muerto *m*, -ta *f* **3** END : fin *m* <the death of civilization : el fin de la civilización>

deathbed [ˈdɛθ,bɛd] *n* : lecho *m* de muerte

deathblow [ˈdɛθ,bloː] *n* : golpe *m* mortal

deathless [ˈdɛθləs] *adj* : eterno, inmortal

deathly [ˈdɛθli] *adj* : de muerte, sepulcral (dícese del silencio), cadavérico (dícese de la palidez)

debacle [dɪˈbɑkəl, -ˈbæ-] *n* : desastre *m*, debacle *m*, fiasco *m*

debar [diˈbɑr] *vt* **-barred; -barring** : excluir, prohibir

debase [diˈbeɪs] *vt* **-based; -basing** : degradar, envilecer

debasement [diˈbeɪsmənt] *n* : degradación *f*, envilecimiento *m*

debatable [diˈbeɪtəbəl] *adj* : discutible

debate[1] [diˈbeɪt] *vt* **-bated; -bating** : debatir, discutir

debate[2] *n* : debate *m*, discusión *f*

debauch [diˈbɔtʃ] *vt* : pervertir, corromper

debauchery [diˈbɔtʃəri] *n, pl* **-eries** : libertinaje *m*, disipación *f*, intemperancia *f*

debilitate [diˈbɪlə,teɪt] *vt* **-tated; -tating** : debilitar

debility [diˈbɪləti] *n, pl* **-ties** : debilidad *f*

debit[1] [ˈdɛbɪt] *vt* : adeudar, cargar, debitar

debit[2] *n* : débito *m*, cargo *m*, debe *m*

debonair [,dɛbəˈnær] *adj* : elegante y desenvuelto, apuesto

debris [dəˈbriː, deɪ-; ˈdeɪ,briː] *n, pl* **-bris** [-ˈbriːz, -,briːz] **1** RUBBLE, RUINS : escombros *mpl*, ruinas *fpl*, restos *mpl* **2** RUBBISH : basura *f*, deshechos *mpl*

debt [ˈdɛt] *n* **1** : deuda *f* <to pay a debt : saldar una deuda> **2** INDEBTEDNESS : endeudamiento *m*

debtor [ˈdɛtər] *n* : deudor *m*, -dora *f*

debunk [diˈbʌŋk] *vt* DISCREDIT : desacreditar, desprestigiar

debut[1] [deɪˈbjuː, ˈdeɪ,bjuː] *vi* : debutar

debut[2] *n* **1** : debut *m* (de un actor), estreno *m* (de una obra) **2** : debut *m*, presentación *f* (en sociedad)

debutante [ˈdɛbjʊ,tɑnt] *n* : debutante *f*

decade [ˈdɛ,keɪd, dɛˈkeɪd] *n* : década *f*

decadence [ˈdɛkədənts] *n* : decadencia *f*

decadent [ˈdɛkədənt] *adj* : decadente

decal [ˈdiː,kæl, diˈkæl] *n* : calcomanía *f*

decamp [di'kæmp] *vi* **:** irse, largarse *fam*

decant [di'kænt] *vt* **:** decantar

decanter [di'kæntər] *n* **:** licorera *f,* garrafa *f*

decapitate [di'kæpə,teɪt] *vt* **-tated; -tating :** decapitar

decay[1] [di'keɪ] *vi* **1** DECOMPOSE **:** descomponerse, pudrirse **2** DETERIORATE **:** deteriorarse **3 :** cariarse (dícese de los dientes)

decay[2] *n* **1** DECOMPOSITION **:** descomposición *f* **2** DECLINE, DETERIORATION **:** decadencia *f,* deterioro *m* **3 :** caries *f* (de los dientes)

decease[1] [di'siːs] *vi* **-ceased; -ceasing :** morir, fallecer

decease[2] *n* **:** fallecimiento *m,* defunción *f,* deceso *m*

deceit [di'siːt] *n* **1** DECEPTION **:** engaño *m* **2** DISHONESTY **:** deshonestidad *f*

deceitful [di'siːtfəl] *adj* **:** falso, embustero, engañoso, mentiroso

deceitfully [di'siːtfəli] *adv* **:** con engaño, con falsedad

deceitfulness [di'siːtfəlnəs] *n* **:** falsedad *f,* engaño *m*

deceive [di'siːv] *vt* **-ceived; -ceiving :** engañar, burlar

deceiver [di'siːvər] *n* **:** impostor *m,* -tora *f*

decelerate [di'sɛlə,reɪt] *vi* **-ated; -ating :** reducir la velocidad, desacelerar

December [di'sɛmbər] *n* **:** diciembre *m*

decency ['disəntsi] *n, pl* **-cies :** decencia *f,* decoro *m*

decent ['diːsənt] *adj* **1** CORRECT, PROPER **:** decente, decoroso, correcto **2** CLOTHED **:** vestido, presentable **3** MODEST **:** púdico, modesto **4** ADEQUATE **:** decente, adecuado <decent wages : paga adecuada>

decently ['diːsəntli] *adv* **:** decentemente

deception [di'sɛpʃən] *n* **:** engaño *m*

deceptive [di'sɛptɪv] *adj* **:** engañoso, falaz — **deceptively** *adv*

decibel ['dɛsəbəl, -,bɛl] *n* **:** decibelio *m*

decide [di'saɪd] *v* **-cided; -ciding** *vt* **1** CONCLUDE **:** decidir, llegar a la conclusión de <he decided what to do : decidió qué iba a hacer> **2** DETERMINE **:** decidir, determinar <one blow decided the fight : un solo golpe determinó la pelea> **3** CONVINCE **:** decidir <her pleas decided me to help : sus súplicas me decidieron a ayudarla> **4** RESOLVE **:** resolver — *vi* **:** decidirse

decided [di'saɪdəd] *adj* **1** UNQUESTIONABLE **:** indudable **2** RESOLUTE **:** decidido, resuelto — **decidedly** *adv*

deciduous [di'sɪdʒʊəs] *adj* **:** caduco, de hoja caduca

decimal[1] ['dɛsəməl] *adj* **:** decimal

decimal[2] *n* **:** número *m* decimal

decipher [di'saɪfər] *vt* **:** descifrar — **decipherable** [-əbəl] *adj*

decision [dɪ'sɪʒən] *n* **:** decisión *f,* determinación *f* <to make a decision : tomar una decisión>

decisive [dɪ'saɪsɪv] *adj* **1** DECIDING **:** decisivo <the decisive vote : el voto decisivo> **2** CONCLUSIVE **:** decisivo, concluyente, contundente <a decisive victory : una victoria contundente> **3** RESOLUTE **:** decidido, resuelto, firme

decisively [dɪ'saɪsɪvli] *adv* **:** con decisión, de manera decisiva

decisiveness [dɪ'saɪsɪvnəs] *n* **1** FORCEFULNESS **:** contundencia *f* **2** RESOLUTION **:** firmeza *f,* decisión *f,* determinación *f*

deck[1] ['dɛk] *vt* **1** FLOOR **:** tumbar, derribar <she decked him with one blow : lo tumbó de un solo golpe> **2 to deck out :** adornar, engalanar

deck[2] *n* **1 :** cubierta *f* (de un barco) **2** *or* **deck of cards :** baraja *f* (de naipes)

declaim [di'kleɪm] *v* **:** declamar

declaration [,dɛklə'reɪʃən] *n* **:** declaración *f,* pronunciamiento *m* (oficial)

declare [di'klær] *vt* **-clared; -claring :** declarar, manifestar <to declare war : declarar la guerra> <they declared their support : manifestaron su apoyo>

decline[1] [di'klaɪn] *v* **-clined; -clining** *vi* **1** DESCEND **:** descender **2** DETERIORATE **:** deteriorarse, decaer <her health is declining : su salud se está deteriorando> **3** DECREASE **:** disminuir, decrecer, decaer **4** REFUSE **:** rehusar — *vt* **1** INFLECT **:** declinar **2** REFUSE, TURN DOWN **:** declinar, rehusar

decline[2] *n* **1** DETERIORATION **:** decadencia *f,* deterioro *m* **2** DECREASE **:** disminución *f,* descenso *m* **3** SLOPE **:** declive *m,* pendiente *f*

decode [di'koːd] *vt* **-coded; -coding :** descifrar (un mensaje), descodificar (una señal)

decompose [,diːkəm'poːz] *v* **-posed; -posing** *vt* **1** BREAK DOWN **:** descomponer **2** ROT **:** descomponer, pudrir — *vi* **:** descomponerse, pudrirse

decomposition [,diː,kɑmpə'zɪʃən] *n* **:** descomposición *f*

decongestant [,diːkən'dʒɛstənt] *n* **:** descongestionante *m*

decor *or* **décor** [deɪ'kɔr, 'deɪ,kɔr] *n* **:** decoración *f*

decorate ['dɛkə,reɪt] *vt* **-rated; -rating 1** ADORN **:** decorar, adornar **2 :** condecorar <he was decorated for bravery : lo condecoraron por valor>

decoration [,dɛkə'reɪʃən] *n* **1** ADORNMENT **:** decoración *f,* adorno *m* **2 :** condecoración *f* (de honor)

decorative ['dɛkərət̬ɪv, -,reɪ-] *adj* **:** decorativo, ornamental, de adorno

decorator ['dɛkə,reɪt̬ər] *n* **:** decorador *m,* -dora *f*

decorum [di'korəm] *n* **:** decoro *m*

decoy[1] [ˈdiːˌkɔɪ, diˈ-] *vt* : atraer (con señuelo)
decoy[2] *n* : señuelo *m,* reclamo *m,* cimbel *m*
decrease[1] [diˈkriːs] *v* **-creased; -creasing** *vi* : decrecer, disminuir, bajar — *vt* : reducir, disminuir
decrease[2] [ˈdiːˌkriːs] *n* : disminución *f,* descenso *m,* bajada *f*
decree[1] [diˈkriː] *vt* **-creed; -creeing** : decretar
decree[2] *n* : decreto *m*
decrepit [diˈkrɛpɪt] *adj* **1** FEEBLE : decrépito, débil **2** DILAPIDATED : deteriorado, ruinoso
decry [diˈkraɪ] *vt* **-cried; -crying** : censurar, criticar
dedicate [ˈdɛdɪˌkeɪt] *vt* **-cated; -cating 1** : dedicar <she dedicated the book to Carlos : le dedicó el libro a Carlos> **2** : consagrar, dedicar <to dedicate one's life : consagrar uno su vida>
dedication [ˌdɛdɪˈkeɪʃən] *n* **1** DEVOTION : dedicación *f,* devoción *f* **2** : dedicatoria *f* (de un libro, una canción, etc.) **3** CONSECRATION : dedicación *f*
deduce [diˈduːs, -ˈdjuːs] *vt* **-duced; -ducing** : deducir, inferir
deduct [diˈdʌkt] *vt* : deducir, descontar, restar
deductible [diˈdʌktəbəl] *adj* : deducible
deduction [diˈdʌkʃən] *n* : deducción *f*
deed[1] [ˈdiːd] *vt* : ceder, transferir
deed[2] *n* **1** ACT : acto *m,* acción *f,* hecho *m* <a good deed : una buena acción> **2** FEAT : hazaña *f,* proeza *f* **3** TITLE : escritura *f,* título *m*
deem [ˈdiːm] *vt* : considerar, juzgar
deep[1] [ˈdiːp] *adv* : hondo, profundamente <to dig deep : cavar hondo>
deep[2] *adj* **1** : hondo, profundo <the deep end : la parte honda> <a deep wound : una herida profunda> **2** WIDE : ancho **3** INTENSE : profundo, intenso **4** DARK : intenso, subido <deep red : rojo subido> **5** LOW : profundo <a deep tone : un tono profundo> **6** ABSORBED : absorto <deep in thought : absorto en la meditación>
deep[3] *n* **1 the deep** : lo profundo, el piélago **2 the deep of night** : lo más profundo de la noche
deepen [ˈdiːpən] *vt* **1** : ahondar, profundizar **2** INTENSIFY : intensificar — *vi* **1** : hacerse más profundo **2** INTENSIFY : intensificarse
deeply [ˈdiːpli] *adv* : hondo, profundamente <I'm deeply sorry : lo siento sinceramente>
deep–seated [ˈdiːpˈsiːtəd] *adj* : profundamente arraigado, enraizado
deer [ˈdɪr] *ns & pl* : ciervo *m,* venado *m*
deerskin [ˈdɪrˌskɪn] *n* : piel *f* de venado
deface [diˈfeɪs] *vt* **-faced; -facing** MAR : desfigurar
defacement [diˈfeɪsmənt] *n* : desfiguración *f*
defamation [ˌdɛfəˈmeɪʃən] *n* : difamación *f*
defamatory [diˈfæməˌtori] *adj* : difamatorio
defame [diˈfeɪm] *vt* **-famed; -faming** : difamar, calumniar
default[1] [diˈfɔlt, ˈdiːˌfɔlt] *vi* **1** : no cumplir (con una obligación), no pagar **2** : no presentarse (en un tribunal)
default[2] *n* **1** NEGLECT : omisión *f,* negligencia *f* **2** NONPAYMENT : impago *m,* falta *f* de pago **3 to win by default** : ganar por abandono
defaulter [diˈfɔltər] *n* : moroso *m,* -sa *f;* rebelde *mf* (en un tribunal)
defeat[1] [diˈfiːt] *vt* **1** FRUSTRATE : frustrar **2** BEAT : vencer, derrotar
defeat[2] *n* : derrota *f,* rechazo *m* (de legislación), fracaso *m* (de planes, etc.)
defecate [ˈdɛfɪˌkeɪt] *vi* **-cated; -cating** : defecar
defect[1] [diˈfɛkt] *vi* : desertar
defect[2] [ˈdiːˌfɛkt, diˈfɛkt] *n* : defecto *m*
defection [diˈfɛkʃən] *n* : deserción *f,* defección *f*
defective [diˈfɛktɪv] *adj* **1** FAULTY : defectuoso **2** DEFICIENT : deficiente
defector [diˈfɛktər] *n* : desertor *m,* -tora *f*
defend [diˈfɛnd] *vt* : defender
defendant [diˈfɛndənt] *n* : acusado *m,* -da *f;* demandado *m,* -da *f*
defender [diˈfɛndər] *n* **1** ADVOCATE : defensor *m,* -sora *f* **2** : defensa *mf* (en deportes)
defense [diˈfɛnts, ˈdiːˌfɛnts] *n* : defensa *f*
defenseless [diˈfɛntsləs] *adj* : indefenso
defensive[1] [diˈfɛntsɪv] *adj* : defensivo
defensive[2] *n* **on the defensive** : a la defensiva
defer [diˈfər] *v* **-ferred; -ferring** *vt* POSTPONE : diferir, aplazar, posponer — *vi* **to defer to** : deferir a
deference [ˈdɛfərənts] *n* : deferencia *f*
deferential [ˌdɛfəˈrɛntʃəl] *adj* : respetuoso
deferment [diˈfərmənt] *n* : aplazamiento *m*
defiance [diˈfaɪənts] *n* : desafío *m*
defiant [diˈfaɪənt] *adj* : desafiante, insolente
deficiency [diˈfɪʃəntsi] *n, pl* **-cies** : deficiencia *f,* carencia *f*
deficient [diˈfɪʃənt] *adj* : deficiente, carente
deficit [ˈdɛfəsɪt] *n* : déficit *m*
defile [diˈfaɪl] *vt* **-filed; -filing 1** DIRTY : ensuciar, manchar **2** CORRUPT : corromper **3** DESECRATE, PROFANE : profanar **4** DISHONOR : deshonrar
defilement [diˈfaɪlmənt] *n* **1** DESECRATION : profanación *f* **2** CORRUPTION

: corrupción *f* **3** CONTAMINATION : contaminación *f*
define [di'faɪn] *vt* **-fined; -fining 1** BOUND : delimitar, demarcar **2** CLARIFY : aclarar, definir **3** : definir <to define a word : definir una palabra>
definite ['dɛfənɪt] *adj* **1** CERTAIN : definido, determinado **2** CLEAR : claro, explícito **3** UNQUESTIONABLE : seguro, incuestionable
definite article *n* : artículo *m* definido
definitely ['dɛfənɪtli] *adv* **1** DOUBTLESSLY : indudablemente, sin duda **2** DEFINITIVELY : definitivamente, seguramente
definition [ˌdɛfə'nɪʃən] *n* : definición *f*
definitive [di'fɪnət̬ɪv] *adj* **1** CONCLUSIVE : definitivo, decisivo **2** AUTHORITATIVE : de autoridad, autorizado
deflate [di'fleɪt] *v* **-flated; -flating** *vt* **1** : desinflar (una llanta, etc.) **2** REDUCE : rebajar <to deflate one's ego : bajarle los humos a uno> — *vi* : desinflarse
deflect [di'flɛkt] *vt* : desviar — *vi* : desviarse
defoliant [di'foːliənt] *n* : defoliante *m*
deform [di'fɔrm] *vt* : deformar
deformed [di'fɔrmd] *adj* : deforme
deformity [di'fɔrmət̬i] *n, pl* **-ties** : deformidad *f*
defraud [di'frɔd] *vt* : estafar, defraudar
defray [di'freɪ] *vt* : sufragar, costear
defrost [di'frɔst] *vt* : descongelar, deshelar — *vi* : descongelarse, deshelarse
deft ['dɛft] *adj* : hábil, diestro — **deftly** *adv*
defunct [di'fʌŋkt] *adj* **1** DECEASED : difunto, fallecido **2** EXTINCT : extinto, fenecido
defy [di'faɪ] *vt* **-fied; -fying 1** CHALLENGE : desafiar, retar **2** DISOBEY : desobedecer **3** RESIST : resistir, hacer imposible, hacer inútil
degenerate¹ [di'dʒɛnəˌreɪt] *vi* **-ated; -ating** : degenerar
degenerate² [di'dʒɛnərət] *adj* : degenerado
degeneration [diˌdʒɛnə'reɪʃən] *n* : degeneración *f*
degradation [ˌdɛgrə'deɪʃən] *n* : degradación *f*
degrade [di'greɪd] *vt* **-graded; -grading 1** : degradar, envilecer **2 to degrade oneself** : rebajarse
degree [di'griː] *n* **1** EXTENT : grado *m* <a third degree burn : una quemadura de tercer grado> **2** : título *m* (de enseñanza superior) **3** : grado *m* (de un círculo, de la temperatura) **4 by degrees** : gradualmente, poco a poco
dehydrate [di'haɪˌdreɪt] *v* **-drated; -drating** *vt* : deshidratar — *vi* : deshidratarse
dehydration [ˌdiːhaɪ'dreɪʃən] *n* : deshidratación *f*
deice [ˌdiː'aɪs] *vt* **-iced; -icing** : deshelar, descongelar
deify ['diːəˌfaɪ, 'deɪ-] *vt* **-fied; -fying** : deificar
deign ['deɪn] *vi* : dignarse, condescender
deity ['diːət̬i, 'deɪ-] *n, pl* **-ties 1 the Deity** : Dios *m* **2** GOD, GODDESS : deidad *f;* dios *m,* diosa *f*
dejected [di'dʒɛktəd] *adj* : abatido, desalentado, desanimado
dejection [di'dʒɛkʃən] *n* : abatimiento *m,* desaliento *m,* desánimo *m*
delay¹ [di'leɪ] *vt* **1** POSTPONE : posponer, postergar **2** HOLD UP : retrasar, demorar — *vi* : tardar, demorar
delay² *n* **1** LATENESS : tardanza *f* **2** HOLDUP : demora *f,* retraso *m*
delectable [di'lɛktəbəl] *adj* **1** DELICIOUS : delicioso, exquisito **2** DELIGHTFUL : encantador
delegate¹ ['dɛlɪˌgeɪt] *v* **-gated; -gating** : delegar
delegate² ['dɛlɪgət, -ˌgeɪt] *n* : delegado *m,* -da *f*
delegation [ˌdɛlɪ'geɪʃən] *n* : delegación *f*
delete [di'liːt] *vt* **-leted; -leting** : suprimir, tachar, eliminar
deletion [di'liːʃən] *n* : supresión *f,* tachadura *f,* eliminación *f*
deliberate¹ [dɪ'lɪbəˌreɪt] *v* **-ated; -ating** *vt* : deliberar sobre, reflexionar sobre, considerar — *vi* : deliberar
deliberate² [dɪ'lɪbərət] *adj* **1** CONSIDERED : reflexionado, premeditado **2** INTENTIONAL : deliberado, intencional **3** SLOW : lento, pausado
deliberately [dɪ'lɪbərətli] *adv* **1** INTENTIONALLY : adrede, a propósito **2** SLOWLY : pausadamente, lentamente
deliberation [dɪˌlɪbə'reɪʃən] *n* **1** CONSIDERATION : deliberación *f,* consideración *f* **2** SLOWNESS : lentitud *f*
delicacy ['dɛlɪkəsi] *n, pl* **-cies 1** : manjar *m,* exquisitez *f* <caviar is a real delicacy : el caviar es un verdadero manjar> **2** FINENESS : delicadeza *f* **3** FRAGILITY : fragilidad *f*
delicate ['dɛlɪkət] *adj* **1** SUBTLE : delicado <a delicate fragrance : una fragancia delicada> **2** DAINTY : delicado, primoroso, fino **3** FRAGILE : frágil **4** SENSITIVE : delicado <a delicate matter : un asunto delicado>
delicately ['dɛlɪkətli] *adv* : delicadamente, con delicadeza
delicatessen [ˌdɛlɪkə'tɛsən] *n* : charcutería *f,* fiambrería *f,* salchichonería *f Mex*
delicious [di'lɪʃəs] *adj* : delicioso, exquisito, rico — **deliciously** *adv*
delight¹ [dɪ'laɪt] *vt* : deleitar, encantar — *vi* **to delight in** : deleitarse con, complacerse en
delight² *n* **1** JOY : placer *m,* deleite *m,* gozo *m* **2** : encanto *m* <your garden is a delight : su jardín es un encanto>

delightful [dɪˈlaɪtfəl] *adj* : delicioso, encantador

delightfully [dɪˈlaɪtfəli] *adv* : de manera encantadora, de maravilla

delineate [diˈlɪni͵eɪt] *vt* **-eated; -eating** : delinear, trazar, bosquejar

delinquency [diˈlɪŋkwən*t*si] *n, pl* **-cies** : delincuencia *f*

delinquent[1] [diˈlɪŋkwənt] *adj* **1** : delincuente **2** OVERDUE : vencido y sin pagar, moroso

delinquent[2] *n* : delincuente *mf* <juvenile delinquent : delincuente juvenil>

delirious [diˈlɪriəs] *adj* : delirante <delirious with joy : loco de alegría>

delirium [diˈlɪriəm] *n* : delirio *m,* desvarío *m*

deliver [diˈlɪvər] *vt* **1** FREE : liberar, librar **2** DISTRIBUTE, HAND : entregar, repartir **3** : asistir en el parto de (un niño) **4** : pronunciar <to deliver a speech : pronunciar un discurso> **5** PROJECT : despachar, lanzar <he delivered a fast ball : lanzó un pelota rápida> **6** DEAL : propinar, asestar <to deliver a blow : asestar un golpe>

deliverance [diˈlɪvərən*t*s] *n* : liberación *f,* rescate *m,* salvación *f*

deliverer [diˈlɪvərər] *n* RESCUER : libertador *m,* -dora *f;* salvador *m,* -dora *f*

delivery [diˈlɪvəri] *n, pl* **-eries 1** LIBERATION : liberación *f* **2** : entrega *f,* reparto *m* <cash on delivery : entrega contra reembolso> <home delivery : servicio a domicilio> **3** CHILDBIRTH : parto *m,* alumbramiento *m* **4** SPEECH : expresión *f* oral, modo *m* de hablar **5** THROW : lanzamiento *m*

dell [ˈdɛl] *n* : hondonada *f,* valle *m* pequeño

delta [ˈdɛltə] *n* : delta *m*

delude [diˈluːd] *vt* **-luded; -luding 1** : engañar **2 to delude oneself** : engañarse

deluge[1] [ˈdɛl͵juːdʒ, -͵juːʒ] *vt* **-uged; -uging 1** FLOOD : inundar **2** OVERWHELM : abrumar <deluged with requests : abrumado de pedidos>

deluge[2] *n* **1** FLOOD : inundación *f* **2** DOWNPOUR : aguacero *m* **3** BARRAGE : aluvión *m*

delusion [diˈluːʒən] *n* **1** : ilusión *f* (falsa) **2 delusions of grandeur** : delirios *mpl* de grandeza

deluxe [diˈlʌks, -ˈlʊks] *adj* : de lujo

delve [ˈdɛlv] *vi* **delved; delving 1** DIG : escarbar **2 to delve into** PROBE : cavar en, ahondar en

demand[1] [diˈmænd] *vt* : demandar, exigir, reclamar

demand[2] *n* **1** REQUEST : petición *f,* pedido *m,* demanda *f* <by popular demand : a petición del público> **2** CLAIM : reclamación *f,* exigencia *f* **3** MARKET : demanda *f* <supply and demand : la oferta y la demanda>

demarcation [͵diː͵mɑrˈkeɪʃən] *n* : demarcación *f,* deslinde *m*

demean [diˈmiːn] *vt* : degradar, rebajar

demeanor [diˈmiːnər] *n* : comportamiento *m,* conducta *f*

demented [diˈmɛntəd] *adj* : demente, loco

demerit [diˈmɛrət] *n* : demérito *m*

demigod [ˈdɛmi͵gɑd, -͵gɔd] *n* : semidiós *m*

demise [dɪˈmaɪz] *n* **1** DEATH : fallecimiento *m,* deceso *m* **2** END : hundimiento *m,* desaparición *f* (de una institución, etc.)

demitasse [ˈdɛmi͵tæs, -͵tɑs] *n* : taza *f* pequeña (de café)

demobilization [di͵moːbələˈzeɪʃən] *n* : desmovilización *f*

demobilize [diˈmoːbə͵laɪz] *vt* **-lized; -lizing** : desmovilizar

democracy [diˈmɑkrəsi] *n, pl* **-cies** : democracia *f*

democrat [ˈdɛmə͵kræt] *n* : demócrata *mf*

democratic [͵dɛməˈkræt̬ɪk] *adj* : democrático — **democratically** [-t̬ɪkli] *adv*

demolish [diˈmɑlɪʃ] *vt* **1** RAZE : demoler, derribar, arrasar **2** DESTROY : destruir, destrozar

demolition [͵dɛməˈlɪʃən, ͵diː-] *n* : demolición *f,* derribo *m*

demon [ˈdiːmən] *n* : demonio *m,* diablo *m*

demonstrably [diˈmɑn*t*strəbli] *adv* : manifiestamente, claramente

demonstrate [ˈdɛmən͵streɪt] *vt* **-strated; -strating 1** SHOW : demostrar **2** PROVE : probar, demostrar **3** EXPLAIN : explicar, ilustrar

demonstration [͵dɛmənˈstreɪʃən] *n* **1** SHOW : muestra *f,* demostración *f* **2** RALLY : manifestación *f*

demonstrative [diˈmɑn*t*strət̬ɪv] *adj* **1** EFFUSIVE : efusivo, expresivo, demostrativo **2** : demostrativo (en lingüística) <demonstrative pronoun : pronombre demostrativo>

demonstrator [ˈdɛmən͵streɪt̬ər] *n* **1** : demostrador *m,* -dora *f* (de productos) **2** PROTESTER : manifestante *mf*

demoralize [diˈmɔrə͵laɪz] *vt* **-ized; -izing** : desmoralizar

demote [diˈmoːt] *vt* **-moted; -moting** : degradar, bajar de categoría

demotion [diˈmoːʃən] *n* : degradación *f,* descenso *m* de categoría

demur [diˈmər] *vi* **-murred; -murring 1** OBJECT : oponerse **2 to demur at** : ponerle objeciones a (algo)

demure [diˈmjʊr] *adj* : recatado, modesto — **demurely** *adv*

den [ˈdɛn] *n* **1** LAIR : cubil *m,* madriguera *f* **2** HIDEOUT : guarida *f* **3** STUDY : estudio *m,* gabinete *m*

denature [diˈneɪtʃər] *vt* **-tured; -turing** : desnaturalizar

denial [diˈnaɪəl] *n* **1** REFUSAL : rechazo *m,* denegación *f,* negativa *f* **2** REPUDIATION : negación *f* (de una creencia, etc.), rechazo *m*

denim [ˈdɛnəm] *n* **1 :** tela *f* vaquera, mezclilla *f Chile, Mex* **2 denims** *npl* → **jeans**

denizen [ˈdɛnəzən] *n* **:** habitante *mf;* morador *m,* -dora *f*

denomination [dɪˌnɑməˈneɪʃən] *n* **1** FAITH **:** confesión *f,* fe *f* **2** VALUE **:** denominación *f,* valor *m* (de una moneda)

denominator [dɪˈnɑməˌneɪt̬ər] *n* **:** denominador *m*

denote [diˈnoːt] *vt* **-noted; -noting 1** INDICATE, MARK **:** indicar, denotar, señalar **2** MEAN **:** significar

denouement [ˌdeɪˌnuːˈmɑ] *n* **:** desenlace *m*

denounce [diˈnaʊnts] *vt* **-nounced; -nouncing 1** CENSURE **:** denunciar, censurar **2** ACCUSE **:** denunciar, acusar, delatar

dense [ˈdɛnts] *adj* **denser; -est 1** THICK **:** espeso, denso <dense vegetation : vegetación densa> <a dense fog : una niebla espesa> **2** STUPID **:** estúpido, burro *fam*

densely [ˈdɛntsli] *adv* **1** THICKLY **:** densamente **2** STUPIDLY **:** torpemente

denseness [ˈdɛntsnəs] *n* **1** → **density 2** STUPIDITY **:** estupidez *f*

density [ˈdɛntsət̬i] *n, pl* **-ties :** densidad *f*

dent[1] [ˈdɛnt] *vt* **:** abollar, mellar

dent[2] *n* **:** abolladura *f,* mella *f*

dental [ˈdɛntəl] *adj* **:** dental

dental floss *n* **:** hilo *m* dental

dentifrice [ˈdɛntəfrɪs] *n* **:** dentífrico *m,* pasta *f* de dientes

dentist [ˈdɛntɪst] *n* **:** dentista *mf*

dentistry [ˈdɛntɪstri] *n* **:** odontología *f*

dentures [ˈdɛntʃərz] *npl* **:** dentadura *f* postiza

denude [diˈnuːd, -ˈnjuːd] *vt* **-nuded; -nuding** STRIP **:** desnudar, despojar

denunciation [diˌnʌntsiˈeɪʃən] *n* **:** denuncia *f,* acusación *f*

deny [diˈnaɪ] *vt* **-nied; -nying 1** REFUTE **:** desmentir, negar **2** DISOWN, REPUDIATE **:** negar, renegar de **3** REFUSE **:** denegar **4 to deny oneself :** privarse, sacrificarse

deodorant [diˈoːdərənt] *n* **:** desodorante *m*

deodorize [diˈoːdəˌraɪz] *vt* **-ized; -izing :** desodorizar

depart [diˈpɑrt] *vt* **:** salirse de — *vi* **1** LEAVE **:** salir, partir, irse **2** DIE **:** morir

department [diˈpɑrtmənt] *n* **1** DIVISION **:** sección *f* (de una tienda, una organización, etc.), departamento *m* (de una empresa, una universidad, etc.), ministerio *m* (del gobierno) **2** PROVINCE, SPHERE **:** esfera *f,* campo *m,* competencia *f*

departmental [diˌpɑrtˈmɛntəl, ˌdiː-] *adj* **:** departamental

department store *n* **:** grandes almacenes *mpl*

departure [diˈpɑrtʃər] *n* **1** LEAVING **:** salida *f,* partida *f* **2** DEVIATION **:** desviación *f*

depend [diˈpɛnd] *vi* **1** RELY **:** contar (con), confiar (en) <depend on me! : ¡cuenta conmigo!> **2 to depend on :** depender de <success depends on hard work : el éxito depende de trabajar duro> **3 that depends :** según, eso depende

dependable [diˈpɛndəbəl] *adj* **:** responsable, digno de confianza, fiable

dependence [diˈpɛndənts] *n* **:** dependencia *f*

dependency [diˈpɛndəntsi] *n, pl* **-cies 1** → **dependence 2 :** posesión *f* (de una unidad política)

dependent[1] [diˈpɛndənt] *adj* **:** dependiente

dependent[2] *n* **:** persona *f* a cargo de alguien

depict [diˈpɪkt] *vt* **1** PORTRAY **:** representar **2** DESCRIBE **:** describir

depiction [diˈpɪkʃən] *n* **:** representación *f,* descripción *f*

deplete [diˈpliːt] *vt* **-pleted; -pleting 1** EXHAUST **:** agotar **2** REDUCE **:** reducir

depletion [diˈpliːʃən] *n* **1** EXHAUSTION **:** agotamiento *m* **2** REDUCTION **:** reducción *f,* disminución *f*

deplorable [diˈplorəbəl] *adj* **1** CONTEMPTIBLE **:** deplorable, despreciable **2** LAMENTABLE **:** lamentable

deplore [diˈplor] *vt* **-plored; -ploring 1** REGRET **:** deplorar, lamentar **2** CONDEMN **:** condenar, deplorar

deploy [diˈplɔɪ] *vt* **:** desplegar

deployment [diˈplɔɪmənt] *n* **:** despliegue *m*

deport [diˈport] *vt* **1** EXPEL **:** deportar, expulsar (de un país) **2 to deport oneself** BEHAVE **:** comportarse

deportment [diˈportmənt] *n* **:** conducta *f,* comportamiento *f*

depose [diˈpoːz] *v* **-posed; -posing** *vt* **:** deponer

deposit[1] [diˈpɑzət] *vt* **-ited; -iting :** depositar

deposit[2] *n* **1 :** depósito *m* (en el banco) **2** DOWN PAYMENT **:** entrega *f* inicial **3 :** depósito *m,* yacimiento *m* (en geología)

depositor [diˈpɑzət̬ər] *n* **:** depositante *mf*

depository [diˈpɑzəˌtori] *n, pl* **-ries :** almacén *m,* depósito *m*

depot [*in sense 1 usu* ˈdɛˌpoː, *2 usu* ˈdiː-] *n* **1** STOREHOUSE **:** almacén *m,* depósito *m* **2** STATION, TERMINAL **:** terminal *mf,* estación *f* (de autobuses, ferrocarriles, etc.)

deprave [diˈpreɪv] *vt* **-praved; -praving :** depravar, pervertir

depraved [diˈpreɪvd] *adj* **:** depravado, degenerado

depravity [diˈprævət̬i] *n, pl* **-ties :** depravación *f*

depreciate [diˈpriːʃiˌeɪt] *v* **-ated; -ating** *vt* **1** DEVALUE **:** depreciar, devaluar 2 DISPARAGE : menospreciar, despreciar — *vi* : depreciarse, devaluarse

depreciation [di,priːʃi'eɪʃən] *n* : depreciación *f,* devaluación *f*

depress [di'prɛs] *vt* **1** PRESS, PUSH : apretar, presionar, pulsar **2** REDUCE : reducir, hacer bajar (precios, ventas, etc.) **3** SADDEN : deprimir, abatir, entristecer **4** DEVALUE : depreciar

depressant[1] [di'prɛsənt] *adj* : depresivo

depressant[2] *n* : depresivo *m*

depressed [di'prɛst] *adj* **1** DEJECTED : deprimido, abatido **2** : deprimido, en crisis (dícese de la economía)

depressing [di'prɛsɪŋ] *adj* : deprimente, triste

depression [di'prɛʃən] *n* **1** DESPONDENCY : depresión *f,* abatimiento *m* **2** : depresión (en una superficie) **3** RECESSION : depresión *f* económica, crisis *f*

deprivation [,dɛprə'veɪʃən] *n* : privación *f*

deprive [di'praɪv] *vt* **-prived; -priving** : privar

depth ['dɛpθ] *n, pl* **depths** ['dɛpθs, 'dɛps] : profundidad *f,* fondo *m* <to study in depth : estudiar a fondo> <in the depths of winter : en pleno invierno>

deputize ['dɛpjʊ,taɪz] *vt* **-tized; -tizing** : nombrar como segundo

deputy ['dɛpjʊti] *n, pl* **-ties** : suplente *mf;* sustituto *m,* -ta *f*

derail [di'reɪl] *v* : descarrilar

derailment [di'reɪlmənt] *n* : descarrilamiento *m*

derange [di'reɪndʒ] *vt* **-ranged; -ranging 1** DISARRANGE : desarreglar, desordenar **2** DISTURB, UPSET : trastornar, perturbar **3** MADDEN : enloquecer, volver loco

derangement [di'reɪndʒmənt] *n* **1** DISTURBANCE, UPSET : trastorno *m* **2** INSANITY : locura *f,* perturbación *f* mental

derby ['dərbi] *n, pl* **-bies 1** : derby *m* <the Kentucky Derby : el Derby de Kentucky> **2** : sombrero *m* hongo

deregulate [di'rɛgjʊ,leɪt] *vt* **-lated; -lating** : desregular

deregulation [di,rɛgjʊ'leɪʃən] *n* : desregularización *f*

derelict[1] ['dɛrə,lɪkt] *adj* **1** ABANDONED : abandonado, en ruinas **2** REMISS : negligente, remiso

derelict[2] *n* **1** : propiedad *f* abandonada **2** VAGRANT : vagabundo *m,* -da *f*

deride [di'raɪd] *vt* **-rided; -riding** : ridiculizar, burlarse de

derision [di'rɪʒən] *n* : escarnio *m,* irrisión *f,* mofa *f*

derisive [di'raɪsɪv] *adj* : burlón

derivative[1] [di'rɪvət̬ɪv] *adj* **1** DERIVED : derivado **2** BANAL : carente de originalidad, banal

derivative[2] *n* : derivado *m*

derive [di'raɪv] *v* **-rived; -riving** *vt* **1** OBTAIN : obtener, sacar **2** DEDUCE : deducir, inferir — *vi* : provenir, derivar, proceder

dermatologist [,dərmə'tɑlədʒɪst] *n* : dermatólogo *m,* -ga *f*

dermatology [,dərmə'tɑlədʒi] *n* : dermatología *f*

derogatory [di'rɑgə,tori] *adj* : despectivo, despreciativo

derrick ['dɛrɪk] *n* **1** CRANE : grúa *f* **2** : torre *f* de perforación (sobre un pozo de petróleo)

descend [di'sɛnd] *vt* : descender, bajar — *vi* **1** : descender, bajar <he descended from the platform : descendió del estrado> **2** DERIVE : descender, provenir **3** STOOP : rebajarse <I descended to his level : me rebajé a su nivel> **4 to descend upon** : caer sobre, invadir

descendant[1] [di'sɛndənt] *adj* : descendente

descendant[2] *n* : descendiente *mf*

descent [di'sɛnt] *n* **1** : bajada *f,* descenso *m* <the descent from the mountain : el descenso de la montaña> **2** ANCESTRY : ascendencia *f,* linaje *f* **3** SLOPE : pendiente *f,* cuesta *f* **4** FALL : caída *f* **5** ATTACK : incursión *f,* ataque *m*

describe [di'skraɪb] *vt* **-scribed; -scribing** : describir

description [di'skrɪpʃən] *n* : descripción *f*

descriptive [di'skrɪptɪv] *adj* : descriptivo <descriptive adjective : adjetivo calificativo>

desecrate ['dɛsɪ,kreɪt] *vt* **-crated; -crating** : profanar

desecration [,dɛsɪ'kreɪʃən] *n* : profanación *f*

desegregate [di'sɛgrə,geɪt] *vt* **-gated; -gating** : eliminar la segregación racial de

desegregation [di,sɛgrə'geɪʃən] *n* : eliminación *f* de la segregación racial

desert[1] [di'zərt] *vt* : abandonar (una persona o un lugar), desertar de (una causa, etc.) — *vi* : desertar

desert[2] ['dɛzərt] *adj* : desierto <a desert island : una isla desierta>

desert[3] *n* **1** ['dɛzərt] : desierto *m* (en geografía) **2** [di'zərt] → **deserts**

deserter [di'zərt̬ər] *n* : desertor *m,* -tora *f*

desertion [di'zərʃən] *n* : abandono *m,* deserción *f* (militar)

deserts [di'zərts] *npl* : merecido *m* <to get one's just deserts : llevarse uno su merecido>

deserve [di'zərv] *vt* **-served; -serving** : merecer, ser digno de

desiccate ['dɛsɪ,keɪt] *vt* **-cated; -cating** : desecar, deshidratar

design[1] [di'zaɪn] *vt* **1** DEVISE : diseñar, concebir, idear **2** PLAN : proyectar **3** SKETCH : trazar, bosquejar

design[2] *n* **1** PLAN, SCHEME : plan *m,* proyecto *m* <by design : a propósito, intencionalmente> **2** SKETCH : diseño *m,* bosquejo *m* **3** PATTERN, STYLE : diseño *m,* estilo *m* **4 designs** *npl* INTENTIONS : propósitos *mpl,* designios *mpl*

designate [ˈdɛzɪg,neɪt] *vt* **-nated; -nating 1** INDICATE, SPECIFY : indicar, especificar **2** APPOINT : nombrar, designar

designation [,dɛzɪgˈneɪʃən] *n* **1** NAMING : designación *f* **2** NAME : denominación *f,* nombre *m* **3** APPOINTMENT : designación *f,* nombramiento *m*

designer [diˈzaɪnər] *n* : diseñador *m,* -dora *f*

desirability [di,zaɪrəˈbɪləti] *n, pl* **-ties 1** ADVISABILITY : conveniencia *f* **2** ATTRACTIVENESS : atractivo *m*

desirable [diˈzaɪrəbəl] *adj* **1** ADVISABLE : conveniente, aconsejable **2** ATTRACTIVE : deseable, atractivo

desire[1] [diˈzaɪr] *vt* **-sired; -siring 1** WANT : desear **2** REQUEST : rogar, solicitar

desire[2] *n* : deseo *m,* anhelo *m,* ansia *m*

desist [diˈsɪst, -ˈzɪst] *vi* **to desist from** : desistir de, abstenerse de

desk [ˈdɛsk] *n* : escritorio *m,* pupitre *m* (en la escuela)

desolate[1] [ˈdɛsə,leɪt, -zə-] *vt* **-lated; -lating** : devastar, desolar

desolate[2] [ˈdɛsələt, -zə-] *adj* **1** BARREN : desolado, desierto, yermo **2** DISCONSOLATE : desconsolado, desolado

desolation [,dɛsəˈleɪʃən, -zə-] *n* : desolación *f*

despair[1] [diˈspær] *vi* : desesperar, perder las esperanzas

despair[2] *n* : desesperación *f,* desesperanza *f*

desperate [ˈdɛspərət] *adj* **1** HOPELESS : desesperado, sin esperanzas **2** RASH : desesperado, precipitado **3** SERIOUS, URGENT : grave, urgente, apremiante <a desperate need : una necesidad apremiante>

desperately [ˈdɛspərətli] *adv* : desesperadamente, urgentemente

desperation [,dɛspəˈreɪʃən] *n* : desesperación *f*

despicable [diˈspɪkəbəl, ˈdɛspɪ-] *adj* : vil, despreciable, infame

despise [diˈspaɪz] *vt* **-spised; -spising** : despreciar

despite [dəˈspaɪt] *prep* : a pesar de, aún con

despoil [diˈspɔɪl] *vt* : saquear

despondency [diˈspɑndəntsi] *n* : desaliento *m,* desánimo *m,* depresión *f*

despondent [diˈspɑndənt] *adj* : desalentado, desanimado

despot [ˈdɛspət, -,pɑt] *n* : déspota *mf;* tirano *m,* -na *f*

despotic [dɛsˈpɑtɪk] *adj* : despótico

despotism [ˈdɛspə,tɪzəm] *n* : despotismo *m*

dessert [diˈzərt] *n* : postre *m*

destination [,dɛstəˈneɪʃən] *n* : destino *m,* destinación *f*

destined [ˈdɛstənd] *adj* **1** FATED : predestinado **2** BOUND : destinado, con destino (a), con rumbo (a)

destiny [ˈdɛstəni] *n, pl* **-nies** : destino *m*

destitute [ˈdɛstə,tuːt, -,tjuːt] *adj* **1** LACKING : carente, desprovisto **2** POOR : indigente, en miseria

destitution [,dɛstəˈtuːʃən, -ˈtjuː-] *n* : indigencia *f,* miseria *f*

destroy [diˈstrɔɪ] *vt* **1** KILL : matar **2** DEMOLISH : destruir, destrozar

destroyer [diˈstrɔɪər] *n* : destructor *m* (buque)

destructible [diˈstrʌktəbəl] *adj* : destructible

destruction [diˈstrʌkʃən] *n* : destrucción *f,* ruina *f*

destructive [diˈstrʌktɪv] *adj* : destructor, destructivo

desultory [ˈdɛsəl,tori] *adj* **1** AIMLESS : sin rumbo, sin objeto **2** DISCONNECTED : inconexo

detach [diˈtætʃ] *vt* : separar, quitar, desprender

detached [diˈtætʃt] *adj* **1** SEPARATE : separado, suelto **2** ALOOF : distante, indiferente **3** IMPARTIAL : imparcial, objetivo

detachment [diˈtætʃmənt] *n* **1** SEPARATION : separación *f* **2** DETAIL : destacamento *m* (de tropas) **3** ALOOFNESS : reserva *f,* indiferencia *f* **4** IMPARTIALITY : imparcialidad *f*

detail[1] [diˈteɪl, ˈdiː,teɪl] *vt* : detallar, exponer en detalle

detail[2] *n* **1** : detalle *m,* pormenor *m* **2** : destacamento *m* (de tropas)

detailed [diˈteɪld, ˈdiː,teɪld] *adj* : detallado, minucioso

detain [diˈteɪn] *vt* **1** HOLD : detener **2** DELAY : entretener, demorar, retrasar

detect [diˈtɛkt] *vt* : detectar, descubrir

detection [diˈtɛkʃən] *n* : descubrimiento *m*

detective [diˈtɛktɪv] *n* : detective *mf* <private detective : detective privado>

detention [diˈtɛntʃən] *n* : detención *m*

deter [diˈtər] *vt* **-terred; -terring** : disuadir, impedir

detergent [diˈtərdʒənt] *n* : detergente *m*

deteriorate [diˈtɪriə,reɪt] *vi* **-rated; -rating** : deteriorarse, empeorar

deterioration [di,tɪriəˈreɪʃən] *n* : deterioro *m,* empeoramiento *m*

determination [dɪ,tərməˈneɪʃən] *n* **1** DECISION : determinación *f,* decisión *f* **2** RESOLUTION : resolución *f,* determinación *f* <with grim determination : con una firme resolución>

determine [diˈtərmən] *vt* **-mined; -mining 1** ESTABLISH : determinar, establecer **2** SETTLE : decidir **3** FIND OUT : averiguar **4** BRING ABOUT : determinar

determined [di'tərmənd] *adj* RESOLUTE : decidido, resuelto
deterrent [di'tərənt] *n* : medida *f* disuasiva
detest [di'tɛst] *vt* : detestar, odiar, aborrecer
detestable [di'tɛstəbəl] *adj* : detestable, odioso, aborrecible
dethrone [di'θro:n] *vt* **-throned; -throning** : destronar
detonate ['dɛtən,eɪt] *v* **-nated; -nating** *vt* : hacer detonar — *vi* : detonar, estallar
detonator ['dɛtən,eɪt̬ər] *n* : detonador *m*
detour[1] ['di:,tʊr, di'tʊr] *vi* : desviarse
detour[2] *n* : desvío *m,* rodeo *m*
detract [di'trækt] *vi* **to detract from** : restarle valor a, quitarle méritos a
detriment ['dɛtrəmənt] *n* : detrimento *m,* perjuicio *m*
detrimental [,dɛtrə'mɛntəl] *adj* : perjudicial — **detrimentally** *adv*
devaluation [di,væljʊ'eɪʃən] *n* : devaluación *f*
devalue [di'væl,ju:] *vt* **-ued; -uing** : devaluar, depreciar
devastate ['dɛvə,steɪt] *vt* **-tated; -tating** : devastar, arrasar, asolar
devastation [,dɛvə'steɪʃən] *n* : devastación *f,* estragos *mpl*
develop [di'vɛləp] *vt* **1** FORM, MAKE : desarrollar, elaborar, formar **2** : revelar (en fotografía) **3** FOSTER : desarrollar, fomentar **4** EXPLOIT : explotar (recursos), urbanizar (un área) **5** ACQUIRE : adquirir <to develop an interest : adquirir un interés> **6** CONTRACT : contraer (una enfermedad) — *vi* **1** GROW : desarrollarse **2** ARISE : aparecer, surgir
developed [di'vɛləpt] *adj* : avanzado, desarrollado
development [di'vɛləpmənt] *n* **1** : desarrollo *m* <physical development : desarrollo físico> **2** : urbanización *f* (de un área), explotación *f* (de recursos), creación *f* (de inventos) **3** EVENT : acontecimiento *m,* suceso *m* <to await developments : esperar acontecimientos>
deviant ['di:viənt] *adj* : desviado, anormal
deviate ['di:vi,eɪt] *v* **-ated; -ating** *vi* : desviarse, apartarse — *vt* : desviar
deviation [,di:vi'eɪʃən] *n* : desviación *f*
device [di'vaɪs] *n* **1** MECHANISM : dispositivo *m,* aparato *m,* mecanismo *m* **2** EMBLEM : emblema *m*
devil[1] ['dɛvəl] *vt* **-iled** *or* **-illed; -iling** *or* **-illing 1** : sazonar con picante y especias **2** PESTER : molestar
devil[2] *n* **1** SATAN : el diablo, Satanás *m* **2** DEMON : diablo *m,* demonio *m* **3** FIEND : persona *f* diabólica; malvado *m,* -da *f*
devilish ['dɛvəlɪʃ] *adj* : diabólico
devilry ['dɛvəlri] *n, pl* **-ries** : diabluras *fpl,* travesuras *fpl*
devious ['di:viəs] *adj* **1** CRAFTY : taimado, artero **2** WINDING : tortuoso, sinuoso
devise [di'vaɪz] *vt* **-vised; -vising 1** INVENT : idear, concebir, inventar **2** PLOT : tramar
devoid [di'vɔɪd] *adj* **~ of** : carente de, desprovisto de
devote [di'vo:t] *vt* **-voted; -voting 1** DEDICATE : consagrar, dedicar <to devote one's life : dedicar uno su vida> **2 to devote oneself** : dedicarse
devoted [di'vo:t̬əd] *adj* **1** FAITHFUL : leal, fiel **2 to be devoted to someone** : tenerle mucho cariño a alguien
devotee [,dɛvə'ti:, -'teɪ] *n* : devoto *m,* -ta *f*
devotion [di'vo:ʃən] *n* **1** DEDICATION : dedicación *f,* devoción *f* **2 devotions** PRAYERS : oraciones *fpl,* devociones *fpl*
devour [di'vaʊər] *vt* : devorar
devout [di'vaʊt] *adj* **1** PIOUS : devoto, piadoso **2** EARNEST, SINCERE : sincero, ferviente — **devoutly** *adv*
devoutness [di'vaʊtnəs] *n* : devoción *f,* piedad *f*
dew ['du:, 'dju:] *n* : rocío *m*
dewlap ['du,læp, 'dju-] *n* : papada *f*
dew point *n* : punto *m* de condensación
dewy ['du:i, 'dju:i] *adj* **dewier; -est** : cubierto de rocío
dexterity [dɛk'stɛrət̬i] *n, pl* **-ties** : destreza *f,* habilidad *f*
dexterous ['dɛkstrəs] *adj* : diestro, hábil
dexterously ['dɛkstrəsli] *adv* : con destreza, con habilidad, hábilmente
dextrose ['dɛk,stro:s] *n* : dextrosa *f*
diabetes [,daɪə'bi:t̬iz] *n* : diabetes *f*
diabetic[1] [,daɪə'bɛt̬ɪk] *adj* : diabético
diabetic[2] *n* : diabético *m,* -ca *f*
diabolic [,daɪə'bɑlɪk] *or* **diabolical** [-lɪkəl] *adj* : diabólico, satánico
diacritical mark [,daɪə'krɪt̬ɪkəl] *n* : signo *m* diacrítico
diadem ['daɪə,dɛm, -dəm] *n* : diadema *f*
diagnose ['daɪɪg,no:s, ,daɪɪg'no:s] *vt* **-nosed; -nosing** : diagnosticar
diagnosis [,daɪɪg'no:sɪs] *n, pl* **-noses** [-'no:,si:z] : diagnóstico *m*
diagnostic [,daɪɪg'nɑstɪk] *adj* : diagnóstico
diagonal[1] [daɪ'ægənəl] *adj* : diagonal, en diagonal
diagonal[2] *n* : diagonal *f*
diagonally [daɪ'ægənəli] *adv* : diagonalmente, en diagonal
diagram[1] ['daɪə,græm] *vt* **-gramed** *or* **-grammed; -graming** *or* **-gramming** : hacer un diagrama de
diagram[2] *n* : diagrama *m,* gráfico *m,* esquema *m*
dial[1] ['daɪl] *v* **dialed** *or* **dialled; dialing** *or* **dialling** : marcar, discar

dial[2] *n* : esfera *f* (de un reloj), dial *m* (de un radio), disco *m* (de un teléfono)
dialect ['daɪəˌlɛkt] *n* : dialecto *m*
dialogue ['daɪəˌlɔg] *n* : diálogo *m*
diameter [daɪ'æmət̬ər] *n* : diámetro *m*
diamond ['daɪmənd, 'daɪə-] *n* **1** : diamante *m,* brillante *m* <a diamond necklace : un collar de brillantes> **2** : rombo *m,* forma *f* de rombo **3** : diamante *m* (en naipes) **4** INFIELD : cuadro *m,* diamante *m* (en béisbol)
diaper ['daɪpər, 'daɪə-] *n* : pañal *m*
diaphragm ['daɪəˌfræm] *n* : diafragma *m*
diarrhea [ˌdaɪə'riːə] *n* : diarrea *f*
diary ['daɪəri] *n, pl* **-ries:** diario *m*
diatribe ['daɪəˌtraɪb] *n* : diatriba *f*
dice[1] ['daɪs] *vt* **diced; dicing** : cortar en cubos
dice[2] *ns & pl* **1** → **die**[2] **2** : dados *mpl* (juego)
dicker ['dɪkər] *vt* : regatear
dictate[1] ['dɪkˌteɪt, dɪk'teɪt] *v* **-tated; -tating** *vt* **1** : dictar <to dictate a letter : dictar una carta> **2** ORDER : mandar, ordenar — *vi* : dar órdenes
dictate[2] ['dɪkˌteɪt] *n* **1** : mandato *m,* orden *f* **2 dictates** *npl* : dictados *mpl* <the dictates of conscience : los dictados de la conciencia>
dictation [dɪk'teɪʃən] *n* : dictado *m*
dictator ['dɪkˌteɪt̬ər] *n* : dictador *m,* -dora *f*
dictatorial [ˌdɪktə'toriəl] *adj* : dictatorial — **dictatorially** *adv*
dictatorship [dɪk'teɪt̬ərˌʃɪp, 'dɪkˌ-] *n* : dictadura *f*
diction ['dɪkʃən] *n* **1** : lenguaje *m,* estilo *m* **2** ENUNCIATION : dicción *f,* articulación *f*
dictionary ['dɪkʃəˌnɛri] *n, pl* **-naries** : diccionario *m*
did → **do**
didactic [daɪ'dæktɪk] *adj* : didáctico
die[1] ['daɪ] *vi* **died** ['daɪd]; **dying** ['daɪɪŋ] **1** : morir **2** CEASE : morir, morirse <a dying civilization : una civilización moribunda> **3** STOP : apagarse, dejar de funcionar <the motor died : el motor se apagó> **4 to die down** SUBSIDE : amainar, disminuir **5 to die out** : extinguirse **6 to be dying for** *or* **to be dying to** : morirse por <I'm dying to leave : me muero por irme>
die[2] ['daɪ] *n, pl* **dice** ['daɪs] : dado *m*
die[3] *n, pl* **dies** ['daɪz] **1** STAMP : troquel *m,* cuño *m* **2** MOLD : matriz *f,* molde *m*
diesel ['diːzəl, -səl] *n* : diesel *m*
diet[1] ['daɪət] *vi* : ponerse a régimen, hacer dieta
diet[2] *n* : régimen *m,* dieta *f*
dietary ['daɪəˌtɛri] *adj* : alimenticio, dietético
dietitian *or* **dietician** [ˌdaɪə'tɪʃən] *n* : dietista *mf*
differ ['dɪfər] *vi* **-ferred; -ferring 1** : diferir, diferenciarse **2** VARY : variar **3** DISAGREE : discrepar, diferir, no estar de acuerdo
difference ['dɪfrənts, 'dɪfərənts] *n* : diferencia *f*
different ['dɪfrənt, 'dɪfərənt] *adj* : distinto, diferente
differentiate [ˌdɪfə'rɛntʃiˌeɪt] *v* **-ated; -ating** *vt* **1** : hacer diferente **2** DISTINGUISH : distinguir, diferenciar — *vi* : distinguir
differentiation [ˌdɪfəˌrɛntʃi'eɪʃən] *n* : diferenciación *f*
differently ['dɪfrəntli, 'dɪfərənt-] *adv* : de otra manera, de otro modo, distintamente
difficult ['dɪfɪˌkʌlt] *adj* : difícil
difficulty ['dɪfɪˌkʌlti] *n, pl* **-ties 1** : dificultad *f* **2** PROBLEM : problema *f,* dificultad *f*
diffidence ['dɪfədənts] *n* **1** SHYNESS : retraimiento *m,* timidez *f,* apocamiento *m* **2** RETICENCE : reticencia *f*
diffident ['dɪfədənt] *adj* **1** SHY : tímido, apocado, inseguro **2** RESERVED : reservado
diffuse[1] [dɪ'fjuːz] *v* **-fused; -fusing** *vt* : difundir, esparcir — *vi* : difundirse, esparcirse
diffuse[2] [dɪ'fjuːs] *adj* **1** WORDY : prolijo, verboso **2** WIDESPREAD : difuso
diffusion [dɪ'juːʒən] *n* : difusión *f*
dig[1] ['dɪg] *v* **dug** ['dʌg]; **digging** *vt* **1** : cavar, excavar <to dig a hole : cavar un hoyo> **2** EXTRACT : sacar <to dig up potatoes : sacar papas del suelo> **3** POKE, THRUST : clavar, hincar <he dug me in the ribs : me dio un codazo en las costillas> **4 to dig up** DISCOVER : descubrir, sacar a luz — *vi* : cavar, excavar
dig[2] *n* **1** POKE : codazo *m* **2** GIBE : pulla *f* **3** EXCAVATION : excavación *f*
digest[1] [daɪ'dʒɛst, dɪ-] *vt* **1** ASSIMILATE : digerir, asimilar **2** : digerir (comida) **3** SUMMARIZE : compendiar, resumir
digest[2] ['daɪˌdʒɛst] *n* : compendio *m,* resumen *m*
digestible [daɪ'dʒɛstəbəl, dɪ-] *adj* : digerible
digestion [daɪ'dʒɛstʃən, dɪ-] *n* : digestión *f*
digestive [daɪ'dʒɛstɪv, dɪ-] *adj* : digestivo <the digestive system : el sistema digestivo>
digit ['dɪdʒət] *n* **1** NUMERAL : dígito *m,* número *m* **2** FINGER, TOE : dedo *m*
digital ['dɪdʒət̬əl] *adj* : digital — **digitally** *adv*
dignified ['dɪgnəˌfaɪd] *adj* : digno, decoroso
dignify ['dɪgnəˌfaɪ] *vt* **-fied; -fying** : dignificar, honrar
dignitary ['dɪgnəˌtɛri] *n, pl* **-taries** : dignatario *m,* -ria *f*
dignity ['dɪgnət̬i] *n, pl* **-ties** : dignidad *f*
digress [daɪ'grɛs, də-] *vi* : desviarse del tema, divagar

digression [daɪˈgrɛʃən, də-] *n* **:** digresión *f*

dike *or* **dyke** [ˈdaɪk] *n* **:** dique *m*

dilapidated [dəˈlæpəˌdeɪt̬əd] *adj* **:** ruinoso, desvencijado, destartalado

dilapidation [dəˌlæpəˈdeɪʃən] *n* **:** deterioro *m,* estado *m* ruinoso

dilate [daɪˈleɪt, ˈdaɪˌleɪt] *v* **-lated; -lating** *vt* **:** dilatar — *vi* **:** dilatarse

dilemma [dɪˈlɛmə] *n* **:** dilema *m*

dilettante [ˈdɪləˌtɑnt, -ˌtænt] *n, pl* **-tantes** [-ˌtɑnts, -ˌtænts] *or* **-tanti** [ˌdɪləˈtɑnti, -ˈtæn-] **:** diletante *mf*

diligence [ˈdɪlədʒənts] *n* **:** diligencia *f,* aplicación *f*

diligent [ˈdɪlədʒənt] *adj* **:** diligente <a diligent search **:** una búsqueda minuciosa> — **diligently** *adv*

dill [ˈdɪl] *n* **:** eneldo *m*

dillydally [ˈdɪliˌdæli] *vi* **-lied; lying :** demorarse, perder tiempo

dilute [daɪˈluːt, də-] *vt* **-luted; -luting :** diluir, aguar

dilution [daɪˈluːʃən, də-] *n* **:** dilución *f*

dim¹ [ˈdɪm] *v* **dimmed; dimming** *vt* **:** atenuar (la luz), nublar (la vista), borrar (la memoria), opacar (una superficie) — *vi* **:** oscurecerse, apagarse

dim² *adj* **dimmer; dimmest 1** FAINT **:** oscuro, tenue (dícese de la luz), nublado (dícese de la vista), borrado (dícese de la memoria) **2** DULL **:** deslustrado **3** STUPID **:** tonto, torpe

dime [ˈdaɪm] *n* **:** moneda *f* de diez centavos

dimension [dəˈmɛntʃən, daɪ-] *n* **1 :** dimensión *f* **2 dimensions** *npl* EXTENT, SCOPE **:** dimensiones *fpl,* extensión *f,* medida *f*

diminish [dəˈmɪnɪʃ] *vt* LESSEN **:** disminuir, reducir, amainar — *vi* DWINDLE, WANE **:** menguar, reducirse

diminutive [dəˈmɪnjʊt̬ɪv] *adj* **:** diminutivo, minúsculo

dimly [ˈdɪmli] *adv* **:** indistintamente, débilmente

dimmer [ˈdɪmər] *n* **:** potenciómetro *m,* conmutador *m* de luces (en automóviles)

dimness [ˈdɪmnəs] *n* **:** oscuridad *f,* debilidad *f* (de la vista), imprecisión *f* (de la memoria)

dimple [ˈdɪmpəl] *n* **:** hoyuelo *m*

din [ˈdɪn] *n* **:** estrépito *m,* estruendo *m*

dine [ˈdaɪn] *vi* **dined; dining :** cenar

diner [ˈdaɪnər] *n* **1 :** comensal *mf* (persona) **2 :** vagón *m* restaurante (en un tren) **3 :** cafetería *f,* restaurante *m* barato

dinghy [ˈdɪŋi, ˈdɪŋgi, ˈdɪŋki] *n, pl* **-ghies :** bote *m*

dinginess [ˈdɪndʒinəs] *n* **1** DIRTINESS **:** suciedad *f* **2** SHABBINESS **:** lo gastado, lo deslucido

dingy [ˈdɪndʒi] *adj* **-gier; -est 1** DIRTY **:** sucio **2** SHABBY **:** gastado, deslucido

dinner [ˈdɪnər] *n* **:** cena *f,* comida *f*

dinosaur [ˈdaɪnəˌsɔr] *n* **:** dinosaurio *m*

dint [ˈdɪnt] *n* **by dint of :** a fuerza de

diocese [ˈdaɪəsəs, -ˌsiːz, -ˌsiːs] *n, pl* **-ceses** [ˈdaɪəsəsəz] **:** diócesis *f*

dip¹ [ˈdɪp] *v* **dipped; dipping** *vt* **1** DUNK, PLUNGE **:** sumergir, mojar, meter **2** LADLE **:** servir con cucharón **3** LOWER **:** bajar, arriar (una bandera) — *vi* **1** DESCEND, DROP **:** bajar en picada, descender **2** SLOPE **:** bajar, inclinarse

dip² *n* **1** SWIM **:** chapuzón *m* **2** DROP **:** descenso *m,* caída *f* **3** SLOPE **:** cuesta *f,* declive *m* **4** SAUCE **:** salsa *f*

diphtheria [dɪfˈθɪriə] *n* **:** difteria *f*

diphthong [ˈdɪfˌθɔŋ] *n* **:** diptongo *m*

diploma [dəˈploːmə] *n, pl* **-mas :** diploma *m*

diplomacy [dəˈploːməsi] *n* **1 :** diplomacia *f* **2** TACT **:** tacto *m,* discreción *f*

diplomat [ˈdɪpləˌmæt] *n* **1 :** diplomático *m,* -ca *f* (en relaciones internacionales) **2 :** persona *f* diplomática

diplomatic [ˌdɪpləˈmæt̬ɪk] *adj* **:** diplomático <diplomatic immunity **:** inmunidad diplomática>

dipper [ˈdɪpər] *n* **1** LADLE **:** cucharón *m,* cazo *m* **2 Big Dipper :** Osa *f* Mayor **3 Little Dipper :** Osa *f* Menor

dire [ˈdaɪr] *adj* **direr; direst 1** HORRIBLE **:** espantoso, terrible, horrendo **2** EXTREME **:** extremo <dire poverty **:** pobreza extrema>

direct¹ [dəˈrɛkt, daɪ-] *vt* **1** ADDRESS **:** dirigir, mandar **2** AIM, POINT **:** dirigir **3** GUIDE **:** indicarle el camino (a alguien), orientar **4** MANAGE **:** dirigir <to direct a film **:** dirigir una película> **5** COMMAND **:** ordenar, mandar

direct² *adv* **:** directamente

direct³ *adj* **1** STRAIGHT **:** directo **2** FRANK **:** franco

direct current *n* **:** corriente *f* continua

direction [dəˈrɛkʃən, daɪ-] *n* **1** SUPERVISION **:** dirección *f* **2** INSTRUCTION, ORDER **:** instrucción *f,* orden *f* **3** COURSE **:** dirección *f,* rumbo *m* <to change direction **:** cambiar de dirección> **4 to ask directions :** pedir indicaciones

directly [dəˈrɛktli, daɪ-] *adv* **1** STRAIGHT **:** directamente <directly north **:** directamente al norte> **2** FRANKLY **:** francamente **3** EXACTLY **:** exactamente, justo <directly opposite **:** justo enfrente> **4** IMMEDIATELY **:** en seguida, inmediatamente

directness [dəˈrɛktnəs, daɪ-] *n* **:** franqueza *f*

director [dəˈrɛktər, daɪ-] *n* **1 :** director *m,* -tora *f* **2 board of directors :** junta *f* directiva, directorio *m*

directory [dəˈrɛktəri, daɪ-] *n, pl* **-ries :** guía *f,* directorio *m* <telephone directory **:** directorio telefónico>

dirge [ˈdərdʒ] *n* **:** canto *m* fúnebre

dirigible [ˈdɪrədʒəbəl, dəˈrɪdʒə-] *n* **:** dirigible *m,* zepelín *m*

dirt [ˈdərt] *n* **1** FILTH **:** suciedad *f,* mugre *f,* porquería *f* **2** SOIL **:** tierra *f*

dirtiness [ˈdərt̬inəs] *n* **:** suciedad *f*

dirty¹ [ˈdərt̬i] *vt* **dirtied; dirtying :** ensuciar, manchar

dirty[2] *adj* **dirtier; -est 1** SOILED, STAINED : sucio, manchado **2** DISHONEST : sucio, deshonesto <a dirty player : un jugador tramposo> <a dirty trick : una mala pasada> **3** INDECENT : indecente, cochino <a dirty joke : un chiste verde>

disability [ˌdɪsəˈbɪləti] *n, pl* **-ties** : minusvalía *f,* discapacidad *f,* invalidez *f*

disable [dɪsˈeɪbəl] *vt* **-abled; -abling** : dejar inválido, inutilizar, incapacitar

disabled [dɪsˈeɪbəld] *adj* : minusválido, discapacitado

disabuse [ˌdɪsəˈbjuːz] *vt* **-bused; -busing** : desengañar, sacar del error

disadvantage [ˌdɪsədˈvæntɪdʒ] *n* : desventaja *f*

disadvantageous [ˌdɪsˌædˌvænˈteɪdʒəs] *adj* : desventajoso, desfavorable

disagree [ˌdɪsəˈgriː] *vi* **1** DIFFER : discrepar, no coincidir **2** DISSENT : disentir, discrepar, no estar de acuerdo

disagreeable [ˌdɪsəˈgriːəbəl] *adj* : desagradable

disagreement [ˌdɪsəˈgriːmənt] *n* **1** : desacuerdo *m* **2** DISCREPANCY : discrepancia *f* **3** ARGUMENT : discusión *f,* altercado *m,* disputa *f*

disappear [ˌdɪsəˈpɪr] *vi* : desaparecer, desvanecerse <to disappear from view : perderse de vista>

disappearance [ˌdɪsəˈpɪrən*t*s] *n* : desaparición *f*

disappoint [ˌdɪsəˈpɔɪnt] *vt* : decepcionar, defraudar, fallar

disappointment [ˌdɪsəˈpɔɪntmənt] *n* : decepción *f,* desilusión *f,* chasco *m*

disapproval [ˌdɪsəˈpruːvəl] *n* : desaprobación *f*

disapprove [ˌdɪsəˈpruːv] *vi* **-proved; -proving** : desaprobar, estar en contra

disapprovingly [ˌdɪsəˈpruːvɪŋli] *adv* : con desaprobación

disarm [dɪsˈɑrm] *vt* : desarmar

disarmament [dɪsˈɑrməmənt] *n* : desarme *m* <nuclear disarmament : desarme nuclear>

disarrange [ˌdɪsəˈreɪndʒ] *vt* **-ranged; -ranging** : desarreglar, desordenar

disarray [ˌdɪsəˈreɪ] *n* : desorden *m,* confusión *f,* desorganización *f*

disaster [dɪˈzæstər] *n* : desastre *m,* catástrofe *f*

disastrous [dɪˈzæstrəs] *adj* : desastroso

disband [dɪsˈbænd] *vt* : disolver — *vi* : disolverse, dispersarse

disbar [dɪsˈbɑr] *vt* **-barred; -barring** : prohibir de ejercer la abogacía

disbelief [ˌdɪsbɪˈliːf] *n* : incredulidad *f*

disbelieve [ˌdɪsbɪˈliːv] *v* **-lieved; -lieving** : no creer, dudar

disburse [dɪsˈbərs] *vt* **-bursed; -bursing** : desembolsar

disbursement [dɪsˈbərsmənt] *n* : desembolso *m*

disc → **disk**

discard [dɪsˈkɑrd, ˈdɪsˌkɑrd] *vt* : desechar, deshacerse de, botar — *vi* : descartarse (en juegos de naipes)

discern [dɪˈsərn, -ˈzərn] *vt* : discernir, distinguir, percibir

discernible [dɪˈsərnəbəl, -ˈzər-] *adj* : perceptible, visible

discernment [dɪˈsərnmənt, -ˈzərn-] *n* : discernimiento *m,* criterio *m*

discharge[1] [dɪsˈtʃɑrdʒ, ˈdɪsˌ-] *v* **-charged; -charging 1** UNLOAD : descargar (carga), desembarcar (pasajeros) **2** SHOOT : descargar, disparar **3** FREE : liberar, poner en libertad **4** DISMISS : despedir **5** EMIT : despedir (humo, etc.), descargar (electricidad) **6** : cumplir con (una obligación), saldar (una deuda) — *vi* **1** : descargarse (dícese de una batería) **2** OOZE : supurar

discharge[2] [ˈdɪsˌtʃɑrdʒ, dɪsˈ-] *n* **1** EMISSION : descarga *f* (de electricidad), emisión *f* (de gases) **2** DISMISSAL : despido *m* (del empleo), baja *f* (del ejército) **3** SECRETION : secreción *f*

disciple [dɪˈsaɪpəl] *n* : discípulo *m,* -la *f*

discipline[1] [ˈdɪsəplən] *vt* **-plined; -plining 1** PUNISH : castigar, sancionar (a los empleados) **2** CONTROL : disciplinar **3 to discipline oneself** : disciplinarse

discipline[2] *n* **1** FIELD : disciplina *f,* campo *m* **2** TRAINING : disciplina *f* **3** PUNISHMENT : castigo *m* **4** SELF-CONTROL : dominio *m* de sí mismo

disc jockey *n* : disc jockey *mf*

disclaim [dɪsˈkleɪm] *vt* DENY : negar

disclose [dɪsˈkloːz] *vt* **-closed; -closing** : revelar, poner en evidencia

disclosure [dɪsˈkloːʒər] *n* : revelación *f*

discolor [dɪsˈkʌlər] *vt* **1** BLEACH : decolorar **2** FADE : desteñir **3** STAIN : manchar — *vi* : decolorarse, desteñirse

discoloration [dɪsˌkʌləˈreɪʃən] *n* **1** FADING : decoloración *f* **2** STAIN : mancha *f*

discomfort [dɪsˈkʌmfərt] *n* **1** PAIN : molestia *f,* malestar *m* **2** UNEASINESS : inquietud *f*

disconcert [ˌdɪskənˈsərt] *vt* : desconcertar

disconnect [ˌdɪskəˈnɛkt] *vt* : desconectar

disconnected [ˌdɪskəˈnɛktəd] *adj* : inconexo

disconsolate [dɪsˈkɑn*t*sələt] *adj* : desconsolado

discontent [ˌdɪskənˈtɛnt] *n* : descontento *m*

discontented [ˌdɪskənˈtɛntəd] *adj* : descontento

discontinue [ˌdɪskənˈtɪnˌjuː] *vt* **-ued; -uing** : suspender, descontinuar

discord [ˈdɪsˌkɔrd] *n* **1** STRIFE : discordia *f,* discordancia *f* **2** : disonancia *f* (en música)

discordant [dɪs'kɔrdənt] *adj* : discordante, discorde — **discordantly** *adv*

discount[1] ['dɪs,kaʊnt, dɪs'-] *vt* **1** REDUCE : descontar, rebajar (precios) **2** DISREGARD : descartar, ignorar

discount[2] ['dɪs,kaʊnt] *n* : descuento *m*, rebaja *f*

discourage [dɪs'kərɪdʒ] *vt* **-aged; -aging 1** DISHEARTEN : desalentar, desanimar **2** DISSUADE : disuadir

discouragement [dɪs'kərɪdʒmənt] *n* : desánimo *m*, desaliento *m*

discourse[1] [dɪs'kors] *vi* **-coursed; -coursing** : disertar, conversar

discourse[2] ['dɪs,kors] *n* **1** TALK : conversación *f* **2** SPEECH, TREATISE : discurso *m*, tratado *m*

discourteous [dɪs'kərt̬iəs] *adj* : descortés — **discourteously** *adv*

discourtesy [dɪs'kərt̬əsi] *n, pl* **-sies** : descortesía *f*

discover [dɪs'kʌvər] *vt* : descubrir

discoverer [dɪs'kʌvərər] *n* : descubridor *m*, -dora *f*

discovery [dɪs'kʌvəri] *n, pl* **-ries** : descubrimiento *m*

discredit[1] [dɪs'krɛdət] *vt* **1** DISBELIEVE : no creer, dudar **2** : desacreditar, desprestigiar, poner en duda <they discredited his research : desacreditaron sus investigaciones>

discredit[2] *n* **1** DISREPUTE : descrédito *m*, desprestigio *m* **2** DOUBT : duda *f*

discreet [dɪs'kriːt] *adj* : discreto — **discreetly** *adv*

discrepancy [dɪs'krɛpəntsi] *n, pl* **-cies** : discrepancia *f*

discretion [dɪs'krɛʃən] *n* **1** CIRCUMSPECTION : discreción *f*, circunspección *f* **2** JUDGMENT : discernimiento *m*, criterio *m*

discriminate [dɪs'krɪmə,neɪt] *v* **-nated; -nating** *vt* DISTINGUISH : distinguir, discriminar, diferenciar — *vi* : discriminar <to discriminate against women : discriminar a las mujeres>

discrimination [dɪs,krɪmə'neɪʃən] *n* **1** PREJUDICE : discriminación *f* **2** DISCERNMENT : discernimiento *m*

discriminatory [dɪs'krɪmənə,tori] *adj* : discriminatorio

discus ['dɪskəs] *n, pl* **-cuses** [-kəsəz] : disco *m*

discuss [dɪs'kʌs] *vt* : hablar de, discutir, tratar (de)

discussion [dɪs'kʌʃən] *n* : discusión *f*, debate *m*, conversación *f*

disdain[1] [dɪs'deɪn] *vt* : desdeñar, despreciar <they disdained to reply : no se dignaron a responder>

disdain[2] *n* : desdén *m*

disdainful [dɪs'deɪnfəl] *adj* : desdeñoso — **disdainfully** *adv*

disease [dɪ'ziːz] *n* : enfermedad *f*, mal *m*, dolencia *f*

diseased [dɪ'ziːzd] *adj* : enfermo

disembark [,dɪsɪm'bɑrk] *v* : desembarcar

disembarkation [dɪs,ɛm,bɑr'keɪʃən] *n* : desembarco *m*, desembarque *m*

disembodied [,dɪsɪm'bɑdid] *adj* : incorpóreo

disenchant [,dɪsɪn'tʃænt] *vt* : desilusionar, desencantar, desengañar

disenchantment [,dɪsɪn'tʃæntmənt] *n* : desencanto *m*, desilusión *f*

disengage [,dɪsɪn'geɪdʒ] *vt* **-gaged; -gaging 1** : soltar, desconectar (un mecanismo) **2 to disengage the clutch** : desembragar

disentangle [,dɪsɪn'tæŋgəl] *vt* **-gled; -gling** UNTANGLE : desenredar, desenmarañar

disfavor [dɪs'feɪvər] *n* : desaprobación *f*

disfigure [dɪs'fɪgjər] *vt* **-ured; -uring** : desfigurar (a una persona), afear (un edificio, un área)

disfigurement [dɪs'fɪgjərmənt] *n* : desfiguración *f*, afeamiento *m*

disfranchise [dɪs'fræn,tʃaɪz] *vt* **-chised; -chising** : privar del derecho a votar

disgrace[1] [dɪ'skreɪs] *vt* **-graced; -gracing** : deshonrar

disgrace[2] *n* **1** DISHONOR : desgracia *f*, deshonra *f* **2** SHAME : vergüenza *f* <he's a disgrace to his family : es una vergüenza para su familia>

disgraceful [dɪ'skreɪsfəl] *adj* : vergonzoso, deshonroso, ignominioso

disgracefully [dɪ'skreɪsfəli] *adv* : vergonzosamente

disgruntle [dɪs'grʌntəl] *vt* **-tled; -tling** : enfadar, contrariar

disguise[1] [dɪ'skaɪz] *vt* **-guised; -guising 1** : disfrazar, enmascarar (el aspecto) **2** CONCEAL : encubrir, disimular

disguise[2] *n* : disfraz *m*

disgust[1] [dɪ'skʌst] *vt* : darle asco (a alguien), asquear, repugnar <eso me da asco : that disgusts me>

disgust[2] *n* : asco *m*, repugnancia *f*

disgusting [dɪ'skʌstɪŋ] *adj* : asqueroso, repugnante — **disgustingly** *adv*

dish[1] ['dɪʃ] *vt* SERVE : servir

dish[2] *n* **1** : plato *m* <the national dish : el plato nacional> **2** PLATE : plato *m* <to wash the dishes : lavar los platos> **3 serving dish** : fuente *f*

dishcloth ['dɪʃ,klɔθ] *n* : paño *m* de cocina (para secar), trapo *m* de fregar (para lavar)

dishearten [dɪs'hɑrtən] *vt* : desanimar, desalentar

dishevel [dɪ'ʃɛvəl] *vt* **-eled** *or* **-elled; -eling** *or* **-elling** : desarreglar, despeinar (el pelo)

disheveled *or* **dishevelled** [dɪ'ʃɛvəld] *adj* : despeinado (dícese del pelo), desarreglado, desaliñado

dishonest [dɪ'sɑnəst] *adj* : deshonesto, fraudulento — **dishonestly** *adv*

dishonesty [dɪ'sɑnəsti] *n, pl* **-ties** : deshonestidad *f*, falta *f* de honradez

dishonor[1] [dɪ'sɑnər] *vt* : deshonrar

dishonor[2] *n* : deshonra *f*
dishonorable [dɪ'sɑnərəbəl] *adj* : deshonroso — **dishonorably** [-bli] *adv*
dishrag ['dɪʃ,ræg] → **dishcloth**
dishwasher ['dɪʃ,wɔʃər] *n* : lavaplatos *m*, lavavajillas *m*
disillusion [,dɪsə'lu:ʒən] *vt* : desilusionar, desencantar, desengañar
disillusionment [,dɪsə'lu:ʒənmənt] *n* : desilusión *f*, desencanto *m*
disinclination [dɪs,ɪnklə'neɪʃən, -,ɪŋ-] *n* : aversión *f*
disinclined [,dɪsɪn'klaɪnd] *adv* : poco dispuesto
disinfect [,dɪsɪn'fɛkt] *vt* : desinfectar
disinfectant[1] [,dɪsɪn'fɛktənt] *adj* : desinfectante
disinfectant[2] *n* : desinfectante *m*
disinherit [,dɪsɪn'hɛrət] *vt* : desheredar
disintegrate [dɪs'ɪntə,greɪt] *v* **-grated; -grating** *vt* : desintegrar, deshacer — *vi* : desintegrarse, deshacerse
disintegration [dɪs,ɪntə'greɪʃən] *n* : desintegración *f*
disinterested [dɪs'ɪntərəstəd, -,rɛs-] *adj* **1** INDIFFERENT : indiferente **2** IMPARTIAL : imparcial, desinteresado
disinterestedness [dɪs'ɪntərəstədnəs, -,rɛs-] *n* : desinterés *m*
disjointed [dɪs'dʒɔɪntəd] *adj* : inconexo, incoherente
disk *or* **disc** ['dɪsk] *n* : disco *m*
dislike[1] [dɪs'laɪk] *vt* **-liked; -liking** : tenerle aversión a (algo), tenerle antipatía (a alguien), no gustarle (algo a uno)
dislike[2] *n* : aversión *f*, antipatía *f*
dislocate ['dɪslo,keɪt, dɪs'lo:-] *vt* **-cated; -cating** : dislocar
dislocation [,dɪslo'keɪʃən] *n* : dislocación *f*
dislodge [dɪs'lɑdʒ] *vt* **-lodged; -lodging** : sacar, desalojar, desplazar
disloyal [dɪs'lɔɪəl] *adj* : desleal
disloyalty [dɪs'lɔɪəlti] *n, pl* **-ties** : deslealtad *f*
dismal ['dɪzməl] *adj* **1** GLOOMY : sombrío, lúgubre, tétrico **2** DEPRESSING : deprimente, triste
dismantle [dɪs'mæntəl] *vt* **-tled; -tling** : desmantelar, desmontar, desarmar
dismay[1] [dɪs'meɪ] *vt* : consternar
dismay[2] *n* : consternación *f*
dismember [dɪs'mɛmbər] *vt* : desmembrar
dismiss [dɪs'mɪs] *vt* **1** : dejar salir, darle permiso (a alguien) para retirarse **2** DISCHARGE : despedir, destituir **3** REJECT : descartar, desechar, rechazar
dismissal [dɪs'mɪsəl] *n* **1** : permiso *m* para retirarse **2** DISCHARGE : despido *m* (de un empleado), destitución *f* (de un funcionario) **3** REJECTION : rechazo *m*
dismount [dɪs'maʊnt] *vi* : desmontar, bajarse, apearse
disobedience [,dɪsə'bi:diənts] *n* : desobediencia *f* — **disobedient** [-ənt] *adj*
disobey [,dɪsə'beɪ] *v* : desobedecer
disorder[1] [dɪs'ɔrdər] *vt* : desordenar, desarreglar
disorder[2] *n* **1** DISARRAY : desorden *m* **2** UNREST : disturbios *mpl*, desórdenes *mpl* **3** AILMENT : afección *f*, indisposición *f*, dolencia *f*
disorderly [dɪs'ɔrdərli] *adj* **1** UNTIDY : desordenado, desarreglado **2** UNRULY : indisciplinado, alborotado **3 disorderly conduct** : conducta *f* escandalosa
disorganization [dɪs,ɔrgənə'zeɪʃən] *n* : desorganización *f*
disorganize [dɪs'ɔrgə,naɪz] *vt* **-nized; -nizing** : desorganizar
disown [dɪs'o:n] *vt* : renegar de, repudiar
disparage [dɪs'pærɪdʒ] *vt* **-aged; -aging** : menospreciar, denigrar
disparagement [dɪs'pærɪdʒmənt] *n* : menosprecio *m*
disparate ['dɪspərət, dɪs'pærət] *adj* : dispar, diferente
disparity [dɪs'pærəṭi] *n, pl* **-ties** : disparidad *f*
dispassionate [dɪs'pæʃənət] *adj* : desapasionado, imparcial — **dispassionately** *adv*
dispatch[1] [dɪs'pætʃ] *vt* **1** SEND : despachar, enviar **2** KILL : despachar, matar **3** HANDLE : despachar
dispatch[2] *n* **1** SENDING : envío *m*, despacho *m* **2** MESSAGE : despacho *m*, reportaje *m* (de un periodista), parte *m* (en el ejército) **3** PROMPTNESS : prontitud *f*, rapidez *f*
dispel [dɪs'pɛl] *vt* **-pelled; -pelling** : disipar, desvanecer
dispensation [,dɪspɛn'seɪʃən] *n* EXEMPTION : exención *m*, dispensa *f*
dispense [dɪs'pɛnts] *v* **-pensed; -pensing** *vt* **1** DISTRIBUTE : repartir, distribuir, dar **2** ADMINISTER, BESTOW : administrar (justicia), conceder (favores, etc.) **3** : preparar y despachar (medicamentos) — *vi* **to dispense with** : prescindir de
dispenser [dɪs'pɛntsər] *n* : dispensador *m*, distibuidor *m* automático
dispersal [dɪs'pərsəl] *n* : dispersión *f*
disperse [dɪs'pərs] *v* **-persed; -persing** *vt* : dispersar, diseminar — *vi* : dispersarse
dispirit [dɪ'spɪrət] *vt* : desalentar, desanimar
displace [dɪs'pleɪs] *vt* **-placed; -placing 1** : desplazar (un líquido, etc.) **2** REPLACE : reemplazar
displacement [dɪs'pleɪsmənt] *n* **1** : desplazamiento *m* (de personas) **2** REPLACEMENT : sustitución *f*, reemplazo *m*
display[1] [dɪs'pleɪ] *vt* : exponer, exhibir, mostrar
display[2] *n* : muestra *f*, exposición *m*, alarde *m*

displease [dɪsˈpliːz] *vt* **-pleased; -pleasing** : desagradar a, disgustar, contrariar

displeasure [dɪsˈplɛʒər] *n* : desagrado *m*

disposable [dɪsˈpoːzəbəl] *adj* **1** : desechable <disposable diapers : pañales desechables> **2** AVAILABLE : disponible

disposal [dɪsˈpoːzəl] *n* **1** PLACEMENT : disposición *f*, colocación *f* **2** REMOVAL : eliminación *f* **3 to have at one's disposal** : disponer de, tener a su disposición

dispose [dɪsˈpoːz] *v* **-posed; -posing** *vt* **1** ARRANGE : disponer, colocar **2** INCLINE : predisponer — *vi* **1 to dispose of** DISCARD : desechar, deshacerse de **2 to dispose of** HANDLE : despachar

disposition [ˌdɪspəˈzɪʃən] *n* **1** ARRANGEMENT : disposición *f* **2** TENDENCY : predisposición *f*, inclinación *f* **3** TEMPERAMENT : temperamento *m*, carácter *m*

disproportion [ˌdɪsprəˈporʃən] *n* : desproporción *f*

disproportionate [ˌdɪsprəˈporʃənət] *adj* : desproporcionado — **disproportionately** *adv*

disprove [dɪsˈpruːv] *vt* **-proved; -proving** : rebatir, refutar

disputable [dɪsˈpjuːt̬əbəl, ˈdɪspjʊt̬əbəl] *adj* : disputable, discutible

dispute[1] [dɪsˈpjuːt] *v* **-puted; -puting** *vt* **1** QUESTION : discutir, cuestionar **2** OPPOSE : combatir, resistir — *vi* ARGUE, DEBATE : discutir

dispute[2] *n* **1** DEBATE : debate *m*, discusión *f* **2** QUARREL : disputa *f*, discusión *f*

disqualification [dɪsˌkwɑləfəˈkeɪʃən] *n* : descalificación *f*

disqualify [dɪsˈkwɑləˌfaɪ] *vt* **-fied; -fying** : descalificar, inhabilitar

disquiet[1] *vt* [dɪsˈkwaɪət̬] : inquietar

disquiet[2] *n* : ansiedad *f*, inquietud *f*

disregard[1] [ˌdɪsrɪˈgɑrd] *vt* : ignorar, no prestar atención a

disregard[2] *n* : indiferencia *f*

disrepair [ˌdɪsrɪˈpær] *n* : mal estado *m*

disreputable [dɪsˈrɛpjʊt̬əbəl] *adj* : de mala fama (dícese de una persona o un lugar), vergonzoso (dícese de la conducta)

disreputably [dɪsˈrɛpjʊt̬əbli] *adv* : vergonzosamente

disrepute [ˌdɪsrɪˈpjuːt] *n* : descrédito *m*, mala fama *f*, deshonra *f*

disrespect [ˌdɪsrɪˈspɛkt] *n* : falta *f* de respeto

disrespectful [ˌdɪsrɪˈspɛktfəl] *adj* : irrespetuoso — **disrespectfully** *adv*

disrobe [dɪsˈroːb] *v* **-robed; -robing** *vt* : desvestir, desnudar — *vi* : desvestirse, desnudarse

disrupt [dɪsˈrʌpt] *vt* : trastornar, perturbar

disruption [dɪsˈrʌpʃən] *n* : trastorno *m*

disruptive [dɪsˈrʌptɪv] *adj* : perjudicial, perturbador — **disruptively** *adv*

dissatisfaction [dɪsˌsæt̬əsˈfækʃən] *n* : descontento *m*, insatisfacción *f*

dissatisfied [dɪsˈsæt̬əsˌfaɪd] *adj* : descontento, insatisfecho

dissatisfy [dɪsˈsæt̬əsˌfaɪ] *vt* **-fied; -fying** : no contentar, no satisfacer

dissect [dɪˈsɛkt] *vt* : disecar

dissemble [dɪˈsɛmbəl] *v* **-bled; -bling** *vt* HIDE : ocultar, disimular — *vi* PRETEND : fingir, disimular

disseminate [dɪˈsɛməˌneɪt] *vt* **-nated; -nating** : diseminar, difundir, divulgar

dissemination [dɪˌsɛməˈneɪʃən] *n* : diseminación *f*, difusión *f*

dissension [dɪˈsɛntʃən] *n* : disensión *f*, desacuerdo *m*

dissent[1] [dɪˈsɛnt] *vi* : disentir

dissent[2] *n* : disentimiento *m*, disensión *f*

dissertation [ˌdɪsərˈteɪʃən] *n* **1** DISCOURSE : disertación *f*, discurso *m* **2** THESIS : tesis *f*

disservice [dɪsˈsərvɪs] *n* : perjuicio *m*

dissident[1] [ˈdɪsədənt] *adj* : disidente

dissident[2] *n* : disidente *mf*

dissimilar [dɪˈsɪmələr] *adj* : distinto, diferente, disímil

dissipate [ˈdɪsəˌpeɪt] *vt* **-pated; -pating 1** DISPERSE : disipar, dispersar **2** SQUANDER : malgastar, desperdiciar, derrochar, disipar

dissipation [ˌdɪsəˈpeɪʃən] *n* : disipación *f*, libertinaje *m*

dissolute [ˈdɪsəˌluːt] *adj* : disoluto

dissolution [ˌdɪsəˈluːʃən] *n* : disolución *f*

dissolve [dɪˈzɑlv] *v* **-solved; -solving** *vt* : disolver — *vi* : disolverse

dissonance [ˈdɪsənənts] *n* : disonancia *f*

dissuade [dɪˈsweɪd] *vt* **-suaded; -suading** : disuadir

distance [ˈdɪstənts] *n* **1** : distancia *f* <the distance between two points : la distancia entre dos puntos> <in the distance : a lo lejos> **2** RESERVE : actitud *f* distante, reserva *f* <to keep one's distance : guardar las distancias>

distant [ˈdɪstənt] *adj* **1** FAR : distante, lejano **2** REMOTE : distante, lejano, remoto **3** ALOOF : distante, frío

distantly [ˈdɪstəntli] *adv* **1** LOOSELY : aproximadamente, vagamente **2** COLDLY : fríamente, con frialdad

distaste [dɪsˈteɪst] *n* : desagrado *m*, aversión *f*

distasteful [dɪsˈteɪstfəl] *adj* : desagradable, de mal gusto

distemper [dɪsˈtɛmpər] *n* : moquillo *m*

distend [dɪsˈtɛnd] *vt* : dilatar, hinchar — *vi* : dilatarse, hincharse

distill [dɪˈstɪl] *vt* : destilar

distillation [ˌdɪstəˈleɪʃən] *n* : destilación *f*

distiller [dɪˈstɪlər] *n* : destilador *m,* -dora *f*
distinct [dɪˈstɪŋkt] *adj* **1** DIFFERENT : distinto, diferente **2** CLEAR, UNMISTAKABLE : marcado, claro, evidente <a distinct possibility : una clara posibilidad>
distinction [dɪˈstɪŋkʃən] *n* **1** DIFFERENTIATION : distinción *f* **2** DIFFERENCE : diferencia *f* **3** EXCELLENCE : distinción *f,* excelencia *f* <a writer of distinction : un escritor destacado>
distinctive [dɪˈstɪŋktɪv] *adj* : distintivo, característico — **distinctively** *adv*
distinctiveness [dɪˈstɪŋktɪvnəs] *n* : peculiaridad *f*
distinctly [dɪˈstɪŋktli] *adv* : claramente, con claridad
distinguish [dɪsˈtɪŋgwɪʃ] *vt* **1** DIFFERENTIATE : distinguir, diferenciar **2** DISCERN : distinguir <he distinguished the sound of the piano : distinguió el sonido del piano> **3 to distinguish oneself** : señalarse, distinguirse — *vi* DISCRIMINATE : distinguir
distinguishable [dɪsˈtɪŋgwɪʃəbəl] *adj* : distinguible
distinguished [dɪsˈtɪŋgwɪʃt] *adj* : distinguido
distort [dɪˈstɔrt] *vt* **1** MISREPRESENT : distorsionar, tergiversar **2** DEFORM : distorsionar, deformar
distortion [dɪˈstɔrʃən] *n* : distorsión *f,* deformación *f,* tergiversación *f*
distract [dɪˈstrækt] *vt* : distraer, entretener
distracted [dɪˈstræktəd] *adj* : distraído
distraction [dɪˈstrækʃən] *n* **1** INTERRUPTION : distracción *f,* interrupción *f* **2** CONFUSION : confusión *f* **3** AMUSEMENT : diversión *f,* entretenimiento *m,* distracción *f*
distraught [dɪˈstrɔt] *adj* : afligido, turbado
distress[1] [dɪˈstrɛs] *vt* : afligir, darle pena (a alguien), hacer sufrir
distress[2] *n* **1** SORROW : dolor *m,* angustia *f,* aflicción *f* **2** PAIN : dolor *m* **3 in ~** : en peligro
distressful [dɪˈstrɛsfəl] *adj* : doloroso, penoso
distribute [dɪˈstrɪˌbjuːt, -bjʊt] *vt* **-uted; -uting** : distribuir, repartir
distribution [ˌdɪstrəˈbjuːʃən] *n* : distribución *f,* reparto *m*
distributive [dɪˈstrɪbjʊt̬ɪv] *adj* : distributivo
distributor [dɪˈstrɪbjʊt̬ər] *n* : distribuidor *m,* -dora *f*
district [ˈdɪsˌtrɪkt] *n* **1** REGION : región *f,* zona *f,* barrio *m* (de una ciudad) **2** : distrito *m* (zona política)
distrust[1] [dɪsˈtrʌst] *vt* : desconfiar de
distrust[2] *n* : desconfianza *f,* recelo *m*
distrustful [dɪsˈtrʌstfəl] *adj* : desconfiado, receloso, suspicaz
disturb [dɪˈstərb] *vt* **1** BOTHER : molestar, perturbar <sorry to disturb you : perdone la molestia> **2** DISARRANGE : desordenar **3** WORRY : inquietar, preocupar **4 to disturb the peace** : alterar el orden público
disturbance [dɪˈstərbən*t*s] *n* **1** COMMOTION : alboroto *m,* disturbio *m* **2** INTERRUPTION : interrupción *f*
disuse [dɪsˈjuːs] *n* : desuso *m*
ditch[1] [ˈdɪtʃ] *vt* **1** : cavar zanjas en **2** DISCARD : deshacerse de, botar
ditch[2] *n* : zanja *f,* fosa *f,* cuneta *f* (en una carretera)
dither [ˈdɪðər] *n* **to be in a dither** : estar nervioso, ponerse como loco
ditto [ˈdɪtoː] *n, pl* **-tos 1** : lo mismo, ídem *m* **2 ditto marks** : comillas *fpl*
ditty [ˈdɪt̬i] *n, pl* **-ties** : canción *f* corta y simple
diurnal [daɪˈərnəl] *adj* **1** DAILY : diario, cotidiano **2** : diurno <a diurnal animal : un animal diurno>
divan [ˈdaɪˌvæn, dɪˈ-] *n* : diván *m*
dive[1] [ˈdaɪv] *vi* **dived** *or* **dove** [ˈdoːv]; **dived; diving 1** PLUNGE : tirarse al agua, zambullirse, dar un clavado **2** SUBMERGE : sumergirse **3** DROP : bajar en picada (dícese de un avión), caer en picada
dive[2] *n* **1** PLUNGE : zambullida *f,* clavado *m* (en el agua) **2** DESCENT : descenso *m* en picada **3** BAR, JOINT : antro *m*
diver [ˈdaɪvər] *n* : saltador *m,* -dora *f;* clavadista *mf*
diverge [dəˈvərdʒ, daɪ-] *vi* **-verged; -verging 1** SEPARATE : divergir, separarse **2** DIFFER : divergir, discrepar
divergence [dəˈvərdʒən*t*s, daɪ-] *n* : divergencia *f* — **divergent** [-ənt] *adj*
diverse [daɪˈvərs, də-, ˈdaɪˌvərs] *adj* : diverso, variado
diversify [daɪˈvərsəˌfaɪ, də-] *vt* **-fied; -fying** : diversificar, variar
diversion [daɪˈvərʒən, də-] *n* **1** DEVIATION : desviación *f* **2** AMUSEMENT, DISTRACTION : diversión *f,* distracción *f,* entretenimiento *m*
diversity [daɪˈvərsət̬i, də-] *n, pl* **-ties** : diversidad *f*
divert [dəˈvərt, daɪ-] *vt* **1** DEVIATE : desviar **2** DISTRACT : distraer **3** AMUSE : divertir, entretener
divest [daɪˈvɛst, də-] *vt* **1** UNDRESS : desnudar, desvestir **2 to divest of** : despojar de
divide [dəˈvaɪd] *v* **-vided; -viding** *vt* **1** HALVE : dividir, partir por la mitad **2** SHARE : repartir, dividir **3** : dividir (números) — *vi* : dividirse, dividir (en matemáticas)
dividend [ˈdɪvəˌdɛnd, -dənd] *n* **1** : dividendo *m* (en finanzas) **2** BONUS : benefício *m,* provecho *m* **3** : dividendo *m* (en matemáticas)
divider [dɪˈvaɪdər] *n* **1** : separador *m* (para ficheros, etc.) **2** *or* **room divider** : mampara *f,* biombo *m*

divine[1] [dəˈvaɪn] *adj* **-viner; -est 1** : divino **2** SUPERB : divino, espléndido — **divinely** *adv*

divine[2] *n* : clérigo *m,* eclesiástico *m*

divinity [dəˈvɪnət̬i] *n, pl* **-ties** : divinidad *f*

divisible [dɪˈvɪzəbəl] *adj* : divisible

division [dɪˈvɪʒən] *n* **1** DISTRIBUTION : división *f,* reparto *m* <division of labor : distribución del trabajo> **2** PART : división *f,* sección *f* **3** : división *f* (en matemáticas)

divisor [dɪˈvaɪzər] *n* : divisor *m*

divorce[1] [dəˈvors] *v* **-vorced; -vorcing** *vt* : divorciar — *vi* : divorciarse

divorce[2] *n* : divorcio *m*

divorcé [dɪˌvorˈseɪ, -ˈsiː; -ˈvorˌ-] *n* : divorciado *m*

divorcée [dɪˌvorˈseɪ, -ˈsiː; -ˈvorˌ-] *n* : divorciada *f*

divulge [dəˈvʌldʒ, daɪ-] *vt* **-vulged; -vulging** : revelar, divulgar

dizzily [ˈdɪzəli] *adv* : vertiginosamente

dizziness [ˈdɪzinəs] *n* : mareo *m,* vahído *m,* vértigo *m*

dizzy [ˈdɪzi] *adj* **dizzier; -est 1** : mareado <I feel dizzy : estoy mareado> **2** : vertiginoso <a dizzy speed : una velocidad vertiginosa>

DNA [ˌdiːˌɛnˈeɪ] *n* : AND *m*

do [ˈduː] *v* **did** [ˈdɪd]; **done** [ˈdʌn]; **doing; does** [ˈdʌz] *vt* **1** CARRY OUT, PERFORM : hacer, realizar, llevar a cabo <she did her best : hizo todo lo posible> **2** PREPARE : preparar, hacer <do your homework : haz tu tarea> **3** ARRANGE : arreglar, peinar (el pelo) **4 to do in** RUIN : estropear, arruinar **5 to do in** KILL : matar, liquidar *fam* — *vi* **1** : hacer <you did well : hiciste bien> **2** FARE : estar, ir, andar <how are you doing? : ¿cómo estás?, ¿cómo te va?> **3** FINISH : terminar <now I'm done : ya terminé> **4** SERVE : servir, ser suficiente, alcanzar <this will do for now : esto servirá por el momento> **5 to do away with** ABOLISH : abolir, suprimir **6 to do away with** KILL : eliminar, matar **7 to do by** TREAT : tratar <he does well by her : él la trata bien> — *v aux* **1** (*used in interrogative sentences and negative statements*) <do you know her? : ¿la conoces?> <I don't like that : a mí no me gusta eso> **2** (*used for emphasis*) <I do hope you'll come : espero que vengas> **3** (*used as a substitute verb to avoid repetition*) <do you speak English? yes, I do : ¿habla inglés? sí>

docile [ˈdɑsəl] *adj* : dócil, sumiso

dock[1] [ˈdɑk] *vt* **1** CUT : cortar **2** : descontar dinero de (un sueldo) — *vi* ANCHOR, LAND : fondear, atracar

dock[2] *n* **1** PIER : atracadero *m* **2** WHARF : muelle *m* **3** : banquillo *m* de los acusados (en un tribunal)

doctor[1] [ˈdɑktər] *vt* **1** TREAT : tratar, curar **2** ALTER : adulterar, alterar, falsificar (un documento)

doctor[2] *n* **1** : doctor *m,* -tora *f* <Doctor of Philosophy : doctor en filosofía> **2** PHYSICIAN : médico *m,* -ca *f;* doctor *m,* -tora *f*

doctrine [ˈdɑktrɪn] *n* : doctrina *f*

document[1] [ˈdɑkjʊˌmɛnt] *vt* : documentar

document[2] [ˈdɑkjʊmənt] *n* : documento *m*

documentary[1] [ˌdɑkjʊˈmɛntəri] *adj* : documental

documentary[2] *n, pl* **-ries** : documental *m*

documentation [ˌdɑkjʊmənˈteɪʃən] *n* : documentación *f*

dodge[1] [ˈdɑdʒ] *v* **dodged; dodging** *vt* : esquivar, eludir, evadir (impuestos) — *vi* : echarse a un lado

dodge[2] *n* **1** RUSE : truco *m,* treta *f,* artimaña *f* **2** EVASION : regate *m,* evasión *f*

dodo [ˈdoːˌdoː] *n, pl* **-does** *or* **-dos** : dodo *m*

doe [ˈdoː] *n, pl* **does** *or* **doe** : gama *f,* cierva *f*

doer [ˈduːər] *n* : hacedor *m,* -dora *f*

does → **do**

doff [ˈdɑf, ˈdɔf] *vt* : quitarse <to doff one's hat : quitarse el sombrero>

dog[1] [ˈdɔg, ˈdɑg] *vt* **dogged; dogging** : seguir de cerca, perseguir, acosar <to dog someone's footsteps : seguir los pasos de alguien> <dogged by bad luck : perseguido por la mala suerte>

dog[2] *n* : perro *m,* -rra *f*

dogcatcher [ˈdɔgˌkætʃər] *n* : perrero *m,* -ra *f*

dog–eared [ˈdɔgˌɪrd] *adj* : con las esquinas dobladas

dogged [ˈdɔgəd] *adj* : tenaz, terco, obstinado

doggy [ˈdɔgi] *n, pl* **doggies** : perrito *m,* -ta *f*

doghouse [ˈdɔgˌhaʊs] *n* : casita *f* de perro

dogma [ˈdɔgmə] *n* : dogma *m*

dogmatic [dɔgˈmæt̬ɪk] *adj* : dogmático

dogmatism [ˈdɔgməˌtɪzəm] *n* : dogmatismo *m*

dogwood [ˈdɔgˌwʊd] *n* : cornejo *m*

doily [ˈdɔɪli] *n, pl* **-lies** : pañito *m*

doings [ˈduːɪŋz] *npl* : eventos *mpl,* actividades *fpl*

doldrums [ˈdoːldrəmz, ˈdɑl-] *npl* **1** : zona *f* de las calmas ecuatoriales **2 to be in the doldrums** : estar abatido (dícese de una persona), estar estancado (dícese de una empresa)

dole [ˈdoːl] *n* **1** ALMS : distribución *f* a los necesitados, limosna *f* **2** : subsidios *mpl* de desempleo

doleful [ˈdoːlfəl] *adj* : triste, lúgubre

dolefully [ˈdoːlfəli] *adv* : con pesar, de manera triste

dole out *vt* **doled out; doling out** : repartir

doll [ˈdɑl, ˈdɔl] *n* : muñeco *m,* -ca *f*

dollar [ˈdɑlər] *n* : dólar *m*

dolly ['dɑli] *n, pl* **-lies 1** → **doll 2** : plataforma *f* rodante
dolphin ['dɑlfən, 'dɔl-] *n* : delfín *m*
dolt ['doːlt] *n* : imbécil *mf;* tonto *m,* -ta *f*
domain [do'meɪn, də-] *n* **1** TERRITORY : dominio *m,* territorio *m* **2** FIELD : campo *m,* esfera *f,* ámbito *m* <the domain of art : el ámbito de las artes>
dome ['doːm] *n* : cúpula *f,* bóveda *f*
domestic[1] [də'mɛstɪk] *adj* **1** HOUSEHOLD : doméstico, casero **2** : nacional, interno <domestic policy : política interna> **3** TAME : domesticado
domestic[2] *n* : empleado *m* doméstico, empleada *f* doméstica
domestically [də'mɛstɪkli] *adv* : domésticamente
domesticate [də'mɛstɪ,keɪt] *vt* **-cated; -cating** : domesticar
domicile ['dɑmə,saɪl, 'doː-; 'dɑməsɪl] *n* : domicilio *m*
dominance ['dɑmənənts] *n* : dominio *m,* dominación *f*
dominant ['dɑmənənt] *adj* : dominante
dominate ['dɑmə,neɪt] *v* **-nated; -nating** : dominar
domination [,dɑmə'neɪʃən] *n* : dominación *f*
domineer [,dɑmə'nɪr] *vt* : dominar sobre, avasallar, tiranizar
Dominican [də'mɪnɪkən] *n* : dominicano *m,* -na *f* — **Dominican** *adj*
dominion [də'mɪnjən] *n* **1** POWER : dominio *m* **2** DOMAIN, TERRITORY : dominio *m,* territorio *m*
domino ['dɑmə,noː] *n, pl* **-noes** *or* **-nos 1** : dominó *m* **2 dominoes** *npl* : dominó *m* (juego)
don ['dɑn] *vt* **donned; donning** : ponerse
donate ['doː,neɪt, doː'-] *vt* **-nated; -nating** : donar, hacer un donativo de
donation [doː'neɪʃən] *n* : donación *f,* donativo *m*
done[1] ['dʌn] → **do**
done[2] *adj* **1** FINISHED : terminado, acabado, concluido **2** COOKED : cocinado
donkey ['dɑŋki, 'dʌŋ-] *n, pl* **-keys** : burro *m,* asno *m*
donor ['doːnər] *n* : donante *mf;* donador *m,* -dora *f*
doodle[1] ['duːdəl] *v* **-dled; -dling** : garabatear
doodle[2] *n* : garabato *m*
doom[1] ['duːm] *vt* : condenar
doom[2] *n* **1** JUDGMENT : sentencia *f,* condena *f* **2** DEATH : muerte *f* **3** FATE : destino *m* **4** RUIN : perdición *f,* ruina *f*
door ['dor] *n* : puerta *f*
doorbell ['dor,bɛl] *n* : timbre *m*
doorknob ['dor,nɑb] *n* : pomo *m,* perilla *f*
doorman ['dormən] *n, pl* **-men** [-mən, -,mɛn] : portero *m*
doormat ['dor,mæt] *n* : felpudo *m*
doorstep ['dor,stɛp] *n* : umbral *m*
doorway ['dor,weɪ] *n* : entrada *f,* portal *m*
dope[1] ['doːp] *vt* **doped; doping** : drogar, narcotizar
dope[2] *n* **1** DRUG : droga *f,* estupefaciente *m,* narcótico *m* **2** IDIOT : idiota *mf;* tonto *m,* -ta *f* **3** INFORMATION : información *f*
dormant ['dɔrmənt] *adj* : inactivo, latente
dormer ['dɔrmər] *n* : buhardilla *f*
dormitory ['dɔrmə,tori] *n, pl* **-ries** : dormitorio *m,* residencia *f* de estudiantes
dormouse ['dɔr,maʊs] *n* : lirón *m*
dorsal ['dɔrsəl] *adj* : dorsal — **dorsally** *adv*
dory ['dori] *n, pl* **-ries** : bote *m* de fondo plano
dosage ['doːsɪdʒ] *n* : dosis *f*
dose[1] ['doːs] *vt* **dosed; dosing** : medicinar
dose[2] *n* : dosis *f*
dot[1] ['dɑt] *vt* **dotted; dotting 1** : poner el punto sobre (una letra) **2** SCATTER : esparcir, salpicar
dot[2] *n* : punto *m* <at six on the dot : a las seis en punto> <dots and dashes : puntos y rayas>
dote ['doːt] *vi* **doted; doting** : chochear
double[1] ['dʌbəl] *v* **-bled; -bling** *vt* **1** : doblar, duplicar (una cantidad), redoblar (esfuerzos) **2** FOLD : doblar, plegar **3 to double one's fist** : apretar el puño — *vi* **1** : doblarse, duplicarse **2 to double over** : retorcerse
double[2] *adj* : doble — **doubly** *adv*
double[3] *n* : doble *mf*
double bass *n* : contrabajo *m*
double–cross [,dʌbəl'krɔs] *vt* : traicionar
double–crosser [,dʌbəl'krɔsər] *n* : traidor *m,* -dora *f*
double–jointed [,dʌbəl'dʒɔintəd] *adj* : con articulaciones dobles
double–talk ['dʌbəl,tɔk] *n* : ambigüedades *fpl,* lenguaje *m* con doble sentido
doubt[1] ['daʊt] *vt* **1** QUESTION : dudar de, cuestionar **2** DISTRUST : desconfiar de **3** : dudar, creer poco probable <I doubt it very much : lo dudo mucho>
doubt[2] *n* **1** UNCERTAINTY : duda *f,* incertidumbre *f* **2** DISTRUST : desconfianza *f* **3** SKEPTICISM : duda *f,* escepticismo *m*
doubtful ['daʊtfəl] *adj* **1** QUESTIONABLE : dudoso **2** UNCERTAIN : dudoso, incierto
doubtfully ['daʊtfəli] *adv* : dudosamente, sin estar convencido
doubtless ['daʊtləs] *or* **doubtlessly** *adv* : sin duda
douche[1] ['duːʃ] *vt* **douched; douching** : irrigar
douche[2] *n* : ducha *f,* irrigación *f*
dough ['doː] *n* : masa *f*

doughnut [ˈdoːˌnʌt] *n* : rosquilla *f*, dona *f Mex*
doughty [ˈdaʊt̬i] *adj* **-tier; -est** : fuerte, valiente
dour [ˈdaʊər, ˈdʊr] *adj* **1** STERN : severo, adusto **2** SULLEN : hosco, taciturno — **dourly** *adv*
douse [ˈdaʊs, ˈdaʊz] *vt* **doused; dousing 1** DRENCH : empapar, mojar **2** EXTINGUISH : extinguir, apagar
dove[1] [ˈdoːv] → **dive**
dove[2] [ˈdʌv] *n* : paloma *f*
dovetail [ˈdʌvˌteɪl] *vi* : encajar, enlazar
dowdy [ˈdaʊdi] *adj* **dowdier; -est** : sin gracia, poco elegante
dowel [ˈdaʊəl] *n* : clavija *f*
down[1] [ˈdaʊn] *vt* **1** FELL : tumbar, derribar, abatir **2** DEFEAT : derrotar
down[2] *adv* **1** DOWNWARD : hacia abajo **2 to lie down :** acostarse, echarse **3 to put down (money) :** pagar un depósito (de dinero) **4 to sit down :** sentarse **5 to take down, to write down** : apuntar, anotar
down[3] *adj* **1** DESCENDING : de bajada <the down elevator : el ascensor de bajada> **2** REDUCED : reducido, rebajado <attendance is down : la concurrencia ha disminuido> **3** DOWNCAST : abatido, deprimido
down[4] *n* : plumón *m*
down[5] *prep* **1** : (hacia) abajo <down the mountain : montaña abajo> <I walked down the stairs : bajé por la escalera> **2** ALONG : por, a lo largo de <we ran down the beach : corrimos por la playa> **3** : a través de <down the years : a través de los años>
downcast [ˈdaʊnˌkæst] *adj* **1** SAD : triste, abatido **2 with downcast eyes** : con los ojos bajos, con los ojos mirando al suelo
downfall [ˈdaʊnˌfɔl] *n* : ruina *f*, perdición *f*
downgrade[1] [ˈdaʊnˌgreɪd] *vt* **-graded; -grading** : bajar de categoría
downgrade[2] *n* : bajada *f*
downhearted [ˈdaʊnˌhɑrt̬əd] *adj* : desanimado, descorazonado
downhill [ˈdaʊnˈhɪl] *adv & adj* : cuesta abajo
down payment *n* : entrega *f* inicial
downpour [ˈdaʊnˌpor] *n* : aguacero *m*, chaparrón *m*
downright[1] [ˈdaʊnˌraɪt] *adv* THOROUGHLY : absolutamente, completamente
downright[2] *adj* : patente, manifiesto, absoluto <a downright refusal : un rechazo categórico>
downstairs[1] [ˈdaʊnˈstærz] *adv* : abajo
downstairs[2] [ˈdaʊnˌstærz] *adj* : del piso de abajo
downstairs[3] [ˈdaʊnˈstærz, -ˌstærz] *n* : planta *f* baja
downstream [ˈdaʊnˈstriːm] *adv* : río abajo
down–to–earth [ˌdaʊntuˈərth] *adj* : práctico, realista
downtown[1] [ˌdaʊnˈtaʊn] *adv* : hacia el centro, al centro, en el centro (de la ciudad)
downtown[2] *adj* : del centro (de la ciudad) <downtown Chicago : el centro de Chicago>
downtown[3] [ˌdaʊnˈtaʊn, ˈdaʊnˌtaʊn] *n* : centro *m* (de la ciudad)
downtrodden [ˈdaʊnˌtrɑdən] *adj* : oprimido
downward [ˈdaʊnwərd] *or* **downwards** [-wərdz] *adv & adj* : hacia abajo
downwind [ˈdaʊnˈwɪnd] *adv & adj* : en la dirección del viento
downy [ˈdaʊni] *adj* **downier; -est 1** : cubierto de plumón, plumoso **2** VELVETY : aterciopelado, velloso
dowry [ˈdaʊri] *n, pl* **-ries** : dote *f*
doze[1] [ˈdoːz] *vi* **dozed; dozing** : dormitar
doze[2] *n* : sueño *m* ligero, cabezada *f*
dozen [ˈdʌzən] *n, pl* **dozens** *or* **dozen** : docena *f*
drab [ˈdræb] *adj* **drabber; drabbest 1** BROWNISH : pardo **2** DULL, LACKLUSTER : monótono, gris, deslustrado
draft[1] [ˈdræft, ˈdraft] *vt* **1** CONSCRIPT : reclutar **2** COMPOSE, SKETCH : hacer el borrador de, redactar
draft[2] *adj* **1** : de barril <draft beer : cerveza de barril> **2** : de tiro <draft horses : caballos de tiro>
draft[3] *n* **1** HAULAGE : tiro *m* **2** DRINK, GULP : trago *m* **3** OUTLINE, SKETCH : bosquejo *m*, borrador *m*, versión *f* **4** : corriente *f* de aire, chiflón *m*, tiro *m* (de una chimenea) **5** CONSCRIPTION : conscripción *f* **6 bank draft :** giro *m* bancario, letra *f* de cambio
draftee [dræfˈtiː] *n* : recluta *mf*
draftsman [ˈdræftsmən] *n, pl* **-men** [-mən, -ˌmɛn] : dibujante *mf*
drafty [ˈdræfti] *adj* **draftier; -est** : con corrientes de aire
drag[1] [ˈdræg] *v* **dragged; dragging** *vt* **1** HAUL : arrastrar, jalar **2** DREDGE : dragar — *vi* **1** TRAIL : arrastrarse **2** LAG : rezagarse **3** : hacerse pesado, hacerse largo <the day dragged on : el día se hizo largo>
drag[2] *n* **1** RESISTANCE : resistencia *f* (aerodinámica) **2** HINDRANCE : traba *f*, estorbo *m* **3** BORE : pesadez *f*, plomo *m fam*
dragnet [ˈdrægˌnɛt] *n* **1** : red *f* barredera (en pesca) **2** : operativo *m* policial de captura
dragon [ˈdrægən] *n* : dragón *m*
dragonfly [ˈdrægənˌflaɪ] *n, pl* **-flies** : libélula *f*
drain[1] [ˈdreɪn] *vt* **1** EMPTY : vaciar, drenar **2** EXHAUST : agotar, consumir — *vi* **1** : escurrir, escurrirse <the dishes are draining : los platos están escurriéndose> **2** EMPTY : desaguar **3 to drain away :** irse agotando

drain[2] *n* **1** : desagüe *m* **2** SEWER : alcantarilla *f* **3** GRATING : sumidero *m,* resumidero *m,* rejilla *f* **4** EXHAUSTION : agotamiento *m,* disminución *f* (de energía, etc.) <to be a drain on : agotar, consumir> **5 to throw down the drain** : tirar por la ventana

drainage [ˈdreɪnɪdʒ] *n* : desagüe *m,* drenaje *m*

drainpipe [ˈdreɪn,paɪp] *n* : tubo *m* de desagüe, caño *m*

drake [ˈdreɪk] *n* : pato *m* (macho)

drama [ˈdrɑmə, ˈdræ-] *n* **1** THEATER : drama *m,* teatro *m* **2** PLAY : obra *f* de teatro, drama *m*

dramatic [drəˈmætɪk] *adj* : dramático — **dramatically** [-tɪkli] *adv*

dramatist [ˈdræmətɪst, ˈdrɑ-] *n* : dramaturgo *m,* -ga *f*

dramatization [ˌdræmət̬əˈzeɪʃən, ˌdrɑ-] *n* : dramatización *f*

dramatize [ˈdræmə,taɪz, ˈdrɑ-] *vt* **-tized; -tizing** : dramatizar

drank → **drink**

drape[1] [ˈdreɪp] *vt* **draped; draping 1** COVER : cubrir (con tela) **2** HANG : drapear, disponer los pliegues de

drape[2] *n* **1** HANG : caída *f* **2 drapes** *npl* : cortinas *fpl*

drapery [ˈdreɪpəri] *n, pl* **-eries 1** CLOTH : pañería *f,* tela *f* para cortinas **2 draperies** *npl* : cortinas *fpl*

drastic [ˈdræstɪk] *adj* **1** HARSH, SEVERE : drástico, severo **2** EXTREME : radical, excepcional — **drastically** [-tɪkli] *adv*

draught [ˈdræft, ˈdraft] → **draft**[3]

draughty [ˈdrafti] → **drafty**

draw[1] [ˈdrɔ] *v* **drew** [ˈdruː]; **drawn** [ˈdrɔn]; **drawing** *vt* **1** PULL : tirar de, jalar, correr (cortinas) **2** ATTRACT : atraer **3** PROVOKE : provocar, suscitar **4** INHALE : aspirar <to draw breath : respirar> **5** EXTRACT : sacar, extraer **6** TAKE : sacar <to draw a number : sacar un número> **7** COLLECT : cobrar, percibir (un sueldo, etc.) **8** BEND : tensar (un arco) **9** TIE : empatar (en deportes) **10** SKETCH : dibujar, trazar **11** FORMULATE : sacar, formular, llegar a <to draw a conclusion : llegar a una conclusión> **12 to draw out** : hacer hablar (sobre algo), hacer salir de sí mismo **13 to draw up** DRAFT : redactar — *vi* **1** SKETCH : dibujar **2** TUG : tirar, jalar **3 to draw near** : acercarse **4 to draw to a close** : terminar, finalizar **5 to draw up** STOP : parar

draw[2] *n* **1** DRAWING, RAFFLE : sorteo *m* **2** TIE : empate *m* **3** ATTRACTION : atracción *f* **4** PUFF : chupada *f* (de un cigarrillo, etc.)

drawback [ˈdrɔ,bæk] *n* : desventaja *f,* inconveniente *m*

drawbridge [ˈdrɔ,bridʒ] *n* : puente *m* levadizo

drawer [ˈdrɔr, ˈdrɔər] *n* **1** ILLUSTRATOR : dibujante *mf* **2** : gaveta *f,* cajón *m* (en un mueble) **3 drawers** *npl* UNDERPANTS : calzones *mpl*

drawing [ˈdrɔɪŋ] *n* **1** LOTTERY : sorteo *m,* lotería *f* **2** SKETCH : dibujo *m,* bosquejo *m*

drawl[1] [ˈdrɔl] *vi* : hablar arrastrando las palabras

drawl[2] *n* : habla *f* lenta y con vocales prolongadas

dread[1] [ˈdrɛd] *vt* : tenerle pavor a, temer

dread[2] *adj* : pavoroso, aterrado

dread[3] *n* : pavor *m,* temor *m*

dreadful [ˈdrɛdfəl] *adj* **1** DREAD : pavoroso **2** TERRIBLE : espantoso, atroz, terrible — **dreadfully** *adv*

dream[1] [ˈdriːm] *v* **dreamed** [ˈdrɛmpt, ˈdriːmd] *or* **dreamt** [ˈdrɛmpt]; **dreaming** *vi* **1** : soñar <to dream about : soñar con> **2** FANTASIZE : fantasear — *vt* **1** : soñar **2** IMAGINE : imaginarse **3 to dream up** : inventar, idear

dream[2] *n* **1** : sueño *m,* ensueño *m* **2 bad dream** NIGHTMARE : pesadilla *f*

dreamer [ˈdriːmər] *n* : soñador *m,* -dora *f*

dreamlike [ˈdriːm,laɪk] *adj* : de ensueño

dreamy [ˈdriːmi] *adj* **dreamier; -est 1** DISTRACTED : soñador, distraído **2** DREAMLIKE : de ensueño **3** MARVELOUS : maravilloso

drearily [ˈdrɪrəli] *adv* : sombríamente

dreary [ˈdrɪri] *adj* **-rier; -est** : deprimente, lóbrego, sombrío

dredge[1] [ˈdrɛdʒ] *vt* **dredged; dredging 1** DIG : dragar **2** COAT : espolvorear, enharinar

dredge[2] *n* : draga *f*

dredger [ˈdrɛdʒər] *n* : draga *f*

dregs [ˈdrɛgz] *npl* **1** LEES : posos *mpl,* heces *fpl* (de un líquido) **2** : heces *fpl,* escoria *f* <the dregs of society : la escoria de la sociedad>

drench [ˈdrɛntʃ] *vt* : empapar, mojar, calar

dress[1] [ˈdrɛs] *vt* **1** CLOTHE : vestir **2** DECORATE : decorar, adornar **3** : preparar (pollo o pescado), aliñar (ensalada) **4** : curar, vendar (una herida) **5** FERTILIZE : abonar (la tierra) — *vi* **1** : vestirse **2 to dress up** : ataviarse, engalanarse, ponerse de etiqueta

dress[2] *n* **1** APPAREL : indumentaria *f,* ropa *f* **2** : vestido *m,* traje *m* (de mujer)

dresser [ˈdrɛsər] *n* : cómoda *f* con espejo

dressing [ˈdrɛsɪŋ] *n* **1** : vestirse *m* **2** : aderezo *m,* aliño *m* (de ensalada), relleno *m* (de pollo) **3** BANDAGE : vendaje *m,* gasa *f*

dressmaker [ˈdrɛs,meɪkər] *n* : modista *mf*

dressmaking [ˈdrɛs,meɪkɪŋ] *n* : costura *f*

dressy [ˈdrɛsi] *adj* **dressier; -est** : de mucho vestir, elegante

drew → **draw**

dribble[1] ['drɪbəl] *vi* **-bled; -bling 1** DRIP : gotear **2** DROOL : babear **3** : driblar (en basquetbol)

dribble[2] *n* **1** TRICKLE : goteo *m,* hilo *m* **2** DROOL : baba *f* **3** : drible *m* (en basquetbol)

drier → **dry**[2], **dryer**

driest → **dry**[2]

drift[1] ['drɪft] *vi* **1** : dejarse llevar por la corriente, ir a la deriva (dícese de un bote), ir sin rumbo (dícese de una persona) **2** ACCUMULATE : amontonarse, acumularse, apilarse

drift[2] *n* **1** DRIFTING : deriva *f* **2** HEAP, MASS : montón *m* (de arena, etc.), ventisquero *m* (de nieve) **3** MEANING : sentido *m*

drifter ['drɪftər] *n* : vagabundo *m,* -da *f*

driftwood ['drɪft,wʊd] *n* : madera *f* flotante

drill[1] ['drɪl] *vt* **1** BORE : perforar, taladrar **2** INSTRUCT : instruir por repetición — *vi* **1** TRAIN : entrenarse **2 to drill for oil** : perforar en busca de petróleo

drill[2] *n* **1** : taladro *m,* barrena *f* **2** EXERCISE, PRACTICE : ejercicio *m,* instrucción *f*

drily → **dryly**

drink[1] ['drɪŋk] *v* **drank** ['dræŋk]; **drunk** ['drʌŋk] *or* **drank; drinking** *vt* **1** IMBIBE : beber, tomar **2 to drink up** ABSORB : absorber — *vi* **1** : beber **2** : beber alcohol, tomar

drink[2] *n* **1** : bebida *f* **2** : bebida *f* alcohólica

drinkable ['drɪŋkəbəl] *adj* : potable

drinker ['drɪŋkər] *n* : bebedor *m,* -dora *f*

drip[1] ['drɪp] *vi* **dripped; dripping** : gotear, chorrear

drip[2] *n* **1** DROP : gota *f* **2** DRIPPING : goteo *m*

drive[1] ['draɪv] *v* **drove** ['dro:v]; **driven** ['drɪvən]; **driving** *vt* **1** IMPEL : impeler, impulsar **2** OPERATE : guiar, conducir, manejar (un vehículo) **3** COMPEL : obligar, forzar **4** : clavar, hincar <to drive a stake : clavar una estaca> **5** *or* **to drive away** : ahuyentar, echar **6 to drive crazy** : volver loco — *vi* : manejar, conducir <do you know how to drive? : ¿sabes manejar?>

drive[2] *n* **1** RIDE : paseo *m* en coche **2** CAMPAIGN : campaña *f* <fund-raising drive : campaña para recaudar fondos> **3** DRIVEWAY : camino *m* de entrada, entrada *f* **4** TRANSMISSION : transmisión *f* <front-wheel drive : tracción delantera> **5** ENERGY : dinamismo *m,* energía *f* **6** INSTINCT, NEED : instinto *m,* necesidad *f* básica

drivel ['drɪvəl] *n* : tontería *f,* estupidez *f*

driver ['draɪvər] *n* : conductor *m,* -tora *f;* chofer *m*

driveway ['draɪv,weɪ] *n* : camino *m* de entrada, entrada *f* (para coches)

drizzle[1] ['drɪzəl] *vi* **-zled; -zling** : lloviznar, garuar

drizzle[2] *n* : llovizna *f,* garúa *f*

droll ['dro:l] *adj* : cómico, gracioso, chistoso — **drolly** *adv*

dromedary ['drɑmə,dɛri] *n, pl* **-daries** : dromedario *m*

drone[1] ['dro:n] *vi* **droned; droning 1** BUZZ : zumbar **2** MURMUR : hablar con monotonía, murmurar

drone[2] *n* **1** : zángano *m* (abeja) **2** FREELOADER : gorrón *m,* -rrona *f fam;* parásito *m,* -ta *f* **3** BUZZ, HUM : zumbido *m,* murmullo *m*

drool[1] ['dru:l] *vi* : babear

drool[2] *n* : baba *f*

droop[1] ['dru:p] *vi* **1** HANG : inclinarse (dícese de la cabeza), encorvarse (dícese de los escombros), marchitarse (dícese de las flores) **2** FLAG : decaer, flaquear <his spirits drooped : se desanimó>

droop[2] *n* : inclinación *f,* caída *f*

drop[1] ['drɑp] *v* **dropped; dropping** *vt* **1** : dejar caer, soltar <she dropped the glass : se le cayó el vaso> <to drop a hint : dejar caer una indirecta> **2** SEND : mandar <drop me a line : mándame unas líneas> **3** ABANDON : abandonar, dejar <to drop the subject : cambiar de tema> **4** LOWER : bajar <he dropped his voice : bajó la voz> **5** OMIT : omitir **6 to drop off** : dejar — *vi* **1** DRIP : gotear **2** FALL : caer(se) **3** DECREASE, DESCEND : bajar, descender <the wind dropped : amainó el viento> **4 to drop back** *or* **to drop behind** : rezagarse, quedarse atrás **5 to drop by** *or* **to drop in** : pasar

drop[2] *n* **1** : gota *f* (de líquido) **2** DECLINE : caída *f,* bajada *f,* descenso *m* **3** INCLINE : caída *f,* pendiente *f* <a 20-foot drop : una caída de 20 pies> **4** SWEET : pastilla *f,* dulce *m* **5 drops** *npl* : gotas *fpl* (de medicina)

droplet ['drɑplət] *n* : gotita *f*

dropper ['drɑpər] *n* : gotero *m,* cuentagotas *m*

dross ['drɑs, 'drɔs] *n* : escoria *f*

drought ['draʊt] *n* : sequía *f*

drove[1] → **drive**

drove[2] ['dro:v] *n* : multitud *f,* gentío *m,* manada *f* (de ganado) <in droves : en manada>

drown ['draʊn] *vt* **1** : ahogar **2** INUNDATE : anegar, inundar **3 to drown out** : ahogar — *vi* : ahogarse

drowse[1] ['draʊz] *vi* **drowsed; drowsing** DOZE : dormitar

drowse[2] *n* : sueño *m* ligero, cabezada *f*

drowsiness ['draʊzinəs] *n* : somnolencia *f,* adormecimiento *m*

drowsy ['draʊzi] *adj* **drowsier; -est** : somnoliento, soñoliento

drub [ˈdrʌb] *vt* **drubbed; drubbing 1** BEAT, THRASH : golpear, apalear **2** DEFEAT : derrotar por completo
drudge[1] [ˈdrʌʤ] *vi* **drudged; drudging** : trabajar como esclavo, trabajar duro
drudge[2] *n* : esclavo *m,* -va *f* del trabajo
drudgery [ˈdrʌʤəri] *n, pl* **-eries** : trabajo *m* pesado
drug[1] [ˈdrʌg] *vt* **drugged; drugging** : drogar, narcotizar
drug[2] *n* **1** MEDICATION : droga *f,* medicina *f,* medicamento *m* **2** NARCOTIC : narcótico *m,* estupefaciente *m,* droga *f*
druggist [ˈdrʌgɪst] *n* : farmacéutico *m,* -ca *f*
drugstore [ˈdrʌgˌstor] *n* : farmacia *f,* botica *f,* droguería *f*
drum[1] [ˈdrʌm] *v* **drummed; drumming** *vt* : meter a fuerza <he drummed it into my head : me lo metió en la cabeza a fuerza> — *vi* : tocar el tambor
drum[2] *n* **1** : tambor *m* **2** : bidón *m* <oil drum : bidón de petróleo>
drummer [ˈdrʌmər] *n* : baterista *mf*
drumstick [ˈdrʌmˌstɪk] *n* **1** : palillo *m* (de tambor), baqueta *f* **2** : muslo *m* de pollo
drunk[1] *pp* → **drink**
drunk[2] [ˈdrʌŋk] *adj* : borracho, embriagado, ebrio
drunk[3] *n* : borracho *m,* -cha *f*
drunkard [ˈdrʌŋkərd] *n* : borracho *m,* -cha *f*
drunken [ˈdrʌŋkən] *adj* : borracho, ebrio <drunken driver : conductor ebrio> <drunken brawl : pleito de borrachos>
drunkenly [ˈdrʌŋkənli] *adv* : como un borracho
drunkenness [ˈdrʌŋkənnəs] *n* : borrachera *f,* embriaguez *f,* ebriedad *f*
dry[1] [ˈdraɪ] *v* **dried; drying** *vt* : secar — *vi* : secarse
dry[2] *adj* **drier; driest 1** : seco **2** THIRSTY : sediento **3** : donde la venta de bebidas alcohólicas está prohibida <a dry county : un condado seco> **4** DULL : aburrido, árido **5** : seco (dícese del vino), brut (dícese de la champaña)
dry–clean [ˈdraɪˌkli:n] *v* : limpiar en seco
dry cleaner *n* : tintorería *f* (servicio)
dry cleaning *n* : limpieza *f* en seco
dryer [ˈdraɪər] *n* **1 hair dryer** : secador *m* **2 clothes dryer** : secadora *f*
dry goods *npl* : artículos *mpl* de confección
dry ice *n* : hielo *m* seco
dryly [ˈdraɪli] *adv* : secamente
dryness [ˈdraɪnəs] *n* : sequedad *f,* aridez *f*
dual [ˈdu:əl, ˈdju:-] *adj* : doble
dub [ˈdʌb] *vt* **dubbed; dubbing 1** CALL : apodar **2** : doblar (una película), mezclar (una grabación)
dubious [ˈdu:biəs, ˈdju:-] *adj* **1** UNCERTAIN : dudoso, indeciso **2** QUESTIONABLE : sospechoso, dudoso, discutible
dubiously [ˈdu:biəsli, ˈdju:-] *adv* **1** UNCERTAINLY : dudosamente, con desconfianza **2** SUSPICIOUSLY : de modo sospechoso, con recelo
duchess [ˈdʌʧəs] *n* : duquesa *f*
duck[1] [ˈdʌk] *vt* **1** LOWER : agachar, bajar (la cabeza) **2** PLUNGE : zambullir **3** EVADE : eludir, evadir — *vi* **to duck down** : agacharse
duck[2] *n, pl* **duck** *or* **ducks** : pato *m,* -ta *f*
duckling [ˈdʌklɪŋ] *n* : patito *m,* -ta *f*
duct [ˈdʌkt] *n* : conducto *m*
ductile [ˈdʌktəl] *adj* : dúctil
dude [ˈdu:d, ˈdju:d] *n* **1** DANDY : dandi *m,* dandy *m* **2** GUY : tipo *m*
due[1] [ˈdu:, ˈdju:] *adv* : justo a, derecho hacia <due north : derecho hacia el norte>
due[2] *adj* **1** PAYABLE : pagadero, sin pagar **2** APPROPRIATE : debido, apropiado <after due consideration : con las debidas consideraciones> **3** EXPECTED : esperado <the train is due soon : esperamos el tren muy pronto, el tren debe llegar pronto> **4 due to** : debido a, por
due[3] *n* **1 to give someone his (her) due** : darle a alguien su merecido **2 dues** *npl* : cuota *f*
duel[1] [ˈdu:əl, ˈdju:-] *vi* : batirse en duelo
duel[2] *n* : duelo *m*
duet [duˈɛt, dju-] *n* : dúo *m*
due to *prep* : debido a
dug *pp* → **dig**
dugout [ˈdʌgˌaʊt] *n* **1** CANOE : piragua *f* **2** SHELTER : refugio *m* subterráneo
duke [ˈdu:k, ˈdju:k] *n* : duque *m*
dull[1] [ˈdʌl] *vt* **1** DIM : opacar, quitar el brillo a, deslustrar **2** BLUNT : embotar (un filo), entorpecer (los sentidos), aliviar (el dolor), amortiguar (sonidos)
dull[2] *adj* **1** STUPID : torpe, lerdo, lento **2** BLUNT : desafilado, despuntado **3** LACKLUSTER : sin brillo, deslustrado **4** BORING : aburrido, soso, pesado — **dully** *adv*
dullness [ˈdʌlnəs] *n* **1** STUPIDITY : estupidez *f* **2** : embotamiento *m* (de los sentidos) **3** MONOTONY : monotonía *f,* insipidez *f* **4** : falta *f* de brillo **5** BLUNTNESS : falta *f* de filo, embotadura *f*
duly [ˈdu:li, ˈdju:-] *adv* PROPERLY : debidamente, a su debido tiempo
dumb [ˈdʌm] *adj* **1** MUTE : mudo **2** STUPID : estúpido, tonto, bobo — **dumbly** *adv*
dumbbell [ˈdʌmˌbɛl] *n* **1** WEIGHT : pesa *f* **2** : estúpido *m,* -da *f*
dumbfound *or* **dumfound** [ˌdʌmˈfaʊnd] *vt* : dejar atónito, dejar sin habla
dummy [ˈdʌmi] *n, pl* **-mies 1** SHAM : imitación *f,* sustituto *m* **2** PUPPET

: muñeco *m* **3** MANNEQUIN : maniquí *m* **4** IDIOT : tonto *m,* -ta *f;* idiota *mf*
dump[1] [ˈdʌmp] *vt* : descargar, verter
dump[2] *n* **1** : vertedero *m,* tiradero *m Mex* **2 down in the dumps** : triste, deprimido
dumpling [ˈdʌmplɪŋ] *n* : bola *f* de masa hervida
dumpy [ˈdʌmpi] *adj* **dumpier; -est** : rechoncho, regordete
dun[1] [ˈdʌn] *vt* **dunned; dunning** : apremiar (a un deudor)
dun[2] *adj* : pardo (color)
dunce [ˈdʌn*t*s] *n* : estúpido *m,* -da *f;* burro *m,* -rra *f fam*
dune [ˈduːn, ˈdjuːn] *n* : duna *f*
dung [ˈdʌŋ] *n* **1** FECES : excrementos *mpl* **2** MANURE : estiércol *m*
dungaree [ˌdʌŋgəˈriː] *n* **1** DENIM : tela *f* vaquera, mezclilla *f Chile, Mex* **2 dungarees** *npl* : pantalones *mpl* de trabajo hechos de tela vaquera
dungeon [ˈdʌndʒən] *n* : mazmorra *f,* calabozo *m*
dunk [ˈdʌŋk] *vt* : mojar, ensopar
duo [ˈduːoː, ˈdjuː-] *n, pl* **duos** : dúo *m,* par *m*
dupe[1] [ˈduːp, djuːp] *vt* **duped; duping** : engañar, embaucar
dupe[2] *n* : inocentón *m,* -tona *f;* simple *mf*
duplex[1] [ˈduːˌplɛks, ˈdjuː-] *adj* : doble
duplex[2] *n* : casa *f* de dos viviendas, dúplex *m*
duplicate[1] [ˈduːplɪˌkeɪt, ˈdjuː-] *vt* **-cated; -cating 1** COPY : duplicar, hacer copias de **2** REPEAT : repetir, reproducir
duplicate[2] [ˈduːplɪkət, ˈdjuː-] *adj* : duplicado <a duplicate invoice : una factura por duplicado>
duplicate[3] [ˈduːplɪkət, ˈdjuː-] *n* : duplicado *m,* copia *f*
duplication [ˌduːplɪˈkeɪʃən, ˌdjuː-] *n* **1** DUPLICATING : duplicación *f,* repetición *f* (de esfuerzos) **2** DUPLICATE : copia *f,* duplicado *m*
duplicity [dʊˈplɪsəṭi, ˌdjuː-] *n, pl* **-ties** : duplicidad *f*
durability [ˌdʊrəˈbɪləṭi, ˌdjʊr-] *n* : durabilidad *f* (de un producto), permanencia *f*
durable [ˈdʊrəbəl, ˈdjʊr-] *adj* : duradero
duration [dʊˈreɪʃən, djʊ-] *n* : duración *f*
duress [dʊˈrɛs, djʊ-] *n* : coacción *f*
during [ˈdʊrɪŋ, ˈdjʊr-] *prep* : durante
dusk [ˈdʌsk] *n* : anochecer *m,* crepúsculo *m*
dusky [ˈdʌski] *adj* **duskier; -est** : oscuro (dícese de los colores)
dust[1] [ˈdʌst] *vt* **1** : quitar el polvo de **2** SPRINKLE : espolvorear
dust[2] *n* : polvo *m*
duster [ˈdʌstər] *n* **1** *or* **dust cloth** : trapo *m* de polvo **2** HOUSECOAT : guardapolvo *m* **3 feather duster** : plumero *m*
dustpan [ˈdʌstˌpæn] *n* : recogedor *m*
dusty [ˈdʌsti] *adj* **dustier; -est** : cubierto de polvo, polvoriento
Dutch[1] [ˈdʌtʃ] *adj* : holandés
Dutch[2] *n* **1** : holandés *m* (idioma) **2 the Dutch** *npl* : los holandeses
Dutch treat *n* : invitación *f* o pago *m* a escote
dutiful [ˈduːṭɪfəl, ˈdjuː-] *adj* : motivado por sus deberes, responsable
duty [ˈduːṭi, ˈdjuː-] *n, pl* **-ties 1** OBLIGATION : deber *m,* obligación *f,* responsabilidad *f* **2** TAX : impuesto *m,* arancel *m*
dwarf[1] [ˈdwɔrf] *vt* **1** STUNT : arrestar el crecimiento de **2** : hacer parecer pequeño
dwarf[2] *n, pl* **dwarfs** [ˈdwɔrfs] *or* **dwarves** [ˈdwɔrvz] : enano *m,* -na *f*
dwell [ˈdwɛl] *vi* **dwelled** *or* **dwelt** [ˈdwɛlt]; **dwelling 1** RESIDE : residir, morar, vivir **2 to dwell on** : pensar demasiado en, insistir en
dweller [ˈdwɛlər] *n* : habitante *mf*
dwelling [ˈdwɛlɪŋ] *n* : morada *f,* vivienda *f,* residencia *f*
dwindle [ˈdwɪndəl] *vi* **-dled; -dling** : menguar, reducirse, disminuir
dye[1] [ˈdaɪ] *vt* **dyed; dyeing** : teñir
dye[2] *n* : tintura *f,* tinte *m*
dying → **die**
dyke → **dike**
dynamic [daɪˈnæmɪk] *adj* : dinámico
dynamite[1] [ˈdaɪnəˌmaɪt] *vt* **-mited; -miting** : dinamitar
dynamite[2] *n* : dinamita *f*
dynamo [ˈdaɪnəˌmoː] *n, pl* **-mos** : dínamo *m,* generador *m* de electricidad
dynasty [ˈdaɪnəsti, -ˌnæs-] *n, pl* **-ties** : dinastía *f*
dysentery [ˈdɪsənˌtɛri] *n, pl* **-teries** : disentería *f*
dystrophy [ˈdɪstrəfi] *n, pl* **-phies 1** : distrofia *f* **2** → **muscular dystrophy**

E

e [ˈiː] *n, pl* **e's** *or* **es** [ˈiːz] : quinta letra del alfabeto inglés
each[1] [ˈiːtʃ] *adv* : cada uno, por persona <they cost $10 each : costaron $10 cada uno>
each[2] *adj* : cada <each student : cada estudiante> <each and every one : todos sin excepción>
each[3] *pron* **1** : cada uno *m,* cada una *f* <each of us : cada uno de nosotros>

2 each other : el uno al otro, mutuamente <we are helping each other : nos ayudamos el uno al otro> <they love each other : se aman>

eager [ˈiːgər] *adj* **1** ENTHUSIASTIC : entusiasta, ávido, deseoso **2** ANXIOUS : ansioso, impaciente

eagerly [ˈiːgərli] *adv* : con entusiasmo, ansiosamente

eagerness [ˈiːgərnəs] *n* : entusiasmo *m,* deseo *m,* impaciencia *f*

eagle [ˈiːgəl] *n* : águila *f*

ear [ˈɪr] *n* **1 :** oído *m,* oreja *f* <inner ear : oído interno> <big ears : orejas grandes> **2 ear of corn :** mazorca *f,* choclo *m*

earache [ˈɪrˌeɪk] *n* : dolor *m* de oído

eardrum [ˈɪrˌdrʌm] *n* : tímpano *m*

earl [ˈərl] *n* : conde *m*

earlobe [ˈɪrˌloːb] *n* : lóbulo *m* de la oreja, perilla *f* de la oreja

early[1] [ˈərli] *adv* **earlier; -est :** temprano, pronto <he arrived early : llegó temprano> <as early as possible : lo más pronto posible, cuanto antes> <ten minutes early : diez minutos de adelanto>

early[2] *adj* **earlier; -est 1** (*referring to a beginning*) : primero <the early stages : las primeras etapas> <in early May : a principios de mayo> **2** (*referring to antiquity*) : primitivo, antiguo <early man : el hombre primitivo> <early painting : la pintura antigua> **3** (*referring to a designated time*) : temprano, antes de la hora, prematuro <he was early : llegó temprano> <early fruit : frutas tempraneras> <an early death : una muerte prematura>

earmark [ˈirˌmɑrk] *vt* : destinar <earmarked funds : fondos destinados>

earn [ˈərn] *vt* **1 :** ganar <to earn money : ganar dinero> **2** DESERVE : ganarse, merecer

earnest[1] [ˈərnəst] *adj* : serio, sincero

earnest[2] *n* **in ~ :** en serio, de verdad <we began in earnest : empezamos de verdad>

earnestly [ˈərnəstli] *adv* **1** SERIOUSLY : con seriedad, en serio **2** FERVENTLY : de todo corazón

earnestness [ˈərnəstnəs] *n* : seriedad *f,* sinceridad *f*

earnings [ˈərnɪŋz] *npl* : ingresos *mpl,* ganancias *fpl,* utilidades *fpl*

earphone [ˈɪrˌfoːn] *n* : audífono *m*

earring [ˈɪrˌrɪŋ] *n* : zarcillo *m,* arete *m,* aro *m Arg, Chile, Uru,* pendiente *m Spain*

earshot [ˈɪrˌʃɑt] *n* : alcance *m* del oído

earth [ˈərθ] *n* **1** LAND, SOIL : tierra *f,* suelo *m* **2 the Earth :** la Tierra

earthen [ˈərθən, -ðən] *adj* : de tierra, de barro

earthenware [ˈərθənˌwær, -ðən-] *n* : loza *f,* vajillas *fpl* de barro

earthly [ˈərθli] *adj* : terrenal, mundano

earthquake [ˈərθˌkweɪk] *n* : terremoto *m,* temblor *m*

earthworm [ˈərθˌwərm] *n* : lombriz *f* (de tierra)

earthy [ˈərθi] *adj* **earthier; -est 1 :** terroso <earthy colors : colores terrosos> **2** DOWN-TO-EARTH : realista, práctico, llano **3** COARSE, CRUDE : basto, grosero, tosco <earthy jokes : chistes groseros>

earwax [ˈɪrˌwæks] → **wax[2]**

earwig [ˈɪrˌwɪg] *n* : tijereta *f*

ease[1] [ˈiːz] *v* **eased; easing** *vt* **1** ALLEVIATE : aliviar, calmar, hacer disminuir **2** LOOSEN, RELAX : aflojar (una cuerda), relajar (restricciones), descargar (tensiones) **3** FACILITATE : facilitar — *vi* : calmarse, relajarse

ease[2] *n* **1** CALM, RELIEF : tranquilidad *f,* comodidad *f,* desahogo *m* **2** FACILITY : facilidad *f* **3 at ~ :** relajado, cómodo <to put someone at ease : tranquilizar a alguien>

easel [ˈiːzəl] *n* : caballete *m*

easily [ˈiːzəli] *adv* **1 :** fácilmente, con facilidad **2** UNQUESTIONABLY : con mucho, de lejos

easiness [ˈiːzinəs] *n* : facilidad *f,* soltura *f*

east[1] [ˈiːst] *adv* : al este

east[2] *adj* : este, del este, oriental <east winds : vientos del este>

east[3] *n* **1 :** este *m* **2 the East :** el Oriente

Easter [ˈiːstər] *n* : Pascua *f* (de Resurrección)

easterly [ˈiːstərli] *adv & adj* : del este

eastern [ˈiːstərn] *adj* **1 :** Oriental, del Este <Eastern Europe : Europa del Este> **2 :** oriental, este

Easterner [ˈiːstərnər] *n* : habitante *mf* del este

eastward [ˈiːstwərd] *adv & adj* : hacia el este

easy [ˈiːzi] *adj* **easier; -est 1 :** fácil **2** LENIENT : indulgente

easygoing [ˌiːziˈgoːɪŋ] *adj* : acomodaticio, tolerante, poco exigente

eat [ˈiːt] *v* **ate** [ˈeɪt]; **eaten** [ˈiːtən]; **eating** *vt* **1 :** comer **2** CONSUME : consumir, gastar, devorar <expenses ate up profits : los gastos devoraron las ganancias> **3** CORRODE : corroer — *vi* **1 :** comer **2 to eat away at** *or* **to eat into :** comerse **3 to eat out :** comer fuera

eatable[1] [ˈiːt̬əbəl] *adj* : comestible, comible *fam*

eatable[2] *n* **1 :** algo para comer **2 eatables** *npl* : comestibles *mpl,* alimentos *mpl*

eater [ˈiːt̬ər] *n* : comedor *m,* -dora *f*

eaves [ˈiːvz] *npl* : alero *m*

eavesdrop [ˈiːvzˌdrɑp] *vi* **-dropped; -dropping :** escuchar a escondidas

eavesdropper [ˈiːvzˌdrɑpər] *n* : persona *f* que escucha a escondidas

ebb[1] [ˈɛb] *vi* **1 :** bajar, menguar (dícese de la marea) **2** DECLINE : decaer, disminuir

ebb[2] *n* **1** : reflujo *m* (de una marea) **2** DECLINE : decadencia *f,* declive *m,* disminución *f*

ebony[1] ['ɛbəni] *adj* **1** : de ébano **2** BLACK : de color ébano, negro

ebony[2] *n, pl* **-nies** : ébano *m*

ebullience [ɪ'bʊljən*t*s, -'bʌl-] *n* : efervescencia *f,* vivacidad *f*

ebullient [ɪ'bʊljənt, -'bʌl-] *adj* : efervescente, vivaz

eccentric[1] [ɪk'sɛntrɪk] *adj* **1** : excéntrico <an eccentric wheel : una rueda excéntrica> **2** ODD, SINGULAR : excéntrico, extraño, raro — **eccentrically** [-trɪkli] *adv*

eccentric[2] *n* : ecéntrico *m,* -ca *f*

eccentricity [ˌɛkˌsɛn'trɪsəṭi] *n, pl* **-ties** : excentricidad *f*

ecclesiastic [ɪˌkliːzi'æstɪk] *n* : eclesiástico *m,* clérigo *m*

ecclesiastical [ɪˌkliːzi'æstɪkəl] *or* **ecclesiastic** *adj* : eclesiástico — **ecclesiastically** *adv*

echelon ['ɛʃəˌlɑn] *n* **1** : escalón *m* (de tropas o aviones) **2** LEVEL : nivel *m,* esfera *f,* estrato *m*

echo[1] ['ɛˌkoː] *v* **echoed; echoing** *vi* : hacer eco, resonar — *vt* : repetir

echo[2] *n, pl* **echoes** : eco *m*

éclair [eɪ'klær, i-] *n* : pastel *m* relleno de crema

eclectic [ɛ'klɛktɪk, ɪ-] *adj* : ecléctico

eclipse[1] [ɪ'klɪps] *vt* **eclipsed; eclipsing** : eclipsar

eclipse[2] *n* : eclipse *m*

ecological *adj* [ˌiːkə'lɑdʒɪkəl, ˌɛkə-] : ecológico — **ecologically** *adv*

ecologist [i'kɑlədʒɪst, ɛ-] *n* : ecólogo *m,* -ga *f*

ecology [i'kɑlədʒi, ɛ-] *n, pl* **-gies** : ecología *f*

economic [ˌiːkə'nɑmɪk, ˌɛkə-] *adj* : económico

economical [ˌiːkə'nɑmɪkəl, ˌɛkə-] *adj* : económico — **economically** *adv*

economics [ˌiːkə'nɑmɪks, ˌɛkə-] *n* : economía *f*

economist [i'kɑnəmɪst] *n* : economista *mf*

economize [i'kɑnəˌmaɪz] *v* **-mized; -mizing** : economizar, ahorrar

economy [i'kɑnəmi] *n, pl* **-mies 1** : economía *f,* sistema *m* económico **2** THRIFT : economía *f,* ahorro *m*

ecosystem ['iːkoˌsɪstəm] *n* : ecosistema *m*

ecru ['ɛˌkruː, 'eɪ-] *n* : color *m* crudo

ecstasy ['ɛkstəsi] *n, pl* **-sies** : éxtasis *m*

ecstatic [ɛk'stæṭɪk, ɪk-] *adj* : extático

ecstatically [ɛk'stæṭɪkli, ɪk-] *adv* : con éxtasis, con gran entusiasmo

Ecuadoran [ˌɛkwə'dorən] *or* **Ecuadorean** *or* **Ecuadorian** [-'doriən] *n* : ecuatoriano *m,* -na *f* — **Ecuadorean** *or* **Ecuadorian** *adj*

ecumenical [ˌɛkjʊ'mɛnɪkəl] *adj* : ecuménico

eczema [ɪg'ziːmə, 'ɛgzəmə, 'ɛksə-] *n* : eczema *m*

eddy[1] ['ɛdi] *vi* **eddied; eddying** : arremolinarse, hacer remolinos

eddy[2] *n, pl* **-dies** : remolino *m*

edema [ɪ'diːmə] *n* : edema *m*

Eden ['iːdən] *n* : Edén *m*

edge[1] ['ɛdʒ] *v* **edged; edging** *vt* **1** BORDER : bordear, ribetear, orlar **2** SHARPEN : afilar, aguzar **3** *or* **to edge one's way** : avanzar poco a poco **4 to edge out** : derrotar por muy poco — *vi* ADVANCE : ir avanzando (poco a poco)

edge[2] *n* **1** : filo *m* (de un cuchillo) **2** BORDER : borde *m,* orilla *f,* margen *m* **3** ADVANTAGE : ventaja *f*

edger ['ɛdʒər] *n* : cortabordes *m*

edgewise ['ɛdʒˌwaɪz] *adv* SIDEWAYS : de lado, de canto

edginess ['ɛdʒinəs] *n* : tensión *f,* nerviosismo *m*

edgy ['ɛdʒi] *adj* **edgier; -est** : tenso, nervioso

edible ['ɛdəbəl] *adj* : comestible

edict ['iːˌdɪkt] *n* : edicto *m,* mandato *m,* orden *f*

edification [ˌɛdəfə'keɪʃən] *n* : edificación *f,* instrucción *f*

edifice ['ɛdəfɪs] *n* : edificio *m*

edify ['ɛdəˌfaɪ] *vt* **-fied; -fying** : edificar

edit ['ɛdɪt] *vt* **1** : editar, redactar, corregir **2** *or* **to edit out** DELETE : recortar, cortar

edition [ɪ'dɪʃən] *n* : edición *f*

editor ['ɛdɪṭər] *n* : editor *m,* -tora *f;* redactor *m,* -tora *f*

editorial[1] [ˌɛdɪ'toriəl] *adj* **1** : de redacción **2** : editorial <an editorial comment : un comentario editorial>

editorial[2] *n* : editorial *m*

editorship ['ɛdəṭərˌʃɪp] *n* : dirección *f*

educable ['ɛdʒəkəbəl] *adj* : educable

educate ['ɛdʒəˌkeɪt] *vt* **-cated; -cating 1** TEACH : educar, enseñar **2** INSTRUCT : formar, educar, instruir **3** INFORM : informar, concientizar

education [ˌɛdʒə'keɪʃən] *n* : educación *f*

educational [ˌɛdʒə'keɪʃənəl] *adj* **1** : docente, de enseñanza <an educational institution : una institución docente> **2** PEDAGOGICAL : pedagógico **3** INSTRUCTIONAL : educativo, instructivo

educator ['ɛdʒəˌkeɪṭər] *n* : educador *m,* -dora *f*

eel ['iːl] *n* : anguila *f*

eerie ['ɪri] *adj* **-rier; -est** : extraño, misterioso, fantasmagórico

eerily ['ɪrəli] *adv* : de manera extraña y misteriosa

efface [ɪ'feɪs, ɛ-] *vt* **-faced; -facing** : borrar

effect[1] [ɪ'fɛkt] *vt* **1** CARRY OUT : efectuar, llevar a cabo **2** ACHIEVE : lograr, realizar

effect[2] *n* **1** RESULT : efecto *m,* resultado *m,* consecuencia *f* <to no effect : sin resultado> **2** MEANING : sentido *m* <something to that effect : algo por el estilo> **3** INFLUENCE : efecto *m,* influencia *f* **4 effects** *npl* BELONGINGS : efectos *mpl*, pertenencias *fpl* **5 to go into effect** : entrar en vigor **6 in ~** REALLY : en realidad, efectivamente

effective [ɪˈfɛktɪv] *adj* **1** EFFECTUAL : efectivo, eficaz **2** OPERATIVE : vigente — **effectively** *adv*

effectiveness [ɪˈfɛktɪvnəs] *n* : eficacia *f*, efectividad *f*

effectual [ɪˈfɛktʃʊəl] *adj* : eficaz, efectivo — **effectually** *adv*

effeminate [əˈfɛmənət] *adj* : afeminado

effervesce [ˌɛfərˈvɛs] *vi* **-vesced; -vescing 1** : estar en efervescencia, burbujear (dícese de líquidos) **2** : estar eufórico, estar muy animado (dícese de las personas)

effervescence [ˌɛfərˈvɛsənts] *n* **1** : efervescencia *f* **2** LIVELINESS : vivacidad *f*

effervescent [ˌɛfərˈvɛsənt] *adj* **1** : efervescente **2** LIVELY, VIVACIOUS : vivaz, animado

effete [ɛˈfiːt, ɪ-] *adj* **1** WORN- OUT : desgastado, agotado **2** DECADENT : decadente **3** EFFEMINATE : afeminado

efficacious [ˌɛfəˈkeɪʃəs] *adj* : eficaz, efectivo

efficacy [ˈɛfɪkəsi] *n, pl* **-cies** : eficacia *f*

efficiency [ɪˈfɪʃəntsi] *n, pl* **-cies** : eficiencia *f*

efficient [ɪˈfɪʃənt] *adj* : eficiente — **efficiently** *adv*

effigy [ˈɛfədʒi] *n, pl* **-gies** : efigie *f*

effluent [ˈɛˌfluːənt, ɛˈfluː-] *n* : efluente *m* — **effluent** *adj*

effort [ˈɛfərt] *n* **1** EXERTION : esfuerzo *m* **2** ATTEMPT : tentativa *f*, intento *m* <it's not worth the effort : no vale la pena>

effortless [ˈɛfərtləs] *adj* : fácil, sin esfuerzo

effortlessly [ˈɛfərtləsli] *adv* : sin esfuerzo, fácilmente

effrontery [ɪˈfrʌntəri] *n, pl* **-teries** : insolencia *f*, desfachatez *f*, descaro *m*

effusion [ɪˈfjuːʒən, ɛ-] *n* : efusión *f*

effusive [ɪˈfjuːsɪv, ɛ-] *adj* : efusivo — **effusively** *adv*

egg[1] [ˈɛg] *vt* **to egg on** : incitar, azuzar, provocar

egg[2] *n* **1** : huevo *m* **2** OVUM : óvulo *m*

eggbeater [ˈɛgˌbiːtər] *n* : batidor *m* (de huevos)

eggnog [ˈɛgˌnɑg] *n* : ponche *m* de huevo, rompope *m CA, Mex*

eggplant [ˈɛgˌplænt] *n* : berenjena *f*

eggshell [ˈɛgˌʃɛl] *n* : cascarón *m*

ego [ˈiːˌgoː] *n, pl* **egos 1** SELF-ESTEEM : amor *m* propio **2** SELF : ego *m*, yo *m*

egocentric [ˌiːgoˈsɛntrɪk] *adj* : egocéntrico

egoism [ˈiːgoˌwɪzəm] *n* : egoísmo *m*

egoist [ˈiːgowɪst] *n* : egoísta *mf*

egoistic [ˌiːˌgoˈwɪstɪk] *adj* : egoísta

egotism [ˈiːgəˌtɪzəm] *n* : egotismo *m*

egotist [ˈiːgətɪst] *n* : egotista *mf*

egotistic [ˌiːgəˈtɪstɪk] *or* **egotistical** [-ˈtɪstɪkəl] *adj* : egotista — **egotistically** *adv*

egregious [ɪˈgriːdʒəs] *adj* : atroz, flagrante, mayúsculo — **egregiously** *adv*

egress [ˈiːˌgrɛs] *n* : salida *f*

egret [ˈiːgrət, -ˌgrɛt] *n* : garceta *f*

eiderdown [ˈaɪdərˌdaʊn] *n* **1** : plumón *m* **2** COMFORTER : edredón *m*

eight[1] *adj* [ˈeɪt] : ocho

eight[2] *n* : ocho *m*

eight hundred[1] *adj* : ochocientos

eight hundred[2] *n* : ochocientos *m*

eighteen[1] [eitˈtiːn] *adj* : dieciocho

eighteen[2] *n* : dieciocho *m*

eighteenth[1] [eɪtˈtiːnθ] *adj* : decimoctavo

eighteenth[2] *n* **1** : decimoctavo *m*, -va *f* (en una serie) **2** : dieciochoavo *m*, dieciochoava parte *f*

eighth[1] [ˈeɪtθ] *adj* : octavo

eighth[2] *n* **1** : octavo *m*, -va *f* (en una serie) **2** : octavo *m*, octava parte *f*

eightieth[1] [ˈeɪt̬iəθ] *adj* : octagésimo

eightieth[2] *n* **1** : octogésimo *m*, -ma *f* (en una serie) **2** : ochentavo *m*, ochentava parte *f*

eighty[1] [ˈeɪt̬i] *adj* : ochenta

eighty[2] *n, pl* **eighties 1** : ochenta *m* **2 the eighties** : los ochenta *mpl*

either[1] [ˈiːðər, ˈaɪ-] *adj* **1** : cualquiera (de los dos) <we can watch either movie : podemos ver cualquiera de las dos películas> **2** : ninguno de los dos <she wasn't in either room : no estaba en ninguna de las dos salas> **3** EACH : cada <on either side of the street : a cada lado de la calle>

either[2] *pron* **1** : cualquiera *mf* (de los dos) <either is fine : cualquiera de los dos está bien> **2** : ninguno *m*, -na *f* (de los dos) <I don't like either : no me gusta ninguno> **3** : algún *m*, alguna *f* <is either of you interested? : ¿está alguno de ustedes (dos) interesado?>

either[3] *conj* **1** : o, u <either David or Daniel could go : puede ir (o) David o Daniel> **2** : ni <we won't watch either this movie or the other : no veremos ni esta película ni la otra>

ejaculate [iˈdʒækjəˌleɪt] *v* **-lated; -lating** *vt* **1** : eyacular **2** EXCLAIM : exclamar — *vi* : eyacular

ejaculation [iˌdʒækjəˈleɪʃən] *n* **1** : eyaculación *f* (en fisiología) **2** EXCLAMATION : exclamación *f*

eject [iˈdʒɛkt] *vt* : expulsar, expeler

ejection [iˈdʒɛkʃən] *n* : expulsión *f*

eke [ˈiːk] *vt* **eked; eking** *or* **to eke out** : ganar a duras penas

elaborate[1] [iˈlæbəˌreɪt] *v* **-rated; -rating** *vt* : elaborar, idear, desarrollar — *vi* **to elaborate on** : ampliar, entrar en detalles

elaborate[2] [iˈlæbərət] *adj* **1** DETAILED : detallado, minucioso, elaborado **2** COMPLICATED : complicado, intrincado, elaborado — **elaborately** *adv*

elaboration [iˌlæbəˈreɪʃən] *n* **:** elaboración *f*
elapse [iˈlæps] *vi* **elapsed; elapsing :** transcurrir, pasar
elastic[1] [iˈlæstɪk] *adj* **:** elástico
elastic[2] *n* **1 :** elástico *m* **2** RUBBER BAND **:** goma *f,* gomita *f,* elástico *m,* liga *f*
elasticity [iˌlæsˈtɪsəṭi, ˌiːˌlæs-] *n, pl* **-ties :** elasticidad *f*
elate [iˈleɪt] *vt* **elated; elating :** alborozar, regocijar
elation [iˈleɪʃən] *n* **:** euforia *f,* júbilo *m,* alborozo *m*
elbow[1] [ˈɛlˌboː] *vt* **:** darle un codazo a
elbow[2] *n* **:** codo *m*
elder[1] [ˈɛldər] *adj* **:** mayor
elder[2] *n* **1 to be someone's elder :** ser mayor que alguien **2 :** anciano *m,* -na *f* (de un pueblo o una tribu) **3 :** miembro *m* del consejo (en varias religiones)
elderberry [ˈɛldərˌbɛri] *n, pl* **-berries :** baya *f* de saúco (fruta), saúco *m* (árbol)
elderly [ˈɛldərli] *adj* **:** mayor, de edad, anciano
eldest [ˈɛldəst] *adj* **:** mayor, de más edad
elect[1] [iˈlɛkt] *vt* **:** elegir
elect[2] *adj* **:** electo <the president-elect : el presidente electo>
elect[3] *npl* **the elect :** los elegidos *mpl*
election [iˈlɛkʃən] *n* **:** elección *f*
elective[1] [iˈlɛktɪv] *adj* **1 :** electivo **2** OPTIONAL **:** facultativo, optativo
elective[2] *n* **:** asignatura *f* electiva
elector [iˈlɛktər] *n* **:** elector *m,* -tora *f*
electoral [iˈlɛktərəl] *adj* **:** electoral
electorate [iˈlɛktərət] *n* **:** electorado *m*
electric [iˈlɛktrɪk] *adj* **1** *or* **electrical** [-trɪkəl] **:** eléctrico **2** THRILLING **:** electrizante, emocionante
electrician [iˌlɛkˈtrɪʃən] *n* **:** electricista *mf*
electricity [iˌlɛkˈtrɪsəṭi] *n, pl* **-ties 1 :** electricidad *f* **2** CURRENT **:** corriente *m* eléctrica
electrification [iˌlɛktrəfəˈkeɪʃən] *n* **:** electrificación *f*
electrify [iˈlɛktrəˌfaɪ] *vt* **-fied; -fying 1 :** electrificar **2** THRILL **:** electrizar, emocionar
electrocardiogram [iˌlɛktroˈkɑrdiəˌgræm] *n* **:** electrocardiograma *m*
electrocardiograph [iˌlɛktroˈkɑrdiəˌgræf] *n* **:** electrocardiógrafo *m*
electrocute [iˈlɛktrəˌkjuːt] *vt* **-cuted; -cuting :** electrocutar
electrocution [iˌlɛktrəˈkjuːʃən] *n* **:** electrocución *f*
electrode [iˈlɛkˌtroːd] *n* **:** electrodo *m*
electrolysis [iˌlɛkˈtrɑləsɪs] *n* **:** electrólisis *f*
electrolyte [iˈlɛktrəˌlaɪt] *n* **:** electrolito *m*
electromagnet [iˌlɛktroˈmægnət] *n* **:** electroimán *m*
electromagnetic [iˌlɛktromægˈnɛṭɪk] *adj* **:** electromagnético **— electromagnetically** [-ṭɪkli] *adv*
electromagnetism [iˌlɛktroˈmægnəˌtɪzəm] *n* **:** electromagnetismo *m*
electron [iˈlɛkˌtrɑn] *n* **:** electrón *m*
electronic [iˌlɛkˈtrɑnɪk] *adj* **:** electrónico **— electronically** [-nɪkli] *adv*
electronic mail *n* **:** correo *m* electrónico
electronics [iˌlɛkˈtrɑnɪks] *n* **:** electrónica *f*
electroplate [iˈlɛktrəˌpleɪt] *vt* **-plated; plating :** galvanizar mediante electrólisis
elegance [ˈɛlɪgən*t*s] *n* **:** elegancia *f*
elegant [ˈɛlɪgənt] *adj* **:** elegante **— elegantly** *adv*
elegy [ˈɛlədʒi] *n, pl* **-gies :** elegía *f*
element [ˈɛləmənt] *n* **1** COMPONENT **:** elemento *m,* factor *m* **2 :** elemento *m* (en la química) **3** MILIEU **:** elemento *m,* medio *m* <to be in one's element : estar en su elemento> **4 elements** *npl* RUDIMENTS **:** elementos *mpl,* rudimentos *mpl,* bases *fpl* **5 the elements** WEATHER **:** los elementos *mpl*
elemental [ˌɛləˈmɛntəl] *adj* **1** BASIC **:** elemental, primario **2 :** elemental (dícese de los elementos químicos)
elementary [ˌɛləˈmɛntri] *adj* **1** SIMPLE **:** elemental, simple, fundamental **2 :** de enseñanza primaria
elementary school *n* **:** escuela *f* primaria
elephant [ˈɛləfənt] *n* **:** elefante *m,* -ta *f*
elevate [ˈɛləˌveɪt] *vt* **-vated; -vating 1** RAISE **:** elevar, levantar, alzar **2** EXALT, PROMOTE **:** elevar, exaltar, ascender **3** ELATE **:** alborozar, regocijar
elevation [ˌɛləˈveɪʃən] *n* **1 :** elevación *f* **2** ALTITUDE **:** altura *f,* altitud *f* **3** PROMOTION **:** ascenso *m*
elevator [ˈɛləˌveɪṭər] *n* **:** ascensor *m,* elevador *m*
eleven[1] [ɪˈlɛvən] *adj* **:** once *m*
eleven[2] *n* **:** once *m*
eleventh[1] [ɪlɛvən*t*θ] *adj* **:** undécimo
eleventh[2] *n* **1 :** undécimo *m,* -ma *f* (en una serie) **2 :** onceavo *m,* onceava parte *f*
elf [ˈɛlf] *n, pl* **elves** [ˈɛlvz] **:** elfo *m,* geniecillo *m,* duende *m*
elfin [ˈɛlfən] *adj* **1 :** de elfo, menudo **2** ENCHANTING, MAGIC **:** mágico, encantador
elfish [ˈɛlfɪʃ] *adj* **1 :** de elfo **2** MISCHIEVOUS **:** travieso
elicit [ɪˈlɪsət] *vt* **:** provocar
eligibility [ˌɛlədʒəˈbɪləṭi] *n, pl* **-ties :** elegibilidad *f*
eligible [ˈɛlədʒəbəl] *adj* **1** QUALIFIED **:** elegible **2** SUITABLE **:** idóneo
eliminate [ɪˈlɪməˌneɪt] *vt* **-nated; -nating :** eliminar
elimination [ɪˌlɪməˈneɪʃən] *n* **:** eliminación *f*
elite [eɪˈliːt, i-] *n* **:** elite *f*

elixir [iˈlɪksər] *n* : elixir *m*
elk [ˈɛlk] *n* : alce *m* (de Europa), uapití *m* (de América)
ellipse [ɪˈlɪps, ɛ-] *n* : elipse *f*
ellipsis [ɪˈlɪpsəs, ɛ-] *n, pl* **-lipses** [-ˌsiːz] **1** : elipsis *f* **2** : puntos *mpl* suspensivos (en la puntuación)
elliptical [ɪˈlɪptɪkəl, ɛ-] *or* **elliptic** [-tɪk] *adj* : elíptico
elm [ˈɛlm] *n* : olmo *m*
elocution [ˌɛləˈkjuːʃən] *n* : elocución *f*
elongate [iˈlɔŋˌgeɪt] *vt* **-gated; -gating** : alargar
elongation [ˌiːˌlɔŋˈgeɪʃən] *n* : alargamiento *m*
elope [iˈloːp] *vi* **eloped; eloping** : fugarse
elopement [iˈloːpmənt] *n* : fuga *f*
eloquence [ˈɛləkwənts] *n* : elocuencia *f*
eloquent [ˈɛləkwənt] *adj* : elocuente — **eloquently** *adv*
El Salvadoran [ˌɛlˌsælvəˈdorən] *n* : salvadoreño *m*, -ña *f* — **El Salvadoran** *adj*
else[1] [ˈɛls] *adv* **1** DIFFERENTLY : de otro modo, de otra manera <how else? : ¿de qué otro modo?> **2** ELSEWHERE : de otro sitio, de otro lugar <where else? : ¿en qué otro sitio?> **3 or else** OTHERWISE : si no, de lo contrario
else[2] *adj* **1** OTHER : otro <anyone else : cualquier otro> <everyone else : todos los demás> <nobody else : ningún otro, nadie más> <somebody else : otra persona> **2** MORE : más <nothing else : nada más> <what else? : ¿qué más?>
elsewhere [ˈɛlsˌhwɛr] *adv* : en otra parte, en otro sitio, en otro lugar
elucidate [iˈluːsəˌdeɪt] *vt* **-dated; -dating** : dilucidar, elucidar, esclarecer
elucidation [iˌluːsəˈdeɪʃən] *n* : elucidación *f*, esclarecimiento *m*
elude [iˈluːd] *vt* **eluded; eluding** : eludir, evadir
elusive [iˈluːsɪv] *adj* **1** EVASIVE : evasivo, esquivo **2** SLIPPERY : huidizo, escurridizo **3** FLEETING, INTANGIBLE : impalpable, fugaz
elusively [iˈluːsɪvli] *adv* : de manera esquiva
elves → **elf**
emaciate [iˈmeɪʃiˌeɪt] *vt* **-ated; -ating** : enflaquecer
emaciation [iˌmeɪsiˈeɪʃən, -ʃi-] *n* : enflaquecimiento *m*, escualidez *f*, delgadez *f* extrema
E–mail [ˈiːˌmeɪl] → **electronic mail**
emanate [ˈɛməˌneɪt] *v* **-nated; -nating** *vi* : emanar, provenir, proceder — *vt* : emanar
emanation [ˌɛməˈneɪʃən] *n* : emanación *f*
emancipate [iˈmæntsəˌpeɪt] *vt* **-pated; -pating** : emancipar
emancipation [iˌmæntsəˈpeɪʃən] *n* : emancipación *f*
emasculate [iˈmæskjəˌleɪt] *vt* **-lated; -lating 1** CASTRATE : castrar, emascular **2** WEAKEN : debilitar
embalm [ɪmˈbɑm, ɛm-, -ˈbɑlm] *vt* : embalsamar
embankment [ɪmˈbæŋkmənt, ɛm-] *n* : terraplén *m*, muro *m* de contención
embargo[1] [ɪmˈbɑrgo, ɛm-] *vt* **-goed; -going** : imponer un embargo sobre
embargo[2] *n, pl* **-goes** : embargo *m*
embark [ɪmˈbɑrk, ɛm-] *vt* : embarcar — *vi* **1** : embarcarse **2 to embark on** START : emprender, embarcarse en
embarkation [ˌɛmˌbɑrˈkeɪʃən] *n* : embarque *m*, embarco *m*
embarrass [ɪmˈbærəs, ɛm-] *vt* : avergonzar, abochornar
embarrassing [ɪmˈbærəsɪŋ, ɛm-] *adj* : embarazoso, violento
embarrassment [ɪmˈbærəsmənt, ɛm-] *n* : vergüenza *f*, pena *f*
embassy [ˈɛmbəsi] *n, pl* **-sies** : embajada *f*
embed [ɪmˈbɛd, ɛm-] *vt* **-bedded; -bedding** : incrustar, empotrar, grabar (en la memoria)
embellish [ɪmˈbɛlɪʃ, ɛm-] *vt* : adornar, embellecer
embellishment [ɪmˈbɛlɪʃmənt, ɛm-] *n* : adorno *m*
ember [ˈɛmbər] *n* : ascua *f*, brasa *f*
embezzle [ɪmˈbɛzəl, ɛm-] *vt* **-zled; -zling** : desfalcar, malversar
embezzlement [ɪmˈbɛzəlmənt, ɛm-] *n* : desfalco *m*, malversación *f*
embezzler [ɪmˈbɛzələr, ɛm-] *n* : desfacador *m*, **-dora** *f*; malversador *m*, -dora *f*
embitter [ɪmˈbɪt̬ər, ɛm-] *vt* : amargar
emblem [ˈɛmbləm] *n* : emblema *m*, símbolo *m*
emblematic [ˌɛmbləˈmæt̬ɪk] *adj* : emblemático, simbólico
embodiment [ɪmˈbɑdɪmənt, ɛm-] *n* : encarnación *f*, personificación *f*
embody [ɪmˈbɑdi, ɛm-] *vt* **-bodied; -bodying** : encarnar, personificar
emboss [ɪmˈbɑs, ɛm-, -ˈbɔs] *vt* : repujar, grabar en relieve
embrace[1] [ɪmˈbreɪs, ɛm-] *vt* **-braced; -bracing 1** HUG : abrazar **2** ADOPT, TAKE ON : adoptar, aceptar **3** INCLUDE : abarcar, incluir
embrace[2] *n* : abrazo *m*
embroider [ɪmˈbrɔɪdər, ɛm-] *vt* : bordar (una tela), adornar (una historia)
embroidery [ɪmˈbrɔɪdəri, ɛm-] *n, pl* **-deries** : bordado *m*
embroil [ɪmˈbrɔɪl, ɛm-] *vt* : embrollar, enredar
embryo [ˈɛmbriˌoː] *n, pl* **embryos** : embrión *m*
embryonic [ˌɛmbriˈɑnɪk] *adj* : embrionario
emend [iˈmɛnd] *vt* : enmendar, corregir

emendation [ˌiːˌmɛnˈdeɪʃən] *n* : enmienda *f*

emerald[1] [ˈɛmrəld, ˈɛmə-] *adj* : verde esmeralda

emerald[2] *n* : esmeralda *f*

emerge [iˈmərdʒ] *vi* **emerged; emerging** : emerger, salir, aparecer, surgir

emergence [iˈmərdʒənts] *n* : aparición *f,* surgimiento *m*

emergency [iˈmərdʒəntsi] *n, pl* **-cies** : emergencia *f*

emergent [iˈmərdʒənt] *adj* : emergente

emery [ˈɛməri] *n, pl* **-eries** : esmeril *m*

emetic[1] [iˈmɛt̬ɪk] *adj* : vomitivo, emético

emetic[2] *n* : vomitivo *m,* emético *m*

emigrant [ˈɛmɪgrənt] *n* : emigrante *mf*

emigrate [ˈɛməˌgreɪt] *vi* **-grated; -grating** : emigrar

emigration [ˌɛməˈgreɪʃən] *n* : emigración *f*

eminence [ˈɛmənənts] *n* **1** PROMINENCE : eminencia *f,* prestigio *m,* renombre *m* **2** DIGNITARY : eminencia *f;* dignatario *m,* -ria *f* <Your Eminence : Su Eminencia>

eminent [ˈɛmənənt] *adj* : eminente, ilustre

eminently [ˈɛmənəntli] *adv* : sumamente

emissary [ˈɛməˌsɛri] *n, pl* **-saries** : emisario *m,* -ria *f*

emission [iˈmɪʃən] *n* : emisión *f*

emit [iˈmɪt] *vt* **emitted; emitting** : emitir, despedir, producir

emote [iˈmoːt] *vi* **emoted; emoting** : exteriorizar las emociones

emotion [iˈmoːʃən] *n* : emoción *f,* sentimiento *m*

emotional [iˈmoːʃənəl] *adj* **1** : emocional, afectivo <an emotional reaction : una reacción emocional> **2** MOVING : emocionante, emotivo, conmovedor

emotionally [iˈmoːʃənəli] *adv* : emocionalmente

emperor [ˈɛmpərər] *n* : emperador *m*

emphasis [ˈɛmfəsɪs] *n, pl* **-phases** [-ˌsiːz] : énfasis *m,* hincapié *m*

emphasize [ˈɛmfəˌsaɪz] *vt* **-sized; -sizing** : enfatizar, destacar, subrayar, hacer hincapié en

emphatic [ɪmˈfætɪk, ɛm-] *adj* : enfático, enérgico, categórico — **emphatically** [-ɪkli] *adv*

empire [ˈɛmˌpaɪr] *n* : imperio *m*

empirical [ɪmˈpɪrɪkəl, ɛm-] *adj* : empírico — **empirically** [-ɪkli] *adv*

employ[1] [ɪmˈplɔɪ, ɛm-] *vt* **1** USE : usar, utilizar **2** HIRE : contratar, emplear **3** OCCUPY : ocupar, dedicar, emplear

employ[2] [ɪmˈplɔɪ, ɛm-; ˈɪmˌ-, ˈɛmˌ-] *n* **1** : puesto *m,* cargo *m,* ocupación *f* **2 to be in the employ of** : estar al servicio de, trabajar para

employee [ɪmˌplɔɪˈiː, ɛm-, -ˈplɔɪˌiː] *n* : empleado *m,* -da *f*

employer [ɪmˈplɔɪər, ɛm-] *n* : patrón *m,* -trona *f;* empleador *m,* -dora *f*

employment [ɪmˈplɔɪmənt, ɛm-] *n* : trabajo *m,* empleo *m*

empower [ɪmˈpaʊər, ɛm-] *vt* : facultar, autorizar, conferirle poder a

empowerment [ɪmˈpaʊərmənt, ɛm-] *n* : autorización *f*

empress [ˈɛmprəs] *n* : emperatriz *f*

emptiness [ˈɛmptinəs] *n* : vacío *m,* vacuidad *f*

empty[1] [ˈɛmpti] *v* **-tied; -tying** *vt* : vaciar — *vi* : desaguar (dícese de un río)

empty[2] *adj* **emptier; -est 1** : vacío **2** VACANT : desocupado, libre **3** MEANINGLESS : vacío, hueco, vano

empty–handed [ˌɛmptiˈhændəd] *adj* : con las manos vacías

empty–headed [ˌɛmptiˈhɛdəd] *adj* : cabeza hueca, tonto

emu [ˈiːˌmjuː] *n* : emú *m*

emulate [ˈɛmjəˌleɪt] *vt* **-lated; -lating** : emular

emulation [ˌɛmjəˈleɪʃən] *n* : emulación *f*

emulsifier [ɪˈmʌlsəˌfaɪər] *n* : emulsionante *m*

emulsify [ɪˈmʌlsəˌfaɪ] *vt* **-fied; -fying** : emulsionar

emulsion [ɪˈmʌlʃən] *n* : emulsión *f*

enable [ɪˈneɪbəl, ɛ-] *vt* **-abled; -abling 1** EMPOWER : habilitar, autorizar, facultar **2** PERMIT : hacer posible, posibilitar, permitar

enact [ɪˈnækt, ɛ-] *vt* **1** : promulgar (un ley o decreto) **2** : representar (un papel en el teatro)

enactment [ɪˈnæktmənt, ɛ-] *n* : promulgación *f*

enamel[1] [ɪˈnæməl] *vt* **-eled** *or* **-elled; -eling** *or* **-elling** : esmaltar

enamel[2] *n* : esmalte *m*

enamor [ɪˈnæmər] *vt* **1** : enamorar **2 to be enamored of** : estar enamorado de (una persona), estar entusiasmado con (algo)

encamp [ɪnˈkæmp, ɛn-] *vi* : acampar

encampment [ɪnˈkæmpmənt, ɛn-] *n* : campamento *m*

encase [ɪnˈkeɪs, ɛn-] *vt* **-cased; -casing** : encerrar, revestir

encephalitis [ɪnˌsɛfəˈlaɪt̬əs, ɛn-] *n, pl* **-litides** [-ˈlɪt̬əˌdiːz] : encefalitis *f*

enchant [ɪnˈtʃænt, ɛn-] *vt* **1** BEWITCH : hechizar, encantar, embrujar **2** CHARM, FASCINATE : cautivar, fascinar, encantar

enchanting [ɪnˈtʃæntɪŋ, ɛn-] *adj* : encantador

enchanter [ɪnˈtʃæntər, ɛn-] *n* SORCERER : mago *m,* encantador *m*

enchantment [ɪnˈtʃæntmənt, ɛn-] *n* **1** SPELL : encanto *m,* hechizo *m* **2** CHARM : encanto *m*

enchantress [ɪnˈtʃæntrəs, ɛn-] *n* **1** SORCERESS : maga *f,* hechicera *f* **2** CHARMER : mujer *f* cautivadora

encircle [ɪnˈsərkəl, ɛn-] *vt* **-cled; -cling** : rodear, ceñir, cercar

enclose [ɪnˈkloːz, ɛn-] *vt* **-closed; -closing 1** SURROUND : encerrar, cercar, rodear **2** INCLUDE : incluir, adjuntar, acompañar <please find enclosed : le enviamos adjunto>

enclosure [ɪn'klo:ʒər, ɛn-] *n* **1** ENCLOSING : encierro *m* **2** : cercado *m* (de terreno), recinto *m* <an enclosure for the press : un recinto para la prensa> **3** ADJUNCT : anexo *m* (con una carta), documento *m* adjunto

encompass [ɪn'kʌmpəs, ɛn-, -'kɑm-] *vt* **1** SURROUND : circundar, rodear **2** INCLUDE : abarcar, comprender

encore ['ɑn,kor] *n* : bis *m*, repetición *f*

encounter[1] [ɪn'kaʊntər, ɛn-] *vt* **1** MEET : encontrar, encontrarse con, toparse con, tropezar con **2** FIGHT : combatir, luchar contra

encounter[2] *n* : encuentro *m*

encourage [ɪn'kərɪdʒ, ɛn-] *vt* **-aged; -aging 1** HEARTEN, INSPIRE : animar, alentar **2** FOSTER : fomentar, promover

encouragement [ɪn'kərɪdʒmənt, ɛn-] *n* : ánimo *m*, aliento *m*

encroach [ɪn'kro:tʃ, ɛn-] *vi* **to encroach on** : invadir, abusar (derechos), quitar (tiempo)

encroachment [ɪn'kro:tʃmənt, ɛn-] *n* : invasión *f*, usurpación *f*

encrust [ɪn'krʌst, ɛn-] *vt* **1** : recubrir con una costra **2** INLAY : incrustar <encrusted with gems : incrustado de gemas>

encumber [ɪn'kʌmbər, ɛn-] *vt* **1** BLOCK : obstruir, estorbar **2** BURDEN : cargar, gravar

encumbrance [ɪn'kʌmbrən*t*s, ɛn-] *n* : estorbo *m*, carga *f*, gravamen *m*

encyclopedia [ɪn,saɪklə'pi:diə, ɛn-] *n* : enciclopedia *f*

encyclopedic [ɪn,saɪklə'pi:dɪk, ɛn-] *adj* : enciclopédico

end[1] ['ɛnd] *vt* **1** STOP : terminar, poner fin a **2** CONCLUDE : concluir, terminar — *vi* : terminar(se), acabar, concluir(se)

end[2] *n* **1** EXTREMITY : extremo *m*, final *m*, punta *f* **2** CONCLUSION : fin *m*, final *m* **3** AIM : fin *m*

endanger [ɪn'deɪndʒər, ɛn-] *vt* : poner en peligro

endear [ɪn'dɪr, ɛn-] *vt* **to endear oneself to** : ganarse la simpatía de, granjearse el cariño de

endearment [ɪn'dɪrmənt, ɛn-] *n* : expresión *f* de cariño

endeavor[1] [ɪn'dɛvər, ɛn-] *vt* : intentar, esforzarse por <he endeavored to improve his work : intentó por mejorar su trabajo>

endeavor[2] *n* : intento *m*, esfuerzo *m*

ending ['ɛndɪŋ] *n* **1** CONCLUSION : final *m*, desenlace *m* **2** SUFFIX : sufijo *m*, terminación *f*

endive ['ɛn,daɪv, ,ɑn'di:v] *n* : endibia *f*, endivia *f*

endless ['ɛndləs] *adj* **1** INTERMINABLE : interminable, inacabable, sin fin **2** INNUMERABLE : innumerable, incontable

endlessly ['ɛndləsli] *adv* : interminablemente, eternamente, sin parar

endocrine ['ɛndəkrən, -,kraɪn, -,kri:n] *adj* : endocrino

endorse [ɪn'dɔrs, ɛn-] *vt* **-dorsed; -dorsing 1** SIGN : endosar, firmar **2** APPROVE : aprobar, sancionar

endorsement [ɪn'dɔrsmənt, ɛn-] *n* **1** SIGNATURE : endoso *m*, firma *f* **2** APPROVAL : aprobación *f*, aval *m*

endow [ɪn'daʊ, ɛn-] *vt* : dotar

endowment [ɪn'daʊmənt, ɛn-] *n* **1** FUNDING : dotación *f* **2** DONATION : donación *f*, legado *m* **3** ATTRIBUTE, GIFT : atributo *m*, dotes *fpl*

endurable [ɪn'dʊrəbəl, ɛn-, -'djʊr-] *adj* : tolerable, soportable

endurance [ɪn'dʊrən*t*s, ɛn-, -'djʊr-] *n* : resistencia *f*, aguante *m*

endure [ɪn'dʊr, ɛn-, -'djʊr] *v* **-dured; -during** *vt* **1** BEAR : resistir, soportar, aguantar **2** TOLERATE : tolerar, soportar — *vi* LAST : durar, perdurar

enema ['ɛnəmə] *n* : enema *m*, lavativa *f*

enemy ['ɛnəmi] *n, pl* **-mies** : enemigo *m*, **-ga** *f*

energetic [,ɛnər'dʒɛtɪk] *adj* : enérgico, vigoroso — **energetically** [-tɪkli] *adv*

energize ['ɛnər,dʒaɪz] *vt* **-gized; -gizing 1** ACTIVATE : activar **2** INVIGORATE : vigorizar

energy ['ɛnərdʒi] *n, pl* **-gies 1** VITALITY : energía *f*, vitalidad *f* **2** EFFORT : esfuerzo *m*, energías *fpl* **3** POWER : energía *f* <atomic energy : energía atómica>

enervate ['ɛnər,veɪt] *vt* **-vated; -vating** : enervar, debilitar

enervation [,ɛnər'veɪʃən] *n* : enervación *f*, debilidad *f*

enfold [ɪn'fo:ld, ɛn-] *vt* : envolver

enforce [ɪn'fors, ɛn-] *vt* **-forced; -forcing 1** : hacer respetar, hacer cumplir (una ley, etc.) **2** IMPOSE : imponer <to enforce obedience : imponer la obediencia>

enforcement [ɪn'forsmənt, ɛn-] *n* : imposición *f*

enfranchise [ɪn'fræn,tʃaɪz, ɛn-] *vt* **-chised; -chising** : conceder el voto a

enfranchisement [ɪn'fræn,tʃaɪzmənt, ɛn-] *n* : concesión *f* del voto

engage [ɪn'geɪdʒ, ɛn-] *v* **-gaged; -gaging** *vt* **1** ATTRACT : captar, atraer, llamar <to engage one's attention : captar la atención> **2** MESH : engranar <to engage the clutch : embragar> **3** COMMIT : comprometer <to get engaged : comprometerse> **4** HIRE : contratar **5** : entablar combate con (un enemigo) — *vi* **1** PARTICIPATE : participar **2 to engage in combat** : entrar en combate

engagement [ɪn'geɪdʒmənt, ɛn-] *n* **1** APPOINTMENT : cita *f,* hora *f* **2** BETROTHAL : compromiso *m*

engaging [ɪn'geɪdʒɪŋ, ɛn-] *adj* : atractivo, encantador, interesante

engender [ɪn'dʒɛndər, ɛn-] *vt* **-dered; -dering** : engendrar

engine ['ɛndʒən] *n* **1** MOTOR : motor *m* **2** LOCOMOTIVE : locomotora *f,* máquina *f*

engineer[1] [ˌɛndʒə'nɪr] *vt* **1** : diseñar, construir (un sistema, un mecanismo, etc.) **2** CONTRIVE : maquinar, tramar, fraguar

engineer[2] *n* **1** : ingeniero *m,* -ra *f* **2** : maquinista *mf* (de locomotoras)

engineering [ˌɛndʒə'nɪrɪŋ] *n* : ingeniería *f*

English[1] ['ɪŋglɪʃ, 'ŋlɪʃ] *adj* : inglés

English[2] *n* **1** : inglés *m* (idioma) **2 the English** : los ingleses

Englishman ['ɪŋglɪʃmən, 'ɪŋlɪʃ-] *n, pl* **-men** [-mən, -ˌmɛn] : inglés *m*

Englishwoman ['ɪŋglɪʃˌwʊmən, 'ɪŋlɪʃ-] *n, pl* **-women** [-ˌwɪmən] : inglesa *f*

engrave [ɪn'greɪv, ɛn-] *vt* **-graved; -graving** : grabar

engraver [ɪn'greɪvər, ɛn-] *n* : grabador *m,* -dora *f*

engraving [ɪn'greɪvɪŋ, ɛn-] *n* : grabado *m*

engross [ɪn'groːs, ɛn-] *vt* : absorber

engrossed [ɪn'groːst, ɛn-] *adj* : absorto

engulf [ɪn'gʌlf, ɛn-] *vt* : envolver, sepultar

enhance [ɪn'hæn*t*s, ɛn-] *vt* **-hanced; -hancing** : realzar, aumentar, mejorar

enhancement [ɪn'hæn*t*smənt, ɛn-] *n* : mejora *f,* realce *m,* aumento *m*

enigma [ɪ'nɪgmə] *n* : enigma *m*

enigmatic [ˌɛnɪg'mæṭɪk, ˌiːnɪg-] *adj* : enigmático — **enigmatically** [-ṭɪkli] *adv*

enjoin [ɪn'dʒɔɪn, ɛn-] *vt* **1** COMMAND : ordenar, imponer **2** FORBID : prohibir, vedar

enjoy [ɪn'dʒɔɪ, ɛn-] *vt* **1** : disfrutar, gozar de <did you enjoy the book? : ¿te gustó el libro?> <to enjoy good health : gozar de buena salud> **2 to enjoy oneself** : divertirse, pasarlo bien

enjoyable [ɪn'dʒɔɪəbəl, ɛn-] *adj* : agradable, placentero, divertido

enjoyment [ɪn'dʒɔɪmənt, ɛn-] *n* : placer *m,* goce *m,* disfrute *m,* deleite *m*

enlarge [ɪn'lɑrdʒ, ɛn-] *v* **-larged; -larging** *vt* : extender, agrandar, ampliar — *vi* **1** : ampliarse **2 to enlarge upon** : extenderse sobre, entrar en detalles sobre

enlargement [ɪn'lɑrdʒmənt, ɛn-] *n* : expansión *f,* ampliación *f* (dícese de fotografías)

enlarger [ɪn'lɑrdʒər, ɛn-] *n* : ampliadora *f*

enlighten [ɪn'laɪtən, ɛn-] *vt* : iluminar, aclarar

enlightenment [ɪn'laɪtənmənt, ɛn-] *n* **1** : ilustración *f* <the Enlightenment : la Ilustración> **2** CLARIFICATION : aclaración *f*

enlist [ɪn'lɪst, ɛn-] *vt* **1** ENROLL : alistar, reclutar **2** SECURE : conseguir <to enlist the support of : conseguir el apoyo de> — *vi* : alistarse

enlisted man [ɪn'lɪstəd, ɛn-] *n* : soldado *m* raso

enlistment [ɪn'lɪstmənt, ɛn-] *n* : alistamiento *m,* reclutamiento *m*

enliven [ɪn'laɪvən, ɛn-] *vt* : animar, alegrar, darle vida a

enmity ['ɛnməṭi] *n, pl* **-ties** : enemistad *f,* animadversión *f*

ennoble [ɪ'noːbəl, ɛ-] *vt* **-bled; -bling** : ennoblecer

ennui [ˌɑn'wiː] *n* : hastío *m,* tedio *m,* fastidio *m,* aburrimiento *m*

enormity [ɪ'nɔrməṭi] *n, pl* **-ties 1** ATROCITY : atrocidad *f,* barbaridad *f* **2** IMMENSITY : enormidad *f,* inmensidad *f*

enormous [ɪ'nɔrməs] *adj* : enorme, inmenso, tremendo — **enormously** *adv*

enough[1] [ɪ'nʌf] *adv* **1** : bastante, suficientemente **2 fair enough!** : ¡está bien!, ¡de acuerdo! **3 strangely enough** : por extraño que parezca **4 sure enough** : en efecto, sin duda alguna **5 well enough** : muy bien, bastante bien

enough[2] *adj* : bastante, suficiente <do we have enough chairs? : ¿tenemos suficientes sillas?>

enough[3] *pron* : (lo) suficiente, (lo) bastante <enough to eat : lo suficiente para comer> <it's not enough : no basta> <I've had enough! : ¡estoy harto!, ¡está bueno ya!>

enquire [ɪn'kwaɪr, ɛn-], **enquiry** ['ɪnˌkwaɪri, 'ɛn-, -kwəri; ɪn'kwaɪri, ɛn'-] → **inquire**, **inquiry**

enrage [ɪn'reɪdʒ, ɛn-] *vt* **-raged; -raging** : enfurecer, encolerizar

enraged [ɪn'reɪdʒd, ɛn-] *adj* : enfurecido, furioso

enrich [ɪn'rɪtʃ, ɛn-] *vt* : enriquecer

enrichment [ɪn'rɪtʃmənt, ɛn-] *n* : enriquecimiento *m*

enroll *or* **enrol** [ɪn'roːl, ɛn-] *v* **-rolled; -rolling** *vt* : matricular, inscribir — *vi* : matricularse, inscribirse

enrollment [ɪn'roːlmənt, ɛn-] *n* : matrícula *f,* inscripción *f*

en route [ɑ'ruːt, ɛn'raʊt] *adv* : de camino, por el camino

ensconce [ɪn'skɑn*t*s, ɛn-] *vt* **-sconced; -sconcing** : acomodar, instalar, establecer cómodamente

ensemble [ɑn'sɑmbəl] *n* : conjunto *m*

enshrine [ɪn'ʃraɪn, ɛn-] *vt* **-shrined; -shrining** : conservar religiosamente, preservar

ensign ['ɛn*t*sən, 'ɛnˌsaɪn] *n* **1** FLAG : enseña *f,* pabellón *m* **2** : alférez *mf* (de fragata)

enslave [ɪn'sleɪv, ɛn-] *vt* **-slaved; -slaving** : esclavizar

enslavement [ɪn'sleɪvmənt, ɛn-] *n* : esclavización *f*

ensnare [ɪn'snær, ɛn-] *vt* **-snared; -snaring** : atrapar

ensue [ɪn'suː, ɛn-] *vi* **-sued; -suing** : seguir, resultar

ensure [ɪn'ʃʊr, ɛn-] *vt* **-sured; -suring** : asegurar, garantizar

entail [ɪn'teɪl, ɛn-] *vt* : implicar, suponer, conllevar

entangle [ɪn'tæŋgəl, ɛn-] *vt* **-gled; -gling** : enredar

entanglement [ɪn'tæŋgəlmənt, ɛn-] *n* : enredo *m*

enter ['ɛntər] *vt* **1** : entrar en, entrar a **2** BEGIN : entrar en, comenzar, iniciar **3** RECORD : anotar, inscribir, dar entrada a **4** JOIN : entrar en, alistarse en, hacerse socio de — *vi* **1** : entrar **2 to enter into** : entrar en, firmar (un acuerdo), entablar (negociaciones, etc.)

enterprise ['ɛntər,praɪz] *n* **1** UNDERTAKING : empresa *f* **2** BUSINESS : empresa *f*, firma *f* **3** INITIATIVE : iniciativa *f*, empuje *m*

enterprising ['ɛntər,praɪzɪŋ] *adj* : emprendedor

entertain [,ɛntər'teɪn] *vt* **1** : recibir, agasajar <to entertain guests : tener invitados> **2** CONSIDER : considerar, contemplar **3** AMUSE : entretener, divertir

entertainer [,ɛntər'teɪnər] *n* : artista *mf*

entertainment [,ɛntər'teɪnmənt] *n* : entretenimiento *m*, diversión *f*

enthrall *or* **enthral** [ɪn'θrɔl, ɛn-] *vt* **-thralled; -thralling** : cautivar, embelesar

enthusiasm [ɪn'θuːzi,æzəm, ɛn-, -'θjuː-] *n* : entusiasmo *m*

enthusiast [ɪn'θuːzi,æst, ɛn-, -'θjuː-, -əst] *n* : entusiasta *mf;* aficionado *m*, -da *f*

enthusiastic [ɪn,θuːzi'æstɪk, ɛn-, -,θjuː-] *adj* : entusiasta, aficionado

enthusiastically [ɪn,θuːzi'æstɪkli, ɛn-, -,θjuː-] *adv* : con entusiasmo

entice [ɪn'taɪs, ɛn-] *vt* **-ticed; -ticing** : atraer, tentar

enticement [ɪn'taɪsmənt, ɛn-] *n* : tentación *f*, atracción *f*, señuelo *m*

entire [ɪn'taɪr, ɛn-] *adj* : entero, completo

entirely [ɪn'taɪrli, ɛn-] *adv* : completamente, totalmente

entirety [ɪn'taɪrti, ɛn-, -'taɪrəti] *n, pl* **-ties** : totalidad *f*

entitle [ɪn'taɪtəl, ɛn-] *vt* **-tled; -tling 1** NAME : titular, intitular **2** : dar derecho a <it entitles you to enter free : le da derecho a entrar gratis> **3 to be entitled to** : tener derecho a

entitlement [ɪn'taɪtəlmənt, ɛn-] *n* RIGHT : derecho *m*

entity ['ɛntəti] *n, pl* **-ties** : entidad *f*, ente *m*

entomologist [,ɛntə'mɑlədʒɪst] *n* : entomólogo *m*, -ga *f*

entomology [,ɛntə'mɑlədʒi] *n* : entomología *f*

entourage [,ɑntʊ'rɑʒ] *n* : séquito *m*

entrails ['ɛn,treɪlz, -trəlz] *npl* : entrañas *fpl*, vísceras *fpl*

entrance[1] [ɪn'trænts, ɛn-] *vt* **-tranced; -trancing** : encantar, embelesar, fascinar

entrance[2] ['ɛntrənts] *n* **1** ENTERING : entrada *f* <to make an entrance : entrar en escena> **2** ENTRY : entrada *f*, puerta *f* **3** ADMISSION : entrada *f*, ingreso *m* <entrance examination : examen de ingreso>

entrant ['ɛntrənt] *n* : candidato *m*, -ta *f* (en un examen); participante *mf* (en un concurso)

entrap [ɪn'træp, ɛn-] *vt* **-trapped; -trapping** : atrapar, entrampar, hacer caer en una trampa

entrapment [ɪn'træpmənt, ɛn-] *n* : captura *f*

entreat [ɪn'triːt, ɛn-] *vt* : suplicar, rogar

entreaty [ɪn'triːti, ɛn-] *n, pl* **-treaties** : ruego *m*, súplica *f*

entrée *or* **entree** ['ɑn,treɪ, ,ɑn'-] *n* : plato *m* principal

entrench [ɪn'trɛntʃ, ɛn-] *vt* **1** FORTIFY : atrincherar (una posición militar) **2** : consolidar, afianzar <firmly entrenched in his job : afianzado en su puesto>

entrepreneur [,ɑntrəprə'nər, -'njʊr] *n* : empresario *m*, -ria *f*

entrust [ɪn'trʌst, ɛn-] *vt* : confiar, encomendar

entry ['ɛntri] *n, pl* **-tries 1** ENTRANCE : entrada *f* **2** NOTATION : entrada *f*, anotación *f*

entwine [ɪn'twaɪn, ɛn-] *vt* **-twined; -twining** : entrelazar, entretejer, entrecruzar

enumerate [ɪ'nuːmə,reɪt, ɛ-, -'njuː-] *vt* **-ated; -ating 1** LIST : enumerar **2** COUNT : contar, enumerar

enumeration [ɪ,nuːmə'reɪʃən, ɛ-, -,njuː-] *n* : enumeración *f*, lista *f*

enunciate [i'nʌntsi,eɪt, ɛ-] *vt* **-ated; -ating 1** STATE : enunciar, decir **2** PRONOUNCE : articular, pronunciar

enunciation [i,nʌntsi'eɪʃən, ɛ-] *n* **1** STATEMENT : enunciación *f*, declaración *f* **2** ARTICULATION : articulación *f*, pronunciación *f*, dicción *f*

envelop [ɪn'vɛləp, ɛn-] *vt* : envolver, cubrir

envelope ['ɛnvə,loːp, 'ɑn-] *n* : sobre *m*

enviable ['ɛnviəbəl] *adj* : envidiable

envious ['ɛnviəs] *adj* : envidioso — **enviously** *adv*

environment [ɪn'vaɪrənmənt, ɛn-, -'vaɪərn-] *n* : medio *m* (ambiente), ambiente *m*, entorno *m*

environmental [ɪn,vaɪrən'mɛntəl, ɛn-, -,vaɪərn-] *adj* : ambiental

environmentalist [ɪn,vaɪrən'mɛntəlɪst, ɛn-, -,vaɪərn-] *n* : ecologista *mf*
environs [ɪn'vaɪrənz, ɛn-, -'vaɪərnz] *npl* : alrededores *mpl*, entorno *m*, inmediaciones *fpl*
envisage [ɪn'vɪzɪdʒ, ɛn-] *vt* **-aged; -aging 1** IMAGINE : imaginarse, concebir **2** FORESEE : prever
envision [ɪn'vɪʒən, ɛn-] *vt* : imaginar
envoy ['ɛn,vɔɪ, 'ɑn-] *n* : enviado *m*, -da *f*
envy[1] ['ɛnvi] *vt* **-vied; -vying** : envidiar
envy[2] *n, pl* **envies** : envidia *f*
enzyme ['ɛn,zaɪm] *n* : enzima *f*
eon ['i:ən, i:,ɑn] → **aeon**
epaulet [,ɛpə'lɛt] *n* : charretera *f*
ephemeral [ɪ'fɛmərəl, -'fi:-] *adj* : efímero, fugaz
epic[1] ['ɛpɪk] *adj* : épico
epic[2] *n* : poema *m* épico, epopeya *f*
epicure ['ɛpɪ,kjʊr] *n* : epicúreo *m*, -rea *f*; gastrónomo *m*, -ma *f*
epicurean [,ɛpɪkjʊ'ri:ən, -'kjʊriən] *adj* : epicúreo
epidemic[1] [,ɛpə'dɛmɪk] *adj* : epidémico
epidemic[2] *n* : epidemia *f*
epidermis [,ɛpə'dərməs] *n* : epidermis *f*
epigram ['ɛpə,græm] *n* : epigrama *m*
epilepsy ['ɛpə,lɛpsi] *n, pl* **-sies** : epilepsia *f*
epileptic[1] [,ɛpə'lɛptɪk] *adj* : epiléptico
epileptic[2] *n* : epiléptico *m*, -ca *f*
episcopal [ɪ'pɪskəpəl] *adj* : episcopal
episode ['ɛpə,so:d] *n* : episodio *m*
episodic [,ɛpə'sɑdɪk] *adj* : episódico
epistle [ɪ'pɪsəl] *n* : epístola *f*, carta *f*
epitaph ['ɛpə,tæf] *n* : epitafio *m*
epithet ['ɛpə,θɛt, -θət] *n* : epíteto *m*
epitome [ɪ'pɪṭəmi] *n* **1** SUMMARY : epítome *m*, resumen *m* **2** EMBODIMENT : personificación *f*
epitomize [ɪ'pɪṭə,maɪz] *vt* **-mized; -mizing 1** SUMMARIZE : resumir **2** EMBODY : ser la personificación de, personificar
epoch ['ɛpək, 'ɛ,pɑk, 'i:,pɑk] *n* : época *f*, era *f*
equable ['ɛkwəbəl, 'i:-] *adj* **1** CALM, STEADY : ecuánime **2** UNIFORM : estable (dícese de la temperatura), constante (dícese del clima), uniforme
equably ['ɛkwəbli, 'i:-] *adv* : con ecuánimidad
equal[1] ['i:kwəl] *vt* **equaled** *or* **equalled; equaling** *or* **equalling 1** : ser igual a <two plus three equals five : dos más tres es igual a cinco> **2** MATCH : igualar
equal[2] *adj* **1** SAME : igual **2** ADEQUATE : adecuado, capaz
equal[3] *n* : igual *mf*
equality [ɪ'kwɑləṭi] *n, pl* **-ties** : igualdad *f*
equalize ['i:kwə,laɪz] *vt* **-ized; -izing** : igualar, equiparar
equally ['i:kwəli] *adv* : igualmente, por igual
equanimity [,i:kwə'nɪməṭi, ,ɛ-] *n, pl* **-ties** : ecuanimidad *f*
equate [ɪ'kweɪt] *vt* **equated; equating** : equiparar, identificar
equation [ɪ'kweɪʒən] *n* : ecuación *f*
equator [ɪ'kweɪṭər] *n* : ecuador *m*
equatorial [,i:kwə'toriəl, ,ɛ-] *adj* : ecuatorial
equestrian[1] [ɪ'kwɛstriən, ɛ-] *adj* : ecuestre
equestrian[2] *n* : jinete *mf*, caballista *mf*
equilateral [,i:kwə'læṭərəl, ,ɛ-] *adj* : equilátero
equilibrium [,i:kwə'lɪbriəm, ,ɛ-] *n, pl* **-riums** *or* **-ria** [-briə] : equilibrio *m*
equine ['i:,kwaɪn, 'ɛ-] *adj* : equino, hípico
equinox ['i:kwə,nɑks, 'ɛ-] *n* : equinoccio *m*
equip [ɪ'kwɪp] *vt* **equipped; equipping 1** FURNISH : equipar **2** PREPARE : preparar
equipment [ɪ'kwɪpmənt] *n* : equipo *m*
equitable ['ɛkwəṭəbəl] *adj* : equitativo, justo, imparcial
equity ['ɛkwəṭi] *n, pl* **-ties 1** FAIRNESS : equidad *f*, imparcialidad *f* **2** VALUE : valor *m* líquido
equivalence [ɪ'kwɪvələnts] *n* : equivalencia *f*
equivalent[1] [ɪ'kwɪvələnt] *adj* : equivalente
equivalent[2] *n* : equivalente *m*
equivocal [ɪ'kwɪvəkəl] *adj* **1** AMBIGUOUS : equívoco, ambiguo **2** QUESTIONABLE : incierto, dudoso, sospechoso
equivocate [ɪ'kwɪvə,keɪt] *vi* **-cated; -cating** : usar lenguaje equívoco, andarse con evasivas
equivocation [ɪ,kwɪvə'keɪʃən] *n* : evasiva *f*, subterfugio *m*
era ['ɪrə, 'ɛrə, 'i:rə] *n* : era *f*, época *f*
eradicate [ɪ'rædə,keɪt] *vt* **-cated; -cating** : erradicar
erase [ɪ'reɪs] *vt* **erased; erasing** : borrar
eraser [ɪ'reɪsər] *n* : goma *f* de borrar, borrador *m*
erasure [ɪ'reɪʃər] *n* : tachadura *f*
ere[1] ['ɛr] *conj* : antes de que
ere[2] *prep* **1** : antes de **2 ere long** : dentro de poco
erect[1] [ɪ'rɛkt] *vt* **1** CONSTRUCT : erigir, construir **2** RAISE : levantar **3** ESTABLISH : establecer
erect[2] *adj* : erguido, derecho, erecto
erection [ɪ'rɛkʃən] *n* **1** : erección *f* (en fisiología) **2** BUILDING : construcción *f*
ermine ['ərmən] *n* : armiño *m*
erode [ɪ'ro:d] *vt* **eroded; eroding** : erosionar (el suelo), corroer (metales)
erosion [ɪ'ro:ʒən] *n* : erosión *f*, corrosión *f*
erotic [ɪ'rɑṭɪk] *adj* : erótico — **erotically** [-ṭɪkli] *adv*

eroticism [ɪˈrɑt̬ə,sɪzəm] *n* : erotismo *m*

err [ˈɛr, ˈər] *vi* : cometer un error, equivocarse, errar

errand [ˈɛrənd] *n* : mandado *m,* encargo *m,* recado *m Spain* <an errand of mercy : una misión de caridad>

errant [ˈɛrənt] *adj* **1** WANDERING : errante **2** ASTRAY : descarriado

erratic [ɪˈræt̬ɪk] *adj* **1** INCONSISTENT : errático, irregular, inconsistente **2** ECCENTRIC : excéntrico, raro

erratically [ɪˈræt̬ɪkli] *adv* : erráticamente, de manera irregular

erroneous [ɪˈroːniəs, ɛ-] *adj* : erróneo — **erroneously** *adv*

error [ˈɛrər] *n* : error *m,* equivocación *f* <to be in error : estar equivocado>

ersatz [ˈɛr,sɑts, ˈər,sæts] *adj* : artificial, sustituto

erstwhile [ˈərst,*h*waɪl] *adj* : antiguo

erudite [ˈɛrə,daɪt, ˈɛrjʊ-] *adj* : erudito, letrado

erudition [,ɛrəˈdɪʃən, ,ɛrjʊ-] *n* : erudición *f*

erupt [ɪˈrʌpt] *vi* **1** : hacer erupción (dícese de un volcán o un sarpullido) **2** : estallar (dícese de la cólera o la violencia)

eruption [ɪˈrʌpʃən] *n* : erupción *f,* estallido *m*

eruptive [ɪˈrʌptɪv] *adj* : eruptivo

escalate [ˈɛskə,leɪt] *v* **-lated; -lating** *vt* : intensificar (un conflicto), aumentar (precios) — *vi* : intensificarse, aumentarse

escalation [,ɛskəˈleɪʃən] *n* : intensificación *f,* escalada *f,* aumento *m,* subida *f*

escalator [ˈɛskə,leɪt̬ər] *n* : escalera *f* mecánica

escapade [ˈɛskə,peɪd] *n* : aventura *f*

escape[1] [ɪˈskeɪp, ɛ-] *v* **-caped; -caping** *vt* : escaparse de, librarse de, evitar — *vi* : escaparse, fugarse, huir

escape[2] *n* **1** FLIGHT : fuga *f,* huida *f,* escapada *f* **2** LEAKAGE : escape *m,* fuga *f* **3** : escapatoria *f,* evasión *f* <to have no escape : no tener escapatoria> <escape from reality : evasión de la realidad>

escapee [ɪ,skeɪˈpiː, ,ɛ-] *n* : fugitivo *m,* -va *f*

escarole [ˈɛskə,roːl] *n* : escarola *f*

escarpment [ɪsˈkɑrpmənt, ɛs-] *n* : escarpa *f,* escarpadura *f*

eschew [ɛˈʃuː, ɪsˈtʃuː] *vt* : evitar, rehuir, abstenerse de

escort[1] [ɪˈskɔrt, ɛ-] *vt* **1** : escoltar <to escort a ship : escoltar un barco> **2** ACCOMPANY : acompañar

escort[2] [ˈɛs,kɔrt] *n* **1** : escolta *f* <armed escort : escolta armada> **2** COMPANION : acompañante *mf;* compañero *m,* -ra *f*

escrow [ˈɛs,kroː] *n* **in escrow** : en depósito, en custodia de un tercero

esophagus [ɪˈsɑfəgəs, iː-] *n, pl* **-gi** [-,gaɪ, -,dʒaɪ] : esófago *m*

esoteric [,ɛsəˈtɛrɪk] *adj* : esotérico, hermético

especially [ɪˈspɛʃəli] *adv* : especialmente, particularmente

espionage [ˈɛspiə,nɑʒ, -,nɑdʒ] *n* : espionaje *m*

espouse [ɪˈspaʊz, ɛ-] *vt* **espoused; espousing** **1** MARRY : casarse con **2** ADOPT, ADVOCATE : apoyar, adherirse a, adoptar

espresso [ɛˈsprɛ,soː] *n, pl* **-sos** : café *m* exprés

essay[1] [ɛˈseɪ, ˈɛ,seɪ] *vt* : intentar, tratar

essay[2] [ˈɛ,seɪ] *n* **1** COMPOSITION : ensayo *m,* trabajo *m* **2** ATTEMPT : intento *m*

essayist [ˈɛ,seɪɪst] *n* : ensayista *mf*

essence [ˈɛsən*t*s] *n* **1** CORE : esencia *f,* núcleo *m,* meollo *m* <in essence : esencialmente> **2** EXTRACT : esencia *f,* extracto *m* **3** PERFUME : esencia *f,* perfume *m*

essential[1] [ɪˈsɛntʃəl] *adj* : esencial, imprescindible, fundamental — **essentially** *adv*

essential[2] *n* : elemento *m* esencial, lo imprescindible

establish [ɪˈstæblɪʃ, ɛ-] *vt* **1** FOUND : establecer, fundar **2** SET UP : establecer, instaurar, instituir **3** PROVE : demostrar, probar

establishment [ɪˈstæblɪʃmənt, ɛ-] *n* **1** ESTABLISHING : establecimiento *m,* fundación *f,* instauración *f* **2** BUSINESS : negocio *m,* establecimiento *m* **3 the Establishment** : la clase dirigente

estate [ɪˈsteɪt, ɛ-] *n* **1** POSSESSIONS : bienes *mpl,* propiedad *f,* patrimonio *m* **2** PROPERTY : hacienda *f,* finca *f,* propiedad *f*

esteem[1] [ɪˈstiːm, ɛ-] *vt* : estimar, apreciar

esteem[2] *n* : estima *f,* aprecio *m*

ester [ˈɛstər] *n* : éster *m*

esthetic [ɛsˈθɛt̬ɪk] → **aesthetic**

estimable [ˈɛstəməbəl] *adj* : estimable

estimate[1] [ˈɛstə,meɪt] *vt* **-mated; -mating** : calcular, estimar

estimate[2] [ˈɛstəmət] *n* **1** : cálculo *m* aproximado <to make an estimate : hacer un cálculo> **2** ASSESSMENT : valoración *f,* estimación *f*

estimation [,ɛstəˈmeɪʃən] *n* **1** JUDGMENT : juicio *m,* opinión *f* <in my estimation : en mi opinión, según mis cálculos> **2** ESTEEM : estima *f,* aprecio *m*

estimator [ˈɛstə,meɪt̬ər] *n* : tasador *m,* -dora *f*

Estonian [ɛˈstoːniən] *n* : estonio *m,* -nia *f* — **Estonian** *adj*

estrange [ɪˈstreɪndʒ, ɛ-] *vt* **-tranged; -tranging** : enajenar, apartar, alejar

estrangement [ɪˈstreɪndʒmənt, ɛ-] *n* : alejamiento *m,* distanciamiento *m*

estrogen [ˈɛstrədʒən] *n* : estrógeno *m*

estrus [ˈɛstrəs] *n* : celo *m*

estuary [ˈɛstʃʊ,wɛri] *n, pl* **-aries** : estuario *m,* -ria *f*

et cetera [ɛt'sɛt̬ərə, -'sɛtrə] : etcétera
etch ['ɛtʃ] *v* : grabar al aguafuerte
etching ['ɛtʃɪŋ] *n* : aguafuerte *m,* grabado *m* al aguafuerte
eternal [ɪ'tərnəl, iː-] *adj* **1** EVERLASTING : eterno **2** INTERMINABLE : constante, incesante
eternally [ɪ'tərnəli, iː-] *adv* : eternamente, para siempre
eternity [ɪ'tərnət̬i, iː-] *n, pl* **-ties** : eternidad *f*
ethane ['ɛˌθeɪn] *n* : etano *m*
ethanol ['ɛθəˌnɔl, -ˌnoːl] *n* : etanol *m*
ether ['iːθər] *n* : éter *m*
ethereal [ɪ'θɪriəl, iː-] *adj* **1** CELESTIAL : etéreo, celeste **2** DELICATE : delicado
ethical ['ɛθɪkəl] *adj* : ético — **ethically** *adv*
ethics ['ɛθɪks] *ns & pl* **1** : ética *f* **2** MORALITY : ética *f,* moral *f,* moralidad *f*
Ethiopian [ˌiːθi'oːpiən] *n* : etíope *mf* — **Ethiopian** *adj*
ethnic ['ɛθnɪk] *adj* : étnico
ethnologist [ɛθ'nɑlədʒɪst] *n* : etnólogo *m,* **-ga** *f*
ethnology [ɛθ'nɑlədʒi] *n* : etnología *f*
etiquette ['ɛt̬ɪkət, -ˌkɛt] *n* : etiqueta *f,* protocolo *m*
etymological [ˌɛt̬əmə'lɑdʒɪkəl] *adj* : etimológico
etymology [ˌɛt̬ə'mɑlədʒi] *n, pl* **-gies** : etimología *f*
eucalyptus [ˌjuːkə'lɪptəs] *n, pl* **-ti** [-ˌtaɪ] *or* **-tuses** [-təsəz] : eucalipto *m*
Eucharist ['juːkərɪst] *n* : Eucaristía *f*
eulogize ['juːləˌdʒaɪz] *vt* **-gized; -gizing** : elogiar, encomiar
eulogy ['juːlədʒi] *n, pl* **-gies** : elogio *m,* encomio *m,* panegírico *m*
eunuch ['juːnək] *n* : eunuco *m*
euphemism ['juːfəˌmɪzəm] *n* : eufemismo *m*
euphemistic [ˌjuːfə'mɪstɪk] *adj* : eufemístico
euphony ['juːfəni] *n, pl* **-nies** : eufonía *f*
euphoria [jʊ'foriə] *n* : euforia *f*
euphoric [jʊ'forɪk] *adj* : eufórico
euthanasia [ˌjuːθə'neɪʒə, -ʒiə] *n* : eutanasia *f*
evacuate [ɪ'vækjʊˌeɪt] *v* **-ated; -ating** *vt* VACATE : evacuar, desalojar — *vi* WITHDRAW : retirarse
evacuation [ɪˌvækjʊ'eɪʃən] *n* : evacuación *f,* desalojo *m*
evade [ɪ'veɪd] *vt* **evaded; evading** : evadir, eludir, esquivar
evaluate [ɪ'væljʊˌeɪt] *vt* **-ated; -ating** : evaluar, valorar, tasar
evaluation [ɪˌvæljʊ'eɪʃən] *n* : evaluación *f,* valoración *f,* tasación *f*
evangelical [ˌiːˌvæn'dʒɛlɪkəl, ˌɛvən-] *adj* : evangélico
evangelist [ɪ'vændʒəlɪst] *n* **1** : evangelista *m* **2** PREACHER : predicador *m,* **-dora** *f*
evaporate [ɪ'væpəˌreɪt] *vi* **-rated; -rating 1** VAPORIZE : evaporarse **2** VANISH : evaporarse, desvanecerse, esfumarse
evaporation [ɪˌvæpə'reɪʃən] *n* : evaporación *f*
evasion [ɪ'veɪʒən] *n* : evasión *f*
evasive [ɪ'veɪsɪv] *adj* : evasivo
evasiveness [ɪ'veɪsɪvnəs] *n* : carácter *m* evasivo
eve ['iːv] *n* **1** : víspera *f* <on the eve of the festivities : en vísperas de las festividades> **2** → **evening**
even[1] ['iːvən] *vt* **1** LEVEL : allanar, nivelar, emparejar **2** EQUALIZE : igualar, equilibrar — *vi* **to even out** : nivelarse, emparejarse
even[2] *adv* **1** : hasta, incluso <even a child can do it : hasta un niño puede hacerlo> <he looked content, even happy : se le veía satisfecho, incluso feliz> **2** (*in negative constructions*) : ni siquiera <he didn't even try : ni siquiera lo intentó> **3** (*in comparisons*) : aún, todavía <even better : aún mejor, todavía mejor> **4 even if** : aunque **5 even so** : aun así **6 even though** : aun cuando, a pesar de que
even[3] *adj* **1** SMOOTH : uniforme, liso, parejo **2** FLAT : plano, llano **3** EQUAL : igual, igualado <an even score : un marcador igualado> **4** REGULAR : regular, constante <an even pace : un ritmo constante> **5** EXACT : exacto, justo **6** : par <even number : número par> **7 to be even** : estar en paz, estar a mano **8 to get even** : desquitarse, vengarse
evening ['iːvnɪŋ] *n* : tarde *f,* noche *f* <in the evening : por la noche>
evenly ['iːvənli] *adv* **1** UNIFORMLY : de modo uniforme, de manera constante **2** FAIRLY : igualmente, equitativamente
evenness ['iːvənnəs] *n* : uniformidad *f,* igualdad *f,* regularidad *f*
event [ɪ'vɛnt] *n* **1** : acontecimiento *m,* suceso *m,* prueba *f* (en deportes) **2 in the event that** : en caso de que
eventful [ɪ'vɛntfəl] *adj* : lleno de incidentes, memorable
eventual [ɪ'vɛntʃʊəl] *adj* : final, consiguiente
eventuality [ɪˌvɛntʃʊ'ælət̬i] *n, pl* **-ties** : eventualidad *f*
eventually [ɪ'vɛntʃʊəli] *adv* : al fin, con el tiempo, algún día
ever ['ɛvər] *adv* **1** ALWAYS : siempre <as ever : como siempre> <ever since : desde entonces> **2** (*in questions*) : alguna vez, algún día <have you ever been to Mexico? : ¿has estado en México alguna vez?> **3** (*in negative constructions*) : nunca <doesn't he ever work? : ¿es que nunca trabaja?> <nobody ever helps me : nadie nunca me ayuda> **4** (*in comparisons*) : nunca <better than ever : mejor que nunca> **5** (*as intensifier*) <I'm ever so happy! : ¡estoy tan y tan feliz!> <he

looks ever so angry : parece estar muy enojado>

evergreen[1] [ˈɛvərˌgriːn] *adj* : de hoja perenne

evergreen[2] *n* : planta *f* de hoja perenne

everlasting [ˌɛvərˈlæstɪŋ] *adj* : eterno, perpetuo, imperecedero

evermore [ˌɛvərˈmor] *adv* : eternamente

every [ˈɛvri] *adj* **1** EACH : cada <every time : cada vez> <every other house : cada dos casas> **2** ALL : todo <every month : todos los meses> <every woman : toda mujer, todas las mujeres> **3** COMPLETE : pleno, entero <to have every confidence : tener plena confianza>

everybody [ˈɛvriˌbʌdi, -ˌbɑ-] *pron* : todos *mpl*, -das *fpl*; todo el mundo

everyday [ˌɛvriˈdeɪ, ˈɛvriˌ-] *adj* : cotidiano, diario, corriente <everyday clothes : ropa de todos los días>

everyone [ˈɛvri ˌwʌn] → **everybody**

everything [ˈɛvriˌθɪŋ] *pron* : todo

everywhere [ˈɛvriˌ*h*wɛr] *adv* : en todas partes, por todas partes, dondequiera <I looked everywhere : busqué en todas partes> <everywhere we go : dondequiera que vayamos>

evict [ɪˈvɪkt] *vt* : desalojar, desahuciar

eviction [ɪˈvɪkʃən] *n* : desalojo *m*, desahucio *m*

evidence [ˈɛvədən*t*s] *n* **1** INDICATION : indicio *m*, señal *m* <to be in evidence : estar a la vista> **2** PROOF : evidencia *f*, prueba *f* **3** TESTIMONY : testimonio *m*, declaración *f* <to give evidence : declarar como testigo, prestar declaración>

evident [ˈɛvidənt] *adj* : evidente, patente, manifiesto

evidently [ˈɛvidəntli, ˌɛviˈdɛntli] *adv* **1** CLEARLY : claramente, obviamente **2** APPARENTLY : aparentemente, evidentemente, al parecer

evil[1] [ˈiːvəl, -vɪl] *adj* **eviler** *or* **eviller; evilest** *or* **evillest 1** WICKED : malvado, malo, maligno **2** HARMFUL : nocivo, dañino, pernicioso **3** UNPLEASANT : desagradable <an evil odor : un olor horrible>

evil[2] *n* **1** WICKEDNESS : mal *m*, maldad *f* **2** MISFORTUNE : desgracia *f*, mal *m*

evildoer [ˌiːvəlˈduːər, ˌiːvɪl-] *n* : malvado *m*, -da *f*

evince [ɪˈvɪn*t*s] *vt* **evinced; evincing** : mostrar, manifestar, revelar

eviscerate [ɪˈvɪsəˌreɪt] *vt* **-ated; -ating** : eviscerar, destripar (un pollo, etc.)

evocation [ˌiːvoˈkeɪʃən, ˌɛ-] *n* : evocación *f*

evocative [iˈvɑkət̬ɪv] *adj* : evocador

evoke [iˈvoːk] *vt* **evoked; evoking** : evocar, provocar

evolution [ˌɛvəˈluːʃən, ˌiː-] *n* : evolución *f*, desarrollo *m*

evolutionary [ˌɛvəˈluːʃəˌnɛri, ˌiː-] *adj* : evolutivo

evolve [iˈvɑlv] *vi* **evolved; evolving** : evolucionar, desarrollarse

ewe [ˈjuː] *n* : oveja *f*

exact[1] [ɪgˈzækt, ɛ-] *vt* : exigir, imponer, arrancar

exact[2] *adj* : exacto, preciso — **exactly** *adv*

exacting [ɪˈzæktɪŋ, ɛg-] *adj* : exigente, riguroso

exactitude [ɪgˈzæktəˌtuːd, ɛg-, -ˌtjuːd] *n* : exactitud *f*, precisión *f*

exaggerate [ɪgˈzædʒəˌreɪt, ɛg-] *v* **-ated; -ating** : exagerar

exaggerated [ɪgˈzædʒəˌreɪt̬əd, ɛg-] *adj* : exagerado — **exaggeratedly** *adv*

exaggeration [ɪgˌzædʒəˈreɪʃən, ɛg-] *n* : exageración *f*

exalt [ɪgˈzɔlt, ɛg-] *vt* : exaltar, ensalzar, glorificar

exaltation [ˌɛgˌzɔlˈteɪʃən, ˌɛkˌsɔl-] *n* : exaltación *f*

exam [ɪgˈzæm, ɛg-] → **examination**

examination [ɪgˌzæməˈneɪʃən, ɛg-] *n* **1** TEST : examen *m* **2** INSPECTION : inspección *f*, revisión *f* **3** INVESTIGATION : examen *m*, estudio *m*

examine [ɪgˈzæmən, ɛg-] *vt* **-ined; -ining 1** TEST : examinar **2** INSPECT : inspeccionar, revisar **3** STUDY : examinar

example [ɪgˈzæmpəl, ɛg-] *n* : ejemplo *m* <for example : por ejemplo> <to set an example : dar ejemplo>

exasperate [ɪgˈzæspəˌreɪt, ɛg-] *vt* **-ated; -ating** : exasperar, sacar de quicio

exasperation [ɪgˌzæspəˈreɪʃən, ɛg-] *n* : exasperación *f*

excavate [ˈɛkskəˌveɪt] *vt* **-vated; -vating** : excavar

excavation [ˌɛkskəˈveɪʃən] *n* : excavación *f*

exceed [ɪkˈsiːd, ɛk-] *vt* **1** SURPASS : exceder, rebasar, sobrepasar **2** : exceder de, sobrepasar <not exceeding two months : que no exceda de dos meses>

exceedingly [ɪkˈsiːdɪŋli, ɛk-] *adv* : extremadamente, sumamente

excel [ɪkˈsɛl, ɛk-] *v* **-celled; -celling** *vi* : sobresalir, descollar, lucirse — *vt* : superar

excellence [ˈɛksələn*t*s] *n* : excelencia *f*

excellency [ˈɛksələn*t*si] *n, pl* **-cies** : excelencia *f* <His Excellency : Su Excelencia>

excellent [ˈɛksələnt] *adj* : excelente, sobresaliente — **excellently** *adv*

except[1] [ɪkˈsɛpt] *vt* : exceptuar, excluir

except[2] *conj* : pero, si no fuera por

except[3] *prep* : excepto, menos, salvo <everyone except Carlos : todos menos Carlos>

exception [ɪkˈsɛpʃən] *n* **1** : excepción *f* **2 to take exception to** : ofenderse por, objetar a

exceptional [ɪkˈsɛpʃənəl] *adj* : excepcional, extraordinario — **exceptionally** *adv*

excerpt[1] [ɛkˈsərpt, ɛɡˈzərpt, ˈɛkˌ-, ˈɛɡˌ-] *vt* : escoger, seleccionar

excerpt[2] [ˈɛkˌsərpt, ˈɛɡˌzərpt] *n* : pasaje *m,* selección *f*

excess[1] [ˈɛkˌsɛs, ɪkˈsɛs] *adj* **1** : excesivo, de sobra **2 excess baggage** : exceso *m* de equipaje

excess[2] [ɪkˈsɛs, ˈɛkˌsɛs] *n* **1** SUPERFLUITY : exceso *m,* superfluidad *f* <an excess of energy : un exceso de energía> **2** SURPLUS : excedente *m,* sobrante *m* <in excess of : superior a>

excessive [ɪkˈsɛsɪv, ɛk-] *adj* : excesivo, exagerado, desmesurado — **excessively** *adv*

exchange[1] [ɪksˈtʃeɪndʒ, ɛks-; ˈɛksˌtʃeɪndʒ] *vt* **-changed; -changing** : cambiar, intercambiar, canjear

exchange[2] *n* **1** : cambio *m,* intercambio *m,* canje *m* **2 stock exchange** : bolsa *f* (de valores)

exchangeable [ɪksˈtʃeɪndʒəbəl, ɛks-] *adj* : canjeable

excise[1] [ɪkˈsaɪz, ɛk-] *vt* **-cised; -cising** : extirpar

excise[2] [ˈɛkˌsaɪz] *n* **excise tax** : impuesto *m* interno, impuesto *m* sobre el consumo

excision [ɪkˈsɪʒən, ɛk-] *n* : extirpación *f,* excisión *f*

excitability [ɪkˌsaɪtəˈbɪlət̬i, ɛk-] *n* : excitabilidad *f*

excitable [ɪkˈsaɪt̬əbəl, ɛk-] *adj* : excitable

excitation [ˌɛkˌsaɪˈteɪʃən] *n* : excitación *f*

excite [ɪkˈsaɪt, ɛk-] *vt* **-cited; -citing 1** AROUSE, STIMULATE : excitar, mover, estimular **2** ANIMATE : entusiasmar, animar **3** EVOKE, PROVOKE : provocar, despertar, suscitar <to excite curiousity : despertar la curiosidad>

excited [ɪkˈsaɪt̬əd, ɛk-] *adj* **1** STIMULATED : excitado, estimulado **2** ENTHUSIASTIC : entusiasmado, emocionado

excitedly [ɪkˈsaɪt̬ədli, ɛk-] *adv* : con excitación, con entusiasmo

excitement [ɪkˈsaɪtmənt, ɛk-] *n* **1** ENTHUSIASM : entusiasmo *m,* emoción *f* **2** AGITATION : agitación *f,* alboroto *m,* conmoción *f* **3** AROUSAL : excitación *f*

exclaim [ɪksˈkleɪm, ɛk-] *v* : exclamar

exclamation [ˌɛkskləˈmeɪʃən] *n* : exclamación *f*

exclamation point *n* : signo *m* de admiración

exclamatory [ɪksˈklæməˌtori, ɛks-] *adj* : exclamativo

exclude [ɪksˈkluːd, ɛks-] *vt* **-cluded; -cluding 1** BAR : excluir, descartar, no admitir **2** EXPEL : expeler, expulsar

exclusion [ɪksˈkluːʒən, ɛks-] *n* : exclusión *f*

exclusive[1] [ɪksˈkluːsɪv, ɛks-] *adj* **1** SOLE : exclusivo, único **2** SELECT : exclusivo, selecto

exclusive[2] *n* : exclusiva *f*

exclusively [ɪksˈkluːsɪvli, ɛks-] *adv* : exclusivamente, únicamente

exclusiveness [ɪksˈkluːsɪvnəs, ɛks-] *n* : exclusividad *f*

excommunicate [ˌɛkskəˈmjuːnəˌkeɪt] *vt* **-cated; -cating** : excomulgar

excommunication [ˌɛkskəˌmjuːnəˈkeɪʃən] *n* : excomunión *f*

excrement [ˈɛkskrəmənt] *n* : excremento *m*

excrete [ɪkˈskriːt, ɛk-] *vt* **-creted; -creting** : excretar

excretion [ɪkˈskriːʃən, ɛk-] *n* : excreción *f*

excruciating [ɪkˈskruːʃiˌeɪt̬ɪŋ, ɛk-] *adj* : insoportable, atroz, terrible — **excruciatingly** *adv*

exculpate [ˈɛkskəlˌpeɪt] *vt* **-pated; -pating** : exculpar

excursion [ɪkˈskərʒən, ɛk-] *n* **1** OUTING : excursión *f,* paseo *m* **2** DIGRESSION : digresión *f*

excuse[1] [ɪkˈskjuːz, ɛk-] *vt* **-cused; -cusing 1** PARDON : disculpar, perdonar <excuse me : con permiso, perdóneme, perdón> **2** EXEMPT : eximir, disculpar **3** JUSTIFY : excusar, justificar

excuse[2] [ɪkˈskjuːs, ɛk-] *n* **1** JUSTIFICATION : excusa *f,* justificación *f* **2** PRETEXT : pretexto *m* **3 to make one's excuses to someone** : pedirle disculpas a alguien

execute [ˈɛksɪˌkjuːt] *vt* **-cuted; -cuting 1** CARRY OUT : ejecutar, llevar a cabo, desempeñar **2** ENFORCE : ejecutar, cumplir (un testamento, etc.) **3** KILL : ejecutar, ajusticiar

execution [ˌɛksɪˈkjuːʃən] *n* **1** PERFORMANCE : ejecución *f,* desempeño *m* **2** IMPLEMENTATION : cumplimiento *m* **3** : ejecución *f* (por un delito)

executioner [ˌɛksɪˈkjuːʃənər] *n* : verdugo *m*

executive[1] [ɪɡˈzɛkjət̬ɪv, ɛɡ-] *adj* : ejecutivo

executive[2] *n* : ejecutivo *m,* -va *f*

executor [ɪɡˈzɛkjət̬ər, ɛɡ-] *n* : albacea *m,* testamentario *m*

executrix [ɪɡˈzɛkjəˌtrɪks, ɛɡ-] *n, pl* **executrices** [-ˌzɛkjəˈtraɪˌsiːz] *or* **executrixes** [-ˈzɛkjəˌtrɪksəz] : albacea *f,* testamentaria *f*

exemplary [ɪɡˈzɛmpləri, ɛɡ-] *adj* : ejemplar

exemplify [ɪɡˈzɛmpləˌfaɪ, ɛɡ-] *vt* **-fied; -fying** : ejemplificar, ilustrar, demostrar

exempt[1] [ɪɡˈzɛmpt, ɛɡ-] *vt* : eximir, dispensar, exonerar

exempt[2] *adj* : exento, eximido

exemption [ɪɡˈzɛmpʃən, ɛɡ-] *n* : exención *f*

exercise[1] [ˈɛksərˌsaɪz] *v* **-cised; -cising** *vt* **1** : ejercitar (el cuerpo) **2** USE : ejercer, hacer uso de — *vi* : hacer ejercicio

exercise[2] *n* **1** : ejercicio *m* **2 exercises** *npl* WORKOUT : ejercicios *mpl* físicos **3 exercises** *npl* CEREMONY : ceremonia *f*

exert [ɪɡˈzərt, ɛɡ-] *vt* **1** : ejercer, emplear **2 to exert oneself** : esforzarse

exertion [ɪg'zərʃən, ɛg-] *n* **1** USE : ejercicio *m* (de autoridad, etc.), uso *m* (de fuerza, etc.) **2** EFFORT : esfuerzo *m,* empeño *m*
exhalation [ˌɛksə'leɪʃən, ˌɛkshə-] *n* : exhalación *f,* espiración *f*
exhale [ɛks'heɪl] *v* **-haled; -haling** *vt* **1** : exhalar, espirar **2** EMIT : exhalar, despedir, emitir — *vi* : espirar
exhaust¹ [ɪg'zɔst, ɛg-] *vt* **1** DEPLETE : agotar **2** TIRE : cansar, fatigar, agotar **3** EMPTY : vaciar
exhaust² *n* **1 exhaust fumes** : gases *mpl* de escape **2 exhaust pipe** : tubo *m* de escape **3 exhaust system** : sistema *m* de escape
exhausted [ɪg'zɔstəd, ɛg-] *adj* : agotado, derrengado
exhausting [ɪg'zɔstɪŋ, ɛg-] *adj* : extenuante, agotador
exhaustion [ɪg'zɔstʃən, ɛg-] *n* : agotamiento *m*
exhaustive [ɪg'zɔstɪv, ɛg-] *adj* : exhaustivo
exhibit¹ [ɪg'zɪbət, ɛg-] *vt* **1** DISPLAY : exhibir, exponer **2** PRODUCE, SHOW : mostrar, presentar
exhibit² *n* **1** OBJECT : objeto *m* expuesto **2** EXHIBITION : exposición *f,* exhibición *f* **3** EVIDENCE : prueba *f* instrumental
exhibition [ˌɛksə'bɪʃən] *n* **1** : exposición *f,* exhibición *f* **2 to make an exhibition of oneself** : dar el espectáculo, hacer el ridículo
exhilarate [ɪg'zɪləˌreɪt, ɛg-] *vt* **-rated; -rating** : alegrar, levantar el ánimo de
exhilaration [ɪgˌzɪlə'reɪʃən, ɛg-] *n* : alegría *f,* regocijo *m,* júbilo *m*
exhort [ɪg'zɔrt, ɛg-] *vt* : exhortar
exhortation [ˌɛkˌsɔr'teɪʃən, -sər-; ˌɛgˌzɔr-] *n* : exhortación *f*
exhumation [ˌɛksju'meɪʃən, -hju-; ˌɛgzu-, -zju-] *n* : exhumación *f*
exhume [ɪg'zuːm, -'zjuːm; ɪks'juːm, -'hjuːm] *vt* **-humed; -huming** : exhumar, desenterrar
exigencies ['ɛksɪdʒən*t*siz, ɪg'zɪdʒənˌsiːz] *npl* : exigencias *fpl*
exile¹ ['ɛgˌzaɪl, 'ɛkˌsaɪl] *vt* **exiled; exiling** : exiliar, desterrar
exile² *n* **1** BANISHMENT : exilio *m,* destierro *m* **2** OUTCAST : exiliado *m,* -da *f;* desterrado *m,* -da *f*
exist [ɪg'zɪst, ɛg-] *vi* **1** BE : existir **2** LIVE : subsistir, vivir
existence [ɪg'zɪstən*t*s, ɛg-] *n* : existencia *f*
existent [ɪg'zɪstənt, ɛg-] *adj* : existente
exit¹ ['ɛgzət, 'ɛksət] *vi* : salir, hacer mutis (en el teatro) — *vt* : salir de
exit² *n* **1** DEPARTURE : salida *f,* partida *f* **2** EGRESS : salida *f* <emergency exit : salida de emergencia>
exodus ['ɛksədəs] *n* : éxodo *m*
exonerate [ɪg'zɑnəˌreɪt, ɛg-] *vt* **-ated; -ating** : exonerar, disculpar, absolver
exoneration [ɪgˌzɑnə'reɪʃən, ɛg-] *n* : exoneración *f*
exorbitant [ɪg'zɔrbətənt, ɛg-] *adj* : exorbitante, excesivo
exorcise ['ɛkˌsɔrˌsaɪz, -sər-] *vt* **-cised; -cising** : exorcizar
exorcism ['ɛksərˌsɪzəm] *n* : exorcismo *m*
exotic¹ [ɪg'zɑtɪk, ɛg-] *adj* : exótico — **exotically** [-ɪkli] *adv*
exotic² *n* : planta *f* exótica
expand [ɪk'spænd, ɛk-] *vt* **1** ENLARGE : expandir, dilatar, aumentar, ampliar **2** EXTEND : extender — *vi* **1** ENLARGE : ampliarse, extenderse **2** : expandirse, dilatarse (dícese de los metales, gases, etc.)
expanse [ɪk'spæn*t*s, ɛk-] *n* : extensión *f*
expansion [ɪk'spæntʃən, ɛk-] *n* **1** ENLARGEMENT : expansión *f,* ampliación *f* **2** EXPANSE : extensión *f*
expansive [ɪk'spæn*t*sɪv, ɛk-] *adj* **1** : expansivo **2** OUTGOING : expansivo, comunicativo **3** AMPLE : ancho, amplio — **expansively** *adv*
expansiveness [ɪk'spæn*t*sɪvnəs, ɛk-] *n* : expansibilidad *f*
expatriate¹ [ɛks'peɪtriˌeɪt] *vt* **-ated; -ating** : expatriar
expatriate² [ɛks'peɪtriət, -ˌeɪt] *adj* : expatriado
expatriate³ [ɛks'peɪtriət, -ˌeɪt] *n* : expatriado *m,* -da *f*
expect [ɪk'spɛkt, ɛk-] *vt* **1** SUPPOSE : suponer, imaginarse **2** ANTICIPATE : esperar **3** COUNT ON, REQUIRE : contar con, esperar — *vi* **to be expecting** : estar embarazada
expectancy [ɪk'spɛktən*t*si, ɛk-] *n, pl* **-cies** : expectativa *f,* esperanza *f*
expectant [ɪk'spɛktənt, ɛk-] *adj* **1** ANTICIPATING : expectante **2** EXPECTING : futuro <expectant mother : futura madre>
expectantly [ɪk'spɛktəntli, ɛk-] *adv* : con expectación
expectation [ˌɛkˌspɛk'teɪʃən] *n* **1** ANTICIPATION : expectación *f* **2** EXPECTANCY : expectativa *f*
expedient¹ [ɪk'spiːdiənt, ɛk-] *adj* : conveniente, oportuno
expedient² *n* : expediente *m,* recurso *m*
expedite ['ɛkspəˌdaɪt] *vt* **-dited; -diting 1** FACILITATE : facilitar, dar curso a **2** HASTEN : acelerar
expedition [ˌɛkspə'dɪʃən] *n* : expedición *f*
expeditious [ˌɛkspə'dɪʃəs] *adj* : pronto, rápido
expel [ɪk'spɛl, ɛk-] *vt* **-pelled; -pelling** : expulsar, expeler
expend [ɪk'spɛnd, ɛk-] *vt* **1** DISBURSE : gastar, desembolsar **2** CONSUME : consumir, agotar
expendable [ɪk'spɛndəbəl, ɛk-] *adj* : prescindible
expenditure [ɪk'spɛndɪtʃər, ɛk-, -ˌtʃʊr] *n* : gasto *m*
expense [ɪk'spɛn*t*s, ɛk-] *n* **1** COST : gasto *m* **2 expenses** *npl* : gastos *mpl,*

expensas *fpl* **3 at the expense of** : a expensas de
expensive [ɪk'spɛntsɪv, ɛk-] *adj* : costoso, caro — **expensively** *adv*
experience[1] [ɪk'spɪriənts, ɛk-] *vt* **-enced; -encing** : experimentar (sentimientos), tener (dificultades), sufrir (una pérdida)
experience[2] *n* : experiencia *f*
experiment[1] [ɪk'spɛrəmənt, ɛk-, -'spɪr-] *vi* : experimentar, hacer experimentos
experiment[2] *n* : experimento *m*
experimental [ɪk,spɛrə'mɛntəl, ɛk-, -,spɪr-] *adj* : experimental — **experimentally** *adv*
experimentation [ɪk,spɛrəmən'teɪʃən, ɛk-, -,spɪr-] *n* : experimentación *f*
expert[1] ['ɛk,spərt, ɪk'spərt] *adj* : experto, de experto, pericial (dícese de un testigo) — **expertly** *adv*
expert[2] ['ɛk,spərt] *n* : experto *m*, -ta *f*; perito *m*, -ta *f*; especialista *mf*
expertise [,ɛkspər'ti:z] *n* : pericia *f*, competencia *f*
expiate ['ɛkspi,eɪt] *vt* **-ated; -ating** : expiar
expiation [,ɛkspi'eɪʃən] *n* : expiación *f*
expiration [,ɛkspə'reɪʃən] *n* **1** EXHALATION : exhalación *f*, espiración *f* **2** DEATH : muerte *f* **3** TERMINATION : vencimiento *m*, caducidad *f*
expire [ɪk'spaɪr, ɛk-] *vi* **-pired; -piring 1** EXHALE : espirar **2** DIE : expirar, morir **3** TERMINATE : caducar, vencer
explain [ɪk'spleɪn, ɛk-] *vt* : explicar
explanation [,ɛksplə'neɪʃən] *n* : explicación *f*
explanatory [ɪk'splænə,tori, ɛk-] *adj* : explicativo, aclaratorio
expletive ['ɛkspləṭɪv] *n* : improperio *m*, palabrota *f fam*, grosería *f*
explicable [ɛk'splɪkəbəl, 'ɛksplɪ-] *adj* : explicable
explicit [ɪk'splɪsət, ɛk-] *adj* : explícito, claro, categórico, rotundo — **explicitly** *adv*
explicitness [ɪk'splɪsətnəs, ɛk-] *n* : claridad *f*, carácter *m* explícito
explode [ɪk'splo:d, ɛk-] *v* **-ploded; -ploding** *vt* **1** BURST : explosionar, hacer explotar **2** REFUTE : rebatir, refutar, desmentir — *vi* **1** BURST : explotar, estallar, reventar **2** SKYROCKET : dispararse
exploit[1] [ɪk'splɔɪt, ɛk-] *vt* : explotar, aprovecharse de
exploit[2] ['ɛk,splɔɪt] *n* : hazaña *f*, proeza *f*
exploitation [,ɛk,splɔɪ'teɪʃən] *n* : explotación *f*
exploration [,ɛksplə'reɪʃən] *n* : exploración *f*
exploratory [ɪk'splorə,tori, ɛk-] *adj* : exploratorio
explore [ɪk'splor, ɛk-] *vt* **-plored; -ploring** : explorar, investigar, examinar
explorer [ɪk'splorər, ɛk-] *n* : explorador *m*, -dora *f*
explosion [ɪk'splo:ʒən, ɛk-] *n* : explosión *f*, estallido *m*
explosive[1] [ɪk'splo:sɪv, ɛk-] *adj* : explosivo, fulminante — **explosively** *adv*
explosive[2] *n* : explosivo *m*
exponent [ɪk'spo:nənt, 'ɛk,spo:-] *n* **1** : exponente *m* **2** ADVOCATE : defensor *m*, -sora *f*; partidario *m*, -ria *f*
exponential [,ɛkspə'nɛntʃəl] *adj* : exponencial — **exponentially** *adv*
export[1] [ɛk'sport, 'ɛk,sport] *vt* : exportar
export[2] ['ɛk,sport] *n* **1** : artículo *m* de exportación **2** → **exportation**
exportation [,ɛk,spor'teɪʃən] *n* : exportación *f*
exporter [ɛk'sportər, 'ɛk,spor-] *n* : exportador *m*, -dora *f*
expose [ɪk'spo:z, ɛk-] *vt* **-posed; -posing 1** : exponer (al peligro, a los elementos, a una enfermedad) **2** : exponer (una película a la luz) **3** DISCLOSE : descubrir, revelar, poner en evidencia **4** UNMASK : desenmascarar
exposé *or* **expose** [,ɛkspo'zeɪ] *n* : exposición *f* (de hechos), relevación *f* (de un escándalo)
exposed [ɪk'spo:zd, ɛk-] *adj* : descubierto, sin protección
exposition [,ɛkspə'zɪʃən] *n* : exposición *f*
exposure [ɪk'spo:ʒər, ɛk-] *n* **1** : exposición *f* **2** CONTACT : exposición *f*, experiencia *f*, contacto *m* **3** UNMASKING : desenmascaramiento *m* **4** ORIENTATION : orientación *f* <a room with a northern exposure : una sala orientada al norte>
expound [ɪk'spaʊnd, ɛk-] *vt* : exponer, explicar — *vi* : hacer comentarios detallados
express[1] [ɪk'sprɛs, ɛk-] *vt* **1** SAY : expresar, comunicar **2** SHOW : expresar, manifestar, externar *Mex* **3** SQUEEZE : exprimir <to express the juice from a lemon : exprimir el jugo de un limón>
express[2] *adv* : por correo exprés, por correo urgente
express[3] *adj* **1** EXPLICIT : expreso, manifiesto **2** SPECIFIC : específico <for that express purpose : con ese fin específico> **3** RAPID : expreso, rápido
express[4] *n* **1** : correo *m* exprés, correo *m* urgente **2** : expreso *m* (tren)
expression [ɪk'sprɛʃən, ɛk-] *n* **1** UTTERANCE : expresión *f* <freedom of expression : libertad de expresión> **2** : expresión *f* (en la matemática) **3** PHRASE : frase *f*, expresión *f* **4** LOOK : expresión *f*, cara *f*, gesto *m* <with a sad expression : con un gesto de tristeza>
expressionless [ɪk'sprɛʃənləs, ɛk-] *adj* : inexpresivo

expressive [ɪk'sprɛsɪv, ɛk-] *adj* : expresivo
expressway [ɪk'sprɛs,weɪ, ɛk-] *n* : autopista *f*
expulsion [ɪk'spʌlʃən, ɛk-] *n* : expulsión *f*
expurgate ['ɛkspər,geɪt] *vt* **-gated; -gating** : expurgar
exquisite [ɛk'skwɪzət, 'ɛk,skwɪ-] *adj* **1** FINE : exquisito, delicado, primoroso **2** INTENSE : intenso, extremo
extant ['ɛkstənt, ɛk'stænt] *adj* : existente
extemporaneous [ɛk,stɛmpə'reɪniəs] *adj* : improvisado — **extemporaneously** *adv*
extend [ɪk'stɛnd, ɛk-] *vt* **1** STRETCH : extender, tender **2** PROLONG : prolongar, prorrogar **3** ENLARGE : agrandar, ampliar, aumentar **4** PROFFER : extender, dar, ofrecer — *vi* : extenderse
extended [ɪk'stɛndəd, ɛk-] *adj* LENGTHY : prolongado, largo
extension [ɪk'stɛntʃən, ɛk-] *n* **1** EXTENDING : extensión *f,* ampliación *f,* prórroga *f,* prolongación *f* **2** ANNEX : ampliación *f,* anexo *m* **3** : extensión *f* (de teléfono)
extensive [ɪk'stɛntsɪv, ɛk-] *adj* : extenso, vasto, amplio — **extensively** *adv*
extent [ɪk'stɛnt, ɛk-] *n* **1** SIZE : extensión *f,* magnitud *f* **2** DEGREE, SCOPE : alcance *m,* grado *m* <to a certain extent : hasta cierto punto>
extenuate [ɪk'stɛnjə,weɪt, ɛk-] *vt* **-ated; -ating** : atenuar, aminorar, mitigar <extenuating circumstances : circunstancias atenuantes>
extenuation [ɪk,stɛnjə'weɪʃən, ɛk-] *n* : atenuación *f,* aminoración *f*
exterior¹ [ɛk'stɪriər] *adj* : exterior
exterior² *n* : exterior *m*
exterminate [ɪk'stərmə,neɪt, ɛk-] *vt* **-nated; -nating** : exterminar
extermination [ɪk,stərmə'neɪʃən, ɛk-] *n* : exterminación *f,* exterminio *m*
exterminator [ɪk'stərmə,neɪṭər, ɛk-] *n* : exterminador *m,* -dora *f*
external [ɪk'stərnəl, ɛk-] *adj* : externo, exterior — **externally** *adv*
extinct [ɪk'stɪŋkt, ɛk-] *adj* : extinto
extinction [ɪk'stɪŋkʃən, ɛk-] *n* : extinción *f*
extinguish [ɪk'stɪŋgwɪʃ, ɛk-] *vt* : extinguir, apagar
extinguisher [ɪk'stɪŋgwɪʃər, ɛk-] *n* : extinguidor *m,* extintor *m*
extirpate ['ɛkstər,peɪt] *vt* **-pated; -pating** : extirpar, exterminar
extol [ɪk'sto:l, ɛk-] *vt* **-tolled; -tolling** : exaltar, ensalzar, alabar
extort [ɪk'stɔrt, ɛk-] *vt* : extorsionar
extortion [ɪk'stɔrʃən, ɛk-] *n* : extorsión *f*
extra¹ ['ɛkstrə] *adv* : extra, más, extremadamente, super <extra special : super especial>
extra² *adj* **1** ADDITIONAL : adicional, suplementario, de más **2** SUPERIOR : superior
extra³ *n* : extra *m*
extract¹ [ɪk'strækt, ɛk-] *vt* : extraer, sacar
extract² ['ɛk,strækt] *n* **1** EXCERPT : pasaje *m,* selección *f,* trozo *m* **2** : extracto *m* <vanilla extract : extracto de vainilla>
extraction [ɪk'strækʃən, ɛk-] *n* : extracción *f*
extractor [ɪk'stræktər, ɛk-] *n* : extractor *m*
extracurricular [,ɛkstrəkə'rɪkjələr] *adj* : extracurricular
extradite ['ɛkstrə,daɪt] *vt* **-dited; -diting** : extraditar
extradition [,ɛkstrə'dɪʃən] *n* : extradición *f*
extramarital [,ɛkstrə'mærəṭəl] *adj* : extramatrimonial
extraneous [ɛk'streɪniəs] *adj* **1** OUTSIDE : extrínseco, externo **2** SUPERFLUOUS : superfluo, ajeno — **extraneously** *adv*
extraordinary [ɪk'strɔrdən,ɛri, ,ɛkstrə'ɔrd-] *adj* : extraordinario, excepcional — **extraordinarily** [ɪk,strɔrdən'ɛrəli, ,ɛkstrə,ɔrd-] *adv*
extrasensory [,ɛkstrə'sɛntsəri] *adj* : extrasensorial
extraterrestrial¹ [,ɛkstrətə'rɛstriəl] *adj* : extraterrestre
extraterrestrial² *n* : extraterrestre *mf*
extravagance [ɪk'strævɪgənts, ɛk-] *n* **1** EXCESS : exceso *m,* extravagancia *f* **2** WASTEFULNESS : derroche *m,* despilfarro *m* **3** LUXURY : lujo *m*
extravagant [ɪk'strævɪgənt, ɛk-] *adj* **1** EXCESSIVE : excesivo, extravagante **2** WASTEFUL : despilfarrador, derrochador, gastador **3** EXORBITANT : costoso, exorbitante
extravagantly [ɪk'strævɪgəntli, ɛk-] *adv* **1** LAVISHLY : a lo grande **2** EXCESSIVELY : exageradamente, desmesuradamente
extravaganza [ɪk,strævə'gænzə, ɛk-] *n* : gran espectáculo *m*
extreme¹ [ɪk'stri:m, ɛk-] *adj* **1** UTMOST : extremo, sumo <of extreme importance : de suma importancia> **2** INTENSE : intenso, extremado <extreme cold : frío extremado> **3** EXCESSIVE : excesivo, extremo <extreme views : opiniones extremas> <extreme measures : medidas excepcionales, medidas drásticas> **4** OUTERMOST : extremo <the extreme north : el norte extremo>
extreme² *n* **1** : extremo *m* **2 in the extreme** : en extremo, en sumo grado
extremely [ɪk'stri:mli, ɛk-] *adv* : sumamente, extremadamente, terriblemente
extremity [ɪk'strɛməṭi, ɛk-] *n, pl* **-ties** **1** EXTREME : extremo *m* **2 extremities** *npl* LIMBS : extremidades *fpl*

extricate [ˈɛkstrəˌkeɪt] *vt* **-cated; -cating :** librar, sacar
extrinsic [ɪkˈstrɪnzɪk, -ˈstrɪntsɪk] *adj* **:** extrínseco
extrovert [ˈɛkstrəˌvərt] *n* **:** extrovertido *m,* -da *f*
extroverted [ˈɛkstrəˌvərṱəd] *adj* **:** extrovertido
extrude [ɪkˈstruːd, ɛk-] *vt* **-truded; -truding :** extrudir, expulsar
exuberance [ɪgˈzuːbərənts, ɛg-] *n* **1** JOYOUSNESS **:** euforia *f,* exaltación *f* **2** VIGOR **:** exuberancia *f,* vigor *m*
exuberant [ɪgˈzuːbərənt, ɛg-] *adj* **1** JOYOUS **:** eufórico **2** LUSH **:** exuberante **— exuberantly** *adv*
exude [ɪgˈzuːd, ɛg-] *vt* **-uded; -uding 1** OOZE **:** rezumar, exudar **2** EMANATE **:** emanar, irradiar
exult [ɪgˈzʌlt, ɛg-] *vi* **:** exultar, regocijarse
exultant [ɪgˈzʌltənt, ɛg-] *adj* **:** exultante, jubiloso **— exultantly** *adv*
exultation [ˌɛksəlˈteɪʃən, ˌɛgzəl-] *n* **:** exultación *f,* júbilo *m,* alborozo *m*
eye[1] [ˈaɪ] *vt* **eyed; eyeing** *or* **eying :** mirar, observar
eye[2] *n* **1 :** ojo *m* **2** VISION **:** visión *f,* vista *f,* ojo *m* <a good eye for bargains : un buen ojo para las gangas> **3** GLANCE **:** mirada *f,* ojeada *f* **4** ATTENTION **:** atención *f* <to catch one's eye : llamar la atención> **5** POINT OF VIEW **:** punto *m* de vista <in the eyes of the law : según la ley> **6 :** ojo *m* (de una aguja, una papa, una tormenta)
eyeball [ˈaɪˌbɔl] *n* **:** globo *m* ocular
eyebrow [ˈaɪˌbraʊ] *n* **:** ceja *f*
eyedropper [ˈaɪˌdrɑpər] *n* **:** cuentagotas *f*
eyeglasses [ˈaɪˌglæsəz] *npl* **:** anteojos *mpl,* lentes *mpl,* espejuelos *mpl,* gafas *fpl*
eyelash [ˈaɪˌlæʃ] *n* **:** pestaña *f*
eyelet [ˈaɪlət] *n* **:** ojete *m*
eyelid [ˈaɪˌlɪd] *n* **:** párpado *m*
eye–opener [ˈaɪˌoːpənər] *n* **:** revelación *f,* sorpresa *f*
eye–opening [ˈaɪˌoːpənɪŋ] *adj* **:** revelador
eyepiece [ˈaɪˌpiːs] *n* **:** ocular *m*
eyesight [ˈaɪˌsaɪt] *n* **:** vista *f,* visión *f*
eyesore [ˈaɪˌsor] *n* **:** monstruosidad *f,* adefesio *m*
eyestrain [ˈaɪˌstreɪn] *n* **:** fatiga *f* visual, vista *f* cansada
eyetooth [ˈaɪˌtuːθ] *n* **:** colmillo *m*
eyewitness [ˈaɪˈwɪtnəs] *n* **:** testigo *mf* ocular, testigo *mf* presencial
eyrie [ˈaɪri] → **aerie**

F

f [ˈɛf] *n, pl* **f's** *or* **fs** [ˈɛfs] **:** sexta letra del alfabeto inglés
fable [ˈfeɪbəl] *n* **:** fábula *f*
fabled [ˈfeɪbəld] *adj* **:** legendario, fabuloso
fabric [ˈfæbrɪk] *n* **1** MATERIAL **:** tela *f,* tejido *m* **2** STRUCTURE **:** estructura *f* <the fabric of society : la estructura de la sociedad>
fabricate [ˈfæbrɪˌkeɪt] *vt* **-cated; -cating 1** CONSTRUCT, MANUFACTURE **:** construir, fabricar **2** INVENT **:** inventar (excusas o mentiras)
fabrication [ˌfæbrɪˈkeɪʃən] *n* **1** LIE **:** mentira *f,* invención *f* **2** MANUFACTURE **:** fabricación *f*
fabulous [ˈfæbjələs] *adj* **1** LEGENDARY **:** fabuloso, legendario **2** INCREDIBLE **:** increíble, fabuloso <fabulous wealth : riqueza fabulosa> **3** WONDERFUL **:** magnífico, estupendo, fabuloso **— fabulously** *adv*
facade [fəˈsɑd] *n* **:** fachada *f*
face[1] [ˈfeɪs] *v* **faced; facing** *vt* **1** LINE **:** recubrir (una superficie), forrar (ropa) **2** CONFRONT **:** enfrentarse a, afrontar, hacer frente a <to face the music : afrontar las consecuencias> <to face the facts : aceptar la realidad> **3 :** estar de cara a, estar enfrente de <she's facing her brother : está de cara a su hermano> **4** OVERLOOK **:** dar a **—** *vi* **:** mirar (hacia), estar orientado (a)
face[2] *n* **1 :** cara *f,* rostro *m* <he told me to my face : me lo dijo a la cara> **2** EXPRESSION **:** cara *f,* expresión *f* <to pull a long face : poner mala cara> **3** GRIMACE **:** mueca *f* <to make faces : hacer muecas> **4** APPEARANCE **:** fisonomía *f,* aspecto *m* <the face of society : la fisonomía de la sociedad> **5** EFFRONTERY **:** desfachatez *f* **6** PRESTIGE **:** prestigio *m* <to lose face : desprestigiarse> **7** FRONT, SIDE **:** cara *f* (de una moneda), esfera *f* (de un reloj), fachada *f* (de un edificio), pared *f* (de una montaña) **8** SURFACE **:** superficie *f,* faz *f* (de la tierra), cara *f* (de la luna) **9 in the face of** DESPITE **:** en medio de, en visto de, ante
facedown [ˈfeɪsˌdaʊn] *adv* **:** boca abajo
faceless [ˈfeɪsləs] *adj* ANONYMOUS **:** anónimo
face–lift [ˈfeɪsˌlɪft] *n* **1 :** estiramiento *m* facial **2** RENOVATION **:** renovación *f,* remozamiento *m*
facet [ˈfæsət] *n* **1 :** faceta *f* (de una piedra) **2** ASPECT **:** faceta *f,* aspecto *m*
facetious [fəˈsiːʃəs] *adj* **:** gracioso, burlón, bromista
facetiously [fəˈsiːʃəsli] *adv* **:** en tono de burla
facetiousness [fəˈsiːʃəsnəs] *n* **:** jocosidad *f*
face–to–face *adv & adj* **:** cara a cara
faceup [ˈfeɪsˈʌp] *adv* **:** boca arriba

face value *n* : valor *m* nominal
facial[1] [ˈfeɪʃəl] *adj* : de la cara, facial
facial[2] *n* : tratamiento *m* facial, limpieza *f* de cutis
facile [ˈfæsəl] *adj* SUPERFICIAL : superficial, simplista
facilitate [fəˈsɪləˌteɪt] *vt* **-tated; -tating** : facilitar
facility [fəˈsɪləṭi] *n, pl* **-ties 1** EASE : facilidad *f* **2** CENTER, COMPLEX : centro *m,* complejo *m* **3 facilities** *npl* AMENITIES : comodidades *fpl*, servicios *mpl*
facing [ˈfeɪsɪŋ] *n* **1** LINING : entretela *f* (de una prenda) **2** : revestimiento *m* (de un edificio)
facsimile [fækˈsɪməli] *n* : facsímile *m,* facsímil *m*
fact [ˈfækt] *n* **1** : hecho *m* <as a matter of fact : de hecho> **2** INFORMATION : información *f,* datos *mpl* <facts and figures : datos y cifras> **3** REALITY : realidad *f* <in fact : en realidad>
faction [ˈfækʃən] *n* : facción *m,* bando *m*
factional [ˈfækʃənəl] *adj* : entre facciones
factious [ˈfækʃəs] *adj* : faccioso, contencioso
factitious [fækˈtɪʃəs] *adj* : artificial, facticio
factor [ˈfæktər] *n* : factor *m*
factory [ˈfæktəri] *n, pl* **-ries** : fábrica *f*
factual [ˈfæktʃʊəl] *adj* : basado en hechos, objetivo
factually [ˈfæktʃʊəli] *adv* : en cuanto a los hechos
faculty [ˈfækəlti] *n, pl* **-ties 1** : facultad *f* <the faculty of sight : las facultades visuales, el sentido de la vista> **2** APTITUDE : aptitud *f,* facilidad *f* **3** TEACHERS : cuerpo *m* docente
fad [ˈfæd] *n* : moda *f* pasajera, manía *f*
fade [ˈfeɪd] *v* **faded; fading** *vi* **1** WITHER : debilitarse (dícese de las personas), marchitarse (dícese de las flores y las plantas) **2** DISCOLOR : desteñirse, decolorarse **3** DIM : apagarse (dícese de la luz), perderse (dícese de los sonidos), fundirse (dícese de las imágenes) **4** VANISH : desvanecerse, decaer — *vt* DISCOLOR : desteñir
fag [ˈfæg] *vt* **fagged; fagging** EXHAUST : cansar, fatigar
fagot *or* **faggot** [ˈfægət] *n* : haz *m* de leña
Fahrenheit [ˈfærənˌhaɪt] *adj* : Fahrenheit
fail[1] [ˈfeɪl] *vi* **1** WEAKEN : fallar, deteriorarse **2** STOP : fallar, detenerse <his heart failed : le falló el corazón> **3** : fracasar, fallar <her plan failed : su plan fracasó> <the crops failed : se perdió la cosecha> **4** : quebrar <a business about to fail : una empresa a punto de quebrar> **5 to fail in** : faltar a, no cumplir con <to fail in one's duties : faltar a sus deberes> — *vt* **1** FLUNK : reprobar (un examen) **2** : fallar <words fail me : las palabras me fallan, no encuentro palabras> **3** DISAPPOINT : fallar, decepcionar <don't fail me! : ¡no me falles!>
fail[2] *n* : fracaso *m*
failing [ˈfeɪlɪŋ] *n* : defecto *m*
failure [ˈfeɪljər] *n* **1** : fracaso *m,* malogro *m* <crop failure : pérdida de la cosecha> <heart failure : insuficiencia cardíaca> <engine failure : falla mecánica> **2** BANKRUPTCY : bancarrota *f,* quiebra *f* **3** : fracaso *m* (persona) <he was a failure as a manager : como gerente, fue un fracaso>
faint[1] [ˈfeɪnt] *vi* : desmayarse
faint[2] *adj* **1** COWARDLY, TIMID : cobarde, tímido **2** DIZZY : mareado <faint with hunger : desfallecido de hambre> **3** SLIGHT : leve, ligero, vago <I haven't the faintest idea : no tengo la más mínima idea> **4** INDISTINCT : tenue, indistinto, apenas perceptible
faint[3] *n* : desmayo *m*
fainthearted [ˈfeɪntˈhɑrṭəd] *adj* : cobarde, pusilánime
faintly [ˈfeɪntli] *adv* : débilmente, ligeramente, levemente
faintness [ˈfeɪntnəs] *n* **1** INDISTINCTNESS : lo débil, falta *f* de claridad **2** FAINTING : desmayo *m,* desfallecimiento *m*
fair[1] [ˈfær] *adj* **1** ATTRACTIVE, BEAUTIFUL : bello, hermoso, atractivo **2** (*relating to weather*) : bueno, despejado <fair weather : tiempo despejado> **3** JUST : justo, imparcial **4** ALLOWABLE : permisible **5** BLOND, LIGHT : rubio (dícese del pelo), blanco (dícese de la tez) **6** ADEQUATE : bastante, adecuado <fair to middling : mediano, regular> **7 fair game** : presa *f* fácil **8 to play fair** : jugar limpio
fair[2] *n* : feria *f*
fairground [ˈfærˌgraʊnd] *n* : parque *m* de diversiones
fairly [ˈfærli] *adv* **1** IMPARTIALLY : imparcialmente, limpiamente, equitativamente **2** QUITE : bastante **3** MODERATELY : medianamente
fairness [ˈfærnəs] *n* **1** IMPARTIALITY : imparcialidad *f,* justicia *f* **2** LIGHTNESS : blancura *f* (de la piel), lo rubio (del pelo)
fairy [ˈfæri] *n, pl* **fairies 1** : hada *f* **2 fairy tale** : cuento *m* de hadas
fairyland [ˈfæriˌlænd] *n* **1** : país *m* de las hadas **2** : lugar *m* encantador
faith [ˈfeɪθ] *n, pl* **faiths** [ˈfeɪθs, ˈfeɪðz] **1** BELIEF : fe *f* **2** ALLEGIANCE : lealtad *f* **3** CONFIDENCE, TRUST : confianza *f,* fe *f* **4** RELIGION : religión *f*
faithful [ˈfeɪθfəl] *adj* : fiel — **faithfully** *adv*
faithfulness [ˈfeɪθfəlnəs] *n* : fidelidad *f*
faithless [ˈfeɪθləs] *adj* **1** DISLOYAL : desleal **2** : infiel (en la religión) — **faithlessly** *adv*

faithlessness [ˈfeɪθləsnəs] *n* **:** deslealtad *f*

fake[1] [ˈfeɪk] *v* **faked; faking** *vt* **1** FALSIFY **:** falsificar, falsear **2** FEIGN **:** fingir — *vi* **1** PRETEND **:** fingir **2 :** hacer un engaño, hacer una finta (en deportes)

fake[2] *adj* **:** falso, fingido, postizo

fake[3] *n* **1** IMITATION **:** imitación *f,* falsificación *f* **2** IMPOSTOR **:** impostor *m,* -tora *f;* charlatán *m,* -tana *f;* farsante *mf* **3** FEINT **:** engaño *m,* finta *f* (en deportes)

faker [ˈfeɪkər] *n* **:** impostor *m,* -tora *f;* charlatán *m,* -tana *f;* farsante *mf*

fakir [fəˈkɪr, ˈfeɪkər] *n* **:** faquir *m*

falcon [ˈfælkən, ˈfɔl-] *n* **:** halcón *m*

falconry [ˈfælkənri, ˈfɔl-] *n* **:** cetrería *f*

fall[1] [ˈfɔl] *vi* **fell** [ˈfɛl]; **fallen** [fɔlən]; **falling 1 :** caer, caerse <to fall out of bed : caer de la cama> <to fall down : caerse> **2** HANG **:** caer **3** DESCEND **:** caer (dícese de la lluvia o de la noche), bajar (dícese de los precios), descender (dícese de la temperatura) **4 :** caer (a un enemigo), rendirse <the city fell : la ciudad se rindió> **5** OCCUR **:** caer <Christmas falls on a Friday : la Navidad cae en viernes> **6 to fall asleep :** dormirse, quedarse dormido **7 to fall from grace** SIN **:** perder la gracia **8 to fall sick :** caer enfermo, enfermarse **9 to fall through :** fracasar, caer en la nada **10 to fall to :** tocar a, corresponder a <the task fell to him : le tocó hacerlo>

fall[2] *n* **1** TUMBLE **:** caída *f* <to break one's fall : frenar uno su caída> <a fall of three feet : una caída de tres pies> **2** FALLING **:** derrumbe *m* (de rocas), aguacero *m* (de lluvia), nevada *f* (de nieve), bajada *f* (de precios), disminución *f* (de cantidades) **3** AUTUMN **:** otoño *m* **4** DOWNFALL **:** caída *f,* ruina *f* **5 falls** *npl* WATERFALL **:** cascada *f,* catarata *f*

fallacious [fəˈleɪʃəs] *adj* **:** erróneo, engañoso, falaz

fallacy [ˈfæləsi] *n, pl* **-cies :** falacia *f*

fall back *vi* **1** RETREAT **:** retirarse, replegarse **2 to fall back on :** recurrir a

fall guy *n* SCAPEGOAT **:** chivo *m* expiatorio

fallible [ˈfæləbəl] *adj* **:** falible

fallout [ˈfɔl,aʊt] *n* **1 :** lluvia *f* radioactiva **2** CONSEQUENCES **:** secuelas *fpl,* consecuencias *fpl*

fallow[1] [ˈfælo] *vt* **:** barbechar

fallow[2] *adj* **to lie fallow :** estar en barbecho

fallow[3] *n* **:** barbecho *m*

false [ˈfɔls] *adj* **falser; falsest 1** UNTRUE **:** falso **2** ERRONEOUS **:** erróneo, equivocado **3** FAKE **:** falso, postizo **4** UNFAITHFUL **:** infiel **5** FRAUDULENT **:** fraudulento <under false pretenses : por fraude>

falsehood [ˈfɔls,hʊd] *n* **:** mentira *f,* falsedad *f*

falsely [ˈfɔlsli] *adv* **:** falsamente, con falsedad

falseness [ˈfɔlsnəs] *n* **:** falsedad *f*

falsetto [fɔlˈsɛt̬oː] *n, pl* **-tos :** falsete *m*

falsification [ˌfɔlsəfəˈkeɪʃən] *n* **:** falsificación *f,* falseamiento *m*

falsify [ˈfɔlsə,faɪ] *vt* **-fied; fying :** falsificar, falsear

falsity [ˈfɔlsət̬i] *n, pl* **-ties :** falsedad *f*

falter [ˈfɔltər] *vi* **-tered; -tering 1** TOTTER **:** tambalearse **2** STAMMER **:** titubear, tartamudear **3** WAVER **:** vacilar

faltering [ˈfɔltərɪŋ] *adj* **:** titubeante, vacilante

fame [ˈfeɪm] *n* **:** fama *f*

famed [ˈfeɪmd] *adj* **:** famoso, célebre, afamado

familial [fəˈmɪljəl, -liəl] *adj* **:** familiar

familiar[1] [fəˈmɪljər] *adj* **1** KNOWN **:** familiar, conocido <to be familiar with : estar familiarizado con> **2** INFORMAL **:** familiar, informal **3** INTIMATE **:** íntimo, de confianza **4** FORWARD **:** confianzudo, atrevido — **familiarly** *adv*

familiar[2] *n* **:** espíritu *m* guardián

familiarity [fə,mɪliˈærət̬i, -,mɪlˈjær-] *n, pl* **-ties 1** KNOWLEDGE **:** conocimiento *m,* familiaridad *f* **2** INFORMALITY, INTIMACY **:** confianza *f,* familiaridad *f* **3** FORWARDNESS **:** exceso *m* de confianza, descaro *m*

familiarize [fəˈmɪljə,raɪz] *vt* **-ized; -izing 1 :** familiarizar **2 to familiarize oneself :** familiarizarse

family [ˈfæmli, ˈfæmə-] *n, pl* **-lies :** familia *f*

family tree *n* **:** árbol *m* genealógico

famine [ˈfæmən] *n* **:** hambre *f,* hambruna *f*

famish [ˈfæmɪʃ] *vi* **to be famished :** estar famélico, estar hambriento, morir de hambre *fam*

famous [ˈfeɪməs] *adj* **:** famoso

famously [ˈfeɪməsli] *adv* **to get on famously :** llevarse de maravilla

fan[1] [ˈfæn] *vt* **fanned; fanning 1 :** abanicar (a una persona), avivar (un fuego) **2** STIMULATE **:** avivar, estimular

fan[2] *n* **1 :** ventilador *m,* abanico *m* **2** ADMIRER, ENTHUSIAST **:** aficionado *m,* -da *f;* entusiasta *mf;* admirador *m,* -dora *f*

fanatic[1] [fəˈnæt̬ɪk] *or* **fanatical** [-t̬ɪkəl] *adj* **:** fanático

fanatic[2] *n* **:** fanático *m,* -ca *f*

fanaticism [fəˈnæt̬ə,sɪzəm] *n* **:** fanatismo *m*

fanciful [ˈfæntsɪfəl] *adj* **1** CAPRICIOUS **:** caprichoso, fantástico, extravagante **2** IMAGINATIVE **:** imaginativo — **fancifully** *adv*

fancy[1] [ˈfæntsi] *vt* **-cied; -cying 1** IMAGINE **:** imaginarse, figurarse <fancy that! : ¡figúrate!, ¡imagínate!> **2** CRAVE **:** apetecer, tener ganas de

fancy[2] *adj* **-cier; -est 1** ELABORATE **:** elaborado **2** LUXURIOUS **:** lujoso, elegante — **fancily** [ˈfæntsəli] *adv*

fancy[3] *n, pl* **-cies 1** LIKING : gusto *m,* afición *f* **2** WHIM : antojo *m,* capricho *m* **3** IMAGINATION : fantasía *f,* imaginación *f*

fandango [fæn'dæŋgo] *n, pl* **-gos** : fandango *m*

fanfare ['fæn,fær] *n* : fanfarria *f*

fang ['fæŋ] *n* : colmillo *m* (de un animal), diente *m* (de una serpiente)

fanlight ['fæn,laɪt] *n* : tragaluz *m*

fantasia [fæn'teɪʒə, -ziə; ,fæntə'ziːə] *n* : fantasía *f*

fantasize ['fæntə,saɪz] *vi* **-sized; -sizing** : fantasear

fantastic [fæn'tæstɪk] *adj* **1** UNBELIEVABLE : fantástico, increíble, extraño **2** ENORMOUS : fabuloso, inmenso <fantastic sums : sumas fabulosas> **3** WONDERFUL : estupendo, fantástico, bárbaro *fam,* macanudo *fam* — **fantastically** [-tɪkli] *adv*

fantasy ['fæntəsi] *n, pl* **-sies** : fantasía *f*

far[1] ['fɑr] *adv* **farther** ['fɑrðər] *or* **further** ['fər-]; **farthest** *or* **furthest** [-ðəst] **1** : lejos <far from here : lejos de aquí> <to go far : llegar lejos> <as far as Chicago : hasta Chicago> <far away : a lo lejos> **2** MUCH : muy, mucho <far bigger : mucho más grande> <far superior : muy superior> <it's by far the best : es con mucho el mejor> **3** (*expressing degree or extent*) <the results are far off : salieron muy inexactos los resultados> <to go so far as : decir tanto como> <to go far enough : tener el alcance necesario> **4** (*expressing progress*) <the work is far advanced : el trabajo está muy avanzado> <to take (something) too far : llevar (algo) demasiado lejos> **5 far and wide** : por todas partes **6 far from it!** : ¡todo lo contrario! **7 so far** : hasta ahora, todavía

far[2] *adj* **farther** *or* **further; farthest** *or* **furthest 1** REMOTE : lejano, remoto <the Far East : el Lejano Oriente, el Extremo Oriente> <a far country : un país lejano> **2** LONG : largo <a far journey : un viaje largo> **3** EXTREME : extremo <the far right : la extrema derecha> <at the far end of the room : en el otro extremo de la sala>

faraway ['fɑrə,weɪ] *adj* : remoto, lejano

farce ['fɑrs] *n* : farsa *f*

farcical ['fɑrsɪkəl] *adj* : absurdo, ridículo

fare[1] ['fær] *vi* **fared; faring** : ir, salir <how did you fare? : ¿cómo te fue?>

fare[2] *n* **1** : pasaje *m,* billete *m,* boleto *m* <half fare : medio pasaje> **2** FOOD : comida *f*

farewell[1] [fær'wɛl] *adj* : de despedida

farewell[2] *n* : despedida *f*

far–fetched ['fɑr'fɛtʃt] *adj* : improbable, exagerado

farina [fə'riːnə] *n* : harina *f*

farm[1] ['fɑrm] *vt* **1** : cultivar, labrar **2** : criar (animales) — *vi* : ser agricultor

farm[2] *n* : granja *f,* hacienda *f,* finca *f,* estancia *f*

farmer ['fɑrmər] *n* : agricultor *m,* granjero *m*

farmhand ['fɑrm,hænd] *n* : peón *m*

farmhouse ['fɑrm,haʊs] *n* : granja *f,* vivienda *f* del granjero, casa *f* de hacienda

farming ['fɑrmɪŋ] *n* : labranza *f,* cultivo *m,* crianza *f* (de animales)

farmland ['fɑrm,lænd] *n* : tierras *fpl* de labranza

farmyard ['fɑrm,jɑrd] *n* : corral *m*

far–off ['fɑr,ɔf, -'ɔf] *adj* : remoto, distante, lejano

far–reaching ['fɑr'riːtʃɪŋ] *adj* : de gran alcance

farsighted ['fɑr,saɪṭəd] *adj* **1** : hipermétrope **2** JUDICIOUS : con visión de futuro, previsor, precavido

farsightedness ['fɑr,saɪṭədnəs] *n* **1** : hipermetropía *f* **2** PRUDENCE : previsión *f*

farther[1] ['fɑrðər] *adv* **1** AHEAD : más lejos (en el espacio), más adelante (en el tiempo) **2** MORE : más

farther[2] *adj* : más lejano, más remoto

farthermost ['fɑrðər,moːst] *adj* : (el) más lejano

farthest[1] ['fɑrðəst] *adv* **1** : lo más lejos <I jumped farthest : salté lo más lejos> **2** : lo más avanzado <he progressed farthest : progresó al punto más avanzado> **3** : más <the farthest developed plan : el plan más desarrollado>

farthest[2] *adj* : más lejano

fascicle ['fæsɪkəl] *n* : fascículo *m*

fascinate ['fæsən,eɪt] *vt* **-nated; -nating** : fascinar, cautivar

fascination [,fæsən'eɪʃən] *n* : fascinación *f*

fascism ['fæʃ,ɪzəm] *n* : fascismo *m*

fascist[1] ['fæʃɪst] *adj* : fascista

fascist[2] *n* : fascista *mf*

fashion[1] ['fæʃən] *vt* : formar, moldear

fashion[2] *n* **1** MANNER : manera *f,* modo *m* **2** CUSTOM : costumbre *f* **3** STYLE : moda *f*

fashionable ['fæʃənəbəl] *adj* : de moda, chic

fashionably ['fæʃənəbli] *adv* : a la moda

fast[1] ['fæst] *vi* : ayunar

fast[2] *adv* **1** SECURELY : firmemente, seguramente <to hold fast : agarrarse bien> **2** RAPIDLY : rápidamente, rápido, de prisa **3** SOUNDLY : profundamente <fast asleep : profundamente dormido>

fast[3] *adj* **1** SECURE : firme, seguro <to make fast : amarrar (un barco)> **2** FAITHFUL : leal <fast friends : amigos leales> **3** RAPID : rápido, veloz **4** : adelantado <10 minutes fast : 10 minutos adelantado> **5** DEEP : profundo <a fast sleep : un sueño pro-

fundo> **6** COLORFAST **:** inalterable, que no destiñe **7** DISSOLUTE **:** extravagante, disipado, disoluto

fast[4] *n* **:** ayuno *m*

fasten [ˈfæsən] *vt* **1** ATTACH **:** sujetar, atar **2** FIX **:** fijar <to fasten one's eyes on : fijar los ojos en> **3** SECURE **:** abrochar (ropa o cinturones), atar (cordones), cerrar (una maleta) — *vi* **:** abrocharse, cerrar

fastener [ˈfæsənər] *n* **:** cierre *m,* sujetador *m*

fastening [ˈfæsənɪŋ] *n* **:** cierre *m,* sujetador *m*

fastidious [fæsˈtɪdiəs] *adj* **:** quisquilloso, exigente — **fastidiously** *adv*

fat[1] [ˈfæt] *adj* **fatter; fattest 1** OBESE **:** gordo, obeso **2** THICK **:** grueso

fat[2] *n* **:** grasa *f*

fatal [ˈfeɪtəl] *adj* **1** DEADLY **:** mortal **2** ILL-FATED **:** malhadado, fatal **3** MOMENTOUS **:** fatídico

fatalism [ˈfeɪtəl,ɪzəm] *n* **:** fatalismo *m*

fatalist [ˈfeɪtəlɪst] *n* **:** fatalista *mf*

fatalistic [,feɪtəlˈɪstɪk] *adj* **:** fatalista

fatality [feɪˈtæləti, fə-] *n, pl* **-ties :** víctima *f* mortal

fatally [ˈfeɪtəli] *adv* **:** mortalmente

fate [ˈfeɪt] *n* **1** DESTINY **:** destino *m* **2** END, LOT **:** final *m,* suerte *f*

fated [ˈfeɪtəd] *adj* **:** predestinado

fateful [ˈfeɪtfəl] *adj* **1** MOMENTOUS **:** fatídico, aciago **2** PROPHETIC **:** profético — **fatefully** *adv*

father[1] [ˈfɑðər] *vt* **:** engendrar

father[2] *n* **1 :** padre *m* <my father and my mother : mi padre y mi madre> <Father Smith : el padre Smith> **2 the Father** GOD **:** el Padre, Dios *m*

fatherhood [ˈfɑðər,hʊd] *n* **:** paternidad *f*

father-in-law [ˈfɑðərɪn,lɔ] *n, pl* **fathers-in-law :** suegro *m*

fatherland [ˈfɑðər,lænd] *n* **:** patria *f*

fatherless [ˈfɑðərləs] *adj* **:** huérfano de padre, sin padre

fatherly [ˈfɑðərli] *adj* **:** paternal

fathom[1] [ˈfæðəm] *vt* UNDERSTAND **:** entender, comprender

fathom[2] *n* **:** braza *f*

fatigue[1] [fəˈtiːg] *vt* **-tigued; -tiguing :** fatigar, cansar

fatigue[2] *n* **:** fatiga *f*

fatness [ˈfætnəs] *n* **:** gordura *f* (de una persona o un animal), grosor *m* (de un objeto)

fatten [ˈfætən] *vt* **:** engordar, cebar

fatty [ˈfæti] *adj* **fattier; -est :** graso, grasoso, adiposo (dícese de los tejidos)

fatuous [ˈfætʃʊəs] *adj* **:** necio, fatuo — **fatuously** *adv*

faucet [ˈfɔsət] *n* **:** llave *f,* canilla *f Arg, Uru,* grifo *m*

fault[1] [ˈfɔlt] *vt* **:** encontrar defectos a

fault[2] *n* **1** SHORTCOMING **:** defecto *m,* falta *f* **2** DEFECT **:** falta *f,* defecto *m,* falla *f* **3** BLAME **:** culpa *f* **4** FRACTURE **:** falla *f* (geológica)

faultfinder [ˈfɔlt,faɪndər] *n* **:** criticón *m,* -cona *f*

faultfinding [ˈfɔlt,faɪndɪŋ] *n* **:** crítica *f*

faultless [ˈfɔltləs] *adj* **:** sin culpa, sin imperfecciones, impecable

faultlessly [ˈfɔltləsli] *adv* **:** impecablemente, perfectamente

faulty [ˈfɔlti] *adj* **faultier; -est :** defectuoso, imperfecto — **faultily** [ˈfɔltəli] *adv*

fauna [ˈfɔnə] *n* **:** fauna *f*

faux pas [,foːˈpɑ] *n, pl* **faux pas** [*same or* -ˈpɑz] **:** metedura *f* de pata *fam*

favor[1] [ˈfeɪvər] *vt* **1** SUPPORT **:** estar a favor de, ser partidario de, apoyar **2** OBLIGE **:** hacerle un favor a **3** PREFER **:** preferir **4** RESEMBLE **:** parecerse a, salir a

favor[2] *n* **:** favor *m* <in favor of : a favor de> <an error in his favor : un error a su favor>

favorable [ˈfeɪvərəbəl] *adj* **:** favorable, propicio

favorably [ˈfeɪvərəbli] *adv* **:** favorablemente, bien

favorite[1] [ˈfeɪvərət] *adj* **:** favorito, preferido

favorite[2] *n* **:** favorito *m,* -ta *f;* preferido *m,* -da *f*

favoritism [ˈfeɪvərə,tɪzəm] *n* **:** favoritismo *m*

fawn[1] [ˈfɔn] *vi* **:** adular, lisonjear

fawn[2] *n* **:** cervato *m*

fax [ˈfæks] *n* **:** facsímil *m,* facsímile *m*

faze [ˈfeɪz] *vt* **fazed; fazing :** desconcertar, perturbar

fear[1] [ˈfɪr] *vt* **:** temer, tener miedo de — *vi* **:** temer

fear[2] *n* **:** miedo *m,* temor *m* <for fear of : por temor a>

fearful [ˈfɪrfəl] *adj* **1** FRIGHTENING **:** espantoso, aterrador, horrible **2** FRIGHTENED **:** temeroso, miedoso

fearfully [ˈfɪrfəli] *adv* **1** EXTREMELY **:** extremadamente, terriblemente **2** TIMIDLY **:** con temor

fearless [ˈfɪrləs] *adj* **:** intrépido, impávido

fearlessly [ˈfɪrləsli] *adv* **:** sin temor

fearlessness [ˈfɪrləsnəs] *n* **:** intrepidez *f,* impavidez *f*

fearsome [ˈfɪrsəm] *adj* **:** aterrador

feasibility [,fiːzəˈbɪləti] *n* **:** viabilidad *f,* factibilidad *f*

feasible [ˈfiːzəbəl] *adj* **:** viable, factible, realizable

feast[1] [ˈfiːst] *vi* **:** banquetear — *vt* **1 :** agasajar, festejar **2 to feast one's eyes on :** regalarse la vista con

feast[2] *n* **1** BANQUET **:** banquete *m,* festín *m* **2** FESTIVAL **:** fiesta *f*

feat [ˈfiːt] *n* **:** proeza *f,* hazaña *f*

feather[1] [ˈfɛðər] *vt* **1 :** emplumar **2 to feather one's nest :** hacer su agosto

feather[2] *n* **1 :** pluma *f* **2 a feather in one's cap :** un triunfo personal

feathered [ˈfɛðərd] *adj* **:** con plumas

feathery [ˈfɛðəri] *adj* **1** DOWNY **:** plumoso **2** LIGHT **:** liviano

feature[1] [ˈfiːtʃər] *v* **-tured; -turing** *vt* **1** IMAGINE : imaginarse **2** PRESENT : presentar — *vi* : figurar

feature[2] *n* **1** CHARACTERISTIC : característica *f*, rasgo *m* **2** : largometraje *m* (en el cine), artículo *m* (en un periódico), documental *m* (en la televisión) **3 features** *npl* : rasgos *mpl*, facciones *fpl* <delicate features : facciones delicadas>

February [ˈfɛbjʊˌɛri, ˈfɛbʊ-, ˈfɛbrʊ-] *n* : febrero *m*

fecal [ˈfiːkəl] *adj* : fecal

feces [ˈfiːˌsiːz] *npl* : heces *fpl*, excrementos *mpl*

feckless [ˈfɛkləs] *adj* : irresponsable

fecund [ˈfɛkənd, ˈfiː-] *adj* : fecundo

fecundity [fɪˈkʌndət̬i, fɛ-] *n* : fecundidad *f*

federal [ˈfɛdrəl, -dərəl] *adj* : federal

federalism [ˈfɛdrəˌlɪzəm, -dərə-] *n* : federalismo *m*

federalist[1] [ˈfɛdrəlɪst, -dərə-] *adj* : federalista

federalist[2] *n* : federalista *mf*

federate [ˈfɛdəˌreɪt] *vt* **-ated; -ating** : federar

federation [ˌfɛdəˈreɪʃən] *n* : federación *f*

fedora [fɪˈdorə] *n* : sombrero *m* flexible de fieltro

fed up *adj* : harto

fee [ˈfiː] *n* **1** : honorarios *mpl* (a un médico, un abogado, etc.) **2 entrance fee** : entrada *f*

feeble [ˈfiːbəl] *adj* **-bler; -blest 1** WEAK : débil, endeble **2** INEFFECTIVE : flojo, pobre, poco convincente

feebleminded [ˌfiːbəlˈmaɪndəd] *adj* **1** : débil mental **2** FOOLISH, STUPID : imbécil, tonto

feebleness [ˈfiːbəlnəs] *n* : debilidad *f*

feebly [ˈfiːbli] *adv* : débilmente

feed[1] [ˈfiːd] *v* **fed** [ˈfɛd]; **feeding** *vt* **1** : dar de comer a, nutrir, alimentar (a una persona) **2** : alimentar (un fuego o una máquina), proveer (información), introducir (datos) — *vi* : comer, alimentarse

feed[2] *n* **1** NOURISHMENT : alimento *m* **2** FODDER : pienso *m*

feel[1] [ˈfiːl] *v* **felt** [ˈfɛlt]; **feeling** *vi* **1** : sentirse, encontrarse <I feel tired : me siento cansada> <he feels hungry : tiene hambre> <she feels like a fool : se siente como una idiota> <to feel like doing something : tener ganas de hacer algo> **2** SEEM : parecer <it feels like spring : parece primavera> **3** THINK : parecerse, opinar, pensar <how does he feel about that? : ¿qué opina él de eso?> — *vt* **1** TOUCH : tocar, palpar **2** SENSE : sentir <to feel the cold : sentir el frío> **3** CONSIDER : sentir, creer, considerar <to feel (it) necessary : creer necesario>

feel[2] *n* **1** SENSATION, TOUCH : sensación *f*, tacto *m* **2** ATMOSPHERE : ambiente *m*, atmósfera *f* **3 to have a feel for** : tener un talento especial para

feeler [ˈfiːlər] *n* : antena *f*, tentáculo *m*

feeling [ˈfiːlɪŋ] *n* **1** SENSATION : sensación *f*, sensibilidad *f* **2** EMOTION : sentimiento *m* **3** OPINION : opinión *f* **4 feelings** *npl* SENSIBILITIES : sentimientos *mpl* <to hurt someone's feelings : herir los sentimientos de alguien>

feet → **foot**

feign [ˈfeɪn] *vt* : simular, aparentar, fingir

feint[1] [ˈfeɪnt] *vi* : fintar, fintear

feint[2] *n* : finta *f*

felicitate [fɪˈlɪsəˌteɪt] *vt* **-tated; -tating** : felicitar, congratular

felicitation [fɪˌlɪsəˈteɪʃən] *n* : felicitación *f*

felicitous [fɪˈlɪsət̬əs] *adj* : acertado, oportuno

feline[1] [ˈfiːˌlaɪn] *adj* : felino

feline[2] *n* : felino *m*, -na *f*

fell[1] [ˈfɛl] *vt* : talar (un árbol), derribar (a una persona)

fell[2] → **fall**

fellow [ˈfɛˌloː] *n* **1** COMPANION : compañero *m*, -ra *f*; camarada *mf* **2** ASSOCIATE : socio *m*, -cia *f* **3** MAN : tipo *m*, hombre *m*

fellowman [ˌfɛloˈmæn] *n*, *pl* **-men** : prójimo *m*, semejante *m*

fellowship [ˈfɛloˌʃɪp] *n* **1** COMPANIONSHIP : camaradería *f*, compañerismo *m* **2** ASSOCIATION : fraternidad *f* **3** GRANT : beca *f* (de investigación)

felon [ˈfɛlən] *n* : malhechor *m*, -chora *f*; criminal *mf*

felonious [fəˈloːniəs] *adj* : criminal

felony [ˈfɛləni] *n*, *pl* **-nies** : delito *m* grave

felt[1] [ˈfɛlt] *n* : fieltro *m*

felt[2] → **feel**

female[1] [ˈfiːˌmeɪl] *adj* : femenino

female[2] *n* **1** : hembra *f* (de animal) **2** WOMAN : mujer *f*

feminine [ˈfɛmənən] *adj* : femenino

femininity [ˌfɛməˈnɪnət̬i] *n* : feminidad *f*, femineidad *f*

feminism [ˈfɛməˌnɪzəm] *n* : feminismo *m*

feminist[1] [ˈfɛmənɪst] *adj* : feminista

feminist[2] *n* : feminista *mf*

femoral [ˈfɛmərəl] *adj* : femoral

femur [ˈfiːmər] *n*, *pl* **femurs** *or* **femora** [ˈfɛmərə] : fémur *m*

fence[1] [ˈfɛnts] *v* **fenced; fencing** *vt* : vallar, cercar — *vi* : hacer esgrima

fence[2] *n* : cerca *f*, valla *f*, cerco *m*

fencer [ˈfɛntsər] *n* : esgrimista *mf*; esgrimidor *m*, -dora *f*

fencing [ˈfɛntsɪŋ] *n* **1** : esgrima *m* (deporte) **2** : materiales *mpl* para cercas **3** ENCLOSURE : cercado *m*

fend [ˈfɛnd] *vt* **to fend off** : rechazar (un enemigo), parar (un golpe), eludir (una pregunta) — *vi* **to fend for oneself** : arreglárselas sólo, valerse por sí mismo

fender [ˈfɛndər] *n* **:** guardabarros *mpl,* salpicadera *f Mex*
fennel [ˈfɛnəl] *n* **:** hinojo *m*
ferment[1] [fərˈmɛnt] *v* **:** fermentar
ferment[2] [ˈfərˌmɛnt] *n* **1 :** fermento *m* (en la química) **2** TURMOIL **:** agitación *f,* conmoción *f*
fermentation [ˌfərmənˈteɪʃən, -ˌmɛn-] *n* **:** fermentación *f*
fern [ˈfərn] *n* **:** helecho *m*
ferocious [fəˈroːʃəs] *adj* **:** feroz — **ferociously** *adv*
ferociousness [fəˈroːʃəsnəs] *n* **:** ferocidad *f*
ferocity [fəˈrɑsət̬i] *n* **:** ferocidad *f*
ferret[1] [ˈfɛrət] *vi* SNOOP **:** hurgar, husmear — *vt* **to ferret out :** descubrir
ferret[2] *n* **:** hurón *m*
ferric [ˈfɛrɪk] *or* **ferrous** [ˈfɛrəs] *adj* **:** férrico
Ferris wheel [ˈfɛrɪs] *n* **:** noria *f*
ferry[1] [ˈfɛri] *vt* **-ried; -rying :** llevar, transportar
ferry[2] *n, pl* **-ries :** transbordador *m,* ferry *m*
ferryboat [ˈfɛriˌboːt] *n* **:** transbordador *m,* ferry *m*
fertile [ˈfərt̬əl] *adj* **:** fértil, fecundo
fertility [fərˈtɪlət̬i] *n* **:** fertilidad *f*
fertilization [ˌfərt̬ələˈzeɪʃən] *n* **:** fertilización *f* (del suelo), fecundación (de un huevo)
fertilize [ˈfərt̬əlˌaɪz] *vt* **-ized; -izing 1 :** fecundar (un huevo) **2 :** fertilizar, abonar (el suelo)
fertilizer [ˈfərt̬əlˌaɪzər] *n* **:** fertilizante *m,* abono *m*
fervent [ˈfərvənt] *adj* **:** ferviente, fervoroso, ardiente — **fervently** *adv*
fervid [ˈfərvɪd] *adj* **:** ardiente, apasionado — **fervidly** *adv*
fervor [ˈfərvər] *n* **:** fervor *m,* ardor *m*
fester [ˈfɛstər] *vi* **:** enconarse, supurar
festival [ˈfɛstəvəl] *n* **:** fiesta *f,* festividad *f,* festival *m*
festive [ˈfɛstɪv] *adj* **:** festivo — **festively** *adv*
festivity [fɛsˈtɪvət̬i] *n, pl* **-ties :** festividad *f,* celebración *f*
festoon[1] [fɛsˈtuːn] *vt* **:** adornar, engalanar
festoon[2] *n* GARLAND **:** guirnalda *f*
fetal [ˈfiːt̬əl] *adj* **:** fetal
fetch [ˈfɛtʃ] *vt* **1** BRING **:** traer, recoger, ir a buscar **2** REALIZE **:** realizar, venderse por <the jewelry fetched $10,000 **:** las joyas se vendieron por $10,000>
fetching [ˈfɛtʃɪŋ] *adj* **:** atractivo, encantador
fête[1] [ˈfeɪt, ˈfɛt] *vt* **fêted; fêting :** festejar, agasajar
fête[2] *n* **:** fiesta *f*
fetid [ˈfɛt̬əd] *adj* **:** fétido
fetish [ˈfɛt̬ɪʃ] *n* **:** fetiche *m*
fetlock [ˈfɛtˌlɑk] *n* **:** espolón *m*
fetter [ˈfɛt̬ər] *vt* **:** encadenar, poner grillos a
fetters [ˈfɛt̬ərz] *npl* **:** grillos *mpl,* grilletes *mpl,* cadenas *fpl*
fettle [ˈfɛt̬əl] *n* **in fine fettle :** en buena forma, en plena forma
fetus [ˈfiːt̬əs] *n* **:** feto *m*
feud[1] [ˈfjuːd] *vi* **:** pelear, contender
feud[2] *n* **:** contienda *f,* enemistad *f* (heredada)
feudal [ˈfjuːdəl] *adj* **:** feudal
feudalism [ˈfjuːdəlˌɪzəm] *n* **:** feudalismo *m*
fever [ˈfiːvər] *n* **:** fiebre *f,* calentura *f*
feverish [ˈfiːvərɪʃ] *adj* **1 :** afiebrado, con fiebre, febril **2** FRANTIC **:** febril, frenético
few[1] [ˈfjuː] *adj* **:** pocos <with few exceptions **:** con pocas excepciones> <a few times **:** varias veces>
few[2] *pron* **1 :** pocos <few (of them) were ready **:** pocos estaban listos> **2 a few :** algunos, unos cuantos **3 few and far between :** contados
fewer [ˈfjuːər] *pron* **:** menos <the fewer the better **:** cuantos menos mejor>
fez [ˈfɛz] *n, pl* **fezzes :** fez *m*
fiancé [ˌfiːˌɑnˈseɪ, ˌfiːˈɑnˌseɪ] *n* **:** prometido *m,* novio *m*
fiancée [ˌfiːˌɑnˈseɪ, ˌfiːˈɑnˌseɪ] *n* **:** prometida *f,* novia *f*
fiasco [fiˈæsˌkoː] *n, pl* **-coes :** fiasco *m,* fracaso *m*
fiat [ˈfiːˌɑt, -ˌæt, -ət; ˈfaɪət, -ˌæt] *n* **:** decreto *m,* orden *m*
fib[1] [ˈfɪb] *vi* **fibbed; fibbing :** decir mentirillas
fib[2] *n* **:** mentirilla *f,* bola *f fam*
fibber [ˈfɪbər] *n* **:** mentirosillo *m,* -lla *f;* cuentista *mf fam*
fiber *or* **fibre** [ˈfaɪbər] *n* **:** fibra *f*
fiberboard [ˈfaɪbərˌbord] *n* **:** cartón *m* madera
fiberglass [ˈfaɪbərˌglæs] *n* **:** fibra *f* de vidrio
fibrillate [ˈfɪbrəˌleɪt, ˈfaɪ-] *vi* **-lated; -lating :** fibrilar
fibrillation [ˌfɪbrəˈleɪʃən, ˌfaɪ-] *n* **:** fibrilación *f*
fibrous [ˈfaɪbrəs] *adj* **:** fibroso
fibula [ˈfɪbjələ] *n, pl* **-lae** [-ˌliː, -ˌlaɪ] *or* **-las :** peroné *m*
fickle [ˈfɪkəl] *adj* **:** inconstante, voluble, veleidoso
fickleness [ˈfɪkəlnəs] *n* **:** volubilidad *f,* inconstancia *f,* veleidad *f*
fiction [ˈfɪkʃən] *n* **:** ficción *f*
fictional [ˈfɪkʃənəl] *adj* **:** ficticio
fictitious [fɪkˈtɪʃəs] *adj* **1** IMAGINARY **:** ficticio, imaginario **2** FALSE **:** falso, ficticio
fiddle[1] [ˈfɪdəl] *vi* **-dled; -dling 1 :** tocar el violín **2 to fiddle with :** juguetear con, toquetear
fiddle[2] *n* **:** violín *m*
fiddler [ˈfɪdlər, ˈfɪdələr] *n* **:** violinista *mf*
fiddlesticks [ˈfɪdəlˌstɪks] *interj* **:** ¡tonterías!
fidelity [fəˈdɛlət̬i, faɪ-] *n, pl* **-ties :** fidelidad *f*

fidget[1] [ˈfɪdʒət] *vi* **1 :** moverse, estarse inquieto **2 to fidget with :** juguetear con
fidget[2] *n* **1 :** persona *f* inquieta **2 fidgets** *npl* RESTLESSNESS **:** inquietud *f*
fidgety [ˈfɪdʒəti] *adj* **:** inquieto
fiduciary[1] [fəˈduːʃiˌɛri, -ˈdjuː-, -ʃəri] *adj* **:** fiduciario
fiduciary[2] *n, pl* **-ries :** fiduciario *m*, -ria *f*
field[1] [ˈfiːld] *vt* **:** interceptar y devolver (una pelota), presentar (un candidato), sortear (una pregunta)
field[2] *adj* **:** de campaña, de campo <field hospital : hospital de campaña> <field goal : gol de campo> <field trip : viaje de estudio>
field[3] *n* **1 :** campo *m* (de cosechas, de batalla, de magnetismo) **2 :** campo *m*, cancha *f* (en deportes) **3 :** campo *m* (de trabajo), esfera *f* (de actividades)
fielder [ˈfiːldər] *n* **:** jugador *m*, -dora *f* de campo; fildeador *m*, -dora *f*
field glasses *n* **:** binoculares *mpl*, gemelos *mpl*
fiend [ˈfiːnd] *n* **1** DEMON **:** demonio *m* **2** EVILDOER **:** persona *f* maligna; malvado *m*, -da *f* **3** FANATIC **:** fanático *m*, -ca *f*
fiendish [ˈfiːndɪʃ] *adj* **:** diabólico — **fiendishly** *adv*
fierce [ˈfɪrs] *adj* **fiercer; -est 1** FEROCIOUS **:** fiero, feroz **2** HEATED **:** acalorado **3** INTENSE **:** intenso, violento, fuerte — **fiercely** *adv*
fierceness [ˈfɪrsnəs] *n* **1** FEROCITY **:** ferocidad *f*, fiereza *f* **2** INTENSITY **:** intensidad *f*, violencia *f*
fieriness [ˈfaɪərinəs] *n* **:** pasión *f*, ardor *m*
fiery [ˈfaɪəri] *adj* **fierier; -est 1** BURNING **:** ardiente, llameante **2** GLOWING **:** encendido **3** PASSIONATE **:** acalorado, ardiente, fogoso
fiesta [fiˈɛstə] *n* **:** fiesta *f*
fife [ˈfaɪf] *n* **:** pífano *m*
fifteen[1] [fɪfˈtiːn] *adj* **:** quince
fifteen[2] *n* **:** quince *m*
fifteenth[1] [fɪfˈtiːnθ] *adj* **:** decimoquinto
fifteenth[2] *n* **1 :** decimoquinto *m*, -ta *f* (en una serie) **2 :** quinceavo *m*, quinceava parte *f*
fifth[1] [ˈfɪfθ] *adj* **:** quinto
fifth[2] *n* **1 :** quinto *m*, -ta *f* (en una serie) **2 :** quinto *m*, quinta parte *f* **3 :** quinta *f* (en la música)
fiftieth[1] [ˈfɪftiəθ] *adj* **:** quincuagésimo
fiftieth[2] *n* **1 :** quincuagésimo *m*, -ma *f* (en una serie) **2 :** cincuentavo *m*, cincuentava parte *f*
fifty[1] [ˈfɪfti] *adj* **:** cincuenta
fifty[2] *n, pl* **-ties :** cincuenta *m*
fifty–fifty[1] [ˌfɪftiˈfɪfti] *adv* **:** a medias, mitad y mitad
fifty–fifty[2] *adj* **to have a fifty–fifty chance :** tener un cincuenta por ciento de posibilidades
fig [ˈfɪg] *n* **:** higo *m*
fight[1] [ˈfaɪt] *v* **fought** [ˈfɔt]; **fighting** *vi* **:** luchar, combatir, pelear — *vt* **:** luchar contra, combatir contra
fight[2] *n* **1** COMBAT **:** lucha *f*, pelea *f*, combate *m* **2** MATCH **:** pelea *f*, combate *m* (en boxeo) **3** QUARREL **:** disputa *f*, pelea *f*, pleito *m*
fighter [ˈfaɪt̬ər] *n* **1** COMBATANT **:** luchador *m*, -dora *f*; combatiente *mf* **2** BOXER **:** boxeador *m*, -dora *f*
figment [ˈfɪgmənt] *n* **figment of the imagination :** producto *m* de la imaginación
figurative [ˈfɪgjərət̬ɪv, -gə-] *adj* **:** figurado, metafórico
figuratively [ˈfɪgjərət̬ɪvli, -gə-] *adv* **:** en sentido figurado, de manera metafórica
figure[1] [ˈfɪgjər, -gər] *v* **-ured; -uring** *vt* **1** CALCULATE **:** calcular **2** ESTIMATE **:** figurarse, calcular <he figured it was possible : se figuró que era posible> — *vi* **1** FEATURE, STAND OUT **:** figurar, destacar **2 that figures! :** ¡obvio!, ¡no me extraña nada!
figure[2] *n* **1** DIGIT **:** número *m*, cifra *f* **2** PRICE **:** precio *m*, cifra *f* **3** PERSONAGE **:** figura *f*, personaje *m* **4 :** figura *f*, tipo *m*, físico *m* <to have a good figure : tener buen tipo, tener un buen físico> **5** DESIGN, OUTLINE **:** figura *f* **6 figures** *npl* **:** aritmética *f*
figurehead [ˈfɪgjərˌhɛd, -gər-] *n* **:** testaferro *m*, líder *mf* sin poder
figure of speech *n* **:** figura *f* retórica, figura *f* de hablar
figure out *vt* **1** UNDERSTAND **:** entender **2** RESOLVE **:** resolver (un problema, etc.)
figurine [ˌfɪgjəˈriːn] *n* **:** estatuilla *f*
Fijian [ˈfiːdʒiən, fɪˈjiːən] *n* **:** fijiano *m*, -na *f* — **Fijian** *adj*
filament [ˈfɪləmənt] *n* **:** filamento *m*
filbert [ˈfɪlbərt] *n* **:** avellana *f*
filch [ˈfɪltʃ] *vt* **:** hurtar, birlar *fam*
file[1] [ˈfaɪl] *v* **filed; filing** *vt* **1** CLASSIFY **:** clasificar **2 :** archivar (documentos) **3** SUBMIT **:** presentar <to file charges : presentar cargos> **4** SMOOTH **:** limar — *vi* **:** desfilar, entrar (o salir) en fila
file[2] *n* **1 :** lima *f* <nail file : lima de uñas> **2** DOCUMENTS **:** archivo *m* **3** LINE **:** fila *f*
filial [ˈfɪliəl, ˈfɪljəl] *adj* **:** filial
filibuster[1] [ˈfɪləˌbʌstər] *vi* **:** practicar el obstruccionismo
filibuster[2] *n* **:** obstruccionismo *m*
filibusterer [ˈfɪləˌbʌstərər] *n* **:** obstruccionista *mf*
filigree [ˈfɪləˌgriː] *n* **:** filigrana *f*
Filipino [ˌfɪləˈpiːnoː] *n* **:** filipino *m*, -na *f* — **Filipino** *adj*
fill[1] [ˈfɪl] *vt* **1 :** llenar, ocupar <to fill a cup : llenar una taza> <to fill a room : ocupar una sala> **2** STUFF **:** rellenar **3** PLUG **:** tapar, rellenar, empastar (un diente) **4** SATISFY **:** cumplir con, satisfacer **5** *or* **to fill out :** llenar, re-

llenar <to fill out a form : rellenar un formulario>

fill[2] *n* **1** FILLING, STUFFING : relleno *m* **2 to eat one's fill** : comer lo suficiente **3 to have one's fill of** : estar harto de

filler ['fɪlər] *n* : relleno *m*

fillet[1] ['fɪlət, fɪ'leɪ, 'fɪˌleɪ] *vt* : cortar en filetes

fillet[2] *n* : filete *m*

fill in *vt* INFORM : informar, poner al corriente — *vi* **to fill in for** : reemplazar a

filling ['fɪlɪŋ] *n* **1** : relleno *m* **2** : empaste *m* (de un diente)

filling station → **service station**

filly ['fɪli] *n, pl* **-lies** : potra *f,* potranca *f*

film[1] ['fɪlm] *vt* : filmar — *vi* : rodar

film[2] *n* **1** COATING : capa *f,* película *f* **2** : película *f* (fotográfica) **3** MOVIE : película *f,* filme *m*

filmy ['fɪlmi] *adj* **filmier; -est 1** GAUZY : diáfano, vaporoso **2** : cubierto de una película

filter[1] ['fɪltər] *vt* : filtrar

filter[2] *n* : filtro *m*

filth ['fɪlθ] *n* : mugre *f,* porquería *f,* roña *f*

filthiness ['fɪlθinəs] *n* : suciedad *f*

filthy ['fɪlθi] *adj* **filthier; -est 1** DIRTY : mugriento, sucio **2** OBSCENE : obsceno, indecente

filtration [fɪl'treɪʃən] *n* : filtración *f*

fin ['fɪn] *n* **1** : aleta *f* **2** : alerón *m* (de un automóvil o un avión)

finagle [fə'neɪgəl] *vt* **-gled; -gling** : arreglárselas para conseguir

final[1] ['faɪnəl] *adj* **1** DEFINITIVE : definitivo, final, inapelable **2** ULTIMATE : final **3** LAST : último, final

final[2] *n* **1** : final *f* (en deportes) **2 finals** *npl* : exámenes *mpl* finales

finale [fɪ'næli, -'nɑ-] *n* : final *m* <grand finale : final triunfal>

finalist ['faɪnəlɪst] *n* : finalista *mf*

finality [faɪ'næləṭi, fə-] *n, pl* **-ties** : finalidad *f*

finalize ['faɪnəlˌaɪz] *vt* **-ized; -izing** : finalizar

finally ['faɪnəli] *adv* **1** LASTLY : por último, finalmente **2** EVENTUALLY : por fin, al final **3** DEFINITIVELY : definitivamente

finance[1] [fə'nænts, 'faɪˌnænts] *vt* **-nanced; -nancing** : financiar

finance[2] *n* **1** : finanzas *fpl* **2 finances** *npl* RESOURCES : recursos *mpl* financieros

financial [fə'næntʃəl, faɪ-] *adj* : financiero, económico

financially [fə'næntʃəli, faɪ-] *adv* : económicamente

financier [ˌfɪnən'sɪr, ˌfaɪˌnæn-] *n* : financiero *m,* -ra *f;* financista *mf*

finch ['fɪntʃ] *n* : pinzón *m*

find[1] ['faɪnd] *vt* **found** ['faʊnd]; **finding 1** LOCATE : encontrar, hallar <I can't find it : no lo encuentro> <to find one's way : encontrar el camino, orientarse> **2** DISCOVER, REALIZE : descubrir, darse cuenta de <he found it difficult : descubrió que era difícil> **3** DECLARE : declarar, hallar <they found him guilty : lo declararon culpable>

find[2] *n* : hallazgo *m*

finder ['faɪndər] *n* : descubridor *m,* -dora *f*

finding ['faɪndɪŋ] *n* **1** FIND : hallazgo *m* **2 findings** *npl* : conclusiones *fpl*

find out *vt* DISCOVER : descubrir, averiguar — *vi* LEARN : enterarse

fine[1] ['faɪn] *vt* **fined; fining** : multar

fine[2] *adj* **finer; -est 1** PURE : puro (dícese del oro y de la plata) **2** THIN : fino, delgado **3** : fino <fine sand : arena fina> **4** SMALL : pequeño, minúsculo <fine print : letras minúsculas> **5** SUBTLE : sutil, delicado **6** EXCELLENT : excelente, magnífico, selecto **7** FAIR : bueno <it's a fine day : hace buen tiempo> **8** EXQUISITE : exquisito, delicado, fino **9 fine arts** : bellas artes *fpl*

fine[3] *n* : multa *f*

finely ['faɪnli] *adv* **1** EXCELLENTLY : con arte **2** ELEGANTLY : elegantemente **3** PRECISELY : con precisión **4 to chop finely** : picar muy fino, picar en trozos pequeños

fineness ['faɪnnəs] *n* **1** EXCELLENCE : excelencia *f* **2** ELEGANCE : elegancia *f,* refinamiento *m* **3** DELICACY : delicadeza *f,* lo fino **4** PRECISION : precisión *f* **5** SUBTLETY : sutileza *f* **6** PURITY : ley *f* (de oro y plata)

finery ['faɪnəri] *n* : galas *fpl,* adornos *mpl*

finesse[1] [fə'nɛs] *vt* **-nessed; -nessing** : ingeniar

finesse[2] *n* **1** REFINEMENT : refinamiento *m,* finura *f* **2** TACT : delicadeza *f,* tacto *m,* diplomacia *f* **3** CRAFTINESS : astucia *f*

finger[1] ['fɪŋgər] *vt* **1** HANDLE : tocar, toquetear **2** ACCUSE : acusar, delatar

finger[2] *n* : dedo *m*

fingerling ['fɪŋgərlɪŋ] *n* : pez *m* pequeño y joven

fingernail ['fɪŋgərˌneɪl] *n* : uña *f*

fingerprint[1] ['fɪŋgərˌprɪnt] *vt* : tomar las huellas digitales a

fingerprint[2] *n* : huella *f* digital

fingertip ['fɪŋgərˌtɪp] *n* : punta *f* del dedo, yema *f* del dedo

finicky ['fɪnɪki] *adj* : maniático, melindroso, mañoso

finish[1] ['fɪnɪʃ] *vt* **1** COMPLETE : acabar, terminar **2** : aplicar un acabado a (muebles, etc.)

finish[2] *n* **1** END : fin *m,* final *m* **2** REFINEMENT : refinamiento *m* **3** : acabado *m* <a glossy finish : un acabado brillante>

finite ['faɪˌnaɪt] *adj* : finito

fink ['fɪŋk] *n* : mequetrefe *mf fam*

Finn ['fɪn] *n* : finlandés *m,* -desa *f*

Finnish[1] ['fɪnɪʃ] *adj* : finlandés

Finnish[2] *n* : finlandés *m* (idioma)

fiord [fi'ɔrd] → **fjord**

fir ['fər] *n* **:** abeto *m*

fire[1] ['faɪr] *vt* **fired; firing 1** IGNITE, KINDLE **:** encender **2** ENLIVEN **:** animar, avivar **3** DISMISS **:** despedir **4** SHOOT **:** disparar **5** BAKE **:** cocer (cerámica)

fire[2] *n* **1 :** fuego *m* **2** BURNING **:** incendio *m* <fire alarm : alarma contra incendios> <to be on fire : estar en llamas> **3** ENTHUSIASM **:** ardor *m,* entusiasmo *m* **4** SHOOTING **:** disparos *mpl*, fuego *m*

firearm ['faɪr,ɑrm] *n* **:** arma *f* de fuego

fireball ['faɪr,bɔl] *n* **1 :** bola *f* de fuego **2** METEOR **:** bólido *m*

firebreak ['faɪr,breɪk] *n* **:** cortafuegos *m*

firebug ['faɪr,bʌg] *n* **:** pirómano *m,* -na *f;* incendiario *m,* -ria *f*

firecracker ['faɪr,krækər] *n* **:** petardo *m*

fire escape *n* **:** escalera *f* de incendios

firefighter ['faɪr,faɪt̬ər] *n* **:** bombero *m,* -ra *f*

firefly ['faɪr,flaɪ] *n, pl* **-flies :** luciérnaga *f*

fireman ['faɪrmən] *n, pl* **-men** [-mən, -,mɛn] **1** FIREFIGHTER **:** bombero *m,* -ra *f* **2** STOKER **:** fogonero *m,* -ra *f*

fireplace ['faɪr,pleɪs] *n* **:** hogar *m,* chimenea *f*

fireproof[1] ['faɪr,pruːf] *vt* **:** hacer incombustible

fireproof[2] *adj* **:** incombustible, ignífugo

fireside[1] ['faɪr,saɪd] *adj* **:** informal <fireside chat : charla informal>

fireside[2] *n* **1** HEARTH **:** chimenea *f,* hogar *m* **2** HOME **:** hogar *m,* casa *f*

firewood ['faɪr,wʊd] *n* **:** leña *f*

fireworks ['faɪr,wərks] *npl* **:** fuegos *mpl* artificiales, pirotecnia *f*

firm[1] ['fərm] *vi* **:** endurecer

firm[2] *adj* **1** VIGOROUS **:** fuerte, vigoroso **2** SOLID, UNYIELDING **:** firme, duro, sólido **3** UNCHANGING **:** firme, inalterable **4** RESOLUTE **:** firme, resuelto

firm[3] *n* **:** empresa *f,* firma *f,* compañía *f*

firmament ['fərməmənt] *n* **:** firmamento *m*

firmly ['fərmli] *adv* **:** firmemente

firmness ['fərmnəs] *n* **:** firmeza *f*

first[1] ['fərst] *adv* **1 :** primero <finish your homework first : primero termina tu tarea> <first and foremost : ante todo> <first of all : en primer lugar> **2 :** por primera vez <I saw it first in Boston : lo vi por primera vez en Boston>

first[2] *adj* **1 :** primero <the first time : la primera vez> <at first sight : a primera vista> <in the first place : en primer lugar> <the first ten applicants : los diez primeros candidatos> **2** FOREMOST **:** principal, primero <first tenor : tenor principal>

first[3] *n* **1 :** primero *m,* -ra *f* (en una serie) **2 :** primero *m,* primera parte *f* **3** *or* **first gear :** primera *f* **4 at ~ :** al principio

first aid *n* **:** primeros auxilios *mpl*

first–class[1] ['fərst'klæs] *adv* **:** en primera <to travel first-class : viajar en primera>

first–class[2] *adj* **:** de primera

first class *n* **:** primera clase *f*

firsthand[1] ['fərst'hænd] *adv* **:** directamente

firsthand[2] *adj* **:** de primera mano

first lieutenant *n* **:** teniente *mf;* teniente primero *m,* teniente primera *f*

firstly ['fərstli] *adv* **:** primeramente, principalmente, en primer lugar

first–rate[1] ['fərst'reɪt] *adv* **:** muy bien

first–rate[2] *adj* **:** de primera, de primera clase

first sergeant *n* **:** sargento *mf*

firth ['fərθ] *n* **:** estuario *m*

fiscal ['fɪskəl] *adj* **:** fiscal — **fiscally** *adv*

fish[1] ['fɪʃ] *vi* **1 :** pescar **2 to fish for** SEEK **:** buscar, rebuscar <to fish for compliments : andar a la caza de cumplidos> — *vt* **:** pescar

fish[2] *n, pl* **fish** *or* **fishes :** pez *m* (vivo), pescado *m* (para comer)

fisherman ['fɪʃərmən] *n, pl* **-men** [-mən, -,mɛn] **:** pescador *m,* -dora *f*

fishery ['fɪʃəri] *n, pl* **-eries 1 → fishing 2 :** zona *f* pesquera, pesquería *f*

fishhook ['fɪʃ,hʊk] *n* **:** anzuelo *m*

fishing ['fɪʃɪŋ] *n* **:** pesca *f,* industria *f* pesquera

fishing pole *n* **:** caña *f* de pescar

fish market *n* **:** pescadería *f*

fishy ['fɪʃi] *adj* **fishier; -est 1 :** a pescado <a fishy taste : un sabor a pescado> **2** QUESTIONABLE **:** dudoso, sospechoso <there's something fishy going on : aquí hay gato encerrado>

fission ['fɪʃən, -ʒən] *n* **:** fisión *f*

fissure ['fɪʃər] *n* **:** fisura *f,* hendidura *f*

fist ['fɪst] *n* **:** puño *m*

fistful ['fɪst,fʊl] *n* **:** puñado *m*

fisticuffs ['fɪstɪ,kʌfs] *npl* **:** lucha *f* a puñetazos

fit[1] ['fɪt] *v* **fitted; fitting** *vt* **1** MATCH **:** corresponder a, coincidir con <the punishment fits the crime : el castigo corresponde al crimen> **2 :** quedar <the dress doesn't fit me : el vestido no me queda> **3** GO **:** caber, encajar en <her key fits the lock : su llave encaja en la cerradura> **4** INSERT, INSTALL **:** poner, colocar **5** ADAPT **:** adecuar, ajustar, adaptar **6** *or* **to fit out** EQUIP **:** equipar — *vi* **1 :** quedar, entallar <these pants don't fit : estos pantalones no me quedan> **2** CONFORM **:** encajar, cuadrar **3 to fit in :** encajar, estar integrado

fit[2] *adj* **fitter; fittest 1** SUITABLE **:** adecuado, apropiado, conveniente **2** QUALIFIED **:** calificado, competente **3** HEALTHY **:** sano, en forma

fit[3] *n* **1** ATTACK **:** ataque *m,* acceso *m,* arranque *m* **2 to be a good fit :** quedar bien **3 to be a tight fit :** ser muy entallado (de ropa), estar apretado (de espacios)

fitful [ˈfɪtfəl] *adj* : irregular, intermitente — **fitfully** *adv*

fitness [ˈfɪtnəs] *n* **1** HEALTH : salud *f*, buena forma *f* (física) **2** SUITABILITY : idoneidad *f*

fitting[1] [ˈfɪtɪŋ] *adj* : adecuado, apropiado

fitting[2] *n* : accesorio *m*

five[1] [ˈfaɪv] *adj* : cinco

five[2] *n* : cinco *m*

five hundred[1] *adj* : quinientos

five hundred[2] *n* : quinientos *m*

fix[1] [ˈfɪks] *vt* **1** ATTACH, SECURE : sujetar, asegurar, fijar **2** ESTABLISH : fijar, concretar, establecer **3** REPAIR : arreglar, reparar **4** PREPARE : preparar <to fix dinner : preparar la cena> **5** : arreglar, amañar <to fix a race : arreglar una carrera> **6** RIVET : fijar (los ojos, la mirada, etc.)

fix[2] *n* **1** PREDICAMENT : aprieto *m*, apuro *m* **2** : posición *f* <to get a fix on : establecer la posición de>

fixate [ˈfɪkˌseɪt] *vi* **-ated; -ating** : obsesionarse

fixation [fɪkˈseɪʃən] *n* : fijación *f*, obsesión *f*

fixed [ˈfɪkst] *adj* **1** STATIONARY : estacionario, inmóvil **2** UNCHANGING : fijo, inalterable **3** INTENT : fijo <a fixed stare : una mirada fija> **4 to be comfortably fixed** : estar en posición acomodada

fixedly [ˈfɪksədli] *adv* : fijamente

fixedness [ˈfɪksədnəs, ˈfikst-] *n* : rigidez *f*

fixture [ˈfɪkstʃər] *n* **1** : parte *f* integrante, elemento *m* fijo **2 fixtures** *npl* : instalaciones *fpl* (de una casa)

fizz[1] [ˈfɪz] *vi* : burbujear

fizz[2] *n* : efervescencia *f*, burbujeo *m*

fizzle[1] [ˈfɪzəl] *vi* **-zled; -zling 1** FIZZ : burbujear **2** FAIL : fracasar

fizzle[2] *n* : fracaso *m*, fiasco *m*

fjord [fiˈɔrd] *n* : fiordo *m*

flab [ˈflæb] *n* : gordura *f*

flabbergast [ˈflæbərˌgæst] *vt* : asombrar, pasmar, dejar atónito

flabby [ˈflæbi] *adj* **-bier; -est** : blando, fofo, aguado *CA, Col, Mex*

flaccid [ˈflæksəd, ˈflæsəd] *adj* : fláccido

flag[1] [ˈflæg] *vi* **flagged; flagging 1** : hacer señales con banderas **2** WEAKEN : flaquear, desfallecer

flag[2] *n* : bandera *f*, pabellón *m*, estandarte *m*

flagon [ˈflægən] *n* : jarra *f* grande

flagpole [ˈflægˌpoːl] *n* : asta *f*, mástil *m*

flagrant [ˈfleɪgrənt] *adj* : flagrante — **flagrantly** *adv*

flagship [ˈflægˌʃɪp] *n* : buque *m* insignia

flagstaff [ˈflægˌstæf] → **flagpole**

flagstone [ˈflægˌstoːn] *n* : losa *f*, piedra *f*

flail[1] [ˈfleɪl] *vt* **1** : trillar (grano) **2** : sacudir, agitar (los brazos)

flail[2] *n* : mayal *m*

flair [ˈflær] *n* : don *m*, facilidad *f*

flak [ˈflæk] *ns & pl* **flak 1** : fuego *m* antiaéreo **2** CRITICISM : críticas *fpl*

flake[1] [ˈfleɪk] *vi* **flaked; flaking** : desmenuzarse, pelarse (dícese de la piel)

flake[2] *n* : copo *m* (de nieve), escama *f* (de la piel), astilla *f* (de madera)

flamboyance [flæmˈbɔɪənts] *n* : extravagancia *f*, rimbombancia *f*

flamboyant [flæmˈbɔɪənt] *adj* : exuberante, extravagante, rimbombante

flame[1] [ˈfleɪm] *vi* **flamed; flaming 1** BLAZE : arder, llamear **2** GLOW : brillar, encenderse

flame[2] *n* BLAZE : llama *f* <to burst into flames : estallar en llamas> <to go up in flame : incendiarse>

flamethrower [ˈfleɪmˌθroːər] *n* : lanzallamas *m*

flamingo [fləˈmɪŋgo] *n, pl* **-gos** : flamenco *m*

flammable [ˈflæməbəl] *adj* : inflamable, flamable

flange [ˈflændʒ] *n* : reborde *m*, pestaña *f*

flank[1] [ˈflæŋk] *vt* **1** : flanquear (para defender o atacar) **2** BORDER, LINE : bordear

flank[2] *n* : ijada *f* (de un animal), costado *m* (de una persona), falda *f* (de una colina), flanco *m* (de un cuerpo de soldados)

flannel [ˈflænəl] *n* : franela *f*

flap[1] [ˈflæp] *v* **flapped; flapping** *vi* **1** : aletear <the bird was flapping (its wings) : el pájaro aleteaba> **2** FLUTTER : ondear, agitarse — *vt* : batir, agitar

flap[2] *n* **1** FLAPPING : aleteo *m*, aletazo *m* (de alas) **2** : soplada *f* (de un sobre), hoja *f* (de una mesa), faldón *m* (de una chaqueta)

flapjack [ˈflæpˌdʒæk] → **pancake**

flare[1] [ˈflær] *vi* **flared; flaring 1** FLAME, SHINE : llamear, brillar **2 to flare up** : estallar, explotar (de cólera)

flare[2] *n* **1** FLASH : destello *m* **2** SIGNAL : (luz *f* de) bengala *f* **3 solar flare** : erupción *f* solar

flash[1] [ˈflæʃ] *vi* **1** SHINE, SPARKLE : destellar, brillar, relampaguear **2** : pasar como un relámpago <an idea flashed through my mind : una idea me cruzó la mente como un relámpago> — *vt* : despedir, lanzar (una luz), transmitir (un mensaje)

flash[2] *adj* SUDDEN : repentino

flash[3] *n* **1** : destello *m* (de luz), fogonazo *m* (de una explosión) **2 flash of lightning** : relámpago *m* **3 in a flash** : de repente, de un abrir y cerrar los ojos

flashiness [ˈflæʃinəs] *n* : ostentación *f*

flashlight [ˈflæʃˌlaɪt] *n* : linterna *f*

flashy [ˈflæʃi] *adj* **flashier; -est** : llamativo, ostentoso

flask [ˈflæsk] *n* : frasco *m*

flat[1] [ˈflæt] *vt* **flatted; flatting 1** FLATTEN : aplanar, achatar **2 :** bajar de tono (en música)
flat[2] *adv* **1** EXACTLY : exactamente <in ten minutes flat : en diez minutos exactos> **2 :** desafinado, demasiado bajo (en la música)
flat[3] *adj* **flatter; flattest 1** EVEN, LEVEL : plano, llano **2** SMOOTH : liso **3** DEFINITE : categórico, rotundo, explícito <a flat refusal : una negativa categórica> **4** DULL : aburrido, soso, monótono (dícese la voz) **5** DEFLATED : desinflado, pinchado, ponchado *Mex* **6 :** bemol (en música) <to sing flat : cantar desafinado>
flat[4] *n* **1** PLAIN : llano *m,* terreno *m* llano **2 :** bemol *m* (en la música) **3** APARTMENT : apartamento *m,* departamento *m* **4** *or* **flat tire :** pinchazo *m,* ponchadura *f Mex*
flatbed [ˈflæt,bɛd] *n* : camión *m* de plataforma
flatcar [ˈflæt,kɑr] *n* : vagón *m* abierto
flatfish [ˈflæt,fɪʃ] *n* : platija *f*
flat–footed [ˈflæt,fʊtəd, ,flætˈ-] *adj* : de pies planos
flatly [ˈflætli] *adv* DEFINITELY : categóricamente, rotundamente
flatness [ˈflætnəs] *n* **1** EVENNESS : lo llano, lisura *f,* uniformidad *f* **2** DULLNESS : monotonía *f*
flat–out [ˈflætˈaʊt] *adj* **1 :** frenético, a toda máquina <a flat-out effort : un esfuerzo frenético> **2** CATEGORICAL : descarado, rotundo, categórico
flatten [ˈflætən] *vt* : aplanar, achatar
flatter [ˈflæṭər] *vt* **1** OVERPRAISE : adular **2** COMPLIMENT : halagar **3 :** favorecer <the photo flatters you : la foto te favorece>
flatterer [ˈflæṭərər] *n* : adulador *m,* -dora *f*
flattering [ˈflæṭərɪŋ] *adj* **1** COMPLIMENTARY : halagador **2** BECOMING : favorecedor
flattery [ˈflæṭəri] *n, pl* **-ries :** halagos *mpl*
flatulence [ˈflætʃələnts] *n* : flatulencia *f,* ventosidad *f*
flatulent [ˈflætʃələnt] *adj* : flatulento
flatware [ˈflæt,wær] *n* : cubertería *f,* cubiertos *mpl*
flaunt[1] [ˈflɔnt] *vt* : alardear, hacer alarde de
flaunt[2] *n* : alarde *m,* ostentación *f*
flavor[1] [ˈfleɪvər] *vt* : dar sabor a, sazonar
flavor[2] *n* **1 :** gusto *m,* sabor *m* **2** FLAVORING : sazón *f,* condimento *m*
flavorful [ˈfleɪvərfəl] *adj* : sabroso
flavoring [ˈfleɪvərɪŋ] *n* : condimento *m,* sazón *f*
flavorless [ˈfleɪvərləs] *adj* : sin sabor
flaw [ˈflɔ] *n* : falla *f,* defecto *m,* imperfección *f*
flawless [ˈflɔləs] *adj* : impecable, perfecto — **flawlessly** *adv*
flax [ˈflæks] *n* : lino *m*
flaxen [ˈflæksən] *adj* : rubio, blondo (dícese del pelo)
flay [ˈfleɪ] *vt* **1** SKIN : desollar, despellejar **2** VILIFY : criticar con dureza, vilipendiar
flea [ˈfliː] *n* : pulga *f*
fleck[1] [ˈflɛk] *vt* : salpicar
fleck[2] *n* : mota *f,* pinta *f*
fledgling [ˈflɛdʒlɪŋ] *n* : polluelo *m,* pollito *m*
flee [ˈfliː] *v* **fled** [ˈflɛd]; **fleeing** *vi* : huir, escapar(se) — *vt* : huir de
fleece[1] [ˈfliːs] *vt* **fleeced; fleecing 1** SHEAR : esquilar, trasquilar **2** SWINDLE : estafar, defraudar
fleece[2] *n* : lana *f,* vellón *m*
fleet[1] [ˈfliːt] *vi* : moverse con rapidez
fleet[2] *adj* SWIFT : rápido, veloz
fleet[3] *n* : flota *f*
fleet admiral *n* : almirante *mf*
fleeting [ˈfliːṭɪŋ] *adj* : fugaz, breve
flesh [ˈflɛʃ] *n* **1 :** carne *f* (de seres humanos y animales) **2 :** pulpa *f* (de frutas)
flesh out *vt* : desarrollar, darle cuerpo a
fleshy [ˈflɛʃi] *adj* **fleshier; -est :** gordo (dícese de las personas), carnoso (dícese de la fruta)
flew → **fly**
flex [ˈflɛks] *vt* : doblar, flexionar
flexibility [,flɛksəˈbɪləṭi] *n, pl* **-ties** : flexibilidad *f,* elasticidad *f*
flexible [ˈflɛksəbəl] *adj* : flexible — **flexibly** [-bli] *adv*
flick[1] [ˈflɪk] *vt* : dar un capirotazo a (con el dedo) <to flick a switch : darle al interruptor> — *vi* **1** FLIT : revolotear **2 to flick through :** hojear (un libro)
flick[2] *n* : coletazo *m* (de una cola), capirotazo *m* (de un dedo)
flicker[1] [ˈflɪkər] *vi* **1** FLUTTER : revolotear, aletear **2** BLINK, TWINKLE : parpadear, titilar
flicker[2] *n* **1 :** parpadeo *m,* titileo *m* **2** HINT, TRACE : indicio *m,* rastro *m* <a flicker of hope : un rayo de esperanza>
flier [ˈflaɪər] *n* **1** AVIATOR : aviador *m,* -dora *f* **2** CIRCULAR : folleto *m* publicitario, circular *f*
flight [ˈflaɪt] *n* **1 :** vuelo *m* (de aves o aviones), trayectoria *f* (de proyectiles) **2** TRIP : vuelo *m* **3** FLOCK, SQUADRON : bandada *f* (de pájaros), escuadrilla *f* (de aviones) **4** ESCAPE : huida *f,* fuga *f* **5 flight of fancy :** ilusiones *fpl,* fantasía *f* **6 flight of stairs :** tramo *m*
flightless [ˈflaɪtləs] *adj* : no volador
flighty [ˈflaɪṭi] *adj* **flightier; -est :** caprichoso, frívolo
flimsy [flɪmzi] *adj* **flimsier; -est 1** LIGHT, THIN : ligero, fino **2** WEAK : endeble, poco sólido **3** IMPLAUSIBLE : pobre, flojo, poco convincente <a flimsy excuse : una excusa floja>
flinch [ˈflɪntʃ] *vi* **1** WINCE : estremecerse **2** RECOIL : recular, retroceder

fling[1] [ˈflɪŋ] *vt* **flung** [ˈflʌŋ]; **flinging 1** THROW : lanzar, tirar, arrojar **2 to fling oneself** : lanzarse, tirarse, precipitarse
fling[2] *n* **1** THROW : lanzamiento *m* **2** ATTEMPT : intento *m* **3** AFFAIR : aventura *f* **4** BINGE : juerga *f*
flint [ˈflɪnt] *n* : pedernal *m*
flinty [ˈflɪnti] *adj* **flintier; -est 1** : de pedernal **2** STERN, UNYIELDING : severo, inflexible
flip[1] [ˈflɪp] *v* **flipped; flipping** *vt* **1** TOSS : tirar <to flip a coin : echar a cara o cruz> **2** OVERTURN : dar la vuelta a, voltear — *vi* **1** : moverse bruscamente **2 to flip through** : hojear (un libro)
flip[2] *adj* : insolente, descarado
flip[3] *n* **1** FLICK : capirotazo *m*, golpe *m* ligero **2** SOMERSAULT : voltereta *f*
flippancy [ˈflɪpəntsi] *n, pl* **-cies** : ligereza *f*, falta *f* de seriedad
flippant [ˈflɪpənt] *adj* : ligero, frívolo, poco serio
flipper [ˈflɪpər] *n* : aleta *f*
flirt[1] [ˈflərt] *vi* **1** : coquetear, flirtear **2** TRIFLE : jugar <to flirt with death : jugar con la muerte>
flirt[2] *n* : coqueto *m*, -ta *f*
flirtation [ˌflərˈteɪʃən] *n* : devaneo *m*, coqueteo *m*
flirtatious [ˌflərˈteɪʃəs] *adj* : insinuante, coqueto
flit [ˈflɪt] *vi* **flitted; flitting 1** : revolotear **2 to flit about** : ir y venir rápidamente
float[1] [ˈfloːt] *vi* **1** : flotar **2** WANDER : vagar, errar — *vt* **1** : poner a flote, hacer flotar (un barco) **2** LAUNCH : hacer flotar (una empresa) **3** ISSUE : emitir (acciones en la bolsa)
float[2] *n* **1** : flotador *m*, corcho *m* (para pescar) **2** BUOY : boya *f* **3** : carroza *f* (en un desfile)
flock[1] [ˈflɑk] *vi* **1** : moverse en rebaño **2** CONGREGATE : congregarse, reunirse
flock[2] *n* : rebaño *m* (de ovejas), bandada *f* (de pájaros)
floe [ˈfloː] *n* : témpano *m* de hielo
flog [ˈflɑg] *vt* **flogged; flogging** : azotar, fustigar
flood[1] [ˈflʌd] *vt* : inundar, anegar
flood[2] *n* **1** INUNDATION : inundación *f* **2** TORRENT : avalancha *f*, diluvio *m*, torrente *m* <a flood of tears : un mar de lágrimas>
floodlight [ˈflʌdˌlaɪt] *n* : foco *m*
floodwater [ˈflʌdˌwɔt̬ər] *n* : crecida *f*, creciente *f*
floor[1] [ˈflor] *vt* **1** : solar, poner suelo a (una casa o una sala) **2** KNOCK DOWN : derribar, echar al suelo **3** NONPLUS : desconcertar, confundir, dejar perplejo
floor[2] *n* **1** : suelo *m*, piso *m* <dance floor : pista de baile> **2** STORY : piso *m*, planta *f* <ground floor : planta baja> <second floor : primer piso> **3** : mínimo *m* (de sueldos, precios, etc.)
floorboard [ˈflorˌbord] *n* : tabla *f* del suelo, suelo *m*, piso *m*
flop[1] [ˈflɑp] *vi* **flopped; flopping 1** FLAP : golpearse, agitarse **2** COLLAPSE : dejarse caer, desplomarse **3** FAIL : fracasar
flop[2] *n* **1** FAILURE : fracaso *m* **2 to take a flop** : caerse
floppy [ˈflɑpi] *adj* **-pier; -est 1** : blando, flexible **2 floppy disk** : diskette *m*, disquete *m*
flora [ˈflorə] *n* : flora *f*
floral [ˈflorəl] *adj* : floral, floreado
florid [ˈflorɪd] *adj* **1** FLOWERY : florido **2** REDDISH : rojizo
florist [ˈflorɪst] *n* : florista *mf*
floss[1] [ˈflɔs] *vi* : limpiarse los dientes con hilo dental
floss[2] *n* **1** : hilo *m* de seda (de brodar) **2** → **dental floss**
flotation [floˈteɪʃən] *n* : flotación *f*
flotilla [floˈtɪlə] *n* : flotilla *f*
flotsam [ˈflɑtsəm] *n* **1** : restos *mpl* flotantes (en el mar) **2 flotsam and jetsam** : desechos *mpl*, restos *mpl*
flounce[1] [ˈflaʊnts] *vi* **flounced; flouncing** : moverse haciendo aspavientos <she flounced into the room : entró en la sala haciendo aspavientos>
flounce[2] *n* **1** RUFFLE : volante *m* **2** FLOURISH : aspaviento *m*
flounder[1] [ˈflaʊndər] *vi* **1** STRUGGLE : forcejear **2** STUMBLE : no saber qué hacer o decir, perder el hilo (en un discurso)
flounder[2] *n, pl* **flounder** *or* **flounders** : platija *f*
flour[1] [ˈflaʊər] *vt* : enharinar
flour[2] *n* : harina *f*
flourish[1] [ˈflərɪʃ] *vi* THRIVE : florecer, prosperar, crecer (dícese de las plantas) — *vt* BRANDISH : blandir
flourish[2] *n* : floritura *f*, floreo *m*
flourishing [ˈflərɪʃɪŋ] *adj* : floreciente, próspero
flout [ˈflaʊt] *vt* : desacatar, burlarse de
flow[1] [ˈfloː] *vi* **1** COURSE : fluir, manar, correr **2** CIRCULATE : circular, correr <traffic is flowing smoothly : el tránsito está circulando con fluidez>
flow[2] *n* **1** FLOWING : flujo *m*, circulación *f* **2** STREAM : corriente *f*, chorro *m*
flower[1] [ˈflaʊər] *vi* : florecer, florear
flower[2] *n* : flor *f*
flowered [ˈflaʊərd] *adj* : florido, floreado
floweriness [ˈflaʊərinəs] *n* : floritura *f*
flowering[1] [ˈflaʊərɪŋ] *adj* : floreciente
flowering[2] *n* : floración *f*, florecimiento *m*
flowerpot [ˈflaʊərˌpɑt] *n* : maceta *f*, tiesto *m*, macetero *m*
flowery [ˈflaʊəri] *adj* **1** : florido **2** FLOWERED : floreado, de flores
flowing [ˈfloːɪŋ] *adj* : fluido, corriente
flown → **fly**
flu [ˈfluː] *n* : gripe *f*, gripa *f Col, Mex*

fluctuate [ˈflʌktʃʊˌeɪt] *vi* **-ated; -ating** : fluctuar
fluctuation [ˌflʌktʃʊˈeɪʃən] *n* : fluctuación *f*
flue [ˈfluː] *n* : tiro *m,* salida *f* de humos
fluency [ˈfluːən*t*si] *n* : fluidez *f,* soltura *f*
fluent [ˈfluːənt] *adj* : fluido
fluently [ˈfluːəntli] *adv* : con soltura, con fluidez
fluff¹ [ˈflʌf] *vt* **1** : mullir <to fluff up the pillows : mullir las almohadas> **2** BUNGLE : echar a perder, equivocarse
fluff² *n* **1** FUZZ : pelusa *f* **2** DOWN : plumón *m*
fluffy [ˈflʌfi] *adj* **fluffier; -est 1** DOWNY : lleno de pelusa, velloso **2** SPONGY : esponjoso
fluid¹ [ˈfluːɪd] *adj* : fluido
fluid² *n* : fluido *m,* líquido *m*
fluidity [fluˈɪdəti] *n* : fluidez *f*
fluid ounce *n* : onza *f* líquida (29.57 mililitros)
fluke [ˈfluːk] *n* : golpe *m* de suerte, chiripa *f,* casualidad *f*
flung → **fling**
flunk [ˈflʌŋk] *vt* FAIL : reprobar — *vi* : salir reprobando
fluorescence [ˌflʊrˈɛsən*t*s, ˌflɔr-] *n* : fluorescencia *f*
fluorescent [ˌflʊrˈɛsənt, ˌflɔr-] *adj* : fluorescente
fluoridate [ˈflɔrəˌdeɪt, ˈflʊr-] *vt* **-dated; -dating** : fluorizar
fluoridation [ˌflɔrəˈdeɪʃən, ˌflʊr-] *n* : fluorización *f,* fluoración *f*
fluoride [ˈflɔrˌaɪd, ˈflʊr-] *n* : fluoruro *m*
fluorine [ˈflʊrˌiːn] *n* : flúor *m*
fluorocarbon [ˌflɔroˈkɑrbən, ˌflʊr-] *n* : fluorocarbono *m*
flurry [ˈfləri] *n, pl* **-ries 1** GUST : ráfaga *f* **2** SNOWFALL : nevisca *f* **3** BUSTLE : frenesí *m,* bullicio *m* **4** BARRAGE : aluvión *m,* oleada *f* <a flurry of questions : un aluvión de preguntas>
flush¹ [ˈflʌʃ] *vt* **1** : limpiar con agua <to flush the toilet : jalar la cadena> **2** RAISE : hacer salir, levantar (en la caza) — *vi* BLUSH : ruborizarse, sonrojarse
flush² *adv* : al mismo nivel, a ras
flush³ *adj* **1** *or* **flushed** [ˈflʌʃt] : colorado, rojo, encendido (dícese de la cara) **2** FILLED : lleno a rebosar **3** ABUNDANT : copioso, abundante **4** AFFLUENT : adinerado **5** ALIGNED, SMOOTH : alineado, liso **6 flush against** : pegado a, contra
flush⁴ *n* **1** FLOW, JET : chorro *m,* flujo *m* rápido **2** SURGE : arrebato *m,* arranque *m* <a flush of anger : un arrebato de cólera> **3** BLUSH : rubor *m,* sonrojo *m* **4** GLOW : resplandor *m,* flor *f* <the flush of youth : la flor de la juventud> <in the flush of victory : en la euforia del triunfo>
fluster¹ [ˈflʌstər] *vt* : poner nervioso, aturdir
fluster² *n* : agitación *f,* confusión *f*
flute [ˈfluːt] *n* : flauta *f*
fluted [ˈfluːtəd] *adj* **1** GROOVED : estriado, acanalado **2** WAVY : ondulado
fluting [ˈfluːtɪŋ] *n* : estrías *fpl*
flutist [ˈfluːtɪst] *n* : flautista *mf*
flutter¹ [ˈflʌtər] *vi* **1** : revolotear (dícese de un pájaro), ondear (dícese de una bandera), palpitar con fuerza (dícese del corazón) **2 to flutter about** : ir y venir, revoltear — *vt* : sacudir, batir
flutter² *n* **1** FLUTTERING : revoloteo *m,* aleteo *m* **2** COMMOTION, STIR : revuelo *m,* agitación *f*
flux [ˈflʌks] *n* **1** : flujo *m* (en física y medicina) **2** CHANGE : cambio *m* <to be in a state of flux : estar cambiando continuamente>
fly¹ [ˈflaɪ] *v* **flew** [ˈfluː]; **flown** [ˈfloːn]; **flying** *vi* **1** : volar (dícese de los pájaros, etc.) **2** TRAVEL : volar (dícese de los aviones), ir en avión (dícese de los pasajeros) **3** FLOAT : flotar, ondear **4** FLEE : huir, escapar **5** RUSH : correr, irse volando **6** PASS : pasar (volando) <how time flies! : ¡cómo pasa el tiempo!> **7 to fly open** : abrir de golpe — *vt* : pilotar (un avión), hacer volar (una cometa)
fly² *n, pl* **flies 1** : mosca *f* <to drop like flies : caer como moscas> **2** : bragueta *f* (de pantalones, etc.)
flyer → **flier**
flying saucer → **UFO**
flypaper [ˈflaɪˌpeɪpər] *n* : papel *m* matamoscas
flyspeck [ˈflaɪˌspɛk] *n* **1** : excremento *m* de mosca **2** SPECK : motita *f,* puntito *m*
flyswatter [ˈflaɪˌswɑtər] *n* : matamoscas *m*
flywheel [ˈflaɪˌ*h*wiːl] *n* : volante *m*
foal¹ [ˈfoːl] *vi* : parir
foal² *n* : potro *m,* -tra *f*
foam¹ [ˈfoːm] *vi* : hacer espuma
foam² *n* : espuma *f*
foamy [ˈfoːmi] *adj* **foamier; -est** : espumoso
focal [ˈfoːkəl] *adj* **1** : focal, central **2 focal point** : foco *m,* punto *m* de referencia
fo'c'sle [ˈfoːksəl] → **forecastle**
focus¹ [ˈfoːkəs] *v* **-cused** *or* **-cussed; -cusing** *or* **-cussing** *vt* **1** : enfocar (un instrumento) **2** CONCENTRATE : concentrar, centrar — *vi* : enfocar, fijar la vista
focus² *n, pl* **-ci** [ˈfoːˌsaɪ, -ˌkaɪ] **1** : foco *m* <to be in focus : estar enfocado> **2** FOCUSING : enfoque *m* **3** CENTER : centro *m,* foco *m*
fodder [ˈfɑdər] *n* : pienso *m,* forraje *m*
foe [ˈfoː] *n* : enemigo *m,* -ga *f*
fog¹ [ˈfɔg, ˈfɑg] *v* **fogged; fogging** *vt* : empañar — *vi* **to fog up** : empañarse
fog² *n* : niebla *f,* neblina *f*
foggy [ˈfɔgi, ˈfɑ-] *adj* **foggier; -est** : nebuloso, brumoso

foghorn ['fɔg,hɔrn, 'fɑg-] *n* **:** sirena *f* de niebla

fogy ['foːgi] *n, pl* **-gies :** carca *mf fam,* persona *f* chapada a la antigua

foible ['fɔɪbəl] *n* **:** flaqueza *f,* debilidad *f*

foil[1] ['fɔɪl] *vt* **:** frustrar, hacer fracasar

foil[2] *n* **1 :** lámina *f* de metal, papel *m* de aluminio **2** CONTRAST **:** contraste *m,* complemento *m* **3** SWORD **:** florete *m* (en esgrima)

foist ['fɔɪst] *vt* **:** encajar, endilgar *fam,* colocar

fold[1] ['foːld] *vt* **1** BEND **:** doblar, plegar **2** CLASP **:** cruzar (brazos), enlazar (manos), plegar (alas) **3** EMBRACE **:** estrechar, abrazar — *vi* **1** FAIL **:** fracasar **2 to fold up :** doblarse, plegarse

fold[2] *n* **1** SHEEPFOLD **:** redil *m* (para ovejas) **2** FLOCK **:** rebaño *m* <to return to the fold : volver al redil> **3** CREASE **:** pliegue *m,* doblez *m*

folder ['foːldər] *n* **1** CIRCULAR **:** circular *f,* folleto *m* **2** BINDER **:** carpeta *f*

foliage ['foːliɪdʒ, -lɪdʒ] *n* **:** follaje *m*

folio ['foːli,oː] *n, pl* **-lios :** folio *m*

folk[1] ['foːk] *adj* **:** popular, folklórico <folk customs : costumbres populares> <folk dance : danza folklórica>

folk[2] *n, pl* **folk** *or* **folks 1** PEOPLE **:** gente *f* **2 folks** *npl* **:** familia *f,* padres *mpl*

folklore ['foːk,lor] *n* **:** folklore *m*

folklorist ['foːk,lorɪst] *n* **:** folklorista *mf*

folksy ['foːksi] *adj* **folksier; -est :** campechano

follicle ['fɑlɪkəl] *n* **:** folículo *m*

follow ['fɑlo] *vt* **1 :** seguir <follow the guide : siga al guía> <she followed the road : siguió el camino, continuó por el camino> **2** PURSUE **:** perseguir, seguir **3** OBEY **:** seguir, cumplir, observar **4** UNDERSTAND **:** entender — *vi* **1 :** seguir **2** UNDERSTAND **:** entender **3 it follows that... :** se deduce que...

follower ['fɑloər] *n* **:** seguidor *m,* -dora *f*

following[1] ['fɑloɪŋ] *adj* NEXT **:** siguiente

following[2] *n* FOLLOWERS **:** seguidores *mpl*

following[3] *prep* AFTER **:** después de

follow through *vi* **to follow through with :** continuar con, realizar

follow up *vt* **:** seguir (una sugerencia, etc.), investigar (una huella)

folly ['fɑli] *n, pl* **-lies :** locura *f,* desatino *m*

foment [fo'mɛnt] *vt* **:** fomentar

fond ['fɑnd] *adj* **1** LOVING **:** cariñoso, tierno **2** PARTIAL **:** aficionado **3** FERVENT **:** ferviente, fervoroso

fondle ['fɑndəl] *vt* **-dled; -dling :** acariciar

fondly ['fɑndli] *adv* **:** cariñosamente, afectuosamente

fondness ['fɑndnəs] *n* **1** LOVE **:** cariño *m* **2** LIKING **:** afición *f*

fondue [fɑn'duː, -'djuː] *n* **:** fondue *f*

font ['fɑnt] *n* **1** *or* **baptismal font :** pila *f* bautismal **2** FOUNTAIN **:** fuente *f*

food ['fuːd] *n* **:** comida *f,* alimento *m*

food chain *n* **:** cadena *f* alimenticia

foodstuffs ['fuːd,stʌfs] *npl* **:** comestibles *mpl*

fool[1] ['fuːl] *vi* **1** JOKE **:** bromear, hacer el tonto **2** TOY **:** jugar, juguetear <don't fool with the computer : no juegues con la computadora> **3 to fool around :** perder el tiempo <he fools around instead of working : pierde el tiempo en vez de trabajar> — *vt* DECEIVE **:** engañar, burlar

fool[2] *n* **1** IDIOT **:** idiota *mf;* tonto *m,* -ta *f;* bobo *m,* -ba *f* **2** JESTER **:** bufón *m,* -fona *f*

foolhardiness ['fuːl,hɑrdinəs] *n* **:** imprudencia *f*

foolhardy ['fuːl,hɑrdi] *adj* RASH **:** imprudente, temerario, precipitado

foolish ['fuːlɪʃ] *adj* **1** STUPID **:** insensato, estúpido **2** SILLY **:** idiota, tonto

foolishly ['fuːlɪʃli] *adv* **:** tontamente

foolishness ['fuːlɪʃnəs] *n* **:** insensatez *f,* estupidez *f,* tontería *f*

foolproof ['fuːl,pruːf] *adj* **:** infalible

foot ['fʊt] *n, pl* **feet** ['fiːt] **:** pie *m*

footage ['fʊtɪdʒ] *n* **:** medida *f* en pies, metraje *m* (en el cine)

football ['fʊt,bɔl] *n* **:** futbol *m* americano, fútbol *m* americano

footbridge ['fʊt,brɪdʒ] *n* **:** pasarela *f,* puente *m* peatonal

foothills ['fʊt,hɪlz] *npl* **:** estribaciones *fpl*

foothold ['fʊt,hoːld] *n* **1 :** punto *m* de apoyo **2 to gain a foothold :** afianzarse en una posición

footing ['fʊtɪŋ] *n* **1** BALANCE **:** equilibrio *m* **2** FOOTHOLD **:** punto *m* de apoyo **3** BASIS **:** base *f* <on an equal footing : en igualdad>

footlights ['fʊt,laɪts] *npl* **:** candilejas *fpl*

footlocker ['fʊt,lɑkər] *n* **:** baúl *m* pequeño, cofre *m*

footloose ['fʊt,luːs] *adj* **:** libre y sin compromiso

footman ['fʊtmən] *n, pl* **-men** [-mən, -,mɛn] **:** lacayo *m*

footnote ['fʊt,noːt] *n* **:** nota *f* al pie de la página

footpath ['fʊt,pæθ] *n* **:** sendero *m,* senda *f,* vereda *f*

footprint ['fʊt,prɪnt] *n* **:** huella *f*

footrace ['fʊt,reɪs] *n* **:** carrera *f* pedestre

footrest ['fʊt,rɛst] *n* **:** apoyapiés *m,* reposapiés *m*

footstep ['fʊt,stɛp] *n* **1** STEP **:** paso *m* **2** FOOTPRINT **:** huella *f*

footstool ['fʊt,stuːl] *n* **:** taburete *m,* escabel *m*

footwear ['fʊt,wær] *n* **:** calzado *m*

footwork ['fʊt,wərk] *n* **:** juego *m* de piernas, juego *m* de pies

fop ['fɑp] *n* **:** petimetre *m,* dandi *m*

for[1] [ˈfɔr] *conj* : puesto que, porque

for[2] *prep* **1** (*indicating purpose*) : para, de <clothes for children : ropa para niños> <it's time for dinner : es la hora de comer> **2** BECAUSE OF : por <for fear of : por miedo de> **3** (*indicating a recipient*) : para, por <a gift for you : un regalo para ti> **4** (*indicating support*) : por <he fought for his country : luchó por su patria> **5** (*indicating a goal*) : por, para <a cure for cancer : una cura para el cáncer> <for your own good : por tu propio bien> **6** (*indicating correspondence or exchange*) : por, para <I bought it for $5 : lo compré por $5> <a lot of trouble for nothing : mucha molestia para nada> **7** AS FOR : para, con respecto a **8** (*indicating duration*) : durante, por <he's going for two years : se va por dos años> <I spoke for ten minutes : hablé (durante) diez minutos> <she has known it for three months : lo sabe desde hace tres meses>

forage[1] [ˈfɔrɪdʒ] *v* **-aged; -aging** *vi* : hurgar (en busca de alimento) — *vt* : buscar (provisiones)

forage[2] *n* : forraje *m*

foray [ˈfɔrˌeɪ] *n* : incursión *f*

forbear[1] [fɔrˈbær] *vi* **-bore** [-ˈbor]; **-borne** [-ˈborn]; **-bearing 1** ABSTAIN : abstenerse **2** : tener paciencia

forbear[2] → **forebear**

forbearance [fɔrˈbærənts] *n* **1** ABSTAINING : abstención *f* **2** PATIENCE : paciencia *f*

forbid [fərˈbɪd] *vt* **-bade** [-ˈbæd, -ˈbeɪd] *or* **-bad** [-ˈbæd]; **-bidden** [-ˈbɪdən]; **-bidding 1** PROHIBIT : prohibir **2** PREVENT : impedir

forbidding [fərˈbɪdɪŋ] *adj* **1** IMPOSING : imponente **2** DISAGREEABLE : desagradable, ingrato **3** GRIM : severo

force[1] [ˈfors] *vt* **forced; forcing 1** COMPEL : obligar, forzar **2** : forzar <to force open the window : forzar la ventana> <to force a lock : forzar una cerradura> **3** IMPOSE : imponer, obligar

force[2] *n* **1** : fuerza *f* **2 by force** : por la fuerza **3 in force** : en vigor, en vigencia

forced [ˈforst] *adj* : forzado, forzoso

forceful [ˈforsfəl] *adj* : fuerte, energético, contundente

forcefully [ˈforsfəli] *adv* : con energía, con fuerza

forcefulness [ˈforsfəlnəs] *n* : contundencia *f*, fuerza *f*

forceps [ˈfɔrsəps, -ˌsɛps] *ns & pl* : fórceps *m*

forcible [ˈforsəbəl] *adj* **1** FORCED : forzoso **2** CONVINCING : contundente, convincente — **forcibly** [-bli] *adv*

ford[1] [ˈford] *vt* : vadear

ford[2] *n* : vado *m*

fore[1] [ˈfor] *adv* **1** FORWARD : hacia adelante **2 fore and aft** : de popa a proa

fore[2] *adj* **1** FORWARD : delantero, de adelante **2** FORMER : anterior

fore[3] *n* **1** : frente *m*, delantera *f* **2 to come to the fore** : empezar a destacar, saltar a primera plana

fore–and–aft [ˈforənˈæft, -ənd-] *adj* : longitudinal

forearm [ˈforˌɑrm] *n* : antebrazo *m*

forebear [ˈforˌbær] *n* : antepasado *m*, -da *f*

foreboding [forˈboːdɪŋ] *n* : premonición *f*, presentimiento *m*

forecast[1] [ˈforˌkæst] *vt* **-cast; -casting** : pronosticar, predecir

forecast[2] *n* : predicción *f*, pronóstico *m*

forecastle [ˈfoːksəl] *n* : castillo *m* de proa

foreclose [forˈkloːz] *vt* **-closed; -closing** : ejecutar (una hipoteca)

forefather [ˈforˌfɑðər] *n* : antepasado *m*, ancestro *m*

forefinger [ˈforˌfɪŋgər] *n* : índice *m*, dedo *m* índice

forefoot [ˈforˌfʊt] *n* : pata *f* delantera

forefront [ˈforˌfrʌnt] *n* : frente *m*, vanguardia *f* <in the forefront : a la vanguardia>

forego [forˈgoː] *vt* **-went; -gone; -going 1** PRECEDE : preceder **2** → **forgo**

foregoing [forˈgoːɪŋ] *adj* : precedente, anterior

foregone [forˈgɔn] *adj* : previsto <a foregone conclusion : un resultado inevitable>

foreground [ˈforˌgraʊnd] *n* : primer plano *m*

forehand[1] [ˈforˌhænd] *adj* : directo, derecho

forehand[2] *n* : golpe *m* del derecho

forehead [ˈfɔrəd, ˈforˌhɛd] *n* : frente *f*

foreign [ˈfɔrən] *adj* **1** : extranjero, exterior <foreign countries : países extranjeros> <foreign trade : comercio exterior> **2** ALIEN : ajeno, extraño <foreign to their nature : ajeno a su carácter> <a foreign body : un cuerpo extraño>

foreigner [ˈfɔrənər] *n* : extranjero *m*, -ra *f*

foreknowledge [forˈnɑlɪdʒ] *n* : conocimiento *m* previo

foreleg [ˈforˌlɛg] *n* : pata *f* delantera

foreman [ˈformən] *n, pl* **-men** [-mən, -ˌmɛn] : capataz *mf* <foreman of the jury : presidente del jurado>

foremost[1] [ˈforˌmoːst] *adv* : en primer lugar

foremost[2] *adj* : más importante, principal, grande

forenoon [ˈforˌnuːn] *n* : mañana *m*

forensic [fəˈrɛntsɪk] *adj* **1** RHETORICAL : retórico, de argumentación **2** : forense <forensic medicine : medicina forense>

foreordain [ˌforɔr'deɪn] *vt* : predestinar, predeterminar
forequarter ['forˌkwɔrt̬ər] *n* : cuarto *m* delantero
forerunner ['forˌrʌnər] *n* : precursor *m*, -sora *f*
foresee [for'siː] *vt* **-saw; -seen; -seeing** : prever
foreseeable [for'siːəbəl] *adj* : previsible <in the foreseeable future : en el futuro inmediato>
foreshadow [for'ʃædoː] *vt* : anunciar, prefigurar
foresight ['forˌsaɪt] *n* : previsión *f*
foresighted ['forˌsaɪt̬əd] *adj* : previsto
forest ['fɔrəst] *n* : bosque *m* (en zonas templadas), selva *f* (en zonas tropicales)
forestall [for'stɔl] *vt* **1** PREVENT : prevenir, impedir **2** PREEMPT : adelantarse a
forested ['fɔrəstəd] *adj* : arbolado
forester ['fɔrəstər] *n* : silvicultor *m*, -tora *f*
forestland ['fɔrəstˌlænd] *n* : zona *f* boscosa
forest ranger → **ranger**
forestry ['fɔrəstri] *n* : silvicultura *f*, ingeniería *f* forestal
foreswear → **forswear**
foretaste[1] ['forˌteɪst] *vt* **-tasted; -tasting** : anticipar
foretaste[2] *n* : anticipo *m*
foretell [for'tɛl] *vt* **-told; -telling** : predecir, pronosticar, profetizar
forethought ['forˌθɔt] *n* : previsión *f*, reflexión *f* previa
forever [fɔr'ɛvər] *adv* **1** PERPETUALLY : para siempre, eternamente **2** CONTINUALLY : siempre, constantemente
forevermore [fɔrˌɛvər'mor] *adv* : por siempre jamás
forewarn [for'wɔrn] *vt* : prevenir, advertir
foreword ['forwərd] *n* : prólogo *m*
forfeit[1] ['fɔrfət] *vt* : perder el derecho a
forfeit[2] *n* **1** FINE, PENALTY : multa *f* **2** : prenda *f* (en un juego)
forge[1] ['fordʒ] *v* **forged; forging** *vt* **1** : forjar (metal o un plan) **2** COUNTERFEIT : falsificar — *vi* **to forge ahead** : avanzar, seguir adelante
forge[2] *n* : forja *f*
forger ['fordʒər] *n* : falsificador *m*, -dora *f*
forgery ['fordʒəri] *n, pl* **-eries** : falsificación *f*
forget [fər'gɛt] *v* **-got** [-'gɑt]; **-gotten** [-'gɑtən] *or* **-got; -getting** *vt* : olvidar — *vi* **to forget about** : olvidarse de, no acordarse de
forgetful [fər'gɛtfəl] *adj* : olvidadizo
forget-me-not [fər'gɛtmiˌnɑt] *n* : nomeolvides *mf*
forgettable [fər'gɛt̬əbəl] *adj* : poco memorable
forgivable [fər'gɪvəbəl] *adj* : perdonable
forgive [fər'gɪv] *vt* **-gave** [-'geɪv]; **-given** [-'gɪvən]; **-giving** : perdonar
forgiveness [fər'gɪvnəs] *n* : perdón *m*
forgiving [fər'gɪvɪŋ] *adj* : indulgente, comprensivo, clemente
forgo *or* **forego** [for'goː] *vt* **-went; -gone; -going** : privarse de, renunciar a
fork[1] ['fɔrk] *vi* : ramificarse, bifurcarse — *vt* **1** : levantar (con un tenedor, una horca, etc.) **2 to fork over** : desembolsar
fork[2] *n* **1** : tenedor *m* (utensilio de cocina) **2** PITCHFORK : horca *f*, horquilla *f* **3** : bifurcación *f* (de un río o camino), horqueta *f* (de un árbol)
forked ['fɔrkt, 'fɔrkəd] *adj* : bífido, ahorquillado
forklift ['fɔrkˌlɪft] *n* : carretilla *f* elevadora
forlorn [fɔr'lɔrn] *adj* **1** DESOLATE : abandonado, desolado, desamparado **2** SAD : triste **3** DESPERATE : desesperado
forlornly [fɔr'lɔrnli] *adv* **1** SADLY : con tristeza **2** HALFHEARTEDLY : sin ánimo
form[1] ['fɔrm] *vt* **1** FASHION, MAKE : formar **2** DEVELOP : moldear, desarrollar **3** CONSTITUTE : constituir, formar **4** ACQUIRE : adquirir (un hábito), formar (una idea) — *vi* : tomar forma, formarse
form[2] *n* **1** SHAPE : forma *f*, figura *f* **2** MANNER : manera *f*, forma *f* **3** DOCUMENT : formulario *m* **4** : forma *f* <in good form : en buena forma> <true to form : en forma consecuente> **5** MOLD : molde *m* **6** KIND, VARIETY : clase *f*, tipo *m* **7** : forma *f* (en gramática) <plural forms : formas plurales>
formal[1] ['fɔrməl] *adj* **1** CEREMONIOUS : formal, de etiqueta, ceremonioso **2** OFFICIAL : formal, oficial, de forma
formal[2] *n* **1** BALL : baile *m* formal, baile *m* de etiqueta **2** *or* **formal dress** : traje *m* de etiqueta
formaldehyde [fɔr'mældəˌhaɪd] *n* : formaldehído *m*
formality [fɔr'mælət̬i] *n, pl* **-ties** : formalidad *f*
formalize ['fɔrməˌlaɪz] *vt* **-ized; -izing** : formalizar
formally ['fɔrməli] *adv* : formalmente
format[1] ['fɔrˌmæt] *vt* **-matted; -matting** : formatear
format[2] *n* : formato *m*
formation [fɔr'meɪʃən] *n* **1** FORMING : formación *f* **2** SHAPE : forma *f* **3 in formation** : en formación
formative ['fɔrmət̬ɪv] *adj* : formativo
former ['fɔrmər] *adj* **1** PREVIOUS : antiguo, anterior <the former president : el antiguo presidente> **2** : primero (de dos)
formerly ['fɔrmərli] *adv* : anteriormente, antes
formidable ['fɔrmədəbəl, fɔr'mɪdə-] *adj* : formidable — **formidably** *adv*

formless [ˈfɔrmləs] *adj* : informe, amorfo
formula [ˈfɔrmjələ] *n, pl* **-las** *or* **-lae** [-ˌliː, -ˌlaɪ] **1** : fórmula *f* **2 baby formula** : preparado *m* para biberón
formulate [ˈfɔrmjəˌleɪt] *vt* **-lated; -lating** : formular, hacer
formulation [ˌfɔrmjəˈleɪʃən] *n* : formulación *f*
fornicate [ˈfɔrnəˌkeɪt] *vi* **-cated; -cating** : fornicar
fornication [ˌfɔrnəˈkeɪʃən] *n* : fornicación *f*
forsake [fərˈseɪk] *vt* **-sook** [-ˈsʊk]; **-saken** [-ˈseɪkən]; **-saking 1** ABANDON : abandonar, desamparar **2** RELINQUISH : renunciar a
forswear [fɔrˈswær] *v* **-swore; -sworn; -swearing** *vt* RENOUNCE : renunciar a — *vi* : perjurar
forsythia [fərˈsɪθiə] *n* : forsitia *f*
fort [ˈfort] *n* **1** STRONGHOLD : fuerte *m,* fortaleza *f,* fortín *m* **2** BASE : base *f* militar
forte [ˈfort, ˈforˌteɪ] *n* : fuerte *m*
forth [ˈforθ] *adv* **1** : adelante <from this day forth : de hoy en adelante> **2 and so forth** : etcétera
forthcoming [forθˈkʌmɪŋ, ˈforθˌ-] *adj* **1** COMING : próximo **2** DIRECT, OPEN : directo, franco, comunicativo
forthright [ˈforθˌraɪt] *adj* : directo, franco — **forthrightly** *adv*
forthrightness [ˈforθˌraɪtnəs] *n* : franqueza *f*
forthwith [forθˈwɪθ, -ˈwɪð] *adv* : inmediatamente, en el acto, enseguida
fortieth[1] [ˈfɔrtiəθ] *adj* : cuadragésimo
fortieth[2] *n* **1** : cuadragésimo *m,* -ma *f* (en una serie) **2** : cuarentavo *m,* cuarentava parte *f*
fortification [ˌfɔrtəfəˈkeɪʃən] *n* : fortificación *f*
fortify [ˈfɔrtəˌfaɪ] *vt* **-fied; -fying** : fortificar
fortitude [ˈfɔrtəˌtuːd, -ˌtjuːd] *n* : fortaleza *f,* valor *m*
fortnight [ˈfortˌnaɪt] *n* : quince días *mpl,* dos semanas *fpl*
fortnightly[1] [ˈfortˌnaɪtli] *adv* : cada quince días
fortnightly[2] *adj* : quincenal
fortress [ˈfɔrtrəs] *n* : fortaleza *f*
fortuitous [fɔrˈtuːətəs, -ˈtjuː-] *adj* : fortuito, accidental
fortunate [ˈfɔrtʃənət] *adj* : afortunado
fortunately [ˈfɔrtʃənətli] *adv* : afortunadamente, con suerte
fortune [ˈfɔrtʃən] *n* **1** : fortuna *f* <to seek one's fortune : buscar uno su fortuna> **2** LUCK : suerte *f,* fortuna *f* **3** DESTINY, FUTURE : destino *m,* buenaventura *f* **4** : dineral *m,* platal *m* <she spent a fortune : se gastó un dineral>
fortune–teller [ˈfɔrtʃənˌtɛlər] *n* : adivino *m,* -na *f*
fortune–telling [ˈfɔrtʃənˌtɛlɪŋ] *n* : adivinación *f*
forty[1] [ˈfɔrti] *adj* : cuarenta
forty[2] *n, pl* **forties** : cuarenta *m*
forum [ˈforəm] *n, pl* **-rums** : foro *m*
forward[1] [ˈfɔrwərd] *vt* **1** PROMOTE : promover, adelantar, fomentar **2** SEND : remitir, enviar
forward[2] *adv* **1** : adelante, hacia adelante <to go forward : irse adelante> **2 from this day forward** : de aquí en adelante
forward[3] *adj* **1** : hacia adelante, delantero **2** BRASH : atrevido, descarado
forward[4] *n* : delantero *m,* -ra *f* (en deportes)
forwarder [ˈfɔrwərdər] *n* : agencia *f* de transportes, agente *mf* expedidor
forwardness [ˈfɔrwərdnəs] *n* : atrevimiento *m,* descaro *m*
forwards [ˈfɔrwərdz] → **forward**[2]
fossil[1] [ˈfɑsəl] *adj* : fósil
fossil[2] *n* : fósil *m*
fossilize [ˈfɑsəˌlaɪz] *vt* **-ized; -izing** : fosilizar — *vi* : fosilizarse
foster[1] [ˈfɔstər] *vt* : promover, fomentar
foster[2] *adj* : adoptivo <foster child : niño adoptivo>
fought → **fight**
foul[1] [ˈfaʊl] *vi* : cometer faltas (en deportes) — *vt* **1** DIRTY, POLLUTE : contaminar, ensuciar **2** TANGLE : enredar
foul[2] *adv* **1** → **foully 2** : contra las reglas
foul[3] *adj* **1** REPULSIVE : asqueroso, repugnante **2** CLOGGED : atascado, obstruido **3** TANGLED : enredado **4** OBSCENE : obsceno **5** BAD : malo <foul weather : mal tiempo> **6** : antirreglamentario (en deportes)
foul[4] *n* : falta *f,* faul *m*
foully [ˈfaʊli] *adv* : asquerosamente
foulmouthed [ˈfaʊlˌmæuːðd, -ˌmaʊθt] *adj* : malhablado
foulness [ˈfaʊlnəs] *n* **1** DIRTINESS : suciedad *f* **2** INCLEMENCY : inclemencia *f* **3** OBSCENITY : obscenidad *f,* grosería *f*
foul play *n* : actos *mpl* criminales
foul–up [ˈfaʊlˌʌp] *n* : lío *m,* confusión *f,* desastre *m*
foul up *vt* SPOIL : estropear, arruinar — *vi* BUNGLE : echar todo a perder
found[1] → **find**
found[2] [ˈfaʊnd] *vt* : fundar, establecer
foundation [faʊnˈdeɪʃən] *n* **1** FOUNDING : fundación *f* **2** BASIS : fundamento *m,* base *f* **3** INSTITUTION : fundación *f* **4** : cimientos *mpl* (de un edificio)
founder[1] [ˈfaʊndər] *vi* SINK : hundirse, irse a pique
founder[2] *n* : fundador *m,* -dora *f*
foundling [ˈfaʊndlɪŋ] *n* : expósito *m,* -ta *f*
foundry [ˈfaʊndri] *n, pl* **-dries** : fundición *f*
fount [ˈfaʊnt] *n* SOURCE : fuente *f,* origen *m*

fountain [ˈfaʊntən] *n* **1** SPRING : fuente *f,* manantial *m* **2** SOURCE : fuente *f,* origen *m* **3** JET : chorro *m* (de agua), surtidor *m*
fountain pen *n* : pluma *f* fuente
four¹ [ˈfor] *adj* : cuatro
four² *n* : cuatro *m*
fourfold [ˈfor,foːld, -ˈfoːld] *adj* : cuadruple
four hundred¹ *adj* : cuatrocientos
four hundred² *n* : cuatrocientos *m*
fourscore [ˈforˈskor] *adj* EIGHTY : ochenta *m*
fourteen¹ [forˈtiːn] *adj* : catorce
fourteen² *n* : catorce *m*
fourteenth¹ [forˈtiːnθ] *adj* : decimocuarto
fourteenth² *n* **1** : decimocuarto *m,* -ta *f* (en una serie) **2** : catorceavo *m,* catorceava parte *f*
fourth¹ [ˈforθ] *adj* : cuarto
fourth² *n* **1** : cuarto *m,* -ta *f* (en una serie) **2** : cuarto *m,* cuarta parte *f*
fowl [ˈfaʊl] *n, pl* **fowl** *or* **fowls** **1** BIRD : ave *f* **2** CHICKEN : pollo *m*
fox¹ [ˈfɑks] *vt* **1** TRICK : engañar **2** BAFFLE : confundir
fox² *n, pl* **foxes** : zorro *m,* -ra *f*
foxglove [ˈfɑks,glʌv] *n* : dedalera *f,* digital *f*
foxhole [ˈfɑks,hoːl] *n* : hoyo *m* para atrincherarse, trinchera *f* individual
foxy [ˈfɑksi] *adj* **foxier; -est** SHREWD : astuto
foyer [ˈfɔɪər, ˈfɔɪ,jeɪ] *n* : vestíbulo *m*
fracas [ˈfreɪkəs, ˈfræ-] *n, pl* **-cases** [-kəsəz] : altercado *m,* pelea *f,* reyerta *f*
fraction [ˈfrækʃən] *n* **1** : fracción *f,* quebrado *m* **2** PORTION : porción *f,* parte *f*
fractional [ˈfrækʃənəl] *adj* **1** : fraccionario **2** TINY : minúsculo, mínimo, insignificante
fractious [ˈfrækʃəs] *adj* **1** UNRULY : rebelde **2** IRRITABLE : malhumorado, irritable
fracture¹ [ˈfræktʃər] *vt* **-tured; -turing** : fracturar
fracture² *n* **1** : fractura *f* (de un hueso) **2** CRACK : fisura *f,* grieta *f,* falla *f* (geológica)
fragile [ˈfrædʒəl, -,dʒaɪl] *adj* : frágil
fragility [frəˈdʒɪləṯi] *n, pl* **-ties** : fragilidad *f*
fragment¹ [ˈfræg,mɛnt] *vt* : fragmentar — *vi* : fragmentarse, hacerse añicos
fragment² [ˈfrægmənt] *n* : fragmento *m,* trozo *m,* pedazo *m*
fragmentary [ˈfrægmən,tɛri] *adj* : fragmentario, incompleto
fragmentation [,frægmənˈteɪʃən, -,mɛn-] *n* : fragmentación *f*
fragrance [ˈfreɪgrən*t*s] *n* : fragancia *f,* aroma *m*
fragrant [ˈfreɪgrənt] *adj* : fragante, aromático — **fragrantly** *adv*
frail [ˈfreɪl] *adj* : débil, delicado
frailty [ˈfreɪlti] *n, pl* **-ties** : debilidad *f,* flaqueza *f*
frame¹ [ˈfreɪm] *vt* **framed; framing** **1** FORMULATE : formular, elaborar **2** BORDER : enmarcar, encuadrar **3** INCRIMINATE : incriminar
frame² *n* **1** BODY : cuerpo *m* **2** : armazón *f* (de un edificio, un barco, o un avión), bastidor *m* (de un automóvil), cuadro *m* (de una bicicleta), marco *m* (de un cuadro, una ventana, una puerta, etc.) **3 frames** *npl* : armazón *mf,* montura *f* (para anteojos) **4 frame of mind** : estado *m* de ánimo
framework [ˈfreɪm,wərk] *n* **1** SKELETON, STRUCTURE : armazón *f,* estructura *f* **2** BASIS : marco *m*
franc [ˈfræŋk] *n* : franco *m*
franchise [ˈfræn,tʃaɪz] *n* **1** LICENSE : licencia *f* exclusiva, concesión *f* (en comercio) **2** SUFFRAGE : sufragio *m*
franchisee [,fræn,tʃaɪˈziː, -tʃə-] *n* : concesionario *m,* -ria *f*
frank¹ [ˈfræŋk] *vt* : franquear
frank² *adj* : franco, sincero, cándido — **frankly** *adv*
frank³ *n* : franqueo *m* (de correo)
frankfurter [ˈfræŋkfərtər, -,fər-] *or* **frankfurt** [-fərt] *n* : salchicha *f* (de Frankfurt, de Viena), perro *m* caliente
frankincense [ˈfræŋkən,sɛn*t*s] *n* : incienso *m*
frankness [ˈfræŋknəs] *n* : franqueza *f,* sinceridad *f,* candidez *f*
frantic [ˈfræntɪk] *adj* : frenético, desesperado — **frantically** *adv*
fraternal [frəˈtərnəl] *adj* : fraterno, fraternal
fraternity [frəˈtərnəṯi] *n, pl* **-ties** : fraternidad *f*
fraternization [,fræṯərnəˈzeɪʃən] *n* : fraternización *f,* confraternización *f*
fraternize [ˈfræṯər,naɪz] *vi* **-nized; -nizing** : fraternizar, confraternizar
fratricidal [,frætrəˈsaɪdəl] *adj* : fratricida
fratricide [ˈfrætrə,saɪd] *n* : fratricidio *m*
fraud [ˈfrɔd] *n* **1** DECEPTION, SWINDLE : fraude *m,* estafa *f,* engaño *m* **2** IMPOSTOR : impostor *m,* -tora *f;* farsante *mf*
fraudulent [ˈfrɔdʒələnt] *adj* : fraudulento — **fraudulently** *adv*
fraught [ˈfrɔt] *adj* **fraught with** : lleno de, cargado de
fray¹ [ˈfreɪ] *vt* **1** WEAR : desgastar, deshilachar **2** IRRITATE : crispar, irritar (los nervios) — *vi* : desgastarse, deshilacharse
fray² *n* : pelea *f,* lucha *f,* refriega *f*
frazzle¹ [ˈfræzəl] *vt* **-zled; -zling** **1** FRAY : desgastar, deshilachar **2** EXHAUST : agotar, fatigar
frazzle² *n* EXHAUSTION : agotamiento *m*
freak [ˈfriːk] *n* **1** ODDITY : ejemplar *m* anormal, fenómeno *m,* rareza *f* **2** ENTHUSIAST : entusiasta *mf*

freakish [ˈfriːkɪʃ] *adj* **:** extraño, estrafalario, raro
freckle[1] [ˈfrɛkəl] *vi* **-led; -ling :** cubrirse de pecas
freckle[2] *n* **:** peca *f*
free[1] [ˈfriː] *vt* **freed; freeing 1** LIBERATE **:** libertar, liberar, poner en libertad **2** RELIEVE, RID **:** librar, eximir **3** RELEASE, UNTIE **:** desatar, soltar **4** UNCLOG **:** desatascar, destapar
free[2] *adv* **1** FREELY **:** libremente **2** GRATIS **:** gratuitamente, gratis
free[3] *adj* **freer; freest 1 :** libre <free as a bird : libre como un pájaro> **2** EXEMPT **:** libre <tax-free : libre de impuestos> **3** GRATIS **:** gratuito, gratis **4** VOLUNTARY **:** espontáneo, voluntario, libre **5** UNOCCUPIED **:** desocupado, libre **6** LOOSE **:** suelto
freebooter [ˈfriːˌbuːtər] *n* **:** pirata *mf*
freeborn [ˈfriːˈbɔrn] *adj* **:** nacido libre
freedom [ˈfriːdəm] *n* **:** libertad *f*
free–for–all [ˈfriːfərˌɔl] *n* **:** pelea *f*, batalla *f* campal
freelance[1] [ˈfriːˌlænts] *vi* **-lanced; -lancing :** trabajar por cuenta propia
freelance[2] *adj* **:** por cuenta propia, independiente
freeload [ˈfriːˌloːd] *vi* **:** gorronear *fam*, gorrear *fam*
freeloader [ˈfriːˌloːdər] *n* **:** gorrón *m*, -rrona *f;* gorrero *m*, -ra *f;* vividor *m*, -dora *f*
freely [ˈfriːli] *adv* **1** FREE **:** libremente **2** GRATIS **:** gratis, gratuitamente
freestanding [ˈfriːˈstændɪŋ] *adj* **:** de pie, no empotrado, independiente
freeway [ˈfriːˌweɪ] *n* **:** autopista *f*
freewill [ˈfriːˌwɪl] *adj* **:** de propia voluntad
free will *n* **:** libre albedrío *m*, propia voluntad *f*
freeze[1] [ˈfriːz] *v* **froze** [ˈfroːz]; **frozen** [ˈfroːzən]; **freezing** *vi* **1 :** congelarse, helarse <the water froze in the lake : el agua se congeló en el lago> <my blood froze : se me heló la sangre> <I'm freezing : me estoy helando> **2** STOP **:** quedarse inmóvil — *vt* **:** helar, congelar (líquidos), congelar (alimentos, precios, activos)
freeze[2] *n* **1** FROST **:** helada *f* **2** FREEZING **:** congelación *f*, congelamiento *m*
freeze–dried [ˈfriːzˈdraɪd] *adj* **:** liofilizado
freeze–dry [ˈfriːzˈdraɪ] *vt* **-dried; -drying :** liofilizar
freezer [ˈfriːzər] *n* **:** congelador *m*
freezing [ˈfriːzɪŋ] *adj* **:** helando <it's freezing! : ¡hace un frío espantoso!>
freezing point *n* **:** punto *m* de congelación
freight[1] [ˈfreɪt] *vt* **:** enviar como carga
freight[2] *n* **1** SHIPPING, TRANSPORT **:** transporte *m*, porte *m*, flete *m* **2** GOODS **:** mercancías *fpl*, carga *f*
freighter [ˈfreɪtər] *n* **:** carguero *m*, buque *m* de carga
French[1] [ˈfrɛntʃ] *adj* **:** francés
French[2] *n* **1 :** francés *m* (idioma) **2 the French** *npl* **:** los franceses
Frenchman [ˈfrɛntʃmən] *n, pl* **-men** [-mən, -ˌmɛn] **:** francés *m*
Frenchwoman [ˈfrɛntʃˌwʊmən] *n, pl* **-women** [-ˌwɪmən] **:** francesa *f*
french fries [ˈfrɛntʃˌfraɪz] *npl* **:** papas *fpl* fritas
frenetic [frɪˈnɛtɪk] *adj* **:** frenético — **frenetically** [-tɪkli] *adv*
frenzied [ˈfrɛnzid] *adj* **:** frenético
frenzy [ˈfrɛnzi] *n, pl* **-zies :** frenesí *m*
frequency [ˈfriːkwəntsi] *n, pl* **-cies :** frecuencia *f*
frequent[1] [friˈkwɛnt, ˈfriːkwənt] *vt* **:** frecuentar
frequent[2] [ˈfriːkwənt] *adj* **:** frecuente — **frequently** *adv*
fresco [ˈfrɛsˌkoː] *n, pl* **-coes :** fresco *m*
fresh [ˈfrɛʃ] *adj* **1 :** dulce <freshwater : agua dulce> **2** PURE **:** puro **3 :** fresco <fresh fruits : frutas frescas> **4** CLEAN, NEW **:** limpio, nuevo <fresh clothes : ropa limpia> <fresh evidence : evidencia nueva> **5** REFRESHED **:** fresco, descansado **6** IMPERTINENT **:** descarado, impertinente
freshen [ˈfrɛʃən] *vt* **:** refrescar, arreglar — *vi* **to freshen up :** arreglarse, lavarse
freshet [ˈfrɛʃət] *n* **:** arroyo *m* desbordado
freshly [ˈfrɛʃli] *adv* **:** recientemente, recién
freshman [ˈfrɛʃmən] *n, pl* **-men** [-mən, -ˌmɛn] **:** estudiante *mf* de primer año universitario
freshness [ˈfrɛʃnəs] *n* **:** frescura *f*
freshwater [ˈfrɛʃˌwɔtər] *n* **:** agua *f* dulce
fret[1] [ˈfrɛt] *vi* **fretted; fretting :** preocuparse, inquietarse
fret[2] *n* **1** VEXATION **:** irritación *f*, molestia *f* **2** WORRY **:** preocupación *f* **3 :** traste *m* (de un instrumento musical)
fretful [ˈfrɛtfəl] *adj* **:** fastidioso, quejoso, neurótico
fretfully [ˈfrɛtfəli] *adv* **:** ansiosamente, fastidiosamente, inquieto
fretfulness [ˈfrɛtfəlnəs] *n* **:** inquietud *f*, irritabilidad *f*
friable [ˈfraɪəbəl] *adj* **:** friable, pulverizable
friar [ˈfraɪər] *n* **:** fraile *m*
fricassee[1] [ˈfrɪkəˌsiː, ˌfrɪkəˈsiː] *vt* **-seed; -seeing :** cocinar al fricasé
fricassee[2] *n* **:** fricasé *m*
friction [ˈfrɪkʃən] *n* **1** RUBBING **:** fricción *f* **2** CONFLICT **:** fricción *f*, roce *m*
Friday [ˈfraɪˌdeɪ, -di] *n* **:** viernes *m*
fridge [ˈfrɪdʒ] → **refrigerator**
friend [ˈfrɛnd] *n* **:** amigo *m*, -ga *f*
friendless [ˈfrɛndləs] *adj* **:** sin amigos
friendliness [ˈfrɛndlinəs] *n* **:** simpatía *f*, amabilidad *f*
friendly [ˈfrɛndli] *adj* **-lier; -est 1 :** simpático, amable, de amigo <a friendly child : un niño simpático> <friendly advice : consejo de amigo>

2 : agradable, acogedor <a friendly atmosphere : un ambiente agradable> 3 GOOD-NATURED : amigable, amistoso <friendly competition : competencia amistosa>

friendship [frɛnd,ʃɪp] *n* : amistad *f*

frieze [ˈfriːz] *n* : friso *m*

frigate [ˈfrɪgət] *n* : fragata *f*

fright [ˈfraɪt] *n* : miedo *m,* susto *m*

frighten [ˈfraitən] *vt* : asustar, espantar

frightened [ˈfraitənd] *adj* : asustado, temeroso

frightening [ˈfraitənɪŋ] *adj* : espantoso, aterrador

frightful [ˈfraɪtfəl] *adj* **1** → **frightening** **2** TREMENDOUS : espantoso, tremendo

frightfully [ˈfraɪtfəli] *adv* : terriblemente, tremendamente

frigid [ˈfrɪdʒɪd] *adj* : glacial, extremadamente frío

frigidity [frɪˈdʒɪdəti] *n* **1** COLDNESS : frialdad *f* **2** : frigidez *f* (sexual)

frill [ˈfrɪl] *n* **1** RUFFLE : volante *m* **2** EMBELLISHMENT : floritura *f,* adorno *m*

frilly [ˈfrɪli] *adj* **frillier; -est** **1** RUFFLY : con volantes **2** OVERDONE : recargado

fringe[1] [ˈfrɪndʒ] *vt* **fringed; fringing** : orlar, bordear

fringe[2] *n* **1** BORDER : fleco *m,* orla *f* **2** EDGE : periferia *f,* margen *m* **3 fringe benefits** : incentivos *mpl*, extras *mpl*

frisk [ˈfrɪsk] *vi* FROLIC : retozar, juguetear — *vt* SEARCH : cachear, registrar

friskiness [ˈfrɪskinəs] *n* : vivacidad *f*

frisky [ˈfrɪski] *adj* **friskier; -est** : retozón, juguetón

fritter[1] [ˈfrɪtər] *vt* : desperdiciar, malgastar <I frittered away the money : malgasté el dinero>

fritter[2] *n* : buñuelo *m*

frivolity [frɪˈvɑləti] *n, pl* **-ties** : frivolidad *f*

frivolous [ˈfrɪvələs] *adj* : frívolo, de poca importancia

frivolously [ˈfrɪvələsli] *adv* : frívolamente, a la ligera

frizz[1] [ˈfrɪz] *vi* : rizarse, encresparse, ponerse chino *Mex*

frizz[2] *n* : rizos *mpl* muy apretados

frizzy [ˈfrɪzi] *adj* **frizzier; -est** : rizado, crespo, chino *Mex*

fro [ˈfroː] *adv* **to and fro** : de aquí para allá, de un lado para otro

frock [ˈfrɑk] *n* DRESS : vestido *m*

frog [ˈfrɔg, ˈfrɑg] *n* **1** : rana *f* **2** FASTENER : alamar *m* 3 **to have a frog in one's throat** : tener carraspera

frogman [ˈfrɔg,mæn, ˈfrɑg-, -mən] *n, pl* **-men** [-mən, -,mɛn] : hombre *m* rana, submarinista *mf*

frolic[1] [ˈfrɑlɪk] *vi* **-icked; -icking** : retozar, juguetear

frolic[2] *n* FUN : diversión *f*

frolicsome [ˈfrɑlɪksəm] *adj* : juguetón

from [ˈfrʌm, ˈfrɑm] *prep* **1** (*indicating a starting point*) : desde, de, a partir de <from Cali to Bogota : de Cali a Bogotá> <where are you from? : ¿de dónde eres?> <from that time onward : desde entonces> <from tomorrow : a partir de mañana> **2** (*indicating a source or sender*) : de <a letter from my friend : una carta de mi amiga> <a quote from Shakespeare : una cita de Shakespeare> **3** (*indicating distance*) : de <10 feet from the entrance : a 10 pies de la entrada> **4** (*indicating a cause*) : de <red from crying : rojos de llorar> <he died from the cold : murió del frío> **5** OFF, OUT OF : de <she took it from the drawer : lo sacó del cajón> **6** (*with adverbs or adverbial phrases*) : de, desde <from above : desde arriba> <from among : de entre>

frond [ˈfrɑnd] *n* : fronda *f,* hoja *f*

front[1] [ˈfrʌnt] *vi* **1** FACE : dar, estar orientado <the house fronts north : la casa da al norte> **2** : servir de pantalla <he fronts for his boss : sirve de pantalla para su jefe>

front[2] *adj* : delantero, de adelante, primero <the front row : la primera fila>

front[3] *n* **1** : frente *m,* parte *f* de adelante, delantera *f* <the front of the class : el frente de la clase> <at the front of the train : en la parte delantera del tren> **2** AREA, ZONE : frente *m,* zona *f* <the Eastern front : el frente oriental> <on the educational front : en el frente de la enseñanza> **3** FACADE : fachada *f* (de un edificio o una persona> **4** : frente *m* (en meteorología)

frontage [ˈfrʌntɪdʒ] *n* : fachada *f,* frente *m*

frontal [ˈfrʌntəl] *adj* : frontal, de frente

frontier [,frʌnˈtɪr] *n* : frontera *f*

frontiersman [,frʌnˈtɪrzmən] *n, pl* **-men** [-mən, -,mɛn] : hombre *m* de la frontera

frontispiece [ˈfrʌntəs,piːs] *n* : frontispicio *m*

frost[1] [ˈfrɔst] *vt* **1** FREEZE : helar **2** ICE : escarchar (pasteles)

frost[2] *n* **1** : helada *f* (en meteorología) **2** : escarcha *f* <frost on the window : escarcha en la ventana>

frostbite [ˈfrɔst,baɪt] *n* : congelación *f*

frostbitten [ˈfrɔst,bɪtən] *adj* : congelado (dícese de una persona), quemado (dícese de una planta)

frosting [ˈfrɔstɪŋ] *n* ICING : glaseado *m,* betún *m Mex*

frosty [ˈfrɔsti] *adj* **frostier; -est** **1** CHILLY : helado, frío **2** COOL, UNFRIENDLY : frío, glacial

froth [ˈfrɔθ] *n, pl* **froths** [ˈfrɔθs, ˈfrɔðz] : espuma *f*

frothy [ˈfrɔθi] *adj* **frothier; -est** : espumoso

frown[1] [ˈfraʊn] *vi* **1** : fruncir el ceño, fruncir el entrecejo **2 to frown at**

: mirar (algo) con ceño, mirar (a alguien) con ceño

frown[2] *n* : ceño *m* (fruncido)

frowsy *or* **frowzy** [ˈfraʊzi] *adj* **frowsier** *or* **frowzier; -est** : desaliñado, desaseado

froze → **freeze**

frozen → **freeze**

frugal [ˈfruːgəl] *adj* : frugal, ahorrativo, parco — **frugally** *adv*

frugality [fruˈgæləṭi] *n* : frugalidad *f*

fruit[1] [ˈfruːt] *vi* : dar fruto

fruit[2] *n* **1** : fruta *f* (término genérico), fruto *m* (término particular) **2 fruits** *npl* REWARDS : frutos *mpl* <the fruits of his labor : los frutos de su trabajo>

fruitcake [ˈfruːtˌkeɪk] *n* : pastel *m* de frutas

fruitful [ˈfruːtfəl] *adj* : fructífero, provechoso

fruition [fruˈɪʃən] *n* **1** : cumplimiento *m*, realización *f* **2 to bring to fruition** : realizar

fruitless [ˈfruːtləs] *adj* : infructuoso, inútil — **fruitlessly** *adv*

fruity [ˈfruːṭi] *adj* **fruitier; -est** : (con sabor) a fruta

frumpy [ˈfrʌmpi] *adj* **frumpier; -est** : anticuado y sin atractivo

frustrate [ˈfrʌsˌtreɪt] *vt* **-trated; -trating** : frustrar

frustrating [ˈfrʌsˌtreɪṭɪŋ] *adj* : frustrante — **frustratingly** *adv*

frustration [ˌfrʌsˈtreɪʃən] *n* : frustración *f*

fry[1] [ˈfraɪ] *vt* **fried; frying** : freír

fry[2] *n, pl* **fries 1** : fritura *f*, plato *m* frito **2** : fiesta *f* en que se sirven frituras **3** *pl* **fry** : alevín *m* (pez)

fuddle [ˈfʌdəl] *vt* **-dled; -dling** : confundir, atontar

fuddy–duddy [ˈfʌdiˌdʌdi] *n, pl* **-dies** : persona *f* chapada a la antigua, carca *mf*

fudge[1] [ˈfʌdʒ] *vt* **fudged; fudging 1** FALSIFY : amañar, falsificar **2** DODGE : esquivar

fudge[2] *n* : dulce *m* blando de chocolate y leche

fuel[1] [ˈfjuːəl] *vt* **-eled** *or* **-elled; -eling** *or* **-elling 1** : abastecer de combustible **2** STIMULATE : estimular

fuel[2] *n* : combustible *m*, carburante *m* (para motores)

fugitive[1] [ˈfjuːdʒəṭɪv] *adj* **1** RUNAWAY : fugitivo **2** FLEETING : efímero, pasajero, fugaz

fugitive[2] *n* : fugitivo *m*, -va *f*

fulcrum [ˈfʊlkrəm, ˈfʌl-] *n, pl* **-crums** *or* **-cra** [-krə] : fulcro *m*

fulfill *or* **fulfil** [fʊlˈfɪl] *vt* **-filled; -filling 1** PERFORM : cumplir con, realizar, llevar a cabo **2** SATISFY : satisfacer

fulfillment [fʊlˈfɪlmənt] *n* **1** PERFORMANCE : cumplimiento *m*, ejecución *f* **2** SATISFACTION : satisfacción *f*, realización *f*

full[1] [ˈfʊl, ˈfʌl] *adv* **1** VERY : muy <full well : muy bien, perfectamente> **2** ENTIRELY : completamente <she swung full around : giró completamente> **3** DIRECTLY : de lleno, directamente <he looked me full in the face : me miró directamente a la cara>

full[2] *adj* **1** FILLED : lleno **2** COMPLETE : completo, detallado **3** MAXIMUM : todo, pleno <at full speed : a toda velocidad> <in full bloom : en plena flor> **4** PLUMP : redondo, llenito *fam*, regordete *fam* <a full face : una cara redonda> <a full figure : un cuerpo llenito> **5** AMPLE : amplio <a full skirt : una falda amplia>

full[3] *n* **1 to pay in full** : pagar en su totalidad **2 to the full** : al máximo

full–fledged [ˈfʊlˈflɛdʒd] *adj* : hecho y derecho

fullness [ˈfʊlnəs] *n* **1** ABUNDANCE : plenitud *f*, abundancia *f* **2** : amplitud *f* (de una falda)

fully [ˈfʊli] *adv* **1** COMPLETELY : completamente, totalmente **2** : al menos, por lo menos <fully half of them : al menos la mitad de ellos>

fulsome [ˈfʊlsəm] *adj* : excesivo, exagerado, efusivo

fumble[1] [ˈfʌmbəl] *v* **-bled; -bling** *vt* **1** : dejar caer, fumblear **2 to fumble one's way** : ir a tientas — *vi* **1** GROPE : hurgar, tantear **2 to fumble with** : manejar con torpeza

fumble[2] *n* : fumble *m* (en futbol americano)

fume[1] [ˈfjuːm] *vi* **fumed; fuming 1** SMOKE : echar humo, humear **2** : enfadarse, enojarse

fume[2] *n* : gas *m*, humo *m*, vapor *m*

fumigate [ˈfjuːməˌgeɪt] *vt* **-gated; -gating** : fumigar

fumigation [ˌfjuːməˈgeɪʃən] *n* : fumigación *m*

fun[1] [ˈfʌn] *adj* : divertido, entretenido

fun[2] *n* **1** AMUSEMENT : diversión *f*, entretenimiento *m* **2** ENJOYMENT : disfrute *m* **3 to have fun** : divertirse **4 to make fun of** : reírse de, burlarse de

function[1] [ˈfʌŋkʃən] *vi* : funcionar, desempeñarse, servir

function[2] *n* **1** PURPOSE : función *f* **2** GATHERING : reunión *f* social, recepción *f* **3** CEREMONY : ceremonia *f*, acto *m*

functional [ˈfʌŋkʃənəl] *adj* : funcional — **functionally** *adv*

functionary [ˈfʌŋkʃəˌnɛri] *n, pl* **-aries** : funcionario *m*, -ria *f*

fund[1] [ˈfʌnd] *vt* : financiar

fund[2] *n* **1** SUPPLY : reserva *f*, cúmulo *m* **2** : fondo *m* <investment fund : fondo de inversiones> **3 funds** *npl* RESOURCES : fondos *mpl*

fundamental[1] [ˌfʌndəˈmɛntəl] *adj* **1** BASIC : fundamental, básico **2** PRINCIPAL : esencial, principal **3** INNATE : innato, intrínseco

fundamental[2] *n* : fundamento *m*

fundamentally [ˌfʌndəˈmɛntəli] *adv* : fundamentalmente, básicamente

funding [ˈfʌndɪŋ] *n* : financiación *f*

funeral[1] [ˈfjuːnərəl] *adj* **1** : funeral, funerario, fúnebre <funeral procession : cortejo fúnebre> **2 funeral home** : funeraria *f*

funeral[2] *n* : funeral *m,* funerales *mpl*

funereal [fjuːˈnɪriəl] *adj* : fúnebre

fungal [ˈfʌŋgəl] *adj* : de hongos, micótico

fungicidal [ˌfʌndʒəˈsaɪdəl, ˌfʌngə-] *adj* : fungicida

fungicide [ˈfʌndʒəˌsaɪd, ˈfʌŋgə-] *n* : fungicida *m*

fungous [ˈfʌŋgəs] *adj* : fungoso

fungus [ˈfʌŋgəs] *n, pl* **fungi** [ˈfʌnˌdʒaɪ, ˈfʌŋˌgaɪ] : hongo *m*

funk [ˈfʌŋk] *n* **1** FEAR : miedo *m* **2** DEPRESSION : depresión *f*

funky [ˈfʌŋki] *adj* **funkier; -est** ODD, QUAINT : raro, extraño, original

funnel[1] [ˈfʌnəl] *vt* **-neled; -neling** CHANNEL : canalizar, encauzar

funnel[2] *n* **1** : embudo *m* **2** SMOKESTACK : chimenea *f* (de un barco o vapor)

funnies [ˈfʌniz] *npl* : tiras *fpl* cómicas

funny [ˈfʌni] *adj* **funnier; -est 1** AMUSING : divertido, cómico **2** STRANGE : extraño, raro

fur[1] [ˈfər] *adj* : de piel

fur[2] *n* **1** : pelaje *m,* piel *f* **2** : prenda *f* de piel

furbish [ˈfərbɪʃ] *vt* : pulir, limpiar

furious [ˈfjʊriəs] *adj* **1** ANGRY : furioso **2** FRANTIC : violento, frenético, vertiginoso (dícese de la velocidad)

furiously [ˈfjʊriəsli] *adv* **1** ANGRILY : furiosamente **2** FRANTICALLY : frenéticamente

furlong [ˈfərˌlɔŋ] *n* : estadio *m* (201.2 m)

furlough[1] [ˈfərˌloː] *vt* : dar permiso a, dar licencia a

furlough[2] *n* LEAVE : permiso *m,* licencia *f*

furnace [ˈfərnəs] *n* : horno *m*

furnish [ˈfərnɪʃ] *vt* **1** SUPPLY : proveer, suministrar **2** : amueblar <furnished apartment : departamento amueblado>

furnishings [ˈfərnɪʃɪŋz] *npl* **1** ACCESSORIES : accesorios *mpl* **2** FURNITURE : muebles *mpl*, mobiliario *m*

furniture [ˈfərnɪtʃər] *n* : muebles *mpl*, mobiliario *m*

furor [ˈfjʊrˌɔr, -ər] *n* **1** RAGE : furia *f,* rabia *f* **2** UPROAR : escándalo *m,* jaleo *m,* alboroto *m*

furrier [ˈfəriər] *n* : peletero *m,* -ra *f*

furrow[1] [ˈfəroː] *vt* **1** : surcar **2 to furrow one's brow** : fruncir el ceño

furrow[2] *n* **1** GROOVE : surco *m* **2** WRINKLE : arruga *f,* surco *m*

furry [ˈfəri] *adj* **furrier; -est** : peludo (dícese de un animal), peluche (dícese de un objeto)

further[1] [ˈfərðər] *vt* : promover, fomentar

further[2] *adv* **1** FARTHER : más lejos, más adelante **2** MOREOVER : además **3** MORE : más <I'll consider it further in the morning : lo consideraré más en la mañana>

further[3] *adj* **1** FARTHER : más lejano **2** ADDITIONAL : adicional, más

furtherance [ˈfərðərənts] *n* : promoción *f,* fomento *m,* adelantamiento *m*

furthermore [ˈfərðərˌmor] *adv* : además

furthermost [ˈfərðərˌmoːst] *adj* : más lejano, más distante

furthest [ˈfərðəst] → **farthest[1], farthest[2]**

furtive [ˈfərtɪv] *adj* : furtivo, sigiloso — **furtively** *adv*

furtiveness [ˈfərtɪvnəs] *n* STEALTH : sigilo *m*

fury [ˈfjʊri] *n, pl* **-ries 1** RAGE : furia *f,* ira *f* **2** VIOLENCE : furia *f,* furor *m*

fuse[1] [ˈfjuːz] *or* **fuze** *vt* **fused** *or* **fuzed; fusing** *or* **fuzing** : equipar con un fusible

fuse[2] *v* **fused; fusing** *vt* **1** SMELT : fundir **2** MERGE : fusionar, fundir — *vi* : fundirse, fusionarse

fuse[3] *n* : fusible *m*

fuselage [ˈfjuːsəˌlɑʒ, -zə-] *n* : fuselage *m*

fusillade [ˈfjuːsəˌlɑd, -ˌleɪd, ˌfjuːsəˈ-, -zə-] *n* : descarga *f* de fusilería

fusion [ˈfjuːʒən] *n* : fusión *f*

fuss[1] [ˈfʌs] *vi* **1** WORRY : preocuparse **2 to fuss with** : juguetear con, toquetear **3 to fuss over** : mimar

fuss[2] *n* **1** COMMOTION : alboroto *m,* escándalo *m* **2** ATTENTION : atenciones *fpl* **3** COMPLAINT : quejas *fpl*

fussbudget [ˈfʌsˌbʌdʒət] *n* : quisquilloso *m,* -sa *f;* melindroso *m,* -sa *f*

fussiness [ˈfʌsinəs] *n* **1** IRRITABILITY : irritabilidad *f* **2** ORNATENESS : lo recargado **3** METICULOUSNESS : meticulosidad *f*

fussy [ˈfʌsi] *adj* **fussier; -est 1** IRRITABLE : irritable, nervioso **2** OVERELABORATE : recargado **3** METICULOUS : meticuloso **4** FASTIDIOUS : quisquilloso, exigente

futile [ˈfjuːtəl, ˈfjuːˌtaɪl] *adj* : inútil, vano

futility [fjuˈtɪləti] *n, pl* **-ties** : inutilidad *f*

future[1] [ˈfjuːtʃər] *adj* : futuro

future[2] *n* : futuro *m*

futuristic [ˌfjuːtʃəˈrɪstɪk] *adj* : futurista

fuze → **fuse[1]**

fuzz [ˈfʌz] *n* : pelusa *f*

fuzziness [ˈfʌzinəs] *n* **1** DOWNINESS : vellosidad *f* **2** INDISTINCTNESS : falta *f* de claridad

fuzzy [ˈfʌzi] *adj* **fuzzier; -est 1** FLUFFY, FURRY : con pelusa, peludo **2** INDISTINCT : indistinto, borroso

G

g [ˈdʒiː] *n, pl* **g's** *or* **gs** [ˈdʒiːz] : séptima letra del alfabeto inglés
gab[1] [ˈgæb] *vi* **gabbed; gabbing** : charlar, cotorrear *fam,* parlotear *fam*
gab[2] *n* CHATTER : cotorreo *m fam,* parloteo *m fam*
gabardine [ˈgæbərˌdiːn] *n* : gabardina *f*
gabby [ˈgæbi] *adj* **gabbier; -est** : hablador, parlanchín
gable [ˈgeɪbəl] *n* : hastial *m,* aguilón *m*
Gabonese [ˌgæbəˈnɪːz, -ˈnɪːs] *n* : gabonés *m,* -nesa *f* — **Gabonese** *adj*
gad [ˈgæd] *vi* **gadded; gadding** WANDER : deambular, vagar, callejear
gadfly [ˈgædˌflaɪ] *n, pl* **-flies 1** : tábano *m* (insecto) **2** FAULTFINDER : criticón *m,* -cona *f fam*
gadget [ˈgædʒət] *n* : artilugio *m,* aparato *m*
gadgetry [ˈgædʒətri] *n* : artilugios *mpl,* aparatos *mpl*
gaff [ˈgæf] *n* **1** : garfio *m* **2** → **gaffe**
gaffe [ˈgæf] *n* : metedura *f* de pata *fam*
gag[1] [ˈgæg] *v* **gagged; gagging** *vt* : amordazar <to tie up and gag : atar y amordazar> — *vi* **1** CHOKE : atragantarse **2** RETCH : hacer arcadas
gag[2] *n* **1** : mordaza *f* (para la boca) **2** JOKE : chiste *m*
gage → **gauge**
gaggle [ˈgægəl] *n* : bandada *f,* manada *f* (de gansos)
gaiety [ˈgeɪəṭi] *n, pl* **-eties 1** MERRYMAKING : juerga *f* **2** MERRIMENT : alegría *f,* regocijo *m*
gaily [ˈgeɪli] *adv* : alegremente
gain[1] [ˈgeɪn] *vt* **1** ACQUIRE, OBTAIN : ganar, obtener, adquirir, conseguir <to gain knowledge : adquirir conocimientos> <to gain a victory : obtener una victoria> **2** REACH : alcanzar, llegar a **3** INCREASE : ganar, aumentar <to gain weight : aumentar de peso> **4** : adelantarse, ganar <the watch gains two minutes a day : el reloj se adelanta dos minutos por día> — *vi* **1** PROFIT : beneficiarse **2** INCREASE : aumentar
gain[2] *n* **1** PROFIT : beneficio *m,* ganancia *f,* lucro *m,* provecho *m* **2** INCREASE : aumento *m*
gainful [ˈgeɪnfəl] *adj* : lucrativo, beneficioso, provechoso <gainful employment : trabajo remunerado>
gait [ˈgeɪt] *n* : paso *m,* andar *m,* manera *f* de caminar
gal [ˈgæl] *n* : muchacha *f*
gala[1] [ˈgeɪlə, ˈgæ-, ˈgɑ-] *adj* : de gala
gala[2] *n* : gala *f,* fiesta *f*
galactic [gəˈlæktɪk] *adj* : galáctico
galaxy [ˈgæləksi] *n, pl* **-axies** : galaxia *f*
gale [ˈgeɪl] *n* **1** WIND : vendaval *f,* viento *m* fuerte **2 gales of laughter** : carcajadas *fpl*
gall[1] [ˈgɔl] *vt* **1** CHAFE : rozar **2** IRRITATE, VEX : irritar, molestar
gall[2] *n* **1** BILE : bilis *f,* hiel *f* **2** INSOLENCE : audacidad *f,* insolencia *f,* descaro *m* **3** SORE : rozadura *f* (de un caballo) **4** : agalla *f* (de una planta)
gallant [ˈgælənt] *adj* **1** BRAVE : valiente, gallardo **2** CHIVALROUS, POLITE : galante, cortés
gallantry [ˈgæləntri] *n, pl* **-ries** : galantería *f,* caballerosidad *f*
gallbladder [ˈgɔlˌblædər] *n* : vesícula *f* biliar
galleon [ˈgæljən] *n* : galeón *m*
gallery [ˈgæləri] *n, pl* **-leries 1** BALCONY : galería *f* (para espectadores) **2** CORRIDOR : pasillo *m,* galería *f,* corredor *m* **3** : galería *f* (para exposiciones)
galley [ˈgæli] *n, pl* **-leys** : galera *f*
gallium [ˈgæliəm] *n* : galio *m*
gallivant [ˈgæləˌvænt] *vi* : callejear
gallon [ˈgælən] *n* : galón *m*
gallop[1] [ˈgæləp] *vi* : galopar
gallop[2] *n* : galope *m*
gallows [ˈgæˌloːz] *n, pl* **-lows** *or* **-lowses** [-ˌloːzəz] : horca *f*
gallstone [ˈgɔlˌstoːn] *n* : cálculo *m* biliar
galore [gəˈlor] *adj* : en abundancia <bargains galore : muchísimas gangas>
galoshes [gəˈlɑʃəz] *n* : galochas *fpl,* chanclos *mpl*
galvanize [ˈgælvənˌaɪz] *vt* **-nized; -nizing 1** STIMULATE : estimular, excitar, impulsar **2** : galvanizar (metales)
Gambian [ˈgæmbiən] *n* : gambiano *m,* -na *f* — **Gambian** *adj*
gambit [ˈgæmbɪt] *n* **1** : gambito *m* (en ajedrez) **2** STRATAGEM : estratagema *f,* táctica *f*
gamble[1] [ˈgæmbəl] *v* **-bled; -bling** *vi* : jugar, arriesgarse — *vt* **1** BET, WAGER : apostar, jugarse **2** RISK : arriesgar
gamble[2] *n* **1** BET : apuesta *f* **2** RISK : riesga *f*
gambler [ˈgæmbələr] *n* : jugador *m,* -dora *f*
gambol [ˈgæmbəl] *vi* **-boled** *or* **-bolled; -boling** *or* **-bolling** FROLIC : retozar, juguetear
game[1] [ˈgeɪm] *adj* **1** READY : listo, dispuesto <we're game for anything : estamos listos para lo que sea> **2** LAME : cojo
game[2] *n* **1** AMUSEMENT : juego *m,* diversión *f* **2** CONTEST : juego *m,* partido *m,* concurso *m* **3** : caza *f* <big game : caza mayor>
gamecock [ˈgeɪmˌkɑk] *n* : gallo *m* de pelea
gamekeeper [ˈgeɪmˌkiːpər] *n* : guardabosque *mf*
gamely [ˈgeɪmli] *adv* : animosamente

gamma ray [ˈgæmə] *n* : rayo *m* gamma

gamut [ˈgæmət] *n* : gama *f,* espectro *m* <to run the gamut : pasar por toda la gama>

gamy *or* **gamey** [ˈgeɪmi] *adj* **gamier; -est** : con sabor de animal de caza, fuerte

gander [ˈgændər] *n* **1** : ganso *m* (animal) **2** GLANCE : mirada *f,* vistazo *m,* ojeada *f*

gang[1] [ˈgæŋ] *vi* **to gang up** : agruparse, unirse

gang[2] *n* : banda *f,* pandilla *f*

gangling [ˈgæŋglɪŋ] *adj* LANKY : larguirucho *fam*

ganglion [ˈgæŋgliən] *n, pl* **-glia** [-gliə] : ganglio *m*

gangplank [ˈgæŋˌplæŋk] *n* : pasarela *f*

gangrene [ˈgæŋˌgriːn, ˈgæn-; gæŋˈ-, gænˈ-] *n* : gangrena *f*

gangrenous [ˈgæŋgrənəs] *adj* : gangrenoso

gangster [ˈgæŋstər] *n* : gángster *mf*

gangway [ˈgæŋˌweɪ] *n* **1** : pasarela *f* **2 gangway!** : ¡abran paso!

gap [ˈgæp] *n* **1** BREACH, OPENING : espacio *m,* brecha *f,* abertura *f* **2** GORGE : desfiladero *m,* barranco *m* **3** : laguna *f* <a gap in my education : una laguna en mi educación> **4** INTERVAL : pausa *f,* intervalo *m* **5** DISPARITY : brecha *f,* disparidad *f*

gape[1] [ˈgeɪp] *vi* **gaped; gaping 1** OPEN : abrirse, estar abierto **2** STARE : mirar fijamente con la boca abierta, mirar boquiabierto

gape[2] *n* **1** OPENING : abertura *f,* brecha *f* **2** STARE : mirada *f* boquiabierta

garage[1] [gəˈrɑʒ, -ˈrɑdʒ] *vt* **-raged; -raging** : dejar en un garaje

garage[2] *n* : garaje *m,* cochera *f*

garb[1] [ˈgɑrb] *vt* : vestir, ataviar

garb[2] *n* : vestimenta *f,* atuendo *f*

garbage [ˈgɑrbɪdʒ] *n* : basura *f,* desechos *mpl*

garbageman [ˈgɑrbɪdʒmən] *n, pl* **-men** [-mən, -ˌmɛn] : basurero *m*

garble [ˈgɑrbəl] *vt* **-bled; -bling** : tergiversar, distorsionar

garbled [ˈgɑrbəld] *adj* : incoherente, incomprensible

garden[1] [ˈgɑrdən] *vi* : trabajar en el jardín

garden[2] *n* : jardín *m*

gardener [ˈgɑrdənər] *n* : jardinero *m,* -ra *f*

gardenia [gɑrˈdiːnjə] *n* : gardenia *f*

gargantuan [gɑrˈgæntʃʊən] *adj* : gigantesco, colosal

gargle[1] [ˈgɑrgəl] *vi* **-gled; -gling** : hacer gárgaras, gargarizar

gargle[2] *n* : gárgara *f*

gargoyle [ˈgɑrˌgɔɪl] *n* : gárgola *f*

garish [ˈgærɪʃ] *adj* GAUDY : llamativo, chillón, charro — **garishly** *adv*

garland[1] [ˈgɑrlənd] *vt* : adornar con guirnaldas

garland[2] *n* : guirnalda *f*

garlic [ˈgɑrlɪk] *n* : ajo *m*

garment [ˈgɑrmənt] *n* : prenda *f*

garner [ˈgɑrnər] *vt* : recoger, cosechar

garnet [ˈgɑrnət] *n* : granate *m*

garnish[1] [ˈgɑrnɪʃ] *vt* : aderezar, guarnecer

garnish[2] *n* : aderezo *m,* guarnición *f*

garret [ˈgærət] *n* : buhardilla *f,* desván *m*

garrison[1] [ˈgærəsən] *vt* **1** QUARTER : acuartelar (tropas) **2** OCCUPY : guarnecer, ocupar (con tropas)

garrison[2] *n* **1** : guarnición *f* (ciudad) **2** FORT : fortaleza *f,* poste *m* militar

garrulous [ˈgærələs] *adj* : charlatán, parlanchín, garlero *Col fam*

garter [ˈgɑrt̬ər] *n* : liga *f*

gas[1] [ˈgæs] *v* **gassed; gassing** *vt* : gasear — *vi* **to gas up** : llenar el tanque con gasolina

gas[2] *n, pl* **gases** [ˈgæsəz] **1** : gas *m* <tear gas : gas lacrimógeno> **2** GASOLINE : gasolina *f*

gaseous [ˈgæʃəs, ˈgæsiəs] *adj* : gaseoso

gash[1] [ˈgæʃ] *vt* : hacer un tajo en, cortar

gash[2] *n* : cuchillada *f,* tajo *m*

gasket [ˈgæskət] *n* : junta *f*

gas mask *n* : máscara *f* antigás

gasoline [ˈgæsəˌliːn, ˌgæsəˈ-] *n* : gasolina *f,* nafta *f*

gasp[1] [ˈgæsp] *vi* **1** : boquear <to gasp with surprise : gritar de asombro> **2** PANT : jadear, respirar con dificultad

gasp[2] *n* **1** : boqueada *f* <a gasp of surprise : un grito sofocado> **2** PANTING : jadeo *m*

gas station → service station

gastric [ˈgæstrɪk] *adj* : gástrico <gastric juice : jugo gástrico>

gastronomic [ˌgæstrəˈnɑmɪk] *adj* : gastronómico

gastronomy [gæsˈtrɑnəmi] *n* : gastronomía *f*

gate [ˈgeɪt] *n* : portón *m,* verja *f,* puerta *f*

gatekeeper [ˈgeɪtˌkiːpər] *n* : guarda *mf;* guardián *m,* -diana *f*

gateway [ˈgeɪtˌweɪ] *n* : puerta *f* (de acceso), entrada *f*

gather [ˈgæðər] *vt* **1** ASSEMBLE : juntar, recoger, reunir **2** HARVEST : recoger, cosechar **3** : fruncir (una tela) **4** INFER : deducir, suponer

gathering [ˈgæðərɪŋ] *n* : reunión *f*

gauche [ˈgoːʃ] *adj* : torpe, falto de tacto

gaudy [ˈgɔdi] *adj* **gaudier; -est** : chillón, llamativo

gauge[1] [ˈgeɪdʒ] *vt* **gauged; gauging 1** MEASURE : medir **2** ESTIMATE, JUDGE : estimar, evaluar, juzgar

gauge[2] *n* **1** : indicador *m* <pressure gauge : indicador de presión> **2** CALIBER : calibre *m* **3** INDICATION : indicio *m,* muestra *f*

gaunt [ˈgɔnt] *adj* : demacrado, enjuto, descarnado
gauntlet [ˈgɔntlət] *n* : guante *m* <to run the gauntlet of : exponerse a>
gauze [ˈgɔz] *n* : gasa *f*
gauzy [ˈgɔzi] *adj* **gauzier; -est** : diáfano, vaporoso
gave → **give**
gavel [ˈgævəl] *n* : martillo *m* (de un juez, un subastador, etc.)
gawk [ˈgɔk] *vi* GAPE : mirar boquiabierto
gawky [ˈgɔki] *adj* **gawkier; -est** : desmañado, torpe, desgarbado
gay [ˈgeɪ] *adj* **1** MERRY : alegre **2** BRIGHT, COLORFUL : vistoso, vivo **3** HOMOSEXUAL : homosexual
gaze[1] [ˈgeɪz] *vi* **gazed; gazing** : mirar (fijamente)
gaze[2] *n* : mirada *f* (fija)
gazelle [gəˈzɛl] *n* : gacela *f*
gazette [gəˈzɛt] *n* : gaceta *f*
gazetteer [ˌgæzəˈtɪr] *n* : diccionario *m* geográfico
gear[1] [ˈgɪr] *vt* ADAPT, ORIENT : adaptar, ajustar, orientar <a book geared to children : un libro adaptado a los niños> — *vi* **to gear up** : prepararse
gear[2] *n* **1** CLOTHING : ropa *f* **2** BELONGINGS : efectos *mpl* personales **3** EQUIPMENT, TOOLS : equipo *m,* aparejo *m,* herramientas *fpl* <fishing gear : aparejo de pescar> <landing gear : tren de aterrizaje> **4** COGWHEEL : rueda *f* dentada **5** : marcha *f,* velocidad *f* (de un vehículo) <to put in gear : poner en marcha> <to change gear(s) : cambiar de velocidad>
gearshift [ˈgɪrˌʃɪft] *n* : palanca *f* de cambio, palanca *f* de velocidad
geese → **goose**
Geiger counter [ˈgaɪgərˌkaʊntər] *n* : contador *m* Geiger
gelatin [ˈdʒɛlətən] *n* : gelatina *f*
gem [ˈdʒɛm] *n* : joya *f,* gema *f,* alhaja *f*
Gemini [ˈdʒɛməˌnaɪ] *n* : Géminis *mf*
gemstone [ˈdʒɛmˌstoːn] *n* : piedra *f* (semipreciosa o preciosa), gema *f*
gender [ˈdʒɛndər] *n* **1** SEX : sexo *m* **2** : género *m* (en la gramática)
gene [ˈdʒiːn] *n* : gen *m,* gene *m*
genealogical [ˌdʒiːniəˈlɑdʒɪkəl] *adj* : genealógico
genealogy [ˌdʒiːniˈɑlədʒi, ˌdʒɛ-, -ˈæ-] *n, pl* **-gies** : genealogía *f*
genera → **genus**
general[1] [ˈdʒɛnrəl, ˈdʒɛnə-] *adj* : general <in general : en general, por lo general>
general[2] *n* : general *mf*
generality [ˌdʒɛnəˈrælət̬i] *n, pl* **-ties** : generalidad *f*
generalization [ˌdʒɛnrələˈzeɪʃən, ˌdʒɛnərə-] *n* : generalización *f*
generalize [ˈdʒɛnrəˌlaɪz, ˈdʒɛnərə-] *v* **-ized; -izing** : generalizar
generally [ˈdʒɛnrəli, ˈdʒɛnərə-] *adv* : generalmente, por lo general, en general
generate [ˈdʒɛnəˌreɪt] *vt* **-ated; -ating** : generar, producir
generation [ˌdʒɛnəˈreɪʃən] *n* : generación *f*
generator [ˈdʒɛnəˌreɪt̬ər] *n* : generador *m*
generic [dʒəˈnɛrɪk] *adj* : genérico
generosity [ˌdʒɛnəˈrɑsət̬i] *n, pl* **-ties** : generosidad *f*
generous [ˈdʒɛnərəs] *adj* **1** OPENHANDED : generoso, dadivoso, desprendido **2** ABUNDANT, AMPLE : abundante, amplio, generoso — **generously** *adv*
genetic [dʒəˈnɛtɪk] *adj* : genético — **genetically** [-t̬ɪkli] *adv*
geneticist [dʒəˈnɛt̬əsɪst] *n* : genetista *mf*
genetics [dʒəˈnɛt̬ɪks] *n* : genética *f*
genial [ˈdʒiːniəl] *adj* GRACIOUS : simpático, cordial, afable — **genially** *adv*
geniality [ˌdʒiːniˈælət̬i] *n* : simpatía *f,* afabilidad *f*
genie [ˈdʒiːni] *n* : genio *m*
genital [ˈdʒɛnət̬əl] *adj* : genital
genitals [ˈdʒɛnət̬əlz] *npl* : genitales *mpl*
genius [ˈdʒiːnjəs] *n* : genio *m*
genocide [ˈdʒɛnəˌsaɪd] *n* : genocidio *m*
genre [ˈʒɑnrə, ˈʒɑr] *n* : género *m*
genteel [dʒɛnˈtiːl] *adj* : cortés, fino, refinado
gentile[1] [ˈdʒɛnˌtaɪl] *adj* : gentil
gentile[2] *n* : gentil *mf*
gentility [dʒɛnˈtɪlət̬i] *n, pl* **-ties 1** : nobleza *f* (de nacimiento) **2** POLITENESS, REFINEMENT : cortesía *f,* refinamiento *m*
gentle [ˈdʒɛntəl] *adj* **-tler; -tlest 1** NOBLE : bien nacido, noble **2** DOCILE : dócil, manso **3** KINDLY : bondadoso, amable **4** MILD : suave, apacible <a gentle breeze : una brisa suave> **5** SOFT : suave (dícese de un sonido), ligero (dícese del tacto) **6** MODERATE : moderado, gradual <a gentle slope : una cuesta gradual>
gentleman [ˈdʒɛntəlmən] *n, pl* **-men** [-mən, -ˌmɛn] : caballero *m,* señor *m*
gentlemanly [ˈdʒɛntəlmənli] *adj* : caballeroso
gentleness [ˈdʒɛntəlnəs] *n* : delicadeza *f,* suavidad *f,* ternura *f*
gentlewoman [ˈdʒɛntəlˌwʊmən] *n, pl* **-women** [-ˌwɪmən] : dama *f,* señora *f*
gently [ˈdʒɛntli] *adv* **1** CAREFULLY, SOFTLY : con cuidado, suavemente, ligeramente **2** KINDLY : amablemente, con delicadeza
gentry [ˈdʒɛntri] *n, pl* **-tries** : aristocracia *f*
genuflect [ˈdʒɛnjʊˌflɛkt] *vi* : doblar la rodilla, hacer una genuflexión
genuflection [ˌdʒɛnjʊˈflɛkʃən] *n* : genuflexión *f*

genuine [ˈdʒɛnjʊwən] *adj* **1** AUTHENTIC, REAL : genuino, verdadero, auténtico **2** SINCERE : sincero — **genuinely** *adv*

genus [ˈdʒiːnəs] *n, pl* **genera** [ˈdʒɛnərə] : género *m*

geographer [dʒiˈɑgrəfər] *n* : geógrafo *m*, -fa *f*

geographical [ˌdʒiːəˈgræfɪkəl] *or* **geographic** [-fɪk] *adj* : geográfico — **geographically** [-fɪkli] *adv*

geography [dʒiˈɑgrəfi] *n, pl* **-phies** : geografía *f*

geologic [ˌdʒiːəˈlɑdʒɪk] *or* **geological** [-dʒɪkəl] *adj* : geológico — **geologically** [-dʒɪkli] *adv*

geologist [dʒiˈɑlədʒɪst] *n* : geólogo *m*, -ga *f*

geology [dʒiˈɑlədʒi] *n* : geología *f*

geometric [ˌdʒiːəˈmɛtrɪk] *or* **geometrical** [-trɪkəl] *adj* : geométrico

geometry [dʒiˈɑmətri] *n, pl* **-tries** : geometría *f*

geranium [dʒəˈreɪniəm] *n* : geranio *m*

gerbil [ˈdʒərbəl] *n* : jerbo *m*, gerbo *m*

geriatric [ˌdʒɛriˈætrɪk] *adj* : geriátrico

geriatrics [ˌdʒɛriˈætrɪks] *n* : geriatría *f*

germ [ˈdʒərm] *n* **1** MICROORGANISM : microbio *m*, germen *m* **2** BEGINNING : germen *m*, principio *m* <the germ of a plan : el germen de un plan>

German [ˈdʒərmən] *n* **1** : alemán *m*, -mana *f* **2** : alemán *m* (idioma) — **German** *adj*

germane [dʒərˈmeɪn] *adj* : relevante, pertinente

germanium [dʒərˈmeɪniəm] *n* : germanio *m*

germ cell *n* : célula *f* germen

germicide [ˈdʒərməˌsaɪd] *n* : germicida *m*

germinate [ˈdʒərməˌneɪt] *v* **-nated; -nating** *vi* : germinar — *vt* : hacer germinar

germination [ˌdʒərməˈneɪʃən] *n* : germinación *f*

gerund [ˈdʒɛrənd] *n* : gerundio *m*

gestation [dʒɛˈsteɪʃən] *n* : gestación *f*

gesture¹ [ˈdʒɛstʃər] *vi* **-tured; -turing** : gesticular, hacer gestos

gesture² *n* **1** : gesto *m*, ademán *m* **2** SIGN, TOKEN : gesto *m*, señal *f* <a gesture of friendship : una señal de amistad>

get [ˈgɛt] *v* **got** [ˈgɑt]; **got** *or* **gotten** [ˈgɑtən]; **getting** *vt* **1** OBTAIN : conseguir, obtener, adquirir **2** RECEIVE : recibir <to get a letter : recibir una carta> **3** EARN : ganar <he gets $10 an hour : gana $10 por hora> **4** FETCH : traer <get me my book : tráigame el libro> **5** CATCH : tomar (un tren, etc.), agarrar (una pelota, una persona, etc.) **6** CONTRACT : contagiarse de, contraer <she got the measles : le dio el sarampión> **7** PREPARE : preparar (una comida) **8** PERSUADE : persuadir, mandar a hacer <I got him to agree : logré convencerlo> **9** (*to cause to be*) <to get one's hair cut : cortarse el pelo> **10** UNDERSTAND : entender <now I get it! : ¡ya entiendo!> **11 to have got** : tener <I've got a headache : tengo un dolor de cabeza> **12 to have got to** : tener que <you've got to come : tienes que venir> — *vi* **1** BECOME : ponerse, volverse, hacerse <to get angry : ponerse furioso, enojarse> **2** GO, MOVE : ir, avanzar <he didn't get far : no avanzó mucho> **3** ARRIVE : llegar <to get home : llegar a casa> **4 to get to be** : llegar a ser <she got to be the director : llegó a ser directora> **5 to get ahead** : adelantarse, progresar **6 to get along** : llevarse bien (con alguien), congeniar **7 to get by** MANAGE : arreglárselas **8 to get over** OVERCOME : superar, consolarse de **9 to get together** MEET : reunirse **10 to get up** : levantarse

getaway [ˈgɛtəˌweɪ] *n* ESCAPE : fuga *f*, huida *f*, escapada *f*

geyser [ˈgaɪzər] *n* : géiser *m*

Ghanaian [ˈgɑniən, ˈgæ-] *n* : ghanés *m*, -nesa *f* — **Ghanaian** *adj*

ghastly [ˈgæstli] *adj* **-lier; -est** **1** HORRIBLE : horrible, espantoso **2** PALE : pálido, cadavérico

gherkin [ˈgərkən] *n* : pepinillo *m*

ghetto [ˈgɛtoː] *n, pl* **-tos** *or* **-toes** : gueto *m*

ghost [ˈgoːst] *n* **1** : fantasma *f*, espectro *m* **2 the Holy Ghost** : el Espíritu Santo

ghostly [ˈgoːstli] *adv* : fantasmal

ghoul [ˈguːl] *n* **1** : demonio *m* necrófago **2** : persona *f* de gustos macabros

GI [ˌdʒiːˈaɪ] *n, pl* **GI's** *or* **GIs** : soldado *m* estadounidense

giant¹ [ˈdʒaɪənt] *adj* : gigante, gigantesco, enorme

giant² *n* : gigante *m*, -ta *f*

gibberish [ˈdʒɪbərɪʃ] *n* : galimatías *m*, jerigonza *f*

gibbon [ˈgɪbən] *n* : gibón *m*

gibe¹ [ˈdʒaɪb] *vi* **gibed; gibing** : mofarse, burlarse

gibe² *n* : pulla *f*, burla *f*, mofa *f*

giblets [ˈdʒɪbləts] *npl* : menudos *mpl*, menudencias *fpl*

giddiness [ˈgɪdinəs] *n* **1** DIZZINESS : vértigo *m*, mareo *m* **2** SILLINESS : frivolidad *f*, estupidez *f*

giddy [ˈgɪdi] *adj* **-dier; -est** **1** DIZZY : mareado, vertiginoso **2** FRIVOLOUS, SILLY : frívolo, tonto

gift [ˈgɪft] *n* **1** TALENT : don *m*, talento *m*, dotes *fpl* **2** PRESENT : regalo *m*, obsequio *m*

gifted [ˈgɪftəd] *adj* TALENTED : talentoso

gigantic [dʒaɪˈgæntɪk] *adj* : gigantesco, enorme, colosal

giggle¹ [ˈgɪgəl] *vi* **-gled; -gling** : reírse tontamente

giggle² *n* : risita *f*, risa *f* tonta

gild [ˈgɪld] *vt* **gilded** *or* **gilt** [ˈgɪlt]; **gilding** : dorar

gill [ˈgɪl] *n* : agalla *f*, branquia *f*

gilt[1] [ˈgɪlt] *adj* : dorado

gilt[2] *n* : dorado *m*

gimlet [ˈgɪmlət] *n* **1** : barrena *f* (herramiento) **2** : bebida *f* de vodka o ginebra y limón

gimmick [ˈgɪmɪk] *n* **1** GADGET : artilugio *m* **2** CATCH : engaño *m,* trampa *f* **3** SCHEME, TRICK : ardid *m,* truco *m*

gin[1] [ˈdʒɪn] *vt* **ginned; ginning** : desmotar (algodón)

gin[2] *n* **1** : desmotadora *f* (de algodón) **2** : ginebra *f* (bebida alcohólica)

ginger [ˈdʒɪndʒər] *n* : jengibre *m*

ginger ale *n* : ginger ale *m,* gaseosa *f* de jengibre

gingerbread [ˈdʒɪndʒərˌbrɛd] *n* : pan *m* de jengibre

gingerly [ˈdʒɪndʒərli] *adv* : con cuidado, cautelosamente

gingham [ˈgɪŋəm] *n* : guinga *f*

ginseng [ˈdʒɪnˌsɪŋ, -ˌsɛŋ] *n* : ginseng *m*

giraffe [dʒəˈræf] *n* : jirafa *f*

gird [ˈgərd] *vt* **girded** *or* **girt** [ˈgərt]; **girding 1** BIND : ceñir, atar **2** ENCIRCLE : rodear **3 to gird oneself** : prepararse

girder [ˈgərdər] *n* : viga *f*

girdle[1] [ˈgərdəl] *vt* **-dled; -dling 1** GIRD : ceñir, atar **2** SURROUND : rodear, circundar

girdle[2] *n* : faja *f*

girl [ˈgərl] *n* **1** : niña *f,* muchacha *f,* chica *f* **2** SWEETHEART : novia *f* **3** DAUGHTER : hija *f*

girlfriend [ˈgərlˌfrɛnd] *n* : novia *f,* amiga *f*

girlhood [ˈgərlˌhʊd] *n* : niñez *f,* juventud *f* (de una muchacha)

girlish [ˈgərlɪʃ] *adj* : de niña

girth [ˈgərθ] *n* **1** : circunferencia *f* (de un árbol, etc.), cintura *f* (de una persona) **2** CINCH : cincha *f* (para caballos, etc.)

gist [ˈdʒɪst] *n* : quid *m,* meollo *m*

give[1] [ˈgɪv] *v* **gave** [ˈgeɪv]; **given** [ˈgɪvən]; **giving** *vt* **1** HAND, PRESENT : dar, regalar, obsequiar <give it to me : dámelo> <they gave him a gold watch : le regalaron un reloj de oro> **2** PAY : dar, pagar <I'll give you $10 for this one : te daré $10 por éste> **3** UTTER : dar, pronunciar <to give a shout : dar un grito> <to give a speech : pronunciar un discurso> <to give a verdict : dictar sentencia> **4** PROVIDE : dar <to give one's word : dar uno su palabra> <to give a party : dar una fiesta> **5** CAUSE : dar, causar, ocasionar <to give trouble : causar problemas> <to give someone to understand : darle a entender a alguien> **6** GRANT : dar, otorgar <to give permission : dar permiso> — *vi* **1** : hacer regalos **2** YIELD : ceder, romperse <it gave under the weight of the crowd : cedió bajo el peso de la muchedumbre> **3 to give in** *or* **to give up** SURRENDER : rendirse, entregarse **4 to give out** : agotarse, acabarse <the supplies gave out : las provisiones se agotaron>

give[2] *n* FLEXIBILITY : flexibilidad *f,* elasticidad *f*

giveaway [ˈgɪvəˌweɪ] *n* **1** : revelación *f* involuntaria **2** GIFT : regalo *m,* obsequio *m*

given [ˈgɪvən] *adj* **1** INCLINED : dado, inclinado <he's given to quarreling : es muy dado a discutir> **2** SPECIFIC : dado, determinado <at a given time : en un momento dado>

given name *n* : nombre *m* de pila

give up *vt* : dejar, renunciar a, abandonar <to give up smoking : dejar de fumar>

gizzard [ˈgɪzərd] *n* : molleja *f*

glacial [ˈgleɪʃəl] *adj* : glacial — **glacially** *adv*

glacier [ˈgleɪʃər] *n* : glaciar *m*

glad [ˈglæd] *adj* **gladder; gladdest 1** PLEASED : alegre, contento <she was glad I came : se alegró de que haya venido> <glad to meet you! : ¡mucho gusto!> **2** HAPPY, PLEASING : feliz, agradable <glad tidings : buenas nuevas> **3** WILLING : dispuesto, gustoso <I'll be glad to do it : lo haré con mucho gusto>

gladden [ˈglædən] *vt* : alegrar

glade [ˈgleɪd] *n* : claro *m*

gladiator [ˈglædiˌeɪt̬ər] *n* : gladiador *m*

gladiolus [ˌglædiˈoːləs] *n, pl* **-li** [-li, -ˌlaɪ] : gladiolo *m,* gladíolo *m*

gladly [ˈglædli] *adv* : con mucho gusto

gladness [ˈglædnəs] *n* : alegría *f,* gozo *m*

glamor *or* **glamour** [ˈglæmər] *n* : atractivo *m,* hechizo *m,* encanto *m*

glamorous [ˈglæmərəs] *adj* : atractivo, encantador

glance[1] [ˈglænts] *vi* **glanced; glancing 1** RICOCHET : rebotar <it glanced off the wall : rebotó en la pared> **2 to glance at** : mirar, echar un vistazo a **3 to glance away** : apartar los ojos

glance[2] *n* : mirada *f,* vistazo *m,* ojeada *f*

gland [ˈglænd] *n* : glándula *f*

glandular [ˈglændʒʊlər] *adj* : glandular

glare[1] [ˈglær] *vi* **glared; glaring 1** SHINE : brillar, relumbrar **2** STARE : mirar con ira, lanzar una mirada feroz

glare[2] *n* **1** BRIGHTNESS : resplandor *m,* luz *f* deslumbrante **2** : mirada *f* feroz

glaring [ˈglærɪŋ] *adj* **1** BRIGHT : deslumbrante, brillante **2** FLAGRANT, OBVIOUS : flagrante, manifiesto <a glaring error : un error que salta a la vista>

glass [ˈglæs] *n* **1** : vidrio *m,* cristal *m* <stained glass : vidrio de color> **2** : vaso *m* <a glass of milk : un vaso de leche> **3 glasses** *npl* SPECTACLES : gafas *fpl,* anteojos *mpl,* lentes *mpl,* espejuelos *mpl*

glassblowing ['glæs,blo:ıŋ] *n* : soplado *m* del vidrio

glassful ['glæs,fʊl] *n* : vaso *m,* copa *f*

glassware ['glæs,wær] *n* : cristalería *f*

glassy ['glæsi] *adj* **glassier; -est 1** VITREOUS : vítreo **2** : vidrioso <glassy eyes : ojos vidriosos>

glaze[1] ['gleız] *vt* **glazed; glazing 1** : ponerle vidrios a (una ventana, etc.) **2** : vidriar (cerámica) **3** : glasear (papel, verduras, etc.)

glaze[2] *n* : vidriado *m,* glaseado *m,* barniz *m*

glazier ['gleıʒər] *n* : vidriero *m,* -ra *f*

gleam[1] ['gli:m] *vi* : brillar, destellar, relucir

gleam[2] *n* **1** LIGHT : luz *f* (oscura) **2** GLINT : destello *m* **3** GLIMMER : rayo *m,* vislumbre *f* <a gleam of hope : un rayo de esperanza>

glean ['gli:n] *vt* : recoger, espigar

glee ['gli:] *n* : alegría *f,* júbilo *m,* regocijo *m*

gleeful ['gli:fəl] *adj* : lleno de alegría

glen ['glɛn] *n* : cañada *f*

glib ['glıb] *adj* **glibber; glibbest 1** : simplista <a glib reply : una respuesta simplista> **2** : con mucha labia (dícese de una persona)

glibly ['glıbli] *adv* : con mucha labia

glide[1] ['glaıd] *vi* **glided; gliding** : deslizarse (en una superficie), planear (en el aire)

glide[2] *n* : planeo *m*

glider ['glaıdər] *n* **1** : planeador *m* (aeronave) **2** : mecedor *m* (tipo de columpio)

glimmer[1] ['glımər] *vi* : brillar con luz trémula

glimmer[2] *n* **1** : luz *f* trémula, luz *f* tenue **2** GLEAM : rayo *m,* vislumbre *f* <a glimmer of understanding : un rayo de entendimiento>

glimpse[1] ['glımps] *vt* **glimpsed; glimpsing** : vislumbrar, entrever

glimpse[2] *n* : mirada *f* breve <to catch a glimpse of : alcanzar a ver, vislumbrar>

glint[1] ['glınt] *vi* GLEAM, SPARKLE : destellar, fulgurar

glint[2] *n* **1** SPARKLE : destello *m,* centelleo *m* **2 to have a glint in one's eye** : chispearle los ojos a uno

glisten[1] ['glısən] *vi* : brillar, centellear

glisten[2] *n* : brillo *m,* centelleo *m*

glitter[1] ['glıţər] *vi* **1** SPARKLE : destellar, relucir, brillar **2** FLASH : relampaguear <his eyes glittered in anger : le relampagueaban los ojos de ira>

glitter[2] *n* **1** BRIGHTNESS : brillo *m* **2** : purpurina *f* (para decoración)

gloat ['glo:t] *vi* **to gloat over** : regodearse en

glob ['glɑb] *n* : plasta *f,* masa *f,* grumo *m*

global ['glo:bəl] *adj* **1** SPHERICAL : esférico **2** WORLDWIDE : global, mundial — **globally** *adv*

globe ['glo:b] *n* **1** SPHERE : esfera *f,* globo *m* **2** EARTH : globo *m,* Tierra *f* **3** : globo *m* terráqueo (modelo de la Tierra)

globe–trotter ['glo:b,trɑţər] *n* : trotamundos *mf*

globular ['glɑbjʊlər] *adj* : globular

globule ['glɑ,bju:l] *n* : glóbulo *m*

gloom ['glu:m] *n* **1** DARKNESS : penumbra *f,* oscuridad *f* **2** MELANCHOLY : melancolía *f,* tristeza *f*

gloomily ['glu:məli] *adv* : tristemente

gloomy ['glu:mi] *adj* **gloomier; -est 1** DARK : oscuro, tenebroso <gloomy weather : tiempo gris> **2** MELANCHOLY : melancólico **3** PESSIMISTIC : pesimista **4** DEPRESSING : deprimente, lúgubre

glorification [,glorəfə'keıʃən] *n* : glorificación *f*

glorify ['glorə,faı] *vt* **-fied; -fying** : glorificar

glorious ['gloriəs] *adj* **1** ILLUSTRIOUS : glorioso, ilustre **2** MAGNIFICENT : magnífico, espléndido, maravilloso — **gloriously** *adv*

glory[1] ['glori] *vi* **-ried; -rying** EXULT : exultar, regocijarse

glory[2] *n, pl* **-ries 1** RENOWN : gloria *f,* fama *f,* honor *m* **2** PRAISE : gloria *f* <glory to God : gloria a Dios> **3** MAGNIFICENCE : magnificencia *f,* esplendor *m,* gloria *f* **4 to be in one's glory** : estar uno en su gloria

gloss[1] ['glɔs, 'glɑs] *vt* **1** EXPLAIN : glosar, explicar **2** POLISH : lustrar, pulir **3 to gloss over** : quitarle importancia a, minimizar

gloss[2] *n* **1** SHINE : lustre *m,* brillo *m* **2** EXPLANATION : glosa *f,* explicación *f* breve **3** → **glossary**

glossary ['glɔsəri, 'glɑ-] *n, pl* **-ries** : glosario *m*

glossy ['glɔsi, 'glɑ-] *adj* **glossier; -est** : brillante, lustroso, satinado (dícese del papel)

glove ['glʌv] *n* : guante *m*

glow[1] ['glo:] *vi* **1** SHINE : brillar, resplandecer **2** BRIM : rebosar <to glow with health : rebosar de salud>

glow[2] *n* **1** BRIGHTNESS : resplandor *m,* brillo *m,* luminosidad *f* **2** FEELING : sensación *f* (de bienestar), oleada *f* (de sentimiento) **3** INCANDESCENCE : incandescencia *f*

glower ['glaʊər] *vi* : fruncir el ceño

glowworm ['glo:,wərm] *n* : luciérnaga *f*

glucose ['glu:,ko:s] *n* : glucosa *f*

glue[1] ['glu:] *vt* **glued; gluing** *or* **glueing** : pegar, encolar

glue[2] *n* : pegamento *m,* cola *f*

gluey ['glu:i] *adj* **gluier; -est** : pegajoso

glum ['glʌm] *adj* **glummer; glummest 1** SULLEN : hosco, sombrío **2** DREARY, GLOOMY : sombrío, triste, melancólico

glut[1] ['glʌt] *vt* **glutted; glutting 1** SATIATE : saciar, hartar **2** : inundar (el mercado)
glut[2] *n* : exceso *m,* superabundancia *f*
glutinous ['glu:tənəs] *adj* STICKY : pegajoso, glutinoso
glutton ['glʌtən] *n* : glotón *m,* -tona *f*
gluttonous ['glʌtənəs] *adj* : glotón
gluttony ['glʌtəni] *n, pl* **-tonies** : glotonería *f,* gula *f*
gnarled ['nɑrld] *adj* **1** KNOTTY : nudoso **2** TWISTED : retorcido
gnash ['næʃ] *vt* : hacer rechinar (los dientes)
gnat ['næt] *n* : jején *m*
gnaw ['nɔ] *vt* : roer
gnome ['no:m] *n* : gnomo *m*
gnu ['nu:, 'nju:] *n, pl* **gnu** *or* **gnus** : ñu *m*
go[1] ['go:] *v* **went** ['wɛnt]; **gone** ['gɔn, 'gɑn]; **going; goes** ['go:z] *vi* **1** PROCEED : ir <to go slow : ir despacio> <to go shopping : ir de compras> **2** LEAVE : irse, marcharse, salir <let's go! : ¡vámonos!> <the train went on time : el tren salió a tiempo> **3** DISAPPEAR : desaparecer, pasarse, irse <her fear is gone : se le ha pasado el miedo> <my pen is gone! : ¡mi pluma desapareció!> **4** EXTEND : ir, extenderse, llegar <this road goes to the river : este camino se extiende hasta el río> <to go from top to bottom : ir de arriba abajo> **5** FUNCTION : funcionar, marchar <the car won't go : el coche no funciona> <to get something going : poner algo en marcha> **6** SELL : venderse <it goes for $15 : se vende por $15> **7** PROGRESS : ir, andar, seguir <my exam went well : me fue bien en el examen> <how did the meeting go? : ¿qué tal la reunión?> **8** BECOME : volverse, quedarse <he's going crazy : está volviéndose loco> <the tire went flat : la llanta se desinfló> **9** FIT : caber <it will go through the door : cabe por la puerta> **10 anything goes!** : ¡todo vale! **11 to go** : faltar <only 10 days to go : faltan sólo 10 días> **12 to go back on** : faltar uno a (su promesa) **13 to go bad** SPOIL : estropearse, echarse a perder **14 to go for** : interesarse uno en, gustarle a uno (algo, alguien) <I don't go for that : eso no me interesa> **15 to go off** EXPLODE : estallar **16 to go with** MATCH : armonizar con, hacer juego con — *v aux* **to be going to** : ir a <I'm going to write a letter : voy a escribir una carta> <it's not going to last : no va a durar>
go[2] *n, pl* **goes 1** ATTEMPT : intento *m* <to have a go at : intentar, probar> **2** SUCCESS : éxito *m* **3** ENERGY : energía *f,* empuje *m* <to be on the go : no parar, no descansar>
goad[1] ['go:d] *vt* : aguijonear (un animal), incitar (a una persona)
goad[2] *n* : aguijón *m*
goal ['go:l] *n* **1** : gol *m* (en deportes) <to score a goal : anotar un gol> **2** *or* **goalposts** : portería *f* **3** AIM, OBJECTIVE : meta *m,* objetivo *m*
goalie ['go:li] → **goalkeeper**
goalkeeper ['go:l,ki:pər] *n* : portero *m,* -ra *f;* guardameta *mf;* arquero *m,* -ra *f*
goaltender ['go:l,tɛndər] → **goalkeeper**
goat ['go:t] *n* **1** : cabra *f* (hembra) **2 billy goat** : macho *m* cabrío, chivo *m*
goatee [go:'ti:] *n* : barbita *f* de chivo, piocha *f Mex*
goatskin ['go:t,skɪn] *n* : piel *f* de cabra
gob ['gɑb] *n* : masa *f,* grumo *m*
gobble ['gɑbəl] *v* **-bled; -bling** *vt* **to gobble up** : tragar, engullir — *vi* : hacer ruidos de pavo
gobbledygook ['gɑbəldi,gʊk, -,gu:k] *n* GIBBERISH : jerigonza *f*
go–between ['go:bɪ,twi:n] *n* : intermediario *m,* -ria *f;* mediador *m,* -dora *f*
goblet ['gɑblət] *n* : copa *f*
goblin ['gɑblən] *n* : duende *m,* trasgo *m*
god ['gɑd, 'gɔd] *n* **1** : dios *m* **2 God** : Dios *m*
godchild ['gɑd,tʃaɪld, 'gɔd-] *n, pl* **-children** : ahijado *m,* -da *f*
goddess ['gɑdəs, 'gɔ-] *n* : diosa *f*
godfather ['gɑd,fɑðər, 'gɔd-] *n* : padrino *m*
godless ['gɑdləs, 'gɔd-] *adj* : ateo
godlike ['gɑd,laɪk, 'gɔd-] *adj* : divino
godly ['gɑdli, 'gɔd-] *adj* **-lier; -est 1** DIVINE : divino **2** DEVOUT, PIOUS : piadoso, devoto, beato
godmother ['gɑd,mʌðər, 'gɔd-] *n* : madrina *f*
godparents ['gɑd,pærənts, 'gɔd-] *npl* : padrinos *mpl*
godsend ['gɑd,sɛnd, 'gɔd-] *n* : bendición *f,* regalo *m* divino
goes → **go**
go–getter ['go:,gɛtər] *n* : persona *f* ambiciosa, buscavidas *mf fam*
goggle ['gɑgəl] *vi* **-gled; -gling** : mirar con ojos desorbitados
goggles ['gɑgəlz] *npl* : gafas *fpl* (protectoras), anteojos *mpl*
goings–on [,go:ɪŋz'ɑn, -'ɔn] *npl* : sucesos *mpl,* ocurrencias *fpl*
goiter ['gɔɪtər] *n* : bocio *m*
gold ['go:ld] *n* : oro *m*
golden ['go:ldən] *adj* **1** : (hecho) de oro **2** : dorado, de color oro <golden hair : pelo rubio> **3** FLOURISHING, PROSPEROUS : dorado, próspero <golden years : años dorados> **4** FAVORABLE : favorable, excelente <a golden opportunity : una excelente oportunidad>
goldenrod ['go:ldən,rɑd] *n* : vara *f* de oro
golden rule *n* : regla *f* de oro
goldfinch ['go:ld,fɪntʃ] *n* : jilguero *m*

goldfish ['goːld,fɪʃ] *n* **:** pez *m* de colores
goldsmith ['goːld,smɪθ] *n* **:** orífice *mf,* orfebre *mf*
golf[1] ['gɑlf, 'gɔlf] *vi* **:** jugar (al) golf
golf[2] *n* **:** golf *m*
golfer ['gɑlfər, 'gɔl-] *n* **:** golfista *mf*
gondola ['gɑndələ, gɑn'doːlə] *n* **:** góndola *f*
gone ['gɔn] *adj* **1** DEAD **:** muerto **2** PAST **:** pasado, ido **3** LOST **:** perdido, desaparecido **4 to be far gone :** estar muy avanzado **5 to be gone on :** estar loco por
goner ['gɔnər] *n* **to be a goner :** estar en las últimas
gong ['gɔŋ, 'gɑŋ] *n* **:** gong *m*
gonorrhea [,gɑnə'riːə] *n* **:** gonorrea *f*
good[1] ['gʊd] *adv* **1** (*used as an intensifier*) **:** bien <a good strong rope **:** una cuerda bien fuerte> **2** WELL **:** bien
good[2] *adj* **better** ['bɛt̬ər]; **best** ['bɛst] **1** PLEASANT **:** bueno, agradable <good news **:** buenas noticias> <to have a good time **:** divertirse> **2** BENEFICIAL **:** bueno, beneficioso <good for a cold **:** beneficioso para los resfriados> <it's good for you **:** es bueno para uno> **3** FULL **:** completo, entero <a good hour **:** una hora entera> **4** CONSIDERABLE **:** bueno, bastante <a good many people **:** muchísima gente, un buen número de gente> **5** ATTRACTIVE, DESIRABLE **:** bueno, bien <a good salary **:** un buen sueldo> <to look good **:** quedar bien> **6** KIND, VIRTUOUS **:** bueno, amable <she's a good person **:** es buena gente> <that's good of you! **:** ¡qué amable!> <good deeds **:** buenas obras> **7** SKILLED **:** bueno, hábil <to be good at **:** tener facilidad para> **8** SOUND **:** bueno, sensato <good advice **:** buenos consejos> **9** (*in greetings*) **:** bueno <good morning **:** buenos días> <good afternoon (evening) **:** buenas tardes> <good night **:** buenas noches>
good[3] *n* **1** RIGHT **:** bien *m* <to do good **:** hacer el bien> **2** GOODNESS **:** bondad *f* **3** BENEFIT **:** bien *m,* provecho *m* <it's for your own good **:** es por tu propio bien> **4 goods** *npl* PROPERTY **:** efectos *mpl* personales, posesiones *fpl* **5 goods** *npl* WARES **:** mercancía *f,* mercadería *f,* artículos *mpl* **6 for ~ :** para siempre
good–bye *or* **good–by** [gʊd'baɪ] *n* **:** adiós *m*
good–for–nothing ['gʊdfər,nʌθɪŋ] *n* **:** inútil *mf;* haragán *m,* -gana *f;* holgazán *m,* -zana *f*
Good Friday *n* **:** Viernes *m* Santo
good–hearted ['gʊd'hɑrt̬əd] *adj* **:** bondadoso, benévolo, de buen corazón
good–looking ['gʊd'lʊkɪŋ] *adj* **:** bello, bonito, guapo
goodly ['gʊdli] *adj* **-lier; -est :** considerable, importante <a goodly number **:** un número considerable>
good–natured ['gʊd'neɪtʃərd] *adj* **:** amigable, amistoso, bonachón *fam*
goodness ['gʊdnəs] *n* **1 :** bondad *f* **2 thank goodness! :** ¡gracias a Dios!, ¡menos mal!
good–tempered ['gʊd'tɛmpərd] *adj* **:** de buen genio
goodwill [,gʊd'wɪl] *n* **1** BENEVOLENCE **:** benevolencia *f,* buena voluntad *f* **2 :** buen nombre *m* (de comercios), renombre *m* comercial
goody ['gʊdi] *n, pl* **goodies :** cosa *f* rica para comer, golosina *f*
gooey ['guːi] *adj* **gooier; gooiest :** pegajoso
goof[1] ['guːf] *vi* **1 to goof off :** holgazanear **2 to goof around :** hacer tonterías **3 to goof up** BLUNDER **:** cometer un error
goof[2] *n* **1 :** bobo *m,* -ba *f;* tonto *m,* -ta *f* **2** BLUNDER **:** error *m,* planchazo *m fam*
goofy ['guːfi] *adj* **goofier; -est** SILLY **:** tonto, bobo
goose ['guːs] *n, pl* **geese** ['giːs] **:** ganso *m,* -sa *f;* ánsar *m;* oca *f*
gooseberry ['guːs,bɛriː, 'guːz-] *n, pl* **-berries :** grosella *f* espinosa
goose bumps *npl* **:** carne *f* de gallina
gooseflesh ['guːs,flɛʃ] → **goose bumps**
goose pimples → **goose bumps**
gopher ['goːfər] *n* **:** taltuza *f*
gore[1] ['gor] *vt* **gored; goring :** cornear
gore[2] *n* BLOOD **:** sangre *f*
gorge[1] ['gɔrdʒ] *vt* **gorged; gorging 1** SATIATE **:** saciar, hartar **2 to gorge oneself :** hartarse, atiborrarse, atracarse *fam*
gorge[2] *n* RAVINE **:** desfiladero *m*
gorgeous ['gɔrdʒəs] *adj* **:** hermoso, espléndido, magnífico
gorilla [gə'rɪlə] *n* **:** gorila *m*
gory ['gori] *adj* **gorier; -est** BLOODY **:** sangriento
gosling ['gɑzlɪŋ, 'gɔz-] *n* **:** ansarino *m*
gospel ['gɑspəl] *n* **1** *or* **Gospel :** evangelio *m* <the four Gospels **:** los cuatro evangelios> **2 the gospel truth :** el evangelio, la pura verdad
gossamer ['gɑsəmər, 'gɑzə-] *adj* **:** tenue, sutil <gossamer wings **:** alas tenues>
gossip[1] ['gɑsɪp] *vi* **:** chismear, contar chismes
gossip[2] *n* **1 :** chismoso *m,* -sa *f* (persona) **2** RUMOR **:** chisme *m,* rumor *m*
gossipy ['gɑsɪpi] *adj* **:** chismoso
got → **get**
Gothic ['gɑθɪk] *adj* **:** gótico
gotten → **get**
gouge[1] ['gaʊdʒ] *vt* **gouged; gouging 1 :** excavar, escoplear (con una gubia) **2** SWINDLE **:** estafar, extorsionar

gouge[2] *n* **1** CHISEL : gubia *f,* formón *m* **2** GROOVE : ranura *f,* hoyo *m* (hecho por un formón)

goulash [ˈguːˌlɑʃ, -ˌlæʃ] *n* : estofado *m,* guiso *m* al estilo húngaro

gourd [ˈgord, ˈgʊrd] *n* : calabaza *f*

gourmand [ˈgʊrˌmɑnd] *n* **1** GLUTTON : glotón *m,* -tona *f* **2** → **gourmet**

gourmet [ˈgʊrˌmeɪ, gʊrˈmeɪ] *n* : gourmet *mf;* gastrónomo *m,* -ma *f*

gout [ˈgaʊt] *n* : gota *f*

govern [ˈgʌvərn] *vt* **1** RULE : gobernar **2** CONTROL, DETERMINE : determinar, controlar, guiar **3** RESTRAIN : dominar (las emociones, etc.) — *vi* : gobernar

governess [ˈgʌvərnəs] *n* : institutriz *f*

government [ˈgʌvərmənt] *n* : gobierno *m*

governmental [ˌgʌvərˈmɛntəl] *adj* : gubernamental, gubernativo

governor [ˈgʌvənər, ˈgʌvərnər] *n* **1** : gobernador *m,* -dora *f* (de un estado, etc.) **2** : regulador *m* (de una máquina)

governorship [ˈgʌvənərˌʃɪp, ˈgʌvərnər-] *n* : cargo *m* de gobernador

gown [ˈgaʊn] *n* **1** : vestido *m* <evening gown : traje de fiesta> **2** : toga *f* (de magistrados, clérigos, etc.)

grab[1] [ˈgræb] *v* **grabbed; grabbing** *vt* SNATCH : agarrar, arrebatar — *vi* : agarrarse

grab[2] *n* **1 to make a grab for** : tratar de agarrar **2 up for grabs** : disponible, libre

grace[1] [ˈgreɪs] *vt* **graced; gracing 1** HONOR : honrar **2** ADORN : adornar, embellecer

grace[2] *n* **1** : gracia *f* <by the grace of God : por la gracia de Dios> **2** BLESSING : bendición *f* (de la mesa) **3** RESPITE : plazo *m,* gracia *f* <a five days' grace (period) : un plazo de cinco días> **4** GRACIOUSNESS : gentileza *f,* cortesía *f* **5** ELEGANCE : elegancia *f,* gracia *f* **6 to be in the good graces of** : estar en buenas relaciones con **7 with good grace** : de buena gana

graceful [ˈgreɪsfəl] *adj* : lleno de gracia, garboso, grácil

gracefully [ˈgreɪsfəli] *adv* : con gracia, con garbo

gracefulness [ˈgreɪsfəlnəs] *n* : gracilidad *f,* apostura *f,* gallardía *f*

graceless [ˈgreɪsləs] *adj* **1** DISCOURTEOUS : descortés **2** CLUMSY, INELEGANT : torpe, desgarbado, poco elegante

gracious [ˈgreɪʃəs] *adj* : cortés, gentil, cordial

graciously [ˈgreɪʃəsli] *adv* : gentilmente

graciousness [ˈgreɪʃəsnəs] *n* : gentileza *f*

gradation [greɪˈdeɪʃən, grə-] *n* : gradación *f*

grade[1] [ˈgreɪd] *vt* **graded; grading 1** SORT : clasificar **2** LEVEL : nivelar **3** : calificar (exámenes, alumnos)

grade[2] *n* **1** QUALITY : categoría *f,* calidad *f* **2** RANK : grado *m,* rango *m* (militar) **3** YEAR : grado *m,* curso *m,* año *m* <sixth grade : el sexto grado> **4** MARK : nota *f,* calificación *f* (en educación) **5** SLOPE : cuesta *f,* pendiente *f,* gradiente *f*

grade school → **elementary school**

gradual [ˈgrædʒʊəl] *adj* : gradual, paulatino

gradually [ˈgrædʒʊəli, ˈgrædʒəli] *adv* : gradualmente, poco a poco

graduate[1] [ˈgrædʒʊˌeɪt] *v* **-ated; -ating** *vi* : graduarse, licenciarse — *vt* : graduar <a graduated thermometer : un termómetro graduado>

graduate[2] [ˈgrædʒʊət] *adj* : de postgrado <graduate course : curso de postgrado>

graduate[3] *n* **1** : licenciado *m,* -da *f;* graduado *m,* -da *f* (de la universidad) **2** : bachiller *mf* (de la escuela secundaria)

graduate student *n* : postgraduado *m,* -da *f*

graduation [ˌgrædʒʊˈeɪʃən] *n* : graduación *f*

graffiti [grəˈfiːti, græ-] *npl* : pintadas *fpl,* graffiti *mpl*

graft[1] [ˈgræft] *vt* : injertar

graft[2] *n* **1** : injerto *m* <skin graft : injerto cutáneo> **2** CORRUPTION : soborno *m* (político), ganancia *f* ilegal

grain [ˈgreɪn] *n* **1** : grano *m* <a grain of corn : un grano de maíz> <like a grain of sand : como grano de arena> **2** CEREALS : cereales *mpl* **3** : veta *f,* vena *f,* grano *m* (de madera) **4** SPECK, TRACE : pizca *f,* ápice *m* <a grain of truth : una pizca de verdad> **5** : grano *m* (unidad de peso)

gram [ˈgræm] *n* : gramo *m*

grammar [ˈgræmər] *n* : gramática *f*

grammar school → **elementary school**

grammatical [grəˈmæt̬ɪkəl] *adj* : gramatical — **grammatically** [-kli] *adv*

granary [ˈgreɪnəri, ˈgræ-] *n, pl* **-ries** : granero *m*

grand [ˈgrænd] *adj* **1** FOREMOST : grande **2** IMPRESSIVE : impresionante, magnífico <a grand view : una vista magnífica> **3** LAVISH : grandioso, suntuoso, lujoso <to live in a grand manner : vivir a lo grande> **4** FABULOUS : fabuloso, magnífico <to have a grand time : pasarlo estupendamente, pasarlo en grande> **5 grand total** : total *m,* suma *f* total

grandchild [ˈgrændˌtʃaɪld] *n, pl* **-children** : nieto *m,* -ta *f*

granddaughter [ˈgrændˌdɔt̬ər] *n* : nieta *f*

grandeur [ˈgrændʒər] *n* : grandiosidad *f,* esplendor *m*

grandfather [ˈgrændˌfɑðər] *n* : abuelo *m*

grandiose [ˈgrændiˌoːs, ˌgrændiˈ-] *adj* **1** IMPOSING : imponente, grandioso **2** POMPOUS : pomposo, presuntuoso

grandmother [ˈgrændˌmʌðər] *n* : abuela *f*
grandparents [ˈgrændˌpærənts] *npl* : abuelos *mpl*
grandson [ˈgrændˌsʌn] *n* : nieto *m*
grandstand [ˈgrændˌstænd] *n* : tribuna *f*
granite [ˈgrænɪt] *n* : granito *m*
grant[1] [ˈgrænt] *vt* **1** ALLOW : conceder <to grant a request : conceder una petición> **2** BESTOW : conceder, dar, otorgar <to grant a favor : otorgar un favor> **3** ADMIT : reconocer, admitir <I'll grant that he's clever : reconozco que es listo> **4 to take for granted** : dar (algo) por sentado
grant[2] *n* **1** GRANTING : concesión *f,* otorgamiento *m* **2** SCHOLARSHIP : beca *f* **3** SUBSIDY : subvención *f*
granular [ˈgrænjʊlər] *adj* : granular
granulated [ˈgrænjʊˌleɪt̬əd] *adj* : granulado
grape [ˈgreɪp] *n* : uva *f*
grapefruit [ˈgreɪpˌfruːt] *n* : toronja *f,* pomelo *m*
grapevine [ˈgreɪpˌvaɪn] *n* **1** : vid *f,* parra *f* **2 through the grapevine** : por vías secretas <I heard it through the grapevine : me lo contaron>
graph [ˈgræf] *n* : gráfica *f,* gráfico *m*
graphic [ˈgræfɪk] *adj* **1** VIVID : vívido, gráfico **2 graphic arts** : artes gráficas
graphically [ˈgræfɪkli] *adv* : gráficamente
graphite [ˈgræˌfaɪt] *n* : grafito *m*
grapnel [ˈgræpnəl] *n* : rezón *m*
grapple [ˈgræpəl] *vi* **-pled; -pling 1** GRIP : agarrar (con un garfio) **2** STRUGGLE : forcejear, luchar (con un problema, etc.)
grasp[1] [ˈgræsp] *vt* **1** GRIP, SEIZE : agarrar, asir **2** COMPREHEND : entender, comprender — *vi* **to grasp at** : aprovechar
grasp[2] *n* **1** GRIP : agarre *m* **2** CONTROL : control *m,* garras *fpl* **3** REACH : alcance *m* <within your grasp : a su alcance> **4** UNDERSTANDING : comprensión *f,* entendimiento *m*
grass [ˈgræs] *n* **1** : hierba *f* (planta) **2** PASTURE : pasto *m,* zacate *m CA, Mex* **3** LAWN : césped *m,* pasto *m*
grasshopper [ˈgræsˌhɑpər] *n* : saltamontes *m*
grassland [ˈgræsˌlænd] *n* : pradera *f*
grassy [ˈgræsi] *adj* **grassier; -est** : cubierto de hierba
grate[1] [ˈgreɪt] *v* **grated; -ing** *vt* **1** : rallar (en cocina) **2** SCRAPE : rascar **3 to grate one's teeth** : hacer rechinar los dientes — *vi* **1** RASP, SQUEAK : chirriar **2** IRRITATE : irritar <to grate on one's nerves : crisparle los nervios a uno>
grate[2] *n* **1** : parrilla *f* (para cocinar) **2** GRATING : reja *f,* rejilla *f,* verja *f* (en una ventana)
grateful [ˈgreɪtfəl] *adj* : agradecido
gratefully [ˈgreɪtfəli] *adv* : con agradecimiento
gratefulness [ˈgreɪtfəlnəs] *n* : gratitud *f,* agradecimiento *m*
grater [ˈgreɪt̬ər] *n* : rallador *m*
gratification [ˌgræt̬əfəˈkeɪʃən] *n* : gratificación *f*
gratify [ˈgræt̬əˌfaɪ] *vt* **-fied; -fying 1** PLEASE : complacer **2** SATISFY : satisfacer, gratificar
grating [ˈgreɪt̬ɪŋ] *n* : reja *f,* rejilla *f*
gratis[1] [ˈgræt̬əs, ˈgreɪ-] *adv* : gratis, gratuitamente
gratis[2] *adj* : gratis, gratuito
gratitude [ˈgræt̬əˌtuːd, -ˌtjuːd] *n* : gratitud *f,* agradecimiento *m*
gratuitous [grəˈtuːət̬əs] *adj* : gratuito
gratuity [grəˈtuːət̬i] *n, pl* **-ities** TIP : propina *f*
grave[1] [ˈgreɪv] *adj* **graver; -est 1** IMPORTANT : grave, de mucha gravedad **2** SERIOUS, SOLEMN : grave, serio
grave[2] *n* : tumba *f,* sepultura *f*
gravel [ˈgrævəl] *n* : grava *f,* gravilla *f*
gravelly [ˈgrævəli] *adj* **1** : de grava **2** HARSH : áspero (dícese de la voz)
gravely [ˈgreɪvli] *adv* : gravemente
gravestone [ˈgreɪvˌstoːn] *n* : lápida *f*
graveyard [ˈgreɪvˌjɑrd] *n* CEMETERY : cementerio *m,* panteón *m,* camposanto *m*
gravitate [ˈgrævəˌteɪt] *vi* **-tated; -tating** : gravitar
gravitation [ˌgrævəˈteɪʃən] *n* : gravitación *f*
gravitational [ˌgrævəˈteɪʃənəl] *adj* : gravitacional
gravity [ˈgrævət̬i] *n, pl* **-ties 1** SERIOUSNESS : gravedad *f,* seriedad *f* **2** : gravedad *f* <the law of gravity : la ley de la gravedad>
gravy [ˈgreɪvi] *n, pl* **-vies** : salsa *f* (preparada con el jugo de la carne asada)
gray[1] [ˈgreɪ] *vt* : hacer gris — *vi* : encanecer, ponerse gris
gray[2] *adj* **1** : gris (dícese del color) **2** : cano, canoso <gray hair : pelo canoso> <to go gray : volverse cano> **3** DISMAL, GLOOMY : gris, triste
gray[3] *n* : gris *m*
grayish [ˈgreɪɪʃ] *adj* : grisáceo
graze [ˈgreɪz] *v* **grazed; grazing** *vi* : pastar, pacer — *vt* **1** : pastorear (ganado) **2** BRUSH : rozar **3** SCRATCH : raspar
grease[1] [ˈgriːs, ˈgriːz] *vt* **greased; greasing** : engrasar, lubricar
grease[2] [ˈgriːs] *n* : grasa *f*
greasy [ˈgriːsi, -zi] *adj* **greasier; -est 1** : grasiento **2** OILY : graso, grasoso
great [ˈgreɪt] *adj* **1** LARGE : grande <a great mountain : una montaña grande> <a great crowd : una gran muchedumbre> **2** INTENSE : intenso, fuerte, grande <great pain : gran dolor> **3** EMINENT : grande, eminente, distinguido <a great poet : un gran poeta> **4** EXCELLENT, TERRIFIC : excelente, estupendo, fabuloso <to have a

great time : pasarlo en grande> **5 a great while** : mucho tiempo

great-aunt [ˌgreɪtˈænt, -ˈant] *n* : tía *f* abuela

greater [ˈgreɪt̬ər] (*comparative of* **great**) : mayor

greatest [ˈgreɪt̬əst] (*superlative of* **great**) : el mayor, la mayor

great–grandchild [ˌgreɪtˈgrænd-ˌtʃaɪld] *n, pl* **-children** [-ˌtʃɪldrən] : bisnieto *m*, -ta *f*

great–grandfather [ˌgreɪtˈgrænd-ˌfɑðər] *n* : bisabuelo *m*

great–grandmother [ˌgreɪtˈgrænd-ˌmʌðər] *n* : bisabuela *f*

greatly [ˈgreɪtli] *adv* **1** MUCH : mucho, sumamente <to be greatly improved : haber mejorado mucho> **2** VERY : muy <greatly superior : muy superior>

greatness [ˈgreɪtnəs] *n* : grandeza *f*

great–uncle [ˌgreɪtˈʌŋkəl] *n* : tío *m* abuelo

grebe [ˈgriːb] *n* : somorgujo *m*

greed [ˈgriːd] *n* **1** AVARICE : avaricia *f*, codicia *f* **2** GLUTTONY : glotonería *f*, gula *f*

greedily [ˈgriːdəli] *adv* : con avaricia, con gula

greediness [ˈgriːdinəs] → **greed**

greedy [ˈgriːdi] *adj* **greedier; -est 1** AVARICIOUS : codicioso, avaricioso **2** GLUTTONOUS : glotón

Greek [ˈgriːk] *n* **1** : griego *m*, -ga *f* **2** : griego *m* (idioma) — **Greek** *adj*

green[1] [ˈgriːn] *adj* **1** : verde (dícese del color) **2** UNRIPE : verde, inmaduro **3** INEXPERIENCED : verde, novato

green[2] *n* **1** : verde *m* **2 greens** *npl* VEGETABLES : verduras *fpl*

greenery [ˈgriːnəri] *n, pl* **-eries** : plantas *fpl* verdes, vegetación *f*

greenhorn [ˈgriːnˌhɔrn] *n* : novato *m*, -ta *f*

greenhouse [ˈgriːnˌhaʊs] *n* : invernadero *m*

greenhouse effect : efecto *m* invernadero

greenish [ˈgriːnɪʃ] *adj* : verdoso

Greenlander [ˈgriːnləndər, -ˌlæn-] *n* : groenlandés *m*, -desa *f*

greenness [ˈgriːnnəs] *n* **1** : verdor *m* **2** INEXPERIENCE : inexperiencia *f*

green thumb *n* **to have a green thumb** : tener buena mano para las plantas

greet [ˈgriːt] *vt* **1** : saludar <to greet a friend : saludar a un amigo> **2** : acoger, recibir <they greeted him with boos : lo recibieron con abucheos>

greeting [ˈgriːt̬ɪŋ] *n* **1** : saludo *m* **2 greetings** *npl* REGARDS : saludos *mpl*, recuerdos *mpl*

gregarious [grɪˈgæriəs] *adj* : gregario (dícese de los animales), sociable (dícese de las personas) — **gregariously** *adv*

gregariousness [grɪˈgæriəsnəs] *n* : sociabilidad *f*

gremlin [ˈgrɛmlən] *n* : duende *m*

grenade [grəˈneɪd] *n* : granada *f*

Grenadian [grəˈneɪdiən] *n* : granadino *m*, -na *f* — **Grenadian** *adj*

grew → **grow**

grey → **gray**

greyhound [ˈgreɪˌhaʊnd] *n* : galgo *m*

grid [ˈgrɪd] *n* **1** GRATING : rejilla *f* **2** NETWORK : red *f* (de electricidad, etc.) **3** : cuadriculado *m* (de un mapa)

griddle [ˈgrɪdəl] *n* : plancha *f*

griddle cake → **pancake**

gridiron [ˈgrɪdˌaɪərn] *n* **1** GRILL : parrilla *f* **2** : campo *m* de futbol americano

grief [ˈgriːf] *n* **1** SORROW : dolor *m*, pena *f* **2** ANNOYANCE, TROUBLE : problemas *mpl*, molestia *f*

grievance [ˈgriːvənts] *n* COMPLAINT : queja *f*

grieve [ˈgriːv] *v* **grieved; grieving** *vt* DISTRESS : afligir, entristecer, apenar — *vi* **1** : sufrir, afligirse **2 to grieve for** *or* **to grieve over** : llorar, lamentar

grievous [ˈgriːvəs] *adj* **1** OPPRESSIVE : gravoso, opresivo, severo **2** GRAVE, SERIOUS : grave, severo, doloroso

grievously [ˈgriːvəsli] *adv* : gravemente, de gravedad

grill[1] [ˈgrɪl] *vt* **1** : asar (a la parrilla) **2** INTERROGATE : interrogar

grill[2] *n* **1** : parrilla *f* (para cocinar) **2** : parrillada *f* (comida) **3** RESTAURANT : grill *m*

grille *or* **grill** [ˈgrɪl] *n* : reja *f*, enrejado *m*

grim [ˈgrɪm] *adj* **grimmer; grimmest 1** CRUEL : cruel, feroz **2** STERN : adusto, severo <a grim expression : un gesto severo> **3** GLOOMY : sombrío, deprimente **4** SINISTER : macabro, siniestro **5** UNYIELDING : inflexible, persistente <with grim determination : con una voluntad de hierro>

grimace[1] [ˈgrɪməs, grɪˈmeɪs] *vi* **-maced; -macing** : hacer muecas

grimace[2] *n* : mueca *f*

grime [ˈgraɪm] *n* : mugre *f*, suciedad *f*

grimly [ˈgrɪmli] *adv* **1** STERNLY : severamente **2** RESOLUTELY : inexorablemente

grimy [ˈgraɪmi] *adj* **grimier; -est** : mugriento, sucio

grin[1] [ˈgrɪn] *vi* **grinned; grinning** : sonreír abiertamente

grin[2] *n* : sonrisa *f* abierta

grind[1] [ˈgraɪnd] *v* **ground** [ˈgraʊnd]; **grinding** *vt* **1** CRUSH : moler, machacar, triturar **2** SHARPEN : afilar **3** POLISH : pulir, esmerilar (lentes, espejos) **4 to grind one's teeth** : rechinarle los dientes a uno **5 to grind down** OPPRESS : oprimir, agobiar — *vi* **1** : funcionar con dificultad, rechinar <to grind to a halt : pararse

poco a poco, llegar a un punto muerto> **2** STUDY : estudiar mucho

grind[2] *n* : trabajo *m* pesado <the daily grind : la rutina diaria>

grinder [ˈgraɪndər] *n* : molinillo *m* <coffee grinder : molinillo de café>

grindstone [ˈgraɪnd,sto:n] *n* : piedra *m* de afilar

grip[1] [ˈgrɪp] *vt* **gripped; gripping 1** GRASP : agarrar, asir **2** HOLD, INTEREST : captar el interés de

grip[2] *n* **1** GRASP : agarre *m,* asidero *m* <to have a firm grip on something : agarrarse bien de algo> **2** CONTROL, HOLD : control *m,* dominio *m* <to lose one's grip on : perder el control de> <inflation tightened its grip on the economy : la inflación se afianzó en su dominio de la economía> **3** UNDERSTANDING : comprensión *f,* entendimiento *m* <to come to grips with : llegar a entender> **4** HANDLE : asidero *m,* empuñadura *f* (de un arma)

gripe[1] [ˈgraɪp] *v* **griped; griping** *vt* IRRITATE, VEX : irritar, fastidiar, molestar — *vi* COMPLAIN : quejarse, rezongar

gripe[2] *n* : queja *f*

grippe [ˈgrɪp] *n* : influenza *f,* gripe *f,* gripa *f Col, Mex*

grisly [ˈgrɪzli] *adj* **-lier; -est** : horripilante, horroroso, truculento

grist [ˈgrɪst] *n* : molienda *f* <it's all grist for the mill : todo ayuda, todo es provechoso>

gristle [ˈgrɪsəl] *n* : cartílago *m*

gristly [ˈgrɪsli] *adj* **-tlier; -est** : cartilaginoso

grit[1] [ˈgrɪt] *vt* **gritted; gritting** : hacer rechinar (los dientes, etc.)

grit[2] *n* **1** SAND : arena *f* **2** GRAVEL : grava *f* **3** COURAGE : valor *m,* coraje *m* **4 grits** *npl* : sémola *f* de maíz

gritty [ˈgrɪṭi] *adj* **-tier; -est 1** : arenoso <a gritty surface : una superficie arenosa> **2** PLUCKY : valiente

grizzled [ˈgrɪzəld] *adj* : entrecano

grizzly bear [ˈgrɪzli] *n* : oso *m* pardo

groan[1] [ˈgro:n] *vi* **1** MOAN : gemir, quejarse **2** CREAK : crujir

groan[2] *n* **1** MOAN : gemido *m,* quejido *m* **2** CREAK : crujido *m*

grocer [ˈgro:sər] *n* : tendero *m,* -ra *f*

grocery [ˈgro:səri, -ʃəri] *n, pl* **-ceries 1** *or* **grocery store** : tienda *f* de comestibles, tienda *f* de abarrotes **2 groceries** *npl* : comestibles *mpl,* abarrotes *mpl*

groggy [ˈgrɑgi] *adj* **-gier; -est** : atontado, grogui, tambaleante

groin [ˈgrɔɪn] *n* : ingle *f*

grommet [ˈgrɑmət, ˈgrʌ-] *n* : arandela *f*

groom[1] [ˈgru:m, ˈgrʊm] *vt* **1** : cepillar, almohazar (un animal) **2** : arreglar, cuidar <well-groomed : bien arreglado> **3** PREPARE : preparar

groom[2] *n* **1** : mozo *m,* -za *f* de cuadra **2** BRIDEGROOM : novio *m*

groove[1] [ˈgru:v] *vt* **grooved; grooving** : acanalar, hacer ranuras en, surcar

groove[2] *n* **1** FURROW, SLOT : ranura *f,* surco *m* **2** RUT : rutina *f*

grope [ˈgro:p] *v* **groped; groping** *vi* : andar a tientas, tantear <he groped for the switch : buscó el interruptor a tientas> — *vt* **to grope one's way** : avanzar a tientas

gross[1] [ˈgro:s] *vt* : tener entrada bruta de, recaudar en bruto

gross[2] *adj* **1** FLAGRANT : flagrante, grave <a gross error : un error flagrante> <a gross injustice : una injusticia grave> **2** FAT : muy gordo, obeso **3** : bruto <gross national product : producto nacional bruto> **4** COARSE, VULGAR : grosero, basto

gross[3] *n* **1** *pl* **gross** : gruesa *f* (12 docenas) **2** *or* **gross income** : ingresos *mpl* brutos

grossly [ˈgro:sli] *adv* **1** EXTREMELY : extremadamente <grossly unfair : totalmente injusto> **2** CRUDELY : groseramente

grotesque [gro:ˈtɛsk] *adj* : grotesco

grotesquely [gro:ˈtɛskli] *adv* : de forma grotesca

grotto [ˈgrɑto:] *n, pl* **-toes** : gruta *f*

grouch[1] [ˈgraʊtʃ] *vi* : refunfuñar, rezongar

grouch[2] *n* **1** COMPLAINT : queja *f* **2** GRUMBLER : gruñón *m,* -ñona *f;* cascarrabias *mf fam*

grouchy [ˈgraʊtʃi] *adj* **grouchier; -est** : malhumorado, gruñon

ground[1] [ˈgraʊnd] *vt* **1** BASE : fundar, basar **2** INSTRUCT : enseñar los conocimientos básicos a <to be well grounded in : ser muy entendido en> **3** : conectar a tierra (un aparato eléctrico) **4** : varar, hacer encallar (un barco) **5** : restringir (un avión o un piloto) a la tierra

ground[2] *n* **1** EARTH, SOIL : suelo *m,* tierra *f* <to dig (in) the ground : cavar la tierra> <to fall to the ground : caerse al suelo> **2** LAND, TERRAIN : terreno *m* <hilly ground : terreno alto> <to lose ground : perder terreno> **3** BASIS, REASON : razón *f,* motivo *m* <grounds for complaint : motivos de queja> **4** BACKGROUND : fondo *m* **5** FIELD : campo *m,* plaza *f* <parade ground : plaza de armas> **6** : tierra *f* (para electricidad) **7 grounds** *npl* PREMISES : recinto *m,* terreno *m* **8 grounds** *npl* DREGS : posos *mpl* (de café)

ground[3] → **grind**

groundhog [ˈgraʊnd,hɔg] *n* : marmota *f* (de América)

groundless [ˈgraʊndləs] *adj* : infundado

groundwork [ˈgraʊnd,wərk] *n* **1** FOUNDATION : fundamento *m,* base *f* **2** PREPARATION : trabajo *m* preparatorio

group[1] [ˈgru:p] *vt* : agrupar

group[2] *n* : grupo *m,* agrupación *f,* conjunto *m,* compañía *f*

grouper [ˈgruːpər] *n* : mero *m*
grouse[1] [ˈgraʊs] *vi* **groused; grousing** : quejarse, rezongar, refunfuñar
grouse[2] *n, pl* **grouse** *or* **grouses** : urogallo *m* (ave)
grout [ˈgraʊt] *n* : lechada *f*
grove [ˈgroːv] *n* : bosquecillo *m,* arboleda *f,* soto *m*
grovel [ˈgrɑvəl, ˈgrʌ-] *vi* **-eled** *or* **-elled; -eling** *or* **-elling 1** CRAWL : arrastrarse **2** : humillarse, postrarse <to grovel before someone : postrarse ante alguien>
grow [ˈgroː] *v* **grew** [ˈgruː]; **grown** [ˈgroːn]; **growing** *vi* **1** : crecer <palm trees grow on the islands : las palmas crecen en las islas> <my hair grows very fast : mi pelo crece muy rápido> **2** DEVELOP, MATURE : desarrollarse, madurar **3** INCREASE : crecer, aumentar **4** BECOME : hacerse, volverse, ponerse <she was growing angry : se estaba poniendo furiosa> <to grow dark : oscurecerse> **5 to grow up** : hacerse mayor <grow up! : ¡no seas niño!> — *vt* **1** CULTIVATE, RAISE : cultivar **2** : dejar crecer <to grow one's hair : dejarse crecer el pelo>
grower [ˈgroːər] *n* : cultivador *m,* -dora *f*
growl[1] [ˈgraʊl] *vi* : gruñir (dícese de un animal), refunfuñar (dícese de una persona)
growl[2] *n* : gruñido *m*
grown–up[1] [ˈgroːnˌəp] *adj* : adulto, mayor
grown–up[2] *n* : adulto *m,* -ta *f;* persona *f* mayor
growth [ˈgroːθ] *n* **1** : crecimiento *m* <to stunt one's growth : detener el crecimiento> **2** INCREASE : aumento *m,* crecimiento *m,* expansión *f* **3** DEVELOPMENT : desarrollo *m* <economic growth : desarrollo económico> <a five days' growth of beard : una barba de cinco días> **4** LUMP, TUMOR : bulto *m,* tumor *m*
grub[1] [ˈgrʌb] *vi* **grubbed; grubbing 1** DIG : escarbar **2** RUMMAGE : hurgar, buscar **3** DRUDGE : trabajar duro
grub[2] *n* **1** : larva *f* <beetle grub : larva del escarabajo> **2** DRUDGE : esclavo *m,* -va *f* del trabajo **3** FOOD : comida *f*
grubby [ˈgrʌbi] *adj* **grubbier; -est** : mugriento, sucio
grudge[1] [ˈgrʌdʒ] *vt* **grudged; grudging** : resentir, envidiar
grudge[2] *n* : rencor *m,* resentimiento *m* <to hold a grudge : guardar rencor>
grueling *or* **gruelling** [ˈgruːlɪŋ, ˈgruːə-] *adj* : extenuante, agotador, duro
gruesome [ˈgruːsəm] *adj* : horripilante, truculento, horroroso
gruff [ˈgrʌf] *adj* **1** BRUSQUE : brusco <a gruff reply : una respuesta brusca> **2** HOARSE : ronco — **gruffly** *adv*
grumble[1] [ˈgrʌmbəl] *vi* **-bled; -bling 1** COMPLAIN : refunfuñar, rezongar, quejarse **2** RUMBLE : hacer un ruido sordo, retumbar (dícese del trueno)
grumble[2] *n* **1** COMPLAINT : queja *f* **2** RUMBLE : ruido *m* sordo, estruendo *m*
grumbler [ˈgrʌmbələr] *n* : gruñón *m,* -ñona *f*
grumpy [ˈgrʌmpi] *adj* **grumpier; -est** : malhumorado, gruñón
grunt[1] [ˈgrʌnt] *vi* : gruñir
grunt[2] *n* : gruñido *m*
guacamole [ˌgwɑkəˈmoːli] *n* : guacamole *m,* guacamol *m*
guarantee[1] [ˌgærənˈtiː] *vt* **-teed; -teeing 1** PROMISE : asegurar, prometer **2** : poner bajo garantía, garantizar (un producto o servicio)
guarantee[2] *n* **1** PROMISE : garantía *f,* promesa *f* <lifetime guarantee : garantía de por vida> **2** → **guarantor**
guarantor [ˌgærənˈtɔr] *n* : garante *mf;* fiador *m,* -dora *f*
guaranty [ˌgærənˈtiː] → **guarantee**
guard[1] [ˈgɑrd] *vt* **1** DEFEND, PROTECT : defender, proteger **2** : guardar, vigilar, custodiar <to guard the frontier : vigilar la frontera> <she guarded my secret well : guardó bien mi secreto> — *vi* **to guard against** : protegerse contra, evitar
guard[2] *n* **1** WATCHMAN : guarda *mf* <security guard : guarda de seguridad> **2** VIGILANCE : guardia *f,* vigilancia *f* <to be on guard : estar en guardia> <to let one's guard down : bajar la guardia> **3** SAFEGUARD : salvaguardia *f,* dispositivo *m* de seguridad (en una máquina) **4** PRECAUTION : precaución *f,* protección *f*
guardhouse [ˈgɑrdˌhaʊs] *n* : cuartel *m* de la guardia
guardian [ˈgɑrdiən] *n* **1** PROTECTOR : guardián *m,* -diana *f;* custodio *m,* -dia *f* **2** : tutor *m,* -tora *f* (de un niño)
guardianship [ˈgɑrdiənˌʃɪp] *n* : custodia *f,* tutela *f*
Guatemalan [ˌgwɑṭəˈmɑlən] *n* : guatemalteco *m,* -ca *f* — **Guatemalan** *adj*
guava [ˈgwɑvə] *n* : guayaba *f*
gubernatorial [ˌguːbənəˈtoriːəl, ˌgjuː-] *adj* : del gobernador
guerrilla *or* **guerilla** [gəˈrɪlə] *n* : guerrillero *m,* -ra *f*
guess[1] [ˈgɛs] *vt* **1** CONJECTURE : adivinar, conjeturar <guess what happened! : ¡adivina lo que pasó!> **2** SUPPOSE : pensar, creer, suponer <I guess so : supongo que sí> **3** : adivinar correctamente, acertar <to guess the answer : acertar la respuesta> — *vi* : adivinar
guess[2] *n* : conjetura *f,* suposición *f*
guesswork [ˈgɛsˌwərk] *n* : suposiciones *fpl,* conjeturas *fpl*
guest [ˈgɛst] *n* : huésped *mf;* invitado *m,* -da *f*
guffaw[1] [gəˈfɔ] *vi* : reírse a carcajadas, carcajearse *fam*

guffaw[2] [gə'fɔ, 'gʌ,fɔ] *n* **:** carcajada *f,* risotada *f*
guidance ['gaɪdənts] *n* **:** orientación *f,* consejos *mpl*
guide[1] ['gaid] *vt* **guided; guiding 1** DIRECT, LEAD **:** guiar, dirigir, conducir **2** ADVISE, COUNSEL **:** aconsejar, orientar
guide[2] *n* **:** guía *f*
guidebook ['gaɪd,bʊk] *n* **:** guía *f* (para viajeros)
guideline ['gaɪd,laɪn] *n* **:** pauta *f,* directriz *f*
guild ['gɪld] *n* **:** gremio *m,* sindicato *m,* asociación *f*
guile ['gaɪl] *n* **:** astucia *f,* engaño *m*
guileless ['gaɪlləs] *adj* **:** inocente, cándido, sin malicia
guillotine[1] ['gɪlə,tiːn, 'giːjə,-] *vt* **-tined; -tining :** guillotinar
guillotine[2] *n* **:** guillotina *f*
guilt ['gɪlt] *n* **:** culpa *f,* culpabilidad *f*
guilty ['gɪlti] *adj* **guiltier; -est :** culpable
guinea fowl ['gɪni] *n* **:** gallina *f* de Guinea
guinea pig *n* **:** conejillo *m* de Indias, cobaya *f*
guise ['gaɪz] *n* **:** apariencia *f,* aspecto *m,* forma *f*
guitar [gə'tɑr, gɪ-] *n* **:** guitarra *f*
gulch ['gʌltʃ] *n* **:** barranco *m,* quebrada *f*
gulf ['gʌlf] *n* **1 :** golfo *m* <the Gulf of Mexico : el Golfo de México> **2** GAP **:** brecha *f* <the gulf between generations : la brecha entre las generaciones> **3** CHASM **:** abismo *m*
gull ['gʌl] *n* **:** gaviota *f*
gullet ['gʌlət] *n* **:** garganta *f*
gullible ['gʌlɪbəl] *adj* **:** crédulo
gully ['gʌli] *n, pl* **-lies :** barranco *m,* hondonada *f*
gulp[1] ['gʌlp] *vt* **1 :** engullir, tragar <he gulped down the whiskey : engulló el whisky> **2** SUPPRESS **:** suprimir, reprimir, tragar <to gulp down a sob : reprimir un sollozo> — *vi* **:** tragar saliva, tener un nudo en la garganta
gulp[2] *n* **:** trago *m*
gum ['gʌm] *n* **1** CHEWING GUM **:** goma *f* de mascar, chicle *m* **2 gums** *npl* **:** encías *fpl*
gumbo ['gʌm,boː] *n* **:** sopa *f* de quingombó
gumdrop ['gʌm,drɑp] *n* **:** pastilla *f* de goma
gummy ['gʌmi] *adj* **gummier; -est :** gomoso
gumption ['gʌmpʃən] *n* **:** iniciativa *f,* agallas *fpl fam*
gun[1] ['gʌn] *vt* **gunned; gunning 1** *or* **to gun down :** matar a tiros, asesinar **2 :** acelerar (rápidamente) <to gun the engine : acelerar el motor>
gun[2] *n* **1** CANNON **:** cañón *m* **2** FIREARM **:** arma *f* de fuego **3** SPRAY GUN **:** pistola *f* **4 to jump the gun :** adelantarse, salir antes de tiempo
gunboat ['gʌn,boːt] *n* **:** cañonero *m*
gunfight ['gʌn,faɪt] *n* **:** tiroteo *m,* balacera *f*
gunfire ['gʌn,faɪr] *n* **:** disparos *mpl*
gunman ['gʌnmən] *n, pl* **-men** [-mən, -,mɛn] **:** pistolero *m,* gatillero *m Mex*
gunner ['gʌnər] *n* **:** artillero *m,* -ra *f*
gunnysack ['gʌni,sæk] *n* **:** saco *m* de yute
gunpowder ['gʌn,paʊdər] *n* **:** pólvora *f*
gunshot ['gʌn,ʃɑt] *n* **:** disparo *m,* tiro *m,* balazo *m*
gunwale ['gʌnəl] *n* **:** borda *f*
guppy ['gʌpi] *n, pl* **-pies :** lebistes *m*
gurgle[1] ['gərgəl] *vi* **-gled; -gling 1 :** borbotar, gorgotear (dícese de un líquido) **2 :** gorjear (dícese de un niño)
gurgle[2] *n* **1 :** borboteo *m,* gorgoteo *m* (de un líquido) **2 :** gorjeo *m* (de un niño)
gush ['gʌʃ] *vi* **1** SPOUT **:** surgir, salir a chorros, chorrear **2 :** hablar con entusiasmo efusivo <she gushed with praise : se deshizo en elogios>
gust ['gʌst] *n* **:** ráfaga *f,* racha *f*
gusto ['gʌs,toː] *n, pl* **gustoes :** entusiasmo *m* <with gusto : con deleite, con ganas>
gusty ['gʌsti] *adj* **gustier; -est :** racheado
gut[1] ['gʌt] *vt* **gutted; gutting 1** EVISCERATE **:** destripar (un pollo, etc.), limpiar (un pescado) **2 :** destruir el interior de (un edificio)
gut[2] *n* **1** INTESTINE **:** intestino *m* **2 guts** *npl* INNARDS **:** tripas *fpl fam,* entrañas *fpl* **3 guts** *npl* COURAGE **:** valentía *f,* agallas *fpl*
gutter ['gʌtər] *n* **1 :** canal *mf,* canaleta *f* (de un techo) **2 :** cuneta *f,* arroyo *m* (de una calle)
guttural ['gʌtərəl] *adj* **:** gutural
guy ['gaɪ] *n* **1** *or* **guyline :** cuerda *f* tensora, cable *m* **2** FELLOW **:** tipo *m,* hombre *m*
guzzle ['gʌzəl] *vt* **-zled; -zling :** chupar, tragarse
gym ['dʒɪm] → **gymnasium**
gymnasium [dʒɪm'neɪziəm, -ʒəm] *n, pl* **-siums** *or* **-sia** [-ziːə, -ʒə] **:** gimnasio *m*
gymnast ['dʒɪmnəst, -,næst] *n* **:** gimnasta *mf*
gymnastic [dʒɪm'næstɪk] *adj* **:** gimnástico
gymnastics [dʒɪm'næstɪks] *ns & pl* **:** gimnasia *f*
gynecologist [,gaɪnə'kɑlədʒɪst, ,dʒɪnə-] *n* **:** ginecólogo *m,* -ga *f*
gynecology [,gaɪnə'kɑlədʒi, ,dʒɪnə-] *n* **:** ginecología *f*
gyp[1] ['dʒɪp] *vt* **gypped; gypping :** estafar, timar
gyp[2] *n* **1** SWINDLER **:** estafador *m,* -dora *f* **2** FRAUD, SWINDLE **:** estafa *f,* timo *m fam*
gypsum ['dʒɪpsəm] *n* **:** yeso *m*

Gypsy [ˈdʒɪpsi] *n, pl* **-sies** : gitano *m,* -na *f*

gyrate [ˈdʒaɪˌreɪt] *vi* **-rated; -rating** : girar, rotar

gyration [dʒaɪˈreɪʃən] *n* : giro *m,* rotación *f*

gyroscope [ˈdʒaɪrəˌskoːp] *n* : giroscopio *m,* giróscopo *m*

H

h [ˈeɪtʃ] *n, pl* **h's** *or* **hs** [ˈeɪtʃəz] : octava letra del alfabeto inglés

haberdashery [ˈhæbərˌdæʃəri] *n, pl* **-eries** : tienda *f* de ropa para caballeros

habit [ˈhæbɪt] *n* **1** CUSTOM : hábito *m,* costumbre *f* **2** : hábito *m* (de un monje o una religiosa) **3** ADDICTION : dependencia *f,* adicción *f*

habitable [ˈhæbɪtəbəl] *adj* : habitable

habitat [ˈhæbɪˌtæt] *n* : hábitat *m*

habitation [ˌhæbɪˈteɪʃən] *n* **1** OCCUPANCY : habitación *f* **2** RESIDENCE : residencia *f,* morada *f*

habit–forming [ˈhæbɪtˌfɔrmɪŋ] *adj* : que crea dependencia

habitual [həˈbɪtʃʊəl] *adj* **1** CUSTOMARY : habitual, acostumbrado **2** INVETERATE : incorregible, empedernido — **habitually** *adv*

habituate [həˈbɪtʃʊˌeɪt] *vt* **-ated; -ating** : habituar, acostumbrar

hack[1] [ˈhæk] *vt* : cortar, tajar <to hack one's way : abrirse paso> — *vi* **1** : hacer tajos **2** COUGH : toser

hack[2] *n* **1** CHOP : hachazo *m,* tajo *m* **2** HORSE : caballo *m* de alquiler **3** WRITER : escritor *m,* -tora *f* a sueldo; escritorzuelo *m,* -la *f* **4** COUGH : tos *f* seca

hackles [ˈhækəlz] *npl* **1** : pluma *f* erizada (de un ave), pelo *m* erizado (de un perro, etc.) **2** **to get one's hackles up** : ponerse furioso

hackney [ˈhækni] *n, pl* **-neys** : caballo *m* de silla, caballo *m* de tiro

hackneyed [ˈhæknid] *adj* TRITE : trillado, gastado

hacksaw [ˈhækˌsɔ] *n* : sierra *f* para metales

had → **have**

haddock [ˈhædək] *ns & pl* : eglefino *m*

hadn't [ˈhædənt] (*contraction of* **had not**) → **have**

haft [ˈhæft] *n* : mango *m,* empuñadura *f*

hag [ˈhæg] *n* **1** WITCH : bruja *f,* hechicera *f* **2** CRONE : vieja *f* fea

haggard [ˈhægərd] *adj* : demacrado, macilento — **haggardly** *adv*

haggle [ˈhægəl] *vi* **-gled; -gling** : regatear

ha–ha [ˌhɑˈhɑ, ˈhɑˈhɑ] *interj* : ¡ja, ja!

hail[1] [ˈheɪl] *vt* **1** GREET : saludar **2** SUMMON : llamar <to hail a taxi : llamar un taxi> — *vi* : granizar (en meteorología)

hail[2] *n* **1** : granizo *m* **2** BARRAGE : aluvión *m,* lluvia *f*

hail[3] *interj* : ¡salve!

hailstone [ˈheɪlˌstoːn] *n* : granizo *m,* piedra *f* de granizo

hailstorm [ˈheɪlˌstɔrm] *n* : granizada *f*

hair [ˈhær] *n* **1** : pelo *m,* cabello *m* <to get one's hair cut : cortarse el pelo> **2** : vello *m* (en las piernas, etc.)

hairbreadth [ˈhærˌbrɛdθ] *or* **hairsbreadth** [ˈhærz-] *n* **by a hairbreadth** : por un pelo

hairbrush [ˈhærˌbrʌʃ] *n* : cepillo *m* (del pelo)

haircut [ˈhærˌkʌt] *n* : corte *m* de pelo

hairdo [ˈhærˌduː] *n, pl* **-dos** : peinado *m*

hairdresser [ˈhærˌdrɛsər] *n* : peluquero *m,* -ra *f*

hairiness [ˈhærinəs] *n* : vellosidad *f*

hairless [ˈhærləs] *adj* : sin pelo, calvo, pelón

hairline [ˈhærˌlaɪn] *n* **1** : línea *f* delgada **2** : nacimiento *m* del pelo <to have a receding hairline : tener entradas>

hairpin [ˈhærˌpɪn] *n* : horquilla *f*

hair–raising [ˈhærˌreɪzɪŋ] *adj* : espeluznante

hairy [ˈhæri] *adj* **hairier; -est** : peludo, velludo

Haitian [ˈheɪʃən, ˈheɪtiən] *n* : haitiano *m,* -na *f* — **Haitian** *adj*

hake [ˈheɪk] *n* : merluza *f*

hale[1] [ˈheɪl] *vt* **haled; haling** : arrastrar, halar <to hale to court : arrastrar al tribunal>

hale[2] *adj* : saludable, robusto

half[1] [ˈhæf, ˈhaf] *adv* : medio, a medias <half cooked : medio cocido>

half[2] *adj* : medio, a medias <a half hour : una media hora> <a half truth : una verdad a medias>

half[3] *n, pl* **halves** [ˈhævz, ˈhavz] **1** : mitad *f* <half of my friends : la mitad de mis amigos> <in half : por la mitad> **2** : tiempo *m* (en deportes)

half brother *n* : medio hermano *m,* hermanastro *m*

halfhearted [ˈhæfˈhɑrtəd] *adj* : sin ánimo, poco entusiasta

halfheartedly [ˈhæfˈhɑrtədli] *adv* : con poco entusiasmo, sin ánimo

half–life [ˈhæfˌlaɪf] *n, pl* **half–lives** : media vida *f*

half sister *n* : media hermana *f,* hermanastra *f*

halfway[1] [ˈhæfˈweɪ] *adv* : a medio camino, a mitad de camino

halfway[2] *adj* : medio, intermedio <a halfway point : un punto intermedio>

half-wit [ˈhæfˌwɪt] *n* : tonto *m,* -ta *f;* imbécil *mf*

half–witted [ˈhæf,wɪt̬əd] *adj* : estúpido
halibut [ˈhælɪbət] *ns & pl* : halibut *m*
hall [ˈhɔl] *n* **1** BUILDING : residencia *f* estudiantil, facultad *f* (de una universidad) **2** VESTIBULE : entrada *f,* vestíbulo *m,* zaguán *m* **3** CORRIDOR : corredor *m,* pasillo *m* **4** AUDITORIUM : sala *f,* salón *m* <concert hall : sala de conciertos> **5 city hall** : ayuntamiento *m*
hallelujah [,hæləˈluːjə, ,hɑ-] *interj* : ¡aleluya!
hallmark [ˈhɔl,mɑrk] *n* : sello *m* (distintivo)
hallow [ˈhæ,loː] *vt* : santificar, consagrar
hallowed [ˈhæ,loːd, ˈhæ,loːəd, ˈhɑ,loːd] *adj* : sagrado
Halloween [,hæləˈwiːn, ,hɑ-] *n* : víspera *f* de Todos los Santos
hallucinate [hæˈluːsən,eɪt] *vi* **-nated; -nating** : alucinar
hallucination [hə,luːsənˈeɪʃən] *n* : alucinación *f*
hallucinatory [həˈluːsənə,tori] *adj* : alucinante
hallucinogen [həˈluːsənədʒən] *n* : alucinógeno *m*
hallucinogenic [hə,luːsənəˈdʒɛnɪk] *adj* : alucinógeno
hallway [ˈhɔl,weɪ] *n* **1** ENTRANCE : entrada *f* **2** CORRIDOR : corredor *m,* pasillo *m*
halo [ˈheɪ,loː] *n, pl* **-los** *or* **-loes** : aureola *f,* halo *m*
halt¹ [ˈhɔlt] *vi* : detenerse, pararse — *vt* **1** STOP : detener, parar (a una persona) **2** INTERRUPT : interrumpir (una actividad)
halt² *n* **1** : alto *m,* parada *f* **2 to come to a halt** : pararse, detenerse
halter [ˈhɔltər] *n* **1** : cabestro *m,* ronzal *m* (para un animal) **2** : blusa *f* sin espalda
halting [ˈhɔltɪŋ] *adj* HESITANT : vacilante, titubeante — **haltingly** *adv*
halve [ˈhæv, ˈhav] *vt* **halved; halving 1** DIVIDE : partir por la mitad **2** REDUCE : reducir a la mitad
halves → **half**
ham [ˈhæm] *n* **1** : jamón *m* **2** *or* **ham actor** : comicastro *m,* -tra *f* **3** *or* **ham radio operator** : radioaficionado *m,* -da *f* **4 hams** *npl* HAUNCHES : ancas *fpl*
hamburger [ˈhæm,bərgər] *or* **hamburg** [-,bərg] *n* **1** : carne *f* molida **2** : hamburguesa *f* (emparedado)
hamlet [ˈhæmlət] *n* VILLAGE : aldea *f,* poblado *m*
hammer¹ [ˈhæmər] *vt* **1** STRIKE : clavar, golpear **2** NAIL : clavar, martillar **3 to hammer out** NEGOTIATE : elaborar, negociar, llegar a — *vi* : martillar, golpear
hammer² *n* **1** : martillo *m* **2** : percusor *m,* percutor *m* (de un arma de fuego)
hammock [ˈhæmək] *n* : hamaca *f*
hamper¹ [ˈhæmpər] *vt* : obstaculizar, dificultar
hamper² *n* : cesto *m,* canasta *f*
hamster [ˈhæmpstər] *n* : hámster *m*
hamstring [ˈhæm,strɪŋ] *vt* **-strung** [-,strʌŋ]; **-stringing 1** : cortarle el tendón del corvejón a (un animal) **2** INCAPACITATE : incapacitar, inutilizar
hand¹ [ˈhænd] *vt* : pasar, dar, entregar
hand² *n* **1** : mano *f* <made by hand : hecho a mano> **2** POINTER : manecilla *f,* aguja *f* (de un reloj o instrumento) **3** SIDE : lado *m* <on the other hand : por otro lado> **4** HANDWRITING : letra *f,* escritura *f* **5** APPLAUSE : aplauso *m* **6** : mano *f,* cartas *fpl* (en juegos de naipes) **7** WORKER : obrero *m,* -ra *f;* trabajador *m,* -dora *f* **8 to ask for someone's hand (in marriage)** : pedir la mano de alguien **9 to lend a hand** : echar una mano
handbag [ˈhænd,bæg] *n* : cartera *f,* bolso *m,* bolsa *f Mex*
handball [ˈhænd,bɔl] *n* : frontón *m*
handbill [ˈhænd,bɪl] *n* : folleto *m,* volante *m*
handbook [ˈhænd,bʊk] *n* : manual *m*
handcuff [ˈhænd,kʌf] *vt* : esposar, ponerle esposas (a alguien)
handcuffs [ˈhænd,kʌfs] *npl* : esposas *fpl*
handful [ˈhænd,fʊl] *n* : puñado *m*
handgun [ˈhænd,gʌn] *n* : pistola *f,* revólver *m*
handicap¹ [ˈhændi,kæp] *vt* **-capped; -capping 1** : asignar un handicap a (en deportes) **2** HAMPER : obstaculizar, poner en desventaja
handicap² *n* **1** DISABILITY : minusvalía *f,* discapacidad *f* **2** DISADVANTAGE : desventaja *f,* handicap *m* (en deportes)
handicapped [ˈhændi,kæpt] *adj* DISABLED : minusválido, discapacitado
handicraft [ˈhændi,kræft] *n* : artesanía *f*
handily [ˈhændəli] *adv* EASILY : fácilmente, con facilidad
handiwork [ˈhændi,wərk] *n* **1** WORK : trabajo *m* **2** CRAFTS : artesanías *fpl*
handkerchief [ˈhæŋkərtʃəf, -,tʃiːf] *n, pl* **-chiefs** : pañuelo *m*
handle¹ [ˈhændəl] *v* **-dled; -dling** *vt* **1** TOUCH : tocar **2** MANAGE : tratar, manejar, despachar **3** SELL : comerciar con, vender — *vi* : responder, conducirse (dícese de un vehículo)
handle² *n* : asa *m,* asidero *m,* mango *m* (de un cuchillo, etc.), pomo *m* (de una puerta), tirador *m* (de un cajón)
handlebars [ˈhændəl,bɑrz] *npl* : manubrio *m,* manillar *m*
handler [ˈhændələr] *n* : cuidador *m,* -dora *f*
handmade [ˈhænd,meɪd] *adj* : hecho a mano
hand–me–downs [ˈhændmi,daʊnz] *npl* : ropa *f* usada

handout [ˈhænd,aʊt] *n* **1** AID : dádiva *f*, limosna *f* **2** LEAFLET : folleto *m*

handpick [ˈhændˈpɪk] *vt* : seleccionar con cuidado

handrail [ˈhænd,reɪl] *n* : pasamanos *m*, barandilla *f*, barandal *m*

handsaw [ˈhænd,sɔ] *n* : serrucho *m*

hands down *adv* **1** EASILY : con facilidad **2** UNQUESTIONABLY : con mucho, de lejos

handshake [ˈhænd,ʃeɪk] *n* : apretón *m* de manos

handsome [ˈhæn*t*səm] *adj* **-somer; -est 1** ATTRACTIVE : apuesto, guapo, atractivo **2** GENEROUS : generoso **3** SIZABLE : considerable

handsomely [ˈhæn*t*səmli] *adv* **1** ELEGANTLY : elegantemente **2** GENEROUSLY : con generosidad

handspring [ˈhænd,sprɪŋ] *n* : voltereta *f*

handstand [ˈhænd,stænd] *n* **to do a handstand** : pararse de manos

hand–to–hand [ˈhænd*t*əˈhænd] *adj* : cuerpo a cuerpo

handwriting [ˈhænd,raɪt̬ɪŋ] *n* : letra *f*, escritura *f*

handwritten [ˈhænd,rɪtən] *adj* : escrito a mano

handy [ˈhændi] *adj* **handier; -est 1** NEARBY : a mano, cercano **2** USEFUL : útil, práctico **3** DEXTEROUS : hábil

hang[1] [ˈhæŋ] *v* **hung** [ˈhʌŋ]; **hanging** *vt* **1** SUSPEND : colgar, tender, suspender **2** (*past tense often* **hanged**) EXECUTE : colgar, ahorcar **3 to hang one's head** : bajar la cabeza — *vi* **1** FALL : caer (dícese de las telas y la ropa) **2** DANGLE : colgar **3** HOVER : flotar, sostenerse en el aire **4** : ser ahorcado **5** DROOP : inclinarse **6 to hang up** : colgar <he hung up on me : me colgó>

hang[2] *n* **1** DRAPE : caída *f* **2 to get the hang of something** : colgarle el truco a algo, lograr entender algo

hangar [ˈhæŋər, ˈhæŋgər] *n* : hangar *m*

hanger [ˈhæŋər] *n* : percha *f*, gancho *m* (para ropa)

hangman [ˈhæŋmən] *n, pl* **-men** [-mən, -,mɛn] : verdugo *m*

hangnail [ˈhæŋ,neɪl] *n* : padrastro *m*

hangout [ˈhæŋ,aʊt] *n* : lugar *m* popular, sitio *m* muy frecuentado

hangover [ˈhæŋ,oːvər] *n* : resaca *f*

hank [ˈhæŋk] *n* : madeja *f*

hanker [ˈhæŋkər] *vi* **to hanker for** : ansiar, anhelar, tener ganas de

hankering [ˈhæŋkərɪŋ] *n* : ansia *f*, anhelo *m*

hansom [ˈhæn*t*səm] *n* : coche *m* de caballos

Hanukkah [ˈxɑnəkə, ˈhɑ-] *n* : Januká, Hanukkah

haphazard [hæpˈhæzərd] *adj* : casual, fortuito, al azar — **haphazardly** *adv*

hapless [ˈhæpləs] *adj* UNFORTUNATE : desafortunado, desventurado — **haplessly**

happen [ˈhæpən] *vi* **1** OCCUR : pasar, ocurrir, suceder, tener lugar **2** BEFALL : pasar, acontecer <what happened to her? : ¿qué le ha pasado?> **3** CHANCE : resultar, ocurrir por casualidad <it happened that I wasn't home : resulta que estaba fuera de casa> <he happens to be right : da la casualidad de que tiene razón>

happening [ˈhæpənɪŋ] *n* : suceso *m*, acontecimiento *m*

happiness [ˈhæpinəs] *n* : felicidad *f*, dicha *f*

happy [ˈhæpi] *adj* **-pier; -est 1** JOYFUL : feliz, contento, alegre **2** FORTUNATE : afortunado, feliz — **happily** [-pəli] *adv*

happy–go–lucky [ˈhæpigoːˈlʌki] *adj* : despreocupado

harangue[1] [həˈræŋ] *vt* **-rangued; -ranguing** : arengar

harangue[2] *n* : arenga *f*

harass [həˈræs, ˈhærəs] *vt* **1** BESIEGE, HOUND : acosar, asediar, hostigar **2** ANNOY : molestar

harassment [həˈræsmənt, ˈhærəsmənt] *n* : acoso *m*, hostigamiento *m* <sexual harrassment : acoso sexual>

harbinger [ˈhɑrbɪndʒər] *n* **1** HERALD : heraldo *m*, precursor *m* **2** OMEN : presagio *m*

harbor[1] [ˈhɑrbər] *vt* **1** SHELTER : dar refugio a, albergar **2** CHERISH, KEEP : abrigar, guardar, albergar <to harbor doubts : guardar dudas>

harbor[2] *n* **1** REFUGE : refugio *m* **2** PORT : puerto *m*

hard[1] [ˈhɑrd] *adv* **1** FORCEFULLY : fuerte, con fuerza <the wind blew hard : el viento sopló fuerte> **2** STRENUOUSLY : duro, mucho <to work hard : trabajar duro> **3 to take something hard** : tomarse algo muy mal, estar muy afectado por algo

hard[2] *adj* **1** FIRM, SOLID : duro, firme, sólido **2** DIFFICULT : difícil, arduo **3** SEVERE : severo, duro <a hard winter : un invierno severo> **4** UNFEELING : insensible, duro **5** DILIGENT : diligente <to be a hard worker : ser muy trabajador> **6 hard liquor** : bebidas *fpl* fuertes **7 hard water** : agua *f* dura

harden [ˈhɑrdən] *vt* : endurecer

hardheaded [,hɑrdˈhɛdəd] *adj* **1** STUBBORN : testarudo, terco **2** REALISTIC : realista, práctico — **hardheadedly** *adv*

hard–hearted [,hɑrdˈhɑrt̬əd] *adj* : despiadado, insensible — **hard–heartedly** *adv*

hard–heartedness [,hɑrdˈhɑrt̬ədnəs] *n* : dureza *f* de corazón

hardly [ˈhɑrdli] *adv* **1** SCARCELY : apenas, casi <I hardly knew her : apenas la conocía> <hardly ever : casi nunca> **2** NOT : difícilmente, poco, no <they can hardly blame me! : ¡difícilmente pueden echarme la culpa!> <it's hardly likely : es poco probable>

hardness [ˈhardnəs] *n* **1** FIRMNESS : dureza *f* **2** DIFFICULTY : dificultad *f* **3** SEVERITY : severidad *f*

hardship [ˈhardˌʃɪp] *n* : dificultad *f,* privación *f*

hardware [ˈhardˌwær] *n* **1** TOOLS : ferretería *f* **2** : hardware *m* (de una computadora)

hardwood [ˈhardˌwʊd] *n* : madera *f* dura, madera *f* noble

hardy [ˈhardi] *adj* **-dier; -est** : fuerte, robusto, resistente (dícese de las plantas) — **hardily** [-dəli] *adv*

hare [ˈhær] *n, pl* **hare** *or* **hares** : liebre *f*

harebrained [ˈhærˌbreɪnd] *adj* : estúpido, absurdo, disparatado

harelip [ˈhærˌlɪp] *n* : labio *m* leporino

harem [ˈhærəm] *n* : harén *m*

hark [ˈhark] *vi* **1** (*used only in the imperative*) LISTEN : escuchar **2 hark back** RETURN : volver **3 hark back** RECALL : recordar

harlequin [ˈharlɪkən, -kwən] *n* : arlequín *m*

harm[1] [ˈharm] *vt* : hacerle daño a, perjudicar

harm[2] *n* : daño *m,* perjuicio *m*

harmful [ˈharmfəl] *adj* : dañino, perjudicial — **harmfully** *adv*

harmless [ˈharmləs] *adj* : inofensivo, inocuo — **harmlessly** *adv*

harmlessness [ˈharmləsnəs] *n* : inocuidad *f*

harmonic [harˈmanɪk] *adj* : armónico — **harmonically** [-nɪkli] *adv*

harmonica [harˈmanɪkə] *n* : armónica *f*

harmonious [harˈmoːniəs] *adj* : armonioso — **harmoniously** *adv*

harmonize [ˈharməˌnaɪz] *v* **-nized; -nizing** : armonizar

harmony [ˈharməni] *n, pl* **-nies** : armonía *f*

harness[1] [ˈharnəs] *vt* **1** : enjaezar (un animal) **2** UTILIZE : utilizar, aprovechar

harness[2] *n* : arreos *mpl,* guarniciones *fpl,* arnés *m*

harp[1] [ˈharp] *vi* **to harp on** : insistir sobre, machacar sobre

harp[2] *n* : arpa *m*

harpist [ˈharpɪst] *n* : arpista *mf*

harpoon[1] [harˈpuːn] *vt* : arponear

harpoon[2] *n* : arpón *m*

harpsichord [ˈharpsɪˌkɔrd] *n* : clavicémbalo *m*

harrow[1] [ˈhærˌoː] *vt* **1** CULTIVATE : gradar, labrar (la tierra) **2** TORMENT : atormentar

harrow[2] *n* : grada *f,* rastra *f*

harry [ˈhæri] *vt* **-ried; -rying** HARASS : acosar, hostigar

harsh [ˈharʃ] *adj* **1** ROUGH : áspero **2** SEVERE : duro, severo **3** : discordante (dícese de los sonidos) — **harshly** *adv*

harshness [ˈharʃnəs] *n* **1** ROUGHNESS : aspereza *f* **2** SEVERITY : dureza *f,* severidad *f*

harvest[1] [ˈharvəst] *v* : cosechar

harvest[2] *n* **1** HARVESTING : siega *f,* recolección *f* **2** CROP : cosecha *f*

harvester [ˈharvəstər] *n* : segador *m,* -dora *f;* cosechadora *f* (máquina)

has → **have**

hash[1] [ˈhæʃ] *vt* **1** MINCE : picar **2 to hash over** DISCUSS : discutir, repasar

hash[2] *n* **1** : picadillo *m* (comida) **2** JUMBLE : revoltijo *m,* fárrago *m*

hasn't [ˈhæzənt] (*contraction of* **has not**) → **has**

hasp [ˈhæsp] *n* : picaporte *m,* pestillo *m*

hassle[1] [ˈhæsəl] *vt* **-sled; -sling** : fastidiar, molestar

hassle[2] *n* **1** ARGUMENT : discusión *f,* disputa *f,* bronca *f* **2** FIGHT : pelea *f,* riña *f* **3** BOTHER, TROUBLE : problemas *mpl,* lío *m*

hassock [ˈhæsək] *n* **1** CUSHION : almohadón *m,* cojín *m* **2** FOOTSTOOL : escabel *m*

haste [ˈheɪst] *n* **1** : prisa *f,* apuro *m* **2 to make haste** : darse prisa, apurarse

hasten [ˈheɪsən] *vt* : acelerar, precipitar — *vi* : apresurarse, apurarse

hasty [ˈheɪsti] *adj* **hastier; -est 1** HURRIED, QUICK : rápido, apresurado, apurado **2** RASH : precipitado — **hastily** [-təli] *adv*

hat [ˈhæt] *n* : sombrero *m*

hatch[1] [ˈhætʃ] *vt* **1** : incubar, empollar (huevos) **2** DEVISE : idear, tramar — *vi* : salir del cascarón

hatch[2] *n* : escotilla *f*

hatchery [ˈhætʃəri] *n, pl* **-ries** : criadero *m*

hatchet [ˈhætʃət] *n* : hacha *f*

hatchway [ˈhætʃˌweɪ] *n* : escotilla *f*

hate[1] [ˈheɪt] *vt* **hated; hating** : odiar, aborrecer, detestar

hate[2] *n* : odio *m*

hateful [ˈheɪtfəl] *adj* : odioso, aborrecible, detestable — **hatefully** *adv*

hatred [ˈheɪtrəd] *n* : odio *m*

hatter [ˈhætər] *n* : sombrerero *m,* -ra *f*

haughtiness [ˈhɔ̌tinəs] *n* : altanería *f,* altivez *f*

haughty [ˈhɔ̌ti] *adj* **-tier; -est** : altanero, altivo — **haughtily** [-ṭəli] *adv*

haul[1] [ˈhɔl] *vt* **1** DRAG, PULL : arrastrar, jalar **2** TRANSPORT : transportar

haul[2] *n* **1** PULL : tirón *m,* jalón *m* **2** CATCH : redada *f* **3** JOURNEY : viaje *m,* trayecto *m* <it's a long haul : es un trayecto largo>

haulage [ˈhɔlɪdʒ] *n* : transporte *m,* tiro *m*

hauler [ˈhɔlər] *n* : transportista *mf*

haunch [ˈhɔntʃ] *n* **1** HIP : cadera *f* **2 haunches** *npl* HINDQUARTERS : ancas *fpl*, cuartos *mpl* traseros

haunt[1] [ˈhɔnt] *vt* **1** : aparecer en (dícese de un fantasma) **2** FREQUENT : frecuentar, rondar **3** PREOCCUPY : perseguir, obsesionar

haunt[2] *n* : guarida *f* (de animales o ladrones), lugar *m* predilecto

haunting [ˈhɔntɪŋ] *adj* : obsesionante, evocador — **hauntingly** *adv*

have [ˈhæv, *in sense 3 as an auxiliary verb usu* ˈhæf] *v* **had** [ˈhæd]; **having; has** [ˈhæz, *in sense 3 as an auxiliary verb usu* ˈhæs] *vt* **1** POSSESS : tener <do you have change? : ¿tienes cambio?> **2** EXPERIENCE, UNDERGO : tener, experimentar, sufrir <I have a toothache : tengo un dolor de muelas> **3** INCLUDE : tener, incluir <April has 30 days : abril tiene 30 días> **4** CONSUME : comer, tomar **5** RECEIVE : tener, recibir <he had my permission : tenía mi permiso> **6** ALLOW : permitir, dejar <I won't have it! : ¡no lo permitiré!> **7** HOLD : hacer <to have a party : dar una fiesta> <to have a meeting : convocar una reunión> **8** HOLD : tener <he had me in his power : me tenía en su poder> **9** BEAR : tener (niños) **10** (*indicating causation*) <she had a dress made : mandó hacer un vestido> <to have one's hair cut : cortarse el pelo> — *v aux* **1** : haber <she has been very busy : ha estado muy ocupada> <I've lived here three years : hace tres años que vivo aquí> **2** (*used in tags*) <you've finished, haven't you? : ha terminado, ¿no?> **3 to have to** : deber, tener que <we have to leave : tenemos que salir>

haven [ˈheɪvən] *n* : refugio *m*

havoc [ˈhævək] *n* **1** DESTRUCTION : estragos *mpl*, destrucción *f* **2** CHAOS, DISORDER : desorden *m*, caos *m*

Hawaiian[1] [həˈwaɪən] *adj* : hawaiano

Hawaiian[2] *n* : hawaiano *m*, -na *f*

hawk[1] [ˈhɔk] *vt* : pregonar, vender (mercancías) en la calle

hawk[2] *n* : halcón *m*

hawker [ˈhɔkər] *n* : vendedor *m*, -dora *f* ambulante

hawthorn [ˈhɔˌθɔrn] *n* : espino *m*

hay [ˈheɪ] *n* : heno *m*

hay fever *n* : fiebre *f* del heno

hayloft [ˈheɪˌlɔft] *n* : pajar *m*

hayseed [ˈheɪˌsiːd] *n* : palurdo *m*, -da *f*

haystack [ˈheɪˌstæk] *n* : almiar *m*

haywire [ˈheɪˌwaɪr] *adj* : descompuesto, desbaratado <to go haywire : estropearse>

hazard[1] [ˈhæzərd] *vt* : arriesgar, aventurar

hazard[2] *n* **1** DANGER : peligro *m*, riesgo *m* **2** CHANCE : azar *m*

hazardous [ˈhæzərdəs] *adj* : arriesgado, peligroso

haze[1] [ˈheɪz] *vt* **hazed; hazing** : abrumar, acosar

haze[2] *n* : bruma *f*, neblina *f*

hazel [ˈheɪzəl] *n* **1** : avellano *m* (árbol) **2** : color *m* avellana

hazelnut [ˈheɪzəlˌnʌt] *n* : avellana *f*

haziness [ˈheɪzinəs] *n* **1** MISTINESS : nebulosidad *f* **2** VAGUENESS : vaguedad *f*

hazy [ˈheɪzi] *adj* **hazier; -est 1** MISTY : brumoso, neblinoso, nebuloso **2** VAGUE : vago, confuso

he [ˈhiː] *pron* : él

head[1] [ˈhɛd] *vt* **1** LEAD : encabezar **2** DIRECT : dirigir — *vi* : dirigirse

head[2] *adj* MAIN : principal <the head office : la oficina central, la sede>

head[3] *n* **1** : cabeza *f* <from head to foot : de pies a cabeza> **2** MIND : mente *f*, cabeza *f* **3** TIP, TOP : cabeza *f* (de un clavo, un martillo, etc.), cabecera *f* (de una mesa o un río), punta *f* (de una flecha), flor *m* (de un repollo, etc.), encabezamiento *m* (de una carta, etc.), espuma *f* (de cerveza) **4** DIRECTOR, LEADER : director *m*, -tora *f*; jefe *m*, -fa *f*; cabeza *f* (de una familia) **5** : cara *f* (de una moneda) <heads or tails : cara o cruz> **6** : cabeza *f* <500 head of cattle : 500 cabezas de ganado> <$10 a head : $10 por cabeza> **7 to come to a head** : llegar a un punto crítico

headache [ˈhɛdˌeɪk] *n* : dolor *m* de cabeza, jaqueca *f*

headband [ˈhɛdˌbænd] *n* : cinta *f* del pelo

headdress [ˈhɛdˌdrɛs] *n* : tocado *m*

headfirst [ˈhɛdˈfərst] *adv* : de cabeza

headgear [ˈhɛdˌgɪr] *n* : gorro *m*, casco *m*, sombrero *m*

heading [ˈhɛdɪŋ] *n* **1** DIRECTION : dirección *f* **2** TITLE : encabezamiento *m*, título *m* **3** : membrete *m* (de una carta)

headland [ˈhɛdlənd, -ˌlænd] *n* : cabo *m*

headlight [ˈhɛdˌlaɪt] *n* : faro *m*, foco *m*, farol *m Mex*

headline [ˈhɛdˌlaɪn] *n* : titular *m*

headlong[1] [ˈhɛdˈlɔŋ] *adv* **1** HEADFIRST : de cabeza **2** HASTILY : precipitadamente

headlong[2] [ˈhɛdˌlɔŋ] *adj* : precipitado

headmaster [ˈhɛdˌmæstər] *n* : director *m*

headmistress [ˈhɛdˌmɪstrəs, -ˈmɪs-] *n* : directora *f*

head–on [ˈhɛdˈɑn, -ˈɔn] *adv & adj* : de frente

headphones [ˈhɛdˌfoːnz] *npl* : audífonos *mpl*, cascos *mpl*

headquarters [ˈhɛdˌkwɔrt̬ərz] *ns & pl* **1** SEAT : oficina *f* central, sede *f* **2** : cuartel *m* general (de los militares)

headrest [ˈhɛdˌrɛst] *n* : apoyacabezas *m*

headship [ˈhɛdˌʃɪp] *n* : dirección *f*

head start *n* : ventaja *f*

headstone [ˈhɛdˌstoːn] *n* : lápida *f*

headstrong [ˈhɛdˈstrɔŋ] *adj* : testarudo, obstinado, empecinado
headwaiter [ˈhɛdˈweɪt̬ər] *n* : jefe *m,* -fa *f* de comedor
headwaters [ˈhɛdˌwɔt̬ərz, -ˌwɑ-] *npl* : cabecera *f*
headway [ˈhɛdˌweɪ] *n* : progreso *m* <to make headway against : avanzar contra>
heady [ˈhɛdi] *adj* **headier; -est 1** INTOXICATING : embriagador, excitante **2** SHREWD : astuto, sagaz
heal [ˈhiːl] *vt* : curar, sanar — *vi* **1** : sanar, curarse **2 to heal up** : cicatrizarse
healer [ˈhiːlər] *n* : curador *m,* -dora *f*
health [ˈhɛlθ] *n* : salud *f*
healthful [ˈhɛlθfəl] *adj* : saludable, salubre — **healthfully** *adv*
healthy [ˈhɛlθi] *adj* **healthier; -est** : sano, bien — **healthily** [-θəli] *adv*
heap[1] [ˈhiːp] *vt* **1** PILE : amontonar, apilar **2** SHOWER : colmar
heap[2] *n* : montón *m,* pila *f*
hear [ˈhɪr] *v* **heard** [ˈhərd]; **hearing** *vt* **1** : oír <do you hear me? : ¿me oyes?> **2** HEED : oír, prestar atención a **3** LEARN : oír, enterarse de — *vi* **1** : oír <to hear about : oír hablar de> **2 to hear from** : tener noticias de
hearing [ˈhɪrɪŋ] *n* **1** : oído *m* <hard of hearing : duro de oído> **2** : vista *f* (en un tribunal) **3** ATTENTION : consideración *f,* oportunidad *f* de expresarse **4** EARSHOT : alcance *m* del oído
hearing aid *n* : audífono *m*
hearken [ˈhɑrkən] *vt* : escuchar
hearsay [ˈhɪrˌseɪ] *n* : rumores *mpl*
hearse [ˈhərs] *n* : coche *m* fúnebre
heart [ˈhɑrt] *n* **1** : corazón *m* **2** CENTER, CORE : corazón *m,* centro *m* <the heart of the matter : el meollo del asunto> **3** FEELINGS : corazón *m,* sentimientos *mpl* <a broken heart : un corazón destrozado> <to have a good heart : tener buen corazón> <to take something to heart : tomarse algo a pecho> **4** COURAGE : valor *m,* corazón *m* <to take heart : animarse, cobrar ánimos> **5 hearts** *npl* : corazones *mpl* (en juegos de naipes) **6 by heart** : de memoria
heartache [ˈhɑrt̬ˌeɪk] *n* : pena *f,* angustia *f*
heart attack *n* : infarto *m,* ataque *m* al corazón
heartbeat [ˈhɑrtˌbiːt] *n* : latido *m* (del corazón)
heartbreak [ˈhɑrtˌbreɪk] *n* : congoja *f,* angustia *f*
heartbreaking [ˈhɑrtˌbreɪkɪŋ] *adj* : desgarrador, que parte el corazón
heartbroken [ˈhɑrtˌbroːkən] *adj* : desconsolado, destrozado
heartburn [ˈhɑrtˌbərn] *n* : acidez *f* estomacal
hearten [ˈhɑrtən] *vt* : alentar, animar
hearth [ˈhɑrθ] *n* : hogar *m,* chimenea *f*
heartily [ˈhɑrt̬əli] *adv* **1** ENTHUSIASTICALLY : de buena gana, con entusiasmo **2** TOTALLY : totalmente, completamente
heartless [ˈhɑrtləs] *adj* : desalmado, despiadado, cruel
heartsick [ˈhɑrtˌsɪk] *adj* : abatido, desconsolado
heartstrings [ˈhɑrtˌstrɪŋz] *npl* : fibras *fpl* del corazón
heartwarming [ˈhɑrtˌwɔrmɪŋ] *adj* : conmovedor, emocionante
hearty [ˈhɑrt̬i] *adj* **heartier; -est 1** CORDIAL, WARM : cordial, caluroso **2** STRONG : fuerte <to have a hearty appetite : ser de buen comer> **3** SUBSTANTIAL : abundante, sustancioso <a hearty breakfast : un desayuno abundante>
heat[1] [ˈhiːt] *vt* : calentar
heat[2] *n* **1** WARMTH : calor *m* **2** HEATING : calefacción *f* **3** EXCITEMENT : calor *m,* entusiasmo *m* <in the heat of the moment : en el calor del momento> **4** ESTRUS : celo *m*
heated [ˈhiːt̬əd] *adj* **1** WARMED : calentado **2** IMPASSIONED : acalorado, apasionado
heater [ˈhiːt̬ər] *n* : calentador *m,* estufa *f,* calefactor *m*
heath [ˈhiːθ] *n* **1** MOOR : brezal *m,* páramo *m* **2** HEATHER : brezo *m*
heathen[1] [ˈhiːðən] *adj* : pagano
heathen[2] *n, pl* **-thens** *or* **-then** : pagano *m,* -na *f;* infiel *mf*
heather [ˈhɛðər] *n* : brezo *m*
heave[1] [ˈhiːv] *v* **heaved** *or* **hove** [ˈhoːv]; **heaving** *vt* **1** LIFT, RAISE : levantar con esfuerzo **2** HURL : lanzar, tirar **3 to heave a sigh** : echar un suspiro, suspirar — *vi* **1** : subir y bajar, palpitar (dícese del pecho) **2 to heave up** RISE : levantarse
heave[2] *n* **1** EFFORT : gran esfuerzo *m* (para levantar algo) **2** THROW : lanzamiento *m*
heaven [ˈhɛvən] *n* **1** : cielo *m* <for heaven's sake : por Dios> **2 heavens** *npl* SKY : cielo *m* <the heavens opened up : empezó a llover a cántaros>
heavenly [ˈhɛvənli] *adj* **1** : celestial, celeste **2** DELIGHTFUL : divino, encantador
heavily [ˈhɛvəli] *adv* **1** : pesadamente, con mucho peso **2** LABORIOUSLY : trabajosamente, penosamente **3** : mucho
heaviness [ˈhɛvinəs] *n* : peso *m,* pesadez *f*
heavy [ˈhɛvi] *adj* **heavier; -est 1** WEIGHTY : pesado **2** DENSE, THICK : denso, espeso, grueso **3** BURDENSOME : oneroso, gravoso **4** PROFOUND : profundo **5** SLUGGISH : lento, tardo **6** STOUT : corpulento **7** SEVERE : severo, duro, fuerte
heavy–duty [ˈhɛviˈduːt̬i, -ˈdjuː-] *adj* : muy resistente, fuerte
heavyweight [ˈhɛviˌweɪt] *n* : peso *m* pesado (en deportes)

Hebrew[1] [ˈhiːˌbruː] *adj* : hebreo

Hebrew[2] *n* **1** : hebreo *m,* -brea *f* **2** : hebreo *m* (idioma)

heckle [ˈhɛkəl] *vt* **-led; -ling** : interrumpir (a un orador)

hectic [ˈhɛktɪk] *adj* : agitado, ajetreado — **hectically** [-tɪkli] *adv*

he'd [ˈhiːd] (*contraction of* **he had** *or* **he would**) → **have, would**

hedge[1] [ˈhɛdʒ] *v* **hedged; hedging** *vt* **1** : cercar con un seto **2 to hedge one's bet** : cubrirse — *vi* **1** : dar rodeos, contestar con evasivas **2 to hedge against** : cubrirse contra, protegerse contra

hedge[2] *n* **1** : seto *m* vivo **2** SAFEGUARD : salvaguardia *f,* protección *f*

hedgehog [ˈhɛdʒˌhɔg, -hɑg] *n* : erizo *m*

heed[1] [ˈhiːd] *vt* : prestar atención a, hacer caso de

heed[2] *n* : atención *f*

heedless [ˈhiːdləs] *adj* : descuidado, despreocupado, inconsciente <to be heedless of : hacer caso omiso de> — **heedlessly** *adv*

heel[1] [ˈhiːl] *vi* : inclinarse

heel[2] *n* : talón *m* (del pie), tacón *m* (de calzado)

heft [ˈhɛft] *vt* : sopesar

hefty [ˈhɛfti] *adj* **heftier; -est** : robusto, fornido, pesado

heifer [ˈhɛfər] *n* : novilla *f*

height [ˈhaɪt] *n* **1** PEAK : cumbre *f,* cima *f,* punto *m* alto <at the height of her career : en la cumbre de su carrera> <the height of stupidity : el colmo de la estupidez> **2** TALLNESS : estatura *f* (de una persona), altura *f* (de un objeto) **3** ALTITUDE : altura *f*

heighten [ˈhaɪtən] *vt* **1** : hacer más alto **2** INTENSIFY : aumentar, intensificar — *vi* : aumentarse, intensificarse

heinous [ˈheɪnəs] *adj* : atroz, abominable, nefando

heir [ˈær] *n* : heredero *m,* -ra *f*

heiress [ˈærəs] *n* : heredera *f*

heirloom [ˈærˌluːm] *n* : reliquia *f* de familia

held → **hold**

helicopter [ˈhɛləˌkɑptər] *n* : helicóptero *m*

helium [ˈhiːliəm] *n* : helio *m*

hell [ˈhɛl] *n* : infierno *m*

he'll [ˈhiːl, ˈhɪl] (*contraction of* **he shall** *or* **he will**) → **shall, will**

hellish [ˈhɛlɪʃ] *adj* : horroroso, infernal

hello [həˈloː, hɛ-] *interj* : ¡hola!

helm [ˈhɛlm] *n* **1** : timón *m* **2 to take the helm** : tomar el mando

helmet [ˈhɛlmət] *n* : casco *m*

help[1] [ˈhɛlp] *vt* **1** AID, ASSIST : ayudar, auxiliar, socorrer, asistir **2** ALLEVIATE : aliviar **3** SERVE : servir <help yourself! : ¡sírvete!> **4** AVOID : evitar <it can't be helped : no lo podemos evitar, no hay más remedio> <I couldn't help smiling : no pude menos que sonreír>

help[2] *n* **1** ASSISTANCE : ayuda *f* <help! : ¡socorro!, ¡auxilio!> **2** STAFF : personal *m* (en una oficina), servicio *m* doméstico

helper [ˈhɛlpər] *n* : ayudante *mf*

helpful [ˈhɛlpfəl] *adj* **1** OBLIGING : servicial, amable, atento **2** USEFUL : útil, práctico — **helpfully** *adv*

helpfulness [ˈhɛlpfəlnəs] *n* **1** KINDNESS : bondad *f,* amabilidad *f* **2** USEFULNESS : utilidad *f*

helping [ˈhɛlpɪŋ] *n* : porción *f*

helpless [ˈhɛlpləs] *adj* **1** POWERLESS : incapaz, impotente **2** DEFENSELESS : indefenso

helplessly [ˈhɛlpləsli] *adv* : en vano, inútilmente

helplessness [ˈhɛlpləsnəs] *n* POWERLESSNESS : incapacidad *f,* impotencia *f*

helter–skelter [ˌhɛltərˈskɛltər] *adv* : atropelladamente, precipitadamente

hem[1] [ˈhɛm] *vt* **hemmed; hemming 1** : dobladillar **2 to hem in** : encerrar

hem[2] *n* : dobladillo *m,* bastilla *f*

hemisphere [ˈhɛməˌsfɪr] *n* : hemisferio *m*

hemispheric [ˌhɛməˈsfɪrɪk, -ˈsfɛr-] *or* **hemispherical** [-ɪkəl] *adj* : hemisférico

hemlock [ˈhɛmˌlɑk] *n* : cicuta *f*

hemoglobin [ˈhiːməˌgloːbən] *n* : hemoglobina *f*

hemophilia [ˌhiːməˈfɪliə] *n* : hemofilia *f*

hemorrhage[1] [ˈhɛmərɪdʒ] *vi* **-rhaged; -rhaging** : sufrir una hemorragia

hemorrhage[2] *n* : hemorragia *f*

hemorrhoids [ˈhɛməˌrɔɪdz, ˈhɛmˌrɔɪdz] *npl* : hemorroides *fpl,* almorranas *fpl*

hemp [ˈhɛmp] *n* : cáñamo *m*

hen [ˈhɛn] *n* : gallina *f*

hence [ˈhɛnts] *adv* **1** : de aquí, de ahí <10 years hence : de aquí a 10 años> <a dog bit me, hence my dislike of animals : un perro me mordió, de ahí mi aversión a los animales> **2** THEREFORE : por lo tanto, por consiguiente

henceforth [ˈhɛntsˌforθ, ˌhɛntsˈ-] *adv* : de ahora en adelante

henchman [ˈhɛntʃmən] *n, pl* **-men** [-mən, -ˌmɛn] : secuaz *mf,* esbirro *m*

henpeck [ˈhɛnˌpɛk] *vt* : dominar (al marido)

hepatitis [ˌhɛpəˈtaɪtəs] *n, pl* **-titides** [-ˈtɪtəˌdiːz] : hepatitis *f*

her[1] [ˈhər] *adj* : su, sus, de ella <her house : su casa, la casa de ella>

her[2] [ˈhər, ər] *pron* **1** (*used as direct object*) : la <I saw her yesterday : la vi ayer> **2** (*used as indirect object*) : le, se <he gave her the book : le dio el libro> <he sent it to her : se lo mandó> **3** (*used as object of a preposition*) : ella <we did it for her : lo hicimos por ella> <taller than her : más alto que ella>

herald[1] [ˈhɛrəld] *vt* ANNOUNCE **:** anunciar, proclamar

herald[2] *n* **1** MESSENGER **:** heraldo *m* **2** HARBINGER **:** precursor *m*

heraldic [hɛˈrældɪk, hə-] *adj* **:** heráldico

heraldry [ˈhɛrəldri] *n, pl* **-ries :** heráldica *f*

herb [ˈərb, ˈhərb] *n* **:** hierba *f*

herbal [ˈərbəl, ˈhər-] *adj* **:** herbario

herbicide [ˈərbəˌsaɪd, ˈhər-] *n* **:** herbicida *m*

herbivore [ˈərbəˌvor, ˈhər-] *n* **:** herbívoro *m*

herbivorous [ˌərˈbɪvərəs, ˌhər-] *adj* **:** herbívoro

herculean [ˌhərkjəˈliːən, ˌhərˈkjuːliən] *adj* **:** hercúleo, sobrehumano

herd[1] [ˈhərd] *vt* **:** reunir en manada, conducir en manada — *vi* **:** ir en manada (dícese de los animales), apiñarse (dícese de la gente)

herd[2] *n* **:** manada *f*

herder [ˈhərdər] → **herdsman**

herdsman [ˈhərdzmən] *n, pl* **-men** [-mən, -ˌmɛn] **:** vaquero *m* (de ganado), pastor *m* (de ovejas)

here [ˈhɪr] *adv* **1 :** aquí, acá <come here! : ¡ven acá!> <right here : aquí mismo> **2** NOW **:** en este momento, ahora, ya <here he comes : ya viene> <here it's three o'clock (already) : ahora son las tres> **3 :** en este punto <here we agree : estamos de acuerdo en este punto> **4 here you are! :** ¡toma!

hereabouts [ˈhɪrəˌbaʊts] *or* **hereabout** [-ˌbaʊt] *adv* **:** por aquí (cerca)

hereafter[1] [hɪrˈæftər] *adv* **1 :** de aquí en adelante, a continuación **2 :** en el futuro

hereafter[2] *n* **the hereafter :** el más allá

hereby [hɪrˈbaɪ] *adv* **:** por este medio

hereditary [həˈrɛdəˌtɛri] *adj* **:** hereditario

heredity [həˈrɛdəṭi] *n* **:** herencia *f*

herein [hɪrˈɪn] *adv* **:** aquí

hereof [hɪrˈʌv] *adv* **:** de aquí

hereon [hɪrˈɑn, -ˈɔn] *adv* **:** sobre esto

heresy [ˈhɛrəsi] *n, pl* **-sies :** herejía *f*

heretic [ˈhɛrəˌtɪk] *n* **:** hereje *mf*

heretical [həˈrɛṭɪkəl] *adj* **:** herético

hereto [hɪrˈtuː] *adv* **:** a esto

heretofore [ˈhɪrṭəˌfor] *adv* HITHERTO **:** hasta ahora

hereunder [hɪrˈʌndər] *adv* **:** a continuación, abajo

hereupon [hɪrəˈpɑn, -ˈpɔn] *adv* **:** con esto, en ese momento

herewith [hɪrˈwɪθ] *adv* **:** adjunto

heritage [ˈhɛrəṭɪdʒ] *n* **:** patrimonio *m* (nacional)

hermaphrodite [hərˈmæfrəˌdaɪt] *n* **:** hermafrodita *mf*

hermetic [hərˈmɛṭɪk] *adj* **:** hermético — **hermetically** [-ṭɪkli] *adv*

hermit [ˈhərmət] *n* **:** ermitaño *m*, -ña *f*; eremita *mf*

hernia [ˈhərniə] *n, pl* **-nias** *or* **-niae** [-niˌiː, -niˌaɪ] **:** hernia *f*

hero [ˈhiːˌroː, ˈhɪrˌoː] *n, pl* **-roes 1 :** héroe *m* **2** PROTAGONIST **:** protagonista *mf*

heroic [hɪˈroːɪk] *adj* **:** heroico — **heroically** [-ɪkli] *adv*

heroics [hɪˈroːɪks] *npl* **:** actos *mpl* heroicos

heroin [ˈhɛroən] *n* **:** heroína *f*

heroine [ˈhɛroən] *n* **1 :** heroína *f* **2** PROTAGONIST **:** protagonista *f*

heroism [ˈhɛroˌɪzəm] *n* **:** heroísmo *m*

heron [ˈhɛrən] *n* **:** garza *f*

herpes [ˈhərˌpiːz] *n* **:** herpes *m*

herpetology [ˌhərpəˈtɑlədʒi] *n* **:** herpetología *f*

herring [ˈhɛrɪŋ] *n, pl* **-ring** *or* **-rings :** arenque *m*

hers [ˈhərz] *pron* **:** suyo, -ya; suyos, -yas; de ella <these shoes are hers : estos zapatos son suyos> <hers are bigger : los de ella son más grandes>

herself [hərˈsɛlf] *pron* **1** (*used reflexively*) **:** se <she dressed herself : se vistió> **2** (*used emphatically*) **:** ella misma <she fixed it herself : lo arregló ella misma, lo arregló por sí sola>

hertz [ˈhərts, ˈhɛrts] *ns & pl* **:** hercio *m*

he's [ˈhiːz] (*contraction of* **he is** *or* **he has**) → **be, have**

hesitancy [ˈhɛzəṭəntsi] *n, pl* **-cies :** vacilación *f*, titubeo *m*, indecisión *f*

hesitant [ˈhɛzəṭənt] *adj* **:** titubeante, vacilante — **hesitantly** *adv*

hesitate [ˈhɛzəˌteɪt] *vi* **-tated; -tating :** vacilar, titubear

hesitation [ˌhɛzəˈteɪʃən] *n* **:** vacilación *f*, indecisión *f*, titubeo *m*

heterogeneous [ˌhɛṭərəˈdʒiːniəs, -njəs] *adj* **:** heterogéneo

heterosexual[1] [ˌhɛṭəroˈsɛkʃʊəl] *adj* **:** heterosexual

heterosexual[2] *n* **:** heterosexual *mf*

heterosexuality [ˌhɛṭəroˌsɛkʃʊˈæləṭi] *n* **:** heterosexualidad *f*

hew [ˈhjuː] *v* **hewed; hewed** *or* **hewn** [ˈhjuːn]; **hewing** *vt* **1** CUT **:** cortar, talar (árboles) **2** SHAPE **:** labrar, tallar — *vi* CONFORM **:** conformarse, ceñirse

hex[1] [ˈhɛks] *vt* **:** hacerle un maleficio (a alguien)

hex[2] *n* **:** maleficio *m*

hexagon [ˈhɛksəˌgɑn] *n* **:** hexágono *m*

hexagonal [hɛkˈsægənəl] *adj* **:** hexagonal

hey [ˈheɪ] *interj* **:** ¡eh!, ¡oye!

heyday [ˈheɪˌdeɪ] *n* **:** auge *m*, apogeo *m*

hi [ˈhaɪ] *interj* **:** ¡hola!

hiatus [haɪˈeɪṭəs] *n* **1 :** hiato *m* **2** PAUSE **:** pausa *f*

hibernate [ˈhaɪbərˌneɪt] *vi* **-nated; -nating :** hibernar, invernar

hibernation [ˌhaɪbərˈneɪʃən] *n* **:** hibernación *f*

hiccup[1] [ˈhɪkəp] *vi* **-cuped; -cuping :** hipar, tener hipo

hiccup[2] *n* : hipo *m* <to have the hiccups : tener hipo>

hick [ˈhɪk] *n* BUMPKIN : palurdo *m*, -da *f*

hickory [ˈhɪkəri] *n*, *pl* **-ries** : nogal *m* americano

hidden [ˈhɪdən] *adj* : oculto

hide[1] [ˈhaɪd] *v* **hid** [ˈhɪd]; **hidden** [ˈhɪdən] *or* **hid; hiding** *vt* **1** CONCEAL : esconder **2** ocultar <to hide one's motives : ocultar uno sus motivos> **3** SCREEN : tapar, no dejar ver — *vi* : esconderse

hide[2] *n* : piel *f*, cuero *m* <to save one's hide : salvar el pellejo>

hide–and–seek [ˈhaɪdəndˈsiːk] *n* **to play hide–and–seek** : jugar a las escondidas

hidebound [ˈhaɪdˌbaʊnd] *adj* : rígido, conservador

hideous [ˈhɪdiəs] *adj* : horrible, horroroso, espantoso — **hideously** *adv*

hideout [ˈhaɪdˌaʊt] *n* : guarida *f*, escondrijo *m*

hierarchical [ˌhaɪəˈrɑrkɪkəl] *adj* : jerárquico

hierarchy [ˈhaɪəˌrɑrki] *n*, *pl* **-chies** : jerarquía *f*

hieroglyphic [ˌhaɪərəˈglɪfɪk] *n* : jeroglífico *m*

hi–fi [ˈhaɪˈfaɪ] *n* **1** → **high fidelity 2** : equipo *m* de alta fidelidad

high[1] [ˈhaɪ] *adv* : alto

high[2] *adj* **1** TALL : alto <a high wall : una pared alta> **2** ELEVATED : alto, elevado <high prices : precios elevados> <high blood pressure : presión alta> **3** GREAT, IMPORTANT : grande, importante, alto <a high number : un número grande> <high society : alta sociedad> <high hopes : grandes esperanzas> **4** : alto (en música) **5** INTOXICATED : borracho, drogado

high[3] *n* **1** : récord *m*, punto *m* máximo <to reach an all-time high : batir el récord> **2** : zona *f* de alta presión (en meteorología) **3** *or* **high gear** : directa *f* **4 on high** : en las alturas

highbrow [ˈhaɪˌbraʊ] *n* : intelectual *mf*

higher [ˈhaɪər] *adj* : superior

high fidelity *n* : alta fidelidad *f*

high–flown [ˈhaɪˈfloːn] *adj* : altisonante

high–handed [ˈhaɪˈhændəd] *adj* : arbitrario

highlands [ˈhaɪləndz] *npl* : tierras *fpl* altas, altiplano *m*

highlight[1] [ˈhaɪˌlaɪt] *vt* **1** EMPHASIZE : destacar, poner en relieve, subrayar **2** : ser el punto culminante de

highlight[2] *n* : punto *m* culminante

highly [ˈhaɪli] *adv* **1** VERY : muy, sumamente **2** FAVORABLY : muy bien <to speak highly of : hablar muy bien de> <to think highly of : tener en mucho a>

highness [ˈhaɪnəs] *n* **1** HEIGHT : altura *f* **2 Highness** : Alteza *f* <Your Royal Highness : Su Alteza Real>

high–rise [ˈhaɪˌraɪz] *adj* : alto, de muchas plantas

high school *n* : escuela *f* superior, escuela *f* secundaria

high seas *npl* : alta mar *f*

high–spirited [ˈhaɪˈspɪrətəd] *adj* : vivaz, muy animado, brioso

high–strung [ˌhaɪˈstrʌŋ] *adj* : nervioso, excitable

highway [ˈhaɪˌweɪ] *n* : carretera *f*

highwayman [ˈhaɪˌweɪmən] *n*, *pl* **-men** [-mən, -ˌmɛn] : salteador *m* (de caminos), bandido *m*

hijack[1] [ˈhaɪˌdʒæk] *vt* : secuestrar

hijack[2] *n* : secuestro *m*

hijacker [ˈhaɪˌdʒækər] *n* : secuestrador *m*, -dora *f*

hike[1] [ˈhaɪk] *v* **hiked; hiking** *vi* : hacer una caminata — *vt* RAISE : subir

hike[2] *n* **1** : caminata *f*, excursión *f* **2** INCREASE : subida *f* (de precios)

hiker [ˈhaɪkər] *n* : excursionista *mf*

hilarious [hɪˈlæriəs, haɪˈ-] *adj* : muy divertido, hilarante

hilarity [hɪˈlærəti, haɪ-] *n* : hilaridad *f*

hill [ˈhɪl] *n* **1** : colina *f*, cerro *m* **2** SLOPE : cuesta *f*, pendiente *f*

hillbilly [ˈhɪlˌbɪli] *n*, *pl* **-lies** : palurdo *m*, -da *f* (de las montañas)

hillock [ˈhɪlək] *n* : loma *f*, altozano *m*, otero *m*

hillside [ˈhɪlˌsaɪd] *n* : ladera *f*, cuesta *f*

hilltop [ˈhɪlˌtɑp] *n* : cima *f*, cumbre *f*

hilly [ˈhɪli] *adj* **hillier; -est** : montañoso, accidentado

hilt [ˈhɪlt] *n* : puño *m*, empuñadura *f*

him [ˈhɪm, əm] *pron* **1** (*used as direct object*) : lo <I found him : lo encontré> **2** (*used as indirect object*) : le, se <we gave him a present : le dimos un regalo> <I sent it to him : se lo mandé> **3** (*used as object of a preposition*) : él <she was thinking of him : pensaba en él> <younger than him : más joven que él>

himself [hɪmˈsɛlf] *pron* **1** (*used reflexively*) : se <he washed himself : se lavó> **2** (*used emphatically*) : él mismo <he did it himself : lo hizo él mismo, lo hizo por sí solo>

hind[1] [ˈhaɪnd] *adj* : trasero, posterior <hind legs : patas traseras>

hind[2] *n* : cierva *f*

hinder [ˈhɪndər] *vt* : dificultar, impedir, estorbar

hindquarters [ˈhaɪndˌkwɔrtərz] *npl* : cuartos *mpl* traseros

hindrance [ˈhɪndrənts] *n* : estorbo *m*, obstáculo *m*, impedimento *m*

hindsight [ˈhaɪndˌsaɪt] *n* : retrospectiva *f* <with the benefit of hindsight : en retrospectiva, con la perspectiva que da la experiencia>

Hindu[1] [ˈhɪnˌduː] *adj* : hindú

Hindu[2] *n* : hindú *mf*

Hinduism [ˈhɪnduːˌɪzəm] *n* : hinduismo *m*

hinge[1] [ˈhɪndʒ] *v* **hinged; hinging** *vt* : unir con bisagras — *vi* **to hinge on** : depender de
hinge[2] *n* : bisagra *f,* gozne *m*
hint[1] [ˈhɪnt] *vt* : insinuar, dar a entender — *vi* : soltar indirectas
hint[2] *n* **1** INSINUATION : insinuación *f,* indirecta *f* **2** TIP : consejo *m,* sugerencia *f* **3** TRACE : pizca *f,* indicio *m*
hinterland [ˈhɪntərˌlænd, -lənd] *n* : interior *m* (de un país)
hip [ˈhɪp] *n* : cadera *f*
hippopotamus [ˌhɪpəˈpɑṭəməs] *n, pl* **-muses** *or* **-mi** [-ˌmaɪ] : hipopótamo *m*
hippo [ˈhɪpoː] *n, pl* **hippos** → **hippopotamus**
hire[1] [ˈhaɪr] *vt* **hired; hiring 1** EMPLOY : contratar, emplear **2** RENT : alquilar, arrendar
hire[2] *n* **1** RENT : alquiler *m* <for hire : se alquila> **2** WAGES : paga *f,* sueldo *m* **3** EMPLOYEE : empleado *m,* -da *f*
his[1] [ˈhɪz, ɪz] *adj* : su, sus, de él <his hat : su sombrero, el sombrero de él>
his[2] *pron* : suyo, -ya; suyos, suyas; de él <the decision is his : la decisión es suya> <it's his, not hers : es de él, no de ella>
Hispanic[1] [hɪˈspænɪk] *adj* : hispano, hispánico
Hispanic[2] *n* : hispano *m,* -na *f;* hispánico *m,* -ca *f*
hiss[1] [ˈhɪs] *vi* : sisear, silbar — *vt* : decir entre dientes
hiss[2] *n* : siseo *m,* silbido *m*
historian [hɪˈstɔriən] *n* : historiador *m,* -dora *f*
historic [hɪˈstɔrɪk] *or* **historical** [-ɪkəl] *adj* : histórico — **historically** [-ɪkli] *adv*
history [ˈhɪstəri] *n, pl* **-ries 1** : historia *f* **2** RECORD : historial *m*
histrionics [ˌhɪstriˈɑnɪks] *ns & pl* : histrionismo *m*
hit[1] [ˈhɪt] *v* **hit; hitting** *vt* **1** STRIKE : golpear, pegar, batear (una pelota) <he hit the dog : le pegó al perro> **2** : chocar contra, dar con, dar en (el blanco) <the car hit a tree : el coche chocó contra un árbol> **3** AFFECT : afectar <the news hit us hard : la noticia nos afectó mucho> **4** ENCOUNTER : tropezar con, toparse con <to hit a snag : tropezar con un obstáculo> **5** REACH : llegar a, alcanzar <the price hit $10 a pound : el precio alcanzó los $10 dólares por libra> <to hit town : llegar a la ciudad> <to hit the headlines : ser noticia> **6 to hit on** *or* **to hit upon** : dar con — *vi* : golpear
hit[2] *n* **1** BLOW : golpe *m* **2** : impacto *m* (de un arma) **3** SUCCESS : éxito *m*
hitch[1] [ˈhɪtʃ] *vt* **1** : mover con sacudidas **2** ATTACH : enganchar, atar, amarriar **3** → **hitchhike 4 to hitch up** : subirse (los pantalones, etc.)
hitch[2] *n* **1** JERK : tirón *m,* jalón *m* **2** OBSTACLE : obstáculo *m,* impedimento *m,* tropiezo *m*
hitchhike [ˈhɪtʃˌhaɪk] *vi* **-hiked; -hiking** : hacer autostop, ir de aventón *Col, Mex fam*
hitchhiker [ˈhɪtʃˌhaɪkər] *n* : autostopista *mf*
hither [ˈhɪðər] *adv* : acá, por aquí
hitherto [ˈhɪðərˌtuː, ˌhɪðərˈ-] *adv* : hasta ahora
hitter [ˈhɪṭər] *n* BATTER : bateador *m,* -dora *f*
HIV [ˌeɪtʃˌaɪˈviː] *n* : VIH *m,* virus *m* del sida
hive [ˈhaɪv] *n* **1** : colmena *f* **2** SWARM : enjambre *m* **3** : lugar *m* muy activo <a hive of activity : un hervidero de actividad>
hives [ˈhaɪvz] *ns & pl* : urticaria *f*
hoard[1] [ˈhord] *vt* : acumular, atesorar
hoard[2] *n* : tesoro *m,* reserva *f,* provisión *f*
hoarfrost [ˈhorˌfrɔst] *n* : escarcha *f*
hoarse [ˈhors] *adj* **hoarser; -est** : ronco — **hoarsely** *adv*
hoarseness [ˈhorsnəs] *n* : ronquera *f*
hoary [ˈhori] *adj* **hoarier; -est 1** : cano, canoso **2** OLD : vetusto, antiguo
hoax[1] [ˈhoːks] *vt* : engañar, embaucar, bromar
hoax[2] *n* : engaño *m,* broma *f*
hobble[1] [ˈhɑbəl] *v* **-bled; -bling** *vi* LIMP : cojear, renguear — *vt* : manear (un animal)
hobble[2] *n* **1** LIMP : cojera *f,* rengo *m* **2** : maniota *f* (para un animal)
hobby [ˈhɑbi] *n, pl* **-bies** : pasatiempo *m,* afición *f*
hobgoblin [ˈhɑbˌgɑblən] *n* : duende *m*
hobnail [ˈhɑbˌneɪl] *n* : tachuela *f*
hobnob [ˈhɑbˌnɑb] *vi* **-nobbed; -nobbing** : codearse
hobo [ˈhoːˌboː] *n, pl* **-boes** : vagabundo *m,* -da *f*
hock[1] [ˈhɑk] *vt* PAWN : empeñar
hock[2] *n* **in hock** : empeñado
hockey [ˈhɑki] *n* : hockey *m*
hod [ˈhɑd] *n* : capacho *m* (de albañil)
hodgepodge [ˈhɑdʒˌpɑdʒ] *n* : mezcolanza *f*
hoe[1] [ˈhoː] *vt* **hoed; hoeing** : azadonar
hoe[2] *n* : azada *f,* azadón *m*
hog[1] [ˈhɔg, ˈhɑg] *vt* **hogged; hogging** : acaparar, monopolizar
hog[2] *n* **1** PIG : cerdo *m,* -da *f* **2** GLUTTON : glotón *m,* -tona *f*
hogshead [ˈhɔgzˌhɛd, ˈhɑgz-] *n* : tonel *m*
hoist[1] [ˈhɔɪst] *vt* : levantar, alzar, izar (una bandera, una vela)
hoist[2] *n* : grúa *f*
hold[1] [ˈhoːld] *v* **held** [ˈhɛld]; **holding** *vt* **1** POSSESS : tener <to hold office : ocupar un puesto> **2** RESTRAIN : detener, controlar <to hold one's temper : controlar su mal genio> **3** CLASP, GRASP : agarrar, coger <to hold hands : agarrarse de la mano> **4** : sujetar,

mantener fijo <hold this nail for me : sujétame este clavo> **5** CONTAIN : contener, dar cabida a **6** SUPPORT : aguantar, sostener **7** REGARD : considerar, tener <he held me responsible : me consideró responsable> **8** CONDUCT : celebrar (una reunión), realizar (un evento), mantener (una conversación) — *vi* **1** : aguantar, resistir <the rope will hold : la cuerda resistirá> **2** : ser válido, valer <my offer still holds : mi oferta todavía es válida> **3 to hold forth** : perorar, arengar **4 to hold to** : mantenerse firme en **5 to hold with** : estar de acuerdo con

hold[2] *n* **1** GRIP : agarre *m,* llave *f* (en deportes) **2** CONTROL : control *m,* dominio *m* <to get hold of oneself : controlarse> **3** DELAY : demora *f* <to put on hold : suspender temporalmente> **4** : bodega *f* (en un barco o un avión) **5 to get hold of** : conseguir, localizar

holder [ˈhoːldər] *n* : poseedor *m,* -dora *f;* titular *mf*

holdings [ˈhoːldɪŋz] *npl* : propiedades *fpl*

hold out *vi* **1** LAST : aguantar, durar **2** RESIST : resistir

holdup [ˈhoːld,ʌp] *n* **1** ROBBERY : atraco *m* **2** DELAY : retraso *m,* demora *f*

hold up *vt* **1** ROB : robarle (a alguien), atracar, asaltar **2** DELAY : retrasar

hole [ˈhoːl] *n* : agujero *m,* hoyo *m*

holiday [ˈhɑlə,deɪ] *n* **1** : día *m* feriado, fiesta *f* **2** VACATION : vacaciones *fpl*

holiness [ˈhoːlinəs] *n* **1** : santidad *f* **2 His Holiness** : Su Santidad

holistic [hoːˈlɪstɪk] *adj* : holístico

holler[1] [ˈhɑlər] *vi* : gritar, chillar

holler[2] *n* : grito *m,* chillido *m*

hollow[1] [ˈhɑ,loː] *vt or* **to hollow out** : ahuecar

hollow[2] *adj* **-lower; -est 1** : hueco, hundido (dícese de las mejillas, etc.), cavernoso (dícese de un sonido) **2** EMPTY, FALSE : vacío, falso

hollow[3] *n* **1** CAVITY : hueco *m,* depresión *f,* cavidad *f* **2** VALLEY : hondonada *f,* valle *m*

hollowness [ˈhɑ,loːnəs] *n* **1** HOLLOW : hueco *m,* cavidad *f* **2** FALSENESS : falsedad *f* **3** EMPTINESS : vacuidad *f*

holly [ˈhɑli] *n, pl* **-lies** : acebo *m*

hollyhock [ˈhɑli,hɑk] *n* : malvarrosa *f*

holocaust [ˈhɑlə,kɔst, ˈhoː-, ˈhɔ-] *n* : holocausto *m*

holster [ˈhoːlstər] *n* : pistolera *f*

holy [ˈhoːli] *adj* **-lier; -est** : santo, sagrado

Holy Ghost → **Holy Spirit**

Holy Spirit *n* **the Holy Spirit** : el Espíritu Santo

homage [ˈɑmɪdʒ, ˈhɑ-] *n* : homenaje *m*

home [ˈhoːm] *n* **1** : casa *f,* hogar *m,* domicilio *m* <to feel at home : sentirse en casa> **2** INSTITUTION : residencia *f,* asilo *m*

homecoming [ˈhoːm,kʌmɪŋ] *n* : regreso *m* (a casa)

homegrown [ˈhoːmˈgroːn] *adj* **1** : de cosecha propia **2** LOCAL : local

homeland [ˈhoːm,lænd] *n* : patria *f,* tierra *f* natal, terruño *m*

homeless [ˈhoːmləs] *adj* : sin hogar, sin techo

homely [ˈhoːmli] *adj* **-lier; -est 1** DOMESTIC : casero, hogareño **2** UGLY : feo, poco atractivo

homemade [ˈhoːmˈmeɪd] *adj* : casero, hecho en casa

homemaker [ˈhoːm,meɪkər] *n* : ama *f* de casa, persona *f* que se ocupa de la casa

home plate *n* : base *f* del bateador

home run *n* : jonrón *m*

homesick [ˈhoːm,sɪk] *adj* : nostálgico <to be homesick : echar de menos a la familia>

homesickness [ˈhoːm,sɪknəs] *n* : nostalgia *f,* morriña *f*

homespun [ˈhoːm,spʌn] *adj* : simple, sencillo

homestead [ˈhoːm,stɛd] *n* : estancia *f,* hacienda *f*

homeward[1] [ˈhoːmwərd] *or* **homewards** [-wərdz] *adv* : de vuelta a casa, hacia casa

homeward[2] *adj* : de vuelta, de regreso

homework [ˈhoːm,wərk] *n* : tarea *f,* deberes *mpl Spain,* asignación *f PRi*

homey [ˈhoːmi] *adj* **homier; -est** : hogareño

homicidal [,hɑməˈsaɪdəl, ,hoː-] *adj* : homicida

homicide [ˈhɑmə,saɪd, ˈhoː-] *n* : homicidio *m*

hominy [ˈhɑməni] *n* : maíz *m* descascarillado

homogeneous [,hoːməˈdʒiːniəs, -njəs] *adj* : homogéneo — **homogeneously** *adv*

homogenize [hoːˈmɑdʒə,naɪz, hə-] *vt* **-nized; -nizing** : homogeneizar

homograph [ˈhɑmə,græf, ˈhoː-] *n* : homógrafo *m*

homonym [ˈhɑmə,nɪm, ˈhoː-] *n* : homónimo *m*

homophone [ˈhɑmə,foːn, ˈhoː-] *n* : homófono *m*

homosexual[1] [,hoːməˈsɛkʃʊəl] *adj* : homosexual

homosexual[2] *n* : homosexual *mf*

homosexuality [,hoːmə,sɛkʃʊˈæləṭi] *n* : homosexualidad *f*

Honduran [hɑnˈdʊrən, -ˈdjʊr-] *n* : hondureño *m,* -ña *f* — **Honduran** *adj*

hone [ˈhoːn] *vt* **honed; honing** : afilar

honest [ˈɑnəst] *adj* : honesto, honrado — **honestly** *adv*

honesty [ˈɑnəsti] *n, pl* **-ties** : honestidad *f,* honradez *f*

honey [ˈhʌni] *n, pl* **-eys** : miel *f*

honeybee [ˈhʌni,biː] *n* : abeja *f*

honeycomb [ˈhʌni,koːm] *n* : panal *m*

honeymoon[1] [ˈhʌni,muːn] *vi* : pasar la luna de miel

honeymoon[2] *n* : luna *f* de miel

honeysuckle [ˈhʌni,sʌkəl] *n* : madreselva *f*

honk[1] [ˈhɑŋk, ˈhɔŋk] *vi* **1** : graznar (dícese del ganso) **2** : tocar la bocina (dícese de un vehículo), pitar

honk[2] *n* : graznido *m* (del ganso), bocinazo *m* (de un vehículo)

honor[1] [ˈɑnər] *vt* **1** RESPECT : honrar **2** : cumplir con <to honor one's word : cumplir con su palabra> **3** : aceptar (un cheque, etc.)

honor[2] *n* **1** : honor *m* <in honor of : en honor de> **2 honors** *npl* AWARDS : honores *mpl*, condecoraciones *fpl* **3 Your Honor** : Su Señoría

honorable [ˈɑnərəbəl] *adj* : honorable, honroso — **honorably** [-bli] *adv*

honorary [ˈɑnə,rɛri] *adj* : honorario

hood [ˈhʊd] *n* **1** : capucha *f* **2** : capó *m*, bonete *m Car* (de un automóvil)

hooded [ˈhʊdəd] *adj* : encapuchado

hoodlum [ˈhʊdləm, ˈhuːd-] *n* THUG : maleante *mf*, matón *m*

hoodwink [ˈhʊd,wɪŋk] *vt* : engañar

hoof [ˈhʊf, ˈhuːf] *n, pl* **hooves** [ˈhʊvz, ˈhuːvz] *or* **hoofs** : pezuña *f*, casco *m*

hoofed [ˈhʊft, ˈhuːft] *adj* : ungulado

hook[1] [ˈhʊk] *vt* : enganchar — *vi* : abrocharse, engancharse

hook[2] *n* : gancho *m*, percha *f*

hookworm [ˈhʊk,wərm] *n* : anquilostoma *m*

hooligan [ˈhuːlɪgən] *n* : gamberro *m*, -rra *f*

hoop [ˈhuːp] *n* : aro *m*

hooray [hʊˈreɪ] → **hurrah**

hoot[1] [ˈhuːt] *vi* **1** SHOUT : gritar <to hoot with laughter : morirse de risa, reírse a carcajadas> **2** : ulular (dícese de un búho), tocar la bocina (dícese de un vehículo), silbar (dícese de un tren o un barco)

hoot[2] *n* **1** : ululato *m* (de un búho), silbido *m* (de un tren), bocinazo *m* (de un vehículo) **2** GUFFAW : carcajada *f*, risotada *f* **3 I don't give a hoot** : me vale un comino, me importa un pito

hop[1] [ˈhɑp] *vi* **hopped; hopping** : brincar, saltar

hop[2] *n* **1** LEAP : salto *m*, brinco *m* **2** FLIGHT : vuelo *m* corto **3** : lúpulo *m* (planta)

hope[1] [ˈhoːp] *v* **hoped; hoping** *vi* : esperar — *vt* : esperar que <we hope she comes : esperamos que venga> <I hope not : espero que no>

hope[2] *n* : esperanza *f*

hopeful [ˈhoːpfəl] *adj* : esperanzado — **hopefully** *adv*

hopeless [ˈhoːpləs] *adj* **1** DESPAIRING : desesperado **2** IMPOSSIBLE : imposible <a hopeless case : un caso perdido>

hopelessly [ˈhoːpləsli] *adv* **1** : sin esperanzas, desesperadamente **2** COMPLETELY : totalmente, completamente **3** IMPOSSIBLY : imposiblemente

hopelessness [ˈhoːpləsnəs] *n* : desesperanza *f*

hopper [ˈhɑpər] *n* : tolva *f*

hopscotch [ˈhɑp,skɑtʃ] *n* : tejo *m*

horde [ˈhord] *n* : horda *f*, multitud *f*

horizon [həˈraɪzən] *n* : horizonte *m*

horizontal [,hɔrəˈzɑntəl] *adj* : horizontal — **horizontally** *adv*

hormone [ˈhɔr,moːn] *n* : hormona *f* — **hormonal** [hɔrˈmoːnəl] *adj*

horn [ˈhɔrn] *n* **1** : cuerno *m* (de un toro, una vaca, etc.) **2** : cuerno *m*, trompa *f* (instrumento musical) **3** : bocina *f*, claxon *m* (de un vehículo)

horned [ˈhɔrnd, ˈhɔrnəd] *adj* : cornudo, astado, con cuernos

hornet [ˈhɔrnət] *n* : avispón *m*

horn of plenty → **cornucopia**

horny [ˈhɔrni] *adj* **hornier; -est** CALLOUS : calloso

horoscope [ˈhɔrə,skoːp] *n* : horóscopo *m*

horrendous [hɔˈrɛndəs] *adj* : horrendo, horroroso, atroz

horrible [ˈhɔrəbəl] *adj* : horrible, espantoso, horroroso — **horribly** [-bli] *adv*

horrid [ˈhɔrɪd] *adj* : horroroso, horrible — **horridly** *adv*

horrify [ˈhɔrə,faɪ] *vt* **-fied; -fying** : horrorizar

horrifying [ˈhɔrə,faɪɪŋ] *adj* : horripilante, horroroso

horror [ˈhɔrər] *n* : horror *m*

hors d'oeuvre [ɔrˈdərv] *n, pl* **hors d'oeuvres** [-ˈdərvz] : entremés *m*

horse [ˈhɔrs] *n* : caballo *m*

horseback [ˈhɔrs,bæk] *n* **on ~** : a caballo

horse chestnut *n* : castaña *f* de Indias

horsefly [ˈhɔrs,flaɪ] *n, pl* **-flies** : tábano *m*

horsehair [ˈhɔrs,hær] *n* : crin *f*

horseman [ˈhɔrsmən] *n, pl* **-men** [-mən, -,mɛn] : jinete *m*, caballista *m*

horsemanship [ˈhɔrsmən,ʃɪp] *n* : equitación *f*

horseplay [ˈhɔrs,pleɪ] *n* : payasadas *fpl*

horsepower [ˈhɔrs,paʊər] *n* : caballo *m* de fuerza

horseradish [ˈhɔrs,rædɪʃ] *n* : rábano *m* picante

horseshoe [ˈhɔrs,ʃuː] *n* : herradura *f*

horsewhip [ˈhɔrs,*h*wɪp] *vt* **-whipped; -whipping** : azotar, darle fuetazos (a alguien)

horsewoman [ˈhɔrs,wʊmən] *n, pl* **-women** [-,wɪmən] : amazona *f*, jinete *f*, caballista *f*

horsey *or* **horsy** [ˈhɔrsi] *adj* **horsier; -est** : relacionado a los caballos, caballar

horticultural [,hɔrtəˈkʌltʃərəl] *adj* : hortícola

horticulture [ˈhɔrtə,kʌltʃər] *n* : horticultura *f*

hose[1] [ˈhoːz] *vt* **hosed; hosing** : regar o lavar con manguera

hose[2] *n* **1** *pl* **hose** SOCKS : calcetines *mpl*, medias *fpl* **2** *pl* **hose** STOCKINGS : medias *fpl* **3** *pl* **hoses** : manguera *f*, manga *f*

hosiery [ˈhoːʒəri, ˈhoːzə-] *n* : calcetería *f*, medias *fpl*

hospice [ˈhɑspəs] *n* : hospicio *m*

hospitable [hɑˈspɪt̬əbəl, ˈhɑsˌpɪ-] *adj* : hospitalario — **hospitably** [-bli] *adv*

hospital [ˈhɑsˌpɪt̬əl] *n* : hospital *m*

hospitality [ˌhɑspəˈtæləti] *n*, *pl* **-ties** : hospitalidad *f*

hospitalization [ˌhɑsˌpɪt̬ələˈzeɪʃən] *n* : hospitalización *f*

hospitalize [ˈhɑsˌpɪt̬əlˌaɪz] *vt* **-ized; -izing** : hospitalizar

host[1] [ˈhoːst] *vt* : presentar (un programa de televisión, etc.)

host[2] *n* **1** : anfitrión *m*, -triona *f* (en la casa, a un evento); presentador *m*, -dora *f* (de un programa de televisión, etc.) **2** *or* **host organism** : huésped *m* **3** TROOPS : huestes *fpl* **4** MULTITUDE : multitud *f* <for a host of reasons : por muchas razones> **5** EUCHARIST : hostia *f*, Eucaristía *f*

hostage [ˈhɑstɪdʒ] *n* : rehén *m*

hostel [ˈhɑstəl] *n* : albergue *m* juvenil

hostess [ˈhoːstɪs] *n* : anfitriona *f* (en la casa), presentadora *f* (de un programa)

hostile [ˈhɑstəl, -ˌtaɪl] *adj* : hostil — **hostilely** *adv*

hostility [hɑsˈtɪləti] *n*, *pl* **-ties** : hostilidad *f*

hot [ˈhɑt] *adj* **hotter; hottest 1** : caliente, cálido, caluroso <hot water : agua caliente> <a hot climate : un clima cálido> <a hot day : un día caluroso> **2** ARDENT, FIERY : ardiente, acalorado <to have a hot temper : tener mal genio> **3** SPICY : picante **4** FRESH : reciente, nuevo <hot news : noticias de última hora> **5** EAGER : ávido **6** STOLEN : robado

hot air *n* : palabrería *f*

hotbed [ˈhɑtˌbɛd] *n* **1** : semillero *m* (de plantas) **2** : hervidero *m*, semillero *m* (de crimen, etc.)

hot dog *n* : perro *m* caliente

hotel [hoːˈtɛl] *n* : hotel *m*

hothead [ˈhɑtˌhɛd] *n* : exaltado *m*, -da *f*

hotheaded [ˈhɑtˈhɛdəd] *adj* : exaltado

hothouse [ˈhɑtˌhaʊs] *n* : invernadero *m*

hot plate *n* : placa *f* (de cocina)

hot rod *n* : coche *m* con motor modificado

hot water *n* **to get into hot water** : meterse en un lío

hound[1] [ˈhaʊnd] *vt* : acosar, perseguir

hound[2] *n* : perro *m* (de caza)

hour [ˈaʊər] *n* : hora *f*

hourglass [ˈaʊərˌglæs] *n* : reloj *m* de arena

hourly [ˈaʊərli] *adv & adj* : cada hora, por hora

house[1] [ˈhaʊz] *vt* **housed; housing** : albergar, alojar, hospedar

house[2] [ˈhaʊs] *n*, *pl* **houses** [ˈhaʊzəz, -səz] **1** HOME : casa *f* **2** : cámara *f* (del gobierno) **3** BUSINESS : casa *f*, empresa *f*

houseboat [ˈhaʊsˌboːt] *n* : casa *f* flotante

housebroken [ˈhaʊsˌbroːkən] *adj* : enseñado

housefly [ˈhaʊsˌflaɪ] *n*, *pl* **-flies** : mosca *f* común

household[1] [ˈhaʊsˌhoːld] *adj* **1** DOMESTIC : doméstico, de la casa **2** FAMILIAR : conocido por todos

household[2] *n* : casa *f*, familia *f*

householder [ˈhaʊsˌhoːldər] *n* : dueño *m*, -ña *f* de casa

housekeeper [ˈhaʊsˌkiːpər] *n* : ama *f* de llaves

housekeeping [ˈhaʊsˌkiːpɪŋ] *n* : gobierno *m* de la casa, quehaceres *mpl* domésticos

housemaid [ˈhaʊsˌmeɪd] *n* : criada *f*, mucama *f*, muchacha *f*, sirvienta *f*

housewarming [ˈhaʊsˌwɔrmɪŋ] *n* : fiesta *f* de estreno de una casa

housewife [ˈhaʊsˌwaɪf] *n*, *pl* **-wives** : ama *f* de casa

housework [ˈhaʊsˌwərk] *n* : faenas *fpl* domésticas, quehaceres *mpl* domésticos

housing [ˈhaʊzɪŋ] *n* **1** HOUSES : vivienda *f* **2** COVERING : caja *f* protectora

hove → **heave**

hovel [ˈhʌvəl, ˈhɑ-] *n* : casucha *f*, tugurio *m*

hover [ˈhʌvər, ˈhɑ-] *vi* **1** : cernerse, sostenerse en el aire **2 to hover about** : rondar

how [ˈhaʊ] *adv* **1** : cómo <how are you? : ¿cómo estas?> <I don't know how to fix it : no se cómo arreglarlo> **2** : qué <how beautiful! : ¡qué bonito!> **3** : cuánto <how old are you? : ¿cuántos años tienes?> **4 how about...?** : ¿qué te parece...?

however[1] [haʊˈɛvər] *adv* **1** : por mucho que, por más que <however hot it is : por mucho calor que haga> **2** NEVERTHELESS : sin embargo, no obstante

however[2] *conj* : comoquiera que, de cualquier manera que

howl[1] [ˈhaʊl] *vi* : aullar

howl[2] *n* : aullido *m*, alarido *m*

hub [ˈhʌb] *n* **1** CENTER : centro *m* **2** : cubo *m* (de una rueda)

hubbub [ˈhʌˌbʌb] *n* : algarabía *f*, alboroto *m*, jaleo *m*

hubcap [ˈhʌbˌkæp] *n* : tapacubos *m*

huckster [ˈhʌkstər] *n* : buhonero *m*, -ra *f*; vendedor *m*, -dora *f* ambulante

huddle[1] [ˈhʌdəl] *vi* **-dled; -dling 1** : apiñarse, amontonarse **2 to huddle together** : acurrucarse

huddle[2] *n* : grupo *m* (cerrado) <to go into a huddle : conferenciar en secreto>

hue [ˈhjuː] *n* : color *m,* tono *m*

huff [ˈhʌf] *n* : enojo *m,* enfado *m* <to be in a huff : estar enojado>

huffy [ˈhʌfi] *adj* **huffier; -est** : enojado, enfadado

hug[1] [ˈhʌg] *vt* **hugged; hugging 1** EMBRACE : abrazar **2** : ir pegado a <the road hugs the river : el camino está pegado al río>

hug[2] *n* : abrazo *m*

huge [ˈhjuːdʒ] *adj* **huger; hugest** : inmenso, enorme — **hugely** *adv*

hulk [ˈhʌlk] *n* **1** : persona *f* fornida **2** : casco *m* (barco), armatoste *m* (edificio, etc.)

hulking [ˈhʌlkɪŋ] *adj* : grandote *fam,* pesado

hull[1] [ˈhʌl] *vt* : pelar

hull[2] *n* **1** HUSK : cáscara *f* **2** : casco *m* (de un barco, un avión, etc.)

hullabaloo [ˈhʌləbəˌluː] *n, pl* **-loos** : alboroto *m,* jaleo *m*

hum[1] [ˈhʌm] *v* **hummed; humming** *vi* **1** BUZZ : zumbar **2** : estar muy activo, moverse <to hum with activity : bullir de actividad> — *vt* : tararear (una melodía)

hum[2] *n* : zumbido *m,* murmullo *m*

human[1] [ˈhjuːmən, ˈjuː-] *adj* : humano — **humanly** *adv*

human[2] *n* : ser *m* humano

humane [hjuːˈmeɪn, ˌjuː-] *adj* : humano, humanitario — **humanely** *adv*

humanism [ˈhjuːməˌnɪzəm, ˈjuː-] *n* : humanismo *m*

humanist [ˈhjuːmənɪst, ˈjuː-] *n* : humanista *mf*

humanitarian[1] [hjuːˌmænəˈtɛriən, juː-] *adj* : humanitario

humanitarian[2] *n* : humanitario *m,* -ria *f*

humanity [hjuːˈmænəṯi, juː-] *n, pl* **-ties** : humanidad *f*

humankind [ˈhjuːmənˈkaɪnd, ˈjuː-] *n* : género *m* humano

humble[1] [ˈhʌmbəl] *vt* **-bled; -bling 1** : humillar **2 to humble oneself** : humillarse

humble[2] *adj* **-bler; -blest** : humilde, modesto — **humbly** [ˈhʌmbli] *adv*

humbug [ˈhʌmˌbʌg] *n* **1** FRAUD : charlatán *m,* -tana *f;* farsante *mf* **2** NONSENSE : patrañas *fpl,* tonterías *fpl*

humdrum [ˈhʌmˌdrʌm] *adj* : monótono, rutinario

humid [ˈhjuːməd, ˈjuː-] *adj* : húmedo

humidifier [hjuːˈmɪdəˌfaɪər, juː-] *n* : humidificador *m*

humidify [hjuːˈmɪdəˌfaɪ, juː-] *vt* **-fied; -fying** : humidificar

humidity [hjuːˈmɪdəṯi, juː-] *n, pl* **-ties** : humedad *f*

humiliate [hjuːˈmɪliˌeɪt, juː-] *vt* **-ated; -ating** : humillar

humiliating [hjuːˈmɪliˌeɪṯɪŋ, juː-] *adj* : humillante

humiliation [hjuːˌmɪliˈeɪʃən, juː-] *n* : humillación *f*

humility [hjuːˈmɪləṯi, juː-] *n* : humildad *f*

hummingbird [ˈhʌmɪŋˌbərd] *n* : colibrí *m,* picaflor *m*

hummock [ˈhʌmək] *n* : montículo *m*

humor[1] [ˈhjuːmər, ˈjuː-] *vt* : seguir el humor a, complacer

humor[2] *n* : humor *m*

humorist [ˈhjuːmərɪst, ˈjuː-] *n* : humorista *mf*

humorless [ˈhjuːmərləs, ˈjuː-] *adj* : sin sentido del humor <a humorless smile : una sonrisa forzada>

humorous [ˈhjuːmərəs, ˈjuː-] *adj* : humorístico, cómico — **humorously** *adv*

hump [ˈhʌmp] *n* : joroba *f,* giba *f*

humpback [ˈhʌmpˌbæk] *n* **1** HUMP : joroba *f,* giba *f* **2** HUNCHBACK : jorobado *m,* -da *f;* giboso *m,* -sa *f*

humpbacked [ˈhʌmpˌbækt] *adj* : jorobado, giboso

humus [ˈhjuːməs, ˈjuː-] *n* : humus *m*

hunch[1] [ˈhʌntʃ] *vt* : encorvar — *vi or* **to hunch up** : encorvarse

hunch[2] *n* PREMONITION : presentimiento *m*

hunchback [ˈhʌntʃˌbæk] *n* **1** HUMP : joroba *f,* giba *f* **2** HUMPBACK : jorobado *m,* -da *f;* giboso *m,* -sa *f*

hunchbacked [ˈhʌntʃˌbækt] *adj* : jorobado, giboso

hundred[1] [ˈhʌndrəd] *adj* : cien, ciento

hundred[2] *n, pl* **-dreds** *or* **-dred** : ciento *m*

hundredth[1] [ˈhʌndrədθ] *adj* : centésimo

hundredth[2] *n* **1** : centésimo *m,* -ma *f* (en una serie) **2** : centésimo *m,* centésima parte *f*

hung → **hang**

Hungarian [hʌŋˈgæriən] *n* **1** : húngaro *m,* -ra *f* **2** : húngaro *m* (idioma) — **Hungarian** *adj*

hunger[1] [ˈhʌŋgər] *vi* **1** : tener hambre **2 to hunger for** : ansiar, anhelar

hunger[2] *n* : hambre *m*

hungrily [ˈhʌŋgrəli] *adv* : ávidamente

hungry [ˈhʌŋgri] *adj* **-grier; -est 1** : hambriento **2 to be hungry** : tener hambre

hunk [ˈhʌŋk] *n* : trozo *m,* pedazo *m*

hunt[1] [ˈhʌnt] *vt* **1** PURSUE : cazar **2 to hunt for** : buscar

hunt[2] *n* **1** PURSUIT : caza *f,* cacería *f* **2** SEARCH : búsqueda *f,* busca *f*

hunter [ˈhʌnṯər] *n* : cazador *m,* -dora *f*

hunting [ˈhʌnṯɪŋ] *n* : caza *f* <to go hunting : ir de caza>

hurdle[1] [ˈhərdəl] *vt* **-dled; -dling** : saltar, salvar (un obstáculo)

hurdle[2] *n* : valla *f* (en deportes), obstáculo *m*

hurl [ˈhərl] *vt* : arrojar, tirar, lanzar

hurrah [hʊˈrɑ, -ˈrɔ] *interj* : ¡hurra!

hurricane [ˈhərəˌkeɪn] *n* : huracán *m*

hurried [ˈhərid] *adj* **:** apresurado, precipitado

hurriedly [ˈhərədli] *adv* **:** apresuradamente, de prisa

hurry[1] [ˈhəri] *v* **-ried; -rying** *vi* **:** apurarse, darse prisa, apresurarse — *vt* **:** apurar, darle prisa (a alguien)

hurry[2] *n* **:** prisa *f,* apuro *f*

hurt[1] [ˈhərt] *v* **hurt; hurting** *vt* **1** INJURE **:** hacer daño a, herir, lastimar <to hurt oneself : hacerse daño> **2** DISTRESS, OFFEND **:** hacer sufrir, ofender, herir — *vi* **:** doler <my foot hurts : me duele el pie>

hurt[2] *n* **1** INJURY **:** herida *f* **2** DISTRESS, PAIN **:** dolor *m,* pena *f*

hurtful [ˈhərtfəl] *adj* **:** hiriente, doloroso

hurtle [ˈhərtəl] *vi* **-tled; -tling :** lanzarse, precipitarse

husband[1] [ˈhʌzbənd] *vt* **:** economizar, bien administrar

husband[2] *n* **:** esposo *m,* marido *m*

husbandry [ˈhʌzbəndri] *n* **1** MANAGEMENT, THRIFT **:** economía *f,* buena administración *f* **2** AGRICULTURE **:** agricultura *f* <animal husbandry : cría de animales>

hush[1] [ˈhʌʃ] *vt* **1** SILENCE **:** hacer callar, acallar **2** CALM **:** calmar, apaciguar

hush[2] *n* **:** silencio *m*

hush–hush [ˈhʌʃˌhʌʃ, ˌhʌʃˈhʌʃ] *adj* **:** muy secreto, confidencial

husk[1] [ˈhʌsk] *vt* **:** descascarar

husk[2] *n* **:** cáscara *f*

huskily [ˈhʌskəli] *adv* **:** con voz ronca

husky[1] [ˈhʌski] *adj* **-kier; -est 1** HOARSE **:** ronco **2** BURLY **:** fornido

husky[2] *n, pl* **-kies :** perro *m,* -rra *f* esquimal

hustle[1] [ˈhəsəl] *v* **-tled; -tling** *vt* **:** darle prisa (a alguien), apurar <they hustled me in : me hicieron entrar a empujones> — *vi* **:** apurarse, ajetrearse

hustle[2] *n* BUSTLE **:** ajetreo *m*

hut [ˈhʌt] *n* **:** cabaña *f,* choza *f,* barraca *f*

hutch [ˈhʌtʃ] *n* **1** CUPBOARD **:** alacena *f* **2 rabbit hutch :** conejera *f*

hyacinth [ˈhaɪəˌsɪnθ] *n* **:** jacinto *m*

hybrid[1] [ˈhaɪbrɪd] *adj* **:** híbrido

hybrid[2] *n* **:** híbrido *m*

hydrant [ˈhaɪdrənt] *n* **:** boca *f* de riego, hidrante *m CA, Col* <fire hydrant : boca de incendios>

hydraulic [haɪˈdrɔlɪk] *adj* **:** hidráulico — **hydraulically** *adv*

hydrocarbon [ˌhaɪdroˈkɑrbən] *n* **:** hidrocarburo *m*

hydrochloric acid [ˌhaɪdroˈklorɪk] *n* **:** ácido *m* clorohídrico

hydroelectric [ˌhaɪdroɪˈlɛktrɪk] *adj* **:** hidroeléctrico

hydrogen [ˈhaɪdrədʒən] *n* **:** hidrógeno *m*

hydrogen bomb *n* **:** bomba *f* de hidrógeno

hydrogen peroxide *n* **:** agua *f* oxigenada, peróxido *m* de hidrógeno

hydrophobia [ˌhaɪdrəˈfoːbiə] *n* **:** hidrofobia *f,* rabia *f*

hydroplane [ˈhaɪdrəˌpleɪn] *n* **:** hidroplano *m*

hyena [haɪˈiːnə] *n* **:** hiena *f*

hygiene [ˈhaɪˌdʒiːn] *n* **:** higiene *f*

hygienic [haɪˈdʒɛnɪk, -ˈdʒiː-; ˌhaɪdʒiˈɛnɪk] *adj* **:** higiénico — **hygienically** [-nɪkli] *adv*

hygienist [haɪˈdʒiːnɪst, -ˈdʒɛ-; ˈhaɪˌdʒiː-] *n* **:** higienista *mf*

hygrometer [haɪˈgrɑmətər] *n* **:** higrómetro *m*

hymn [ˈhɪm] *n* **:** himno *m*

hymnal [ˈhɪmnəl] *n* **:** himnario *m*

hype [ˈhaɪp] *n* **:** bombo *m* publicitario

hyperactive [ˌhaɪpərˈæktɪv] *adj* **:** hiperactivo

hyperbole [haɪˈpərbəli] *n* **:** hipérbole *f*

hypercritical [ˌhaɪpərˈkrɪtəkəl] *adj* **:** hipercrítico

hypersensitivity [ˌhaɪpərˌsɛntsəˈtɪvəti] *n* **:** hipersensibilidad *f*

hypertension [ˈhaɪpərˌtɛntʃən] *n* **:** hipertensión *f*

hyphen [ˈhaɪfən] *n* **:** guión *m*

hyphenate [ˈhaɪfənˌeɪt] *vt* **-ated; -ating :** escribir con guión

hypnosis [hɪpˈnoːsɪs] *n, pl* **-noses** [-ˌsiːz] **:** hipnosis *f*

hypnotic [hɪpˈnɑtɪk] *adj* **:** hipnótico, hipnotizador

hypnotism [ˈhɪpnəˌtɪzəm] *n* **:** hipnotismo *m*

hypnotize [ˈhɪpnəˌtaɪz] *vt* **-tized; -tizing :** hipnotizar

hypochondria [ˌhaɪpəˈkɑndriə] *n* **:** hipocondría *f*

hypochondriac [ˌhaɪpəˈkɑndriˌæk] *n* **:** hipocondríaco *m,* -ca *f*

hypocrisy [hɪpˈɑkrəsi] *n, pl* **-sies :** hipocresía *f*

hypocrite [ˈhɪpəˌkrɪt] *n* **:** hipócrita *mf*

hypocritical [ˌhɪpəˈkrɪtɪkəl] *adj* **:** hipócrita

hypodermic[1] [ˌhaɪpəˈdərmɪk] *adj* **:** hipodérmico

hypodermic[2] *n* **:** aguja *f* hipodérmica

hypotenuse [haɪˈpɑtənˌuːs, -ˌuːz, -ˌjuːs, -ˌjuːz] *n* **:** hipotenusa *f*

hypothesis [haɪˈpɑθəsɪs] *n, pl* **-eses** [-ˌsiːz] **:** hipótesis *f*

hypothetical [ˌhaɪpəˈθɛtɪkəl] *adj* **:** hipotético — **hypothetically** [-tɪkli] *adv*

hysteria [hɪsˈtɛriə, -tɪr-] *n* **:** histeria *f,* histerismo *m*

hysterical [hɪsˈtɛrɪkəl] *adj* **:** histérico — **hysterically** [-ɪkli] *adv*

hysterics [hɪsˈtɛrɪks] *n* **:** histeria *f,* histerismo *m*

I

i [ˈaɪ] *n, pl* **i's** *or* **is** [ˈaɪz] : novena letra del alfabeto inglés
I [ˈaɪ] *pron* : yo
ibis [ˈaɪbəs] *n, pl* **ibis** *or* **ibises** : ibis *f*
ice[1] [ˈaɪs] *v* **iced; icing** *vt* **1** FREEZE : congelar, helar **2** CHILL : enfriar **3 to ice a cake** : escarchar un pastel — *vi* : helarse, congelarse
ice[2] *n* **1** : hielo *m* **2** SHERBET : sorbete *m,* nieve *f Cuba, Mex, PRi*
iceberg [ˈaɪsˌbərg] *n* : iceberg *m*
icebox [ˈaɪsˌbɑks] → **refrigerator**
icebreaker [ˈaɪsˌbreɪkər] *n* : rompehielos *m*
ice cap *n* : casquete *m* glaciar
ice–cold [ˈaɪsˈkoːld] *adj* : helado
ice cream *n* : helado *m,* mantecado *m PRi*
Icelander [ˈaɪsˌlændər, -lən-] *n* : islandés *m,* -desa *f*
Icelandic[1] [aɪsˈlændɪk] *adj* : islandés
Icelandic[2] *n* : islandés *m* (idioma)
ice–skate [ˈaɪsˌskeɪt] *vi* **-skated; -skating** : patinar
ice skater *n* : patinador *m,* -dora *f*
ichthyology [ˌɪkthiˈɑlədʒi] *n* : ictiología *f*
icicle [ˈaɪˌsɪkəl] *n* : carámbano *m*
icily [ˈaɪsəli] *adv* : fríamente, con frialdad <he stared at me icily : me fijó la mirada con mucha frialdad>
icing [ˈaɪsɪŋ] *n* : glaseado *m,* betún *m Mex*
icon [ˈaɪˌkɑn, -kən] *n* : icono *m*
iconoclasm [aɪˈkɑnəˌklæzəm] *n* : iconoclasia *f*
iconoclast [aɪˈkɑnəˌklæst] *n* : iconoclasta *mf*
icy [ˈaɪsi] *adj* **icier; -est 1** : cubierto de hielo <an icy road : una carretera cubierta de hielo> **2** FREEZING : helado, gélido, glacial **3** ALOOF : frío, distante
id [ˈɪd] *n* : id *m*
I'd [ˈaɪd] (*contraction of* **I should** *or* **I would**) → **should, would**
idea [aɪˈdiːə] *n* : idea *f*
ideal[1] [aɪˈdiːəl] *adj* : ideal
ideal[2] *n* : ideal *m*
idealism [aɪˈdiːəˌlɪzəm] *n* : idealismo *m*
idealist [aɪˈdiːəlɪst] *n* : idealista *mf*
idealistic [aɪˌdiːəˈlɪstɪk] *adj* : idealista
idealistically [aɪˌdiːəˈlɪstɪkli] *adv* : con idealismo
idealization [aɪˌdiːələˈzeɪʃən] *n* : idealización *f*
idealize [aɪˈdiːəˌlaɪz] *vt* **-ized; -izing** : idealizar
ideally [aɪˈdiːəli] *adv* : perfectamente
identical [aɪˈdɛntɪkəl] *adj* : idéntico — **identically** [-tɪkli] *adv*
identifiable [aɪˌdɛntəˈfaɪəbəl] *adj* : identificable
identification [aɪˌdɛntəfəˈkeɪʃən] *n* **1** : identificación *f* **2 identification card** : carnet *m,* cédula *f* de identidad, identificación *f*
identify [aɪˈdɛntəˌfaɪ] *v* **-fied; -fying** *vt* : identificar — *vi* **to identify with** : identificarse con
identity [aɪˈdɛntət̬i] *n, pl* **-ties** : identidad *f*
ideological [ˌaɪdiəˈlɑdʒɪkəl, ˌɪ-] *adj* : ideológico — **ideologically** [-dʒɪkli] *adv*
ideology [ˌaɪdiˈɑlədʒi, ˌɪ-] *n, pl* **-gies** : ideología *f*
idiocy [ˈɪdiəsi] *n, pl* **-cies 1** : idiotez *f* **2** NONSENSE : estupidez *f,* tontería *f*
idiom [ˈɪdiəm] *n* **1** LANGUAGE : lenguaje *m* **2** EXPRESSION : modismo *m,* expresión *f* idiomática
idiomatic [ˌɪdiəˈmæt̬ɪk] *adj* : idiomático
idiosyncrasy [ˌɪdioˈsɪŋkrəsi] *n, pl* **-sies** : idiosincrasia *f*
idiosyncratic [ˌɪdiosɪnˈkræt̬ɪk] *adj* : idiosincrásico — **idiosyncratically** [-t̬ɪkli] *adv*
idiot [ˈɪdiət] *n* **1** : idiota *mf* (en medicina) **2** FOOL : idiota *mf;* tonto *m,* -ta *f;* imbécil *mf fam*
idiotic [ˌɪdiˈɑt̬ɪk] *adj* : estúpido, idiota
idiotically [ˌɪdiˈɑt̬ɪkli] *adv* : estúpidamente
idle[1] [ˈaɪdəl] *v* **idled; idling** *vi* **1** LOAF : holgazanear, flojear, haraganear **2** : andar al ralentí (dícese de un automóvil), marchar en vacío (dícese de una máquina) — *vt* : dejar sin trabajo
idle[2] *adj* **idler; idlest 1** VAIN : frívolo, vano, infundado <idle curiosity : pura curiosidad> **2** INACTIVE : inactivo, parado, desocupado **3** LAZY : holgazán, haragán, perezoso
idleness [ˈaɪdəlnəs] *n* **1** INACTIVITY : inactividad *f,* ociosidad *f* **2** LAZINESS : holgazanería *f,* flojera *f,* pereza *f*
idler [ˈaɪdələr] *n* : haragán *m,* -gana *f;* holgazán *m,* -zana *f*
idly [ˈaɪdəli] *adv* : ociosamente
idol [ˈaɪdəl] *n* : ídolo *m*
idolater *or* **idolator** [aɪˈdɑlət̬ər] *n* : idólatra *mf*
idolatrous [aɪˈdɑlətrəs] *adj* : idólatra
idolatry [aɪˈdɑlətri] *n, pl* **-tries** : idolatría *f*
idolize [ˈaɪdəlaɪz] *vt* **-ized; -izing** : idolatrar
idyll [ˈaɪdəl] *n* : idilio *m*
idyllic [aɪˈdɪlɪk] *adj* : idílico
if [ˈɪf] *conj* **1** : si <I would do it if I could : lo haría si pudiera> <if so : si es así> <as if : como si> <if I were you : yo que tú> **2** WHETHER : si <I don't know if they're ready : no sé si están listos> **3** THOUGH : aunque, si bien <it's pretty, if somewhat old-fashioned : es lindo aunque algo anticuado>
igloo [ˈɪˌgluː] *n, pl* **-loos** : iglú *m*

ignite [ɪg'naɪt] *v* **-nited; -niting** *vt* : prenderle fuego a, encender — *vi* : prender, encenderse

ignition [ɪg'nɪʃən] *n* **1** IGNITING : ignición *f,* encendido *m* **2** *or* **ignition switch** : encendido *m,* arranque *m* <to turn on the ignition : arrancar el motor>

ignoble [ɪg'noːbəl] *adj* : innoble — **ignobly** *adv*

ignominious [ˌɪgnə'mɪniəs] *adj* : ignominioso, deshonroso — **ignominiously** *adv*

ignominy ['ɪgnəˌmɪni] *n, pl* **-nies** : ignominia *f*

ignoramus [ˌɪgnə'reɪməs] *n* : ignorante *mf;* bestia *mf;* bruto *m,* -ta *f*

ignorance ['ɪgnərən*t*s] *n* : ignorancia *f*

ignorant ['ɪgnərənt] *adj* **1** : ignorante **2 to be ignorant of** : no ser consciente de, desconocer, ignorar

ignorantly ['ɪgnərəntli] *adv* : ignorantemente, con ignorancia

ignore [ɪg'nor] *vt* **-nored; -noring** : ignorar, hacer caso omiso de, no hacer caso de

iguana [ɪ'gwɑnə] *n* : iguana *f,* garrobo *f CA*

ilk ['ɪlk] *n* : tipo *m,* clase *f,* índole *f*

ill[1] ['ɪl] *adv* **worse** ['wərs]; **worst** ['wərst] : mal <to speak ill of : hablar mal de> <he can ill afford to fail : mal puede permitirse el lujo de fracasar>

ill[2] *adj* **worse; worst 1** SICK : enfermo **2** BAD : malo <ill luck : mala suerte>

ill[3] *n* **1** EVIL : mal *m* **2** MISFORTUNE : mal *m,* desgracia *f* **3** AILMENT : enfermedad *f*

I'll ['aɪl] (*contraction of* **I shall** *or* **I will**) → **shall, will**

illegal [ɪl'liːgəl] *adj* : ilegal — **illegally** *adv*

illegality [ɪli'gæləṭi] *n* : ilegalidad *f*

illegibility [ɪlˌlɛdʒə'bɪləṭi] *n, pl* **-ties** : ilegibilidad *f*

illegible [ɪl'lɛdʒəbəl] *adj* : ilegible — **illegibly** [-bli] *adv*

illegitimacy [ˌɪlɪ'dʒɪṭəməsi] *n* : ilegitimidad *f*

illegitimate [ˌɪlɪ'dʒɪṭəmət] *adj* **1** BASTARD : ilegítimo, bastardo **2** UNLAWFUL : ilegítimo, ilegal — **illegitimately** *adv*

ill–fated ['ɪl'feɪṭəd] *adj* : malhadado, infortunado, desventurado

illicit [ɪl'lɪsət] *adj* : ilícito — **illicitly** *adv*

illiteracy [ɪl'lɪṭərəsi] *n, pl* **-cies** : analfabetismo *m*

illiterate[1] [ɪl'lɪṭərət] *adj* : analfabeto

illiterate[2] *n* : analfabeto *m,* -ta *f*

ill–mannered [ˌɪl'manərd] *adj* : descortés, maleducado

ill–natured [ˌɪl'neɪtʃərd] *adj* : desagradable, de mal genio

ill–naturedly [ˌɪl'neɪtʃərdli] *adv* : desagradablemente

illness ['ɪlnəs] *n* : enfermedad *f*

illogical [ɪl'lɑdʒɪkəl] *adj* : ilógico — **illogically** [-kli] *adv*

ill–tempered [ˌɪl'tempərd] → **ill–natured**

ill–treat [ˌɪl'triːt] *vt* : maltratar

ill–treatment [ˌɪl'triːtmənt] *n* : maltrato *m*

illuminate [ɪ'luːməˌneɪt] *vt* **-nated; -nating 1** : iluminar, alumbrar **2** ELUCIDATE : esclarecer, elucidar

illumination [ɪˌluːmə'neɪʃən] *n* **1** LIGHTING : iluminación *f,* luz *f* **2** ELUCIDATION : esclarecimiento *m,* elucidación *f*

ill–use ['ɪl'juːz] → **ill–treat**

illusion [ɪ'luːʒən] *n* : ilusión *f*

illusory [ɪ'luːsəri, -zəri] *adj* : engañoso, ilusorio

illustrate ['ɪləsˌtreɪt] *v* **-trated; -trating** : ilustrar

illustration [ˌɪlə'streɪʃən] *n* **1** PICTURE : ilustración *f* **2** EXAMPLE : ejemplo *m,* ilustración *f*

illustrative [ɪ'lʌstrəṭɪv, 'ɪləˌstreɪṭɪv] *adj* : ilustrativo — **illustratively** *adv*

illustrator ['ɪləˌstreɪṭər] *n* : ilustrador *m,* -dora *f;* dibujante *mf*

illustrious [ɪ'lʌstriəs] *adj* : ilustre, eminente, glorioso

illustriousness [ɪ'lʌstriəsnəs] *n* : eminencia *f,* prestigio *m*

ill will *n* : animosidad *f,* malquerencia *f,* mala voluntad *f*

I'm ['aɪm] (*contraction of* **I am**) → **be**

image[1] ['ɪmɪdʒ] *vt* **-aged; -aging** : imaginar, crear una imagen de

image[2] *n* : imagen *f*

imagery ['ɪmɪdʒri] *n, pl* **-eries 1** IMAGES : imágenes *fpl* **2** : imaginería *f* (en el arte)

imaginable [ɪ'mædʒənəbəl] *adj* : imaginable — **imaginably** [-bli] *adv*

imaginary [ɪ'mædʒəˌnɛri] *adj* : imaginario

imagination [ɪˌmædʒə'neɪʃən] *n* : imaginación *f*

imaginative [ɪ'mædʒənəṭɪv, -əˌneɪṭɪv] *adj* : imaginativo — **imaginatively** *adv*

imagine [ɪ'mædʒən] *vt* **-ined; -ining** : imaginar(se)

imbalance [ɪm'bælən*t*s] *n* : desajuste *m,* desbalance *m,* desequilibrio *m*

imbecile[1] ['ɪmbəsəl, -ˌsɪl] *or* **imbecilic** [ˌɪmbə'sɪlɪk] *adj* : imbécil, estúpido

imbecile[2] *n* **1** : imbécil *mf* (en medicina) **2** FOOL : idiota *mf;* imbécil *mf fam;* estúpido *m,* -da *f*

imbecility [ˌɪmbə'sɪləṭi] *n, pl* **-ties** : imbecilidad *f*

imbibe [ɪm'baɪb] *v* **-bibed; -bibing** *vt* **1** DRINK : beber **2** ABSORB : absorber, embeber — *vi* : beber

imbue [ɪm'bjuː] *vt* **-bued; -buing** : imbuir

imitate ['ɪməˌteɪt] *vt* **-tated; -tating** : imitar, remedar

imitation[1] [ˌɪmə'teɪʃən] *adj* : de imitación, artificial

imitation[2] *n* : imitación *f*

imitative ['ɪməˌteɪṭɪv] *adj* : imitativo, imitador, poco original

imitator ['ɪməˌteɪṭər] *n* : imitador *m*, -dora *f*

immaculate [ɪ'mækjələt] *adj* **1** PURE : inmaculado, puro **2** FLAWLESS : impecable, intachable — **immaculately** *adv*

immaterial [ˌɪmə'tɪriəl] *adj* **1** INCORPOREAL : incorpóreo **2** UNIMPORTANT : irrelevante, sin importancia

immature [ˌɪmə'tʃʊr, -'tjʊr, -'tʊr] *adj* : inmaduro, verde (dícese de la fruta)

immaturity [ˌɪmə'tʃʊrəṭi, -'tjʊr-, -'tʊr-] *n, pl* **-ties** : inmadurez *f*, falta *f* de madurez

immeasurable [ɪ'mɛʒərəbəl] *adj* : inconmensurable, incalculable — **immeasurably** [-bli] *adv*

immediate [ɪ'mi:diət] *adj* **1** INSTANT : inmediato, instantáneo <immediate relief : alivio instantáneo> **2** DIRECT : inmediato, directo <the immediate cause of death : la causa directa de la muerte> **3** URGENT : urgente, apremiante **4** CLOSE : cercano, próximo, inmediato <her immediate family : sus familiares más cercanos> <in the immediate vicinity : en los alrededores, en las inmediaciones>

immediately [ɪ'mi:diətli] *adv* : inmediatamente, enseguida

immemorial [ˌɪmə'moriəl] *adj* : inmemorial

immense [ɪ'mɛnts] *adj* : inmenso, enorme — **immensely** *adv*

immensity [ɪ'mɛntsəṭi] *n, pl* **-ties** : inmensidad *f*

immerse [ɪ'mərs] *vt* **-mersed; -mersing 1** SUBMERGE : sumergir **2 to immerse oneself in** : enfrascarse en

immersion [ɪ'mərʒən] *n* **1** : inmersión *f* (en un líquido) **2** : enfrascamiento *m* (en una actividad)

immigrant ['ɪmɪgrənt] *n* : inmigrante *mf*

immigrate ['ɪməˌgreɪt] *vi* **-grated; -grating** : inmigrar

immigration [ˌɪmə'greɪʃən] *n* : inmigración *f*

imminence ['ɪmənənts] *n* : inminencia *f*

imminent ['ɪmənənt] *adj* : inminente — **imminently** *adv*

immobile [ɪm'o:bəl] *adj* **1** FIXED, IMMOVABLE : inmovible, fijo **2** MOTIONLESS : inmóvil

immobility [ˌɪmo'bɪləṭi] *n, pl* **-ties** : inmovilidad *f*

immobilize [ɪ'mo:bəˌlaɪz] *vt* **-lized; -lizing** : inmovilizar, paralizar

immoderate [ɪ'mɑdərət] *adj* : inmoderado, desmesurado, desmedido, excesivo — **immoderately** *adv*

immodest [ɪ'mɑdəst] *adj* **1** INDECENT : inmodesto, indecente, impúdico **2** CONCEITED : inmodesto, presuntuoso, engreído — **immodestly** *adv*

immodesty [ɪ'mɑdəsti] *n* : inmodestia *f*

immoral [ɪ'mɔrəl] *adj* : inmoral

immorality [ˌɪmɔ'ræləṭi, ˌɪmə-] *n, pl* **-ties** : inmoralidad *f*

immorally [ɪ'mɔrəli] *adv* : de manera inmoral

immortal[1] [ɪ'mɔrtəl] *adj* : inmortal

immortal[2] *n* : inmortal *mf*

immortality [ˌɪˌmɔr'tæləṭi] *n* : inmortalidad *f*

immortalize [ɪ'mɔrtəlˌaɪz] *vt* **-ized; -izing** : inmortalizar

immovable [ɪ'mu:vəbəl] *adj* **1** FIXED : fijo, inmovible **2** UNYIELDING : inflexible

immune [ɪ'mju:n] *adj* **1** : inmune <immune to smallpox : inmune a la viruela> **2** EXEMPT : exento, inmune

immune system *n* : sistema *m* inmunológico

immunity [ɪ'mju:nəṭi] *n, pl* **-ties 1** : inmunidad *f* **2** EXEMPTION : exención *f*

immunization [ˌɪmjʊnə'zeɪʃən] *n* : inmunización *f*

immunize ['ɪmjʊˌnaɪz] *vt* **-nized; -nizing** : inmunizar

immunology [ˌɪmjʊ'nɑlədʒi] *n* : inmunología *f*

immutable [ɪ'mju:ṭəbəl] *adj* : inmutable

imp ['ɪmp] *n* RASCAL : diablillo *m*; pillo *m*, -lla *f*

impact[1] [ɪm'pækt] *vt* **1** STRIKE : chocar con, impactar **2** AFFECT : afectar, impactar, impresionar — *vi* **1** STRIKE : hacer impacto, golpear **2 to impact on** : tener un impacto sobre

impact[2] ['ɪmˌpækt] *n* **1** COLLISION : impacto *m*, choque *m*, colisión *f* **2** EFFECT : efecto *m*, impacto *m*, consecuencias *fpl*

impacted [ɪm'pæktəd] *adj* : impactado, incrustado (dícese de los dientes)

impair [ɪm'pær] *vt* : perjudicar, dañar, afectar

impairment [ɪm'pærmənt] *n* : perjuicio *m*, daño *m*

impala [ɪm'pɑlə, -'pæ-] *n, pl* **impalas** *or* **impala** : impala *m*

impale [ɪm'peɪl] *vt* **-paled; -paling** : empalar

impanel [ɪm'pænəl] *vt* **-eled** *or* **-elled; -eling** *or* **-elling** : elegir (un jurado)

impart [ɪm'pɑrt] *vt* **1** CONVEY : impartir, dar, conferir **2** DISCLOSE : revelar, divulgar

impartial [ɪm'pɑrʃəl] *adj* : imparcial — **impartially** *adv*

impartiality [ɪmˌpɑrʃi'æləṭi] *n, pl* **-ties** : imparcialidad *f*

impassable [ɪm'pæsəbəl] *adj* : infranqueable, intransitable — **impassably** [-bli] *adv*

impasse [ˈɪm,pæs] *n* **1** DEADLOCK : impasse *m*, punto *m* muerto **2** DEAD END : callejón *m* sin salida

impassioned [ɪmˈpæʃənd] *adj* : apasionado, vehemente

impassive [ɪmˈpæsɪv] *adj* : impasible, indiferente

impassively [ɪmˈpæsɪvli] *adv* : impasiblemente, sin emoción

impatience [ɪmˈpeɪʃən*t*s] *n* : impaciencia *f*

impatient [ɪmˈpeɪʃənt] *adj* : impaciente — **impatiently** *adv*

impeach [ɪmˈpiːtʃ] *vt* : destituir (a un funcionario) de su cargo

impeachment [ɪmˈpiːtʃmənt] *n* **1** ACCUSATION : acusación *f* **2** DISMISSAL : destitución *f*

impeccable [ɪmˈpɛkəbəl] *adj* : impecable — **impeccably** [-bli] *adv*

impecunious [,ɪmpɪˈkjuːniəs] *adj* : falto de dinero

impede [ɪmˈpiːd] *vt* **-peded; -peding** : impedir, dificultar, obstaculizar

impediment [ɪmˈpɛdəmənt] *n* **1** HINDRANCE : impedimento *m*, obstáculo *m* **2 speech impediment** : defecto *m* del habla

impel [ɪmˈpɛl] *vt* **-pelled; -pelling** : impeler

impend [ɪmˈpɛnd] *vi* : ser inminente

impenetrable [ɪmˈpɛnətrəbəl] *adj* **1** : impenetrable <an impenetrable forest : una selva impenetrable> **2** INSCRUTABLE : incomprensible, inescrutable, impenetrable — **impenetrably** [-bli] *adv*

impenitent [ɪmˈpɛnətənt] *adj* : impenitente

imperative[1] [ɪmˈpɛrət̬ɪv] *adj* **1** AUTHORITATIVE : imperativo, imperioso **2** NECESSARY : imprescindible — **imperatively** *adv*

imperative[2] *n* : imperativo *m*

imperceptible [,ɪmpərˈsɛptəbəl] *adj* : imperceptible — **imperceptibly** [-bli] *adv*

imperfect [ɪmˈpərfɪkt] *adj* : imperfecto, defectuoso — **imperfectly** *adv*

imperfection [ɪm,pərˈfɛkʃən] *n* : imperfección *f*, defecto *m*

imperial [ɪmˈpɪriəl] *adj* **1** : imperial **2** SOVEREIGN : soberano **3** IMPERIOUS : imperioso, señorial

imperialism [ɪmˈpɪriə,lɪzəm] *n* : imperialismo *m*

imperialist[1] [ɪmˈpɪriəlɪst] *adj* : imperialista

imperialist[2] *n* : imperialista *mf*

imperialistic [ɪm,pɪriːəˈlɪstɪk] *adj* : imperialista

imperil [ɪmˈpɛrəl] *vt* **-iled** *or* **-illed; -iling** *or* **-illing** : poner en peligro

imperious [ɪmˈpɪriəs] *adj* : imperioso — **imperiously** *adv*

imperishable [ɪmˈpɛrɪʃəbəl] *adj* : imperecedero

impermanent [ɪmˈpərmənənt] *adj* : pasajero, inestable, efímero — **impermanently** *adv*

impermeable [ɪmˈpərmiəbəl] *adj* : impermeable

impersonal [ɪmˈpərsənəl] *adj* : impersonal — **impersonally** *adv*

impersonate [ɪmˈpərsən,eɪt] *vt* **-ated; -ating** : hacerse pasar por, imitar

impersonation [ɪm,pərsənˈeɪʃən] *n* : imitación *f*

impersonator [ɪmˈpərsən,eɪt̬ər] *n* : imitador *m*, -dora *f*

impertinence [ɪmˈpərtənən*t*s] *n* : impertinencia *f*

impertinent [ɪmˈpərtənənt] *adj* **1** IRRELEVANT : impertinente, irrelevante **2** INSOLENT : impertinente, insolente

impertinently [ɪmˈpərtənəntli] *adv* : con impertinencia, impertinentemente

imperturbable [,ɪmpərˈtərbəbəl] *adj* : imperturbable

impervious [ɪmˈpərviəs] *adj* **1** IMPENETRABLE : impermeable **2** INSENSITIVE : insensible <impervious to criticism : insensible a la crítica>

impetuosity [ɪm,pɛtʃʊˈɑsət̬i] *n, pl* **-ties** : impetuosidad *f*

impetuous [ɪmˈpɛtʃʊəs] *adj* : impetuoso, impulsivo

impetuously [ɪmˈpɛtʃʊəsli] *adv* : de manera impulsiva, impetuosamente

impetus [ˈɪmpət̬əs] *n* : ímpetu *m*, impulso *m*

impiety [ɪmˈpaɪət̬i] *n, pl* **-ties** : impiedad *f*

impinge [ɪmˈpɪndʒ] *vi* **-pinged; -pinging 1 to impinge on** AFFECT : afectar a, incidir en **2 to impinge on** VIOLATE : violar, vulnerar

impious [ˈɪmpiəs, ɪmˈpaɪəs] *adj* : impío, irreverente

impish [ˈɪmpɪʃ] *adj* MISCHIEVOUS : pícaro, travieso

impishly [ˈɪmpɪʃli] *adv* : con picardía

implacable [ɪmˈplækəbəl] *adj* : implacable — **implacably** [-bli] *adv*

implant[1] [ɪmˈplænt] *vt* **1** INCULCATE, INSTILL : inculcar, implantar **2** INSERT : implantar, insertar

implant[2] [ˈɪm,plænt] *n* : implante *m* (de pelo), injerto *m* (de piel)

implantation [,ɪm,plænˈteɪʃən] *n* : implantación *f*

implausibility [ɪm,plɔzəˈbɪlət̬i] *n, pl* **-ties** : inverosimilitud *f*

implausible [ɪmˈplɔzəbəl] *adj* : inverosímil, poco convincente

implement[1] [ˈɪmplə,mɛnt] *vt* : poner en práctica, implementar

implement[2] [ˈɪmpləmənt] *n* : utensilio *m*, instrumento *m*, implemento *m*

implementation [,ɪmpləmənˈteɪʃən] *n* : implementación *f*, ejecución *f*, cumplimiento *m*

implicate [ˈɪmplə,keɪt] *vt* **-cated; -cating** : implicar, involucrar

implication [ˌɪmpləˈkeɪʃən] *n* **1** CONSEQUENCE : implicación *f,* consecuencia *f* **2** INFERENCE : insinuación *f,* inferencia *f*

implicit [ɪmˈplɪsət] *adj* **1** IMPLIED : implícito, tácito **2** ABSOLUTE : absoluto, completo <implicit faith : fe ciega> — **implicitly** *adv*

implied [ɪmˈplaɪd] *adj* : implícito, tácito

implode [ɪmˈploːd] *vi* **-ploded; -ploding** : implosionar

implore [ɪmˈplor] *vt* **-plored; -ploring** : implorar, suplicar

imply [ɪmˈplaɪ] *vt* **-plied; -plying 1** SUGGEST : insinuar, dar a entender **2** INVOLVE : implicar, suponer <rights imply obligations : los derechos implican unas obligaciones>

impolite [ˌɪmpəˈlaɪt] *adj* : descortés, maleducado

impoliteness [ˌɪmpəˈlaɪtnəs] *n* : descortesía *f,* falta *f* de educación

impolitic [ɪmˈpɑləˌtɪk] *adj* : imprudente, poco político

imponderable[1] [ɪmˈpɑndərəbəl] *adj* : imponderable

imponderable[2] *n* : imponderable *m*

import[1] [ɪmˈport] *vt* **1** SIGNIFY : significar **2** : importar <to import foreign cars : importar autos extranjeros>

import[2] [ˈɪmˌport] *n* **1** SIGNIFICANCE : importancia *f,* significación *f* **2** → **importation**

importance [ɪmˈportənts] *n* : importancia *f*

important [ɪmˈpɔrtənt] *adj* : importante

importantly [ɪmˈpɔrtəntli] *adv* **1** : con importancia **2 more importantly** : lo que es más importante

importation [ˌɪmˌpɔrˈteɪʃən] *n* : importación *f*

importer [ɪmˈportər] *n* : importador *m,* -dora *f*

importunate [ɪmˈpɔrtʃənət] *adj* : importuno, insistente

importune [ˌɪmpərˈtuːn, -ˈtjuːn; ɪmˈpɔrtʃən] *vt* **-tuned; -tuning** : importunar, implorar

impose [ɪmˈpoːz] *v* **-posed; -posing** *vt* : imponer <to impose a tax : imponer un impuesto> — *vi* **to impose on** : abusar de, molestar <to impose on her kindness : abusar de su bondad>

imposing [ɪmˈpoːzɪŋ] *adj* : imponente, impresionante

imposition [ˌɪmpəˈzɪʃən] *n* : imposición *f*

impossibility [ɪmˌpɑsəˈbɪləṭi] *n, pl* **-ties** : imposibilidad *f*

impossible [ɪmˈpɑsəbəl] *adj* **1** : imposible <an impossible task : una tarea imposible> <to make life impossible for : hacerle la vida imposible a> **2** UNACCEPTABLE : inaceptable

impossibly [ɪmˈpɑsəbli] *adv* : imposiblemente, increíblemente

impostor *or* **imposter** [ɪmˈpɑstər] *n* : impostor *m,* -tora *f*

imposture [ɪmˈpɑstʃər] *n* : impostura *f*

impotence [ˈɪmpətənts] *n* : impotencia *f*

impotency [ˈɪmpətəntsi] → **impotence**

impotent [ˈɪmpətənt] *adj* : impotente

impound [ɪmˈpaʊnd] *vt* : incautar, embargar, confiscar

impoverish [ɪmˈpɑvərɪʃ] *vt* : empobrecer

impoverishment [ɪmˈpɑvərɪʃmənt] *n* : empobrecimiento *m*

impracticable [ɪmˈpræktɪkəbəl] *adj* : impracticable

impractical [ɪmˈpræktɪkəl] *adj* : poco práctico

imprecise [ˌɪmprɪˈsaɪs] *adj* : impreciso

imprecisely [ˌɪmprɪˈsaɪsli] *adv* : con imprecisión

impreciseness [ˌɪmprɪˈsaɪsnəs] → **imprecision**

imprecision [ˌɪmprɪˈsɪʒən] *n* : imprecisión *f,* falta de precisión *f*

impregnable [ɪmˈprɛgnəbəl] *adj* : inexpugnable, impenetrable, inconquistable

impregnate [ɪmˈprɛgˌneɪt] *vt* **-nated; -nating 1** FERTILIZE : fecundar **2** PERMEATE, SATURATE : impregnar, empapar, saturar

impresario [ˌɪmprəˈsɑriˌo, -ˈsær-] *n, pl* **-rios** : empresario *m,* -ria *f*

impress [ɪmˈprɛs] *vt* **1** IMPRINT : imprimir, estampar **2** : impresionar, causar impresión a <I was not impressed : no me hizo buena impresión> **3 to impress (something) on someone** : recalcarle (algo) a alguien — *vi* : impresionar, hacer una impresión

impression [ɪmˈprɛʃən] *n* **1** IMPRINT : marca *f,* huella *f,* molde *m* (de los dientes) **2** EFFECT : impresión *f,* efecto *m,* impacto *m* **3** PRINTING : impresión *f* **4** NOTION : impresión *f,* noción *f*

impressionable [ɪmˈprɛʃənəbəl] *adj* : impresionable

impressive [ɪmˈprɛsɪv] *adj* : impresionante — **impressively** *adv*

impressiveness [ɪmˈprɛsɪvnəs] *n* : calidad de ser impresionante

imprint[1] [ɪmˈprɪnt, ˈɪmˌ-] *vt* : imprimir, estampar

imprint[2] [ˈɪmˌprɪnt] *n* : marca *f,* huella *f*

imprison [ɪmˈprɪzən] *vt* **1** JAIL : encarcelar, aprisionar **2** CONFINE : recluir, encerrar

imprisonment [ɪmˈprɪzənmənt] *n* : encarcelamiento *m*

improbability [ɪmˌprɑbəˈbɪləṭi] *n, pl* **-ties** : improbabilidad *f,* inverosimilitud *f*

improbable [ɪmˈprɑbəbəl] *adj* : improbable, inverosímil

impromptu[1][ɪm'prɑmp,tu:, -,tju:] *adv* : sin preparación, espontáneamente

impromptu[2] *adj* : espontáneo, improvisado

impromptu[3] *n* : improvisación *f*

improper [ɪm'prɑpər] *adj* **1** INCORRECT : incorrecto, impropio **2** INDECOROUS : indecoroso

improperly [ɪm'prɑpərli] *adv* : incorrectamente, indebidamente

impropriety [,ɪmprə'praɪəṭi] *n, pl* **-eties 1** INDECOROUSNESS : indecoro *m,* falta *f* de decoro **2** ERROR : impropiedad *f,* incorrección *f*

improve [ɪm'pru:v] *v* **-proved; -proving** : mejorar

improvement [ɪm'pru:vmənt] *n* : mejoramiento *m,* mejora *f*

improvidence [ɪm'prɑvədən*t*s] *n* : imprevisión *f*

improvident [ɪm'prɑvədənt] *adj* : sin previsión, imprevisor

improvisation [ɪm,prɑvə'zeɪʃən, ,ɪmprəvə-] *n* : improvisación *f*

improvise ['ɪmprə,vaɪz] *v* **-vised; -vising** : improvisar

imprudence [ɪm'pru:dən*t*s] *n* : imprudencia *f,* indiscreción *f*

imprudent [ɪm'pru:dənt] *adj* : imprudente, indiscreto

impudence ['ɪmpjədən*t*s] *n* : insolencia *f,* descaro *m*

impudent ['ɪmpjədənt] *adj* : insolente, descarado — **impudently** *adv*

impugn [ɪm'pju:n] *vt* : impugnar

impulse ['ɪm,pʌls] *n* **1** : impulso *m* **2 on impulse** : sin reflexionar

impulsive [ɪm'pʌlsɪv] *adj* : impulsivo — **impulsively** *adv*

impulsiveness [ɪm'pʌlsɪvnəs] *n* : impulsividad *f*

impunity [ɪm'pju:nəṭi] *n* **1** : impunidad *f* **2 with impunity** : impunemente

impure [ɪm'pjʊr] *adj* **1** : impuro <impure thoughts : pensamientos impuros> **2** CONTAMINATED : con impurezas, impuro

impurity [ɪm'pjʊrəṭi] *n, pl* **-ties** : impureza *f*

impute [ɪm'pju:t] *vt* **-puted; -puting** ATTRIBUTE : imputar, atribuir

in[1] ['ɪn] *adv* **1** INSIDE : dentro, adentro <let's go in : vamos adentro> **2** HARVESTED : recogido <the crops are in : las cosechas ya están recogidas> **3 to be in** : estar <is Linda in? : ¿está Linda?> **4 to be in** : estar en poder <the Democrats are in : los demócratas están en el poder> **5 to be in for** : ser objeto de, estar a punto de <they're in for a treat : los van a agasajar> <he's in for a surprise : se va a llevar una sorpresa> **6 to be in on** : participar en, tomar parte en

in[2] *adj* **1** INSIDE : interior <the in part : la parte interior> **2** FASHIONABLE : de moda

in[3] *prep* **1** (*indicating location or position*) <in the lake : en el lago> <a pain in the leg : un dolor en la pierna> <in the sun : al sol> <in the rain : bajo la lluvia> <the best restaurant in Buenos Aires : el mejor restaurante de Buenos Aires> **2** INTO : en, a <he broke it in pieces : lo rompió en pedazos> <she went in the house : se metió a la casa> **3** DURING : por, durante <in the afternoon : por la tarde> **4** WITHIN : dentro de <I'll be back in a week : vuelvo dentro de una semana> **5** (*indicating manner*) : en, con, de <in Spanish : en español> <written in pencil : escrito con lápiz> <in this way : de esta manera> **6** (*indicating states or circumstances*) <to be in luck : tener suerte> <to be in love : estar enamorado> <to be in a hurry : tener prisa> **7** (*indicating purpose*) : en <in reply : en respuesta, como réplica>

inability [,ɪnə'bɪləṭi] *n, pl* **-ties** : incapacidad *f*

inaccessibility [,ɪnɪk,sɛsə'bɪləṭi] *n, pl* **-ties** : inaccesibilidad *f*

inaccessible [,ɪnɪk'sɛsəbəl] *adj* : inaccesible

inaccuracy [ɪn'ækjərəsi] *n, pl* **-cies 1** : inexactitud *f* **2** MISTAKE : error *m*

inaccurate [ɪn'ækjərət] *n* : inexacto, erróneo, incorrecto

inaccurately [ɪn'ækjərətli] *adv* : incorrectamente, con inexactitud

inaction [ɪn'ækʃən] *n* : inactividad *f,* inacción *f*

inactive [ɪn'æktɪv] *n* : inactivo

inactivity [,ɪn,æk'tɪvəṭi] *n, pl* **-ties** : inactividad *f,* ociosidad *f*

inadequacy [ɪn'ædɪkwəsi] *n, pl* **-cies 1** INSUFFICIENCY : insuficiencia *f* **2** INCOMPETENCE : ineptitud *f,* incompetencia *f*

inadequate [ɪn'ædɪkwət] *adj* **1** INSUFFICIENT : insuficiente, inadecuado **2** INCOMPETENT : inepto, incompetente

inadmissible [,ɪnæd'mɪsəbəl] *adj* : inadmisible

inadvertent [,ɪnəd'vərtənt] *adj* : inadvertido, involuntario — **inadvertently** *adv*

inadvisable [,ɪnæd'vaɪzəbəl] *adj* : desaconsejable

inalienable [ɪn'eɪljənəbəl, -'eɪliənə-] *adj* : inalienable

inane [ɪ'neɪn] *adj* **inaner; -est** : estúpido, idiota, necio

inanimate [ɪn'ænəmət] *adj* : inanimado, exánime

inanity [ɪ'nænəṭi] *n, pl* **-ties 1** STUPIDITY : estupidez *f* **2** NONSENSE : idiotez *f,* disparate *m*

inapplicable [ɪn'æplɪkəbəl, ,ɪnə'plɪkəbəl] *adj* IRRELEVANT : inaplicable, irrelevante

inappreciable [,ɪnə'pri:ʃəbəl] *adj* : inapreciable, imperceptible

inappropriate [,ɪnə'pro:priət] *adj* : inapropiado, inadecuado, impropio

inappropriateness [ˌɪnəˈproːpriətnəs] *n* : lo inapropiado, impropiedad *f*

inapt [ɪnˈæpt] *adj* **1** UNSUITABLE : inadecuado, inapropiado **2** INEPT : inepto

inarticulate [ˌɪnɑrˈtɪkjələt] *adj* : inarticulado, incapaz de expresarse

inarticulately [ˌɪnɑrˈtɪkjələtli] *adv* : inarticuladamente

inasmuch as [ˌɪnæzˈmʌtʃæz] *conj* : ya que, dado que, puesto que

inattention [ˌɪnəˈtɛntʃən] *n* : falta *f* de atención, distracción *f*

inattentive [ˌɪnəˈtɛntɪv] *adj* : distraído, despistado

inattentively [ˌɪnəˈtɛntɪvli] *adv* : distraídamente, sin prestar atención

inaudible [ɪnˈɔdəbəl] *adj* : inaudible

inaudibly [ɪnˈɔdəbli] *adv* : de forma inaudible

inaugural[1] [ɪˈnɔgjərəl, -gərəl] *adj* : inaugural, de investidura

inaugural[2] *n* **1** *or* **inaugural address** : discurso *m* de investidura **2** INAUGURATION : investidura *f* (de una persona)

inaugurate [ɪˈnɔgjəˌreɪt, -gə-] *vt* **-rated; -rating 1** BEGIN : inaugurar **2** INDUCT : investir <to inaugurate the president : investir al presidente>

inauguration [ɪˌnɔgjəˈreɪʃən, -gə-] *n* **1** : inauguración *f* (de un edificio, un sistema, etc.) **2** : investidura *f* (de una persona)

inauspicious [ˌɪnɔˈspɪʃəs] *adj* : desfavorable, poco propicio

inborn [ˈɪnˌbɔrn] *adj* **1** CONGENITAL, INNATE : innato, congénito **2** HEREDITARY : hereditario

inbred [ˈɪnˌbrɛd] *adj* **1** : engendrado por endogamia **2** INNATE : innato

inbreed [ˈɪnˌbriːd] *vt* **-bred; -breeding** : engendrar por endogamia

inbreeding [ˈɪnˌbriːdɪŋ] *n* : endogamia *f*

incalculable [ɪnˈkælkjələbəl] *adj* : incalculable — **incalculably** [-bli] *adv*

incandescence [ˌɪnkənˈdɛsənts] *n* : incandescencia *f*

incandescent [ˌɪnkənˈdɛsənt] *adj* **1** : incandescente **2** BRILLIANT : brillante

incantation [ˌɪnˌkænˈteɪʃən] *n* : conjuro *m*, ensalmo *m*

incapable [ɪnˈkeɪpəbəl] *adj* : incapaz

incapacitate [ˌɪnkəˈpæsəˌteɪt] *vt* **-tated; -tating** : incapacitar

incapacity [ˌɪnkəˈpæsəti] *n, pl* **-ties** : incapacidad *f*

incarcerate [ɪnˈkɑrsəˌreɪt] *vt* **-ated; -ating** : encarcelar

incarceration [ɪnˌkɑrsəˈreɪʃən] *n* : encarcelamiento *m*, encarcelación *f*

incarnate[1] [ɪnˈkɑrˌneɪt] *vt* **-nated; -nating** : encarnar

incarnate[2] [ɪnˈkɑrnət, -ˌneɪt] *adj* : encarnado

incarnation [ˌɪnˌkɑrˈneɪʃən] *n* : encarnación *f*

incendiary[1] [ɪnˈsɛndiˌɛri] *adj* : incendiario

incendiary[2] *n, pl* **-aries** : incendiario *m*, -ria *f*; pirómano *m*, -na *f*

incense[1] [ɪnˈsɛnts] *vt* **-censed; -censing** : indignar, enfadar, enfurecer

incense[2] [ˈɪnˌsɛnts] *n* : incienso *m*

incentive [ɪnˈsɛntɪv] *n* : incentivo *m*, aliciente *m*, motivación *f*, acicate *m*

inception [ɪnˈsɛpʃən] *n* : comienzo *m*, principio *m*

incessant [ɪnˈsɛsənt] *adj* : incesante, continuo — **incessantly** *adv*

incest [ˈɪnˌsɛst] *n* : incesto *m*

incestuous [ɪnˈsɛstʃʊəs] *adj* : incestuoso

inch[1] [ˈɪntʃ] *v* : avanzar poco a poco

inch[2] *n* **1** : pulgada *f* **2 every inch** : absoluto, seguro <every inch a winner : un seguro ganador> **3 within an inch of** : a punto de

incidence [ˈɪntsədənts] *n* **1** FREQUENCY : frecuencia *f*, índice *m* <a high incidence of crime : un alto índice de crímenes> **2 angle of incidence** : ángulo *m* de incidencia

incident[1] [ˈɪntsədənt] *adj* : incidente

incident[2] *n* : incidente *m*, incidencia *f*, episodio *m* (en una obra de ficción)

incidental[1] [ˌɪntsəˈdɛntəl] *adj* **1** SECONDARY : incidental, secundario **2** ACCIDENTAL : casual, fortuito

incidental[2] *n* **1** : algo incidental **2 incidentals** *npl* : imprevistos *mpl*

incidentally [ˌɪntsəˈdɛntəli, -ˈdɛntli] *adv* **1** BY CHANCE : incidentalmente, casualmente **2** BY THE WAY : a propósito, por cierto

incinerate [ɪnˈsɪnəˌreɪt] *vt* **-ated; -ating** : incinerar

incinerator [ɪnˈsɪnəˌreɪtər] *n* : incinerador *m*

incipient [ɪnˈsɪpiənt] *adj* : incipiente, naciente

incise [ɪnˈsaɪz] *vt* **-cised; -cising 1** ENGRAVE : grabar, cincelar, inscribir **2** : hacer una incisión en

incision [ɪnˈsɪʒən] *n* : incisión *f*

incisive [ɪnˈsaɪsɪv] *adj* : incisivo, penetrante

incisively [ɪnˈsaɪsɪvli] *adv* : con agudeza

incisor [ɪnˈsaɪzər] *n* : incisivo *m*

incite [ɪnˈsaɪt] *vt* **-cited; -citing** : incitar, instigar

incitement [ɪnˈsaɪtmənt] *n* : incitación *f*

inclemency [ɪnˈklɛməntsi] *n, pl* **-cies** : inclemencia *f*

inclement [ɪnˈklɛmənt] *adj* : inclemente, tormentuoso

inclination [ˌɪnkləˈneɪʃən] *n* **1** PROPENSITY : inclinación *f*, tendencia *f* **2** DESIRE : deseo *m*, ganas *fpl* **3** BOW : inclinación *f*

incline[1] [ɪnˈklaɪn] *v* **-clined; -clining** *vi* **1** SLOPE : inclinarse **2** TEND : inclinarse, tender <he is inclined to be late : tiende a llegar tarde> — *vt* **1** LOWER : inclinar, bajar <to incline one's head

: bajar la cabeza> 2 SLANT : inclinar 3 PREDISPOSE : predisponer

incline[2] [ˈɪn,klaɪn] *n* : inclinación *f*, pendiente *f*

inclined [ɪnˈklaɪnd] *adj* 1 SLOPING : inclinado 2 PRONE : prono, dispuesto, dado

inclose, inclosure → **enclose, enclosure**

include [ɪnˈklu:d] *vt* **-cluded; -cluding** : incluir, comprender

inclusion [ɪnˈklu:ʒən] *n* : inclusión *f*

inclusive [ɪnˈklu:sɪv] *adj* : inclusivo

incognito [,ɪn,kɑgˈni:to, ɪnˈkɑgnə,to:] *adv & adj* : de incógnito

incoherence [,ɪnkoˈhɪrən*t*s, -ˈhɛr-] *n* : incoherencia *f*

incoherent [,ɪnkoˈhɪrənt, -ˈhɛr-] *adj* : incoherente — **incoherently** *adv*

incombustible [,ɪnkəmˈbʌstəbəl] *adj* : incombustible

income [ˈɪn,kʌm] *n* : ingresos *mpl*, entradas *fpl*

income tax *n* : impuesto *m* sobre la renta

incoming [ˈɪn,kʌmɪŋ] *adj* 1 ARRIVING : que se recibe (dícese del correo), que llega (dícese de las personas), ascendente (dícese de la marea) 2 NEW : nuevo, entrante <the incoming president : el nuevo presidente> <the incoming year : el año entrante>

incommunicado [,ɪnkə,mju:nəˈkɑdo] *adj* : incomunicado

incomparable [ɪnˈkɑmpərəbəl] *adj* : incomparable, sin igual

incompatible [,ɪnkəmˈpæt̬əbəl] *adj* : incompatible

incompetence [ɪnˈkɑmpət̬ən*t*s] *n* : incompetencia *f*, impericia *f*, ineptitud *f*

incompetent [ɪnˈkɑmpət̬ənt] *adj* : incompetente, inepto, incapaz

incomplete [,ɪnkəmˈpli:t] *adj* : incompleto — **incompletely** *adv*

incomprehensible [,ɪn,kɑmpriˈhɛn*t*səbəl] *adj* : incomprensible

inconceivable [,ɪnkənˈsi:vəbəl] *adj* 1 INCOMPREHENSIBLE : incomprensible 2 UNBELIEVABLE : inconcebible, increíble

inconceivably [,ɪnkənˈsi:vəbli] *adv* : inconcebiblemente, increíblemente

inconclusive [,ɪnkənˈklu:sɪv] *adj* : inconcluyente, no decisivo

incongruity [,ɪnkənˈgru:ət̬i, -,kɑn-] *n, pl* **-ties** : incongruencia *f*

incongruous [ɪnˈkɑŋgrʊəs] *adj* : incongruente, inapropiado, fuera de lugar

incongruously [ɪnˈkɑŋgrʊəsli] *adv* : de manera incongruente, inapropiadamente

inconsequential [,ɪn,kɑnsəˈkwɛntʃəl] *adj* : intrascendente, de poco importancia

inconsiderable [,ɪnkənˈsɪdərəbəl] *adj* : insignificante

inconsiderate [,ɪnkənˈsɪdərət] *adj* : desconsiderado, sin consideración — **inconsiderately** *adv*

inconsistency [,ɪnkənˈsɪstən*t*si] *n, pl* **-cies** : inconsecuencia *f*, inconsistencia *f*

inconsistent [,ɪnkənˈsɪstənt] *adj* : inconsecuente, inconsistente

inconsolable [,ɪnkənˈso:ləbəl] *adj* : inconsolable — **inconsolably** [-bli] *adv*

inconspicuous [,ɪnkənˈspɪkjʊəs] *adj* : discreto, no conspicuo, que no llama la atención

inconspicuously [,ɪnkənˈspɪkjʊəsli] *adv* : discretamente, sin llamar la atención

incontestable [,ɪnkənˈtɛstəbəl] *adj* : incontestable, indiscutible — **incontestably** [-bli] *adv*

incontinence [ɪnˈkɑntənən*t*s] *n* : incontinencia *f*

incontinent [ɪnˈkɑntənənt] *adj* : incontinente

inconvenience[1] [,ɪnkənˈvi:njən*t*s] **-nienced; -niencing** *vt* : importunar, incomodar, molestar

inconvenience[2] *n* : incomodidad *f*, molestia *f*

inconvenient [,ɪnkənˈvi:njənt] *adj* : inconveniente, importuno, incómodo — **inconveniently** *adv*

incorporate [ɪnˈkɔrpə,reɪt] *vt* **-rated; -rating** 1 INCLUDE : incorporar, incluir 2 : incorporar, constituir en sociedad (dícese de un negocio)

incorporation [ɪn,kɔrpəˈreɪʃən] *n* : incorporación *f*

incorporeal [,ɪn,kɔrˈporiəl] *adj* : incorpóreo

incorrect [,ɪnkəˈrɛkt] *adj* 1 INACCURATE : incorrecto 2 WRONG : equivocado, erróneo 3 IMPROPER : impropio — **incorrectly** *adv*

incorrigible [ɪnˈkɔrədʒəbəl] *adj* : incorregible

incorruptible [,ɪnkəˈrʌptəbəl] *adj* : incorruptible

increase[1] [ɪnˈkri:s, ˈɪn,kri:s] *v* **-creased; -creasing** *vi* GROW : aumentar, crecer, subir (dícese de los precios) — *vt* AUGMENT : aumentar, acrecentar

increase[2] [ˈɪn,kri:s, ɪnˈkri:s] *n* : aumento *m*, incremento *m*, subida *f* (de precios)

increasing [ɪnˈkri:sɪŋ, ˈɪn,kri:sɪŋ] *adj* : creciente

increasingly [ɪnˈkri:sɪŋli] *adv* : cada vez más

incredible [ɪnˈkrɛdəbəl] *adj* : increíble — **incredibly** [-bli] *adv*

incredulity [,ɪnkrɪˈdu:lət̬i, -ˈdju:-] *n* : incredulidad *f*

incredulous [ɪnˈkrɛdʒələs] *adj* : incrédulo, escéptico

incredulously [ɪnˈkrɛdʒələsli] *adv* : con incredulidad

increment [ˈɪŋkrəmənt, ˈɪn-] *n* : incremento *m*, aumento *m*

incremental [,ɪŋkrəˈmɛntəl, ,ɪn-] *adj* : de incremento

incriminate [ɪn'krɪmə,neɪt] *vt* **-nated; -nating** : incriminar
incrimination [ɪn,krɪmə'neɪʃən] *n* : incriminación *f*
incriminatory [ɪn'krɪmənə,tori] *adj* : incriminatorio
incubate ['ɪŋkjʊ,beɪt, 'ɪn-] *v* **-bated; -bating** *vt* : incubar, empollar — *vi* : incubar(se), empollar
incubation [,ɪŋkjʊ'beɪʃən, ,ɪn-] *n* : incubación *f*
incubator ['ɪŋkjʊ,beɪtər, 'ɪn-] *n* : incubadora *f*
inculcate [ɪn'kʌl,keɪt, 'ɪn,kʌl-] *vt* **-cated; -cating** : inculcar
incumbency [ɪn'kʌmbəntsi] *n, pl* **-cies** 1 OBLIGATION : incumbencia *f* 2 : mandato *m* (en la política)
incumbent¹ [ɪn'kʌmbənt] *adj* : obligatorio
incumbent² *n* : titular *mf*
incur [ɪn'kər] *vt* **incurred; incurring** : provocar (al enojo), incurrir en (gastos, obligaciones)
incurable [ɪn'kjʊrəbəl] *adj* : incurable, sin remedio
incursion [ɪn'kərʒən] *n* : incursión *f*
indebted [ɪn'dɛtəd] *adj* 1 : endeudado 2 **to be indebted to** : estar en deuda con, estarle agracido a
indebtedness [ɪn'dɛtədnəs] *n* : endeudamiento *m*
indecency [ɪn'diːsəntsi] *n, pl* **-cies** : indecencia *f*
indecent [ɪn'diːsənt] *adj* : indecente — **indecently** *adv*
indecipherable [,ɪndɪ'saɪfərəbəl] *adj* : indescifrable
indecision [,ɪndɪ'sɪʒən] *n* : indecisión *f*, irresolución *f*
indecisive [,ɪndɪ'saɪsɪv] *adj* 1 INCONCLUSIVE : indeciso, que no es decisivo 2 IRRESOLUTE : indeciso, irresoluto, vacilante 3 INDEFINITE : indefinido — **indecisively** *adv*
indecorous [ɪn'dɛkərəs, ,ɪndɪ'korəs] *adj* : indecoroso — **indecorously** *adv*
indecorousness [ɪn'dɛkərəsnəs, ,ɪndɪ'korəs-] *n* : indecoro *m*
indeed [ɪn'diːd] *adv* 1 TRULY : verdaderamente, de veras 2 (*used as intensifier*) <thank you very much indeed : muchísimas gracias> 3 OF COURSE : claro, por supuesto
indefatigable [,ɪndɪ'fætɪgəbəl] *adj* : incansable, infatigable — **indefatigably** [-bli] *adv*
indefensible [,ɪndɪ'fɛntsəbəl] *adj* 1 VULNERABLE : indefendible, vulnerable 2 INEXCUSABLE : inexcusable
indefinable [,ɪndɪ'faɪnəbəl] *adj* : indefinible
indefinite [ɪn'dɛfənət] *adj* 1 : indefinido, indeterminado <indefinite pronouns : pronombres indefinidos> 2 VAGUE : vago, impreciso
indefinitely [ɪn'dɛfənətli] *adv* : indefinidamente, por un tiempo indefinido
indelible [ɪn'dɛləbəl] *adj* : indeleble, imborrable — **indelibly** [-bli] *adv*
indelicacy [ɪn'dɛləkəsi] *n* : falta *f* de delicadeza
indelicate [ɪn'dɛlɪkət] *adj* 1 IMPROPER : indelicado, indecoroso 2 TACTLESS : indiscreto, falto de tacto
indemnify [ɪn'dɛmnə,faɪ] *vt* **-fied; -fying** 1 INSURE : asegurar 2 COMPENSATE : indemnizar, compensar
indemnity [ɪn'dɛmnəti] *n, pl* **-ties** 1 INSURANCE : indemnidad *f* 2 COMPENSATION : indemnización *f*
indent [ɪn'dɛnt] *vt* : sangrar (un párrafo)
indentation [,ɪn,dɛn'teɪʃən] *n* 1 NOTCH : muesca *f*, mella *f* 2 INDENTING : sangría *f* (de un párrafo)
indenture¹ [ɪn'dɛntʃər] *vt* **-tured; -turing** : ligar por contrato
indenture² *n* : contrato de aprendizaje
independence [,ɪndə'pɛndənts] *n* : independencia *f*
Independence Day *n* : día *m* de la Independencia (4 de julio en los EE.UU.)
independent¹ [,ɪndə'pɛndənt] *adj* : independiente — **independently** *adv*
independent² *n* : independiente *mf*
indescribable [,ɪndɪ'skraɪbəbəl] *adj* : indescriptible, incalificable — **indescribably** [-bli] *adv*
indestructibility [,ɪndɪ,strʌktə'bɪləti] *n* : indestructibilidad *f*
indestructible [,ɪndɪ'strʌktəbəl] *adj* : indestructible
indeterminate [,ɪndɪ'tərmənət] *adj* 1 VAGUE : vago, impreciso, indeterminado 2 INDEFINITE : indeterminado, indefinido
index¹ ['ɪn,dɛks] *vt* 1 : ponerle un índice a (un libro o una revista) 2 : incluir en un índice <all proper names are indexed : todos los nombres propios están incluidos en el índice> 3 INDICATE : indicar, señalar 4 REGULATE : indexar, indiciar <to index prices : indiciar los precios>
index² *n, pl* **-dexes** *or* **-dices** ['ɪndə,siːz] 1 : índice *m* (de un libro, de precios) 2 INDICATION : indicio *m*, índice *m*, señal *f* <an index of her character : una señal de su carácter>
index finger *n* FOREFINGER : dedo *m* índice
Indian ['ɪndiən] *n* 1 : indio *m*, -dia *f* 2 → **American Indian** — **Indian** *adj*
indicate ['ɪndə,keɪt] *vt* **-cated; -cating** 1 POINT OUT : indicar, señalar 2 SHOW, SUGGEST : ser indicio de, ser señal de 3 EXPRESS : expresar, señalar 4 REGISTER : marcar, poner (una medida, etc.)
indication [,ɪndə'keɪʃən] *n* : indicio *m*, señal *f*
indicative [ɪn'dɪkətɪv] *adj* : indicativo

indicator [ˈɪndəˌkeɪt̬ər] *n* : indicador *m*
indict [ɪnˈdaɪt] *vt* : acusar, procesar (por un crímen)
indictment [ɪnˈdaɪtmənt] *n* : acusación *f*
indifference [ɪnˈdɪfrən*t*s, -ˈdɪfə-] *n* : indiferencia *f*
indifferent [ɪnˈdɪfrənt, -ˈdɪfə-] *adj* **1** UNCONCERNED : indiferente **2** MEDIOCRE : mediocre
indifferently [ɪnˈdɪfrəntli, -ˈdɪfə-] *adv* **1** : con indiferencia, indiferentemente **2** SO-SO : de modo regular, más o menos
indigence [ˈɪndɪdʒən*t*s] *n* : indigencia *f*
indigenous [ɪnˈdɪdʒənəs] *adj* : indígena, nativo
indigent [ˈɪndɪdʒənt] *adj* : indigente, pobre
indigestible [ˌɪndaɪˈdʒɛstəbəl, -dɪ-] *adj* : difícil de digerir
indigestion [ˌɪndaɪˈdʒɛstʃən, -dɪ-] *n* : indigestión *f*, empacho *m*
indignant [ɪnˈdɪgnənt] *adj* : indignado
indignantly [ɪnˈdɪgnəntli] *adv* : con indignación
indignation [ˌɪndɪgˈneɪʃən] *n* : indignación *f*
indignity [ɪnˈdɪgnət̬i] *n, pl* **-ties** : indignidad *f*
indigo [ˈɪndɪˌgoː] *n, pl* **-gos** *or* **-goes** : añil *m*, índigo *m*
indirect [ˌɪndəˈrɛkt, -daɪ-] *adj* : indirecto — **indirectly** *adv*
indiscernible [ˌɪndɪˈsərnəbəl, -ˈzər-] *adj* : imperceptible
indiscreet [ˌɪndɪˈskriːt] *adj* : indiscreto, imprudente — **indiscreetly** *adv*
indiscretion [ˌɪndɪˈskrɛʃən] *n* : indiscreción *f*, imprudencia *f*
indiscriminate [ˌɪndɪˈskrɪmənət] *adj* : indiscriminado
indiscriminately [ˌɪndɪˈskrɪmənətli] *adv* : sin discriminación, sin discernimiento
indispensable [ˌɪndɪˈspɛn*t*səbəl] *adj* : indispensable, necesario, imprescindible — **indispensably** [-bli] *adv*
indisposed [ˌɪndɪˈspoːzd] *adj* **1** ILL : indispuesto, enfermo **2** AVERSE, DISINCLINED : opuesto, reacio <to be indisposed toward working : no tener ganas de trabajar>
indisputable [ˌɪndɪˈspjuːt̬əbəl, ɪnˈdɪspjʊt̬ə-] *adj* : indiscutible, incuestionable, incontestable — **indisputably** [-bli] *adv*
indistinct [ˌɪndɪˈstɪŋkt] *adj* : indistinto — **indistinctly** *adv*
indistinctness [ˌɪndɪˈstɪŋktnəs] *n* : falta *f* de claridad
individual[1] [ˌɪndəˈvɪdʒʊəl] *adj* **1** PERSONAL : individual, personal <individual traits : características personales> **2** SEPARATE : individual, separado **3** PARTICULAR : particular, propio
individual[2] *n* : individuo *m*
individualist [ˌɪndəˈvɪdʒʊəlɪst] *n* : individualista *mf*
individuality [ˌɪndəˌvɪdʒʊˈælət̬i] *n, pl* **-ties** : individualidad *f*
individually [ˌɪndəˈvɪdʒʊəli, -dʒəli] *adv* : individualmente
indivisible [ˌɪndɪˈvɪzəbəl] *adj* : indivisible
indoctrinate [ɪnˈdɑktrəˌneɪt] *vt* **-nated; -nating 1** TEACH : enseñar, instruir **2** PROPAGANDIZE : adoctrinar
indoctrination [ɪnˌdɑktrəˈneɪʃən] *n* : adoctrinamiento *m*
indolence [ˈɪndələn*t*s] *n* : indolencia *f*
indolent [ˈɪndələnt] *adj* : indolente
indomitable [ɪnˈdɑmət̬əbəl] *adj* : invencible, indomable, indómito — **indomitably** [-bli] *adv*
Indonesian [ˌɪndoˈniːʒən, -ʃən] *n* : indonesio *m*, -sia *f* — **Indonesian** *adj*
indoor [ˈɪnˈdor] *adj* : interior (dícese de las plantas), para estar en casa (dícese de la ropa), cubierto (dícese de las piscinas, etc.), bajo techo (dícese de los deportes)
indoors [ˈɪnˈdorz] *adv* : adentro, dentro
indubitable [ɪnˈduːbət̬əbəl, -ˈdjuː-] *adj* : indudable, incuestionable, indiscutible
indubitably [ɪnˈduːbət̬əbli, -ˈdjuː-] *adv* : indudablemente
induce [ɪnˈduːs, -ˈdjuːs] *vt* **-duced; -ducing 1** PERSUADE : persuadir, inducir **2** CAUSE : inducir, provocar <to induce labor : provocar un parto>
inducement [ɪnˈduːsmənt, -ˈdjuːs-] *n* **1** INCENTIVE : incentivo *m*, aliciente *m* **2** : inducción *f*, provocación *f* (de un parto)
induct [ɪnˈdʌkt] *vt* **1** INSTALL : instalar, investir **2** ADMIT : admitir (como miembro) **3** CONSCRIPT : reclutar (al servicio militar)
inductee [ˌɪnˌdʌkˈtiː] *n* : recluta *mf*, conscripto *m*, -ta *f*
induction [ɪnˈdʌkʃən] *n* **1** INTRODUCTION : iniciación *f*, introducción *f* **2** : inducción *f* (en la lógica o la electricidad)
inductive [ɪnˈdʌktɪv] *adj* : inductivo
indulge [ɪnˈdʌldʒ] *v* **-dulged; -dulging** *vt* **1** GRATIFY : gratificar, satisfacer **2** SPOIL : consentir, mimar — *vi* **to indulge in** : permitirse
indulgence [ɪnˈdʌldʒən*t*s] *n* **1** SATISFYING : satisfacción *f*, gratificación *f* **2** HUMORING : complacencia *f*, indulgencia *f* **3** SPOILING : consentimiento *m* **4** : indulgencia *f* (en la religión)
indulgent [ɪŋˈdʌldʒənt] *adj* : indulgente, consentido — **indulgently** *adv*
industrial [ɪnˈdʌstriəl] *adj* : industrial — **industrially** *adv*
industrialist [ɪnˈdʌstriəlɪst] *n* : industrial *mf*

industrialization [ɪn,dʌstriələ'zeɪʃən] *n* : industrialización *f*

industrialize [ɪn'dʌstriə,laɪz] *vt* **-ized; -izing** : industrializar

industrious [ɪn'dʌstriəs] *adj* : diligente, industrioso, trabajador

industriously [ɪn'dʌstriəsli] *adv* : con diligencia, con aplicación

industriousness [ɪn'dʌstriəsnəs] *n* : diligencia *f,* aplicación *f*

industry ['ɪndəstri] *n, pl* **-tries 1** DILIGENCE : diligencia *f,* aplicación *f* **2** : industria *f* <the steel industry : la industria siderúrgica>

inebriated [ɪ'ni:bri,eɪt̬əd] *adj* : ebrio, embriagado

inebriation [ɪ,ni:bri'eɪʃən] *n* : ebriedad *f,* embriaguez *f*

ineffable [ɪn'ɛfəbəl] *adj* : inefable — **ineffably** [-bli] *adv*

ineffective [,ɪnɪ'fɛktɪv] *adj* **1** INEFFECTUAL : ineficaz, inútil **2** INCAPABLE : incompetente, ineficiente, incapaz

ineffectively [,ɪnɪ'fɛktɪvli] *adv* : ineficazmente, infructuosamente

ineffectual [,ɪnɪ'fɛktʃʊəl] *adj* : inútil, ineficaz — **ineffectually** *adv*

inefficiency [,ɪnɪ'fɪʃəntsi] *n, pl* **-cies** : ineficiencia *f,* ineficacia *f*

inefficient [,ɪnɪ'fɪʃənt] *adj* **1** : ineficiente, ineficaz **2** INCAPABLE, INCOMPETENT : incompetente, incapaz — **inefficiently** *adv*

inelegance [ɪn'ɛləgənts] *n* : inelegancia *f*

inelegant [ɪn'ɛləgənt] *adj* : inelegante, poco elegante

ineligibility [ɪn,ɛlədʒə'bɪlət̬i] *n* : inelegibilidad *f*

ineligible [ɪn'ɛlədʒəbəl] *adj* : inelegible

inept [ɪ'nɛpt] *adj* : inepto <inept at : incapaz para>

ineptitude [ɪ'nɛptə,tu:d, -,tju:d] *n* : ineptitud *f,* incompetencia *f,* incapacidad *f*

inequality [,ɪnɪ'kwɑlət̬i] *n, pl* **-ties** : desigualdad *f*

inert [ɪ'nərt] *adj* **1** INACTIVE : inerte, inactivo **2** SLUGGISH : lento

inertia [ɪ'nərʃə] *n* : inercia *f*

inescapable [,ɪnɪ'skeɪpəbəl] *adj* : inevitable, ineludible — **inescapably** [-bli] *adv*

inessential [,ɪnɪ'sɛntʃəl] *adj* : que no es esencial, innecesario

inestimable [ɪn'ɛstəməbəl] *adj* : inestimable, inapreciable

inevitability [ɪn,ɛvət̬ə'bɪlət̬i] *n, pl* **-ties** : inevitabilidad *f*

inevitable [ɪn'ɛvət̬əbəl] *adj* : inevitable — **inevitably** [-bli] *adv*

inexact [,ɪnɪg'zækt] *adj* : inexacto

inexactly [,ɪnɪg'zæktli] *adv* : sin exactitud

inexcusable [,ɪnɪk'skju:zəbəl] *adj* : inexcusable, imperdonable — **inexcusably** [-bli] *adv*

inexhaustible [,ɪnɪg'zɔstəbəl] *adj* **1** INDEFATIGABLE : infatigable, incansable **2** ENDLESS : inagotable — **inexhaustibly** [-bli] *adv*

inexorable [ɪn'ɛksərəbəl] *adj* : inexorable — **inexorably** [-bli] *adv*

inexpensive [,ɪnɪk'spɛntsɪv] *adj* : barato, económico

inexperience [,ɪnɪk'spɪriənts] *n* : inexperiencia *f*

inexperienced [,ɪnɪk'spɪriəntst] *adj* : inexperto, novato

inexplicable [,ɪnɪk'splɪkəbəl] *adj* : inexplicable — **inexplicably** [-bli] *adv*

inexpressible [,ɪnɪk'sprɛsəbəl] *adj* : inexpresable, inefable

inextricable [,ɪnɪk'strɪkəbəl, ɪ'nɛk,strɪ-] *adj* : inextricable — **inextricably** [-bli] *adv*

infallibility [ɪn,fælə'bɪlət̬i] *n* : infalibilidad *f*

infallible [ɪn'fæləbəl] *adj* : infalible — **infallibly** [-bli] *adv*

infamous ['ɪnfəməs] *adj* : infame — **infamously** *adv*

infamy ['ɪnfəmi] *n, pl* **-mies** : infamia *f*

infancy ['ɪnfəntsi] *n, pl* **-cies** : infancia *f*

infant ['ɪnfənt] *n* : bebé *m;* niño *m,* -ña *f*

infantile ['ɪnfən,taɪl, -təl, -,ti:l] *adj* : infantil, pueril

infantile paralysis → **poliomyelitis**

infantry ['ɪnfəntri] *n, pl* **-tries** : infantería *f*

infatuated [ɪn'fætʃʊ,eɪt̬əd] *adj* **to be infatuated with** : estar encaprichado con

infatuation [ɪn,fætʃʊ'eɪʃən] *n* : encaprichamiento *m,* enamoramiento *m*

infect [ɪn'fɛkt] *vt* : infectar, contagiar

infection [ɪn'fɛkʃən] *n* : infección *f,* contagio *m*

infectious [ɪn'fɛkʃəs] *adj* : infeccioso, contagioso

infer [ɪn'fər] *vt* **inferred; inferring 1** DEDUCE : deducir, inferir **2** SURMISE : concluir, suponer, tener entendido **3** IMPLY : sugerir, insinuar

inference ['ɪnfərənts] *n* : deducción *f,* inferencia *f,* conclusión *f*

inferior[1] [ɪn'fɪriər] *adj* : inferior, malo

inferior[2] *n* : inferior *mf*

inferiority [ɪn,fɪri'ɔrət̬i] *n, pl* **-ties** : inferioridad *f* <inferiority complex : complejo de inferioridad>

infernal [ɪn'fərnəl] *adj* **1** : infernal <infernal fires : fuegos infernales> **2** DIABOLICAL : infernal, diabólico **3** DAMNABLE : maldito, condenado

inferno [ɪn'fər,no:] *n, pl* **-nos** : infierno *m*

infertile [ɪn'fərt̬əl, -,taɪl] *adj* : estéril, infecundo

infertility [,ɪnfər'tɪlət̬i] *n* : esterilidad *f,* infecundidad *f*

infest [ɪn'fɛst] *vt* : infestar, plagar

infidel ['ɪnfədəl, -,dɛl] *n* : infiel *mf*

infidelity [ˌɪnfəˈdɛləṭi, -faɪ-] *n, pl* **-ties** **1** UNFAITHFULNESS **:** infidelidad *f* **2** DISLOYALTY **:** deslealtad *f*
infield [ˈɪnˌfiːld] *n* **:** cuadro *m,* diamante *m*
infiltrate [ɪnˈfɪlˌtreɪt, ˈɪnfɪl-] *v* **-trated; -trating** *vt* **:** infiltrar — *vi* **:** infiltrarse
infiltration [ˌɪnfɪlˈtreɪʃən] *n* **:** infiltración *f*
infinite [ˈɪnfənət] *adj* **1** LIMITLESS **:** infinito, sin límites **2** VAST **:** infinito, vasto, extenso
infinitely [ˈɪnfənətli] *adv* **:** infinitamente
infinitesimal [ˌɪnˌfɪnəˈtɛsəməl] *adj* **:** infinitésimo, infinitesimal — **infinitesimally** *adv*
infinitive [ɪnˈfɪnəṭɪv] *n* **:** infinitivo *m*
infinitude [ɪnˈfɪnəˌtuːd, -tjuːd] *n* **:** infinitud *f*
infinity [ɪnˈfɪnəṭi] *n, pl* **-ties** **1 :** infinito *m* (en matemáticas, etc.) **2 :** infinidad *f* <an infinity of stars : una infinidad de estrellas>
infirm [ɪnˈfərm] *adj* **1** FEEBLE **:** enfermizo, endeble **2** INSECURE **:** inseguro
infirmary [ɪnˈfərməri] *n, pl* **-ries :** enfermería *f,* hospital *m*
infirmity [ɪnˈfərməṭi] *n, pl* **-ties** **1** FRAILTY **:** debilidad *f,* endeblez *f* **2** AILMENT **:** enfermedad *f,* dolencia *f* <the infirmities of age : los achaques de la vejez>
inflame [ɪnˈfleɪm] *v* **-flamed; -flaming** *vt* **1** KINDLE **:** inflamar, encender **2 :** inflamar (una herida) **3** STIR UP **:** encender, provocar, inflamar — *vi* **:** inflamarse
inflammable [ɪnˈflæməbəl] *adj* **1** FLAMMABLE **:** inflamable **2** IRASCIBLE **:** irascible, explosivo
inflammation [ˌɪnfləˈmeɪʃən] *n* **:** inflamación *f*
inflammatory [ɪnˈflæməˌtori] *adj* **:** inflamatorio, incendiario
inflatable [ɪnˈfleɪṭəbəl] *adj* **:** inflable
inflate [ɪnˈfleɪt] *vt* **-flated; -flating** **:** inflar, hinchar
inflation [ɪnˈfleɪʃən] *n* **:** inflación *f*
inflationary [ɪnˈfleɪʃəˌnɛri] *adj* **:** inflacionario, inflacionista
inflect [ɪnˈflɛkt] *vt* **1** CONJUGATE, DECLINE **:** conjugar, declinar **2** MODULATE **:** modular (la voz)
inflection [ɪnˈflɛkʃən] *n* **:** inflexión *f*
inflexibility [ɪnˌflɛksəˈbɪləṭi] *n, pl* **-ties** **:** inflexibilidad *f*
inflexible [ɪnˈflɛksɪbəl] *adj* **:** inflexible
inflict [ɪnˈflɪkt] *vt* **1 :** infligir, causar, imponer **2 to inflict oneself on :** imponer uno su presencia (a alguien)
infliction [ɪnˈflɪkʃən] *n* **:** imposición *f*
influence[1] [ˈɪnˌfluːənts, ɪnˈfluːənts] *vt* **-enced; -encing** **:** influenciar, influir en
influence[2] *n* **1 :** influencia *f,* influjo *m* <to exert influence over : ejercer influencia sobre> <the influence of gravity : el influjo de la gravidad> **2 under the influence :** bajo la influencia del alcohol, embriagado
influential [ˌɪnfluˈɛntʃəl] *adj* **:** influyente
influenza [ˌɪnfluˈɛnzə] *n* **:** gripe *f,* influenza *f,* gripa *f Col, Mex*
influx [ˈɪnˌflʌks] *n* **:** afluencia *f* (de gente), entrada *f* (de mercancías), llegada *f* (de ideas)
inform [ɪnˈfɔrm] *vt* **:** informar, notificar, avisar — *vi* **to inform on :** delatar, denunciar
informal [ɪnˈfɔrməl] *adj* **1** UNCEREMONIOUS **:** sin ceremonia, sin etiqueta **2** CASUAL **:** informal, familiar (dícese del lenguaje) **3** UNOFFICIAL **:** extraoficial
informality [ˌɪnfɔrˈmæləṭi, -fər-] *n, pl* **-ties :** informalidad *f,* familiaridad *f,* falta *f* de ceremonia
informally [ɪnˈfɔrməli] *adv* **:** sin ceremonias, de manera informal, informalmente
informant [ɪnˈfɔrmənt] *n* **:** informante *mf;* informador *m,* -dora *f*
information [ˌɪnfərˈmeɪʃən] *n* **:** información *f*
informative [ɪnˈfɔrməṭɪv] *adj* **:** informativo, instructivo
informer [ɪnˈfɔrmər] *n* **:** informante *mf;* informador *m,* -dora *f*
infraction [ɪnˈfrækʃən] *n* **:** infracción *f,* violación *f,* transgresión *f*
infrared [ˌɪnfrəˈrɛd] *adj* **:** infrarrojo
infrastructure [ˈɪnfrəˌstrʌktʃər] *n* **:** infraestructura *f*
infrequent [ɪnˈfriːkwənt] *adj* **:** infrequente, raro
infrequently [ɪnˈfriːkwəntli] *adv* **:** raramente, con poca frecuencia
infringe [ɪnˈfrɪndʒ] *v* **-fringed; -fringing** *vt* **:** infringir, violar — *vi* **to infringe on :** abusar de, violar
infringement [ɪnˈfrɪndʒmənt] *n* **1** VIOLATION **:** violación *f* (de la ley), incumplimiento *m* (de un contrato) **2** ENCROACHMENT **:** usurpación *f* (de derechos, etc.)
infuriate [ɪnˈfjʊriˌeɪt] *vt* **-ated; -ating** **:** enfurecer, poner furioso
infuriating [ɪnˈfjʊriˌeɪṭɪŋ] *adj* **:** indignante, exasperante
infuse [ɪnˈfjuːz] *vt* **-fused; -fusing** **1** INSTILL **:** infundir **2** STEEP **:** hacer una infusión de
infusion [ɪnˈfjuːʒən] *n* **:** infusión *f*
ingenious [ɪnˈdʒiːnjəs] *adj* **:** ingenioso — **ingeniously** *adv*
ingenue *or* **ingénue** [ˈɑndʒəˌnuː, ˈæn-; ˈæʒə-, ˈɑ-] *n* **:** ingenua *f*
ingenuity [ˌɪndʒəˈnuːəṭi, -ˈnjuː-] *n, pl* **-ities :** ingenio
ingenuous [ɪnˈdʒɛnjʊəs] *adj* **1** FRANK **:** cándido, franco **2** NAIVE **:** ingenuo — **ingenuously** *adv*
ingenuousness [ɪnˈdʒɛnjʊəsnəs] *n* **1** FRANKNESS **:** candidez *f,* candor *m* **2** NAÏVETÉ **:** ingenuidad *f*

ingest [ɪn'dʒɛst] *vt* : ingerir

inglorious [ɪn'gloriəs] *adj* : deshonroso, ignominioso

ingot ['ɪŋgət] *n* : lingote *m*

ingrained [ɪn'greɪnd] *adj* : arraigado

ingrate ['ɪn,greɪt] *n* : ingrato *m*, -ta *f*

ingratiate [ɪn'greɪʃi,eɪt] *vt* **-ated; -ating** : conseguir la benevolencia de <to ingratiate oneself with someone : congraciarse con alguien>

ingratiating [ɪn'greɪʃi,eɪṭɪŋ] *adj* : halagador, zalamero, obsequioso

ingratitude [ɪn'grætə,tu:d, -,tju:d] *n* : ingratitud *f*

ingredient [ɪn'gri:diənt] *n* : ingrediente *m*, componente *m*

ingrown ['ɪn,gro:n] *adj* **1** : crecido hacia adentro **2 ingrown toenail** : uña *f* encarnada

inhabit [ɪn'hæbət] *vt* : vivir en, habitar, ocupar

inhabitable [ɪn'hæbəṭəbəl] *adj* : habitable

inhabitant [ɪn'hæbəṭənt] *n* : habitante *mf*

inhalant [ɪn'heɪlənt] *n* : inhalante *m*

inhalation [,ɪnhə'leɪʃən, ,ɪnə-] *n* : inhalación *f*

inhale [ɪn'heɪl] *v* **-haled; -haling** *vt* : inhalar, aspirar — *vi* : inspirar

inhaler [ɪn'heɪlər] *n* : inhalador *m*

inhere [ɪn'hɪr] *vi* **-hered; -hering** : ser inherente

inherent [ɪn'hɪrənt, -'hɛr-] *adj* : inherente, intrínseco — **inherently** *adv*

inherit [ɪn'hɛrət] *vt* : heredar

inheritance [ɪn'hɛrəṭənts] *n* : herencia *f*

inheritor [ɪn'hɛrəṭər] *n* : heredero *m*, -da *f*

inhibit [ɪn'hɪbət] *vt* IMPEDE : inhibir, impedir

inhibition [,ɪnhə'bɪʃən, ,ɪnə-] *n* : inhibición *f*, cohibición *f*

inhuman [ɪn'hju:mən, -'ju:-] *adj* : inhumano, cruel — **inhumanly** *adv*

inhumane [,ɪnhju'meɪn, -ju-] *adj* INHUMAN : inhumano, cruel

inhumanity [,ɪnhju'mænəṭi, -ju-] *n, pl* **-ties** : inhumanidad *f*, crueldad *f*

inimical [ɪ'nɪmɪkəl] *adj* **1** UNFAVORABLE : adverso, desfavorable **2** HOSTILE : hostil — **inimically** *adv*

inimitable [ɪ'nɪməṭəbəl] *adj* : inimitable

iniquitous [ɪ'nɪkwəṭəs] *adj* : inicuo, malvado

iniquity [ɪ'nɪkwəṭi] *n, pl* **-ties** : iniquidad *f*

initial[1] [ɪ'nɪʃəl] *vt* **-tialed** *or* **-tialled; -tialing** *or* **-tialling** : poner las iniciales a, firmar con las iniciales

initial[2] *adj* : inicial, primero — **initially** *adv*

initial[3] *n* : inicial *f*

initiate[1] [ɪ'nɪʃi,eɪt] *vt* **-ated; -ating 1** BEGIN : comenzar, iniciar **2** INDUCT : instruir **3** INTRODUCE : introducir, instruir

initiate[2] [ɪ'nɪʃiət] *n* : iniciado *m*, -da *f*

initiation [ɪ,nɪʃi'eɪʃən] *n* : iniciación *f*

initiative [ɪ'nɪʃəṭɪv] *n* : iniciativa *f*

initiatory [ɪ'nɪʃiə,tori] *adj* **1** INTRODUCTORY : introductorio **2** : de iniciación <initiatory rites : ritos de iniciación>

inject [ɪn'dʒɛkt] *vt* : inyectar

injection [ɪn'dʒɛkʃən] *n* : inyección *f*

injudicious [,ɪndʒʊ'dɪʃəs] *adj* : imprudente, indiscreto, poco juicioso

injunction [ɪn'dʒʌŋkʃən] *n* **1** ORDER : orden *f*, mandato *m* **2** COURT ORDER : mandamiento *m* judicial

injure ['ɪndʒər] *vt* **-jured; -juring 1** WOUND : herir, lesionar **2** HURT : lastimar, dañar, herir **3 to injure oneself** : hacerse daño

injurious [ɪn'dʒʊriəs] *adj* : perjudicial <injurious to one's health : perjudicial a la salud>

injury ['ɪndʒəri] *n, pl* **-ries 1** WRONG : mal *m*, injusticia *f* **2** DAMAGE, HARM : herida *f*, daño *m*, perjuicio *m*

injustice [ɪn'dʒʌstəs] *n* : injusticia *f*

ink[1] ['ɪŋk] *vt* : entintar

ink[2] *n* : tinta *f*

inkling ['ɪŋklɪŋ] *n* : presentimiento *m*, indicio *m*, sospecho *m*

inkwell ['ɪŋk,wɛl] *n* : tintero *m*

inky ['ɪŋki] *adj* **1** : manchado de tinta **2** BLACK : negro, impenetrable <inky darkness : negra oscuridad>

inland[1] ['ɪn,lænd, -lənd] *adv* : hacia el interior, tierra adentro

inland[2] *adj* : interior

inland[3] *n* : interior *m*

in–law ['ɪn,lɔ] *n* **1** : pariente *m* político **2 in–laws** *npl* : suegros *mpl*

inlay[1] [ɪn'leɪ, 'ɪn,leɪ] *vt* **-laid** [-'leɪd, -,leɪd]; **-laying** : incrustar, taracear

inlay[2] ['ɪn,leɪ] *n* **1** : incrustación *f* **2** : empaste *m* (de un diente)

inlet ['ɪn,lɛt, -lət] *n* : cala *f*, ensenada *f*

inmate ['ɪn,meɪt] *n* : paciente *mf* (en un hospital); preso *m*, -sa *f* (en una prisión); interno *m*, -na *f* (en un asilo)

in memoriam [,ɪnmə'moriəm] *prep* : en memoria de

inmost ['ɪn,mo:st] → **innermost**

inn ['ɪn] *n* **1** : posada *f*, hostería *f*, fonda *f* **2** TAVERN : taberna *f*

innards ['ɪnərdz] *npl* : entrañas *fpl*, tripas *fpl fam*

innate [ɪ'neɪt] *adj* **1** INBORN : innato **2** INHERENT : inherente

inner ['ɪnər] *adj* : interior, interno

innermost ['ɪnər,mo:st] *adj* : más íntimo, más profundo

innersole ['ɪnər'so:l] → **insole**

inning ['ɪnɪŋ] *n* : entrada *f*

innkeeper ['ɪn,ki:pər] *n* : posadero *m*, -ra *f*

innocence ['ɪnəsənts] *n* : inocencia *f*

innocent[1] ['ɪnəsənt] *adj* : inocente — **innocently** *adv*

innocent[2] *n* : inocente *mf*

innocuous [ɪ'nɑkjəwəs] *adj* **1** HARMLESS : inocuo **2** INOFFENSIVE : inofensivo

innovate ['ɪnə,veɪt] *vi* **-vated; -vating** : innovar

innovation [,ɪnə'veɪʃən] *n* : innovación *f,* novedad *f*

innovative ['ɪnə,veɪt̬ɪv] *adj* : innovador

innovator ['ɪnə,veɪt̬ər] *n* : innovador *m,* -dora *f*

innuendo [,ɪnjʊ'ɛndo] *n, pl* **-dos** *or* **-does** : insinuación *f,* indirecta *f*

innumerable [ɪ'nu:mərəbəl, -'nju:-] *adj* : innumerable

inoculate [ɪ'nɑkjə,leɪt] *vt* **-lated; -lating** : inocular

inoculation [ɪ,nɑkjə'leɪʃən] *n* : inoculación *f*

inoffensive [,ɪnə'fɛntsɪv] *adj* : inofensivo

inoperable [ɪn'ɑpərəbəl] *adj* : inoperable

inoperative [ɪn'ɑpərət̬ɪv, -,reɪ-] *adj* : inoperante

inopportune [ɪn,ɑpər'tu:n, -'tju:n] *adj* : inoportuno — **inopportunely** *adv*

inordinate [ɪn'ɔrdənət] *adj* : excesivo, inmoderado, desmesurado — **inordinately** *adv*

inorganic [,ɪn,ɔr'gænɪk] *adj* : inorgánico

inpatient ['ɪn,peɪʃənt] *n* : paciente *mf* hospitalizado

input[1] ['ɪn,pʊt] *vt* **inputted** *or* **input; inputting** : entrar (datos, información)

input[2] *n* **1** CONTRIBUTION : aportación *f,* contribución *f* **2** ENTRY : entrada *f* (de datos) **3** ADVICE, OPINION : consejos *mpl,* opinión *f*

inquest ['ɪn,kwɛst] *n* INQUIRY, INVESTIGATION : investigación *f,* averiguación *f,* pesquisa *f* (judicial)

inquire [ɪn'kwaɪr] *v* **-quired; -quiring** *vt* : preguntar, informarse de, inquirir <he inquired how to get in : preguntó como entrar> — *vi* **1** ASK : preguntar, informarse <to inquire about : informarse sobre> <to inquire after (someone) : preguntar por (alguien)> **2 to inquire into** INVESTIGATE : investigar, inquirir sobre

inquirer [ɪn'kwaɪrər] *n* : inquiridor *m,* -dora *f;* investigador *m,* -dora *f*

inquiringly [ɪn'kwaɪrɪŋli] *adv* : inquisitivamente

inquiry ['ɪn,kwaɪri, ɪn'kwaɪri; 'ɪnkwəri, 'ɪŋ-] *n, pl* **-ries 1** QUESTION : pregunta *f* <to make inquiries about : pedir información sobre> **2** INVESTIGATION : investigación *f,* inquisición *f,* pesquisa *f*

inquisition [,ɪnkwə'zɪʃən, ,ɪŋ-] *n* **1** : inquisición *f,* interrogatorio *m,* investigación *f* **2 the Inquisition** : la Inquisición *f*

inquisitive [ɪn'kwɪzət̬ɪv] *adj* : inquisidor, inquisitivo, curioso — **inquisitively** *adv*

inquisitiveness [ɪn'kwɪzət̬ɪvnəs] *n* : curiosidad *f*

inquisitor [ɪn'kwɪzət̬ər] *n* : inquisidor *m,* -dora *f;* interrogador *m,* -dora *f*

inroad ['ɪn,ro:d] *n* **1** ENCROACHMENT, INVASION : invasión *f,* incursión *f* **2 to make inroads into** : ocupar parte de (un tiempo), agotar parte de (ahorros, recursos), invadir (un territorio)

insane [ɪn'seɪn] *adj* **1** MAD : loco, demente <to go insane : volverse loco> **2** ABSURD : absurdo, insensato <an insane scheme : un proyecto insensato>

insanely [ɪn'seɪnli] *adv* : como un loco <insanely suspicious : loco de recelo>

insanity [ɪn'sænət̬i] *n, pl* **-ties 1** MADNESS : locura *f* **2** FOLLY : locura *f,* insensatez *f*

insatiable [ɪn'seɪʃəbəl] *adj* : insaciable — **insatiably** [-bli] *adv*

inscribe [ɪn'skraɪb] *vt* **-scribed; -scribing 1** ENGRAVE : inscribir, grabar **2** ENROLL : inscribir **3** DEDICATE : dedicar (un libro)

inscription [ɪn'skrɪpʃən] *n* : inscripción *f* (en un monumento), dedicación *f* (en un libro), leyenda *f* (de una ilustración, etc.)

inscrutable [ɪn'skru:t̬əbəl] *adj* : inescrutable, misterioso — **inscrutably** [-bli] *adv*

inseam ['ɪn,si:m] *n* : entrepierna *f*

insect ['ɪn,sɛkt] *n* : insecto *m*

insecticidal [ɪn,sɛktə'saɪdəl] *adj* : insecticida

insecticide [ɪn'sɛktə,saɪd] *n* : insecticida *m*

insecure [,ɪnsɪ'kjʊr] *adj* : inseguro, poco seguro — **insecurely** *adv*

insecurely [,ɪnsɪ'kjʊrli] *adv* : inseguramente

insecurity [,ɪnsɪ'kjʊrət̬i] *n, pl* **-ties** : inseguridad *f*

inseminate [ɪn'sɛmə,neɪt] *vt* **-nated; -nating** : inseminar

insemination [ɪn,sɛmə'neɪʃən] *n* : inseminación *f*

insensibility [ɪn,sɛntsə'bɪlət̬i] *n, pl* **-ties** : insensibilidad *f*

insensible [ɪn'sɛntsəbəl] *adj* **1** UNCONSCIOUS : inconsciente, sin conocimiento **2** NUMB : insensible, entumecido **3** UNAWARE : inconsciente

insensitive [ɪn'sɛntsət̬ɪv] *adj* : insensible

insensitivity [ɪn,sɛntsə'tɪvət̬i] *n, pl* **-ties** : insensibilidad *f*

inseparable [ɪn'sɛpərəbəl] *adj* : inseparable

insert[1] [ɪn'sərt] *vt* **1** : insertar, introducir, poner, meter <insert your key in the lock : mete tu llave en la cerradura> **2** INTERPOLATE : interpolar, intercalar

insert[2] [ˈɪnˌsərt] *n* **:** inserción *f,* hoja *f* insertada (en una revista, etc.)

insertion [ɪnˈsərʃən] *n* **:** inserción *f*

inset [ˈɪnˌsɛt] *n* **:** página *f* intercalada (en un libro), entredós *m* (de encaje en la ropa)

inshore[1] [ˈɪnˈʃor] *adv* **:** hacia la costa

inshore[2] *adj* **:** cercano a la costa, costero <inshore fishing **:** pesca costera>

inside[1] [ɪnˈsaɪd, ˈɪnˌsaɪd] *adv* **:** adentro, dentro <to run inside **:** correr para adentro> <inside and out **:** por dentro y por fuera>

inside[2] *adj* **1 :** interior, de adentro, de dentro <the inside lane **:** el carril interior> **2 :** confidencial <inside information **:** información confidencial>

inside[3] *n* **1 :** interior *m,* parte *f* de adentro **2 insides** *npl* BELLY, GUTS **:** tripas *fpl fam* **3 inside out :** al revés

inside[4] *prep* **1** INTO **:** al interior de **2** WITHIN **:** dentro de **3** (*referring to time*) **:** en menos de <inside an hour **:** en menos de una hora>

inside of *prep* INSIDE **:** dentro de

insider [ɪnˈsaɪdər] *n* **:** persona *f* enterada

insidious [ɪnˈsɪdiəs] *adj* **:** insidioso — **insidiously** *adv*

insidiousness [ɪnˈsɪdiəsnəs] *n* **:** insidia *f*

insight [ˈɪnˌsaɪt] *n* **:** perspicacia *f,* penetración *f*

insightful [ɪnˈsaɪtfəl] *adj* **:** perspicaz

insignia [ɪnˈsɪgniə] *or* **insigne** [-ˌniː] *n, pl* **-nia** *or* **-nias :** insignia *f,* enseña *f*

insignificance [ˌɪnsɪgˈnɪfɪkən*t*s] *n* **:** insignificancia *f*

insignificant [ˌɪnsɪgˈnɪfɪkənt] *adj* **:** insignificante

insincere [ˌɪnsɪnˈsɪr] *adj* **:** insincero, poco sincero

insincerely [ˌɪnsɪnˈsɪrli] *adv* **:** con poca sinceridad

insincerity [ˌɪnsɪnˈsɛrət̬i, -ˈsɪr-] *n, pl* **-ties :** insinceridad *f*

insinuate [ɪnˈsɪnjʊˌeɪt] *vt* **-ated; -ating :** insinuar

insinuation [ɪnˌsɪnjʊˈeɪʃən] *n* **:** insinuación *f*

insipid [ɪnˈsɪpəd] *adj* **:** insípido

insist [ɪnˈsɪst] *v* **:** insistir

insistence [ɪnˈsɪstən*t*s] *n* **:** insistencia *f*

insistent [ɪnˈsɪstənt] *adj* **:** insistente — **insistently** *adv*

insofar as [ˌɪnsoˈfɑræz] *conj* **:** en la medida en que, en tanto que, en cuanto a

insole [ˈɪnˌsoːl] *n* **:** plantilla *f*

insolence [ˈɪn*t*sələn*t*s] *n* **:** insolencia *f*

insolent [ˈɪn*t*sələnt] *adj* **:** insolente

insolubility [ɪnˌsɑljʊˈbɪlət̬i] *n* **:** insolubilidad *f*

insoluble [ɪnˈsɑljʊbəl] *adj* **:** insoluble

insolvency [ɪnˈsɑlvən*t*si] *n, pl* **-cies :** insolvencia *f*

insolvent [ɪnˈsɑlvənt] *adj* **:** insolvente

insomnia [ɪnˈsɑmniə] *n* **:** insomnio *m*

insomuch as [ˌɪnsoˈmʌtʃæz] → **inasmuch as**

insomuch that *conj* SO **:** así que, de manera que

inspect [ɪnˈspɛkt] *vt* **:** inspeccionar, examinar, revisar

inspection [ɪnˈspɛkʃən] *n* **:** inspección *f,* examen *m,* revisión *f,* revista *f* (de tropas)

inspector [ɪnˈspɛktər] *n* **:** inspector *m,* -tora *f*

inspiration [ˌɪn*t*spəˈreɪʃən] *n* **:** inspiración *f*

inspirational [ˌɪn*t*spəˈreɪʃənəl] *adj* **:** inspirador

inspire [ɪnˈspaɪr] *v* **-spired; -spiring** *vt* **1** INHALE **:** inhalar, aspirar **2** STIMULATE **:** estimular, animar, inspirar **3** INSTILL **:** inspirar, infundir — *vi* **:** inspirar

instability [ˌɪn*t*stəˈbɪlət̬i] *n, pl* **-ties :** inestabilidad *f*

install [ɪnˈstɔl] *vt* **-stalled; -stalling 1 :** instalar <to install the new president **:** instalar el presidente nuevo> <to install a fan **:** montar un abanico> **2 to install oneself :** instalarse

installation [ˌɪn*t*stəˈleɪʃən] *n* **:** instalación *f*

installment [ɪnˈstɔlmənt] *n* **1 :** plazo *m,* cuota *f* <to pay in four installments **:** pagar a cuatro plazos> **2 :** entrega *f* (de una publicación o telenovela) **3** INSTALLATION **:** instalación *f*

instance [ˈɪn*t*stən*t*s] *n* **1** INSTIGATION **:** instancia *f* **2** EXAMPLE **:** ejemplo *m* <for instance **:** por ejemplo> **3** OCCASION **:** instancia *f,* caso *m,* ocasión *f* <he prefers, in this instance, to remain anonymous **:** en este caso prefiere quedarse anónimo>

instant[1] [ˈɪn*t*stənt] *adj* **1** IMMEDIATE **:** inmediato, instantáneo <an instant reply **:** una respuesta inmediata> **2 :** instantáneo <instant coffee **:** café instantáneo>

instant[2] *n* **:** momento *m,* instante *m*

instantaneous [ˌɪn*t*stənˈteɪniəs] *adj* **:** instantáneo

instantaneously [ˌɪn*t*stənˈteɪniəsli] *adv* **:** instantáneamente, al instante

instantly [ˈɪn*t*stəntli] *adv* **:** al instante, instantáneamente

instead [ɪnˈstɛd] *adv* **1 :** en cambio, en lugar de eso, en su lugar <Dad was going, but Mom went instead **:** papá iba a ir, pero mamá fue en su lugar> **2** RATHER **:** al contrario

instead of *prep* **:** en vez de, en lugar de

instep [ˈɪnˌstɛp] *n* **:** empeine *m*

instigate [ˈɪn*t*stəˌgeɪt] *vt* **-gated; -gating** INCITE, PROVOKE **:** instigar, incitar, provocar, fomentar

instigation [ˌɪn*t*stəˈgeɪʃən] *n* **:** instancia *f,* incitación *f*

instigator [ˈɪn*t*stəˌgeɪt̬ər] *n* **:** instigador *m,* -dora *f;* incitador *m,* -dora *f*

instill [ɪn'stɪl] *vt* **-stilled; -stilling** : inculcar, infundir

instinct ['ɪn,stɪŋkt] *n* **1** TALENT : instinto *m,* don *m* <an instinct for the right word : un don para escoger la palabra apropiada> **2** : instinto *m* <maternal instincts : instintos maternales>

instinctive [ɪn'stɪŋktɪv] *adj* : instintivo

instinctively [ɪn'stɪŋktɪvli] *adv* : instintivamente, por instinto

instinctual [ɪn'stɪŋktʃʊəl] *adj* : instintivo

institute[1] ['ɪntstə,tu:t, -,tju:t] *vt* **-tuted; -tuting 1** ESTABLISH: establecer, instituir, fundar **2** INITIATE : iniciar, empezar, entablar

institute[2] *n* : instituto *m*

institution [,ɪntstə'tu:ʃən, -'tju:-] *n* **1** ESTABLISHING : institución *f,* establecimiento *m* **2** CUSTOM : institución *f,* tradición *f* <the institution of marriage : la institución del matrimonio> **3** ORGANIZATION : institución *f,* organismo *m* **4** ASYLUM : asilo *m*

institutional [,ɪntstə'tu:ʃənəl, -'tju:-] *adj* : institucional

institutionalize [,ɪntstə'tu:ʃənə,laɪz, -'tju:-] *vt* **-ized; -izing 1** : institucionalizar <institutionalized values : valores institucionalizados> **2** : internar <institutionalized orphans : huérfanos internados>

instruct [ɪn'strʌkt] *vt* **1** TEACH, TRAIN : instruir, adiestrar, enseñar **2** COMMAND : mandar, ordenar, dar instrucciones a

instruction [ɪn'strʌkʃən] *n* **1** TEACHING : instrucción *f,* enseñanza *f* **2** COMMAND : orden *f,* instrucción *f* **3 instructions** *npl* DIRECTIONS : instrucciones *fpl,* modo *m* de empleo

instructional [ɪn'strʌkʃənəl] *adj* : instructivo, educativo

instructive [ɪn'strʌktɪv] *adj* : instructivo

instructor [ɪn'strʌktər] *n* : instructor *m,* -tora *f*

instrument ['ɪntstrəmənt] *n* : instrumento *m*

instrumental [,ɪntstrə'mɛntəl] *adj* : instrumental

instrumentalist [,ɪntstrə'mɛntəlɪst] *n* : instrumentista *mf*

insubordinate [,ɪnsə'bɔrdənət] *adj* : insubordinado

insubordination [,ɪnsə,bɔrdən'eɪʃən] *n* : insubordinación *f*

insubstantial [,ɪnsəb'stæntʃəl] *adj* : insustancial, poco nutritivo (dícese de una comida), poco sólido (dícese de una estructura o un argumento)

insufferable [ɪn'sʌfərəbəl] *adj* UNBEARABLE : insufrible, intolerable, inaguantable, insoportable — **insufferably** [-bli] *adv*

insufficiency [,ɪnsə'fɪʃəntsi] *n, pl* **-cies** : insuficiencia *f*

insufficient [,ɪnsə'fɪʃənt] *adj* : insuficiente — **insufficiently** *adv*

insular ['ɪntsʊlər, -sjʊ-] *adj* **1** : isleño (dícese de la gente), insular (dícese del clima) <insular residents : residentes de la isla> **2** NARROW-MINDED : de miras estrechas

insularity [,ɪntsʊ'lærəṭi, -sjʊ-] *n* : insularidad *f*

insulate ['ɪntsə,leɪt] *vt* **-lated; -lating** : aislar

insulation [,ɪntsə'leɪʃən] *n* : aislamiento *m*

insulator ['ɪntsə,leɪṭər] *n* : aislante *m,* aislador *m*

insulin ['ɪntsələn] *n* : insulina *f*

insult[1] [ɪn'sʌlt] *vt* : insultar, ofender, injuriar

insult[2] ['ɪn,sʌlt] *n* : insulto *m,* injuria *f,* agravio *m*

insulting [ɪn'sʌltɪŋ] *adj* : ofensivo, injurioso, insultante

insultingly [ɪn'sʌltɪŋli] *adv* : ofensivamente, de manera insultante

insuperable [ɪn'su:pərəbəl] *adj* : insuperable — **insuperably** [-bli] *adv*

insurable [ɪn'ʃʊrəbəl] *adj* : asegurable

insurance [ɪn'ʃʊrənts, 'ɪn,ʃʊr-] *n* : seguro *m* <life insurance : seguro de vida> <insurance company : compañía de seguros>

insure [ɪn'ʃʊr] *vt* **-sured; -suring 1** UNDERWRITE : asegurar **2** ENSURE : asegurar, garantizar

insured [ɪn'ʃʊrd] *n* : asegurado *m,* -da *f*

insurer [ɪn'ʃʊrər] *n* : asegurador *m,* -dora *f*

insurgent[1] [ɪn'sərdʒənt] *adj* : insurgente

insurgent[2] *n* : insurgente *mf*

insurmountable [,ɪnsər'maʊntəbəl] *adj* : insuperable, insalvable — **insurmountably** [-bli] *adv*

insurrection [,ɪnsə'rɛkʃən] *n* : insurrección *f,* levantamiento *m,* alzamiento *m*

intact [ɪn'tækt] *adj* : intacto

intake ['ɪn,teɪk] *n* **1** OPENING : entrada *f,* toma *f* <fuel intake : toma de combustible> **2** : entrada *f* (de agua o aire), consumo *m* (de sustancias nutritivas) **3 intake of breath** : inhalación *f*

intangible [ɪn'tændʒəbəl] *adj* : intangible, impalpable — **intangibly** [-bli] *adv*

integer ['ɪntɪdʒər] *n* : entero *m*

integral ['ɪntɪgrəl] *adj* : integral, esencial

integrate ['ɪntə,greɪt] *v* **-grated; -grating** *vt* **1** UNITE : integrar, unir **2** DESEGREGATE : eliminar la segregación de — *vi* : integrarse

integration [,ɪntə'greɪʃən] *n* : integración *f*

integrity [ɪn'tɛgrəṭi] *n* : integridad *f*

intellect ['ɪntəl,ɛkt] *n* : intelecto *m,* inteligencia *f,* capacidad *f* intelectual

intellectual[1] [ˌɪntəˈlɛktʃʊəl] *adj* : intelectual — **intellectually** *adv*
intellectual[2] *n* : intelectual *mf*
intellectualism [ˌɪntəˈlɛktʃʊəˌlɪzəm] *n* : intelectualismo *m*
intelligence [ɪnˈtɛləʤənts] *n* **1** : inteligencia *f* **2** INFORMATION, NEWS : inteligencia *f,* información *f,* noticias *fpl*
intelligent [ɪnˈtɛləʤənt] *adj* : inteligente — **intelligently** *adv*
intelligibility [ɪnˌtɛləʤəˈbɪləṱi] *n* : inteligibilidad *f*
intelligible [ɪnˈtɛləʤəbəl] *adj* : inteligible, comprensible — **intelligibly** [-bli] *adv*
intemperance [ɪnˈtɛmpərənts] *n* : inmoderación *f,* intemperancia *f*
intemperate [ɪnˈtɛmpərət] *adj* : excesivo, inmoderado, desmedido
intend [ɪnˈtɛnd] *vt* **1** MEAN : querer decir <that's not what I intended : eso no es lo que quería decir> **2** PLAN : tener planeado, proyectar, proponerse <I intend to finish by Thursday : me propongo acabar para el jueves>
intended [ɪnˈtɛndəd] *adj* **1** PLANNED : previsto, proyectado **2** INTENTIONAL : intencional, deliberado
intense [ɪnˈtɛnts] *adj* **1** EXTREME : intenso, extremo <intense pain : dolor intenso> **2** : profundo, intenso <to my intense relief : para mi alivio profundo> <intense enthusiasm : entusiasmo ardiente>
intensely [ɪnˈtɛntsli] *adv* : sumamente, profundamente, intensamente
intensification [ɪnˌtɛntsəfəˈkeɪʃən] *n* : intensificación *f*
intensify [ɪnˈtɛntsəˌfaɪ] *v* **-fied; -fying** *vt* **1** STRENGTHEN : intensificar, redoblar <to intensify one's efforts : redoblar uno sus esfuerzos> **2** SHARPEN : intensificar, agudizar (dolor, ansiedad) — *vi* : intensificarse, hacerse más intenso
intensity [ɪnˈtɛntsəṱi] *n, pl* **-ties** : intensidad *f*
intensive [ɪnˈtɛntsɪv] *adj* : intensivo — **intensively** *adv*
intent[1] [ɪnˈtɛnt] *adj* **1** FIXED : concentrado, fijo <an intent stare : una mirada fija> **2 intent on** *or* **intent upon** : resuelto a, atento a
intent[2] *n* **1** PURPOSE : intención *f,* propósito *m* **2 for all intents and purposes** : a todos los efectos, prácticamente
intention [ɪnˈtɛntʃən] *n* : intención *f,* propósito *m*
intentional [ɪnˈtɛntʃənəl] *adj* : intencional, deliberado
intentionally [ɪnˈtɛntʃənəli] *adv* : a propósito, adrede
intently [ɪnˈtɛntli] *adv* : atentamente, fijamente
inter [ɪnˈtər] *vt* **-terred; -terring** : enterrar, inhumar
interact [ˌɪntərˈækt] *vi* : interactuar, actuar recíprocamente, relacionarse
interaction [ˌɪntərˈækʃən] *n* : interacción *f,* interrelación *f*
interactive [ˌɪntərˈæktɪv] *adj* : interactivo
interbreed [ˌɪntərˈbriːd] *v* **-bred** [-ˈbrɛd]; **-breeding** *vt* : cruzar — *vi* : cruzarse
intercalate [ɪnˈtərkəˌleɪt] *vt* **-lated; -lating** : intercalar
intercede [ˌɪntərˈsiːd] *vi* **-ceded; -ceding** : interceder
intercept [ˌɪntərˈsɛpt] *vt* : interceptar
interception [ˌɪntərˈsɛpʃən] *n* : intercepción *f*
intercession [ˌɪntərˈsɛʃən] *n* : intercesión *f*
interchange[1] [ˌɪntərˈtʃeɪnʤ] *vt* **-changed; -changing** : intercambiar
interchange[2] [ˈɪntərˌtʃeɪnʤ] *n* **1** EXCHANGE : intercambio *m,* cambio *m* **2** JUNCTION : empalme *m,* enlace *m* de carreteras
interchangeable [ˌɪntərˈtʃeɪnʤəəl] *adj* : intercambiable
intercity [ˈɪntərˈsɪṱi] *adj* : interurbano
intercollegiate [ˌɪntərkəˈliːʤət, -ʤiət] *adj* : interuniversitario
intercontinental [ˌɪntərˌkɑntənˈɛntəl] *adj* : intercontinental
intercourse [ˈɪntərˌkors] *n* **1** RELATIONS : relaciones *fpl,* trato *m* **2** COPULATION : acto *m* sexual, relaciones *fpl* sexuales, coito *m*
interdenominational [ˌɪntərdɪˌnɑməˈneɪʃənəl] *adj* : interconfesional
interdepartmental [ˌɪntərdɪˌpɑrtˈmɛntəl, -ˌdiː-] *adj* : interdepartamental
interdependence [ˌɪntərdɪˈpɛndənts] *n* : interdependencia *f*
interdependent [ˌɪntərdɪˈpɛndənt] *adj* : interdependiente
interdict [ˌɪntərˈdɪkt] *vt* **1** PROHIBIT : prohibir **2** : cortar (las líneas de comunicación o provisión del enemigo)
interest[1] [ˈɪntrəst, -təˌrɛst] *vt* : interesar
interest[2] *n* **1** SHARE, STAKE : interés *m,* participación *f* **2** BENEFIT : provecho *m,* beneficio *m,* interés *m* <in the public interest : en el interés público> **3** CHARGE : interés *m,* cargo *m* <compound interest : interés compuesto> **4** CURIOSITY : interés *m,* curiosidad *f* **5** COLOR : color *m,* interés *m* <places of local interest : lugares de color local> **6** HOBBY : afición *f*
interesting [ˈɪntrəstɪŋ, -təˌrɛstɪŋ] *adj* : interesante — **interestingly** *adv*
interface [ˈɪntərˌfeɪs] *n* **1** : punto *m* de contacto <oil-water interface : punto de contacto entre el agua y el aceite> **2** : interfase *f,* interfaz *f* (de una computadora)
interfere [ˌɪntərˈfɪr] *vi* **-fered; -fering** **1** INTERPOSE : interponerse, hacer in-

terferencia <to interfere with a play : obstruir una jugada> **2** MEDDLE : entrometerse, interferir, intervenir **3 to interfere with** DISRUPT : afectar (una actividad), interferir (la radiotransmisión) **4 to interfere with** TOUCH : tocar <someone interfered with my papers : alguien tocó mis papeles>

interference [ˌɪntərˈfɪrənts] *n* : interferencia *f,* intromisión *f*

intergalactic [ˌɪntərgəˈlæktɪk] *adj* : intergaláctico

intergovernmental [ˌɪntərˌgʌvərˈmɛntəl, -vərn-] *adj* : intergubernamental

interim¹ [ˈɪntərəm] *adj* : interino, provisional

interim² *n* **1** : interín *m,* intervalo *m* **2 in the interim** : en el interín, mientras tanto

interior¹ [ɪnˈtɪriər] *adj* : interior

interior² *n* : interior *m*

interject [ˌɪntərˈdʒɛkt] *vt* : interponer, agregar

interjection [ˌɪntərˈdʒɛkʃən] *n* **1** : interjección *f* (en lingüística) **2** EXCLAMATION : exclamación *f* **3** INTERPOSITION, INTERRUPTION : interposición *f,* interrupción *f*

interlace [ˌɪntərˈleɪs] *vt* **-laced; -lacing 1** INTERWEAVE : entrelazar **2** INTERSPERSE : intercalar

interlock [ˌɪntərˈlɑk] *vt* **1** UNITE : trabar, unir **2** ENGAGE, MESH : engranar — *vi* : entrelazarse, trabarse

interloper [ˌɪntərˈloːpər] *n* **1** INTRUDER : intruso *m,* -sa *f* **2** MEDDLER : entrometido *m,* -da *f*

interlude [ˈɪntərˌluːd] *n* **1** INTERVAL : intervalo *m,* intermedio *m* (en el teatro) **2** : interludio *m* (en música)

intermarriage [ˌɪntərˈmærɪdʒ] *n* **1** : matrimonio *m* mixto (entre miembros de distintas razas o religiones) **2** : matrimonio *m* entre miembros del mismo grupo

intermarry [ˌɪntərˈmæri] *vi* **-married; -marrying 1** : casarse (con miembros de otros grupos) **2** : casarse entre sí (con miembros del mismo grupo)

intermediary¹ [ˌɪntərˈmiːdiˌɛri] *adj* : intermediario

intermediary² *n, pl* **-aries** : intermediario *m,* -ria *f*

intermediate¹ [ˌɪntərˈmiːdiət] *adj* : intermedio

intermediate² *n* GO-BETWEEN : intermediario *m,* -ria *f;* mediador *m,* -dora *f*

interment [ɪnˈtərmənt] *n* : entierro *m*

interminable [ɪnˈtərmənəbəl] *adj* : interminable, constante — **interminably** [-bli] *adv*

intermingle [ˌɪntərˈmɪŋgəl] *vt* **-mingled; -mingling** : entremezclar, mezclar — *vi* : entremezclarse

intermission [ˌɪntərˈmɪʃən] *n* : intermisión *f,* intervalo *m,* intermedio *m*

intermittent [ˌɪntərˈmɪtənt] *adj* : intermitente — **intermittently** *adv*

intermix [ˌɪntərˈmɪks] *vt* : entremezclar

intern¹ [ˈɪnˌtərn, ɪnˈtərn] *vt* : confinar (durante la guerra) — *vi* : servir de interno, hacer las prácticas

intern² [ˈɪnˌtərn] *n* : interno *m,* -na *f*

internal [ɪnˈtərnəl] *adj* : interno, interior <internal bleeding : hemorragia interna> <internal affairs : asuntos interiores, asuntos domésticos> — **internally** *adv*

international [ˌɪntərˈnæʃənəl] *adj* : internacional — **internationally** *adv*

internationalize [ˌɪntərˈnæʃənəˌlaɪz] *vt* **-ized; -izing** : internacionalizar

internee [ˌɪnˌtərˈniː] *n* : interno *m,* -na *f*

internist [ˈɪnˌtərnɪst] *n* : internista *mf*

interpersonal [ˌɪntərˈpərsənəl] *adj* : interpersonal

interplay [ˈɪntərˌpleɪ] *n* : interacción *f,* juego *m*

interpolate [ɪnˈtərpəˌleɪt] *vt* **-lated; -lating** : interpolar

interpose [ˌɪntərˈpoːz] *v* **-posed; -posing** *vt* : interponer, interrumpir con — *vi* : interponerse

interposition [ˌɪntərpəˈzɪʃən] *n* : interposición *f*

interpret [ɪnˈtərprət] *vt* : interpretar

interpretation [ɪnˌtərprəˈteɪʃən] *n* : interpretación *f*

interpretative [ɪnˈtərprəˌteɪt̬ɪv] *adj* : interpretativo

interpreter [ɪnˈtərprət̬ər] *n* : intérprete *mf*

interpretive [ɪnˈtərprət̬ɪv] *adj* : interpretativo

interracial [ˌɪntərˈreɪʃəl] *adj* : interracial

interrelate [ˌɪntərɪˈleɪt] *vi* **-related; -relating** : interelacionar

interrelationship [ˌɪntərɪˈleɪʃənˌʃɪp] *n* : interrelación *f*

interrogate [ɪnˈtɛrəˌgeɪt] *vt* **-gated; -gating** : interrogar, someter a un interrogatorio

interrogation [ɪnˌtɛrəˈgeɪʃən] *n* : interrogación *f*

interrogative¹ [ˌɪntəˈrɑgət̬ɪv] *adj* : interrogativo

interrogative² *n* : interrogativo *m*

interrogator [ɪnˈtɛrəˌgeɪt̬ər] *n* : interrogador *m,* -dora *f*

interrogatory [ˌɪntəˈrɑgəˌtɔri] → **interrogative¹**

interrupt [ˌɪntəˈrʌpt] *v* : interrumpir

interruption [ˌɪntəˈrʌpʃən] *n* : interrupción *f*

intersect [ˌɪntərˈsɛkt] *vt* : cruzar, cortar — *vi* : cruzarse (dícese de los caminos), intersectarse (dícese de las líneas o figuras), cortarse

intersection [ˌɪntərˈsɛkʃən] *n* : intersección *f,* cruce *m*

intersperse [ˌɪntərˈspərs] *vt* **-spersed; -spersing** : intercalar, entremezclar

interstate [ˌɪntərˈsteɪt] *adj* : interestatal

interstellar [ˌɪntərˈstɛlər] *adj* : interestelar

interstice [ɪnˈtərstəs] *n, pl* **-stices** [-stəˌsiːz, -stəsəz] : intersticio *m*

intertwine [ˌɪntərˈtwaɪn] *vi* **-twined; -twining** : entrelazarse

interval [ˈɪntərvəl] *n* : intervalo *m*

intervene [ˌɪntərˈviːn] *vi* **-vened; -vening 1** ELAPSE : transcurrir, pasar <the intervening years : los años intermediarios> **2** INTERCEDE : intervenir, interceder, mediar

intervention [ˌɪntərˈvɛntʃən] *n* : intervención *f*

interview[1] [ˈɪntərˌvjuː] *vt* : entrevistar — *vi* : hacer entrevistas

interview[2] *n* : entrevista *f*

interviewer [ˈɪntərˌvjuːər] *n* : entrevistador *m*, -dora *f*

interweave [ˌɪntərˈwiːv] *v* **-wove** [-ˈwoːv]; **-woven** [-ˈwoːvən]; **-weaving** *vt* : entretejer, entrelazar — *vi* INTERTWINE : entrelazarse, entretejerse

interwoven [ˌɪntərˈwoːvən] *adj* : entretejido

intestate [ɪnˈtɛsˌteɪt, -tət] *adj* : intestado

intestinal [ɪnˈtɛstənəl] *adj* : intestinal

intestine [ɪnˈtɛstən] *n* **1** : intestino *m* **2 small intestine** : intestino *m* delgado **3 large intestine** : intestino *m* grueso

intimacy [ˈɪntəməsi] *n, pl* **-cies 1** CLOSENESS : intimidad *f* **2** FAMILIARITY : familiaridad *f*

intimate[1] [ˈɪntəˌmeɪt] *vt* **-mated; -mating** : insinuar, dar a entender

intimate[2] [ˈɪntəmət] *adj* **1** CLOSE : íntimo, de confianza <intimate friends : amigos íntimos> **2** PRIVATE : íntimo, privado <intimate clubs : clubes íntimos> **3** INNERMOST, SECRET : íntimo, secreto <intimate fantasies : fantasías secretas>

intimate[3] *n* : amigo *m* íntimo, amiga *f* íntima

intimidate [ɪnˈtɪməˌdeɪt] *vt* **-dated; -dating** : intimidar

intimidation [ɪnˌtɪməˈdeɪʃən] *n* : intimidación *f*

into [ˈɪnˌtuː] *prep* **1** (*indicating motion*) : en, a, contra, dentro de <she got into bed : se metió en la cama> <to get into a plane : subir a un avión> <he crashed into the wall : chocó contra la pared> <looking into the sun : mirando al sol> **2** (*indicating state or condition*) : a, en <to burst into tears : echarse a llorar> <the water turned into ice : el agua se convirtió en hielo> <to translate into English : traducir al inglés> **3** (*indicating time*) <far into the night : hasta bien entrada la noche> <he's well into his eighties : tiene los ochenta bien cumplidos> **4** (*in mathematics*) <3 into 12 is 4 : 12 dividido por 3 es 4>

intolerable [ɪnˈtɑlərəbəl] *adj* : intolerable — **intolerably** [-bli] *adv*

intolerance [ɪnˈtɑlərənts] *n* : intolerancia *f*

intolerant [ɪnˈtɑlərənt] *adj* : intolerante

intonation [ˌɪntoˈneɪʃən] *n* : intonación *f*

intone [ɪnˈtoːn] *vt* **-toned; -toning** : entonar

intoxicant [ɪnˈtɑksɪkənt] *n* : bebida *f* alcohólica

intoxicate [ɪnˈtɑksəˌkeɪt] *vt* **-cated; -cating** : emborrachar, embriagar

intoxicated [ɪnˈtɑksəˌkeɪt̬əd] *adj* : borracho, embriagado

intoxicating [ɪnˈtɑksəˌkeɪt̬ɪŋ] *adj* : embriagador

intoxication [ɪnˌtɑksəˈkeɪʃən] *n* : embriaguez *f*

intractable [ɪnˈtræktəbəl] *adj* : obstinado, intratable

intramural [ˌɪntrəˈmjʊrəl] *adj* : interno, dentro de la universidad

intransigence [ɪnˈtræntsədʒənts, -ˈtrænzə-] *n* : intransigencia *f*

intransigent [ɪnˈtræntsədʒənt, -ˈtrænzə-] *adj* : intransigente

intravenous [ˌɪntrəˈviːnəs] *adj* : intravenoso — **intravenously** *adv*

intrepid [ɪnˈtrɛpəd] *adj* : intrépido

intricacy [ˈɪntrɪkəsi] *n, pl* **-cies** : complejidad *f*, lo intrincado

intricate [ˈɪntrɪkət] *adj* : intrincado, complicado — **intricately** *adv*

intrigue[1] [ɪnˈtriːg] *v* **-trigued; -triguing** : intrigar

intrigue[2] [ˈɪnˌtriːg, ɪnˈtriːg] *n* : intriga *f*

intriguing [ɪnˈtriːgɪŋli] *adj* : intrigante, fascinante

intrinsic [ɪnˈtrɪnzɪk, -ˈtrɪntsɪk] *adj* : intrínseco, esencial — **intrinsically** [-zɪkli, -sɪ-] *adv*

introduce [ˌɪntrəˈduːs, -ˈdjuːs] *vt* **-duced; -ducing 1** : presentar <let me introduce my father : permítame presentar a mi padre> **2** : introducir (algo nuevo), lanzar (un producto), presentar (una ley), proponer (una idea o un tema)

introduction [ˌɪntrəˈdʌkʃən] *n* : introducción *f*, presentación *f*

introductory [ˌɪntrəˈdʌktəri] *adj* : introductorio, preliminar, de introducción

introspection [ˌɪntrəˈspɛkʃən] *n* : introspección *f*

introspective [ˌɪntrəˈspɛktɪv] *adj* : introspectivo — **introspectively** *adv*

introvert [ˈɪntrəˌvərt] *n* : introvertido *m*, -da *f*

introverted [ˈɪntrəˌvərt̬əd] *adj* : introvertido

intrude [ɪnˈtruːd] *v* **-truded; -truding** *vi* **1** INTERFERE : inmiscuirse, entrometerse **2** DISTURB, INTERRUPT : molestar, estorbar, interrumpir — *vt* : introducir por fuerza

intruder [ɪn'tru:dər] *n* : intruso *m,* -sa *f*

intrusion [ɪn'tru:ʒən] *n* : intrusión *f*

intrusive [ɪn'tru:sɪv] *adj* : intruso

intuit [ɪn'tu:ɪt, -'tju:-] *vt* : intuir

intuition [ˌɪntʊ'ɪʃən, -tjʊ-] *n* : intuición *f*

intuitive [ɪn'tu:ət̬ɪv, -'tju:-] *adj* : intuitivo — **intuitively** *adv*

inundate ['ɪnənˌdeɪt] *vt* **-dated; -dating** : inundar

inundation [ˌɪnən'deɪʃən] *n* : inundación *f*

inure [ɪ'nʊr, -'njʊr] *vt* **-ured; -uring** : acostumbrar, habituar

invade [ɪn'veɪd] *vt* **-vaded; -vading** : invadir

invader [ɪn'veɪdər] *n* : invasor *m,* -sora *f*

invalid[1] [ɪn'væləd] *adj* : inválido, nulo

invalid[2] ['ɪnvələd] *adj* : inválido, discapacitado

invalid[3] ['ɪnvələd] *n* : inválido *m,* -da *f*

invalidate [ɪn'væləˌdeɪt] *vt* **-dated; -dating** : invalidar

invalidity [ˌɪnvə'lɪdət̬i] *n, pl* **-ties** : invalidez *f,* falta de validez *f*

invaluable [ɪn'væljəbəl, -'væljʊə-] *adj* : invalorable, inestimable, inapreciable

invariable [ɪn'væriəbəl] *adj* : invariable, constante — **invariably** [-bli] *adv*

invasion [ɪn'veɪʒən] *n* : invasión *f*

invasive [ɪn'veɪsɪv] *adj* : invasivo

invective [ɪn'vɛktɪv] *n* : invectiva *f,* improperio *m,* vituperio *m*

inveigh [ɪn'veɪ] *vi* **to inveigh against** : arremeter contra, lanzar invectivas contra

inveigle [ɪn'veɪgəl, -'vi:-] *vt* **-gled; -gling** : engatusar, embaucar, persuadir con engaños

invent [ɪn'vɛnt] *vt* : inventar

invention [ɪn'vɛntʃən] *n* : invención *f,* invento *m*

inventive [ɪn'vɛntɪv] *adj* : inventivo

inventiveness [ɪn'vɛntɪvnəs] *n* : ingenio *m,* inventiva *f*

inventor [ɪn'vɛntər] *n* : inventor *m,* -tora *f*

inventory[1] ['ɪnvənˌtɔri] *vt* **-ried; -rying** : inventariar

inventory[2] *n, pl* **-ries 1** LIST : inventario *m* **2** STOCK : existencias *fpl*

inverse[1] [ɪn'vərs, 'ɪnˌvərs] *adj* : inverso — **inversely** *adv*

inverse[2] *n* : inverso *m*

inversion [ɪn'vɛrʒən] *n* : inversión *f*

invert [ɪn'vərt] *vt* : invertir

invertebrate[1] [ɪn'vərt̬əbrət, -ˌbreɪt] *adj* : invertebrado

invertebrate[2] *n* : invertebrado *m*

invest [ɪn'vɛst] *vt* **1** AUTHORIZE : investir, autorizar **2** CONFER : conferir **3** : invertir, dedicar <he invested his savings in stocks : invirtió sus ahorros en acciones> <to invest one's time : dedicar uno su tiempo>

investigate [ɪn'vɛstəˌgeɪt] *v* **-gated; -gating** : investigar

investigation [ɪnˌvɛstə'geɪʃən] *n* : investigación *f,* estudio *m*

investigative [ɪn'vɛstəˌgeɪt̬ɪv] *adj* : investigador

investigator [ɪn'vɛstəˌgeɪt̬ər] *n* : investigador *m,* -dora *f*

investiture [ɪn'vɛstəˌtʃʊr, -tʃər] *n* : investidura *f*

investment [ɪn'vɛstmənt] *n* : inversión *f*

investor [ɪn'vɛstər] *n* : inversor *m,* -sora *f;* inversionista *mf*

inveterate [ɪn'vɛt̬ərət] *adj* **1** DEEP-SEATED : inveterado, enraizado **2** HABITUAL : empedernido, incorregible

invidious [ɪn'vɪdiəs] *adj* **1** OBNOXIOUS : repugnante, odioso **2** UNJUST : injusto — **invidiously** *adv*

invigorate [ɪn'vɪgəˌreɪt] *vt* **-rated; -rating** : vigorizar, animar

invigorating [ɪn'vɪgəˌreɪt̬ɪŋ] *adj* : vigorizante, estimulante

invigoration [ɪnˌvɪgə'reɪʃən] *n* : animación *f*

invincibility [ɪnˌvɪntsə'bɪlət̬i] *n* : invencibilidad *f*

invincible [ɪn'vɪntsəbəl] *adj* : invencible — **invincibly** [-bli] *adv*

inviolable [ɪn'vaɪələbəl] *adj* : inviolable

inviolate [ɪn'vaɪələt] *adj* : inviolado, puro

invisibility [ɪnˌvɪzə'bɪlət̬i] *n* : invisibilidad *f*

invisible [ɪn'vɪzəbəl] *adj* : invisible — **invisibly** [-bli] *adv*

invitation [ˌɪnvə'teɪʃən] *n* : invitación *f*

invite [ɪn'vaɪt] *vt* **-vited; -viting 1** ATTRACT : atraer, tentar <a book that invites interest : un libro que atrae el interés> **2** PROVOKE : provocar, buscar <to invite trouble : buscarse problemas> **3** ASK : invitar <we invited them for dinner : los invitamos a cenar> **4** SOLICIT : solicitar, buscar (preguntas, comentarios, etc.)

inviting [ɪn'vaɪt̬ɪŋ] *adj* : atractivo, atrayente

invocation [ˌɪnvə'keɪʃən] *n* : invocación *f*

invoice[1] ['ɪnˌvɔɪs] *vt* **-voiced; -voicing** : facturar

invoice[2] *n* : factura *f*

invoke [ɪn'vo:k] *vt* **-voked; -voking 1** : invocar, apelar a <she invoked our aid : apeló a nuestra ayuda> **2** CITE : invocar, citar <to invoke a precedent : invocar un precedente> **3** CONJURE UP : hacer aparecer, invocar

involuntary [ɪn'vɑlənˌtɛri] *adj* : involuntario — **involuntarily** [ɪnˌvɑlən'tɛrəli] *adv*

involve [ɪn'vɑlv] *vt* **-volved; -volving** **1** ENGAGE : ocupar <workers involved in construction : trabajadores ocupados con la construcción> **2** IMPLICATE : involucrar, enredar, implicar <to be involved in a crime : estar involucrado en un crimen> **3** CONCERN : concernir, afectar **4** CONNECT : conectar, relacionar **5** ENTAIL, INCLUDE : suponer, incluir, consistir en <what does the job involve? : ¿en qué consiste el trabajo?> **6 to be involved with someone** : tener una relación (amorosa) con alguien

involved [ɪn'vɑlvd] *adj* **1** COMPLEX, INTRICATE : complicado, complejo, enrevesado **2** CONCERNED : interesado, afectado

involvement [ɪn'vɑlvmənt] *n* **1** PARTICIPATION : participación *f*, complicidad *f* **2** RELATIONSHIP : relación *f*

invulnerable [ɪn'vʌlnərəbəl] *adj* : invulnerable

inward[1] ['ɪnwərd] *or* **inwards** [-wərdz] *adv* : hacia adentro, hacia el interior

inward[2] *adj* INSIDE : interior, interno

inwardly ['ɪnwərdli] *adv* **1** MENTALLY, SPIRITUALLY : por dentro **2** INTERNALLY : internamente, interiormente **3** PRIVATELY : para sus adentros, para sí

iodide ['aɪəˌdaɪd] *n* : yoduro *m*

iodine ['aɪəˌdaɪn, -dən] *n* : yodo *m*, tintura *f* de yodo

iodize ['aɪəˌdaɪz] *vt* **-dized; -dizing** : yodar

ion ['aɪən, 'aɪˌɑn] *n* : ion *m*

ionic [aɪ'ɑnɪk] *adj* : iónico

ionize ['aɪəˌnaɪz] *v* **ionized; ionizing** : ionizar

ionosphere [aɪ'ɑnəˌsfɪr] *n* : ionosfera *f*

iota [aɪ'oːt̬ə] *n* : pizca *f*, ápice *m*

IOU [ˌaɪˌo'juː] *n* : pagaré *m*, vale *m*

Iranian [ɪ'reɪniən, -'ræ-, -'rɑ-; aɪ'-] *n* : iraní *mf* — **Iranian** *adj*

Iraqi [ɪ'rakiː] *n* : iraquí *mf* — **Iraqi** *adj*

irascibility [ɪˌræsə'bɪlət̬i] *n* : irascibilidad *f*

irascible [ɪ'ræsəbəl] *adj* : irascible

irate [aɪ'reɪt] *adj* : furioso, airado, iracundo — **irately** *adv*

ire ['aɪr] *n* : ira *f*, cólera *f*

iridescence [ˌɪrə'dɛsənts] *n* : iridiscencia *f*

iridescent [ˌɪrə'dɛsənt] *adj* : iridiscente

iris ['aɪrəs] *n, pl* **irises** *or* **irides** ['aɪrəˌdiːz, 'ɪr-] **1** : iris *m* (del ojo) **2** : lirio *m* (planta)

Irish[1] ['aɪrɪʃ] *adj* : irlandés

Irish[2] **1** : irlandés *m* (idioma) **2 the Irish** *npl* : los irlandeses

Irishman ['aɪrɪʃmən] *n* : irlandés *m*

Irishwoman ['aɪrɪʃˌwʊmən] *n* : irlandesa *f*

irk ['ərk] *vt* : fastidiar, irritar, preocupar

irksome ['ərksəm] *adj* : irritante, fastidioso — **irksomely** *adv*

iron[1] ['aɪərn] *v* : planchar

iron[2] *n* **1** : hierro *m*, fierro *m* <a will of iron : una voluntad de hierro, una voluntad férrea> **2** : plancha *f* (para planchar la ropa)

ironclad ['aɪərn'klæd] *adj* **1** : acorazado, blindado **2** STRICT : riguroso, estricto

ironic [aɪ'rɑnɪk] *or* **ironical** [-nɪkəl] *adj* : irónico — **ironically** [-kli] *adv*

ironing ['aɪərnɪŋ] *n* **1** PRESSING : planchada *f* **2** : ropa *f* para planchar

ironing board *n* : tabla *f* (de planchar)

ironwork ['aɪərnˌwərk] *n* **1** : obra *f* de hierro **2 ironworks** *npl* : fundición *f*

ironworker ['aɪərnˌwərkər] *n* : fundidor *m*, -dora *f*

irony ['aɪrəni] *n, pl* **-nies** : ironía *f*

irradiate [ɪ'reɪdiˌeɪt] *vt* **-ated; -ating** : irradiar, radiar

irradiation [ɪˌreɪdi'eɪʃən] *n* : irradiación *f*, radiación *f*

irrational [ɪ'ræʃənəl] *adj* : irracional — **irrationally** *adv*

irrationality [ɪˌræʃə'nælət̬i] *n, pl* **-ties** : irracionalidad *f*

irreconcilable [ɪˌrɛkən'saɪləbəl] *adj* : irreconciliable

irrecoverable [ˌɪrɪ'kʌvərəbəl] *adj* : irrecuperable — **irrecoverably** [-bli] *adv*

irredeemable [ˌɪrɪ'diːməbəl] *adj* **1** : irredimible (dícese de un bono) **2** HOPELESS : irremediable, irreparable

irreducible [ˌɪrɪ'duːsəbəl, -'djuː-] *adj* : irreducible — **irreducibly** [-bli] *adv*

irrefutable [ˌɪrɪ'fjuːt̬əbəl, ɪr'ɛfjə-] *adj* : irrefutable

irregular[1] [ɪ'rɛgjələr] *adj* : irregular — **irregularly** *adv*

irregular[2] *n* **1** : soldado *m* irregular **2 irregulars** *npl* : artículos *mpl* defectuosos

irregularity [ɪˌrɛgjə'lærət̬i] *n, pl* **-ties** : irregularidad *f*

irrelevance [ɪ'rɛləvənts] *n* : irrelevancia *f*

irrelevant [ɪ'rɛləvənt] *adj* : irrelevante

irreligious [ˌɪrɪ'lɪdʒəs] *adj* : irreligioso

irreparable [ɪ'rɛpərəbəl] *adj* : irreparable

irreplaceable [ˌɪrɪ'pleɪsəbəl] *adj* : irreemplazable, insustituible

irrepressible [ˌɪrɪ'prɛsəbəl] *adj* : incontenible, incontrolable

irreproachable [ɪrɪ'proːtʃəbəl] *adj* : irreprochable, intachable

irresistible [ˌɪrɪ'zɪstəbəl] *adj* : irresistible — **irresistibly** [-bli] *adv*

irresolute [ɪ'rɛzəˌluːt] *adj* : irresoluto, indeciso

irresolutely [ɪ'rɛzəˌluːtli, -ˌrɛzə'luːt-] *adv* : de manera indecisa

irresolution [ɪˌrɛzə'luːʃən] *n* : irresolución *f*

irrespective of [ˌɪrɪˈspɛktɪvəv] *prep* : sin tomar en consideración, sin tener en cuenta
irresponsibility [ˌɪrɪˌspɑntsəˈbɪləṭi] *n, pl* **-ties** : irresponsabilidad *f,* falta *f* de responsabilidad
irresponsible [ˌɪrɪˈspɑntsəbəl] *adj* : irresponsable — **irresponsibly** [-bli] *adv*
irretrievable [ˌɪrɪˈtriːvəbəl] *adj* IRRECOVERABLE : irrecuperable
irreverence [ɪˈrɛvərənts] *n* : irreverencia *f,* falta *f* de respeto
irreverent [ɪˈrɛvərənt] *adj* : irreverente, irrespetuoso
irreversible [ˌɪrɪˈvərsəbəl] *adj* : irreversible
irrevocable [ɪˈrɛvəkəbəl] *adj* : irrevocable — **irrevocably** [-bli] *adv*
irrigate [ˈɪrəˌgeɪt] *vt* **-gated; -gating** : irrigar, regar
irrigation [ˌɪrəˈgeɪʃən] *n* : irrigación *f,* riego *m*
irritability [ˌɪrəṭəˈbɪləṭi] *n, pl* **-ties** : irritabilidad *f*
irritable [ˈɪrəṭəbəl] *adj* : irritable, colérico
irritably [ˈɪrəṭəbli] *adv* : con irritación
irritant[1] [ˈɪrəṭənt] *adj* : irritante
irritant[2] *n* : agente *m* irritante
irritate [ˈɪrəˌteɪt] *vt* **-tated; -tating 1** ANNOY : irritar, molestar **2** : irritar (en medicina)
irritating [ˈɪrəˌteɪṭɪŋ] *adj* : irritante
irritatingly [ˈɪrəˌteɪṭɪŋli] *adv* : de modo irritante, fastidiosamente
irritation [ˌɪrəˈteɪʃən] *n* : irritación *f*
is → **be**
Islam [ɪsˈlɑm, ɪz-, -ˈlæm; ˈɪsˌlɑm, ˈɪz-, -ˌlæm] *n* : el Islam
Islamic [ɪsˈlɑmɪk, ɪz-, -ˈlæ-] *adj* : islámico
island [ˈaɪlənd] *n* : isla *f*
islander [ˈaɪləndər] *n* : isleño *m,* -ña *f*
isle [ˈaɪl] *n* : isla *f,* islote *m*
islet [ˈaɪlət] *n* : islote *m*
isolate [ˈaɪsəˌleɪt] *vt* **-lated; -lating** : aislar
isolated [ˈaɪsəˌleɪṭəd] *adj* : aislado, solo
isolation [ˌaɪsəˈleɪʃən] *n* : aislamiento *m*
isometric [ˌaɪsəˈmɛtrɪk] *adj* : isométrico
isometrics [ˌaɪsəˈmɛtrɪks] *ns & pl* : isometría *f*
isosceles [aɪˈsɑsəˌliːz] *adj* : isósceles
isotope [ˈaɪsəˌtoːp] *n* : isótopo *m*
Israeli [ɪzˈreɪli] *n* : israelí *mf* — **Israeli** *adj*
issue[1] [ˈɪˌʃuː] *v* **-sued; -suing** *vi* **1** EMERGE : emerger, salir, fluir **2** DESCEND : descender (dícese de los padres o antepasados específicos) **3** EMANATE, RESULT : emanar, surgir, resultar — *vt* **1** EMIT : emitir **2** DISTRIBUTE : emitir, distribuir <to issue a new stamp : emitir un sello nuevo> **3** PUBLISH : publicar
issue[2] *n* **1** EMERGENCE, FLOW : emergencia *f,* flujo *m* **2** PROGENY : descendencia *f,* progenie *f* **3** OUTCOME, RESULT : desenlace *m,* resultado *m,* consecuencia *f* **4** MATTER, QUESTION : asunto *m,* cuestión *f* **5** PUBLICATION : publicación *f,* distribución *f,* emisión *f* **6** : número *m* (de un periódico o una revista)
isthmus [ˈɪsməs] *n* : istmo *m*
it [ˈɪt] *pron* **1** (*as subject; generally omitted*) : él, ella, ello <it's a big building : es un edificio grande> <who was it? : ¿quién era?> **2** (*as indirect object*) : le <I'll give it some water : voy a darle agua> **3** (*as direct object*) : lo, la <give it to me : dámelo> **4** (*as object of a preposition; generally omitted*) : él, ella, ello <behind it : detrás, detrás de él> **5** (*in impersonal constructions*) <it's raining : está lloviendo> <it's 8 o'clock : son las ocho> **6** (*as the implied subject or object of a verb*) <it is necessary to study : es necesario estudiar> <to give it all one's got : dar lo mejor de sí>
Italian [ɪˈtæliən, aɪ-] *n* **1** : italiano *m,* -na *f* **2** : italiano *m* (idioma) — **Italian** *adj*
italic[1] [ɪˈtælɪk, aɪ-] *adj* : en cursiva, en bastardilla
italic[2] *n* : cursiva *f,* bastardilla *f*
italicize [ɪˈtæləˌsaɪz, aɪ-] *vt* **-cized; -cizing** : poner en cursiva
itch[1] [ˈɪtʃ] *vi* **1** : picar <her arm itched : le pica el brazo> **2** : morirse <they were itching to go outside : se morían por salir> — *vt* : dar picazón, hacer picar
itch[2] *n* **1** ITCHING : picazón *f,* picor *m,* comezón *f* **2** RASH : sarpullido *m,* erupción *f* **3** DESIRE : ansia *f,* deseo *m*
itchy [ˈɪtʃi] *adj* **itchier; -est** : que pica, que da comezón
it'd [ˈɪṭəd] (*contraction of* **it had** *or* **it would**) → **have, would**
item [ˈaɪṭəm] *n* **1** OBJECT : artículo *m,* pieza *f* <item of clothing : prenda de vestir> **2** : punto *m* (en una agenda), número *m* (en el teatro), ítem *m* (en un documento) **3 news item** : noticia *f*
itemize [ˈaɪṭəˌmaɪz] *vt* **-ized; -izing** : detallar, enumerar, listar
itinerant [aɪˈtɪnərənt] *adj* : itinerante, ambulante
itinerary [aɪˈtɪnəˌrɛri] *n, pl* **-aries** : itinerario *m*
it'll [ˈɪṭəl] (*contraction of* **it shall** *or* **it will**) → **shall, will**
its [ˈɪts] *adj* : su, sus <its kennel : su perrera> <a city and its inhabitants : una ciudad y sus habitantes>
it's [ˈɪts] (*contraction of* **it is** *or* **it has**) → **be, have**
itself [ɪtˈsɛlf] *pron* **1** (*used reflexively*) : se <the cat gave itself a bath : el gato se bañó> **2** (*used for emphasis*) : (él) mismo, (ella) misma, sí (mismo), solo <he is courtesy itself : es la misma cortesía> <in and of itself : por sí

mismo> <it opened by itself : se abrió solo>

I've ['aɪv] (*contraction of* **I have**) → **have**

ivory ['aɪvəri] *n, pl* **-ries 1 :** marfil *m* **2 :** color *m* de marfil

ivy ['aɪvi] *n, pl* **ivies 1 :** hiedra *f,* yedra *f* **2** → **poison ivy**

J

j ['dʒeɪ] *n, pl* **j's** *or* **js** ['dʒeɪz] **:** décima letra del alfabeto inglés

jab[1] ['dʒæb] *v* **jabbed; jabbing** *vt* **1** PUNCTURE **:** clavar, pinchar **2** POKE **:** dar, golpear (con la punta de algo) <he jabbed me in the ribs : me dio un codazo en las costillas> — *vi* **to jab at :** dar, golpear

jab[2] *n* **1** PRICK **:** pinchazo *m* **2** POKE **:** golpe *m* abrupto

jabber[1] ['dʒæbər] *v* **:** farfullar

jabber[2] *n* **:** galimatías *m,* farfulla *f*

jack[1] ['dʒæk] *vt* **to jack up 1 :** levantar (con un gato) **2** INCREASE **:** subir, aumentar

jack[2] *n* **1 :** gato *m,* cric *m* <hydraulic jack : gato hidráulico> **2** FLAG **:** pabellón *m* **3** SOCKET **:** enchufe *m* hembra **4 :** jota *f,* valet *m* <jack of hearts : jota de corazones> **5 jacks** *npl* **:** cantillos *mpl*

jackal ['dʒækəl] *n* **:** chacal *m*

jackass ['dʒæk,æs] *n* **:** asno *m,* burro *m*

jacket ['dʒækət] *n* **1 :** chaqueta *f* **2** COVER **:** sobrecubierta *f* (de un libro), carátula *f* (de un disco)

jackhammer ['dʒæk,hæmər] *n* **:** martillo *m* neumático

jack–in–the–box ['dʒækɪnðə,bɑks] *n* **:** caja *f* de sorpresa

jackknife[1] ['dʒæk,naɪf] *vi* **-knifed; -knifing :** doblarse como una navaja, plegarse

jackknife[2] *n* **:** navaja *f*

jack–of–all–trades *n* **:** persona *f* que sabe un poco de todo, persona *f* de muchos oficios

jack–o'–lantern ['dʒækə,læntərn] *n* **:** linterna *f* hecha de una calabaza

jackpot ['dʒæk,pɑt] *n* **1 :** primer premio *m,* gordo *m* **2 to hit the jackpot :** sacarse la lotería, sacarse el gordo

jackrabbit ['dʒæk,ræbət] *n* **:** liebre *f* grande de Norteamérica

jade ['dʒeɪd] *n* **:** jade *m*

jaded ['dʒeɪdəd] *adj* **1** TIRED **:** agotado **2** BORED **:** hastiado

jagged ['dʒægəd] *adj* **:** dentado, mellado

jaguar ['dʒæg,wɑr, 'dʒægjʊ,wɑr] *n* **:** jaguar *m*

jai alai ['haɪ,laɪ] *n* **:** jai alai *m,* pelota *f* vasca

jail[1] ['dʒeɪl] *vt* **:** encarcelar

jail[2] *n* **:** cárcel *f*

jailbreak ['dʒeɪl,breɪk] *n* **:** fuga *f,* huida *f* (de la cárcel)

jailer *or* **jailor** ['dʒeɪlər] *n* **:** carcelero *m,* -ra *f*

jalapeño [,hɑlə'peɪnjo, ,hæ-, -'pi:no] *n* **:** jalapeño *m*

jalopy [dʒə'lɑpi] *n, pl* **-lopies :** cacharro *m fam,* carro *m* destartalado

jalousie ['dʒæləsi] *n* **:** celosía *f*

jam[1] ['dʒæm] *v* **jammed; jamming** *vt* **1** CRAM **:** apiñar, embutir **2** BLOCK **:** atascar, atorar **3 to jam on the brakes :** frenar en seco — *vi* STICK **:** atascarse, atrancarse

jam[2] *n* **1** *or* **traffic jam :** atasco *m,* embotellamiento *m* (de tráfico) **2** PREDICAMENT **:** lío *m,* aprieto *m,* apuro *m* **3 :** mermelada *f* <strawberry jam : mermelada de fresa>

jamb ['dʒæm] *n* **:** jamba *f*

jamboree [,dʒæmbə'ri:] *n* **:** fiesta *f* grande

jangle[1] ['dʒæŋgəl] *v* **-gled; -gling** *vi* **:** hacer un ruido metálico — *vt* **1 :** hacer sonar **2 to jangle one's nerves :** irritar, crispar

jangle[2] *n* **:** ruido *m* metálico

janitor ['dʒænətər] *n* **:** portero *m,* -ra *f;* conserje *mf*

January ['dʒænjʊ,ɛri] *n* **:** enero *m*

Japanese [,dʒæpə'ni:z, -'ni:s] *n* **1 :** japonés *m,* -nesa *f* **2 :** japonés *m* (idioma) — **Japanese** *adj*

jar[1] ['dʒɑr] *v* **jarred; jarring** *vi* **1** GRATE **:** chirriar **2** CLASH **:** desentonar **3** SHAKE **:** sacudirse **4 to jar on :** crispar, enervar — *vt* JOLT **:** sacudir

jar[2] *n* **1** GRATING **:** chirrido *m* **2** JOLT **:** vibración *f,* sacudida *f* **3 :** tarro *m,* bote *m,* pote *m* <a jar of honey : un tarro de miel>

jargon ['dʒɑrgən] *n* **:** jerga *f*

jasmine ['dʒæzmən] *n* **:** jazmín *m*

jasper ['dʒæspər] *n* **:** jaspe *m*

jaundice ['dʒɔndɪs] *n* **:** ictericia *f*

jaundiced ['dʒɔndɪst] *adj* **1 :** ictérico **2** EMBITTERED, RESENTFUL **:** amargado, resentido, negativo <with a jaundiced eye : con una actitud de cinismo>

jaunt ['dʒɔnt] *n* **:** excursión *f,* paseo *m*

jauntily ['dʒɔntəli] *adv* **:** animadamente

jauntiness ['dʒɔntinəs] *n* **:** animación *f,* vivacidad *f*

jaunty ['dʒɔnti] *adj* **-tier; -est 1** SPRIGHTLY **:** animado, alegre **2** RAKISH **:** desenvuelto, desenfadado

javelin ['dʒævələn] *n* **:** jabalina *f*

jaw[1] ['dʒɔ] *vi* GAB **:** cotorrear *fam,* parlotear *fam*

jaw[2] *n* **1 :** mandíbula *f,* quijada *f* **2 :** mordaza *f* (de una herramienta) **3 the jaws of death :** las garras *f* de la muerte

jawbone ['dʒɔ,bo:n] *n* : mandíbula *f*
jay ['dʒeɪ] *n* : arrendajo *m,* chara *f Mex,* azulejo *m Mex*
jaybird ['dʒeɪ,bərd] → **jay**
jaywalk ['dʒeɪ,wɔk] *vi* : cruzar la calle sin prudencia
jaywalker ['dʒeɪ,wɔkər] *n* : peatón *m* imprudente
jazz[1] ['dʒæz] *vt* **to jazz up** : animar, alegrar
jazz[2] *n* : jazz *m*
jazzy ['dʒæzi] *adj* **jazzier; -est 1** : con ritmo de jazz **2** FLASHY, SHOWY : llamativo, ostentoso
jealous ['dʒɛləs] *adj* : celoso, envidioso — **jealously** *adv*
jealousy ['dʒɛləsi] *n* : celos *mpl,* envidia *f*
jeans ['dʒi:nz] *npl* : jeans *mpl,* vaqueros *mpl*
jeep ['dʒi:p] *n* : jeep *m*
jeer[1] ['dʒɪr] *vi* **1** BOO : abuchear **2** SCOFF : mofarse, burlarse — *vt* RIDICULE : mofarse de, burlarse de
jeer[2] *n* **1** : abucheo *m* **2** TAUNT : mofa *f,* burla *f*
Jehovah [dʒɪ'ho:və] *n* : Jehová *m*
jell ['dʒɛl] *vi* **1** SET : gelificarse, cuajar **2** FORM : cuajar, formarse (una idea, etc.)
jelly[1] ['dʒɛli] *v* **jellied; jellying** *vi* **1** JELL : gelificarse, cuajar **2** : hacer jalea — *vt* : gelificar
jelly[2] *n, pl* **-lies 1** : jalea *f* **2** GELATIN : gelatina *f*
jellyfish ['dʒɛli,fɪʃ] *n* : medusa *f*
jeopardize ['dʒɛpər,daɪz] *vt* **-dized; -dizing** : arriesgar, poner en peligro
jeopardy ['dʒɛpərdi] *n* : peligro *m,* riesgo *m*
jerk[1] ['dʒərk] *vt* **1** JOLT : sacudir **2** TUG, YANK : darle un tirón a — *vi* JOLT : dar sacudidas <the train jerked along : el tren iba moviéndose a sacudidas>
jerk[2] *n* **1** TUG : tirón *m,* jalón *m* **2** JOLT : sacudida *f* brusca **3** FOOL : estúpido *m,* -da *f;* idiota *mf*
jerkin ['dʒərkən] *n* : chaqueta *f* sin mangas, chaleco *m*
jerky ['dʒərki] *adj* **jerkier; -est 1** : espasmódico (dícese de los movimientos) **2** CHOPPY : inconexo (dícese de la prosa) — **jerkily** [-kəli] *adv*
jerry–built ['dʒɛri,bɪlt] *adj* : mal construido, chapucero
jersey ['dʒərzi] *n, pl* **-seys** : jersey *m*
jest[1] ['dʒɛst] *vi* : bromear
jest[2] *n* : broma *f,* chiste *m*
jester ['dʒɛstər] *n* : bufón *m,* -fona *f*
Jesus ['dʒi:zəs, -zəz] *n* : Jesús *m*
jet[1] ['dʒɛt] *v* **jetted; jetting** *vt* SPOUT : arrojar a chorros — *vi* **1** GUSH : salir a chorros, chorrear **2** FLY : viajar en avión, volar
jet[2] *n* **1** STREAM : chorro *m* **2** *or* **jet airplane** : avión *m* a reacción, reactor *m* **3** : azabache *m* (mineral) **4 jet engine** : reactor *m,* motor *m* a reacción **5 jet lag** : desajuste *m* de horario (debido a un vuelo largo)
jet–propelled *adj* : a reacción
jetsam ['dʒɛtsəm] *n* **flotsam and jetsam** : restos *mpl,* desechos *mpl*
jettison ['dʒɛtəsən] *vt* **1** : echar al mar **2** DISCARD : desechar, deshacerse de
jetty ['dʒɛti] *n, pl* **-ties 1** PIER, WHARF : desembarcadero *m,* muelle *m* **2** BREAKWATER : malecón *m,* rompeolas *m*
Jew ['dʒu:] *n* : judío *m,* **-día** *f*
jewel ['dʒu:əl] *n* **1** : joya *f,* alhaja *f* **2** GEM : piedra *f* preciosa, gema *f* **3** : rubí *m* (de un reloj) **4** TREASURE : joya *f,* tesoro *m*
jeweler *or* **jeweller** ['dʒu:ələr] *n* : joyero *m,* -ra *f*
jewelry ['dʒu:əlri] *n* : joyas *fpl,* alhajas *fpl*
Jewish ['dʒu:ɪʃ] *adj* : judío
jib ['dʒɪb] *n* : foque *m* (de un barco)
jibe ['dʒaɪb] *vi* **jibed; jibing** AGREE : concordar
jiffy ['dʒɪfi] *n, pl* **-fies** : santiamén *m,* segundo *m,* momento *m*
jig[1] ['dʒɪg] *vi* **jigged; jigging** : bailar la giga
jig[2] *n* **1** : giga *f* **2 the jig is up** : se acabó la fiesta
jigger ['dʒɪgər] *n* : medida de 1 a 2 onzas (para licores)
jiggle[1] ['dʒɪgəl] *v* **-gled; -gling** *vt* : agitar o sacudir ligeramente — *vi* : agitarse, vibrar
jiggle[2] *n* : sacudida *f,* vibración *f*
jigsaw ['dʒɪg,sɔ] *n* **1** : sierra *f* de vaivén **2 jigsaw puzzle** : rompecabezas *m*
jilt ['dʒɪlt] *vt* : dejar plantado, dar calabazas a
jimmy[1] ['dʒɪmi] *vt* **-mied; -mying** : forzar con una palanqueta
jimmy[2] *n, pl* **-mies** : palanqueta *f*
jingle[1] ['dʒɪŋgəl] *v* **-gled; -gling** *vi* : tintinear — *vt* : hacer sonar
jingle[2] *n* **1** TINKLE : tintineo *m,* retintín *m* **2** : canción *f* rimada
jingoism ['dʒɪŋgo,ɪzəm] *n* : jingoísmo *m,* patriotería *f*
jingoistic [,dʒɪŋgo'ɪstɪk] *or* **jingoist** ['dʒɪŋgoɪst] *adj* : jingoísta, patriotero
jinx[1] ['dʒɪŋks] *vt* : traer mala suerte a, salar *CoRi, Mex*
jinx[2] *n* **1** : cenizo *m,* -za *f* **2 to put a jinx on** : echarle el mal de ojo a
jitters ['dʒɪtərz] *npl* : nervios *mpl* <he got the jitters : se puso nervioso>
jittery ['dʒɪtəri] *adj* : nervioso
job ['dʒɑb] *n* **1** : trabajo *m* <he did odd jobs for her : le hizo algunos trabajos> **2** CHORE, TASK : tarea *f,* quehacer *m* **3** EMPLOYMENT : trabajo *m,* empleo *m,* puesto *m*
jobber ['dʒɑbər] *n* MIDDLEMAN : intermediario *m,* -ria *f*
jockey[1] ['dʒɑki] *v* **-eyed; -eying** *vt* **1** MANIPULATE : manipular **2** MANEUVER

: maniobrar — *vi* **to jockey for position** : maniobrar para conseguir algo

jockey[2] *n, pl* **-eys** : jockey *mf*

jocose [dʒoˈkoːs] *adj* : jocoso

jocular [ˈdʒɑkjʊlər] *adj* : jocoso — **jocularly** *adv*

jocularity [ˌdʒɑkjʊˈlærət̬i] *n* : jocosidad *f*

jodhpurs [ˈdʒɑdpərz] *npl* : pantalones *mpl* de montar

jog[1] [ˈdʒɑg] *v* **jogged; jogging** *vt* **1** NUDGE : dar, empujar, codear **2 to jog one's memory** : refrescar la memoria — *vi* **1** RUN : correr despacio, trotar, hacer footing (como ejercicio) **2** TRUDGE : andar a trote corto

jog[2] *n* **1** PUSH, SHAKE : empujoncito *m,* sacudida *f* leve **2** TROT : trote *m* corto, footing *m* (en deportes) **3** TWIST : recodo *m,* vuelta *f,* curva *f*

jogger [ˈdʒɑgər] *n* : persona *f* que hace footing

join [ˈdʒɔɪn] *vt* **1** CONNECT, LINK : unir, juntar <to join in marriage : unir en matrimonio> **2** ADJOIN : lindar con, colindar con **3** MEET : reunirse con, encontrarse con <we joined them for lunch : nos reunimos con ellos para almorzar> **4** : hacerse socio de (una organización), afiliarse a (un partido), entrar en (una empresa) — *vi* **1** UNITE : unirse **2** MERGE : empalmar (dícese de las carreteras), confluir (dícese de los ríos) **3 to join up** : hacerse socio, enrolarse

joiner [ˈdʒɔɪnər] *n* **1** CARPENTER : carpintero *m,* -ra *f* **2** : persona *f* que se une a varios grupos

joint[1] [ˈdʒɔɪnt] *adj* : conjunto, colectivo, mutuo <a joint effort : un esfuerzo conjunto> — **jointly** *adv*

joint[2] *n* **1** : articulación *f,* coyuntura *f* <out of joint : dislocado> **2** ROAST : asado *m* **3** JUNCTURE : juntura *f,* unión *f* **4** DIVE : antro *m,* tasca *f*

joist [ˈdʒɔɪst] *n* : viga *f*

joke[1] [ˈdʒoːk] *vi* **joked; joking** : bromear

joke[2] *n* **1** STORY : chiste *m* **2** PRANK : broma *f*

joker [ˈdʒoːkər] *n* **1** PRANKSTER : bromista *mf* **2** : comodín *m* (en los naipes)

jokingly [ˈdʒoːkɪŋli] *adv* : en broma

jollity [ˈdʒɑlət̬i] *n, pl* **-ties** MERRIMENT : alegría *f,* regocijo *m*

jolly [ˈdʒɑli] *adj* **-lier; -est** : alegre, jovial

jolt[1] [ˈdʒoːlt] *vi* JERK : dar tumbos, dar sacudidas — *vt* : sacudir

jolt[2] *n* **1** JERK : sacudida *f* brusca **2** SHOCK : golpe *m* (emocional)

jonquil [ˈdʒɑnkwɪl] *n* : junquillo *m*

Jordanian [dʒɔrˈdeɪniən] *n* : jordano *m,* -na *f* — **Jordanian** *adj*

josh [ˈdʒɑʃ] *vt* TEASE : tomarle el pelo (a alguien) — *vi* JOKE : bromear

jostle [ˈdʒɑsəl] *v* **-tled; -tling** *vi* **1** SHOVE : empujar, dar empellones **2** CONTEND : competir — *vt* **1** SHOVE : empujar **2 to jostle one's way** : abrirse paso a empellones

jot[1] [ˈdʒɑt] *vt* **jotted; jotting** : anotar, apuntar <jot it down : apúntalo>

jot[2] *n* BIT : ápice *m,* jota *f,* pizca *f*

jounce[1] [ˈdʒæʊnts] *v* **jounced; jouncing** *vt* JOLT : sacudir — *vi* : dar tumbos, dar sacudidas

jounce[2] *n* JOLT : sacudida *f,* tumbo *m*

journal [ˈdʒərnəl] *n* **1** DIARY : diario *m* **2** PERIODICAL : revista *f,* publicación *f* periódica **3** NEWSPAPER : periódico *m,* diario *m*

journalism [ˈdʒərnəlˌɪzəm] *n* : periodismo *m*

journalist [ˈdʒərnəlɪst] *n* : periodista *mf*

journalistic [ˌdʒərnəlˈɪstɪk] *adj* : periodístico

journey[1] [ˈdʒərni] *vi* **-neyed; -neying** : viajar

journey[2] *n, pl* **-neys** : viaje *m*

journeyman [ˈdʒərnimən] *n, pl* **-men** [-mən, -ˌmɛn] : oficial *m*

joust[1] [ˈdʒæʊst] *vi* : justar

joust[2] *n* : justa *f*

jovial [ˈdʒoːviəl] *adj* : jovial — **jovially** *adv*

joviality [ˌdʒoːviˈælət̬i] *n* : jovialidad *f*

jowl [ˈdʒæʊl] *n* **1** JAW : mandíbula *f* **2** CHEEK : mejilla *f,* cachete *m*

joy [ˈdʒɔɪ] *n* **1** HAPPINESS : gozo *m,* alegría *f,* felicidad *f* **2** DELIGHT : placer *m,* deleite *m* <the child is a real joy : el niño es un verdadero placer>

joyful [ˈdʒɔɪfəl] *adj* : gozoso, alegre, feliz — **joyfully** *adv*

joyless [ˈdʒɔɪləs] *adj* : sin alegría, triste

joyous [ˈdʒɔɪəs] *adj* : alegre, feliz, eufórico — **joyously** *adv*

joyousness [ˈdʒɔɪəsnəs] *n* : alegría *f,* felicidad *f,* euforia *f*

joyride [ˈdʒɔɪˌraɪd] *n* : paseo *m* temerario e irresponsable (en coche)

jubilant [ˈdʒuːbələnt] *adj* : jubiloso, alborozado — **jubilantly** *adv*

jubilation [ˌdʒuːbəˈleɪʃən] *n* : júbilo *m*

jubilee [ˈdʒuːbəˌliː] *n* **1** : quincuagésimo aniversario *m* **2** CELEBRATION : celebración *f,* festejos *mpl*

Judaic [dʒʊˈdeɪɪk] *adj* : judaico

Judaism [ˈdʒuːdəˌɪzəm, ˈdʒuːdi-, ˈdʒuːˌdeɪ-] *n* : judaísmo *m*

judge[1] [ˈdʒʌdʒ] *vt* **judged; judging 1** ASSESS : evaluar, juzgar **2** DEEM : juzgar, considerar **3** TRY : juzgar (ante el tribuno) **4 judging by** : a juzgar por

judge[2] *n* **1** : juez *mf,* jueza *f* **2 to be a good judge of** : saber juzgar a, entender mucho de

judgment *or* **judgement** [ˈdʒʌdʒmənt] *n* **1** RULING : fallo *m,* sentencia *f* **2** OPINION : opinión *f* **3** DISCERNMENT : juicio *m,* discernimiento *m*

judgmental [ˌdʒʌdʒˈmɛnt̬əl] *adj* : crítico — **judgmentally** *adv*

judicature [ˈdʒuːdɪkəˌtʃʊr] *n* : judicatura *f*

judicial [dʒʊˈdɪʃəl] *adj* : judicial — **judicially** *adv*

judiciary[1] [dʒʊˈdɪʃiˌɛri, -ˈdɪʃəri] *adj* : judicial

judiciary[2] *n* **1** JUDICATURE : judicatura *f* **2** : poder *m* judicial

judicious [dʒʊˈdɪʃəs] *adj* SOUND, WISE : juicioso, sensato — **judiciously** *adv*

judo [ˈdʒuːˌdoː] *n* : judo *m*

jug [ˈdʒʌg] *n* **1** : jarra *f,* jarro *m,* cántaro *m* **2** JAIL : cárcel *f,* chirona *f fam*

juggernaut [ˈdʒʌgərˌnɔt] *n* : gigante *m,* fuerza *f* irresistible <a political juggernaut : un gigante político>

juggle [ˈdʒʌgəl] *v* **-gled; -gling** *vt* **1** : hacer juegos malabares con **2** MANIPULATE : manipular, jugar con — *vi* : hacer juegos malabares

juggler [ˈdʒʌgələr] *n* : malabarista *mf*

jugular [ˈdʒʌgjʊlər] *adj* : yugular <jugular vein : vena yugular>

juice [ˈdʒuːs] *n* **1** : jugo *m* (de carne, de frutas) *m,* zumo *m* (de frutas) **2** ELECTRICITY : electricidad *f,* luz *f*

juicer [ˈdʒuːsər] *n* : exprimidor *m*

juiciness [ˈdʒuːsinəs] *n* : jugosidad *f*

juicy [ˈdʒuːsi] *adj* **juicier; -est 1** SUCCULENT : jugoso, suculento **2** PROFITABLE : jugoso, lucrativo **3** RACY : picante

jukebox [ˈdʒuːkˌbɑks] *n* : rocola *f,* máquina *f* de discos

julep [ˈdʒuːləp] *n* : bebida *f* hecha con whisky americano y menta

July [dʒʊˈlaɪ] *n* : julio *m*

jumble[1] [ˈdʒʌmbəl] *vt* **-bled; -bling** : mezclar, revolver

jumble[2] *n* : revoltijo *m,* fárrago *m,* embrollo *m*

jumbo[1] [ˈdʒʌmˌboː] *adj* : gigante, enorme, de tamaño extra grande

jumbo[2] *n, pl* **-bos** : coloso *m,* cosa *f* de tamaño extra grande

jump[1] [ˈdʒʌmp] *vi* **1** LEAP : saltar, brincar **2** START : levantarse de un salto, sobresaltarse **3** MOVE, SHIFT : moverse, pasar <to jump from job to job : pasar de un empleo a otro> **4** INCREASE, RISE : dar un salto, aumentarse de golpe, subir bruscamente **5** BUSTLE : animarse, ajetrearse **6 to jump to conclusions** : sacar conclusiones precipitadas — *vt* **1** : saltar <to jump a fence : saltar una valla> **2** SKIP : saltarse **3** ATTACK : atacar, asaltar **4 to jump the gun** : precipitarse

jump[2] *n* **1** LEAP : salto *m* **2** START : sobresalto *m,* respingo *m* **3** INCREASE : subida *f* brusca, aumento *m* **4** ADVANTAGE : ventaja *f* <we got the jump on them : les llevamos la ventaja>

jumper [ˈdʒʌmpər] *n* **1** : saltador *m,* -dora *f* (en deportes) **2** : jumper *m,* vestido *m* sin mangas

jumpy [ˈdʒʌmpi] *adj* **jumpier; -est** : asustadizo, nervioso

junction [ˈdʒʌŋkʃən] *n* **1** JOINING : unión *f* **2** : cruce *m* (de calles), empalme *m* (de un ferrocarril), confluencia *f* (de ríos)

juncture [ˈdʒʌŋktʃər] *n* **1** UNION : juntura *f,* unión *f* **2** MOMENT, POINT : coyuntura *f* <at this juncture : en esta coyuntura, en este momento>

June [ˈdʒuːn] *n* : junio *m*

jungle [ˈdʒʌŋgəl] *n* : jungla *f,* selva *f*

junior[1] [ˈdʒuːnjər] *adj* **1** YOUNGER : más joven <John Smith, Junior : John Smith, hijo> **2** SUBORDINATE : subordinado, subalterno

junior[2] *n* **1** : persona *f* de menor edad <she's my junior : es menor que yo> **2** SUBORDINATE : subalterno *m,* -na *f;* subordinado *m,* -da *f* **3** : estudiante *mf* de penúltimo año

juniper [ˈdʒuːnəpər] *n* : enebro *m*

junk[1] [ˈdʒʌŋk] *vt* : echar a la basura

junk[2] *n* **1** RUBBISH : desechos *mpl,* desperdicios *mpl* **2** STUFF : trastos *mpl fam,* cachivaches *mpl fam* **3 piece of junk** : cacharro *m,* porquería *f*

junket [ˈdʒʌŋkət] *n* : viaje *m* (pagado con dinero público)

junta [ˈhʊntə, ˈdʒʌn-, ˈhʌn-] *n* : junta *f* militar

Jupiter [ˈdʒuːpətər] *n* : Júpiter *m*

jurisdiction [ˌdʒʊrəsˈdɪkʃən] *n* : jurisdicción *f*

jurisprudence [ˌdʒʊrəsˈpruːdənts] *n* : jurisprudencia *f*

jurist [ˈdʒʊrɪst] *n* : jurista *mf;* magistrado *m,* -da *f*

juror [ˈdʒʊrər] *n* : jurado *m,* -da *f*

jury [ˈdʒʊri] *n, pl* **-ries** : jurado *m*

just[1] [ˈdʒʌst] *adv* **1** EXACTLY : justo, precisamente, exactamente **2** POSSIBLY : posiblemente <it just might work : tal vez resulte> **3** BARELY : justo, apenas <just in time : justo a tiempo> **4** ONLY : sólo, solamente, nada más <just us : sólo nosotros> **5** QUITE : muy, simplemente <it's just horrible! : ¡qué horrible!> **6 to have just (done something)** : acabar de (hacer algo) <he just called : acaba de llamar>

just[2] *adj* : justo — **justly** *adv*

justice [ˈdʒʌstɪs] *n* **1** : justicia *f* **2** JUDGE : juez *mf,* jueza *f*

justification [ˌdʒʌstəfəˈkeɪʃən] *n* : justificación *f*

justify [ˈdʒʌstəˌfaɪ] *vt* **-fied; -fying** : justificar — **justifiable** [ˌdʒʌstəˈfaɪəbəl] *adj*

jut [ˈdʒʌt] *vi* **jutted; jutting** : sobresalir

jute [ˈdʒuːt] *n* : yute *m*

juvenile[1] [ˈdʒuːvəˌnaɪl, -vənəl] *adj* **1** : juvenil <juvenile delinquent : delincuente juvenil> <juvenile court : tribunal de menores> **2** CHILDISH : infantil

juvenile[2] *n* : menor *mf*

juxtapose [ˈdʒʌkstəˌpoːz] *vt* **-posed; -posing** : yuxtaponer

juxtaposition [ˌdʒʌkstəpəˈzɪʃən] *n* : yuxtaposición *f*

K

k [ˈkeɪ] *n, pl* **k's** *or* **ks** [ˈkeɪz] : undécima letra del alfabeto inglés
kaiser [ˈkaɪzər] *n* : káiser *m*
kale [ˈkeɪl] *n* : col *f* rizada
kaleidoscope [kəˈlaɪdəˌsko:p] *n* : calidoscopio *m*
kangaroo [ˌkæŋgəˈru:] *n, pl* **-roos** : canguro *m*
kaolin [ˈkeɪələn] *n* : caolín *m*
karat [ˈkærət] *n* : quilate *m*
karate [kəˈrɑti] *n* : karate *m*
katydid [ˈkeɪt̮iˌdɪd] *n* : saltamontes *m*
kayak [ˈkaɪˌæk] *n* : kayac *m,* kayak *m*
keel[1] [ˈki:l] *vi* **to keel over** : volcar (dícese de un barco), desplomarse (dícese de una persona)
keel[2] *n* : quilla *f*
keen [ˈki:n] *adj* **1** SHARP : afilado, filoso <a keen blade : una hoja afilada> **2** PENETRATING : cortante, penetrante <a keen wind : un viento cortante> **3** ENTHUSIASTIC : entusiasta **4** ACUTE : agudo, fino <keen hearing : oído fino> <keen intelligence : inteligencia aguda>
keenly [ˈki:nli] *adv* **1** ENTHUSIASTICALLY : con entusiasmo **2** INTENSELY : vivamente, profundamente <keenly aware of : muy consciente de>
keenness [ˈki:nnəs] *n* **1** SHARPNESS : lo afilado, lo filoso **2** ENTHUSIASM : entusiasmo *m* **3** ACUTENESS : agudeza *f*
keep[1] [ˈki:p] *v* **kept** [ˈkɛpt]; **keeping** *vt* **1** : cumplir (la palabra a uno), acudir a (una cita) **2** OBSERVE : observar (una fiesta) **3** GUARD : guardar, cuidar **4** CONTINUE : mantener <to keep silence : mantener silencio> **5** SUPPORT : mantener (una familia) **6** RAISE : criar (animales) **7** : llevar, escribir (un diario, etc.) **8** RETAIN : guardar, conservar, quedarse con **9** STORE : guardar **10** DETAIN : hacer quedar, detener **11** PRESERVE : guardar <to keep a secret : guardar un secreto> — *vi* **1** : conservarse (dícese de los alimentos) **2** CONTINUE : seguir, no dejar <he keeps on pestering us : no deja de molestarnos> **3 to keep from** : abstenerse de <I couldn't keep from laughing : no podía contener la risa>
keep[2] *n* **1** TOWER : torreón *m* (de un castillo), torre *f* del homenaje **2** SUSTENANCE : manutención *f,* sustento *m* **3 for keeps** : para siempre
keeper [ˈki:pər] *n* **1** : guarda *mf* (en un zoológico); conservador *m,* -dora *f* (en un museo) **2** GAMEKEEPER : guardabosque *mf*
keeping [ˈki:pɪŋ] *n* **1** CONFORMITY : conformidad *f,* acuerdo *m* <in keeping with : de acuerdo con> **2** CARE : cuidado *m* <in the keeping of : al cuidado de>
keepsake [ˈki:pˌseɪk] *n* : recuerdo *m*
keep up *vt* CONTINUE, MAINTAIN : mantener, seguir con — *vi* **1** : mantenerse al corriente <he kept up with the news : se mantenía al tanto de las noticias> **2** CONTINUE : continuar **3 to keep up with someone** : mantener contacto con alguien
keg [ˈkɛg] *n* : barril *m*
kelp [ˈkɛlp] *n* : alga *f* marina
ken [ˈkɛn] *n* **1** SIGHT : vista *f,* alcance *m* de la vista **2** UNDERSTANDING : comprensión *f,* alcance *m* del conocimiento <it's beyond his ken : no lo puede entender>
kennel [ˈkɛnəl] *n* : caseta *f* para perros, perrera *f*
Kenyan [ˈkɛnjən, ˈki:n-] *n* : keniano *m,* -na *f* — **Kenyan** *adj*
kept → **keep**
kerchief [ˈkərtʃəf, -ˌtʃi:f] *n* : pañuelo *m*
kernel [ˈkərnəl] *n* **1** : almendra *f* (de semillas y nueces) **2** : grano *m* (de cereales) **3** CORE : meollo *m* <a kernel of truth : un fondo de verdad>
kerosene *or* **kerosine** [ˈkɛrəˌsi:n, ˌkɛrəˈ-] *n* : queroseno *m,* kerosén *m,* kerosene *m*
ketchup [ˈkɛtʃəp, ˈkæ-] *n* : salsa *f* catsup
kettle [ˈkɛtəl] *n* **1** : hervidor *m,* pava *f Arg, Bol, Chile* **2** → **teakettle**
kettledrum [ˈkɛtəlˌdrʌm] *n* : timbal *m*
key[1] [ˈki:] *vt* **1** ATTUNE : adaptar, adecuar **2 to key up** : poner nervioso, inquietar
key[2] *adj* : clave, fundamental
key[3] *n* **1** : llave *f* **2** SOLUTION : clave *f,* soluciones *fpl* **3** : tecla *f* (de un piano o una máquina) **4** : tono *m,* tonalidad *f* (en la música) **5** ISLET, REEF : cayo *m,* islote *m*
keyboard [ˈki:ˌbord] *n* : teclado *m*
keyhole [ˈki:ˌho:l] *n* : bocallave *f,* ojo *m* (de una cerradura)
keynote[1] [ˈki:ˌno:t] *vt* **-noted; -noting** **1** : establecer la tónica de (en música) **2** : pronunciar el discurso principal de
keynote[2] *n* **1** : tónica *f* (en música) **2** : idea *f* fundamental
keystone [ˈki:ˌsto:n] *n* : clave *f,* dovela *f*
khaki [ˈkæki, ˈkɑ-] *n* : caqui *m*
khan [ˈkɑn, ˈkæn] *n* : kan *m*
kibbutz [kəˈbʊts, -ˈbu:ts] *n, pl* **-butzim** [-ˌbʊtˈsi:m, -ˌbu:t-] : kibutz *m*
kibitz [ˈkɪbɪts] *vi* : dar consejos molestos
kibitzer [ˈkɪbɪtsər, kɪˈbɪt-] *n* : persona *f* que da consejos molestos
kick[1] [ˈkɪk] *vi* **1** : dar patadas (dícese de una persona), cocear (dícese de un animal) **2** PROTEST : patalear, protestar **3** RECOIL : dar un culatazo (dícese de

un arma de fuego) — *vt* **:** patear, darle una patada (a alguien)
kick[2] *n* **1 :** patada *f,* puntapié *m,* coz *f* (de un animal) **2** RECOIL **:** culatazo *m* (de un arma de fuego) **3 :** fuerza *f* <a drink with a kick : una bebida fuerte>
kicker [ˈkɪkər] *n* **:** pateador *m,* -dora *f* (en deportes)
kickoff [ˈkɪkˌɔf] *n* **:** saque *m* (inicial)
kick off *vi* **1 :** hacer el saque inicial (en deportes) **2** BEGIN **:** empezar — *vt* **:** empezar
kid[1] [ˈkɪd] *v* **kidded; kidding** *vt* **1** FOOL **:** engañar **2** TEASE **:** tomarle el pelo (a alguien) — *vi* JOKE **:** bromear <I'm only kidding : lo digo en broma>
kid[2] *n* **1 :** chivo *m,* -va *f;* cabrito *m,* -ta *f* **2** CHILD **:** chico *m,* -ca *f;* niño *m,* -ña *f*
kidder [ˈkɪdər] *n* **:** bromista *mf*
kiddingly [ˈkɪdɪŋli] *adv* **:** en broma
kidnap [ˈkɪdˌnæp] *vt* **-napped** *or* **-naped** [-ˌnæpt]; **-napping** *or* **-naping** [-ˌnæpɪŋ] **:** secuestrar, raptar
kidnapper *or* **kidnaper** [ˈkɪdˌnæpər] *n* **:** secuestrador *m,* -dora *f;* raptor *m,* -tora *f*
kidney [ˈkɪdni] *n, pl* **-neys :** riñón *m*
kidney bean *n* **:** frijol *m*
kill[1] [ˈkɪl] *vt* **1 :** matar **2** END **:** acabar con, poner fin a **3 to kill time :** matar el tiempo
kill[2] *n* **1** KILLING **:** matanza *f* **2** PREY **:** presa *f*
killer [ˈkɪlər] *n* **:** asesino *m,* -na *f*
kiln [ˈkɪl, ˈkɪln] *n* **:** horno *m*
kilo [ˈkiːˌloː] *n, pl* **-los :** kilo *m*
kilocycle [ˈkɪləˌsaɪkəl] *n* **:** kilociclo *m*
kilogram [ˈkɪləˌgræm, ˈkiː-] *n* **:** kilogramo *m*
kilohertz [ˈkɪləˌhərts] *n* **:** kilohertzio *m*
kilometer [kɪˈlɑmət̬ər, ˈkɪləˌmiː-] *n* **:** kilómetro *m*
kilowatt [ˈkɪləˌwɑt] *n* **:** kilovatio *m*
kilt [ˈkɪlt] *n* **:** falda *f* escocesa
kilter [ˈkɪltər] *n* **1** ORDER **:** buen estado *m* **2 out of kilter :** descompuesto, estropeado
kimono [kəˈmoːno, -nə] *n, pl* **-nos :** kimono *m,* quimono *m*
kin [ˈkɪn] *n* **:** familiares *mpl*, parientes *mpl*
kind[1] [ˈkaɪnd] *adj* **:** amable, bondadoso, benévolo
kind[2] *n* **1** ESSENCE **:** esencia *f* <a difference in degree, not in kind : una diferencia cuantitativa y no cualitativa> **2** CATEGORY **:** especie *f,* género *m* **3** TYPE **:** clase *f,* tipo *m,* índole *f*
kindergarten [ˈkɪndərˌgɑrtən, -dən] *n* **:** kinder *m,* kindergarten *m,* jardín *m* de infantes, jardín *m* de niños *Mex*
kindhearted [ˌkaɪndˈhɑrt̬əd] *adj* **:** bondadoso, de buen corazón
kindle [ˈkɪndəl] *v* **-dled; -dling** *vt* **1** IGNITE **:** encender **2** AROUSE **:** despertar, suscitar — *vi* **:** encenderse
kindliness [ˈkaɪndlinəs] *n* **:** bondad *f*
kindling [ˈkɪndlɪŋ, ˈkɪndlən] *n* **:** astillas *fpl,* leña *f*
kindly[1] [ˈkaɪndli] *adv* **1** AMIABLY **:** amablemente, bondadosamente **2** COURTEOUSLY **:** cortésmente, con cortesía <we kindly ask you not smoke : les rogamos que no fumen> **3** PLEASE **:** por favor **4 to take kindly to :** aceptar de buena gana
kindly[2] *adj* **-lier; -est :** bondadoso, amable
kindness [ˈkaɪndnəs] *n* **:** bondad *f*
kind of *adv* SOMEWHAT **:** un tanto, algo
kindred[1] [ˈkɪndrəd] *adj* SIMILAR **:** similar, afín <kindred spirits : almas gemelas>
kindred[2] *n* **1** FAMILY **:** familia *f,* parentela *f* **2 → kin**
kinfolk [ˈkɪnˌfoːk] *or* **kinfolks** [-ˌfoːks] *npl* **→ kin**
king [ˈkɪŋ] *n* **:** rey *m*
kingdom [ˈkɪŋdəm] *n* **:** reino *m*
kingfisher [ˈkɪŋˌfɪʃər] *n* **:** martín *m* pescador
kingly [ˈkɪŋli] *adj* **-lier; -est :** regio, real
king–size [ˈkɪŋˌsaɪz] *or* **king–sized** [-ˌsaɪzd] *adj* **:** de tamaño muy grande, extra largo (dícese de cigarillos)
kink [ˈkɪŋk] *n* **1 :** rizo *m* (en el pelo), vuelta *f* (en una cuerda) **2** CRAMP **:** calambre *m* <to have a kink in the neck : tener tortícolis>
kinky [ˈkɪŋki] *adj* **-kier; -est :** rizado (dícese del pelo), enroscado (dícese de una cuerda)
kinship [ˈkɪnˌʃɪp] *n* **:** parentesco *m*
kinsman [ˈkɪnzmən] *n, pl* **-men** [-mən, -ˌmɛn] **:** familiar *m,* pariente *m*
kinswoman [ˈkɪnzˌwʊmən] *n, pl* **-women** [-ˌwɪmən] **:** familiar *f,* pariente *f*
kipper [ˈkɪpər] *n* **:** arenque *m* ahumado
kiss[1] [ˈkɪs] *vt* **:** besar — *vi* **:** besarse
kiss[2] *n* **:** beso *m*
kit [ˈkɪt] *n* **1** SET **:** juego *m,* kit *m* **2** CASE **:** estuche *m,* caja *f* **3 first–aid kit :** botiquín *m* **4 tool kit :** caja *f* de herramientas **5 travel kit :** neceser *m*
kitchen [ˈkɪtʃən] *n* **:** cocina *f*
kite [ˈkaɪt] *n* **1 :** milano *m* (ave) **2 :** cometa *f,* papalote *m Mex* <to fly a kite : hacer volar una cometa>
kith [ˈkɪθ] *n* **:** amigos *mpl* <kith and kin : amigos y parientes>
kitten [ˈkɪtən] *n* **:** gatito *m,* -ta *f*
kitty [ˈkɪt̬i] *n, pl* **-ties 1** FUND, POOL **:** bote *m,* fondo *m* común **2** CAT **:** gato *m,* gatito *m*
kitty–corner [ˈkɪt̬iˌkɔrnər] *or* **kitty–cornered** [-nərd] **→ catercorner**
kiwi [ˈkiːˌwiː] *n* **:** kiwi *m*
kleptomania [ˌklɛptəˈmeɪniə] *n* **:** cleptomanía *f*
kleptomaniac [ˌklɛptəˈmeɪniˌæk] *n* **:** cleptómano *m,* -na *f*
knack [ˈnæk] *n* **:** maña *f,* facilidad *f*
knapsack [ˈnæpˌsæk] *n* **:** mochila *f,* morral *m*

knave [ˈneɪv] *n* **:** bellaco *m,* pícaro *m*

knead [ˈniːd] *vt* **1 :** amasar, sobar **2** MASSAGE **:** masajear

knee [ˈniː] *n* **:** rodilla *f*

kneecap [ˈniːˌkæp] *n* **:** rótula *f*

kneel [ˈniːl] *vi* **knelt** [ˈnɛlt] *or* **kneeled** [ˈniːld]; **kneeling :** arrodillarse, ponerse de rodillas

knell [ˈnɛl] *n* **:** doble *m,* toque *m* <death knell : toque de difuntos>

knew → **know**

knickers [ˈnɪkərz] *npl* **:** pantalones *mpl* bombachos de media pierna

knickknack [ˈnɪkˌnæk] *n* **:** chuchería *f,* baratija *f*

knife[1] [ˈnaɪf] *vt* **knifed** [ˈnaɪft]; **knifing :** acuchillar, apuñalar

knife[2] *n, pl* **knives** [ˈnaɪvz] **:** cuchillo *m*

knight[1] [ˈnaɪt] *vt* **:** conceder el título de *Sir* a

knight[2] *n* **1 :** caballero *m* <knight errant : caballero andante> **2 :** caballo *m* (en ajedrez) **3 :** uno que tiene el título de *Sir*

knighthood [ˈnaɪtˌhʊd] *n* **1 :** caballería *f* **2 :** título *m* de *Sir*

knightly [ˈnaɪtli] *adj* **:** caballeresco

knit[1] [ˈnɪt] *v* **knit** *or* **knitted** [ˈnɪt̬əd]; **knitting** *vt* **1** UNITE **:** unir, enlazar **2 :** tejer <to knit a sweater : tejer un suéter> **3 to knit one's brows :** fruncir el ceño — *vi* **1 :** tejer **2 :** soldarse (dícese de los huesos)

knit[2] *n* **:** prenda *f* tejida

knitter [ˈnɪt̬ər] *n* **:** tejedor *m,* -dora *f*

knob [ˈnɑb] *n* **1** LUMP **:** bulto *m,* protuberancia *f* **2** HANDLE **:** perilla *f,* tirador *m,* botón *m*

knobbed [ˈnɑbd] *adj* **1** KNOTTY **:** nudoso **2 :** que tiene perilla o botón

knobby [ˈnɑbi] *adj* **knobbier; -est 1** KNOTTY **:** nudoso **2 knobby knees :** rodillas *fpl* huesudas

knock[1] [ˈnɑk] *vt* **1** HIT, RAP **:** golpear, golpetear **2 :** hacer chocar <they knocked heads : se dieron en la cabeza> **3** CRITICIZE **:** criticar — *vi* **1** RAP **:** dar un golpe, llamar (a la puerta) **2** COLLIDE **:** darse, chocar

knock[2] *n* **:** golpe *m,* llamada *f* (a la puerta), golpeteo *m* (de un motor)

knock down *vt* **:** derribar, echar al suelo

knocker [ˈnɑkər] *n* **:** aldaba *f,* llamador *m*

knock–kneed [ˈnɑkˈniːd] *adj* **:** patizambo

knock out *vt* **:** dejar sin sentido, poner fuera de combate (en el boxeo)

knoll [ˈnoːl] *n* **:** loma *f,* otero *m,* montículo *m*

knot[1] [ˈnɑt] *v* **knotted; knotting** *vt* **:** anudar — *vi* **:** anudarse

knot[2] *n* **1 :** nudo *m* (en cordel o madera), nódulo *m* (en los músculos) **2** CLUSTER **:** grupo *m* **3 :** nudo *m* (unidad de velocidad)

knotty [ˈnɑt̬i] *adj* **-tier; -est 1** GNARLED **:** nudoso **2** COMPLEX **:** espinoso, enredado, complejo

know [ˈnoː] *v* **knew** [ˈnuː, ˈnjuː]; **known** [ˈnoːn]; **knowing** *vt* **1 :** saber <he knows the answer : sabe la respuesta> **2 :** conocer (a una persona, un lugar) <do you know Julia? : ¿conoces a Julia?> **3** RECOGNIZE **:** reconocer **4** DISCERN, DISTINGUISH **:** distinguir, discernir **5 to know how to :** saber <I don't know how to dance : no sé bailar> — *vi* **:** saber

knowable [ˈnoːəbəl] *adj* **:** conocible

knowing [ˈnoːɪŋ] *adj* **1** KNOWLEDGEABLE **:** informado <a knowing look : una mirada de complicidad> **2** ASTUTE **:** astuto **3** DELIBERATE **:** deliberado, intencional

knowingly [ˈnoːɪŋli] *adv* **1 :** con complicidad <she smiled knowingly : sonrió con una mirada de complicidad> **2** DELIBERATELY **:** a sabiendas, adrede, a propósito

know–it–all [ˈnoːɪt̬ˌɔl] *n* **:** sabelotodo *mf fam*

knowledge [ˈnɑlɪdʒ] *n* **1** AWARENESS **:** conocimiento *m* **2** LEARNING **:** conocimientos *mpl,* saber *m*

knowledgeable [ˈnɑlɪdʒəbəl] *adj* **:** informado, entendido, enterado

known [ˈnoːn] *adj* **:** conocido, familiar

knuckle [ˈnʌkəl] *n* **:** nudillo *m*

koala [koˈwɑlə] *n* **:** koala *m*

kohlrabi [ˌkoːlˈrɑbi, -ˈræ-] *n, pl* **-bies :** colinabo *m*

Koran [kəˈrɑn, -ˈræn] *n* **the Koran :** el Corán

Korean [kəˈriːən] *n* **:** coreano *m,* -na *f* — **Korean** *adj*

kosher [ˈkoːʃər] *adj* **:** aprobado por la ley judía

kowtow [ˌkaʊˈtaʊ, ˈkaʊˌtaʊ] *vi* **to kowtow to :** humillarse ante, doblegarse ante

krypton [ˈkrɪpˌtɑn] *n* **:** criptón *m*

kudos [ˈkjuːˌdɑs, ˈkuː-, -ˌdoːz] *n* **:** fama *f,* renombre *m*

kumquat [ˈkʌmˌkwɑt] *n* **:** naranjita *f* china

Kuwaiti [kʊˈweɪt̬i] *n* **:** kuwaití *mf* — **Kuwaiti** *adj*

L

l [ˈɛl] *n, pl* **l's** *or* **ls** [ˈɛlz] **:** duodécima letra del alfabeto inglés

lab [ˈlæb] → **laboratory**

label[1] [ˈleɪbəl] *vt* **-beled** *or* **-belled; -beling** *or* **-belling 1 :** etiquetar, poner etiqueta a **2** BRAND, CATEGORIZE

: calificar, tildar, tachar <they labeled him as a fraud : lo calificaron de farsante>

label[2] *n* **1** : etiqueta *f,* rótulo *m* **2** DESCRIPTION : calificación *f,* descripción *f* **3** BRAND : marca *f*

labial [ˈleɪbiəl] *adj* : labial

labor[1] [ˈleɪbər] *vi* **1** WORK : trabajar **2** STRUGGLE : avanzar penosamente (dícese de una persona), funcionar con dificultad (dícese de un motor) **3 to labor under a delusion** : hacerse ilusiones, tener una falsa impresión — *vt* BELABOR : insistir en, extenderse sobre

labor[2] *n* **1** EFFORT, WORK : trabajo *m,* esfuerzos *mpl* **2** : parto *m* <to be in labor : estar de parto> **3** TASK : tarea *f,* labor *m* **4** WORKERS : mano *f* de obra

laboratory [ˈlæbrəˌtori, ləˈbɔrə-] *n, pl* **-ries** : laboratorio *m*

Labor Day *n* : Día *m* del Trabajo

laborer [ˈleɪbərər] *n* : peón *m;* trabajador *m,* -dora *f*

laborious [ləˈboriəs] *adj* : laborioso, difícil

laboriously [ləˈboriəsli] *adv* : laboriosamente, trabajosamente

labor union → **union**

labyrinth [ˈlæbəˌrɪnθ] *n* : laberinto *m*

lace[1] [ˈleɪs] *vt* **laced; lacing 1** TIE : acordonar, atar los cordones de **2** : adornar de encaje <I laced the dress in white : adorné el vestido de encaje blanco> **3** SPIKE : echar licor a

lace[2] *n* **1** : encaje *m* **2** SHOELACE : cordón *m* (de zapatos), agujeta *f Mex*

lacerate [ˈlæsəˌreɪt] *vt* **-ated; -ating** : lacerar

laceration [ˌlæsəˈreɪʃən] *n* : laceración *f*

lack[1] [ˈlæk] *vt* : carecer de, no tener <she lacks patience : carece de paciencia> — *vi* : faltar <they lack for nothing : no les falta nada>

lack[2] *n* : falta *f,* carencia *f*

lackadaisical [ˌlækəˈdeɪzɪkəl] *adj* : apático, indiferente, lánguido — **lackadaisically** [-kli] *adv*

lackey [ˈlæki] *n, pl* **-eys 1** FOOTMAN : lacayo *m* **2** TOADY : adulador *m,* -dora *f*

lackluster [ˈlækˌlʌstər] *adj* **1** DULL : sin brillo, apagado, deslustrado **2** MEDIOCRE : deslucido, mediocre

laconic [ləˈkɑnɪk] *adj* : lacónico — **laconically** [-nɪkli] *adv*

lacquer[1] [ˈlækər] *vt* : laquear, pintar con laca

lacquer[2] *n* : laca *f*

lacrosse [ləˈkrɔs] *n* : lacrosse *f*

lactic acid [ˈlæktɪk] *n* : ácido *m* láctico

lacuna [ləˈkuːnə, -ˈkjuː-] *n, pl* **-nae** [-ˌniː, -ˌnaɪ] *or* **-nas** : laguna *f*

lacy [ˈleɪsi] *adj* **lacier; -est** : de encaje, como de encaje

lad [ˈlæd] *n* : muchacho *m,* niño *m*

ladder [ˈlædər] *n* : escalera *f*

laden [ˈleɪdən] *adj* : cargado

ladle[1] [ˈleɪdəl] *vt* **-dled; -dling** : servir con cucharón

ladle[2] *n* : cucharón *m,* cazo *m*

lady [ˈleɪdi] *n, pl* **-dies 1** : señora *f,* dama *f* **2** WOMAN : mujer *f*

ladybird [ˈleɪdiˌbərd] → **ladybug**

ladybug [ˈleɪdiˌbʌg] *n* : mariquita *f*

lag[1] [ˈlæg] *vi* **lagged; lagging** : quedarse atrás, retrasarse, rezagarse

lag[2] *n* **1** DELAY : retraso *m,* demora *f* **2** INTERVAL : lapso *m,* intervalo *m*

lager [ˈlɑgər] *n* : cerveza *f* rubia

laggard[1] [ˈlægərd] *adj* : retardado, retrasado

laggard[2] *n* : rezagado *m,* -da *f*

lagoon [ləˈguːn] *n* : laguna *f*

laid *pp* → **lay**

lain *pp* → **lie**

lair [ˈlær] *n* : guarida *f,* madriguera *f*

laissez–faire [ˌlɛˌseɪˈfær, ˌleɪˌzeɪ-] *n* : liberalismo *m* económico

laity [ˈleɪəṱi] *n* **the laity** : los laicos, el laicado

lake [ˈleɪk] *n* : lago *m*

lama [ˈlɑmə] *n* : lama *m*

lamb [ˈlæm] *n* **1** : cordero *m,* borrego *m* (animal) **2** : carne *f* de cordero

lambaste [læmˈbeɪst] *or* **lambast** [-ˈbæst] *vt* **-basted; -basting 1** BEAT, THRASH : golpear, azotar, darle una paliza (a alguien) **2** CENSURE : arremeter contre, censurar

lame[1] [ˈleɪm] *vt* **lamed; laming** : lisiar, hacer cojo

lame[2] *adj* **lamer; lamest 1** : cojo, renco, rengo **2** WEAK : pobre, débil, poco convincente <a lame excuse : una excusa débil>

lamé [lɑˈmeɪ, læ-] *n* : lamé *m*

lame duck *n* : persona *f* sin poder <a lame-duck President : un presidente saliente>

lamely [ˈleɪmli] *adv* : sin convicción

lameness [ˈleɪmnəs] *n* **1** : cojera *f,* renquera *f* **2** : falta *f* de convicción, debilidad *f,* pobreza *f* <the lameness of her response : la pobreza de su respuesta>

lament[1] [ləˈmɛnt] *vt* **1** MOURN : llorar, llorar por **2** DEPLORE : lamentar, deplorar — *vi* : llorar

lament[2] *n* : lamento *m*

lamentable [ˈlæməntəbəl, ləˈmɛntə-] *adj* : lamentable, deplorable — **lamentably** [-bli] *adv*

lamentation [ˌlæmənˈteɪʃən] *n* : lamentación *f,* lamento *m*

laminate[1] [ˈlæməˌneɪt] *vt* **-nated; -nating** : laminar

laminate[2] [ˈlæmənət] *n* : laminado *m*

laminated [ˈlæməˌneɪṱəd] *adj* : laminado

lamp [ˈlæmp] *n* : lámpara *f*

lampoon[1] [læmˈpuːn] *vt* : satirizar

lampoon[2] *n* : sátira *f*

lamprey [ˈlæmpri] *n, pl* **-preys** : lamprea *f*

lance[1] [ˈlænts] *vt* **lanced; lancing** : abrir con lanceta, sajar

lance[2] *n* : lanza *f*

lance corporal *n* : cabo *m* interino, soldado *m* de primera clase

lancet [ˈlæntsət] *n* : lanceta *f*

land[1] [ˈlænd] *vt* **1** : desembarcar (pasajeros de un barco), hacer aterrizar (un avión) **2** CATCH : pescar, sacar (un pez) del agua **3** GAIN, SECURE : conseguir, ganar <to land a job : conseguir empleo> **4** DELIVER : dar, asestar <he landed a punch : asestó un puñetazo> — *vi* **1** : aterrizar, tomar tierra, atracar <the plane just landed : el avión acaba de aterrizar> <the ship landed an hour ago : el barco atracó hace una hora>**2** ALIGHT : posarse, aterrizar <to land on one's feet : caer de pie>

land[2] *n* **1** GROUND : tierra *f* <dry land : tierra firme> **2** TERRAIN : terreno *m* **3** NATION : país *m,* nación *f* **4** DOMAIN : mundo *m,* dominio *m* <the land of dreams : el mundo de los sueños>

landfill [ˈlænd͵fɪl] *n* : vertadero *m* (de basuras)

landing [ˈlændɪŋ] *n* **1** : aterrizaje *m* (de aviones), desembarco *m* (de barcos) **2** : descansillo *m* (de una escalera)

landing field *n* : campo *m* de aterrizaje

landing strip → **airstrip**

landlady [ˈlænd͵leɪdi] *n, pl* **-dies** : casera *f,* dueña *f,* arrendadora *f*

landless [ˈlændləs] *adj* : sin tierra

landlocked [ˈlænd͵lɑkt] *adj* : sin salida al mar

landlord [ˈlænd͵lɔrd] *n* : dueño *m,* casero *m,* arrendador *m*

landlubber [ˈlænd͵lʌbər] *n* : marinero *m* de agua dulce

landmark [ˈlænd͵mɑrk] *n* **1** : señal *f* (geográfica), punto *m* de referencia **2** MILESTONE : hito *m* <a landmark in our history : un hito en nuestra historia> **3** MONUMENT : monumento *m* histórico

landowner [ˈlænd͵oːnər] *n* : hacendado *m,* -da *f;* terrateniente *mf*

landscape[1] [ˈlænd͵skeɪp] *vt* **-scaped; -scaping** : ajardinar

landscape[2] *n* : paisaje *m*

landslide [ˈlænd͵slaɪd] *n* **1** : desprendimiento *m* de tierras, derrumbe *m* **2 landslide victory** : victoria *f* arrolladora

landward [ˈlændwərd] *adv* : en dirección de la tierra, hacia tierra

lane [ˈleɪn] *n* **1** PATH, WAY : camino *m,* sendero *m* **2** : carril *m* (de una carretera)

language [ˈlæŋgwɪdʒ] *n* **1** : idioma *m,* lengua *f* <the English language : el idioma inglés> **2** : lenguaje *m* <body language : lenguaje corporal>

languid [ˈlæŋgwɪd] *adj* : lánguido — **languidly** *adv*

languish [ˈlæŋgwɪʃ] *vi* **1** WEAKEN : languidecer, debilitarse **2** PINE : consumirse, suspirar (por) <to languish for love : suspirar por el amor> <he languished in prison : estuvo pudriéndose en la cárcel>

languor [ˈlæŋgər] *n* : languidez *f*

languorous [ˈlæŋgərəs] *adj* : lánguido — **languorously** *adv*

lank [ˈlæŋk] *adj* **1** THIN : delgado, larguirucho *fam* **2** LIMP : lacio

lanky [ˈlæŋki] *adj* **lankier; -est** : delgado, larguirucho *fam*

lanolin [ˈlænəlɪn] *n* : lanolina *f*

lantern [ˈlæntərn] *n* : linterna *f,* farol *m*

Laotian [leɪˈoːʃən, ˈlaʊʃən] *n* : laosiano *m,* -na *f* — **Laotian** *adj*

lap[1] [ˈlæp] *v* **lapped; lapping** *vt* **1** FOLD : plegar, doblar **2** WRAP : envolver **3** : lamer, besar <waves were lapping the shore : las olas lamían la orilla> **4 to lap up** : beber a lengüetadas (como un gato) — *vi* OVERLAP : traslaparse

lap[2] *n* **1** : falda *f,* regazo *m* (del cuerpo) **2** OVERLAP : traslapo *m* **3** : vuelta *f* (en deportes) **4** STAGE : etapa *f* (de un viaje)

lapdog [ˈlæp͵dɔg] *n* : perro *m* faldero

lapel [ləˈpɛl] *n* : solapa *f*

Lapp [ˈlæp] *n* : lapón *m,* -pona *f* — **Lapp** *adj*

lapse[1] [ˈlæps] *vi* **lapsed; lapsing 1** FALL, SLIP : caer <to lapse into bad habits : caer en malos hábitos> <to lapse into unconsciousness : perder el conocimiento> <to lapse into silence : quedarse callado> **2** FADE : decaer, desvanecerse <her dedication lapsed : su dedicación se desvaneció> **3** CEASE : cancelarse, perderse **4** ELAPSE : transcurrir, pasar **5** EXPIRE : caducar

lapse[2] *n* **1** SLIP : lapsus *m,* deliz *m,* falla *f* <a lapse of memory : una falla de memoria> **2** INTERVAL : lapso *m,* intervalo *m,* período *m* **3** EXPIRATION : caducidad *f*

laptop [ˈlæp͵tɑp] *adj* : portátil, laptop

larboard [ˈlɑrbərd] *n* : babor *m*

larcenous [ˈlɑrsənəs] *adj* : de robo

larceny [ˈlɑrsəni] *n, pl* **-nies** : robo *m,* hurto *m*

larch [ˈlɑrtʃ] *n* : alerce *f*

lard [ˈlɑrd] *n* : manteca *f* de cerdo

larder [ˈlɑrdər] *n* : despensa *f,* alacena *f*

large [ˈlɑrdʒ] *adj* **larger; largest 1** BIG : grande **2** COMPREHENSIVE : amplio, extenso **3 by and large** : por lo general

largely [ˈlɑrdʒli] *adv* : en gran parte, en su mayoría

largeness [ˈlɑrdʒnəs] *n* : lo grande

largesse *or* **largess** [lɑrˈʒɛs, -ˈdʒɛs] *n* : generosidad *f,* largueza *f*

lariat [ˈlæriət] *n* : lazo *m*

lark [ˈlɑrk] *n* **1** FUN : diversión *f* <what a lark! : ¡qué divertido!> **2** : alondra *f* (pájaro)

larva [ˈlɑrvə] *n, pl* **-vae** [-͵viː, -͵vaɪ] : larva *f* — **larval** [-vəl] *adj*

laryngitis [͵lærənˈdʒaɪtəs] *n* : laringitis *f*

larynx [ˈlærɪŋks] *n, pl* **-rynges** [ləˈrɪn,ʤiːz] *or* **-ynxes** [ˈlærɪŋksəz] : laringe *f*

lasagna [ləˈzɑnjə] *n* : lasaña *f*

lascivious [ləˈsɪviəs] *adj* : lascivo

lasciviousness [ləˈsɪviəsnəs] *n* : lascivia *f*, lujuria *f*

laser [ˈleɪzər] *n* : láser *m*

lash[1] [ˈlæʃ] *vt* **1** WHIP : azotar **2** BIND : atar, amarrar

lash[2] *n* **1** WHIP : látigo *m* **2** STROKE : latigazo *m* **3** EYELASH : pestaña *f*

lass [ˈlæs] *or* **lassie** [ˈlæsi] *n* : muchacha *f*, chica *f*

lassitude [ˈlæsə,tuːd, -,tjuːd] *n* : lasitud *f*

lasso[1] [ˈlæ,soː, læˈsuː] *vt* : lazar

lasso[2] *n, pl* **-sos** *or* **-soes** : lazo *m*, reata *f Mex*

last[1] [ˈlæst] *vi* **1** CONTINUE : durar <how long will it last? : ¿cuánto durará?> **2** ENDURE : aguantar, durar **3** SURVIVE : durar, sobrevivir **4** SUFFICE : durar, bastar — *vt* **1** : durar <it will last a lifetime : durará toda la vida> **2 to last out** : aguantar

last[2] *adv* **1** : en último lugar, al último <we came in last : llegamos en último lugar> **2** : por última vez, la última vez <I saw him last in Bogota : lo vi por última vez en Bogotá> **3** FINALLY : por último, en conclusión

last[3] *adj* **1** FINAL : último, final **2** PREVIOUS : pasado <last year : el año pasado>

last[4] *n* **1** : el último, la última, lo último <at last : por fin, al fin, finalmente> **2** : horma *f* (de zapatero)

lasting [ˈlæstɪŋ] *adj* : perdurable, duradero, estable

lastly [ˈlæstli] *adv* : por último, finalmente

latch[1] [ˈlætʃ] *vt* : cerrar con picaporte

latch[2] *n* : picaporte *m*, pestillo *m*, pasador *m*

late[1] [ˈleɪt] *adv* **later; latest 1** : tarde <to arrive late : llegar tarde> <to sleep late : dormir hasta tarde> **2** : a última hora, a finales <late in the month : a finales del mes> **3** RECENTLY : recién, últimamente <as late as last year : todavía en el año pasado>

late[2] *adj* **later; latest 1** TARDY : tardío, de retraso <to be late : llegar tarde> **2** : avanzado <because of the late hour : a causa de la hora avanzada> **3** DECEASED : difunto, fallecido **4** RECENT : reciente, último <our late quarrel : nuestra última pelea>

latecomer [ˈleɪt,kʌmər] *n* : rezagado *m*, -da *f*

lately [ˈleɪtli] *adv* : recientemente, últimamente

lateness [ˈleɪtnəs] *n* **1** DELAY : retraso *m*, atraso *m*, tardanza *f* **2** : lo avanzado (de la hora)

latent [ˈleɪtənt] *adj* : latente — **latently** *adv*

lateral [ˈlætərəl] *adj* : lateral — **laterally** *adv*

latex [ˈleɪ,tɛks] *n, pl* **-tices** [ˈleɪtə,siːz, ˈlætə-] *or* **-texes** : látex *m*

lath [ˈlæθ, ˈlæð] *n, pl* **laths** *or* **lath** : listón *m*

lathe [ˈleɪð] *n* : torno *m*

lather[1] [ˈlæðər] *vt* : enjabonar — *vi* : espumar, hacer espuma

lather[2] *n* **1** : espuma *f* (de jabón) **2** : sudor *m* (de caballo) **3 to get into a lather** : ponerse histérico

Latin[1] *adj* : latino

Latin[2] *n* **1** : latín *m* (idioma) **2** → **Latin American**

Latin–American [ˈlætənəˈmɛrikən] *adj* : latinoamericano

Latin American *n* : latinoamericano *m*, -na *f*

latitude [ˈlætə,tuːd, -,tjuːd] *n* : latitud *f*

latrine [ləˈtriːn] *n* : letrina *f*

latter[1] [ˈlætər] *adj* **1** SECOND : segundo **2** LAST : último

latter[2] *pron* **the latter** : éste, ésta, éstos *pl*, éstas *pl*

lattice [ˈlætəs] *n* : enrejado *m*, celosía *f*

Latvian [ˈlætviən] *n* : letón *m*, -tona *f* — **Latvian** *adj*

laud[1] [ˈlɔd] *vt* : alabar, loar

laud[2] *n* : alabanza *f*, loa *f*

laudable [ˈlɔdəbəl] *adj* : loable — **laudably** [-bli] *adv*

laugh[1] [ˈlæf] *vi* : reír, reírse

laugh[2] *n* **1** LAUGHTER : risa *f* **2** JOKE : chiste *m*, broma *f* <he did it for a laugh : lo hizo en broma, lo hizo para divertirse>

laughable [ˈlæfəbəl] *adj* : risible, de risa

laughingstock [ˈlæfɪŋ,stɑk] *n* : hazmerreír *m*

laughter [ˈlæftər] *n* : risa *f*, risas *fpl*

launch[1] [ˈlɔntʃ] *vt* **1** HURL : lanzar **2** : botar (un barco) **3** START : iniciar, empezar

launch[2] *n* **1** : lancha *f* (bote) **2** LAUNCHING : lanzamiento *m*

launder [ˈlɔndər] *vt* **1** : lavar y planchar (ropa) **2** : blanquear, lavar (dinero)

launderer [ˈlɔndərər] *n* : lavandero *m*, -ra *f*

laundress [ˈlɔndrəs] *n* : lavandera *f*

laundry [ˈlɔndri] *n, pl* **laundries 1** : ropa *f* sucia, ropa *f* para lavar <to do the laundry : lavar la ropa> **2** : lavandería *f* (servicio de lavar)

laureate [ˈlɔriət] *n* : laureado *m*, -da *f* <poet laureate : poeta laureado>

laurel [ˈlɔrəl] *n* **1** : laurel *m* (planta) **2 laurels** *npl* : laureles *mpl* <to rest on one's laurels : dormirse uno en sus laureles>

lava [ˈlɑvə, ˈlæ-] *n* : lava *f*

lavatory [ˈlævə,tori] *n, pl* **-ries** : baño *m*, cuarto *m* de baño

lavender [ˈlævəndər] *n* : lavanda *f,* espliego *m*

lavish[1] [ˈlævɪʃ] *vt* : prodigar (a), colmar (de)

lavish[2] *adj* **1** EXTRAVAGANT : pródigo, generoso, derrochador **2** ABUNDANT : abundante **3** LUXURIOUS : lujoso, espléndido

lavishly [ˈlævɪʃli] *adv* : con generosidad, espléndidamente <to live lavishly : vivir a lo grande>

lavishness [ˈlævɪʃnəs] *n* : generosidad *f,* esplendidez *f*

law [ˈlɔ] *n* **1** : ley *f* <to break the law : violar la ley> **2** : derecho *m* <criminal law : derecho criminal> **3** : abogacía *f* <to practice law : ejercer la abogacía>

law–abiding [ˈlɔəˌbaɪdɪŋ] *adj* : observante de la ley

lawbreaker [ˈlɔˌbreɪkər] *n* : infractor *m,* -tora *f* de la ley

lawful [ˈlɔfəl] *adj* : legal, legítimo, lícito — **lawfully** *adv*

lawgiver [ˈlɔˌgɪvər] *n* : legislador *m,* -dora *f*

lawless [ˈlɔləs] *adj* : anárquico, ingobernable — **lawlessly** *adv*

lawlessness [ˈlɔləsnəs] *n* : anarquía *f,* desorden *m*

lawmaker [ˈlɔˌmeɪkər] *n* : legislador *m,* -dora *f*

lawman [ˈlɔmən] *n, pl* **-men** [-mən, -ˌmɛn] : agente *m* del orden

lawn [ˈlɔn] *n* : césped *m,* pasto *m*

lawn mower *n* : cortadora *f* de césped

lawsuit [ˈlɔˌsuːt] *n* : pleito *m,* litigio *m,* demanda *f*

lawyer [ˈlɔɪər, ˈlɔjər] *n* : abogado *m,* -da *f*

lax [ˈlæks] *adj* : laxo, relajado — **laxly** *adv*

laxative [ˈlæksət̬ɪv] *n* : laxante *m*

laxity [ˈlæksət̬i] *n* : relajación *f,* descuido *m,* falta *f* de rigor

lay[1] [ˈleɪ] *vt* **laid** [ˈleɪd]; **laying 1** PLACE, PUT : poner, colocar <she laid it on the table : lo puso en la mesa> <to lay eggs : poner huevos> **2** : hacer <to lay a bet : hacer una apuesta> **3** IMPOSE : imponer <to lay a tax : imponer un impuesto> <to lay the blame on : echarle la culpa a> **4 to lay out** PRESENT : presentar, exponer <he laid out his plan : presentó su proyecto> **5 to lay out** DESIGN : diseñar (el trazado de)

lay[2] *pp* → **lie**

lay[3] *adj* SECULAR : laico, lego

lay[4] *n* **1** : disposición *f,* configuración *f* <the lay of the land : la configuración del terreno> **2** BALLAD : romance *m,* balada *f*

layer [ˈleɪər] *n* **1** : capa *f* (de pintura, etc.), estrato *m* (de roca) **2** : gallina *f* ponedora

layman [ˈleɪmən] *n, pl* **-men** [-mən, -ˌmɛn] : laico *m,* lego *m*

layoff [ˈleɪˌɔf] *n* : despido *m*

lay off *vt* : despedir

layout [ˈleɪˌaʊt] *n* : disposición *f,* distribución *f* (de una casa, etc.), trazado *m* (de una ciudad)

lay up *vt* **1** STORE : guardar, almacenar **2 to be laid up** : estar enfermo, tener que guardar cama

laywoman [ˈleɪˌwʊmən] *n, pl* **-women** [-ˌwɪmən] : laica *f,* lega *f*

laziness [ˈleɪzinəs] *n* : pereza *f,* flojera *f*

lazy [ˈleɪzi] *adj* **-zier; -est** : perezoso, holgazán — **lazily** [ˈleɪzəli] *adv*

leach [ˈliːtʃ] *vt* : filtrar

lead[1] [ˈliːd] *vt* **led** [ˈlɛd]; **leading 1** GUIDE : conducir, llevar, guiar **2** DIRECT : dirigir **3** HEAD : encabezar, ir al frente de **4 to lead to** : resultar en, llevar a <it only leads to trouble : sólo resulta en problemas>

lead[2] *n* : delantera *f,* primer lugar *m* <to take the lead : tomar la delantera>

lead[3] [ˈlɛd] *n* **1** : plomo *m* (metal) **2** : mina *f* (de lápiz) **3 lead poisoning** : saturnismo *m*

leaden [ˈlɛdən] *adj* **1** : plomizo <a leaden sky : un ciel plomizo> **2** HEAVY : pesado

leader [ˈliːdər] *n* : jefe *m,* -fa *f;* líder *mf;* dirigente *mf;* gobernante *mf*

leadership [ˈliːdərˌʃɪp] *n* : mando *m,* dirección *f*

leaf[1] [ˈliːf] *vi* **1** : echar hojas (dícese de un árbol) **2 to leaf through** : hojear (un libro)

leaf[2] *n, pl* **leaves** [ˈliːvz] **1** : hoja *f* (de plantas o libros) **2 to turn over a new leaf** : hacer borrón y cuenta nueva

leafless [ˈliːfləs] *adj* : sin hojas, pelado

leaflet [ˈliːflət] *n* : folleto *m*

leafy [ˈliːfi] *adj* **leafier; -est** : frondoso

league[1] [ˈliːg] *v* **leagued; leaguing** *vt* : aliar, unir — *vi* : aliarse, unirse

league[2] *n* **1** : legua *f* (medida de distancia) **2** ASSOCIATION : alianza *f,* sociedad *f,* liga *f*

leak[1] [ˈliːk] *vt* **1** : perder, dejar escapar (un líquido o un gas) **2** : filtrar (información) — *vi* **1** : gotear, escaparse, fugarse (dícese de un líquido o un gas) **2** : hacer agua (dícese de un bote) **3** : filtrarse, divulgarse (dícese de información)

leak[2] *n* **1** HOLE : agujero *m* (en recipientes), gotera *f* (en un tejado) **2** ESCAPE : fuga *f,* escape *m* **3** : filtración *f* (de información)

leakage [ˈliːkɪdʒ] *n* : escape *m,* fuga *f*

leaky [ˈliːki] *adj* **leakier; -est** : agujereado (dícese de un recipiente), que hace agua (dícese de un bote), con goteras (dícese de un tejado)

lean[1] [ˈliːn] *vi* **1** BEND : inclinarse, ladearse **2** RECLINE : reclinarse **3** RELY : apoyarse (en), depender (de) **4** INCLINE, TEND : inclinarse, tender — *vt* : apoyar

lean[2] *adj* 1 THIN : delgado, flaco 2 : sin grasa, magro (dícese de la carne)

leanness [ˈliːnnəs] *n* : delgadez *f*

lean–to [ˈliːnˌtuː] *n* : cobertizo *m*

leap[1] [ˈliːp] *vi* **leapt** *or* **leaped** [ˈliːpt, ˈlɛpt]; **leaping** : saltar, brincar

leap[2] *n* : salto *m*, brinco *m*

leap year *n* : año *m* bisiesto

learn [ˈlərn] *vt* 1 : aprender <to learn to sing : aprender a cantar> 2 MEMORIZE : aprender de memoria 3 DISCOVER : saber, enterarse de — *vi* 1 : aprender <to learn from experience : aprender por experiencia> 2 FIND OUT : enterarse, saber

learned [ˈlərnəd] *adj* : erudito

learner [ˈlərnər] *n* : principiante *mf*, estudiante *mf*

learning [ˈlərnɪŋ] *n* : erudición *f*, saber *m*

lease[1] [ˈliːs] *vt* **leased; leasing** : arrendar

lease[2] *n* : contrato *m* de arrendamiento

leash[1] [ˈliːʃ] *vt* : atraillar (un animal)

leash[2] *n* : traílla *f*

least[1] [ˈliːst] *adv* : menos <when least expected : cuando menos se espera>

least[2] *adj* (*superlative of* **little**) : menor, más mínimo

least[3] *n* 1 : lo menos <at least : por lo menos> 2 **to say the least** : por no decir más

leather [ˈlɛðər] *n* : cuero *m*

leathery [ˈlɛðəri] *adj* : curtido (dícese de la piel), correoso (dícese de la carne)

leave[1] [ˈliːv] *v* **left** [ˈlɛft]; **leaving** *vt* 1 BEQUEATH : dejar, legar 2 DEPART : dejar, salir(se) de 3 ABANDON : abandonar, dejar 4 FORGET : dejar, olvidarse de <I left the books at the library : dejé los libros en la biblioteca> 5 **to be left** : quedar <it's all I have left : es todo lo que me queda> 6 **to be left over** : sobrar 7 **to leave out** : omitir, excluir — *vi* : irse, salir, partir, marcharse <she left yesterday morning : se fue ayer por la mañana>

leave[2] *n* 1 PERMISSION : permiso *m* <by your leave : con su permiso> 2 *or* **leave of absence** : permiso *m*, licencia *f* <maternity leave : licencia por maternidad> 3 **to take one's leave** : despedirse

leaven [ˈlɛvən] *n* : levadura *f*

leaves → **leaf**[2]

leaving [ˈliːvɪŋ] *n* 1 : salida *f*, partida *f* 2 **leavings** *npl* : restos *mpl*, sobras *fpl*

Lebanese [ˌlɛbəˈniːz, -ˈniːs] *n* : libanés *m*, -nesa *f* — **Lebanese** *adj*

lecherous [ˈlɛtʃərəs] *adj* : lascivo, libidinoso — **lecherously** *adv*

lechery [ˈlɛtʃəri] *n* : lascivia *f*, lujuria *f*

lecture[1] [ˈlɛktʃər] *v* **-tured; -turing** *vi* : dar clase, dictar clase, dar una conferencia — *vt* SCOLD : sermonear, echar una reprimenda a, regañar

lecture[2] *n* 1 : conferencia *f* 2 REPRIMAND : reprimenda *f*

led *pp* → **lead**[1]

ledge [ˈlɛdʒ] *n* : repisa *f* (de una pared), antepecho *m* (de una ventana), saliente *m* (de una montaña)

ledger [ˈlɛdʒər] *n* : libro *m* mayor, libro *m* de contabilidad

lee[1] [ˈliː] *adj* : de sotavento

lee[2] *n* : sotavento *m*

leech [ˈliːtʃ] *n* : sanguijuela *f*

leek [ˈliːk] *n* : puerro *m*

leer[1] [ˈlɪr] *vi* : mirar con lascivia

leer[2] *n* : mirada *f* lasciva

leery [ˈlɪri] *adj* : receloso

lees [ˈliːz] *npl* : posos *mpl*, heces *fpl*

leeward[1] [ˈliːwərd, ˈluːərd] *adj* : de sotavento

leeward[2] *n* : sotavento *m*

leeway [ˈliːˌweɪ] *n* : libertad *f*, margen *m*

left[1] [ˈlɛft] *adv* : hacia la izquierda

left[2] *pp* → **leave**

left[3] *adj* : izquierdo

left[4] *n* : izquierda *f* <on the left : a la izquierda>

left–hand [ˈlɛftˈhænd] *adj* 1 : de la izquierda 2 → **left–handed**

left–handed [ˈlɛftˈhændəd] *adj* 1 : zurdo (dícese de una persona) 2 : con doble sentido <a left-handed compliment : un cumplido a medias>

leftovers [ˈlɛftˌoːvərz] *npl* : restos *mpl*, sobras *fpl*

left wing *n* **the left wing** : la izquierda

left–winger [ˈlɛftˈwɪŋər] *n* : izquierdista *mf*

leg [ˈlɛg] *n* 1 : pierna *f* (de una persona, de carne, de ropa), pata *f* (de un animal, de muebles) 2 STAGE : etapa *f* (de un viaje), vuelta *f* (de una carrera)

legacy [ˈlɛgəsi] *n, pl* **-cies** : legado *m*, herencia *f*

legal [ˈliːgəl] *adj* 1 : legal, jurídico <legal advisor : asesor jurídico> <the legal profession : la abogacía> 2 LAWFUL : legítimo, legal

legalistic [ˌliːgəˈlɪstɪk] *adj* : legalista

legality [liˈgæləṭi] *n, pl* **-ties** : legalidad *f*

legalize [ˈliːgəˌlaɪz] *vt* **-ized; -izing** : legalizar

legally [ˈliːgəli] *adv* : legalmente

legate [ˈlɛgət] *n* : legado *m*

legation [lɪˈgeɪʃən] *n* : legación *f*

legend [ˈlɛdʒənd] *n* 1 STORY : leyenda *f* 2 INSCRIPTION : leyenda *f*, inscripción *f* 3 : signos *mpl* convencionales (en un mapa)

legendary [ˈlɛdʒənˌdɛri] *adj* : lengendario

legerdemain [ˌlɛdʒərdəˈmeɪn] → **sleight of hand**

leggings [ˈlɛgɪŋz, ˈlɛgənz] *npl* : mallas *fpl*

legibility [ˌlɛdʒəˈbɪləṭi] *n* : legibilidad *f*

legible [ˈlɛdʒəbəl] *adj* : legible

legibly [ˈlɛdʒəbli] *adv* : de manera legible

legion [ˈliːdʒən] *n* : legión *f*

legionnaire [ˌliːdʒəˈnær] *n* : legionario *m*, -ria *f*

legislate [ˈlɛdʒəsˌleɪt] *vi* **-lated; -lating** : legislar

legislation [ˌlɛdʒəsˈleɪʃən] *n* : legislación *f*

legislative [ˈlɛdʒəsˌleɪt̬ɪv] *adj* : legislativo, legislador

legislator [ˈlɛdʒəsˌleɪt̬ər] *n* : legislador *m*, -dora *f*

legislature [ˈlɛdʒəsˌleɪtʃər] *n* : asamblea *f* legislativa

legitimacy [lɪˈdʒɪt̬əməsi] *n* : legitimidad *f*

legitimate [lɪˈdʒɪt̬əmət] *adj* **1** VALID : legítimo, válido, justificado **2** LAWFUL : legítimo, legal

legitimately [lɪˈdʒɪt̬əmətli] *adv* : legítimamente

legitimize [lɪˈdʒɪt̬əˌmaɪz] *vt* **-mized; -mizing** : legitimar, hacer legítimo

legume [ˈlɛˌgjuːm, lɪˈgjuːm] *n* : legumbre *f*

leisure [ˈliːʒər, ˈlɛ-] *n* **1** : ocio *m*, tiempo *m* libre <a life of leisure : una vida de ocio>**2 to take one's leisure** : reposar **3 at your leisure** : cuando te venga bien, cuando tengas tiempo

leisurely [ˈliːʒərli, ˈlɛ-] *adj & adv* : lento, sin prisas

lemming [ˈlɛmɪŋ] *n* : lemming *m*

lemon [ˈlɛmən] *n* : limón *m*

lemonade [ˌlɛməˈneɪd] *n* : limonada *f*

lemony [ˈlɛməni] *adj* : a limón

lend [ˈlɛnd] *vt* **lent** [ˈlɛnt]; **lending 1** : prestar <to lend money : prestar dinero> **2** GIVE : dar <it lends force to his criticism : da fuerza a su crítica> **3 to lend oneself to** : prestarse a

length [ˈlɛŋkθ] *n* **1** : longitud *f*, largo *m* <10 feet in length : 10 pies de largo> **2** DURATION : duración *f* **3** : trozo *m* (de madera), corte *m* (de tela) **4 to go to any lengths** : hacer todo lo posible **5 at ~** : extensamente <to speak at length : hablar largo y tendido>

lengthen [ˈlɛŋkθən] *vt* **1** : alargar <can they lengthen the dress? : ¿se puede alargar el vestido?> **2** EXTEND, PROLONG : prolongar, extender — *vi* : alargarse, crecer <the days are lengthening : los días están creciendo>

lengthways [ˈlɛŋkθˌweɪz] → **lengthwise**

lengthwise [ˈlɛŋkθˌwaɪz] *adv* : a lo largo, longitudinalmente

lengthy [ˈlɛŋkθi] *adj* **lengthier; -est 1** OVERLONG : largo y pesado **2** EXTENDED : prolongado, largo

leniency [ˈliːniəntsi] *n, pl* **-cies** : lenidad *f*, indulgencia *f*

lenient [ˈliːniənt] *adj* : indulgente, poco severo

leniently [ˈliːniəntli] *adv* : con lenidad, con indulgencia

lens [ˈlɛnz] *n* **1** : cristalino *m* (del ojo) **2** : lente *mf* (de un instrumento o una cámara) **3** → **contact lens**

lent → **lend**

Lent [ˈlɛnt] *n* : Cuaresma *f*

lentil [ˈlɛntəl] *n* : lenteja *f*

Leo [ˈliːoː] *n* : Leo *mf*

leopard [ˈlɛpərd] *n* : leopardo *m*

leotard [ˈliːəˌtɑrd] *n* : leotardo *m*, malla *f*

leper [ˈlɛpər] *n* : leproso *m*, -sa *f*

leprechaun [ˈlɛprəˌkɑn] *n* : duende *m* (irlandés)

leprosy [ˈlɛprəsi] *n* : lepra *f* — **leprous** [ˈlɛprəs] *adj*

lesbian[1] [ˈlɛzbiən] *adj* : lesbiano

lesbian[2] *n* : lesbiana *f*

lesbianism [ˈlɛzbiəˌnɪzəm] *n* : lesbianismo *m*

lesion [ˈliːʒən] *n* : lesión *f*

less[1] [ˈlɛs] *adv* (*comparative of* **little**[1]) : menos <the less you know, the better : cuanto menos sepas, mejor> <less and less : cada vez menos>

less[2] *adj* (*comparative of* **little**[2]) : menos <less than three : menos de tres> <less money : menos dinero> <nothing less than perfection : nada menos que la perfección>

less[3] *pron* : menos <I'm earning less : estoy ganando menos>

less[4] *prep* : menos <one month less two days : un mes menos dos días>

lessee [lɛˈsiː] *n* : arrendatario *m*, -ria *f*

lessen [ˈlɛsən] *vt* : disminuir, reducir — *vi* : disminuir, reducirse

lesser [ˈlɛsər] *adj* : menor <to a lesser degree : en menor grado>

lesson [ˈlɛsən] *n* **1** CLASS : clase *f*, curso *m* **2** : lección *f* <the lessons of history : las lecciones de la historia>

lessor [ˈlɛˌsɔr, lɛˈsɔr] *n* : arrendador *m*, -dora *f*

lest [ˈlɛst] *conj* : para (que) no <lest we forget : para que no olvidemos>

let [ˈlɛt] *vt* **let; letting 1** ALLOW : dejar, permitir <let me see it : déjame verlo> **2** MAKE : hacer <let me know : házmelo saber, avísame> <let them wait : que esperen, haz que esperen> **3** RENT : alquilar **4** (*used in the first person plural imperative*) <let's go! : ¡vamos!, ¡vámonos!> <let us pray : oremos> **5 to let down** DISAPPOINT : fallar **6 to let off** FORGIVE : perdonar **7 to let out** REVEAL : revelar **8 to let up** ABATE : amainar, disminuir <the pace never lets up : el ritmo nunca disminuye>

letdown *n* : chasco *m*, decepción *f*

lethal [ˈliːθəl] *adj* : letal — **lethally** *adv*

lethargic [lɪˈθɑrdʒɪk] *adj* : letárgico

lethargy [ˈlɛθərdʒi] *n* : letargo *m*

let on *vi* **1** ADMIT : reconocer <don't let on! : ¡no digas nada!> **2** PRETEND : fingir

let's [ˈlɛts] (*contraction of* **let us**) → **let**

letter[1] [ˈlɛt̬ər] *vt* : marcar con letras, inscribir letras en

letter[2] *n* **1** : letra *f* (del alfabeto) **2** : carta *f* <a letter to my mother : una carta a mi madre> **3 letters** *npl* ARTS : letras *fpl* **4 to the letter** : al pie de la letra

lettering [ˈlɛt̬ərɪŋ] *n* : letra *f*

lettuce [ˈlɛt̬əs] *n* : lechuga *f*

leukemia [luːˈkiːmiə] *n* : leucemia *f*

levee [ˈlɛvi] *n* : dique *m*

level[1] [ˈlɛvəl] *vt* **-eled** *or* **-elled; -eling** *or* **-elling 1** FLATTEN : nivelar, aplanar **2** AIM : apuntar (una pistola), dirigir (una acusación) **3** RAZE : rasar, arrasar

level[2] *adj* **1** EVEN : llano, plano, parejo **2** CALM : tranquilo <to keep a level head : no perder la cabeza>

level[3] *n* : nivel *m*

leveler [ˈlɛvələr] *n* : nivelador *m*, -dora *f*

levelheaded [ˈlɛvəlˈhɛdəd] *adj* : sensato, equilibrado

levelly [ˈlɛvəli] *adv* CALMLY : con ecuanimidad *f*, con calma

levelness [ˈlɛvəlnəs] *n* : uniformidad *f*

lever [ˈlɛvər, ˈliː-] *n* : palanca *f*

leverage [ˈlɛvərɪdʒ, ˈliː-] *n* **1** : apalancamiento *m* (en física) **2** INFLUENCE : influencia *f*, palanca *f fam*

leviathan [lɪˈvaɪəθən] *n* : leviatán *m*, gigante *m*

levity [ˈlɛvət̬i] *n* : ligereza *f*, frivolidad *f*

levy[1] [ˈlɛvi] *vt* **levied; levying 1** IMPOSE : imponer, exigir, gravar (un impuesto) **2** COLLECT : recaudar (un impuesto)

levy[2] *n, pl* **levies** : impuesto *m*, gravamen *m*

lewd [ˈluːd] *adj* : lascivo — **lewdly** *adv*

lewdness [ˈluːdnəs] *n* : lascivia *f*

lexicographer [ˌlɛksəˈkɑgrəfər] *n* : lexicógrafo *m*, -fa *f*

lexicographical [ˌlɛksəkoˈgræfɪkəl] *or* **lexicographic** [-ˈgræfɪk] *adj* : lexicográfico

lexicography [ˌlɛksəˈkɑgrəfi] *n* : lexicografía *f*

lexicon [ˈlɛksɪˌkɑn] *n, pl* **-ica** [-kə] *or* **-icons** : léxico *m*, lexicón *m*

liability [ˌlaɪəˈbɪlət̬i] *n, pl* **-ties 1** RESPONSIBILITY : responsabilidad *f* **2** SUSCEPTIBILITY : propensión *f* **3** DRAWBACK : desventaja *f* **4 liabilities** *npl* DEBTS : deudas *fpl*, pasivo *m*

liable [ˈlaɪəbəl] *adj* **1** RESPONSIBLE : responsable **2** SUSCEPTIBLE : propenso **3** PROBABLE : probable <it's liable to happen : es probable que suceda>

liaison [ˈliːəˌzɑn, liˈeɪ-] *n* **1** CONNECTION : enlace *m*, relación *f* **2** AFFAIR : amorío *m*, aventura *f*

liar [ˈlaɪər] *n* : mentiroso *m*, -sa *f*; embustero *m*, -ra *f*

libel[1] [ˈlaɪbəl] *vt* **-beled** *or* **-belled; -beling** *or* **-belling** : difamar, calumniar

libel[2] *n* : difamación *f*, calumnia *f*

libeler [ˈlaɪbələr] *n* : difamador *m*, -dora *f*; calumniador *m*, -dora *f*; libelista *mf*

libelous *or* **libellous** [ˈlaɪbələs] *adj* : difamatorio, calumnioso, injurioso

liberal[1] [ˈlɪbrəl, ˈlɪbərəl] *adj* **1** TOLERANT : liberal, tolerante **2** GENEROUS : generoso **3** ABUNDANT : abundante **4 liberal arts** : humanidades *fpl*, artes *fpl* liberales

liberal[2] *n* : liberal *mf*

liberalism [ˈlɪbrəˌlɪzəm, ˈlɪbərə-] *n* : liberalismo *m*

liberality [ˌlɪbəˈrælət̬i] *n, pl* **-ties** : liberalidad *f*, generosidad *f*

liberalize [ˈlɪbrəˌlaɪz, ˈlɪbərə-] *vt* **-ized; -izing** : liberalizar

liberally [ˈlɪbrəli, ˈlɪbərə-] *adv* **1** GENEROUSLY : generosamente **2** ABUNDANTLY : abundantemente **3** FREELY : libremente

liberate [ˈlɪbəˌreɪt] *vt* **-ated; -ating** : liberar, libertar

liberation [ˌlɪbəˈreɪʃən] *n* : liberación *f*

liberator [ˈlɪbəˌreɪt̬ər] *n* : libertador *m*, -dora *f*

Liberian [laɪˈbɪriən] *n* : liberiano *m*, -na *f* — **Liberian** *adj*

libertine [ˈlɪbərˌtiːn] *n* : libertino *m*, -na *f*

liberty [ˈlɪbərt̬i] *n, pl* **-ties 1** : libertad *f* **2 to take the liberty of** : tomarse la libertad de **3 to take liberties with** : tomarse confianzas con, tomarse libertades con

libido [ləˈbiːdoː, -ˈbaɪ-] *n, pl* **-dos** : libido *f* — **libidinous** [ləˈbɪdənəs] *adj*

Libra [ˈliːbrə] *n* : Libra *mf*

librarian [laɪˈbrɛriən] *n* : bibliotecario *m*, -ria *f*

library [ˈlaɪˌbrɛri] *n, pl* **-braries** : biblioteca *f*

librettist [lɪˈbrɛtɪst] *n* : libretista *mf*

libretto [lɪˈbrɛt̬o] *n, pl* **-tos** *or* **-ti** [-tiː] : libreto *m*

Libyan [ˈlɪbiən] *n* : libio *m*, -bia *f* — **Libyan** *adj*

lice → **louse**

license[1] [ˈlaɪsənts] *vt* **licensed; licensing** : licenciar, autorizar, dar permiso a

license[2] *or* **licence** *n* **1** PERMISSION : licencia *f*, permiso *m* **2** PERMIT : licencia *f*, carnet *m Spain* <driver's license : licencia de conducir> **3** FREEDOM : libertad *f* **4** LICENTIOUSNESS : libertinaje *m*

licentious [laɪˈsɛntʃəs] *adj* : licencioso, disoluto — **licentiously** *adv*

licentiousness [laɪˈsɛntʃəsnəs] *n* : libertinaje *m*

lichen [ˈlaɪkən] *n* : liquen *m*

licit [ˈlɪsət] *adj* : lícito

lick[1] [ˈlɪk] *vt* **1** : lamer **2** BEAT : darle una paliza (a alguien)

lick[2] *n* : lamida *f,* lengüetada *f* <a lick of paint : una mano de pintura> **2** BIT : pizca *f,* ápice *m* **3 a lick and a promise** : una lavada a la carrera
licorice [ˈlɪkərɪʃ, -rəs] *n* : regaliz *m,* dulce *m* de regaliz
lid [ˈlɪd] *n* **1** COVER : tapa *f* **2** EYELID : párpado *m*
lie[1] [ˈlaɪ] *vi* **lay** [ˈleɪ]; **lain** [ˈleɪn]; **lying** [ˈlaɪɪŋ] **1** : acostarse, echarse <I lay down : me acosté> **2** : estar, estar situado, encontrarse <the book lay on the table : el libro estaba en la mesa> <the city lies to the south : la ciudad se encuentra al sur> **3** CONSIST : consistir **4 to lie in** : residir en <the power lies in the people : el poder reside en el pueblo>
lie[2] *vi* **lied; lying** [ˈlaɪɪŋ] : mentir
lie[3] *n* **1** UNTRUTH : mentira *f* <to tell lies : decir mentiras> **2** POSITION : posición *f*
liege [ˈliːdʒ] *n* : señor *m* feudal
lien [ˈliːn, ˈliːən] *n* : derecho *m* de retención
lieutenant [luːˈtɛnənt] *n* : teniente *mf*
lieutenant colonel *n* : teniente *mf* coronel
lieutenant commander *n* : capitán *m,* -tana *f* de corbeta
lieutenant general *n* : teniente *mf* general
life [ˈlaɪf] *n, pl* **lives** [ˈlaɪvz] **1** : vida *f* <plant life : la vida vegetal> **2** EXISTENCE : vida *f,* existencia *f* **3** BIOGRAPHY : biografía *f,* vida *f* **4** DURATION : duración *f,* vida *f* **5** LIVELINESS : vivacidad *f,* animación *f*
lifeblood [ˈlaɪf,blʌd] *n* : parte *f* vital, sustento *m*
lifeboat [ˈlaɪf,boːt] *n* : bote *m* salvavidas
lifeguard [ˈlaɪf,gɑrd] *n* : socorrista *mf,* salvavidas *mf*
lifeless [ˈlaɪfləs] *adj* : sin vida, muerto
lifelike [ˈlaɪf,laɪk] *adj* : que parece vivo, natural, verosímil
lifelong [ˈlaɪfˈlɔŋ] *adj* : de toda la vida <a lifelong friend : un amigo de toda la vida>
life preserver *n* : salvavidas *m*
lifesaver [ˈlaɪf,seɪvər] *n* **1** : salvación *f* **2** → **lifeguard**
lifesaving [ˈlaɪf,seɪvɪŋ] *n* : socorrismo *m*
lifestyle [ˈlaɪf,staɪl] *n* : estilo *m* de vida
lifetime [ˈlaɪf,taɪm] *n* : vida *f,* curso *m* de la vida
lift[1] [ˈlɪft] *vt* **1** RAISE : levantar, alzar, subir **2** END : levantar <to lift a ban : levantar una prohibición> — *vi* **1** RISE : levantarse, alzarse **2** CLEAR UP : despejar <the fog lifted : se disipó la niebla>
lift[2] *n* **1** LIFTING : levantamiento *m,* alzamiento *m* **2** BOOST : impulso *m,* estímulo *m* **3 to give someone a lift** : llevar en coche a alguien
liftoff [ˈlɪft,ɔf] *n* : despegue *m*
ligament [ˈlɪgəmənt] *n* : ligamento *m*
ligature [ˈlɪgə,tʃʊr, -tʃər] *n* : ligadura *f*
light[1] [ˈlaɪt] *v* **lit** [ˈlɪt] *or* **lighted; lighting** *vt* **1** ILLUMINATE : iluminar, alumbrar **2** IGNITE : encender, prenderle fuego a — *vi* : encenderse, prender
light[2] *vi* **lighted** *or* **lit** [ˈlɪt]; **lighting 1** LAND, SETTLE : posarse **2** DISMOUNT : bajarse, apearse
light[3] [ˈlaɪt] *adv* **1** LIGHTLY : suavemente, ligeramente **2 to travel light** : viajar con poco equipaje
light[4] *adj* **1** LIGHTWEIGHT : ligero, liviano, poco pesado **2** EASY : fácil, ligero, liviano <light reading : lectura fácil> <light work : trabajo liviano> **3** GENTLE, MILD : fino, suave, leve <a light breeze : una brisa suave> <a light rain : una lluvia fina> **4** FRIVOLOUS : de poca importancia, superficial **5** BRIGHT : bien iluminado, claro **6** PALE : claro (dícese de los colores), rubio (dícese del pelo)
light[5] *n* **1** ILLUMINATION : luz *f* **2** DAYLIGHT : luz *f* del día **3** DAWN : amanecer *m,* madrugada *f* **4** LAMP : lámpara *f* <to turn on off the light : apagar la luz> **5** ASPECT : aspecto *m* <in a new light : con otros ojos> <in the light of : en vista de, a la luz de> **6** MATCH : fósforo *m,* cerillo *m* **7 to bring to light** : sacar a (la) luz
lightbulb [ˈlaɪt,bʌlb] *n* : bombilla *f,* foco *m,* bombillo *m CA, Col, Ven*
lighten [ˈlaɪtən] *vt* **1** ILLUMINATE : iluminar, dar más luz a **2** : aclararse (el pelo) **3** : aligerar (una carga, etc.) **4** RELIEVE : aliviar **5** GLADDEN : alegrar <it lightened his heart : alegró su corazón>
lighter [ˈlaɪt̬ər] *n* : encendedor *m*
lighthearted [ˈlaɪtˈhɑrt̬əd] *adj* : alegre, despreocupado, desenfadado — **lightheartedly** *adv*
lightheartedness [ˈlaɪtˈhɑrt̬ədnəs] *n* : desenfado *m,* alegría *f*
lighthouse [ˈlaɪt,haʊs] *n* : faro *m*
lighting [ˈlaɪt̬ɪŋ] *n* : iluminación *f*
lightly [ˈlaɪtli] *adv* **1** GENTLY : suavemente **2** SLIGHTLY : ligeramente **3** FRIVOLOUSLY : a la ligera **4 to let off lightly** : tratar con indulgencia
lightness [ˈlaɪtnəs] *n* **1** BRIGHTNESS : luminosidad *f,* claridad *f* **2** GENTLENESS : ligereza *f,* suavidad *f,* delicadeza *f* **3** : ligereza *f,* liviandad *f* (de peso)
lightning [ˈlaɪtnɪŋ] *n* : relámpago *m,* rayo *m*
lightning bug → **firefly**
lightproof [ˈlaɪt,pruːf] *adj* : impenetrable por la luz, opaco
lightweight [ˈlaɪtˈweɪt] *adj* : ligero, liviano, de poco peso
light–year [ˈlaɪt,jɪr] *n* : año *m* luz
lignite [ˈlɪg,naɪt] *n* : lignito *m*
likable *or* **likeable** [ˈlaɪkəbəl] *adj* : simpático, agradable

like[1] [ˈlaɪk] *v* **liked; liking** *vt* **1 :** agradar, gustarle (algo a uno) <he likes rice : le gusta el arroz> <she doesn't like flowers : a ella no le gustan las flores> <I like you : me caes bien> **2** WANT **:** querer, desear <I'd like a hamburger : quiero una hamburguesa> <he would like more help : le gustaría tener más ayuda> — *vi* **:** querer <do as you like : haz lo que quieras>

like[2] *adj* **:** parecido, semejante, similar

like[3] *n* **1** PREFERENCE **:** preferencia *f,* gusto *m* **2 the like :** cosa *f* parecida, cosas *fpl* por el estilo <I've never seen the like : nunca he visto cosa parecida>

like[4] *conj* **1** AS IF **:** como si <they looked at me like I was crazy : se me quedaron mirando como si estuviera loca> **2** AS **:** como, igual que <she doesn't love you like I do : ella no te quiere como yo>

like[5] *prep* **1 :** como, parecido a <she acts like my mother : se comporta como mi madre> <he looks like me : se parece a mí> **2 :** propio de, típico de <that's just like her : eso es muy típico de ella> **3 :** como <animals like cows : animales como vacas> **4 like this, like that :** así <do it like that : hazlo así>

likelihood [ˈlaɪkli,hʊd] *n* **:** probabilidad *f* <in all likelihood : con toda probabilidad>

likely[1] [ˈlaɪkli] *adv* **:** probablemente <most likely he's sick : lo más probable es que esté enfermo> <they're likely to come : es probable que vengan>

likely[2] *adj* **-lier; -est 1** PROBABLE **:** probable <to be likely to : ser muy probable que> **2** SUITABLE **:** apropiado, adecuado **3** BELIEVABLE **:** verosímil, creíble **4** PROMISING **:** prometedor

liken [ˈlaɪkən] *vt* **:** comparar

likeness [ˈlaɪknəs] *n* **1** SIMILARITY **:** semejanza *f,* parecido *m* **2** PORTRAIT **:** retrato *m*

likewise [ˈlaɪk,waɪz] *adv* **1** SIMILARLY **:** de la misma manera, asimismo **2** ALSO **:** también, además, asimismo

liking [ˈlaɪkɪŋ] *n* **1** FONDNESS **:** afición *f* (por una cosa), simpatía *f* (por una persona) **2** TASTE **:** gusto *m* <is it to your liking? : ¿te gusta?>

lilac [ˈlaɪlək, -,læk, -,lɑk] *n* **:** lila *f*

lilt [ˈlɪlt] *n* **:** cadencia *f,* ritmo *m* alegre

lily [ˈlɪli] *n, pl* **lilies 1 :** lirio *m,* azucena *f* **2 lily of the valley :** lirio *m* de los valles, muguete *m*

lima bean [ˈlaɪmə] *n* **:** frijol *m* de media luna

limb [ˈlɪm] *n* **1** APPENDAGE **:** miembro *m,* extremidad *f* **2** BRANCH **:** rama *f*

limber[1] [ˈlɪmbər] *vi or* **to limber up :** calentarse, prepararse

limber[2] *adj* **:** ágil (dícese de las personas), flexible (dícese de los objetos)

limbo [ˈlɪm,boː] *n, pl* **-bos 1 :** limbo *m* (en la religión) **2** OBLIVION **:** olvido *m* <the project is in limbo : el proyecto ha caído en el olvido>

lime [ˈlaɪm] *n* **1 :** cal *f* (óxido) **2 :** lima *f* (fruta), limón *m* verde *Mex*

limelight [ˈlaɪm,laɪt] *n* **to be in the limelight :** ser el centro de atención, estar en el candelero

limerick [ˈlɪmərɪk] *n* **:** poema *m* jocoso de cinco versos

limestone [ˈlaɪm,stoːn] *n* **:** piedra *f* caliza, caliza *f*

limit[1] [ˈlɪmət] *vt* **:** limitar, restringir

limit[2] *n* **1** MAXIMUM **:** límite *m,* máximo *m* <speed limit : límite de velocidad> **2 limits** *npl* **:** límites *mpl,* confines *mpl* <city limits : límites de la ciudad> **3 that's the limit! :** ¡eso es el colmo!

limitation [,lɪməˈteɪʃən] *n* **:** limitación *f,* restricción *f*

limited [ˈlɪmət̬əd] *adj* **:** limitado, restringido

limitless [ˈlɪmətləs] *adj* **:** ilimitado, sin límites

limousine [ˈlɪmə,ziːn, ,lɪməˈ-] *n* **:** limusina *f*

limp[1] [ˈlɪmp] *vi* **:** cojear

limp[2] *adj* **1** FLACCID **:** fláccido **2** LANK **:** lacio (dícese del pelo) **3** WEAK **:** débil <to feel limp : sentirse desfallecer, sentirse sin fuerzas>

limp[3] *n* **:** cojera *f*

limpid [ˈlɪmpəd] *adj* **:** límpido, claro

limply [ˈlɪmpli] *adv* **:** sin fuerzas

limpness [ˈlɪmpnəs] *n* **:** flaccidez *f,* debilidad *f*

linden [ˈlɪndən] *n* **:** tilo *m*

line[1] [ˈlaɪn] *v* **lined; lining** *vt* **1 :** forrar, cubrir <to line a dress : forrar un vestido> <to line the walls : cubrir las paredes> **2** MARK **:** rayar, trazar líneas en **3** BORDER **:** bordear **4** ALIGN **:** alinear — *vi* **to line up :** ponerse in fila, hacer cola

line[2] *n* **1** CORD, ROPE **:** cuerda *f* **2** WIRE **:** cable *m* <power line : cable eléctrico> **3 :** línea *f* (de teléfono) **4** ROW **:** fila *f,* hilera *f* **5** NOTE **:** nota *f,* líneas *fpl* <drop me a line : mándame unas líneas> **6** COURSE **:** línea *f* <line of inquiry : línea de investigación> **7** AGREEMENT **:** conformidad *f* <to be in line with : ser conforme a> <to fall into line : estar de acuerdo> **8** OCCUPATION **:** ocupación *f,* rama *f,* especialidad *f* **9** LIMIT **:** línea *f,* límite *m* <dividing line : línea divisoria> <to draw the line : fijar límites> **10** SERVICE **:** línea *f* <bus line : línea de autobuses> **11** MARK **:** línea *f,* arruga *f* (de la cara)

lineage [ˈlɪniɪdʒ] *n* **:** linaje *m,* abolengo *m*

lineal [ˈlɪniəl] *adj* **:** en línea directa

lineaments [ˈlɪniəmənts] *npl* **:** facciones *fpl* (de la cara), rasgos *mpl*

linear [ˈlɪniər] *adj* **:** lineal

linen [ˈlɪnən] *n* : lino *m*

liner [ˈlaɪnər] *n* **1** LINING : forro *m* **2** SHIP : buque *m,* transatlántico *m*

lineup [ˈlaɪn,əp] *n* **1** : fila *f* de sospechosos **2** : formación *f* (en deportes) **3** ALIGNMENT : alineación *f*

linger [ˈlɪŋgər] *vi* **1** TARRY : quedarse, entretenerse, rezagarse **2** PERSIST : persistir, sobrevivir

lingerie [,lɑndʒəˈreɪ, ,læʒəˈriː] *n* : ropa *f* íntima femenina, lencería *f*

lingo [ˈlɪŋgo] *n, pl* **-goes 1** LANGUAGE : idioma *m* **2** JARGON : jerga *f*

linguist [ˈlɪŋgwɪst] *n* : lingüista *mf*

linguistic [lɪŋˈgwɪstɪk] *adj* : lingüístico

linguistics [lɪŋˈgwɪstɪks] *n* : lingüística *f*

liniment [ˈlɪnəmənt] *n* : linimento *m*

lining [ˈlaɪnɪŋ] *n* : forro *m*

link[1] [ˈlɪŋk] *vt* : unir, enlazar, conectar — *vi* **to link up** : unirse, conectar

link[2] *n* **1** : eslabón *m* (de una cadena) **2** BOND : conexión *f,* lazo *m,* vínculo *m*

linkage [ˈlɪŋkɪdʒ] *n* : conexión *f,* unión *f,* enlace *m*

linoleum [ləˈnoːliəm] *n* : linóleo *m*

linseed oil [ˈlɪn,siːd] *n* : aceite *m* de linaza

lint [ˈlɪnt] *n* : pelusa *f*

lintel [ˈlɪntəl] *n* : dintel *m*

lion [ˈlaɪən] *n* : león *m*

lioness [ˈlaɪənɪs] *n* : leona *f*

lionize [ˈlaɪə,naɪz] *vt* **-ized; -izing** : tratar a una persona como muy importante

lip [ˈlɪp] *n* **1** : labio *m* **2** EDGE, RIM : pico *m* (de una jarra), borde *m* (de una taza)

lipreading [ˈlɪp,riːdɪŋ] *n* : lectura *f* de los labios

lipstick [ˈlɪp,stɪk] *n* : lápiz *m* de labios, barra *f* de labios

liquefy [ˈlɪkwə,faɪ] *v* **-fied; -fying** *vt* : licuar — *vi* : licuarse

liqueur [lɪˈkʊr, -ˈkər, -ˈkjʊr] *n* : licor *m*

liquid[1] [ˈlɪkwəd] *adj* : líquido

liquid[2] *n* : líquido *m*

liquidate [ˈlɪkwə,deɪt] *vt* **-dated; -dating** : liquidar

liquidation [,lɪkwəˈdeɪʃən] *n* : liquidación *f*

liquidity [lɪkˈwɪdət̬i] *n* : liquidez *f*

liquor [ˈlɪkər] *n* : alcohol *m,* bebidas *fpl* alcohólicas, licor *m*

lisp[1] [ˈlɪsp] *vi* : cecear

lisp[2] *n* : ceceo *m*

lissome [ˈlɪsəm] *adj* **1** FLEXIBLE : flexible **2** LITHE : ágil y grácil

list[1] [ˈlɪst] *vt* **1** ENUMERATE : hacer una lista de, enumerar **2** INCLUDE : poner en una lista, incluir — *vi* : escorar (dícese de un barco)

list[2] *n* **1** ENUMERATION : lista *f* **2** SLANT : escora *f,* inclinación *f*

listen [ˈlɪsən] *vi* **1** : escuchar, oír **2 to listen to** HEED : prestar atención a, hacer caso de, escuchar **3 to listen to reason** : atender a razones

listener [ˈlɪsənər] *n* : oyente *mf,* persona *f* que sabe escuchar

listless [ˈlɪstləs] *adj* : lánguido, apático — **listlessly** *adv*

listlessness [ˈlɪstləsnəs] *n* : apatía *f,* languidez *f,* desgana *f*

lit [ˈlɪt] *pp* → **light**

litany [ˈlɪt̬əni] *n, pl* **-nies** : letanía *f*

liter [ˈliːt̬ər] *n* : litro *m*

literacy [ˈlɪt̬ərəsi] *n* : alfabetismo *m*

literal [ˈlɪt̬ərəl] *adj* : literal — **literally** *adv*

literary [ˈlɪt̬ə,rɛri] *adj* : literario

literate [ˈlɪt̬ərət] *adj* : alfabetizado

literature [ˈlɪt̬ərə,tʃʊr, -tʃər] *n* : literatura *f*

lithe [ˈlaɪð, ˈlaɪθ] *adj* : ágil y grácil

lithesome [ˈlaɪðsəm, ˈlaɪθ-] → **lissome**

lithograph [ˈlɪθə,græf] *n* : litografía *f*

lithographer [lɪˈθɑgrəfər, ˈlɪθə,græfər] *n* : litógrafo *m,* -fa *f*

lithography [lɪˈθɑgrəfi] *n* : litografía *f*

litigant [ˈlɪtɪgənt] *n* : litigante *mf*

litigate [ˈlɪt̬ə,geɪt] *vi* **-gated; -gating** : litigar

litigation [,lɪt̬əˈgeɪʃən] *n* : litigio *m*

litmus paper [ˈlɪtməs] *n* : papel *m* de tornasol

litter[1] [ˈlɪt̬ər] *vt* : tirar basura en, ensuciar — *vi* : tirar basura

litter[2] *n* **1** : camada *f,* cría *f* <a litter of kittens : una cría de gatitos> **2** STRETCHER : camilla *f* **3** RUBBISH : basura *f* **4** : arena *f* higiénica (para gatos)

little[1] [ˈlɪt̬əl] *adv* **less** [ˈlɛs]; **least** [ˈliːst] **1** : poco <she sings very little : canta muy poco> **2 little did I know that...** : no tenía la menor idea de que ... **3 as little as possible** : lo menos posible

little[2] *adj* **littler** *or* **less** [ˈlɛs] *or* **lesser** [ˈlɛsər]; **littlest** *or* **least** [ˈliːst] **1** SMALL : pequeño **2** : poco <they speak little Spanish : hablan poco español> <little by little : poco a poco> **3** TRIVIAL : sin importancia, trivial

little[3] *n* **1** : poco *m* <little has changed : poco ha cambiado> **2 a little** : un poco, algo <it's a little surprising : es algo sorprendente>

Little Dipper → **dipper**

liturgical [ləˈtərdʒɪkəl] *adj* : litúrgico — **liturgically** [-kli] *adv*

liturgy [ˈlɪt̬ərdʒi] *n, pl* **-gies** : liturgia *f*

livable [ˈlɪvəbəl] *adj* : habitable

live[1] [ˈlɪv] *vi* **lived; living 1** EXIST : vivir <as long as I live : mientras viva> <to live from day to day : vivir al día> **2** : llevar una vida, vivir <he lived simply : llevó una vida sencilla> **3** SUBSIST : mantenerse, vivir **4** RESIDE : vivir, residir

live[2] [ˈlaɪv] *adj* **1** LIVING : vivo **2** BURNING : encendido <a live coal : una brasa> **3** : con corriente <live wires

: cables con corriente> **4** : cargado, sin estallar <a live bomb : una bomba sin estallar> **5** CURRENT : de actualidad <a live issue : un asunto de actualidad> **6** : en vivo, en directo <a live interview : una entrevista en vivo>

livelihood ['laɪvli,hʊd] *n* : sustento *m,* vida *f,* medio *m* de vida

liveliness ['laɪvlinəs] *n* : animación *f,* vivacidad *f*

livelong ['lɪv'lɔŋ] *adj* : entero, completo

lively ['laɪvli] *adj* **-lier; -est** : animado, vivaz, vivo, enérgico

liven ['laɪvən] *vt* : animar — *vi* : animarse

liver ['lɪvər] *n* : hígado *m*

livery ['lɪvəri] *n, pl* **-eries** : librea *f*

lives → **life**

livestock ['laɪv,stɑk] *n* : ganado *m*

live wire *n* : persona *f* vivaz y muy activa

livid ['lɪvəd] *adj* **1** BLACK-AND-BLUE : amoratado **2** PALE : lívido **3** ENRAGED : furioso

living[1] ['lɪvɪŋ] *adj* : vivo

living[2] *n* **to make a living** : ganarse la vida

living room *n* : living *m,* sala *f* de estar

lizard ['lɪzərd] *n* : lagarto *m*

llama ['lɑmə, 'jɑ-] *n* : llama *f*

load[1] ['lo:d] *vt* : cargar, embarcar

load[2] *n* **1** CARGO : carga *f* **2** WEIGHT : peso *m* **3** BURDEN : carga *f,* peso *m* **4 loads** *npl* : montón *m,* pila *f,* cantidad *f* <loads of work : un montón de trabajo>

loaf[1] ['lo:f] *vi* : holgazanear, flojear, haraganear

loaf[2] *n, pl* **loaves** ['lo:vz] **1** : pan *m,* pan *m* de molde, barra *f* de pan **2 meat loaf** : pan *m* de carne

loafer ['lo:fər] *n* : holgazán *m,* -zana *f;* haragán *m,* -gana *f;* vago *m,* -ga *f*

loam ['lo:m] *n* : marga *f,* suelo *m*

loan[1] ['lo:n] *vt* : prestar

loan[2] *n* : préstamo *m,* empréstito *m* (del banco)

loath ['lo:θ, 'lo:ð] *adj* : poco dispuesto <I am loath to say it : me resisto a decirlo>

loathe ['lo:ð] *vt* **loathed; loathing** : odiar, aborrecer

loathing ['lo:ðɪŋ] *n* : aversión *f,* odio *m,* aborrecimiento *m*

loathsome ['lo:θsəm, 'lo:ð-] *adj* : odioso, repugnante

lob[1] ['lɑb] *vt* **lobbed; lobbing** : hacerle un globo (a otro jugador)

lob[2] *n* : globo *m* (en deportes)

lobby[1] ['lɑbi] *v* **-bied; -bying** *vt* : presionar, ejercer presión sobre — *vi* **to lobby for** : presionar para (lograr algo)

lobby[2] *n, pl* **-bies 1** FOYER : vestíbulo *m* **2** LOBBYISTS : grupo *m* de presión, lobby *m*

lobbyist ['lɑbiɪst] *n* : miembro *m* de un lobby

lobe ['lo:b] *n* : lóbulo *m*

lobed ['lo:bd] *adj* : lobulado

lobotomy [lə'bɑt̬əmi, lo-] *n, pl* **-mies** : lobotomía *f*

lobster ['lɑbstər] *n* : langosta *f*

local[1] ['lo:kəl] *adj* : local

local[2] *n* **1** : anestesia *f* local **2 the locals** : los vecinos del lugar, los habitantes

locale [lo'kæl] *n* : lugar *m,* escenario *m*

locality [lo'kælət̬i] *n, pl* **-ties** : localidad *f*

localize ['lo:kə,laɪz] *vt* **-ized; -izing** : localizar

locally ['lo:kəli] *adv* : en la localidad, en la zona

locate ['lo:,keɪt, lo'keɪt] *v* **-cated; -cating** *vt* **1** POSITION : situar, ubicar **2** FIND : localizar, ubicar — *vi* SETTLE : establecerse

location [lo'keɪʃən] *n* **1** POSITION : posición *f,* emplazamiento *m,* ubicación *f* **2** PLACE : lugar *m,* sitio *m*

lock[1] ['lɑk] *vt* **1** FASTEN : cerrar **2** CONFINE : encerrar <they locked me in the room : me encerraron en la sala> **3** IMMOBILIZE : bloquear (una rueda) — *vi* **1** : cerrarse (dícese de una puerta) **2** : trabarse, bloquearse (dícese de una rueda)

lock[2] *n* **1** : mechón *m* (de pelo) **2** FASTENER : cerradura *f,* cerrojo *m,* chapa *f* **3** : esclusa *f* (de un canal)

locker ['lɑkər] *n* : armario *m,* cajón *m* con llave, lócker *m*

locket ['lɑkət] *n* : medallón *m,* guardapelo *m,* relicario *m*

lockjaw ['lɑk,ʤɔ] *n* : tétano *m*

lockout ['lɑk,aʊt] *n* : cierre *m* patronal, lockout *m*

locksmith ['lɑk,smɪθ] *n* : cerrajero *m,* -ra *f*

lockup ['lɑk,ʌp] *n* JAIL : cárcel *f*

locomotion [,lo:kə'mo:ʃən] *n* : locomoción *f*

locomotive[1] [,lo:kə'mo:t̬ɪv] *adj* : locomotor

locomotive[2] *n* : locomotora *f*

locust ['lo:kəst] *n* **1** : langosta *f,* chapulín *m CA, Mex* **2** CICADA : cigarra *f,* chicharra *f* **3** : acacia *f* blanca (árbol)

locution [lo'kju:ʃən] *n* : locución *f*

lode ['lo:d] *n* : veta *f,* vena *f,* filón *m*

lodestar ['lo:d,stɑr] *n* : estrella *f* polar

lodestone ['lo:d,sto:n] *n* : piedra *f* imán

lodge[1] ['lɑʤ] *v* **lodged; lodging** *vt* **1** HOUSE : hospedar, alojar **2** FILE : presentar <to lodge a complaint : presentar una demanda> — *vi* **1** : posarse, meterse <the bullet lodged in the door : la bala se incrustó en la puerta> **2** STAY : hospedarse, alojarse

lodge[2] *n* **1** : pabellón *m,* casa *f* de campo <hunting lodge : refugio de caza> **2** : madriguera *f* (de un castor) **3** : logia *f* <Masonic lodge : logia masónica>

lodger [ˈlɑʤər] *n* : inquilino *m*, -na *f*; huésped *m*, -peda *f*

lodging [ˈlɑʤɪŋ] *n* **1** : alojamiento *m* **2 lodgings** *npl* ROOMS : habitaciones *fpl*

loft [ˈlɔft] *n* **1** ATTIC : desván *m*, ático *m*, buhardilla *f* **2** : loft *m* (en un depósito comercial) **3** HAYLOFT : pajar *m* **4** : galería *f* <choir loft : galería del coro>

loftily [ˈlɔftəli] *adv* : altaneramente, con altivez

loftiness [ˈlɔftinəs] *n* **1** NOBILITY : nobleza *f* **2** ARROGANCE : altanería *f*, arrogancia *f* **3** HEIGHT : altura *f*, elevación *f*

lofty [ˈlɔfti] *adj* **loftier; -est 1** NOBLE : noble, elevado **2** HAUGHTY : altivo, arrogante, altanero **3** HIGH : majestuoso, elevado

log[1] [ˈlɔg, ˈlɑg] *vi* **logged; logging 1** : talar (árboles) **2** RECORD : registrar, anotar **3 to log on** : entrar (al sistema) **4 to log off** : salir (del sistema)

log[2] *n* **1** : tronco *m*, leño *m* **2** RECORD : diario *m*

logarithm [ˈlɔgəˌrɪðəm, ˈlɑ-] *n* : logaritmo *m*

logger [ˈlɔgər, ˈlɑ-] *n* : leñador *m*, -dora *f*

loggerhead [ˈlɔgərˌhɛd, ˈlɑ-] *n* **1** : tortuga *f* boba **2 to be at loggerheads** : estar en pugna, estar en desacuerdo

logic [ˈlɑʤɪk] *n* : lógica *f* — **logical** [ˈlɑʤɪkəl] *adj* — **logically** [-kli] *adv*

logistic [ləˈʤɪstɪk, lo-] *adj* : logístico

logistics [ləˈʤɪstɪks, lo-] *ns & pl* : logística *f*

logo [ˈloːˌgoː] *n, pl* **logos** [-ˌgoːz] : logotipo *m*

loin [ˈlɔɪn] *n* **1** : lomo *m* <pork loin : lomo de cerdo> **2 loins** *npl* : lomos *mpl* <to gird one's loins : prepararse para la lucha>

loiter [ˈlɔɪt̬ər] *vi* : vagar, perder el tiempo

loll [ˈlɑl] *vi* **1** SLOUCH : repantigarse **2** IDLE : holgazanear, hacer el vago

lollipop *or* **lollypop** [ˈlɑliˌpɑp] *n* : dulce *m* en palito, chupete *m Chile, Peru,* paleta *f CA, Mex*

lone [ˈloːn] *adj* **1** SOLITARY : solitario **2** ONLY : único

loneliness [ˈloːnlinəs] *n* : soledad *f*

lonely [ˈloːnli] *adj* **-lier; -est 1** SOLITARY : solitario, aislado **2** LONESOME : solo <to feel lonely : sentirse muy solo>

loner [ˈloːnər] *n* : solitario *m*, -ria *f*; recluso *m*, -sa *f*

lonesome [ˈloːnsəm] *adj* : solo, solitario

long[1] [ˈlɔŋ] *vi* **1 to long for** : añorar, desear, anhelar **2 to long to** : anhelar, estar deseando <they longed to see her : estaban deseando verla, tenían muchas ganas de verla>

long[2] *adv* **1** : mucho, mucho tiempo <it didn't take long : no llevó mucho tiempo> <will it last long? : ¿va a durar mucho?> **2 all day long** : todo el día **3 as long as** *or* **so long as** : mientras, con tal que **4 long before** : mucho antes **5 so long!** : ¡hasta luego!, ¡adiós!

long[3] *adj* **longer** [ˈlɔŋgər]; **longest** [ˈlɔŋgəst] **1** (*indicating length*) : largo <the dress is too long : el vestido es demasiado largo> <a long way from : bastante lejos de> <in the long run : a la larga> **2** (*indicating time*) : largo, prolongado <a long illness : una enfermedad prolongada> <a long walk : un paseo largo> <at long last : por fin> **3 to be long on** : estar cargado de

long[4] *n* **1 before long** : dentro de poco **2 the long and the short** : lo esencial, lo fundamental

longevity [lɑnˈʤɛvət̬i] *n* : longevidad *f*

longhand [ˈlɔŋˌhænd] *n* : escritura *f* a mano, escritura *f* cursiva

longhorn [ˈlɔŋˌhɔrn] *n* : longhorn *mf*

longing [lɔŋɪŋ] *n* : vivo deseo *m*, ansia *f*, anhelo *m*

longingly [lɔŋɪŋlli] *adv* : ansiosamente, con ansia

longitude [ˈlɑnʤəˌtuːd, -ˌtjuːd] *n* : longitud *f*

longitudinal [ˌlɑnʤəˈtuːdənəl, -ˈtjuː-] *adj* : longitudinal — **longitudinally** *adv*

longshoreman [ˈlɔŋˈʃormən] *n, pl* **-men** [-mən, -ˌmɛn] : estibador *m*, -dora *f*

long–suffering [ˈlɔŋˈsʌfərɪŋ] *adj* : paciente, sufrido

look[1] [ˈlʊk] *vi* **1** GLANCE : mirar <to look out the window : mirar por la ventana> **2** INVESTIGATE : buscar, mirar <look in the closet : busca en el closet> <look before you leap : mira lo que haces> **3** SEEM : parecer <he looks happy : parece estar contento> <I look like my mother : me parezco a mi madre> **4 to look after** : cuidar, cuidar de **5 to look for** EXPECT : esperar **6 to look for** SEEK : buscar — *vt* : mirar

look[2] *n* **1** GLANCE : mirada *f* **2** EXPRESSION : cara *f* <a look of disapproval : una cara de desaprobación> **3** ASPECT : aspecto *m*, apariencia *f*, aire *m*

lookout [ˈlʊkˌaʊt] *n* **1** : centinela *mf*, vigía *mf* **2 to be on the lookout for** : estar al acecho de, andar a la caza de

loom[1] [ˈluːm] *vi* **1** : aparecer, surgir <the city loomed up in the distance : la ciudad surgió en la distancia> **2** IMPEND : amenazar, ser inminente **3 to loom large** : cobrar mucha importancia

loom[2] *n* : telar *m*

loon [ˈluːn] *n* : somorgujo *m*, somormujo *m*

loony *or* **looney** [ˈluːni] *adj* **-nier; -est** : loco, chiflado *fam*

loop[1] [ˈluːp] *vt* **1 :** hacer lazadas con **2 to loop around :** pasar alrededor de — *vi* **1 :** rizar el rizo (dícese de un avión) **2 :** serpentear (dícese de una carretera)

loop[2] *n* **1 :** lazada *f* (en hilo o cuerda) **2** BEND **:** curva *f* **3** CIRCUIT **:** circuito *m* cerrado **4 :** rizo *m* (en la aviación) <to loop the loop : rizar el rizo>

loophole [ˈluːpˌhoːl] *n* **:** escapatoria *f,* pretexto *m*

loose[1] [ˈluːs] *vt* **loosed; loosing 1** RELEASE **:** poner en libertad, soltar **2** UNTIE **:** deshacer, desatar **3** DISCHARGE, UNLEASH **:** descargar, desatar

loose[2] → **loosely**

loose[3] *adj* **looser; -est 1** INSECURE **:** flojo, suelto, poco seguro <a loose tooth : un diente flojo> **2** ROOMY **:** suelto, holgado <loose clothing : ropa holgada> **3** OPEN **:** suelto, abierto <loose soil : suelo suelto> <a loose weave : una tejida abierta> **4** FREE **:** suelto <to break loose : soltarse> **5** SLACK **:** flojo, flexible **6** APPROXIMATE **:** libre, aproximado <a loose translation : una traducción aproximada>

loosely [ˈluːsli] *adv* **1 :** sin apretar **2** ROUGHLY **:** aproximadamente, más o menos

loosen [ˈluːsən] *vt* **:** aflojar

loose–leaf [ˈluːsˈliːf] *adj* **:** de hojas sueltas

looseness [ˈluːsnəs] *n* **1 :** aflojamiento *m,* holgura *f* (de ropa) **2** IMPRECISION **:** imprecisión *f*

loot[1] [ˈluːt] *vt* **:** saquear, robar

loot[2] *n* **:** botín *m*

looter [ˈluːtər] *n* **:** saqueador *m,* -dora *f*

lop [ˈlɑp] *vt* **lopped; lopping :** cortar, podar

lope[1] [ˈloːp] *vi* **loped; loping :** correr a paso largo

lope[2] *n* **:** paso *m* largo

lopsided [ˈlɑpˌsaɪdəd] *adj* **1** CROOKED **:** torcido, chueco, ladeado **2** ASYMETRICAL **:** asimétrico

loquacious [loˈkweɪʃəs] *adj* **:** locuaz

lord [ˈlɔrd] *n* **1 :** señor *m,* noble *m* **2 :** lord *m* (en la Gran Bretaña) **3 the Lord :** el Señor **4 good Lord! :** ¡Dios mío!

lordly [ˈlɔrdli] *adj* **-lier; -est** HAUGHTY **:** arrogante, altanero

lordship [ˈlɔrdˌʃɪp] *n* **:** señoría *f*

Lord's Supper *n* **:** Eucaristía *f*

lore [ˈlor] *n* **:** saber *m* popular, tradición *f*

lose [ˈluːz] *v* **lost** [ˈlɔst]; **losing** [ˈluːzɪŋ] *vt* **1 :** perder <I lost my umbrella : perdí mi paraguas> <to lose blood : perder sangre> <to lose one's voice : quedarse afónico> <to have nothing to lose : no tener nada que perder> <to lose no time : no perder tiempo> <to lose weight : perder peso, adelgazar> <to lose one's temper : perder los estribos, enojarse, enfadarse> <to lose sight of : perder de vista> **2 :** costar, hacer perder <the errors lost him his job : los errores le costaron su empleo> **3 :** atrasar <my watch loses 5 minutes a day : mi reloj atrasa 5 minutos por día> **4 to lose oneself :** perderse, ensimismarse — *vi* **1 :** perder <we lost to the other team : perdimos contra el otro equipo> **2 :** atrasarse <the clock loses time : el reloj se atrasa>

loser [ˈluːzər] *n* **:** perdedor *m,* -dora *f*

loss [ˈlɔs] *n* **1** LOSING **:** pérdida *f* <loss of memory : pérdida de memoria> <to sell at a loss : vender con pérdida> <to be at a loss to : no saber como> **2** DEFEAT **:** derrota *f,* juego *m* perdido **3 losses** *npl* DEATHS **:** muertos *mpl*

lost [ˈlɔst] *adj* **1 :** perdido <a lost cause : una causa perdida> <lost in thought : absorto> **2 to get lost :** perderse **3 to make up for lost time :** recuperar el tiempo perdido

lot [ˈlɑt] *n* **1** DRAWING **:** sorteo *m* <by lot : por sorteo> **2** SHARE **:** parte *f,* porción *f* **3** FATE **:** suerte *f* **4** LAND, PLOT **:** terreno *m,* solar *m,* lote *m,* parcela *f* **5 a lot of** *or* **lots of :** mucho, un montón de, bastante <lots of books : un montón de libros, muchos libros> <a lot of people : mucha gente>

loth [ˈloːθ, ˈloːð] → **loath**

lotion [ˈloːʃən] *n* **:** loción *f*

lottery [ˈlɑtəri] *n, pl* **-teries :** lotería *f*

lotus [ˈloːtəs] *n* **:** loto *m*

loud[1] [ˈlaʊd] *adv* **:** alto, fuerte <out loud : en voz alta>

loud[2] *adj* **1 :** alto, fuerte <a loud voice : una voz alta> **2** NOISY **:** ruidoso <a loud party : una fiesta ruidosa> **3** FLASHY **:** llamativo, chillón

loudly [ˈlaʊdli] *adv* **:** alto, fuerte, en voz alta

loudness [ˈlaʊdnəs] *n* **:** volumen *m,* fuerza *f* (del ruido)

loudspeaker [ˈlaʊdˌspiːkər] *n* **:** altavoz *m,* altoparlante *m*

lounge[1] [ˈlaʊndʒ] *vi* **lounged; lounging :** holgazanear, gandulear

lounge[2] *n* **:** salón *m,* sala *f* de estar

louse [ˈlaʊs] *n, pl* **lice** [ˈlaɪs] **:** piojo *m*

lousy [ˈlaʊzi] *adj* **lousier; -est 1 :** piojoso, lleno de piojos **2** BAD **:** pésimo, muy malo

lout [ˈlaʊt] *n* **:** bruto *m,* patán *m*

louver *or* **louvre** [ˈluːvər] *n* **:** persiana *f,* listón *m* de persiana

lovable [ˈlʌvəbəl] *adj* **:** adorable, amoroso, encantador

love[1] [ˈlʌv] *v* **loved; loving** *vt* **1 :** querer, amar <I love you : te quiero> **2** ENJOY **:** encantarle a alguien, ser (muy) aficionado a, gustarle mucho a uno (algo) <she loves flowers : le encantan las flores> <he loves golf : es muy aficionado al golf> <I'd love

to go with you : me gustaría mucho acompañarte> — *vi* : querer, amar
love[2] *n* **1** : amor *m,* cariño *m* <to be in love with : estar enamorado de> <to fall in love with : enamorarse de> **2** ENTHUSIASM, INTEREST : amor *m,* afición *m,* gusto *m* <love of music : afición a la música> **3** BELOVED : amor *m;* amado *m,* -da *f;* enamorado *m,* -da *f*
loveless [ˈlʌvləs] *adj* : sin amor
loveliness [ˈlʌvlinəs] *n* : belleza *f,* hermosura *f*
lovelorn [ˈlʌvˌlɔrn] *adj* : herido de amor, perdidamente enamorado
lovely [ˈlʌvli] *adj* **-lier; -est** : hermoso, bello, lindo, precioso
lover [ˈlʌvər] *n* : amante *mf* (de personas); aficionado *m,* -da *f* (a alguna actividad)
loving [ˈlʌvɪŋ] *adj* : amoroso, cariñoso
lovingly [ˈlʌvɪŋli] *adv* : cariñosamente
low[1] [ˈloː] *vi* : mugir
low[2] *adv* : bajo, profundo <to aim low : apuntar bajo> <to lie low : mantenerse escondido> <to turn the lights down low : bajar las luces>
low[3] *adj* **lower** [ˈloːər]; **-est 1** : bajo <a low building : un edificio bajo> <a low bow : una profunda reverencia> **2** SOFT : bajo, suave <in a low voice : en voz baja> **3** SHALLOW : bajo, poco profundo **4** HUMBLE : humilde, modesto **5** DEPRESSED : deprimido, bajo de moral **6** INFERIOR : bajo, inferior **7** UNFAVORABLE : mal <to have a low opinion of him : tener un mal concepto de él> **8 to be low on** : tener poco de, estar escaso de
low[4] *n* **1** : punto *m* bajo <to reach an all-time low : estar más bajo que nunca> **2** *or* **low gear** : primera velocidad *f* **3** : mugido *m* (de una vaca)
lowbrow [ˈloːˌbraʊ] *n* : persona *f* inculta
lower[1] [ˈloːər] *vt* **1** DROP : bajar <to lower one's voice : bajar la voz> **2** : arriar, bajar <to lower the flag : arriar la bandera> **3** REDUCE : reducir, bajar **4 to lower oneself** : rebajarse
lower[2] [ˈloːər] *adj* : inferior, más bajo, de abajo
lowland [ˈloːlənd, -ˌlænd] *n* : tierras *fpl* bajas
lowly [ˈloːli] *adj* **-lier; -est** : humilde, modesto
loyal [ˈlɔɪəl] *adj* : leal, fiel — **loyally** *adv*
loyalist [ˈlɔɪəlɪst] *n* : partidario *m,* -ria *f* del régimen
loyalty [ˈlɔɪəlti] *n, pl* **-ties** : lealtad *f,* fidelidad *f*
lozenge [ˈlɑzəndʒ] *n* : pastilla *f*
LSD [ˌɛlˌɛsˈdiː] *n* : LSD *m*
lubricant [ˈluːbrɪkənt] *n* : lubricante *m*
lubricate [ˈluːbrɪˌkeɪt] *vt* **-cated; -cating** : lubricar — **lubrication** [ˌluːbrɪˈkeɪʃən] *n*
lucid [ˈluːsəd] *adj* : lúcido, claro — **lucidly** *adv*
lucidity [luːˈsɪdəṭi] *n* : lucidez *f*
luck [ˈlʌk] *n* **1** : suerte *f* **2 to have bad luck** : tener mala suerte **3 good luck!** : ¡(buena) suerte!
luckily [ˈlʌkəli] *adv* : afortunadamente, por suerte
luckless [ˈlʌkləs] *adj* : desafortunado
lucky [ˈlʌki] *adj* **luckier; -est 1** : afortunado, que tiene suerte <a lucky woman : una mujer afortunada **2** FORTUITOUS : fortuito, de suerte **3** OPPORTUNE : oportuno **4** : de (la) suerte <lucky number : número de la suerte>
lucrative [ˈluːkrəṭɪv] *adj* : lucrativo, provechoso — **lucratively** *adv*
ludicrous [ˈluːdəkrəs] *adj* : ridículo, absurdo — **ludicrously** *adv*
ludicrousness [ˈluːdəkrəsnəs] *n* : ridiculez *f,* absurdo *m*
lug [ˈlʌg] *vt* **lugged; lugging** : arrastrar, transportar con dificultad
luggage [ˈlʌgɪdʒ] *n* : equipaje *m*
lugubrious [lʊˈguːbriəs] *adj* : lúgubre — **lugubriously** *adv*
lukewarm [ˈluːkˈwɔrm] *adj* **1** TEPID : tibio **2** HALFHEARTED : poco entusiasta
lull[1] [ˈlʌl] *vt* **1** CALM, SOOTHE : calmar, sosegar **2 to lull to sleep** : arrullar, adormecer
lull[2] *n* : calma *f,* pausa *f*
lullaby [ˈlʌləˌbaɪ] *n, pl* **-bies** : canción *f* de cuna, arrullo *m,* nana *f*
lumbago [ˌlʌmˈbeɪgo] *n* : lumbago *m*
lumber[1] [ˈlʌmbər] *vt* : aserrar (madera) — *vi* : moverse pesadamente
lumber[2] *n* : madera *f*
lumberjack [ˈlʌmbərˌdʒæk] *n* : leñador *m,* -dora *f*
lumberyard [ˈlʌmbərˌjɑrd] *n* : almacén *m* de maderas
luminary [ˈluːməˌnɛri] *n, pl* **-naries** : lumbrera *f,* luminaria *f*
luminescence [ˌluːməˈnɛsənts] *n* : luminiscencia *f* — **luminescent** [-ˈnɛsənt] *adj*
luminosity [ˌluːməˈnɑsəṭi] *n, pl* **-ties** : luminosidad *f*
luminous [ˈluːmənəs] *adj* : luminoso — **luminously** *adv*
lump[1] [ˈlʌmp] *vt or* **to lump together** : juntar, agrupar, amontonar — *vi* CLUMP : agruparse, aglutinarse
lump[2] *n* **1** GLOB : grumo *m* **2** PIECE : pedazo *m,* trozo *m,* terrón *m* <a lump of coal : un trozo de carbón> <a lump of sugar : un terrón de azúcar> **3** SWELLING : bulto *m,* hinchazón *f,* protuberancia *f* **4 to have a lump in one's throat** : tener un nudo en la garganta
lumpy [ˈlʌmpi] *adj* **lumpier; -est 1** : lleno de grumos (dícese de una salsa) **2** UNEVEN : desigual, disparejo
lunacy [ˈluːnəsi] *n, pl* **-cies** : locura *f*
lunar [ˈluːnər] *adj* : lunar
lunatic[1] [ˈluːnəˌtɪk] *adj* : lunático, loco

lunatic[2] *n* **:** loco *m,* -ca *f*
lunch[1] [ˈlʌntʃ] *vi* **:** almorzar, comer
lunch[2] *n* **:** almuerzo *m,* comida *f,* lonche *m*
luncheon [ˈlʌntʃən] *n* **1 :** comida *f,* almuerzo *m* **2 luncheon meat :** fiambres *fpl*
lung [ˈlʌŋ] *n* **:** pulmón *m*
lunge[1] [ˈlʌndʒ] *vi* **lunged; lunging 1** THRUST **:** atacar (en la esgrima) **2 to lunge forward :** arremeter, lanzarse
lunge[2] *n* **1 :** arremetida *f,* embestida *f* **2 :** estocada *f* (en la esgrima)
lurch[1] [ˈlərtʃ] *vi* **1** PITCH **:** cabecear, dar bandazos, dar sacudidas **2** STAGGER **:** tambalearse
lurch[2] *n* **1 :** sacudida *f,* bandazo *m* (de un vehículo) **2 :** tambaleo *m* (de una persona)
lure[1] [ˈlʊr] *vt* **lured; luring :** atraer
lure[2] *n* **1** ATTRACTION **:** atractivo *m* **2** ENTICEMENT **:** señuelo *m,* aliciente *m* **3** BAIT **:** cebo *m* artificial (en la pesca)
lurid [ˈlʊrəd] *adj* **1** GRUESOME **:** espeluznante, horripilante **2** SENSATIONAL **:** sensacionalista, chocante **3** GAUDY **:** chillón
lurk [ˈlərk] *vi* **:** estar al acecho
luscious [ˈlʌʃəs] *adj* **1** DELICIOUS **:** delicioso, exquisito **2** SEDUCTIVE **:** seductor, cautivador
lush [ˈlʌʃ] *adj* **1** LUXURIANT **:** exuberante, lozano **2** LUXURIOUS **:** suntuoso, lujoso
lust[1] [ˈlʌst] *vi* **to lust after :** desear (a una persona), codiciar (riquezas, etc.)
lust[2] *n* **1** LASCIVIOUSNESS **:** lujuria *f,* lascivia *f* **2** CRAVING **:** deseo *m,* ansia *f,* anhelo *m*
luster *or* **lustre** [ˈlʌstər] *n* **1** GLOSS, SHEEN **:** lustre *m,* brillo *m* **2** SPLENDOR **:** lustre *m,* esplendor *m*
lusterless [ˈlʌstərləs] *adj* **:** deslustrado, sin brillo
lustful [ˈlʌstfəl] *adj* **:** lujurioso, lascivo, lleno de deseo
lustrous [ˈlʌstrəs] *adj* **:** brillante, brilloso, lustroso
lusty [ˈlʌsti] *adj* **lustier; -est :** fuerte, robusto, vigoroso — **lustily** [ˈlʌstəli] *adv*
lute [ˈluːt] *n* **:** laúd *m*
luxuriant [ˌlʌgˈʒʊriənt, ˌlʌkˈʃʊr-] *adj* **1 :** exuberante, lozano (dícese de las plantas) **2 :** abundante y hermoso (dícese del pelo) — **luxuriantly** *adv*
luxuriate [ˌlʌgˈʒʊriˌeɪt, ˌlʌkˈʃʊr-] *vi* **-ated; -ating 1 :** disfrutar **2 to luxuriate in :** deleitarse con
luxurious [ˌlʌgˈʒʊriəs, ˌlʌkˈʃʊr-] *adj* **:** lujoso, suntuoso — **luxuriously** *adv*
luxury [ˈlʌkʃəri, ˈlʌgʒə-] *n, pl* **-ries :** lujo *m*
lye [ˈlaɪ] *n* **:** lejía *f*
lying → **lie**[1], **lie**[2]
lymph [ˈlɪmpf] *n* **:** linfa *f*
lymphatic [lɪmˈfætɪk] *adj* **:** linfático
lynch [ˈlɪntʃ] *vt* **:** linchar
lynx [ˈlɪŋks] *n, pl* **lynx** *or* **lynxes :** lince *m*
lyre [ˈlaɪr] *n* **:** lira *f*
lyric[1] [ˈlɪrɪk] *adj* **:** lírico
lyric[2] *n* **1 :** poema *m* lírico **2 lyrics** *npl* **:** letra *f* (de una canción)
lyrical [ˈlɪrɪkəl] *adj* **:** lírico, elocuente

M

m [ˈɛm] *n, pl* **m's** *or* **ms** [ˈɛmz] **:** decimotercera letra del alfabeto inglés
ma'am [ˈmæm] → **madam**
macabre [məˈkɑb, -ˈkɑbər, -ˈkɑbrə] *adj* **:** macabro
macadam [məˈkædəm] *n* **:** macadán *m*
macaroni [ˌmækəˈroːni] *n* **:** macarrones *mpl*
macaroon [ˌmækəˈruːn] *n* **:** macarrón *m,* mostachón *m*
macaw [məˈkɔ] *n* **:** guacamayo *m*
mace [ˈmeɪs] *n* **1 :** maza *f* (arma o símbolo) **2 :** macis *f* (especia)
machete [məˈʃɛti] *n* **:** machete *m*
machination [ˌmækəˈneɪʃən, ˌmæʃə-] *n* **:** maquinación *f,* intriga *f*
machine[1] [məˈʃiːn] *vt* **-chined; -chining :** trabajar a máquina
machine[2] *n* **1 :** máquina *f* <machine shop : taller de máquinas> <machine language : lenguaje de la máquina> **2 :** aparato *m,* maquinaria *f* (en política)
machine gun *n* **:** ametralladora *f*
machinery [məˈʃiːnəri] *n, pl* **-eries 1 :** maquinaria *f* **2** WORKS **:** mecanismo *m*
machinist [məˈʃiːnɪst] *n* **:** maquinista *mf*
mackerel [ˈmækərəl] *n, pl* **-el** *or* **-els :** caballa *f*
mackinaw [ˈmækəˌnɔ] *n* **:** chaqueta *f* escocesa de lana
mad [ˈmæd] *adj* **madder; maddest 1** INSANE **:** loco, demente **2** RABID **:** rabioso **3** FOOLISH **:** tonto, insensato **4** ANGRY **:** enojado, furioso **5** CRAZY **:** loco <I'm mad about you : estoy loco por ti>
Madagascan [ˌmædəˈgæskən] *n* **:** malgache *mf* — **Madagascan** *adj*
madam [ˈmædəm] *n, pl* **mesdames** [meɪˈdɑm, -ˈdæm] **:** señora *f*
madcap[1] [ˈmædˌkæp] *adj* ZANY **:** alocado, disparatado
madcap[2] *n* **:** alocado *m,* -da *f*
madden [ˈmædən] *vt* **:** enloquecer, enfurecer
maddeningly [ˈmædənɪŋli] *adv* **:** irritantemente <maddeningly vague : tan vago que te exaspera>

made → **make**[1]
madhouse [ˈmæd,haʊs] *n* **:** manicomio *m* <the office was a madhouse **:** la oficina parecía una casa de locos>
madly [ˈmædli] *adv* **:** como un loco, locamente
madman [ˈmæd,mæn, -mən] *n, pl* **-men** [-mən, -,mɛn] **:** loco *m,* demente *m*
madness [ˈmædnəs] *n* **:** locura *f,* demencia *f*
madwoman [ˈmæd,wʊmən] *n, pl* **-women** [-,wɪmən] **:** loca *f,* demente *f*
maelstrom [ˈmeɪlstrəm] *n* **:** remolino *m,* vorágine *f*
maestro [ˈmaɪ,stroː] *n, pl* **-stros** *or* **-stri** [-,striː] **:** maestro *m*
Mafia [ˈmɑfiə] *n* **:** Mafia *f*
magazine [ˈmægə,ziːn] *n* **1** STOREHOUSE **:** almacén *m,* polvorín *m* (de explosivos) **2** PERIODICAL **:** revista *f* **3 :** cargador *m* (de un arma de fuego)
magenta [məˈdʒɛntə] *n* **:** magenta *f,* color *m* magenta
maggot [ˈmægət] *n* **:** gusano *m*
magic[1] [ˈmædʒɪk] *or* **magical** [ˈmædʒɪkəl] *adj* **:** mágico
magic[2] *n* **:** magia *f*
magically [ˈmædʒɪkli] *adv* **:** mágicamente <they magically appeared **:** aparecieron como por arte de magia>
magician [məˈdʒɪʃən] *n* **1** SORCERER **:** mago *m,* -ga *f* **2** CONJURER **:** prestidigitador *m,* -dora *f;* mago *m,* -ga *f*
magistrate [ˈmædʒə,streɪt] *n* **:** magistrado *m,* -da *f*
magma [ˈmægmə] *n* **:** magma *m*
magnanimity [,mægnəˈnɪməṭi] *n, pl* **-ties :** magnanimidad *f*
magnanimous [mægˈnænəməs] *adj* **:** magnánimo, generoso — **magnanimously** *adv*
magnate [ˈmæg,neɪt, -nət] *n* **:** magnate *mf*
magnesium [mægˈniːziəm, -ʒəm] *n* **:** magnesio *m*
magnet [ˈmægnət] *n* **:** imán *m*
magnetic [mægˈnɛtɪk] *adj* **:** magnético — **magnetically** [-tɪkli] *adv*
magnetic field *n* **:** campo *m* magnético
magnetism [ˈmægnə,tɪzəm] *n* **:** magnetismo *m*
magnetize [ˈmægnə,taɪz] *vt* **-tized; -tizing 1 :** magnetizar, imantar **2** ATTRACT **:** magnetizar, atraer
magnification [,mægnəfəˈkeɪʃən] *n* **:** aumento *m,* ampliación *f*
magnificence [mægˈnɪfəsənts] *n* **:** magnificencia *f*
magnificent [mægˈnɪfəsənt] *adj* **:** magnífico — **magnificently** *adv*
magnify [ˈmægnə,faɪ] *vt* **-fied; -fying 1** ENLARGE **:** ampliar **2** EXAGGERATE **:** magnificar, exagerar
magnifying glass *n* **:** lupa *f*
magnitude [ˈmægnə,tuːd, -,tjuːd] *n* **1** GREATNESS **:** magnitud *f,* grandeza *f* **2** QUANTITY **:** cantidad *f* **3** IMPORTANCE **:** magnitud *f,* envergadura *f*
magnolia [mægˈnoːljə] *n* **:** magnolia *f* (flor), magnolio *m* (árbol)
magpie [ˈmæg,paɪ] *n* **:** urraca *f*
mahogany [məˈhɑgəni] *n, pl* **-nies :** caoba *f*
maid [ˈmeɪd] *n* **1** MAIDEN **:** doncella *f* **2** *or* **maidservant** [ˈmeɪd,sərvənt] **:** sirvienta *f,* muchacha *f,* mucama *f,* criada *f*
maiden[1] [ˈmeɪdən] *adj* **1** UNMARRIED **:** soltera **2** FIRST **:** primero <maiden voyage **:** primera travesía>
maiden[2] *n* **:** doncella *f*
maidenhood [ˈmeɪdən,hʊd] *n* **:** doncellez *f*
maiden name *n* **:** nombre *m* de soltera
mail[1] [ˈmeɪl] *vt* **:** enviar por correo, echar al correo
mail[2] *n* **1 :** correo *m* <airmail **:** correo aéreo> **2 :** malla *f* <coat of mail **:** cota de malla>
mailbox [ˈmeɪl,bɑks] *n* **:** buzón *m*
mailman [ˈmeɪl,mæn, -mən] *n, pl* **-men** [-mən, -,mɛn] **:** cartero *m*
maim [ˈmeɪm] *vt* **:** mutilar, desfigurar, lisiar
main[1] [ˈmeɪn] *adj* **:** principal, central <the main office **:** la oficina central>
main[2] *n* **1** HIGH SEAS **:** alta mar *f* **2 :** tubería *f* principal (de agua o gas), cable *m* principal (de un circuito) **3 with might and main :** con todas sus fuerzas
mainframe [ˈmeɪn,freɪm] *n* **:** mainframe *m,* computadora *f* central
mainland [ˈmeɪn,lænd, -lənd] *n* **:** continente *m*
mainly [ˈmeɪnli] *adv* **1** PRINCIPALLY **:** principalmente, en primer lugar **2** MOSTLY **:** principalmente, en la mayor parte
mainstay [ˈmeɪn,steɪ] *n* **:** pilar *m,* sostén *m* principal
mainstream[1] [ˈmeɪn,striːm] *adj* **:** dominante, corriente, convencional
mainstream[2] *n* **:** corriente *f* principal
maintain [meɪnˈteɪn] *vt* **1** SERVICE **:** dar mantenimiento a (una máquina) **2** PRESERVE **:** mantener, conservar <to maintain silence **:** guardar silencio> **3** SUPPORT **:** mantener, sostener **4** ASSERT **:** mantener, sostener, afirmar
maintenance [ˈmeɪntənənts] *n* **:** mantenimiento *m*
maize [ˈmeɪz] *n* **:** maíz *m*
majestic [məˈdʒɛstɪk] *adj* **:** majestuoso — **majestically** [-tɪkli] *adv*
majesty [ˈmædʒəsti] *n, pl* **-ties 1 :** majestad *f* <Your Majesty **:** su Majestad> **2** SPLENDOR **:** majestuosidad *f,* esplendor *m*
major[1] [ˈmeɪdʒər] *vi* **-jored; -joring :** especializarse

major[2] *adj* **1** GREATER : mayor **2** NOTEWORTHY : mayor, notable **3** SERIOUS : grave **4** : mayor (en la música)

major[3] *n* **1** : mayor *mf,* comandante *mf* (en las fuerzas armadas) **2** : especialidad *f* (universitaria)

Majorcan [mɑˈdʒɔrkən, mə-, -ˈjɔr-] *n* : mallorquín *m,* -quina *f* — **Majorcan** *adj*

major general *n* : general *mf* de división

majority [məˈdʒɔrət̬i] *n, pl* **-ties** **1** ADULTHOOD : mayoría *f* de edad **2** : mayoría *f,* mayor parte *f* <the vast majority : la inmensa mayoría>

make[1] [ˈmeɪk] *v* **made** [ˈmeɪd]; **making** *vt* **1** CREATE : hacer <to make noise : hacer ruido> **2** FASHION, MANUFACTURE : hacer, fabricar <she made a dress : hizo un vestido> **3** DEVISE, FORM : desarrollar, elaborar, formar **4** CONSTITUTE : hacer, constituir <made of stone : hecho de piedra> **5** PREPARE : hacer, preparar **6** RENDER : hacer, poner <it makes him nervous : lo pone nervioso> <to make someone happy : hacer feliz a alguien> <it made me sad : me dio pena> **7** PERFORM : hacer <to make a gesture : hacer un gesto> **8** COMPEL : hacer, forzar, obligar **9** EARN : ganar <to make a living : ganarse la vida> — *vi* **1** HEAD : ir, dirigirse <we made for home : nos fuimos a casa> **2 to make do** : arreglárselas **3 to make good** REPAY : pagar **4 to make good** SUCCEED : tener éxito

make[2] *n* BRAND : marca *f*

make–believe[1] [ˌmeɪkbəˈliːv] *adj* : imaginario

make–believe[2] *n* : fantasía *f,* invención *f* <a world of make-believe : un mundo de ensueño>

make out *vt* **1** WRITE : hacer (un cheque) **2** DISCERN : distinguir, divisar **3** UNDERSTAND : comprender, entender — *vi* : arreglárselas <how did you make out? : ¿qué tal te fue?>

maker [ˈmeɪkər] *n* : fabricante *mf*

makeshift [ˈmeɪkˌʃɪft] *adj* : provisional, improvisado

makeup [ˈmeɪkˌʌp] *n* **1** COMPOSITION : composición *f* **2** CHARACTER : carácter *m,* temperamento *m* **3** COSMETICS : maquillaje *m*

make up *vt* **1** INVENT : inventar **2** : recuperar <she made up the time : recuperó las horas perdidas> — *vi* RECONCILE : hacer las paces, reconciliarse

maladjusted [ˌmæləˈdʒʌstəd] *adj* : inadaptado

malady [ˈmælədi] *n, pl* **-dies** : dolencia *f,* enfermedad *f,* mal *m*

malaise [məˈleɪz, mæ-] *n* : malestar *m*

malapropism [ˈmæləˌprɑˌpɪzəm] *n* : uso *m* incorrecto y cómico de una palabra

malaria [məˈlɛriə] *n* : malaria *f,* paludismo *m*

malarkey [məˈlɑrki] *n* : tonterías *fpl,* estupideces *fpl*

Malawian [məˈlɑwiən] *n* : malauiano *m,* -na *f* — **Malawian** *adj*

Malay [məˈleɪ, ˈmeɪˌleɪ] *n* **1** *or* **Malayan** [məˈleɪən, meɪ-; ˈmeɪˌleɪən] : malayo *m,* -ya *f* **2** : malayo *m* (idioma) — **Malay** *or* **Malayan** *adj*

male[1] [ˈmeɪl] *adj* **1** : macho **2** MASCULINE : masculino

male[2] *n* : macho *m* (de animales o plantas), varón *m* (de personas)

malefactor [ˈmæləˌfæktər] *n* : malhechor *m,* -chora *f*

maleness [ˈmeɪlnəs] *n* : masculinidad *f*

malevolence [məˈlɛvələnts] *n* : malevolencia *f*

malevolent [məˈlɛvələnt] *adj* : malévolo

malformation [ˌmælfɔrˈmeɪʃən] *n* : malformación *f*

malformed [mælˈfɔrmd] *adj* : mal formado, deforme

malfunction[1] [mælˈfʌŋkʃən] *vi* : funcionar mal

malfunction[2] *n* : mal funcionamiento *m*

malice [ˈmælɪs] *n* **1** : malicia *f,* malevolencia *f* **2 with malice aforethought** : con premeditación

malicious [məˈlɪʃəs] *adj* : malicioso, malévolo — **maliciously** *adv*

malign[1] [məˈlaɪn] *vt* : calumniar, difamar

malign[2] *adj* : maligno

malignancy [məˈlɪgnəntsi] *n, pl* **-cies** : malignidad *f*

malignant [məˈlɪgnənt] *adj* : maligno

malinger [məˈlɪŋgər] *vi* : fingirse enfermo

malingerer [məˈlɪŋgərər] *n* : uno que se finge enfermo

mall [ˈmɔl] *n* **1** PROMENADE : alameda *f,* paseo *m* (arbolado) **2** : centro *m* comercial <shopping mall : galería comercial>

mallard [ˈmælərd] *n, pl* **-lard** *or* **-lards** : pato *m* real, ánade *mf* real

malleable [ˈmæliəbəl] *adj* : maleable

mallet [ˈmælət] *n* : mazo *m*

malnourished [mælˈnərɪʃt] *adj* : desnutrido, malnutrido

malnutrition [ˌmælnʊˈtrɪʃən, -njʊ-] *n* : desnutrición *f,* malnutrición *f*

malodorous [mælˈoːdərəs] *adj* : maloliente

malpractice [ˌmælˈpræktəs] *n* : mala práctica *f,* negligencia *f*

malt [ˈmɔlt] *n* : malta *f*

maltreat [mælˈtriːt] *vt* : maltratar

mama *or* **mamma** [ˈmɑmə] *n* : mamá *f*

mammal [ˈmæməl] *n* : mamífero *m*

mammalian [məˈmeɪliən, mæ-] *adj* : mamífero

mammary [ˈmæməri] *adj* **1** : mamario **2 mammary gland** : glándula mamaria

mammogram ['mæmə,græm] *n* : mamografía *f*

mammoth[1] ['mæməθ] *adj* : colosal, gigantesco

mammoth[2] *n* : mamut *m*

man[1] ['mæn] *vt* **manned; manning** : tripular (un barco o avión), encargarse de (un servicio)

man[2] *n, pl* **men** ['mɛn] **1** PERSON : hombre *m,* persona *f* **2** MALE : hombre *m* **3** MANKIND : humanidad *f*

manacles ['mænɪkəlz] *npl* HANDCUFFS : esposas *fpl*

manage ['mænɪdʒ] *v* **-aged; -aging** *vt* **1** HANDLE : controlar, manejar **2** DIRECT : administrar, dirigir **3** CONTRIVE : lograr, ingeniárselas para — *vi* COPE : arreglárselas

manageable ['mænɪdʒəbəl] *adj* : manejable

management ['mænɪdʒmənt] *n* **1** DIRECTION : administración *f,* gestión *f,* dirección *f* **2** HANDLING : manejo *m* **3** MANAGERS : dirección *f,* gerencia *f*

manager ['mænɪdʒər] *n* : director *m,* -tora *f;* gerente *mf;* administrador *m,* -dora *f*

managerial [,mænə'dʒɪriəl] *adj* : directivo, gerencial

mandarin ['mændərən] *n* **1** : mandarín *m* **2** *or* **mandarin orange** : mandarina *f*

mandate ['mæn,deɪt] *n* : mandato *m*

mandatory ['mændə,tori] *adj* : obligatorio

mandible ['mændəbəl] *n* : mandíbula *f*

mandolin [,mændə'lɪn, 'mændələn] *n* : mandolina *f*

mane ['meɪn] *n* : crin *f* (de un caballo), melena *f* (de un león o una persona)

maneuver[1] [mə'nu:vər, -'nju:-] *vt* **1** PLACE, POSITION : maniobrar, posicionar, colocar **2** MANIPULATE : manipular, maniobrar — *vi* : maniobrar

maneuver[2] *n* : maniobra *f*

manfully ['mænfəli] *adj* : valientemente

manganese ['mæŋgə,ni:z, -,ni:s] *n* : manganeso *m*

mange ['meɪndʒ] *n* : sarna *f*

manger ['meɪndʒər] *n* : pesebre *m*

mangle ['mæŋgəl] *vt* **-gled; -gling** **1** CRUSH, DESTROY : aplastar, despedazar, destrozar **2** MUTILATE : mutilar <to mangle a text : mutilar un texto>

mango ['mæŋ,go:] *n, pl* **-goes** : mango *m*

mangrove ['mæn,gro:v, 'mæŋ-] *n* : mangle *m*

mangy ['meɪndʒi] *adj* **mangier; -est** **1** : sarnoso **2** SHABBY : gastoso

manhandle ['mæn,hændəl] *vi* **-dled; -dling** : maltratar, tratar con poco cuidado

manhole ['mæn,ho:l] *n* : boca *f* de alcantarilla

manhood ['mæn,hʊd] *n* **1** : madurez *f* (de un hombre) **2** COURAGE, MANLINESS : hombría *f,* valor *m* **3** MEN : hombres *mpl*

manhunt ['mæn,hʌnt] *n* : búsqueda *f* (de un criminal)

mania ['meɪniə, -njə] *n* : manía *f*

maniac ['meɪni,æk] *n* : maníaco *m,* -ca *f;* maniático *m,* -ca *f*

maniacal [mə'naɪəkəl] *adj* : maníaco, maniaco

manicure[1] ['mænə,kjʊr] *vt* **-cured; -curing** **1** : hacer la manicura a **2** TRIM : recortar

manicure[2] *n* : manicura *f*

manicurist ['mænə,kjʊrɪst] *n* : manicuro *m,* -ra *f*

manifest[1] ['mænə,fɛst] *vt* : manifestar

manifest[2] *adj* : manifiesto, patente — **manifestly** *adv*

manifestation [,mænəfə'steɪʃən] *n* : manifestación *f*

manifesto [,mænə'fɛs,to:] *n, pl* **-tos** *or* **-toes** : manifiesto *m*

manifold[1] ['mænə,fo:ld] *adj* : diverso, variado

manifold[2] *n* : colector *m* (de escape)

manipulate [mə'nɪpjə,leɪt] *vt* **-lated; -lating** : manipular

manipulation [mə,nɪpjə'leɪʃən] *n* : manipulación *f*

manipulative [mə'nɪpjə,leɪt̬ɪv, -lət̬ɪv] *adj* : manipulador

mankind ['mæn'kaɪnd, ,kaɪnd] *n* : género *m* humano, humanidad *f*

manliness ['mænlinəs] *n* : hombría *f,* masculinidad *f*

manly ['mænli] *adj* **-lier; -est** : varonil, viril

man–made ['mæn'meɪd] *adj* : artificial <man-made fabrics : telas sintéticas>

manna ['mænə] *n* : maná *m*

mannequin ['mænɪkən] *n* **1** DUMMY : maniquí *m* **2** MODEL : modelo *mf*

manner ['mænər] *n* **1** KIND, SORT : tipo *m,* clase *f* **2** WAY : manera *f,* modo *m* **3** STYLE : estilo *m* (artístico) **4 manners** *npl* CUSTOMS : costumbres *fpl* <Victorian manners : costumbres victorianas> **5 manners** *npl* ETIQUETTE : modales *mpl,* educación *f,* etiqueta *f* <good manners : buenos modales>

mannered ['mænərd] *adj* **1** AFFECTED, ARTIFICIAL : amanerado, afectado **2** **well–mannered** : educado, cortés **3** → **ill–mannered**

mannerism ['mænə,rɪzəm] *n* : peculiaridad *f,* gesto *m* particular

mannerly ['mænərli] *adj* : cortés, bien educado

mannish ['mænɪʃ] *adj* : masculino, hombruno

man–of–war [,mænə'wɔr, -əv'wɔr] *n, pl* **men–of–war** [,mɛn-] WARSHIP : buque *m* de guerra

manor ['mænər] *n* **1** : casa *f* solariega, casa *f* señorial **2** ESTATE : señorío *m*

manpower ['mæn,paʊər] *n* **:** personal *m,* mano *f* de obra
mansion ['mæntʃən] *n* **:** mansión *f*
manslaughter ['mæn,slɔtər] *n* **:** homicidio *m* sin premeditación
mantel ['mæntəl] *n* **:** repisa *f* de chimenea
mantelpiece ['mæntəl,pi:s] → **mantel**
mantis ['mæntəs] *n, pl* **-tises** *or* **-tes** ['mæn,ti:z] **:** mantis *f* religiosa
mantle ['mæntəl] *n* **:** manto *m*
manual[1] ['mænjʊəl] *adj* **:** manual — **manually** *adv*
manual[2] *n* **:** manual *m*
manufacture[1] [,mænjə'fæktʃər] *vt* **-tured; -turing :** fabricar, manufacturar, confeccionar (ropa), elaborar (comestibles)
manufacture[2] *n* **:** manufactura *f,* fabricación *f,* confección *f* (de ropa), elaboración *f* (de comestibles)
manufacturer [,mænjə'fæktʃərər] *n* **:** fabricante *m;* manufacturero *m,* -ra *f*
manure [mə'nʊr, -'njʊr] *n* **:** estiércol *m*
manuscript ['mænjə,skrɪpt] *n* **:** manuscrito *m*
many[1] ['mɛni] *adj* **more** ['mor]; **most** ['mo:st] **:** muchos
many[2] *pron* **:** muchos *pl,* -chas *pl*
map[1] ['mæp] *vt* **mapped; mapping 1 :** trazar el mapa de **2** PLAN **:** planear, proyectar <to map out a program : planear un programa>
map[2] *n* **:** mapa *m*
maple ['meɪpəl] *n* **:** arce *m*
mar ['mɑr] *vt* **marred; marring 1** SPOIL **:** estropear, echar a perder **2** DEFACE **:** desfigurar
maraschino [,mærə'ski:no:, -'ʃi:-] *n, pl* **-nos :** cereza *f* al marrasquino
marathon ['mærə,θɑn] *n* **1** RACE **:** maratón *m* **2** CONTEST **:** competencia *f* de resistencia
maraud [mə'rɔd] *vi* **:** merodear
marauder [mə'rɔdər] *n* **:** merodeador *m,* -dora *f*
marble ['mɑrbəl] *n* **1 :** mármol *m* **2 :** canica *f* <to play marbles : jugar a las canicas>
march[1] ['mɑrtʃ] *vi* **1 :** marchar, desfilar <they marched past the grandstand : desfilaron ante la tribuna> **2 :** caminar con resolución <she marched right up to him : se le acercó sin vacilación>
march[2] *n* **1** MARCHING **:** marcha *f* **2** PASSAGE **:** paso *m* (del tiempo) **3** PROGRESS **:** avance *m,* progreso *m* **4 :** marcha *f* (en música)
March ['mɑrtʃ] *n* **:** marzo *m*
marchioness ['mɑrʃənɪs] *n* **:** marquesa *f*
Mardi Gras ['mɑrdi,grɑ] *n* **:** martes *m* de Carnaval
mare ['mær] *n* **:** yegua *f*
margarine ['mɑrdʒərən] *n* **:** margarina *f*
margin ['mɑrdʒən] *n* **:** margen *m*
marginal ['mɑrdʒənəl] *adj* **1 :** marginal **2** MINIMAL **:** mínimo — **marginally** *adv*
marigold ['mærə,go:ld] *n* **:** maravilla *f,* caléndula *f*
marijuana [,mærə'*h*wɑnə] *n* **:** marihuana *f*
marina [mə'ri:nə] *n* **:** puerto *m* deportivo
marinate ['mærə,neɪt] *vt* **-nated; -nating :** marinar
marine[1] [mə'ri:n] *adj* **1 :** marino <marine life : vida marina> **2** NAUTICAL **:** náutico, marítimo **3 :** de la infantería de marina
marine[2] *n* **:** soldado *m* de marina
mariner ['mærɪnər] *n* **:** marinero *m,* marino *m*
marionette [,mæriə'nɛt] *n* **:** marioneta *f,* títere *m*
marital ['mærətəl] *adj* **1 :** matrimonial **2 marital status :** estado *m* civil
maritime ['mærə,taɪm] *adj* **:** marítimo
marjoram ['mɑrdʒərəm] *n* **:** mejorana *f*
mark[1] ['mɑrk] *vt* **1 :** marcar **2** CHARACTERIZE **:** caracterizar **3** SIGNAL **:** señalar **4** NOTICE **:** prestar atención a, hacer caso de **5 to mark off :** demarcar, delimitar
mark[2] *n* **1** TARGET **:** blanco *m* **2 :** marca *f,* señal *f* <put a mark where you left off : pon una señal donde terminaste> **3** INDICATION **:** señal *f,* indicio *m* **4** GRADE **:** nota *f* **5** IMPRINT **:** huella *f,* marca *f* **6** BLEMISH **:** marca *f,* imperfección *f*
marked ['mɑrkt] *adj* **:** marcado, notable — **markedly** ['mɑrkədli] *adv*
marker ['mɑrkər] *n* **:** marcador *m*
market[1] ['mɑrkət] *vt* **:** poner en venta, comercializar
market[2] *n* **1** MARKETPLACE **:** mercado *m* <the open market : el mercado libre> **2** DEMAND **:** demanda *f,* mercado *m* **3** STORE **:** tienda *f* **4** → **stock market**
marketable ['mɑrkətəbəl] *adj* **:** vendible
marketplace ['mɑrkət,pleɪs] *n* **:** mercado *m*
marksman ['mɑrksmən] *n, pl* **-men** [-mən, -,mɛn] **:** tirador *m*
marksmanship ['mɑrksmən,ʃɪp] *n* **:** puntería *f*
marlin ['mɑrlɪn] *n* **:** marlín *m*
marmalade ['mɑrmə,leɪd] *n* **:** mermelada *f*
marmoset ['mɑrmə,sɛt] *n* **:** tití *m*
marmot ['mɑrmət] *n* **:** marmota *f*
maroon[1] [mə'ru:n] *vt* **:** abandonar, aislar
maroon[2] *n* **:** rojo *m* oscuro, granate *m*
marquee [mɑr'ki:] *n* **:** marquesina *f*
marquess ['mɑrkwɪs] *or* **marquis** ['mɑrkwɪs, mɑr'ki:] *n, pl* **-quesses** *or* **-quises** [-'ki:z, -'ki:zəz] *or* **-quis** [-'ki:, -'ki:z] **:** marqués *m*
marquise [mɑr'ki:z] → **marchioness**

marriage ['mærɪdʒ] *n* **1 :** matrimonio *m* **2** WEDDING **:** casamiento *m,* boda *f*

marriageable ['mærɪdʒəbəl] *adj* **of marriageable age :** de edad de casarse

married ['mærid] *adj* **1 :** casado **2 to get married :** casarse

marrow ['mæroː] *n* **:** médula *f,* tuétano *m*

marry ['mæri] *vt* **-ried; -rying 1 :** casar <the priest married them : el cura los casó> **2 :** casarse con <she married John : se casó con John>

Mars ['mɑrz] *n* **:** Marte *m*

marsh ['mɑrʃ] *n* **1 :** pantano *m* **2 salt marsh :** marisma *f*

marshal[1] ['mɑrʃəl] *vt* **-shaled** *or* **-shalled; -shaling** *or* **-shalling 1 :** poner en orden, reunir **2** USHER **:** conducir

marshal[2] *n* **1 :** maestro *m* de ceremonias **2 :** mariscal *m* (en el ejército); jefe *m,* -fa *f* (de la policía, de los bomberos, etc.)

marshmallow ['mɑrʃˌmɛloː, -ˌmæloː] *n* **:** malvavisco *m*

marshy ['mɑrʃi] *adj* **marshier; -est :** pantanoso

marsupial [mɑr'suːpiəl] *n* **:** marsupial *m*

mart ['mɑrt] *n* MARKET **:** mercado *m*

marten ['mɑrtən] *n, pl* **-ten** *or* **-tens :** marta *f*

martial ['mɑrʃəl] *adj* **:** marcial

martin ['mɑrtən] *n* **1** SWALLOW **:** golondrina *f* **2** SWIFT **:** vencejo *m*

martyr[1] ['mɑrtər] *vt* **:** martirizar

martyr[2] *n* **:** mártir *mf*

martyrdom ['mɑrtərdəm] *n* **:** martirio *m*

marvel[1] ['mɑrvəl] *vi* **-veled** *or* **-velled; -veling** *or* **-velling :** maravillarse

marvel[2] *n* **:** maravilla *f*

marvelous ['mɑrvələs] *or* **marvellous** *adj* **:** maravilloso — **marvelously** *adv*

Marxism ['mɑrkˌsɪzəm] *n* **:** marxismo *m*

Marxist[1] ['mɑrksɪst] *adj* **:** marxista

Marxist[2] *n* **:** marxista *mf*

mascara [mæs'kærə] *n* **:** rímel *m,* rimel *m*

mascot ['mæsˌkɑt, -kət] *n* **:** mascota *f*

masculine ['mæskjələn] *adj* **:** masculino

masculinity [ˌmæskjə'lɪnəṱi] *n* **:** masculinidad *f*

mash[1] ['mæʃ] *vt* **1 :** hacer puré de (papas, etc.) **2** CRUSH **:** aplastar, majar

mash[2] *n* **1** FEED **:** afrecho *m* **2 :** malta *f* (para hacer bebidas alcohólicas) **3** PASTE, PULP **:** papilla *f,* pasta *f*

mask[1] ['mæsk] *vt* **1** CONCEAL, DISGUISE **:** enmascarar, ocultar **2** COVER **:** cubrir, tapar

mask[2] *n* **:** máscara *f,* careta *f,* mascarilla *f* (de un cirujano o dentista)

masochism ['mæsəˌkɪzəm, 'mæzə-] *n* **:** masoquismo *m*

masochist ['mæsəˌkɪst, 'mæzə-] *n* **:** masoquista *mf*

masochistic [ˌmæsə'kɪstɪk, ˌmæzə-] *adj* **:** masoquista

mason ['meɪsən] *n* **1** BRICKLAYER **:** albañil *mf* **2** *or* **stonemason** ['stoːnˌ-] **:** mampostero *m,* cantero *m*

masonry ['meɪsənri] *n, pl* **-ries 1** BRICKLAYING **:** albañería *f* **2** *or* **stonemasonry** ['stoːnˌ-] **:** mampostería *f*

masquerade[1] [ˌmæskə'reɪd] *vi* **-aded; -ading 1 :** disfrazarse (de), hacerse pasar (por) **2 :** asistir a una mascarada

masquerade[2] *n* **1 :** mascarada *f,* baile *m* de disfraces **2** FACADE **:** farsa *f,* fachada *f*

mass[1] ['mæs] *vi* **:** concentrarse, juntarse en masa — *vt* **:** concentrar

mass[2] *n* **1 :** masa *f* <atomic mass : masa atómica> **2** BULK **:** mole *f,* volumen *m* **3** MULTITUDE **:** cantidad *f,* montón *m* (de cosas), multitud *f* (de gente) **4 the masses :** las masas, el pueblo, el populacho

Mass ['mæs] *n* **:** misa *f*

massacre[1] ['mæsɪkər] *vt* **-cred; -cring :** masacrar

massacre[2] *n* **:** masacre *f*

massage[1] [mə'sɑʒ, -'sɑdʒ] *vt* **-saged; -saging :** masajear

massage[2] *n* **:** masaje *m*

masseur [mæ'sər] *n* **:** masajista *m*

masseuse [mæ'søz, -'suːz] *n* **:** masajista *f*

massive ['mæsɪv] *adj* **1** BULKY **:** voluminoso, macizo **2** HUGE **:** masivo, enorme — **massively** *adv*

mast ['mæst] *n* **:** mástil *m,* palo *m*

master[1] ['mæstər] *vt* **1** SUBDUE **:** dominar **2 :** llegar a dominar <she mastered French : llegó a dominar el francés>

master[2] *n* **1** TEACHER **:** maestro *m,* profesor *m* **2** EXPERT **:** experto *m,* -ta *f;* maestro *m,* -tra *f* **3 :** amo *m* (de animales o esclavos), señor *m* (de la casa) **4 master's degree :** maestría *f*

masterful ['mæstərfəl] *adj* **1** IMPERIOUS **:** autoritario, imperioso, dominante **2** SKILLFUL **:** magistral — **masterfully** *adv*

masterly ['mæstərli] *adj* **:** magistral

masterpiece ['mæstərˌpiːs] *n* **:** obra *f* maestra

masterwork ['mæstərˌwərk] → **masterpiece**

mastery ['mæstəri] *n* **1** DOMINION **:** dominio *m,* autoridad *f* **2** SUPERIORITY **:** superioridad *f* **3** EXPERTISE **:** maestría *f*

masticate ['mæstəˌkeɪt] *v* **-cated; -cating :** masticar

mastiff ['mæstɪf] *n* **:** mastín *m*

mastodon ['mæstəˌdɑn] *n* **:** mastodonte *m*

masturbate ['mæstərˌbeɪt] *v* **-bated; bating** *vi* **:** masturbarse — *vt* **:** masturbar

masturbation [ˌmæstər'beɪʃən] *n* **:** masturbación *f*

mat[1] [ˈmæt] *v* **matted; matting** *vt* TANGLE : enmarañar — *vi* : enmarañarse

mat[2] *n* **1** : estera *f* **2** TANGLE : maraña *f* **3** PAD : colchoneta *f* (de gimnasia) **4** *or* **matt** *or* **matte** [ˈmæt] FRAME : marco *m* (de cartón)

mat[3] → **matte**

matador [ˈmæt̬əˌdɔr] *n* : matador *m*

match[1] [ˈmætʃ] *vt* **1** PIT : enfrentar, oponer **2** EQUAL, FIT : igualar, corresponder a, coincidir con **3** : combinar con, hacer juego con <her shoes match her dress : sus zapatos hacen juego con su vestido> — *vi* **1** CORRESPOND : concordar, coincidir **2** : hacer juego <with a tie to match : con una corbata que hace juego>

match[2] *n* **1** EQUAL : igual *mf* <he's no match for her : no puede competir con ella> **2** FIGHT, GAME : partido *m,* combate *m* (en boxeo) **3** MARRIAGE : matrimonio *m,* casamiento *m* **4** : fósforo *m,* cerilla *f,* cerillo *m* (*in various countries*) <he lit a match : encendió un fósforo> **5 to be a good match** : hacer buena pareja (dícese de las personas), hacer juego (dícese de la ropa)

matchless [ˈmætʃləs] *adj* : sin igual, sin par

matchmaker [ˈmætʃˌmeɪkər] *n* : casamentero *m,* -ra *f*

mate[1] [ˈmeɪt] *v* **mated; mating** *vi* **1** FIT : encajar **2** PAIR : emparejarse **3** (*relating to animals*) : aparearse, copular — *vt* : aparear, acoplar (animales)

mate[2] *n* **1** COMPANION : compañero *m,* -ra *f;* camarada *mf* **2** : macho *m,* hembra *f* (de animales) **3** : oficial *mf* (de un barco) <first mate : primer oficial> **4** : compañero *m,* -ra *f;* pareja *f* (de un zapato, etc.)

material[1] [məˈtɪriəl] *adj* **1** PHYSICAL : material, físico <the material world : el mundo material> <material needs : necesidades materiales> **2** IMPORTANT : importante, esencial **3 material evidence** : prueba *f* sustancial

material[2] *n* **1** : material *m* **2** CLOTH : tejido *m,* tela *f*

materialism [məˈtɪriəˌlɪzəm] *n* : materialismo *m*

materialist [məˈtɪriəlɪst] *n* : materialista *mf*

materialistic [məˌtɪriəˈlɪstɪk] *adj* : materialista

materialize [məˈtɪriəˌlaɪz] *v* **-ized; -izing** *vt* : materializar, hacer aparecer — *vi* : materializarse, aparecer

maternal [məˈtərnəl] *adj* MOTHERLY : maternal — **maternally** *adv*

maternity[1] [məˈtərnət̬i] *adj* : de maternidad <maternity clothes : ropa de futura mamá> <maternity leave : licencia por maternidad>

maternity[2] *n, pl* **-ties** : maternidad *f*

math [ˈmæθ] → **mathematics**

mathematical [ˌmæθəˈmæt̬ɪkəl] *adj* : matemático — **mathematically** *adv*

mathematician [ˌmæθəməˈtɪʃən] *n* : matemático *m,* -ca *f*

mathematics [ˌmæθəˈmæt̬ɪks] *ns & pl* : matemáticas *fpl,* matemática *f*

matinee *or* **matinée** [ˌmætənˈeɪ] *n* : matiné *f*

matriarch [ˈmeɪtriˌɑrk] *n* : matriarca *f*

matriarchy [ˈmeɪtriˌɑrki] *n, pl* **-chies** : matriarcado *m*

matriculate [məˈtrɪkjəˌleɪt] *v* **-lated; -lating** *vt* : matricular — *vi* : matricularse

matriculation [məˌtrɪkjəˈleɪʃən] *n* : matrícula *f,* matriculación *f*

matrimony [ˈmætrəˌmoːni] *n* : matrimonio *m* — **matrimonial** [ˌmætrəˈmoːniəl] *adj*

matrix [ˈmeɪtrɪks] *n, pl* **-trices** [ˈmeɪtrəˌsiːz, ˈmæ-] *or* **-trixes** [ˈmeɪtrɪksəz] : matriz *f*

matron [ˈmeɪtrən] *n* : matrona *f*

matronly [ˈmeɪtrənli] *adj* : de matrona, matronal

matte [ˈmæt] *adj* : mate, de acabado mate

matter[1] [ˈmæt̬ər] *vi* : importar <it doesn't matter : no importa>

matter[2] *n* **1** QUESTION : asunto *m,* cuestión *f* <a matter of taste : una cuestión de gusto> **2** SUBSTANCE : materia *f,* sustancia *f* **3 matters** *npl* CIRCUMSTANCES : situación *f,* cosas *fpl* <to make matters worse : para colmo de males> **4 to be the matter** : pasar <what's the matter? : ¿qué pasa?> **5 as a matter of fact** : en efecto, en realidad **6 for that matter** : de hecho **7 no matter how much** : por mucho que

matter–of–fact [ˈmæt̬ərəvˈfækt] *adj* : práctico, realista

mattress [ˈmætrəs] *n* : colchón *m*

mature[1] [məˈtʊr, -ˈtjʊr, -ˈtʃʊr] *vi* **-tured; -turing 1** : madurar **2** : vencer <when does the loan mature? : ¿cuándo vence el préstamo?>

mature[2] *adj* **-turer; -est 1** : maduro **2** DUE : vencido

maturity [məˈtʊrət̬i, -ˈtjʊr-, -ˈtʃʊr-] *n* : madurez *f*

maudlin [ˈmɔdlɪn] *adj* : sensiblero

maul[1] [ˈmɔl] *vt* **1** BEAT : golpear, pegar **2** MANGLE : mutilar **3** MANHANDLE : maltratar

maul[2] *n* MALLET : mazo *m*

Mauritanian [ˌmɔrəˈteɪniən] *n* : mauritano *m,* -na *f* — **Mauritanian** *adj*

mausoleum [ˌmɔsəˈliːəm, ˌmɔzə-] *n, pl* **-leums** *or* **-lea** [-ˈliːə] : mausoleo *m*

mauve [ˈmoːv, ˈmɔv] *n* : malva *m*

maven *or* **mavin** [ˈmeɪvən] *n* EXPERT : experto *m,* -ta *f*

maverick [ˈmævrɪk, ˈmævə-] *n* **1** : ternero *m* sin marcar **2** NONCONFORMIST : inconformista *mf,* disidente *mf*

mawkish [ˈmɔkɪʃ] *adj* : sensiblero

maxim [ˈmæksəm] *n* : máxima *f*

maximize [ˈmæksəˌmaɪz] *vt* **-mized; -mizing** : maximizar, llevar al máximo

maximum[1] [ˈmæksəməm] *adj* : máximo

maximum[2] *n, pl* **-ma** [ˈmæksəmə] *or* **-mums** : máximo *m*

may [ˈmeɪ] *v aux, past* **might** [ˈmaɪt]; *present s & pl* **may 1** (*expressing permission*) : poder <you may go : puedes ir> **2** (*expressing possibility or probability*) : poder <you may be right : puede que tengas razón> <it may happen occasionally : puede pasar de vez en cuando> **3** (*expressing desires, intentions, or contingencies*) <may the best man win : que gane el mejor> <I laugh that I may not weep : me río para no llorar> <come what may : pase lo que pase>

May [ˈmeɪ] *n* : mayo *m*

maybe [ˈmeɪbi] *adv* PERHAPS : quizás, tal vez

mayfly [ˈmeɪˌflaɪ] *n, pl* **-flies** : efímera *f*

mayhem [ˈmeɪˌhɛm, ˈmeɪəm] *n* **1** MUTILATION : mutilación *f* **2** DEVASTATION : estragos *mpl*

mayonnaise [ˈmeɪəˌneɪz] *n* : mayonesa *f*

mayor [ˈmeɪər, ˈmɛr] *n* : alcalde *m*, -desa *f*

mayoral [ˈmeɪərəl, ˈmɛrəl] *adj* : de alcalde

maze [ˈmeɪz] *n* : laberinto *m*

me [ˈmiː] *pron* **1** : me <she called me : me llamó> <give it to me : dámelo> **2** (*after a preposition*) : mí <for me : para mí> <with me : conmigo> **3** (*after conjunctions and verbs*) : yo <it's me : soy yo> <as big as me : tan grande como yo> **4** (*emphatic use*) : yo <me, too! : ¡yo también!> <who, me? : ¿quién, yo?>

meadow [ˈmɛdoː] *n* : prado *m*, pradera *f*

meadowland [ˈmɛdoˌlænd] *n* : pradera *f*

meadowlark [ˈmɛdoˌlɑrk] *n* : pájaro *m* cantor con el pecho amarillo

meager *or* **meagre** [ˈmiːgər] *adj* **1** THIN : magro, flaco **2** POOR, SCANTY : exiguo, escaso, pobre

meagerly [ˈmiːgərli] *adv* : pobremente

meagerness [ˈmiːgərnəs] *n* : escasez *f*, pobreza *f*

meal [ˈmiːl] *n* **1** : comida *f* <a hearty meal : una comida sustanciosa> **2** : harina *f* (de maíz, etc.)

mealtime [ˈmiːlˌtaɪm] *n* : hora *f* de comer

mean[1] [ˈmiːn] *vt* **meant** [ˈmɛnt]; **meaning 1** INTEND : querer, pensar, tener la intención de <I didn't mean to do it : lo hice sin querer> <what do you mean to do? : ¿qué piensas hacer?> **2** SIGNIFY : querer decir, significar <what does that mean? : ¿qué quiere decir eso?> **3** : importar <health means everything : lo que más importa es la salud>

mean[2] *adj* **1** HUMBLE : humilde **2** NEGLIGIBLE : despreciable <it's no mean feat : no es poca cosa> **3** STINGY : mezquino, tacaño **4** CRUEL : malo, cruel <to be mean to someone : tratar mal a alguien> **5** AVERAGE, MEDIAN : medio

mean[3] *n* **1** MIDPOINT : término *m* medio **2** AVERAGE : promedio *m*, media *f* aritmética **3 means** *npl* WAY : medio *m*, manera *f*, vía *f* **4 means** *npl* RESOURCES : medios *mpl*, recursos *mpl* **5 by all means** : por supuesto, cómo no **6 by means of** : por medio de **7 by no means** : de ninguna manera, de ningún modo

meander [miˈændər] *vi* **-dered; -dering 1** WIND : serpentear **2** WANDER : vagar, andar sin rumbo fijo

meaning [ˈmiːnɪŋ] *n* **1** : significado *m*, sentido *m* <double meaning : doble sentido> **2** INTENT : intención *f*, propósito *m*

meaningful [ˈmiːnɪŋfəl] *adj* : significativo — **meaningfully** *adv*

meaningless [ˈmiːnɪŋləs] *adj* : sin sentido

meanness [ˈmiːnnəs] *n* **1** CRUELTY : crueldad *f*, mezquindad *f* **2** STINGINESS : tacañería *f*

meantime[1] [ˈmiːnˌtaɪm] *adv* → **meanwhile**[1]

meantime[2] *n* **1** : interín *m* **2 in the meantime** : entretanto, mientras tanto

meanwhile[1] [ˈmiːnˌ*h*waɪl] *adv* : entretanto, mientras tanto

meanwhile[2] *n* → **meantime**[2]

measles [ˈmiːzəlz] *ns & pl* : sarampión *m*

measly [ˈmiːzli] *adj* **-slier; -est** : miserable, mezquino

measurable [ˈmɛʒərəbəl, ˈmeɪ-] *adj* : mensurable — **measurably** [-bli] *adv*

measure[1] [ˈmɛʒər, ˈmeɪ-] *v* **-sured; -suring** : medir <he measured the table : midió la mesa> <it measures 15 feet tall : mide 15 pies de altura>

measure[2] *n* **1** AMOUNT : medida *f*, cantidad *f* <in large measure : en gran medida> <a full measure : una cantidad exacta> <a measure of proficiency : una cierta competencia> <for good measure : de ñapa, por añadidura> **2** DIMENSIONS, SIZE : medida *f*, tamaño *m* **3** RULER : regla *f* <tape measure : cinta métrica> **4** MEASUREMENT : medida *f* <cubic measure : medida de capacidad> **5** MEASURING : medición *f* **6 measures** *npl* : medidas *fpl* <security measures : medidas de seguridad>

measureless [ˈmɛʒərləs, ˈmeɪ-] *adj* : inmensurable

measurement [ˈmɛʒərmənt, ˈmeɪ-] *n* **1** MEASURING : medición *f* **2** DIMENSION : medida *f*

measure up *vi* **to measure up to** : estar a la altura de

meat ['mi:t] *n* **1** FOOD : comida *f* **2** : carne *f* <meat and fish : carne y pescado> **3** SUBSTANCE : sustancia *f*, esencia *f* <the meat of the story : la sustancia del cuento>

meatball ['mi:t,bɔl] *n* : albóndiga *f*

meaty ['mi:ṭi] *adj* **meatier; -est** : con mucha carne, carnoso

mechanic [mɪ'kænɪk] *n* : mecánico *m*, -ca *f*

mechanical [mɪ'kænɪkəl] *adj* : mecánico — **mechanically** *adv*

mechanics [mɪ'kænɪks] *ns & pl* **1** : mecánica *f* <fluid mechanics : la mecánica de fluidos> **2** MECHANISMS : mecanismos *mpl*, aspectos *mpl* prácticos

mechanism ['mɛkə,nɪzəm] *n* : mecanismo *m*

mechanization [,mɛkənə'zeɪʃən] *n* : mecanización *f*

mechanize ['mɛkə,naɪz] *vt* **-nized; -nizing** : mecanizar

medal ['mɛdəl] *n* : medalla *f*, condecoración *f*

medalist ['mɛdəlɪst] *or* **medallist** *n* : medallista *mf*

medallion [mə'dæljən] *n* : medallón *m*

meddle ['mɛdəl] *vi* **-dled; -dling** : meterse, entrometerse

meddler ['mɛdələr] *n* : entrometido *m*, -da *f*

meddlesome ['mɛdəlsəm] *adj* : entrometido

media ['mi:diə] *npl* : medios *mpl* de comunicación

median[1] ['mi:diən] *adj* : medio

median[2] *n* : valor *m* medio

mediate ['mi:di,eɪt] *vi* **-ated; -ating** : mediar

mediation [,mi:di'eɪʃən] *n* : mediación *f*

mediator ['mi:di,eɪṭər] *n* : mediador *m*, -dora *f*

medical ['mɛdɪkəl] *adj* : médico

medicate ['mɛdə,keɪt] *vt* **-cated; -cating** : medicar <medicated powder : polvos medicinales>

medication [,mɛdə'keɪʃən] *n* **1** TREATMENT : tratamiento *m*, medicación *f* **2** MEDICINE : medicamento *m* <to be on medication : estar medicado>

medicinal [mə'dɪsənəl] *adj* : medicinal

medicine ['mɛdəsən] *n* **1** MEDICATION : medicina *f*, medicamento *m* **2** : medicina *f* <he's studying medicine : estudia medicina>

medicine man *n* : hechicero *m*

medieval *or* **mediaeval** [mɪ'di:vəl, ,mi:-, ,mɛ-, -di'i:vəl] *adj* : medieval

mediocre [,mi:di'o:kər] *adj* : mediocre

mediocrity [,mi:di'ɑkrəṭi] *n, pl* **-ties** : mediocridad *f*

meditate ['mɛdə,teɪt] *vi* **-tated; -tating** : meditar

meditation [,mɛdə'teɪʃən] *n* : meditación *f*

meditative ['mɛdə,teɪṭɪv] *adj* : meditabundo

medium[1] ['mi:diəm] *adj* : mediano <of medium height : de estatura mediana, de estatura regular>

medium[2] *n, pl* **-diums** *or* **-dia** ['mi:diə] **1** MEAN : punto *m* medio, término *m* medio <happy medium : justo medio> **2** MEANS : medio *m* **3** SUBSTANCE : medio *m*, sustancia *f* <a viscous medium : un medio viscoso> **4** : medio *m* de comunicación **5** : medio *m* (artístico)

medley ['mɛdli] *n, pl* **-leys** : popurrí *m* (de canciones)

meek ['mi:k] *adj* **1** LONG-SUFFERING : paciente, sufrido **2** SUBMISSIVE : sumiso, dócil, manso

meekly ['mi:kli] *adv* : dócilmente

meekness ['mi:knəs] *n* : mansedumbre *f*, docilidad *f*

meet[1] ['mi:t] *v* **met** ['mɛt]; **meeting** *vt* **1** ENCOUNTER : encontrarse con **2** JOIN : unirse con **3** CONFRONT : enfrentarse a **4** SATISFY : satisfacer, cumplir con <to meet costs : pagar los gastos> **5** : conocer <I met his sister : conocí a su hermana> — *vi* ASSEMBLE : reunirse, congregarse

meet[2] *n* : encuentro *m*

meeting ['mi:ṭɪŋ] *n* **1** : reunión *f* <to open the meeting : abrir la sesión> **2** ENCOUNTER : encuentro *m* **3** : entrevista *f* (formal)

meetinghouse ['mi:ṭɪŋ,haʊs] *n* : iglesia *f* (de ciertas confesiones protestantes)

megabyte ['mɛgə,baɪt] *n* : megabyte *m*

megahertz ['mɛgə,hərts, -,hɛrts] *n* : megahercio *m*

megaphone ['mɛgə,fo:n] *n* : megáfono *m*

melancholy[1] ['mɛlən,kɑli] *adj* : melancólico, triste, sombrío

melancholy[2] *n, pl* **-cholies** : melancolía *f*

melanoma [,mɛlə'no:mə] *n, pl* **-mas** : melanoma *m*

melee ['meɪ,leɪ, meɪ'leɪ] *n* BRAWL : reyerta *f*, riña *f*, pelea *f*

meliorate ['mi:ljə,reɪt, 'mi:liə-] → **ameliorate**

mellow[1] ['mɛlo:] *vt* : suavizar, endulzar — *vi* : suavizarse, endulzarse

mellow[2] *adj* **1** RIPE : maduro **2** MILD : apacible <a mellow character : un carácter apacible> <mellow wines : vinos añejos> **3** : suave, dulce <mellow colors : colores suaves> <mellow tones : tonos dulces>

mellowness ['mɛlonəs] *n* : suavidad *f*, dulzura *f*

melodic [mə'lɑdɪk] *adj* : melódico — **melodically** [-dɪkli] *adv*

melodious [mə'lo:diəs] *adj* : melodioso — **melodiously** *adv*

melodiousness [mə'lo:diəsnəs] *n* : calidad *f* de melódico

melodrama ['mɛlə,drɑmə, -,dræ-] *n* : melodrama *m*

melodramatic [,mɛlədrə'mæţɪk] *adj* : melodramático — **melodramatically** [-ţɪkli] *adv*

melody ['mɛlədi] *n, pl* **-dies** : melodía *f,* tonada *f*

melon ['mɛlən] *n* : melón *m*

melt ['mɛlt] *vt* **1** : derretir, disolver **2** SOFTEN : ablandar <it melted his heart : ablandó su corazón> — *vi* **1** : derretirse, disolverse **2** SOFTEN : ablandarse **3** DISAPPEAR : desvanecerse, esfumarse <the clouds melted away : las nubes se desvanecieron>

melting point *n* : punto *m* de fusión

member ['mɛmbər] *n* **1** LIMB : miembro *m* **2** : miembro *m* (de un grupo); socio *m,* -cia *f* (de un club) **3** PART : miembro *m,* parte *f*

membership ['mɛmbər,ʃɪp] *n* **1** : membresía *f* <application for membership : solicitud de entrada> **2** MEMBERS : membresía *f,* miembros *mpl,* socios *mpl*

membrane ['mɛm,breɪn] *n* : membrana *f* — **membranous** ['mɛmbrənəs] *adj*

memento [mɪ'mɛn,to:] *n, pl* **-tos** *or* **-toes** : recuerdo *m*

memo ['mɛmo:] *n, pl* **memos** : memorándum *m*

memoirs ['mɛm,wɑrz] *npl* : memorias *fpl,* autobiografía *f*

memorabilia [,mɛmərə'biliə, -'bɪljə] *npl* **1** : objetos *mpl* de interés histórico **2** MEMENTOS : recuerdos *mpl*

memorable ['mɛmərəbəl] *adj* : memorable, notable — **memorably** [-bli] *adv*

memorandum [,mɛmə'rændəm] *n, pl* **-dums** *or* **-da** [-də] : memorándum *m*

memorial[1] [mə'moriəl] *adj* : conmemorativo

memorial[2] *n* : monumento *m* conmemorativo

Memorial Day *n* : el último lunes de mayo (observado en Estados Unidos como día feriado para conmemorar a los caídos en guerra)

memorialize [mə'moriə,laɪz] *vt* **-ized; -izing** COMMEMORATE : conmemorar

memorization [,mɛmərə'zeɪʃən] *n* : memorización *f*

memorize ['mɛmə,raɪz] *vt* **-rized; -rizing** : memorizar, aprender de memoria

memory ['mɛmri, 'mɛmə-] *n, pl* **-ries** **1** : memoria *f* <he has a good memory : tiene buena memoria> **2** RECOLLECTION : recuerdo *m* **3** COMMEMORATION : memoria *f,* conmemoración *f*

men → **man**[2]

menace[1] ['mɛnəs] *vt* **-aced; -acing** **1** THREATEN : amenazar **2** ENDANGER : poner en peligro

menace[2] *n* : amenaza *f*

menacing ['mɛnəsɪŋli] *adj* : amenazador, amenazante

menagerie [mə'nædʒəri, -'næʒəri] *n* : colección *f* de animales salvajes

mend[1] ['mɛnd] *vt* **1** CORRECT : enmendar, corregir <to mend one's ways : enmendarse> **2** REPAIR : remendar, arreglar, reparar — *vi* HEAL : curarse

mend[2] *n* : remiendo *m*

mendicant ['mɛndɪkənt] *n* BEGGAR : mendigo *m,* -ga *f*

menhaden [mɛn'heɪdən, mən-] *ns & pl* : pez *m* de la misma familia que los arenques

menial[1] ['mi:niəl] *adj* : servil, bajo

menial[2] *n* : sirviente *m,* -ta *f*

meningitis [,mɛnən'dʒaɪţəs] *n, pl* **-gitides** [-'dʒɪţə,di:z] : meningitis *f*

menopause ['mɛnə,pɔz] *n* : menopausia *f*

menorah [mə'norə] *n* : candelabro *m* (usado en los oficios religiosos judíos)

menstrual ['mɛntstrʊəl] *adj* : menstrual

menstruate ['mɛntstrʊ,eɪt] *vi* **-ated; -ating** : menstruar

menstruation [,mɛntstrʊ'eɪʃən] *n* : menstruación *f*

mental ['mɛntəl] *adj* : mental <mental hospital : hospital psiquiátrico> — **mentally** *adv*

mentality [mɛn'tæləţi] *n, pl* **-ties** : mentalidad *f*

menthol ['mɛn,θɔl, -,θo:l] *n* : mentol *m*

mentholated [,mɛntθə,leɪţəd] *adj* : mentolado

mention[1] ['mɛntʃən] *vt* : mencionar, mentar, referirse a <don't mention it! : ¡de nada!, ¡no hay de qué!>

mention[2] *n* : mención *f*

mentor ['mɛn,tɔr, 'mɛntər] *n* : mentor *m*

menu ['mɛn,ju:] *n* **1** : menú *m,* carta *f* (en un restaurante) **2** : menú *m* (de computadoras)

meow[1] [mi:'aʊ] *vi* : maullar

meow[2] *n* : maullido *m,* miau *m*

mercantile ['mərkən,ti:l, -,taɪl] *adj* : mercantil

mercenary[1] ['mərsən,ɛri] *adj* : mercenario

mercenary[2] *n, pl* **-naries** : mercenario *m,* -ria *f*

merchandise ['mərtʃən,daɪz, -,daɪs] *n* : mercancía *f,* mercadería *f*

merchandiser ['mərtʃən,daɪzər] *n* : comerciante *mf;* vendedor *m,* -dora *f*

merchant ['mərtʃənt] *n* : comerciante *mf*

merchant marine *n* : marina *f* mercante

merciful ['mərsɪfəl] *adj* : misericordioso, clemente

mercifully ['mərsɪfli] *adv* **1** : con misericordia, con compasión **2** FORTUNATELY : afortunadamente

merciless ['mərsɪləs] *adj* : despiadado — **mercilessly** *adv*
mercurial [,mər'kjʊriəl] *adj* TEMPERAMENTAL : temperamental, volátil
mercury ['mərkjəri] *n, pl* **-ries** : mercurio *m*
Mercury *n* : Mercurio *m*
mercy ['mərsi] *n, pl* **-cies 1** CLEMENCY : misericordia *f,* clemencia *f* **2** BLESSING : bendición *f*
mere ['mɪr] *adj, superlative* **merest** : mero, simple
merely ['mɪrli] *adv* : solamente, simplemente
merge ['mərdʒ] *v* **merged; merging** *vi* : unirse, fusionarse (dícese de las compañías), confluir (dícese de los ríos, las calles, etc.) — *vt* : unir, fusionar, combinar
merger ['mərdʒər] *n* : unión *f,* fusión *f*
meridian [mə'rɪdiən] *n* : meridiano *m*
meringue [mə'ræŋ] *n* : merengue *m*
merino [mə'ri:no] *n, pl* **-nos 1** : merino *m,* -na *f* **2** *or* **merino wool** : lana *f* merino
merit[1] ['mɛrət] *vt* : merecer, ser digno de
merit[2] *n* : mérito *m,* valor *m*
meritorious [,mɛrə'toriəs] *adj* : meritorio
mermaid ['mər,meɪd] *n* : sirena *f*
merriment ['mɛrɪmənt] *n* : alegría *f,* júbilo *m,* regocijo *m*
merry ['mɛri] *adj* **-rier; -est** : alegre — **merrily** ['mɛrəli] *adv*
merry–go–round ['mɛrigo,raʊnd] *n* : carrusel *m,* tiovivo *m*
merrymaker ['mɛri,meɪkər] *n* : juerguista *mf*
merrymaking ['mɛri,meɪkɪŋ] *n* : juerga *f*
mesa ['meɪsə] *n* : mesa *f*
mesdames → **madam, Mrs.**
mesh[1] ['mɛʃ] *vi* **1** ENGAGE : engranar (dícese de las piezas mecánicas) **2** TANGLE : enredarse **3** COORDINATE : coordinarse, combinar
mesh[2] *n* **1** : malla *f* <wire mesh : malla metálica> **2** NETWORK : red *f* **3** MESHING : engranaje *m* <in mesh : engranado>
mesmerize ['mɛzmə,raɪz] *vt* **-ized; -izing 1** HYPNOTIZE : hipnotizar **2** FASCINATE : cautivar, embelesar, fascinar
mess[1] ['mɛs] *vt* **1** SOIL : ensuciar **2 to mess up** DISARRANGE : desordenar, desarreglar **3 to mess up** BUNGLE : echar a perder — *vi* **1** PUTTER : entretenerse **2** INTERFERE : meterse, entrometerse <don't mess with me : no te metas conmigo>
mess[2] *n* **1** : rancho *m* (para soldados, etc.) **2** DISORDER : desorden *m* <your room is a mess : tienes el cuarto hecho un desastre> **3** CONFUSION, TURMOIL : confusión *f,* embrollo *m,* lío *m fam*
message ['mɛsɪdʒ] *n* : mensaje *m,* recado *m*
messenger ['mɛsəndʒər] *n* : mensajero *m,* -ra *f*
Messiah [mə'saɪə] *n* : Mesías *m*
Messrs. → **Mr.**
messy ['mɛsi] *adj* **messier; -est** UNTIDY : desordenado, sucio
met → **meet**
metabolic [,mɛt̬ə'bɑlɪk] *adj* : metabólico
metabolism [mə'tæbə,lɪzəm] *n* : metabolismo *m*
metabolize [mə'tæbə,laɪz] *vt* **-lized; -lizing** : metabolizar
metal ['mɛt̬əl] *n* : metal *m*
metallic [mə'tælɪk] *adj* : metálico
metallurgical [,mɛt̬əl'ərdʒɪkəl] *adj* : metalúrgico
metallurgy ['mɛt̬əl,ərdʒi] *n* : metalurgia *f*
metalwork ['mɛt̬əl,wərk] *n* : objeto *m* de metal
metalworking ['mɛt̬əl,wərkɪŋ] *n* : metalistería *f*
metamorphosis [,mɛt̬ə'mɔrfəsɪs] *n, pl* **-phoses** [-,si:z] : metamorfosis *f*
metaphor ['mɛt̬ə,fɔr, -fər] *n* : metáfora *f*
metaphoric [,mɛt̬ə'fɔrɪk] *or* **metaphorical** [-ɪkəl] *adj* : metafórico
metaphysical [,mɛt̬ə'fɪzəkəl] *adj* : metafísico
metaphysics [,mɛt̬ə'fɪzɪks] *n* : metafísica *f*
mete ['mi:t] *vt* **meted; meting** ALLOT : repartir, distribuir <to mete out punishment : imponer castigos>
meteor ['mi:t̬iər, -t̬i:,ɔr] *n* : meteoro *m*
meteoric [,mi:t̬i'ɔrɪk] *adj* : meteórico
meteorite ['mi:t̬iə,raɪt] *n* : meteorito *m*
meteorologic [,mi:t̬i,ɔrə'lɑdʒɪk] *or* **meteorological** [-'lɑdʒɪkəl] *adj* : meteorológico
meteorologist [,mi:t̬iə'rɑlədʒɪst] *n* : meteorólogo *m,* -ga *f*
meteorology [,mi:t̬iə'rɑlədʒi] *n* : meteorología *f*
meter ['mi:t̬ər] *n* **1** : metro *m* <it measures 2 meters : mide 2 metros> **2** : contador *m,* medidor *m* (de electricidad, etc.) <parking meter : parquímetro> **3** : metro *m* (en literatura o música)
methane ['mɛ,θeɪn] *n* : metano *m*
method ['mɛθəd] *n* : método *m*
methodical [mə'θɑdɪkəl] *adj* : metódico — **methodically** *adv*
meticulous [mə'tɪkjələs] *adj* : meticuloso — **meticulously** *adv*
meticulousness [mə'tɪkjələsnəs] *n* : meticulosidad *f*
metric ['mɛtrɪk] *or* **metrical** [-trɪkəl] *adj* : métrico
metric system *n* : sistema *m* métrico
metronome ['mɛtrə,no:m] *n* : metrónomo *m*
metropolis [mə'trɑpələs] *n* : metrópoli *f,* metrópolis *f*
metropolitan [,mɛtrə'pɑlətən] *adj* : metropolitano

mettle [ˈmɛtəl] *n* : temple *m,* valor *m* <on one's mettle : dispuesto a mostrar su valía>
Mexican [ˈmɛksɪkən] *n* : mexicano *m,* -na *f* — **Mexican** *adj*
mezzanine [ˈmɛzəˌniːn, ˌmɛzəˈniːn] *n* **1** : entrepiso *m,* entresuelo *m* **2** : primer piso *m* (de un teatro)
miasma [maɪˈæzmə] *n* : miasma *m*
mica [ˈmaɪkə] *n* : mica *f*
mice → **mouse**
micro [ˈmaɪkro] *adj* : muy pequeño, microscópico
microbe [ˈmaɪˌkroːb] *n* : microbio *m*
microbiology [ˌmaɪkrobaɪˈɑlədʒi] *n* : microbiología *f*
microcomputer [ˈmaɪkrokəmˌpjuːtər] *n* : microcomputadora *f*
microcosm [ˈmaɪkroˌkɑzəm] *n* : microcosmo *m*
microfilm [ˈmaɪkroˌfɪlm] *n* : microfilm *m*
micrometer [maɪˈkrɑmətər] *n* : micrómetro *m*
micron [ˈmaɪˌkrɑn] *n* : micrón *m*
microorganism [ˌmaɪkroˈɔrgəˌnɪzəm] *n* : microorganismo *m,* microbio *m*
microphone [ˈmaɪkrəˌfoːn] *n* : micrófono *m*
microprocessor [ˈmaɪkroˌprɑˌsɛsər] *n* : microprocesador *m*
microscope [ˈmaɪkrəˌskoːp] *n* : microscopio *m*
microscopic [ˌmaɪkrəˈskɑpɪk] *adj* : microscópico
microscopy [maɪˈkrɑskəpi] *n* : microscopía *f*
microwave [ˈmaɪkrəˌweɪv] *n* **1** : microonda *f* **2** *or* **microwave oven** : microondas *m*
mid [ˈmɪd] *adj* : medio <mid morning : a media mañana> <in mid-August : a mediados de agosto> <in mid ocean : en alta mar>
midair [ˈmɪdˈær] *n* **in ~** : en el aire <to catch in midair : agarrar al vuelo>
midday [ˈmɪdˈdeɪ] *n* NOON : mediodía *m*
middle[1] [ˈmɪdəl] *adj* **1** CENTRAL : medio, del medio, de en medio **2** INTERMEDIATE : intermedio, mediano <middle age : la mediana edad>
middle[2] *n* **1** CENTER : medio *m,* centro *m* <fold it down the middle : dóblalo por la mitad> **2 in the middle of** : en medio de (un espacio), a mitad de (una actividad) <in the middle of the month : a mediados del mes>
Middle Ages *npl* : Edad *f* Media
middle class *n* : clase *f* media
middleman [ˈmɪdəlˌmæn] *n, pl* **-men** [-mən, -ˌmɛn] : intermediario *m,* -ria *f*
middling [ˈmɪdlɪŋ, -lən] *adj* **1** MEDIUM, MIDDLE : mediano **2** MEDIOCRE : mediocre, regular
midge [ˈmɪdʒ] *n* : mosca *f* pequeña
midget [ˈmɪdʒət] *n* **1** : enano *m,* -na *f* (persona) **2** : cosa *f* diminuta
midland [ˈmɪdlənd, -ˌlænd] *n* : región *f* central (de un país)
midnight [ˈmɪdˌnaɪt] *n* : medianoche *f*
midpoint [ˈmɪdˌpɔɪnt] *n* : punto *m* medio, término *m* medio
midriff [ˈmɪdˌrɪf] *n* : diafragma *m*
midshipman [ˈmɪdˌʃɪpmən, ˌmɪdˈʃɪp-] *n, pl* **-men** [-mən, -ˌmɛn] : guardiamarina *m*
midst[1] [ˈmɪdst] *n* : medio *m* <in our midst : entre nosotros> <in the midst of : en medio de>
midst[2] *prep* : entre
midstream [ˈmɪdˈstriːm, -ˌstriːm] *n* : medio *m* de la corriente <in the midstream of his career : en medio de su carrera>
midsummer [ˈmɪdˈsʌmər, -ˌsʌ-] *n* : pleno verano *m*
midtown [ˈmɪdˌtaʊn] *n* : centro *m* (de una ciudad)
midway [ˈmɪdˌweɪ] *adv* HALFWAY : a mitad de camino
midweek [ˈmɪdˌwiːk] *n* : medio *m* de la semana <in midweek : a media semana>
midwife [ˈmɪdˌwaɪf] *n, pl* **-wives** [-ˌwaɪvz] : partera *f,* comadrona *f*
midwinter [ˈmɪdˈwɪntər, -ˌwin-] *n* : pleno invierno *m*
midyear [ˈmɪdˌjɪr] *n* : medio *m* del año <at midyear : a mediados del año>
mien [ˈmiːn] *n* : aspecto *m,* porte *m,* semblante *m*
miff [ˈmɪf] *vt* : ofender
might[1] [ˈmaɪt] (*used to express permission or possibility or as a polite alternative to* **may**) → **may** <it might be true : podría ser verdad> <might I speak with Sarah? : ¿se puede hablar con Sarah?>
might[2] *n* : fuerza *f,* poder *m*
mightily [ˈmaɪtəli] *adv* : con mucha fuerza, poderosamente
mighty[1] [ˈmaɪti] *adv* VERY : muy <mighty good : muy bueno, buenísimo>
mighty[2] *adj* **mightier; -est 1** POWERFUL : poderoso, potente **2** GREAT : grande, imponente
migraine [ˈmaɪˌgreɪn] *n* : jaqueca *f,* migraña *f*
migrant [ˈmaɪgrənt] *n* : trabajador *m,* -dora *f* ambulante
migrate [ˈmaɪˌgreɪt] *vi* **-grated; -grating** : emigrar
migration [maɪˈgreɪʃən] *n* : migración *f*
migratory [ˈmaɪgrəˌtori] *adj* : migratorio
mild [ˈmaɪld] *adj* **1** GENTLE : apacible, suave <a mild disposition : un temperamento suave> **2** LIGHT : leve, ligero <a mild punishment : un castigo leve, un castigo poco severo> **3** TEMPERATE : templado (dícese del clima) — **mildly** *adv*

mildew[1] [ˈmɪl,duː, -,djuː] *vi* : enmohecerse
mildew[2] *n* : moho *m*
mildness [ˈmaɪldnəs] *n* : apacibilidad *f,* suavidad *f*
mile [ˈmaɪl] *n* : milla *f*
mileage [ˈmaɪlɪdʒ] *n* **1** ALLOWANCE : viáticos *mpl* (pagados por milla recorrida) **2** : distancia *f* recorrida (en millas), kilometraje *m*
milestone [ˈmaɪl,stoːn] *n* LANDMARK : hito *m,* jalón *m* <a milestone in his life : un hito en su vida>
milieu [miːlˈjuː, -ˈjø] *n, pl* **-lieus** *or* **-lieux** [-ˈjuːz, -ˈjø] SURROUNDINGS : entorno *m,* medio *m,* ambiente *m*
militant[1] [ˈmɪlətənt] *adj* : militante, combativo
militant[2] *n* : militante *mf*
militarism [ˈmɪlətə,rɪzəm] *n* : militarismo *m*
militaristic [,mɪlətəˈrɪstɪk] *adj* : militarista
military[1] [ˈmɪlə,tɛri] *adj* : militar
military[2] *n* **the military** : las fuerzas armadas
militia [məˈlɪʃə] *n* : milicia *f*
milk[1] [ˈmɪlk] *vt* **1** : ordeñar (una vaca, etc.) **2** EXPLOIT : explotar
milk[2] *n* : leche *f*
milkman [ˈmɪlk,mæn, -mən] *n, pl* **-men** [-mən, -,mɛn] : lechero *m*
milk shake *n* : batido *m,* licuado *m*
milkweed [ˈmɪlk,wiːd] *n* : algodoncillo *m*
milky [ˈmɪlki] *adj* **milkier; -est** : lechoso
Milky Way *n* : Vía *f* Láctea
mill[1] [ˈmɪl] *vt* : moler (granos), fresar (metales), acordonar (monedas) — *vi* **to mill about** : arremolinarse
mill[2] *n* **1** : molino *m* (para moler granos) **2** FACTORY : fábrica *f* <textile mill : fábrica textil> **3** GRINDER : molinillo *m*
millennium [məˈlɛniəm] *n, pl* **-nia** [-niə] *or* **-niums** : milenio *m*
miller [ˈmɪlər] *n* : molinero *m,* -ra *f*
millet [ˈmɪlət] *n* : mijo *m*
milligram [ˈmɪlə,græm] *n* : miligramo *m*
milliliter [ˈmɪlə,liːtər] *n* : mililitro *m*
millimeter [ˈmɪlə,miːtər] *n* : milímetro *m*
milliner [ˈmɪlənər] *n* : sombrerero *m,* -ra *f* (de señoras)
millinery [ˈmɪlə,nɛri] *n* : sombreros *mpl* de señora
million[1] [ˈmɪljən] *adj* **a million** : un millón de
million[2] *n, pl* **millions** *or* **million** : millón *m*
millionaire [,mɪljəˈnær, ˈmɪljə,nær] *n* : millonario *m,* -ria *f*
millionth[1] [ˈmɪljənθ] *adj* : millonésimo
millionth[2] *n* : millonésimo *m*
millipede [ˈmɪlə,piːd] *n* : milpiés *m*
millstone [ˈmɪl,stoːn] *n* : rueda *f* de molino, muela *f*
mime[1] [ˈmaɪm] *v* **mimed; miming** *vt* MIMIC : imitar, remedar — *vi* PANTOMIME : hacer la mímica
mime[2] *n* **1** : mimo *mf* **2** PANTOMIME : pantomima *f*
mimeograph [ˈmɪmiə,græf] *n* : mimeógrafo *m*
mimic[1] [ˈmɪmɪk] *vt* **-icked; -icking** : imitar, remedar
mimic[2] *n* : imitador *m,* -dora *f*
mimicry [ˈmɪmɪkri] *n, pl* **-ries** : mímica *f,* imitación *f*
minaret [,mɪnəˈrɛt] *n* : alminar *m,* minarete *m*
mince [ˈmɪnts] *v* **minced; mincing** *vt* **1** CHOP : picar, moler (carne) **2 not to mince one's words** : no tener uno pelos en la lengua — *vi* : caminar de manera afectada
mincemeat [ˈmɪnts,miːt] *n* : mezcla *f* de fruta picada, sebo, y especias
mind[1] [ˈmaɪnd] *vt* **1** TEND : cuidar, atender <mind the children : cuida a los niños> **2** OBEY : obedecer **3** : preocuparse por, sentirse molestado por <I don't mind his jokes : sus bromas no me molestan> **4** : tener cuidado con <mind the ladder! : ¡cuidado con la escalera!> — *vi* **1** OBEY : obedecer **2** CARE : importarle a uno <I don't mind : no me importa, me es igual>
mind[2] *n* **1** MEMORY : memoria *f,* recuerdo *m* <keep it in mind : téngalo en cuenta> **2** : mente *f* <the mind and the body : la mente y el cuerpo> **3** INTENTION : intención *f,* propósito *m* <to have a mind to do something : tener intención de hacer algo> **4** : razón *f* <he's out of his mind : está loco> **5** OPINION : opinión *f* <to change one's mind : cambiar de opinión> **6** INTELLECT : capacidad *f* intelectual
minded [ˈmaɪndəd] *adj* **1** (*used in combination*) <narrow-minded : de mentalidad cerrada> <health-minded : preocupado por la salud> **2** INCLINED : inclinado
mindful [ˈmaɪndfəl] *adj* AWARE : consciente — **mindfully** *adv*
mindless [ˈmaɪndləs] *adj* **1** SENSELESS : estúpido, sin sentido <mindless violence : violencia sin sentido> **2** HEEDLESS : inconsciente
mindlessly [ˈmaɪndləsli] *adv* **1** SENSELESSLY : sin sentido **2** HEEDLESSLY : inconscientemente
mine[1] [ˈmaɪn] *vt* **mined; mining 1** : extraer (oro, etc.) **2** : minar (con artefactos explosivos)
mine[2] *n* : mina *f* <gold mine : mina de oro>
mine[3] *pron* : mío, mía <that one's mine : ése es el mío> <some friends of mine : unos amigos míos>
minefield [ˈmaɪn:fiːld] *n* : campo *m* de minas
miner [ˈmaɪnər] *n* : minero *m,* -ra *f*

mineral [ˈmɪnərəl] *n* : mineral *m* — **mineral** *adj*

mineralogy [ˌmɪnəˈrɑlədʒi, -ˈræ-] *n* : mineralogía *f*

mingle [ˈmɪŋgəl] *v* **-gled; -gling** *vt* MIX : mezclar — *vi* **1** MIX : mezclarse **2** CIRCULATE : circular

miniature[1] [ˈmɪniəˌtʃʊr, ˈmɪnɪˌtʃʊr, -tʃər] *adj* : en miniatura, diminuto

miniature[2] *n* : miniatura *f*

minibus [ˈmɪniˌbʌs] *n* : microbús *m*, pesera *f Mex*

minicomputer [ˈmɪnikəmˌpjuːṭər] *n* : minicomputadora *f*

minimal [ˈmɪnəməl] *adj* : mínimo

minimally [ˈmɪnəməli] *adv* : en grado mínimo

minimize [ˈmɪnəˌmaɪz] *vt* **-mized; -mizing** : minimizar

minimum[1] [ˈmɪnəməm] *adj* : mínimo

minimum[2] *n, pl* **-ma** [ˈmɪnəmə] *or* **-mums** : mínimo *m*

miniskirt [ˈmɪniˌskərt] *n* : minifalda *f*

minister[1] [ˈmɪnəstər] *vi* **to minister to** : cuidar (de), atender a

minister[2] *n* **1** : pastor *m*, -tora *f* (de una iglesia) **2** : ministro *m*, -tra *f* (en política)

ministerial [ˌmɪnəˈstɪriəl] *adj* : ministerial

ministry [ˈmɪnəstri] *n, pl* **-tries 1** : ministerio *m* (en política) **2** : sacerdocio *m* (en el catolicismo), clerecía *f* (en el protestantismo)

minivan [ˈmɪniˌvæn] *n* : minivan *f*

mink [ˈmɪŋk] *n, pl* **mink** *or* **minks** : visón *m*

minnow [ˈmɪnoː] *n, pl* **-nows** : pececillo *m* de agua dulce

minor[1] [ˈmaɪnər] *adj* : menor

minor[2] *n* **1** : menor *mf* (de edad) **2** : asignatura *f* secundaria (de estudios)

minority [məˈnɔrəṭi, maɪ-] *n, pl* **-ties** : minoría *f*

minstrel [ˈmɪn*t*strəl] *n* : juglar *m*, trovador *m* (en el medioevo)

mint[1] [ˈmɪnt] *vt* : acuñar

mint[2] *adj* : sin usar <in mint condition : como nuevo>

mint[3] *n* **1** : menta *f* <mint tea : té de menta> **2** : pastilla *f* de menta **3** : casa *f* de la moneda <the U.S. Mint : la casa de la moneda de los EE.UU.> **4** FORTUNE : dineral *m*, fortuna *f*

minuet [ˌmɪnjʊˈɛt] *n* : minué *m*

minus[1] [ˈmaɪnəs] *n* **1** : cantidad *f* negativa **2 minus sign** : signo *m* de menos

minus[2] *prep* **1** : menos <four minus two : cuatro menos dos> **2** WITHOUT : sin <minus his hat : sin su sombrero>

minuscule *or* **miniscule** [ˈmɪnəsˌkjuːl, mɪˈnʌs-] *adj* : minúsculo

minute[1] [maɪˈnuːt, mɪ-, -ˈnjuːt] *adj* **-nuter; -est 1** TINY : diminuto, minúsculo **2** DETAILED : minucioso

minute[2] [ˈmɪnət] *n* **1** : minuto *m* <ten minutes late : diez minutos de retraso> **2** MOMENT : momento *m* **3 minutes** *npl* : actas *fpl* (de una reunión)

minutely [maɪˈnuːtli, mɪ-, -ˈnjuːt-] *adv* : minuciosamente

miracle [ˈmɪrɪkəl] *n* : milagro *m*

miraculous [məˈrækjələs] *adj* : milagroso — **miraculously** *adv*

mirage [mɪˈrɑʒ, *chiefly Brit* ˈmɪrˌɑʒ] *n* : espejismo *m*

mire[1] [ˈmaɪr] *vi* **mired; miring** : atascarse

mire[2] *n* : lodo *m*, barro *m*, fango *m*

mirror[1] [ˈmɪrər] *vt* : reflejar

mirror[2] *n* : espejo *m*

mirth [ˈmərθ] *n* : alegría *f*, regocijo *m*

mirthful [ˈmərθfəl] *adj* : alegre, regocijado

misanthrope [ˈmɪsənˌθroːp] *n* : misántropo *m*, -pa *f*

misanthropic [ˌmɪsənˈθrɑpɪk] *adj* : misantrópico

misanthropy [mɪˈsænθrəpi] *n* : misantropía *f*

misapprehend [ˌmɪsˌæprəˈhɛnd] *vt* : entender mal

misapprehension [ˌmɪsˌæprəˈhɛntʃən] *n* : malentendido *m*

misappropriate [ˌmɪsəˈproːpriˌeɪt] *vt* **-ated; -ating** : malversar

misbegotten [ˌmɪsbiˈgɑtən] *adj* **1** ILLEGITIMATE : ilegítimo **2** : mal concebido <misbegotten laws : leyes mal concebidas>

misbehave [ˌmɪsbiˈheɪv] *vi* **-haved; -having** : portarse mal

misbehavior [ˌmɪsbiˈheɪvjər] *n* : mala conducta *f*

miscalculate [mɪsˈkælkjəˌleɪt] *v* **-lated; -lating** : calcular mal

miscalculation [mɪsˌkælkjəˈleɪʃən] *n* : error *m* de cálculo, mal cálculo *m*

miscarriage [ˌmɪsˈkærɪdʒ, ˈmɪsˌkærɪdʒ] *n* **1** : aborto *m* **2** FAILURE : fracaso *m*, malogro *m* <a miscarriage of justice : una injusticia, un error judicial>

miscarry [ˌmɪsˈkæri, ˈmɪsˌkæri] *vi* **-ried; -rying 1** ABORT : abortar **2** FAIL : malograrse, fracasar

miscellaneous [ˌmɪsəˈleɪniəs] *adj* : misceláneo

miscellany [ˈmɪsəˌleɪni] *n, pl* **-nies** : miscelánea *f*

mischance [mɪsˈtʃæn*t*s] *n* : desgracia *f*, infortunio *m*, mala suerte *f*

mischief [ˈmɪstʃəf] *n* : diabluras *fpl*, travesuras *fpl*

mischievous [ˈmɪstʃəvəs] *adj* : travieso, pícaro

mischievously [ˈmɪstʃəvəsli] *adv* : de manera traviesa

misconception [ˌmɪskənˈsɛpʃən] *n* : concepto *m* erróneo, idea *f* falsa

misconduct [mɪsˈkɑndəkt] *n* : mala conducta *f*

misconstrue [ˌmɪskənˈstruː] *vt* **-strued; -struing** : malinterpretar

misdeed [mɪsˈdiːd] *n* : fechoría *f*

misdemeanor [ˌmɪsdɪˈmiːnər] *n* : delito *m* menor

miser [ˈmaɪzər] *n* : avaro *m*, -ra *f*; tacaño *m*, -ña *f*

miserable [ˈmɪzərəbəl] *adj* **1** UNHAPPY : triste, desdichado **2** WRETCHED : miserable, desgraciado <a miserable hut : una choza miserable> **3** UNPLEASANT : desagradable, malo <miserable weather : tiempo malísimo> **4** CONTEMPTIBLE : despreciable, mísero <for a miserable $10 : por unos míseros diez dólares>

miserably [ˈmɪzərəbli] *adv* **1** SADLY : tristemente **2** WRETCHEDLY : miserablemente, lamentablemente **3** UNFORTUNATELY : desgraciadamente

miserly [ˈmaɪzərli] *adj* : avaro, tacaño

misery [ˈmɪzəri] *n, pl* **-eries** : miseria *f*, sufrimiento *m*

misfire [mɪsˈfaɪr] *vi* **-fired; -firing** : fallar

misfit [ˈmɪsˌfɪt] *n* : inadaptado *m*, -da *f*

misfortune [mɪsˈfɔrtʃən] *n* : desgracia *f*, desventura *f*, infortunio *m*

misgiving [mɪsˈgɪvɪŋ] *n* : duda *f*, recelo *m*

misguided [mɪsˈgaɪdəd] *adj* : desacertado, equivocado, mal informado

mishap [ˈmɪsˌhæp] *n* : contratiempo *m*, percance *m*, accidente *m*

misinform [ˌmɪsɪnˈfɔrm] *vt* : informar mal

misinterpret [ˌmɪsɪnˈtərprət] *vt* : malinterpretar

misinterpretation [ˌmɪsɪnˌtərprəˈteɪʃən] *n* : mala interpretación *f*, malentendido *m*

misjudge [mɪsˈdʒʌdʒ] *vt* **-judged; -judging** : juzgar mal

mislay [mɪsˈleɪ] *vt* **-laid** [-leɪd]; **-laying** : extraviar, perder

mislead [mɪsˈliːd] *vt* **-led** [-ˈlɛd]; **-leading** : engañar

misleading [mɪsˈliːdɪŋ] *adj* : engañoso

mismanage [mɪsˈmænɪdʒ] *vt* **-aged; -aging** : administrar mal

mismanagement [mɪsˈmænɪdʒmənt] *n* : mala administración *f*

misnomer [mɪsˈnoːmər] *n* : nombre *m* inapropiado

misogynist [mɪˈsɑdʒənɪst] *n* : misógino *m*

misplace [mɪsˈpleɪs] *vt* **-placed; -placing** : extraviar, perder

misprint [ˈmɪsˌprɪnt, mɪsˈ-] *n* : errata *f*, error *m* de imprenta

mispronounce [ˌmɪsprəˈnaʊnts] *vt* **-nounced; -nouncing** : pronunciar mal

mispronunciation [ˌmɪsprəˌnʌntsiˈeɪʃən] *n* : pronunciación *f* incorrecta

misquote [mɪsˈkwoːt] *vt* **-quoted; -quoting** : citar incorrectamente

misread [mɪsˈriːd] *vt* **-read; -reading** **1** : leer mal <she misread the sentence : leyó mal la frase> **2** MISUNDERSTAND : malinterpretar <they misread his intention : malinterpretaron su intención>

misrepresent [ˌmɪsˌrɛprɪˈzɛnt] *vt* : distorsionar, falsear, tergiversar

misrule[1] [mɪsˈruːl] *vt* **-ruled; -ruling** : gobernar mal

misrule[2] *n* : mal gobierno *m*

miss[1] [ˈmɪs] *vt* **1** : errar, faltar <to miss the target : no dar en el blanco> **2** : no encontrar, perder <they missed each other : no se encontraron> <I missed the plane : perdí el avión> **3** : echar de menos, extrañar <we miss him a lot : lo echamos mucho de menos> **4** OVERLOOK : pasar por alto, perder (una oportunidad, etc.) **5** AVOID : evitar <they just missed hitting the tree : por muy poco chocan contra el árbol> **6** OMIT : saltarse <he missed breakfast : se saltó el desayuno>

miss[2] *n* **1** : fallo *m* (de un tiro, etc.) **2** FAILURE : fracaso *m* **3** : señorita *f* <Miss Jones : la señorita Jones> <excuse me, miss : perdone, señorita>

missal [ˈmɪsəl] *n* : misal *m*

misshapen [mɪˈʃeɪpən] *adj* : deforme

missile [ˈmɪsəl] *n* **1** : misil *m* <guided missile : misil guiado> **2** PROJECTILE : proyectil *m*

missing [ˈmɪsɪŋ] *adj* **1** ABSENT : ausente <who's missing? : ¿quién falta?> **2** LOST : perdido, desaparecido <missing persons : los desaparecidos>

mission [ˈmɪʃən] *n* **1** : misión *f* (mandada por una iglesia) **2** DELEGATION : misión *f*, delegación *f*, embajada *f* **3** TASK : misión *f*

missionary[1] [ˈmɪʃəˌnɛri] *adj* : misionero

missionary[2] *n, pl* **-aries** : misionero *m*, -ra *f*

missive [ˈmɪsɪv] *n* : misiva *f*

misspell [mɪsˈspɛl] *vt* : escribir mal

misspelling [mɪsˈspɛlɪŋ] *n* : falta *f* de ortografía

misstep [ˈmɪsˌstɛp] *n* : traspié *m*, tropezón *m*

mist [ˈmɪst] *n* **1** HAZE : neblina *f*, niebla *f* **2** SPRAY : rocío *m*

mistake[1] [mɪˈsteɪk] *vt* **-took** [-ˈstʊk]; **-taken** [-ˈsteɪkən]; **-taking** **1** MISINTERPRET : malinterpretar **2** CONFUSE : confundir <he mistook her for Clara : la confundió con Clara>

mistake[2] *n* **1** MISUNDERSTANDING : malentendido *m*, confusión *f* **2** ERROR : error *m* <I made a mistake : me equivoqué, cometí un error>

mistaken [mɪˈsteɪkən] *adj* WRONG : equivocado — **mistakenly** *adv*

mister [ˈmɪstər] *n* : señor *m* <watch out, mister : cuidado, señor>

mistiness [ˈmɪstinəs] *n* : nebulosidad *f*

mistletoe [ˈmɪsəlˌtoː] *n* : muérdago *m*

mistreat [mɪsˈtriːt] *vt* : maltratar

mistreatment [mɪsˈtriːtmənt] *n* : maltrato *m*, abuso *m*

mistress [ˈmɪstrəs] *n* **1** : dueña *f,* señora *f* (de una casa) **2** LOVER : amante *f*

mistrust[1] [mɪsˈtrʌst] *vt* : desconfiar de

mistrust[2] *n* : desconfianza *f*

mistrustful [mɪsˈtrʌstfəl] *adj* : desconfiado

misty [ˈmɪsti] *adj* **mistier; -est 1** : neblinoso, nebuloso **2** TEARFUL : lloroso

misunderstand [ˌmɪsˌʌndərˈstænd] *vt* **-stood** [-ˈstʊd]; **-standing 1** : entender mal **2** MISINTERPRET : malinterpretar <don't misunderstand me : no me malinterpretes>

misunderstanding [ˌmɪsˌʌndərˈstændɪŋ] *n* **1** MISINTERPRETATION : malentendido *m* **2** DISAGREEMENT, QUARREL : disputa *f,* discusión *f*

misuse[1] [mɪsˈjuːz] *vt* **-used; -using 1** : emplear mal **2** ABUSE, MISTREAT : abusar de, maltratar

misuse[2] [mɪsˈjuːs] *n* **1** : mal empleo *m,* mal uso *m* **2** WASTE : derroche *m,* despilfarro *m* **3** ABUSE : abuso *m*

mite [ˈmaɪt] *n* **1** : ácaro *m* **2** BIT : poco *m* <a mite tired : un poquito cansado>

miter *or* **mitre** [ˈmaɪt̬ər] *n* **1** : mitra *f* (de un obispo) **2** *or* **miter joint** : inglete *m*

mitigate [ˈmɪt̬əˌgeɪt] *vt* **-gated; -gating** : mitigar, aliviar

mitigation [ˌmɪt̬əˈgeɪʃən] *n* : mitigación *f,* alivio *m*

mitosis [maɪˈtoːsɪs] *n, pl* **-toses** [-ˌsiːz] : mitosis *f*

mitt [ˈmɪt] *n* : manopla *f,* guante *m* (de béisbol)

mitten [ˈmɪtən] *n* : manopla *f,* mitón *m*

mix[1] [ˈmɪks] *vt* **1** COMBINE : mezclar **2** STIR : remover, revolver **3 to mix up** CONFUSE : confundir — *vi* : mezclarse

mix[2] *n* : mezcla *f*

mixer [ˈmɪksər] *n* **1** : batidora *f* (de la cocina) **2 cement mixer** : hormigonera *f*

mixture [ˈmɪkstʃər] *n* : mezcla *f*

mix–up [ˈmɪksˌʌp] *n* CONFUSION : confusión *f,* lío *m fam*

mnemonic [nɪˈmɑnɪk] *adj* : mnemónico

moan[1] [ˈmoːn] *vi* : gemir

moan[2] *n* : gemido *m*

moat [ˈmoːt] *n* : foso *m*

mob[1] [ˈmɑb] *vt* **mobbed; mobbing 1** ATTACK : atacar en masa **2** HOUND : acosar, rodear

mob[2] *n* **1** THRONG : multitud *f,* turba *f,* muchedumbre *f* **2** GANG : pandilla *f*

mobile[1] [ˈmoːbəl, -ˌbiːl, -ˌbaɪl] *adj* : móvil <mobile home : caravana, casa rodante>

mobile[2] [ˈmoˌbiːl] *n* : móvil *m*

mobility [moˈbɪlət̬i] *n* : movilidad *f*

mobilize [ˈmoːbəˌlaɪz] *vt* **-lized; -lizing** : movilizar

moccasin [ˈmɑkəsən] *n* **1** : mocasín *m* **2** *or* **water moccasin** : serpiente *f* venenosa de Norteamérica

mocha [ˈmoːkə] *n* **1** : mezcla *f* de café y chocolate **2** : color *m* chocolate

mock[1] [ˈmɑk, ˈmɔk] *vt* **1** RIDICULE : burlarse de, mofarse de **2** MIMIC : imitar, remedar (de manera burlona)

mock[2] *adj* **1** SIMULATED : simulado **2** PHONY : falso

mockery [ˈmɑkəri, ˈmɔ-] *n, pl* **-eries 1** JEER, TAUNT : burla *f,* mofa *f* <to make a mockery of : burlarse de> **2** FAKE : imitación *f* (burlona)

mockingbird [ˈmɑkɪŋˌbərd, ˈmɔ-] *n* : sinsonte *m*

mode [ˈmoːd] *n* **1** FORM : modo *m,* forma *f* **2** MANNER : modo *m,* manera *f,* estilo *m* **3** FASHION : moda *f*

model[1] [ˈmɑdəl] *v* **-eled** *or* **-elled; -eling** *or* **-elling** *vt* SHAPE : modelar — *vi* : trabajar de modelo

model[2] *adj* **1** EXEMPLARY : modelo, ejemplar <a model student : un estudiante modelo> **2** MINIATURE : en miniatura

model[3] *n* **1** PATTERN : modelo *m* **2** MINIATURE : modelo *m,* miniatura *f* **3** EXAMPLE : modelo *m,* ejemplo *m* **4** MANNEQUIN : modelo *mf* **5** DESIGN : modelo *m* <the '97 model : el modelo '97>

modem [ˈmoːdəm, -ˌdɛm] *n* : módem *m*

moderate[1] [ˈmɑdəˌreɪt] *v* **-ated; -ating** *vt* : moderar, temperar — *vi* **1** CALM : moderarse, calmarse **2** : fungir como moderador (en un debate, etc.)

moderate[2] [ˈmɑdərət] *adj* : moderado

moderate[3] [ˈmɑdərət] *n* : moderado *m,* -da *f*

moderately [ˈmɑdərətli] *adv* **1** : con moderación **2** FAIRLY : medianamente

moderation [ˌmɑdəˈreɪʃən] *n* : moderación *f*

moderator [ˈmɑdəˌreɪt̬ər] *n* : moderador *m,* -dora *f*

modern [ˈmɑdərn] *adj* : moderno

modernity [məˈdərnət̬i] *n* : modernidad *f*

modernization [ˌmɑdərnəˈzeɪʃən] *n* : modernización *f*

modernize [ˈmɑdərˌnaɪz] *v* **-ized; -izing** *vt* : modernizar — *vi* : modernizarse

modest [ˈmɑdəst] *adj* **1** HUMBLE : modesto **2** DEMURE : recatado, pudoroso **3** MODERATE : modesto, moderado — **modestly** *adv*

modesty [ˈmɑdəsti] *n* : modestia *f*

modicum [ˈmɑdɪkəm] *n* : mínimo *m,* pizca *f*

modification [ˌmɑdəfəˈkeɪʃən] *n* : modificación *f*

modifier [ˈmɑdəˌfaɪər] *n* : modificante *m,* modificador *m*

modify [ˈmɑdəˌfaɪ] *vt* **-fied; -fying** : modificar, calificar (en gramática)

modish [ˈmoːdɪʃ] *adj* STYLISH : a la moda, de moda

modular [ˈmɑdʒələr] *adj* : modular

modulate [ˈmɑdʒəˌleɪt] *vt* **-lated; -lating** : modular

modulation [ˌmɑdʒəˈleɪʃən] *n* : modulación *f*
module [ˈmɑˌdʒuːl] *n* : módulo *m*
mogul [ˈmoːgəl] *n* : magnate *mf;* potentado *m,* -da *f*
mohair [ˈmoːˌhær] *n* : mohair *m*
moist [ˈmɔɪst] *adj* : húmedo
moisten [ˈmɔɪsən] *vt* : humedecer
moistness [ˈmɔɪstnəs] *n* : humedad *f*
moisture [ˈmɔɪstʃər] *n* : humedad *f*
moisturize [ˈmɔɪstʃəˌraɪz] *vt* **-ized; -izing** : humedecer (el aire), humectar (la piel)
moisturizer [ˈmɔɪtʃəˌraɪzər] *n* : crema *f* hidratante, crema *f* humectante
molar [ˈmoːlər] *n* : muela *f,* molar *m*
molasses [məˈlæsəz] *n* : melaza *f*
mold[1] [ˈmoːld] *vt* : moldear, formar (carácter, etc.) — *vi* : enmohecerse <the bread will mold : el pan se enmohecerá>
mold[2] *n* **1** *or* **leaf mold** : mantillo *m* **2** FORM : molde *m* <to break the mold : romper el molde> **3** FUNGUS : moho *m*
molder [ˈmoːldər] *vi* CRUMBLE : desmoronarse
molding [ˈmoːldɪŋ] *n* : moldura *f* (en arquitectura)
moldy [ˈmoːldi] *adj* **moldier; -est** : mohoso
mole [ˈmoːl] *n* **1** : lunar *m* (en la piel) **2** : topo *m* (animal)
molecule [ˈmɑlɪˌkjuːl] *n* : molécula *f* — **molecular** [məˈlɛkjələr] *adj*
molehill [ˈmoːlˌhɪl] *n* : topera *f*
molest [məˈlɛst] *vt* **1** ANNOY, DISTURB : molestar **2** : abusar (sexualmente)
mollify [ˈmɑləˌfaɪ] *vt* **-fied; -fying** : apaciguar, aplacar
mollusk *or* **mollusc** [ˈmɑləsk] *n* : molusco *m*
mollycoddle [ˈmɑliˌkɑdəl] *vt* **-dled; -dling** PAMPER : consentir, mimar
molt [ˈmoːlt] *vi* : mudar, hacer la muda
molten [ˈmoːltən] *adj* : fundido
mom [ˈmɑm, ˈmʌm] *n* : mamá *f*
moment [ˈmoːmənt] *n* **1** INSTANT : momento *m* <one moment, please : un momento, por favor> **2** TIME : momento *m* <at the moment : de momento, actualmente> <from that moment : desde entonces> **3** IMPORTANCE : importancia *f* <of great moment : de gran importancia>
momentarily [ˌmoːmənˈtɛrəli] *adv* **1** : momentáneamente **2** SOON : dentro de poco, pronto
momentary [ˈmoːmənˌtɛri] *adj* : momentáneo
momentous [moˈmɛntəs] *adj* : de suma importancia, fatídico
momentum [moˈmɛntəm] *n, pl* **-ta** [-tə] *or* **-tums 1** : momento *m* (en física) **2** IMPETUS : ímpetu *m,* impulso *m*
monarch [ˈmɑˌnɑrk, -nərk] *n* : monarca *mf*
monarchism [ˈmɑˌnɑrˌkɪzəm, -nər-] *n* : monarquismo *m*
monarchist [ˈmɑˌnɑrkɪst, -nər-] *n* : monárquico *m,* -ca *f*
monarchy [ˈmɑˌnɑrki, -nər-] *n, pl* **-chies** : monarquía *f*
monastery [ˈmɑnəˌstɛri] *n, pl* **-teries** : monasterio *m*
monastic [məˈnæstɪk] *adj* : monástico — **monastically** [-tɪkli] *adv*
Monday [ˈmʌnˌdeɪ, -di] *n* : lunes *m*
monetary [ˈmɑnəˌtɛri, ˈmʌnə-] *adj* : monetario
money [ˈmʌni] *n, pl* **-eys** *or* **-ies** [ˈmʌniz] : dinero *m,* plata *f*
moneyed [ˈmʌnid] *adj* : adinerado
moneylender [ˈmʌniˌlɛndər] *n* : prestamista *mf*
money order *n* : giro *m* postal
Mongolian [mɑnˈgoːliən, mɑŋ-] *n* : mongol *m,* -gola *f* — **Mongolian** *adj*
mongoose [ˈmɑnˌguːs, ˈmɑŋ-] *n, pl* **-gooses** : mangosta *f*
mongrel [ˈmɑŋgrəl, ˈmʌŋ-] *n* **1** : perro *m* mestizo, perro *m* corriente *Mex* **2** HYBRID : híbrido *m*
monitor[1] [ˈmɑnət̬ər] *vt* : controlar, monitorear
monitor[2] *n* **1** : ayudante *mf* (en una escuela) **2** : monitor *m* (de una computadora, etc.)
monk [ˈmʌŋk] *n* : monje *m*
monkey[1] [ˈmʌŋki] *vi* **-keyed; -keying 1 to monkey around** : hacer payasadas, payasear **2 to monkey with** : juguetear con
monkey[2] *n, pl* **-keys** : mono *m,* -na *f*
monkeyshines [ˈmʌŋkiˌʃaɪnz] *npl* PRANKS : picardías *fpl,* travesuras *fpl*
monkey wrench *n* : llave *f* inglesa
monkshood [ˈmʌŋksˌhʊd] *n* : acónito *m*
monocle [ˈmɑnɪkəl] *n* : monóculo *m*
monogamous [məˈnɑgəməs] *adj* : monógamo
monogamy [məˈnɑgəmi] *n* : monogamia *f*
monogram[1] [ˈmɑnəˌgræm] *vt* **-grammed; -gramming** : marcar con monograma <monogrammed towels : toallas con monograma>
monogram[2] *n* : monograma *m*
monograph [ˈmɑnəˌgræf] *n* : monografía *f*
monolingual [ˌmɑnəˈlɪŋgwəl] *adj* : monolingüe
monolith [ˈmɑnəˌlɪθ] *n* : monolito *m*
monolithic [ˌmɑnəˈlɪθɪk] *adj* : monolítico
monologue [ˈmɑnəˌlɔg] *n* : monólogo *m*
monoplane [ˈmɑnəˌpleɪn] *n* : monoplano *m*
monopolize [məˈnɑpəˌlaɪz] *vt* **-lized; -lizing** : monopolizar
monopoly [məˈnɑpəli] *n, pl* **-lies** : monopolio *m*
monosyllabic [ˌmɑnosəˈlæbɪk] *adj* : monosilábico

monosyllable [ˈmɑnoˌsɪləbəl] *n* : monosílabo *m*
monotheism [ˈmɑnoθiːˌɪzəm] *n* : monoteísmo *m*
monotheistic [ˌmɑnoθiːˈɪstɪk] *adj* : monoteísta
monotone [ˈmɑnəˌtoːn] *n* : voz *f* monótona
monotonous [məˈnɑtənəs] *adj* : monótono — **monotonously** *adv*
monotony [məˈnɑtəni] *n* : monotonía *f*, uniformidad *f*
monoxide [məˈnɑkˌsaɪd] *n* : monóxido *m*
monsoon [mɑnˈsuːn] *n* : monzón *m*
monster [ˈmɑntstər] *n* : monstruo *m*
monstrosity [mɑnˈstrɑsəti] *n, pl* **-ties** : monstruosidad *f*
monstrous [ˈmɑntstrəs] *adj* : monstruoso — **monstrously** *adv*
montage [mɑnˈtɑʒ] *n* : montaje *m*
month [ˈmʌnθ] *n* : mes *m*
monthly[1] [ˈmʌnθli] *adv* : mensualmente
monthly[2] *adj* : mensual
monthly[3] *n, pl* **-lies** : publicación *f* mensual
monument [ˈmɑnjəmənt] *n* : monumento *m*
monumental [ˌmɑnjəˈmɛntəl] *adj* : monumental — **monumentally** *adv*
moo[1] [ˈmuː] *vi* : mugir
moo[2] *n* : mugido *m*
mood [ˈmuːd] *n* : humor *m* <to be in a good mood : estar de buen humor> <to be in the mood for : tener ganas de> <to be in no mood for : no estar para>
moodiness [ˈmuːdinəs] *n* **1** SADNESS : melancolía *f*, tristeza *f* **2** : cambios *mpl* de humor, carácter *m* temperamental
moody [ˈmuːdi] *adj* **moodier; -est 1** GLOOMY : melancólico, deprimido **2** TEMPERAMENTAL : temperamental, de humor variable
moon [ˈmuːn] *n* : luna *f*
moonbeam [ˈmuːnˌbiːm] *n* : rayo *m* de luna
moonlight[1] [ˈmuːnˌlaɪt] *vi* : estar pluriempleado
moonlight[2] *n* : claro *m* de luna, luz *f* de la luna
moonlit [ˈmuːnˌlɪt] *adj* : iluminado por la luna <a moonlit night : una noche de luna>
moonshine [ˈmuːnˌʃaɪn] *n* **1** MOONLIGHT : luz *f* de la luna **2** NONSENSE : disparates *mpl*, tonterías *fpl* **3** : whiskey *m* destilado ilegalmente
moor[1] [ˈmʊr, ˈmɔr] *vt* : amarrar
moor[2] *n* : brezal *m*, páramo *m*
mooring [ˈmʊrɪŋ, ˈmɔr-] *n* DOCK : atracadero *m*
moose [ˈmuːs] *ns & pl* : alce *m* (norteamericano)
moot [ˈmuːt] *adj* DEBATABLE : discutible
mop[1] [ˈmɑp] *vt* **mopped; mopping** : trapear
mop[2] *n* : trapeador *m*
mope [ˈmoːp] *vi* **moped; moping** : andar deprimido, quedar abatido
moped [ˈmoːˌpɛd] *n* : ciclomotor *m*
moral[1] [ˈmɔrəl] *adj* : moral <moral judgment : juicio moral> <moral support : apoyo moral> — **morally** *adv*
moral[2] *n* **1** : moraleja *f* (de un cuento, etc.) **2 morals** *npl* : moral *f*, moralidad *f*
morale [məˈræl] *n* : moral *f*
morality [məˈræləti] *n, pl* **-ties** : moralidad *f*
morass [məˈræs] *n* **1** SWAMP : ciénaga *f*, pantano *m* **2** CONFUSION, MESS : lío *m fam*, embrollo *m*
moratorium [ˌmɔrəˈtoriəm] *n, pl* **-riums** *or* **-ria** [-iə] : moratoria *f*
moray [ˈmɔrˌeɪ, məˈreɪ] *n* : morena *f*
morbid [ˈmɔrbɪd] *adj* **1** : mórbido, morboso (en medicina) **2** GRUESOME : morboso, horripilante
morbidity [mɔrˈbɪdəti] *n* : morbosidad *f*
more[1] [ˈmor] *adv* : más <what more can I say? : ¿qué más puedo decir?> <more important : más importante> <once more : una vez más>
more[2] *adj* : más <nothing more than that : nada más que eso> <more work : más trabajo>
more[3] *n* : más *m* <the more you eat, the more you want : cuanto más comes, tanto más quieres>
more[4] *pron* : más <more were found : se encontraron más>
moreover [morˈoːvər] *adv* : además
mores [ˈmɔrˌeɪz, -iːz] *npl* CUSTOMS : costumbres *fpl*, tradiciones *fpl*
morgue [ˈmɔrg] *n* : morgue *f*
moribund [ˈmɔrəˌbʌnd] *adj* : moribundo
morn [ˈmɔrn] → **morning**
morning [ˈmɔrnɪŋ] *n* : mañana *f* <good morning! : ¡buenos días!>
Moroccan [məˈrɑkən] *n* : marroquí *mf* — **Moroccan** *adj*
moron [ˈmorˌɑn] *n* **1** : retrasado *m*, -da *f* mental **2** DUNCE : estúpido *m*, -da *f*; tonto *m*, -ta *f*
morose [məˈroːs] *adj* : hosco, sombrío — **morosely** *adv*
moroseness [məˈroːsnəs] *n* : malhumor *m*
morphine [ˈmɔrˌfiːn] *n* : morfina *f*
morrow [ˈmɑroː] *n* : día *m* siguiente
Morse code [ˈmɔrs] *n* : código *m* morse
morsel [ˈmɔrsəl] *n* **1** BITE : bocado *m* **2** FRAGMENT : pedazo *m*
mortal[1] [ˈmɔrtəl] *adj* : mortal <mortal blow : golpe mortal> <mortal fear : miedo mortal> — **mortally** *adv*
mortal[2] *n* : mortal *mf*
mortality [mɔrˈtæləti] *n* : mortalidad *f*
mortar [ˈmɔrtər] *n* **1** : mortero *m*, molcajete *m Mex* <mortar and pestle

: mortero y maja> **2** : mortero *m* <mortar shell : granada de mortero> **3** CEMENT : mortero *m,* argamasa *f*

mortgage[1] ['mɔrgɪdʒ] *vt* **-gaged; -gaging** : hipotecar

mortgage[2] *n* : hipoteca *f*

mortification [ˌmɔrt̬əfə'keɪʃən] *n* **1** : mortificación *f* **2** HUMILIATION : humillación *f,* vergüenza *f*

mortify ['mɔrt̬əˌfaɪ] *vt* **-fied; -fying 1** : mortificar (en religión) **2** HUMILIATE : humillar, avergonzar

mortuary ['mɔrtʃəˌwɛri] *n, pl* **-aries** FUNERAL HOME : funeraria *f*

mosaic [mo'zeɪɪk] *n* : mosaico *m*

Moslem ['mɑzləm] → **Muslim**

mosque ['mɑsk] *n* : mezquita *f*

mosquito [mə'skiːt̬o] *n, pl* **-toes** : mosquito *m,* zancudo *m*

moss ['mɔs] *n* : musgo *m*

mossy ['mɔsi] *adj* **-ier; -est** : musgoso

most[1] ['moːst] *adv* : más <the most interesting book : el libro más interesante>

most[2] *adj* **1** : la mayoría de, la mayor parte de <most people : la mayoría de la gente> **2** GREATEST : más (dícese de los números), mayor (dícese de las cantidades) <the most ability : la mayor capacidad>

most[3] *n* : más *m,* máximo *m* <the most I can do : lo más que puedo hacer> <three weeks at the most : tres semanas como máximo>

most[4] *pron* : la mayoría, la mayor parte <most will go : la mayoría irá>

mostly ['moːstli] *adv* MAINLY : en su mayor parte, principalmente

mote ['moːt] *n* SPECK : mota *f*

motel [mo'tɛl] *n* : motel *m*

moth ['mɔθ] *n* : palomilla *f,* polilla *f*

mother[1] ['mʌðər] *vt* **1** BEAR : dar a luz a **2** PROTECT : cuidar de, proteger

mother[2] *n* : madre *f*

motherhood ['mʌðərˌhʊd] *n* : maternidad *f*

mother–in–law ['mʌðərɪnˌlɔ] *n, pl* **mothers–in–law** : suegra *f*

motherland ['mʌðərˌlænd] *n* : patria *f*

motherly ['mʌðərli] *adj* : maternal

mother–of–pearl [ˌmʌðərəv'pərl] *n* : nácar *m,* madreperla *f*

motif [mo'tiːf] *n* : motivo *m*

motion[1] ['moːʃən] *vt* : hacerle señas (a alguien) <she motioned us to come in : nos hizo señas para que entráramos>

motion[2] *n* **1** MOVEMENT : movimiento *m* <to set in motion : poner en marcha> **2** PROPOSAL : moción *f* <to second a motion : apoyar una moción>

motionless ['moːʃənləs] *adj* : inmóvil, quieto

motion picture *n* MOVIE : película *f*

motivate ['moːt̬əˌveɪt] *vt* **-vated; -vating** : motivar, mover, inducir

motivation [ˌmoːt̬ə'veɪʃən] *n* : motivación *f*

motive[1] ['moːtɪv] *adj* : motor <motive power : fuerza motriz>

motive[2] *n* : motivo *m,* móvil *m*

motley ['mɑtli] *adj* : abigarrado, variopinto

motor[1] ['moːt̬ər] *vi* : viajar en coche

motor[2] *n* : motor *m*

motorbike ['moːt̬ərˌbaɪk] *n* : motocicleta *f* (pequeña), moto *f*

motorboat ['moːt̬ərˌboːt] *n* : bote *m* a motor, lancha *f* motora

motorcar ['moːt̬ərˌkɑr] *n* : automóvil *m*

motorcycle ['moːt̬ərˌsaɪkəl] *n* : motocicleta *f*

motorcyclist ['moːt̬ərˌsaɪkəlɪst] *n* : motociclista *mf*

motorist ['moːt̬ərɪst] *n* : automovilista *mf,* motorista *mf*

mottle ['mɑtəl] *vt* **-tled; -tling** : manchar, motear <mottled skin : piel manchada> <a mottled surface : una superficie moteada>

motto ['mɑt̬oː] *n, pl* **-toes** : lema *m*

mould ['moːld] → **mold**

mound ['maʊnd] *n* **1** PILE : montón *m* **2** KNOLL : montículo *m* **3 burial mound** : túmulo *m*

mount[1] ['maʊnt] *vt* **1** : montar a (un caballo), montar en (una bicicleta), subir a **2** : montar (artillería, etc.) — *vi* INCREASE : aumentar

mount[2] *n* **1** SUPPORT : soporte *m* **2** HORSE : caballería *f,* montura *f* **3** MOUNTAIN : monte *m,* montaña *f*

mountain ['maʊntən] *n* : montaña *f*

mountaineer [ˌmaʊntən'ɪr] *n* : alpinista *mf;* montañero *m,* -ra *f*

mountainous ['maʊntənəs] *adj* : montañoso

mountaintop ['maʊntənˌtɑp] *n* : cima *f,* cumbre *f*

mourn ['morn] *vt* : llorar (por), lamentar <to mourn the death of : llorar la muerte de> — *vi* : llorar, estar de luto

mourner ['mornər] *n* : doliente *mf*

mournful ['mornfəl] *adj* **1** SORROWFUL : lloroso, plañidero, triste **2** GLOOMY : deprimente, entristecedor — **mournfully** *adv*

mourning ['mornɪŋ] *n* : duelo *m,* luto *m*

mouse ['maʊs] *n, pl* **mice** ['maɪs] **1** : ratón *m,* -tona *f* **2** : ratón *m* (de una computadora)

mousetrap ['maʊsˌtræp] *n* : ratonera *f*

moustache ['mʌˌstæʃ, mə'stæʃ] → **mustache**

mouth[1] ['maʊð] *vt* **1** : decir con poca sinceridad, repetir sin comprensión **2** : articular en silencio <she mouthed the words : formó las palabras con los labios>

mouth[2] ['maʊθ] *n* : boca *f* (de una persona o un animal), entrada *f* (de un túnel), desembocadura *f* (de un río)

mouthful ['maʊθˌfʊl] *n* : bocado *m* (de comida), bocanada *f* (de líquido o humo)

mouthpiece [ˈmaʊθˌpiːs] *n* : boquilla *f* (de un instrumento musical)
movable [ˈmuːvəbəl] *or* **moveable** *adj* : movible, móvil
move[1] [ˈmuːv] *v* **moved; moving** *vi* **1** GO : ir **2** RELOCATE : mudarse, trasladarse **3** STIR : moverse <¡no te muevas! : don't move!> **4** ACT : actuar — *vt* **1** : mover <move it over there : ponlo allí> <he kept moving his feet : no dejaba de mover los pies> **2** INDUCE, PERSUADE : inducir, persuadir, mover **3** TOUCH : conmover <it moved him to tears : lo hizo llorar> **4** PROPOSE : proponer
move[2] *n* **1** MOVEMENT : movimiento *m* **2** RELOCATION : mudanza *f* (de casa), traslado *m* **3** STEP : paso *m* <a good move : un paso acertado>
movement [ˈmuːvmənt] *n* : movimiento *m*
mover [ˈmuːvər] *n* : persona *f* que hace mudanzas
movie [ˈmuːvi] *n* **1** : película *f* **2 movies** *npl* : cine *m*
moving [ˈmuːvɪŋ] *adj* **1** : en movimiento <a moving target : un blanco móvil> **2** TOUCHING : conmovedor, emocionante
mow[1] [ˈmoː] *vt* **mowed; mowed** *or* **mown** [ˈmoːn]; **mowing** : cortar (la hierba)
mow[2] [ˈmaʊ] *n* : pajar *m*
mower [ˈmoːər] → **lawn mower**
Mr. [ˈmɪstər] *n, pl* **Messrs.** [ˈmɛsərz] : señor *m*
Mrs. [ˈmɪsəz, -səs, *esp South* ˈmɪzəz, -zəs] *n, pl* **Mesdames** [meɪ-ˈdɑm, -ˈdæm] : señora *f*
Ms. [ˈmɪz] *n* : señora *f,* señorita *f*
much[1] [ˈmʌtʃ] *adv* **more** [ˈmor]; **most** [ˈmoːst] : mucho <I'm much happier : estoy mucho más contenta> <she talks as much as I do : habla tanto como yo>
much[2] *adj* **more; most** : mucho <it has much validity : tiene mucha validez> <too much time : demasiado tiempo>
much[3] *pron* : mucho, -cha <I don't need much : no necesito mucho>
mucilage [ˈmjuːsəlɪdʒ] *n* : mucílago *m*
muck [ˈmʌk] *n* **1** MANURE : estiércol *m* **2** DIRT, FILTH : mugre *f,* suciedad *f* **3** MIRE, MUD : barro *m,* fango *m,* lodo *m*
mucous [ˈmjuːkəs] *adj* : mucoso <mucous membrane : membrana mucosa>
mucus [ˈmjuːkəs] *n* : mucosidad *f*
mud [ˈmʌd] *n* : barro *m,* fango *m,* lodo *m*
muddle[1] [ˈmʌdəl] *v* **-dled; -dling** *vt* **1** CONFUSE : confundir **2** BUNGLE : echar a perder, malograr — *vi* : andar confundido <to muddle through : arreglárselas>
muddle[2] *n* : confusión *f,* embrollo *m,* lío *m*
muddleheaded [ˌmʌdəlˈhɛdəd, ˈmʌdəlˌ-] *adj* CONFUSED : confuso, despistado
muddy[1] [ˈmʌdi] *vt* **-died; -dying** : llenar de barro
muddy[2] *adj* **-dier; -est** : barroso, fangoso, lodoso, enlodado <you're all muddy : estás cubierto de barro>
muff[1] [ˈmʌf] *vt* BUNGLE : echar a perder, fallar (un tiro, etc.)
muff[2] *n* : manguito *m*
muffin [ˈmʌfən] *n* : magdalena *f,* mantecada *f Mex*
muffle [ˈmʌfəl] *vt* **-fled; -fling 1** ENVELOP : cubrir, tapar **2** DEADEN : amortiguar (un sonido)
muffler [ˈmʌflər] *n* **1** SCARF : bufanda *f* **2** : silenciador *m,* mofle *m CA, Mex* (de un automóvil)
mug[1] [ˈmʌg] *v* **mugged; mugging** *vi* : posar (con afectación), hacer muecas <mugging for the camera : haciendo muecas para la cámara> — *vt* ASSAULT : asaltar, atracar
mug[2] *n* CUP : tazón *m*
mugger [ˈmʌgər] *n* : atracador *m,* -dora *f*
mugginess [ˈmʌginəs] *n* : bochorno *m*
muggy [ˈmʌgi] *adj* **-gier; -est** : bochornoso
mulatto [mʊˈlɑto, -ˈlæ-] *n, pl* **-toes** *or* **-tos** : mulato *m,* -ta *f*
mulberry [ˈmʌlˌbɛri] *n, pl* **-ries** : morera *f* (árbol), mora *f* (fruta)
mulch[1] [ˈmʌltʃ] *vt* : cubrir con pajote
mulch[2] *n* : pajote *m*
mule [ˈmjuːl] *n* **1** : mula *f* **2** : obstinado *m,* -da *f;* terco *m,* -ca *f*
mulish [ˈmjuːlɪʃ] *adj* : obstinado, terco
mull [ˈmʌl] *vt* **to mull over** : reflexionar sobre
mullet [ˈmʌlət] *n, pl* **-let** *or* **-lets** : mújol *m,* múgil *m*
multicolored [ˌmʌltiˈkʌlərd, ˌmʌltaɪ-] *adj* : multicolor, abigarrado
multifaceted [ˌmʌltiˈfæsət̬əd, ˌmʌltaɪ-] *adj* : multifacético
multifamily [ˌmʌltiˈfæmli, ˌmʌltaɪ-] *adj* : multifamiliar
multifarious [ˌmʌltəˈfæriəs] *adj* DIVERSE : diverso, variado
multilateral [ˌmʌltiˈlæt̬ərəl, ˌmʌltaɪ-] *adj* : multilateral
multimedia [ˌmʌltiˈmiːdiə, ˌmʌltaɪ-] *adj* : multimedia
multimillionaire [ˌmʌltiˌmɪljəˈnær, ˌmʌltaɪ-, -ˈmɪljəˌnær] *adj* : multimillonario
multinational [ˌmʌltiˈnæʃənəl, ˌmʌltaɪ-] *adj* : multinacional
multiple[1] [ˈmʌltəpəl] *adj* : múltiple
multiple[2] *n* : múltiplo *m*
multiple sclerosis [skləˈroːsɪs] *n* : esclerosis *f* múltiple
multiplication [ˌmʌltəpləˈkeɪʃən] *n* : multiplicación *f*
multiplicity [ˌmʌltəˈplɪsət̬i] *n, pl* **-ties** : multiplicidad *f*
multiplier [ˈmʌltəˌplaɪər] *n* : multiplicador *m* (en matemáticas)

multiply [ˈmʌltəˌplaɪ] *v* **-plied; -plying** *vt* : multiplicar — *vi* : multiplicarse

multipurpose [ˌmʌltiˈpərpəs, ˌmʌlˌtaɪ-] *adj* : multiuso

multitude [ˈmʌltəˌtuːd, -ˌtjuːd] *n* **1** CROWD : multitud *f,* muchedumbre *f* **2** HOST : multitud *f,* gran cantidad *f* <a multitude of ideas : numerosas ideas>

multivitamin [ˌmʌltiˈvaɪt̬əmən, ˌmʌltaɪ-] *adj* : multivitamínico

mum[1] [ˈmʌm] *adj* SILENT : callado

mum[2] *n* → **chrysanthemum**

mumble[1] [ˈmʌmbəl] *v* **-bled; -bling** *vt* : mascullar, musitar — *vi* : mascullar, hablar entre dientes, murmurar

mumble[2] *n* **to speak in a mumble** : hablar entre dientes

mummy [ˈmʌmi] *n, pl* **-mies** : momia *f*

mumps [ˈmʌmps] *ns & pl* : paperas *fpl*

munch [ˈmʌntʃ] *v* : mascar, masticar

mundane [ˌmʌnˈdeɪn, ˈmʌnˌ-] *adj* **1** EARTHLY, WORLDLY : mundano, terrenal **2** COMMONPLACE : rutinario, ordinario

municipal [mjʊˈnɪsəpəl] *adj* : municipal

municipality [mjʊˌnɪsəˈpæləṱi] *n, pl* **-ties** : municipio *m*

munitions [mjʊˈnɪʃənz] *npl* : municiones *fpl*

mural[1] [ˈmjʊrəl] *adj* : mural

mural[2] [ˈmjʊrəlɪst] *n* : mural *m*

murder[1] [ˈmərdər] *vt* : asesinar, matar — *vi* : matar

murder[2] *n* : asesinato *m,* homicidio *m*

murderer [ˈmərdərər] *n* : asesino *m,* -na *f;* homicida *mf*

murderess [ˈmərdərɪs, -dəˌrɛs, -dərəs] *n* : asesina *f,* homicida *f*

murderous [ˈmərdərəs] *adj* : asesino, homicida

murk [ˈmərk] *n* DARKNESS : oscuridad *f,* tinieblas *fpl*

murkiness [ˈmərkinəs] *n* : oscuridad *f,* tenebrosidad *f*

murky [ˈmərki] *adj* **-kier; -est** : oscuro, tenebroso

murmur[1] [ˈmərmər] *vi* **1** DRONE : mumurar **2** GRUMBLE : refunfuñar, regañar, rezongar — *vt* MUMBLE : murmurar

murmur[2] *n* **1** COMPLAINT : queja *f* **2** DRONE : murmullo *m,* rumor *m*

muscle[1] [ˈmʌsəl] *vi* **-cled; -cling** : meterse <to muscle in on : meterse por la fuerza en, entrometerse en>

muscle[2] *n* **1** : músculo *m* **2** STRENGTH : fuerza *f*

muscular [ˈmʌskjələr] *adj* **1** : muscular <muscular tissue : tejido muscular> **2** BRAWNY : musculoso

muscular dystrophy *n* : distrofia *f* muscular

musculature [ˈmʌskjələˌtʃʊr, -tʃər] *n* : musculatura *f*

muse[1] [ˈmjuːz] *vi* **mused; musing** PONER, REFLECT : cavilar, meditar, reflexionar

muse[2] *n* : musa *f*

museum [mjʊˈziːəm] *n* : museo *m*

mush [ˈmʌʃ] *n* **1** : gachas *fpl* (de maíz) **2** SENTIMENTALITY : sensiblería *f*

mushroom[1] [ˈmʌʃˌruːm, -ˌrʊm] *vi* GROW, MULTIPLY : crecer rápidamente, multiplicarse

mushroom[2] *n* : hongo *m,* champiñón *m,* seta *f*

mushy [ˈmʌʃi] *adj* **mushier; -est 1** SOFT : blando **2** MAWKISH : sensiblero

music [ˈmjuːzɪk] *n* : música *f*

musical[1] [ˈmjuːzɪkəl] *adj* : musical, de música — **musically** *adv*

musical[2] *n* : comedia *f* musical

music box *n* : cajita *f* de música

musician [mjʊˈzɪʃən] *n* : músico *m,* -ca *f*

musk [ˈmʌsk] *n* : almizcle *m*

musket [ˈmʌskət] *n* : mosquete *m*

musketeer [ˌmʌskəˈtɪr] *n* : mosquetero *m*

muskrat [ˈmʌskˌræt] *n, pl* **-rat** *or* **-rats** : rata *f* almizclera

Muslim[1] [ˈmʌzləm, ˈmʊs-, ˈmʊz-] *adj* : musulmán

Muslim[2] *n* : musulmán *m,* -mana *f*

muslin [ˈmʌzlən] *n* : muselina *f*

muss[1] [ˈmʌs] *vt* : desordenar, despeinar (el pelo)

muss[2] *n* : desorden *m*

mussel [ˈmʌsəl] *n* : mejillón *m*

must[1] [ˈmʌst] *v aux* **1** (*expressing obligation or necessity*) : deber, tener que <you must stop : debes parar> <we must obey : tenemos que obedecer> **2** (*expressing probability*) : deber (de), haber de <you must be tired : debes de estar cansado> <it must be late : ha de ser tarde>

must[2] *n* : necesidad *f* <exercise is a must : el ejercicio es imprescindible>

mustache [ˈmʌˌstæʃ, mʌˈstæʃ] *n* : bigote *m,* bigotes *mpl*

mustang [ˈmʌˌstæŋ] *n* : mustang *m*

mustard [ˈmʌstərd] *n* : mostaza *f*

muster[1] [ˈmʌstər] *vt* **1** ASSEMBLE : reunir **2 to muster up** : armarse de, cobrar (valor, fuerzas, etc.)

muster[2] *n* **1** INSPECTION : revista *f* (de tropas) <it didn't pass muster : no resistió un examen minucioso> **2** COLLECTION : colección *f*

mustiness [ˈmʌstinəs] *n* : lo mohoso

musty [ˈmʌsti] *adj* **mustier; -est** : mohoso, que huele a moho, que huele a encerrado

mutant[1] [ˈmjuːtənt] *adj* : mutante

mutant[2] *n* : mutante *m*

mutate [ˈmjuːˌteɪt] *vi* **-tated; -tating 1** : mutar (genéticamente) **2** CHANGE : transformarse

mutation [mjuːˈteɪʃən] *n* : mutación *f* (genética)

mute[1] [ˈmjuːt] *vt* **muted; muting** MUFFLE : amortiguar, ponerle sordina a (un instrumento musical)
mute[2] *adj* **muter; mutest** : mudo — **mutely** *adv*
mute[3] *n* **1** : mudo *m,* -da *f* (persona) **2** : sordina *f* (para un instrumento musical)
mutilate [ˈmjuːt̬əˌleɪt] *vt* **-lated; -lating** : mutilar
mutilation [ˌmjuːt̬əˈleɪʃən] *n* : mutilación *f*
mutineer [ˌmjuːtənˈɪr] *n* : amotinado *m,* -da *f*
mutinous [ˈmjuːtənəs] *adj* : amotinado
mutiny[1] [ˈmjuːtəni] *vi* **-nied; -nying** : amotinarse
mutiny[2] *n, pl* **-nies** : amotinamiento *m,* motín *m*
mutt [ˈmʌt] *n* MONGREL : perro *m* mestizo, perro *m* corriente *Mex*
mutter [ˈmʌt̬ər] *vi* **1** MUMBLE : mascullar, hablar entre dientes, murmurar **2** GRUMBLE : refunfuñar, regañar, rezongar
mutton [ˈmʌtən] *n* : carne *f* de carnero
mutual [ˈmjuːtʃʊəl] *adj* **1** : mutuo <mutual respect : respeto mutuo> **2** COMMON : común <a mutual friend : un amigo común>
mutually [ˈmjuːtʃʊəli, -tʃəli] *adv* **1** : mutuamente <mutually beneficial : mutuamente beneficioso> **2** JOINTLY : conjuntamente
muzzle[1] [ˈmʌzəl] *vt* **-zled; -zling** : ponerle un bozal a (un animal), amordazar
muzzle[2] *n* **1** SNOUT : hocico *m* **2** : bozal *m* (para un perro, etc.) **3** : boca *f* (de un arma de fuego)
my[1] [ˈmaɪ] *adj* : mi <my parents : mis padres>
my[2] *interj* : ¡caramba!, ¡Dios mío!
myopia [maɪˈoːpiə] *n* : miopía *f*
myopic [maɪˈoːpɪk, -ˈɑ-] *adj* : miope
myriad[1] [ˈmɪriəd] *adj* INNUMERABLE : innumerable
myriad[2] *n* : miríada *f*
myrrh [ˈmər] *n* : mirra *f*
myrtle [ˈmərt̬əl] *n* : mirto *m,* arrayán *m*
myself [maɪˈsɛlf] *pron* **1** (*used reflexively*) : me <I washed myself : me lavé> **2** (*used for emphasis*) : yo mismo, yo misma <I did it myself : lo hice yo mismo>
mysterious [mɪˈstɪriəs] *adj* : misterioso — **mysteriously** *adv*
mysteriousness [mɪˈstɪriəsnəs] *n* : lo misterioso
mystery [ˈmɪstəri] *n, pl* **-teries** : misterio *m*
mystic[1] [ˈmɪstɪk] *adj* : místico
mystic[2] *n* : místico *m,* -ca *f*
mystical [ˈmɪstɪkəl] *adj* : místico — **mystically** *adv*
mysticism [ˈmɪstəˌsɪzəm] *n* : misticismo *m*
mystify [ˈmɪstəˌfaɪ] *vt* **-fied; -fying** : dejar perplejo, confundir
mystique [mɪˈstiːk] *n* : aura *f* de misterio
myth [ˈmɪθ] *n* : mito *m*
mythical [ˈmɪθɪkəl] *adj* : mítico
mythological [ˌmɪθəˈlɑdʒɪkəl] *adj* : mitológico
mythology [mɪˈθɑlədʒi] *n, pl* **-gies** : mitología *f*

N

n [ˈɛn] *n, pl* **n's** *or* **ns** [ˈɛnz] : decimocuarta letra del alfabeto inglés
nab [ˈnæb] *vt* **nabbed; nabbing** : prender, pillar *fam,* pescar *fam*
nadir [ˈneɪdər, ˈneɪˌdɪr] *n* : nadir *m,* punto *m* más bajo
nag[1] [ˈnæg] *v* **nagged; nagging** *vi* **1** COMPLAIN : quejarse, rezongar **2 to nag at** HASSLE : molestar, darle (la) lata (a alguien) — *vt* **1** PESTER : molestar, fastidiar **2** SCOLD : regañar, estarle encima a *fam*
nag[2] *n* **1** GRUMBLER : gruñón *m,* -ñona *f* **2** HORSE : jamelgo *m*
naiad [ˈneɪəd, ˈnaɪ-, -ˌæd] *n, pl* **-iads** *or* **-iades** [-əˌdiːz] : náyade *f*
nail[1] [ˈneɪl] *vt* : clavar, sujetar con clavos
nail[2] *n* **1** FINGERNAIL : uña *f* <nail file : lima (de uñas)> <nail polish : laca de uñas> **2** : clavo *m* <to hit the nail on the head : dar en el clavo>
naive *or* **naïve** [nɑˈiːv] *adj* **-iver; -est** **1** INGENUOUS : ingenuo, cándido **2** GULLIBLE : crédulo
naively [nɑˈiːvli] *adv* : ingenuamente
naïveté [ˌnɑˌiːvəˈteɪ, nɑˈiːvəˌ-] *n* : ingenuidad *f*
naked [ˈneɪkəd] *adj* **1** UNCLOTHED : desnudo **2** UNCOVERED : desenvainado (dícese de una espada), pelado (dícese de los árboles), expuesto al aire (dícese de una llama) **3** OBVIOUS, PLAIN : manifiesto, puro, desnudo <the naked truth : la pura verdad> **4 to the naked eye** : a simple vista
nakedly [ˈneɪkədli] *adv* : manifiestamente
nakedness [ˈneɪkədnəs] *n* : desnudez *f*
name[1] [ˈneɪm] *vt* **named; naming** **1** CALL : llamar, bautizar, ponerle nombre a **2** MENTION : mentar, mencionar, dar el nombre de <they have named a suspect : han dado el nombre de un

sospechoso> **3** APPOINT : nombrar **4 to name a price** : fijar un precio

name[2] *adj* **1** KNOWN : de nombre <name brand : marca conocida> **2** PROMINENT : de renombre, de prestigio

name[3] *n* **1** : nombre *m* <what is your name : ¿cómo se llama?> **2** SURNAME : apellido *m* **3** EPITHET : epíteto *m* <to call somebody names : llamar a alguien de todo> **4** REPUTATION : fama *f,* reputación *f* <to make a name for oneself : darse a conocer, hacerse famoso>

nameless [ˈneɪmləs] *adj* **1** ANONYMOUS : anónimo **2** INDESCRIBABLE : indecible, indescriptible

namelessly [ˈneɪmləsli] *adv* : anónimamente

namely [ˈneɪmli] *adv* : a saber

namesake [ˈneɪmˌseɪk] *n* : tocayo *m,* -ya *f;* homónimo *m,* -ma *f*

Namibian [nəˈmɪbiən] *n* : namibio *m,* -bia *f* — **Namibian** *adj*

nap[1] [ˈnæp] *vi* **napped; napping 1** : dormir, dormir la siesta **2 to be caught napping** : estar desprevenido

nap[2] *n* **1** SLEEP : siesta *f* <to take a nap : echarse una siesta> **2** FUZZ, PILE : pelo *m,* pelusa *f* (de telas)

nape [ˈneɪp, ˈnæp] *n* : nuca *f,* cerviz *f,* cogote *m*

naphtha [ˈnæfθə] *n* : nafta *f*

napkin [ˈnæpkən] *n* : servilleta *f*

narcissism [ˈnɑrsəˌsɪzəm] *n* : narcisismo *m*

narcissist [ˈnɑrsəsɪst] *n* : narcisista *mf*

narcissistic [ˌnɑrsəˈsɪstɪk] *adj* : narcisista

narcissus [nɑrˈsɪsəs] *n, pl* **-cissus** *or* **-cissuses** *or* **-cissi** [-ˈsɪˌsaɪ, -ˌsiː] : narciso *m*

narcotic[1] [nɑrˈkɑtɪk] *adj* : narcótico

narcotic[2] *n* : narcótico *m,* estupefaciente *m*

narrate [ˈnærˌeɪt] *vt* **-rated; -rating** : narrar, relatar

narration [næˈreɪʃən] *n* : narración *f*

narrative[1] [ˈnærət̬ɪv] *adj* : narrativo

narrative[2] *n* : narración *f,* narrativa *f,* relato *m*

narrator [ˈnærˌeɪt̬ər] *n* : narrador *m,* -dora *f*

narrow[1] [ˈnærˌoː] *vi* : estrecharse, angostarse <the river narrowed : el río se estrechó> — *vt* **1** : estrechar, angostar **2** LIMIT : restringir, limitar <to narrow the search : limitar la búsqueda>

narrow[2] *adj* **1** : estrecho, angosto **2** LIMITED : estricto, limitado <in the narrowest sense of the word : en el sentido más estricto de la palabra> **3 to have a narrow escape** : escapar por un pelo

narrowly [ˈnæroli] *adv* **1** BARELY : por poco **2** CLOSELY : de cerca

narrow–minded [ˌnæroˈmaɪndəd] *adj* : de miras estrechas

narrowness [ˈnæronəs] *n* : estrechez *f*

narrows [ˈnæroːz] *npl* STRAIT : estrecho *m*

narwhal [ˈnɑrˌhwɑl, ˈnɑrwəl] *n* : narval *m*

nasal [ˈneɪzəl] *adj* : nasal, gangoso <a nasal voice : una voz gangosa>

nasally [ˈneɪzəli] *adv* **1** : por la nariz **2** : con voz gangosa

nastily [ˈnæstəli] *adv* : con maldad, cruelmente

nastiness [ˈnæstinəs] *n* : porquería *f*

nasturtium [nəˈstərʃəm, næ-] *n* : capuchina *f*

nasty [ˈnæsti] *adj* **-tier; -est 1** FILTHY : sucio, mugriento **2** OBSCENE : obsceno **3** MEAN, SPITEFUL : malo, malicioso **4** UNPLEASANT : desagradable, feo **5** REPUGNANT : asqueroso, repugnante <a nasty smell : un olor asqueroso>

natal [ˈneɪt̬əl] *adj* : natal

nation [ˈneɪʃən] *n* : nación *f*

national[1] [ˈnæʃənəl] *adj* : nacional

national[2] *n* : ciudadano *m,* -na *f;* nacional *mf*

nationalism [ˈnæʃənəˌlɪzəm] *n* : nacionalismo *m*

nationalist[1] [ˈnæʃənəlɪst] *adj* : nacionalista

nationalist[2] *n* : nacionalista *mf*

nationalistic [ˌnæʃənəˈlɪstɪk] *adj* : nacionalista

nationality [ˌnæʃəˈnælət̬i] *n, pl* **-ties** : nacionalidad *f*

nationalization [ˌnæʃənələˈzeɪʃən] *n* : nacionalización *f*

nationalize [ˈnæʃənəˌlaɪz] *vt* **-ized; -izing** : nacionalizar

nationally [ˈnæʃənəli] *adv* : a escala nacional, a nivel nacional

nationwide [ˈneɪʃənˈwaɪd] *adj* : en toda la nación, por todo el país

native[1] [ˈneɪt̬ɪv] *adj* **1** INNATE : innato **2** : natal <her native city : su ciudad natal> **3** INDIGENOUS : indígeno, autóctono

native[2] *n* **1** ABORIGINE : nativo *m,* -va *f;* indígena *mf* **2** : natural *m* <he's a native of Mexico : es natural de México>

Native American → **American Indian**

nativity [nəˈtɪvət̬i, neɪ-] *n, pl* **-ties 1** BIRTH : navidad *f* **2 the Nativity** : la Natividad, la Navidad

natty [ˈnæt̬i] *adj* **-tier; -est** : elegante, garboso

natural[1] [ˈnætʃərəl] *adj* **1** : natural, de la naturaleza <natural woodlands : bosques naturales> <natural childbirth : parto natural> **2** INNATE : innato, natural **3** UNAFFECTED : natural, sin afectación **4** LIFELIKE : natural, vivo

natural[2] *n* **to be a natural** : tener un talento innato (para algo)

natural gas *n* : gas *m* natural

natural history *n* : historia *f* natural

naturalist [ˈnætʃərəlɪst] *n* : naturalista *mf*
naturalization [ˌnætʃərələˈzeɪʃən] *n* : naturalización *f*
naturalize [ˈnætʃərəˌlaɪz] *vt* **-ized; -izing** : naturalizar
naturally [ˈnætʃərəli] *adv* **1** INHERENTLY : naturalmente, intrínsecamente **2** UNAFFECTEDLY : de manera natural **3** OF COURSE : por supuesto, naturalmente
naturalness [ˈnætʃərəlnəs] *n* : naturalidad *f*
natural science *n* : ciencias *fpl* naturales
nature [ˈneɪtʃər] *n* **1** : naturaleza *f* <the laws of nature : las leyes de la naturaleza> **2** KIND, SORT : índole *f*, clase *f* <things of this nature : cosas de esta índole> **3** DISPOSITION : carácter *m*, natural *m*, naturaleza *f* <it is his nature to be friendly : es de natural simpático> <human nature : la naturaleza humana>
naught [ˈnɔt] *n* **1** : nada *f* <to come to naught : reducirse a nada, fracasar> **2** ZERO : cero *m*
naughtily [ˈnɔt̬əli] *adv* : traviesamente, con malicia
naughtiness [ˈnɔt̬inəs] *n* : mala conducta *f*, travesuras *fpl*, malicia *f*
naughty [ˈnɔt̬i] *adj* **-tier; -est 1** MISCHIEVOUS : travieso, pícaro **2** RISQUÉ : picante, subido de tono
nausea [ˈnɔziə, ˈnɔʃə] *n* **1** SICKNESS : náuseas *fpl* **2** DISGUST : asco *m*
nauseate [ˈnɔziˌeɪt, -ʒi-, -si-, -ʃi-] *vt* **-ated; -ating 1** SICKEN : darle náuseas (a alguien) **2** DISGUST : asquear, darle asco (a alguien)
nauseating *adj* : nauseabundo, repugnante
nauseatingly [ˈnɔziˌeɪt̬ɪŋli, -ʒi-, -si-, -ʃi-] *adv* : hasta el punto de dar asco <nauseatingly sweet : tan dulce que da asco>
nauseous [ˈnɔʃəs, -ziəs] *adj* **1** SICK : mareado, con náuseas **2** SICKENING : nauseabundo
nautical [ˈnɔt̬ɪkəl] *adj* : náutico
nautilus [ˈnɔt̬ələs] *n, pl* **-luses** *or* **-li** [-ˌlaɪ, -ˌliː] : nautilo *m*
naval [ˈneɪvəl] *adj* : naval
nave [ˈneɪv] *n* : nave *f*
navel [ˈneɪvəl] *n* : ombligo *m*
navigability [ˌnævɪgəˈbɪlət̬i] *n* : navegabilidad *f*
navigable [ˈnævɪgəbəl] *adj* : navegable
navigate [ˈnævəˌgeɪt] *v* **-gated; -gating** *vi* : navegar — *vt* **1** STEER : gobernar (un barco), pilotar (un avión) **2** : navegar por (un río, etc.)
navigation [ˌnævəˈgeɪʃən] *n* : navegación *f*
navigator [ˈnævəˌgeɪt̬ər] *n* : navegante *mf*
navy [ˈneɪvi] *n, pl* **-vies 1** FLEET : flota *f* **2** : marina *f* de guerra, armada *f* <the United States Navy : la armada de los Estados Unidos> **3** *or* **navy blue** : azul *m* marino
nay[1] [ˈneɪ] *adv* : no
nay[2] *n* : no *m*, voto *m* en contra
Nazi [ˈnɑtsi, ˈnæt-] *n* : nazi *mf*
Nazism [ˈnɑtˌsɪzəm, ˈnæt-] *or* **Naziism** [ˈnɑtsiˌɪzəm, ˈnæt-] *n* : nazismo *m*
Neanderthal man [niˈændərˌθɔl, -ˌtɔl] *n* : hombre *m* de Neanderthal
near[1] [ˈnɪr] *vt* **1** : acercarse a <the ship is nearing port : el barco se está acercando al puerto> **2** : estar a punto de <she is nearing graduation : está a punto de graduarse>
near[2] *adv* **1** CLOSE : cerca <my family lives quite near : mi familia vive muy cerca> **2** NEARLY : casi <I came near to finishing : casi terminé>
near[3] *adj* **1** CLOSE : cercano, próximo **2** SIMILAR : parecido, semejante
near[4] *prep* : cerca de
nearby[1] [nɪrˈbaɪ, ˈnɪrˌbaɪ] *adv* : cerca
nearby[2] *adj* : cercano
nearly [ˈnɪrli] *adv* **1** ALMOST : casi <nearly asleep : casi dormido> **2 not nearly** : ni con mucho, ni mucho menos <it was not nearly so bad as I had expected : no fue ni con mucho tan malo como esperaba>
nearness [ˈnɪrnəs] *n* : proximidad *f*
nearsighted [ˈnɪrˌsaɪt̬əd] *adj* : miope, corto de vista
nearsightedly [ˈnɪrˌsaɪt̬ədli] *adv* : con miopía
nearsightedness [ˈnɪrˌsaɪt̬ədnəs] *n* : miopía *f*
neat [ˈniːt] *adj* **1** CLEAN, ORDERLY : ordenado, pulcro, limpio **2** UNDILUTED : solo, sin diluir **3** SIMPLE, TASTEFUL : sencillo y de buen gusto **4** CLEVER : hábil, ingenioso <a neat trick : un truco ingenioso>
neatly [ˈniːtli] *adv* **1** TIDILY : ordenadamente **2** CLEVERLY : ingeniosamente
neatness [ˈniːtnəs] *n* : pulcritud *f*, limpieza *f*, orden *m*
nebula [ˈnɛbjʊlə] *n, pl* **-lae** [-ˌliː, -ˌlaɪ] : nebulosa *f*
nebulous [ˈnɛbjʊləs] *adj* : nebuloso, vago
necessarily [ˌnɛsəˈsɛrəli] *adv* : necesariamente, forzosamente
necessary[1] [ˈnɛsəˌsɛri] *adj* **1** INEVITABLE : inevitable **2** COMPULSORY : necesario, obligatorio **3** ESSENTIAL : imprescindible, preciso, necesario
necessary[2] *n, pl* **-saries** : lo esencial, lo necesario
necessitate [nɪˈsɛsəˌteɪt] *vt* **-tated; -tating** : necesitar, requerir
necessity [nɪˈsɛsət̬i] *n, pl* **-ties 1** NEED : necesidad *f* **2** REQUIREMENT : requisito *m* indispensable **3** POVERTY : indigencia *f*, necesidad *f* **4** INEVITABILITY : inevitabilidad *f*
neck[1] [ˈnɛk] *vi* : besuquearse

neck[2] *n* **1 :** cuello *m* (de una persona), pescuezo *m* (de un animal) **2** COLLAR **:** cuello *m* **3 :** cuello *m* (de una botella), mástil *m* (de una guitarra)
neckerchief [ˈnɛkərtʃəf, -ˌtʃiːf] *n, pl* **-chiefs** [-tʃəfs, -ˌtʃiːfs] **:** pañuelo *m* (para el cuello), mascada *f Mex*
necklace [ˈnɛkləs] *n* **:** collar *m*
neckline [ˈnɛkˌlaɪn] *n* **:** escote *m*
necktie [ˈnɛkˌtaɪ] *n* **:** corbata *f*
nectar [ˈnɛktər] *n* **:** néctar *m*
nectarine [ˌnɛktəˈriːn] *n* **:** nectarina *f*
née *or* **nee** [ˈneɪ] *adj* **:** de soltera <Mrs. Smith, née Whitman : la señora Smith, de soltera Whitman>
need[1] [ˈniːd] *vt* **1 :** necesitar <I need your help : necesito su ayuda> <I need money : me falta dinero> **2** REQUIRE **:** requerir, exigir <that job needs patience : ese trabajo exige paciencia> **3 to need to :** tener que <he needs to study : tiene que estudiar> <they need to be scolded : hay que reprenderlos> — *v aux* **1** MUST **:** tener que, deber <need you shout? : ¿tienes que gritar?> **2 to be needed :** hacer falta <you needn't worry : no hace falta que te preocupes, no hay por qué preocuparse>
need[2] *n* **1** NECESSITY **:** necesidad *f* <in case of need : en caso de necesidad> **2** LACK **:** falta *f* <the need for better training : la falta de mejor capacitación> <to be in need : necesitar> **3** POVERTY **:** necesidad *f,* indigencia *f* **4 needs** *npl* **:** requisitos *mpl*, carencias *fpl*
needful [ˈniːdfəl] *adj* **:** necesario
needle[1] [ˈniːdəl] *vt* **-dled; -dling :** pinchar
needle[2] *n* **1 :** aguja *f* <to thread a needle : enhebrar una aguja> <knitting needle : aguja de tejer> **2** POINTER **:** aguja *f,* indicador *m*
needlepoint [ˈniːdəlˌpɔɪnt] *n* **1** LACE **:** encaje *m* de mano **2** EMBROIDERY **:** bordado *m* en cañamazo
needless [ˈniːdləs] *adj* **:** innecesario
needlessly [ˈniːdləsli] *adv* **:** sin ninguna necesidad, innecesariamente
needlework [ˈniːdəlˌwərk] *n* **:** bordado *m*
needn't [ˈniːdənt] (*contraction of* **need not**) → **need**
needy[1] [ˈniːdi] **needier; -est** *adj* **:** necesitado
needy[2] *n* **the needy :** los necesitados *mpl*
nefarious [nɪˈfæriəs] *adj* **:** nefario, nefando, infame
negate [nɪˈgeɪt] *vt* **-gated; -gating 1** DENY **:** negar **2** NULLIFY **:** invalidar, anular
negation [nɪˈgeɪʃən] *n* **:** negación *f*
negative[1] [ˈnɛgət̬ɪv] *adj* **:** negativo
negative[2] *n* **1 :** negación *f* (en lingüística) **2 :** negativa *f* <to answer in the negative : contestar con una negativa> **3 :** término *m* negativo (en matemáticas) **4 :** negativo *m,* imagen *f* en negativo (en fotografía)
negatively [ˈnɛgət̬ɪvli] *adv* **:** negativamente
neglect[1] [nɪˈglɛkt] *vt* **1 :** desatender, descuidar <to neglect one's health : descuidar la salud> **2 :** no cumplir con, faltar a <to neglect one's obligations : faltar uno a sus obligaciones> <he neglected to tell me : omitió decírmelo>
neglect[2] *n* **1 :** negligencia *f,* descuido *m,* incumplimiento *m* <through neglect : por negligencia> <neglect of duty : incumplimiento del deber> **2 in a state of neglect :** abandonado, descuidado
neglectful [nɪˈglɛktfəl] *adj* **:** descuidado *m*
negligee [ˌnɛgləˈʒeɪ] *n* **:** negligé *m*
negligence [ˈnɛglɪdʒən*t*s] *n* **:** descuido *m,* negligencia *f*
negligent [ˈnɛglɪdʒənt] *adj* **:** negligente, descuidado — **negligently** *adv*
negligible [ˈnɛglɪdʒəbəl] *adj* **:** insignificante, despreciable
negotiable [nɪˈgoːʃəbəl, -ʃiə-] *adj* **:** negociable
negotiate [nɪˈgoːʃiˌeɪt] *v* **-ated; -ating** *vi* **:** negociar — *vt* **1 :** negociar, gestionar <to negotiate a treaty : negociar un trato> **2 :** salvar, franquear <they negotiated the obstacles : salvaron los obstáculos> <to negotiate a turn : tomar una curva>
negotiation [nɪˌgoːʃiˈeɪʃən, -siˈeɪ-] *n* **:** negociación *f*
negotiator [nɪˈgoːʃiˌeɪt̬ər, -siˌeɪ-] *n* **:** negociador *m,* -dora *f*
Negro [ˈniːˌgroː] *n, pl* **-groes :** negro *m,* -gra *f*
neigh[1] [ˈneɪ] *vi* **:** relinchar
neigh[2] *n* **:** relincho *m*
neighbor[1] [ˈneɪbər] *vt* **:** ser vecino de, estar junto a <her house neighbors mine : su casa está junto a la mía> — *vi* **:** estar cercano, lindar, colindar <her land neighbors on mine : sus tierras lindan con las mías>
neighbor[2] *n* **1 :** vecino *m,* -na *f* **2 love thy neighbor :** ama a tu prójimo
neighborhood [ˈneɪbərˌhʊd] *n* **1 :** barrio *m,* vecindad *f,* vecindario *m* **2 in the neighborhood of :** alrededor de, cerca de
neighborly [ˈneɪbərli] *adv* **:** amable, de buena vecindad
neither[1] [ˈniːðər, ˈnaɪ-] *adj* **:** ninguno (de los dos)
neither[2] *conj* **1 :** ni <neither asleep nor awake : ni dormido ni despierto> **2** NOR **:** ni (tampoco) <I'm not asleep — neither am I : no estoy dormido — ni yo tampoco>
neither[3] *pron* **:** ninguno
nemesis [ˈnɛməsɪs] *n, pl* **-eses** [-ˌsiːz] **1** RIVAL **:** rival *mf* **2** RETRIBUTION **:** justo castigo *m*

neologism [ni'ɑlə,dʒɪzəm] *n* : neologismo *m*

neon[1] ['ni:,ɑn] *adj* : de neón <neon sign : letrero de neón>

neon[2] *n* : neón *m*

Nepali [nə'pɔli, -'pɑ-, -'pæ-] *n* : nepalés *m,* -lesa *f* — **Nepali** *adj*

neophyte ['ni:ə,faɪt] *n* : neófito *m,* -ta *f*

nephew ['nɛ,fju:, *chiefly British* 'nɛ,vju:] *n* : sobrino *m*

nepotism ['nɛpə,tɪzəm] *n* : nepotismo *m*

Neptune ['nɛp,tu:n, -,tju:n] *n* : Neptuno *m*

nerd ['nərd] *n* : ganso *m,* -sa *f*

nerve ['nərv] *n* **1** : nervio *m* **2** COURAGE : coraje *m,* valor *m,* fuerza *f* de la voluntad <to lose one's nerve : perder el valor> **3** AUDACITY, GALL : atrevimiento *m,* descaro *m* <of all the nerve! : ¡qué descaro!> **4 nerves** *npl* : nervios *mpl* <a fit of nerves : un ataque de nervios>

nervous ['nərvəs] *adj* **1** : nervioso <the nervous system : el sistema nervioso> **2** EXCITABLE : nervioso, excitable <to get nervous : excitarse, ponerse nervioso> **3** FEARFUL : miedoso, temeroso

nervously ['nərvəsli] *adv* : nerviosamente

nervousness ['nərvəsnəs] *n* : nerviosismo *m,* nerviosidad *f,* ansiedad *f*

nervy ['nərvi] *adj* **nervier; -est 1** COURAGEOUS : valiente **2** IMPUDENT : atrevido, descarado, fresco *fam* **3** NERVOUS : nervioso

nest[1] ['nɛst] *vi* : anidar

nest[2] *n* **1** : nido *m* (de un ave), avispero *m* (de una avispa), madriguera *f* (de un animal) **2** REFUGE : nido *m,* refugio *m* **3** SET : juego *m* <a nest of tables : un juego de mesitas>

nestle ['nɛsəl] *vi* **-tled; -tling** : acurrucarse, arrimarse cómodamente

net[1] ['nɛt] *vt* **netted; netting 1** CATCH : pescar, atrapar con una red **2** CLEAR : ganar neto <they netted $5000 : ganaron $5000 netos> **3** YIELD : producir neto

net[2] *adj* : neto <net weight : peso neto> <net gain : ganancia neta>

net[3] *n* : red *f,* malla *f*

nether ['nɛðər] *adj* **1** : inferior, más bajo **2 the nether regions** : el infierno

nettle[1] ['nɛt̬əl] *vt* **-tled; -tling** : irritar, provocar, molestar

nettle[2] *n* : ortiga *f*

network ['nɛt,wərk] *n* **1** SYSTEM : red *f* **2** CHAIN : cadena *f* <a network of supermarkets : una cadena de supermercados>

neural ['nʊrəl, 'njʊr-] *adj* : neural

neuralgia [nʊ'rældʒə, njʊ-] *n* : neuralgia *f*

neuritis [nʊ'raɪt̬əs, njʊ-] *n, pl* **-ritides** [-'rɪt̬ə,di:z] *or* **-ritises** : neuritis *f*

neurological [,nʊrə'lɑdʒɪkəl, ,njʊr-] *or* **neurologic** [,nʊrə'lɑdʒɪk, ,njʊr-] *adj* : neurológico

neurologist [nʊ'rɑlədʒɪst, njʊ-] *n* : neurólogo *m,* -ga *f*

neurology [nʊ'rɑlədʒi, njʊ-] *n* : neurología *f*

neurosis [nʊ'ro:sɪs, njʊ-] *n, pl* **-roses** [-,si:z] : neurosis *f*

neurotic[1] [nʊ'rɑt̬ɪk, njʊ-] *adj* : neurótico

neurotic[2] *n* : neurótico *m,* -ca *f*

neuter[1] ['nu:t̬ər, 'nju:-] *vt* : castrar

neuter[2] *adj* : neutro

neutral[1] ['nu:trəl, 'nju:-] *adj* **1** IMPARTIAL : neutral, imparcial <to remain neutral : permanecer neutral> **2** : neutro <a neutral color : un color neutro> **3** : neutro (en la química o la electricidad)

neutral[2] *n* : punto *m* muerto (de un automóvil)

neutrality [nu:'trælət̬i:, nju:-] *n* : neutralidad *f*

neutralization [,nu:trələ'zeɪʃən, ,nju:-] *n* : neutralización *f*

neutralize ['nu:trə,laɪz, 'nju:-] *vt* **-ized; -izing** : neutralizar

neutron ['nu:,trɑn, 'nju:-] *n* : neutrón *m*

never ['nɛvər] *adv* **1** : nunca, jamás <he never studies : nunca estudia> **2 never again** : nunca más, nunca jamás **3 never mind** : no importa

nevermore [,nɛvər'mor] *adv* : nunca más

nevertheless [,nɛvərðə'lɛs] *adv* : sin embargo, no obstante

new ['nu:, 'nju:] *adj* **1** : nuevo <a new dress : un vestido nuevo> **2** RECENT : nuevo, reciente <what's new? : ¿qué hay de nuevo?> <a new arrival : un recién llegado> **3** DIFFERENT : nuevo, distinto <this problem is new : este problema es distinto> <new ideas : ideas nuevas> **4 like new** : como nuevo

newborn ['nu:,bɔrn, 'nju:-] *adj* : recién nacido

newcomer ['nu:,kʌmər, 'nju:-] *n* : recién llegado *m,* recién llegada *f*

newfangled ['nu:'fæŋgəld, 'nju:-] *adj* : novedoso

newfound ['nu:'faʊnd, 'nju:-] *adj* : recién descubierto

newly ['nu:li, 'nju:-] *adv* : recién, recientemente

newlywed ['nu:li,wɛd, 'nju:-] *n* : recién casado *m,* -da *f*

new moon *n* : luna *f* nueva

newness ['nu:nəs, 'nju:-] *n* : novedad *f*

news ['nu:z, 'nju:z] *n* : noticias *fpl*

newscast ['nu:z,kæst, 'nju:z-] *n* : noticiero *m,* informativo *m*

newscaster ['nu:z,kæstər, 'nju:z-] *n* : presentador *m,* -dora *f;* locutor *m,* -tora *f*

newsletter ['nuːz,lɛt̬ər, 'njuːz-] *n* : boletín *m* informativo

newsman ['nuːzmən, 'njuːz-, -ˌmæn] *n, pl* **-men** [-mən, -ˌmɛn] : periodista *m,* reportero *m*

newspaper ['nuːzˌpeɪpər, 'njuːz-] *n* : periódico *m,* diario *m*

newspaperman ['nuːzˌpeɪpərˌmæn, 'njuːz-] *n, pl* **-men** [-mən, -ˌmɛn] **1** REPORTER : periodista *m,* reportero *m* **2** : dueño *m* de un periódico

newsprint ['nuːzˌprɪnt, 'njuːz-] *n* : papel *m* de prensa

newsstand ['nuːzˌstænd, 'njuːz-] *n* : quiosco *m,* puesto *m* de periódicos

newswoman ['nuːzˌwʊmən, 'njuːz-] *n, pl* **-women** [-ˌwɪmən] : periodista *f,* reportera *f*

newsworthy ['nuːzˌwərði, 'njuːz-] *adj* : de interés periodístico

newsy ['nuːziː, 'njuː-] *adj* **newsier; -est** : lleno de noticias

newt ['nuːt, 'njuːt] *n* : tritón *m*

New Year *n* : Año *m* Nuevo

New Year's Day *n* : día *m* del Año Nuevo

New Yorker [nuː'jɔrkər, njuː-] *n* : neoyorquino *m,* -na *f*

New Zealander [nuː'ziːləndər, njuː-] *n* : neozelandés *m,* -desa *f*

next[1] ['nɛkst] *adv* **1** AFTERWARD : después, luego <what will you do next? : ¿qué harás después?> **2** NOW : después, ahora, entonces <next I will sing a song : ahora voy a cantar una canción> **3** : la próxima vez <when next we meet : la próxima vez que nos encontremos>

next[2] *adj* **1** ADJACENT : contiguo, de al lado **2** COMING : que viene, próximo <next Friday : el viernes que viene> **3** FOLLOWING : siguiente <the next year : el año siguiente>

next–door ['nɛkst'dor] *adj* : de al lado

next to[1] *adv* ALMOST : casi, prácticamente <next to impossible : casi imposible>

next to[2] *prep* : junto a, al lado de

nib ['nɪb] *n* : plumilla *f*

nibble[1] ['nɪbəl] *v* **-bled; -bling** *vt* : pellizcar, mordisquear, picar — *vi* : picar

nibble[2] *n* : mordisco *m*

Nicaraguan [ˌnɪkə'rɑgwən] *n* : nicaragüense *mf* — **Nicaraguan** *adj*

nice ['naɪs] *adj* **nicer; nicest 1** REFINED : pulido, refinado **2** SUBTLE : fino, sutil **3** PLEASING : agradable, bueno, lindo <nice weather : buen tiempo> **4** RESPECTABLE : bueno, decente **5 nice and** : bien, muy <nice and hot : bien caliente> <nice and slow : despacito>

nicely ['naɪsli] *adv* **1** KINDLY : amablemente **2** POLITELY : con buenos modales **3** ATTRACTIVELY : de buen gusto

niceness ['naɪsnəs] *n* : simpatía *f,* amabilidad *f*

nicety ['naɪsət̬i] *n, pl* **-ties 1** DETAIL, SUBTLETY : sutileza *f,* detalle *m* **2 niceties** *npl* : lujos *mpl,* detalles *mpl*

niche ['nɪtʃ] *n* **1** RECESS : nicho *m,* hornacina *f* **2** : nicho *m,* hueco *m* <to make a niche for oneself : hacerse un hueco, encontrarse una buena posición>

nick[1] ['nɪk] *vt* : cortar, hacer una muesca en

nick[2] *n* **1** CUT : corte *m,* muesca *f* **2 in the nick of time** : en el momento crítico, justo a tiempo

nickel ['nɪkəl] *n* **1** : níquel *m* **2** : moneda *f* de cinco centavos

nickname[1] ['nɪkˌneɪm] *vt* **-named; -naming** : apodar

nickname[2] *n* : apodo *m,* mote *m,* sobrenombre *m*

nicotine ['nɪkəˌtiːn] *n* : nicotina *f*

niece ['niːs] *n* : sobrina *f*

Nigerian [naɪ'dʒɪriən] *n* : nigeriano *m,* -na *f* — **Nigerian** *adj*

niggardly ['nɪgərdli] *adj* : mezquino, tacaño

niggling ['nɪgəlɪŋ] *adj* **1** PETTY : insignificante **2** PERSISTENT : constante, persistente <a niggling doubt : una duda constante>

nigh[1] ['naɪ] *adv* **1** NEARLY : casi **2 to draw nigh** : acercarse, avecinarse

nigh[2] *adj* : cercano, próximo

night[1] ['naɪt] *adj* : nocturno, de la noche <the night sky : el cielo nocturno> <night shift : turno de la noche>

night[2] *n* **1** EVENING : noche *f* <at night : de noche> <last night : anoche> <tomorrow night : mañana por la noche> **2** DARKNESS : noche *f,* oscuridad *f* <night fell : cayó la noche>

nightclothes ['naɪtˌkloːðz, -ˌkloːz] *npl* : ropa *f* de dormir

nightclub ['naɪtˌklʌb] *n* : cabaret *m,* club *m* nocturno

night crawler ['naɪtˌkrɔlər] *n* EARTHWORM : lombriz *f* (de tierra)

nightfall ['naɪtˌfɔl] *n* : anochecer *m*

nightgown ['naɪtˌgaʊn] *n* : camisón *m* (de noche)

nightingale ['naɪtənˌgeɪl, 'naɪt̬ɪŋ-] *n* : ruiseñor *m*

nightly[1] ['naɪtli] *adv* : cada noche, todas las noches

nightly[2] *adj* : de todas las noches

nightmare ['naɪtˌmær] *n* : pesadilla *f*

nightmarish ['naɪtˌmærɪʃ] *adj* : de pesadilla

night owl *n* : noctámbulo *m,* -la *f*

nightshade ['naɪtˌʃeɪd] *n* : hierba *f* mora

nightshirt ['naɪtˌʃərt] *n* : camisa *f* de dormir

nightstick ['naɪtˌstɪk] *n* : porra *f*

nighttime ['naɪtˌtaɪm] *n* : noche *f*

nil ['nɪl] *n* : nada *f,* cero *m*

nimble ['nɪmbəl] *adj* **-bler; -blest 1** AGILE : ágil **2** CLEVER : hábil, ingenioso

nimbleness ['nɪmbəlnəs] *n* : agilidad *f*

nimbly [ˈnɪmbli] *adv* : con agilidad, ágilmente
nincompoop [ˈnɪnkəmˌpuːp, ˈnɪŋ-] *n* FOOL : tonto *m*, -ta *f;* bobo *m*, -ba *f*
nine[1] [ˈnaɪn] *adj* **1** : nueve **2 nine times out of ten** : casi siempre
nine[2] *n* : nueve *m*
nine hundred[1] *adj* : novecientos
nine hundred[2] *n* : novecientos *m*
ninepins [ˈnaɪnˌpɪnz] *n* : bolos *mpl*
nineteen[1] [naɪnˈtiːn] *adj* : diecinueve
nineteen[2] *n* : diecinueve *m*
nineteenth[1] [naɪnˈtiːnθ] *adj* : decimoveno, decimonono <the nineteenth century : el siglo diecinueve>
nineteenth[2] *n* : decimonoveno *m*, -na *f;* decimonono *m*, -na *f* (en una serie) **2** : diecinueveavo *m*, diecinueveava parte *f*
ninetieth[1] [ˈnaɪntiəθ] *adj* : nonagésimo
ninetieth[2] *n* **1** : nonagésimo *m*, -ma *f* (en una serie) **2** : noventavo *m*, noventava parte *f*
ninety[1] [ˈnaɪnti] *adj* : noventa
ninety[2] *n, pl* **-ties** : noventa *m*
ninth[1] [ˈnaɪnθ] *adj* : noveno
ninth[2] *n* **1** : noveno *m*, -na *f* (en una serie) **2** : noveno *m*, novena parte *f*
ninny [ˈnɪni] *n, pl* **ninnies** FOOL : tonto *m*, -ta *f;* bobo *m*, -ba *f*
nip[1] [ˈnɪp] *vt* **nipped; nipping 1** PINCH : pellizcar **2** BITE : morder, mordisquear **3 to nip in the bud** : cortar de raíz
nip[2] *n* **1** TANG : sabor *m* fuerte **2** PINCH : pellizco *m* **3** NIBBLE : mordisco *m* **4** SWALLOW : trago *m*, traguito *m* **5 there's a nip in the air** : hace fresco
nipple [ˈnɪpəl] *n* : pezón *m* (de una mujer), tetilla *f* (de un hombre)
nippy [ˈnɪpi] *adj* **-pier; -est 1** SHARP : fuerte, picante **2** CHILLY : frío <it's nippy today : hoy hace frío>
nit [ˈnɪt] *n* : liendre *f*
nitrate [ˈnaɪˌtreɪt] *n* : nitrato *m*
nitric acid [ˈnaɪtrɪk] *n* : ácido *m* nítrico
nitrite [ˈnaɪˌtraɪt] *n* : nitrito *m*
nitrogen [ˈnaɪtrədʒən] *n* : nitrógen *m*
nitroglycerin *or* **nitroglycerine** [ˌnaɪtroˈglɪsərən] *n* : nitroglicerina *f*
nitwit [ˈnɪtˌwɪt] *n* : zonzo *m*, -za *f;* bobo *m*, -ba *f*
no[1] [ˈnoː] *adv* : no <are you leaving?—no : ¿te vas?—no> <no less than : no menos de> <to say no : decir que no> <like it or no : quieras o no quieras>
no[2] *adj* **1** : ninguno <it's no trouble : no es ningún problema> <she has no money : no tiene dinero> **2** (*indicating a small amount*) <we'll be there in no time : llegamos dentro de poco, no tardamos nada> **3** (*expressing a negation*) <he's no liar : no es mentiroso>
no[3] *n, pl* **noes** *or* **nos** [ˈnoːz] **1** DENIAL : no *m* <I won't take no for an answer : no aceptaré un no por respuesta> **2** : vota *f* en contra <the noes have it : se ha rechazado la moción>
nobility [noˈbɪləti] *n* : nobleza *f*
noble[1] [ˈnoːbəl] *adj* **-bler; -blest 1** ILLUSTRIOUS : noble, glorioso **2** ARISTOCRATIC : noble **3** STATELY : majestuoso, magnífico **4** LOFTY : noble, elevado <noble sentiments : sentimientos elevados>
noble[2] *n* : noble *mf,* aristócrata *mf*
nobleman [ˈnoːbəlmən] *n, pl* **-men** [-mən, -ˌmɛn] : noble *m,* aristócrata *m*
nobleness [ˈnoːbəlnəs] *n* : nobleza *f*
noblewoman [ˈnoːbəlˌwʊmən] *n, pl* **-women** [-ˌwɪmən] : noble *f,* aristócrata *f*
nobly [ˈnoːbli] *adv* : noblemente
nobody[1] [ˈnoːbədi, -ˌbɑdi] *n, pl* **-bodies** : don nadie *m* <he's a mere nobody : es un don nadie>
nobody[2] *pron* : nadie
nocturnal [nɑkˈtərnəl] *adj* : nocturno
nocturne [ˈnɑkˌtərn] *n* : nocturno *m*
nod[1] [ˈnɑd] *v* **nodded; nodding** *vi* **1** : saludar con la cabeza, asentir con la cabeza **2 to nod off** : dormirse, quedarse dormido — *vt* : inclinar (la cabeza) <to nod one's head in agreement : asentir con la cabeza>
nod[2] *n* : saludo *m* con la cabeza, señal *m* con la cabeza, señal *m* de asentimiento
node [ˈnoːd] *n* : nudo *m* (de una planta)
nodule [ˈnɑˌdʒuːl] *n* : nódulo *m*
noel [noˈɛl] *n* **1** CAROL : villancico *m* de Navidad **2 Noel** CHRISTMAS : Navidad *f*
noes → **no**[3]
noise[1] [ˈnɔɪz] *vt* **noised; noising** : rumorear, publicar
noise[2] *n* : ruido *m*
noiseless [ˈnɔɪzləs] *adj* : silencioso, sin ruido
noiselessly [ˈnɔɪzləsli] *adv* : silenciosamente
noisemaker [ˈnɔɪzˌmeɪkər] *n* : matraca *f*
noisiness [ˈnɔɪzinəs] *n* : ruido *m*
noisome [ˈnɔɪsəm] *adj* : maloliente, fétido
noisy [ˈnɔɪzi] *adj* **noisier; -est** : ruidoso — **noisily** [ˈnɔɪzəli] *adv*
nomad[1] [ˈnoːˌmæd] → **nomadic**
nomad[2] *n* : nómada *mf*
nomadic [noˈmædɪk] *adj* : nómada
nomenclature [ˈnoːmənˌkleɪtʃər] *n* : nomenclatura *f*
nominal [ˈnɑmənəl] *adj* **1** : nominal <the nominal head of his party : el jefe nominal de su partido> **2** TRIFLING : insignificante
nominally [ˈnɑmənəli] *adv* : sólo de nombre, nominalmente
nominate [ˈnɑməˌneɪt] *vt* **-nated; -nating 1** PROPOSE : proponer (como candidato), nominar **2** APPOINT : nombrar

nomination [ˌnɑməˈneɪʃən] *n* **1** PROPOSAL : propuesta *f,* postulación *f* **2** APPOINTMENT : nombramiento *m*

nominative[1] [ˈnɑmənət̬ɪv] *adj* : nominativo

nominative[2] *n or* **nominative case** : nominativo *m*

nominee [ˌnɑməˈniː] *n* : candidato *m,* -ta *f*

nonaddictive [ˌnɑnəˈdɪktɪv] *adj* : que no crea dependencia

nonalcoholic [ˌnɑnˌælkəˈhɔlɪk] *adj* : sin alcohol, no alcohólico

nonaligned [ˌnɑnəˈlaɪnd] *adj* : no alineado

nonbeliever [ˌnɑnbəˈliːvər] *n* : no creyente *mf*

nonbreakable [ˌnɑnˈbreɪkəbəl] *adj* : irrompible

nonce [ˈnɑnts] *n* **for the nonce** : por el momento

nonchalance [ˌnɑnʃəˈlɑnts] *n* : indiferencia *f,* despreocupación *f*

nonchalant [ˌnɑnʃəˈlɑnt] *adj* : indiferente, despreocupado, impasible

nonchalantly [ˌnɑnʃəˈlɑntli] *adv* : con aire despreocupado, con indiferencia

noncombatant [ˌnɑnkəmˈbætənt, -ˈkɑmbə-] *adj* : no combatiente *mf*

noncommissioned officer [ˌnɑnkəˈmɪʃənd] *n* : suboficial *mf*

noncommittal [ˌnɑnkəˈmɪt̬əl] *adj* : evasivo, que no se compromete

nonconductor [ˌnɑnkənˈdʌktər] *n* : aislante *m*

nonconformist [ˌnɑnkənˈfɔrmɪst] *n* : inconformista *mf,* inconforme *mf*

nonconformity [ˌnɑnkənˈfɔrmət̬i] *n* : inconformidad *f,* no conformidad *f*

noncontagious [ˌnɑnkənˈteɪdʒəs] *adj* : no contagioso

nondenominational [ˌnɑndɪˌnɑməˈneɪʃənəl] *adj* : no sectario

nondescript [ˌnɑndɪˈskrɪpt] *adj* : anodino, soso

nondiscriminatory [ˌnɑndɪˈskrɪmənəˌtori] *adj* : no discriminatorio

nondrinker [ˌnɑnˈdrɪŋkər] *n* : abstemio *m,* -mia *f*

none[1] [ˈnʌn] *adv* : de ninguna manera, de ningún modo, nada <he was none too happy : no se sintió nada contento> <I'm none the worse for it : no estoy peor por ello> <none too soon : a buena hora>

none[2] *pron* : ninguno, ninguna

nonentity [ˌnɑnˈɛntət̬i] *n, pl* **-ties** : persona *f* insignificante, nulidad *f*

nonessential [ˌnɑnɪˈsɛntʃəl] *adj* : secundario, no esencial

nonessentials [ˌnɑnɪˈsɛntʃəlz] *npl* : cosas *fpl* secundarias, cosas *fpl* accesorias

nonetheless [ˌnʌnðəˈlɛs] *adv* : sin embargo, no obstante

nonexistence [ˌnɑnɪgˈzɪstənts] *n* : inexistencia *f*

nonexistent [ˌnɑnɪgˈzɪstənt] *adj* : inexistente

nonfat [ˌnɑnˈfæt] *adj* : sin grasa

nonfattening [ˌnɑnˈfætənɪŋ] *adj* : que no engorda

nonfiction [ˌnɑnˈfɪkʃən] *n* : no ficción *f*

nonflammable [ˌnɑnˈflæməbəl] *adj* : no inflamable

nonintervention [ˌnɑnˌɪntərˈvɛntʃən] *n* : no intervención *f*

nonmalignant [ˌnɑnməˈlɪgnənt] *adj* : no maligno, benigno

nonnegotiable [ˌnɑnnɪˈgoːʃəbəl, -ʃiə-] *adj* : no negociable

nonpareil[1] [ˌnɑnpəˈrɛl] *adj* : sin parangón, sin par

nonpareil[2] *n* : persona *f* sin igual, cosa *f* sin par

nonpartisan [ˌnɑnˈpɑrt̬əzən, -sən] *adj* : imparcial

nonpaying [ˌnɑnˈpeɪɪŋ] *adj* : que no paga

nonpayment [ˌnɑnˈpeɪmənt] *n* : impago *m,* falta *f* de pago

nonperson [ˌnɑnˈpərsən] *n* : persona *f* sin derechos

nonplus [ˌnɑnˈplʌs] *vt* **-plussed; -plussing** : confundir, desconcertar, dejar perplejo

nonprescription [ˌnɑnprɪˈskrɪpʃən] *adj* : disponible sin receta del médico

nonproductive [ˌnɑnprəˈdʌktɪv] *adj* : improductivo

nonprofit [ˌnɑnˈprɑfət] *adj* : sin fines lucrativos

nonproliferation [ˌnɑnprəˌlɪfəˈreɪʃən] *adj* : no proliferación

nonresident [ˌnɑnˈrɛzədənt, -ˌdɛnt] *n* : no residente *mf*

nonscheduled [ˌnɑnˈskɛˌdʒuːld] *adj* : no programado, no regular

nonsectarian [ˌnɑnˌsɛkˈtæriən] *adj* : no sectario

nonsense [ˈnɑnˌsɛnts, ˈnɑntsənts] *n* : tonterías *fpl,* disparates *mpl*

nonsensical [nɑnˈsɛntsɪkəl] *adj* ABSURD : absurdo, disparatado — **nonsensically** [-kli] *adv*

nonsmoker [ˌnɑnˈsmoːkər] *n* : no fumador *m,* -dora *f;* persona *f* que no fuma

nonstandard [ˌnɑnˈstændərd] *adj* : no regular, no estándar

nonstick [ˌnɑnˈstɪk] *adj* : antiadherente

nonstop[1] [ˌnɑnˈstɑp] *adv* : sin parar <he talked nonstop : habló sin parar>

nonstop[2] *adj* : directo, sin escalas <nonstop flight : vuelo directo>

nonsupport [ˌnɑnsəˈport] *n* : falta *f* de manutención

nontaxable [ˌnɑnˈtæksəbəl] *adj* : exento de impuestos

nontoxic [ˌnɑnˈtɑksɪk] *adj* : no tóxico

nonviolence [ˌnɑnˈvaɪlənts, -ˈvaɪə-] *n* : no violencia *f*

nonviolent [ˌnɑnˈvaɪlənt, -ˈvaɪə-] *adj* : pacífico, no violento

noodle [ˈnuːdəl] *n* : fideo *m,* tallarín *m*

nook [ˈnʊk] *n* : rincón *m,* recoveco *m,* escondrijo *m* <in every nook and cranny : en todos los rincones>
noon [ˈnuːn] *n* : mediodía *m*
noonday [ˈnuːn,deɪ] *n* : mediodía *m* <the noonday sun : el sol de mediodía>
no one *pron* NOBODY : nadie
noontime [ˈnuːn,taɪm] *n* : mediodía *m*
noose [ˈnuːs] *n* **1** LASSO : lazo *m* **2 hangman's noose:** dogal *m,* soga *f*
nor [ˈnɔr] *conj* : ni <neither good nor bad : ni bueno ni malo> <nor I! : ¡ni yo tampoco!>
Nordic [ˈnɔrdɪk] *adj* : nórdico
norm [ˈnɔrm] *n* **1** STANDARD : norma *f,* modelo *m* **2** CUSTOM, RULE : regla *f* general, lo normal
normal [ˈnɔrməl] *adj* : normal — **normally** *adv*
normalcy [ˈnɔrməlsi] *n* : normalidad *f*
normality [nɔrˈmæləṭi] *n* : normalidad *f*
normalize [ˈnɔrmə,laɪz] *vt* : normalizar
Norse [ˈnɔrs] *adj* : nórdico
north¹ [ˈnɔrθ] *adv* : al norte
north² *adj* : norte, del norte <the north coast : la costa del norte>
north³ *n* **1** : norte *m* **2 the North** : el Norte *m*
northbound [ˈnɔrθ,baʊnd] *adv* : con rumbo al norte
North American *n* : norteamericano *m,* -na *f* — **North American** *adj*
northeast¹ [nɔrθˈiːst] *adv* : hacia el nordeste
northeast² *adj* : nordeste, del nordeste
northeast³ *n* : nordeste *m,* noreste *m*
northeasterly¹ [nɔrθˈiːstərli] *adv* : hacia el nordeste
northeasterly² *adj* : nordeste, del nordeste
northeastern [nɔrθˈiːstərn] *adj* : nordeste, del nordeste
northerly¹ [ˈnɔrðərli] *adv* : hacia el norte
northerly² *adj* : del norte <a northerly wind : un viento del norte>
northern [ˈnɔrðərn] *adj* : norte, norteño, septentrional
Northerner [ˈnɔrðərnər] *n* : norteño *m,* -ña *f*
northern lights → **aurora borealis**
North Pole : Polo *m* Norte
North Star *n* : estrella *f* polar
northward [ˈnɔrθwərd] *adv & adj* : hacia el norte
northwest¹ [nɔrθˈwɛst] *adv* : hacia el noroeste
northwest² *adj* : del noroeste
northwest³ *n* : noroeste *m*
northwesterly¹ [nɔrθˈwɛstərli] *adv* : hacia el noroeste
northwesterly² *adj* : del noroeste
northwestern [nɔrθˈwɛstərn] *adj* : noroeste, del noroeste
Norwegian [nɔrˈwiːdʒən] *n* **1** : noruego *m,* -ga *f* **2** : noruego *m* (idioma) — **Norwegian** *adj*
nose¹ [ˈnoːz] *v* **nosed; nosing** *vt* **1** SMELL : olfatear **2** : empujar con el hocico <the dog nosed open the bag : el perro abrió el saco con el hocico> **3** EDGE, MOVE : mover poco a poco — *vi* **1** PRY : entrometerse, meter las narices **2** EDGE : avanzar poco a poco
nose² *n* **1** : nariz *f* (de una persona), hocico *m* (de un animal) <to blow one's nose : sonarse las narices> **2** SMELL : olfato *m,* sentido *m* del olfato **3** FRONT : parte *f* delantera, nariz *f* (de un avión), proa *f* (de un barco) **4 to follow one's nose** : dejarse guiar por el instinto
nosebleed [ˈnoːz,bliːd] *n* : hemorragia *f* nasal
nosedive [ˈnoːz,daɪv] *n* **1** : descenso *m* en picada (de un avión) **2** : caída *f* súbita (de precios, etc.)
nose–dive [ˈnoːz,daɪv] *vi* : descender en picada, caer en picada
nostalgia [nɑˈstældʒə, nə-] *n* : nostalgia *f*
nostalgic [nɑˈstældʒɪk, nə-] *adj* : nostálgico
nostril [ˈnɑstrəl] *n* : ventana *f* de la nariz
nostrum [ˈnɑstrəm] *n* : panacea *f*
nosy *or* **nosey** [ˈnoːzi] *adj* **nosier; -est** : entrometido
not [ˈnɑt] *adv* **1** (*used to form a negative*) : no <she is not tired : no está cansada> <not to say something would be wrong : no decir nada sería injusto> **2** (*used to replace a negative clause*) : no <are we going or not? : ¿vamos a ir o no?> <of course not! : ¡claro que no!>
notable¹ [ˈnoːṭəbəl] *adj* **1** NOTEWORTHY : notable, de notar **2** DISTINGUISHED, PROMINENT : distinguido, destacado
notable² *n* : persona *f* importante, personaje *m*
notably [ˈnoːṭəbli] *adv* : notablemente, particularmente
notarize [ˈnoːṭə,raɪz] *vt* **-rized; -rizing** : autenticar, autorizar
notary public [ˈnoːṭəri] *n, pl* **-ries public** *or* **-ry publics** : notario *m,* -ria *f;* escribano *m,* -na *f*
notation [noˈteɪʃən] *n* **1** NOTE : anotación *f,* nota *f* **2** : notación *f* <musical notation : notación musical>
notch¹ [ˈnɑtʃ] *vt* : hacer una muesca en, cortar
notch² *n* : muesca *f,* corte *m*
note¹ [ˈnoːt] *vt* **noted; noting 1** NOTICE : notar, observar, tomar nota de **2** RECORD : anotar, apuntar
note² *n* **1** : nota *f* (musical) **2** COMMENT : nota *f,* comentario *m* **3** LETTER : nota *f,* cartita *f* **4** PROMINENCE : prestigio *m* <a musician of note : un músico destacado> **5** ATTENTION : atención *f* <to take note of : prestar atención a>

notebook [ˈnoːtˌbʊk] *n* : libreta *f,* cuaderno *m*

noted [ˈnoːtəd] *adj* EMINENT : renombrado, eminente, celebrado

noteworthy [ˈnoːtˌwərðiː] *adj* : notable, de notar, de interés

nothing[1] [ˈnʌθɪŋ] *adv* **1** : de ninguna manera <nothing daunted, we carried on : sin amilanarnos, seguimos adelante> **2 nothing like** : no...en nada <he's nothing like his brother : no se parece en nada a su hermano>

nothing[2] *n* **1** NOTHINGNESS : nada *f* **2** ZERO : cero *m* **3** : persona *f* de poca importancia, cero *m* **4** TRIFLE : nimiedad *f*

nothing[3] *pron* : nada <there's nothing better : no hay nada mejor> <nothing else : nada más> <nothing but : solamente> <they mean nothing to me : ellos me son indiferentes>

nothingness [ˈnʌθɪŋnəs] *n* **1** VOID : vacío *m,* nada *f* **2** NONEXISTENCE : inexistencia *f* **3** TRIFLE : nimiedad *f*

notice[1] [ˈnoːtɪs] *vt* **-ticed; -ticing** : notar, observar, advertir, darse cuenta de

notice[2] *n* **1** NOTIFICATION : aviso *m,* notificación *f* **2** ATTENTION : atención *f* <to take notice of : prestar atención a>

noticeable [ˈnoːtɪsəbəl] *adj* : evidente, perceptible — **noticeably** [-bli] *adv*

notification [ˌnoːtəfəˈkeɪʃən] *n* : notificación *f,* aviso *m*

notify [ˈnoːtəˌfaɪ] *vt* **-fied; -fying** : notificar, avisar

notion [ˈnoːʃən] *n* **1** IDEA : idea *f,* noción *f* **2** WHIM : capricho *m,* antojo *m* **3 notions** *npl* : artículos *mpl* de mercería

notoriety [ˌnoːtəˈraɪəti] *n* : mala fama *f,* notoriedad *f*

notorious [noˈtoːriəs] *adj* : de mala fama, célebre, bien conocido

notwithstanding[1] [ˌnɑtwɪθˈstændɪŋ, -wɪð-] *adv* NEVERTHELESS : no obstante, sin embargo

notwithstanding[2] *conj* : a pesar de que

notwithstanding[3] *prep* : a pesar de, no obstante

nougat [ˈnuːgət] *n* : turrón *m*

nought [ˈnɔt, ˈnɑt] → **naught**

noun [ˈnaʊn] *n* : nombre *m,* sustantivo *m*

nourish [ˈnərɪʃ] *vt* **1** FEED : alimentar, nutrir, sustentar **2** FOSTER : fomentar, alentar

nourishing [ˈnərɪʃɪŋ] *adj* : alimenticio, nutritivo

nourishment [ˈnərɪʃmənt] *n* : nutrición *f,* alimento *m,* sustento *m*

novel[1] [ˈnɑvəl] *adj* : original, novedoso

novel[2] *n* : novela *f*

novelist [ˈnɑvəlɪst] *n* : novelista *mf*

novelty [ˈnɑvəlti] *n, pl* **-ties 1** : novedad *f* **2 novelties** *npl* TRINKETS : baratijas *fpl,* chucherías *fpl*

November [noˈvɛmbər] *n* : noviembre *m*

novice [ˈnɑvɪs] *n* : novato *m,* -ta *f;* principiante *mf;* novicio *m,* -cia *f*

now[1] [ˈnaʊ] *adv* **1** PRESENTLY : ahora, ya, actualmente <from now on : de ahora en adelante> <long before now : ya hace tiempo> <now and then : de vez en cuando> **2** IMMEDIATELY : ahora (mismo), inmediatamente <do it right now! : ¡hazlo ahora mismo!> **3** THEN : ya, entonces <now they were ready : ya estaban listos> **4** (*used to introduce a statement, a question, a command, or a transition*) <now hear this! : ¡presten atención!> <now what do you think of that? : ¿qué piensas de eso?>

now[2] *n* (*indicating the present time*) <until now : hasta ahora> <by now : ya> <ten years from now : dentro de 10 años>

now[3] *conj* **now that** : ahora que, ya que

nowadays [ˈnaʊəˌdeɪz] *adv* : hoy en día, actualmente, en la actualidad

nowhere[1] [ˈnoːˌhwɛr] *adv* **1** : en ninguna parte, a ningún lado <nowhere to be found : en ninguna parte, por ningún lado> <you're going nowhere : no estás yendo a ningún lado, no estás yendo a ninguna parte> **2 nowhere near** : ni con mucho, nada cerca <it's nowhere near here : no está nada cerca de aquí>

nowhere[2] *n* **1** : ninguna parte *f* **2 out of nowhere** : de la nada

noxious [ˈnɑkʃəs] *adj* : nocivo, dañino, tóxico

nozzle [ˈnɑzəl] *n* : boca *f*

nuance [ˈnuːˌɑnts, ˈnjuː-] *n* : matiz *m*

nub [ˈnʌb] *n* **1** KNOB, LUMP : protuberancia *f,* nudo *m* **2** GIST : quid *m,* meollo *m*

nuclear [ˈnuːkliər, ˈnjuː-] *adj* : nuclear

nucleus [ˈnuːkliəs, ˈnjuː-] *n, pl* **-clei** [-kliˌaɪ] : núcleo *m*

nude[1] [ˈnuːd, ˈnjuːd] *adj* **nuder; nudest** : desnudo

nude[2] *n* : desnudo *m*

nudge[1] [ˈnʌdʒ] *vt* **nudged; nudging** : darle con el codo (a alguien)

nudge[2] *n* : toque *m* que se da con el codo

nudism [ˈnuːˌdɪzəm, ˈnjuː-] *n* : nudismo *m*

nudist [ˈnuːdɪst, ˈnjuː-] *n* : nudista *mf*

nudity [ˈnuːdəti, ˈnjuː-] *n* : desnudez *f*

nugget [ˈnʌgət] *n* : pepita *f*

nuisance [ˈnuːsənts, ˈnjuː-] *n* **1** BOTHER : fastidio *m,* molestia *f,* lata *f* **2** PEST : peste *f;* pesado *m,* -da *f fam*

null [ˈnʌl] *adj* : nulo <null and void : nulo y sin efecto>

nullify [ˈnʌləˌfaɪ] *vt* **-fied; -fying** : invalidar, anular

numb[1] [ˈnʌm] *vt* : entumecer, adormecer

numb[2] *adj* : entumecido, dormido <numb with fear : paralizado de miedo>

number[1] [ˈnʌmbər] *vt* **1** COUNT, INCLUDE : contar, incluir **2** : numerar <number the pages : numera las páginas> **3** TOTAL : ascender a, sumar

number[2] *n* **1** : número *m* <in round numbers : en números redondos> <telephone number : número de teléfono> **2 a number of** : varios, unos pocos, unos cuantos

numberless [ˈnʌmbərləs] *adj* : innumerable, sin número

numbness [ˈnʌmnəs] *n* : entumecimiento *m*

numeral [ˈnuːmərəl, ˈnjuː-] *n* : número *m* <Roman numeral : número romano>

numerator [ˈnuːməˌreɪt̬ər, ˈnjuː-] *n* : numerador *m*

numeric [nʊˈmɛrɪk, njʊ-] *adj* : numérico

numerical [nʊˈmɛrɪkəl, njʊ-] *adj* : numérico — **numerically** [-kli] *adv*

numerous [ˈnuːmərəs, ˈnjuː-] *adj* : numeroso

numismatics [ˌnuːməzˈmæt̬ɪks, ˌnjuː-] *n* : numismática *f*

numskull [ˈnʌmˌskʌl] *n* : tonto *m*, -ta *f*; mentecato *m*, -ta *f*; zoquete *m fam*

nun [ˈnʌn] *n* : monja *f*

nuptial [ˈnʌpʃəl] *adj* : nupcial

nuptials [ˈnʌpʃəlz] *npl* WEDDING : nupcias *fpl*, boda *f*

nurse[1] [ˈnərs] *vt* **nursed; nursing 1** SUCKLE : amamantar **2** : cuidar (de), atender <to nurse the sick : cuidar a los enfermos> <to nurse a cold : curarse de un resfriado>

nurse[2] *n* **1** : enfermero *m*, -ra *f* **2** → **nursemaid**

nursemaid [ˈnərsˌmeɪd] *n* : niñera *f*

nursery [ˈnərsəri] *n, pl* **-eries 1** *or* **day nursery** : guardería *f* **2** : vivero *m* (de plantas)

nursing home *n* : hogar *m* de ancianos, clínica *f* de reposo

nurture[1] [ˈnərtʃər] *vt* **-tured; -turing 1** FEED, NOURISH : nutrir, alimentar **2** EDUCATE : criar, educar **3** FOSTER : alimentar, fomentar

nurture[2] *n* **1** UPBRINGING : crianza *f*, educación *f* **2** FOOD : alimento *m*

nut [ˈnʌt] *n* **1** : nuez *f* **2** : tuerca *f* <nuts and bolts : tuercas y tornillos> **3** LUNATIC : loco *m*, -ca *f*; chiflado *m*, -da *f fam* **4** ENTHUSIAST : fanático *m*, -ca *f*; entusiasta *mf*

nutcracker [ˈnʌtˌkrækər] *n* : cascanueces *m*

nuthatch [ˈnʌtˌhætʃ] *n* : trepador *m*

nutmeg [ˈnʌtˌmɛg] *n* : nuez *f* moscada

nutrient [ˈnuːtriənt, ˈnjuː-] *n* : nutriente *m*, alimento *m* nutritivo

nutriment [ˈnuːtrəmənt, ˈnjuː-] *n* : nutrimento *m*

nutrition [nʊˈtrɪʃən, njʊ-] *n* : nutrición *f*

nutritional [nʊˈtrɪʃənəl, njʊ-] *adj* : alimenticio

nutritious [nʊˈtrɪʃəs, njʊ-] *adj* : nutritivo, alimenticio

nuts [ˈnʌts] *adj* **1** FANATICAL : fanático **2** CRAZY : loco, chiflado *fam*

nutshell [ˈnʌtˌʃɛl] *n* **1** : cáscara *f* de nuez **2 in a nutshell** : en pocas palabras

nutty [ˈnʌt̬i] *adj* **-tier; -tiest** : loco, chiflado *fam*

nuzzle [ˈnʌzəl] *v* **-zled; -zling** *vi* NESTLE : acurrucarse, arrimarse — *vt* : acariciar con el hocico

nylon [ˈnaɪˌlɑn] *n* **1** : nilón *m* **2 nylons** *npl* : medias *fpl* de nilón

nymph [ˈnɪmpf] *n* : ninfa *f*

O

o [ˈoː] *n, pl* **o's** *or* **os** [ˈoːz] **1** : decimoquinta letra del alfabeto inglés **2** ZERO : cero *m*

O [ˈoː] → **oh**

oaf [ˈoːf] *n* : zoquete *m*; bruto *m*, -ta *f*

oafish [ˈoːfɪʃ] *adj* : torpe, lerdo

oak [ˈoːk] *n, pl* **oaks** *or* **oak** : roble *m*

oaken [ˈoːkən] *adj* : de roble

oar [ˈor] *n* : remo *m*

oarlock [ˈorˌlɑk] *n* : tolete *m*, escálamo *m*

oasis [oˈeɪsɪs] *n, pl* **oases** [-ˌsiːz] : oasis *m*

oat [ˈoːt] *n* : avena *f*

oath [ˈoːθ] *n, pl* **oaths** [ˈoːðz, ˈoːθs] **1** : juramento *m* <to take an oath : prestar juramento> **2** SWEARWORD : mala palabra *f*, palabrota *f*

oatmeal [ˈoːtˌmiːl] *n* : avena *f* <instant oatmeal : avena instantánea>

obdurate [ˈɑbdʊrət, -djʊ-] *adj* : inflexible, firme, obstinado

obedience [oˈbiːdiənts] *n* : obediencia *f*

obedient [oˈbiːdiənt] *adj* : obediente — **obediently** *adv*

obelisk [ˈɑbəˌlɪsk] *n* : obelisco *m*

obese [oˈbiːs] *adj* : obeso

obesity [oˈbiːsət̬i] *n* : obesidad *f*

obey [oˈbeɪ] *v* **obeyed; obeying** : obedecer <to obey the law : cumplir la ley>

obfuscate [ˈɑbfəˌskeɪt] *vt* **-cated; -cating** : ofuscar, confundir

obituary [əˈbɪtʃʊˌɛri] *n, pl* **-aries** : obituario *m*, necrología *f*

object[1] [əbˈdʒɛkt] *vt* : objetar — *vi* : oponerse, poner reparos, hacer objeciones

object[2] [ˈɑbdʒɪkt] *n* **1** : objeto *m* **2** OBJECTIVE, PURPOSE : objetivo *m*, pro-

pósito *m* **3** : complemento *m* (en gramática)
objection [əb'dʒɛkʃən] *n* : objeción *f*
objectionable [əb'dʒɛkʃənəbəl] *adj* : ofensivo, indeseable — **objectionably** [-bli] *adv*
objective[1] [əb'dʒɛktɪv] *adj* **1** IMPARTIAL : objetivo, imparcial **2** : de complemento, directo (en gramática)
objective[2] *n* **1** : objetivo *m* **2** *or* **objective case** : acusativo *m*
objectively [əb'dʒɛktɪvli] *adv* : objetivamente
objectivity [ˌɑbˌdʒɛk'tɪvəṭi] *n, pl* **-ties** : objetividad *f*
obligate ['ɑbləˌgeɪt] *vt* **-gated; -gating** : obligar
obligation [ˌɑblə'geɪʃən] *n* : obligación *f*
obligatory [ə'blɪgəˌtori] *adj* : obligatorio
oblige [ə'blaɪdʒ] *vt* **obliged; obliging** **1** COMPEL : obligar **2** : hacerle un favor (a alguien), complacer <to oblige a friend : hacerle un favor a un amigo> **3 to be much obliged** : estar muy agradecido
obliging [ə'blaɪdʒɪŋ] *adj* : servicial, complaciente — **obligingly** *adv*
oblique [o'bliːk] *adj* **1** SLANTING : oblicuo **2** INDIRECT : indirecto — **obliquely** *adv*
obliterate [ə'blɪṭəˌreɪt] *vt* **-ated; -ating** **1** ERASE : obliterar, borrar **2** DESTROY : destruir, eliminar
obliteration [əˌblɪṭə'reɪʃən] *n* : obliteración *f*
oblivion [ə'blɪviən] *n* : olvido *m*
oblivious [ə'blɪviəs] *adj* : inconsciente — **obliviously** *adv*
oblong[1] ['ɑˌblɔŋ] *adj* : oblongo
oblong[2] *n* : figura *f* oblonga, rectángulo *m*
obnoxious [ɑb'nɑkʃəs, əb-] *adj* : repugnante, odioso — **obnoxiously** *adv*
oboe ['oːˌboː] *n* : oboe *m*
oboist ['oˌboɪst] *n* : oboe *mf*
obscene [ɑb'siːn, əb-] *adj* : obsceno, indecente — **obscenely** *adv*
obscenity [ɑb'sɛnəṭi, əb-] *n, pl* **-ties** : obscenidad *f*
obscure[1] [ɑb'skjʊr, əb-] *vt* **-scured; -scuring** **1** CLOUD, DIM : oscurecer, nublar **2** HIDE : ocultar
obscure[2] *adj* **1** DIM : oscuro **2** REMOTE, SECLUDED : recóndito **3** VAGUE : oscuro, confuso, vago **4** UNKNOWN : desconocido <an obscure poet : un poeta desconocido> — **obscurely** *adv*
obscurity [ɑb'skjʊrəṭi, əb-] *n, pl* **-ties** : oscuridad *f*
obsequious [əb'siːkwiəs] *adj* : servil, excesivamente atento
observable [əb'zərvəbəl] *adj* : observable, perceptible
observance [əb'zərvənts] *n* **1** FULFILLMENT : observancia *f*, cumplimiento *m* **2** PRACTICE : práctica *f*
observant [əb'zərvənt] *adj* : observador
observation [ˌɑbsər'veɪʃən, -zər-] *n* : observación *f*
observatory [əb'zərvəˌtori] *n, pl* **-ries** : observatorio *m*
observe [əb'zərv] *v* **-served; -serving** *vt* **1** OBEY : observar, obedecer **2** CELEBRATE : celebrar, guardar (una práctica religiosa) **3** WATCH : observar, mirar **4** REMARK : observar, comentar — *vi* LOOK : mirar
obsess [əb'sɛs] *vt* : obsesionar
obsession [ɑb'sɛʃən, əb-] *n* : obsesión *f*
obsessive [ɑb'sɛsɪv, əb-] *adj* : obsesivo — **obsessively** *adv*
obsolescence [ˌɑbsə'lɛsənts] *n* : obsolescencia *f*
obsolescent [ˌɑbsə'lɛsənt] *adj* : obsolescente <to become obsolescent : caer en desuso>
obsolete [ˌɑbsə'liːt, 'ɑbsəˌ-] *adj* : obsoleto, anticuado
obstacle ['ɑbstɪkəl] *n* : obstáculo *m*, impedimento *m*
obstetric [əb'stɛtrɪk] *or* **obstetrical** [-trɪkəl] *adj* : obstétrico
obstetrician [ˌɑbstə'trɪʃən] *n* : obstetra *mf;* tocólogo *m*, -ga *f*
obstetrics [əb'stɛtrɪks] *ns & pl* : obstetricia *f*, tocología *f*
obstinacy ['ɑbstənəsi] *n, pl* **-cies** : obstinación *f*, terquedad *f*
obstinate ['ɑbstənət] *adj* : obstinado, terco — **obstinately** *adv*
obstreperous [əb'strɛpərəs] *adj* **1** CLAMOROUS : ruidoso, clamoroso **2** UNRULY : rebelde, indisciplinado
obstruct [əb'strʌkt] *vt* : obstruir, bloquear
obstruction [əb'strʌkʃən] *n* : obstrucción *f*, bloqueo *m*
obstructive [əb'strəktɪv] *adj* : obstructor
obtain [əb'teɪn] *vt* : obtener, conseguir — *vi* PREVAIL : imperar, prevalecer
obtainable [əb'teɪnəbəl] *adj* : obtenible, asequible
obtrude [əb'truːd] *v* **-truded; -truding** *vt* **1** EXTRUDE : expulsar **2** IMPOSE : imponer — *vi* INTRUDE : inmiscuirse, entrometerse
obtrusive [əb'truːsɪv] *adj* **1** IMPERTINENT, MEDDLESOME : impertinente, entrometido **2** PROTRUDING : prominente
obtuse [ɑb'tuːs, əb-, -'tjuːs] *adj* : obtuso, torpe
obtuse angle *n* : ángulo obtuso
obviate ['ɑbviˌeɪt] *vt* **-ated; -ating** : obviar, evitar
obvious ['ɑbviəs] *adj* : obvio, evidente, manifiesto
obviously ['ɑbviəsli] *adv* **1** CLEARLY : obviamente, evidentemente **2** OF COURSE : claro, por supuesto
occasion[1] [ə'keɪʒən] *vt* : ocasionar, causar

occasion[2] *n* **1** OPPORTUNITY : oportunidad *f,* ocasión *f* **2** CAUSE : motivo *m,* razón *f* **3** INSTANCE : ocasión *f* **4** EVENT : ocasión *f,* acontecimiento *m* **5 on ~** : de vez en cuando, ocasionalmente

occasional [ə'keɪʒənəl] *adj* : ocasional

occasionally [ə'keɪʒənəli] *adv* : de vez en cuando, ocasionalmente

occidental [ˌɑksə'dɛntəl] *adj* : oeste, del oeste, occidental

occult[1] [ə'kʌlt, 'ɑˌkʌlt] *adj* **1** HIDDEN, SECRET : oculto, secreto **2** ARCANE : arcano, esotérico

occult[2] *n* **the occult** : las ciencias ocultas

occupancy ['ɑkjəpən*t*si] *n, pl* **-cies** : ocupación *f,* habitación *f*

occupant ['ɑkjəpənt] *n* : ocupante *mf*

occupation [ˌɑkjə'peɪʃən] *n* : ocupación *f,* profesión *f,* oficio *m*

occupational [ˌɑkjə'peɪʃənəl] *adj* : ocupacional

occupy ['ɑkjəˌpaɪ] *vt* **-pied; -pying** : ocupar

occur [ə'kər] *vi* **occurred; occurring** **1** EXIST : encontrarse, existir **2** HAPPEN : ocurrir, acontecer, suceder, tener lugar **3** : ocurrirse <it occurred to him that. . . : se le ocurrió que. . .>

occurrence [ə'kərən*t*s] *n* : acontecimiento *m,* suceso *m,* ocurrencia *f*

ocean ['oːʃən] *n* : océano *m*

oceanic [ˌoːʃi'ænɪk] *adj* : oceánico

oceanography [ˌoːʃə'nɑgrəfi] *n* : oceanografía *f*

ocelot ['ɑsəˌlɑt,'oː-] *n* : ocelote *m*

ocher *or* **ochre** ['oːkər] *n* : ocre *m*

o'clock [ə'klɑk] *adv* (*used in telling time*) <it's ten o'clock : son las diez> <at six o'clock : a las seis>

octagon ['ɑktəˌgɑn] *n* : octágono *m*

octagonal [ɑk'tægənəl] *adj* : octagonal

octave ['ɑktɪv] *n* : octava *f*

October [ɑk'toːbər] *n* : octubre *m*

octopus ['ɑktəˌpʊs, -pəs] *n, pl* **-puses** *or* **-pi** [-ˌpaɪ] : pulpo *m*

ocular ['ɑkjələr] *adj* : ocular

oculist ['ɑkjəlɪst] *n* **1** OPHTHALMOLOGIST : oftalmólogo *m,* -ga *f;* oculista *mf* **2** OPTOMETRIST : optometrista *mf*

odd ['ɑd] *adj* **1** : sin pareja, suelto <an odd sock : un calcetín sin pareja> **2** UNEVEN : impar <odd numbers : números impares> **3** : y pico, y tantos <forty odd years ago : hace cuarenta y pico años> **4** : alguno, uno que otro <odd jobs : algunos trabajos> **5** STRANGE : extraño, raro

oddball ['ɑdˌbɔl] *n* : excéntrico *m,* -ca *f;* persona *f* rara

oddity ['ɑdəṱi] *n, pl* **-ties** : rareza *f,* cosa *f* rara

oddly ['ɑdli] *adv* : de manera extraña

oddness ['ɑdnəs] *n* : rareza *f,* excentricidad *f*

odds ['ɑdz] *npl* **1** CHANCES : probabilidades *fpl* **2** : puntos *mpl* de ventaja (de una apuesta) **3 to be at odds** : estar en desacuerdo

odds and ends *npl* : costillas *fpl,* cosas *fpl* sueltas, cachivaches *mpl*

ode ['oːd] *n* : oda *f*

odious ['oːdiəs] *adj* : odioso — **odiously** *adv*

odor ['oːdər] *n* : olor *m*

odorless ['oːdərləs] *adj* : inodoro, sin olor

odorous ['oːdərəs] *adj* : oloroso

odyssey ['ɑdəsi] *n, pl* **-seys** : odisea *f*

o'er ['or] → **over**

of ['ʌv, 'ɑv] *prep* **1** FROM : de <a man of the city : un hombre de la ciudad> **2** (*indicating character or background*) : de <a woman of great ability : una mujer de gran capacidad> **3** (*indicating cause*) : de <he died of the flu : murió de la gripe> **4** BY : de <the works of Shakespeare : las obras de Shakespeare> **5** (*indicating contents, material or quantity*) : de <a house of wood : una casa de madera> <a glass of water : un vaso de agua> **6** (*indicating belonging or connection*) : de <the front of the house : el frente de la casa> **7** ABOUT : sobre, de <tales of the West : los cuentos del Oeste> **8** (*indicating a particular example*) : de <the city of Caracas : la ciudad de Caracas> **9** FOR : por, a <love of country : amor por la patria> **10** (*indicating time or date*) <five minutes of ten : las diez menos cinco> <the eighth of April : el ocho de abril>

off[1] ['ɔf] *adv* **1** (*indicating change of position or state*) <to march off : marcharse> <he dozed off : se puso a dormir> **2** (*indicating distance in space or time*) <some miles off : a varias millas> <the holiday is three weeks off : faltan tres semanas para la fiesta> **3** (*indicating removal*) <the knob came off : se le cayó el pomo> **4** (*indicating termination*) <shut the television off : apaga la televisión> **5** (*indicating suspension of work*) <to take a day off : tomarse un día de descanso> **6 off and on** : de vez en cuando

off[2] *adj* **1** FARTHER : más remoto, distante <the off side of the building : el lado distante del edificio> **2** STARTED : empezado <to be off on a spree : irse de juerga> **3** OUT : apagado <the light is off : la luz está apagada> **4** CANCELED : cancelado, suspendido **5** INCORRECT : erróneo, incorrecto **6** REMOTE : remoto, lejano <an off chance : una posibilidad remota> **7** FREE : libre <I'm off today : hoy estoy libre> **8 to be well off** : vivir con desahogo, tener bastante dinero

off[3] *prep* **1** (*indicating physical separation*) : de <she took it off the table : lo tomó de la mesa> <a shop off the main street : una tienda al lado de la calle principal> **2** : a la costa de, a expensas de <he lives off his sister : vive a expensas de su hermana> **3** (*indicating the suspension of an activity*) <to be off duty : estar libre> <he's off liquor : ha dejado el alcohol> **4** BELOW : por debajo de <he's off his game : está por debajo de su juego normal>

offal [ˈɔfəl] *n* **1** RUBBISH, WASTE : desechos *mpl*, desperdicios *mpl* **2** VISCERA : vísceras *fpl*, asaduras *fpl*

offend [əˈfɛnd] *vt* **1** VIOLATE : violar, atentar contra **2** HURT : ofender <to be easily offended : ser muy susceptible>

offender [əˈfɛndər] *n* : delincuente *mf;* infractor *m*, -tora *f*

offense *or* **offence** [əˈfɛnts, ˈɔˌfɛnts] *n* **1** INSULT : ofensa *f*, injuria *f*, agravio *m* <to take offense : ofenderse> **2** ASSAULT : ataque *m* **3** : ofensiva *f* (en deportes) **4** CRIME, INFRACTION : infracción *f*, delito *m*

offensive[1] [əˈfɛntsɪv, ˈɔˌfɛnt-] *adj* : ofensivo — **offensively** *adv*

offensive[2] *n* : ofensiva *f*

offer[1] [ˈɔfər] *vt* **1** : ofrecer <they offered him the job : le ofrecieron el puesto> **2** PROPOSE : proponer, sugerir **3** SHOW : ofrecer, mostrar <to offer resistance : ofrecer resistencia>

offer[2] *n* : oferta *f*, ofrecimiento *m*, propuesta *f*

offering [ˈɔfərɪŋ] *n* : ofrenda *f*

offhand[1] [ˈɔfˈhænd] *adv* : sin preparación, sin pensarlo

offhand[2] *adj* **1** IMPROMPTU : improvisado **2** ABRUPT : brusco

office [ˈɔfəs] *n* **1** : cargo *m* <to run for office : presentarse como candidato> **2** : oficina *f*, despacho *m*, gabinete *m* (en la casa) <office hours : horas de oficina>

officeholder [ˈɔfəsˌhoːldər] *n* : titular *mf*

officer [ˈɔfəsər] *n* **1** *or* **police officer** : policía *mf*, agente *mf* de policía **2** OFFICIAL : oficial *mf;* funcionario *m*, -ria *f;* director *m*, -tora *f* (en una empresa) **3** COMMISSIONED OFFICER : oficial *mf*

official[1] [əˈfɪʃəl] *adj* : oficial — **officially** *adv*

official[2] *n* : funcionario *m*, -ria *f;* oficial *mf*

officiate [əˈfɪʃiˌeɪt] *v* **-ated; -ating** *vi* **1** : arbitrar (en deportes) **2 to officiate at** : oficiar, celebrar — *vt* : arbitrar

officious [əˈfɪʃəs] *adj* : oficioso

offing [ˈɔfɪŋ] *n* **in the offing** : en perspectiva

offset [ˈɔfˌsɛt] *vt* **-set; -setting** : compensar

offshoot [ˈɔfˌʃuːt] *n* **1** OUTGROWTH : producto *m*, resultado *m* **2** BRANCH, SHOOT : retoño *m*, rama *f*, vástago *m* (de una planta)

offshore[1] [ˈɔfˈʃor] *adv* : a una distancia de la costa

offshore[2] *adj* **1** : de (la) tierra <an offshore wind : un viento que sopla de tierra> **2** : (de) costa afuera, cercano a la costa <an offshore island : una isla costera>

offspring [ˈɔfˌsprɪŋ] *ns & pl* **1** YOUNG : crías *fpl* (de los animales) **2** PROGENY : prole *f*, progenie *f*

off-the-road [ˈɔfðəˈroːd] *adj* : extraoficial

often [ˈɔfən, ˈɔftən] *adv* : muchas veces, a menudo, seguido

oftentimes [ˈɔfənˌtaɪmz, ˈɔftən-] *or* **ofttimes** [ˈɔftˌtaɪms] → **often**

ogle [ˈoːgəl] *vt* **ogled; ogling** : comerse con los ojos, quedarse mirando a

ogre [ˈoːgər] *n* : ogro *m*

oh [ˈoː] *interj* : ¡oh!, ¡ah!, ¡ay! <oh, of course : ah, por supuesto> <oh no! : ¡ay no!> <oh really? : ¿de veras?>

ohm [ˈoːm] *n* : ohm *m*, ohmio *m*

oil[1] [ˈɔɪl] *vt* : lubricar, engrasar, aceitar

oil[2] *n* **1** : aceite *m* **2** PETROLEUM : petróleo *m* **3** *or* **oil painting** : óleo *m*, pintura *f* al óleo **4** *or* **oil paint(s)** : óleo *m*

oilcloth [ˈɔɪlˌklɔθ] *n* : hule *m*

oiliness [ˈɔɪlinəs] *n* : lo aceitoso

oilskin [ˈɔɪlˌskɪn] *n* **1** : hule *m* **2 oilskins** *npl* : impermeable *m*

oily [ˈɔɪli] *adj* **oilier; -est** : aceitoso, grasiento, grasoso <oily fingers : dedos grasientos>

ointment [ˈɔɪntmənt] *n* : ungüento *m*, pomada *f*

OK[1] [ˌoːˈkeɪ] *vt* **OK'd** *or* **okayed** [ˌoːˈkeɪd]; **OK'ing** *or* **okaying** APPROVE, AUTHORIZE : dar el visto bueno a, autorizar, aprobar

OK[2] *or* **okay** [ˌoːˈkeɪ] *adv* **1** WELL : bien **2** YES : sí, por supuesto

OK[3] *adj* : bien <he's OK : está bien> <it's OK with me : estoy de acuerdo>

OK[4] *n* : autorización *f*, visto *m* bueno

okra [ˈoːkrə, *South also* -kri] *n* : quingombó *m*

old[1] [ˈoːld] *adj* **1** ANCIENT : antiguo <old civilizations : civilizaciones antiguas> **2** FAMILIAR : viejo <old friends : viejos amigos> <the same old story : el mismo cuento> **3** (*indicating a certain age*) <he's ten years old : tiene diez años (de edad)> **4** AGED : viejo, anciano <an old woman : una anciana> **5** FORMER : antiguo <her old neighborhood : su antiguo barrio> **6** WORN-OUT : viejo, gastado

old[2] *n* **1 the old** : los viejos, los ancianos **2 in the days of old** : antaño, en los tiempos antiguos

olden [ˈoːldən] *adj* : de antaño, de antigüedad

old–fashioned [ˈoːldˈfæʃənd] *adj* : anticuado, pasado de moda

old maid *n* **1** SPINSTER : soltera *f* **2** FUSSBUDGET : maniático *m*, -ca *f;* melindroso *m*, -sa *f*

old–time [ˈoːldˈtaɪm] *adj* : antiguo

old–timer [ˈoːldˈtaɪmər] *n* **1** VETERAN : veterano *m,* -na *f* **2** *or* **oldster** : anciano *m,* -na *f*

old–world [ˈoːldˈwərld] *adj* : pintoresco (de antaño)

oleander [ˈoːli,ændər] *n* : adelfa *f*

oleomargarine [,oːlioˈmɑrdʒərən] → **margarine**

olfactory [ɑlˈfæktəri,ol-] *adj* : olfativo

oligarchy [ˈɑlə,gɑrki, ˈoːlə-] *n, pl* **-chies** : oligarquía *f*

olive [ˈɑlɪv, -ləv] *n* **1** : aceituna *f,* oliva *f* (fruta) **2** : olivo *m* (árbol) **3** *or* **olive green** : color *m* aceituna, verde *m* oliva

Olympic Games [oˈlɪmpɪk] *npl* : Juegos *mpl* Olímpicos

Omani [oˈmɑni, -ˈmæ-] *n* : omaní *mf* — **Omani** *adj*

ombudsman [ˈɑm,bʊdzmən, ɑmˈbʊdz-] *n, pl* **-men** [-mən, -,mɛn] : ombudsman *m*

omelet *or* **omelette** [ˈɑmlət, ˈɑmə-] *n* : omelette *mf,* tortilla *f* de huevo

omen [ˈoːmən] *n* : presagio *m,* augurio *m,* agüero *m*

ominous [ˈɑmənəs] *adj* : ominoso, agorero, de mal agüero

ominously [ˈɑmənəsli] *adv* : de manera amenazadora

omission [oˈmɪʃən] *n* : omisión *f*

omit [oˈmɪt] *vt* **omitted; omitting 1** LEAVE OUT : omitir, excluir **2** NEGLECT : omitir <they omitted to tell us : omitieron decírnoslo>

omnipotence [ɑmˈnɪpətənts] *n* : omnipotencia *f* — **omnipotent** [ɑmˈnɪpətənt] *adj*

omnipresent [,ɑmnɪˈprɛzənt] *adj* : omnipresente

omniscient [ɑmˈnɪʃənt] *adj* : omnisciente

omnivorous [ɑmˈnɪvərəs] *adj* **1** : omnívoro **2** AVID : ávido, voraz

on[1] [ˈɑn, ˈɔn] *adv* **1** (*indicating contact with a surface*) <put the top on : pon la tapa> <he has a hat on : lleva un sombrero puesto> **2** (*indicating forward movement*) <from that moment on : a partir de ese momento> <farther on : más adelante> **3** (*indicating operation or an operating position*) <turn the light on : prende la luz>

on[2] *adj* **1** (*being in operation*) <the radio is on : el radio está prendido> **2** (*taking place*) <the game is on : el juego ha comenzado> **3 to be on to** : estar enterado de

on[3] *prep* **1** (*indicating position*) : en, sobre, encima de <on the table : en (sobre, encima de) la mesa> <shadows on the wall : sombras en la pared> <on horseback : a caballo> **2** AT, TO : a <on the right : a la derecha> **3** ABOARD, IN : en, a <on the plane : en el avión> <he got on the train : subió al tren> **4** (*indicating time*) <she worked on Saturdays : trabajaba los sábados> <every hour on the hour : a la hora en punto> **5** (*indicating means or agency*) : por <he cut himself on a tin can : se cortó con una lata> <to talk on the telephone : hablar por teléfono> **6** (*indicating a state or process*) : en <on fire : en llamas> <on the increase : en aumento> **7** (*indicating connection or membership*) : en <on a committee : en una comisión> **8** (*indicating an activity*) <on vacation : de vacaciones> <on a diet : a dieta> **9** ABOUT, CONCERNING : sobre <a book on insects : un libro sobre insectos> <reflect on that : reflexiona sobre eso>

once[1] [ˈwʌnts] *adv* **1** : una vez <once a month : una vez al mes> <once and for all : de una vez por todas> **2** EVER : alguna vez **3** FORMERLY : antes, anteriormente

once[2] *adj* FORMER : antiguo

once[3] *n* **1** : una vez **2 at ~** SIMULTANEOUSLY : al mismo tiempo, simultáneamente **3 at ~** IMMEDIATELY : inmediatamente, en seguida

once[4] *conj* : una vez que, tan pronto como

once–over [,wʌntsˈoːvər, ˈwʌnts,-] *n* **to give someone the once–over** : echarle un vistazo a alguien

oncoming [ˈɑn,kʌmɪŋ, ˈɔn-] *adj* : que viene

one[1] [ˈwʌn] *adj* **1** (*being a single unit*) : un, una <he only wants one apple : sólo quiere una manzana> **2** (*being a particular one*) : un, una <he arrived early one morning : llegó temprano una mañana> **3** (*being the same*) : mismo, misma <they're all members of one team : todos son miembros del mismo equipo> <one and the same thing : la misma cosa> **4** SOME : alguno, alguna; un, una <I'll see you again one day : algún día te veré otra vez> <at one time or another : en una u otra ocasión>

one[2] *n* **1** : uno *m* (número) **2** (*indicating the first of a set or series*) <from day one : desde el primer momento> **3** (*indicating a single person or thing*) <the one (girl) on the right : la de la derecha> <he has the one but needs the other : tiene uno pero necesita el otro>

one[3] *pron* **1** : uno, una <one of his friends : una de sus amigas> <one never knows : uno nunca sabe, nunca se sabe> <to cut one's finger : cortarse el dedo> **2 one and all** : todos, todo el mundo **3 one another** : el uno al otro, se <they loved one another : se amaban> **4 that one** : aquél, aquella **5 which one?** : ¿cuál?

onerous [ˈɑnərəs, ˈoːnə-] *adj* : oneroso, gravoso

oneself [,wʌnˈsɛlf] *pron* **1** (*used reflexively or for emphasis*) : se, sí mismo, uno mismo <to control oneself : controlarse> <to talk to oneself

: hablarse a sí mismo> <to do it oneself : hacérselo uno mismo> **2 by ~** : solo

one–sided [ˈwʌnˈsaɪdəd] *adj* **1** : de un solo lado **2** LOPSIDED : asimétrico **3** BIASED : parcial, tendencioso **4** UNILATERAL : unilateral

onetime [ˈwʌnˈtaɪm] *adj* FORMER : antiguo

one–way [ˈwʌnˈweɪ] *adj* **1** : de sentido único, de una sola dirección <a one-way street : una calle de sentido único> **2** : de ida, sencillo <a one-way ticket : un boleto de ida>

ongoing [ˈɑnˌgoːɪŋ] *adj* **1** CONTINUING : en curso, corriente **2** DEVELOPING : en desarrollo

onion [ˈʌnjən] *n* : cebolla *f*

only[1] [ˈoːnli] *adv* **1** MERELY : sólo, solamente, nomás <for only two dollars : por tan sólo dos dólares> <only once : sólo una vez, no más de una vez> <I only did it to help : lo hice por ayudar nomás> **2** SOLELY : únicamente, sólo, solamente <only he knows it : solamente él lo sabe> **3** (*indicating a result*) <it will only cause him problems : no hará más que crearle problemas> **4 if only** : ojalá, por lo menos <if only it were true! : ¡ojalá sea cierto!> <if he could only dance : si por lo menos pudiera bailar>

only[2] *adj* : único <an only child : un hijo único> <the only chance : la única oportunidad>

only[3] *conj* BUT : pero <I would go, only I'm sick : iría, pero estoy enfermo>

onset [ˈɑnˌsɛt] *n* : comienzo *m,* llegada *f*

onslaught [ˈɑnˌslɔt, ˈɔn-] *n* : arremetida *f,* embestida *f,* embate *m*

onto [ˈɑnˌtuː, ˈɔn-] *prep* : sobre

onus [ˈoːnəs] *n* : responsabilidad *f,* carga *f*

onward[1] [ˈɑnwərd, ˈɔn-] *or* **onwards** *adv* FORWARD : adelante, hacia adelante

onward[2] *adj* : hacia adelante

onyx [ˈɑnɪks] *n* : ónix *m*

ooze[1] [ˈuːz] *v* **oozed; oozing** *vi* : rezumar — *vt* **1** : rezumar **2** EXUDE : irradiar, rebosar <to ooze confidence : irradiar confianza>

ooze[2] *n* SLIME : cieno *m,* limo *m*

opal [ˈoːpəl] *n* : ópalo *m*

opaque [oˈpeɪk] *adj* **1** : opaco **2** UNCLEAR : poco claro

open[1] [ˈoːpən] *vt* **1** : abrir <open the door : abre la puerta> **2** UNCOVER : destapar **3** UNFOLD : desplegar, abrir **4** CLEAR : abrir (un camino, etc.) **5** INAUGURATE : abrir (una tienda), inaugurar (una exposición, etc.) **6** INITIATE : initiar, entablar, abrir <to open the meeting : abrir la sesión> <to open a discussion : entablar un debate> — *vi* **1** : abrirse **2** BEGIN : empezar, comenzar

open[2] *adj* **1** : abierto <an open window : una ventana abierta> **2** FRANK : abierto, franco, directo **3** UNCOVERED : descubierto, abierto **4** EXTENDED : extendido, abierto <with open arms : con los brazos abiertos> **5** UNRESTRICTED : libre, abierto **6** UNDECIDED : pendiente, por decidir, sin resolver <an open question : una cuestión pendiente> **7** AVAILABLE : vacante, libre <the job is open : el puesto está vacante>

open[3] *n* **in the open 1** OUTDOORS : al aire libre **2** KNOWN : conocido, sacado a la luz

open-air [ˈoːpənˈær] *adj* OUTDOOR : al aire libre

open-and-shut [ˈoːpənəndˈʃʌt] *adj* : claro, evidente <an open-and-shut case : un caso muy claro>

opener [ˈoːpənər] *n* : destapador *m,* abrelatas *m,* abridor *m*

openhanded [ˌoːpənˈhændəd] *adj* : generoso, liberal

openhearted [ˌoːpənˈhɑrt̬əd] *adj* **1** FRANK : franco, sincero **2** : generoso, de gran corazón

opening [ˈoːpənɪŋ] *n* **1** BEGINNING : comienzo *m,* principio *m,* apertura *f* **2** APERTURE : abertura *f,* brecha *f,* claro *m* (en el bosque) **3** OPPORTUNITY : oportunidad *f*

openly [ˈoːpənli] *adv* **1** FRANKLY : abiertamente, francamente **2** PUBLICLY : públicamente, declaradamente

openness [ˈoːpənnəs] *n* : franqueza *f*

opera [ˈɑprə, ˈɑpərə] *n* **1** : ópera *f* **2** → **opus**

opera glasses *npl* : gemelos *mpl* de teatro

operate [ˈɑpəˌreɪt] *v* **-ated; -ating** *vi* **1** ACT, FUNCTION : operar, funcionar, actuar **2 to operate on (someone)** : operar a (alguien) — *vt* **1** WORK : operar, manejar, hacer funcionar (una máquina) **2** MANAGE : manejar, administrar (un negocio)

operatic [ˌɑpəˈræt̬ɪk] *adj* : operístico

operation [ˌɑpəˈreɪʃən] *n* **1** FUNCTIONING : funcionamiento *m* **2** USE : uso *m,* manejo *m* (de máquinas) **3** SURGERY : operación *f,* intervención *f* quirúrgica

operational [ˌɑpəˈreɪʃənəl] *adj* : operacional, de operación

operative [ˈɑpərət̬ɪv, -ˌreɪ-] *adj* **1** OPERATING : vigente, en vigor **2** WORKING : operativo **3** SURGICAL : quirúrgico

operator [ˈɑpəˌreɪt̬ər] *n* : operador *m,* -dora *f*

operetta [ˌɑpəˈrɛt̬ə] *n* : opereta *f*

ophthalmologist [ˌɑfˌθælˈmɑlədʒɪst, -θəˈmɑ-] *n* : oftalmólogo *m,* -ga *f*

ophthalmology [ˌɑfˌθælˈmɑlədʒi, -θəˈmɑ-] *n* : oftalmología *f*

opiate [ˈoːpiət, -piˌeɪt] *n* : opiato *m*

opinion [əˈpɪnjən] *n* : opinión *f*

opinionated [əˈpɪnjəˌneɪt̬əd] *adj* : testarudo, dogmático

opium ['oːpiəm] *n* : opio *m*

opossum [ə'pɑsəm] *n* : zarigüeya *f,* oposum *m*

opponent [ə'poːnənt] *n* : oponente *mf;* opositor *m,* -tora *f;* contrincante *mf* (en deportes)

opportune [ˌɑpər'tuːn, -'tjuːn] *adj* : oportuno — **opportunely** *adv*

opportunist [ˌɑpər'tuːnɪst, -'tjuː-] *n* : oportunista *mf*

opportunity [ˌɑpər'tuːnəti, -'tjuː-] *n, pl* **-ties** : oportunidad *f,* ocasión *f,* chance *m,* posibilidades *fpl*

oppose [ə'poːz] *vt* **-posed; -posing 1** : ir en contra de, oponerse a <good opposes evil : el bien se opone al mal> **2** COMBAT : luchar contra, combatir, resistir

opposite[1] ['ɑpəzət] *adv* : enfrente

opposite[2] *adj* **1** FACING : de enfrente <the opposite side : el lado de enfrente> **2** CONTRARY : opuesto, contrario <in opposite directions : en direcciones contrarias> <the opposite sex : el sexo opuesto, el otro sexo>

opposite[3] *n* : lo contrario, lo opuesto

opposite[4] *prep* : enfrente de, frente a

opposition [ˌɑpə'zɪʃən] *n* **1** : oposición *f,* resistencia *f* **2 in opposition to** AGAINST : en contra de

oppress [ə'prɛs] *vt* **1** PERSECUTE : oprimir, perseguir **2** BURDEN : oprimir, agobiar

oppression [ə'prɛʃən] *n* : opresión *f*

oppressive [ə'prɛsɪv] *adj* **1** HARSH : opresivo, severo **2** STIFLING : agobiante, sofocante <oppressive heat : calor sofocante>

oppressor [ə'prɛsər] *n* : opresor *m,* -sora *f*

opprobrium [ə'proːbriəm] *n* : oprobio *m*

opt ['ɑpt] *vi* : optar

optic ['ɑptɪk] *or* **optical** [-tɪkəl] *adj* : óptico

optician [ɑp'tɪʃən] *n* : óptico *m,* -ca *f*

optics ['ɑptɪks] *npl* : óptica *f*

optimal ['ɑptəməl] *adj* : óptimo

optimism ['ɑptəˌmɪzəm] *n* : optimismo *m*

optimist ['ɑptəmɪst] *n* : optimista *mf*

optimistic [ˌɑptə'mɪstɪk] *adj* : optimista

optimistically [ˌɑptə'mɪstɪkli] *adv* : con optimismo, positivamente

optimum[1] ['ɑptəməm] *adj* → **optimal**

optimum[2] *n, pl* **-ma** ['ɑptəmə] : lo óptimo, lo ideal

option ['ɑpʃən] *n* : opción *f* <she has no option : no tiene más remedio>

optional ['ɑpʃənəl] *adj* : facultativo, optativo

optometrist [ɑp'tɑmətrɪst] *n* : optometrista *mf*

optometry [ɑp'tɑmətri] *n* : optometría *f*

opulence ['ɑpjələnts] *n* : opulencia *f*

opulent ['ɑpjələnt] *adj* : opulento

opus ['oːpəs] *n, pl* **opera** ['oːpərə, 'ɑpə-] : opus *m,* obra *f* (de música)

or ['ɔr] *conj* **1** (*indicating an alternative*) : o (u *before words beginning with* o *or* ho) <coffee or tea : café o té> <one day or another : un día u otro> **2** (*following a negative*) : ni <he didn't have his keys or his wallet : no llevaba ni sus llaves ni su billetera>

oracle ['ɔrəkəl] *n* : oráculo *m*

oral ['orəl] *adj* : oral — **orally** *adv*

orange ['ɔrɪndʒ] *n* **1** : naranja *f,* china *f PRi* (fruto) **2** : naranja *m* (color), color *m* de china *PRi*

orangeade [ˌɔrɪndʒ'eɪd] *n* : naranjada *f*

orangutan [ə'ræŋəˌtæŋ, -'ræŋgə-, -ˌtæn] *n* : orangután *m*

oration [ə'reɪʃən] *n* : oración *f,* discurso *m*

orator ['ɔrət̬ər] *n* : orador *m,* -dora *f*

oratorio [ˌɔrə'toriˌoː] *n, pl* **-rios** : oratorio *m*

oratory ['ɔrəˌtori] *n, pl* **-ries** : oratoria *f*

orb ['ɔrb] *n* : orbe *m*

orbit[1] ['ɔrbət] *vt* **1** CIRCLE : girar alrededor de **2** : poner en órbita (un satélite, etc.) — *vi* : orbitar

orbit[2] *n* : órbita *f*

orbital ['ɔrbət̬əl] *adj* : orbital

orchard ['ɔrtʃərd] *n* : huerto *m*

orchestra ['ɔrkəstrə] *n* : orquesta *f*

orchestral [ɔr'kɛstrəl] *adj* : orquestal

orchestrate ['ɔrkəˌstreɪt] *vt* **-trated; -trating 1** : orquestar, instrumentar (en música) **2** ORGANIZE : arreglar, organizar

orchestration [ˌɔrkə'streɪʃən] *n* : orquestación *f*

orchid ['ɔrkɪd] *n* : orquídea *f*

ordain [ɔr'deɪn] *vt* **1** : ordenar (en religión) **2** DECREE : decretar, ordenar

ordeal [ɔr'diːl, 'ɔrˌdiːl] *n* : prueba *f* dura, experiencia *f* terrible

order[1] ['ɔrdər] *vt* **1** ORGANIZE : arreglar, ordenar, poner en orden **2** COMMAND : ordenar, mandar **3** REQUEST : pedir, encargar <to order a meal : pedir algo de comer> — *vi* : hacer un pedido

order[2] *n* **1** : orden *f* <a religious order : una orden religiosa> **2** COMMAND : orden *f,* mandato *m* <to give an order : dar una orden> **3** REQUEST : orden *f,* pedido *m* <purchase order : orden de compra> **4** ARRANGEMENT : orden *m* <in chronological order : por orden cronológico> **5** DISCIPLINE : orden *m* <law and order : el orden público> **6 in order to** : para **7 out of order** : descompuesto, averiado **8 orders** *npl or* **holy orders** : órdenes *fpl* sagradas

orderliness ['ɔrdərlinəs] *n* : orden *m*

orderly[1] ['ɔrdərli] *adj* **1** METHODICAL : ordenado, metódico **2** PEACEFUL : pacífico, disciplinado

orderly[2] *n, pl* **-lies 1** : ordenanza *m* (en el ejército) **2** : camillero *m* (en un hospital)

ordinal [ˈɔrdənəl] *n or* **ordinal number** : ordinal *m,* número *m* ordinal
ordinance [ˈɔrdənənts] *n* : ordenanza *f,* reglamento *m*
ordinarily [ˌɔrdənˈɛrəli] *adv* : ordinariamente, por lo general
ordinary [ˈɔrdənˌɛri] *adj* **1** NORMAL, USUAL : normal, usual **2** AVERAGE : común y corriente, normal **3** MEDIOCRE : mediocre, ordinario
ordination [ˌɔrdənˈeɪʃən] *n* : ordenación *f*
ordnance [ˈɔrdnənts] *n* : artillería *f*
ore [ˈor] *n* : mineral *m* (metalífero), mena *f*
oregano [əˈrɛgəˌnoː] *n* : orégano *m*
organ [ˈɔrgən] *n* **1** : órgano *m* (instrumento) **2** : órgano *m* (del cuerpo) **3** PERIODICAL : publicación *f* periódica, órgano *m*
organic [ɔrˈgænɪk] *adj* : orgánico — **organically** *adv*
organism [ˈɔrgəˌnɪzəm] *n* : organismo *m*
organist [ˈɔrgənɪst] *n* : organista *mf*
organization [ˌɔrgənəˈzeɪʃən] *n* **1** ORGANIZING : organización *f* **2** BODY : organización *f,* organismo *m*
organizational [ˌɔrgənəˈzeɪʃənəl] *adj* : organizativo
organize [ˈɔrgəˌnaɪz] *vt* **-nized; -nizing** : organizar, arreglar, poner en orden
organizer [ˈɔrgəˌnaɪzər] *n* : organizador *m,* -dora *f*
orgasm [ˈɔrˌgæzəm] *n* : orgasmo *m*
orgy [ˈɔrdʒi] *n, pl* **-gies** : orgía *f*
orient [ˈoriˌɛnt] *vt* : orientar
Orient *n* **the Orient** : el Oriente
oriental [ˌoriˈɛntəl] *adj* : del Oriente, oriental
Oriental *n* : oriental *mf*
orientation [ˌoriənˈteɪʃən] *n* : orientación *f*
orifice [ˈɔrəfəs] *n* : orificio *m*
origin [ˈɔrədʒən] *n* **1** ANCESTRY : origen *m,* ascendencia *f* **2** SOURCE : origen *m,* raíz *f,* fuente *f*
original[1] [əˈrɪdʒənəl] *adj* : original
original[2] *n* : original *m*
originality [əˌrɪdʒəˈnæləti] *n* : originalidad *f*
originally [əˈrɪdʒənəli] *adv* **1** AT FIRST : al principio, originariamente **2** CREATIVELY : originalmente, con originalidad
originate [əˈrɪdʒəˌneɪt] *v* **-nated; -nating** *vt* : originar, iniciar, crear — *vi* **1** BEGIN : originarse, empezar **2** COME : provenir, proceder, derivarse
originator [əˈrɪdʒəˌneɪtər] *n* : creador *m,* -dora *f;* inventor *m,* -tora *f*
oriole [ˈoriˌoːl, -iəl] *n* : oropéndola *f*
ornament[1] [ˈɔrnəmənt] *vt* : adornar, decorar, ornamentar
ornament[2] *n* : ornamento *m,* adorno *m,* decoración *f*
ornamental [ˌɔrnəˈmɛntəl] *adj* : ornamental, de adorno, decorativo
ornamentation [ˌɔrnəmənˈteɪʃən, -mɛn-] *n* : ornamentación *f*
ornate [ɔrˈneɪt] *adj* : elaborado, recargado
ornery [ˈɔrnəri, ˈɑrnəri] *adj* **ornerier; -est** : de mal genio, malhumorado
ornithologist [ˌɔrnəˈθɑlədʒɪst] *n* : ornitólogo *m,* -ga *f*
ornithology [ˌɔrnəˈθɑlədʒi] *n, pl* **-gies** : ornitología *f*
orphan[1] [ˈɔrfən] *vt* : dejar huérfano
orphan[2] *n* : huérfano *m,* -na *f*
orphanage [ˈɔrfənɪdʒ] *n* : orfelinato *m,* orfanato *m*
orthodontics [ˌɔrθəˈdɑntɪks] *n* : ortodoncia *f*
orthodontist [ˌɔrθəˈdɑntɪst] *n* : ortodoncista *mf*
orthodox [ˈɔrθəˌdɑks] *adj* : ortodoxo
orthodoxy [ˈɔrθəˌdɑksi] *n, pl* **-doxies** : ortodoxia *f*
orthographic [ˌɔrθəˈgræfɪk] *adj* : ortográfico
orthography [ɔrˈθɑgrəfi] *n, pl* **-phies** SPELLING : ortografía *f*
orthopedic [ˌɔrθəˈpiːdɪk] *adj* : ortopédico
orthopedics [ˌɔrθəˈpiːdɪks] *ns & pl* : ortopedia *f*
orthopedist [ˌɔrθəˈpiːdɪst] *n* : ortopedista *mf*
oscillate [ˈɑsəˌleɪt] *vi* **-lated; -lating** : oscilar
oscillation [ˌɑsəˈleɪʃən] *n* : oscilación *f*
osmosis [ɑzˈmoːsɪs, ɑs-] *n* : ósmosis *f,* osmosis *f*
ostensible [ɑˈstɛntsəbəl] *adj* APPARENT : aparente, ostensible — **ostensibly** [-bli] *adv*
ostentation [ˌɑstənˈteɪʃən] *n* : ostentación *f,* boato *m*
ostentatious [ˌɑstənˈteɪʃəs] *adj* : ostentoso — **ostentatiously** *adv*
osteopath [ˈɑstiəˌpæθ] *n* : osteópata *f*
osteopathy [ˌɑstiˈɑpəθi] *n* : osteopatía *f*
osteoporosis [ˌɑstiopəˈroːsɪs] *n, pl* **-roses** [-ˌsiːz] : osteoporosis *f*
ostracism [ˈɑstrəˌsɪzəm] *n* : ostracismo *m*
ostracize [ˈɑstrəˌsaɪz] *vt* **-cized; -cizing** : condenar al ostracismo, marginar, aislar
ostrich [ˈɑstrɪtʃ, ˈɔs-] *n* : avestruz *m*
other[1] [ˈʌðər] *adv* **other than** : aparte de, fuera de
other[2] *adj* : otro <the other boys : los otros muchachos> <smarter than other people : más inteligente que los demás> <on the other hand : por otra parte, por otro lado> <every other day : cada dos días>
other[3] *pron* : otro, otra <one in front of the other : uno tras otro> <myself and three others : yo y tres otros, yo y tres más> <somewhere or other : en alguna parte>

otherwise[1] [ˈʌðər͵waɪz] *adv* **1** DIFFERENTLY **:** de otro modo, de manera distinta <he could not act otherwise : no pudo actuar de manera distinta> **2 :** eso aparte, por lo demás <I'm dizzy, but otherwise I'm fine : estoy mareado pero, por lo demás, estoy bien> **3** OR ELSE **:** de lo contario, si no <do what I tell you, otherwise you'll be sorry : haz lo que te digo, de lo contario, te arrepentirás>

otherwise[2] *adj* **:** diferente, distinto <the facts are otherwise : la realidad es diferente>

otter [ˈɑt̬ər] *n* **:** nutria *f*

ought [ˈɔt] *v aux* **:** deber <you ought to take care of yourself : deberías cuidarte>

oughtn't [ˈɔtənt] (*contraction of* **ought not**) → **ought**

ounce [ˈaʊnts] *n* **:** onza *f*

our [ˈɑr, ˈaʊr] *adj* **:** nuestro

ours [ˈaʊrz, ˈɑrz] *pron* **:** nuestro, nuestra <a cousin of ours : un primo nuestro>

ourselves [ɑrˈsɛlvz, aʊr-] *pron* **1** (*used reflexively*) **:** nos, nosotros <we amused ourselves : nos divertimos> <we were always thinking of ourselves : siempre pensábamos en nosotros> **2** (*used for emphasis*) **:** nosotros mismos, nosotras mismas <we did it ourselves : lo hicimos nosotros mismos>

oust [ˈaʊst] *vt* **:** desbancar, expulsar

ouster [ˈaʊstər] *n* **:** expulsión *f* (de un país, etc.), destitución *f* (de un puesto)

out[1] [ˈaʊt] *vi* **:** revelarse, hacerse conocido

out[2] *adv* **1** (*indicating direction or movement*) **:** para afuera <she opened the door and looked out : abrió la puerta y miró para afuera> **2** (*indicating a location away from home or work*) **:** fuera, afuera <to eat out : comer afuera> **3** (*indicating loss of control or possession*) <they let the secret out : sacaron el secreto a la luz> **4** (*indicating completion or discontinuance*) <his money ran out : se le acabó el dinero> <to turn out the light : apagar la luz> **5** OUTSIDE **:** fuera, afuera <out in the garden : afuera en el jardín> **6** ALOUD **:** en voz alta, en alto <to cry out : gritar>

out[3] *adj* **1** EXTERNAL **:** externo, exterior **2** OUTLYING **:** alejado, distante <the out islands : las islas distantes> **3** ABSENT **:** ausente **4** UNFASHIONABLE **:** fuera de moda **5** EXTINGUISHED **:** apagado

out[4] *prep* **1** (*used to indicate an outward movement*) **:** por <I looked out the window : miré por la ventana> <she ran out the door : corrió por la puerta> **2** → **out of**

out-and-out [ˈaʊtənˈaʊt] *adj* UTTER **:** redomado, absoluto

outboard motor [ˈaʊt͵bord] *n* **:** motor *m* fuera de borde

outbound [ˈaʊt͵baʊnd] *adj* **:** que sale, de salida

outbreak [ˈaʊt͵breɪk] *n* **:** brote *m* (de una enfermedad), comienzo *m* (de guerra), ola *f* (de violencia), erupción *f* (de granos)

outbuilding [ˈaʊt͵bɪldɪŋ] *n* **:** edificio *m* anexo

outburst [ˈaʊt͵bərst] *n* **:** arranque *m*, arrebato *m*

outcast [ˈaʊt͵kæst] *n* **:** marginado *m*, -da *f;* paria *mf*

outcome [ˈaʊt͵kʌm] *n* **:** resultado *m*, desenlace *m*, consecuencia *f*

outcrop [ˈaʊt͵krɑp] *n* **:** afloramiento *m*

outcry [ˈaʊt͵kraɪ] *n, pl* **-cries :** clamor *m*, protesta *f*

outdated [͵aʊtˈdeɪt̬əd] *adj* **:** anticuado, fuera de moda

outdistance [͵aʊtˈdɪstənts] *vt* **-tanced; -tancing :** aventajar, dejar atrás

outdo [͵aʊtˈduː] *vt* **-did** [-ˈdɪd]; **-done** [-ˈdʌn]; **-doing**; **-does** [-ˈdʌz] **:** superar

outdoor [ˈaʊtˈdor] *adj* **:** al aire libre <outdoor sports : deportes al aire libre> <outdoor clothing : ropa de calle>

outdoors[1] [ˈaʊtˈdorz] *adv* **:** afuera, al aire libre

outdoors[2] *n* **:** aire *m* libre

outer [ˈaʊt̬ər] *adj* **1 :** exterior, externo **2 outer space :** espacio *m* exterior

outermost [ˈaʊt̬ər͵moːst] *adj* **:** más remoto, más exterior, extremo

outfield [ˈaʊt͵fiːld] *n* **the outfield :** los jardines

outfielder [ˈaʊt͵fiːldər] *n* **:** jardinero *m*, -ra *f*

outfit[1] [ˈaʊt͵fɪt] *vt* **-fitted; -fitting** EQUIP **:** equipar

outfit[2] *n* **1** EQUIPMENT **:** equipo *m* **2** COSTUME, ENSEMBLE **:** traje *m*, conjunto *m* **3** GROUP **:** conjunto *m*

outgo [ˈaʊt͵goː] *n, pl* **outgoes :** gasto *m*

outgoing [ˈaʊt͵goːɪŋ] *adj* **1** OUTBOUND **:** que sale **2** DEPARTING **:** saliente <an outgoing president : un presidente saliente> **3** EXTROVERTED **:** extrovertido, expansivo

outgrow [͵aʊtˈgroː] *vt* **-grew** [-ˈgruː]; **-grown** [-ˈgroːn]; **-growing 1 :** crecer más que <that tree outgrew all the others : ese árbol creció más que todos los otros> **2 to outgrow one's clothes :** quedarle pequeña la ropa a uno

outgrowth [ˈaʊt͵groːθ] *n* **1** OFFSHOOT **:** brote *m*, vástago *m* (de una planta) **2** CONSEQUENCE **:** consecuencia *f*, producto *m*, resultado *m*

outing [ˈaʊt̬ɪŋ] *n* **:** excursión *f*

outlandish [aʊtˈlændɪʃ] *adj* **:** descabellado, muy extraño

outlast [͵aʊtˈlæst] *vt* **:** durar más que

outlaw[1] [ˈaʊt͵lɔ] *vt* **:** hacerse ilegal, declarar fuera de la ley, prohibir

outlaw[2] *n* **:** bandido *m,* -da *f;* bandolero *m,* -ra *f;* forajido *m,* -da *f*

outlay [ˈaʊtˌleɪ] *n* **:** gasto *m,* desembolso *m*

outlet [ˈaʊtˌlɛt, -lət] *n* **1** EXIT **:** salida *f,* escape *m* <electrical outlet : toma de corriente> **2** RELIEF **:** desahogo *m* **3** MARKET **:** mercado *m,* salida *f*

outline[1] [ˈaʊtˌlaɪn] *vt* **-lined; -lining 1** SKETCH **:** diseñar, esbozar, bosquejar **2** DEFINE, EXPLAIN **:** perfilar, delinear, explicar <she outlined our responsibilities : delineó nuestras responsabilidades>

outline[2] *n* **1** PROFILE **:** perfil *m,* silueta *f,* contorno *m* **2** SKETCH **:** bosquejo *m,* boceto *m* **3** SUMMARY **:** esquema *m,* resumen *m,* sinopsis *m* <an outline of world history : un esquema de la historia mundial>

outlive [ˌaʊtˈlɪv] *vt* **-lived; -living :** sobrevivir a

outlook [ˈaʊtˌlʊk] *n* **1** VIEW **:** vista *f,* panorama *f* **2** POINT OF VIEW **:** punto *m* de vista **3** PROSPECTS **:** perspectivas *fpl*

outlying [ˈaʊtˌlaɪɪŋ] *adj* **:** alejado, distante, remoto <the outlying areas : las afueras>

outmoded [ˌaʊtˈmoːdəd] *adj* **:** pasado de moda, anticuado

outnumber [ˌaʊtˈnʌmbər] *vt* **:** superar en número a, ser más numeroso de

out of *prep* **1** (*indicating direction or movement from within*) **:** de, por <we ran out of the house : salimos corriendo de la casa> <to look out of the window : mirar por la ventana> **2** (*being beyond the limits of*) <out of control : fuera de control> <to be out of sight : desaparecer de vista> **3** OF **:** de <one out of four : uno de cada cuatro> **4** (*indicating absence or loss*) **:** sin <out of money : sin dinero> <we're out of matches : nos hemos quedado sin fósforos> **5** BECAUSE OF **:** por <out of curiosity : por curiosidad> **6** FROM **:** de <made out of plastic : hecho de plástico>

out–of–date [ˌaʊt̬əvˈdeɪt] *adj* **:** anticuado, obsoleto, pasado de moda

out-of-door [ˌaʊt̬əvˈdor] *or* **out-of-doors** [-ˈdorz] *adj* → **outdoor**

out-of-doors *n* → **outdoors**

outpatient [ˈaʊtˌpeɪʃənt] *n* **:** paciente *m* externo, paciente *f* externa

outpost [ˈaʊtˌpoːst] *n* **:** puesto *m* avanzado

output[1] [ˈaʊtˌpʊt] *vt* **-putted** *or* **-put; -putting :** producir

output[2] *n* **:** producción *f* (de una fábrica), rendimiento *m* (de una máquina), productividad *f* (de una persona)

outrage[1] [ˈaʊtˌreɪdʒ] *vt* **-raged; -raging 1** INSULT **:** ultrajar, injuriar **2** INFURIATE **:** indignar, enfurecer

outrage[2] *n* **1** ATROCITY **:** atropello *m,* atrocidad *f,* atentado *m* **2** SCANDAL **:** escándalo *m* **3** ANGER **:** ira *f,* furia *f*

outrageous [ˌaʊtˈreɪdʒəs] *adj* **1** SCANDALOUS **:** escandaloso, ofensivo, atroz **2** UNCONVENTIONAL **:** poco convencional, extravagante **3** EXORBITANT **:** exorbitante, excesivo (dícese de los precios, etc.)

outright[1] [ˌaʊtˈraɪt] *adv* **1** COMPLETELY **:** por completo, totalmente <to sell outright : vender por completo> <he refused it outright : lo rechazó rotundamente> **2** DIRECTLY **:** directamente, sin reserva **3** INSTANTLY **:** al instante, en el acto

outright[2] [ˈaʊtˌraɪt] *adj* **1** COMPLETE **:** completo, absoluto, categórico <an outright lie : una mentira absoluta> **2** **:** sin reservas <an outright gift : un regalo sin reservas>

outset [ˈaʊtˌsɛt] *n* **:** comienzo *m,* principio *m*

outshine [ˌaʊtˈʃaɪn] *vt* **-shone** [-ˈʃoːn, -ˈʃɒn] *or* **-shined; -shining :** eclipsar

outside[1] [ˌaʊtˈsaɪd, ˈaʊtˌ-] *adv* **:** fuera, afuera

outside[2] *adj* **1 :** exterior, externo <the outside edge : el borde exterior> <outside influences : influencias externas> **2** REMOTE **:** remoto <an outside chance : una posibilidad remota>

outside[3] *n* **1** EXTERIOR **:** parte *f* de afuera, exterior *m* **2** MOST **:** máximo *m* <three weeks at the outside : tres semanas como máximo> **3 from the outside :** desde afuera, desde fuera

outside[4] *prep* **:** fuera de, afuera de <outside my window : fuera de mi ventana> <outside regular hours : fuera del horario normal> <outside the law : afuera de la ley>

outside of *prep* **1** → **outside**[4] **2** → **besides**[2]

outsider [ˌaʊtˈsaɪdər] *n* **:** forastero *m,* -ra *f*

outskirts [ˈaʊtˌskərts] *npl* **:** afueras *fpl,* alrededores *mpl*

outsmart [ˌaʊtˈsmɑrt] → **outwit**

outspoken [ˌaʊtˈspoːkən] *adj* **:** franco, directo

outstanding [ˌaʊtˈstændɪŋ] *adj* **1** UNPAID **:** pendiente **2** NOTABLE **:** destacado, notable, excepcional, sobresaliente

outstandingly [ˌaʊtˈstændɪŋli] *adv* **:** excepcionalmente

outstrip [ˌaʊtˈstrɪp] *vt* **-stripped** *or* **-stript** [-ˈstrɪpt]; **-stripping 1 :** aventajar, dejar atrás <he outstripped the other runners : aventajó a los otros corredores> **2** SURPASS **:** aventajar, sobrepasar

outward[1] [ˈaʊtwərd] *or* **outwards** [-wərdz] *adv* **:** hacia afuera, hacia el exterior

outward[2] *adj* **1 :** hacia afuera <an outward flow : un flujo hacia afuera> **2** **:** externo, external <outward beauty : belleza externa>

outwardly [ˈaʊtwərdli] *adv* **1** EXTERNALLY : externalmente **2** APPARENTLY : aparentemente <outwardly friendly : aparentemente simpático>

outwit [ˌaʊtˈwɪt] *vt* **-witted; -witting** : ser más listo que

ova → **ovum**

oval[1] [ˈoːvəl] *adj* : ovalado, oval

oval[2] *n* : óvalo *m*

ovary [ˈoːvəri] *n, pl* **-ries** : ovario *m*

ovation [oˈveɪʃən] *n* : ovación *f*

oven [ˈʌvən] *n* : horno *m*

over[1] [ˈoːvər] *adv* **1** (*indicating movement across*) <he flew over to London : voló a Londres> <come on over! : ¡ven acá!> **2** (*indicating an additional amount*) <the show ran 10 minutes over : el espectáculo terminó 10 minutos de tarde> **3** ABOVE, OVERHEAD : por encima **4** AGAIN : otra vez, de nuevo <over and over : una y otra vez> <to start over : volver a empezar> **5 all over** EVERYWHERE : por todas partes **6 to fall over** : caerse **7 to turn over** : poner boca abajo, voltear

over[2] *adj* **1** HIGHER, UPPER : superior **2** REMAINING : sobrante, que sobra **3** ENDED : terminado, acabado <the work is over : el trabajo está terminado>

over[3] *prep* **1** ABOVE : encima de, arriba de, sobre <over the fireplace : encima de la chimenea> <the hawk flew over the hills : el halcón voló sobre los cerros> **2** : más de <over $50 : más de $50> **3** ALONG : por, sobre <to glide over the ice : deslizarse sobre el hielo> **4** (*indicating motion through a place or thing*) <they showed me over the house : me mostraron la casa> **5** ACROSS : por encima de, sobre <he jumped over the ditch : saltó por encima de la zanja> **6** UPON : sobre <a cape over my shoulders : una capa sobre los hombros> **7** ON : por <to speak over the telephone : hablar por teléfono> **8** DURING : en, durante <over the past 25 years : durante los últimos 25 años> **9** BECAUSE OF : por <they fought over the money : se pelearon por el dinero>

overabundance [ˌoːvərəˈbʌndən*t*k] *n* : superabundancia *f*

overabundant [ˌoːvərəˈbʌndənt] *adj* : superabundante

overactive [ˌoːvərˈæktɪv] *adj* : hiperactivo

overall [ˌoːvərˈɔl] *adj* : total, global, de conjunto

overalls [ˈoːvərˌɔlz] *npl* : overol *m*

overawe [ˌoːvərˈɔ] *vt* **-awed; -awing** : intimidar, impresionar

overbearing [ˌoːvərˈbærɪŋ] *adj* : dominante, imperioso, prepotente

overboard [ˈoːvərˌbord] *adv* : por la borda, al agua

overburden [ˌoːvərˈbərdən] *vt* : sobrecargar, agobiar

overcast [ˈoːvərˌkæst] *adj* CLOUDY : nublado

overcharge [ˌoːvərˈtʃɑrdʒ] *vt* **-charged; -charging** : cobrarle de más (a alguien)

overcoat [ˈoːvərˌkoːt] *n* : abrigo *m*

overcome [ˌoːvərˈkʌm] *v* **-came** [-ˈkeɪm]; **-come; -coming** *vt* **1** CONQUER : vencer, derrotar, superar **2** OVERWHELM : abrumar, agobiar — *vi* : vencer

overconfidence [ˌoːvərˈkɑnfədən*t*s] *n* : exceso *m* de confianza

overconfident [ˌoːvərˈkɑnfədənt] *adj* : demasiado confiado

overcook [ˌoːvərˈkʊk] *vt* : recocer, cocer demasiado

overcrowded [ˌoːvərˈkraʊdəd] *adj* **1** PACKED : abarrotado, atestado de gente **2** OVERPOPULATED : superpoblado

overdo [ˌoːvərˈduː] *vt* **-did** [-ˈdɪd]; **-done** [-ˈdʌn]; **-doing; -does** [-ˈdʌz] **1** : hacer demasiado **2** EXAGGERATE : exagerar **3** OVERCOOK : recocer

overdose [ˈoːvərˌdoːs] *n* : sobredosis *f*

overdraft [ˈoːvərˌdræft] *n* : sobregiro *m*, descubierto *m*

overdraw [ˌoːvərˈdrɔ] *vt* **-drew** [-ˈdruː]; **-drawn** [-ˈdrɔn]; **-drawing 1** : sobregirar <my account is overdrawn : tengo la cuenta en descubierto> **2** EXAGGERATE : exagerar

overdue [ˌoːvərˈduː] *adj* **1** UNPAID : vencido y sin pagar **2** TARDY : de retraso, tardío

overeat [ˌoːvərˈiːt] *vi* **-ate** [-ˈeɪt]; **-eaten** [-ˈiːtən]; **-eating** : comer demasiado

overelaborate [ˌoːvərɪˈlæbərət] *adj* : recargado

overestimate [ˌoːvərˈɛstəˌmeɪt] *vt* **-mated; -mating** : sobreestimar

overexcited [ˌoːvərɪkˈsaɪt̬əd] *adj* : sobreexcitado

overexpose [ˌoːvərɪkˈspoːz] *vt* **-posed; -posing** : sobreexponer

overfeed [ˌoːvərˈfiːd] *vt* **-fed** [-ˈfɛd]; **-feeding** : sobrealimentar

overflow[1] [ˌoːvərˈfloː] *vt* **1** : desbordar **2** INUNDATE : inundar — *vi* : desbordarse, rebosar

overflow[2] [ˈoːvərˌfloː] *n* **1** : derrame *m*, desbordamiento *m* (de un río) **2** SURPLUS : exceso *m*, excedente *m*

overfly [ˌoːvərˈflaɪ] *vt* **-flew** [-ˈfluː]; **-flown** [-ˈfloːn]; **-flying** : sobrevolar

overgrown [ˌoːvərˈgroːn] *adj* **1** : cubierto <overgrown with weeds : cubierto de malas hierbas> **2** : demasiado grande

overhand[1] [ˈoːvərˌhænd] *adv* : por encima de la cabeza

overhand[2] *adj* : por lo alto (tirada)

overhang[1] [ˌoːvərˈhæŋ] *v* **-hung** [-ˈhʌŋ]; **-hanging** *vt* **1** : sobresalir por encima de **2** THREATEN : amenazar — *vi* : sobresalir

overhang[2] [ˈoːvərˌhæŋ] *n* : saliente *mf*

overhaul [ˌoːvərˈhɔl] *vt* **1** : revisar <to overhaul an engine : revisar un motor> **2** OVERTAKE : adelantar

overhead[1] [ˌoːvərˈhɛd] *adv* : por encima, arriba, por lo alto

overhead[2] [ˈoːvərˌhɛd] *adj* : de arriba

overhead[3] [ˈoːvərˌhɛd] *n* : gastos *mpl* generales

overhear [ˌoːvərˈhɪr] *vt* **-heard; -hearing** : oír por casualidad

overheat [ˌoːvərˈhiːt] *vt* : recalentar, sobrecalentar, calentar demasiado

overjoyed [ˌoːvərˈdʒɔɪd] *adj* : rebosante de alegría

overkill [ˈoːvərˌkɪl] *n* : exceso *m,* excedente *m*

overland[1] [ˈoːvərˌlænd, -lənd] *adv* : por tierra

overland[2] *adj* : terrestre, por tierra

overlap[1] [ˌoːvərˈlæp] *v* **-lapped; -lapping** *vt* : traslapar — *vi* : traslaparse, solaparse

overlap[2] [ˈoːvərˌlæp] *n* : traslapo *m*

overlay[1] [ˌoːvərˈleɪ] *vt* **-laid** [-ˈleɪd]; **-laying** : recubrir, revestir

overlay[2] [ˈoːvərˌleɪ] *n* : revestimiento *m*

overload [ˌoːvərˈloːd] *vt* : sobrecargar

overlong [ˌoːvərˈlɔŋ] *adj* : excesivamente largo, largo y pesado

overlook [ˌoːvərˈlʊk] *vt* **1** INSPECT : inspeccionar, revisar **2** : tener vista a, dar a <a house overlooking the valley : una casa que tiene vista al valle> **3** MISS : pasar por alto **4** EXCUSE : dejar pasar, disculpar

overly [ˈoːvərli] *adv* : demasiado

overnight[1] [ˌoːvərˈnaɪt] *adv* **1** : por la noche, durante la noche **2** : de la noche a la mañana <we can't do it overnight : no podemos hacerlo de la noche a la mañana>

overnight[2] [ˈoːvərˈnaɪt] *adj* **1** : de noche <an overnight stay : una estancia de una noche> <an overnight bag : una bolsa de viaje> **2** SUDDEN : repentino

overpass [ˈoːvərˌpæs] *n* : paso *m* elevado, paso *m* a desnivel *Mex*

overpopulated [ˌoːvərˈpɑpjəˌleɪt̬əd] *adj* : sobrepoblado

overpower [ˌoːvərˈpaʊər] *vt* **1** CONQUER, SUBDUE : vencer, superar **2** OVERWHELM : abrumar, agobiar <overpowered by the heat : sofocado por el calor>

overpraise [ˌoːvərˈpreɪz] *vt* **-praised; -praising** : adular

overrate [ˌoːvərˈreɪt] *vt* **-rated; -rating** : sobrevalorar, sobrevaluar

override [ˌoːvərˈraɪd] *vt* **-rode** [-ˈroːd]; **-ridden** [-ˈrɪdən]; **-riding 1** : predominar sobre, contar más que <hunger overrode our manners : el hambre predominó sobre los modales> **2** ANNUL : anular, invalidar <to override a veto : anular un veto>

overrule [ˌoːvərˈruːl] *vt* **-ruled; -ruling** : anular (una decisión), desautorizar (una persona), denegar (un pedido)

overrun [ˌoːvərˈrʌn] *v* **-ran** [-ˈræn]; **-running** *vt* **1** INVADE : invadir **2** INFEST : infestar, plagar **3** EXCEED : exceder, rebasar — *vi* : rebasar el tiempo previsto

overseas[1] [ˌoːvərˈsiːz] *adv* : en el extranjero <to travel overseas : viajar al extranjero>

overseas[2] [ˈoːvərˌsiːz] *adj* : extranjero, exterior

oversee [ˌoːvərˈsiː] *vt* **-saw** [-ˈsɔ]; **-seen** [-ˈsiːn]; **-seeing** SUPERVISE : supervisar

overseer [ˈoːvərˌsiːər] *n* : supervisor *m,* -sora *f;* capataz *mf*

overshadow [ˌoːvərˈʃæˌdoː] *vt* **1** DARKEN : oscurecer, ensombrecer **2** ECLIPSE, OUTSHINE : eclipsar

overshoe [ˈoːvərˌʃuː] *n* : chanclo *m*

overshoot [ˌoːvərˈʃuːt] *vt* **-shot** [-ˈʃɑt]; **-shooting** : pasarse de <to overshoot the mark : pasarse de la raya>

oversight [ˈoːvərˌsaɪt] *n* : descuido *m,* inadvertencia *f*

oversleep [ˌoːvərˈsliːp] *vi* **-slept** [-ˈslɛpt]; **-sleeping** : no despertarse a tiempo, quedarse dormido

overspread [ˌoːvərˈsprɛd] *vt* **-spread; -spreading** : extenderse sobre

overstaffed [ˌoːvərˈstæft] *adj* : con exceso de personal

overstate [ˌoːvərˈsteɪt] *vt* **-stated; -stating** EXAGGERATE : exagerar

overstatement [ˌoːvərˈsteɪtmənt] *n* : exageración *f*

overstep [ˌoːvərˈstɛp] *vt* **-stepped; -stepping** EXCEED : sobrepasar, traspasar, exceder

overt [oˈvərt, ˈoːˌvərt] *adj* : evidente, manifiesto, patente

overtake [ˌoːvərˈteɪk] *vt* **-took** [-ˈtʊk]; **-taken** [-ˈteɪkən]; **-taking** : pasar, adelantar, rebasar *Mex*

overthrow[1] [ˌoːvərˈθroː] *vt* **-threw** [-ˈθruː]; **-thrown** [-ˈθroːn]; **-throwing 1** OVERTURN : dar la vuelta a, volcar **2** DEFEAT, TOPPLE : derrocar, derribar, deponer

overthrow[2] [ˈoːvərˌθroː] *n* : derrocamiento *m,* caída *f*

overtime [ˈoːvərˌtaɪm] *n* **1** : horas *fpl* extras (de trabajo) **2** : prórroga *f* (en deportes)

overtly [oˈvərtli, ˈoːˌvərt-] *adv* OPENLY : abiertamente

overtone [ˈoːvərˌtoːn] *n* **1** : armónico *m* (en música) **2** HINT, SUGGESTION : tinte *m,* insinuación *f*

overture [ˈoːvərˌtʃʊr, -tʃər] *n* **1** PROPOSAL : propuesta *f* **2** : obertura *f* (en música)

overturn [ˌoːvərˈtərn] *vt* **1** UPSET : dar la vuelta a, volcar **2** NULLIFY : anular, invalidar — *vi* TURN OVER : volcar, dar un vuelco

overuse [ˌoːvərˈjuːz] *vt* **-used; -using** : abusar de
overview [ˈoːvərˌvjuː] *n* : resumen *m,* visión *f* general
overweening [ˌoːvərˈwiːnɪŋ] *adj* **1** ARROGANT : arrogante, soberbio **2** IMMODERATE : desmesurado
overweight [ˌoːvərˈweɪt] *adj* : demasiado gordo, demasiado pesado
overwhelm [ˌoːvərˈhwɛlm] *vt* **1** CRUSH, DEFEAT : aplastar, arrollar **2** SUBMERGE : inundar, sumergir **3** OVERPOWER : abrumar, agobiar <overwhelmed by remorse : abrumado de remordimiento>
overwhelming [ˌoːvərˈhwɛlmɪŋ] *adj* **1** CRUSHING : abrumador, apabullante **2** SWEEPING : arrollador, aplastante <an overwhelming majority : una mayoría aplastante>
overwork [ˌoːvərˈwərk] *vt* **1** : hacer trabajar demasiado **2** OVERUSE : abusar de — *vi* : trabajar demasiado
overwrought [ˌoːvərˈrɔt] *adj* : alterado, sobreexcitado
ovoid [ˈoːˌvɔɪd] *or* **ovoidal** [oˈvɔɪdəl] *adj* : ovoide
ovulate [ˈɑvjəˌleɪt, ˈoː-] *vi* **-lated; -lating** : ovular
ovulation [ˌɑvjəˈleɪʃən, ˌoː-] *n* : ovulación *f*
ovum [ˈoːvəm] *n, pl* **ova** [-və] : óvulo *m*
owe [ˈoː] *vt* **owed; owing** : deber <you owe me $10 : me debes $10> <he owes his wealth to his father : le debe su riqueza a su padre>
owing to *prep* : debido a
owl [ˈaʊl] *n* : búho *m,* lechuza *f,* tecolote *m Mex*
own[1] *v* [ˈoːn] *vt* **1** POSSESS : poseer, tener, ser dueño de **2** ADMIT : reconocer, admitir — *vi* **to own up** : reconocer (algo), admitir (algo)
own[2] *adj* : propio, personal, particular <his own car : su propio coche>
own[3] *pron* **my (your, his/her, our, their) own** : el mío, la mía; el tuyo, la tuya; el suyo, la suya; el nuestro, la nuestra <to each his own : cada uno a lo suyo> <money of my own : mi propio dinero> <to be on one's own : estar solo>
owner [ˈoːnər] *n* : dueño *m,* -ña *f;* propietario *m,* -ria *f*
ownership [ˈoːnərˌʃɪp] *n* : propiedad *f*
ox [ˈɑks] *n, pl* **oxen** [ˈɑksən] : buey *m*
oxidation [ˌɑksəˈdeɪʃən] *n* : oxidación *f*
oxide [ˈɑkˌsaɪd] *n* : óxido *m*
oxidize [ˈɑksəˌdaɪz] *vt* **-dized; -dizing** : oxidar
oxygen [ˈɑksɪdʒən] *n* : oxígeno *m*
oyster [ˈɔɪstər] *n* : ostra *f,* ostión *m Mex*
ozone [ˈoːˌzoːn] *n* : ozono *m*

P

p [ˈpiː] *n, pl* **p's** *or* **ps** [ˈpiːz] : decimosexta letra del alfabeto inglés
pace[1] [ˈpeɪs] *v* **paced; pacing** *vi* : caminar, ir y venir — *vt* **1** : caminar por <she paced the floor : caminaba de un lado a otro del cuarto> **2 to pace a runner** : marcarle el ritmo a un corredor
pace[2] *n* **1** STEP : paso *m* **2** RATE : paso *m,* ritmo *m* <to set the pace : marcar el paso, marcar la pauta>
pacemaker [ˈpeɪsˌmeɪkər] *n* : marcapasos *m*
pacific [pəˈsɪfɪk] *adj* : pacífico
pacifier [ˈpæsəˌfaɪər] *n* : chupete *m,* chupón *m,* mamila *f Mex*
pacifism [ˈpæsəˌfɪzəm] *n* : pacifismo *m*
pacifist [ˈpæsəfɪst] *n* : pacifista *mf*
pacify [ˈpæsəˌfaɪ] *vt* **-fied; -fying 1** SOOTHE : apaciguar, pacificar **2** : pacificar (un país, una región, etc.)
pack[1] [ˈpæk] *vt* **1** PACKAGE : empaquetar, embalar, envasar **2** : empacar, meter (en una maleta) <to pack one's bag : hacer la maleta> **3** FILL : llenar, abarrotar <a packed theater : un teatro abarrotado> **4 to pack off** SEND : mandar — *vi* : empacar, hacer las maletas
pack[2] *n* **1** BUNDLE : bulto *m,* fardo *m* **2** BACKPACK : mochila *f* **3** PACKAGE : paquete *m,* cajetilla *f* (de cigarillos, etc.) **4** : manada *f* (de lobos, etc.), jauría *f* (de perros) <a pack of thieves : una pandilla de ladrones>
package[1] [ˈpækɪdʒ] *vt* **-aged; -aging** : empaquetar, embalar
package[2] *n* : paquete *m,* bulto *m*
packer [ˈpækər] *n* : empacador *m,* -dora *f*
packet [ˈpækət] *n* : paquete *m*
pact [ˈpækt] *n* : pacto *m,* acuerdo *m*
pad[1] [ˈpæd] *vt* **padded; padding 1** FILL, STUFF : rellenar, acolchar (una silla, una pared) **2** : meter paja en, rellenar <to pad a speech : rellenar un discurso>
pad[2] *n* **1** CUSHION : almohadilla *f* <a shoulder pad : una hombrera> **2** TABLET : bloc *m* (de papel) **3** *or* **lily pad** : hoja *f* grande (de un nenúfar) **4 ink pad** : tampón *m* **5 launching pad** : plataforma *f* (de lanzamiento)
padding [ˈpædɪŋ] *n* **1** FILLING : relleno *m* **2** : paja *f* (en un discurso, etc.)
paddle[1] [ˈpædəl] *v* **-dled; -dling** *vt* **1** : hacer avanzar (una canoa) con canalete **2** HIT : azotar, darle nalgadas a (con una pala o paleta) — *vi* **1** : remar (en una canoa) **2** SPLASH : chapotear, mojarse los pies

paddle[2] *n* **1 :** canalete *m,* zagual *m* (de una canoa, etc.) **2 :** pala *f,* paleta *f* (en deportes)

paddock [ˈpædək] *n* **1** PASTURE **:** potrero *m* **2 :** paddock *m,* cercado *m* (en un hipódromo)

paddy [ˈpædi] *n, pl* **-dies :** arrozal *m*

padlock[1] [ˈpæd,lɑk] *vt* **:** cerrar con candado

padlock[2] *n* **:** candado *m*

pagan[1] [ˈpeɪgən] *adj* **:** pagano

pagan[2] *n* **:** pagano *m,* -na *f*

paganism [ˈpeɪgən,ɪzəm] *n* **:** paganismo *m*

page[1] [ˈpeɪdʒ] *vt* **paged; paging :** llamar por altavoz

page[2] *n* **1** BELLHOP **:** botones *m* **2 :** página *f* (de un libro, etc.)

pageant [ˈpædʒənt] *n* **1** SPECTACLE **:** espectáculo *m* **2** PROCESSION **:** desfile *m*

pageantry [ˈpædʒəntri] *n* **:** pompa *f,* fausto *m*

pagoda [pəˈgoːdə] *n* **:** pagoda *f*

paid → **pay**

pail [ˈpeɪl] *n* **:** balde *m,* cubo *m,* cubeta *f Mex*

pailful [ˈpeɪl,fʊl] *n* **:** balde *m,* cubo *m,* cubeta *f Mex*

pain[1] [ˈpeɪn] *vt* **:** doler

pain[2] *n* **1** PENALTY **:** pena *f* <under pain of death : so pena de muerte> **2** SUFFERING **:** dolor *m,* malestar *m,* pena *f* (mental) **3 pains** *npl* EFFORT **:** esmero *m,* esfuerzo *m* <to take pains : esmerarse>

painful [ˈpeɪnfəl] *adj* **:** doloroso — **painfully** *adv*

painkiller [ˈpeɪn,kɪlər] *n* **:** analgésico *m*

painless [ˈpeɪnləs] *adj* **:** indoloro, sin dolor

painlessly [ˈpeɪnləsli] *adv* **:** sin dolor

painstaking [ˈpeɪn,steɪkɪŋ] *adj* **:** esmerado, cuidadoso, meticuloso — **painstakingly** *adv*

paint[1] [ˈpeɪnt] *v* **:** pintar

paint[2] *n* **:** pintura *f*

paintbrush [ˈpeɪnt,brʌʃ] *n* **:** pincel *m* (de un artista), brocha *f* (para pintar casas, etc.)

painter [ˈpeɪntər] *n* **:** pintor *m,* -tora *f*

painting [ˈpeɪntɪŋ] *n* **:** pintura *f*

pair[1] [ˈpær] *vt* **:** emparejar, poner en parejas — *vi* **:** emparejarse

pair[2] *n* **:** par *m* (de objetos), pareja *f* (de personas o animales) <a pair of scissors : unas tijeras>

pajamas [pəˈdʒɑməz, -ˈdʒæ-] *npl* **:** pijama *m,* piyama *mf*

Pakistani [,pækɪˈstæni, ,pɑkɪˈstɑni] *n* **:** paquistaní *mf* — **Pakistani** *adj*

pal [ˈpæl] *n* **:** amigo *m,* -ga *f;* compinche *mf fam;* chamo *m,* -ma *f Ven fam;* cuate *m,* -ta *f Mex*

palace [ˈpæləs] *n* **:** palacio *m*

palatable [ˈpælətəbəl] *adj* **:** sabroso

palate [ˈpælət] *n* **1 :** paladar *m* (de la boca) **2** TASTE **:** paladar *m,* gusto *m*

palatial [pəˈleɪʃəl] *adj* **:** suntuoso, espléndido

palaver [pəˈlævər, -ˈlɑ-] *n* **:** palabrería *f*

pale[1] [ˈpeɪl] *v* **paled; paling** *vi* **:** palidecer — *vt* **:** hacer pálido

pale[2] *adj* **paler; palest 1 :** pálido <to turn pale : palidecer, ponerse pálido> **2 :** claro (dícese de los colores)

paleness [ˈpeɪlnəs] *n* **:** palidez *f*

Palestinian [,pæləˈstɪniən] *n* **:** palestino *m,* -na *f* — **Palestinian** *adj*

palette [ˈpælət] *n* **:** paleta *f* (para mezclar pigmentos)

palisade [,pæləˈseɪd] *n* **1** FENCE **:** empalizada *f,* estacada *f* **2** CLIFFS **:** acantilado *m*

pall[1] [ˈpɔl] *vi* **:** perder su sabor, dejar de gustar

pall[2] *n* **1 :** paño *m* mortuario (sobre un ataúd) **2** COVER **:** cortina *f* (de humo, etc.) **3 to cast a pall over :** ensombrecer

pallbearer [ˈpɔl,bɛrər] *n* **:** portador *m,* -dora *f* del féretro

pallet [ˈpælət] *n* **1** BED **:** camastro *m* **2** PLATFORM **:** plataforma *f* de carga

palliative [ˈpæli,eɪtɪv, ˈpæljətɪv] *adj* **:** paliativo

pallid [ˈpæləd] *adj* **:** pálido

pallor [ˈpælər] *n* **:** palidez *f*

palm[1] [ˈpɑm, ˈpɑlm] *vt* **1** CONCEAL **:** escamotear (un naipe, etc.) **2 to palm off :** encajar, endilgar *fam* <he palmed it off on me : me lo endilgó>

palm[2] *n* **1** *or* **palm tree :** palmera *f* **2 :** palma *f* (de la mano)

Palm Sunday *n* **:** Domingo *m* de Ramos

palomino [,pæləˈmiː,noː] *n, pl* **-nos :** caballo *m* de color dorado

palpable [ˈpælpəbəl] *adj* **:** palpable — **palpably** [-bli] *adv*

palpitate [ˈpælpə,teɪt] *vi* **-tated; -tating :** palpitar

palpitation [,pælpəˈteɪʃən] *n* **:** palpitación *f*

palsy [ˈpɔlzi] *n, pl* **-sies 1 :** parálisis *f* **2** → **cerebral palsy**

paltry [ˈpɔltri] *adj* **-trier; -est :** mísero, mezquino, insignificante <a paltry excuse : una mala excusa>

pampas [ˈpæmpəz, ˈpɑmpəs] *npl* **:** pampa *f*

pamper [ˈpæmpər] *vt* **:** mimar, consentir, chiquear *Mex*

pamphlet [ˈpæm*p*flət] *n* **:** panfleto *m,* folleto *m*

pan[1] [ˈpæn] *vt* **panned; panning** CRITICIZE **:** poner por los suelos — *vi* **to pan for gold :** cribar el oro con batea, lavar oro

pan[2] *n* **1 :** cacerola *f,* cazuela *f* **2 frying pan :** sartén *mf,* freidera *f Mex*

panacea [,pænəˈsiːə] *n* **:** panacea *f*

Panamanian [,pænəˈmeɪniən] *n* **:** panameño *m,* -ña *f* — **Panamanian** *adj*

pancake [ˈpæn,keɪk] *n* **:** panqueque *m*

pancreas [ˈpæŋkriəs, ˈpæn-] *n* **:** páncreas *m*

panda [ˈpændə] *n* **:** panda *mf*

pandemonium [ˌpændəˈmoːniəm] *n* **:** pandemonio *m,* pandemónium *m*

pander [ˈpændər] *vi* **to pander to :** satisfacer, complacer (a alguien) <to pander to popular taste : satisfacer el gusto popular>

pane [ˈpeɪn] *n* **:** cristal *m,* vidrio *m*

panel[1] [ˈpænəl] *vt* **-eled** *or* **-elled; -eling** *or* **-elling :** adornar con paneles

panel[2] *n* **1 :** lista *f* de nombres (de un jurado, etc.) **2** GROUP **:** panel *m,* grupo *m* <discussion panel : panel de discusión> **3 :** panel *m* (de una pared, etc.) **4 instrument panel :** tablero *m* de instrumentos

paneling [ˈpænəlɪŋ] *n* **:** paneles *mpl*

pang [ˈpæŋ] *n* **:** puntada *f,* punzada *f*

panic[1] [ˈpænɪk] *v* **-icked; -icking** *vt* **:** llenar de pánico — *vi* **:** ser presa de pánico

panic[2] *n* **:** pánico *m*

panicky [ˈpænɪki] *adj* **:** presa de pánico

panorama [ˌpænəˈræmə, -ˈrɑ-] *n* **:** panorama *m*

panoramic [ˌpænəˈræmɪk, -ˈrɑ-] *adj* **:** panorámico

pansy [ˈpænzi] *n, pl* **-sies :** pensamiento *m*

pant[1] [ˈpænt] *vi* **:** jadear, resoplar

pant[2] *n* **:** jadeo *m,* resoplo *m*

pantaloons [ˌpæntəˈluːnz] → **pants**

panther [ˈpænθər] *n* **:** pantera *f*

panties [ˈpæntiz] *npl* **:** calzones *mpl,* pantaletas *fpl*

pantomime[1] [ˈpæntəˌmaɪm] *v* **-mimed; -miming** *vt* **:** representar mediante la pantomima — *vi* **:** hacer la mímica

pantomime[2] *n* **:** pantomima *f*

pantry [ˈpæntri] *n, pl* **-tries :** despensa *f*

pants [ˈpænts] *npl* **1** TROUSERS **:** pantalón *m,* pantalones *mpl* **2** → **panties**

pap [ˈpæp] *n* **:** papilla *f* (para bebés, etc.)

papal [ˈpeɪpəl] *adj* **:** papal

papaya [pəˈpaɪə] *n* **:** papaya *f* (fruta)

paper[1] [ˈpeɪpər] *vt* WALLPAPER **:** empapelar

paper[2] *adj* **:** de papel

paper[3] *n* **1 :** papel *m* <a piece of paper : un papel> **2** DOCUMENT **:** papel *m,* documento *m* **3** NEWSPAPER **:** periódico *m,* diario *m*

paperback [ˈpeɪpərˌbæk] *n* **:** libro *m* en rústica

paper clip *n* **:** clip *m,* sujetapapeles *m*

paperweight [ˈpeɪpərˌweɪt] *n* **:** pisapapeles *m*

papery [ˈpeɪpəri] *adj* **:** parecido al papel

papier–mâché [ˌpeɪpərməˈʃeɪ, ˌpæˌpjeɪmæˈʃeɪ] *n* **:** papel *m* maché

papoose [pæˈpuːs, pə-] *n* **:** niño *m,* -ña *f* de los indios norteamericanos

paprika [pəˈpriːkə, pæ-] *n* **:** pimentón *m,* paprika *f*

papyrus [pəˈpaɪrəs] *n, pl* **-ruses** *or* **-ri** [-ri, -ˌraɪ] **:** papiro *m*

par [ˈpɑr] *n* **1** VALUE **:** valor *m* (nominal), par *f* <below par : debajo de la par> **2** EQUALITY **:** igualdad *f* <to be on a par with : estar al mismo nivel que> **3 :** par *m* (en golf)

parable [ˈpærəbəl] *n* **:** parábola *f*

parachute[1] [ˈpærəˌʃuːt] *vi* **-chuted; -chuting :** lanzarse en paracaídas

parachute[2] *n* **:** paracaídas *m*

parachutist [ˈpærəˌʃuːṭɪst] *n* **:** paracaidista *mf*

parade[1] [pəˈreɪd] *vi* **-raded; -rading 1** MARCH **:** desfilar **2** SHOW OFF **:** pavonearse, lucirse

parade[2] *n* **1** PROCESSION **:** desfile *m* **2** DISPLAY **:** alarde *m*

paradigm [ˈpærəˌdaɪm] *n* **:** paradigma *m*

paradise [ˈpærəˌdaɪs, -ˌdaɪz] *n* **:** paraíso *m*

paradox [ˈpærəˌdɑks] *n* **:** paradoja *f*

paradoxical [ˌpærəˈdɑksɪkəl] *adj* **:** paradójico — **paradoxically** *adv*

paraffin [ˈpærəfən] *n* **:** parafina *f*

paragraph[1] [ˈpærəˌgræf] *vt* **:** dividir en párrafos

paragraph[2] *n* **:** párrafo *m,* acápite *m*

Paraguayan [ˌpærəˈgwaɪən, -ˈgweɪ-] *n* **:** paraguayo *m,* -ya *f* — **Paraguayan** *adj*

parakeet [ˈpærəˌkiːt] *n* **:** periquito *m*

parallel[1] [ˈpærəˌlɛl, -ləl] *vt* **1** MATCH, RESEMBLE **:** ser paralelo a, ser análogo a, corresponder con **2 :** extenderse en línea paralela con <the road parallels the river : el camino se extiende a lo largo del río>

parallel[2] *adj* **:** paralelo

parallel[3] *n* **1 :** línea *f* paralela, superficie *f* paralela **2 :** paralelo *m* (en geografía) **3** SIMILARITY **:** paralelismo *m,* semejanza *f*

parallelogram [ˌpærəˈlɛləˌgræm] *n* **:** paralelogramo *m*

paralysis [pəˈræləsɪs] *n, pl* **-yses** [-ˌsiːz] **:** parálisis *f*

paralyze [ˈpærəˌlaɪz] *vt* **-lyzed; -lyzing :** paralizar

parameter [pəˈræməṭər] *n* **:** parámetro *m*

paramount [ˈpærəˌmaʊnt] *adj* **:** supremo <of paramount importance : de suma importancia>

paranoia [ˌpærəˈnɔɪə] *n* **:** paranoia *f*

paranoid [ˈpærəˌnɔɪd] *adj* **:** paranoico

parapet [ˈpærəpət, -ˌpɛt] *n* **:** parapeto *m*

paraphernalia [ˌpærəfəˈneɪljə, -fər-] *ns & pl* **:** parafernalia *f*

paraphrase[1] [ˈpærəˌfreɪz] *vt* **-phrased; -phrasing :** parafrasear

paraphrase[2] *n* **:** paráfrasis *f*

paraplegic[1] [ˌpærəˈpliːdʒɪk] *adj* **:** parapléjico

paraplegic[2] *n* **:** parapléjico *m,* -ca *f*

parasite [ˈpærəˌsaɪt] *n* : parásito *m*
parasitic [ˌpærəˈsɪtɪk] *adj* : parasitario
parasol [ˈpærəˌsɔl] *n* : sombrilla *f,* quitasol *m,* parasol *m*
paratrooper [ˈpærəˌtruːpər] *n* : paracaidista *mf* (militar)
parboil [ˈpɑrˌbɔɪl] *vt* : sancochar, cocer a medias
parcel[1] [ˈpɑrsəl] *vt* **-celed** *or* **-celled; -celing** *or* **-celling** *or* **to parcel out** : repartir, parcelar (tierras)
parcel[2] *n* **1** LOT : parcela *f,* lote *m* **2** PACKAGE : paquete *m,* bulto *m*
parch [ˈpɑrtʃ] *vt* : resecar
parchment [ˈpɑrtʃmənt] *n* : pergamino *m*
pardon[1] [ˈpɑrdən] *vt* **1** FORGIVE : perdonar, disculpar <pardon me! : ¡perdone!, ¡disculpe la molestia!> **2** REPRIEVE : indultar (a un delincuente)
pardon[2] *n* **1** FORGIVENESS : perdón *m* **2** REPRIEVE : indulto *m*
pardonable [ˈpɑrdənəbəl] *adj* : perdonable, disculpable
pare [ˈpær] *vt* **pared; paring 1** PEEL : pelar **2** TRIM : recortar **3** REDUCE : reducir <he pared it (down) to 50 pages : lo redujo a 50 páginas>
parent [ˈpærənt] *n* **1** : madre *f,* padre *m* **2 parents** *npl* : padres *mpl*
parentage [ˈpærəntɪdʒ] *n* : linaje *m,* abolengo *m,* origen *m*
parental [pəˈrɛntəl] *adj* : de los padres
parenthesis [pəˈrɛnθəsɪs] *n, pl* **-theses** [-ˌsiːz] : paréntesis *m*
parenthetic [ˌpærənˈθɛt̬ɪk] *or* **parenthetical** [-tɪkəl] *adj* : parentético — **parenthetically** [-t̬ɪkli] *adv*
parenthood [ˈpærəntˌhʊd] *n* : paternidad *f*
parfait [pɑrˈfeɪ] *n* : postre *m* elaborado con frutas y helado
pariah [pəˈraɪə] *n* : paria *mf*
parish [ˈpærɪʃ] *n* : parroquia *f*
parishioner [pəˈrɪʃənər] *n* : feligrés *m,* -gresa *f*
parity [ˈpærət̬i] *n, pl* **-ties** : paridad *f*
park[1] [ˈpɑrk] *vt* : estacionar, parquear, aparcar *Spain* — *vi* : estacionarse, parquearse, aparcar *Spain*
park[2] *n* : parque *m*
parka [ˈpɑrkə] *n* : parka *f*
parkway [ˈpɑrkˌweɪ] *n* : carretera *f* ajardinada, bulevar *m*
parley[1] [ˈpɑrli] *vi* : parlamentar, negociar
parley[2] *n, pl* **-leys** : negociación *f,* parlamento *m*
parliament [ˈpɑrləmənt, ˈpɑrljə-] *n* : parlamento *m*
parliamentary [ˌpɑrləˈmɛntəri, ˌpɑrljə-] *adj* : parlamentario
parlor [ˈpɑrlər] *n* **1** : sala *f,* salón *m* (en una casa) **2** : salón *m* <beauty parlor : salón de belleza> **3 funeral parlor** : funeraria *f*
parochial [pəˈroːkiəl] *adj* **1** : parroquial **2** PROVINCIAL : pueblerino, de miras estrechas
parody[1] [ˈpærədi] *vt* **-died; -dying** : parodiar
parody[2] *n, pl* **-dies** : parodia *f*
parole [pəˈroːl] *n* : libertad *f* condicional
paroxysm [ˈpærəkˌsɪzəm, pəˈrɑk-] *n* : paroxismo *m*
parquet [ˈpɑrˌkeɪ, pɑrˈkeɪ] *n* : parquet *m,* parqué *m*
parrakeet → **parakeet**
parrot [ˈpærət] *n* : loro *m,* papagayo *m*
parry[1] [ˈpæri] *v* **-ried; -rying** *vi* : parar un golpe — *vt* EVADE : esquivar (una pregunta, etc.)
parry[2] *n, pl* **-ries** : parada *f*
parsimonious [ˌpɑrsəˈmoːniəs] *adj* : tacaño, mezquino
parsley [ˈpɑrsli] *n* : perejil *m*
parsnip [ˈpɑrsnɪp] *n* : chirivía *f*
parson [ˈpɑrsən] *n* : pastor *m,* -tora *f;* clérigo *m*
parsonage [ˈpɑrsənɪdʒ] *n* : rectoría *f,* casa *f* del párroco
part[1] [ˈpɑrt] *vi* **1** SEPARATE : separarse, despedirse <we should part as friends : debemos separarnos amistosamente> **2** OPEN : abrirse <the curtains parted : las cortinas se abrieron> **3 to part with** : dehacerse de — *vt* **1** SEPARATE : separar **2 to part one's hair** : hacerse la raya, peinarse con raya
part[2] *n* **1** SECTION, SEGMENT : parte *f,* sección *f* **2** PIECE : pieza *f* (de una máquina, etc.) **3** ROLE : papel *m* **4** : raya *f* (del pelo)
partake [pɑrˈteɪk, pər-] *vi* **-took** [-ˈtʊk]; **-taken** [-ˈteɪkən]; **-taking 1 to partake of** CONSUME : comer, beber, tomar **2 to partake in** : participar en (una actividad, etc.)
partial [ˈpɑrʃəl] *adj* **1** BIASED : parcial, tendencioso **2** INCOMPLETE : parcial, incompleto **3 to be partial to** : ser aficionado a
partiality [ˌpɑrʃiˈælət̬i] *n, pl* **-ties** : parcialidad *f*
partially [ˈpɑrʃəli] *adv* : parcialmente
participant [pərˈtɪsəpənt, pɑr-] *n* : participante *mf*
participate [pərˈtɪsəˌpeɪt, pɑr-] *vi* **-pated; -pating** : participar
participation [pərˌtɪsəˈpeɪʃən, pɑr-] *n* : participación *f*
participle [ˈpɑrt̬əˌsɪpəl] *n* : participio *m*
particle [ˈpɑrt̬ɪkəl] *n* : partícula *f*
particular[1] [pɑrˈtɪkjələr] *adj* **1** SPECIFIC : particular, en particular <this particular person : esta persona en particular> **2** SPECIAL : particular, especial <with particular emphasis : con un énfasis especial> **3** FUSSY : exigente, maniático <to be very particular : ser muy especial> <I'm not particular : me da igual>
particular[2] *n* **1** DETAIL : detalle *m,* sentido *m* **2 in particular** : en particular, en especial

particularly [pɑr'tɪkjələrli] *adv* **1** ESPECIALLY : particularmente, especialmente **2** SPECIFICALLY : específicamente, en especial

partisan ['pɑrtəzən, -sən] *n* **1** ADHERENT : partidario *m,* -ria *f* **2** GUERRILLA : partisano *m,* -na *f;* guerrillero *m,* -ra *f*

partition[1] [pər'tɪʃən, pɑr-] *vt* : dividir <to partition off (a room) : dividir con un tabique>

partition[2] *n* **1** DISTRIBUTION : partición *f,* división *f,* reparto *m* **2** DIVIDER : tabique *m,* mampara *f,* biombo *m*

partly ['pɑrtli] *adv* : en parte, parcialmente

partner ['pɑrtnər] *n* **1** COMPANION : compañero *m,* -ra *f* **2** : pareja *f* (en un juego, etc.) <dancing partner : pareja de baile> **3** SPOUSE : cónyuge *mf* **4** *or* **business partner** : socio *m,* -cia *f;* asociado *m,* -da *f*

partnership ['pɑrtnər,ʃɪp] *n* **1** ASSOCIATION : asociación *f,* compañerismo *m* **2** : sociedad *f* (de negociantes) <to form a partnership : asociarse>

part of speech : categoría *f* gramatical

partridge ['pɑrtrɪdʒ] *n, pl* **-tridge** *or* **-tridges** : perdiz *f*

party ['pɑrti] *n, pl* **-ties 1** : partido *m* (político) **2** PARTICIPANT : parte *f,* participante *mf* **3** GROUP : grupo *m* (de personas) **4** GATHERING : fiesta *f* <to throw a party : dar una fiesta>

parvenu ['pɑrvə,nu:, -,nju:] *n* : advenedizo *m,* -za *f*

pass[1] ['pæs] *vi* **1** : pasar, cruzarse <a car passed by : pasó un coche> <we passed in the hallway : nos cruzamos en el pasillo> **2** CEASE : pasarse <the pain passed : se pasó el dolor> **3** ELAPSE : pasar, transcurrir **4** PROCEED : pasar <let me pass : déjame pasar> **5** HAPPEN : pasar, ocurrir **6** : pasar, aprobar (en un examen) **7** RULE : fallar <the jury passed on the case : el jurado falló en el caso> **8** *or* **to pass down** : pasar <the throne passed to his son : el trono pasó a su hijo> **9 to let pass** OVERLOOK : pasar por alto **10 to pass as** : pasar por **11 to pass away** *or* **to pass on** DIE : fallecer, morir — *vt* **1** : pasar por <they passed the house : pasaron por la casa> **2** OVERTAKE : pasar, adelantar **3** SPEND : pasar (tiempo) **4** HAND : pasar <pass me the salt : pásame la sal> **5** : aprobar (un examen, una ley)

pass[2] *n* **1** CROSSING, GAP : paso *m,* desfiladero *m,* puerto *m* <mountain pass : puerto de montaña> **2** PERMIT : pase *m,* permiso *m* **3** : pase *m* (en deportes) **4** SITUATION : situación *f* (difícil) <things have come to a pretty pass! : ¡hasta dónde hemos llegado!>

passable ['pæsəbəl] *adj* **1** ADEQUATE : adecuado, pasable **2** : transitable (dícese de un camino, etc.)

passably ['pæsəbli] *adv* : pasablemente

passage ['pæsɪdʒ] *n* **1** PASSING : paso *m* <the passage of time : el paso del tiempo> **2** PASSAGEWAY : pasillo *m* (dentro de un edificio), pasaje *m* (entre edificios) **3** VOYAGE : travesía *f* (por el mar), viaje *m* <to grant safe passage : dar un salvoconducto> **4** SECTION : pasaje *m* (en música o literatura)

passageway ['pæsɪdʒ,weɪ] *n* : pasillo *m,* pasadizo *m,* corredor *m*

passbook ['pæs,bʊk] *n* BANKBOOK : libreta *f* de ahorros

passé [pæ'seɪ] *adj* : pasado de moda

passenger ['pæsəndʒər] *n* : pasajero *m,* -ra *f*

passerby [,pæsər'baɪ, 'pæsər,-] *n, pl* **passersby** : transeúnte *mf*

passing ['pæsɪŋ] *n* DEATH : fallecimiento *m*

passion ['pæʃən] *n* : pasión *f,* ardor *m*

passionate ['pæʃənət] *adj* **1** IRASCIBLE : irascible, iracundo **2** ARDENT : apasionado, ardiente, ferviente, fogoso

passionately ['pæʃənətli] *adv* : apasionadamente, fervientemente, con pasión

passive[1] ['pæsɪv] *adj* : pasivo — **passively** *adv*

passive[2] *n* : voz *f* pasiva (en gramática)

Passover ['pæs,o:vər] *n* : Pascua *f* (en el judaísmo)

passport ['pæs,port] *n* : pasaporte *m*

password ['pæs,wərd] *n* : contraseña *f*

past[1] ['pæst] *adv* : por delante <he drove past : pasamos en coche>

past[2] *adj* **1** AGO : hace <10 years past : hace 10 años> **2** LAST : último <the past few months : los últimos meses> **3** BYGONE : pasado <in past times : en tiempos pasados> **4** : pasado (en gramática)

past[3] *n* : pasado *m*

past[4] *prep* **1** BY : por, por delante de <he ran past the house : pasó por la casa corriendo> **2** BEYOND : más allá de <just past the corner : un poco más allá de la esquina> <we went past the exit : pasamos la salida> **3** AFTER : despúes de <past noon : después del mediodía> <half past two : las dos y media>

pasta ['pɑstə, 'pæs-] *n* : pasta *f*

paste[1] ['peɪst] *vt* **pasted; pasting** : pegar (con engrudo)

paste[2] *n* **1** : pasta *f* <tomato paste : pasta de tomate> **2** : engrudo *m* (para pegar)

pasteboard ['peɪst,bord] *n* : cartón *m,* cartulina *f*

pastel [pæ'stɛl] *n* : pastel *m* — **pastel** *adj*

pasteurization [,pæstʃərə'zeɪʃən, ,pæstjə-] *n* : pasteurización *f*

pasteurize ['pæstʃə,raɪz, 'pæstjə-] *vt* **-ized; -izing** : pasteurizar

pastime ['pæs,taɪm] *n* : pasatiempo *m*

pastor ['pæstər] *n* : pastor *m,* -tora *f*

pastoral [ˈpæstərəl] *adj* : pastoral

past participle *n* : participio *m* pasado

pastry [ˈpeɪstri] *n, pl* **-ries** 1 DOUGH : pasta *f,* masa *f* 2 **pastries** *npl* : pasteles *mpl*

pasture[1] [ˈpæstʃər] *v* **-tured; -turing** *vi* GRAZE : pacer, pastar — *vt* : apacentar, pastar

pasture[2] *n* : pastizal *m,* potrero *m,* pasto *m*

pasty [ˈpeɪsti] *adj* **pastier; -est** 1 : pastoso (en consistencia) 2 PALLID : pálido

pat[1] [ˈpæt] *vt* **patted; patting** : dar palmaditas a, tocar

pat[2] *adv* : de memoria <to have down pat : saberse de memoria>

pat[3] *adj* 1 APT : apto, apropiado 2 GLIB : fácil 3 UNYIELDING : firme <to stand pat : mantenerse firme>

pat[4] *n* 1 TAP : golpecito *m,* palmadita *f* <a pat on the back : una palmadita en la espalda> 2 CARESS : caricia *f* 3 : porción *f* <a pat of butter : una porción de mantequilla>

patch[1] [ˈpætʃ] *vt* 1 MEND, REPAIR : remender, parchar, ponerle un parche a 2 **to patch together** IMPROVISE : confeccionar, improvisar 3 **to patch up** : arreglar <they patched things up : hicieron las paces>

patch[2] *n* 1 : parche *m,* remiendo *m* (para la ropa) <eye patch : parche para el ojo> 2 PIECE : mancha *f,* trozo *m* <a patch of sky : un trozo de cielo> 3 PLOT : parcela *f,* terreno *m* <cabbage patch : parcela de repollos>

patchwork [ˈpætʃˌwərk] *n* : labor *f* de retazos

patchy [ˈpætʃi] *adj* **patchier; -est** 1 IRREGULAR : irregular, desigual 2 INCOMPLETE : parcial, incompleto

patent[1] [ˈpætənt] *vt* : patentar

patent[2] *adj* [ˈpætənt, ˈpeɪt-] 1 OBVIOUS : patente, evidente 2 [ˈpæt-] PATENTED : patentado

patent[3] [ˈpætənt] *n* : patente *f*

patently [ˈpætəntli] *adv* : patentemente, evidentemente

paternal [pəˈtərnəl] *adj* 1 FATHERLY : paternal 2 : paterno <paternal grandfather : abuelo paterno>

paternity [pəˈtərnət̬i] *n* : paternidad *f*

path [ˈpæθ, ˈpɑθ] *n* 1 TRACK, TRAIL : camino *m,* sendero *m,* senda *f* 2 COURSE, ROUTE : recorrido *m,* trayecto *m,* trayectoria *f*

pathetic [pəˈθɛt̬ɪk] *adj* : patético — **pathetically** [-t̬ɪkli] *adv*

pathological [ˌpæθəˈlɑdʒɪkəl] *adj* : patológico

pathologist [pəˈθɑlədʒɪst] *n* : patólogo *m,* -ga *f*

pathology [pəˈθɑlədʒi] *n, pl* **-gies** : patología *f*

pathos [ˈpeɪˌθɑs, ˈpæ-, -ˌθɔs] *n* : patetismo *m*

pathway [ˈpæθˌweɪ] *n* : camino *m,* sendero *m,* senda *f,* vereda *f*

patience [ˈpeɪʃənts] *n* : paciencia *f*

patient[1] [ˈpeɪʃənt] *adj* : paciente — **patiently** *adv*

patient[2] *n* : paciente *mf*

patio [ˈpæt̬iˌoː] *n, pl* **-tios** : patio *m*

patriarch [ˈpeɪtriˌɑrk] *n* : patriarca *m*

patrimony [ˈpætrəˌmoːni] *n, pl* **-nies** : patrimonio *m*

patriot [ˈpeɪtriət] *n* : patriota *mf*

patriotic [ˌpeɪtriˈɑt̬ɪk] *adj* : patriótico — **patriotically** *adv*

patriotism [ˈpeɪtriəˌtɪzəm] *n* : patriotismo *m*

patrol[1] [pəˈtroːl] *v* **-trolled; -trolling** : patrullar

patrol[2] *n* : patrulla *f*

patrolman [pəˈtroːlmən] *n, pl* **-men** [-mən, -ˌmɛn] : policía *mf,* guardia *mf*

patron [ˈpeɪtrən] *n* 1 SPONSOR : patrocinador *m,* -dora *f* 2 CUSTOMER : cliente *m,* -ta *f* 3 *or* **patron saint** : patrono *m,* -na *f*

patronage [ˈpeɪtrənɪdʒ, ˈpæ-] *n* 1 SPONSORSHIP : patrocinio *m* 2 CLIENTELE : clientela *f* 3 : influencia *f* (política)

patronize [ˈpeɪtrəˌnaɪz, ˈpæ-] *vt* **-ized; -izing** 1 SPONSOR : patrocinar 2 : ser cliente de (un negocio) 3 : tratar con condescendencia

patter[1] [ˈpæt̬ər] *vi* 1 TAP : golpetear, tamborilear (dícese de la lluvia) 2 **to patter about** : corretear (con pasos ligeros)

patter[2] *n* 1 TAPPING : golpeteo *m,* tamborileo *m* (de la lluvia), correteo *m* (de pies) 2 CHATTER : palabrería *f,* parloteo *m fam*

pattern[1] [ˈpæt̬ərn] *vt* 1 BASE : basar (en un modelo) 2 **to pattern after** : hacer imitación de

pattern[2] *n* 1 MODEL : modelo *m,* patrón *m* (de costura) 2 DESIGN : diseño *m,* dibujo *m,* estampado *m* (de tela) 3 NORM, STANDARD : pauta *f,* norma *f,* patrón *m*

patty [ˈpæt̬i] *n, pl* **-ties** : porción *f* de carne picada (u otro alimento) en forma de ruedita <a hamburger patty : una hamburguesa>

paucity [ˈpɔsət̬i] *n* : escasez *f*

paunch [ˈpɔntʃ] *n* : panza *f,* barriga *f*

pauper [ˈpɔpər] *n* : pobre *mf,* indigente *mf*

pause[1] [ˈpɔz] *vi* **paused; pausing** : hacer una pausa, pararse (brevemente)

pause[2] *n* : pausa *f*

pave [ˈpeɪv] *vt* **paved; paving** : pavimentar <to pave with stones : empedrar>

pavement [ˈpeɪvmənt] *n* : pavimento *m,* empedrado *m*

pavilion [pəˈvɪljən] *n* : pabellón *m*

paving [ˈpeɪvɪŋ] → **pavement**

paw[1] [ˈpɔ] *vt* : tocar, manosear, sobar

paw[2] *n* : pata *f,* garra *f,* zarpa *f*

pawn[1] [ˈpɔn] *vt* : empeñar, prendar

pawn[2] *n* **1** PLEDGE, SECURITY **:** prenda *f* **2** PAWNING **:** empeño *m* **3 :** peón *m* (en ajedrez)

pawnbroker [ˈpɔnˌbroːkər] *n* **:** prestamista *mf*

pawnshop [ˈpɔnˌʃɑp] *n* **:** casa *f* de empeños, monte *m* de piedad

pay[1] [ˈpeɪ] *v* **paid** [ˈpeɪd]; **paying** *vt* **1 :** pagar (una cuenta, a un empleado, etc.) **2 to pay attention :** poner atención, prestar atención, hacer caso **3 to pay back :** pagar, devolver <she paid them back : les devolvió el dinero> <I'll pay you back for what you did! : ¡me las pagarás!> **4 to pay off** SETTLE **:** saldar, cancelar (una deuda, etc.) **5 to pay one's respects :** presentar uno sus respetos **6 to pay a visit :** hacer una visita — *vi* **:** valer la pena <crime doesn't pay : no hay crimen sin castigo>

pay[2] *n* **:** paga *f*

payable [ˈpeɪəbəl] *adj* DUE **:** pagadero

paycheck [ˈpeɪˌtʃɛk] *n* **:** sueldo *m,* cheque *m* del sueldo

payee [peɪˈiː] *n* **:** beneficiario *m,* -ria *f* (de un cheque, etc.)

payment [ˈpeɪmənt] *n* **1 :** pago *m* **2** INSTALLMENT **:** plazo *m,* cuota *f* **3** REWARD **:** recompensa *f*

payroll [ˈpeɪˌroːl] *n* **:** nómina *f*

PC [ˌpiːˈsiː] *n, pl* **PCs** *or* **PC's :** PC *mf,* computadora *f* personal

pea [ˈpiː] *n* **:** chícharo *m,* guisante *m,* arveja *f*

peace [ˈpiːs] *n* **1 :** paz *f* <peace treaty : tratado de paz> <peace and tranquillity : paz y tranquilidad> **2** ORDER **:** orden *m* (público)

peaceable [ˈpiːsəbəl] *adj* **:** pacífico — **peaceably** [-bli] *adv*

peaceful [ˈpiːsfəl] *adj* **1** PEACEABLE **:** pacífico **2** CALM, QUIET **:** tranquilo, sosegado — **peacefully** *adv*

peacemaker [ˈpiːsˌmeɪkər] *n* **:** conciliador *m,* -dora *f;* mediador *m,* -dora *f*

peach [ˈpiːtʃ] *n* **:** durazno *m,* melocotón *m*

peacock [ˈpiːˌkɑk] *n* **:** pavo *m* real

peak[1] [ˈpiːk] *vi* **:** alcanzar su nivel máximo

peak[2] *adj* **:** máximo

peak[3] *n* **1** POINT **:** punta *f* **2** CREST, SUMMIT **:** cima *f,* cumbre *f* **3** APEX **:** cúspide *f,* apogeo *m,* nivel *m* máximo

peaked [ˈpiːkəd] *adj* SICKLY **:** pálido

peal[1] [ˈpiːl] *vi* **:** repicar

peal[2] *n* **:** repique *m,* tañido *m* (de campanada) <peals of laughter : carcajadas>

peanut [ˈpiːˌnʌt] *n* **:** maní *m,* cacahuate *m Mex,* cacahuete *m Spain*

pear [ˈpær] *n* **:** pera *f*

pearl [ˈpərl] *n* **:** perla *f*

pearly [ˈpərli] *adj* **pearlier; -est :** nacarado

peasant [ˈpɛzənt] *n* **:** campesino *m,* -na *f*

peat [ˈpiːt] *n* **:** turba *f*

pebble [ˈpɛbəl] *n* **:** piedrita *f,* piedrecita *f,* guijarro *m*

pecan [pɪˈkɑn, -ˈkæn, ˈpiːˌkæn] *n* **:** pacana *f,* nuez *f Mex*

peccadillo [ˌpɛkəˈdɪlo] *n, pl* **-loes** *or* **-los :** pecadillo *m*

peccary [ˈpɛkəri] *n, pl* **-ries :** pécari *m,* pecarí *m*

peck[1] [ˈpɛk] *vt* **:** picar, picotear

peck[2] *n* **1 :** medida *f* de áridos equivalente a 8.810 litros **2 :** picotazo *m* (de un pájaro) <a peck on the cheek : un besito en la mejilla>

pectoral [ˈpɛktərəl] *adj* **:** pectoral

peculiar [pɪˈkjuːljər] *adj* **1** DISTINCTIVE **:** propio, peculiar, característico <peculiar to this area : propio de esta zona> **2** STRANGE **:** extraño, raro — **peculiarly** *adv*

peculiarity [pɪˌkjuːlˈjærət̬i, -ˌkjuːliˈær-] *n, pl* **-ties 1** DISTINCTIVENESS **:** peculiaridad *f* **2** ODDITY, QUIRK **:** rareza *f,* idiosincrasia *f,* excentricidad *f*

pecuniary [pɪˈkjuːniˌɛri] *adj* **:** pecuniario

pedagogical [ˌpɛdəˈgɑdʒɪkəl, -ˈgoː-] *adj* **:** pedagógico

pedagogy [ˈpɛdəˌgoːdʒi, -ˌgɑ-] *n* **:** pedagogía *f*

pedal[1] [ˈpɛdəl] *v* **-aled** *or* **-alled; -aling** *or* **-alling** *vi* **:** pedalear — *vt* **:** darle a los pedales de

pedal[2] *n* **:** pedal *m*

pedant [ˈpɛdənt] *n* **:** pedante *mf*

pedantic [pɪˈdæntɪk] *adj* **:** pedante

pedantry [ˈpɛdəntri] *n, pl* **-ries :** pedantería *f*

peddle [ˈpɛdəl] *vt* **-dled; -dling :** vender (en las calles)

peddler [ˈpɛdlər] *n* **:** vendedor *m,* -dora *f* ambulante; mercachifle *m*

pedestal [ˈpɛdəstəl] *n* **:** pedestal *m*

pedestrian[1] [pəˈdɛstriən] *adj* **1** COMMONPLACE **:** pedestre, ordinario **2 :** de peatón <pedestrian crossing : paso de peatones>

pedestrian[2] *n* **:** peatón *m,* -tona *f*

pediatric [ˌpiːdiˈætrɪk] *adj* **:** pediátrico

pediatrician [ˌpiːdiəˈtrɪʃən] *n* **:** pediatra *mf*

pediatrics [ˌpiːdiˈætrɪks] *ns & pl* **:** pediatría *f*

pedigree [ˈpɛdəˌgriː] *n* **1** FAMILY TREE **:** árbol *m* genealógico **2** LINEAGE **:** pedigrí *m* (de un animal), linaje *m* (de una persona)

peek[1] [ˈpiːk] *vi* **1** PEEP **:** espiar, mirar furtivamente **2** GLANCE **:** echar un vistazo

peek[2] *n* **1 :** miradita *f* (furtiva) **2** GLANCE **:** vistazo *m,* ojeada *f*

peel[1] [ˈpiːl] *vt* **1 :** pelar (fruta, etc.) **2** *or* **to peel away :** quitar — *vi* **:** pelarse (dícese de la piel), desconcharse (dícese de la pintura)

peel[2] *n* **:** cáscara *f*

peep[1] [ˈpiːp] *vi* **1** PEEK **:** espiar, mirar furtivamente **2** CHEEP **:** piar **3 to peep out** SHOW **:** asomarse
peep[2] *n* **1** CHEEP **:** pío *m* (de un pajarito) **2** GLANCE **:** vistazo *m,* ojeada *f*
peer[1] [ˈpɪr] *vi* **:** mirar detenidamente, mirar con atención
peer[2] *n* **1** EQUAL **:** par *m,* igual *mf* **2** NOBLE **:** noble *mf*
peerage [ˈpɪrɪdʒ] *n* **:** nobleza *f*
peerless [ˈpɪrləs] *adj* **:** sin par, incomparable
peeve[1] [ˈpiːv] *vt* **peeved; peeving :** fastidiar, irritar, molestar
peeve[2] *n* **:** queja *f*
peevish [ˈpiːvɪʃ] *adj* **:** quejoso, fastidioso — **peevishly** *adv*
peevishness [ˈpiːvɪʃnəs] *n* **:** irritabilidad *f*
peg[1] [ˈpɛg] *vt* **pegged; pegging 1** PLUG **:** tapar (con una clavija) **2** FASTEN, FIX **:** sujetar (con estaquillas) **3 to peg out** MARK **:** marcar (con estaquillas)
peg[2] *n* **:** estaquilla *f* (para clavar), clavija *f* (para tapar)
pejorative [pɪˈdʒɔrət̬ɪv] *adj* **:** peyorativo — **pejoratively** *adv*
pelican [ˈpɛlɪkən] *n* **:** pelícano *m*
pellagra [pəˈlægrə, -ˈleɪ-] *n* **:** pelagra *f*
pellet [ˈpɛlət] *n* **1** BALL **:** bolita *f* <food pellet **:** bolita de comida> **2** SHOT **:** perdigón *m*
pell–mell [ˈpɛlˈmɛl] *adv* **:** desordenadamente, atropelladamente
pelt[1] [ˈpɛlt] *vt* **1** THROW **:** lanzar, tirar (algo a alguien) **2 to pelt with stones :** apedrear — *vi* BEAT **:** golpear con fuerza <the rain was pelting down **:** llovía a cántaros>
pelt[2] *n* **:** piel *f,* pellejo *m*
pelvic [ˈpɛlvɪk] *adj* **:** pélvico
pelvis [ˈpɛlvɪs] *n, pl* **-vises** *or* **-ves** [ˈpɛlˌviːz] **:** pelvis *f*
pen[1] [ˈpɛn] *vt* **penned; penning 1** *or* **pen in :** encerrar (animales) **2** WRITE **:** escribir
pen[2] *n* **1** CORRAL **:** corral *m,* redil *m* (para ovejas) **2 :** pluma *f* <fountain pen **:** pluma fuente> <ballpoint pen **:** bolígrafo>
penal [ˈpiːnəl] *adj* **:** penal
penalize [ˈpiːnəlˌaɪz, ˈpɛn-] *vt* **-ized; -izing :** penalizar, sancionar, penar
penalty [ˈpɛnəlti] *n, pl* **-ties 1** PUNISHMENT **:** pena *f,* castigo *m* **2** DISADVANTAGE **:** desventaja *f,* castigo *m,* penalty *m* (en deportes) **3** FINE **:** multa *f*
penance [ˈpɛnənts] *n* **:** penitencia *f*
pence → **penny**
penchant [ˈpɛntʃənt] *n* **:** inclinación *f,* afición *f*
pencil[1] [ˈpɛntsəl] *vt* **-ciled** *or* **-cilled; -ciling** *or* **-cilling :** escribir con lápiz, dibujar con lápiz
pencil[2] *n* **:** lápiz *m*
pendant [ˈpɛndənt] *n* **:** colgante *m*
pending[1] [ˈpɛndɪŋ] *adj* **:** pendiente
pending[2] *prep* **1** DURING **:** durante **2** AWAITING **:** en espera de
pendulum [ˈpɛndʒələm, -djʊləm] *n* **:** péndulo *m*
penetrate [ˈpɛnəˌtreɪt] *vt* **-trated; -trating :** penetrar
penetrating [ˈpɛnəˌtreɪt̬ɪŋ] *adj* **:** penetrante, cortante
penetration [ˌpɛnəˈtreɪʃən] *n* **:** penetración *f*
penguin [ˈpɛŋgwɪn, ˈpɛn-] *n* **:** pingüino *m*
penicillin [ˌpɛnəˈsɪlən] *n* **:** penicilina *f*
peninsula [pəˈnɪntsələ, -ˈnɪntʃʊlə] *n* **:** península *f*
penis [ˈpiːnəs] *n, pl* **-nes** [-ˌniːz] *or* **-nises :** pene *m*
penitence [ˈpɛnət̬ənts] *n* **:** arrepentimiento *m,* penitencia *f*
penitent[1] [ˈpɛnət̬ənt] *adj* **:** arrepentido, penitente
penitent[2] *n* **:** penitente *mf*
penitentiary [ˌpɛnəˈtɛntʃəri] *n, pl* **-ries :** penitenciaría *f,* prisión *m,* presidio *m*
penmanship [ˈpɛnmənˌʃɪp] *n* **:** escritura *f,* caligrafía *f*
pen name *n* **:** seudónimo *m*
pennant [ˈpɛnənt] *n* **:** gallardete *m* (de un barco), banderín *m*
penniless [ˈpɛniləs] *adj* **:** sin un centavo
penny [ˈpɛni] *n, pl* **-nies** *or* **pence** [ˈpɛnts] **1 :** penique *m* (del Reino Unido) **2** *pl* **-nies** CENT **:** centavo *m* (de los Estados Unidos)
pension[1] [ˈpɛntʃən] *vt or* **to pension off :** jubilar
pension[2] *n* **:** pensión *m,* jubilación *f*
pensive [ˈpɛntsɪv] *adj* **:** pensativo, meditabundo — **pensively** *adv*
pent [ˈpɛnt] *adj* **:** encerrado <pent-up feelings **:** emociones reprimidas>
pentagon [ˈpɛntəˌgɑn] *n* **:** pentágono *m*
pentagonal [pɛnˈtægənəl] *adj* **:** pentagonal
penthouse [ˈpɛntˌhaʊs] *n* **:** ático *m,* penthouse *m*
penury [ˈpɛnjəri] *n* **:** penuria *f,* miseria *f*
peon [ˈpiːˌɑn, -ən] *n, pl* **-ons** *or* **-ones** [peɪˈoːniːz] **:** peón *m*
peony [ˈpiːəni] *n, pl* **-nies :** peonía *f*
people[1] [ˈpiːpəl] *vt* **-pled; -pling :** poblar
people[2] *ns & pl* **1 people** *npl* **:** gente *f,* personas *fpl* <people like him **:** él le cae bien a la gente> <many people **:** mucha gente, muchas personas> **2** *pl* **peoples :** pueblo *m* <the Cuban people **:** el pueblo cubano>
pep[1] [ˈpɛp] *vt* **pepped; pepping** *or* **to pep up :** animar
pep[2] *n* **:** energía *f,* vigor *m*
pepper[1] [ˈpɛpər] *vt* **1 :** añadir pimienta a **2** RIDDLE **:** acribillar (a balazos) **3** SPRINKLE **:** salpicar <peppered with quotations **:** salpicado de citas>

pepper[2] *n* **1 :** pimienta *f* (condimento) **2 :** pimiento *m,* pimentón *m* (fruta) **3** → **chili**
peppermint [ˈpɛpərˌmɪnt] *n* **:** menta *f*
peppery [ˈpɛpəri] *adj* **:** picante
peppy [ˈpɛpi] *adj* **peppier; -est :** lleno de energía, vivaz
peptic [ˈpɛptɪk] *adj* **peptic ulcer :** úlcera *f* estomacal
per [ˈpər] *prep* **1 :** por <miles per hour : millas por hora> **2** ACCORDING TO **:** según <per his specifications : según sus especificaciones>
per annum [pərˈænəm] *adv* **:** al año, por año
percale [ˌpərˈkeɪl, ˈpər-ˌ; ˌpərˈkæl] *n* **:** percal *m*
per capita [pərˈkæpɪt̬ə] *adv & adj* **:** per cápita
perceive [pərˈsiːv] *vt* **-ceived; -ceiving 1** REALIZE **:** percatarse de, concientizarse de, darse cuenta de **2** NOTE **:** percibir, notar
percent[1] [pərˈsɛnt] *adv* **:** por ciento
percent[2] *n, pl* **-cent** *or* **-cents 1 :** por ciento <10 percent of the population : el 10 por ciento de la población> **2** → **percentage**
percentage [pərˈsɛntɪdʒ] *n* **:** porcentaje *m*
perceptible [pərˈsɛptəbəl] *adj* **:** perceptible — **perceptibly** [-bli] *adv*
perception [pərˈsɛpʃən] *n* **1 :** percepción *f* <color perception : la percepción de los colores> **2** INSIGHT **:** perspicacia *f* **3** IDEA **:** idea *f,* imagen *f*
perceptive [pərˈsɛptɪv] *adj* **:** perspicaz
perceptively [pərˈsɛptɪvli] *adv* **:** con perspicacia
perch[1] [ˈpərtʃ] *vi* **1** ROOST **:** posarse **2** SIT **:** sentarse (en un sitio elevado) — *vt* PLACE **:** posar, colocar
perch[2] *n* **1** ROOST **:** percha *f* (para los pájaros) **2** *pl* **perch** *or* **perches :** perca *f* (pez)
percolate [ˈpərkəˌleɪt] *vi* **-lated; -lating :** colarse, filtrarse <percolated coffee : café filtrado>
percolator [ˈpərkəˌleɪt̬ər] *n* **:** cafetera *f* de filtro
percussion [pərˈkʌʃən] *n* **1** STRIKING **:** percusión *f* **2** *or* **percussion instruments :** instrumentos *mpl* de percusión
peremptory [pəˈrɛmptəri] *adj* **:** perentorio
perennial[1] [pəˈrɛniəl] *adj* **1 :** perenne, vivaz <perennial flowers : flores perennes> **2** RECURRENT **:** perenne, continuo <a perennial problem : un problema eterno>
perennial[2] *n* **:** planta *f* perenne, planta *f* vivaz
perfect[1] [pərˈfɛkt] *vt* **:** perfeccionar
perfect[2] [ˈpərfɪkt] *adj* **:** perfecto — **perfectly** *adv*
perfection [pərˈfɛkʃən] *n* **:** perfección *f*
perfectionist [pərˈfɛkʃənɪst] *n* **:** perfeccionista *mf*
perfidious [pərˈfɪdiəs] *adj* **:** pérfido
perforate [ˈpərfəˌreɪt] *vt* **-rated; -rating :** perforar
perforation [ˌpərfəˈreɪʃən] *n* **:** perforación *f*
perform [pərˈfɔrm] *vt* **1** CARRY OUT **:** realizar, hacer, desempeñar **2** PRESENT **:** representar, dar (una obra teatral, etc.) — *vi* **:** actuar (en una obra teatral), cantar (en una ópera, etc.), tocar (en un concierto, etc.), bailar (en un ballet, etc.)
performance [pərˈfɔrmənts] *n* **1** EXECUTION **:** ejecución *f,* realización *f,* desempeño *m,* rendimiento *m* **2** INTERPRETATION **:** interpretación *f* <his performance of Hamlet : su interpretación de Hamlet> **3** PRESENTATION **:** representación *f* (de una obra teatral), función *f*
performer [pərˈfɔrmər] *n* **:** artista *mf;* actor *m,* -triz *f;* intérprete *mf* (de música)
perfume[1] [pərˈfjuːm, ˈpərˌ-] *vt* **-fumed; -fuming :** perfumar
perfume[2] [ˈpərˌfjuːm, pərˈ-] *n* **:** perfume *m*
perfunctory [pərˈfʌŋktəri] *adj* **:** mecánico, superficial, somero
perhaps [pərˈhæps] *adv* **:** tal vez, quizá, quizás
peril [ˈpɛrəl] *n* **:** peligro *m*
perilous [ˈpɛrələs] *adj* **:** peligroso — **perilously** *adv*
perimeter [pəˈrɪmət̬ər] *n* **:** perímetro *m*
period [ˈpɪriəd] *n* **1 :** punto *m* (en puntuación) **2 :** período *m* <a two-hour period : un período de dos horas> **3** STAGE **:** época *f* (histórica), fase *f,* etapa *f*
periodic [ˌpɪriˈɑdɪk] *or* **periodical** [-dɪkəl] *adj* **:** periódico — **periodically** [-dɪkli] *adv*
periodical [ˌpɪriˈɑdɪkəl] *n* **:** publicación *f* periódica, revista *f*
peripheral [pəˈrɪfərəl] *adj* **:** periférico
periphery [pəˈrɪfəri] *n, pl* **-eries :** periferia *f*
periscope [ˈpɛrəˌskoːp] *n* **:** periscopio *m*
perish [ˈpɛrɪʃ] *vi* DIE **:** perecer, morirse
perishable[1] [ˈpɛrɪʃəbəl] *adj* **:** perecedero
perishable[2] *n* **:** producto *m* perecedero
perjure [ˈpərdʒər] *vt* **-jured; -juring** (*used in law*) **to perjure oneself :** perjurar, perjurarse
perjury [ˈpərdʒəri] *n* **:** perjurio *m*
perk[1] [ˈpərk] *vt* **1 :** levantar (las orejas, etc.) **2** *or* **to perk up** FRESHEN **:** arreglar — *vi* **to perk up :** animarse, reanimarse
perk[2] *n* **:** extra *m*
perky [ˈpərki] *adj* **perkier; -est :** animado, alegre, lleno de vida
permanence [ˈpərmənənts] *n* **:** permanencia *f*

permanent[1] [ˈpərmənənt] *adj* : permanente — **permanently** *adv*
permanent[2] *n* : permanente *f*
permeable [ˈpərmiəbəl] *adj* : permeable
permeate [ˈpərmiˌeɪt] *v* **-ated; -ating** *vt* **1** PENETRATE : penetrar, impregnar **2** PERVADE : penetrar, difundirse por — *vi* : penetrar
permissible [pərˈmɪsəbəl] *adj* : permisible, lícito
permission [pərˈmɪʃən] *n* : permiso *m*
permissive [pərˈmɪsɪv] *adj* : permisivo
permit[1] [pərˈmɪt] *vt* **-mitted; -mitting** : permitir, dejar <weather permitting : si el tiempo lo permite>
permit[2] [ˈpərˌmɪt, pərˈ-] *n* : permiso *m,* licencia *f*
pernicious [pərˈnɪʃəs] *adj* : pernicioso
peroxide [pəˈrɑkˌsaɪd] *n* **1** : peróxido *m* **2** → **hydrogen peroxide**
perpendicular[1] [ˌpərpənˈdɪkjələr] *adj* **1** VERTICAL : vertical **2** : perpendicular <perpendicular lines : líneas perpendiculares> — **perpendicularly** *adv*
perpendicular[2] *n* : perpendicular *f*
perpetrate [ˈpərpəˌtreɪt] *vt* **-trated; -trating** : perpetrar, cometer (un delito)
perpetrator [ˈpərpəˌtreɪt̬ər] *n* : autor *m,* -tora *f* (de un delito)
perpetual [pərˈpɛtʃʊəl] *adj* **1** EVERLASTING : perpetuo, eterno **2** CONTINUAL : perpetuo, continuo, constante
perpetually [pərˈpɛtʃʊəli, -tʃəli] *adv* : para siempre, eternamente
perpetuate [pərˈpɛtʃʊˌeɪt] *vt* **-ated; -ating** : perpetuar
perpetuity [ˌpərpəˈtuːət̬i, -ˈtjuː-] *n, pl* **-ties** : perpetuidad *f*
perplex [pərˈplɛks] *vt* : dejar perplejo, confundir
perplexed [pərˈplɛkst] *adj* : perplejo
perplexity [pərˈplɛksət̬i] *n, pl* **-ties** : perplejidad *f,* confusión *f*
persecute [ˈpərsɪˌkjuːt] *vt* **-cuted; -cuting** : perseguir
persecution [ˌpərsɪˈkjuːʃən] *n* : persecución *f*
perseverance [ˌpərsəˈvɪrən*t*s] *n* : perseverancia *f*
persevere [ˌpərsəˈvɪr] *vi* **-vered; -vering** : perseverar
Persian [ˈpərʒən] *n* **1** : persa *mf* **2** : persa *m* (idioma) — **Persian** *adj*
persist [pərˈsɪst] *vi* : persistir
persistence [pərˈsɪstən*t*s] *n* **1** CONTINUATION : persistencia *f* **2** TENACITY : perseverancia *f,* tenacidad *f*
persistent [pərˈsɪstənt] *adj* : persistente — **persistently** *adv*
person [ˈpərsən] *n* **1** HUMAN, INDIVIDUAL : persona *f,* individuo *m,* ser *m* humano **2** : persona *f* (en gramática) **3 in person** : en persona
personable [ˈpərsənəbəl] *adj* : agradable
personage [ˈpərsənɪdʒ] *n* : personaje *m*
personal [ˈpərsənəl] *adj* **1** OWN, PRIVATE : personal, particular, privado <for personal reasons : por razones personales> **2** : en persona <to make a personal appearance : presentarse en persona, hacerse acto de presencia> **3** : íntimo, personal <personal hygiene : higiene personal> **4** INDISCREET, PRYING : indiscreto, personal
personality [ˌpərsənˈælət̬i] *n, pl* **-ties** **1** DISPOSITION : personalidad *f,* temperamento *m* **2** CELEBRITY : personalidad *f,* personaje *m,* celebridad *f*
personalize [ˈpərsənəˌlaɪz] *vt* **-ized; -izing** : personalizar
personally [ˈpərsənəli] *adv* **1** : personalmente, en persona <I'll do it personally : lo haré personalmente> **2** : como persona <personally she's very amiable : como persona es muy amable> **3** : personalmente <personally, I don't believe it : yo, personalmente, no me lo creo>
personification [pərˌsɑnəfəˈkeɪʃən] *n* : personificación *f*
personify [pərˈsɑnəˌfaɪ] *vt* **-fied; -fying** : personificar
personnel [ˌpərsənˈɛl] *n* : personal *m*
perspective [pərˈspɛktɪv] *n* : perspectiva *f*
perspicacious [ˌpərspəˈkeɪʃəs] *adj* : perspicaz
perspiration [ˌpərspəˈreɪʃən] *n* : transpiración *f,* sudor *m*
perspire [pərˈspaɪr] *vi* **-spired; -spiring** : transpirar, sudar
persuade [pərˈsweɪd] *vt* **-suaded; -suading** : persuadir, convencer
persuasion [pərˈsweɪʒən] *n* : persuasión *f*
persuasive [pərˈsweɪsɪv, -zɪv] *adj* : persuasivo — **persuasively** *adv*
persuasiveness [pərˈsweɪsɪvnəs, -zɪv-] *n* : persuasión *f*
pert [ˈpərt] *adj* **1** SAUCY : descarado, impertinente **2** JAUNTY : alegre, animado <a pert little hat : un sombrero coqueto>
pertain [pərˈteɪn] *vi* **1** BELONG : pertenecer (a) **2** RELATE : estar relacionado (con)
pertinence [ˈpərtənən*t*s] *n* : pertinencia *f*
pertinent [ˈpərtənənt] *adj* : pertinente
perturb [pərˈtərb] *vt* : perturbar
perusal [pəˈruːzəl] *n* : lectura *f* cuidadosa
peruse [pəˈruːz] *vt* **-rused; -rusing** **1** READ : leer con cuidado **2** SCAN : recorrer con la vista <he perused the newspaper : echó un vistazo al periódico>
Peruvian [pəˈruːviən] *n* : peruano *m,* -na *f* — **Peruvian** *adj*
pervade [pərˈveɪd] *vt* **-vaded; -vading** : penetrar, difundirse por
pervasive [pərˈveɪsɪv, -zɪv] *adj* : penetrante

perverse [pərˈvərs] *adj* **1** CORRUPT : perverso, corrompido **2** STUBBORN : obstinado, porfiado, terco (sin razón) — **perversely** *adv*

perversion [pərˈvərʒən] *n* : perversión *f*

perversity [pərˈvərsət̬i] *n, pl* **-ties 1** CORRUPTION : corrupción *f* **2** STUBBORNNESS : obstinación *f,* terquedad *f*

pervert[1] [pərˈvərt] *vt* **1** DISTORT : pervertir, distorsionar **2** CORRUPT : pervertir, corromper

pervert[2] [ˈpərˌvərt] *n* : pervertido *m,* -da *f*

peso [ˈpeɪˌsoː] *n, pl* **-sos** : peso *m*

pessimism [ˈpɛsəˌmɪzəm] *n* : pesimismo *m*

pessimist [ˈpɛsəmɪst] *n* : pesimista *mf*

pessimistic [ˌpɛsəˈmɪstɪk] *adj* : pesimista

pest [ˈpɛst] *n* **1** NUISANCE : peste *f;* latoso *m,* -sa *f fam* <to be a pest : dar (la) lata> **2** : insecto *m* nocivo, animal *m* nocivo <the squirrels were pests : las ardillas eran una plaga>

pester [ˈpɛstər] *vt* **-tered; -tering** : molestar, fastidiar

pesticide [ˈpɛstəˌsaɪd] *n* : pesticida *m*

pestilence [ˈpɛstələn*t*s] *n* : pestilencia *f,* peste *f*

pestle [ˈpɛsəl, ˈpɛstəl] *n* : mano *f* de mortero, mazo *m,* maja *f*

pet[1] [ˈpɛt] *vt* **petted; petting** : acariciar

pet[2] *n* **1** : animal *m* doméstico **2** FAVORITE : favorito *m,* -ta *f*

petal [ˈpɛt̬əl] *n* : pétalo *m*

petite [pəˈtiːt] *adj* : pequeña, menuda, chiquita

petition[1] [pəˈtɪʃən] *vt* : peticionar

petition[2] *n* : petición *f*

petitioner [pəˈtɪʃənər] *n* : peticionario *m,* -ria *f*

petrify [ˈpɛtrəˌfaɪ] *vt* **-fied; -fying** : petrificar

petroleum [pəˈtroːliəm] *n* : petróleo *m*

petticoat [ˈpɛt̬iˌkoːt] *n* : enagua *f,* fondo *m Mex*

pettiness [ˈpɛt̬inəs] *n* **1** INSIGNIFICANCE : insignificancia *f* **2** MEANNESS : mezquindad *f*

petty [ˈpɛt̬i] *adj* **-tier; -est 1** MINOR : menor <petty cash : dinero para gastos menores> **2** INSIGNIFICANT : insignificante, trivial, nimio **3** MEAN : mezquino

petty officer *n* : suboficial *mf*

petulance [ˈpɛtʃələn*t*s] *n* : irritabilidad *f,* mal genio *m*

petulant [ˈpɛtʃələnt] *adj* : irritable, de mal genio

petunia [pɪˈtuːnjə, -ˈtjuː-] *n* : petunia *f*

pew [ˈpjuː] *n* : banco *m* (de iglesia)

pewter [ˈpjuːt̬ər] *n* : peltre *m*

pH [ˌpiːˈeɪtʃ] *n* : pH *m*

phallic [ˈfælɪk] *adj* : fálico

phallus [ˈfæləs] *n, pl* **-li** [ˈfæˌlaɪ] *or* **-luses** : falo *m*

phantasy [ˈfæntəsi] → **fantasy**

phantom [ˈfæntəm] *n* : fantasma *m*

pharaoh [ˈfɛrˌoː, ˈfeɪˌroː] *n* : faraón *m*

pharmaceutical [ˌfɑrməˈsuːt̬ɪkəl] *adj* : farmacéutico

pharmacist [ˈfɑrməsɪst] *n* : farmacéutico *m,* -ca *f*

pharmacology [ˌfɑrməˈkɑlədʒi] *n* : farmacología *f*

pharmacy [ˈfɑrməsi] *n, pl* **-cies** : farmacia *f*

pharynx [ˈfærɪŋks] *n, pl* **pharynges** [fəˈrɪnˌdʒiːz] : faringe *f*

phase[1] [ˈfeɪz] *vt* **phased; phasing 1** SYNCHRONIZE : sincronizar, poner en fase **2** STAGGER : escalonar **3 to phase in** : introducir progresivamente **4 to phase out** : retirar progresivamente, dejar de producir

phase[2] *n* **1** : fase *f* (de la luna, etc.) **2** STAGE : fase *f,* etapa *f*

pheasant [ˈfɛzənt] *n, pl* **-ant** *or* **-ants** : faisán *m*

phenomenal [fɪˈnɑmənəl] *adj* : extraordinario, excepcional

phenomenon [fɪˈnɑməˌnɑn, -nən] *n, pl* **-na** [-nə] *or* **-nons 1** : fenómeno *m* **2** *pl* **-nons** PRODIGY : fenómeno *m,* prodigio *m*

philanthropic [ˌfɪlənˈθrɑpɪk] *adj* : filantrópico

philanthropist [fəˈlæn*t*θrəpɪst] *n* : filántropo *m,* -pa *f*

philanthropy [fəˈlæn*t*θrəpi] *n, pl* **-pies** : filantropía *f*

philately [fəˈlæt̬əli] *n* : filatelia *f*

philodendron [ˌfɪləˈdɛndrən] *n, pl* **-drons** *or* **-dra** [-drə] : arácea *f*

philosopher [fəˈlɑsəfər] *n* : filósofo *m,* -fa *f*

philosophic [ˌfɪləˈsɑfɪk] *or* **philosophical** [-fɪkəl] *adj* : filosófico — **philosophically** [-kli] *adv*

philosophize [fəˈlɑsəˌfaɪz] *vi* **-phized; -phizing** : filosofar

philosophy [fəˈlɑsəfi] *n, pl* **-phies** : filosofía *f*

phlebitis [flɪˈbaɪt̬əs] *n* : flebitis *f*

phlegm [ˈflɛm] *n* : flema *f*

phlox [ˈflɑks] *n, pl* **phlox** *or* **phloxes** : polemonio *m*

phobia [ˈfoːbiə] *n* : fobia *f*

phoenix [ˈfiːnɪks] *n* : fénix *m*

phone[1] [ˈfoːn] *v* → **telephone**[1]

phone[2] *n* → **telephone**[2]

phoneme [ˈfoːˌniːm] *n* : fonema *m*

phonetic [fəˈnɛt̬ɪk] *adj* : fonético

phonetics [fəˈnɛt̬ɪks] *n* : fonética *f*

phonics [ˈfɑnɪks] *n* : método *m* fonético de aprender a leer

phonograph [ˈfoːnəˌgræf] *n* : fonógrafo *m,* tocadiscos *m*

phony[1] *or* **phoney** [ˈfoːni] *adj* **-nier; -est** : falso

phony[2] *or* **phoney** *n, pl* **-nies** : farsante *mf;* charlatán *m,* -tana *f*

phosphate [ˈfɑsˌfeɪt] *n* : fosfato *m*

phosphorescence [ˌfɑsfəˈrɛsən*t*s] *n* : fosforescencia *f*

phosphorescent [ˌfɑsfəˈrɛsənt] *adj* : fosforescente — **phosphorescently** *adv*

phosphorus [ˈfɑsfərəs] *n* : fósforo *m*

photo [ˈfoːt̬oː] *n, pl* **-tos** : foto *f*

photocopier [ˈfoːt̬oˌkɑpiər] *n* : fotocopiadora *f*

photocopy[1] [ˈfoːt̬oˌkɑpi] *vt* **-copied; -copying** : fotocopiar

photocopy[2] *n, pl* **-copies** : fotocopia *f*

photoelectric [ˌfoːt̬oɪˈlɛktrɪk] *adj* : fotoeléctrico

photogenic [ˌfoːt̬əˈdʒɛnɪk] *adj* : fotogénico

photograph[1] [ˈfoːt̬əˌgræf] *vt* : fotografiar

photograph[2] *n* : fotografía *f*, foto *f* <to take a photograph of : tomarle una fotografía a, tomar una fotografía de>

photographer [fəˈtɑgrəfər] *n* : fotógrafo *m*, -fa *f*

photographic [ˌfoːt̬əˈgræfɪk] *adj* : fotográfico — **photographically** [-fɪkli] *adv*

photography [fəˈtɑgrəfi] *n* : fotografía *f*

photosynthesis [ˌfoːt̬oˈsɪn*t*θəsɪs] *n* : fotosíntesis *f*

photosynthetic [ˌfoːt̬osɪnˈθɛt̬ɪk] *adj* : fotosintético, de fotosíntesis

phrase[1] [ˈfreɪz] *vt* **phrased; phrasing** : expresar

phrase[2] *n* : frase *f*, locución *f* <to coin a phrase : para decirlo así>

phylum [ˈfaɪləm] *n, pl* **-la** [-lə] : phylum *m*

physical[1] [ˈfɪzɪkəl] *adj* **1** : físico <physical laws : leyes físicas> **2** MATERIAL : material, físico **3** BODILY : físico, corpóreo — **physically** [-kli] *adv*

physical[2] *n* CHECKUP : chequeo *m*, reconocimiento *m* médico

physician [fəˈzɪʃən] *n* : médico *m*, -ca *f*

physicist [ˈfɪzəsɪst] *n* : físico *m*, -ca *f*

physics [ˈfɪzɪks] *ns & pl* : física *f*

physiognomy [ˌfɪziˈɑgnəmi] *n, pl* **-mies** : fisonomía *f*

physiological [ˈfɪziəˈlɑdʒɪkəl] *or* **physiologic** [-dʒɪk] *adj* : fisiológico

physiologist [ˌfɪziˈɑlədʒɪst] *n* : fisiólogo *m*, -ga *f*

physiology [ˌfɪziˈɑlədʒi] *n* : fisiología *f*

physique [fəˈziːk] *n* : físico *m*

pi [ˈpaɪ] *n, pl* **pis** [ˈpaɪz] : pi *f*

pianist [piˈænɪst, ˈpiːənɪst] *n* : pianista *mf*

piano [piˈænoː] *n, pl* **-anos** : piano *m*

piazza [piˈæzə, -ˈɑtsə] *n, pl* **-zas** *or* **-ze** [-ˈɑtˌseɪ] : plaza *f*

picayune [ˌpɪkiˈjuːn] *adj* : trivial, nimio, insignificante

piccolo [ˈpɪkəˌloː] *n, pl* **-los** : flautín *m*

pick[1] [ˈpɪk] *vt* **1** : picar, labrar (con un pico) <he picked the hard soil : picó la tierra dura> **2** : quitar, sacar (poco a poco) <to pick meat off the bones : quitar pedazos de carne de los huesos> **3** : recoger, arrancar (frutas, flores, etc.) **4** SELECT : escoger, elegir **5** PROVOKE : provocar <to pick a quarrel : buscar pleito, buscar pelea> **6 to pick a lock** : forzar una cerradura **7 to pick someone's pocket** : robarle algo del bolsillo de alguien <someone picked my pocket! : ¡me robaron la cartera del bolsillo!> — *vi* **1** NIBBLE : picar, picotear **2 to pick and choose** : ser exigente **3 to pick at** : tocar, rascarse (una herida, etc.) **4 to pick on** TEASE : mofarse de, atormentar

pick[2] *n* **1** CHOICE : selección *f* **2** BEST : lo mejor <the pick of the crop : la crema y nata> **3** → **pickax**

pickax [ˈpɪkˌæks] *n* : pico *m*, zapapico *m*, piqueta *f*

pickerel [ˈpɪkərəl] *n, pl* **-el** *or* **-els** : lucio *m* pequeño

picket[1] [ˈpɪkət] *v* : piquetear

picket[2] *n* **1** STAKE : estaca *f* **2** STRIKER : huelguista *mf*, integrante *mf* de un piquete

pickle[1] [ˈpɪkəl] *vt* **-led; -ling** : encurtir, escabechar

pickle[2] *n* **1** BRINE : escabeche *m* **2** GHERKIN : pepinillo *m* (encurtido) **3** JAM, TROUBLE : lío *m*, apuro *m*

pickpocket [ˈpɪkˌpɑkət] *n* : carterista *mf*

pickup [ˈpɪkˌəp] *n* **1** IMPROVEMENT : mejora *f* **2** *or* **pickup truck** : camioneta *f*

pick up *vt* **1** LIFT : levantar **2** TIDY : arreglar, ordenar — *vi* IMPROVE : mejorar

picnic[1] [ˈpɪkˌnɪk] *vi* **-nicked; -nicking** : ir de picnic

picnic[2] *n* : picnic *m*

pictorial [pɪkˈtoriəl] *adj* : pictórico

picture[1] [ˈpɪktʃər] *vt* **-tured; -turing 1** DEPICT : representar **2** IMAGINE : imaginarse <can you picture it? : ¿te lo puedes imaginar?>

picture[2] *n* **1** : cuadro *m* (pintado o dibujado), ilustración *f*, fotografía *f* **2** DESCRIPTION : descripción *f* **3** IMAGE : imagen *f* <he's the picture of his father : es la viva imagen de su padre> **4** MOVIE : película *f*

picturesque [ˌpɪktʃəˈrɛsk] *adj* : pintoresco

pie [ˈpaɪ] *n* : pastel *m* (con fruta o carne), empanada *f* (con carne)

piebald [ˈpaɪˌbɔld] *adj* : picazo, pío

piece[1] [ˈpiːs] *vt* **pieced; piecing 1** PATCH : parchar, arreglar **2 to piece together** : construir pieza por pieza

piece[2] *n* **1** FRAGMENT : trozo *m*, pedazo *m* **2** COMPONENT : pieza *f* <a three-piece suit : un traje de tres piezas> **3** UNIT : pieza *f* <a piece of fruit : una (pieza de) fruta> **4** WORK : obra *f*, pieza *f* (de música, etc.) **5** (*in board games*) : ficha *f*, pieza *f*, figura *f* (en ajedrez)

piecemeal[1] [ˈpiːsˌmiːl] *adv* **:** poco a poco, por partes
piecemeal[2] *adj* **:** hecho poco a poco, poco sistemático
pied [ˈpaɪd] *adj* **:** pío
pier [ˈpɪr] *n* **1 :** pila *f* (de un puente) **2** WHARF **:** muelle *m,* atracadero *m,* embarcadero *m* **3** PILLAR **:** pilar *m*
pierce [ˈpɪrs] *vt* **pierced; piercing 1** PENETRATE **:** atravesar, traspasar, penetrar (en) <the bullet pierced his leg : la bala le atravesó la pierna> <to pierce one's heart : traspasarle el corazón a uno> **2** PERFORATE **:** perforar, agujerear (las orejas, etc.) **3 to pierce the silence :** desgarrar el silencio
piety [ˈpaɪəti] *n, pl* **-eties :** piedad *f*
pig [ˈpɪg] *n* **1** HOG, SWINE **:** cerdo *m,* -da *f;* puerco *m,* -ca *f* **2** SLOB **:** persona *f* desaliñada; cerdo *m,* -da *f* **3** GLUTTON **:** glotón *m,* -tona *f* **4** *or* **pig iron :** lingote *m* de hierro
pigeon [ˈpɪdʒən] *n* **:** paloma *f*
pigeonhole [ˈpɪdʒənˌhoːl] *n* **:** casilla *f*
pigeon–toed [ˈpɪdʒənˌtoːd] *adj* **:** patituerto
piggish [ˈpɪgɪʃ] *adj* **1** GREEDY **:** glotón **2** DIRTY **:** cochino, sucio
piggyback [ˈpɪgiˌbæk] *adv & adj* **:** a cuestas
pigheaded [ˈpɪgˌhɛdəd] *adj* **:** terco, obstinado
piglet [ˈpɪglət] *n* **:** cochinillo *m;* lechón *m,* -chona *f*
pigment [ˈpɪgmənt] *n* **:** pigmento *m*
pigmentation [ˌpɪgmənˈteɪʃən] *n* **:** pigmentación *f*
pigmy → **pygmy**
pigpen [ˈpɪgˌpɛn] *n* **:** chiquero *m,* pocilga *f*
pigsty [ˈpɪgˌstaɪ] → **pigpen**
pigtail [ˈpɪgˌteɪl] *n* **:** coleta *f,* trenza *f*
pike [ˈpaɪk] *n, pl* **pike** *or* **pikes 1 :** lucio *m* (pez) **2** LANCE **:** pica *f* **3** → **turnpike**
pile[1] [ˈpaɪl] *v* **piled; piling** *vt* **:** amontonar, apilar — *vi* **to pile up :** amontonarse, acumularse
pile[2] *n* **1** STAKE **:** pilote *m* **2** HEAP **:** montón *m,* pila *f* **3** NAP **:** pelo *m* (de telas)
piles [ˈpaɪlz] *npl* HEMORRHOIDS **:** hemorroides *fpl,* almorranas *fpl*
pilfer [ˈpɪlfər] *vt* **:** robar (cosas pequeñas), ratear
pilgrim [ˈpɪlgrəm] *n* **:** peregrino *m,* -na *f*
pilgrimage [ˈpɪlgrəmɪdʒ] *n* **:** peregrinación *f*
pill [ˈpɪl] *n* **:** pastilla *f,* píldora *f*
pillage[1] [ˈpɪlɪdʒ] *vt* **-laged; -laging :** saquear
pillage[2] *n* **:** saqueo *m*
pillar [ˈpɪlər] *n* **:** pilar *m,* columna *f*
pillory [ˈpɪləri] *n, pl* **-ries :** picota *f*
pillow [ˈpɪˌloː] *n* **:** almohada *f*
pillowcase [ˈpɪˌloːˌkeɪs] *n* **:** funda *f*
pilot[1] [ˈpaɪlət] *vt* **:** pilotar, pilotear
pilot[2] *n* **:** piloto *mf*
pilot light *n* **:** piloto *m*
pimento [pəˈmɛnˌtoː] → **pimiento**
pimiento [pəˈmɛnˌtoː, -ˈmjɛn-] *n, pl* **-tos :** pimiento *m* morrón
pimp [ˈpɪmp] *n* **:** proxeneta *m*
pimple [ˈpɪmpəl] *n* **:** grano *m*
pimply [ˈpɪmpəli] *adj* **-plier; -est :** cubierto de granos
pin[1] [ˈpɪn] *vt* **pinned; pinning 1** FASTEN **:** prender, sujetar (con alfileres) **2** HOLD, IMMOBILIZE **:** inmovilizar, sujetar **3 to pin one's hopes on :** poner sus esperanzas en
pin[2] *n* **1 :** alfiler *m* <safety pin : alfiler de gancho> <a bobby pin : una horquilla> **2** BROOCH **:** alfiler *m,* broche *m,* prendedor *m* **3** *or* **bowling pin :** bolo *m*
pinafore [ˈpɪnəˌfor] *n* **:** delantal *m*
pincer [ˈpɪntsər] *n* **1** CLAW **:** pinza *f* (de una langosta, etc.) **2 pincers** *npl* **:** pinzas *fpl,* tenazas *fpl,* tenaza *f*
pinch[1] [ˈpɪntʃ] *vt* **1 :** pellizcar <she pinched my cheek : me pellizcó el cachete> **2** STEAL **:** robar — *vi* **:** apretar <my shoes pinch : me aprietan los zapatos>
pinch[2] *n* **1** EMERGENCY **:** emergencia *f* <in a pinch : en caso necesario> **2** PAIN **:** dolor *m,* tormento *m* **3** SQUEEZE **:** pellizco *m* (con los dedos) **4** BIT **:** pizca *f,* pellizco *m* <a pinch of cinnamon : una pizca de canela>
pinch hitter *n* **1** SUBSTITUTE **:** sustituto *m,* -ta *f* **2 :** bateador *m* emergente (en beisbol)
pincushion [ˈpɪnˌkʊʃən] *n* **:** acerico *m,* alfiletero *m*
pine[1] [ˈpaɪn] *vi* **pined; pining 1 to pine away :** languidecer, consumirse **2 to pine for :** añorar, suspirar por
pine[2] *n* **1 :** pino *m* (árbol) **2 :** madera *f* de pino
pineapple [ˈpaɪnˌæpəl] *n* **:** piña *f,* ananá *m,* ananás *m*
pinion[1] [ˈpɪnjən] *vt* **:** sujetar los brazos de, inmovilizar
pinion[2] *n* **:** piñón *m*
pink[1] [ˈpɪŋk] *adj* **:** rosa, rosado
pink[2] *n* **1 :** clavelito *m* (flor) **2 :** rosa *m,* rosado *m* (color) **3 to be in the pink :** estar en plena forma, rebosar de salud
pinkeye [ˈpɪŋkˌaɪ] *n* **:** conjuntivitis *f* aguda
pinkish [ˈpɪŋkɪʃ] *adj* **:** rosáceo
pinnacle [ˈpɪnɪkəl] *n* **1 :** pináculo *m* (de un edificio) **2** PEAK **:** cima *f,* cumbre *f* (de una montaña) **3** ACME **:** pináculo *m,* cúspide *f,* apogeo *m*
pinpoint [ˈpɪnˌpɔɪnt] *vt* **:** precisar, localizar con precisión
pint [ˈpaɪnt] *n* **:** pinta *f*
pinto [ˈpɪnˌtoː] *n, pl* **pintos :** caballo *m* pinto
pinworm [ˈpɪnˌwərm] *n* **:** oxiuro *m*
pioneer[1] [ˌpaɪəˈnɪr] *vt* **:** promover, iniciar, introducir
pioneer[2] *n* **:** pionero *m,* -ra *f*

pious [ˈpaɪəs] *adj* **1** DEVOUT : piadoso, devoto **2** SANCTIMONIOUS : beato

piously [ˈpaɪəsli] *adv* **1** DEVOUTLY : piadosamente **2** SANCTIMONIOUSLY : santurronamente

pipe[1] [ˈpaɪp] *v* **piped; piping** *vi* : hablar en voz chillona — *vt* **1** PLAY : tocar (el caramillo o la flauta) **2** : conducir por tuberías <to pipe water : transportar el agua por tubería>

pipe[2] *n* **1** : caramillo *m* (instrumento musical) **2** BAGPIPE : gaita *f* **3** : tubo *m,* caño *m* <gas pipes : tubería de gas> **4** : pipa *f* (para fumar)

pipeline [ˈpaɪpˌlaɪn] *n* **1** : conducto *m,* oleoducto *m* (para petróleo), gasoducto *m* (para gas) **2** CONDUIT : vía *f* (de información, etc.)

piper [ˈpaɪpər] *n* : músico *m,* -ca *f* que toca el caramillo o la gaita

piping [ˈpaɪpɪŋ] *n* **1** : música *f* del caramillo o de la gaita **2** TRIM : cordoncillo *m,* ribete *m* con cordón

piquant [ˈpiːkənt, ˈpɪkwənt] *adj* **1** SPICY : picante **2** INTRIGUING : intrigante, estimulante

pique[1] [ˈpiːk] *vt* **piqued; piquing 1** IRRITATE : picar, irritar **2** AROUSE : despertar (la curiosidad, etc.)

pique[2] *n* : pique *m,* resentimiento *m*

piracy [ˈpaɪrəsi] *n, pl* **-cies** : piratería *f*

piranha [pəˈrɑnə, -ˈrɑnjə, -ˈrænjə] *n* : piraña *f*

pirate [ˈpaɪrət] *n* : pirata *mf*

pirouette [ˌpɪrəˈwɛt] *n* : pirueta *f*

pis → **pi**

Pisces [ˈpaɪˌsiːz, ˈpɪ-; ˈpɪsˌkeɪs] *n* : Piscis *mf*

pistachio [pəˈstæʃiˌoː, -ˈstɑ-] *n, pl* **-chios** : pistacho *m*

pistil [ˈpɪstəl] *n* : pistilo *m*

pistol [ˈpɪstəl] *n* : pistola *f*

piston [ˈpɪstən] *n* : pistón *m,* émbolo *m*

pit[1] [ˈpɪt] *v* **pitted; pitting** *vt* **1** : marcar de hoyos, picar (una superficie) **2** : deshuesar (una fruta) **3 to pit against** : enfrentar a, oponer a — *vi* : quedar marcado

pit[2] *n* **1** HOLE : fosa *f,* hoyo *m* <a bottomless pit : un pozo sin fondo> **2** MINE : mina *f* **3** : foso *m* <orchestra pit : foso orquestal> **4** POCKMARK : marca *f* (en la cara), cicatriz *f* de viruela **5** STONE : hueso *m,* pepa *f* (de una fruta) **6 pit of the stomach** : boca *f* del estómago

pitch[1] [ˈpɪtʃ] *vt* **1** SET UP : montar, armar (una tienda) **2** THROW : lanzar, arrojar **3** ADJUST, SET : dar el tono de (un discurso, un instrumento musical) — *vi* **1** *or* **pitch forward** FALL : caerse **2** LURCH : cabecear (dícese de un barco o un avión), dar bandazos

pitch[2] *n* **1** LURCHING : cabezada *f,* cabeceo *m* (de un barco o un avión) **2** SLOPE : (grado de) inclinación *f,* pendiente *f* **3** : tono *m* (en música) <perfect pitch : oído absoluto> **4** THROW : lanzamiento *m* **5** DEGREE : grado *m,* nivel *m,* punto *m* <the excitement reached a high pitch : la excitación llegó a un punto culminante> **6** *or* **sales pitch** : presentación *f* (de un vendedor) **7** TAR : pez *f,* brea *f*

pitcher [ˈpɪtʃər] *n* **1** JUG : jarra *f,* jarro *m,* cántaro *m,* pichel *m* **2** : lanzador *m,* -dora *f* (en béisbol, etc.)

pitchfork [ˈpɪtʃˌfɔrk] *n* : horquilla *f,* horca *f*

piteous [ˈpɪt̬iəs] *adj* : lastimoso, lastimero — **piteously** *adv*

pitfall [ˈpɪtˌfɔl] *n* : peligro *m* (poco obvio), dificultad *f*

pith [ˈpɪθ] *n* **1** : médula *f* (de una planta) **2** CORE : meollo *m,* entraña *f*

pithy [ˈpɪθi] *adj* **pithier; -est** : conciso y sustancioso <pithy comments : comentarios sucintos>

pitiable [ˈpɪt̬iəbəl] → **pitiful**

pitiful [ˈpɪt̬ɪfəl] *adj* **1** LAMENTABLE : lastimero, lastimoso, lamentable **2** CONTEMPTIBLE : despreciable, lamentable — **pitifully** [-fli] *adv*

pitiless [ˈpɪt̬ɪləs] *adj* : despiadado — **pitilessly** *adv*

pittance [ˈpɪtənts] *n* : miseria *f*

pituitary [pəˈtuːəˌtɛri, -ˈtjuː-] *adj* : pituitario

pity[1] [ˈpɪt̬i] *vt* **pitied; pitying** : compadecer, compadecerse de

pity[2] *n, pl* **pities 1** COMPASSION : compasión *f,* piedad *f* **2** SHAME : lástima *f,* pena *f* <what a pity! : ¡qué lástima!>

pivot[1] [ˈpɪvət] *vi* **1** : girar sobre un eje **2 to pivot on** : girar sobre, depender de

pivot[2] *n* : pivote *m*

pivotal [ˈpɪvət̬əl] *adj* : fundamental, central

pixie *or* **pixy** [ˈpɪksi] *n, pl* **pixies** : elfo *m,* hada *f*

pizza [ˈpiːtsə] *n* : pizza *f*

pizzazz *or* **pizazz** [pəˈzæz] *n* **1** GLAMOR : encanto *m* **2** VITALITY : animación *f,* vitalidad *f*

placard [ˈplækərd, -ˌkɑrd] *n* POSTER : cartel *m,* póster *m,* afiche *m*

placate [ˈpleɪˌkeɪt, ˈplæ-] *vt* **-cated; -cating** : aplacar, apaciguar

place[1] [ˈpleɪs] *vt* **placed; placing 1** PUT, SET : poner, colocar **2** SITUATE : situar, ubicar, emplazar <to be well placed : estar bien situado> <to place in a job : colocar en un trabajo> **3** IDENTIFY, RECALL : identificar, ubicar, recordar <I can't place him : no lo ubico> **4 to place an order** : hacer un pedido

place[2] *n* **1** SPACE : sitio *m,* lugar *m* <there's no place to sit : no hay sitio para sentarse> **2** LOCATION, SPOT : lugar *m,* sitio *m,* parte *f* <place of work : lugar de trabajo> <our summer place : nuestra casa de verano> <all over the place : por todas partes> **3** RANK : lugar *m,* puesto *m* <he took first place : ganó el primer lugar> **4**

POSITION : lugar *m* <everything in its place : todo en su debido lugar> <to feel out of place : sentirse fuera de lugar> **5** SEAT : asiento *m,* cubierto *m* (a la mesa) **6** JOB : puesto *m* **7** ROLE : papel *m,* lugar *m* <to change places : cambiarse los papeles> **8 to take place :** tener lugar **9 to take the place of :** sustituir a

placebo [plə'siːˌboː] *n, pl* **-bos :** placebo *m*

placement ['pleɪsmənt] *n* : colocación *f*

placenta [plə'sɛntə] *n, pl* **-tas** *or* **-tae** [-ti, -ˌtaɪ] : placenta *f*

placid ['plæsəd] *adj* : plácido, tranquilo — **placidly** *adv*

plagiarism ['pleɪdʒəˌrɪzəm] *n* : plagio *m*

plagiarist ['pleɪdʒərɪst] *n* : plagiario *m,* -ria *f*

plagiarize ['pleɪdʒəˌraɪz] *vt* **-rized; -rizing :** plagiar

plague[1] ['pleɪg] *vt* **plagued; plaguing** **1** AFFLICT : plagar, afligir **2** HARASS : acosar, atormentar

plague[2] *n* **1 :** plaga *f* (de insectos, etc.) **2 :** peste *f* (en medicina)

plaid[1] ['plæd] *adj* : escocés, de cuadros <a plaid skirt : una falda escocesa>

plaid[2] *n* TARTAN : tela *f* escocesa, tartán *m*

plain[1] ['pleɪn] *adj* **1** SIMPLE, UNADORNED : liso, sencillo, sin adornos **2** CLEAR : claro <in plain language : en palabras claras> **3** FRANK : franco, puro <the plain truth : la pura verdad> **4** HOMELY : ordinario, poco atractivo **5 in plain sight :** a la vista de todos

plain[2] *n* : llanura *f,* llano *m,* planicie *f*

plainly ['pleɪnli] *adv* **1** CLEARLY : claramente **2** FRANKLY : francamente, con franqueza **3** SIMPLY : sencillamente

plaintiff ['pleɪntɪf] *n* : demandante *mf*

plaintive ['pleɪntɪv] *adj* MOURNFUL : lastimero, plañidero

plait[1] ['pleɪt, 'plæt] *vt* **1** PLEAT : plisar **2** BRAID : trenzar

plait[2] *n* **1** PLEAT : pliegue *m* **2** BRAID : trenza *f*

plan[1] ['plæn] *v* **planned; planning** *vt* **1 :** planear, proyectar, planificar <to plan a trip : planear un viaje> <to plan a city : planificar una ciudad> **2** INTEND : tener planeado, proyectar — *vi* : hacer planes

plan[2] *n* **1** DIAGRAM : plano *m,* esquema *m* **2** SCHEME : plan *m,* proyecto *m,* programa *m* <to draw up a plan : elaborar un proyecto>

plane[1] ['pleɪn] *vt* **planed; planing** : cepillar (madera)

plane[2] *adj* : plano

plane[3] *n* **1 :** plano *m* (en matemáticas, etc.) **2** LEVEL : nivel *m* **3 :** cepillo *m* (de carpintero) **4** → **airplane**

planet ['plænət] *n* : planeta *f*

planetarium [ˌplænə'tɛriəm] *n, pl* **-iums** *or* **-ia** [-iə] : planetario *m*

planetary ['plænəˌtɛri] *adj* : planetario

plank ['plæŋk] *n* **1** BOARD : tablón *m,* tabla *f* **2 :** artículo *m,* punto *m* (de una plataforma política)

plankton ['plæŋktən] *n* : plancton *m*

plant[1] ['plænt] *vt* **1 :** plantar (flores, árboles), sembrar (semillas) **2** PLACE : plantar, colocar <to plant an idea : inculcar una idea>

plant[2] *n* **1 :** planta *f* <leafy plants : plantas frondosas> **2** FACTORY : planta *f,* fábrica *f* <hydroelectric plant : planta hidroeléctrica> **3** MACHINERY : maquinaria *f,* equipo *m*

plantain ['plæntən] *n* **1 :** llantén *m* (mala hierba) **2 :** plátano *m,* plátano *m* macho *Mex* (fruta)

plantation [plæn'teɪʃən] *n* : plantación *f,* hacienda *f* <a coffee plantation : un cafetal>

planter ['plæntər] *n* **1 :** hacendado *m,* -da *f* (de una hacienda) **2** FLOWERPOT : tiesto *m,* maceta *f*

plaque ['plæk] *n* **1** TABLET : placa *f* **2** : placa *f* (dental)

plasma ['plæzmə] *n* : plasma *m*

plaster[1] ['plæstər] *vt* **1 :** enyesar, revocar (con yeso) **2** COVER : cubrir, llenar <a wall plastered with notices : una pared cubierta de avisos>

plaster[2] *n* **1 :** yeso *m,* revoque *m* (para paredes, etc.) **2 :** escayola *f,* yeso *m* (en medicina) **3 plaster of Paris** ['pærɪs] : yeso *m* mate

plaster cast *n* : vaciado *m* de yeso

plasterer ['plæstərər] *n* : revocador *m,* -dora *f*

plastic[1] ['plæstɪk] *adj* **1 :** de plástico **2** PLIABLE : plástico, flexible **3 plastic surgery :** cirugía *f* plástica

plastic[2] *n* : plástico *m*

plate[1] ['pleɪt] *vt* **plated; plating** : chapar (en metal)

plate[2] *n* **1** PLAQUE, SHEET : placa *f* <a steel plate : una placa de acero> **2** UTENSILS : vajilla *f* (de metal) <silver plate : vajilla de plata> **3** DISH : plato *m* **4** DENTURES : dentadura *f* postiza **5** ILLUSTRATION : lámina *f* (en un libro) **6 license plate :** matrícula *f,* placa *f* de matrícula

plateau [plæ'toː] *n, pl* **-teaus** *or* **-teaux** [-'toːz] : meseta *f*

platform ['plætˌfɔrm] *n* **1** STAGE : plataforma *f,* estrado *m,* tribuna *f* **2** : andén *m* (de una estación de ferrocarril) **3 political platform** : plataforma *f* política, programa *m* electoral

plating ['pleɪtɪŋ] *n* **1 :** enchapado *m* **2 silver plating :** plateado *m*

platinum ['plætənəm] *n* : platino *m*

platitude ['plætəˌtuːd, -ˌtjuːd] *n* : lugar *m* común, perogrullada *f*

platoon [plə'tuːn] *n* : sección *f* (en el ejército)

platter ['plætər] *n* : fuente *f*

platypus [ˈplætɪpəs, -ˌpʊs] *n, pl* **platypuses** *or* **platypi** [-ˌpaɪ, -ˌpiː] : ornitorrinco *m*

plausibility [ˌplɔzəˈbɪləṭi] *n, pl* **-ties** : credibilidad *f,* verosimilitud *f*

plausible [ˈplɔzəbəl] *adj* : creíble, convincente, verosímil — **plausibly** [-bli] *adv*

play[1] [ˈpleɪ] *vi* **1** : jugar <to play with a doll : jugar con una muñeca> <to play with an idea : darle vueltas a una idea> **2** FIDDLE, TOY : jugar, juguetear <don't play with your food : no juegues con la comida> **3** : tocar <to play in a band : tocar en un grupo> **4** : actuar (en una obra de teatro) — *vt* **1** : jugar (un deporte, etc.), jugar a (un juego), jugar contra (un contrincante) **2** : tocar (música o un instrumento) **3** PERFORM : interpretar, hacer el papel de (un carácter), representar (una obra de teatro) <she plays the lead : hace el papel principal>

play[2] *n* **1** GAME, RECREATION : juego *m* <children at play : niños jugando> <a play on words : un juego de palabras> **2** ACTION : juego *m* <the ball is in play : la pelota está en juego> <to bring into play : poner en juego> **3** DRAMA : obra *f* de teatro, pieza *f* (de teatro) **4** MOVEMENT : juego *m* (de la luz, una brisa, etc.) **5** SLACK : juego *m* <there's not enough play in the wheel : la rueda no da lo suficiente>

playacting [ˈpleɪˌæktɪŋ] *n* : actuación *f,* teatro *m*

player [ˈpleɪər] *n* **1** : jugador *m,* -dora *f* (en un juego) **2** ACTOR : actor *m,* actriz *f* **3** MUSICIAN : músico *m,* -ca *f*

playful [ˈpleɪfəl] *adj* **1** FROLICSOME : juguetón **2** JOCULAR : jocoso — **playfully** *adv*

playfulness [ˈpleɪfəlnəs] *n* : lo juguetón, jocosidad *f,* alegría *f*

playground [ˈpleɪˌgraʊnd] *n* : patio *m* de recreo, jardín *m* para jugar

playhouse [ˈpleɪˌhaʊs] *n* **1** THEATER : teatro *m* **2** : casita *f* de juguete

playing card *n* : naipe *m,* carta *f*

playmate [ˈpleɪˌmeɪt] *n* : compañero *m,* -ra *f* de juego

play-off [ˈpleɪˌɔf] *n* : desempate *m*

playpen [ˈpleɪˌpɛn] *n* : corral *m* (para niños)

plaything [ˈpleɪˌθɪŋ] *n* : juguete *m*

playwright [ˈpleɪˌraɪt] *n* : dramaturgo *m,* -ga *f*

plaza [ˈplæzə, ˈplɑ-] *n* **1** SQUARE : plaza *f* **2 shopping plaza** MALL : centro *m* comercial

plea [ˈpliː] *n* **1** : acto *m* de declararse <he entered a plea of guilty : se declaró culpable> **2** APPEAL : ruego *m,* súplica *f*

plead [ˈpliːd] *v* **pleaded** *or* **pled** [ˈplɛd]; **pleading** *vi* **1** : declararse (culpable o inocente) **2 to plead for** : suplicar, implorar — *vt* **1** : alegar, pretextar <he pleaded illness : pretextó la enfermedad> **2 to plead a case** : defender un caso

pleasant [ˈplɛzənt] *adj* : agradable, grato, bueno — **pleasantly** *adv*

pleasantness [ˈplɛzəntnəs] *n* : lo agradable, amenidad *f*

pleasantries [ˈplɛzəntriz] *npl* : cumplidos *mpl,* cortesías *fpl* <to exchange pleasantries : intercambiar cumplidos>

please[1] [ˈpliːz] *v* **pleased; pleasing** *vt* **1** GRATIFY : complacer <please yourself! : ¡cómo quieras!> **2** SATISFY : contentar, satisfacer — *vi* **1** SATISFY : complacer, agradar <anxious to please : deseoso de complacer> **2** LIKE : querer <do as you please : haz lo que quieras, haz lo que te parezca>

please[2] *adv* : por favor

pleased [ˈpliːzd] *adj* : contento, satisfecho, alegre

pleasing [ˈpliːzɪŋ] *adj* : agradable — **pleasingly** *adv*

pleasurable [ˈplɛʒərəbəl] *adj* PLEASANT : agradable

pleasure [ˈplɛʒər] *n* **1** WISH : deseo *m,* voluntad *f* <at your pleasure : cuando guste> **2** ENJOYMENT : placer *m,* disfrute *m,* goce *m* <with pleasure : con mucho gusto> **3** : placer *m,* gusto *m* <it's a pleasure to be here : me da gusto estar aquí> <the pleasures of reading : los placeres de leer>

pleat[1] [ˈpliːt] *vt* : plisar

pleat[2] *n* : pliegue *m*

plebeian [plɪˈbiən] *adj* : ordinario, plebeyo

pledge[1] [ˈplɛdʒ] *vt* **pledged; pledging 1** PAWN : empeñar, prendar **2** PROMISE : prometer, jurar

pledge[2] *n* **1** SECURITY : garantía *f,* prenda *f* **2** PROMISE : promesa *f*

plenteous [ˈplɛntiəs] *adj* : copioso, abundante

plentiful [ˈplɛntɪfəl] *adj* : abundante — **plentifully** [-fli] *adv*

plenty [ˈplɛnti] *n* : abundancia *f* <plenty of time : tiempo de sobra> <plenty of visitors : muchos visitantes>

plethora [ˈplɛθərə] *n* : plétora *f*

pleurisy [ˈplʊrəsi] *n* : pleuresía *f*

pliable [ˈplaɪəbəl] *adj* : flexible, maleable

pliant [ˈplaɪənt] → **pliable**

pliers [ˈplaɪərz] *npl* : alicates *mpl,* pinzas *fpl*

plight [ˈplaɪt] *n* : situación *f* difícil, apuro *m*

plod [ˈplɑd] *vi* **plodded; plodding 1** TRUDGE : caminar pesadamente y lentamente **2** DRUDGE : trabajar laboriosamente

plot[1] [ˈplɑt] *v* **plotted; plotting** *vt* **1** DEVISE : tramar **2 to plot out** : trazar, determinar (una posición, etc.) — *vi* CONSPIRE : conspirar

plot[2] *n* **1** LOT : terreno *m,* parcela *f,* lote *m* **2** STORY : argumento *m* (en el teatro), trama *f* (en un libro, etc.) **3** CONSPIRACY, INTRIGUE **:** complot *m,* intriga *f*

plotter [ˈplɑt̬ər] *n* **:** conspirador *m,* -dora *f;* intrigante *mf*

plow[1] *or* **plough** [ˈplaʊ] *vt* **1 :** arar (la tierra) **2 to plow the seas :** surcar los mares

plow[2] *or* **plough** *n* **1 :** arado *m* **2 →** **snowplow**

plowshare [ˈplaʊˌʃɛr] *n* **:** reja *f* del arado

ploy [ˈplɔɪ] *n* **:** estratagema *f,* maniobra *f*

pluck[1] [ˈplʌk] *vt* **1** PICK **:** arrancar **2 :** desplumar (un pollo, etc.) — *vi* **to pluck at :** tirar de

pluck[2] *n* **1** TUG **:** tirón *m* **2** COURAGE, SPIRIT **:** valor *m,* ánimo *m*

plucky [ˈplʌki] *adj* **pluckier; -est :** valiente, animoso

plug[1] [ˈplʌg] *vt* **plugged; plugging 1** BLOCK **:** tapar **2** PROMOTE **:** hacerle publicidad a, promocionar **3 to plug in :** enchufar

plug[2] *n* **1** STOPPER **:** tapón *m* **2 :** enchufe *m* (eléctrico) **3** ADVERTISEMENT **:** publicidad *f,* propaganda *f*

plum [ˈplʌm] *n* **1 :** ciruela *f* (fruta) **2 :** color *m* ciruela **3** PRIZE **:** premio *m,* algo muy atractivo

plumage [ˈpluːmɪdʒ] *n* **:** plumaje *m*

plumb[1] [ˈplʌm] *vt* **1 :** aplomar <to plumb a wall : aplomar una pared> **2** SOUND **:** sondear, sondar

plumb[2] *adv* **1** VERTICALLY **:** a plomo, verticalmente **2** EXACTLY **:** justo, exactamente **3** COMPLETELY **:** completamente, absolutamente <plumb crazy : loco de remate>

plumb[3] *adj* **:** a plomo

plumb[4] *n or* **plumb line :** plomada *f*

plumber [ˈplʌmər] *n* **:** plomero *m,* -ra *f;* fontanero *m,* -ra *f*

plumbing [ˈplʌmɪŋ] *n* **1 :** plomería *f,* fontanería *f* (trabajo del plomero) **2** PIPES **:** cañería *f,* tubería *f*

plume [ˈpluːm] *n* **1** FEATHER **:** pluma *f* **2** TUFT **:** penacho *m* (en un sombrero, etc.)

plumed [ˈpluːmd] *adj* **:** con plumas <white-plumed birds : aves de plumaje blanco>

plummet [ˈplʌmət] *vi* **:** caer en picada, desplomarse

plump[1] [ˈplʌmp] *vi or* **to plump down :** dejarse caer (pesadamente)

plump[2] *adv* **1** STRAIGHT **:** a plomo **2** DIRECTLY **:** directamente, sin rodeos <he ran plump into the door : dio de cara con la puerta>

plump[3] *adj* **:** llenito *fam,* regordete *fam,* rechoncho *fam*

plumpness [ˈplʌmpnəs] *n* **:** gordura *f*

plunder[1] [ˈplʌndər] *vi* **:** saquear, robar

plunder[2] *n* **:** botín *m*

plunderer [ˈplʌndərər] *n* **:** saqueador *m,* -dora *f*

plunge[1] [ˈplʌndʒ] *v* **plunged; plunging** *vt* **1** IMMERSE **:** sumergir **2** THRUST **:** hundir, clavar — *vi* **1** DIVE **:** zambullirse (en el agua) **2 :** meterse precipitadamente o violentamente <they plunged into war : se enfrascaron en una guerra> <he plunged into depression : cayó en la depresión> **3** DESCEND **:** descender en picada <the road plunges dizzily : la calle desciende vertiginosamente>

plunge[2] *n* **1** DIVE **:** zambullida *f* **2** DROP **:** descenso *m* abrupto <the plunge in prices : el desplome de los precios>

plural[1] [ˈplʊrəl] *adj* **:** plural

plural[2] *n* **:** plural *m*

plurality [plʊˈræləṭi] *n, pl* **-ties :** pluralidad *f*

pluralize [ˈplʊrəˌlaɪz] *vt* **-ized; -izing :** pluralizar

plus[1] [ˈplʌs] *adj* **1** POSITIVE **:** positivo <a plus factor : un factor positivo> **2** (*indicating a quantity in addition*) <a grade of C plus : una calificación entre C y B> <a salary of $30,000 plus : un sueldo de más de $30,000>

plus[2] *n* **1** *or* **plus sign :** más *m,* signo *m* de más **2** ADVANTAGE **:** ventaja *f*

plus[3] *prep* **:** más (en matemáticas)

plus[4] *conj* AND **:** y

plush[1] [ˈplʌʃ] *adj* **1 :** afelpado **2** LUXURIOUS **:** lujoso

plush[2] *n* **:** felpa *f,* peluche *m*

plushy [ˈplʌʃi] *adj* **plushier; -est :** lujoso

Pluto [ˈpluːt̬oː] *n* **:** Plutón *m*

plutocracy [pluːˈtɑkrəsi] *n, pl* **-cies :** plutocracia *f*

plutonium [pluːˈtoːniəm] *n* **:** plutonio *m*

ply[1] [ˈplaɪ] *v* **plied; plying** *vt* **1** USE, WIELD **:** manejar <to ply an ax : manejar un hacha> **2** PRACTICE **:** ejercer <to ply a trade : ejercer un oficio> **3 to ply with questions :** acosar con preguntas

ply[2] *n, pl* **plies 1** LAYER **:** chapa *f* (de madera), capa *f* (de papel) **2** STRAND **:** cabo *m* (de hilo, etc.)

plywood [ˈplaɪˌwʊd] *n* **:** contrachapado *m*

pneumatic [nʊˈmæṭɪk, njʊ-] *adj* **:** neumático

pneumonia [nʊˈmoːnjə, njʊ-] *n* **:** pulmonía *f,* neumonía *f*

poach [ˈpoːtʃ] *vt* **1 :** cocer a fuego lento <to poach an egg : escalfar un huevo> **2 to poach game :** cazar ilegalmente — *vi* **:** cazar ilegalmente

poacher [ˈpoːtʃər] *n* **:** cazador *m* furtivo, cazadora *f* furtiva

pock [ˈpɑk] *n* **1** PUSTULE **:** pústula *f* **2 →** **pockmark**

pocket[1] [ˈpɑkət] *vt* **1 :** meterse en el bolsillo <he pocketed the pen : se metió la pluma en el bolsillo> **2** STEAL **:** embolsarse

pocket[2] *n* **1 :** bolsillo *m,* bolsa *f Mex* <a coat pocket : el bolsillo de un abrigo>

<air pockets : bolsas de aire> **2** CENTER : foco *m,* centro *m* <a pocket of resistance : un foco de resistencia>

pocketbook [ˈpɑkətˌbʊk] *n* **1** PURSE : cartera *f,* bolso *m,* bolsa *f Mex* **2** MEANS : recursos *mpl*

pocketknife [ˈpɑkətˌnaɪf] *n, pl* **-knives** : navaja *f*

pocket-size [ˈpɑkətˈsaɪz] *adj* : de bolsillo

pockmark [ˈpɑkˌmɑrk] *n* : cicatriz *f* de viruela, viruela *f*

pod [ˈpɑd] *n* : vaina *f* <pea pod : vaina de guisantes>

podiatrist [pəˈdaɪətrɪst, po-] *n* : podólogo *m,* -ga *f*

podiatry [pəˈdaɪətri, po-] *n* : podología *f,* podiatría *f*

podium [ˈpoːdiəm] *n, pl* **-diums** *or* **-dia** [-diə] : podio *m,* estrado *m,* tarima *f*

poem [ˈpoːəm] *n* : poema *m,* poesía *f*

poet [ˈpoːət] *n* : poeta *mf*

poetic [poˈɛt̬ɪk] *or* **poetical** [-t̬ɪkəl] *adj* : poético

poetry [ˈpoːətri] *n* : poesía *f*

pogrom [ˈpoːgrəm, pəˈgrɑm, ˈpɑgrəm] *n* : pogrom *m*

poignancy [ˈpɔɪnjəntsi] *n, pl* **-cies** : lo conmovedor

poignant [ˈpɔɪnjənt] *adj* **1** PAINFUL : penoso, doloroso <poignant grief : profundo dolor> **2** TOUCHING : conmovedor, emocionante

poinsettia [pɔɪnˈsɛt̬iə, -ˈsɛt̬ə] *n* : flor *f* de Nochebuena

point[1] [ˈpɔɪnt] *vt* **1** SHARPEN : afilar (la punta de) **2** INDICATE : señalar, indicar <to point the way : señalar el camino> **3** AIM : apuntar **4 to point out** : señalar, indicar — *vi* **1 to point at** : señalar (con el dedo) **2 to point to** INDICATE : señalar, indicar

point[2] *n* **1** ITEM : punto *m* <the main points : los puntos principales> **2** QUALITY : cualidad *f* <her good points : sus buenas cualidades> <it's not his strong point : no es su (punto) fuerte> **3** (*indicating a chief idea or meaning*) <it's beside the point : no viene al caso> <to get to the point : ir al grano> <to stick to the point : no salirse del tema> **4** PURPOSE : fin *m,* propósito *m* <there's no point to it : no vale la pena, no sirve para nada> **5** PLACE : punto *m,* lugar *m* <points of interest : puntos interesantes> **6** : punto *m* (en una escala) <boiling point : punto de ebullición> **7** MOMENT : momento *m,* coyuntura *f* <at this point : en este momento> **8** TIP : punta *f* **9** HEADLAND : punta *f,* cabo *m* **10** PERIOD : punto *m* (marca de puntuación) **11** UNIT : punto *m* <he scored 15 points : ganó 15 puntos> <shares fell 10 points : las acciones bajaron 10 enteros> **12 compass points** : puntos *mpl* cardinales **13 decimal point** : punto *m* decimal, coma *f*

point-blank[1] [ˈpɔɪntˈblæŋk] *adv* **1** : a quemarropa <to shoot point-blank : disparar a quemarropa> **2** BLUNTLY, DIRECTLY : a bocajarro, sin rodeos, francamente

point-blank[2] *adj* **1** : a quemarropa <point-blank shots : disparos a quemarropa> **2** BLUNT, DIRECT : directo, franco

pointedly [ˈpɔɪntədli] *adv* : intencionadamente, directamente

pointer [ˈpɔɪntər] *n* **1** STICK : puntero *m* (para maestros, etc.) **2** INDICATOR, NEEDLE : indicador *m,* aguja *f* **3** : perro *m* de muestra **4** HINT, TIP : consejo *m*

pointless [ˈpɔɪntləs] *adj* : inútil, ocioso, vano <it's pointless to continue : no tiene sentido continuar>

point of view *n* : perspectiva *f,* punto *m* de vista

poise[1] [ˈpɔɪz] *vt* **poised; poising** BALANCE : equilibrar, balancear

poise[2] *n* : aplomo *m,* compostura *f*

poison[1] [ˈpɔɪzən] *vt* **1** : envenenar, intoxicar **2** CORRUPT : corromper

poison[2] *n* : veneno *m*

poison ivy *n* : hiedra *f* venenosa

poisonous [ˈpɔɪzənəs] *adj* : venenoso, tóxico, ponzoñoso

poke[1] [ˈpoːk] *v* **poked; poking** *vt* **1** JAB : golpear (con la punta de algo), dar <he poked me with his finger : me dio con el dedo> **2** THRUST : introducir, asomar <I poked my head out the window : asomé la cabeza por la ventana> — *vi* **1 to poke around** RUMMAGE : hurgar **2 to poke along** DAWDLE : demorarse, entretenerse

poke[2] *n* : golpe *m* abrupto (con la punta de algo)

poker [ˈpoːkər] *n* **1** : atizador *m* (para el fuego) **2** : póker *m,* poker *m* (juego de naipes)

polar [ˈpoːlər] *adj* : polar

polar bear *n* : oso *m* blanco

Polaris [poˈlærɪs, -ˈlɑr-] → **North Star**

polarize [ˈpoːləˌraɪz] *vt* **-ized; -izing** : polarizar

pole [ˈpoːl] *n* **1** : palo *m,* poste *m,* vara *f* <telephone pole : poste de teléfonos> **2** : polo *m* <the South Pole : el Polo Sur> **3** : polo *m* (eléctrico o magnético)

Pole [ˈpoːl] *n* : polaco *m,* -ca *f*

polecat [ˈpoːlˌkæt] *n, pl* **polecats** *or* **polecat 1** : turón *m* (de Europa) **2** SKUNK : mofeta *f,* zorrillo *m*

polemical [pəˈlɛmɪkəl] *adj* : polémico

polemics [pəˈlɛmɪks] *ns & pl* : polémica *f*

polestar [ˈpoːlˌstɑr] → **North Star**

police[1] [pəˈliːs] *vt* **-liced; -licing** : mantener el orden en <to police the streets : patrullar las calles>

police[2] *ns & pl* **1** : policía *f* (organización) **2** POLICE OFFICERS : policías *mfpl*

policeman [pəˈliːsmən] *n, pl* **-men** [-mən, -ˌmɛn] : policía *m*

police officer *n* : policía *mf,* agente *mf* de policía
policewoman [pə'liːsˌwʊmən] *n, pl* **-women** [-ˌwɪmən] : policía *f,* mujer *f* policía
policy ['pɑləsi] *n, pl* **-cies 1** : política *f* <foreign policy : política exterior> **2** *or* **insurance policy** : póliza *f* de seguros, seguro *m*
polio[1] ['poːliˌoː] *adj* : de polio <polio vaccine : vacuna contra la polio>
polio[2] *n* → **poliomyelitis**
poliomyelitis [ˌpoːliˌoːˌmaɪə'laɪt̬əs] *n* : poliomielitis *f,* polio *f*
polish[1] ['pɑlɪʃ] *vt* **1** : pulir, lustrar, sacar brillo a <to polish one's nails : pintarse las uñas> **2** REFINE : pulir, perfeccionar
polish[2] *n* **1** LUSTER : brillo *m,* lustre *m* **2** REFINEMENT : refinamiento *m* **3** : betún *m* (para zapatos), cera *f* (para suelos y muebles), esmalte *m* (para las uñas)
Polish[1] ['poːlɪʃ] *adj* : polaco
Polish[2] *n* : polaco *m* (idioma)
polite [pə'laɪt] *adj* **-liter; -est** : cortés, correcto, educado
politely [pə'laɪtli] *adv* : cortésmente, correctamente, con buenos modales
politeness [pə'laɪtnəs] *n* : cortesía *f*
politic ['pɑləˌtɪk] *adj* : diplomático, prudente
political [pə'lɪtɪkəl] *adj* : político — **politically** [-tɪkli] *adv*
politician [ˌpɑlə'tɪʃən] *n* : político *m,* -ca *f*
politics ['pɑləˌtɪks] *ns & pl* : política *f*
polka ['poːlkə, 'poːkə] *n* : polka *f*
polka dot ['poːkəˌdɑt] *n* : lunar *m* (en un diseño)
poll[1] ['poːl] *vt* **1** : obtener (votos) <she polled over 1000 votes : obtuvo más de 1000 votos> **2** CANVASS : encuestar, sondear — *vi* : obtener votos
poll[2] *n* **1** SURVEY : encuesta *f,* sondeo *m* **2 polls** *npl* : urnas *fpl* <to go to the polls : acudir a las urnas, ir a votar>
pollen ['pɑlən] *n* : polen *m*
pollinate ['pɑləˌneɪt] *vt* **-nated; -nating** : polinizar
pollination [ˌpɑlə'neɪʃən] *n* : polinización *f*
pollster ['poːlstər] *n* : encuestador *m,* -dora *f*
pollutant [pə'luːtənt] *n* : contaminante *m*
pollute [pə'luːt] *vt* **-luted; -luting** : contaminar
pollution [pə'luːʃən] *n* : contaminación *f*
pollywog *or* **polliwog** ['pɑliˌwɔg] *n* TADPOLE : renacuajo *m*
polo ['poːˌloː] *n* : polo *m*
poltergeist ['poːltərˌgaɪst] *n* : poltergeist *m,* fantasma *m* travieso
polyester ['pɑliˌɛstər, ˌpɑli'-] *n* : poliéster *m*
polygamous [pə'lɪgəməs] *adj* : polígamo
polygamy [pə'lɪgəmi] *n* : poligamia *f*
polygon ['pɑliˌgɑn] *n* : polígono *m*
polymer ['pɑləmər] *n* : polímero *m*
polyunsaturated [ˌpɑliˌʌn'sætʃəˌreɪt̬əd] *adj* : poliinsaturado
pomegranate ['pɑməˌgrænət, 'pɑmˌgrænət] *n* : granada *f* (fruta)
pommel[1] ['pʌməl] *vt* → **pummel**
pommel[2] ['pʌməl, 'pɑ-] *n* **1** : pomo *m* (de una espada) **2** : perilla *f* (de una silla de montar)
pomp ['pɑmp] *n* **1** SPLENDOR : pompa *f,* esplendor *m* **2** OSTENTATION : boato *m,* ostentación *f*
pom-pom ['pɑmˌpɑm] *n* : borla *f,* pompón *m*
pomposity [pɑm'pɑsət̬i] *n, pl* **-ties** : pomposidad *f*
pompous ['pɑmpəs] *adj* : pomposo — **pompously** *adv*
poncho ['pɑnˌtʃoː] *n, pl* **-chos** : poncho *m*
pond ['pɑnd] *n* : charca *f* (natural), estanque *m* (artificial)
ponder ['pɑndər] *vt* : reflexionar, considerar — *vi* **to ponder over** : reflexionar sobre, sopesar
ponderous ['pɑndərəs] *adj* : pesado
pontiff ['pɑntɪf] *n* POPE : pontífice *m*
pontificate [pɑn'tɪfəˌkeɪt] *vi* **-cated; -cating** : pontificar
pontoon [pɑn'tuːn] *n* : pontón *m*
pony ['poːni] *n, pl* **-nies** : poni *m,* poney *m,* jaca *f*
ponytail ['poːniˌteɪl] *n* : cola *f* de caballo, coleta *f*
poodle ['puːdəl] *n* : caniche *m*
pool[1] ['puːl] *vt* : mancomunar, hacer un fondo común de
pool[2] *n* **1** : charca *f* <a swimming pool : una piscina> **2** PUDDLE : charco *m* **3** RESERVE, SUPPLY : fondo *m* común (de recursos), reserva *f* **4** : billar *m* (juego)
poor ['pʊr, 'por] *adj* **1** : pobre <poor people : los pobres> **2** SCANTY : pobre, escaso <poor attendance : baja asistencia> **3** UNFORTUNATE : pobre <poor thing! : ¡pobrecito!> **4** BAD : malo <to be in poor health : estar mal de salud>
poorly ['pʊrli, 'por-] *adv* : mal
pop[1] ['pɑp] *v* **popped; popping** *vi* **1** BURST : reventarse, estallar **2** : ir, venir, o aparecer abruptamente <he popped into the house : se metió en la casa> <a menu pops up : aparece un menú> **3 to pop out** PROTRUDE : salirse, saltarse <my eyes popped out of my head : se me saltaban los ojos> — *vt* **1** BURST : reventar **2** : hacer o meter abruptamente <he popped it into his mouth : se lo metió en la boca>
pop[2] *adj* : popular <pop music : música popular>
pop[3] *n* **1** : estallido *m* pequeño (de un globo, etc.) **2** SODA : refresco *m,* gaseosa *f*

popcorn [ˈpɑpˌkɔrn] *n* : palomitas *fpl* (de maíz)
pope [ˈpoːp] *n* : papa *m* <Pope John : el Papa Juan>
poplar [ˈpɑplər] *n* : álamo *m*
poplin [ˈpɑplɪn] *n* : popelín *m*, popelina *f*
poppy [ˈpɑpi] *n, pl* **-pies** : amapola *f*
populace [ˈpɑpjələs] *n* **1** MASSES : pueblo *m* **2** POPULATION : población *f*
popular [ˈpɑpjələr] *adj* **1** : popular <the popular vote : el voto popular> **2** COMMON : generalizado, común <popular beliefs : creencias generalizadas> **3** : popular, de gran popularidad <a popular singer : un cantante popular>
popularity [ˌpɑpjəˈlærət̬i] *n* : popularidad *f*
popularize [ˈpɑpjələˌraɪz] *vt* **-ized; -izing** : popularizar
popularly [ˈpɑpjələrli] *adv* : popularmente, vulgarmente
populate [ˈpɑpjəˌleɪt] *vt* **-lated; -lating** : poblar
population [ˌpɑpjəˈleɪʃən] *n* : población *f*
populous [ˈpɑpjələs] *adj* : populoso
porcelain [ˈpɔrsələn] *n* : porcelana *f*
porch [ˈportʃ] *n* : porche *m*
porcupine [ˈpɔrkjəˌpaɪn] *n* : puerco *m* espín
pore¹ [ˈpor] *vi* **pored; poring 1** GAZE : mirar (con atención) **2 to pore over** : leer detenidamente, estudiar
pore² *n* : poro *m*
pork [ˈpork] *n* : carne *f* de cerdo, carne *f* de puerco
pornographic [ˌpɔrnəˈgræfɪk] *adj* : pornográfico
pornography [pɔrˈnɑgrəfi] *n* : pornografía *f*
porous [ˈporəs] *adj* : poroso
porpoise [ˈpɔrpəs] *n* **1** : marsopa *f* **2** DOLPHIN : delfín *m*
porridge [ˈpɔrɪdʒ] *n* : sopa *f* espesa de harina, gachas *fpl*
port¹ [ˈport] *adj* : de babor <on the port side : a babor>
port² *n* **1** HARBOR : puerto *m* **2** ORIFICE : orificio *m* (de una válvula, etc.) **3** : puerto *m* (de una computadora) **4** PORTHOLE : portilla *f* **5** *or* **port side** : babor *m* (de un barco) **6** : oporto *m* (vino)
portable [ˈport̬əbəl] *adj* : portátil
portal [ˈport̬əl] *n* : portal *m*
portend [pɔrˈtɛnd] *vt* : presagiar, augurar
portent [ˈpɔrˌtɛnt] *n* : presagio *m*, augurio *m*
portentous [pɔrˈtɛntəs] *adj* : profético, que presagia
porter [ˈport̬ər] *n* : maletero *m*, mozo *m* (de estación)
portfolio [portˈfoːliˌo] *n, pl* **-lios 1** FOLDER : cartera *f* (para llevar papeles), carpeta *f* **2** : cartera *f* (diplomática) **3 investment portfolio** : cartera de inversiones
porthole [ˈportˌhoːl] *n* : portilla *f* (de un barco), ventanilla *f* (de un avión)
portico [ˈport̬ɪˌko] *n, pl* **-coes** *or* **-cos** : pórtico *m*
portion¹ [ˈporʃən] *vt* DISTRIBUTE : repartir
portion² *n* PART, SHARE : porción *f*, parte *f*
portly [ˈportli] *adj* **-lier; -est** : corpulento
portrait [ˈportrət, -ˌtreɪt] *n* : retrato *m*
portray [porˈtreɪ] *vt* **1** DEPICT : representar, retratar **2** DESCRIBE : describir **3** PLAY : interpretar (un personaje)
portrayal [porˈtreɪəl] *n* **1** REPRESENTATION : representación *f* **2** PORTRAIT : retrato *m*
Portuguese [ˌportʃəˈgiːz, -ˈgiːs] *n* **1** : portugués *m*, -guesa *f* (persona) **2** : portugués *m* (idioma) — **Portuguese** *adj*
pose¹ [ˈpoːz] *v* **posed; posing** *vt* PRESENT : plantear (una pregunta, etc.), representar (una amenaza) — *vi* **1** : posar (para una foto, etc.) **2 to pose as** : hacerse pasar por
pose² *n* **1** : pose *f* <to strike a pose : asumir una pose> **2** PRETENSE : pose *f*, afectación *f*
posh [ˈpɑʃ] *adj* : elegante, de lujo
position¹ [pəˈzɪʃən] *vt* : colocar, situar, ubicar
position² *n* **1** APPROACH, STANCE : posición *f*, postura *f*, planteamiento *m* **2** LOCATION : posición *f*, ubicación *f* **3** STATUS : posición *f* (en una jerarquía) **4** JOB : puesto *m*
positive [ˈpɑzət̬ɪv] *adj* **1** DEFINITE : incuestionable, inequívoco <positive evidence : pruebas irrefutables> **2** CONFIDENT : seguro **3** : positivo (en gramática, matemáticas, y física) **4** AFFIRMATIVE : positivo, afirmativo <a positive response : una respuesta positiva>
positively [ˈpɑzət̬ɪvli] *adv* **1** FAVORABLY : favorablemente **2** OPTIMISTICALLY : positivamente **3** DEFINITELY : definitivamente, en forma concluyente **4** (*used for emphasis*) : realmente, verdaderamente <it's positively awful! : ¡es verdaderamente malo!>
possess [pəˈzɛs] *vt* **1** HAVE, OWN : poseer, tener **2** SEIZE : apoderarse de <he was possessed by fear : el miedo se apoderó de él>
possession [pəˈzɛʃən] *n* **1** POSSESSING : posesión *f* **2** : posesión *f* (por un demonio, etc.) **3 possessions** *npl* PROPERTY : bienes *mpl*, propiedad *f*
possessive¹ [pəˈzɛsɪv] *adj* **1** : posesivo (en gramática) **2** JEALOUS : posesivo, celoso
possessive² *n or* **possessive case** : posesivo *m*

possessor [pə'zɛsər] *n* : poseedor *m*, -dora *f*
possibility [ˌpɑsə'bɪləṭi] *n, pl* **-ties** : posibilidad *f*
possible ['pɑsəbəl] *adj* : posible
possibly ['pɑsəbli] *adv* **1** CONCEIVABLY : posiblemente <it can't possibly be true! : ¡no puede ser!> **2** PERHAPS : quizás, posiblemente
possum ['pɑsəm] → **opossum**
post[1] ['po:st] *vt* **1** MAIL : echar al correo, mandar por correo **2** ANNOUNCE : anunciar <they've posted the grades : han anunciado las notas> **3** AFFIX : fijar, poner (noticias, etc.) **4** STATION : apostar **5 to keep (someone) posted** : tener al corriente (a alguien)
post[2] *n* **1** POLE : poste *m*, palo *m* **2** STATION : puesto *m* **3** CAMP : puesto *m* (militar) **4** JOB, POSITION : puesto *m*, empleo *m*, cargo *m*
postage ['po:stɪdʒ] *n* : franqueo *m*
postal ['po:stəl] *adj* : postal
postcard ['po:stˌkɑrd] *n* : postal *f*, tarjeta *f* postal
poster ['po:stər] *n* : póster *m*, cartel *m*, afiche *m*
posterior[1] [pɑ'stɪriər, po-] *adj* : posterior
posterior[2] *n* BUTTOCKS : trasero *m*, nalgas *fpl*, asentaderas *fpl*
posterity [pɑ'stɛrəṭi] *n* : posteridad *f*
postgraduate[1] [ˌpo:st'grædʒʊət] *adj* : de postgrado
postgraduate[2] *n* : postgraduado *m*, -da *f*
posthaste ['po:st'heɪst] *adv* : a toda prisa
posthumous ['pɑstʃəməs] *adj* : póstumo — **posthumously** *adv*
postman ['po:stmən, -ˌmæn] → **mailman**
postmark[1] ['po:stˌmɑrk] *vt* : matasellar
postmark[2] *n* : matasellos *m*
postmaster ['po:stˌmæstər] *n* : administrador *m*, -dora *f* de correos
postmortem [ˌpo:st'mɔrṭəm] *n* : autopsia *f*
postnatal [ˌpo:st'neɪṭəl] *adj* : postnatal <postnatal depression : depresión posparto>
post office *n* : correo *m*, oficina *f* de correos
postoperative [ˌpo:st'ɑpərəṭɪv, -ˌreɪ-] *adj* : posoperatorio
postpaid [ˌpo:st'peɪd] *adv* : con franqueo pagado
postpone [ˌpo:st'po:n] *vt* **-poned; -poning** : postergar, aplazar, posponer
postponement [ˌpo:st'po:nmənt] *n* : postergación *f*, aplazamiento *m*
postscript ['po:stˌskrɪpt] *n* : postdata *f*, posdata *f*
postulate ['pɑstʃəˌleɪt] *vt* **-lated; -lating** : postular
posture[1] ['pɑstʃər] *vi* **-tured; -turing** : posar, asumir una pose
posture[2] *n* : postura *f*
postwar [ˌpo:st'wɔr] *adj* : de (la) posguerra
posy ['po:zi] *n, pl* **-sies 1** FLOWER : flor *f* **2** BOUQUET : ramo *m*, ramillete *m*
pot[1] ['pɑt] *vt* **potted; potting** : plantar (en una maceta)
pot[2] *n* **1** : olla *f* (de cocina) **2 pots and pans** : cacharros *mpl*
potable ['po:ṭəbəl] *adj* : potable
potash ['pɑtˌæʃ] *n* : potasa *f*
potassium [pə'tæsiəm] *n* : potasio *m*
potato [pə'teɪṭo] *n, pl* **-toes** : papa *f*, patata *f Spain*
potato chips *npl* : papas *fpl* fritas (de bolsa)
potbellied ['pɑtˌbɛlid] *adj* : panzón, barrigón *fam*
potbelly ['pɑtˌbɛli] *n* : panza *f*, barriga *f*
potency ['po:tənṭsi] *n, pl* **-cies 1** POWER : fuerza *f*, potencia *f* **2** EFFECTIVENESS : eficacia *f*
potent ['po:tənt] *adj* **1** POWERFUL : potente, poderoso **2** EFFECTIVE : eficaz <a potent medicine : una medicina bien fuerte>
potential[1] [pə'tɛntʃəl] *adj* : potencial, posible
potential[2] *n* **1** : potencial *m* <growth potential : potencial de crecimiento> <a child with potential : un niño que promete> **2** : potencial *m* (eléctrico) — **potentially** *adv*
potful ['pɑtˌfʊl] *n* : contenido *m* de una olla <a potful of water : una olla de agua>
pothole ['pɑtˌho:l] *n* : bache *m*
potion ['po:ʃən] *n* : brebaje *m*, poción *f*
potluck ['pɑtˌlʌk] *n* **to take potluck** : tomar lo que haya
potpourri [ˌpo:pʊ'ri:] *n* : popurrí *m*
potshot ['pɑtˌʃɑt] *n* **1** : tiro *m* al azar <to take potshots at : disparar al azar a> **2** CRITICISM : crítica *f* (hecha al azar)
potter ['pɑṭər] *n* : alfarero *m*, -ra *f*
pottery ['pɑṭəri] *n, pl* **-teries** : cerámica *f*
pouch ['paʊtʃ] *n* **1** BAG : bolsa *f* pequeña **2** : bolsa *f* (de un animal)
poultice ['po:lṭəs] *n* : emplasto *m*, cataplasma *f*
poultry ['po:ltri] *n* : aves *fpl* de corral
pounce ['paʊnṭs] *vi* **pounced; pouncing** : abalanzarse
pound[1] ['paʊnd] *vt* **1** CRUSH : machacar, machucar, majar **2** BEAT : golpear, machacar <she pounded the lessons into them : les machacaba las lecciones> <he pounded home his point : les hizo entender su razonamiento> — *vi* **1** BEAT : palpitar (dícese del corazón) **2** RESOUND : retumbar, resonar **3** : andar con paso pesado <we pounded through the mud : caminamos pesadamente por el barro>

pound[2] *n* **1 :** libra *f* (unidad de peso) **2 :** libra *f* (unidad monetaria) **3 dog pound :** perrera *f*

pour ['por] *vt* **1 :** echar, verter, servir (bebidas) <pour it into a pot : viértalo en una olla> **2 :** proveer con abundancia <they poured money into it : le invirtieron mucho dinero> **3 to pour out :** dar salida a <he poured out his feelings to her : se desahogó con ella> — *vi* **1** FLOW **:** manar, fluir, salir <blood was pouring from the wound : la sangre le salía de la herida> **2 it's pouring (outside) :** está lloviendo a cántaros

pout[1] ['paʊt] *vi* **:** hacer pucheros

pout[2] *n* **:** puchero *m*

poverty ['pɑvərt̬i] *n* **:** pobreza *f,* indigencia *f*

powder[1] ['paʊdər] *vt* **1 :** empolvar <to powder one's face : empolvarse la cara> **2** PULVERIZE **:** pulverizar

powder[2] *n* **:** polvo *m,* polvos *mpl*

powdery ['paʊdəri] *adj* **:** polvoriento, como polvo

power[1] ['paʊər] *vt* **:** impulsar, propulsar

power[2] *n* **1** AUTHORITY **:** poder *m,* autoridad *f* <executive powers : poderes ejecutivos> **2** ABILITY **:** capacidad *f,* poder *m* **3 :** potencia *f* (política) <foreign powers : potencias extranjeras> **4** STRENGTH **:** fuerza *f* **5 :** potencia *f* (en física y matemáticas)

powerful ['paʊərfəl] *adj* **:** poderoso, potente — **powerfully** *adv*

powerhouse ['paʊər,haʊs] *n* **:** persona *f* dinámica

powerless ['paʊərləs] *adj* **:** impotente

power plant *n* **:** central *f* eléctrica

powwow ['paʊ,waʊ] *n* **:** conferencia *f*

pox ['pɑks] *n, pl* **pox** *or* **poxes 1** CHICKEN POX **:** varicela *f* **2** SYPHILIS **:** sífilis *f*

practicable ['præktɪkəbəl] *adj* **:** practicable, viable, factible

practical ['præktɪkəl] *adj* **:** práctico

practicality [,præktɪ'kæləti] *n, pl* **-ties :** factibilidad *f,* viabilidad *f*

practical joke *n* **:** broma *f* (pesada)

practically ['præktɪkli] *adv* **1 :** de manera práctica **2** ALMOST **:** casi, prácticamente

practice[1] *or* **practise** ['præktəs] *vt* **-ticed** *or* **-tised; -ticing** *or* **-tising 1 :** practicar <he practiced his German on us : practicó el alemán con nosotros> <to practice politeness : practicar la cortesía> **2 :** ejercer <to practice medicine : ejercer la medicina>

practice[2] *n* **1** USE **:** práctica *f* <to put into practice : poner en práctica> **2** CUSTOM **:** costumbre *f* <it's a common practice here : por aquí se acostumbra hacerlo> **3** TRAINING **:** práctica *f* **4 :** ejercicio *m* (de una profesión)

practitioner [præk'tɪʃənər] *n* **1 :** profesional *mf* **2 general practitioner :** médico *m,* -ca *f*

pragmatic [præg'mæt̬ɪk] *adj* **:** pragmático — **pragmatically** *adv*

pragmatism ['prægmə,tɪzəm] *n* **:** pragmatismo

prairie ['prɛri] *n* **:** pradera *f,* llanura *f*

praise[1] ['preɪz] *vt* **praised; praising :** elogiar, alabar <to praise God : alabar a Dios>

praise[2] *n* **:** elogio *m,* alabanza *f*

praiseworthy ['preɪz,wərði] *adj* **:** digno de alabanza, loable

prance[1] ['prænts] *vi* **pranced; prancing 1 :** hacer cabriolas, cabriolar <a prancing horse : un caballo haciendo cabriolas> **2** SWAGGER **:** pavonearse

prance[2] *n* **:** cabriola *f*

prank ['præŋk] *n* **:** broma *f,* travesura *f*

prankster ['præŋkstər] *n* **:** bromista *mf*

prattle[1] ['prætəl] *vt* **-tled; -tling :** parlotear *fam,* cotorrear *fam,* balbucear (como un niño)

prattle[2] *n* **:** parloteo *m fam,* cotorreo *m fam,* cháchara *f fam*

prawn ['prɔn] *n* **:** langostino *m,* camarón *m,* gamba *f*

pray ['preɪ] *vt* ENTREAT **:** rogar, suplicar — *vi* **:** rezar

prayer ['prɛr] *n* **1 :** plegaria *f,* oración *f* <to say one's prayers : orar, rezar> <the Lord's Prayer : el Padrenuestro> **2** PRAYING **:** rezo *m,* oración *f* <to kneel in prayer : arrodillarse para rezar>

praying mantis → **mantis**

preach ['pri:tʃ] *vi* **:** predicar — *vt* ADVOCATE **:** abogar por <to preach cooperation : promover la cooperación>

preacher ['pri:tʃər] *n* **1 :** predicador *m,* -dora *f* **2** MINISTER **:** pastor *m,* -tora *f*

preamble ['pri:,æmbəl] *n* **:** preámbulo *m*

prearrange [,pri:ə'reɪndʒ] *vt* **-ranged; -ranging :** arreglar de antemano

precarious [pri'kæriəs] *adj* **:** precario — **precariously** *adv*

precariousness [pri'kæriəsnəs] *n* **:** precariedad *f*

precaution [pri'kɔʃən] *n* **:** precaución *f*

precautionary [pri'kɔʃə,nɛri] *adj* **:** preventivo, cautelar, precautorio

precede [pri'si:d] *v* **-ceded; -ceding :** preceder a

precedence ['prɛsədənts, prɪ'si:dənts] *n* **:** precedencia *f*

precedent ['prɛsədənt] *n* **:** precedente *m*

precept ['pri:,sɛpt] *n* **:** precepto *m*

precinct ['pri:,sɪŋkt] *n* **1** DISTRICT **:** distrito *m* (policial, electoral, etc.) **2 precincts** *npl* PREMISES **:** recinto *m,* predio *m,* límites *mpl* (de una ciudad)

precious ['prɛʃəs] *adj* **1 :** precioso <precious gems : piedras preciosas> **2** DEAR **:** querido **3** AFFECTED **:** afectado

precipice ['prɛsəpəs] *n* **:** precipicio *m*

precipitate [pri'sɪpə,teɪt] *v* **-tated; -tating** *vt* **1** HASTEN, PROVOKE **:** precipitar, provocar **2** HURL **:** arrojar **3**

: precipitar (en química) — *vi* : precipitarse (en química), condensarse (en meteorología)

precipitation [pri,sɪpə'teɪʃən] *n* **1** HASTE : precipitación *f,* prisa *f* **2** : precipitaciones *fpl* (en meteorología)

precipitous [pri'sɪpət̬əs] *adj* **1** HASTY, RASH : precipitado **2** STEEP : escarpado, empinado <a precipitous drop : una caída vertiginosa>

précis [preɪ'siː] *n, pl* **précis** [-'siːz] : resumen *m*

precise [pri'saɪs] *adj* **1** DEFINITE : preciso, explícito **2** EXACT : exacto, preciso <precise calculations : cálculos precisos> — **precisely** *adv*

preciseness [pri'saɪsnəs] *n* : precisión *f,* exactitud *f*

precision [pri'sɪʒən] *n* : precisión *f*

preclude [pri'kluːd] *vt* **-cluded; -cluding** : evitar, impedir, excluir (una posibilidad, etc.)

precocious [pri'koːʃəs] *adj* : precoz — **precociously** *adv*

precocity [pri'kɑsət̬i] *n* : precocidad *f*

preconceive [,priːkən'siːv] *vt* **-ceived; -ceiving** : preconcebir

preconception [,priːkən'sɛpʃən] *n* : idea *f* preconcebida

precondition [,priːkən'dɪʃən] *n* : precondición *f,* condición *f* previa

precook [,priː'kʊk] *vt* : precocinar

precursor [pri'kərsər] *n* : precursor *m,* -sora *f*

predator ['prɛdət̬ər] *n* : depredador *m,* -dora *f*

predatory ['prɛdə,tori] *adj* : depredador

predecessor ['prɛdə,sɛsər, 'priː-] *n* : antecesor *m,* -sora *f;* predecesor *m,* -sora *f*

predestination [pri,dɛstə'neɪʃən] *n* : predestinación *f*

predestine [pri'dɛstən] *vt* **-tined; -tining** : predestinar

predetermine [,priːdɪ'tərmən] *vt* **-mined; -mining** : predeterminar

predicament [pri'dɪkəmənt] *n* : apuro *m,* aprieto *m*

predicate¹ ['prɛdə,keɪt] *vt* **-cated; -cating 1** AFFIRM : afirmar, aseverar **2 to be predicated on** : estar basado en

predicate² ['prɛdɪkət] *n* : predicado *m*

predict [pri'dɪkt] *vt* : pronosticar, predecir

predictable [pri'dɪktəbəl] *adj* : previsible — **predictably** [-bli] *adv*

prediction [pri'dɪkʃən] *n* : pronóstico *m,* predicción *f*

predilection [,prɛdəl'ɛkʃən, ,priː-] *n* : predilección *f*

predispose [,priːdɪ'spoːz] *vt* **-posed; -posing** : predisponer

predominance [pri'dɑmənənts] *n* : predominio *m*

predominant [pri'dɑmənənt] *adj* : predominante — **predominantly** *adv*

predominate [pri'dɑmə,neɪt] *vi* **-nated; -nating 1** : predominar (en cantidad) **2** PREVAIL : prevalecer

preeminence [pri'ɛmənənts] *n* : preeminencia *f*

preeminent [pri'ɛmənənt] *adj* : preeminente

preeminently [pri'ɛmənəntli] *adv* : especialmente

preempt [pri'ɛmpt] *vt* **1** APPROPRIATE : apoderarse de, apropriarse de **2** : reemplazar (un programa de televisión, etc.) **3** FORESTALL : adelantarse a (un ataque, etc.)

preen ['priːn] *vt* : arreglarse (el pelo, las plumas, etc.)

prefabricated [,priː'fæbrə,keɪt̬əd] *adj* : prefabricado

preface ['prɛfəs] *n* : prefacio *m,* prólogo *m*

prefatory ['prɛfə,tori] *adj* : preliminar

prefer [pri'fər] *vt* **-ferred; -ferring 1** : preferir <I prefer coffee : prefiero café> **2 to prefer charges against** : presentar cargos contra

preferable ['prɛfərəbəl] *adj* : preferible

preferably ['prɛfərəbli] *adv* : preferentemente, de preferencia

preference ['prɛfrənts, 'prɛfər-] *n* : preferencia *f,* gusto *m*

preferential [,prɛfə'rɛntʃəl] *adj* : preferencial, preferente

prefigure [pri'fɪgjər] *vt* **-ured; -uring** FORESHADOW : prefigurar, anunciar

prefix ['priː,fɪks] *n* : prefijo *m*

pregnancy ['prɛgnəntsi] *n, pl* **-cies** : embarazo *m,* preñez *f*

pregnant ['prɛgnənt] *adj* **1** : embarazada (dícese de una mujer), preñada (dícese de un animal) **2** MEANINGFUL : significativo

preheat [,priː'hiːt] *vt* : precalentar

prehensile [pri'hɛntsəl, -'hɛn,saɪl] *adj* : prensil

prehistoric [,priːhɪs'tɔrɪk] *or* **prehistorical** [-ɪkəl] *adj* : prehistórico

prejudge [,priː'dʒʌdʒ] *vt* **-judged; -judging** : prejuzgar

prejudice¹ ['prɛdʒədəs] *vt* **-diced; -dicing 1** DAMAGE : perjudicar **2** BIAS : predisponer, influir en

prejudice² *n* **1** DAMAGE : perjuicio *m* (en derecho) **2** BIAS : prejuicio *m*

prelate ['prɛlət] *n* : prelado *m*

preliminary¹ [pri'lɪmə,nɛri] *adj* : preliminar

preliminary² *n, pl* **-naries 1** : preámbulo *m,* preludio *m* **2 preliminaries** *npl* : preliminares *mpl*

prelude ['prɛ,luːd, 'prɛl,juːd; 'preɪ,luːd, 'priː-] *n* : preludio *m*

premarital [,priː'mærət̬əl] *adj* : prematrimonial

premature [,priːmə'tʊr, -'tjʊr, -'tʃʊr] *adj* : prematuro — **prematurely** *adv*

premeditate [pri'mɛdə,teɪt] *vt* **-tated; -tating** : premeditar

premeditation [pri,mɛdə'teɪʃən] *n* : premeditación *f*
premenstrual [pri'mɛntstruəl] *adj* : premenstrual
premier[1] [pri'mɪr, -'mjɪr; 'pri:miər] *adj* : principal
premier[2] *n* PRIME MINISTER : primer ministro *m,* primera ministra *f*
premiere[1] [prɪ'mjɛr, -'mɪr] *vt* **-miered; -miering** : estrenar
premiere[2] *n* : estreno *m*
premise ['prɛmɪs] *n* **1** : premisa *f* <the premise of his arguments : la premisa de sus argumentos> **2 premises** *npl* : recinto *m,* local *m*
premium ['pri:miəm] *n* **1** BONUS : prima *f* **2** SURCHARGE : recargo *m* <to sell at a premium : vender (algo) muy caro> **3 insurance premium** : prima *f* (de seguros) **4 to set a premium on** : darle un gran valor (a algo)
premonition [,pri:mə'nɪʃən, ,prɛmə-] *n* : presentimiento *m,* premonición *f*
prenatal [,pri:'neɪṭəl] *adj* : prenatal
preoccupation [pri,ɑkjə'peɪʃən] *n* : preocupación *f*
preoccupied [pri'ɑkjə,paɪd] *adj* : abstraído, ensimismado, preocupado
preoccupy [pri'ɑkjə,paɪ] *vt* **-pied; -pying** : preocupar
preparation [,prɛpə'reɪʃən] *n* **1** PREPARING : preparación *f* **2** MIXTURE : preparado *m* <a preparation for burns : un preparado para quemaduras> **3 preparations** *npl* ARRANGEMENTS : preparativos *mpl*
preparatory [pri'pærə,tori] *adj* : preparatorio
prepare [pri'pær] *v* **-pared; -paring** *vt* : preparar — *vi* : prepararse
prepay [,pri:'peɪ] *vt* **-paid; -paying** : pagar por adelantado
preponderance [pri'pɑndərənts] *n* : preponderancia *f*
preponderant [pri'pɑndərənt] *adj* : preponderante — **preponderantly** *adv*
preposition [,prɛpə'zɪʃən] *n* : preposición *f*
prepositional [,prɛpə'zɪʃənəl] *adj* : preposicional
prepossessing [,pri:pə'zɛsɪŋ] *adj* : atractivo, agradable
preposterous [pri'pɑstərəs] *adj* : absurdo, ridículo
prerequisite[1] [pri'rɛkwəzət] *adj* : necesario, esencial
prerequisite[2] *n* : condición *f* necesario, requisito *m* previo
prerogative [pri'rɑgəṭɪv] *n* : prerrogativa *f*
presage ['prɛsɪdʒ, pri'seɪdʒ] *vt* **-saged; -saging** : presagiar
preschool ['pri:,sku:l] *adj* : preescolar <preschool students : estudiantes de preescolar>
prescribe [pri'skraɪb] *vt* **-scribed; -scribing 1** ORDAIN : prescribir, ordenar **2** : recetar (medicinas, etc.)
prescription [pri'skrɪpʃən] *n* : receta *f*
presence ['prɛzənts] *n* : presencia *f*
present[1] [pri'zɛnt] *vt* **1** INTRODUCE : presentar <to present oneself : presentarse> **2** : presentar (una obra de teatro, etc.) **3** GIVE : entregar (un regalo, etc.), regalar, obsequiar **4** SHOW : presentar, ofrecer <it presents a lovely view : ofrece una vista muy linda>
present[2] ['prɛzənt] *adj* **1** : actual <present conditions : condiciones actuales> **2** : presente <all the students were present : todos los estudiantes estaban presentes>
present[3] ['prɛzənt] *n* **1** GIFT : regalo *m,* obsequio *m* **2** : presente *m* <at present : en este momento> **3** *or* **present tense** : presente *m*
presentation [,pri:,zɛn'teɪʃən, ,prɛzən-] *n* : presentación *f* <presentation ceremony : ceremonia de entrega>
presentiment [pri'zɛntəmənt] *n* : presentimiento *m,* premonición *f*
presently ['prɛzəntli] *adv* **1** SOON : pronto, dentro de poco **2** NOW : actualmente, ahora
present participle *n* : participio *m* presente, participio *m* activo
preservation [,prɛzər'veɪʃən] *n* : conservación *f,* preservación *f*
preservative [pri'zərvəṭɪv] *n* : conservante *m*
preserve[1] [pri'zərv] *vt* **-served; -serving 1** PROTECT : proteger, preservar **2** : conservar (los alimentos, etc.) **3** MAINTAIN : conservar, mantener
preserve[2] *n* **1** *or* **preserves** *npl* : conserva *f* <peach preserves : duraznos en conserva> **2** : coto *m* <game preserve : coto de caza>
preside [pri'zaɪd] *vi* **-sided; -siding 1 to preside over** : presidir <he presided over the meeting : presidió la reunión> **2 to preside over** : supervisar <she presides over the department : dirige el departamento>
presidency ['prɛzədəntsi] *n, pl* **-cies** : presidencia *f*
president ['prɛzədənt] *n* : presidente *m,* -ta *f*
presidential [,prɛzə'dɛntʃəl] *adj* : presidencial
press[1] ['prɛs] *vt* **1** PUSH : apretar **2** SQUEEZE : apretar, prensar (frutas, flores, etc.) **3** IRON : planchar (ropa) **4** URGE : instar, apremiar <he pressed me to come : insistió en que viniera> — *vi* **1** PUSH : apretar <press hard : aprieta con fuerza> **2** CROWD : apiñarse **3** : abrirse paso <I pressed through the crowd : me abrí paso entre el gentío> **4** URGE : presionar
press[2] *n* **1** CROWD : multitud *f* **2** : imprenta *f,* prensa *f* <to go to press : entrar en prensa> **3** URGENCY : urgencia *f,* prisa *f* **4** PRINTER, PUBLISHER : imprenta *f,* editorial *f* **5 the press** : la

prensa <freedom of the press : libertad de prensa>

pressing [ˈprɛsɪŋ] *adj* URGENT : urgente

pressure[1] [ˈprɛʃər] *vt* **-sured; -suring** : presionar, apremiar

pressure[2] *n* **1** : presión *f* <to be under pressure : estar bajo presión> **2** → **blood pressure**

pressurize [ˈprɛʃəˌraɪz] *vt* **-ized; -izing** : presurizar

prestige [prɛˈstiːʒ, -ˈstiːdʒ] *n* : prestigio *m*

prestigious [prɛˈstɪdʒəs] *adj* : prestigioso

presto [ˈprɛsˌtoː] *adv* : de pronto

presumably [priˈzuːməbli] *adv* : es de suponer, supuestamente <presumably, he's guilty : supone que es culpable>

presume [priˈzuːm] *vt* **-sumed; -suming 1** ASSUME, SUPPOSE : suponer, asumir, presumir **2 to presume to** : atreverse a, osar

presumption [priˈzʌmpʃən] *n* **1** AUDACITY : atrevimiento *m,* osadía *f* **2** ASSUMPTION : presunción *f,* suposición *f*

presumptuous [priˈzʌmptʃʊəs] *adj* : descarado, atrevido

presuppose [ˌpriːsəˈpoːz] *vt* **-posed; -posing** : presuponer

pretend [priˈtɛnd] *vt* **1** CLAIM : pretender **2** FEIGN : fingir, simular — *vi* : fingir

pretense *or* **pretence** [ˈpriːˌtɛnts, priˈtɛnts] *n* **1** CLAIM : afirmación *f* (falsa), pretensión *f* **2** FEIGNING : fingimiento *m,* simulación *f* <to make a pretense of doing something : fingir hacer algo> <a pretense of order : una apariencia de orden> **3** PRETEXT : pretexto *m* <under false pretenses : con pretextos falsos, de manera fraudulenta>

pretension [priˈtɛntʃən] *n* **1** CLAIM : pretensión *f,* afirmación *f* **2** ASPIRATION : aspiración *f,* ambición *f* **3** PRETENTIOUSNESS : pretensiones *fpl,* presunción *f*

pretentious [priˈtɛntʃəs] *adj* : pretencioso

pretentiousness [priˈtɛntʃəsnəs] *n* : presunción *f,* pretenciones *fpl*

pretext [ˈpriːˌtɛkst] *n* : pretexto *m,* excusa *f*

prettily [ˈprɪtəli] *adv* : atractivamente

prettiness [ˈprɪtinəs] *n* : lindeza *f*

pretty[1] [ˈprɪti] *adv* : bastante, bien <it's pretty obvious : está bien claro> <it's pretty much the same : es más o menos igual>

pretty[2] *adj* **-tier; -est** : bonito, lindo, guapo <a pretty girl : una muchacha guapa> <what a pretty dress! : ¡qué vestido más lindo!>

pretzel [ˈprɛtsəl] *n* : galleta *f* salada (en forma de nudo)

prevail [priˈveɪl] *vi* **1** TRIUMPH : prevalecer **2** PREDOMINATE : predominar **3 to prevail upon** : persuadir, convencer <I prevailed upon her to sing : la convencí para que cantara>

prevalence [ˈprɛvələnts] *n* : preponderancia *f,* predominio *m*

prevalent [ˈprɛvələnt] *adj* **1** COMMON : común y corriente, general **2** WIDESPREAD : extendido

prevaricate [priˈværəˌkeɪt] *vi* **-cated; -cating** LIE : mentir

prevarication [priˌværəˈkeɪʃən] *n* : mentira *f*

prevent [priˈvɛnt] *vt* **1** AVOID : prevenir, evitar <steps to prevent war : medidas para evitar la guerra> **2** HINDER : impedir

preventable [priˈvɛntəbəl] *adj* : evitable

preventative [priˈvɛntət̬ɪv] → **preventive**

prevention [priˈvɛntʃən] *n* : prevención *f*

preventive [priˈvɛntɪv] *adj* : preventivo

preview [ˈpriːˌvju] *n* : preestreno *m*

previous [ˈpriːviəs] *adj* : previo, anterior <previous knowledge : conocimientos previos> <the previous day : el día anterior> <in the previous year : en el año pasado>

previously [ˈpriːviəsli] *adv* : antes

prewar [ˌpriːˈwɔr] *adj* : de antes de la guerra

prey [ˈpreɪ] *n, pl* **preys** : presa *f*

prey on *vt* **1** : cazar, alimentarse de <it preys on fish : se alimenta de peces> **2 to prey on one's mind** : hacer presa en alguien, atormentar a alguien

price[1] [ˈpraɪs] *vt* **priced; pricing** : poner un precio a

price[2] *n* : precio *m* <peace at any price : la paz a toda costa>

priceless [ˈpraɪsləs] *adj* : inestimable, inapreciable

prick[1] [ˈprɪk] *vt* **1** : pinchar **2 to prick up one's ears** : levantar las orejas — *vi* : pinchar

prick[2] *n* **1** STAB : pinchazo *m* <a prick of conscience : un remordimiento> **2** → **pricker**

pricker [ˈprɪkər] *n* THORN : espina *f*

prickle[1] [ˈprɪkəl] *vi* **-led; -ling** : sentir un cosquilleo, tener un hormigueo

prickle[2] *n* **1** : espina *f* (de una planta) **2** TINGLE : cosquilleo *m,* hormigueo *m*

prickly [ˈprɪkəli] *adj* **1** THORNY : espinoso **2** : que pica <a prickly sensation : un hormigueo>

prickly pear *n* : tuna *f*

pride[1] [ˈpraɪd] *vt* **prided; priding** : estar orgulloso de <to pride oneself on : preciarse de, enorgullecerse de>

pride[2] *n* : orgullo *m*

priest [ˈpriːst] *n* : sacerdote *m,* cura *m*

priestess [ˈpriːstɪs] *n* : sacerdotisa *f*

priesthood [ˈpriːstˌhʊd] *n* : sacerdocio *m*

priestly [ˈpriːstli] *adj* : sacerdotal

prig [ˈprɪg] *n* : mojigato *m,* -ta *f;* gazmoño *m,* -ña *f*

prim ['prɪm] *adj* **primmer; primmest** 1 PRISSY : remilgado 2 PRUDISH : mojigato, gazmoño
primarily [praɪ'mɛrəli] *adv* : principalmente, fundamentalmente
primary[1] ['praɪ,mɛri, 'praɪməri] *adj* 1 FIRST : primario 2 PRINCIPAL : principal 3 BASIC : fundamental
primary[2] *n, pl* **-ries** : elección *f* primaria
primary color *n* : color *m* primario
primary school → **elementary school**
primate *n* 1 ['praɪ,meɪt, -mət] : primado *m* (obispo) 2 [-,meɪt] : primate *m* (animal)
prime[1] ['praɪm] *vt* **primed; priming** 1 : cebar <to prime a pump : cebar una bomba> 2 PREPARE : preparar (una superficie para pintar) 3 COACH : preparar (a un testigo, etc.)
prime[2] *adj* 1 CHIEF, MAIN : principal, primero 2 EXCELLENT : de primera (categoría), excelente
prime[3] *n* **the prime of one's life** : la flor de la vida
prime minister *n* : primer ministro *m*, primera ministra *f*
primer[1] ['prɪmər] *n* 1 READER : cartilla *f* 2 MANUAL : manual *m*
primer[2] ['praɪmər] *n* 1 : cebo *m* (para explosivos) 2 : base *f* (de pintura)
primeval [praɪ'mi:vəl] *adj* : primitivo, primigenio
primitive ['prɪmət̬ɪv] *adj* : primitivo
primly ['prɪmli] *adv* : mojigatamente
primness ['prɪmnəs] *n* : mojigatería *f*, gazmoñería *f*
primordial [praɪ'mɔrdiəl] *adj* : primordial, fundamental
primp ['prɪmp] *vi* : arreglarse, acicalarse
primrose ['prɪm,ro:z] *n* : primavera *f*, prímula *f*
prince ['prɪnts] *n* : príncipe *m*
princely ['prɪntsli] *adj* : principesco
princess ['prɪntsəs, 'prɪn,sɛs] *n* : princesa *f*
principal[1] ['prɪntsəpəl] *adj* : principal — **principally** *adv*
principal[2] *n* 1 PROTAGONIST : protagonista *mf* 2 : director *m*, -tora *f* (de una escuela) 3 CAPITAL : principal *m*, capital *m* (en finanzas)
principality [,prɪntsə'pælət̬i] *n, pl* **-ties** : principado *m*
principle ['prɪntsəpəl] *n* : principio *m*
print[1] ['prɪnt] *vt* : imprimir (libros, etc.) — *vi* : escribir con letra de molde
print[2] *n* 1 IMPRESSION : marca *f*, huella *f*, impresión *f* 2 : texto *m* impreso <to be out of print : estar agotado> 3 LETTERING : letra *f* 4 ENGRAVING : grabado *m* 5 : copia *f* (en fotografía) 6 : estampado *m* (de tela)
printer ['prɪntər] *n* 1 : impresor *m*, -sora *f* (persona) 2 : impresora *f* (máquina)
printing ['prɪntɪŋ] *n* 1 : impresión *f* (acto) <the third printing : la tercera tirada> 2 : imprenta *f* (profesión) 3 LETTERING : letras *fpl* de molde
printing press *n* : prensa *f*
print out *vt* : imprimir (de una computadora)
printout ['prɪnt,aʊt] *n* : copia *f* impresa (de una computadora)
prior ['praɪər] *adj* 1 : previo 2 **prior to** : antes de
priority [praɪ'ɔrət̬i] *n, pl* **-ties** : prioridad *f*
priory ['praɪəri] *n, pl* **-ries** : priorato *m*
prism ['prɪzəm] *n* : prisma *m*
prison ['prɪzən] *n* : prisión *f*, cárcel *f*
prisoner ['prɪzənər] *n* : preso *m*, -sa *f*; recluso *m*, -sa *f* <prisoner of war : prisionero de guerra>
prissy ['prɪsi] *adj* **-sier; -est** : remilgado, melindroso
pristine ['prɪs,ti:n, prɪs'-] *adj* : puro, prístino
privacy ['praɪvəsi] *n, pl* **-cies** : privacidad *f*
private[1] ['praɪvət] *adj* 1 PERSONAL : privado, particular <private property : propiedad privada> 2 INDEPENDENT : privado, independiente <private studies : estudios privados> 3 SECRET : secreto 4 SECLUDED : aislado, privado — **privately** *adv*
private[2] *n* : soldado *m* raso
privateer [,praɪvə'tɪr] *n* : corsario *m*
privation [praɪ'veɪʃən] *n* : privación *f*
privilege ['prɪvlɪdʒ, 'prɪvə-] *n* : privilegio *m*
privileged ['prɪvlɪdʒd, 'prɪvə-] *adj* : privilegiado
privy[1] ['prɪvi] *adj* **to be privy to** : estar enterado de
privy[2] *n, pl* **privies** : excusado *m*, retrete *m* (exterior)
prize[1] ['praɪz] *vt* **prized; prizing** : valorar, apreciar
prize[2] *adj* 1 : premiado <a prize stallion : un semental premiado> 2 OUTSTANDING : de primera, excepcional
prize[3] *n* 1 AWARD : premio *m* <third prize : el tercer premio> 2 : joya *f*, tesoro *m* <he's a real prize : es un tesoro>
prizefighter ['praɪz,faɪt̬ər] *n* : boxeador *m*, -dora *f* profesional
prizewinning ['praɪz,wɪnɪŋ] *adj* : premiado
pro[1] ['pro:] *adv* : a favor
pro[2] *adj* → **professional**[1]
pro[3] *n* 1 : pro *m* <the pros and cons : los pros y los contras> 2 → **professional**[2]
probability [,prɑbə'bɪlət̬i] *n, pl* **-ties** : probabilidad *f*
probable ['prɑbəbəl] *adj* : probable — **probably** [-bli] *adv*
probate[1] ['pro:,beɪt] *vt* **-bated; -bating** : autenticar (un testamento)
probate[2] *n* : autenticación *f* (de un testamento)

probation [pro'beɪʃən] *n* **1 :** período *m* de prueba (para un empleado, etc.) **2 :** libertad *f* condicional (para un preso)

probationary [pro'beɪʃəˌnɛri] *adj* **:** de prueba

probe[1] ['pro:b] *vt* **probed; probing 1 :** sondar (en medicina y tecnología) **2** INVESTIGATE **:** investigar, sondear

probe[2] *n* **1 :** sonda *f* (en medicina, etc.) <space probe : sonda espacial> **2** INVESTIGATION **:** investigación *f,* sondeo *m*

probity ['pro:bət̬i] *n* **:** probidad *f*

problem[1] ['prɑbləm] *adj* **:** difícil

problem[2] *n* **:** problema *m*

problematic [ˌprɑblə'mæt̬ɪk] *or* **problematical** [-tɪkəl] *adj* **:** problemático

proboscis [prə'bɑsɪs] *n, pl* **-cises** *also* **-cides** [-səˌdi:z] **:** probóscide *f*

procedural [prə'si:dʒərəl] *adj* **:** de procedimiento

procedure [prə'si:dʒər] *n* **:** procedimiento *m* <administrative procedures : trámites administrativos>

proceed [pro'si:d] *vi* **1 :** proceder <to proceed to do something : proceder a hacer algo> **2** CONTINUE **:** continuar, proseguir, seguir <he proceeded to the next phase : pasó a la segunda fase> **3** ADVANCE **:** avanzar <as the conference proceeded : mientras seguía avanzando la conferencia> <the road proceeds south : la calle sigue hacia el sur>

proceeding [pro'si:dɪŋ] *n* **1** PROCEDURE **:** procedimiento *m* **2 proceedings** *npl* EVENTS **:** acontecimientos *mpl* **3 proceedings** *npl* MINUTES **:** actas *fpl* (de una reunión, etc.)

proceeds ['pro:ˌsi:dz] *npl* **:** ganancias *fpl*

process[1] ['prɑˌsɛs, 'pro:-] *vt* **:** procesar, tratar

process[2] *n, pl* **-cesses** ['prɑˌsɛsəz, 'pro:-, -səsəz, -səˌsi:z] **1 :** proceso *m* <the process of elimination : el proceso de eliminación> **2** METHOD **:** proceso *m,* método *m* <manufacturing processes : procesos industriales> **3 :** acción *f* judicial <due process of law : el debido proceso (de la ley)> **4** SUMMONS **:** citación *f* **5** PROJECTION **:** protuberancia *f* (anatómica) **6 in the process of :** en vías de <in the process of repair : en reparaciones>

procession [prə'sɛʃən] *n* **:** procesión *f,* desfile *m* <a funeral procession : un cortejo fúnebre>

processional [prə'sɛʃənəl] *n* **:** himno *m* para una procesión

processor ['prɑˌsɛsər, 'pro:-, -səsər] *n* **1 :** procesador *m* (de una computadora) **2 food processor :** procesador *m* de alimentos

proclaim [pro'kleɪm] *vt* **:** proclamar

proclamation [ˌprɑklə'meɪʃən] *n* **:** proclamación *f*

proclivity [pro'klɪvət̬i] *n, pl* **-ties :** proclividad *f*

procrastinate [prə'kræstəˌneɪt] *vi* **-nated; -nating :** demorar, aplazar las responsabilidades

procrastination [prəˌkræstə'neɪʃən] *n* **:** aplazamiento *m,* demora *f,* dilación *f*

procreate ['pro:kriˌeɪt] *vi* **-ated; -ating :** procrear

procreation [ˌpro:kri'eɪʃən] *n* **:** procreación *f*

proctor[1] ['prɑktər] *vt* **:** supervisar (un examen)

proctor[2] *n* **:** supervisor *m,* -sora *f* (de un examen)

procure [prə'kjʊr] *vt* **-cured; -curing 1** OBTAIN **:** procurar, obtener **2** BRING ABOUT **:** provocar, lograr, conseguir

procurement [prə'kjʊrmənt] *n* **:** obtención *f*

prod[1] ['prɑd] *vt* **prodded; prodding 1** JAB, POKE **:** pinchar, golpear (con la punta de algo) **2** GOAD **:** incitar, estimular

prod[2] *n* **1** JAB, POKE **:** golpe *m* (con la punta de algo), pinchazo *m* **2** STIMULUS **:** estímulo *m* **3 cattle prod :** picana *f,* aguijón *m*

prodigal[1] ['prɑdɪgəl] *adj* SPENDTHRIFT **:** pródigo, despilfarrador, derrochador

prodigal[2] *n* **:** pródigo *m,* -ga *f;* derrochador *m,* -dora *f*

prodigious [prə'dɪdʒəs] *adj* **1** MARVELOUS **:** prodigioso, maravilloso **2** HUGE **:** enorme, vasto <prodigious sums : muchísimo dinero> **— prodigiously** *adv*

prodigy ['prɑdədʒi] *n, pl* **-gies :** prodigio *m* <child prodigy : niño prodigio>

produce[1] [prə'du:s, -'dju:s] *vt* **-duced; -ducing 1** EXHIBIT **:** presentar, mostrar **2** YIELD **:** producir **3** CAUSE **:** producir, causar **4** CREATE **:** producir <to produce a poem : escribir un poema> **5 :** poner en escena (una obra de teatro), producir (una película)

produce[2] ['prɑˌdu:s, 'pro:-, -ˌdju:s] *n* **:** productos *mpl* agrícolas

producer [prə'du:sər, -'dju:-] *n* **:** productor *m,* -tora *f*

product ['prɑˌdʌkt] *n* **:** producto *m*

production [prə'dʌkʃən] *n* **:** producción *f*

productive [prə'dʌktɪv] *adj* **:** productivo

productivity [ˌpro:ˌdʌk'tɪvət̬i, ˌprɑ-] *n* **:** productividad *f*

profane[1] [pro'feɪn] *vt* **-faned; -faning :** profanar

profane[2] *adj* **1** SECULAR **:** profano **2** IRREVERENT **:** irreverente, impío

profanity [pro'fænət̬i] *n, pl* **-ties 1** IRREVERENCE **:** irreverencia *f,* impiedad *f* **2 :** blasfemias *fpl,* obscenidades *fpl* <don't use profanity : no digas blasfemias>

profess [prə'fɛs] *vt* **1** DECLARE **:** declarar, manifestar **2** CLAIM **:** pretender **3 :** profesar (una religión, etc.)

professedly [prəˈfɛsədli] *adv* **1** OPENLY : declaradamente **2** ALLEGEDLY : supuestamente
profession [prəˈfɛʃən] *n* : profesión *f*
professional[1] [prəˈfɛʃənəl] *adj* : profesional — **professionally** *adv*
professional[2] *n* : profesional *mf*
professionalism [prəˈfɛʃənəˌlizəm] *n* : profesionalismo *m*
professor [prəˈfɛsər] *n* : profesor *m* (universitario), profesora *f* (universitaria); catedrático *m,* -ca *f*
proffer [ˈprɑfər] *vt* **-fered; -fering** : ofrecer, dar
proficiency [prəˈfɪʃən*t*si] *n* : competencia *f,* capacidad *f*
proficient [prəˈfɪʃənt] *adj* : competente, experto — **proficiently** *adv*
profile [ˈproːˌfaɪl] *n* : perfil *m* <a portrait in profile : un retrato de perfil> <to keep a low profile : no llamar la atención, hacerse pasar desapercibido>
profit[1] [ˈprɑfət] *vi* : sacar provecho (de), beneficiarse (de)
profit[2] *n* **1** ADVANTAGE : provecho *m,* partido *m,* beneficio *m* **2** GAIN : beneficio *m,* utilidad *f,* ganancia *f* <to make a profit : sacar beneficios>
profitable [ˈprɑfət̬əbəl] *adj* : rentable, lucrativo — **profitably** [-bli] *adv*
profitless [ˈprɑfətləs] *adj* : infructuoso, inútil
profligate [ˈprɑflɪgət, -ˌgeɪt] *adj* **1** DISSOLUTE : disoluto, licencioso **2** SPENDTHRIFT : despilfarrador, derrochador, pródigo
profound [prəˈfaʊnd] *adj* : profundo
profoundly [prəˈfaʊndli] *adv* : profundamente, en profundidad
profundity [prəˈfʌndət̬i] *n, pl* **-ties** : profundidad *f*
profuse [prəˈfjuːs] *adj* **1** COPIOUS : profuso, copioso **2** LAVISH : pródigo — **profusely** *adv*
profusion [prəˈfjuːʒən] *n* : abundancia *f,* profusión *f*
progeny [ˈprɑdʒəni] *n, pl* **-nies** : progenie *f*
progesterone [proˈdʒɛstəˌroːn] *n* : progesterona *f*
prognosis [prɑgˈnoːsɪs] *n, pl* **-noses** [-ˌsiːz] : pronóstico *m* (médico)
program[1] [ˈproːˌgræm, -grəm] *vt* **-grammed** *or* **-gramed; -gramming** *or* **-graming** : programar
program[2] *n* : programa *m*
programmer [ˈproːˌgræmər] *n* : programador *m,* -dora *f*
programming [ˈproːˌgræmɪŋ] *n* : programación *f*
progress[1] [prəˈgrɛs] *vi* **1** PROCEED : progresar, adelantar **2** IMPROVE : mejorar
progress[2] [ˈprɑgrəs, -ˌgrɛs] *n* **1** ADVANCE : progreso *m,* adelanto *m,* avance *m* <to make progress : hacer progresos> **2** BETTERMENT : mejora *f,* mejoramiento *m*
progression [prəˈgrɛʃən] *n* **1** ADVANCE : avance *m* **2** SEQUENCE : desarrollo *m* (de eventos)
progressive [prəˈgrɛsɪv] *adj* **1** : progresista <a progressive society : una sociedad progresista> **2** : progresivo <a progressive disease : una enfermedad progresiva> **3** *or* **Progressive** : progresista (en política) **4** : progresivo (en gramática)
progressively [prəˈgrɛsɪvli] *adv* : progresivamente, poco a poco
prohibit [proˈhɪbət] *vt* : prohibir
prohibition [ˌproːəˈbɪʃən, ˌproːhə-] *n* : prohibición *f*
prohibitive [proˈhɪbət̬ɪv] *adj* : prohibitivo
project[1] [prəˈdʒɛkt] *vt* **1** PLAN : proyectar, planear **2** : proyectar (imágenes, misiles, etc.) — *vi* PROTRUDE : sobresalir, salir
project[2] [ˈprɑˌdʒɛkt, -dʒɪkt] *n* : proyecto *m,* trabajo *m* (de un estudiante) <research project : proyecto de investigación>
projectile [prəˈdʒɛktəl, -ˌtaɪl] *n* : proyectil *m*
projection [prəˈdʒɛkʃən] *n* **1** PLAN : plan *m,* proyección *f* **2** : proyección *f* (de imágenes, misiles, etc.) **3** PROTRUSION : saliente *m*
projector [prəˈdʒɛktər] *n* : proyector *m*
proletarian[1] [ˌproːləˈtɛriən] *adj* : proletario
proletarian[2] *n* : proletario *m,* -ria *f*
proletariat [ˌproːləˈtɛriət] *n* : proletariado *m*
proliferate [prəˈlɪfəˌreɪt] *vi* **-ated; -ating** : proliferar
proliferation [prəˌlɪfəˈreɪʃən] *n* : proliferación *f*
prolific [prəˈlɪfɪk] *adj* : prolífico
prologue [ˈproːˌlɔg] *n* : prólogo *m*
prolong [prəˈlɔŋ] *vt* : prolongar
prolongation [ˌproːˌlɔŋˈgeɪʃən] *n* : prolongación *f*
prom [ˈprɑm] *n* : baile *m* formal (de un colegio)
promenade[1] [ˌprɑməˈneɪd, -ˈnɑd] *vi* **-naded; -nading** : pasear, pasearse, dar un paseo
promenade[2] *n* : paseo *m*
prominence [ˈprɑmənən*t*s] *n* **1** PROJECTION : prominencia *f* **2** EMINENCE : eminencia *f,* prestigio *m*
prominent [ˈprɑmənənt] *adj* **1** OUTSTANDING : prominente, destacado **2** PROJECTING : prominente, saliente
prominently [ˈprɑmənəntli] *adv* : destacadamente, prominentemente
promiscuity [ˌprɑmɪsˈkjuːət̬i] *n, pl* **-ties** : promiscuidad *f*
promiscuous [prəˈmɪskjʊəs] *adj* : promiscuo — **promiscuously** *adv*
promise[1] [ˈprɑməs] *v* **-ised; -ising** : prometer

promise[2] *n* **1 :** promesa *f* <he kept his promise : cumplió su promesa> **2 to show promise :** prometer

promising [ˈprɑməsɪŋ] *adj* **:** prometedor

promissory [ˈprɑməˌsori] *adj* **:** que promete <a promissory note : un pagaré>

promontory [ˈprɑmənˌtori] *n, pl* **-ries :** promontorio *m*

promote [prəˈmoːt] *vt* **-moted; -moting 1 :** ascender (a un alumno o un empleado) **2** ADVERTISE **:** promocionar, hacerle publicidad a **3** FURTHER **:** promover, fomentar

promoter [prəˈmoːt̬ər] *n* **:** promotor *m,* -tora *f;* empresario *m,* -ria *f* (en deportes)

promotion [prəˈmoːʃən] *n* **1 :** ascenso *m* (de un alumno o un empleado) **2** FURTHERING **:** promoción *f,* fomento *m* **3** ADVERTISING **:** publicidad *f,* propaganda *f*

promotional [prəˈmoːʃənəl] *adj* **:** promocional

prompt[1] [ˈprɑmpt] *vt* **1** INDUCE **:** provocar (una cosa), inducir (a una persona) <curiosity prompted me to ask you : la curiosidad me indujo a preguntarle> **2 :** apuntar (a un actor, etc.)

prompt[2] *adj* **:** pronto, rápido <prompt payment : pago puntual>

prompter [ˈprɑmptər] *n* **:** apuntador *m,* -dora *f* (en teatro)

promptly [ˈprɑmptli] *adv* **:** inmediatamente, rápidamente

promptness [ˈprɑmptnəs] *n* **:** prontitud *f,* rapidez *f*

prone [ˈproːn] *adj* **1** LIABLE **:** propenso, proclive <accident-prone : propenso a los accidentes> **2 :** boca abajo, decúbito prono <in a prone position : en decúbito prono>

prong [ˈprɔŋ] *n* **:** punta *f,* diente *m*

pronoun [ˈproːˌnaʊn] *n* **:** pronombre *m*

pronounce [prəˈnaʊnts] *vt* **-nounced; -nouncing 1 :** pronunciar <how do you pronounce your name? : ¿cómo se pronuncia su nombre?> **2** DECLARE **:** declarar **3 to pronounce sentence :** dictar sentencia, pronunciar un fallo

pronounced [prəˈnaʊntst] *adj* MARKED **:** pronunciado, marcado

pronouncement [prəˈnaʊntsmənt] *n* **:** declaración *f*

pronunciation [prəˌnʌntsiˈeɪʃən] *n* **:** pronunciación *f*

proof[1] [ˈpruːf] *adj* **:** a prueba <proof against tampering : a prueba de manipulación>

proof[2] *n* **:** prueba *f*

proofread [ˈpruːfˌriːd] *v* **-read; -reading** *vt* **:** corregir — *vi* **:** corregir pruebas

proofreader [ˈpruːfˌriːdər] *n* **:** corrector *m,* -tora *f* (de pruebas)

prop[1] [ˈprɑp] *vt* **propped; propping 1 to prop against :** apoyar contra **2 to prop up** SUPPORT **:** apoyar, apuntalar, sostener **3 to prop up** SUSTAIN **:** alentar (a alguien), darle ánimo (a alguien)

prop[2] *n* **1** SUPPORT **:** puntal *m,* apoyo *m,* soporte *m* **2 :** accesorio *m* (en teatro)

propaganda [ˌprɑpəˈgændə, ˌproː-] *n* **:** propaganda *f*

propagandize [ˌprɑpəˈgænˌdaɪz, ˌproː-] *v* **-dized; -dizing** *vt* **:** someter a propaganda — *vi* **:** hacer propaganda

propagate [ˈprɑpəˌgeɪt] *v* **-gated; -gating** *vi* **:** propagarse — *vt* **:** propagar

propagation [ˌprɑpəˈgeɪʃən] *n* **:** propagación *f*

propane [ˈproːˌpeɪn] *n* **:** propano *m*

propel [prəˈpɛl] *vt* **-pelled; -pelling :** impulsar, propulsar, impeler

propellant *or* **propellent** [prəˈpɛlənt] *n* **:** propulsor *m*

propeller [prəˈpɛlər] *n* **:** hélice *f*

propensity [prəˈpɛntsət̬i] *n, pl* **-ties :** propensión *f,* tendencia *f,* inclinación *f*

proper [ˈprɑpər] *adj* **1** RIGHT, SUITABLE **:** apropiado, adecuado **2 :** propio, mismo <the city proper : la propia ciudad> **3** CORRECT **:** correcto **4** GENTEEL **:** fino, refinado, cortés **5** OWN, SPECIAL **:** propio <proper name : nombre propio> — **properly** *adv*

property [ˈprɑpərt̬i] *n, pl* **-ties 1** CHARACTERISTIC **:** característica *f,* propiedad *f* **2** POSSESSIONS **:** propiedad *f* **3** BUILDING **:** inmueble *m* **4** LAND, LOT **:** terreno *m,* lote *m,* parcela *f* **5** PROP **:** accesorio *m* (en teatro)

prophecy [ˈprɑfəsi] *n, pl* **-cies :** profecía *f,* vaticinio *m*

prophesy [ˈprɑfəˌsaɪ] *v* **-sied; -sying** *vt* **1** FORETELL **:** profetizar (como profeta) **2** PREDICT **:** profetizar, predecir, vaticinar — *vi* **:** hacer profecías

prophet [ˈprɑfət] *n* **:** profeta *m,* profetisa *f*

prophetic [prəˈfɛt̬ɪk] *or* **prophetical** [-t̬ɪkəl] *adj* **:** profético — **prophetically** [-t̬ɪkli] *adv*

propitiate [proˈpɪʃiˌeɪt] *vt* **-ated; -ating :** propiciar

propitious [prəˈpɪʃəs] *adj* **:** propicio

proponent [prəˈpoːnənt] *n* **:** defensor *m,* -sora *f;* partidario *m,* -ria *f*

proportion[1] [prəˈporʃən] *vt* **:** proporcionar <well-proportioned : de buenas proporciones>

proportion[2] *n* **1** RATIO **:** proporción *f* **2** SYMMETRY **:** proporción *f,* simetría *f* <out of proportion : desproporcionado> **3** SHARE **:** parte *f* **4 proportions** *npl* SIZE **:** dimensiones *fpl*

proportional [prəˈporʃənəl] *adj* **:** proporcional — **proportionally** *adv*

proportionate [prəˈporʃənət] *adj* **:** proporcional — **proportionately** *adv*

proposal [prəˈpoːzəl] *n* **1** PROPOSITION **:** propuesta *f,* proposición *f* <marriage

proposal : propuesta de matrimonio> 2 PLAN : proyecto *m,* propuesta *f*

propose [prə'po:z] *v* **-posed; -posing** *vi* : proponer matrimonio — *vt* **1** INTEND : pensar, proponerse **2** SUGGEST : proponer

proposition [ˌprɑpə'zɪʃən] *n* **1** PROPOSAL : proposición *f,* propuesta *f* **2** STATEMENT : proposición *f*

propound [prə'paʊnd] *vt* : proponer, exponer

proprietary [prə'praɪəˌtɛri] *adj* : propietario, patentado

proprietor [prə'praɪət̬ər] *n* : propietario *m,* -ria *f*

propriety [prə'praɪət̬i] *n, pl* **-eties 1** DECORUM : decencia *f,* decoro *m* **2 proprieties** *npl* CONVENTIONS : convenciones *fpl,* cánones *mpl* sociales

propulsion [prə'pʌlʃən] *n* : propulsión *f*

prosaic [pro'zeɪɪk] *adj* : prosaico

proscribe [pro'skraɪb] *vt* **-scribed; -scribing** : proscribir

prose ['pro:z] *n* : prosa *f*

prosecute ['prɑsɪˌkju:t] *vt* **-cuted; -cuting 1** CARRY OUT : llevar a cabo **2** : procesar, enjuiciar <prosecuted for fraud : procesado por fraude>

prosecution [ˌprɑsɪ'kju:ʃən] *n* **1** : procesamiento *m* <the prosecution of forgers : el procesamiento de falsificadores> **2** PROSECUTORS : acusación *f* <witness for the prosecution : testigo de cargo>

prosecutor ['prɑsɪˌkju:t̬ər] *n* : acusador *m,* -dora *f;* fiscal *mf*

prospect[1] ['prɑˌspɛkt] *vi* : prospectar (el terreno) <to prospect for gold : buscar oro>

prospect[2] *n* **1** VISTA : vista *f,* panorama *m* **2** POSSIBILITY : posibilidad *f* **3** OUTLOOK : perspectiva *f* **4** : posible cliente *m,* -ta *f* <a salesman looking for prospects : un vendedor buscando nuevos clientes>

prospective [prə'spɛktɪv, 'prɑˌspɛk-] *adj* **1** EXPECTANT : futuro <prospective mother : futura madre> **2** POTENTIAL : potencial, posible <prospective employee : posible empleado>

prospector ['prɑˌspɛktər, prɑ'spɛk-] *n* : prospector *m,* -tora *f;* explorador *m,* -dora *f*

prospectus [prə'spɛktəs] *n* : prospecto *m*

prosper ['prɑspər] *vi* : prosperar

prosperity [prɑ'spɛrət̬i] *n* : prosperidad *f*

prosperous ['prɑspərəs] *adj* : próspero

prostate ['prɑˌsteɪt] *n* : próstata *f*

prosthesis [prɑs'θi:sɪs, 'prɑsθə-] *n, pl* **-theses** [-ˌsi:z] : prótesis *f*

prostitute[1] ['prɑstəˌtu:t, -ˌtju:t] *vt* **-tuted; -tuting 1** : prostituir **2 to prostitute oneself** : prostituirse

prostitute[2] *n* : prostituto *m,* -ta *f*

prostitution [ˌprɑstə'tu:ʃən, -'tju:-] *n* : prostitución *f*

prostrate[1] ['prɑˌstreɪt] *vt* **-trated; -trating 1** : postrar **2 to prostrate oneself** : postrarse

prostrate[2] *adj* : postrado

prostration [prɑ'streɪʃən] *n* : postración *f*

protagonist [pro'tægənɪst] *n* : protagonista *mf*

protect [prə'tɛkt] *vt* : proteger

protection [prə'tɛkʃən] *n* : protección *f*

protective [prə'tɛktɪv] *adj* : protector

protector [prə'tɛktər] *n* **1** : protector *m,* -tora *f* (persona) **2** GUARD : protector *m* (aparato)

protectorate [prə'tɛktərət] *n* : protectorado *m*

protégé ['pro:t̬əˌʒeɪ] *n* : protegido *m,* -da *f*

protein ['pro:ˌti:n] *n* : proteína *f*

protest[1] [pro'tɛst] *vt* **1** ASSERT : afirmar, declarar **2** : protestar <they protested the decision : protestaron (por) la decisión> — *vi* **to protest against** : protestar contra

protest[2] ['pro:ˌtɛst] *n* **1** DEMONSTRATION : manifestación *f* (de protesta) <a public protest : una manifestación pública> **2** COMPLAINT : queja *f,* protesta *f*

Protestant ['prɑt̬əstənt] *n* : protestante *mf*

Protestantism ['prɑt̬əstənˌtɪzəm] *n* : protestantismo *m*

protocol ['pro:t̬əˌkɔl] *n* : protocolo *m*

proton ['proˌtɑn] *n* : protón *m*

protoplasm ['pro:t̬əˌplæzəm] *n* : protoplasma *m*

prototype ['pro:t̬əˌtaɪp] *n* : prototipo *m*

protozoan [ˌpro:t̬ə'zo:ən] *n* : protozoario *m,* protozoo *m*

protract [pro'trækt] *vt* : prolongar

protractor [pro'træktər] *n* : transportador *m* (instrumento)

protrude [pro'tru:d] *vi* **-truded; -truding** : salir, sobresalir

protrusion [pro'tru:ʒən] *n* : protuberancia *f,* saliente *m*

protuberance [pro'tu:bərənts, -'tju:-] *n* : protuberancia *f*

proud ['praʊd] *adj* **1** HAUGHTY : altanero, orgulloso, arrogante **2** : orgulloso <she was proud of her work : estaba orgullosa de su trabajo> <too proud to beg : demasiado orgulloso para rogar> **3** GLORIOUS : glorioso — **proudly** *adv*

prove ['pru:v] *v* **proved; proved** *or* **proven** ['pru:vən]; **proving** *vt* **1** TEST : probar **2** DEMONSTRATE : probar, demostrar — *vi* : resultar <it proved effective : resultó efectivo>

Provençal [ˌpro:vɑn'sɑl, ˌprɑvən-] *n* **1** : provenzal *mf* **2** : provenzal *m* (idioma) — **Provençal** *adj*

proverb ['prɑ,vərb] *n* : proverbio *m*, refrán *m*

proverbial [prə'vərbiəl] *adj* : proverbial

provide [prə'vaɪd] *v* **-vided; -viding** *vt* **1** STIPULATE : estipular **2 to provide with** : proveer de, proporcionar — *vi* **1** : proveer <the Lord will provide : el Señor proveerá> **2 to provide for** SUPPORT : mantener **3 to provide for** ANTICIPATE : hacer previsiones para, prever

provided [prə'vaɪdəd] *or* **provided that** *conj* : con tal (de) que, siempre que

providence ['prɑvədənts] *n* **1** PRUDENCE : previsión *f*, prudencia *f* **2** *or* **Providence** : providencia *f* <divine providence : la Divina Providencia> **3 Providence** GOD : Providencia *f*

provident ['prɑvədənt] *adj* **1** PRUDENT : previsor, prudente **2** FRUGAL : frugal, ahorrativo

providential [,prɑvə'dɛntʃəl] *adj* : providencial

providing that → **provided**

province ['prɑvɪnts] *n* **1** : provincia *f* (de un país) <to live in the provinces : vivir en las provincias> **2** FIELD, SPHERE : campo *m*, competencia *f* <it's not in my province : no es de mi competencia>

provincial [prə'vɪntʃəl] *adj* **1** : provincial <provincial government : gobierno provincial> **2** : provinciano, pueblerino <a provincial mentality : una mentalidad provinciana>

provision[1] [prə'vɪʒən] *vt* : aprovisionar, abastecer

provision[2] *n* **1** PROVIDING : provisión *f*, suministro *m* **2** STIPULATION : condición *f*, salvedad *f*, estipulación *f* **3 provisions** *npl* : despensa *f*, víveres *mpl*, provisiones *fpl*

provisional [prə'vɪʒənəl] *adj* : provisional, provisorio — **provisionally** *adv*

proviso [prə'vaɪ,zo:] *n*, *pl* **-sos** *or* **-soes** : condición *f*, salvedad *f*, estipulación *f*

provocation [,prɑvə'keɪʃən] *n* : provocación *f*

provocative [prə'vɑkət̬ɪv] *adj* : provocador, provocativo <a provocative article : un artículo que hace pensar>

provoke [prə'vo:k] *vt* **-voked; -voking** : provocar

prow ['praʊ] *n* : proa *f*

prowess ['praʊəs] *n* **1** VALOR : valor *m*, valentía *f* **2** SKILL : habilidad *f*, destreza *f*

prowl ['praʊl] *vi* : merodear, rondar — *vt* : rondar por

prowler ['praʊlər] *n* : merodeador *m*, -dora *f*

proximity [prɑk'sɪmət̬i] *n* : proximidad *f*

proxy ['prɑksi] *n*, *pl* **proxies 1** : poder *m* (de actuar en nombre de alguien) <by proxy : por poder> **2** AGENT : apoderado *m*, -da *f*; representante *mf*

prude ['pru:d] *n* : mojigato *m*, -ta *f*; gazmoño *m*, -ña *f*

prudence ['pru:dənts] *n* **1** SHREWDNESS : prudencia *f*, sagacidad *f* **2** CAUTION : prudencia *f*, cautela *f* **3** THRIFTINESS : frugalidad *f*

prudent ['pru:dənt] *adj* **1** SHREWD : prudente, sagaz **2** CAUTIOUS, FARSIGHTED : prudente, previsor, precavido **3** THRIFTY : frugal, ahorrativo — **prudently** *adv*

prudery ['pru:dəri] *n*, *pl* **-eries** : mojigatería *f*, gazmoñería *f*

prudish ['pru:dɪʃ] *adj* : mojigato, gazmoño

prune[1] ['pru:n] *vt* **pruned; pruning** : podar (arbustos, etc.), acortar (un texto), recortar (gastos, etc.)

prune[2] *n* : ciruela *f* pasa

prurient ['prʊriənt] *adj* : lascivo

pry ['praɪ] *v* **pried; prying** *vi* : curiosear, huronear <to pry into other people's business : meterse uno en lo que no le importa> — *vt or* **to pry open** : abrir (con una palanca), apalancar

psalm ['sɑm, 'sɑlm] *n* : salmo *m*

pseudonym ['su:də,nɪm] *n* : seudónimo *m*

psoriasis [sə'raɪəsɪs] *n* : soriasis *f*, psoriasis *f*

psyche ['saɪki] *n* : psique *f*, psiquis *f*

psychiatric [,saɪki'ætrɪk] *adj* : psiquiátrico, siquiátrico

psychiatrist [sə'kaɪətrɪst, saɪ-] *n* : psiquiatra *mf*, siquiatra *mf*

psychiatry [sə'kaɪətri, saɪ-] *n* : psiquiatría *f*, siquiatría *f*

psychic[1] ['saɪkɪk] *adj* **1** : psíquico, síquico (en psicología) **2** CLAIRVOYANT : clarividente

psychic[2] *n* : vidente *mf*, clarividente *mf*

psychoanalysis [,saɪkoə'næləsɪs] *n*, *pl* **-yses** : psicoanálisis *m*, sicoanálisis *m*

psychoanalyst [,saɪko'ænəlɪst] *n* : psicoanalista *mf*, sicoanalista *mf*

psychoanalytic [,saɪko,ænəl'ɪt̬ɪk] *adj* : psicoanalítico, sicoanalítico

psychoanalyze [,saɪko'ænəl,aɪz] *vt* **-lyzed; -lyzing** : psicoanalizar, sicoanalizar

psychological [,saɪkə'lɑdʒɪkəl] *adj* : psicológico, sicológico — **psychologically** *adv*

psychologist [saɪ'kɑlədʒɪst] *n* : psicólogo *m*, -ga *f*; sicólogo *m*, -ga *f*

psychology [saɪ'kɑlədʒi] *n*, *pl* **-gies** : psicología *f*, sicología *f*

psychopath ['saɪkə,pæθ] *n* : psicópata *mf*, sicópata *mf*

psychopathic [,saɪkə'pæθɪk] *adj* : psicopático, sicopático

psychosis [saɪ'ko:sɪs] *n*, *pl* **-choses** [-'ko:,si:z] : psicosis *f*, sicosis *f*

psychosomatic [,saɪkəsə'mæt̬ɪk] *adj* : psicosomático, sicosomático

psychotherapist [,saɪko'θɛrəpɪst] *n* : psicoterapeuta *mf*, sicoterapeuta *mf*

psychotherapy [ˌsaɪkoˈθɛrəpi] *n, pl* **-pies** : psicoterapia *f,* sicoterapia *f*

psychotic[1] [saɪˈkɑt̬ɪk] *adj* : psicótico, sicótico

psychotic[2] *n* : psicótico *m,* -ca *f;* sicótico *m,* -ca *f*

puberty [ˈpjuːbərt̬i] *n* : pubertad *f*

pubic [ˈpjuːbɪk] *adj* : pubiano, púbico

public[1] [ˈpʌblɪk] *adj* : público — **publicly** *adv*

public[2] *n* : público *m*

publication [ˌpʌbləˈkeɪʃən] *n* : publicación *f*

publicist [ˈpʌbləsɪst] *n* : publicista *mf*

publicity [pəˈblɪsət̬i] *n* : publicidad *f*

publicize [ˈpʌbləˌsaɪz] *vt* **-cized; -cizing** : publicitar

public school *n* : escuela *f* pública

publish [ˈpʌblɪʃ] *vt* : publicar

publisher [ˈpʌblɪʃər] *n* : casa *f* editorial (compañía); editor *m,* -tora *f* (persona)

pucker[1] [ˈpʌkər] *vt* : fruncir, arrugar — *vi* : arrugarse

pucker[2] *n* : arruga *f,* frunce *m,* fruncido *m*

pudding [ˈpʊdɪŋ] *n* : budín *m,* pudín *m*

puddle [ˈpʌdəl] *n* : charco *m*

pudgy [ˈpʌdʒi] *adj* **pudgier; -est** : regordete *fam,* rechoncho *fam,* gordinflón *fam*

puerile [ˈpjʊrəl] *adj* : pueril

Puerto Rican[1] [ˌpwɛrt̬əˈriːkən, ˌport̬ə-] *adj* : puertorriqueño

Puerto Rican[2] *n* : puertorriqueño *m,* -ña *f*

puff[1] [ˈpʌf] *vi* **1** BLOW : soplar **2** PANT : resoplar, jadear **3 to puff up** SWELL : hincharse — *vt* **1** BLOW : soplar <to puff smoke : echar humo> **2** INFLATE : inflar, hinchar <to puff out one's cheeks : inflar las mejillas>

puff[2] *n* **1** GUST : soplo *m,* ráfaga *f,* bocanada *f* (de humo) **2** DRAW : chupada *f* (a un cigarrillo) **3** SWELLING : hinchazón *f* **4 cream puff** : pastelito *m* de crema **5 powder puff** : borla *f*

puffy [ˈpʌfi] *adj* **puffier; -est 1** SWOLLEN : hinchado, inflado **2** SPONGY : esponjoso, suave

pug [ˈpʌg] *n* **1** : doguillo *m* (perro) **2** *or* **pug nose** : nariz *f* achatada

pugnacious [ˌpʌgˈneɪʃəs] *adj* : pugnaz, agresivo

puke [ˈpjuːk] *vi* **puked; puking** : vomitar, devolver

pull[1] [ˈpʊl, ˈpʌl] *vt* **1** DRAW, TUG : tirar de, jalar **2** EXTRACT : sacar, extraer <to pull teeth : sacar muelas> <to pull a gun on : amenazar a (alguien) con pistola> **3** TEAR : desgarrarse (un músculo, etc.) **4 to pull down** : bajar, echar abajo, derribar (un edificio) **5 to pull in** ATTRACT : atraer (una muchedumbre, etc.) <to pull in votes : conseguir votos> **6 to pull off** REMOVE : sacar, quitar **7 to pull oneself together** : calmarse, tranquilizarse **8 to pull up** RAISE : levantar, subir — *vi* **1** DRAW, TUG : tirar, jalar **2** (*indicating movement in a specific direction*) <they pulled in front of us : se nos metieron delante> <to pull to a stop : pararse> **3 to pull through** RECOVER : recobrarse, reponerse **4 to pull together** COOPERATE : trabajar juntos, cooperar

pull[2] *n* **1** TUG : tirón *m,* jalón *m* <he gave it a pull : le dio un tirón> **2** ATTRACTION : atracción *f,* fuerza *f* <the pull of gravity : la fuerza de la gravedad> **3** INFLUENCE : influencia *f* **4** HANDLE : tirador *m* (de un cajón, etc.) **5 bell pull** : cuerda *f*

pullet [ˈpʊlət] *n* : polla *f,* gallina *f* (joven)

pulley [ˈpʊli] *n, pl* **-leys** : polea *f*

pullover [ˈpʊlˌoːvər] *n* : suéter *m*

pulmonary [ˈpʊlməˌnɛri, ˈpʌl-] *adj* : pulmonar

pulp [ˈpʌlp] *n* **1** : pulpa *f* (de una fruta, etc.) **2** MASH : papilla *f,* pasta *f* <wood pulp : pasta de papel, pulpa de papel> <to beat to a pulp : hacer papilla (a alguien)> **3** : pulpa *f* (de los dientes)

pulpit [ˈpʊlˌpɪt] *n* : púlpito *m*

pulsate [ˈpʌlˌseɪt] *vi* **-sated; -sating 1** BEAT : latir, palpitar **2** VIBRATE : vibrar

pulsation [ˌpʌlˈseɪʃən] *n* : pulsación *f*

pulse [ˈpʌls] *n* : pulso *m*

pulverize [ˈpʌlvəˌraɪz] *vt* **-ized; -izing** : pulverizar

puma [ˈpuːmə, ˈpjuː-] *n* : puma *m;* león *m,* leona *f* (in various countries)

pumice [ˈpʌməs] *n* : piedra *f* pómez

pummel [ˈpʌməl] *vt* **-meled; -meling** : aporrear, apalear

pump[1] [ˈpʌmp] *vt* **1** : bombear <to pump water : bombear agua> <to pump (up) a tire : inflar una llanta> **2** : mover (una manivela, un pedal, etc.) de arriba abajo <to pump someone's hand : darle un fuerte apretón de manos (a alguien)> **3 to pump out** : sacar, vaciar (con una bomba)

pump[2] *n* **1** : bomba *f* <water pump : bomba de agua> **2** SHOE : zapato *m* de tacón

pumpernickel [ˈpʌmpərˌnɪkəl] *n* : pan *m* negro de centeno

pumpkin [ˈpʌmpkɪn, ˈpʌŋkən] *n* : calabaza *f,* zapallo *m Arg, Chile, Peru, Uru*

pun[1] [ˈpʌn] *vi* **punned; punning** : hacer juegos de palabras

pun[2] *n* : juego *m* de palabras, albur *m Mex*

punch[1] [ˈpʌntʃ] *vt* **1** HIT : darle un puñetazo (a alguien), golpear <she punched him in the nose : le dio un puñetazo en la nariz> **2** PERFORATE : perforar (papel, etc.), picar (un boleto)

punch[2] *n* **1** : perforadora *f* <paper punch : perforadora de papel> **2** BLOW : golpe *m,* puñetazo *m* **3** : ponche *m* <fruit punch : ponche de frutas>

punctilious [pəŋk'tɪliəs] *adj* **:** puntilloso
punctual ['pʌŋktʃʊəl] *adj* **:** puntual
punctuality [ˌpʌŋktʃʊ'æləṭi] *n* **:** puntualidad *f*
punctually ['pʌŋktʃʊəli] *adv* **:** puntualmente, a tiempo
punctuate ['pʌŋktʃʊˌeɪt] *vt* **-ated; -ating :** puntuar
punctuation [ˌpʌŋktʃʊ'eɪʃən] *n* **:** puntuación *f*
puncture[1] ['pʌŋktʃər] *vt* **-tured; -turing :** pinchar, punzar, perforar, ponchar *Mex*
puncture[2] *n* **:** pinchazo *m,* ponchadura *f Mex*
pundit ['pʌndɪt] *n* **:** experto *m,* -ta *f*
pungency ['pʌndʒən*t*si] *n* **:** acritud *f,* acrimonia *f*
pungent ['pʌndʒənt] *adj* **:** acre
punish ['pʌnɪʃ] *vt* **:** castigar
punishable ['pʌnɪʃəbəl] *adj* **:** punible
punishment ['pʌnɪʃmənt] *n* **:** castigo *m*
punitive ['pjuːnəṭɪv] *adj* **:** punitivo
punt[1] ['pʌnt] *vt* **:** impulsar (un barco) con una pértiga — *vi* **:** despejar (en deportes)
punt[2] *n* **1 :** batea *f* (barco) **2 :** patada *f* de despeje (en deportes)
puny ['pjuːni] *adj* **-nier; -est :** enclenque, endeble
pup ['pʌp] *n* **:** cachorro *m,* -rra *f* (de un perro); cría *f* (de otros animales)
pupa ['pjuːpə] *n, pl* **-pae** [-pi, -ˌpaɪ] *or* **-pas :** crisálida *f,* pupa *f*
pupil ['pjuːpəl] *n* **1 :** alumno *m,* -na *f* (de colegio) **2 :** pupila *f* (del ojo)
puppet ['pʌpət] *n* **:** títere *m,* marioneta *f*
puppy ['pʌpi] *n, pl* **-pies :** cachorro *m,* -rra *f*
purchase[1] ['pərtʃəs] *vt* **-chased; -chasing :** comprar
purchase[2] *n* **1** PURCHASING **:** compra *f,* adquisición *f* **2 :** compra *f* <last-minute purchases : compras de última hora> **3** GRIP **:** agarre *m,* asidero *m* <she got a firm purchase on the wheel : se agarró bien del volante>
purchase order *n* **:** orden *f* de compra
pure ['pjʊr] *adj* **purer; purest :** puro
puree[1] [pjʊ'reɪ, -'riː] *vt* **-reed; -reeing :** hacer un puré con
puree[2] *n* **:** puré *m*
purely ['pjʊrli] *adv* **1** WHOLLY **:** puramente, completamente <purely by chance : por pura casualidad> **2** SIMPLY **:** sencillamente, meramente
purgative ['pərgəṭɪv] *n* **:** purgante *m*
purgatory ['pərgəˌtori] *n, pl* **-ries :** purgatorio *m*
purge[1] ['pərdʒ] *vt* **purged; purging :** purgar
purge[2] *n* **:** purga *f*
purification [ˌpjʊrəfə'keɪʃən] *n* **:** purificación *f*
purify ['pjʊrəˌfaɪ] *vt* **-fied; -fying :** purificar
puritan ['pjʊrətən] *n* **:** puritano *m,* -na *f*
puritanical [ˌpjuːrə'tænɪkəl] *adj* **:** puritano
purity ['pjʊrəṭi] *n* **:** pureza *f*
purl[1] ['pərl] *v* **:** tejer al revés, tejer del revés
purl[2] *n* **:** punto *m* del revés
purloin [pər'lɔɪn, 'pərˌlɔɪn] *vt* **:** hurtar, robar
purple ['pərpəl] *n* **:** morado *m,* color *m* púrpura
purport [pər'port] *vt* **:** pretender <to purport to be : pretender ser>
purpose ['pərpəs] *n* **1** INTENTION **:** propósito *m,* intención *f* <on purpose : a propósito, adrede> **2** FUNCTION **:** función *f* **3** RESOLUTION **:** resolución *f,* determinación *f*
purposeful ['pərpəsfəl] *adj* **:** determinado, decidido, resuelto
purposefully ['pərpəsfəli] *adv* **:** decididamente, resueltamente
purposely ['pərpəsli] *adv* **:** intencionadamente, a propósito, adrede
purr[1] ['pər] *vi* **:** ronronear
purr[2] *n* **:** ronroneo *m*
purse[1] ['pərs] *vt* **pursed; pursing :** fruncir <to purse one's lips : fruncir la boca>
purse[2] *n* **1** HANDBAG **:** cartera *f,* bolso *m,* bolsa *f Mex* <a change purse : un monedero> **2** FUNDS **:** fondos *mpl* **3** PRIZE **:** premio *m*
pursue [pər'suː] *vt* **-sued; -suing 1** CHASE **:** perseguir **2** SEEK **:** buscar, tratar de encontrar <to pursue pleasure : buscar el placer> **3** FOLLOW **:** seguir <the road pursues a northerly course : el camino sigue hacia el norte> **4 :** dedicarse a <to pursue a hobby : dedicarse a un pasatiempo>
pursuer [pər'suːər] *n* **:** perseguidor *m,* -dora *f*
pursuit [pər'suːt] *n* **1** CHASE **:** persecución *f* **2** SEARCH **:** búsqueda *f,* busca *f* **3** ACTIVITY **:** actividad *f,* pasatiempo *m*
purveyor [pər'veɪər] *n* **:** proveedor *m,* -dora *f*
pus ['pʌs] *n* **:** pus *m*
push[1] ['pʊʃ] *vt* **1** SHOVE **:** empujar **2** PRESS **:** apretar, pulsar <push that button : aprieta ese botón> **3** PRESSURE, URGE **:** presionar **4 to push around** BULLY **:** intimidar, mangonear — *vi* **1** SHOVE **:** empujar **2** INSIST **:** insistir, presionar **3 to push off** LEAVE **:** marcharse, irse, largarse *fam* **4 to push on** PROCEED **:** seguir
push[2] *n* **1** SHOVE **:** empujón *m* **2** DRIVE **:** empuje *m,* energía *f,* dinamismo *m* **3** EFFORT **:** esfuerzo *m*
push-button ['pʊʃ'bʌṭən] *adj* **:** de botones
pushcart ['pʊʃˌkɑrt] *n* **:** carretilla *f* de mano
pushy ['pʊʃi] *adj* **pushier; -est :** mandón, prepotente

pussy [ˈpʊsi] *n, pl* **pussies :** gatito *m,* -ta *f;* minino *m,* -na *f*
pussy willow *n* **:** sauce *m* blanco
pustule [ˈpʌs,tʃuːl] *n* **:** pústula *f*
put [ˈpʊt] *v* **put; putting** *vt* **1** PLACE **:** poner, colocar <put it on the table : ponlo en la mesa> **2** INSERT **:** meter **3** (*indicating causation of a state or feeling*) **:** poner <it put her in a good mood : la puso de buen humor> <to put into effect : poner en práctica> **4** IMPOSE **:** imponer <they put a tax on it : lo gravaron con un impuesto> **5** SUBJECT **:** someter, poner <to put to the test : poner a prueba> <to put to death : ejecutar> **6** EXPRESS **:** expresar, decir <he put it simply : lo dijo sencillamente> **7** APPLY **:** aplicar <to put one's mind to something : proponerse hacer algo> 8 SET **:** poner <I put him to work : lo puse a trabajar> **9** ATTACH **:** dar <to put a high value on : dar gran valor a> **10** PRESENT **:** presentar, exponer <to put a question to someone : hacer una pregunta a alguien> — *vi* **1 to put to sea :** hacerse a la mar **2 to put up with :** aguantar, soportar
put away *vt* **1** KEEP **:** guardar **2** *or* **to put aside :** dejar a un lado
put by *vt* SAVE **:** ahorrar
put down *vt* **1** SUPPRESS **:** aplastar, suprimir **2** ATTRIBUTE **:** atribuir <she put it down to luck : lo atribuyó a la suerte>
put in *vi* **:** presentarse <I've put in for the position : me presenté para el puesto> — *vt* DEVOTE **:** dedicar (unas horas, etc.)
put off *vt* DEFER **:** aplazar, posponer
put on *vt* **1** ASSUME **:** afectar, adoptar **2** PRODUCE **:** presentar (una obra de teatro, etc.) **3** WEAR **:** ponerse
put out *vt* INCONVENIENCE **:** importunar, incomodar
putrefy [ˈpjuːtrə,faɪ] *v* **-fied; -fying** *vt* **:** pudrir — *vi* **:** pudrirse
putrid [ˈpjuːtrɪd] *adj* **:** putrefacto, pútrido
putter [ˈpʌt̬ər] *vi or* **to putter around :** entretenerse
putty[1] [ˈpʌt̬i] *vt* **-tied; -tying :** poner masilla en
putty[2] *n, pl* **-ties :** masilla *f*
put up *vt* **1** LODGE **:** alojar **2** CONTRIBUTE **:** contribuir, pagar
puzzle[1] [ˈpʌzəl] *vt* **-zled; -zling 1** CONFUSE **:** confundir, dejar perplejo **2 to puzzle out :** dar vueltas a, tratar de resolver
puzzle[2] *n* **1 :** rompecabezas *m* <a crossword puzzle : un crucigrama> **2** MYSTERY **:** misterio *m,* enigma *m*
puzzlement [ˈpʌzəlmənt] *n* **:** desconcierto *m,* perplejidad *f*
pygmy[1] [ˈpɪgmi] *adj* **:** enano, pigmeo
pygmy[2] *n, pl* **-mies 1** DWARF **:** enano *m,* -na *f* **2 Pygmy :** pigmeo *m,* -mea *f*
pylon [ˈpaɪ,lɑn, -lən] *n* **1 :** torre *f* de conducta eléctrica **2 :** pilón *m* (de un puente)
pyramid [ˈpɪrə,mɪd] *n* **:** pirámide *f*
pyre [ˈpaɪr] *n* **:** pira *f*
pyromania [,paɪroˈmeɪniə] *n* **:** piromanía *f*
pyromaniac [,paɪroˈmeɪni,æk] *n* **:** pirómano *m,* -na *f*
pyrotechnics [,paɪrəˈtɛknɪks] *npl* **1** FIREWORKS **:** fuegos *mpl* artificiales **2** DISPLAY, SHOW **:** espectáculo *m,* muestra *f* de virtuosismo <computer pyrotechnics : efectos especiales hechos por computadora>
python [ˈpaɪ,θɑn, -θən] *n* **:** pitón *f,* serpiente *f* pitón

Q

q [ˈkjuː] *n, pl* **q's** *or* **qs** [ˈkjuːz] **:** decimoséptima letra del alfabeto inglés
quack[1] [ˈkwæk] *vi* **:** graznar
quack[2] *n* **1 :** graznido *m* (de pato) **2** CHARLATAN **:** curandero *m,* -ra *f;* matasanos *m fam*
quadrangle [ˈkwɑ,dræŋgəl] *n* **1** COURTYARD **:** patio *m* interior **2** → **quadrilateral**
quadrant [ˈkwɑdrənt] *n* **:** cuadrante *m*
quadrilateral [,kwɑdrəˈlæt̬ərəl] *n* **:** cuadrilátero *m*
quadruped [ˈkwɑdrə,pɛd] *n* **:** cuadrúpedo *m*
quadruple [kwɑˈdruːpəl, -ˈdrʌ-; ˈkwɑdrə-] *v* **-pled; -pling** *vt* **:** cuadruplicar — *vi* **:** cuadruplicarse
quadruplet [kwɑˈdruːplət, -ˈdrʌ-; ˈkwɑdrə-] *-n* **:** cuatrillizo *m,* -za *f*
quagmire [ˈkwæg,maɪr, ˈkwɑg-] *n* **:** cenagal *m,* lodazal *m*
quail[1] [ˈkweɪl] *vi* **:** encogerse, acobardarse
quail[2] *n, pl* **quail** *or* **quails :** codorniz *f*
quaint [ˈkweɪnt] *adj* **1** ODD **:** extraño, curioso **2** PICTURESQUE **:** pintoresco — **quaintly** *adv*
quaintness [ˈkweɪntnəs] *n* **:** rareza *f,* lo curioso
quake[1] [ˈkweɪk] *vi* **quaked; quaking :** temblar
quake[2] *n* **:** temblor *m,* terremoto *m*
qualification [,kwɑləfəˈkeɪʃən] *n* **1** LIMITATION, RESERVATION **:** reserva *f,* limitación *f* <without qualification : sin reservas> **2** REQUIREMENT **:** requisito *m* **3 qualifications** *npl* ABILITY **:** aptitud *f,* capacidad *f*
qualified [ˈkwɑlə,faɪd] *adj* **:** competente, capacitado
qualify [ˈkwɑlə,faɪ] *v* **-fied; -fying** *vt* **1 :** matizar <to qualify a statement

: matizar una declaración> **2** MODIFY : calificar (en gramática) **3** : habilitar <the certificate qualified her to teach : el certificado la habilitó para enseñar> — *vi* **1** : obtener el título, recibirse <to qualify as an engineer : recibirse de ingeniero> **2** : clasificarse (en deportes)

quality [ˈkwɑlət̬i] *n, pl* **-ties** **1** NATURE : carácter *m* **2** ATTRIBUTE : cualidad *f* **3** GRADE : calidad *f* <of good quality : de buena calidad>

qualm [ˈkwɑm, ˈkwɑlm, ˈkwɔm] *n* **1** MISGIVING : duda *f,* aprensión *f* **2** RESERVATION, SCRUPLE : escrúpulo *m,* reparo *m*

quandary [ˈkwɑndri] *n, pl* **-ries** : dilema *m*

quantity [ˈkwɑntət̬i] *n, pl* **-ties** : cantidad *f*

quantum theory [ˈkwɑntəm] *n* : teoría *f* cuántica

quarantine¹ [ˈkwɔrənˌtiːn] *vt* **-tined; -tining** : poner en cuarentena

quarantine² *n* : cuarentena *f*

quarrel¹ [ˈkwɔrəl] *vi* **-reled** *or* **-relled; -reling** *or* **-relling** : pelearse, reñir, discutir

quarrel² *n* : pelea *f,* riña *f,* disputa *f*

quarrelsome [ˈkwɔrəlsəm] *adj* : pendenciero, discutidor

quarry¹ [ˈkwɔri] *vt* **quarried; quarrying** **1** EXTRACT : extraer, sacar <to quarry marble : extraer mármol> **2** EXCAVATE : excavar <to quarry a hill : excavar un cerro>

quarry² *n, pl* **quarries** **1** PREY : presa *f* **2** *or* **stone quarry** : cantera *f*

quart [ˈkwɔrt] *n* : cuarto *m* de galón

quarter¹ [ˈkwɔrt̬ər] *vt* **1** : dividir en cuatro partes **2** LODGE : alojar, acuartelar (tropas)

quarter² *n* **1** : cuarto *m,* cuarta parte *f* <a foot and a quarter : un pie y cuarto> <a quarter after three : las tres y cuarto> **2** : moneda *f* de 25 centavos, cuarto *m* de dólar **3** DISTRICT : barrio *m* <business quarter : barrio comercial> **4** PLACE : parte *f* <from all quarters : de todas partes> <at close quarters : de muy cerca> **5** MERCY : clemencia *f,* cuartel *m* <to give no quarter : no dar cuartel> **6 quarters** *npl* LODGING : alojamiento *m,* cuartel *m* (militar)

quarterly¹ [ˈkwɔrt̬ərli] *adv* : cada tres meses, trimestralmente

quarterly² *adj* : trimestral

quarterly³ *n, pl* **-lies** : publicación *f* trimestral

quartermaster [ˈkwɔrt̬ərˌmæstər] *n* : intendente *mf*

quartet [kwɔrˈtɛt] *n* : cuarteto *m*

quartz [ˈkwɔrts] *n* : cuarzo *m*

quash [ˈkwɑʃ, ˈkwɔʃ] *vt* **1** ANNUL : anular **2** QUELL : sofocar, aplastar

quaver¹ [ˈkweɪvər] *vi* **1** SHAKE : temblar <her voice was quavering : su voz temblaba> **2** TRILL : trinar

quaver² *n* : temblor *m* (de la voz)

quay [ˈkiː, ˈkeɪ, ˈkweɪ] *n* : muelle *m*

queasiness [ˈkwiːzinəs] *n* : mareo *m,* náusea *f*

queasy [ˈkwiːzi] *adj* **-sier; -est** : mareado

queen [ˈkwiːn] *n* : reina *f*

queenly [ˈkwiːnli] *adj* **-lier; -est** : de reina, regio

queer [ˈkwɪr] *adj* : extraño, raro, curioso — **queerly** *adv*

quell [ˈkwɛl] *vt* : aplastar, sofocar

quench [ˈkwɛntʃ] *vt* **1** EXTINGUISH : apagar, sofocar **2** SATISFY : saciar, satisfacer (la sed)

querulous [ˈkwɛrələs, ˈkwɛrjələs, ˈkwɪr-] *adj* : quejumbroso, quejoso — **querulously** *adv*

query¹ [ˈkwɪri, ˈkwɛr-] *vt* **-ried; -rying** **1** ASK : preguntar, interrogar <we queried the professor : preguntamos al profesor> **2** QUESTION : cuestionar, poner en duda <to query a matter : cuestionar un asunto>

query² *n, pl* **-ries** **1** QUESTION : pregunta *f* **2** DOUBT : duda *f*

quest¹ [ˈkwɛst] *v* : buscar

quest² *n* : búsqueda *f*

question¹ [ˈkwɛstʃən] *vt* **1** ASK : preguntar **2** DOUBT : poner en duda, cuestionar **3** INTERROGATE : interrogar — *vi* INQUIRE : inquirir, preguntar

question² *n* **1** QUERY : pregunta *f* **2** ISSUE : asunto *m,* problema *f,* cuestión *f* **3** POSSIBILITY : posibilidad *f* <it's out of the question : es indiscutible> **4** DOUBT : duda *f* <to call into question : poner en duda>

questionable [ˈkwɛstʃənəbəl] *adj* : dudoso, discutible, cuestionable <questionable results : resultados discutibles> <questionable motives : motivos sospechosos>

questioner [ˈkwɛstʃənər] *n* : interrogador *m,* -dora *f*

question mark *n* : signo *m* de interrogación

questionnaire [ˌkwɛstʃəˈnær] *n* : cuestionario *m*

queue¹ [ˈkjuː] *vi* **queued; queuing** *or* **queueing** : hacer cola

queue² *n* **1** PIGTAIL : coleta *f,* trenza *f* **2** LINE : cola *f,* fila *f*

quibble¹ [ˈkwɪbəl] *vi* **-bled; -bling** : quejarse por nimiedades, andar con sutilezas

quibble² *n* : objeción *f* de poca monta, queja *f* insignificante

quick¹ [ˈkwɪk] *adv* : rápidamente

quick² *adj* **1** RAPID : rápido **2** ALERT, CLEVER : listo, vivo, agudo **3 a quick temper** : un genio vivo

quick³ *n* **1** FLESH : carne *f* viva **2 to cut someone to the quick** : herir a alguien en lo más vivo

quicken [ˈkwɪkən] *vt* **1** REVIVE : resucitar **2** AROUSE : estimular, despertar **3** HASTEN : acelerar <she quickened her pace : aceleró el paso>

quickly [ˈkwɪkli] *adv* : rápidamente, rápido, de prisa
quickness [ˈkwɪknəs] *n* : rapidez *f*
quicksand [ˈkwɪkˌsænd] *n* : arena *f* movediza
quicksilver [ˈkwɪkˌsɪlvər] *n* : mercurio *m,* azogue *m*
quick–tempered [ˈkwɪkˈtɛmpərd] *adj* : irascible, de genio vivo
quick–witted [ˈkwɪkˈwɪt̬əd] *adj* : agudo
quiet[1] *v* [ˈkwaɪət] *vt* **1** SILENCE : hacer callar, acallar **2** CALM : calmar, tranquilizar — *vi* **to quiet down** : calmarse, tranquilizarse
quiet[2] *adv* : silenciosamente <a quiet-running engine : un motor silencioso>
quiet[3] *adj* **1** CALM : tranquilo, calmoso **2** MILD : sosegado, suave <a quiet disposition : un temperamento sosegado> **3** SILENT : silencioso **4** UNOBTRUSIVE : discreto **5** SECLUDED : aislado <a quiet nook : un rincón aislado> — **quietly** *adv*
quiet[4] *n* **1** CALM : calma *f,* tranquilidad *f* **2** SILENCE : silencio *m*
quietness [ˈkwaɪətnəs] *n* : suavidad *f,* tranquilidad *f,* quietud *f*
quietude [ˈkwaɪəˌtuːd, -ˌtjuːd] *n* : quietud *f,* reposo *m*
quill [ˈkwɪl] *n* **1** SPINE : púa *f* (de un puerco espín) **2** : pluma *f* (para escribir)
quilt[1] [ˈkwɪlt] *vt* : acolchar
quilt[2] *n* : colcha *f,* edredón *m*
quince [ˈkwɪnts] *n* : membrillo *m*
quinine [ˈkwaɪˌnaɪn] *n* : quinina *f*
quintessence [kwɪnˈtɛsənts] *n* : quintaesencia *f*
quintet [kwɪnˈtɛt] *n* : quinteto *m*
quintuple [kwɪnˈtuːpəl, -ˈtjuː-, -ˈtʌ-; ˈkwɪntə-] *adj* : quíntuplo
quintuplet [kwɪnˈtʌplət, -ˈtuː-, -ˈtjuː-; ˈkwɪntə-] *n* : quintillizo *m,* -za *f*
quip[1] [ˈkwɪp] *vi* **quipped; quipping** : bromear
quip[2] *n* : ocurrencia *f,* salida *f*
quirk [ˈkwərk] *n* : peculiaridad *f,* rareza *f* <a quirk of fate : un capricho del destino>
quirky [ˈkwərki] *adj* **-kier; -est** : peculiar, raro
quit [ˈkwɪt] *v* **quit; quitting** *vt* : dejar, abandonar <to quit smoking : dejar de fumar> — *vi* **1** STOP : parar **2** RESIGN : dimitir, renunciar
quite [ˈkwaɪt] *adv* **1** COMPLETELY : completamente, totalmente **2** RATHER : bastante <quite near : bastante cerca>
quits [ˈkwɪts] *adj* **to call it quits** : quedar en paz
quitter [ˈkwɪt̬ər] *n* : derrotista *mf*
quiver[1] [ˈkwɪvər] *vi* : temblar, estremecerse, vibrar
quiver[2] *n* **1** : carcaj *m,* aljaba *f* (para flechas) **2** TREMBLING : temblor *m,* estremecimiento *m*
quixotic [kwɪkˈsɑt̬ɪk] *adj* : quijotesco
quiz[1] [ˈkwɪz] *vt* **quizzed; quizzing** : interrogar, hacer una prueba a (en el colegio)
quiz[2] *n, pl* **quizzes** : examen *m* corto, prueba *f*
quizzical [ˈkwɪzɪkəl] *adj* **1** TEASING : burlón **2** CURIOUS : curioso, interrogativo
quorum [ˈkworəm] *n* : quórum *m*
quota [ˈkwoːt̬ə] *n* : cuota *f,* cupo *m*
quotable [ˈkwoːt̬əbəl] *adj* : citable
quotation [kwoˈteɪʃən] *n* **1** CITATION : cita *f* **2** ESTIMATE : presupuesto *m,* estimación *f* **3** PRICE : cotización *f*
quotation marks *npl* : comillas *fpl*
quote[1] [ˈkwoːt] *vt* **quoted; quoting 1** CITE : citar **2** VALUE : cotizar (en finanzas)
quote[2] *n* **1** → **quotation 2 quotes** *npl* → **quotation marks**
quotient [ˈkwoːʃənt] *n* : cociente *m*

R

r [ˈɑr] *n, pl* **r's** *or* **rs** [ˈɑrz] : decimoctava letra del alfabeto inglés
rabbi [ˈræˌbaɪ] *n* : rabino *m,* -na *f*
rabbit [ˈræbət] *n, pl* **-bit** *or* **-bits** : conejo *m,* -ja *f*
rabble [ˈræbəl] *n* **1** MASSES : populacho *m* **2** RIFFRAFF : chusma *f,* gentuza *f*
rabid [ˈræbɪd] *adj* **1** : rabioso, afectado con la rabia **2** FURIOUS : furioso **3** FANATIC : fanático
rabies [ˈreɪbiːz] *ns & pl* : rabia *f*
raccoon [ræˈkuːn] *n, pl* **-coon** *or* **-coons** : mapache *m*
race[1] [ˈreɪs] *vi* **raced; racing 1** : correr, competir (en una carrera) **2** RUSH : ir a toda prisa, ir corriendo
race[2] *n* **1** CURRENT : corriente *f* (de agua) **2** : carrera *f* <dog race : carrera de perros> <the presidential race : la carrera presidential> **3** : raza *f* <the black race : la raza negra> <the human race : el género humano>
racecourse [ˈreɪsˌkors] *n* : pista *f* (de carreras)
racehorse [ˈreɪsˌhors] *n* : caballo *m* de carreras
racer [ˈreɪsər] *n* : corredor *m,* -dora *f*
racetrack [ˈreɪsˌtræk] *n* : pista *f* (de carreras)
racial [ˈreɪʃəl] *adj* : racial — **racially** *adv*
racism [ˈreɪˌsɪzəm] *n* : racismo *m*
racist [ˈreɪsɪst] *n* : racista *mf*

rack[1] ['ræk] *vt* **1** : atormentar <racked with pain : atormentado por el dolor> **2 to rack one's brains** : devanarse los sesos

rack[2] *n* **1** SHELF, STAND : estante *m* <a luggage rack : un portaequipajes> <a coatrack : un perchero, una percha> **2** : potro *m* (instrumento de la tortura)

racket ['rækət] *n* **1** : raqueta *f* (en deportes) **2** DIN : estruendo *m,* bulla *f,* jaleo *m fam* **3** SWINDLE : estafa *f,* timo *m fam*

racketeer [ˌrækə'tɪr] *n* : estafador *m,* -dora *f*

raconteur [ˌræˌkɑn'tər] *n* : anecdotista *mf*

racy ['reɪsi] *adj* **racier; -est** : subido de tono, picante

radar ['reɪˌdɑr] *n* : radar *m*

radial ['reɪdiəl] *adj* : radial

radiance ['reɪdiən*t*s] *n* : resplandor *m*

radiant ['reɪdiənt] *adj* : radiante — **radiantly** *adv*

radiate ['reɪdiˌeɪt] *v* **-ated; -ating** *vt* : irradiar, emitir <to radiate heat : irradiar el calor> <to radiate happiness : rebosar de alegría> — *vi* **1** : irradiar **2** SPREAD : salir, extenderse <to radiate (out) from the center : salir del centro>

radiation [ˌreɪdi'eɪʃən] *n* : radiación *f*

radiator ['reɪdiˌeɪt̬ər] *n* : radiador *m*

radical[1] ['rædɪkəl] *adj* : radical — **radically** [-kli] *adv*

radical[2] *n* : radical *mf*

radii → **radius**

radio[1] ['reɪdiˌoː] *v* : llamar por radio, transmitir por radio

radio[2] *n, pl* **-dios** : radio *m* (aparato), radio *f* (emisora, radiodifusión)

radioactive ['reɪdio'æktɪv] *adj* : radiactivo, radioactivo

radioactivity [ˌreɪdioˌæk'tɪvət̬i] *n, pl* **-ties** : radiactividad *f,* radioactividad *f*

radiologist [ˌreɪdi'ɑlədʒɪst] *n* : radiólogo *m,* -ga *f*

radiology [ˌreɪdi'ɑlədʒi] *n* : radiología *f*

radish ['rædɪʃ] *n* : rábano *m*

radium ['reɪdiəm] *n* : radio *m*

radius ['reɪdiəs] *n, pl* **radii** [-diˌaɪ] : radio *m*

radon ['reɪˌdɑn] *n* : radón *m*

raffle[1] ['ræfəl] *vt* **-fled; -fling** : rifar, sortear

raffle[2] *n* : rifa *f,* sorteo *m*

raft ['ræft] *n* **1** : balsa *f* <rubber rafts : balsas de goma> **2** LOT, SLEW : montón *m* <a raft of documents : un montón de documentos>

rafter ['ræftər] *n* : par *m,* viga *f*

rag ['ræg] *n* **1** CLOTH : trapo *m* **2 rags** *npl* TATTERS : harapos *mpl,* andrapos *mpl*

ragamuffin ['rægəˌmʌfən] *n* : pilluelo *m,* -la *f*

rage[1] ['reɪdʒ] *vi* **raged; raging 1** : estar furioso, rabiar <to fly into a rage : enfurecerse> **2** : bramar, hacer estragos <the wind was raging : el viento bramaba> <flu raged through the school : la gripe hizo estragos por el colegio>

rage[2] *n* **1** ANGER : furia *f,* ira *f,* cólera *f* **2** FAD : moda *f,* furor *m*

ragged ['rægəd] *adj* **1** UNEVEN : irregular, desigual **2** TORN : hecho jirones **3** TATTERED : andrajoso, harapiento

ragout [ræ'guː] *n* : ragú *m,* estofado *m*

ragtime ['rægˌtaɪm] *n* : ragtime *m*

ragweed ['rægˌwiːd] *n* : ambrosía *f*

raid[1] ['reɪd] *vt* **1** : invadir, hacer una incursión en <raided by enemy troops : invadido por tropas enemigas> **2** : asaltar, atracar <the gang raided the warehouse : la pandilla asaltó el almacén> **3** : allanar, hacer una redada en <police raided the house : la policía allanó la vivienda>

raid[2] *n* **1** : invasión *f* (militar) **2** : asalto *m* (por delincuentes) **3** : redada *f,* allanamiento *m* (por la policía)

raider ['reɪdər] *n* **1** ATTACKER : asaltante *mf;* invasor *m,* -sora *f* **2 corporate raider** : tiburón *m*

rail[1] ['reɪl] *vi* **1 to rail against** REVILE : denostar contra **2 to rail at** SCOLD : regañar, reprender

rail[2] *n* **1** BAR : barra *f,* barrera *f* **2** HANDRAIL : pasamanos *m,* barandilla *f* **3** TRACK : riel *m* (para ferrocarriles) **4** RAILROAD : ferrocarril *m*

railing ['reɪlɪŋ] *n* **1** : baranda *f* (de un balcón, etc.) **2** RAILS : verja *f*

raillery ['reɪləri] *n, pl* **-leries** : bromas *fpl*

railroad ['reɪlˌroːd] *n* : ferrocarril *m*

railway ['reɪlˌweɪ] → **railroad**

raiment ['reɪmənt] *n* : vestiduras *fpl*

rain[1] ['reɪn] *vi* **1** : llover <it's raining : está lloviendo> **2 to rain down** SHOWER : llover <insults rained down on him : le llovieron los insultos>

rain[2] *n* : lluvia *f*

rainbow ['reɪnˌboː] *n* : arco *m* iris

raincoat ['reɪnˌkoːt] *n* : impermeable *m*

raindrop ['reɪnˌdrɑp] *n* : gota *f* de lluvia

rainfall ['reɪnˌfɔl] *n* : lluvia *f,* precipitación *f*

rainstorm ['reɪnˌstɔrm] *n* : temporal *m* (de lluvia)

rainwater ['reɪnˌwɔt̬ər] *n* : agua *f* de lluvia

rainy ['reɪni] *adj* **rainier; -est** : lluvioso

raise[1] ['reɪz] *vt* **raised; raising 1** LIFT : levantar, subir, alzar <to raise one's spirits : levantarle el ánimo a alguien> **2** ERECT : levantar, erigir **3** COLLECT : recaudar <to raise money : recaudar dinero> **4** REAR : criar <to raise one's children : criar uno a sus niños> **5** GROW : cultivar **6** INCREASE : aumentar, subir **7** PROMOTE : ascender **8** PROVOKE : provocar <it raised

a laugh : provocó una risa> **9** BRING UP : sacar (temas, objeciones, etc.)

raise[2] *n* : aumento *m*

raisin [ˈreɪzən] *n* : pasa *f*

raja *or* **rajah** [ˈrɑdʒə, -ˌdʒɑ, -ˌʒɑ] *n* : rajá *m*

rake[1] [ˈreɪk] *v* **raked; raking** *vt* **1** : rastrillar <to rake leaves : rastrillar las hojas> **2** SWEEP : barrer <raked with gunfire : barrido con metralla> — *vi* **to rake through** : revolver, hurgar en

rake[2] *n* **1** : rastrillo *m* **2** LIBERTINE : libertino *m*, -na *f;* calavera *m*

rakish [ˈreɪkɪʃ] *adj* **1** JAUNTY : desenvuelto, desenfadado **2** DISSOLUTE : libertino, disoluto

rally[1] [ˈræli] *v* **-lied; -lying** *vi* **1** MEET, UNITE : reunirse, congregarse **2** RECOVER : recuperarse — *vt* **1** ASSEMBLE : reunir (tropas, etc.) **2** RECOVER : recobrar (la fuerza, el ánimo, etc.)

rally[2] *n, pl* **-lies** : reunión *f,* mitin *m,* manifestación *f*

ram[1] [ˈræm] *v* **rammed; ramming** *vt* **1** DRIVE : hincar, clavar <he rammed it into the ground : lo hincó en la tierra> **2** SMASH : estrellar, embestir — *vi* COLLIDE : chocar (contra), estrellarse

ram[2] *n* **1** : carnero *m* (animal) **2 battering ram** : ariete *m*

RAM [ˈræm] *n* : RAM *f*

ramble[1] [ˈræmbəl] *vi* **-bled; -bling 1** WANDER : pasear, deambular **2 to ramble on** : divagar, perder el hilo **3** SPREAD : trepar (dícese de una planta)

ramble[2] *n* : paseo *m,* excursión *f*

rambler [ˈræmblər] *n* **1** WALKER : excursionista *mf* **2** ROSE : rosa *f* trepadora

rambunctious [ræmˈbʌŋkʃəs] *adj* UNRULY : alborotado

ramification [ˌræməfəˈkeɪʃən] *n* : ramificación *f*

ramify [ˈræməˌfaɪ] *vi* **-fied; -fying** : ramificarse

ramp [ˈræmp] *n* : rampa *f*

rampage[1] [ˈræmˌpeɪdʒ, ræmˈpeɪdʒ] *vi* **-paged; -paging** : andar arrasando todo, correr destrozando

rampage[2] [ˈræmˌpeɪdʒ] *n* : alboroto *m,* frenesí *m* (de violencia)

rampant [ˈræmpənt] *adj* : desenfrenado

rampart [ˈræmˌpɑrt] *n* : terraplén *m,* muralla *f*

ramrod [ˈræmˌrɑd] *n* : baqueta *f*

ramshackle [ˈræmˌʃækəl] *adj* : destartalado

ran → **run**

ranch [ˈræntʃ] *n* **1** : hacienda *f,* rancho *m,* finca *f* ganadera **2** FARM : granja *f* <fruit ranch : granja de frutas>

rancher [ˈræntʃər] *n* : estanciero *m,* -ra *f;* ranchero *m,* -ra *f*

rancid [ˈræntsɪd] *adj* : rancio

rancor [ˈræŋkər] *n* : rencor *m*

random [ˈrændəm] *adj* **1** : fortuito, aleatorio **2 at ~** : al azar — **randomly** *adv*

rang → **ring**

range[1] [ˈreɪndʒ] *v* **ranged; ranging** *vt* ARRANGE : alinear, ordenar, arreglar — *vi* **1** ROAM : deambular <to range through the town : deambular por el pueblo> **2** EXTEND : extenderse <the results range widely : los resultados se extienden mucho> **3** VARY : variar <discounts range from 20% to 40% : los descuentos varían entre 20% y 40%>

range[2] *n* **1** ROW : fila *f,* hilera *f* <a mountain range : una cordillera> **2** GRASSLAND : pradera *f,* pampa *f* **3** STOVE : cocina *f* **4** VARIETY : variedad *f,* gama *f* **5** SPHERE : ámbito *m,* esfera *f,* campo *m* **6** REACH : registro *m* (de la voz), alcance *m* (de un arma de fuego) **7 shooting range** : campo *m* de tiro

ranger [ˈreɪndʒər] *n or* **forest ranger** : guardabosque *mf*

rangy [ˈreɪndʒi] *adj* **rangier; -est** : alto y delgado

rank[1] [ˈræŋk] *vt* **1** RANGE : alinear, ordenar, poner en fila **2** CLASSIFY : clasificar — *vi* **1 to rank above** : ser superior a **2 to rank among** : encontrarse entre, figurar entre

rank[2] *adj* **1** LUXURIANT : lozano, exuberante (dícese de una planta) **2** SMELLY : fétido, maloliente **3** OUTRIGHT : completo, absoluto <a rank injustice : una injusticia manifiesta>

rank[3] *n* **1** LINE, ROW : fila *f* <to close ranks : cerrar filas> **2** GRADE, POSITION : grado *m,* rango *m* (militar) <to pull rank : abusar de su autoridad> **3** CLASS : categoría *f,* clase *f* **4 ranks** *npl* : soldados *mpl* rasos

rank and file *n* **1** RANKS : soldados *mpl* rasos **2** : bases *fpl* (de un partido, etc.)

rankle [ˈræŋkəl] *v* **-kled; -kling** *vi* : doler — *vt* : irritar, herir

ransack [ˈrænˌsæk] *vt* : revolver, desvalijar, registrar de arriba abajo

ransom[1] [ˈræntsəm] *vt* : rescatar, pagar un rescate por

ransom[2] *n* : rescate *m*

rant [ˈrænt] *vi or* **to rant and rave** : despotricar, desvariar

rap[1] [ˈræp] *v* **rapped; rapping** *vt* **1** KNOCK : golpetear, dar un golpe en **2** CRITICIZE : criticar — *vi* **1** CHAT : charlar, cotorrear *fam* **2** KNOCK : dar un golpe

rap[2] *n* **1** BLOW, KNOCK : golpe *m,* golpecito *m* **2** CHAT : charla *f* **3** *or* **rap music** : rap *m* **4 to take the rap** : pagar el pato *fam*

rapacious [rəˈpeɪʃəs] *adj* **1** GREEDY : avaricioso, codicioso **2** PREDATORY : rapaz, de rapiña **3** RAVENOUS : voraz

rape[1] [ˈreɪp] *vt* **raped; raping** : violar

rape[2] *n* **1** : colza *f* (planta) **2** : violación *f* (de una persona)

rapid [ˈræpɪd] *adj* : rápido — **rapidly** *adv*

rapidity [rəˈpɪdəṭi] *n* : rapidez *f*

rapids [ˈræpɪdz] *npl* : rápidos *mpl*

rapier [ˈreɪpiər] *n* : estoque *m*

rapist [ˈreɪpɪst] *n* : violador *m*, -dora *f*

rapport [ræˈpor] *n* : relación *f* armoniosa, entendimiento *m*

rapt [ˈræpt] *adj* : absorto, embelesado

rapture [ˈræptʃər] *n* : éxtasis *m*

rapturous [ˈræptʃərəs] *adj* : extasiado, embelesado

rare [ˈrær] *adj* **rarer; rarest 1** RAREFIED : enrarecido **2** FINE : excelente, excepcional <a rare talent : un talento excepcional> **3** UNCOMMON : raro, poco común **4** : poco cocido (dícese de la carne)

rarefy [ˈrærəˌfaɪ] *vt* **-fied; -fying** : rarificar, enrarecer

rarely [ˈrærli] *adv* SELDOM : pocas veces, rara vez

raring [ˈrærən, -ɪŋ] *adj* : lleno de entusiasmo, con muchas ganas

rarity [ˈrærəṭi] *n, pl* **-ties** : rareza *f*

rascal [ˈræskəl] *n* : pillo *m*, -lla *f*; pícaro *m*, -ra *f*

rash[1] [ˈræʃ] *adj* : imprudente, precipitado — **rashly** *adv*

rash[2] *n* : sarpullido *m*, erupción *f*

rashness [ˈræʃnəs] *n* : precipitación *f*, impetuosidad *f*

rasp[1] [ˈræsp] *vt* **1** SCRAPE : raspar, escofinar **2 to rasp out** : decir en voz áspera

rasp[2] *n* : escofina *f*

raspberry [ˈræzˌbɛri] *n, pl* **-ries** : frambuesa *f*

rat [ˈræt] *n* : rata *f*

ratchet [ˈrætʃət] *n* : trinquete *m*

rate[1] [ˈreɪt] *vt* **rated; rating 1** CONSIDER, REGARD : considerar, estimar **2** DESERVE : merecer

rate[2] *n* **1** PACE, SPEED : velocidad *f*, ritmo *m* <at this rate : a este paso> **2** : índice *m*, tasa *f* <birth rate : índice de natalidad> <interest rate : tasa de interés> **3** CHARGE, PRICE : precio *m*, tarifa *f*

rather [ˈræðər, ˈrʌ-, ˈrɑ-] *adv* **1** (*indicating preference*) <she would rather stay in the house : preferiría quedarse en casa> <I'd rather not : mejor que no> **2** (*indicating preciseness*) <my father, or rather my stepfather : mi padre, o mejor dicho mi padrastro> **3** INSTEAD : sino que, más que, al contrario <I'm not pleased; rather I'm disappointed : no estoy satisfecho, sino desilusionado> **4** SOMEWHAT : algo, un tanto <rather strange : un poco extraño> **5** QUITE : bastante <rather difficult : bastante difícil>

ratification [ˌræṭəfəˈkeɪʃən] *n* : ratificación *f*

ratify [ˈræṭəˌfaɪ] *vt* **-fied; -fying** : ratificar

rating [ˈreɪṭɪŋ] *n* **1** STANDING : clasificación *f*, posición *f* **2 ratings** *npl* : índice *m* de audiencia

ratio [ˈreɪʃio] *n, pl* **-tios** : proporción *f*, relación *f*

ration[1] [ˈræʃən, ˈreɪʃən] *vt* : racionar

ration[2] *n* **1** : ración *f* **2 rations** *npl* PROVISIONS : víveres *mpl*

rational [ˈræʃənəl] *adj* : racional, razonable, lógico — **rationally** *adv*

rationale [ˌræʃəˈnæl] *n* **1** EXPLANATION : explicación *f* **2** BASIS : base *f*, razones *fpl*

rationalization [ˌræʃənələˈzeɪʃən] *n* : racionalización *f*

rationalize [ˈræʃənəˌlaɪz] *vt* **-ized; -izing** : racionalizar

rattle[1] [ˈræṭəl] *v* **-tled; -tling** *vi* **1** CLATTER : traquetear, hacer ruido **2 to rattle on** CHATTER : parlotear *fam* — *vt* **1** : hacer sonar, agitar <the wind rattled the door : el viento sacudió la puerta> **2** DISCONCERT, WORRY : desconcertar, poner nervioso **3 to rattle off** : despachar, recitar, decir de corrido

rattle[2] *n* **1** CLATTER : traqueteo *m*, ruido *m* **2** *or* **baby's rattle** : sonajero *m* **3** : cascabel *m* (de una culebra)

rattler [ˈræṭələr] → **rattlesnake**

rattlesnake [ˈræṭəlˌsneɪk] *n* : serpiente *f* de cascabel

ratty [ˈræṭi] *adj* **rattier; -est** : raído, andrajoso

raucous [ˈrɔkəs] *adj* **1** HOARSE : ronco **2** BOISTEROUS : escandaloso, bullicioso — **raucously** *adv*

ravage[1] [ˈrævɪdʒ] *vt* **-aged; -aging** : devastar, arrasar, hacer estragos

ravage[2] *n* : destrozo *m*, destrucción *f* <the ravages of war : los estragos de la guerra>

rave [ˈreɪv] *vi* **raved; raving 1** : delirar, desvariar <to rave like a maniac : desvariar como un loco> **2 to rave about** : hablar con entusiasmo sobre, entusiasmarse por

ravel [ˈrævəl] *v* **-eled** *or* **-elled; -eling** *or* **-elling** *vt* UNRAVEL : desenredar, desenmarañar — *vi* FRAY : deshilacharse

raven [ˈreɪvən] *n* : cuervo *m*

ravenous [ˈrævənəs] *adj* : hambriento, voraz — **ravenously** *adv*

ravine [rəˈviːn] *n* : barranco *m*, quebrada *f*

ravish [ˈrævɪʃ] *vt* **1** PLUNDER : saquear **2** ENCHANT : embelesar, cautivar, encantar

raw [ˈrɔ] *adj* **rawer; rawest 1** UNCOOKED : crudo **2** UNTREATED : sin tratar, sin refinar, puro <raw data : datos en bruto> <raw materials : materias primas> **3** INEXPERIENCED : novato, inexperto **4** OPEN : abierto, en carne viva <a raw sore : una llaga abierta> **5** : frío y húmedo <a raw day : un día crudo> **6** UNFAIR : injusto <a raw deal : un trato injusto, una injusticia>

rawhide [ˈrɔˌhaɪd] *n* : cuero *m* sin curtir

ray [ˈreɪ] *n* **1** : rayo *m* (de la luz, etc.) <a ray of hope : un resquicio de esperanza> **2** : raya *f* (pez)

rayon [ˈreɪˌɑn] *n* : rayón *m*

raze [ˈreɪz] *vt* **razed; razing** : arrasar, demoler

razor [ˈreɪzər] *n* **1 straight razor** : navaja *f* (de afeitar) **2 safety razor** : maquinilla *f* de afeitar, rastrillo *m Mex*

reach[1] [ˈriːtʃ] *vt* **1** EXTEND : extender, alargar <to reach out one's hand : extender la mano> **2** : alcanzar <I couldn't reach the apple : no pude alcanzar la manzana> **3** : llegar a, llegar hasta <the shadow reached the wall : la sombra llegó hasta la pared> **4** CONTACT : contactar, ponerse en contacto con — *vi* **1** *or* **to reach out** : extender la mano **2** STRETCH : extenderse **3 to reach for** : tratar de agarrar

reach[2] *n* : alcance *m,* extensión *f*

react [riˈækt] *vi* : reaccionar

reaction [riˈækʃən] *n* : reacción *f*

reactionary[1] [riˈækʃəˌnɛri] *adj* : reaccionario

reactionary[2] *n, pl* **-ries** : reaccionario *m,* -ria *f*

reactor [riˈæktər] *n* : reactor *m* <nuclear reactor : reactor nuclear>

read[1] [ˈriːd] *v* **read** [ˈrɛd]; **reading** *vt* **1** : leer <to read a story : leer un cuento> **2** INTERPRET : interpretar <it can be read two ways : se puede interpretar de dos maneras> **3** : decir, poner <the sign read "No smoking" : el letrero decía "No Fumar"> **4** : marcar <the thermometer reads 70° : el termómetro marca 70°> — *vi* **1** : leer <he can read : sabe leer> **2** SAY : decir <the list reads as follows : la lista dice lo siguiente>

read[2] *n* **to be a good read** : ser una lectura amena

readable [ˈriːdəbəl] *adj* : legible — **readably** [-bli] *adv*

reader [ˈriːdər] *n* : lector *m,* -tora *f*

readily [ˈrɛdəli] *adv* **1** WILLINGLY : de buena gana, con gusto **2** EASILY : fácilmente, con facilidad

readiness [ˈrɛdinəs] *n* **1** WILLINGNESS : buena disposición *f* **2 to be in readiness** : estar preparado

reading [ˈriːdɪŋ] *n* : lectura *f*

readjust [ˌriːəˈdʒʌst] *vt* : reajustar — *vi* : volverse a adaptar

readjustment [ˌriːəˈdʒʌstmənt] *n* : reajuste *m*

ready[1] [ˈrɛdi] *vt* **readied; readying** : preparar

ready[2] *adj* **readier; -est 1** PREPARED : listo, preparado **2** WILLING : dispuesto **3** : a punto de <ready to cry : a punto de llorar> **4** AVAILABLE : disponible <ready cash : efectivo> **5** QUICK : vivo, agudo <a ready wit : un ingenio agudo>

ready–made [ˈrɛdiˈmeɪd] *adj* : preparado, confeccionado

reaffirm [ˌriːəˈfərm] *vt* : reafirmar

real[1] [ˈriːl] *adv* VERY : muy <we had a real good time : lo pasamos muy bien>

real[2] *adj* **1** : inmobilario <real property : bien inmueble, bien raíz> **2** GENUINE : auténtico, genuino **3** ACTUAL, TRUE : real, verdadero <a real friend : un verdadero amigo> **4 for real** SERIOUSLY : de veras, de verdad

real estate *n* : propiedad *f* inmobiliaria, bienes *mpl* raíces

realign [ˌriːəˈlaɪn] *vt* : realinear

realignment [ˌriːəˈlaɪnmənt] *n* : realineamiento *m*

realism [ˈriːəˌlɪzəm] *n* : realismo *m*

realist [ˈriːəlɪst] *n* : realista *mf*

realistic [ˌriːəˈlɪstɪk] *adj* : realista

realistically [ˌriːəˈlɪstɪkli] *adv* : de manera realista

reality [riˈæləṭi] *n, pl* **-ties** : realidad *f*

realization [ˌriːələˈzeɪʃən] *n* : realización *f*

realize [ˈriːəˌlaɪz] *vt* **-ized; -izing 1** ACCOMPLISH : realizar, llevar a cabo **2** GAIN : obtener, realizar, sacar <to realize a profit : realizar beneficios> **3** UNDERSTAND : darse cuenta de, saber

really [ˈrɪli, ˈriː-] *adv* **1** ACTUALLY : de verdad, en realidad **2** TRULY : verdaderamente, realmente **3** FRANKLY : francamente, en serio

realm [ˈrɛlm] *n* **1** KINGDOM : reino *m* **2** SPHERE : esfera *f,* campo *m*

ream[1] [ˈriːm] *vt* : escariar

ream[2] *n* **1** : resma *f* (de papel) **2 reams** *npl* LOADS : montones *mpl*

reap [ˈriːp] *v* : cosechar

reaper [ˈriːpər] *n* **1** : cosechador *m,* -dora *f* (persona) **2** : cosechadora *f* (máquina)

reappear [ˌriːəˈpɪr] *vi* : reaparecer

reappearance [ˌriːəˈpɪrənts] *n* : reaparición *f*

rear[1] [ˈrɪr] *vt* **1** LIFT, RAISE : levantar **2** BREED, BRING UP : criar — *vi or* **to rear up** : encabritarse

rear[2] *adj* : trasero, posterior, de atrás

rear[3] *n* **1** BACK : parte *f* de atrás <to bring up the rear : cerrar la marcha> **2** *or* **rear end** : trasero *m*

rear admiral *n* : contraalmirante *mf*

rearrange [ˌriːəˈreɪndʒ] *vt* **-ranged; -ranging** : colocar de otra manera, volver a arreglar, reorganizar

reason[1] [ˈriːzən] *vt* THINK : pensar — *vi* : razonar <I can't reason with her : no puedo razonar con ella>

reason[2] *n* **1** CAUSE, GROUND : razón *f,* motivo *m* <the reason for his trip : el motivo de su viaje> <for this reason : por esta razón, por lo cual> <the reason why : la razón por la cual, el porqué> **2** SENSE : razón *f* <to lose

one's reason : perder los sesos> <to listen to reason : avenirse a razones>

reasonable ['riːzənəbəl] *adj* **1** SENSIBLE : razonable **2** INEXPENSIVE : barato, económico

reasonably ['riːzənəbli] *adv* **1** SENSIBLY : razonablemente **2** FAIRLY : bastante

reasoning ['riːzənɪŋ] *n* : razonamiento *m,* raciocinio *m,* argumentos *mpl*

reassess [ˌriːə'sɛs] *vt* : revaluar, reconsiderar

reassurance [ˌriːə'ʃʊrən*t*s] *n* : consuelo *m,* palabras *fpl* alentadoras

reassure [ˌriːə'ʃʊr] *vt* **-sured; -suring** : tranquilizar

reawaken [ˌriːə'weɪkən] *vt* : volver a despertar, reavivar

rebate ['riːˌbeɪt] *n* : reembolso *m,* devolución *f*

rebel[1] [rɪ'bɛl] *vi* **-belled; -belling** : rebelarse, sublevarse

rebel[2] ['rɛbəl] *adj* : rebelde

rebel[3] ['rɛbəl] *n* : rebelde *mf*

rebellion [rɪ'bɛljən] *n* : rebelión *f*

rebellious [rɪ'bɛljəs] *adj* : rebelde

rebelliousness [rɪ'bɛljəsnəs] *n* : rebeldía *f*

rebirth [ˌriː'bərθ] *n* : renacimiento *m*

rebound[1] ['riːˌbaʊnd, ˌriː'baʊnd] *vi* : rebotar

rebound[2] ['riːˌbaʊnd] *n* : rebote *m*

rebuff[1] [ri'bʌf] *vt* : desairar, rechazar

rebuff[2] *n* : desaire *m,* rechazo *m*

rebuild [ˌriː'bɪld] *vt* **-built** [-'bɪlt]; **-building** : reconstruir

rebuke[1] [ri'bjuːk] *vt* **-buked; -buking** : reprender, regañar

rebuke[2] *n* : reprimenda *f,* reproche *m*

rebut [ri'bʌt] *vt* **-butted; -butting** : rebatir, refutar

rebuttal [ri'bʌtəl] *n* : refutación *f*

recalcitrant [ri'kælsətrənt] *adj* : recalcitrante

recall[1] [ri'kɔl] *vt* **1** : llamar, retirar <recalled to active duty : llamado al servicio activo> **2** REMEMBER : recordar, acordarse de **3** REVOKE : revocar

recall[2] [ri'kɔl, 'riːˌkɔl] *n* **1** : retirada *f* (de personas o mercancías) **2** MEMORY : memoria *f* <to have total recall : poder recordar todo>

recant [ri'kænt] *vt* : retractarse de — *vi* : retractarse, renegar

recapitulate [ˌriːkə'pɪtʃəˌleɪt] *v* **-lated; -lating** : resumir, recapitular

recapture [ˌriː'kæptʃər] *vt* **-tured; -turing 1** REGAIN : volver a tomar, reconquistar **2** RELIVE : revivir (la juventud, etc.)

recede [ri'siːd] *vi* **-ceded; -ceding 1** WITHDRAW : retirarse, retroceder **2** FADE : desvanecerse, alejarse **3** SLANT : inclinarse **4 to have a receding hairline** : tener entradas

receipt [ri'siːt] *n* **1** : recibo *m* **2 receipts** *npl* : ingresos *mpl*, entradas *fpl*

receivable [ri'siːvəbəl] *adj* **accounts receivable** : cuentas por cobrar

receive [ri'siːv] *vt* **-ceived; -ceiving 1** GET : recibir <to receive a letter : recibir una carta> <to receive a blow : recibir un golpe> **2** WELCOME : acoger, recibir <to receive guests : tener invitados> **3** : recibir, captar (señales de radio)

receiver [ri'siːvər] *n* **1** : receptor *m,* -tora *f* (en futbol americano) **2** : receptor *m* (de radio o televisión) **3 telephone receiver** : auricular *m*

recent ['riːsənt] *adj* : reciente — **recently** *adv*

receptacle [ri'sɛptɪkəl] *n* : receptáculo *m,* recipiente *m*

reception [ri'sɛpʃən] *n* : recepción *f*

receptionist [ri'sɛpʃənɪst] *n* : recepcionista *mf*

receptive [ri'sɛptɪv] *adj* : receptivo

receptivity [ˌriːˌsɛp'tɪvət̬i] *n* : receptividad *f*

recess[1] ['riːˌsɛs, rɪ'sɛs] *vt* **1** : poner en un hueco <recessed lighting : iluminación empotrada> **2** ADJOURN : suspender, levantar

recess[2] *n* **1** ALCOVE : hueco *m,* nicho *m* **2** BREAK : receso *m,* descanso *m,* recreo *m* (en el colegio)

recession [ri'sɛʃən] *n* : recesión *f,* depresión *f* económica

recessive [ri'sɛsɪv] *adj* : recesivo

recharge [ˌriː'tʃɑrdʒ] *vt* **-charged; -charging** : recargar

rechargeable [ˌriː'tʃɑrdʒəbəl] *adj* : recargable

recipe ['rɛsəˌpiː] *n* : receta *f*

recipient [ri'sɪpiənt] *n* : recipiente *mf*

reciprocal [ri'sɪprəkəl] *adj* : recíproco

reciprocate [ri'sɪprəˌkeɪt] *vi* **-cated; -cating** : reciprocar

reciprocity [ˌrɛsə'prɑsət̬i] *n, pl* **-ties** : reciprocidad *f*

recital [ri'saɪt̬əl] *n* **1** PERFORMANCE : recital *m* **2** ENUMERATION : relato *m*, enumeración *f*

recitation [ˌrɛsə'teɪʃən] *n* : recitación *f*

recite [ri'saɪt] *vt* **-cited; -citing 1** : recitar (un poema, etc.) **2** RECOUNT : narrar, relatar, enumerar

reckless ['rɛkləs] *adj* : imprudente, temerario — **recklessly** *adv*

recklessness ['rɛkləsnəs] *n* : imprudencia *f,* temeridad *f*

reckon ['rɛkən] *vt* **1** CALCULATE : calcular, contar **2** CONSIDER : considerar

reckoning ['rɛkənɪŋ] *n* **1** CALCULATION : cálculo *m* **2** SETTLEMENT : ajuste *m* de cuentas <day of reckoning : día del juicio final>

reclaim [ri'kleɪm] *vt* **1** : ganar, sanear <to reclaim marshy land : sanear las tierras pantanosas> **2** RECOVER : recobrar, reciclar <to reclaim old tires : reciclar llantas desechadas> **3** REGAIN : reclamar, recuperar <to reclaim one's rights : reclamar uno sus derechos>

recline [ri'klaɪn] *vi* **-clined; -clining 1** LEAN : reclinarse **2** REPOSE : recostarse

recluse ['rɛ,klu:s, ri'klu:s] *n* : solitario *m,* -ria *f*

recognition [,rɛkɪg'nɪʃən] *n* : reconocimiento *m*

recognizable ['rɛkəg,naɪzəbəl] *adj* : reconocible

recognize ['rɛkɪg,naɪz] *vt* **-nized; -nizing** : reconocer

recoil[1] [ri'kɔɪl] *vi* : retroceder, dar un culatazo

recoil[2] ['ri:,kɔɪl, ri'-] *n* : retroceso *m,* culatazo *m*

recollect [,rɛkə'lɛkt] *v* : recordar

recollection [,rɛkə'lɛkʃən] *n* : recuerdo *m*

recommend [,rɛkə'mɛnd] *vt* **1** : recomendar <she recommended the medicine : recomendó la medicina> **2** ADVISE, COUNSEL : aconsejar, recomendar

recommendation [,rɛkəmən'deɪʃən] *n* : recomendación *f*

recompense[1] ['rɛkəm,pɛnts] *vt* **-pensed; -pensing** : indemnizar, recompensar

recompense[2] *n* : indemnización *f,* compensación *f*

reconcile ['rɛkən,saɪl] *v* **-ciled; -ciling** *vt* **1** : reconciliar (personas), conciliar (ideas, etc.) **2 to reconcile oneself to** : resignarse a — *vi* MAKE UP : reconciliarse, hacer las paces

reconciliation [,rɛkən,sɪli'eɪʃən] *n* : reconciliación *f* (con personas), conciliación *f* (con ideas, etc.)

recondite ['rɛkən,daɪt, ri'kɑn-] *adj* : recóndito, abstruso

recondition [,ri:kən'dɪʃən] *vt* : reacondicionar

reconnaissance [ri'kɑnəzənts, -sənts] *n* : reconocimiento *m*

reconnoiter *or* **reconnoitre** [,ri:kə'nɔɪtər, ,rɛkə-] *v* **-tered** *or* **-tred; -tering** *or* **-tring** *vt* : reconocer — *vi* : hacer un reconocimiento

reconsider [,ri:kən'sɪdər] *vt* : reconsiderar, repensar

reconsideration [,ri:kən,sɪdə'reɪʃən] *n* : reconsideración *f*

reconstruct [,ri:kən'strʌkt] *vt* : reconstruir

record[1] [ri'kɔrd] *vt* **1** WRITE DOWN : anotar, apuntar **2** REGISTER : registrar, hacer constar **3** INDICATE : marcar (una temperatura, etc.) **4** TAPE : grabar

record[2] ['rɛkərd] *n* **1** DOCUMENT : registro *m,* documento *m* oficial **2** HISTORY : historial *m* <a good academic record : un buen historial académico> <criminal record : antecedentes penales> **3** : récord *m* <the world record : el récord mundial> **4** : disco *m* (de música, etc.) <to make a record : grabar un disco>

recorder [ri'kɔrdər] *n* **1** : flauta *f* dulce (instrumento de viento) **2 tape recorder** : grabadora *f*

recount[1] [ri'kaʊnt] *vt* **1** NARRATE : narrar, relatar **2** : volver a contar (votos, etc.)

recount[2] ['ri:,kaʊnt, ,ri'-] *n* : recuento *m*

recoup [ri'ku:p] *vt* : recuperar, recobrar

recourse ['ri:,kors, ri'-] *n* : recurso *m* <to have recourse to : recurrir a>

recover [ri'kʌvər] *vt* REGAIN : recobrar — *vi* RECUPERATE : recuperarse

recovery [ri'kʌvəri] *n, pl* **-eries** : recuperación *f*

re–create [,ri:kri'eɪt] *vt* **-ated; -ating** : recrear

recreation [,rɛkri'eɪʃən] *n* : recreo *m,* esparcimiento *m,* diversión *f*

recreational [,rɛkri'eɪʃənəl] *adj* : recreativo, de recreo

recrimination [ri,krɪmə'neɪʃən] *n* : recriminación *f*

recruit[1] [ri'kru:t] *vt* : reclutar

recruit[2] *n* : recluta *mf*

recruitment [ri'kru:tmənt] *n* : reclutamiento *m,* alistamiento *m*

rectal ['rɛktəl] *adj* : rectal

rectangle ['rɛk,tæŋgəl] *n* : rectángulo *m*

rectangular [rɛk'tæŋgjələr] *adj* : rectangular

rectify ['rɛktə,faɪ] *vt* **-fied; -fying** : rectificar

rectitude ['rɛktə,tu:d, -,tju:d] *n* : rectitud *f*

rector ['rɛktər] *n* : rector *m,* -tora *f*

rectory ['rɛktəri] *n, pl* **-ries** : rectoría *f*

rectum ['rɛktəm] *n, pl* **-tums** *or* **-ta** [-tə] : recto *m*

recuperate [ri'ku:pə,reɪt, -'kju:-] *v* **-ated; -ating** *vt* : recuperar — *vi* : recuperarse, restablecerse

recuperation [ri,ku:pə'reɪʃən, -,kju:-] *n* : recuperación *f*

recur [ri'kər] *vi* **-curred; -curring** : volver a ocurrir, volver a producirse, repetirse

recurrence [ri'kərənts] *n* : repetición *f,* reaparición *f*

recurrent [ri'kərənt] *adj* : recurrente, que se repite

recycle [ri'saɪkəl] *vt* **-cled; -cling** : reciclar

red[1] ['rɛd] *adj* **1** : rojo, colorado <to be red in the face : ponerse colorado> <to have red hair : ser pelirrojo> **2** COMMUNIST : rojo, comunista

red[2] *n* **1** : rojo *m,* colorado *m* **2 Red** COMMUNIST : comunista *mf*

red blood cell *n* : glóbulo *m* rojo

red–blooded ['rɛd'blʌdəd] *adj* : vigoroso

redcap ['rɛd,kæp] → **porter**

redden ['rɛdən] *vt* : enrojecer — *vi* BLUSH : enrojecerse, ruborizarse

reddish ['rɛdɪʃ] *adj* : rojizo

redecorate [,ri:'dɛkə,reɪt] *vt* **-rated; -rating** : renovar, pintar de nuevo

redeem [ri'di:m] *vt* **1** RESCUE, SAVE : rescatar, salvar **2** : desempeñar <she redeemed it from the pawnshop : lo desempeñó de la casa de empeños> **3** : redimir (en religión) **4** : canjear, vender <to redeem coupons : canjear cupones>
redeemer [ri'di:mər] *n* : redentor *m*, -tora *f*
redemption [ri'dɛmpʃən] *n* : redención *f*
redesign [ˌri:di'zaɪn] *vt* : rediseñar
red–handed ['rɛd'hændəd] *adj* : con las manos en la masa
redhead ['rɛdˌhɛd] *n* : pelirrojo *m*, -ja *f*
red–hot ['rɛd'hɑt] *adj* **1** : candente **2** ARDENT : ardiente, fervoroso
rediscover [ˌri:di'skʌvər] *vt* : redescubrir
redistribute [ˌri:di'strɪˌbju:t] *vt* **-uted; -uting** : redistribuir
red–letter ['rɛd'lɛt̬ər] *adj* **red–letter day** : día *m* memorable
redness ['rɛdnəs] *n* : rojez *f*
redo [ˌri:'du:] *vt* **-did** [-dɪd]; **-done** [-'dʌn]; **-doing 1** : hacer de nuevo **2** → **redecorate**
redolence ['rɛdələnts] *n* : fragancia *f*
redolent ['rɛdələnt] *adj* **1** FRAGRANT : fragante, oloroso **2** SUGGESTIVE : evocador
redouble [ri'dʌbəl] *vt* **-bled; -bling** : redoblar, intensificar (esfuerzos, etc.)
redoubtable [rɛ'daʊt̬əbəl] *adj* : temible
redress [ri'drɛs] *vt* : reparar, remediar, enmendar
red snapper *n* : pargo *m*, huachinango *m Mex*
red tape *n* : papeleo *m*
reduce [ri'du:s, -'dju:s] *v* **-duced; -ducing** *vt* **1** LESSEN : reducir, disminuir, rebajar (precios) **2** DEMOTE : bajar de categoría, degradar **3 to be reduced to** : verse rebajado a, verse forzado a **4 to reduce someone to tears** : hacer llorar a alguien — *vi* SLIM : adelgazar
reduction [ri'dʌkʃən] *n* : reducción *f*, rebaja *f*
redundant [ri'dʌndənt] *adj* : superfluo, redundante
redwood ['rɛdˌwʊd] *n* : secoya *f*
reed ['ri:d] *n* **1** : caña *f*, carrizo *m*, junco *m* **2** : lengüeta *f* (para instrumentos de viento)
reef ['ri:f] *n* : arrecife *m*, escollo *m*
reek[1] ['ri:k] *vi* : apestar
reek[2] *n* : hedor *m*
reel ['ri:l] *vt* **1 to reel in** : enrollar, sacar (un pez) del agua **2 to reel off** : recitar de un tirón — *vi* **1** SPIN, WHIRL : girar, dar vueltas **2** STAGGER : tambalearse
reel[2] *n* **1** : carrete *m* (de pescar etc.), rollo *m* (de fotos) **2** : baile *m* escocés **3** STAGGER : tambaleo *m*
reelect [ˌri:ɪ'lɛkt] *vt* : reelegir
reenact [ˌri:ɪ'nækt] *vt* : representar de nuevo, reconstruir
reenter [ˌri:'ɛntər] *vt* : volver a entrar
reestablish [ˌri:ɪ'stæblɪʃ] *vt* : restablecer
reevaluate [ˌri:ɪ'væljʊˌeɪt] *vt* **-ated; -ating** : revaluar
reevaluation [ˌri:ɪˌvæljʊ'eɪʃən] *n* : revaluación *f*
reexamine [ˌri:ɪg'zæmən, -ɛg-] *vt* **-ined; -ining** : volver a examinar, reexaminar
refer [ri'fər] *v* **-ferred; -ferring** *vt* DIRECT, SEND : remitir, enviar <to refer a patient to a specialist : enviar a un paciente a un especialista> — *vi* **to refer to** MENTION : referirse a, aludir a
referee[1] [ˌrɛfə'ri:] *v* **-eed; -eeing** : arbitrar
referee[2] *n* : árbitro *m*, -tra *f*; réferi *mf*
reference ['rɛfrənts, 'rɛfə-] *n* **1** ALLUSION : referencia *f*, alusión *f* <to make reference to : hacer referencia a> **2** CONSULTATION : consulta *f* <for future reference : para futuras consultas> **3** *or* **reference book** : libro *m* de consulta **4** TESTIMONIAL : informe *m*, referencia *f*, recomendación *f*
referendum [ˌrɛfə'rɛndəm] *n*, *pl* **-da** [-də] *or* **-dums** : referéndum *m*
refill[1] [ˌri:'fɪl] *vt* : rellenar
refill[2] ['ri:ˌfɪl] *n* : recambio *m*
refinance [ˌri:'faɪˌnænts] *vt* **-nanced; -nancing** : refinanciar
refine [ri'faɪn] *vt* **-fined; -fining 1** : refinar (azúcar, petróleo, etc.) **2** PERFECT : perfeccionar, pulir
refined [ri'faɪnd] *adj* **1** : refinado (dícese del azúcar, etc.) **2** CULTURED : culto, educado, refinado
refinement [ri'faɪnmənt] *n* : refinamiento *m*, fineza *f*, finura *f*
refinery [ri'faɪnəri] *n*, *pl* **-eries** : refinería *f*
reflect [ri'flɛkt] *vt* **1** : reflejar <to reflect light : reflejar la luz> <happiness is reflected in her face : la felicidad se refleja en su cara> **2 to reflect that** : pensar que, considerar que — *vi* **1 to reflect on** : reflexionar sobre **2 to reflect badly on** : desacreditar, perjudicar
reflection [ri'flɛkʃən] *n* **1** : reflexión *f*, reflejo *m* (de la luz, de imágenes, etc.) **2** THOUGHT : reflexión *f*, meditación *f*
reflective [ri'flɛktɪv] *adj* **1** THOUGHTFUL : reflexivo, pensativo **2** : reflectante (en física)
reflector [ri'flɛktər] *n* : reflector *m*
reflex ['ri:ˌflɛks] *n* : reflejo *m*
reflexive [ri'flɛksɪv] *adj* : reflexivo <a reflexive verb : un verbo reflexivo>
reform[1] [ri'fɔrm] *vt* : reformar — *vi* : reformarse
reform[2] *n* : reforma *f*
reformation [ˌrɛfər'meɪʃən] *n* : reforma *f* <the Reformation : la Reforma>

reformatory [ri'fɔrmə,tori] *n, pl* **-ries** : reformatorio *m*
reformer [ri'fɔrmər] *n* : reformador *m*, -dora *f*
refract [ri'frækt] *vt* : refractar — *vi* : refractarse
refraction [ri'frækʃən] *n* : refracción *f*
refractory [ri'fræktəri] *adj* OBSTINATE : refractario, obstinado
refrain[1] [ri'freɪn] *vi* **to refrain from** : abstenerse de
refrain[2] *n* : estribillo *m* (en música)
refresh [ri'frɛʃ] *vt* : refrescar <to refresh one's memory : refrescarle la memoria a uno>
refreshment [ri'frɛʃmənt] *n* **1** : refresco *m* **2 refreshments** *npl* : refrigerio *m*
refrigerate [ri'frɪdʒə,reɪt] *vt* **-ated; -ating** : refrigerar
refrigeration [ri,frɪdʒə'reɪʃən] *n* : refrigeración *f*
refrigerator [ri'frɪdʒə,reɪt̬ər] *n* : refrigerador *mf*, nevera *f*
refuel [ri:'fju:əl] *v* **-eled** *or* **-elled; -eling** *or* **-elling** *vi* : repostar — *vt* : llenar de combustible
refuge ['rɛ,fju:dʒ] *n* : refugio *m*
refugee [,rɛfjʊ'dʒi:] *n* : refugiado *m*, -da *f*
refund[1] [ri'fʌnd, 'ri:,fʌnd] *vt* : reembolsar, devolver
refund[2] ['ri:,fʌnd] *n* : reembolso *m*, devolución *f*
refundable [ri'fʌndəbəl] *adj* : reembolsable
refurbish [ri'fərbɪʃ] *vt* : renovar, restaurar
refusal [ri'fju:zəl] *n* : negativa *f*, rechazo *m*, denegación *f* (de una petición)
refuse[1] [ri'fju:z] *vt* **-fused; -fusing 1** REJECT : rechazar, rehusar **2** DENY : negar, rehusar, denegar <to refuse permission : negar el permiso> **3 to refuse to** : negarse a
refuse[2] ['rɛ,fju:s, -,fju:z] *n* : basura *f*, desechos *mpl*, desperdicios *m*
refutation [,rɛfjʊ'teɪʃən] *n* : refutación *f*
refute [ri'fju:t] *vt* **-futed; -futing 1** DENY : desmentir, negar **2** DISPROVE : refutar, rebatir
regain [ri:'geɪn] *vt* **1** RECOVER : recuperar, recobrar **2** REACH : alcanzar <to regain the shore : llegar a la tierra>
regal ['ri:gəl] *adj* : real, regio
regale [ri'geɪl] *vt* **-galed; -galing 1** ENTERTAIN : agasajar, entretener **2** AMUSE, DELIGHT : deleitar, divertir
regalia [ri'geɪljə] *npl* : ropaje *m*, vestiduras *fpl*, adornos *mpl*
regard[1] [ri'gɑrd] *vt* **1** OBSERVE : observar, mirar **2** HEED : tener en cuenta, hacer caso de **3** CONSIDER : considerar **4** RESPECT : respetar <highly regarded : muy estimado> **5 as regards** : en cuanto a, en lo que se refiere a
regard[2] *n* **1** CONSIDERATION : consideración *f* **2** ESTEEM : respeto *m*, estima *f* **3** PARTICULAR : aspecto *m*, sentido *m* <in this regard : en este sentido> **4 regards** *npl* : saludos *mpl*, recuerdos *mpl* **5 with regard to** : con relación a, con respecto a
regarding [ri'gɑrdɪŋ] *prep* : con respecto a, en cuanto a
regardless [ri'gɑrdləs] *adv* : a pesar de todo
regardless of *prep* : a pesar de, sin tener en cuenta <regardless of our mistakes : a pesar de nuestros errores> <regardless of age : sin tener en cuenta la edad>
regenerate [ri'dʒɛnə,reɪt] *v* **-ated; -ating** *vt* : regenerar — *vi* : regenerarse
regeneration [ri,dʒɛnə'reɪʃən] *n* : regeneración *f*
regent ['ri:dʒənt] *n* **1** RULER : regente *mf* **2** : miembro *m* de la junta directiva (de una universidad, etc.)
regime [reɪ'ʒi:m, rɪ-] *n* : régimen *m*
regimen ['rɛdʒəmən] *n* : régimen *m*
regiment[1] ['rɛdʒə,mɛnt] *vt* : reglamentar
regiment[2] ['rɛdʒəmənt] *n* : regimiento *m*
region ['ri:dʒən] *n* **1** : región *f* **2 in the region of** : alrededor de
regional ['ri:dʒənəl] *adj* : regional — **regionally** *adv*
register[1] ['rɛdʒəstər] *vt* **1** RECORD : registrar, inscribir **2** INDICATE : marcar (temperatura, medidas, etc.) **3** REVEAL : manifestar, acusar <to register surprise : acusar sorpresa> **4** : certificar (correo) — *vi* ENROLL : inscribirse, matricularse
register[2] *n* : registro *m*
registrar ['rɛdʒə,strɑr] *n* : registrador *m*, -dora *f* oficial
registration [,rɛdʒə'streɪʃən] *n* **1** REGISTERING : inscripción *f*, matriculación *f*, registro *m* **2** *or* **registration number** : matrícula *f*, número *m* de matrícula
registry ['rɛdʒəstri] *n, pl* **-tries** : registro *m*
regress [ri'grɛs] *vi* : retroceder
regression [ri'grɛʃən] *n* : retroceso *m*, regresión *f*
regressive [ri'grɛsɪv] *adj* : regresivo
regret[1] [ri'grɛt] *vt* **-gretted; -gretting** : arrepentirse de, lamentar <he regrets nothing : no se arrepiente de nada> <I regret to tell you : lamento decirle>
regret[2] *n* **1** REMORSE : arrepentimiento *m*, remordimientos *mpl* **2** SADNESS : pesar *m*, dolor *m* **3 regrets** *npl* : excusas *fpl* <to send one's regrets : excusarse>
regretful [ri'grɛtfəl] *adj* : arrepentido, pesaroso
regretfully [ri'grɛtfəli] *adv* : con pesar
regrettable [ri'grɛtəbəl] *adj* : lamentable — **regrettably** [-bli] *adv*

regular[1] [ˈrɛgjələr] *adj* **1** NORMAL : regular, normal, usual **2** STEADY : uniforme, regular <a regular pace : un paso regular> **3** CUSTOMARY, HABITUAL : habitual, de costumbre

regular[2] *n* : cliente *mf* habitual

regularity [ˌrɛgjəˈlærət̬i] *n, pl* **-ties** : regularidad *f*

regularly [ˈrɛgjələrli] *adv* : regularmente, con regularidad

regulate [ˈrɛgjəˌleɪt] *vt* **-lated; -lating** : regular

regulation [ˌrɛgjəˈleɪʃən] *n* **1** REGULATING : regulación *f* **2** RULE : regla *f,* reglamento *m,* norma *f* <safety regulations : reglas de seguridad>

regurgitate [riˈgərdʒəˌteɪt] *v* **-tated; -tating** : regurgitar, vomitar

rehabilitate [ˌriːhəˈbɪləˌteɪt, ˌriːə-] *vt* **-tated; -tating** : rehabilitar

rehabilitation [ˌriːhəˌbɪləˈteɪʃən, ˌriːə-] *n* : rehabilitación *f*

rehearsal [riˈhərsəl] *n* : ensayo *m*

rehearse [riˈhərs] *v* **-hearsed; -hearsing** : ensayar

reheat [ˌriːˈhiːt] *vt* : recalentar

reign[1] [ˈreɪn] *vi* **1** RULE : reinar **2** PREVAIL : reinar, predominar

reign[2] *n* : reinado *m*

reimburse [ˌriːəmˈbərs] *vt* **-bursed; -bursing** : reembolsar

reimbursement [ˌriːəmˈbərsmənt] *n* : reembolso *m*

rein[1] [ˈreɪn] *vt* : refrenar (un caballo)

rein[2] *n* **1** : rienda *f* <to give free rein to : dar rienda suelta a> **2** CHECK : control *m* <to keep a tight rein on : llevar un estricto control de>

reincarnation [ˌriːɪnˌkɑrˈneɪʃən] *n* : reencarnación *f*

reindeer [ˈreɪnˌdɪr] *n* : reno *m*

reinforce [ˌriːənˈfors] *vt* **-forced; -forcing** : reforzar

reinforcement [ˌriːənˈforsmənt] *n* : refuerzo *m*

reinstate [ˌriːənˈsteɪt] *vt* **-stated; -stating 1** : reintegrar, restituir (una persona) **2** RESTORE : restablecer (un servicio, etc.)

reinstatement [ˌriːənˈsteɪtmənt] *n* : reintegración *f,* restitución *f,* restablecimiento *m*

reiterate [riˈɪt̬əˌreɪt] *vt* **-ated; -ating** : reiterar, repetir

reiteration [riˌɪt̬əˈreɪʃən] *n* : reiteración *f,* repetición *f*

reject[1] [riˈdʒɛkt] *vt* : rechazar

reject[2] [ˈriːˌdʒɛkt] *n* : desecho *m* (cosa), persona *f* rechazada

rejection [riˈdʒɛkʃən] *n* : rechazo *m*

rejoice [riˈdʒɔɪs] *vi* **-joiced; -joicing** : alegrarse, regocijarse

rejoin *vt* [ˌriːˈdʒɔɪn] **1** : reincorporarse a, reintegrarse a <he rejoined the firm : se reincorporó a la firma> **2** [riˈ-] REPLY, RETORT : replicar

rejoinder [riˈdʒɔɪndər] *n* : réplica *f*

rejuvenate [riˈdʒuːvəˌneɪt] *vt* **-nated; -nating** : rejuvenecer

rejuvenation [riˌdʒuːvəˈneɪʃən] *n* : rejuvenecimiento *m*

rekindle [ˌriːˈkɪndəl] *vt* **-dled; -dling** : reavivar

relapse[1] [riˈlæps] *vi* **-lapsed; -lapsing** : recaer, volver a caer

relapse[2] [ˈriːˌlæps, riˈlæps] *n* : recaída *f*

relate [riˈleɪt] *v* **-lated; -lating** *vt* **1** TELL : relatar, contar **2** ASSOCIATE : relacionar, asociar <to relate crime to poverty : relacionar la delincuencia a la pobreza> — *vi* **1** CONNECT : conectar, estar relacionado (con) **2** INTERACT : relacionarse (con), llevarse bien (con) **3 to relate to** UNDERSTAND : identificarse con, simpatizar con

related [riˈleɪt̬əd] *adj* : emparentado <to be related to : ser pariente de>

relation [riˈleɪʃən] *n* **1** NARRATION : relato *m,* narración *f* **2** RELATIVE : pariente *mf,* familiar *mf* **3** RELATIONSHIP : relación *f* <in relation to : en relación con, con relación a> **4 relations** *npl* : relaciones *fpl* <public relations : relaciones públicas>

relationship [riˈleɪʃənˌʃɪp] *n* **1** CONNECTION : relación *f* **2** KINSHIP : parentesco *m*

relative[1] [ˈrɛlət̬ɪv] *adj* : relativo — **relatively** *adv*

relative[2] *n* : pariente *mf,* familiar *mf*

relativity [ˌrɛləˈtɪvət̬i] *n, pl* **-ties** : relatividad *f*

relax [riˈlæks] *vt* : relajar, aflojar — *vi* : relajarse

relaxation [ˌriːˌlækˈseɪʃən] *n* **1** RELAXING : relajación *f,* aflojamiento *m* **2** DIVERSION : esparcimiento *m,* distracción *f*

relay[1] [ˈriːˌleɪ, riˈleɪ] *vt* **-layed; -laying** : transmitir

relay[2] [ˈriːˌleɪ] *n* **1** : relevo *m* **2** *or* **relay race** : carrera de relevos

release[1] [riˈliːs] *vt* **-leased; -leasing 1** FREE : liberar, poner en libertad **2** LOOSEN : soltar, aflojar <to release the brake : soltar el freno> **3** RELINQUISH : renunciar a, ceder **4** ISSUE : publicar (un libro), estrenar (una película), sacar (un disco)

release[2] *n* **1** LIBERATION : liberación *f,* puesta *f* en libertad **2** RELINQUISHMENT : cesión *f* (de propiedad, etc.) **3** ISSUE : estreno *m* (de una película), puesta *f* en venta (de un disco), publicación *f* (de un libro) **4** ESCAPE : escape *m,* fuga *f* (de un gas)

relegate [ˈrɛləˌgeɪt] *vt* **-gated; -gating** : relegar

relent [riˈlɛnt] *vi* : ablandarse, ceder

relentless [riˈlɛntləs] *adj* : implacable, sin tregua

relentlessly [riˈlɛntləsli] *adv* : implacablemente

relevance [ˈrɛləvən*t*s] *n* : pertinencia *f,* relación *f*

relevant [ˈrɛləvənt] *adj* : pertinente — **relevantly** *adv*

reliability [riˌlaɪəˈbɪləti] *n, pl* **-ties 1** : fiabilidad *f,* seguridad *f* (de una cosa) **2** : formalidad *f,* seriedad *f* (de una persona)

reliable [riˈlaɪəbəl] *adj* : confiable, fiable, fidedigno, seguro

reliably [riˈlaɪəbli] *adv* : sin fallar <to be reliably informed : saber (algo) de fuentes fidedignas>

reliance [riˈlaɪənts] *n* **1** DEPENDENCE : dependencia *f* **2** CONFIDENCE : confianza *f*

reliant [riˈlaɪənt] *adj* : confiable, dependente

relic [ˈrɛlɪk] *n* **1** : reliquia *f* **2** VESTIGE : vestigio *m*

relief [riˈliːf] *n* **1** : alivio *m,* desahogo *m* <relief from pain : alivio del dolor> **2** AID, WELFARE : ayuda *f* (benéfica), asistencia *f* social **3** : relieve *m* (en la escultura) <relief map : mapa en relieve> **4** REPLACEMENT : relevo *m*

relieve [riˈliːv] *vt* **-lieved; -lieving 1** ALLEVIATE : aliviar, mitigar <to feel relieved : sentirse aliviado> **2** FREE : liberar, eximir <to relieve someone of responsibility for : eximir a alguien de la responsabilidad de> **3** REPLACE : relevar (a un centinela, etc.) **4** BREAK : romper <to relieve the monotony : romper la monotonía>

religion [riˈlɪdʒən] *n* : religión *f*

religious [riˈlɪdʒəs] *adj* : religioso — **religiously** *adv*

relinquish [riˈlɪŋkwɪʃ, -ˈlɪn-] *vt* **1** GIVE UP : renunciar a, abandonar **2** RELEASE : soltar

relish[1] [ˈrɛlɪʃ] *vt* : saborear (comida), disfrutar con (una idea, una perspectiva, etc.)

relish[2] *n* **1** ENJOYMENT : gusto *m,* deleite *m* **2** : salsa *f* (condimento)

relive [ˌriːˈlɪv] *vt* **-lived; -living** : revivir

relocate [ˌriːˈloːˌkeɪt, ˌriːloˈkeɪt] *v* **-cated; -cating** *vt* : reubicar, trasladar — *vi* : trasladarse

relocation [ˌriːloˈkeɪʃən] *n* : reubicación *f,* traslado *m*

reluctance [riˈlʌktənts] *n* : renuencia *f,* reticencia *f,* desgana *f*

reluctant [riˈlʌktənt] *adj* : renuente, reacio, reticente

reluctantly [riˈlʌktəntli] *adv* : a regañadientes

rely [riˈlaɪ] *vi* **-lied; -lying 1** DEPEND : depender (de), contar (con) **2** TRUST : confiar (en)

remain [riˈmeɪn] *vi* **1** : quedar <very little remains : queda muy poco> <the remaining 10 minutes : los 10 minutos que quedan> **2** STAY : quedarse, permanecer **3** CONTINUE : continuar, seguir <to remain the same : continuar siendo igual> **4 to remain to** : quedar por <to remain to be done : quedar por hacer> <it remains to be seen : está por ver>

remainder [riˈmeɪndər] *n* : resto *m,* remanente *m*

remains [riˈmeɪnz] *npl* : restos *mpl* <mortal remains : restos mortales>

remark[1] [riˈmɑrk] *vt* **1** NOTICE : observar **2** SAY : comentar, observar — *vi* **to remark on** : hacer observaciones sobre

remark[2] *n* : comentario *m,* observación *f*

remarkable [riˈmɑrkəbəl] *adj* : extraordinario, notable — **remarkably** [-bli] *adv*

rematch [ˈriːˌmætʃ] *n* : revancha *f*

remedial [riˈmiːdiəl] *adj* : correctivo <remedial classes : clases para alumnos atrasados>

remedy[1] [ˈrɛmədi] *vt* **-died; -dying** : remediar

remedy[2] *n, pl* **-dies** : remedio *m,* medicamento *m*

remember [riˈmɛmbər] *vt* **1** RECOLLECT : acordarse de, recordar **2** : no olvidar <remember my words : no olvides mis palabras> <to remember to : acordarse de> **3** : dar saludos, dar recuerdos <remember me to her : dale saludos de mi parte> **4** COMMEMORATE : recordar, conmemorar

remembrance [riˈmɛmbrənts] *n* **1** RECOLLECTION : recuerdo *m* <in remembrance of : en conmemoración de> **2** MEMENTO : recuerdo *m*

remind [riˈmaɪnd] *vt* : recordar <remind me to do it : recuérdame que lo haga> <she reminds me of Clara : me recuerda de Clara>

reminder [riˈmaɪndər] *n* : recuerdo *m*

reminisce [ˌrɛməˈnɪs] *vi* **-nisced; -niscing** : rememorar los viejos tiempos

reminiscence [ˌrɛməˈnɪsənts] *n* : recuerdo *m,* reminiscencia *f*

reminiscent [ˌrɛməˈnɪsənt] *adj* **1** NOSTALGIC : reminiscente, nostálgico **2** SUGGESTIVE : evocador, que recuerda — **reminiscently** *adv*

remiss [riˈmɪs] *adj* : negligente, descuidado, remiso

remission [riˈmɪʃən] *n* : remisión *f*

remit [riˈmɪt] *vt* **-mitted; -mitting 1** PARDON : perdonar **2** SEND : remitir, enviar (dinero)

remittance [riˈmɪtənts] *n* : remesa *f*

remnant [ˈrɛmnənt] *n* : restos *mpl,* vestigio *m*

remodel [riˈmɑdəl] *vt* **-eled** *or* **-elled; -eling** *or* **-elling** : remodelar, reformar

remonstrate [riˈmɑnˌstreɪt] *vi* **-strated; -strating** : protestar <to remonstrate with someone : quejarse a alguien>

remorse [riˈmɔrs] *n* : remordimiento *m*

remorseful [riˈmɔrsfəl] *adj* : arrepentido, lleno de remordimiento

remorseless [riˈmɔrsləs] *adj* **1** PITILESS : despiadado **2** RELENTLESS : implacable

remote [ri'mo:t] *adj* **-moter; -est 1** FAR-OFF : lejano, remoto <remote countries : países remotos> <in the remote past : en el pasado lejano> **2** SECLUDED : recóndito **3** : a distancia, remoto <remote control : control remoto> **4** SLIGHT : remoto **5** ALOOF : distante

remotely [ri'mo:tli] *adv* **1** SLIGHTLY : remotamente **2** DISTANTLY : en un lugar remoto, muy lejos

remoteness [ri'mo:tnəs] *n* : lejanía *f*

removable [ri'mu:vəbəl] *adj* : movible, separable

removal [ri'mu:vəl] *n* : separación *f,* extracción *f,* supresión *f* (en algo escrito), eliminación *f* (de problemas, etc.)

remove [ri'mu:v] *vt* **-moved; -moving 1** : quitar, quitarse <remove the lid : quite la tapa> <to remove one's hat : quitarse el sombrero> **2** EXTRACT : sacar, extraer <to remove the contents of : sacar el contenido de> **3** ELIMINATE : eliminar, disipar

remunerate [ri'mju:nə,reɪt] *vt* **-ated; -ating** : remunerar

remuneration [ri,mju:nə'reɪʃən] *n* : remuneración *f*

remunerative [ri'mju:nərəṭɪv, -,reɪ-] *adj* : remunerativo

renaissance [,rɛnə'sɑnts, -'zɑnts; 'rɛnə,-] *n* : renacimiento *m* <the Renaissance : el Renacimiento>

renal ['ri:nəl] *adj* : renal

rename [,ri:'neɪm] *vt* **-named; -naming** : ponerle un nombre nuevo a

rend ['rɛnd] *vt* **rent** ['rɛnt]; **rending** : desgarrar

render ['rɛndər] *vt* **1** : derretir <to render lard : derretir la manteca> **2** GIVE : prestar, dar <to render aid : prestar ayuda> **3** MAKE : hacer, volver, dejar <it rendered him helpless : lo dejó incapacitado> **4** TRANSLATE : traducir, verter <to render into English : traducir al inglés>

rendezvous ['rɑndɪ,vu:, -deɪ-] *ns & pl* : encuentro *m,* cita *f*

rendition [rɛn'dɪʃən] *n* : interpretación *f*

renegade ['rɛnɪ,geɪd] *n* : renegado *m,* -da *f*

renege [ri'nɪg, -'nɛg] *vi* **-neged; -neging** : no cumplir con (una promesa, etc.)

renew [ri'nu:, -'nju:] *vt* **1** REVIVE : renovar, reavivar <to renew the sentiments of youth : renovar los sentimientos de la juventud> **2** RESUME : reanudar **3** EXTEND : renovar <to renew a subscription : renovar una suscripción>

renewable [ri'nu:əbəl, -'nju:-] *adj* : renovable

renewal [ri'nu:əl, -'nju:-] *n* : renovación *f*

renounce [ri'naʊnts] *vt* **-nounced; -nouncing** : renunciar a

renovate ['rɛnə,veɪt] *vt* **-vated; -vating** : restaurar, renovar

renovation [,rɛnə'veɪʃən] *n* : restauración *f,* renovación *f*

renown [ri'naʊn] *n* : renombre *m,* fama *f,* celebridad *f*

renowned [ri'naʊnd] *adj* : renombrado, célebre, famoso

rent¹ ['rɛnt] *vt* : rentar, alquilar

rent² *n* **1** : renta *f,* alquiler *m* <for rent : se alquila> **2** RIP : rasgadura *f*

rental¹ ['rɛntəl] *adj* RENT : de alquiler

rental² *n* : alquiler *m*

renter ['rɛntər] *n* : arrendatario *m,* -ria *f*

renunciation [ri,nʌntsi'eɪʃən] *n* : renuncia *f*

reopen [,ri:'o:pən] *vt* : volver a abrir

reorganization [,ri:,ɔrgənə'zeɪʃən] *n* : reorganización *f*

reorganize [,ri:'ɔrgən,aɪz] *vt* **-nized; -nizing** : reorganizar

repair¹ [ri'pær] *vt* : reparar, arreglar, refaccionar

repair² *n* **1** : reparación *f,* arreglo *m* **2** CONDITION : estado *m* <in bad repair : en mal estado>

reparation [,rɛpə'reɪʃən] *n* **1** AMENDS : reparación *f* **2 reparations** *npl* COMPENSATION : indemnización *f*

repartee [,rɛpər'ti:, -,pɑr-, -'teɪ] *n* : intercambio *m* de réplicas ingeniosas

repast [ri'pæst, 'ri:,pæst] *n* : comida *f*

repatriate [ri'peɪtri,eɪt] *vt* **-ated; -ating** : repatriar

repay [ri'peɪ] *vt* **-paid; -paying** : pagar, devolver, reembolsar

repeal¹ [ri'pi:l] *vt* : abrogar, revocar

repeal² *n* : abrogación *f,* revocación *f*

repeat¹ [ri'pi:t] *vt* : repetir

repeat² *n* : repetición *f*

repeatedly [ri'pi:ṭədli] *adv* : repetidamente, repetidas veces

repel [ri'pɛl] *vt* **-pelled; -pelling 1** REPULSE : repeler (un enemigo, etc.) **2** RESIST : repeler **3** REJECT : rechazar, repeler **4** DISGUST : repugnar, darle asco (a alguien)

repellent *or* **repellant** [ri'pɛlənt] *n* : repelente *m*

repent [ri'pɛnt] *vi* : arrepentirse

repentance [ri'pɛntənts] *n* : arrepentimiento *m*

repentant [ri'pɛntənt] *adj* : arrepentido

repercussion [,ri:pər'kʌʃən, ,rɛpər-] *n* : repercusión *f*

repertoire ['rɛpər,twɑr] *n* : repertorio *m*

repertory ['rɛpər,tori] *n, pl* **-ries** : repertorio *m*

repetition [,rɛpə'tɪʃən] *n* : repetición *f*

repetitious [,rɛpə'tɪʃəs] *adj* : repetitivo, reiterativo — **repetitiously** *adv*

repetitive [ri'pɛtət̬ɪv] *adj* : repetitivo, reiterativo

replace [ri'pleɪs] *vt* **-placed; -placing 1** : volver a poner <replace it in the drawer : vuelve a ponerlo en el cajón> **2** SUBSTITUTE : reemplazar, sustituir **3** : reponer <to replace the worn carpet : reponer la alfombra raída>

replaceable [ri'pleɪsəbəl] *adj* : reemplazable

replacement [ri'pleɪsmənt] *n* **1** SUBSTITUTION : reemplazo *m,* sustitución *f* **2** SUBSTITUTE : sustituto *m,* -ta *f;* suplente *mf* (persona) **3 replacement part** : repuesto *m,* pieza *f* de recambio

replenish [ri'plɛnɪʃ] *vt* : rellenar, llenar de nuevo

replenishment [ri'plɛnɪʃmənt] *n* : reabastecimiento *m*

replete [ri'pliːt] *adj* : repleto, lleno

replica ['rɛplɪkə] *n* : réplica *f,* reproducción *f*

reply[1] [ri'plaɪ] *vi* **-plied; -plying** : contestar, responder

reply[2] *n, pl* **-plies** : respuesta *f,* contestación *f*

report[1] [ri'port] *vt* **1** ANNOUNCE : relatar, anunciar **2** : dar parte de, informar de, reportar <he reported an accident : dio parte de un accidente> <to report a crime : denunciar un delito> **3** : informar acerca de (en un periódico, la televisión, etc.) — *vi* **1** : hacer un informe, informar **2 to report for duty** : presentarse, reportarse

report[2] *n* **1** RUMOR : rumor *m* **2** REPUTATION : reputación *f* <people of evil report : personas de mala fama> **3** ACCOUNT : informe *m,* reportaje *m* (en un periódico, etc.) **4** BANG : estallido *m* (de un arma de fuego)

report card *n* : boletín *m* de calificaciones, boletín *m* de notas

reportedly [ri'portədli] *adv* : según se dice, según se informa

reporter [ri'portər] *n* : periodista *mf;* reportero *m,* -ra *f*

repose[1] [ri'poːz] *vi* **-posed; -posing** : reposar, descansar

repose[2] *n* **1** : reposo *m,* descanso *m* **2** CALM : calma *f,* tranquilidad *f*

repository [ri'pɑzə,tori] *n, pl* **-ries** : depósito *m*

repossess [,riːpə'zɛs] *vt* : recuperar, recobrar la posesión de

reprehensible [,rɛpri'hɛntsəbəl] *adj* : reprensible — **reprehensibly** *adv*

represent [,rɛprɪ'zɛnt] *vt* **1** SYMBOLIZE : representar <the flag represents our country : la bandera representa a nuestro país> **2** : representar, ser un representante de <an attorney who represents his client : un abogado que representa su cliente> **3** PORTRAY : presentar <he represents himself as a friend : se presenta como amigo>

representation [,rɛprɪ,zɛn'teɪʃən, -zən-] *n* : representación *f*

representative[1] [,rɛprɪ'zɛntət̬ɪv] *adj* : representativo

representative[2] *n* **1** : representante *mf* **2** : diputado *m,* -da *f* (en la política)

repress [ri'prɛs] *vt* : reprimir

repression [ri'prɛʃən] *n* : represión *f*

repressive [ri'prɛsɪv] *adj* : represivo

reprieve[1] [ri'priːv] *vt* **-prieved; -prieving** : indultar

reprieve[2] *n* : indulto *m*

reprimand[1] ['rɛprə,mænd] *vt* : reprender

reprimand[2] *n* : reprimenda *f*

reprint[1] [ri'prɪnt] *vt* : reimprimir

reprint[2] ['riː,prɪnt, ri'prɪnt] *n* : reedición *f*

reprisal [ri'praɪzəl] *n* : represalia *f*

reproach[1] [ri'proːtʃ] *vt* : reprochar

reproach[2] *n* **1** DISGRACE : deshonra *f* **2** REBUKE : reproche *m,* recriminación *f*

reproachful [ri'proːtʃfəl] *adj* : de reproche

reproduce [,riːprə'duːs, -'djuːs] *v* **-duced; -ducing** *vt* : reproducir — *vi* BREED : reproducirse

reproduction [,riːprə'dʌkʃən] *n* : reproducción *f*

reproductive [,riːprə'dʌktɪv] *adj* : reproductor

reproof [ri'pruːf] *n* : reprobación *f,* reprimenda *f,* reproche *m*

reprove [ri'pruːv] *vt* **-proved; -proving** : reprender, censurar

reptile ['rɛp,taɪl] *n* : reptil *m*

republic [ri'pʌblɪk] *n* : república *f*

republican[1] [ri'pʌblɪkən] *adj* : republicano

republican[2] *n* : republicano *m,* -na *f*

repudiate [ri'pjuːdi,eɪt] *vt* **-ated; -ating 1** REJECT : rechazar **2** DISOWN : repudiar, renegar de

repudiation [ri,pjuːdi'eɪʃən] *n* : rechazo *m,* repudio *m*

repugnance [ri'pʌgnənts] *n* : repugnancia *f*

repugnant [ri'pʌgnənt] *adj* : repugnante, asqueroso

repulse[1] [ri'pʌls] *vt* **-pulsed; -pulsing 1** REPEL : repeler **2** REBUFF : desairar, rechazar

repulse[2] *n* : rechazo *m*

repulsive [ri'pʌlsɪv] *adj* : repulsivo, repugnante, asqueroso — **repulsively** *adv*

reputable ['rɛpjətəbəl] *adj* : acreditado, de buena reputación

reputation [,rɛpjə'teɪʃən] *n* : reputación *f,* fama *f*

repute [ri'pjuːt] *n* : reputación *f,* fama *f*

reputed [ri'pjuːt̬əd] *adj* : reputado, supuesto <she's reputed to be the best : tiene fama de ser la mejor>

reputedly [ri'pjuːtədli] *adv* : supuestamente, según se dice

request[1] [ri'kwɛst] *vt* : pedir, solicitar, rogar <to request assistance : solicitar asistencia, pedir ayuda> <I requested him to do it : le pedí que lo hiciera>

request[2] *n* **:** petición *f,* solicitud *f,* pedido *m*
requiem [ˈrɛkwiəm, ˈreɪ-] *n* **:** réquiem *m*
require [riˈkwaɪr] *vt* **-quired; -quiring 1** CALL FOR, DEMAND **:** requerir, exigir <if required : si se requiere> <to require that something be done : exigir que algo se haga> **2** NEED **:** necesitar, requerir
requirement [riˈkwaɪrmənt] *n* **1** NECESSITY **:** necesidad *f* **2** DEMAND **:** requisito *m,* demanda *f*
requisite[1] [ˈrɛkwəzɪt] *adj* **:** esencial, necesario
requisite[2] *n* **:** requisito *m,* necesidad *f*
requisition[1] [ˌrɛkwəˈzɪʃən] *vt* **:** requisar
requisition[2] *n* **:** requisición *f,* requisa *f*
reread [ˌriːˈriːd] *vt* **-read; -reading :** releer
reroute [ˌriːˈruːt, -ˈraʊt] *vt* **-routed; -routing :** desviar
resale [ˈriːˌseɪl, ˌriːˈseɪl] *n* **:** reventa *f* <resale price : precio de venta>
rescind [riˈsɪnd] *vt* **1** CANCEL **:** rescindir, cancelar **2** REPEAL **:** abrogar, revocar
rescue[1] [ˈrɛsˌkjuː] *vt* **-cued; -cuing :** rescatar, salvar
rescue[2] *n* **:** rescate *m*
rescuer [ˈrɛskjuər] *n* **:** salvador *m,* -dora *f*
research[1] [riˈsərtʃ, ˈriːˌsərtʃ] *v* **:** investigar
research[2] *n* **:** investigación *f*
researcher [riˈsərtʃər, ˈriːˌ-] *n* **:** investigador *m,* -dora *f*
resemblance [riˈzɛmbləntˢ] *n* **:** semejanza *f,* parecido *m*
resemble [riˈzɛmbəl] *vt* **-sembled; -sembling :** parecerse a, asemejarse a
resent [riˈzɛnt] *vt* **:** resentirse de, ofenderse por
resentful [riˈzɛntfəl] *adj* **:** resentido, rencoroso — **resentfully** *adv*
resentment [riˈzɛntmənt] *n* **:** resentimiento *m*
reservation [ˌrɛzərˈveɪʃən] *n* **1 :** reservación *f,* reserva *f* <to make a reservation : hacer una reservación> **2** DOUBT, MISGIVING **:** reserva *f,* duda *f* <without reservations : sin reservas> **3 :** reserva *f* (de indios americanos)
reserve[1] [riˈzərv] *vt* **-served; -serving :** reservar
reserve[2] *n* **1** STOCK **:** reserva *f* <to keep in reserve : guardar en reserva> **2** RESTRAINT **:** reserva *f,* moderación *f* **3 reserves** *npl* **:** reservas *fpl* (militares)
reserved [riˈzərvd] *adj* **:** reservado
reservoir [ˈrɛzərˌvwɑr, -ˌvwɔr, -ˌvɔr] *n* **:** embalse *m*
reset [ˌriːˈsɛt] *vt* **-set; -setting :** reajustar, poner en hora (un reloj), reinicializar (una computadora)
reside [riˈzaɪd] *vi* **-sided; -siding 1** DWELL **:** residir **2** LIE **:** radicar, residir <the power resides in the presidency : el poder radica en la presidencia>
residence [ˈrɛzədəntˢ] *n* **:** residencia *f*
resident[1] [ˈrɛzədənt] *adj* **:** residente
resident[2] *n* **:** residente *mf*
residential [ˌrɛzəˈdɛntʃəl] *adj* **:** residencial
residual [riˈzɪdʒʊəl] *adj* **:** residual
residue [ˈrɛzəˌduː, -ˌdjuː] *n* **:** residuo *m,* resto *m*
resign [riˈzaɪn] *vt* **1** QUIT **:** dimitir, renunciar **2 to resign oneself :** aguantarse, resignarse
resignation [ˌrɛzɪgˈneɪʃən] *n* **:** resignación *f*
resignedly [riˈzaɪnədli] *adv* **:** con resignación
resilience [riˈzɪljəntˢ] *n* **1 :** capacidad *f* de recuperación, adaptabilidad *f* **2** ELASTICITY **:** elasticidad *f*
resiliency [riˈzɪljəntˢi] → **resilience**
resilient [riˈzɪljənt] *adj* **1** STRONG **:** resistente, fuerte **2** ELASTIC **:** elástico
resin [ˈrɛzən] *n* **:** resina *f*
resist [riˈzɪst] *vt* **1** WITHSTAND **:** resistir <to resist heat : resistir el calor> **2** OPPOSE **:** oponerse a
resistance [riˈzɪstəntˢ] *n* **:** resistencia *f*
resistant [riˈzɪstənt] *adj* **:** resistente
resolute [ˈrɛzəˌluːt] *adj* **:** firme, resuelto, decidido
resolutely [ˈrɛzəˌluːtli, ˌrɛzəˈ-] *adv* **:** resueltamente, firmemente
resolution [ˌrɛzəˈluːʃən] *n* **1** SOLUTION **:** solución *f* **2** RESOLVE **:** resolución *f,* determinación *f* **3** DECISION **:** propósito *m,* decisión *f* <New Year's resolutions : propósitos para el Año Nuevo> **4** MOTION, PROPOSAL **:** moción *f,* resolución *f* (legislativa)
resolve[1] [riˈzɑlv] *vt* **-solved; -solving 1** SOLVE **:** resolver, solucionar **2** DECIDE **:** resolver <she resolved to get more sleep : resolvió dormir más>
resolve[2] *n* **:** resolución *f,* determinación *f*
resonance [ˈrɛzənəntˢ] *n* **:** resonancia *f*
resonant [ˈrɛzənənt] *adj* **:** resonante, retumbante
resort[1] [riˈzɔrt] *vi* **to resort to :** recurrir <to resort to force : recurrir a la fuerza>
resort[2] *n* **1** RECOURSE **:** recurso *m* <as a last resort : como último recurso> **2** HANGOUT **:** lugar *m* popular, lugar *m* muy frecuentado **3 :** lugar *m* de vacaciones <tourist resort : centro turístico>
resound [riˈzaʊnd] *vi* **:** retumbar, resonar
resounding [riˈzaʊndɪŋ] *adj* **1** RESONANT **:** retumbante, resonante **2** ABSOLUTE, CATEGORICAL **:** rotundo, tremendo <a resounding success : un éxito rotundo>
resource [ˈriːˌsɔrs, riˈsɔrs] *n* **1** RESOURCEFULNESS **:** ingenio *m,* recursos *mpl* **2 resources** *npl* **:** recursos *mpl*

<natural resources : recursos naturales> **3 resources** *npl* MEANS : recursos *mpl*, medios *mpl*, fondos *mpl*

resourceful [ri'sorsfəl, -'zors-] *adj* : ingenioso

resourcefulness [ri'sorsfəlnəs, -'zors-] *n* : ingenio *m*, recursos *mpl*, inventiva *f*

respect[1] [ri'spɛkt] *vt* : respetar, estimar

respect[2] *n* **1** REFERENCE : relación *f*, respeto *m* <with respect to : en lo que respecta a> **2** ESTEEM : respeto *m*, estima *f* **3** DETAIL, PARTICULAR : detalle *m*, sentido *m*, respeto *m* <in some respects : en algunos sentidos> **4 respects** *npl* : respetos *mpl* <to pay one's respects : presentar uno sus respetos>

respectability [ri,spɛktə'bɪləti] *n* : respetabilidad *f*

respectable [ri'spɛktəbəl] *adj* **1** PROPER : respetable, decente **2** CONSIDERABLE : considerable, respetable <a respectable amount : una cantidad respetable> — **respectably** [-bli] *adv*

respectful [ri'spɛktfəl] *adj* : respetuoso — **respectfully** *adv*

respectfulness [ri'spɛktfəlnəs] *n* : respetuosidad *f*

respective [ri'spɛktɪv] *adj* : respectivo <their respective homes : sus casas respectivas> — **respectively** *adv*

respiration [,rɛspə'reɪʃən] *n* : respiración *f*

respirator ['rɛspə,reɪtər] *n* : respirador *m*

respiratory ['rɛspərə,tori, rɪ'spaɪrə-] *adj* : respiratorio

respite ['rɛspɪt, rɪ'spaɪt] *n* : respiro *m*, tregua *f*

resplendent [ri'splɛndənt] *adj* : resplandeciente — **resplendently** *adv*

respond [ri'spɑnd] *vi* **1** ANSWER : contestar, responder **2** REACT : responder, reaccionar <to respond to treatment : responder al tratamiento>

response [ri'spɑnts] *n* : respuesta *f*

responsibility [ri,spɑntsə'bɪləti] *n, pl* **-ties** : responsabilidad *f*

responsible [ri'spɑntsəbəl] *adj* : responsable — **responsibly** [-bli] *adv*

responsive [ri'spɑntsɪv] *adj* **1** ANSWERING : que responde **2** SENSITIVE : sensible, receptivo

responsiveness [ri'spɑntsɪvnəs] *n* : receptividad *f*, sensibilidad *f*

rest[1] ['rɛst] *vi* **1** REPOSE : reposar, descansar **2** RELAX : quedarse tranquilo **3** STOP : pararse, detenerse **4** DEPEND : basarse (en), descansar (sobre), depender (de) <the decision rests with her : la decisión pesa sobre ella> **5 to rest on** : apoyarse en, descansar sobre <to rest on one's arm : apoyarse en el brazo> — *vt* **1** RELAX : descansar **2** SUPPORT : apoyar **3 to rest one's eyes on** : fijar la mirada en

rest[2] *n* **1** RELAXATION, REPOSE : reposo *m*, descanso *m* **2** SUPPORT : soporte *m*, apoyo *m* **3** : silencio *m* (en música) **4** REMAINDER : resto *m* **5 to come to rest** : pararse

restatement [,riː'steɪtmənt] *n* : repetición *f*

restaurant ['rɛstə,rɑnt, -rənt] *n* : restaurante *m*

restful ['rɛstfəl] *adj* **1** RELAXING : relajante **2** PEACEFUL : tranquilo, sosegado

restitution [,rɛstə'tuːʃən, -'tjuː-] *n* : restitución *f*

restive ['rɛstɪv] *adj* : inquieto, nervioso

restless ['rɛstləs] *adj* **1** FIDGETY : inquieto, agitado **2** IMPATIENT : impaciente **3** SLEEPLESS : desvelado <a restless night : una noche en blanco>

restlessly ['rɛstləsli] *adv* : nerviosamente

restlessness ['rɛstləsnəs] *n* : inquietud *f*, agitación *f*

restoration [,rɛstə'reɪʃən] *n* : restauración *f*, restablecimiento *m*

restore [ri'stor] *vt* **-stored; -storing 1** RETURN : volver **2** REESTABLISH : restablecer **3** REPAIR : restaurar

restrain [ri'streɪn] *vt* **1** : refrenar, contener **2 to restrain oneself** : contenerse

restrained [ri'streɪnd] *adj* : comedido, templado, contenido

restraint [ri'streɪnt] *n* **1** RESTRICTION : restricción *f*, limitación *f*, control *m* **2** CONFINEMENT : encierro *m* **3** RESERVE : reserva *f*, control *m* de sí mismo

restrict [ri'strɪkt] *vt* : restringir, limitar, constreñir

restricted [ri'strɪktəd] *adj* **1** LIMITED : limitado, restringido **2** CLASSIFIED : secreto, confidencial

restriction [ri'strɪkʃən] *n* : restricción *f*

restrictive [ri'strɪktɪv] *adj* : restrictivo — **restrictively** *adv*

restructure [ri'strʌktʃər] *vt* **-tured; -turing** : reestructurar

result[1] [ri'zʌlt] *vi* : resultar <to result in : resultar en, tener por resultado>

result[2] *n* : resultado *m*, consecuencia *f* <as a result of : como consecuencia de>

resultant [ri'zʌltənt] *adj* : resultante

resume [ri'zuːm] *v* **-sumed; -suming** *vt* : reanudar — *vi* : reanudarse

résumé *or* **resume** *or* **resumé** ['rɛzə,meɪ, ,rɛzə'-] *n* **1** SUMMARY : resumen *m* **2** CURRICULUM VITAE : currículum *m*, currículo *m*

resumption [ri'zʌmpʃən] *n* : reanudación *f*

resurface [,riː'sərfəs] *v* **-faced; -facing** *vt* : pavimentar (una carretera) de nuevo — *vi* : volver a salir en la superficie

resurgence [ri'sərdʒənts] *n* : resurgimiento *m*

resurrect [ˌrɛzəˈrɛkt] *vt* : resucitar, desempolvar
resurrection [ˌrɛzəˈrɛkʃən] *n* : resurrección *f*
resuscitate [riˈsʌsəˌteɪt] *vt* **-tated; -tating** : resucitar, revivir
retail[1] [ˈriːˌteɪl] *vt* : vender al por menor, vender al detalle
retail[2] *adv* : al por menor, al detalle
retail[3] *adj* : detallista, minorista
retail[4] *n* : venta *f* al detalle, venta *f* al por menor
retailer [ˈriːˌteɪlər] *n* : detallista *mf,* minorista *mf*
retain [riˈteɪn] *vt* : retener, conservar, guardar
retainer [riˈteɪnər] *n* **1** SERVANT : criado *m,* -da *f* **2** ADVANCE : anticipo *m*
retaliate [riˈtæliˌeɪt] *vi* **-ated; -ating** : responder, contraatacar, tomar represalias
retaliation [riˌtæliˈeɪʃən] *n* : represalia *f,* retaliación *f*
retard [riˈtɑrd] *vt* : retardar, retrasar
retarded [riˈtɑrdəd] *adj* : retrasado
retch [ˈrɛtʃ] *vi* : hacer arcadas
retention [riˈtɛntʃən] *n* : retención *f*
retentive [riˈtɛntɪv] *adj* : retentivo
reticence [ˈrɛtəsənts] *n* : reticencia *f*
reticent [ˈrɛtəsənt] *adj* : reticente
retina [ˈrɛtənə] *n, pl* **-nas** *or* **-nae** [-əni, -ənˌaɪ] : retina *f*
retinue [ˈrɛtənˌuː, -ˌjuː] *n* : séquito *m,* comitiva *f,* cortejo *m*
retire [riˈtaɪr] *vi* **-tired; -tiring 1** RETREAT, WITHDRAW : retirarse, retraerse **2** : retirarse, jubilarse (de su trabajo) **3** : acostarse, irse a dormir
retiree [riˌtaɪˈriː] *n* : jubilado *m,* -da *f*
retirement [riˈtaɪrmənt] *n* : jubilación *f*
retiring [riˈtaɪrɪŋ] *adj* SHY : retraído
retort[1] [riˈtɔrt] *vt* : replicar
retort[2] *n* : réplica *f*
retrace [ˌriːˈtreɪs] *vt* **-traced; -tracing** : volver sobre, desandar <to retrace one's steps : volver uno sobre sus pasos>
retract [riˈtrækt] *vt* **1** TAKE BACK, WITHDRAW : retirar, retractarse de **2** : retraer (las garras) — *vi* : retractarse
retractable [riˈtræktəbəl] *adj* : retractable
retrain [ˌriːˈtreɪn] *vt* : reciclar, reconvertir
retreat[1] [riˈtriːt] *vi* : retirarse
retreat[2] *n* **1** WITHDRAWAL : retirada *f,* repliegue *m,* retiro *m* <to beat a retreat : batirse en retirada> **2** REFUGE : retiro *m,* refugio *m*
retrench [riˈtrɛntʃ] *vt* : reducir (gastos) — *vi* : economizar
retribution [ˌrɛtrəˈbjuːʃən] *n* PUNISHMENT : castigo *m,* pena *f* merecida
retrieval [riˈtriːvəl] *n* : recuperación *f* <beyond retrieval : irrecuperable> <data retrieval : recuperación de datos>
retrieve [riˈtriːv] *vt* **-trieved; -trieving 1** : cobrar <to retrieve game : cobrar la caza> **2** RECOVER : recuperar
retriever [riˈtriːvər] *n* : perro *m* cobrador
retroactive [ˌrɛtroˈæktɪv] *adj* : retroactivo — **retroactively** *adv*
retrograde [ˈrɛtrəˌgreɪd] *adj* : retrógrado
retrospect [ˈrɛtrəˌspɛkt] *n* **in retrospect** : mirando hacia atrás, retrospectivamente
retrospective [ˌrɛtrəˈspɛktɪv] *adj* : retrospectivo
return[1] [riˈtərn] *vi* **1** : volver, regresar <to return home : regresar a casa> **2** REAPPEAR : reaparecer, resurgir **3** ANSWER : responder — *vt* **1** REPLACE, RESTORE : devolver, volver (a poner), restituir <to return something to its place : volver a poner algo en su lugar> **2** YIELD : producir, redituar, rendir **3** REPAY : pagar, devolver <to return a compliment : devolver un cumplido>
return[2] *adj* : de vuelta
return[3] *n* **1** RETURNING : regreso *m,* vuelta *f,* retorno *m* **2** *or* **tax return** : declaración *f* de impuestos **3** YIELD : rédito *m,* rendimiento *m,* ganancia *f* **4 returns** *npl* DATA, RESULTS : resultados *mpl,* datos *mpl*
reunion [riˈjuːnjən] *n* : reunión *f,* reencuentro *m*
reunite [ˌriːjʊˈnaɪt] *v* **-nited; -niting** *vt* : (volver a) reunir — *vi* : (volver a) reunirse
reusable [riˈjuːzəbəl] *adj* : reutilizable
reuse [riˈjuːz] *vt* **-used; -using** : reutilizar, usar de nuevo
revamp [ˌriˈvæmp] *vt* : renovar
reveal [riˈviːl] *vt* **1** DIVULGE : revelar, divulgar <to reveal a secret : revelar un secreto> **2** SHOW : manifestar, mostrar, dejar ver
reveille [ˈrɛvəli] *n* : toque *m* de diana
revel[1] [ˈrɛvəl] *vi* **-eled** *or* **-elled; -eling** *or* **-elling 1** CAROUSE : ir de juerga **2 to revel in** : deleitarse en
revel[2] *n* : juerga *f,* parranda *f fam*
revelation [ˌrɛvəˈleɪʃən] *n* : revelación *f*
reveler *or* **reveller** [ˈrɛvələr] *n* : juerguista *mf*
revelry [ˈrɛvəlri] *n, pl* **–ries** : juerga *f,* parranda *f fam,* jarana *f fam*
revenge[1] [riˈvɛndʒ] *vt* **-venged; -venging** : vengar <to revenge oneself on : vengarse de>
revenge[2] *n* : venganza *f*
revenue [ˈrɛvəˌnuː, -ˌnjuː] *n* : ingresos *mpl,* rentas *fpl*
reverberate [riˈvərbəˌreɪt] *vi* **-ated; -ating** : reverberar
reverberation [riˌvərbəˈreɪʃən] *n* : reverberación *f*
revere [riˈvɪr] *vt* **-vered; -vering** : reverenciar, venerar

reverence ['rɛvərənts] *n* : reverencia *f,* veneración *f*

reverend ['rɛvərənd] *adj* : reverendo <the Reverend John Chapin : el reverendo John Chapin>

reverent ['rɛvərənt] *adj* : reverente — **reverently** *adv*

reverie ['rɛvəri] *n, pl* **-eries** : ensueño *m*

reversal ['rɛvərsəl] *n* **1** INVERSION : inversión *f* (del orden normal) **2** CHANGE : cambio *m* total **3** SETBACK : revés *m,* contratiempo *m*

reverse[1] [ri'vərs] *v* **-versed; -versing** *vt* **1** INVERT : invertir **2** CHANGE : cambiar totalmente **3** ANNUL : anular, revocar — *vi* : dar marcha atrás

reverse[2] *adj* **1** : inverso <in reverse order : en orden inverso> <the reverse side : el reverso> **2** OPPOSITE : contrario, opuesto

reverse[3] *n* **1** OPPOSITE : lo contrario, lo opuesto **2** SETBACK : revés *m,* contratiempo *m* **3** BACK : reverso *m,* dorso *m,* revés *m* **4** *or* **reverse gear** : marcha *f* atrás, reversa *f Col, Mex*

reversible [ri'vərsəbəl] *adj* : reversible

reversion [ri'vərʒən] *n* : reversión *f,* vuelta *f*

revert [ri'vərt] *vi* : revertir

review[1] [ri'vjuː] *vt* **1** REEXAMINE : volver a examinar, repasar (una lección) **2** CRITICIZE : reseñar, hacer una crítica de **3** EXAMINE : examinar, analizar <to review one's life : examinar su vida> **4 to review the troops** : pasar revista a las tropas

review[2] *n* **1** INSPECTION : revista *f* (de tropas) **2** ANALYSIS, OVERVIEW : resumen *m,* análisis *m* <a review of current affairs : un análisis de las actualidades> **3** CRITICISM : reseña *f,* crítica *f* (de un libro, etc.) **4** : repaso *m* (para un examen) **5** REVUE : revista *f* (musical)

reviewer [ri'vjuːər] *n* : crítico *m,* -ca *f*

revile [ri'vaɪl] *vt* **-viled; -viling** : injuriar, denostar

revise [ri'vaɪz] *vt* **-vised; -vising** : revisar, corregir, refundir <to revise a dictionary : corregir un diccionario>

revision [ri'vɪʒən] *n* : revisión *f*

revival [ri'vaɪvəl] *n* **1** : renacimiento *m* (de ideas, etc.), restablecimiento *m* (de costumbres, etc.), reactivación *f* (de la economía) **2** : reanimación *f,* resucitación *f* (en medicina) **3** *or* **revival meeting** : asamblea *f* evangelista

revive [ri'vaɪv] *v* **-vived; -viving** *vt* **1** REAWAKEN : reavivar, reanimar, reactivar (la economía), resucitar (a un paciente) **2** REESTABLISH : restablecer — *vi* **1** : renacer, reanimarse, reactivarse **2** COME TO : recobrar el sentido, volver en sí

revoke [ri'voːk] *vt* **-voked; -voking** : revocar

revolt[1] [ri'voːlt] *vi* **1** REBEL : rebelarse, sublevarse **2 to revolt at** : sentir repugnancia por — *vt* DISGUST : darle asco (a alguien), repugnar

revolt[2] *n* REBELLION : rebelión *f,* revuelta *f,* sublevación *f*

revolting [ri'voːltɪŋ] *adj* : asqueroso, repugnante

revolution [ˌrɛvə'luːʃən] *n* : revolución *f*

revolutionary[1] [ˌrɛvə'luːʃənˌɛri] *adj* : revolucionario

revolutionary[2] *n, pl* **-aries** : revolucionario *m,* -ria *f*

revolutionize [ˌrɛvə'luːʃənˌaɪz] *vt* **-ized; -izing** : cambiar radicalmente, revolucionar

revolve [ri'vɑlv] *v* **-volved; -volving** *vt* ROTATE : hacer girar — *vi* **1** ROTATE : girar <to revolve around : girar alrededor de> **2 to revolve in one's mind** : darle vueltas en la cabeza a alguien

revolver [ri'vɑlvər] *n* : revólver *m*

revue [ri'vjuː] *n* : revista *f* (musical)

revulsion [ri'vʌlʃən] *n* : repugnancia *f*

reward[1] [ri'wɔrd] *vt* : recompensar, premiar

reward[2] *n* : recompensa *f*

rewrite [ˌriː'raɪt] *vt* **-wrote; -written; -writing** : escribir de nuevo, volver a escribir

rhapsody ['ræpsədi] *n, pl* **-dies 1** : elogio *m* excesivo <to go into rhapsodies over : extasiarse por> **2** : rapsodia *f* (en música)

rhetoric ['rɛt̬ərɪk] *n* : retórica *f*

rhetorical [rɪ'tɔrɪkəl] *adj* : retórico

rheumatic [rʊ'mæt̬ɪk] *adj* : reumático

rheumatism ['ruːməˌtɪzəm, 'rʊ-] *n* : reumatismo *m*

rhinestone ['raɪnˌstoːn] *n* : diamante *m* de imitación

rhino ['raɪˌnoː] *n, pl* **rhino** *or* **rhinos** → **rhinoceros**

rhinoceros [raɪ'nɑsərəs] *n, pl* **-eroses** *or* **-eros** *or* **-eri** [-ˌraɪ] : rinoceronte *m*

rhododendron [ˌroːdə'dɛndrən] *n* : rododendro *m*

rhombus ['rɑmbəs] *n, pl* **-buses** *or* **-bi** [-ˌbaɪ, -bi] : rombo *m*

rhubarb ['ruːˌbɑrb] *n* : ruibarbo *m*

rhyme[1] ['raɪm] *vi* **rhymed; rhyming** : rimar

rhyme[2] *n* **1** : rima *f* **2** VERSE : verso *m* (en rima)

rhythm ['rɪðəm] *n* : ritmo *m*

rhythmic ['rɪðmɪk] *or* **rhythmical** [-mɪkəl] *adj* : rítmico — **rhythmically** [-mɪkli] *adv*

rib[1] ['rɪb] *vt* **ribbed; ribbing 1** : hacer en canalé <a ribbed sweater : un suéter en canalé> **2** TEASE : tomarle el pelo (a alguien)

rib[2] *n* **1** : costilla *f* (de una persona o un animal) **2** : nervio *m* (de una bóveda o una hoja), varilla *f* (de un paraguas), canalé *m* (de una prenda tejida)

ribald [ˈrɪbəld] *adj* : escabroso, procaz

ribbon [ˈrɪbən] *n* **1** : cinta *f* **2 to tear to ribbons** : hacer jirones

rice [ˈraɪs] *n* : arroz *m*

rich [ˈrɪtʃ] *adj* **1** WEALTHY : rico **2** SUMPTUOUS : suntuoso, lujoso **3** : pesado <rich foods : comida pesada> **4** ABUNDANT : abundante **5** : vivo, intenso <rich colors : colores vivos> **6** FERTILE : fértil, rico

riches [ˈrɪtʃəz] *npl* : riquezas *fpl*

richly [ˈrɪtʃli] *adv* **1** SUMPTUOUSLY : suntuosamente, ricamente **2** ABUNDANTLY : abundantemente **3 richly deserved** : bien merecido

richness [ˈrɪtʃnəs] *n* : riqueza *f*

rickets [ˈrɪkəts] *n* : raquitismo *m*

rickety [ˈrɪkət̬i] *adj* : desvencijado, destartalado

ricksha *or* **rickshaw** [ˈrɪkˌʃɔ] *n* : cochecillo *m* tirado por un hombre

ricochet[1] [ˈrɪkəˌʃeɪ] *vi* **-cheted** [-ˌʃeɪd] *or* **-chetted** [-ˌʃɛt̬əd]; **-cheting** [-ˌʃeɪɪŋ] *or* **-chetting** [-ˌʃɛt̬ɪŋ] : rebotar

ricochet[2] *n* : rebote *m*

rid [ˈrɪd] *vt* **rid; ridding 1** FREE : librar <to rid the city of thieves : librar la ciudad de ladrones> **2 to rid oneself of** : desembarazarse de

riddance [ˈrɪdənts] *n* : libramiento *m* <good riddance! : ¡adiós y buen viaje!, ¡vete con viento fresco!>

riddle[1] [ˈrɪdəl] *vt* **-dled; -dling** : acribillar <riddled with bullets : acribillado a balazos> <riddled with errors : lleno de errores>

riddle[2] *n* : acertijo *m,* adivinanza *f*

ride[1] [ˈraɪd] *v* **rode** [ˈroːd]; **ridden** [ˈrɪdən]; **riding** *vt* **1** : montar, ir, andar <to ride a horse : montar a caballo> <to ride a bicycle : montar en bicicleta, andar en bicicleta> <to ride the bus : ir en autobús> **2** TRAVERSE : recorrer <he rode 5 miles : recorrió 5 millas> **3** TEASE : burlarse de, ridiculizar **4** CARRY : llevar **5** WEATHER : capear <they rode out the storm : capearon el temporal> **6 to ride the waves** : surcar los mares — *vi* **1** : montar a caballo, cabalgar **2** TRAVEL : ir, viajar (en coche, en bicicleta, etc.) **3** RUN : andar, marchar <the car rides well : el coche anda bien> **4 to ride at anchor** : estar fondeado **5 to let things ride** : dejar pasar las cosas

ride[2] *n* **1** : paseo *m,* vuelta *f* (en coche, en bicicleta, a caballo) <to go for a ride : dar una vuelta> <to give someone a ride : llevar en coche a alguien> **2** : aparato *m* (en un parque de diversiones)

rider [ˈraɪdər] *n* **1** : jinete *mf* <the rider fell off his horse : el jinete se cayó de su caballo> **2** CYCLIST : ciclista *mf* **3** MOTORCYCLIST : motociclista *mf* **4** CLAUSE : cláusula *f* añadida

ridge [ˈrɪdʒ] *n* **1** CHAIN : cadena *f* (de montañas o cerros) **2** : caballete *m* (de un techo), cresta *f* (de una ola o una montaña), cordoncillo *m* (de telas)

ridicule[1] [ˈrɪdəˌkjuːl] *vt* **-culed; -culing** : burlarse de, mofarse de, ridiculizar

ridicule[2] *n* : burlas *fpl*

ridiculous [rəˈdɪkjələs] *adj* : ridículo, absurdo

ridiculously [rəˈdɪkjələsli] *adv* : de forma ridícula

rife [ˈraɪf] *adj* : abundante, común <to be rife with : estar plagado de>

riffraff [ˈrɪfˌræf] *n* : chusma *f,* gentuza *f*

rifle[1] [ˈraɪfəl] *v* **-fled; -fling** *vt* RANSACK : desvalijar, saquear — *vi* : **to rifle through** : revolver

rifle[2] *n* : rifle *m,* fusil *m*

rift [ˈrɪft] *n* **1** FISSURE : grieta *f,* fisura *f* **2** BREAK : ruptura *f* (entre personas), división *f* (dentro de un grupo)

rig[1] [ˈrɪg] *vt* **rigged; rigging 1** : aparejar (un barco) **2** EQUIP : equipar **3** FIX : amañar (una elección, etc.) **4 to rig up** CONSTRUCT : construir, erigir **5 to rig oneself out as** : vestirse de

rig[2] *n* **1** : aparejo *m* (de un barco) **2** *or* **oil rig** : torre *f* de perforación, plataforma *f* petrolífera

rigging [ˈrɪgɪŋ, -gən] *n* : jarcia *f,* aparejo *m*

right[1] [ˈraɪt] *vt* **1** FIX, RESTORE : reparar <to right the economy : reparar la economía> **2** STRAIGHTEN : enderezar

right[2] *adv* **1** : bien <to live right : vivir bien> **2** PRECISELY : precisamente, justo <right in the middle : justo en medio> **3** DIRECTLY, STRAIGHT : derecho, directamente <he went right home : fue derecho a casa> **4** IMMEDIATELY : inmediatamente <right after lunch : inmediatamente después del almuerzo> **5** COMPLETELY : completamente <he felt right at home : se sintió completamente cómodo> **6** : a la derecha <to look left and right : mirar a la izquierda y a la derecha>

right[3] *adj* **1** UPRIGHT : bueno, honrado <right conduct : conducta honrada> **2** CORRECT : correcto <the right answer : la respuesta correcta> **3** APPROPRIATE : apropiado, adecuado, debido <the right man for the job : el hombre perfecto para el trabajo> **4** STRAIGHT : recto <a right line : una línea recta> **5** : derecho <the right hand : la mano derecha> **6** SOUND : bien <he's not in his right mind : no está bien de la cabeza>

right[4] *n* **1** GOOD : bien *m* <to do right : hacer el bien> **2** : derecha *f* <on the right : a la derecha> **3** *or* **right hand** : mano *f* derecha **4** ENTITLEMENT : derecho *m* <the right to vote : el derecho a votar> <women's rights : los derechos de la mujer> **5 the Right** : la derecha (en la política)

right angle *n* **:** ángulo *m* recto
right–angled [ˈraɪtˈæŋgəld] *or* **right–angle** [-gəl] *adj* **1 :** en ángulo recto **2 right–angled triangle :** triángulo *m* rectángulo
righteous [ˈraɪtʃəs] *adj* **:** recto, honrado — **righteously** *adv*
righteousness [ˈraɪtʃəsnəs] *n* **:** rectitud *f,* honradez *f*
rightful [ˈraɪtfəl] *adj* **1** JUST **:** justo **2** LAWFUL **:** legítimo — **rightfully** *adv*
right–hand [ˈraɪtˈhænd] *adj* **1 :** situado a la derecha **2** RIGHT-HANDED **:** para la mano derecha, con la mano derecha **3 right–hand man :** brazo *m* derecho
right–handed [ˈraɪtˈhændəd] *adj* **1 :** diestro <a right-handed pitcher **:** un lanzador diestro> **2 :** para la mano derecha, con la mano derecha **3** CLOCKWISE **:** en la dirección de las manecillas del reloj
rightly [ˈraɪtli] *adv* **1** JUSTLY **:** justamente, con razón **2** PROPERLY **:** debidamente, apropiadamente **3** CORRECTLY **:** correctamente
right–of–way [ˈraɪtəˈweɪ, -əv-] *n, pl* **rights–of–way 1 :** preferencia (del tráfico) **2** ACCESS **:** derecho *m* de paso
rightward [ˈraɪtwərd] *adj* **:** a la derecha, hacia la derecha
right–wing [ˈraɪtˈwɪŋ] *adj* **:** derechista
right wing *n* **the right wing :** la derecha
right–winger [ˈraɪtˈwɪŋər] *n* **:** derechista *mf*
rigid [ˈrɪdʒɪd] *adj* **:** rígido — **rigidly** *adv*
rigidity [rɪˈdʒɪdəti] *n, pl* **-ties :** rigidez *f*
rigmarole [ˈrɪgməˌroːl, ˈrɪgə-] *n* **1** NONSENSE **:** galimatías *m,* disparates *mpl* **2** PROCEDURES **:** trámites *mpl*
rigor [ˈrɪgər] *n* **:** rigor *m*
rigor mortis [ˌrɪgərˈmɔrtəs] *n* **:** rigidez *f* cadavérica
rigorous [ˈrɪgərəs] *adj* **:** rigoroso — **rigorously** *adv*
rile [ˈraɪl] *vt* **riled; riling :** irritar
rill [ˈrɪl] *n* **:** riachuelo *m*
rim [ˈrɪm] *n* **1** EDGE **:** borde *m* **2 :** llanta *f,* rin *m Col, Mex* (de una rueda) **3** FRAME **:** montura *f* (de anteojos)
rime [ˈraɪm] *n* **:** escarcha *f*
rind [ˈraɪnd] *n* **:** corteza *f*
ring[1] [ˈrɪŋ] *v* **rang** [ˈræŋ]; **rung** [ˈrʌŋ]; **ringing** *vi* **1 :** sonar <the doorbell rang **:** el timbre sonó> <to ring for **:** llamar> **2** RESOUND **:** resonar **3** SEEM **:** parecer <to ring true **:** parecer cierto> — *vt* **1 :** tocar, hacer sonar (un timbre, una alarma, etc.) **2** SURROUND **:** cercar, rodear
ring[2] *n* **1 :** anillo *m,* sortija *f* <wedding ring **:** anillo de matrimonio> **2** BAND **:** aro *m,* anillo *m* <piston ring **:** aro de émbolo> **3** CIRCLE **:** círculo *m* **4** ARENA **:** arena *f,* ruedo *m* <a boxing ring **:** un cuadrilátero, un ring> **5** GANG **:** banda *f* (de ladrones, etc.) **6** SOUND **:** timbre *m,* sonido *m* **7** CALL **:** llamada *f* (por teléfono)
ringer [ˈrɪŋər] *n* **to be a dead ringer for :** ser un vivo retrato de
ringleader [ˈrɪŋˌliːdər] *n* **:** cabecilla *mf*
ringlet [ˈrɪŋlət] *n* **:** sortija *f,* rizo *m*
ringworm [ˈrɪŋˌwərm] *n* **:** tiña *f*
rink [ˈrɪŋk] *n* **:** pista *f* <skating rink **:** pista de patinaje>
rinse[1] [ˈrɪnts] *vt* **rinsed; rinsing :** enjuagar <to rinse out one's mouth **:** enjuagarse la boca>
rinse[2] *n* **:** enjuague *m*
riot[1] [ˈraɪət] *vi* **:** amotinarse
riot[2] *n* **:** motín *m,* tumulto *m,* alboroto *m*
rioter [ˈraɪətər] *n* **:** alborotador *m,* -dora *f*
riotous [ˈraɪətəs] *adj* **1** UNRULY, WILD **:** desenfrenado, alborotado **2** ABUNDANT **:** abundante
rip[1] [ˈrɪp] *v* **ripped; ripping** *vt* **:** rasgar, arrancar, desgarrar — *vi* **:** rasgarse, desgarrarse
rip[2] *n* **:** rasgón *m,* desgarrón *m*
ripe [ˈraɪp] *adj* **riper; ripest 1** MATURE **:** maduro <ripe fruit **:** fruta madura> **2** READY **:** listo, preparado
ripen [ˈraɪpən] *v* **:** madurar
ripeness [ˈraɪpnəs] *n* **:** madurez *f*
rip–off [ˈrɪpˌɔf] *n* **1** THEFT **:** robo *m* **2** SWINDLE **:** estafa *f,* timo *m fam*
ripple[1] [ˈrɪpəl] *v* **-pled; -pling** *vi* **:** rizarse, ondear, ondular — *vt* **:** rizar
ripple[2] *n* **:** onda *f,* ondulación *f*
rise[1] [ˈraɪz] *vi* **rose** [ˈroːz]; **risen** [ˈrɪzən]; **rising 1** GET UP **:** levantarse <to rise to one's feet **:** ponerse de pie> **2 :** elevarse, alzarse <the mountains rose to the west **:** las montañas se elevaron al oeste> **3 :** salir (dícese del sol y de la luna) **4 :** subir (dícese de las aguas, del humo, etc.) <the river rose **:** las aguas subieron de nivel> **5** INCREASE **:** aumentar, subir **6** ORIGINATE **:** nacer, proceder **7 to rise in rank :** ascender **8 to rise up** REBEL **:** sublevarse, rebelarse
rise[2] *n* **1** ASCENT **:** ascensión *f,* subida *f* **2** ORIGIN **:** origen *m* **3** ELEVATION **:** elevación *f* **4** INCREASE **:** subida *f,* aumento *m,* alzamiento *m* **5** SLOPE **:** pendiente *f,* cuesta *f*
riser [ˈraɪzər] *n* **1 :** contrahuella *f* (de una escalera) **2 early riser :** madrugador *m,* -dora *f* **3 late riser :** dormilón *m,* -lona *f*
risk[1] [ˈrɪsk] *vt* **:** arriesgar
risk[2] *n* **:** riesgo *m,* peligro *m* <at risk **:** en peligro> <at your own risk **:** por su cuenta y riesgo>
risky [ˈrɪski] *adj* **riskier; -est :** arriesgado, peligroso, riesgoso
risqué [rɪˈskeɪ] *adj* **:** escabroso, picante, subido de tono
rite [ˈraɪt] *n* **:** rito *m*

ritual[1] [ˈrɪtʃʊəl] *adj* : ritual — **ritually** *adv*
ritual[2] *n* : ritual *m*
rival[1] [ˈraɪvəl] *vt* **-valed** *or* **-valled; -valing** *or* **-valling** : rivalizar con, competir con
rival[2] *adj* : competidor, rival
rival[3] *n* : rival *mf;* competidor *m,* -dora *f*
rivalry [ˈraɪvəlri] *n, pl* **-ries** : rivalidad *f,* competencia *f*
river [ˈrɪvər] *n* : río *m*
riverbank [ˈrɪvər,bæŋk] *n* : ribera *f,* orilla *f*
riverbed [ˈrɪvər,bɛd] *n* : cauce *m,* lecho *m*
riverside [ˈrɪvər,saɪd] *n* : ribera *f,* orilla *f*
rivet[1] [ˈrɪvət] *vt* **1** : remachar **2** FIX : fijar (los ojos, etc.) **3** FASCINATE : fascinar, cautivar
rivet[2] *n* : remache *m*
rivulet [ˈrɪvjələt] *n* : arroyo *m,* riachuelo *m* <rivulets of sweat : gotas de sudor>
roach [ˈroːtʃ] → **cockroach**
road [ˈroːd] *n* **1** : carretera *f,* calle *f,* camino *m* **2** PATH : camino *m,* sendero *m,* vía *f* <on the road to a solution : en vías de una solución>
roadblock [ˈroːd,blɑk] *n* : control *m*
roadrunner [ˈroːd,rʌnər] *n* : correcaminos *m*
roadside [ˈroːd,saɪd] *n* : borde *m* de la carretera
roadway [ˈroːd,weɪ] *n* : carretera *f,* calzada *f*
roam [ˈroːm] *vi* : vagar, deambular, errar — *vt* : vagar por
roan[1] [ˈroːn] *adj* : ruano
roan[2] *n* : caballo *m* ruano
roar[1] [ˈror] *vi* : rugir, bramar <to roar with laughter : reírse a carcajadas> — *vt* : decir a gritos
roar[2] *n* **1** : rugido *m,* bramido *m* (de un animal) **2** DIN : clamor *m* (de gente), fragor *m* (del trueno), estruendo *m* (del tráfico, etc.)
roast[1] [ˈroːst] *vt* : asar (carne, papas), tostar (café, nueces) — *vi* : asarse
roast[2] *adj* **1** : asado <roast chicken : pollo asado> **2 roast beef** : rosbif *m*
roast[3] *n* : asado *m*
rob [ˈrɑb] *v* **robbed; robbing** *vt* **1** STEAL : robar **2** DEPRIVE : privar, quitar — *vi* : robar
robber [ˈrɑbər] *n* : ladrón *m,* -drona *f*
robbery [ˈrɑbəri] *n, pl* **-beries** : robo *m*
robe[1] [ˈroːb] *vt* **robed; robing** : vestirse
robe[2] *n* **1** : toga *f* (de magistrados, etc.), sotana *f* (de eclesiásticos) <robe of office : traje de ceremonias> **2** BATHROBE : bata *f*
robin [ˈrɑbən] *n* : petirrojo *m*
robot [ˈroː,bɑt, -bət] *n* : robot *m*
robust [roˈbʌst, ˈroː,bʌst] *adj* : robusto, fuerte — **robustly** *adv*
rock[1] [ˈrɑk] *vt* **1** : acunar (a un niño), mecer (una cuna) **2** SHAKE : sacudir — *vi* SWAY : mecerse, balancearse
rock[2] *adj* : de rock
rock[3] *n* **1** ROCKING : balanceo *m* **2** *or* **rock music** : rock *m,* música *f* rock **3** : roca *f* (substancia) **4** STONE : piedra *f*
rock and roll *n* : rock and roll *m*
rocker [ˈrɑkər] *n* **1** : balancín *m* **2** *or* **rocking chair** : mecedora *f,* balancín *m* **3 to be off one's rocker** : estar chiflado, estar loco
rocket[1] [ˈrɑkət] *vi* : dispararse, subir rápidamente
rocket[2] *n* : cohete *m*
rocking horse *n* : caballito *m* (de balancín)
rock salt *n* : sal *f* gema
rocky [ˈrɑki] *adj* **rockier; -est 1** : rocoso, pedregoso **2** UNSTEADY : inestable
rod [ˈrɑd] *n* **1** BAR : barra *f,* varilla *f,* vara *f* (de madera) <a fishing rod : una caña (de pescar)> **2** : medida *f* de longitud equivalente a 5.03 metros (5 yardas)
rode → **ride**[1]
rodent [ˈroːdənt] *n* : roedor *m*
rodeo [ˈroːdi,oː, roˈdeɪ,oː] *n, pl* **-deos** : rodeo *m*
roe [ˈroː] *n* : hueva *f*
roe deer *n* : corzo *m*
rogue [ˈroːg] *n* SCOUNDREL : pícaro *m,* -ra *f;* pillo *m,* -lla *f*
roguish [ˈroːgɪʃ] *adj* : pícaro, travieso
role [ˈroːl] *n* : papel *m,* función *f,* rol *m*
roll[1] [ˈroːl] *vt* **1** : hacer rodar <to roll the ball : hacer rodar la pelota> <to roll one's eyes : poner los ojos en blanco> **2** : liar (un cigarillo) **3** *or* **to roll up** : enrollar <to roll (oneself) up into a ball : hacerse una bola> **4** FLATTEN : estirar (masa), laminar (metales), pasar el rodillo por (el césped) **5 to roll up one's sleeves** : arremangarse — *vi* **1** : rodar <the ball kept on rolling : la pelota siguió rodando> **2** SWAY : balancearse <the ship rolled in the waves : el barco se balanceó en las olas> **3** REVERBERATE, SOUND : tronar (dícese del trueno), redoblar (dícese de un tambor) **4 to roll along** PROCEED : ponerse en marcha **5 to roll around** : revolcarse **6 to roll by** : pasar **7 to roll over** : dar una vuelta
roll[2] *n* **1** LIST : lista *f* <to call the roll : pasar lista> <to have on the roll : tener inscrito> **2** *or* **bread roll** : panecito *m,* bolillo *m Mex* **3** : rollo *m* (de papel, de tela, etc.) <a roll of film : un carrete> <a roll of bills : un fajo> **4** : redoble *m* (de tambores), retumbo *m* (del trueno, etc.) **5** ROLLING, SWAYING : balanceo *m*
roller [ˈroːlər] *n* **1** : rodillo *m* **2** CURLER : rulo *m*
roller coaster [ˈroːlər,koːstər] *n* : montaña *f* rusa

roller–skate ['roːlər,skeɪt] *vi* **-skated; -skating** : patinar (sobre ruedas)
roller skate *n* : patín *m* (de ruedas)
rollicking ['rɑlɪkɪŋ] *adj* : animado, alegre
rolling pin *n* : rodillo *m*
Roman[1] ['roːmən] *adj* : romano
Roman[2] *n* : romano *m*, -na *f*
Roman Catholic *n* : católico *m*, -ca *f* — **Roman Catholic** *adj*
Roman Catholicism *n* : catolicismo *m*
romance[1] [ro'mænts, 'roː,mænts] *vi* **-manced; -mancing** FANTASIZE : fantasear
romance[2] *n* **1** : romance *m*, novela *f* de caballerías **2** : novela *f* de amor, novela *f* romántica **3** AFFAIR : romance *m*, amorío *m*
Romanian [rʊ'meɪniən, ro-] *n* **1** : rumano *m*, -na *f* **2** : rumano *m* (idioma) — **Romanian** *adj*
Roman numeral *n* : número *m* romano
romantic [ro'mæntɪk] *adj* : romántico — **romantically** [-tɪkli] *adv*
romp[1] ['rɑmp] *vi* FROLIC : retozar, jugetear
romp[2] *n* : retozo *m*
roof[1] ['ruːf, 'rʊf] *vt* : techar
roof[2] *n, pl* **roofs** ['ruːfs, 'rʊfs; 'ruːvz, 'rʊvz] **1** : techo *m*, tejado *m*, techado *m* **2 roof of the mouth** : paladar *m*
roofing ['ruːfɪŋ, 'rʊfɪŋ] *n* : techumbre *f*
rooftop ['ruːf,tɑp, 'rʊf-] *n* ROOF : tejado *m*
rook[1] ['rʊk] *vt* CHEAT : defraudar, estafar, timar
rook[2] *n* **1** : grajo *m* (ave) **2** : torre *f* (en ajedrez)
rookie ['rʊki] *n* : novato *m*, -ta *f*
room[1] ['ruːm, 'rʊm] *vi* LODGE : alojarse, hospedarse
room[2] *n* **1** SPACE : espacio *m*, sitio *m*, lugar *m* <to make room for : hacer lugar para> **2** : cuarto *m*, habitación *f* (en una casa), sala *f* (para reuniones, etc.) **3** BEDROOM : dormitorio *m*, habitación *f*, pieza *f* **4** (*indicating possibility or opportunity*) <room for improvement : posibilidad de mejorar> <there's no room for error : no hay lugar para errores>
roomer ['ruːmər, 'rʊmər] *n* : inquilino *m*, -na *f*
rooming house *n* : pensión *f*
roommate ['ruːm,meɪt, 'rʊm-] *n* : compañero *m*, -ra *f* de cuarto
roomy ['ruːmi, 'rʊmi] *adj* **roomier; -est 1** SPACIOUS : espacioso, amplio **2** LOOSE : suelto, holgado <a roomy blouse : una blusa holgada>
roost[1] ['ruːst] *vi* : posarse, dormir (en una percha)
roost[2] *n* : percha *f*
rooster ['ruːstər, 'rʊs-] *n* : gallo *m*
root[1] ['ruːt, 'rʊt] *vi* **1** : arraigar <the plant rooted easily : la planta arraigó con facilidad> <deeply rooted traditions : tradiciones profundamente arraigadas> **2** : hozar (dícese de los cerdos) <to root around in : hurgar en> **3 to root for** : apoyar a, alentar — *vt* **to root out** *or* **to root up** : desarraigar (plantas), extirpar (problemas, etc.)
root[2] *n* **1** : raíz *f* (de una planta) **2** ORIGIN : origen *m*, raíz *f* **3** CORE : centro *m*, núcleo *m* <to get to the root of the matter : ir al centro del asunto>
rootless ['ruːtləs, 'rʊt-] *adj* : desarraigado
rope[1] ['roːp] *vt* **roped; roping 1** TIE : amarrar, atar **2** LASSO : lazar **3 to rope off** : acordonar
rope[2] *n* : soga *f*, cuerda *f*
rosary ['roːzəri] *n, pl* **-ries** : rosario *m*
rose[1] → **rise[1]**
rose[2] ['roːz] *adj* : rosa, color de rosa
rose[3] *n* **1** : rosal *m* (planta), rosa *f* (flor) **2** : rosa *m* (color)
rosebush ['roːz,bʊʃ] *n* : rosal *m*
rosemary ['roːz,mɛri] *n, pl* **-maries** : romero *m*
rosette [ro'zɛt] *n* : escarapela *f* (hecho de cintas), roseta *f* (en arquitectura)
Rosh Hashanah [,rɑʃhɑ'ʃɑnə, ,roːʃ-] *n* : el Año Nuevo judío
rosin ['rɑzən] *n* : colofonia *f*
roster ['rɑstər] *n* : lista *f*
rostrum ['rɑstrəm] *n, pl* **-trums** *or* **-tra** [-trə] : tribuna *f*, estrado *m*
rosy ['roːzi] *adj* **rosier; -est 1** : sonrosado, de color rosa **2** PROMISING : prometedor, halagüeno
rot[1] ['rɑt] *v* **rotted; rotting** *vi* : pudrirse, descomponerse — *vt* : pudrir, descomponer
rot[2] *n* : putrefacción *f*, descomposición *f*, podredumbre *f*
rotary[1] ['roːtəri] *adj* : rotativo, rotatorio
rotary[2] *n, pl* **-ries 1** : máquina *f* rotativa **2** TRAFFIC CIRCLE : rotonda *f*, glorieta *f*
rotate ['roː,teɪt] *v* **-tated; -tating** *vi* REVOLVE : girar, rotar — *vt* **1** TURN : hacer girar, darle vueltas a **2** ALTERNATE : alternar
rotation [ro'teɪʃən] *n* : rotación *f*
rote ['roːt] *n* **to learn by rote** : aprender de memoria
rotor ['roːtər] *n* : rotor *m*
rotten ['rɑtən] *adj* **1** PUTRID : podrido, putrefacto **2** CORRUPT : corrompido **3** BAD : malo <a rotten day : un día malísimo>
rottenness ['rɑtənnəs] *n* : podredumbre *f*
rotund [ro'tʌnd] *adj* **1** ROUNDED : redondeado **2** PLUMP : regordete *fam*, llenito *fam*
rouge ['ruːʒ, 'ruːdʒ] *n* : colorete *m*
rough[1] ['rʌf] *vt* **1** ROUGHEN : poner áspero **2 to rough out** SKETCH : esbozar, bosquejar **3 to rough up** BEAT : darle una paliza (a alguien) **4 to rough it** : vivir sin comodidades

rough[2] *adj* **1** COARSE **:** áspero, basto **2** UNEVEN **:** desigual, escabroso, accidentado (dícese del terreno) **3 :** agitado (dícese del mar), tempestuoso (dícese del tiempo), violento (dícese del viento) **4** VIOLENT **:** violento, brutal <a rough neighborhood : un barrio peligroso> **5** DIFFICULT **:** duro, difícil **6** CRUDE **:** rudo, tosco, burdo <a rough cottage : una casita tosca> <a rough draft : un borrador> <a rough sketch : un bosquejo> **7** APPROXIMATE **:** aproximado <a rough idea : una idea aproximada>

rough[3] *n* **1 the rough :** el rough (en golf) **2 in the rough :** en borrador

roughage [ˈrʌfɪdʒ] *n* **:** fibra *f*

roughen [ˈrʌfən] *vt* **:** poner áspero — *vi* **:** ponerse áspero

roughly [ˈrʌfli] *adv* **1 :** bruscamente <to treat roughly : maltratar> **2** CRUDELY **:** burdamente **3** APPROXIMATELY **:** aproximadamente, más o menos

roughneck [ˈrʌfˌnɛk] *n* **:** matón *m*

roughness [ˈrʌfnəs] *n* **:** rudeza *f,* aspereza *f*

roulette [ruːˈlɛt] *n* **:** ruleta *f*

round[1] [ˈraʊnd] *vt* **1 :** redondear <she rounded the edges : redondeó los bordes> **2** TURN **:** doblar <to round the corner : dar la vuelta a la esquina> **3 to round off :** redondear (un número) **4 to round off** *or* **to round out** COMPLETE **:** rematar, terminar **5 to round up** GATHER **:** reunir

round[2] *adv* → **around**[1]

round[3] *adj* **1 :** redondo <a round table : una mesa redonda> <in round numbers : en números redondos> <round shoulders : espaldas cargadas> **2 round trip :** viaje *m* de ida y vuelta

round[4] *n* **1** CIRCLE **:** círculo *m* **2** SERIES **:** serie *f,* sucesión *f* <a round of talks : una ronda de negociaciones> <the daily round : la rutina cotidiana> **3 :** asalto *m* (en boxeo), recorrido *m* (en golf), vuelta *f* (en varios juegos) **4 :** salva *f* (de aplausos) **5 round of drinks :** ronda *f* **6 round of ammunition :** disparo *m,* cartucho *m* **7 rounds** *npl* **:** recorridos *mpl* (de un cartero), rondas *fpl* (de un vigilante), visitas *fpl* (de un médico) <to make the rounds : hacer visitas>

round[5] *prep* → **around**[2]

roundabout [ˈraʊndəˌbaʊt] *adj* **:** indirecto <to speak in a roundabout way : hablar con rodeos>

roundly [ˈraʊndli] *adv* **1** THOROUGHLY **:** completamente **2** BLUNTLY **:** francamente, rotundamente **3** VIGOROUSLY **:** con vigor

roundness [ˈraʊndnəs] *n* **:** redondez *f*

roundup [ˈraʊndˌʌp] *n* **1 :** rodeo *m* (de animales), redada *f* (de delincuentes, etc.) **2** SUMMARY **:** resumen *m*

round up *vt* **1 :** rodear (ganado), reunir (personas) **2** SUMMARIZE **:** hacer un resumen de

roundworm [ˈraʊndˌwərm] *n* **:** lombriz *f* intestinal

rouse [ˈraʊz] *vt* **roused; rousing 1** AWAKE **:** despertar **2** EXCITE **:** excitar <it roused him to fury : lo enfureció>

rout[1] [ˈraʊt] *vt* **1** DEFEAT **:** derrotar, aplastar **2 to rout out :** hacer salir

rout[2] *n* **1** DISPERSAL **:** desbandada *f,* dispersión *f* **2** DEFEAT **:** derrota *f* aplastante

route[1] [ˈruːt, ˈraʊt] *vt* **routed; routing :** dirigir, enviar, encaminar

route[2] *n* **:** camino *m,* ruta *f,* recorrido *m*

routine[1] [ruːˈtiːn] *adj* **:** rutinario — **routinely** *adv*

routine[2] *n* **:** rutina *f*

rove [ˈroːv] *v* **roved; roving** *vi* **:** vagar, errar — *vt* **:** errar por

rover [ˈroːvər] *n* **:** vagabundo *m,* -da *f*

row[1] [ˈroː] *vt* **1 :** avanzar a remo <to row a boat : remar> **2 :** llevar a remo <he rowed me to shore : me llevó hasta la orilla> — *vi* **:** remar

row[2] [ˈraʊ] *n* **1 :** paseo *m* en barca <to go for a row : salir a remar> **2** LINE, RANK **:** fila *f,* hilera *f* **3** SERIES **:** serie *f* <three days in a row : tres días seguidos> **4** RACKET **:** estruendo *m,* bulla *f* **5** QUARREL **:** pelea *f,* riña *f*

rowboat [ˈroːˌboːt] *n* **:** bote *m* de remos

rowdiness [ˈraʊdinəs] *n* **:** bulla *f*

rowdy[1] [ˈraʊdi] *adj* **-dier; -est :** escandaloso, alborotador

rowdy[2] *n, pl* **-dies :** alborotador *m,* -dora *f*

royal[1] [ˈrɔɪəl] *adj* **:** real — **royally** *adv*

royal[2] *n* **:** persona de linaje real, miembro de la familia real

royalty [ˈrɔɪəlti] *n, pl* **-ties 1 :** realeza *f* (posición) **2 :** miembros *mpl* de la familia real **3 royalties** *npl* **:** derechos *mpl* de autor

rub[1] [ˈrʌb] *v* **rubbed; rubbing** *vt* **1 :** frotar, restregar <to rub one's hands together : frotarse las manos> **2** MASSAGE **:** friccionar, masajear **3** CHAFE **:** rozar **4** POLISH **:** frotar, pulir **5** SCRUB **:** fregar **6 to rub elbows with :** codarse con **7 to rub someone the wrong way :** sacar de quicio a alguien, caerle mal a alguien — *vi* **to rub against :** rozar

rub[2] *n* **1** RUBBING **:** frotamiento *m,* fricción *f* **2** DIFFICULTY **:** problema *m*

rubber [ˈrʌbər] *n* **1 :** goma *f,* caucho *m,* hule *m Mex* **2 rubbers** *npl* OVERSHOES **:** chanclos *mpl*

rubber band *n* **:** goma *f* (elástica), gomita *f*

rubber–stamp [ˈrʌbərˈstæmp] *vt* **1** APPROVE **:** aprobar, autorizar **2** STAMP **:** sellar

rubber stamp *n* **:** sello *m* (de goma)

rubbery [ˈrʌbəri] *adj* **:** gomoso

rubbish ['rʌbɪʃ] *n* : basura *f*, desechos *mpl*, desperdicios *mpl*
rubble ['rʌbəl] *n* : escombros *mpl*, ripio *m*
ruble ['ru:bəl] *n* : rublo *m*
ruby ['ru:bi] *n, pl* **-bies 1** : rubí *m* (gema) **2** : color *m* de rubí
rudder ['rʌdər] *n* : timón *m*
ruddy ['rʌdi] *adj* **-dier; -est** : rubicundo (dícese de la cara, etc.), rojizo (dícese del cielo)
rude ['ru:d] *adj* **ruder; rudest 1** CRUDE : tosco, rústico **2** IMPOLITE : grosero, descortés, maleducado **3** ABRUPT : brusco <a rude awakening : una sorpresa desagradable>
rudely ['ru:dli] *adv* : groseramente
rudeness ['ru:dnəs] *n* **1** IMPOLITENESS : grosería *f*, descortesía *f*, falta *f* de educación **2** ROUGHNESS : tosquedad *f* **3** SUDDENNESS : brusquedad *f*
rudiment ['ru:dəmənt] *n* : rudimento *m*, noción *f* básica <the rudiments of Spanish : los rudimentos del español>
rudimentary [ˌru:də'mɛntəri] *adj* : rudimentario, básico
rue ['ru:] *vt* **rued; ruing** : lamentar, arrepentirse de
rueful ['ru:fəl] *adj* **1** PITIFUL : lastimoso **2** REGRETFUL : arrepentido, pesaroso
ruffian ['rʌfiən] *n* : matón *m*
ruffle[1] ['rʌfəl] *vt* **-fled; -fling 1** AGITATE : agitar, rizar (agua) **2** RUMPLE : arrugar (ropa), despeinar (pelo) **3** ERECT : erizar (plumas) **4** VEX : alterar, irritar, perturbar **5** : fruncir volantes en (tela)
ruffle[2] *n* FLOUNCE : volante *m*
ruffly ['rʌfəli] *adj* : con volantes
rug ['rʌg] *n* : alfombra *f*, tapete *m*
rugged ['rʌgəd] *adj* **1** ROUGH, UNEVEN : accidentado, escabroso <rugged mountains : montañas accidentadas> **2** HARSH : duro, severo **3** ROBUST, STURDY : robusto, fuerte
ruin[1] ['ru:ən] *vt* **1** DESTROY : destruir, arruinar **2** BANKRUPT : arruinar, hacer quebrar
ruin[2] *n* **1** : ruina *f* <to fall into ruin : caer en ruinas> **2** : ruina *f*, perdición *f* <to be the ruin of : ser la perdición de> **3 ruins** *npl* : ruinas *fpl*, restos *mpl* <the ruins of the ancient temple : las ruinas del templo antiguo>
ruinous ['ru:ənəs] *adj* : ruinoso
rule[1] ['ru:l] *v* **ruled; ruling** *vt* **1** CONTROL, GOVERN : gobernar (un país), controlar (las emociones) **2** DECIDE : decidir, fallar <the judge ruled that... : el juez falló que...> **3** DRAW : trazar con una regla — *vi* **1** GOVERN : gobernar, reinar **2** PREVAIL : prevalecer, imperar **3 to rule against** : fallar en contra de
rule[2] *n* **1** REGULATION : regla *f*, norma *f* **2** CUSTOM, HABIT : regla *f* general <as a rule : por lo general> **3** GOVERNMENT : gobierno *m*, dominio *m* **4** RULER : regla *f* (para medir)
ruler ['ru:lər] *n* **1** LEADER, SOVEREIGN : gobernante *mf;* soberano *m*, -na *f* **2** : regla *f* (para medir)
ruling ['ru:lɪŋ] *n* : resolución *f*, fallo *m*
rum ['rʌm] *n* : ron *m*
Rumanian [rʊ'meɪniən] → **Romanian**
rumble[1] ['rʌmbəl] *vi* **-bled; -bling** : retumbar, hacer ruidos (dícese del estómago)
rumble[2] *n* : estruendo *m*, ruido *m* sordo, retumbo *m*
ruminant[1] ['ru:mənənt] *adj* : rumiante
ruminant[2] *n* : rumiante *m*
ruminate ['ru:məˌneɪt] *vi* **-nated; -nating 1** : rumiar (en zoología) **2** REFLECT : reflexionar, rumiar
rummage ['rʌmɪdʒ] *v* **-maged; -maging** *vi* : hurgar — *vt* RANSACK : revolver <they rummaged the attic : revolvieron el ático>
rummy ['rʌmi] *n* : rummy *m* (juego de naipes)
rumor[1] ['ru:mər] *vt* : rumorear <it is rumored that. . . : se rumorea que. . . , se dice que. . .>
rumor[2] *n* : rumor *m*
rump ['rʌmp] *n* **1** : ancas *fpl*, grupa *f* (de un animal) **2** : cadera *f* <rump steak : filete de cadera>
rumple ['rʌmpəl] *vt* **-pled; -pling** : arrugar (ropa, etc.), despeinar (pelo)
rumpus ['rʌmpəs] *n* : lío *m*, jaleo *m* *fam*
run[1] ['rʌn] *v* **ran** ['ræn]; **run; running** *vi* **1** : correr <she ran to catch the bus : corrió para alcanzar el autobús> <run and fetch the doctor : corre a buscar al médico> **2** : circular, correr <the train runs between Detroit and Chicago : el tren circula entre Detroit y Chicago> <to run on time : ser puntual> **3** FUNCTION : funcionar, ir <the engine runs on gasoline : el motor funciona con gasolina> <to run smoothly : ir bien> **4** FLOW : correr, ir **5** LAST : durar <the movie runs for two hours : la película dura dos horas> <the contract runs for three years : el contrato es válido por tres años> **6** : desteñir, despintar (dícese de los colores) **7** EXTEND : correr, extenderse **8 to run for office** : postularse, presentarse — *vt* **1** : correr <to run 10 miles : correr 10 millas> <to run errands : hacer los mandados> <to run out of town : hacer salir del pueblo> **2** PASS : pasar **3** DRIVE : llevar en coche **4** OPERATE : hacer funcionar (un motor, etc.) **5** : echar <to run water : echar agua> **6** MANAGE : dirigir, llevar (un negocio, etc.) **7** EXTEND : tender (un cable, etc.) **8 to run a risk** : correr un riesgo
run[2] *n* **1** : carrera *f* <at a run : a la carrera, corriendo> <to go for a run : ir a correr> **2** TRIP : vuelta *f*, paseo *m* (en coche), viaje *m* (en avión) **3** SERIES : serie *f* <a run of disappointments : una serie de desilusiones> <in

the long run : a la larga> <in the short run : a corto plazo> 4 DEMAND : gran demanda *f* <a run on the banks : una corrida bancaria> **5** (*used for theatrical productions and films*) <to have a long run : mantenerse mucho tiempo en la cartelera> **6** TYPE : tipo *m* <the average run of students : el tipo más común de estudiante> **7** : carrera *f* (en béisbol) **8** : carrera *f* (en una media) **9 to have the run of** : tener libre acceso de (una casa, etc.) **10 ski run** : pista *f* (de esquí)

runaway[1] [ˈrʌnəˌweɪ] *adj* **1** FUGITIVE : fugitivo **2** UNCONTROLLABLE : incontrolable, fuera de control <runaway inflation : inflación desenfrenada> <a runaway success : un éxito aplastante>

runaway[2] *n* : fugitivo *m*, -va *f*

rundown [ˈrʌnˌdaʊn] *n* SUMMARY : resumen *m*

run–down [ˈrʌnˈdaʊn] *adj* **1** DILAPIDATED : ruinoso, destartalado **2** SICKLY, TIRED : cansado, débil

rung[1] → **ring**[1]

rung[2] [ˈrʌŋ] *n* : peldaño *m*, escalón *m*

run–in [ˈrʌnˌɪn] *n* : disputa *f*, altercado *m*

runner [ˈrʌnər] *n* **1** RACER : corredor *m*, -dora *f* **2** MESSENGER : mensajero *m*, -ra *f* **3** TRACK : riel *m* (de un cajón, etc.) **4** : patín *m* (de un trineo), cuchilla *f* (de un patín) **5** : estolón *m* (planta)

runner–up [ˌrʌnərˈʌp] *n, pl* **runners–up** : subcampeón *m*, -peona *f*

running [ˈrʌnɪŋ] *adj* **1** FLOWING : corriente <running water : agua corriente> **2** CONTINUOUS : continuo <a running battle : una lucha continua> **3** CONSECUTIVE : seguido <six days running : por seis días seguidos>

run over *vt* : atropellar — *vi* OVERFLOW : rebosar

runt [ˈrʌnt] *n* : animal *m* pequeño <the runt of the litter : el más pequeño de la camada>

runway [ˈrʌnˌweɪ] *n* : pista *f* de aterrizaje

rupee [ruːˈpiː, ˈruːˌ-] *n* : rupia *f*

rupture[1] [ˈrʌptʃər] *v* **-tured; -turing** *vt* **1** BREAK, BURST : romper, reventar **2** : causar una hernia en — *vi* : reventarse

rupture[2] *n* **1** BREAK : ruptura *f* **2** HERNIA : hernia *f*

rural [ˈrʊrəl] *adj* : rural, campestre

ruse [ˈruːs, ˈruːz] *n* : treta *f*, ardid *m*, estratagema *f*

rush[1] [ˈrʌʃ] *vi* : correr, ir de prisa <to rush around : correr de un lado a otro> <to rush off : irse corriendo> — *vt* **1** HURRY : apresurar, apurar **2** ATTACK : abalanzarse sobre, asaltar

rush[2] *adj* : urgente

rush[3] *n* **1** HASTE : prisa *f*, apuro *m* **2** SURGE : ráfaga *f* (de aire), torrente *m* (de aguas), avalancha *f* (de gente) **3** DEMAND : demanda *f* <a rush on sugar : una gran demanda para el azúcar> **4** : carga *f* (en futbol americano) **5** : junco *m* (planta)

russet [ˈrʌsət] *n* : color *m* rojizo

Russian [ˈrʌʃən] *n* **1** : ruso *m*, -sa *f* **2** : ruso *m* (idioma) — **Russian** *adj*

rust[1] [ˈrʌst] *vi* : oxidarse — *vt* : oxidar

rust[2] *n* **1** : herrumbre *f*, orín *m*, óxido *m* (en los metales) **2** : roya *f* (en las plantas)

rustic[1] [ˈrʌstɪk] *adj* : rústico, campestre — **rustically** [-tɪkli] *adv*

rustic[2] *n* : rústico *m*, -ca *f*; campesino *m*, -na *f*

rustle[1] [ˈrʌsəl] *v* **-tled; -tling** *vt* **1** : hacer susurrar, hacer crujir <to rustle a newspaper : hacer crujir un periódico> **2** STEAL : robar (ganado) — *vi* : susurrar, crujir

rustle[2] *n* : murmullo *m*, susurro *m*, crujido *m*

rustler [ˈrʌsələr] *n* : ladrón *m*, -drona *f* de ganado

rusty [ˈrʌsti] *adj* **rustier; -est** : oxidado, herrumbroso

rut [ˈrʌt] *n* **1** GROOVE, TRACK : rodada *f*, surco *m* **2 to be in a rut** : ser esclavo de la rutina

ruthless [ˈruːθləs] *adj* : despiadado, cruel — **ruthlessly** *adv*

ruthlessness [ˈruːθləsnəs] *n* : crueldad *f*, falta *f* de piedad

Rwandan [rʊˈɑndən] *n* : ruandés *m*, -desa *f* — **Rwandan** *adj*

rye [ˈraɪ] *n* **1** : centeno *m* **2** *or* **rye whiskey** : whisky *m* de centeno

S

s [ˈɛs] *n, pl* **s's** *or* **ss** [ˈɛsəz] : decimonovena letra del alfabeto inglés

Sabbath [ˈsæbəθ] *n* **1** : sábado *m* (en el judaísmo) **2** : domingo *m* (en el cristianismo)

saber [ˈseɪbər] *n* : sable *m*

sable [ˈseɪbəl] *n* **1** BLACK : negro *m* **2** : marta *f* cebellina (animal)

sabotage[1] [ˈsæbəˌtɑʒ] *vt* **-taged; -taging** : sabotear

sabotage[2] *n* : sabotaje *m*

sac [ˈsæk] *n* : saco *m* (anatómico)

saccharin [ˈsækərən] *n* : sacarina *f*

saccharine *adj* [ˈsækərən, -ˌriːn, -ˌraɪn] : meloso, empalagoso

sachet [sæˈʃeɪ] *n* : bolsita *f* (perfumada)

sack[1] [ˈsæk] *vt* **1** FIRE : echar (del trabajo), despedir **2** PLUNDER : saquear

sack[2] *n* BAG : saco *m*

sacrament [ˈsækrəmənt] *n* : sacramento *m*

sacramental [ˌsækrəˈmɛntəl] *adj* : sacramental
sacred [ˈseɪkrəd] *adj* **1** RELIGIOUS : sagrado, sacro <sacred texts : textos sagrados> **2** HOLY : sagrado **3 sacred to** : consagrado a
sacrifice[1] [ˈsækrəˌfaɪs] *vt* **-ficed; -ficing 1** : sacrificar **2 to sacrifice oneself** : sacrificarse
sacrifice[2] *n* : sacrificio *m*
sacrilege [ˈsækrəlɪdʒ] *n* : sacrilegio *m*
sacrilegious [ˌsækrəˈlɪdʒəs, -ˈliː-] *adj* : sacrílego
sacrosanct [ˈsækroˌsæŋkt] *adj* : sacrosanto
sad [ˈsæd] *adj* **sadder; saddest** : triste — **sadly** *adv*
sadden [ˈsædən] *vt* : entristecer
saddle[1] [ˈsædəl] *vt* **-dled; -dling** : ensillar
saddle[2] *n* : silla *f* (de montar)
sadism [ˈseɪˌdɪzəm, ˈsæ-] *n* : sadismo *m*
sadist [ˈseɪdɪst, ˈsæ-] *n* : sádico *m*, -ca *f*
sadistic [səˈdɪstɪk] *adj* : sádico — **sadistically** [-tɪkli] *adv*
sadness [ˈsædnəs] *n* : tristeza *f*
safari [səˈfɑri, -ˈfær-] *n* : safari *m*
safe[1] [ˈseɪf] *adj* **safer; safest 1** UNHARMED : ileso <safe and sound : sano y salvo> **2** SECURE : seguro **3 to be on the safe side** : para mayor seguridad **4 to play it safe** : ir a la segura
safe[2] *n* : caja *f* fuerte
safeguard[1] [ˈseɪfˌgɑrd] *vt* : salvaguardar, proteger
safeguard[2] *n* : salvaguarda *f*, protección *f*
safekeeping [ˈseɪfˈkiːpɪŋ] *n* : custodia *f*, protección *f* <to put into safekeeping : poner en buen recaudo>
safely [ˈseɪfli] *adv* **1** UNHARMED : sin incidentes, sin novedades <they landed safely : aterrizaron sin novedades> **2** SECURELY : con toda seguridad, sin peligro
safety [ˈseɪfti] *n, pl* **-ties** : seguridad *f*
safety belt *n* : cinturón *m* de seguridad
safety pin *n* : alfiler *m* de gancho, alfiler *m* de seguridad, imperdible *m Spain*
saffron [ˈsæfrən] *n* : azafrán *m*
sag[1] [ˈsæg] *vi* **sagged; sagging 1** DROOP, SINK : combarse, hundirse, inclinarse **2** : colgar, caer <his jowls sagged : le colgaban las mejillas> **3** FLAG : flaquear, decaer <his spirits sagged : se le flaqueó el ánimo>
sag[2] *n* : combadura *f*
saga [ˈsɑgə, ˈsæ-] *n* : saga *f*
sagacious [səˈgeɪʃəs] *adj* : sagaz
sage[1] [ˈseɪdʒ] *adj* **sager; -est** : sabio — **sagely** *adv*
sage[2] *n* **1** : sabio *m*, -bia *f* **2** : salvia *f* (planta)
sagebrush [ˈseɪdʒˌbrʌʃ] *n* : artemisa *f*
Sagittarius [ˌsædʒəˈtɛriəs] *n* : Sagitario *mf*
said → **say**
sail[1] [ˈseɪl] *vi* **1** : navegar (en un barco) **2** : ir fácilmente <we sailed right in : entramos sin ningún problema> — *vt* **1** : gobernar (un barco) **2 to sail the seas** : cruzar los mares
sail[2] *n* **1** : vela *f* (de un barco) **2** : viaje *m* en velero <to go for a sail : salir a navegar>
sailboat [ˈseɪlˌboːt] *n* : velero *m*, barco *m* de vela
sailfish [ˈseɪlˌfɪʃ] *n* : pez *m* vela
sailor [ˈseɪlər] *n* : marinero *m*
saint [ˈseɪnt, *before a name* ˌseɪnt *or* sənt] *n* : santo *m*, -ta *f* <Saint Francis : San Francisco> <Saint Rose : Santa Rosa>
saintliness [ˈseɪntlinəs] *n* : santidad *f*
saintly [ˈseɪntli] *adj* **saintlier; -est** : santo
sake [ˈseɪk] *n* **1** BENEFIT : bien *m* <for the children's sake : por el bien de los niños> **2** (*indicating an end or a purpose*) <art for art's sake : el arte por el arte> <let's say, for argument's sake, that he's wrong : pongamos que está equivocado> **3 for goodness' sake!** : ¡por (el amor de) Dios!
salable *or* **saleable** [ˈseɪləbəl] *adj* : vendible
salacious [səˈleɪʃəs] *adj* : salaz — **salaciously** *adv*
salad [ˈsæləd] *n* : ensalada *f*
salamander [ˈsæləˌmændər] *n* : salamandra *f*
salami [səˈlɑmi] *n* : salami *m*
salary [ˈsæləri] *n, pl* **-ries** : sueldo *m*
sale [ˈseɪl] *n* **1** SELLING : venta *f* **2** : liquidación *f*, rebajas *fpl* <on sale : de rebaja> **3 sales** *npl* : ventas *fpl* <to work in sales : trabajar en ventas>
salesman [ˈseɪlzmən] *n, pl* **-men** [-mən, -ˌmɛn] **1** : vendedor *m*, dependiente *m* (en una tienda) **2 traveling salesman** : viajante *m*, representante *m*
salesperson [ˈseɪlzˌpərsən] *n* : vendedor *m*, -dora *f*; dependiente *m*, -ta *f* (en una tienda)
saleswoman [ˈseɪlzˌwʊmən] *n, pl* **-women** [-ˌwɪmən] **1** : vendedora *f*, dependienta *f* (en una tienda) **2 traveling saleswoman** : viajante *f*, representante *f*
salient [ˈseɪljənt] *adj* : saliente, sobresaliente
saline [ˈseɪˌliːn, -ˌlaɪn] *adj* : salino
saliva [səˈlaɪvə] *n* : saliva *f*
salivary [ˈsæləˌvɛri] *adj* : salival <salivary gland : glándula salival>
salivate [ˈsæləˌveɪt] *vi* **-vated; -vating** : salivar
sallow [ˈsæloː] *adj* : amarillento, cetrino
sally[1] [ˈsæli] *vi* **-lied; -lying** SET OUT : salir, hacer una salida
sally[2] *n, pl* **-lies 1** : salida *f* (militar), misión *f* **2** QUIP : salida *f*, ocurrencia *f*

salmon ['sæmən] *ns & pl* **1** : salmón *m* (pez) **2** : color *m* salmón

salon [sə'lɑn, 'sæ,lɑn, sæ'lɔ̃] *n* : salón *m* <beauty salon : salón de belleza>

saloon [sə'lu:n] *n* **1** HALL : salón *m* (en un barco) **2** BARROOM : bar *m*

salsa ['sɔlsə, 'sɑl-] *n* : salsa *f* mexicana, salsa *f* picante

salt[1] ['sɔlt] *vt* : salar, echarle sal a

salt[2] *adj* : salado

salt[3] *n* : sal *f*

saltwater ['sɔlt,wɔt̬ər, -,wɑ-] *adj* : de agua salada

salty ['sɔlt̬i] *adj* **saltier; -est** : salado

salubrious [sə'lu:briəs] *adj* : salubre

salutary ['sæljə,tɛri] *adj* : saludable, salubre

salutation [,sæljə'teɪʃən] *n* : saludo *m*, salutación *f*

salute[1] [sə'lu:t] *v* **-luted; -luting** *vt* **1** : saludar (con gestos o ceremonias) **2** ACCLAIM : reconocer, aclamar — *vi* : hacer un saludo

salute[2] *n* **1** : saludo *m* (gesto), salva *f* (de cañonazos) **2** TRIBUTE : reconocimiento *m*, homenaje *m*

salvage[1] ['sælvɪdʒ] *vt* **-vaged; -vaging** : salvar, rescatar

salvage[2] *n* **1** SALVAGING : salvamento *m*, rescate *m* **2** : objetos *mpl* salvados

salvation [sæl'veɪʃən] *n* : salvación *f*

salve[1] ['sæv, 'sav] *vt* **salved; salving** : calmar, apaciguar <to salve one's conscience : aliviarse la conciencia>

salve[2] *n* : ungüento *m*

salvo ['sæl,vo:] *n, pl* **-vos** *or* **-voes** : salva *f*

same[1] ['seɪm] *adj* : mismo, igual <the results are the same : los resultados son iguales> <he said the same thing as you : dijo lo mismo que tú>

same[2] *pron* : mismo <it's all the same to me : me da lo mismo> <the same to you! : ¡igualmente!>

sameness ['seɪmnəs] *n* **1** SIMILARITY : identidad *f*, semejanza *f* **2** MONOTONY : monotonía *f*

sample[1] ['sæmpəl] *vt* **-pled; -pling** : probar

sample[2] *n* : muestra *f*, prueba *f*

sampler ['sæmplər] *n* : dechado *m* (en bordado)

sanatorium [,sænə'toriəm] *n, pl* **-riums** *or* **-ria** [-iə] : sanatorio *m*

sanctify ['sæŋktə,faɪ] *vt* **-fied; -fying** : santificar

sanctimonious [,sæŋktə'mo:niəs] *adj* : beato, santurrón

sanction[1] ['sæŋkʃən] *vt* : sancionar, aprobar

sanction[2] *n* **1** AUTHORIZATION : sanción *f*, autorización *f* **2 sanctions** *npl* : sanciones *fpl* <to impose sanctions on : imponer sanciones a>

sanctity ['sæŋktət̬i] *n, pl* **-ties** : santidad *f*

sanctuary ['sæŋktʃʊ,ɛri] *n, pl* **-aries 1** : presbiterio *m* (en una iglesia) **2** REFUGE : refugio *m*, asilo *m*

sand[1] ['sænd] *vt* : lijar (madera)

sand[2] *n* : arena *f*

sandal ['sændəl] *n* : sandalia *f*

sandbank ['sænd,bæŋk] *n* : banco *m* de arena

sandpaper *n* : papel *m* de lija

sandpiper ['sænd,paɪpər] *n* : andarríos *m*

sandstone ['sænd,sto:n] *n* : arenisca *f*

sandstorm ['sænd,stɔrm] *n* : tormenta *f* de arena

sandwich[1] ['sænd,wɪtʃ] *vt* : intercalar, encajonar, meter (entre dos cosas)

sandwich[2] *n* : sandwich *m*, emparedado *m*, bocadillo *m Spain*

sandy ['sændi] *adj* **sandier; -est** : arenoso

sane ['seɪn] *adj* **saner; sanest 1** : cuerdo **2** SENSIBLE : sensato, razonable

sang → **sing**

sanguine ['sæŋgwən] *adj* **1** RUDDY : sanguíneo, rubicundo **2** HOPEFUL : optimista

sanitarium [,sænə'tɛriəm] *n, pl* **-iums** *or* **-ia** [-iə] → **sanatorium**

sanitary ['sænətɛri] *adj* **1** : sanitario <sanitary measures : medidas sanitarias> **2** HYGIENIC : higiénico **3 sanitary napkin** : compresa *f*, paño *m* higiénico

sanitation [,sænə'teɪʃən] *n* : sanidad *f*

sanity ['sænət̬i] *n* : cordura *f*, razón *f* <to lose one's sanity : perder el juicio>

sank → **sink**

Santa Claus ['sæntə,klɔz] *n* : Papá Noel, San Nicolás

sap[1] ['sæp] *vt* **sapped; sapping 1** UNDERMINE : socavar **2** WEAKEN : minar, debilitar

sap[2] *n* **1** : savia *f* (de una planta) **2** SUCKER : inocentón *m*, -tona *f*

sapling ['sæplɪŋ] *n* : árbol *m* joven

sapphire ['sæ,faɪr] *n* : zafiro *m*

sarcasm ['sɑr,kæzəm] *n* : sarcasmo *m*

sarcastic [sɑr'kæstɪk] *adj* : sarcástico — **sarcastically** [-tɪkli] *adv*

sarcophagus [sɑr'kɑfəgəs] *n, pl* **-gi** [-,gaɪ, -,dʒaɪ] : sarcófago *m*

sardine [sɑr'di:n] *n* : sardina *f*

sardonic [sɑr'dɑnɪk] *adj* : sardónico — **sardonically** [-nɪkli] *adv*

sarsaparilla [,sæspə'rɪlə, ,sɑrs-] *n* : zarzaparrilla *f*

sash ['sæʃ] *n* **1** : faja *f* (de un vestido), fajín *m* (de un uniforme) **2** *pl* **sash** : marco *m* (de una ventana)

sassafras ['sæsə,fræs] *n* : sasafrás *m*

sassy ['sæsi] *adj* **sassier; -est** → **saucy**

sat → **sit**

Satan ['seɪtən] *n* : Satanás *m*, Satán *m*

satanic [sə'tænɪk, seɪ-] *adj* : satánico — **satanically** [-nɪkli] *adv*

satchel ['sætʃəl] *n* : cartera *f*, saco *m*

sate ['seɪt] *vt* **sated; sating** : saciar

satellite [ˈsæt̬əˌlaɪt] *n* : satélite *m* <spy satellite : satélite espía>
satiate [ˈseɪʃiˌeɪt] *vt* **-ated; -ating** : saciar, hartar
satin [ˈsætən] *n* : raso *m*, satín *m*, satén *m*
satire [ˈsæˌtaɪr] *n* : sátira *f*
satiric [səˈtɪrɪk] *or* **satirical** [-ɪkəl] *adj* : satírico
satirize [ˈsæt̬əˌraɪz] *vt* **-rized; -rizing** : satirizar
satisfaction [ˌsæt̬əsˈfækʃən] *n* : satisfacción *f*
satisfactory [ˌsæt̬əsˈfæktəri] *adj* : satisfactorio, bueno — **satisfactorily** [-rəli] *adv*
satisfy [ˈsæt̬əsˌfaɪ] *v* **-fied; -fying** *vt* **1** PLEASE : satisfacer, contentar **2** CONVINCE : convencer **3** FULFILL : satisfacer, cumplir con, llenar **4** SETTLE : pagar, saldar (una cuenta) — *vi* SUFFICE : bastar
saturate [ˈsætʃəˌreɪt] *vt* **-rated; -rating 1** SOAK : empapar **2** FILL : saturar
saturation [ˌsætʃəˈreɪʃən] *n* : saturación *f*
Saturday [ˈsæt̬ərˌdeɪ, -di] *n* : sábado *m*
Saturn [ˈsæt̬ərn] *n* : Saturno *m*
satyr [ˈseɪt̬ər, ˈsæ-] *n* : sátiro *m*
sauce [ˈsɔs] *n* : salsa *f*
saucepan [ˈsɔsˌpæn] *n* : cacerola *f*, cazo *m*, cazuela *f*
saucer [ˈsɔsər] *n* : platillo *m*
sauciness [ˈsɔsinəs] *n* : descaro *m*, frescura *f*
saucy [ˈsɔsi] *adj* **saucier; -est** IMPUDENT : descarado, fresco *fam* — **saucily** *adv*
sauna [ˈsɔnə, ˈsaʊnə] *n* : sauna *mf*
saunter [ˈsɔntər, ˈsɑn-] *vi* : pasear, parsearse
sausage [ˈsɔsɪdʒ] *n* : salchicha *f*, embutido *m*
sauté [sɔˈteɪ, soː-] *vt* **-téed** *or* **-téd; -téing** : saltear, sofreír
savage[1] [ˈsævɪdʒ] *adj* : salvaje, feroz — **savagely** *adv*
savage[2] *n* : salvaje *mf*
savagery [ˈsævɪdʒri, -dʒəri] *n, pl* **-ries 1** FEROCITY : ferocidad *f* **2** WILDNESS : salvajismo *m*
save[1] [ˈseɪv] *vt* **saved; saving 1** RESCUE : salvar, rescatar **2** PRESERVE : preservar, conservar **3** KEEP : guardar, ahorrar (dinero), almacenar (alimentos)
save[2] *prep* EXCEPT : salvo, excepto, menos
savior [ˈseɪvjər] *n* **1** : salvador *m*, -dora *f* **2 the Savior** : el Salvador *m*
savor[1] [ˈseɪvər] *vt* : saborear
savor[2] *n* : sabor *m*
savory [ˈseɪvəri] *adj* : sabroso
saw[1] → **see**
saw[2] [ˈsɔ] *vt* **sawed; sawed** *or* **sawn** [ˈsɔn]; **sawing** : serrar, cortar (con sierra)
saw[3] *n* : sierra *f*
sawdust [ˈsɔˌdʌst] *n* : aserrín *m*, serrín *m*
sawhorse [ˈsɔˌhɔrs] *n* : caballete *m*, burro *m* (en carpintería)
sawmill [ˈsɔˌmɪl] *n* : aserradero *m*
saxophone [ˈsæksəˌfoːn] *n* : saxofón *m*
say[1] [ˈseɪ] *v* **said** [ˈsɛd]; **saying; says** [ˈsɛz] *vt* **1** EXPRESS, UTTER : decir, expresar <to say no : decir que no> <that goes without saying : ni que decir tiene> <no sooner said than done : dicho y hecho> <to say again : repetir> <to say one's prayers : rezar> **2** INDICATE : marcar, poner <my watch says three o'clock : mi reloj marca las tres> <what does the sign say? : ¿qué pone el letrero?> **3** ALLEGE : decir <it's said that she's pretty : se dice que es bonita> — *vi* : decir
say[2] *n, pl* **says** [ˈseɪz] : voz *f*, opinión *f* <to have no say : no tener ni voz ni voto> <to have one's say : dar uno su opinión>
saying [ˈseɪɪŋ] *n* : dicho *m*, refrán *m*
scab [ˈskæb] *n* **1** : costra *f*, postilla *f* (en una herida) **2** STRIKEBREAKER : rompehuelgas *mf*, esquirol *mf*
scabbard [ˈskæbərd] *n* : vaina *f* (de una espada), funda *f* (de un puñal, etc.)
scabby [ˈskæbi] *adj* **scabbier; -est** : lleno de costras
scaffold [ˈskæfəld, -ˌfoːld] *n* **1** *or* **scaffolding** : andamio *m* (para obreros, etc.) **2** : patíbulo *m*, cadalso *m* (para ejecuciones)
scald [ˈskɔld] *vt* **1** BURN : escaldar **2** HEAT : calentar (hasta el punto de ebullición)
scale[1] [ˈskeɪl] *v* **scaled; scaling** *vt* **1** : escamar (un pescado) **2** CLIMB : escalar (un muro, etc.) **3 to scale down** : reducir — *vi* WEIGH : pesar <he scaled in at 200 pounds : pesó 200 libras>
scale[2] *n* **1** *or* **scales** : balanza *f*, báscula *f* (para pesar) **2** : escama *f* (de un pez, etc.) **3** EXTENT : escala *f*, proporción *f* <wage scale : escala salarial> **4** : escala *f* (en música, en cartografía, etc.) <to draw to scale : dibujar a escala>
scallion [ˈskæljən] *n* : cebollino *m*, cebolleta *f*
scallop [ˈskɑləp, ˈskæ-] *n* **1** : vieira *f* (molusco) **2** : festón *m* (decoración)
scalp[1] [ˈskælp] *vt* : arrancar la cabellera a
scalp[2] *n* : cuero *m* cabelludo
scalpel [ˈskælpəl] *n* : bisturí *m*, escalpelo *m*
scaly [ˈskeɪli] *adj* **scalier; -est** : escamoso
scam [ˈskæm] *n* : estafa *f*, timo *m fam*, chanchullo *m fam*
scamp [ˈskæmp] *n* : bribón *m*, -bona *f*; granuja *mf*; travieso *m*, -sa *f*
scamper [ˈskæmpər] *vi* : corretear

scan[1] [ˈskæn] *vt* **scanned; scanning 1** : escandir (versos) **2** SCRUTINIZE : escudriñar, escrutar <to scan the horizon : escudriñar el horizonte> **3** PERUSE : echarle un vistazo a (un periódico, etc.) **4** EXPLORE : explorar (con radar), hacer un escáner de (en ecografía) **5** : escanear (una imagen)

scan[2] *n* **1** : ecografía *f,* examen *m* ultrasónico (en medicina) **2** : imagen *f* escaneada (en una computadora)

scandal [ˈskændəl] *n* **1** DISGRACE, OUTRAGE : escándalo *m* **2** GOSSIP : habladurías *fpl,* chismes *mpl*

scandalize [ˈskændəlˌaɪz] *vt* **-ized; -izing** : escandalizar

scandalous [ˈskændələs] *adj* : de escándalo

Scandinavian[1] [ˌskændəˈneɪviən] *adj* : escandinavo

Scandinavian[2] *n* : escandinavo *m,* -va *f*

scanner [ˈskænər] *n* : escáner *m,* scanner *m*

scant [ˈskænt] *adj* : escaso

scanty [ˈskænti] *adj* **scantier; -est** : exiguo, escaso <a scanty meal : una comida insuficiente> — **scantily** [-təli] *adv*

scapegoat [ˈskeɪpˌgoːt] *n* : chivo *m* expiatorio, cabeza *f* de turco

scapula [ˈskæpjələ] *n, pl* **-lae** [-ˌliː, -ˌlaɪ] *or* **-las** → **shoulder blade**

scar[1] [ˈskɑr] *v* **scarred; scarring** *vt* : dejar una cicatriz en — *vi* : cicatrizar

scar[2] *n* : cicatriz *f,* marca *f*

scarab [ˈskærəb] *n* : escarabajo *m*

scarce [ˈskɛrs] *adj* **scarcer; -est** : escaso

scarcely [ˈskɛrsli] *adv* **1** BARELY : apenas **2** : ni mucho menos, ni nada que se le parezca <he's scarcely an expert : ciertamente no es experto>

scarcity [ˈskɛrsəṭi] *n, pl* **-ties** : escasez *f*

scare[1] [ˈskɛr] *vt* **scared; scaring** : asustar, espantar

scare[2] *n* **1** FRIGHT : susto *m,* sobresalto *m* **2** ALARM : pánico *m*

scarecrow [ˈskɛrˌkroː] *n* : espantapájaros *m,* espantajo *m*

scarf [ˈskɑrf] *n, pl* **scarves** [ˈskɑrvz] *or* **scarfs 1** MUFFLER : bufanda *f* **2** KERCHIEF : pañuelo *m*

scarlet [ˈskɑrlət] *n* : escarlata *f* — **scarlet** *adj*

scarlet fever *n* : escarlatina *f*

scary [ˈskɛri] *adj* **scarier; -est** : espantoso, pavoroso

scathing [ˈskeɪðɪŋ] *adj* : mordaz, cáustico

scatter [ˈskæṭər] *vt* : esparcir, desparramar — *vi* DISPERSE : dispersarse

scavenge [ˈskævəndʒ] *v* **-venged; -venging** *vt* : rescatar (de la basura), pepenar *CA, Mex* — *vi* : rebuscar, hurgar en la basura <to scavenge for food : andar buscando comida>

scavenger [ˈskævəndʒər] *n* **1** : persona *f* que rebusca en las basuras; pepenador *m,* -dora *f CA, Mex* **2** : carroñero *m,* -ra *f* (animal)

scenario [səˈnæriˌoː, -ˈnɑr-] *n, pl* **-ios 1** PLOT : argumento *m* (en teatro), guión *m* (en cine) **2** SITUATION : situación *f* hipotética <in the worst-case scenario : en el peor de los casos>

scene [ˈsiːn] *n* **1** : escena *f* (en una obra de teatro) **2** SCENERY : decorado *m* (en el teatro) **3** VIEW : escena *f* **4** LOCALE : escenario *m* **5** COMMOTION, FUSS : escándalo *m,* escena *f* <to make a scene : armar un escándalo>

scenery [ˈsiːnəri] *n, pl* **-eries 1** : decorado *m* (en el teatro) **2** LANDSCAPE : paisaje *m*

scenic [ˈsiːnɪk] *adj* : pintoresco

scent[1] [ˈsɛnt] *vt* **1** SMELL : oler, olfatear **2** PERFUME : perfumar **3** SENSE : sentir, percibir

scent[2] *n* **1** ODOR : olor *m,* aroma *m* **2** : olfato *m* <a dog with a keen scent : un perro con un buen olfato> **3** PERFUME : perfume *m*

scented [ˈsɛntəd] *adj* : perfumado

scepter [ˈsɛptər] *n* : cetro *m*

sceptic [ˈskɛptɪk] → **skeptic**

schedule[1] [ˈskɛˌdʒuːl, -dʒəl, *esp Brit* ˈʃɛdˌjuːl] *vt* **-uled; -uling** : planear, programar

schedule[2] *n* **1** PLAN : programa *m,* plan *m* <on schedule : según lo previsto> <behind schedule : atrasado, con retraso> **2** TIMETABLE : horario *m*

scheme[1] [ˈskiːm] *vi* **schemed; scheming** : intrigar, conspirar

scheme[2] *n* **1** PLAN : plan *m,* proyecto *m* **2** PLOT, TRICK : intriga *f,* ardid *m* **3** FRAMEWORK : esquema *f* <a color scheme : una combinación de colores>

schemer [ˈskiːmər] *n* : intrigante *mf*

schism [ˈsɪzəm, ˈskɪ-] *n* : cisma *m*

schizophrenia [ˌskɪtsəˈfriːniə, ˌskɪzə-, -ˈfrɛ-] *n* : esquizofrenia *f*

schizophrenic [ˌskɪtsəˈfrɛnɪk, ˌskɪzə-] *n* : esquizofrénico *m,* -ca *f* — **schizophrenic** *adj*

scholar [ˈskɑlər] *n* **1** STUDENT : escolar *mf;* alumno *m,* -na *f* **2** EXPERT : especialista *mf*

scholarly [ˈskɑlərli] *adj* : erudito

scholarship [ˈskɑlərˌʃɪp] *n* **1** LEARNING : erudición *f* **2** GRANT : beca *f*

scholastic [skəˈlæstɪk] *adj* : académico

school[1] [ˈskuːl] *vt* : instruir, enseñar

school[2] *n* **1** : escuela *f,* colegio *m* (institución) **2** : estudiantes *mfpl* y profesores *mpl* (de una escuela) **3** : escuela *f* (en pintura, etc.) <the Flemish school : la escuela flamenca> **4 school of fish** : banco *m,* cardumen *m*

schoolboy [ˈskuːlˌbɔɪ] *n* : escolar *m,* colegial *m*

schoolgirl [ˈskuːlˌgərl] *n* : escolar *f,* colegiala *f*

schoolhouse ['sku:l,haʊs] *n* : escuela *f*
schoolmate ['sku:l,meɪt] *n* : compañero *m,* -ra *f* de escuela
schoolroom ['sku:l,ru:m, -,rʊm] → **classroom**
schoolteacher ['sku:l,ti:tʃər] *n* : maestro *m,* -tra *f;* profesor *m,* -sora *f*
schooner ['sku:nər] *n* : goleta *f*
science ['saɪənts] *n* : ciencia *f*
scientific [,saɪən'tɪfɪk] *adj* : científico — **scientifically** [-fɪkli] *adv*
scientist ['saɪəntɪst] *n* : científico *m,* -ca *f*
scintillating ['sɪntə,leɪṭɪŋ] *adj* : chispeante, brillante
scissors ['sɪzərz] *npl* : tijeras *fpl*
scoff ['skɑf] *vi* **to scoff at** : burlarse de, mofarse de
scold ['sko:ld] *vt* : regañar, reprender, reñir
scoop[1] ['sku:p] *vt* **1** : sacar (con pala o cucharón) **2 to scoop out** HOLLOW : vaciar, ahuecar
scoop[2] *n* : pala *f* (para harina, etc.), cucharón *m* (para helado, etc.)
scoot ['sku:t] *vi* : ir rápidamente <she scooted around the corner : volvió la esquina a toda prisa>
scooter ['sku:ṭər] *n* : patineta *f,* monopatín *m,* patinete *m*
scope ['sko:p] *n* **1** RANGE : alcance *m,* ámbito *m,* extensión *f* **2** OPPORTUNITY : posibilidades *fpl,* libertad *f*
scorch ['skɔrtʃ] *vt* : chamuscar, quemar
score[1] ['skor] *v* **scored; scoring** *vt* **1** RECORD : anotar **2** MARK, SCRATCH : marcar, rayar **3** : marcar, meter (en deportes) **4** GAIN : ganar, apuntarse **5** GRADE : calificar (exámenes, etc.) **6** : instrumentar, orquestar (música) — *vi* **1** : marcar (en deportes) **2** : obtener una puntuación (en un examen)
score[2] *n, pl* **scores 1** *or pl* **score** TWENTY : veintena *f* **2** LINE, SCRATCH : línea *f,* marca *f* **3** : resultado *m* (en deportes) <what's the score? : ¿cómo va el marcador?> **4** GRADE, POINTS : calificación *f* (en un examen), puntuación *f* (en un concurso) **5** ACCOUNT : cuenta *f* <to settle a score : ajustar una cuenta> <on that score : a ese respecto> **6** : partitura *f* (musical)
scorn[1] ['skɔrn] *vt* : despreciar, menospreciar, desdeñar
scorn[2] *n* : desprecio *m,* menosprecio *m,* desdén *m*
scornful ['skɔrnfəl] *adj* : desdeñoso, despreciativo — **scornfully** *adv*
Scorpio ['skɔrpi,o:] *n* : Escorpio *mf,* Escorpión *mf*
scorpion ['skɔrpiən] *n* : alacrán *m,* escorpión *m*
Scot ['skɑt] *n* : escocés *m,* -cesa *f*
Scotch[1] ['skɑtʃ] *adj* → **Scottish[1]**
Scotch[2] *npl* **the Scotch** : los escoceses
scot–free ['skɑt'fri:] *adj* **to get off scot–free** : salir impune, quedar sin castigo
Scots ['skɑts] *n* : escocés *m* (idioma)
Scottish[1] ['skɑṭɪʃ] *adj* : escocés
Scottish[2] *n* → **Scots**
scoundrel ['skaʊndrəl] *n* : sinvergüenza *mf;* bellaco *m,* -ca *f*
scour ['skaʊər] *vt* **1** EXAMINE, SEARCH : registrar (un área), revisar (documentos, etc.) **2** SCRUB : fregar, restregar
scourge[1] ['skərdʒ] *vt* **scourged; scourging** : azotar
scourge[2] *n* : azote *m*
scout[1] ['skaʊt] *vi* **1** RECONNOITER : reconocer **2 to scout around for** : explorar en busca de
scout[2] *n* **1** : explorador *m,* -dora *f* **2** *or* **talent scout** : cazatalentos *mf*
scow ['skaʊ] *n* : barcaza *f,* gabarra *f*
scowl[1] ['skaʊl] *vi* : fruncir el ceño
scowl[2] *n* : ceño *m* fruncido
scram ['skræm] *vi* **scrammed; scramming** : largarse
scramble[1] ['skræmbəl] *v* **-bled; -bling** *vi* **1** : trepar, gatear (con torpeza) <he scrambled over the fence : se trepó a la cerca con dificultad> **2** STRUGGLE : pelearse (por) <they scrambled for seats : se pelearon por los asientos> — *vt* **1** JUMBLE : mezclar **2 to scramble eggs** : hacer huevos revueltos
scramble[2] *n* : rebatiña *f,* pelea *f*
scrap[1] ['skræp] *v* **scrapped; scrapping** *vt* DISCARD : desechar — *vi* FIGHT : pelearse
scrap[2] *n* **1** FRAGMENT : pedazo *m,* trozo *m* **2** FIGHT : pelea *f* **3** *or* **scrap metal** : chatarra *f* **4 scraps** *npl* LEFTOVERS : restos *mpl,* sobras *fpl*
scrapbook ['skræp,bʊk] *n* : álbum *m* de recortes
scrape[1] ['skreɪp] *v* **scraped; scraping** *vt* **1** GRAZE, SCRATCH : rozar, rascar <to scrape one's knee : rasparse la rodilla> **2** CLEAN : raspar <to scrape carrots : raspar zanahorias> **3 to scrape off** : raspar (pintura, etc.) **4 to scrape up** *or* **to scrape together** : juntar, reunir poco a poco — *vi* **1** RUB : rozar **2 to scrape by** : arreglárselas, ir tirando
scrape[2] *n* **1** SCRAPING : raspadura *f* **2** SCRATCH : rasguño *m* **3** PREDICAMENT : apuro *m,* aprieto *m*
scratch[1] ['skrætʃ] *vt* **1** : arañar, rasguñar <to scratch an itch : rascarse> **2** MARK : rayar, marcar **3 to scratch out** : tachar
scratch[2] *n* **1** : rasguño *m,* arañazo *m* (en la piel), rayón *m* (en un mueble, etc.) **2** : sonido *m* rasposo <I heard a scratch at the door : oí como que raspaban a la puerta>
scratchy ['skrætʃi] *adj* **scratchier; -est** : áspero, que pica <a scratchy sweater : un suéter que pica>
scrawl[1] ['skrɔl] *v* : garabatear
scrawl[2] *n* : garabato *m*

scrawny [ˈskrɔni] *adj* **scrawnier; -est** : flaco, escuálido
scream[1] [ˈskriːm] *vi* : chillar, gritar
scream[2] *n* : chillido *m,* grito *m*
screech[1] [ˈskriːtʃ] *vi* : chillar (dícese de las personas o de los animales), chirriar (dícese de los frenos, etc.)
screech[2] *n* 1 : chillido *m,* grito *m* (de una persona o un animal) **2** : chirrido *m* (de frenos, etc.)
screen[1] [ˈskriːn] *vt* **1** SHIELD : proteger **2** CONCEAL : tapar, ocultar **3** EXAMINE : someter a una revisión, hacerle un chequeo (a un paciente) **4** SIEVE : cribar
screen[2] *n* **1** PARTITION : biombo *m,* pantalla *f* **2** SIEVE : criba *f* **3** : pantalla *f* (de un televisor, una computadora, etc.) **4** MOVIES : cine *m* **5** *or* **window screen** : ventana *f* de tela metálica
screw[1] [ˈskruː] *vt* : atornillar — *vi* **to screw in** : atornillarse
screw[2] *n* **1** : tornillo *m* (para fijar algo) **2** TWIST : vuelta *f* **3** PROPELLER : hélice *f*
screwdriver [ˈskruːˌdraɪvər] *n* : destornillador *m,* desarmador *m Mex*
scribble[1] [ˈskrɪbəl] *v* **-bled; -bling** : garabatear
scribble[2] *n* : garabato *m*
scribe [ˈskraɪb] *n* : escriba *m*
scrimp [ˈskrɪmp] *vi* **1 to scrimp on** : escatimar **2 to scrimp and save** : hacer economías
script [ˈskrɪpt] *n* **1** HANDWRITING : letra *f,* escritura *f* **2** : guión *m* (de una película, etc.)
scriptural [ˈskrɪptʃərəl] *adj* : bíblico
scripture [ˈskrɪptʃər] *n* **1** : escritos *mpl* sagrados (de una religión) **2 the Scriptures** *npl* : las Sagradas Escrituras
scroll [ˈskroːl] *n* **1** : rollo *m* (de pergamino, etc.) **2** : voluta *f* (adorno en arquitectura)
scrotum [ˈskroːtəm] *n, pl* **scrota** [-tə] *or* **scrotums** : escroto *m*
scrounge [ˈskraʊndʒ] *v* **scrounged; scrounging** *vt* **1** BUM : gorrear *fam,* sablear *fam* (dinero) **2 to scrounge around for** : buscar, andar a la busca de — *vi* **to scrounge off someone** : vivir a costa de alguien
scrub[1] [ˈskrʌb] *vt* **scrubbed; scrubbing** : restregar, fregar
scrub[2] *n* **1** THICKET, UNDERBRUSH : maleza *f,* matorral *m,* matorrales *mpl* **2** SCRUBBING : fregado *m,* restregadura *f*
scrubby [ˈskrʌbi] *adj* **-bier; -est 1** STUNTED : achaparrado **2** : cubierto de maleza
scruff [ˈskrʌf] *n* **by the scruff of the neck** : por el cogote, por el pescuezo
scrumptious [ˈskrʌmpʃəs] *adj* : delicioso, muy rico
scruple [ˈskruːpəl] *n* : escrúpulo *m*
scrupulous [ˈskruːpjələs] *adj* : escrupuloso — **scrupulously** *adv*
scrutinize [ˈskruːtənˌaɪz] *vt* **-nized; -nizing** : escrutar, escudriñar
scrutiny [ˈskruːtəni] *n, pl* **-nies** : escrutinio *m,* inspección *f*
scuff [ˈskʌf] *vt* : rayar, raspar <to scuff one's feet : arrastrar los pies>
scuffle[1] [ˈskʌfəl] *vi* **-fled; -fling 1** TUSSLE : pelearse **2** SHUFFLE : caminar arrastrando los pies
scuffle[2] *n* **1** TUSSLE : refriega *f,* pelea *f* **2** SHUFFLE : arrastre *m* de los pies
scull[1] [ˈskʌl] *vi* : remar (con espadilla)
scull[2] *n* OAR : espadilla *f*
sculpt [ˈskʌlpt] *v* : esculpir
sculptor [ˈskʌlptər] *n* : escultor *m,* -tora *f*
sculpture[1] [ˈskʌlptʃər] *vt* **-tured; -turing** : esculpir
sculpture[2] *n* : escultura *f*
scum [ˈskʌm] *n* **1** FROTH : espuma *f,* nata *f* **2** : verdín *m* (encima de un líquido)
scurrilous [ˈskərələs] *adj* : difamatorio, calumnioso, injurioso
scurry [ˈskəri] *vi* **-ried; -rying** : corretear
scurvy [ˈskərvi] *n* : escorbuto *m*
scuttle[1] [ˈskʌtəl] *v* **-tled; -tling** *vt* : hundir (un barco) — *vi* SCAMPER : corretear
scuttle[2] *n* : cubo *m* (para carbón)
scythe [ˈsaɪð] *n* : guadaña *f*
sea[1] [ˈsiː] *adj* : del mar
sea[2] *n* **1** : mar *mf* <the Black Sea : el Mar Negro> <on the high seas : en alta mar> <heavy seas : mar gruesa, mar agitada> **2** MASS : mar *m,* multitud *f* <a sea of faces : un mar de rostros>
seabird [ˈsiːˌbərd] *n* : ave *f* marina
seacoast [ˈsiːˌkoːst] *n* : costa *f,* litoral *m*
seafarer [ˈsiːˌfærər] *n* : marinero *m*
seafaring[1] [ˈsiːˌfærɪŋ] *adj* : marinero
seafaring[2] *n* : navegación *f*
seafood [ˈsiːˌfuːd] *n* : mariscos *mpl*
seagull [ˈsiːˌgʌl] *n* : gaviota *f*
sea horse [ˈsiːˌhɔrs] *n* : hipocampo *m,* caballito *m* de mar
seal[1] [ˈsiːl] *vt* **1** CLOSE : sellar, cerrar <to seal a letter : cerrar una carta> <to seal an agreement : sellar un acuerdo> **2 to seal up** : tapar, rellenar (una grieta, etc.)
seal[2] *n* **1** : foca *f* (animal) **2** : sello *m* <seal of approval : sello de aprobación> **3** CLOSURE : cierre *m,* precinto *m*
sea level *n* : nivel *m* del mar
sea lion *n* : león *m* marino
sealskin [ˈsiːlˌskɪn] *n* : piel *f* de foca
seam[1] [ˈsiːm] *vt* **1** STITCH : unir con costuras **2** MARK : marcar
seam[2] *n* **1** STITCHING : costura *f* **2** LODE, VEIN : veta *f,* filón *m*
seaman [ˈsiːmən] *n, pl* **-men** [-mən, -ˌmɛn] **1** SAILOR : marinero *m* **2** : marino *m* (en la armada)
seamless [ˈsiːmləs] *adj* **1** : sin costuras, de una pieza **2** : perfecto <a seamless transition : una transición fluida>

seamstress [ˈsiːmpstrəs] *n* : costurera *f*

seamy [ˈsiːmi] *adj* **seamier; -est** : sórdido

séance [ˈseɪˌɑnts] *n* : sesión *f* de espiritismo

seaplane [ˈsiːˌpleɪn] *n* : hidroavión *m*

seaport [ˈsiːˌport] *n* : puerto *m* marítimo

sear [ˈsɪr] *vt* **1** PARCH, WITHER : secar, resecar **2** SCORCH : chamuscar, quemar

search[1] [ˈsərtʃ] *vt* : registrar (un edificio, un área), cachear (a una persona), buscar en — *vi* **to search for** : buscar

search[2] *n* : búsqueda *f*, registro *m* (de un edificio, etc.), cacheo *m* (de una persona)

searchlight [ˈsərtʃˌlaɪt] *n* : reflector *m*

seashell [ˈsiːˌʃɛl] *n* : concha *f* (marina)

seashore [ˈsiːˌʃor] *n* : orilla *f* del mar

seasick [ˈsiːˌsɪk] *adj* : mareado <to get seasick : marearse>

seasickness [ˈsiːˌsɪknəs] *n* : mareo *m*

seaside → **seacoast**

season[1] [ˈsiːzən] *vt* **1** FLAVOR, SPICE : sazonar, condimentar **2** CURE : curar, secar <seasoned wood : madera seca> <a seasoned veteran : un veterano avezado>

season[2] *n* **1** : estación *f* (del año) **2** : temporada *f* (en deportes, etc.) <baseball season : temporada de beisbol>

seasonable [ˈsiːzənəbəl] *adj* **1** : propio de la estación (dícese del tiempo, de las temperaturas, etc.) **2** TIMELY : oportuno

seasonal [ˈsiːzənəl] *adj* : estacional — **seasonally** *adv*

seasoning [ˈsiːzənɪŋ] *n* : condimento *m*, sazón *f*

seat[1] [ˈsiːt] *vt* **1** SIT : sentar <please be seated : siéntense, por favor> **2** HOLD : tener cabida para <the stadium seats 40,000 : el estadio tiene 40,000 asientos>

seat[2] *n* **1** : asiento *m*, plaza *f* (en un vehículo) <take a seat : tome asiento> **2** BOTTOM : fondillos *mpl* (de la ropa), trasero *m* (del cuerpo) **3** : sede *f* (de un gobierno, etc.)

seat belt *n* : cinturón *m* de seguridad

sea urchin *n* : erizo *m* de mar

seawall [ˈsiːˌwɑl] *n* : rompeolas *m*, dique *m* marítimo

seawater [ˈsiːˌwɔt̬ər, -ˌwɑ-] *n* : agua *f* de mar

seaweed [ˈsiːˌwiːd] *n* : alga *f* marina

seaworthy [ˈsiːˌwərði] *adj* : en condiciones de navegar

secede [sɪˈsiːd] *vi* **-ceded; -ceding** : separarse (de una nación, etc.)

seclude [sɪˈkluːd] *vt* **-cluded; -cluding** : aislar

seclusion [sɪˈkluːʒən] *n* : aislamiento *m*

second[1] [ˈsɛkənd] *vt* : secundar, apoyar (una moción)

second[2] *or* **secondly** [ˈsɛkəndli] *adv* : en segundo lugar

second[3] *adj* : segundo

second[4] *n* **1** : segundo *m*, -da *f* (en una serie) **2** : segundo *m*, segunda parte *f* **3** : segundo *m*, ayudante *m* (en deportes) **4** MOMENT : segundo *m*, momento *m*

secondary [ˈsɛkənˌdɛri] *adj* : secundario

secondhand [ˈsɛkəndˈhænd] *adj* : de segunda mano

second lieutenant *n* : alférez *mf*, subteniente *mf*

second–rate [ˈsɛkəndˈreɪt] *adj* : mediocre, de segunda categoría

secrecy [ˈsiːkrəsi] *n, pl* **-cies** : secreto *m*

secret[1] [ˈsiːkrət] *adj* : secreto — **secretly** *adv*

secret[2] *n* : secreto *m*

secretarial [ˌsɛkrəˈtɛriəl] *adj* : de secretario, de oficina

secretariat [ˌsɛkrəˈtɛriət] *n* : secretaría *f*, secretariado *m*

secretary [ˈsɛkrəˌtɛri] *n, pl* **-taries 1** : secretario *m*, -ria *f* (en una oficina, etc.) **2** : ministro *m*, -tra *f;* secretario *m*, -ria *f* <Secretary of State : Secretario de Estado>

secrete [sɪˈkriːt] *vt* **-creted; -creting 1** : secretar, segregar (en fisiología) **2** HIDE : ocultar

secretion [sɪˈkriːʃən] *n* : secreción *f*

secretive [ˈsiːkrət̬ɪv, sɪˈkriːt̬ɪv] *adj* : reservado, callado, secreto

sect [ˈsɛkt] *n* : secta *f*

sectarian [sɛkˈtɛriən] *adj* : sectario

section [ˈsɛkʃən] *n* : sección *f*, parte *f* (de un mueble, etc.), sector *m* (de la población), barrio *m* (de una ciudad)

sectional [ˈsɛkʃənəl] *adj* **1** : en sección, en corte <a sectional diagram : un gráfico en corte> **2** FACTIONAL : de grupo, entre facciones **3** : modular <sectional furniture : muebles modulares>

sector [ˈsɛktər] *n* : sector *m*

secular [ˈsɛkjələr] *adj* **1** : secular, laico <secular life : la vida secular> **2** : seglar (dícese de los sacerdotes, etc.)

secure[1] [sɪˈkjʊr] *vt* **-cured; -curing 1** FASTEN : asegurar (una puerta, etc.), sujetar **2** GET : conseguir

secure[2] *adj* **-curer; -est** : seguro — **securely** *adv*

security [sɪˈkjʊrət̬i] *n, pl* **-ties 1** SAFETY : seguridad *f* **2** GUARANTEE : garantía *f* **3 securities** *npl* : valores *mpl*

sedan [sɪˈdæn] *n* **1** *or* **sedan chair** : silla *f* de manos **2** : sedán *m* (automóvil)

sedate[1] [sɪˈdeɪt] *vt* **-dated; -dating** : sedar

sedate[2] *adj* : sosegado — **sedately** *adv*

sedation [sɪˈdeɪʃən] *n* : sedación *f*

sedative[1] [ˈsɛdət̬ɪv] *adj* : sedante

sedative[2] *n* : sedante *m*, calmante *m*

sedentary ['sɛdən,tɛri] *adj* : sedentario

sedge ['sɛdʒ] *n* : juncia *f*

sediment ['sɛdəmənt] *n* : sedimento *m* (geológico), poso *m* (en un líquido)

sedimentary [,sɛdə'mɛntəri] *adj* : sedimentario

sedition [sɪ'dɪʃən] *n* : sedición *f*

seditious [sɪ'dɪʃəs] *adj* : sedicioso

seduce [sɪ'du:s, -'dju:s] *vt* **-duced; -ducing** : seducir

seduction [sɪ'dʌkʃən] *n* : seducción *f*

seductive [sɪ'dʌktɪv] *adj* : seductor, seductivo

see[1] ['si:] *v* **saw** ['sɔ]; **seen** ['si:n]; **seeing** *vt* **1** : ver <I saw a dog : vi un perro> <see you later! : ¡hasta luego!> **2** EXPERIENCE : ver, conocer **3** UNDERSTAND : ver, entender **4** ENSURE : asegurarse <see that it's correct : asegúrese de que sea correcto> **5** ACCOMPANY : acompañar **6 to see off** : despedir, despedirse de — *vi* **1** : ver <seeing is believing : ver para creer> **2** UNDERSTAND : entender, ver <now I see! : ¡ya entiendo!> **3** CONSIDER : ver <let's see : vamos a ver> **4 to see to** : ocuparse de

see[2] *n* : sede *f* <the Holy See : la Santa Sede>

seed[1] ['si:d] *vt* **1** SOW : sembrar **2** : despepitar, quitarle las semillas a

seed[2] *n, pl* **seed** *or* **seeds 1** : semilla *f*, pepita *f* (de una fruta) **2** SOURCE : germen *m*, semilla *f*

seedless ['si:dləs] *adj* : sin semillas

seedling ['si:dlɪŋ] *n* : plantón *m*

seedpod ['si:d,pɑd] → **pod**

seedy ['si:di] *adj* **seedier; -est 1** : lleno de semillas **2** SHABBY : raído (dícese de la ropa) **3** RUN-DOWN : ruinoso (dícese de los edificios, etc.), sórdido

seek ['si:k] *v* **sought** ['sɔt]; **seeking** *vt* **1** : buscar <to seek an answer : buscar una solución> **2** REQUEST : solicitar, pedir **3 to seek to** : tratar de, intentar de — *vi* SEARCH : buscar

seem ['si:m] *vi* : parecer

seeming ['si:mɪŋ] *adj* : aparente, ostensible

seemingly ['si:mɪŋli] *adv* : aparentemente, según parece

seemly ['si:mli] *adj* **seemlier; -est** : apropiado, decoroso

seep ['si:p] *vi* : filtrarse

seer ['si:ər] *n* : vidente *mf*, clarividente *mf*

seesaw[1] ['si:,sɔ] *vi* **1** : jugar en un subibaja **2** VACILLATE : vacilar, oscilar

seesaw[2] *n* : balancín *m*, subibaja *m*

seethe ['si:ð] *vi* **seethed; seething 1** : bullir, hervir **2 to seethe with anger** : rabiar, estar furioso

segment ['sɛgmənt] *n* : segmento *m*

segmented ['sɛg,mɛntəd, sɛg'mɛn-] *adj* : segmentado

segregate ['sɛgrɪ,geɪt] *vt* **-gated; -gating** : segregar

segregation [,sɛgrɪ'geɪʃən] *n* : segregación *f*

seismic ['saɪzmɪk, 'saɪs-] *adj* : sísmico

seize ['si:z] *v* **seized; seizing** *vt* **1** CAPTURE : capturar, tomar, apoderarse de **2** ARREST : detener **3** CLUTCH, GRAB : agarrar, coger, aprovechar (una oportunidad) **4 to be seized with** : estar sobrecogido por — *vi or* **to seize up** : agarrotarse

seizure ['si:ʒər] *n* **1** CAPTURE : toma *f*, captura *f* **2** ARREST : detención *f* **3** : ataque *m* <an epileptic seizure : un ataque epiléptico>

seldom ['sɛldəm] *adv* : pocas veces, rara vez, casi nunca

select[1] [sə'lɛkt] *vt* : escoger, elegir, seleccionar (a un candidato, etc.)

select[2] *adj* : selecto

selection [sə'lɛkʃən] *n* : selección *f*, elección *f*

selective [sə'lɛktɪv] *adj* : selectivo

selenium [sə'li:niəm] *n* : selenio *m*

self ['sɛlf] *n, pl* **selves** ['sɛlvz] **1** : ser *m*, persona *f* <the self : el yo> <with his whole self : con todo su ser> <her own self : su propia persona> **2** SIDE : lado (de la personalidad) <his better self : su lado bueno>

self–addressed [,sɛlfə'drɛst] *adj* : con la dirección del remitente <include a self-addressed envelope : incluya un sobre con su nombre y dirección>

self–appointed [,sɛlfə'pɔɪntəd] *adj* : autoproclamado, autonombrado

self–assurance [,sɛlfə'ʃʊrənts] *n* : seguridad *f* en sí mismo

self–assured [,sɛlfə'ʃʊrd] *adj* : seguro de sí mismo

self–centered [,sɛlf'sɛntərd] *adj* : egocéntrico

self–confidence [,sɛlf'kɑnfədənts] *n* : confianza *f* en sí mismo

self–confident [,sɛlf'kɑnfədənt] *adj* : seguro de sí mismo

self–conscious [,sɛlf'kɑntʃəs] *adj* : cohibido, tímido

self–consciously [,sɛlf'kɑntʃəsli] *adv* : de manera cohibida

self–consciousness [,sɛlf'kɑntʃəsnəs] *n* : vergüenza *f*, timidez *f*

self–contained [,sɛlfkən'teɪnd] *adj* **1** INDEPENDENT : independiente **2** RESERVED : reservado

self–control [,sɛlfkən'tro:l] *n* : autocontrol *m*, control *m* de sí mismo

self–defense [,sɛlfdɪ'fɛnts] *n* : defensa *f* propia, defensa *f* personal <to act in self-defense : actuar en defensa propia> <self-defense class : clase de defensa personal>

self–denial [,sɛlfdɪ'naɪəl] *n* : abnegación *f*

self–destructive [,sɛlfdɪ'strʌktɪv] *adj* : autodestructivo

self–determination [,sɛlfdɪ,tərmə'neɪʃən] *n* : autodeterminación *f*

self–discipline [,sɛlf'dɪsəplən] *n* : autodisciplina *f*

self–employed [ˌsɛlfɪm'plɔɪd] *adj* : que trabaja por cuenta propia, autónomo
self–esteem [ˌsɛlfɪ'stiːm] *n* : autoestima *f,* amor *m* propio
self–evident [ˌsɛlf'ɛvədənt] *adj* : evidente, manifiesto
self–explanatory [ˌsɛlfɪk'splænəˌtori] *adj* : fácil de entender, evidente
self–expression [ˌsɛlfɪk'sprɛʃən] *n* : expresión *f* personal
self–government [ˌsɛlf'gʌvərmənt, -vərn-] *n* : autogobierno *m*
self–help [ˌsɛlf'hɛlp] *n* : autoayuda *f*
self–important [ˌsɛlfɪm'pɔrtənt] *adj* **1** VAIN : vanidoso, presumido **2** ARROGANT : arrogante
self–indulgent [ˌsɛlfɪn'dʌldʒənt] *adj* : que se permite excesos
self–inflicted [ˌsɛlfɪn'flɪktəd] *adj* : autoinfligido
self–interest [ˌsɛlf'ɪntrəst, -təˌrɛst] *n* : interés *m* personal
selfish ['sɛlfɪʃ] *adj* : egoísta
selfishly ['sɛlfɪʃli] *adv* : de manera egoísta
selfishness ['sɛlfɪʃnəs] *n* : egoísmo *m*
selfless ['sɛlfləs] *adj* UNSELFISH : desinteresado
self–made [ˌsɛlf'meɪd] *adj* : próspero gracias a sus propios esfuerzos
self–pity [ˌsɛlf'pɪt̬i] *n, pl* **-ties** : autocompasión *f*
self–portrait [ˌsɛlf'pɔrtrət] *n* : autorretrato *m*
self–propelled [ˌsɛlfpro'pɛld] *adj* : autopropulsado
self–reliance [ˌsɛlfri'laɪən*t*s] *n* : independencia *f,* autosuficiencia *f*
self–respect [ˌsɛlfri'spɛkt] *n* : autoestima *f,* amor *m* propio
self–restraint [ˌsɛlfri'streɪnt] *n* : autocontrol *m,* moderación *f*
self–righteous [ˌsɛlf'raɪtʃəs] *adj* : santurrón, moralista
self–sacrifice [ˌsɛlf'sækrəˌfaɪs] *n* : abnegación *f*
selfsame ['sɛlfˌseɪm] *adj* : mismo
self–service [ˌsɛlf'sərvɪs] *adj* **1** : de autoservicio **2 self-service restaurant** : autoservicio *m*
self–sufficiency [ˌsɛlfsə'fɪʃən*t*si] *n* : autosuficiencia *f*
self–sufficient [ˌsɛlfsə'fɪʃənt] *adj* : autosuficiente
self–taught [ˌsɛlf'tɔt] *adj* : autodidacto
sell ['sɛl] *v* **sold** ['soːld]; **selling** *vt* : vender — *vi* : venderse
seller ['sɛlər] *n* : vendedor *m,* -dora *f*
selves → **self**
semantics [sɪ'mæntɪks] *ns & pl* : semántica *f*
semaphore ['sɛməˌfor] *n* : semáforo *m*
semblance ['sɛmblən*t*s] *n* : apariencia *f*
semen ['siːmən] *n* : semen *m*
semester [sə'mɛstər] *n* : semestre *m*
semicolon ['sɛmiˌkoːlən, 'sɛˌmaɪ-] *n* : punto y coma *m*
semiconductor ['sɛmikənˌdʌktər, 'sɛˌmaɪ-] *n* : semiconductor *m*
semifinal ['sɛmiˌfaɪnəl, 'sɛˌmaɪ-] *n* : semifinal *f*
seminar ['sɛməˌnɑr] *n* : seminario *m*
seminary ['sɛməˌnɛri] *n, pl* **-naries** : seminario *m*
senate ['sɛnət] *n* : senado *m*
senator ['sɛnət̬ər] *n* : senador *m,* -dora *f*
send ['sɛnd] *vt* **sent** ['sɛnt]; **sending 1** : mandar, enviar <to send a letter : mandar una carta> <to send word : avisar, mandar decir> **2** PROPEL : mandar, lanzar <he sent it into left field : lo mandó al jardín izquierdo> <to send up dust : alzar polvo> **3 to send into a rage** : poner furioso
sender ['sɛndər] *n* : remitente *mf* (de una carta, etc.)
Senegalese [ˌsɛnəgə'liːz, -'liːs] *n* : senegalés *m,* -lesa *f* — **Senegalese** *adj*
senile ['siːˌnaɪl] *adj* : senil
senility [sɪ'nɪlət̬i] *n* : senilidad *f*
senior[1] ['siːnjər] *adj* **1** ELDER : mayor <John Doe, Senior : John Doe, padre> **2** : superior (en rango), más antiguo (en años de servicio) <a senior official : un alto oficial>
senior[2] *n* **1** : superior *m* (en rango) **2 to be someone's senior** : ser mayor que alguien <she's two years my senior : me lleva dos años>
seniority [ˌsiː'njɔrət̬i] *n* : antigüedad *f* (en años de servicio)
sensation [sɛn'seɪʃən] *n* : sensación *f*
sensational [sɛn'seɪʃənəl] *adj* : que causa sensación <sensational stories : historias sensacionalistas>
sense[1] ['sɛn*t*s] *vt* **sensed; sensing** : sentir <he sensed danger : se dio cuenta del peligro>
sense[2] *n* **1** MEANING : sentido *m,* significado *m* **2** : sentido *m* <the sense of smell : el sentido del olfato> **3 to make sense** : tener sentido
senseless ['sɛn*t*sləs] *adj* **1** MEANINGLESS : sin sentido, sin razón **2** UNCONSCIOUS : inconsciente
senselessly ['sɛn*t*sləsli] *adv* : sin sentido
sensibility [ˌsɛn*t*sə'bɪlət̬i] *n, pl* **-ties** : sensibilidad *f*
sensible ['sɛn*t*səbəl] *adj* **1** PERCEPTIBLE : sensible, perceptible **2** AWARE : consciente **3** REASONABLE : sensato <a sensible man : un hombre sensato> <sensible shoes : zapatos prácticos> — **sensibly** [-bli] *adv*
sensibleness ['sɛn*t*səbəlnəs] *n* : sensatez *f,* solidez *f*
sensitive ['sɛn*t*sət̬ɪv] *adj* **1** : sensible, delicado <sensitive skin : piel sensible> **2** IMPRESSIONABLE : sensible, impresionable **3** TOUCHY : susceptible

sensitiveness [ˈsɛntsət̬ɪvnəs] → **sensitivity**
sensitivity [ˌsɛntsəˈtɪvət̬i] *n, pl* **-ties** : sensibilidad *f*
sensor [ˈsɛnˌsɔr, ˈsɛntsər] *n* : sensor *m*
sensory [ˈsɛntsəri] *adj* : sensorial
sensual [ˈsɛntʃʊəl] *adj* : sensual — **sensually** *adv*
sensuous [ˈsɛntʃʊəs] *adj* : sensual
sent → **send**
sentence[1] [ˈsɛntənts, -ənz] *vt* **-tenced; -tencing** : sentenciar
sentence[2] *n* **1** JUDGMENT : sentencia *f* **2** : oración *f*, frase *f* (en gramática)
sentiment [ˈsɛntəmənt] *n* **1** BELIEF : opinión *f* **2** FEELING : sentimiento *m* **3** → **sentimentality**
sentimental [ˌsɛntəˈmɛntəl] *adj* : sentimental
sentimentality [ˌsɛntəˌmɛnˈtæləti] *n, pl* **-ties** : sentimentalismo *m*, sensiblería *f*
sentinel [ˈsɛntənəl] *n* : centinela *mf*, guardia *mf*
sentry [ˈsɛntri] *n, pl* **-tries** : centinela *mf*
sepal [ˈsiːpəl, ˈsɛ-] *n* : sépalo *m*
separable [ˈsɛpərəbəl] *adj* : separable
separate[1] [ˈsɛpəˌreɪt] *v* **-rated; -rating** *vt* **1** DETACH, SEVER : separar **2** DISTINGUISH : diferenciar, distinguir — *vi* PART : separarse
separate[2] [ˈsɛprət, ˈsɛpə-] *adj* **1** INDIVIDUAL : separado, aparte <a separate state : un estado separado> <in a separate envelope : en un sobre aparte> **2** DISTINCT : distinto
separately [ˈsɛprətli, ˈsɛpə-] *adv* : por separado, separadamente, aparte
separation [ˌsɛpəˈreɪʃən] *n* : separación *f*
sepia [ˈsiːpiə] *n* : color *m* sepia
September [sɛpˈtɛmbər] *n* : septiembre *m*, setiembre *m*
sepulchre [ˈsɛpəlkər] *n* : sepulcro *m*
sequel [ˈsiːkwəl] *n* **1** CONSEQUENCE : secuela *f*, consecuencia *f* **2** : continuación *f* (de una película, etc.)
sequence [ˈsiːkwənts] *n* **1** SERIES : serie *f*, sucesión *f*, secuencia *f* (matemática o musical) **2** ORDER : orden *m*
sequester [sɪˈkwɛstər] *vt* : aislar
sequin [ˈsiːkwən] *n* : lentejuela *f*
sequoia [sɪˈkwɔɪə] *n* : secoya *f*, secuoya *f*
sera → **serum**
Serb [ˈsərb] *or* **Serbian** [ˈsərbiən] *n* : serbio *m*, -bia *f* — **Serb** *or* **Serbian** *adj*
Serbo–Croatian [ˌsərbokroˈeɪʃən] *n* : serbocroata *m* (idioma) — **Serbo–Croatian** *adj*
serenade[1] [ˌsɛrəˈneɪd] *vt* **-naded; -nading** : darle una serenata (a alguien)
serenade[2] *n* : serenata *f*
serene [səˈriːn] *adj* : sereno — **serenely** *adv*
serenity [səˈrɛnət̬i] *n* : serenidad *f*
serf [ˈsərf] *n* : siervo *m*, -va *f*
serge [ˈsərdʒ] *n* : sarga *f*
sergeant [ˈsɑrdʒənt] *n* : sargento *mf*
serial[1] [ˈsɪriəl] *adj* : seriado
serial[2] *n* : serie *f*, serial *m* (de radio o televisión), publicación *f* por entregas
serially [ˈsɪriəli] *adv* : en serie
series [ˈsɪrˌiːz] *n, pl* **series** : serie *f*, sucesión *f*
serious [ˈsɪriəs] *adj* **1** SOBER : serio **2** DEDICATED, EARNEST : serio, dedicado <to be serious about something : tomar algo en serio> **3** GRAVE : serio, grave <serious problems : problemas graves>
seriously [ˈsɪriəsli] *adv* **1** EARNESTLY : seriamente, con seriedad, en serio **2** SEVERELY : gravemente
seriousness [ˈsɪriəsnəs] *n* : seriedad *f*, gravedad *f*
sermon [ˈsərmən] *n* : sermón *m*
serpent [ˈsərpənt] *n* : serpiente *f*
serrated [səˈreɪt̬əd, ˈsɛrˌeɪt̬əd] *adj* : dentado, serrado
serum [ˈsɪrəm] *n, pl* **serums** *or* **sera** [ˈsɪrə] : suero *m*
servant [ˈsərvənt] *n* : criado *m*, -da *f*; sirviente *m*, -ta *f*
serve [ˈsərv] *v* **served; serving** *vi* **1** : servir <to serve in the navy : servir en la armada> <to serve on a jury : ser miembro de un jurado> **2** DO, FUNCTION : servir <to serve as : servir de, servir como> **3** : sacar (en deportes) — *vt* **1** : servir <to serve God : servir a Dios> **2** HELP : servir <it serves no purpose : no sirve para nada> **3** : servir (comida o bebida) <dinner is served : la cena está servida> **4** SUPPLY : abastecer **5** CARRY OUT : cumplir, hacer <to serve time : servir una pena> **6 to serve a summons** : entregar una citación
server [ˈsərvər] *n* **1** : camarero *m*, -ra *f*; mesero *m*, -ra *f* (en un restaurante) **2** *or* **serving dish** : fuente *f* (para servir comida)
service[1] [ˈsərvəs] *vt* **-viced; -vicing 1** MAINTAIN : darle mantenimiento a (una máquina), revisar **2** REPAIR : arreglar, reparar
service[2] *n* **1** HELP, USE : servicio *m* <to do someone a service : hacerle un servicio a alguien> <at your service : a sus órdenes> <to be out of service : no funcionar> **2** CEREMONY : oficio *m* (religioso) **3** DEPARTMENT, SYSTEM : servicio *m* <social services : servicios sociales> <train service : servicio de trenes> **4** SET : juego *m*, servicio *m* <tea service : juego de té> **5** MAINTENANCE : mantenimiento *m*, revisión *f*, servicio *m* **6** : saque *m* (en deportes) **7 armed services** : fuerzas *fpl* armadas
serviceable [ˈsərvəsəbəl] *adj* **1** USEFUL : útil **2** DURABLE : duradero
serviceman [ˈsərvəsˌmæn, -mən] *n, pl* **-men** [-mən, -ˌmɛn] : militar *m*

service station *n* : estación *f* de servicio

servicewoman [ˈsərvəs͵wʊmən] *n, pl* **-women** [-͵wɪmən] : militar *f*

servile [ˈsərvəl, -͵vaɪl] *adj* : servil

serving [ˈsərvɪŋ] *n* HELPING : porción *f,* ración *f*

servitude [ˈsərvə͵tuːd, -͵tjuːd] *n* : servidumbre *f*

sesame [ˈsɛsəmi] *n* : ajonjolí *m,* sésamo *m*

session [ˈsɛʃən] *n* : sesión *f*

set[1] [ˈsɛt] *v* **set; setting** *vt* **1** SEAT : sentar **2** *or* **to set down** PLACE : poner, colocar **3** ARRANGE : fijar, establecer <to set the date : poner la fecha> <he set the agenda : estableció la agenda> **4** ADJUST : poner (un reloj, etc.) **5** (*indicating the causing of a certain condition*) <to set fire to : prenderle fuego a> <she set it free : lo soltó> **6** MAKE, START : poner, hacer <I set them working : los puse a trabajar> — *vi* **1** SOLIDIFY : fraguar (dícese del cemento, etc.), cuajar (dícese de la gelatina, etc.) **2** : ponerse (dícese del sol o de la luna)

set[2] *adj* **1** ESTABLISHED, FIXED : fijo, establecido **2** RIGID : inflexible <to be set in one's ways : tener costumbres muy arraigadas> **3** READY : listo, preparado

set[3] *n* **1** COLLECTION : juego *m* <a set of dishes : un juego de platos, una vajilla> <a tool set : una caja de herramientas> **2** *or* **stage set** : decorado *m* (en el teatro), plató *m* (en el cine) **3** APPARATUS : aparato *m* <a television set : un televisor> **4** : conjunto *m* (en matemáticas)

setback [ˈsɛt͵bæk] *n* : revés *m,* contratiempo *m*

set in *vi* BEGIN : comenzar, empezar

set off *vt* **1** PROVOKE : provocar **2** EXPLODE : hacer estallar (una bomba, etc.) — *vi or* **to set forth** : salir

set out *vi* : salir (de viaje) — *vt* INTEND : proponerse

settee [sɛˈtiː] *n* : sofá *m*

setter [ˈsɛt̬ər] *n* : setter *mf* <Irish setter : setter irlandés>

setting [ˈsɛt̬ɪŋ] *n* **1** : posición *f,* ajuste *m* (de un control) **2** : engaste *m,* montura *f* (de una gema) **3** SCENE : escenario *m* (de una novela, etc.) **4** SURROUNDINGS : ambiente *m,* entorno *m,* marco *m*

settle [ˈsɛt̬əl] *v* **settled; settling** *vi* **1** ALIGHT, LAND : posarse (dícese de las aves), depositarse (dícese del polvo) **2** SINK : asentarse (dícese de los edificios) <he settled into the chair : se arrellanó en la silla> **3** : instalarse (en una casa), establecerse (en una ciudad o región) **4 to settle down** : calmarse, tranquilizarse <settle down! : ¡tranquilízate!, ¡cálmate!> **5 to settle down** : sentar cabeza, hacerse sensato <to marry and settle down : casarse y sentar cabeza> — *vt* **1** ARRANGE, DECIDE : fijar, decidir, acordar (planes, etc.) **2** RESOLVE : resolver, solucionar <to settle an argument : resolver una discusión> **3** PAY : pagar <to settle an account : saldar una cuenta> **4** CALM : calmar (los nervios), asentar (el estómago) **5** COLONIZE : colonizar **6 to settle oneself** : acomodarse, hacerse cómodo

settlement [ˈsɛt̬əlmənt] *n* **1** PAYMENT : pago *m,* liquidación *f* **2** COLONY : asentamiento *m* **3** RESOLUTION : acuerdo *m*

settler [ˈsɛt̬ələr] *n* : poblador *m,* -dora *f;* colono *m,* -na *f*

set up *vt* **1** ASSEMBLE : montar, armar **2** ERECT : levantar, erigir **3** ESTABLISH : establecer, fundar, montar (un negocio) **4** CAUSE : armar <they set up a clamor : armaron un alboroto>

seven[1] [ˈsɛvən] *adj* : siete

seven[2] *n* : siete *m*

seven hundred[1] *adj* : setecientos

seven hundred[2] *n* : setecientos *m*

seventeen[1] [͵sɛvənˈtiːn] *adj* : diecisiete

seventeen[2] *n* : diecisiete *m*

seventeenth[1] [͵sɛvənˈtiːnθ] *adj* : decimoséptimo

seventeenth[2] *n* **1** : decimoséptimo *m,* -ma *f* (en una serie) **2** : diecisieteavo *m,* diecisieteava parte *f*

seventh[1] [ˈsɛvənθ] *adj* : séptimo

seventh[2] *n* **1** : séptimo *m,* -ma *f* (en una serie) **2** : séptimo *m,* séptima parte *f*

seventieth[1] [ˈsɛvəntiəθ] *adj* : septuagésimo

seventieth[2] *n* **1** : septuagésimo *m,* -ma *f* (en una serie) **2** : setentavo *m,* setentava parte *f,* septuagésima parte *f*

seventy[1] [ˈsɛvənt̬i] *adj* : setenta

seventy[2] *n, pl* **-ties** : setenta *m*

sever [ˈsɛvər] *vt* **-ered; -ering** : cortar, romper

several[1] [ˈsɛvrəl, ˈsɛvə-] *adj* **1** DISTINCT : distinto **2** SOME : varios <several weeks : varias semanas>

several[2] *pron* : varios, varias

severance [ˈsɛvrən*t*s, sɛvə-] *n* **1** : ruptura *f* (de relaciones, etc.) **2 severance pay** : indemnización *f* (por despido)

severe [səˈvɪr] *adj* **severer; -est 1** STRICT : severo **2** AUSTERE : sobrio, austero **3** SERIOUS : grave <a severe wound : una herida grave> <severe aches : dolores fuertes> **4** DIFFICULT : duro, difícil — **severely** *adv*

severity [səˈvɛrət̬i] *n* **1** HARSHNESS : severidad *f* **2** AUSTERITY : sobriedad *f,* austeridad *f* **3** SERIOUSNESS : gravedad *f* (de una herida, etc.)

sew [ˈsoː] *v* **sewed; sewn** [ˈsoːn] *or* **sewed; sewing** : coser

sewage [ˈsuːɪdʒ] *n* : aguas *fpl* negras, aguas *fpl* residuales

sewer[1] [ˈsoːər] *n* : uno que cose

sewer[2] [ˈsuːər] *n* : alcantarilla *f,* cloaca *f*

sewing [ˈsoːɪŋ] *n* : costura *f*

sex [ˈsɛks] *n* **1** : sexo *m* <the opposite sex : el sexo opuesto> **2** COPULATION : relaciones *fpl* sexuales

sexism [ˈsɛkˌsɪzəm] *n* : sexismo *m*

sexist[1] [ˈsɛksɪst] *adj* : sexista

sexist[2] *n* : sexista *mf*

sextant [ˈsɛkstənt] *n* : sextante *m*

sextet [sɛkˈstɛt] *n* : sexteto *m*

sexton [ˈsɛkstən] *n* : sacristán *m*

sexual [ˈsɛkʃʊəl] *adj* : sexual — **sexually** *adv*

sexuality [ˌsɛkʃʊˈæləṱi] *n* : sexualidad *f*

sexy [ˈsɛksi] *adj* **sexier; -est** : sexy

shabbily [ˈʃæbəli] *adv* **1** : pobremente <shabbily dressed : pobremente vestido> **2** UNFAIRLY : mal, injustamente

shabbiness [ˈʃæbinəs] *n* **1** : lo gastado (de ropa, etc.) **2** : lo mal vestido (de personas) **3** UNFAIRNESS : injusticia *f*

shabby [ˈʃæbi] *adj* **shabbier; -est 1** : gastado (dícese de la ropa, etc.) **2** : mal vestido (dícese de las personas) **3** UNFAIR : malo, injusto <shabby treatment : mal trato>

shack [ˈʃæk] *n* : choza *f,* rancho *m*

shackle[1] [ˈʃækəl] *vt* **-led; -ling** : ponerle grilletes (a alguien)

shackle[2] *n* : grillete *m*

shad [ˈʃæd] *n* : sábalo *m*

shade[1] [ˈʃeɪd] *v* **shaded; shading** *vt* **1** SHELTER : proteger (del sol o de la luz) **2** *or* **to shade in** : matizar los colores de — *vi* : convertirse gradualmente <his irritation shaded into rage : su irritación iba convirtiéndose en furia>

shade[2] *n* **1** : sombra *f* <to give shade : dar sombra> **2** : tono *m* (de un color) **3** NUANCE : matiz *m* **4** : pantalla *f* (de una lámpara), persiana *f* (de una ventana)

shadow[1] [ˈʃædoː] *vt* **1** DARKEN : ensombrecer **2** TRAIL : seguir de cerca, seguirle la pista (a alguien)

shadow[2] *n* **1** : sombra *f* **2** DARKNESS : oscuridad *f* **3** TRACE : sombra *f,* atisbo *m,* indicio *m* <without a shadow of a doubt : sin sombra de duda, sin lugar a dudas> **4 to cast a shadow over** : ensombrecer

shadowy [ˈʃædowi] *adj* **1** INDISTINCT : vago, indistinto **2** DARK : oscuro

shady [ˈʃeɪdi] *adj* **shadier; -est 1** : sombreado (dícese de un lugar), que da sombra (dícese de un árbol) **2** DISREPUTABLE : sospechoso (dícese de una persona), turbio (dícese de un negocio, etc.)

shaft [ˈʃæft] *n* **1** : asta *f* (de una lanza), astil *m* (de una flecha), mango *m* (de una herramienta) **2** *or* **mine shaft** : pozo *m*

shaggy [ˈʃægi] *adj* **shaggier; -est 1** HAIRY : peludo <a shaggy dog : un perro peludo> **2** UNKEMPT : enmarañado, despeinado (dícese del pelo, de las barbas, etc.)

shake[1] [ˈʃeɪk] *v* **shook** [ˈʃʊk]; **shaken** [ˈʃeɪkən]; **shaking** *vt* **1** : sacudir, agitar, hacer temblar <he shook his head : negó con la cabeza> **2** WEAKEN : debilitar, hacer flaquear <it shook her faith : debilitó su confianza> **3** UPSET : afectar, alterar **4 to shake hands with someone** : darle la mano a alguien, estrecharle la mano a alguien — *vi* : temblar, sacudirse

shake[2] *n* : sacudida *f,* apretón *m* (de manos)

shaker [ˈʃeɪkər] *n* **1 salt shaker** : salero *m* **2 pepper shaker** : pimentero *m* **3 cocktail shaker** : coctelera *f*

shake–up [ˈʃeɪkˌʌp] *n* : reorganización *f*

shakily [ˈʃeɪkəli] *adv* : temblorosamente

shaky [ˈʃeɪki] *adj* **shakier; -est 1** SHAKING : tembloroso **2** UNSTABLE : poco firme, inestable **3** PRECARIOUS : precario, incierto **4** QUESTIONABLE : dudoso, cuestionable <shaky arguments : argumentos discutibles>

shale [ˈʃeɪl] *n* : esquisto *m*

shall [ˈʃæl] *v aux, past* **should** [ˈʃʊd]; *present s & pl* **shall 1** (*used to express a command*) <you shall do as I say : harás lo que te digo> **2** (*used to express futurity*) <we shall see : ya veremos> <when shall we expect you? : ¿cuándo te podemos esperar?> **3** (*used to express determination*) <you shall have the money : tendrás el dinero> **4** (*used to express a condition*) <if he should die : si muriera> <if they should call, tell me : si llaman, dímelo> **5** (*used to express obligation*) <he should have said it : debería haberlo dicho> **6** (*used to express probability*) <they should arrive soon : deben (de) llegar pronto> <why should he lie? : ¿porqué ha de mentir?>

shallow [ˈʃæloː] *adj* **1** : poco profundo (dícese del agua, etc.) **2** SUPERFICIAL : superficial

shallows [ˈʃæloːz] *npl* : bajío *m,* bajos *mpl*

sham[1] [ˈʃæm] *v* **shammed; shamming** : fingir

sham[2] *adj* : falso, fingido

sham[3] *n* **1** FAKE, PRETENSE : farsa *f,* simulación *f,* imitación *f* **2** FAKER : impostor *m,* -tora *f;* farsante *mf*

shamble [ˈʃæmbəl] *vi* **-bled; -bling** : caminar arrastrando los pies

shambles [ˈʃæmbəlz] *ns & pl* : caos *m,* desorden *m,* confusión *f*

shame[1] [ˈʃeɪm] *vt* **shamed; shaming 1** : avergonzar <he was shamed by their words : sus palabras le dieron vergüenza> **2** DISGRACE : deshonrar

shame[2] *n* **1** : vergüenza *f* <to have no shame : no tener vergüenza> **2** DISGRACE : vergüenza *f,* deshonra *f* **3** PITY : lástima *f,* pena *f* <what a shame! : ¡qué pena!>

shamefaced [ˈʃeɪm,feɪst] *adj* : avergonzado

shameful [ˈʃeɪmfəl] *adj* : vergonzoso — **shamefully** *adv*

shameless [ˈʃeɪmləs] *adj* : descarado, desvergonzado — **shamelessly** *adv*

shampoo[1] [ʃæmˈpuː] *vt* : lavar (el pelo)

shampoo[2] *n, pl* **-poos** : champú *m*

shamrock [ˈʃæm,rɑk] *n* : trébol *m*

shank [ˈʃæŋk] *n* : parte *f* baja de la pierna

shan't [ˈʃænt] (*contraction of* **shall not**) → **shall**

shanty [ˈʃænti] *n, pl* **-ties** : choza *f,* rancho *m*

shape[1] [ˈʃeɪp] *v* **shaped; shaping** *vt* **1** : dar forma a, modelar (arcilla, etc.), tallar (madera, piedra), formar (carácter) <to be shaped like : tener forma de> **2** DETERMINE : decidir, determinar — *vi or* **to shape up** : tomar forma

shape[2] *n* **1** : forma *f,* figura *f* <in the shape of a circle : en forma de círculo> **2** CONDITION : estado *m,* condiciones *fpl,* forma *f* (física) <to get in shape : ponerse en forma>

shapeless [ˈʃeɪpləs] *adj* : informe

shapely [ˈʃeɪpli] *adj* **shapelier; -est** : curvilíneo, bien proporcionado

shard [ˈʃɑrd] *n* : fragmento *m,* casco *m* (de cerámica, etc.)

share[1] [ˈʃɛr] *v* **shared; sharing** *vt* **1** APPORTION : dividir, repartir **2** : compartir <they share a room : comparten una habitación> — *vi* : compartir

share[2] *n* **1** PORTION : parte *f,* porción *f* <one's fair share : lo que le corresponde a uno> **2** : acción *f* (en una compañía) <to hold shares : tener acciones>

sharecropper [ˈʃɛr,krɑpər] *n* : aparcero *m,* -ra *f*

shareholder [ˈʃɛr,hoːldər] *n* : accionista *mf*

shark [ˈʃɑrk] *n* : tiburón *m*

sharp[1] [ˈʃɑrp] *adv* : en punto <at two o'clock sharp : a las dos en punto>

sharp[2] *adj* **1** : afilado, filoso <a sharp knife : un cuchillo afilado> **2** PENETRATING : cortante, fuerte **3** CLEVER : agudo, listo, perspicaz **4** ACUTE : agudo <sharp eyesight : vista aguda> **5** HARSH, SEVERE : duro, severo, agudo <a sharp rebuke : una reprimenda mordaz> **6** STRONG : fuerte <sharp cheese : queso fuerte> **7** ABRUPT : brusco, repentino **8** DISTINCT : nítido, definido <a sharp image : una imagen bien definida> **9** ANGULAR : anguloso (dícese de la cara) **10** : sostenido (en música)

sharp[3] *n* : sostenido *m* (en música)

sharpen [ˈʃɑrpən] *vt* : afilar, aguzar <to sharpen a pencil : sacarle punta a un lápiz> <to sharpen one's wits : aguzar el ingenio>

sharpener [ˈʃɑrpənər] *n* : afilador *m* (para cuchillos, etc.), sacapuntas *m* (para lápices)

sharply [ˈʃɑrpli] *adv* **1** ABRUPTLY : bruscamente **2** DISTINCTLY : claramente, marcadamente

sharpness [ˈʃɑrpnəs] *n* **1** : lo afilado (de un cuchillo, etc.) **2** ACUTENESS : agudeza *f* (de los sentidos o de la mente) **3** INTENSITY : intensidad *f,* agudeza *f* (de dolores, etc.) **4** HARSHNESS : dureza *f,* severidad *f* **5** ABRUPTNESS : brusquedad *f* **6** CLARITY : nitidez *f*

sharpshooter [ˈʃɑrp,ʃuːṭər] *n* : tirador *m,* -dora *f* de primera

shatter [ˈʃæṭər] *vt* **1** : hacer añicos <to shatter the silence : romper el silencio> **2 to be shattered by** : quedar destrozado por — *vi* : hacerse añicos, romperse en pedazos

shave[1] [ˈʃeɪv] *v* **shaved; shaved** *or* **shaven** [ˈʃeɪvən]; **shaving** *vt* **1** : afeitar, rasurar <she shaved her legs : se rasuró las piernas> <they shaved (off) his beard : le afeitaron la barba> **2** SLICE : cortar (en pedazos finos) — *vi* : afeitarse, rasurarse

shave[2] *n* : afeitada *f,* rasurada *f*

shaver [ˈʃeɪvər] *n* : afeitadora *f,* máquina *f* de afeitar, rasuradora *f*

shawl [ˈʃɔl] *n* : chal *m,* mantón *m,* rebozo *m*

she [ˈʃiː] *pron* : ella

sheaf [ˈʃiːf] *n, pl* **sheaves** [ˈʃiːvz] : gavilla *f* (de cereales), haz *m* (de flechas), fajo *m* (de papeles)

shear [ˈʃɪr] *vt* **sheared; sheared** *or* **shorn** [ˈʃorn]; **shearing 1** : esquilar, trasquilar <to shear sheep : trasquilar ovejas> **2** CUT : cortar (el pelo, etc.)

shears [ˈʃɪrz] *npl* : tijeras *fpl* (grandes)

sheath [ˈʃiːθ] *n, pl* **sheaths** [ˈʃiːðz, ˈʃiːθs] : funda *f,* vaina *f*

sheathe [ˈʃiːð] *vt* **sheathed; sheathing** : envainar, enfundar

shed[1] [ˈʃɛd] *vt* **shed; shedding 1** : derramar (sangre o lágrimas) **2** EMIT : emitir (luz) <to shed light on : aclarar> **3** DISCARD : mudar (la piel, etc.) <to shed one's clothes : quitarse uno la ropa>

shed[2] *n* : cobertizo *m*

she'd [ˈʃiːd] (*contraction of* **she had** *or* **she would**) → **have, would**

sheen [ˈʃiːn] *n* : brillo *m,* lustre *m*

sheep [ˈʃiːp] *ns & pl* : oveja *f*

sheepfold [ˈʃiːp,foːld] *n* : redil *m*

sheepish [ˈʃiːpɪʃ] *adj* : avergonzado

sheepskin [ˈʃiːp,skɪn] *n* : piel *f* de oveja, piel *f* de borrego

sheer[1] [ˈʃɪr] *adv* **1** COMPLETELY : completamente, totalmente **2** VERTICALLY : verticalmente

sheer[2] *adj* **1** TRANSPARENT : vaporoso, transparente **2** ABSOLUTE, UTTER : puro <by sheer luck : por pura suerte> **3** STEEP : escarpado, vertical

sheet [ˈʃiːt] *n* **1** *or* **bedsheet** [ˈbɛd,ʃiːt] : sábana *f* **2** : hoja *f* (de papel) **3**

: capa *f* (de hielo, etc.) **4** : lámina *f,* placa *f* (de vidrio, metal, etc.), plancha *f* (de metal, madera, etc.) <baking sheet : placa de horno>

sheikh *or* **sheik** [ˈʃiːk, ˈʃeɪk] *n* : jeque *m*

shelf [ˈʃɛlf] *n, pl* **shelves** [ˈʃɛlvz] **1** : estante *m,* anaquel *m* (en una pared) **2** : banco *m,* arrecife *m* (en geología) <continental shelf : plataforma continental>

shell[1] [ˈʃɛl] *vt* **1** : desvainar (chícharos), pelar (nueces, etc.) **2** BOMBARD : bombardear

shell[2] *n* **1** SEASHELL : concha *f* **2** : cáscara *f* (de huevos, nueces, etc.), vaina *f* (de chícharos, etc.), caparazón *m* (de crustáceos, tortugas, etc.) **3** : cartucho *m,* casquillo *m* <a .45 caliber shell : un cartucho calibre .45> **4** *or* **racing shell** : bote *m* (para hacer regatas de remos)

she'll [ˈʃiːl, ˈʃɪl] (*contraction of* **she shall** *or* **she will**) → **shall, will**

shellac[1] [ʃəˈlæk] *vt* **-lacked; -lacking 1** : laquear (madera, etc.) **2** DEFEAT : darle una paliza (a alguien), derrotar

shellac[2] *n* : laca *f*

shellfish [ˈʃɛlˌfɪʃ] *n* : marisco *m*

shelter[1] [ˈʃɛltər] *vt* **1** PROTECT : proteger, abrigar **2** HARBOR : dar refugio a, albergar

shelter[2] *n* : refugio *m,* abrigo *m* <to take shelter : refugiarse>

shelve [ˈʃɛlv] *vt* **shelved; shelving 1** : poner en estantes **2** DEFER : dar carpetazo a

shenanigans [ʃəˈnænɪgənz] *npl* **1** TRICKERY : artimañas *fpl* **2** MISCHIEF : travesuras *fpl*

shepherd[1] [ˈʃɛpərd] *vt* **1** : cuidar (ovejas, etc.) **2** GUIDE : conducir, guiar

shepherd[2] *n* : pastor *m*

shepherdess [ˈʃɛpərdəs] *n* : pastora *f*

sherbet [ˈʃərbət] *or* **sherbert** [-bərt] *n* : sorbete *m,* nieve *f Cuba, Mex, PRi*

sheriff [ˈʃɛrɪf] *n* : sheriff *mf*

sherry [ˈʃɛri] *n, pl* **-ries** : jerez *m*

she's [ˈʃiːz] (*contraction of* **she is** *or* **she has**) → **be, have**

shield[1] [ˈʃiːld] *vt* **1** PROTECT : proteger **2** CONCEAL : ocultar <to shield one's eyes : taparse los ojos>

shield[2] *n* **1** : escudo *m* (armadura) **2** PROTECTION : protección *f,* blindaje *m* (de un cable)

shier, shiest → **shy**

shift[1] [ˈʃɪft] *vt* **1** CHANGE : cambiar <to shift gears : cambiar de velocidad> **2** MOVE : mover **3** TRANSFER : transferir <to shift the blame : echarle la culpa (a otro)> — *vi* **1** CHANGE : cambiar **2** MOVE : moverse **3 to shift for oneself** : arreglárselas solo

shift[2] *n* **1** CHANGE, TRANSFER : cambio *m* <a shift in priorities : un cambio de prioridades> **2** : turno *m* <night shift : turno de noche> **3** DRESS : vestido *m* (suelto) **4** → **gearshift**

shiftless [ˈʃɪftləs] *adj* : perezoso, vago, holgazán

shifty [ˈʃɪfti] *adj* **shiftier; -est** : taimado, artero <a shifty look : una mirada huidiza>

shilling [ˈʃɪlɪŋ] *n* : chelín *m*

shimmer [ˈʃɪmər] *vi* GLIMMER : brillar con luz trémula

shin[1] [ˈʃɪn] *vi* **shinned; shinning** : trepar, subir <she shinned up the pole : subió al poste>

shin[2] *n* : espinilla *f,* canilla *f*

shine[1] [ˈʃaɪn] *v* **shone** [ˈʃoːn, *esp Brit and Canadian* ˈʃɒn] *or* **shined; shining** *vi* **1** : brillar, relucir <the stars were shining : las estrellas brillaban> **2** EXCEL : brillar, lucirse — *vt* **1** : alumbrar <he shined the flashlight at it : lo alumbró con la linterna> **2** POLISH : sacarle brillo a, lustrar

shine[2] *n* : brillo *m,* lustre *m*

shingle[1] [ˈʃɪŋgəl] *vt* **-gled; -gling** : techar

shingle[2] *n* : tablilla *f* (para techar)

shingles [ˈʃɪŋgəlz] *npl* : herpes *m*

shinny [ˈʃɪni] *vi* **-nied; -nying** → **shin**[1]

shiny [ˈʃaɪni] *adj* **shinier; -est** : brillante

ship[1] [ˈʃɪp] *vt* **shipped; shipping 1** LOAD : embarcar (en un barco) **2** SEND : transportar (en barco), enviar <to ship by air : enviar por avión>

ship[2] *n* **1** : barco *m,* buque *m* **2** → **spaceship**

shipboard [ˈʃɪpˌbord] *n* **on ~** : a bordo

shipbuilder [ˈʃɪpˌbɪldər] *n* : constructor *m,* -tora *f* naval

shipment [ˈʃɪpmənt] *n* **1** SHIPPING : transporte *m,* embarque *m* **2** : envío *m,* remesa *f* <a shipment of medicine : un envío de medicina>

shipping [ˈʃɪpɪŋ] *n* **1** SHIPS : barcos *mpl,* embarcaciones *fpl* **2** TRANSPORTATION : transporte *m* (de mercancías)

shipshape [ˈʃɪpˈʃeɪp] *adj* : ordenado

shipwreck[1] [ˈʃɪpˌrɛk] *vt* **to be shipwrecked** : naufragar

shipwreck[2] *n* : naufragio *m*

shipyard [ˈʃɪpˌjɑrd] *n* : astillero *m*

shirk [ˈʃərk] *vt* : eludir, rehuir <to shirk one's responsibilities : esquivar uno sus responsabilidades>

shirt [ˈʃərt] *n* : camisa *f*

shiver[1] [ˈʃɪvər] *vi* **1** : tiritar (de frío) **2** TREMBLE : estremecerse, temblar

shiver[2] *n* : escalofrío *m,* estremecimiento *m*

shoal [ˈʃoːl] *n* : banco *m,* bajío *m*

shock[1] [ˈʃɑk] *vt* **1** UPSET : conmover, conmocionar **2** STARTLE : asustar, sobresaltar **3** SCANDALIZE : escandalizar **4** : darle una descarga eléctrica a

shock[2] *n* **1** COLLISION, JOLT : choque *m,* sacudida *f* **2** UPSET : conmoción *f,* golpe *m* emocional **3** : shock *m* (en medicina) **4** *or* **electric shock** : descarga *f* eléctrica **5** SHEAVES : gavillas *fpl* **6 shock of hair** : mata *f* de pelo

shock absorber *n* **:** amortiguador *m*

shoddy [ˈʃɑdi] *adj* **shoddier; -est :** de mala calidad <a shoddy piece of work : un trabajo chapucero>

shoe[1] [ˈʃuː] *vt* **shod** [ˈʃɑd]; **shoeing :** herrar (un caballo)

shoe[2] *n* **1 :** zapato *m* <the shoe industry : la industria del calzado> **2** HORSESHOE **:** herradura *f* **3 brake shoe :** zapata *f*

shoelace [ˈʃuːˌleɪs] *n* **:** cordón *m* (de zapatos)

shoemaker [ˈʃuːˌmeɪkər] *n* **:** zapatero *m,* -ra *f*

shone → **shine**

shook → **shake**

shoot[1] [ˈʃuːt] *v* **shot** [ˈʃɑt]; **shooting** *vt* **1 :** disparar, tirar <to shoot a bullet : tirar una bala> **2 :** pegarle un tiro a, darle un balazo a <he shot her : le pegó un tiro> <they shot and killed him : lo mataron a balazos> **3** THROW **:** lanzar (una pelota, etc.), echar (una mirada) **4** PHOTOGRAPH **:** fotografiar **5** FILM **:** filmar — *vi* **1 :** disparar (con un arma de fuego) **2** DART **:** ir rápidamente <it shot past : pasó como una bala>

shoot[2] *n* **:** brote *m,* retoño *m,* vástago *m*

shooting star *n* **:** estrella *f* fugaz

shop[1] [ˈʃɑp] *vi* **shopped; shopping :** hacer compras <to go shopping : ir de compras>

shop[2] *n* **1** WORKSHOP **:** taller *m* **2** STORE **:** tienda *f*

shopkeeper [ˈʃɑpˌkiːpər] *n* **:** tendero *m,* -ra *f*

shoplift [ˈʃɑpˌlɪft] *vi* **:** hurtar mercancía (de una tienda) — *vt* **:** hurtar (de una tienda)

shoplifter [ˈʃɑpˌlɪftər] *n* **:** ladrón *m,* -drona *f* (que roba en una tienda)

shopper [ˈʃɑpər] *n* **:** comprador *m,* -dora *f*

shore[1] [ˈʃor] *vt* **shored; shoring :** apuntalar <they shored up the wall : apuntalaron la pared>

shore[2] *n* **1 :** orilla *f* (del mar, etc.) **2** PROP **:** puntal *m*

shoreline [ˈʃorˌlaɪn] *n* **:** orilla *f*

shorn → **shear**

short[1] [ˈʃɔrt] *adv* **1** ABRUPTLY **:** repentinamente, súbitamente <the car stopped short : el carro se paró en seco> **2 to fall short :** no alcanzar, quedarse corto

short[2] *adj* **1 :** corto (de medida), bajo (de estatura) **2** BRIEF **:** corto <short and sweet : corto y bueno> <a short time ago : hace poco> **3** CURT **:** brusco, cortante, seco **4 :** corto (de tiempo, de dinero) <I'm one dollar short : me falta un dólar>

short[3] *n* **1 shorts** *npl* **:** shorts *mpl,* pantalones *mpl* cortos **2** → **short circuit**

shortage [ˈʃɔrtɪdʒ] *n* **:** falta *f,* escasez *f,* carencia *f*

shortcake [ˈʃɔrtˌkeɪk] *n* **:** tarta *f* de fruta

shortchange [ˈʃɔrtˈtʃeɪndʒ] *vt* **-changed; -changing :** darle mal el cambio (a alguien)

short circuit *n* **:** cortocircuito *m,* corto *m* (eléctrico)

shortcoming [ˈʃɔrtˌkʌmɪŋ] *n* **:** defecto *m*

shortcut [ˈʃɔrtˌkʌt] *n* **1 :** atajo *m* <to take a shortcut : cortar camino> **2 :** alternativa *f* fácil, método *m* rápido

shorten [ˈʃɔrtən] *vt* **:** acortar — *vi* **:** acortarse

shorthand [ˈʃɔrtˌhænd] *n* **:** taquigrafía *f*

short–lived [ˈʃɔrtˈlɪvd, -ˈlaɪvd] *adj* **:** efímero

shortly [ˈʃɔrtli] *adv* **1** BRIEFLY **:** brevemente <to put it shortly : para decirlo en pocas palabras> **2** SOON **:** dentro de poco

shortness [ˈʃɔrtnəs] *n* **1 :** lo corto <shortness of stature : estatura baja> **2** BREVITY **:** brevedad *f* **3** CURTNESS **:** brusquedad *f* **4** SHORTAGE **:** falta *f,* escasez *f,* carencia *f*

shortsighted [ˈʃɔrtˌsaɪt̬əd] → **nearsighted**

shot [ˈʃɑt] *n* **1 :** disparo *m,* tiro *m* <to fire a shot : disparar> **2** PELLETS **:** perdigones *mpl* **3 :** tiro *m* (en deportes) **4** ATTEMPT **:** intento *m,* tentativa *f* <to have a shot at : hacer un intento por> **5** RANGE **:** alcance *m* <a long shot : una posibilidad remota> **6** PHOTOGRAPH **:** foto *f* **7** INJECTION **:** inyección *f* **8 :** trago *m* (de licor)

shotgun [ˈʃɑtˌgʌn] *n* **:** escopeta *f*

should → **shall**

shoulder[1] [ˈʃoːldər] *vt* **1** JOSTLE **:** empujar (con el hombro) **2 :** ponerse al hombro (una mochila, etc.) **3 :** cargar con (la responsabilidad, etc.)

shoulder[2] *n* **1 :** hombro *m* <to shrug one's shoulders : encogerse los hombros> **2 :** arcén *m* (de una carretera)

shoulder blade *n* **:** omóplato *m,* omoplato *m,* escápula *f*

shouldn't [ˈʃʊdənt] (*contraction of* **should not**) → **should**

shout[1] [ˈʃaʊt] *v* **:** gritar, vocear

shout[2] *n* **:** grito *m*

shove[1] [ˈʃʌv] *v* **shoved; shoving :** empujar bruscamente

shove[2] *n* **:** empujón *m,* empellón *m*

shovel[1] [ˈʃʌvəl] *vt* **-veled** *or* **-velled; -veling** *or* **-velling 1 :** mover con (una) pala <they shoveled the dirt out : sacaron la tierra con palas> **2** DIG **:** cavar (con una pala)

shovel[2] *n* **:** pala *f*

show[1] [ˈʃoː] *v* **showed; shown** [ˈʃoːn] *or* **showed; showing** *vt* **1** DISPLAY **:** mostrar, enseñar **2** REVEAL **:** demostrar, manifestar, revelar <he showed himself to be a coward : se reveló como cobarde> **3** TEACH **:** enseñar **4** PROVE **:** demostrar, probar **5** CON-

DUCT, DIRECT : llevar, acompañar <to show someone the way : indicarle el camino a alguien> **6** : proyectar (una película), dar (un programa de televisión) — *vi* **1** : notarse, verse <the stain doesn't show : la mancha no se ve> **2** APPEAR : aparecer, dejarse ver

show[2] *n* **1** : demostración *f* <a show of force : una demostración de fuerza> **2** EXHIBITION : exposición *f,* exhibición *f* <flower show : exposición de flores> <to be on show : estar expuesto> **3** : espectáculo *m* (teatral), programa *m* (de televisión, etc.) <to go to a show : ir al teatro>

showcase [ˈʃoːˌkeɪs] *n* : vitrina *f*

showdown [ˈʃoːˌdaʊn] *n* : confrontación *f* (decisiva)

shower[1] [ˈʃaʊər] *vt* **1** SPRAY : regar, mojar **2** HEAP : colmar <they showered him with gifts : lo colmaron de regalos, le llovieron los regalos> — *vi* **1** BATHE : ducharse, darse una ducha **2** RAIN : llover

shower[2] *n* **1** : chaparrón *m,* chubasco *m* <a chance of showers : una posibilidad de chaparrones> **2** : ducha *f* <to take a shower : ducharse> **3** PARTY : fiesta *f* <a bridal shower : una despedida de soltera>

show off *vt* : hacer alarde de, ostentar — *vi* : lucirse

show up *vi* APPEAR : aparecer — *vt* EXPOSE : revelar

showy [ˈʃoːi] *adj* **showier; -est** : llamativo, ostentoso — **showily** *adv*

shrank → **shrink**

shrapnel [ˈʃræpnəl] *ns & pl* : metralla *f*

shred[1] [ˈʃrɛd] *vt* **shredded; shredding** : hacer trizas, desmenuzar (con las manos), triturar (con una máquina) <to shred vegetables : cortar verduras en tiras>

shred[2] *n* **1** STRIP : tira *f,* jirón *m* (de tela) **2** BIT : pizca *f* <not a shred of evidence : ni la mínima prueba>

shrew [ˈʃruː] *n* **1** : musaraña *f* (animal) **2** : mujer *f* regañona, arpía *f*

shrewd [ˈʃruːd] *adj* : astuto, inteligente, sagaz — **shrewdly** *adv*

shrewdness [ˈʃruːdnəs] *n* : astucia *f*

shriek[1] [ˈʃriːk] *vi* : chillar, gritar

shriek[2] *n* : chillido *m,* alarido *m,* grito *m*

shrill [ˈʃrɪl] *adj* : agudo, estridente

shrilly [ˈʃrɪli] *adv* : agudamente

shrimp [ˈʃrɪmp] *n* : camarón *m,* langostino *m*

shrine [ˈʃraɪn] *n* **1** TOMB : sepulcro *m* (de un santo) **2** SANCTUARY : lugar *m* sagrado, santuario *m*

shrink [ˈʃrɪŋk] *vi* **shrank** [ˈʃræŋk]; **shrunk** [ˈʃrʌŋk] *or* **shrunken** [ˈʃrʌŋkən]; **shrinking 1** RECOIL : retroceder <he shrank back : se echó para atrás> **2** : encogerse (dícese de la ropa)

shrinkage [ˈʃrɪŋkɪdʒ] *n* : encogimiento *m* (de ropa, etc.), contracción *f,* reducción *f*

shrivel [ˈʃrɪvəl] *vi* **-veled** *or* **-velled; -veling** *or* **-velling** : arrugarse, marchitarse

shroud[1] [ˈʃraʊd] *vt* : envolver

shroud[2] *n* **1** : sudario *m,* mortaja *f* **2** VEIL : velo *m* <wrapped in a shroud of mystery : envuelto en un aura de misterio>

shrub [ˈʃrʌb] *n* : arbusto *m,* mata *f*

shrubbery [ˈʃrʌbəri] *n, pl* **-beries** : arbustos *mpl,* matas *fpl*

shrug [ˈʃrʌg] *vi* **shrugged; shrugging** : encogerse de hombros

shrunk → **shrink**

shuck[1] [ˈʃʌk] *vt* : pelar (mazorcas, etc.), abrir (almejas, etc.)

shuck[2] *n* **1** HUSK : cascarilla *f,* cáscara *f* (de una nuez, etc.), hojas *fpl* (de una mazorca) **2** SHELL : concha *f* (de una almeja, etc.)

shudder[1] [ˈʃʌdər] *vi* : estremecerse

shudder[2] *n* : estremecimiento *m,* escalofrío *m*

shuffle[1] [ˈʃʌfəl] *v* **-fled; -fling** *vt* MIX : mezclar, revolver, barajar (naipes) — *vi* : caminar arrastrando los pies

shuffle[2] *n* **1** : acto *m* de revolver <each player gets a shuffle : a cada jugador le toca barajar> **2** JUMBLE : revoltijo *m* **3** : arrastramiento *m* de los pies

shun [ˈʃʌn] *vi* **shunned; shunning** : evitar, esquivar, eludir

shunt [ˈʃʌnt] *vt* : desviar, cambiar de vía (un tren)

shut [ˈʃʌt] *v* **shut; shutting** *vt* **1** CLOSE : cerrar <shut the lid : tápalo> **2 to shut out** EXCLUDE : excluir, dejar fuera a (personas), no dejar que entre (luz, ruido, etc.) **3 to shut up** CONFINE : encerrar — *vi* : cerrarse <the factory shut down : la fábrica cerró sus puertas>

shut–in [ˈʃʌtˌɪn] *n* : inválido *m,* -da *f* (que no puede salir de casa)

shutter [ˈʃʌt̬ər] *n* **1** : contraventana *f,* postigo *m* (de una ventana o puerta) **2** : obturador *m* (de una cámara)

shuttle[1] [ˈʃʌt̬əl] *v* **-tled; -tling** *vt* : transportar <she shuttled him back and forth : lo llevaba de acá para allá> — *vi* : ir y venir

shuttle[2] *n* **1** : lanzadera *f* (para tejer) **2** : vehículo *m* que hace recorridos cortos **3** → **space shuttle**

shuttlecock [ˈʃʌt̬əlˌkɑk] *n* : volante *m*

shut up *vi* : callarse <shut up! : ¡cállate (la boca)!>

shy[1] [ˈʃaɪ] *vi* **shied; shying** : retroceder, asustarse

shy[2] *adj* **shier** *or* **shyer** [ˈʃaɪər]; **shiest** *or* **shyest** [ˈʃaɪəst] **1** TIMID : tímido **2** WARY : cauteloso <he's not shy about asking : no vacila en preguntar> **3** SHORT : corto (de dinero, etc.) <I'm two dollars shy : me faltan dos dólares>

shyly [ˈʃaɪli] *adv* : tímidamente

shyness [ˈʃaɪnəs] *n* : timidez *f*

sibling [ˈsɪblɪŋ] *n* : hermano *m,* hermana *f*

Sicilian [səˈsɪljən] *n* : siciliano *m,* -na *f* — **Sicilian** *adj*

sick [ˈsɪk] *adj* **1** : enfermo **2** NAUSEOUS : mareado, con náuseas <to get sick : vomitar> **3** : para uso de enfermos <sick day : día de permiso (por enfermedad)>

sickbed [ˈsɪk,bɛd] *n* : lecho *m* de enfermo

sicken [ˈsɪkən] *vt* **1** : poner enfermo **2** REVOLT : darle asco (a alguien) — *vi* : enfermar(se), caer enfermo

sickening [ˈsɪkənɪŋ] *adj* : asqueroso, repugnante, nauseabundo

sickle [ˈsɪkəl] *n* : hoz *f*

sickly [ˈsɪkli] *adj* **sicklier; -est 1** : enfermizo **2** → **sickening**

sickness [ˈsɪknəs] *n* **1** : enfermedad *f* **2** NAUSEA : náuseas *fpl*

side [ˈsaɪd] *n* **1** : lado *m,* costado *m* (de una persona), ijada *f* (de un animal) **2** : lado *m,* cara *f* (de una moneda, etc.) **3** : lado *m,* parte *f* <he's on my side : está de mi parte> <to take sides : tomar partido>

sideboard [ˈsaɪd,bord] *n* : aparador *m*

sideburns [ˈsaɪd,bərnz] *npl* : patillas *fpl*

sided [ˈsaɪdəd] *adj* : que tiene lados <one-sided : de un lado>

side effect *n* : efecto *m* secundario

sideline [ˈsaɪd,laɪn] *n* **1** : línea *f* de banda (en deportes) **2** : actividad *f* suplementaria (en negocios) **3 to be on the sidelines** : estar al margen

sidelong [ˈsaɪd,lɔŋ] *adj* : de reojo, de soslayo

sideshow [ˈsaɪd,ʃoː] *n* : espectáculo *m* secundario, atracción *f* secundaria

sidestep [ˈsaɪd,stɛp] *v* **-stepped; -stepping** *vi* : dar un paso hacia un lado — *vt* AVOID : esquivar, eludir

sidetrack [ˈsaɪd,træk] *vt* : desviar (una conversación, etc.), distraer (a una persona)

sidewalk [ˈsaɪd,wɔk] *n* : acera *f,* vereda *f,* andén *m CA, Col,* banqueta *f Mex*

sideways[1] [ˈsaɪd,weɪz] *adv* **1** : hacia un lado <it leaned sideways : se inclinaba hacia un lado> **2** : de lado, de costado <lie sideways : acuéstese de costado>

sideways[2] *adj* : hacia un lado <a sideways glance : una mirada de reojo>

siding [ˈsaɪdɪŋ] *n* **1** : apartadero *m* (para trenes) **2** : revestimiento *m* exterior (de un edificio)

sidle [ˈsaɪdəl] *vi* **-dled; -dling** : moverse furtivamente

siege [ˈsiːdʒ, ˈsiːʒ] *n* : sitio *m* <to be under siege : estar sitiado>

siesta [siːˈɛstə] *n* : siesta *f*

sieve [ˈsɪv] *n* : tamiz *m,* cedazo *m,* criba *f* (en minerología)

sift [ˈsɪft] *vt* **1** : tamizar, cerner <sift the flour : tamice la harina> **2** *or* **sift through** : examinar cuidadosamente, pasar por el tamiz

sifter [ˈsɪftər] *n* : tamiz *m,* cedazo *m*

sigh[1] [ˈsaɪ] *vi* : suspirar

sigh[2] *n* : suspiro *m*

sight[1] [ˈsaɪt] *vt* : ver (a una persona), divisar (la tierra, un barco)

sight[2] *n* **1** : vista *f* (facultad) <out of sight : fuera de vista> **2** : algo visto <it's a familiar sight : se ve con frecuencia> <she's a sight for sore eyes : da gusto verla> **3** : lugar *m* de interés (para turistas, etc.) **4** : mira *f* (de un rifle, etc.) **5** GLIMPSE : mirada *f* breve <I caught sight of her : la divisé, alcancé a verla>

sightless [ˈsaɪtləs] *adj* : invidente, ciego

sightseer [ˈsaɪt,siːər] *n* : turista *mf*

sign[1] [ˈsaɪn] *vt* **1** : firmar <to sign a check : firmar un cheque> **2** *or* **to sign on** HIRE : contratar (a un empleado), fichar (a un jugador) — *vi* **1** : hacer una seña <she signed for him to stop : le hizo una seña para que se parara> **2** : comunicarse por señas

sign[2] *n* **1** SYMBOL : símbolo *m,* signo *m* <minus sign : signo de menos> **2** GESTURE : seña *f,* señal *f,* gesto *m* **3** : letrero *m,* cartel *m* <neon sign : letrero de neón> **4** TRACE : señal *f,* indicio *m*

signal[1] [ˈsɪgnəl] *vt* **-naled** *or* **-nalled; -naling** *or* **-nalling 1** : hacerle señas (a alguien) <she signaled me to leave : me hizo señas para que saliera> **2** INDICATE : señalar, indicar — *vi* : hacer señas, comunicar por señas

signal[2] *adj* NOTABLE : señalado, notable

signal[3] *n* : señal *f*

signature [ˈsɪgnə,tʃʊr] *n* : firma *f*

signet [ˈsɪgnət] *n* : sello *m*

significance [sɪgˈnɪfɪkən*t*s] *n* **1** MEANING : significado *m* **2** IMPORTANCE : importancia *f*

significant [sɪgˈnɪfɪkənt] *adj* **1** IMPORTANT : importante **2** MEANINGFUL : significativo — **significantly** *adv*

signify [ˈsɪgnə,faɪ] *vt* **-fied; -fying 1** : indicar <he signified his desire for more : haciendo señas indicó que quería más> **2** MEAN : significar

sign language *n* : lenguaje *m* por señas

signpost [ˈsaɪn,poːst] *n* : poste *m* indicador

silence[1] [ˈsaɪlən*t*s] *vt* **-lenced; -lencing** : silenciar, acallar

silence[2] *n* : silencio *m*

silent [ˈsaɪlənt] *adj* **1** : callado <to remain silent : quedarse callado, guardar silencio> **2** QUIET, STILL : silencioso **3** MUTE : mudo <a silent letter : una letra muda>

silently [ˈsaɪləntli] *adv* : silenciosamente, calladamente

silhouette[1] [,sɪləˈwɛt] *vt* **-etted; -etting** : destacar la silueta de <it was

silhouetted against the sky : se perfilaba contra el cielo>
silhouette[2] *n* : silueta *f*
silica [ˈsɪlɪkə] *n* : sílice *f*
silicon [ˈsɪlɪkən, -ˌkɑn] *n* : silicio *m*
silk [ˈsɪlk] *n* : seda *f*
silken [ˈsɪlkən] *adj* **1** : de seda <a silken veil : un velo de seda> **2** SILKY : sedoso <silken hair : cabellos sedosos>
silkworm [ˈsɪlkˌwərm] *n* : gusano *m* de seda
silky [ˈsɪlki] *adj* **silkier; -est** : sedoso
sill [ˈsɪl] *n* : alféizar *m* (de una ventana), umbral *m* (de una puerta)
silliness [ˈsɪlinəs] *n* : tontería *f*, estupidez *f*
silly [ˈsɪli] *adj* **sillier; -est** : tonto, estúpido, ridículo
silo [ˈsaɪˌloː] *n, pl* **silos** : silo *m*
silt [ˈsɪlt] *n* : cieno *m*
silver[1] [ˈsɪlvər] *adj* **1** : de plata <a silver spoon : una cuchara de plata> **2** → **silvery**
silver[2] *n* **1** : plata *f* **2** COINS : monedas *fpl* **3** → **silverware 4** : color *m* plata
silverware [ˈsɪlvərˌwær] *n* **1** : artículos *mpl* de plata, platería *f* **2** FLATWARE : cubertería *f*
silvery [ˈsɪlvəri] *adj* : plateado
similar [ˈsɪmələr] *adj* : similar, parecido, semejante
similarity [ˌsɪməˈlærət̬i] *n, pl* **-ties** : semejanza *f*, parecido *m*
similarly [ˈsɪmələrli] *adv* : de manera similar
simile [ˈsɪməˌliː] *n* : símil *m*
simmer [ˈsɪmər] *v* : hervir a fuego lento
simper[1] [ˈsɪmpər] *vi* : sonreír como un tonto
simper[2] *n* : sonrisa *f* tonta
simple [ˈsɪmpəl] *adj* **simpler; -plest 1** INNOCENT : inocente **2** PLAIN : sencillo, simple **3** EASY : simple, sencillo, fácil **4** STRAIGHTFORWARD : puro, simple <the simple truth : la pura verdad> **5** NAIVE : ingenuo, simple
simpleton [ˈsɪmpəltən] *n* : bobo *m*, -ba *f*; tonto *m*, -ta *f*
simplicity [sɪmˈplɪsət̬i] *n* : simplicidad *f*, sencillez *f*
simplification [ˌsɪmpləfəˈkeɪʃən] *n* : simplificación *f*
simplify [ˈsɪmpləˌfaɪ] *vt* **-fied; -fying** : simplificar
simply [ˈsɪmpli] *adv* **1** PLAINLY : sencillamente **2** SOLELY : simplemente, sólo **3** REALLY : absolutamente
simulate [ˈsɪmjəˌleɪt] *vt* **-lated; -lating** : simular
simultaneous [ˌsaɪməlˈteɪniəs] *adj* : simultáneo — **simultaneously** *adv*
sin[1] [ˈsɪn] *vi* **sinned; sinning** : pecar
sin[2] *n* : pecado *m*
since[1] [ˈsɪnts] *adv* **1** : desde entonces <they've been friends ever since : desde entonces han sido amigos> <she's since become mayor : más tarde se hizo alcalde> **2** AGO : hace <he's long since dead : murió hace mucho>
since[2] *conj* **1** : desde que <since he was born : desde que nació> **2** INASMUCH AS : ya que, puesto que, dado que
since[3] *prep* : desde
sincere [sɪnˈsɪr] *adj* **-cerer; -est** : sincero — **sincerely** *adv*
sincerity [sɪnˈsɛrət̬i] *n* : sinceridad *f*
sinew [ˈsɪnˌjuː, ˈsɪˌnuː] *n* **1** TENDON : tendón *m*, nervio *m* (en la carne) **2** POWER : fuerza *f*
sinewy [ˈsɪnjʊi, ˈsɪnʊi] *adj* **1** STRINGY : fibroso **2** STRONG, WIRY : fuerte, nervudo
sinful [ˈsɪnfəl] *adj* : pecador (dícese de las personas), pecaminoso
sing [ˈsɪŋ] *v* **sang** [ˈsæŋ] *or* **sung** [ˈsʌŋ]; **sung; singing** : cantar
singe [ˈsɪndʒ] *vt* **singed; singeing** : chamuscar, quemar
singer [ˈsɪŋər] *n* : cantante *mf*
single[1] [ˈsɪŋgəl] *vt* **-gled; -gling** *or* **to single out 1** SELECT : escoger **2** DISTINGUISH : señalar
single[2] *adj* **1** UNMARRIED : soltero **2** SOLE : solo <a single survivor : un solo sobreviviente> <every single one : cada uno, todos>
single[3] *n* **1** : soltero *m*, -ra *f* <for married couples and singles : para los matrimonios y los solteros> **2** *or* **single room** : habitación *f* individual **3** DOLLAR : billete *m* de un dólar
single–handed [ˈsɪŋgəlˈhændəd] *adj* : sin ayuda, solo
singly [ˈsɪŋgli] *adv* : individualmente, uno por uno
singular[1] [ˈsɪŋgjələr] *adj* **1** : singular (en gramática) **2** OUTSTANDING : singular, sobresaliente **3** STRANGE : singular, extraño
singular[2] *n* : singular *m*
singularly [ˈsɪŋgjələrli] *adv* : singularmente
sinister [ˈsɪnəstər] *adj* : siniestro
sink[1] [ˈsɪŋk] *v* **sank** [ˈsæŋk] *or* **sunk** [ˈsʌŋk]; **sunk; sinking** *vi* **1** : hundirse (dícese de un barco) **2** DROP, FALL : descender, caer <to sink into a chair : dejarse caer en una silla> <her heart sank : se le cayó el alma a los pies> **3** DECREASE : bajar — *vt* **1** : hundir (un barco, etc.) **2** EXCAVATE : excavar (un pozo para minar), perforar (un pozo de agua) **3** PLUNGE, STICK : clavar, hincar **4** INVEST : invertir (fondos)
sink[2] *n* **1 kitchen sink** : fregadero *m*, lavaplatos *m Chile, Col, Mex* **2 bathroom sink** : lavabo *m*, lavamanos *m*
sinner [ˈsɪnər] *n* : pecador *m*, -dora *f*
sinuous [ˈsɪnjʊəs] *adj* : sinuoso — **sinuously** *adv*
sinus [ˈsaɪnəs] *n* : seno *m*
sip[1] [ˈsɪp] *v* **sipped; sipping** *vt* : sorber — *vi* : beber a sorbos
sip[2] *n* : sorbo *m*
siphon[1] [ˈsaɪfən] *vt* : sacar con sifón

siphon[2] *n* : sifón *m*

sir [ˈsər] *n* **1** (*in titles*) : sir *m* **2** (*as a form of address*) : señor *m* <Dear Sir : Muy señor mío> <yes sir! : ¡sí, señor!>

sire[1] [ˈsaɪr] *vt* **sired; siring** : engendrar, ser el padre de

sire[2] *n* : padre *m*

siren [ˈsaɪrən] *n* : sirena *f*

sirloin [ˈsərˌlɔɪn] *n* : solomillo *m*

sirup → **syrup**

sisal [ˈsaɪsəl, -zəl] *n* : sisal *m*

sissy [ˈsɪsi] *n, pl* **-sies** : mariquita *f fam*

sister [ˈsɪstər] *n* : hermana *f*

sisterhood [ˈsɪstərˌhʊd] *n* **1** : condición *f* de ser hermana **2** : sociedad *f* de mujeres

sister-in-law [ˈsɪstərɪnˌlɔ] *n, pl* **sisters-in-law** : cuñada *f*

sisterly [ˈsɪstərli] *adj* : de hermana

sit [ˈsɪt] *v* **sat** [ˈsæt]; **sitting** *vi* **1** : sentarse, estar sentado <he sat down : se sentó> **2** ROOST : posarse **3** : sesionar <the legislature is sitting : la legislatura está en sesión> **4** POSE : posar (para un retrato) **5** LIE, REST : estar (ubicado) <the house sits on a hill : la casa está en una colina> — *vt* SEAT : sentar, colocar <I sat him on the sofa : lo senté en el sofá>

site [ˈsaɪt] *n* 1 PLACE : sitio *m*, lugar *m* **2** LOCATION : emplazamiento *m*, ubicación *f*

sitting room → **living room**

sitter [ˈsɪtər] → **baby-sitter**

situated [ˈsɪtʃʊˌeɪtəd] *adj* LOCATED : ubicado, situado

situation [ˌsɪtʃʊˈeɪʃən] *n* **1** LOCATION : situación *f*, ubicación *f*, emplazamiento *m* **2** CIRCUMSTANCES : situación *f* **3** JOB : empleo *m*

six[1] [ˈsɪks] *adj* : seis

six[2] *n* : seis *m*

six-gun [ˈsɪksˌgʌn] *n* : revólver *m* (con seis cámaras)

six hundred[1] *adj* : seiscientos

six hundred[2] *n* : seiscientos *m*

six-shooter [ˈsɪksˌʃuːtər] → **six-gun**

sixteen[1] [sɪksˈtiːn] *adj* : dieciséis

sixteen[2] *n* : dieciséis *m*

sixteenth[1] [sɪksˈtiːnθ] *adj* : decimosexto

sixteenth[2] *n* **1** : decimosexto *m*, -ta *f* (en una serie) **2** : dieciseisavo *m*, dieciseisava parte *f*

sixth[1] [ˈsɪksθ, ˈsɪkst] *adj* : sexto

sixth[2] *n* **1** : sexto *m*, -ta *f* (en una serie) **2** : sexto *m*, sexta parte *f*

sixtieth[1] [ˈsɪkstiəθ] *adj* : sexagésimo

sixtieth[2] *n* **1** : sexagésimo *m*, -ma *f* (en una serie) **2** : sesentavo *m*, sesentava parte *f*

sixty[1] [ˈsɪksti] *adj* : sesenta

sixty[2] *n, pl* **-ties** : sesenta *m*

sizable *or* **sizeable** [ˈsaɪzəbəl] *adj* : considerable

size[1] [ˈsaɪz] *vt* **sized; sizing 1** : clasificar según el tamaño **2 to size up** : evaluar, apreciar

size[2] *n* **1** DIMENSIONS : tamaño *m*, talla *f* (de ropa), número *m* (de zapatos) **2** MAGNITUDE : magnitud *f*

sizzle [ˈsɪzəl] *vi* **-zled; -zling** : chisporrotear

skate[1] [ˈskeɪt] *vi* **skated; skating** : patinar

skate[2] *n* **1** : patín *m* <roller skate : patín de ruedas> **2** : raya *f* (pez)

skateboard [ˈskeɪtˌbord] *n* : monopatín *m*

skater [ˈskeɪtər] *n* : patinador *m*, -dora *f*

skein [ˈskeɪn] *n* : madeja *f*

skeletal [ˈskɛlətəl] *adj* **1** : óseo (en anatomía) **2** EMACIATED : esquelético

skeleton [ˈskɛlətən] *n* **1** : esqueleto *m* (anatómico) **2** FRAMEWORK : armazón *mf*

skeptic [ˈskɛptɪk] *n* : escéptico *m*, -ca *f*

skeptical [ˈskɛptɪkəl] *adj* : escéptico

skepticism [ˈskɛptəˌsɪzəm] *n* : escepticismo *m*

sketch[1] [ˈskɛtʃ] *vt* : bosquejar — *vi* : hacer bosquejos

sketch[2] *n* **1** DRAWING, OUTLINE : esbozo *m*, bosquejo *m* **2** ESSAY : ensayo *m*

sketchy [ˈskɛtʃi] *adj* **sketchier; -est** : incompleto, poco detallado

skewer[1] [ˈskjuːər] *vt* : ensartar (carne, etc.)

skewer[2] *n* : brocheta *f*, broqueta *f*

ski[1] [ˈskiː] *vi* **skied; skiing** : esquiar

ski[2] *n, pl* **skis** : esquí *m*

skid[1] [ˈskɪd] *vi* **skidded; skidding** : derrapar, patinar

skid[2] *n* : derrape *m*, patinazo *m*

skier [ˈskiːər] *n* : esquiador *m*, -dora *f*

skiff [ˈskɪf] *n* : esquife *m*

skill [ˈskɪl] *n* **1** DEXTERITY : habilidad *f*, destreza *f* **2** CAPABILITY : capacidad *f*, arte *m*, técnica *f* <organizational skills : la capacidad para organizar>

skilled [ˈskɪld] *adj* : hábil, experto

skillet [ˈskɪlət] *n* : sartén *mf*

skillful [ˈskɪlfəl] *adj* : hábil, diestro

skillfully [ˈskɪlfəli] *adv* : con habilidad, con destreza

skim[1] [ˈskɪm] *vt* **skimmed; skimming 1** *or* **to skim off** : espumar, descremar (leche) **2** : echarle un vistazo a (un libro, etc.), pasar rozando (un superficie)

skim[2] *adj* : descremado <skim milk : leche descremada>

skimp [ˈskɪmp] *vi* **to skimp on** : escatimar

skimpy [ˈskɪmpi] *adj* **skimpier; -est** : exiguo, escaso, raquítico

skin[1] [ˈskɪn] *vt* **skinned; skinning** : despellejar, desollar

skin[2] *n* **1** : piel *f*, cutis *m* (de la cara) <dark skin : piel morena> **2** RIND : piel *f*

skin diving *n* : buceo *m*, submarinismo *m*

skinflint [ˈskɪnˌflɪnt] *n* : tacaño *m*, -ña *f*

skinned [ˈskɪnd] *adj* : de piel <tough-skinned : de piel dura>

skinny [ˈskɪni] *adj* **skinnier; -est** : flaco

skip[1] [ˈskɪp] *v* **skipped; skipping** *vi* : ir dando brincos — *vt* : saltarse

skip[2] *n* : brinco *m,* salto *m*

skipper [ˈskɪpər] *n* : capitán *m,* -tana *f*

skirmish[1] [ˈskərmɪʃ] *vi* : escaramuzar

skirmish[2] *n* : escaramuza *f,* refriega *f*

skirt[1] [ˈskərt] *vt* **1** BORDER : bordear **2** EVADE : evadir, esquivar

skirt[2] *n* : falda *f,* pollera *f*

skit [ˈskɪt] *n* : sketch *m* (teatral)

skittish [ˈskɪt̬ɪʃ] *adj* : asustadizo, nervioso

skulk [ˈskʌlk] *vi* : merodear

skull [ˈskʌl] *n* **1** : cráneo *m,* calavera *f* **2 skull and crossbones** : calavera *f* (bandera pirata)

skunk [ˈskʌŋk] *n* : zorrillo *m,* mofeta *f*

sky [ˈskaɪ] *n, pl* **skies** : cielo *m*

skylark [ˈskaɪˌlɑrk] *n* : alondra *f*

skylight [ˈskaɪˌlaɪt] *n* : claraboya *f,* tragaluz *m*

skyline [ˈskaɪˌlaɪn] *n* : horizonte *m*

skyrocket [ˈskaɪˌrɑkət] *vi* : dispararse

skyscraper [ˈskaɪˌskreɪpər] *n* : rascacielos *m*

slab [ˈslæb] *n* : losa *f* (de piedra), tabla *f* (de madera), pedazo *m* grueso (de pan, etc.)

slack[1] [ˈslæk] *adj* **1** CARELESS : descuidado, negligente **2** LOOSE : flojo **3** SLOW : de poco movimiento

slack[2] *n* **1** : parte *f* floja <to take up the slack : tensar (una cuerda, etc.)> **2 slacks** *npl* : pantalones *mpl*

slacken [ˈslækən] *vt* : aflojar — *vi* : aflojarse

slag [ˈslæg] *n* : escoria *f*

slain → **slay**

slake [ˈsleɪk] *vt* **slaked; slaking** : saciar (la sed), satisfacer (la curiosidad)

slam[1] [ˈslæm] *v* **slammed; slamming** *vt* **1** : cerrar de golpe <he slammed the door : dio un portazo> **2** : tirar o dejar caer de golpe <he slammed down the book : dejó caer el libro de un golpe> — *vi* **1** : cerrarse de golpe **2 to slam into** : chocar contra

slam[2] *n* : golpe *m,* portazo *m* (de una puerta)

slander[1] [ˈslændər] *vt* : calumniar, difamar

slander[2] *n* : calumnia *f,* difamación *f*

slanderous [ˈslændərəs] *adj* : difamatorio, calumnioso

slang [ˈslæŋ] *n* : argot *m,* jerga *f*

slant[1] [ˈslænt] *vi* : inclinarse, ladearse — *vt* **1** SLOPE : inclinar **2** ANGLE : sesgar, orientar, dirigir <a story slanted towards youth : un artículo dirigido a los jóvenes>

slant[2] *n* **1** INCLINE : inclinación *f* **2** PERSPECTIVE : perspectiva *f,* enfoque *m*

slap[1] [ˈslæp] *vt* **slapped; slapping** : bofetear, cachetear, dar una palmada (en la espalda, etc.)

slap[2] *n* : bofetada *f,* cachetada *f,* palmada *f*

slash[1] [ˈslæʃ] *vt* **1** GASH : cortar, hacer un tajo en **2** REDUCE : reducir, rebajar (precios)

slash[2] *n* : tajo *m,* corte *m*

slat [ˈslæt] *n* : tablilla *f,* listón *m*

slate [ˈsleɪt] *n* **1** : pizarra *f* <a slate roof : un techo de pizarra> **2** : lista *f* de candidatos (políticos)

slaughter[1] [ˈslɔt̬ər] *vt* **1** BUTCHER : matar (animales) **2** MASSACRE : masacrar (personas)

slaughter[2] *n* **1** : matanza *f* (de animales) **2** MASSACRE : masacre *f,* carnicería *f*

slaughterhouse [ˈslɔt̬ərˌhaʊs] *n* : matadero *m*

Slav [ˈslɑv, ˈslæv] *n* : eslavo *m,* -va *f*

slave[1] [ˈsleɪv] *vi* **slaved; slaving** : trabajar como un burro

slave[2] *n* : esclavo *m,* -va *f*

slaver [ˈslævər, ˈsleɪ-] *vi* : babear

slavery [ˈsleɪvəri] *n* : esclavitud *f*

Slavic [ˈslɑvɪk, ˈslæ-] *adj* : eslavo

slavish [ˈsleɪvɪʃ] *adj* **1** SERVILE : servil **2** IMITATIVE : poco original

slay [ˈsleɪ] *vt* **slew** [ˈsluː]; **slain** [ˈsleɪn]; **slaying** : asesinar, matar

slayer [ˈsleɪər] *n* : asesino *m,* -na *f*

sleazy [ˈsliːzi] *adj* **sleazier; -est 1** SHODDY : chapucero, de mala calidad **2** DILAPIDATED : ruinoso **3** DISREPUTABLE : de mala fama

sled[1] [ˈslɛd] *v* **sledded; sledding** *vi* : ir en trineo — *vt* : transportar en trineo

sled[2] *n* : trineo *m*

sledge [ˈslɛdʒ] *n* **1** : trineo *m* (grande) **2** → **sledgehammer**

sledgehammer [ˈslɛdʒˌhæmər] *n* : almádena *f,* combo *m Chile, Peru*

sleek[1] [ˈsliːk] *vt* SLICK : alisar

sleek[2] *adj* : liso y brillante

sleep[1] [ˈsliːp] *vi* **slept** [ˈslɛpt]; **sleeping** : dormir

sleep[2] *n* **1** : sueño *m* **2 to go to sleep** : dormirse

sleeper [ˈsliːpər] *n* **1** : durmiente *mf* <to be a light sleeper : tener el sueño ligero> **2** *or* **sleeping car** : coche *m* cama, coche *m* dormitorio

sleepily [ˈsliːpəli] *adv* : de manera somnolienta

sleepiness [ˈsliːpinəs] *n* : somnolencia *f*

sleepless [ˈsliːpləs] *adj* : sin dormir, desvelado <to have a sleepless night : pasar la noche en blanco>

sleepwalker [ˈsliːpˌwɔkər] *n* : sonámbulo *m,* -la *f*

sleepy [ˈsliːpi] *adj* **sleepier; -est 1** DROWSY : somnoliento, soñoliento <to be sleepy : tener sueño> **2** LETHARGIC : aletargado, letárgico

sleet[1] [ˈsliːt] *vi* **to be sleeting** : caer aguanieve

sleet[2] *n* : aguanieve *f*

sleeve [ˈsliːv] *n* : manga *f* (de una camisa, etc.)

sleeveless [ˈsliːvləs] *adj* : sin mangas

sleigh[1] [ˈsleɪ] *vi* : ir en trineo

sleigh[2] *n* : trineo *m* (tirado por caballos)

sleight of hand [ˌslaɪtəvˈhænd] : prestidigitación *f*, juegos *mpl* de manos

slender [ˈslɛndər] *adj* **1** SLIM : esbelto, delgado **2** SCANTY : exiguo, escaso <a slender hope : una esperanza lejana>

sleuth [ˈsluːθ] *n* : detective *mf;* sabueso *m*, -sa *f*

slew → slay

slice[1] [ˈslaɪs] *vt* **sliced; slicing** : cortar

slice[2] *n* : rebanada *f*, tajada *f*, lonja *f* (de carne, etc.), rodaja *f* (de una verdura, fruta, etc.), trozo *m* (de pastel, etc.)

slick[1] [ˈslɪk] *vt* : alisar

slick[2] *adj* **1** SLIPPERY : resbaladizo, resbaloso **2** CRAFTY : astuto, taimado

slicker [ˈslɪkər] *n* : impermeable *m*

slide[1] [ˈslaɪd] *v* **slid** [ˈslɪd]; **sliding** [ˈslaɪdɪŋ] *vi* **1** SLIP : resbalar **2** GLIDE : deslizarse **3** DECLINE : bajar <to let things slide : dejar pasar las cosas> — *vt* : correr, deslizar

slide[2] *n* **1** SLIDING : deslizamiento *m* **2** SLIP : resbalón *m* **3** : tobogán *m* (para niños) **4** : TRANSPARENCY : diapositiva *f* (fotográfica) **5** DECLINE : descenso *m*

slier, sliest → sly

slight[1] [ˈslaɪt] *vt* : desairar, despreciar

slight[2] *adj* **1** SLENDER : esbelto, delgado **2** FLIMSY : endeble **3** TRIFLING : leve, insignificante <a slight pain : un leve dolor> **4** SMALL : pequeño, ligero <not in the slightest : en absoluto>

slight[3] *n* SNUB : desaire *m*

slightly [ˈslaɪtli] *adv* : ligeramente, un poco

slim[1] [ˈslɪm] *v* **slimmed; slimming** : adelgazar

slim[2] *adj* **slimmer; slimmest 1** SLENDER : esbelto, delgado **2** SCANTY : exiguo, escaso

slime [ˈslaɪm] *n* **1** : baba *f* (secretado por un animal) **2** MUD, SILT : fango *m*, cieno *m*

slimy [ˈslaɪmi] *adj* **slimier; -est** : viscoso

sling[1] [ˈslɪŋ] *vt* **slung** [ˈslʌŋ]; **slinging 1** THROW : lanzar, tirar **2** HANG : colgar

sling[2] *n* **1** : honda *f* (arma) **2** : cabestrillo *m* <my arm is in a sling : llevo el brazo en cabestrillo>

slingshot [ˈslɪŋˌʃɑt] *n* : tiragomas *m*, resortera *f Mex*

slink [ˈslɪŋk] *vi* **slunk** [ˈslʌŋk]; **slinking** : caminar furtivamente

slip[1] [ˈslɪp] *v* **slipped; slipping** *vi* **1** STEAL : ir sigilosamente <to slip away : escabullirse> <to slip out the door : escaparse por la puerta> **2** SLIDE : resbalarse, deslizarse **3** LAPSE : caer <to slip into error : equivocarse> **4 to let slip** : dejar escapar **5 to slip into** PUT ON : ponerse — *vt* **1** PUT : meter, poner **2** PASS : pasar <she slipped me a note : me pasó una nota> **3 to slip one's mind** : olvidársele a uno

slip[2] *n* **1** PIER : atracadero *m* **2** MISHAP : percance *m*, contratiempo *m* **3** MISTAKE : error *m*, desliz *m* <a slip of the tongue : un lapsus> **4** PETTICOAT : enagua *f* **5** : injerto *m*, esqueje *m* (de una planta) **6 slip of paper** : papelito *m*

slipper [ˈslɪpər] *n* : zapatilla *f*, pantufla *f*

slipperiness [ˈslɪpərinəs] *n* **1** : lo resbaloso, lo resbaladizo **2** TRICKINESS : astucia *f*

slippery [ˈslɪpəri] *adj* **slipperier; -est 1** : resbaloso, resbaladizo <a slippery road : un camino resbaloso> **2** TRICKY : artero, astuto, taimado **3** ELUSIVE : huidizo, escurridizo

slipshod [ˈslɪpˌʃɑd] *adj* : descuidado, chapucero

slip up *vi* : equivocarse

slit[1] [ˈslɪt] *vt* **slit; slitting** : cortar, abrir por lo largo

slit[2] *n* **1** OPENING : abertura *f*, rendija *f* **2** CUT : corte *m*, raja *f*, tajo *m*

slither [ˈslɪðər] *vi* : deslizarse

sliver [ˈslɪvər] *n* : astilla *f*

slob [ˈslɑb] *n* : persona *f* desaliñada <what a slob! : ¡qué cerdo!>

slobber[1] [ˈslɑbər] *vi* : babear

slobber[2] *n* : baba *f*

slogan [ˈsloːgən] *n* : lema *m*, eslogan *m*

sloop [ˈsluːp] *n* : balandra *f*

slop[1] [ˈslɑp] *v* **slopped; slopping** *vt* : derramar — *vi* : derramarse

slop[2] *n* : bazofia *f*

slope[1] [ˈsloːp] *vi* **sloped; sloping** : inclinarse <the road slopes upward : el camino sube (en pendiente)>

slope[2] *n* : inclinación *f*, pendiente *f*, declive *m*

sloppy [ˈslɑpi] *adj* **sloppier; -est 1** MUDDY, SLUSHY : lodoso, fangoso **2** UNTIDY : descuidado (en el trabajo, etc.), desaliñado (de aspecto)

slot [ˈslɑt] *n* : ranura *f*

sloth [ˈslɔθ, ˈsloːθ] *n* **1** LAZINESS : pereza *f* **2** : perezoso *m* (animal)

slouch[1] [ˈslaʊtʃ] *vi* : andar con los hombros caídos, repantigarse (en un sillón)

slouch[2] *n* **1** SLUMPING : mala postura *f* **2** BUNGLER, IDLER : haragán *m*, -gana *f;* inepto *m*, -ta *f* <to be no slouch : no quedarse atrás>

slough[1] [ˈslʌf] *vt* : mudar de (piel)

slough[2] [ˈsluː, ˈslaʊ] *n* SWAMP : ciénaga *f*

Slovak [ˈsloːˌvɑk, -ˌvæk] *or* **Slovakian** [sloːˈvɑkiən, -ˈvæ-] *n* : eslovaco *m*, -ca *f* — **Slovak** *or* **Slovakian** *adj*

Slovene [ˈsloːˌviːn] *or* **Slovenian** [sloːˈviːniən] *n* : esloveno *m*, -na *f* — **Slovene** *or* **Slovenian** *adj*

slovenly [ˈslɑvənli, ˈslʌv-] *adj* : descuidado (en el trabajo, etc.), desaliñado (de aspecto)

slow[1] [sloː] *vt* : retrasar, reducir la marcha de — *vi* : ir más despacio

slow[2] *adv* : despacio, lentamente

slow[3] *adj* **1** : lento <a slow process : un proceso lento> **2** : atrasado <my watch is slow : mi reloj está atrasado, mi reloj se atrasa> **3** SLUGGISH : lento, poco activo **4** STUPID : lento, torpe, corto de alcances

slowly [sloːli] *adv* : lentamente, despacio

slowness [sloːnəs] *n* : lentitud *f,* torpeza *f*

sludge [ˈslʌdʒ] *n* : aguas *fpl* negras, aguas *fpl* residuales

slug[1] [ˈslʌg] *vt* **slugged; slugging** : pegarle un porrazo (a alguien)

slug[2] *n* **1** : babosa *f* (molusco) **2** BULLET : bala *f* **3** TOKEN : ficha *f* **4** BLOW : porrazo *m,* puñetazo *m*

sluggish [ˈslʌgɪʃ] *adj* : aletargado, lento

sluice[1] [ˈsluːs] *vt* **sluiced; sluicing** : lavar en agua corriente

sluice[2] *n* : canal *m*

slum [ˈslʌm] *n* : barriada *f,* barrio *m* bajo

slumber[1] [ˈslʌmbər] *vi* : dormir

slumber[2] *n* : sueño *m*

slump[1] [ˈslʌmp] *vi* **1** DECLINE, DROP : disminuir, bajar **2** SLOUCH : encorvarse, dejarse caer (en una silla, etc.)

slump[2] *n* : bajón *m,* declive *m* (económico)

slung → **sling**

slunk → **slink**

slur[1] [ˈslər] *vt* **slurred; slurring** : ligar (notas musicales), tragarse (las palabras)

slur[2] *n* **1** : ligado *m* (en música), mala pronunciación *f* (de las palabras) **2** ASPERSION : calumnia *f,* difamación *f*

slurp[1] [ˈslərp] *vi* : beber o comer haciendo ruido — *vt* : sorber ruidosamente

slurp[2] *n* : sorbo *m* (ruidoso)

slush [ˈslʌʃ] *n* : nieve *f* medio derretida

slut [ˈslʌt] *n* PROSTITUTE : ramera *f,* fulana *f*

sly [ˈslaɪ] *adj* **slier** [ˈslaɪər]; **sliest** [ˈslaɪəst] **1** CUNNING : astuto, taimado **2** UNDERHANDED : soplado — **slyly** *adv*

slyness [ˈslaɪnəs] *n* : astucia *f*

smack[1] [ˈsmæk] *vi* **to smack of** : oler a, saber a — *vt* **1** KISS : besar, plantarle un beso (a alguien) **2** SLAP : pegarle una bofetada (a alguien) **3 to smack one's lips** : relamerse

smack[2] *adv* : justo, exactamente <smack in the face : en plena cara>

smack[3] *n* **1** TASTE, TRACE : sabor *m,* indicio *m* **2** : chasquido *m* (de los labios) **3** SLAP : bofetada *f* **4** KISS : beso *m*

small [ˈsmɔl] *adj* **1** : pequeño, chico <a small house : una casa pequeña> <small change : monedas de poco valor> **2** TRIVIAL : pequeño, insignificante

smallness [ˈsmɔlnəs] *n* : pequeñez *f*

smallpox [ˈsmɔlˌpɑks] *n* : viruela *f*

smart[1] [ˈsmɑrt] *vi* **1** STING : escocer, picar, arder **2** HURT : dolerse, resentirse <to smart under a rejection : dolerse ante un rechazo>

smart[2] *adj* **1** BRIGHT : listo, vivo, inteligente **2** STYLISH : elegante — **smartly** *adv*

smart[3] *n* : escozor *m,* dolor *m*

smartness [ˈsmɑrtnəs] *n* **1** INTELLIGENCE : inteligencia *f* **2** ELEGANCE : elegancia *f*

smash[1] [ˈsmæʃ] *vt* **1** BREAK : romper, quebrar, hacer pedazos **2** WRECK : destrozar, arruinar **3** CRASH : estrellar, chocar — *vi* **1** SHATTER : hacerse pedazos, hacerse añicos **2** COLLIDE, CRASH : estrellarse, chocar

smash[2] *n* **1** BLOW : golpe *m* **2** COLLISION : choque *m* **3** BANG, CRASH : estrépito *m*

smattering [ˈsmæt̬ərɪŋ] *n* **1** : nociones *fpl* <she has a smattering of programming : tiene nociones de programación> **2** : un poco, unos cuantos <a smattering of spectators : unos cuantos espectadores>

smear[1] [ˈsmɪr] *vt* **1** DAUB : embadurnar, untar (mantequilla, etc.) **2** SMUDGE : emborronar **3** SLANDER : calumniar, difamar

smear[2] *n* **1** SMUDGE : mancha *f* **2** SLANDER : calumnia *f*

smell[1] [ˈsmɛl] *v* **smelled** *or* **smelt** [ˈsmɛlt]; **smelling** *vt* : oler, olfatear <to smell danger : olfatear el peligro> — *vi* : oler <to smell good : oler bien>

smell[2] *n* **1** : olfato *m,* sentido *m* del olfato **2** ODOR : olor *m*

smelly [ˈsmɛli] *adj* **smellier; -est** : maloliente

smelt[1] [ˈsmɛlt] *vt* : fundir

smelt[2] *n, pl* **smelts** *or* **smelt** : eperlano *m* (pez)

smile[1] [ˈsmaɪl] *vi* **smiled; smiling** : sonreír

smile[2] *n* : sonrisa *f*

smirk[1] [ˈsmərk] *vi* : sonreír con suficiencia

smirk[2] *n* : sonrisa *f* satisfecha

smite [ˈsmaɪt] *vt* **smote** [ˈsmoːt]; **smitten** [ˈsmɪtən] *or* **smote; smiting 1** STRIKE : golpear **2** AFFLICT : afligir

smith [ˈsmɪθ] *n* : herrero *m,* -ra *f*

smithy [ˈsmɪθi] *n, pl* **smithies** : herrería *f*

smock [ˈsmɑk] *n* : bata *f,* blusón *m*

smog [ˈsmɑg, ˈsmɔg] *n* : smog *m*

smoke[1] [ˈsmoːk] *v* **smoked; smoking** *vi* **1** : echar humo, humear <a smoking chimney : una chimenea que echa humo> **2** : fumar <I don't smoke : no fumo> — *vt* : ahumar (carne, etc.)

smoke[2] *n* : humo *m*

smoke detector [dɪˈtɛktər] *n* : detector *m* de humo

smoker [ˈsmoːkər] *n* : fumador *m*, -dora *f*

smokestack [ˈsmoːkˌstæk] *n* : chimenea *f*

smoky [ˈsmoːki] *adj* **smokier; -est 1** SMOKING : humeante **2** : a humo <a smoky flavor : un sabor a humo> **3** : lleno de humo <a smoky room : un cuarto lleno de humo>

smolder [ˈsmoːldər] *vi* **1** : arder sin llama **2** : arder (en el corazón) <his anger smoldered : su rabia ardía>

smooth[1] [ˈsmuːð] *vt* : alisar

smooth[2] *adj* **1** : liso (dícese de una superficie) <smooth skin : piel lisa> **2** : suave (dícese de un movimiento) <a smooth landing : un aterrizaje suave> **3** : sin grumos <a smooth sauce : una salsa sin grumos> **4** : fluido <smooth writing : escritura fluida>

smoothly [ˈsmuːðli] *adv* **1** GENTLY, SOFTLY : suavemente **2** EASILY : con facilidad, sin problemas

smoothness [ˈsmuːðnəs] *n* : suavidad *f*

smother [ˈsmʌðər] *vt* **1** SUFFOCATE : ahogar, sofocar **2** COVER : cubrir **3** SUPPRESS : contener — *vi* : asfixiarse

smudge[1] [ˈsmʌdʒ] *v* **smudged; smudging** *vt* : emborronar — *vi* : correrse

smudge[2] *n* : mancha *f*, borrón *m*

smug [ˈsmʌg] *adj* **smugger; smuggest** : suficiente, pagado de sí mismo

smuggle [ˈsmʌgəl] *vt* **-gled; -gling** : contrabandear, pasar de contrabando

smuggler [ˈsmʌgələr] *n* : contrabandista *mf*

smugly [ˈsmʌgli] *adv* : con suficiencia

smut [ˈsmʌt] *n* **1** SOOT : tizne *m*, hollín *m* **2** FUNGUS : tizón *m* **3** OBSCENITY : obscenidad *f*, inmundicia *f*

smutty [ˈsmʌti] *adj* **smuttier; -est 1** SOOTY : tiznado **2** OBSCENE : obsceno, indecente

snack [ˈsnæk] *n* : refrigerio *m*, bocado *m*, tentempié *m fam* <an afternoon snack : una merienda>

snag[1] [ˈsnæg] *v* **snagged; snagging** *vt* : enganchar — *vi* : engancharse

snag[2] *n* : problema *m*, inconveniente *m*

snail [ˈsneɪl] *n* : caracol *m*

snake [ˈsneɪk] *n* : culebra *f*, serpiente *f*

snakebite [ˈsneɪkˌbaɪt] *n* : mordedura *f* de serpiente

snap[1] [ˈsnæp] *v* **snapped; snapping** *vi* **1** : intentar morder (dícese de un perro, etc.), picar (dícese de un pez) **2** : hablar con severidad <he snapped at me! : ¡me gritó!> **3** BREAK : romperse, quebrarse (haciendo un chasquido) — *vt* **1** BREAK : partir (en dos), quebrar **2** : hacer (algo) de un golpe <to snap open : abrir de golpe> **3** RETORT : decir bruscamente **4** CLICK : chasquear <to snap one's fingers : chasquear los dedos>

snap[2] *n* **1** CLICK, CRACK : chasquido *m* **2** FASTENER : broche *m* **3** CINCH : cosa *f* fácil <it's a snap : es facilísimo>

snapdragon [ˈsnæpˌdrægən] *n* : dragón *m* (flor)

snapper [ˈsnæpər] → **red snapper**

snappy [ˈsnæpi] *adj* **snappier; -est 1** FAST : rápido <make it snappy! : ¡date prisa!> **2** LIVELY : vivaz **3** CHILLY : frío **4** STYLISH : elegante

snapshot [ˈsnæpˌʃɑt] *n* : instantánea *f*

snare[1] [ˈsnær] *vt* **snared; snaring** : atrapar

snare[2] *n* : trampa *f*, red *f*

snare drum *n* : tambor *m* con bordón

snarl[1] [ˈsnɑrl] *vi* **1** TANGLE : enmarañar, enredar **2** GROWL : gruñir

snarl[2] *n* **1** TANGLE : enredo *m*, maraña *f* **2** GROWL : gruñido *m*

snatch[1] [ˈsnætʃ] *vt* : arrebatar

snatch[2] *n* : fragmento *m*

sneak[1] [ˈsniːk] *vi* : ir a hurtadillas — *vt* : hacer furtivamente <to sneak a look : mirar con disimulo> <he sneaked a smoke : fumó un cigarrillo a escondidas>

sneak[2] *n* : soplón *m*, -plona *f*

sneakers [ˈsniːkərz] *npl* : tenis *mpl*, zapatillas *fpl*

sneaky [ˈsniːki] *adj* **sneakier; -est** : solapado

sneer[1] [ˈsnɪr] *vi* : sonreír con desprecio

sneer[2] *n* : sonrisa *f* de desprecio

sneeze[1] [ˈsniːz] *vi* **sneezed; sneezing** : estornudar

sneeze[2] *n* : estornudo *m*

snicker[1] [ˈsnɪkər] *vi* : reírse disimuladamente

snicker[2] *n* : risita *f*

snide [ˈsnaɪd] *adj* : sarcástico

sniff[1] [ˈsnɪf] *vi* **1** SMELL : oler, husmear (dícese de los animales) **2 to sniff at** : despreciar, desdeñar — *vt* **1** SMELL : oler **2 to sniff out** : olerse, husmear

sniff[2] *n* **1** SNIFFING : aspiración *f* por la nariz **2** SMELL : olor *m*

sniffle [ˈsnɪfəl] *vi* **-fled; -fling** : respirar con la nariz congestionada

sniffles [ˈsnɪfəlz] *npl* : resfriado *m*

snip[1] [ˈsnɪp] *vt* **snipped; snipping** : cortar (con tijeras)

snip[2] *n* : tijeretada *f*, recorte *m*

snipe[1] [ˈsnaɪp] *vi* **sniped; sniping** : disparar

snipe[2] *n, pl* **snipes** *or* **snipe** : agachadiza *f*

sniper [ˈsnaɪpər] *n* : francotirador *m*, -dora *f*

snivel [ˈsnɪvəl] *vi* **-veled** *or* **-velled; -veling** *or* **-velling 1** → **snuffle 2** WHINE : lloriquear

snob [ˈsnɑb] *n* : esnob *mf*, snob *mf*

snobbery [ˈsnɑbəri] *n, pl* **-beries** : esnobismo *m*

snobbish [ˈsnɑbɪʃ] *adj* : esnob, snob

snobbishness [ˈsnɑbɪʃnəs] *n* : esnobismo *m*

snoop[1] [ˈsnuːp] *vi* : husmear, curiosear

snoop[2] *n* : fisgón *m*, -gona *f*

snooze[1] [ˈsnuːz] *vi* **snoozed; snoozing** : dormitar
snooze[2] *n* : siestecita *f,* siestita *f*
snore[1] [ˈsnor] *vi* **snored; snoring** : roncar
snore[2] *n* : ronquido *m*
snort[1] [ˈsnɔrt] *vi* : bufar, resoplar
snort[2] *n* : bufido *m,* resoplo *m*
snout [ˈsnaʊt] *n* : hocico *m,* morro *m*
snow[1] [ˈsnoː] *vi* **1** : nevar <I'm snowed in : estoy aislado por la nieve> **2 to be snowed under** : estar inundado
snow[2] *n* : nieve *f*
snowball [ˈsnoːˌbɔl] *n* : bola *f* de nieve
snowdrift [ˈsnoːˌdrɪft] *n* : ventisquero *m*
snowfall [ˈsnoːˌfɔl] *n* : nevada *f*
snowplow [ˈsnoːˌplaʊ] *n* : quitanieves *m*
snowshoe [ˈsnoːˌʃuː] *n* : raqueta *f* (para nieve)
snowstorm [ˈsnoːˌstɔrm] *n* : tormenta *f* de nieve, ventisca *f*
snowy [ˈsnoːi] *adj* **snowier; -est** : nevoso <a snowy road : un camino nevado>
snub[1] [ˈsnʌb] *vi* **snubbed; snubbing** : desairar
snub[2] *n* : desaire *m*
snub–nosed [ˈsnʌbˌnoːzd] *adj* : de nariz respingada
snuff[1] [ˈsnʌf] *vt* **1** : apagar (una vela) **2** : sorber (algo) por la nariz
snuff[2] *n* : rapé *m*
snuffle [ˈsnʌfəl] *vi* **-fled; -fling** : respirar con la nariz congestionada
snug [ˈsnʌg] *adj* **snugger; snuggest 1** COMFORTABLE : cómodo **2** TIGHT : ajustado, ceñido <snug pants : pantalones ajustados>
snuggle [ˈsnʌgəl] *vi* **-gled; -gling** : acurrucarse <to snuggle up to someone : arrimársele a alguien>
snugly [ˈsnʌgli] *adv* **1** COMFORTABLY : cómodamente **2** : de manera ajustada <the shirt fits snugly : la camisa queda ajustada>
so[1] [ˈsoː] *adv* **1** (*referring to something indicated or suggested*) <do you think so? : ¿tú crees?> <so it would seem : eso parece> <I told her so : se lo dije> <he's ready, or so he says : según dice, está listo> <it so happened that. . . : resultó que. . .> <do it like so : hazlo así> <so be it : así sea> **2** ALSO : también <so do I : yo también> **3** THUS : así, de esta manera **4** : tan <he'd never been so happy : nunca había estado tan contento> **5** CONSEQUENTLY : por lo tanto
so[2] *conj* **1** THEREFORE : así que **2** *or* **so that** : para que, así que, de manera que **3 so what?** : ¿y qué?
soak[1] [ˈsoːk] *vi* : estar en remojo — *vt* **1** : poner en remojo **2 to soak up** ABSORB : absorber
soak[2] *n* : remojo *m*
soap[1] [ˈsoːp] *vt* : enjabonar
soap[2] *n* : jabón *m*
soapsuds [ˈsoːpˌsʌdz] → **suds**
soapy [ˈsoːpi] **soapier; -est** *adj* : jabonoso <a soapy taste : un gusto a jabón> <a soapy texture : una textura de jabón>
soar [ˈsor] *vi* **1** FLY : volar **2** RISE : remontar el vuelo (dícese de las aves) <her hopes soared : su esperanza renació> <prices are soaring : los precios están subiendo vertiginosamente>
sob[1] [ˈsɑb] *vi* **sobbed; sobbing** : sollozar
sob[2] *n* : sollozo *m*
sober [ˈsoːbər] *adj* **1** : sobrio <he's not sober enough to drive : está demasiado borracho para manejar> **2** SERIOUS : serio
soberly [ˈsoːbərli] *adv* **1** : sobriamente **2** SERIOUSLY : seriamente
sobriety [səˈbraɪəṭi, so-] *n* **1** : sobriedad *f* <sobriety test : prueba de alcoholemia> **2** SERIOUSNESS : seriedad *f*
so–called [ˈsoːˈkɔld] *adj* : supuesto, presunto <the so-called experts : los expertos, así llamados>
soccer [ˈsɑkər] *n* : futbol *m,* fútbol *m*
sociable [ˈsoːʃəbəl] *adj* : sociable
social[1] [ˈsoːʃəl] *adj* : social — **socially** *adv*
social[2] *n* : reunión *f* social
socialism [ˈsoːʃəˌlɪzəm] *n* : socialismo *m*
socialist[1] [ˈsoːʃəlɪst] *adj* : socialista
socialist[2] *n* : socialista *mf*
socialize [ˈsoːʃəˌlaɪz] *v* **-ized; -izing** *vt* **1** NATIONALIZE : nacionalizar **2** : socializar (en psicología) — *vi* : alternar, circular <to socialize with friends : alternar con amigos>
social work *n* : asistencia *f* social
society [səˈsaɪəṭi] *n, pl* **-eties 1** COMPANIONSHIP : compañía *f* **2** : sociedad *f* <a democratic society : una sociedad democrática> <high society : alta sociedad> **3** ASSOCIATION : sociedad *f,* asociación *f*
sociology [ˌsoːsiˈɑləʤi] *n* : sociología *f*
sociological [ˌsoːsiəˈlɑʤɪkəl] *adj* : sociológico
sociologist [ˌsoːsiˈɑləʤɪst] *n* : sociólogo *m,* -ga *f*
sock[1] [ˈsɑk] *vt* : pegar, golpear, darle un puñetazo a
sock[2] *n* **1** *pl* **socks** *or* **sox** [ˈsɑks] : calcetín *m,* media *f* <shoes and socks : zapatos y calcetines> **2** *pl* **socks** [ˈsɑks] PUNCH : puñetazo *m*
socket [ˈsɑkət] *n* **1** *or* **electric socket** : enchufe *m,* toma *f* de corriente **2** : glena *f* (de una articulación) <shoulder socket : glena del hombro> **3 eye socket** : órbita *f,* cuenca *f*
sod[1] [ˈsɑd] *vt* **sodded; sodding** : cubrir de césped
sod[2] *n* TURF : césped *m,* tepe *m*

soda [ˈsoːdə] *n* **1** *or* **soda water :** soda *f* **2** *or* **soda pop :** gaseosa *f*, refresco *m* **3** *or* **ice–cream soda :** refresco *m* con helado
sodden [ˈsɑdən] *adj* SOGGY **:** empapado
sodium [ˈsoːdiəm] *n* **:** sodio *m*
sodium bicarbonate *n* **:** bicarbonato *m* de soda
sodium chloride → salt
sofa [ˈsoːfə] *n* **:** sofá *m*
soft [ˈsɔft] *adj* **1 :** blando <a soft pillow **:** una almohada blanda> **2** SMOOTH **:** suave (dícese de las texturas, de los sonidos, etc.) **3** NONALCOHOLIC **:** no alcohólico <a soft drink **:** un refresco>
softball [ˈsɔftˌbɔl] *n* **:** softbol *m*
soften [ˈsɔfən] *vt* **:** ablandar (algo sólido), suavizar (la piel, un golpe, etc.), amortiguar (un impacto) — *vi* **:** ablandarse, suavizarse
softly [ˈsɔftli] *adv* **:** suavemente <she spoke softly **:** habló en voz baja>
softness [ˈsɔftnəs] *n* **1 :** blandura *f*, lo blando (de una almohada, de la mantequilla, etc.) **2** SMOOTHNESS **:** suavidad *f*
software [ˈsɔftˌwær] *n* **:** software *m*
soggy [ˈsɑgi] *adj* **soggier; -est :** empapado
soil[1] [ˈsɔɪl] *vt* **:** ensuciar — *vi* **:** ensuciarse
soil[2] *n* **1** DIRTINESS **:** suciedad *f* **2** DIRT, EARTH **:** suelo *m*, tierra *f* **3** COUNTRY **:** patria *f* <her native soil **:** su tierra natal>
sojourn[1] [ˈsoːˌdʒərn, soːˈdʒərn] *vi* **:** pasar una temporada
sojourn[2] *n* **:** estadía *f*, estancia *f*, permanencia *f*
solace [ˈsɑləs] *n* **:** consuelo *m*
solar [ˈsoːlər] *adj* **:** solar <the solar system **:** el sistema solar>
sold → sell
solder[1] [ˈsɑdər, ˈsɔ-] *vt* **:** soldar
solder[2] *n* **:** soldadura *f*
soldier[1] [ˈsoːldʒər] *vi* **:** servir como soldado
soldier[2] *n* **:** soldado *mf*
sole[1] [ˈsoːl] *adj* **:** único
sole[2] *n* **1 :** suela *f* (de un zapato) **2 :** lenguado *m* (pez)
solely [ˈsoːli] *adv* **:** únicamente, sólo
solemn [ˈsɑləm] *adj* **:** solemne, serio — **solemnly** *adv*
solemnity [səˈlɛmnəṭi] *n, pl* **-ties :** solemnidad *f*
solicit [səˈlɪsət] *vt* **:** solicitar
solicitous [səˈlɪsəṭəs] *adj* **:** solícito
solicitude [səˈlɪsəˌtuːd, -ˌtjuːd] *n* **:** solicitud *f*
solid[1] [ˈsɑləd] *adj* **1 :** macizo <a solid rubber ball **:** una bola maciza de caucho> **2** CUBIC **:** tridimensional **3** COMPACT **:** compacto, denso **4** STURDY **:** sólido **5** CONTINUOUS **:** seguido, continuo <two solid hours **:** dos horas seguidas> <a solid line **:** una línea continua> **6** UNANIMOUS **:** unánime **7** DEPENDABLE **:** serio, fiable **8** PURE **:** macizo, puro <solid gold **:** oro macizo>
solid[2] *n* **:** sólido *m*
solidarity [ˌsɑləˈdærəṭi] *n* **:** solidaridad *f*
solidify [səˈlɪdəˌfaɪ] *v* **-fied; -fying** *vt* **:** solidificar — *vi* **:** solidificarse
solidity [səˈlɪdəṭi] *n, pl* **-ties :** solidez *f*
solidly [ˈsɑlədli] *adv* **1 :** sólidamente **2** UNANIMOUSLY **:** unánimemente
soliloquy [səˈlɪləkwi] *n, pl* **-quies :** soliloquio *m*
solitaire [ˈsɑləˌtɛr] *n* **:** solitario *m*
solitary [ˈsɑləˌtɛri] *adj* **1** ALONE **:** solitario **2** SECLUDED **:** apartado, retirado **3** SINGLE **:** solo
solitude [ˈsɑləˌtuːd, -ˌtjuːd] *n* **:** soledad *f*
solo[1] [ˈsoːˌloː] *vi* **:** volar en solitario (dícese de un piloto)
solo[2] *adv & adj* **:** en solitario, a solas
solo[3] *n, pl* **solos :** solo *m*
soloist [ˈsoːloɪst] *n* **:** solista *mf*
solstice [ˈsɑlstɪs] *n* **:** solsticio *m*
soluble [ˈsɑljəbəl] *adj* **:** soluble
solution [səˈluːʃən] *n* **:** solución *f*
solve [ˈsɑlv] *vt* **solved; solving :** resolver, solucionar
solvency [ˈsɑlvəntsi] *n* **:** solvencia *f*
solvent [ˈsɑlvənt] *n* **:** solvente *m*
Somali [soˈmɑli, sə-] *n* **:** somalí *mf* — **Somali** *adj*
somber [ˈsɑmbər] *adj* **1** DARK **:** sombrío, oscuro <somber colors **:** colores oscuros> **2** GRAVE **:** sombrío, serio **3** MELANCHOLY **:** sombrío, lúgubre
sombrero [səmˈbrɛrˌoː] *n, pl* **-ros :** sombrero *m* (mexicano)
some[1] [ˈsʌm] *adj* **1 :** un, algún <some lady stopped me **:** una mujer me detuvo> <some distant galaxy **:** alguna galaxia lejana> **2 :** algo de, un poco de <he drank some water **:** tomó (un poco de) agua> **3 :** unos <do you want some apples? **:** ¿quieres unas manzanas?> <some years ago **:** hace varios años>
some[2] *pron* **1 :** algunos <some went, others stayed **:** algunos se fueron, otros se quedaron> **2 :** un poco, algo <there's some left **:** queda un poco> <I have gum; do you want some? **:** tengo chicle, ¿quieres?>
somebody [ˈsʌmbədi, -ˌbɑdi] *pron* **:** alguien
someday [ˈsʌmˌdeɪ] *adv* **:** algún día
somehow [ˈsʌmˌhaʊ] *adv* **1 :** de alguna manera, de algún modo <I'll do it somehow **:** lo haré de alguna manera> **2 :** por alguna rázon <somehow I don't trust her **:** por alguna razón no me fío de ella>
someone [ˈsʌmˌwʌn] *pron* **:** alguien
somersault[1] [ˈsʌmərˌsɔlt] *vi* **:** dar volteretas, dar un salto mortal
somersault[2] *n* **:** voltereta *f*, salto *m* mortal

something [ˈsʌmθɪŋ] *pron* : algo <I want something else : quiero otra cosa> <she's writing a novel or something : está escribiendo una novela o no sé qué>
sometime [ˈsʌm,taɪm] *adv* : algún día, en algún momento <sometime next month : durante el mes que viene>
sometimes [ˈsʌm,taɪmz] *adv* : a veces, algunas veces, de vez en cuando
somewhat [ˈsʌm,hwʌt, -,hwɑt] *adv* : algo, un tanto
somewhere [ˈsʌm,*h*wɛr] *adv* **1** : en alguna parte, a algún lugar **2 somewhere else** : en otro sitio
son [ˈsʌn] *n* : hijo *m*
sonar [ˈsoː,nɑr] *n* : sonar *m*
sonata [səˈnɑt̬ə] *n* : sonata *f*
song [ˈsɔŋ] *n* : canción *f,* canto *m* (de un pájaro)
songbird [ˈsɔŋ,bərd] *n* : pájaro *m* cantor
sonic [ˈsɑnɪk] *adj* **1** : sónico **2 sonic boom** : estampido *m* sónico
son-in-law [ˈsʌnɪn,lɔ] *n, pl* **sons-in-law** : yerno *m,* hijo *m* político
sonnet [ˈsɑnət] *n* : soneto *m*
sonorous [ˈsɑnərəs, səˈnorəs] *adj* : sonoro
soon [ˈsuːn] *adv* **1** : pronto, dentro de poco <he'll arrive soon : llegará pronto> **2** QUICKLY : pronto <as soon as possible : lo más pronto posible> <the sooner the better : cuanto antes mejor>
soot [ˈsʊt, ˈsuːt, ˈsʌt] *n* : hollín *m,* tizne *m*
soothe [ˈsuːð] *vt* **soothed; soothing 1** CALM : calmar, tranquilizar **2** RELIEVE : aliviar
soothsayer [ˈsuːθ,seɪər] *n* : adivino *m,* -na *f*
sooty [ˈsʊt̬i, ˈsuː-, ˈsʌ-] *adj* **sootier; -est** : cubierto de hollín, tiznado
sop[1] [ˈsɑp] *vt* **sopped; sopping 1** DIP : mojar **2** SOAK : empapar **3 to sop up** : rebañar, absorber
sop[2] *n* **1** CONCESSION : concesión *f* **2** BRIBE : soborno *m*
sophisticated [səˈfɪstə,keɪt̬əd] *adj* **1** COMPLEX : complejo **2** WORLDLY-WISE : sofisticado
sophistication [sə,fɪstəˈkeɪʃən] *n* **1** COMPLEXITY : complejidad *f* **2** URBANITY : sofisticación *f*
sophomore [ˈsɑf,mor, ˈsɑfə,mor] *n* : estudiante *mf* de segundo año
soporific [,sɑpəˈrɪfɪk, ,soː-] *adj* : soporífero
soprano [səˈpræ,noː] *n, pl* **-nos** : soprano *mf*
sorcerer [ˈsɔrsərər] *n* : hechicero *m,* brujo *m,* mago *m*
sorceress [ˈsɔrsərəs] *n* : hechicera *f,* bruja *f,* maga *f*
sorcery [ˈsɔrsəri] *n* : hechicería *f,* brujería *f*
sordid [ˈsɔrdɪd] *adj* : sórdido
sore[1] [ˈsor] *adj* **sorer; sorest 1** PAINFUL : dolorido, doloroso <I have a sore throat : me duele la garganta> **2** ACUTE, SEVERE : extremo, grande <in sore straits : en grandes apuros> **3** ANGRY : enojado, enfadado
sore[2] *n* : llaga *f*
sorely [ˈsorli] *adv* : muchísimo <it was sorely needed : se necesitaba urgentemente> <she was sorely missed : la echaban mucho de menos>
soreness [ˈsornəs] *n* : dolor *m*
sorghum [ˈsɔrgəm] *n* : sorgo *m*
sorority [səˈrɔrət̬i] *n, pl* **-ties** : hermandad *f* (de estudiantes femeninas)
sorrel [ˈsɔrəl] *n* **1** : alazán *m* (color o animal) **2** : acedera *f* (hierba)
sorrow [ˈsɑr,oː] *n* : pesar *m,* dolor *m,* pena *f*
sorrowful [ˈsɑrofəl] *adj* : triste, afligido, apenado
sorrowfully [ˈsɑrofəli] *adv* : con tristeza
sorry [ˈsɑri] *adj* **sorrier; -est 1** PITIFUL : lastimero, lastimoso **2 to be sorry** : sentir, lamentar <I'm sorry : lo siento> **3 to feel sorry for** : compadecer <I feel sorry for him : me da pena>
sort[1] [ˈsɔrt] *vt* : clasificar
sort[2] *n* **1** KIND : tipo *m,* clase *f* <a sort of writer : una especie de escritor> **2** NATURE : índole *f* **3 out of sorts** : de mal humor
sortie [ˈsɔrt̬i, sɔrˈtiː] *n* : salida *f*
SOS [,ɛs,oːˈɛs] *n* : SOS *m*
so-so [ˈsoːˈsoː] *adj & adv* : así así, de modo regular
soufflé [suːˈfleɪ] *n* : suflé *m*
sought → **seek**
soul [ˈsoːl] *n* **1** SPIRIT : alma *f* **2** ESSENCE : esencia *f* **3** PERSON : persona *f,* alma *f*
soulful [ˈsoːlfəl] *adj* : conmovedor, lleno de emoción
sound[1] [ˈsaʊnd] *vt* **1** : sondar (en navegación) **2** *or* **to sound out** PROBE : sondear **3** : hacer sonar, tocar (una trompeta, etc.) — *vi* **1** : sonar <the alarm sounded : la alarma sonó> **2** SEEM : parecer
sound[2] *adj* **1** HEALTHY : sano <safe and sound : sano y salvo> <of sound mind and body : en pleno uso de sus facultades> **2** FIRM, SOLID : sólido **3** SENSIBLE : lógico, sensato **4** DEEP : profundo <a sound sleep : un sueño profundo>
sound[3] *n* **1** : sonido *m* <the speed of sound : la velocidad del sonido> **2** NOISE : sonido *m,* ruido *m* <I heard a sound : oí un sonido> **3** CHANNEL : brazo *m* de mar, canal *m* (ancho)
soundless [ˈsaʊndləs] *adj* : sordo
soundlessly [ˈsaʊndləsli] *adv* : silenciosamente
soundly [ˈsaʊndli] *adv* **1** SOLIDLY : sólidamente **2** SENSIBLY : lógicamente, sensatamente **3** DEEPLY : profunda-

mente <sleeping soundly : durmiendo profundamente>
soundness ['saʊndnəs] *n* **1** SOLIDITY : solidez *f* **2** SENSIBLENESS : sensatez *f*, solidez *f*
soundproof ['saʊnd,pru:f] *adj* : insonorizado
sound wave *n* : onda *f* sonora
soup ['su:p] *n* : sopa *f*
sour[1] ['saʊər] *vi* : agriarse, cortarse (dícese de la leche) — *vt* : agriar, cortar (leche)
sour[2] *adj* **1** ACID : agrio, ácido (dícese de la fruta, etc.), cortado (dícese de la leche) **2** DISAGREEABLE : desagradable, agrio
source ['sors] *n* : fuente *f*, origen *m*, nacimiento *m* (de un río)
sourness ['saʊərnəs] *n* : acidez *f*
south[1] ['saʊθ] *adv* : al sur, hacia el sur <the window looks south : la ventana mira al sur> <she continued south : continuó hacia el sur>
south[2] *adj* : sur, del sur <the south entrance : la entrada sur> <South America : Sudamérica, América del Sur>
south[3] *n* : sur *m*
South African *n* : sudafricano *m*, -na *f* — **South African** *adj*
South American[1] *adj* : sudamericano, suramericano
South American[2] *n* : sudamericano *m*, -na *f*; suramericano *m*, -na *f*
southbound ['saʊθ,baʊnd] *adj* : con rumbo al sur
southeast[1] [saʊ'θi:st] *adj* : sureste, sudeste, del sureste
southeast[2] *n* : sureste *m*, sudeste *m*
southeasterly [saʊ'θi:stərli] *adv & adj* **1** : del sureste (dícese del viento) **2** : hacia el sureste
southeastern [saʊ'θi:stərn] → **southeast**[1]
southerly ['sʌðərli] *adv & adj* : del sur
southern ['sʌðərn] *adj* : sur, sureño, meridional, austral <a southern city : una ciudad del sur del país, una ciudad meridional> <the southern side : el lado sur>
Southerner ['sʌðərnər] *n* : sureño *m*, -ña *f*
South Pole : Polo *m* Sur
southward ['saʊθwərd] *or* **southwards** [-wərdz] *adv & adj* : hacia el sur
southwest[1] [saʊθ'wɛst, *as a nautical term often* saʊ'wɛst] *adj* : suroeste, sudoeste, del suroeste
southwest[2] *n* : suroeste *m*, sudoeste *m*
southwesterly [saʊθ'wɛstərli] *adv & adj* **1** : del suroeste (dícese del viento) **2** : hacia el suroeste
southwestern [saʊθ'wɛstərn] → **southwest**[1]
souvenir [,su:və'nɪr, 'su:və,-] *n* : recuerdo *m*, souvenir *m*
sovereign[1] ['sɑvərən] *adj* : soberano
sovereign[2] *n* **1** : soberano *m*, -na *f* (monarca) **2** : soberano *m* (moneda)
sovereignty ['sɑvərənti] *n, pl* **-ties** : soberanía *f*
Soviet ['so:vi,ɛt, 'sɑ-, -viət] *adj* : soviético
sow[1] ['so:] *vt* **sowed; sown** ['so:n] *or* **sowed; sowing 1** PLANT : sembrar **2** SCATTER : esparcir
sow[2] ['saʊ] *n* : cerda *f*
sox → **sock**
soybean ['sɔɪ,bi:n] *n* : soya *f*, soja *f*
spa ['spɑ] *n* : balneario *m*
space[1] ['speɪs] *vt* **spaced; spacing** : espaciar
space[2] *n* **1** PERIOD : espacio *m*, lapso *m*, período *m* **2** ROOM : espacio *m*, sitio *m*, lugar *m* <is there space for me? : ¿hay sitio para mí?> **3** : espacio *m* <blank space : espacio en blanco> **4** : espacio *m* (en física) **5** PLACE : plaza *f*, sitio *m* <to reserve space : reservar plazas> <parking space : sitio para estacionarse>
spacecraft ['speɪs,kræft] *n* : nave *f* espacial
spaceflight ['speɪs,flaɪt] *n* : vuelo *m* espacial
spaceman ['speɪsmən, -,mæn] *n, pl* **-men** [-mən, -,mɛn] : astronauta *m*, cosmonauta *m*
spaceship ['speɪs,ʃɪp] *n* : nave *f* espacial
space shuttle *n* : transbordador *m* espacial
space suit *n* : traje *m* espacial
spacious ['speɪʃəs] *adj* : espacioso, amplio
spade[1] ['speɪd] *v* **spaded; spading** *vt* : palear — *vi* : usar una pala
spade[2] *n* **1** SHOVEL : pala *f* **2** : pica *f* (naipe)
spaghetti [spə'gɛti] *n* : espagueti *m*, espaguetis *mpl*, spaghetti *mpl*
span[1] ['spæn] *vt* **spanned; spanning** : abarcar (un período de tiempo), extenderse sobre (un espacio)
span[2] *n* **1** : lapso *m*, espacio *m* (de tiempo) <life span : duración de la vida> **2** : luz *f* (entre dos soportes)
spangle ['spæŋgəl] *n* : lentejuela *f*
Spaniard ['spænjərd] *n* : español *m*, -ñola *f*
spaniel ['spænjəl] *n* : spaniel *m*
Spanish[1] ['spænɪʃ] *adj* : español
Spanish[2] *n* **1** : español *m* (idioma) **2 the Spanish** *npl* : los españoles
spank ['spæŋk] *vt* : darle nalgadas (a alguien)
spar[1] ['spɑr] *vi* **sparred; sparring** : entrenarse (en boxeo)
spar[2] *n* : palo *m*, verga *f* (de un barco)
spare[1] ['spær] *vt* **spared; sparing 1** : perdonar <to spare someone's life : perdonarle la vida a alguien> **2** SAVE : ahorrar, evitar <I'll spare you the trouble : le evitaré la molestia> **3** : prescindir de <I can't spare her : no puedo prescindir de ella> <can you

spare a dollar? : ¿me das un dólar?> **4** STINT : escatimar <they spared no expense : no repararon en gastos> **5 to spare** : de sobra

spare[2] *adj* **1** : de repuesto, de recambio <spare tire : llanta de repuesto> **2** EXCESS : de más, de sobra <spare time : tiempo libre> **3** LEAN : delgado

spare[3] *n or* **spare part** : repuesto *m,* recambio *m*

sparing [ˈspærɪŋ] *adj* : parco, económico — **sparingly** *adv*

spark[1] [ˈspɑrk] *vi* : chispear, echar chispas — *vt* PROVOKE : despertar, provocar <to spark interest : despertar interés>

spark[2] *n* **1** : chispa *f* <to throw off sparks : echar chispas> **2** GLIMMER, TRACE : destello *m,* pizca *f*

sparkle[1] [ˈspɑrkəl] *vi* **-kled; -kling 1** FLASH, SHINE : destellar, centellear, brillar **2** : estar muy animado (dícese de una conversación, etc.)

sparkle[2] *n* : destello *m,* centelleo *m*

sparkler [ˈspɑrklər] *n* : luz *f* de bengala

spark plug *n* : bujía *f*

sparrow [ˈspæroː] *n* : gorrión *m*

sparse [ˈspɑrs] *adj* **sparser; -est** : escaso — **sparsely** *adv*

spasm [ˈspæzəm] *n* **1** : espasmo *m* (muscular) **2** BURST, FIT : arrebato *m*

spasmodic [spæzˈmɑdɪk] *adj* **1** : espasmódico **2** SPORADIC : irregular, esporádico — **spasmodically** [-dɪkli] *adv*

spastic [ˈspæstɪk] *adj* : espástico

spat[1] → **spit[1]**

spat[2] [ˈspæt] *n* : discusión *f,* disputa *f,* pelea *f*

spatial [ˈspeɪʃəl] *adj* : espacial

spatter[1] [ˈspæt̬ər] *v* : salpicar

spatter[2] *n* : salpicadura *f*

spatula [ˈspætʃələ] *n* : espátula *f,* paleta *f* (para servir)

spawn[1] [ˈspɔn] *vi* : desovar, frezar — *vt* GENERATE : generar, producir

spawn[2] *n* : hueva *f,* freza *f*

spay [ˈspeɪ] *vt* : esterilizar (una perra, etc.)

speak [ˈspiːk] *v* **spoke** [ˈspoːk]; **spoken** [ˈspoːkən]; **speaking** *vi* **1** TALK : hablar <to speak to someone : hablar con alguien> <who's speaking? : ¿de parte de quien?> <so to speak : por así decirlo> **2 to speak out** : hablar claramente **3 to speak out against** : denunciar **4 to speak up** : hablar en voz alta **5 to speak up for** : defender — *vt* **1** SAY : decir <she spoke her mind : habló con franqueza> **2** : hablar (un idioma)

speaker [ˈspiːkər] *n* **1** : hablante *mf* <a native speaker : un hablante nativo> **2** : orador *m,* -dora *f* <the keynote speaker : el orador principal> **3** LOUDSPEAKER : altavoz *m,* altoparlante *m*

spear[1] [ˈspɪr] *vt* : atravesar con una lanza

spear[2] *n* : lanza *f*

spearhead[1] [ˈspɪrˌhɛd] *vt* : encabezar

spearhead[2] *n* : punta *f* de lanza

spearmint [ˈspɪrmɪnt] *n* : menta *f* verde

special [ˈspɛʃəl] *adj* : especial <nothing special : nada en especial, nada en particular> — **specially** *adv*

specialist [ˈspɛʃəlɪst] *n* : especialista *mf*

specialization [ˌspɛʃələˈzeɪʃən] *n* : especialización *f*

specialize [ˈspɛʃəˌlaɪz] *vi* **-ized; -izing** : especializarse

specialty [ˈspɛʃəlt̬i] *n, pl* **-ties** : especialidad *f*

species [ˈspiːˌʃiːz, -ˌsiːz] *ns & pl* : especie *f*

specific [spɪˈsɪfɪk] *adj* : específico, determinado — **specifically** [-fɪkli] *adv*

specification [ˌspɛsəfəˈkeɪʃən] *n* : especificación *f*

specify [ˈspɛsəˌfaɪ] *vt* **-fied; -fying** : especificar

specimen [ˈspɛsəmən] *n* **1** SAMPLE : espécimen *m,* muestra *f* **2** EXAMPLE : espécimen *m,* ejemplar *m*

speck [ˈspɛk] *n* **1** SPOT : manchita *f* **2** BIT, TRACE : mota *f,* pizca *f,* ápice *m*

speckled [ˈspɛkəld] *adj* : moteado

spectacle [ˈspɛktɪkəl] *n* **1** : espectáculo *m* **2 spectacles** *npl* GLASSES : lentes *fpl,* gafas *fpl,* anteojos *mpl,* espejuelos *mpl*

spectacular [spɛkˈtækjələr] *adj* : espectacular

spectator [ˈspɛkˌteɪt̬ər] *n* : espectador *m,* -dora *f*

specter *or* **spectre** [ˈspɛktər] *n* : espectro *m,* fantasma *m*

spectrum [ˈspɛktrəm] *n, pl* **spectra** [-trə] *or* **spectrums 1** : espectro *m* (de colores, etc.) **2** RANGE : gama *f,* abanico *m*

speculate [ˈspɛkjəˌleɪt] *vi* **-lated; -lating 1** : especular (en finanza) **2** WONDER : preguntarse, hacer conjeturas

speculation [ˌspɛkjəˈleɪʃən] *n* : especulación *f*

speculative [ˈspɛkjəˌleɪt̬ɪv] *adj* : especulativo

speculator [ˈspɛkjəˌleɪt̬ər] *n* : especulador *m,* -dora *f*

speech [ˈspiːtʃ] *n* **1** : habla *f,* modo *m* de hablar, expresión *f* **2** ADDRESS : discurso *m*

speechless [ˈspiːtʃləs] *adj* : enmudecido, estupefacto

speed[1] [ˈspiːd] *v* **sped** [ˈspɛd] *or* **speeded; speeding** *vi* **1** : ir a toda velocidad, correr a toda prisa <he sped off : se fue a toda velocidad> **2** : conducir a exceso de velocidad <a ticket for speeding : una multa por exceso de velocidad> — *vt* **to speed up** : acelerar

speed[2] *n* **1** SWIFTNESS : rapidez *f* **2** VELOCITY : velocidad *f*

speedboat [ˈspiːdˌboːt] *n* : lancha *f* motora
speed bump *n* : badén *m*
speed limit *n* : velocidad *f* máxima, límite *m* de velocidad
speedometer [spɪˈdɑmət̬ər] *n* : velocímetro *m*
speedup [ˈspiːdˌʌp] *n* : aceleracion *f*
speedy [ˈspiːdi] *adj* **speedier, -est** : rápido — **speedily** [-dəli] *adv*
spell[1] [ˈspɛl] *vt* **1** : escribir, deletrear (verbalmente) <how do you spell it? : ¿cómo se escribe?, ¿cómo se deletrea?> **2** MEAN : significar <that could spell trouble : eso puede significar problemas> **3** RELIEVE : relevar
spell[2] *n* **1** TURN : turno *m* **2** PERIOD, TIME : período *m* (de tiempo) **3** ENCHANTMENT : encanto *m,* hechizo *m,* maleficio *m*
spellbound [ˈspɛlˌbaʊnd] *adj* : embelesado
speller [ˈspɛlər] *n* : persona *f* que escribe <she's a good speller : tiene buena ortografía>
spelling [ˈspɛlɪŋ] *n* : ortografía *f*
spend [ˈspɛnd] *vt* **spent** [ˈspɛnt]; **spending 1** : gastar (dinero, etc.) **2** PASS : pasar (el tiempo) <to spend time on : dedicar tiempo a>
spendthrift [ˈspɛndˌθrɪft] *n* : derrochador *m,* -dora *f;* despilfarrador *m,* -dora *f*
sperm [ˈspərm] *n, pl* **sperm** *or* **sperms** : esperma *mf*
spew [ˈspjuː] *vi* : salir a chorros — *vt* : vomitar, arrojar (lava, etc.)
sphere [ˈsfɪr] *n* : esfera *f*
spherical [ˈsfɪrɪkəl, ˈsfɛr-] *adj* : esférico
spice[1] [ˈspaɪs] *vt* **spiced; spicing 1** SEASON : condimentar, sazonar **2** *or* **to spice up** : salpimentar, hacer más interesante
spice[2] *n* **1** : especia *f* **2** FLAVOR, INTEREST : sabor *m* <the spice of life : la sal de la vida>
spick-and-span [ˈspɪkəndˈspæn] *adj* : limpio y ordenado
spicy [ˈspaɪsi] *adj* **spicier; -est 1** SPICED : condimentado, sazonado **2** HOT : picante **3** RACY : picante
spider [ˈspaɪdər] *n* : araña *f*
spigot [ˈspɪgət, -kət] *n* : llave *f,* grifo *m,* canilla *Arg, Uru*
spike[1] [ˈspaɪk] *vt* **spiked; spiking 1** FASTEN : clavar (con clavos grandes) **2** PIERCE : atravesar **3** : añadir alcohol a <he spiked her drink with rum : le puso ron a la bebida>
spike[2] *n* : clavo *m* grande
spill[1] [ˈspɪl] *vt* **1** SHED : derramar, verter <to spill blood : derrame sangre> **2** DIVULGE : revelar, divulgar — *vi* : derramarse
spill[2] *n* **1** SPILLING : derrame *m,* vertido *m* <oil spill : derrame de petróleo> **2** FALL : caída *f*
spin[1] [ˈspɪn] *v* **spun** [ˈspʌn]; **spinning** *vi* **1** : hilar **2** TURN : girar **3** REEL : dar vueltas <my head is spinning : la cabeza me está dando vueltas> — *vt* **1** : hilar (hilo, etc.) **2** : tejer <to spin a web : tejer una telaraña> **3** TWIRL : hacer girar
spin[2] *n* : vuelta *f,* giro *m* <to go for a spin : dar una vuelta (en coche)>
spinach [ˈspɪnɪtʃ] *n* : espinacas *fpl,* espinaca *f*
spinal column [ˈspaɪnəl] *n* BACKBONE : columna *f* vertebral
spinal cord *n* : médula *f* espinal
spindle [ˈspɪndəl] *n* **1** : huso *m* (para hilar) **2** : eje *m* (de un mecanismo)
spindly [ˈspɪndli] *adj* : larguirucho *fam,* largo y débil (dícese de una planta)
spine [ˈspaɪn] *n* **1** BACKBONE : columna *f* vertebral, espina *f* dorsal **2** QUILL : púa *f* (de un animal) **3** THORN : espina *f* **4** : lomo *m* (de un libro)
spineless [ˈspaɪnləs] *adj* **1** : sin púas, sin espinas **2** INVERTEBRATE : invertebrado **3** WEAK : débil (de carácter)
spinet [ˈspɪnət] *n* : espineta *f*
spinster [ˈspɪntstər] *n* : soltera *f*
spiny [ˈspaɪni] *adj* **spinier; -est** : con púas (dícese de los animales), espinoso (dícese de las plantas)
spiral[1] [ˈspaɪrəl] *vi* **-raled** *or* **-ralled; -raling** *or* **-ralling** : ir en espiral
spiral[2] *adj* : espiral, en espiral <a spiral staircase : una escalera de caracol>
spiral[3] *n* : espiral *f*
spire [ˈspaɪr] *n* : aguja *f*
spirit[1] [ˈspɪrət] *vt* **to spirit away** : hacer desaparecer
spirit[2] *n* **1** : espíritu *m* <body and spirit : cuerpo y espíritu> **2** GHOST : espíritu *m,* fantasma *m* **3** MOOD : espíritu *m,* humor *m* <in the spirit of friendship : en el espíritu de amistad> <to be in good spirits : estar de buen humor> **4** ENTHUSIASM, VIVACITY : espíritu *m,* ánimo *m,* brío *m* **5 spirits** *npl* : licores *mpl*
spirited [ˈspɪrət̬əd] *adj* : animado, energético
spiritless [ˈspɪrətləs] *adj* : desanimado
spiritual[1] [ˈspɪrɪtʃʊəl, -tʃəl] *adj* : espiritual — **spiritually** *adv*
spiritual[2] *n* : espiritual *m* (canción)
spiritualism [ˈspɪrɪtʃʊəˌlɪzəm, -tʃə-] *n* : espiritismo *m*
spirituality [ˌspɪrɪtʃʊˈælət̬i] *n, pl* **-ties** : espiritualidad *f*
spit[1] [ˈspɪt] *v* **spit** *or* **spat** [ˈspæt]; **spitting** : escupir
spit[2] *n* **1** SALIVA : saliva *f* **2** ROTISSERIE : asador *m* **3** POINT : lengua *f* (de tierra)
spite[1] [ˈspaɪt] *vt* **spited; spiting** : fastidiar, molestar
spite[2] *n* **1** : despecho *m,* rencor *m* **2 in spite of** : a pesar de (que), pese a (que)

spiteful ['spaɪtfəl] *adj* : malicioso, rencoroso

spitting image *n* **to be the spitting image of** : ser el vivo retrato de

spittle ['spɪtəl] *n* : saliva *f*

splash[1] ['splæʃ] *vt* : salpicar — *vi* **1** : salpicar **2 to splash around** : chapotear

splash[2] *n* **1** SPLASHING : salpicadura *f* **2** SQUIRT : chorrito *m* **3** SPOT : mancha *f*

splatter ['splætər] → **spatter**

splay ['spleɪ] *vt* : extender (hacia afuera) <to splay one's fingers : abrir los dedos> — *vi* : extenderse (hacia afuera)

spleen ['spli:n] *n* **1** : bazo *m* (órgano) **2** ANGER, SPITE : ira *f*, rencor *m*

splendid ['splɛndəd] *adj* : espléndido — **splendidly** *adv*

splendor ['splɛndər] *n* : esplendor *m*

splice[1] ['splaɪs] *vt* **spliced; splicing** : empalmar, unir

splice[2] *n* : empalme *m*, unión *f*

splint ['splɪnt] *n* : tablilla *f*

splinter[1] ['splɪntər] *vt* : astillar — *vi* : astillarse

splinter[2] *n* : astilla *f*

split[1] ['splɪt] *v* **split; splitting** *vt* **1** CLEAVE : partir, hender <to split wood : partir madera> **2** BURST : romper, rajar <to split open : abrir> **3** DIVIDE, SHARE : dividir, repartir — *vi* **1** : partirse (dícese de la madera, etc.) **2** BURST, CRACK : romperse, rajarse **3** *or* **to split up** : dividirse

split[2] *n* **1** CRACK : rajadura *f* **2** TEAR : rotura *f* **3** DIVISION : división *f*, escisión *f*

splurge[1] ['splərdʒ] *v* **splurged; splurging** *vt* : derrochar — *vi* : derrochar dinero

splurge[2] *n* : derroche *m*

spoil[1] ['spɔɪl] *v* **spoiled** *or* **spoilt** ['spɔɪlt]; **spoiling** *vt* **1** PILLAGE : saquear **2** RUIN : estropear, arruinar **3** PAMPER : consentir, mimar — *vi* : estropearse, echarse a perder

spoil[2] *n* PLUNDER : botín *m*

spoke[1] → **speak**

spoke[2] ['spo:k] *n* : rayo *m* (de una rueda)

spoken → **speak**

spokesman ['spo:ksmən] *n, pl* **-men** [-mən, -ˌmɛn] : portavoz *mf*; vocero *m*, -ra *f*

spokeswoman ['spo:ksˌwʊmən] *n, pl* **-women** [-ˌwɪmən] : portavoz *f*, vocera *f*

sponge[1] ['spʌndʒ] *vt* **sponged; sponging** : limpiar con una esponja

sponge[2] *n* : esponja *f*

spongy ['spʌndʒi] *adj* **spongier; -est** : esponjoso

sponsor[1] ['spɑntsər] *vt* : patrocinar, auspiciar, apadrinar (a una persona)

sponsor[2] *n* : patrocinador *m*, -dora *f*; padrino *m*, madrina *f*

sponsorship ['spɑntsərˌʃɪp] *n* : patrocinio *m*, apadrinamiento *m*

spontaneity [ˌspɑntə'ni:əṭi, -'neɪ-] *n* : espontaneidad *f*

spontaneous [spɑn'teɪniəs] *adj* : espontáneo — **spontaneously** *adv*

spoof ['spu:f] *n* : burla *f*, parodia *f*

spook[1] ['spu:k] *vt* : asustar

spook[2] *n* : fantasma *m*, espíritu *m*, espectro *m*

spooky ['spu:ki] *adj* **spookier; -est** : que da miedo, espeluzante

spool ['spu:l] *n* : carrete *m*

spoon[1] ['spu:n] *vt* : comer, servir, o echar con cuchara

spoon[2] *n* : cuchara *f*

spoonful ['spu:nˌfʊl] *n* : cucharada *f* <by the spoonful : a cucharadas>

spoor ['spʊr, 'spor] *n* : rastro *m*, pista *f*

sporadic [spə'rædɪk] *adj* : esporádico — **sporadically** [-dɪkli] *adv*

spore ['spor] *n* : espora *f*

sport[1] ['sport] *vi* FROLIC : retozar, juguetear — *vt* SHOW OFF : lucir, ostentar

sport[2] *n* **1** : deporte *m* <outdoor sports : deportes al aire libre> **2** JEST : broma *f* **3 to be a good sport** : tener espíritu deportivo

sportsman ['sportsmən] *n, pl* **-men** [-mən, -ˌmɛn] : deportista *m*

sportsmanship ['sportsmənˌʃɪp] *n* : espíritu *m* deportivo, deportividad *f Spain*

sportswoman ['sportsˌwʊmən] *n, pl* **-women** [-ˌwɪmən] : deportista *f*

sporty ['sporṭi] *adj* **sportier; -est** : deportivo

spot[1] ['spɑt] *v* **spotted; spotting** *vt* **1** STAIN : manchar **2** RECOGNIZE, SEE : ver, reconocer <to spot an error : descubrir un error> — *vi* : mancharse

spot[2] *adj* : hecho al azar <a spot check : un vistazo, un control aleatorio>

spot[3] *n* **1** STAIN : mancha *f* **2** DOT : punto *m* **3** PIMPLE : grano *m* <to break out in spots : salirle granos a alguien> **4** PREDICAMENT : apuro *m*, aprieto *m*, lío *m* <in a tight spot : en apuros> **5** PLACE : lugar *m*, sitio *m* <to be on the spot : estar en el lugar>

spotless ['spɑtləs] *adj* : impecable, inmaculado — **spotlessly** *adv*

spotlight[1] ['spɑtˌlaɪt] *vt* **-lighted** *or* **-lit** [-ˌlɪt]; **-lighting 1** LIGHT : iluminar (con un reflector) **2** HIGHLIGHT : destacar, poner en relieve

spotlight[2] *n* **1** : reflector *m*, foco *m* **2 to be in the spotlight** : ser el centro de atención

spotty ['spɑṭi] *adj* **spottier; -est** : irregular, desigual

spouse ['spaʊs] *n* : cónyuge *mf*

spout[1] ['spaʊt] *vt* **1** : lanzar chorros de **2** DECLAIM : declamar — *vi* : salir a chorros

spout[2] *n* **1** : pico *m* (de una jarra, etc.) **2** STREAM : chorro *m*

sprain[1] ['spreɪn] *vt* : sufrir un esguince en

sprain² *n* : esguince *m,* torcedura *f*

sprawl¹ ['sprɔl] *vi* **1** LIE : tumbarse, echarse, despatarrarse **2** EXTEND : extenderse

sprawl² *n* **1** : postura *f* despatarrada **2** SPREAD : extensión *f,* expansión *f*

spray¹ ['spreɪ] *vt* : rociar (una superficie), pulverizar (un líquido)

spray² *n* **1** BOUQUET : ramillete *m* **2** MIST : rocío *m* **3** ATOMIZER : atomizador *m,* pulverizador *m*

spray gun *n* : pistola *f*

spread¹ ['sprɛd] *v* **spread; spreading** *vt* **1** *or* **to spread out** : desplegar, extender **2** SCATTER, STREW : esparcir **3** SMEAR : untar (mantequilla, etc.) **4** DISSEMINATE : difundir, sembrar, propagar — *vi* **1** : difundirse, correr, propagarse **2** EXTEND : extenderse

spread² *n* **1** EXTENSION : extensión *f,* difusión *f* (de noticias, etc.), propagación *f* (de enfermedades, etc.) **2** : colcha *f* (para una cama), mantel *m* (para una mesa) **3** PASTE : pasta *f* <cheese spread : pasta de queso>

spreadsheet ['sprɛd,ʃi:t] *n* : hoja *f* de cálculo

spree ['spri] *n* **1** : acción *f* desenfrenada <to go on a shopping spree : comprar como loco> **2** BINGE : parranda *f,* juerga *f* <on a spree : de parranda, de juerga>

sprig ['sprɪg] *n* : ramita *f,* ramito *m*

sprightly ['spraɪtli] *adj* **sprightlier; -est** : vivo, animado <with a sprightly step : con paso ligero>

spring¹ ['sprɪŋ] *v* **sprang** ['spræŋ] *or* **sprung** ['sprʌŋ]; **sprung; springing** *vi* **1** LEAP : saltar **2** : mover rápidamente <the lid sprang shut : la tapa se cerró de un golpe> <he sprang to his feet : se paró de un salto> **3 to spring up** : brotar (dícese de las plantas), surgir **4 to spring from** : surgir de — *vt* **1** RELEASE : soltar (de repente) <to spring the news on someone : sorprender a alguien con las noticias> <to spring a trap : hacer saltar una trampa> **2** ACTIVATE : accionar (un mecanismo) **3 to spring a leak** : hacer agua

spring² *n* **1** SOURCE : fuente *f,* origen *m* **2** : manantial *m,* fuente *f* <hot spring : fuente termal> **3** : primavera *f* <spring and summer : la primavera y el verano> **4** : resorte *m,* muelle *m* (de metal, etc.) **5** LEAP : salto *m,* brinco *m* **6** RESILIENCE : elasticidad *f*

springboard ['sprɪŋ,bord] *n* : trampolín *m*

springtime ['sprɪŋ,taɪm] *n* : primavera *f*

springy ['sprɪŋi] *adj* **springier; -est 1** RESILIENT : elástico **2** LIVELY : enérgico

sprinkle¹ ['sprɪŋkəl] *vt* **-kled; -kling** : rociar (con agua), espolvorear (con azúcar, etc.), salpicar

sprinkle² *n* : llovizna *f*

sprinkler ['sprɪŋkələr] *n* : rociador *m,* aspersor *m*

sprint¹ ['sprɪnt] *vi* : echar la carrera, esprintar (en deportes)

sprint² *n* : esprint *m* (en deportes)

sprite ['spraɪt] *n* : hada *f,* elfo *m*

sprocket ['sprɑkət] *n* : diente *m* (de una rueda dentada)

sprout¹ ['spraʊt] *vi* : brotar

sprout² *n* : brote *m,* retoño *m,* vástago *m*

spruce¹ ['spru:s] *v* **spruced; sprucing** *vt* : arreglar — *vi or* **to spruce up** : arreglarse, acicalarse

spruce² *adj* **sprucer; sprucest** : pulcro, arreglado

spruce³ *n* : picea *f* (árbol)

spry ['spraɪ] *adj* **sprier** *or* **spryer** ['spraɪər]; **spriest** *or* **spryest** ['spraɪəst] : ágil, activo

spun → **spin**

spunk ['spʌŋk] *n* : valor *m,* coraje *m,* agallas *fpl fam*

spunky ['spʌŋki] *adj* **spunkier; -est** : animoso, corajudo

spur¹ ['spər] *vt* **spurred; spurring** *or* **to spur on** : espolear (un caballo), motivar (a una persona, etc.)

spur² *n* **1** : espuela *f,* acicate *m* **2** STIMULUS : acicate *m* **3** : espolón *m* (de aves gallináceas)

spurious ['spjʊriəs] *adj* : espurio

spurn ['spərn] *vt* : desdeñar, rechazar

spurt¹ ['spərt] *vt* SQUIRT : lanzar un chorro de — *vi* SPOUT : salir a chorros

spurt² *n* **1** : actividad *f* repentina <a spurt of energy : una explosión de energía> <to do in spurts : hacer por rachas> **2** JET : chorro *m* (de agua, etc.)

sputter¹ ['spʌtər] *vi* **1** JABBER : farfullar **2** : chisporrotear (dícese de la grasa, etc.), petardear (dícese de un motor)

sputter² *n* **1** JABBER : farfulla *f* **2** : chisporroteo *m* (de grasa, etc.), petardeo *m* (de un motor)

spy¹ ['spaɪ] *v* **spied; spying** *vt* SEE : ver, divisar — *vi* : espiar <to spy on someone : espiar a alguien>

spy² *n* : espía *mf*

squab ['skwɑb] *n, pl* **squabs** *or* **squab** : pichón *m*

squabble¹ ['skwɑbəl] *vi* **-bled; -bling** : reñir, pelearse, discutir

squabble² *n* : riña *f,* pelea *f,* discusión *f*

squad ['skwɑd] *n* : pelotón *m* (militar), brigada *f* (de policías), cuadrilla *f* (de obreros, etc.)

squadron ['skwɑdrən] *n* : escuadrón *m* (de militares), escuadrilla *f* (de aviones), escuadra *f* (de naves)

squalid ['skwɑlɪd] *adj* : miserable

squall ['skwɔl] *n* **1** : aguacero *m* tormentoso, chubasco *m* tormentoso **2** **snow squall** : tormenta *f* de nieve

squalor ['skwɑlər] *n* : miseria *f*

squander ['skwɑndər] *vt* : derrochar (dinero, etc.), desaprovechar (una oportunidad, etc.), desperdiciar (talentos, energías, etc.)

square[1] ['skwær] *vt* **squared; squaring 1 :** cuadrar **2 :** elevar al cuadrado (en matemáticas) **3** CONFORM **:** conciliar (con), ajustar (con) **4** SETTLE **:** saldar (una cuenta) <I squared it with him : lo arreglé con él>

square[2] *adj* **squarer; -est 1 :** cuadrado <a square house : una casa cuadrada> **2** RIGHT-ANGLED **:** a escuadra, en ángulo recto **3 :** cuadrado (en matemáticas) <a square mile : una milla cuadrada> **4** HONEST **:** justo <a square deal : un buen acuerdo> <fair and square : en buena lid>

square[3] *n* **1 :** escuadra *f* (instrumento) **2 :** cuadrado *m,* cuadro *m* <to fold into squares : plegar en cuadrados> **3 :** plaza *f* (de una ciudad) **4 :** cuadrado *m* (en matemáticas)

squarely ['skwærli] *adv* **1** EXACTLY **:** exactamente, directamente, justo **2** HONESTLY **:** honradamente, justamente

square root *n* **:** raíz *f* cuadrada

squash[1] ['skwɑʃ, 'skwɔʃ] *vt* **1** CRUSH **:** aplastar **2** SUPPRESS **:** acallar (protestas), sofocar (una rebelión)

squash[2] *n* **1** *pl* **squashes** *or* **squash :** calabaza *f* (vegetal) **2** *or* **squash racquets :** squash *m* (deporte)

squat[1] ['skwɑt] *vi* **squatted; squatting 1** CROUCH **:** agacharse, ponerse en cuclillas **2 :** ocupar un lugar sin derecho

squat[2] *adj* **squatter; squattest :** bajo y ancho, rechoncho *fam* (dícese de una persona)

squat[3] *n* **1 :** posición *f* en cuclillas **2 :** ocupación *f* ilegal (de un lugar)

squaw ['skwɔ] *n* **:** india *f* (norteamericana)

squawk[1] ['skwɔk] *vi* **:** graznar (dícese de las aves), chillar

squawk[2] *n* **:** graznido *m* (de un ave), chillido *m*

squeak[1] ['skwiːk] *vi* **:** chillar (dícese de un animal), chirriar (dícese de un objeto)

squeak[2] *n* **:** chillido *m,* chirrido *m*

squeaky ['skwiːki] *adj* **squeakier; -est :** chirriante <a squeaky voice : una voz chillona>

squeal[1] ['skwiːl] *vi* **1 :** chillar (dícese de las personas o los animales), chirriar (dícese de los frenos, etc.) **2** PROTEST **:** quejarse

squeal[2] *n* **1 :** chillido *m* (de una persona o un animal) **2** SCREECH **:** chirrido *m* (de frenos, etc.)

squeamish ['skwiːmɪʃ] *adj* **:** impresionable, sensible <he's squeamish about cockroaches : las cucarachas le dan asco>

squeeze[1] ['skwiːz] *vt* **squeezed; squeezing 1** PRESS **:** apretar, exprimir (naranjas, etc.) **2** EXTRACT **:** extraer (jugo, etc.)

squeeze[2] *n* **:** apretón *m*

squelch ['skwɛltʃ] *vt* **:** aplastar (una rebelión, etc.)

squid ['skwɪd] *n, pl* **squid** *or* **squids :** calamar *m*

squint[1] ['skwɪnt] *vi* **:** mirar con los ojos entornados

squint[2] *adj* *or* **squint-eyed** ['skwɪnt,aɪd] **:** bizco

squint[3] *n* **:** ojos *mpl* bizcos, bizquera *f*

squire ['skwaɪr] *n* **:** hacendado *m,* -da *f;* terrateniente *mf*

squirm ['skwərm] *vi* **:** retorcerse

squirrel ['skwərəl] *n* **:** ardilla *f*

squirt[1] ['skwərt] *vt* **:** lanzar un chorro de — *vi* SPURT **:** salir a chorros

squirt[2] *n* **:** chorrito *m*

stab[1] [stæb] *vt* **stabbed; stabbing 1** KNIFE **:** acuchillar, apuñalar **2** STICK **:** clavar (con una aguja, etc.), golpear (con el dedo, etc.)

stab[2] *n* **1 :** puñalada *f,* cuchillada *f* **2** JAB **:** pinchazo *m* (con una aguja, etc.), golpe *m* (con un dedo, etc.) **3 to take a stab at :** intentar

stability [stə'bɪləti] *n, pl* **-ties :** estabilidad *f*

stabilize ['steɪbə,laɪz] *v* **-lized; -lizing** *vt* **:** estabilizar — *vi* **:** estabilizarse

stable[1] ['steɪbəl] *vt* **-bled; -bling :** poner (ganado) en un establo, poner (caballos) en una caballeriza

stable[2] *adj* **-bler; -blest 1** FIXED, STEADY **:** fijo, sólido, estable **2** LASTING **:** estable, perdurable <a stable government : un gobierno estable> **3 :** estacionario (en medicina), equilibrado (en psicología)

stable[3] *n* **:** establo *m* (para ganado), caballeriza *f* o cuadra *f* (para caballos)

staccato [stə'kɑtoː] *adj* **:** staccato

stack[1] ['stæk] *vt* **1** PILE **:** amontonar, apilar **2** COVER **:** cubrir, llenar <he stacked the table with books : cubrió la mesa de libros>

stack[2] *n* **1** PILE **:** montón *m,* pila *f* **2** SMOKESTACK **:** chimenea *f*

stadium ['steɪdiəm] *n, pl* **-dia** [-diə] *or* **-diums :** estadio *m*

staff[1] ['stæf] *vt* **:** proveer de personal

staff[2] *n, pl* **staffs** ['stæfs, stævz] *or* **staves** ['stævz, 'steɪvz] **1 :** bastón *m* (de mando), báculo *m* (de obispo) **2** *pl* **staffs** PERSONNEL **:** personal *m* **3** *pl* **staffs :** pentagrama *m* (en música)

stag[1] ['stæg] *adv* **:** solo, sin pareja <to go stag : ir solo>

stag[2] *adj* **:** sólo para hombres

stag[3] *n, pl* **stags** *or* **stag :** ciervo *m,* venado *m*

stage[1] ['steɪdʒ] *vt* **staged; staging :** poner en escena (una obra de teatro)

stage[2] *n* **1** PLATFORM **:** estrado *m,* tablado *m,* escenario *m* (de un teatro) **2** PHASE, STEP **:** fase *f,* etapa *f* <stage of development : fase de desarrollo> <in stages : por etapas> **3 the stage :** el teatro *m*

stagecoach ['steɪdʒ,koːtʃ] *n* **:** diligencia *f*

stagger[1] [ˈstægər] *vi* TOTTER **:** tambalearse **—** *vt* **1** ALTERNATE **:** alternar, escalonar (turnos de trabajo) **2 :** hacer tambalear <to be staggered by **:** quedarse estupefacto por>

stagger[2] *n* **:** tambaleo *m*

staggering [ˈstægərɪŋli] *adj* **:** asombroso

stagnant [ˈstægnənt] *adj* **:** estancado

stagnate [ˈstæg͵neɪt] *vi* **-nated; -nating :** estancarse

staid [ˈsteɪd] *adj* **:** serio, sobrio

stain[1] [ˈsteɪn] *vt* **1** DISCOLOR **:** manchar **2** DYE **:** teñir (madera, etc.) **3** SULLY **:** manchar, empañar

stain[2] *n* **1** SPOT **:** mancha *f* **2** DYE **:** tinte *m,* tintura *f* **3** BLEMISH **:** mancha *f,* mácula *f*

stainless [ˈsteɪnləs] *adj* **:** sin mancha <stainless steel **:** acero inoxidable>

stair [ˈstær] *n* **1** STEP **:** escalón *m,* peldaño *m* **2 stairs** *npl* **:** escalera *f,* escaleras *fpl*

staircase [ˈstær͵keɪs] *n* **:** escalera *f,* escaleras *fpl*

stairway [ˈstær͵weɪ] *n* **:** escalera *f,* escaleras *fpl*

stake[1] [ˈsteɪk] *vt* **staked; staking 1 :** estacar, marcar con estacas (una propiedad) **2** BET **:** jugarse, apostar **3 to stake a claim to :** reclamar, reivindicar

stake[2] *n* **1** POST **:** estaca *f* **2** BET **:** apuesta *f* <to be at stake **:** estar en juego> **3** INTEREST, SHARE **:** interés *m,* participación *f*

stalactite [stəˈlæk͵taɪt] *n* **:** estalactita *f*

stalagmite [stəˈlæg͵maɪt] *n* **:** estalagmita *f*

stale [ˈsteɪl] *adj* **staler; stalest :** viejo <stale bread **:** pan duro> <stale news **:** viejas noticias>

stalemate [ˈsteɪl͵meɪt] *n* **:** punto *m* muerto, impasse *m*

stalk[1] [ˈstɔk] *vt* **:** acechar **—** *vi* **:** caminar rígidamente (por orgullo, ira, etc.)

stalk[2] *n* **:** tallo *m* (de una planta)

stall[1] [ˈstɔl] *vt* **1 :** parar (un motor) **2** DELAY **:** entretener (a una persona), demorar **—** *vi* **1 :** pararse (dícese de un motor) **2** DELAY **:** demorar, andar con rodeos

stall[2] *n* **1 :** compartimiento *m* (de un establo) **2 :** puesto *m* (en un mercado, etc.)

stallion [ˈstæljən] *n* **:** caballo *m* semental

stalwart [ˈstɔlwərt] *adj* **1** STRONG **:** fuerte <a stalwart supporter **:** un firme partidario> **2** BRAVE **:** valiente, valeroso

stamen [ˈsteɪmən] *n* **:** estambre *m*

stamina [ˈstæmənə] *n* **:** resistencia *f*

stammer[1] [ˈstæmər] *vi* **:** tartamudear, titubear

stammer[2] *n* **:** tartamudeo *m,* titubeo *m*

stamp[1] [ˈstæmp] *vt* **1 :** pisotear (con los pies) <to stamp one's feet **:** patear, dar una patada> **2** IMPRESS, IMPRINT **:** sellar (una factura, etc.), acuñar (monedas) **3 :** franquear, ponerle estampillas a (correo)

stamp[2] *n* **1 :** sello *m* (para documentos, etc.) **2** DIE **:** cuño *m* (para monedas) **3** *or* **postage stamp :** sello *m,* estampilla *f,* timbre *m CA, Mex*

stampede[1] [stæmˈpiːd] *vi* **-peded; -peding :** salir en estampida

stampede[2] *n* **:** estampida *f*

stance [ˈstænts] *n* **:** postura *f*

stanch [ˈstɔntʃ, ˈstɑntʃ] *vt* **:** detener, estancar (un líquido)

stand[1] [ˈstænd] *v* **stood** [ˈstʊd]; **standing** *vi* **1 :** estar de pie, estar parado <I was standing on the corner **:** estaba parada en la esquina> **2** *or* **to stand up :** levantarse, pararse, ponerse de pie **3** *(indicating a specified position or location)* <they stand third in the country **:** ocupan el tercer lugar en el país> <the machines are standing idle **:** las máquinas están paradas> **4** *(referring to an opinion)* <how does he stand on the matter ? **:** ¿cuál es su postura respecto al asunto?> **5** BE **:** estar <the house stands on a hill **:** la casa está en una colina> **6** CONTINUE **:** seguir <the order still stands **:** el mandato sigue vigente> **—** *vt* **1** PLACE, SET **:** poner, colocar <he stood them in a row **:** los colocó en hilera> **2** TOLERATE **:** aguantar, soportar <he can't stand her **:** no la puede tragar> **3 to stand firm :** mantenerse firme **4 to stand guard :** hacer la guardia

stand[2] *n* **1** RESISTANCE **:** resistencia *f* <to make a stand against **:** resistir a> **2** BOOTH, STALL **:** stand *m,* puesto *m,* kiosko *m* (para vender periódicos, etc.) **3** BASE **:** pie *m,* base *f* **4 :** grupo *m* (de árboles, etc.) **5** POSITION **:** posición *f,* postura *f* **6 stands** *npl* GRANDSTAND **:** tribuna *f*

standard[1] [ˈstændərd] *adj* **1** ESTABLISHED **:** estándar, oficial <standard measures **:** medidas oficiales> <standard English **:** el inglés estándar> **2** NORMAL **:** normal, estándar, común **3** CLASSIC **:** estándar, clásico <a standard work **:** una obra clásica>

standard[2] *n* **1** BANNER **:** estandarte *m* **2** CRITERION **:** criterio *m* **3** RULE **:** estándar *m,* norma *f,* regla *f* **4** LEVEL **:** nivel *m* <standard of living **:** nivel de vida> **5** SUPPORT **:** poste *m,* soporte *m*

standardize [ˈstændər͵daɪz] *vt* **-ized; -izing :** estandarizar

standard time *n* **:** hora *f* oficial

stand by *vt* **:** atenerse a, cumplir con (una promesa, etc.) **—** *vi* **1 :** mantenerse aparte <to stand by and do nothing **:** mirar sin hacer nada> **2 :** estar preparado, estar listo (para un anuncio, un ataque, etc.)

stand for *vt* **1** REPRESENT **:** significar **2** PERMIT, TOLERATE **:** permitir, tolerar

standing [ˈstændɪŋ] *n* **1** POSITION, RANK **:** posición *f* **2** DURATION **:** duración *f*

stand out *vi* **1 :** destacar(se) <she stands out from the rest : se destaca entre los otros> **2 to stand out against** RESIST **:** oponerse a
standpoint [ˈstændˌpɔint] *n* **:** punto *m* de vista
standstill [ˈstændˌstɪl] *n* **1** STOP **:** detención *f,* paro *m* <to come to a standstill : pararse> **2** DEADLOCK **:** punto *m* muerto, impasse *m*
stand up *vt* **:** dejar plantado <he stood me up again : otra vez me dejó plantado> — *vi* **1** ENDURE **:** durar, resistir **2 to stand up for :** defender **3 to stand up to :** hacerle frente (a alguien)
stank → **stink**
stanza [ˈstænzə] *n* **:** estrofa *f*
staple[1] [ˈsteɪpəl] *vt* **-pled; -pling :** engrapar, grapar
staple[2] *adj* **:** principal, básico <a staple food : un alimento básico>
staple[3] *n* **1 :** producto *m* principal **2 :** grapa *f* (para engrapar papeles)
stapler [ˈsteɪplər] *n* **:** engrapadora *f,* grapadora *f*
star[1] [ˈstɑr] *v* **starred; starring** *vt* **1 :** marcar con una estrella o un asterisco **2** FEATURE **:** ser protagonizado por — *vi* **:** tener el papel principal <to star in : protagonizar>
star[2] *n* **:** estrella *f*
starboard [ˈstɑrbərd] *n* **:** estribor *m*
starch[1] [ˈstɑrtʃ] *vt* **:** almidonar
starch[2] *n* **:** almidón *m,* fécula *f* (comida)
starchy [ˈstɑrtʃi] *adj* **starchier; -est :** lleno de almidón <a starchy diet : una dieta feculenta>
stardom [ˈstɑrdəm] *n* **:** estrellato *m*
stare[1] [ˈstær] *vi* **stared; staring :** mirar fijamente
stare[2] *n* **:** mirada *f* fija
starfish [ˈstɑrˌfɪʃ] *n* **:** estrella *f* de mar
stark[1] [ˈstɑrk] *adv* **:** completamente <stark raving mad : loco de remate> <stark naked : completamente desnudo>
stark[2] *adj* **1** ABSOLUTE **:** absoluto **2** BARREN, DESOLATE **:** desolado, desierto **3** BARE **:** desnudo **4** HARSH **:** severo, duro
starlight [ˈstɑrˌlaɪt] *n* **:** luz *f* de las estrellas
starling [ˈstɑrlɪŋ] *n* **:** estornino *m*
starry [ˈstɑri] *adj* **starrier; -est :** estrellado
start[1] [ˈstɑrt] *vi* **1** JUMP **:** levantarse de un salto, sobresaltarse, dar un respingo **2** BEGIN **:** empezar, comenzar **3** SET OUT **:** salir (de viaje, etc.) **4 :** arrancar (dícese de un motor) — *vt* **1** BEGIN **:** empezar, comenzar, iniciar **2** CAUSE **:** provocar, causar **3** ESTABLISH **:** fundar, montar, establecer <to start a business : montar un negocio> **4 :** arrancar, poner en marcha, encender <to start the car : arrancar el motor>
start[2] *n* **1** JUMP **:** sobresalto *m,* respingo *m* **2** BEGINNING **:** principio *m,* comienzo *m* <to get an early start : salir temprano>
starter [ˈstɑrt̬ər] *n* **1** ENTRANT **:** participante *mf* (en deportes) **2** APPETIZER **:** entremés *m,* aperitivo *m* **3 :** motor *m* de arranque (de un vehículo)
startle [ˈstɑrt̬əl] *vt* **-tled; -tling :** asustar, sobresaltar
starvation [stɑrˈveɪʃən] *n* **:** inanición *f,* hambre *f*
starve [ˈstɑrv] *v* **starved; starving** *vi* **:** morirse de hambre — *vt* **:** privar de comida
stash [ˈstæʃ] *vt* **:** esconder, guardar (en un lugar secreto)
state[1] [ˈsteɪt] *vt* **stated; stating 1** REPORT **:** puntualizar, exponer (los hechos, etc.) <state your name : diga su nombre> **2** ESTABLISH, FIX **:** establecer, fijar
state[2] *n* **1** CONDITION **:** estado *m,* condición *f* <a liquid state : un estado líquido> <state of mind : estado de ánimo> <in a bad state : en malas condiciones> **2** NATION **:** estado *m,* nación *f* **3 :** estado *m* (dentro de un país) <the States : los Estados Unidos>
stateliness [ˈsteɪtlinəs] *n* **:** majestuosidad *f*
stately [ˈsteɪtli] *adj* **statelier; -est :** majestuoso
statement [ˈsteɪtmənt] *n* **1** DECLARATION **:** declaración *f,* afirmación *f* **2** *or* **bank statement :** estado *m* de cuenta
stateroom [ˈsteɪtˌruːm, -ˌrʊm] *n* **:** camarote *m*
statesman [ˈsteɪtsmən] *n, pl* **-men** [-mən, -ˌmɛn] **:** estadista *mf*
static[1] [ˈstæt̬ɪk] *adj* **:** estático
static[2] *n* **:** estática *f,* interferencia *f*
station[1] [ˈsteɪʃən] *vt* **:** apostar, estacionar
station[2] *n* **1 :** estación *f* (de trenes, etc.) **2** RANK, STANDING **:** condición *f* (social) **3 :** canal *m* (de televisión), estación *f* o emisora *f* (de radio) **4 police station :** comisaría *f* **5 fire station :** estación *f* de bomberos, cuartel *m* de bomberos
stationary [ˈsteɪʃəˌnɛri] *adj* **1** IMMOBILE **:** estacionario, inmovible **2** UNCHANGING **:** inmutable, inalterable
stationery [ˈsteɪʃəˌnɛri] *n* **:** papel *m* y sobres *mpl* (para correspondencia)
station wagon *n* **:** camioneta *f* guayín, camioneta *f* ranchera
statistic [stəˈtɪstɪk] *n* **:** estadística *f* <according to statistics : según las estadísticas>
statistical [stəˈtɪstɪkəl] *adj* **:** estadístico
statue [ˈstæˌtʃuː] *n* **:** estatua *f*
statuesque [ˌstætʃʊˈɛsk] *adj* **:** escultural
statuette [ˌstætʃʊˈɛt] *n* **:** estatuilla *f*
stature [ˈstætʃər] *n* **1** HEIGHT **:** estatura *f,* talla *f* **2** PRESTIGE **:** talla *f,* prestigio *m*

status [ˈsteɪtəs, ˈstæ-] *n* **:** condición *f,* situación *f,* estatus *m* (social) <marital status : estado civil>
statute [ˈstæˌtʃuːt] *n* **:** ley *f,* estatuto *m*
staunch [ˈstɔntʃ] *adj* **:** acérrimo, incondicional, leal <a staunch supporter : un partidario incondicional> — **staunchly** *adv*
stave[1] [ˈsteɪv] *vt* **staved** *or* **stove** [ˈstoːv]; **staving 1 to stave in : romper 2 to stave off :** evitar (un ataque), prevenir (un problema)
stave[2] *n* **:** duela *f* (de un barril)
staves → staff
stay[1] [ˈsteɪ] *vi* **1** REMAIN **:** quedarse, permanecer <to stay in : quedarse en casa> <he stayed in the city : permaneció en la ciudad> **2** CONTINUE **:** seguir, quedarse <it stayed cloudy : siguió nublado> <to stay awake : mantenerse despierto> **3** LODGE **:** hospedarse, alojarse (en un hotel, etc.) — *vt* **1** HALT **:** detener, suspender (una ejecución, etc.) **2 to stay the course :** aguantar hasta el final
stay[2] *n* **1** SOJOURN **:** estadía *f,* estancia *f,* permanencia *f* **2** SUSPENSION **:** suspensión *f* (de una sentencia) **3** SUPPORT **:** soporte *m*
stead [ˈstɛd] *n* **1 :** lugar *m* <she went in his stead : fue en su lugar> **2 to stand (someone) in good stead :** ser muy útil a, servir de mucho a
steadfast [ˈstɛdˌfæst] *adj* **:** firme, resuelto <a steadfast friend : un fiel amigo> <a steadfast refusal : una negativa categórica>
steadily [ˈstɛdəli] *adv* **1** CONSTANTLY **:** continuamente, sin parar **2** FIRMLY **:** con firmeza **3** FIXEDLY **:** fijamente
steady[1] [ˈstɛdi] *v* **steadied; steadying** *vt* **:** sujetar <she steadied herself : recobró el equilibrio> — *vi* **:** estabilizarse
steady[2] *adj* **steadier; -est 1** FIRM, SURE **:** seguro, firme <to have a steady hand : tener buen pulso> **2** FIXED, REGULAR **:** fijo <a steady income : ingresos fijos> **3** CALM **:** tranquilo, ecuánime <she has steady nerves : es imperturbable> **4** DEPENDABLE **:** responsable, fiable **5** CONSTANT **:** constante
steak [ˈsteɪk] *n* **:** bistec *m,* filete *m,* churrasco *m,* bife *m Arg, Chile, Uru*
steal [ˈstiːl] *v* **stole** [ˈstoːl]; **stolen** [ˈstoːlən]; **stealing** *vt* **:** robar, hurtar — *vi* **1 :** robar, hurtar **2 :** ir sigilosamente <to steal away : escabullirse>
stealth [ˈstɛlθ] *n* **:** sigilo *m*
stealthily [ˈstɛlθəli] *adv* **:** furtivamente
stealthy [ˈstɛlθi] *adj* **stealthier; -est :** furtivo, sigiloso
steam[1] [ˈstiːm] *vi* **:** echar vapor <to steam away : moverse echando vapor> — *vt* **1 :** cocer al vapor (en cocina) **2 to steam open :** abrir con vapor
steam[2] *n* **1 :** vapor *m* **2 to let off steam :** desahogarse
steamboat [ˈstiːmˌboːt] **→ steamship**
steam engine *n* **:** motor *m* de vapor
steamroller [ˈstiːmˌroːlər] *n* **:** apisonadora *f*
steamship [ˈstiːmˌʃɪp] *n* **:** vapor *m,* barco *m* de vapor
steamy [ˈstiːmi] *adj* **steamier; -est 1 :** lleno de vapor **2** EROTIC **:** erótico <a steamy romance : un tórrido romance>
steed [ˈstiːd] *n* **:** corcel *m*
steel[1] [ˈstiːl] *vt* **to steel oneself :** armarse de valor
steel[2] *adj* **:** de acero
steel[3] *n* **:** acero *m*
steely [ˈstiːli] *adj* **steelier; -est :** como acero <a steely gaze : una mirada fría> <steely determination : determinación férrea>
steep[1] [ˈstiːp] *vt* **:** remojar, dejar (té, etc.) en infusión
steep[2] *adj* **1 :** empinado, escarpado <a steep cliff : un precipicio escarpado> **2** CONSIDERABLE **:** considerable, marcado **3** EXCESSIVE **:** excesivo <steep prices : precios muy altos>
steeple [ˈstiːpəl] *n* **:** aguja *f,* campanario *m*
steeplechase [ˈstiːpəlˌtʃeɪs] *n* **:** carrera *f* de obstáculos
steeply [ˈstiːpli] *adv* **:** abruptamente
steer[1] [ˈstɪr] *vt* **1 :** conducir (un coche), gobernar (un barco) **2** GUIDE **:** dirigir, guiar
steer[2] *n* **:** buey *m*
steering wheel *n* **:** volante *m*
stein [ˈstaɪn] *n* **:** jarra *f* (para cerveza)
stellar [ˈstɛlər] *adj* **:** estelar
stem[1] [ˈstɛm] *v* **stemmed; stemming** *vt* **:** detener, contener, parar <to stem the tide : detener el curso> — *vi* **to stem from :** provenir de, ser el resultado de
stem[2] *n* **:** tallo *m* (de una planta)
stench [ˈstɛntʃ] *n* **:** hedor *m,* mal olor *m*
stencil[1] [ˈstɛn*t*səl] *vt* **-ciled** *or* **-cilled; -ciling** *or* **-cilling :** marcar utilizando una plantilla
stencil[2] *n* **:** plantilla *f* (para marcar)
stenographer [stəˈnɑgrəfər] *n* **:** taquígrafo *m,* -fa *f*
stenographic [ˌstɛnəˈgræfɪk] *adj* **:** taquigráfico
stenography [stəˈnɑgrəfi] *n* **:** taquigrafía *f*
step[1] [ˈstɛp] *vi* **stepped; stepping 1 :** dar un paso <step this way, please : pase por aquí, por favor> <he stepped outside : salió> **2 to step on :** pisar
step[2] *n* **1 :** paso *m* <step by step : paso por paso> **2** STAIR **:** escalón *m,* peldaño *m* **3** RUNG **:** escalón *m,* travesaño *m* **4** MEASURE, MOVE **:** medida *f,* paso *m* <to take steps : tomar medidas> **5** STRIDE **:** paso *m* <with a quick step : con paso rápido>

stepbrother [ˈstɛpˌbrʌðər] *n* **:** hermanastro *m*

stepdaughter [ˈstɛpˌdɔt̬ər] *n* **:** hijastra *f*

stepfather [ˈstɛpˌfɑðər, -ˌfa-] *n* **:** padrastro *m*

stepladder [ˈstɛpˌlædər] *n* **:** escalera *f* de tijera

stepmother [ˈstɛpˌmʌðər] *n* **:** madrastra *f*

steppe [ˈstɛp] *n* **:** estepa *f*

stepping-stone [ˈstɛpɪŋˌstoːn] *n* **:** pasadera *f* (en un río, etc.), trampolín *m* (al éxito)

stepsister [ˈstɛpˌsɪstər] *n* **:** hermanastra *f*

stepson [ˈstɛpˌsʌn] *n* **:** hijastro *m*

step up *vt* INCREASE **:** aumentar

stereo[1] [ˈstɛriˌoː, ˈstɪr-] *adj* **:** estéreo

stereo[2] *n, pl* **stereos :** estéreo *m*

stereophonic [ˌstɛrioˈfɑnɪk, ˌstɪr-] *adj* **:** estereofónico

stereotype[1] [ˈstɛrioˌtaɪp, ˈstɪr-] *vt* **-typed; -typing :** estereotipar

stereotype[2] *n* **:** estereotipo *m*

sterile [ˈstɛrəl] *adj* **:** estéril

sterility [stəˈrɪlət̬i] *n* **:** esterilidad *f*

sterilization [ˌstɛrələˈzeɪʃən] *n* **:** esterilización *f*

sterilize [ˈstɛrəˌlaɪz] *vt* **-ized; -izing :** esterilizar

sterling [ˈstərlɪŋ] *adj* **1 :** de ley <sterling silver : plata de ley> **2** EXCELLENT **:** excelente

stern[1] [ˈstərn] *adj* **:** severo, adusto — **sternly** *adv*

stern[2] *n* **:** popa *f*

sternness [ˈstərnnəs] *n* **:** severidad *f*

sternum [ˈstərnəm] *n, pl* **sternums** *or* **sterna** [-nə] **:** esternón *m*

stethoscope [ˈstɛθəˌskoːp] *n* **:** estetoscopio *m*

stevedore [ˈstiːvəˌdor] *n* **:** estibador *m*, -dora *f*

stew[1] [ˈstuː, ˈstjuː] *vt* **:** estofar, guisar — *vi* **1 :** cocer (dícese de la carne, etc.) **2** FRET **:** preocuparse

stew[2] *n* **1 :** estofado *m,* guiso *m* **2 to be in a stew :** estar agitado

steward [ˈstuːərd, ˈstjuː-] *n* **1** MANAGER **:** administrador *m* **2 :** auxiliar *m* de vuelo (en un avión), camarero *m* (en un barco)

stewardess [ˈstuːərdəs, ˈstjuː-] *n* **1** MANAGER **:** administradora *f* **2 :** camarera *f* (en un barco) **3 :** auxiliar *f* de vuelo, azafata *f,* aeromoza *f* (en un avión)

stick[1] [ˈstɪk] *v* **stuck** [ˈstʌk]; **sticking** *vt* **1** STAB **:** clavar **2** ATTACH **:** pegar **3** PUT **:** poner **4 to stick out :** sacar (la lengua, etc.), extender (la mano) — *vi* **1** ADHERE **:** pegarse, adherirse **2** JAM **:** atascarse **3 to stick around :** quedarse **4 to stick out** PROJECT **:** sobresalir (de una superficie), asomar (por detrás o debajo de algo) **5 to stick to :** no abandonar <stick to your guns : manténgase firme> **6 to stick up :** estar parado (dícese del pelo, etc.), sobresalir (de una superficie) **7 to stick with :** serle fiel a (una persona), seguir con (una cosa) <I'll stick with what I know : prefiero lo conocido>

stick[2] *n* **1** BRANCH, TWIG **:** ramita *f* **2 :** palo *m,* vara *f* <a walking stick : un bastón>

sticker [ˈstɪkər] *n* **:** etiqueta *f* adhesiva

stickler [ˈstɪklər] *n* **:** persona *f* exigente <to be a stickler for : insistir mucho en>

sticky [ˈstɪki] *adj* **stickier; -est 1** ADHESIVE **:** pegajoso, adhesivo **2** MUGGY **:** bochornoso **3** DIFFICULT **:** difícil

stiff [ˈstɪf] *adj* **1** RIGID **:** rígido, tieso <a stiff dough : una masa firme> **2 :** agarrotado, entumecido <stiff muscles : músculos entumecidos> **3** STILTED **:** acartonado, poco natural **4** STRONG **:** fuerte (dícese del viento, etc.) **5** DIFFICULT, SEVERE **:** severo, difícil, duro

stiffen [ˈstɪfən] *vt* **1** STRENGTHEN **:** fortalecer, reforzar (tela, etc.) **2 :** hacer más duro (un castigo, etc.) — *vi* **1** HARDEN **:** endurecerse **2 :** entumecerse (dícese de los músculos)

stiffly [ˈstɪfli] *adv* **1** RIGIDLY **:** rígidamente **2** COLDLY **:** con frialdad

stiffness [ˈstɪfnəs] *n* **1** RIGIDITY **:** rigidez *f* **2** COLDNESS **:** frialdad *f* **3** SEVERITY **:** severidad *f*

stifle [ˈstaɪfəl] *vt* **-fled; -fling** SMOTHER, SUPPRESS **:** sofocar, reprimir, contener <to stifle a yawn : reprimir un bostezo>

stigma [ˈstɪgmə] *n, pl* **stigmata** [stɪgˈmɑt̬ə, ˈstɪgmət̬ə] *or* **stigmas :** estigma *m*

stigmatize [ˈstɪgməˌtaɪz] *vt* **-tized; -tizing :** estigmatizar

stile [ˈstaɪl] *n* **:** escalones *mpl* para cruzar un cerco

stiletto [stəˈlɛˌt̬oː] *n, pl* **-tos** *or* **-toes :** estilete *m*

still[1] [ˈstɪl] *vt* CALM **:** pacificar, apaciguar — *vi* **:** pacificarse, apaciguarse

still[2] *adv* **1** QUIETLY **:** quieto <sit still! : ¡quédate quieto!> **2 :** de todos modos, aún, todavía <she still lives there : aún vive allí> <it's still the same : sigue siendo lo mismo> **3** IN ANY CASE **:** de todos modos, aún así <he still has doubts : aún así le quedan dudas> <I still prefer that you stay : de todos modos prefiero que te quedes>

still[3] *adj* **1** MOTIONLESS **:** quieto, inmóvil **2** SILENT **:** callado

still[4] *n* **1** SILENCE **:** quietud *f,* calma *f* **2 :** alambique *m* (para destilar alcohol)

stillborn [ˈstɪlˌbɔrn] *adj* **:** nacido muerto

stillness [ˈstɪlnəs] *n* **:** calma *f,* silencio *m*

stilt [ˈstɪlt] *n* **:** zanco *m*

stilted [ˈstɪltəd] *adj* **:** afectado, poco natural

stimulant [ˈstɪmjələnt] *n* **:** estimulante *m* — **stimulant** *adj*

stimulate [ˈstɪmjəˌleɪt] *vt* **-lated; -lating :** estimular

stimulation [ˌstɪmjəˈleɪʃən] *n* **1** STIMULATING **:** estimulación *f* **2** STIMULUS **:** estímulo *m*

stimulus [ˈstɪmjələs] *n, pl* **-li** [-ˌlaɪ] **1 :** estímulo *m* **2** INCENTIVE **:** acicate *m*

sting[1] [ˈstɪŋ] *v* **stung** [ˈstʌŋ]; **stinging** *vt* **1 :** picar <a bee stung him : le picó una abeja> **2** HURT **:** hacer escocer (físicamente), herir (emocionalmente) — *vi* **1 :** picar (dícese de las abejas, etc.) **2** SMART **:** escocer, arder

sting[2] *n* **:** picadura *f* (herida), escozor *m* (sensación)

stinger [ˈstɪŋər] *n* **:** aguijón *m* (de una abeja, etc.)

stinginess [ˈstɪndʒinəs] *n* **:** tacañería *f*

stingy [ˈstɪndʒi] *adj* **stingier; -est 1** MISERLY **:** tacaño, avaro **2** PALTRY **:** mezquino, mísero

stink[1] [ˈstɪŋk] *vi* **stank** [ˈstæŋk] *or* **stunk** [ˈstʌŋk]; **stunk; stinking :** apestar, oler mal

stink[2] *n* **:** hedor *m,* mal olor *m,* peste *f*

stint[1] [ˈstɪnt] *vt* **:** escatimar <to stint oneself of : privarse de> — *vi* **to stint on :** escatimar

stint[2] *n* **:** período *m*

stipend [ˈstaɪˌpɛnd, -pənd] *n* **:** estipendio *m*

stipulate [ˈstɪpjəˌleɪt] *vt* **-lated; -lating :** estipular

stipulation [ˌstɪpjəˈleɪʃən] *n* **:** estipulación *f*

stir[1] [ˈstər] *v* **stirred; stirring** *vt* **1** AGITATE **:** mover, agitar **2** MIX **:** revolver, remover **3** INCITE **:** incitar, impulsar, motivar **4** *or* **to stir up** AROUSE **:** despertar (memorias, etc.), provocar (ira, etc.) — *vi* **:** moverse, agitarse

stir[2] *n* **1** MOTION **:** movimiento *m* **2** COMMOTION **:** revuelo *m*

stirrup [ˈstərəp, ˈstɪr-] *n* **:** estribo *m*

stitch[1] [ˈstɪtʃ] *vt* **:** coser, bordar (para decorar) — *vi* **:** coser

stitch[2] *n* **1 :** puntada *f* **2** TWINGE **:** punzada *f,* puntada *f*

stock[1] [ˈstɑk] *vt* **:** surtir, abastecer, vender — *vi* **to stock up :** abastecerse

stock[2] *n* **1** SUPPLY **:** reserva *f,* existencias *fpl* (en comercio) <to be out of stock : estar agotadas las existencias> **2** SECURITIES **:** acciones *fpl,* valores *mpl* **3** LIVESTOCK **:** ganado *m* **4** ANCESTRY **:** linaje *m,* estirpe *f* **5** BROTH **:** caldo *m* **6 to take stock :** evaluar

stockade [stɑˈkeɪd] *n* **:** estacada *f*

stockbroker [ˈstɑkˌbroːkər] *n* **:** corredor *m,* -dora *f* de bolsa

stockholder [ˈstɑkˌhoːldər] *n* **:** accionista *mf*

stocking [ˈstɑkɪŋ] *n* **:** media *f* <a pair of stockings : unas medias>

stock market *n* **:** bolsa *f*

stockpile[1] [ˈstɑkˌpaɪl] *vt* **-piled; -piling :** acumular, almacenar

stockpile[2] *n* **:** reservas *fpl*

stocky [ˈstɑki] *adj* **stockier; -est :** robusto, fornido

stockyard [ˈstɑkˌjɑrd] *n* **:** corral *m*

stodgy [ˈstɑdʒi] *adj* **stodgier; -est 1** DULL **:** aburrido, pesado **2** OLD-FASHIONED **:** anticuado

stoic[1] [ˈstoːɪk] *or* **stoical** [-ɪkəl] *adj* **:** estoico — **stoically** [-ɪkli] *adv*

stoic[2] *n* **:** estoico *m,* -ca *f*

stoicism [ˈstoːəˌsɪzəm] *n* **:** estoicismo *m*

stoke [ˈstoːk] *vt* **stoked; stoking :** atizar (un fuego), echarle carbón a (un horno)

stole[1] → **steal**

stole[2] [ˈstoːl] *n* **:** estola *f*

stolen → **steal**

stolid [ˈstɑlɪd] *adj* **:** impasible, imperturbable — **stolidly** *adv*

stomach[1] [ˈstʌmɪk] *vt* **:** aguantar, soportar

stomach[2] *n* **1 :** estómago *m* **2** BELLY **:** vientre *m,* barriga *f,* panza *f* **3** DESIRE **:** ganas *fpl* <he had no stomach for a fight : no quería pelea>

stomachache [ˈstʌmɪkˌeɪk] *n* **:** dolor *m* de estómago

stomp [ˈstɑmp, ˈstɔmp] *vt* **:** pisotear — *vi* **:** pisar fuerte

stone[1] [ˈstoːn] *vt* **stoned; stoning :** apedrear, lapidar

stone[2] *n* **1 :** piedra *f* **2** PIT **:** hueso *m,* pepa *f* (de una fruta)

Stone Age *n* **:** Edad *f* de Piedra

stony [ˈstoːni] *adj* **stonier; -est 1** ROCKY **:** pedregoso **2** UNFEELING **:** insensible, frío <a stony stare : una mirada glacial>

stood → **stand**

stool [ˈstuːl] *n* **1** SEAT **:** taburete *m,* banco *m* **2** FOOTSTOOL **:** escabel *m* **3** FECES **:** deposición *f* de heces

stoop[1] [ˈstuːp] *vi* **1** CROUCH **:** agacharse **2 to stoop to :** rebajarse a

stoop[2] *n* **1 :** espaldas *fpl* encorvadas <to have a stoop : ser encorvado> **2 :** entrada *f* (de una casa)

stop[1] [ˈstɑp] *v* **stopped; stopping** *vt* **1** PLUG **:** tapar **2** PREVENT **:** impedir, evitar <she stopped me from leaving : me impidió que saliera> **3** HALT **:** parar, detener **4** CEASE **:** dejar de <he stopped talking : dejó de hablar> — *vi* **1** HALT **:** detenerse, parar **2** CEASE **:** cesar, terminar <the rain won't stop : no deja de llover> **3** STAY **:** quedarse <she stopped with friends : se quedó en casa de unos amigos> **4 to stop by :** visitar

stop[2] *n* **1** STOPPER **:** tapón *m* **2** HALT **:** parada *f,* alto *m* <to come to a stop : pararse, detenerse> <to put a stop to : poner fin a> **3 :** parada *f* <bus stop : parada de autobús>

stopgap [ˈstɑpˌgæp] *n* **:** arreglo *m* provisorio

stoplight [ˈstɑpˌlaɪt] *n* **:** semáforo *m*

stoppage [ˈstɑpɪdʒ] *n* : acto *m* de parar <a work stoppage : un paro>

stopper [ˈstɑpər] *n* : tapón *m*

storage [ˈstorɪdʒ] *n* : almacenamiento *m,* almacenaje *m*

storage battery *n* : acumulador *m*

store[1] [ˈstor] *vt* **stored; storing :** guardar, almacenar

store[2] *n* **1** RESERVE, SUPPLY : reserva *f* **2** SHOP : tienda *f* <grocery store : tienda de comestibles>

storehouse [ˈstorˌhaʊs] *n* : almacén *m,* depósito *m*

storekeeper [ˈstorˌkiːpər] *n* : tendero *m,* -ra *f*

storeroom [ˈstorˌruːm, -ˌrʊm] *n* : almacén *m,* depósito *m*

stork [ˈstɔrk] *n* : cigüeña *f*

storm[1] [ˈstɔrm] *vi* **1** : llover o nevar tormentosamente **2** RAGE : ponerse furioso, vociferar **3 to storm out :** salir echando pestes — *vt* ATTACK : asaltar

storm[2] *n* **1** : tormenta *f,* tempestad *f* **2** UPROAR : alboroto *m,* revuelo *m,* escándalo *m* <a storm of abuse : un torrente de abusos>

stormy [ˈstɔrmi] *adj* **stormier; -est** : tormentoso

story [ˈstori] *n, pl* **stories 1** NARRATIVE : cuento *m,* relato *m* **2** ACCOUNT : historia *f,* relato *m* **3** : piso *m,* planta *f* (de un edificio) <first story : planta baja>

stout [ˈstaʊt] *adj* **1** FIRM, RESOLUTE : firme, resuelto **2** STURDY : fuerte, robusto, sólido **3** FAT : corpulento, gordo

stove[1] [ˈstoːv] *n* : cocina *f* (para cocinar), estufa *f* (para calentar)

stove[2] → **stave**[1]

stow [ˈstoː] *vt* **1** STORE : poner, meter, guardar **2** LOAD : cargar — *vi* **to stow away :** viajar de polizón

stowaway [ˈstoːəˌweɪ] *n* : polizón *m*

straddle [ˈstrædəl] *vt* **-dled; -dling** : sentarse a horcajadas sobre

straggle [ˈstrægəl] *vi* **-gled; -gling** : rezagarse, quedarse atrás

straggler [ˈstrægələr] *n* : rezagado *m,* -da *f*

straight[1] [ˈstreɪt] *adv* **1** : derecho, directamente <go straight, then turn right : sigue derecho, luego gira a la derecha> **2** HONESTLY : honestamente <to go straight : enmendarse> **3** CLEARLY : con claridad **4** FRANKLY : francamente, con franqueza

straight[2] *adj* **1** : recto (dícese de las líneas, etc.), derecho (dícese de algo vertical), lacio (dícese del pelo) **2** HONEST, JUST : honesto, justo **3** NEAT, ORDERLY : arreglado, ordenado

straighten [ˈstreɪtən] *vt* **1** : enderezar, poner derecho **2 to straighten up** : arreglar, ordenar <he straightened up the house : arregló la casa>

straightforward [streɪtˈfɔrwərd] *adj* **1** FRANK : franco, sincero **2** CLEAR, PRECISE : puro, simple, claro

straightway [ˈstreɪtˈweɪ, -ˌweɪ] *adv* : inmediatamente

strain[1] [ˈstreɪn] *vt* **1** EXERT : forzar (la vista, la voz) <to strain oneself : hacer un gran esfuerzo> **2** FILTER : colar, filtrar **3** INJURE : lastimarse, hacerse daño en <to strain a muscle : sufrir un esguince>

strain[2] *n* **1** LINEAGE : linaje *m,* abolengo *m* **2** STREAK, TRACE : veta *f* **3** VARIETY : tipo *m,* variedad *f* **4** STRESS : tensión *f,* presión *f* **5** SPRAIN : esguince *m,* torcedura *f* (del tobillo, etc.) **6 strains** *npl* TUNE : melodía *f,* acordes *mpl,* compases *fpl*

strainer [ˈstreɪnər] *n* : colador *m*

strait [ˈstreɪt] *n* **1** : estrecho *m* **2 straits** *npl* DISTRESS : aprietos *mpl,* apuros *mpl* <in dire straits : en serios aprietos>

straitened [ˈstreɪtənd] *adj* **in straitened circumstances :** en apuros económicos

strand[1] [ˈstrænd] *vt* **1** : varar **2 to be left stranded :** quedar(se) varado, quedar colgado <they left me stranded : me dejaron abandonado>

strand[2] *n* **1** : hebra *f* (de hilo, etc.) <a strand of hair : un pelo> **2** BEACH : playa *f*

strange [ˈstreɪndʒ] *adj* **stranger; -est 1** QUEER, UNUSUAL : extraño, raro **2** UNFAMILIAR : desconocido, nuevo

strangely [ˈstreɪndʒli] *adv* ODDLY : de manera extraña <to behave strangely : portarse de una manera rara> <strangely, he didn't call : curiosamente, no llamó>

strangeness [ˈstreɪndʒnəs] *n* **1** ODDNESS : rareza *f* **2** UNFAMILIARITY : lo desconocido

stranger [ˈstreɪndʒər] *n* : desconocido *m,* -da *f;* extraño *m,* -ña *f*

strangle [ˈstræŋgəl] *vt* **-gled; -gling** : estrangular

strangler [ˈstræŋglər] *n* : estrangulador *m,* -dora *f*

strap[1] [ˈstræp] *vt* **strapped; strapping 1** FASTEN : sujetar con una correa **2** FLOG : azotar (con una correa)

strap[2] *n* **1** : correa *f* **2 shoulder strap** : tirante *m*

strapless [ˈstræpləs] *n* : sin tirantes

strapping [ˈstræpɪŋ] *adj* : robusto, fornido

stratagem [ˈstrætədʒəm, -ˌdʒɛm] *n* : estratagema *f,* artimaña *f*

strategic [strəˈtiːdʒɪk] *adj* : estratégico

strategy [ˈstrætədʒi] *n, pl* **-gies** : estrategia *f*

stratified [ˈstrætəˌfaɪd] *adj* : estratificado

stratosphere [ˈstrætəˌsfɪr] *n* : estratosfera *f*

stratum [ˈstreɪtəm, ˈstræ-] *n, pl* **strata** [-tə] : estrato *m,* capa *f*

straw *n* **1** : paja *f* <the last straw : el colmo> **2** *or* **drinking straw :** pajita *f,* popote *m Mex*

strawberry [ˈstrɔˌbɛri] *n, pl* **-ries** : fresa *f*

stray[1] [ˈstreɪ] *vi* **1** WANDER : alejarse, extraviarse <the cattle strayed away : el ganado se descarrió> **2** DIGRESS : desviarse, divagar

stray[2] *adj* : perdido, callejero (dícese de un perro o un gato), descarriado (dícese del ganado)

stray[3] *n* : animal *m* perdido, animal *m* callejero

streak[1] [ˈstriːk] *vt* : hacer rayas en <blue streaked with grey : azul veteado con gris> — *vi* : ir como una flecha

streak[2] *n* **1** : raya *f*, veta *f* (en mármol, queso, etc.), mechón *m* (en el pelo) **2** : rayo *m* (de luz) **3** TRACE : veta *f* **4** : racha *f* <a streak of luck : una racha de suerte>

stream[1] [ˈstriːm] *vi* : correr, salir a chorros <tears streamed from his eyes : las lágrimas brotaban de sus ojos> — *vt* : derramar, dejar correr <to stream blood : derramar sangre>

stream[2] *n* **1** BROOK : arroyo *m*, riachuelo *m* **2** RIVER : río *m* **3** FLOW : corriente *f*, chorro *m*

streamer [ˈstriːmər] *n* **1** PENNANT : banderín *m* **2** RIBBON : serpentina *f* (de papel), cinta *f* (de tela)

streamlined [ˈstriːmˌlaɪnd] *adj* **1** : aerodinámico (dícese de los automóviles, etc.) **2** EFFICIENT : eficiente, racionalizado

street [ˈstriːt] *n* : calle *f*

streetcar [ˈstriːtˌkɑr] *n* : tranvía *m*

strength [ˈstrɛŋkθ] *n* **1** POWER : fuerza *f* **2** SOLIDITY, TOUGHNESS : solidez *f*, resistencia *f*, dureza *f* **3** INTENSITY : intensidad *f* (de emociones, etc.), lo fuerte (de un sabor, etc.) **4** : punto *m* fuerte <strengths and weaknesses : virtudes y defectos> **5** NUMBER : número *m*, complemento *m* <in full strength : en gran número>

strengthen [ˈstrɛŋkθən] *vt* **1** : fortalecer (los músculos, el espíritu, etc.) **2** REINFORCE : reforzar **3** INTENSIFY : intensificar, redoblar (esfuerzos, etc.) — *vi* **1** : fortalecerse, hacerse más fuerte **2** INTENSIFY : intensificarse

strenuous [ˈstrɛnjʊəs] *adj* **1** VIGOROUS : vigoroso, enérgico **2** ARDUOUS : duro, riguroso

strenuously [ˈstrɛnjʊəsli] *adv* : vigorosamente, duro

stress[1] [ˈstrɛs] *vt* **1** : someter a tensión (física) **2** EMPHASIZE : enfatizar, recalcar **3 to stress out** : estresar

stress[2] *n* **1** : tensión *f* (en un material) **2** EMPHASIS : énfasis *m*, acento *m* (en lingüística) **3** TENSION : tensión *f* (nerviosa), estrés *m*

stressful [ˈstrɛsfəl] *adj* : estresante

stretch[1] [ˈstrɛtʃ] *vt* **1** EXTEND : estirar, extender, desplegar (alas) **2 to stretch the truth** : forzar la verdad, exagerar — *vi* : estirarse

stretch[2] *n* **1** STRETCHING : extensión *f*, estiramiento *m* (de músculos) **2** ELASTICITY : elasticidad *f* **3** EXPANSE : tramo *m*, trecho *m* <the home stretch : la recta final> **4** PERIOD : período *m* (de tiempo)

stretcher [ˈstrɛtʃər] *n* : camilla *f*

strew [ˈstruː] *vt* **strewed; strewed** *or* **strewn** [ˈstruːn]; **strewing 1** SCATTER : esparcir (semillas, etc.), desparramar (papeles, etc.) **2 to strew with** : cubrir de

stricken [ˈstrɪkən] *adj* **stricken with** : aquejado de (una enfermedad), afligido por (tristeza, etc.)

strict [ˈstrɪkt] *adj* : estricto — **strictly** *adv*

strictness [ˈstrɪktnəs] *n* : severidad *f*, lo estricto

stricture [ˈstrɪktʃər] *n* : crítica *f*, censura *f*

stride[1] [ˈstraɪd] *vi* **strode** [ˈstroːd]; **stridden** [ˈstrɪdən]; **striding** : ir dando trancos, ir dando zancadas

stride[2] *n* : tranco *m*, zancada *f*

strident [ˈstraɪdənt] *adj* : estridente

strife [ˈstraɪf] *n* : conflictos *mpl*, disensión *f*

strike[1] [ˈstraɪk] *v* **struck** [ˈstrʌk]; **struck; striking** *vt* **1** HIT : golpear (a una persona) <to strike a blow : pegar un golpe> **2** DELETE : suprimir, tachar **3** COIN, MINT : acuñar (monedas) **4** : dar (la hora) **5** AFFLICT : sobrevenir <he was stricken with a fever : le sobrevino una fiebre> **6** IMPRESS : impresionar, parecer <her voice struck me : su voz me impresionó> <it struck him as funny : le pareció chistoso> **7** : encender (un fósforo) **8** FIND : descubrir (oro, petróleo) **9** ADOPT : adoptar (una pose, etc.) — *vi* **1** HIT : golpear <to strike against : chocar contra> **2** ATTACK : atacar **3** : declararse en huelga

strike[2] *n* **1** BLOW : golpe *m* **2** : huelga *f*, paro *m* <to be on strike : estar en huelga> **3** ATTACK : ataque *m*

strikebreaker [ˈstraɪkˌbreɪkər] *n* : rompehuelgas *mf*, esquirol *mf*

strike out *vi* **1** HEAD : salir (para) **2** : ser ponchado (en béisbol) <the batter struck out : poncharon al bateador>

striker [ˈstraɪkər] *n* : huelgista *mf*

strike up *vt* START : entablar, empezar

striking [ˈstraɪkɪŋ] *adj* : notable, sorprendente, llamativo <a striking beauty : una belleza imponente> — **strikingly** *adv*

string[1] [ˈstrɪŋ] *vt* **strung** [ˈstrʌŋ]; **stringing 1** THREAD : ensartar <to string beads : ensartar cuentas> **2** HANG : colgar (con un cordel)

string[2] *n* **1** : cordel *m*, cuerda *f* **2** SERIES : serie *f*, sarta *f* (de insultos, etc.) **3 strings** *npl* : cuerdas *fpl* (en música)

string bean *n* : judía *f*, ejote *m Mex*

stringent [ˈstrɪndʒənt] *adj* : estricto, severo

stringy ['strɪŋi] *adj* **stringier; -est** : fibroso
strip[1] ['strɪp] *v* **stripped; stripping** *vt* : quitar (ropa, pintura, etc.), desnudar, despojar — *vi* UNDRESS : desnudarse
strip[2] *n* : tira *f* <a strip of land : una faja>
stripe[1] ['straɪp] *vt* **striped** ['straɪpt]; **striping** : marcar con rayas o listas
stripe[2] *n* **1** : raya *f,* lista *f* **2** BAND : franja *f*
striped ['straɪpt, 'straɪpəd] *adj* : a rayas, de rayas, rayado, listado
strive ['straɪv] *vi* **strove** ['stro:v]; **striven** ['strɪvən] *or* **strived; striving 1 to strive for** : luchar por lograr **2 to strive to** : esforzarse por
strode → **stride**
stroke[1] ['stro:k] *vt* **stroked; stroking** : acariciar
stroke[2] *n* : golpe *m* <a stroke of luck : un golpe de suerte>
stroll[1] ['stro:l] *vi* : pasear, pasearse, dar un paseo
stroll[2] *n* : paseo *m*
stroller ['stro:lər] *n* : cochecito *m* (para niños)
strong ['strɔŋ] *adj* **1** : fuerte **2** HEALTHY : sano **3** ZEALOUS : ferviente
stronghold ['strɔŋˌho:ld] *n* : fortaleza *f,* fuerte *m,* bastión *m* <a cultural stronghold : un baluarte de la cultura>
strongly ['strɔŋli] *adv* **1** POWERFULLY : fuerte, con fuerza **2** STURDILY : fuertemente, sólidamente **3** INTENSELY : intensamente, profundamente **4** WHOLEHEARTEDLY : totalmente
struck → **strike**[1]
structural ['strʌktʃərəl] *adj* : estructural
structure[1] ['strʌktʃər] *vt* **-tured; -turing** : estructurar
structure[2] *n* **1** BUILDING : construcción *f* **2** ARRANGEMENT, FRAMEWORK : estructura *f*
struggle[1] ['strʌgəl] *vi* **-gled; -gling 1** CONTEND : forcejear (físicamente), luchar, contender **2** : hacer con dificultad <she struggled forward : avanzó con dificultad>
struggle[2] *n* : lucha *f,* pelea *f* (física)
strum ['strʌm] *vt* **strummed; strumming** : rasguear
strung → **string**[1]
strut[1] ['strʌt] *vi* **strutted; strutting** : pavonearse
strut[2] *n* **1** : pavoneo *m* <he walked with a strut : se pavoneaba> **2** : puntal *m* (en construcción, etc.)
strychnine ['strɪkˌnaɪn, -nən, -ˌni:n] *n* : estricnina *f*
stub[1] ['stʌb] *vt* **stubbed; stubbing 1 to stub one's toe** : darse en el dedo (del pie) **2 to stub out** : apagarse
stub[2] *n* : colilla *f* (de un cigarrillo), cabo *m* (de un lápiz, etc.), talón *m* (de un cheque)
stubble ['stʌbəl] *n* **1** : rastrojo *m* (de plantas) **2** BEARD : barba *f*
stubborn ['stʌbərn] *adj* **1** OBSTINATE : terco, obstinado, empecinado **2** PERSISTENT : pertinaz, persistente — **stubbornly** *adv*
stubbornness ['stʌbərnnəs] *n* **1** OBSTINACY : terquedad *f,* obstinación *f* **2** PERSISTENCE : persistencia *f*
stubby ['stʌbi] *adj* **stubbier; -est** : corto y grueso <stubby fingers : dedos regordetes>
stucco ['stʌko:] *n, pl* **stuccos** *or* **stuccoes** : estuco *m*
stuck → **stick**[1]
stuck–up ['stʌk'ʌp] *adj* : engreído, creído *fam*
stud[1] ['stʌd] *vt* **studded; studding** : tachonar, salpicar
stud[2] *n* **1** *or* **stud horse** : semental *m* **2** : montante *m* (en construcción) **3** HOBNAIL : tachuela *f,* tachón *m*
student ['stu:dənt, 'stju:-] *n* : estudiante *mf;* alumno *m,* -na *f* (de un colegio)
studied ['stʌdid] *adj* : intencionado, premeditado
studio ['stu:diˌo:, 'stju:-] *n, pl* **studios** : estudio *m*
studious ['stu:diəs, 'stju:-] *adj* : estudioso — **studiously** *adv*
study[1] ['stʌdi] *v* **studied; studying 1** : estudiar **2** EXAMINE : examinar, estudiar
study[2] *n, pl* **studies 1** STUDYING : estudio *m* **2** OFFICE : estudio *m,* gabinete *m* (en una casa) **3** RESEARCH : investigación *f,* estudio *m*
stuff[1] ['stʌf] *vt* : rellenar, llenar, atiborrar
stuff[2] *n* **1** POSSESSIONS : cosas *fpl* **2** ESSENCE : esencia *f* **3** SUBSTANCE : cosa *f,* cosas *fpl* <some sticky stuff : una cosa pegajosa> <she knows her stuff : es experta>
stuffing ['stʌfɪŋ] *n* : relleno *m*
stuffy ['stʌfi] *adj* **stuffier; -est 1** CLOSE : viciado, cargado <a stuffy room : una sala mal ventilada> <stuffy weather : tiempo bochornoso> **2** : tapado (dícese de la nariz) **3** STODGY : pesado, aburrido
stumble[1] ['stʌmbəl] *vi* **-bled; -bling 1** TRIP : tropezar, dar un traspié **2** FLOUNDER : quedarse sin saber qué hacer o decir **3 to stumble across** *or* **to stumble upon** : dar con, tropezar con
stumble[2] *n* : tropezón *m,* traspié *m*
stump[1] ['stʌmp] *vt* : dejar perplejo <to be stumped : no tener respuesta>
stump[2] *n* **1** : muñón *m* (de un brazo o una pierna) **2** *or* **tree stump** : cepa *f,* tocón *m* **3** STUB : cabo *m*
stun ['stʌn] *vt* **stunned; stunning 1** : aturdir (con un golpe) **2** ASTONISH, SHOCK : dejar estupefacto, dejar atónito, aturdir
stung → **sting**[1]
stunk → **stink**[1]

stunning [ˈstʌnɪŋ] *adj* **1** ASTONISHING : asombroso, pasmoso, increíble **2** STRIKING : imponente, impresionante (dícese de la belleza)
stunt[1] [ˈstʌnt] *vt* : atrofiar
stunt[2] *n* : proeza *f* (acrobática)
stupefy [ˈstuːpəˌfaɪ, ˈstjuː-] *vt* **-fied; -fying 1** : aturdir, atontar (con drogas, etc.) **2** AMAZE : dejar estupefacto, dejar atónito
stupendous [stʊˈpɛndəs, stjʊ-] *adj* **1** MARVELOUS : estupendo, maravilloso **2** TREMENDOUS : tremendo — **stupendously** *adv*
stupid [ˈstuːpəd, ˈstjuː-] *adj* **1** IDIOTIC, SILLY : tonto, bobo, estúpido **2** DULL, OBTUSE : lento, torpe, lerdo
stupidity [stʊˈpɪdət̬i, stjʊ-] *n* : tontería *f*, estupidez *f*
stupidly [ˈstuːpədli, ˈstjuː-] *adv* **1** IDIOTICALLY : estúpidamente, tontamente **2** DENSELY : torpemente
stupor [ˈstuːpər, ˈstjuː-] *n* : estupor *m*
sturdily [ˈstərdəli] *adv* : sólidamente
sturdiness [ˈstərdinəs] *n* : solidez *f* (de muebles, etc.), robustez *f* (de una persona)
sturdy [ˈstərdi] *adj* **sturdier; -est** : fuerte, robusto, sólido
sturgeon [ˈstərdʒən] *n* : esturión *m*
stutter[1] [ˈstʌt̬ər] *vi* : tartamudear
stutter[2] *n* STAMMER : tartamudeo *m*
sty [ˈstaɪ] *n* **1** *pl* **sties** PIGPEN : chiquero *m*, polcilga *f* **2** *pl* **sties** *or* **styes** : orzuelo *m* (en el ojo)
style[1] [ˈstaɪl] *vt* **styled; styling 1** NAME : llamar **2** : peinar (pelo), diseñar (vestidos, etc.) <carefully styled prose : prosa escrita con gran esmero>
style[2] *n* **1** : estilo *m* <that's just his style : él es así> <to live in style : vivir a lo grande> **2** FASHION : moda *f*
stylish [ˈstaɪlɪʃ] *adj* : de moda, elegante, chic
stylishly [ˈstaɪlɪʃli] *adv* : con estilo
stylishness [ˈstaɪlɪʃnəs] *n* : estilo *m*
stylize [ˈstaɪˌlaɪz, ˈstaɪə-] *vt* : estilizar
stylus [ˈstaɪləs] *n, pl* **styli** [ˈstaɪˌlaɪ] **1** PEN : estilo *m* **2** NEEDLE : aguja *f* (de un tocadiscos)
stymie [ˈstaɪmi] *vt* **-mied; -mieing** : obstaculizar
suave [ˈswɑv] *adj* : fino, urbano
sub[1] [ˈsʌb] *vi* **subbed; subbing** → **substitute**[1]
sub[2] *n* **1** → **substitute**[2] **2** → **submarine**
subcommittee [ˈsʌbkəˌmɪt̬i] *n* : subcomité *m*
subconscious[1] [səbˈkɑntʃəs] *adj* : subconsciente — **subconsciously** *adv*
subconscious[2] *n* : subconsciente *m*
subcontract [ˌsʌbˈkɑnˌtrækt] *vt* : subcontratar
subdivide [ˌsʌbdəˈvaɪd, ˈsʌbdəˌvaɪd] *vt* **-vided; -viding** : subdividir
subdivision [ˈsʌbdəˌvɪʒən] *n* : subdivisión *f*
subdue [səbˈduː, -ˈdjuː] *vt* **-dued; -duing 1** OVERCOME : sojuzgar (a un enemigo), vencer, superar **2** CONTROL : dominar **3** SOFTEN : suavizar, atenuar (luz, etc.), moderar (lenguaje)
subhead [ˈsʌbˌhɛd] *or* **subheading** [-ˌhɛdɪŋ] *n* : subtítulo *m*
subject[1] [səbˈdʒɛkt] *vt* **1** CONTROL, DOMINATE : controlar, dominar **2** : someter <they subjected him to pressure : lo sometieron a presiones>
subject[2] [ˈsʌbdʒɪkt] *adj* **1** : subyugado, sometido <a subject nation : una nación subyugada> **2** PRONE : sujeto, propenso <subject to colds : sujeto a resfriarse> **3 subject to** : sujeto a <subject to congressional approval : sujeto a la aprobación del congreso>
subject[3] [ˈsʌbdʒɪkt] *n* **1** : súbdito *m*, -ta *f* (de un gobierno) **2** TOPIC : tema *m* **3** : sujeto *m* (en gramática)
subjection [səbˈdʒɛkʃən] *n* : sometimiento *m*
subjective [səbˈdʒɛktɪv] *adj* : subjetivo — **subjectively** *adv*
subjectivity [ˌsʌbˌdʒɛkˈtɪvət̬i] *n* : subjetividad *f*
subjugate [ˈsʌbdʒɪˌgeɪt] *vt* **-gated; -gating** : subyugar, someter, sojuzgar
subjunctive [səbˈdʒʌŋktɪv] *n* : subjuntivo *m* — **subjunctive** *adj*
sublet [ˈsʌbˌlɛt] *vt* **-let; -letting** : subarrendar
sublime [səˈblaɪm] *adj* : sublime
sublimely [səˈblaɪmli] *adv* **1** : de manera sublime **2** UTTERLY : absolutamente, completamente
submarine[1] [ˈsʌbməˌriːn, ˌsʌbməˈ-] *adj* : submarino
submarine[2] *n* : submarino *m*
submerge [səbˈmərdʒ] *v* **-merged; -merging** *vt* : sumergir — *vi* : sumergirse
submission [səbˈmɪʃən] *n* **1** YIELDING : sumisión *f* **2** PRESENTATION : presentación *f*
submissive [səbˈmɪsɪv] *adj* : sumiso, dócil
submit [səbˈmɪt] *v* **-mitted; -mitting** *vi* YIELD : rendirse <to submit to : someterse a> — *vt* PRESENT : presentar
subnormal [ˌsʌbˈnɔrməl] *adj* : por debajo de lo normal
subordinate[1] [səˈbɔrdənˌeɪt] *vt* **-nated; -nating** : subordinar
subordinate[2] [səˈbɔrdənət] *adj* : subordinado <a subordinate clause : una oración subordinada>
subordinate[3] *n* : subordinado *m*, -da *f*; subalterno *m*, -na *f*
subordination [səˌbɔrdənˈeɪʃən] *n* : subordinación *f*
subpoena[1] [səˈpiːnə] *vt* **-naed; -naing** : citar
subpoena[2] *n* : citación *f*, citatorio *m*
subscribe [səbˈskraɪb] *vi* **-scribed; -scribing 1** : suscribirse (a una revista, etc.) **2 to subscribe to** : sus-

cribir (una opinión, etc.), estar de acuerdo con
subscriber [səb'skraɪbər] *n* : suscriptor *m,* -tora *f* (de una revista, etc.); abonado *m,* -da *f* (de un servicio)
subscription [səb'skrɪpʃən] *n* : suscripción *f*
subsequent ['sʌbsɪkwənt, -sə,kwɛnt] *adj* : subsiguiente <subsequent to : posterior a>
subsequently ['sʌb,kwɛntli, -kwənt-] *adv* : posteriormente
subservient [səb'sərviənt] *adj* : servil
subside [səb'saɪd] *vi* **-sided; -siding 1** SINK : hundirse, descender **2** ABATE : calmarse (dícese de las emociones), amainar (dícese del viento, etc.)
subsidiary[1] [səb'sɪdi,ɛri] *adj* : secundario
subsidiary[2] *n, pl* **-ries** : filial *f,* subsidiaria *f*
subsidize ['sʌbsə,daɪz] *vt* **-dized; -dizing** : subvencionar, subsidiar
subsidy ['sʌbsədi] *n, pl* **-dies** : subvención *f,* subsidio *m*
subsist [səb'sɪst] *vi* : subsistir, mantenerse, vivir
subsistence [səb'sɪstən*t*s] *n* : subsistencia *f*
substance ['sʌbstən*t*s] *n* **1** ESSENCE : sustancia *f,* esencia *f* **2** : sustancia *f* <a toxic substance : una sustancia tóxica> **3** WEALTH : riqueza *f* <a woman of substance : una mujer acaudalada>
substandard [,sʌb'stændərd] *adj* : inferior, deficiente
substantial [səb'stæntʃəl] *adj* **1** ABUNDANT : sustancioso <a substantial meal : una comida sustanciosa> **2** CONSIDERABLE : considerable, apreciable **3** SOLID, STURDY : sólido
substantially [səb'stæntʃəli] *adv* : considerablemente
substantiate [səb'stæntʃi,eɪt] *vt* **-ated; -ating** : confirmar, probar, justificar
substitute[1] ['sʌbstə,tu:t, -,tju:t] *v* **-tuted; -tuting** *vt* : sustituir — *vi* **to substitute for** : sustituir
substitute[2] *n* **1** : sustituto *m,* -ta *f;* suplente *mf* (persona) **2** : sucedáneo *m* <sugar substitute : sucedáneo de azúcar>
substitute teacher *n* : profesor *m,* -sora *f* suplente
substitution [,sʌbstə'tu:ʃən, -'tju:-] *n* : sustitución *f*
subterfuge ['sʌbtər,fju:dʒ] *n* : subterfugio *m*
subterranean [,sʌbtə'reɪniən] *adj* : subterráneo
subtitle ['sʌb,taɪtəl] *n* : subtítulo *m*
subtle ['sʌtəl] *adj* **-tler; -tlest 1** DELICATE, ELUSIVE : sutil, delicado **2** CLEVER : sutil, ingenioso
subtlety ['sʌtəlti] *n, pl* **-ties** : sutileza *f*
subtly ['sʌtəli] *adv* : sutilmente
subtotal ['sʌb,to:təl] *n* : subtotal *m*
subtract [səb'trækt] *vt* : restar, sustraer
subtraction [səb'trækʃən] *n* : resta *f,* sustracción *f*
suburb ['sʌ,bərb] *n* : municipio *m* periférico, suburbio *m*
suburban [sə'bərbən] *adj* : de las afueras (de una ciudad), suburbano
subversion [səb'vərʒən] *n* : subversión *f*
subversive [səb'vərsɪv] *adj* : subversivo
subway ['sʌb,weɪ] *n* : metro *m,* subterráneo *m Arg, Uru*
succeed [sək'si:d] *vt* FOLLOW : suceder a — *vi* : tener éxito (dícese de las personas), dar resultado (dícese de los planes, etc.) <she succeeded in finishing : logró terminar>
success [sək'sɛs] *n* : éxito *m*
successful [sək'sɛsfəl] *adj* : exitoso, logrado — **successfully** *adv*
succession [sək'sɛʃən] *n* : sucesión *f* <in succesion : sucesivamente>
successive [sək'sɛsɪv] *adj* : sucesivo, consecutivo — **successively** *adv*
successor [sək'sɛsər] *n* : sucesor *m,* -sora *f*
succinct [sək'sɪŋkt, sə'sɪŋkt] *adj* : sucinto — **succinctly** *adv*
succor[1] ['sʌkər] *vt* : socorrer
succor[2] *n* : socorro *m*
succotash ['sʌkə,tæʃ] *n* : guiso *m* de maíz y frijoles
succulent[1] ['sʌkjələnt] *adj* : suculento, jugoso
succulent[2] *n* : suculenta *f* (planta)
succumb [sə'kʌm] *vi* : sucumbir
such[1] ['sʌtʃ] *adv* **1** SO : tan <such tall buildings : edificios tan grandes> **2** VERY : muy <he's not in such good shape : anda un poco mal> **3 such that** : de tal manera que
such[2] *adj* : tal <there's no such thing : no existe tal cosa> <in such cases : en tales casos> <animals such as cows and sheep : animales como vacas y ovejas>
such[3] *pron* **1** : tal <such was the result : tal fue el resultado> <he's a child, and acts as such : es un niño, y se porta como tal> **2** : algo o alguien semejante <books, papers and such : libros, papeles y cosas por el estilo>
suck ['sʌk] *vi* **1** : chupar (por la boca), aspirar (dícese de las máquinas) **2** SUCKLE : mamar — *vt* : sorber (bebidas), chupar (dulces, etc.)
sucker ['sʌkər] *n* **1** : ventosa *f* (de un insecto, etc.) **2** : chupón *m* (de una planta) **3** → **lollipop 4** FOOL : tonto *m,* -ta *f;* idiota *mf*
suckle ['sʌkəl] *v* **-led; -ling** *vt* : amamantar — *vi* : mamar
suckling ['sʌklɪŋ] *n* : lactante *mf*
sucrose ['su:,kro:s, -,kro:z] *n* : sacarosa *f*
suction ['sʌkʃən] *n* : succión *f*

Sudanese [ˌsuːdən'iːz, -'iːs] *n* : sudanés *m,* -nesa *f* — **Sudanese** *adj*

sudden ['sʌdən] *adj* **1** : repentino, súbito <all of a sudden : de pronto, de repente> **2** UNEXPECTED : inesperado, improvisto **3** ABRUPT, HASTY : precipitado, brusco

suddenly ['sʌdənli] *adv* **1** : de repente, de pronto **2** ABRUPTLY : bruscamente

suddenness ['sʌdənnəs] *n* **1** : lo repentino **2** ABRUPTNESS : brusquedad *f* **3** HASTINESS : lo precipitado

suds ['sʌdz] *npl* : espuma *f* (de jabón)

sue ['suː] *v* **sued; suing** *vt* : demandar — *vi* **to sue for** : demandar por (daños, etc.)

suede ['sweɪd] *n* : ante *m,* gamuza *f*

suet ['suːət] *n* : sebo *m*

suffer ['sʌfər] *vi* : sufrir — *vt* **1** : sufrir, padecer (dolores, etc.) **2** PERMIT : permitir, dejar

sufferer ['sʌfərər] *n* : persona que padece (una enfermedad, etc.)

suffering ['sʌfərɪŋ] *n* : sufrimiento *m*

suffice [sə'faɪs] *vi* **-ficed; -ficing** : ser suficiente, bastar

sufficient [sə'fɪʃənt] *adj* : suficiente

sufficiently [sə'fɪʃəntli] *adv* : (lo) suficientemente, bastante

suffix ['sʌˌfɪks] *n* : sufijo *m*

suffocate ['sʌfəˌkeɪt] *v* **-cated; -cating** *vt* : asfixiar, ahogar — *vi* : asfixiarse, ahogarse

suffocation [ˌsʌfə'keɪʃən] *n* : asfixia *f,* ahogo *m*

suffrage ['sʌfrɪdʒ] *n* : sufragio *m,* derecho *m* al voto

suffuse [sə'fjuːz] *vt* **-fused; -fusing** : impregnar (de olores, etc.), bañar (de luz), teñir (de colores), llenar (de emociones)

sugar[1] ['ʃʊgər] *vt* : azucarar

sugar[2] *n* : azúcar *mf*

sugarcane ['ʃʊgərˌkeɪn] *n* : caña *f* de azúcar

sugary ['ʃʊgəri] *adj* **1** : azucarado <sugary desserts : postres azucarados> **2** SACCHARINE : empalagoso

suggest [səg'dʒɛst, sə-] *vt* **1** PROPOSE : sugerir **2** IMPLY : indicar, dar a entender

suggestible [səg'dʒɛstəbəl, sə-] *adj* : influenciable

suggestion [səg'dʒɛstʃən, sə-] *n* **1** PROPOSAL : sugerencia *f* **2** INDICATION : indicio *m* **3** INSINUATION : insinuación *f*

suggestive [səg'dʒɛstɪv, sə-] *adj* : insinuante — **suggestively** *adv*

suicidal [ˌsuːə'saɪdəl] *adj* : suicida

suicide ['suːəˌsaɪd] *n* **1** : suicidio *m* (acto) **2** : suicida *mf* (persona)

suit[1] ['suːt] *vt* **1** ADAPT : adaptar **2** BEFIT : convenir a, ser apropiado a **3** BECOME : favorecer, quedarle bien (a alguien) <the dress suits you : el vestido te queda bien> **4** PLEASE : agradecer, satisfacer, convenirle bien (a alguien) <does Friday suit you? : ¿le conviene el viernes?> <suit yourself! : ¡como quieras!>

suit[2] *n* **1** LAWSUIT : pleito *m,* litigio *m* **2** : traje *m* (ropa) **3** : palo *m* (de naipes)

suitability [ˌsuːṭə'bɪləṭi] *n* : idoneidad *f,* lo apropiado

suitable ['suːṭəbəl] *adj* : apropiado, idóneo — **suitably** [-bli] *adv*

suitcase ['suːtˌkeɪs] *n* : maleta *f,* valija *f,* petaca *f Mex*

suite ['swiːt, *for 2 also* 'suːt] *n* **1** : suite *f* (de habitaciones) **2** SET : juego *m* (de muebles)

suitor ['suːṭər] *n* : pretendiente *m*

sulfur ['sʌlfər] *n* : azufre *m*

sulfuric acid [ˌsʌl'fjʊrɪk] *adj* : ácido *m* sulfúrico

sulfurous [ˌsʌl'fjʊrəs, 'sʌlfərəs, 'sʌlfjə-] *adj* : sulfuroso

sulk[1] ['sʌlk] *vi* : estar de mal humor, enfurruñarse *fam*

sulk[2] *n* : mal humor *m*

sulky ['sʌlki] *adj* **sulkier; -est** : malhumorado, taimado *Chile*

sullen ['sʌlən] *adj* **1** MOROSE : hosco, taciturno **2** DREARY : sombrío, deprimente

sullenly ['sʌlənli] *adv* **1** MOROSELY : hoscamente **2** GLOOMILY : sombríamente

sully ['sʌli] *vt* **sullied; sullying** : manchar, empañar

sultan ['sʌltən] *n* : sultán *m*

sultry ['sʌltri] *adj* **sultrier; -est 1** : bochornoso <sultry weather : tiempo sofocante, tiempo bochornoso> **2** SENSUAL : sensual, seductor

sum[1] ['sʌm] *vt* **summed; summing 1** : sumar (números) **2** → **sum up**

sum[2] *n* **1** AMOUNT : suma *f,* cantidad *f* **2** TOTAL : suma *f,* total *f* **3** : suma *f,* adición *f* (en matemáticas)

sumac ['ʃuːˌmæk, 'suː-] *n* : zumaque *m*

summarize ['sʌməˌraɪz] *v* **-rized; -rizing** : resumir, compendiar

summary[1] ['sʌməri] *adj* **1** CONCISE : breve, conciso **2** IMMEDIATE : inmediato <a summary dismissal : un despido inmediato>

summary[2] *n, pl* **-ries** : resumen *m,* compendio *m*

summer ['sʌmər] *n* : verano *m*

summery ['sʌməri] *adj* : veraniego

summit ['sʌmət] *n* **1** : cumbre *f,* cima *f* (de una montaña) **2** *or* **summit conference** : cumbre *f*

summon ['sʌmən] *vt* **1** CALL : convocar (una reunión, etc.), llamar (a una persona) **2** : citar (en derecho) **3 to summon up** : armarse de (valor, etc.) <to summon up one's strength : reunir fuerzas>

summons ['sʌmənz] *n, pl* **summonses 1** SUBPOENA : citación *f,* citatorio *m Mex* **2** CALL : llamada *f,* llamamiento *m*

sumptuous ['sʌmptʃʊəs] *adj* : suntuoso

sum up *vt* **1** SUMMARIZE : resumir **2** EVALUATE : evaluar — *vi* : recapitular
sun[1] ['sʌn] *vt* **sunned; sunning 1** : poner al sol **2 to sun oneself** : asolearse, tomar el sol
sun[2] *n* **1** : sol *m* **2** SUNSHINE : luz *f* del sol
sunbeam ['sʌn,biːm] *n* : rayo *m* de sol
sunblock ['sʌn,blɑk] *n* : filtro *m* solar
sunburn[1] ['sʌn,bərn] *vi* **-burned** [-,bərnd] *or* **-burnt** [-,bərnt]; **-burning** : quemarse por el sol
sunburn[2] ['sʌn,bərn] *n* : quemadura *f* de sol
sundae ['sʌndi] *n* : sundae *m*
Sunday ['sʌn,deɪ, -di] *n* : domingo *m*
sundial ['sʌn,daɪl] *n* : reloj *m* de sol
sundown ['sʌn,daʊn] → **sunset**
sundries ['sʌndriz] *npl* : artículos *mpl* diversos
sundry ['sʌndri] *adj* : varios, diversos
sunflower ['sʌn,flaʊər] *n* : girasol *m*, mirasol *m*
sung → **sing**
sunglasses ['sʌn,glæsəz] *npl* : gafas *fpl* de sol, lentes *mpl* de sol
sunk → **sink**[1]
sunken ['sʌŋkən] *adj* : hundido
sunlight ['sʌn,laɪt] *n* : sol *m*, luz *f* del sol
sunny ['sʌni] *adj* **sunnier; -est** : soleado
sunrise ['sʌn,raɪz] *n* : salida *f* del sol
sunset ['sʌn,sɛt] *n* : puesta *f* del sol
sunshine ['sʌn,ʃaɪn] *n* : sol *m*, luz *f* del sol
sunspot ['sʌn,spɑt] *n* : mancha *f* solar
sunstroke ['sʌn,stroːk] *n* : insolación *f*
suntan ['sʌn,tæn] *n* : bronceado *m*
sup ['sʌp] *vi* **supped; supping** : cenar
super ['suːpər] *adj* : súper <super! : ¡fantástico!>
superabundance [,suːpərə'bʌndənts] *n* : superabundancia *f*
superb [sʊ'pərb] *adj* : magnífico, espléndido — **superbly** *adv*
supercilious [,suːpər'sɪliəs] *adj* : altivo, altanero, desdeñoso
supercomputer ['suːpərkəm,pjuːtər] *n* : supercomputadora *f*
superficial [,suːpər'fɪʃəl] *adj* : superficial — **superficially** *adv*
superfluous [sʊ'pərflʊəs] *adj* : superfluo
superhighway ['suːpər,haɪ,weɪ, ,suːpər'-] *n* : autopista *f*
superhuman [,suːpər'*h*juːmən] *adj* **1** SUPERNATURAL : sobrenatural **2** HERCULEAN : sobrehumano
superimpose [,suːpərɪm'poːz] *vt* **-posed; -posing** : superponer, sobreponer
superintend [,suːpərɪn'tɛnd] *vt* : supervisar
superintendent [,suːpərɪn'tɛndənt] *n* : portero *m*, -ra *f* (de un edificio); director *m*, -tora *f* (de una escuela, etc.); superintendente *mf* (de policía)
superior[1] [sʊ'pɪriər] *adj* **1** BETTER : superior **2** HAUGHTY : altivo, altanero
superior[2] *n* : superior *m*
superiority [sʊ,pɪri'ɔrət̬i] *n, pl* **-ties** : superioridad *f*
superlative[1] [sʊ'pərlət̬ɪv] *adj* **1** : superlativo (en gramática) **2** SUPREME : supremo **3** EXCELLENT : excelente, excepcional
superlative[2] *n* : superlativo *m*
supermarket ['suːpər,mɑrkət] *n* : supermercado *m*
supernatural [,suːpər'nætʃərəl] *adj* : sobrenatural
supernaturally [,suːpər'nætʃərəli] *adv* : de manera sobrenatural
superpower ['suːpər,paʊər] *n* : superpotencia *f*
supersede [,suːpər'siːd] *vt* **-seded; -seding** : suplantar, reemplazar, sustituir
supersonic [,suːpər'sɑnɪk] *adj* : supersónico
superstition [,suːpər'stɪʃən] *n* : superstición *f*
superstitious [,suːpər'stɪʃəs] *adj* : supersticioso
superstructure ['suːpər,strʌktʃər] *n* : superestructura *f*
supervise ['suːpər,vaɪz] *vt* **-vised; -vising** : supervisar, dirigir
supervision [,suːpər'vɪʒən] *n* : supervisión *f*, dirección *f*
supervisor ['suːpər,vaɪzər] *n* : supervisor *m*, -sora *f*
supervisory [,suːpər'vaɪzəri] *adj* : de supervisor
supine [sʊ'paɪn] *adj* **1** : en decúbito supino, en decúbito dorsal **2** ABJECT, INDIFFERENT : indiferente, apático
supper ['sʌpər] *n* : cena *f*, comida *f*
supplant [sə'plænt] *vt* : suplantar
supple ['sʌpəl] *adj* **-pler; -plest** : flexible
supplement[1] ['sʌplə,mɛnt] *vt* : complementar, completar
supplement[2] ['sʌpləmənt] *n* **1** : complemento *m* <dietary supplement : complemento alimenticio> **2** : suplemento *m* (de un libro o periódico)
supplementary [,sʌplə'mɛntəri] *adj* : suplementario
supplicate ['sʌplə,keɪt] *v* **-cated; -cating** *vi* : rezar — *vt* : suplicar
supplier [sə'plaɪər] *n* : proveedor *m*, -dora *f*; abastecedor *m*, -dora *f*
supply[1] [sə'plaɪ] *vt* **-plied; -plying** : suministrar, proveer de, proporcionar
supply[2] *n, pl* **-plies 1** PROVISION : provisión *f*, suministro *m* <supply and demand : la oferta y la demanda> **2** STOCK : reserva *f*, existencias *fpl* (de un negocio) **3 supplies** *npl* PROVISIONS : provisiones *fpl*, víveres *mpl*, despensa *f*
support[1] [sə'port] *vt* **1** BACK : apoyar, respaldar **2** MAINTAIN : mantener, sos-

tener, sustentar **3** PROP UP **:** sostener, apoyar, apuntalar, soportar

support[2] *n* **1 :** apoyo *m* (moral), ayuda *f* (económica) **2** PROP **:** soporte *m,* apoyo *m*

supporter [sə'portər] *n* **:** partidario *m,* -ria *f*

suppose [sə'po:z] *vt* **-posed; -posing 1** ASSUME **:** suponer, imaginarse **2** BELIEVE **:** suponer, creer **3 to be supposed to :** tener que, deber

supposition [ˌsʌpə'zɪʃən] *n* **:** suposición *f*

suppository [sə'pɑzəˌtori] *n, pl* **-ries :** supositorio *m*

suppress [sə'prɛs] *vt* **1** SUBDUE **:** sofocar, suprimir, reprimir (una rebelión, etc.) **2 :** suprimir, ocultar (información) **3** REPRESS **:** reprimir, contener <to suppress a yawn **:** reprimir un bostezo>

suppression [sə'prɛʃən] *n* **1** SUBDUING **:** represión *f* **2 :** supresión *f* (de información) **3** REPRESSION **:** represión *f,* inhibición *f*

supremacy [sʊ'prɛməsi] *n, pl* **-cies :** supremacía *f*

supreme [sʊ'pri:m] *adj* **:** supremo

Supreme Being *n* **:** Ser *m* Supremo

supremely [sʊ'pri:mli] *adv* **:** totalmente, sumamente

surcharge ['sərˌtʃɑrdʒ] *n* **:** recargo *m*

sure[1] ['ʃʊr] *adv* **1** ALL RIGHT **:** por supuesto, claro **2** *(used as an intensifier)* <it sure is hot! **:** ¡hace tanto calor!> <she sure is pretty! **:** ¡qué linda es!>

sure[2] *adj* **surer; -est :** seguro <to be sure about something **:** estar seguro de algo> <a sure sign **:** una clara señal> <for sure **:** seguro, con seguridad>

surely ['ʃʊrli] *adv* **1** CERTAINLY **:** seguramente **2** (*used as an intensifier*) <you surely don't mean that! **:** ¡no me digas que estás hablando en serio!>

sureness ['ʃʊrnəs] *n* **:** certeza *f,* seguridad *f*

surety ['ʃʊrəti] *n, pl* **-ties :** fianza *f,* garantía *f*

surf ['sərf] *n* **1** WAVES **:** oleaje *m* **2** FOAM **:** espuma *f*

surface[1] ['sərfəs] *v* **-faced; -facing** *vi* **:** salir a la superficie — *vt* **:** revestir (una carretera)

surface[2] *n* **1 :** superficie *f* **2 on the surface :** en apariencia

surfboard ['sərfˌbord] *n* **:** tabla *f* de surf, tabla *f* de surfing

surfeit ['sərfət] *n* **:** exceso *m*

surfing ['sərfɪŋ] *n* **:** surf *m,* surfing *m*

surge[1] ['sərdʒ] *vi* **surged; surging 1 :** hincharse (dícese del mar), levantarse (dícese de las olas) **2** SWARM **:** salir en tropel (dícese de la gente, etc.)

surge[2] *n* **1 :** oleaje *m* (del mar), oleada *f* (de gente) **2** FLUSH **:** arranque *m,* arrebato *m* (de ira, etc.) **3** INCREASE **:** aumento *m* (súbito)

surgeon ['sərdʒən] *n* **:** cirujano *m,* -na *f*

surgery ['sərdʒəri] *n, pl* **-geries :** cirugía *f*

surgical ['sərdʒɪkəl] *adj* **:** quirúrgico — **surgically** [-kli] *adv*

surly ['sərli] *adj* **surlier; -est :** hosco, arisco

surmise[1] [sər'maɪz] *vt* **-mised; -mising :** conjeturar, suponer, concluir

surmise[2] *n* **:** conjetura *f*

surmount [sər'maʊnt] *vt* **1** OVERCOME **:** superar, vencer, salvar **2** CLIMB **:** escalar **3** CAP, TOP **:** coronar

surname ['sərˌneɪm] *n* **:** apellido *m*

surpass [sər'pæs] *vt* **:** superar, exceder, rebasar, sobrepasar

surplus ['sərˌplʌs] *n* **:** excedente *m,* sobrante *m,* superávit *m* (de dinero)

surprise[1] [sə'praɪz, sər-] *vt* **-prised; -prising :** sorprender

surprise[2] *n* **:** sorpresa *f* <to take by surprise **:** sorprender>

surprising [sə'praɪzɪŋ, sər-] *adj* **:** sorprendente — **surprisingly** *adv*

surrender[1] [sə'rɛndər] *vt* **1 :** entregar, rendir **2 to surrender oneself :** entregarse — *vi* **:** rendirse

surrender[2] *n* **:** rendición *m* (de una ciudad, etc.), entrega *f* (de posesiones)

surreptitious [ˌsərəp'tɪʃəs] *adj* **:** subrepticio — **surreptitiously** *adv*

surrogate ['sərəgət, -ˌgeɪt] *n* **:** sustituto *m*

surround [sə'raʊnd] *vt* **:** rodear

surroundings [sə'raʊndɪŋz] *npl* **:** ambiente *m,* entorno *m*

surveillance [sər'veɪlənts, -'veɪljənts, -'veɪənts] *n* **:** vigilancia *f*

survey[1] [sər'veɪ] *vt* **-veyed; -veying 1 :** medir (un terreno) **2** EXAMINE **:** inspeccionar, examinar, revisar **3** POLL **:** hacer una encuesta de, sondear

survey[2] ['sərˌveɪ] *n, pl* **-veys 1** INSPECTION **:** inspección *f,* revisión *f* **2 :** medición *f* (de un terreno) **3** POLL **:** encuesta *f,* sondeo *m*

surveyor [sər'veɪər] *n* **:** agrimensor *m,* -sora *f*

survival [sər'vaɪvəl] *n* **:** supervivencia *f,* sobrevivencia *f*

survive [sər'vaɪv] *v* **-vived; -viving** *vi* **:** sobrevivir — *vt* OUTLIVE **:** sobrevivir a

survivor [sər'vaɪvər] *n* **:** superviviente *mf,* sobreviviente *mf*

susceptibility [səˌsɛptə'bɪləti] *n, pl* **-ties :** vulnerabilidad *f,* propensión *f* (a enfermedades, etc.)

susceptible [sə'sɛptəbəl] *adj* **1** VULNERABLE **:** vulnerable, sensible <susceptible to flattery **:** sensible a halagos> **2** PRONE **:** propenso <susceptible to colds **:** propenso a resfriarse>

suspect[1] [sə'spɛkt] *vt* **1** DISTRUST **:** dudar de **2 :** sospechar (algo), sospechar de (una persona) **3** IMAGINE, THINK **:** imaginarse, creer

suspect[2] ['sʌs͵pɛkt, sə'spɛkt] *adj* : sospechoso, dudoso, cuestionable
suspect[3] ['sʌs͵pɛkt] *n* : sospechoso *m*, -sa *f*
suspend [sə'spɛnd] *vt* : suspender
suspenders [sə'spɛndərz] *npl* : tirantes *mpl*
suspense [sə'spɛn*t*s] *n* : incertidumbre *f*, suspenso *m* (en una película, etc.)
suspenseful [sə'spɛn*t*sfəl] *adj* : de suspenso
suspension [sə'spɛntʃən] *n* : suspensión *f*
suspicion [sə'spɪʃən] *n* **1** : sospecha *f* **2** TRACE : pizca *f*, atisbo *m*
suspicious [sə'spɪʃəs] *adj* **1** QUESTIONABLE : sospechoso, dudoso **2** DISTRUSTFUL : suspicaz, desconfiado
suspiciously [sə'spɪʃəsli] *adv* : de modo sospechoso, con recelo
sustain [sə'steɪn] *vt* **1** NOURISH : sustentar **2** PROLONG : sostener **3** SUFFER : sufrir **4** SUPPORT, UPHOLD : apoyar, respaldar, sostentar
sustenance ['sʌstənən*t*s] *n* **1** NOURISHMENT : sustento *m* **2** SUPPORT : sostén *m*
svelte ['sfɛlt] *adj* : esbelto
swab[1] ['swɑb] *vt* **swabbed; swabbing** **1** CLEAN : lavar, limpiar **2** : aplicar a (con hisopo)
swab[2] *n or* **cotton swab** : hisopo *m* (para aplicar medicinas, etc.)
swaddle ['swɑdəl] *vt* **-dled; -dling** ['swɑdəlɪŋ] : envolver (en pañales)
swagger[1] ['swægər] *vi* : pavonearse
swagger[2] *n* : pavoneo *m*
swallow[1] ['swɑloː] *vt* **1** : tragar (comida, etc.) **2** ENGULF : tragarse, envolver **3** REPRESS : tragarse (insultos, etc.) — *vi* : tragar
swallow[2] *n* **1** : golondrina *f* (pájaro) **2** GULP : trago *m*
swam → **swim**[1]
swamp[1] ['swɑmp] *vt* : inundar
swamp[2] *n* : pantano *m*, ciénaga *f*
swampy ['swɑmpi] *adj* **swampier; -est** : pantanoso, cenagoso
swan ['swɑn] *n* : cisne *f*
swap[1] ['swɑp] *vt* **swapped; swapping** : cambiar, intercambiar <to swap places : cambiarse de sitio>
swap[2] *n* : cambio *m*, intercambio *m*
swarm[1] ['swɔrm] *vi* : enjambrar
swarm[2] *n* : enjambre *m*
swarthy ['swɔrði, -θi] *adj* **swarthier; -est** : moreno
swashbuckling ['swɑʃ͵bʌklɪŋ] *adj* : de aventurero
swat[1] ['swɑt] *vt* **swatted; swatting** : aplastar (un insecto), darle una palmada (a alguien)
swat[2] *n* : palmada *f* (con la mano), golpe *m* (con un objeto)
swatch ['swɑtʃ] *n* : muestra *f*
swath ['swɑθ, 'swɔθ] *or* **swathe** ['swɑð, 'swɔð, 'sweɪð] *n* : franja *f* (de grano segado)
swathe ['swɑð, 'swɔð, 'sweɪð] *vt* **swathed; swathing** : envolver
swatter ['swɑtər] → **flyswatter**
sway[1] ['sweɪ] *vi* : balancearse, mecerse — *vt* INFLUENCE : influir en, convencer
sway[2] *n* **1** SWINGING : balanceo *m* **2** INFLUENCE : influjo *m*
swear ['swær] *v* **swore** ['swor]; **sworn** ['sworn]; **swearing** *vi* **1** VOW : jurar **2** CURSE : decir palabrotas — *vt* : jurar
swearword ['swær͵wərd] *n* : mala palabra *f*, palabrota *f*
sweat[1] ['swɛt] *vi* **sweat** *or* **sweated; sweating** **1** PERSPIRE : sudar, transpirar **2** OOZE : rezumar **3 to sweat over** : sudar la gota gorda por
sweat[2] *n* : sudor *m*, transpiración *f*
sweater ['swɛtər] *n* : suéter *m*
sweatshirt ['swɛt͵ʃərt] *n* : sudadera *f*
sweaty ['swɛti] *adj* **sweatier; -est** : sudoroso, sudado, transpirado
Swede ['swiːd] *n* : sueco *m*, -ca *f*
Swedish[1] ['swiːdɪʃ] *adj* : sueco
Swedish[2] *n* **1** : sueco *m* (idioma) **2 the Swedish** *npl* : los suecos
sweep[1] ['swiːp] *v* **swept** ['swɛpt]; **sweeping** *vt* **1** : barrer (el suelo, etc.), limpiar (suciedad, etc.) <he swept the books aside : apartó los libros de un manotazo> **2** *or* **to sweep through** : extenderse por (dícese del fuego, etc.), azotar (dícese de una tormenta) — *vi* **1** : barrer, limpiar **2** : extenderse (en una curva), describir una curva <the sun swept across the sky : el sol describía una curva en el cielo>
sweep[2] *n* **1** : barrido *m*, barrida *f* (con una escoba) **2** : movimiento *m* circular **3** SCOPE : alcance *m*
sweeper ['swiːpər] *n* : barrendero *m*, -ra *f*
sweeping ['swiːpɪŋ] *adj* **1** WIDE : amplio (dícese de un movimiento) **2** EXTENSIVE : extenso, radical **3** INDISCRIMINATE : indiscriminado, demasiado general **4** OVERWHELMING : arrollador, aplastante
sweepstakes ['swiːp͵steɪks] *ns & pl* **1** : carrera *f* (en que el ganador se lleva el premio entero) **2** LOTTERY : lotería *f*
sweet[1] ['swiːt] *adj* **1** : dulce <sweet desserts : postres dulces> **2** FRESH : fresco **3** : sin sal (dícese de la mantequilla, etc.) **4** PLEASANT : dulce, agradable **5** DEAR : querido
sweet[2] *n* : dulce *m*
sweeten ['swiːtən] *vt* : endulzar
sweetener ['swiːtənər] *n* : endulzante *m*
sweetheart ['swiːt͵hɑrt] *n* : novio *m*, -via *f* <thanks, sweetheart : gracias, cariño>
sweetly ['swiːtli] *adv* : dulcemente
sweetness ['swiːtnəs] *n* : dulzura *f*
sweet potato *n* : batata *f*, boniato *m*
swell[1] ['swɛl] *vi* **swelled; swelled** *or* **swollen** ['swoːlən, 'swʌl-]; **swelling** **1** *or* **to swell up** : hincharse <her

ankle swelled : se le hinchó el tobillo> 2 *or* **to swell out** : inflarse, hincharse (dícese de las velas, etc.) 3 INCREASE : aumentar, crecer

swell[2] *n* **1** : oleaje *m* (del mar) **2** → **swelling**

swelling [ˈswɛlɪŋ] *n* : hinchazón *f*

swelter [ˈswɛltər] *vi* : sofocarse de calor

swept → **sweep**[1]

swerve[1] [ˈswərv] *vi* **swerved; swerving** : virar bruscamente

swerve[2] *n* : viraje *m* brusco

swift[1] [ˈswɪft] *adj* **1** FAST : rápido, veloz **2** SUDDEN : repentino, súbito — **swiftly** *adv*

swift[2] *n* : vencejo *m* (pájaro)

swiftness [ˈswɪftnəs] *n* : rapidez *f,* velocidad *f*

swig[1] [ˈswɪg] *vi* **swigged; swigging** : tomar a tragos, beber a tragos

swig[2] *n* : trago *m*

swill[1] [ˈswɪl] *vt* : chupar, beber a tragos grandes

swill[2] *n* **1** SLOP : bazofia *f* **2** GARBAGE : basura *f*

swim[1] [ˈswɪm] *vi* **swam** [ˈswæm]; **swum** [ˈswʌm]; **swimming 1** : nadar **2** FLOAT : flotar **3** REEL : dar vueltas <his head was swimming : la cabeza le daba vueltas>

swim[2] *n* : baño *m,* chapuzón *m* <to go for a swim : ir a nadar>

swimmer [ˈswɪmər] *n* : nadador *m,* -dora *f*

swindle[1] [ˈswɪndəl] *vt* **-dled; -dling** : estafar, timar

swindle[2] *n* : estafa *f,* timo *m fam*

swindler [ˈswɪndələr] *n* : estafador *m,* -dora *f;* timador *m,* -dora *f*

swine [ˈswaɪn] *ns & pl* : cerdo *m,* -da *f*

swing[1] [ˈswɪŋ] *v* **swung** [ˈswʌŋ]; **swinging** *vt* **1** : describir una curva con <he swung the ax at the tree : le dio al arbol con el hacha> **2** : balancear (los brazos, etc.), hacer oscilar **3** SUSPEND : colgar — *vi* **1** SWAY : balancearse (dícese de los brazos, etc.), oscilar (dícese de un objeto), columpiarse, mecerse (en un columpio) **2** SWIVEL : girar (en un pivote) <the door swung shut : la puerta se cerró> **3** CHANGE : virar, cambiar (dícese de las opiniones, etc.)

swing[2] *n* **1** SWINGING : vaivén *m,* balanceo *m* **2** CHANGE, SHIFT : viraje *m,* movimiento *m* **3** : columpio *m* (para niños) **4 to take a swing at someone** : intentar pegarle a alguien

swipe[1] [ˈswaɪp] *vt* **swiped; swiping 1** STRIKE : dar, pegar (con un movimiento amplio) **2** WIPE : limpiar **3** STEAL : birlar *fam,* robar

swipe[2] *n* BLOW : golpe *m*

swirl[1] [ˈswərl] *vi* : arremolinarse

swirl[2] *n* **1** EDDY : remolino *m* **2** SPIRAL : espiral *f*

swish[1] [ˈswɪʃ] *vt* : mover (produciendo un sonido) <she swished her skirt : movía la falda> — *vi* : moverse (produciendo un sonido) <the cars swished by : se oían pasar los coches>

swish[2] *n* : silbido *m* (de un látigo, etc.), susurro *m* (de agua), crujido *m* (de ropa, etc.)

Swiss [ˈswɪs] *n* : suizo *m,* -za *f* — **Swiss** *adj*

swiss chard *n* : acelga *f*

switch[1] [ˈswɪtʃ] *vt* **1** LASH, WHIP : azotar **2** CHANGE : cambiar de **3** EXCHANGE : intercambiar **4 to switch on** : encender, prender **5 to switch off** : apagar — *vi* **1** : moverse de un lado al otro **2** CHANGE : cambiar **3** SWAP : intercambiarse

switch[2] *n* **1** WHIP : vara *f* **2** CHANGE, SHIFT : cambio *m* **3** : interruptor *m,* llave *f* (de la luz, etc.)

switchboard [ˈswɪtʃˌbord] *n* : conmutador *m,* centralita *f*

swivel[1] [ˈswɪvəl] *vi* **-veled** *or* **-velled; -veling** *or* **-velling** : girar (sobre un pivote)

swivel[2] *n* : base *f* giratoria

swollen → **swell**[1]

swoon[1] [ˈswuːn] *vi* : desvanecerse, desmayarse

swoon[2] *n* : desvanecimiento *m,* desmayo *m*

swoop[1] [ˈswuːp] *vi* : abatirse (dícese de las aves), descender en picada (dícese de un avión)

swoop[2] *n* : descenso *m* en picada

sword [ˈsɔrd] *n* : espada *f*

swordfish [ˈsɔrdˌfɪʃ] *n* : pez *m* espada

swore, sworn → **swear**

swum → **swim**[1]

swung → **swing**[1]

sycamore [ˈsɪkəˌmor] *n* : sicomoro *m*

sycophant [ˈsɪkəfənt, -ˌfænt] *n* : adulador *m,* -dora *f*

syllabic [səˈlæbɪk] *adj* : silábico

syllable [ˈsɪləbəl] *n* : sílaba *f*

syllabus [ˈsɪləbəs] *n, pl* **-bi** [-ˌbaɪ] *or* **-buses** : programa *m* (de estudios)

symbol [ˈsɪmbəl] *n* : símbolo *m*

symbolic [sɪmˈbɑlɪk] *adj* : simbólico — **symbolically** [-kli] *adv*

symbolism [ˈsɪmbəˌlɪzəm] *n* : simbolismo *m*

symbolize [ˈsɪmbəˌlaɪz] *vt* **-ized; -izing** : simbolizar

symmetrical [səˈmɛtrɪəl] *or* **symmetric** [-trɪk] *adj* : simétrico — **symmetrically** [-trɪkli] *adv*

symmetry [ˈsɪmətri] *n, pl* **-tries** : simetría *f*

sympathetic [ˌsɪmpəˈθɛt̬ɪk] *adj* **1** PLEASING : agradable **2** RECEPTIVE : receptivo, favorable **3** COMPASSIONATE, UNDERSTANDING : comprensivo, compasivo

sympathetically [ˌsɪmpəˈθɛt̬ɪkli] *adv* : con compasión, con comprensión

sympathize [ˈsɪmpəˌθaɪz] *vi* **-thized; -thizing** : compadecer <I sympathize with you : te compadezco>

sympathy [ˈsɪmpəθi] *n, pl* **-thies 1** COMPASSION : compasión *f* **2** UNDERSTANDING : comprensión *f* **3** AGREEMENT : solidaridad *f* <in sympathy with : de acuerdo con> **4** CONDOLENCES : pésame *m,* condolencias *fpl*

symphonic [sɪmˈfɑnɪk] *adj* : sinfónico

symphony [ˈsɪmpfəni] *n, pl* **-nies** : sinfonía *f*

symposium [sɪmˈpoːziəm] *n, pl* **-sia** [-ziə] *or* **-siums** : simposio *m*

symptom [ˈsɪmptəm] *n* : síntoma *m*

symptomatic [ˌsɪmptəˈmæṯɪk] *adj* : sintomático

synagogue [ˈsɪnəˌgɑg, -ˌgɔg] *n* : sinagoga *f*

synchronize [ˈsɪŋkrəˌnaɪz, ˈsɪn-] *v* **-nized; -nizing** *vi* : estar sincronizado — *vt* : sincronizar

syncopate [ˈsɪŋkəˌpeɪt, ˈsɪn-] *vt* **-pated; -pating** : sincopar

syncopation [ˌsɪŋkəˈpeɪʃən, ˌsɪn-] *n* : síncopa *f*

syndicate[1] [ˈsɪndəˌkeɪt] *vi* **-cated; -cating** : formar una asociación

syndicate[2] [ˈsɪndɪkət] *n* : asociación *f,* agrupación *f*

syndrome [ˈsɪnˌdroːm] *n* : síndrome *m*

synonym [ˈsɪnəˌnɪm] *n* : sinónimo *m*

synonymous [səˈnɑnəməs] *adj* : sinónimo

synopsis [səˈnɑpsɪs] *n, pl* **-opses** [-ˌsiːz] : sinopsis *f*

syntax [ˈsɪnˌtæks] *n* : sintaxis *f*

synthesis [ˈsɪnθəsɪs] *n, pl* **-theses** [-ˌsiːz] : síntesis *f*

synthesize [ˈsɪnθəˌsaɪz] *vt* **-sized; -sizing** : sintetizar

synthetic[1] [sɪnˈθɛṯɪk] *adj* : sintético, artificial — **synthetically** [-ṯɪkli] *adv*

synthetic[2] *n* : producto *m* sintético

syphilis [ˈsɪfələs] *n* : sífilis *f*

Syrian [ˈsɪriən] *n* : sirio *m,* -ria *f* — **Syrian** *adj*

syringe [səˈrɪndʒ, ˈsɪrɪndʒ] *n* : jeringa *f,* jeringuilla *f*

syrup [ˈsərəp, ˈsɪrəp] *n* : jarabe *m,* almíbar *m* (de azúcar y agua)

system [ˈsɪstəm] *n* **1** METHOD : sistema *m,* método *m* **2** APPARATUS : sistema *m,* instalación *f,* aparato *m* <electrical system : instalación eléctrica> <digestive system : aparato digestivo> **3** BODY : organismo *m,* cuerpo *m* <diseases that affect the whole system : enfermedades que afectan el organismo entero> **4** NETWORK : red *f*

systematic [ˌsɪstəˈmæṯɪk] *adj* : sistemático — **systematically** [-ṯɪkli] *adv*

systematize [ˈsɪstəməˌtaɪz] *vt* **-tized; -tizing** : sistematizar

systemic [sɪsˈtɛmɪk] *adj* : sistémico

T

t [ˈtiː] *n, pl* **t's** *or* **ts** [ˈtiːz] : vigésima letra del alfabeto inglés

tab [ˈtæb] *n* **1** FLAP, TAG : lengüeta *f* (de un sobre, una caja, etc.), etiqueta *f* (de ropa) **2** → **tabulator 3** BILL, CHECK : cuenta *f* **4 to keep tabs on** : tener bajo vigilancia

tabby [ˈtæbi] *n, pl* **-bies 1** *or* **tabby cat** : gato *m* atigrado **2** : gata *f*

tabernacle [ˈtæbərˌnækəl] *n* : tabernáculo *m*

table [ˈteɪbəl] *n* **1** : mesa *f* <a table for two : una mesa para dos> **2** LIST : tabla *f* <multiplication table : tabla de multiplicar> **3 table of contents** : índice *m* de materias

tableau [tæˈbloː, ˈtæˌ-] *n, pl* **-leaux** [-ˈbloːz, -ˌbloːz] : retablo *m,* cuadro *m* vivo (en teatro)

tablecloth [ˈteɪbəlˌklɔθ] *n* : mantel *m*

tablespoon [ˈteɪbəlˌspuːn] *n* **1** : cuchara *f* (de mesa) **2** → **tablespoonful**

tablespoonful [ˈteɪbəlˌspuːnˌfʊl] *n* : cucharada *f*

tablet [ˈtæblət] *n* **1** PLAQUE : placa *f* **2** PAD : bloc *m* (de papel) **3** PILL : tableta *f,* pastilla *f,* píldora *f* <an aspirin tablet : una tableta de aspirina>

table tennis *n* : tenis *m* de mesa

tableware [ˈteɪbəlˌwær] *n* : vajillas *fpl,* cubiertos *mpl* (de mesa)

tabloid [ˈtæˌblɔɪd] *n* : tabloide *m*

taboo[1] [təˈbuː, tæ-] *adj* : tabú

taboo[2] *n* : tabú *m*

tabular [ˈtæbjələr] *adj* : tabular

tabulate [ˈtæbjəˌleɪt] *vt* **-lated; -lating** : tabular

tabulator [ˈtæbjəˌleɪṯər] *n* : tabulador *m*

tacit [ˈtæsɪt] *adj* : tácito, implícito — **tacitly** *adv*

taciturn [ˈtæsɪˌtərn] *adj* : taciturno

tack[1] [ˈtæk] *vt* **1** : sujetar con tachuelas **2 to tack on** ADD : añadir, agregar

tack[2] *n* **1** : tachuela *f* **2** COURSE : rumbo *m* <to change tack : cambiar de rumbo>

tackle[1] [ˈtækəl] *vt* **-led; -ling 1** : taclear (en futbol americano) **2** CONFRONT : abordar, enfrentar, emprender (un problema, un trabajo, etc.)

tackle[2] *n* **1** EQUIPMENT, GEAR : equipo *m,* aparejo *m* **2** : aparejo *m* (de un buque) **3** : tacleada *f* (en futbol americano)

tacky [ˈtæki] *adj* **tackier; -est 1** STICKY : pegajoso **2** CHEAP, GAUDY : de mal gusto, naco *Mex*

tact [ˈtækt] *n* : tacto *m,* delicadeza *f,* discreción *f*

tactful [ˈtæktfəl] *adj* : discreto, diplomático, de mucho tacto
tactfully [ˈtæktfəli] *adv* : discretamente, con mucho tacto
tactic [ˈtæktɪk] *n* : táctica *f*
tactical [ˈtæktɪkəl] *adj* : táctico, estratégico
tactics [ˈtæktɪks] *ns & pl* : táctica *f,* estrategia *f*
tactile [ˈtæktəl, -ˌtaɪl] *adj* : táctil
tactless [ˈtæktləs] *adj* : indiscreto, poco delicado
tactlessly [ˈtæktləsli] *adv* : rudamente, sin tacto
tadpole [ˈtædˌpoːl] *n* : renacuajo *m*
taffeta [ˈtæfətə] *n* : tafetán *m,* tafeta *f Arg, Mex, Uru*
taffy [ˈtæfi] *n, pl* **-fies** : caramelo *m* de melaza, chicloso *m Mex*
tag[1] [ˈtæg] *v* **tagged; tagging** *vt* **1** LABEL : etiquetar **2** TAIL : seguir de cerca **3** TOUCH : tocar (en varios juegos) — *vi* **to tag along** : pegarse, acompañar
tag[2] *n* **1** LABEL : etiqueta *f* **2** SAYING : dicho *m,* refrán *m*
tail[1] [ˈteɪl] *vt* FOLLOW : seguir de cerca, pegarse
tail[2] *n* **1** : cola *f,* rabo *m* (de un animal) **2** : cola *f,* parte *f* posterior <a comet's tail : la cola de un cometa> **3 tails** *npl* : cruz *f* (de una moneda) <heads or tails : cara o cruz>
tailed [ˈteɪld] *adj* : que tiene cola
tailgate[1] [ˈteɪlˌgeɪt] *vi* **-gated; -gating** : seguir a un vehículo demasiado de cerca
tailgate[2] *n* : puerta *f* trasera (de un vehículo)
taillight [ˈteɪlˌlaɪt] *n* : luz *f* trasera (de un vehículo), calavera *f Mex*
tailor[1] [ˈteɪlər] *vt* **1** : confeccionar o alterar (ropa) **2** ADAPT : adaptar, ajustar
tailor[2] *n* : sastre *m,* -tra *f*
tailpipe [ˈteɪlˌpaɪp] *n* : tubo *m* de escape
tailspin [ˈteɪlˌspɪn] *n* : barrena *f*
taint[1] [ˈteɪnt] *vt* : contaminar, corromper
taint[2] *n* : corrupción *f,* impureza *f*
take[1] [ˈteɪk] *v* **took** [ˈtʊk]; **taken** [ˈteɪkən]; **taking** *vt* **1** CAPTURE : capturar, apresar **2** GRASP : tomar, agarrar <to take the bull by the horns : tomar al toro por los cuernos> **3** CATCH : tomar, agarrar <taken by surprise : tomado por sorpresa> **4** CAPTIVATE : encantar, fascinar **5** INGEST : tomar, ingerir <take two pills : tome dos píldoras> **6** REMOVE : sacar, extraer <take an orange : saca una naranja> **7** : tomar, coger (un tren, un autobús, etc.) **8** NEED, REQUIRE : tomar, requirir <these things take time : estas cosas toman tiempo> **9** BRING, CARRY : llevar, sacar, cargar <take them with you : llévalos contigo> <take the trash out : saca la basura> **10** BEAR, ENDURE : soportar, aguantar (dolores, etc.) **11** ACCEPT : aceptar (un cheque, etc.), seguir (consejos), asumir (la responsabilidad) **12** SUPPOSE : suponer <I take it that... : supongo que...> **13** (*indicating an action or an undertaking*) <to take a walk : dar un paseo> <to take a class : tomar una clase> **14 to take place** HAPPEN : tener lugar, suceder, ocurrir — *vi* : agarrar (dícese de un tinte), prender (dícese de una vacuna)
take[2] *n* **1** PROCEEDS : recaudación *f,* ingresos *mpl,* ganancias *fpl* **2** : toma *f* (de un rodaje o una grabación)
take back *vt* : retirar (palabras, etc.)
take in *vt* **1** : tomarle a, achicar (un vestido, etc.) **2** INCLUDE : incluir, abarcar **3** ATTEND : ir a <to take in a movie : ir al cine> **4** GRASP, UNDERSTAND : captar, entender **5** DECEIVE : engañar
takeoff [ˈteɪkˌɔf] *n* **1** PARODY : parodia *f* **2** : despegue *m* (de un avión o cohete)
take off *vt* REMOVE : quitar <take off your hat : quítate el sombrero> — *vi* **1** : despegar (dícese de un avión o un cohete) **2** LEAVE : irse, partir
take on *vt* **1** TACKLE : abordar, emprender (problemas, etc.) **2** ACCEPT : aceptar, encargarse de, asumir (una responsabilidad) **3** CONTRACT : contratar (trabajadores) **4** ASSUME : adoptar, asumir, adquirir <the neighborhood took on a dingy look : el barrio asumió una apariencia deprimente>
takeover [ˈteɪkˌoːvər] *n* : toma *f* (de poder o de control), adquisición *f* (de una empresa por otra)
take over *vt* : tomar el poder de, tomar las riendas de — *vi* : asumir el mando
taker [ˈteɪkər] *n* : persona *f* interesada <available to all takers : disponible a cuantos estén interesados>
take up *vt* **1** LIFT : levantar **2** SHORTEN : acortar (una falda, etc.) **3** BEGIN : empezar, dedicarse a (un pasatiempo, etc.) **4** OCCUPY : ocupar, llevar (tiempo, espacio) **5** PURSUE : volver a (una cuestión, un asunto) **6** CONTINUE : seguir con
talc [ˈtælk] *n* : talco *m*
talcum powder [ˈtælkəm] *n* : talco *m,* polvos *mpl* de talco
tale [ˈteɪl] *n* **1** ANECDOTE, STORY : cuento *m,* relato *m,* anécdota *f* **2** FALSEHOOD : cuento *m,* mentira *f*
talent [ˈtælənt] *n* : talento *m,* don *m*
talented [ˈtæləntəd] *adj* : talentoso
talisman [ˈtælɪsmən, -lɪz-] *n, pl* **-mans** : talismán *m*
talk[1] [ˈtɔk] *vi* **1** : hablar <he talks for hours : se pasa horas hablando> **2** CHAT : charlar, platicar — *vt* **1** SPEAK : hablar <to talk French : hablar francés> <to talk business : hablar de negocios> **2** PERSUADE : influenciar, convencer <she talked me out of it : me convenció que no lo hiciera> **3**

to talk over DISCUSS **:** hablar de, discutir

talk[2] *n* **1** CONVERSATION **:** charla *f,* plática *f,* conversación *f* **2** GOSSIP, RUMOR **:** chisme *m,* rumores *mpl*

talkative [ˈtɔkət̬ɪv] *adj* **:** locuaz, parlanchín, charlatán

talker [ˈtɔkər] *n* **:** conversador *m,* -dora *f;* hablador *m,* -dora *f*

tall [ˈtɔl] *adj* **:** alto <how tall is he? **:** ¿cuánto mide?>

tallness [ˈtɔlnəs] *n* HEIGHT **:** estatura *f* (de una persona), altura *f* (de un objeto)

tallow [ˈtæloː] *n* **:** sebo *m*

tally[1] [ˈtæli] *v* **-lied; -lying** *vt* RECKON **:** contar, hacer una cuenta de — *vi* MATCH **:** concordar, corresponder, cuadrar

tally[2] *n, pl* **-lies :** cuenta *f* <to keep a tally **:** llevar la cuenta>

talon [ˈtælən] *n* **:** garra *f* (de un ave de rapiña)

tambourine [ˌtæmbəˈriːn] *n* **:** pandero *m,* pandereta *f*

tame[1] [ˈteɪm] *vt* **tamed; taming :** domar, amansar, domesticar

tame[2] *adj* **tamer; -est 1** DOMESTICATED **:** domesticado, manso **2** DOCILE **:** manso, dócil **3** DULL **:** aburrido, soso

tamely [ˈteɪmli] *adv* **:** mansamente, dócilmente

tamer [ˈteɪmər] *n* **:** domador *m,* -dora *f*

tamp [ˈtæmp] *vt* **:** apisonar

tamper [ˈtæmpər] *vi* **to tamper with :** adulterar (una sustancia), forzar (un sello, una cerradura), falsear (documentos), manipular (una máquina)

tampon [ˈtæmˌpɑn] *n* **:** tampón *m*

tan[1] [ˈtæn] *v* **tanned; tanning** *vt* **1 :** curtir (pieles) **2 :** broncear — *vi* **:** broncearse

tan[2] *n* **1** SUNTAN **:** bronceado *m* <to get a tan **:** broncearse> **2 :** color *m* canela, color *m* café con leche

tandem[1] [ˈtændəm] *adv or* **in tandem :** en tándem

tandem[2] *n* **:** tándem *m* (bicicleta)

tang [ˈtæŋ] *n* **:** sabor *m* fuerte

tangent [ˈtændʒənt] *n* **:** tangente *f* <to go off on a tangent **:** irse por la tangente>

tangerine [ˈtændʒəˌriːn, ˌtændʒəˈ-] *n* **:** mandarina *f*

tangible [ˈtændʒəbəl] *adj* **:** tangible, palpable — **tangibly** [-bli] *adv*

tangle[1] [ˈtæŋgəl] *v* **-gled; -gling** *vt* **:** enredar, enmarañar — *vi* **:** enredarse

tangle[2] *n* **:** enredo *m,* maraña *f*

tango[1] [ˈtæŋˌgoː] *vi* **:** bailar el tango

tango[2] *n, pl* **-gos :** tango *m*

tangy [ˈtæŋi] *adj* **tangier; -est :** que tiene un sabor fuerte

tank [ˈtæŋk] *n* **:** tanque *m,* depósito *m* <fuel tank **:** depósito de combustibles>

tankard [ˈtæŋkərd] *n* **:** jarra *f*

tanker [ˈtæŋkər] *n* **:** buque *m* cisterna, camión *m* cisterna, avión *m* cisterna <an oil tanker **:** un petrolero>

tanner [ˈtænər] *n* **:** curtidor *m,* -dora *f*

tannery [ˈtænəri] *n, pl* **-neries :** curtiduría *f,* tenería *f*

tannin [ˈtænən] *n* **:** tanino *m*

tantalize [ˈtæntəˌlaɪz] *vt* **-lized; -lizing :** tentar, atormentar (con algo inasequible)

tantalizing [ˈtæntəˌlaɪzɪŋ] *adj* **:** tentador, seductor

tantamount [ˈtæntəˌmaʊnt] *adj* **:** equivalente

tantrum [ˈtæntrəm] *n* **:** rabieta *f,* berrinche *m* <to throw a tantrum **:** hacer un berrinche>

tap[1] [ˈtæp] *vt* **tapped; tapping 1 :** ponerle una espita a, sacar líquido de (un barril, un tanque, etc.) **2 :** intervenir (una línea telefónica) **3** PAT, TOUCH **:** tocar, golpear ligeramente <he tapped me on the shoulder **:** me tocó en el hombro>

tap[2] *n* **1** FAUCET **:** llave *f,* grifo *m* <beer on tap **:** cerveza de barril> **2 :** extracción *f* (de líquido) <a spinal tap **:** una punción lumbar> **3** PAT, TOUCH **:** golpecito *m,* toque *m*

tape[1] [ˈteɪp] *vt* **taped; taping 1 :** sujetar o mendar con cinta adhesiva **2** RECORD **:** grabar

tape[2] *n* **1 :** cinta *f* (adhesiva, magnética, etc.) **2** → **tape measure**

tape measure *n* **:** cinta *f* métrica

taper[1] [ˈteɪpər] *vi* **1 :** estrecharse gradualmente <its tail tapers towards the tip **:** su cola va estrechándose hacia la punta> **2** *or* **to taper off :** disminuir gradualmente

taper[2] *n* **1** CANDLE **:** vela *f* larga y delgada **2** TAPERING **:** estrechamiento *m* gradual

tapestry [ˈtæpəstri] *n, pl* **-tries :** tapiz *m*

tapeworm [ˈteɪpˌwərm] *n* **:** solitaria *f,* tenia *f*

tapioca [ˌtæpiˈoːkə] *n* **:** tapioca *f*

tar[1] [ˈtɑr] *vt* **tarred; tarring :** alquitranar

tar[2] *n* **:** alquitrán *m,* brea *f,* chapopote *m Mex*

tarantula [təˈræntʃələ, -ˈræntələ] *n* **:** tarántula *f*

tardiness [ˈtɑrdinəs] *n* **:** tardanza *f,* retraso *m*

tardy [ˈtɑrdi] *adj* **-dier; -est** LATE **:** tardío, de retraso

target[1] [ˈtɑrgət] *vt* **:** fijar como objetivo, dirigir, destinar

target[2] *n* **1 :** blanco *m* <target practice **:** tiro al blanco> **2** GOAL, OBJECTIVE **:** meta *f,* objetivo *m*

tariff [ˈtærɪf] *n* DUTY **:** tarifa *f,* arancel *m*

tarnish[1] [ˈtɑrnɪʃ] *vt* **1** DULL **:** deslustrar **2** SULLY **:** empañar, manchar (una reputación, etc.) — *vi* **:** deslustrarse

tarnish[2] *n* **:** deslustre *m*

tarpaulin [tɑr'pɔlən, 'tɑrpə-] *n* : lona *f* (impermeable)

tarry[1] ['tæri] *vi* **-ried; -rying** : demorarse, entretenerse

tarry[2] ['tɑri] *adj* **1** : parecido al alquitrán **2** : cubierto de alquitrán

tart[1] ['tɑrt] *adj* **1** SOUR : ácido, agrio **2** CAUSTIC : mordaz, acrimonioso — **tartly** *adv*

tart[2] *n* : tartaleta *f*

tartan ['tɑrtən] *n* : tartán *m*

tartar ['tɑrt̬ər] *n* **1** : tártaro *m* <tartar sauce : salsa tártara> **2** : sarro *m* (dental)

tartness ['tɑrtnəs] *n* **1** SOURNESS : acidez *f* **2** ACRIMONY, SHARPNESS : mordacidad *f,* acrimonia *f,* acritud *f*

task ['tæsk] *n* : tarea *f,* trabajo *m*

taskmaster ['tæsk,mæstər] *n* **to be a hard taskmaster** : ser exigente, ser muy estricto

tassel ['tæsəl] *n* : borla *f*

taste[1] ['teɪst] *v* **tasted; tasting** *vt* : probar (alimentos), degustar, catar (vinos) <taste this soup : prueba esta sopa> — *vi* : saber <this tastes good : esto sabe bueno>

taste[2] *n* **1** SAMPLE : prueba *f,* bocado *m* (de comida), trago *m* (de bebidas) **2** FLAVOR : gusto *m,* sabor *m* **3** : gusto *m* <she has good taste : tiene buen gusto> <in bad taste : de mal gusto>

taste bud *n* : papila *f* gustativa

tasteful ['teɪstfəl] *adj* : de buen gusto

tastefully ['teɪstfəli] *adv* : con buen gusto

tasteless ['teɪstləs] *adj* **1** FLAVORLESS : sin sabor, soso, insípido **2** : de mal gusto <a tasteless joke : un chiste de mal gusto>

taster ['teɪstər] *n* : degustador *m,* -dora *f;* catador *m,* -dora *f* (de vinos)

tastiness ['teɪstinəs] *n* : lo sabroso

tasty ['teɪsti] *adj* **tastier; -est** : sabroso, gustoso

tatter ['tæt̬ər] *n* **1** SHRED : tira *f,* jirón *m* (de tela) **2 tatters** *npl* : andrajos *mpl,* harapos *mpl* <to be in tatters : estar por los suelos>

tattered ['tæt̬ərd] *adj* : andrajoso, en jirones

tattle ['tæt̬əl] *vi* **-tled; -tling 1** CHATTER : parlotear *fam,* cotorrear *fam* **2 to tattle on someone** : acusar a alguien

tattletale ['tæt̬əl,teɪl] *n* : soplón *m,* -plona *f fam*

tattoo[1] [tæ'tuː] *vt* : tatuar

tattoo[2] *n* : tatuaje *m* <to get a tattoo : tatuarse>

taught → **teach**

taunt[1] ['tɔnt] *vt* MOCK : mofarse de, burlarse de

taunt[2] *n* : mofa *f,* burla *f*

Taurus ['tɔrəs] *n* : Tauro *mf*

taut ['tɔt] *adj* : tirante, tenso — **tautly** *adv*

tautness ['tɔtnəs] *n* : tirantez *f,* tensión *f*

tavern ['tævərn] *n* : taberna *f*

tawdry ['tɔdri] *adj* **-drier; -est** : chabacano, vulgar

tawny ['tɔni] *adj* **-nier; -est** : leonado

tax[1] ['tæks] *vt* **1** : gravar, cobrar un impuesto sobre **2** CHARGE : acusar <they taxed him with neglect : fue acusado de incumplimiento> **3 to tax someone's strength** : ponerle a prueba las fuerzas (a alguien)

tax[2] *n* **1** : impuesto *m,* tributo *m* **2** BURDEN : carga *f*

taxable ['tæksəbəl] *adj* : sujeto a un impuesto

taxation [tæk'seɪʃən] *n* : impuestos *mpl*

tax–exempt ['tæksɪg'zɛmpt, -ɛg-] *adj* : libre de impuestos

taxi[1] ['tæksi] *vi* **taxied; taxiing** *or* **taxying; taxis** *or* **taxies 1** : ir en taxi **2** : rodar sobre la pista de aterrizaje (dícese de un avión)

taxi[2] *n, pl* **taxis** : taxi *m,* libre *m Mex*

taxicab ['tæksi,kæb] → **taxi[2]**

taxidermist ['tæksə,dərmɪst] *n* : taxidermista *mf*

taxidermy ['tæksə,dərmi] *n* : taxidermia *f*

taxpayer ['tæks,peɪər] *n* : contribuyente *mf,* causante *mf Mex*

TB [,tiː'biː] → **tuberculosis**

tea ['tiː] *n* **1** : té *m* (planta y bebida) **2** : merienda *f,* té *m* (comida)

teach ['tiːtʃ] *v* **taught** ['tɔt]; **teaching** *vt* : enseñar, dar clases de <she teaches math : da clases de matemáticas> <she taught me everything I know : me enseñó todo lo que sé> — *vi* : enseñar, dar clases

teacher ['tiːtʃər] *n* : maestro *m,* -tra *f* (de enseñanza primaria); profesor *m,* -sora *f* (de enseñanza secundaria)

teaching ['tiːtʃɪŋ] *n* : enseñanza *f*

teacup ['tiː,kʌp] *n* : taza *f* para té

teak ['tiːk] *n* : teca *f*

teakettle ['tiː,kɛtəl] *n* : tetera *f*

teal ['tiːl] *n, pl* **teal** *or* **teals** : cerceta *f* (pato)

team[1] ['tiːm] *vi or* **to team up 1** : formar un equipo (en deportes) **2** COLLABORATE : asociarse, juntarse, unirse

team[2] *adj* : de equipo

team[3] *n* **1** : tiro *m* (de caballos), yunta *f* (de bueyes o mulas) **2** : equipo *m* (en deportes, etc.)

teammate ['tiːm,meɪt] *n* : compañero *m,* -ra *f* de equipo

teamster ['tiːmstər] *n* : camionero *m,* -ra *f*

teamwork ['tiːm,wərk] *n* : trabajo *m* en equipo, cooperación *f*

teapot ['tiː,pɑt] *n* : tetera *f*

tear[1] ['tær] *v* **tore** ['tor]; **torn** ['torn]; **tearing** *vt* **1** RIP : desgarrar, romper, rasgar (tela) <to tear to pieces : hacer pedazos> **2** *or* **to tear apart** DIVIDE : dividir **3** REMOVE : arrancar <torn from his family : arrancado de su familia> **4 to tear down** : derribar — *vi* **1** RIP : desgarrarse, romperse **2** RUSH

: ir a gran velocidad <she went tearing down the street : se fue como rayo por la calle>

tear[2] *n* : desgarradura *f,* rotura *f,* desgarro *m* (muscular)

tear[3] ['tɪr] *n* : lágrima *f*

teardrop ['tɪr,drɑp] → **tear[3]**

tearful ['tɪrfəl] *adj* : lloroso, triste — **tearfully** *adv*

tease[1] ['ti:z] *vt* **teased; teasing 1** MOCK : burlarse de, mofarse de **2** ANNOY : irritar, fastidiar

tease[2] *n* **1** TEASING : burla *f,* mofa *f* **2** : bromista *mf;* guasón *m,* -sona *f*

teaspoon ['ti:,spu:n] *n* **1** : cucharita *f* **2** → **teaspoonful**

teaspoonful ['ti:,spu:n,fʊl] *n, pl* **-spoonfuls** [-,fʊlz] *or* **-spoonsful** [-,spu:nz,fʊl] : cucharadita *f*

teat ['ti:t] *n* : tetilla *f*

technical ['tɛknɪkəl] *adj* : técnico — **technically** [-kli] *adv*

technicality [,tɛknə'kæləṭi] *n, pl* **-ties** : detalle *m* técnico

technician [tɛk'nɪʃən] *n* : técnico *m,* -ca *f*

technique [tɛk'ni:k] *n* : técnica *f*

technological [,tɛknə'lɑdʒɪkəl] *adj* : tecnológico

technology [tɛk'nɑlədʒi] *n, pl* **-gies** : tecnología *f*

teddy bear ['tɛdi] *n* : oso *m* de peluche

tedious ['ti:diəs] *adj* : aburrido, pesado, monótono — **tediously** *adv*

tediousness ['ti:diəsnəs] *n* : lo aburrido, lo pesado

tedium ['ti:diəm] *n* : tedio *m,* pesadez *f*

tee ['ti:] *n* : tee *mf*

teem ['ti:m] *vi* **to teem with** : estar repleto de, estar lleno de

teenage ['ti:n,eɪdʒ] *or* **teenaged** [-eɪdʒd] *adj* : adolescente, de adolescencia

teenager ['ti:n,eɪdʒər] *n* : adolescente *mf*

teens ['ti:nz] *npl* : adolescencia *f*

teepee → **tepee**

teeter[1] ['ti:ṭər] *vi* : balancearse, tambalearse

teeter[2] *n or* **teeter–totter** ['ti:ṭər-,tɑṭər] → **seesaw**

teeth → **tooth**

teethe ['ti:ð] *vi* **teethed; teething** : formársele a uno los dientes <the baby's teething : le están saliendo los dientes al niño>

telecast[1] ['tɛlə,kæst] *vt* **-cast; -casting** : televisar, transmitir por televisión

telecast[2] *n* : transmisión *f* por televisión

telecommunication ['tɛləkə,mju:nə'keɪʃən] *n* : telecomunicación *f*

telegram ['tɛlə,græm] *n* : telegrama *m*

telegraph[1] ['tɛlə,græf] *v* : telegrafiar

telegraph[2] *n* : telégrafo *m*

telepathic [,tɛlə'pæθɪk] *adj* : telepático — **telepathically** [-θɪkli] *adv*

telepathy [tə'lɛpəθi] *n* : telepatía *f*

telephone[1] ['tɛlə,fo:n] *v* **-phoned; -phoning** *vt* : llamar por teléfono a, telefonear — *vi* : telefonear

telephone[2] *n* : teléfono *m*

telescope[1] ['tɛlə,sko:p] *vi* **-scoped; -scoping** : plegarse (como un telescopio)

telescope[2] *n* : telescopio *m*

telescopic [,tɛlə'skɑpɪk] *adj* : telescópico

televise ['tɛlə,vaɪz] *vt* **-vised; -vising** : televisar

television ['tɛlə,vɪʒən] *n* : televisión *f*

tell ['tɛl] *v* **told** ['to:ld]; **telling** *vt* **1** COUNT : contar, enumerar <all told : en total> **2** INSTRUCT : decir <he told me how to fix it : me dijo cómo arreglarlo> <they told her to wait : le dijeron que esperara> **3** RELATE : contar, relatar, narrar <to tell a story : contar una historia> **4** DIVULGE, REVEAL : revelar, divulgar <he told me everything about her : me contó todo acerca de ella> **5** DISCERN : discernir, notar <I can't tell the difference : no noto la diferencia> — *vi* **1** SAY : decir <I won't tell : no voy a decírselo a nadie> **2** KNOW : saber <you never can tell : nunca se sabe> **3** SHOW : notarse, hacerse sentir <the strain is beginning to tell : la tensión se empieza a notar>

teller ['tɛlər] *n* **1** NARRATOR : narrador *m,* -dora *f* **2** *or* **bank teller** : cajero *m,* -ra *f*

temerity [tə'mɛrəṭi] *n, pl* **-ties** : temeridad *f*

temp ['tɛmp] *n* : empleado *m,* -da *f* temporal

temper[1] ['tɛmpər] *vt* **1** MODERATE : moderar, temperar **2** ANNEAL : templar (acero, etc.)

temper[2] *n* **1** DISPOSITION : carácter *m,* genio *m* **2** HARDNESS : temple *m,* dureza *f* (de un metal) **3** COMPOSURE : calma *f,* serenidad *f* <to lose one's temper : perder los estribos> **4** RAGE : furia *f* <to fly into a temper : ponerse furioso>

temperament ['tɛmpərmənt, -prə-, -pərə-] *n* : temperamento *m*

temperamental [,tɛmpər'mɛntəl, -prə-, -pərə-] *adj* : temperamental

temperance ['tɛmprənts] *n* : templanza *f,* temperancia *f*

temperate ['tɛmpərət] *adj* : templado (dícese del clima, etc.), moderado

temperature ['tɛmpər,tʃʊr, -prə-, -pərə-, -tʃər] *n* **1** : temperatura *f* **2** FEVER : calentura *f,* fiebre *f*

tempest ['tɛmpəst] *n* : tempestad *f*

tempestuous [tɛm'pɛstʃʊəs] *adj* : tempestuoso

temple ['tɛmpəl] *n* **1** : templo *m* (en religión) **2** : sien *f* (en anatomía)

tempo ['tɛm,po:] *n, pl* **-pi** [-,pi:] *or* **-pos** : ritmo *m,* tempo *m* (en música)

temporal ['tɛmpərəl] *adj* : temporal

temporarily [,tɛmpə'rɛrəli] *adv* : temporalmente, provisionalmente

temporary ['tɛmpə,rɛri] *adj* : temporal, provisional, provisorio

tempt ['tɛmpt] *vt* : tentar

temptation [tɛmp'teɪʃən] *n* : tentación *f*

tempter ['tɛmptər] *n* : tentador *m*

temptress ['tɛmptrəs] *n* : tentadora *f*

ten[1] ['tɛn] *adj* : diez

ten[2] *n* **1** : diez *m* (número) **2** : decena *f* <tens of thousands : decenas de millares>

tenable ['tɛnəbəl] *adj* : sostenible, defendible

tenacious [tə'neɪʃəs] *adj* : tenaz

tenacity [tə'næsəṭi] *n* : tenacidad *f*

tenancy ['tɛnəntsi] *n, pl* **-cies** : tenencia *f,* inquilinato *m* (de un inmueble)

tenant ['tɛnənt] *n* : inquilino *m,* -na *f;* arrendatario *m,* -ria *f*

tend ['tɛnd] *vt* : atender, cuidar (de), ocuparse de — *vi* : tender <it tends to benefit the consumer : tiende a beneficiar al consumidor>

tendency ['tɛndəntsi] *n, pl* **-cies** : tendencia *f,* proclividad *f,* inclinación *f*

tender[1] ['tɛndər] *vt* : entregar, presentar <I tendered my resignation : presenté mi renuncia>

tender[2] *adj* **1** : tierno, blando <tender steak : bistec tierno> **2** AFFECTIONATE, LOVING : tierno, cariñoso, afectuoso **3** DELICATE : tierno, sensible, delicado

tender[3] *n* **1** OFFER : propuesta *f,* oferta *f* (en negocios) **2 legal tender** : moneda *f* de curso legal

tenderize ['tɛndə,raɪz] *vt* **-ized; -izing** : ablandar (carnes)

tenderloin ['tɛndɛr,lɔɪn] *n* : lomo *f* (de res o de puerco)

tenderly ['tɛndərli] *adv* : tiernamente, con ternura

tenderness ['tɛndərnəs] *n* : ternura *f*

tendon ['tɛndən] *n* : tendón *m*

tendril ['tɛndrɪl] *n* : zarcillo *m*

tenement ['tɛnəmənt] *n* : casa *f* de vecindad

tenet ['tɛnət] *n* : principio *m*

tennis ['tɛnəs] *n* : tenis *m*

tenor ['tɛnər] *n* **1** PURPORT : tenor *m,* significado *m* **2** : tenor *m* (en música)

tenpins ['tɛn,pɪnz] *npl* : bolos *mpl,* boliche *m*

tense[1] ['tɛnts] *v* **tensed; tensing** *vt* : tensar — *vi* : tensarse, ponerse tenso

tense[2] *adj* **tenser; tensest 1** TAUT : tenso, tirante **2** NERVOUS : tenso, nervioso

tense[3] *n* : tiempo *m* (de un verbo)

tensely ['tɛntsli] *adv* : tensamente

tenseness ['tɛntsnəs] → **tension**

tension ['tɛntʃən] *n* **1** TAUTNESS : tensión *f,* tirantez *f* **2** STRESS : tensión *f,* nerviosismo *m,* estrés *m*

tent ['tɛnt] *n* : tienda *f* de campaña

tentacle ['tɛntɪkəl] *n* : tentáculo *m*

tentative ['tɛntəṭɪv] *adj* **1** HESITANT : indeciso, vacilante **2** PROVISIONAL : sujeto a cambios, provisional

tentatively ['tɛntəṭɪvli] *adv* : provisionalmente

tenth[1] ['tɛnθ] *adj* : décimo

tenth[2] *n* **1** : décimo *m,* -ma *f* (en una serie) **2** : décimo *m,* décima parte *f*

tenuous ['tɛnjʊəs] *adj* : tenue, débil <tenuous reasons : razones poco convincentes>

tenuously ['tɛnjʊəsli] *adv* : tenuemente, ligeramente

tenure ['tɛnjər] *n* : tenencia *f* (de un cargo o una propiedad), titularidad *f* (de un puesto académico)

tepee ['tiː,piː] *n* : tipi *m*

tepid ['tɛpɪd] *adj* : tibio

term[1] ['tərm] *vt* : calificar de, llamar, nombrar

term[2] *n* **1** PERIOD : término *m,* plazo *m,* período *m* **2** : término *m* (en matemáticas) **3** WORD : término *m,* vocablo *m* <legal terms : términos legales> **4 terms** *npl* CONDITIONS : términos *mpl,* condiciones *fpl* **5 terms** *npl* RELATIONS : relaciones *fpl* <to be on good terms with : tener buenas relaciones con> **6 in terms of** : con respecto a, en cuanto a

terminal[1] ['tərmənəl] *adj* : terminal

terminal[2] *n* **1** : terminal *m,* polo *m* (en electricidad) **2** : terminal *m* (de una computadora) **3** STATION : terminal *f,* estación *f* (de transporte público)

terminate ['tərmə,neɪt] *v* **-nated; -nating** *vi* : terminar(se), concluirse — *vt* : terminar, poner fin a

termination [,tərmə'neɪʃən] *n* : cese *m,* terminación *f*

terminology [,tərmə'nɑlədʒi] *n, pl* **-gies** : terminología *f*

terminus ['tərmənəs] *n, pl* **-ni** [-,naɪ] *or* **-nuses 1** END : término *m,* fin *m* **2** : terminal *f* (de transporte público)

termite ['tər,maɪt] *n* : termita *f*

tern ['tərn] *n* : golondrina *f* de mar

terrace[1] ['tɛrəs] *vt* **-raced; -racing** : formar en terrazas, disponer en bancales

terrace[2] *n* **1** PATIO : terraza *f,* patio *m* **2** : terraplén *m,* terraza *f,* bancal *m* (en agricultura)

terra–cotta [,tɛrə'kɑṭə] *n* : terracota *f*

terrain [tə'reɪn] *n* : terreno *m*

terrapin ['tɛrəpɪn] *n* : galápago *m* norteamericano

terrarium [tə'ræriəm] *n, pl* **-ia** [-iə] *or* **-iums** : terrario *m*

terrestrial [tə'rɛstriəl] *adj* : terrestre

terrible ['tɛrəbəl] *adj* : atroz, horrible, terrible

terribly ['tɛrəbli] *adv* **1** BADLY : muy mal **2** EXTREMELY : terriblemente, extremadamente

terrier ['tɛriər] *n* : terrier *mf*

terrific [tə'rɪfɪk] *adj* **1** FRIGHTFUL : aterrador **2** EXTRAORDINARY : extraordinario, excepcional **3** EXCELLENT : excelente, estupendo

terrify ['tɛrə,faɪ] *vt* **-fied; -fying** : aterrorizar, aterrar, espantar

terrifying [ˈtɛrəˌfaɪɪŋ] *adj* : espantoso, aterrador

territory [ˈtɛrəˌtori] *n, pl* **-ries** : territorio *m* — **territorial** [ˌtɛrəˈtoriəl] *adj*

terror [ˈtɛrər] *n* : terror *m*

terrorism [ˈtɛrərˌɪzəm] *n* : terrorismo *m*

terrorist[1] [ˈtɛrərɪst] *adj* : terrorista

terrorist[2] *n* : terrorista *mf*

terrorize [ˈtɛrərˌaɪz] *vt* **-ized; -izing** : aterrorizar

terry [ˈtɛri] *n, pl* **-ries** *or* **terry cloth** : (tela de) toalla *f*

terse [ˈtərs] *adj* **terser; tersest** : lacónico, conciso, seco — **tersely** *adv*

tertiary [ˈtərʃiˌɛri] *adj* : terciario

test[1] [ˈtɛst] *vt* : examinar, evaluar — *vi* : hacer pruebas

test[2] *n* : prueba *f*, examen *m*, test *m* <to put to the test : poner a prueba>

testament [ˈtɛstəmənt] *n* **1** WILL : testamento *m* **2** : Testamento *m* (en la Biblia) <the Old Testament : el Antiguo Testamento>

testicle [ˈtɛstɪkəl] *n* : testículo *m*

testify [ˈtɛstəˌfaɪ] *v* **-fied; -fying** *vi* : testificar, atestar, testimoniar — *vt* : testificar

testimonial [ˌtɛstəˈmoːniəl] *n* **1** REFERENCE : recomendación *f* **2** TRIBUTE : homenaje *m*, tributo *m*

testimony [ˈtɛstəˌmoːni] *n, pl* **-nies** : testimonio *m*, declaración *f*

test tube *n* : probeta *f*, tubo *m* de ensayo

testy [ˈtɛsti] *adj* **-tier; -est** : irritable

tetanus [ˈtɛtənəs] *n* : tétano *m*, tétanos *m*

tête-à-tête [ˌtɛt̬əˈtɛt, ˌteɪt̬əˈteɪt] *n* : conversación *f* en privado

tether[1] [ˈtɛðər] *vt* : atar (con una cuerda), amarrar

tether[2] *n* : atadura *f*, cadena *f*, correa *f*

text [ˈtɛkst] *n* **1** : texto *m* **2** TOPIC : tema *m* **3** → **textbook**

textbook [ˈtɛkstˌbʊk] *n* : libro *m* de texto

textile [ˈtɛkˌstaɪl, ˈtɛkstəl] *n* : textil *m*, tela *f* <the textile industry : la industria textil>

textual [ˈtɛkstʃʊəl] *adj* : textual

texture [ˈtɛkstʃər] *n* : textura *f*

than[1] [ˈðæn] *conj* : que, de <it's worth more than that : vale más que eso> <more than you think : más de lo que piensas>

than[2] *prep* : que, de <you're better than he is : eres mejor que él> <more than once : más de una vez>

thank [ˈθæŋk] *vt* : agradecer, darle (las) gracias (a alguien) <thank you! : ¡gracias!> <I thanked her for the present : le di las gracias por el regalo> <I thank you for your help : le agradezco su ayuda>

thankful [ˈθæŋkfəl] *adj* : agradecido

thankfully [ˈθæŋkfəli] *adv* **1** GRATEFULLY : con agradecimiento **2** FORTUNATELY : afortunadamente, por suerte <thankfully, it's over : se acabó, gracias a Dios>

thankfulness [ˈθæŋkfəlnəs] *n* : agradecimiento *m*, gratitud *f*

thankless [ˈθæŋkləs] *adj* : ingrato <a thankless task : un trabajo ingrato>

thanks [ˈθæŋks] *npl* **1** : agradecimiento *m* **2 thanks!** : ¡gracias!

Thanksgiving [θæŋksˈgɪvɪŋ, ˈθæŋksˌ-] *n* : el día de Acción de Gracias (fiesta estadounidense)

that[1] [ˈðæt] *adv* (*in negative constructions*) : tan <it's not that expensive : no es tan caro> <not that much : no tanto>

that[2] *adj, pl* **those** : ese, esa, aquel, aquella <do you see those children? : ¿ves a aquellos niños?>

that[3] *conj & pron* : que <he said that he was afraid : dijo que tenía miedo> <the book that he wrote : el libro que escribió>

that[4] *pron, pl* **those** [ˈðoːz] **1** : ése, ésa, eso <that's my father : ése es mi padre> <those are the ones he likes : ésos son los que le gustan> <what's that? : ¿qué es eso?> **2** (*referring to more distant objects or time*) : aquél, aquélla, aquello <those are maples and these are elms : aquéllos son arces y éstos son olmos> <that came to an end : aquello se acabó>

thatch[1] [ˈθætʃ] *vt* : cubrir o techar con paja

thatch[2] *n* : paja *f* (usada para techos)

thaw[1] [ˈθɔ] *vt* : descongelar — *vi* : derretirse (dícese de la nieve), descongelarse (dícese de los alimentos)

thaw[2] *n* : deshielo *m*

the[1] [ðə, *before vowel sounds usu* ðiː] *adv* **1** (*used to indicate comparison*) <the sooner the better : cuanto más pronto, mejor> <she likes this one the best : éste es el que más le gusta> **2** (*used as a conjunction*) : cuanto <the more I learn, the less I understand : cuanto más aprendo, menos entiendo>

the[2] *art* : el, la, los, las <the gloves : los guantes> <the suitcase : la maleta> <forty cookies to the box : cuarenta galletas por caja>

theater *or* **theatre** [ˈθiːət̬ər] *n* **1** : teatro *m* (edificio) **2** DRAMA : teatro *m*, drama *m*

theatrical [θiˈætrɪkəl] *adj* : teatral, dramático

thee [ˈðiː] *pron* : te, ti

theft [ˈθɛft] *n* : robo *m*, hurto *m*

their [ˈðɛr] *adj* : su <their friends : sus amigos>

theirs [ˈðɛrz] *pron* : (el) suyo, (la) suya, (los) suyos, (las) suyas <they came for theirs : vinieron por el suyo> <theirs is bigger : la suya es más grande, la de ellos es más grande> <a brother of theirs : un hermano suyo, un hermano de ellos>

them [ˈðɛm] *pron* **1** (*as a direct object*) : los (*Spain sometimes* les), las <I know them : los conozco> **2** (*as indirect object*) : les, se <I sent them a letter : les mandé una carta> <give it to them : dáselo (a ellos)> **3** (*as object of a preposition*) : ellos, ellas <go with them : ve con ellos> **4** (*for emphasis*) : ellos, ellas <I wasn't expecting them : no los esperaba a ellos>

theme [ˈθiːm] *n* **1** SUBJECT, TOPIC : tema *m* **2** COMPOSITION : composición *f,* trabajo *m* (escrito) **3** : tema *m* (en música)

themselves [ðəmˈsɛlvz, ðɛm-] *pron* **1** (*as a reflexive*) : se, sí <they enjoyed themselves : se divirtieron> <they divided it among themselves : lo repartieron entre sí, se lo repartieron> **2** (*for emphasis*) : ellos mismos, ellas mismas <they built it themselves : ellas mismas lo construyeron>

then[1] [ˈðɛn] *adv* **1** : entonces, en ese tiempo <I was sixteen then : tenía entonces dieciséis años> <since then : desde entonces> **2** NEXT : después, luego <we'll go to Toronto, then to Winnipeg : iremos a Toronto, y luego a Winnipeg> **3** BESIDES : además, aparte <then there's the tax : y aparte está el impuesto> **4** : entonces, en ese caso <if you like music, then you should attend : si te gusta la música, entonces deberías asistir>

then[2] *adj* : entonces <the then governor of Georgia : el entonces gobernador de Georgia>

thence [ˈðɛnts, ˈθɛnts] *adv* : de ahí, de ahí en adelante

theologian [ˌθiːəˈloːdʒən] *n* : teólogo *m,* -ga *f*

theological [ˌθiːəˈlɑdʒɪkəl] *adj* : teológico

theology [θiˈɑlədʒi] *n, pl* **-gies** : teología *f*

theorem [ˈθiːərəm, ˈθɪrəm] *n* : teorema *m*

theoretical [ˌθiːəˈrɛtɪkəl] *adj* : teórico — **theoretically** *adv*

theorize [ˈθiːəˌraɪz] *vi* **-rized; -rizing** : teorizar

theory [ˈθiːəri, ˈθɪri] *n, pl* **-ries** : teoría *f*

therapeutic [ˌθɛrəˈpjuːtɪk] *adj* : terapéutico — **therapeutically** *adv*

therapist [ˈθɛrəpɪst] *n* : terapeuta *mf*

therapy [ˈθɛrəpi] *n, pl* **-pies** : terapia *f*

there[1] [ˈðær] *adv* **1** : ahí, allí, allá <stand over there : párate ahí> <over there : por allí, por allá> <who's there? : ¿quién es?> **2** : ahí, en esto, en eso <there is where we disagree : en eso es donde no estamos de acuerdo>

there[2] *pron* **1** (*introducing a sentence or clause*) <there comes a time to decide : llega un momento en que tiene uno que decidir> **2 there is, there are** : hay <there are many children here : aquí hay muchos niños> <there's a good hotel downtown : hay un buen hotel en el centro>

thereabouts [ðærəˈbaʊts, ˈðærəˌ-] *or* **thereabout** [-ˈbaʊt, -ˌbaʊt] *adv* **or thereabouts** : por ahí, más o menos <at five o'clock or thereabouts : por ahí de las cinco>

thereafter [ðærˈæftər] *adv* : después <shortly thereafter : poco después>

thereby [ðærˈbaɪ, ˈðærˌbaɪ] *adv* : de tal modo, de ese manera, así

therefore [ˈðærˌfor] *adv* : por lo tanto, por consiguiente

therein [ðærˈɪn] *adv* **1** : allí adentro, ahí adentro <the contents therein : lo que allí se contiene> **2** : allí, en ese aspecto <therein lies the problem : allí está el problema>

thereof [ðærˈʌv, -ˈɑv] *adv* : de eso, de esto

thereupon [ˈðærəˌpɑn, -ˌpɔn; ˌðærəˈpɑn, -ˈpɔn] *adv* : acto seguido, inmediatamente (después)

therewith [ðærˈwɪð, -ˈwɪθ] *adv* : con eso, con ello

thermal [ˈθərməl] *adj* **1** : térmico (en física) **2** HOT : termal

thermodynamics [ˌθərmodaɪˈnæmɪks] *ns & pl* : termodinámica *f*

thermometer [θərˈmɑmətər] *n* : termómetro *m*

thermos [ˈθərməs] *n* : termo *m*

thermostat [ˈθərməˌstæt] *n* : termostato *m*

thesaurus [θɪˈsɔrəs] *n, pl* **-sauri** [-ˈsɔrˌaɪ] *or* **-sauruses** [-ˈsɔrəsəz] : diccionario *m* de sinónimos

these → **this**

thesis [ˈθiːsɪs] *n, pl* **theses** [ˈθiːˌsiːz] : tesis *f*

they [ˈðeɪ] *pron* : ellos, ellas <they are here : están aquí> <they don't know : ellos no saben>

they'd [ˈðeɪd] (*contraction of* **they had** *or* **they would**) → **have, would**

they'll [ˈðeɪl, ˈðɛl] (*contraction of* **they shall** *or* **they will**) → **shall, will**

they're [ˈðɛr] (*contraction of* **they are**) → **be**

they've [ˈðeɪv] (*contraction of* **they have**) → **have**

thiamine [ˈθaɪəmɪn, -ˌmiːn] *n* : tiamina *f*

thick[1] [ˈθɪk] *adj* **1** : grueso <a thick plank : una tabla gruesa> **2** : espeso, denso <thick syrup : jarabe espeso> — **thickly** *adv*

thick[2] *n* **1 in the thick of** : en medio de <in the thick of the battle : en lo más reñido de la batalla> **2 through thick and thin** : a las duras y a las maduras

thicken [ˈθɪkən] *vt* : espesar (un líquido) — *vi* : espesarse

thickener [ˈθɪkənər] *n* : espesante *m*

thicket [ˈθɪkət] *n* : matorral *m,* maleza *f,* espesura *f*

thickness [ˈθɪknəs] *n* : grosor *m,* grueso *m,* espesor *m*

thickset [ˈθɪkˈsɛt] *adj* STOCKY : robusto, fornido

thick–skinned [ˈθɪkˈskɪnd] *adj* : poco sensible, que no se ofende fácilmente

thief [ˈθiːf] *n, pl* **thieves** [ˈθiːvz] : ladrón *m,* -drona *f*

thieve [ˈθiːv] *v* **thieved; thieving** : hurtar, robar

thievery [ˈθiːvəri] *n* : hurto *m,* robo *m,* latrocinio *m*

thigh [ˈθaɪ] *n* : muslo *m*

thighbone [ˈθaɪˌboːn] *n* : fémur *m*

thimble [ˈθɪmbəl] *n* : dedal *m*

thin[1] [ˈθɪn] *v* **thinned; thinning** *vt* : hacer menos denso, diluir, aguar (un líquido), enrarecer (un gas) — *vi* : diluirse, aguarse (dícese de un líquido), enrarecerse (dícese de un gas)

thin[2] *adj* **thinner; -est** **1** LEAN, SLIM : delgado, esbelto, flaco **2** SPARSE : ralo, escaso <a thin beard : una barba rala> **3** WATERY : claro, aguado, diluido **4** FINE : delgado, fino <thin slices : rebanadas finas>

thing [ˈθɪŋ] *n* **1** AFFAIR, MATTER : cosa *f,* asunto *m* <don't talk about those things : no hables de esas cosas> <how are things? : ¿cómo van las cosas?> **2** ACT, EVENT : cosa *f,* suceso *m,* evento *m* <the flood was a terrible thing : la inundación fue una cosa terrible> **3** OBJECT : cosa *f,* objeto *m* <don't forget your things : no olvides tus cosas>

think [ˈθɪŋk] *v* **thought** [ˈθɔt]; **thinking** *vt* **1** : pensar <I thought to return early : pensaba regresar temprano> **2** BELIEVE : pensar, creer, opinar **3** PONDER : pensar, reflexionar **4** CONCEIVE : ocurrirse, concebir <we've thought up a plan : se nos ha ocurrido un plan> — *vi* **1** REASON : pensar, razonar **2** CONSIDER : pensar, considerar <think of your family first : primero piensa en tu familia>

thinker [ˈθɪŋkər] *n* : pensador *m,* -dora *f*

thinly [ˈθɪnli] *adv* **1** LIGHTLY : ligeramente **2** SPARSELY : escasamente <thinly populated : poco populado> **3** BARELY : apenas

thinness [ˈθɪnnəs] *n* : delgadez *f*

thin–skinned [ˈθɪnˈskɪnd] *adj* : susceptible, muy sensible

third[1] [ˈθərd] *or* **thirdly** [-li] *adv* : en tercer lugar <she came in third : llegó en tercer lugar>

third[2] *adj* : tercero <the third day : el tercer día>

third[3] *n* **1** : tercero *m,* -ra *f* (en una serie) **2** : tercero *m,* tercera parte *f*

third world *n* **the Third World** : el Tercer Mundo *m*

thirst[1] [ˈθərst] *vi* **1** : tener sed **2 to thirst for** DESIRE : tener sed de, estar sediento de

thirst[2] *n* : sed *f*

thirsty [ˈθərsti] *adj* **thirstier; -est** : sediento, que tiene sed <I'm thirsty : tengo sed>

thirteen[1] [ˌθərˈtiːn] *adj* : trece

thirteen[2] *n* : trece *m*

thirteenth[1] [ˌθərˈtiːnθ] *adj* : décimo tercero

thirteenth[2] *n* **1** : decimotercero *m,* -ra *f* (en una serie) **2** : treceavo *m,* treceava parte *f*

thirtieth[1] [ˈθərt̬iəθ] *adj* : trigésimo

thirtieth[2] *n* **1** : trigésimo *m,* -ma *f* (en una serie) **2** : treintavo *m,* treintava parte *f*

thirty[1] [ˈθərt̬i] *adj* : treinta

thirty[2] *n, pl* **thirties** : treinta *m*

this[1] [ˈðɪs] *adv* : así, a tal punto <this big : así de grande>

this[2] *adj, pl* **these** [ˈðiːz] : este <these things : estas cosas> <read this book : lee este libro>

this[3] *pron, pl* **these** : esto <what's this? : ¿qué es esto?> <this wasn't here yesterday : esto no estaba aquí ayer>

thistle [ˈθɪsəl] *n* : cardo *m*

thong [ˈθɔŋ] *n* **1** STRAP : correa *f,* tira *f* **2** *or* **thong sandal** : chancla *f,* chancleta *f*

thorax [ˈθorˌæks] *n, pl* **-raxes** *or* **-races** [ˈθorəˌsiːz] : tórax *m*

thorn [ˈθɔrn] *n* : espina *f*

thorny [ˈθɔrni] *adj* **thornier; -est** : espinoso

thorough [ˈθəroː] *adj* **1** CONSCIENTIOUS : concienzudo, meticuloso **2** COMPLETE : absoluto, completo — **thoroughly** *adv*

thoroughbred [ˈθəroˌbrɛd] *adj* : de pura sangre (dícese de un caballo)

Thoroughbred *n or* **Thoroughbred horse** : pura sangre *mf*

thoroughfare [ˈθəroˌfær] *n* : vía *f* pública, carretera *f*

thoroughness [ˈθəronəs] *n* : esmero *m,* meticulosidad *f*

those → **that**

thou [ˈðaʊ] *pron* : tú

though[1] [ˈðoː] *adv* **1** HOWEVER, NEVERTHELESS : sin embargo, no obstante **2 as ~** : como si <as though nothing had happened : como si nada hubiera pasado>

though[2] *conj* : aunque, a pesar de <though it was raining, we went out : salimos a pesar de la lluvia>

thought[1] → **think**

thought[2] [ˈθɔt] *n* **1** THINKING : pensamiento *m,* ideas *fpl* <Western thought : el pensamiento occidental> **2** COGITATION : pensamiento *m,* reflexión *f,* raciocinio *m* **3** IDEA : idea *f,* ocurrencia *f* <it was just a thought : fue sólo una idea>

thoughtful [ˈθɔtfəl] *adj* **1** PENSIVE : pensativo, meditabundo **2** CONSIDERATE : considerado, atento, cortés — **thoughtfully** *adv*

thoughtfulness [ˈθɔtfəlnəs] *n* : consideración *f,* atención *f,* cortesía *f*

thoughtless [ˈθɔtləs] *adj* **1** CARELESS : descuidado, negligente **2** INCONSIDERATE : desconsiderado — **thoughtlessly** *adv*

thousand[1] [ˈθaʊzənd] *adj* : mil

thousand[2] *n, pl* **-sands** *or* **-sand** : mil *m*

thousandth[1] [ˈθaʊzəntθ] *adj* : milésimo

thousandth[2] *n* **1** : milésimo *m,* -ma *f* (en una serie) **2** : milésimo *m,* milésima parte *f*

thrash [ˈθræʃ] *vt* **1** → **thresh 2** BEAT : golpear, azotar, darle una paliza (a alguien) **3** FLAIL : sacudir, agitar bruscamente

thread[1] [ˈθrɛd] *vt* **1** : enhilar, enhebrar (una aguja) **2** STRING : ensartar (cuentas en un hilo) **3 to thread one's way** : abrirse paso

thread[2] *n* **1** : hilo *m,* hebra *f* <needle and thread : aguja e hilo> <the thread of an argument : el hilo de un debate> **2** : rosca *f,* filete *m* (de un tornillo)

threadbare [ˈθrɛdˈbær] *adj* **1** SHABBY, WORN : raído, gastado **2** TRITE : trillado, tópico, manido

threat [ˈθrɛt] *n* : amenaza *f*

threaten [ˈθrɛtən] *v* : amenazar

threatening [ˈθrɛtənɪŋ] *adj* : amenazador — **threateningly** *adv*

three[1] [ˈθri:] *adj* : tres

three[2] *n* : tres *m*

threefold [ˈθri:ˌfo:ld] *adj* TRIPLE : triple

three hundred[1] *adj* : trescientos

three hundred[2] *n* : trescientos *m*

threescore [ˈθri:ˈskor] *adj* SIXTY : sesenta

thresh [ˈθrɛʃ] *vt* : trillar (grano)

thresher [ˈθrɛʃər] *n* : trilladora *f*

threshold [ˈθrɛʃˌho:ld, -ˌo:ld] *n* : umbral *m*

threw → **throw**[1]

thrice [ˈθraɪs] *adv* : tres veces

thrift [ˈθrɪft] *n* : economía *f,* frugalidad *f*

thriftless [ˈθrɪftləs] *adj* : despilfarrador, manirroto

thrifty [ˈθrɪfti] *adj* **thriftier; -est** : económico, frugal — **thriftily** [ˈθrɪftəli] *adv*

thrill[1] [ˈθrɪl] *vt* : emocionar — *vi* **to thrill to** : dejarse conmover por, estremecerse con

thrill[2] *n* : emoción *f*

thriller [ˈθrɪlər] *n* **1** : evento *m* emocionante **2** : obra *f* de suspenso

thrilling [ˈθrɪlɪŋ] *adj* : emocionante, excitante

thrive [ˈθraɪv] *vi* **throve** [ˈθro:v] *or* **thrived; thriven** [ˈθrɪvən] **1** FLOURISH : florecer, crecer abundantemente **2** PROSPER : prosperar

throat [ˈθro:t] *n* : garganta *f*

throaty [ˈθro:ti] *adj* **throatier; -est** : ronco (dícese de la voz)

throb[1] [ˈθrɑb] *vi* **throbbed; throbbing** : palpitar, latir (dícese del corazón), vibrar (dícese de un motor, etc.)

throb[2] *n* : palpitación *f,* latido *m,* vibración *f*

throe [ˈθro:] *n* **1** PAIN, SPASM : espasmo *m,* dolor *m* <the throes of childbirth : los dolores de parto> **2 throes** *npl* : lucha *f* larga y ardua <in the throes of : en el medio de>

throne [ˈθro:n] *n* : trono *m*

throng[1] [ˈθrɔŋ] *vt* CROWD : atestar, atiborrar, llenar — *vi* : aglomerarse, amontonarse

throng[2] *n* : muchedumbre *f,* gentío *m,* multitud *f*

throttle[1] [ˈθrɑtəl] *vt* **-tled; -tling 1** STRANGLE : estrangular, ahogar **2 to throttle down** : desacelerar (un motor)

throttle[2] *n* **1** : válvula *f* reguladora **2 at full throttle** : a toda máquina

through[1] [ˈθru:] *adv* **1** : a través, de un lado a otro <let them through : déjenlos pasar> **2** : de principio a fin <she read the book through : leyó el libro de principio a fin> **3** COMPLETELY : completamente <soaked through : completamente empapado>

through[2] *adj* **1** DIRECT : directo <a through train : un tren directo> **2** FINISHED : terminado, acabado <we're through : hemos terminado>

through[3] *prep* **1** : a través de, por <through the door : por la puerta> <a road through the woods : un camino que atraviesa el bosque> **2** BETWEEN : entre <a path through the trees : un sendero entre los árboles> **3** BECAUSE OF : a causa de, como consecuencia de **4** (*in expressions of time*) <through the night : durante la noche> <to go through an experience : pasar por una experiencia> **5** : a, hasta <from Monday through Friday : de lunes a viernes>

throughout[1] [θru:ˈaʊt] *adv* **1** EVERYWHERE : por todas partes **2** THROUGH : desde el principio hasta el fin de (algo)

throughout[2] *prep* **1** : en todas partes de, a través de <throughout the United States : en todo Estados Unidos> **2** : de principio a fin de, durante <throughout the winter : durante todo el invierno>

throve → **thrive**

throw[1] [ˈθro:] *vt* **threw** [ˈθru:]; **thrown** [ˈθro:n]; **throwing 1** TOSS : tirar, lanzar, echar, arrojar, aventar *Col, Mex* <to throw a ball : tirar una pelota> **2** UNSEAT : desmontar (a un jinete) **3** CAST : proyectar <it threw a long shadow : proyectó una sombra larga> **4 to throw a party** : dar una fiesta **5 to throw into confusion** : desconcertar **6 to throw out** DISCARD : botar, tirar (en la basura)

throw[2] *n* TOSS **:** tiro *m,* tirada *f,* lanzamiento *m,* lance *m* (de dados)

thrower [ˈθroːər] *n* **:** lanzador *m,* -dora *f*

throw up *v* VOMIT **:** vomitar, devolver

thrush [ˈθrʌʃ] *n* **:** tordo *m,* zorzal *m*

thrust[1] [ˈθrʌst] *vt* **thrust; thrusting 1** SHOVE **:** empujar bruscamente **2** PLUNGE, STAB **:** apuñalar, clavar <he thrust a dagger into her heart **:** la apuñaló en el corazón> **3 to thrust one's way :** abrirse paso **4 to thrust upon :** imponer a

thrust[2] *n* **1** PUSH, SHOVE **:** empujón *m,* empellón *m* **2** LUNGE **:** estocada *f* (en esgrima) **3** IMPETUS **:** ímpetu *m,* impulso *m,* propulsión *f* (de un motor)

thud[1] [ˈθʌd] *vi* **thudded; thudding :** producir un ruido sordo

thud[2] *n* **:** ruido *m* sordo (que produce un objeto al caer)

thug [ˈθʌg] *n* **:** matón *m*

thumb[1] [ˈθʌm] *vt* **:** hojear (con el pulgar)

thumb[2] *n* **:** pulgar *m,* dedo *m* pulgar

thumbnail [ˈθʌm,neɪl] *n* **:** uña *f* del pulgar

thumbtack [ˈθʌm,tæk] *n* **:** tachuela *f,* chinche *f*

thump[1] [ˈθʌmp] *vt* POUND **:** golpear, aporrear — *vi* **:** latir con vehemencia (dícese del corazón)

thump[2] *n* THUD **:** ruido *m* sordo

thunder[1] [ˈθʌndər] *vi* **1 :** tronar <it rained and thundered all night **:** llovió y tronó durante la noche> **2** BOOM **:** retumbar, bramar, resonar — *vt* ROAR, SHOUT **:** decir a gritos, vociferar

thunder[2] *n* **:** truenos *mpl*

thunderbolt [ˈθʌndər,boːlt] *n* **:** rayo *m*

thunderclap [ˈθʌndər,klæp] *n* **:** trueno *m*

thunderous [ˈθʌndərəs] *adj* **:** atronador, ensordecedor, estruendoso

thundershower [ˈθʌndər,ʃaʊər] *n* **:** lluvia *f* con truenos y relámpagos

thunderstorm [ˈθʌndər,stɔrm] *n* **:** tormenta *f* con truenos y relámpagos

thunderstruck [ˈθʌndər,strʌk] *adj* **:** atónito

Thursday [ˈθərz,deɪ, -di] *n* **:** jueves *m*

thus [ˈðʌs] *adv* **1 :** así, de esta manera **2** SO **:** hasta (cierto punto) <the weather's been nice thus far **:** hasta ahora ha hecho buen tiempo> **3** HENCE **:** por consiguiente, por lo tanto

thwart [ˈθwɔrt] *vt* **:** frustrar

thy [ˈðaɪ] *adj* **:** tu

thyme [ˈtaɪm, ˈθaɪm] *n* **:** tomillo *m*

thyroid [ˈθaɪ,rɔɪd] *n or* **thyroid gland :** tiroides *mf,* glándula *f* tiroidea

thyself [ðaɪˈsɛlf] *pron* **:** ti, ti mismo

tiara [tiˈærə, -ˈɑr-] *n* **:** diadema *f*

tibia [ˈtɪbiə] *n, pl* **-iae** [-bi,iː] **:** tibia *f*

tic [ˈtɪk] *n* **:** tic *m*

tick[1] [ˈtɪk] *vi* **1 :** hacer tictac **2** OPERATE, RUN **:** operar, andar (dícese de un mecanismo) <what makes him tick? **:** ¿qué es lo que lo mueve?> — *vt or* **to tick off** CHECK **:** marcar

tick[2] *n* **1 :** tictac *m* (de un reloj) **2** CHECK **:** marca *f* **3 :** garrapata *f* (insecto)

ticket[1] [ˈtɪkət] *vt* LABEL **:** etiquetar

ticket[2] *n* **1 :** boleto *m,* entrada *f* (de un espectáculo), pasaje *m* (de avión, tren, etc.) **2** SLATE **:** lista *f* de candidatos

tickle[1] [ˈtɪkəl] *v* **-led; -ling** *vt* **1** AMUSE **:** divertir, hacerle gracia (a alguien) **2 :** hacerle cosquillas (a alguien) <don't tickle me! **:** ¡no me hagas cosquillas!> — *vi* **:** picar

tickle[2] *n* **:** cosquilla *f*

ticklish [ˈtɪkəlɪʃ] *adj* **1 :** cosquilloso (dícese de una persona) **2** DELICATE, TRICKY **:** delicado, peliagudo

tidal [ˈtaɪdəl] *adj* **:** de marea, relativo a la marea

tidal wave *n* **:** maremoto *m*

tidbit [ˈtɪd,bɪt] *n* **1** BITE, SNACK **:** bocado *m,* golosina *f* **2 :** dato *m* o noticia *f* interesante <useful tidbits of information **:** informaciones útiles>

tide[1] [ˈtaɪd] *vt* **tided; tiding** *or* **to tide over :** proveer lo necesario para aguantar una dificultad <this money will tide you over until you find work **:** este dinero te mantendrá hasta que encuentres empleo>

tide[2] *n* **1 :** marea *f* **2** CURRENT **:** corriente *f* (de eventos, opiniones, etc.)

tidily [ˈtaɪdəli] *adv* **:** ordenadamente

tidiness [ˈtaɪdinəs] *n* **:** aseo *m,* limpieza *f,* orden *m*

tidings [ˈtaɪdɪŋz] *npl* **:** nuevas *fpl*

tidy[1] [ˈtaɪdi] *vt* **-died; -dying :** asear, limpiar, poner en orden

tidy[2] *adj* **-dier; -est 1** CLEAN, NEAT **:** limpio, aseado, en orden **2** SUBSTANTIAL **:** grande, considerable <a tidy sum **:** una suma considerable>

tie[1] [ˈtaɪ] *v* **tied; tying** *or* **tieing** *vt* **1 :** atar, amarrar <to tie a knot **:** atar un nudo> <to tie one's shoelaces **:** atarse los cordones> **2** BIND, UNITE **:** ligar, atar **3 :** empatar <they tied the score **:** empataron el marcador> — *vi* **:** empatar <the two teams were tied **:** los dos equipos empataron>

tie[2] *n* **1 :** ligadura *f,* cuerda *f,* cordón *m* (para atar algo) **2** BOND, LINK **:** atadura *f,* ligadura *f,* vínculo *m,* lazo *m* <family ties **:** lazos familiares> **3** *or* **railroad tie :** traviesa *f* **4** DRAW **:** empate *m* (en deportes) **5** NECKTIE **:** corbata *f*

tier [ˈtɪr] *n* **:** hilera *f,* escalón *m*

tiff [ˈtɪf] *n* **:** disgusto *m,* disputa *f*

tiger [ˈtaɪgər] *n* **:** tigre *m*

tight[1] [ˈtaɪt] *adv* TIGHTLY **:** bien, fuerte <shut it tight **:** ciérralo bien>

tight[2] *adj* **1 :** bien cerrado, hermético <a tight seal **:** un cierre hermético> **2** STRICT **:** estricto, severo **3** TAUT **:** tirante, tenso **4** SNUG **:** apretado, ajustado, ceñido <a tight dress **:** un vestido ceñido> **5** DIFFICULT **:** difícil <to be in a tight spot **:** estar en un aprieto> **6** STINGY **:** apretado, avaro, agarrado

fam **7** CLOSE : reñido <a tight game : un juego reñido> **8** SCARCE : escaso <money is tight : escasea el dinero>
tighten ['taɪtən] *vt* : tensar (una cuerda, etc.), apretar (un nudo, un tornillo, etc.), apretarse (el cinturón), reforzar (las reglas)
tightly ['taɪtli] *adv* : bien, fuerte
tightness ['taɪtnəs] *n* : lo apretado, lo tenso, tensión *f*
tightrope ['taɪt,ro:p] *n* : cuerda *f* floja
tights ['taɪts] *npl* : leotardo *m,* malla *f*
tightwad ['taɪt,wɑd] *n* : avaro *m,* -ra *f;* tacaño *m,* -ña *f*
tigress ['taɪgrəs] *n* : tigresa *f*
tile[1] ['taɪl] *vt* **tiled; tiling** : embaldosar (un piso), revestir de azulejos (una pared), tejar (un techo)
tile[2] *n* **1** *or* **floor tile** : losa *f,* baldosa *f,* mosaico *m Mex* (de un piso) **2** : azulejo *m* (de una pared) **3** : teja *f* (de un techo)
till[1] ['tɪl] *vt* : cultivar, labrar
till[2] *n* : caja *f,* caja *f* registradora
till[3] *prep & conj* → **until**
tiller ['tɪlər] *n* **1** : cultivador *m,* -dora *f* (de la tierra) **2** : caña *f* del timón (de un barco)
tilt[1] ['tɪlt] *vt* : ladear, inclinar — *vi* : ladearse, inclinarse
tilt[2] *n* **1** SLANT : inclinación *f* **2 at full tilt** : a toda velocidad
timber ['tɪmbər] *n* **1** : madera *f* (para construcción) **2** BEAM : viga *f*
timberland ['tɪmbər,lænd] *n* : bosque *m* maderero
timbre ['tæmbər, 'tɪm-] *n* : timbre *m*
time[1] ['taɪm] *vt* **timed; timing 1** SCHEDULE : fijar la hora de, calcular el momento oportuno para **2** CLOCK : cronometrar, medir el tiempo de (una competencia, etc.)
time[2] *n* **1** : tiempo *m* <the passing of time : el paso del tiempo> <she doesn't have time : no tiene tiempo> **2** MOMENT : tiempo *m,* momento *m* <this is not the time to bring it up : no es el momento de sacar el tema> **3** : vez *f* <she called you three times : te llamó tres veces> <three times greater : tres veces mayor> **4** AGE : tiempo *m,* era *f* <in your grandparents' time : en el tiempo de tus abuelos> **5** TEMPO : tiempo *m,* ritmo *m* (en música) **6** : hora *f* <what time is it? : ¿qué hora es?> <at the usual time : a la hora acostumbrada> <to keep time : ir a la hora> <to lose time : atrasar> **7** EXPERIENCE : rato *m,* experiencia *f* <we had a nice time together : pasamos juntos un rato agradable> <to have a rough time : pasarlo mal> <have a good time! : ¡que se diviertan!> **8 at times** SOMETIMES : a veces **9 for the time being** : por el momento, de momento **10 from time to time** OCCASIONALLY : de vez en cuando **11 in time** PUNCTUALLY : a tiempo **12 in time** EVENTUALLY : con el tiempo **13 time after time** : una y otra vez
timekeeper ['taɪm,ki:pər] *n* : cronometrador *m,* -dora *f*
timeless ['taɪmləs] *adj* : eterno
timely ['taɪmli] *adj* **-lier; -est** : oportuno
timepiece ['taɪm,pi:s] *n* : reloj *m*
timer ['taɪmər] *n* : temporizador *m,* cronómetro *m*
times ['taɪmz] *prep* : por <3 times 4 is 12 : 3 por 4 son 12>
timetable ['taɪm,teɪbəl] *n* : horario *m*
timid ['tɪmɪd] *adj* : tímido — **timidly** *adv*
timidity [tə'mɪdəti] *n* : timidez *f*
timorous ['tɪmərəs] *adj* : timorato, miedoso
timpani ['tɪmpəni] *npl* : timbales *mpl*
tin ['tɪn] *n* **1** : estaño *m,* hojalata *f* (metal) **2** CAN : lata *f,* bote *m,* envase *m*
tincture ['tɪŋktʃər] *n* : tintura *f*
tinder ['tɪndər] *n* : yesca *f*
tine ['taɪn] *n* : diente *m* (de un tenedor, etc.)
tinfoil ['tɪn,fɔɪl] *n* : papel *m* (de) aluminio
tinge[1] ['tɪndʒ] *vt* **tinged; tingeing** *or* **tinging** ['tɪndʒɪŋ] TINT : matizar, teñir ligeramente
tinge[2] *n* **1** TINT : matiz *m,* tinte *m* sutil **2** TOUCH : dejo *m,* sensación *f* ligera
tingle[1] ['tɪŋgəl] *vi* **-gled; -gling** : sentir (un) hormigueo, sentir (un) cosquilleo
tingle[2] *n* : hormigueo *m,* cosquilleo *m*
tinker ['tɪŋkər] *vi* **to tinker with** : arreglar con pequeños ajustes, toquetear (con intento de arreglar)
tinkle[1] ['tɪŋkəl] *vi* **-kled; -kling** : tintinear
tinkle[2] *n* : tintineo *m*
tinsel ['tɪntsəl] *n* : oropel *m*
tint[1] ['tɪnt] *vt* : teñir, colorar
tint[2] *n* : tinte *m*
tiny ['taɪni] *adj* **-nier; -est** : diminuto, minúsculo
tip[1] ['tɪp] *v* **tipped; tipping** *vt* **1** *or* **to tip over** : volcar, voltear, hacer caer **2** TILT : ladear, inclinar <to tip one's hat : saludar con el sombrero> **3** TAP : tocar, golpear ligeramente **4** : darle una propina (a un mesero, etc.) <I tipped him $5 : le di $5 de propina> **5** : adornar o cubrir la punta de <wings tipped in red : alas que tienen las puntas rojas> **6 to tip off** : dar información a — *vi* TILT : ladearse, inclinarse
tip[2] *n* **1** END, POINT : punta *f,* extremo *m* <on the tip of one's tongue : en la punta de la lengua> **2** GRATUITY : propina *f* **3** ADVICE, INFORMATION : consejo *m,* información *f* (confidencial)
tip–off ['tɪp,ɔf] *n* **1** SIGN : indicación *f,* señal *f* **2** TIP : información *f* (confidencial)

tipple [ˈtɪpəl] *vi* **-pled; -pling** : tomarse unas copas
tipsy [ˈtɪpsi] *adj* **-sier; -est** : achispado
tiptoe[1] [ˈtɪpˌtoː] *vi* **-toed; -toeing** : caminar de puntillas
tiptoe[2] *adv* : de puntillas
tiptoe[3] *n* : punta *f* del pie
tip–top[1] [ˈtɪpˈtɑp, -ˌtɑp] *adj* EXCELLENT : excelente
tip–top[2] *n* SUMMIT : cumbre *f*, cima *f*
tirade [ˈtaɪˌreɪd] *n* : diatriba *f*
tire[1] [ˈtaɪr] *v* **tired; tiring** *vt* : cansar, agotar, fatigar — *vi* : cansarse
tire[2] *n* : llanta *f*, neumático *m*, goma *f*
tired [ˈtaɪrd] *adj* : cansado, agotado, fatigado <to get tired : cansarse>
tireless [ˈtaɪrləs] *adj* : incansable, infatigable — **tirelessly** *adv*
tiresome [ˈtaɪrsəm] *adj* : fastidioso, pesado, tedioso — **tiresomely** *adv*
tissue [ˈtɪˌʃuː] *n* **1** : pañuelo *m* de papel **2** : tejido *m* <lung tissue : tejido pulmonar>
titanic [taɪˈtænɪk, tə-] *adj* GIGANTIC : titánico, gigantesco
titanium [taɪˈteɪniəm, tə-] *n* : titanio *m*
titillate [ˈtɪtəlˌeɪt] *vt* **-lated; -lating** : excitar, estimular placenteramente
title[1] [ˈtaɪtəl] *vt* **-tled; -tling** : titular, intitular
title[2] *n* : título *m*
titter[1] [ˈtɪtər] *vi* GIGGLE : reírse tontamente
titter[2] *n* : risita *f*, risa *f* tonta
tizzy [ˈtɪzi] *n, pl* **tizzies** : estado *m* agitado o nervioso <I'm all in a tizzy : estoy todo alterado>
TNT [ˌtiːˌɛnˈtiː] *n* : TNT *m*
to[1] [ˈtuː] *adv* **1** : a un estado consciente <to come to : volver en sí> **2 to and fro** : de aquí para allá, de un lado para otro
to[2] *prep* **1** (*indicating a place*) : a <to go to the doctor : ir al médico> <I'm going to John's : voy a la casa de John> **2** TOWARD : a, hacia <two miles to the south : dos millas hacia el sur> **3** ON : en, sobre <apply salve to the wound : póngale ungüento a la herida> **4** UP TO : hasta, a <to a degree : hasta cierto grado> <from head to toe : de pies a cabeza> **5** (*in expressions of time*) <it's quarter to seven : son las siete menos cuarto> **6** UNTIL : a, hasta <from May to December : de mayo a diciembre> **7** (*indicating belonging or possession*) : de, a <the key to the lock : la llave del candado> **8** (*indicating response*) : a <dancing to the rhythm : bailando al compás> **9** (*indicating comparison or proportion*) : a <it's similar to mine : es parecido al mío> <they won 4 to 2 : ganaron 4 a 2> **10** (*indicating agreement or conformity*) : a, de acuerdo con <made to order : hecho a la orden> <to my knowledge : a mi saber> **11** (*indicating inclusion*) : en cada, por <twenty to the box : veinte por caja> **12** (*used to form the infinitive*) <to understand : entender> <to go away : irse>
toad [ˈtoːd] *n* : sapo *m*
toadstool [ˈtoːdˌstuːl] *n* : hongo *m* (no comestible)
toady [ˈtoːdi] *n, pl* **toadies** : adulador *m*, -dora *f*
toast[1] [ˈtoːst] *vt* **1** : tostar (pan) **2** : brindar por <to toast the victors : brindar por los vencedores> **3** WARM : calentar <to toast oneself : calentarse>
toast[2] *n* **1** : pan *m* tostado, tostadas *fpl* **2** : brindis *m* <to propose a toast : proponer un brindis>
toaster [ˈtoːstər] *n* : tostador *m*
tobacco [təˈbækoː] *n, pl* **-cos** : tabaco *m*
toboggan[1] [təˈbɑgən] *vi* : deslizarse en tobogán
toboggan[2] *n* : tobogán *m*
today[1] [təˈdeɪ] *adv* **1** : hoy <she arrives today : hoy llega> **2** NOWADAYS : hoy en día
today[2] *n* : hoy *m* <today is a holiday : hoy es día de fiesta>
toddle [ˈtɑdəl] *vi* **-dled; -dling** : hacer pininos, hacer pinitos
toddler [ˈtɑdələr] *n* : niño *m* pequeño, niña *f* pequeña (que comienza a caminar)
to–do [təˈduː] *n, pl* **to–dos** [-ˈduːz] FUSS : lío *m*, alboroto *m*
toe [ˈtoː] *n* : dedo *m* del pie
toenail [ˈtoːˌneɪl] *n* : uña *f* del pie
toffee *or* **toffy** [ˈtɔfi, ˈtɑ-] *n, pl* **toffees** *or* **toffies** : caramelo *m* elaborado con azúcar y mantequilla
toga [ˈtoːgə] *n* : toga *f*
together [təˈgɛðər] *adv* **1** : juntamente, juntos (el uno con el otro) <Susan and Sarah work together : Susan y Sarah trabajan juntas> **2 ~ with** : junto con
togetherness [təˈgɛðərnəs] *n* : unión *f*, compañerismo *m*
togs [ˈtɑgz, ˈtɔgz] *npl* : ropa *f*
toil[1] [ˈtɔɪl] *vi* : trabajar arduamente
toil[2] *n* : trabajo *m* arduo
toilet [ˈtɔɪlət] *n* **1** : arreglo *m* personal **2** BATHROOM : (cuarto de) baño *m*, servicios *mpl* (públicos), sanitario *m Col, Mex, Ven* **3** : inodoro *m* <to flush the toilet : jalar la cadena>
toilet paper *n* : papel *m* higiénico
toiletries [ˈtɔɪlətriz] *npl* : artículos *mpl* de tocador
token [ˈtoːkən] *n* **1** PROOF, SIGN : prueba *f*, muestra *f*, señal *m* **2** SYMBOL : símbolo *m* **3** SOUVENIR : recuerdo *m* **4** : ficha *f* (para transporte público, etc.)
told → **tell**
tolerable [ˈtɑlərəbəl] *adj* : tolerable — **tolerably** [-bli] *adv*
tolerance [ˈtɑlərənts] *n* : tolerancia *f*
tolerant [ˈtɑlərənt] *adj* : tolerante — **tolerantly** *adv*

tolerate [ˈtɑləˌreɪt] *vt* **-ated; -ating 1** ACCEPT : tolerar, aceptar **2** BEAR, ENDURE : tolerar, aguantar, soportar

toleration [ˌtɑləˈreɪʃən] *n* : tolerancia *f*

toll[1] [ˈtoːl] *vt* : tañer, sonar (una campana) — *vi* : sonar, doblar (dícese de las campanas)

toll[2] *n* **1** : peaje *m* (de una carretera, un puente, etc.) **2** CASUALTIES : pérdida *f*, número *m* de víctimas **3** TOLLING : tañido *m* (de campanas)

tollbooth [ˈtoːlˌbuːθ] *n* : caseta *f* de peaje

tollgate [ˈtoːlˌgeɪt] *n* : barrera *f* de peaje

tomahawk [ˈtɑməˌhɔk] *n* : hacha *f* de guerra (de los indígenas norteamericanos)

tomato [təˈmeɪto, -ˈmɑ-] *n, pl* **-toes** : tomate *m*

tomb [ˈtuːm] *n* : sepulcro *m*, tumba *f*

tomboy [ˈtɑmˌbɔɪ] *n* : marimacho *mf;* niña *f* que se porta como muchacho

tombstone [ˈtuːmˌstoːn] *n* : lápida *f*

tomcat [ˈtɑmˌkæt] *n* : gato *m* (macho)

tome [ˈtoːm] *n* : tomo *m*

tomorrow[1] [təˈmɑro] *adv* : mañana

tomorrow[2] *n* : mañana *m*

tom–tom [ˈtɑmˌtɑm] *n* : tam-tam *m*

ton [ˈtən] *n* : tonelada *f*

tone[1] [ˈtoːn] *vt* **toned; toning 1** *or* **to tone down** : atenuar, suavizar, moderar **2** *or* **to tone up** STRENGTHEN : tonificar, vigorizar

tone[2] *n* : tono *m* <in a friendly tone : en tono amistoso> <a greyish tone : un tono grisáceo>

tongs [ˈtɑŋz, ˈtɔŋz] *npl* : tenazas *fpl*

tongue [ˈtʌŋ] *n* **1** : lengua *f* **2** LANGUAGE : lengua *f*, idioma *m*

tongue–tied [ˈtʌŋˌtaɪd] *adj* **to get tongue–tied** : trabársele la lengua a uno

tonic[1] [ˈtɑnɪk] *adj* : tónico

tonic[2] *n* **1** : tónico *m* **2** *or* **tonic water** : tónica *f*

tonight[1] [təˈnaɪt] *adv* : esta noche

tonight[2] *n* : esta noche *f*

tonsil [ˈtɑn*t*səl] *n* : amígdala *f*, angina *f Mex*

tonsillitis [ˌtɑn*t*səˈlaɪtəs] *n* : amigdalitis *f*, anginas *fpl Mex*

too [ˈtuː] *adv* **1** ALSO : también **2** EXCESSIVELY : demasiado <it's too hot in here : aquí hace demasiado calor>

took → **take**[1]

tool[1] [ˈtuːl] *vt* **1** : fabricar, confeccionar (con herramientas) **2** EQUIP : instalar maquinaria en (una fábrica)

tool[2] *n* : herramienta *f*

toolbox [ˈtuːlˌbɑks] *n* : caja *f* de herramientas

toot[1] [ˈtuːt] *vt* : sonar (un claxon o un pito)

toot[2] *n* : pitido *m*, bocinazo *m* (de un claxon)

tooth [ˈtuːθ] *n, pl* **teeth** [ˈtiːθ] : diente *m*

toothache [ˈtuːθˌeɪk] *n* : dolor *m* de muelas

toothbrush [ˈtuːθˌbrʌʃ] *n* : cepillo *m* de dientes

toothless [ˈtuːθləs] *adj* : desdentado

toothpaste [ˈtuːθˌpeɪst] *n* : pasta *f* de dientes, crema *f* dental, dentífrico *m*

toothpick [ˈtuːθˌpɪk] *n* : palillo *m* (de dientes), mondadientes *m*

top[1] [ˈtɑp] *vt* **topped; topping 1** COVER : cubrir, coronar **2** SURPASS : sobrepasar, superar **3** CLEAR : pasar por encima de

top[2] *adj* : superior <the top shelf : la repisa superior> <one of the top lawyers : uno de los mejores abogados>

top[3] *n* **1** : parte *f* superior, cumbre *f*, cima *f* (de un monte, etc.) <to climb to the top : subir a la cumbre> **2** COVER : tapa *f*, cubierta *f* **3** : trompo *m* (juguete) **4 on top of** : encima de

topaz [ˈtoːˌpæz] *n* : topacio *m*

topcoat [ˈtɑpˌkoːt] *n* : sobretodo *m*, abrigo *m*

topic [ˈtɑpɪk] *n* : tema *f*, tópico *m*

topical [ˈtɑpɪkəl] *adj* : de interés actual

topmost [ˈtɑpˌmoːst] *adj* : más alto

top–notch [ˈtɑpˈnɑʧ] *adj* : de lo mejor, de primera categoría

topographic [ˌtɑpəˈgræfɪk,] *or* **topographical** [-fɪkəl] *adj* : topográfico

topography [təˈpɑgrəfi] *n, pl* **-phies** : topografía *f*

topple [ˈtɑpəl] *v* **-pled; -pling** *vi* : caerse, venirse abajo — *vt* : volcar, derrocar (un gobierno, etc.)

topsoil [ˈtɑpˌsɔɪl] *n* : capa *f* superior del suelo

topsy–turvy [ˌtɑpsiˈtərvi] *adv & adj* : patas arriba, al revés

torch [ˈtɔrʧ] *n* : antorcha *f*

tore → **tear**[1]

torment[1] [tɔrˈmɛnt, ˈtɔrˌ-] *vt* : atormentar, torturar, martirizar

torment[2] [ˈtɔrˌmɛnt] *n* : tormento *m*, suplicio *m*, martirio *m*

tormentor [tɔrˈmɛntər] *n* : atormentador *m*, -dora *f*

torn → **tear**[1]

tornado [tɔrˈneɪdo] *n, pl* **-does** *or* **-dos** : tornado *m*

torpedo[1] [tɔrˈpiːdo] *vt* : torpedear

torpedo[2] *n, pl* **-does** : torpedo *m*

torpid [ˈtɔrpɪd] *adj* **1** SLUGGISH : aletargado **2** APATHETIC : apático

torpor [ˈtɔrpər] *n* : letargo *m*, apatía *f*

torrent [ˈtɔrənt] *n* : torrente *m*

torrential [tɔˈrɛnʧəl, tə-] *adj* : torrencial

torrid [ˈtɔrɪd] *adj* : tórrido

torso [ˈtɔrˌsoː] *n, pl* **-sos** *or* **-si** [-ˌsiː] : torso *m*

tortilla [tɔrˈtiːjə] *n* : tortilla *f*

tortoise [ˈtɔrtəs] *n* : tortuga *f* (terrestre)

tortoiseshell [ˈtɔrtəsˌʃɛl] *n* : carey *m*, concha *f*

tortuous [ˈtɔrʧʊəs] *adj* : tortuoso

torture[1] [ˈtɔrtʃər] *vt* **-tured; -turing** : torturar, atormentar

torture[2] *n* : tortura *f,* tormento *m* <it was sheer torture! : ¡fue un verdadero suplicio!>

torturer [ˈtɔrtʃərər] *n* : torturador *m,* -dora *f*

toss[1] [ˈtɔs, ˈtɑs] *vt* **1** AGITATE, SHAKE : sacudir, agitar, mezclar (una ensalada) **2** THROW : tirar, echar, lanzar — *vi* : sacudirse, moverse agitadamente <to toss and turn : dar vueltas>

toss[2] *n* THROW : lanzamiento *m,* tiro *m,* tirada *f,* lance *m* (de dados, etc.)

toss–up [ˈtɔsˌʌp] *n* : posibilidad *f* igual <it's a toss-up : quizá sí, quizá no>

tot [ˈtɑt] *n* : pequeño *m,* -ña *f*

total[1] [ˈtoːtəl] *vt* **-taled** *or* **-talled; -taling** *or* **-talling 1** *or* **to total up** ADD : sumar, totalizar **2** AMOUNT TO : ascender a, llegar a

total[2] *adj* : total, completo, absoluto — **totally** *adv*

total[3] *n* : total *m*

totalitarian [toːˌtæləˈtɛriən] *adj* : totalitario

totalitarianism [toːˌtæləˈtɛriəˌnɪzəm] *n* : totalitarismo *m*

totality [toːˈtæləṭi] *n, pl* **-ties** : totalidad *f*

tote [ˈtoːt] *vt* **toted; toting** : cargar, llevar

totem [ˈtoːtəm] *n* : tótem *m*

totter [ˈtɑtər] *vi* : tambalearse

touch[1] [ˈtʌtʃ] *vt* **1** FEEL, HANDLE : tocar, tentar **2** AFFECT, MOVE : conmover, afectar, tocar <his gesture touched our hearts : su gesto nos tocó el corazón> — *vi* : tocarse

touch[2] *n* **1** : tacto *m* (sentido) **2** DETAIL : toque *m,* detalle *m* <a touch of color : un toque de color> **3** BIT : pizca *f,* gota *f,* poco *m* **4** ABILITY : habilidad *f* <to lose one's touch : perder la habilidad> **5** CONTACT : contacto *m,* comunicación *f* <to keep in touch : mantenerse en contacto>

touchdown [ˈtʌtʃˌdaʊn] *n* : touchdown *m* (en futbol americano)

touch up *vt* : retocar

touchy [ˈtʌtʃi] *adj* **touchier; -est 1** : sensible, susceptible (dícese de una persona) **2** : delicado <a touchy subject : un tema delicado>

tough[1] [ˈtʌf] *adj* **1** STRONG : fuerte, resistente (dícese de materiales) **2** LEATHERY : correoso <a tough steak : un bistec duro> **3** HARDY : fuerte, robusto (dícese de una persona) **4** STRICT : severo, exigente **5** DIFFICULT : difícil **6** STUBBORN : terco, obstinado

tough[2] *n* : matón *m,* persona *f* ruda y brusca

toughen [ˈtʌfən] *vt* : fortalecer, endurecer — *vi* : endurecerse, hacerse más fuerte

toughness [ˈtʌfnəs] *n* : dureza *f*

toupee [tuːˈpeɪ] *n* : peluquín *m,* bisoñé *m*

tour[1] [ˈtʊr] *vi* : tomar una excursión, viajar — *vt* : recorrer, hacer una gira por

tour[2] *n* **1** : gira *f,* tour *m,* excursión *f* **2 tour of duty** : período *m* de servicio

tourist [ˈtʊrɪst, ˈtər-] *n* : turista *mf*

tournament [ˈtərnəmənt, ˈtʊr-] *n* : torneo *m*

tourniquet [ˈtərnɪkət, ˈtʊr-] *n* : torniquete *m*

tousle [ˈtaʊzəl] *vt* **-sled; -sling** : desarreglar, despeinar (el cabello)

tout [ˈtaʊt] *vt* : promocionar, elogiar (con exageración)

tow[1] [ˈtoː] *vt* : remolcar

tow[2] *n* : remolque *m*

toward [ˈtord, təˈwɔrd] *or* **towards** [ˈtordz, təˈwɔrdz] *prep* **1** (*indicating direction*) : hacia, rumbo a <heading toward town : dirigiéndose rumbo al pueblo> <efforts towards peace : esfuerzos hacia la paz> **2** (*indicating time*) : alrededor de <toward midnight : alrededor de la medianoche> **3** REGARDING : hacia, con respecto a <his attitude toward life : su actitud hacia la vida> **4** FOR : para, como pago parcial de (una compra o deuda)

towel [ˈtaʊəl] *n* : toalla *f*

tower[1] [ˈtaʊər] *vi* **to tower over** : descollar sobre, elevarse sobre, dominar

tower[2] *n* : torre *f*

towering [ˈtaʊərɪŋ] *adj* : altísimo, imponente

town [ˈtaʊn] *n* : pueblo *m,* ciudad *f* (pequeña)

township [ˈtaʊnˌʃɪp] *n* : municipio *m*

tow truck [ˈtoːˌtrʌk] *n* : grúa *f*

toxic [ˈtɑksɪk] *adj* : tóxico

toxicity [tɑkˈsɪsəṭi] *n, pl* **-ties** : toxicidad *f*

toxin [ˈtɑksɪn] *n* : toxina *f*

toy[1] [ˈtɔɪ] *vi* : juguetear, jugar

toy[2] *adj* : de juguete <a toy rifle : un rifle de juguete>

toy[3] *n* : juguete *m*

trace[1] [ˈtreɪs] *vt* **traced; tracing 1** : calcar (un dibujo, etc.) **2** OUTLINE : delinear, trazar (planes, etc.) **3** TRACK : describir (un curso, una historia) **4** FIND : localizar, ubicar

trace[2] *n* **1** SIGN, TRACK : huella *f,* rastro *m,* indicio *m,* vestigio *m* <he disappeared without a trace : desapareció sin dejar rastro> **2** BIT, HINT : pizca *f,* ápice *m,* dejo *m*

trachea [ˈtreɪkiə] *n, pl* **-cheae** [-kiˌiː] : tráquea *f*

tracing paper *n* : papel *m* de calcar

track[1] [ˈtræk] *vt* **1** TRAIL : seguir la pista de, rastrear **2** : dejar huellas de <he tracked mud all over : dejó huellas de lodo por todas partes>

track[2] *n* **1** : rastro *m,* huella *f* (de animales), pista *f* (de personas) **2** PATH : pista *f,* sendero *m,* camino *m* **3** *or* **railroad track** : vía *f* (férrea) **4** → **racetrack 5** : oruga *f* (de un tanque,

etc.) **6** : pista *f* (deporte) **7 to keep track of** : llevar la cuenta de
track–and–field [ˈtrækəndˈfiːld] *adj* : de pista y campo
tract [ˈtrækt] *n* **1** AREA : terreno *m*, extensión *f*, área *f* **2** : tracto *m* <digestive tract : tracto digestivo> **3** PAMPHLET : panfleto *m*, folleto *m*
traction [ˈtrækʃən] *n* : tracción *f*
tractor [ˈtræktər] *n* **1** : tractor *m* (vehículo agrícola) **2** TRUCK : camión *m* (con remolque)
trade[1] [ˈtreɪd] *v* **traded; trading** *vi* : comerciar, negociar — *vt* EXCHANGE : intercambiar, canjear
trade[2] *n* **1** OCCUPATION : oficio *m*, profesión *f*, ocupación *f* <a carpenter by trade : carpintero de oficio> **2** COMMERCE : comercio *m*, industria *f* <free trade : libre comercio> <the book trade : la industria del libro> **3** EXCHANGE : intercambio *m*, canje *m*
trade–in [ˈtreɪdˌɪn] *n* : artículo *m* que se canjea por otro
trademark [ˈtreɪdˌmɑrk] *n* **1** : marca *f* registrada **2** CHARACTERISTIC : sello *m* característico (de un grupo, una persona, etc.)
trader [ˈtreɪdər] *n* : negociante *mf*, tratante *mf*, comerciante *mf*
tradesman [ˈtreɪdzmən] *n*, *pl* **-men** [-mən, -ˌmɛn] **1** CRAFTSMAN : artesano *m*, -na *f* **2** SHOPKEEPER : tendero *m*, -ra *f*; comerciante *mf*
trade wind *n* : viento *m* alisio
tradition [trəˈdɪʃən] *n* : tradición *f*
traditional [trəˈdɪʃənəl] *adj* : tradicional — **traditionally** *adv*
traffic[1] [ˈtræfɪk] *vi* **trafficked; trafficking** : traficar (en)
traffic[2] *n* **1** COMMERCE : tráfico *m*, comercio *m* <the drug traffic : el narcotráfico> **2** : tráfico *m*, tránsito *m*, circulación *f* (de vehículos, etc.)
traffic circle *n* : rotonda *f*, glorieta *f*
trafficker [ˈtræfɪkər] *n* : traficante *mf*
traffic light *n* : semáforo *m*, luz *f* (de tránsito)
tragedy [ˈtrædʒədi] *n*, *pl* **-dies** : tragedia *f*
tragic [ˈtrædʒɪk] *adj* : trágico — **tragically** *adv*
trail[1] [ˈtreɪl] *vi* **1** DRAG : arrastrarse **2** LAG : quedarse atrás, retrasarse **3 to trail away** *or* **to trail off** : disminuir, menguar, desvanecerse — *vt* **1** DRAG : arrastrar **2** PURSUE : perseguir, seguir la pista de
trail[2] *n* **1** TRACK : rastro *m*, huella *f*, pista *f* <a trail of blood : un rastro de sangre> **2** : cola *f*, estela *f* (de un meteoro) **3** PATH : sendero *m*, camino *m*, vereda *f*
trailer [ˈtreɪlər] *n* **1** : remolque *m*, tráiler *m* (de un camión) **2** : caravana *f* (vivienda ambulante)
train[1] [ˈtreɪn] *vt* **1** : entrenar (atletas), capacitar (empleados), adiestrar, amaestrar (animales) **2** POINT : apuntar (un arma, etc.) — *vi* : entrenar(se) (físicamente), prepararse (profesionalmente) <she's training at the gym : se está entrenando en el gimnasio>
train[2] *n* **1** : cola *f* (de un vestido) **2** RETINUE : cortejo *m*, séquito *m* **3** SERIES : serie *f* (de eventos) **4** : tren *m* <passenger train : tren de pasajeros>
trainee [treɪˈniː] *n* : aprendiz *m*, -diza *f*
trainer [ˈtreɪnər] *n* : entrenador *m*, -dora *f*
traipse [ˈtreɪps] *vi* **traipsed; traipsing** : andar de un lado para otro, vagar
trait [ˈtreɪt] *n* : rasgo *m*, característica *f*
traitor [ˈtreɪtər] *n* : traidor *m*, -dora *f*
traitorous [ˈtreɪtərəs] *adj* : traidor
trajectory [trəˈdʒɛktəri] *n*, *pl* **-ries** : trayectoria *f*
tramp[1] [ˈtræmp] *vi* : caminar (a paso pesado) — *vt* : deambular por, vagar por <to tramp the streets : vagar por las calles>
tramp[2] *n* **1** VAGRANT : vagabundo *m*, -da *f* **2** HIKE : caminata *f*
trample [ˈtræmpəl] *vt* **-pled; -pling** : pisotear, hollar
trampoline [ˌtræmpəˈliːn, ˈtræmpəˌ-] *n* : trampolín *m*, cama *f* elástica
trance [ˈtrænts] *n* : trance *m*
tranquil [ˈtræŋkwəl] *adj* : calmo, tranquilo, sereno — **tranquilly** *adv*
tranquilize [ˈtræŋkwəˌlaɪz] *vt* **-ized; -izing** : tranquilizar
tranquilizer [ˈtræŋkwəˌlaɪzər] *n* : tranquilizante *m*
tranquillity *or* **tranquility** [træŋˈkwɪləti] *n* : sosiego *m*, tranquilidad *f*
transact [trænˈzækt] *vt* : negociar, gestionar, hacer (negocios)
transaction [trænˈzækʃən] *n* **1** : transacción *f*, negocio *m*, operación *f* **2 transactions** *npl* RECORDS : actas *fpl*
transatlantic [ˌtræntsətˈlæntɪk, ˌtrænz-] *adj* : transatlántico
transcend [trænˈsɛnd] *vt* : trascender, sobrepasar
transcribe [trænˈskraɪb] *vt* **-scribed; -scribing** : transcribir
transcript [ˈtrænˌskrɪpt] *n* : copia *f* oficial
transcription [trænˈskrɪpʃən] *n* : transcripción *f*
transfer[1] [træntsˈfər, ˈtræntsˌfər] *v* **-ferred; -ferring** *vt* **1** : trasladar (a una persona), transferir (fondos) **2** : transferir, traspasar, ceder (propiedad) **3** PRINT : imprimir (un diseño) — *vi* **1** MOVE : trasladarse, cambiarse **2** CHANGE : transbordar, cambiar (de un transporte a otro) <she transferred at E Street : hizo un transborde a la calle E>
transfer[2] [ˈtræntsˌfər] *n* **1** TRANSFERRING : transferencia *f* (de fondos, de

propiedad, etc.), traslado *m* (de una persona) **2** DECAL **:** calcomanía *f* **3 :** boleto *m* (para cambiar de un avión, etc., a otro)

transferable [trænts'fərəbəl] *adj* **:** transferible

transference [trænts'fərənts] *n* **:** transferencia *f*

transfigure [trænts'fɪgjər] *vt* **-ured; -uring :** transfigurar, transformar

transfix [trænts'fɪks] *vt* **1** PIERCE **:** traspasar, atravesar **2** IMMOBILIZE **:** paralizar

transform [trænts'fɔrm] *vt* **:** transformar

transformation [ˌtræntsfər'meɪʃən] *n* **:** transformación *f*

transformer [trænts'fɔrmər] *n* **:** transformador *m*

transfusion [trænts'fjuːʒən] *n* **:** transfusión *f*

transgress [trænts'grɛs, trænz-] *vt* **:** transgredir, infringir

transgression [trænts'grɛʃən, trænz-] *n* **:** transgresión *f*

transient[1] ['træntʃənt, 'trænsiənt] *adj* **:** pasajero, transitorio **— transiently** *adv*

transient[2] *n* **:** transeúnte *mf*

transistor [træn'zɪstər, -'sɪs-] *n* **:** transistor *m*

transit ['træntsɪt, 'trænzɪt] *n* **1** PASSAGE **:** pasaje *m,* tránsito *m* <in transit : en tránsito> **2** TRANSPORTATION **:** transporte *m* (público) **3 :** teodolito *m* (instrumento topográfico)

transition [træn'sɪʃən, -'zɪʃ-] *n* **:** transición *f*

transitional [træn'sɪʃənəl, -'zɪʃ-] *adj* **:** de transición

transitive ['træntsət̬ɪv, 'trænzə-] *adj* **:** transitivo

transitory ['træntsəˌtori, 'trænzə-] *adj* **:** transitorio

translate [trænts'leɪt, trænz-; 'træntsˌ-, 'trænsˌ-] *vt* **-lated; -lating :** traducir

translation [trænts'leɪʃən, trænz-] *n* **:** traducción *f*

translator [trænts'leɪt̬ər, trænz-; 'træntsˌ-, 'trænsˌ-] *n* **:** traductor *m,* -tora *f*

translucent [trænts'luːsənt, trænz-] *adj* **:** translúcido

transmission [trænts'mɪʃən, trænz-] *n* **:** transmisión *f*

transmit [trænts'mɪt, trænz-] *vt* **-mitted; -mitting :** transmitir

transmitter [trænts'mɪt̬ər, trænz-; 'træntsˌ-, 'trænsˌ-] *n* **:** transmisor *m,* emisor *m*

transom ['træntsəm] *n* **:** montante *m* (de una puerta), travesaño *m* (de una ventana)

transparency [trænts'pærəntsi] *n, pl* **-cies :** transparencia *f*

transparent [trænts'pærənt] *adj* **1 :** transparente, traslúcido <a transparent fabric : una tela transparente> **2** OBVIOUS **:** transparente, obvio, claro **— transparently** *adv*

transpiration [ˌtræntspə'reɪʃən] *n* **:** transpiración *f*

transpire [trænts'paɪr] *vi* **-spired; -spiring 1 :** transpirar (en biología y botanía) **2** TURN OUT **:** resultar **3** HAPPEN **:** suceder, ocurrir, tener lugar

transplant[1] [trænts'plænt] *vt* **:** trasplantar

transplant[2] ['træntsˌplænt] *n* **:** trasplante *m*

transport[1] [trænts'port, 'træntsˌ-] *vt* **1** CARRY **:** transportar, acarrear **2** ENRAPTURE **:** transportar, extasiar

transport[2] ['træntsˌport] *n* **1** TRANSPORTATION **:** transporte *m,* transportación *f* **2** RAPTURE **:** éxtasis *m* **3** *or* **transport ship :** buque *m* de transporte (de personal militar)

transportation [ˌtræntspər'teɪʃən] *n* **:** transporte *m,* transportación *f*

transpose [trænts'poːz] *vt* **-posed; -posing :** trasponer, trasladar, transportar (una composición musical)

transverse [trænts'vərs, trænz-] *adj* **:** transversal, transverso, oblicuo **— transversely** *adv*

trap[1] ['træp] *vt* **trapped; trapping :** atrapar, apresar (en una trampa)

trap[2] *n* **:** trampa *f* <to set a trap : tender una trampa>

trapdoor ['træp'dor] *n* **:** trampilla *f,* escotillón *m*

trapeze [træ'piːz] *n* **:** trapecio *m*

trapezoid ['træpəˌzɔɪd] *n* **:** trapezoide *m,* trapecio *m*

trapper ['træpər] *n* **:** trampero *m,* -ra *f;* cazador *m,* -dora *f* (que usa trampas)

trappings ['træpɪŋz] *npl* **1 :** arreos *mpl,* jaeces *mpl* (de un caballo) **2** ADORNMENTS **:** adornos *mpl,* pompa *f*

trash ['træʃ] *n* **:** basura *f*

trauma ['trɔmə, 'traʊ-] *n* **:** trauma *m*

traumatic [trə'mæt̬ɪk, trɔ-, traʊ-] *adj* **:** traumático

travel[1] ['trævəl] *vi* **-eled** *or* **-elled; -eling** *or* **-elling 1** JOURNEY **:** viajar **2** GO, MOVE **:** desplazarse, moverse, ir <the waves travel at uniform speed : las ondas se desplazan a una velocidad uniforme>

travel[2] *n* **:** viajes *mpl*

traveler *or* **traveller** ['trævələr] *n* **:** viajero *m,* -ra *f*

traverse [trə'vərs, træ'vərs, 'trævərs] *vt* **-versed; -versing** CROSS **:** atravesar, extenderse a través de, cruzar

travesty ['trævəsti] *n, pl* **-ties :** parodia *f*

trawl[1] ['trɔl] *vi* **:** pescar con red de arrastre, rastrear

trawl[2] *n or* **trawl net :** red *f* de arrastre

trawler ['trɔlər] *n* **:** barco *m* de pesca (utilizado para rastrear)

tray ['treɪ] *n* **:** bandeja *f,* charola *f Bol, Mex, Peru*

treacherous [ˈtrɛtʃərəs] *adj* **1** TRAITOROUS : traicionero, traidor **2** DANGEROUS : peligroso
treacherously [ˈtrɛtʃərəsli] *adv* : a traición
treachery [ˈtrɛtʃəri] *n, pl* **-eries** : traición *f*
tread[1] [ˈtrɛd] *v* **trod** [ˈtrɑd]; **trodden** [ˈtrɑdən] *or* **trod; treading** *vt* TRAMPLE : pisotear, hollar — *vi* **1** WALK : caminar, andar **2 to tread on** : pisar
tread[2] *n* **1** STEP : paso *m,* andar *m* **2** : banda *f* de rodadura (de un neumático, etc.) **3** : escalón *m* (de una escalera)
treadle [ˈtrɛdəl] *n* : pedal *m* (de una máquina)
treadmill [ˈtrɛd͵mɪl] *n* **1** : rueda *f* de andar **2** ROUTINE : rutina *f*
treason [ˈtriːzən] *n* : traición *f* (a la patria, etc.)
treasure[1] [ˈtrɛʒər, ˈtreɪ-] *vt* **-sured; -suring** : apreciar, valorar
treasure[2] *n* : tesoro *m*
treasurer [ˈtrɛʒərər, ˈtreɪ-] *n* : tesorero *m,* -ra *f*
treasury [ˈtrɛʒəri, ˈtreɪ-] *n, pl* **-suries** : tesorería *f,* tesoro *m*
treat[1] [ˈtriːt] *vt* **1** DEAL WITH : tratar (un asunto) <the article treats of poverty : el artículo trata de la pobreza> **2** HANDLE : tratar (a una persona), manejar (un objeto) <to treat something as a joke : tomar(se) algo a broma> **3** INVITE : invitar, convidar <he treated me to a meal : me invitó a comer> **4** : tratar, atender (en medicina) **5** PROCESS : tratar <to treat sewage : tratar las aguas negras>
treat[2] *n* : gusto *m,* placer *m* <it was a treat to see you : fue un placer verte> <it's my treat : yo invito>
treatise [ˈtriːtɪs] *n* : tratado *m,* estudio *m*
treatment [ˈtriːtmənt] *n* : trato *m,* tratamiento *m* (médico)
treaty [ˈtriːti] *n, pl* **-ties** : tratado *m,* convenio *m*
treble[1] [ˈtrɛbəl] *vt* **-bled; -bling** : triplicar
treble[2] *adj* **1** → **triple 2** : de tiple, soprano (en música) **3 treble clef** : clave *f* de sol
treble[3] *n* : tiple *m,* parte *f* soprana
tree [ˈtriː] *n* : árbol *m*
treeless [ˈtriːləs] *adj* : carente de árboles
trek[1] [ˈtrɛk] *vi* **trekked; trekking** : hacer un viaje largo y difícil
trek[2] *n* : viaje *m* largo y difícil
trellis [ˈtrɛlɪs] *n* : enrejado *m,* espaldera *f,* celosía *f*
tremble [ˈtrɛmbəl] *vi* **-bled; -bling** : temblar
tremendous [trɪˈmɛndəs] *adj* : tremendo — **tremendously** *adv*
tremor [ˈtrɛmər] *n* : temblor *m*
tremulous [ˈtrɛmjələs] *adj* : trémulo, tembloroso
trench [ˈtrɛntʃ] *n* **1** DITCH : zanja *f* **2** : trinchera *f* (militar)
trenchant [ˈtrɛntʃənt] *adj* : cortante, mordaz
trend[1] [ˈtrɛnd] *vi* : tender, inclinarse
trend[2] *n* **1** TENDENCY : tendencia *f* **2** FASHION : moda *f*
trendy [ˈtrɛndi] *adj* **trendier; -est** : de moda
trepidation [͵trɛpəˈdeɪʃən] *n* : inquietud *f,* ansiedad *f*
trespass[1] [ˈtrɛspəs, -͵pæs] *vi* **1** SIN : pecar, transgredir **2** : entrar ilegalmente (en propiedad ajena)
trespass[2] *n* **1** SIN : pecado *m,* transgresión *f* <forgive us our trespasses : perdónanos nuestras deudas> **2** : entrada *f* ilegal (en propiedad ajena)
tress [ˈtrɛs] *n* : mechón *m*
trestle [ˈtrɛsəl] *n* **1** : caballete *m* (armazón) **2** *or* **trestle bridge** : puente *m* de caballete
triad [ˈtraɪ͵æd] *n* : tríada *f*
trial[1] [ˈtraɪəl] *adj* : de prueba <trial period : período de prueba>
trial[2] *n* **1** : juicio *m,* proceso *m* <to stand trial : ser sometido a juicio> **2** AFFLICTION : aflicción *f,* tribulación *f* **3** TEST : prueba *f,* ensayo *m*
triangle [ˈtraɪ͵æŋgəl] *n* : triángulo *m*
triangular [traɪˈæŋgjələr] *adj* : triangular
tribal [ˈtraɪbəl] *adj* : tribal
tribe [ˈtraɪb] *n* : tribu *f*
tribesman [ˈtraɪbzmən] *n, pl* **-men** [-mən, -͵mɛn] : miembro *m* de una tribu
tribulation [͵trɪbjəˈleɪʃən] *n* : tribulación *f*
tribunal [traɪˈbjuːnəl, trɪ-] *n* : tribunal *m,* corte *f*
tributary [ˈtrɪbjə͵tɛri] *n, pl* **-taries** : afluente *m*
tribute [ˈtrɪb͵juːt] *n* : tributo *m*
trick[1] [ˈtrɪk] *vt* : engañar, embaucar
trick[2] *n* **1** RUSE : trampa *f,* treta *f,* artimaña *f* **2** PRANK : broma *f* <we played a trick on her : le gastamos una broma> **3** : truco *m* <magic tricks : trucos de magia> <the trick is to wait five minutes : el truco está en esperar cinco minutos> **4** MANNERISM : peculiaridad *f,* manía *f* **5** : baza *f* (en juegos de naipes)
trickery [ˈtrɪkəri] *n* : engaños *mpl,* trampas *fpl*
trickle[1] [ˈtrɪkəl] *vi* **-led; -ling** : gotear, chorrear
trickle[2] *n* : goteo *m,* hilo *m*
trickster [ˈtrɪkstər] *n* : estafador *m,* -dora *f;* embaucador *m,* -dora *f*
tricky [ˈtrɪki] *adj* **trickier; -est** **1** SLY : astuto, taimado **2** DIFFICULT : delicado, peliagudo, difícil
tricycle [ˈtraɪsəkəl, -͵sɪkəl] *n* : triciclo *m*
trident [ˈtraɪdənt] *n* : tridente *m*
triennial [traɪˈɛniəl] *adj* : trienal
trifle[1] [ˈtraɪfəl] *vi* **-fled; -fling** : jugar, juguetear

trifle² *n* : nimiedad *f,* insignificancia *f*
trifling [ˈtraɪflɪŋ] *adj* : trivial, insignificante
trigger¹ [ˈtrɪgər] *vt* : causar, provocar
trigger² *n* : gatillo *m*
trigonometry [ˌtrɪgəˈnɑmətri] *n* : trigonometría *f*
trill¹ [ˈtrɪl] *vi* QUAVER : trinar, gorjear — *vt* : vibrar <to trill the *r* : vibrar la *r*>
trill² *n* **1** QUAVER : trino *m,* gorjeo *m* **2** : vibración *f* (en fonología)
trillion [ˈtrɪljən] *n* : billón *m*
trilogy [ˈtrɪlədʒi] *n, pl* **-gies** : trilogía *f*
trim¹ [ˈtrɪm] *vt* **trimmed; trimming 1** DECORATE : adornar, decorar **2** CUT : recortar **3** REDUCE : recortar, reducir <to trim the excess : recortar el exceso>
trim² *adj* **trimmer; trimmest 1** SLIM : esbelto **2** NEAT : limpio y arreglado, bien cuidado
trim³ *n* **1** CONDITION : condición *f,* estado *m* <to keep in trim : mantenerse en buena forma> **2** CUT : recorte *m* **3** TRIMMING : adornos *mpl*
trimming [ˈtrɪmɪŋ] *n* : adornos *mpl,* accesorios *mpl*
Trinity [ˈtrɪnəti] *n* : Trinidad *f*
trinket [ˈtrɪŋkət] *n* : chuchería *f,* baratija *f*
trio [ˈtriːˌoː] *n, pl* **trios** : trío *m*
trip¹ [ˈtrɪp] *v* **tripped; tripping** *vi* **1** : caminar (a paso ligero) **2** STUMBLE : tropezar **3 to trip up** ERR : equivocarse, cometer un error — *vt* **1** : hacerle una zancadilla (a alguien) <you tripped me on purpose! : ¡me hiciste la zancadilla a propósito!> **2** ACTIVATE : activar (un mecanismo) **3 to trip up** : hacer equivocar (a alguien)
trip² *n* **1** JOURNEY : viaje *m* <to take a trip : hacer un viaje> **2** STUMBLE : tropiezo *m,* traspié *m*
tripartite [traɪˈpɑrˌtaɪt] *adj* : tripartito
tripe [ˈtraɪp] *n* **1** : mondongo *m,* callos *mpl,* pancita *f Mex* **2** TRASH : porquería *f*
triple¹ [ˈtrɪpəl] *vt* **-pled; -pling** : triplicar
triple² *adj* : triple
triple³ *n* : triple *m*
triplet [ˈtrɪplət] *n* **1** : terceto *m* (en poesía, música, etc.) **2** : trillizo *m,* -za *f* (persona)
triplicate [ˈtrɪplɪkət] *n* : triplicado *m*
tripod [ˈtraɪˌpɑd] *n* : trípode *m*
trite [ˈtraɪt] *adj* **triter; tritest** : trillado, tópico, manido
triumph¹ [ˈtraɪəmpf] *vi* : triunfar
triumph² *n* : triunfo *m*
triumphal [traɪˈʌmpfəl] *adj* : triunfal
triumphant [traɪˈʌmpfənt] *adj* : triunfante, triunfal — **triumphantly** *adv*
trivia [ˈtrɪviə] *ns & pl* : trivialidades *fpl,* nimiedades *fpl*
trivial [ˈtrɪviəl] *adj* : trivial, intrascendente, insignificante
triviality [ˌtrɪviˈæləti] *n, pl* **-ties** : trivialidad *f*
trod, trodden → **tread¹**
troll [ˈtroːl] *n* : duende *m* o gigante *m* de cuentos folklóricos
trolley [ˈtrɑli] *n, pl* **-leys** : tranvía *m*
trombone [trɑmˈboːn] *n* : trombón *m*
trombonist [trɑmˈboːnɪst] *n* : trombón *m*
troop¹ [ˈtruːp] *vi* : desfilar, ir en tropel
troop² *n* **1** : escuadrón *m* (de caballería) **2** GROUP : grupo *m,* banda *f* (de personas) **3 troops** *npl* SOLDIERS : tropas *fpl,* soldados *mpl*
trooper [ˈtruːpər] *n* **1** : soldado *m* (de caballería) **2** : policía *m* montado **3** : policía *m* (estatal)
trophy [ˈtroːfi] *n, pl* **-phies** : trofeo *m*
tropic¹ [ˈtrɑpɪk] *or* **tropical** [-pɪkəl] *adj* : tropical
tropic² *n* **1** : trópico *m* <tropic of Cancer : trópico de Cáncer> **2 the tropics** : el trópico
trot¹ [ˈtrɑt] *vi* **trotted; trotting** : trotar
trot² *n* : trote *m*
trouble¹ [ˈtrʌbəl] *v* **-bled; -bling** *vt* **1** DISTURB, WORRY : molestar, perturbar, inquietar **2** AFFLICT : afligir, afectar — *vi* : molestarse, hacer un esfuerzo <they didn't trouble to come : no se molestaron en venir>
trouble² *n* **1** PROBLEMS : problemas *mpl,* dificultades *fpl* <to be in trouble : estar en un aprieto> <heart trouble : problemas de corazón> **2** EFFORT : molestia *f,* esfuerzo *m* <to take the trouble : tomarse la molestia> <it's not worth the trouble : no vale la pena>
troublemaker [ˈtrʌbəlˌmeɪkər] *n* : agitador *m,* -dora *f;* alborotador *m,* -dora *f*
troublesome [ˈtrʌbəlsəm] *adj* : problemático, dificultoso — **troublesomely** *adv*
trough [ˈtrɔf] *n, pl* **troughs** [ˈtrɔfs, ˈtrɔvz] **1** : comedero *m,* bebedero *m* (de animales) **2** CHANNEL, HOLLOW : depresión *f* (en el suelo), seno *m* (de olas)
trounce [ˈtraʊnts] *vt* **trounced; trouncing 1** THRASH : apalear, darle una paliza (a alguien) **2** DEFEAT : derrotar contundentemente
troupe [ˈtruːp] *n* : troupe *f*
trousers [ˈtraʊzərz] *npl* : pantalón *m,* pantalones *mpl*
trout [ˈtraʊt] *n, pl* **trout** : trucha *f*
trowel [ˈtraʊəl] *n* **1** : llana *f,* paleta *f* (de albañil) **2** : desplantador *m* (de jardinero)
truant [ˈtruːənt] *n* : alumno *m,* -na *f* que falta a clase sin permiso
truce [ˈtruːs] *n* : tregua *f,* armisticio *m*
truck¹ [ˈtrʌk] *vt* : transportar en camión
truck² *n* **1** : camión *m* (vehículo automóvil), carro *m* (manual) **2** DEAL-

INGS : tratos *mpl* <to have no truck with : no tener nada que ver con>
trucker ['trʌkər] *n* : camionero *m*, -ra *f*
truculent ['trʌkjələnt] *adj* : agresivo, beligerante
trudge ['trʌdʒ] *vi* **trudged; trudging** : caminar a paso pesado
true[1] ['tru:] *vt* **trued; trueing** : aplomar (algo vertical), nivelar (algo horizontal), centrar (una rueda)
true[2] *adv* **1** TRUTHFULLY : lealmente, sinceramente **2** ACCURATELY : exactamente, certeramente
true[3] *adj* **truer; truest 1** LOYAL : fiel, leal **2** : cierto, verdadero, verídico <it's true : es cierto, es la verdad> <a true story : una historia verídica> **3** GENUINE : auténtico, genuino — **truly** *adv*
true–blue ['tru:'blu:] *adj* LOYAL : leal, fiel
truffle ['trʌfəl] *n* : trufa *f*
truism ['tru:ˌɪzəm] *n* : perogrullada *f*, verdad *f* obvia
trump[1] ['trʌmp] *vt* : matar (en juegos de naipes)
trump[2] *n* : triunfo *m* (en juegos de naipes)
trumped–up ['trʌmpt'ʌp] *adj* : inventado, fabricado <trumped-up charges : falsas acusaciones>
trumpet[1] ['trʌmpət] *vi* **1** : sonar una trompeta **2** : berrear, bramar (dícese de un animal) — *vt* : proclamar a los cuatro vientos
trumpet[2] *n* : trompeta *f*
trumpeter ['trʌmpət̬ər] *n* : trompetista *mf*
truncate ['trʌŋˌkeɪt, 'trʌn-] *vt* **-cated; -cating** : truncar
trundle ['trʌndəl] *v* **-dled; -dling** *vi* : rodar lentamente — *vt* : hacer rodar, empujar lentamente
trunk ['trʌŋk] *n* **1** : tronco *m* (de un árbol o del cuerpo) **2** : trompa *f* (de un elefante) **3** CHEST : baúl *m* **4** : maletero *m*, cajuela *f Mex* (de un auto) **5 trunks** *npl* : traje *m* de baño (de caballero)
truss[1] ['trʌs] *vt* : atar (con fuerza)
truss[2] *n* **1** FRAMEWORK : armazón *m* (de una estructura) **2** : braguero *m* (en medicina)
trust[1] ['trʌst] *vi* : confiar, esperar <to trust in God : confiar en Dios> — *vt* **1** ENTRUST : confiar, encomendar **2** : confiar en, tenerle confianza a <I trust you : te tengo confianza>
trust[2] *n* **1** CONFIDENCE : confianza *f* **2** HOPE : esperanza *f*, fe *f* **3** CREDIT : crédito *m* <to sell on trust : fiar> **4** : fideicomiso *m* <to hold in trust : guardar en fideicomiso> **5** : trust *m* (consorcio empresarial) **6** CUSTODY : responsabilidad *f*, custodia *f*
trustee [ˌtrʌs'ti:] *n* : fideicomisario *m*, -ria *f*; fiduciario *m*, -ria *f*
trustful ['trʌstfəl] *adj* : confiado — **trustfully** *adv*
trustworthiness ['trəstˌwərðinəs] *n* : integridad *f*, honradez *f*
trustworthy ['trəstˌwərði] *adj* : digno de confianza, confiable
trusty ['trəsti] *adj* **trustier; -est** : fiel, confiable
truth ['tru:θ] *n*, *pl* **truths** ['tru:ðz, 'tru:θs] : verdad *f*
truthful ['tru:θfəl] *adj* : sincero, veraz — **truthfully** *adv*
truthfulness ['tru:θfəlnəs] *n* : sinceridad *f*, veracidad *f*
try[1] ['traɪ] *v* **tried; trying** *vt* **1** : enjuiciar, juzgar, procesar <he was tried for murder : fue procesado por homicidio> **2** : probar <did you try the salad? : ¿probaste la ensalada?> **3** TEST : tentar, poner a prueba <to try one's patience : tentarle la paciencia a uno> **4** ATTEMPT : tratar (de), intentar **5** *or* **to try on** : probarse (ropa) — *vi* : tratar, intentar
try[2] *n*, *pl* **tries** : intento *m*, tentativa *f*
tryout ['traɪˌaʊt] *n* : prueba *f*
tsar ['zɑr, 'tsɑr, 'sɑr] → **czar**
T–shirt ['ti:ˌʃərt] *n* : camiseta *f*
tub ['tʌb] *n* **1** CASK : cuba *f*, barril *m*, tonel *m* **2** CONTAINER : envase *m* (de plástico, etc.) <a tub of margarine : un envase de margarina> **3** BATHTUB : tina *f* (de baño), bañera *f*
tuba ['tu:bə, 'tju:-] *n* : tuba *f*
tube ['tu:b, 'tju:b] *n* **1** PIPE : tubo *m* **2** : tubo *m* (de dentífrico, etc.) **3** *or* **inner tube** : cámara *f* **4** : tubo *m* (de un aparato electrónico) **5** : trompa *f* (en anatomía)
tubeless ['tu:bləs, 'tju:b-] *adj* : sin cámara (dícese de una llanta)
tuber ['tu:bər, 'tju:-] *n* : tubérculo *m*
tubercular [tʊ'bərkjələr, tjʊ-] → **tuberculous**
tuberculosis [tʊˌbərkjə'lo:sɪs, tjʊ-] *n*, *pl* **-loses** [-ˌsi:z] : tuberculosis *f*
tuberculous [tʊ'bərkjələs, tjʊ-] *adj* : tuberculoso
tuberous ['tu:bərəs, 'tju:-] *adj* : tuberoso
tubing ['tu:bɪŋ, 'tju:-] *n* : tubería *f*
tubular ['tu:bjələr, 'tju:-] *adj* : tubular
tuck[1] ['tʌk] *vt* **1** PLACE, PUT : meter, colocar <tuck in your shirt : métete la camisa> **2** : guardar, esconder <to tuck away one's money : guardar uno bien su dinero> **3** COVER : arropar (a un niño en la cama)
tuck[2] *n* : pliegue *m*, alforza *f*
Tuesday ['tu:zˌdeɪ, 'tju:z-, -di] *n* : martes *m*
tuft ['tʌft] *n* : penacho *m* (de plumas), copete *m* (de pelo)
tug[1] ['tʌg] *v* **tugged; tugging** *vi* : tirar, jalar, dar un tirón — *vt* : jalar, arrastrar, remolcar (con un barco)
tug[2] *n* **1** : tirón *m*, jalón *m* **2** → **tugboat**
tugboat ['tʌgˌbo:t] *n* : remolcador *m*
tug–of–war [ˌtʌgə'wɔr] *n*, *pl* **tugs–of–war** : tira y afloja *m*
tulip ['tu:lɪp, 'tju:-] *n* : tulipán *m*

tumble[1] ['tʌmbəl] *v* **-bled; -bling** *vi* **1** : dar volteretas (en acrobacia) **2** FALL : caerse, venirse abajo — *vt* **1** TOPPLE : volcar **2** TOSS : hacer girar

tumble[2] *n* : voltereta *f,* caída *f*

tumbler ['tʌmblər] *n* **1** ACROBAT : acróbata *mf,* saltimbanqui *mf* **2** GLASS : vaso *m* (de mesa) **3** : clavija *f* (de una cerradura)

tummy ['tʌmi] *n, pl* **-mies** BELLY : panza *f,* vientre *m*

tumor ['tu:mər 'tju:-] *n* : tumor *m*

tumult ['tu:ˌmʌlt 'tju:-] *n* : tumulto *m,* alboroto *m*

tumultuous [tʊ'mʌltʃʊəs, tju:-] *adj* : tumultuoso

tuna ['tu:nə 'tju:-] *n, pl* **-na** *or* **-nas** : atún *m*

tundra ['tʌndrə] *n* : tundra *f*

tune[1] ['tu:n, 'tju:n] *v* **tuned; tuning** *vt* **1** ADJUST : ajustar, hacer más preciso, afinar (un motor) **2** : afinar (un instrumento musical) **3** : sintonizar (un radio o televisor) — *vi* **to tune in** : sintonizar (con una emisora)

tune[2] *n* **1** MELODY : tonada *f,* canción *f,* melodía *f* **2 in tune** : afinado (dícese de un instrumento o de la voz), sintonizado, en sintonía

tuneful ['tu:nfəl, 'tju:n-] *adj* : armonioso, melódico

tuner ['tu:nər, 'tju:-] *n* : afinador *m,* -dora *f* (de instrumentos); sintonizador *m* (de un radio o un televisior)

tungsten ['tʌŋkstən] *n* : tungsteno *m*

tunic ['tu:nɪk, 'tju:-] *n* : túnica *f*

tuning fork *n* : diapasón *m*

Tunisian [tu:'ni:ʒən, tju:'nɪziən] *n* : tunecino *m,* -na *f* — **Tunisian** *adj*

tunnel[1] ['tʌnəl] *vi* **-neled** *or* **-nelled; -neling** *or* **-nelling** : hacer un túnel

tunnel[2] *n* : túnel *m*

turban ['tərbən] *n* : turbante *m*

turbid ['tərbɪd] *adj* : turbio

turbine ['tərbən, -ˌbaɪn] *n* : turbina *f*

turboprop ['tərbo:ˌprɑp] *n* : turbopropulsor *m* (motor), avión *m* turbopropulsado

turbulence ['tərbjələnts] *n* : turbulencia *f*

turbulent ['tərbjələnt] *adj* : turbulento — **turbulently** *adv*

tureen [tə'ri:n, tjʊ-] *n* : sopera *f*

turf ['tərf] *n* SOD : tepe *m*

turgid ['tərdʒɪd] *adj* **1** SWOLLEN : turgente **2** : ampuloso, hinchado <turgid style : estilo ampuloso>

turkey ['tərki] *n, pl* **-keys** : pavo *m*

turmoil ['tərˌmɔɪl] *n* : agitación *f,* desorden *m,* confusión *f*

turn[1] ['tərn] *vt* **1** : girar, voltear, volver <to turn one's head : voltear la cabeza> <she turned her chair toward the fire : giró su asiento hacia la hoguera> **2** ROTATE : darle vuelta a, hacer girar <turn the handle : dale vuelta a la manivela> **3** SPRAIN, WRENCH : dislocar, torcer **4** UPSET : revolver (el estómago) **5** TRANSFORM : convertir <to turn water into wine : convertir el agua en vino> **6** SHAPE : tornear (en carpintería) — *vi* **1** ROTATE : girar, dar vueltas **2** : girar, doblar, dar una vuelta <turn left : doble a la izquierda> <to turn around : dar la media vuelta> **3** BECOME : hacerse, volverse, ponerse **4** SOUR : agriarse, cortarse (dícese de la leche) **5 to turn to** : recurrir a <they have no one to turn to : no tienen quien les ayude>

turn[2] *n* **1** : vuelta *f,* giro *m* <a sudden turn : una vuelta repentina> **2** CHANGE : cambio *m* **3** CURVE : curva *f* (en un camino) **4** : turno *m* <they're awaiting their turn : están esperando su turno> <whose turn is it? : ¿a quién le toca?>

turncoat ['tərnˌko:t] *n* : traidor *m,* -dora *f*

turn down *vt* **1** REFUSE : rehusar, rechazar <they turned down our invitation : rehusaron nuestra invitación> **2** LOWER : bajar (el volumen)

turn in *vt* : entregar <to turn in one's work : entregar uno su trabajo> <they turned in the suspect : entregaron al sospechoso> — *vi* : acostarse, irse a la cama

turnip ['tərnəp] *n* : nabo *m*

turn off *vt* : apagar (la luz, la radio, etc.)

turn on *vt* : prender (la luz, etc.), encender (un motor, etc.)

turnout ['tərnˌaʊt] *n* : concurrencia *f*

turn out *vt* **1** EVICT, EXPEL : expulsar, echar, desalojar **2** PRODUCE : producir **3** → **turn off** — *vi* **1** : concurrir, presentarse <many turned out to vote : muchos concurrieron a votar> **2** PROVE, RESULT : resultar

turnover ['tərnˌo:vər] *n* **1** : tarta *f* (rellena de fruta) **2** : volumen *m* (de ventas) **3** : rotación *f* (de personal) <a high turnover : un alto nivel de rotación>

turn over *vt* **1** TRANSFER : entregar, transferir (un cargo o una responsabilidad) **2** : voltear, darle la vuelta a <turn the cassette over : voltea el cassette>

turnpike ['tərnˌpaɪk] *n* : carretera *f* de peaje

turnstile ['tərnˌstaɪl] *n* : torniquete *m* (de acceso)

turntable ['tərnˌteɪbəl] *n* : tornamesa *mf*

turn up *vi* **1** APPEAR : aparecer, presentarse **2** HAPPEN : ocurrir, suceder (inesperadamente) — *vt* : subir (el volumen)

turpentine ['tərpənˌtaɪn] *n* : aguarrás *m,* trementina *f*

turquoise ['tərˌkɔɪz, -ˌkwɔɪz] *n* : turquesa *f*

turret ['tərət] *n* **1** TOWER : torre *f* pequeña **2** : torreta *f* (de un tanque, un avión, etc.)

turtle ['tərṭəl] *n* : tortuga *f* (marina)

turtledove [ˈtərt̮əlˌdʌv] *n* **:** tórtola *f*
turtleneck [ˈtərt̮əlˌnɛk] *n* **:** cuello *m* de tortuga, cuello *m* alto
tusk [ˈtʌsk] *n* **:** colmillo *m*
tussle[1] [ˈtʌsəl] *vi* **-sled; -sling** SCUFFLE **:** pelearse, reñir
tussle[2] *n* **:** riña *f,* pelea *f*
tutor[1] [ˈtuːt̮ər, ˈtjuː-] *vt* **:** darle clases particulares (a alguien)
tutor[2] *n* **:** tutor *m,* -tora *f;* maestro *m,* -tra *f* (particular)
tuxedo [ˌtəkˈsiːˌdoː] *n, pl* **-dos** *or* **-does :** esmoquin *m,* smoking *m*
TV [ˌtiːˈviː, ˈtiːˌviː] → **television**
twain [ˈtweɪn] *n* **:** dos *m*
twang[1] [ˈtwæŋ] *vt* **:** pulsar la cuerda de (una guitarra) — *vi* **:** hablar en tono nasal
twang[2] *n* **1 :** tañido *m* (de una cuerda de guitarra) **2 :** tono *m* nasal (de voz)
tweak[1] [ˈtwiːk] *vt* **:** pellizcar
tweak[2] *n* **:** pellizco *m*
tweed [ˈtwiːd] *n* **:** tweed *m*
tweet[1] [ˈtwiːt] *vi* **:** piar
tweet[2] *n* **:** gorjeo *m,* pío *m*
tweezers [ˈtwiːzərz] *npl* **:** pinzas *fpl*
twelfth[1] [ˈtwɛlfθ] *adj* **:** duodécimo
twelfth[2] *n* **1 :** duodécimo *m,* -ma *f* (en una serie) **2 :** doceavo *m,* doceava parte *f*
twelve[1] [ˈtwɛlv] *adj* **:** doce
twelve[2] *n* **:** doce *m*
twentieth[1] [ˈtwʌntiəθ, ˈtwɛn-] *adj* **:** vigésimo
twentieth[2] *n* **1 :** vigésimo *m,* -ma *f* (en una serie) **2 :** veinteavo *m,* veinteava parte *f*
twenty[1] [ˈtwʌnti, ˈtwɛn-] *adj* **:** veinte
twenty[2] *n, pl* **-ties :** veinte *m*
twice [ˈtwaɪs] *adv* **:** dos veces <twice a day : dos veces al día> <it costs twice as much : cuesta el doble>
twig [ˈtwɪg] *n* **:** ramita *f*
twilight [ˈtwaɪˌlaɪt] *n* **:** crepúsculo *m*
twill [ˈtwɪl] *n* **:** sarga *f,* tela *f* cruzada
twin[1] [ˈtwɪn] *adj* **:** gemelo, mellizo
twin[2] *n* **:** gemelo *m,* -la *f;* mellizo *m,* -za *f*
twine[1] [ˈtwaɪn] *v* **twined; twining** *vt* **:** entrelazar, entrecruzar — *vi* **:** enroscarse (alrededor de algo)
twine[2] *n* **:** cordel *m,* cuerda *f,* mecate *m CA, Mex, Ven*
twinge[1] [ˈtwɪndʒ] *vi* **twinged; twinging** *or* **twingeing :** sentir punzadas
twinge[2] *n* **:** punzada *f,* dolor *m* agudo
twinkle[1] [ˈtwɪŋkəl] *vi* **-kled; -kling 1 :** centellear, titilar (dícese de las estrellas o de la luz) **2 :** chispear, brillar (dícese de los ojos)
twinkle[2] *n* **:** centelleo *m* (de las estrellas), brillo *m* (de los ojos)
twirl[1] [ˈtwərl] *vt* **:** girar, darle vueltas a — *vi* **:** girar, dar vueltas (rápidamente)
twirl[2] *n* **:** giro *m,* vuelta *f*
twist[1] [ˈtwɪst] *vt* **:** torcer, retorcer <he twisted my arm : me torció el brazo> — *vi* **:** retorcerse, enroscarse, serpentear (dícese de un río, un camino, etc.)
twist[2] *n* **1** BEND **:** vuelta *f,* recodo *m* (en el camino, el río, etc.) **2** TURN **:** giro *m* <give it a twist : hazlo girar> **3** SPIRAL **:** espiral *f* <a twist of lemon : una rodajita de limón> **4 :** giro *m* inesperado (de eventos, etc.)
twister [ˈtwɪstər] **1** → **tornado 2** → **waterspout**
twitch[1] [ˈtwɪtʃ] *vi* **:** moverse nerviosamente, contraerse espasmódicamente (dícese de un músculo)
twitch[2] *n* **:** espasmo *m,* sacudida *f* <a nervous twitch : un tic nervioso>
twitter[1] [ˈtwɪt̮ər] *vi* CHIRP **:** gorjear, cantar (dícese de los pájaros)
twitter[2] *n* **:** gorjeo *m*
two[1] [ˈtuː] *adj* **:** dos
two[2] *n, pl* **twos :** dos *m*
twofold[1] [ˈtuːˈfoːld] *adv* **:** al doble
twofold[2] [ˈtuːˌfoːld] *adj* **:** doble
two hundred[1] *adj* **:** doscientos
two hundred[2] *n* **:** doscientos *m*
twosome [ˈtuːsəm] *n* COUPLE **:** pareja *f*
tycoon [taɪˈkuːn] *n* **:** magnate *mf*
tying → **tie**[1]
type[1] [ˈtaɪp] *v* **typed; typing** *vt* **1** TYPEWRITE **:** escribir a máquina, pasar (un texto) a máquina **2** CATEGORIZE **:** categorizar, identificar — *vi* **:** escribir a máquina
type[2] *n* **1** KIND **:** tipo *m,* clase *f,* categoría *f* **2** *or* **printing type :** tipo *m*
typewrite [ˈtaɪpˌraɪt] *v* **-wrote; -written :** escribir a máquina
typewriter [ˈtaɪpˌraɪt̮ər] *n* **:** máquina *f* de escribir
typhoid[1] [ˈtaɪˌfɔɪd, taɪˈ-] *adj* **:** relativo al tifus o a la tifoidea
typhoid[2] *n or* **typhoid fever :** tifoidea *f*
typhoon [taɪˈfuːn] *n* **:** tifón *m*
typhus [ˈtaɪfəs] *n* **:** tifus *m,* tifo *m*
typical [ˈtɪpɪkəl] *adj* **:** típico, característico — **typically** *adv*
typify [ˈtɪpəˌfaɪ] *vt* **-fied; -fying :** ser típico o representativo de (un grupo, una clase, etc.)
typist [ˈtaɪpɪst] *n* **:** mecanógrafo *m,* -fa *f*
typographic [ˌtaɪpəˈgræfɪk] *or* **typographical** [-fɪkəl] *adj* **:** tipográfico — **typographically** [-fɪkli] *adv*
typography [taɪˈpɑgrəfi] *n* **:** tipografía *f*
tyrannical [təˈrænɪkəl, taɪ-] *adj* **:** tiránico — **tyrannically** [-nɪkli] *adv*
tyrannize [ˈtɪrəˌnaɪz] *vt* **-nized; -nizing :** tiranizar
tyranny [ˈtɪrəni] *n, pl* **-nies :** tiranía *f*
tyrant [ˈtaɪrənt] *n* **:** tirano *m,* -na *f*
tzar [ˈzɑr, ˈtsɑr, ˈsɑr] → **czar**

U

u [ˈjuː] *n, pl* **u's** *or* **us** [ˈjuːz] **:** vigésima primera letra del alfabeto inglés
ubiquitous [juːˈbɪkwət̬əs] *adj* **:** ubicuo, omnipresente
udder [ˈʌdər] *n* **:** ubre *f*
UFO [ˌjuːˌɛfˈoː, ˈjuːˌfoː] *n, pl* **UFO's** *or* **UFOs** (*unidentified flying object*) **:** ovni *m,* OVNI *m*
Ugandan [juːˈgændən, -ˈgɑn-; uːˈgɑn-] *n* **:** ugandés *m,* -desa *f* — **Ugandan** *adj*
ugliness [ˈʌglinəs] *n* **:** fealdad *f*
ugly [ˈʌgli] *adj* **uglier; -est 1** UNATTRACTIVE **:** feo **2** DISAGREEABLE **:** desagradable, feo <ugly weather : tiempo feo> <to have an ugly temper : tener mal genio>
Ukrainian [juːˈkreɪniən, -ˈkraɪ-] *n* **:** ucraniano *m,* -na *f* — **Ukrainian** *adj*
ukulele [ˌjuːkəˈleɪli] *n* **:** ukelele *m*
ulcer [ˈʌlsər] *n* **:** úlcera *f* (interna), llaga *f* (externa)
ulcerate [ˈʌlsəˌreɪt] *vi* **-ated; -ating :** ulcerarse
ulceration [ˌʌlsəˈreɪʃən] *n* **1 :** ulceración *f* **2** ULCER **:** úlcera *f,* llaga *f*
ulcerous [ˈʌlsərəs] *adj* **:** ulceroso
ulna [ˈʌlnə] *n* **:** cúbito *m*
ulterior [ˌʌlˈtɪriər] *adj* **:** oculto <ulterior motive : motivo oculto, segunda intención>
ultimate [ˈʌltəmət] *adj* **1** FINAL **:** último, final **2** SUPREME **:** supremo, máximo **3** FUNDAMENTAL **:** fundamental, esencial
ultimately [ˈʌltəmətli] *adv* **1** FINALLY **:** por último, finalmente **2** EVENTUALLY **:** a la larga, con el tiempo
ultimatum [ˌʌltəˈmeɪt̬əm, -ˈmɑ-] *n, pl* **-tums** *or* **-ta** [-t̬ə] **:** ultimátum *m*
ultraviolet [ˌʌltrəˈvaɪələt] *adj* **:** ultravioleta
umbilical cord [ˌʌmˈbɪlɪkəl] *adj* **:** cordón umbilical
umbrage [ˈʌmbrɪdʒ] *n* **to take umbrage at :** ofenderse por
umbrella [ˌʌmˈbrɛlə] *n* **1 :** paraguas *m* **2 beach umbrella :** sombrilla *f*
umpire[1] [ˈʌmˌpaɪr] *v* **-pired; -piring :** arbitrar
umpire[2] *n* **:** árbitro *m,* -tra *f*
umpteenth [ˌʌmpˈtiːnθ] *adj* **:** enésimo
unable [ˌʌnˈeɪbəl] *adj* **:** incapaz <to be unable to : no poder>
unabridged [ˌʌnəˈbrɪdʒd] *adj* **:** íntegro
unacceptable [ˌʌnɪkˈsɛptəbəl] *adj* **:** inaceptable
unaccompanied [ˌʌnəˈkʌmpənid] *adj* **:** solo, sin acompañamiento (en música)
unaccountable [ˌʌnəˈkaʊntəbəl] *adj* **:** inexplicable, incomprensible — **unaccountably** [-bli] *adv*
unaccustomed [ˌʌnəˈkʌstəmd] *adj* **1** UNUSUAL **:** desacostumbrado, inusual **2** UNUSED **:** inhabituado <unaccustomed to noise : inhabituado al ruido>
unacquainted [ˌʌnəˈkweɪntəd] *adj* **to be unacquainted with :** desconocer, ignorar
unadorned [ˌʌnəˈdɔrnd] *adj* **:** sin adornos, puro y simple
unadulterated [ˌʌnəˈdʌltəˌreɪt̬əd] *adj* **1** PURE **:** puro <unadulterated food : comida pura> **2** ABSOLUTE **:** completo, absoluto
unaffected [ˌʌnəˈfɛktəd] *adj* **1 :** no afectado, indiferente **2** NATURAL **:** sin afectación, natural
unaffectedly [ˌʌnəˈfɛktədli] *adv* **:** de manera natural
unafraid [ˌʌnəˈfreɪd] *adj* **:** sin miedo
unaided [ˌʌnˈeɪdəd] *adj* **:** sin ayuda, solo
unambiguous [ˌʌnæmˈbɪgjʊəs] *adj* **:** inequívoco
unanimity [ˌjuːnəˈnɪmət̬i] *n* **:** unanimidad *f*
unanimous [jʊˈnænəməs] *adj* **:** unánime — **unanimously** *adv*
unannounced [ˌʌnəˈnaʊnst] *adj* **:** sin dar aviso
unanswered [ˌʌnˈæntsərd] *adj* **:** sin contestar
unappealing [ˌʌnəˈpiːlɪŋ] *adj* **:** desagradable
unappetizing [ˌʌnˈæpəˌtaɪzɪŋ] *adj* **:** poco apetitoso, poco apetecible
unarmed [ˌʌnˈɑrmd] *adj* **:** sin armas, desarmado
unassisted [ˌʌnəˈsɪstəd] *adj* **:** sin ayuda
unassuming [ˌʌnəˈsuːmɪŋ] *adj* **:** modesto, sin pretensiones
unattached [ˌʌnəˈtætʃt] *adj* **1** LOOSE **:** suelto **2** INDEPENDENT **:** independiente **3 :** solo (ni casado ni prometido)
unattractive [ˌʌnəˈtræktɪv] *adj* **:** poco atractivo
unauthorized [ˌʌnˈɔθəˌraɪzd] *adj* **:** sin autorización, no autorizado
unavailable [ˌʌnəˈveɪləbəl] *adj* **:** no disponible
unavoidable [ˌʌnəˈvɔɪdəbəl] *adj* **:** inevitable, ineludible
unaware[1] [ˌʌnəˈwær] *adv* → **unawares**
unaware[2] *adj* **:** inconsciente
unawares [ˌʌnəˈwærz] *adv* **1 :** por sorpresa <to catch someone unawares : agarrar a alguien desprevenido> **2** UNINTENTIONALLY **:** inconscientemente, inadvertidamente
unbalanced [ˌʌnˈbæləntst] *adj* **:** desequilibrado
unbearable [ˌʌnˈbærəbəl] *adj* **:** insoportable, inaguantable — **unbearably** [-bli] *adv*
unbecoming [ˌʌnbɪˈkʌmɪŋ] *adj* **1** UNSEEMLY **:** impropio, indecoroso **2** UNFLATTERING **:** poco favorecedor

unbelievable [ˌʌnbəˈliːvəbəl] *adj* : increíble — **unbelievably** [-bli] *adv*
unbend [ˌʌnˈbɛnd] *vi* **-bent** [-ˈbɛnt]; **-bending** RELAX : relajarse
unbending [ˌʌnˈbɛndɪŋ] *adj* : inflexible
unbiased [ˌʌnˈbaɪəst] *adj* : imparcial, objetivo
unbind [ˌʌnˈbaɪnd] *vt* **-bound** [-ˈbaʊnd]; **-binding 1** UNFASTEN, UNTIE : desatar, desamarrar **2** RELEASE : liberar
unbolt [ˌʌnˈboːlt] *vt* : abrir el cerrojo de, descorrer el pestillo de
unborn [ˌʌnˈbɔrn] *adj* : aún no nacido, que va a nacer
unbosom [ˌʌnˈbʊzəm, -ˈbuː-] *vt* : revelar, divulgar
unbreakable [ˌʌnˈbreɪkəbəl] *adj* : irrompible
unbridled [ˌʌnˈbraɪdəld] *adj* : desenfrenado
unbroken [ˌʌnˈbroːkən] *adj* **1** INTACT : intacto, sano **2** CONTINUOUS : continuo, ininterrumpido
unbuckle [ˌʌnˈbʌkəl] *vt* **-led; -ling** : desabrochar
unburden [ˌʌnˈbərdən] *vt* **1** UNLOAD : descargar **2 to unburden oneself** : desahogarse
unbutton [ˌʌnˈbʌtən] *vt* : desabrochar, desabotonar
uncalled–for [ˌʌnˈkɔldˌfɔr] *adj* : inapropiado, innecesario
uncanny [ənˈkæni] *adj* **-nier; -est 1** STRANGE : extraño **2** EXTRAORDINARY : raro, extraordinario — **uncannily** [-ˈkænəli] *adv*
unceasing [ˌʌnˈsiːsɪŋ] *adj* : incesante, continuo — **unceasingly** *adv*
unceremonious [ˌʌnˌsɛrəˈmoːniəs] *adj* **1** INFORMAL : sin ceremonia, sin pompa **2** ABRUPT : abrupto, brusco — **unceremoniously** *adv*
uncertain [ˌʌnˈsərtən] *adj* **1** INDEFINITE : indeterminado **2** UNSURE : incierto, dudoso **3** CHANGEABLE : inestable, variable <uncertain weather : tiempo inestable> **4** HESITANT : indeciso **5** VAGUE : poco claro
uncertainly [ˌʌnˈsərtənli] *adv* : dudosamente, con desconfianza
uncertainty [ˌʌnˈərtənti] *n, pl* **-ties** : duda *f,* incertidumbre *f*
unchangeable [ˌʌnˈtʃeɪndʒəbəl] *adj* : inalterable, inmutable
unchanged [ˌʌnˈtʃeɪndʒd] *adj* : sin cambiar
unchanging [ˌʌnˈtʃeɪdʒɪŋ] *adj* : inalterable, inmutable, firme
uncharacteristic [ˌʌnˌkærɪktəˈrɪstɪk] *adj* : inusual, desacostumbrado
uncharged [ˌʌnˈtʃɑrdʒd] *adj* : sin carga (eléctrica)
uncivilized [ˌʌnˈsɪvəˌlaɪzd] *adj* **1** BARBAROUS : incivilizado, bárbaro **2** WILD : salvaje
uncle [ˈʌŋkəl] *n* : tío *m*
unclean [ˌʌnˈkliːn] *adj* **1** IMPURE : impuro **2** DIRTY : sucio
unclear [ˌʌnˈklɪr] *adj* : confuso, borroso, poco claro
Uncle Sam [ˈsæm] *n* : el Tío Sam
unclog [ˌʌnˈklɑg] *vt* **-clogged; -clogging** : desatascar, destapar
unclothed [ˌʌnˈkloːðd] *adj* : desnudo
uncomfortable [ˌʌnˈkʌmpfərṭəbəl] *adj* **1** : incómodo (dícese de una silla, etc.) **2** UNEASY : inquieto, incómodo
uncommitted [ˌʌnkəˈmɪṭəd] *adj* : sin compromisos
uncommon [ˌʌnˈkɑmən] *adj* **1** UNUSUAL : raro, poco común **2** REMARKABLE : excepcional, extraordinario
uncommonly [ˌʌnˈkɑmənli] *adv* : extraordinariamente
uncompromising [ˌʌnˈkɑmprəˌmaɪzɪŋ] *adj* : inflexible, intransigente
unconcerned [ˌʌnkənˈsərnd] *adj* : indiferente — **unconcernedly** [-ˈsərnədli] *adv*
unconditional [ˌʌnkənˈdɪʃənəl] *adj* : incondicional — **unconditionally** *adv*
unconscious[1] [ˌʌnˈkɑntʃəs] *adj* : inconsciente — **unconsciously** *adv*
unconscious[2] *n* : inconsciente *m*
unconsciousness [ˌʌnˈkɑntʃəsnəs] *n* : inconsciencia *f*
unconstitutional [ˌʌnˌkɑntstəˈtuːʃənəl, -ˈtjuː-] *adj* : inconstitucional
uncontrollable [ˌʌnkənˈtroːləbəl] *adj* : incontrolable, incontenible — **uncontrollably** [-bli] *adv*
uncontrolled [ˌʌnkənˈtroːld] *adj* : incontrolado
unconventional [ˌʌnkənˈvɛntʃənəl] *adj* : poco convencional
unconvincing [ˌʌnkənˈvɪntsɪŋ] *adj* : poco convincente
uncouth [ˌʌnˈkuːθ] *adj* CRUDE, ROUGH : grosero, rudo
uncover [ˌʌnˈkʌvər] *vt* **1** : destapar (un objeto), dejar al descubierto **2** EXPOSE, REVEAL : descubrir, revelar, exponer
uncultivated [ˌʌnˈkʌltəˌveɪṭəd] *adj* : inculto
uncurl [ˌʌnˈkərl] *vt* UNROLL : desenrollar — *vi* : desenrollarse, desrizarse (dícese del pelo)
uncut [ˌʌnˈkʌt] *adj* **1** : sin cortar <uncut grass : hierba sin cortar> **2** : sin tallar, en bruto <an uncut diamond : un diamante en bruto> **3** UNABRIDGED : completo, íntegro
undaunted [ˌʌnˈdɔntəd] *adj* : impávido
undecided [ˌʌndiˈsaɪdəd] *adj* **1** IRRESOLUTE : indeciso, irresoluto **2** UNRESOLVED : pendiente, no resuelto
undefeated [ˌʌndiˈfiːṭəd] *adj* : invicto
undeniable [ˌʌndiˈnaɪəbəl] *adj* : innegable — **undeniably** [-bli] *adv*
under[1] [ˈʌndər] *adv* **1** LESS : menos <$10 or under : $10 o menos> **2** UNDERWATER : debajo del agua **3** : bajo los efectos de la anestesia

under² *adj* **1** LOWER : (más) bajo, inferior **2** SUBORDINATE : inferior **3** : insuficiente <an under dose of medicine : una dosis insuficiente de medicina>

under³ *prep* **1** BELOW, BENEATH : debajo de, abajo de <under the table : abajo de la mesa> <we walked under the arch : pasamos por debajo del arco> <under the sun : bajo el sol> **2** : menos de <in under 20 minutes : en menos de 20 minutos> **3** (*indicating rank or authority*) : bajo <under the command of : bajo las órdenes de> **4** SUBJECT TO : bajo <under suspicion : bajo sospecha> <under the circumstances : dadas las circunstancias> **5** ACCORDING TO : según, de acuerdo con, conforme a <under the present laws : según las leyes actuales>

underage [ˌʌndərˈeɪdʒ] *adj* : menor de edad

underbrush [ˈʌndərˌbrəʃ] *n* : maleza *f*

underclothes [ˈʌndərˌklo:z, -ˌklo:ðz] → **underwear**

underclothing [ˈʌndərˌklo:ðɪŋ] → **underwear**

undercover [ˌʌndərˈkʌvər] *adj* : secreto, clandestino

undercurrent [ˈʌndərˌkərənt] *n* **1** : corriente *f* submarina **2** UNDERTONE : corriente *f* oculta, trasfondo *m*

undercut [ˌʌndərˈkʌt] *vt* **-cut; -cutting** : vender más barato que

underdeveloped [ˌʌndərdɪˈvɛləpt] *adj* : subdesarrollado, atrasado

underdog [ˈʌndərˌdɔg] *n* : persona *f* que tiene menos posibilidades

underdone [ˌʌndərˈdʌn] *adj* RARE : poco cocido

underestimate [ˌʌndərˈɛstəˌmeɪt] *vt* **-mated; -mating** : subestimar, menospreciar

underexposed [ˌʌndərɪkˈspo:zd] *adj* : subexpuesto (en fotografía)

underfoot [ˌʌndərˈfʊt] *adv* **1** : bajo los pies <to trample underfoot : pisotear> **2 to be underfoot** : estorbar <they're always underfoot : están siempre estorbando>

undergarment [ˈʌndərˌgɑrmənt] *n* : prenda *f* íntima

undergo [ˌʌndərˈgo:] *vt* **-went** [-ˈwɛnt;]; **-gone** [-ˈgɔn]; **-going** : sufrir, experimentar <to undergo an operation : someterse a una intervención quirúrgica>

undergraduate [ˌʌndərˈgrædʒʊət] *n* : estudiante *m* universitario, estudiante *f* universitaria

underground¹ [ˌʌndərˈgraʊnd] *adv* **1** : bajo tierra **2** SECRETLY : clandestinamente, en secreto <to go underground : pasar a la clandestinidad>

underground² [ˈʌndərˌgraʊnd] *adj* **1** SUBTERRANEAN : subterráneo **2** SECRET : secreto, clandestino

underground³ [ˈʌndərˌgraʊnd] *n* : movimiento *m* o grupo *m* clandestino

undergrowth [ˈʌndərˈgro:θ] *n* : maleza *f*, broza *f*

underhand¹ [ˈʌndərˌhænd] *adv* **1** SECRETLY : de manera clandestina **2** *or* **underhanded** : sin levantar el brazo por encima del hombro (en deportes)

underhand² *adj* **1** SLY : solapado **2** : por debajo del hombro (en deportes)

underhanded [ˌʌndərˈhændəd] *adj* **1** SLY : solapado **2** SHADY : turbio, poco limpio

underline [ˈʌndərˌlaɪn] *vt* **-lined; -lining 1** : subrayar **2** EMPHASIZE : subrayar, acentuar, hacer hincapié en

underlying [ˌʌndərˈlaɪɪŋ] *adj* **1** : subyacente <the underlying rock : la roca subyacente> **2** FUNDAMENTAL : fundamental, esencial

undermine [ˌʌndərˈmaɪn] *vt* **-mined; -mining 1** : socavar (una estructura, etc.) **2** SAP, WEAKEN : minar, debilitar

underneath¹ [ˌʌndərˈni:θ] *adv* : debajo, abajo <the part underneath : la parte de abajo>

underneath² *prep* : debajo de, abajo de

undernourished [ˌʌndərˈnərɪʃt] *adj* : desnutrido

underpants [ˈʌndərˌpænts] *npl* : calzoncillos *mpl*, calzones *mpl*

underpass [ˈʌndərˌpæs] *n* : paso *m* a desnivel

underprivileged [ˌʌndərˈprɪvlɪdʒd] *adj* : desfavorecido

underrate [ˌʌndərˈreɪt] *vt* **-rated; -rating** : subestimar, menospreciar

underscore [ˈʌndərˌskor] *vt* **-scored; -scoring** → **underline**

undersea¹ [ˌʌndərˈsi:] *or* **underseas** [-ˈsi:z] *adv* : bajo la superficie del mar

undersea² *adj* : submarino

undersecretary [ˌʌndərˈsɛkrəˌtɛri] *n, pl* **-ries** : subsecretario *m*, -ria *f*

undersell [ˌʌndərˈsɛl] *vt* **-sold; -selling** : vender más barato que

undershirt [ˈʌndərˌʃərt] *n* : camiseta *f*

undershorts [ˈʌndərˌʃɔrts] *npl* : calzoncillos *mpl*

underside [ˈʌndərˌsaɪd, ˌʌndərˈsaɪd] *n* : parte *f* de abajo

undersized [ˌʌndərˈsaɪzd] *adj* : más pequeño de lo normal

understand [ˌʌndərˈstænd] *v* **-stood** [-ˈstʊd;]; **-standing** *vt* **1** COMPREHEND : comprender, entender <I don't understand it : no lo entiendo> <that's understood : eso se comprende> <to make oneself understood : hacerse entender> **2** BELIEVE : entender <to give someone to understand : dar a alguien a entender> **3** INFER : tener entendido <I understand that she's leaving : tengo entendido que se va> — *vi* : comprender, entender

understandable [ˌʌndərˈstændəbəl] *adj* : comprensible

understanding[1] [ˌʌndərˈstændɪŋ] *adj* : comprensivo, compasivo
understanding[2] *n* **1** GRASP : comprensión *f,* entendimiento *m* **2** SYMPATHY : comprensión *f* (mutua) **3** INTERPRETATION : interpretación *f* <it's my understanding that... : tengo la impresión de que..., tengo entendido que...> **4** AGREEMENT : acuerdo *m,* arreglo *m*
understate [ˌʌndərˈsteɪt] *vt* **-stated; -stating** : minimizar, subestimar
understatement [ˌʌndərˈsteɪtmənt] *n* : atenuación *f* <that's an understatement : decir sólo eso es quedarse corto>
understudy [ˈʌndərˌstʌdi] *n, pl* **-dies** : sobresaliente *mf,* suplente *mf* (en el teatro)
undertake [ˌʌndərˈteɪk] *vt* **-took** [-ˈtʊk]; **-taken** [-ˈteɪkən]; **-taking 1** : emprender (una tarea), asumir (una responsabilidad) **2** PROMISE : comprometerse (a hacer algo)
undertaker [ˈʌndərˌteɪkər] *n* : director *m,* -tora *f* de funeraria
undertaking [ˈʌndərˌteɪkɪŋ, ˌʌndərˈ-] *n* **1** ENTERPRISE, TASK : empresa *f,* tarea *f* **2** PLEDGE : promesa *f,* garantía *f*
undertone [ˈʌndərˌtoːn] *n* **1** : voz *f* baja <to speak in an undertone : hablar en voz baja> **2** HINT, UNDERCURRENT : trasfondo *m,* matiz *m*
undertow [ˈʌndərˌtoː] *n* : resaca *f*
undervalue [ˌʌndərˈvælˌjuː] *vt* **-ued; -uing** : menospreciar, subestimar
underwater[1] [ˌʌndərˈwɔt̬ər, -ˈwɑ-] *adv* : debajo (del agua)
underwater[2] *adj* : submarino
under way [ˌʌndərˈweɪ] *adv* : en marcha, en camino <to get under way : ponerse en marcha>
underwear [ˈʌndərˌwær] *n* : ropa *f* interior, ropa *f* íntima
underworld [ˈʌndərˌwərld] *n* **1** HELL : infierno *m* **2 the underworld** CRIMINALS : la hampa, los bajos fondos
underwrite [ˈʌndərˌraɪt, ˌʌndərˈ-] *vt* **-wrote** [-ˌroːt, -ˈroːt]; **-written** [-ˌrɪtən, -ˈrɪtən]; **-writing 1** INSURE : asegurar **2** FINANCE : financiar **3** BACK, ENDORSE : suscribir, respaldar
underwriter [ˈʌndərˌraɪt̬ər, ˌʌndərˈ-] *n* INSURER : asegurador *m,* -dora *f*
undeserving [ˌʌndiˈzərvɪŋ] *adj* : indigno
undesirable[1] [ˌʌndiˈzaɪrəbəl] *adj* : indeseable
undesirable[2] *n* : indeseable *mf*
undeveloped [ˌʌndiˈvɛləpt] *adj* : sin desarrollar, sin revelar (dícese de una película)
undies [ˈʌndiːz] → **underwear**
undignified [ˌʌnˈdɪgnəfaɪd] *adj* : indecoroso
undiluted [ˌʌndaɪˈluːtəd, -də-] *adj* : sin diluir, concentrado
undiscovered [ˌʌndɪˈskʌvərd] *adj* : no descubierto
undisputed [ˌʌndɪˈspjuːt̬əd] *adj* : indiscutible
undisturbed [ˌʌndɪˈstərbd] *adj* : tranquilo (dícese de una persona), sin tocar (dícese de un objeto)
undivided [ˌʌndɪˈvaɪdəd] *adj* : íntegro, completo
undo [ˌʌnˈduː] *vt* **-did** [-ˈdɪd]; **-done** [-ˈdʌn]; **-doing 1** UNFASTEN : desabrochar, desatar, abrir **2** ANNUL : anular **3** REVERSE : deshacer, reparar (daños, etc.) **4** RUIN : arruinar, destruir
undoing [ˌʌnˈduːɪŋ] *n* : ruina *f,* perdición *f*
undoubted [ˌʌnˈdaʊt̬əd] *adj* : cierto, indudable — **undoubtedly** *adv*
undress [ˌʌnˈdrɛs] *vt* : desvestir, desabrigar, desnudar — *vi* : desvestirse, desnudarse
undrinkable [ˌʌnˈdrɪŋkəbəl] *adj* : no potable
undue [ˌʌnˈduː, -ˈdjuː] *adj* : excesivo, indebido — **unduly** *adv*
undulate [ˈʌndʒəˌleɪt] *vi* **-lated; -lating** : ondular
undulation [ˌʌndʒəˈleɪʃən] *n* : ondulación *f*
undying [ˌʌnˈdaɪɪŋ] *adj* : perpetuo, imperecedero
unearth [ˌʌnˈərθ] *vt* **1** EXHUME : desenterrar, exhumar **2** DISCOVER : descubrir
unearthly [ˌʌnˈərθli] *adj* **-lier; -est** : sobrenatural, de otro mundo
uneasily [ˌʌnˈiːzəli] *adv* : inquietamente, con inquietud
uneasiness [ˌʌnˈiːzinəs] *n* : inquietud *f*
uneasy [ˌʌnˈiːzi] *adj* **-easier; -est 1** AWKWARD : incómodo **2** WORRIED : preocupado, inquieto **3** RESTLESS : inquieto, agitado
uneducated [ˌʌnˈɛdʒəˌkeɪt̬əd] *adj* : inculto, sin educación
unemployed [ˌʌnɪmˈplɔɪd] *adj* : desempleado
unemployment [ˌʌnɪmˈplɔɪmənt] *n* : desempleo *m*
unending [ˌʌnˈɛndɪŋ] *adj* : sin fin, interminable
unendurable [ˌʌnɪnˈdʊrəbəl, -ɛn-, -ˈdjʊr-] *adj* : insoportable, intolerable
unequal [ˌʌnˈiːkwəl] *adj* **1** : desigual **2** INADEQUATE : incapaz, incompetente <to be unequal to a task : no estar a la altura de una tarea>
unequaled *or* **unequalled** [ˌʌnˈiːkwəld] *adj* : sin igual
unequivocal [ˌʌnɪˈkwɪvəkəl] *adj* : inequívoco, claro — **unequivocally** *adv*
unerring [ˌʌnˈɛrɪŋ, -ˈər-] *adj* : infalible
unethical [ˌʌnˈɛθɪkəl] *adj* : poco ético
uneven [ˌʌnˈiːvən] *adj* **1** ODD : impar (dícese de un número) **2** : desigual, desnivelado (dícese de una superficie) <uneven terrain : terreno accidentado> **3** IRREGULAR : irregular, poco uniforme **4** UNEQUAL : desigual

unevenly [ˌʌnˈiːvənli] *adv* : desigualmente, irregularmente
uneventful [ˌʌnɪˈvɛntfəl] *adj* : sin incidentes, tranquilo
unexpected [ˌʌnɪkˈspɛktəd] *adj* : imprevisto, inesperado — **unexpectedly** *adv*
unfailing [ˌʌnˈfeɪlɪŋ] *adj* **1** CONSTANT : constante **2** INEXHAUSTIBLE : inagotable **3** SURE : a toda prueba, indefectible
unfair [ˌʌnˈfær] *adj* : injusto — **unfairly** *adv*
unfairness [ˌʌnˈfærnəs] *n* : injusticia *f*
unfaithful [ˌʌnˈfeɪθfəl] *adj* : desleal, infiel — **unfaithfully** *adv*
unfaithfulness [ˌʌnˈfeɪθfəlnəs] *n* : infidelidad *f*, deslealtad *f*
unfamiliar [ˌʌnfəˈmɪljər] *adj* **1** STRANGE : desconocido, extraño <an unfamiliar place : un lugar nuevo> **2 to be unfamiliar with** : no estar familiarizado con, desconocer
unfamiliarity [ˌʌnfəˌmɪliˈærət̬i] *n* : falta *f* de familiaridad
unfashionable [ˌʌnˈfæʃənəbəl] *adj* : fuera de moda
unfasten [ˌʌnˈfæsən] *vt* : desabrochar, desatar (una cuerda, etc.), abrir (una puerta)
unfavorable [ˌʌnˈfeɪvərəbəl] *adj* : desfavorable, mal — **unfavorably** [-bli] *adv*
unfeeling [ˌʌnˈfiːlɪŋ] *adj* : insensible — **unfeelingly** *adv*
unfinished [ˌʌnˈfɪnɪʃd] *adj* : inacabado, incompleto
unfit [ˌʌnˈfɪt] *adj* **1** UNSUITABLE : inadecuado, impropio **2** UNSUITED : no apto, incapaz **3** : incapacitado (físicamente) <to be unfit : no estar en forma>
unflappable [ˌʌnˈflæpəbəl] *adj* : imperturbable
unflattering [ˌʌnˈflæt̬ərɪŋ] *adj* : poco favorecedor
unfold [ˌʌnˈfoːld] *vt* **1** EXPAND : desplegar, desdoblar, extender <to unfold a map : desplegar un mapa> **2** DISCLOSE, REVEAL : revelar, exponer (un plan, etc.) — *vi* **1** DEVELOP : desarrollarse, desenvolverse <the story unfolded : el cuento se desarrollaba> **2** EXPAND : extenderse, desplegarse
unforeseeable [ˌʌnforˈsiːəbəl] *adj* : imprevisible
unforeseen [ˌʌnforˈsiːn] *adj* : imprevisto
unforgettable [ˌʌnfərˈgɛt̬əbəl] *adj* : inolvidable, memorable — **unforgettably** [-bli] *adv*
unforgivable [ˌʌnfərˈgɪvəbəl] *adj* : imperdonable
unfortunate[1] [ˌʌnˈfɔrtʃənət] *adj* **1** UNLUCKY : desgraciado, infortunado, desafortunado <how unfortunate! : ¡qué mala suerte!> **2** INAPPROPRIATE : inoportuno <an unfortunate comment : un comentario poco feliz>
unfortunate[2] *n* : desgraciado *m*, -da *f*
unfortunately [ˌʌnˈfɔrtʃənətli] *adv* : desafortunadamente
unfounded [ˌʌnˈfaʊndəd] *adj* : infundado
unfreeze [ˌʌnˈfriːz] *v* **-froze** [-ˈfroːz]; **-frozen** [-ˈfroːzən]; **-freezing** *vt* : descongelar — *vi* : descongelarse
unfriendliness [ˌʌnˈfrɛndlinəs] *n* : hostilidad *f*, antipatía *f*
unfriendly [ˌʌnˈfrɛndli] *adj* **-lier; -est** : poco amistoso, hostil
unfurl [ˌʌnˈfərl] *vt* : desplegar, desdoblar — *vi* : desplegarse
unfurnished [ˌʌnˈfərnɪʃt] *adj* : desamueblado
ungainly [ˌʌnˈgeɪnli] *adj* : desgarbado
ungodly [ˌʌnˈgɔdli, -ˈgɑd-] *adj* **1** IMPIOUS : impío **2** OUTRAGEOUS : atroz, terrible <at an ungodly hour : a una hora intempestiva>
ungrateful [ˌʌnˈgreɪtfəl] *adj* : desagradecido, ingrato — **ungratefully** *adv*
ungratefulness [ˌʌnˈgreɪtfəlnəs] *n* : ingratitud *f*
unhappily [ˌʌnˈhæpəli] *adv* **1** SADLY : tristemente **2** UNFORTUNATELY : desafortunadamente, lamentablemente
unhappiness [ˌʌnˈhæpinəs] *n* : infelicidad *f*, tristeza *f*, desdicha *f*
unhappy [ˌʌnˈhæpi] *adj* **-pier; -est 1** UNFORTUNATE : desafortunado, desventurado **2** MISERABLE, SAD : infeliz, triste, desdichado **3** INOPPORTUNE : inoportuno, poco feliz
unharmed [ˌʌnˈhɑrmd] *adj* : salvo, ileso
unhealthy [ˌʌnˈhɛlθi] *adj* **-thier; -est 1** UNWHOLESOME : insalubre, malsano, nocivo a la salud <an unhealthy climate : un clima insalubre> **2** SICKLY : de mala salud, enfermizo
unheard–of [ˌʌnˈhərdəv] *adj* : sin precedente, inaudito, insólito
unhinge [ˌʌnˈhɪndʒ] *vt* **-hinged; -hinging 1** : desquiciar (una puerta, etc.) **2** DISRUPT, UNSETTLE : trastornar, perturbar
unholy [ˌʌnˈhoːli] *adj* **-lier; -est 1** : profano, impío **2** UNGODLY : atroz, terrible
unhook [ˌʌnˈhʊk] *vt* **1** : desenganchar, descolgar (de algo) **2** UNDO : desabrochar
unhurt [ˌʌnˈhərt] *adj* : ileso
unicorn [ˈjuːnəˌkɔrn] *n* : unicornio *m*
unidentified [ˌʌnaɪˈdɛntəˌfaɪd] *adj* : no identificado <unidentified flying object : objeto volador no identificado>
unification [ˌjuːnəfəˈkeɪʃən] *n* : unificación *f*
uniform[1] [ˈjuːnəˌfɔrm] *adj* : uniforme, homogéneo, constante
uniform[2] *n* : uniforme *m*
uniformity [ˌjuːnəˈfɔrmət̬i] *n, pl* **-ties** : uniformidad *f*

unify [ˈjuːnəˌfaɪ] *vt* **-fied; -fying** : unificar, unir

unilateral [ˌjuːnəˈlætərəl] *adj* : unilateral — **unilaterally** *adv*

unimaginable [ˌʌnɪˈmædʒənəbəl] *adj* : inimaginable, inconcebible

unimportant [ˌʌnɪmˈpɔrtənt] *adj* : intrascendente, insignificante, sin importancia

uninhabited [ˌʌnɪnˈhæbət̬əd] *adj* : deshabitado, desierto, despoblado

uninhibited [ˌʌnɪnˈhɪbət̬əd] *adj* : desenfadado, desinhibido, sin reservas

uninjured [ˌʌnˈindʒərd] *adj* : ileso

unintelligent [ˌʌnɪnˈtɛlədʒənt] *adj* : poco inteligente

unintelligible [ˌʌnɪnˈtɛlədʒəbəl] *adj* : ininteligible, incomprensible

unintentional [ˌʌnɪnˈtɛntʃənəl] *adj* : no deliberado, involuntario

unintentionally [ˌʌnɪnˈtɛntʃənəli] *adv* : involuntariamente, sin querer

uninterested [ˌʌnˈɪntəˌrɛstəd, -trəstəd] *adj* : indiferente

uninteresting [ˌʌnˈɪntəˌrɛstɪŋ, -trəstɪŋ] *adj* : poco interesante, sin interés

uninterrupted [ˌʌnˌɪntəˈrʌptəd] *adj* : ininterrumpido, continuo

union [ˈjuːnjən] *n* **1** : unión *f* **2** *or* **labor union** : sindicato *m*, gremio *m*

unionize [ˈjuːnjəˌnaɪz] *v* **-ized; -izing** *vt* : sindicalizar, sindicar — *vi* : sindicalizarse

unique [jʊˈniːk] *adj* **1** SOLE : único, solo **2** UNUSUAL : extraordinario

uniquely [jʊˈniːkli] *adv* **1** EXCLUSIVELY : exclusivamente **2** EXCEPTIONALLY : excepcionalmente

unison [ˈjuːnəsən, -zən] *n* **1** : unísono *m* (en música) **2** CONCORD : acuerdo *m*, armonía *f*, concordia *f* **3 in ~** SIMULTANEOUSLY : simultáneamente, al unísono

unit [ˈjuːnɪt] *n* **1** : unidad *f* **2** : módulo *m* (de un mobiliario)

unite [jʊˈnaɪt] *v* **united; uniting** *vt* : unir, juntar, combinar — *vi* : unirse, juntarse

unity [ˈjuːnət̬i] *n, pl* **-ties 1** UNION : unidad *f*, unión *f* **2** HARMONY : armonía *f*, acuerdo *m*

universal [ˌjuːnəˈvərsəl] *adj* **1** GENERAL : general, universal <a universal rule : una regla universal> **2** WORLDWIDE : universal, mundial — **universally** *adv*

universe [ˈjuːnəˌvərs] *n* : universo *m*

university [ˌjuːnəˈvərsət̬i] *n, pl* **-ties** : universidad *f*

unjust [ˌʌnˈdʒʌst] *adj* : injusto — **unjustly** *adv*

unjustifiable [ˌʌnˌdʒʌstəˈfaɪəbəl] *adj* : injustificable

unjustified [ˌʌnˈdʒʌstəˌfaɪd] *adj* : injustificado

unkempt [ˌʌnˈkɛmpt] *adj* : descuidado, desaliñado, despeinado (dícese del pelo)

unkind [ˌʌnˈkaɪnd] *adj* : poco amable, cruel — **unkindly** *adv*

unkindness [ˌʌnˈkaɪndnəs] *n* : crueldad *f*, falta *f* de amabilidad

unknowing [ˌʌnˈnoːɪŋ] *adj* : inconsciente, ignorante — **unknowingly** *adv*

unknown [ˌʌnˈnoːn] *adj* : desconocido

unlawful [ˌʌnˈlɔfəl] *adj* : ilícito, ilegal — **unlawfully** *adv*

unleash [ˌʌnˈliːʃ] *vt* : soltar, desatar

unless [ənˈlɛs] *conj* : a menos que, salvo que, a no ser que

unlike[1] [ˌʌnˈlaɪk] *adj* **1** DIFFERENT : diferente, distinto **2** UNEQUAL : desigual

unlike[2] *prep* **1** : diferente de, distinto de <unlike the others : distinto a los demás> **2** : a diferencia de <unlike her sister, she is shy : a diferencia de su hermana, es tímida>

unlikelihood [ˌʌnˈlaɪkliˌhʊd] *n* : improbabilidad *f*

unlikely [ˌʌnˈlaɪkli] *adj* **-lier; -est 1** IMPROBABLE : improbable, poco probable **2** UNPROMISING : poco prometedor

unlimited [ˌʌnˈlɪmət̬əd] *adj* : ilimitado

unload [ˌʌnˈloːd] *vt* **1** REMOVE : descargar, desembarcar (mercancías o pasajeros) **2** : descargar (un avión, un camión, etc.) **3** DUMP : deshacerse de — *vi* : descargar (dícese de un avión, un camión, etc.)

unlock [ˌʌnˈlɑk] *vt* **1** : abrir (con llave) **2** DISCLOSE, REVEAL : revelar

unluckily [ˌʌnˈlʌkəli] *adv* : desgraciadamente

unlucky [ˌʌnˈlʌki] *adj* **-luckier; -est 1** : de mala suerte, desgraciado, desafortunado <an unlucky year : un año de mala suerte> **2** INAUSPICIOUS : desfavorable, poco propicio **3** REGRETTABLE : lamentable

unmanageable [ˌʌnˈmænɪdʒəbəl] *adj* : difícil de controlar, poco manejable, ingobernable

unmarried [ˌʌnˈmærid] *adj* : soltero

unmask [ˌʌnˈmæsk] *vt* EXPOSE : desenmascarar

unmerciful [ˌʌnˈmərsɪfəl] *adj* MERCILESS : despiadado — **unmercifully** *adv*

unmistakable [ˌʌnmɪˈsteɪkəbəl] *adj* : evidente, inconfundible, obvio — **unmistakably** [-bli] *adv*

unmoved [ˌʌnˈmuːvd] *adj* : impasible <to be unmoved by : permanecer impasible ante>

unnatural [ˌʌnˈnætʃərəl] *adj* **1** ABNORMAL, UNUSUAL : anormal, poco natural, poco normal **2** AFFECTED : afectado, forzado <an unnatural smile : una sonrisa forzada> **3** PERVERSE : perverso, antinatural

unnecessary [ˌʌnˈnɛsəˌsɛri] *adj* : innecesario — **unnecessarily** [-ˌnɛsəˈsɛrəli] *adv*

unnerve [ˌʌnˈnərv] *vt* **-nerved; -nerving** : turbar, desconcertar, poner nervioso
unnoticed [ˌʌnˈnoːt̬əst] *adj* : inadvertido <to go unnoticed : pasar inadvertido>
unobstructed [ˌʌnəbˈstrʌktəd] *adj* : libre, despejado
unobtainable [ˌʌnəbˈteɪnəbəl] *adj* : inasequible
unobtrusive [ˌʌnəbˈstruːsɪv] *adj* : discreto
unoccupied [ˌʌnˈɑkjəˌpaɪd] *adj* **1** IDLE : desempleado, desocupado **2** EMPTY : desocupado, libre, deshabitado
unofficial [ˌʌnəˈfɪʃəl] *adj* : extraoficial, oficioso, no oficial
unorganized [ˌʌnˈɔrgəˌnaɪzd] *adj* : desorganizado
unorthodox [ˌʌnˈɔrθəˌdɑks] *adj* : poco ortodoxo, poco convencional
unpack [ˌʌnˈpæk] *vt* : desempacar — *vi* : desempacar, deshacer las maletas
unpaid [ˌʌnˈpeɪd] *adj* : no remunerado, no retribuido <an unpaid bill : una cuenta pendiente>
unparalleled [ˌʌnˈpærəˌlɛld] *adj* : sin igual
unpatriotic [ˌʌnˌpeɪtriˈɑt̬ɪk] *adj* : antipatriótico
unpleasant [ˌʌnˈplɛzənt] *adj* : desagradable — **unpleasantly** *adv*
unplug [ˌʌnˈplʌg] *vt* **-plugged; -plugging 1** UNCLOG : destapar, desatascar **2** DISCONNECT : desconectar, desenchufar
unpopular [ˌʌnˈpɑpjələr] *adj* : impopular, poco popular
unpopularity [ˌʌnˌpɑpjəˈlærət̬i] *n* : impopularidad *f*
unprecedented [ˌʌnˈprɛsəˌdɛntəd] *adj* : sin precedentes, inaudito, nuevo
unpredictable [ˌʌnpriˈdɪktəbəl] *adj* : impredecible
unprejudiced [ˌʌnˈprɛdʒədəst] *adj* : imparcial, objetivo
unprepared [ˌʌnpriˈpærd] *adj* : no preparado <an unprepared speech : un discurso improvisado>
unpretentious [ˌʌnpriˈtɛntʃəs] *adj* : modesto, sin pretensiones
unprincipled [ˌʌnˈprɪntsəpəld] *adj* : sin principios, carente de escrúpulos
unproductive [ˌʌnprəˈdʌktɪv] *adj* : improductivo
unprofitable [ˌʌnˈprɑfət̬əbəl] *adj* : no rentable, poco provechoso
unpromising [ˌʌnˈprɑməsɪŋ] *adj* : poco prometedor
unprotected [ˌʌnprəˈtɛktəd] *adj* : sin protección, desprotegido
unprovoked [ˌʌnprəˈvoːkt] *adj* : no provocado
unpunished [ˌʌnˈpʌnɪʃt] *adj* : impune <to go unpunished : escapar sin castigo>
unqualified [ˌʌnˈkwɑləˌfaɪd] *adj* **1** : no calificado, sin título **2** COMPLETE : completo, absoluto <an unqualified denial : una negación incondicional>
unquestionable [ˌʌnˈkwɛstʃənəbəl] *adj* : incuestionable, indudable, indiscutible — **unquestionably** [-bli] *adv*
unquestioning [ˌʌnˈkwɛstʃənɪŋ] *adj* : incondicional, absoluto, ciego
unravel [ˌʌnˈrævəl] *v* **-eled** *or* **-elled; -eling** *or* **-elling** *vt* **1** DISENTANGLE : desenmarañar, desenredar **2** SOLVE : aclarar, desenmarañar, desentrañar — *vi* : deshacerse
unreal [ˌʌnˈriːl] *adj* : irreal
unrealistic [ˌʌnˌriːəˈlɪstɪk] *adj* : poco realista
unreasonable [ˌʌnˈriːzənəbəl] *adj* **1** IRRATIONAL : poco razonable, irrazonable, irracional **2** EXCESSIVE : excesivo <unreasonable prices : precios excesivos>
unreasonably [ˌʌnˈriːzənəbli] *adv* **1** IRRATIONALLY : irracionalmente, de manera irrazonable **2** EXCESSIVELY : excesivamente
unrefined [ˌʌnriˈfaɪnd] *adj* **1** : no refinado, sin refinar (dícese del azúcar, de la harina, etc.) **2** : poco refinado, inculto (dícese de una persona)
unrelated [ˌʌnriˈleɪt̬əd] *adj* : no relacionado, inconexo
unrelenting [ˌʌnriˈlɛntɪŋ] *adj* **1** STERN : severo, inexorable **2** CONSTANT, RELENTLESS : constante, implacable
unreliable [ˌʌnriˈlaɪəbəl] *adj* : que no es de fiar, de poca confianza, inestable (dícese del tiempo)
unrepentant [ˌʌnriˈpɛntənt] *adj* : impenitente
unresolved [ˌʌnriˈzɑlvd] *adj* : pendiente, no resuelto
unrest [ˌʌnˈrɛst] *n* : inquietud *f*, malestar *m* <political unrest : disturbios políticos>
unrestrained [ˌʌnriˈstreɪnd] *adj* : desenfrenado, incontrolado
unrestricted [ˌʌnriˈstrɪktəd] *adj* : sin restricción <unrestricted access : libre acceso>
unrewarding [ˌʌnriˈwɔrdɪŋ] *adj* THANKLESS : ingrato
unripe [ˌʌnˈraɪp] *adj* : inmaduro, verde
unrivaled *or* **unrivalled** [ˌʌnˈraɪvəld] *adj* : incomparable
unroll [ˌʌnˈroːl] *vt* : desenrollar — *vi* : desenrollarse
unruffled [ˌʌnˈrʌfəld] *adj* **1** SERENE : sereno, tranquilo **2** SMOOTH : tranquilo, liso <unruffled waters : aguas tranquilas>
unruliness [ˌʌnˈruːlinəs] *n* : indisciplina *f*
unruly [ˌʌnˈruːli] *adj* : indisciplinado, díscolo, rebelde
unsafe [ˌʌnˈseɪf] *adj* : inseguro
unsaid [ˌʌnˈsɛd] *adj* : sin decir <to leave unsaid : quedar por decir>
unsanitary [ˌʌnˈsænəˌtɛri] *adj* : antihigiénico

unsatisfactory [ˌʌnˌsæt̬əsˈfæktəri] *adj* : insatisfactorio
unsatisfied [ˌʌnˈsæt̬əsˌfaɪd] *adj* : insatisfecho
unscathed [ˌʌnˈskeɪðd] *adj* UNHARMED : ileso
unscheduled [ˌʌnˈskɛˌdʒuːld] *adj* : no programado, imprevisto
unscientific [ˌʌnˌsaɪənˈtɪfɪk] *adj* : poco científico
unscrupulous [ˌʌnˈskruːpjələs] *adj* : inescrupuloso, sin escrúpulos — **unscrupulously** *adv*
unseal [ˌʌnˈsiːl] *vt* : abrir, quitarle el sello a
unseasonable [ˌʌnˈsiːzənəbəl] *adj* **1** : extemporáneo <unseasonable rain : lluvia extemporánea> **2** UNTIMELY : extemporáneo, inoportuno
unseemly [ˌʌnˈsiːmli] *adj* **-lier; -est 1** INDECOROUS : indecoroso **2** INAPPROPRIATE : impropio, inapropiado
unseen [ˌʌnˈsiːn] *adj* **1** UNNOTICED : inadvertido **2** INVISIBLE : oculto, invisible
unselfish [ˌʌnˈsɛlfɪʃ] *adj* : generoso, desinteresado — **unselfishly** *adv*
unselfishness [ˌʌnˈsɛlfɪʃnəs] *n* : generosidad *f,* desinterés *m*
unsettle [ˌʌnˈsɛt̬əl] *vt* **-tled; -tling** DISTURB : trastornar, alterar, perturbar
unsettled [ˌʌnˈsɛt̬əld] *adj* **1** CHANGEABLE : inestable, variable <unsettled weather : tiempo inestable> **2** DISTURBED : agitado, inquieto <unsettled waters : aguas agitadas> **3** UNDECIDED : pendiente (dícese de un asunto), indeciso (dícese de una persona) **4** UNPAID : sin saldar, pendiente **5** UNINHABITED : despoblado, no colonizado
unshaped [ˌʌnˈʃeɪpt] *adj* : sin forma, informe
unsightly [ˌʌnˈsaɪtli] *adj* UGLY : feo, de aspecto malo
unskilled [ˌʌnˈskɪld] *adj* : no calificado
unskillful [ˌʌnˈskɪlfəl] *adj* : inexperto, poco hábil
unsnap [ˌʌnˈsnæp] *vt* **-snapped; -snapping** : desabrochar
unsociable *adj* : poco sociable
unsolved [ˌʌnˈsɔlvd] *adj* : no resuelto, sin resolver
unsophisticated [ˌʌnsəˈfɪstəˌkeɪt̬əd] *adj* **1** NAIVE, UNWORLDLY : ingenuo, de poco mundo **2** SIMPLE : simple, poco sofisticado, rudimentario
unsound [ˌʌnˈsaʊnd] *adj* **1** UNHEALTHY : enfermizo, de mala salud **2** : poco sólido, defectuoso (dícese de una estructura, etc.) **3** INVALID : inválido, erróneo **4 of unsound mind** : mentalmente incapacitado
unspeakable [ˌʌnˈspiːkəbəl] *adj* **1** INDESCRIBABLE : indecible, inexpresable, incalificable **2** HEINOUS : atroz, nefando, abominable — **unspeakably** [-bli] *adv*
unspecified [ˌʌnˈspɛsəˌfaɪd] *adj* : indeterminado, sin especificar
unspoiled [ˌʌnˈspɔɪld] *adj* **1** : conservado, sin estropear (dícese de un lugar) **2** : que no está mimado (dícese de un niño)
unstable [ˌʌnˈsteɪbəl] *adj* **1** CHANGEABLE : variable, inestable, cambiable <an unstable pulse : un pulso irregular> **2** UNSTEADY : inestable, poco sólido (dícese de una estructura)
unsteadily [ˌʌnˈstɛdəli] *adv* : de modo inestable
unsteadiness [ˌʌnˈstɛdinəs] *n* : inestabilidad *f,* inseguridad *f*
unsteady [ˌʌnˈstɛdi] *adj* **1** UNSTABLE : inestable, variable **2** SHAKY : tembloroso
unstoppable [ˌʌnˈstɑpəbəl] *adj* : irrefrenable, incontenible
unsubstantiated [ˌʌnsəbˈstæntʃiˌeɪt̬əd] *adj* : no corroborado, no demostrado
unsuccessful [ˌʌnsəkˈsɛsfəl] *adj* : fracasado, infructuoso
unsuitable [ˌʌnˈsuːt̬əbəl] *adj* : inadecuado, impropio, inapropiado <an unsuitable time : una hora inconveniente>
unsuited [ˌʌnˈsuːt̬əd] *adj* : inadecuado, inepto
unsung [ˌʌnˈsʌŋ] *adj* : olvidado
unsure [ˌʌnˈʃʊr] *adj* : incierto, dudoso
unsurpassed [ˌʌnsərˈpæst] *adj* : sin par, sin igual
unsuspecting [ˌʌnsəˈspɛktɪŋ] *adj* : desprevenido, desapercibido, confiado
unsympathetic [ˌʌnˌsɪmpəˈθɛtɪk] *adj* : poco comprensivo, indiferente
untangle [ˌʌnˈteɪŋgəl] *vt* **-gled; -gling** : desenmarañar, desenredar
unthinkable [ˌʌnˈθɪŋkəbəl] *adj* : inconcebible, impensable
unthinking [ˌʌnˈθɪŋkɪŋ] *adj* : irreflexivo, inconsciente — **unthinkingly** *adv*
untidy [ˌʌnˈtaɪdi] *adj* **1** SLOVENLY : desaliñado **2** DISORDERLY : desordenado, desarreglado
untie [ˌʌnˈtaɪ] *vt* **-tied; -tying** *or* **-tieing** : desatar, deshacer
until¹ [ˌʌnˈtɪl] *prep* : hasta <until now : hasta ahora>
until² *conj* : hasta que <until they left : hasta que salieron> <don't answer until you're sure : no contestes hasta que (no) estés seguro>
untimely [ˌʌnˈtaɪmli] *adj* **1** PREMATURE : prematuro <an untimely death : una muerte prematura> **2** INOPPORTUNE : inoportuno, intempestivo
untold [ˌʌnˈtoːld] *adj* **1** : nunca dicho <the untold secret : el secreto sin contar> **2** INCALCULABLE : incalculable, indecible
untouched [ˌʌnˈtʌtʃt] *adj* **1** INTACT : intacto, sin tocar, sin probar (dícese de la comida) **2** UNAFFECTED : insensible, indiferente

untoward [ˌʌnˈtɔrd, -ˈtoːərd, -təˈwɔrd] *adj* **1** : indecoroso, impropio (dícese del comportamiento) **2** ADVERSE, UNFORTUNATE : desafortunado, adverso <untoward effects : efectos perjudiciales> **3** UNSEEMLY : indecoroso

untrained [ˌʌnˈtreɪnd] *adj* : inexperto, no capacitado

untreated [ˌʌnˈtriːtəd] *adj* : no tratado (dícese de una enfermedad, etc.), sin tratar (dícese de un material)

untroubled [ˌʌnˈtrʌbəld] *adj* : tranquilo <to be untroubled by : no estar afectado por>

untrue [ˌʌnˈtruː] *adj* **1** UNFAITHFUL : infiel **2** FALSE : falso

untrustworthy [ˌʌnˈtrʌstˌwərði] *adj* : de poca confianza (dícese de una persona), no fidedigno (dícese de la información)

untruth [ˌʌnˈtruːθ, ˈʌnˌ-] *n* : mentira *f,* falsedad *f*

untruthful [ˌʌnˈtruːθfəl] *adj* : mentiroso, falso

unusable [ˌʌnˈjuːzəbəl] *adj* : inútil, inservible

unused [ˌʌnˈjuːzd, *in sense 1 usually* -ˈjuːst] *adj* **1** UNACCUSTOMED : inhabituado **2** NEW : nuevo **3** IDLE : no utilizado (dícese de la tierra) **4** REMAINING : restante <the unused portion : la porción restante>

unusual [ˌʌnˈjuːʒʊəl] *adj* : inusual, poco común, raro

unusually [ˌʌnˈjuːʒʊəli, -ˈjuːʒəli] *adv* : excepcionalmente, extraordinariamente, fuera de lo común

unwanted [ˌʌnˈwɑntəd] *adj* : superfluo, de sobre

unwarranted [ˌʌnˈwɔrəntəd] *adj* : injustificado

unwary [ˌʌnˈwæri] *adj* : incauto

unwavering [ˌʌnˈweɪvərɪŋ] *adj* : firme, inquebrantable <an unwavering gaze : una mirada fija>

unwelcome [ˌʌnˈwɛlkəm] *adj* : importuno, molesto

unwell [ˌʌnˈwɛl] *adj* : enfermo, mal

unwholesome [ˌʌnˈhoːlsəm] *adj* **1** UNHEALTHY : malsano, insalubre **2** PERNICIOUS : pernicioso **3** LOATHSOME : repugnante, muy desagradable

unwieldy [ˌʌnˈwiːldi] *adj* CUMBERSOME : difícil de manejar, torpe y pesado

unwilling [ˌʌnˈwɪlɪŋ] *adj* : poco dispuesto <to be unwilling to : no estar dispuesto a>

unwillingly [ˌʌnˈwɪlɪŋli] *adv* : a regañadientes, de mala gana

unwind [ˌʌnˈwaɪnd] *v* **-wound** [-ˈwaʊnd]; **-winding** *vt* **1** UNROLL : desenrollar **2** RELAX : relajar — *vi* : desenrollarse

unwise [ˌʌnˈwaɪz] *adj* : imprudente, desacertado, poco aconsejable

unwisely [ˌʌnˈwaɪzli] *adv* : imprudentemente

unwitting [ˌʌnˈwɪtɪŋ] *adj* **1** UNAWARE : inconsciente **2** INADVERTENT : involuntario, inadvertido <an unwitting mistake : un error inadvertido> — **unwittingly** *adv*

unworthiness [ˌʌnˈwərðinəs] *n* : falta *f* de valía

unworthy [ˌʌnˈwərði] *adj* **1** UNDESERVING : indigno <to be unworthy of : no ser digno de> **2** UNMERITED : inmerecido

unwrap [ˌʌnˈræp] *vt* **-wrapped; -wrapping** : desenvolver, deshacer

unwritten [ˌʌnˈrɪtən] *adj* : no escrito

unyielding [ˌʌnˈjiːldɪŋ] *adj* : firme, inflexible, rígido

unzip [ˌʌnˈzɪp] *vt* **-zipped; -zipping** : abrir el cierre de

up[1] [ˈʌp] *v* **upped** [ˈʌpt]; **upping; ups** *vt* INCREASE : aumentar, subir <they upped the prices : aumentaron los precios> — *vi* **to up and** : agarrar y *fam* <she up and left : agarró y se fue>

up[2] *adv* **1** ABOVE : arriba, en lo alto <up in the mountains : arriba en las montañas> **2** UPWARDS : hacia arriba <push it up : empújalo hacia arriba> <the sun came up : el sol salió> <prices went up : los precios subieron> **3** (*indicating an upright position or waking state*) <to sit up : ponerse derecho> <they got up late : se levantaron tarde> <I stayed up all night : pasé toda la noche sin dormir> **4** (*indicating volume or intensity*) <to speak up : hablar más fuerte> **5** (*indicating a northerly direction*) <the climate up north : el clima del norte> <I'm going up to Canada : voy para Canadá> **6** (*indicating the appearance or existence of something*) <the book turned up : el libro apareció> **7** (*indicating consideration*) <she brought the matter up : mencionó el asunto> **8** COMPLETELY : completamente <eat it up : cómetelo todo> **9** : en pedazos <he tore it up : lo rompió en pedazos> **10** (*indicating a stopping*) <the car pulled up to the curb : el carro paró al borde de la acera> **11** (*indicating an even score*) <the game was 10 up : empataron a 10>

up[3] *adj* **1** (*risen above the horizon*) <the sun is up : ha salido el sol> **2** (*being above a normal or former level*) <prices are up : los precios han aumentado> <the river is up : las aguas están altas> **3** : despierto, levantado <up all night : despierto toda la noche> **4** BUILT : construido <the house is up : la casa está construida> **5** OPEN : abierto <the windows are up : las ventanas están abiertas> **6** (*moving or going upward*) <the up staircase : la escalera para subir> **7** ABREAST : enterado, al día, al corriente <to be up on the news : estar al corriente de las noticias> **8** PREPARED : preparado <we were up for the test

: estuvimos preparados para el examen> **9** FINISHED : terminado, acabado <time is up : se ha terminado el tiempo permitido> **10 to be up :** pasar <what's up? : ¿qué pasa?>

up[4] *prep* **1** (*to, toward, or at a higher point of*) <he went up the stairs : subió la escalera> **2** (*to or toward the source of*) <to go up the river : ir río arriba> **3** ALONG : a lo largo, por <up the coast : a lo largo de la costa> <just up the way : un poco más adelante> <up and down the city : por toda la ciudad>

upbraid [ˌʌpˈbreɪd] *vt* : reprender, regañar

upbringing [ˈʌpˌbrɪŋɪŋ] *n* : crianza *f,* educación *f*

upcoming [ˌʌpˈkʌmɪŋ] *adj* : próximo

update[1] [ˌʌpˈdeɪt] *vt* **-dated; -dating** : poner al día, poner al corriente, actualizar

update[2] [ˈʌpˌdeɪt] *n* : actualización *f,* puesta *f* al día

upend [ˌʌpˈɛnd] *vt* **1** : poner vertical **2** OVERTURN : volcar

upgrade[1] [ˈʌpˌgreɪd, ˌʌpˈ-] *vt* **-graded; -grading** : elevar la categoría de (un puesto, etc.), implementar mejoras a (una facilidad, etc.)

upgrade[2] [ˈʌpˌgreɪd] *n* **1** SLOPE : cuesta *f,* pendiente *f* **2** RISE : aumento *m* de categoría (de un puesto), ascenso *m* (de un empleado)

upheaval [ˌʌpˈhiːvəl] *n* **1** : levantamiento *m* (en geología) **2** DISTURBANCE, UPSET : trastorno *m,* agitación *f,* conmoción *f*

uphill[1] [ˌʌpˈhɪl] *adv* : cuesta arriba

uphill[2] [ˈʌpˌhɪl] *adj* **1** ASCENDING : en subida **2** DIFFICULT : difícil, arduo

uphold [ˌʌpˈhoːld] *vt* **-held; -holding** **1** SUPPORT : sostener, apoyar, mantener **2** RAISE : levantar **3** CONFIRM : confirmar (una decisión judicial)

upholster [ˌʌpˈhoːlstər] *vt* : tapizar

upholsterer [ˌʌpˈhoːlstərər] *n* : tapicero *m,* -ra *f*

upholstery [ˌʌpˈhoːlstəri] *n, pl* **-steries** : tapicería *f*

upkeep [ˈʌpˌkiːp] *n* : mantenimiento *m*

upland [ˈʌplənd, -ˌlænd] *n* : altiplanicie *f,* altiplano *m*

uplift[1] [ˌʌpˈlɪft] *vt* **1** RAISE : elevar, levantar **2** ELEVATE : elevar, animar (el espíritu, la mente, etc.)

uplift[2] [ˈʌpˌlɪft] *n* : elevación *f*

upon [əˈpɔn, əˈpɑn] *prep* : en, sobre <upon the desk : sobre el escritorio> <upon leaving : al salir> <questions upon questions : pregunta tras pregunta>

upper[1] [ˈʌpər] *adj* **1** HIGHER : superior <the upper classes : las clases altas> **2 :** alto (en geografía) <the upper Mississippi : el alto Mississippi>

upper[2] *n* : parte *f* superior (del calzado, etc.)

uppercase [ˌʌpərˈkeɪs] *adj* : mayúsculo

upper hand *n* : ventaja *f,* dominio *m*

uppermost [ˈʌpərˌmoːst] *adj* : más alto <it was uppermost in his mind : era lo que más le preocupaba>

upright[1] [ˈʌpˌraɪt] *adj* **1** VERTICAL : vertical **2** ERECT : erguido, derecho <to sit upright : sentarse derecho>**3** JUST : recto, honesto, justo

upright[2] *n* : montante *m,* poste *m,* soporte *m*

uprising [ˈʌpˌraɪzɪŋ] *n* : insurrección *f,* revuelta *f,* alzamiento *m*

uproar [ˈʌpˌror] *n* COMMOTION : alboroto *m,* jaleo *m,* escándalo *m*

uproarious [ˌʌpˈroriəs] *adj* **1** CLAMOROUS : estrepitoso, clamoroso **2** HILARIOUS : muy divertido, hilarante — **uproariously** *adv*

uproot [ˌʌpˈruːt, -ˈrʊt] *vt* : desarraigar

upset[1] [ˌʌpˈsɛt] *vt* **-set; -setting** **1** OVERTURN : volcar **2** SPILL : derramar **3** DISTURB : perturbar, disgustar, inquietar, alterar **4** SICKEN : sentar mal a <it upsets my stomach : me sienta mal al estómago> **5** DISRUPT : trastornar, desbaratar (planes, etc.) **6** DEFEAT : derrotar (en deportes)

upset[2] *adj* **1** DISPLEASED, DISTRESSED : disgustado, alterado **2 to have an upset stomach** : estar mal del estómago, estar descompuesto (de estómago)

upset[3] [ˈʌpˌsɛt] *n* **1** OVERTURNING : vuelco *m* **2** DISRUPTION : trastorno *m* (de planes, etc.) **3** DEFEAT : derrota *f* (en deportes)

upshot [ˈʌpˌʃɑt] *n* : resultado *m* final

upside–down [ˌʌpˌsaɪdˈdaʊn] *adj* : al revés

upside down [ˌʌpˌsaɪdˈdaʊn] *adv* **1** : al revés **2** : en confusión, en desorden

upstairs[1] [ˌʌpˈstærz] *adv* : arriba, en el piso superior

upstairs[2] [ˈʌpˌstærz, ˌʌpˈ-] *adj* : de arriba

upstairs[3] [ˈʌpˌstærz, ˌʌpˈ-] *ns & pl* : piso *m* de arriba, planta *f* de arriba

upstanding [ˌʌpˈstændɪŋ, ˈʌpˌ-] *adj* HONEST, UPRIGHT : honesto, íntegro, recto

upstart [ˈʌpˌstɑrt] *n* : advenedizo *m,* -za *f*

upswing [ˈʌpˌswɪŋ] *n* : alza *f,* mejora *f* notable <to be on the upswing : estar mejorándose>

uptight [ˌʌpˈtaɪt] *adj* : tenso, nervioso

up to *prep* **1** : hasta <up to a year : hasta un año> <in mud up to my ankles : en barro hasta los tobillos> **2 to be up to :** estar a la altura de <I'm not up to going : no estoy en condiciones de ir> **3 to be up to :** depender de <it's up to the director : depende del director>

up–to–date [ˌʌptəˈdeɪt] *adj* **1** CURRENT : corriente, al día <to keep up-to-date

: mantenerse al corriente> 2 MODERN : moderno

uptown [ˈʌpˈtaʊn] *adv* : hacia la parte alta de la ciudad, hacia el distrito residencial

upturn [ˈʌpˌtərn] *n* : mejora *f,* auge *m* (económico)

upward[1] [ˈʌpwərd] *or* **upwards** [-wərdz] *adv* : hacia arriba

upward[2] *adj* : ascendente, hacia arriba

upwind [ˌʌpˈwɪnd] *adv & adj* : contra el viento

uranium [jʊˈreɪniəm] *n* : uranio *m*

Uranus [jʊˈreɪnəs, ˈjʊrənəs] *n* : Urano *m*

urban [ˈərbən] *adj* : urbano

urbane [ˌərˈbeɪn] *adj* : urbano, cortés

urchin [ˈərtʃən] *n* **1** SCAMP : granuja *mf;* pillo *m,* -lla *f* **2 sea urchin** : erizo *m* de mar

urethra [jʊˈriːθrə] *n, pl* **-thras** *or* **-thrae** [-ˌθriː] : uretra *f*

urge[1] [ˈərdʒ] *vt* **urged; urging 1** PRESS : instar, apremiar, insistir <we urged him to come : insistimos en que viniera> **2** ADVOCATE : recomendar, abogar por **3 to urge on** : animar, alentar

urge[2] *n* : impulso *m,* ganas *fpl,* compulsión *f*

urgency [ˈərdʒəntsi] *n, pl* **-cies** : urgencia *f*

urgent [ˈərdʒənt] *adj* **1** PRESSING : urgente, apremiante **2** INSISTENT : insistente **3 to be urgent** : urgir

urgently [ˈərdʒəntli] *adv* : urgentemente

urinal [ˈjʊrənəl, *esp Brit* jʊˈraɪnəl] *n* : orinal *m* (recipiente), urinario *m* (lugar)

urinary [ˈjʊrəˌnɛri] *adj* : urinario

urinate [ˈjʊrəˌneɪt] *vi* **-nated; -nating** : orinar

urination [ˌjʊrəˈneɪʃən] *n* : orinación *f*

urine [ˈjʊrən] *n* : orina *f*

urn [ˈərn] *n* **1** VASE : urna *f* **2** : recipiente *m* (para servir café, etc.)

Uruguayan [ˌʊrəˈgwaɪən, ˌjʊr-, -ˈgweɪ-] *n* : uruguayo *m,* -ya *f* — **Uruguayan** *adj*

us [ˈʌs] *pron* **1** (*as direct object*) : nos <they were visiting us : nos visitaban> **2** (*as indirect object*) : nos <he gave us a present : nos dio un regalo> **3** (*as object of preposition*) : nosotros, nosotras <stay with us : quédese con nosotros> <both of us : nosotros dos> **4** (*for emphasis*) : nosotros <it's us! : ¡somos nosotros!>

usable [ˈjuːzəbəl] *adj* : utilizable

usage [ˈjuːsɪdʒ, -zɪdʒ] *n* **1** HABIT : costumbre *f,* hábito *m* **2** USE : uso *m*

use[1] [ˈjuːz] *v* **used** [ˈjuːzd, *in phrase "used to" usually* ˈjuːstuː]; **using** *vt* **1** EMPLOY : emplear, usar **2** CONSUME : consumir, tomar (drogas, etc.) **3** UTILIZE : usar, utilizar <to use tact : usar tacto> <he used his friends to get ahead : usó a sus amigos para mejorar su posición> **4** TREAT : tratar <they used the horse cruelly : maltrataron al caballo> **5 to use up** : agotar, consumir, gastar — *vi* (*used in the past with* **to** *to indicate a former fact or state*) : soler, acostumbrar <winters used to be colder : los inviernos solían ser más fríos, los inviernos eran más fríos> <she used to dance : acostumbraba bailar>

use[2] [ˈjuːs] *n* **1** APPLICATION, EMPLOYMENT : uso *m,* empleo *m,* utilización *f* <out of use : en desuso> <ready for use : listo para usar> <to be in use : usarse, estar funcionando> <to make use of : servirse de, aprovechar> **2** USEFULNESS : utilidad *f* <to be of no use : no servir (para nada)> <it's no use! : ¡es inútil!> **3 to have the use of** : poder usar, tener acceso a **4 to have no use for** : no necesitar <she has no use for poetry : a ella no le gusta la poesía>

used [ˈjuːzd] *adj* **1** SECONDHAND : usado, de segunda mano <used cars : coches usados> **2 used to** ACCUSTOMED : acostumbrado <used to the heat : acostumbrado al calor>

useful [ˈjuːsfəl] *adj* : útil, práctico — **usefully** *adv*

usefulness [ˈjuːsfəlnəs] *n* : utilidad *f*

useless [ˈjuːsləs] *adj* : inútil — **uselessly** *adv*

uselessness [ˈjuːsləsnəs] *n* : inutilidad *f*

user [ˈjuːzər] *n* : usuario *m,* -ria *f*

usher[1] [ˈʌʃər] *vt* **1** ESCORT : acompañar, conducir **2 to usher in** : hacer pasar (a alguien) <to usher in a new era : anunciar una nueva época>

usher[2] *n* : acomodador *m,* -dora *f*

usherette [ˌʌʃəˈrɛt] *n* : acomodadora *f*

usual [ˈjuːʒʊəl] *adj* **1** NORMAL : usual, normal **2** CUSTOMARY : acostumbrado, habitual, de costumbre **3** ORDINARY : ordinario, típico

usually [ˈjuːʒʊəli, ˈjuːʒəli] *adv* : usualmente, normalmente

usurp [jʊˈsərp, -ˈzərp] *vt* : usurpar

usurper [jʊˈsərpər, -ˈzər-] *n* : usurpador *m,* -dora *f*

utensil [jʊˈtɛntsəl] *n* **1** : utensilio *m* (de cocina) **2** IMPLEMENT : implemento *m,* útil *m* (de labranza, etc.)

uterus [ˈjuːtərəs] *n, pl* **uteri** [-ˌraɪ] : útero *m,* matriz *f*

utilitarian [juːˌtɪləˈtɛriən] *adj* : utilitario

utility [juːˈtɪləti] *n, pl* **-ties 1** USEFULNESS : utilidad *f* **2 public utility** : empresa *f* de servicio público

utilization [ˌjuːtələˈzeɪʃən] *n* : utilización *f*

utilize [ˈjuːtəlˌaɪz] *vt* **-lized; -lizing** : utilizar, hacer uso de

utmost[1] [ˈʌtˌmoːst] *adj* **1** FARTHEST : extremo, más lejano **2** GREATEST : sumo, mayor <of the utmost importance : de suma importancia>

utmost[2] *n* : lo más posible <to the utmost : al máximo>
utopia [jʊˈtoːpiə] *n* : utopía *f*
utopian [jʊˈtoːpiən] *adj* : utópico
utter[1] [ˈʌtər] *vt* : decir, articular, pronunciar (palabras)
utter[2] *adj* : absoluto — **utterly** *adv*
utterance [ˈʌtərən*t*s] *n* : declaración *f,* articulación *f*

V

v [ˈviː] *n, pl* **v's** *or* **vs** [ˈviːz] : vigésima segunda letra del alfabeto inglés
vacancy [ˈveɪkən*t*si] *n, pl* **-cies 1** EMPTINESS : vacío *m,* vacuidad *f* **2** : vacante *f,* puesto *m* vacante <to fill a vacancy : ocupar un puesto> **3** : habitación *f* libre (en un hotel) <no vacancies : completo>
vacant [ˈveɪkənt] *adj* **1** EMPTY : libre, desocupado (dícese de los edificios, etc.) **2** : vacante (dícese de los puestos) **3** BLANK : vacío, ausente <a vacant stare : una mirada ausente>
vacate [ˈveɪˌkeɪt] *vt* **-cated; -cating** : desalojar, desocupar
vacation[1] [veɪˈkeɪʃən, və-] *vi* : pasar las vacaciones, vacacionar *Mex*
vacation[2] *n* : vacaciones *fpl* <to be on vacation : estar de vacaciones>
vacationer [veɪˈkeɪʃənər, və-] *n* : turista *mf,* veraneante *mf,* vacacionista *mf CA, Mex*
vaccinate [ˈvæksəˌneɪt] *vt* **-nated; -nating** : vacunar
vaccination [ˌvæksəˈneɪʃən] *n* : vacunación *f*
vaccine [vækˈsiːn, ˈvækˌ-] *n* : vacuna *f*
vacillate [ˈvæsəˌleɪt] *vi* **-lated; -lating 1** HESITATE : vacilar **2** SWAY : oscilar
vacillation [ˌvæsəˈleɪʃən] *n* : indecisión *f,* vacilación *f*
vacuous [ˈvækjʊəs] *adj* **1** EMPTY : vacío **2** INANE : vacuo, necio, estúpido
vacuum[1] [ˈvæˌkjuːm, -kjəm] *vt* : limpiar con aspiradora, pasar la aspiradora por
vacuum[2] *n, pl* **vacuums** *or* **vacua** [ˈvækjʊə] : vacío *m*
vacuum cleaner *n* : aspiradora *f*
vagabond[1] [ˈvægəˌbɑnd] *adj* : vagabundo
vagabond[2] *n* : vagabundo *m,* -da *f*
vagary [ˈveɪgəri, vəˈgɛri] *n, pl* **-ries** : capricho *m*
vagina [vəˈdʒaɪnə] *n, pl* **-nae** [-ˌniː, -ˌnaɪ] *or* **-nas** : vagina *f*
vagrancy [ˈveɪgrən*t*si] *n* : vagancia *f*
vagrant[1] [ˈveɪgrənt] *adj* : vagabundo
vagrant[2] *n* : vagabundo *m,* -da *f*
vague [ˈveɪg] *adj* **vaguer; -est 1** IMPRECISE : vago, impreciso <a vague feeling : una sensación indefinida> <I haven't the vaguest idea : no tengo la más remota idea> **2** UNCLEAR : borroso, poco claro <a vague outline : un perfil indistinto> **3** ABSENTMINDED : distraído
vaguely [ˈveɪgli] *adv* : vagamente, de manera imprecisa
vagueness [ˈveɪgnəs] *n* : vaguedad *f,* imprecisión *f*
vain [ˈveɪn] *adj* **1** WORTHLESS : vano **2** FUTILE : vano, inútil <in vain : en vano> **3** CONCEITED : vanidoso, presumido
vainly [ˈveɪnli] *adv* : en vano, vanamente, inútilmente
valance [ˈvælən*t*s, ˈveɪ-] *n* **1** FLOUNCE : volante *m* (de una cama, etc.) **2** : galería *f* de cortina (sobre una ventana)
vale [ˈveɪl] *n* : valle *m*
valedictorian [ˌvæləˌdɪkˈtoriən] *n* : estudiante *mf* que pronuncia el discurso de despedida en ceremonia de graduación
valedictory [ˌvæləˈdɪktəri] *adj* : de despedida
valentine [ˈvælənˌtaɪn] *n* : tarjeta *f* que se manda el Día de los Enamorados (el 14 de febrero)
Valentine's Day *n* : Día *m* de los Enamorados
valet [ˈvæˌleɪ, væˈleɪ, ˈvælət] *n* : ayuda *m* de cámara
valiant [ˈvæljənt] *adj* : valiente, valeroso
valiantly [ˈvæljəntli] *adv* : con valor, valientemente
valid [ˈvæləd] *adj* : válido
validate [ˈvæləˌdeɪt] *vt* **-dated; -dating** : validar, dar validez a
validity [vəˈlɪdət̬i, væ-] *n* : validez *f*
valise [vəˈliːs] *n* : maleta *f* (de mano)
valley [ˈvæli] *n, pl* **-leys** : valle *m*
valor [ˈvælər] *n* : valor *m,* valentía *f*
valorous [ˈvælərəs] *adj* : valeroso, valiente
valuable[1] [ˈvæljʊəbəl, ˈvæljəbəl] *adj* **1** EXPENSIVE : valioso, de valor **2** WORTHWHILE : valioso, apreciable
valuable[2] *n* : objeto *m* de valor
valuation [ˌvæljʊˈeɪʃən] *n* **1** APPRAISAL : valoración *f,* tasación *f* **2** VALUE : valuación *f*
value[1] [ˈvælˌjuː] *vt* **-ued; -uing 1** APPRAISE : valorar, avaluar, tasar **2** APPRECIATE : valorar, apreciar
value[2] *n* **1** : valor *m* <of little value : de poco valor> <to be a good value : estar bien de precio, tener buen precio> <at face value : en su sentido literal>

2 values *npl* : valores *mpl* (morales), principios *mpl*
valueless [ˈvæljuːləs] *adj* : sin valor
valve [ˈvælv] *n* : válvula *f*
vampire [ˈvæm,paɪr] *n* **1** : vampiro *m* **2** *or* **vampire bat** : vampiro *m*
van[1] [ˈvæn] → **vanguard**
van[2] *n* : furgoneta *f*, camioneta *f*
vanadium [vəˈneɪdiəm] *n* : vanadio *m*
vandal [ˈvændəl] *n* : vándalo *m*
vandalism [ˈvændəl,ɪzəm] *n* : vandalismo *m*
vandalize [ˈvændəl,aɪz] *vt* : destrozar, destruir, estropear
vane [ˈveɪn] *n or* **weather vane** : veleta *f*
vanguard [ˈvæn,gɑrd] *n* : vanguardia *f*
vanilla [vəˈnɪlə, -ˈnɛ-] *n* : vainilla *f*
vanish [ˈvænɪʃ] *vi* : desaparecer, disiparse, desvanecerse
vanity [ˈvænəti] *n, pl* **-ties 1** : vanidad *f* **2** *or* **vanity table** : tocador *m*
vanquish [ˈvæŋkwɪʃ, ˈvæn-] *vt* : vencer, conquistar
vantage point [ˈvæntɪdʒ] *n* : posición *f* ventajosa
vapid [ˈvæpəd, ˈveɪ-] *adj* : insípido, insulso
vapor [ˈveɪpər] *n* : vapor *m*
vaporize [ˈveɪpə,raɪz] *v* **-rized; -rizing** *vt* : vaporizar — *vi* : vaporizarse, evaporarse
vaporizer [ˈveɪpə,raɪzər] *n* : vaporizador *m*
variability [,vɛriəˈbɪləti] *n, pl* **-ties** : variabilidad *f*
variable[1] [ˈvɛriəbəl] *adj* : variable <variable cloudiness : nubosidad variable>
variable[2] *n* : variable *f*, factor *m*
variance [ˈvɛriənts] *n* **1** DISCREPANCY : varianza *f*, discrepancia *f* **2** DISAGREEMENT : desacuerdo *m* <at variance with : en desacuerdo con>
variant[1] [ˈvɛriənt] *adj* : variante, divergente
variant[2] *n* : variante *f*
variation [,vɛriˈeɪʃən] *n* : variación *f*, diferencias *fpl*
varicose [ˈværə,koːs] *adj* : varicoso
varicose veins *npl* : varices *fpl*, várices *fpl*
varied [ˈvɛrid] *adj* : variado, dispar, diferente
variegated [ˈvɛriə,geɪtəd] *adj* : abigarrado, multicolor
variety [vəˈraɪəti] *n, pl* **-ties 1** DIVERSITY : diversidad *f*, variedad *f* **2** ASSORTMENT : surtido *m* <for a variety of reasons : por diversas razones> **3** SORT : clase *f* **4** BREED : variedad *f* (de plantas)
various [ˈvɛriəs] *adj* : varios, diversos
varnish[1] [ˈvɑrnɪʃ] *vt* : barnizar
varnish[2] *n* : barniz *f*
varsity [ˈvɑrsəti] *n, pl* **-ties** : equipo *m* universitario
vary [ˈvɛri] *v* **varied; varying** *vt* : variar, diversificar — *vi* **1** CHANGE : variar, cambiar **2** DEVIATE : desviarse
vascular [ˈvæskjələr] *adj* : vascular
vase [ˈveɪs, ˈveɪz, ˈvɑz] *n* : jarrón *m*, florero *m*
vassal [ˈvæsəl] *n* : vasallo *m*, -lla *f*
vast [ˈvæst] *adj* : inmenso, enorme, vasto
vastly [ˈvæstli] *adv* : enormemente
vastness [ˈvæstnəs] *n* : vastedad *f*, inmensidad *f*
vat [ˈvæt] *n* : cuba *f*, tina *f*
vaudeville [ˈvɔdvəl, -,vɪl; ˈvɔdə,vɪl] *n* : vodevil *m*
vault[1] [ˈvɔlt] *vi* LEAP : saltar
vault[2] *n* **1** JUMP : salto *m* <pole vault : salto de pértiga, salto con garrocha> **2** DOME : bóveda *f* **3** : bodega *f* (para vino), bóveda *f* de seguridad (de un banco) **4** CRYPT : cripta *f*
vaulted [ˈvɔltəd] *adj* : abovedado
vaunted [ˈvɔntəd] *adj* : cacareado, alardeado <a much vaunted wine : un vino muy alardeado>
VCR [,viː,siːˈɑr] *n* : video *m*, videocasetera *f*
veal [ˈviːl] *n* : ternera *f*, carne *f* de ternera
veer [ˈvɪr] *vi* : virar (dícese de un barco), girar (dícese de un coche), torcer (dícese de un camino)
vegetable[1] [ˈvɛdʒtəbəl, ˈvɛdʒətə-] *adj* : vegetal
vegetable[2] *n* **1** : vegetal *m* <the vegetable kingdom : el reino vegetal> **2** : verdura *f*, hortaliza *f* (para comer)
vegetarian [,vɛdʒəˈtɛriən] *n* : vegetariano *mf*
vegetarianism [,vɛdʒəˈtɛriə,nɪzəm] *n* : vegetarianismo *m*
vegetate [ˈvɛdʒə,teɪt] *vi* **-tated; -tating** : vegetar
vegetation [,vɛdʒəˈteɪʃən] *n* : vegetación *f*
vehemence [ˈviːəmənts] *n* : intensidad *f*, vehemencia *f*
vehement [ˈviːəmənt] *adj* : intenso, vehemente
vehemently [ˈviːəməntli] *adv* : vehementemente, con vehemencia
vehicle [ˈviːəkəl, ˈviː,hɪkəl] *n* **1** *or* **motor vehicle** : vehículo *m* **2** MEDIUM : vehículo *m*, medio *m*
vehicular [viˈhɪkjələr, və-] *adj* : vehicular <vehicular homicide : muerte por atropello>
veil[1] [ˈveɪl] *vt* **1** CONCEAL : velar, disimular **2** : cubrir con un velo <to veil one's face : cubrirse con un velo>
veil[2] *n* : velo *m* <bridal veil : velo de novia>
vein [ˈveɪn] *n* **1** : vena *f* (en anatomía, botánica, etc.) **2** LODE : veta *f*, vena *f*, filón *m* **3** STYLE : vena *f* <in a humorous vein : en vena humorística>
veined [ˈveɪnd] *adj* : veteado (dícese del queso, de los minerales, etc.)

velocity [vəˈlɑsət̬i] *n, pl* **-ties** : velocidad *f*
velour [vəˈlʊr] *or* **velours** [-ˈlʊrz] *n* : velour *m*
velvet[1] [ˈvɛlvət] *adj* **1** : de terciopelo **2** → **velvety**
velvet[2] *n* : terciopelo *m*
velvety [ˈvɛlvət̬i] *adj* : aterciopelado
venal [ˈviːnəl] *adj* : venal, sobornable
vend [ˈvɛnd] *vt* : vender
vendetta [vɛnˈdɛt̬ə] *n* : vendetta *f*
vendor [ˈvɛndər] *n* : vendedor *m,* -dora *f;* puestero *m,* -ra *f*
veneer[1] [vəˈnɪr] *vt* : enchapar, chapar
veneer[2] *n* **1** : enchapado *m,* chapa *f* **2** APPEARANCE : apariencia *f,* barniz *m* <a veneer of culture : un barniz de cultura>
venerable [ˈvɛnərəbəl] *adj* : venerable
venerate [ˈvɛnəˌreɪt] *vt* **-ated; -ating** : venerar
veneration [ˌvɛnəˈreɪʃən] *n* : veneración *f*
venereal disease [vəˈnɪriəl] *n* : enfermedad *f* venérea
venetian blind [vəˈniːʃən] *n* : persiana *f* veneciana
Venezuelan [ˌvɛnəˈzweɪlən, -zʊˈeɪ-] *n* : venezolano *m,* -na *f* — **Venezuelan** *adj*
vengeance [ˈvɛndʒən*t*s] *n* : venganza *f* <to take vengeance on : vengarse de>
vengeful [ˈvɛndʒfəl] *adj* : vengativo
venial [ˈviːniəl] *adj* : venial <a venial sin : un pecado venial>
venison [ˈvɛnəsən, -zən] *n* : venado *m,* carne *f* de venado
venom [ˈvɛnəm] *n* **1** : veneno *m* **2** MALICE : veneno *m,* malevolencia *f*
venomous [ˈvɛnəməs] *adj* : venenoso
vent[1] [ˈvɛnt] *vt* : desahogar, dar salida a <to vent one's feelings : desahogarse>
vent[2] *n* **1** OPENING : abertura *f* (de escape), orificio *m* **2** *or* **air vent** : respiradero *m,* rejilla *f* de ventilación **3** OUTLET : desahogo *m* <to give vent to one's anger : desahogar la ira>
ventilate [ˈvɛntəlˌeɪt] *vt* **-lated; -lating** : ventilar
ventilation [ˌvɛntəlˈeɪʃən] *n* : ventilación *f*
ventilator [ˈvɛntəlˌeɪt̬ər] *n* : ventilador *m*
ventricle [ˈvɛntrɪkəl] *n* : ventrículo *m*
ventriloquism [vɛnˈtrɪləˌkwɪzəm] *n* : ventriloquia *f*
ventriloquist [vɛnˈtrɪləˌkwɪst] *n* : ventrílocuo *m,* -cua *f*
venture[1] [ˈvɛntʃər] *v* **-tured; -turing** *vt* **1** RISK : arriesgar **2** OFFER : aventurar <to venture an opinion : aventurar una opinión> — *vi* : arriesgarse, atreverse, aventurarse
venture[2] *n* **1** UNDERTAKING : empresa *f* **2** GAMBLE, RISK : aventura *f,* riesgo *m*
venturesome [ˈvɛntʃərsəm] *adj* **1** ADVENTUROUS : audaz, atrevido **2** RISKY : arriesgado
venue [ˈvɛnˌjuː] *n* **1** PLACE : lugar *m* **2** : jurisdicción *f* (en derecho)
Venus [ˈviːnəs] *n* : Venus *m*
veracity [vəˈræsət̬i] *n, pl* **-ties** : veracidad *f*
veranda *or* **verandah** [vəˈrændə] *n* : terraza *f,* veranda *f*
verb [ˈvərb] *n* : verbo *m*
verbal [ˈvərbəl] *adj* : verbal
verbalize [ˈvərbəˌlaɪz] *vt* **-ized; -izing** : expresar con palabras, verbalizar
verbally [ˈvərbəli] *adv* : verbalmente, de palabra
verbatim[1] [vərˈbeɪt̬əm] *adv* : palabra por palabra, textualmente
verbatim[2] *adj* : literal, textual
verbose [vərˈboːs] *adj* : verboso, prolijo
verdant [ˈvərdənt] *adj* : verde, verdeante
verdict [ˈvərdɪkt] *n* **1** : veredicto *m* (de un jurado) **2** JUDGMENT, OPINION : juicio *m,* opinión *f*
verge[1] [ˈvərdʒ] *vi* **verged; verging** : estar al borde, rayar <it verges on madness : raya en la locura>
verge[2] *n* **1** EDGE : borde *m* **2 to be on the verge of** : estar a pique de, estar al borde de, estar a punto de
verification [ˌvɛrəfəˈkeɪʃən] *n* : verificación *f*
verify [ˈvɛrəˌfaɪ] *vt* **-fied; -fying** : verificar, comprobar, confirmar
veritable [ˈvɛrət̬əbəl] *adj* : verdadero — **veritably** *adv*
vermicelli [ˌvərməˈtʃɛli, -ˈsɛli] *n* : fideos *mpl* finos
vermin [ˈvərmən] *ns & pl* : alimañas *fpl,* bichos *mpl,* sabandijas *fpl*
vermouth [vərˈmuːth] *n* : vermut *m*
vernacular[1] [vərˈnækjələr] *adj* : vernáculo
vernacular[2] *n* : lengua *f* vernácula
versatile [ˈvərsət̬əl] *adj* : versátil
versatility [ˌvərsəˈtɪlət̬i] *n* : versatilidad *f*
verse [ˈvərs] *n* **1** LINE, STANZA : verso *m,* estrofa *f* **2** POETRY : poesía *f* **3** : versículo *m* (en la Biblia)
versed [ˈvərst] *adj* : versado <to be well versed in : ser muy versado en>
version [ˈvərʒən] *n* : versión *f*
versus [ˈvərsəs] *prep* : versus
vertebra [ˈvərt̬əbrə] *n, pl* **-brae** [-ˌbreɪ, -ˌbriː] *or* **-bras** : vértebra *f*
vertebrate[1] [ˈvərt̬əbrət, -ˌbreɪt] *adj* : vertebrado
vertebrate[2] *n* : vertebrado *m*
vertex [ˈvərˌtɛks] *n, pl* **vertices** [ˈvərt̬əˌsiːz] **1** : vértice *m* (en matemáticas y anatomía) **2** SUMMIT, TOP : ápice *m,* cumbre *f,* cima *f*
vertical[1] [ˈvərt̬ɪkəl] *adj* : vertical — **verticalmente** *adv*
vertical[2] *n* : vertical *f*
vertigo [ˈvərt̬ɪˌgoː] *n, pl* **-goes** *or* **-gos** : vértigo *m*
verve [ˈvərv] *n* : brío *m*

very[1] [ˈvɛri] *adv* **1** EXTREMELY : muy, sumamente <very few : muy pocos> <I am very sorry : lo siento mucho> **2** (*used for emphasis*) <at the very least : por lo menos, como mínimo> <the same dress : el mismo vestido>
very[2] *adj* **verier; -est 1** EXACT, PRECISE : mismo, exacto <at that very moment : en ese mismo momento> <it's the very thing : es justo lo que hacía falta> **2** BARE, MERE : solo, mero <the very thought of it : sólo pensarlo> **3** EXTREME : extremo, de todo <at the very top : arriba de todo>
vespers [ˈvɛspərz] *npl* : vísperas *fpl*
vessel [ˈvɛsəl] *n* **1** CONTAINER : vasija *f*, recipiente *m* **2** BOAT, CRAFT : nave *f*, barco *m*, buque *m* **3** : vaso *m* <blood vessel : vaso sanguíneo>
vest[1] [ˈvɛst] *vt* **1** CONFER : conferir <to vest authority in : conferirle la autoridad a> **2** CLOTHE : vestir
vest[2] *n* **1** : chaleco *m* **2** UNDERSHIRT : camiseta *f*
vestibule [ˈvɛstəˌbjuːl] *n* : vestíbulo *m*
vestige [ˈvɛstɪdʒ] *n* : vestigio *m*, rastro *m*
vestment [ˈvɛstmənt] *n* : vestidura *f*
vestry [ˈvɛstri] *n, pl* **-tries** : sacristía *f*
vet [ˈvɛt] *n* **1** → **veterinarian 2** → **veteran**[2]
veteran[1] [ˈvɛtərən, ˈvɛtrən] *adj* : veterano
veteran[2] *n* : veterano *m*, -na *f*
Veterans Day *n* : día *m* del Armisticio (celebrado el 11 de noviembre en los Estados Unidos)
veterinarian [ˌvɛtərəˈnɛriən, ˌvɛtəˈnɛr-] *n* : veterinario *m*, -ria *f*
veterinary [ˈvɛtərəˌnɛri] *adj* : veterinario
veto[1] [ˈviːto] *vt* **1** FORBID : prohibir **2** : vetar <to veto a bill : vetar un proyecto de ley>
veto[2] *n, pl* **-toes 1** : veto *m* <the power of veto : el derecho de veto> **2** BAN : veto *m*, prohibición *f*
vex [ˈvɛks] *vt* : contrariar, molestar, irritar
vexation [vɛkˈseɪʃən] *n* : contrariedad *f*, irritación *f*
via [ˈvaɪə, ˈviːə] *prep* : por, vía
viability [ˌvaɪəˈbɪləti] *n* : viabilidad *f*
viable [ˈvaɪəbəl] *adj* : viable
viaduct [ˈvaɪəˌdʌkt] *n* : viaducto *m*
vial [ˈvaɪəl] *n* : frasco *m*
vibrant [ˈvaɪbrənt] *adj* **1** LIVELY : vibrante, animado, dinámico **2** BRIGHT : fuerte, vivo (dícese de los colores)
vibrate [ˈvaɪˌbreɪt] *vi* **-brated; -brating 1** OSCILLATE : vibrar, oscilar **2** THRILL : bullir <to vibrate with excitement : bullir de emoción>
vibration [vaɪˈbreɪʃən] *n* : vibración *f*
vicar [ˈvɪkər] *n* : vicario *m*, -ria *f*
vicarious [vaɪˈkæriːəs, vɪ-] *adj* : indirecto — **vicariously** *adv*
vice [ˈvaɪs] *n* : vicio *m*
vice admiral *n* : vicealmirante *mf*
vice president *n* : vicepresidente *m*, -ta *f*
viceroy [ˈvaɪsˌrɔɪ] *n* : virrey *m*, -rreina *f*
vice versa [ˌvaɪsɪˈvərsə, ˌvaɪsˈvər-] *adv* : viceversa
vicinity [vəˈsɪnəti] *n, pl* **-ties 1** NEIGHBORHOOD : vecindad *f*, inmediaciones *fpl* **2** NEARNESS : proximidad *f*
vicious [ˈvɪʃəs] *adj* **1** DEPRAVED : depravado, malo **2** SAVAGE : malo, fiero, salvaje <a vicious dog : un perro feroz> **3** MALICIOUS : malicioso
viciously [ˈvɪʃəsli] *adv* : con saña, brutalmente
viciousness [ˈvɪʃəsnəs] *n* : brutalidad *f*, ferocidad *f* (de un animal), malevolencia *f* (de un comentario, etc.)
vicissitudes [vəˈsɪsəˌtuːdz, vaɪ-, -ˌtjuːdz] *npl* : vicisitudes *fpl*
victim [ˈvɪktəm] *n* : víctima *f*
victimize [ˈvɪktəˌmaɪz] *vt* **-mized; -mizing** : tomar como víctima, perseguir, victimizar *Arg, Mex*
victor [ˈvɪktər] *n* : vencedor *m*, -dora *f*
Victorian [vɪkˈtoːriən] *adj* : victoriano
victorious [vɪkˈtoːriəs] *adj* : victorioso — **victoriously** *adv*
victory [ˈvɪktəri] *n, pl* **-ries** : victoria *f*, triunfo *m*
victuals [ˈvɪtəlz] *npl* : víveres *mpl*, provisiones *fpl*
video[1] [ˈvɪdiˌoː] *adj* : de video <video recording : grabación de video>
video[2] *n* **1** : video *m* (medio o grabación) **2** → **videotape**[2]
videocassette [ˌvɪdiokəˈsɛt] *n* : videocasete *m*, videocassette *m*
videocassette recorder → **VCR**
videotape[1] [ˈvɪdioˌteɪp] *vt* **-taped; -taping** : grabar en video, videograbar
videotape[2] *n* : videocinta *f*
vie [ˈvaɪ] *vi* **vied; vying** [ˈvaɪɪŋ] : competir, rivalizar
Vietnamese [viˌɛtnəˈmiːz, -ˈmiːs] *n* : vietnamita *mf* — **Vietnamese** *adj*
view[1] [ˈvjuː] *vt* **1** OBSERVE : mirar, ver, observar **2** CONSIDER : considerar, contemplar
view[2] *n* **1** SIGHT : vista *f* <to come into view : aparecer> **2** ATTITUDE, OPINION : opinión *f*, parecer *m*, actitud *f* <in my view : en mi opinión> **3** SCENE : vista *f*, panorama *f* **4** INTENTION : idea *f*, vista *f* <with a view to : con vistas a, con la idea de> **5 in view of** : dado que, en vista de (que)
viewer [ˈvjuːər] *n or* **television viewer** : telespectador *m*, -dora *f*; televidente *mf*
viewpoint [ˈvjuːˌpɔɪnt] *n* : punto *m* de vista
vigil [ˈvɪdʒəl] *n* **1** : vigilia *f*, vela *f* **2 to keep vigil** : velar
vigilance [ˈvɪdʒələnts] *n* : vigilancia *f*
vigilant [ˈvɪdʒələnt] *adj* : vigilante

vigilante [ˌvɪdʒəˈlænˌtiː] *n* : integrante *mf* de un comité de vigilancia (que actúa como policía)
vigilantly [ˈvɪdʒələntli] *adv* : con vigilancia
vigor [ˈvɪgər] *n* : vigor *m,* energía *f,* fuerza *f*
vigorous [ˈvɪgərəs] *adj* : vigoroso, enérgico — **vigorously** *adv*
Viking [ˈvaɪkɪŋ] *n* : vikingo *m,* -ga *f*
vile [ˈvaɪl] *adj* **viler; vilest 1** WICKED : vil, infame **2** REVOLTING : asqueroso, repugnante **3** TERRIBLE : horrible, atroz <vile weather : tiempo horrible> <to be in a vile mood : estar de un humor de perros>
vilify [ˈvɪləˌfaɪ] *vt* **-fied; -fying** : vilipendiar, denigrar, difamar
villa [ˈvɪlə] *n* : casa *f* de campo, quinta *f*
village [ˈvɪlɪdʒ] *n* : pueblo *m* (grande), aldea *f* (pequeña)
villager [ˈvɪlɪdʒər] *n* : vecino *m,* -na *f* (de un pueblo); aldeano *m,* -na *f* (de una aldea)
villain [ˈvɪlən] *n* : villano *m,* -na *f;* malo *m,* -la *f* (en ficción, películas, etc.)
villainess [ˈvɪlənɪs, -nəs] *n* : villana *f*
villainous [ˈvɪlənəs] *adj* : infame, malvado
villainy [ˈvɪləni] *n, pl* **-lainies** : vileza *f,* maldad *f*
vim [ˈvɪm] *n* : brío *m,* vigor *m,* energía *f*
vindicate [ˈvɪndəˌkeɪt] *vt* **-cated; -cating 1** EXONERATE : vindicar, disculpar **2** JUSTIFY : justificar
vindication [ˌvɪndəˈkeɪʃən] *n* : vindicación *f,* justificación *f*
vindictive [vɪnˈdɪktɪv] *adj* : vengativo
vine [ˈvaɪn] *n* **1** GRAPEVINE : vid *f,* parra *f* **2** : planta *f* trepadora, enredadera *f*
vinegar [ˈvɪnɪgər] *n* : vinagre *m*
vinegary [ˈvɪnɪgəri] *adj* : avinagrado
vineyard [ˈvɪnjərd] *n* : viña *f,* viñedo *m*
vintage[1] [ˈvɪntɪdʒ] *adj* **1** : añejo (dícese de un vino) **2** CLASSIC : clásico, de época
vintage[2] *n* **1** : cosecha *f* <the 1947 vintage : la cosecha de 1947> **2** ERA : época *f,* era *f* <slang of recent vintage : argot de la época reciente>
vinyl [ˈvaɪnəl] *n* : vinilo
viola [viːˈoːlə] *n* : viola *f*
violate [ˈvaɪəˌleɪt] *vt* **-lated; -lating 1** BREAK : infringir, violar, quebrantar <to violate the rules : violar las reglas> **2** RAPE : violar **3** DESECRATE : profanar
violation [ˌvaɪəˈleɪʃən] *n* **1** : violación *f,* infracción *f* (de una ley) **2** DESECRATION : profanación *f*
violence [ˈvaɪlənts, ˈvaɪə-] *n* : violencia *f*
violent [ˈvaɪlənt, ˈvaɪə-] *adj* : violento
violently [ˈvaɪləntli, ˈvaɪə-] *adv* : violentamente, con violencia
violet [ˈvaɪlət, ˈvaɪə-] *n* : violeta *f*
violin [ˌvaɪəˈlɪn] *n* : violín *m*
violinist [ˌvaɪəˈlɪnɪst] *n* : violinista *mf*
violoncello [ˌvaɪələnˈtʃɛloː, ˌviː-] → **cello**
VIP [ˌviːˌaɪˈpiː] *n, pl* **VIPs** [-ˈpiːz] : VIP *mf,* persona *f* de categoría
viper [ˈvaɪpər] *n* : víbora *f*
viral [ˈvaɪrəl] *adj* : viral, vírico <viral pneumonia : pulmonía viral>
virgin[1] [ˈvərdʒən] *adj* **1** CHASTE : virginal <the virgin birth : el alumbramiento virginal> **2** : virgen, intacto <a virgin forest : una selva virgen> <virgin wool : lana virgen>
virgin[2] *n* : virgen *mf*
virginity [vərˈdʒɪnət̬i] *n* : virginidad *f*
Virgo [ˈvərˌgoː, ˈvɪr-] *n* : Virgo *mf*
virile [ˈvɪrəl, -ˌaɪl] *adj* : viril, varonil
virility [vəˈrɪlət̬i] *n* : virilidad *f*
virtual [ˈvərtʃʊəl] *adj* : virtual <a virtual dictator : un virtual dictador> <virtual reality : realidad virtual>
virtually [ˈvərtʃʊəli, ˈvərtʃəli] *adv* : en realidad, de hecho, casi
virtue [ˈvərˌtʃuː] *n* **1** : virtud *f* **2 by virtue of** : en virtud de, debido a
virtuosity [ˌvərtʃʊˈɑsət̬i] *n, pl* **-ties** : virtuosismo *m*
virtuoso [ˌvərtʃʊˈoːsoː, -zoː] *n, pl* **-sos** *or* **-si** [-ˌsiː, -ˌziː] : virtuoso *m,* -sa *f*
virtuous [ˈvərtʃʊəs] *adj* : virtuoso, bueno — **virtuously** *adv*
virulence [ˈvɪrələnts, ˈvɪrjə-] *n* : virulencia *f*
virulent [ˈvɪrələnt, ˈvɪrjə-] *adj* : virulento
virus [ˈvaɪrəs] *n* : virus *m*
visa [ˈviːzə, -sə] *n* : visa *f*
vis-à-vis [ˌviːzəˈviː, -sə-] *prep* : con relación a, con respecto a
viscera [ˈvɪsərə] *npl* : vísceras *fpl*
visceral [ˈvɪsərəl] *adj* : visceral
viscosity [vɪsˈkɑsət̬i] *n, pl* **-ties** : viscosidad *f*
viscount [ˈvaɪˌkæʊnt] *n* : vizconde *m*
viscountess [ˈvaɪˌkæʊntɪs] *n* : vizcondesa *f*
viscous [ˈvɪskəs] *adj* : viscoso
vise [ˈvaɪs] *n* : torno *m* de banco, tornillo *m* de banco
visibility [ˌvɪzəˈbɪlət̬i] *n, pl* **-ties** : visibilidad *f*
visible [ˈvɪzəbəl] *adj* **1** : visible <the visible stars : las estrellas visibles> **2** OBVIOUS : evidente, patente
visibly [ˈvɪzəbli] *adv* : visiblemente
vision [ˈvɪʒən] *n* **1** EYESIGHT : vista *f,* visión *f* **2** APPARITION : visión *f,* aparición *f* **3** FORESIGHT : visión *f* (del futuro), previsión *f* **4** IMAGE : imagen *f* <she had visions of a disaster : se imaginaba un desastre>
visionary[1] [ˈvɪʒəˌnɛri] *adj* **1** FARSIGHTED : visionario, con visión de futuro **2** UTOPIAN : utópico, poco realista
visionary[2] *n, pl* **-ries** : visionario *m,* -ria *f*

visit[1] [ˈvɪzət] *vt* **1** : visitar, ir a ver **2** AFFLICT : azotar, afligir <visited by troubles : afligido con problemas> — *vi* : hacer (una) visita

visit[2] *n* : visita *f*

visitor [ˈvɪzət̬ər] *n* : visitante *mf* (a una ciudad, etc.), visita *f* (a una casa)

visor [ˈvaɪzər] *n* : visera *f*

vista [ˈvɪstə] *n* : vista *f*

visual [ˈvɪʒʊəl] *adj* : visual <the visual arts : las artes visuales> — **visually** *adv*

visualize [ˈvɪʒʊəˌlaɪz] *vt* **-ized; -izing** : visualizar, imaginarse, hacerse una idea de

vital [ˈvaɪt̬əl] *adj* **1** : vital <vital organs : órganos vitales> **2** CRUCIAL : esencial, crucial, decisivo <of vital importance : de suma importancia> **3** LIVELY : enérgico, lleno de vida, vital

vitality [vaɪˈtælət̬i] *n, pl* **-ties** : vitalidad *f*, energía *f*

vitally [ˈvaɪt̬əli] *adv* : sumamente

vital statistics *npl* : estadísticas *fpl* demográficas

vitamin [ˈvaɪt̬əmən] *n* : vitamina *f* <vitamin deficiency : carencia vitamínica>

vitreous [ˈvɪtriəs] *adj* : vítreo

vitriolic [ˌvɪtriˈɑlɪk] *adj* : mordaz, virulento

vituperation [vaɪˌtuːpəˈreɪʃən, -ˌtjuː-] *n* : vituperio *m*

vivacious [vəˈveɪʃəs, vaɪ-] *adj* : vivaz, animado, lleno de vida

vivaciously [vəˈveɪʃəsli, vaɪ-] *adv* : con vivacidad, animadamente

vivacity [vəˈvæsət̬i, vaɪ-] *n* : vivacidad *f*

vivid [ˈvɪvəd] *adj* **1** LIVELY : lleno de vitalidad **2** BRILLIANT : vivo, intenso <vivid colors : colores vivos> **3** INTENSE, SHARP : vívido, gráfico <a vivid dream : un sueño vívido>

vividly [ˈvɪvədli] *adv* **1** BRIGHTLY : con colores vivos **2** SHARPLY : vívidamente

vividness [ˈvɪvədnəs] *n* **1** BRIGHTNESS : intensidad *f*, viveza *f* **2** SHARPNESS : lo gráfico, nitidez *f*

vivisection [ˌvɪvəˈsɛkʃən, ˈvɪvəˌ-] *n* : vivisección *f*

vixen [ˈvɪksən] *n* : zorra *f*, raposa *f*

vocabulary [voːˈkæbjəˌlɛri] *n, pl* **-laries 1** : vocabulario *m* **2** LEXICON : léxico *m*

vocal [ˈvoːkəl] *adj* **1** : vocal **2** LOUD, OUTSPOKEN : ruidoso, muy franco

vocal cords *npl* : cuerdas *fpl* vocales

vocalist [ˈvoːkəlɪst] *n* : cantante *mf*, vocalista *mf*

vocalize [ˈvoːkəlˌaɪz] *vt* **-ized; -izing** : vocalizar

vocation [voˈkeɪʃən] *n* : vocación *f* <to have a vocation for : tener vocación de>

vocational [voˈkeɪʃənəl] *adj* : profesional <vocational guidance : orientación profesional>

vociferous [voˈsɪfərəs] *adj* : ruidoso, vociferante

vodka [ˈvɑdkə] *n* : vodka *m*

vogue [ˈvoːg] *n* : moda *f*, boga *f* <to be in vogue : estar de moda, estar en boga>

voice[1] [ˈvɔɪs] *vt* **voiced; voicing** : expresar

voice[2] *n* **1** : voz *f* <in a low voice : en voz baja> <to lose one's voice : quedarse sin voz> <the voice of the people : la voz del pueblo> **2 to make one's voice heard** : hacerse oír

voice box → **larynx**

voiced [ˈvɔɪst] *adj* : sonoro

void[1] [ˈvɔɪd] *vt* : anular, invalidar <to void a contract : anular un contrato>

void[2] *adj* **1** EMPTY : vacío, desprovisto <void of content : desprovisto de contenido> **2** INVALID : inválido, nulo

void[3] *n* : vacío *m*

volatile [ˈvɑlət̬əl] *adj* : volátil, inestable

volatility [ˌvɑləˈtɪlət̬i] *n* : volatilidad *f*, inestabilidad *f*

volcanic [vɑlˈkænɪk] *adj* : volcánico

volcano [vɑlˈkeɪˌnoː] *n, pl* **-noes** *or* **-nos** : volcán *m*

vole [ˈvoːl] *n* : campañol *m*

volition [voˈlɪʃən] *n* : volición *f*, voluntad *f* <of one's own volition : por voluntad propia>

volley [ˈvɑli] *n, pl* **-leys 1** : descarga *f* (de tiros) **2** : torrente *m*, lluvia *f* (de insultos, etc.) **3** : salva *f* (de aplausos) **4** : volea *f* (en deportes)

volleyball [ˈvɑliˌbɔl] *n* : voleibol *m*

volt [ˈvoːlt] *n* : voltio *m*

voltage [ˈvoːltɪdʒ] *n* : voltaje *m*

volubility [ˌvɑljəˈbɪlət̬i] *n* : locuacidad *f*

voluble [ˈvɑljəbəl] *adj* : locuaz

volume [ˈvɑljəm, -ˌjuːm] *n* **1** BOOK : volumen *m*, tomo *m* **2** SPACE : capacidad *f*, volumen *m* (en física) **3** AMOUNT : cantidad *f*, volumen *m* **4** LOUDNESS : volumen *m*

voluminous [vəˈluːmənəs] *adj* : voluminoso

voluntary [ˈvɑlənˌtɛri] *adj* : voluntario — **voluntarily** [ˌvɑlənˈtɛrəli] *adv*

volunteer[1] [ˌvɑlənˈtɪr] *vt* : ofrecer, dar <to volunteer one's assistance : ofrecer la ayuda> — *vi* : ofrecerse, alistarse como voluntario

volunteer[2] *n* : voluntario *m*, -ria *f*

voluptuous [vəˈlʌptʃʊəs] *adj* : voluptuoso

vomit[1] [ˈvɑmət] *v* : vomitar

vomit[2] *n* : vómito *m*

voodoo [ˈvuːˌduː] *n, pl* **voodoos** : vudú *m*

voracious [vɔˈreɪʃəs, və-] *adj* : voraz

voraciously [vɔˈreɪʃəsli, və-] *adv* : vorazmente, con voracidad

vortex [ˈvɔrˌtɛks] *n, pl* **vortices** [ˈvɔrtəˌsiːz] : vórtice *m*

vote[1] [ˈvoːt] *vi* **voted; voting :** votar <to vote Democratic : votar por los demócratas>
vote[2] *n* **1 :** voto *m* **2** SUFFRAGE **:** sufragio *m,* derecho *m* al voto
voter [ˈvoːtər] *n* **:** votante *mf*
voting [ˈvoːtɪŋ] *n* **:** votación *f*
vouch [ˈvæʊtʃ] *vi* **to vouch for :** garantizar (algo), responder de (algo), responder por (alguien)
voucher [ˈvæʊtʃər] *n* **1** RECEIPT **:** comprobante *m* **2 :** vale *m* <travel voucher : vale de viajar>
vow[1] [væʊ] *vt* **:** jurar, prometer, hacer voto de
vow[2] *n* **:** promesa *f,* voto *m* (en la religión) <a vow of poverty : un voto de pobreza>
vowel [ˈvæʊəl] *n* **:** vocal *m*
voyage[1] [ˈvɔɪɪdʒ] *vi* **-aged; -aging :** viajar
voyage[2] *n* **:** viaje *m*
voyager [ˈvɔɪɪdʒər] *n* **:** viajero *m,* -ra *f*
vulcanize [ˈvʌlkəˌnaɪz] *vt* **-nized; -nizing :** vulcanizar
vulgar [ˈvʌlgər] *adj* **1** COMMON, PLEBIAN **:** ordinario, populachero, del vulgo **2** COARSE, CRUDE **:** grosero, de mal gusto, majadero *Mex* **3** INDECENT **:** indecente, colorado (dícese de un chiste, etc.)
vulgarity [ˌvʌlˈgærət̬i] *n, pl* **-ties :** grosería *f,* vulgaridad *f*
vulgarly [ˈvʌlgərli] *adv* **:** vulgarmente, groseramente
vulnerability [ˌvʌlnərəˈbɪlət̬i] *n, pl* **-ties :** vulnerabilidad *f*
vulnerable [ˈvʌlnərəbəl] *adj* **:** vulnerable
vulture [ˈvʌltʃər] *n* **:** buitre *m,* zopilote *m CA, Mex*
vying → **vie**

W

w [ˈdʌbəlˌjuː] *n, pl* **w's** *or* **ws** [-ˌjuːz] **:** vigésima tercera letra del alfabeto inglés
wad[1] [ˈwɑd] *vt* **wadded; wadding 1 :** hacer un taco con, formar en una masa **2** STUFF **:** rellenar
wad[2] *n* **:** taco *m* (de papel), bola *f* (de algodón, etc.), fajo *m* (de billetes)
waddle[1] [ˈwɑdəl] *vi* **-dled; -dling :** andar como un pato
waddle[2] *n* **:** andar *m* de pato
wade [ˈweɪd] *v* **waded; wading** *vi* **1 :** caminar por el agua **2 to wade through :** leer (algo) con dificultad — *vt or* **to wade across :** vadear
wading bird *n* **:** zancuda *f,* ave *f* zancuda
wafer [ˈweɪfər] *n* **:** barquillo *m,* galleta *f* de barquillo
waffle [ˈwɑfəl] *n* **1 :** wafle *m* **2 waffle iron :** waflera *f*
waft [ˈwɑft, ˈwæft] *vt* **:** llevar por el aire — *vi* **:** flotar
wag[1] [ˈwæg] *v* **wagged; wagging** *vt* **:** menear — *vi* **:** menearse, moverse
wag[2] *n* **1 :** meneo *m* (de la cola) **2** JOKER, WIT **:** bromista *mf*
wage[1] [ˈweɪdʒ] *vt* **waged; waging :** hacer, librar <to wage war : hacer la guerra>
wage[2] *n or* **wages** *npl* **:** sueldo *m,* salario *m* <minimum wage : salario mínimo>
wager[1] [ˈweɪdʒər] *v* **:** apostar
wager[2] *n* **:** apuesta *f*
waggish [ˈwægɪʃ] *adj* **:** burlón, bromista (dícese de una persona), chistoso (dícese de un comentario)
waggle [ˈwægəl] *vt* **-gled; -gling :** menear, mover (de un lado a otro)
wagon [ˈwægən] *n* **1 :** carro *m* (tirado por caballos) **2** CART **:** carrito *m* **3** → **station wagon**
waif [ˈweɪf] *n* **:** niño *m* abandonado, animal *m* sin hogar
wail[1] [ˈweɪl] *vi* **:** gemir, lamentarse
wail[2] *n* **:** gemido *m,* lamento *m*
wainscot [ˈweɪnskət, -ˌskɑt, -ˌskoːt] *or* **wainscoting** [-skət̬ɪŋ, -ˌskɑ-, -ˌskoː-] *n* **:** boiserie *f,* revestimiento *m* de paneles de madera
waist [ˈweɪst] *n* **:** cintura *f* (del cuerpo humano), talle *m* (de ropa)
waistline [ˈweɪstˌlaɪn] → **waist**
wait[1] [ˈweɪt] *vi* **:** esperar <to wait for something : esperar algo> <wait and see! : ¡espera y verás!> <I can't wait : me muero de ganas> — *vt* **1** AWAIT **:** esperar **2** DELAY **:** retrasar <don't wait lunch : no retrase el almuerzo> **3** SERVE **:** servir, atender <to wait tables : servir (a la mesa)>
wait[2] *n* **1 :** espera *f* **2 to lie in wait :** estar al acecho
waiter [ˈweɪt̬ər] *n* **:** mesero *m,* camarero *m,* mozo *m Arg, Chile, Col, Peru*
waiting room *n* **:** sala *f* de espera
waitress [ˈweɪtrəs] *n* **:** mesera *f,* camarera *f,* moza *f Arg, Chile, Col, Peru*
waive [ˈweɪv] *vt* **waived; waiving :** renunciar a <to waive one's rights : renunciar a sus derechos> <to waive the rules : no aplicar las reglas>
waiver [ˈweɪvər] *n* **:** renuncia *f*
wake[1] [ˈweɪk] *v* **woke** [ˈwoːk]; **woken** [ˈwoːkən] *or* **waked; waking** *vi or* **to wake up :** despertar(se) <he woke at noon : se despertó al mediodía> <wake up! : ¡despiértate!> — *vt* **:** despertar
wake[2] *n* **1** VIGIL **:** velatorio *m,* velorio *m* (de un difunto) **2** TRAIL **:** estela *f* (de un barco, un huracán, etc.) **3** AFTERMATH **:** consecuencias *fpl* <in the wake of : tras, como consecuencia de>

wakeful [ˈweɪkfəl] *adj* **1** SLEEPLESS **:** desvelado **2** VIGILANT **:** alerta, vigilante

waken [ˈweɪkən] → **awake**

walk[1] [ˈwɔk] *vi* **1 :** caminar, andar, pasear <you're walking too fast : estás caminando demasiado rápido> <to walk around the city : pasearse por la ciudad> **2 :** ir andando, ir a pie <we had to walk home : tuvimos que ir a casa a pie> **3 :** darle base por bolas (a un bateador) **—** *vt* **1 :** recorrer, caminar <she walked two miles : caminó dos millas> **2** ACCOMPANY **:** acompañar **3 :** sacar a pasear (a un perro)

walk[2] *n* **1 :** paseo *m,* caminata *f* <to go for a walk : ir a caminar, dar un paseo> **2** PATH **:** camino *m* **3** GAIT **:** andar *m* **4 :** marcha *f* (en beisbol) **5 walk of life :** esfera *f,* condición *f*

walker [ˈwɔkər] *n* **1 :** paseante *mf;* andador *m,* -dora *f* **2** HIKER **:** excursionista *mf* **3** *or* **baby walker :** andador *m*

walking stick *n* **:** bastón *m*

walkout [ˈwɔkˌaʊt] *n* STRIKE **:** huelga *f*

walk out *vi* **1** STRIKE **:** declararse en huelga **2** LEAVE **:** salir, irse **3 to walk out on :** abandonar, dejar

wall[1] [ˈwɔl] *vt* **1 to wall in :** cercar con una pared o un muro, tapiar, amurallar **2 to wall off :** separar con una pared o un muro **3 to wall up :** tapiar, condenar (una ventana, etc.)

wall[2] *n* **1 :** muro *m* (exterior) <the walls of the city : las murallas de la ciudad> **2 :** pared *f* (interior) **3** BARRIER **:** barrera *f* <a wall of mountains : una barrera de montañas> **4 :** pared *f* (en anatomía)

wallaby [ˈwɑləbi] *n, pl* **-bies :** ualabí *m*

walled [ˈwɔld] *adj* **:** amurallado

wallet [ˈwɑlət] *n* **:** billetera *f,* cartera *f*

wallflower [ˈwɔlˌflaʊər] *n* **1 :** alhelí *m* (flor) **2 to be a wallflower :** comer pavo

wallop[1] [ˈwɑləp] *vt* **1** TROUNCE **:** darle una paliza (a alguien) **2** SOCK **:** pegar fuerte

wallop[2] *n* **:** golpe *m* fuerte, golpazo *m*

wallow[1] [ˈwɑˌloː] *vi* **1 :** revolcarse <to wallow in the mud : revolcarse en el lodo> **2** DELIGHT **:** deleitarse <to wallow in luxury : nadar en lujos>

wallow[2] *n* **:** revolcadero *m* (para animales)

wallpaper[1] [ˈwɔlˌpeɪpər] *vt* **:** empapelar

wallpaper[2] *n* **:** papel *m* pintado

walnut [ˈwɔlˌnʌt] *n* **1 :** nuez *f* (fruta) **2 :** nogal *m* (árbol y madera)

walrus [ˈwɔlrəs, ˈwɑl-] *n, pl* **-rus** *or* **-ruses :** morsa *f*

waltz[1] [ˈwɔlts] *vi* **1 :** valsar, bailar el vals **2** BREEZE **:** pasar con ligereza <to waltz in : entrar tan campante>

waltz[2] *n* **:** vals *m*

wan [ˈwɑn] *adj* **wanner; -est 1** PALLID **:** pálido **2** DIM **:** tenue <wan light : luz tenue> **3** LANGUID **:** lánguido <a wan smile : una sonrisa lánguida> **— wanly** *adv*

wand [ˈwɑnd] *n* **:** varita *f* (mágica)

wander [ˈwɑndər] *vi* **1** RAMBLE **:** deambular, vagar, vagabundear **2** STRAY **:** alejarse, desviarse, divagar <she let her mind wander : dejó vagar la imaginación> **—** *vt* **:** recorrer <to wander the streets : vagar por las calles>

wanderer [ˈwɑndərər] *n* **:** vagabundo *m,* -da *f;* viajero *m,* -ra *f*

wanderlust [ˈwɑndərˌlʌst] *n* **:** pasión *f* por viajar

wane[1] [ˈweɪn] *vi* **waned; waning 1 :** menguar (dícese de la luna) **2** DECLINE **:** disminuir, decaer, menguar

wane[2] *n* **on the wane :** decayendo, en decadencia

wangle [ˈwæŋgəl] *vt* **-gled; -gling** FINAGLE **:** arreglárselas para conseguir

want[1] [ˈwɑnt, ˈwɔnt] *vt* **1** LACK **:** faltar **2** REQUIRE **:** requerir, necesitar **3** DESIRE **:** querer, desear

want[2] *n* **1** LACK **:** falta *f* **2** DESTITUTION **:** indigencia *f,* miseria *f* **3** DESIRE, NEED **:** deseo *m,* necesidad *f*

wanting [ˈwɑntɪŋ, ˈwɔn-] *adj* **1** ABSENT **:** ausente **2** DEFICIENT **:** deficiente <he's wanting in common sense : le falta sentido común>

wanton [ˈwɑntən, ˈwɔn-] *adj* **1** LEWD, LUSTFUL **:** lascivo, lujurioso, licencioso **2** INHUMANE, MERCILESS **:** despiadado <wanton cruelty : crueldad despiadada>

wapiti [ˈwɑpəti] *n, pl* **-ti** *or* **-tis :** uapití *m*

war[1] [ˈwɔr] *vi* **warred; warring :** combatir, batallar, hacer la guerra

war[2] *n* **:** guerra *f* <to go to war : entrar en guerra>

warble[1] [ˈwɔrbəl] *vi* **-bled; -bling :** gorjear, trinar

warble[2] *n* **:** trino *m,* gorjeo *m*

warbler [ˈwɔrblər] *n* **:** pájaro *m* gorjeador, curruca *f*

ward[1] [ˈwɔrd] *vt* **to ward off :** desviar, protegerse contra

ward[2] *n* **1 :** sala *f* (de un hospital, etc.) <maternity ward : sala de maternidad> **2 :** distrito *m* electoral o administrativo (de una ciudad) **3 :** pupilo *m,* -la *f* (de un tutor, etc.)

warden [ˈwɔrdən] *n* **1** KEEPER **:** guarda *mf;* guardián *m,* -diana *f* <game warden : guardabosque> **2** *or* **prison warden :** alcaide *m*

wardrobe [ˈwɔrdˌroːb] *n* **1** CLOSET **:** armario *m* **2** CLOTHES **:** vestuario *m,* guardarropa *f*

ware [ˈwær] *n* **1** POTTERY **:** cerámica *f* **2 wares** *npl* GOODS **:** mercancía *f,* mercadería *f*

warehouse [ˈwærˌhaʊs] *n* **:** depósito *m,* almacén *m,* bodega *f Chile, Col, Mex*

warfare [ˈwɔrˌfær] *n* **1** WAR : guerra *f* **2** STRUGGLE : lucha *f* <the warfare against drugs : la lucha contra las drogas>
warhead [ˈwɔrˌhɛd] *n* : ojiva *f,* cabeza *f* (de un misil)
warily [ˈwærəli] *adv* : cautelosamente, con cautela
wariness [ˈwærinəs] *n* : cautela *f*
warlike [ˈwærˌlaɪk] *adj* : belicoso, guerrero
warm¹ [ˈwɔrm] *vt* **1** HEAT : calentar, recalentar **2 to warm one's heart** : reconfortar a uno, alegrar el corazón **3 to warm up** : calentar (los músculos, un automóvil, etc.) — *vi* **1** : calentarse **2 to warm to** : tomarle simpatía (a alguien), entusiasmarse con (algo)
warm² *adj* **1** LUKEWARM : tibio, templado **2** : caliente, cálido, caluroso <a warm wind : un viento cálido> <a warm day : un día caluroso, un día de calor> <warm hands : manos calientes> **3** : caliente, que abriga <warm clothes : ropa de abrigo> <I feel warm : tengo calor> **4** CARING, CORDIAL : cariñoso, cordial **5** : cálido (dícese de colores) **6** FRESH : fresco, reciente <a warm trail : un rastro reciente> **7** (*used for riddles*) : caliente
warm–blooded [ˈwɔrmˈblʌdəd] *adj* : de sangre caliente
warmhearted [ˈwɔrmˈhɑrt̬əd] *adj* : cariñoso
warmly [ˈwɔrmli] *adv* **1** AFFECTIONATELY : calurosamente, afectuosamente **2 to dress warmly** : abrigarse
warmonger [ˈwɔrˌmɑŋgər, -ˌmʌŋ-] *n* : belicista *mf*
warmth [ˈwɔrmpθ] *n* **1** : calor *m* **2** AFFECTION : cariño *m,* afecto *m* **3** ENTHUSIASM : ardor *m,* entusiasmo *m*
warm–up [ˈwɔrmˌʌp] *n* : calentamiento *m*
warn [ˈwɔrn] *vt* **1** CAUTION : advertir, alertar **2** INFORM : avisar, informar
warning [ˈwɔrnɪŋ] *n* **1** ADVICE : advertencia *f,* aviso *m* **2** ALERT : alerta *f,* alarma *f*
warp¹ [ˈwɔrp] *vt* **1** : alabear, combar **2** PERVERT : pervertir, deformar — *vi* : pandearse, alabearse, combarse
warp² *n* **1** : urdimbre *f* <the warp and the weft : la urdimbre y la trama> **2** : alabeo *m* (en la madera, etc.)
warrant¹ [ˈwɔrənt] *vt* **1** ASSURE : asegurar, garantizar **2** GUARANTEE : garantizar **3** JUSTIFY, MERIT : justificar, merecer
warrant² *n* **1** AUTHORIZATION : autorización *f,* permiso *m* <an arrest warrant : una orden de detención> **2** JUSTIFICATION : justificación *f*
warranty [ˈwɔrənti, ˌwɔrənˈtiː] *n, pl* **-ties** : garantía *f*
warren [ˈwɔrən] *n* : madriguera *f* (de conejos)
warrior [ˈwɔriər] *n* : guerrero *m,* -ra *f*
warship [ˈwɔrˌʃɪp] *n* : buque *m* de guerra
wart [ˈwɔrt] *n* : verruga *f*
wartime [ˈwɔrˌtaɪm] *n* : tiempo *m* de guerra
wary [ˈwæri] *adj* **warier; -est** : cauteloso, receloso <to be wary of : desconfiar de>
was → **be**
wash¹ [ˈwɔʃ, ˈwɑʃ] *vt* **1** CLEAN : lavar(se), limpiar, fregar <to wash the dishes : lavar los platos> <to wash one's hands : lavarse las manos> **2** DRENCH : mojar **3** LAP : bañar <waves were washing the shore : las olas bañaban la orilla> **4** CARRY, DRAG : arrastrar **5 to wash away** : llevarse (un puente, etc.) — *vi* **1** : lavarse (dícese de una persona o la ropa) <the dress washes well : el vestido se lava bien> **2 to wash against** *or* **to wash over** : bañar
wash² *n* **1** : lavado *m* <to give something a wash : lavar algo> **2** LAUNDRY : artículos *mpl* para lavar, ropa *f* sucia **3** : estela *f* (de un barco)
washable [ˈwɔʃəbəl, ˈwɑ-] *adj* : lavable
washboard [ˈwɔʃˌbord, ˈwɑʃ-] *n* : tabla *f* de lavar
washbowl [ˈwɔʃˌboːl, ˈwɑʃ-] *n* : lavabo *m,* lavamanos *m*
washcloth [ˈwɔʃˌklɔθ, ˈwɑʃ-] *n* : toallita *f* (para lavarse)
washed–out [ˈwɔʃtˈaʊt, ˈwɑʃt-] *adj* **1** : desvaído (dícese de colores) **2** EXHAUSTED : agotado, desanimado
washed–up [ˈwɔʃtˈʌp, ˈwɑʃt-] *adj* : acabado (dícese de una persona), fracasado (dícese de un negocio, etc.)
washer [ˈwɔʃər, ˈwɑ-] *n* **1** → **washing machine 2** : arandela *f* (de una llave, etc.)
washing [ˈwɔʃɪŋ, ˈwɑ-] *n* WASH : ropa *f* para lavar
washing machine *n* : máquina *f* de lavar, lavadora *f*
washout [ˈwɔʃˌaʊt, ˈwɑʃ-] *n* **1** : erosión *f* (de la tierra) **2** FAILURE : fracaso *m* <she's a washout : es un desastre>
washroom [ˈwɔʃˌruːm, ˈwɑʃ-, -ˌrʊm] *n* : servicios *mpl* (públicos), baño *m,* sanitario *m Col, Mex, Ven*
wasn't [ˈwʌzənt] (*contraction of* **was not**) → **be**
wasp [ˈwɑsp] *n* : avispa *f*
waspish [ˈwɑspɪʃ] *adj* **1** IRRITABLE : irritable, irascible **2** CAUSTIC : cáustico, mordaz
waste¹ [ˈweɪst] *v* **wasted; wasting** *vt* **1** DEVASTATE : arrasar, arruinar, devastar **2** SQUANDER : desperdiciar, despilfarrar, malgastar <to waste time : perder tiempo> — *vi or* **to waste away** : consumirse, chuparse
waste² *adj* **1** BARREN : yermo, baldío **2** DISCARDED : de desecho **3** EXCESS : sobrante

waste[3] *n* **1** → **wasteland** **2** MISUSE **:** derroche *m,* desperdicio *m,* despilfarro *m* <a waste of time : una pérdida de tiempo> **3** RUBBISH **:** basura *f,* desechos *mpl,* desperdicios *mpl* **4** EXCREMENT **:** excremento *m*

wastebasket [ˈweɪstˌbæskət] *n* **:** cesto *m* (de basura), papelera *f,* zafacón *m Car*

wasteful [ˈweɪstfəl] *adj* **:** despilfarrador, derrochador, pródigo

wastefulness [ˈweɪstfəlnəs] *n* **:** derroche *m,* despilfarro *m*

wasteland [ˈweɪstˌlænd, -lənd] *n* **:** baldío *m,* yermo *m,* desierto *m*

watch[1] [ˈwɑtʃ] *vi* **1** *or* **to keep watch** **:** velar **2** OBSERVE **:** mirar, ver, observar **3 to watch for** AWAIT **:** esperar, quedar a la espera de **4 to watch out** **:** tener cuidado <watch out! : ¡ten cuidado!, ¡ojo!> — *vt* **1** OBSERVE **:** mirar, observar **2** *or* **to watch over** **:** vigilar, cuidar **3 :** tener cuidado de <watch what you do : ten cuidado con lo que haces>

watch[2] *n* **1 :** guardia *f* <to be on watch : estar de guardia> **2** SURVEILLANCE **:** vigilancia *f* **3** LOOKOUT **:** guardia *mf,* centinela *f,* vigía *mf* **4** TIMEPIECE **:** reloj *m*

watchdog [ˈwɑtʃˌdɔg] *n* **:** perro *m* guardián

watcher [ˈwɑtʃər] *n* **:** observador *m,* -dora *f*

watchful [ˈwɑtʃfəl] *adj* **:** alerta, vigilante, atento

watchfulness [ˈwɑtʃfəlnəs] *n* **:** vigilancia *f*

watchman [ˈwɑtʃmən] *n, pl* **-men** [-mən, -ˌmɛn] **:** vigilante *m,* guarda *m*

watchword [ˈwɑtʃˌwərd] *n* **1** PASSWORD **:** contraseña *f* **2** SLOGAN **:** lema *m,* eslogan *m*

water[1] [ˈwɔt̬ər, ˈwɑ-] *vt* **1 :** regar (el jardín, etc.) **2 to water down** DILUTE **:** diluir, aguar — *vi* **:** lagrimar (dícese de los ojos), hacérsele agua la boca a uno <my mouth is watering : se me hace agua la boca>

water[2] *n* **:** agua *f*

water buffalo *n* **:** búfalo *m* de agua

watercolor [ˈwɔt̬ərˌkʌlər, ˈwɑ-] *n* **:** acuarela *f*

watercourse [ˈwɔt̬ərˌkors, ˈwɑ-] *n* **:** curso *m* de agua

watercress [ˈwɔt̬ərˌkrɛs, ˈwɑ-] *n* **:** berro *m*

waterfall [ˈwɔt̬ərˌfɔl, ˈwɑ-] *n* **:** cascada *f,* salto *m* de agua, catarata *f*

waterfowl [ˈwɔt̬ərˌfaʊl, ˈwɑ-] *n* **:** ave *f* acuática

waterfront [ˈwɔt̬ərˌfrʌnt, ˈwɑ-] *n* **1 :** tierra *f* que bordea un río, un lago, o un mar **2** WHARF **:** muelle *m*

water lily *n* **:** nenúfar *m*

waterlogged [ˈwɔt̬ərˌlɔgd, ˈwɑt̬ərˌlɑgd] *adj* **:** lleno de agua, empapado, inundado (dícese del suelo)

watermark [ˈwɔt̬ərˌmɑrk, ˈwɑ-] *n* **1 :** marca *f* del nivel de agua **2 :** filigrana *f* (en el papel)

watermelon [ˈwɔt̬ərˌmɛlən, ˈwɑ-] *n* **:** sandía *f*

water moccasin → **moccasin**

waterpower [ˈwɔt̬ərˌpaʊər, ˈwɑ-] *n* **:** energía *f* hidráulica

waterproof[1] [ˈwɔt̬ərˌpruːf, ˈwɑ-] *vt* **:** hacer impermeable, impermeabilizar

waterproof[2] *adj* **:** impermeable, a prueba de agua

watershed [ˈwɔt̬ərˌʃɛd, ˈwɑ-] *n* **1 :** línea *f* divisoria de aguas **2** BASIN **:** cuenca *f* (de un río)

waterskiing [ˈwɔt̬ərˌskiːɪŋ, ˈwɑ-] *n* **:** esquí *m* acuático

waterspout [ˈwɔt̬ərˌspaʊt, ˈwɑ-] *n* WHIRLWIND **:** tromba *f* marina

watertight [ˈwɔt̬ərˌtaɪt, ˈwɑ-] *adj* **1 :** hermético **2** IRREFUTABLE **:** irrebatible, irrefutable <a watertight contract : un contrato sin lagunas>

waterway [ˈwɔt̬ərˌweɪ, ˈwɑ-] *n* **:** vía *f* navegable

waterworks [ˈwɔt̬ərˌwərks, ˈwɑ-] *npl* **:** central *f* de abastecimiento de agua

watery [ˈwɔt̬əri, ˈwɑ-] *adj* **1 :** acuoso, como agua **2 :** aguado, diluido <watery soup : sopa aguada> **3 :** lloroso <watery eyes : ojos llorosos> **4** WASHED-OUT **:** desvaído (dícese de colores)

watt [ˈwɑt] *n* **:** vatio *m*

wattage [ˈwɑt̬ɪdʒ] *n* **:** vataje *m*

wattle [ˈwɑt̬əl] *n* **:** carúncula *f* (de un ave, etc.)

wave[1] [ˈweɪv] *v* **waved; waving** *vi* **1 :** saludar con la mano, hacer señas con la mano <she waved at him : lo saludó con la mano> **2** FLUTTER, SHAKE **:** ondear, agitarse **3** UNDULATE **:** ondular — *vt* **1** SHAKE **:** agitar **2** BRANDISH **:** blandir **3** CURL **:** ondular, marcar (el pelo) **4** SIGNAL **:** hacerle señas a (con la mano) <he waved farewell : se despidió con la mano>

wave[2] *n* **1 :** ola *f* (de agua) **2** CURL **:** onda *f* (en el pelo) **3 :** onda *f* (en física) **4** SURGE **:** oleada *f* <a wave of enthusiasm : una oleada de entusiasmo> **5** GESTURE **:** señal *f* con la mano, saludo *m* con la mano

wavelength [ˈweɪvˌlɛŋkθ] *n* **:** longitud *f* de onda

waver [ˈweɪvər] *vi* **1** VACILLATE **:** vacilar, fluctuar **2** FLICKER **:** parpadear, titilar, oscilar **3** FALTER **:** flaquear, tambalearse

wavy [ˈweɪvi] *adj* **wavier; -est :** ondulado

wax[1] [ˈwæks] *vi* **1 :** crecer (dícese de la luna) **2** BECOME **:** volverse, ponerse <to wax indignant : indignarse> — *vt* **:** encerar

wax[2] *n* **1** BEESWAX **:** cera *f* de abejas **2 :** cera *f* <floor wax : cera para el piso>

3 *or* **earwax** [ˈɪrˌwæks] : cerilla *f,* cerumen *m*

waxen [ˈwæksən] *adj* : de cera

waxy [ˈwæksi] *adj* **waxier; -est** : ceroso

way [ˈweɪ] *n* **1** PATH, ROAD : camino *m,* vía *f* **2** ROUTE : camino *m,* ruta *f* <to go the wrong way : equivocarse de camino> <I'm on my way : estoy de camino> **3** : línea *f* de conducta, camino *m* <he chose the easy way : optó por el camino fácil> **4** MANNER, MEANS : manera *f,* modo *m,* forma *f* <in the same way : del mismo modo, igualmente> <there are no two ways about it : no cabe la menor duda> **5** (*indicating a wish*) <have it your way : como tú quieras> <to get one's own way : salirse uno con la suya> **6** STATE : estado *m* <things are in a bad way : las cosas marchan mal> **7** RESPECT : aspecto *m,* sentido *m* **8** CUSTOM : costumbre *f* <to mend one's ways : dejar las malas costumbres> **9** PASSAGE : camino *m* <to get in the way : meterse en el camino> **10** DISTANCE : distancia *f* <to come a long way : hacer grandes progresos> **11** DIRECTION : dirección *f* <come this way : venga por aquí> <which way did he go? : ¿por dónde fue?> **12 by the way** : a propósito, por cierto **13 by way of** VIA : vía, pasando por **14 out of the way** REMOTE : remoto, recóndito **15** → **under way**

wayfarer [ˈweɪˌfærər] *n* : caminante *mf*

waylay [ˈweɪˌleɪ] *vt* **-laid** [-ˌleɪd]; **-laying** ACCOST : abordar

wayside [ˈweɪˌsaɪd] *n* : borde *m* del camino

wayward [ˈweɪwərd] *adj* **1** UNRULY : díscolo, rebelde **2** UNTOWARD : adverso

we [ˈwiː] *pron* : nosotros, nosotras

weak [ˈwiːk] *adj* **1** FEEBLE : débil, endeble **2** : flojo, pobre <a weak excuse : una excusa poco convincente> **3** DILUTED : aguado, diluido <weak tea : té poco cargado> **4** FAINT : tenue (dícese de los colores, las luces, los sonidos, etc.)

weaken [ˈwiːkən] *vt* : debilitar — *vi* : debilitarse, flaquear

weakling [ˈwiːklɪŋ] *n* : alfeñique *m fam;* debilucho *m,* -cha *f*

weakly[1] [ˈwiːkli] *adv* : débilmente

weakly[2] *adj* **weaklier; -est** : débil, enclenque

weakness [ˈwiːknəs] *n* **1** FEEBLENESS : debilidad *f* **2** FAULT, FLAW : flaqueza *f,* punto *m* débil

wealth [ˈwɛlθ] *n* **1** RICHES : riqueza *f* **2** PROFUSION : abundancia *f,* profusión *f*

wealthy [ˈwɛlθi] *adj* **wealthier; -est** : rico, acaudalado, adinerado

wean [ˈwiːn] *vt* **1** : destetar (a los niños o las crías) **2 to wean someone away from** : quitarle a alguien la costumbre de

weapon [ˈwɛpən] *n* : arma *f*

weaponless [ˈwɛpənləs] *adj* : desarmado

wear[1] [ˈwær] *v* **wore** [ˈwor]; **worn** [ˈworn]; **wearing** *vt* **1** : llevar (ropa, un reloj, etc.), calzar (zapatos) <to wear a happy smile : sonreír alegremente> **2** *or* **to wear away** : desgastar, erosionar (rocas, etc.) **3 to wear out** : gastar <he wore out his shoes : gastó sus zapatos> **4 to wear out** EXHAUST : agotar, fatigar <to wear oneself out : agotarse> — *vi* **1** LAST : durar **2 to wear off** DIMINISH : disminuir **3 to wear out** : gastarse

wear[2] *n* **1** USE : uso *m* <for everyday wear : para todos los días> **2** CLOTHING : ropa *f* <children's wear : ropa de niños> **3** DETERIORATION : desgaste *m* <to be the worse for wear : estar deteriorado>

wearable [ˈwærəbəl] *adj* : que puede ponerse (dícese de una prenda)

wear and tear *n* : desgaste *m*

weariness [ˈwɪrinəs] *n* : fatiga *f,* cansancio *m*

wearisome [ˈwɪrisəm] *adj* : aburrido, pesado, cansado

weary[1] [ˈwɪri] *v* **-ried; -rying** *vt* **1** TIRE : cansar, fatigar **2** BORE : hastiar, aburrir — *vi* : cansarse

weary[2] *adj* **-rier; -est 1** TIRED : cansado **2** FED UP : harto **3** BORED : aburrido

weasel [ˈwiːzəl] *n* : comadreja *f*

weather[1] [ˈwɛðər] *vt* **1** WEAR : erosionar, desgastar **2** ENDURE : aguantar, sobrellevar, capear <to weather the storm : capear el temporal>

weather[2] *n* : tiempo *m*

weather–beaten [ˈwɛðərˌbiːtən] *adj* : curtido

weatherman [ˈwɛðərˌmæn] *n, pl* **-men** [-mən, -ˌmɛn] METEOROLOGIST : meteorólogo *m,* -ga *f*

weatherproof [ˈwɛðərˌpruːf] *adj* : que resiste a la intemperie, impermeable

weather vane → **vane**

weave[1] [ˈwiːv] *v* **wove** [ˈwoːv] *or* **weaved; woven** [ˈwoːvən] *or* **weaved; weaving** *vt* **1** : tejer (tela) **2** INTERLACE : entretejer, entrelazar **3 to weave one's way through** : abrirse camino por — *vi* **1** : tejer **2** WIND : serpentear, zigzaguear

weave[2] *n* : tejido *m,* trama *f*

weaver [ˈwiːvər] *n* : tejedor *m,* -dora *f*

web[1] [ˈwɛb] *vt* **webbed; webbing** : cubrir o proveer con una red

web[2] *n* **1** COBWEB, SPIDERWEB : telaraña *f,* tela *f* de araña **2** ENTANGLEMENT, SNARE : red *f,* enredo *m* <a web of intrigue : una red de intriga> **3** : membrana *f* interdigital (de aves) **4** NETWORK : red *f* <a web of highways : una red de carreteras>

webbed ['wɛbd] *adj* : palmeado <webbed feet : patas palmeadas>

wed ['wɛd] *vt* **wedded; wedding 1** MARRY : casarse con **2** UNITE : ligar, unir

we'd ['wiːd] (*contraction of* **we had, we should,** *or* **we would**) → **have, should, would**

wedding ['wɛdɪŋ] *n* : boda *f,* casamiento *m*

wedge[1] ['wɛdʒ] *vt* **wedged; wedging 1** : apretar (con una cuña) <to wedge open : mantener abierto con una cuña> **2** CRAM : meter, embutir

wedge[2] *n* **1** : cuña *f* **2** PIECE : porción *f,* trozo *m*

wedlock ['wɛd,lɑk] → **marriage**

Wednesday ['wɛnz,deɪ, -di] *n* : miércoles *m*

wee ['wiː] *adj* : pequeño, minúsculo <in the wee hours : a las altas horas>

weed[1] ['wiːd] *vt* **1** : desherbar, desyerbar **2 to weed out** : eliminar, quitar

weed[2] *n* : mala hierba *f*

weedy ['wiːdi] *adj* **weedier; -est 1** : cubierto de malas hierbas **2** LANKY, SKINNY : flaco, larguirucho *fam*

week ['wiːk] *n* : semana *f*

weekday ['wiːk,deɪ] *n* : día *m* laborable

weekend ['wiːk,ɛnd] *n* : fin *m* de semana

weekly[1] ['wiːkli] *adv* : semanalmente

weekly[2] *adj* : semanal

weekly[3] *n, pl* **-lies** : semanario *m*

weep ['wiːp] *v* **wept** ['wɛpt]; **weeping** : llorar

weeping willow *n* : sauce *m* llorón

weepy ['wiːpi] *adj* **weepier; -est** : lloroso, triste

weevil ['wiːvəl] *n* : gorgojo *m*

weft ['wɛft] *n* : trama *f*

weigh ['weɪ] *vt* **1** : pesar **2** CONSIDER : considerar, sopesar **3 to weigh anchor** : levar anclas **4 to weigh down** : sobrecargar (con una carga), abrumar (con preocupaciones, etc.) — *vi* **1** : pesar <it weighs 10 pounds : pesa 10 libras> **2** COUNT : tener importancia, contar **3 to weigh on one's mind** : preocuparle a uno

weight[1] ['weɪt] *vt* **1** : poner peso en, sujetar con un peso **2** BURDEN : cargar, oprimir

weight[2] *n* **1** HEAVINESS : peso *m* <to lose weight : bajar de peso, adelgazar> **2** : peso *m* <weights and measures : pesos y medidas> **3** : pesa *f* <to lift weights : levantar pesas> **4** BURDEN : peso *m,* carga *f* <to take a weight off one's mind : quitarle un peso de encima a uno> **5** IMPORTANCE : peso *m* **6** INFLUENCE : influencia *f,* autoridad *f* <to throw one's weight around : hacer sentir su influencia>

weighty ['weɪti] *adj* **weightier; -est 1** HEAVY : pesado **2** IMPORTANT : importante, de peso

weird ['wɪrd] *adj* **1** MYSTERIOUS : misterioso **2** STRANGE : extraño, raro — **weirdly** *adv*

welcome[1] ['wɛlkəm] *vt* **-comed; -coming** : darle la bienvenida a, recibir

welcome[2] *adj* : bienvenido <to make someone welcome : acoger bien a alguien> <you're welcome! : ¡de nada!, ¡no hay de qué!>

welcome[3] *n* : bienvenida *f,* recibimiento *m,* acojida *f*

weld[1] ['wɛld] *v* : soldar

weld[2] *n* : soldadura *f*

welder ['wɛldər] *n* : soldador *m,* -dora *f*

welfare ['wɛl,fær] *n* **1** WELL-BEING : bienestar *m* **2** : asistencia *f* social

well[1] ['wɛl] *vi or* **to well up** : brotar, manar

well[2] *adv* **better** ['bɛt̬ər]; **best** ['bɛst] **1** RIGHTLY : bien, correctamente **2** SATISFACTORILY : bien <to turn out well : resultar bien, salir bien> **3** COMPLETELY : completamente <well-hidden : completamente escondido> **4** INTIMATELY : bien <I knew him well : lo conocía bien> **5** CONSIDERABLY, FAR : muy, bastante <well ahead : muy adelante> <well before the deadline : bastante antes de la fecha> **6 as well** ALSO : también **7** → **as well as**

well[3] *adj* **1** SATISFACTORY : bien <all is well : todo está bien> **2** DESIRABLE : conveniente <it would be well if you left : sería conveniente que te fueras> **3** HEALTHY : bien, sano

well[4] *n* **1** : pozo *m* (de agua, petróleo, gas, etc.), aljibe *m* (de agua) **2** SOURCE : fuente *f* <a well of information : una fuente de información> **3** *or* **stairwell** : caja *f,* hueco *m* (de la escalera)

well[5] *interj* **1** (*used to introduce a remark*) : bueno **2** (*used to express surprise*) : ¡vaya!

we'll ['wiːl, wɪl] (*contraction of* **we shall** *or* **we will**) → **shall, will**

well–balanced ['wɛl'bælənst] *adj* : equilibrado

well–being ['wɛl'biːɪŋ] *n* : bienestar *m*

well–bred ['wɛl'brɛd] *adj* : fino, bien educado

well–done ['wɛl'dʌn] *adj* **1** : bien hecho <well-done! : ¡bravo!> **2** : bien cocido

well–known ['wɛl'noːn] *adj* : famoso, bien conocido

well–meaning ['wɛl'miːnɪŋ] *adj* : bienintencionado, que tiene buenas intenciones

well–nigh ['wɛl'naɪ] *adv* : casi <well-nigh impossible : casi imposible>

well–off ['wɛl'ɔf] → **well–to–do**

well–rounded ['wɛl'raʊndəd] *adj* : completo, equilibrado

well–to–do [,wɛltə'duː] *adj* : próspero, adinerado, rico

welt [ˈwɛlt] *n* **1 :** vira *f* (de un zapato) **2** WHEAL **:** verdugón *m*
welter [ˈwɛltər] *n* **:** fárrago *m,* revoltijo *m* <a welter of data : un fárrago de datos>
wend [ˈwɛnd] *vi* **to wend one's way :** ponerse en camino, encaminar sus pasos
went → **go**
wept → **weep**
were → **be**
we're [ˈwɪr, ˈwər, ˈwiːər] (*contraction of* **we are**) → **be**
werewolf [ˈwɪrˌwʊlf, ˈwɛr-, ˈwər-, -ˌwʌlf] *n, pl* **-wolves** [-ˌwʊlvz, -ˌwʌlvz] **:** hombre *m* lobo
west[1] [ˈwɛst] *adv* **:** al oeste
west[2] *adj* **:** oeste, del oeste, occidental <west winds : vientos del oeste>
west[3] *n* **1 :** oeste *m* **2 the West :** el Oeste, el Occidente
westerly [ˈwɛstərli] *adv* & *adj* **:** del oeste
western [ˈwɛstərn] *adj* **1 :** Occidental, del Oeste **2 :** occidental, oeste
Westerner [ˈwɛstərnər] *n* **:** habitante *mf* del oeste
West Indian *n* **:** antillano *m,* -na *f* — **West Indian** *adj*
westward [ˈwɛstwərd] *adv & adj* **:** hacia el oeste
wet[1] [ˈwɛt] *vt* **wet** *or* **wetted; wetting :** mojar, humedecer
wet[2] *adj* **wetter; wettest 1 :** mojado, húmedo <wet clothes : ropa mojada> **2** RAINY **:** lluvioso **3 wet paint :** pintura *f* fresca
wet[3] *n* **1** MOISTURE **:** humedad *f* **2** RAIN **:** lluvia *f*
we've [ˈwiːv] (*contraction of* **we have**) → **have**
whack[1] [ˈ*h*wæk] *vt* **:** golpear (fuertemente), aporrear
whack[2] *n* **1 :** golpe *m* fuerte, porrazo *m* **2** ATTEMPT **:** intento *m,* tentativa *f*
whale[1] [ˈ*h*weɪl] *vi* **whaled; whaling :** cazar ballenas
whale[2] *n, pl* **whales** *or* **whale :** ballena *f*
whaleboat [ˈ*h*weɪlˌboːt] *n* **:** ballenero *m*
whalebone [ˈ*h*weɪlˌboːn] *n* **:** barba *f* de ballena
whaler [ˈ*h*weɪlər] *n* **1 :** ballenero *m,* -ra *f* **2** → **whaleboat**
wharf [ˈ*h*wɔrf] *n, pl* **wharves** [ˈ*h*wɔrvz] **:** muelle *m,* embarcadero *m*
what[1] [ˈ*h*wɑt, ˈ*h*wʌt] *adv* **1** HOW **:** cómo, cúanto <what he suffered! : ¡cómo sufría!> **2 what with :** entre <what with one thing and another : entre una cosa y otra>
what[2] *adj* **1** (*used in questions*) **:** qué <what more do you want? : ¿qué más quieres?> <what color is it? : ¿de qué color es?> **2** (*used in exclamations*) **:** qué <what an idea! : ¡qué idea!> **3** ANY, WHATEVER **:** cualquier <give what help you can : da cualquier contribución que puedas>
what[3] *pron* **1** (*used in direct questions*) **:** qué <what happened? : ¿qué pasó?> <what does it cost? : ¿cuánto cuesta?> **2** (*used in indirect statements*) **:** lo que, que <I don't know what to do : no sé que hacer> <do what I tell you : haz lo que te digo> **3 what for** WHY **:** porqué **4 what if :** y si <what if he knows? : ¿y si lo sabe?>
whatever[1] [*h*wɑṭˈɛvər, ˌ*h*wʌṭ-] *adj* **1** ANY **:** cualquier, cualquier...que <whatever way you prefer : de cualquier manera que prefiera, como prefiera> **2** (*in negative constructions*) <there's no chance whatever : no hay ninguna posibilidad> <nothing whatever : nada en absoluto>
whatever[2] *pron* **1** ANYTHING **:** (todo) lo que <I'll do whatever I want : haré lo que quiera> **2** (*no matter what*) <whatever it may be : sea lo que sea> **3** WHAT **:** qué <whatever do you mean? : ¿qué quieres decir?>
whatsoever[1] [ˌ*h*wɑtsoˈɛvər, ˌ*h*wʌṭ-] *adj* → **whatever**[1]
whatsoever[2] *pron* → **whatever**[2]
wheal [ˈ*h*wiːl] *n* **:** verdugón *m*
wheat [ˈ*h*wiːt] *n* **:** trigo *m*
wheaten [ˈ*h*wiːtən] *adj* **:** de trigo
wheedle [ˈ*h*wiːdəl] *vt* **-dled; -dling** CAJOLE **:** engatusar <to wheedle something out of someone : sonsacarle algo a alguien>
wheel[1] [ˈ*h*wiːl] *vt* **:** empujar (una bicicleta, etc.), mover (algo sobre ruedas) — *vi* **1** ROTATE **:** girar, rotar **2 to wheel around** TURN **:** darse la vuelta
wheel[2] *n* **1 :** rueda *f* **2** *or* **steering wheel :** volante *m* (de automóviles, etc.), timón *m* (de barcos o aviones) **3 wheels** *npl* **:** maquinaria *f,* fuerza *f* impulsora <the wheels of government : la maquinaria del gobierno>
wheelbarrow [ˈ*h*wiːlˌbærˌoː] *n* **:** carretilla *f*
wheelchair [ˈ*h*wiːlˌtʃær] *n* **:** silla *f* de ruedas
wheeze[1] [ˈ*h*wiːz] *vi* **wheezed; wheezing :** resollar, respirar con dificultad
wheeze[2] *n* **:** resuello *m*
whelk [ˈ*h*wɛlk] *n* **:** buccino *m*
whelp[1] [ˈ*h*wɛlp] *vi* **:** parir
whelp[2] *n* **:** cachorro *m,* -rra *f*
when[1] [ˈ*h*wɛn] *adv* **:** cuándo <when will you return? : ¿cuándo volverás?> <he asked me when I would be home : me preguntó cuándo estaría en casa>
when[2] *conj* **1** (*referring to a particular time*) **:** cuando, en que <when you are ready : cuando estés listo> <the days when I clean the house : los días en que limpio la casa> **2** IF **:** cuando, si <how can I go when I have no money? : ¿cómo voy a ir si no tengo dinero?> **3** ALTHOUGH **:** cuando <you said it was big when actually it's

small : dijiste que era grande cuando en realidad es pequeño>
when[3] *pron* : cuándo <since when are you the boss? : ¿desde cuándo eres el jefe?>
whence [ˈ*h*wɛnts] *adv* : de donde
whenever[1] [*h*wɛnˈɛvər] *adv* **1** : cuando sea <tomorrow or whenever : manaña o cuando sea> **2** (*in questions*) : cuándo
whenever[2] *conj* **1** : siempre que, cada vez que <whenever I go, I'm disappointed : siempre que voy, quedo desilusionado> **2** WHEN : cuando <whenever you like : cuando quieras>
where[1] [ˈ*h*wɛr] *adv* : dónde, adónde <where is he? : ¿dónde está?> <where did they go? : ¿adónde fueron?>
where[2] *conj* : donde, adonde <she knows where the house is : sabe donde está la casa> <she goes where she likes : va adonde quiera>
where[3] *pron* : donde <Chicago is where I live : Chicago es donde vivo>
whereabouts[1] [ˈ*h*wɛrəˌbaʊts] *adv* : dónde, por dónde <whereabouts is the house? : ¿dónde está la casa?>
whereabouts[2] *ns & pl* : paradero *m*
whereas [*h*wɛrˈæz] *conj* **1** : considerando que (usado en documentos legales) **2** : mientras que <I like the white one whereas she prefers the black : me gusta el blanco mientras que ella prefiere el negro>
whereby [*h*wɛrˈbaɪ] *adv* : por lo cual
wherefore [ˈ*h*wɛrˌfor] *adv* : por qué
wherein [*h*wɛrˈɪn] *adv* : en el cual, en el que
whereof [*h*wɛrˈʌv, -ɑv] *conj* : de lo cual
whereupon [ˈ*h*wɛrəˌpɑn, -ˌpɔn] *conj* : con lo cual, después de lo cual
wherever[1] [*h*wɛrˈɛvər] *adv* **1** WHERE : dónde, adónde **2** : en cualquier parte <or wherever : o donde sea>
wherever[2] *conj* : dondequiera que, donde sea <wherever you go : dondequiera que vayas>
wherewithal [ˈ*h*wɛrwɪˌðɔl, -ˌθɔl] *n* : medios *mpl*, recursos *mpl*
whet [ˈ*h*wɛt] *vt* **whetted; whetting 1** SHARPEN : afilar **2** STIMULATE : estimular <to whet the appetite : estimular el apetito>
whether [ˈ*h*wɛðər] *conj* **1** : si <I don't know whether it is finished : no sé si está acabado> <we doubt whether he'll show up : dudamos que aparezca> **2** (*used in comparisons*) <whether I like it or not : tanto si quiero como si no> <whether he comes or he doesn't : venga o no>
whetstone [ˈ*h*wɛtˌsto:n] *n* : piedra *f* de afilar
whey [ˈ*h*weɪ] *n* : suero *m* (de la leche)
which[1] [ˈ*h*wɪtʃ] *adj* : qué, cuál <which tie do you prefer? : ¿cuál corbata prefieres?> <which ones? : ¿cuáles?> <tell me which house is yours : dime qué casa es la tuya>
which[2] *pron* **1** : cuál <which is the right answer? : ¿cuál es la respuesta correcta?> **2** : que, el (la) cual <the cup which broke : la taza que se quebró> <the house, which is made of brick : la casa, la cual es de ladrillo>
whichever[1] [*h*wɪtʃˈɛvər] *adj* : el (la) que, cualquiera que <whichever book you like : cualquier libro que te guste>
whichever[2] *pron* : el (la) que, cualquiera que <take whichever you want : toma el que quieras> <whichever I choose : cualquiera que elija>
whiff[1] [ˈ*h*wɪf] *v* PUFF : soplar
whiff[2] *n* **1** PUFF : soplo *m*, ráfaga *f* **2** SNIFF : olor *m* **3** HINT : dejo *m*, pizca *f*
while[1] [ˈ*h*waɪl] *vt* **whiled; whiling** : pasar <to while away the time : matar el tiempo>
while[2] *n* **1** TIME : rato *m*, tiempo *m* <after a while : después de un rato> <in a while : dentro de poco> **2 to be worth one's while** : valer la pena
while[3] *conj* **1** : mientras <whistle while you work : silba mientras trabajas> **2** WHEREAS : mientras que **3** ALTHOUGH : aunque <while it's very good, it's not perfect : aunque es muy bueno, no es perfecto>
whim [ˈ*h*wɪm] *n* : capricho *m*, antojo *m*
whimper[1] [ˈ*h*wɪmpər] *vi* : lloriquear, gimotear
whimper[2] *n* : quejido *m*
whimsical [ˈ*h*wɪmzɪkəl] *adj* **1** CAPRICIOUS : caprichoso, fantasioso **2** ERRATIC : errático — **whimsically** *adv*
whine[1] [ˈ*h*waɪn] *vi* **whined; whining 1** : lloriquear, gimotear, gemir **2** COMPLAIN : quejarse
whine[2] *n* : quejido *m*, gemido *m*
whinny[1] [ˈ*h*wɪni] *vi* **-nied; -nying** : relinchar
whinny[2] *n*, *pl* **-nies** : relincho *m*
whip[1] [ˈ*h*wɪp] *v* **whipped; whipping** *vt* **1** SNATCH : sacar (rápidamente), arrebatar <she whipped the cloth off the table : arrebató el mantel de la mesa> **2** LASH : azotar **3** DEFEAT : vencer, derrotar **4** INCITE : incitar, despertar <to whip up enthusiasm : despertar el entusiasmo> **5** BEAT : batir (huevos, crema, etc.) — *vi* FLAP : agitarse
whip[2] *n* **1** : látigo *m*, azote *m*, fusta *f* (de jinete) **2** : miembro *m* de un cuerpo legislativo encargado de disciplina
whiplash [ˈ*h*wɪpˌlæʃ] *n* or **whiplash injury** : traumatismo *m* cervical
whippet [ˈ*h*wɪpət] *n* : galgo *m* pequeño, galgo *m* inglés
whippoorwill [ˈ*h*wɪpərˌwɪl] *n* : chotacabras *mf*
whir[1] [ˈ*h*wər] *vi* **whirred; whirring** : zumbar
whir[2] *n* : zumbido *m*

whirl[1] [ˈhwərl] *vi* **1** SPIN **:** dar vueltas, girar <my head is whirling **:** la cabeza me está dando vueltas> **2 to whirl about :** arremolinarse, moverse rápidamente

whirl[2] *n* **1** SPIN **:** giro *m,* vuelta *f,* remolino *m* (dícese del polvo, etc.) **2** BUSTLE **:** bullicio *m,* torbellino *m* (de actividad, etc.) **3 to give it a whirl :** intentar hacer, probar

whirlpool [ˈhwərl,pu:l] *n* **:** vorágine *f,* remolino *m*

whirlwind [ˈhwərl,wɪnd] *n* **:** remolino *m,* torbellino *m,* tromba *f*

whisk[1] [ˈhwɪsk] *vt* **1 :** llevar <she whisked the children off to bed **:** llevó a los niños a la cama> **2 :** batir <to whisk eggs **:** batir huevos> **3 to whisk away** *or* **to whisk off :** sacudir

whisk[2] *n* **1** WHISKING **:** sacudida *f* (movimiento) **2 :** batidor *m* (para batir huevos, etc.)

whisk broom *n* **:** escobilla *f*

whisker [ˈhwɪskər] *n* **1 :** pelo *m* (de la barba o el bigote) **2 whiskers** *npl* **:** bigotes *mpl* (de animales)

whiskey *or* **whisky** [ˈhwɪski] *n, pl* **-keys** *or* **-kies :** whisky *m*

whisper[1] [ˈhwɪspər] *vi* **:** cuchichear, susurrar — *vt* **:** decir en voz baja, susurrar

whisper[2] *n* **1** WHISPERING **:** susurro *m,* cuchicheo *m* **2** RUMOR **:** rumor *m* **3** TRACE **:** dejo *m,* pizca *f*

whistle[1] [ˈhwɪsəl] *v* **-tled; -tling** *vi* **:** silbar, chiflar, pitar (dícese de un tren, etc.) — *vt* **:** silbar <to whistle a tune **:** silbar una melodía>

whistle[2] *n* **1** WHISTLING **:** chiflido *m,* silbido *m* **2 :** silbato *m,* pito *m* (instrumento)

whit [ˈhwɪt] *n* BIT **:** ápice *m,* pizca *f*

white[1] [ˈhwaɪt] *adj* **whiter; -est :** blanco

white[2] *n* **1 :** blanco *m* (color) **2 :** clara *f* (de huevos) **3** *or* **white person :** blanco *m,* -ca *f*

white blood cell *n* **:** glóbulo *m* blanco

whitecaps [ˈhwaɪt,kæps] *npl* **:** cabrillas *fpl*

white–collar [ˈhwaɪtˈkɑlər] *adj* **1 :** de oficina **2 white–collar worker :** oficinista *mf*

whitefish [ˈhwaɪt,fɪʃ] *n* **:** pescado *m* blanco

whiten [ˈhwaɪtən] *vt* **:** blanquear — *vi* **:** ponerse blanco

whiteness [ˈhwaɪtnəs] *n* **:** blancura *f*

white–tailed deer [ˈhwaɪtˈteɪld] *n* **:** ciervo *f* de Virginia

whitewash[1] [ˈhwaɪt,wɔʃ] *vt* **1 :** enjalbegar, blanquear <to whitewash a fence **:** enjalbegar una valla> **2** CONCEAL **:** encubrir (un escándalo, etc.)

whitewash[2] *n* **1 :** jalbegue *m,* lechada *f* **2** COVER-UP **:** encubrimiento *m*

whither [ˈhwɪðər] *adv* **:** adónde

whiting [ˈhwaɪtɪŋ] *n* **:** merluza *f,* pescadilla *f* (pez)

whitish [ˈhwaɪtɪʃ] *adj* **:** blancuzco

whittle [ˈhwɪtəl] *vt* **-tled; -tling 1 :** tallar (madera) **2 to whittle down :** reducir, recortar <to whittle down expenses **:** reducir los gastos>

whiz[1] *or* **whizz** [ˈhwɪz] *vi* **whizzed; whizzing 1** BUZZ **:** zumbar **2 to whiz by :** pasar muy rápido, pasar volando

whiz[2] *or* **whizz** *n, pl* **whizzes 1** BUZZ **:** zumbido *m* **2 to be a whiz :** ser un prodigio, ser muy hábil

who [ˈhu:] *pron* **1** (*used in direct and indirect questions*) **:** quién <who is that? **:** ¿quién es ése?> <who did it? **:** ¿quién lo hizo?> <we know who they are **:** sabemos quiénes son> **2** (*used in relative clauses*) **:** que, quien <the lady who lives there **:** la señora que vive allí> <for those who wait **:** para los que esperan, para quienes esperan>

whodunit [hu:ˈdʌnɪt] *n* **:** novela *f* policíaca

whoever [hu:ˈɛvər] *pron* **1 :** quienquiera que, quien <whoever did it **:** quienquiera que lo hizo> <give it to whoever you want **:** dalo a quien quieras> **2** (*used in questions*) **:** quién <whoever could that be? **:** ¿quién podría ser?>

whole[1] [ˈho:l] *adj* **1** UNHURT **:** ileso **2** INTACT **:** intacto, sano **3** ENTIRE **:** entero, íntegro <the whole island **:** toda la isla> <whole milk **:** leche entera> **4 a whole lot :** muchísimo

whole[2] *n* **1 :** todo *m* **2 as a whole :** en conjunto **3 on the whole :** en general

wholehearted [ˈho:lˈhɑrtəd] *adj* **:** sin reservas, incondicional

whole number *n* **:** entero *m*

wholesale[1] [ˈho:l,seɪl] *v* **-saled; -saling** *vt* **:** vender al por mayor — *vi* **:** venderse al por mayor

wholesale[2] *adv* **:** al por mayor

wholesale[3] *adj* **1 :** al por mayor <wholesale grocer **:** tendero al por mayor> **2** TOTAL **:** total, absoluto <wholesale slaughter **:** matanza sistemática>

wholesale[4] *n* **:** mayoreo *m*

wholesaler [ˈho:l,seɪlər] *n* **:** mayorista *mf*

wholesome [ˈho:lsəm] *adj* **1 :** sano <wholesome advice **:** consejo sano> **2** HEALTHY **:** sano, saludable

whole wheat *adj* **:** de trigo integral

wholly [ˈho:li] *adv* **1** COMPLETELY **:** completamente **2** SOLELY **:** exclusivamente, únicamente

whom [ˈhu:m] *pron* **1** (*used in direct questions*) **:** a quién <whom did you choose? **:** ¿a quién elegiste?> **2** (*used in indirect questions*) **:** de quién, con quién, en quién <I don't know whom to consult **:** no sé con quién consultar> **3** (*used in relative clauses*) **:** que, a quien <the lawyer whom I recommended to you **:** el abogado que te recomendé>

whomever [huːm'ɛvər] *pron* : a quienquiera que, a quien

whoop[1] ['*h*wuːp, '*h*wʊp] *vi* : gritar, chillar

whoop[2] *n* : grito *m*

whooping cough *n* : tos *f* ferina

whopper ['*h*wɑpər] *n* **1** : cosa *f* enorme **2** LIE : mentira *f* colosal

whopping ['*h*wɑpɪŋ] *adj* : enorme

whore ['hor] *n* : puta *f*, ramera *f*

whorl ['*h*wɔrl, '*h*wərl] *n* : espiral *f*, espira *f* (de una concha), línea *f* (de una huella digital)

whose[1] ['huːz] *adj* **1** (*used in questions*) : de quién <whose truck is that? : ¿de quién es ese camión?> **2** (*used in relative clauses*) : cuyo <the person whose work is finished : la persona cuyo trabajo está terminado>

whose[2] *pron* : de quién <tell me whose it was : dime de quién era>

why[1] ['*h*waɪ] *adv* : por qué <why did you do it? : ¿por qué lo hizo?>

why[2] *n, pl* **whys** REASON : porqué *m*, razón *f*

why[3] *conj* : por qué <I know why he left : yo sé por qué salió> <there's no reason why it should exist : no hay razón para que exista>

why[4] *interj* (*used to express surprise*) : ¡vaya!, ¡mira!

wick ['wɪk] *n* : mecha *f*

wicked ['wɪkəd] *adj* **1** EVIL : malo, malvado **2** MISCHIEVOUS : travieso, pícaro <a wicked grin : una sonrisa traviesa> **3** TERRIBLE : terrible, horrible <a wicked storm : una tormenta horrible>

wickedly ['wɪkədli] *adv* : con maldad

wickedness ['wɪkədnəs] *n* : maldad *f*

wicker[1] ['wɪkər] *adj* : de mimbre

wicker[2] *n* **1** : mimbre *m* **2** → **wickerwork**

wickerwork ['wɪkər,wərk] *n* : artículos *mpl* de mimbre

wicket ['wɪkət] *n* **1** WINDOW : ventanilla *f* **2** *or* **wicket gate** : postigo *m* **3** : aro *m* (en croquet), palos *mpl* (en críquet)

wide[1] ['waɪd] *adv* **wider; widest 1** WIDELY : por todas partes <to travel far and wide : viajar por todas partes> **2** COMPLETELY : completamente, totalmente <wide open : abierto de par en par> **3 wide apart** : muy separados

wide[2] *adj* **wider; widest 1** VAST : vasto, extensivo <a wide area : una área extensiva> **2** : ancho <three meters wide : tres metros de ancho> **3** BROAD : ancho, amplio **4** *or* **wide–open** : muy abierto **5 wide of the mark** : desviado, lejos del blanco

wide–awake ['waɪdə'weɪk] *adj* : (completamente) despierto

wide–eyed ['waɪd'aɪd] *adj* **1** : con los ojos muy abiertos **2** NAIVE : inocente, ingenuo

widely ['waɪdli] *adv* : extensivamente, por todas partes

widen ['waɪdən] *vt* : ampliar, ensanchar — *vi* : ampliarse, ensancharse

widespread ['waɪd'sprɛd] *adj* : extendido, extenso, difuso

widow[1] ['wɪ,doː] *vt* : dejar viuda <to be widowed : enviudar>

widow[2] *n* : viuda *f*

widower ['wɪdowər] *n* : viudo *m*

width ['wɪdθ] *n* : ancho *m*, anchura *f*

wield ['wiːld] *vt* **1** USE : usar, manejar <to wield a broom : usar una escoba> **2** EXERCISE : ejercer <to wield influence : influir>

wiener ['wiːnər] → **frankfurter**

wife ['waɪf] *n, pl* **wives** ['waɪvz] : esposa *f*, mujer *f*

wifely ['waɪfli] *adj* : de esposa, conyugal

wig ['wɪg] *n* : peluca *f*

wiggle[1] ['wɪgəl] *v* **-gled; -gling** *vt* : menear, contonear <to wiggle one's hips : contonearse> — *vi* : menearse

wiggle[2] *n* : meneo *m*, contoneo *m*

wiggly ['wɪgəli] *adj* **-glier; -est 1** : que se menea **2** WAVY : ondulado

wigwag ['wɪg,wæg] *vi* **-wagged; -wagging** : comunicar por señales

wigwam ['wɪg,wɑm] *n* : wigwam *m*

wild[1] ['waɪld] *adv* **1** → **wildly 2 to run wild** : descontrolarse

wild[2] *adj* **1** : salvaje, silvestre, cimarrón <wild horses : caballos salvajes> <wild rice : arroz silvestre> **2** DESOLATE : yermo, agreste **3** UNRULY : desenfrenado **4** CRAZY : loco, fantástico <wild ideas : ideas locas> **5** BARBAROUS : salvaje, bárbaro **6** ERRATIC : errático <a wild throw : un tiro errático>

wild[3] *n* → **wilderness**

wildcat ['waɪld,kæt] *n* **1** : gato *m* montés **2** BOBCAT : lince *m* rojo

wilderness ['wɪldərnəs] *n* : yermo *m*, desierto *m*

wildfire ['waɪld,faɪr] *n* **1** : fuego *m* descontrolado **2 to spread like wildfire** : propagarse como un reguero de pólvora

wildflower ['waɪld,flaʊər] *n* : flor *f* silvestre

wildfowl ['waɪld,faʊl] *n* : ave *f* de caza

wildlife ['waɪld,laɪf] *n* : fauna *f*

wildly ['waɪldli] *adv* **1** FRANTICALLY : frenéticamente, como un loco **2** EXTREMELY : extremadamente <wildly happy : loco de felicidad>

wile[1] ['waɪl] *vt* **wiled; wiling** LURE : atraer

wile[2] *n* : ardid *m*, artimaña *f*

will[1] ['wɪl] *v past* **would** ['wʊd]; *pres sing & pl* **will** *vi* WISH : querer <do what you will : haz lo que quieras> — *v aux* **1** (*expressing willingness*) <no one would take the job : nadie aceptaría el trabajo> <I won't do it : no lo haré> **2** (*expressing habitual action*) <he will get angry over nothing : se pone furioso por cualquier cosa> **3** (*forming the future tense*)

<tomorrow we will go shopping : mañana iremos de compras> **4** (*expressing capacity*) <the couch will hold three people : en el sofá cabrán tres personas> **5** (*expressing determination*) <I will go despite them : iré a pesar de ellos> **6** (*expressing probability*) <that will be the mailman : eso ha de ser el cartero> **7** (*expressing inevitability*) <accidents will happen : los accidentes ocurrirán> **8** (*expressing a command*) <you will do as I say : harás lo que digo>

will[2] *vt* **1** ORDAIN : disponer, decretar <if God wills it : si Dios lo dispone, si Dios quiere> **2** : lograr a fuerza de voluntad <they were willing him to succeed : estaban deseando que tuviera éxito> **3** BEQUEATH : legar

will[3] *n* **1** DESIRE : deseo *m,* voluntad *f* **2** VOLITION : voluntad *f* <free will : libre albedrío> **3** WILLPOWER : voluntad *f,* fuerza *f* de voluntad <a will of iron : una voluntad férrea> **4** : testamento *m* <to make a will : hacer testamento>

willful *or* **wilful** [ˈwɪlfəl] *adj* **1** OBSTINATE : obstinado, terco **2** INTENTIONAL : intencionado, deliberado — **willfully** *adv*

willing [ˈwɪlɪŋ] *adj* **1** INCLINED, READY : listo, dispuesto **2** OBLIGING : servicial, complaciente

willingly [ˈwɪlɪŋli] *adv* : con gusto

willingness [ˈwɪlɪŋnəs] *n* : buena voluntad *f*

willow [ˈwɪˌloː] *n* : sauce *m*

willowy [ˈwɪlowi] *adj* : esbelto

willpower [ˈwɪlˌpaʊər] *n* : voluntad *f,* fuerza *f* de voluntad

wilt [ˈwɪlt] *vi* **1** : marchitarse (dícese de las flores) **2** LANGUISH : debilitarse, languidecer

wily [ˈwaɪli] *adj* **wilier; -est** : artero, astuto

win[1] [ˈwɪn] *v* **won** [ˈwʌn]; **winning** *vi* : ganar — *vt* **1** : ganar, conseguir **2 to win over** : ganarse a **3 to win someone's heart** : conquistar a alguien

win[2] *n* : triunfo *m,* victoria *f*

wince[1] [ˈwɪnts] *vi* **winced; wincing** : estremecerse, hacer una mueca de dolor

wince[2] *n* : mueca *f* de dolor

winch [ˈwɪntʃ] *n* : torno *m*

wind[1] [ˈwɪnd] *vt* : dejar sin aliento <to be winded : quedarse sin aliento>

wind[2] [ˈwaɪnd] *v* **wound** [ˈwaʊnd]; **winding** *vi* MEANDER : serpentear — *vt* **1** COIL, ROLL : envolver, enrollar **2** TURN : hacer girar <to wind a clock : darle cuerda a un reloj>

wind[3] [ˈwɪnd] *n* **1** : viento *m* <against the wind : contra el viento> **2** BREATH : aliento *m* **3** FLATULENCE : flatulencia *f,* ventosidad *f* **4 to get wind of** : enterarse de

wind[4] [ˈwaɪnd] *n* **1** TURN : vuelta *f* **2** BEND : recodo *m,* curva *f*

windbreak [ˈwɪndˌbreɪk] *n* : barrera *f* contra el viento, abrigadero *m*

windfall [ˈwɪndˌfɔl] *n* **1** : fruta *f* caída **2** : beneficio *m* imprevisto

wind instrument *n* : instrumento *m* de viento

windlass [ˈwɪndləs] *n* : cabrestante *m*

windmill [ˈwɪndˌmɪl] *n* : molino *m* de viento

window [ˈwɪnˌdoː] *n* **1** : ventana *f* (de un edificio o una computadora), ventanilla *f* (de un vehículo o avión), vitrina *f* (de una tienda) **2** → **windowpane**

windowpane [ˈwɪnˌdoːˌpeɪn] *n* : vidrio *m*

window–shop [ˈwɪndoˌʃɑp] *vi* **-shopped; -shopping** : mirar las vitrinas

windpipe [ˈwɪndˌpaɪp] *n* : tráquea *f*

windshield [ˈwɪndˌʃiːld] *n* **1** : parabrisas *m* **2 windshield wiper** : limpiaparabrisas *m*

windup [ˈwaɪndˌʌp] *n* : conclusión *f*

wind up *vt* END : terminar, concluir — *vi* : terminar, acabar

windward[1] [ˈwɪndwərd] *adj* : de barlovento

windward[2] *n* : barlovento *m*

windy [ˈwɪndi] *adj* **windier; -est 1** : ventoso <it's windy : hace viento> **2** VERBOSE : verboso, prolijo

wine[1] [ˈwaɪn] *v* **wined; wining** *vi* : beber vino — *vt* **to wine and dine** : agasajar

wine[2] *n* : vino *m*

wing[1] [ˈwɪŋ] *vi* FLY : volar

wing[2] *n* **1** : ala *f* (de un ave, un avión, o un edificio) **2** FACTION : ala *f* <the right wing of the party : el ala derecha del partido> **3 wings** *npl* : bastidores *mpl* (de un teatro) **4 on the wing** : al vuelo, volando **5 under one's wing** : bajo el cargo de uno

winged [ˈwɪŋd, ˈwɪŋəd] *adj* : alado

wink[1] [ˈwɪŋk] *vi* **1** : guiñar el ojo **2** BLINK : pestañear, parpadear **3** FLICKER : parpadear, titilar

wink[2] *n* **1** : guiño *m* (del ojo) **2** NAP : siesta *f* <not to sleep a wink : no pegar el ojo>

winner [ˈwɪnər] *n* : ganador *m,* -dora *f*

winning [ˈwɪnɪŋ] *adj* **1** VICTORIOUS : ganador **2** CHARMING : encantador

winnings [ˈwɪnɪŋz] *npl* : ganancias *fpl*

winnow [ˈwɪˌnoː] *vt* : aventar (el grano, etc.)

winsome [ˈwɪnsəm] *adj* CHARMING : encantador

winter[1] [ˈwɪntər] *adj* : invernal, de invierno

winter[2] *n* : invierno *m*

wintergreen [ˈwɪntərˌgriːn] *n* : gaulteria *f*

wintertime [ˈwɪntərˌtaɪm] *n* : invierno *m*

wintry [ˈwɪntri] *adj* **wintrier; -est 1** WINTER : invernal, de invierno **2** COLD

: frío <she gave us a wintry greeting : nos saludó fríamente>

wipe[1] [ˈwaɪp] *vt* **wiped; wiping 1** : limpiar, pasarle un trapo a <to wipe one's feet : limpiarse los pies> **2 to wipe away** : enjugar (lágrimas), borrar (una memoria) **3 to wipe out** ANNIHILATE : aniquilar, destruir

wipe[2] *n* : pasada *f* (con un trapo, etc.)

wire[1] [ˈwaɪr] *vt* **-wired; wiring 1** : instalar el cableado en (una casa, etc.) **2** BIND : atar con alambre **3** TELEGRAPH : telegrafiar, mandarle un telegrama (a alguien)

wire[2] *n* **1** : alambre *m* <barbed wire : alambre de púas> **2** : cable *m* (eléctrico o telefónico) **3** CABLEGRAM, TELEGRAM : telegrama *m,* cable *m*

wireless [ˈwaɪrləs] *adj* : inalámbrico

wiretapping [ˈwaɪrˌtæpɪŋ] *n* : intervención *f* electrónica

wiring [ˈwaɪrɪŋ] *n* : cableado *m*

wiry [ˈwaɪri] *adj* **wirier; -est 1** : hirsuto, tieso (dícese del pelo) **2** : esbelto y musculoso (dícese del cuerpo)

wisdom [ˈwɪzdəm] *n* **1** KNOWLEDGE : sabiduría *f* **2** JUDGMENT, SENSE : sensatez *f*

wisdom tooth *n* : muela *f* de juicio

wise[1] [ˈwaɪz] *adj* **wiser; wisest 1** LEARNED : sabio **2** SENSIBLE : sabio, sensato, prudente **3** KNOWLEDGEABLE : entendido, enterado <they're wise to his tricks : conocen muy bien sus mañas>

wise[2] *n* : manera *f,* modo *m* <in no wise : de ninguna manera>

wisecrack [ˈwaɪzˌkræk] *n* : broma *f,* chiste *m*

wisely [ˈwaɪzli] *adv* : sabiamente, sensatamente

wish[1] [ˈwɪʃ] *vt* **1** WANT : desear, querer **2 to wish (something) for** : desear <they wished me well : me desearon lo mejor> — *vi* **1** : pedir (como deseo) **2** : querer <as you wish : como quieras>

wish[2] *n* **1** : deseo *m* <to grant a wish : conceder un deseo> **2 wishes** *npl* : saludos *mpl*, recuerdos *mpl* <to send best wishes : mandar muchos recuerdos>

wishbone [ˈwɪʃˌboːn] *n* : espoleta *f*

wishful [ˈwɪʃfəl] *adj* **1** HOPEFUL : deseoso, lleno de esperanza **2 wishful thinking** : ilusiones *fpl*

wishy–washy [ˈwɪʃiˌwɔʃi, -ˌwɑʃi] *adj* : insípido, soso

wisp [ˈwɪsp] *n* **1** BUNCH : manojo *m* (de paja) **2** STRAND : mechón *m* (de pelo) **3** : voluta *f* (de humo)

wispy [ˈwɪspi] *adj* **wispier; -est** : tenue, ralo (dícese del pelo)

wisteria [wɪsˈtɪriə] *n* : glicinia *f*

wistful [ˈwɪstfəl] *adj* : añorante, anhelante, melancólico — **wistfully** *adv*

wistfulness [ˈwɪstfəlnəs] *n* : añoranza *f,* melancolía *f*

wit [ˈwɪt] *n* **1** INTELLIGENCE : inteligencia *f* **2** CLEVERNESS : ingenio *m,* gracia *f,* agudeza *f* **3** HUMOR : humorismo *m* **4** JOKER : chistoso *m,* -sa *f* **5 wits** *npl* : razón *f,* buen juicio *m* <scared out of one's wits : muerto de miedo> <to be at one's wits' end : estar desesperado>

witch [ˈwɪtʃ] *n* : bruja *f*

witchcraft [ˈwɪtʃˌkræft] *n* : brujería *f,* hechicería *f*

witch doctor *n* : hechicero *m,* -ra *f*

witchery [ˈwɪtʃəri] *n, pl* **-eries 1** → **witchcraft 2** CHARM : encanto *m*

witch–hunt [ˈwɪtʃˌhʌnt] *n* : caza *f* de brujas

with [ˈwɪð, ˈwɪθ] *prep* **1** : con <I'm going with you : voy contigo> <coffee with milk : café con leche> **2** AGAINST : con <to argue with someone : discutir con alguien> **3** (*used in descriptions*) : con, de <the girl with red hair : la muchacha de pelo rojo> **4** (*indicating manner, means, or cause*) : con <to cut with a knife : cortar con un cuchillo> <fix it with tape : arréglalo con cinta> <with luck : con suerte> **5** DESPITE : a pesar de, aún con <with all his work, the business failed : a pesar de su trabajo, el negocio fracasó> **6** REGARDING : con respecto a, con <the trouble with your plan : el problema con su plan> **7** ACCORDING TO : según <it varies with the season : varía según la estación> **8** (*indicating support or understanding*) : con <I'm with you all the way : estoy contigo hasta el fin>

withdraw [wɪðˈdrɔ, wɪθ-] *v* **-drew** [-ˈdruː]; **-drawn** [-ˈdrɔn]; **-drawing** *vt* **1** REMOVE : retirar, apartar, sacar (dinero) **2** RETRACT : retractarse de — *vi* : retirarse, recluirse (de la sociedad)

withdrawal [wɪðˈdrɔəl, wɪθ-] *n* **1** : retirada *f,* retiro *m* (de fondos, etc.), retraimiento *m* (social) **2** RETRACTION : retractación *f* **3 withdrawal symptoms** : síndrome *m* de abstinencia

withdrawn [wɪðˈdrɔn, wɪθ-] *adj* : retraído, reservado, introvertido

wither [ˈwɪðər] *vt* : marchitar, agostar — *vi* **1** WILT : marchitarse **2** WEAKEN : decaer, debilitarse

withhold [wɪθˈhoːld, wɪð-] *vt* **-held** [-ˈhɛld]; **-holding** : retener (fondos), aplazar (una decisión), negar (permiso, etc.)

within[1] [wɪðˈɪn, wɪθ-] *adv* : dentro

within[2] *prep* **1** : dentro de <within the limits : dentro de los límites> **2** (*in expressions of distance*) : a menos de <within 10 miles of the ocean : a menos de 10 millas del mar> **3** (*in expressions of time*) : dentro de <within an hour : dentro de una hora> <within a month of her birthday : a poco menos de un mes de su cumpleaños>

without[1] [wɪð'aʊt, wɪθ-] *adv* **1** OUTSIDE : fuera **2 to do without** : pasar sin algo

without[2] *prep* **1** OUTSIDE : fuera de **2** : sin <without fear : sin temor> <he left without his briefcase : se fue sin su portafolios>

withstand [wɪθ'stænd, wɪð-] *vt* **-stood** [-'stʊd]; **-standing 1** BEAR : aguantar, soportar **2** RESIST : resistir, resistirse a

witless ['wɪtləs] *adj* : estúpido, tonto

witness[1] ['wɪtnəs] *vt* **1** SEE : presenciar, ver, ser testigo de **2** : atestiguar (una firma, etc.) — *vi* TESTIFY : atestiguar, testimoniar

witness[2] *n* **1** TESTIMONY : testimonio *m* <to bear witness : atestiguar, testimoniar> **2** : testigo *mf* <witness for the prosecution : testigo de cargo>

witticism ['wɪt̬əˌsɪzəm] *n* : agudeza *f,* ocurrencia *f*

witty ['wɪt̬i] *adj* **-tier; -est** : ingenioso, ocurrente, gracioso

wives → **wife**

wizard ['wɪzərd] *n* **1** SORCERER : mago *m,* brujo *m,* hechicero *m* **2** : genio *m* <a math wizard : un genio en matemáticas>

wizened ['wɪzənd, 'wiː-] *adj* : arrugado, marchito

wobble[1] ['wɑbəl] *vi* **-bled; -bling** : bambolearse, tambalearse, temblar (dícese de la voz)

wobble[2] *n* : tambaleo *m,* bamboleo *m*

wobbly ['wɑbəli] *adj* : bamboleante, tambaleante, inestable

woe ['woː] *n* **1** GRIEF, MISFORTUNE : desgracia *f,* infortunio *m,* aflicción *f* **2 woes** *npl* TROUBLES : penas *fpl,* males *mpl*

woeful ['woːfəl] *adj* **1** SORROWFUL : afligido, apenado, triste **2** UNFORTUNATE : desgraciado, infortunado **3** DEPLORABLE : lamentable

woke, woken → **wake**[1]

wolf[1] ['wʊlf] *vt or* **to wolf down** : engullir

wolf[2] *n, pl* **wolves** ['wʊlvz] : lobo *m,* -ba *f*

wolfram ['wʊlfrəm] → **tungsten**

wolverine [ˌwʊlvə'riːn] *n* : glotón *m* (animal)

woman ['wʊmən] *n, pl* **women** ['wɪmən] : mujer *f*

womanhood ['wʊmənˌhʊd] *n* **1** : condición *f* de mujer **2** WOMEN : mujeres *fpl*

womanly ['wʊmənli] *adj* : femenino

womb ['wuːm] *n* : útero *m,* matriz *f*

won → **win**

wonder[1] ['wʌndər] *vi* **1** SPECULATE : preguntarse, pensar <to wonder about : preguntarse por> **2** MARVEL : asombrarse, maravillarse — *vt* : preguntarse <I wonder if they're coming : me pregunto si vendrán>

wonder[2] *n* **1** MARVEL : maravilla *f,* milagro *m* <to work wonders : hacer maravillas> **2** AMAZEMENT : asombro *m*

wonderful ['wʌndərfəl] *adj* : maravilloso, estupendo

wonderfully ['wʌndərfəli] *adv* : maravillosamente, de maravilla

wonderland ['wʌndərˌlænd, -lənd] *n* : país *m* de las maravillas

wonderment ['wʌndərmənt] *n* : asombro *m*

wondrous ['wʌndrəs] → **wonderful**

wont[1] ['wɔnt, 'woːnt, 'wɑnt] *adj* : acostumbrado, habituado

wont[2] *n* : hábito *m,* costumbre *f*

won't ['woːnt] (*contraction of* **will not**) → **will**[1]

woo ['wuː] *vt* **1** COURT : cortejar **2** : buscar el apoyo de (clientes, votantes, etc.)

wood[1] ['wʊd] *adj* : de madera

wood[2] *n* **1** *or* **woods** *npl* FOREST : bosque *m* **2** : madera *f* (materia) **3** FIREWOOD : leña *f*

woodchuck ['wʊdˌtʃʌk] *n* : marmota *f* de América

woodcut ['wʊdˌkʌt] *n* **1** : plancha *f* de madera (para imprimir imágenes) **2** : grabado *m* en madera

woodcutter ['wʊdˌkʌt̬ər] *n* : leñador *m,* -dora *f*

wooded ['wʊdəd] *adj* : arbolado, boscoso

wooden ['wʊdən] *adj* **1** : de madera <a wooden cross : una cruz de madera> **2** STIFF : rígido, inexpresivo (dícese del estilo, de la cara, etc.)

woodland ['wʊdlənd, -ˌlænd] *n* : bosque *m*

woodpecker ['wʊdˌpɛkər] *n* : pájaro *m* carpintero

woodshed ['wʊdˌʃɛd] *n* : leñera *f*

woodsman ['wʊdzmən] → **woodcutter**

woodwind ['wʊdˌwɪnd] *n* : instrumento *m* de viento de madera

woodworking ['wʊdˌwərkɪŋ] *n* : carpintería *f*

woody ['wʊdi] *adj* **woodier; -est 1** → **wooded 2** : leñoso <woody plants : plantas leñosas> **3** : leñoso (dícese de la textura), a madera (dícese del aroma, etc.)

woof ['wʊf] → **weft**

wool ['wʊl] *n* : lana *f*

woolen[1] *or* **woollen** ['wʊlən] *adj* : de lana

woolen[2] *or* **woollen** *n* **1** : lana *f* (tela) **2 woolens** *npl* : prendas *fpl* de lana

woolly ['wʊli] *adj* **-lier; -est 1** : lanudo **2** CONFUSED : confuso, vago

woozy ['wuːzi] *adj* **-zier; -est** : mareado

word[1] ['wərd] *vt* : expresar, formular, redactar

word[2] *n* **1** : palabra *f,* vocablo *m,* voz *f* <word for word : palabra por palabra> <in one's own words : en sus

propias palabras> <words fail me : me quedo sin habla> **2** REMARK : palabra *f* <by word of mouth : de palabra> <to have a word with : hablar (dos palabras) con> **3** COMMAND : orden *f* <to give the word : dar la orden> <just say the word : no tienes que decirlo> **4** MESSAGE, NEWS : noticias *fpl* <is there any word from her? : ¿hay noticias de ella?> <to send word : mandar un recado> **5** PROMISE : palabra *f* <to keep one's word : cumplir uno su palabra> **6 words** *npl* QUARREL : palabra *f,* riña *f* <to have words with : tener unas palabras con, reñir con> **7 words** *npl* TEXT : letra *f* (de una canción, etc.)

wordiness [ˈwərdinəs] *n* : verbosidad *f*

wording [ˈwərdɪŋ] *n* : redacción *f,* lenguaje *m* (de un documento)

word processing *n* : procesamiento *m* de textos

word processor *n* : procesador *m* de textos

wordy [ˈwərdi] *adj* **wordier; -est** : verboso, prolijo

wore → **wear**[1]

work[1] [ˈwərk] *v* **worked** [ˈwərkt] *or* **wrought** [ˈrɔt]; **working** *vt* **1** OPERATE : trabajar, operar <to work a machine : operar una máquina> **2** : lograr, conseguir (algo) con esfuerzo <to work one's way up : lograr subir por sus propios esfuerzos> **3** EFFECT : efectuar, llevar a cabo, obrar (milagros) **4** MAKE, SHAPE : elaborar, fabricar, formar <a beautifully wrought vase : un florero bellamente elaborado> **5 to work up** : estimular, excitar <don't get worked up : no te agites> — *vi* **1** LABOR : trabajar <to work full-time : trabajar a tiempo completo> **2** FUNCTION : funcionar, servir

work[2] *adj* : laboral

work[3] *n* **1** LABOR : trabajo *m,* labor *f* **2** EMPLOYMENT : trabajo *m,* empleo *m* **3** TASK : tarea *f,* faena *f* **4** DEED : obra *f,* labor *f* <works of charity : obras de caridad> **5** : obra *f* (de arte o literatura) **6** → **workmanship 7 works** *npl* FACTORY : fábrica *f* **8 works** *npl* MECHANISM : mecanismo *m*

workable [ˈwərkəbəl] *adj* **1** : explotable (dícese de una mina, etc.) **2** FEASIBLE : factible, realizable

workaday [ˈwərkəˌdeɪ] *adj* : ordinario, banal

workbench [ˈwərkˌbɛntʃ] *n* : mesa *f* de trabajo

workday [ˈwərkˌdeɪ] *n* **1** : jornada *f* laboral **2** WEEKDAY : día *m* hábil, día *m* laborable

worker [ˈwərkər] *n* : trabajador *m,* -dora *f;* obrero *m,* -ra *f*

working [ˈwərkɪŋ] *adj* **1** : que trabaja <working mothers : madres que trabajan> <the working class : la clase obrera> **2** : de trabajo <working hours : horas de trabajo> **3** FUNCTIONING : que funciona, operativo **4** SUFFICIENT : suficiente <a working majority : una mayoría suficiente> <working knowledge : conocimientos básicos>

workingman [ˈwərkɪŋˌmæn] *n, pl* **-men** [-mən, -ˌmɛn] : obrero *m*

workman [ˈwərkmən] *n, pl* **-men** [-mən, -ˌmɛn] **1** → **workingman 2** ARTISAN : artesano *m*

workmanlike [ˈwərkmənˌlaɪk] *adj* : bien hecho, competente

workmanship [ˈwərkmənˌʃɪp] *n* **1** WORK : ejecución *f,* trabajo *m* **2** CRAFTSMANSHIP : artesanía *f,* destreza *f*

workout [ˈwərkˌaʊt] *n* : ejercicios *mpl* físicos, entrenamiento *m*

work out *vt* **1** DEVELOP, PLAN : idear, planear, desarrollar **2** RESOLVE : solucionar, resolver <to work out the answer : calcular la solución> — *vi* **1** TURN OUT : resultar **2** SUCCEED : lograr, dar resultado, salir bien **3** EXERCISE : hacer ejercicio

workroom [ˈwərkˌruːm, -ˌrʊm] *n* : taller *m*

workshop [ˈwərkˌʃɑp] *n* : taller *m* <ceramics workshop : taller de cerámica>

world[1] [ˈwərld] *adj* : mundial, del mundo <world championship : campeonato mundial>

world[2] *n* : mundo *m* <around the world : alrededor del mundo> <a world of possibilities : un mundo de posibilidades> <to think the world of someone : tener a alguien en alta estima> <to be worlds apart : no tener nada que ver (uno con otro)>

worldly [ˈwərldli] *adj* **1** : mundano <wordly goods : bienes materiales> **2** SOPHISTICATED : sofisticado, de mundo

worldwide[1] [ˈwərldˈwaɪd] *adv* : mundialmente, en todo el mundo

worldwide[2] *adj* : global, mundial

worm[1] [ˈwərm] *vi* **1** CRAWL : arrastrarse, deslizarse (como gusano) <to worm one's way into someone's confidence : ganarse la confianza de alguien> **2 to worm something out of someone** : sonsacarle algo a alguien — *vt* : desparasitar (un animal)

worm[2] *n* **1** : gusano *m,* lombriz *f* **2 worms** *npl* : lombrices *fpl* (parásitos)

wormy [ˈwərmi] *adj* **wormier; -est** : infestado de gusanos

worn → **wear**[1]

worn–out [ˈwornˈaʊt] *adj* **1** USED : gastado, desgastado **2** TIRED : agotado

worried [ˈwərid] *adj* : inquieto, preocupado

worrier [ˈwəriər] *n* : persona *f* que se preocupa mucho

worrisome [ˈwərisəm] *adj* **1** DISTURBING : preocupante, inquietante **2** : que se preocupa mucho (dícese de una persona)

worry[1] [ˈwəri] *v* **-ried; -rying** *vt* : preocupar, inquietar — *vi* : preocuparse, inquietarse, angustiarse

worry[2] *n, pl* **-ries** : preocupación *f,* inquietud *f,* angustia *f*
worse[1] [ˈwərs] *adv* (*comparative of* **bad** *or of* **ill**) : peor <to feel worse : sentirse peor>
worse[2] *adj* (*comparative of* **bad** *or of* **ill**) : peor <from bad to worse : de mal en peor> <to get worse : empeorar>
worse[3] *n* : estado *m* peor <to take a turn for the worse : ponerse peor> <so much the worse : tanto peor>
worsen [ˈwərsən] *vt* : empeorar — *vi* : empeorar(se)
worship[1] [ˈwərʃəp] *v* **-shiped** *or* **-shipped; -shiping** *or* **-shipping** *vt* : adorar, venerar <to worship God : adorar a Dios> — *vi* : practicar una religión
worship[2] *n* : adoración *f,* culto *m*
worshiper *or* **worshipper** [ˈwərʃəpər] *n* : devoto *m,* -ta *f;* adorador *m,* -dora *f*
worst[1] [ˈwərst] *vt* DEFEAT : derrotar
worst[2] *adv* (*superlative of* **ill** *or of* **bad** *or* **badly**) : peor <the worst dressed of all : el peor vestido de todos>
worst[3] *adj* (*superlative of* **bad** *or of* **ill**) : peor <the worst movie : la peor película>
worst[4] *n* **the worst** : lo peor, el (la) peor <the worst is over : ya ha pasado lo peor>
worsted [ˈwʊstəd, ˈwərstəd] *n* : estambre *m*
worth[1] [ˈwərθ] *n* **1** : valor *m* (monetario) <ten dollars' worth of gas : diez dólares de gasolina> **2** MERIT : valor *m,* mérito *m,* valía *f* <an employee of great worth : un empleado de gran valía>
worth[2] *prep* **to be worth** : valer <her holdings are worth a fortune : sus propiedades valen una fortuna> <it's not worth it : no vale la pena>
worthiness [ˈwərðinəs] *n* : mérito *m*
worthless [ˈwərθləs] *adj* **1** : sin valor <worthless trinkets : chucherías sin valor> **2** USELESS : inútil
worthwhile [wərθˈ*h*waɪl] *adj* : que vale la pena
worthy [ˈwərði] *adj* **-thier; -est 1** : digno <worthy of promotion : digno de un ascenso> **2** COMMENDABLE : meritorio, encomiable
would [ˈwʊd] *past of* **will 1** (*expressing preference*) <I would rather go alone than with her : preferiría ir sola que con ella> **2** (*expressing intent*) <those who would ban certain books : aquellos que prohibirían ciertos libros> **3** (*expressing habitual action*) <he would often take his kids to the park : solía llevar a sus hijos al parque> **4** (*expressing contingency*) <I would go if I had the money : iría yo si tuviera el dinero> **5** (*expressing probability*) <she would have won if she hadn't tripped : habría ganado si no hubiera tropezado> **6** (*expressing a request*) <would you kindly help me with this? : ¿tendría la bondad de ayudarme con esto?>
would–be [ˈwʊdˈbiː] *adj* : potencial <a would-be celebrity : un aspirante a celebridad>
wouldn't [ˈwʊdˈənt] (*contraction of* **would not**) → **would**
wound[1] [ˈwuːnd] *vt* : herir
wound[2] *n* : herida *f*
wound[3] [ˈwaʊnd] → **wind**[2]
wove, woven → **weave**[1]
wrangle[1] [ˈræŋgəl] *vi* **-gled; -gling** : discutir, reñir <to wrangle over : discutir por>
wrangle[2] *n* : riña *f,* disputa *f*
wrap[1] [ˈræp] *v* **wrapped; wrapping** *vt* **1** COVER : envolver, cubrir <to wrap a package : envolver un paquete> <wrapped in mystery : envuelto en misterio> **2** ENCIRCLE : rodear, ceñir <to wrap one's arms around someone : estrechar a alguien> **3 to wrap up** FINISH : darle fin a (algo) — *vi* **1** COIL : envolverse, enroscarse **2 to wrap up** DRESS : abrigarse <wrap up warmly : abrígate bien>
wrap[2] *n* **1** WRAPPER : envoltura *f* **2** : prenda *f* que envuelve (como un chal, una bata, etc.)
wrapper [ˈræpər] *n* : envoltura *f,* envoltorio *m*
wrapping [ˈræpɪŋ] *n* : envoltura *f,* envoltorio *m*
wrath [ˈræθ] *n* : ira *f,* cólera *f*
wrathful [ˈræθfəl] *adj* : iracundo
wreak [ˈriːk] *vt* : infligir, causar <to wreak havoc : crear caos, causar estragos>
wreath [ˈriːθ] *n, pl* **wreaths** [ˈriːðz, ˈriːθs] : corona *f* (de flores, etc.)
wreathe [ˈriːð] *vt* **wreathed; wreathing 1** ADORN : coronar (de flores, etc.) **2** ENVELOP : envolver <wreathed in mist : envuelto en niebla>
wreck[1] [ˈrɛk] *vt* : destruir, arruinar, estrellar (un automóvil), naufragar (un barco)
wreck[2] *n* **1** WRECKAGE : restos *mpl* (de un buque naufragado, un avión siniestrado, etc.) **2** RUIN : ruina *f,* desastre *m* <this place is a wreck! : ¡este lugar está hecho un desastre!> <to be a nervous wreck : tener los nervios destrozados>
wreckage [ˈrɛkɪdʒ] *n* : restos *mpl* (de un buque naufragado, un avión siniestrado, etc.), ruinas *fpl* (de un edificio)
wrecker [ˈrɛkər] *n* **1** TOW TRUCK : grúa *f* **2** : desguazador *m* (de autos, barcos, etc.), demoledor *m* (de edificios)
wren [ˈrɛn] *n* : chochín *m*
wrench[1] [ˈrɛntʃ] *vt* **1** PULL : arrancar (de un tirón) **2** SPRAIN, TWIST : torcerse (un tobillo, un músculo, etc.)
wrench[2] *n* **1** TUG : tirón *m,* jalón *m* **2** SPRAIN : torcedura *f* **3** *or* **monkey wrench** : llave *f* inglesa

wrest [ˈrɛst] *vt* : arrancar
wrestle[1] [ˈrɛsəl] *v* **-tled; -tling** *vi* **1** : luchar, practicar la lucha (en deportes) **2** STRUGGLE : luchar <to wrestle with a dilemma : lidiar con un dilema> — *vt* : luchar contra
wrestle[2] *n* STRUGGLE : lucha *f*
wrestler [ˈrɛsələr] *n* : luchador *m*, -dora *f*
wrestling [ˈrɛsəlɪŋ] *n* : lucha *f*
wretch [ˈrɛtʃ] *n* : infeliz *mf;* desgraciado *m*, -da *f*
wretched [ˈrɛtʃəd] *adj* **1** MISERABLE, UNHAPPY : desdichado, afligido <I feel wretched : me siento muy mal> **2** UNFORTUNATE : miserable, desgraciado, lastimoso <wretched weather : tiempo espantoso> **3** INFERIOR : inferior, malo
wretchedly [ˈrɛtʃədli] *adv* : miserablemente, lamentablemente
wriggle [ˈrɪgəl] *vi* **-gled; -gling** : retorcerse, menearse
wring [ˈrɪŋ] *vt* **wrung** [ˈrʌŋ]; **wringing** **1** *or* **to wring out** : escurrir, exprimir (el lavado) **2** EXTRACT : arrancar, sacar (por la fuerza) **3** TWIST : torcer, retorcer **4 to wring someone's heart** : partirle el corazón a alguien
wringer [ˈrɪŋər] *n* : escurridor *m*
wrinkle[1] [ˈrɪŋkəl] *v* **-kled; -kling** *vt* : arrugar — *vi* : arrugarse
wrinkle[2] *n* : arruga *f*
wrinkly [ˈrɪŋkəli] *adj* **wrinklier; -est** : arrugado
wrist [ˈrɪst] *n* **1** : muñeca *f* (en anatomía) **2** *or* **wristband** [ˈrɪstˌbænd] CUFF : puño *m*
writ [ˈrɪt] *n* : orden *f* (judicial)
write [ˈraɪt] *v* **wrote** [ˈroːt]; **written** [ˈrɪtən]; **writing** : escribir
write down *vt* : apuntar, anotar
write off *vt* CANCEL : cancelar
writer [ˈraɪtər] *n* : escritor *m*, -tora *f*
writhe [ˈraɪð] *vi* **writhed; writhing** : retorcerse
writing [ˈraɪtɪŋ] *n* : escritura *f*
wrong[1] [ˈrɔŋ] *vt* **wronged; wronging** : ofender, ser injusto con
wrong[2] *adv* : mal, incorrectamente
wrong[3] *adj* **wronger** [ˈrɔŋər]; **wrongest** [ˈrɔŋəst] **1** EVIL, SINFUL : malo, injusto, inmoral **2** IMPROPER, UNSUITABLE : inadecuado, inapropiado, malo **3** INCORRECT : incorrecto, erróneo, malo <a wrong answer : una mala respuesta> **4 to be wrong** : equivocarse, estar equivocado
wrong[4] *n* **1** INJUSTICE : injusticia *f*, mal *m* **2** OFFENSE : ofensa *f*, agravio *m* (en derecho) **3 to be in the wrong** : haber hecho mal, estar equivocado
wrongdoer [ˈrɔŋˌduːər] *n* : malhechor *m*, -chora *f*
wrongdoing [ˈrɔŋˌduːɪŋ] *n* : fechoría *f*, maldad *f*
wrongful [ˈrɔŋfəl] *adj* **1** UNJUST : injusto **2** UNLAWFUL : ilegal
wrongly [ˈrɔŋli] *adv* **1** : injustamente **2** INCORRECTLY : erróneamente, incorrectamente
wrote → **write**
wrought [ˈrɔt] *adj* **1** SHAPED : formado, forjado <wrought iron : hierro forjado> **2** *or* **wrought up** : agitado, excitado
wrung → **wring**
wry [ˈraɪ] *adj* **wrier** [ˈraɪər]; **wriest** [ˈraɪəst] **1** TWISTED : torcido <a wry neck : un cuello torcido> **2** : irónico, sardónico (dícese del humor)

X

x[1] *n, pl* **x's** *or* **xs** [ˈɛksəz] **1** : vigésima cuarta letra del alfabeto inglés **2** : incógnita *f* (en matemáticas)
x[2] [ˈɛks] *vt* **x–ed** [ˈɛkst]; **x–ing** *or* **x'ing** [ˈɛksiŋ] DELETE : tachar
xenon [ˈziːˌnɑn, ˈzɛ-] *n* : xenón *m*
xenophobia [ˌzɛnəˈfoːbiə, ˌziː-] *n* : xenofobia *f*
Xmas [ˈkrɪsməs] *n* : Navidad *f*
x–ray [ˈɛksˌreɪ] *vt* : radiografiar
X ray [ˈɛksˌreɪ] *n* **1** : rayo *m* X **2** *or* **X–ray photograph** : radiografía *f*
xylophone [ˈzaɪləˌfoːn] *n* : xilófono *m*

Y

y [ˈwaɪ] *n, pl* **y's** *or* **ys** [ˈwaɪz] : vigésima quinta letra del alfabeto inglés
yacht[1] [ˈjɑt] *vi* : navegar (a vela), ir en yate <to go yachting : irse a navegar>
yacht[2] *n* : yate *m*
yak [ˈjæk] *n* : yac *m*
yam [ˈjæm] *n* **1** : ñame *m* **2** SWEET POTATO : batata *f*, boniato *m*
yank[1] [ˈjæŋk] *vt* : tirar de, jalar, darle un tirón a
yank[2] *n* : tirón *m*
Yankee [ˈjæŋki] *n* : yanqui *mf*
yap[1] [ˈjæp] *vi* **yapped; yapping** **1** BARK, YELP : ladrar, gañir **2** CHATTER : cotorrear *fam*, parlotear *fam*
yap[2] *n* : ladrido *m*, gañido *m*

yard [ˈjɑrd] *n* **1** : yarda *f* (medida) **2** SPAR : verga *f* (de un barco) **3** COURTYARD : patio *m* **4** : jardín *m* (de una casa) **5** : depósito *m* (de mercancías, etc.)
yardage [ˈjɑrdɪdʒ] *n* : medida *f* en yardas
yardarm [ˈjɑrdˌɑrm] *n* : penol *m*
yardstick [ˈjɑrdˌstɪk] *n* **1** : vara *f* **2** CRITERION : criterio *m,* norma *f*
yarn [ˈjɑrn] *n* **1** : hilado *m* **2** TALE : historia *f,* cuento *m* <to spin a yarn : inventar una historia>
yawl [ˈjɔl] *n* : yola *f*
yawn[1] [ˈjɔn] *vi* **1** : bostezar **2** OPEN : abrirse
yawn[2] *n* : bostezo *m*
ye [ˈjiː] *pron* : vosotros, vosotras
yea[1] [ˈjeɪ] *adv* YES : sí
yea[2] *n* : voto *m* a favor
year [ˈjɪr] *n* **1** : año *m* <last year : el año pasado> <he's ten years old : tiene diez años> **2** : curso *m,* año *m* (escolar) **3 years** *npl* AGES : siglos *mpl,* años *mpl* <I haven't seen them in years : hace siglos que no los veo>
yearbook [ˈjɪrˌbʊk] *n* : anuario *m*
yearling [ˈjɪrlɪŋ, ˈjərlən] *n* : animal *m* menor de dos año
yearly[1] [ˈjɪrli] *adv* : cada año, anualmente
yearly[2] *adj* : anual
yearn [ˈjərn] *vi* : anhelar, ansiar
yearning [ˈjərnɪŋ] *n* : anhelo *m*
yeast [ˈjiːst] *n* : levadura *f*
yell[1] [ˈjɛl] *vi* : gritar, chillar — *vt* : gritar
yell[2] *n* : grito *m,* alarido *m* <to let out a yell : dar un grito>
yellow[1] [ˈjɛlo] *vi* : ponerse amarillo, volverse amarillo
yellow[2] *adj* **1** : amarillo **2** COWARDLY : cobarde
yellow[3] *n* : amarillo *m*
yellow fever *n* : fiebre *f* amarilla
yellowish [ˈjɛloɪʃ] *adj* : amarillento
yellow jacket *n* : avispa *f* (con rayas amarillas)
yelp[1] [ˈjɛlp] *vi* : dar un gañido (dícese de un animal), dar un grito (dícese de una persona)
yelp[2] *n* : gañido *m* (de un animal), grito *m* (de una persona)
yen [ˈjɛn] *n* **1** DESIRE : deseo *m,* ganas *fpl* **2** : yen *m* (moneda japonesa)
yeoman [ˈjoːmən] *n, pl* **-men** [-mən, -mɛn] : suboficial *mf* de marina
yes[1] [ˈjɛs] *adv* : sí <to say yes : decir que sí>
yes[2] *n* : sí *m*
yesterday[1] [ˈjɛstərˌdeɪ, -di] *adv* : ayer
yesterday[2] *n* **1** : ayer *m* **2 the day before yesterday** : anteayer
yet[1] [ˈjɛt] *adv* **1** BESIDES, EVEN : aún <yet more problems : más problemas aún> <yet again : otra vez> **2** SO FAR : aún, todavía <not yet : todavía no> <as yet : hasta ahora, todavía> **3** : ya <has he come yet? : ¿ya ha venido?> **4** EVENTUALLY : todavía, algún día **5** NEVERTHELESS : sin embargo
yet[2] *conj* : pero
yew [ˈjuː] *n* : tejo *m*
yield[1] [ˈjiːld] *vt* **1** SURRENDER : ceder <to yield the right of way : ceder el paso> **2** PRODUCE : producir, dar, rendir (en finanzas) — *vi* **1** GIVE : ceder <to yield under pressure : ceder por la presión> **2** GIVE IN, SURRENDER : ceder, rendirse, entregarse
yield[2] *n* : rendimiento *m,* rédito *m* (en finanzas)
yodel[1] [ˈjoːdəl] *vi* **-deled** *or* **-delled; -deling** *or* **-delling** : cantar al estilo tirolés
yodel[2] *n* : canción *f* al estilo tirolés
yoga [ˈjoːgə] *n* : yoga *m*
yogurt [ˈjoːgərt] *n* : yogur *m,* yogurt *m*
yoke[1] [ˈjoːk] *vt* **yoked; yoking** : uncir (animales)
yoke[2] *n* **1** : yugo *m* (para uncir animales) <the yoke of oppression : el yugo de la opresión> **2** TEAM : yunta *f* (de bueyes) **3** : canesú *m* (de ropa)
yokel [ˈjoːkəl] *n* : palurdo *m,* -da *f*
yolk [ˈjoːk] *n* : yema *f* (de un huevo)
Yom Kippur [ˌjoːmkɪˈpʊr, ˌjɑm-, -ˈkɪpər] *n* : el Día *m* del Perdón, Yom Kippur
yon [ˈjɑn] → **yonder**
yonder[1] [ˈjɑndər] *adv* : allá <over yonder : allá lejos>
yonder[2] *adj* : aquel <yonder hill : aquella colina>
yore [ˈjoːr] *n* **in days of yore** : antaño
you [ˈjuː] *pron* **1** (*used as subject — familiar*) : tú; vos (*in some Latin American countries*); ustedes *pl;* vosotros, vosotras *pl Spain* **2** (*used as subject — formal*) : usted, ustedes *pl* **3** (*used as indirect object — familiar*) : te, les *pl* (se *before lo, la, los, las*), os *pl Spain* <he told it to you : te lo contó> <I gave them to (all of, both of) you : se los di> **4** (*used as indirect object — formal*) : lo (*Spain sometimes* le), la; los (*Spain sometimes* les), las *pl* **5** (*used after a preposition — familiar*) : ti; vos (*in some Latin American countries*); ustedes *pl;* vosotros, vosotras *pl Spain* **6** (*used after a preposition — formal*) : usted, ustedes *pl* **7** (*used as an impersonal subject*) <you never know : nunca se sabe> <you have to be aware : hay que ser consciente> <you mustn't do that : eso no se hace> **8 with you** (*familiar*) : contigo; con ustedes *pl;* con vosotros, con vosotras *pl Spain* **9 with you** (*formal*) : con usted, con ustedes *pl*
you'd [ˈjuːd, ˈjʊd] (*contraction of* **you had** *or* **you would**) → **have, would**
you'll [ˈjuːl, ˈjʊl] (*contraction of* **you shall** *or* **you will**) → **shall, will**
young[1] [ˈjʌŋ] *adj* **younger** [ˈjʌŋgər]; **youngest** [-gəst] **1** : joven, pequeño, menor <young people : los jóvenes>

<my younger brother : mi hermano menor> <she is the youngest : es la más pequeña> **2** FRESH, NEW : tierno (dícese de las verduras), joven (dícese del vino) **3** YOUTHFUL : joven, juvenil

young[2] *npl* : jóvenes *mfpl* (de los humanos), crías *fpl* (de los animales)

youngster [ˈjʌŋkstər] *n* **1** YOUTH : joven *mf* **2** CHILD : chico *m,* -ca *f;* niño *m,* -ña *f*

your [ˈjʊr, ˈjoːr, jər] *adj* **1** (*familiar singular*) : tu <your cat : tu gato> <your books : tus libros> <wash your hands : lávate las manos> **2** (*familiar plural*) su, vuestro *Spain* <your car : su coche, el coche de ustedes> **3** (*formal*) : su <your houses : sus casas> **4** (*impersonal*) : el, la, los, las <on your left : a la izquierda>

you're [ˈjʊr, ˈjoːr, ˈjər, ˈjuːər] (*contraction of* **you are**) → **be**

yours [ˈjʊrz, ˈjoːrz] *pron* **1** (*belonging to one person — familiar*) : (el) tuyo, (la) tuya, (los) tuyos, (las) tuyas <those are mine; yours are there : ésas son mías; las tuyas están allí> <is this one yours? : ¿éste es tuyo?> **2** (*belonging to more than one person — familiar*) : (el) suyo, (la) suya, (los) suyos, (las) suyas; (el) vuestro, (la) vuestra, (los) vuestros, (las) vuestras *Spain* <our house and yours : nuestra casa y la suya> **3** (*formal*) : (el) suyo, (la) suya, (los) suyos, (las) suyas

yourself [jərˈsɛlf] *pron, pl* **yourselves** [-ˈsɛlvz] **1** (*used reflexively — familiar*) : te, se *pl,* os *pl Spain* <wash yourself : lávate> <you dressed yourselves : se vistieron, os vestisteis> **2** (*used reflexively — formal*) : se <did you hurt yourself? : ¿se hizo daño?> <you've gotten yourselves dirty : se ensuciaron> **3** (*used for emphasis*) : tú mismo, tú misma; usted mismo, usted misma; ustedes mismos, ustedes mismas *pl;* vosotros mismos, vosotras mismas *pl Spain* <you did it yourselves? : ¿lo hicieron ustedes mismos?, ¿lo hicieron por sí solos?>

youth [ˈjuːθ] *n, pl* **youths** [ˈjuːðz, ˈjuːθs] **1** : juventud *f* <in her youth : en su juventud> **2** BOY : joven *m* **3** : jóvenes *mfpl,* juventud *f* <the youth of our city : los jóvenes de nuestra ciudad>

youthful [ˈjuːθfəl] *adj* **1** : de juventud **2** YOUNG : joven **3** JUVENILE : juvenil

youthfulness [ˈjuːθfəlnəs] *n* : juventud *f*

you've [ˈjuːv] (*contraction of* **you have**) → **have**

yowl[1] [ˈjæʊl] *vi* : aullar

yowl[2] *n* : aullido *m*

yo–yo [ˈjoːˌjoː] *n, pl* **-yos** : yoyo *m,* yoyó *m*

yucca [ˈjʌkə] *n* : yuca *f*

Yugoslavian [ˌjuːgoˈslɑviən] *n* : yugoslavo *m,* -va *f* — **Yugoslavian** *adj*

yule [ˈjuːl] *n* CHRISTMAS : Navidad *f*

yuletide [ˈjuːlˌtaɪd] *n* : Navidades *fpl*

Z

z [ˈziː] *n, pl* **z's** *or* **zs** : vigésima sexta letra del alfabeto inglés

Zambian [ˈzæmbiən] *n* : zambiano *m,* -na *f* — **Zambian** *adj*

zany[1] [ˈzeɪni] *adj* **-nier; -est** : alocado, disparatado

zany[2] *n, pl* **-nies** : bufón *m,* -fona *f*

zeal [ˈziːl] *n* : fervor *m,* celo *m,* entusiasmo *m*

zealot [ˈzɛlət] *n* : fanático *m,* -ca *f*

zealous [ˈzɛləs] *adj* : celoso — **zealously** *adv*

zebra [ˈziːbrə] *n* : cebra *f*

zenith [ˈziːnəθ] *n* **1** : cenit *m* (en astronomía) **2** PEAK : apogeo *m,* cenit *m* <at the zenith of his career : en el apogeo de su carrera>

zephyr [ˈzɛfər] *n* : céfiro *m*

zeppelin [ˈzɛplən, -pəlɪn] *n* : zepelín *m*

zero[1] [ˈziːro, ˈzɪro] *vi* **to zero in on** : apuntar hacia, centrarse en (un problema, etc.)

zero[2] *adj* : cero, nulo <zero degrees : cero grados> <zero opportunities : oportunidades nulas>

zero[3] *n, pl* **-ros** : cero *m* <below zero : bajo cero>

zest [ˈzɛst] *n* **1** GUSTO : entusiasmo *m,* brío *m* **2** FLAVOR : sabor *m,* sazón *f*

zestful [ˈzɛstfəl] *adj* : brioso

zigzag[1] [ˈzɪgˌzæg] *vi* **-zagged; -zagging** : zigzaguear

zigzag[2] *adv & adj* : en zigzag

zigzag[3] *n* : zigzag *m*

Zimbabwean [zɪmˈbɑbwiən, -bweɪ-] *n* : zimbabuense *mf* — **Zimbabwean** *adj*

zinc [ˈzɪŋk] *n* : cinc *m,* zinc *m*

zing [ˈzɪŋ] *n* **1** HISS, HUM : zumbido *m,* silbido *m* **2** ENERGY : brío *m*

zinnia [ˈzɪniə, ˈziː-, -njə] *n* : zinnia *f*

Zionism [ˈzaɪəˌnɪzəm] *n* : sionismo *m*

Zionist [ˈzaɪənɪst] *n* : sionista *mf*

zip[1] [ˈzɪp] *v* **zipped; zipping** *vt or* **to zip up** : cerrar el cierre de — *vi* **1** SPEED : pasarse volando <the day zipped by : el día se pasó volando> **2** HISS, HUM : silbar, zumbar

zip[2] *n* **1** ZING : zumbido *m,* silbido *m* **2** ENERGY : brío *m*

zip code *n* : código *m* postal

zipper [ˈzɪpər] *n* : cierre *m,* cremallera *f,* zíper *m CA, Mex*

zippy [ˈzɪpi] *adj* **-pier; -est** : brioso

zircon [ˈzər,kɑn] *n* **:** circón *m,* zircón *m*
zirconium [,zərˈkoːniəm] *n* **:** circonio *m*
zither [ˈzɪðər, -θər] *n* **:** cítara *f*
zodiac [ˈzoːdi,æk] *n* **:** zodíaco *m*
zombie [ˈzɑmbi] *n* **:** zombi *mf,* zombie *mf*
zone[1] [ˈzoːn] *vt* **zoned; zoning 1 :** dividir en zonas **2** DESIGNATE **:** declarar <to zone for business **:** declarar como zona comercial>
zone[2] *n* **:** zona *f*
zoo [ˈzuː] *n, pl* **zoos :** zoológico *m,* zoo *m*
zoological [,zoːəˈlɑdʒɪkəl, ,zuːə-] *adj* **:** zoológico
zoologist [zoˈɑlədʒɪst, zuː-] *n* **:** zoólogo *m,* -ga *f*
zoology [zoˈɑlədʒi, zuː-] *n* **:** zoología *f*
zoom[1] [ˈzuːm] *vi* **1 :** zumbar, ir volando <to zoom past **:** pasar volando> **2** CLIMB **:** elevarse <the plane zoomed up **:** el avión se elevó>
zoom[2] *n* **1 :** zumbido *m* <the zoom of an engine **:** el zumbido de un motor> **2 :** subida *f* vertical (de un avión, etc.) **3** *or* **zoom lens :** zoom *m*
zucchini [zʊˈkiːni] *n, pl* **-ni** *or* **-nis :** calabacín *m,* calabacita *f Mex*
zygote [ˈzaɪ,goːt] *n* **:** zigoto *m,* cigoto *m*

Common Spanish Abbreviations
Abreviaturas comunes en español

SPANISH ABBREVIATION AND EXPANSION		ENGLISH EQUIVALENT	
abr.	abril	**Apr.**	April
A.C., a.C.	antes de Cristo	**BC**	before Christ
a. de J.C.	antes de Jesucristo	**BC**	before Christ
admon., admón.	administración	—	administration
a/f	a favor	—	in favor
ago.	agosto	**Aug.**	August
Apdo.	apartado (de correos)	—	P.O. box
aprox.	aproximadamente	**approx.**	approximately
Aptdo.	apartado (de correos)	—	P.O. box
Arq.	arquitecto	**arch.**	architect
A.T.	Antiguo Testamento	**O. T.**	Old Testament
atte.	atentamente	—	sincerely
atto., atta.	atento, atenta	—	kind, courteous
av., avda.	avenida	**ave.**	avenue
a/v.	a vista	—	on receipt
BID	Banco Interamericano de Desarrollo	**IDB**	Interamerican Development Bank
B^{0}	banco	—	bank
BM	Banco Mundial		World Bank
c/, C/	calle	**st.**	street
C	centígrado, Celsius	**C**	centigrade, Celsius
C.	compañía	**Co.**	company
CA	corriente alterna	**AC**	alternating current
cap.	capítulo	**ch., chap.**	chapter
c/c	cuenta corriente	—	current account, checking account
c.c.	centímetros cúbicos	**cu. cm**	cubic centimeters
CC	corriente continua	**DC**	direct current
c/d	con descuento	—	with discount
Cd.	ciudad	—	city
CE	Comunidad Europea	**EC**	European Community
CEE	Comunidad Económica Europea	**EEC**	European Economic Community
cf.	confróntese	**cf.**	compare
cg.	centígramo	**cg**	centigram
CGT	Confederación General de Trabajadores *or* del Trabajo	—	confederation of workers, workers' union
CI	coeficiente intelectual *or* de inteligencia	**IQ**	intelligence quotient
Cía.	compañía	**Co.**	company
cm.	centímetro	**cm**	centimeter

SPANISH ABBREVIATION AND EXPANSION		ENGLISH EQUIVALENT	
Cnel.	coronel	**Col.**	colonel
col.	columna	**col.**	column
Col. *Mex*	Colonia	—	—
Com.	comandante	**Cmdr.**	commander
comp.	compárese	**comp.**	compare
Cor.	coronel	**Col.**	colonel
C.P.	código postal	—	zip code
CSF, c.s.f.	coste, seguro y flete	**c.i.f.**	cost, insurance, and freight
cta.	cuenta	**ac., acct.**	account
cte.	corriente	**cur.**	current
c/u	cada uno, cada una	**ea.**	each
CV	caballo de vapor	**hp**	horsepower
D.	Don	—	—
Da., D.ª	Doña	—	—
d.C.	después de Cristo	**AD**	anno Domini (in the year of our Lord)
dcha.	derecha	—	right
d. de J.C.	después de Jesucristo	**AD**	anno Domini (in the year of our Lord)
dep.	departamento	**dept.**	department
DF, D.F.	Distrito Federal	—	Federal District
dic.	diciembre	**Dec.**	December
dir.	director, directora	**dir.**	director
dir.	dirección	—	address
Dña.	Doña	—	—
do.	domingo	**Sun.**	Sunday
dpto.	departamento	**dept.**	department
Dr.	doctor	**Dr.**	doctor
Dra.	doctora	**Dr.**	doctor
dto.	descuento	—	discount
E, E.	Este, este	**E**	East, east
Ed.	editorial	—	publishing house
Ed., ed.	edición	**ed.**	edition
edif.	edificio	**bldg.**	building
edo.	estado	**st.**	state
EEUU, EE.UU.	Estados Unidos	**US, U.S.**	United States
ej.	por ejemplo	**e.g.**	for example
E.M.	esclerosis multiple	**MS**	multiple sclerosis
ene.	enero	**Jan.**	January
etc.	etcétera	**etc.**	et cetera
ext.	extensión	**ext.**	extension
F	Fahrenheit	**F**	Fahrenheit
f.a.b.	franco a bordo	**f.o.b.**	free on board
FC	ferrocarril	**RR**	railroad
feb.	febrero	**Feb.**	February
FF AA, FF.AA.	Fuerzas Armadas	—	armed forces
FMI	Fondo Monetario Internacional	**IMF**	International Monetary Fund
g.	gramo	**g., gm, gr.**	gram
G.P.	giro postal	**M.O.**	money order
gr.	gramo	**g., gm, gr.**	gram

SPANISH ABBREVIATION AND EXPANSION		ENGLISH EQUIVALENT	
Gral.	general	**Gen.**	general
h.	hora	**hr.**	hour
Hnos.	hermanos	**Bros.**	brothers
I + D, I & D, I y D	investigación y desarrollo	**R & D**	research and development
i.e.	esto es, es decir	**i.e.**	that is
incl.	inclusive	**incl.**	inclusive, inclusively
Ing.	ingeniero, ingeniera	**eng.**	engineer
IPC	indice de precios al consumo	**CPI**	consumer price index
IVA	impuesto al valor agregado	**VAT**	value-added tax
izq.	izquierda	**l.**	left
juev.	jueves	**Thurs.**	Thursday
jul.	julio	**Jul.**	July
jun.	junio	**Jun.**	June
kg.	kilogramo	**kg**	kilogram
km.	kilómetro	**km**	kilometer
km/h	kilómetros por hora	**kph**	kilometers per hour
kv, kV	kilovatio	**kw, kW**	kilowatt
l.	litro	**l, lit.**	liter
Lic.	licenciado, licenciada	—	*usually indicates a college graduate*
Ltda.	limitada	**Ltd.**	limited
lun.	lunes	**Mon.**	Monday
m	masculino	**m**	masculine
m	metro	**m**	meter
m	minuto	**m**	minute
mar.	marzo	**Mar.**	March
mart.	martes	**Tues.**	Tuesday
mg.	miligramo	**mg**	milligram
miérc.	miércoles	**Wednes.**	Wednesday
min	minuto	**min.**	minute
mm.	milímetro	**mm**	millimeter
M-N, m/n	moneda nacional	—	national currency
Mons.	monseñor	**Msgr.**	monsignor
Mtro.	maestro	—	teacher
Mtra.	maestra	—	teacher
N, N.	Norte, norte	**N, no.**	North, north
n/	nuestro	—	our
n.º	número	**no.**	number
N. de (la) R.	nota de (la) redacción	—	editor's note
NE	nordeste	**NE**	northeast
NN.UU.	Naciones Unidas	**UN**	United Nations
NO	noroeste	**NW**	northwest
nov.	noviembre	**Nov.**	November
N.T.	Nuevo Testamento	**N.T.**	New Testament
ntra., ntro.	nuestra, nuestro	—	our
NU	Naciones Unidas	**UN**	United Nations
núm.	número	**num.**	number
O, O.	Oeste, oeste	**W**	West, west
oct.	octubre	**Oct.**	October
OEA, O.E.A.	Organización de Estados Americanos	**OAS**	Organization of American States

SPANISH ABBREVIATION AND EXPANSION		ENGLISH EQUIVALENT	
OMS	Organización Mundial de la Salud	**WHO**	World Health Organization
ONG	organización no gubernamental	**NGO**	non-governmental organization
ONU	Organización de las Naciones Unidas	**UN**	United Nations
OTAN	Organización del Tratado del Atlántico Norte	**NATO**	North Atlantic Treaty Organization
p.	página	**p.**	page
P, P.	padre (*in religion)*	**Fr.**	father
pág.	página	**pg.**	page
pat.	patente	**pat.**	patent
PCL	pantalla de cristal líquido	**LCD**	liquid crystal display
P.D.	postdata	**P.S.**	postscript
p. ej.	por ejemplo	**e.g.**	for example
PNB	Producto Nacional Bruto	**GNP**	gross national product
P^{o}	paseo	**Ave.**	avenue
p.p.	porte pagado	**ppd.**	postpaid
PP, p.p.	por poder, por poderes	**p.p.**	by proxy
prom.	promedio	**av., avg.**	average
ptas., pts.	pesetas	—	—
q.e.p.d.	que en paz descanse	**R.I.P.**	may he/she rest in peace
R, R/	remite	—	sender
RAE	Real Academia Española	—	—
ref., ref.^{a}	referencia	**ref.**	reference
rep.	república	**rep.**	republic
r.p.m.	revoluciones por minuto	**rpm.**	revolutions per minute
rte.	remite, remitente	—	sender
s.	siglo	**c., cent.**	century
s/	su, sus	—	his, her, your, their
S, S.	Sur, sur	**S, so.**	South, south
S.	san, santo	**St.**	saint
S.A.	sociedad anónima	**Inc.**	incorporated (company)
sáb.	sábado	**Sat.**	Saturday
s/c	su cuenta	—	your account
SE	sudeste, sureste	**SE**	southeast
seg.	segundo, segundos	**sec.**	second, seconds
sep., sept.	septiembre	**Sept.**	September
s.e.u.o.	salvo error u omisión	—	errors and omissions excepted
Sgto.	sargento	**Sgt.**	sergeant
S.L.	sociedad limitada	**Ltd.**	limited (corporation)
S.M.	Su Majestad	**HM**	His Majesty, Her Majesty
s/n	sin número	—	no (street) number
s.n.m.	sobre el nivel de mar	**a.s.l.**	above sea level
SO	sudoeste/suroeste	**SW**	southwest

SPANISH ABBREVIATION AND EXPANSION		ENGLISH EQUIVALENT	
S.R.C.	se ruega contestación	**R.S.V.P.**	please reply
ss.	siguientes	—	the following ones
SS, S.S.	Su Santidad	**H.H.**	His Holiness
Sta.	santa	**St.**	saint
Sto.	santo	**St.**	saint
t, t.	tonelada	**t., tn.**	ton
TAE	tasa anual efectiva	**APR**	annual percentage rate
tb.	también	—	also
tel., Tel.	teléfono	**tel.**	telephone
Tm.	tonelada métrica	**MT**	metric ton
Tn.	tonelada	**t., tn.**	ton
trad.	traducido	**tr., trans., transl.**	translated
UE	Unión Europea	**EU**	European Union
Univ.	universidad	**Univ., U.**	university
UPC	unidad procesadora central	**CPU**	central processing unit
Urb.	urbanización	—	residential area
v	versus	**v., vs.**	versus
v	verso	**v., ver., vs.**	verse
v.	véase	**vid.**	see
Vda.	viuda	—	widow
v.g., v.gr.	verbigracia	**e.g.**	for example
vier., viern.	viernes	**Fri.**	Friday
V.M.	Vuestra Majestad	—	Your Majesty
$V^{o}B^{o}$, $V.^{o}B.^{o}$	visto bueno	—	OK, approved
vol, vol.	volumen	**vol.**	volume
vra., vro.	vuestra, vuestro	—	your

Common English Abbreviations
Abreviaturas comunes en inglés

ENGLISH ABBREVIATION AND EXPANSION		SPANISH EQUIVALENT	
AAA	American Automobile Association	—	—
AD	anno Domini (in the year of our Lord)	**d.C., d. de J.C.**	después de Cristo, después de Jesucristo
AK	Alaska	—	Alaska
AL, Ala.	Alabama	—	Alabama
Alas.	Alaska	—	Alaska
a.m., AM	ante meridiem (before noon)	**a.m.**	ante meridiem (de la mañana)
Am., Amer.	America, American	—	América, americano
amt.	amount	—	cantidad
anon.	anonymous	—	anónimo
ans.	answer	—	respuesta
Apr.	April	**abr.**	abril
AR	Arkansas	—	Arkansas
Ariz.	Arizona	—	Arizona
Ark.	Arkansas	—	Arkansas
asst.	assistant	**ayte.**	ayudante
atty.	attorney	—	abogado, -da
Aug.	August	**ago.**	agosto
ave.	avenue	**av., avda.**	avenida
AZ	Arizona	—	Arizona
BA	Bachelor of Arts	**Lic.**	Licenciado, -da en Filosofía y Letras
BA	Bachelor of Arts (degree)	—	Licenciatura en Filosofía y Letras
BC	before Christ	**a.C., A.C., a. de J.C.**	antes de Cristo, antes de Jesucristo
BCE	before the Christian Era, before the Common Era	—	antes de la era cristiana, antes de la era común
bet.	between	—	entre
bldg.	building	**edif.**	edificio
blvd.	boulevard	**blvar., br.**	bulevar
Br., Brit.	Britain, British	—	Gran Bretaña, británico
Bro(s).	brother(s)	**Hno(s),**	hermano(s)
BS	Bachelor of Science	**Lic.**	Licenciado, -da en Ciencias
BS	Bachelor of Science (degree)	—	Licenciatura en Ciencias
c	carat	—	quilate
c	cent	—	centavo

ENGLISH ABBREVIATION AND EXPANSION		SPANISH EQUIVALENT	
c	centimeter	**cm.**	centímetro
c	century	**s.**	siglo
c	cup	—	taza
C	Celsius, centigrade	**C**	Celsius, centígrado
CA, Cal., Calif.	California	—	California
Can., Canad.	Canada, Canadian	—	Canadá, canadiense
cap.	capital	—	capital
cap.	capital	—	mayúscula
Capt.	captain	—	capitán
cent.	century	**s.**	siglo
CEO	chief executive officer	—	presidente, -ta (de una corporación)
ch., chap.	chapter	**cap.**	capítulo
CIA	Central Intelligence Agency	—	—
cm	centimeter	**cm.**	centímetro
Co.	company	**C., Cía.**	compañía
co.	county	—	condado
CO	Colorado	—	Colorado
c/o	care of	**a/c**	a cargo de
COD	cash on delivery, collect on delivery	—	(pago) contra reembolso
col.	column	**col.**	columna
Col., Colo.	Colorado	—	Colorado
Conn.	Connecticut	—	Connecticut
corp.	corporation	—	corporación
CPR	cardiopulmonary resuscitation	**RCP**	reanimación cardiopulmonar, resucitación cardiopulmonar
ct.	cent	—	centavo
CT	Connecticut	—	Connecticut
D.A.	district attorney	—	fiscal (del distrito)
DC	District of Columbia	—	—
DDS	Doctor of Dental Surgery	—	doctor de cirugía dental
DE	Delaware	—	Delaware
Dec.	December	**dic.**	diciembre
Del.	Delaware	—	Delaware
DJ	disc jockey		disc-jockey
dept.	department	**dep., dpto.**	departamento
DMD	Doctor of Dental Medicine	—	doctor de medicina dental
doz.	dozen	—	docena
Dr.	doctor	**Dr., Dra.**	doctor, doctora
DST	daylight saving time	—	—
DVM	Doctor of Veterinary Medicine	—	doctor de medicina veterinaria
E	East, east	**E, E.**	Este, este
ea.	each	**c/u**	cada uno, cada una
e.g.	for example	**v.g., v.gr.**	verbigracia

ENGLISH ABBREVIATION AND EXPANSION		SPANISH EQUIVALENT	
EMT	emergency medical technician	—	técnico, -ca en urgencias médicas
Eng.	England, English	—	Inglaterra, inglés
esp.	especially	—	especialmente
EST	eastern standard time	—	—
etc.	et cetera	**etc.**	etcétera
f	false	—	falso
f	female	**f**	femenino
F	Fahrenheit	**F**	Fahrenheit
FBI	Federal Bureau of Investigation	—	—
Feb.	February	**feb.**	febrero
fem.	feminine	—	femenino
FL, Fla.	Florida	—	Florida
Fri.	Friday	**vier., viern.**	viernes
ft.	feet, foot	—	pie(s)
g	gram	**g., gr.**	gramo
Ga., GA	Georgia	—	Georgia
gal.	gallon	—	galón
Gen.	general	**Gral.**	general
gm	gram	**g., gr.**	gramo
gov.	governor	—	gobernador, -dora
govt.	government	—	gobierno
gr.	gram	**g., gr.**	gramo
HI	Hawaii	—	Hawai, Hawaii
hr.	hour	**h.**	hora
HS	high school	—	colegio secundario
ht.	height	—	altura
Ia., IA	Iowa	—	Iowa
ID	Idaho	—	Idaho
i.e.	id est (that is)	**i.e.**	id est (esto es, es decir)
IL, Ill	Illinois	—	Illinois
in.	inch	—	pulgada
IN	Indiana	—	Indiana
Inc.	incorporated (company)	**S.A.**	sociedad anónima
Ind.	Indian, Indiana	—	Indiana
Jan.	January	**ene.**	enero
Jul.	July	**jul.**	julio
Jun.	June	**jun.**	junio
Jr., Jun.	Junior	**Jr.**	Júnior
Kan., Kans.	Kansas	—	Kansas
kg	kilogram	**kg.**	kilogramo
km	kilometer	**km.**	kilómetro
KS	Kansas	—	Kansas
Ky., KY	Kentucky	—	Kentucky
l	liter	**l.**	litro
l.	left	**izq.**	izquierda
L	large	**G**	(talla) grande
La, LA	Louisiana	—	Luisiana, Louisiana
lb.	pound	—	libra

ENGLISH ABBREVIATION AND EXPANSION		SPANISH EQUIVALENT	
Ltd.	limited (corporation)	**S.L.**	sociedad limitada
m	male	**m**	masculino
m	meter	**m**	metro
m	mile	—	milla
M	medium	**M**	(talla) mediana
MA	Massachusetts	—	Massachusetts
Maj.	major	—	mayor
Mar.	March	**mar.**	marzo
masc.	masculine	—	masculino
Mass.	Massachusetts	—	Massachusetts
Md., MD	Maryland	—	Maryland
M.D.	Doctor of Medicine	—	doctor de medicina
Me., ME	Maine	—	Maine
Mex.	Mexican, Mexico	**Méx.**	mexicano, México
mg	milligram	**mg.**	miligramo
mi.	mile	—	milla
MI, Mich.	Michigan	—	Michigan
min.	minute	**min**	minuto
Minn.	Minnesota	—	Minnesota
Miss.	Mississippi	—	Mississippi, Misisipí
ml	mililiter	**ml.**	mililitro
mm	millimeter	**mm.**	milímetro
MN	Minnesota	—	Minnesota
mo.	month	—	mes
Mo., MO	Missouri	—	Missouri
Mon.	Monday	**lun.**	lunes
Mont.	Montana	—	Montana
mpg	miles per gallon	—	millas pør galón
mph	miles per hour	—	millas por hora
MS	Mississippi	—	Mississippi, Misisipí
mt.	mount, mountain	—	monte, montaña
MT	Montana	—	Montana
mtn.	mountain	—	montaña
N	North, north	**N**	Norte, norte
NASA	National Aeronautics and Space Administration	—	—
NC	North Carolina	—	Carolina del Norte, North Carolina
ND, N. Dak.	North Dakota	—	Dakota del Norte, North Dakota
NE	northeast	**NE**	nordeste
NE, Neb., Nebr.	Nebraska	—	Nebraska
Nev.	Nevada	—	Nevada
NH	New Hampshire	—	New Hampshire
NJ	New Jersey	—	Nueva Jersey, New Jersey
NM., N. Mex.	New Mexico	—	Nuevo México, New Mexico
no.	north	**N**	norte
no.	number	**n.º**	número
Nov.	November	**nov.**	noviembre
N.T.	New Testament	**N.T.**	Nuevo Testamento

ENGLISH ABBREVIATION	AND EXPANSION	SPANISH EQUIVALENT	
NV	Nevada	—	Nevada
NW	northwest	**NO**	noroeste
NY	New York	**NY**	Nueva York, New York
O	Ohio	—	Ohio
Oct.	October	**oct.**	octubre
OH	Ohio	—	Ohio
OK, Okla.	Oklahoma	—	Oklahoma
OR, Ore., Oreg.	Oregon	—	Oregon
O.T.	Old Testament	**A.T.**	Antiguo Testamento
oz.	ounce, ounces	—	onza, onzas
p.	page	**p.**	página
Pa., PA	Pennsylvania	—	Pennsylvania, Pensilvania
pat.	patent	**pat.**	patente
PD	police department	—	departamento de policía
PE	physical education	—	educación física
Penn., Penna.	Pennsylvania	—	Pennsylvania, Pensilvania
pg.	page	**pág.**	página
PhD	Doctor of Philosophy	—	doctor, -tora (en filosofía)
pkg.	package	—	paquete
p.m., PM	post meridiem (afternoon)	**p.m.**	post meridiem (de la tarde)
P.O.	post office	—	oficina de correos, correo
pp.	pages	**págs.**	páginas
PR	Puerto Rico	**PR**	Puerto Rico
pres.	present	—	presente
pres.	president		presidente, -ta
prof.	professor	—	profesor, -sora
P.S.	postscript	**P.D.**	postdata
P.S.	public school	—	escuela pública
pt.	pint	—	pinta
pt.	point	**pto.**	punto
PTA	Parent-Teacher Association	—	—
PTO	Parent-Teacher Organization	—	—
q, qt.	quart	—	cuarto de galón
r.	right	**dcha.**	derecha
rd.	road	**c/, C/**	calle
RDA	recommended daily allowance	—	consumo diario recomendado
recd.	received	—	recibido
Rev.	reverend	**Rdo.**	reverendo
RI	Rhode Island	—	Rhode Island
rpm	revolutions per minute	**r.p.m.**	revoluciones por minuto
RR	railroad	**FC**	ferrocarril

ENGLISH ABBREVIATION AND EXPANSION		SPANISH EQUIVALENT	
R.S.V.P	please reply (répondez s'il vous plaît)	**S.R.C.**	se ruega contestación
rt.	right	**dcha.**	derecha
rte.	route	—	ruta
S	small	**P**	(talla) pequeña
S	South, south	**S**	Sur, sur
S.A.	South America	—	Sudamérica, América del Sur
Sat.	Saturday	**sáb.**	sábado
SC	South Carolina	—	Carolina del Sur, South Carolina
SD, S. Dak.	South Dakota	—	Dakota del Sur, South Dakota
SE	southeast	**SE**	sudeste, sureste
Sept.	September	**sep., sept.**	septiembre
so.	south	**S**	sur
sq.	square		cuadrado
Sr.	Senior	**Sr.**	Sénior
Sr.	sister (*in religion*)	—	sor
st.	state	—	estado
st.	street	**c/, C/**	calle
St.	saint	**S., Sto., Sta.**	santo, santa
Sun.	Sunday	**dom.**	domingo
SW	southwest	**SO**	sudoeste, suroeste
t.	teaspoon	—	cucharadita
T, tb., tbsp.	tablespoon	—	cucharada (grande)
Tenn.	Tennessee	—	Tennessee
Tex.	Texas	—	Texas
Thu., Thur., Thurs.	Thursday	**juev.**	jueves
TM	trademark	—	marca (de un producto)
TN	Tennessee	—	Tennessee
tsp.	teaspoon	—	cucharadita
Tue., Tues.	Tuesday	**mart.**	martes
TX	Texas	—	Texas
UN	United Nations	**NU, NN.UU.**	Naciones Unidas
US	United States	**EEUU, EE.UU.**	Estados Unidos
USA	United States of America	**EEUU, EE.UU.**	Estados Unidos de América
usu.	usually	—	usualmente
UT	Utah	—	Utah
v.	versus	**v**	versus
Va., VA	Virginia	—	Virginia
vol.	volume	**vol.**	volumen
VP	vice president	—	vicepresidente, -ta
vs.	versus	**v**	versus
Vt., VT	Vermont	—	Vermont

ENGLISH ABBREVIATION AND EXPANSION		SPANISH EQUIVALENT	
W	West, west	**O**	Oeste, oeste
WA, Wash.	Washington (state)	—	Washington
Wed.	Wednesday	**miérc.**	miércoles
WI, Wis., Wisc.	Wisconsin	—	Wisconsin
wt.	weight	—	peso
WV, W. Va.	West Virginia	—	Virginia del Oeste, West Virginia
WY, Wyo.	Wyoming	—	Wyoming
yd.	yard	—	yarda
yr.	year	—	año

Metric System : Conversions
Sistema métrico : conversiones

Length

unit	number of meters	approximate U.S. equivalents	
millimeter	0.001	0.039	inch
centimeter	0.01	0.39	inch
meter	1	39.37	inches
kilometer	1,000	0.62	mile

Longitud

unidad	número de metros	equivalentes aproximados de los EE.UU.	
milímetro	0.001	0.039	pulgada
centímetro	0.01	0.39	pulgada
metro	1	39.37	pulgadas
kilómetro	1,000	0.62	milla

Area

unit	number of square meters	approximate U.S. equivalents	
square centimeter	0.0001	0.155	square inch
square meter	1	10.764	square feet
hectare	10,000	2.47	acres
square kilometer	1,000,000	0.3861	square mile

Superficie

unidad	número de metros cuadrados	equivalentes aproximados de los EE.UU.	
centímetro cuadrado	0.0001	0.155	pulgada cuadrada
metro cuadrado	1	10.764	pies cuadrados
hectárea	10,000	2.47	acres
kilómetro cuadrado	1,000,000	0.3861	milla cuadrada

Volume

unit	number of cubic meters	approximate U.S. equivalents	
cubic centimeter	0.000001	0.061	cubic inch
cubic meter	1	1.307	cubic yards

Volumen

unidad	número de metros cúbicos	equivalentes aproximados de los EE.UU	
centímetro cúbico	0.000001	0.061	pulgada cúbica
metro cúbico	1	1.307	yardas cúbicas

Capacity

unit	number of liters	approximate U.S. equivalents		
		CUBIC	DRY	LIQUID
liter	1	61.02 cubic inches	0.908 quart	1.057 quarts

Capacidad

unidad	número de litros	equivalentes aproximados de los EE.UU.		
		CÚBICO	SECO	LIQUIDO
litro	1	61.02 pulgadas cúbicas	0.908 cuarto	1.057 cuartos

Mass and Weight

unit	number of grams	approximate U.S. equivalents	
milligram	0.001	0.015	grain
centigram	0.01	0.154	grain
gram	1	0.035	ounce
kilogram	1,000	2.2046	pounds
metric ton	1,000,000	1.102	short tons

Masa y peso

unidad	número de gramos	equivalentes aproximados de los EE.UU.	
miligramo	0.001	0.015	grano
centigramo	0.01	0.154	grano
gramo	1	0.035	onza
kilogramo	1.000	2.2046	libras
tonelada métrica	1,000,000	1.102	toneladas cortas